AGE, WEIGHT & DISTANCE TABLE

For use with Chase and Hurdle races

Distance	Age	Jan	Feb	Mar	Apr	May	June
2m	5	12—7	12—7	12—7	12—7	12—7	12—7
	4	11–13	12—0	12—1	12—2	12—3	12—4
2¼m	5	12—7	12—7	12—7	12—7	12—7	12—7
	4	11–12	11–13	12—0	12—1	12—2	12—3
2½m	5	12—7	12—7	12—7	12—7	12—7	12—7
	4	11–11	11–12	11–13	12—0	12—1	12—2
2¾m	5	12—6	12—7	12—7	12—7	12—7	12—7
	4	11–10	11–11	11–12	11–13	12—0	12—1
3m	5	12—6	12—6	12—7	12—7	12—7	12—7
	4	11—8	11–10	11–11	11–12	11–13	12—0

Distance	Age	July	Aug	Sep	Oct	Nov	Dec
2m	5	12—7	12—7	12—7	12—7	12—7	12—7
	4	12—4	12—5	12—5	12—6	12—6	12—7
	3	11—5	11—6	11—8	11—9	11–11	11–12
2¼m	5	12—7	12—7	12—7	12—7	12—7	12—7
	4	12—3	12—4	12—5	12—5	12—6	12—6
	3	11—4	11—5	11—7	11—8	11—9	11–10
2½m	5	12—7	12—7	12—7	12—7	12—7	12—7
	4	12—2	12—3	12—4	12—5	12—6	12—6
	3		11—4	11—6	11—7	11—8	11—9
2¾m	5	12—7	12—7	12—7	12—7	12—7	12—7
	4	12—2	12—3	12—4	12—5	12—5	12—6
	3					11—7	11—8
3m	5	12—7	12—7	12—7	12—7	12—7	12—7
	4	12—1	12—2	12—3	12—4	12—5	12—5
	3				11—5	11—6	11—7

For 6-y-o's and older, use 12-7 in all cases

Note Race distances in the above tables are shown only at ¼-mile intervals. For races of 2m1f use the 2¼-mile table weights; for races of 2m3f use 2½ miles; and so forth. For races over odd distances, the nearest distance shown in the table should be used. Races over distances longer than 3 miles should be treated as 3-mile races.

National Hunt Flat races A separate age, weight & distance table is used for NH Flat races but there is no weight-for-age allowance for 5-y-o's; over 2 miles from January to November the allowance for 4-y-o's is 1 lb less than it is over jumps.

CHASERS & HURDLERS 2004/05

Price £66.00

A TIMEFORM PUBLICATION

A Timeform Publication

Compiled and produced by

G. Greetham (Director), D. P. Cleary (Editor), M. S. Rigg (Handicapper), J. Ingles, P. Morrell and E. K. Wilkinson (essays), P. E. Turner (additional research), D. W. Johnson (short commentaries), P. A. Muncaster (short commentaries and proof checking), H. Brewer, M. Hall, D. Holdsworth, W. Muncaster, A-M. Stevens and R. Todd (production).

ISBN 1 901570 52 5

CONTENTS

The age, weight and distance table, for use in applying the ratings in races involving horses of different ages, appears on the end paper at the front of the book

3
UINNESS

30th EDITION

Chasers & Hurdlers 2004/05

Introduction

Is jumping enjoying a 'golden age' of steeplechasing to compare with the era of Arkle, Flyingbolt, Mill House and Dunkirk? The latest season was unique in the era of *Chasers & Hurdlers* in featuring four horses, all chasers, rated over 180. The highest-rated horse for the second year running is **Moscow Flyer**, a phenomenon among chasers and now winner of nineteen of his twenty completed starts over fences. Only Desert Orchid has stronger claims to the mantle 'greatest steeplechaser since Arkle'. The extended entry on one of Moscow Flyer's great rivals **Azertyuiop** reveals some similarities between the latest season and the 1965/6 season. Questioning the fairness of water jumps is another topic in the essay, Azertyuiop's bad mistake at the water costing him his chance of a second successive Queen Mother Champion Chase in which, as well as Moscow Flyer, the presence of one of the new young stars of steeplechasing **Well Chief** contributed to making the two-mile championship the race of the Festival for many, a re-run of what turned out to be the race of the season between the three in the Tingle Creek at Sandown in December. A burst blood vessel which sidelined three-times Gold Cup winner **Best Mate** robbed the Cheltenham Festival meeting of its focal point. Whether a fit and well Best Mate would have won a fourth Gold Cup, however, is at least debatable. He would certainly have had his work cut out against another young star **Kicking King**. Kicking King raced regularly from October right through to the Punchestown Festival, shortly after the end of the British season. He won both the King George VI Chase and the Cheltenham Gold Cup, running to a higher level of form at Kempton despite a last-fence blunder there, and is only the third since Arkle (after Desert Orchid and Best Mate) to win the two races in the same season. A meeting between Kicking King and Best Mate is scheduled for the new Betfair Chase at Haydock in November, a race which carries a £1m bonus if the winner also goes on to collect the King George (to be staged temporarily at Sandown while Kempton is redeveloped) and the Gold Cup.

The essay on **Hardy Eustace**, who won his second Champion Hurdle, recalls the 'golden age of hurdling', from the first of Persian War's three

Most of the emphasis in the jumping season is put on the period from mid-March to the end of April but the race of the latest season took place at Sandown in December. The Tingle Creek turned into a three-way battle between three of the best two-mile chasers in the history of the sport, Moscow Flyer pictured (top) leading at the last from Well Chief (white face) and Azertyuiop. The season's top staying chaser was Kicking King, winner of both the King George VI Chase and the Cheltenham Gold Cup, as well as the Punchestown Gold Cup (bottom picture). All four chasers ended the season with Timeform ratings higher than 180, the first time there have been as many as four horses rated over 180 in the thirty-year history of this Annual.

Calamity almost overtook the season's top staying chaser Kicking King in the King George VI Chase. He recovered from this bad mistake at the last to record one of the best performances seen in the race since Desert Orchid's day

Champion Hurdle wins to the second of Sea Pigeon's victories in the same race. Parallels were drawn between the latest edition and Monksfield's second Champion Hurdle victory over Sea Pigeon, though any similarities apply only to the way the two races unfolded. The latest Champion Hurdle is likely to be remembered as much for being a race that the runner-up **Harchibald** lost, as for being one which Hardy Eustace won. The winning margin was the smallest in the race since 1955, the controversy over Paul Carberry's riding of Harchibald given a full airing in the essay. The first five in the Champion Hurdle were all trained in Ireland whose leading hurdlers dominated the important races at up to two and a half miles. Harchibald won the 'Fighting Fifth' at Newcastle and the Christmas Hurdle at Kempton, the Champion Hurdle third **Brave Inca** went on to win the Emo Oil Champion Hurdle at Punchestown, the Champion Hurdle fifth **Macs Joy** won the December Festival Hurdle and the AIG Europe Champion Hurdle, and **Back In Front** won the Bula. The other Irish-trained Champion Hurdle runners also made their mark: **Accordion Etoile** (Greatwood Hurdle) and **Essex** (Pierse Hurdle and totesport Trophy) landed valuable handicaps, while **Al Eile** went on to win the Aintree Hurdle. Another of Ireland's top hurdlers the tough and game mare **Solerina** didn't make it to Cheltenham but added to her fine record with another four wins, including the McManus Memorial Hurdle at Tipperary and the Hatton's Grace at Fairyhouse.

Irish-trained horses won nine races at the newly-expanded Cheltenham Festival, one more than their previous record of eight in 1957/8, which led directly to a rule change after the Irish victories included four of the six handicaps at the meeting. Irish horses could be handicapped in Britain at that time provided they had run a minimum of three times in Ireland and the *Bloodstock Breeders' Review* noted that 'the apparent improvement made by some of these horses over their Irish form did not pass without comment.' In October that year, the stewards of the National Hunt Committee brought its rules into line with those of the Jockey Club, which allotted Irish horses top weight unless they had run three times in Britain or, in the case of more valuable events, had taken part in their own country in races of a certain minimum value. The Irish, incidentally, had no runners in the Gold Cup and only one in the Champion Hurdle at the 1958 Festival. The handicappers at the BHB and their Irish counterparts nowadays keep their assessments more or less in line—the Turf Club marks of many Irish-trained hurdlers, for example, were raised after the latest season—so that Irish challengers now mostly race off their domestic marks in Britain and vice versa.

Ireland's prosperous economy and the strong support of the Irish government for the thoroughbred industries is largely responsible for the renaissance of Irish jumping, which went through a period not so long ago of being something of a nursery whose best prospects were regularly sold to British stables. Ireland's strong hand at Cheltenham was mirrored at Aintree where **Hedgehunter** became the fourth Irish-trained winner of the Grand National in seven years. He was one of eight Irish-trained winners at the meeting where Moscow Flyer and Fota Island both followed up Cheltenham victories (though neither managed the hat-trick at Punchestown, a feat last achieved by Istabraq in 1999). The additional day at Cheltenham, where the new races worked well in general (as outlined in the entries on **Thisthatandtother** and **Trabolgan** with related comment on **Another Rum** and **Dabiroun**), ensured a new record crowd total. The first three days attracted 55,184, 54,850 and 54,817 (around 15% down on the average individual daily total the previous year) but the Gold Cup day attendance was 66,767, bringing the four-day total to 231,618

The season's most controversial race—halfway up the run-in in the Champion Hurdle and Harchibald and Paul Carberry are apparently cruising alongside the hard-ridden Hardy Eustace

(compared to 197,111 for the three days the year before). Aintree's official total for its three days was 151,660, with 70,739 attending on National day. A new paddock and weighing room are among changes planned before the next National meeting. BBC television viewing figures for the Grand National were also healthy at 9.5m (almost 2m more than watched the royal wedding on the same day), while the Channel 4 audience of 1.3m for the Cheltenham Gold Cup was, perhaps understandably, down more than 400,000 on the figure for Best Mate's third Gold Cup (the figures held steady at 1.2m and 1.1m on the Tuesday and Wednesday, though only 800,000 tuned in to the third day). The fall in television viewers on Gold Cup day was actually greater than stated, as the previous year up to 200,000 had tuned in to Cheltenham coverage on the original free-to-air attheraces, a dedicated satellite and cable horseracing channel which closed at the end of March 2004 after the collapse of an original ten-year deal which was over-reliant on making a success of interactive betting.

Racing's need for dedicated daily TV coverage was illustrated by a worrying fall in credit and internet betting turnover which was not reversed even after a revamped At The Races (Channel 4 withdrawing as a partner) and the rival Racing UK (which became a subscription-based service) were launched by June. Later in the year, Channel 4 coverage beyond 2005 looked in doubt after the terrestrial company sought an £8m subsidy or sponsorship which they said was needed to cover costs of the rights and of production, as well as compensation for revenue allegedly lost by showing racing. The BHB called a meeting of racecourse and betting industry representatives, the result of which was a decision that no subsidy would be offered because of 'the precedent such action would set'. A planned change in broadcasting rules, which gave more flexibility for advertising opportunities and sponsorship within television programmes, was eventually used to find a way out of the impasse. A programme sponsorship package was settled for 2006 at £4.8m (£800,000 of it being money Channel 4 will no longer have to pay racecourses for TV rights). The biggest slice, £3m, was created after a re-evaluation of its overall racing

The Grand National jockeys pose for the traditional photograph in front of Aintree's historical weatherboarded unsaddling enclosure and weighing room which was used for the last time

The finish of the (Brit Insurance) Spa Hurdle, one of four new races at the Cheltenham Festival; the new four-day format generally worked well

sponsorship by totesport, whose scoop6 jackpot-type bet relies heavily on its promotion on Channel 4. Surprisingly, the Levy Board made available £1m to the racecourses, justifying the payment by saying the Channel 4 deal would protect racing's public profile and thereby the levy income, though some bookmakers pointed out that totesport was being given an unfair opportunity to promote its products at their expense (around 90% of the levy is raised through bookmakers).

Though the exact relationship is a little more complex, and no serious research has been done for some time, when a race is shown on terrestrial television, phone and internet betting is reckoned to be between two and three times as much as if there was only satellite coverage. Sponsorship would also be lost without terrestrial coverage, the Horseracing Sponsors' Association estimating the sum, if Channel 4 stopped broadcasting racing, at between £7m-£8m of the annual total £17m-£18m that sponsors contribute to prize money. While the BBC, and possibly BSkyB and ITV, would have been in the market for some of the gems—notably the Cheltenham Festival—this would have been, with the BBC, partly at the cost of some existing scheduled televised fixtures. Also believed to be at stake was the space given to racing in the media, including the mass-circulation tabloid Saturday racing pullouts which focus largely on the televised meetings. That said, the proposed seventy-five or so days of live racing action (including every Saturday) to be covered by Channel 4 in 2006 may prove even more costly if the deal becomes a permanent model. Racing would have received media rights revenue from the BBC (or Sky or ITV) for the Cheltenham Festival and other fixtures, revenue temporarily waived. The current BBC deal has one year left and, though it could not, at present, enter a commercial deal for sponsorship, the BBC might consider whether it should receive a subsidy of some sort from racing. The bookmakers pay over £30m a year to show racing in betting shops and may also feel that the climate has changed. As well as raising questions about the value of racing's picture rights, the deal with Channel 4 also potentially cost Racing UK a number of additional viewers, though only a fraction of any audience migrates when a sport switches from terrestrial to digital (in successive nights of

Chairman Peter Jones presenting the trophy to the connections of Essex, Irish-trained winner of Britain's top handicap hurdle, the totesport Trophy at Newbury; totesport's £3m contribution to a sponsorship package helped to ensure Channel 4's continued racing coverage in 2006

Champions League football in 2005, for example, 1.2m watched Chelsea play Liverpool on Sky, as against 4.9m who had watched Arsenal's game on ITV the previous night). Most of the racing at risk was also covered by Racing UK which, along with At The Races, provides significantly wider coverage—all British and Irish racing—than was provided by the original attheraces alone which had only forty-nine of the fifty-nine British courses and no Irish racing. Whilst clearly recognising the need for racing to have a wide audience, the courses which own Racing UK have waived their picture rights to a terrestrial broadcaster, while continuing to charge the current 32,500 customers of its own channel £20 a month. Racing UK and At The Races (available with the minimum Sky subscription of around £20 a month) both claim to be doing well, Racing UK already having more viewers than the Racing Channel which ran from 1995 to 2003 and At The Races having 1.2m unique viewers a month (including Ireland). Racing UK's research shows that 22,750 of its subscribers watch at some time each day; At The Races has 200,000 individual viewers each day. Racing's ultimate aim, regardless of terrestrial television considerations, must be to show every race free-to-air, though, without cutting back the current level of coverage, that would not be possible now on one channel. Subscriptions to Racing UK reportedly yield around £7m, not a lot more than the sponsorship secured by Channel 4 in 2006, and both Racing UK and At The Races are sure to be looking at sponsorship prospects for their live racing programmes. Bookmakers, some of whom were prepared to discuss sponsorship with Channel 4, seem an obvious source. Interestingly, the bookmakers would have been due to pay around an additional £1.5m a year if Channel 4 had ceased its coverage; under current arrangements, they do not pay picture rights for races shown on terrestrial television. One final point on the subject: the latest research by Ofcom shows that more than 60% of UK households now receive digital television and that, by 2010, the number of households able to view television over broadband is likely to exceed the number of households dependent on analogue terrestrial broadcasts for their television viewing.

To return to the Cheltenham Festival, home-trained runners generally kept the Irish at bay in the novice events, **Penzance**, **Faasel** (who went on to win the upgraded Anniversary Hurdle, part of a first-day treble for trainer Nicky Richards at Aintree) and **Akilak** landing a one, two, three in the Triumph Hurdle. Penzance wasn't the only leading juvenile to end the campaign unbeaten, British-trained **United**, who missed Cheltenham, taking her record to three out of three when landing the Champion Four Year Old Hurdle at Punchestown. The best of the Irish juveniles were Dabiroun, winner of the inaugural Fred Winter Juvenile Novices' Handicap at the Cheltenham Festival, and **Strangely Brown**, sixth in the Triumph, third in the Anniversary and second to United at Punchestown before winning the top race for juvenile hurdlers in France. Faasel and Strangely Brown were purchased off the Flat at the Newmarket Autumn Sales, as was the Royal & SunAlliance Hurdle winner **No Refuge**, one of three Cheltenham Festival winners for the owner/trainer/jockey combination of Andrea and Graham Wylie, Howard Johnson and Graham Lee which also enjoyed success with **Arcalis** in the Supreme Novices' Hurdle and **Inglis Drever** in the World Hurdle (formerly the Stayers'). The entry on Inglis Drever looks at the present-day World Hurdle compared to the 'eighties and appeals for it to be made more of a race for true stayers by extending its distance to that of the Gold Cup. The Inglis Drever essay also looks at the impact of the inaugural BHB order of merit. **Baracouda**, twice a winner of the Stayers', had to be content with the runners-up spot for the second year running, ahead of the versatile **Rule Supreme** who is capable of switching between hurdles and fences in top company and won the Hennessy at Leopardstown from **Beef Or Salmon** who took the scalps of both Best Mate and Kicking King in the latest season. Baracouda had won the Long Distance Hurdle at Newbury for the second time and the Long Walk (transferred temporarily from Ascot to Windsor) for the fourth. It was a lucrative season for French-trained raiders generally, Baracouda's stable winning good prizes with the likes of **Blue Canyon**, **Kelami**, **L'Ami** and **Moulin Riche**, while Arnaud Chaille-Chaille, trainer of **Cyrlight**, the most exciting jumper in France, would have had a leading contender for the Royal & SunAlliance Hurdle had **Ambobo** not suffered a minor leg injury.

Six of Timeform's top twenty novice hurdlers at the time failed to make it to the Festival, as did thirteen of the top twenty bumper performers (**Missed That** provided his trainer Willie Mullins with a fifth success in the Champion Bumper). It was a similar story with the season's leading novice chasers, nine of the top twenty in Timeform's pre-Cheltenham list being among the absentees. Injuries to the Nigel Twiston-Davies-trained trio **Fundamentalist**, **Baron Windrush** and **Ollie Magern** (whose write-up looks at the restructuring of the novice chase programme to make it more competitive) robbed the Festival of three novice chasers capable of making a major impact, as did the unfortunate injury suffered by **Kauto Star** (whose entry debates the pros and cons of remounting). **El Vaquero**, who gave Best Mate's stable its most prestigious success of the season in the Scilly Isles Novices' Chase at Sandown, was another notable by his absence. He was bought privately by the Wylies in the summer and will be trained in 2005/6 by Howard Johnson. It was a measure of the strength of the Wylies' team, incidentally, that just about the pick of the novice hurdlers to carry their colours, the ex-Flat **Mephisto**, stayed at home while Arcalis and No Refuge carried off the two biggest novice hurdles at Cheltenham.

Trabolgan's Royal & SunAlliance Chase victory was one of three at Cheltenham for trainer Nicky Henderson but even his excellent haul of Festival winners over the years falls short of that of Martin Pipe who is now on thirty-four and edging closer to Fulke Walwyn's record of forty. **Contraband** provided Pipe and his principal patron David Johnson with their fourth winner of the Arkle Challenge Trophy in the last eight runnings. The essay on Well Chief summarises Johnson's tremendous season, in which he became the first owner to win a hundred races and top the £1m mark in 1,2,3 prize money in a jumping season. The essay on **Comply Or Die** gives an insight into changes that have taken place in his buying policy, while the review of **Celestial Gold** outlines the progress of Johnson's new jockey Timmy Murphy. The Johnson horses played a big part in securing Pipe's fifteenth trainers' championship—and his tenth in a row—in a second successive nip-and-tuck battle with Paul Nicholls who has now finished second in the table in each of the last seven seasons. The last few weeks of the campaign revolved around the championship, with the narrow defeat of the Nicholls-trained **Cornish Rebel** in the Scottish National making a difference of £43,448, as well as denying Ruby Walsh a fourth major National of the campaign (though the essay points out that, when it comes to Nationals, Walsh was just scratching the surface).

Pipe's eventual success in the trainers' championship was accompanied by apparent official concerns over some of his tactics, a point enlarged on in the commentary on **Commercial Flyer**, running for the third time in as many days when one of ten runners declared by the stable in the valuable handicap that opened Sandown's card on the final day. The Nicholls stable has run horses on consecutive days numerous times in the past, including Lake Kariba, Kadarann (twice) and Venn Ottery at the Scottish National meeting, and there are plenty of other precedents, among those springing immediately to mind Irish-trained

Despite the loss of Tony McCoy's services, it was business as usual for champion owner and trainer David Johnson and Martin Pipe; they are pictured returning with Contraband (Timmy Murphy), their fourth winner of the Arkle Trophy in the last eight runnings

Feroda winning on successive days at Aintree in 1989 and Generosa winning what is now the Pertemps Final at Cheltenham in 1999 before finishing third in the Coral Cup less than twenty-four hours later. The write-up on progressive chaser **Oneway** recounts that his dam is a half-sister to Threadbare who, at the age of ten in 1973, won a hurdle, a chase and a Flat race in the space of three racing days.

The competitive instincts of both Pipe and Nicholls were illustrated by the string of horses they ran in the closing weeks. They were the only two trainers represented—Pipe had five runners, Nicholls four—in the Celebration Chase at Sandown in which Well Chief's victory over Azertyuiop, fittingly a duel between the stables' respective best horses, finally put the title out of Nicholls' reach. In the Betfred Gold Cup, won by Irish-trained **Jack High**, Pipe saddled seven runners, all of them owned by David Johnson. Pipe's £2,613,666 in 1,2,3 prize money for the season narrowly surpassed his previous highest total achieved in 2001/2, while Nicholls with £2,557,665 was over £1.1m ahead of third-placed Philip Hobbs. Both Pipe and Nicholls publicly declared that winning the title was not a major priority, Pipe reportedly saying at one point 'I'm sure Mr Nicholls will win the championship one day . . . I don't have that many left to run.' The statement brought a retort from Nicholls of 'That's absolute bollocks, he'll have double the amount of runners I've got in every race, trying to cancel us out.' Nicholls also revealed that one of his owners had caught a glimpse of Pipe's *Racing Post* at the track one day and noticed that the Nicholls runners were highlighted in yellow. Illustrating how seriously both took the pursuit of the title, Pipe ran thirty-four horses on the penultimate day of the season, Nicholls ran fourteen. Nicholls trained his thousandth winner in Britain when Noble Action won a bumper at Folkestone in November, reaching the total just fourteen years after taking out a trainer's licence. Pipe, by the way, was among the first to experience the court-room atmosphere of an open hearing of the Jockey Club disciplinary panel (see the entry on **Celtic Son**), the decision to allow the media to attend some hearings coinciding with the Jockey Club's move from its offices in Portman Square to new premises in Shaftesbury Avenue.

The Cheltenham Festival wins of **King Harald** and **Idole First** (whose entry contains more detail) produced a ticklish situation for Jockey Club officials. King Harald's jockey had been fined £2,500 the week before Cheltenham for deliberately misleading Jockey Club officials investigating race-fixing and Idole First's owner was in a standoff about handing over telephone records in another potential case. The much publicised 'huge investigation' by City of London police into criminal activity involving so-called 'fixing' of races rumbled on, though most of its activity revolved around Flat racing. The investigation is thought to centre on the laying, on betting exchanges, of horses allegedly prevented from winning. In a separate, long-running case, bloodstock agent and former jockey Graham Bradley began a five-year ban in October for passing information for reward and other offences when a jockey (he lost a last-ditch bid to the Court of Appeal in July).

In contrast to the nail-biting finish to the trainers' championship, the jockeys' title was sewn up a long time before the end of the season. Tony McCoy, that paragon of skill, strength and consistency, celebrated a tenth jockeys' championship, reaching 200 winners for the sixth time in his career despite the interrupted season at Jackdaws Castle (see **Iris's Gift**) to which McCoy had switched after a long and successful association with Martin Pipe at Pond House. Timmy Murphy, the new number one at Pond House, finished second in the table by number of winners, fifty-seven behind McCoy and eight ahead of third-placed Richard Johnson, but Murphy topped the prize-money tables (from Ruby Walsh, with McCoy third). The very promising Paddy Brennan, based with Philip Hobbs, took the conditional jockeys' title and finished ninth overall by number of winners. His season is covered in the essay on Maghull Novices' Chase winner **Ashley Brook**.

The campaign to outlaw foxhunting, pledged by Labour in its 1997 election manifesto, finally reached fruition with the passing—by use of the Parliament Act—of the Hunting Act 2004 which came into force in February 2005. Leaving aside the issue of all those table mats, sporting prints and inn signs depicting what is now a criminal activity, the hunts have largely managed to continue by using a variety of methods to kill foxes legally, under permitted exemptions, or, reportedly in some cases, by hunting illegally where they have found police unavailable to enforce the ban. Either way, apocalyptic warnings that a hunting ban would sound the death knell for point-to-pointing look like proving wide of the mark. Over two hundred fixtures have been scheduled for 2006. There were maximum fields for the Foxhunter at Cheltenham and the Fox Hunters' at Aintree, the popularity of hunter chases and points with owners highlighted in the essay on **Sleeping Night** who went on to win a handicap at the Grand National meeting after winning the Foxhunter at Cheltenham. The Festival also staged its first cross-country race, won by **Spot Thedifference** who had won

Leading conditional jockey Paddy Brennan made his mark and is a name for the future; Jim Culloty, who won three Gold Cups on Best Mate, took the sport by surprise when announcing his retirement from the saddle

the two events over the course earlier in the season. The mare **Registana**, twice winner of the Velka Pardubicka, the most famous cross-country race in the world, would have beaten Spot Thedifference at the Open meeting in November but for taking the wrong course before two out. Mares and fillies are generally up against it in National Hunt racing. Along with Solerina and United, **Like-A-Butterfly** proved a notable exception in Britain and Ireland in the latest season, winning the Powers Gold Cup at Fairyhouse and the Mildmay Novices' Chase at Aintree in a belated novice chasing campaign. Twenty-two years after the legendary Dawn Run gained important wins in her novice hurdling season at Aintree—where, incidentally, she ran on consecutive days—and Punchestown, the novice **Asian Maze** was sent out from the same yard to follow in her footsteps, winning championship events at Aintree (Dawn Run's win had come in a handicap) and Punchestown. Asian Maze also won the Grade 3 Mares Novices' Hurdle Championship Final at Fairyhouse, one of the few opportunities for mares to compete for a good prize against just their own sex, a subject discussed in the entry on **Senorita Rumbalita**, who took the inaugural running of a listed mares' bumper at the Grand National meeting. On the human female front, the review of **Forest Gunner** discusses the publicity surrounding Carrie Ford's participation in the Grand National and recalls some of the most successful and notable lady riders.

The most significant—and surprising—retirement from the ranks of the jockeys was that announced some time after the end of the latest season of Best Mate's regular rider Jim Culloty whose other career highlights included winning the Grand National on Bindaree and the King George VI Chase on Edredon Bleu (whose retirement was also confirmed). Culloty had felt dazed after some recent heavy falls and said he had to 'put my health before my career'. There are reminders every day of the dangers that jump jockeys face and it is sad to have to record the death of twenty-year-old conditional Tom Halliday, based with Sue Smith, who was killed in a fall at Market Rasen in the early part of the 2005/6 season. Halliday was the first jump jockey to die as a result of an accident on a British racecourse for nine years, since Richard Davis was killed in a fall at Southwell.

As is customary, the horses whose names are highlighted in bold in this introduction are among the hundred or so that are the subject of extended entries in this edition of *Chasers & Hurdlers*. The Timeform essays are written to inform and entertain and, in conjunction with the extensive photographic coverage of the season's big races and best horses, help to fulfil one of the original aims of the series to provide an accurate, authoritative and permanent record of the jumping year, this particular issue covering a vintage one which we hope will be brought vividly to life for those who pick up *Chasers & Hurdlers 2004/5* to browse in years to come. In the immediate future, the wealth of facts, analysis and informed opinion should prove of practical value in the new season. More than 9,250 jumpers are dealt with individually, including the pick of the Irish-trained performers not seen out in Britain in the latest season. *Chasers & Hurdlers 2004/05* covers comprehensively the British season, which ran from April 25th 2004 to April 23rd 2005, and in detail the Irish one which ran from May 2nd 2004 to April 30th 2005. For technical reasons the form figures at the start of the commentaries relate only to races taking place during the British season. The review of French jumping—Timeform 'Top Horses In France'—makes its second appearance, complementing the coverage of those French-trained horses which appear in the main body of the book. The coverage of racing over jumps in France is from July 2004 to June 2005.

September 2005

TIMEFORM CHAMPIONS OF 2004/05

CHAMPION JUMPER & BEST TWO-MILE CHASER – RATED AT 184+

MOSCOW FLYER

11 b.g. Moscow Society – Meelick Lady (Duky)

Owner Mr Brian Kearney   Trainer Mrs J. Harrington

BEST STAYING CHASER – RATED AT 182

KICKING KING

7 b.g. Old Vic – Fairy Blaze (Good Thyne)

Owner Mr Conor Clarkson   Trainer T. J. Taaffe

BEST TWO-MILE HURDLER — RATED AT 165

HARDY EUSTACE

8 b.g. Archway – Sterna Star (Corvaro)

Owner Mr Laurence Byrne   Trainer D. T. Hughes

BEST STAYING HURDLER — RATED AT 162

INGLIS DREVER

6 b.g. In The Wings – Cormorant Creek (Gorytus)

Owner Andrea & Graham Wylie   Trainer J. Howard Johnson

BEST NOVICE CHASERS — RATED AT 154+, 154p and 154

ASHLEY BROOK

7 ch.g. Magical Wonder – Seamill (Lafontaine)
Owner Mrs E. K. Ellis Trainer K. Bishop

FUNDAMENTALIST

7 b.g. Supreme Leader – Run For Shelter (Strong Gale)
Owner Gripen Trainer N. A. Twiston-Davies

OLLIE MAGERN

7 b.g. Alderbrook – Outfield (Monksfield)
Owner Mr Roger Nicholls Trainer N. A. Twiston-Davies

BEST PERFORMANCE IN A HUNTER CHASE – RATED AT 137*

SLEEPING NIGHT

9 b.g. Sleeping Car – Doll Night (Karkour)
Owner D. J. & F. A. Jackson Trainer P. F. Nicholls

BEST NOVICE HURDLER – RATED AT 149+

AMBOBO

5 b.g. Kingmambo – Bold Bold (Sadler's Wells)
Owner Mr S. Mulryan Trainer A Chaille-Chaille

BEST JUVENILE HURDLERS – RATED AT 144p

FAASEL

4 b.g. Unfuwain – Waqood (Riverman)
Owner Mr Jim Ennis Trainer N. G. Richards

PENZANCE

4 ch.g. Pennekamp – Kalinka (Soviet Star)
Owner Elite Racing Club Trainer A. King

BEST BUMPER PERFORMER – RATED AT 128

KARANJA

6 b.g. Karinga Bay – Proverbial Rose (Proverb)
Owner Mr D. G. Staddon Trainer V. R. A. Dartnall

* NB achieved a higher rating in a handicap

THE TIMEFORM 'TOP 100' CHASERS AND HURDLERS

Hurdlers

165 Hardy Eustace
164§ Harchibald
163 Brave Inca
163 Macs Joy
162 Inglis Drever
162 Rooster Booster
161 Back In Front
160 Accordion Etoile
160 Monet's Garden
159 Al Eile
159 Baracouda
159 Rule Supreme
158 Exotic Dancer
158 Intersky Falcon
158 Korelo
158 Patriarch Express
157§ Westender
157 Solerina
156 Crystal d'Ainay
155 It Takes Time
153 Royal Shakespeare
153 Self Defense
152+ Essex
152 Mistanoora
151 Mr Ed
149+ Ambobo
149 Big Moment
149 Emotional Moment
149 Perouse
148p Cyrlight
148p Mephisto
148 Monkerhostin
147p No Refuge
147 Blue Canyon
147 Brewster
147 Geos
147 Lough Derg
147 Rigmarole
146p Racing Demon
146+ Genghis
146 Moulin Riche
146 Royal Emperor
145 Claymore
144 Arcalis
144 Dancing Bay
144 Gold Medallist
144 Hawadeth
144 Idole First
144 King Revo
144 My Way de Solzen
144 Our Ben
144 Over The Creek
144 Pole Star
144 Rosaker
144 Royal Rosa
144 Sh Boom
144 Tamarinbleu
143 Albuhera
143 Commercial Flyer
143 Reveillez
143 The Bajan Bandit
143 Tumbling Dice
142p Asian Maze
142? Chivalry
142 Mister McGoldrick
141 Adamant Approach
141 Chief Yeoman
141 Power Elite
141 Supreme Prince
141 The French Furze
141 Turpin Green
140+ Quick
140 Carlys Quest
140 Georges Girl
140 Howle Hill
140 Telemoss
140 Trouble At Bay
140 Unleash
140 Yogi
139 Dalaram
139 Justified
139 Risk Accessor
138p Mighty Man
138 Batman Senora
138 Hirvine
138 Kadoun
138 Sixo
138 Turtle Soup
138 Wild Passion
138 Yes Sir
137+ Royal Paradise
137 Copeland
137 Dusky Warbler
137 Holland Park
137 Impek
137 Marcel
137 Silvertown
136p Knowhere
136+ Kauto Star
136 Almaydan
136 Distant Prospect
136 Florida Coast
136 Kasthari
136 Ladalko
136 Mansony
136 Roman Ark
136 Torrid Kentavr

Chasers

184+ Moscow Flyer
182 Azertyuiop
182 Kicking King
182 Well Chief
175 Kingscliff
171 Beef Or Salmon
168 Grey Abbey
167x Rule Supreme
165+ Best Mate
165 Harbour Pilot
164 Keen Leader
163x Take The Stand
162 Farmer Jack
162 Le Roi Miguel
161 Celestial Gold
161 Strong Flow
160 Thisthatandtother
159 First Gold
159 Oneway
158 Our Vic
158 Rathgar Beau
157+ Hedgehunter
157 Armaturk
157 Cenkos
157 Fondmort
157 Irish Hussar
157 Sir Rembrandt
156 Hand Inn Hand
156 Mister McGoldrick
156 Royal Auclair
155+ One Knight
155 Therealbandit
154p Fundamentalist
154+ Ashley Brook
154x Pizarro
154x Seebald
154 Chives
154 It Takes Time
154 Native Upmanship
154 Ollie Magern
153 Central House
153 Trabolgan
151p Fota Island
151 Calling Brave
151 Cloudy Bays
151 Kadarann
151 Native Scout
151 Strong Run
150p Cyrlight
150p Kauto Star
150p Lord Transcend
150x Lord Sam
150 Contraband
150 Ground Ball
149 Ballycassidy
149 Lacdoudal
149 Murphy's Cardinal
149 Ulaan Baatar
149 War of Attrition
148p Lord of Illusion
148+ Watson Lake

148x Horus
148 Comply Or Die
148 D'Argent
148 Forget The Past
148 Sleeping Night
147§ Upgrade
147 Brooklyn Breeze
147 Caracciola
146? Spot Thedifference
146x Truckers Tavern
146§ Stormez
146 Bindaree
146 Cornish Rebel
146 Hot Shots
146 Impek
146 Supreme Prince
145p Colonel Frank
145p Foreman
145 Baron Windrush
145 Joly Bey
145 L'Ami
145 Risk Accessor
145 River City
144x Redemption
144 Great Travel
144 Jazz d'Estruval
144 Joes Edge
144 Monkerhostin
143+ El Vaquero
143+ Patches
143 Iznogoud
143 Nil Desperandum
143 Palarshan
142+ Full Irish
142 Distant Thunder
142 Golden Alpha
142 Mouseski
142 Tikram
141§ Le Duc
141 Ad Hoc
141 Barrow Drive
141 Claymore
141 Colca Canyon
141 Kadount
141 Kelami
141 Knife Edge
141 Le Passing
141 Limerick Boy
141 Lord Noelie
141 Takagi

THE TIMEFORM TOP JUVENILES, NOVICES, HUNTER CHASERS AND NH FLAT HORSES

Juvenile Hurdlers
144p Faasel
144p Penzance
136 Akilak
136 Dabiroun
135p United
135 Cerium
134 Phar Bleu
133 Strangely Brown
130 Admiral
130 Diego Cao
129 Arch Rebel
129 Don't Be Shy
129 New Rock
129 Yankeedoodledandy
128 Miss Academy
128 Voy Por Ustedes
127 Bonbon Rose
126 Barati
126 Dont Call Me Derek
126 Sky's The Limit

Novice Hurdlers
149+ Ambobo
148p Cyrlight
148p Mephisto
147p No Refuge
147 Brewster
146p Racing Demon
146+ Genghis
146 Moulin Riche
144 Arcalis
144 Gold Medallist
144 My Way de Solzen
144 Our Ben
144 Over The Creek
144 Pole Star
143 Commercial Flyer
143 Reveillez
142p Asian Maze
141 Turpin Green
140 Carlys Quest
139 Justified

Novice Chasers
154p Fundamentalist
154+ Ashley Brook
154 Ollie Magern
153 Trabolgan
151p Fota Island
150p Kauto Star
150 Contraband
149 Lacdoudal
149 Ulaan Baatar
149 War of Attrition
148p Lord of Illusion
148+ Watson Lake
148 Comply Or Die
148 Forget The Past
146 Cornish Rebel
145p Foreman
145 Baron Windrush
145 L'Ami
145 River City
144 Jazz d'Estruval
144 Joes Edge

National Hunt Flat Horses
128 Karanja
123 Missed That
123 Travino
122 De Soto
122 Rasharrow
122 The Mick Weston
121 Be Be King
121 Refinement
120 Oscar Park
118 Clew Bay Cove
118 Dawadari
118 Lennon
118 Manners
117p Firth of Forth
117 There Is No Doubt
116 Buena Vista
116 The Cool Guy
115 Itsmyboy
115 Sweet Kiln
114 Earth Man
114 Mister Top Notch
114 Some Touch

Hunter Chasers
148 Sleeping Night*
142 Mouseski*
136 Foly Pleasant
132 Venn Ottery*
131 Katarino
128 Bright Approach
128 Placid Man
126 Mister Friday
123 Caught At Dawn
121+ Lord Atterbury
121§ Montifault
120 Torduff Express
119p Industrious
118x General Montcalm
118x Gun N'Roses II
118 Cantarinho
118 Sikander A Azam
117x Silence Reigns
117 Earthmover
117 Monty's Quest
117 Right To Reply

*NB * indicates best performance achieved in a race other than a hunter chase*

2004/05 STATISTICS

The following tables show the leading owners, trainers, jockeys, sires of winners and horses over jumps in Britain during 2004/05. The prize-money statistics, compiled by *Timeform*, relate to win-money and to first-three prize money. Win money has traditionally been used to decide the trainers' championship, though since 1994 the BHB and the National Trainers' Federation have recognised championships decided by total prize money as determined by the *Racing Post*. The jockeys' championship has traditionally been decided by the number of winners.

OWNERS (1,2,3 earnings)	*Horses*	*Indiv'l Wnrs*	*Races Won*	*Runs*	*%*	*Stakes £*
1 Mr D A Johnson	82	46	111	465	23.8	1,677,153
2 Mr Trevor Hemmings	48	25	38	189	20.1	975,259
3 Mr John P McManus	108	41	58	325	17.8	751,195
4 Andrea & Graham Wylie	39	21	36	123	29.2	716,870
5 Mrs J Stewart	14	11	18	80	22.5	379,890
6 Mr Conor Clarkson	1	1	2	2	100.0	328,268
7 Mr Brian Kearney	1	1	3	3	100.0	306,750
8 Mr Clive D Smith	5	4	4	21	19.0	267,316
9 Mr C G Roach	6	3	5	20	25.0	249,345
10 Mr J Hales	12	6	9	37	24.3	238,784

OWNERS (by win-money)	*Horses*	*Indiv'l Wnrs*	*Races Won*	*Runs*	*%*	*Stakes £*
1 Mr D A Johnson	82	46	111	465	23.8	1,280,242
2 Mr Trevor Hemmings	48	25	38	189	20.1	777,302
3 Andrea & Graham Wylie	39	21	36	123	29.2	579,253
4 Mr John P McManus	108	41	58	325	17.8	564,740
5 Mr Conor Clarkson	1	1	2	2	100.0	328,268
6 Mr Brian Kearney	1	1	3	3	100.0	306,750
7 Mrs J Stewart	14	11	18	80	22.5	244,698
8 Mr Laurence Byrne	2	1	1	2	50.0	174,000
9 Mrs Karola Vann	7	5	10	38	26.3	151,358
10 Elite Racing Club	12	7	13	49	26.5	147,941

TRAINERS (1,2,3 earnings)	*Horses*	*Indiv'l Wnrs*	*Races Won*	*Runs*	*%*	*Stakes £*
1 M C Pipe	230	101	193	1168	16.5	2,613,666
2 P F Nicholls	158	88	153	709	21.5	2,557,665
3 P J Hobbs	140	76	121	616	19.6	1,448,363
4 J Howard Johnson	98	38	68	316	21.5	1,188,521
5 Jonjo O'Neill	156	68	96	521	18.4	839,242
6 Miss Venetia Williams	122	46	80	529	15.1	818,672
7 N A Twiston-Davies	96	42	69	384	17.9	753,978
8 A King	98	38	66	362	18.2	738,940
9 N J Henderson	120	43	53	362	14.6	695,642
10 Mrs S J Smith	98	34	60	464	12.9	660,896
11 N G Richards	70	33	50	230	21.7	600,075
12 P Bowen	45	19	40	202	19.8	586,247

TRAINERS (by win-money)	*Horses*	*Indiv'l Wnrs*	*Races Won*	*Runs*	*%*	*Stakes £*
1 M C Pipe	230	101	193	1168	16.5	1,798,032
2 P F Nicholls	158	88	153	709	21.5	1,627,991
3 P J Hobbs	140	76	121	616	19.6	1,032,181
4 J Howard Johnson	98	38	68	316	21.5	999,386
5 N A Twiston-Davies	96	42	69	384	17.9	555,258
6 Miss Venetia Williams	122	46	80	529	15.1	551,525
7 Jonjo O'Neill	156	68	96	521	18.4	515,022

TRAINERS (with 100+ winners)	*Horses*	*Indiv'l Wnrs*	*Races Won*	*2nd*	*3rd*	*Runs*	*%*
M C Pipe	230	101	193	134	100	1168	16.5
P F Nicholls	158	88	153	104	92	709	21.5
P J Hobbs	140	76	121	95	77	616	19.6

JOCKEYS (by winners)	*1st*	*2nd*	*3rd*	*Unpl*	*Total Mts*	*%*
1 A P McCoy	200	144	92	385	821	24.3
2 T J Murphy	143	90	73	387	693	20.6
3 R Johnson	135	111	100	468	814	16.5
4 A Dobbin	115	82	66	333	596	19.2
5 G Lee	100	87	71	312	570	17.5
6 R Thornton	97	85	70	384	636	15.2
7 R Walsh	81	57	45	128	311	26.0
8 C Llewellyn	72	54	48	356	530	13.5
9 P J Brennan	67	59	56	335	517	12.9
10 M A Fitzgerald	65	63	59	338	525	12.3
11 Christian Williams	59	59	50	288	456	12.9
12 J Tizzard	58	58	67	342	525	11.0

JOCKEYS (1,2,3 earnings)	*Races Won*	*Rides*	*%*	*Stakes £*
1 T J Murphy	143	693	20.6	2,068,120
2 R Walsh	81	311	26.0	2,064,047
3 A P McCoy	200	821	24.3	1,993,178
4 G Lee	100	570	17.5	1,409,040
5 R Johnson	135	814	16.5	1,309,455
6 A Dobbin	115	596	19.2	1,164,141
7 R Thornton	97	636	15.2	1,119,581
8 B J Geraghty	10	71	14.0	854,755
9 M A Fitzgerald	65	525	12.3	767,403
10 C Llewellyn	72	530	13.5	760,615
11 Christian Williams	59	456	12.9	735,109
12 A Thornton	54	522	10.3	698,568

JOCKEYS (by win-money)	*Races Won*	*Rides*	*%*	*Stakes £*
1 T J Murphy	143	693	20.6	1,586,174
2 R Walsh	81	311	26.0	1,469,434
3 A P McCoy	200	821	24.3	1,445,621
4 G Lee	100	570	17.5	1,068,868
5 R Johnson	135	814	16.5	945,206
6 A Dobbin	115	596	19.2	803,624
7 B J Geraghty	10	71	14.0	756,283
8 R Thornton	97	636	15.2	755,828

CONDITIONAL JOCKEYS	*1st*	*2nd*	*3rd*	*Unpl*	*Total Mts*	*%*
1 P J Brennan	67	59	56	335	517	12.9
2 S Thomas	55	51	60	269	435	12.6
3 K Mercer	40	24	39	202	305	13.1

AMATEUR RIDERS	*1st*	*2nd*	*3rd*	*Unpl*	*Total Mts*	*%*
1 Mr T Greenall	31	33	24	131	219	14.1
2 Mr N Williams	16	6	11	47	80	20.0
3 Mr D Jacob	8	3	6	22	39	20.5

SIRES OF WINNERS (1,2,3 earnings)	*Races Won*	*Runs*	*%*	*Stakes £*
1 Roselier (by Misti IV)	98	629	15.5	1,000,840
2 Supreme Leader (by Bustino)	86	517	16.6	939,963
3 Montelimar (by Alleged)	23	198	11.6	725,693
4 Old Vic (by Sadler's Wells)	37	207	17.8	606,236
5 Sadler's Wells (by Northern Dancer)	44	320	13.7	484,831
6 Lord Americo (by Lord Gayle)	44	414	10.6	459,593
7 Moscow Society (by Nijinsky)	23	130	17.6	430,588
8 Alderbrook (by Ardross)	25	197	12.6	429,125
9 Un Desperado (by Top Ville)	31	211	14.6	416,494
10 In The Wings (by Sadler's Wells)	15	93	16.1	399,428
11 Alflora (by Niniski)	34	338	10.0	376,831
12 Bob Back (by Roberto)	24	172	13.9	358,530
13 Garde Royale (by Mill Reef)	7	70	10.0	344,167
14 King's Ride (by Rarity)	25	188	13.2	314,988
15 Phardante (by Pharly)	32	295	10.8	314,985

SIRES OF WINNERS (by win-money)	*Horses*	*Indiv'l Wnrs*	*Races Won*	*Stakes £*
1 Supreme Leader (by Bustino)	151	54	86	704,848
2 Roselier (by Misti IV)	159	57	98	683,915
3 Montelimar (by Alleged)	56	16	23	636,203
4 Old Vic (by Sadler's Wells)	57	25	37	503,864
5 Moscow Society (by Nijinsky)	36	12	23	394,740
6 Sadler's Wells (by Northern Dancer)	67	26	44	382,619

LEADING HORSES (1,2,3 earnings)	*Races Won*	*Runs*	*Stakes £*
1 Hedgehunter 9 b.g Montelimar–Aberedw	1	1	406,000
2 Kicking King 7 b.g Old Vic–Fairy Blaze	2	2	328,268
3 Moscow Flyer 11 b.g Moscow Society–Meelick Lady	3	3	306,750
4 Inglis Drever 6 b.g In The Wings–Cormorant Creek	3	6	242,900
5 Royal Auclair 8 ch.g Garde Royale–Carmonera	1	8	238,900
6 Well Chief 6 ch.g. Night Shift–Wellesiena	2	7	210,350
7 Grey Abbey 11 gr.g Nestor–Tacovaon	3	4	183,750
8 Take The Stand 9 b.g Witness Box–Denys Daughter	2	11	176,408
9 Hardy Eustace 8 b.g Archway–Sterna Star	1	1	174,000
10 Azertyuiop 8 b.g Baby Turk–Temara	2	6	171,500

EXPLANATORY NOTES

'Chasers & Hurdlers 2004/05' deals individually, in alphabetical sequence, with every horse that ran over the sticks or in National Hunt Flat races in Britain during the 2004/5 season, plus a number of foreign-trained horses that did not race here. For each of these horses is given (1) its age, colour and sex, (2) its breeding and, where this information has not been given in a previous Chasers & Hurdlers or Racehorses Annual, a family outline (3) a form summary giving its Timeform rating—or ratings—at the end of the previous season, followed by the details of all its performances during the past season, (4) a Timeform rating—or ratings—of its merit (which appears in the margin), (5) a Timeform commentary on its racing or general characteristics as a racehorse, with some suggestions, perhaps, regarding its prospects for 2005/6 and (6) the name of the trainer in whose charge it was on the last occasion it ran.

The book is published with a twofold purpose. Firstly, it is intended to have permanent value as a review of the exploits and achievements of the more notable of our chasers and hurdlers in the 2004/5 season. Thus, while the commentaries upon the vast majority of the horses are, of necessity, in note form, the best horses are more critically examined. The text is illustrated by half-tone portraits of the most notable horses (where these are available) and photographs of the major races. Secondly, the book is designed to help the punter to analyse races, and the notes which follow contain instructions for using the data.

TIMEFORM RATINGS

The Timeform Rating of a horse is simply the merit of the horse expressed in pounds and is arrived at by careful examination of its running against other horses using a scale of weight for distance beaten. Timeform maintains a 'running' handicap of all horses in training throughout the season.

THE LEVEL OF THE RATINGS

At the close of each season the ratings of all the horses that have raced are re-examined, and, if necessary, the general level of the handicap is adjusted so that all the ratings are kept at the same standard level from year to year. Some of the ratings may, therefore, be different from those in the final issue of the 2004/5 Timeform Chasing Black Book series.

RATINGS AND WEIGHT-FOR-AGE

The reader has, in the ratings in this book, a universal handicap embracing all the horses in training it is possible to weigh up, ranging from tip-top performers, with ratings from 170 upwards, down to the meanest platers, rated around the 60 mark. All the ratings are at weight-for-age, so that equal ratings mean horses of equal merit. In using Timeform to assess the prospects of various runners, allowance should be made for any difference specified by the Age, Weight and Distance Table at the front.

Steeplechase ratings, preceded by c, should not be confused with hurdle ratings, preceded by h. Where a horse has raced over fences and also over hurdles its ratings as a chaser and hurdler are printed one above the other, the steeplechase rating (c) being placed above the hurdle rating (h).

Thus with REGALITY c157
h143

the top figure, 157, is the rating to be used in steeplechases, and the one below, 143, is for use only in hurdle races. Where a horse has a rating based on its performance in a National Hunt Flat race (usually referred to in the text as a bumper) it is preceded by 'F'. The procedure for making age and weight adjustments to the ratings (i.e. for the calculation of Race Ratings) is as follows:

A. Horses of the Same Age

If the horses all carry the same weight there are no adjustments to be made, and the horses with the highest ratings have the best chances. If the horses carry different weights, jot down their ratings, and to the rating of each horse add one point for every pound the horse is set to carry less than 12st 7lb, or subtract one point for every pound it has to carry more than 12st 7lb. When the ratings have been adjusted in this way the highest resultant figure indicates the horse with the best chance at the weights.

Example (any distance: any month of the season)

Teucer	5 yrs (11-0) ..	Rating 140 ..	add 21	161
Kiowa	5 yrs (10-7) ..	Rating 125 ..	add 28	153
Golden Age	5 yrs (10-4) ..	Rating 120 ..	add 31	151

Teucer has the best chance, and Golden Age the worst

B. Horses of Different Ages

In this case, reference must be made to the Age, Weight and Distance Table at the front. Use the Table for steeplechasers and hurdlers alike. Treat each horse separately, and compare the weight it has to carry with the weight prescribed for it in the table, according to the age of the horse, the distance of the race and the month of the year. Then, add one point to the rating for each pound the horse has to carry less than the weight given in the table: or, subtract one point from the rating for every pound it has to carry more than the weight prescribed by the table. The highest resultant figure indicates the horse most favoured by the weights.

Example (2¾m steeplechase in January)

(Table Weights: 8-y-o 12-7; 7-y-o 12-7; 5-y-o 12-6)

Black Book	8 yrs (12-8) ..	Rating 140 ..	subtract 1 ..	139
Pressman	7 yrs (12-3) ..	Rating 132 ..	add 4	136
Copyright	5 yrs (12-7) ..	Rating 150 ..	subtract 1 ..	149

Copyright has the best chance, and Pressman the worst

Example (3m hurdle race in March)

(Table Weights: 9-y-o 12-7; 5-y-o 12-7; 4-y-o 11-11)

Oxer	9 yrs (10-12) ..	Rating 110 ..	add 23 ..	133
Clairval	5 yrs (10-7) ..	Rating 119 ..	add 28	147
Gallette	4 yrs (10-7) ..	Rating 128 ..	add 18 ..	146

Clairval has the best chance, and Oxer the worst

C. Horses in National Hunt Flat races

The procedure for calculating Race Ratings in National Hunt Flat races is precisely the same as in (A) or (B).

Example (2m N.H. Flat in February)

(Table Weights: 6-y-o 12-7; 5-y-o 12-7; 4-y-o 12-1)

Squall	6 yrs (10-12) ..	Rating 88 ..	add 23	111
Lupin	5 yrs (11-3) ..	Rating 97 ..	add 18	115
Chariot	4 yrs (10-9) ..	Rating 84 ..	add 20	104

Lupin has the best chance, and Chariot the worst

The National Hunt Flat ratings are on a scale comparable with that used for hurdlers and chasers. The ratings can therefore be used not only within the context of National Hunt Flat races themselves, but also as an indication of the potential form of such horses in their first few starts over jumps.

JOCKEYSHIP AND RIDERS' ALLOWANCES

For the purposes of rating calculations it should, in general, be assumed that the allowance the rider is able to claim (3 lb, 5 lb, or 7 lb) is nullified by his or her inexperience. Therefore, the *weight adjustments to the ratings should be calculated on the weight allotted by the handicapper, or determined by the conditions of the race,* and no extra addition should be made to a rating because the horse's rider claims an allowance. This is the general routine procedure; but, of course, after the usual adjustments have been made the quality of jockeyship is still an important factor to be considered when deciding between horses with similar chances.

WEIGHING UP A RACE

The ratings tell which horses in a particular race are most favoured by the weights; but complete analysis demands that the racing character of each horse is also studied carefully to see if there is any reason why the horse might be expected not to run up to its rating. It counts for little that a horse is thrown in at the weights if it has no pretensions whatever to staying the distance, or is unable to act on the prevailing going. Suitability of distance and going are no doubt the most important points to be considered, but there are others. For example, the ability of a horse to accommodate itself to the conformation of the track. There is also the matter of a horse's ability and dependability as a jumper and of its temperament: nobody would be in a hurry to take a short price about a horse with whom it is always an even chance whether it will get round or not, or whether it will consent to race.

A few minutes spent checking up on these matters in the commentaries upon the horses concerned will sometimes put a very different complexion on a race from that which is put upon it by the ratings alone. We repeat, therefore, that the correct way to use Timeform, or this annual volume, in the analysis of individual races is, first to use the ratings to discover which horses are most favoured by the weights, and second, to check through the comments on the horse to see what factors other than weight might also affect the outcome of the race.

THE FORM SUMMARIES

The form summaries enclosed in the brackets list each horse's performances in the last season in sequence, showing, for each race, its distance in furlongs, the state of the going and the horse's placing at the finish. Steeplechase form figures are prefixed by the letter 'c' and N.H. Flat race (bumper) form figures by the letter 'F', the others relating to form over hurdles.

The going is symbolised as follows: f–firm, m–good to firm, g–good, d–good to soft/dead, s–soft, v–heavy.

Placings are indicated up to sixth place, by superior figures, an asterisk denoting a win; and superior letters are used to convey what happened to the horse during the race: F–fell (F^3 denotes remounted and finished third); pu–pulled up; ur–unseated rider; bd–brought down; R–refused; rtr–refused to race; su–slipped up; ro–ran out; co–carried out; wd–withdrawn; dis–disqualified.

Thus, [2004/5 h82, F80: 16g 16s* c18g^{pu} 16f^2 c20v^F Apr 10] states that the horse was rated 82 over hurdles and 80 in bumpers at the end of the previous season. In the 2004/5 jumping season the horse ran five times; unplaced in a 2m hurdle race on good going, winning a 2m hurdle race on soft going, being pulled up in a 2¼m steeplechase on good going, running second in a 2m hurdle race on firm going and falling in a 2½m steeplechase on heavy going. Its last race was on April 10th.

Where sale prices are given they are in guineas unless otherwise stated. The prefix IR denotes Irish guineas, IR £ denotes Irish punts, $ refers to American dollars, francs refers to French francs and € indicates the euro. Any other currencies are converted into pounds sterling at the prevailing exchange rate.

THE RATING SYMBOLS

The following symbols, attached to the ratings, are to be interpreted as stated:-

p	likely to improve.
P	capable of *much* better form.
+	the horse may be better than we have rated it.
d	the horse appears to have deteriorated, and might no longer be capable of running to the rating given.
§	unreliable (for temperamental or other reasons).
§§	so temperamentally unsatisfactory as to be not worth a rating.
x	poor jumper.
xx	a very bad jumper, so bad as to be not worth a rating.
?	the horse's rating is suspect or, used without a rating, the horse can't be assessed with confidence or, if used in the in-season Timeform publications, that the horse is out of form.

CHASERS & HURDLERS 2004/05

Horse	*Commentary*	*Rating*

ABA GOLD (IRE) 5 b.m. Darnay – Abadila (IRE) (Shernazar) [2004/5 F16g Feb 27] fifth foal: half-sister to Irish bumper winner Abadair (by Forest Wind): dam twice-raced half-sister to smart French hurdler Chinese Gordon and one-time useful 2m chaser Abalvino: well held in bumper on debut. *Mrs L. B. Normile* — **F–**

ABALVINO (FR) 11 ch.g. Sillery (USA) – Abalvina (FR) (Abdos) [2004/5 c119, h–: c16d^4 c16d^4 c17s^3 c19v^2 c19v^{pu} c16s^4 Mar 5] quite good-topped gelding: useful handicap chaser at one time, on the downgrade: stays 19f: acts on heavy going: tried in cheek-pieces: tongue tied: front runner: unreliable. *P. R. Webber* — **c111 § h–**

ABBEYKNOCK BOY (IRE) 8 b. or br.g. Alphabatim (USA) – Haha Dash (IRE) (Lord Ha Ha) [2004/5 c–, h–: c21d^{pu} Feb 18] winning pointer: poor maiden hurdler/chaser: stays 3m: acts on good to soft going: tried visored/tongue tied: none too genuine. *B. J. Clarke* — **c– h–**

ABBEY PRINCESS 5 b.m. Prince Daniel (USA) – Riverain (Bustino) [2004/5 F16s F16v 19d 17s 21v^4 Mar 28] small mare: fourth foal: half-sister to prolific Italian sprinter Matthias (by Superpower): dam, won 2m hurdle, also 2-y-o 7f winner, from family of Champion Four Year Old Hurdle winner Shaunies Lady: sign of ability only in bumper on debut. *J. Howard Johnson* — **h– F74**

ABERDARE 6 b.m. Overbury (IRE) – Temple Heights (Shirley Heights) [2004/5 F80: 22v^{pu} 22s* 20d^3 20s^{ro} 20v^3 23v^4 22s^4 24s* Apr 20] small, angular mare: fair novice hurdler: won at Ayr in November and Perth in April: will stay beyond 3m: raced on good going or softer (acts on heavy). *J. R. Bewley* — **h100**

ABER GALE 6 gr.m. Thethingaboutitis (USA) – Twablade (IRE) (Strong Gale) [2004/5 F17s F16s^6 20m^F Apr 10] rather unfurnished mare: first foal: dam of little account over hurdles: well held in 2 bumpers: fell second hurdling debut. *Mrs S. M. Johnson* — **h– F–**

ABIGAIL 5 gr.m. Simply Great (FR) – Stormy Gal (IRE) (Strong Gale) [2004/5 F–: F16s F16d 19g Dec 16] small mare: well held in bumpers and novice hurdle. *T. D. Easterby* — **h– F–**

ABILITY 6 b.g. Alflora (IRE) – Beatle Song (Song) [2004/5 h–: 16g 17g^6 16g Jun 10] no form over hurdles: tried tongue tied. *S. C. Burrough* — **h–**

A BIT OF FUN 4 ch.g. Unfuwain (USA) – Horseshoe Reef (Mill Reef (USA)) [2004/5 17g^3 16s^5 16g* 16d^3 16g^2 16g^2 16m^5 Apr 17] medium-sized gelding: poor on Flat (stays 9.4f): fair hurdler: won seller at Doncaster in December: sold out of J. Quinn's stable 10,000 gns Doncaster March Sales after sixth outing: raced around 2m: acts on good to soft and good to firm going. *J. T. Stimpson* — **h103**

ABRAGANTE (IRE) 4 b.g. Saddlers' Hall (IRE) – Joli's Girl (Mansingh (USA)) [2004/5 F16s* Mar 22] €56,000 3-y-o: good-topped gelding: half-brother to useful performer up to 1m Joli's Princess (by Prince Sabo) and bad 2m hurdler/1¾m winner Side Bar (by Mummy's Game): dam, winner up to 2¾m over hurdles/9f winner on Flat, half-sister to good 2m hurdler Osric and useful hurdler around 2½m Forager: won 21-runner bumper at Wetherby on debut by ½ length from Autograph: sold to join M. Pipe £90,000 Cheltenham April Sales. *R. D. E. Woodhouse* — **F98**

ABRAHAM SMITH 5 b.g. Lord Americo – Alice Smith (Alias Smith (USA)) [2004/5 F–: F17g 16v 17s^4 16d^5 21d^4 24s^5 Apr 16] well held in 2 bumpers: modest maiden hurdler: should stay 3m: acts on soft ground: sold 20,000 gns Doncaster May Sales. *B. J. Eckley* — **h94 F–**

ABROGATE (IRE) 4 b.g. Revoque (IRE) – Czarina's Sister (Soviet Lad (USA)) [2004/5 16g 17m^6 Aug 6] modest maiden on Flat (stays 1m): well held in juvenile hurdles. *P. C. Haslam* — **h–**

ABSOLUT POWER (GER) 4 ch.g. Acatenango (GER) – All Our Dreams (Caerleon (USA)) [2004/5 16g^2 16s^3 20d^5 Feb 26] ex-German gelding: useful on Flat (stays 1½m), successful at Milan and Baden-Baden in 2004: left A. Wohler after last of 7 in German St Leger: fair form over hurdles: stays 2½m: joined J. Geake. *C. R. Egerton* — **h101**

ABZUSON 8 b.g. Abzu – Mellouise (Handsome Sailor) [2004/5 h96: 20s 20d 24d 24d^2 24v* 24v^2 24s^3 24s 24s^R Apr 10] big gelding: fair hurdler: won novice at Towcester in January: tired in third when refused last final start: stays 3m: acts on heavy going. *J. R. Norton* **h105**

ACACIA AVENUE (IRE) 5 b.g. Shardari – Ennel Lady (IRE) (Erin's Hope) [2004/5 F16s^5 F17d Mar 26] good-topped gelding: third foal: dam unraced half-sister to very smart 2m to 3m chaser Opera Hat: won 4-y-o maiden Irish point in October: best effort in bumpers (ran twice for F. Flood in 2003/4) when fifth of 15 at Sandown on reappearance. *Ian Williams* **F92**

ACCELERATION (IRE) 5 b.g. Groom Dancer (USA) – Overdrive (Shirley Heights) [2004/5 h80§: 16m 16m 16d^{pu} 22s^F 20m^5 20s^4 20d^5 16v^6 16d^4 17s^6 20s Apr 22] tall gelding: poor maiden hurdler: stays 2½m: acts on soft and good to firm going: sometimes wears headgear: ungenuine. *R. Allan* **h80 §**

ACCEPTING 8 b.g. Mtoto – D'Azy (Persian Bold) [2004/5 h99: 26g^{pu} 24m^5 23d* 26d^2 27d^4 25g^3 24d 26s Feb 10] compact gelding: unreliable on Flat: fair handicap hurdler: won at Haydock in November: stays 27f: acts on good to firm and good to soft going: has worn cheekpieces, blinkered nowadays. *J. Mackie* **h104**

ACCESS OVERSEAS 8 b.m. Access Ski – Access Advantage (Infantry) [2004/5 h68: 16g c16s^{pu} 16m 16m^4 16g 19g^4 17m^5 16v^{pu} Nov 25] rather sparely-made mare: poor hurdler: no show on chasing debut: stays easy 2¾m: acts on firm and good to soft going. *J. D. Frost* **c–** **h65**

ACCORDELLO (IRE) 4 b.f. Accordion – Marello (Supreme Leader) [2004/5 F12g^2 F16s^2 F16g^5 F17s^2 Apr 7] neat filly: first foal: dam high-class hurdler up to 25f: useful form in bumpers: best effort when ½-length second to Senorita Rumbalita, pair clear, in listed mares event at Aintree final start, leading 3f out and staying on well as winner idled. *K. G. Reveley* **F109**

ACCORDING TO BILLY (IRE) 6 b.g. Accordion – Graphic Lady (IRE) (Phardante (FR)) [2004/5 F100: F16m^4 16s* Dec 5] fairly useful form in bumpers: won 20-runner maiden at Punchestown on hurdling debut by 1½ lengths from Johnston's Swallow: will stay beyond 2m: likely to improve. *E. J. O'Grady, Ireland* **h112 p** **F100**

ACCORDING TO PETE 4 b.g. Accordion – Magic Bloom (Full of Hope) [2004/5 F17g^3 Mar 19] second foal: dam, fair chaser, stayed 25f: 7 lengths third to Rimsky in bumper at Bangor on debut. *J. M. Jefferson* **F90**

ACCORDION ETOILE (IRE) 6 b.g. Accordion – Royal Thimble (IRE) (Prince Rupert (FR)) [2004/5 h122, F89: 16m* 16g* 16s^2 16d* 16v^5 16g^4 20d^6 Apr 9] **h160**

Trainer Paul Nolan, who has held a licence since 1995, is now well established in his native Ireland and finished sixth in the trainers' championship there in 2004/5. He was only twenty-six when he started training, though he had already

Betdaq.com Hurdle, Tipperary—
Accordion Etoile and John Cullen are not extended to land this valuable summer prize

Greatwood Handicap Hurdle, Cheltenham—the Irish raider enters the Champion Hurdle picture with victory over Westender (blinkers), Perouse (No.6) and Rooster Booster (grey)

had one sporting career before that, having played hurling to quite a high standard and helped Wexford win the junior all-Ireland Final in 1992. In the latest season Nolan's name also became more familiar in Britain thanks to Accordion Etoile and Dabiroun. The pair won valuable handicap hurdles at Cheltenham, Dabiroun at the Festival meeting where Accordion Etoile finished fourth in the Champion Hurdle. Nolan might have had even more to cheer about at the Festival if a minor injury had not kept his promising Cloone River out of the Arkle Challenge Trophy. Cloone River had landed a gamble in the Galway Hurdle in July and looked destined for much better things over fences after successes on his first two starts in chases.

A far more serious setback had threatened to end Accordion Etoile's career midway through the 2003/4 season, by which time he had won a bumper at Clonmel, a maiden hurdle at Roscommon and a Grade 3 novice hurdle at Navan. Thankfully, the operation to remove a malignant growth on a fetlock joint proved successful, so much so that Accordion Etoile was off the course only six months and returned to complete a full season, one in which he made remarkable progress. The winner of minor events at Punchestown and Tipperary on his first two outings in 2004/5, Accordion Etoile then finished a good second to Solerina in the Grade 1 McManus Memorial at Tipperary before making the first of what turned out to be three appearances in Britain, in the Greatwood Handicap Hurdle at Cheltenham in November. The Greatwood, promoted to Grade 3 for the first time, attracted a slightly smaller field than usual but it was still a cracking renewal, Accordion Etoile's eight rivals including the three previous winners of the race, Westender, Rooster Booster and Rigmarole. Accordion Etoile, set to receive weight from all three, looked to have been let in lightly off a BHB mark of 149 and, sent off favourite, didn't need to improve to capture the £40,600 first prize. There was a lot to like about the manner of his victory too. Held up in a race which didn't begin in earnest until three out and seemed to favour those who raced prominently, Accordion Etoile made headway two out, travelling very strongly, led and quickened turning into the straight and ran on well to win by three lengths from the pacesetter Westender, looking to have something to spare.

There was an overreaction to Accordion Etoile's performance in some quarters and he was as low as 6/1 in the ante-post betting on the Champion Hurdle. He started at 14/1 in March, having finished well held in the meantime in the AIG Europe Champion Hurdle at Leopardstown, where the ground was heavy. The far less testing conditions which prevailed at the Cheltenham Festival suited Accordion Etoile much better, and he showed high-class form in fourth behind Hardy

Eustace, Harchibald and Brave Inca, looking a big danger two out after travelling very strongly once again under a patient ride, but appearing awkward when coming under pressure in the straight and unable to quicken. Accordion Etoile had been raced only at two miles since winning over two and a half on his hurdling debut and wasn't suited by the return to the latter trip on his only appearance after the Champion Hurdle, in the Aintree Hurdle, managing only sixth to Al Eile having pulled hard in a falsely-run race.

Accordion Etoile (IRE) (b.g. 1999)	Accordion (b 1986)	Sadler's Wells (b 1981)	Northern Dancer
			Fairy Bridge
		Sound of Success (ch 1969)	Successor
			Belle Musique
	Royal Thimble (IRE) (b 1991)	Prince Rupert (b 1984)	Prince Tenderfoot
			Carrozzella
		Tootsie Roll (b 1983)	Comedy Star
			Just Kidding

Accordion Etoile is the second foal of Royal Thimble and her only winner to date, although her third foal French Accordion, a brother to Accordion Etoile and also a stable companion, has shown enough over hurdles to suggest that it should not be too long before he opens his account. Royal Thimble was a fair performer who won five races, including over an extended seven furlongs and a mile and a quarter on the Flat. Raced only at around two miles on good ground or firmer over hurdles, Royal Thimble was successful in a novice event at Plumpton and handicaps at Worcester and Hereford. Accordion Etoile's grandam Tootsie Roll, a lightly-raced maiden, is out of Just Kidding, a very smart stakes winner at up to a mile in the United States. The strong, lengthy Accordion Etoile usually impresses in appearance and was clearly the pick of the paddock before the Champion Hurdle.

Banjo Syndicate's "Accordion Etoile"

He is certainly very much a chasing type, and if he turns up at the next Cheltenham Festival it may well be as a leading contender for the Arkle. While he does have form on very soft ground, Accordion Etoile is better under less testing conditions and acts on good to firm. *Paul Nolan, Ireland*

ACE COMING 4 b.g. First Trump – Tarry (Salse (USA)) [2004/5 17s³ 16s 16s Mar 6] medium-sized gelding: fair on Flat (stays 9f), successful twice in 2004, sold out of D. Eddy's stable 12,000 gns Doncaster November Sales: no form over hurdles: blinkered final start. *D. B. Feek* **h–**

ACERTACK (IRE) 8 b.g. Supreme Leader – Ask The Madam (Strong Gale) [2004/5 c80, h–: c17d⁶ c17g* c17d² c18g⁵ c20d² c17sᵘʳ c17v² c17v* c21s⁴ c22gᵘʳ c20d³ Apr 18] lengthy gelding: modest chaser: won novice handicaps at Plumpton in October and January: may prove best up to 2½m: raced on good going or softer (acts on heavy): tends to make odd mistake. *R. Rowe* **c93 h–**

ACES FOUR (IRE) 6 ch.g. Fourstars Allstar (USA) – Special Trix (IRE) (Peacock (FR)) [2004/5 F96: F16s Nov 4] medium-sized gelding: fairly useful at best in bumpers, tailed off only outing in 2004/5: tends to hang left. *W. McKeown* **F–**

ACHILLES WINGS (USA) 9 b.g. Irish River (FR) – Shirley Valentine (Shirley Heights) [2004/5 h109: c19s 19s⁴ 19d⁶ 20s 19d³ 19g² Apr 12] leggy gelding: fair handicap hurdler: well held on chasing debut: stays easy 2¾m: acts on soft going: wears cheekpieces over hurdles nowadays. *Miss K. M. George* **c– h100**

ACQUIRED (IRE) 7 b. or br.m. Presenting – The Scarlet Dragon (Oats) [2004/5 F75: 21g May 8] modest form in mares bumpers in 2003/4: soundly beaten on hurdling debut: sold 1,700 gns Doncaster August Sales. *Mrs H. Dalton* **h–**

ACQUISITOR (FR) 5 b.g. Cadoudal (FR) – La Domengere (FR) (Dom Pasquini (FR)) [2004/5 16s 17g 20v 24g Feb 27] lengthy gelding: fourth foal: dam unraced half-sister to smart chaser Artic Jack (by Cadoudal), stays 3½m: no form over hurdles, jumping with little fluency. *M. Todhunter* **h–**

ACROSS THE WATER 11 b.m. Slip Anchor – Stara (Star Appeal) [2004/5 c–, h–: 16d 17s Nov 30] leggy mare: winning pointer: no form in hunter chases or over hurdles. *G. H. Jones* **c– h–**

ACT IN TIME (IRE) 13 b.g. Actinium (FR) – Anvil Chorus (Levanter) [2004/5 c107d, h90: c26d² c20g Feb 17] good-topped gelding: twice-raced hurdler: veteran chaser: left T. George, won point in February: stays 29f: acts on heavy and good to firm going: tried in visor/cheekpieces: hard ride. *Mrs H. J. Houghton* **c85 h–**

ACTUAL 5 b.g. Factual (USA) – Tugra (FR) (Baby Turk) [2004/5 F16g⁶ 21v⁶ Mar 28] third foal: dam winning pointer: soundly beaten in bumper and novice hurdle. *P. D. Niven* **h– F–**

ACUTEANGLE (IRE) 9 b. or br.m. Cataldi – Sharp Mama VII (Damsire Unregistered) [2004/5 c–, h–: c21mᵖᵘ May 19] no form in points or hunter chases since 2002. *Mrs S. Wall* **c– h–**

ADALAR (IRE) 5 br.g. Grand Lodge (USA) – Adalya (IRE) (Darshaan) [2004/5 16g Oct 7] fair on Flat (stays 1¼m): well held in seller on hurdling debut. *P. D. Evans* **h–**

ADALIE 11 b.m. Absalom – Allied Newcastle (Crooner) [2004/5 c93, h–: 17d 16s⁶ 16v 16s c24d c20vᵖᵘ c24m² Mar 14] sturdy mare: winning hurdler: modest chaser: trained first 3 starts by Miss G. Browne, fourth by J. Joseph: stays 3m: acts on good to firm and heavy going: not a fluent jumper. *J. D. Frost* **c91 x h–**

ADALPOUR (IRE) 7 b.g. Kahyasi – Adalya (IRE) (Darshaan) [2004/5 h81: 17d 16d 21gᶠ 20g⁴ 22m 22m² 22g² 24g² 20g Aug 14] poor maiden hurdler: stays 3m: acts on soft and good to firm going: tried in cheekpieces. *C. W. Moore* **h75**

ADAMANT APPROACH (IRE) 11 b.g. Mandalus – Crash Approach (Crash Course) [2004/5 c141, h127: c20sᵖᵘ 16v⁴ 16v⁴ 19v⁴ 16v Mar 6] sturdy gelding: useful hurdler/chaser: best effort in 2004/5 when fourth to Essex in Pierse Hurdle (Handicap) at Leopardstown third start: best around 2m: acts on heavy going, probably on good to firm: tongue tied last 4 outings. *W. P. Mullins, Ireland* **c– h141**

ADAM'S BELLE (IRE) 5 b.m. Fourstars Allstar (USA) – Electric Belle (IRE) (Electric) [2004/5 F18f² F16mᵖᵘ Sep 24] €1,600 3-y-o: first foal: dam unraced: fell in maiden Irish point in 2004: much better effort in bumpers when second at Limerick: sold out of R. Rath's stable 13,000 gns Doncaster August Sales. *N. B. King* **F85**

ADAMS WINE (IRE) 6 b.g. Hubbly Bubbly (USA) – Glen Fuel (IRE) (Meneval (USA)) [2004/5 19f^F 16f 24f^3 24g^3 22d 22g^3 c21m^6 Jul 26] second foal: brother to winning pointer Three Mill: dam unraced: winning pointer: modest maiden hurdler: well held on chasing debut: blinkered 3 of last 4 starts. *E. J. O'Grady, Ireland* **c– h94**

ADARMA (IRE) 7 b.m. Topanoora – Overtime (IRE) (Executive Perk) [2004/5 h115: c20s^{ur} c17s* c16s^2 c20s* c16s^3 c17v* Apr 2] rangy mare: fairly useful hurdler: similar form in novice chases, successful in listed mares events at Cork in December and Thurles in January and 5-runner contest at Navan in April: stays 2½m: raced on going softer than good (acts on heavy). *C. Roche, Ireland* **c114 h–**

ADELE 5 b.m. Cloudings (IRE) – Sharp Practice (Broadsword (USA)) [2004/5 F–: F16m Apr 25] leggy mare: well held in bumpers. *J. G. O'Neill* **F–**

ADELPHI BOY (IRE) 9 ch.g. Ballad Rock – Toda (Absalom) [2004/5 h105: 20m^F 16m^F Sep 4] lengthy gelding: lightly-raced winning hurdler: fell both starts in 2004/5: should stay beyond 2m. *M. Todhunter* **h100 ?**

ADELPHIE LASS 5 b.m. Theatrical Charmer – Miss Adventure (Adonijah) [2004/5 F–: F18g^6 17d^5 16d 21d 22s^2 20g 16v^2 22g^6 21d^{pu} Apr 18] well held in 2 bumpers: poor novice hurdler: claimed out of M. Hoad's stable £6,000 seventh start: stays 2¾m: raced on good going or softer: wore cheekpieces sixth outing. *D. B. Feek* **h79 F–**

ADELPHI THEATRE (USA) 8 b.g. Sadler's Wells (USA) – Truly Bound (USA) (In Reality) [2004/5 20d Apr 20] useful-looking gelding: winning hurdler, lightly raced and very little form since 2001: stays 2½m: acts on good to soft going. *R. Rowe* **h–**

ADEYON 5 b.m. Presenting – Relkissimo (Relkino) [2004/5 F16s Mar 22] tall mare: fifth foal: half-sister to winning pointer by Strong Gale: dam, poor maiden, half-sister to high-class 2m hurdler Past Glories: well held in bumper on debut. *P. Beaumont* **F–**

AD HOC (IRE) 11 b.g. Strong Gale – Knockarctic (Quayside) [2004/5 c141, h–: 25d^5 c29d^4 c24g c36d^F Apr 9] lengthy gelding: very smart handicap chaser at best, just useful form since 2002/3: failed to complete in Grand National at Aintree for third time when falling second Becher's (reportedly suffered minor ligament damage): very lightly raced over hurdles, fifth to The Dark Lord in listed handicap at Cheltenham on reappearance: effective at 3m to 33f: acts on good to firm and heavy going. *P. F. Nicholls* **c141 h127 +**

ADIOS (GER) 6 b.g. Lagunas – Aerope (Celestial Storm (USA)) [2004/5 16g^{pu} Feb 27] successful 3 times up to 11f from 9 starts on Flat in Germany at 3/4 yrs for H. Blume: no show in maiden on hurdling debut. *P. D. Niven* **h–**

ADIYSHA (IRE) 8 b.m. Namaqualand (USA) – Adira (IRE) (Ballad Rock) [2004/5 h75: 17m^6 17g 17d^F Aug 1] poor maiden hurdler: stays easy 19f: best on good going or firmer (acts on firm): blinkered once. *D. A. Rees* **h–**

ADJAMI (IRE) 4 b.g. Entrepreneur – Adjriyna (Top Ville) [2004/5 17d^4 16s^5 17s^3 Jan 20] half-brother to several winners, including 17f chase winner Adjiram (by Be My Guest): runner-up twice from 5 starts up to 1¼m on Flat in 2004 for A. de Royer Dupre: fair form over hurdles, third to Medison in novice at Taunton. *A. King* **h106**

ADJAWAR (IRE) 7 b.g. Ashkalani (IRE) – Adjriyna (Top Ville) [2004/5 16s^3 16s^4 16s 16v 16g 17m* Apr 9] sturdy gelding: fairly useful on Flat (stays 1½m) at 5 yrs, well beaten since: modest hurdler: easily won seller at Hereford in April: raced around 2m: acts on soft and good to firm going. *J. J. Quinn* **h91**

ADJIRAM (IRE) 9 b.g. Be My Guest (USA) – Adjriyna (Top Ville) [2004/5 h59§: 19g^2 19g^3 17g^6 22m^3 c17g* c17g^2 Oct 18] sturdy gelding: maiden hurdler, improved into modest performer in 2004/5: similar form over fences, making all in novice handicap at Plumpton in October on debut: finished lame next time: barely stays 2¾m: acts on firm going: has looked ungenuine (did nothing wrong in 2004/5). *A. W. Carroll* **c86 h86**

ADLESTROP 5 ch.m. Alderbrook – Lady Buck (Pollerton) [2004/5 F16s^6 Mar 13] 12,500 3-y-o: half-sister to several winners, including fairly useful chaser Shining Willow (by Strong Gale), stayed 3m, and fair 2m hurdler Lord Buckingham (by Carroll House): dam unraced half-sister to top-class 2m to 2½m jumper Buck House: favourite, raced freely when sixth of 18 in mares maiden bumper at Warwick on debut. *R. T. Phillips* **F81**

ADMIRAL (IRE) 4 b.c. Alhaarth (IRE) – Coast Is Clear (IRE) (Rainbow Quest (USA)) [2004/5 16d^5 16g* 17g 17g* 16g* Apr 16] tall colt: fairly useful on Flat (stays 1½m), successful twice in 2004, sold out of Sir Michael Stoute's stable 60,000 gns Newmarket Autumn Sales: developed into useful juvenile hurdler, winning at Musselburgh **h130**

Purvis Marquees Juvenile Novices' Hurdle, Ayr—
a third hurdling win for Admiral, who makes all to beat Afrad

(maiden, easily) in February and Market Rasen and Ayr (made all to beat Afrad 3 lengths) in April: likely to prove best around 2m: races freely: may be capable of better still. *R. C. Guest*

ADMIRAL PEARY (IRE) 9 b. or br.g. Lord Americo – Arctic Brief (Buckskin (FR)) [2004/5 h100x: 22d^2 25v^2 Dec 31] smallish, close-coupled gelding: fair handicap hurdler: ran well both starts after 19-month lay-off: probably best at 2¾m+: acts on heavy and good to firm going: sketchy jumper: free-going sort, effective held up or forcing pace. *C. R. Egerton* **h108**

ADOLPHUS (IRE) 8 b.g. Tidaro (USA) – Coxtown Queen (IRE) (Corvaro (USA)) [2004/5 c24g c20g^2 c24m^4 c20f^3 c16v^5 c21f^4 Oct 7] good-topped gelding: maiden hurdler: modest handicap chaser: possibly best around 2½m: acts on firm and good to soft going: tried tongue tied/in headgear: held up: sold 7,200 gns Doncaster October Sales, won points in February and March for C. Storey. *A. J. Martin, Ireland* **c88 h–**

ADOPTED HERO (IRE) 5 b.g. Sadler's Wells (USA) – Lady Liberty (NZ) (Noble Bijou (USA)) [2004/5 h120: 16g 16s Dec 17] smallish, good-topped gelding: useful on Flat at best, poor efforts at Nad Al Sheba early in 2005: fairly useful form in juvenile hurdles in 2003/4: stiff tasks in handicaps in 2004/5: raced around 2m on good going or softer: sent to Spain. *G. L. Moore* **h117**

A DOUBLE EWE BEE 4 b.f. Kingsinger (IRE) – Some Dream (Vitiges (FR)) [2004/5 16s* 17s^3 16g^{pu} Jan 19] dam winning 17f hurdler: no form on Flat: 66/1, won 10-runner juvenile seller at Ludlow in December on hurdling debut: better form next time, ran as if amiss final start: likely to stay 2½m. *W. G. M. Turner* **h78**

ADVANCE EAST 13 b.g. Polish Precedent (USA) – Startino (Bustino) [2004/5 c16d^3 c16d^4 c20v* c16v^2 c16s^4 c20v^{pu} Mar 1] workmanlike gelding: has been hobdayed: poor handicap chaser: won at Uttoxeter in December: stays 21f: acts on any going: tried blinkered. *M. J. M. Evans* **c76 h–**

ADVENT GIRL 6 ch.m. Bollin William – Advent Lady (Kemal (FR)) [2004/5 F16g May 1] first foal: dam poor pointer: tailed off in bumper on debut. *P. R. Wood* **F–**

AEGEAN KNIGHT 6 b.g. Prince Sabo – Load Line (High Line) [2004/5 aF16g^6 Oct 30] half-brother to 3 winners, including fair chaser Quattro (by Robellino), stayed 3m: **F–**

dam unraced sister to Park Hill winner Quay Line, from family of high-class miler Soviet Line: reportedly lame in bumper on debut. *Miss Gay Kelleway*

AEGEAN PIRATE (IRE) 8 b.g. Polykratis – Rusheen Na Corra (IRE) (Burslem) [2004/5 F–: 16g^{pu} May 16] no form. *C. J. Hemsley* **h–**

AELRED 12 b.g. Ovac (ITY) – Sponsorship (Sparkler) [2004/5 c118?, h–: c22v c20d^{6} c20s^{5} c20v^{6} c16s 17v^{4} c24v* Mar 19] sturdy gelding: lightly raced over hurdles: fair handicap chaser: tried again in cheekpieces, first form in 2004/5 when making all in weak event at Newcastle: stays 3m: acts on heavy and good to firm going: has had tongue tied: has won or been placed in 13 of 17 races at Newcastle: usually races prominently. *R. Johnson* **c106 h81**

AFAIR PROMISE (NZ) 5 br.g. Vain Promise (AUS) – Diamond Fair (NZ) (Diamante D) [2004/5 F16d^{6} Dec 29] tall, leggy gelding: 10½ lengths sixth of 15 to Earth Man in Grade 2 bumper at Newbury on debut. *A. King* **F99**

AFDAL (IRE) 5 b.g. Grand Lodge (USA) – Afragha (IRE) (Darshaan) [2004/5 F16d Nov 6] smallish, angular gelding: second foal: half-brother to 11f winners Afreen (by Entrepreneur) and Afrad (by Linamix), latter fairly useful 2m hurdle winner: dam, 1¼m winner, closely related to useful 2m to 2½m hurdler Afarad and half-sister to fairly useful hurdler up to 3m Afarka: sold unraced out of A. de Royer Dupre's stable €2,200 Goffs (France) July (2003) Sale: tailed off in bumper on debut. *Miss Venetia Williams* **F–**

AFEEF (USA) 6 br.g. Dayjur (USA) – Jah (USA) (Relaunch (USA)) [2004/5 h74: 16d^{pu} 16d 18s^{2} 22d^{3} 21d* 21d^{2} c21s^{F} Jan 18] good-topped gelding: modest hurdler: won seller at Sedgefield in November: fell first on chasing debut: stays 2¾m: acts on soft ground: wore cheekpieces and tongue strap last 5 starts. *R. T. Phillips* **c– h88**

A FEW BOB BACK (IRE) 9 b.g. Bob Back (USA) – Kottna (USA) (Lyphard (USA)) [2004/5 c97, h112: 19d^{5} 23s^{4} 20v 25d^{5} c25s^{pu} 24s* 24s^{2} c24d* c24v^{3} Apr 17] smallish gelding: fair handicap hurdler: trained until after third start by D. Eddy: back to best when winning at Market Rasen in March: improved effort over fences (jumped much better) when winning novice at Carlisle later in month: stays 25f: acts on soft and good to firm going: usually wears headgear: sold 20,000 gns Doncaster May Sales. *Karen McLintock* **c105 h113**

A FEW KIND WORDS (IRE) 4 b.g. Darazari (IRE) – Aussieannie (IRE) (Arapahos (FR)) [2004/5 F16v^{2} F16v^{6} Mar 29] €120,000 3-y-o: first foal: dam, lightly raced in points, sister to fairly useful chaser Call Me Dara and fairly useful hurdler Be Home Early, both effective around 3m: much better effort in bumpers when second of 16 to Dancing Partner at Uttoxeter. *Miss K. Marks* **F92**

AFISTFULLOFDOLLARS (IRE) 7 b.g. Be My Native (USA) – Myra Gaye (Buckskin (FR)) [2004/5 F105: 18v* 18s^{3} 24s* Mar 28] useful in bumpers in 2003/4: successful twice from 3 starts over hurdles, in maiden at Navan in February and minor event at Fairyhouse in March, beating Bright Gas a length in latter: will stay beyond 3m: type to improve further. *N. Meade, Ireland* **h121 p**

AFRAD (FR) 4 gr.g. Linamix (FR) – Afragha (IRE) (Darshaan) [2004/5 16g^{3} 16g* 16g^{2} Apr 16] leggy gelding: third foal: half-brother to 11f winner Afreen (by Entrepreneur): dam, 1¼m winner, closely related to useful 2m to 2½m hurdler Afarad and half-sister to fairly useful hurdler up to 3m Afarka: fairly useful on Flat (stays 1½m), successful in June, sold out of A. de Royer Dupre's stable €25,000 Goffs (France) October Sale: won juvenile hurdle at Newbury in December: much better form when second to Admiral at Ayr and Strides of Fire at Punchestown in April: tends to carry head awkwardly: may do better still in handicaps. *N. J. Henderson* **h124**

AFRICAN SUNSET (IRE) 5 b.g. Danehill Dancer (IRE) – Nizamiya (Darshaan) [2004/5 h–: 16d 17m^{5} Jul 26] poor form over hurdles: raced around 2m. *J. Howard Johnson* **h80**

AFTER EIGHT (GER) 5 b.g. Sir Felix (FR) – Amrei (Ardross) [2004/5 h112: 20v^{3} 20v^{6} 16d^{5} 21g^{5} 20d 20m Apr 23] small, compact gelding: fairly useful hurdler: off a year, ran well in handicaps most starts in 2004/5: stays 21f: acts on any going. *Miss Venetia Williams* **h122**

AFTER GALWAY (IRE) 9 b.g. Camden Town – Money For Honey (New Brig) [2004/5 h72: 16g* 20s Apr 22] lightly-raced gelding: easily best effort over hurdles when dead-heating with Vitelli in novice at Hexham in May: should stay 2½m. *Miss V. Scott* **h99**

AFTER ME BOYS 11 b.g. Arzanni – Realm Wood (Precipice Wood) [2004/5 h120: 24g^{3} 22d^{6} 24s Apr 16] workmanlike gelding: fairly useful handicap hurdler, lightly raced: effective at 2½m to 3m: acts on any going. *Mrs S. J. Smith* **h116**

AFTER THE BLUE (IRE) 8 b.g. Last Tycoon – Sudden Interest (FR) (Highest Honor (FR)) [2004/5 h–: 20dpu 20g 19m May 23] compact gelding: winning 2½m hurdler, no form since early-2002/3: tried blinkered/visored: used to have tongue tied. *K. G. Wingrove* **h–**

AFZAL ROSE 5 b.m. Afzal – Fortria Rosie Dawn (Derring Rose) [2004/5 F–: F17g6 20spu 20v5 19vpu 21s6 Mar 10] no form in bumpers or mares novice hurdles. *M. Scudamore* **h– F–**

AGGI MAC 4 b.f. Defacto (USA) – Giffoine (Timeless Times (USA)) [2004/5 16d Nov 27] poor maiden on Flat (stays 6f): well beaten in juvenile hurdle. *Andrew Turnell* **h–**

AGINCOURT (IRE) 9 b.g. Alphabatim (USA) – Miss Brantridge (Riboboy (USA)) [2004/5 c96§, h–: c25g5 c24s5 c24g c27vpu Mar 28] workmanlike gelding: staying handicap chaser, no form since winning on 2003/4 reappearance: blinkered once: often gets behind: one to leave alone. *John R. Upson* **c– § h– §**

A GLASS IN THYNE (IRE) 7 br.g. Glacial Storm (USA) – River Thyne (IRE) (Good Thyne (USA)) [2004/5 h106: c24v* c24d4 Dec 11] leggy gelding: fairly useful form when runner-up on second of 2 outings in novice hurdles: won maiden at Bangor in November on chasing debut by 18 lengths from Fullards: made a couple of mistakes when fourth to L'Ami in Grade 2 novice at Lingfield: will stay beyond 3m: acts on heavy ground. *B. N. Pollock* **c123 h–**

AGNESE 5 ch.m. Abou Zouz (USA) – Efizia (Efisio) [2004/5 F79: F17d5 F16m* 16d3 17d5 20d4 20d Jan 7] sturdy mare: modest form in bumpers: won 4-runner maiden at Wetherby in May: poor form over hurdles: may prove best around 2m: tried in cheekpieces. *G. M. Moore* **h79 F79**

AGOSTINI (GER) 4 ch.c. Platini (GER) – Ariostea (FR) (Tagel (USA)) [2004/5 16g5 16dpu 17g 19m3 Apr 2] close-coupled ex-German colt: successful twice around 1m from 6 starts on Flat, claimed from M. Hofer €23,500 in September: modest form in juvenile hurdles: stays 19f: acts on good to firm going: saddle slipped second start. *Miss Venetia Williams* **h88**

AH YEAH (IRE) 8 b.g. Roselier (FR) – Serena Bay (Furry Glen) [2004/5 c79, h85, F85: c25m2 c21dpu c16s2 Jan 7] close-coupled gelding: winning pointer: modest maiden hurdler/chaser: stays 25f, effective at much shorter: acts on soft and good to firm going: sometimes wears cheekpieces: temperament under suspicion: sold 6,000 gns Doncaster May Sales. *K. C. Bailey* **c85 h–**

AIDE DE CAMP (FR) 6 b.g. Saint Preuil (FR) – Baraka de Thaix II (FR) (Olmeto) [2004/5 F89: 20s Dec 17] won maiden bumper at Newton Abbot on debut: still looked inexperienced when well held in maiden hurdle at Windsor 8 months later. *P. F. Nicholls* **h– p**

AIMEES MARK (IRE) 9 b. or br.g. Jolly Jake (NZ) – Wee Mite (Menelek) [2004/5 c22v* c20s c22v* c24vur c24vpu Dec 27] good-topped gelding: fair chaser: won maiden at Listowel in September and intermediate handicap at Galway in October: failed to complete in valuable handicaps at Navan, Leopardstown and Punchestown, still to be asked for effort when unseating 5 out in novice event at last-named in late-April: stays 3m: raced on good going or softer (acts on heavy). *F. Flood, Ireland* **c110 h–**

AIN'T THAT A SHAME (IRE) 5 ch.g. Broken Hearted – Alvinru (Sandalay) [2004/5 F17s2 F17s* F16d3 Feb 19] tall gelding: has scope: sixth foal: half-brother to winning pointer by Lord Americo: dam, bumper winner, half-sister to fairly useful hurdler/winning chaser up to 3m Manaree, dam of Refinement: fairly useful form in bumpers, landing odds in 17-runner maiden at Exeter in January. *P. F. Nicholls* **F103**

AIR ATTACHE (USA) 10 b.g. Sky Classic (CAN) – Diplomatic Cover (USA) (Roberto (USA)) [2004/5 c113, h–: c17mF May 22] fairly useful hurdler in 2000: fair chaser: fell fatally at Stratford: stayed 21f: acted on firm going (not discredited on good to soft): tongue tied. *K. R. Pearce* **c– h–**

AIR OF AFFECTION 4 b.f. Air Express (IRE) – Auntie Gladys (Great Nephew) [2004/5 F14g6 F16s4 F16s3 Apr 10] 2,800F: lengthy filly: fifth foal: half-sister to useful Family Man (by Indian Ridge) and Bishopstone Man (by Piccolo), both 7f/1m winners: dam poor maiden half-sister to useful 6f performer Simon Rattle: modest form in bumpers. *J. R. Turner* **F82**

AITCH DOUBLEYOU (IRE) 5 ch.g. Classic Memory – Bucksreward (IRE) (Buckskin (FR)) [2004/5 F16d Nov 28] strong gelding: second foal: dam maiden Irish pointer: tailed off in bumper on debut. *P. L. Clinton* **F–**

AKARUS (FR) 10 b.g. Labus (FR) – Meris (FR) (Amarko (FR)) [2004/5 c135, h–: c29v c29s Jan 15] useful handicap chaser at best: first completion since 2002/3, respectable seventh of 17 to Silver Birch in Welsh National at Chepstow: ran poorly in visor following month: stays 4¼m: acts on heavy going: has worn blinkers. *M. C. Pipe* **c125 h–**

AKHTARI (IRE) 5 b.g. In The Wings – Akishka (Nishapour (FR)) [2004/5 h114p: 16s 16s 16v* 16g 20s[5] Mar 28] rangy gelding: fair form over hurdles: won 22-runner maiden at Punchestown in February by 3½ lengths from Tycoon Hall: well held after in Grade 1 novice at Cheltenham and useful minor event at Fairyhouse: should stay 2½m: acts on heavy going. *D. T. Hughes, Ireland* **h114**

AKILAK (IRE) 4 br.g. Charnwood Forest (IRE) – Akilara (IRE) (Kahyasi) [2004/5 17s* 16s* 17g[3] Mar 18] **h136**

The boat came in for County Durham-based trainer Howard Johnson and his jockey Graham Lee on the first three days of the Festival, with Arcalis at 20/1, No Refuge at 15/2 and Inglis Drever at 5/1 giving them the biggest catch of the Festival as trainer and rider with their victories on Tuesday, Wednesday and Thursday respectively (though Robert Thornton also rode three winners). Only on Friday were the pair left empty-handed. Grey Abbey managed only fifth at 15/2 in the Gold Cup on a card which opened with defeat for the stable's shortest-priced runner of the week Akilak, who had to settle for third when 7/2 favourite for the Triumph.

Akilak shot to the fore in the Triumph Hurdle betting with a most impressive first appearance over jumps under Lee in the Wragge & Co Juvenile Novices' Hurdle over course and distance in January. In what was just about the strongest line-up for a juvenile event in Britain prior to the Festival, Akilak started at 50/1 in a field of sixteen, which included the promising Miss Academy and the unbeaten French-trained Danaw. Akilak belied his inexperience emphatically in the end, joining the leaders on the bridle going to the last and storming away to beat the useful Yankeedoodledandy by six lengths. Akilak seemed well suited by the emphasis the strong gallop and soft ground put on stamina at Cheltenham and he was less impressive when landing odds of 9/4-on in a steadily-run race for the Victor Ludorum Hurdle at Haydock on his only other outing prior to the Festival. In a field of six at Haydock, he needed to be shaken up on the run-in to get the better of Karelian by a length and a half.

Back in a far larger field, Akilak seemed likely to have things run to suit in the Triumph, and he duly got a more well-run race. However, with ground conditions much less testing than he had encountered, he took a while to warm to his task after being short of room briefly three out, staying on to be nearest at the line, eight lengths behind close finishers Penzance and Faasel, running his best race all the same. Akilak had testing conditions for his only run after the Festival and started

Wragge & Co Finesse Juvenile Novices' Hurdle, Cheltenham—
50/1 hurdling debutant Akilak claims the unbeaten record of Yankeedoodledandy (noseband)

Victor Ludorum Juvenile Novices' Hurdle, Haydock—
victory over Karelian (noseband) cements Akilak's position as ante-post favourite for the Triumph

13/8-on in a field of seven for the Champion Four Year Old Hurdle at Punchestown in April, shortly after the end of the British season, but he seemed past his best, not fluent at times and managing only third behind twelve-length winner United, beaten half a length for second by Triumph sixth Strangely Brown.

Akilak (IRE) (br.g. 2001)	Charnwood Forest (IRE) (b or br 1992)	Warning (b 1985)	Known Fact
			Slightly Dangerous
		Dance of Leaves (b 1987)	Sadler's Wells
			Fall Aspen
	Akilara (IRE) (br 1992)	Kahyasi (b 1985)	Ile de Bourbon
			Kadissya
		Akishka (b or br 1988)	Nishapour
			Akiyda

In common with Dabiroun, winner of the inaugural Fred Winter Juvenile Novices' Hurdle at the Festival, Akilak was bred by the Aga Khan, who has been no stranger to producing successful jumpers over the years, including several others to have taken high rank as juvenile hurdlers, Triumph winner Shawiya among them, as well as Mounamara and Zafarabad, both winners of the Champion Four Year Old Hurdle at Punchestown in their time. Another Triumph winner Paddy's Return is by Kahyasi out of a mare bred by the Aga Khan. Akilak's third dam is Akiyda, successful in the Arc de Triomphe in the Aga Khan's colours. Akilak's dam Akilara was a winner over nine furlongs on the Flat and has also produced Akshar (by Danehill), a smart performer at up to a mile and a quarter before making a useful novice over hurdles in the latest season, finishing ninth in the Supreme Novices' Hurdle at Cheltenham. Akilara is a half-sister to another useful hurdler, Akasian, who stayed three miles. Akilak showed fairly useful form in four races on the Flat at two and three, winning a maiden over a mile before finishing second in a handicap over a mile and a quarter, and was bought out of John Oxx's stable for €100,000 at the Goffs Horses In Training Sale in Ireland in October, eventually ending up in a partnership including Newcastle United and former England footballer Alan

ADA Partnership's "Akilak"

Shearer. A well-made gelding, Akilak was one of the more striking sorts physically in the field at Cheltenham, where he was also the pick of the paddock in condition. The still lightly-raced Akilak may progress further in 2005/6 and is the type that could do well in good handicaps. His sire Charnwood Forest, a high-class performer at seven furlongs to a mile, got better with age. Likely to prove suited by testing conditions at around two miles, Akilak will be at least as effective over further. Held up to date and already a sound jumper, he has raced only on good ground or softer over hurdles, but his win on the Flat came on good to firm. *J. Howard Johnson*

AKSHAR (IRE) 6 b.g. Danehill (USA) – Akilara (IRE) (Kahyasi) [2004/5 16v* 16v⁴ 16g Mar 15] compact gelding: half-brother to smart juvenile hurdler Akilak (by Charnwood Forest): dam half-sister to useful hurdler up to 3m Akasian: smart at 4 yrs on Flat (stays 10.5f) for Sir Michael Stoute, useful form at best in 4 starts in 2004: won maiden at Leopardstown in December on hurdling debut by neck from Ocras Mor: didn't find much off bridle when ninth to Arcalis in Grade 1 novice at Cheltenham and fourth to Snoopy Loopy in well-contested novice at Punchestown 6 weeks later: will prove best at 2m. *D. K. Weld, Ireland* **h127**

ALAARED (USA) 5 b.g. King of Kings (IRE) – Celtic Loot (USA) (Irish River (FR)) [2004/5 h–: 16m 22m⁶ 21m⁴ Jun 8] angular gelding: has only one eye and wears eyecover: no worthwhile form over hurdles. *D. R. Gandolfo* **h–**

ALAFDAL (USA) 5 b. or br.g. Gone West (USA) – Aqaarid (USA) (Nashwan (USA)) [2004/5 16gᵖᵘ 16gᵖᵘ Feb 27] disappointing maiden on Flat: pulled up both starts over hurdles. *R. Allan* **h–**

ALAGON (IRE) 5 b.g. Alzao (USA) – Forest Lair (Habitat) [2004/5 21d⁵ 22s² 22v⁴ 19d² 24g* 22m* Apr 17] good-topped ex-French gelding: half-brother to fairly useful 2m **h109**

hurdler Munif (by Caerleon): maiden on Flat: fair hurdler: won handicap at Bangor in March and novice at Stratford in April: stays 3m: acts on soft and good to firm going: effective visored or not. *Ian Williams*

ALAIPOUR (IRE) 6 b.g. Kahyasi – Alaiyda (USA) (Shahrastani (USA)) [2004/5 16m^{5} 18m^{3} 20f^{2} 16f^{6} 16d^{6} Jun 29] maiden on Flat: poor maiden hurdler: stays 2½m: acts on firm and good to soft going: usually wears cheekpieces, pulled hard in blinkers fourth start: has had tongue tied. *Lindsay Woods, Ireland* **h82**

ALAKDAR (CAN) 11 ch.g. Green Dancer (USA) – Population (General Assembly (USA)) [2004/5 c90, h–: c19m^{pu} c21s^{pu} c23m c26g^{5} c26g^{3} Aug 2] good-topped gelding: poor chaser: stays 3m: acts on firm and soft going: tried in headgear. *C. J. Down* **c70 h–**

ALAM (USA) 6 b.g. Silver Hawk (USA) – Ghashtah (USA) (Nijinsky (CAN)) [2004/5 h105: 17d* 22v^{2} 20s^{3} c16v* c21v^{4} c16v^{2} c17v^{5} 16s^{4} Mar 19] sturdy gelding: fairly useful handicap hurdler: had run of race when winning conditional jockeys event at Carlisle in October: won maiden at Hexham in December on chasing debut by 5 lengths from Edmo Yewkay: let down by jumping 2 of next 3 starts: effective around 2m to 2¾m: raced on going softer than good (acts on heavy). *P. Monteith* **c117 h119**

ALASIL (USA) 5 b.g. Swain (IRE) – Asl (USA) (Caro) [2004/5 h87: 17g^{2} 21g^{4} 16g 18s^{3} 20s 16s^{F} 18s^{5} 17m Mar 14] strong, compact gelding: modest form at best over hurdles: should stay 2½m: wore cheekpieces/blinkers 4 of last 5 starts. *Mrs N. Smith* **h87**

ALASKAN FIZZ 4 ch.f. Efisio – Anchorage (IRE) (Slip Anchor) [2004/5 F13s^{3} Jan 31] seventh foal: half-sister to several winners, including fairly useful hurdler Barneys Lyric (by Hector Protector), stays 3m, and 2m winner Lord Alaska (by Sir Harry Lewis): dam, 1½m winner, half-sister to smart dual-purpose performer Brunico: 3¼ lengths third to Wishin And Jokin in bumper at Exeter on debut, staying on well. *R. T. Phillips* **F84**

ALAYZEASS (IRE) 6 b.m. Aahsaylad – In Reverse (IRE) (Cardinal Flower) [2004/5 F–: F16g F18g May 9] modest form on second of 3 starts in bumpers: sold £1,600 Ascot October Sales: pulled up in point in February. *J. S. Moore* **F80**

ALBANY (IRE) 5 ch.g. Alhaarth (IRE) – Tochar Ban (USA) (Assert) [2004/5 h115: 24d^{5} Nov 20] sturdy gelding: fairly useful juvenile hurdler in 2003/4: tailed-off last of 5 finishers in handicap at Aintree on return, travelling strongly long way and not punished when beaten: stays 3m: acts on soft going. *J. Howard Johnson* **h–**

ALBA ROSE 6 gr.m. Overbury (IRE) – Belle Rose (IRE) (Roselier (FR)) [2004/5 F–: F16f^{6} 22v^{pu} 20s^{pu} 20m Dec 12] no sign of ability. *J. N. R. Billinge* **h– F–**

ALBERT HOUSE (IRE) 7 ch.g. Carroll House – Action Plan (Creative Plan (USA)) [2004/5 h98: c24g^{2} Oct 5] workmanlike gelding: modest form over hurdles: several mistakes when second of 3 in novice at Huntingdon on chasing debut: stays 3m. *R. H. Alner* **c103 h–**

ALBERT MOONEY (IRE) 5 b.h. Dr Massini (IRE) – Prudent Rose (IRE) (Strong Gale) [2004/5 F16s* F16d* Nov 27] tall horse: seventh foal: half-brother to 2 winners, including hurdler up to 2¾m Phar Glory (by Phardante): dam unraced half-sister to useful 2m to 2¾m hurdler/chaser King Wah Glory: improved form in bumpers in 2004/5, winning at Naas in October and Fairyhouse in November, beating Celtic Sammy comfortably by 2 lengths at latter: will stay beyond 2m: useful prospect. *D. Wachman, Ireland* **F112**

ALBUHERA (IRE) 7 b.g. Desert Style (IRE) – Morning Welcome (IRE) (Be My Guest (USA)) [2004/5 h138: 16d^{4} 16g^{2} Nov 27] good-topped gelding: useful hurdler: easily better effort in 2004/5 when ½-length second to Distant Prospect in quite valuable handicap at Newbury: will prove best around 2m with emphasis on speed: acts on firm and good to soft going: tongue tied: held up. *P. F. Nicholls* **h143**

ALCAPONE (IRE) 11 b.g. Roselier (FR) – Ann's Cap (IRE) (Cardinal Flower) [2004/5 c146, h–: c16g^{6} c20s^{5} c20s^{3} c16s c18d^{2} c21d^{pu} Apr 8] workmanlike gelding: useful chaser: best effort in 2004/5 when third to Rathgar Beau in Grade 2 at Clonmel in November: has form at 3m, at least as effective at shorter: acts on good to firm and heavy going: has had tongue tied: not fluent when pulled up both starts over National fences at Aintree. *M. F. Morris, Ireland* **c137 h–**

ALCATRAS (IRE) 8 b. or br.g. Corrouge (USA) – Kisco (IRE) (Henbit (USA)) [2004/5 c85+, h–§: c23m^{2} c23m^{F} c23d^{4} c24g c23s^{pu} c24s^{3} c25s^{F} c24d^{pu} c24g^{5} Apr 15] workmanlike gelding: modest maiden chaser: stays 3m: acts on good to firm going: blinkered last 5 starts: often let down by jumping: has been reluctant to race, and one to treat with caution. *B. J. M. Ryall* **c85 x h– §**

ALCHEMYSTIC (IRE) 5 b.g. In The Wings – Kama Tashoof (Mtoto) [2004/5 h102: 19g c16d^{4} 18d^{pu} 24g^{pu} Mar 19] well-made gelding: winning hurdler: no show in **c– h–**

2004/5, including on chasing debut, sold out of G. L. Moore's stable £10,000 Ascot December Sales before third start (tongue tied): stays 19f: has carried head high/hung left. *M. A. Barnes*

ALCOPOP 6 b.g. Alderbrook – Albaciyna (Hotfoot) [2004/5 F92: 20s^6 16g^5 17s^3 17g c16g^4 c16s^F c16g* c16g^{ur} c20s* Mar 31] useful-looking gelding: modest hurdler: better over fences, winning handicaps at Doncaster (novice) and Ludlow in March: stays 2½m: acts on soft going: blinkered sixth outing: carries head high. *Miss Venetia Williams* **c102 h85 §**

ALCRIS 6 b. or br.g. Alderbrook – One of Those Days (Soviet Lad (USA)) [2004/5 F84: F17v^4 20s^6 16g Nov 15] unfurnished gelding: better effort in 2 bumpers on debut: poor form in novice hurdles. *Jonjo O'Neill* **h76 F75**

ALDERBROOK GIRL (IRE) 5 b. or br.m. Alderbrook – Trassey Bridge (Strong Gale) [2004/5 F17d^3 F18s^5 F16m Apr 2] lengthy, angular mare: second foal: dam, fair chaser who stayed 2½m, half-sister to useful staying chaser Southern Star: best effort in bumpers (modest form) on debut. *R. Curtis* **F79**

ALDERBURN 6 b.g. Alderbrook – Threewaygirl (Orange Bay) [2004/5 F96: 16d 20s* 20v^3 22s^3 20d^6 21m^2 Apr 13] tall, good-topped gelding: fairly useful novice hurdler: won maiden at Windsor in December: ran well all 4 starts after, second to Prins Willem at Cheltenham final one: barely stays testing 2¾m: acts on heavy and good to firm going: has taken good hold: type to do well over fences in 2005/6. *H. D. Daly* **h120**

ALDERMAN ROSE 5 b.g. Alderbrook – Rose Ravine (Deep Run) [2004/5 F16g Apr 19] half-brother to several winners, including smart staying hurdler/chaser Frosty Canyon (by Arctic Lord) and winning hurdler/fairly useful chaser Alvino (by Alflora), stays 21f: dam won 1985 Stayers' Hurdle: ninth of 17 in maiden bumper at Towcester on debut: likely to be suited by further than 2m. *R. T. Phillips* **F84**

ALDIRUOS (IRE) 5 ch.g. Bigstone (IRE) – Ball Cat (FR) (Cricket Ball (USA)) [2004/5 h69: 16m^5 17g^3 17g 16g* 19g* 16d* 16d 20s* 20g^3 22d^6 Mar 11] rather sparely-made gelding: fair hurdler: left P. Hobbs after second outing: much improved after, winning novice handicaps at Worcester and Lingfield in October and Wetherby in November and December: best effort when third to Pretty Star in similar event at Sandown penultimate start: probably stays 2¾m: acts on soft going: tried blinkered: has had tongue tied: tough and consistent. *A. W. Carroll* **h104**

ALEEMDAR (IRE) 8 b.g. Doyoun – Aleema (Red God) [2004/5 h–: 17d May 17] winning hurdler: no form since 2002/3: best at sharp 2m: acts on soft and good to firm going: tried blinkered/visored: has had tongue tied. *A. E. Jones* **h–**

AL EILE (IRE) 5 b.g. Alzao (USA) – Kilcsem Eile (IRE) (Commanche Run) [2004/5 h131: 16g 16s^6 16v^3 16d^3 16g 20d* Apr 9] **h159**

Al Eile pulled off a surprise for the second successive year at the Grand National meeting. Twelve months after landing the Anniversary Hurdle at 25/1 from Triumph Hurdle winner Made In Japan, he was returned to Aintree and took the Scottish And Newcastle Aintree Hurdle, a Grade 1 contest that attracted half a dozen who had run in the Champion Hurdle, including Brave Inca, Accordion Etoile, Macs Joy and Intersky Falcon, all of whom had finished in front of seventh-placed Al Eile at Cheltenham. Also in the Aintree Hurdle line-up was the World Hurdle winner Inglis Drever and the seventh in that race, Exotic Dancer. Brave Inca and Inglis Drever dominated the betting, starting at 2/1 and 9/4 respectively, with 7/1-shot Macs Joy the only other in the nine-strong field at single-figure odds. An 11/1-shot, Al Eile travelled smoothly throughout—held up as usual—and hit the front near the line after being produced to challenge at the last. He had a neck and three quarters of a length to spare over Inglis Drever and 50/1-shot Exotic Dancer, the first three clear of Macs Joy. Al Eile would probably have had more to do if Brave Inca, still to be asked for his effort and looking sure to play a part in the finish, had not parted company with his rider three out. Back at two miles, Al Eile will still have something to find with the likes of Brave Inca, Macs Joy and Accordion Etoile—not to mention the Champion Hurdle first and second Hardy Eustace and Harchibald—and, now that his stamina is proven, he is likely to enjoy more success campaigned at around two and a half miles, and possibly further.

Al Eile didn't win over hurdles between his two Aintree victories and his improvement for the step up in distance—the Aintree Hurdle was his first attempt at two and a half miles—had also been hard to predict. A mile seemed to be Al Eile's optimum trip as a three-year-old on the Flat and nothing he achieved as a

Scottish And Newcastle Aintree Hurdle—a first success since the previous year's meeting for Al Eile (left), who gets the better of Exotic Dancer (centre) and Inglis Drever in a muddling race

juvenile hurdler suggested he would be anything but a two-miler over timber. The first intimation that Al Eile possessed hitherto-hidden reserves of stamina came when he won a handicap at Navan over a mile and a quarter on soft ground on his return to the Flat in October 2004. Al Eile followed up that month with victories at a mile and three quarters and at two miles (November Handicap under top weight of 9-7), both at Leopardstown, on each occasion showing improved form. Al Eile had run well below his Anniversary Hurdle form in the Champion Four Year Old Hurdle at Punchestown in late-April and never got into contention behind Macs Joy when resuming his hurdling career in the December Festival Hurdle at Leopardstown.

In all honesty, Al Eile didn't look up to taking on top company at this stage and it was something of a surprise to see the Champion Hurdle chosen as his Cheltenham Festival target, rather than the County Hurdle. A 25/1-shot in the Champion, Al Eile would have been among the County Hurdle favourites on the strength of good efforts behind his compatriot Essex in two of the season's major handicaps, the Pierse Hurdle at Leopardstown in January and the totesport Trophy at Newbury in February. Al Eile returned to something like his Anniversary form at Leopardstown where he stayed on very strongly to snatch third after having far too much to do in the straight. The early pace in the Pierse was unusually steady for a race of its type which counted against Al Eile. It was a similar story at Newbury where Al Eile was still towards the rear turning for home and did well to finish three lengths and a head behind Essex, who gave him 6 lb, and one of the lightweights Bongo Fury. Neither Essex nor Al Eile proved up to the task in a Champion Hurdle dominated by Irish-trained horses, but the keeping-on Al Eile appeared to put up a markedly improved effort, splitting the first two British-trained finishers Intersky Falcon and Rooster Booster. Al Eile was seven lengths behind third-placed Brave Inca, four behind Accordion Etoile and two and a half behind Macs Joy.

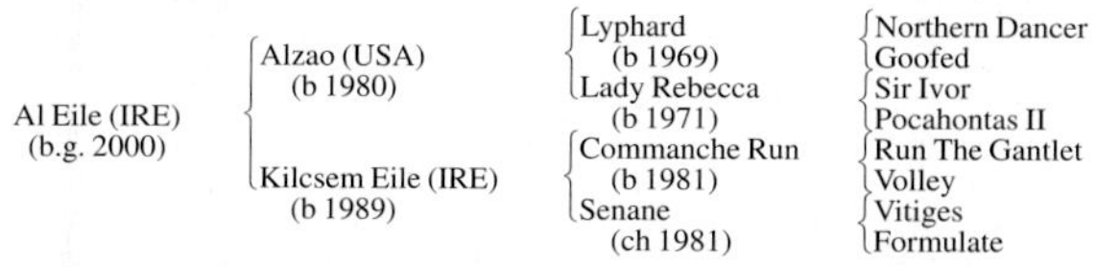

Al Eile (IRE) (b.g. 2000)	Alzao (USA) (b 1980)	Lyphard (b 1969)	Northern Dancer
			Goofed
		Lady Rebecca (b 1971)	Sir Ivor
			Pocahontas II
	Kilcsem Eile (IRE) (b 1989)	Commanche Run (b 1981)	Run The Gantlet
			Volley
		Senane (ch 1981)	Vitiges
			Formulate

The rather leggy Al Eile, who was outstanding in appearance at Aintree, is by Alzao, a successful stallion much better known for his Flat performers who include the multiple Group 1-winning sisters Albanova and Alborada, the Nassau winner Last Second (a half-sister to the dam of Albanova and Alborada), the Sussex Stakes winner Second Set, Irish classic winners Matiya and Winona, and Epsom

Mr M. A. Ryan's "Al Eile"

Oaks winner Shahtoush, among many others. Not that Al Eile is Alzao's only notable jumper—he is also the sire of the smart hurdler and useful chaser Hawthorn Blaze, the smart chaser Desert Mountain and the useful hurdlers Alzulu, Beaucadeau and Stompin. Apart from Hawthorn Blaze, who stayed twenty-one furlongs, they were all best at around two miles. Shahtoush is a half-sister to Al Eile's grandam Senane, a fairly useful performer for Henry Cecil who gained her only win over a mile at two. Formulate, the dam of Senane and Shahtoush, was also trained by Cecil and was the top staying two-year-old filly of her year; the Oaks runner-up Game Plan, dam of good Flat performers Strategic and Sobieski, is another of her daughters. This is a good Flat-racing family, which, further back, produced triple classic winner Meld and her Derby-winning son Charlottown, as well as two American classic runners-up in Twice A Prince and Play The Red. Al Eile is the only winner out of Kilcsem Eile, who showed nothing in a total of seven starts on the Flat and over hurdles. Before Al Eile came along, Kilcsem Eile's main claim to fame was being a half-sister to Bunbury Cup winner Crumpton Hill. Al Eile, who finished third in the Queen Alexandra Stakes over two and three quarter miles on the Flat in June, acts on heavy and good to firm going. *J. Queally, Ireland*

ALERON (IRE) 7 b.g. Sadler's Wells (USA) – High Hawk (Shirley Heights) [2004/5 19s^2 16d* 19g^2 16g* 17g^5 16g^5 16g^3 19m^2 Apr 23] quite good-topped gelding: half-brother to winning pointer by Kings Lake: fair up to 2m on Flat: useful novice hurdler: won at Wetherby in November and Musselburgh in January: best effort when 10½ lengths fifth of 20 to Arcalis in Supreme Novices' Hurdle at Cheltenham sixth start: stays 19f: acts on good to firm going, probably on soft: wore cheekpieces final outing: usually races prominently. *J. J. Quinn* **h133**

ALESSANDRO SEVERO 6 gr.g. Brief Truce (USA) – Altaia (FR) (Sicyos (USA)) [2004/5 h–: 24v^{pu} 16v^{pu} 19v^{5} 19d^{5} 20d 16s^{2} 20s^{2} Apr 16] angular gelding: poor maiden hurdler: stays 2½m: acts on soft going: visored last 5 outings: tried tongue tied. *Mrs D. A. Hamer* **h75**

ALETHEA GEE 7 b.m. Sure Blade (USA) – Star Flower (Star Appeal) [2004/5 17g 17m^{6} 16d Oct 9] lengthy mare: half-sister to 3 winning hurdlers, including fairly useful around 2m Country Orchid (by Town And Country): no form on Flat or over hurdles. *K. G. Reveley* **h–**

ALEXANDER BANQUET (IRE) 12 b.g. Glacial Storm (USA) – Black Nancy (Monksfield) [2004/5 c141, h–: 24s 20s c29s^{pu} Mar 28] strong gelding: top-class chaser at one time, largely well below best since 2001/2: winning hurdler: better effort in handicaps in 2004/5 when seventh in listed race at Navan second start: stays 3¼m: has form on good to firm going, used to go particularly well on soft/heavy. *W. P. Mullins, Ireland* **c–** **h114**

ALEXANDER MUSICAL (IRE) 7 b. or br.g. Accordion – Love For Lydia (IRE) (Law Society (USA)) [2004/5 h76, F–: 22g 19f 21g^{pu} 19s^{pu} 24d 25s^{pu} c16d^{6} c19v^{pu} c16m^{4} Mar 21] tall, angular gelding: little form: tried blinkered/visored. *S. T. Lewis* **c–** **h–**

ALEXANDER NEVSKY 9 b.g. Be My Native (USA) – Tsarella (Mummy's Pet) [2004/5 c26m^{pu} May 19] big, rangy gelding: poor pointer nowadays. *D. S. Dennis* **c–** **h–**

ALEXANDERTHEGREAT (IRE) 7 b.g. Supreme Leader – Sandy Jayne (IRE) (Royal Fountain) [2004/5 h141: c23d* c24d^{F} c25s^{2} c24d^{5} Feb 12] lengthy gelding: useful novice hurdler in 2003/4: won novice at Exeter in November on chasing debut: every chance when fell 2 out in Grade 2 novice at Lingfield won by L'Ami: disappointing last 2 starts: stays 25f: acts on soft going: sold 30,000 gns Doncaster May Sales. *P. F. Nicholls* **c132** **h–**

ALFADORA 5 ch.g. Alflora (IRE) – Dorazine (Kalaglow) [2004/5 16s 19m Apr 9] sixth foal: half-brother to modest 6f winner Rileys Dream (by Rudimentary): dam, fair 7f to 10.5f winner, out of half-sister to 1975 St Leger winner Bruni: well held over hurdles. *M. F. Harris* **h–**

ALFANO (IRE) 7 b.g. Priolo (USA) – Sartigila (Efisio) [2004/5 16g^{4} 16d^{3} Feb 3] fair on Flat (stays 1½m), sold out of E. James's stable £1,100 Ascot December (2003) Sales: better effort in novice hurdles when third to Faasel at Kelso: will stay beyond 2m. *Mrs R. L. Elliot* **h89**

ALFASONIC 5 b.g. Alflora (IRE) – Lady Solstice (Vital Season) [2004/5 F16v^{4} F16s^{3} 20d Mar 19] sturdy gelding: sixth foal: half-brother to winning pointer by Scorpio: dam unraced, out of sister to smart Irish chaser Corrie-Vacoul: fair form when in frame in 2 bumpers at Warwick: well held in novice at Uttoxeter on hurdling debut. *A. King* **h84** **F90**

ALFA SUNRISE 8 b.g. Alflora (IRE) – Gipsy Dawn (Lighter) [2004/5 h96: 24s* 24s c22s^{3} c20s^{pu} c20d^{5} c24g^{5} Mar 3] angular gelding: fair novice hurdler: won at Towcester in October: hasn't convinced with jumping and little form over fences: stays 3m well: acts on soft going. *R. H. Buckler* **c95** **h101**

ALFHALA (IRE) 4 b.f. Acatenango (GER) – Maid of Kashmir (IRE) (Dancing Brave (USA)) [2004/5 16d^{3} 16d^{6} 16d 16g^{2} 16g^{pu} Mar 4] lengthy filly: half-sister to winning 2m hurdler Shaalyn (by In The Wings): behind in 1m maiden on Flat for A. Stewart: modest form over hurdles: wore cheekpieces on debut. *M. J. Gingell* **h84**

ALFIE BRIGHT 7 ch.g. Alflora (IRE) – Candlebright (Lighter) [2004/5 h–: c20d^{pu} Nov 29] well-made gelding: no sign of ability. *Mrs L. B. Normile* **c–** **h–**

ALFIE'S CONNECTION 4 ch.g. Danzig Connection (USA) – Lady Warninglid (Ela-Mana-Mou) [2004/5 F13g F16m^{4} F16g^{5} Feb 27] half-brother to several winners, including Tees Components (by Risk Me), useful on Flat and up to 3m over hurdles, and fair stayer La Brief (by Law Society): dam unraced: form in bumpers only when fourth at Musselburgh (tended to hang left). *K. G. Reveley* **F88**

ALFIE'S SUN 6 b.g. Alflora (IRE) – Sun Dante (IRE) (Phardante (FR)) [2004/5 F97: 21d* 24d^{3} 20d 24m^{3} Apr 10] big, rangy gelding: will make a chaser: fair form in novice hurdles: well backed, won at Huntingdon in October: best effort when third at Windsor next time: stays 3m: possibly unsuited by good to firm going. *D. E. Cantillon* **h106**

ALFIE VALENTINE 9 b.g. Alflora (IRE) – My Aisling (John de Coombe) [2004/5 h–: 26d^{pu} 24s^{pu} Oct 30] no sign of ability. *Mrs P. Ford* **h–**

ALFLORIANO 6 b.g. Alflora (IRE) – Swallowfield (Wattlefield) [2004/5 F–: 22g^{pu} May 7] workmanlike gelding: no show in bumper or novice hurdle (jumped poorly): sold 1,200 gns Doncaster August Sales. *O. Sherwood* **h–**

ALFORMASI 6 b.g. Alflora (IRE) – Anamasi (Idiot's Delight) [2004/5 F17g^6 May 11] eighth foal: half-brother to winning hurdler/one-time fairly useful chaser Navarone (by Gunner B), stays 3m: dam, lightly-raced hurdler, half-sister to dual Scottish Grand National winner Androma and useful staying chaser Bigsun: sixth to Red Georgie in bumper at Hereford on debut. *P. F. Nicholls* **F82**

ALFRED THE GREY 8 gr.g. Environment Friend – Ranyah (USA) (Our Native (USA)) [2004/5 c26g^2 c26s^3 c25g^4 c24d^F c26d^4 c26d^2 c24d^6 c26v^{pu} c26m^2 Apr 21] leggy gelding: poor chaser: stays 3¼m: acts on good to firm going, probably on soft: tried blinkered: not one to trust. *G. L. Moore* **c76 §** **h–**

ALF'S SPINNEY 5 ch.g. Anshan – Netherdrom (Netherkelly) [2004/5 F16d^4 F16g Apr 19] rather unfurnished gelding: fifth foal: dam winning pointer: better effort in bumpers when fourth to Yaboya at Wincanton. *Ian Williams* **F86**

ALFY RICH 9 b.g. Alflora (IRE) – Weareagrandmother (Prince Tenderfoot (USA)) [2004/5 h76: 20s^2 20d* 24d* c20s^2 c20s^2 c21s^{bd} c25v^3 c27v^{pu} c24s^{pu} Feb 9] tall gelding: modest hurdler: claimed from P. Rich £6,000 first start: improved form when winning handicaps at Hexham (conditional jockeys seller) and Perth in June: similar form when placed all 3 completed starts over fences: stays 25f: acts on heavy and good to firm going. *M. Todhunter* **c98** **h92**

ALGENON (DEN) 5 br.g. Asaasy (USA) – La Natte (FR) (Native Guile (USA)) [2004/5 F95: F16g 21m^3 May 19] unfurnished gelding: best effort in bumpers when third at Haydock on debut: poor form on hurdling debut: sold 26,000 gns Doncaster May Sales. *Ferdy Murphy* **h70** **F72**

ALGYMO 5 b.m. Tamure (IRE) – Red Point (Reference Point) [2004/5 h–, F–: 19g^{pu} 17g^5 19g^5 18s 19d^4 24s^6 22d 17s^2 24g^4 Apr 7] poor hurdler: stays 3m: acts on soft going: has worn cheekpieces, usually blinkered: tried tongue tied. *S. C. Burrough* **h75**

ALHERI 14 gr.g. Puget (USA) – Miss Haddon (Free Boy) [2004/5 c25s^6 c21m^2 c25m^2 24s Oct 21] workmanlike gelding: winning pointer: poor maiden hurdler/chaser: stays 3¼m: raced mainly on good going or firmer (acts on firm): tried tongue tied: makes mistakes. *J. A. T. de Giles* **c78** **h–**

ALIANNA (FR) 4 b.f. Anabaa (USA) – Ambassadrice (FR) (Be My Guest (USA)) [2004/5 17m^F Nov 25] no form on Flat or on hurdling debut. *S. Dow* **h–**

ALI BRUCE 5 b.g. Cadeaux Genereux – Actualite (Polish Precedent (USA)) [2004/5 F–: F16g May 13] well held in bumpers: successful 4 times from 6f to 1m on all-weather on Flat, last 3 for G. L. Moore having been claimed for £12,000. *D. E. Cantillon* **F–**

ALICE JONES (IRE) 7 b. or br.m. King's Ride – Alice Brennan (IRE) (Good Thyne (USA)) [2004/5 F17g F16d 23d^{pu} 23v^{pu} Jan 3] €36,000 4-y-o: sturdy mare: first foal: dam, poor maiden hurdler, sister to useful 2m hurdler New York Rainbow and half-sister to useful chaser around 2½m All The Aces and dam of useful 2m chaser Cable Beach: no form in bumpers or over hurdles. *J. Mackie* **h–** **F–**

ALICE'S OLD ROSE 8 b.m. Broadsword (USA) – Rosie Marchioness (Neltino) [2004/5 17g^4 16d 20d^6 17m^4 20g^3 20d^2 22s^2 Dec 5] sister to winning pointer: dam, winning hurdler, half-sister to useful chaser up to 3¼m Kelly's Honor: tailed off only completed start in points: poor maiden hurdler: stays 2¾m: acts on soft ground. *Mrs H. O. Graham* **h78**

ALIKAT (IRE) 4 b.f. Alhaarth (IRE) – Be Crafty (USA) (Crafty Prospector (USA)) [2004/5 16m^3 17m^4 16g^2 16d 19s 19s* 16s^3 16g^6 19g* 22m^2 Apr 21] leggy filly: maiden on Flat: developed into fairly useful hurdler: trained on debut by J. J. Murphy: won handicaps at Taunton in February and April: stays 2¾m: acts on soft and good to firm ground: visored fifth start. *M. C. Pipe* **h119**

ALI SHUFFLE (IRE) 6 b.g. Ali-Royal (IRE) – Ediyrna (IRE) (Doyoun) [2004/5 20m^F 16s^3 20g 18s 17d 17d^5 16s^{pu} 16v Dec 27] half-brother to winning 2m hurdler Swift Spirit (by Lake Coniston): poor maiden hurdler: left R. Roberts after fourth outing: form only around 2m: acts on soft going. *J. J. Lambe, Ireland* **h80**

ALITTLEBITOPOWER 8 ch.g. Alflora (IRE) – What A Moppet (IRE) (Torus) [2004/5 c25m^3 c20d^2 c25g^{pu} Mar 9] second foal: dam lightly-raced half-sister to useful Irish hurdler I've Topped It: winning pointer: poor form when placed in hunter chases. *C. Storey* **c73**

ALIZARIN (IRE) 6 b.m. Tagula (IRE) – Persian Empress (IRE) (Persian Bold) [2004/5 h–: c21g^{pu} Apr 30] of no account. *P. Cartmell* **c–** **h–**

ALLAHRAKHA 14 ch.g. Aragon – Bernigra Girl (Royal Match) [2004/5 c19d^{pu} Oct 2] sparely-made gelding: winning hurdler: no form over fences: off over 6 years prior to reappearance. *O. J. Carter* **c–** **h–**

ALL BLEEVABLE 8 b.g. Presidium – Eve's Treasure (Bustino) [2004/5 h96: 17d 17g^{5} 17g^{6} 17d^{3} 19g^{F} 16g^{2} 16g^{6} Mar 18] close-coupled gelding: modest handicap hurdler: best around 2m: acts on good to firm and heavy going: races prominently. *Mrs S. Lamyman* **h96**

ALLBORN LAD (IRE) 5 b.g. Fourstars Allstar (USA) – Billeragh Girl (Normandy) [2004/5 F16d Jan 6] €35,000 4-y-o: half-brother to useful chaser Second Schedual (by Golden Love), stayed 25f: dam unraced half-sister to dam of Farmer Jack: well held in bumper on debut. *C. J. Mann* **F–**

ALLEGEDLY RED 6 ch.m. Sabrehill (USA) – Tendency (Ballad Rock) [2004/5 h75: 20d 16g^{2} 20m^{4} 17g^{5} 20g 16m* 16m^{5} 17s* Apr 2] leggy mare: modest hurdler: won seller at Hexham (for Mrs A. Duffield) in October and mares claimer at Bangor in April: best form around 2m: acts on firm and soft going: effective tongue tied or not. *R. Johnson* **h91**

ALLEGEDLY SO (IRE) 4 b.g. Flemensfirth (USA) – Celtic Lace (Celtic Cone) [2004/5 F17s^{5} F16s* Apr 10] sixth foal: dam little sign of ability: better effort in bumpers when winning maiden at Hexham by short head from Rathowen. *D. W. Whillans* **F95**

ALLEGED SLAVE (IRE) 10 ch.g. Husyan (USA) – Lek Dawn (Menelek) [2004/5 c107, h–: c17d^{2} c16d* May 8] workmanlike gelding: thrice-raced hurdler: fair chaser: made all in handicap at Southwell: stays 2½m: raced on good going or softer. *A. King* **c110** **h–**

ALLERTON BOY 6 ch.g. Beveled (USA) – Darakah (Doulab (USA)) [2004/5 17m^{6} 19m^{4} 17s^{6} 17m^{6} 16m 16g^{pu} Oct 4] half-brother to fair 2m to 3m hurdler Bodfari Signet (by King's Signet): poor maiden on Flat (stays 6f) nowadays, sold out of R. Hodges' stable £1,000 Ascot April Sales: non-stayer over hurdles: tongue tied fifth outing. *Evan Williams* **h–**

ALLEZ MOUSSON 7 b.g. Hernando (FR) – Rynechra (Blakeney) [2004/5 h79?: 20g^{F} 20s^{pu} Oct 24] fair at best on Flat (best at 2m+), well held in 2004: little form over hurdles. *A. Bailey* **h–**

ALLEZ PETIT LUIS (FR) 7 br.g. Grand Tresor (FR) – Galissima (FR) (Sicyos (USA)) [2004/5 F18m 22m 16f^{5} 24f^{3} 16s 24v^{pu} 20d^{6} 16s* 16s* 16v* 16s^{2} 20s^{5} 18s^{2} Mar 13] third foal: half-brother to winning French hurdler/chaser around 2½m Ajaccio (by Caerwent) and 11f Flat winner Houla Hoop (by Snurge): dam, 1½m winner/winning 17f hurdler, half-sister to smart Flat stayer Ethan Frome: fair form in bumpers: progressive handicap hurdler: left F. Kavanagh after sixth outing: won at Wexford in November and Clonmel and Thurles (novice) in December: best effort when second over 2¼m at Naas in March: probably stays 2½m: acts on heavy going. *C. A. Murphy, Ireland* **h115** **F92**

ALLEZ SCOTIA 6 ch.m. Minster Son – Allez (Move Off) [2004/5 h67, F77: 17g 24m^{3} 20s^{6} 22s^{4} 17d^{3} 20s^{3} 16g^{2} 20g^{5} 16v Mar 17] leggy mare: poor maiden hurdler: stays 3m: acts on soft and good to firm going. *R. Nixon* **h83**

ALLEZ TOUJOURS (IRE) 10 b.g. Castle Keep – Adapan (Pitpan) [2004/5 c–, h–: c24s* c24s^{3} Nov 13] lengthy gelding: maiden hurdler: poor form over fences, winning handicap at Uttoxeter in October: stays 3m: acts on soft going: tried blinkered. *M. Sheppard* **c68** **h–**

ALL FOR A REASON (IRE) 6 gr.g. Zaffaran (USA) – Cyrano Imperial (IRE) (Cyrano de Bergerac) [2004/5 19g Dec 8] €46,000 3-y-o: tall gelding: second foal: half-brother to fairly useful bumper winner Beyond The Pale (by Be My Native): dam unraced: well held in novice hurdle on debut. *P. J. Hobbs* **h–**

ALLFRIENDS 6 b. or br.g. Alflora (IRE) – Three Friends (IRE) (The Parson) [2004/5 F–: 23v^{pu} 20s^{pu} Mar 22] leggy gelding: no form in bumper or over hurdles: tongue tied final start. *H. P. Hogarth* **h–**

ALL HEART 4 ch.f. Alhaarth (IRE) – Meznh (IRE) (Mujtahid (USA)) [2004/5 16s^{4} 16s 16s^{3} 16v^{3} 16s* 16v^{4} Jan 15] modest maiden on Flat (stays 9.5f): fair juvenile hurdler: won at Thurles in January: good fourth to Strangely Brown in Grade 3 at Punchestown later in month. *Thomas Mullins, Ireland* **h113**

ALL HONEY (IRE) 8 ch.m. Fourstars Allstar (USA) – A Bit of Honey (The Parson) [2004/5 c–, h71: 20g Jul 14] leggy mare: failed to complete in 2 chases: poor hurdler: stays 2¾m: acts on heavy going: blinkered once. *Miss K. Marks* **c–** **h–**

ALLIED IMPERIAL 9 b.m. Morpeth – Super Sarena (IRE) (Taufan (USA)) [2004/5 c16d^{6} c16g 19g^{ur} 27d Aug 21] maiden hurdler: no show in 2 chases: tried tongue tied. *J. D. Frost* **c– h–**

ALLINJIM (IRE) 6 b.g. Turtle Island (IRE) – Bounayya (USA) (Al Nasr (FR)) [2004/5 21d^{pu} 16d 17s Feb 9] sturdy gelding: fairly useful on Flat (stays 15f) at 4 yrs: no form in novice hurdles. *J. A. Glover* **h–**

ALL IN THE STARS (IRE) 7 ch.g. Fourstars Allstar (USA) – Luton Flyer (Condorcet (FR)) [2004/5 h106: c23g^{3} c26d* c26d* c25d^{2} c25v^{pu} c24d^{3} Mar 5] smallish, sturdy gelding: fair maiden hurdler: fairly useful novice chaser: won twice at Plumpton in November, handicap on first occasion: better form when placed both completed starts after: stays 3¼m: acts on soft going: twice visored in 2003/4. *D. P. Keane* **c122 h–**

ALL MARQUE (IRE) 5 b.m. Saddlers' Hall (IRE) – Buzzing Beauty (Junius (USA)) [2004/5 F16s^{4} F16d F17s Jan 18] lengthy mare: fourth foal: dam unraced: no form in bumpers. *S. Gollings* **F–**

ALL ON MY OWN (USA) 10 ch.g. Unbridled (USA) – Some For All (USA) (One For All (USA)) [2004/5 c–, h56: 17v^{4} 16s^{4} 16g^{6} 16s 16d^{2} 16g^{4} 16d^{5} Mar 28] close-coupled gelding: well held only outing over fences: bad maiden hurdler: raced mainly around 2m on good going or softer: tried blinkered, visored last 3 starts. *I. W. McInnes* **c– h57**

ALL ROCK HARD (NZ) 7 ch.g. Bigstone (IRE) – My Lady Gray (NZ) (Otehi Bay (AUS)) [2004/5 h89: 17g 20d^{5} c20g^{2} c16g c16m c16g^{2} c16m^{pu} Aug 6] modest maiden hurdler/chaser: lame final outing: probably stays 2½m: acts on firm going: usually wears blinkers/cheekpieces. *R. C. Guest* **c91 h–**

ALL SONSILVER (FR) 8 b.g. Son of Silver – All Licette (FR) (Native Guile (USA)) [2004/5 c109, h–: c24g^{pu} Aug 14] useful-looking gelding: fair handicap chaser: left M. Todhunter, ran poorly only outing in 2004/5: stays 25f: acts on heavy going: has folded tamely. *P. Kelsall* **c– h–**

ALL STAR (GER) 5 b.g. Lomitas – Alte Garde (FR) (Garde Royale) [2004/5 16g^{pu} 17m^{2} 16g 17g* 16s^{6} 16d^{4} 16d^{6} Mar 12] angular gelding: successful once around 1¼m (at 3 yrs) from 8 starts on Flat in Germany for P. Schiergen: fairly useful hurdler: won handicap at Taunton in December: ran well after when fourth in well-contested similar events at Newbury and Punchestown: likely to prove best around 2m: acts on good to soft going, possibly not on soft. *N. J. Henderson* **h117**

ALLSTAR LEADER (IRE) 8 b.g. Fourstars Allstar (USA) – Rugged Leader (Supreme Leader) [2004/5 h79: 21d Dec 7] leggy gelding: poor hurdler: off 16 months, soundly beaten only outing in 2004/5: stays easy 3m: acts on firm going. *J. J. Lambe, Ireland* **h–**

ALLSTARS BLAZING (IRE) 5 b.g. Fourstars Allstar (USA) – Heather Blazing (IRE) (Paean) [2004/5 16d^{pu} Nov 24] seventh foal: half-brother to bumper winner Watts Hill (by Old Vic): dam unraced: no show in novice hurdle on debut. *Mrs P. Sly* **h–**

ALL THINGS EQUAL (IRE) 6 b.g. Supreme Leader – Angel's Dream (King's Ride) [2004/5 F95: F17g^{3} 19g^{4} 17s^{4} Feb 17] lengthy, useful-looking gelding: won maiden Irish point: fair form when placed in bumpers, virtually ran off course on bend into straight at Aintree only start on left-handed track: off over 7 months, found little under pressure when fourth in novice company over hurdles at Taunton. *S. E. H. Sherwood* **h97 F95**

ALLUDE (IRE) 6 b.g. Darshaan – Ahliyat (USA) (Irish River (FR)) [2004/5 h104: 16s^{2} 16d^{pu} Jan 1] strong, lengthy gelding: fair hurdler in 2003/4: bought out of C. Mann's stable £3,400 Ascot August Sales: off 16 months, second in seller (claimed from N. Rossiter £6,000) at Leicester on reappearance: ran poorly in handicap next time: will stay beyond 2m: acts on soft and good to firm going: usually wears cheekpieces. *M. A. Buckley* **h97**

ALLUMEE 6 ch.g. Alflora (IRE) – Coire Vannich (Celtic Cone) [2004/5 F95: 16d^{4} 16g^{2} 17s^{2} 16d^{5} 16d^{2} 16g^{2} Apr 17] sturdy gelding: fair novice hurdler: raced around 2m on good going or softer. *P. J. Hobbs* **h110**

ALLY SHRIMP 4 b.g. Tamure (IRE) – Minigale (Strong Gale) [2004/5 F16g^{5} F17d^{4} Mar 26] strong gelding: fifth foal: half-brother to modest chaser up to 3m Windle Brook (by Gildoran) and fair hurdler/chaser up to 3m Ahraydoubleyou (by Teenoso): dam unraced half-sister to high-class staying chaser By The Way: fair form in bumpers: will be suited by further. *T. P. Tate* **F89**

ALMA BAY 5 ch.m. Karinga Bay – Almanot (Remainder Man) [2004/5 F17m^{5} Sep 1] fourth foal: dam placed in bumper: well beaten in bumper on debut. *R. Curtis* **F–**

AL MABROOK (IRE) 10 b.g. Rainbows For Life (CAN) – Sky Lover (Ela-Mana-Mou) [2004/5 h89: 21g[3] 21g* 21m 20g[2] 22m 22v 21v[pu] 21v 20s Apr 10] close-coupled gelding: modest handicap hurdler: won at Sedgefield (third course success) in May: lost form after fourth outing: stays 21f: acts on any going: tried in cheekpieces/visor. *N. G. Richards* **h93 d**

ALMAH (SAF) 7 b.m. Al Mufti (USA) – Jazz Champion (SAF) (Dancing Champ (USA)) [2004/5 18s[2] 16s* 16d* 16d[6] 19s* 16v[2] 24s[3] 21g Apr 14] fairly useful on Flat (stays 2m), successful 5 times in South Africa: similar standard over hurdles: landed odds in novices at Towcester in November, Leicester in December and Exeter in January, first 2 mares events: should stay at least 2½m: acts on heavy going. *Miss Venetia Williams* **h118**

ALMANOSO 9 b.m. Teenoso (USA) – Almanot (Remainder Man) [2004/5 c–§, h58§: 25g[pu] May 9] jumped poorly only start over fences: bad maiden hurdler: stays 3¼m: acts on soft going: wore blinkers/cheekpieces last 4 starts: unreliable: sold £1,100 Ascot June Sales. *R. Curtis* **c– §** **h– §**

ALMARAVIDE (GER) 9 ch.g. Orfano (GER) – Allerleirauh (GER) (Espresso) [2004/5 h122: 20s Dec 4] smallish gelding: fairly useful handicap hurdler, lightly raced: last of 15 finishers in valuable event at Haydock, only outing in 2004/5: should stay beyond 2½m: acts on heavy going, not discredited on firm. *M. Bradstock* **h–**

ALMAYDAN 7 b.g. Marju (IRE) – Cunning (Bustino) [2004/5 h129: 16m[4] 16g[4] c16d* c16d[3] c16v* c16d* c16g c16g[2] Apr 14] strong gelding: useful hurdler: good fourth in handicaps at Haydock and Aintree in May: similar form over fences: won maiden at Huntingdon in October and novices at Warwick in December and Huntingdon in January: easily better effort in handicaps at Cheltenham when second to Andreas: raced mainly around 2m: acts on heavy and good to firm going: sound jumper. *R. Lee* **c137** **h136**

ALMENARA 6 ch.m. Weld – Dishcloth (Fury Royal) [2004/5 F16s F16v Jan 15] half-sister to fairly useful chaser Parahandy (by Lancastrian), stayed 29f: dam fairly useful 2m hurdler/winning chaser: well beaten in bumpers. *G. M. Moore* **F–**

ALMIRE DU LIA (FR) 7 ch.g. Beyssac (FR) – Lita (FR) (Big John (FR)) [2004/5 c104, h–: c25m[4] May 19] big gelding: winning hurdler: fair chaser: ran as if amiss last 2 outings: stays 25f: acts on firm and soft going: usually wears cheekpieces/visor. *Mrs S. C. Bradburne* **c–** **h–**

ALMNADIA (IRE) 6 b.m. Alhaarth (IRE) – Mnaafa (IRE) (Darshaan) [2004/5 h103: 20g* 19d* 21g[pu] Apr 14] smallish mare: fair handicap hurdler: won at Uttoxeter (mares event) and Market Rasen early in season: soon behind after blundering seventh in listed mares handicap at Cheltenham 8 months later: stays 3m: acts on firm and good to soft going: reliable. *S. Gollings* **h112**

ALMOST BROKE 8 ch.g. Nearly A Hand – Teletex (Pollerton) [2004/5 c26d* c19v* c25s[5] c21d* c20d[6] c20s* Apr 20] tall gelding: modest novice hurdler in 2002/3: took really well to fences after 18-month absence, winning handicaps at Newton Abbot (readily), Chepstow (jumped right), Wincanton and Perth (beat Powder Creek a neck in 4-way finish despite idling): has won at 3¼m, best form over shorter: acts on heavy going. *P. F. Nicholls* **c127** **h–**

ALPH 8 b.g. Alflora (IRE) – Royal Birthday (St Paddy) [2004/5 h85: 17d[5] May 15] tall, lengthy, rather sparely-made gelding: well held in 2 novice hurdles: fourth over 1½m on Flat in August (refused to enter stall intended next outing). *R. Ingram* **h–**

ALPHABETIC 8 ch.g. Alflora (IRE) – Incamelia (St Columbus) [2004/5 h93: c19d[F] c25d[3] Mar 10] well-made gelding: modest form in novice hurdles: off 14 months, would have finished second but for falling 2 out in maiden at Chepstow on chasing debut: found nothing next time: should stay beyond 2½m: acts on good to firm and good to soft going. *N. J. Henderson* **c107** **h–**

ALPHA GAMBLE (IRE) 5 ch.g. Alphabatim (USA) – Caher Cross (IRE) (Phardante (FR)) [2004/5 17d[4] 20s[6] Dec 17] €3,400 3-y-o: first foal: dam unraced, from family of top-class chaser up to 2½m Leap Frog: won maiden on second of 2 starts in 4-y-o Irish points in 2004: better effort over hurdles when fourth in novice at Folkestone: should be suited by 2½m+. *R. Rowe* **h93**

ALPHA GIOCONDA (IRE) 8 b.g. Alphabatim (USA) – Rio Dulce (Rio Carmelo (FR)) [2004/5 h–p: 20d[3] 21s* 17d Jan 1] angular gelding: off 5½ months, best effort in novice hurdles when winning at Kempton in November: will stay beyond 21f: sold 5,000 gns Doncaster May Sales. *N. J. Henderson* **h99**

ALPHAGRAN (IRE) 5 b.g. Alphabatim (USA) – Grannie No (Brave Invader (USA)) [2004/5 F18m Apr 21] €7,000 4-y-o: half-brother to several winners, including **F–**

useful chaser Blue Irish, stayed 27f, and fairly useful hurdler/fair chaser Celtic Pride (both by Roselier), stays 3m: dam, lightly-raced maiden, half-sister to useful chaser up to 21f Freeline Finishing: well held in bumper on debut. *Miss A. M. Newton-Smith*

ALPHA IMAGE (IRE) 6 b.g. Alphabatim (USA) – Happy Image (Le Moss) [2004/5 h–: c23m^{6} c21m^{4} c21g^{pu} c26g^{pu} c17d^{2} c18m^{4} c16d^{F} Oct 3] rather leggy gelding: pulled up both starts over hurdles: poor maiden chaser: should stay beyond 21f: wore cheekpieces/ blinkers last 3 starts. *Mrs L. Williamson* **c73 h–**

ALPHA JULIET (IRE) 4 b.f. Victory Note (USA) – Zara's Birthday (IRE) (Waajib) [2004/5 16d^{4} 16d^{3} 16d 16s^{F} 16s^{ur} Mar 1] leggy filly: poor form in maidens on Flat and in juvenile hurdles. *G. M. Moore* **h71**

ALPHA LEATHER 14 gr.g. Zambrano – Harvey's Choice (Whistlefield) [2004/5 c–, h–: c25s^{pu} Apr 28] tall gelding: no longer of any account: tried visored. *M. J. Grassick* **c– h–**

ALPHASUPREME (IRE) 8 ch.m. Alphabatim (USA) – Railway Rabbit (IRE) (Supreme Leader) [2004/5 F–: 22g^{5} 19m^{F} 19f^{4} 26d Oct 17] little sign of ability. *Mrs P. N. Dutfield* **h–**

ALPHECCA (USA) 4 b.g. Kingmambo (USA) – Limbo (USA) (A P Indy (USA)) [2004/5 16g Apr 16] useful form on Flat (will probably stay 1½m), sold out of Sir Michael Stoute's stable 24,000 gns Newmarket Autumn Sales: well held in juvenile on hurdling debut. *K. G. Reveley* **h–**

ALPINE HIDEAWAY (IRE) 12 b.g. Tirol – Arbour (USA) (Graustark) [2004/5 c–, h75: 17m^{2} 17m^{3} 19g^{2} 17d^{4} 17v^{2} Oct 17] angular gelding: modest handicap hurdler: stays 19f: acts on any going: tried blinkered/visored, wears cheekpieces nowadays. *J. S. Wainwright* **c– h88**

ALPINE SLAVE 8 ch.g. Alflora (IRE) – Celtic Slave (Celtic Cone) [2004/5 c105, h–: c25d^{F} c25g c26d^{5} Apr 18] sturdy gelding: fair chaser in 2003/4: off 11 months, below form in 2004/5: stays 3¼m: raced on good going or softer (acts on soft). *N. J. Gifford* **c85 h–**

ALPINE STAR 8 ch.g. Alflora (IRE) – Northwood Star (IRE) (Henbit (USA)) [2004/5 16g 16s^{4} 17g^{pu} 17d^{3} Jan 1] stocky gelding: fairly useful form when third in bumper on debut: off 2½ years before reappearance: best effort over hurdles in novice handicap on final start: will stay beyond 17f. *N. J. Gifford* **h112**

ALRAFID (IRE) 6 ch.g. Halling (USA) – Ginger Tree (USA) (Dayjur (USA)) [2004/5 17g* 16d^{2} 16d^{5} 17g^{2} 16g^{2} Mar 14] medium-sized gelding: useful on Flat (stays 1¼m): fair hurdler: won novice at Taunton in October: will prove best around 2m with emphasis on speed: takes strong hold. *G. L. Moore* **h111**

ALRIDA (IRE) 6 b.g. Ali-Royal (IRE) – Ride Bold (USA) (J O Tobin (USA)) [2004/5 h94p: 17d^{2} 17m* 17d* 22d Aug 22] angular gelding: fairly useful at best on Flat (stays 21f): similar standard over hurdles: won novice at Market Rasen in June and valuable handicap there (beat Wet Lips 5 lengths) in July: should stay 2½m+. *R. A. Fahey* **h121**

ALRIGHT NOW M'LAD (IRE) 5 b.g. Supreme Leader – Chattering (Le Bavard (FR)) [2004/5 F16d^{5} 16s^{4} Mar 5] medium-sized gelding: fifth foal: half-brother to winning 2½m chaser Bandon Valley (by Montelimar): dam, modest hurdler/chaser who stayed 3m, sister to dam of high-class staying hurdler Marello: fifth of 20 in bumper at Huntingdon on debut: 23 lengths fourth to Valley Ride in novice hurdle there 3 months later: capable of better, particularly at 2½m+. *Jonjo O'Neill* **h83 p F90**

ALROYAL (GER) 6 ch.g. Royal Solo (IRE) – Alamel (USA) (Shadeed (USA)) [2004/5 16d^{4} 16g* 17d* 16d^{pu} 16m^{5} 16m* 17d^{pu} Oct 3] rangy, useful-looking ex-German gelding: won at 1m on Flat for H. J. Groschel: fair novice hurdler: won at Uttoxeter in July, Market Rasen in August and Plumpton in September: likely to prove best around 2m: acts on good to firm and good to soft going. *C. J. Mann* **h112**

ALSKA (FR) 12 b. or br.m. Leading Counsel (USA) – Kolkwitzia (FR) (The Wonder (FR)) [2004/5 c94, h–: c33s^{4} c25g^{3} c31m^{4} c24g^{4} c25s^{pu} c24g^{6} Apr 15] angular mare: fair hunter chaser: below form in 2005: stays 33f: acts on any going: tried blinkered/visored, not for long time: moody. *P. L. Southcombe* **c91 § h–**

ALSTON HOUSE 10 gr.g. Gran Alba (USA) – Pablena (Pablond) [2004/5 c26g^{pu} c21m^{pu} Jun 27] maiden pointer: no show in 2 chases, blinkered in second. *J. L. Spearing* **c–**

ALSYATI 7 ch.g. Salse (USA) – Rubbiyati (Cadeaux Genereux) [2004/5 h79+: 16m^{2} Apr 25] lengthy gelding: poor hurdler: no form in points in 2005: raced around 2m: acts on good to firm going. *D. Burchell* **h84**

ALTESSE DE SOU (FR) 5 gr.m. Saint Preuil (FR) – Pretty Point (Crystal Glitters (USA)) [2004/5 c18s c18s c18d^{4} 18d 18s* 17d^{4} 17v^{3} 17g^{5} Dec 15] leggy mare: fifth foal: half-sister to 4 winners, including useful 2m hurdler/chaser Tysou (by Ajdayt) and 8.5f to 1¼m winner Souscription (by Script Ohio): dam winning hurdler around 2m: maiden chaser: modest hurdler: won 4-y-o claimer at Auteuil (claimed from M. Rolland €18,600) in September: raced around 2m: acts on soft ground: tried blinkered. *M. C. Pipe* **c91 h97**

ALTHREY DANDY (IRE) 10 ch.g. Good Thyne (USA) – Hawthorn Dandy (Deep Run) [2004/5 c24d* c24d^{6} c26g^{F} Apr 14] lengthy gelding: won both starts in points in 2004: made most to win hunter chase at Bangor in May: little impact in similar events after 10-month absence: should stay beyond 3m: acts on good to soft going: started very slowly second outing: one to treat with caution. *Miss C. J. Goodall* **c99 §**

ALTITUDE DANCER (IRE) 5 b.g. Sadler's Wells (USA) – Height of Passion (Shirley Heights) [2004/5 h89: 16v^{4} 16g^{5} 19m^{3} 21g* 19m^{3} 21d^{5} Apr 18] smallish gelding: modest hurdler: claimed from P. Blockley £6,000 third start: won handicap at Plumpton in March: stays 21f: acts on good to firm going: blinkered second and third starts: not one to trust. *Mrs A. M. Thorpe* **h89 §**

ALTO FICO (IRE) 5 ch.g. Un Desperado (FR) – Barberstown's Last (Le Bavard (FR)) [2004/5 F16s F16m Apr 2] very tall gelding: sixth foal: half-brother to winning pointer Valtorus (by Torus): dam unraced: no show in 2 bumpers. *Miss H. C. Knight* **F–**

ALTREGAN BOY (IRE) 13 b.g. Lancastrian – Please Oblige (Le Levanstell) [2004/5 c32m^{ur} c30d^{4} c23m c26g^{pu} Jul 15] workmanlike gelding: poor chaser: left D. Broad in Ireland after second start: thorough stayer: acts on heavy going: has been blinkered, also tried in cheekpieces: tried tongue tied. *C. N. Kellett* **c86 h–**

ALVA GLEN (USA) 8 b.g. Gulch (USA) – Domludge (USA) (Lyphard (USA)) [2004/5 h87d: 16d^{4} 17m^{4} 20m 16s 17m 16g^{F} 16d* Apr 3] modest hurdler: sold out of Miss V. Williams' stable 6,500 gns Doncaster November Sales after third start: won handicap at Wincanton in April: stays 2½m: acts on good to firm and good to soft going: headstrong: looked temperamental at times for former stable. *B. J. Llewellyn* **h94**

ALVARO (IRE) 8 ch.g. Priolo (USA) – Gezalle (Shareef Dancer (USA)) [2004/5 c75, h73: 21m* 22f^{5} c19s^{2} c25g^{6} 20s* 20s^{2} c24v^{2d} c25v^{pu} c24d^{pu} Apr 22] workmanlike gelding: modest hurdler: won selling handicaps at Plumpton in September and Leicester in December: best effort when second in claimer at Leicester sixth start: poor form over fences: stays 27f: acts on heavy and good to firm going: blinkered/in cheekpieces in 2004/5. *B. J. Llewellyn* **c79 h99**

*totesport Summer Hurdle (Handicap), Market Rasen—
the novice Alrida has had things sewn up from some way out*

ALWAYS 6 b.g. Dynaformer (USA) – Love And Affection (USA) (Exclusive Era (USA)) [2004/5 h115: 20g c17m* c16m* c17g^{2} c17s* c17g^{2} c20s^{3} c16d* c18d^{5} Nov 13] leggy gelding: fairly useful hurdler: good first season over fences, winning maiden at Fairyhouse and novices at Punchestown, Cork (made all in 3-runner race) and Roscommon (Grade 3 event, beat Old Flame by ¾ length): fell heavily fifth in handicap at Punchestown in late-April: stays 2½m: acts on soft and good to firm going: tried blinkered/tongue tied: usually races prominently: reliable. *N. Meade, Ireland* **c120 h103**

ALWAYS BELIEVE (USA) 9 b.g. Carr de Naskra (USA) – Wonder Mar (USA) (Fire Dancer (USA)) [2004/5 h–: 16d 16g Dec 9] small gelding: no show in 3 novice hurdles: tried tongue tied. *Mrs P. Ford* **h–**

ALWAYS FLYING (USA) 4 ch.g. Fly So Free (USA) – Dubiously (USA) (Jolie Jo (USA)) [2004/5 16m^{3} 16g^{2} 17g^{6} Feb 16] tall, leggy gelding: modest on Flat (stays 1½m): modest form in juvenile hurdles. *N. Wilson* **h92**

ALWAYS IN DEBT (IRE) 6 b.g. Norwich – Forever In Debt (Pragmatic) [2004/5 F83: 20s^{4} 20v^{3} 24v 20g 20d^{pu} Apr 20] well-made gelding: modest form at best over hurdles. *P. J. Hobbs* **h88**

ALWAYS RAINBOWS (IRE) 7 b. or br.g. Rainbows For Life (CAN) – Maura's Guest (IRE) (Be My Guest (USA)) [2004/5 c–, h92: 16m c20d^{ur} c17m^{5} c20m^{5} 17d^{5} 20g 17d^{6} 16d^{5} 20s^{2} 20d^{4} 23d^{4} 21d^{2} 19g^{3} Dec 11] useful-looking gelding: no form over fences (poor jumper): poor hurdler nowadays: seems to stay 23f: acts on heavy going: usually wears headgear: difficult ride. *B. S. Rothwell* **c– § h80 §**

ALWAYS WAINING (IRE) 4 b.c. Unfuwain (USA) – Glenarff (USA) (Irish River (FR)) [2004/5 16g^{4} 16d^{4} 16v* 17d* 20v* Feb 19] sturdy colt: useful on Flat (should stay 1¼m), successful 3 times in 2004, claimed from M. Johnston £30,000 in October: fairly useful juvenile hurdler: won at Uttoxeter in January and Market Rasen and Uttoxeter in February, left clear last (disputing lead with Lord Olympia at time) in novice at last-named: stays 2½m: acts on heavy going. *P. L. Clinton* **h116**

ALYSSIA MIA 4 br.f. Bob's Return (IRE) – Amazon (IRE) (Petorius) [2004/5 aF16g Feb 19] first foal: dam thrice-raced maiden: ran as if amiss in bumper on debut. *M. R. Bosley* **F–**

AMADEUS (AUS) 8 ch.g. Brief Truce (USA) – Amazaan (NZ) (Zamazaan (FR)) [2004/5 16g* 16g^{2} c16s* c16s* c16s^{6} c16s^{2} 19v^{3} c16s^{pu} c16d^{2} c20d^{4} Apr 20] angular gelding: left J. M. Bradley/off 2½ years, first form over hurdles when winning novice handicap at Plumpton in October: modest handicap chaser: won novice events at Hexham and Chepstow in November: best efforts when second: best form at 2m: acts on soft going. *M. Scudamore* **c97 h74**

AMALFI STORM 4 b.f. Slip Anchor – Mayroni (Bustino) [2004/5 F16s^{4} F17g^{2} Apr 3] sister to bumper winner Caulkleys Bank and half-sister to winners abroad by Batshoof and Glint of Gold: dam, placed at 1¾m, sister to very smart 1½m winner Bustomi and half-sister to dam of useful chaser up to 21f Scots Grey: better effort in bumpers when second to Rosita Bay in steadily-run mares event at Market Rasen. *M. W. Easterby* **F88**

AMANDARI (FR) 9 ch.g. Petit Loup (USA) – Baby Sitting (FR) (Son of Silver) [2004/5 h–: 20d 21g 27m^{4} 26g^{6} 22g^{5} 22g 21m^{pu} 22d^{2} 24m^{2} Oct 1] rather leggy gelding: bad maiden hurdler: probably stays 3m: wears cheekpieces nowadays. *J. K. Hunter* **h57**

AMARULA RIDGE (IRE) 4 b.g. Indian Ridge – Mail Boat (Formidable (USA)) [2004/5 17s^{2} 17v^{4} 16s^{2} 16g Mar 15] rather leggy gelding: useful on Flat (stays 9f) at 3 yrs, sold out of K. Prendergast's stable 21,000 gns Newmarket Autumn Sales: fairly useful juvenile hurdler: best effort when eighth of 24 to Dabiroun in valuable handicap at Cheltenham: likely to prove best around 2m with emphasis on speed. *P. J. Hobbs* **h114**

AMBER DAWN 6 ch.m. Weld – Scrambird (Dubassoff (USA)) [2004/5 F–: F16g^{5} 20v 19v 20m^{5} Apr 10] angular mare: signs of a little ability in bumpers (for B. Llewellyn) and over hurdles. *J. Gallagher* **h74 F71**

AMBER GO GO 8 ch.m. Rudimentary (USA) – Plaything (High Top) [2004/5 c–, h52: 20d 21g 17g^{3} 17d^{5} 20g^{2} 16m 22s^{5} c20v^{6} 21d^{3} 25g 21v^{pu} 19d^{6} 27v^{4} 17d Apr 5] lengthy mare: poor handicap hurdler: stays 27f: acts on soft going: tried in cheekpieces. *James Moffatt* **c– h65**

AMBERLEIGH HOUSE (IRE) 13 br.g. Buckskin (FR) – Chancy Gal (Al Sirat) [2004/5 c146, h105: 23d c20s^{4} c27s^{5} c20s^{4} c24g c36d Apr 9] lengthy gelding: winning hurdler: smart handicap chaser at best: very good record over National fences at Aintree (in frame 5 out of 8 completed starts), won Martell Cognac Grand National in 2004: **c140 h–**

always well off pace in race year later: best effort in 2004/5 when fifth to Silver Birch in Becher Chase at same course in November: stays 4½m: acts on good to firm and heavy going: sound jumper. *D. McCain*

AMBER MOSS 10 ch.g. Phardante (FR) – Queen's Darling (Le Moss) [2004/5 c–§, h76§: 24d 27m^{pu} May 19] workmanlike gelding: winning hurdler/maiden chaser: stays 27f, at least when emphasis is on speed: wears cheekpieces: ungenuine. *Mrs C. J. Kerr* **c– § h– §**

AMBERSONG 7 ch.g. Hernando (FR) – Stygian (USA) (Irish River (FR)) [2004/5 16g* 16s^6 16g^3 16g* 16g^5 16d Mar 24] modest on Flat (stays 1¾m): modest hurdler: won seller in October and novice claimer in December, both at Ludlow: likely to stay beyond 2m. *A. W. Carroll* **h85**

AMBER STARLIGHT 7 b.m. Binary Star (USA) – Stupid Cupid (Idiot's Delight) [2004/5 h81p: 20s^2 22s^{pu} 21m^{pu} Apr 2] rather leggy mare: easily best effort over hurdles when second to Inch Pride in mares novice at Fontwell: likely to stay 3m. *R. Rowe* **h102**

AMBITION ROYAL (FR) 5 ch.g. Cyborg (FR) – Before Royale (FR) (Dauphin du Bourg (FR)) [2004/5 F98: F16g F16g 16s^2 16s^3 16v^2 16s^4 16s^4 Apr 22] strong, stocky gelding: bumper winner, left Mrs L. Normile after first start: fair maiden hurdler: will stay beyond 2m: acts on heavy going. *Miss Lucinda V. Russell* **h100 F–**

AMBOBO (USA) 5 b.g. Kingmambo (USA) – Bold Bold (IRE) (Sadler's Wells (USA)) [2004/5 17g* 17s* 17d* 18s^2 17s* 20s* Jan 29] **h149 +**

Trainer Arnaud Chaille-Chaille and owner Sean Mulryan opted against their unbeaten chaser Cyrlight's taking his chance in the King George VI Chase at Kempton, for a season at least, but a month after Christmas the stable's very first runner in Britain was successful when Ambobo, one of three in the stable's raiding party, won the Grade 2 Royal Gloucestershire Hussars Novices' Hurdle at Cheltenham. Formerly known as the Persian War Novices' Hurdle, and more recently the Classic Novices' Hurdle—still the registered name of the race—it was previously run at Chepstow and then Uttoxeter and had been won in recent seasons by the likes of Monsignor, Keen Leader and Iris's Gift. Monsignor went on to win the Royal & SunAlliance Hurdle at the Festival and by mid-March Ambobo was favourite to do the same. But just four days before the race, Ambobo was ruled out by an injury to his off-fore sustained during a gallop at home.

Ambobo was a 14/1-chance at Cheltenham in January—only three others in the field of ten were sent off at longer odds—but he put up an improved performance to win with authority, showing a combination of speed and stamina, the latter something which could only have been taken on trust beforehand as it was his first attempt at two and a half miles. Handy throughout and jumping fluently, Ambobo was rousted clear after two out and ran on strongly up the hill for a two-and-a-half-length victory over the favourite and Challow Hurdle winner Brewster, with the Ebor winner Mephisto making a promising hurdling debut eight lengths back in third. Mephisto clearly improved a good deal in winning his three subsequent races

Royal Gloucestershire Hussars Classic Novices' Hurdle, Cheltenham—
French raider Ambobo (noseband) comes out on top from Brewster in a strong field

but Brewster, who was placed over three miles at Cheltenham and Aintree, Ladalko and Moulin Riche, fifth and sixth respectively, all upheld or boosted the form. There wasn't a better performance in a novice hurdle all season than Ambobo's at Cheltenham and he would clearly have been a major factor in the Royal & SunAlliance Hurdle.

Ambobo brought a fine record in France with him to Cheltenham. He had been beaten there only once in five starts over hurdles, taking on only fellow four-year-olds before the turn of the year and campaigned for the most part in the Provinces. His only defeat had come when giving weight to the Guillaume Macaire-trained Rigoureux at Bordeaux on his fourth start, but Ambobo had the same rival back in fourth at level weights when winning a listed race at Enghien in November on his final start before Cheltenham. For the record, Ambobo's first three wins came at Gramat, Clairefontaine and Cholet, and, as a matter of interest, the second of those wins came at the expense of another horse who was to show useful form in novice hurdles in Britain later in the season, My Way de Solzen.

Ambobo is on the small side for a hurdler, but sturdy, and he was bred to excel on the Flat. He is bred on similar lines to the leading three-year-old fillies Divine Proportions and Virginia Waters, by Kingmambo out of a Sadler's Wells mare, and comes from the same family as the top-class milers Polish Precedent, Zilzal and Intikhab. Polish Precedent is his closest relative among that trio, being a half-brother to Ambobo's grandam, the minor American stakes winner Jasmina. As it was, Ambobo showed form verging on useful for Criquette Head-Maarek, winning a minor event at Deauville over an extended mile and a half before being sold for €65,000 at the Goffs Arc Sale in 2003. He then had two starts for his owner's Flat trainer Eric Libaud (blinkered for the last of them) before being sent hurdling.

Ambobo (USA) (b.g. 2000)	Kingmambo (USA) (b 1990)	Mr Prospector (b 1970)	Raise A Native
			Gold Digger
		Miesque (b 1984)	Nureyev
			Pasadoble
	Bold Bold (IRE) (b 1993)	Sadler's Wells (b 1981)	Northern Dancer
			Fairy Bridge
		Jasmina (ch 1985)	Forli
			Past Example

Ambobo's dam Bold Bold won at a mile and a quarter at Saint-Cloud and has bred two other winners, the fairly useful French winner at around the same trip, True Wooman (by Capote), and the middle-distance winner Trompette (by Bahri). Ambobo isn't the first in his family to win a good prize over hurdles, however, as that honour went to his dam's brother Sabadilla, winner of the 2003 Galway Hurdle. Sabadilla isn't as good a hurdler as Ambobo, but he was a better Flat horse in his prime, showing smart form when his wins included the November Handicap. Ambobo's year-younger half-brother Boldini (by Atticus) showed little in three starts over hurdles for Martin Pipe in the latest season.

Having shown his proficiency over British hurdles, Ambobo will no doubt be sent on more cross-Channel raids in future, when he could be joined by the likes of Cyrlight and the same connections' leading juvenile hurdler Kiko. Chaille-Chaille, a neighbour of Macaire's on the south-west coast of France, has had growing success in recent seasons, reaching third place by races won over jumps in France in 2003 and the same position by prize money won in 2004. Ambobo, who stays two and a half miles and has raced only on good ground or softer, may still be capable of better. *A. Chaille-Chaille, France*

AMBRY 8 b.g. Machiavellian (USA) – Alkaffeyeh (IRE) (Sadler's Wells (USA)) **h116 §** [2004/5 h119: 23m 20m^{6} 24d^{4} 24m^{2} 21d Nov 9] compact gelding: fairly useful handicap hurdler: stays 25f: acts on heavy and good to firm going: used to be blinkered/visored: usually races lazily. *Mrs S. J. Smith*

AMBUSHED (IRE) 9 b.g. Indian Ridge – Surprise Move (IRE) (Simply Great (FR)) **c90** [2004/5 c91, h99: c16g^{3} c16d^{pu} 16g c20m^{pu} c17g^{6} c16m^{5} c16s^{F} 16d^{5} Sep 22] modest **h80** hurdler/maiden chaser, below form in 2004/5 after first outing: best around 2m: acts on soft and good to firm going: fell heavily when visored seventh start. *P. Monteith*

AMERAS (IRE) 7 b.m. Hamas (IRE) – Amerindian (Commanche Run) [2004/5 h71: **c71** 16d 16s^{5} c16g^{4} c16v^{3} c16s^{2} Apr 10] angular mare: poor novice hurdler: similar form over **h63**

fences: raced mainly around 2m: acts on heavy going: tried tongue tied: races freely. *Miss S. E. Forster*

AMERICAN PRESIDENT (IRE) 9 br.g. Lord Americo – Deceptive Response (Furry Glen) [2004/5 19g^{ro} 16s^{F} 19g^{3} 16v Jan 26] sturdy gelding: fair novice hurdler: ran out on reappearance: should stay 2½m+: free-going sort: has given trouble in preliminaries. *O. Brennan* **h101**

AMICELLI (GER) 6 b.g. Goofalik (USA) – Arratonia (GER) (Arratos (FR)) [2004/5 h106: 21m^{5} Apr 25] useful-looking gelding: fair form in novice/maiden hurdles: let down by jumping in handicap only start in 2004/5: stays 21f: joined P. Hobbs. *C. J. Mann* **h–**

AMID THE CHAOS (IRE) 5 ch.g. Nashwan (USA) – Celebrity Style (USA) (Seeking The Gold (USA)) [2004/5 h110: 16g^{2} 20g^{F} 16m* 16m* 20s^{2} Sep 16] well-made gelding: fair hurdler: won maiden at Kilbeggan in August and minor event at Down Royal in September: stays 2½m: yet to race on firm going, acts on any other: blinkered in 2004/5: tongue tied once. *D. K. Weld, Ireland* **h110**

AMIR ZAMAN 7 ch.g. Salse (USA) – Colorvista (Shirley Heights) [2004/5 16g Apr 26] sturdy gelding: fair up to 2m on Flat: thrice-raced over hurdles, easily best effort when second in maiden in 2002/3: will stay 2½m. *J. R. Jenkins* **h–**

AMIWORTHIT (IRE) 6 ch.m. Flying Spur (AUS) – Chief's Princess (Be My Chief (USA)) [2004/5 F16v Feb 19] second foal: dam poor maiden: tailed off in bumper on debut. *K. G. Wingrove* **F–**

AMJAD 8 ch.g. Cadeaux Genereux – Babita (Habitat) [2004/5 c77?, h–: 17g^{3} 17g 16g c16m 17m^{5} 16m^{pu} 17d^{6} 20s^{6} Nov 5] leggy gelding: poor hurdler/maiden chaser: best around 2m: acts on firm and good to soft going: pulls hard: not a fluent jumper. *Miss Kate Milligan* **c– h74 x**

AMMONIAS (GER) 6 b.h. Monsun (GER) – Augreta (GER) (Simply Great (FR)) [2004/5 h115: 20m* 22d^{3} 24d^{4} Jan 29] good-topped horse: fair novice hurdler: idled when landing odds at Wetherby in October: reportedly distressed when disappointing next time: stays at least 21f (stiffish task at 3m): unraced on extremes of going: tongue tied last 2 starts. *C. J. Mann* **h107**

AMNESTY 6 ch.g. Salse (USA) – Amaranthus (Shirley Heights) [2004/5 16s^{6} 16g 16v 16s^{ur} 16s^{6} 16d^{2} 18g Mar 20] angular gelding: fair on Flat (stays 9.7f): modest novice hurdler: will prove best at 2m with emphasis on speed. *G. L. Moore* **h93**

AMONG EQUALS 8 b.g. Sadler's Wells (USA) – Epicure's Garden (USA) (Affirmed (USA)) [2004/5 h108: 20g^{rtr} May 1] angular gelding: fair hurdler in 2003/4: refused to race at Uttoxeter in May (also did so on Flat previous month): will stay beyond 2¼m: acts on heavy going: one to leave alone. *M. Meade* **h– §**

A MONK SWIMMING (IRE) 4 br.g. Among Men (USA) – Sea Magic (IRE) (Distinctly North (USA)) [2004/5 16d 16d Feb 4] lengthy gelding: poor maiden on Flat (stays 1½m): well beaten in juvenile hurdles: sold £800 Ascot April Sales. *John Berry* **h–**

AMPLIFI (IRE) 8 b.g. Phardante (FR) – Season's Delight (Idiot's Delight) [2004/5 c87x, h84: 22d^{2} May 17] medium-sized gelding: modest maiden hurdler/chaser: stays 2¾m: acts on good to soft going: generally let down by jumping over fences: sold 10,000 gns Doncaster May Sales. *P. J. Hobbs* **c– x h95**

AMPTINA (IRE) 10 b.g. Shardari – Cotton Gale (Strong Gale) [2004/5 c75, h–: c16g c16m c17g^{5} c21d^{5} c21d^{2} c16m Sep 19] poor chaser: stays 21f: acts on good to firm and good to soft going: has had tongue tied: weak finisher. *Mrs S. J. Smith* **c69 § h– §**

AMRITSAR 8 ch.g. Indian Ridge – Trying For Gold (USA) (Northern Baby (CAN)) [2004/5 h69: 16m^{5} 20g^{pu} 17d^{4} 20m 19d^{5} Oct 5] angular gelding: poor maiden hurdler: best efforts around 2m: tried in cheekpieces: has had tongue tied. *K. G. Wingrove* **h62**

AMYROSEISUPPOSE 6 b.m. Classic Cliche (IRE) – Fishki (Niniski (USA)) [2004/5 F17s^{ur} Nov 29] £2,000 4-y-o: half-sister to 3 winners, including modest hurdlers Fishki's Lad (by Casteddu) and Green 'N' Gold (by Cloudings): dam winning jumper, stayed 25f: well held when unseating 4f out in mares bumper on debut. *D. Flood* **F–**

ANAKA FLIGHT 4 b.f. Missed Flight – Hamanaka (USA) (Conquistador Cielo (USA)) [2004/5 F16s^{pu} Feb 5] third foal: dam winning 2m hurdler: breathing problem in bumper on debut. *I. McMath* **F–**

ANALOGY (IRE) 5 ch.g. Bahhare (USA) – Anna Comnena (IRE) (Shareef Dancer (USA)) [2004/5 h129: 24g* May 13] lengthy gelding: fairly useful hurdler: in cheek- **h128**

pieces, won handicap at Ludlow in May: stays easy 3m: acts on firm and good to soft going: blinkered once: usually tongue tied. *C. J. Mann*

ANALYZE (FR) 7 b.g. Anabaa (USA) – Bramosia (Forzando) [2004/5 h99: 16g 17m6 Aug 6] compact gelding: fairly useful miler on Flat, successful 3 times in 2004: claimed to join A. Reid £6,000 in February: modest form at best over hurdles, generally jumping none too fluently: needs sharp 2m. *B. G. Powell* **h–**

ANATAR (IRE) 7 b.g. Caerleon (USA) – Anaza (Darshaan) [2004/5 h111: c20m4 c20g3 c16g6 20s* 21g 20m Apr 23] leggy gelding: has failed to impress with jumping and attitude over fences: fairly useful handicap hurdler: won at Sandown in February: well held in stronger races after: stays 2½m: acts on heavy going. *M. C. Pipe* **c89 h125**

AN CAPALL DUBH (IRE) 9 b. or br.g. Air Display (USA) – Lady of Wales (Welsh Pageant) [2004/5 c25d2 c21s5 Apr 7] tall ex-Irish gelding: thrice-raced over hurdles: fairly useful pointer/hunter chaser: stayed on after getting outpaced when fifth to Katarino in Fox Hunters' at Aintree: stays 25f: acts on soft going: tried tongue tied. *Mrs Edward Crow* **c107 h–**

ANDALEER (IRE) 10 b.m. Phardante (FR) – Dunleer Duchess (Our Mirage) [2004/5 c–, h–: c18m3 16m3 c16grtr 17m5 19g6 20m c21m4 Sep 28] good-topped mare: poor maiden hurdler/chaser: stays 19f: acts on firm and good to soft going: tongue tied: ungenuine: sold 2,400 gns Doncaster October Sales. *Mrs H. Dalton* **c82 § h69 §**

ANDREAS (FR) 5 b.g. Marchand de Sable (USA) – Muscova Dancer (FR) (Muscovite (USA)) [2004/5 h?: 17dF c16m* c16g* c16sF Apr 22] **c134 P h–**

At the time it seemed likely to mirror the outcome of the trainers' championship: the Paul Nicholls-trained Andreas came cruising to the last, going clear, in a novice chase at Perth on the penultimate day of the season, when he fell and let in the Martin Pipe-trained Sardagna. Whether the 2005/6 title will be quite so

Nicholson Holman Cup Handicap Chase, Cheltenham—Andreas (hooped cap) goes into many a notebook with a facile success over fellow novice Almaydan (centre)

Mr Mark Tincknell's "Andreas"

keenly fought remains to be seen but there is a good chance that Andreas will be a significant contributor to Nicholls' haul. Andreas had won his two starts over fences prior to Perth, a maiden at Taunton in March and a handicap at Cheltenham in April. Andreas could hardly fail to beat two negligible opponents at Taunton but his performance at Cheltenham was of an altogether higher order. Off a stiff-looking mark, one hardly justified on his form over hurdles nor on his run at Taunton, he bolted up, sauntering clear after leading on the bridle at the second last and beating the useful novice Almaydan by seven lengths, value for considerably more.

As a hurdler, Andreas hadn't been easy to assess, though wins at Divonne-les-Bains and Cagnes-sur-Mer from five starts in France and a last-of-ten placing in a juvenile hurdle at Ayr on his British debut hardly suggested a horse with the potential he went on to show at Cheltenham or Perth. The initial view wasn't really challenged by his reappearance effort either. Starting at 20/1, he would have finished well held in an ordinary handicap hurdle at Exeter in December had he not fallen heavily when weakening two from home. Perhaps Andreas took time to come to himself after arriving in Britain, though it is more likely that fences suit him much better than hurdles. Until his fall at Perth he had jumped really well and that mishap is likely to represent a rare lapse. Andreas is a half-brother to a winning cross country chaser at around two and three quarter miles but he is likely to prove at his most effective at around two miles. He won on good to firm going at Taunton but has otherwise raced on good or softer. He wore a tongue strap on all three starts over fences. *P. F. Nicholls*

ANDRE CHENIER (IRE) 4 b.g. Perugino (USA) – Almada (GER) (Lombard (GER)) [2004/5 16d 16v^{5} 16s^{5} 16v* 16s* Apr 3] useful-looking gelding: successful once (over 1½m) from 12 starts on Flat for Frau J. Mayer in Germany: fair form over hurdles: won juveniles at Kelso in March and April: raced around 2m on going softer than good, will be at least as effective under less testing conditions: likely to do better still. *P. Monteith* **h108 p**

ANDREWJAMES (IRE) 11 gr.g. Van Der Linden (FR) – Tolaytala (Be My Guest (USA)) [2004/5 c24g* c21v^{4} c24v^{5} c20s* c31d Mar 15] workmanlike gelding: modest chaser on balance: won cross-country event at Punchestown very early in season and conditional jockeys handicap at Down Royal in February: probably stays 31f: acts on good to firm and heavy going: usually blinkered prior to 2004/5: inconsistent. *P. D. McCreery, Ireland* **c86 h–**

ANDSUEPHI (IRE) 13 b.g. Montelimar (USA) – Butler's Daughter (Rhett Butler) [2004/5 c25s^{pu} Feb 15] lengthy gelding: veteran chaser, lightly raced nowadays, including in points: stays 3m, at least when conditions aren't testing: acts on good to firm and heavy going. *Mrs S. A. Hodge* **c– h–**

ANDY GIN (FR) 6 b.g. Ski Chief (USA) – Love Love Kate (FR) (Saint Andrews (FR)) [2004/5 h–: 17d 20g^{5} 16g^{pu} 16s^{3} 16s^{pu} 16s^{3} Mar 27] leggy gelding: winning hurdler, modest nowadays: sold out of P. Hobbs's stable 3,000 gns Doncaster May Sales after first outing, left M. Harris after third: raced mainly around 2m on good going or softer: tried visored: unreliable. *Miss E. M. England* **h96 §**

ANDY'S LAD (IRE) 13 br.g. Versailles Road (USA) – Ah Ye Know (Wolverlife) [2004/5 20d c24s^{pu} c19v^{pu} c21g^{2} Apr 10] neat gelding: winning hurdler/chaser: stays 21f: probably acts on any going: blinkered once in 1998/9 (won). *D. Burchell* **c86 h–**

ANFLORA 8 b.m. Alflora (IRE) – Ancella (Tycoon II) [2004/5 F73: c24g^{pu} 24s 23s^{5} c24v^{F} 24g 26s^{3} Jan 5] lengthy mare: winning pointer, little form otherwise: left C. Roberts after fourth start. *B. J. Llewellyn* **c– h64**

ANGEL DELIGHT 9 gr.m. Seymour Hicks (FR) – Bird's Custard (Birdbrook) [2004/5 c96, h–: c21g^{F4} c20d^{3} c20s^{4} c16d^{3} c16g^{3} c24d^{3} c25s^{pu} c20d* c20g^{2} c20g^{5} c19g^{6} Apr 15] plain, angular mare: modest chaser: won mares novice at Ludlow in March: barely stays 3m: acts on good to firm and good to soft going: wore cheekpieces seventh start. *J. L. Spearing* **c98 h–**

ANGIE'S DOUBLE 5 ch.m. Double Trigger (IRE) – Arch Angel (IRE) (Archway (IRE)) [2004/5 17s^{4} 16s^{F} 19g 16s 22v^{4} 16d 21g 16g^{5} Apr 19] little form on Flat at 2/3 yrs for D. ffrench Davis: poor form over hurdles: left G. Charles-Jones after fourth start: likely to prove best short of 2¾m. *M. Scudamore* **h63**

ANGUILLA 10 b.g. Rudimentary (USA) – More Wise (Ballymore) [2004/5 h71: 20d^{5} 24m^{pu} Jun 5] workmanlike gelding: bad maiden hurdler. *P. T. Dalton* **h58**

ANIMAL MAGIC 5 b.m. Shareef Dancer (USA) – Blessed Lass (HOL) (Good Times (ITY)) [2004/5 h–: 16m^{4} 16m^{F} Jun 29] small mare: no form over hurdles. *C. J. Down* **h–**

ANISETTE 4 b.f. Abou Zouz (USA) – Natural Gold (USA) (Gold Meridian (USA)) [2004/5 16d Oct 31] modest maiden around 1¼m on Flat: eighth of 18 in juvenile maiden on hurdling debut. *Julian Poulton* **h78**

ANKLES BACK (IRE) 8 b.g. Seclude (USA) – Pedalo (Legal Tender) [2004/5 c104, h–: c23d^{pu} c20s^{pu} c24g* Mar 28] close-coupled, workmanlike gelding: pulled up only outing over hurdles: fair chaser: back to form when winning handicap at Huntingdon: stays 3m: acts on good to firm going: forces pace: has found little: unreliable. *H. D. Daly* **c105 § h–**

ANNA GAYLE 4 ch.f. Dr Fong (USA) – Urban Dancer (IRE) (Generous (IRE)) [2004/5 18s^{pu} Oct 12] no form on Flat (for Mrs A. Perrett) or on hurdling debut. *R. Rowe* **h–**

ANNAKITA 5 b.m. Unfuwain (USA) – Cuban Reef (Dowsing (USA)) [2004/5 17g^{6} 16d 16s^{2} Feb 24] modest on Flat (stayed 2m), successful in April: similar form over hurdles: dead. *W. J. Musson* **h92**

ANNA WALHAAN (IRE) 6 b.g. Green Desert (USA) – Queen's Music (USA) (Dixieland Band (USA)) [2004/5 h87: 16m^{6} 16g^{5} 17g Aug 14] close-coupled gelding: fair on Flat at 5 yrs: poor form over hurdles: barely stays 2m: visored/blinkered last 2 starts. *Ian Williams* **h82**

ANNIE BIRD (IRE) 6 ch.m. Flying Spur (AUS) – Magic Bird (IRE) (Bluebird (USA)) [2004/5 F16m F16d F16s F17d 16d 16v^{pu} Feb 19] ex-Irish mare: third foal: dam **h– F–**

poor maiden: of no account, left Mrs A. Naughton after fourth start: tried tongue tied. *K. G. Wingrove*

ANNIE BYERS 9 ch.m. Sula Bula – Tuneful Flutter (Orchestra) [2004/5 c105, h91+: c21d* 20d^{3} c21v^{5} c24d^{pu} Nov 6] rather leggy mare: fair handicap hurdler: similar form over fences, winning listed mares handicap at Uttoxeter in May: stayed 2¾m: acted on good to firm and heavy going: dead. *J. G. Portman* **c108 h101**

ANNIE DIPPER 10 ch.m. Weld – Honey Dipper (Golden Dipper) [2004/5 c66: c23s^{ur} c21g^{3} c26v^{pu} Apr 22] maiden chaser: placed in point and hunter in 2005. *P. F. Popham* **c85 ?**

ANNIES THEME 7 b.m. Weld – Metannee (The Brianstan) [2004/5 F–: F16v Dec 28] rather leggy mare: no form in points or bumpers. *Dr J. R. J. Naylor* **F–**

ANNIJAZ 8 b.m. Alhijaz – Figment (Posse (USA)) [2004/5 16g^{pu} 17d^{pu} Oct 17] angular mare: modest on Flat (stays 1m): no form over hurdles. *J. M. Bradley* **h–**

ANNIVERSARY GUEST (IRE) 6 b. or br.m. Desert King (IRE) – Polynesian Goddess (IRE) (Salmon Leap (USA)) [2004/5 20g^{3} 22g^{pu} Jul 12] half-sister to 3m hurdle winner Sea Squirt (by Fourstars Allstar): poor maiden on Flat (stays 2¼m): similar form on first of 2 starts over hurdles. *Mrs Lucinda Featherstone* **h79**

ANOTHER ACE (IRE) 8 b.g. Synefos (USA) – Another Space (Brave Invader (USA)) [2004/5 c26g^{pu} c24d^{2} Aug 24] well-made gelding: won maiden Irish point in 2002: poor form on completed start in chases: sold 1,400 gns Doncaster October Sales. *P. D. Niven* **c65**

ANOTHER ARTISTE (IRE) 9 b.g. Montelimar (USA) – Another Space (Brave Invader (USA)) [2004/5 24m 24g c24g c23f^{pu} Sep 5] lengthy gelding: winning Irish pointer: modest maiden hurdler/chaser: left E. O'Grady, no form in 2004/5: stays 3m: acts on heavy going: has worn cheekpieces. *H. D. Daly* **c– h–**

ANOTHER BALLY 9 br.g. Neltino – Michele My Belle (Lochnager) [2004/5 c–, h–: c17g^{pu} Apr 30] maiden pointer: no form otherwise. *Mrs H. Dalton* **c– h–**

ANOTHER BARGAIN (IRE) 6 b.g. Mister Lord (USA) – Flashy Treasure (Crash Course) [2004/5 20d^{pu} 16s 16d Apr 11] €12,000 4-y-o: good-topped gelding: sixth foal: half-brother to winning pointer Treasulier (by Roselier): dam unraced half-sister to useful chaser around 2½m Tildarg: no show over hurdles. *N. G. Richards* **h–**

ANOTHER CHANCE 10 b.g. Golden Heights – Lapopie (Deep Run) [2004/5 c100, h109: c23d^{3} c22v^{F} c24d^{pu} 24d Jan 31] rangy gelding: winning hurdler/maiden chaser, no form in 2004/5: stays 3m: acts on heavy going: tried in cheekpieces. *J. M. Jefferson* **c– h–**

ANOTHER CLUB ROYAL 6 b.g. Overbury (IRE) – Miss Club Royal (Avocat) [2004/5 h74: 24g^{pu} c20s^{5} c21v^{2} Oct 29] winning hurdler: twice raced in chases: much improved in points in 2005, successful in April. *D. McCain* **c66 h–**

ANOTHER CONQUEST 6 b.m. El Conquistador – Kellys Special (Netherkelly) [2004/5 h76, F–: 27g 22d^{3} c25d^{pu} c22s^{4} c22s^{2} c24v* c24s^{2} c26g^{4} Apr 10] poor maiden hurdler: better over fences despite poor jumping, winning maiden at Towcester in February: thorough stayer: raced on good going or softer (acts on heavy). *J. W. Mullins* **c94 x h85**

ANOTHER COPPER 9 ch.g. Bandmaster (USA) – Letitica (Deep Run) [2004/5 c74§, h86§: c25g 24d^{pu} May 12] compact gelding: poor chaser/novice hurdler, won point in April: stays 3¼m: acts on any going: often blinkered: unreliable. *C. J. Down* **c– § h– §**

ANOTHERCOPPERCOAST (IRE) 5 ch.g. Presenting – Parsee (IRE) (Persian Mews) [2004/5 F16s^{3} F16d^{6} Mar 19] 14,000 3-y-o: smallish gelding: second foal: dam won 19f hurdle: won maiden point on debut in January: better effort in bumpers when third of 20 at Fairyhouse. *Paul A. Roche, Ireland* **F96**

ANOTHER DECKIE (IRE) 7 b.g. Naheez (USA) – Merry Friends (King's Ride) [2004/5 16m^{3} 18g^{5} 17d^{bd} 20g^{2} 16g* Feb 27] €14,000 4-y-o: good-topped ex-Irish gelding: fourth foal: dam lightly raced over hurdles/in points: fair hurdler: left B. Jones after second outing: won handicap at Musselburgh in February: stays 2½m: acts on soft and good to firm going. *L. Lungo* **h113**

ANOTHER DIAMOND (IRE) 7 b.m. First Trump – Rockin' Rosie (Song) [2004/5 17g^{pu} 20m^{pu} 24g^{6} 19s 17g^{4} Mar 3] poor hurdler: stays 2¾m: acts on good to firm and heavy going: usually blinkered: tried tongue tied. *C. J. Down* **h84**

ANOTHER DOLLAR (IRE) 7 b.m. Supreme Leader – Deep Dollar (Deep Run) [2004/5 20g^{bd} c20s^{4} c16s* c20v^{F3} c20s^{3} c21v^{5} c21d^{pu} Mar 19] sturdy mare: fair hurdler in 2003/4: similar form over fences, winning 4-runner mares novice at Gowran in December: stays 2½m: acts on soft going. *Mrs J. Harrington, Ireland* **c108 h–**

ANOTHER DUDE (IRE) 8 br.g. Shardari – Gemma's Fridge (Frigid Aire) [2004/5 h112: 18m^{3} c17v^{F} c16s^{F} 16m* 17g^{pu} Mar 18] lengthy gelding: fairly useful handicap hurdler: better than ever when winning at Musselburgh in February: let down by jumping both starts over fences: stays 19f: acts on good to firm and heavy going: blinkered once (raced freely). *J. Howard Johnson* **c– h125**

ANOTHER GENERAL (IRE) 10 ch.g. Glacial Storm (USA) – Whats In A Name (IRE) (Le Moss) [2004/5 c–, h–: c24g^{pu} c24v^{pu} 24g^{pu} Mar 19] angular gelding: winning hurdler/chaser: hasn't completed since 2002/3: should stay beyond 25f: acts on heavy going. *R. T. Phillips* **c– h–**

ANOTHER GRADUATE (IRE) 7 ch.g. Naheez (USA) – Another Daisy (Major Point) [2004/5 h–: 21d 19s 20d 24m^{pu} Apr 10] smallish gelding: no sign of ability. *John R. Upson* **h–**

ANOTHER JAMESON (IRE) 5 b.m. Good Thyne (USA) – Another Grouse (Pragmatic) [2004/5 F16s F16s Feb 10] €52,000 3-y-o: second foal: dam fairly useful staying chaser: little impact in 2 mares bumpers. *J. M. Jefferson* **F–**

ANOTHER JOKER 10 b.g. Commanche Run – Just For A Laugh (Idiot's Delight) [2004/5 c107, h–: c17m^{2} c19m* c17v* c21d^{F} c16d^{4} Dec 4] lengthy, workmanlike gelding: maiden hurdler: fairly useful handicap chaser: much improved in 2004/5, winning at Hereford in September and Stratford (3 ran) in October: stays 19f: acts on any going: bold-jumping front runner. *J. L. Needham* **c124 h–**

ANOTHER NATIVE (IRE) 7 b.g. Be My Native (USA) – Lancastrians Wine (IRE) (Lancastrian) [2004/5 16v^{2} 20s c19s^{4} Jan 3] €30,000 4-y-o: well-made gelding: third foal: dam unraced: bumper winner: modest novice hurdler: sold out of F. Flood's stable 20,000 Doncaster November Sales after second outing: shaped quite well when fourth in maiden at Exeter on chasing debut: should stay 2½m: raced mainly on going softer than good. *C. J. Mann* **c95 p h94**

ANOTHER PROMISE (IRE) 6 b.g. Presenting – Snape (IRE) (Strong Gale) [2004/5 h90: 19g^{4} 22d 19v* 20s^{5} 19s^{2} Mar 10] rangy gelding: chasing type: modest handicap hurdler: won at Warwick in December: should be suited by 2½m+: raced on good going or softer (acts on heavy). *J. A. Supple* **h97**

ANOTHER RALEAGH (IRE) 11 b.g. Be My Native (USA) – Caffra Mills (Pitpan) [2004/5 c20d^{F} c20g^{pu} c20d^{5} Jan 15] tall gelding: useful chaser in 2002/3: off 21 months, let down by jumping on return: stays 2½m: acts on heavy going. *A. Ennis* **c122 ? h–**

ANOTHER RUM (IRE) 7 b.g. Zaffaran (USA) – Sharp Fashion VII (Bustineto) [2004/5 h121, F84: c20s^{2} c25d^{2} c24v^{F} c24v^{4} c33g* c33g^{3} Apr 16] **c131 h–**

The National Hunt Chase is a race which embodies the very history of the sport. Taking its name from the committee which ran jump racing in Britain until 1968, first run in 1860 and staged at Cheltenham since 1911, the National Hunt Chase Challenge Cup was, until the Second World War, the most prestigious race at what was then the National Hunt meeting at Cheltenham (the Festival is a much later innovation). Traditionally, it was for horses which were maidens at starting, ridden by amateur riders. Later, it was open to those which, at the start of the season, had not won a race of any description. But the conditions were changed in 2002, opening up the event to a better quality of runner (i.e. those that had won over hurdles in the previous seasons). In the process, the race lost that which had made it distinctive, for all that Timbera and Celestial Gold have been among those placed. It now seems neither a race worth preserving purely for its tradition, nor a race worth its place in the Festival programme on its own merits. Indeed, there are clear signs that the race in its new form is attracting runners who might otherwise contest the Royal & SunAlliance Chase. Cheltenham's managing director Edward Gillespie reported after the latest Festival that the race was under review, and there is clearly pressure for at least one of the amateur rider races at the fixture to be dropped. The Kim Muir Fulke Walwyn, which needs something to differentiate it from the William Hill Handicap, and the Foxhunter, likely to be unaffected by the ban on hunting with dogs, look less vulnerable than the National Hunt Chase. Running the race as a four-mile novice handicap, open to all riders, would still give the race a unique character, though such a change has the disadvantage of losing almost completely the tradition of the original race. Reverting to the conditions pre-2002, but opening the race to professional riders, would be the option that would cover as many of the objectives as possible, though that would not satisfy those who think every race at the Festival should be either of championship standard or an ultra-competitive handicap.

Twenty went to post for the latest National Hunt Chase, as many as six of them plausible candidates for a place in the SunAlliance. Two, Control Man and Keepatem, were representing owners with a runner in the other race, while Sixo and Your A Gassman were from stables with a runner in the SunAlliance. The favourite was Point Barrow, who had been good enough to win the Grade 3 Ten Up Novices' Chase at Navan the previous month. Fourth in that event and also behind the favourite in a maiden chase at Fairyhouse in December, had been Another Rum, who was also in the National Hunt Chase field, sent off a 40/1-chance. Another Rum's form was better than might have been indicated by the fact that he had still to win after four races over fences, having, in addition to his two runs against Point Barrow, finished second to Joes Edge in a novice at Ayr and fallen at halfway in a Grade 1 novice at Leopardstown.

The latest renewal of the National Hunt Chase was an example of why the race is not satisfactory as it stands, the problems made worse by a switch to the New Course, with a slightly longer trip and three more fences to jump. With many of the leading contenders not certain to get the trip in a well-run race, the majority were patiently ridden and the 100/1-chance Go White Lightning pottered along in front. It was some indication of the way the race was run that second favourite Keepatem was still in contention three out despite a very poor round of jumping. Plenty of others were poised as the pace finally picked up. Another Rum, who had raced more handily than the majority of the more fancied runners, was the one to quicken decisively after leading two out, drawing seven lengths clear. The 150/1-chance Caislean Ui Cuain got the best of the bunched finish for second, with Control Man third and Go White Lightning holding on to fourth. Point Barrow could finish no better than fifth, lacking the speed to challenge after being hunted round.

The novelist and writer B.S. Johnson once wrote that 'It is just so much wasted effort, to attempt to understand anything.' While that would be a bleak view for students of form, there is no denying that time spent trying to make sense of the outcome of the latest National Hunt Chase could be better utilised. For what it is worth, the view that most of the fancied runners had run well below their best seemed the most sensible one to take. One aspect of the race which has not altered with the change in conditions is the apparent difficulty the winners have in scoring afterwards. None of the first three winners since the conditions changed has won since, though Celestial Gold and Silver Birch were second and fourth in 2004. Another Rum did not win on his only subsequent start either but he acquitted himself well, and had he been able to run off his proper mark, instead of from 17 lb

National Hunt Chase Challenge Cup (Amateur Riders' Novices' Chase), Cheltenham—outsiders to the fore as Another Rum lands a muddling race

out of the handicap, he would, in theory at least, have won the Scottish Grand National at Ayr, as he finished a short head and ten lengths behind fellow novices and close-finishers Joes Edge (who was also out of the weights) and Cornish Rebel. He had run his best race over hurdles at the previous year's Scottish National meeting and had won twice there over hurdles, the track clearly suiting him well.

Another Rum (IRE) (b.g. 1998)	Zaffaran (USA) (b 1985)	Assert (b 1979)	Be My Guest
			Irish Bird
		Sweet Alliance (b 1974)	Sir Ivor
			Mrs Peterkin
	Sharp Fashion VII (b 1986)	Bustineto (b 1978)	Bustino
			Pepita
		Cloughaun Lady (br 1977)	Baragoi
			Fashion's Frill

The good-topped Another Rum clearly stays very well and, though he has won on good to firm going and has form on soft, his best efforts have been on good. Presumably, another tilt at the Scottish Grand National could be on the agenda in 2005/6. Another Rum is not the only Cheltenham Festival winner in his family as his grandam Cloughaun Lady is a half-sister to the dam of Katabatic, the 1991 Queen Mother Champion Chase winner and a top-class performer at up to two and a half miles. Other notable names in the family are the dual Irish Grand National runner-up Height o'Fashion, who was a half-sister to the third dam Fashion's Frill, and the Great Yorkshire Chase winner Get Out of Me Way, who was a half-brother to Cloughaun Lady. Another Rum's dam Sharp Fashion VII has produced two other winners, the pointer Changing Fashion (by Jamesmead) and Another Rum's bumper-winning sister Bealtaine. *I. A. Duncan, Ireland*

ANOTHER SUPERMAN (IRE) 6 b.g. Beneficial – Royal Broderick (IRE) (Lancastrian) [2004/5 F16g F16m F16m^{4} F16m F16g^{2} 17v^{4} 16g 20s^{6} 20m^{6} 25g^{pu} Dec 28] €16,000 4-y-o: sturdy gelding: second foal: half-brother to winning pointer by Muharib: dam unraced half-sister to useful 2m chaser Black Amber out of half-sister to Cheltenham Gold Cup winner Davy Lad: fair form in bumpers: form over hurdles only on debut: sold out of P. Roche's stable €15,000 Goffs October Sale after eighth start. *Lindsay Woods, Ireland* **h89 F89**

ANOTHER TAIPAN (IRE) 5 b.g. Taipan (IRE) – Sheeghee (IRE) (Noalto) [2004/5 F16v^{5} F16g Apr 16] 4,000 3-y-o: second foal: dam, winning pointer, out of sister to smart staying chaser Sea Captain: little encouragement in 2 bumpers. *A. C. Whillans* **F–**

ANOTHER WINDFALL 6 gr.m. Executive Perk – Rymolbreese (Rymer) [2004/5 F16d F17s 16s 16d 25s^{pu} Mar 13] 9,200 4-y-o: third foal: half-sister to winning 2m hurdler/chaser Seymour Breese (by Seymour Hicks): dam poor novice hurdler/chaser: no show in bumpers/over hurdles. *C. P. Morlock* **h– F–**

ANSAR (IRE) 9 b.g. Kahyasi – Anaza (Darshaan) [2004/5 c128, h–: c22m* 21f^{5} 16v^{3} 21g Mar 16] leggy gelding: useful chaser: won Galway Plate (Handicap) in July by 1½ lengths from Risk Accessor: one-time smart hurdler: well held last 3 starts, including in Grade 1 in USA and Coral Cup at Cheltenham (blinkered): will stay 3m: acts on soft and good to firm going. *D. K. Weld, Ireland* **c130 h124**

ANSHABIL (IRE) 6 br.g. Anshan – Billeragh Thyne (IRE) (Good Thyne (USA)) [2004/5 F91: 21s 19s^{4} 19g 22d^{pu} Apr 17] useful-looking gelding: fair form in bumpers: form over hurdles only when fourth in novice at Hereford: should stay beyond 19f. *A. King* **h98**

ANTIGIOTTO (IRE) 4 ch.g. Desert Story (IRE) – Rofool (IRE) (Fools Holme (USA)) [2004/5 16g^{5} 16s^{4} 18s Jan 24] sturdy gelding: fair maiden on Flat (stays 1¼m), sold out of L. Cumani's stable 22,000 gns Newmarket Autumn Sales: modest form first 2 starts in juvenile hurdles: may prove best at bare 2m. *P. Bowen* **h97**

ANTINOMY (IRE) 5 ch.m. Anshan – Ardentinny (Ardross) [2004/5 F17s^{4} F16d^{3} F17g Apr 14] €12,000 4-y-o: leggy mare: first foal: dam, fair bumper winner, from family of very smart 2½m to 4½m chaser The Tsarevich: easily best effort in bumpers when third in mares event at Fakenham. *N. J. Henderson* **F83**

ANTONINE 5 ch.g. Selkirk (USA) – Eversince (USA) (Foolish Pleasure (USA)) [2004/5 F89: F16d May 8] leggy gelding: fair form on first of 2 outings in bumpers: sold 3,500 gns Doncaster May Sales: well beaten in point in March. *C. J. Mann* **F–**

ANTONY EBENEEZER 6 ch.h. Hurricane Sky (AUS) – Captivating (IRE) (Wolfhound (USA)) [2004/5 h93: 16m^{4} 16g^{5} 16g^{6} 17d^{3} 16m^{3} 16d* 20s^{2} 16s^{3} 20s^{5} 16d^{5} 16g^{pu} 16s^{pu} 19d^{6} Mar 14] leggy horse: modest hurdler: won seller at Uttoxeter in October: best around 2m: acts on soft and good to firm going: tried in cheekpieces: has had tongue tied: free-going sort, sometimes finds little. *C. R. Dore* **h88**

ANXIOUS MOMENTS (IRE) 10 b.g. Supreme Leader – Ms Brooks (IRE) (Lord Ha Ha) [2004/5 c132, h–: c16s^{F} c18d^{2} c17d 16s^{5} Mar 6] tall, close-coupled gelding: winning hurdler: fairly useful handicap chaser: easily best effort in 2004/5 when second to Mistletoeandwine at Punchestown in November: jumped with little confidence after bad mistake second at Fairyhouse later in month: best around 2m: raced on good going or softer (acts on soft): held up. *C. F. Swan, Ireland* **c129 h102 +**

ANY NEWS 8 ch.g. Karinga Bay – D'Egliere (FR) (Port Etienne (FR)) [2004/5 h–: 19g^{pu} 17g^{F} 17d^{pu} 16d^{6} Oct 3] leggy gelding: poor maiden hurdler: raced mainly around 2m: tongue tied last 3 starts. *Miss M. E. Rowland* **h73**

ANYPORTINASTORM (IRE) 7 b.g. Glacial Storm (USA) – Port Alley (Torus) [2004/5 F102: F18m* 16s 16s^{5} 16d^{3} 16d* 20s^{6} 16v^{2} Dec 28] strong gelding: will make a chaser: fairly useful in bumpers, successful at Punchestown in May: fairly useful novice hurdler: won maiden at Fairyhouse in November: better form both subsequent starts, sixth to Petertheknot in Grade 2 at Navan and second to easy winner Blazing Liss in minor event at Leopardstown: bred to stay beyond 2½m: acts on heavy going (bumper winner on good to firm). *Thomas Mullins, Ireland* **h123 F102**

ANZAL (IRE) 7 b.g. Kahyasi – Anazara (USA) (Trempolino (USA)) [2004/5 h92: 20g^{pu} Jul 14] small, leggy gelding: modest handicap hurdler in early-2003/4: no show last 4 starts: should stay beyond 2½m: acts on good to soft and good to firm going: tried blinkered/tongue tied. *D. R. Gandolfo* **h–**

AONINCH 5 ch.m. Inchinor – Willowbank (Gay Fandango (USA)) [2004/5 17d^{6} Nov 2] half-sister to fairly useful hurdler/fair chaser Kimberley (by Shareef Dancer), stays 3m: dam half-sister to Imperial Cup winner Travel Mystery: fair on Flat (stays 1¾m): sixth of 9 in mares novice at Folkestone on hurdling debut. *Mrs P. N. Dutfield* **h75**

APADI (USA) 9 ch.g. Diesis – Ixtapa (USA) (Chief's Crown (USA)) [2004/5 c–§, h88§: 17d^{2} 16d^{4} c16g^{F} c17g^{2} c17g^{5} c17g^{5} c17d* 17d^{5} c16d^{2} c16s^{6} c16s^{F} c17s^{3} c16s^{5} c16v^{2} c17s^{4} c17d^{ur} Apr 11] sturdy gelding: modest hurdler/chaser: made all in novice handicap over fences at Cartmel in August: barely stays 19f: acts on any going: tried in cheekpieces: headstrong: has refused/looked reluctant to race: not one to trust. *R. C. Guest* **c89 § h89 §**

A PIECE OF CAKE (IRE) 12 gr.g. Roselier (FR) – Boreen Bro (Boreen (FR)) [2004/5 c–, h–: c22v^{6} c33g^{pu} Apr 16] good-topped gelding: useful handicap chaser in 2002/3: lightly raced and no form since: stays 4m: has won on good to firm going, raced mainly on softer (acts on heavy). *J. S. Goldie* **c– h–**

APOLLO THEATRE 7 b.g. Sadler's Wells (USA) – Threatening (Warning) [2004/5 h102: 19s* 20s^{6} 20s^{pu} 21d^{4} 22d^{5} 19g^{4} Apr 12] useful-looking gelding: fair hurdler: won novice at Lingfield in November: stays 2¾m: raced on good going or softer: tongue tied last 3 starts. *R. Rowe* **h106**

APOLLO VICTORIA (FR) 8 b.g. Sadler's Wells (USA) – Dame Solitaire (CAN) (Halo (USA)) [2004/5 h98: c21d^{F} c19v^{pu} c21g^{pu} Apr 10] well held only completed start over jumps. *L. Corcoran* **c– h–**

A POUND DOWN (IRE) 8 b.g. Treasure Hunter – Ann's Queen (IRE) (Rhoman Rule (USA)) [2004/5 c–: c21g^{F} c19d^{5} c23g^{5} c21g^{5} c21g^{pu} 22s^{pu} c24d^{pu} c19m^{3} c16s c19g^{pu} Dec 9] tall gelding: poor maiden chaser: no show on hurdling debut: stays 21f. *N. G. Ayliffe* **c74 h–**

APPACH (FR) 6 gr.g. Riche Mare (FR) – Simply Red (FR) (R B Chesne) [2004/5 17m^{pu} 19d^{2} 20d 17m^{3} 17g Apr 12] ex-French gelding: first foal: half-brother to 7.5f winner Rossinante (by Calling Collect): dam winning hurdler around 2m: maiden on Flat: maiden hurdler/chaser: left C. Gourdain, poor form over hurdles in Britain. *Mrs H. M. Bridges* **c? h76**

APPLEADAY (IRE) 4 gr.g. Beneficial – Hello Aris (IRE) (Aristocracy) [2004/5 F16s^{6} Mar 23] €22,000 3-y-o: second foal: dam unraced, from family of smart hurdler/very smart chaser Lord Transcend (by Aristocracy), stays 3¼m: sixth of 14 in bumper at Chepstow on debut. *P. R. Webber* **F77**

APPLE JOE 9 b.g. Sula Bula – Hazelwain (Hard Fact) [2004/5 c82, h–: c24s c20s^{3} c26d^{3} c26s^{3} c29s^{2} Jan 2] lengthy gelding: no form over hurdles: modest handicap chaser: stays 29f: acts on heavy going: usually wears cheekpieces nowadays. *A. J. Whiting* **c85 h–**

APPROACHING LAND (IRE) 10 ch.g. Dry Dock – Crash Approach (Crash Course) [2004/5 23d^{3} 24d^{6} 16m 16d^{5} 21v^{5} 20s^{6} Apr 10] angular gelding: winning pointer: form over hurdles only when third in maiden at Wetherby. *M. W. Easterby* **h93**

APRIL'S PAST 7 br.m. Past Glories – April's Crook (Crozier) [2004/5 c19g^{pu} May 12] fourth foal: half-sister to winning 2¾m chaser Westwinds (by Vital Season): dam winning pointer: no form in points or hunter chase: temperamental. *R. Atkinson* **c– §**

APRIL SPIRIT 10 b.m. Nomination – Seraphim (FR) (Lashkari) [2004/5 c92, h–: c23f c25m^{6} Oct 1] leggy, sparely-made mare: modest handicap chaser: well held both starts in 2004/5: stays 3¼m: acts on any going. *Mrs S. J. Smith* **c– h–**

APSARA 4 br.f. Groom Dancer (USA) – Ayodhya (IRE) (Astronef) [2004/5 16d 16d 19s^{5} Mar 1] angular filly: half-sister to 2m hurdle winner Astronomer (by Ardkinglass): fairly useful on Flat (should stay 1½m) at 3 yrs for H. Cecil: modest form at best in novice hurdles: whipped round start on debut. *G. M. Moore* **h90**

AQRIBAA (IRE) 7 b. or br.g. Pennekamp (USA) – Karayb (IRE) (Last Tycoon) [2004/5 h–: 17g^{pu} 17m^{pu} Sep 28] maiden hurdler. *A. J. Lockwood* **h–**

ARABIAN KNIGHT (IRE) 5 ch.g. Fayruz – Cheerful Knight (IRE) (Mac's Imp (USA)) [2004/5 16v^{pu} Oct 16] close-coupled gelding: modest and ungenuine sprinter on Flat: no show in seller on hurdling debut. *R. J. Hodges* **h–**

ARABIAN MOON (IRE) 9 ch.g. Barathea (IRE) – Excellent Alibi (USA) (Exceller (USA)) [2004/5 c105d, h115d: c21g 24m 20m* Aug 6] compact gelding: modest on Flat (stays 21f): winning chaser (went with little enthusiasm on reappearance): modest hurdler nowadays: won claimer (claimed by R. Brotherton £6,000) at Worcester in August: stays 3m: has won on good to soft going, best form on good or firmer: tried in cheekpieces/visor. *M. C. Pipe* **c– § h93**

ARABIE 7 b.g. Polish Precedent (USA) – Always Friendly (High Line) [2004/5 16g^{6} 16d^{ur} Mar 3] dam half-sister to fairly useful hurdler up to easy 3m Hawkes Run: fairly useful on Flat (stays 1¼m), successful in April: no form in 2 novice hurdles, pulling very hard. *Ian Williams* **h–**

ARADNAK (IRE) 5 b.m. Son of Sharp Shot (IRE) – Kandara (FR) (Dalsaan) [2004/5 F18m May 26] half-sister to winners in USA by Star de Naskra and Eastern Echo: dam, fairly useful 5f/6f winner at 2 yrs, half-sister to high-class US 1m/1¼m performer In Excess: tailed off in bumper on debut. *C. J. Hemsley* **F–**

ARAGLIN 6 b.g. Sadler's Wells (USA) – River Cara (USA) (Irish River (FR)) [2004/5 h89: 20m^{pu} 20g^{2} 20m^{6} 22g^{2} 20g^{2} 20d^{3} 22g^{F} 20d^{3} 19g^{5} 21g Mar 28] small, sturdy gelding: modest handicap hurdler: stays 2¾m: acts on good to firm and good to soft going: tried blinkered: consistent. *Miss S. J. Wilton* **h94**

ARAGON'S BOY 5 ch.g. Aragon – Fancier Bit (Lion Cavern (USA)) [2004/5 16v^{pu} 16d Nov 24] tall gelding: fair on Flat (stays 1m) at 4 yrs: no form over hurdles. *T. D. Easterby* **h–**

ARCALIS 5 gr.g. Lear Fan (USA) – Aristocratique (Cadeaux Genereux) [2004/5 16s* 16g* 16g^{4} 16d^{3} 16g* Mar 15] **h144**

Home-trained runners offered scant resistance to the Irish challenge in the Champion Hurdle as defending champion Hardy Eustace led home an unprecedented clean sweep of the first five places for runners from Ireland. There was some consolation for the future for British-trained horses, however, in the results of the novice events over hurdles at Cheltenham. Among the juveniles, Penzance, Faasel and Akilak provided a one, two, three for British-trained runners in the Triumph Hurdle, following on from the successes of Arcalis in the Supreme Novices' Hurdle and No Refuge in the Royal And SunAlliance Novices' Hurdle. Of course, all of them have a way to go to be up to challenging Hardy Eustace, Harchibald and company in 2005/6, but, with Intersky Falcon and Rooster Booster, best of the British in the latest Champion Hurdle in sixth and eighth respectively, seemingly with their best days behind them, there should be plenty of opportunities to earn more prize money in the run-up to the Festival at least.

Letheby & Christopher Supreme Novices' Hurdle, Cheltenham—
Arcalis collars Wild Passion (noseband) at the last and launches a memorable meeting for connections

Arcalis had a crack at the best hurdlers prior to Cheltenham. Successful on both starts after joining Howard Johnson on the Flat in the summer, including in the John Smith's Cup at York in July, when he had shown smart form, Arcalis was stepped up sharply in class over hurdles after winning novice events impressively in quick succession at Ayr and Newcastle in December. Such was the impression he had made that Arcalis started third favourite at 15/2 for the Christmas Hurdle at Kempton, but his inexperience proved too much for him to overcome, forced into mistakes at the third and two out before coming home twenty-two lengths fourth of eight to Harchibald and Rooster Booster. Arcalis was beaten almost as far into third returned to novice company at Newbury when next seen in February, again making a bad mistake early on. As a result, he started at 20/1 in one of the most open-looking renewals for many years for the Letheby & Christopher Supreme Novices' Hurdle. Few of the runners had attained the standard normally required to win, Martin Pipe's Marcel going off favourite at 13/2 followed by the Irish-trained Justified at 7/1 and another home-trained runner My Way de Solzen at 8/1. The market proved an unreliable guide. Several of those with the better form looked more long-term chasing than hurdling prospects in the paddock, and Arcalis had too much finishing speed for all of them. Held up as usual, his hurdling stood up to the test this time and, after improving going well to chase Wild Passion on the turn, he jumped to the front at the last and ran on strongly to draw clear. Wild Passion held second six lengths back, with Dusky Warbler half a length further away in third and Prins Willem another four lengths behind. Arcalis' winning time compared quite favourably with that recorded by Hardy Eustace in the Champion Hurdle later on the card, though that was as much a reflection of the stronger early pace in the Supreme Novices' rather than the fact that the form was out of the ordinary by the standards of the contest.

Bought privately by current connections out of Lynda Ramsden's stable at the end of his three-year-old season, Arcalis cost 32,000 guineas when originally purchased as a foal. His dam Aristocratique, a fair sprint maiden in Ireland on the Flat, has bred only one other winner to date, the fairly useful Noble Academy (by Royal Academy), her first foal, successful over five furlongs. Aristocratique's dam Well Off was of little account but did quite a lot better at stud, producing the fairly useful nine-furlong winner Jiggery Pokery and the useful six- and seven-furlong

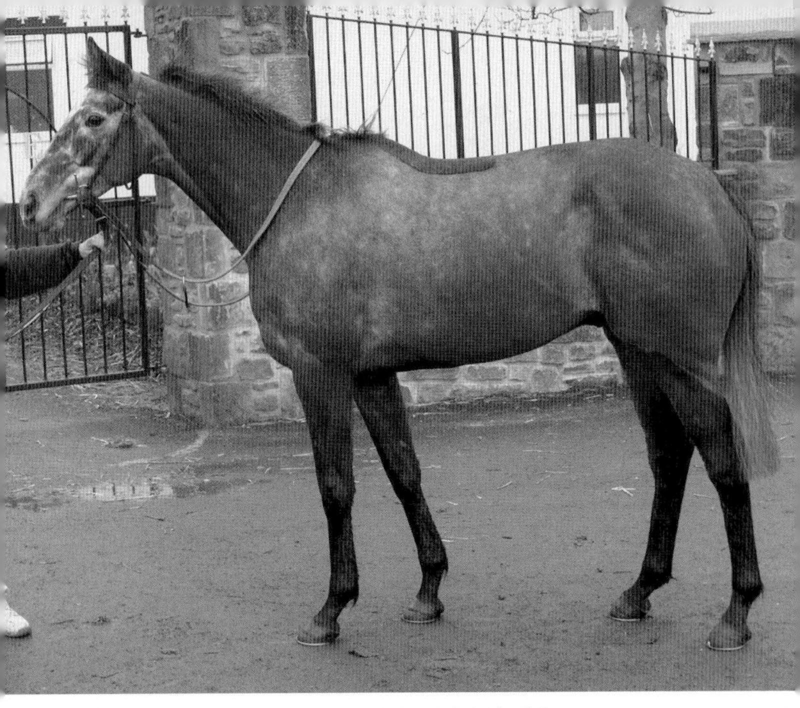

Andrea & Graham Wylie's "Arcalis"

Arcalis (gr.g. 2000)	Lear Fan (USA) (b 1981)	Roberto (b 1969)	Hail To Reason
			Bramalea
		Wac (b 1969)	Lt Stevens
			Belthazar
	Aristocratique (gr 1993)	Cadeaux Genereux (ch 1985)	Young Generation
			Smarten Up
		Well Off (gr 1974)	Welsh Pageant
			Rockney

winner Royal Loft. Royal Loft herself is the dam of plenty of winners as well, including the fair hurdlers Sulawesi and Welcome To Unos. Arcalis' sire Lear Fan was a high-class miler on the Flat, in which sphere he has also had a reasonably successful career at stud, though Arcalis isn't his first good jumper, another of his sons Vaporetto having won the Grade 1 Grand Course de Haies d'Auteuil over twenty-five furlongs. The close-coupled Arcalis, who stays a mile and a half on the Flat, will probably prove best at around two miles over hurdles. It bears repeating that his form still has a long way to go to be up with that of the best hurdlers, but there is probably more improvement in him, particularly given the standard he reached on the Flat. His jumping should help him bridge the gap. Although inclined to make mistakes at times in his first season, on occasions Arcalis also showed the fluency usually associated with those that make it in the top flight as two-milers. A genuine sort, he has raced only on good ground or softer over hurdles, though he was a winner on firm on the Flat. *J. Howard Johnson*

ARC EN CIEL (GER) 5 b.h. Daun (GER) – Amarna (GER) (Nebos (GER)) [2004/5 **h116**
20d 20v^{3} 16v^{2} 20s^{2} 20s^{3} 16s^{5} 20v^{2} 16s* 22v^{3} 20s^{6} 16d* 16v* 19s Mar 27] successful 3

times up to 11f on Flat in Germany for H. Blume: fairly useful hurdler: won minor event at Thurles in January and novices at Wexford (handicap) and Thurles in March: stays 2¾m: raced on going softer than good (acts on heavy): held up. *Gerard Cully, Ireland*

ARCEYE 8 b.g. Weld – Flower of Tintern (Free State) [2004/5 h–, F–: c16m^{5} Apr 25] won maiden point in January, no form otherwise. *M. G. Rimell* **c– h–**

ARCHENKO 5 b.g. Weldnaas (USA) – Silverdale Rose (Nomination) [2004/5 F–: 17d 16d^{pu} Jun 20] no sign of ability. *A. Berry* **h–**

ARCHIAS (GER) 6 b.g. Darshaan – Arionette (Lombard (GER)) [2004/5 h91: 16d^{F} 16d^{4} 16d^{3} 16m* 16m^{6} c17m^{2} c20m^{ur} Jun 12] leggy, angular gelding: modest hurdler: won handicap at Wetherby in May: similar form when runner-up in maiden at Market Rasen on chasing debut: raced mainly at 2m: yet to race on extremes of going: has worn cheek-pieces: tongue tied final 2003/4 outing: headstrong. *R. C. Guest* **c90 h91**

ARCHIE BABE (IRE) 9 ch.g. Archway (IRE) – Frensham Manor (Le Johnstan) [2004/5 h110: 16d^{5} 19d 19g 17s^{6} 16s* Mar 10] workmanlike gelding: fair on Flat (stays 1½m): fair handicap hurdler: won at Towcester in March: should stay beyond 2m: acts on soft ground. *J. J. Quinn* **h112**

ARCHIE CLARKE (GER) 5 b.g. Taishan (GER) – Anthela (GER) (Orfano (GER)) [2004/5 16d^{pu} Jan 7] well beaten in 2 races on Flat in 2004: no show in novice on hurdling debut. *J. Gallagher* **h–**

ARCHIRONDEL 7 b.g. Bin Ajwaad (IRE) – Penang Rose (NZ) (Kingdom Bay (NZ)) [2004/5 h–: 17m^{2} 17m^{3} 16m 16g^{pu} Dec 28] smallish gelding: fair on Flat (stays 1½m), successful in April: modest novice hurdler: raced mainly around 2m. *M. D. Hammond* **h85**

ARCH REBEL (USA) 4 b.g. Arch (USA) – Sheba's Step (USA) (Alysheba (USA)) [2004/5 16v* 16s^{3} Feb 6] good-topped gelding: useful on Flat (stays 1½m): good start over hurdles, winning Grade 2 Durkan New Homes Juvenile Hurdle at Leopardstown (travelled smoothly and led last when beating Don't Be Bitin 5 lengths) in December and 5½ lengths third of 6 to Strangely Brown there 6 weeks later: may do better. *N. Meade, Ireland* **h129**

ARCTIC BLUE 5 b.g. Polar Prince (IRE) – Miss Sarajane (Skyliner) [2004/5 h–: 17d^{pu} 16s* Mar 23] left M. Gingell and off 8 months, much improved when 200/1-winner of novice hurdle at Chepstow in March: tried in cheekpieces. *P. R. Rodford* **h113**

ARCTIC CHALLENGE (IRE) 11 b.g. Glacial Storm (USA) – Ruckinge Girl (Eborneezer) [2004/5 c124, h–: c21d^{pu} c21s^{ur} Apr 7] rather leggy gelding: fairly useful handicap chaser in 2003/4 for K. Burke: no show in hunters on return: stays 21f: acts on good to firm and heavy going: tried in cheekpieces. *David M. Easterby* **c– h–**

ARCTIC COPPER (IRE) 11 b.g. Montelimar (USA) – Miss Penguin (General Assembly (USA)) [2004/5 c142§, h–: c20s^{6} 20d c16s^{2} c20s c16s c17s^{6} c36d Apr 9] good-topped gelding: useful chaser: form in 2004/5 (including over hurdles) only when remote second of 4 finishers to Moscow Flyer in Grade 2 at Navan in November: effective at 2m to 29f: acts on any going: usually wears blinkers/cheekpieces: has had tongue tied: not one to trust: sold 17,000 gns Doncaster May Sales. *N. Meade, Ireland* **c131 § h–**

ARCTIC ECHO 6 b.g. Alderbrook – Arctic Oats (Oats) [2004/5 F16g* F16m* F17d^{3} F16d Apr 20] sturdy gelding: fifth foal: dam, fair hurdler, stayed 3m: fairly useful form in bumpers, winning at Hexham in September and October. *G. A. Swinbank* **F99**

ARCTIC GAMBLE 13 b.g. Arctic Lord – Honey Gamble (Gambling Debt) [2004/5 c–: c25m^{pu} c26g^{4} Jun 7] workmanlike gelding: poor handicap chaser: stays 25f: best efforts on good going or firmer. *L. G. Cottrell* **c80**

ARCTIC GLOW 6 ch.m. Weld – Arctic Mission (The Parson) [2004/5 h–: 17s^{5} 19d^{6} 24g* 22s^{pu} 24s^{4} 25g^{2} Mar 14] poor hurdler: won selling handicap at Taunton in December: stays 25f: acts on soft ground. *Mrs H. Pudd* **h68**

ARCTIC KING 12 b.g. Arctic Lord – Dunsilly Bell (London Bells (CAN)) [2004/5 c75, h–: c21g^{ur} c23g^{3} c26v^{6} Apr 22] rangy gelding: winning pointer: modest hunter chaser: stays 23f: acts on soft going: tried blinkered: sketchy jumper. *M. Frieze* **c84 x h–**

ARCTIC LAGOON (IRE) 6 ch.g. Bering – Lake Pleasant (IRE) (Elegant Air) [2004/5 c93, h78: c16f^{5} c25d 20d c22m^{5} c25s^{2} c20g 24g^{3} 24v^{4} 24g^{2} 24s^{F} 24s^{4} Apr 20] good-topped gelding: maiden hurdler/chaser, modest at best: stays 3m: acts on soft going: tried visored: has had tongue tied. *Mrs S. C. Bradburne* **c79 h85**

ARCTIC MINSTER 6 ch.g. Minster Son – Celtic Tern (Celtic Cone) [2004/5 F16s F16s^{2} F17d^{5} Mar 26] lengthy, workmanlike gelding: third foal: dam, maiden pointer, **F91**

from family of Grand National winners Anglo and Red Alligator: best effort in bumpers when second to Harry Flashman at Ayr: will be suited by greater test of stamina. *G. A. Harker*

ARCTIC MOSS (IRE) 6 ch.m. Moscow Society (USA) – Arctic Match (Royal Match) [2004/5 F94: F17v* F16g* F16d Mar 12] tall, rather unfurnished mare: fairly useful form in bumpers, winning mares events at Sedgefield in January and Musselburgh in February. *E. W. Tuer* — **F100**

ARCTIC SPIRIT 10 b.g. Arctic Lord – Dickies Girl (Saxon Farm) [2004/5 c–, h74: 16g^{2} c16m* 16s c16d^{2} c16d c16s* c18d c17d^{2} Feb 8] close-coupled gelding: poor maiden hurdler: fair handicap chaser: won at Towcester in May and December: barely stays 19f: probably acts on any going: tried visored: usually races prominently. *R. Dickin* — **c102 h76**

ARCTIC TIMES (IRE) 9 ch.g. Montelimar (USA) – Miss Penguin (General Assembly (USA)) [2004/5 c98, h–: c25g^{bd} c24m^{3} c21s^{F} Apr 7] good-topped gelding: fair hunter chaser: won 3 times in points in 2005 before end of April: stays 25f: acts on good to firm and heavy going: tried in cheekpieces. *Eugene M. O'Sullivan, Ireland* — **c94 h–**

ARDAGHEY (IRE) 6 b. or br.g. Lord Americo – Mrs Pepper (Lancastrian) [2004/5 F16s* F16g^{4} 21d^{4} 20v* Feb 2] good-topped gelding: type to make a chaser: second foal: brother to winning pointer Sub Contract: dam unraced: won maiden Irish point on debut in 2004: fairly useful form in 2 bumpers, making all at Uttoxeter in October: also made promising start over hurdles, winning 3-runner novice at Leicester by head from The Listener: will stay 3m: capable of further improvement. *N. A. Twiston-Davies* — **h122 p F107**

ARDASHIR (FR) 6 b.g. Simon du Desert (FR) – Antea (FR) (Esprit du Nord (USA)) [2004/5 h122: 23d^{2} 16g* c20d^{5} c16g^{2} c20d^{F} c21d^{pu} c21s^{5} c22s^{4} c33g^{F} c23v 24g Apr 14] leggy gelding: fairly useful hurdler: won novice at Perth in September: fair form over fences, often let down by jumping: stays 3m: acts on soft going, probably on good to firm: has broken blood vessels. *N. A. Twiston-Davies* — **c111 x h121**

ARDEN HILLS (IRE) 11 b.g. Supreme Leader – Pisa (IRE) (Carlingford Castle) [2004/5 c–, h84: 22g^{pu} Jun 7] winning pointer: well held both completed starts in chases: poor handicap hurdler: should stay 3m: acts on good to firm and heavy going. *J. D. Frost* — **c– h–**

ARDENT SCOUT 13 b.g. Ardross – Vidette (Billion (USA)) [2004/5 c129, h–: c25d^{pu} c30d^{3} c26s^{2} c27s^{ur} c26d^{5} c28v^{pu} c25v^{3} c22d^{pu} Feb 3] rangy gelding: fairly useful handicap chaser: well below best in 2004/5 except when ½-length second to Grattan Lodge at Carlisle in October: stays 4m: acts on good to firm and heavy going: usually sound jumper. *Mrs S. J. Smith* — **c125 d h–**

ARD SOLUS (IRE) 8 b.g. Supreme Leader – Red Bit (IRE) (Henbit (USA)) [2004/5 16v* Oct 16] IR 31,000 3-y-o: strong gelding: fourth foal: half-brother to bumper winner The Beeches (by Be My Native): dam unraced half-sister to top-class 2m to 2½m chaser Waterloo Boy: bumper winner: thrice-raced over hurdles, off 17 months prior to winning seller at Stratford in October: well held only start over fences: raced around 2m on good ground or softer: clearly difficult to train: sold 2,100 gns Doncaster May Sales. *C. Roche, Ireland* — **c– h81**

ARDWELSHIN (FR) 7 b.g. Ajdayt (USA) – Reem Dubai (IRE) (Nashwan (USA)) [2004/5 h67: 17g 16m^{3} 20m^{pu} 20g^{pu} 16g^{pu} Jul 29] workmanlike gelding: little form over hurdles: tried blinkered/in cheekpieces. *C. J. Down* — **h–**

ARDYNAGH (IRE) 6 b.g. Aahsaylad – Night Matron (IRE) (Hatim (USA)) [2004/5 16v^{3} Dec 15] €12,000 4-y-o: third foal: brother to fairly useful hurdler Major Burns, stays 2½m well: dam, showed some ability in bumpers, out of half-sister to top-class hurdler/chaser Night Nurse: sixth on completed start in Irish points in 2004: 21½ lengths third to Dance Party in novice at Hexham on hurdling debut: likely to be suited by further. *J. Howard Johnson* — **h81 p**

ARGAMIA (GER) 9 b.m. Orfano (GER) – Arkona (GER) (Aspros (GER)) [2004/5 c16d^{ur} 16g c18m^{4} Apr 2] rather leggy mare: modest at best on Flat: lightly-raced maiden jumper. *P. J. McBride* — **c– h–**

ARGENTO 8 b.g. Weldnaas (USA) – Four M'S (Majestic Maharaj) [2004/5 c110, h–: c16s^{2} c16d^{2} c16d^{F} c16d^{2} c17d^{3} c19g Mar 5] leggy gelding: fairly useful handicap chaser: raced mainly around 2m: acts on any going: front runner/races prominently: jumps boldly, but is prone to mistakes. *G. M. Moore* — **c118 h–**

ARGENT OU OR (FR) 4 b.g. Mansonnien (FR) – Gold Or Silver (FR) (Glint of Gold) [2004/5 F18d* Apr 18] fourth foal: brother to 3 fairly useful jumpers in France, including hurdler Belle Manson, stayed 2½m: dam successful around 1¼m: favourite, — **F96**

signs of greenness when winning maiden bumper at Plumpton on debut by 1½ lengths from Earl of Forestry. *M. C. Pipe*

ARGY BARGY (IRE) 8 b.g. Lord Americo – Bargy Fancy (Crash Course) [2004/5 20s Oct 31] no show in bumper/novice hurdle 2 years apart. *J. Wade* **h–**

ARICOVAIR (IRE) 5 ch.g. Desert Prince (IRE) – Linoise (FR) (Caerwent) [2004/5 16s^{pu} Mar 23] no sign of ability on Flat or on hurdling debut. *Mrs A. J. Bowlby* **h–**

ARIJAZ 8 b.g. Teenoso (USA) – Zajira (IRE) (Ela-Mana-Mou) [2004/5 h80, F–: 20d 18g^4 16f c20m 20m^{pu} Feb 6] poor handicap hurdler: lame final start: weakened quickly on chasing debut time before: possibly best short of 3m: acts on firm going. *Mrs L. B. Normile* **c–** **h86**

ARIMERO (GER) 5 b.g. Monsun (GER) – Averna (Heraldiste (USA)) [2004/5 h104: 16f 16m^6 16d 17g^3 17s^5 18s 16s 17g^3 Apr 12] leggy, useful-looking gelding: modest maiden hurdler: sold out of C. Swan's stable 17,000 gns Doncaster August Sales after second start: raced around 2m: best efforts on good going or firmer: tried blinkered/in cheekpieces. *J. G. Portman* **h95**

ARISTOXENE (FR) 5 b.g. Start Fast (FR) – Petite Folie (Salmon Leap (USA)) [2004/5 h107: c20d^3 c20v* c24d^4 c25g^5 Apr 16] good-topped gelding: fair form in juvenile hurdles for G. Macaire in 2003/4: better over fences, winning 4-runner novice handicap at Haydock in December: stays 3m: raced on good going or softer: room for improvement in jumping. *N. J. Henderson* **c123** **h–**

ARIZONA DESERT (IRE) 5 b.g. Desert Story (IRE) – Happy Tidings (Hello Gorgeous (USA)) [2004/5 F17m^{pu} Jun 25] half-brother to several winners, including useful 2-y-o 1¼m winners Eldorado and Trigger Happy (both by Ela-Mana-Mou): dam unraced half-sister to St Leger winner Snurge: broke leg in bumper on debut. *W. S. Cunningham* **F–**

ARIZONA (IRE) 7 b.g. Sadler's Wells (USA) – Marie de Beaujeu (FR) (Kenmare (FR)) [2004/5 16d Jun 23] little show in 2 novice hurdles 15 months apart. *Mark Campion* **h–**

ARJAY 7 b.g. Shaamit (IRE) – Jenny's Call (Petong) [2004/5 h–: 17d^5 17m 20m^{pu} 19s 19d 19s 17g^3 Apr 3] workmanlike gelding: poor hurdler: sold out of A. Turnell's stable 5,500 gns Doncaster August Sales after reappearance: blinkered last 3 starts. *S. B. Clark* **h68**

ARJAYPEAR (IRE) 6 b.g. Petardia – Lila Pedigo (IRE) (Classic Secret (USA)) [2004/5 h84: 16s Dec 22] poor maiden hurdler: left A. King, well held only 2004/5 start: stays easy 2½m: acts on firm going: tried blinkered. *D. Burchell* **h–**

ARK ADMIRAL 6 b.g. Inchinor – Kelimutu (Top Ville) [2004/5 h86: 16d^{ro} 16f^2 17g^4 16g Jul 29] poor maiden hurdler: left P. Nicholls after second start: raced around 2m: acts on firm going: tongue tied: temperamental: poor form on Flat in 2005. *C. L. Tizzard* **h82 §**

ARKHOLME 4 b.g. Robellino (USA) – Free Spirit (IRE) (Caerleon (USA)) [2004/5 16s^F 16d^5 17d^5 Nov 15] useful-looking gelding: fairly useful on Flat (should stay at least 1¼m), successful twice in 2004: best effort over hurdles when fifth of 18 in juvenile maiden at Huntingdon on second start: tried in cheekpieces. *P. Winkworth* **h91**

ARLEQUIN DE SOU (FR) 11 b.g. Sir Brink (FR) – Colombine (USA) (Empery (USA)) [2004/5 c68, h–: c21d Apr 28] lengthy, useful-looking gelding: fairly useful handicap chaser at best: on downgrade in hunters and points: stays 3m: acts on good to firm and heavy going: blinkered. *Miss Polly Curling* **c–** **h–**

ARLEY MIST 6 b.m. Environment Friend – Hilly-Down Lass (Deep Run) [2004/5 F16d May 6] ninth foal: half-sister to modest staying hurdler Hanover Square (by Le Moss): dam, maiden pointer, half-sister to dam of useful staying jumpers Brackenfield and Brackenheath: well held in bumper on debut. *T. H. Caldwell* **F–**

ARMAGEDDON 8 b.g. Deploy – Arusha (IRE) (Dance of Life (USA)) [2004/5 c24s^{pu} Apr 2] tall gelding: lightly raced: disappointing over hurdles: pulled up on chasing debut. *O. Sherwood* **c–** **h–**

ARMAGH SOUTH (IRE) 6 ch.g. Topanoora – Mogen (Adonijah) [2004/5 h79, F76: 16s 24m^2 Nov 26] poor form over hurdles: stays 3m: joined J. Tuck. *J. Howard Johnson* **h80**

ARM AND A LEG (IRE) 10 ch.g. Petardia – Ikala (Lashkari) [2004/5 17d^3 17d^3 17g^5 17g* 17m^2 16g 16g* 16d* 17d* 18m^2 16g Sep 12] leggy gelding: fair handicap hurdler: much improved in first half of 2004/5, winning at Newton Abbot, Uttoxeter, Stratford and Newton Abbot again: best around 2m: acts on soft and good to firm going: takes good hold: races prominently. *Mrs D. A. Hamer* **c–** **h102**

ARMARIVER (FR) 5 ch.g. River Mist (USA) – Armalita (FR) (Goodland (FR)) [2004/5 aF16g^5 F18s^3 17d^4 Feb 11] 25,000 3-y-o: fourth foal: half-brother to very smart **h105 p** **F95**

chaser Armaturk (by Baby Turk), stays 21f: dam winning hurdler/chaser up to 19f: easily better effort in bumpers when third at Plumpton: 5½ lengths fourth to Rebel Rhythm in novice at Bangor on hurdling debut: should improve. *P. F. Nicholls*

ARMATURK (FR) 8 ch.g. Baby Turk – Armalita (FR) (Goodland (FR)) [2004/5 c149, h–: c16g* c16d* c21d^{4} c16v^{3} c16s c17d^{3} c16g c16g^{3} c16g^{6} Apr 23] tall, angular gelding: very smart handicap chaser: reportedly had breathing operation after 2003/4: successful first 2 starts on return, beating Bleu Superbe 4 lengths in listed event at Lingfield in October and Well Chief by head at Cheltenham in November: respectable efforts at best after next outing: effective at 2m to 21f: acts on good to firm and heavy going: has had tongue tied. *P. F. Nicholls* **c157** **h–**

ARMEN (FR) 8 b.g. Kaldoun (FR) – Anna Edes (FR) (Fabulous Dancer (USA)) [2004/5 c93, h–: c21g^{2} c23g^{F} c26g^{2} Jun 7] workmanlike gelding: winning hurdler: let down by jumping and modest form at best over fences: probably stays 3¼m: acts on heavy going: visored last 4 starts. *M. C. Pipe* **c93 x** **h–**

ARMENTIERES 4 b.f. Robellino (USA) – Perfect Poppy (Shareef Dancer (USA)) [2004/5 16d 16g^{3} 16v^{2} 16d* 16v^{3} 16s 16s^{3} 16v^{pu} 16s Apr 3] close-coupled filly: modest on Flat (best form at 7f/1m): poor hurdler: made all in seller (sold from J. Spearing 5,200 gns) at Catterick in January: raced around 2m on good going or softer (acts on heavy): blinkered/visored: ungenuine. *Mrs E. Slack* **h79 §**

ARNISTON LOVER 7 ch.g. Tigani – Chelwood (Kala Shikari) [2004/5 17d^{pu} Nov 9] well beaten in 2 maidens around 6f at 3 yrs on Flat for B. Ellison: very free when pulled up in novice on hurdling debut. *L. R. James* **h–**

ARNOLD LAYNE (IRE) 6 gr.g. Roselier (FR) – Cotton Gale (Strong Gale) [2004/5 F17s* Apr 2] €48,000 4-y-o: brother to fairly useful hurdler Absolutly Equiname, stayed 25f, and half-brother to poor chaser Amptina (by Shardari), stays 21f: dam won 2¼m hurdle in Ireland: won bumper at Bangor on debut by 17 lengths from Willy Furnley, leading on bridle 4f out and coasting clear: will stay at least 2½m: useful prospect. *R. T. Phillips* **F101 p**

A ROMP TOO FAR (IRE) 9 b.g. Eurobus – Saxa Princess (IRE) (Lancastrian) [2004/5 c–, h–: c24s^{F} c23g^{F} Apr 12] medium-sized gelding: first past post in maiden point in 2004, little form otherwise: tried in cheekpieces. *M. Ranger* **c– x** **h–**

ARONDELLA 6 b.m. Fourstars Allstar (USA) – Persian Dream (IRE) (Mazaad) [2004/5 F16s F17m^{6} Nov 11] unfurnished mare: first foal: half-sister to bumper winner She's No Muppet (by Teenoso): dam winning 2m hurdler: tailed off in 2 bumpers. *N. R. Mitchell* **F–**

AROUND BEFORE (IRE) 8 ch.g. Be My Native (USA) – Glynn Cross (IRE) (Mister Lord (USA)) [2004/5 c105, h94+: c28g^{4} c24m* Jun 13] winning hurdler: fair chaser: won weak handicap at Stratford in June: stays 3¼m: acts on firm and good to soft going: tried in cheekpieces: tongue tied nowadays. *Jonjo O'Neill* **c113** **h–**

ARRAYOU (FR) 4 b.g. Valanjou (FR) – Cavatine (FR) (Spud (FR)) [2004/5 15s^{3} 15s^{3} 17s^{5} 16s^{4} 16s* 16s^{2} 16v 16s^{3} 18s 16g^{5} 21d^{2} 16d* Apr 20] good-topped ex-French gelding: second foal: half-brother to fair 15f hurdle winner Creatif (by Ecologist): dam, placed around 2m over hurdles, half-sister to useful chaser up to 21f Creative: once-raced on Flat: fairly useful hurdler: left J. Bertran de Balanda after third start: won juvenile at Leicester in December and novice at Worcester (best effort when beating Cherub by length) in April: best efforts around 2m: acts on soft ground: blinkered/visored 5 of last 6 outings: held up. *O. Sherwood* **h120 +**

ART AFFAIR (GER) 4 b.f. Germany (USA) – A Real Work of Art (IRE) (Keen) [2004/5 16v 16s^{5} 16g* Mar 28] tall filly: maiden on Flat (stays 1¼m) for W. Himmel in Germany: clearly best effort over hurdles when winning maiden at Plumpton in March: likely to prove best at 2m with emphasis on speed. *Mrs L. Wadham* **h99**

ARTANE BOYS 8 b.g. Saddlers' Hall (IRE) – Belleminette (IRE) (Simply Great (FR)) [2004/5 16m^{3} 17g^{2} 16m^{3} 17g* 16m^{3} 20m^{3} c16d^{5} Nov 23] lengthy ex-Irish gelding: first foal: dam, fair at 7f/1m, sister to one-time useful hurdler up to 2¾m General Cloney: bumper winner: fair hurdler: left C. Roche after 2003/4: won maiden at Market Rasen in August: looked in need of experience when fifth of 7 in handicap at Warwick on chasing debut: raced mainly around 2m: acts on good to firm and heavy going: has worn cheekpieces: tried in tongue strap: held up (has found little): should improve over fences. *Jonjo O'Neill* **c96 p** **h105**

ARTEEA (IRE) 6 b.g. Oscar (IRE) – Merric (IRE) (Electric) [2004/5 F99: F16g F16v 16v^{6} 16s 18d^{3} 16s^{2} 19v* 20v^{2} 20v^{3} 16s* 16s^{4} Mar 28] close-coupled, deep-girthed geld- **h127** **F–**

ing: fairly useful bumper winner in 2003/4: fairly useful hurdler: won maiden at Limerick in December and novice at Naas in February: good fourth to Wild Passion in Grade 1 novice at Punchestown in late-April: stays 2½m: raced on good going or softer (acts on heavy): patiently ridden. *M. Hourigan, Ireland*

ARTEMISE (FR) 7 b.m. Cyborg (FR) – Articule (FR) (Art Francais (USA)) [2004/5 h93: 20g 18mpu Aug 19] leggy mare: handicap hurdler, modest at best in 2003/4: will prove suited by further than 2m: raced mainly on good going or softer. *A. King* **h–**

ARTHUR-K 8 ch.g. Greensmith – Classy Miss (Homeboy) [2004/5 22s6 26s Feb 10] compact gelding: no form over hurdles or in points. *Mrs H. R. J. Nelmes* **h–**

ARTHURS KINGDOM (IRE) 9 b.g. Roi Danzig (USA) – Merrie Moment (IRE) (Taufan (USA)) [2004/5 c79§, h–§: 21g Apr 30] lengthy gelding: poor hurdler/chaser: stays 27f: acts on good to firm and heavy going: often wears headgear: unreliable. *Miss Kate Milligan* **c– § h– §**

ARTHUR SYMONS 7 b.g. River Falls – Anchor Inn (Be My Guest (USA)) [2004/5 17dpu 17spu Nov 18] half-brother to several winners, including useful hurdler/very smart chaser Mister McGoldrick (by Sabrehill), stays 2½m: well beaten in 4 maidens on Flat at 3 yrs for J. M. Jefferson: no show over hurdles: gave plenty of trouble in preliminaries both starts. *Miss Kariana Key* **h–**

ARTIC JACK (FR) 9 b.g. Cadoudal (FR) – Si Jamais (FR) (Arctic Tern (USA)) [2004/5 c150, h–: c25spu c27s c26g c26dur c24dpu c33d c25gpu Apr 8] big, rangy gelding: smart chaser at best: badly out of sorts in 2004/5: stays 3½m: acts on good to firm and heavy going. *Mrs S. J. Smith* **c– h–**

ART POINT (GER) 6 b.g. Dashing Blade – A Real Work of Art (IRE) (Keen) [2004/5 17d 19d2 19g3 Aug 21] angular gelding: half-brother to 2m hurdle winner Art Afair (by Germany): successful around 9f on Flat in Germany at 3 yrs: won around 2m at Vittel both starts in juvenile hurdles in France in 2002 for M. Hofer: fair form when placed in handicaps in Britain: stays 19f. *Mrs L. Wadham* **h104**

ARUBA DAM (IRE) 7 br.m. Be My Native (USA) – Arumah (Arapaho) [2004/5 h68, F–: 16s Feb 24] little show in bumpers or over hurdles. *B. G. Powell* **h–**

ARUMUN (IRE) 4 b.g. Posidonas – Adwoa (IRE) (Eurobus) [2004/5 F16d5 F16g* Mar 26] tall gelding: has scope: second foal: dam unraced: better effort in bumpers when winning at Haydock (sweating and on toes) by 3 lengths from Bumper, racing freely dictating pace. *M. Scudamore* **F99**

ARVI'S WAY 8 b.g. Alflora (IRE) – Gentle Madam (Camden Town) [2004/5 16g Jan 24] lengthy gelding: twice-raced in bumpers: well held in maiden on hurdling debut: will be suited by 2½m+. *Mrs S. J. Smith* **h–**

ARZILLO 9 b.g. Forzando – Titania's Dance (IRE) (Fairy King (USA)) [2004/5 h79: 16m Sep 24] poor maiden hurdler: needs sharp 2m: raced on good/good to firm going: has worn cheekpieces. *G. H. Yardley* **h–**

ASCARI 9 br.g. Presidium – Ping Pong (Petong) [2004/5 c–, h74: 20d 16m 17v* 17g Apr 3] angular gelding: poor hurdler: won selling handicap at Market Rasen in October: raced mainly around 2m: acts on heavy going: in cheekpieces last 2 starts: has pulled hard. *A. L. Forbes* **c– h73**

ASCENMOOR 5 b.g. Mistertopogigo (IRE) – Asmarina (Ascendant) [2004/5 F17d F16g Nov 11] third foal: half-brother to 1m winner Ace-Ma-Vana (by Savahra Sound): dam, 9.4f winner, half-sister to one-time useful sprinter First Maite: blinkered, well beaten in 2 bumpers and on Flat debut. *S. R. Bowring* **F–**

ASH BRANCH (IRE) 11 ch.g. Shardari – Etnas Princess (The Parson) [2004/5 24gpu Jun 10] rangy gelding: winning hurdler: no sign of retaining ability. *Sir John Barlow Bt* **h–**

ASHDOWN KING 8 ch.g. Nearly A Hand – Rose Mulholland (Lombard (GER)) [2004/5 c22spu Oct 12] sixth foal: dam, behind in bumpers and fell only outing over hurdles, out of half-sister to smart chaser up to 3m Kissane: no form in maiden points and maiden chase. *N. R. Mitchell* **c–**

ASHFIELD ORCHESTRA (IRE) 9 b.m. Orchestra – Colour Clown (Random Shot) [2004/5 20dur c22s2 c26v5 c23vur c24v4 Feb 20] IR 1,000 4-y-o: medium-sized mare: seventh foal: half-sister to winning pointers by Le Bavard and Good Thyne: dam unraced: winning pointer: modest novice chaser: should stay 3m: raced on going softer than good: makes mistakes. *M. Brown* **c90 h–**

ASHGAN (IRE) 12 br.g. Yashgan – Nicky's Dilemma (Kambalda) [2004/5 c20g^{4} 20m 22g 20m^{3} 26d c20g c16d c31d 25v 16d 20d^{6} 22g Mar 20] lengthy gelding: winning hurdler/chaser, poor nowadays: sold out of A. Dalton's stable 3,000 gns Doncaster May Sales after first start: best around 2½m on good going or firmer: tried blinkered/visored. *Dr P. Pritchard* **c– h80**

ASHGAR (USA) 9 ch.g. Bien Bien (USA) – Ardisia (USA) (Affirmed (USA)) [2004/5 c–§, h83§: 20m^{3} May 20] quite good-topped gelding: winning chaser: poor hurdler: stays 3¼m: acts on any going: usually blinkered: ungenuine: sold 3,500 gns Doncaster May Sales, in frame in points in 2005. *M. D. Hammond* **c– § h83 §**

ASHGREEN 8 b.g. Afzal – Space Kate (Space King) [2004/5 c90, h–: c25s^{6} c25v^{2} c24s^{pu} c24s^{6} Mar 23] poor handicap chaser: barely stays 25f when conditions are testing: acts on heavy going: tried blinkered/in cheekpieces. *Miss Venetia Williams* **c84 h–**

ASH LADDIE (IRE) 5 ch.g. Ashkalani (IRE) – Lady Ellen (Horage) [2004/5 17g Aug 21] modest maiden up to 9f on Flat for E. Alston: no show on hurdling debut. *J. S. Wainwright* **h–**

ASHLEYBANK HOUSE (IRE) 8 b.g. Lord Americo – Deep Perk (IRE) (Deep Run) [2004/5 h108+: c22s^{4} c22s^{pu} 23s 22v^{6} Mar 5] well-made gelding: fair hurdler at best, below form in 2004/5: jumped poorly both starts over fences: stays 3m: acts on heavy going (unraced on firmer than good): sold 7,500 gns Doncaster May Sales. *L. Lungo* **c– h92**

ASHLEY BROOK (IRE) 7 ch.g. Magical Wonder (USA) – Seamill (IRE) (Lafontaine (USA)) [2004/5 h121: c17s* c21d* c16v^{2} c20g^{4} c16g^{2} c16d* Apr 9] **c154 + h–**

An exciting new talent came to the fore among the younger riders in 2004/5 in Paddy Brennan, who took the conditional jockeys' championship with sixty-seven wins, twelve more than nearest-rival Sam Thomas. Based at Philip Hobbs's yard, Brennan proved a more than able deputy for the stable's number one Richard Johnson at times, memorably when completing a four-timer at Doncaster in December, three of his winners trained by Hobbs. What was particularly impressive was the way Brennan got fluent rounds out of the chasers he rode on a day when the demanding Doncaster fences were exacting a stiff toll otherwise. Brennan struck up a notable partnership with the leading novice chaser Ashley Brook, winning the Grade 1 John Smith Maghull Novices' Chase on him at Aintree, though afterwards he was full of praise for fellow jockey Rodi Greene, who had got him the ride in the first place. Greene, a stalwart of the Martin Pipe stable and also a long-time rider for Ashley Brook's trainer Kevin Bishop, had announced his retirement in February. Brennan had still been claiming 3 lb when twice successfully stepping in for the injured Greene on Ashley Brook in November and took over again following Greene's retirement. Greene returned to race-riding in unusual circumstances on the last two days of the season. Having continued to ride work, he was asked to lend a hand when Pipe faced a jockey shortage as he pulled out all the stops to retain the trainers' championship. Greene had four mounts in all and continued race-riding into the 2005/6 season. Had he not temporarily retired, Greene would have continued to ride Ashley Brook and victory in the Maghull would have given him a first Grade 1 success in a career stretching back to the late-'eighties.

Ashley Brook began his career in bumpers in 2002/3, dead-heating for first in one at Ludlow, and the following season showed himself a fairly useful novice hurdler, winning at Exeter and Taunton. He made his first appearance over fences in a novice event in which the then ante-post favourite for the Arkle, Sporazene, started at 5/2-on to follow up a recent course victory. Ashley Brook, a 9/1-shot in a field of six, showed no signs of his inexperience as he attacked his fences and, under an enterprising ride from Brennan, established a clear lead. Sporazene was cutting into it but still eight lengths down when falling four out, leaving Ashley Brook to win by twenty-five lengths. It was a similar story two weeks later in another six-runner novice chase, this time at Newton Abbot, Ashley Brook again impressing with his jumping as he landed the odds by a distance. Greene was back on board when Ashley Brook took on much stronger opposition on his next two starts, Ashley Brook acquitting himself well when a half-length second to My Will, four lengths clear of third-placed Contraband, at Uttoxeter and fourth of five, blundering at each of the last two fences, to El Vaquero in the Scilly Isles Novices' Chase at Sandown, on what was supposed to be Greene's final day in the saddle.

John Smith's Maghull Novices' Chase, Aintree—champion conditional jockey Paddy Brennan conjures another memorable leap from the front-running Ashley Brook

Ashley Brook's jumping was spot on when he and Brennan were reunited in March, in the Arkle Trophy at Cheltenham, where he ran a cracking race to finish a length second to Contraband, setting a good pace, not losing the lead until pitching on landing at the last then having to be switched right after the winner crossed him early on the run-in.

The Arkle first and second, along with third-placed River City, War of Attrition, Made In Japan and Mambo des Mottes all met again in the Maghull Novices' Chase, which attracted ten runners in all. War of Attrition was again sent off favourite, at 11/4, with Ashley Brook (3/1), River City (7/2) and Contraband (4/1) next in the betting, 11/1 bar the four. With Contraband running no sort of race and River City also well below par, it was Ashley Brook and War of Attrition who upheld the Arkle form, finishing first and second. Indeed, in winning by sixteen lengths Ashley Brook not only bettered his Arkle performance but also produced form just about as good as was seen all season in the two-mile novice chase division. He made the running once again, setting a good pace, and, although joined in the back straight by the useful Dempsey, Ashley Brook had seen him off by four out. War of Attrition moved into second at the next but Ashley Brook, continuing to run on strongly, soon put him in his place. Ashley Brook's jumping was breath-taking at times. The ability to jump quickly and accurately is something that will stand him in good stead when he goes into open company, though whether it will be enough to help him trouble the top two-mile chasers is another matter. There will be plenty of opportunities for Ashley Brook to avoid Moscow Flyer and Well Chief and pick up more good prizes in 2005/6, especially as he is also effective over as far as twenty-one furlongs and may stay even further than that. Brennan himself is of the opinion that Ashley Brook will definitely get three miles.

Ashley Brook, a strong gelding who is very much a chaser in appearance, doesn't, however, have a jumping pedigree, though there are a few jumpers in his family and his dam Seamill is by Lafontaine, latterly a jumping sire. Ashley Brook's sire Magical Wonder was a high-class performer on the Flat in France,

Mrs E. K. Ellis' "Ashley Brook"

Ashley Brook (IRE) (ch.g. 1998)	Magical Wonder (USA) (ch 1983)	Storm Bird (b 1978)	Northern Dancer
			South Ocean
		Flama Ardiente (ch 1972)	Crimson Satan
			Royal Rafale
	Seamill (IRE) (b 1989)	Lafontaine (b 1977)	Sham
			Valya
		Pearl Reef (ch 1983)	Main Reef
			Pearl Grey

gaining his most important success in the nine-furlong Prix Jean Prat, while Seamill won once at ten furlongs and twice at eleven in Ireland. Seamill was also given a couple of runs over hurdles but showed no promise. Ashley Brook is her second foal and only winner to date. The next two dams were also winners in Ireland, Pearl Reef in a seven-furlong maiden at two and Pearl Grey in a mile-and-a-half maiden at three. Pearl Reef foaled a winning hurdler, Lucy Con, while Pearl Grey is half-sister to the dam of the useful two-mile hurdler Relevant, who won the Victor Ludorum. Ashley Brook, thoroughly game and reliable, acts on heavy going. He wasn't at his best on the only occasion he raced on ground firmer than good, on his final outing over hurdles, and, given that he is said to have had a problem with sore shins in the latest season, it is unlikely he will be risked on such a surface again. *K. Bishop*

ASHLEY MARSH 7 b.g. Alflora (IRE) – Annapuma (Rakaposhi King) [2004/5 h–: c16d² c16mpu Jun 8] no show over hurdles: poor form on completed start (jumped right) in chases: in frame in points in 2005. *T. R. George* **c63 h–**

ASHNAYA (FR) 7 b.m. Ashkalani (IRE) – Upend (Main Reef) [2004/5 h86: 16d² 16v c16d⁴ c25s⁴ c21v² c20m² Apr 23] sturdy mare: modest handicap hurdler: similar form **c92 h93**

over fences: stays 25f: acts on soft and good to firm going: tried blinkered, often wears cheekpieces. *G. M. Moore*

ASHTAROUTE (USA) 5 b.m. Holy Bull (USA) – Beating The Buzz (IRE) (Bluebird (USA)) [2004/5 h–: 22g² 24m⁵ 16g 16g 19d Jan 13] small mare: modest maiden on Flat (stays 1½m): poor maiden hurdler: probably stays 3m. *M. C. Chapman* **h78**

ASHTON VALE 6 ch.g. Ashkalani (IRE) – My Valentina (Royal Academy (USA)) [2004/5 h–: 16m 16mpu Jun 12] sturdy gelding: fair juvenile hurdler in 2002/3 for P. Nicholls, no form since: raced around 2m: acts on firm and good to soft going: tongue tied. *M. A. Barnes* **h–**

ASIAN MAZE (IRE) 6 ch.m. Anshan – Mazuma (IRE) (Mazaad) [2004/5 F17d⁴ F20g² F16m³ 16g⁵ 16g 16s² 18s* 20v* 24s* 20v* 20v² 20s* 24d* Apr 8] **h142 p** **F88**

Twenty-two years after Dawn Run crowned her novice hurdle season with wins at both Aintree and Punchestown, a mare from the same yard emerged to gain Grade 1 successes at both Festivals. If Asian Maze's form isn't on a par with Dawn Run's at this stage, she has many of the same qualities and the potential to improve quite a bit further. In her novice season, Dawn Run won five of her ten races, including a competitive handicap at Liverpool (as Aintree was then officially known) and the two-mile Champion Novices' Hurdle at Punchestown; Asian Maze was kept even busier, running sixteen times between her debut in a bumper in March 2004 and her success in the Menolly Homes Champion Novices' Hurdle at Punchestown thirteen months later. Dawn Run ran two of her best races that season in defeat, when runner-up to Sabin du Loir in the Sun Alliance Novices' Hurdle at Cheltenham and to the Champion Hurdle winner Gaye Brief in the Sun Templegate Hurdle (now the Aintree Hurdle), but Asian Maze, once she broke her duck on her fourth start over hurdles, was beaten just the once. And just as Dawn Run made her mark as a very tough and genuine front runner, so Asian Maze's progress coincided with a switch to front-running tactics. It would be fanciful to suggest Asian Maze can come close to matching the subsequent exploits of her predecessor, but there are certainly good races to be won with her and it would be no surprise if she returned to Aintree with a leading chance in the Aintree Hurdle itself next spring.

There was little in Asian Maze's early efforts to indicate the heights she might reach. She made the frame in the four bumpers she contested after her debut, though they were ordinary races, and the pick of her first three outings over hurdles, a second placing in a maiden at Listowel, represented just modest form. Asian Maze made the running for the first time in her next race, a mares novice at Punchestown in October which she won by half a length, and by the end of the year she had completed a four-timer, landing novices at Galway and Cork and a listed hurdle for mares back at Punchestown. As well as the change in tactics, Asian Maze may well also have been helped by a step up in trip (she raced at two and a half

John Smith's NUSSL Sefton Novices' Hurdle, Aintree—
front-running pair Asian Maze and Brewster (checks) pull well clear of a competitive-looking field

Menolly Homes Champion Novices' Hurdle, Punchestown—
win number seven as a novice for this remarkable mare;
Kerryhead Windfarm (hooped cap) and Washington Lad (left) lead the remainder home

miles or further after her first win), though she's by no means a sluggard and it was suggested at the end of the campaign that she might be tried in a good race at two miles.

After the turn of the year, Asian Maze's form continued to progress, though she met defeat on her next start, conceding 5 lb to the promising Washington Lad in the Golden Cygnet at Leopardstown and going down by a length and a half. That turned out to be Asian Maze's final outing for Paddy Mullins, who handed over the licence at his County Kilkenny stables to son Thomas at the end of February. Paddy Mullins, who trained his first winner in 1953, gained notable successes on the Flat, including winning the 2003 Irish Oaks with Vintage Tipple and the 1973 Champion Stakes with Hurry Harriet, but Dawn Run was the greatest horse he trained. His other good jumping winners included four in the Irish Grand National (Vulpine, Herring Gull, Dim Wit and Luska), four in the Galway Hurdle and three in the Galway Plate. Mullins trained Redundant Pal to win two successive runnings of the Ladbroke but many of his best runners were mares or fillies, with Grabel, Minorette's Girl and Mounamara among them in addition to Dawn Run and Asian Maze. A setback kept Asian Maze off for two months and she was forced to miss Cheltenham, returning for the Irish Stallion Farms EBF Mares Novices' Hurdle Championship Final at Fairyhouse at the end of March, in which she gained her most impressive success to that point, coasting home by twelve lengths from the fairly useful Mrs Wallensky.

Even better was to come. Twelve days later Asian Maze was sent to Aintree for an altogether more demanding contest, the Grade 1 John Smith's Nussl Sefton Novices' Hurdle, a race which didn't exist in Dawn Run's day. The pick of Asian Maze's opponents looked to be the smart novices Moulin Riche and Brewster, who had been first and third in the (Brit Insurance) Spa Hurdle at Cheltenham, the Royal & SunAlliance fifth Gold Medallist and the well-regarded Bewley's Berry, though of that quartet only Brewster gave his running. As Asian Maze increased the tempo four out, only Brewster could go with her after the outsider Football Crazy hit three out, but, determined as that rival was, Asian Maze kept on far too stoutly, winning by two and a half lengths, the pair finishing twenty-five lengths ahead of the third. There was no rival with Brewster's ability in the line-up for the Grade 1 Champion Novices' Hurdle at Punchestown later in April, shortly after the end of the British season, and Asian Maze made short work of her ten opponents, quickening an already sound pace three out and around twelve lengths up on the bridle when her rider started to ease her down going to the last; she won by five lengths from the unconsidered Kerryhead Windfarm with Washington Lad, conceding weight this time, third, though the margin in truth could have been a good deal further had her rider wished.

Asian Maze was one of two notable winners for her sire Anshan that afternoon at Punchestown, Pay It Forward landing the valuable novice handicap chase just over half an hour earlier. Asian Maze is the third foal of Mazuma, the second, Torosay (by Presenting), winning two points in 2005. Mazuma was also trained by Paddy Mullins, winning a two-mile maiden hurdle, as was her half-brother Fabulist who was a fair two-mile hurdler who also won at two and a half miles. The grandam Mag produced ten winners in all, the best of them the

Mrs C. A. Moore's "Asian Maze"

Asian Maze (IRE) (ch.m. 1999)	Anshan (ch 1987)	Persian Bold (br 1975)	Bold Lad
			Relkarunner
		Lady Zi (b 1980)	Manado
			Exbury Grace
	Mazuma (IRE) (b 1990)	Mazaad (b 1983)	Auction Ring
			Sweet Relations
		Mag (b 1968)	Noble Jay
			Orestia

useful juvenile hurdler Lir, who won the Aurelius Hurdle at Ascot. Several of Mag's daughters have produced above-average jumpers who showed more stamina than Lir and Fabulist, among them the fairly useful three-mile hurdler Tribune and the out-and-out staying chaser The Malakarma. The leggy, close-coupled Asian Maze has raced mainly on going softer than good over hurdles and acts on heavy. *Thomas Mullins, Ireland*

ASK AGAIN 6 ch.g. Rakaposhi King – Boreen's Glory (Boreen (FR)) [2004/5 25s^5 Dec 18] ninth foal: half-brother to winning pointer by Duky: dam, placed fourth in point, out of half-sister to top-class staying chaser The Dikler: won completed start in maiden points in 2004: bought 23,000 gns Doncaster May Sales: well beaten in novice on hurdling debut. *D. G. Bridgwater* **h–**

ASK ANDREA 5 ch.m. Busy Flight – Craberi Flash Foot (Lighter) [2004/5 F18s 20d^{pu} Feb 26] first foal: dam unraced: no form in bumper or maiden hurdle. *N. R. Mitchell* **h–** **F–**

ASK FOR LUCK (IRE) 8 b.g. Camden Town – French Thistle (Kemal (FR)) [2004/5 h75: 26d^5 22s^2 c21g^4 May 21] workmanlike gelding: poor maiden hurdler: well beaten on chasing debut: should stay beyond 3m: acts on soft going. *J. G. Portman* **c–** **h84**

ASK HENRY (IRE) 9 b. or br.g. Jolly Jake (NZ) – Pineway VII (Damsire Unregistered) [2004/5 c23s^3 c26g^5 c28s^3 c24g^3 Feb 17] tall gelding: fairly useful handicap chaser: off 18 months, placed 3 of 4 starts in 2004/5: stays 3½m: raced mainly on good ground or softer: tried tongue tied. *P. F. Nicholls* **c122**

ASK ME NOT (IRE) 7 b.m. Shernazar – Cabin Glory (The Parson) [2004/5 24d^{pu} May 9] IR £1,000 3-y-o: fourth foal: half-sister to 3m hurdle winner Simple Glory (by Simply Great): dam never ran: winning Irish pointer: showed nothing in maiden on hurdling debut. *F. Lloyd* **h–**

ASK ME WHAT (IRE) 8 b.m. Shernazar – Laffan's Bridge (IRE) (Mandalus) [2004/5 c–, h99: c20d^4 20m^6 20g* 24m^3 20m^3 22g^6 c21m^3 c21m^5 c26m^{pu} 20d^5 20s^3 Oct 13] lengthy mare: modest handicap hurdler: sold out of Miss V. Williams' stable 4,500 gns Doncaster May Sales before second start: won at Worcester in July: poor form over fences, usually makes mistakes: stays 3m: acts on good to firm and heavy going: tried blinkered. *Mrs A. M. Thorpe* **c78 x h97**

ASK THE DRIVER 4 b.g. Ashkalani (IRE) – Tithcar (Cadeaux Genereux) [2004/5 16f Oct 7] modest maiden on Flat (stays 1¼m): well held in juvenile on hurdling debut: sold 7,000 gns Newmarket Autumn Sales. *D. J. S. ffrench Davis* **h–**

ASK THE NATIVES (IRE) 11 br.g. Be My Native (USA) – Ask The Lady (Over The River (FR)) [2004/5 c26s* c24s* Apr 16] useful-looking gelding: fairly useful hurdler/chaser at best: won both starts in points in 2004 (reportedly fractured pelvis subsequently): did well on return, winning hunters at Warwick in March and Bangor (by ½ length from Yeoman Sailor) in April: stays 3¼m: acts on heavy going. *Miss C. Roddick* **c115 h–**

ASK THE UMPIRE (IRE) 10 b.g. Boyne Valley – Ask Breda (Ya Zaman (USA)) [2004/5 c16f^{pu} c20s^4 c16d^4 c20d^5 21d 21s c22s 20d^4 c19v* c20d^5 Apr 20] leggy ex-Irish gelding: bumper winner: poor hurdler/chaser: sold out of J. Dreaper's stable 4,400 gns Doncaster August Sales, subsequently had several trainers: best effort in 2004/5 when winning selling handicap chase at Chepstow in March: stays 2½m: acts on any going: often wears cheekpieces/blinkers: tried tongue tied. *B. J. Llewellyn* **c84 h73**

ASPARAGUS (IRE) 11 b.g. Roselier (FR) – Arctic Bead (IRE) (Le Moss) [2004/5 c118, h–: c19s^2 c20s^2 c21d^2 c19s^F c29v^6 Dec 28] smallish gelding: fairly useful handicap chaser: good sixth to Silver Birch in Welsh National at Chepstow (collapsed after line): stayed 29f: raced on good going or softer (acted on heavy): tongue tied: usually raced prominently: tremendously tough and consistent (in frame on 23 of 24 completed outings): dead. *M. Sheppard* **c124 h–**

ASPIRING ACTOR (IRE) 5 b.g. Old Vic – Stasias Dream (IRE) (Montelimar (USA)) [2004/5 F18s^5 F17d^2 F18d^2 Feb 20] useful-looking gelding: first foal: dam poor maiden hurdler: fairly useful form in bumpers, second to Nice Horse at Fontwell final start. *P. F. Nicholls* **F97**

ASSIGNATION 5 b.g. Compton Place – Hug Me (Shareef Dancer (USA)) [2004/5 h–: 17d 19m 16f^{ur} 17d 17m^3 16g^F Nov 18] close-coupled gelding: poor hurdler: wore cheekpieces last 4 starts. *Miss M. Bragg* **h63**

ASSOON 6 b.g. Ezzoud (IRE) – Handy Dancer (Green God) [2004/5 h112, F89: 16m* 19g^3 Sep 30] rather leggy gelding: fair maiden on Flat (stays 2¼m): fair form over hurdles: won maiden at Huntingdon in August: likely to be suited by 2½m+. *G. L. Moore* **h99**

ASSUMETHEPOSITION (FR) 5 gr.g. Cyborg (FR) – Jeanne Grey (FR) (Fast Topaze (USA)) [2004/5 F80: 20d^4 16g^4 16g^6 21g^5 16v^2 20v* 17v^2 20g Mar 26] unfurnished gelding: modest hurdler: won handicap at Newcastle in February: should stay beyond 2½m: raced on good going or softer (acts on heavy): wore cheekpieces last 3 starts. *R. C. Guest* **h91**

ASSUMPTALINA 5 b.m. Primitive Rising (USA) – New Broom (IRE) (Brush Aside (USA)) [2004/5 F16g Mar 26] unfurnished mare: third foal: half-sister to winning 2m hurdler Witch's Brew (by Simply Great): dam, no sign of ability, half-sister to top-class chaser up to 25f Simply Dashing: well held in bumper on debut. *R. T. Phillips* **F–**

ASTAFORT (FR) 6 ch.g. Kendor (FR) – Tres Chic (USA) (Northern Fashion (USA)) [2004/5 h81: 16d^F May 12] good-topped gelding: poor maiden hurdler: fell fatally at Perth: stayed 2½m: acted on heavy going. *A. C. Whillans* **h–**

ASTLEY GOLD (IRE) 11 ch.g. Big Sink Hope (USA) – Ascot Princess (Prince Hansel) [2004/5 c21d^{pu} May 15] big, rangy gelding: maiden hurdler/chaser: won point in January. *G. Whisker* **c– h–**

ASTON LAD 4 b.c. Bijou d'Inde – Fishki (Niniski (USA)) [2004/5 17s^4 18d^3 17g^5 16s^2 16s^{pu} Apr 10] half-brother to modest hurdlers Fishki's Lad (by Casteddu) and Green 'N' Gold (by Cloudings): dam winning jumper, stayed 25f: modest maiden on Flat (should stay 1½m): fair form in juvenile hurdles: would have won but for being pulled up (reportedly lame) on run-in at Hexham final start: raced around 2m on good going or softer. *M. D. Hammond* **h103**

ASTON MARA 8 b.g. Bering – Coigach (Niniski (USA)) [2004/5 h96d: 22d^{pu} 22g 20m Aug 30] neat gelding: modest handicap hurdler at best, has lost his form. *M. A. Buckley* **h–**

ASTONVILLE (FR) 11 b.g. Top Ville – Astonishing (BRZ) (Vacilante (ARG)) [2004/5 c18s 20s^4 20d^5 20v c24s^{pu} 16g c26g c36d^{pu} Apr 9] lengthy ex-French gelding: one-time very smart hurdler/useful chaser: claimed from M. Rolland €8,000 second start: highly tried and no form for M. Scudamore in Britain: tailed off when refused in Grand Steeple-Chase de Paris at Auteuil after end of British season: stays 25f: acts on heavy going: tried visored. *R. Chotard, France* **c–** **h108**

ASTORMYDAYISCOMING 7 b.g. Alhaatmi – Valentine Song (Pas de Seul) [2004/5 h–: 16s^3 20d^5 20v c16v^{pu} 19d^{pu} 16v Feb 20] leggy gelding: poor maiden hurdler: no show on chasing debut: stays 2½m: acts on soft and good to firm going: has worn blinkers/cheekpieces: tried tongue tied. *C. N. Kellett* **c–** **h65**

ASTRAL AFFAIR (IRE) 6 br.m. Norwich – Jupiters Jill (Jupiter Pluvius) [2004/5 h–, F76: 20m 20d 24g^4 Jul 7] unfurnished mare: placed in maiden Irish point: modest form in bumpers: form over hurdles only on final start. *P. A. Pritchard* **h70**

ASTRAL DANCER (IRE) 5 b.g. Fourstars Allstar (USA) – Walk N'Dance (IRE) (Pennine Walk) [2004/5 F64: F16d F17d^4 F16s 17d Feb 11] rather unfurnished gelding: modest form once in 4 starts in bumpers: well held in novice hurdle. *J. Mackie* **h–** **F82**

ASTRAL PRINCE 7 ch.g. Efisio – Val d'Erica (Ashmore (FR)) [2004/5 c67, h–: c21m* c21g^F c21g^{pu} Jul 16] lengthy gelding: maiden hurdler: poor chaser: won weak novice at Sedgefield in May: stays 21f: acts on soft and good to firm going: usually blinkered/in cheekpieces: tried tongue tied. *Mrs K. Walton* **c84 ?** **h–**

ASTRONOMIC 5 b.g. Zafonic (USA) – Sky Love (USA) (Nijinsky (CAN)) [2004/5 17d* 16s* 16d^F 16v^5 16d^{pu} Apr 8] strong, close-coupled gelding: useful on Flat (stays 1¼m), sold out of A. Fabre's stable 190,000 gns Newmarket Autumn (2003) Sales, well held only outing in 2004: good start over hurdles, winning novices at Sedgefield in November and Haydock (fairly useful form, beat below-par Marcel 1½ lengths in listed event) in December: lost action final outing: raced around 2m on going softer than good (ran poorly on heavy). *J. Howard Johnson* **h125**

ASTYANAX (IRE) 5 b.g. Hector Protector (USA) – Craigmill (Slip Anchor) [2004/5 16s 16g^6 21d^3 23d^4 24g^5 Apr 1] sturdy gelding: fairly useful on Flat (stays 2m), successful twice in 2004, sold out of Sir Mark Prescott's stable 75,000 gns Newmarket Autumn Sales: modest form over hurdles: has jumped none too fluently. *N. J. Henderson* **h95**

ATAHUELPA 5 b.g. Hernando (FR) – Certain Story (Known Fact (USA)) [2004/5 h108d: 16g 17g* 16m^3 16d* 16s^3 16d^2 16d* 16d 16d^3 16d Apr 9] leggy gelding: fairly useful hurdler: left M. Harris after reappearance and much improved: won novices at Bangor (handicap) in August and Chepstow in October and handicap at Windsor in November: likely to prove best around 2m: acts on soft going, probably on good to firm: tried tongue tied: sold 11,000 gns Doncaster May Sales. *A. King* **h121**

Quattro Rubber Products Newton Novices' Hurdle, Haydock—
Astronomic becomes the first to defeat the prolific Marcel (spotted cap) in Britain

ATHENRY GENT (IRE) 6 ch.g. Fourstars Allstar (USA) – Covette (Master Owen) [2004/5 h–: 27m 20g 24d Oct 9] workmanlike gelding: well beaten over hurdles: third on completed start in points. *J. Howard Johnson* **h–**

ATHLUMNEY LAD (IRE) 6 b.g. Mujadil (USA) – Simouna (Ela-Mana-Mou) [2004/5 16m* 16g^{4} 16s* 16s* 16v Jan 9] fairly useful at 1½m on Flat: fairly useful handicap hurdler: won at Galway in July, Gowran in October and Down Royal in November: raced at 2m: acts on soft and good to firm going. *N. Meade, Ireland* **h121**

ATHNOWEN (IRE) 13 b.g. Lord Americo – Lady Bluebird (Arapaho) [2004/5 c96§, h–§: c17d* c21d^{4} c20s^{3} c23s^{ur} c24s^{4} c19v^{pu} c19d^{rtr} Feb 1] sturdy gelding: fair handicap chaser: won at Exeter in May: effective at 2m to 3m: acts on soft and good to firm going: visored once: sketchy jumper: often gives trouble at start, refused to race final outing. *J. R. Payne* **c106 x h– §**

ATHOLLBROSE (USA) 4 b.g. Mister Baileys – Knightly Cut Up (USA) (Gold Crest (USA)) [2004/5 16m^{6} 16m 16s^{4} 16v^{2} 16d 16v^{6} 16s^{pu} 20s^{pu} Apr 20] leggy gelding: modest maiden on Flat (stays 1½m): poor juvenile hurdler, sold out of T. Easterby's stable 4,100 gns Doncaster October Sales after second start: raced mainly around 2m. *Mrs C. J. Kerr* **h71**

ATLANTIC CITY 4 ch.g. First Trump – Pleasuring (Good Times (ITY)) [2004/5 16d 16g* Mar 28] compact gelding: fair on Flat (stays 1½m), successful in January: easily better effort in juvenile hurdles when winning at Plumpton in March. *Mrs L. Richards* **h103**

ATLANTIC CROSSING (IRE) 8 b.g. Roselier (FR) – Ocean Mist (IRE) (Crash Course) [2004/5 c87x, h–: 20g^{4} 22d^{pu} May 9] leggy, quite good-topped gelding: modest handicap hurdler: in frame in points in 2005: should stay beyond 2½m: raced on good going or softer: tried blinkered: makes mistakes over fences. *P. Beaumont* **c– x h92**

ATLANTIC HAWK 7 b.g. Daar Alzamaan (IRE) – Pyewacket (Belfort (FR)) [2004/5 h–: 20d Nov 13] well-made gelding: poor form only completion over hurdles: hard ride. *Mrs S. J. Smith* **h82**

ATLANTIC TERN 4 b.c. Atraf – Great Tern (Simply Great (FR)) [2004/5 16g Jul 18] modest maiden on Flat (stays 1¼m): tailed off in juvenile hurdle. *N. M. Babbage* **h–**

ATLANTICUS (IRE) 9 b.g. Kings Lake (USA) – Amazonia (GER) (Alpenkonig (GER)) [2004/5 c–, h–: 20d Jun 20] lengthy, angular gelding: winning hurdler: little form over fences: stays 2½m: acts on soft going: visored once: has had tongue tied. *K. W. Hogg, Isle of Man* **c– h–**

ATLANTIS (HOL) 6 ch.g. No Ski – File Moon (HOL) (Man In The Moon (USA)) [2004/5 16d^{5} 18s^{3} 16s^{pu} 16g^{4} 17s^{4} 20s^{2} 21g 20g Feb 5] good-topped gelding: successful 7 times up to around 1¼m on Flat in Germany and Holland: modest maiden hurdler: moody efforts in blinkers last 2 starts: stays 2½m: raced on good ground or softer (acts on soft): ungenuine. *G. L. Moore* **h90 §**

A TOI A MOI (FR) 5 ch.g. Cyborg (FR) – Peperonelle (FR) (Dom Pasquini (FR)) [2004/5 h105: 19g^{2} 17v* 16s^{ur} Dec 13] tall, lengthy gelding: fair novice hurdler: won at Bangor in November: stays 19f: raced on good going or softer. *Miss Venetia Williams* **h111 +**

ATOMIC BREEZE (IRE) 11 b. or br.g. Strong Gale – Atomic Lady (Over The River (FR)) [2004/5 c64§, h–: c27g^{pu} c27m^{2} c28d^{pu} c25m^{4} c20m^{5} c25g^{pu} Dec 28] plain gelding: poor handicap chaser: stays 3½m: acts on firm and good to soft going: unreliable. *D. M. Forster* **c64 § h–**

ATTACK 9 gr.g. Sabrehill (USA) – Butsova (Formidable (USA)) [2004/5 c–, h–: c24d^{pu} Mar 28] angular gelding: winning hurdler in 2002/3: little other form, including in points: tried in blinkers/cheekpieces: tongue tied. *Mrs Julie Read* **c– h–**

AT THE DOUBLE 9 b.g. Sure Blade (USA) – Moheli (Ardross) [2004/5 18d^{4} 21s^{3} 16d c16s^{pu} 16s^{4} 21v* 22v 20s 22s* 20s^{6} 16g^{3} Apr 19] poor hurdler: won sellers at Plumpton in January and Fontwell (handicap) in March: pulled up after mistake fourth on chasing debut: stays 3m: raced on good going or softer: usually visored/blinkered: not one to trust. *P. Winkworth* **c– h81 §**

ATTICUS FINCH (IRE) 8 b.g. Witness Box (USA) – Dramatic Loop (IRE) (Balinger) [2004/5 c95x, h81: 26g^{pu} c20g^{pu} 26f* 26d c25s^{4} c24s^{3} c25s^{5} Mar 22] workmanlike gelding: trained third/fourth starts by G. Harker: poor hurdler: won handicap at Huntingdon in September: modest handicap chaser: stayed easy 3¼m: acted on firm and soft going: tried in cheekpeices: free-going sort, prone to mistakes: dead. *Mrs M. Stirk* **c96 x h80**

ATTITUDE 4 ch.f. Riverwise (USA) – Came Cottage (Nearly A Hand) [2004/5 F17g Apr 3] eighth foal: sister to top-class 2m hurdler Rooster Booster and 2¼m bumper **F–**

winner Cockatoo Ridge: dam fairly useful pointer: never in contention in mares bumper on debut. *A. King*

ATTORNEY GENERAL (IRE) 6 b.g. Sadler's Wells (USA) – Her Ladyship (Polish Precedent (USA)) [2004/5 h109: 20g^{3} 20s^{F} 24d^{2} 24d^{2} 22g^{4} 24g Mar 17] medium-sized gelding: improved into useful handicap hurdler: ran well when in frame, particularly so when second to Korelo at Cheltenham and fourth to Supreme Serenade at Sandown fourth and fifth starts: will stay beyond 3m: raced on good going or softer: not a straightforward ride. *J. A. B. Old* **h134**

ATUM RE (IRE) 8 br.g. Be My Native (USA) – Collopy's Cross (Pragmatic) [2004/5 c132, h–: c20s^{ur} c20s^{pu} c16d^{4} c16d^{6} c16g c20g^{6} Apr 22] tall, good-topped gelding: useful chaser in 2003/4: below best in 2004/5: likely to prove best up to 2½m: acts on soft and good to firm going: visored last 3 starts: usually sound jumper: free-going sort: joined P. Nicholls. *P. R. Webber* **c124 h–**

AT YOUR REQUEST 4 gr.g. Bering – Requesting (Rainbow Quest (USA)) [2004/5 16s^{6} 16s^{4} 16d^{2} 16v^{2} 16s* 16g^{2} 17m^{4} Apr 13] lengthy gelding: fair maiden on Flat (stays 1½m), sold out of E. Dunlop's stable 32,000 gns Newmarket July Sales: fairly useful juvenile hurdler: won quite valuable event at Huntingdon in February: good second of 24 to Dabiroun in valuable handicap at Cheltenham next time: raced around 2m: acts on soft and good to firm going: carries head awkwardly/flashes tail. *Ian Williams* **h122**

AUBURN DUKE 5 ch.g. Inchinor – Dakota Girl (Northern State (USA)) [2004/5 F–: F16d May 6] well held in 2 bumpers. *W. Jenks* **F–**

AUBURN SPIRIT 10 ch.g. Teamster – Spirit of Youth (Kind of Hush) [2004/5 c104, h80: c26d^{3} c30d* c32d^{3} c30s^{2} c24d c30s^{4} c29v* c29s^{4} c28s^{pu} Apr 3] tall gelding: poor hurdler: fair handicap chaser: won at Huntingdon in November and Warwick in February: stays 4m: acts on good to firm and heavy going: tried visored: tough, though sometimes takes plenty of driving. *M. D. I. Usher* **c110 h–**

AUDIOSTREETDOTCOM 8 ch.g. Risk Me (FR) – Ballagarrow Girl (North Stoke) [2004/5 c–§, h95§: 22d^{pu} 20g^{4} 26d^{3} 22m* 19d 20v^{2} 22d^{ur} 25v^{pu} 20v^{3} 19s^{pu} 22v Feb 15] lengthy gelding: little show in 3 chases: modest hurdler: left G. Balding after first outing: didn't have to be near best to win seller at Newton Abbot in September: left N. Berry after sixth start: stays 2¾m: raced mainly on good going or softer (acts on heavy): usually wears blinkers/cheekpieces (has worn hood): ungenuine. *R. A. Harris* **c– § h91 §**

AUDITOR 6 b.g. Polish Precedent (USA) – Annaba (IRE) (In The Wings) [2004/5 c–, h–: c17f^{ur} c16m^{4} c23g^{pu} c16g^{3} c19s^{2} c16d* c16s^{pu} c16s^{pu} c19s^{3} c21g^{pu} Apr 14] rather sparely-made gelding: no form over hurdles: poor chaser: 23 lb out of weights, won very weak handicap at Towcester in November: best around 2m: acts on good to soft going, probably on good to firm: blinkered once: none too genuine. *S. T. Lewis* **c85 § h–**

AUDITTY (IRE) 12 b.g. Montelimar (USA) – Tax Code (Workboy) [2004/5 c103, h–: c16m^{5} c16m^{pu} c21d^{pu} Oct 3] lengthy gelding: fair handicap chaser in 2003/4: no form in 2004/5, including in points: stays 2½m: very best efforts on good going or firmer (acts on firm). *W. Jenks* **c– h–**

AUGHERSKEA (IRE) 6 b.g. Oscar (IRE) – Closing Thyne (IRE) (Good Thyne (USA)) [2004/5 F114: F16g^{3} 16s* 18d^{2} 20s 18s^{3} 20s^{4} Feb 20] rangy, well-made gelding: useful bumper winner: similar standard over hurdles: won maiden at Down Royal in November: best efforts when second to Mossy Green in minor event at Fairyhouse and third to Royal Paradise in Grade 1 novice at Leopardstown: should stay beyond 2¼m: acts on soft going: tried tongue tied: has hung left. *N. Meade, Ireland* **h130**

AUGUST ROSE (IRE) 5 b. or br.m. Accordion – Lockersleybay (IRE) (Orchestra) [2004/5 F16s 16d^{R} Apr 11] second foal: dam unraced half-sister to dam of useful staying chaser St Mellion Fairway: no show in bumper or novice hurdle. *J. Barclay* **h– F–**

AUK 10 ch.g. Absalom – Lady Stock (Crofter (USA)) [2004/5 16g^{6} Apr 19] sturdy gelding: bad hurdler: raced mainly around 2m on going softer than good (acts on heavy). *Mrs P. Robeson* **c– h54**

AULD THYNES SAKE (IRE) 8 b.g. Good Thyne (USA) – La Fairy (IRE) (Lafontaine (USA)) [2004/5 h74: 19d^{3} 20s^{pu} Dec 17] workmanlike gelding: poor maiden hurdler: should stay at least 2½m. *Mrs Merrita Jones* **h76**

AUNTIE JACHINTA 7 b.m. Governor General – Hopeful Alda (Kambalda) [2004/5 F70: aF16g Oct 30] well held in 3 bumpers. *J. A. Supple* **F–**

AURAZURE (IRE) 7 gr.g. Roselier (FR) – Siul Currach (Deep Run) [2004/5 F96: 24d^{3} 21d^{5} Dec 7] fairly useful form when fourth in bumpers in 2003/4: better effort in novice hurdles when third at Southwell. *C. R. Egerton* **h96**

AUTOGRAPH 4 b.f. Polar Prince (IRE) – Seraphim (FR) (Lashkari) [2004/5 F16s^{2} F17m^{4} Apr 23] tall, useful-looking filly: fourth foal: half-sister to winning hurdler/ modest staying chaser April Spirit (by Nomination) and fairly useful 11f winner/modest hurdler Miss Holly (by Makbul): dam, modest hurdler, 13f winner on Flat: better effort in bumpers when second of 21 to Abragante at Wetherby. *Mrs S. J. Smith* **F91**

AUTUMN MIST (IRE) 10 br.g. Phardante (FR) – Sprinkling Star (Strong Gale) [2004/5 c24f^{2} c25f^{6} c23m^{3} c24f^{4} c21g^{4} c22f^{2} c24s^{4} c22g^{4} 24s c24d^{2} c20d^{2} c26d* c24s c26v^{2} c30s Feb 11] winning hurdler: modest handicap chaser: left E. Sheehy after tenth outing: made all at Plumpton in December: stays 3¼m: acts on any going: blinkered/ visored: often tongue tied: front runner. *M. Scudamore* **c90 h–**

AUTUMN RAIN (USA) 8 br.g. Dynaformer (USA) – Edda (USA) (Ogygian (USA)) [2004/5 h–: c20s^{ur} 26s c24d^{pu} Jan 31] workmanlike gelding: maiden jumper: no form since 2002/3. *D. L. Williams* **c– h–**

AUTUMN RED (IRE) 5 ch.g. Zaffaran (USA) – Ballygullen River (IRE) (Over The River (FR)) [2004/5 F16d^{2} F17g^{2} Mar 19] 16,000 3-y-o, 20,000 4-y-o: big gelding: chasing type: third foal: dam unraced half-sister to dam of useful 2m to 21f chaser Full Irish: fairly useful form when runner-up in bumpers, beaten neck by Rimsky at Bangor second time: will be suited by stiffer test of stamina. *P. R. Webber* **F98**

AVADI (IRE) 7 b.g. Un Desperado (FR) – Flamewood (Touching Wood (USA)) [2004/5 h87, F77: c23d^{pu} c22v^{F2} Oct 17] useful-looking gelding: modest form over hurdles: similar form in novice handicap chase at Market Rasen (6 lengths clear when fell last): stays 3m: acts on heavy going. *Mrs H. Dalton* **c89 h–**

AVALANCHE (FR) 8 gr.g. Highest Honor (FR) – Fairy Gold (Golden Fleece (USA)) [2004/5 c141, h107+: c20g 16d^{ur} c20g Apr 22] big, workmanlike gelding: maiden hurdler: useful handicap chaser in 2003/4: little show in 2004/5: stays 21f: unraced on firm going, acts on any other: usually races prominently: pulls hard: sound jumper. *J. R. Best* **c– h–**

AVANTI 9 gr.g. Reprimand – Dolly Bevan (Another Realm) [2004/5 24d 19d 20s^{3} 19v 21g^{ur} 18s^{6} 22d Mar 26] sturdy gelding: poor novice hurdler: seems to stay 2½m: visored last 2 starts. *Dr J. R. J. Naylor* **h62**

AVANTI TIGER (IRE) 6 b. or br.g. Supreme Leader – Reign of Terror (IRE) (Orchestra) [2004/5 h–, F84: 20v 20v^{pu} 22v Feb 15] medium-sized gelding: no form over hurdles. *C. C. Bealby* **h–**

AVAS DELIGHT (IRE) 7 b.g. Ajraas (USA) – Whothatis (Creative Plan (USA)) [2004/5 h87+, F84: 16d^{3} 20s^{5} 16d^{5} 16d^{ur} 16d^{2} 16s 19g^{3} 19g^{3} Apr 15] modest handicap hurdler: stays 2½m: raced on good going or softer. *R. H. Alner* **h98**

AVEBURY 9 b.g. Fairy King (USA) – Circle of Chalk (FR) (Kris) [2004/5 c89, h–: c16g^{6} c16f^{4} Jun 6] winning hurdler: modest form in novice chases: raced around 2m: acts on firm and good to soft going: usually tongue tied: sold 1,000 gns Doncaster August Sales, resold 500 gns Doncaster October Sales. *G. M. Moore* **c84 h–**

AVENCHES (GER) 5 ch.m. Dashing Blade – Altja (GER) (Acatenango (GER)) [2004/5 16v 19m^{6} 19s^{pu} 16d^{pu} Apr 18] ran 25 times on Flat in Germany, succesful twice around 1¼m in 2004: no form over hurdles: claimed from C. Von Der Recke £6,000 on debut: trained by Mrs L. Jewell next start. *M. J. McGrath* **h–**

AVERSE (USA) 6 b.m. Lord Avie (USA) – Averti (USA) (Known Fact (USA)) [2004/5 F88: 16d^{2} 17d^{4} 16v^{6} Dec 18] big, angular mare: runner-up in bumper on debut: best effort over hurdles when second in mares intermediate at Perth: will prove best around 2m. *N. G. Richards* **h90**

AVESOMEOFTHAT (IRE) 4 b.g. Lahib (USA) – Lacinia (Groom Dancer (USA)) [2004/5 17m^{3} 16f^{2} 16g^{6} 16g^{5} 16d^{3} 19m Apr 2] lengthy gelding: fair maiden at best on Flat (stays 1m): modest juvenile hurdler: likely to prove best around 2m: tongue tied after fourth outing. *Mrs P. N. Dutfield* **h92**

AVITTA (IRE) 6 b.m. Pennekamp (USA) – Alinova (USA) (Alleged (USA)) [2004/5 h109§: 16g^{3} 16s* 16s^{3} 17g 16s^{pu} 16g^{6} 21g Apr 14] rangy mare: fair handicap hurdler: won weak mares event at Haydock in November: best around 2m: acts on heavy going: ungenuine. *Miss Venetia Williams* **h114 §**

AVOCA MIST (IRE) 5 b. or br.m. Luso – Apicat (Buckskin (FR)) [2004/5 F16s^2 F16s^2 F16d* F16s* F17d Apr 9] small, angular mare: half-sister to several winners, including useful chaser Boneyarrow (by Over The River), stays 21f, and useful staying hurdler Friendship (by Strong Gale): dam unraced half-sister to high-class staying chaser Simon Legree: useful in bumpers: won at Thurles and Fairyhouse in March, beating La Marianne by neck at latter: easily better effort in graded events subsequently when seventh to The Cool Guy at Aintree next time. *W. P. Mullins, Ireland* **F105**

AWAKEN 4 b.f. Zafonic (USA) – Dawna (Polish Precedent (USA)) [2004/5 17d 16g 16g Mar 9] small filly: half-sister to bumper winner Golden Measure (by Rainbow Quest): modest maiden on Flat: no form over hurdles. *G. A. Swinbank* **h–**

AWESOME WELLS (IRE) 11 b.g. Sadler's Wells (USA) – Shadywood (Habitat) [2004/5 h72: 20g^{pu} 20s^6 May 5] strong gelding: poor hurdler: no form in 2004/5, including in points: stays 2½m: acts on soft going: often tongue tied. *D. J. Wintle* **h–**

AWWAL MARRA (USA) 5 ch.m. King of Kings (IRE) – Secretariat Lass (USA) (Secretariat (USA)) [2004/5 17d 16s^5 19g Dec 16] good-topped mare: second in 2-y-o maiden for M. Johnston, well held on Flat in 2004: signs of ability over hurdles only on second start. *E. W. Tuer* **h72**

AXFORD LORD 5 gr.g. Petong – Bellyphax (Bellypha) [2004/5 16g^{pu} 20d^{pu} Oct 9] modest 6f winner at 2 yrs, no form on Flat in 2004: no show in 2 novice hurdles. *A. C. Whillans* **h–**

AYE AYE POPEYE (IRE) 7 ch.g. Imperial Frontier (USA) – Boskovice (IRE) (Flash of Steel) [2004/5 h114: 16g c16d^2 c16s^2 c16s^4 c17v^F Dec 26] compact gelding: fair hurdler: similar form in maiden chases, second to impressive Royal Alphabet at Thurles and Like-A-Butterfly at Naas in November: best at 2m: acts on heavy going: tried blinkered. *Mrs J. Harrington, Ireland* **c114 h114**

AZERTYUIOP (FR) 8 b.g. Baby Turk – Temara (FR) (Rex Magna (FR)) [2004/5 c182, h–: c17s* c16d^2 c24g^3 c17d* c16g^3 c16g^2 Apr 23] **c182 h–**

The use of the adjective golden implies both rarity and preciousness, some near-ideal or almost perfect state. It may be premature to talk of a 'golden age' for steeplechasing to compare with the era of Arkle, Flyingbolt, Mill House and Dunkirk in the 'sixties, but these are certainly golden days for the two-milers, a group that has traditionally tended to be among the 'cinderella' horses of the jumping scene. Azertyuiop, Moscow Flyer and Well Chief rightly received the recognition they deserved for some memorable performances in the latest season. All three are truly outstanding chasers, their ratings bettered among the specialist two-milers of Timeform's experience only by the legendary Dunkirk. The very versatile Flyingbolt romped home by fifteen lengths in the 1966 Two-Mile Champion Chase but his Timeform rating (like that of another notably versatile tip-top chaser Desert Orchid) came from his performances over longer distances, including tremendous weight-carrying victories that season in the Massey-Ferguson Gold Cup over two and a half miles, the Thyestes Handicap Chase and the Irish Grand National.

Though Flyingbolt and Dunkirk were contemporaries, they never met. Dunkirk scored a facile twenty-length victory in the Two-Mile Champion Chase in 1965 when Flyingbolt gained his Cheltenham Festival success in the Cotswold Chase, one of five victories in an unbeaten campaign as a novice. Dunkirk was dead by the time the 1966 Cheltenham Festival came around, killed in a fall running over his wrong trip against Arkle in the King George VI Chase at Kempton, having won both his starts that season, beating Mill House by fifteen lengths over two miles in the Frogmore Chase at Ascot and then justifying short-priced favouritism under 12-7 in the Mackeson Gold Cup (run over two miles and a few yards). The 1965/6 season saw Arkle win his third successive Gold Cup but his career was ended the following season by a broken bone in a foot sustained in the King George VI Chase. The 1965/6 season also turned out to be the peak of Flyingbolt's career. Aged only seven, he was struck down by brucellosis, a bacterial disease, and never regained his true form. Mill House, winner of the 1963 Gold Cup and runner-up in 1964 and 1965, broke down while being prepared for the 1966 Gold Cup but did recover to contest the 1967 renewal in which he was three lengths in front and moving well when falling at the seventeenth. He also fell at the fifteenth when favourite for the 1968 renewal.

William Hill Haldon Gold Cup Chase (Limited Handicap), Exeter—a fine reappearance by Azertyuiop, who gives 18 lb and a comprehensive beating to both Seebald and Kadarann

The exhilarating Dunkirk, a natural front-runner, was only eight at the time of his death. He achieved a Timeform rating of 186, compared to Flyingbolt's 210 and Arkle's 212. Mill House was rated 191 at his peak (in the 1963/4 season) but was still rated 177 in the final *Timeform Black Book* of the 1965/6 season. When racing historians look back, they will find some similarities between the 2004/5 season and 1965/6. The infection which sidelined triple Gold Cup winner Best Mate (Timeform 182 at his best) robbed the Cheltenham Festival of its focal point, but even a top-form Best Mate would have had his work cut out against Kicking King, who had a magnificent season, also winning the King George VI Chase and the Punchestown Gold Cup, in the process earning a Timeform rating of 182, the same as Azertyuiop and Well Chief and 2 lb below the highest-rated horse of the season, Moscow Flyer.

The latest season was unique in having four such highly-rated steeplechasers at the top of the end-of-season rankings, but one of them, Azertyuiop, may not be around in 2005/6. He suffered a bad overreach when beaten four lengths by Well Chief in the Celebration Chase at Sandown on the last day of the British season, an injury that looks set to keep him off the course for twelve months. Azertyuiop's season ended in something of an anti-climax as he also returned injured—with pulled abdominal muscles—after finishing a below-form third, beaten two lengths and thirteen lengths by Moscow Flyer and Well Chief in the Queen Mother Champion Chase. To his credit, Azertyuiop kept on gamely at Cheltenham but any chance of victory was effectively ended with a bad mistake at the sixth fence, the water jump, hitting the fence and then dropping his hind legs in the water. There are around twenty fewer courses with water jumps than there used to be, no bad thing considering that the obstacle is arguably unfair, something of a trap as the horses cannot see the ditch on the landing side. Horses can be injured through no fault of their own, although, mercifully, the days when chasers sometimes ended up breaking their backs have long gone, with ditches being much shallower nowadays. That said, unless a water jump is in front of the stands—providing a spectacle as it does at Aintree and Newbury, for example—there seems little justification for having it. Cheltenham's is in the back straight.

The Queen Mother Champion Chase and the Celebration Chase are the only two races in which Azertyuiop has finished behind Well Chief. Azertyuiop came off the better in the Tingle Creek Chase at Sandown in December and in the totepool Game Spirit Chase at Newbury in February. He was warmed up—for an eagerly-anticipated Tingle Creek clash with Moscow Flyer—in the William Hill Haldon Gold Cup, a limited handicap, at Exeter in November. A first fence casualty in the race the previous year, Azertyuiop put up a tip-top performance when easily conceding weight all round, winning by five lengths from Seebald, who was receiving 18 lb. Azertyuiop's performance, running off a BHB mark of 174, was worth a Timeform rating of 177 on the bare result. He had earned his Timeform rating of 182 in *Chasers & Hurdlers 2003/04* with a cracking effort when beaten a neck by Isio, to whom he was conceding 19 lb, in the Victor Chandler Chase at Ascot, showing form that was 10 lb in advance of that of the Queen Mother Champion Chase which Azertyuiop won in tremendous fashion, jumping well and drawing clear to win by nine lengths after Moscow Flyer (who had won the race the previous year and then beaten Azertyuiop in the Tingle Creek) parted company with his rider four out.

The betting public somewhat surprisingly sided with Azertyuiop in the latest renewal of the Tingle Creek, sending him off at odds on against Moscow Flyer in what was seen as a virtual match, the previous year's Arkle winner Well Chief looking to have plenty to find on the two best chasers in training. In a race that lived right up to its billing—if anything surpassing it—Azertyuiop went down by a length and a half, beaten fairly and squarely by Moscow Flyer, with Well Chief a short head away third and a gap of twenty-five lengths back to the high-class Cenkos, a previous winner of the race. Azertyuiop's owner John Hales's suggestion afterwards that the horse might have done better had his rider pressed on earlier in the race received plenty of comment afterwards, a matter touched on in the essay on Harchibald. The Tingle Creek represented outstanding form, Well Chief franking it in no uncertain terms when winning the Victor Chandler under top weight in late-January (transferred to Cheltenham because of redevelopment at Ascot). There had been a possibility for a time that Azertyuiop and Well Chief would meet in the Castleford Chase at Wetherby over Christmas but Azertyuiop became a surprise late runner in the King George after weather doubts arose (Well Chief fell when odds on for the rescheduled Castleford in early-January). Azertyuiop's form in finishing third in a vintage King George VI Chase, beaten two and a half lengths

totepool Game Spirit Chase, Newbury—
Azertyuiop confirms Tingle Creek placings despite meeting Well Chief (white face) on terms 4 lb worse

and a length and a quarter by Kicking King and Kingscliff, would have been good enough to have won six of the eight previous runnings. Even so, the longer trip almost certainly told in the end on Azertyuiop, who was outstayed for second after being the only runner able to go with Kicking King when he went on at the twelfth and soon had most of his rivals stone cold.

Azertyuiop was tackling three miles for the first time in the King George VI Chase as, incidentally, among previous winners, was Desert Orchid. Edredon Bleu, another regarded until Kempton as an unlikely stayer, was running in the race for the second time when winning in 2003. Other similar types, Barnbrook Again, Remittance Man and Deep Sensation, didn't suffer any lasting ill-effects from tackling the King George, all going on to win the same season's Queen Mother Champion Chase, nor did Royal Relief who fell at the fourteenth in the 1971 King George before winning that season's Champion Chase. Travado (a faller at Kempton) went on to finish second at Cheltenham and dual King George winner One Man won the Queen Mother Champion Chase after being beaten into fifth when attempting a King George hat-trick. Azertyuiop still seemed very much on course to put up a stout defence of his title at Cheltenham where he was unbeaten in three starts, having also won the November Chase and the Arkle there as a novice. Azertyuiop completed his preparation in exemplary style in the Game Spirit Chase, successfully conceding 4 lb to Well Chief, ridden out from the last to hold on by two and a half lengths, with twenty-three lengths further back to third-placed Armaturk. Well Chief was weighted to turn the tables on Azertyuiop at Newbury on their Tingle Creek form, but Azertyuiop's superior jumping always looked like winning the day after he moved up to dispute the lead with Castleford Chase winner Mister McGoldrick at the eighth.

The scene seemed set for a battle royal with Moscow Flyer at Cheltenham, Azertyuiop's trainer saying that the winner would be 'stronger and tighter' for the Champion Chase (he was reportedly six kilos heavier at Newbury than his best racing weight). It now seems unlikely, however, that racegoers will have a further opportunity to see another duel between Azertyuiop and Moscow Flyer who is rising twelve. The score between them stands at 3-1 in Moscow Flyer's favour, Moscow Flyer crucially winning their two meetings in the Tingle Creek, which has more than proved its worth as a mid-season championship since its elevation from Grade 2 limited handicap status in the 1994/5 season. The score between Azertyuiop and Well Chief, incidentally, is 2-2.

Azertyuiop (FR) (b.g. 1997)	Baby Turk (b 1982)	Northern Baby (b 1976)	Northern Dancer
			Two Rings
		Vieille Villa (b 1974)	Kashmir II
			Vielle Demeure
	Temara (FR) (b 1985)	Rex Magna (br 1974)	Right Royal V
			Chambre d'Amour
		Charabia (b 1976)	Bazin
			Kachabia

There is speculation that, if and when Azertyuiop returns to action, he may be campaigned more regularly over longer distances. His trainer described him in the latest season as 'a staying two-miler who just keeps galloping and needs to be ridden aggressively to be at his best.' There is stamina on both sides of Azertyuiop's pedigree—his sire won the Grand Prix de Deauville over thirteen and a half furlongs and his dam is by a Prix Royal-Oak winner—and, of course, he showed top-class form when third in the King George. Azertyuiop's half-brother Bipbap (by Dom Pasquini), the best French four-year-old chaser of 1998, stayed well, his record including a good third in the Prix La Haye Jousselin over nearly three and a half miles. Azertyuiop's owner, incidentally, was also represented in the latest season by another member of the family, bumper winner Cracboumwiz, by Azertyuiop's sire out of Azertyuiop's winning half-sister Ellapampa (successful over hurdles and fences at up to nineteen furlongs in France). The tall, good-topped Azertyuiop usually takes the eye in the paddock, though he spoiled his appearance by sweating before his last two starts. He is a consistent performer and a fine jumper who acts on soft and good to firm going (not discredited on his only outing on heavy). *P. F. Nicholls*

AZZEMOUR (FR) 6 ch.g. Morespeed – Tarde (FR) (Kashtan (FR)) [2004/5 F85p: F18g 22d^{4} 19d^{6} 22s^{4} 23d^{2} 21d 22m^{2} Apr 23] fourth in bumper on debut: modest novice hurdler: stays 23f: acts on soft and good to firm going: tongue tied final start: takes good hold, and has finished weakly. *P. F. Nicholls* **h99 F–**

B

BAAWRAH 4 ch.g. Cadeaux Genereux – Kronengold (USA) (Golden Act (USA)) [2004/5 16d 16s 16s^{5} 16v^{3} Nov 17] strong gelding: fair on Flat (stays 1¼m), sold out of M. Channon's stable 27,000 gns Newmarket July Sales: no form over hurdles: wore cheekpieces final start. *M. Todhunter* **h–**

BABA MIA 5 b.m. Gothenberg (IRE) – Kagram Queen (Prince Ragusa) [2004/5 17d^{pu} Aug 30] little form on Flat at 3 yrs: gave deal of trouble and very slowly away on hurdling debut. *N. Wilson* **h–**

BABS WHEAL 9 b.m. Petoski – Releta (Relkino) [2004/5 20m Jun 5] lengthy mare: no form outside points (won maiden in 2004). *D. J. Wintle* **h–**

BABY GEE 11 ch.m. King Among Kings – Market Blues (Porto Bello) [2004/5 h92: 18d^{6} 16g^{3} 16s^{6} 16g^{6} Apr 15] small mare: modest handicap hurdler: stays 21f: unraced on firm going, acts on any other: game. *D. W. Whillans* **h89**

BABY RUN (FR) 5 b.g. Baby Turk – Run For Laborie (FR) (Lesotho (USA)) [2004/5 F105: 17g^{2} 16d^{2} 16v* 16v^{2} Jan 22] quite good-topped gelding: bumper winner: fairly useful novice hurdler: landed odds at Haydock in December: better form when runner-up on other starts, to Escompteur at Bangor and Marcel and Roman Ark in Grade 2 events at Cheltenham and Haydock respectively: likely to prove best around 2m for time being: raced on good going or softer (acts on heavy): free-going sort. *N. A. Twiston-Davies* **h128**

BABY SISTER 6 ch.m. King Among Kings – Market Blues (Porto Bello) [2004/5 F87: F16d F16g^{6} 20s^{6} 17d 20s Apr 20] smallish, leggy mare: runner-up once from 4 starts in bumpers: poor form over hurdles: likely to prove best around 2m for time being. *D. W. Whillans* **h82 F79**

BACARDI BOY (IRE) 9 b.g. Lord Americo – Little Welly (Little Buskins) [2004/5 c96, h–: c24d^{3} c24m^{6} c23m^{5} c23d^{5} Apr 20] sturdy gelding: winning hurdler: maiden chaser, poor form in 2004/5: left T. George after first outing: stays 3¼m: acts on heavy going: weak finisher: sold 3,800 gns Doncaster May Sales. *J. M. Bradley* **c82 h–**

BACCARAT (IRE) 11 b.g. Bob Back (USA) – Sarahlee (Sayyaf) [2004/5 c–x, h–: c24g^{4} Mar 9] strong, robust gelding: of little account nowadays: has had tongue tied. *Lady Susan Brooke* **c– x h–**

BACK AMONG FRIENDS 6 b.g. Bob Back (USA) – Betty's Girl (Menelek) [2004/5 F16v* F16v^{5} F16s^{4} Mar 23] 17,000 4-y-o: medium-sized gelding: fourth foal: half-brother to winning pointer by Broken Hearted: dam winning staying chaser: best effort in bumpers (fairly useful form) when winning at Uttoxeter on debut in December: failed to settle both subsequent starts. *J. A. B. Old* **F100**

BACKBEAT (IRE) 8 ch.g. Bob Back (USA) – Pinata (Deep Run) [2004/5 c–, h–: c17s^{2} c19d* c19d* c24g^{F} c24g^{pu} Mar 16] sturdy gelding: winning hurdler: useful novice chaser: won at Exeter in November (handicap) and December, beating Liverpool Echo by 5 lengths in latter: let down by jumping in Grade 1 novices last 2 starts, sold out of D. Elsworth's stable £50,000 Ascot February Sales in between: should stay 3m: raced on good ground or softer: blinkered (jumped badly right) on chasing debut: tends to sweat. *J. Howard Johnson* **c134 h–**

BACK DE BAY (IRE) 5 b.g. Bob Back (USA) – Baybush (Boreen (FR)) [2004/5 20s^{pu} Nov 14] €22,000 4-y-o: brother to winning 2½m hurdler Our Dream, and half-brother to several other winners, including smart chaser Sparky Gayle (by Strong Gale), stayed 25f: dam, winning 2m hurdler, half-sister to high-class chaser up to 3m Golden Freeze: no show in novice hurdle on debut. *J. R. Cornwall* **h–**

BACK IN FRONT (IRE) 8 br.g. Bob Back (USA) – Storm Front (IRE) (Strong Gale) [2004/5 h152: 16d^{2} 17d* 16g Mar 15] **h161**

If asked to choose whether the 2003 Supreme Novices' winner Back In Front or the winner of the Royal & SunAlliance at that year's Festival, Hardy Eustace, was the more likely to go on to Champion Hurdle success, most of the votes at that stage of their careers would probably have gone to Back In Front. Back In Front's ten-length defeat of Kicking King showed all the qualities of a potential Champion Hurdle horse. Back In Front's two subsequent outings at the Punchestown Festival did nothing to diminish his prospects of developing into a leading challenger to title-holder Rooster Booster the following season. But Back In Front never made it to the 2004 Champion Hurdle. After an unconvincing win in the Morgiana Hurdle at Punchestown and a rather lazy performance in fifth in the December Festival Hurdle at Leopardstown, a succession of setbacks prevented Back In Front from being seen out again that season. A fibrillating heart and lameness in his near-fore disrupted his preparation for the Champion and then a bout of flu ruled him out of a return at Punchestown.

Back In Front therefore had something to prove on his return in the latest season, particularly as he re-entered the fray at a time when Irish candidates for the Champion Hurdle were queuing up for the race. He reappeared in a two-mile maiden on the Flat at Navan in October, a race which Hardy Eustace had won the year before incidentally. Back In Front's debut on the Flat was a winning one, with another good hurdler Macs Joy in third, and the pair met again in what was widely expected to be a virtual match in the Morgiana Hurdle at Punchestown in November. Barry Geraghty had been in the saddle for Back In Front's win twelve months earlier but chose to partner Macs Joy—who had defeated Brave Inca at Down Royal in the meantime—on this occasion, that decision seemingly the factor in Macs Joy's shading Back In Front for favouritism. Back In Front's intended rider David Casey broke a leg in a fall two days before, Davy Russell taking over the ride. As the betting suggested, there was little between Back In Front and Macs Joy, Back In Front emerging the better by a head (giving 8 lb), but both were upstaged by Harchibald who ran out an impressive winner, produced at the final flight. Conceding 5 lb to the winner as well, Back In Front put up a better effort in defeat than when winning the race the year before and, when Harchibald followed up with a win over Inglis Drever in the 'Fighting Fifth' at Newcastle a fortnight later, Back In Front's effort looked all the more creditable.

Back In Front was also sent to Britain for his next start, in the totesport Bula Hurdle at Cheltenham. He already had a good record at the track, having won a bumper there and finished third behind Pizarro and Rhinestone Cowboy in the Champion Bumper in the season before his Supreme Novices' win. Back In Front was sent off the 5/2 favourite for the Bula, with Inglis Drever and the first two from the 2003 Champion Hurdle, Rooster Booster and Westender, the others close up in the betting. With Rooster Booster setting a strong pace, the race was set up ideally

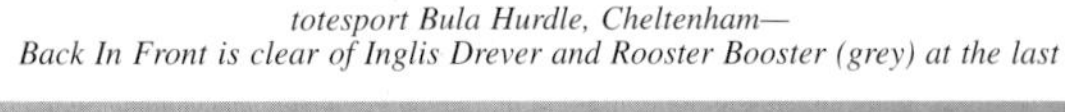

totesport Bula Hurdle, Cheltenham—
Back In Front is clear of Inglis Drever and Rooster Booster (grey) at the last

for Back In Front who took his time to cut back Rooster Booster's clear lead down the hill before eventually taking over approaching the last for a four-length win over Inglis Drever, with an uncooperative Westender still managing to pass Rooster Booster for third. High-class effort though it was from Back In Front, the result was widely interpreted as a compliment to Harchibald, rather than a strong endorsement of his own claims.

It was three months before Back In Front was seen out again, returned to Cheltenham for the Champion Hurdle, though there was nothing untoward about his absence this time. His trainer was reluctant to take him to Leopardstown again —likening the inside hurdles track used for the big races there to Chester—and didn't want to run him on heavy ground at Gowran, the only other alternative in Ireland. Although other Irish horses advanced their Champion Hurdle claims while Back In Front sat out the big pre-Cheltenham hurdles, Back In Front shared favouritism with Hardy Eustace come the big race, Ruby Walsh picking up the ride this time at the expense of Davy Russell. With conditions less testing than they had been for the Bula (run on the stiffer New Course) and the pace only picking up from after the third last, Back In Front was outpaced from that point and finished only ninth in the end, running some way below his best.

As earlier Annuals have pointed out, the workmanlike Back In Front's pedigree is nothing out of the ordinary, though, as a first foal, his own exploits have naturally aroused plenty of interest in his younger siblings in the sale-ring. Indeed, a brother set a record for a store foal in Ireland when knocked down for €110,000 at Tattersalls (Ireland) November National Hunt Sale in 2003. A year later at the same venue, Back In Front's unraced half-sister Storm In Front (by Fourstars Allstar, and in foal to Back In Front's sire Bob Back) fetched €125,000 on the same day that Back In Front finished second in the Morgiana. Their dam Storm Front's only other runner so far is the five-year-old mare Bobbies Storm (also by Bob Back), who showed fair form at best in three bumpers in Ireland in the latest season. Also coming through are a four-year-old by Accordion and a three-year-old by Darnay.

Back In Front (IRE) (br.g. 1997)	Bob Back (USA) (br 1981)	Roberto (b 1969)	Hail To Reason
			Bramalea
		Toter Back (ch 1967)	Carry Back
			Romantic Miss
	Storm Front (IRE) (br 1988)	Strong Gale (br 1975)	Lord Gayle
			Sterntau
		Tuneful (b 1971)	Reliance II
			Song of The Coral

Storm Front was a useful hurdler and fairly useful chaser in Ireland at around two and a half miles. Back In Front has been tried only once at that trip to date, winning an ordinary novice at Limerick impressively on his start prior to the Supreme Novices', and it could be a move worth repeating. On the other hand, he is not that far behind the best over two miles and just needs things to go his way, as they did in the Bula, to win another good race. Back In Front has raced mainly on good ground or softer, but has not encountered heavy ground since finishing second to Hardy Eustace on his hurdles debut; he has also won a bumper on good to firm. *E. J. O'Grady, Ireland*

BACK NINE (IRE) 8 b.g. Bob Back (USA) – Sylvia Fox (Deep Run) [2004/5 20d* 22d* 24g^{pu} Apr 14] strong ex-Irish gelding: half-brother to fair 2m hurdler Buffalo Bill and fairly useful 2m and 2½m hurdle winner Masteroffoxhounds (both by Be My Native): dam, 2m winner on Flat/over hurdles, half-sister to fairly useful 2m chaser Belstone Fox: won bumper at Navan in 2002/3: left A. Moore and off 15 months, improved form over hurdles when winning handicaps at Sandown in February (novice) and March: should stay 3m: acts on heavy going: type to do well over fences in 2005/6. *R. H. Alner* **h116**

BACKSCRATCHER 11 b.g. Backchat (USA) – Tiernee Quintana (Artaius (USA)) [2004/5 c76§, h70§: c25m^{pu} 20s^{pu} c23d 26s 24v^{pu} c20m^{2} Apr 10] rather leggy gelding: poor hurdler/chaser: stays 3m: acts on soft and good to firm going: usually blinkered nowadays: not one to rely on. *John R. Upson* **c72 §** **h– §**

BACK TO BEN ALDER (IRE) 8 b. or br.g. Bob Back (USA) – Winter Fox (Martinmas) [2004/5 h113: 16g 16s^{5} 16d^{6} 24d Apr 8] good sort: chaser in appearance: **h117**

fairly useful hurdler: should stay beyond 2m: room for improvement in jumping. *N. J. Henderson*

BACK TO FAVOUR (IRE) 6 b.m. Bob Back (USA) – Fortune And Favour (IRE) (Homo Sapien) [2004/5 F17g² F17g³ May 23] second foal: dam unraced half-sister to top-class hurdler up to 2½m Fortune And Fame: better effort in bumpers when 2½ lengths second to Red Georgie at Hereford on debut. *C. Tinkler* **F97**

BADEN VUGIE (IRE) 8 bl.g. Hamas (IRE) – Bag Lady (Be My Guest (USA)) [2004/5 c–, h–: c16g⁶ c20m³ c19mᶠ c17mᵖᵘ c26dᵖᵘ c16m Mar 21] sturdy, lengthy gelding: little sign of ability. *S. T. Lewis* **c– h–**

BADGERS GLORY 9 b. or gr.g. Neltino – Shedid (St Columbus) [2004/5 c–, h–: c20m³ c23mᵘʳ c18m⁵ Aug 19] third in weakly-contested novice chase at Fontwell early in season: won points in March and April: tried blinkered. *G. P. Enright* **c64 h–**

BADSEY BOY 7 b.g. Another Hoarwithy – Nicky's Choice (Baron Blakeney) [2004/5 22gᵖᵘ Aug 15] workmanlike gelding: first foal: dam well beaten in bumpers: showed nothing in novice hurdle on debut. *A. W. Carroll* **h–**

BAFFLE 4 b.f. Selkirk (USA) – Elude (Slip Anchor) [2004/5 16d Feb 11] leggy filly: fair on Flat (likely to stay at least 1¼m), sold out of J. Dunlop's stable 8,000 gns Newmarket Autumn Sales: tailed off in juvenile hurdle. *M. J. Ryan* **h–**

BAFFLING SECRET (FR) 5 gr.g. Kizitca (FR) – Kadroulienne (FR) (Kadrou (FR)) [2004/5 F16d⁶ F17d³ F16m F16v² Jan 10] second foal: dam lightly-raced maiden on Flat: best effort in bumpers when runner-up at Newcastle. *L. Lungo* **F91**

BAGAN (FR) 6 b.h. Rainbow Quest (USA) – Maid of Erin (USA) (Irish River (FR)) [2004/5 17g⁴ 21d* 21d* 19g* 21g 20g² Apr 15] strong, rangy horse: half-brother to fairly useful hurdler Mizyan (by Melyno), stayed 3m: fairly useful on Flat (stays 1½m), sold out of H. Cecil's stable 26,000 gns Newmarket Autumn Sales: fairly useful novice hurdler: won at Ludlow (maiden) and Kempton in January and Doncaster (again idled) in March: no match for Mephisto in 3-runner event at Ayr in April: respectable fifth to Asian Maze in Grade 1 at Punchestown later in month: stays 21f: raced on good/good to soft going. *C. J. Mann* **h129**

BAHAMIAN FRONTIER 5 b.m. Bahamian Bounty – My Discovery (IRE) (Imperial Frontier (USA)) [2004/5 F17s Oct 19] long-backed mare: second foal: half-sister to 7f winner Geespot (by Pursuit of Love): dam unraced: well beaten in bumper. *J. D. Frost* **F–**

BAIE DES SINGES 11 b.g. Royal Vulcan – Mikey's Monkey (Monksfield) [2004/5 c–x, h–: c16g⁴ c19d⁴ c20s² c20dᶠ c17s² c20g³ c16s³ Mar 23] workmanlike gelding: poor maiden chaser: effective at 2m to 3m: acts on soft going: tried blinkered: sketchy jumper. *M. J. M. Evans* **c74 x h–**

BAIKALINE (FR) 6 b.m. Cadoudal (FR) – Advantage (FR) (Antheus (USA)) [2004/5 c–, h–: 16s³ 21s² c20s⁴ c20g* c20d⁴ Apr 18] leggy mare: modest maiden hurdler: similar form over fences: won maiden at Plumpton in March: likely to stay beyond 21f: acts on heavy going. *Ian Williams* **c89 h97**

BAILEY CONTRACT 7 b.m. Contract Law (USA) – Megabucks (Buckskin (FR)) [2004/5 h–, F–: 16mᵘʳ Apr 28] jumped badly both starts over hurdles. *A. C. Whillans* **h– x**

BAILEY MILL 7 b.m. Overbury (IRE) – Strong Tempo (IRE) (Strong Gale) [2004/5 F16d F16f 20dᵖᵘ Jun 30] fourth foal: dam, lightly-raced maiden, from family of Night Nurse: no sign of ability in bumpers or maiden hurdle. *A. C. Whillans* **h– F–**

BAILEYS PRIZE (USA) 8 ch.g. Mister Baileys – Mar Mar (USA) (Forever Casting (USA)) [2004/5 c–, h82§: 16d⁶ 22s May 11] medium-sized gelding: tailed off in maiden chase: poor maiden hurdler: stays 19f: acts on soft going: tried in headgear: ungenuine. *B. J. Llewellyn* **c– h83 §**

BAILY BREEZE (IRE) 6 b.g. Zaffaran (USA) – Mixed Blends (The Parson) [2004/5 20d 16d 24s² 20s* Nov 21] €85,000 3-y-o: sixth living foal (all by Zaffaran): brother to fairly useful chaser/fair hurdler Baily Mist, stays 3m: dam, useful hurdler/chaser who stayed 2½m, half-sister to dual Whitbread Gold Cup winner Topsham Bay: fairly useful novice hurdler: won maiden at Cork in November: good second to Asian Maze in listed event there earlier in month: will stay beyond 3m. *M. F. Morris, Ireland* **h115**

BAILY MIST (IRE) 8 b.m. Zaffaran (USA) – Mixed Blends (The Parson) [2004/5 c111, h108: c22dᶠ c20s⁶ c24s* c24sᶠ c24v c22v c20v³ Apr 2] medium-sized mare: fair hurdler: fairly useful chaser: won minor event at Thurles in December: stays 3m: acts on heavy going: tried in cheekpieces. *M. F. Morris, Ireland* **c116 h–**

BAJAN GIRL (FR) 5 b.m. Emperor Jones (USA) – Lovely Noor (USA) (Fappiano (USA)) [2004/5 F83: 22g^{pu} 17g^{ur} 22m^{5} 19m^{3} 17g^{5} 17g* 17g^{4} 16g 16d^{6} 18s^{4} Dec 21] leggy, unfurnished mare: poor hurdler, claimed from M. Pipe £6,000 third start: won novice handicap at Hereford in September: best form around 2m: acts on good to soft ground, below form on soft final outing: tried visored. *D. Brace* **h81**

BAKER OF OZ 4 b.g. Pursuit of Love – Moorish Idol (Aragon) [2004/5 16s 16d 16s 17m^{5} 17g Apr 3] angular, plain gelding: fair on Flat (stays 1m), successful in June, sold out of R. Hannon's stable 5,500 gns Newmarket Autumn Sales: poor maiden hurdler. *D. Burchell* **h65**

BAK ON BOARD 9 b.g. Sula Bula – Kirstins Pride (Silly Prices) [2004/5 c–, h–: c26g^{pu} c26v^{3} Apr 22] workmanlike gelding: maiden hurdler/chaser: winning pointer, including in 2005: stays 3¼m: acts on any going: tried blinkered. *A. J. Tizzard* **c83 h–**

BAK TO BILL 10 b.g. Nicholas Bill – Kirstins Pride (Silly Prices) [2004/5 c106, h114: c21s^{4} c23s^{2} c24d^{ur} c24s* c26d^{3} c23s^{4} c24s* c24d^{4} c24d^{5} c24d^{4} Mar 24] lengthy gelding: fair chaser: won novices at Uttoxeter in November and Ludlow (handicap) in January: stays 3¼m: acts on any going: tried in cheekpieces: usually ridden by Miss L. Gardner. *Mrs S. Gardner* **c109 h–**

BALALAIKA TUNE (IRE) 6 b.m. Lure (USA) – Bohemienne (USA) (Polish Navy (USA)) [2004/5 16m^{pu} 17d^{pu} 16v 21d^{pu} Nov 9] poor maiden on Flat (stays 2m): no show over hurdles: sold 700 gns Doncaster November Sales. *W. Storey* **h–**

BALAPOUR (IRE) 7 b.g. Kahyasi – Balaniya (USA) (Diesis) [2004/5 h131: 20g 20d^{2} 20g* 16g c17d^{F} 20s c17s^{6} c20d^{3} c17d^{6} c16s^{ur} c20s* c24s^{pu} 17g Mar 18] smallish gelding: fairly useful hurdler: won minor event at Ballinrobe in July: better efforts previous and final starts: fair form over fences, winning maiden at Down Royal in February: stays 2½m: acts on firm and soft going: tongue tied: not one to rely on. *P. O. Brady, Ireland* **c107 § h128 §**

BALIGRUNDLE 5 b.g. Moshaajir (USA) – Masirah (Dunphy) [2004/5 F16m^{6} Jun 12] half-brother to 3 winners, including temperamental winning hurdler Ibn Masirah (by Crowning Honors): dam modest maiden: sixth of 17 in bumper at Hexham on debut. *W. S. Coltherd* **F86**

BALINAHINCH CASTLE (IRE) 8 b.g. Good Thyne (USA) – Emerald Flair (Flair Path) [2004/5 h–: c25d^{3} c24g^{4} Mar 4] useful-looking gelding: won first 2 starts over hurdles for J. O'Neill in 2002/3: little form since, including in maiden chases. *Mrs L. B. Normile* **c90 ? h–**

BALINDOOLEY (FR) 5 b.g. Sheyrann – Rose Des Ifs (FR) (Herodias (FR)) [2004/5 F16m F16m^{4} Nov 26] second foal: dam once-raced: better effort in bumpers when fourth in maiden at Musselburgh. *C. F. Swan, Ireland* **F80**

BALINOVA (IRE) 8 b.g. Lord Americo – Shuil Comeragh (Laurence O) [2004/5 c25s^{2} c24s* Feb 24] half-brother to winning 2½m hurdler Shuil Saor (by Fairbairn): dam, winning hurdler/chaser up to 3m in Ireland, half-sister to useful staying chaser Baronet and to dam of very smart hurdler Liss A Paoraigh: winning pointer: better effort in hunters when winning at Huntingdon by 2½ lengths from Lancastrian Jet: will stay beyond 25f: should do better. *C. J. Bennett* **c109 p**

BALISTEROS (FR) 16 b.g. Bad Conduct (USA) – Oldburry (FR) (Fin Bon) [2004/5 c100, h–: c24d^{su} c25g^{pu} May 20] workmanlike gelding: prolific winning pointer/hunter chaser: stayed 3½m: acted on heavy and good to firm going: ran badly only start in visor: not a straightforward ride: reportedly retired. *Mrs B. K. Thomson* **c– h–**

BALKIRK 8 ch.g. Selkirk (USA) – Balenare (Pharly (FR)) [2004/5 h–: c19m c20d^{ur} Dec 7] angular gelding: maiden hurdler: no form over fences: tried blinkered/in cheekpieces: has had tongue tied. *Mrs H. M. Bridges* **c– h–**

BALLA D'AIRE (IRE) 10 b. or br.g. Balla Cove – Silius (Junius (USA)) [2004/5 c73, h–: c20g^{3} c24m^{pu} c21s^{2} Oct 22] leggy gelding: maiden hurdler: poor chaser: stays easy 23f: acts on firm and soft going: blinkered once. *K. F. Clutterbuck* **c68 h–**

BALLADEER (IRE) 7 b.g. King's Theatre (IRE) – Carousel Music (On Your Mark) [2004/5 h105: 22d c19m^{3} c20d^{F} Sep 10] close-coupled gelding: fair hurdler: similar form both starts in novice chases: should stay 3m: acts on firm and soft going: usually races prominently. *Miss H. C. Knight* **c105 h–**

BALLARDS BOY (FR) 6 b.g. Sleeping Car (FR) – Anita (FR) (Olmeto) [2004/5 h–: 19g 16s 16v 17v^{4} 16g Mar 5] lengthy, unfurnished gelding: no sign of ability: tried tongue tied. *N. J. Pomfret* **h–**

BALLARE (IRE) 6 b.g. Barathea (IRE) – Raindancing (IRE) (Tirol) [2004/5 16g Oct 3] angular gelding: modest on Flat (stays 1¼m): well held on hurdling debut. *Bob Jones* **h–**

BALL GAMES 7 b.g. Mind Games – Deb's Ball (Glenstal (USA)) [2004/5 h75§: 17d^{4} 16m* 17g^{ur} 16d^{pu} Apr 11] close-coupled gelding: poor hurdler: won selling handicap at Catterick in December: raced around 2m: acts on good to firm going: tried visored/in cheekpieces: has looked moody. *James Moffatt* **h77**

BALLINCLAY KING (IRE) 11 b.g. Asir – Clonroche Artic (Pauper) [2004/5 c135§, h–: c22v^{3} c25s* c25s^{4} c22v^{R} c20v^{4} Jan 22] tall, rather leggy gelding: fairly useful handicap chaser nowadays: won 3-runner event at Kelso in November: stays 25f: acts on heavy going: tried in cheekpieces: has broken blood vessels: moody. *Ferdy Murphy* **c117 § h– §**

BALLINRUANE (IRE) 6 br.g. Norwich – Katie Dick (IRE) (Roselier (FR)) [2004/5 F16s 20s 19d 16v Feb 15] tall gelding: fourth foal: dam unraced: tailed off in bumper and novice hurdles. *B. S. Rothwell* **h– F–**

BALL IN THE NET 12 b.g. Arctic Lord – Courtlands Girl (Crimson Beau) [2004/5 c24g c23m^{pu} Jun 16] successful 3 times in points in February and March: no form otherwise. *B. G. Powell* **c– h–**

BALLINTRA BOY (IRE) 6 b.g. Oscar (IRE) – Super Leg (Super Slip) [2004/5 F16s* Mar 29] lengthy, rather unfurnished gelding: sixth known foal: half-brother to 2 winners, including fairly useful hurdler/chaser Roses of Picardy (by Roselier), probably stayed 3m: dam, placed over hurdles, half-sister to smart hurdler Random Leg and useful staying chaser Daltmore: won 22-runner maiden bumper at Fairyhouse on debut by 2 lengths from Limestream, travelling well in mid-field and weaving through to lead over 1f out: well held in Grade 1 bumper at Punchestown late following month. *N. Meade, Ireland* **F105**

BALLINURE BOY (IRE) 12 b.g. Meneval (USA) – Sweet Cahore (General Ironside) [2004/5 c84: c25m^{pu} May 19] winning pointer/hunter chaser, amiss at Folkestone in May. *Mrs S. J. Hickman* **c–**

BALLISTIC BOY 8 ch.g. First Trump – Be Discreet (Junius (USA)) [2004/5 h–: 22m 20m Jun 5] good-topped gelding: winning hurdler: lightly raced and no form since 2001. *R. W. Thomson* **h–**

BALLISTIGO (IRE) 6 br.g. Executive Perk – Herballistic (Rolfe (USA)) [2004/5 F16d F16d^{5} F16s 21m^{6} Apr 13] 45,000 5-y-o: lengthy gelding: second foal: half-brother to winning 2¾m hurdler Miniballist (by Tragic Role): dam, behind in 2 bumpers, half-sister to top-class staying chaser Go Ballistic: best effort in bumpers when fifth to Hobbs Hill at Kempton: still green when sixth to Prins Willem in novice hurdle at Cheltenham: likely to improve. *A. King* **h101 p F89**

BALLOCH 4 ch.f. Wootton Rivers (USA) – Balayer (Balidar) [2004/5 16s Nov 21] eighth foal: half-sister to winning pointer by Le Coq d'Or: dam poor plater: tailed off in juvenile hurdle on debut. *Mary Meek* **h–**

BALL O MALT (IRE) 9 b.g. Star Quest – Vera Dodd (IRE) (Riot Helmet) [2004/5 22v^{2} 16d c16g* c16v^{2} c16d^{3} 20v^{4} c21g^{F} Mar 17] big, lengthy gelding: fair novice hurdler: fairly useful form over fences: won novice at Catterick in December by 3½ lengths from Waterspray: effective at 2m to 3m: raced on good going or softer over jumps (acts on heavy). *R. A. Fahey* **c120 h112**

BALLYAAHBUTT (IRE) 6 b.g. Good Thyne (USA) – Lady Henbit (IRE) (Henbit (USA)) [2004/5 F–: 20m^{6} 20d 21g Apr 1] useful-looking gelding: little sign of ability. *B. G. Powell* **h–**

BALLYAGRAN (IRE) 5 b.g. Pierre – Promalady (IRE) (Homo Sapien) [2004/5 F16s* Apr 21] lengthy, useful-looking gelding: second foal: dam unraced: won 18-runner bumper at Gowran on debut: useful form when 2½ lengths second to Silent Oscar at Punchestown week later, staying on well. *N. Meade, Ireland* **F111**

BALLYALBANY (IRE) 7 b.g. Lord Americo – Raisin Turf (IRE) (Phardante (FR)) [2004/5 h–, F84: 23d^{5} 17g^{4} 16d^{3} 16g^{5} 17d 21d^{3} 22d Mar 11] sturdy gelding: fair maiden hurdler: stays 21f: raced on good going or softer. *Mrs Susan Nock* **h102**

BALLYAMBER (IRE) 10 b.g. Glacial Storm (USA) – El Scarsdale (Furry Glen) [2004/5 c133, h–: c18g* c22m c20v^{2} Aug 26] tall, good sort: useful chaser: not seen out after creditable second of 5 to Splendour in handicap at Tralee: effective at 2m to 3m: acts on heavy going. *W. P. Mullins, Ireland* **c136 h–**

BALLYBAWN HOUSE 4 b.f. Tamure (IRE) – Squeaky Cottage (True Song) [2004/5 F12g F12d F16v^{2} F16v^{3} F16d^{6} Mar 12] 9,000 3-y-o: eighth foal: half-sister to fairly useful hurdler/novice chaser Copsale Lad (by Karinga Bay), stays 21f, and winning 2m chaser Fantasmic (by Broadsword): dam once-raced half-sister to useful 2m to 2½m hurdler Charlie's Cottage: modest form in bumpers: will stay 2½m. *J. C. Fox* **F83**

BALLYBAY DEMENSE (IRE) 9 b. or br.g. Bob Back (USA) – Coach Road (Brave Invader (USA)) [2004/5 c24s^{pu} c26v^{pu} c24d^{pu} c26d^{ur} Nov 23] big gelding: maiden chaser: no form in 2004/5: in cheekpieces last 3 starts: sketchy jumper. *Mrs J. Candlish* **c– x**

BALLY BOLSHOI (IRE) 5 b.m. Bob Back (USA) – Moscow Money (IRE) (Moscow Society (USA)) [2004/5 19d 17v^{5} 22g Apr 12] second foal: dam unraced: no worthwhile form in novice hurdles. *Mrs S. D. Williams* **h–**

BALLYBOUGH JACK (IRE) 5 b.g. Shernazar – Lunar Approach (IRE) (Mandalus) [2004/5 F16d^{2} F17g^{2} Apr 12] third foal: half-brother to winning pointer by Over The River: dam, runner-up in Irish point, sister to smart 2m hurdler/useful chaser Adamant Approach: thrice-raced in maiden Irish points in 2004, winning in December: fairly useful form in bumpers at Wincanton and Exeter, behind Clyffe Hanger at latter. *B. G. Powell* **F98**

BALLYBOUGH RASHER (IRE) 10 b.g. Broken Hearted – Chat Her Up (Proverb) [2004/5 c148x, h116: c25d^{ur} 24d^{4} 24g^{2} c24g^{pu} c36d^{R} Apr 9] sturdy gelding: fairly useful hurdler: smart chaser in 2003/4: failed to complete all 3 starts over fences in 2004/5: effective at 2½m to 4m: acts on soft and good to firm going: often let down by jumping over fences. *J. Howard Johnson* **c– x h120**

BALLYBROPHY (IRE) 10 gr.g. Roselier (FR) – Bavardmore (Le Bavard (FR)) [2004/5 c124, h–: c26s c24s^{6} c24v c24d^{6} c24s^{pu} c26s^{6} c26g^{2} c26d^{pu} Apr 18] workmanlike gelding: fairly useful staying chaser in 2003/4, has deteriorated considerably: acts on heavy going: usually wears headgear: tried tongue tied. *G. Brown* **c78 h–**

BALLYCASSIDY (IRE) 9 br.g. Insan (USA) – Bitofabreeze (IRE) (Callernish) [2004/5 c140, h–: c27d^{2} c25s^{5} c24d^{pu} c26g c36d^{ur} c29g^{5} Apr 23] strong, lengthy gelding: smart chaser: good second to Stormez in valuable handicap at Cheltenham on reappearance: generally let down by jumping after: effective at 2½m to 27f: acts on firm and good to soft going, unsuited by softer: blinkered once: often leads. *P. Bowen* **c149 h–**

BALLYFIN (IRE) 7 b.g. Lord Americo – Scar Stream (Paddy's Stream) [2004/5 22v c24g^{F} c20d* Mar 17] IR £11,000 3-y-o: sixth foal: dam placed in bumpers: twice-raced over hurdles: unbeaten in 3 points in 2004: fair form in hunters, winning at Down Royal on completed start. *I. R. Ferguson, Ireland* **c98 h–**

BALLYGOE (IRE) 6 b.g. Flemensfirth (USA) – Handy Lady (Nearly A Hand) [2004/5 F16v^{3} Jan 15] fourth known living foal: dam once-raced, out of half-sister to top-class chaser up to 2½m Artifice: raced 4 times in points, winning both outings in October: second favourite, 1¼ lengths third of 11 to Be My Leader in bumper at Punchestown. *W. P. Mullins, Ireland* **F103**

BALLYHALE (IRE) 7 br.g. Mister Lord (USA) – Deep Inagh (Deep Run) [2004/5 F16d^{6} 20d^{5} Nov 29] useful-looking gelding: third foal: half-brother to fairly useful hurdler/fair chaser The Culdee (by Phardante), stays 25f, and fair 2m hurdle winner Giolla De (by Glacial Storm): dam, useful 2m hurdler, from family of top-class 2m to 3m chaser Lough Inagh: won maiden Irish point on debut in February 2004: sixth to Manners in listed bumper at Cheltenham: didn't see race out when fifth in novice at Newcastle on hurdling debut: should do better. *P. D. Niven* **h81 p F93**

BALLYHOO (IRE) 5 b.m. Supreme Leader – Ballyhouraprincess (IRE) (Mulhollande (USA)) [2004/5 F16g^{4} F18s^{2} F17s^{pu} Jan 20] €6,500 4-y-o: third foal: dam placed in bumper and over hurdles: shaped very much like a stayer first 2 starts in bumpers, distressed final one. *J. W. Mullins* **F82**

BALLYJOHNBOY LORD (IRE) 6 b.g. Arctic Lord – Mount Sackville (Whistling Deer) [2004/5 F16s^{3} F16v 19v 16v^{ur} 16s^{3} 18d^{5} 16s^{2} 19s^{2} Mar 27] ex-Irish gelding: first foal: dam unraced half-sister to one-time very smart staying chaser/smart hurdler Sackville: third on first of 2 starts in bumpers: fair maiden hurdler: left E. Sheehy after seventh start: probably better suited by 19f than shorter, and will stay further. *M. Scudamore* **h104 F92**

BALLYKETTRAIL (IRE) 9 b.g. Catrail (USA) – Ballykett Lady (USA) (Sir Ivor (USA)) [2004/5 h–: 22d^{pu} 19d^{5} May 17] well-made gelding: fairly useful hurdler at one time: better effort in 2004/5 on second start: stays 2½m: raced mainly on good going or softer: tried blinkered/in cheekpieces: has had tongue tied. *Jonjo O'Neill* **h106**

BALLYLESSON (IRE) 10 b.g. Erdelistan (FR) – Three Dieu (Three Dons) [2004/5 20m Sep 24] winning pointer: little other form. *N. B. King* **c– h–**

BALLYLUSKY (IRE) 8 b.g. Lord Americo – Blackbushe Place (IRE) (Buckskin (FR)) [2004/5 c107+, h130: c25d* c25d^F 24d^{pu} Apr 8] well-made gelding: useful handicap hurdler in 2003/4: fair chaser: successful at Aintree in 4-runner handicap in November: effective at 2½m to 25f: acts on good to firm and heavy going: usually front runner over hurdles (ridden more patiently over fences): poor jumper of fences: sold 30,000 gns Doncaster May Sales. *Jonjo O'Neill* **c109 x h–**

BALLYMENA 4 b.f. Saddlers' Hall (IRE) – Ace Gunner (Gunner B) [2004/5 F16v F14m^6 F16m Apr 10] first foal: dam modest form in bumpers: poor form in bumpers. *C. Roberts* **F74**

BALLYNATTIN BUCK (IRE) 9 b.g. Buckskin (FR) – Dikler Gale (IRE) (Strong Gale) [2004/5 c20f* c20f^2 c24f^4 c20d^2 c20g^6 c24d* c21v^F c24v c24s^5 Mar 26] rangy gelding: maiden hurdler: fairly useful chaser: won maiden at Limerick in May and listed handicap at Wexford (easily beat Ira Hayes 7 lengths) in November: well held subsequently: stays 3m: probably acts on any going: tongue tied. *A. L. T. Moore, Ireland* **c117 h–**

BALLYNURE (IRE) 7 b. or br.g. Roselier (FR) – Fresh Partner (IRE) (Yashgan) [2004/5 20d 24d^5 24v c25d^{pu} c23s^6 c25s^{pu} 22s^5 Apr 3] €45,000 4-y-o: third foal: dam unraced half-sister to fairly useful staying hurdler Will of The People: won maiden Irish point in 2003, well beaten in 2004: bought 4,000 gns Doncaster May (2004) Sales: no solid form over hurdles/fences or in chases. *Mrs L. B. Normile* **c– h89 ?**

BALLYROBERT (IRE) 8 b. or br.g. Bob's Return (IRE) – Line Abreast (High Line) [2004/5 c103, h–: c20d^2 c19s^4 Nov 18] good-bodied gelding: fair chaser: would have made successful reappearance in handicap at Huntingdon but for blundering last when 6 lengths clear: let down by jumping next time: stays 2½m: raced on good going or softer: prone to mistakes. *C. R. Egerton* **c112 x h–**

BALLY'S BAK 7 ch.m. Bob Back (USA) – Whatagale (Strong Gale) [2004/5 h85: 20m^2 22g^2 21d^4 20g^F 20d^2 19d^4 c20d^6 Dec 9] sturdy mare: modest maiden hurdler: would have won mares novice at Bangor in August but for falling 2 out: last of 6 finishers in mares novice on chasing debut: stays 3m: acts on good to firm and heavy going. *Mrs S. J. Smith* **c86 h97**

BALLYSICYOS (FR) 10 b.g. Nikos – Bally Duke (FR) (Iron Duke (FR)) [2004/5 c26g^{ur} Mar 18] tall, angular gelding: useful pointer nowadays, successful 3 times in February and March: will stay beyond 25f: acts on soft and firm going: blinkered once: usually let down by jumping in chases. *Mrs O. C. Jackson* **c– x h–**

BALLYSTONE (IRE) 12 ch.g. Roselier (FR) – Gusserane Princess (Paddy's Stream) [2004/5 c115, h104: c25g^5 May 14] well-made gelding: fair staying handicap hurdler/chaser: well beaten in point in 2005: acts on heavy and good to firm going: tried in visor/cheekpieces. *L. Lungo* **c107 h–**

BALLYVADDY (IRE) 9 gr.g. Roselier (FR) – Bodalmore Kit (Bargello) [2004/5 c94p, h125: c24m* c24d* c24d^4 c25d^3 c24g Mar 28] sturdy gelding: fairly useful handicap hurdler in 2003/4: similar form over fences, successful in handicaps at Fakenham in May and Chepstow (final start for G. Balding, stayed on strongly to beat Lord Noelie 1¼ lengths) in October: off 4 months, soon off bridle when below form final start: will be suited by further than 25f: acts on good to firm and heavy going: tried visored/in cheekpieces: usually held up. *J. A. Geake* **c119 h–**

BALLYWALTER (IRE) 9 ch.g. Commanche Run – Call Me Honey (Le Bavard (FR)) [2004/5 c–, h–: c25v^5 c19v c24d^4 Mar 12] lengthy gelding: winning pointer: maiden hurdler: trained by C. Egerton first start only: 100/1, apparently easily best effort in chases when fourth (possibly flattered in steadily-run event) in maiden at Chepstow: stays 25f: acts on good to firm and heavy going. *Dr P. Pritchard* **c97 ? h–**

BALMORAL QUEEN 5 br.m. Wizard King – Balmoral Princess (Thethingaboutitis (USA)) [2004/5 h–, F–: 21g^4 19s^{ur} Dec 18] stocky mare: no sign of ability. *D. McCain* **h–**

BALOO 9 b.g. Morpeth – Moorland Nell (Neltino) [2004/5 c86, h105: c21g^3 c21d^2 c26m^6 24g^5 Dec 9] small gelding: modest handicap hurdler/maiden chaser: stays 27f: probably acts on any going: has had tongue tied. *J. D. Frost* **c91 h99**

BAMBI DE L'ORME (FR) 6 gr.g. True Brave (USA) – Princesse Ira (FR) (Less Ice) [2004/5 c116, h122: c16s^{ur} c17g^{ro} c16d^2 c16d^{ur} c16s^F c16g^2 c16s^3 Apr 7] tall gelding: useful handicap chaser: good placed efforts on completed starts in 2004/5, running particularly well behind Fota Island in Grand Annual at Cheltenham and another valuable **c136 h–**

event at Aintree last 2: stays 19f: raced on good ground or softer: free-going sort, usually waited with. *Ian Williams*

BAMBY (IRE) 5 b.m. Glacial Storm (USA) – Ardfallon (IRE) (Supreme Leader) [2004/5 F16g^{6} F16d Feb 18] €25,000 4-y-o: unfurnished mare: fifth foal: dam, fourth in bumper, from family of useful chasers up to 3m Bells Life and Indian Tonic: better effort in bumpers on debut. *D. J. Wintle* **F79**

BAMFORD CASTLE (IRE) 10 b.g. Scenic – Allorette (Ballymore) [2004/5 16g^{3} 22g^{pu} May 26] smallish ex-Irish gelding: useful hurdler at one time: sold out of P. Mullins' stable 8,000 gns Newmarket Autumn (2001) Sales: third in seller on completed start in early-2004/5: should stay beyond 2m: acts on good to firm and heavy going: inconsistent. *R. Ford* **h78**

BANALUSO (IRE) 5 b.g. Luso – Trembling Lass (IRE) (Tremblant) [2004/5 F17d^{4} F16s 16g 19v 22g Apr 12] good-topped gelding: second foal: dam unraced: better effort in bumpers on debut: well held over hurdles: sold 18,000 gns Doncaster May Sales. *Miss H. C. Knight* **h–** **F91**

BANANA RIDGE 7 ch.m. Primitive Rising (USA) – Madison Girl (Last Fandango) [2004/5 F83: c21g* c20d^{4} c28g^{pu} c20g^{pu} c16s^{2} c16m^{4} 19g c24g^{ur} c24m^{F} Feb 6] well held only outing over hurdles: poor chaser: won hunter at Sedgefield in April 2004: stays 21f: acts on good to firm going: tried tongue tied. *P. Maddison* **c76** **h–**

BANASAN (IRE) 7 b.g. Marju (IRE) – Banaja (IRE) (Sadler's Wells (USA)) [2004/5 c125, h120: c18g^{3} 20g^{2} c22m^{6} 16g^{2} c24v* Sep 22] leggy gelding: fairly useful hurdler/ chaser: won Guinness Kerry National Handicap Chase at Listowel in September by 1½ lengths from Fatherofthebride: effective at 2m to 3m: acts on any going: tried blinkered/ in cheekpieces. *M. J. P. O'Brien, Ireland* **c128** **h120**

BANCHORY TWO (IRE) 5 b.g. Un Desperado (FR) – Theyllallwin (IRE) (Le Bavard (FR)) [2004/5 F17d^{5} F16d^{3} F17d^{4} 19g^{3} 22s^{6} 22g^{4} Apr 12] good-topped gelding: sixth foal: brother to 2½m hurdle winner Fiddlers Bar: dam unraced: fair form in bumpers: best effort in novice hurdles when fourth to Standin Obligation at Exeter, travelling strongly under patient ride and not unduly knocked about: type to do better in handicaps. *P. F. Nicholls* **h106 p** **F95**

BANDIT BROWN (IRE) 9 b.g. Supreme Leader – Parkroe Lady (IRE) (Deep Run) [2004/5 c93, h–: c20s^{ur} c25g^{6} c25s^{pu} c21s^{4} c20s^{ur} c20g^{pu} Mar 14] modest novice chaser: form in 2004/5 only on fourth start: stays 2¾m: acts on soft going. *P. Winkworth* **c90** **h–**

BAN DUBH 6 b.m. Syrtos – Hatherley (Deep Run) [2004/5 F–: F17d 24g^{pu} Jun 3] no form in bumpers or maiden hurdle: runner-up in point in 2005. *J. Rudge* **h–** **F–**

BANG AND BLAME (IRE) 9 b.g. Be My Native (USA) – Miss Lucille (Fine Blade (USA)) [2004/5 23d^{pu} 20m^{pu} 24m^{pu} 24g^{5} c21m c21m^{3} c25g^{5} c20g^{5} c25d^{2} Oct 9] workmanlike gelding: no form over hurdles: poor maiden chaser: stays 25f. *M. W. Easterby* **c76** **h–**

Guinness Kerry National Handicap Chase, Listowel—
Ruby Walsh needs to be at his strongest as Banasan (No.8) holds off Fatherofthebride (blinkers) and Barrow Drive (stars cap)

Sunbury Handicap Chase, Kempton—
Banker Count's Indian summer continues with a hat-trick win over the much younger Zeta's River

BANJO HILL 11 b.g. Arctic Lord – Just Hannah (Macmillion) [2004/5 c112, h–: c23m5 c28gpu c26gpu Apr 14] lengthy, good-bodied gelding: fair chaser at best: below form in 2004/5: stays 23f: acts on firm and good to soft going: tried visored: has had tongue tied. *Miss E. C. Lavelle* **c93 h–**

BANKER COUNT 13 b.g. Lord Bud – Gilzie Bank (New Brig) [2004/5 c128, h–: c20gur c20g5 c20g5 c20d2 c21d3 c20s* c19v* c20d* c24s3 c21g2 c24m5 Apr 2] big gelding: useful handicap chaser: revitalized in 2004/5, winning at Leicester in December, Towcester in January and Kempton (beat Zeta's River by 8 lengths) in February: again jumped well when running creditably in valuable events ninth and tenth starts, third to Farmer Jack at Kempton and second to Liberthine at Cheltenham: effective at 2½m to 25f: acts on good to firm and heavy going: usually ridden prominently nowadays. *Miss Venetia Williams* **c134 h–**

BANKERSDRAFT 10 ch.g. Mazaad – Overdraft (Bustino) [2004/5 c–, h–: c20spu Mar 11] compact gelding: winning pointer: little other form: has worn cheekpieces: tried tongue tied: sold 1,000 gns Doncaster May Sales. *Mrs Sylvia Robinson* **c– h–**

BANKIT 12 ch.g. Gildoran – Game Trust (National Trust) [2004/5 c22v3 May 10] fair pointer. *M. G. Hazell* **c–**

BANNINGHAM BLAZE 5 b.m. Averti (IRE) – Ma Pavlova (USA) (Irish River (FR)) [2004/5 h80: 17d May 9] compact mare: modest on Flat (stays easy 2m), successful 3 times in 2004, last 2 for A. Carroll: poor hurdler: barely stays 19f: acts on firm going: tried blinkered/visored. *C. R. Dore* **h–**

BANNISTER LANE 5 b.g. Overbury (IRE) – Miss Club Royal (Avocat) [2004/5 F16d Feb 24] seventh foal: brother to 2m hurdle winner Another Club Royal and half-brother to 2 winners, including 2½m and 3m chase winner Mister Club Royal (by Alflora): dam fair staying hurdler/chaser: well held in bumper on debut. *D. McCain* **F81**

BANNOW STRAND (IRE) 5 b.g. Luso – Bid For Fun (IRE) (Auction Ring (USA)) [2004/5 21dF 20s5 16v3 21m 16d6 Apr 22] big gelding: has plenty of scope: will make a **h91 p**

chaser: sixth foal: half-brother to winning 2m hurdler Hardycomestohardy (by Be My Native): dam unraced half-sister to dam of top-class staying hurdler Bannow Bay and very smart hurdler Mighty Moss: won 4-y-o maiden Irish point on debut in 2004: starting to tire when falling heavily 3 out in Grade 1 novice at Newbury won by Brewster on hurdling debut: modest form at best but not knocked about after: remains capable of better. *M. C. Pipe*

BARABASCHI 9 b.g. Elmaamul (USA) – Hills' Presidium (Presidium) [2004/5 17dpu May 29] no sign of ability. *R. N. Bevis* **h–**

BARACOUDA (FR) 10 b.g. Alesso (USA) – Peche Aubar (FR) (Zino) [2004/5 h171: 24g* 25s* 24g² Mar 17] **h159**

Having shown top-class form and proven almost invincible in four seasons of competition in Britain, Baracouda began the latest campaign with the top staying hurdles once again seemingly at his mercy—still looking the big fish in quite a small pond with Iris's Gift set to go novice chasing. Rising ten years of age, Baracouda was reported by his trainer never to have been so well at the beginning of a season. Iris's Gift had prevented Baracouda from completing a hat-trick of wins in the Stayers' Hurdle, and another potential stumbling-block was taken away when Rhinestone Cowboy, who had beaten Iris's Gift in the Champion Stayers at Punchestown in the spring, was ruled out for the rest of the season with a leg injury.

That left Crystal d'Ainay, thirteen lengths behind Baracouda in third in the Stayers' Hurdle, but a five-year-old with time on his side, looking Baracouda's main rival, at least among the staying hurdlers trained in Britain. The first of their three encounters in the latest season took place in the Ballymore Properties Long Distance Hurdle at Newbury at the end of November, with Baracouda 9/4-on to make a winning reappearance in the race for the second year running. Crystal d'Ainay started at 5/1, having had the benefit of an outing when second at Wetherby to Telemoss, who was also in the field. After the two rank outsiders had built up a clear lead and then come back to their field, Baracouda and Crystal d'Ainay duly came to the fore, Baracouda typically idling in front and having only three quarters of a length to spare at the line. For the first time since his hurdling debut, Baracouda was without Thierry Doumen in the saddle. Doumen had retired from riding in the summer to concentrate on his training career after a shoulder operation, leaving Tony McCoy, as retained rider to owner J. P. McManus, to take his place. Newbury may have been McCoy's first experience of riding Baracouda in a race, but he was

Ballymore Properties Long Distance Hurdle, Newbury—
Tony McCoy begins his association with Baracouda (hoops) on a winning note, though Crystal d'Ainay pushes them close

well acquainted with the horse from numerous rides against him on Martin Pipe-trained hurdlers over the years. One memorable encounter had come in the 2002 Ascot Hurdle when McCoy poached a huge lead on Mr Cool, one which Baracouda clawed back only at the death to win by a neck. Similar tactics by McCoy on Deano's Beeno in the Long Walk Hurdle at Ascot a month later had paid off, and Baracouda's defeat at 11/4-on remains his only reverse on British soil outside the Cheltenham Festival.

Baracouda had proved time and again that he was very hard to beat in a straight fight, and it was now McCoy's job to ensure that that continued, while other riders had the task of working out how best to bring about Baracouda's downfall. There was no better demonstration of tactical manoeuvring at work than when Baracouda and Crystal d'Ainay next met in the Long Walk Hurdle. Sponsored by Telectronics Systems, the Long Walk was one of the most high-profile races among those transferred to Windsor during Ascot's redevelopment. As well as Crystal d'Ainay, the third and fifth at Newbury, Kadara and It Takes Time, took Baracouda on again, while an interesting new rival was the Irish-trained winner of the Grande Course de Haies d'Auteuil in the summer, Rule Supreme. Baracouda started 13/8-on to land his fourth Long Walk, with Crystal d'Ainay and Rule Supreme sharing second favouritism at 11/2. Kadara stole a lead at the start but by halfway the pace had slackened and, going to the third last, the field of eight was still tightly grouped. Crystal d'Ainay's rider Robert Thornton had felt he had set up the Newbury race for Baracouda by giving him a lead into the closing stages and was determined that the roles would be reversed this time, especially as Crystal d'Ainay shares Baracouda's tendency to idle in front. Jumping the third last, Crystal d'Ainay took the lead from Kadara, with Baracouda stalking him on the bridle. Approaching two out, with the field still bunched, Thornton glanced to his left to see Baracouda and McCoy moving upsides. Thornton promptly checked his mount, but McCoy immediately did the same, Baracouda tossing his head around as McCoy restrained him. Sh Boom, in contrast under the whip, briefly gave the pair a lead over the second last, but they were soon disputing it again, though neither rider was yet willing to commit and leave himself in front. Running down to the final flight, the first two began to pull clear and Thornton steered Crystal d'Ainay away from Baracouda, allowing the latter to take a fractional advantage. A couple of strides after the last, Baracouda stumbled but recovered quickly, and, with both riders finally asking their partners for everything, it was Baracouda who pulled out extra to go three quarters of a length up by the line, though clearly neither he nor Crystal d'Ainay was putting everything in. Behind them, Rule Supreme, who had been unable to go with the first two initially, finished best of all, failing by a short head to catch Crystal d'Ainay for second, and passing both him and Baracouda just strides after the line. It Takes Time was only a further length back in fourth, also closing as the leaders idled. Crystal d'Ainay's trainer Alan King summed up the race neatly: 'We tried to see if we could get Baracouda in front of us at some stage, but unfortunately it was at the line.'

The race lacked nothing in entertainment value but it was a far cry from the manner of Baracouda's three other successes in the Long Walk. In 2000, as a novice and making his British debut, he slammed Deano's Beeno by fourteen lengths. A year later he landed odds of 5/2-on by twenty-four lengths, and, following Deano's Beeno's narrow revenge in 2002, Baracouda gave another imperious display in 2003 with a thirty-length beating of Mr Cool at 7/2-on. After his Long Walk victories in both 2001 and 2003, Baracouda had been given another race before going to Cheltenham, winning the Rendlesham Hurdle at Kempton on the first occasion and the Sandown Hurdle, a handicap in which all his rivals were out of the weights, on the second. This time, he was sent directly to Cheltenham without another run, as he had been following his Long Walk defeat in 2002.

By the time of the World Hurdle, as the Stayers' had now become, Baracouda was 6/5 to regain his crown, his chief rivals once again including Crystal d'Ainay and Rule Supreme. But Baracouda was denied by the unknown quantity in the field Inglis Drever, who had been campaigned through the winter as a Champion Hurdle horse. For the first time, Baracouda gave the impression that his best days were behind him. His muddling wins earlier in the season had made it hard to gauge for sure whether Baracouda retained all his considerable ability, but his three-length defeat by Inglis Drever seemed to suggest that he might be on the downgrade. Not that Baracouda ran a bad race though. Gradually closing from the rear (his pacemaker Knife Edge being virtually ignored), Baracouda looked the likely winner into the straight but didn't respond in quite the expected manner when shaken up, though he still finished three quarters of a length ahead of Rule Supreme, while Crystal d'Ainay ran a rare poor race and was pulled up.

Although twice now a beaten favourite in the staying hurdlers' championship race at the Festival, Baracouda's tally of two wins and two second places gives him the best overall record in the race since it took its current form in 1972 (his record might have been even better had he not been denied a run in the race in the foot and mouth interrupted 2000/1 season). The previous holders of the best record were Crimson Embers and Galmoy who between them contested ten consecutive Stayers' Hurdles from 1982 to 1991. Crimson Embers' final appearance when fifth as a twelve-year-old in 1987 coincided with the first of Galmoy's wins. Had Baracouda managed to win back his stayers' crown, he would have been the first horse to do so since Crimson Embers, whose wins came four years apart in 1982 and 1986, and he would also have been the oldest winner since eleven-year-old Crimson Embers won his second Stayers' Hurdle. Between his victories, Crimson Embers finished fourth, fifth and second, though was particularly unlucky not to be awarded the race on the last of those occasions when badly hampered by his stable-companion Rose Ravine. As for Galmoy, he followed up his debut success

Telectronics Systems Long Walk Hurdle, Windsor—
Baracouda gains his fourth win in the race in another closely-run thing with Crystal d'Ainay after a last-flight stumble

in the race with another win in 1988, and finished second, eleventh and fifth in subsequent attempts. For all their admirable records, neither Galmoy (rated 165 at his best) nor Crimson Embers (162) reached a level of form that Baracouda attained at his best (175), Crimson Embers incidentally not reaching his peak until the season in which he turned eleven.

Baracouda (FR) (b.g. 1995)	Alesso (USA) (b 1983)	Alleged (b 1974)	Hoist The Flag
			Princess Pout
		Leandra (b 1978)	Luthier
			Ady Endre
	Peche Aubar (FR) (b 1984)	Zino (b 1979)	Welsh Pageant
			Cyriana
		Salto Mortale (ch 1971)	Hul A Hul
			Dover Lassie

The tall, leggy Baracouda's pedigree has been discussed in previous editions of *Chasers & Hurdlers*. He has raced only on good ground or softer, and acts on heavy. Plans to send Baracouda chasing have been mooted in the past, but it seems most unlikely that that will be an option he will be asked to take up at this stage of his career. Baracouda may not be the outstanding hurdler he once was, but, even with younger rivals around, he should still be competitive in the top staying hurdles for at least another season; a fifth Long Walk (back at Windsor again) would be some achievement. His trainer's knack of keeping his horses at the top of their form season after season is something we have mentioned before, citing Jim And Tonic on the Flat, as well as The Fellow and First Gold (the latter still capable of very smart form over fences at the age of twelve in the latest season) as other good examples. Baracouda's record may never read more impressively than it stands at present, so perhaps the best tribute to both him and his trainer is simply to state that Baracouda has now won fourteen of his seventeen races in Britain and has finished second in the three others. His career record over hurdles as a whole now stands at eighteen wins and six seconds from twenty-five starts. His only finish outside the first two was when fifth at Auteuil on his hurdling debut (wearing blinkers), after which he joined the Doumen stable. By the way, the winner of that particular Auteuil contest, in addition to his defeat of Baracouda, secured another claim to fame, albeit a more dubious one, when he turned up at Cheltenham in the latest season. That horse was none other than Astonville, who, now a shadow of his former self in France, trailed round in the Champion Hurdle and three days later 'accomplished' the same feat in the Gold Cup, starting at 500/1 on both occasions. *F. Doumen, France*

BARANOOK (IRE) 4 b.c. Barathea (IRE) – Gull Nook (Mill Reef (USA)) [2004/5 16v^{2} 17m^{5} 16d^{5} Apr 22] sturdy colt: lightly-raced maiden up to 1½m on Flat, sold out of P. Harris' stable 42,000 gns Newmarket Autumn Sales: best effort over hurdles when second in maiden at Chepstow. *B. J. Llewellyn* **h92**

BARATI (IRE) 4 b.g. Sadler's Wells (USA) – Oriane (Nashwan (USA)) [2004/5 16v^{F} 16v^{3} 16s^{2} 17g Mar 18] lengthy gelding: useful on Flat (will stay 1¾m) for J. Oxx: fairly useful form when placed behind Strangely Brown in graded juveniles at Punchestown and Leopardstown: well held in Triumph Hurdle at Cheltenham. *M. J. P. O'Brien, Ireland* **h126**

BARBER OF SEVILLE 7 ch.g. Kris – Carte Blanche (Cadeaux Genereux) [2004/5 F17m^{pu} Sep 8] 6,000Y, 2,000 4-y-o, 2,500 6-y-o: third foal: dam modest 1m winner at 4 yrs: no show in bumper on debut. *G. F. Bridgwater* **F–**

BARBILYRIFLE (IRE) 4 b.g. Indian Rocket – Age of Elegance (Troy) [2004/5 16d 16d^{pu} 16s^{pu} Dec 22] leggy gelding: fair but unreliable on Flat (stays 6f), sold out of H. Morrison's stable £2,400 Ascot June Sales: no form in juvenile hurdles: tried in cheekpieces. *H. H. G. Owen* **h–**

BARBURY HILL (IRE) 9 b.g. Rashar (USA) – Supreme Rehearsal (IRE) (Supreme Leader) [2004/5 16d 19d^{5} 22d^{5} Dec 2] medium-sized gelding: poor maiden hurdler: stays 2¾m: acts on good to firm and good to soft ground. *A. King* **h70**

BARCELONA 8 b.g. Barathea (IRE) – Pipitina (Bustino) [2004/5 h112: 22g^{5} 20m^{5} 22d 21d 20g 18m^{4} Sep 5] compact gelding: fairly useful handicap hurdler at best, generally out of sorts in 2004/5: stays 2¾m: acts on firm and soft going: usually blinkered/in cheekpieces: often tongue tied: sold only £1,600 Ascot November Sales, fourth in 2 points in 2005. *G. L. Moore* **h104 d**

BARCHAM AGAIN (IRE) 8 b.g. Aristocracy – Dante's Thatch (IRE) (Phardante (FR)) [2004/5 c93, h81: c24d* May 6] good-topped gelding: maiden hurdler: modest handicap chaser: won novice event at Ludlow in May: stays 25f: raced on good going or softer: wears cheekpieces: has been let down by jumping over fences: sold 5,500 gns Doncaster May Sales. *K. C. Bailey* **c99 h–**

BARCLAY BOY 6 b.g. Terimon – Nothings Forever (Oats) [2004/5 F18g^{4} F17s^{3} F16s^{2} 20v^{5} 21m Apr 13] rather unfurnished gelding: first foal: dam never ran: in frame all 3 starts in bumpers: fair form both outings over hurdles, seventh to Prins Willem in novice at Cheltenham. *A. J. Lidderdale* **h100 F89**

BARD OF DRUMCOO (IRE) 10 ch.g. Orange Reef – Sporting Houdini (Monseigneur (USA)) [2004/5 c61: c24d^{4} May 5] prolific winning pointer in 2004: poor form in hunter chases. *D. J. Kemp* **c76**

BAREME (FR) 6 b.g. Homme de Loi (IRE) – Roxa (FR) (Kenmare (FR)) [2004/5 16d^{5} Nov 6] rangy, useful-looking gelding: lightly-raced winning hurdler: off 21 months and favourite, fifth of 10 in handicap at Sandown: raced at 2m on good to soft going. *N. J. Henderson* **h113**

BARGAIN HUNT (IRE) 4 b.g. Foxhound (USA) – Atisayin (USA) (Al Nasr (FR)) [2004/5 16d 16m^{5} 16m^{6} 19d^{6} 16d^{2} 16s^{4} Apr 3] smallish gelding: poor maiden on Flat (stays 9f): modest juvenile hurdler: best effort on soft ground. *W. Storey* **h86**

BAR GAYNE (IRE) 6 ch.g. Good Thyne (USA) – Annie's Alkali (Strong Gale) [2004/5 F16v* 22s^{5} 21g 16s Mar 23] €4,000 4-y-o: fifth foal: brother to bumper winner Anniesthyne and winning pointer Thyne Express and half-brother to modest 2m hurdler Croi Bhriste (by Broken Hearted): dam, placed in bumper, half-sister to fairly useful hurdler Fairwood Present, stays 21f: won 9-runner bumper at Uttoxeter on debut in January: poor form over hurdles. *T. R. George* **h77 F87**

BARMAN (USA) 6 ch.g. Atticus (USA) – Blue Tip (FR) (Tip Moss (FR)) [2004/5 21d^{4} Feb 9] fairly useful on Flat (stays 1¾m), sold out of P. Cole's stable 21,000 gns Newmarket Autumn Sales: tongue tied, found little when fourth in novice at Ludlow on hurdling debut. *C. J. Mann* **h77**

BARNA DREAM (IRE) 9 b.g. Torus – Barna Beauty (Gala Performance) [2004/5 16g* 16m* 16m^{2} 20m^{3} Aug 8] lengthy gelding: off nearly 2 years before reappearance: fair hurdler: won maiden at Ballinrobe and handicap at Cork in July: raced mainly at 2m: acts on good to firm going. *V. T. O'Brien, Ireland* **h110**

BARNARDS GREEN (IRE) 7 ch.g. Florida Son – Pearly Castle (IRE) (Carlingford Castle) [2004/5 c84?, h–: c19m^{4} c16m c19g* c16g^{4} c19m^{4} c20d^{3} c19g c16g^{4} c18s^{5} c16d^{4} c19g Apr 15] lengthy gelding: poor chaser: dictated pace when winning handicap at Taunton in October: stays 2½m: acts on good to soft and good to firm going: tried visored: has often shaped as if amiss/finished weakly. *R. H. Alner* **c81 § h– §**

BARNEY MCALL (IRE) 5 b.g. Grand Lodge (USA) – Persian Song (Persian Bold) [2004/5 16g^{6} 16d 17g* Apr 7] leggy gelding: fairly useful on Flat (stays 10.5f), successful twice in 2003, sold out of Mrs A. Perrett's stable 95,000 gns Newmarket July Sales later in year: tongue tied, easily best effort over hurdles when winning maiden at Taunton in April: very stiff task when pulled up at Punchestown later in month: raced around 2m on good/good to soft ground. *R. T. Phillips* **h102**

BARNEYS LYRIC 5 ch.g. Hector Protector (USA) – Anchorage (IRE) (Slip Anchor) [2004/5 h115: 19v* 24s^{2} 21d Nov 14] angular gelding: fairly useful hurdler: improved form when winning handicap at Stratford in October by 8 lengths from Cool Roxy: also ran well when second to L'Aventure in similar event at Chepstow: stays at least 3m: acts on heavy going: effective making running or ridden more patiently: sold only 6,200 gns Doncaster May Sales. *N. A. Twiston-Davies* **h131**

BARNEYS PRINCE 5 b.g. Prince of Peace – Baashful Blaze (Shaab) [2004/5 F17g^{6} F16d Nov 6] lengthy, rather unfurnished gelding: first foal: dam maiden pointer: little show in 2 bumpers. *C. J. Down* **F–**

BARNEYS REFLECTION 5 b.g. Petoski – Annaberg (IRE) (Tirol) [2004/5 h77, F–: 19s^{4} 21d^{6} 19v^{4} 20g 16d* 17g* Apr 3] close-coupled gelding: modest hurdler: visored, much improved when winning selling handicaps at Fakenham and Market Rasen (sold to join A. Crook 9,000 gns) in space of week: best efforts around 2m: raced on good going or softer. *Mrs L. Wadham* **h96**

BARON ALLFOURS 13 gr.g. Baron Blakeney – Georgian Quickstep (Dubassoff (USA)) [2004/5 c77, h–: c24d^{pu} Nov 3] veteran staying chaser: acts on firm and good to soft going: sometimes finishes weakly. *Miss Z. C. Davison* **c– h–**

BARON ARON (IRE) 10 br.g. Lord Americo – Eleika (Camden Town) [2004/5 c96d, h96: 21g May 9] good-topped gelding: winning hurdler/chaser, modest at best: raced mainly around 2m: acts on heavy going: tried blinkered. *B. N. Pollock* **c– h–**

BARON DE FEYPO (IRE) 7 b.g. Simply Great (FR) – Fete Champetre (Welsh Pageant) [2004/5 16s 16s 18v* 16v 19v* 20v^{4} 20s 16d* Mar 14] angular gelding: fair handicap hurdler: won at Leopardstown in December, Naas in January and Stratford in March: ran well after on Flat and in competitive event won by Stutter at Punchestown in late-April: stays 2½m: acts on heavy going: tried blinkered/in cheekpieces: held up. *P. O. Brady, Ireland* **h111**

BARON HALEBOP 8 b.g. Baron Blakeney – Lunar Missile (Cruise Missile) [2004/5 c19g^{6} c16m^{ur} c16m^{6} c22m Jun 25] first foal: dam ran once: no form in novice company over fences: won maiden point in March. *J. W. Payne* **c–**

BARON MONTY (IRE) 7 b.g. Supreme Leader – Lady Shoco (Montekin) [2004/5 20v^{pu} 20v* 20d* 20g^{4} Mar 26] strong gelding: will make a chaser: traces of stringhalt: dual bumper winner: fairly useful novice hurdler, off 18 months before reappearance: won at Haydock in January and February: good fourth to Kilgowan in handicap at same course: will stay beyond 2½m: acts on heavy ground. *C. Grant* **h121**

BARONS KNIGHT 4 ch.g. Lahib (USA) – Red Barons Lady (IRE) (Electric) [2004/5 F16d Apr 20] tall gelding: seventh foal: half-brother to fair 2m hurdler Cristoforo (by Perugino), also fairly useful up to 1½m on Flat, and 7f and 9f winner Black Turtle (by Turtle Island): dam maiden: well held in bumper on debut. *P. R. Webber* **F–**

BARON'S PHARAOH (IRE) 10 b.g. Phardante (FR) – Katomi (Monksfield) [2004/5 h79: 24d^{pu} c19m^{5} c20m^{2} c21m^{F} Jun 27] quite good-topped gelding: winning hurdler: modest form over fences: should stay beyond 19f: acts on good to firm and good to soft going. *A. W. Carroll* **c94 h–**

BARON STEANE (IRE) 6 b.g. Lord Americo – Lottosprite (IRE) (Sandalay) [2004/5 F83: 20d^{5} May 15] useful-looking gelding: fair form on first of 2 outings in bumpers: well held in novice on hurdling debut. *Lady Connell* **h–**

BARON WINDRUSH 7 b.g. Alderbrook – Dame Scarlet (Blakeney) [2004/5 h118: c24v* c20g^{ur} c24d^{ur} c25s* c25d^{6} c26d^{2} c29s* c28s^{6} Feb 19] **c145 h–**

Alderbrook, the first winner of the Champion Hurdle since Monksfield to become available as a stallion, was always going to be an interesting sire of jumpers and has made quite an impact already, his initial crop including the likes of smart hurdlers Perouse and Sh Boom and stable-companions Baron Windrush and Ollie Magern, two of the best novice chasers of 2004/5. Alderbrook was no stayer him-

totesport Classic Chase (Handicap), Warwick—
the novice Baron Windrush (nearest camera) proves well suited by this longer trip as he defeats D'Argent

The Double Octagon Partnership's "Baron Windrush"

self, either on the Flat or over hurdles, though he is by the influence for stamina Ardross and generally his offspring appear to stay pretty well. While Perouse is a two-miler, his three other named representatives, as well as plenty of others, stay at least three miles. Indeed, that distance is a bare minimum for Baron Windrush, who put up his best performance when winning the totesport Classic Chase, a very valuable handicap run over three miles five furlongs on testing ground at Warwick in January.

Baron Windrush showed fairly useful form, winning novice events at Market Rasen and Wetherby in his first season over hurdles in 2003/4, and he was successful on his first two completed outings over fences. As his sire's offspring tend to, he races freely, and Baron Windrush made most of the running in a maiden at Stratford in October, jumping well in the main to win by eighteen lengths from Limerick Leader. He gave a similar display when winning a three-runner novice event at Aintree the following month by a distance from Joes Edge. Yet Baron Windrush's jumping twice let him down at Cheltenham in between—he unseated his rider each time—and he was far from fluent when a creditable second to Lord of Illusion in a handicap there on New Year's Day. So there was a question mark about just how effective Baron Windrush would be around Warwick, a course where sound jumping is at a premium. The least experienced of the sixteen who lined up for the Classic Chase, a race worth over £66,000 to the winner and the richest ever staged at Warwick, Baron Windrush was ridden with a lot more restraint than usual and coped well enough with the tricky fences. Benefiting from the stiffer test of stamina, Baron Windrush showed improved form to win by two and a half lengths from D'Argent, he and the runner-up pulling well clear of the remainder from the home turn. Baron Windrush finally gained the upper hand after the last and might have had a bit more to spare had he not pecked on landing two out. The Scottish National was nominated as the main target for Baron Windrush later in the season, but he made his only appearance subsequently at Haydock in February, starting favourite but finishing a remote sixth in the Red Square Vodka Gold Cup to Forest Gunner after jumping slowly. Baron Windrush was still 4/1 favourite for the National Hunt Chase when the following month brought an announcement that Baron Windrush would miss the remainder of the season after picking up an injury. He should be back in action in 2005/6, when races such as the Welsh and Scottish Nationals will surely be on his agenda. The Grand National could also come into the reckoning. His stable has won it twice, with Earth Summit and Bindaree, the latter successful when an eight-year-old in his second season as a chaser.

Baron Windrush (b.g. 1998)	Alderbrook (b 1989)	Ardross (b 1976)	Run The Gantlet
			Le Melody
		Twine (ch 1981)	Thatching
			House Tie
	Dame Scarlet (b 1982)	Blakeney (b 1966)	Hethersett
			Windmill Girl
		Noble Duty (b 1970)	Reliance II
			Noble Countess

Baron Windrush is the ninth foal of Dame Scarlet, an unraced sister to the Sun Alliance Novices' Hurdle winner Fealty. The next dam Noble Duty won over thirteen furlongs in France. Dame Scarlet has bred four other winners, the most recent of those being Ceeawayhome (by Nomadic Way) who was successful in a bumper in Ireland in 2003. Two others have won over jumps, the modest hurdler and fair chaser at up to two and a half miles Balleswhidden (by Robellino) and the fairly useful performer in Ireland Good Glow (by Jalmood), successful twice in two-mile hurdles and a hunter chase over twenty-five furlongs. Baron Windrush, a tall gelding, will stay beyond twenty-nine furlongs. He acts on heavy going and is untried on firmer than good. *N. A. Twiston-Davies*

BARRACAT (IRE) 8 b.g. Good Thyne (USA) – Helens Fashion (IRE) (Over The River (FR)) [2004/5 h–: 19d 21d 22g^{pu} Apr 17] smallish gelding: bumper winner: no solid form over hurdles: sold 4,000 gns Doncaster May Sales. *Miss G. Browne* **h–**

BARRACK BUSTER 6 b.m. Bigstone (IRE) – Tarkhana (IRE) (Dancing Brave (USA)) [2004/5 h114: 18m^{4} 24m^{4} 19f* 22m^{6} 19m* 16g* 16s* 16s^{3} 16s Mar 29] sparely-made mare: useful hurdler: won handicaps at Kilbeggan in June and August (fourth course win from as many starts at track) and minor event and intermediate at Punchestown in autumn: best form up to 19f: acts on firm and soft going. *Martin Brassil, Ireland* **h133**

BARRANCO (IRE) 4 b.g. Sadler's Wells (USA) – Belize Tropical (IRE) (Baillamont (USA)) [2004/5 16d 18s 16d 16g^{4} 21g^{6} 17m^{2} Apr 9] compact gelding: brother to 2m hurdle winner Deauville: twice-raced on Flat in France, won 13f event at Liseaux in May: sold out of A. Fabre's stable 4,500 gns Newmarket July Sales: poor maiden hurdler: best efforts around 2m with emphasis on speed: blinkered last 4 outings. *G. L. Moore* **h83**

BARRELBIO (IRE) 10 b.g. Elbio – Esther (Persian Bold) [2004/5 20g 22g^{pu} May 26] good-topped gelding: handicap hurdler: no form since 2001/2: blinkered once. *F. P. Murtagh* **c– h–**

BARREN LANDS 10 b.g. Green Desert (USA) – Current Raiser (Filiberto (USA)) [2004/5 c–, h–: 19g^{5} 17d^{3} 16d^{5} 17d^{4} 17g c19d^{3} c24s^{4} c24s^{pu} 19g 20d^{5} Apr 20] compact gelding: winning hurdler/chaser, fair form at best in 2004/5: stays 19f: acts on soft and good to firm going. *K. Bishop* **c104 h104**

BARRONS PIKE 6 ch.g. Jumbo Hirt (USA) – Bromley Rose (Rubor) [2004/5 F–: 24g c25d^{ur} Apr 11] runner-up in points in 2005: no other form. *B. Storey* **c– h–**

BARROW BROOK 7 b.m. Seymour Hicks (FR) – Weldcome (Weld) [2004/5 F16m^{2} F16s^{2} Nov 5] first foal: dam unraced half-sister to smart staying chaser High Edge Grey: runner-up in bumpers at Hexham: will be suited by further than 2m. *Mrs S. J. Smith* **F87**

BARROW DRIVE 9 b.g. Gunner B – Fille de Soleil (Sunyboy) [2004/5 c142, h–: c24v^{3} c24s^{ur} c20s^{pu} c24v^{pu} c20v^{2} 18s* 18s 20d Apr 9] sturdy gelding: useful chaser: placed in valuable handicap at Listowel and Grade 2 at Gowran: fairly useful hurdler: won minor event at Thurles in February: stays 25f, effective at much shorter: probably **c141 h127**

acts on any going: wore cheekpieces 3 of last 4 starts: usually tongue tied, effective when not: usually races prominently. *Anthony Mullins, Ireland*

BARROW (SWI) 8 br.g. Caerleon (USA) – Bestow (Shirley Heights) [2004/5 h–: 19s 16s 20s^{6} 17d^{ur} Apr 5] angular gelding: winning hurdler: off nearly 2 years, little impact in 2004/5: will stay 3m: acts on soft and good to firm going. *Ferdy Murphy* **h88**

BARRYS ARK (IRE) 7 b. or br.g. Commanche Run – Hand Me Down (Cheval) [2004/5 F16g F17s* 20v^{4} 19s* Mar 27] €22,000 4-y-o: rangy ex-Irish gelding: half-brother to winning 2m hurdler Bramblehill-Beauty (by Glacial Storm): dam winning pointer/modest staying hurdler: winning pointer in 2004: left W. Harney, better effort in bumpers when winning at Hereford in November: shaped encouragingly on hurdling debut, and month later won maiden at Towcester by 1½ lengths from Ballyjohnboy Lord: will stay beyond 2½m: remains open to improvement. *J. A. B. Old* **h105 p** **F97**

BARRYSCOURT LAD (IRE) 11 b.g. Glacial Storm (USA) – Clonana (Le Bavard (FR)) [2004/5 c24g^{4} c32v^{pu} Mar 5] tall, workmanlike gelding: useful form when winning Great Yorkshire Chase at Doncaster in 2002/3 (returned lame): off 2 years and left M. Pipe, not knocked about when fourth in amateur event at Sandown: mistake ninth and soon behind in handicap next time: stays 33f: acts on good to firm and heavy going: not easiest of rides. *R. D. E. Woodhouse* **c98 +**

BARTON BANDIT 9 ch.g. Sula Bula – Yamrah (Milford) [2004/5 c–, h–: c24d^{pu} Apr 22] medium-sized gelding: maiden chaser: no form outside points for long time: has been tongue tied. *Miss Sarah Kent* **c–** **h–**

BARTON BARON (IRE) 7 b.g. Phardante (FR) – Boolavogue (IRE) (Torus) [2004/5 h–: c16s* c17v^{pu} c20g^{3} c19s^{pu} c20m^{3} Apr 10] big, well-made gelding: modest novice handicap chaser: won weak event at Towcester in October: stays 2½m: acts on soft ground. *D. P. Keane* **c86** **h–**

BARTON BEAU (IRE) 6 b.g. Kylian (USA) – Hetty Green (Bay Express) [2004/5 22s 20s 17s 16v^{6} 16v* 16d^{F} Feb 26] sturdy gelding: tailed off in maidens on Flat at 3 yrs, sold out of T. Easterby's stable £2,000 Ascot October (2003) Sales: first form over hurdles when winning selling handicap at Towcester in February: running well when falling 2 out next time: should stay beyond 2m: acts on heavy going: usually blinkered. *Simon Earle* **h82**

BARTON FLOWER 4 br.f. Danzero (AUS) – Iota (Niniski (USA)) [2004/5 16g^{3} Apr 17] poor maiden on Flat (probably stays 1¾m, tried blinkered) at 3 yrs for M. Easterby: third of 9 in novice at Wincanton on hurdling debut, poorly placed after early mistakes: may do better. *D. P. Keane* **h78**

BARTON GATE 7 b.g. Rock Hopper – Ruth's River (Young Man (FR)) [2004/5 h100: c16s^{2} c19s^{3} Nov 24] tall, close-coupled gelding: fair hurdler: similar form when second in novice at Newton Abbot on chasing debut: ran as if amiss next time: best efforts at 2m: acts on soft going: usually blinkered/visored. *D. P. Keane* **c99** **h–**

BARTON HILL 8 b.g. Nicholas Bill – Home From The Hill (IRE) (Jareer (USA)) [2004/5 h90: c24s^{pu} c18g^{2} c18g^{2} c19v^{pu} c18s^{2} c21s^{3} c19d* c16d^{2} c20g Apr 22] leggy gelding: modest hurdler: fair novice chaser: won at Exeter in March: stays at least 19f: acts on heavy going: blinkered last 4 outings. *D. P. Keane* **c106** **h–**

BARTON LEGEND 5 b.g. Midnight Legend – Home From The Hill (IRE) (Jareer (USA)) [2004/5 F16s^{4} F16d* Mar 19] rather unfurnished gelding: fourth foal: half-brother to winning hurdler/fair chaser around 2½m Barton Hill (by Nicholas Bill): dam fairly useful 2m hurdler, also won up to 1½m on Flat: fair form in bumpers, beating Mars Rock 1½ lengths in steadily-run event at Uttoxeter. *D. P. Keane* **F94**

BARTON MAY 6 ch.m. Midnight Legend – Yamrah (Milford) [2004/5 h82: c20s^{F} c21d* c20v^{2} c20d^{5} c21d^{pu} c21d^{2} c25d* Apr 3] lengthy mare: poor maiden hurdler: fair chaser: won handicaps at Folkestone (novice) in November and Wincanton in April: stays 25f: acts on heavy going: effective tongue tied or not. *D. P. Keane* **c103** **h–**

BARTON NIC 12 b.g. Nicholas Bill – Dutch Majesty (Homing) [2004/5 c78+, h111: 16g^{2} 16d* 16d c21s^{3} c17v* c16v* c16d^{2} c16v^{pu} 16d c16s^{pu} Mar 7] workmanlike gelding: fairly useful hurdler: better than ever first 2 starts, winning handicap at Sandown in November: took advantage of much lower mark over fences when winning at Plumpton and Chepstow in January: has won at 3m, best form around 2m: acts on heavy going: wears headgear: patiently ridden. *D. P. Keane* **c96** **h120**

BARTON PARK 5 b.g. Most Welcome – William's Bird (USA) (Master Willie) [2004/5 F16s^{2} F16v 16s^{3} Feb 18] tall gelding: has scope: ninth foal: half-brother to 3 **h78 p** **F95**

winners on Flat, including fairly useful 1997 2-y-o 1m winner Chim Chiminey (by Sabrehill) and 1¼m winner Erith's Chill Wind (by Be My Chief): dam useful 2-y-o 5f and 7f winner: better effort in bumpers when second to Crashtown Leader at Uttoxeter: free to post and in race when well-held third in novice at Sandown on hurdling debut: open to improvement over hurdles, but needs to settle. *D. P. Keane*

BARTON SAINT (NZ) 10 ch.g. St Hilarion (USA) – Aquatramp (NZ) (Pevero) [2004/5 c26g^{pu} c23g^{4} c23m^{5} c23g^{4} c24g^{pu} Apr 7] leggy, angular gelding: winning pointer: poor maiden chaser, left P. Rodford after fourth outing: stays easy 3¼m: acts on good to firm going: tried tongue tied: temperamental. *B. G. Parsons*
c84 § **h– §**

BARTON SUN (IRE) 6 b.g. Indian Ridge – Sun Screen (Caerleon (USA)) [2004/5 F–: F16d F16v 16d 17s^{pu} 20d 24d^{4} 24d^{pu} Apr 20] good-topped gelding: modest form in bumpers: little worthwhile form over hurdles. *R. N. Bevis*
h73 **F82**

BARUM BELLE 5 b.m. Thowra (FR) – La Belle Shyanne (Shy Groom (USA)) [2004/5 F16d F16s Mar 23] rather unfurnished mare: second foal: dam bad maiden on Flat, out of 2-y-o 5f winner: well held in bumpers. *Mrs S. D. Williams*
F–

BASIL 12 br.g. Lighter – Thrupence (Royal Highway) [2004/5 c79x, h–: c24d^{pu} c27d^{pu} c25v^{pu} c25d^{pu} c29s^{pu} Mar 12] tall gelding: poor handicap chaser, no form in 2004/5: stays 29f: best efforts on going softer than good (acts on heavy): usually makes mistakes. *J. N. R. Billinge*
c– x **h–**

BASILEA STAR (IRE) 8 b.g. Fourstars Allstar (USA) – Swiss Castle (IRE) (Carlingford Castle) [2004/5 20s^{6} 20s^{ur} 22s* 22s* 25g* 20v* 24d^{3} 24g 22g^{2} Apr 16] well-made gelding: type to make a chaser: second foal: half-brother to 2m hurdle winner Roman Native (by Be My Native): dam, placed in bumper, half-sister to fairly useful hurdler around 2½m Potential Pin: won both starts in Irish points in 2004: sold out of J. Kiely's stable 15,000 gns Doncaster May Sales: useful hurdler: won handicaps at Kelso (2), Catterick and Uttoxeter (beat Celtic Son by 1¾ lengths) between November and January: remained in form, third to stable-companion Carlys Quest in substandard Grade 1 at Punchestown in late-April: stays 25f: acts on heavy going: usually tongue tied. *Ferdy Murphy*
h133

BASINET 7 b.g. Alzao (USA) – Valiancy (Grundy) [2004/5 h91: 16d^{3} 17m^{2} 17d* Aug 28] modest on Flat (stays 9f): modest novice hurdler: won handicap at Cartmel in convincing style: likely to prove best around 2m: acts on good to firm and good to soft going. *J. J. Quinn*
h95

BASSANO (USA) 11 b.g. Alwasmi (USA) – Marittima (USA) (L'Emigrant (USA)) [2004/5 c68, h–: c22g^{3} c24g^{pu} Jun 10] stocky, lengthy gelding: poor maiden chaser: stays 23f: acts on heavy and good to firm going: tongue tied last 4 outings: has found little/jumped right: sold £950 Ascot April Sales. *S. C. Burrough*
c68 **h–**

BASSETT TIGER (IRE) 9 b.g. Shardari – Bassett Girl (Brigadier Gerard) [2004/5 c21g^{4} c22f^{2} c20g* c24f* c24s^{6} c22g^{5} c24v^{pu} c28s^{pu} Nov 7] fair chaser: won 2 handicaps at Wexford in July: stays 3m: acts on any going: sometimes tongue tied. *W. P. Mullins, Ireland*
c112 **h–**

BATANG (GER) 6 br.h. Grand Lodge (USA) – Bejaria (GER) (Konigsstuhl (GER)) [2004/5 16m* 16m^{4} 20f* 16d* 17d^{2} 16g Jul 29] half-brother to one-time useful 2m hurdler/winning chaser Bernardon (by Suave Dancer): won over 1m at 3 yrs on Flat in Germany: fair hurdler: won maiden at Wexford in May and novices at Clonmel and Limerick in summer: stays 2½m: acts on firm and good to soft going. *Gerard Cully, Ireland*
h111

BATHWICK ANNIE 9 ch.m. Sula Bula – Lily Mab (FR) (Prince Mab (FR)) [2004/5 c120, h87: c24d^{6} c25d^{pu} c25s* c25s* c25d^{2} c33d^{pu} Mar 19] workmanlike mare: maiden hurdler: fairly useful chaser: back in form after turn of year, winning handicaps at Wincanton in January, making all to beat Zaffamore by 8 lengths in quite valuable event on second occasion: should stay beyond 25f: acts on soft going: usually bold-jumping front runner, though has tendency to go right. *D. P. Keane*
c127 **h–**

BATMAN SENORA (FR) 9 b.g. Chamberlin (FR) – Cartza (FR) (Carmarthen (FR)) [2004/5 c148, h140: 20v* c29s^{6} 25d 25s^{6} 20v^{5} c23g Jan 9] rangy gelding: smart chaser/useful hurdler at Auteuil, winning minor hurdle in May: thrice-raced in Britain and Ireland, well beaten in Grade 2 hurdle at Wetherby fourth outing: left I. Williams, behind when pulled up lame in Grande Steeple-Chase de Paris in May: effective around 2½m and stays 29f: best efforts on soft/heavy going: usually blinkered: races prominently. *J. Ortet, France*
c124 **h138**

BATOKA (UAE) 4 b.g. Hennessy (USA) – Zambezi (USA) (Rahy (USA)) [2004/5 F13d Nov 28] 600 2-y-o: first foal: dam, French 1m winner, half-sister to smart performer
F70

up to 1m Zoning, from family of Oh So Sharp: favourite, eighth of 15 in 3-y-o bumper at Doncaster on debut: joined Mrs S. Smith. *G. A. Harker*

BATON CHARGE (IRE) 7 b.g. Gildoran – Frizzball (IRE) (Orchestra) [2004/5 c88, F–: c16g^{F} c24d^{F} c20d^{5} c20s^{pu} Dec 22] rangy, angular gelding: maiden chaser, well held on completed outing in 2004/5. *T. R. George* **c73**

BATOUTOFTHEBLUE 12 br.g. Batshoof – Action Belle (Auction Ring (USA)) [2004/5 c–, h–: 24f^{2} 24d^{5} 27m^{2} 26d* c22d* Oct 3] quite good-topped gelding: fair hurdler: successful in claimer at Southwell in August: won maiden at Market Rasen (reportedly finished lame) on completed start in chases: stays 27f: acts on firm and good to soft going: wears cheekpieces: not an easy ride. *R. Johnson* **c99 h108**

BATSWING 10 b.g. Batshoof – Magic Milly (Simply Great (FR)) [2004/5 c121d, h101: c18s^{3} c20g^{6} c16s^{2} c17s* 16d^{3} c16g Mar 18] lengthy gelding: fairly useful handicap chaser: won at Plumpton in January: fair hurdler: barely stays 21f: acts on heavy and good to firm going: tried in blinkers/cheekpieces: has had tongue tied: irresolute. *G. L. Moore* **c123 § h101 §**

BATTEN DOWN (IRE) 7 b.g. Glacial Storm (USA) – Dikler Gale (IRE) (Strong Gale) [2004/5 17g^{pu} c21g^{3} c21d^{3} c24g* c24g^{pu} c24d^{4} Sep 10] rather leggy gelding: thrice-raced maiden hurdler: best effort in chases when winning handicap at Stratford in August, making most under excellent ride from A. McCoy: likely to prove better at 3m+ than shorter: acts on good to soft going: visored/blinkered last 3 starts: has had tongue tied: takes plenty of driving. *Jonjo O'Neill* **c87 h–**

BATTIES DEN (IRE) 5 br.g. Corrouge (USA) – Miners Society (Miner's Lamp) [2004/5 F16s Mar 1] €15,000 4-y-o: good-topped gelding: fifth foal: half-brother to winning pointer by Durgam: dam maiden half-sister to fairly useful hurdler/chaser up to 3m Dr Bones and fairly useful 2m hurdler Spirit of Park: looked to need run when seventh of 16 in maiden bumper at Catterick on debut. *P. D. Niven* **F81**

BAUDOLINO 8 br.g. Bin Ajwaad (IRE) – Stos (IRE) (Bluebird (USA)) [2004/5 16g 20s^{5} 17g 16d 20d^{pu} Jan 26] third foal: dam unraced, from family of 2000 Guineas and Irish Derby winner El Gran Senor: no form over hurdles. *R. J. Price* **h–**

BAYADERE (GER) 5 b.m. Lavirco (GER) – Brangane (IRE) (Anita's Prince) [2004/5 16g Apr 19] successful over 7f at 2 yrs in Germany, soundly beaten on Flat in Britain in 2004, sold out of V. Smith's stable 3,000 gns Newmarket February Sales: well beaten in novice on hurdling debut. *K. F. Clutterbuck* **h–**

BAYFORD BOY 5 b.g. Miner's Lamp – Emma's Vision (IRE) (Vision (USA)) [2004/5 F17g^{4} F16d Jun 23] third foal: half-brother to winning pointer by General Gambul: dam of no account: modest form on first of 2 starts in bumpers. *K. Bishop* **F83**

BAY ISLAND (IRE) 9 b. or br.g. Treasure Hunter – Wild Deer (Royal Buck) [2004/5 c26s^{pu} Apr 28] tall gelding: modest chaser in 2002/3 for Mrs H. Dalton: won point in 2004, pulled up on hunter debut: stays 3¼m: acts on soft and good to firm going: usually tongue tied: front runner: tends to jump right. *B. Perkins* **c– h–**

BAY KENNY 7 b.g. Karinga Bay – Erica Superba (Langton Heath) [2004/5 h117, F93: 22g^{2} 20d^{pu} c26d^{pu} c20g^{4} c20d^{4} Jan 25] well-made gelding: fairly useful hurdler at best in 2003/4: no encouragement in 3 starts over fences: should stay beyond 3m: acts on good to soft going (won bumper on good to firm). *K. C. Bailey* **c– h101**

BAY LEGEND (IRE) 7 b.g. Toulon – Kabarda (Relkino) [2004/5 22g 22d^{pu} c16g^{pu} Jul 14] no form in varied events. *M. Pitman* **c– h–**

BAY OF MAGENTA 4 b.f. El Conquistador – Lady Magenta (Rolfe (USA)) [2004/5 16m Sep 19] half-sister to winning pointer Travelling Jack (by Lyphento): dam plater, form only around 1¼m: showed nothing in juvenile hurdle on debut. *A. J. Whiting* **h–**

BAY OF PLENTY 11 b.m. Teenoso (USA) – Bara Peg (Random Shot) [2004/5 19s^{5} Mar 23] lengthy, good-topped mare: maiden hurdler: no show only outing since 2002. *K. Bishop* **h–**

BAYOSS (IRE) 9 b.g. Commanche Run – Baylough Lady (IRE) (Lancastrian) [2004/5 c24g^{3} c21s^{pu} c24g c22s^{2} Mar 23] 9,500 4-y-o: third foal: half-brother to bumper winner Mr Lundy (by Ore): dam unraced: winning pointer: form in 4 chases only when second in maiden at Towcester: should stay beyond 2¾m. *Mrs Tracey Barfoot-Saunt* **c84**

BAYOU PRINCESS 4 ch.f. Bluegrass Prince (IRE) – Josifina (Master Willie) [2004/5 16s^{2} 16d^{5} 17s^{4} 17d^{6} 16s 19s^{5} 19v^{pu} 16s^{pu} Mar 27] leggy filly: dam fair 2m hurdler: lightly-raced maiden on Flat: best effort over hurdles when second in juvenile maiden at **h88**

Kempton on debut: sold out of B. de Haan's stable £6,800 Ascot November Sales after next start, lame final outing: should stay beyond 17f. *S. T. Lewis*

BAYSIDE 4 ch.g. Docksider (USA) – Sister Sophie (USA) (Effervescing (USA)) [2004/5 F12g F16d* F16g* F16g^{2} Mar 9] leggy gelding: closely related to smart hurdler/winning chaser Hasty Prince (by Halling), stays 2½m, and half-brother to several winners, including smart 6f (at 2 yrs) to 9f winner Port Lucaya (by Sharpo): dam, 1¼m winner in USA, half-sister to Diminuendo (by Diesis): fairly useful form in bumpers: won at Catterick and Musselburgh (beat Double Gem by ¾ length) in January. *K. G. Reveley* **F102**

BAY SOLITAIRE 4 b.g. Charnwood Forest (IRE) – Golden Wings (USA) (Devil's Bag (USA)) [2004/5 16m^{4} 16m^{3} 16s Nov 4] lengthy, useful-looking gelding: well held on Flat: best effort in juvenile hurdles when third at Wetherby. *T. D. Easterby* **h88**

BDELLIUM 7 b.m. Royal Vulcan – Kelly's Logic (Netherkelly) [2004/5 c92?, h–: 25m^{2} 24s^{2} 26s^{3} c24v^{4d} c20d^{4} 25g* 24d^{2} Apr 20] sturdy mare: modest hurdler: won handicap at Plumpton in March: similar form over fences: stays 3¼m: acts on soft and good to firm going: consistent. *B. I. Case* **c87 h85**

BEACHCOMBER 10 b.g. Kuwait Beach (USA) – Miss Rupert (Solar Topic) [2004/5 c–: c24g Apr 30] winning pointer: fair form completed start in hunters. *J. Groucott* **c88**

BEACHCOMBER BAY (IRE) 10 ch.g. Un Desperado (FR) – Beachcomber Lass (Day Is Done) [2004/5 c135, h–: c20g c21s^{ur} Apr 7] lengthy gelding: useful chaser in 2003/4: left N. Meade, successful in point in March: stays 2½m: raced on good going or softer (acts on heavy): tried blinkered. *I. J. Keeling, Ireland* **c– h–**

BEAMISH PRINCE 6 ch.g. Bijou d'Inde – Unconditional Love (IRE) (Polish Patriot (USA)) [2004/5 h85: 17m^{2} 16d* 16d^{F} 16s^{4} 16s* 16s^{4} 16v^{2} 16g^{2} 19m^{6} Apr 23] leggy gelding: fairly useful hurdler: won conditional jockeys handicap at Haydock in October and novice at Wetherby in December: will prove best around 2m: acts on good to firm and heavy going: consistent. *G. M. Moore* **h116**

BEANNEY (ARG) 5 gr.h. Handsome Halo (ARG) – Little Wing (ARG) (Ringaro (USA)) [2004/5 16g^{5} 16d* 19s^{pu} 17s^{F} Mar 19] smallish horse: successful 3 times up to around 1¼m on Flat, including at Cologne in August: won novice hurdle at Catterick in January: unsuited by stiffer test of stamina next time. *C. Von Der Recke, Germany* **h94**

BEARAWAY (IRE) 8 b.g. Fourstars Allstar (USA) – Cruiseaway (Torus) [2004/5 h96, F101: c16g^{2} c17m^{3} c19m* c16m c16d^{2} c16d* c16g^{pu} c16s^{pu} c16g Dec 28] useful-looking gelding: bumper winner: fair hurdler: similar form over fences, winning novice at Hereford in June and handicap at Warwick in November: ran as if amiss after: stays 19f: acts on firm and good to soft going: tried in cheekpieces: tongue tied nowadays. *Mrs H. Dalton* **c104 h–**

BEARE NECESSITIES (IRE) 6 ch.g. Presenting – Lady Laburnum (Carlingford Castle) [2004/5 h88p: 21g^{3} May 8] modest form in novice hurdles at Exeter and Warwick over 5 months apart: looked capable of better but not seen out again. *A. Ennis* **h99 p**

BEAR ON BOARD (IRE) 10 b.g. Black Monday – Under The River (Over The River (FR)) [2004/5 c130, h–: c28v^{6} Dec 18] well-made gelding: useful handicap chaser: won 3 times in 2003/4: reportedly retired after breaking down on reappearance: thorough stayer: acted on good to firm and heavy going: game and reliable. *A. King* **c– h–**

BEAT THE HEAT (IRE) 7 b.g. Salse (USA) – Summer Trysting (USA) (Alleged (USA)) [2004/5 h115: 20d^{3} 20g c16s^{3} c20d^{F} c16v^{4} c19d^{5} 20s^{6} 18s Apr 3] angular gelding: fair handicap hurdler: similar form when in frame over fences: stays 2½m: acts on good to firm and heavy going: blinkered once: tongue tied second outing: held up. *Jedd O'Keeffe* **c109 h112**

BEAU ARTISTE 5 ch.g. Peintre Celebre (USA) – Belle Esprit (Warning) [2004/5 h94: 17m^{3} 16g^{2} 16d 17v 16m Feb 6] fair novice hurdler: raced around 2m: tried in blinkers/cheekpieces: raced around 2m. *J. Howard Johnson* **h101**

BEAUCHAMP GIGI (IRE) 7 b.m. Bob Back (USA) – Beauchamp Grace (Ardross) [2004/5 F97: 20m* 20g^{3} Jan 21] bumper winner: successful in maiden at Musselburgh on hurdling debut: better form when third to Golden Odyssey in mares event there following month: will stay beyond 2½m: remains open to improvement. *J. Howard Johnson* **h101 p**

BEAUCHAMP ORACLE 8 gr.g. Mystiko (USA) – Beauchamp Cactus (Niniski (USA)) [2004/5 c21d^{2} c24s^{5} c23s^{4} c23g^{2} Apr 12] lengthy gelding: winning pointer: fair maiden hunter chaser: stays 3m: acts on soft going. *S. Flook* **c89**

BEAUCHAMP PRINCE (IRE) 4 gr.g. Beauchamp King – Katie Baggage (IRE) (Brush Aside (USA)) [2004/5 16m4 16s 17v* 16v5 21v4 17s 20d3 16g Mar 15] tall gelding: has scope: third foal: dam unraced: fair juvenile hurdler: won at Bangor in November: should stay at least 2½m: acts on good to firm and heavy ground: has hung left. *M. Scudamore* **h104**

BEAUCHAMP QUEST 6 b.g. Pharly (FR) – Beauchamp Kate (Petoski) [2004/5 F–: F16g F17g 17gur 16d 16gpu 16d 17spu Feb 17] smallish gelding: no sign of ability: sold out of P. Jones's stable £2,200 Ascot July Sales after first outing, left W. Goldsworthy after sixth: tried blinkered (hung badly). *G. F. Bridgwater* **h–** **F–**

BEAUCHAMP RIBBON 5 b.m. Vettori (IRE) – Beauchamp Kate (Petoski) [2004/5 16m 16gpu 16m Aug 30] compact mare: fair on Flat (stays 11.7f, wears headgear) at 3 yrs, tailed off in 3 starts in 2004: no show in maiden hurdles: tried blinkered. *A. J. Chamberlain* **h–**

BEAUCHAMP VALLEY (IRE) 4 b.g. Beauchamp King – Valley of Time (FR) (In Fijar (USA)) [2004/5 F16g Apr 16] first foal: dam 7f winner/poor novice hurdler: tailed off in bumper on debut. *F. Jestin* **F–**

BEAU COUP 8 b.g. Toulon – Energance (IRE) (Salmon Leap (USA)) [2004/5 h76: 22s* 23m4 c24dpu 22g3 Apr 3] fair hurdler: improved form when winning novice handicap at Newton Abbot in May: ran as if amiss on chasing debut: stays 2¾m: acts on soft going, below form on good to firm: none too consistent. *John R. Upson* **c–** **h100**

BEAU DE TURGEON (FR) 4 b.g. Turgeon (USA) – Beluda (FR) (Beyssac (FR)) [2004/5 F13g6 F16s 20d Apr 20] rather unfurnished gelding: fourth foal: half-brother to winning hurdler around 2m Beluborg (by Cyborg): dam winning chaser up to around 2¾m: better effort in bumpers on debut: never dangerous in maiden on hurdling debut. *Ian Williams* **h–** **F83**

BEAUGENCY (NZ) 7 br.g. Prized (USA) – Naiades (NZ) (Beaufort Sea (USA)) [2004/5 12sF 16d2 16g3 20v5 20sF Feb 10] useful-looking gelding: successful once over 1m from 22 starts up to around 1¼m on Flat in New Zealand: fell in maiden on hurdling debut there in August for K. Myers: modest form in Britain: stays 2½m. *R. C. Guest* **h89**

BEAULY (IRE) 10 b.g. Beau Sher – Woodland Theory (Sheer Grit) [2004/5 h79: 16d5 17g4 17m 21mbd 19g* 18spu Oct 12] good-topped gelding: poor handicap hurdler: won conditional jockeys seller (sold from J. O'Shea 5,500 gns) at Exeter in October: fatally injured 6 days later: stayed 19f: acted on firm and good to soft going. *M. C. Pipe* **h77**

BEAU PEAK 6 ch.m. Meadowbrook – Peak A Boo (Le Coq d'Or) [2004/5 F17d6 Mar 26] leggy mare: first foal: dam, signs of only a little ability over hurdles, half-sister to fair staying chaser Peter (by Meadowbrook): never a threat in bumper on debut. *D. W. Whillans* **F71**

BEAU ROBERTO 11 b.g. Robellino (USA) – Night Jar (Night Shift (USA)) [2004/5 21gpu Apr 30] maiden hurdler: off 17 months and left J. Goldie, showed little only 2004/5 start. *Miss P. Robson* **h–**

BEAU SADDLER 4 b.g. Accondy (IRE) – Wand of Youth (Mandamus) [2004/5 F16g F16s Mar 12] seventh foal: half-brother to winning pointer by Lancastrian: dam, lightly-raced, out of very smart staying chaser Young Ash Leaf: tailed off in bumpers. *A. R. Dicken* **F–**

BEAUSEJOUR (USA) 7 ch.m. Diesis – Libeccio (NZ) (Danzatore (CAN)) [2004/5 h86: 21g6 18m 20m6 20g6 Jul 30] smallish mare: poor handicap hurdler: left J. Gallagher before lame final start: stays 21f: acts on good to firm going, possibly not on softer than good: sometimes wears cheekpieces: often none too fluent. *B. P. J. Baugh* **h81**

BEAU SUPREME (IRE) 8 b.g. Supreme Leader – Miss Sabreur (Avocat) [2004/5 h102: c25s3 c21d3 c20s* c24s2 c24d* c24d2 Mar 19] useful-looking gelding: fair maiden hurdler: much better over fences: won handicaps at Ludlow in January and March: will stay beyond 25f: raced on good going or softer (acts on soft). *C. J. Down* **c121** **h–**

BEAUTIFUL ROSA 4 ch.f. Bien Bien (USA) – Starosta (Soviet Star (USA)) [2004/5 F12g Nov 10] third foal: dam unraced half-sister to very smart stayer Weld: mid-field in 3-y-o bumper at Newbury on debut, tenderly handled throughout. *G. A. Huffer* **F75 +**

BEAUTIFUL VISION (IRE) 5 ch.g. Moscow Society (USA) – Rumi (Nishapour (FR)) [2004/5 F16v6 F16v* F16g Mar 16] good-topped gelding: second foal: dam fair middle-distance winner/poor novice hurdler: useful form in bumpers when winning at Leopardstown in January by 8 lengths from Extra Pickins: well held in Grade 1 at Cheltenham final start. *T. J. Taaffe, Ireland* **F104**

BEAU TORERO (FR) 7 gr.g. True Brave (USA) – Brave Lola (FR) (Dom Pasquini (FR)) [2004/5 c–, h86: c16m4 Aug 30] lengthy, useful-looking gelding: modest hurdler: twice-raced over fences, dismounted after line on reappearance: stays easy 19f: acts on good to firm and good to soft going. *B. N. Pollock* **c76 h–**

BEAVER (AUS) 6 b.g. Bite The Bullet (USA) – Mahenge (AUS) (Twig Moss (FR)) [2004/5 16g3 Jan 24] successful 3 times from 7f to around 1¼m from 28 starts on Flat in Australia: third in maiden at Southwell on hurdling debut (not fluent): should improve. *R. C. Guest* **h100 p**

BEBE FACTUAL (GER) 4 b.c. So Factual (USA) – Bebe Kamira (GER) (Kamiros II) [2004/5 16dpu 17g6 Apr 15] successful twice on Flat in Germany in 2004 over 9f and 1m for C. Sprengel: well held in juvenile hurdles. *J. D. Frost* **h–**

BE BE KING (IRE) 6 b.g. Bob Back (USA) – Trimar Gold (Goldhill) [2004/5 F16d* F16d2 20d5 Mar 19] 46,000 3-y-o: lengthy gelding: seventh foal: half-brother to 3 winners, including fairly useful hurdler/useful chaser up to 4¼m Ackzo and fair chaser around 2m Count Karmuski (both by Ardross): dam fair jumper up to 2½m: looked smart prospect both starts in bumpers, winning at Wincanton on debut in December most impressively by 11 lengths from Sea The Light and 3½ lengths second to Karanja in Grade 2 at Newbury in February: not fluent when fifth to Halcon Genelardais in novice at Uttoxeter on hurdling debut: will stay beyond 2½m: sure to improve and win races over hurdles. *P. F. Nicholls* **h98 p F121**

BE BOP BENTLEY 10 br.g. Arms And The Man – Playful Touch (Lepanto (GER)) [2004/5 c–: c24gur Apr 30] of little account. *P. Maskill* **c–**

BEBOPSKIDDLY 4 b.g. Robellino (USA) – Adarama (IRE) (Persian Bold) [2004/5 16g 17d Nov 15] leggy gelding: modest maiden on Flat (should be suited by 1¼m+): well held over hurdles: tried blinkered. *B. G. Powell* **h–**

BECKLEY (IRE) 9 b.g. Phardante (FR) – Baybush (Boreen (FR)) [2004/5 16m Oct 3] tall gelding: modest hurdler in 2002/3: well held only subsequent start: stays 2½m: has pulled hard. *C. Grant* **h–**

BED BUG (FR) 7 b.g. Double Bed (FR) – Cotation (FR) (Recitation (USA)) [2004/5 h102: c21dpu c17mpu 21m3 Jul 2] tall, leggy gelding: fair handicap hurdler: reportedly lame final outing: none too fluent in novice chases: stays 21f: acts on good to firm going: tried blinkered: sold 3,500 gns Doncaster August Sales. *N. J. Henderson* **c– h102**

BEE AN BEE (IRE) 8 b.g. Phardante (FR) – Portia's Delight (IRE) (The Parson) [2004/5 c125, h–: 23d c22d2 c24d c25vpu c24g5 c24m2 Apr 2] well-made gelding: winning hurdler: fairly useful handicap chaser: creditable efforts in 2004/5 only when runner-up at Newbury, beaten 1½ lengths by Red Devil Robert on second occasion: will stay beyond 25f: acts on heavy and good to firm going: tried in blinkers/visor: has found little. *T. R. George* **c123 h91**

BEECHCOURT 8 b.g. Son Pardo – Calametta (Oats) [2004/5 h111: c17s2 c19v2 c19vur 16v 16s* 17g Mar 18] tall gelding: fairly useful handicap hurdler: won at Leopardstown in February: heavily-backed favourite, only eleventh of 30 in valuable event at Cheltenham following month: similar form when runner-up on completed starts over fences: probably best around 2m: raced on good going or softer: has hung left and doesn't always find much. *M. J. P. O'Brien, Ireland* **c121 h124**

BEECHWOOD 7 b.g. Fraam – Standard Rose (Ile de Bourbon (USA)) [2004/5 h76: 17g6 Apr 10] lengthy, good sort: poor form over hurdles: needs emphasis on speed at 2m. *P. R. Rodford* **h–**

BEEF OR SALMON (IRE) 9 ch.g. Cajetano (USA) – Farinella (IRE) (Salmon Leap (USA)) [2004/5 c171+, h–: c25g* c24s5 c24s* c20s3 c24v* c24s2 c26gpu Mar 18] **c171 h–**

'Where's the beef?' No matter how impressive the overall record of a top-class staying chaser may be, if he hasn't passed the acid test for such a horse and won a Cheltenham Gold Cup by the end of his career, then he runs the risk of having the substance of his claims to top-class status being questioned, or even of being considered something of an under-achiever. Florida Pearl tended to suffer in that regard, and his immediate successor as Ireland's best staying chaser, Beef Or Salmon, is in danger of suffering a similar fate. Like Florida Pearl, Beef Or Salmon has now tried and failed three times in the Gold Cup. He could be excused an early fall when second favourite in 2003 as he was still a novice at the time, and his staying-on fourth after a more careful round of jumping twelve months later suggested it could possibly prove a case of third time lucky. With Best Mate out of the picture and another three Grade 1 prizes in Ireland under his belt since the 2004 Gold Cup, Beef Or Salmon's Cheltenham claims had never looked stronger prior to his latest bid. But he ran an abysmal race, getting reminders as early as the sixth and soon toiling on the final circuit before being pulled up. A reproduction of Beef Or Salmon's best form would, in theory, have been sufficient to win what turned out to be a far from vintage Gold Cup, but the title of Ireland's top staying chaser has already passed to the winner, Kicking King, and it will be a very hard task indeed for Beef Or Salmon to win it back. The Gold Cup itself may have eluded Beef Or Salmon, but he did at least take the scalp of the Gold Cup winners Best Mate and Kicking King during the latest season, a campaign in which his fortunes ebbed and flowed.

Having ended his previous campaign with an impressive defeat of the dual Gold Cup third Harbour Pilot in the Heineken Punchestown Gold Cup in April, Beef Or Salmon made his return five and a half months later in the Munster National at his local track, Limerick. This was his first, and so far, only appearance in a handicap, carrying 12-0 and giving upwards of 23 lb to some useful and largely in-form rivals who had the benefit of more recent outings. In the circumstances, those firms who pushed out Beef Or Salmon's odds for the Gold Cup following his defeat—he was beaten over fifteen lengths into fifth behind Colca Canyon—seemed to be overreacting. That certainly looked the case when an evidently fitter Beef Or Salmon returned to his best in the James Nicholson Wine Merchant Champion Chase at Down Royal in November. Taking on Colca Canyon at level weights this time, in a field which also included Harbour Pilot and Glenelly Gale (who had won a much weaker renewal of the same race the year before), Beef Or Salmon's jumping wasn't always spot-on, but the steady pace meant that wasn't much of a handicap and, after challenging two out, he ran on too well for the second favourite, Kicking King, winning by three and a half lengths.

Beef Or Salmon returned from Down Royal with what was described by his trainer as a 'nasty' overreach, but he was out again just a month later, starting odds on for a rematch with Kicking King in the Punchestown Chase, a race Beef Or

James Nicholson Wine Merchant Champion Chase, Down Royal—
Beef Or Salmon (noseband) claims his only verdict over Kicking King in three meetings in 2004/5

Lexus Chase, Leopardstown—
another notable scalp, with a below-par Best Mate having to settle for second

Salmon had won with a fluent round of jumping the year before. It turned out to be the race which signalled a shift in the balance of power from Beef Or Salmon to his younger rival. Whilst Kicking King won with authority, jumping well in the lead, Beef Or Salmon gave the distinct impression he hadn't fully recovered from his setback, soon needing reminders and jumping less than fluently, making no impression from four out and eventually beaten seventeen lengths into third.

This defeat had to be taken more seriously than his reverse at Limerick, and it looked like being a struggle for Beef Or Salmon to return to the top of his form at Leopardstown's Christmas meeting little more than three weeks later. Beef Or Salmon had won the Ericsson Chase in 2002 but the anticipated showdown with Best Mate the following season had failed to meet expectations when Beef Or Salmon finished a below-par third, reported by his rider to have gurgled. Now under new sponsorship, the Lexus Chase, as the Ericsson had become, drew a field of six, with Best Mate (10/9-on) and Beef Or Salmon (9/4) dominating the betting for the second year running. Rule Supreme, back over fences for the first time since finishing fifth to Beef Or Salmon at Punchestown in the spring, Pizarro and Cloudy Bays (third and fifth respectively in the Tommy Whittle Chase at Haydock last time) and outsider Barrow Drive completed the line-up. With Harbour Pilot an absentee, Paul Carberry was free to deputise for Timmy Murphy who had riding commitments in Britain the same day. Murphy had been Beef Or Salmon's partner throughout his chasing career except when Carberry had been in the saddle for his debut over fences.

Once again, the hoped-for head-to-head between Beef Or Salmon and Best Mate failed to materialise, and this time it was Best Mate's connections who were left looking for excuses. With the ground heavy and the pace steady, conditions played to Beef Or Salmon's strengths rather than to those of his chief rival, and he bounced right back to form. Making his move slightly earlier than usual under his new rider, Beef Or Salmon was upsides Best Mate going to three out and quickened into a decisive lead at the next, soon leaving Best Mate toiling. Kept up to his work on the run-in, Beef Or Salmon had a seven-length advantage over Best Mate at the line, though Rule Supreme had been challenging for the runner-up spot when coming down at the last, leaving Pizarro to take a remote third. Incidentally, Carberry's 'hurry-up' hand gestures to Jim Culloty on the runner-up earned him a caution from the stewards that such antics 'would not be tolerated in future.'

Carberry kept the ride on Beef Or Salmon for his two remaining races. The partnership was maintained for the Hennessy Cognac Gold Cup back at Leopardstown in February, in anticipation that Murphy would also be unavailable at Cheltenham. Beef Or Salmon looked to have a second Hennessy at his mercy in the absence of Kicking King and he held main rivals Pizarro and Rule Supreme on Lexus form, but his in-and-out season took another turn for the worse. Even before he was hampered by Pizarro's fall five out, Beef Or Salmon did not look to be going quite so well as Rule Supreme, and a mistake at the last sealed his fate, Beef Or Salmon crossing the line fourteen lengths behind the winner. Carberry reported afterwards that Beef Or Salmon had gurgled during the race, and he was subsequently found to be suffering from a respiratory infection, though a scope in early-March gave him the all-clear to take his chance at Cheltenham. When galloping-companion Arteea gave the Hourigan stable only its second winner since the turn of the year (and its first placed horse since the Hennessy) five days before the Gold Cup, Beef Or Salmon was promoted to favouritism with some firms as other leading contenders fell by the wayside. Beef Or Salmon was not seen out again after Cheltenham (a post-race scope revealing an infection) but will presumably have races like the Lexus and Hennessy as main targets again in 2005/6.

Beef Or Salmon (IRE) (ch.g. 1996)	Cajetano (USA) (b 1986)	Run The Gantlet (b 1968)	Tom Rolfe
			First Feather
		Intensive (1979)	Sir Wiggle
			Flying Legs
	Farinella (IRE) (ch 1988)	Salmon Leap (ch 1980)	Northern Dancer
			Fish-Bar
		Boldella (b 1977)	Bold Lad
			Ardelle

Beef Or Salmon may well prove to be the only winner out of his once-raced dam Farinella who died in 2000. His dam's final foal, a mare by Saddlers' Hall, is now a five-year-old and has been named Dining Hall, though she has never raced. Further details of Beef Or Salmon's pedigree have appeared in previous Annuals. A strong gelding, he stays three and a quarter miles, though doesn't need that much of a test, the shorter distance not being a reason for his poor showing at Punchestown in December. Indeed, Beef Or Salmon has two wins in the two-mile Hilly Way Chase to his name, the second gained from Rathgar Beau. He has still to race on ground firmer than good. Beef Or Salmon's jumping technique is more likely to result in his losing ground at his fences, rather than actually falling, and while that might not be too serious a flaw in a steadily-run race with a small field, in a race like the Cheltenham Gold Cup Beef Or Salmon's lack of fluency is a much more serious handicap. On his day, an in-form Beef Or Salmon is still a top-class chaser with a good turn of foot. His days as Ireland's main Gold Cup hope, however, now look to be behind him. *M. Hourigan, Ireland*

BEEFY NOVA 13 ch.g. Ra Nova – Cherry Sip (Nearly A Hand) [2004/5 c75, h–: c20v^{pu} c21s^{pu} Jan 3] workmanlike gelding: poor handicap chaser: no show in 2004/5: stays 3m: acts on good to firm and heavy going. *G. H. Yardley* **c–** **h–**

BEEHAWK 6 b.g. Gunner B – Cupids Bower (Owen Dudley) [2004/5 19d 17v^{3} 17g 24d^{ur} Apr 20] rangy gelding: will make a chaser: brother to one-time useful but irresolute chaser Irbee, stays 3¼m, and half-brother to modest chaser Kingsmoor (by Regal Embers), stays 2½m: dam, winning hurdler, stayed 25f: runner-up on second of 2 outings in maiden points in 2004: tongue tied, much improved form in conditional jockeys novice handicap hurdle at Worcester final start, travelling strongly and 8 lengths clear when stumbling and unseating last: stays 3m. *P. F. Nicholls* **h102**

BEET DE BOB (IRE) 7 b. or br.g. Bob Back (USA) – Beet Statement (IRE) (Strong Statement (USA)) [2004/5 24m^{5} Apr 10] first foal: dam, winning chaser up to 21f, half-sister to fairly useful chaser up to 3m River Cora: winning Irish pointer: bought 20,000 gns Doncaster August Sales: fifth in novice at Worcester on hurdling debut. *Mrs S. E. Busby* **h79**

BE FAIR 7 br.g. Blushing Flame (USA) – Tokyo (Mtoto) [2004/5 h122: 20g^{4} c16d^{2} Oct 31] well-made gelding: fairly useful novice hurdler in 2003/4: promising second to Almaydan in maiden at Huntingdon on chasing debut: stays 21f: unraced on extremes of going: has awkward head carriage. *D. E. Cantillon* **c114 p** **h122**

BEHAVINGBADLY (IRE) 10 b.g. Lord Americo – Audrey's Turn (Strong Gale) [2004/5 c105x, h–: c22v c28s* c30v^{4} c24v^{4} c25v^{pu} c29s^{4} c28s^{3} c31s Apr 22] good-topped gelding: winning hurdler: fair handicap chaser: won 5-runner event at Kelso in November: stays 31f: raced on good going or softer (acts on heavy): usually let down by jumping over fences. *A. Parker* **c103 x** **h–**

BEKSTAR 10 b.m. Nicholas Bill – Murex (Royalty) [2004/5 h–: 22g^{6} 22m^{5} 22f* 24g^{6} 18s* Nov 5] lengthy, rather sparely-made mare: poor hurdler: won handicap at Wincanton in October and minor event at Fontwell (awarded race on technical grounds) in November: probably best short of 3m: acts on firm and soft going. *J. C. Tuck* **h79**

BELCARO (GER) 6 b.g. Dashing Blade – Bella Carolina (GER) (Surumu (GER)) [2004/5 h96: 17g^{5} 16m^{6} 17g^{pu} 17g^{4} 18m^{4} Aug 19] rather leggy gelding: modest hurdler: **h92**

raced around 2m on good/good to firm going: blinkered third outing (folded tamely). *C. J. Mann*

BELISARIO (IRE) 11 b. or br.g. Distinctly North (USA) – Bold Kate (Bold Lad (IRE)) [2004/5 c122, h–: c20s^{F} c24v^{F} Dec 30] big, leggy gelding: fairly useful handicap chaser, won only start in 2003/4: failed to complete in 2004/5: stays 3m: acts on heavy and good to firm going. *M. W. Easterby* **c– h–**

BELISCO (USA) 4 b.g. Royal Academy (USA) – A Mean Fit (USA) (Fit To Fight (USA)) [2004/5 19m^{pu} Apr 23] modest up to 1¼m on Flat (often wears headgear/tongue strap): jumped poorly on hurdling debut. *C. A. Dwyer* **h–**

BELLA MARY 10 b.m. Derrylin – Pro-Token (Proverb) [2004/5 c70, h63: c26d^{3} c21g^{3} c22g^{ro} 22m 26m^{4} Jul 2] workmanlike mare: poor maiden hurdler/chaser: stays 3¼m: acts on soft going, probably on good to firm. *C. T. Pogson* **c78 h59**

BELLANEY JEWEL (IRE) 6 gr.m. Roselier (FR) – Sister of Gold (The Parson) [2004/5 F16g^{6} 24s* Apr 10] rather leggy mare: seventh foal: half-sister to modest chaser Twotensforafive (by Arctic Lord), stays 3m, and modest hurdler/winning chaser Cardinal Mark (by Ardross), stays 3¼m: dam unraced sister to useful hurdler Book of Gold, stayed 2½m: won completed start in maiden Irish points in 2004: sixth of 14 in bumper: upped markedly in trip, won novice at Hexham on hurdling debut: will prove suited by test of stamina. *J. J. Quinn* **h101 F70**

BELLAPORT GIRL 7 b.m. Supreme Leader – Derry Nell (Derrylin) [2004/5 F–: F16s 20d 26s^{pu} Jan 5] leggy mare: no form in bumpers or over hurdles: sold £1,250 Ascot April Sales. *Dr J. R. J. Naylor* **h– F–**

BELL LANE (IRE) 5 ch.g. Wakashan – Demoiselle (Midyan (USA)) [2004/5 F17g Jul 12] second foal: half-brother to 5f winner Pat The Builder (by Common Grounds): dam ran twice: failed to stay in bumper on debut. *B. G. Powell* **F–**

BEL OMBRE (FR) 5 b.g. Nikos – Danse du Soleil (FR) (Morespeed) [2004/5 F–: F17d^{5} 16g 16d 16d^{ur} Feb 12] good-topped gelding: no form in 2 bumpers: not a factor in above-average novice company over hurdles. *O. Sherwood* **h93 F–**

BELSKI 12 br.g. Arctic Lord – Bellekino (Relkino) [2004/5 c105: c24g^{5} c31d c26d^{4} c25d^{4} c23s^{4} c25s^{pu} c24s^{pu} Mar 23] tall gelding: veteran chaser: should stay beyond 25f: unraced on firm going, acts on any other: visored final outing. *C. L. Tizzard* **c89**

BELTANE 7 b.g. Magic Ring (IRE) – Sally's Trust (IRE) (Classic Secret (USA)) [2004/5 19s^{pu} Mar 7] modest and unreliable on Flat (stays 1m), successful early in 2004: no show in novice hurdle. *W. de Best-Turner* **h–**

BELTER 5 b.g. Terimon – Bellinote (FR) (Noir Et Or) [2004/5 F16d F16g^{6} F17s^{6} Feb 7] compact gelding: half-brother to 1¼m winner Patrita Park (by Flying Tyke): dam maiden half-sister to smart 1981 French 2-y-o stayer Beau Pretender: poor form in bumpers. *N. Wilson* **F68**

BELUGA (IRE) 6 gr.g. John French – Mesena (Pals Passage) [2004/5 F85: F16d^{4} F18g^{4} Oct 18] good-topped gelding: modest form at best in bumpers. *M. Pitman* **F74**

BELVENTO (IRE) 13 b.g. Strong Gale – Salufair (Salluceva) [2004/5 c99§, h–: c25m^{2} May 19] good sort: fair pointer/hunter chaser: won point in April: stays 3¼m: best efforts on good/good to firm ground: inconsistent. *Miss Rachel Deakin* **c95 § h–**

BE MERRY (IRE) 6 ch.m. Broken Hearted – Charlies Rising (IRE) (Rising) [2004/5 F83: F16v F16s^{4} F16v 16s^{pu} Mar 11] small mare: signs of only a little ability in bumpers: looked temperamental on hurdling debut. *I. A. Gault, Ireland* **h– F73**

BE MY BETTER HALF (IRE) 10 b.g. Be My Native (USA) – The Mrs (Mandalus) [2004/5 c114, h–: c20d^{2} c20s^{2} c20v* c24s^{pu} c21d Apr 8] big, workmanlike gelding: fairly useful chaser: won handicap at Limerick in December: little impact in much more competitive events after: stays 2¾m: acts on heavy going: front runner. *A. L. T. Moore, Ireland* **c126 h–**

BE MY DREAM (IRE) 10 b.g. Be My Native (USA) – Dream Toi (Carlburg) [2004/5 c91, h–: c24s^{3} Mar 27] tall gelding: winning pointer, including in 2005: fair hunter chaser: suited by 3m+: acts on heavy going: tried in visor/cheekpieces. *Ms C. Steele* **c99 h–**

BE MY FRIEND (IRE) 9 ch.g. Be My Native (USA) – Miss Lamb (Relkino) [2004/5 c–, h–: 17g^{pu} Apr 30] winning hurdler: won point in March. *Mrs H. Dalton* **c– h–**

BE MY MANAGER (IRE) 10 b.g. Be My Native (USA) – Fahy Quay (Quayside) [2004/5 c136, h–: c24s^{pu} c24v^{5} c24g^{6} c22d^{pu} Feb 3] tall gelding: useful handicap chaser **c– h–**

in 2003/4, out of form in 2004/5: stays 3m: acts on any going: tried in cheekpieces/ blinkers: reportedly difficult to train. *M. Todhunter*

BE MY ROYAL (IRE) 11 b.g. Be My Native (USA) – Royal Rehearsal (Pamroy) [2004/5 24s^3 c29v^F c25v^5 c22v^{pu} c24d Mar 5] tall gelding: useful hurdler/chaser at one time for W. Mullins, suffered serious tendon injury when first past post in Hennessy Gold Cup at Newbury (subsequently disqualified) final start in 2002/3: well held on completed outings over fences in 2004/5: best at 3m+: raced on good going or softer over jumps (acts on heavy): makes mistakes over fences. *T. R. George* **c110 x** **h123**

BE MY VALENTINE (IRE) 7 b.m. Be My Native (USA) – Valantonia (IRE) (Over The River (FR)) [2004/5 h–, F81: 20g^2 Jun 10] neat mare: modest form in 2 bumpers: better effort over hurdles on only start in 2004/5. *C. R. Egerton* **h83**

BEN BELLESHOT 6 gr.g. Vague Shot – Ballygriffin Belle (Another Realm) [2004/5 F18d F16s Mar 6] £1,800 5-y-o: sturdy gelding: second foal: half-brother to fair 7f winner Ballygriffin Kid (by Komaite): dam ran 3 times: no form in bumpers. *P. W. Hiatt* **F–**

BENBOW 8 ch.g. Gunner B – Juno Away (Strong Gale) [2004/5 h–: c24d^{ur} May 15] maiden jumper, including in points. *G. L. Edwards* **c–** **h–**

BEN BRITTEN 6 ch.g. Sabrehill (USA) – Golden Panda (Music Boy) [2004/5 h–: 16d 16s^6 16v Dec 27] workmanlike gelding: best effort in novice hurdles when sixth at Kelso. *N. G. Richards* **h84**

BENBYAS 8 b.g. Rambo Dancer (CAN) – Light The Way (Nicholas Bill) [2004/5 h139: c16v^{ur} c16v^{pu} Jan 10] medium-sized gelding: useful handicap hurdler in 2003/4: off 8 months (reportedly suffered from knee trouble and a bout of laminitis), failed to complete both outings over fences (lost action second time): best around 2m: raced mainly on good going or softer (acts on heavy): usually forces pace: superb jumper of hurdles: most genuine. *D. Carroll* **c–** **h–**

BENEFIT 11 b.g. Primitive Rising (USA) – Sobriquet (Roan Rocket) [2004/5 c72, h84: c23d^2 c25g* c23m^2 c25g^2 c25d^2 c27d^4 c27d^4 c26d^{pu} 24d c24g* c24d^2 c24d^6 c25g c25s^3 c25m* Apr 23] small, lengthy gelding: winning hurdler: poor chaser: won novice handicaps at Hexham in May, Fakenham in January and Market Rasen in April: stays 25f: unraced on firm going, acts on any other: wore cheekpieces (none too keen) eighth outing. *Miss L. C. Siddall* **c84** **h–**

BENEKING 5 b. or br.g. Wizard King – Gagajulu (Al Hareb (USA)) [2004/5 17d Nov 30] modest maiden on Flat (barely stays 1¼m), sold out of R. Hollinshead's stable 3,000 gns Doncaster October Sales: well beaten in novice on hurdling debut, far from fluent. *P. Bowen* **h–**

BEN FROM KETTON 10 b.g. Cruise Missile – Saucy Girl (Saucy Kit) [2004/5 c–: c27g* May 25] fair pointer, successful in March: first form in 3 hunter chases when winning at Sedgefield: stays 27f. *S. J. Robinson* **c96**

BENGAL BULLET 8 b.g. Infantry – Indian Cruise (Cruise Missile) [2004/5 c26g* c19g* c28g^{ur} c24d^F c25s^2 c19v^2 Mar 30] 1,400 5-y-o: second foal: dam, winning chaser, stayed 2¾m: useful hunter chaser: won novices at Newton Abbot and Exeter (simple task) very early in season: better form when twice second at Exeter in March: stays 3¼m: acts on heavy going. *C. Blank* **c113**

BENGO (IRE) 5 b.g. Beneficial – Goforroad (IRE) (Mister Lord (USA)) [2004/5 F16d 20v^3 21d* 20d^4 20d^2 Apr 22] rangy gelding: has plenty of scope: second foal: half-brother to 2½m bumper winner Ballysheedy (by Moscow Society): dam unraced, from family of smart 2m to 2½m chaser Leotard: fourth in 4-y-o maiden Irish point on debut: backward when well held in bumper: dead-heated with Il Duce in 17-runner novice at Newbury in March: similar form in frame all other starts over hurdles: will stay 3m: interesting chasing prospect. *B. De Haan* **h115** **F79**

BEN LOMAND 5 ch.g. Inchinor – Benjarong (Sharpo) [2004/5 16g Dec 8] sturdy gelding: fairly useful on Flat (best at 6f) at 3 yrs, well below best in 2004: broke blood vessel on hurdling debut (wore eyecover). *B. W. Duke* **h–**

BENNIE'S PRIDE (IRE) 9 b.g. Welsh Term – Mugs Away (Mugatpura) [2004/5 c120, h–: 24g 20d^3 24s^2 c24v c24v^F Jan 9] well-made gelding: fair handicap hurdler: fairly useful handicap chaser: stays 3m: acts on good to firm and heavy going: in cheekpieces final outing (fell third time last 7 starts over fences). *M. J. P. O'Brien, Ireland* **c121** **h106**

BENNY 4 b.g. New Frontier (IRE) – Drumkilly Lilly (IRE) (Executive Perk) [2004/5 F16s^2 F16m Apr 10] 1,700 3-y-o: second foal: dam unraced: better effort in bumpers when second to Calusa Charlie at Towcester. *R. H. York* **F85**

BENO (IRE) 6 b.g. Ridgewood Ben – Future Romance (Distant Relative) [2004/5 h–, F–: 20d^{pu} 18g^{5} 16m^{pu} Jun 5] angular gelding: no sign of ability. *Mrs H. O. Graham* **h–**

BENOVA BOY 13 ch.g. Ra Nova – Alithorne (Kinglet) [2004/5 c60: c24m^{3} c23m^{pu} c24g^{3} Jul 11] lengthy gelding: winning pointer: poor maiden chaser: stays 3m: usually wears headgear. *S. J. Gilmore* **c–**

BENRAJAH (IRE) 8 b.g. Lord Americo – Andy's Fancy (IRE) (Andretti) [2004/5 c112, h–: c22g^{2} c28g^{pu} c20d^{2} c20d^{pu} c20v^{3} c20d* c21d^{5} c25g^{2} c20d^{4} c20g* Apr 17] well-made gelding: fair handicap chaser: won at Newcastle in November and Stratford in April: effective at 2½m to 3¼m: second in bumper on soft going, raced mainly under less testing conditions (simple task on firm): usually races up with pace: genuine. *M. Todhunter* **c114 h–**

BENSON (IRE) 10 b. or br.g. Hawkstone (IRE) – Erin St Helen (IRE) (Seclude (USA)) [2004/5 c–, h–: c19m 21g May 9] workmanlike gelding: winning chaser/maiden hurdler: poor pointer nowadays: tried visored. *J. W. Mullins* **c– h–**

BEN'S REVENGE 5 b.g. Emperor Jones (USA) – Bumble Boogie (IRE) (Bluebird (USA)) [2004/5 F16d F17g F17m F16d Jun 23] 2,400Y, 1,200 3-y-o: second foal: half-brother to 1¼m winner Limbo Lad (by Millkom): dam unraced, from family of very smart stayer Persian Punch: well held in bumpers: poor on Flat. *M. Wellings* **F–**

BEN THE BRAVE (IRE) 6 b.g. Ridgewood Ben – Shoot The Dealer (IRE) (Common Grounds) [2004/5 F16v F16g Jan 24] €9,000 3-y-o, €15,500 4-y-o: fourth foal: dam modest 5f winner: tailed off in bumpers: sold £1,300 Ascot February Sales. *Mrs A. M. Thorpe* **F–**

BENTYHEATH LANE 8 b.g. Puissance – Eye Sight (Roscoe Blake) [2004/5 c–, h71: 16g 16g c17m^{ur} c17g^{6} c21m^{pu} 16g 16d c20d^{6} Apr 20] lengthy, angular gelding: no longer of any account: tried in cheekpieces. *M. Mullineaux* **c– h–**

BENVOLIO 8 br.g. Cidrax (FR) – Miss Capulet (Commanche Run) [2004/5 c–, h–: c20g c21d^{4} c20g c16s^{pu} Oct 29] smallish gelding: of little account: tried in headgear: dead. *I. W. McInnes* **c– h–**

BE OFF WITH YOU 6 b.m. Nalchik (USA) – Tilstock Maid (Rolfe (USA)) [2004/5 F–: F17g 21g Nov 11] well beaten in bumpers and maiden hurdle. *B. R. Foster* **h– F–**

BE POSITIVE 5 b.g. Petoski – Go Positive (Profilic) [2004/5 F16v F16d^{6} Apr 20] rather unfurnished gelding: first foal: dam modest maiden who stayed 1½m: better effort in bumpers when never-nearer sixth of 17 at Worcester. *C. J. Down* **F83**

BERENGARIO (IRE) 5 b.g. Mark of Esteem (IRE) – Ivrea (Sadler's Wells (USA)) [2004/5 h67, F–: 17g^{4} 16f^{3} 16g* 16d^{4} 16g* 21g 16s^{3} 20s 19s 16d^{2} 16d^{4} Apr 3] unfurnished gelding: fair handicap hurdler: won at Wincanton in October and November (novice): best other efforts at same course: best around 2m: acts on soft going: tried blinkered: has carried head awkwardly. *S. C. Burrough* **h105**

BERGAMO 9 b.g. Robellino (USA) – Pretty Thing (Star Appeal) [2004/5 h95§: 21g^{2} 22d^{2} 21g^{5} 24f 17d 24m^{3} 25g^{4} 25g^{4} Dec 28] small gelding: modest handicap hurdler: stays easy 3m: acts on soft and good to firm going: wears headgear: irresolute. *B. Ellison* **h95 §**

BERGERAC (NZ) 7 b.g. Just A Dancer (NZ) – Guiding Star (NZ) (Star Wolf) [2004/5 13d^{ur} 16d^{5} Feb 3] runner-up 3 times up to around 1¼m from 10 starts on Flat in New Zealand: unseated on hurdling debut there: patiently ridden and kept on not unduly knocked about when fifth to Seeyaaj in novice at Kelso on British debut: will do better. *R. C. Guest* **h80 p**

BERING GIFTS (IRE) 10 b.g. Bering – Bobbysoxer (Valiyar) [2004/5 c–§, h–§: c26m May 19] workmanlike gelding: winning hurdler/pointer: maiden chaser: stays easy 21f: acts on firm going: needs waiting tactics: temperamental. *Mrs T. J. Hill* **c– § h– §**

BERKELEY HEIGHTS 5 b.m. Hector Protector (USA) – Dancing Heights (IRE) (High Estate) [2004/5 17s^{5} 24s^{F} Apr 16] poor on Flat (seems to stay 2m): well beaten on completed start over hurdles: tried in cheekpieces. *Mrs J. Candlish* **h–**

BERKLEY (IRE) 8 b.g. Arctic Lord – Coach Road (Brave Invader (USA)) [2004/5 c25g^{6} c20d* c25f^{2} c23m^{4} c22m c24s c18d c22d^{2} c24s* c24v^{2} c25v^{3} c28v^{6} c22v^{2} c28d^{2} c25s^{5} c24v* Apr 10] compact gelding: fair handicap chaser: won at Kilbeggan in May, Thurles in November and Limerick in April: stays 3½m: acts on any going: blinkered: usually races prominently: tough and consistent. *P. Verling, Ireland* **c110 h–**

BERNARDON (GER) 9 b.g. Suave Dancer (USA) – Bejaria (GER) (Konigsstuhl (GER)) [2004/5 h118: c17m* c16g^{4} c16g^{pu} c16m^{2} c16d^{2} c17m* 16g^{pu} 17d 17d c17d^{3} **c117 d h108 §**

c16d^{6} c16d^{5} 17s^{2} c22s^{pu} c16d^{F} c16s^{pu} 16v^{6} c21d^{5} c20d^{6} 19m Apr 17] close-coupled gelding: fairly useful hurdler in 2003/4: similar form over fences in early part of 2004/5, winning novice at Kelso and handicap at Southwell: deteriorated markedly after, sold out of R. C. Guest's stable 2,800 gns Doncaster October Sales after twelfth start: raced mainly around 2m: acts on soft and good to firm going: tried visored, usually wears cheekpieces nowadays: takes good hold, and usually held up: one to treat with caution. *A. J. Deakin*

BERNINI (IRE) 5 b.g. Grand Lodge (USA) – Alsahah (IRE) (Unfuwain (USA)) [2004/5 h102: 16d^{pu} 19g 16d c16s^{2} c20d^{pu} c16s^{6} 19d Mar 4] good-topped gelding: disappointing maiden hurdler: form over fences only when second in novice handicap at Hereford: should stay beyond 2m: acts on soft going: tried blinkered. *N. J. Henderson* **c89 h–**

BERRYWHITE (IRE) 7 ch.g. Barathea (IRE) – Berryville (USA) (Hatchet Man (USA)) [2004/5 h–: 16s 23d^{pu} Nov 13] stocky gelding: poor form on Flat in Britain in 2004: no form over hurdles. *C. Grant* **h–**

BERTIE ARMS 5 gr.m. Cloudings (IRE) – Pugilistic (Hard Fought) [2004/5 F–: F17g^{6} F16g 19g 16d 16g^{6} 16s 19g Mar 9] sturdy mare: well held in bumpers and over hurdles. *J. M. Jefferson* **h– F–**

BERTIE O'TOOLE 11 b.g. Jendali (USA) – Young Mary (Young Generation) [2004/5 c–, h–: c21g^{pu} c25g^{pu} May 20] no form outside points: tongue tied: poor jumper. *Mrs R. L. Elliot* **c– x h–**

BERTOCELLI 4 ch.g. Vettori (IRE) – Dame Jude (Dilum (USA)) [2004/5 16d 16g Jan 24] plain gelding: modest on Flat (stays 1¼m): showed little in 2 starts over hurdles. *G. G. Margarson* **h–**

BESEIGED (USA) 8 ch.g. Cadeaux Genereux – Munnaya (USA) (Nijinsky (CAN)) [2004/5 h107: 17s 16d^{2} 20s^{5} 16d 17g 16m^{6} 16d Mar 14] workmanlike gelding: fair handicap hurdler: easily best effort in 2004/5 on second outing: stays 19f, at least when conditions aren't testing: acts on good to firm and good to soft going. *R. A. Fahey* **h113**

BEST ACCOLADE 6 b.g. Oscar (IRE) – Made of Talent (Supreme Leader) [2004/5 F16v^{3} Jan 10] first foal: dam winning pointer: won both starts in points in 2004: shaped like a stayer when third of 6 in bumper at Newcastle. *J. Howard Johnson* **F87**

BEST ACTOR (IRE) 6 b.g. Oscar (IRE) – Supreme Princess (IRE) (Supreme Leader) [2004/5 F17d* F16d Dec 29] good-topped gelding: chasing type: first foal: dam unraced: looked useful prospect when winning bumper at Folkestone on debut by 21 lengths from Jackie Boy: ran as if amiss in Grade 2 at Newbury following month. *M. Pitman* **F102**

BESTAM 6 b.g. Selkirk (USA) – Showery (Rainbow Quest (USA)) [2004/5 16d 16s^{2} 16d^{3} 16g Mar 5] leggy gelding: useful winner over 1m at 2/3 yrs, well beaten in 3 races on Flat in UAE at 4 yrs for D. Watson: modest form at best in novice hurdles: likely to prove best over sharp 2m: has taken strong hold. *G. C. Bravery* **h90**

BEST CHINA (IRE) 5 b.g. West China – Knights Pleasure (IRE) (Gallant Knight) [2004/5 F18s F16v c27v^{5} c20s c25s^{4} Mar 11] €5,800 3-y-o: second foal: dam, winning pointer, half-sister to useful staying chaser Howyanow: won maiden point in 2004: well beaten in bumpers/maiden chases. *Liam Lennon, Ireland* **c– F–**

BEST FLIGHT 5 gr.g. Sheikh Albadou – Bustling Nelly (Bustino) [2004/5 20m^{2} 20g^{4} 16g^{3} Feb 27] half-brother to several winners, including fair 2m hurdler Borora (by Shareef Dancer) and fairly useful hurdler/chaser Silk Degrees (by Dunbeath), stayed 3m: fair on Flat (stays 1¼m), sold out of B. Hills's stable 16,500 gns Newmarket Autumn Sales: modest form when placed in maiden hurdles: may prove best short of 2½m. *N. Wilson* **h91**

BEST MATE (IRE) 10 b.g. Un Desperado (FR) – Katday (FR) (Miller's Mate) [2004/5 c176+, h–: c23d* c24v^{2} Dec 28] **c165 + h–**

There was no fourth Cheltenham Gold Cup success for Best Mate. 'At eight thirty yesterday morning all our dreams were destroyed in a mere handful of gallop strides . . . My husband Terry and I watched in utter dismay as our champion faltered on the beautiful downland turf . . . A terrible numb feeling came over me . . . The shock to the system was indescribable.' On the Thursday before the Cheltenham Festival, in the final stages of his preparation for the blue riband of steeplechasing, Best Mate burst a blood vessel. His trainer Henrietta Knight, who again contributed a column to *The Daily Telegraph*, painted a vivid picture of what happened: 'His rider, his devoted lass Jackie Jenner sensed immediately something was wrong and allowed him to stop. We were with her in a flash . . . Her face was etched with agony . . . There were flecks of blood on her clothes and Matey's nostrils were ominously red.' Later in the column, the trainer managed to view things more phlegmatically, looking forward to Best Mate's return in the autumn, and other members of the team took a similar line. Rider Jim Culloty, in his column in *The Guardian*, said: 'It could have been a lot worse, after all.' Meanwhile owner Jim Lewis, interviewed on At The Races, put matters in a proper perspective: 'I have had people coming in here crying their eyes out. You would think it was a disaster, well it isn't a disaster, a tsunami is a disaster.' The *Racing Post* was in the happy position of being able to provide a dramatic eye-witness account by their photographer Edward Whitaker. Elsewhere, Greg Wood in *The Guardian* was among those journalists to seek medical advice. Under an article headlined 'Broken blood vessel need not spell end says Club vet', Wood quoted not only Peter Webbon, the Jockey Club veterinary director, but also Dr David Martin, head of physiology at the Animal Health Trust. Others looked at what Best Mate's non-appearance would mean to the Gold Cup itself. *The Independent*, for example, carried the headline: 'Whoever wins will feel they won because he was not there.' It was obviously not felt necessary to state who he was.

The sense that Best Mate had some automatic right to win the Cheltenham Gold Cup, because he had won the race in the three previous seasons, was all too apparent in the coverage but, while it would be absurd to suggest the race was not the poorer for his absence, there are clear grounds for thinking that even Best Mate at the top of his game might have had his work cut out to cope with Kicking King. Three appearances in 2004 had not seen Best Mate perform to anything like his best. The first of those had been his third Gold Cup, when, in contrast to the easy victories of the two preceding years, Best Mate had had to work quite hard to beat Sir Rembrandt and Harbour Pilot. Best Mate's 2004/5 campaign began in the William Hill Chase at Exeter in November, in a race put on as a one-off, specially as a warm-up for him, over a little short of three miles. The presence of Best Mate certainly drew the crowds to Exeter that Friday and the BBC showed it during

William Hill Chase, Exeter—
substitute jockey Timmy Murphy takes over the reins for Best Mate's sole win of 2004/5

There was no Cheltenham roar for Best Mate (pictured at home earlier in the season with Edredon Bleu); an infection prevented a bid for a fourth Gold Cup

coverage from Windsor the same afternoon, though whether the race should have been staged at all is arguable. Leaving that aside, Best Mate appeared to have one meaningful opponent in Sir Rembrandt, with Seebald and the long-absent Frenchman's Creek seemingly making up the numbers. When Sir Rembrandt turned in a dismal performance, it looked as if Best Mate could win as his rider Timmy Murphy liked and his aim seemed to be to get home first with as little exertion as possible. In the end, however, Best Mate was forced to work hard, much harder than might have been expected, given that he looked pretty fit beforehand, to see off Seebald by a short head after the pace picked up only at the second last. Murphy, incidentally, was on board as Culloty was sidelined with an injured thumb. Murphy was given the nod ahead of Tony McCoy, who rode Best Mate to beat Marlborough in the 2002 King George. Knight has written: 'To me, Tony McCoy is not the ideal jockey for Best Mate and never will be.'

This was a performance well short of Best Mate's best. In his defence the Exeter race was effectively a glorified schooling session and clearly not an event on which to base a judgement on how good Best Mate was, or might still be. The trouble is, neither was his only subsequent appearance, in the Lexus Chase at Leopardstown just after Christmas. As in the previous year, connections gave the King George VI Chase at Kempton a miss in favour of the slightly less valuable and less prestigious Grade 1 two days later. In 2003, Best Mate had put up a most impressive performance in defeating Le Coudray in what was then the Ericsson Chase, connections also landing the King George with Edredon Bleu. In 2004, Best Mate was comprehensively defeated by Beef Or Salmon, unable to quicken two out (after the winner had had first run) in a steadily-run race on particularly testing ground. The conditions at Leopardstown offered a valid excuse for Best Mate's substandard effort and a further one was forthcoming when it emerged that Best Mate had cut himself on the journey to Ireland ('sustained a nasty gash to his head during a nightmare crossing' were his trainer's words), but it was doubtful—especially in the light of Kicking King's top-class performance in the King George—whether Best Mate still deserved to hold his position as Gold Cup favourite. Best Mate was reported to be coughing shortly afterwards, though he would not, in any case, have run between Leopardstown and Cheltenham, nor would he in all likelihood have run after Cheltenham, even without his bursting a blood vessel. A season cut short.

Best Mate (IRE) (b.g. 1995)	Un Desperado (FR) (b 1983)	Top Ville (b 1976)	High Top
			Sega Ville
		White Lightning (gr 1970)	Baldric II
			Rough Sea
	Katday (FR) (br 1987)	Miller's Mate (b 1982)	Mill Reef
			Primatie
		Kanara (b 1973)	Hauban
			Alika

As Peter Webbon suggested, Best Mate should return none the worse in the autumn. At one point Miss Knight hinted (teased, perhaps) that Best Mate might have his initial run of the campaign in the Hennessy at Newbury as he might no longer have to carry top weight, but that looks an unlikely prospect now with the advent of a new Grade 1 three-mile chase at Haydock in November, one which carries a massive bonus if the winner goes on to land the King George and Cheltenham Gold Cup. Haydock presumably is deemed a suitable course for Best Mate's requirements, even though his connections have not taken the opportunity in the past to take in the Edward Hanmer (a race lost to the calendar, along with the Tommy Whittle, as a result of the new chase). With the King George at Sandown rather than Kempton in 2005, connections may well forego a third trip to Leopardstown for Best Mate's second start. Then should come a delayed date with destiny at Cheltenham in March, though the Gold Cup hasn't been won by a horse aged over ten since What A Myth in 1969 (Tied Cottage, a twelve-year-old like What A Myth, was first past the post in 1980 but was disqualified). This all raises the tantalising prospect of three clashes between Best Mate and Kicking King. Tantalising, for after five seasons and fifteen races over fences, it is still not clear quite how good Best Mate is. Best Mate and Kicking King may well be the two best three-mile chasers since Desert Orchid. Tantalus, of course, never got hold of the fruit, but it is profoundly to be hoped that one of the three races at least will show just how good this pair of top-notch chasers really are. *Miss H. C. Knight*

BEST OF THE BLUES 5 b.g. Whittingham (IRE) – Gold And Blue (IRE) (Bluebird (USA)) [2004/5 F14m Mar 21] brother to several winners, including fair 6f to 9f winner Blue Star, and half-brother to 2 others: dam lightly-raced Irish maiden: well held in maiden bumper on debut, reportedly hanging left: modest form in maidens on Flat following month. *J. W. Unett* **F–**

BE TELLING (IRE) 6 b.g. Oscar (IRE) – Manhattan King (IRE) (King's Ride) [2004/5 16d Jan 26] third foal: dam unraced half-sister to fairly useful staying chaser Captain Brandy: won maiden Irish point on debut in January 2004: green, well beaten in novice at Huntingdon on hurdling debut: should do better. *B. J. Curley* **h– p**

BE THE TOPS (IRE) 7 br.g. Topanoora – Be The One (IRE) (Supreme Leader) [2004/5 c–§, h97§: c23d^{3} c26g^{F} c21m* c22g^{2} c23m* c24g^{3} Aug 14] winning hurdler: fair chaser: won handicaps at Southwell and Worcester in July: stays 3m: acts on good to firm and heavy going: wears headgear: has looked temperamental. *Jonjo O'Neill* **c106 § h– §**

BETTER DAYS (IRE) 9 b.g. Supreme Leader – Kilkilrun (Deep Run) [2004/5 c125, h–: c20g^{2} c20d^{pu} c19g^{4} c24g^{3} 19d^{5} 20d^{4} 20d^{5} c21d Apr 8] useful-looking gelding: fair handicap hurdler: fairly useful handicap chaser: stays 21f: acts on soft and good to firm going: usually front runner/races prominently. *Mrs S. J. Smith* **c129 h109**

BETTER MOMENT (IRE) 8 b.g. Turtle Island (IRE) – Snoozeandyoulose (IRE) (Scenic) [2004/5 c–§, h98§: 19v^{3} Apr 22] smallish gelding: modest hurdler: off 20 months before only outing in 2004/5: probably stays 19f: probably acts on any going: tried blinkered, visored nowadays: tried tongue tied: often looks none too keen. *M. C. Pipe* **c– § h88 §**

BETTERWARE BOY 5 ch.g. Barathea (IRE) – Crystal Drop (Cadeaux Genereux) [2004/5 h–: 17g 19m 16g^{6} 21g^{3} Dec 9] workmanlike gelding: maiden on Flat: left P. Phelan, first form over hurdles when third in amateur handicap at Ludlow: stays 21f. *A. P. Jones* **h76**

BEULAH 4 b.f. Perpendicular – Ewe Lamb (Free State) [2004/5 F12g F16m Apr 10] leggy filly: half-sister to winning 2¾m hurdler Romney (by Timeless Times): dam winning 2m hurdler: well held in bumpers. *Mrs P. Sly* **F–**

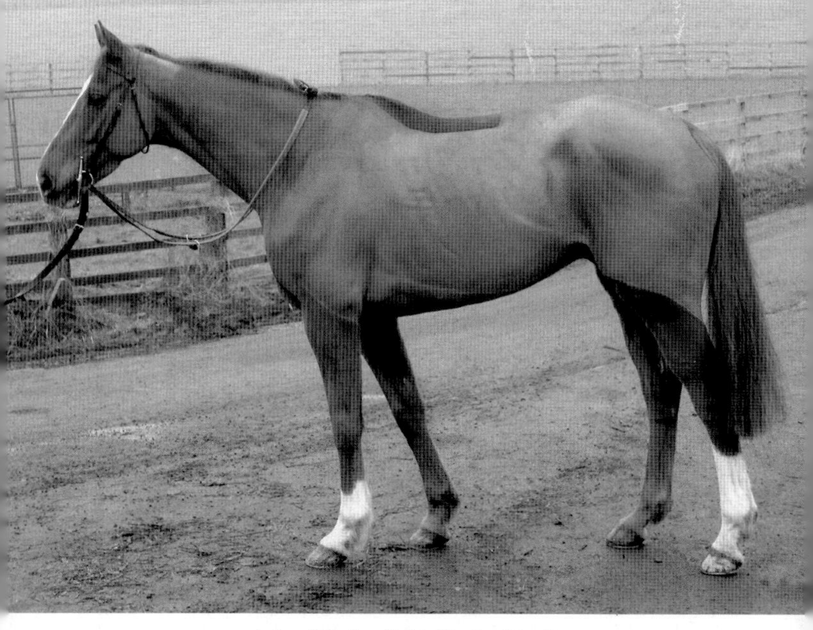

Andrea & Graham Wylie's "Bewleys Berry"

BE UPSTANDING 10 ch.g. Hubbly Bubbly (USA) – Two Travellers (Deep Run) [2004/5 c101§, h–: c28g^{4} c24m^{4} c24s^{pu} c26s^{pu} c20v^{4} c23d^{2} c25d^{2} c24d^{2} c25m^{5} c26v^{2} c31s^{4} Apr 22] big gelding: modest handicap chaser: trained third to fifth starts by N. Pomfret: stays 31f: acts on heavy going, probably on good to firm: sometimes wears headgear: often let down by jumping/temperament. *Ferdy Murphy* **c92 § h–**

BE WISE GIRL 4 ch.f. Fleetwood (IRE) – Zabelina (USA) (Diesis) [2004/5 16s 16v^{2} 16g^{5} 16d^{pu} 17d* Mar 26] modest on Flat (stays 1¼m), sold out of J. Given's stable 4,000 gns Doncaster November Sales: poor hurdler: won mares maiden at Newton Abbot in March, making most and getting back up after runner-up lost ground avoiding omitted final flight: raced around 2m: tends to flash tail. *A. W. Carroll* **h84**

BEWLEYS BERRY (IRE) 7 ch.g. Shernazar – Approach The Dawn (IRE) (Orchestra) [2004/5 F99P: 16v* 20v^{2} 24d* 24g^{F} 24d^{pu} Apr 8] lengthy, workmanlike gelding: chasing type: successful 3 times in Irish points: created good impression over hurdles when landing odds in novice at Hexham in December and Grade 2 River Don Novices' at Doncaster (beat Indy Mood easily by 10 lengths) in January: raced too freely final start: stays 3m: raced mainly on going softer than good. *J. Howard Johnson* **h129**

BEWLEYS GUEST (IRE) 6 b.g. Presenting – Pedigree Corner (Pollerton) [2004/5 F16d 24g^{pu} 19s^{pu} 17s^{6} 22g^{5} Apr 17] €15,000 3-y-o: half-brother to 3 winning pointers: dam, lightly raced in bumpers/points, half-sister to useful hurdler/chaser Mac's Chariot, stayed 25f: successful 3 times in Irish points, including twice in 2004: no form in bumper or over hurdles. *Miss Venetia Williams* **h– F–**

BEYOND BORDERS (USA) 7 b.g. Pleasant Colony (USA) – Welcome Proposal (Be My Guest (USA)) [2004/5 h90§: 20s 16d 16s^{4} 21d^{2} 22s^{2} 21d^{4} 19s^{ur} 19g^{3} 16s^{3} 16s 20g 16v^{3} 16v^{pu} 19s^{pu} Mar 10] compact gelding: modest maiden hurdler: stays 2¾m: probably acts on any going: usually wears blinkers/cheekpieces: ungenuine. *S. Gollings* **h85 §**

BEYOND THE PALE (IRE) 7 b.g. Be My Native (USA) – Cyrano Imperial (IRE) (Cyrano de Bergerac) [2004/5 16d^{F} 16d^{4} 16d 16d^{pu} Mar 5] tall, angular gelding: fair form **h105**

over hurdles, off nearly 2 years before reappearance: raced at 2m on good ground or softer. *Noel T. Chance*

BEYOND THE POLE (USA) 7 b.g. Ghazi (USA) – North of Sunset (USA) (Northern Baby (CAN)) [2004/5 h–: 18m^5 16g 16d^{pu} Apr 18] little form over hurdles: tried tongue tied. *B. R. Johnson* **h79**

BEYONDTHEREALM 7 b.g. Morpeth – Workamiracle (Teamwork) [2004/5 h93, F89: 22d^4 May 17] medium-sized gelding: winning pointer: modest form on first of 2 starts over hurdles: should stay beyond 2m. *J. D. Frost* **h–**

BEZWELL BLUE 6 ch.m. Bluebird (USA) – Willisa (Polar Falcon (USA)) [2004/5 F16f^5 Jun 6] little show in 2 bumpers. *Mrs J. C. McGregor* **F–**

BHAYDALKO (FR) 5 b.g. Kadalko (FR) – Bhaydana (Sassafras (FR)) [2004/5 F16m Apr 2] compact gelding: half-brother to several winners, including winning hurdler/chaser up to around 2½m Bellayana (by Nice Havrais) and 2m hurdler Dana Royale (by Garde Royale): dam won 3 times up to 1½m on Flat in France: twelfth of 21 in bumper at Newbury on debut. *Ms Bridget Nicholls* **F–**

BICKWELL 7 br.m. Afzal – Flying Cherub (Osiris) [2004/5 F16d F16v Feb 5] fifth foal: dam, fair 2m hurdler, sister to fairly useful staying chaser Flying God: well beaten in bumpers. *Mrs J. G. Retter* **F–**

BID FOR FAME (USA) 8 b. or br.g. Quest For Fame – Shroud (USA) (Vaguely Noble) [2004/5 h112: 19g^4 22s^5 21d^6 c20g Apr 3] leggy gelding: fair hurdler: never a factor in maiden on chasing debut: stays 21f: acts on good to firm and good to soft going: has jumped none too fluently. *C. G. Cox* **c–** **h101**

BID SPOTTER (IRE) 6 b.g. Eagle Eyed (USA) – Bebe Auction (IRE) (Auction Ring (USA)) [2004/5 h71: 16g* 21g 16m^3 16m 17m^{pu} 16g^{pu} 16s c20v^3 Jan 15] smallish, stocky gelding: poor hurdler: won handicap at Towcester very early in season: 17 lengths third of 4 finishers in novice at Wetherby on chasing debut: stays 2½m: acts on heavy and good to firm going: often runs as if amiss. *Mrs Lucinda Featherstone* **c90** **h74**

BIG BERTHA 7 ch.m. Dancing Spree (USA) – Bertrade (Homeboy) [2004/5 16d Nov 24] half-sister to winning 2½m hurdler Homestead (by Indian Ridge): fair on Flat (stays easy 2m), successful in January: soundly beaten in mares novice on hurdling debut. *John Berry* **h–**

BIG BONE (FR) 5 b.g. Zayyani – Bone Crasher (FR) (Cadoudal (FR)) [2004/5 F94: 16s^4 19g* 22s^3 19v 20s^5 Mar 23] lengthy gelding: fair form over hurdles, winning novice at Taunton in December: should stay beyond 19f. *P. J. Hobbs* **h108**

BIG E (IRE) 8 ch.g. Port Lucaya – Lucayan Sunshine (USA) (Sunshine Forever (USA)) [2004/5 20d^{pu} Jun 20] leggy gelding: showed nothing in 2 starts over hurdles nearly 4 years apart. *K. W. Hogg, Isle of Man* **h–**

BIG KING (IRE) 9 b.g. Phardante (FR) – La Maree (Tumble Wind) [2004/5 22m^5 20m^2 20f 20g* 20m 20g c23d* c20s^2 c24g* Nov 10] big, rangy gelding: brother to useful 2m hurdler Lady Arpel and half-brother to winning hurdlers by Barathea and Soviet Lad: dam maiden hurdler: fair hurdler: won maiden at Limerick in July: fairly useful form over fences, winning maiden at Downpatrick in October and novice handicap at Newbury in November: stays 3m: acts on soft and good to firm ground. *G. O'Leary, Ireland* **c119** **h102**

BIG LUGS 9 ch.g. Rakaposhi King – Winnowing (IRE) (Strong Gale) [2004/5 16s 16v 21s^{pu} Feb 7] compact gelding: no sign of ability. *J. S. Haldane* **h–**

BIG MAX 10 b.g. Rakaposhi King – Edwina's Dawn (Space King) [2004/5 c90, h98: c19d^4 c21d^{ur} c19s^6 c24s^5 24d 19s^6 Mar 7] well-made gelding: modest hurdler/maiden chaser: let down by jumping over fences in 2004/5: stays 3m: unraced on firm going, acts on any other. *Miss K. M. George* **c74 x** **h90**

BIG MOMENT 7 ch.g. Be My Guest (USA) – Petralona (USA) (Alleged (USA)) [2004/5 h147: 20s^2 20d^2 20d Feb 20] smallish gelding: useful on Flat (stays 18.7f): smart hurdler: good efforts first 2 starts, beaten 1½ lengths by Mistanoora in valuable handicap at Chepstow and 9 lengths by Westender in minor event at Cheltenham: favourite, ran poorly in Grade 2 at Fontwell: will stay 3m: raced on good going or softer (acts on heavy) over hurdles: has jumped none too fluently. *Mrs A. J. Perrett* **h149**

BIG QUICK (IRE) 10 ch.g. Glacial Storm (USA) – Furryvale (Furry Glen) [2004/5 h–: 22g Mar 20] modest handicap hurdler in 2002/3: ran poorly both subsequent starts 22 months apart: best at 3m+: unraced on heavy going, acts on any other. *L. Wells* **h–**

BIG ROB (IRE) 6 b.g. Bob Back (USA) – Native Shore (IRE) (Be My Native (USA)) [2004/5 h85, F87: 21s^{4} c18g* c16v* c16d^{2} c21g^{F} Mar 17] tall, good-topped gelding: modest novice hurdler: much better over fences, winning novice handicaps impressively at Newbury in November and Wetherby in January: fairly useful form when beating Caribbean Cove 11 lengths at latter: still travelling well when falling 4 out in valuable novice handicap won by King Harald at Cheltenham: will probably stay 3m: raced on good going or softer: remains open to improvement over fences. *B. G. Powell* **c121 p h88**

BIG SMOKE (IRE) 5 gr.g. Perugino (USA) – Lightning Bug (Prince Bee) [2004/5 h–: 16m 21m^{5} May 19] tailed off all starts over hurdles. *J. Howard Johnson* **h–**

BIG STAR (IRE) 8 ro.g. Fourstars Allstar (USA) – Dame Blakeney (IRE) (Blakeney) [2004/5 h–, F–: c17m^{ur} c21m^{6} c20g^{4} May 29] little sign of ability: tried tongue tied: sold 5,700 gns Doncaster August Sales. *M. A. Barnes* **c– h–**

BIG WHEEL 10 ch.g. Mujtahid (USA) – Numuthej (USA) (Nureyev (USA)) [2004/5 c–, h108: c16f^{F} c16m^{6} 17m^{4} Sep 28] angular gelding: lightly raced over fences: fair hurdler, well held final start: barely stays 21f: acts on firm and soft going: tried blinkered. *N. G. Richards* **c– h–**

BILL BROWN 7 b.g. North Briton – Dickies Girl (Saxon Farm) [2004/5 h–, F–: 16d^{3} 17v* 16d^{6} 16s^{5} Mar 13] leggy gelding: modest novice hurdler: won handicap at Hereford in February: should stay 2½m: acts on heavy going. *R. Dickin* **h86**

BILLIE JOHN (IRE) 10 ch.g. Boyne Valley – Lovestream (Sandy Creek) [2004/5 c108, h93: 16d^{5} c17m^{3} c16g^{4} c17m^{F} c16m* c17g* 16d^{pu} Oct 16] modest hurdler: fair handicap chaser: won at Uttoxeter (left in front 2 out) and Bangor in August: best around 2m: acts on firm going: takes strong hold: usually races prominently. *Mrs K. Walton* **c108 h93**

BILL ME UP (IRE) 9 b.g. Shardari – Little Credit (Little Buskins) [2004/5 c99, h–: c21d^{5} c21d^{2} c26g^{2} May 27] prolific winning pointer: maiden hunter chaser: should stay 3m+. *J. Heard* **c83 h–**

BILL OWEN 9 ch.g. Nicholas Bill – Pollys Owen (Master Owen) [2004/5 c80: c18m^{3} c16g^{4} c16g* c16g^{pu} c16g* c16g^{3} c19g* c21d^{3} c16g^{pu} Apr 17] medium-sized gelding: modest handicap chaser: won at Newton Abbot in July, Wincanton in October and Taunton in December: stays 19f: acts on firm going: wears cheekpieces/blinkers nowadays: front runner. *D. P. Keane* **c94**

BILL'S ECHO 6 br.g. Double Eclipse (IRE) – Bit On Edge (Henbit (USA)) [2004/5 c98, h97: c17g* c16d^{3} c17g* c16d^{5} c16s^{4} Nov 7] leggy gelding: modest maiden hurdler: fair handicap chaser: won at Bangor in April (novice) and October: barely stays 19f: acts on good to soft going: sometimes finds little. *R. C. Guest* **c111 h–**

BILLYANDI (IRE) 5 ch.g. Zaffaran (USA) – Top Dart (Whistling Top) [2004/5 F16s* F16s^{4} Mar 31] seventh foal: half-brother to winning pointer by Florida Son: dam of little account: fair form in bumpers, winning at Towcester on debut in March. *N. A. Twiston-Davies* **F85**

BILLY BALLBREAKER (IRE) 9 b.g. Good Thyne (USA) – Droichead Dhamhile (IRE) (The Parson) [2004/5 c–, h86: c22m^{6} Apr 21] leggy gelding: modest maiden hurdler: poor jumper and no form over fences: stays 3m: acts on soft going: has worn visor. *C. L. Tizzard* **c– h–**

BILLY BONNIE (IRE) 8 ch.g. Anshan – Sinology (Rainbow Quest (USA)) [2004/5 h116: 24g 24m* 22m^{5} Jul 31] medium-sized gelding: fairly useful handicap hurdler: successful at Navan in May: ran well at Galway next time: stays 3m: acts on good to firm and heavy going: blinkered last 2 outings: tried tongue tied: below form on Flat after final start. *N. Meade, Ireland* **h121**

BILLY COLEMAN (IRE) 7 b.g. Hollow Hand – Little Treat (Miner's Lamp) [2004/5 F16v 19s 17s Jan 10] lengthy gelding: fourth foal: half-brother to fair chaser Three Days Reign (by Camden Town), stays 3m, and useful pointer Evan's Collier Boy (by Supreme Leader): dam once-raced, from family of top-class staying chaser Carvill's Hill: fourth in maiden point in 2004: no form in bumper or novice hurdles. *D. Brace* **h– F–**

BILLY FLYNN (IRE) 4 b.g. General Monash (USA) – Word of Honor (FR) (Highest Honor (FR)) [2004/5 16g^{pu} Mar 16] poor maiden on Flat: breathing problem on hurdling debut. *Miss D. Mountain* **h–**

BILLY TWO RIVERS (IRE) 6 ch.g. Woodborough (USA) – Good Visibility (IRE) (Electric) [2004/5 h74: 16g^{5} 20d 20d^{2} 20d^{3} 24s* 24g^{2} 22m^{pu} Oct 3] poor hurdler: won weak conditional jockeys handicap at Perth in August: lame final start: stays 3m: acts on soft going: usually wears cheekpieces nowadays. *D. R. MacLeod* **h77**

BILLYVODDAN (IRE) 6 b.g. Accordion – Derryclare (Pollerton) [2004/5 h99, F92: 20d* 21d^2 20s^2 20v^3 19d* 20d^2 20d^4 Apr 9] strong, lengthy gelding: fairly useful novice hurdler: won at Uttoxeter in May and Doncaster in January: further improvement in valuable handicaps after, head second to Julius Caesar at Sandown (novice) and fourth to Genghis at Aintree: will stay 3m: acts on heavy going: genuine: type to do well over fences in 2005/6. *H. D. Daly* **h127**

BINDAREE (IRE) 11 ch.g. Roselier (FR) – Flowing Tide (Main Reef) [2004/5 c157, h–: c29v^5 c24v^6 c36d Apr 9] leggy gelding: very smart handicap chaser at best: won Grand National at Aintree in 2002 and Welsh National at Chepstow in 2003: form in 2004/5 only when 5½ lengths fifth to Silver Birch in latter race: stays 4½m: unraced on firm going, acts on any other: tried blinkered: usually jumps soundly. *N. A. Twiston-Davies* **c146 h–**

BINNY BAY 9 b.m. Karinga Bay – Binny Grove (Sunyboy) [2004/5 c77§, h–§: 20d^4 19m^{bd} 16g^6 22m 22g^{ur} 22m Sep 4] leggy mare: winning hurdler/chaser: little form in 2004/5: stays 21f: acts on good to firm and heavy going: tried blinkered: tongue tied: ungenuine. *D. McCain* **c– § h64 §**

BINT SESARO (IRE) 4 b.f. Sesaro (USA) – Crazed Rainbow (USA) (Graustark) [2004/5 F16g Feb 27] sixth foal: half-sister to modest stayer Flying Colours (by Fairy King): dam, ran once in France, half-sister to very smart miler King of Clubs: little show in bumper on debut. *Mrs L. B. Normile* **F–**

BINT ST JAMES 10 b.m. Shareef Dancer (USA) – St James's Antigua (IRE) (Law Society (USA)) [2004/5 h–: 20g^{pu} 19g^{pu} 17g Apr 3] angular mare: of little account nowadays: left W. Clay after reappearance: tried in visor. *J. T. Stimpson* **h–**

BIRCHALL (IRE) 6 b.g. Priolo (USA) – Ballycuirke (Taufan (USA)) [2004/5 16d^6 16s c16g 16s Mar 13] good-topped gelding: half-brother to fair hurdler Kildare Chiller (by Shahrastani), stayed 21f: modest on Flat (stays 1½m) at 4 yrs, generally below form in 2004: poor maiden hurdler: little show on chasing debut. *Ian Williams* **c– h84**

BIRDWATCH 7 b.g. Minshaanshu Amad (USA) – Eider (Niniski (USA)) [2004/5 h–p, F93: 20d^6 20s 20s 16v^5 24v^3 24v^{pu} 24s^{ur} Mar 11] sturdy gelding: clearly best effort over hurdles (modest form) when third in novice handicap at Ayr: better suited by 3m than shorter: raced on good ground or softer over hurdles. *K. G. Reveley* **h91**

BIRKWOOD 6 b.g. Presidium – Wire Lass (New Brig) [2004/5 c24g^{pu} Feb 16] 6,500 4-y-o: second foal: dam winning pointer: fair pointer, successful in January and February. *Ian Stark* **c–**

BIRTLEY BOY 6 ch.g. Le Moss – City Lighter (Lighter) [2004/5 F16g Sep 12] second foal: dam, of little account, out of useful chaser up to 3m Another City: well beaten in bumper on debut, hanging. *R. Johnson* **F–**

BISCAR TWO (IRE) 4 b.g. Daggers Drawn (USA) – Thoughtful Kate (Rock Hopper) [2004/5 16d^4 16d^3 16d^3 17d^4 16s^3 16v^2 17s^5 16s^4 17g Mar 18] leggy, angular gelding: modest on Flat (stays 1¼m), sold out of R. Whitaker's stable £5,200 Ascot August Sales: fairly useful juvenile hurdler: ran well when second to Phar Bleu in Grade 1 at Chepstow and fifth to Akilak in Grade 2 at Cheltenham, and when ninth of 23 to Penzance in Triumph Hurdle: will stay beyond 17f: raced on good going or softer (acts on heavy): blinkered last 5 outings: hard ride, usually soon off bridle. *B. J. Llewellyn* **h114**

BISCAY WIND (IRE) 5 ch.m. Anshan – La Bise (Callernish) [2004/5 F16d 20d Dec 9] €6,000 3-y-o: sparely-made mare: eleventh foal: half-sister to winning hurdler/fairly useful staying chaser Jultara (by Strong Statement): dam twice-raced in Irish points: no form in bumper or mares novice hurdle. *T. R. George* **h– F–**

BISHOP'S BLADE 8 b.g. Sure Blade (USA) – Myrtilla (Beldale Flutter (USA)) [2004/5 h–: 26m^{pu} 22g 27g^2 19g Aug 10] winning pointer: form over hurdles only when runner-up in handicap at Newton Abbot: tried blinkered. *E. Retter* **h71**

BISHOP'S BRIDGE (IRE) 7 b.g. Norwich – River Swell (IRE) (Over The River (FR)) [2004/5 F98: c16g^6 16g^4 19d^3 22s^5 21g^5 16m Apr 17] tall gelding: tailed off in novice on chasing debut: fair novice hurdler: stays 19f: tried in cheekpieces: has hung right/found little. *Andrew Turnell* **c– h107**

BISHOPS STRAND (IRE) 8 ch.g. Fourstars Allstar (USA) – Deep Captain (Deep Run) [2004/5 20d^{pu} Apr 25] IR 5,400 3-y-o: sturdy gelding: seventh foal: dam unraced **h–**

half-sister to useful 2½m chase winner Pin's Pride, out of sister to top-class chaser Captain Christy: no show in novice hurdle on debut. *O. Brennan*

BISON KING (IRE) 8 b.g. King's Ride – Valantonia (IRE) (Over The River (FR)) [2004/5 h105: 22d4 24g3 27dpu 24dpu Jan 12] big, rangy gelding: chasing type: fair hurdler: stays 3¼m: raced on good going or softer: tried blinkered (looked temperamental): usually races prominently: poor jumper. *C. R. Egerton* **h102 x**

BIT OF A GIFT 7 b.g. Henbit (USA) – Saxon Gift (Saxon Farm) [2004/5 F16m4 F16d2 F16v* Apr 17] good-bodied gelding: fifth foal: dam unraced: best effort in bumpers (useful form) when winning 20-runner event at the Curragh by 1½ lengths from Nicanor, staying on dourly: almost certainly hadn't recovered when well held in Grade 1 event at Punchestown 10 days later. *Thomas Mullins, Ireland* **F108**

BITOFAMIXUP (IRE) 14 br.g. Strong Gale – Geeaway (Gala Performance) [2004/5 c117d, h–: c24mpu May 16] tall, rangy gelding: veteran chaser: placed twice in points in 2005: stays 3½m: acts on firm and soft going: tried blinkered: often tongue tied. *M. J. Roberts* **c– h–**

BITTA DASH 5 ch.g. Bandmaster (USA) – Letitica (Deep Run) [2004/5 F16d Feb 19] 8,500 4-y-o: sturdy gelding: brother to unreliable hurdler/winning chaser Another Copper, stays 3¼m, and half-brother to 2 winners, including fairly useful hurdler/chaser Let's Be Frank (by Malaspina), stays 21f: dam of little account: well held in bumper on debut. *A. J. Wilson* **F–**

BIZET (IRE) 9 b.g. Zaffaran (USA) – Annie Sue VI (Snuff Matter) [2004/5 c16s6 c25v* c24v3 c18v* c21g Mar 17] workmanlike gelding: half-brother to fair staying chaser Woodlands Boy (by Hawaiian Return): dam won 4¼m hunter chase: fair hurdler: fairly useful chaser: much improved after leaving A. Martin after reappearance, winning handicap at Fairyhouse in January and minor event at Clonmel in February: better than ever when ½-length second to Livingstonebramble in novice at Punchestown in late-April: stays 25f: raced mainly on going softer than good: has worn tongue strap: sometimes let down by jumping. *F. Flood, Ireland* **c123 h–**

BLACK APALACHI (IRE) 6 b.g. Old Vic – Hattons Dream (IRE) (Be My Native (USA)) [2004/5 F96p: F16v2 F16v 18s* 24v3 18s6 20s* 21g 24d Apr 8] leggy, angular gelding: useful in bumpers: useful novice hurdler: won maiden at Downpatrick (by 20 lengths) in December and Grade 2 at Naas (beat Homer Wells 2 lengths) in February: much better effort in Grade 1 events after when eighth in Royal & SunAlliance Novices' Hurdle at Cheltenham: should stay beyond 21f: raced mainly on soft/heavy going. *P. J. Rothwell, Ireland* **h130 F106**

BLACKBERRY WAY 11 ch.m. Almoojid – Prickly Path (Royal Match) [2004/5 c91, h–: c21gpu c23d4 c24m3 c21vF Oct 29] tall mare: fair chaser: left Ms L. Cullen after second start: would have won handicap at Uttoxeter but for falling when clear 2 out: probably stays 25f: acts on heavy and good to firm going: has had tongue tied. *J. W. Mullins* **c104 h–**

BLACK BOB (IRE) 8 b.g. Good Thyne (USA) – Midsummer Blends (IRE) (Duky) [2004/5 h–: c20spu c25spu Mar 1] big, lengthy gelding: no sign of ability. *J. S. Haldane* **c– h–**

BLACK BULLET (NZ) 12 br.g. Silver Pistol (AUS) – Monte d'Oro (NZ) (Cache of Gold (USA)) [2004/5 c–, h–: c17s3 c16dpu c16g2 c17dpu c16s3 c16spu Apr 21] tall, angular gelding: fair handicap chaser: in-and-out form in 2004/5: stays 2½m: acts on good to firm and heavy going: races prominently. *Mrs J. Candlish* **c111 h–**

BLACK CHALK (IRE) 7 br.g. Roselier (FR) – Ann's Cap (IRE) (Cardinal Flower) [2004/5 20sF Mar 19] sixth foal: brother to winning hurdler/smart chaser Alcapone, stays 3m: dam unraced half-sister to dam of top-class chaser Carvill's Hill (by Roselier): no form over hurdles, though showed up well long way when well backed in novice handicap at Newcastle after 13-month absence, only start in 2004/5. *Bernard Jones, Ireland* **h–**

BLACKCHURCH MIST (IRE) 8 b.m. Erins Isle – Diandra (Shardari) [2004/5 c106, h109: 22g 22d 24f5 22mpu 20m4 22g 20m 21d5 19m 22m4 22g3 22f* 20d 20d6 22dpu c16d c21d 21g Jan 14] angular mare: winning chaser, usually let down by jumping: modest hurdler: won weak minor event at Wincanton in October: stays 2¾m: acts on firm and good to soft going: tried in cheekpieces: tongue tied. *B. W. Duke* **c– h94**

BLACK COLLAR 6 br.m. Bob's Return (IRE) – Rosemoss (Le Moss) [2004/5 F77: 16s Oct 24] won both starts in points in 2004: modest form in bumper for T. Walford: seventh of 15 in mares novice on hurdling debut, not knocked about: likely to be suited by further than 2m. *K. C. Bailey* **h77**

BLACK DOT COM (IRE) 9 br.m. Black Monday – Mile Tree (Kambalda) [2004/5 20v 22s^{6} 24s 24s* 24v c24s^{pu} Feb 10] won maiden Irish point in 2004: poor hurdler: best effort when winning conditional jockeys handicap at Thurles in January: jumped poorly on chasing debut: stays 3m: acts on soft going. *Mrs A. O'Connor, Ireland* **c–** **h75**

BLACKERGREEN 6 b.g. Zaffaran (USA) – Ballinderry Moss (Le Moss) [2004/5 F93+: F16g 20d 21d^{4} 19g 21v^{pu} 24v^{3} 25s^{2} 26g^{3} 24s 27s^{2} Apr 22] well-made gelding: runner-up on first of 2 starts in bumpers: modest maiden hurdler: stays 27f: raced on good going or softer (acts on heavy): wore cheekpieces final outing. *K. G. Reveley* **h93** **F73**

BLACK FROST (IRE) 9 ch.g. Glacial Storm (USA) – Black Tulip (Pals Passage) [2004/5 c120, h–: c20s* c20s^{5} c19v^{5} c24d^{pu} c24g Mar 5] sturdy gelding: useful handicap chaser: won at Haydock in November: below form after: stays 2¾m: acts on good to firm and heavy going: has been let down by jumping. *Mrs S. J. Smith* **c131** **h–**

BLACK HILLS 6 b.g. Dilum (USA) – Dakota Girl (Northern State (USA)) [2004/5 F16d^{3} F16s^{2} Mar 23] big gelding: chasing sort: second foal: half-brother to modest hurdler Westernmost (by Most Welcome), stays 21f: dam, fair hurdler, stayed 3m: fair form when placed in bumpers at Huntingdon and Chepstow. *J. A. Geake* **F93**

BLACK JACK KETCHUM (IRE) 6 b.g. Oscar (IRE) – Cailin Supreme (IRE) (Supreme Leader) [2004/5 F16m* F16m* Jul 21] €50,000 3-y-o: first foal: dam, useful hurdler up to 2½m, sister to smart hurdler up to 3m Castlekellyleader: looked useful prospect when landing odds in bumpers at Worcester in June and July, impressive when beating Call Me Anything 8 lengths on second occasion. *Jonjo O'Neill* **F111**

BLACK LEGEND (IRE) 6 b.g. Marju (IRE) – Lamping (Warning) [2004/5 h85: 17d 16g^{4} 16m 16g^{5} 16g Jul 29] angular gelding: poor maiden on Flat and over hurdles: best form at 2m on good ground: blinkered last 2 outings: often tongue tied: sold £2,800 Ascot October Sales. *R. Lee* **h82**

BLACK LEOPARD (IRE) 6 b. or br.g. Presenting – Glen Laura (Kambalda) [2004/5 h–: 20d^{pu} Apr 25] tall gelding: has scope: never a factor in novice hurdles: runner-up in points in 2005. *P. D. Niven* **h–**

BLACKOUT (IRE) 10 b.g. Black Monday – Fine Bess (Fine Blade (USA)) [2004/5 c–, h–: c24d^{3} c24m^{5} 24v c23s^{4} c29s^{5} c26v^{pu} Apr 17] poor maiden hurdler/chaser: stays 3m. *J. Barclay* **c–** **h–**

BLACK SAINT 8 br.g. Perpendicular – Fool's Errand (Milford) [2004/5 h–: 19g^{pu} 17g^{4} Aug 21] good-bodied gelding: no solid form over hurdles: tongue tied. *P. Wegmann* **h–**

BLACK SHAN (IRE) 5 br.g. Anshan – Singing Forever (Chief Singer) [2004/5 F16m Apr 2] rather unfurnished gelding: fourth foal: dam, winning hurdler who stayed 2½m, half-sister to smart 5f to 7f filly Blue Siren: 12 lengths ninth of 21 in bumper at Newbury on debut. *A. Ennis* **F89**

BLACK SMOKE (IRE) 8 gr.g. Ala Hounak – Korean Citizen (IRE) (Mister Lord (USA)) [2004/5 c94, h–: c25g^{bd} c26d^{4} c28s^{F} c30d^{3} c25v^{4} c24s^{5} c23d c24d^{4} c28g* Mar 26] good-topped gelding: well held in 2 novice hurdles: modest chaser: won handicap at Haydock: stays 3¾m: raced on good going or softer. *R. C. Guest* **c90** **h–**

BLACK SWAN (IRE) 5 b.g. Nashwan (USA) – Sea Spray (IRE) (Royal Academy (USA)) [2004/5 h–: 17g^{6} 21g 22s^{pu} 19s^{5} 17s 19g 20d^{pu} Mar 12] lengthy gelding: little form: blinkered final start. *G. A. Ham* **h–**

BLACKTHORN 6 ch.g. Deploy – Balliasta (USA) (Lyphard (USA)) [2004/5 17g^{2} 17m^{3} 16m^{5} Oct 1] modest on Flat (stays 1½m) at 5 yrs: modest form when placed first 2 starts over hurdles: sold to join R. Ford 10,000 gns Newmarket Autumn Sales. *Mrs J. R. Ramsden* **h87**

BLACK TORRINGTON (IRE) 7 b.g. Norwich – Sylvies Missiles (IRE) (Buckskin (FR)) [2004/5 F16g^{6} F16g^{6} 20s^{5} 16v^{pu} Nov 17] fourth foal: half-brother to 27f chase winner Sylviesbuck (by Kasmayo): dam maiden: sixth in bumpers: much better effort in novice hurdles when fifth of 12 at Hexham. *G. M. Moore* **h93** **F80**

BLAIRGOWRIE (IRE) 6 b.g. Supreme Leader – Parsons Term (IRE) (The Parson) [2004/5 F98: 20s* 27v^{F} 23s^{3} 21d* Apr 5] fair form in novice hurdles: won at Hexham in November and Sedgefield in April: let down by jumping both starts in between: should stay beyond 21f. *J. Howard Johnson* **h109 +**

BLAISE WOOD (USA) 4 b.g. Woodman (USA) – Castellina (USA) (Danzig Connection (USA)) [2004/5 18m^{3} 17d^{4} 16m^{4} 17g 17d^{2} 16s* 16g^{3} 20v^{pu} 19d Feb 4] stocky gelding: half-brother to modest 2m hurdler Castle River (by Irish River): poor maiden **h77**

on Flat (stays 1¼m): poor hurdler: won novice seller at Towcester in November: left G. L. Moore after next outing: should stay 2½m: acts on soft and good to firm going: tried in cheekpieces. *A. L. Forbes*

BLAKENEY COAST (IRE) 8 b.g. Satco (FR) – Up To More Trix (IRE) (Torus) [2004/5 c98, h80: c21d^{pu} c18d^{pu} c21d c17v^{4} c25s^{pu} c20g^{3} Mar 27] good sort: winning chaser: out of form in 2004/5: stays 2½m: acts on good to firm going: tried in cheekpieces: has had tongue tied. *C. L. Tizzard* — **c–** **h–**

BLAKENEY RUN 5 gr.g. Commanche Run – Lady Blakeney (Baron Blakeney) [2004/5 F16d^{6} F16d Mar 10] £5,400 4-y-o: workmanlike gelding: second foal: dam winning chaser, stayed 25f: better effort in bumpers when sixth of 16 at Wincanton. *Miss M. Bragg* — **F76**

BLAKES ROAD (IRE) 8 b. or br.g. Be My Native (USA) – Joyau (IRE) (Roselier (FR)) [2004/5 F–: c21m^{5} May 19] no form in bumpers or hunter chase: placed in points in 2005. *Ms Lisa Stock* — **c–**

BLAME THE REF (IRE) 8 ch.g. Aahsaylad – Nags Head (IRE) (Aristocracy) [2004/5 c22d^{2} c25v^{3} c24s^{pu} c28s^{5} c25v^{4} Jan 3] workmanlike gelding: winning hurdler: fair maiden chaser: stays 25f: acts on good to firm and heavy going. *C. C. Bealby* — **c101** **h–**

BLANDINGS CASTLE 4 b.g. Cloudings (IRE) – Country House (Town And Country) [2004/5 17d 16d 16d Nov 13] good-topped gelding: first foal: dam fairly useful hurdler around 2½m: well beaten in juvenile hurdles. *Nick Williams* — **h–**

BLANK CANVAS (IRE) 7 b.g. Presenting – Strong Cloth (IRE) (Strong Gale) [2004/5 F76: 16d^{2} 22s^{pu} 24d^{4} Nov 19] useful-looking gelding: modest form in 2 bumpers and on completed starts over hurdles. *K. C. Bailey* — **h92**

BLASKET SOUND (IRE) 13 b.g. Lancastrian – June's Friend (Laurence O) [2004/5 c–, h91: 27s^{3} 27m^{4} 24g^{3} Jul 14] rather sparely-made gelding: winning chaser: modest handicap hurdler: in frame in points in 2005: stays 27f: acts on good to firm and heavy going: tried blinkered. *D. J. Wintle* — **c–** **h88**

BLAU GRAU (GER) 8 b.g. Neshad (USA) – Belle Orfana (GER) (Orfano (GER)) [2004/5 h60: 16s 16g^{pu} 16s Nov 28] non-stayer over hurdles: sold out of K. Morgan's stable £1,200 Ascot June Sales before reappearance. *N. E. Berry* — **h–**

BLAZEAWAY (USA) 5 b. or br.g. Hansel (USA) – Alessia's Song (USA) (Air Forbes Won (USA)) [2004/5 h71: 16g 18m^{4} 17g 16m^{4} 22g^{pu} 19d^{5} 16f^{3} 17f Sep 28] angular gelding: poor maiden hurdler: will prove best around 2m: best efforts on firm/good to firm going: tried blinkered/in cheekpieces: ungenuine. *R. S. Brookhouse* — **h74 §**

BLAZE ON 6 ch.g. Minster Son – Clova (Move Off) [2004/5 F16d^{3} F16g 24d^{4} 22g^{2} 24f^{6} 22g^{ur} Sep 12] leggy gelding: first foal: dam unraced half-sister to fairly useful staying hurdler Linlathen: third in bumper on debut: form over hurdles only when distant second in novice at Stratford: unbeaten in 3 points in 2005: should stay 3m. *R. H. York* — **h73 +** **F77**

BLAZING BATMAN 12 ch.g. Shaab – Cottage Blaze (Sunyboy) [2004/5 c100, h67: 24s^{5} c31d c16d^{6} c16d^{5} c21d^{pu} c19v^{6} c16v^{pu} 23s 24s^{4} c24g 24d^{pu} Apr 8] sturdy gelding: winning chaser/maiden hurdler: stays 29f: acts on any going: blinkered (pulled up) once: has looked unenthusiastic. *Dr P. Pritchard* — **c– §** **h– §**

BLAZING COURT (IRE) 8 ch.g. Roselier (FR) – The Blazing Star (Proverb) [2004/5 24g^{pu} Oct 14] leggy gelding: no show in varied events, including point. *D. J. Wintle* — **h–**

BLAZING FIDDLE (IRE) 6 b.g. Anshan – Second Violin (IRE) (Cataldi) [2004/5 F–: F16m^{5} F17v 20s 20v^{pu} 19g Mar 4] rather unfurnished gelding: little sign of ability, sold out of J. M. Jefferson's stable 2,100 gns Doncaster November Sales after third outing: resold £1,300 Ascot April Sales. *R. J. Armson* — **h–** **F75**

BLAZING FIRE 8 b.g. Derrylin – Shean Deas (Le Moss) [2004/5 22d^{pu} 24g^{5} c24g^{pu} c22s^{ur} Mar 23] angular gelding: second foal: dam, fair pointer, out of half-sister to smart 2½m chaser Winter Rain: no sign of ability. *M. Wellings* — **c–** **h–**

BLAZING HILLS 9 ch.g. Shaab – Cottage Blaze (Sunyboy) [2004/5 c81, h–: c25g^{2} c26d^{3} c24m^{4} c24g* c23m^{5} c21g^{4} c26d^{2} c24m* c24f^{3} c24g^{pu} c24d Nov 12] good-bodied gelding: fair handicap chaser: won at Uttoxeter in June and Stratford in September: thorough stayer: acts on any going: has worn blinkers: sometimes let down by jumping. *P. T. Dalton* — **c101** **h–**

Bewleys Hotels European Breeders Fund Mares Hurdle, Punchestown—
the favourite Blazing Liss signs off for the paddocks with a win

BLAZING LISS (IRE) 6 b.m. Supreme Leader – Liss de Paor (IRE) (Phardante (FR)) [2004/5 F109: F16g^{2} 18s^{F} 16v^{2} 20v^{4} 16s* 16v* 16v^{2} 16d* 16s^{3} Mar 29] small, stocky mare: useful bumper performer: fairly useful hurdler: won maiden at Cork and minor event at Leopardstown in December and listed mares races at Limerick (novice) in March and Punchestown (beat Mags Benefit 2½ lengths) in late-April: effective at 2m, will stay beyond 2½m: raced on going softer than good over hurdles (won bumper on good to firm): reportedly covered by Flemensfirth. *J. E. Kiely, Ireland* — **h125 F107**

BLAZING SADDLES (IRE) 6 b.g. Sadler's Wells (USA) – Dalawara (IRE) (Top Ville) [2004/5 h–: 22m^{pu} 26m^{pu} 21g Jul 16] little form over hurdles: wears headgear. *Mrs J. Candlish* — **h–**

BLAZING SKY (IRE) 5 b.m. Beneficial – Blazing Comet (Deroulede) [2004/5 F16v F16s^{6} Mar 28] €19,000 4-y-o: unfurnished mare: fourth foal: half-sister to winning hurdlers Blazing Missile (by Durgam), at 2½m, and Halley's Comet (by Roselier), stays 3m: dam, winning 2m chaser, from family of useful 2m to 2½m hurdler/chaser Double Symphony: easily best effort in bumpers when winning very valuable restricted mares event at Punchestown in late-April easily by 14 lengths from Stepping Out Well. *F. F. McGuinness, Ireland* — **F99 +**

BLAZING THE TRAIL (IRE) 5 ch.g. Indian Ridge – Divine Pursuit (Kris) [2004/5 17s^{6} 16g Mar 18] fair on Flat (probably stays 1½m), successful in 2004, sold out of J. Hills's stable 18,000 gns Newmarket Autumn Sales: poor form in 2 maiden hurdles: tongue tied second start. *C. J. Mann* — **h81**

BLENCATHRA 6 b.m. Midnight Legend – April City (Lidhame) [2004/5 F–: F17g^{5} F17m^{6} 19d Nov 28] well held in bumpers and mares novice hurdle. *C. Smith* — **h– F–**

BLESS YOURSELF (IRE) 9 b.g. Shardari – Wee Madge (Apollo Eight) [2004/5 c21d^{F} May 15] no sign of ability: blinkered final outing: sold £1,800 Ascot August Sales. *D. McCain Jnr* — **c– x h–**

BLEU SUPERBE (FR) 10 b.g. Epervier Bleu – Brett's Dream (FR) (Pharly (FR)) [2004/5 c138x, h–: c16g^{2} c20g c16d^{2} c16d^{F} c16g^{6} c16g c16s c16g^{2} Apr 16] rather sparely-made gelding: useful handicap chaser: creditable efforts when second at Lingfield, Sandown and Ayr and when eighth to Fota Island in Grand Annual at Cheltenham sixth start: ideally suited by 2m: acts on good to firm and heavy going: tried tongue tied: usually races prominently: often let down by jumping. *Miss Venetia Williams* — **c138 x h–**

BLOW ME DOWN 6 b.m. Overbury (IRE) – Chinook's Daughter (IRE) (Strong Gale) [2004/5 h–, F73: 21m^{4} 21s^{pu} 20s^{F} 16d^{pu} Jan 6] leggy mare: of little account. *F. Jordan* — **h–**

BLUE AMERICO (IRE) 7 br.g. Lord Americo – Princess Menelek (Menelek) [2004/5 h111: 16g^{F} 21d^{su} 20d* 22d^{4} 20v^{F} 21g^{F} c16s^{6} c20s^{pu} 21m 20s^{4} Apr 21] tall, — **c86 h115 x**

useful-looking gelding: fairly useful handicap hurdler: won at Huntingdon in November: found nothing on completed start in maiden chases: should stay 2¾m: acts on soft and good to firm going: held up, and takes good hold: makes mistakes: needs treating with caution. *P. F. Nicholls*

BLUE AWAY (IRE) 7 b. or br.g. Blues Traveller (IRE) – Lomond Heights (IRE) (Lomond (USA)) [2004/5 h112: 17g* 20d5 21d 20s6 16s Mar 29] lengthy gelding: fair handicap hurdler: won at Killarney in July: stays 21f: yet to race on firm going, acts on any other: has won in visor, tried blinkered: held up. *P. Hughes, Ireland* **h111**

BLUEBELL HILL 8 b.m. Puget (USA) – Fooling With Fire (Idiot's Delight) [2004/5 19m Sep 8] lengthy mare: of little account: sold £1,400 Ascot October Sales. *D. Burchell* **h–**

BLUEBERRY BOY (IRE) 6 b.g. Old Vic – Glenair Lady (Golden Love) [2004/5 F16dpu F16v* F16v3 F16s3 Mar 27] sturdy gelding: sixth reported foal: half-brother to winning pointer by Phardante: dam fair hurdler up to 21f: won bumper at Leopardstown in December: better form when third in similar events at Naas (6¾ lengths behind Missed That) and Fairyhouse (beaten 2¼ lengths by Avoca Mist) subsequently: will stay 2½m. *Paul Stafford, Ireland* **F110**

BLUEBERRY ICE (IRE) 7 b. or br.m. Glacial Storm (USA) – Call Me Honey (Le Bavard (FR)) [2004/5 F17m3 20d5 16d 20s Jan 24] €9,000 4-y-o: lengthy mare: fifth foal: half-sister to bumper winner The Uilleann Piper (by Lord Americo) and winning pointer by Commanche Run: dam unraced half-sister to useful staying hurdler Jakarrdi: modest form in bumper: form over hurdles only when fifth in mares novice at Huntingdon. *B. G. Powell* **h85 F80**

BLUE BROOK 6 ch.g. Alderbrook – Connaught's Pride (Hubbly Bubbly (USA)) [2004/5 F68: 16dF 17d 17g 18spu 19g Mar 3] useful-looking gelding: no form over hurdles, left Mrs S. Williams after third start: tongue tied (folded tamely) final outing. *P. F. Nicholls* **h–**

BLUE BUSINESS 7 br.g. Roselier (FR) – Miss Redlands (Dubassoff (USA)) [2004/5 h100, F85: 27g4 24g4 22s* 24d* 22d* 24g* Apr 14] useful-looking gelding: type to make a chaser: progressive over hurdles, winning novices at Wincanton and Taunton and handicaps at Wincanton and Cheltenham between January and April: useful form when beating Idaho d'Ox 13 lengths at last-named: should stay beyond 3m: acts on soft going: blinkered final 2 outings. *P. F. Nicholls* **h132**

BLUE BUSTER 5 b.g. Young Buster (IRE) – Lazybird Blue (IRE) (Bluebird (USA)) [2004/5 F86: F17d* F17d2 F16m* Dec 12] tall, good sort: fairly useful form in bumpers, winning at Sedgefield (maiden) in October and Musselburgh (beat Rogues Gallery ½ length) in December: second to easy winner Refinement at Aintree in between. *M. W. Easterby* **F102**

BLUE CANYON (FR) 7 b.g. Bering – Nini Princesse (IRE) (Niniski (USA)) [2004/5 18s* 19s5 16g 20v* 20d* 20d Apr 9] **h147**

Two horses named Blue Canyon saw action in Britain in the latest season, and, to make the potential for confusion between the two even greater, they are the same age. In practice, however, it would be long odds against their ever turning up in the same race; there's a wide gulf between the pair in terms of ability. The Irish-bred Blue Canyon was well behind when falling in a maiden chase at Hereford early in the season on his only outing, while his French-bred namesake made his British debut at the other end of the scale in the Grade 1 Christmas Hurdle. There was not a lot of promise in his last-place finish at Kempton, though two miles was too sharp for him and the company a little too strong. Stepped up to two and a half miles for the totesport Hurdle, a Grade 2 limited handicap at Haydock the following month, Blue Canyon produced a smart effort, one which bettered anything he had shown in France. In extremely testing conditions (the meeting had been in doubt), Blue Canyon saved ground by being kept to the inside throughout and asserted from the last. The favourite and top weight Patriarch Express fell four out when still going very well behind the leaders, and it was that horse's stable-companion Royal Emperor who stayed on for second, beaten two lengths. This contest replaced Haydock's long-standing Premier Stayers' Hurdle, a three-mile event which was forced out when Cheltenham's Cleeve Hurdle, run a week later, was extended from two and a half miles to three. The Haydock authorities evidently felt they had drawn the short straw, and expressed their displeasure by registering the new race (prior to

totesport Hurdle (Limited Handicap) (Co Cup), Haydock—
Blue Canyon (partially hidden) comes to tackle Royal Emperor (grey) two out;
also pictured is the weakening Polar Red

totesport putting their name to it) as the Co Cup—presumably to rhyme with 'lock up' rather than 'soak up'.

The National Spirit Hurdle at Fontwell in February, also sponsored by totesport, was Blue Canyon's next race, one which had seen the same connections' Baracouda scramble home by a neck four years earlier. Starting the 3/1 second favourite and giving weight all round, Blue Canyon's win was gained much more smoothly, improving to track the leader Copeland two out and soon having the race won after leading before the last. Copeland was four lengths back, just holding on for second ahead of Le Duc, while the favourite, Big Moment, spoiled his chance with a bad mistake early on. With Baracouda in the World Hurdle and the Champion Hurdle not an option, Blue Canyon's only Festival entry was in the Coral Cup, but he missed Cheltenham altogether in favour of the Aintree Hurdle. Against the World Hurdle winner Inglis Drever and several who had run well in the Champion Hurdle, Blue Canyon faced a stiffish task, but he ran creditably to finish seventh of eight finishers in what was admittedly a muddling race.

The Christmas Hurdle had been Blue Canyon's first race in the colours of J. P. McManus; his latest outings in France had been in the colours of the Doumens' stud, the Haras d'Ecouves. Blue Canyon had had plenty of racing on the Flat, and had already won four races in the Provinces prior to joining the Doumen stable as a five-year-old. He showed fairly useful form in staying handicaps on the Flat for his new yard without adding to his wins, but soon proved useful over hurdles, winning twice at Auteuil. Blue Canyon had two runs at Enghien in the autumn prior to the Christmas Hurdle, winning a listed event before finishing fifth in the track's Grande Course de Haies.

Blue Canyon (FR) (b.g. 1998)	Bering (ch 1983)	Arctic Tern (ch 1973)	Sea Bird II
			Bubbling Beauty
		Beaune (ch 1974)	Lyphard
			Barbra
	Nini Princesse (IRE) (b 1989)	Niniski (b 1976)	Nijinsky
			Virginia Hills
		Princesse Timide (br 1980)	Blushing Groom
			Rigid Princess

Blue Canyon is one of six winners out of his dam Nini Princesse. All the others have won on the Flat, mostly in France, but the best of them is Miss Honorine (by Highest Honor), a useful winner of three listed races in Ireland from a mile to a mile and a quarter. Nini Princesse won six races at up to around a mile and a quarter in France, and is one of nine winners out of the useful French filly at up to a mile and a quarter Princesse Timide. Those nine also include Nini Princesse's brother, Louis Cyphre, a very smart French performer at up to a mile and a half who later won at Grade 1 level in the States, the smart French sprinter/miler Psychobabble, and a stakes winner in Japan, Star King Man, as well as the fairly useful two-mile hurdler Majesty. Despite his Flat background, the good-topped Blue Canyon may be best exploited over fences from now on, ranking as he does a little behind the best hurdlers. Knowing his owner, he will no doubt continue to be campaigned in Britain from now on. Blue Canyon has never raced beyond two and a half miles, but he was a stayer on the Flat and shapes as though he will get further. He has raced only on good going or softer over hurdles and coped extremely well with heavy ground at Haydock. *F. Doumen, France*

BLUE CANYON (IRE) 7 b.g. Phardante (FR) – Miss Gosling (Prince Bee) [2004/5 h80: c19m^F May 11] strong, lengthy gelding: poor form over hurdles: fell chasing debut: tried tongue tied. *B. De Haan* **c– h–**

BLUE DANCE 6 b.g. Danzig Connection (USA) – Blues Player (Jaazeiro (USA)) [2004/5 h–p: 17g^5 May 11] modest form on second of 2 outings over hurdles. *N. A. Twiston-Davies* **h90**

BLUE ENDEAVOUR (IRE) 7 b.g. Endeavour (USA) – Jingle Bells (FR) (In The Mood (FR)) [2004/5 h104, F87: 19s^2 22d^4 22s^5 17s* Mar 22] good-topped gelding: fair hurdler: 5/1-on, well below best when winning novice seller at Exeter in March, hanging left: stays 2¾m: acts on soft going (bumper form on good to firm): hard ride, and one to avoid. *P. F. Nicholls* **h104 §**

BLUE ETTE (IRE) 5 b.g. Blues Traveller (IRE) – Princess Roxanne (Prince Tenderfoot (USA)) [2004/5 F–: F17d^{pu} F16g Dec 29] quite good-topped gelding: no sign of ability. *G. A. Swinbank* **F–**

BLUE HAWK (IRE) 8 ch.g. Prince of Birds (USA) – Classic Queen (IRE) (Classic Secret (USA)) [2004/5 h93: 20d^{pu} 19g 16s^{pu} 17g Apr 3] angular gelding: modest hurdler: no form in 2004/5, left Miss L. Davis after reappearance: should stay beyond 17f: acts on firm going. *P. T. Midgley* **h–**

BLUE JAR 7 b.g. Royal Abjar (USA) – Artist's Glory (Rarity) [2004/5 h–: c24g^{pu} c20m^{pu} Apr 10] of little account. *M. Mullineaux* **c– h–**

BLUELAND (IRE) 6 b.m. Bigstone (IRE) – Legally Delicious (Law Society (USA)) [2004/5 F20m^{su} F16g^4 F18s^2 F16s^3 Mar 13] ex-Irish mare: third foal: half-sister to 6f winner Turtles Reprisal (by Turtle Island): dam fair 1m winner: best effort in bumpers (fair form) when short-head second at Limerick in October, final start for K. Purcell. *Noel T. Chance* **F91**

BLUE LEADER (IRE) 6 b.g. Cadeaux Genereux – Blue Duster (USA) (Danzig (USA)) [2004/5 h82: c17g^{pu} 20s^{pu} 17g 16d^3 16s* 16d^2 c16g 16d 16g^2 16d Mar 24] tall gelding: sold out of G. Brown's stable £5,500 Ascot October Sales after first outing: modest handicap hurdler: won seller at Ludlow in January: bled from nose final start: let down by jumping both starts over fences: best around 2m: acts on soft going: tried in cheekpieces, tongue tied nowadays. *W. K. Goldsworthy* **c– h98**

BLUE MAINE (IRE) 8 b.m. Doubletour (USA) – Bluejama (Windjammer (USA)) [2004/5 h–, F–: 24m^5 20m^6 Jun 27] first sign of ability in maiden hurdle at Uttoxeter final start. *N. A. Twiston-Davies* **h75**

BLUE MARINER 5 b.g. Marju (IRE) – Mazarine Blue (Bellypha) [2004/5 16d Jan 26] fair on Flat (stays 1¼m): well held in novice on hurdling debut, racing freely. *J. Jay* **h–**

BLUE MORNING 7 b.m. Balnibarbi – Bad Start (USA) (Bold Bidder) [2004/5 h–, F–: 20g^{pu} 16v* 20s 18s 16v^6 16v^4 16s^5 22s Apr 3] poor hurdler: won seller at Kelso in October: should stay beyond 2m: acts on heavy going: wears cheekpieces nowadays. *Mrs J. C. McGregor* **h75**

BLUE NUN 4 b.f. Bishop of Cashel – Matisse (Shareef Dancer (USA)) [2004/5 16s^{pu} 17s 17d^6 17s Feb 17] close-coupled filly: no form on Flat (for Mrs A. Duffield) or over hurdles: wore cheekpieces final start. *G. F. H. Charles-Jones* **h–**

BLUE PLANET (IRE) 7 b.g. Bluebird (USA) – Millie Musique (Miller's Mate) [2004/5 h79: 21d Apr 18] workmanlike gelding: modest maiden hurdler: well held only start in 2004/5: stays 21f: acts on soft going: tried tongue tied. *P. G. Murphy* **h–**

BLUE RIDE (IRE) 8 b.m. King's Ride – Charmere's Beauty (IRE) (Phardante (FR)) [2004/5 h125: 22d^{pu} Nov 6] lengthy, rather sparely-made mare: fairly useful hurdler, lightly raced: off nearly a year, no show only start in 2004/5: probably stays 25f: acts on firm and good to soft going, probably on soft: difficult ride. *P. F. Nicholls* **h–**

BLUE RISING 4 gr.g. Primitive Rising (USA) – Pollytickle (Politico (USA)) [2004/5 F13d^{6} F14g 16v^{4} 18d^{4} 16v^{2} Feb 15] third foal: dam no form in 3 races over hurdles: modest form in 3-y-o bumpers: best effort over hurdles when second to easy winner Dont Call Me Derek in juvenile at Newcastle: will stay 2½m. *Ferdy Murphy* **h86** **F78**

BLUE SAVANNA 5 ch.g. Bluegrass Prince (IRE) – Dusk In Daytona (Beveled (USA)) [2004/5 h75: 16d^{5} 18m^{5} May 26] leggy gelding: little form over hurdles: modest form at best on Flat in 2004: in blinkers/cheekpieces since debut. *J. G. Portman* **h–**

BLUES STORY (FR) 7 b.g. Pistolet Bleu (IRE) – Herbe Sucree (FR) (Tiffauges) [2004/5 c–, h96d: 20d^{pu} 17d 19g 16d^{pu} 19d Mar 26] lengthy gelding: well held completed start over fences: maiden hurdler: no form in 2004/5, sold from R. Ford £2,500 Ascot August Sales after reappearance: stays 2½m: acts on good to soft going. *N. G. Ayliffe* **c–** **h–**

BLUESTONE LAD (IRE) 7 b. or br.g. Lord Americo – Killbally Castle (IRE) (Over The River (FR)) [2004/5 20d 16g^{6} 24d^{6} 24s^{3} 24v^{5} 20s* 20d^{2} 20v* 20v* 24s Feb 19] angular gelding: second foal: dam unraced: fair hurdler: won handicaps at Fairyhouse in November and January (2): probably stays 3m: raced on good going or softer (acts on heavy). *P. A. Fahy, Ireland* **h114**

BLUE STREAK (IRE) 8 ch.g. Bluebird (USA) – Fleet Amour (USA) (Afleet (CAN)) [2004/5 h97: 17m 20m^{pu} 18m^{3} 21g^{2} 16g^{4} Oct 18] angular gelding: modest hurdler: below best in 2004/5, generally failing to impress with attitude: joined K. Bell, never dangerous returned to Flat in April: stays 21f: acts on good to firm and heavy going: usually blinkered nowadays. *G. L. Moore* **h90 §**

BLUETORIA 4 b.f. Vettori (IRE) – Blue Birds Fly (Rainbow Quest (USA)) [2004/5 16d 16g^{5} 21d 16v 17s^{5} 20d^{pu} 16g Mar 28] workmanlike filly: fair maiden on Flat (stays 1¼m), though has given plenty of trouble at start: little form over hurdles: claimed from J. Glover £6,000 second start: visored last 4 outings. *Miss Victoria Roberts* **h69**

BLUE TUNE (FR) 4 b.g. Green Tune (USA) – Anvers (FR) (Ganges (USA)) [2004/5 16g Oct 26] sturdy gelding: first foal: dam 5.5f winner: maiden on Flat (stays 12.5f) for E. Denel: in cheekpieces, always behind in juvenile on hurdling debut. *R. Rowe* **h–**

BLUE WING 4 b.g. Bluebird (USA) – Warbler (Warning) [2004/5 F13d^{2} F14d^{3} F16v^{6} Feb 2] 2,500 3-y-o: third foal: half-brother to 1m winner Reed Minder (by Zamindar) and 1¼m winner Trill (by Highest Honor), both useful in France: dam smart 10.5f and 11.5f winner who stayed 15f well: fair form when placed in 3-y-o bumpers: blinkered final outing: well held on Flat debut later in February: sold 5,000 gns Doncaster May Sales. *M. W. Easterby* **F82**

BLUE YONDER 5 b.m. Terimon – Areal (IRE) (Roselier (FR)) [2004/5 F–: 20m 17d^{ur} 16s 16s^{pu} 16g Nov 11] unfurnished mare: no form in bumper or novice hurdles: tried tongue tied. *Evan Williams* **h–**

BLUNHAM 5 b.g. Danzig Connection (USA) – Relatively Sharp (Sharpen Up) [2004/5 h–: 16d 16d Jan 13] leggy, close-coupled gelding: poor on Flat (stays 1m): well held all 3 starts over hurdles. *M. C. Chapman* **h–**

BLUNHAM HILL (IRE) 7 ch.g. Over The River (FR) – Bronach (Beau Charmeur (FR)) [2004/5 c97, h95: c22s^{2} c22s^{F} c22v^{6} c26d^{3} c24s^{ur} c29s^{2} Mar 13] quite good-topped gelding: maiden hurdler: modest handicap chaser: stays 29f: acts on heavy going. *John R. Upson* **c91** **h–**

BLUSHING BULL 6 b.g. Makbul – Blush (Gildoran) [2004/5 F107: F16s* 20s* 20v^{2} 22v* 20v 24s^{3} Apr 21] good-topped gelding: useful form in bumpers: won at Chepstow in May: fairly useful novice hurdler: won at Chepstow (impressive) in November and Uttoxeter (10/3-on, had to work much harder to beat In Accord a neck) in January: stays 3m: raced only on soft/heavy going over hurdles. *P. F. Nicholls* **h118** **F103**

BLUSHING PRINCE (IRE) 7 b.g. Priolo (USA) – Eliade (IRE) (Flash of Steel) [2004/5 h85: 20s Jan 19] winning hurdler: pulled hard only outing in 2004/5: likely to prove best at 2m: acts on firm going: tongue tied. *R. C. Guest* **h–**

BLYTH BROOK 13 b.g. Meadowbrook – The Bean-Goose (King Sitric) [2004/5 c105, h–: c24g^{3} c21s^{pu} Mar 11] leggy gelding: fairly useful hunter chaser: stays 27f: acts on good to firm going, probably on good to soft (no form on softer): often let down by jumping. *W. T. Reed* **c105 x** **h–**

BOANERGES (IRE) 8 br.g. Caerleon (USA) – Sea Siren (Slip Anchor) [2004/5 16d^{pu} Oct 3] smallish gelding: sprinter on Flat, on downgrade: no potential as a hurdler. *J. M. Bradley* **h–**

BOARDROOM DANCER (IRE) 8 b.g. Executive Perk – Dancing Course (IRE) (Crash Course) [2004/5 c88, h–: c26d^{pu} Apr 18] lengthy, workmanlike gelding: winning chaser, lightly raced: stays 3m. *Miss I. E. Craig* **c– h–**

BOARDROOM FIDDLE (IRE) 6 ch.g. Executive Perk – Opera Time (IRE) (Orchestra) [2004/5 F16g May 1] €19,000 4-y-o: sturdy gelding: third foal: dam unraced half-sister to dam of Hennessy winner What's Up Boys: tailed off in bumper on debut. *Miss E. C. Lavelle* **F–**

BOBALONG (IRE) 8 b.g. Bob's Return (IRE) – Northern Wind (Northfields (USA)) [2004/5 h104?: c26v^{pu} Dec 31] workmanlike gelding: form only when making all in slowly-run 3m maiden hurdle in 2003/4: tried tongue tied. *C. P. Morlock* **c– h–**

BOB AR AGHAIDH (IRE) 9 b.g. Bob Back (USA) – Shuil Ar Aghaidh (The Parson) [2004/5 h114: 24d^{5} 20s^{4} c22s^{6} c25s^{F} c24s^{2} Feb 17] sturdy gelding: fair hurdler on his day: jumped better than previously over fences when second in maiden at Taunton: stays 3m: acts on heavy going. *C. Tinkler* **c105 h105 x**

BOBBI ROSE RED 8 ch.m. Bob Back (USA) – Lady Rosanna (Kind of Hush) [2004/5 c64, h72: c20d^{pu} c20v^{pu} 19s^{5} 20s^{6} 16g Apr 19] lengthy, sparely-made mare: poor maiden hurdler/chaser: probably stays 25f: acts on good to soft going: wore cheekpieces last 4 starts. *P. T. Dalton* **c– h66**

BOBBLE WONDER 4 b.f. Classic Cliche (IRE) – Wonderfall (FR) (The Wonder (FR)) [2004/5 F16s Mar 13] first foal: dam poor 2m hurdler: behind in mares bumper on debut. *D. G. Bridgwater* **F–**

BOB BOB BOBBIN 6 gr.g. Bob Back (USA) – Absalom's Lady (Absalom) [2004/5 F109: F16s* F16d^{2} 19g^{3} 21s^{3} 22v* 19v* 24g^{4} Mar 18] **h134 F110**

It is very hard to fault the record so far of the promising young jumper Bob Bob Bobbin. Four runs in bumpers yielded a win at Chepstow in October and three appearances in the frame in Grade 2 and listed events, the last a second to Manners at the Open meeting at Cheltenham. Five runs over hurdles have seen him finish no worse than fourth, the highlights being two wins and a fourth place in the (Brit

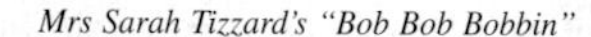

Mrs Sarah Tizzard's "Bob Bob Bobbin"

Insurance) Spa Hurdle at the Cheltenham Festival. If ever there were the horse for whom everything over hurdles was a bonus it is Bob Bob Bobbin, who looks every inch a chaser and is likely to be a leading candidate for the Royal & SunAlliance Chase at the next Festival if all goes to plan.

Bob Bob Bobbin's best effort in four appearances before Cheltenham came in a Grade 2 novice at Warwick in January when he finished third to No Refuge and Lady Zephyr. He was dropped in class and won his next two starts, ordinary novices at Folkestone and back at Warwick, but he was not especially impressive either time. For his second win particularly, the nineteen-furlong trip looked on the short side, even on testing ground, and it was no surprise that a step up to three miles in the Spa brought about a fair amount of improvement. Travelling well up with the pace, he belied odds of 20/1 and was still bang in contention into the straight but couldn't quicken and finished under six lengths fourth to Moulin Riche, clear of the remainder.

Bob Bob Bobbin was well bought for 15,000 guineas as a four-year-old, his dam's next two foals, Big Business (by Slip Anchor) and War General (by Classic Cliche), having made €58,000 and 130,000 guineas as three-year-olds respectively. They are both in training with Tom Taaffe and have yet to trouble the judge. Bob Bob Bobbin's dam Absalom's Lady was one of the better racemares of the last twenty years, showing very smart form over hurdles and smart form over fences, her victories including the New Year's Day Hurdle at Windsor, the Christmas Hurdle at Kempton and the Haldon Gold Cup at Exeter. *C. L. Tizzard*

BOBBY BLAKENEY 10 gr.g. Baron Blakeney – Coming Out (Fair Season) [2004/5 h–: 22dpu 26dpu Oct 17] no form in points or over hurdles. *Miss L. V. Davis* **h–**

BOBBY BROWN (IRE) 5 b.g. Insan (USA) – Miss Sally Knox (IRE) (Erdelistan (FR)) [2004/5 F16g 19m 24d5 25spu Mar 13] deep-girthed gelding: first foal: dam unraced, out of useful hurdler up to 2½m Miss Bobby Bennett: no sign of ability, left M. Appleby after second start: tried tongue tied. *Mrs H. Dalton* **h– F–**

BOBBY DAZZLER 6 b.g. Bob's Return (IRE) – Preachers Popsy (The Parson) [2004/5 h109, F–: 20d* 24g* Sep 23] good-topped gelding: fair hurdler: won novices at Chepstow in May and Perth (left with simple task) in September: stays 3m: raced on good going or softer. *N. A. Twiston-Davies* **h114**

BOBBY GAYLE (IRE) 5 ch.m. Bob Back (USA) – Elite (Lord Gayle (USA)) [2004/5 F17d6 F17spu Jan 3] rather unfurnished mare: sixth foal: sister to useful bumper winner Captain Sunshine and a winner in Italy: dam won at 1¼m: sixth of 7 in slowly-run bumper on debut: tailed off some way out next time. *Mrs S. D. Williams* **F80**

BOBBY ICATA 4 b.g. I'm Supposin (IRE) – Its My Turn (Palm Track) [2004/5 F16v F16v Feb 19] half-brother to several winners, including fair hurdler up to 2½m Silverdale Lad (by Presidium) and modest staying hurdler Prince Nicholas (by Midyan): dam fair miler: tailed off in bumpers. *K. W. Hogg, Isle of Man* **F–**

BOBERELLE (IRE) 5 gr.m. Bob Back (USA) – Zephyrelle (IRE) (Celio Rufo) [2004/5 F16g* F16d3 Mar 12] lengthy, unfurnished mare: third foal: dam, fair form in bumpers, sister to useful 2m hurdlers Winter Squall and Zephyrus and half-sister to smart 2m hurdler Carobee and useful hurdler Alekhine: fairly useful form in mares bumpers, winning at Ludlow in December and third to Funny Times in listed event at Sandown. *C. Tinkler* **F99**

BOB JUSTICE (IRE) 9 b.g. Bob Back (USA) – Bramdean (Niniski (USA)) [2004/5 c–, h133: 24g5 c20d5 21s6 c20sF c19v4 c19v6 c22v5 c20s c20d Apr 3] rather leggy gelding: useful hurdler: winning chaser, fair form at best in 2004/5: effective at 2m to easy 3m: acts on heavy going: blinkered after sixth outing: sold 23,000 gns Doncaster May Sales. *T. M. Walsh, Ireland* **c115 h–**

BOB NICKEL (IRE) 8 ch.g. Bob's Return (IRE) – Nickel Run (Deep Run) [2004/5 c20spu Mar 11] poor maiden pointer. *M. Keighley* **c–**

BOBOSH 9 b.g. Devil's Jump – Jane Craig (Rapid Pass) [2004/5 h–: c21g3 c18m4 c20m4 c20g2 c20d* c16d* c16s2 c16g6 c20d5 c19m2 c20m5 Apr 23] leggy gelding: winning hurdler: fair novice chaser: won at Market Rasen in July and Hereford in October: stays 21f: acts on soft and good to firm going: visored once (tried to run out), tried in cheekpieces: often front runner. *R. Dickin* **c107 h–**

BOBSBEST (IRE) 9 b.g. Lashkari – Bobs (Warpath) [2004/5 c–, h84: c20g² c16s³ c20s³ c19gF c20g* c24d⁴ c20vur c20s⁴ c18m³ c21g⁵ c20d³ Apr 20] small, angular gelding: poor hurdler: modest handicap chaser: won at Huntingdon in January: stays 3m: acts on soft and good to firm going. *R. J. Price* **c87 h–**

BOB'S BUSTER 9 b.g. Bob's Return (IRE) – Saltina (Bustino) [2004/5 c103, h–: c17v⁶ c16d³ c16d⁶ c16g³ c16s⁵ c17s² Apr 2] sturdy gelding: modest handicap chaser: raced around 2m: acts on heavy and good to firm going: wears cheekpieces: held up: headstrong. *R. Johnson* **c94 h–**

BOB'S GONE (IRE) 7 ch.g. Eurobus – Bob's Girl (IRE) (Bob Back (USA)) [2004/5 h104: 22m² 22g⁶ 20g* 20s² 24d 23dF 24v 16d 23v 20v Jan 10] leggy gelding: fair hurdler: made all in claimer at Perth in July: no form in handicaps after next outing: stays 2¾m: acts on soft and good to firm going. *N. G. Richards* **h111 d**

BOB'S LAD 8 b.g. Weldnaas (USA) – Porte Belloch (Belfort (FR)) [2004/5 22g⁴ c18m³ c25g³ c24spu Oct 20] 500 4-y-o: first foal: dam 1m winner: winning pointer: failed to see race out in maiden hurdle and on chasing debut, ran poorly after. *Evan Williams* **c83 h92**

BOBSLEIGH 6 b.g. Robellino (USA) – Do Run Run (Commanche Run) [2004/5 h111: 21v² 25s⁴ 22d⁵ Feb 20] angular gelding: fair on Flat (stays 21f): fair hurdler: should stay beyond 2¾m: acts on heavy ground. *H. Morrison* **h113**

BOBSOUROWN (IRE) 6 b.g. Parthian Springs – Suir Queen (Deep Run) [2004/5 F17d² 16s 20v 20vpu 20g⁶ 21vpu Mar 28] €8,000 3-y-o: sixth foal: dam winning pointer: won maiden Irish point in 2004: bought 7,500 gns Doncaster May Sales: second of 14 in maiden bumper at Sedgefield: little worthwhile form in novice hurdles. *F. P. Murtagh* **h81 F91**

BOB'S SHERIE 6 b.m. Bob's Return (IRE) – Sheraton Girl (Mon Tresor) [2004/5 h–: 22dpu 19mpu Jun 9] sturdy mare: of no account: tried in cheekpieces. *M. Mullineaux* **h–**

BOB'S TEMPTATION 6 br.g. Bob's Return (IRE) – Temptation (IRE) (Clearly Bust) [2004/5 F–: F16d Dec 5] tailed off in bumpers. *A. J. Wilson* **F–**

BOB'S THE BUSINESS (IRE) 11 b.g. Bob Back (USA) – Kiora (Camden Town) [2004/5 c101: c24d³ c25gpu c28s³ c32d² c28s⁵ c32vpu Mar 5] rangy gelding: fair handicap chaser: thorough stayer: acts on soft going. *Ian Williams* **c104**

BOB THE BUILDER 6 b.g. Terimon – True Clown (True Song) [2004/5 24s⁵ 21d⁵ 24d⁴ Mar 5] big gelding: will make a chaser: fifth foal: half-brother to 3 winners by Teenoso, including fairly useful 2m chaser Percy Parkeeper and modest hurdler/chaser up to 25f Brambly Hedge: dam, winning chaser, stayed 3¼m: easily best effort in novice hurdles when fourth to Ferimon at Newbury: will stay beyond 3m. *N. A. Twiston-Davies* **h98**

BOB THE PILER 9 b.g. Jendali (USA) – Laxay (Laxton) [2004/5 h111: c16s³ c16s² Dec 6] medium-sized gelding: fair hurdler: modest form both starts in maiden chases, far from fluent on second occasion: stays 2½m: raced on good going or softer (acts on heavy). *N. G. Richards* **c95 h–**

BO DANCER (IRE) 11 ch.g. Magical Wonder (USA) – Pitty Pal (USA) (Caracolero (USA)) [2004/5 17d³ 20g⁶ 17d 20s⁴ 22spu Nov 18] tall gelding: handicap hurdler: off nearly 2 years, well below best in 2004/5: stays 27f: acts on any going. *Mrs E. Slack* **h70**

BODDIDLEY (IRE) 7 b.g. Be My Native (USA) – Boardwalker (IRE) (Waajib) [2004/5 21g⁵ 24s⁴ 22g³ Apr 17] 40,000 4-y-o: first foal: dam, middle-distance maiden, half-sister to useful 2m hurdler Crowded House: won 2½m maiden on completed outing in points in 2004, placed both starts in 2005: best effort in novice hurdles when third of 5 finishers to Shining Lights at Wincanton. *P. F. Nicholls* **h92**

BODFARI CREEK 8 ch.g. In The Wings – Cormorant Creek (Gorytus (USA)) [2004/5 h112: 22mpu 22g⁴ 22m Sep 21] fair hurdler at best: shaped as if amiss all 3 starts in 2004/5, tongue tied last 2: stays 3m: raced mainly on good going or firmer (acts on firm). *J. G. Portman* **h88**

BODFARI ROSE 6 ch.m. Indian Ridge – Royale Rose (FR) (Bering) [2004/5 h86: 20spu Apr 16] modest maiden hurdler at best, off 19 months before only outing in 2004/5: form only around 2m: acts on soft and good to firm going: tried blinkered, wore cheekpieces in 2003/4. *A. Bailey* **h–**

BODFARI SAUVAGE 5 b.g. Loup Sauvage (USA) – Petite Sonnerie (Persian Bold) [2004/5 F16gpu F17s Nov 30] rangy gelding: sixth foal: half-brother to several winners, including useful performer around 1¼m Petite Speciale (by Atticus) and 3 winners in USA: dam, placed in Britain, later successful in USA, including at 8.5f: shaped as if amiss both starts in bumpers: sold 1,800 gns Doncaster March Sales. *P. R. Webber* **F–**

BODFARI SIGNET 9 ch.g. King's Signet (USA) – Darakah (Doulab (USA)) [2004/5 h107: 20m^5 c20d^4 24d 16g^5 22m^5 22v 21d^4 16m* 20m^2 17g^4 16m^3 17g^F 16g^6 Feb 27] leggy gelding: fair handicap hurdler: won at Musselburgh (third course win) in November: never a factor after blundering second on chasing debut (not knocked about): effective at 2m to easy 3m: acts on firm and soft going, not at best on heavy: tried in headgear: usually waited with. *Mrs S. C. Bradburne* **c79 +** **h108**

BODIAM (IRE) 5 b.m. Mukaddamah (USA) – Partenza (USA) (Red Ransom (USA)) [2004/5 17g^{pu} Dec 14] well beaten in 3 starts at 2 yrs for J. M. Bradley: no aptitude for hurdling in novice on debut. *Mrs L. P. Baker* **h–**

BODKIN BOY (IRE) 5 b.g. Darnay – Kristar (Kris) [2004/5 F16v^4 F16s^6 16s^{pu} Apr 22] brother to 8.5f winner Market Minstrel and half-brother to 7f winner Impulse (by Imp Society): dam, Italian 1m winner, out of useful 7f to 1¼m filly Guest Night: signs of ability in 2 bumpers at Ayr, on both occasions dictating pace long way: struggling at halfway in weak maiden on hurdling debut. *Mrs S. C. Bradburne* **h–** **F85**

BOGUS DREAMS (IRE) 8 ch.g. Lahib (USA) – Dreams Are Free (IRE) (Caerleon (USA)) [2004/5 c16s^5 16g^4 16s* Mar 11] well-made gelding: useful on Flat (best around 1¼m) at 4 yrs for S. Woods: no form in 4 starts over hurdles in Ireland for B. Jones in 2002: never dangerous fifth of 8 in novice handicap at Hexham on chasing debut: favourite over hurdles last 2 starts, easily winning novice handicap at Ayr: likely to prove best at 2m: capable of better over hurdles and fences. *L. Lungo* **c80 p** **h109 p**

BOHEMIAN BOY (IRE) 7 gr.g. Roselier (FR) – Right Hand (Oats) [2004/5 h116: 24v^{pu} 21d^2 22d 24s^2 Apr 16] compact gelding: fair hurdler: will stay beyond 3m: raced on going softer than good. *M. Pitman* **h112**

BOHEMIAN SPIRIT (IRE) 7 b.g. Eagle Eyed (USA) – Tuesday Morning (Sadler's Wells (USA)) [2004/5 c104: c21d* c25g* c28g^5 c24v^{ur} c22d^{pu} c21s^3 Mar 11] fairly useful hunter chaser: successful at Cheltenham and Aintree (novice) early in 2004/5: left M. Brown, won point in February: effective at 21f to 25f: acts on heavy ground. *Miss M. A. Neill* **c108**

BOING BOING (IRE) 5 b.g. King's Theatre (IRE) – Limerick Princess (IRE) (Polish Patriot (USA)) [2004/5 h97: 17d^6 16g^{pu} 16s 20s^3 19d^{pu} 19g^3 16s^{pu} Dec 22] sturdy gelding: modest handicap hurdler: stays 2½m: acts on soft and good to firm going: wore cheekpieces third outing: free-going sort: unreliable. *Miss S. J. Wilton* **h92 §**

BOLD AFFAIR 6 ch.g. Bold Arrangement – So Curious (Gildoran) [2004/5 F–: 17g^{pu} 16m^{pu} Aug 6] leggy gelding: no sign of ability. *Mrs L. Williamson* **h–**

BOLD BISHOP (IRE) 8 b.g. Religiously (USA) – Ladybojangles (IRE) (Buckskin (FR)) [2004/5 h139: c16g^2 16d^{pu} Mar 12] rangy gelding: useful hurdler in 2003/4: no show in valuable handicap at Sandown in March: promising 3 lengths second to Supreme Developer in novice at Newcastle on chasing debut 3 months earlier: should stay 2½m: acts on soft and good to firm going: blinkered once in bumpers: sure to improve over fences. *Jonjo O'Neill* **c125 p** **h–**

BOLD CLASSIC (IRE) 12 b.g. Persian Bold – Bay Street (Grundy) [2004/5 c93?, h–: c22s^5 c26g^{pu} Jul 15] close-coupled gelding: modest chaser: out of form early in 2004/5: stays 3¼m: acts on heavy and good to firm going: tried in cheekpieces. *C. Grant* **c–** **h–**

BOLD HUNTER 11 b.g. Polish Precedent (USA) – Pumpona (USA) (Sharpen Up) [2004/5 c–, h63: 20s^{pu} c16f^4 c19m^3 May 28] sturdy gelding: poor hurdler/chaser, little form for long time: tried blinkered. *M. J. M. Evans* **c–** **h–**

BOLDINI (USA) 4 ch.g. Atticus (USA) – Bold Bold (IRE) (Sadler's Wells (USA)) [2004/5 18m^F 17d^3 17g Oct 14] half-brother to smart hurdler Ambobo (by Kingmambo): dam, 1¼m winner, sister to Galway Hurdle winner Sabadilla: close third in claimer (claimed from Mme C. Head-Maarek €30,000) at Maisons-Laffitte in June, poor form on Flat in Britain for S. Liddiard: disputing lead when falling heavily 2 out in juvenile at Fontwell on hurdling debut: disappointed after, claimed £5,000 final start: visored: sold £700 Ascot February Sales. *M. C. Pipe* **h85**

BOLD INVESTOR 8 b.g. Anshan – Shirlstar Investor (Some Hand) [2004/5 c20s^F 21d c24g^{ur} Mar 16] workmanlike gelding: useful chaser/fairly useful handicap hurdler at best: off 18 months, little sign of retaining ability in 2004/5: stays 3m: raced mainly on good going or softer (acts on soft). *Jonjo O'Neill* **c–** **h–**

BOLD LEADER 8 b.g. Tragic Role (USA) – Swift Messenger (Giolla Mear) [2004/5 17g^5 16m 18m Sep 21] 3,800 5-y-o: good-topped gelding: sixth foal: half-brother to fairly **h75**

useful staying chaser Hermes Harvest (by Oats): dam, winning hurdler/chaser, stayed well: poor form over hurdles. *D. L. Williams*

BOLD MOMENTO 6 b.g. Never So Bold – Native of Huppel (IRE) (Be My Native (USA)) [2004/5 F–: 16g[6] 20v[pu] 20d[6] Apr 20] angular gelding: signs of a little ability: tried in blinkers/cheekpieces. *B. De Haan* **h81 ?**

BOLD NAVIGATOR 15 b.g. Lighter – Drummond Lass (Peacock (FR)) [2004/5 c89: c24d[3] Sep 22] veteran chaser: won point in February: stays 27f: acts on soft going. *A. M. Crow* **c81**

BOLD TACTICS (IRE) 9 br.g. Jurado (USA) – Bold Lyndsey (Be My Native (USA)) [2004/5 c96: c20s[3] Mar 11] fair hunter chaser: lost chance with bad mistake sixth (water) in maiden at Leicester in March: may prove best around 2½m: acts on soft going. *Nick Shutts* **c82**

BOLEYKNOWSBEST (IRE) 7 b.g. Camden Town – Barrys Best (IRE) (King Luthier) [2004/5 h116, F–: 16g* 16s 16d[3] 16v[bd] 16v 16s 16d[6] Apr 9] medium-sized gelding: fairly useful hurdler: raced around 2m: best efforts on good/good to soft going: usually waited with. *R. P. Burns, Ireland* **h116**

BOLLIN ANNABEL 4 b.f. King's Theatre (IRE) – Bollin Magdalene (Teenoso (USA)) [2004/5 16d[4] 16s* 16d[3] 16v[6] 16d[5] 19s[3] 16v* 20s[2] 20s Apr 22] leggy filly: dam fairly useful hurdler up to 3m: modest maiden on Flat (stays 1¾m): fair hurdler: won juvenile at Haydock in November and conditional jockeys mares handicap at Hexham in March: stays 2½m: raced on going softer than good (acts on heavy). *T. D. Easterby* **h106**

BOLLIN THOMAS 7 b.g. Alhijaz – Bollin Magdalene (Teenoso (USA)) [2004/5 19v[5] 16v[2] 16d[4] 20v 16d[3] 20s[4] Mar 10] compact gelding: half-brother to fair hurdler Bollin Annabel (by King's Theatre), stays 2½m: dam fairly useful hurdler up to 3m: fairly useful on Flat (stays 2m): fair form over hurdles: stays 2½m: raced on going softer than good (acts on heavy): blinkered final outing. *T. D. Easterby* **h100**

BOLLITREE BOB 4 b.g. Bob's Return (IRE) – Lady Prunella (IRE) (Supreme Leader) [2004/5 F12d Jan 1] tall gelding: first foal: dam once-raced half-sister to useful staying chaser Latent Talent: ninth of 12 finishers in listed bumper at Cheltenham on debut. *M. Scudamore* **F81**

BOLSHOI BALLET 7 b.g. Dancing Spree (USA) – Broom Isle (Damister (USA)) [2004/5 h99: 16m[4] 16g* 16s[6] 16d[3] 16d[3] Jan 1] quite good-topped gelding: fair handicap hurdler: won at Uttoxeter in May: should stay 2½m: acts on good to firm and heavy going: wears cheekpieces/blinkers nowadays. *J. Mackie* **h106**

BOLTON BARRIE (IRE) 7 b.g. Broken Hearted – Ballyduggan Queen (IRE) (King Luthier) [2004/5 c–, h94: c21g* c25d May 9] sturdy gelding: modest handicap hurdler: easily best effort over fences when winning novice handicap at Southwell in May: stays 25f: acts on firm and good to soft going: tried in cheekpieces (ran poorly). *R. C. Guest* **c93 h–**

BOLTON FOREST (IRE) 12 b.g. Be My Native (USA) – Tickenor Wood (Le Bavard (FR)) [2004/5 c–, h–: c16g[pu] May 1] tall gelding: winning hurdler/chaser: lightly raced and little form since early-2000/1: tried in tongue strap. *Miss S. E. Forster* **c– h–**

BONBON ROSE (FR) 4 ch.c. Mansonnien (FR) – Rose Angevine (FR) (Master Thatch) [2004/5 16s* 17s* 15s* 18v* 17s[6] 17g Mar 18] **c131 p h127**

British racegoers certainly didn't see the best of Bonbon Rose. In two visits to Cheltenham, Bonbon Rose finished sixth to Akilak in the Finesse Hurdle and twentieth to Penzance in the Triumph Hurdle. On both occasions he travelled well, in the Finesse looking the likely winner turning into the straight but not really lasting home in a very well-run race. In the Triumph, Bonbon Rose's rider was very easy on him once he lost ground going to two out. In France, it was a different story. Bonbon Rose won all four starts over hurdles prior to his Cheltenham runs and all three starts over fences after. As those wins came after the end of the British season, Bonbon Rose is still a novice in British terms and would be a very interesting challenger were connections to be tempted across the Channel again, something that is, however, reportedly unlikely.

Bonbon Rose's four wins over hurdles, a debut success at Royan La Palmyre in his trainer's backyard and three victories at Auteuil, showed him a fairly useful performer, but he looked even better when sent over fences. The first two races he won were just minor events, though there was a lot to like about the way he won them, but the third win came in the top chase for his age group, the Group 1

*Gras Savoye Cinema Prix Ferdinand Dufaure, Auteuil—
Bonbon Rose makes all to beat outsider Anglican*

Prix Ferdinand Dufaure. Those opponents who had contested the main trial races looked below the standard expected and Bonbon Rose, who was sent off at evens on the pari mutuel, ran out a comfortable winner, making all, again jumping fluently and quickening when shaken up on the flat to defeat the outsider Anglican by six lengths with a further five to Willdance, winner of the main trial race. Bonbon Rose gave his trainer Arnaud Chaille-Chaille his fourth successive win in the Dufaure, following Karly Flight, Ice Mood and Cyrlight. Like Karly Flight, Bonbon Rose was returned to hurdling after the Dufaure, sent off at odds on for the championship four-year-old hurdle, the Prix Alain du Breil, but he ran as if past his best and could finish only seventh to Strangely Brown. Bonbon Rose is smallish and sturdy in appearance; still a colt, he may be retired to stud in 2006. In the meantime he will stay beyond two and a half miles. He has raced mainly on soft or heavy ground, though the Dufaure was, very unusually for Auteuil, run on ground which the times suggest was good. *A. Chaille-Chaille, France*

BONEYARROW (IRE) 9 ch.g. Over The River (FR) – Apicat (Buckskin (FR)) [2004/5 c136, h–: c29d^{pu} c24s c24v c18v^{2} c20v Feb 3] sturdy gelding: useful chaser in 2003/4: form in 2004/5 only when second of 5 to easy winner Scarthy Lad in minor event at Thurles in January (final start for W. Mullins): bred to stay 3m+: raced on good going or softer (acts on heavy). *E. Griffin, Ireland* **c127 h–**

BONFIRE NIGHT (IRE) 9 b.m. Air Display (USA) – Smokey Path (IRE) (Scallywag) [2004/5 c54x, h66: c16g^{3} c16f* c22m^{3} Jun 25] workmanlike mare: maiden hurdler: poor chaser: made all in weak handicap at Towcester in May: effective at 2m to 2¾m: acts on firm and good to soft going. *R. Dickin* **c73 x h–**

BONGO FURY (FR) 6 b.m. Sillery (USA) – Nativelee (FR) (Giboulee (CAN)) [2004/5 16d 17d^{5} 17g^{ur} 16d* 16d* 16d^{2} 17g 16g^{5} Apr 15] sparely-made mare: useful handicap hurdler: won mares races at Sandown and Doncaster (again idled in front) in January: best effort when 3 lengths second of 25 to Essex in valuable event at Newbury: raced around 2m: has won on firm going, best efforts on good or softer (acts on heavy): visored since debut. *M. C. Pipe* **h132**

BONJOUR BOND (IRE) 4 ro.g. Portrait Gallery (IRE) – Musical Essence (Song) [2004/5 17g^{pu} Apr 15] poor maiden on Flat (stays 1½m), sold out of B. Smart's stable 4,000 gns Doncaster October Sales: showed little in juvenile on hurdling debut. *J. G. M. O'Shea* **h–**

BONNE NOEL'S (IRE) 5 b.g. Saddlers' Hall (IRE) – Mursuma (Rarity) [2004/5 NR] rather unfurnished gelding: half-brother to 7 winners, including top-class 2m to 2½m chaser/useful hurdler Direct Route (by Executive Perk) and smart 2m hurdlers Joe Mac (by Topanoora) and Penny A Day (by Supreme Leader): dam, 1m winner, half-sister to high-class hurdler/smart chaser Youlneverwalkalone, effective at 2m to 3m, and high-class staying hurdler Galmoy: 20/1 and on weak side, highly promising 6 lengths third to **F101 p**

Silent Oscar in bumper at Punchestown on debut in late-April: sure to do better. *C. Roche, Ireland*

BONNET'S PIECES 6 b.m. Alderbrook – Chichell's Hurst (Oats) [2004/5 h–, F–: 16s³ 16s² 19gF 17s⁴ 16v⁴ 16g Mar 16] medium-sized mare: modest novice hurdler: will stay 2½m: acts on heavy ground: has raced freely: often makes running. *Mrs P. Sly* **h86**

BONNIE FLORA 9 b.m. Then Again – My Minnie (Kind of Hush) [2004/5 h–: 17g* 19m⁵ c16s* c17gro c16g³ Aug 2] poor form over hurdles: won novice at Exeter in April 2004: won 2-finisher novice at Newton Abbot on chasing debut in June: may prove best around 2m: acts on soft going: forces pace. *J. W. Mullins* **c92 h75**

BONNY GREY 7 gr.m. Seymour Hicks (FR) – Sky Wave (Idiot's Delight) [2004/5 F88: F16g² F17g 16g⁶ 21s⁵ 16d² 16s² 19m⁴ 16d* Apr 22] leggy mare: bumper winner: fair hurdler: won maiden at Chepstow in April: should stay 2½m: acts on soft and good to firm going. *P. D. Evans* **h105 F92**

BONNY GROVE 5 b.g. Bonny Scot (IRE) – Binny Grove (Sunyboy) [2004/5 F–: F16g F16s Feb 3] lengthy gelding: no form in bumpers. *H. J. Evans* **F–**

BONNY JAGO 4 ch.g. Bonny Scot (IRE) – Bold Honey (IRE) (Nearly A Nose (USA)) [2004/5 F12g Nov 10] first foal: dam ran twice over hurdles: ninth of 23 in 3-y-o bumper at Newbury on debut. *John Allen* **F82**

BONNYJO (FR) 6 br.g. Cyborg (FR) – Argument Facile (FR) (Argument (FR)) [2004/5 F79: 16g⁵ 16s 19d⁵ 25v 20d⁶ Jan 26] rather leggy gelding: poor form over hurdles: stays 2½m. *P. R. Webber* **h74**

BON TEMPS ROULER (FR) 6 b.g. Hero's Honor (USA) – Top Nue (FR) (Treasure Kay) [2004/5 16d³ 16s 16s 16s* Mar 29] lengthy gelding: has scope: second foal: dam French 7f and 9f winner: much improved over hurdles when making all in Menolly Homes Handicap Hurdle at Fairyhouse in March, beating Mansony ¾ length: raced at 2m on good to soft/soft going. *A. L. T. Moore, Ireland* **h113**

ladbrokesgames.com Mares' Only Handicap Hurdle, Sandown—
the old firm of Pipe and McCoy team up successfully as Bongo Fury beats stable-companion La Lambertine

Jenny Mould Memorial Handicap Chase, Cheltenham—
Bonus Bridge has taken Latalomne's measure at the last

BONUS BRIDGE (IRE) 10 b.g. Executive Perk – Corivia (Over The River (FR)) [2004/5 c128, h–: c16d^{4} c17g^{pu} c16d* c16g c16s^{4} c16g^{F} Apr 16] tall gelding: useful handicap chaser: won at Cheltenham in December by 12 lengths from Latalomne, ridden more patiently than usual: best effort after when fourth to Fota Island in valuable event at Aintree: races mainly around 2m, probably stays 2½m: acts on soft and good to firm going: usually races prominently: has wandered/finished weakly. *H. D. Daly* **c138 h–**

BONUS TRIX (IRE) 9 b.g. Executive Perk – Black Trix (Peacock (FR)) [2004/5 h85: 19d^{6} May 4] good-topped gelding: modest hurdler at best, lightly raced nowadays: should stay at least 2½m: usually suffers breathing problems (tried tongue tied). *C. Tinkler* **h–**

BOOK'S WAY 9 br.g. Afzal – In A Whirl (USA) (Island Whirl (USA)) [2004/5 c–, h65: 19m* 20d 26m^{4} 22m^{2} 24d^{4} 20d 20s^{2} 24m^{6} 19g 20m 16g^{6} 20d^{4} Mar 28] sparely-made gelding: little form over fences: poor handicap hurdler: won seller at Market Rasen in June: stays 3¼m: acts on firm and soft going: tried visored/in cheekpieces. *D. W. Thompson* **c– h72**

BOOM OR BUST (IRE) 6 ch.g. Entrepreneur – Classic Affair (USA) (Trempolino (USA)) [2004/5 h81: 17d 17m 16m 19g^{6} c19d^{4} 17m Nov 11] angular gelding: maiden hurdler: no form in 2004/5, including on chasing debut: raced mainly around 2m: acts on soft and good to firm going: tried blinkered, often wears cheekpieces. *Miss K. M. George* **c– h–**

BOOZY DOUZ 5 ch.m. Abou Zouz (USA) – Ackcontent (USA) (Key To Content (USA)) [2004/5 h–: 19g^{pu} Jun 15] no form on Flat or over hurdles. *H. S. Howe* **h–**

BORDER ARTIST 6 ch.g. Selkirk (USA) – Aunt Tate (Tate Gallery (USA)) [2004/5 16g 16f^{5} 17d^{6} 16s^{5} Nov 21] fair on Flat (stays 1m) for D. Nicholls: poor novice hurdler: will prove best over sharp 2m. *K. G. Reveley* **h75**

BORDER CRAIC (IRE) 5 ch.g. Glacial Storm (USA) – Clare Maid (IRE) (Fidel) [2004/5 F16s Mar 12] €17,000 4-y-o: second foal: dam, 2m hurdle winner, sister to very smart hurdler Fidway: tailed off in bumper on debut. *B. Mactaggart* **F–**

BORDER STAR (IRE) 8 b.g. Parthian Springs – Tengello (Bargello) [2004/5 c–, h78: 16m^{5} 19d^{3} Oct 5] lengthy gelding: no show only start over fences: poor hurdler: stays 2¾m: acts on soft and good to firm going: wears cheekpieces/blinkers: tried tongue tied. *J. M. Jefferson* **c– h75**

BORDER TALE 5 b.g. Selkirk (USA) – Likely Story (IRE) (Night Shift (USA)) [2004/5 h108: 18d^{6} 16m 16d^{5} 16g 16s 20g Mar 26] sturdy gelding: fair hurdler: raced mainly around 2m: acts on good to firm going, possibly not on soft: has suffered breathing problems. *N. A. Twiston-Davies* **h103**

BOREHILL JOKER 9 ch.g. Pure Melody (USA) – Queen Matilda (Castle Keep) [2004/5 c79, h82: 16m^{pu} 16v^{3} 19s* 20s^{3} c19g* 19s^{2} c20d^{ur} 19d^{4} c20g^{4} c19s^{bd} c20s^{5} Feb 10] sparely-made gelding: modest handicap hurdler/chaser: left E. Haddock after second start: won conditional jockeys selling hurdle at Market Rasen and over fences at Catterick in December: stays 2½m: acts on heavy going: tried blinkered: usually tongue tied for former stable: genuine. *J. L. Spearing* **c91 h98**

BORING GORING (IRE) 11 b.g. Aristocracy – Coolrusk (IRE) (Millfontaine) [2004/5 c82x, h–: 21g 22m c23m Jul 21] rangy gelding: poor hurdler/maiden chaser, no form since reappearance in 2003/4: tried blinkered: usually tongue tied: poor jumper of fences. *Miss A. M. Newton-Smith* **c– x h–**

BORORA 6 gr.g. Shareef Dancer (USA) – Bustling Nelly (Bustino) [2004/5 h101: 17g^{2} 16g* 17g* 17d^{3} 16d^{2} 16d^{4} 16d 17g^{3} 16g^{3} Apr 1] close-coupled gelding: useful handicap hurdler: won at Worcester and Newton Abbot in July: 200/1, excelled himself when 4 lengths third to Fontanesi in valuable 30-runner event at Cheltenham eighth start: best around 2m: acts on good to firm and good to soft going. *R. Lee* **h130**

BOSCO (IRE) 4 br.g. Petardia – Classic Goddess (IRE) (Classic Secret (USA)) [2004/5 16s^{pu} 16v^{6} 19s Feb 6] modest on Flat (stays 1¼m), successful in June for R. Hannon, sold out of P. McEntee's stable £1,900 Ascot November Sales: no form over hurdles: free-going sort. *I. R. Brown* **h–**

BOSS ROYAL 8 ch.g. Afzal – Born Bossy (Eborneezer) [2004/5 c78x, h–: c19m^{F} c21g^{pu} 19s c24s^{pu} c19s^{pu} c19s^{pu} c25v^{pu} Feb 13] workmanlike gelding: winning hurdler/ maiden chaser: no form in 2004/5: stays easy 2½m: acts on soft and good to firm going: usually tongue tied: poor jumper. *G. A. Ham* **c– x h–**

BOSTON LASS 8 br.m. Terimon – Larksmore (Royal Fountain) [2004/5 c72, h–: c25g* c26d^{2} May 29] close-coupled mare: poor chaser: won novice at Hexham in May: stays 27f: acts on heavy and good to firm going: sometimes wears cheekpieces. *R. D. E. Woodhouse* **c83 h–**

BOSTON STRONG BOY (IRE) 5 ch.g. Pennekamp (USA) – Cossack Princess (IRE) (Lomond (USA)) [2004/5 F16g^{2} Oct 5] fourth foal: half-brother to fairly useful 1m winner My Very Own (by Persian Bold): dam fourth at 1¼m in Ireland: 2½ lengths second to Midnight Spur in bumper at Huntingdon on debut. *C. Tinkler* **F92**

BOSUNS MATE 12 ch.g. Yachtsman (USA) – Langton Lass (Nearly A Hand) [2004/5 c95x, h–: c23s^{pu} c22g^{pu} Apr 1] useful-looking gelding: veteran chaser, no sign of retaining ability in 2005: often wears headgear: poor jumper. *M. Keighley* **c– x h–**

BOSWORTH BOURN (IRE) 5 b.g. Aahsaylad – Pastinas Lass (Bargello) [2004/5 F16s 21s 19s 19s 22s 22d^{6} 21g Mar 28] rather unfurnished gelding: half-brother to 2 winning hurdlers, notably useful stayer Rosin The Bow (by Roselier): dam, placed once at 5 yrs, half-sister to high-class Irish hurdler Slaney Idol: no form: has been visored/ blinkered. *Miss J. S. Davis* **h– F–**

BOSWORTH BOY 7 b.g. Deploy – Krill (Kris) [2004/5 h–: 16d Nov 21] good-topped gelding: soundly beaten all 3 outings over hurdles, sold out of J. Gallagher's stable £4,600 Ascot October Sales. *A. J. Chamberlain* **h–**

BOTTOM DRAWER 5 b.g. My Best Valentine – Little Egret (Carwhite) [2004/5 17s 16d Apr 20] good-topped gelding: well beaten in 2 maidens at 3 yrs for D. ffrench Davis, and on both starts over hurdles. *Mrs D. A. Hamer* **h–**

BOUGOURE (IRE) 6 b.g. Oscar (IRE) – Jasmine Melody (Jasmine Star) [2004/5 F16s^{5} F16d F16d^{2} F16s* Mar 1] €30,000 4-y-o: sturdy gelding: ninth foal: half-brother to winning hurdlers Very Tasty (by Be My Native), around 2m, and Desert Melody (by Carlingford Castle), at 21f: dam, winning 2m hurdler in Ireland, half-sister to useful 2½m chaser Bibendum: fairly useful form when second to Buena Vista in bumper at Doncaster in January: didn't have to run quite to same level to win maiden at Catterick by ½ length from Brave Fellow: will stay 2½m. *Mrs S. J. Smith* **F100**

BOULTA (IRE) 11 ch.g. Commanche Run – Boulta View (Beau Chapeau) [2004/5 c92: c25m* c25g^{pu} c24v^{pu} c25s^{pu} Apr 3] fair hunter chaser: made all in 4-runner event at Kelso very early in season: no subsequent form, left Mrs C. Moore after next outing: stays 25f: acts on good to firm ground: has worn cheekpieces: tried tongue tied. *W. Amos* **c97**

BOUNCE AGAIN (FR) 5 b.g. Jeune Homme (USA) – Lattaquie (FR) (Fast Topaze (USA)) [2004/5 F81: 16g 17s 16g 22s 17v^{2} c19m^{5} c26g^{3} c22s^{pu} c24d^{4} Apr 22] workmanlike gelding: no form over hurdles: poor form over fences: may prove best short of 3m: visored last 6 starts: sold 5,000 gns Doncaster May Sales. *M. C. Pipe* **c68 h–**

BOUNCE BACK (USA) 9 ch.g. Trempolino (USA) – Lattaquie (FR) (Fast Topaze (USA)) [2004/5 c128x, h–: c25d^{ur} c24d c29d^{5} 22d Dec 26] tall gelding: smart hurdler/ chaser at one time, has deteriorated considerably: stays 29f: acts on heavy and good to firm going: tried blinkered/visored: makes mistakes: often soon off bridle. *M. C. Pipe* **c114 x h–**

BOUND 7 b.g. Kris – Tender Moment (IRE) (Caerleon (USA)) [2004/5 h127: c17m* c16g^{3} c17s^{ur} c16g^{F} Jan 19] tall gelding: fairly useful handicap hurdler: easily landed **c108 h–**

odds in maiden at Market Rasen on chasing debut in June: well held only subsequent completed start: best around 2m: acts on soft and good to firm going: sometimes tongue tied: races freely: has found little. *Mrs L. Wadham*

BOUNDARY HOUSE 7 ch.g. Alflora (IRE) – Preacher's Gem (The Parson) [2004/5 h–, F87: 21s 16s^4 19v^5 c19s^F c19s^2 c19d^{pu} Apr 22] leggy, sparely-made gelding: poor form over hurdles and fences: should be suited by 2½m+: raced on good going or softer. *J. A. B. Old* — **c82 h75**

BOURBON MANHATTAN 7 b.g. Alflora (IRE) – Vanina II (FR) (Italic (FR)) [2004/5 h134: c20s^F Oct 28] rangy, useful-looking gelding: useful novice hurdler in 2003/4: didn't convince with jumping and fell eighth in maiden at Stratford on chasing debut (reportedly suffered fractures to right shoulder): should prove at least as effective at 2½m as shorter: acts on good to firm and soft going, below form on heavy. *A. King* — **c– h–**

BOURNEAGAINKRISTEN 7 ch.m. Afzal – Miss Lawn (FR) (Lashkari) [2004/5 F16v 16d 16d^{pu} Mar 24] third foal: dam, fair hurdler, stayed 2½m: no sign of ability. *D. Burchell* — **h– F–**

BOWD LANE JOE 6 gr.g. Mazaad – Race To The Rhythm (Deep Run) [2004/5 h–: 16g c16g^5 c16s^3 c16g^6 Mar 28] tall, unfurnished gelding: well held over hurdles: poor form over fences: raced mainly at 2m on good ground or softer. *A. W. Carroll* — **c70 h–**

BOWLEAZE (IRE) 6 br.g. Right Win (IRE) – Mrs Cullen (Over The River (FR)) [2004/5 h94: 16s 21s 22s^2 19d^3 24g* 24g^{pu} Apr 14] rangy gelding: will make a chaser: fairly useful novice hurdler: won at Newbury in April by 3½ lengths from Dancing Rock, still on bridle last: laboured effort 2 weeks later: best effort at 3m: acts on soft and good to firm ground. *R. H. Alner* — **h116**

BOWLING GREEN (IRE) 9 b.g. Bowling Pin – Fraulein Koln (IRE) (Mandalus) [2004/5 20f^5 20d 20m^3 20g^5 22f* 22f^F Oct 7] ex-Irish gelding: well held both completed starts over fences (fell twice): modest hurdler: left P. Lenihan, improved form when winning amateur handicap at Exeter in September: stays 2¾m: acts on firm going. *Jonjo O'Neill* — **c– h94**

BOW STRADA 8 ch.g. Rainbow Quest (USA) – La Strada (Niniski (USA)) [2004/5 c–, h–: 22g^4 c24m^3 24d c22g* Sep 25] angular, close-coupled gelding: fairly useful hurdler: useful chaser: best effort when winning valuable handicap at Market Rasen by 16 lengths from Tango Royal, setting good pace and soon clear: stays 3m: acts on firm and good to soft going. *P. J. Hobbs* — **c136 + h122**

BOXCLEVER 4 b.g. Accordion – Pugilistic (Hard Fought) [2004/5 F16s Apr 22] half-brother to 3 winners by Gunner B, including fair hurdler/chaser up to 2¾m Gunner Marc: dam unraced half-sister to smart 2m hurdler Jobroke: seventh of 18 in bumper at Perth on debut, staying on when hampered final 1f. *J. M. Jefferson* — **F82**

BOX OF TRICKS (IRE) 5 ch.g. Barathea (IRE) – Chocolate Box (Most Welcome) [2004/5 F–: 16g 16m^{pu} Jun 6] no form in bumper (tongue tied) or 2 starts over hurdles. *Mrs B. E. Matthews* — **h–**

BOX ON (IRE) 8 b. or br.g. Un Desperado (FR) – Party Dancer (Be My Guest (USA)) [2004/5 20g^2 20s^4 20d^6 24v^{pu} Jan 29] IR £21,000 4-y-o: big, heavy-topped gelding: half-brother to winning pointer by Montelimar: dam ran twice: won maiden Irish point in 2003: modest form first 2 starts over hurdles: should stay 3m+. *Miss V. Scott* — **h97**

BOYACKASHA (IRE) 7 b.g. Executive Perk – Lady Pauper (IRE) (Le Moss) [2004/5 c21g^2 c20d^2 c22v^3 c23d^4 c21d^6 c22v^{pu} 19s Mar 27] €4,700 4-y-o: strong, lengthy gelding: eighth foal: half-brother to several winning pointers: dam unraced, from family of high-class 2m to 2½m hurdler King Credo: won maiden point in 2004: fair form in maiden chases second and third starts: disappointing after, including over hurdles: stays 2¾m: acts on heavy going. *E. McNamara, Ireland* — **c101 h–**

BOYNE BANKS (IRE) 10 ch.g. Boyne Valley – Pallatess (Pall Mall) [2004/5 c–, h–: c21d Apr 28] winning pointer: little other form: tried blinkered. *Mrs Sarah Stafford* — **c– h–**

BOY'S HURRAH (IRE) 9 b.g. Phardante (FR) – Gorryelm (Arctic Slave) [2004/5 c106: c28g^6 c25v^2 c25v^2 c24d* c24d* c24g^F c24d^2 c21d c29g^{pu} Apr 23] strong gelding: fair handicap chaser: won at Sandown in December and January: best effort when second there seventh outing: stays 25f: acts on any going: bold jumper: often front runner. *J. Howard Johnson* — **c115**

BOYSTEROUS (IRE) 5 b.g. Lord Americo – Hells Angel (IRE) (Kambalda) [2004/5 F17g^6 Apr 7] 19,000 4-y-o: second foal: dam unraced: sixth of 12 in bumper at Taunton on debut. *Mrs H. Dalton* — **F77**

BRAD 7 b.g. Deploy – Celia Brady (Last Tycoon) [2004/5 c–, h70, F85: c19g^4 Apr 26] lengthy gelding: little form in 2 starts over hurdles and fences: sold 4,200 gns Doncaster May Sales, resold 2,500 gns Doncaster October Sales. *P. R. Webber* **c– h–**

BRADY BOYS (USA) 8 b.g. Cozzene (USA) – Elvia (USA) (Roberto (USA)) [2004/5 c81, h76: c21g^4 c20m^{pu} c19m^{ur} c16s c20s^{pu} c19g^F c25s^6 c20v^4 c25m^4 c24g^6 Apr 15] lengthy gelding: poor hurdler: maiden chaser: no form in 2004/5: has worn visor/cheekpieces. *J. G. M. O'Shea* **c– h–**

BRAEBURN 10 b.g. Petoski – Great Granny Smith (Fine Blue) [2004/5 c82: c26g^{pu} May 23] useful-looking gelding: maiden chaser, modest at best: won points in February and March. *R. T. Phillips* **c– h–**

BRAGADINO 6 b.g. Zilzal (USA) – Graecia Magna (USA) (Private Account (USA)) [2004/5 16m 16m^5 Dec 12] half-brother to 3 winners over jumps, including useful 2m chaser Theseus (by Danehill) and fairly useful hurdler/chaser Polydamas (by Last Tycoon), stayed 2½m: useful at one time on Flat (stays 9f), has deteriorated considerably: poor form in 2 starts over hurdles, tongue tied second time (hung right). *Lindsay Woods, Ireland* **h81**

BRAMANTINO (IRE) 5 b.g. Perugino (USA) – Headrest (Habitat) [2004/5 16d 16s^6 16v^4 16v 16g^5 17v^2 16d Apr 11] half-brother to modest hurdler Kasid (by Caerleon), stays 2¾m: fair on Flat (stays 1½m), successful 3 times in 2004: poor maiden hurdler: raced around 2m on good going or softer: effective blinkered or not. *R. A. Fahey* **h80**

BRAMBLEHILL DUKE (IRE) 13 b.g. Kambalda – Scat-Cat (Furry Glen) [2004/5 c113x, h–: c25g c25g^6 c21d^6 c26d^F c25d^{bd} c28s^{pu} c25s c21g^R Apr 10] medium-sized gelding: one-time fairly useful handicap chaser, very much on the downgrade: stays 27f: acts on good to firm and heavy going: usually let down by jumping. *Miss Venetia Williams* **c90 x h–**

BRAMLYNN BROOK (FR) 7 ch.g. Apple Tree (FR) – Sainte Lys (FR) (Don Roberto (USA)) [2004/5 h104, F103: 26g 24s^2 24g^2 24d^6 Jan 1] big, lengthy gelding: fair hurdler: several mistakes and dismounted after line final start: should stay beyond 3m: acts on heavy going. *Miss Venetia Williams* **h112**

bet@bluesquare.com Handicap Chase, Market Rasen—
front-running tactics work very well for wide-margin winner Bow Strada

BRANDY BAY 4 ch.f. Karinga Bay – Ower Farm (Coronash) [2004/5 F16v^4 F16d F16v Mar 29] second foal: dam unraced: poor form in bumpers. *C. L. Tizzard* **F74**

BRANDY WINE (IRE) 7 b.g. Roselier (FR) – Sakonnet (IRE) (Mandalus) [2004/5 h–, F83: 16v^5 16d 24v* Feb 13] rangy gelding: will make a chaser: upped in trip, much improved effort over hurdles when winning amateur handicap at Ayr in February: should do better again. *L. Lungo* **h96 p**

BRANKLEY BOY 7 ch.g. Afzal – Needwood Fortune (Tycoon II) [2004/5 17d^3 19s^2 Mar 7] won bumper on debut in 2003: off 2 years, fair form when placed both starts in novice hurdles: will stay beyond 19f: should improve and win a race over hurdles. *N. J. Henderson* **h110 p**

BRASILIA PRINCE 6 ch.g. Karinga Bay – Cappuccino Girl (Broadsword (USA)) [2004/5 21d^F 21s^{pu} 16g 22m^3 Apr 21] second foal: dam modest staying hurdler: well held both completed starts in novice hurdles: tried visored. *G. P. Enright* **h–**

BRAVE CARADOC (IRE) 7 b.g. Un Desperado (FR) – Drivers Bureau (Proverb) [2004/5 h90: c25g c22d^2 c22s^F Dec 21] tall gelding: modest form over hurdles/fences: should be suited by 3m+: acts on soft going: sold £1,200 Ascot February Sales. *G. L. Moore* **c92 h–**

BRAVE DANE (IRE) 7 b.g. Danehill (USA) – Nuriva (USA) (Woodman (USA)) [2004/5 h92+: 16g* 16m* 16g^4 Oct 14] long-backed gelding: fairly useful on Flat (stays 11.7f), successful 3 times in 2004: modest hurdler: won novice handicaps at Ludlow and Stratford in May: raced around 2m: acts on good to firm and good to soft going. *A. W. Carroll* **h92**

BRAVE EFFECT (IRE) 9 br.g. Bravefoot – Crupney Lass (Ardoon) [2004/5 c90, h93: c25g^{pu} c21m^3 21m^{pu} 19m^4 19g^4 21v 16v^3 16m^2 16g^2 16s^3 Mar 22] well-made gelding: modest handicap hurdler: left M. Todhunter after third start: generally let down by jumping over fences: stays 21f: acts on firm and good to soft going, below best on softer: tried in cheekpieces, visored last 3 starts: tongue tied once: has finished weakly. *Mrs Dianne Sayer* **c85 x h98**

BRAVE INCA (IRE) 7 b.g. Good Thyne (USA) – Wigwam Mam (IRE) (Commanche Run) [2004/5 h148p: 16g* 16s^2 20d^2 16s^2 16v^2 16g^3 20d^{ur} Apr 9] **h163**

Thank goodness for Punchestown. By the end of April, all of Ireland's leading hurdlers, with the exception of Brave Inca, had picked up at least one good prize in the course of the season. If Brave Inca had missed out, it certainly wouldn't have been for the lack of trying, so his success at Punchestown was deserved, his gameness and reliability finally rewarded. Those qualities turned out to be decisive against an equally good but less resolute rival. Twelve months earlier, Brave Inca had been enjoying a feast, rather than enduring a famine. A battling short-head victory over Royal Shakespeare in the Evening Herald Champion Novices' Hurdle at the Punchestown Festival had been his seventh win in a row and his third in Grade 1 company after the Deloitte Novices' Hurdle at Leopardstown and the Letheby & Christopher Supreme Novices' at Cheltenham, the latter gained by a neck from War of Attrition in a thrilling race.

In the latest season, Brave Inca swapped a succession of wins for a series of placed efforts. The mare Solerina proved six lengths too good for Brave Inca in the Hatton's Grace Hurdle at Fairyhouse in November, before Macs Joy came between him and a couple of big prizes. The weights were very much against Brave Inca when he made his return in the autumn against a race-fit Macs Joy in an intermediate event at Down Royal earlier in November, Brave Inca going down by a length, conceding 10 lb to the winner. The pair met again twice more during the winter at Leopardstown, both times on level terms, but Brave Inca was beaten three lengths in the December Festival Hurdle, after getting outpaced, and finished a short head behind Macs Joy when they reopposed in the AIG Europe Champion Hurdle the following month. This was the first of three thrilling three-way finishes Brave Inca was involved in, the third party on this occasion being Hardy Eustace. Looking only fourth-best at one stage, Brave Inca stayed on to tremendous effect, so well that his rider believed he had got up. Brave Inca did finally come out on top in his fourth clash with Macs Joy in the Champion Hurdle at Cheltenham, only to go down in another tight finish, this time beaten a neck and the same behind Hardy Eustace and Harchibald. Brave Inca looked very well at Cheltenham—he had been

Emo Oil Champion Hurdle, Punchestown—
a Tony McCoy-inspired Brave Inca gets the better of Harchibald (right) and Macs Joy (centre)

trained for the race all year—but it was still slightly surprising that he ran his best race yet, coping much better than might have been imagined with a pace that wasn't stepped up until after the third last. Always prominent, Brave Inca held every chance at the last but couldn't quite get his head in front up the hill. Another feature of Brave Inca's Cheltenham performance was his better than usual round of jumping. His jumping had let him down behind Solerina at Fairyhouse and he had been fortunate to get away with going down on his nose at the third flight in the AIG Europe. On his next outing after Cheltenham, however, Brave Inca's luck ran out. Starting favourite for the Aintree Hurdle (before which he didn't take the eye quite so much), he was still to be asked for his effort, looking likely to play a major role in the finish, when diving at the third-last flight and all but falling, giving his rider no chance of staying in the saddle.

And so to Punchestown. If the events of the preceding months had shown anything, it was that there was precious little between Brave Inca and his chief rivals Macs Joy and Harchibald, though the betting for the five-runner Emo Oil Champion Hurdle suggested otherwise, Harchibald starting at 6/4-on, Brave Inca at 2/1 and Macs Joy at 11/2. Useful novice Publican and rank outsider Bob What completed the field. While the race was to provide consolation for Brave Inca's efforts during the season, there was none for his regular rider Barry Cash who had to make way for Tony McCoy. The new partnership was an instant success. McCoy set a slow pace but Brave Inca was under the whip to raise the tempo from three out where Macs Joy, Harchibald and even Publican were all still close up and seemingly travelling better. With Brave Inca giving a willing response to a typically forceful ride from McCoy, he was still bang there at the last with Macs Joy upsides, while Harchibald was produced at the same time to make a line of three. Macs Joy was the first to crack on the run-in and Harchibald initially looked like gaining the upper hand, but Brave Inca proved the more resolute, battling back to lead again near the line and prevailing by a head from Harchibald with Macs Joy just a length behind them.

Novices Syndicate's "Brave Inca"

Brave Inca (IRE) (b.g. 1998)	Good Thyne (USA) (br 1977)	Herbager (b 1956)	Vandale II
			Flagette
		Foreseer (b or br 1969)	Round Table
			Regal Gleam
	Wigwam Mam (IRE) (ch 1993)	Commanche Run (b 1981)	Run The Gantlet
			Volley
		Rozifer (ch 1978)	Lucifer
			Rozeen

It will be a surprise if Brave Inca has to wait until the next Punchestown Festival before getting his head in front again, though connections will have to decide whether he remains over hurdles or is switched to fences. He is certainly a chasing type on looks, being a strong, good-bodied gelding, and has the potential to make a first-rate novice. There has already been a top-class chaser among Brave Inca's immediate family—Merry Gale is out of a half-sister to Brave Inca's grandam Rozifer—and another good chaser a bit further back in dual Champion Chase winner Skymas. First foal Brave Inca remains the only runner so far out of his unraced dam Wigwam Mam. Her four-year-old gelding by Mister Mat fetched 50,000 guineas at the Doncaster May Sales.

Brave Inca has often given the impression that he would prove better at two and a half miles than two (he has already won at the longer trip), but two miles is where most of the top prizes over hurdles are, and his record at that trip is hard to fault, as he showed at both Cheltenham and Punchestown even though the emphasis wasn't on stamina. He acts on heavy ground and has yet to race on firmer than good. Whether Brave Inca is campaigned towards another Champion Hurdle or goes novice chasing, his reliability and gameness will stand him in good stead. Given the heights he has now reached, it seems all the more remarkable that he finished no nearer than seventh on the first four starts of his career, showing no better than poor form. *C. A. Murphy, Ireland*

BRAVE LORD (IRE) 8 ch.g. Mister Lord (USA) – Artic Squaw (IRE) (Buckskin (FR)) [2004/5 h85: 23d^pu 20v c20s* c24d³ Mar 26] strong, lengthy gelding: maiden hurdler: much improved when winning maiden at Carlisle in March on chasing debut: better form again when third in handicap there 2 weeks later: will stay beyond 3m: acts on soft going. *L. Lungo* **c113 h–**

BRAVE REBELLION 6 b.g. Primitive Rising (USA) – Grand Queen (Grand Conde (FR)) [2004/5 F16d³ F16s² F16g* Mar 28] 9,500 4-y-o: sturdy gelding: fifth foal: brother to fair hurdler/chaser Harfdecent, stayed 25f: dam bad Flat maiden: fairly useful form in bumpers: won 8-runner event at Huntingdon by 1½ lengths from Knighton Lad, making most: will be suited by stiffer test of stamina. *K. G. Reveley* **F95**

BRAVE SPIRIT (FR) 7 b.g. Legend of France (USA) – Guerre Ou Paix (FR) (Comrade In Arms) [2004/5 c76, h78?: c25m² c24s⁴ c24d^ur c26s* c24s* c23d² c26d* c28s* c27s* c25v² c24d⁴ c24g⁶ c23v Mar 30] rather leggy gelding: sold out of I. Williams' stable 16,000 gns Doncaster May Sales after first outing: had fine run over fences between November and February, winning handicaps at Fontwell (3), Lingfield (novice) and Taunton: even better form tenth and eleventh starts, fourth of 6 in Grade 2 novice at Lingfield on second occasion: stays 3½m: acts on soft and good to firm going: usually wears cheekpieces: tried tongue tied. *C. L. Tizzard* **c129 h–**

BRAVE THOUGHT (IRE) 10 b.g. Commanche Run – Bristol Fairy (Smartset) [2004/5 c104, h–: 17v⁶ c16d* c20g³ c16v³ c16s³ Mar 12] sturdy gelding: winning hurdler: fair chaser: won handicap at Newcastle in December: stays 2½m: raced mainly on going softer than good (acts on heavy). *P. Monteith* **c115 h–**

BRAVE VISION 9 b.g. Clantime – Kinlet Vision (IRE) (Vision (USA)) [2004/5 17s 16d* 16d* 16d* 16v³ 16g^ur Mar 26] sturdy gelding: fair handicap hurdler: returned from 20-month absence an improved performer, winning 3 times at Newcastle in quick succession (amateur event on first occasion): best around 2m: acts on good to firm and heavy going. *A. C. Whillans* **h107**

BRAVURA 7 ch.g. Never So Bold – Sylvan Song (Song) [2004/5 h89: 16g⁶ Mar 14] modest on all-weather on Flat (stays easy 1½m) on return from long absence in 2005: modest form on first (in cheekpieces) of 2 starts in novice hurdles. *G. L. Moore* **h–**

BREAKING BALL (IRE) 5 ch.g. Erins Isle – Noorajo (IRE) (Ahonoora) [2004/5 F18f* F16m 22g^pu 22m³ 20m⁴ 21g^pu Oct 6] ex-Irish gelding: sixth foal: brother to winning hurdler up to 2¾m Traditional: dam placed at 1m: won bumper at Limerick on debut in May for E. Griffin: poor form over hurdles: in cheekpieces/blinkers last 3 starts. *Miss Venetia Williams* **h72 F91**

BREAKING BREEZE (IRE) 10 b.g. Mandalus – Knockacool Breeze (Buckskin (FR)) [2004/5 c–, h–: c17d³ c19m⁴ c21g⁵ c25g³ c25g c19m⁴ c19g* c24g² c24d⁵ Nov 9] lengthy gelding: fair handicap chaser: back to best when making all in seller at Hereford in September: stays 3m, at least when conditions aren't testing: acts on good to firm and good to soft going: free-going sort who usually races up with pace. *J. S. King* **c103 h–**

BREATHOFFRESHAIR (IRE) 8 ch.g. Fresh Breeze (USA) – Carl Louise (Invited (USA)) [2004/5 h–, F–: 19s 21d^pu c22g^ur Apr 19] no sign of ability: trained by N. Twiston-Davies on reappearance: tried blinkered. *J. Gallagher* **c– h–**

BREEMA DONNA 7 b.m. Sir Harry Lewis (USA) – Donna Del Lago (Kings Lake (USA)) [2004/5 F–: F16d 16s^F 16d 16g^F 16s³ 20s Feb 24] leggy mare: form only in mares novice hurdle on penultimate outing: should stay beyond 2m. *R. Dickin* **h64 F–**

BREEZER 5 b.g. Forzando – Lady Lacey (Kampala) [2004/5 h91: 16d 19d 16d 16d 19s^pu 20s 19g* 19g 17g Apr 12] angular gelding: modest hurdler: won selling handicap at Taunton in March: stays 19f: acts on good to firm going: tried visored: not one to rely on. *J. A. Geake* **h86 §**

BREEZY BOY 6 gr.g. Terimon – Wordy's Wind (Strong Gale) [2004/5 20m^pu May 16] first foal: dam, poor maiden hurdler, stayed 3m: no show in novice hurdle on debut. *Mrs C. A. Dunnett* **h–**

BREFFNI FLYER (IRE) 9 b.g. Namaqualand (USA) – Lyphard's Lady (Lyphard's Special (USA)) [2004/5 18g c20m² c20f* c20f² c20f* c22f³ 20g 20s 22s c20d^F 22s Nov 25] smallish, rather sparely-made gelding: fair chaser: won maiden at Kilbeggan in May and handicap at Wexford in June: winning hurdler, only poor form in 2004/5: stays 2¾m: acts on any going: tried blinkered/in cheekpieces. *Patrick Martin, Ireland* **c103 h79**

BREKNEN LE NOIR (FR) 7 b.g. Pelder (IRE) – Roziyna (Reform) [2004/5 h113: c20s^F Oct 28] good-topped gelding: fair hurdler: upsides winner when falling last in **c103 h–**

maiden at Stratford on chasing debut: stays 2½m: acts on heavy going (yet to race on firmer than good): blinkered last 6 starts: front runner: jumps none too fluently. *P. J. Hobbs*

BRETTON 4 b.g. Polar Prince (IRE) – Understudy (In The Wings) [2004/5 16d Nov 6] modest on Flat (stays 1½m), successful in January: in cheekpieces, eighth of 11 in juvenile at Sandown on hurdling debut. *B. A. Pearce* **h76**

BREWSTER (IRE) 8 b.g. Roselier (FR) – Aelia Paetina (Buckskin (FR)) [2004/5 h130: 20s^4 21d* 24d* 21d* 20s^2 24g^3 24d^2 Apr 8] **h147**

Prior to the latest season, Winston Run, a 100/1-shot when third to Barton in the 1999 Royal & SunAlliance Novices' Hurdle, was the only one of Ian Williams' twenty-three runners to have been placed at the Cheltenham Festival. All the more reason for Williams to feel delighted when three of the four horses he sent to Cheltenham in March came either second or third. However, it would also be understandable if the trainer was somewhat disappointed not to have saddled his first Festival winner. At Your Request (33/1) and Bambi de L'Orme (16/1) excelled themselves in finishing runner-up in the Fred Winter Juvenile Handicap Hurdle and the Grand Annual Chase respectively, but Brewster didn't quite run up to his best, despite being beaten less than three lengths in finishing third to Moulin Riche when favourite for the Brit Insurance Novices' Hurdle, registered as the Spa Novices' Hurdle. On going less testing than he encountered in his other races during the season, Brewster was just found wanting for speed after leading from the eighth to two out. Next time out, on softer ground, Brewster easily turned the tables on Moulin Riche in the Sefton Novices' Hurdle at Aintree, running right up to his best in finishing two and a half lengths second to Asian Maze.

Brewster won a bumper at Sligo for Ian Buchanan on his only start before joining his present stable in 2002, and was lightly raced in his first two seasons over hurdles. It wasn't until November that he finally got off the mark in that sphere, in a novice event at Cheltenham. He followed up a month later in the Grade 2 Bristol Novices' Hurdle, also sponsored by Brit Insurance, on the same course, beating Jackson by twelve lengths, and just over two weeks after that completed his hat-trick in the Grade 1 stanjamesuk.com Challow Novices' Hurdle at Newbury. It wasn't the strongest renewal of the Challow Hurdle and Brewster didn't need to improve to win it by a length and three quarters from Ladalko, pulling clear with

stanjamesuk.com Challow Novices' Hurdle, Newbury—
the game Brewster (checks) outstays Ladalko to complete a hat-trick

the runner-up from two out, losing the lead at the last but soon back in front. Brewster was sent off favourite to complete a four-timer when returned to Cheltenham for a Grade 2 contest at the end of January but, although he showed further improvement, he had to settle for second place, two and a half lengths behind Ambobo. As on the occasion of his three wins, Brewster was ridden by David Dennis, who was replaced by Richard Johnson at the Festival. Dennis was back on board at Aintree, though.

Brewster (IRE) (b.g. 1997)	Roselier (FR) (b 1973)	Misti IV (br 1958)	Medium
			Mist
		Peace Rose (br 1959)	Fastnet Rock
			La Paix
	Aelia Paetina (ch 1983)	Buckskin (b 1973)	Yelapa
			Bete A Bon Dieu
		Mariamne (ch 1977)	Deep Run
			Agrippina

Brewster, who fetched IR £22,000 as an unraced four-year-old at the Derby Sale, is the sixth foal of Aelia Paetina, a sister to the smart chaser Buck Rogers, who won the John Durkan Memorial and the Leopardstown Chase in 1999/00. Aelia Paetina, who finished second in a point-to-point in Ireland, has produced two winners of similar events in Britain, Mefein Boy (by Royal Fountain) and Eagle Hill (by Mandalus). The next dam Mariamne, an unraced half-sister to the useful jumper Drusus, is out of the Irish Cesarewitch winner and winning hurdler Agrippina. Another of Agrippina's daughters Claudia Pulchra is the grandam of the useful three-mile chaser Killusty, a third Tender Eyes is the grandam of the Kim Muir Chase winner Stop The Waller. Agrippina is a half-sister to the useful hurdler and middle-distance stayer Humdoleila. As expected given his pedigree, stamina is Brewster's forte and he will prove very well suited by further than three miles. While he has shown his form on going ranging from good to firm to heavy, the more emphasis the ground places on stamina the more effective Brewster will be. Brewster could well be sent over fences in 2005/6, and if he takes well to chasing there is every reason to think he will be turning up at the next Cheltenham Festival as a leading contender for the Royal & SunAlliance Chase. The rather leggy Brewster is by no means a chaser in appearance, though clearly there are several notable chasers in his family and he is a sound jumper of hurdles. He is said by his trainer to have schooled well over fences at home. He certainly has the right racing character, being thoroughly reliable and also game, all in all a most likeable individual. *Ian Williams*

BRIAR (CZE) 6 b.g. House Rules (USA) – Bright Angel (AUT) (Antuco (GER)) [2004/5 h81: c25s^pu Feb 5] leggy, close-coupled gelding: winning hurdler: little impact in point/hunter chase: stays 2½m: acts on heavy going: usually wears cheekpieces (tried in eyeshield). *David Ibbotson* **c– h–**

BRIAREUS 5 ch.g. Halling (USA) – Lower The Tone (IRE) (Phone Trick (USA)) [2004/5 16v² 16s* 16m* Apr 2] tall, good-topped gelding: fairly useful on Flat (stays 1½m): promising start over hurdles, winning novices at Kempton and Newbury: jumped well and again made running when beating Forthright 11 lengths at latter: not certain to stay much beyond 2m: useful hurdler in the making. *A. M. Balding* **h124 p**

BRIAR'S MIST (IRE) 8 gr.g. Roselier (FR) – Claycastle (IRE) (Carlingford Castle) [2004/5 c25s³ c25s³ c25v² c27d³ c24v* c30v³ c24v^3d c24s⁴ c29s* c28g⁴ c27g⁴ Apr 15] good-topped gelding: twice-raced hurdler: modest chaser: trained in Ireland in 2003/4 by E. O'Sullivan (won 2 points in 2004): won handicaps at Uttoxeter (novice) in December and Ayr in March: stays 29f: raced on good going or softer (acts on heavy): wears cheekpieces/blinkers: usually races prominently. *C. Grant* **c96 h–**

BRICKETSTOWN KING (IRE) 9 br.g. Mandalus – Laurel Walk (Buckskin (FR)) [2004/5 c23d⁴ c22d^pu c20g⁶ c23d⁴ Dec 2] first foal: dam, winning Irish pointer, half-sister to smart staying chaser Broadheath: won maiden Irish point in 2004: little form in chases. *Mark Campion* **c–**

BRIDEPARK TWO 5 b.m. Rakaposhi King – Bridepark Rose (IRE) (Kemal (FR)) [2004/5 16d^pu 21d^pu Nov 23] rather leggy mare: second foal: dam winning hurdler around 2½m: no show over hurdles. *Mrs H. Dalton* **h–**

BRIDGE HOTEL (IRE) 10 b.g. Beau Sher – Lady Dorcet (Condorcet (FR)) [2004/5 20f³ 22d³ 22m³ c21s³ c22g⁴ 24s Oct 8] fair handicap hurdler: fair form on second of 2 starts in novice company over fences: stays 3m: acts on firm and soft going. *Paul A. Roche, Ireland* **c103 + h112**

BRIDGE PAL 5 ch.m. First Trump – White Domino (Sharpen Up) [2004/5 16s⁵ 17d⁵ 16s⁴ 16v³ 16s⁴ 16v⁵ 16s² 16v⁵ 16d Apr 11] smallish, compact mare: half-sister to winning 2m hurdler Pinkerton's Pal (by Dominion): fair maiden on Flat (stays 1½m) at 3 yrs for W. Jarvis, showed nothing in 2 starts in 2004: modest form over hurdles: raced around 2m on going softer than good. *P. Monteith* **h85**

BRIERY FOX (IRE) 7 ch.g. Phardante (FR) – Briery Gale (Strong Gale) [2004/5 F16d* 19s⁴ 20d* 20d³ Mar 19] lengthy, useful-looking gelding: will make a chaser: first foal: dam poor novice hurdler: won maiden on last of 5 starts in points in 2004: won bumper at Wincanton in November: fairly useful form in novice hurdles, winning at Fakenham in February by ¾ length from Reel Missile: stays 2½m. *H. D. Daly* **h115 F102**

BRIERY LANE (IRE) 4 ch.g. Tagula (IRE) – Branston Berry (IRE) (Mukaddamah (USA)) [2004/5 F16g Mar 9] lengthy gelding: first foal: dam fairly useful 5f to 8.5f winner: well held in bumper on debut. *Mrs K. Walton* **F–**

BRIERY MEC 10 b.g. Ron's Victory (USA) – Briery Fille (Sayyaf) [2004/5 h–: 17d⁶ 16mᵖᵘ May 27] of little account on Flat nowadays: little impact in 3 starts over hurdles. *H. J. Collingridge* **h76**

BRIGADIER BENSON (IRE) 5 b.g. Fourstars Allstar (USA) – Decent Enough (Decent Fellow) [2004/5 16g⁶ 17d⁵ 17d 16d³ 17g² Apr 12] eighth foal: half-brother to fair 3m hurdle winner By Degree (by Roselier) and 2½m hurdle winner Mallardstown (by Buckskin): dam, dual bumper winner, half-sister to smart staying hurdler/useful chaser Gillan Cove: modest novice hurdler: will stay at least 2½m. *R. H. Alner* **h95**

BRIGADIER BROWN (IRE) 8 b.g. Satco (FR) – Tarasandy (IRE) (Arapahos (FR)) [2004/5 24f* 24m³ 24f 24m c21s⁴ c22v⁴ 24s⁴ 21d² 25d⁴ 24v 24v Feb 15] IR 8,600 3-y-o: lengthy gelding: third foal: half-brother to 2m hurdle winner Lala Nova (by Zaffaran): dam, unraced: modest form when fourth in maiden chases at Cork and Listowel: fairly useful handicap hurdler: won at Limerick in May: best effort when fourth to The Dark Lord in listed handicap at Cheltenham ninth start: stays 25f: acts on any going. *John Joseph Murphy, Ireland* **c98 p h116**

BRIGADIER DU BOIS (FR) 6 gr.g. Apeldoorn (FR) – Artic Night (FR) (Kaldoun (FR)) [2004/5 h82: c16d² c16d² c16s⁴ c17v² c19v² c20v⁴ Mar 1] lengthy gelding: poor maiden hurdler/chaser: stays 19f: raced on good going or softer (acts on heavy): tried blinkered: sometimes tongue tied. *Mrs L. Wadham* **c82 h–**

BRIGHT APPROACH (IRE) 12 gr.g. Roselier (FR) – Dysart Lady (King's Ride) [2004/5 c126: c23d⁵ c28m³ c32m³ c24g² c27d⁶ c31d c30d c25m⁴ Apr 13] smallish gelding: fairly useful chaser: best effort when third to Take The Stand in valuable handicap at Uttoxeter third start: suited by thorough test of stamina: has form on good to soft going, best efforts on good or firmer (acts on firm). *J. G. Cann* **c128**

BRIGHT BEACON 11 br.g. Lighter – Pennulli (Sir Nulli) [2004/5 c24sᶠ May 5] winning pointer: broke leg in second hunter chase. *Mrs C. Williams* **c–**

BRIGHT DAWN (IRE) 6 bl.m. Norwich – Bright Day (IRE) (Phardante (FR)) [2004/5 F16s 20dᵖᵘ Feb 18] €5,000 3-y-o, 7,500 4-y-o: first foal: dam unraced, out of sister to useful staying chaser Von Trappe: well beaten on completed start in maiden points in 2004: no form in bumper or novice hurdle. *P. Beaumont* **h– F–**

BRIGHT EAGLE (IRE) 5 ch.g. Eagle Eyed (USA) – Lumiere (USA) (Northjet) [2004/5 h–: 17m³ 16d³ 16d² Nov 23] small, leggy gelding: fair novice hurdler: raced around 2m: acts on good to soft going. *R. Lee* **h103**

BRIGHT GAS 6 b.m. Spectrum (IRE) – Kirsten (Kris) [2004/5 22s³ 22d² 20s² 22v* 22s³ 24s³ 24s² Mar 28] leggy, lengthy mare: sixth foal: half-sister to several winners, including one-time fairly useful hurdler Kattegat (by Slip Anchor): dam, 1½m winner, half-sister to top-class 1½m performer Petoski: fairly useful novice hurdler: won at Navan (maiden) in January and Punchestown (awarded race after being beaten neck by Orchestral Dream) in late-April: stays 3m: raced on going softer than good (acts on heavy): consistent. *R. P. Burns, Ireland* **h115**

BRIGHT GREEN 6 b.g. Green Desert (USA) – Shining High (Shirley Heights) [2004/5 h98: 21g⁶ c16sᵖᵘ c19m⁵ Nov 11] modest hurdler: sold out of J. Old's stable **c– h–**

£6,300 Ascot June Sales after reappearance: mistakes both starts over fences: should stay beyond 2m: acts on heavy going. *C. J. Gray*

BRIGHT PRESENT (IRE) 7 b. or br.g. Presenting – Bright Rose (Skyliner) [2004/5 c24g^{ur} c23v^{pu} c24g^{pu} Mar 18] fifth foal: dam unraced: successful twice in Irish points, including in 2004: no form in maiden chases, let down by jumping first 2 starts. *B. N. Pollock* **c–**

BRIGHT SPIRIT 4 b.g. Petoski – Lunabelle (Idiot's Delight) [2004/5 F16d^{3} F17g Apr 7] lengthy, useful-looking gelding: fifth foal: half-brother to fairly useful bumper winners Moonstream (by Terimon) and Sorrento (by Neltino) and modest hurdlers September Moon (by Bustino) and Moon Spinner (by Elmaamul): dam, winning 2m hurdler/chaser, half-sister to dam of useful hurdler up to 2½m Easter Ross: better effort in bumpers (fairly useful form) when third of 18 to Sworn In at Newbury. *N. J. Henderson* **F95**

BRIGHT STEEL (IRE) 8 gr.g. Roselier (FR) – Ikeathy (Be Friendly) [2004/5 h–: 17d^{5} 20d^{3} 24s^{3} 20v^{2} 20s^{3} Nov 21] rather leggy gelding: poor maiden hurdler: stays 3m: acts on heavy ground. *M. Todhunter* **h75**

BRIGHT TIMES AHEAD (IRE) 7 ch.m. Rainbows For Life (CAN) – Just A Second (Jimsun) [2004/5 F–: 21g^{pu} 20s^{pu} 22s^{pu} Feb 10] more signs of temperament than ability. *C. J. Drewe* **h– §**

BRISBANE ROAD (IRE) 8 b.g. Blues Traveller (IRE) – Eva Fay (IRE) (Fayruz) [2004/5 16d 21g^{2} 24d^{pu} Apr 20] workmanlike gelding: modest maiden hurdler: should stay 3m: acts on soft going: tried visored/in cheekpieces: has had tongue tied. *B. J. Llewellyn* **h86**

BRITESAND (IRE) 5 ch.g. Humbel (USA) – The Hollow Beach (IRE) (Beau Sher) [2004/5 F16s^{5} F17s^{4} 22s^{5} Mar 9] €900 3-y-o: first foal: dam unraced: better effort in bumpers on debut: jumped poorly when tailed off in novice on hurdling debut. *J. S. Moore* **h–** **F85**

BROADBROOK LASS 11 ch.m. Broadsword (USA) – Netherbrook Lass (Netherkelly) [2004/5 c86: c21s^{F} c21m^{F} 21d^{4} c24s* c20d^{2} c22v* c24v^{6} 24s^{pu} c24s^{6} Mar 5] has been to stud and had 2 foals: fair handicap chaser: jumped better than usual when winning at Fakenham in November and Uttoxeter in January: little show in 2 outings over hurdles: stays 3m: acts on good to firm and heavy ground: usually tongue tied: front runner: tail flasher. *Mrs H. Dalton* **c100** **h79**

BROADGATE FLYER (IRE) 11 b.g. Silver Kite (USA) – Fabulous Pet (Somethingfabulous (USA)) [2004/5 c93, h–: c25m^{pu} c24d^{4} c25g^{2} c27g^{5} c20m^{2} c25m^{4} c21g c21d* c26s^{4} Aug 25] medium-sized gelding: modest handicap chaser: made virtually all when winning at Southwell in August: stays 25f: acts on firm and good to soft going, not on softer: poor efforts in blinkers/cheekpieces: tongue tied: not one to rely on. *Miss Lucinda V. Russell* **c94 §** **h–**

BROADWAY SCORE (USA) 7 b.g. Theatrical – Brocaro (USA) (Mr Prospector (USA)) [2004/5 17d^{2} 17d^{2} 16d^{5} 17d Dec 7] useful at one time on Flat (stays 10.5f) for J. Hills, badly out of sorts in 2004: poor form over hurdles: lame final outing: has raced freely. *M. W. Easterby* **h83**

BROCHRUA (IRE) 5 b.m. Hernando (FR) – Severine (USA) (Trempolino (USA)) [2004/5 h63: 17g^{4} 16g^{pu} 16m 19g^{5} 17d^{5} 16g^{2} 16s 19g* 16g^{4} 17s^{6} 17g 19d Mar 14] modest hurdler: won seller at Taunton in December: stays 2½m: best efforts on good going: blinkered fourth start (saddle slipped). *J. D. Frost* **h86**

BROCTUNE MELODY 6 b. or br.g. Merdon Melody – Eider (Niniski (USA)) [2004/5 F83: F16g^{6} 22m^{6} 20d Oct 9] workmanlike gelding: modest form at best in bumpers: tailed off in 2 novice hurdles: sold 1,700 gns Doncaster November Sales, well held in point. *K. G. Reveley* **h–** **F–**

BRODICK CASTLE 6 gr.g. Arzanni – Celtic Comma (Celtic Cone) [2004/5 F17v^{F} Feb 13] 4,500 4-y-o: chunky gelding: first foal: dam no sign of ability: behind when falling fatally in bumper. *J. A. B. Old* **F–**

BROGUESTOWN BREEZE (IRE) 12 b.g. Montelimar (USA) – Spin A Coin (Torus) [2004/5 c–, h–: c25g c25v^{4} c28g^{5} c26g^{pu} Mar 28] workmanlike gelding: winning chaser: no longer of any account: tried in cheekpieces. *R. Dean* **c–** **h–**

BROKEN DREAM (IRE) 8 b.g. Broken Hearted – A Little Further (Mandalus) [2004/5 c94, h–: c21s^{2} c26g^{3} c23g^{pu} Oct 6] modest novice chaser: stays 3¼m: acts on heavy going (unraced on firmer than good): amateur ridden nowadays. *P. R. Rodford* **c94** **h–**

BROKEN KNIGHTS (IRE) 8 ch.g. Broken Hearted – Knight's Row (Le Bavard (FR)) [2004/5 20v^2 23s^F 20s* 24s* Apr 2] well-made gelding: will make a chaser: fairly useful hurdler: off 20 months before reappearance: not out of first 2 in 7 completed starts, in 2004/5 winning handicaps at Ayr (by 5 lengths from Red Man) in March and Bangor (by ½ length from Will of The People) in April: stays 3m: raced on good going or softer (acts on heavy). *N. G. Richards* **h128**

BROKEN MAGIC (IRE) 5 b.g. Broken Hearted – Allaracket (IRE) (The Parson) [2004/5 F16g^2 F16s 16g^{pu} Nov 11] second foal: half-brother to fair 2m hurdler Travellers Heir (by Montelimar): dam, Irish bumper winner, half-sister to smart staying hurdler Kristenson: form in bumpers only when second at Down Royal: no show in novice hurdle. *D. M. Fogarty, Ireland* **h–** **F88**

BROKE ROAD (IRE) 9 b.g. Deploy – Shamaka (Kris) [2004/5 16g^5 16s* 16d* 16d Mar 14] leggy gelding: fair handicap hurdler: off 28 months prior to reappearance: won at Wincanton in February and Kempton in March: raced around 2m: acts on soft and good to firm going (pulled up on heavy): visored once: has had tongue tied. *Mrs H. Dalton* **c–** **h110**

BROMLEY ABBEY 7 ch.m. Minster Son – Little Bromley (Riberetto) [2004/5 F–: F16s^5 16d 17d 24s^{pu} Apr 10] lengthy mare: signs of ability only in bumper on reappearance. *Miss S. E. Forster* **h–** **F78**

BROMLEY MOSS 6 ch.g. Le Moss – Little Bromley (Riberetto) [2004/5 F16d 17s^{pu} 22s 16d Apr 11] workmanlike gelding: third foal: dam fairly useful 2m hurdler: no form in bumper or novice hurdles. *Miss S. E. Forster* **h–** **F–**

BRONCO CHARLIE (IRE) 7 b.g. Be My Native (USA) – Cockney Bug (Torus) [2004/5 F16m* F17g^4 Sep 25] €74,000 4-y-o: half-brother to fair hurdler up to 19f Westfield Cockney (by Mulhollande): dam maiden half-sister to dam of high-class hurdler Cockney Lad: better effort in bumpers (fairly useful form) when winning at Galway (trained by A. O'Brien) in July by 2 lengths from Arctic Bear: amateur ridden both starts. *Jonjo O'Neill* **F99**

BRONHALLOW 12 b.g. Belmez (USA) – Grey Twig (Godswalk (USA)) [2004/5 c86, h–: c21m^{pu} 22d^5 26d^6 c24d c26d^{ur} 26s 21g Jan 14] angular gelding: winning hurdler/chaser: no form in 2004/5: usually wears headgear and tongue strap. *Mrs Barbara Waring* **c–** **h–**

BRONZESMITH 9 b.g. Greensmith – Bronze Age (Celtic Cone) [2004/5 c106§, h–: c19m* c16g* c20m^{pu} Jun 5] lengthy gelding: fairly useful chaser: won novice at Hereford and handicap at Newton Abbot in May: stays 19f: acts on soft and good to firm going (bumper form on heavy): tried tongue tied. *B. J. M. Ryall* **c115 +** **h–**

BROOKLANDS LAD 8 b.g. North Col – Sancal (Whistlefield) [2004/5 c75, h78: c16s^{pu} c19v^5 c16g^3 c19m^2 c16d* Apr 3] workmanlike gelding: maiden hurdler: poor chaser: made all in novice handicap at Wincanton, despite jumping left last 3 fences: should stay beyond 19f: acts on good to firm and good to soft going: tried tongue tied. *J. W. Mullins* **c81** **h–**

BROOKLYN BREEZE (IRE) 8 b. or br.g. Be My Native (USA) – Moss Gale (Strong Gale) [2004/5 c131p, h–: 24v^5 20s c21s c16d^3 c21g^4 c20g* Apr 15] rangy, useful-looking gelding: winning hurdler: smart handicap chaser: won at Ayr by 7 lengths from Tango Royal: also ran well time before when fourth to Libertine in valuable event at Cheltenham, looking likely winner 3 out but tiring before last (reportedly suffered breathing problem): effective at 2m (given a test) to 3m: acts on good to firm and good to soft going: may be capable of better yet. *L. Lungo* **c147 +** **h–**

BROOKLYN BROWNIE (IRE) 6 b.g. Presenting – In The Brownies (IRE) (Lafontaine (USA)) [2004/5 F90: 20d^3 20g^2 19g^6 Jul 29] good-bodied gelding: bumper winner: easily best effort over hurdles when second in novice at Uttoxeter in July. *J. M. Jefferson* **h109**

BROOKLYN'S GOLD (USA) 10 b.g. Seeking The Gold (USA) – Brooklyn's Dance (FR) (Shirley Heights) [2004/5 c102, h114: 16s^5 16d 20d 17g^2 16d Jan 15] close-coupled gelding: twice-raced over fences: fairly useful handicap hurdler: clearly best effort in 2004/5 when second to Silvertown at Musselburgh in December: best form around 2m: has won on soft going, best form on good/good to firm: usually races prominently. *Ian Williams* **c–** **h115**

BROOKS 9 b.g. Minster Son – Melody Moon (Philip of Spain) [2004/5 c93: c21g^F c19m^{pu} Jun 9] fair maiden chaser, lightly raced: lame final start: stays 2½m: free-going sort. *John R. Upson* **c102**

BROOKSIE 10 b.g. Efisio – Elkie Brooks (Relkino) [2004/5 h76: 20s^{pu} 16m^{pu} 22m 16g^{6} 16d Dec 2] angular gelding: poor hurdler: trained first 3 starts by Dr P. Pritchard: stays 2¾m: acts on any going: usually visored/blinkered: has had tongue tied: has found little/been reluctant to race. *Miss K. M. George* **h– §**

BROOKSY DOVE 7 ch.g. Alderbrook – Coney Dove (Celtic Cone) [2004/5 h–: 24g^{pu} Oct 14] no sign of ability, even in points. *A. E. Price* **h–**

BROOMERS HILL (IRE) 5 b.g. Sadler's Wells (USA) – Bella Vitessa (IRE) (Thatching) [2004/5 F81: 16v^{5} 16s 20s^{pu} 20s^{pu} 20d 26s Feb 10] sturdy gelding: modest in bumpers: no show over hurdles after debut: wore cheekpieces and tongue strap last 3 starts. *L. A. Dace* **h79 ?**

BRORA SUTHERLAND (IRE) 6 b.g. Synefos (USA) – Downtotheswallows (IRE) (Boreen (FR)) [2004/5 F16s 16g^{pu} 20s 17d Mar 26] big, good-topped gelding: second foal: dam unraced, from family of useful chaser Colnel Rayburn: no form in bumper or novice hurdles. *Miss Lucinda V. Russell* **h–** **F–**

BROSIE 4 b.f. Opening Verse (USA) – Sveltissima (Dunphy) [2004/5 F16s Apr 22] seventh foal: half-sister to fair 2m hurdler Royal Measure (by Inchinor): dam, 7f/1m winner, half-sister to fairly useful 2m hurdler Bifocal: soundly beaten in bumper on debut. *L. Lungo* **F–**

BROTHER CADFAEL 4 ch.g. So Factual (USA) – High Habit (Slip Anchor) [2004/5 17s Dec 2] modest on Flat (stays 1¾m), successful in January: well held in juvenile on hurdling debut. *John A. Harris* **h–**

BROTHER TED 8 b.g. Henbit (USA) – Will Be Wanton (Palm Track) [2004/5 h–: 17g^{6} 16v^{2} 16s 16v^{pu} Feb 19] leggy gelding: form over hurdles only when second in seller: tried tongue tied. *J. K. Cresswell* **h81**

BROUGHTON BOY 5 br.g. Alhaatmi – Metabolic Melody (Creetown) [2004/5 F17g F16v F16s 20d^{pu} 20d Apr 20] tall gelding: first foal: dam unraced: no sign of ability. *G. J. Smith* **h–** **F–**

Hillhouse Quarry Handicap Chase, Ayr—Brooklyn Breeze puts up an improved performance

BROUGHTONS MILL 10 gr.g. Ron's Victory (USA) – Sandra's Desire (Grey Desire) [2004/5 h53: 16m^{6} 19m Jun 9] close-coupled gelding: poor maiden on Flat: bad maiden hurdler: raced mainly around 2m: wore cheekpieces last 4 outings. *J. A. Supple* **h51**

BROWNEYES BLUE (IRE) 7 b.g. Satco (FR) – Bawnard Lady (Ragapan) [2004/5 F71: 22s^{pu} 16s 20s^{5} 24v^{ur} 24v Jan 10] no form over hurdles: tongue tied second start. *D. R. MacLeod* **h–**

BROWN FLYER 8 gr.g. Baron Blakeney – Brown Veil (Don't Look) [2004/5 h–: 26d Apr 29] no form in 4 starts over hurdles: placed in points in 2005. *H. D. Daly* **h–**

BROWN TEDDY 8 b.g. Afzal – Quadrapol (Pollerton) [2004/5 h104: c17d* c16v^{3} c20d^{2} c20d^{4} c16s^{2} c17g^{2} Mar 19] lengthy gelding: fair hurdler: won maiden at Kelso on chasing debut in October: better form when placed after, though inclined to make mistakes: stays 2½m: acts on heavy going, probably on good to firm. *R. Ford* **c108 h–**

BROWNY BOY (GER) 5 b.g. Platini (GER) – Beautys Girl (GER) (Grauer Wicht (GER)) [2004/5 16v^{3} 16s* Mar 3] won from 7f to 8.5f on Flat at 3 yrs for T. Gibson in Germany: well-backed favourite after promising debut over hurdles, won 16-runner maiden at Limerick in March in good style by 12 lengths from Ponmeoath: open to improvement. *P. J. F. Hassett, Ireland* **h113 p**

BRUERN (IRE) 8 b.g. Aahsaylad – Bob's Girl (IRE) (Bob Back (USA)) [2004/5 h–, F–: c24s^{pu} Dec 18] quite good-topped gelding: no sign of ability. *Mrs Mary Hambro* **c– h–**

BRUNATE 6 b.g. Chaddleworth (IRE) – Dawn Call (Rymer) [2004/5 F17d Nov 2] third foal: dam twice-raced half-sister to fairly useful 2m hurdler Three Scholars: showed nothing in bumper on debut. *T. R. George* **F–**

BRUNDEANLAWS 4 b.f. Endoli (USA) – The Respondant (Respect) [2004/5 F14s Feb 9] leggy filly: second foal: dam unraced: tailed off in bumper on debut. *Mrs H. O. Graham* **F–**

BRUSH A KING 10 b.g. Derrylin – Colonial Princess (Roscoe Blake) [2004/5 c–, h89: 24d^{6} 21g^{3} 27m* 21d* 24g^{2} 25d^{4} 23d^{pu} 24g 24s^{pu} Apr 16] plain gelding: tailed off both starts over fences: fair handicap hurdler: much improved in 2004/5, winning at Stratford in June and Southwell in August: poor efforts last 3 outings: stays 27f: acts on good to firm and good to soft going: tried blinkered: claimer ridden: takes good hold and races prominently. *C. T. Pogson* **c– h110**

BRUSH THE ARK 11 b.m. Brush Aside (USA) – Expensive Lark (Sir Lark) [2004/5 h83: 20d* 20d^{3} 26g^{4} May 31] small, lengthy mare: modest hurdler: won mares handicap at Fakenham in May: reluctant to line up final start: stays 3¼m: raced on good going or softer (acts on soft). *J. S. Smith* **h93**

BRUTHUINNE (IRE) 10 ch.g. Vaquillo (USA) – Portane Miss (Salluceva) [2004/5 c–§, h–: c25s^{3} c25s^{3} Mar 22] strong gelding: winning chaser: modest pointer nowadays: stays easy 3¼m: acts on soft and good to firm going: often front runner: one to treat with caution. *J. H. Berwick* **c82 § h–**

BUALADHBOS (IRE) 6 b.g. Royal Applause – Goodnight Girl (IRE) (Alzao (USA)) [2004/5 h–: 21d^{pu} 16d Jan 26] workmanlike gelding: no form over hurdles. *F. Jordan* **h–**

BUBBA BOY (IRE) 5 b. or br.g. Anshan – Royal Patrol (IRE) (Phardante (FR)) [2004/5 F91: F18g* F16g 19s^{F} 20s^{5} 22s Dec 21] sturdy gelding: fairly useful form when winning maiden bumper at Plumpton in October by 10 lengths from Oscar Bill: no form over hurdles, jumping less than fluently: should stay 2½m: raced only on soft going over hurdles, bumper form on good. *M. C. Pipe* **h– F101**

BUBBLE BOY (IRE) 6 ch.g. Hubbly Bubbly (USA) – Cool Charm (Beau Charmeur (FR)) [2004/5 F83: F18d c22s* c24d^{pu} c23v^{2} c25m^{4} Apr 13] tall, rather unfurnished gelding: better effort in bumpers when fifth on debut: fairly useful novice chaser: 100/1, won maiden at Fontwell in January, beating below-form Distant Thunder ½ length: stays 23f: acts on heavy going: races prominently. *B. G. Powell* **c117 F–**

BUBBLE BROOK 7 b.g. Alderbrook – Leinster Girl (Don) [2004/5 F–: 24d 20s^{pu} Dec 4] workmanlike gelding: no sign of ability, even in points: tried visored. *H. J. Manners* **h–**

BUCKBY LANE 9 b.g. Nomadic Way (USA) – Buckby Folly (Netherkelly) [2004/5 c131p, h–: c21s* c20d Mar 5] tall, useful-looking gelding: winning hurdler: off over a year and only third start over fences, useful form when winning Ladbrokes Trophy Chase **c139 h–**

Ladbrokes Trophy Chase (Handicap), Cheltenham—
the bold-jumping Buckby Lane makes a winning return after thirteen months off

(Handicap) at Cheltenham in January by 1¼ lengths from Kandjar d'Allier: respectable tenth, weakening only last, to Supreme Prince in similar event at Newbury next time (reportedly suffering from sore shins): should stay 3m: acts on soft and good to firm going: bold-jumping front runner. *P. R. Webber*

BUCKLAND GOLD (IRE) 5 b.g. Lord Americo – Beann Ard (IRE) (Mandalus) [2004/5 17v 21g³ 20sᶠ Mar 30] 9,000 4-y-o, resold 13,000 4-y-o: second foal: dam unraced sister to one-time very smart staying chaser Macgeorge: form over hurdles only when 3¾ lengths third of 7 in steadily-run novice at Plumpton, jumping sketchily. *D. B. Feek* **h85**

BUCKLAND KNIGHT (IRE) 9 b. or br.g. Commanche Run – Myra Gaye (Buckskin (FR)) [2004/5 c114?, h–: c26sᵖᵘ Mar 13] lengthy gelding: winning hurdler: has failed to complete in hunter chases and points: stays 3¼m: acts on heavy going: tried blinkered. *Mrs Laura J. Young* **c– h–**

BUCKSAREBACK (IRE) 9 b.g. Buckskin (FR) – Town of Trees (IRE) (Lancastrian) [2004/5 c25sᵖᵘ c24d³ Nov 27] brother to winning 3m chaser Carnival Buck: placed in maiden Irish points in 2003: no form in novice company over fences. *R. Johnson* **c–**

BUCKSKIN LAD (IRE) 10 b. or br.g. Buckskin (FR) – Loverush (Golden Love) [2004/5 h–: c24vᶠ 22s⁵ Mar 9] winning hurdler: fell first on chasing debut: stays 3¼m: acts on soft going: tried in cheekpieces. *Mrs N. S. Sharpe* **c– h–**

BUCK WHALEY (IRE) 5 ch.g. Fleetwood (IRE) – Kayzarana (IRE) (Generous (IRE)) [2004/5 F16m⁵ F16f⁶ F16d² 16d 20v* 16d⁴ Dec 9] rather unfurnished gelding: fair form in bumpers: left A. Mullins after hurdling debut: won novice at Uttoxeter in November: stays 2½m: acts on heavy going. *Jonjo O'Neill* **h104 F94**

BUDDY GIRIE 12 b.g. Lord Bud – Hatsu-Girie (Ascertain (USA)) [2004/5 c91, h–: c21g² c25d⁴ May 6] fair hunter chaser: won point in April: stays 27f: acts on soft going. *P. Cornforth* **c86 h–**

BUDE 6 gr.g. Environment Friend – Gay Da Cheen (IRE) (Tenby) [2004/5 c–, h85§: 21m 23d 24d^{pu} c20s^{pu} Dec 22] angular gelding: modest handicap hurdler at best, no form in 2004/5: let down by jumping over fences: stays easy 3m: acts on good to firm and good to soft going: tried blinkered/in cheekpieces: not one to trust. *S. A. Brookshaw* **c– § h– §**

BUDLE BAY 9 b.g. Gran Alba (USA) – Sunylyn (Sunyboy) [2004/5 c27d^{pu} c23d^{5} Jan 11] tall gelding: won maiden point in 2003: no show in 2 chases: tried tongue tied. *R. Lee* **c–**

BUENA VISTA (IRE) 4 b.g. In The Wings – Park Special (Relkino) [2004/5 F12g^{6} F12d^{4} F16d* F16g^{6} Mar 16] 675,000Y: leggy gelding: brother to Central Park, very smart up to 2m, and Lancashire Oaks winner Mellow Park and half-brother to 3 winners, including fair 2m hurdler Majal (by Caerleon) and useful Velvet Moon (by Shaadi), herself dam of Dubai World Cup winner Moon Ballad: dam Irish 1¼m winner: unraced on Flat for A. P. O'Brien: progressed into smart bumper performer: won maiden at Doncaster in January by 8 lengths from Bougoure: best effort when 6¼ lengths sixth to Missed That in Grade 1 at Cheltenham in March. *M. C. Pipe* **F116**

BUFFALO BILL (IRE) 9 ch.g. Be My Native (USA) – Sylvia Fox (Deep Run) [2004/5 16f^{3} 16d^{6} 16m^{4} 16m^{6} 16d* 16d^{2} Dec 11] angular gelding: dual bumper winner for A. O'Brien: fair hurdler: left D. Wachman after first start: won handicap at Warwick in December: raced at 2m: acts on firm and good to soft going (unraced on softer): tongue tied fourth outing: has finished weakly. *A. M. Hales* **h103**

BUFFY 5 b.m. Classic Cliche (IRE) – Annie Kelly (Oats) [2004/5 F16m^{3} F16g F16s Apr 22] 8,000 4-y-o: third foal: dam modest 2m hurdler/chaser: modest form first 2 starts in bumpers. *B. Mactaggart* **F75**

BUGLE MAJOR (IRE) 6 b.g. Anshan – Pit Runner (Deep Run) [2004/5 F16d* 19s^{pu} Jan 3] sturdy gelding: fifth foal: dam, 2m hurdle winner, half-sister to fairly useful chaser around 2½m Visible Difference, out of half-sister to high-class 2m to 2½m chaser Travado: won maiden Irish point in 2004: second start in bumpers (trained by Mrs P. Curling on first), won at Huntingdon in December by 2½ lengths from Wellpict One: prominent to 4 out in novice at Exeter on hurdling debut: should do better. *N. J. Henderson* **h– p F98**

BULGARIA MOON 5 ch.g. Groom Dancer (USA) – Gai Bulga (Kris) [2004/5 h–: 22g^{pu} 20s^{5} Aug 25] little form on Flat, none over hurdles: has bled from nose. *C. Grant* **h–**

BULLFINCH 12 ch.g. Anshan – Lambay (Lorenzaccio) [2004/5 c33s^{pu} c24s c24s^{pu} Mar 27] sparely-made gelding: modest pointer nowadays: no form in hunter chases. *D. Frankland* **c– h–**

BULLIES ACRE (IRE) 5 b.g. Arctic Cider (USA) – Clonminch Lady (Le Bavard (FR)) [2004/5 F17d 16g 16v 21s^{pu} Feb 7] €3,000 3-y-o, 6,200 4-y-o: second foal: dam bumper winner: well beaten in bumper and over hurdles. *F. P. Murtagh* **h– F–**

BULLYRAG 4 b.g. Makbul – Dusk In Daytona (Beveled (USA)) [2004/5 F12g F16s 17g^{pu} Apr 15] good-topped gelding: third foal: half-brother to fairly useful 6f/7f winner Mistral Sky (by Hurricane Sky) and 1½m winner Blue Savanna (by Bluegrass Prince): dam won around 7f: well held in 2 bumpers: downed tools after halfway in juvenile on hurdling debut: tried in cheekpieces/visor: has had tongue tied: ungenuine: sold £2,500 Ascot April Sales. *J. G. Portman* **h– § F–**

BUMPER (FR) 4 b.g. Cadoudal (FR) – Dame Blonde (FR) (Pampabird) [2004/5 F12d F18s* F16g^{2} Mar 26] unfurnished gelding: third foal: dam, won 2m hurdle, also successful up to around 11f on Flat: fairly useful form in bumpers: won at Fontwell in February by head from Matelot, pair long way clear. *M. C. Pipe* **F103**

BUNJERRY 7 b.m. Rock City – Strawberry Split (Anax) [2004/5 22v^{pu} 17s^{pu} Apr 2] medium-sized mare: fourth foal: dam won 2m selling hurdle: no sign of ability. *P. L. Clinton* **h–**

BUNKUM 7 b.g. Robellino (USA) – Spinning Mouse (Bustino) [2004/5 c107, h107: c23g* c23g^{2} c22s^{2} c20s^{3} c20v^{F} 25s 20v c20s^{5} c21g Apr 14] good-topped gelding: winning hurdler: fairly useful chaser: won maiden at Worcester in May by 7 lengths from Undeniable: lost form after third outing: stays 23f: acts on heavy ground. *R. Lee* **c117 h–**

BUNRATTY CASTLE (IRE) 10 b.g. Supreme Leader – Shannon Foam (Le Bavard (FR)) [2004/5 c25d^{2} c25d^{3} c26v* Apr 22] lengthy, rather leggy gelding: winning hurdler: fairly useful chaser: off 2 years before reappearance: won handicap at Newton Abbot in April by 6 lengths from Latitude: stays 3¼m: acts on any going: sold 8,500 gns Doncaster May Sales. *P. F. Nicholls* **c122 h–**

BUNRATTY'S SOLE (IRE) 7 br.g. Phardante (FR) – Bucks Gift (IRE) (Buckley) [2004/5 c–: c26m May 19] winning pointer, including in January: in cheekpieces, well beaten both outings in hunters. *N. M. Bloom* **c–**

BUNTER BARLOW (SAF) 9 b.g. Fine Edge – Jungle Creature (SAF) (Jungle Cove (USA)) [2004/5 16m 17g Oct 6] won 9 times up to around 1¼m from 36 starts on Flat (has been blinkered) in South Africa: well beaten in novice hurdles. *Miss Venetia Williams* **h–**

BURLEY DON CARLOS 9 b.g. Neltino – Burley Bianca (Kinglet) [2004/5 c–: c26g Apr 27] winning pointer: little show on completed start in hunter chases: tried in cheekpieces. *D. Pipe* **c–**

BURNING GOLD 7 b.g. Gildoran – Regan (USA) (Lear Fan (USA)) [2004/5 h–: c21gpu c16sur c16d4 c21gpu Jul 12] little form, including in points. *Mrs S. D. Williams* **c– h–**

BURNING QUESTION 7 ch.g. Alderbrook – Give Me An Answer (True Song) [2004/5 20sur 20vpu 18vpu 20s 22spu Apr 3] third foal: brother to fair hurdler/fairly useful chaser Naunton Brook, stays 25f: dam, winning hurdler/twice-raced chaser, stayed 21f: no show over hurdles. *J. S. Haldane* **h–**

BURNING SHORE (IRE) 5 b.m. Desert King (IRE) – Gerante (USA) (Private Account (USA)) [2004/5 h85: 20d3 24g* May 14] modest hurdler: best effort when winning novice handicap at Aintree: stays 3m: unraced on extremes of going: reliable. *Mrs L. Wadham* **h91**

BURNING TRUTH (USA) 11 ch.g. Known Fact (USA) – Galega (Sure Blade (USA)) [2004/5 c113, h111: c20m4 20m2 c24mpu c21mpu c19d2 Oct 17] good-topped gelding: winning hurdler: fair chaser: stays 2½m: acts on firm and good to soft going. *M. Sheppard* **c108 h87**

BURNS BELLE 4 b.f. Hawkstone (IRE) – Thorntoun Belle (IRE) (Rainbows For Life (CAN)) [2004/5 F14g F16d F16v Jan 29] small filly: first foal: dam little form on Flat: poor form in bumpers. *R. C. Guest* **F72**

BURNSIDE PLACE 5 b.m. Alderbrook – Knowing (Lochnager) [2004/5 F16v F16s Feb 10] 3,200 4-y-o: first foal: dam, of little account, half-sister to one-time useful jumpers Byron Lamb and Lord Lamb and useful 2m hurdler Mr Lamb: no sign of ability. *C. C. Bealby* **F–**

BURNT COPPER (IRE) 5 b.g. College Chapel – Try My Rosie (Try My Best (USA)) [2004/5 h81: 16g 17gpu Sep 25] smallish gelding: modest on Flat (stays 1½m): poor hurdler: no show in 2004/5. *J. R. Best* **h–**

BURNTOAKBOY 7 b.g. Sir Harry Lewis (USA) – Sainte Martine (Martinmas) [2004/5 h113, F95: 16g6 17g3 20d2 18s4 20s4 24v4 24v 20s 20s2 Apr 13] leggy gelding: fairly useful handicap hurdler: mainly creditable efforts when in frame in 2004/5: stays 2½m: acts on soft going. *N. Nelson, Ireland* **h122**

BURNT OUT (IRE) 6 ch.m. Anshan – Lantern Lover (Be My Native (USA)) [2004/5 h110, F85: 24m3 24mF 24s 20d 20s* 20v5 20sF 22s Mar 28] unfurnished mare: fairly useful hurdler: apparently much improved when making nearly all in mares handicap at Gowran in December: no other form after first outing: stays 3m: acts on soft and good to firm going. *J. A. O'Connell, Ireland* **h121**

BURUNDI (IRE) 11 b.g. Danehill (USA) – Sofala (Home Guard (USA)) [2004/5 c110, h–: c20m c24g6 22g5 16g Apr 1] tall gelding: fairly useful hurdler/fair chaser at best, well below form in 2004/5: stays 2¾m: acts on soft and good to firm going, possibly not on heavy: fell only run in blinkers: held up. *A. W. Carroll* **c– h–**

BURWOOD BREEZE (IRE) 9 b.g. Fresh Breeze (USA) – Shuil Le Cheile (Quayside) [2004/5 c110, h–: c25m2 c24d2 c24m2 c20d* c22v2 c20v2 c21dro c24d5 Mar 5] workmanlike gelding: fairly useful handicap chaser: won at Lingfield (amateurs) in December: stays 3m: acts on heavy and good to firm going: patiently ridden: has hung left and often finds little. *T. R. George* **c118 § h–**

BUSH HILL BANDIT (IRE) 10 b. or br.g. Executive Perk – Baby Isle (Menelek) [2004/5 c92, h–: c25m3 May 19] fair hunter chaser: successful twice in points in 2005: barely stays 3½m: acts on soft and good to firm going. *Mrs Anne-Marie Hays* **c92 h–**

BUSHIDO (IRE) 6 br.g. Brief Truce (USA) – Pheopotstown (Henbit (USA)) [2004/5 h112: 20m* 22d* 20g4 Aug 24] small gelding: fairly useful handicap hurdler: won at Wetherby in May and Market Rasen in July: stays 2¾m: acts on soft and good to firm going: front runner: tends to hang left, and has gone in snatches. *Mrs S. J. Smith* **h117**

BUSH PARK (IRE) 10 b.g. Be My Native (USA) – By All Means (Pitpan) [2004/5 c109§, h99: c20d^4 c21g^3 c26g^5 c23f^4 Sep 28] strong, lengthy gelding: winning hurdler: fair handicap chaser: effective around 2½m and stays 25f: acts on any going: tried blinkered/visored: has had tongue tied: lazy. *R. H. Alner* — **c106 §** **h–**

BUSINESS CLASS (NZ) 13 b.g. Accountant (NZ) – Fury's Princess (NZ) (Our Kungfu (NZ)) [2004/5 c98, h–: 16g 21m c21d^5 c24g^{pu} Oct 26] lengthy gelding: winning chaser/maiden hurdler: no show in 2004/5: lame final outing: stays 2¾m: acts on firm and good to soft going: tried in cheekpieces. *Dr P. Pritchard* — **c–** **h–**

BUSINESSMONEY JAKE 4 b.g. Petoski – Cloverjay (Lir) [2004/5 F12g 16s 17s^3 16d^5 22d^5 Mar 26] first foal: dam unraced: tenth of 23 in 3-y-o bumper on debut: modest form over hurdles, often let down by jumping. *V. R. A. Dartnall* — **h89 x** **F82**

BUSINESS TRAVELLER (IRE) 5 ch.g. Titus Livius (FR) – Dancing Venus (Pursuit of Love) [2004/5 h98: 20m 20d^6 20s 19d^4 19g 24d^{ur} 22d 17g^{pu} 24s^4 Jan 10] smallish gelding: modest handicap hurdler: form in 2004/5 only when twice fourth at Taunton: barely stays 3m: acts on soft going: held up. *R. J. Price* — **h93**

BUSTISU 8 b.m. Rakaposhi King – Tasmin Gayle (IRE) (Strong Gale) [2004/5 h71: 19s^{pu} 19v^{ur} Feb 13] poor hurdler: stays 21f: difficult ride. *D. J. Wintle* — **h–**

BUTLER'S CABIN (FR) 5 b.g. Poliglote – Strictly Cool (USA) (Bering) [2004/5 F17d^2 F16d^2 Nov 28] fourth foal: half-brother to useful 2m hurdler/winning chaser Heezapistol (by Pistolet Bleu) and fairly useful 7f winner Highest Cool (by Highest Honor): dam French 2-y-o 9f winner: fairly useful form when runner-up in bumpers, tended to hang left when beaten 4 lengths by Lutea at Newbury on second occasion. *Jonjo O'Neill* — **F102**

BUTTERWICK CHIEF 8 b.g. Be My Chief (USA) – Swift Return (Double Form) [2004/5 17d 16d Apr 11] good-topped gelding: temperamental maiden on Flat: lightly raced and little form over hurdles: tried blinkered. *R. A. Fahey* — **h–**

BUTTRESS 6 b.g. Zamindar (USA) – Furnish (Green Desert (USA)) [2004/5 F89: F16m^2 16g 16g Feb 27] strong gelding: placed on 3 of 4 starts in bumpers: well held both outings over hurdles, though soon plenty to do and not knocked about second time: will prove best at sharp 2m. *M. W. Easterby* — **h– p** **F95**

BUZYBAKSON (IRE) 8 b. or br.g. Bob Back (USA) – Middle Verde (USA) (Sham (USA)) [2004/5 c103, h–: c20g^4 c22s^3 c19s^3 c24s^3 c24v^2 c28s* c23g^5 c28v^4 c24d c30s c24d^{pu} c28g^6 c25m^{pu} Apr 13] leggy gelding: winning hurdler: fair novice chaser: won handicap at Market Rasen in December: thorough stayer: acts on heavy going: tried blinkered: often let down by jumping. *J. R. Cornwall* — **c101 x** **h–**

BY ALL MEN (IRE) 5 b.g. Among Men (USA) – Bellinzona (Northfields (USA)) [2004/5 20m^{pu} 16m^{pu} 16g^{ur} 16m^6 17m 17f^{pu} 19g^{pu} Oct 6] half-brother to fairly useful 2m hurdler Maralinga (by Simply Great): little form on Flat, none over hurdles: tried tongue tied. *B. Llewellyn* — **h–**

BY DEGREE (IRE) 9 gr.g. Roselier (FR) – Decent Enough (Decent Fellow) [2004/5 c23s^2 c21d^{pu} c21d^{ur} 22g^5 Apr 10] sturdy gelding: fair novice hurdler in 2002/3: off 19 months, promising start over fences when ½-length second to Willie John Daly in maiden at Exeter: let down by jumping third start, finished lame final one: will stay beyond 3m: acts on heavy going. *R. J. Hodges* — **c114** **h–**

BYGONE 7 b.g. Past Glories – Meltonby (Sayf El Arab (USA)) [2004/5 F84: F17g^6 19m^{pu} Sep 8] modest form at best in bumpers: sold out of J. Hetherton's stable 4,200 gns Doncaster May Sales after first outing: ran as if amiss on hurdling debut. *K. F. Clutterbuck* — **h–** **F–**

BYLAND 5 b.g. Danzig (USA) – Coxwold (USA) (Cox's Ridge (USA)) [2004/5 F87: aF16g F16g Dec 16] best effort in bumpers on debut, no show in 2004/5. *K. A. Morgan* — **F–**

BY MY SIDE (IRE) 11 b. or br.g. Brush Aside (USA) – Stay As You Are (Buckskin (FR)) [2004/5 c21g^{pu} c23g^6 c26v^{pu} Apr 22] fair pointer, successful in March: little form in novice hunter chases: often blinkered. *M. J. Lethbridge* — **c64** **h–**

BYWAY 8 b.m. Nearly A Hand – Wenvoe Lane (Tom Noddy) [2004/5 20m 24g^{pu} Aug 18] first foal: dam never ran: no sign of ability: sold £2,000 Ascot November Sales. *J. W. Tudor* — **h–**

BYWELL BEAU (IRE) 6 b.g. Lord Americo – Early Dalus (IRE) (Mandalus) [2004/5 F92: F16d F16d 23v^3 23s^4 20d^2 24s^3 Apr 10] sturdy gelding: fair form in bumpers: best effort over hurdles when second in novice at Carlisle: should stay beyond 2½m. *J. I. A. Charlton* — **h94** **F84**

C

CABALLE (USA) 8 ch.m. Opening Verse (USA) – Attirance (FR) (Crowned Prince (USA)) [2004/5 h–: 16v^{4} 16d^{4} 16s* 16g c16g^{4} Apr 19] workmanlike mare: modest handicap hurdler: won conditional jockeys event at Plumpton in February: poor form on chasing debut: should stay 2½m: acts on heavy going: tried blinkered. *M. Scudamore* **c73 h86**

CABER (IRE) 5 b.g. Celtic Swing – Arusha (IRE) (Dance of Life (USA)) [2004/5 h80, F–: 24d May 9] poor form on first of 2 starts in maiden hurdles: sold 7,000 gns Doncaster May Sales, won maiden point in March. *O. Sherwood* **h–**

CADEAUX ROUGE (IRE) 4 ch.f. Croco Rouge (IRE) – Gift of Glory (FR) (Niniski (USA)) [2004/5 17d Sep 10] half-sister to fairly useful hurdler up to 2½m Seixo Branco (by Saddlers' Hall): modest form at best on Flat: well held in juvenile on hurdling debut: sold £500 Ascot November Sales. *Mrs P. N. Dutfield* **h–**

CADTAURI (FR) 4 b. or br.g. Alpha Tauri (FR) – Cadmina (FR) (Cadoudal (FR)) [2004/5 F13s F16s Feb 18] useful-looking gelding: has scope: fifth foal: half-brother to fairly useful hurdler up to 2½m Cadminka (by Saint Preuil): dam little sign of ability: well held in bumpers. *Miss H. C. Knight* **F–**

CAESAREAN HUNTER (USA) 6 ch.g. Jade Hunter (USA) – Grey Fay (USA) (Grey Dawn II) [2004/5 h–: 20g^{6} 22s^{4} 17g Apr 12] lengthy gelding: little form over hurdles: likely to prove best short of 2¾m: tried tongue tied. *R. T. Phillips* **h–**

CAESAR'S PALACE (GER) 8 ch.g. Lomitas – Caraveine (FR) (Nikos) [2004/5 h101: 24d^{4} 24f^{6} 17d^{F} 24s* 24v^{4} 24d^{4} 24d^{4} 24g^{6} 22s^{4} 24s^{4} 24g^{4} Apr 15] workmanlike gelding: fair handicap hurdler: well backed, won at Aintree in October: stays 27f: probably acts on any going: effective with or without headgear: front runner/races prominently: lazy. *Miss Lucinda V. Russell* **h102**

CAHER SOCIETY (IRE) 13 ch.g. Moscow Society (USA) – Dame's Delight (Ballymoss) [2004/5 c83x, h–: c20s^{ur} c16v^{4} c20s^{4} c20s^{pu} Mar 31] lengthy gelding: fairly useful hunter chaser at one time, on downgrade: stays 3m: acts on heavy going: sketchy jumper. *J. R. Holt* **c78 x h–**

CAIPIROSKA 6 b.g. Petoski – Caipirinha (IRE) (Strong Gale) [2004/5 20s 20s 27v^{pu} Dec 31] third foal: dam 3m hurdle winner: thrice-raced in points in 2004, winning both completed starts: bought 65,000 gns Doncaster May Sales: no form in 3 novice hurdles: tongue tied final start. *Ferdy Murphy* **h–**

CAISHILL (IRE) 6 b. or br.g. Dolphin Street (FR) – Pretonic (Precocious) [2004/5 c117, h108: c18g^{pu} 24m 16s^{4} 20s 22v 17v 20v c18v^{2} 18s c20g^{5} Mar 19] useful-looking gelding: fairly useful hurdler/chaser at best, largely well below form in 2004/5: very best form at 2m: probably acts on any going: often blinkered. *Joseph Crowley, Ireland* **c111 h94**

CAISLEAN UI CUAIN (IRE) 9 b.g. Satco (FR) – Poundworld (IRE) (Orchestra) [2004/5 26g* 24d^{2} c26g^{6} 24s^{3} c26d* c24d^{pu} 24g^{3} c22s^{5} c27d^{5} 27d^{3} 22s c20v^{6} 20v c28d c23g c33g^{2} Mar 17] strong, workmanlike gelding: winning pointer: modest hurdler/chaser on balance of form, successful at Cartmel in handicap hurdle in May and 2-runner novice chase in August: 150/1, appeared to step up long way on previous form when 7 lengths second to Another Rum in National Hunt Chase at Cheltenham in March: tailed off in amateur riders handicap chase at Punchestown in late-April: evidently well suited by thorough test of stamina: acts on soft going: tried blinkered. *J. J. Lambe, Ireland* **c112 ? h88**

CAKE IT EASY (IRE) 5 ch.m. Kendor (FR) – Diese Memory (USA) (Diesis) [2004/5 h92: 16d^{F} 16d^{4} 20v^{2} 20d* 19s^{2} 16d Mar 20] tall mare: modest hurdler: won mares novice at Newcastle in December: sold out of K. Reveley's stable 9,000 gns Doncaster January Sales before next start: stays 2½m: acts on heavy going. *E. McNamara, Ireland* **h95**

CALAMINTHA 5 b.m. Mtoto – Calendula (Be My Guest (USA)) [2004/5 h107: 16d 16s^{F} 24d Jan 1] medium-sized mare: fairly useful on Flat (will stay 2½m), successful in April: similar merit over hurdles: in front when fell 2 out in mares handicap at Haydock: should stay beyond 2¼m: acts on soft ground: visored last 3 starts in 2003/4: not a fluent jumper: has shown signs of temperament. *M. C. Pipe* **h116**

CALAMITYCHARACTER 6 b.m. Tragic Role (USA) – Shaa Spin (Shaadi (USA)) [2004/5 F17d 16d 16s^{4} 16s^{ur} Apr 22] first foal: half-sister to winning pointer by Puissance: dam, maiden, half-sister to Ebor winner Vicious Circle: well held in bumper and on completed starts over hurdles. *I. McMath* **h– F–**

CALATAGAN (IRE) 6 ch.g. Danzig Connection (USA) – Calachuchi (Martinmas) [2004/5 h117: 16g* 16d 16d 17g 16g Apr 16] good-topped gelding: fair on Flat (best up to 1½m): fairly useful handicap hurdler: best effort when winning 21-runner conditional jockeys event at Cheltenham in October: will prove best at 2m: acts on good to soft going: free-going sort: races prominently/makes running. *J. M. Jefferson* **h129**

CALCAR (IRE) 5 b.g. Flying Spur (AUS) – Poscimur (IRE) (Prince Rupert (FR)) [2004/5 16g 16v 20v^{pu} Jan 3] good-topped gelding: modest maiden at best on Flat (stays 13f): little impact in 3 novice hurdles. *Mrs S. Lamyman* **h–**

CALCOT FLYER 7 br.g. Anshan – Lady Catcher (Free Boy) [2004/5 h84: c23d^{5} c23s^{2} c24d^{pu} c23d* Apr 20] rather leggy gelding: maiden hurdler: modest form over fences: won novice handicap at Worcester in April: likely to prove best at 3m+: raced on good going or softer. *A. King* **c97 h–**

CALDBECK 8 ch.m. Jumbo Hirt (USA) – My Goddess (Palm Track) [2004/5 16g^{pu} May 8] seventh foal: dam winning pointer: no sign of ability, including in points. *D. A. Nolan* **h–**

CALIBAN (IRE) 7 ch.g. Rainbows For Life (CAN) – Amour Toujours (IRE) (Law Society (USA)) [2004/5 16d 19m 19d 17g^{2} 19g^{6} 17d* 19s^{6} 17g^{4} 17m 19m Apr 17] neat gelding: fair handicap hurdler: won at Bangor in February: stays 2½m: acts on soft and good to firm going: visored/blinkered 4 of last 5 starts: front runner/races prominently: carries head high. *Ian Williams* **h103 §**

CALIES OLD VIC (IRE) 6 b.g. Old Vic – Calishee (IRE) (Callernish) [2004/5 F16s* F20g^{3} Sep 7] third foal: brother to fairly useful chaser/fair hurdler Calvic, stays 3¼m, and half-brother to 2½m bumper/point winner Calithyne (by Good Thyne): dam winning pointer: pulled up in point on debut: fairly useful form in bumpers at Cork (won impressively) in August and Galway (2 lengths third to Sans Souci Boy) in September: will stay beyond 2½m. *J. E. Kiely, Ireland* **F100**

CALLADINE (IRE) 9 b.g. Erins Isle – Motus (Anfield) [2004/5 20g^{F} c17g^{5} c23d^{2} c24s* c24v^{ur} Jan 20] close-coupled gelding: useful hurdler at best, off 14 months before reappearance: fairly useful form in maiden chases, winning at Clonmel in December: best effort when second to Keepatem at Downpatrick: best around 3m: acts on soft going (pulled too hard on good to firm). *C. Roche, Ireland* **c122 h–**

CALLED TO THE BAR 12 b.g. Legal Bwana – Miss Gaylord (Cavo Doro) [2004/5 24s^{2} 26s 24g^{2} Apr 7] workmanlike gelding: lightly raced: modest handicap hurdler: stays 3½m: acts on soft and good to firm going: wore cheekpieces final outing. *Evan Williams* **c– h87**

CALLING BRAVE (IRE) 9 ch.g. Bob Back (USA) – Queenie Kelly (The Parson) [2004/5 c145+, h142: c24d^{2} c24g^{pu} Dec 26] well-made gelding: useful hurdler: smart chaser: best effort when second of 5 to Colonel Frank in intermediate at Sandown on reappearance, challenging when blundering last: struggling long way out in King George VI Chase at Kempton: stays 25f: acts on soft and good to firm going. *N. J. Henderson* **c151 h–**

CALL ME ANYTHING (IRE) 6 br.g. Oscar (IRE) – Beaudel (Fidel) [2004/5 F16m^{6} F16m^{5} F16g^{2} F16m^{2} 16g^{3} Oct 26] €6,500 4-y-o: angular ex-Irish gelding: third foal: dam winning pointer: best efforts in bumpers (trained by J. Mangan on debut) when second at Worcester: third to Chockdee in maiden at Cheltenham on hurdling debut: will be suited by further than 2m. *D. Brace* **h109 F93**

CALL ME BOBBI 6 b.m. Executive Perk – Call-Me-Dinky (Mart Lane) [2004/5 F17s^{4} F16d Mar 14] second foal: half-sister to winning pointer by Henbit: dam winning pointer: poor form on first of 2 outings in bumpers. *Mrs S. M. Johnson* **F72**

CALLMECOZMO (IRE) 7 ch.g. Zaffaran (USA) – Call Me Connie (IRE) (Combine Harvester) [2004/5 F105: F16s c16v^{4} c24g* c24s^{ur} Mar 23] lengthy gelding: useful form when winning bumper on debut in 2003/4: upped long way in trip, easily best effort over fences when making all in maiden at Doncaster in January: stays 3m: possibly unsuited by soft/heavy ground. *P. R. Webber* **c101 F–**

CALL ME JACK (IRE) 9 b.g. Lord Americo – Tawney Rose (Tarqogan) [2004/5 c87x, h90: c17g^{5} c17d^{3} c16s^{2} Mar 11] rangy gelding: poor novice chaser: left J. Hetherton after second start: raced mainly around 2m: acts on heavy going: tried in cheekpieces: has had tongue tied: often front runner: poor jumper. *Mrs C. A. Coward* **c77 x h–**

CALL OSCAR (IRE) 6 b.g. Oscar (IRE) – Athy Princess (IRE) (Over The River (FR)) [2004/5 F16v^{4} F16d* Mar 14] first foal: dam, winning pointer, half-sister to top-class chaser Imperial Call: won maiden bumper at Stratford by head from Lannigans Lock: bred to be suited by further than 2m. *C. Tinkler* **F95**

CALLOW LAKE (IRE) 5 b.g. Bahhare (USA) – Sharayif (IRE) (Green Desert (USA)) [2004/5 h120: 17g^{3} 16g Jul 29] fairly useful on Flat (stays 17f): fairly useful hurdler: better effort in handicaps early in 2004/5 when third to Blue Away at Killarney: left D. Wachman, creditable third in similar event at Punchestown in late-April: will stay beyond 17f: acts on soft going. *Mrs J. Harrington, Ireland* **h120**

CAL MAC 6 b.g. Botanic (USA) – Shifting Mist (Night Shift (USA)) [2004/5 h84: 16g^{pu} 17d^{2} 17d^{6} c16f^{5} c17g^{pu} 16m^{6} c20g* Oct 4] sparely-made gelding: poor maiden hurdler: only one not to fall when winning 3-runner maiden chase at Plumpton: raced mainly around 2m: acts on firm and good to soft going: tried in cheekpieces: temperamental: sold 1,600 gns Doncaster October Sales, second over 1½m on Flat in Sweden in March. *M. J. Gingell* **c81 §** **h84 §**

CALOMERIA 4 b.f. Groom Dancer (USA) – Calendula (Be My Guest (USA)) [2004/5 16d* 16s* 16d^{6} 16d* 16d^{5} 16v^{pu} 16s^{6} 16g^{pu} Mar 4] close-coupled filly: half-sister to winning hurdler around 2m Calamintha (by Mtoto): fair maiden on Flat (stays 2m), claimed from R. Beckett £5,000 in October: fair juvenile hurdler: won at Haydock, Wetherby (listed event, by 1½ lengths from Iron Man) and Sandown (beat Papini ½ length) before turn of year: ran poorly last 3 outings: will stay beyond 2m: acts on soft going: flashes tail. *D. McCain* **h111**

CALON LAN (IRE) 14 b.g. Bustineto – Cherish (Bargello) [2004/5 c66§, h–: c18m* c20d* c17m^{5} c20g* c19m^{pu} c20m^{3} c19g c16v^{3} c18s^{6} Feb 4] poor handicap chaser: won at Fontwell (seller), Worcester and Bangor in summer: left R. Williams after seventh start: stays 21f: acts on any going: tried blinkered: sometimes looks none too keen. *P. M. Rich* **c80 §** **h–**

CALUSA CHARLIE (IRE) 6 b.g. Old Vic – Star Cream (Star Appeal) [2004/5 F16s* Mar 27] 23,000 4-y-o: half-brother to several winners, including useful 2m hurdler Tropical Lake (by Lomond) and fairly useful 2m to 2½m hurdler I Remember It Well (by Don't Forget Me): dam ran twice: won bumper at Towcester on debut by 7 lengths from Benny. *B. G. Powell* **F94**

CALVIC (IRE) 7 ch.g. Old Vic – Calishee (IRE) (Callernish) [2004/5 h100: c23g^{5} c22s* c22s^{F} c25s^{2} c21s* c26s* Feb 14] fair hurdler: fairly useful novice chaser: won at Haydock in November, Wincanton in January and Plumpton (beat Sonnant 5 lengths) in February: stays 3¼m: acts on heavy going. *T. R. George* **c119** **h–**

CAMADERRY (IRE) 7 ch.g. Dr Devious (IRE) – Rathvindon (Realm) [2004/5 h–: 16d 17g^{pu} May 25] sturdy gelding: maiden hurdler, no form in 2004: tried in cheekpieces. *Mrs A. M. Naughton* **h–**

CAMARADERIE 9 b.g. Most Welcome – Secret Valentine (Wollow) [2004/5 c–§, h–§: 17s^{pu} 20s^{pu} Dec 2] winning but unreliable 2m hurdler: lightly raced and no form since 2002/3: unseated only outing over fences: successful with or without blinkers. *A. G. Juckes* **c– §** **h– §**

CAMBO (FR) 4 b. or br.g. Mansonnien (FR) – Royal Lie (FR) (Garde Royale) [2004/5 16s^{pu} Nov 6] ex-French gelding: sixth foal: brother to 2 winners, including one-time fair hurdler/fairly useful chaser Mercato, stays 3m, and half-brother to fair chaser around 2m San Martino (by Snurge): dam, placed over 1½m, half-sister to dam of Le Coudray: fair on Flat (stays 2m), successful in February for Miss S. West: jumped poorly on hurdling debut. *R. Ford* **h–**

CAMBRIAN DAWN 11 b.g. Danehill (USA) – Welsh Daylight (Welsh Pageant) [2004/5 c20v^{F} 23s^{pu} c25s^{pu} Apr 3] sturdy gelding: one-time fair hurdler: left J. O'Neill and off 2 years, no sign of retaining ability in 2004/5: stays 25f: acts on heavy going: tongue tied once in bumpers. *Mrs L. B. Normile* **c–** **h–**

CAMDENATION (IRE) 9 b.g. Camden Town – Out The Nav (IRE) (Over The River (FR)) [2004/5 h84: 24s^{pu} 20v 20s c24d c22s^{4} c22g* Apr 19] compact gelding: modest hurdler at best, sold out of N. Gifford's stable £3,000 Ascot August Sales after first outing: first form over fences when winning maiden at Towcester: should stay 3m: acts on soft going. *J. R. Jenkins* **c84** **h–**

CAMDEN BELLA 5 b.m. Sir Harry Lewis (USA) – Camden Grove (Uncle Pokey) [2004/5 F17g^{6} Apr 3] fifth foal: dam, poor 2m novice hurdler, from family of smart 2m chaser Somerled and very smart staying chaser Young Ash Leaf: never-nearer sixth of 15 in mares bumper at Market Rasen on debut. *N. G. Richards* **F81 +**

CAMDEN CARRIG (IRE) 10 b. or br.g. Camden Town – Tinnecarrig Grove (Boreen (FR)) [2004/5 c24s* c25g^{F} May 14] fairly useful pointer: won novice hunter chase at Chepstow impressively by 28 lengths: about to be headed when falling heavily 2 out at Aintree 9 days later. *Simon Bloss* **c100**

CAMERON BRIDGE (IRE) 9 b.g. Camden Town – Arctic Raheen (Over The River (FR)) [2004/5 c129, h108: c20d^{2} c21g* c20g^{2} c20g c20d^{F} Jan 15] useful-looking gelding: winning hurdler: useful handicap chaser: off 5½ months, won at Wincanton in October by 4 lengths from Kelrev: stays 21f: acts on soft and good to firm going: usually held up. *P. J. Hobbs* **c130 h–**

CAMERON JACK 10 b.g. Elmaamul (USA) – Ile de Reine (Ile de Bourbon (USA)) [2004/5 c–x, h92: 22m^{pu} Apr 28] lengthy, angular gelding: usually let down by jumping over fences: modest hurdler: lame only outing in 2004/5: stays 3¼m: acts on good to firm and heavy going: has flashed tail under pressure. *Miss Kate Milligan* **c– x h–**

CAMPAIGN CHARLIE 5 b.g. Rakaposhi King – Inesdela (Wolver Hollow) [2004/5 F16s^{2} Mar 5] ninth foal: half-brother to fairly useful staying chaser Roberty Bob (by Bob Back) and fairly useful 1990 2-y-o sprint winner Seneca Reef (by Simply Great): dam unraced: green, short-headed by Liathroidisneachta in 5-runner bumper at Huntingdon on debut, hanging right. *H. D. Daly* **F90**

CAMPAIGN TRAIL (IRE) 7 b.g. Sadler's Wells (USA) – Campestral (USA) (Alleged (USA)) [2004/5 h134: 24s^{pu} 22s^{6} c26d^{2} c22s* c26v^{4} Feb 25] good-topped gelding: useful handicap hurdler, below form first 2 starts in 2004/5: fairly useful form when second in maiden at Warwick on chasing debut: made hard work of simpler task at Towcester 8 days later, hanging left: will stay beyond 3¼m: acts on soft going: edgy sort (tends to sweat): patiently ridden. *Jonjo O'Neill* **c123 h117**

CAMPESINO (IRE) 6 b.g. Entrepreneur – Campestral (USA) (Alleged (USA)) [2004/5 F16v^{3} F16d^{4} F16s^{3} F16g^{3} Apr 16] rangy, good sort: closely related to 4 winners by Sadler's Wells, including useful staying hurdler/winning chaser Campaign Trail and smart middle-distance stayer Camporese, and half-brother to 1m winner by Bigstone: dam fairly useful 2-y-o 7f winner who stayed 11.5f: in frame all 4 starts in bumpers, best effort when third of 21 to Abragante at Wetherby on third: will stay beyond 2m: sold to join Mrs H. Dalton 50,000 gns Doncaster May Sales. *G. A. Swinbank* **F98**

CAMP HILL 11 gr.g. Ra Nova – Baytino (Neltino) [2004/5 c85§, h–: 22s^{5} 24s^{5} c25s^{pu} Dec 6] angular gelding: winning chaser: maiden hurdler: formerly best around 2½m on soft/heavy going: inconsistent. *J. S. Haldane* **c– § h–**

CAMPING SITE 5 br.g. Desert King (IRE) – House Hunting (Zafonic (USA)) [2004/5 F16g Sep 23] 3,500 3-y-o: first foal: dam unraced, out of Poule d'Essai des Pouliches winner Houseproud: tailed off in bumper on debut. *Mrs L. B. Normile* **F–**

CANACHAM 6 ch.m. Beveled (USA) – Austral Jane (Dominion) [2004/5 F16d F18s^{pu} Jan 1] lengthy mare: third foal: dam, little form over hurdles, fair maiden up to around 1m on Flat: no show in 2 bumpers or on Flat. *D. L. Williams* **F–**

CANADIAN STORM 4 gr.g. With Approval (CAN) – Sheer Gold (USA) (Cutlass (USA)) [2004/5 16g^{2} 16m^{6} 16g^{4} 16m^{ur} 17m^{6} Mar 21] neat gelding: fair on Flat (stays 1¼m), claimed from M. Tompkins £10,000 after winning in July: headstrong, and went wrong way after hurdling debut: one to treat with caution. *Miss Venetia Williams* **h89 §**

CANATRICE (IRE) 5 gr.m. Brief Truce (USA) – Cantata (IRE) (Saddlers' Hall (IRE)) [2004/5 h81: 18m^{4} 16m^{2} 16g^{6} Oct 6] good-topped mare: poor maiden hurdler: best efforts around 2m: acts on good to firm going: wears cheekpieces. *T. D. McCarthy* **h80**

CA NA TRONA (IRE) 6 b.g. Accordion – Sterna Star (Corvaro (USA)) [2004/5 h96, F80: 22s^{3} 24m* Nov 11] good-topped gelding: fair form over hurdles: made all in novice at Taunton: will stay beyond 3m: acts on soft and good to firm going. *C. J. Mann* **h103**

CANAVAN (IRE) 6 gr.g. Bob Back (USA) – Silver Glen (IRE) (Roselier (FR)) [2004/5 F16s^{5} 20d^{F} 24d^{3} 24v 20v Jan 22] €35,000 4-y-o: good-topped gelding: first foal: dam unraced from family of high-class hurdler around 2m Colonel Yeager: fifth in bumper at Ayr: poor form in novice hurdles, jumping less than fluently. *Ferdy Murphy* **h78 F80**

CAN CAN FLYER (IRE) 4 ch.g. In The Wings – Can Can Lady (Anshan) [2004/5 16d 19s Mar 1] leggy gelding: half-brother to winning hurdler Robbie Can Can (by Robellino): fair on Flat (will stay 2m), sold out of M. Johnston's stable 26,000 gns Newmarket Autumn Sales: poor form on first of 2 starts in novice hurdles: joined J. Tuck. *J. Howard Johnson* **h79**

CANCUN CARIBE (IRE) 8 ch.g. Port Lucaya – Miss Tuko (Good Times (ITY)) [2004/5 h97+: 19d^{pu} May 17] dual hurdle winner up to 19f: lame only outing in 2004/5. *Evan Williams* **h–**

CANDARLI (IRE) 9 ch.g. Polish Precedent (USA) – Calounia (IRE) (Pharly (FR)) [2004/5 h104: 17d 16s^{2} 19g* 20d 16d 16d Mar 10] rather sparely-made gelding: fair **h110**

handicap hurdler: dictated pace when winning at Newbury in November: stays 19f: acts on soft going, probably on good to firm: has run as if amiss more than once. *D. R. Gandolfo*

CANDELLO 7 b.m. Supreme Leader – Oubava (FR) (Groom Dancer (USA)) [2004/5 F98p: F16v* F16d Mar 12] useful-looking mare: landed odds first 2 starts in mares bumpers, in very weak event at Haydock in January on second occasion: all but pulled up and finished distressed final outing. *N. J. Henderson* — **F98**

CANE BRAKE (IRE) 6 b.g. Sadler's Wells (USA) – Be My Hope (IRE) (Be My Native (USA)) [2004/5 h115: c22v* c22d^{ur} c20s* c20s* c20v* c21v^{4} c24v^{6} Jan 22] fairly useful hurdler: successful first 4 completed outings over fences, showing useful form, in maiden at Galway in October and novices at Cork in November and Navan and Limerick in December: in command when left distance clear by Old Flame's last-fence fall in Grade 2 at last-named: mistakes last 2 outings: stays 2¾m: raced on going softer than good (acts on heavy). *D. Wachman, Ireland* — **c130 x** **h–**

CANLIS 6 b.g. Halling (USA) – Fajjoura (IRE) (Fairy King (USA)) [2004/5 16d May 5] disappointing maiden on Flat, sold out of K. Ryan's stable 1,200 gns Doncaster October Sales: showed nothing in seller on hurdling debut. *D. W. Thompson* — **h–**

CANNI THINKAAR (IRE) 4 b.g. Alhaarth (IRE) – Cannikin (IRE) (Lahib (USA)) [2004/5 16f^{6} 17g^{3} 16s^{5} 17d^{4} 16s^{4} 18d^{5} 16d^{4} 16s^{5} 17s* 16s^{6} 16g^{2} 19m^{4} 21d^{4} Apr 18] small gelding: modest maiden on Flat (stays 1¼m): modest juvenile hurdler: dictated pace when winning maiden at Folkestone in January: stays 19f: acts on soft and good to firm going: wore cheekpieces/visor after debut: hasn't convinced with attitude. *P. Butler* — **h88**

CANNON FIRE (FR) 4 ch.c. Grand Lodge (USA) – Muirfield (FR) (Crystal Glitters (USA)) [2004/5 18m^{3} 16d^{5} 16m^{3} 16d Dec 26] angular colt: fair maiden up to 1¼m at 2 yrs: sold out of M. Channon's stable 15,000 gns Doncaster August Sales: modest form over hurdles: well held in visor final start. *Evan Williams* — **h93**

CANON BARNEY (IRE) 10 b. or br.g. Salluceva – Debbies Candy (Candy Cane) [2004/5 c–x, h101: 22d^{6} c22s^{5} c24s^{3} c30d^{F} Mar 8] sturdy gelding: fair handicap hurdler/chaser: form in 2004/5 only on third outing: stays 3¼m: raced on going softer than good: wore cheekpieces last 2 starts in 2003/4: poor jumper of fences. *Jonjo O'Neill* — **c103 x** **h–**

CANSALRUN (IRE) 6 b.m. Anshan – Monamandy (IRE) (Mandalus) [2004/5 h81, F76: 19d 17s^{6} 19s^{pu} 17m^{2} 22d^{3} 18m^{2} Apr 21] rather unfurnished mare: modest novice hurdler: stays 2¾m: acts on good to firm and good to soft going: tried tongue tied. *R. H. Alner* — **h88**

CANTARINHO 7 b.g. Alderbrook – Hot Hostess (Silly Season) [2004/5 c110: c26d^{4} c20d* c28g* c21d^{2} c24g^{3} c26g Mar 18] useful-looking gelding: useful hunter chaser: won novices at Huntingdon and Stratford (valuable event, by 3 lengths from News Flash) in May: tongue tied, close up long way when eighth in Foxhunter at Cheltenham final start: effective at 2½m to 3½m: acts on soft going: usually travels strongly up with pace. *D. J. Kemp* — **c118**

CAN'T BE SCRABBLE 12 b.g. Gargoor – Scribble Along (Supergrey) [2004/5 c–§, h89§: c23m^{F} 22g^{6} 22g^{pu} 22g Aug 15] sturdy gelding: winning pointer: fell both starts in chases: modest hurdler: no form in 2004/5: stays easy 3m: acts on good to firm going: headstrong front runner: temperamental. *C. J. Down* — **c– §** **h– §**

CANTEMERLE (IRE) 5 b.m. Bluebird (USA) – Legally Delicious (Law Society (USA)) [2004/5 16s 16d^{3} 16g 19v^{pu} Dec 31] compact mare: modest maiden on Flat (stays 1½m): form over hurdles only when third in seller at Ludlow: looked uncooperative when blinkered next start. *W. M. Brisbourne* — **h70**

CANTERBURY BELL 5 b.m. Bishop of Cashel – Old Flower (Persian Bold) [2004/5 F16s Jan 19] 1,400 4-y-o: rangy, rather unfurnished mare: second foal: dam unraced sister to fairly useful 2m hurdler Suivez: well held in mares bumper on debut. *P. D. Niven* — **F–**

CANTGETON (IRE) 5 b.g. Germany (USA) – Lahana (IRE) (Rising) [2004/5 F16v^{2} F16v F16s F17g^{5} 20d* Apr 20] tall, leggy gelding: second foal: dam twice-raced sister to fairly useful chaser up to 3m Hakkinen: fairly useful form in bumpers, ½-length second to Notaproblem at Wetherby on debut: won maiden at Worcester on hurdling debut in April by head from Stern, hanging left: should prove as effective at 2m as at 2½m. *M. C. Pipe* — **h114** **F97**

CANTORIS 5 b.g. Unfuwain (USA) – Choir Mistress (Chief Singer) [2004/5 h–: 22g^{pu} 20s^{pu} 24g Jul 7] close-coupled gelding: no form over hurdles: blinkered: tried tongue tied. *C. L. Popham* — **h–**

CANTYS BRIG (IRE) 8 gr.g. Roselier (FR) – Call Catherine (IRE) (Strong Gale) [2004/5 h–: 20d4 24g c21d c25spu c27dpu c19gF 19g Mar 4] lengthy gelding: no solid form: tried blinkered. *Miss L. C. Siddall* **c– h–**

CANUSEUS (USA) 4 b.g. Theatrical – Charmer's Gift (USA) (Blushing John (USA)) [2004/5 F13g Jan 17] good-bodied gelding: fifth foal: half-brother to winner in USA by Diazo: dam never ran: eighth of 18 in bumper at Doncaster on debut: sold 800 gns Doncaster May Sales. *T. P. Tate* **F80**

CAPER 5 b.g. Salse (USA) – Spinning Mouse (Bustino) [2004/5 16s3 16s3 16g4 16dpu 16d 19m* 26m6 Apr 9] half-brother to fairly useful hurdler/chaser Bunkum (by Robellino), stays 23f: bad maiden on Flat: poor novice hurdler: won seller at Hereford in March: stays 19f: acts on soft and good to good to firm going: wore cheekpieces last 2 starts. *R. Hollinshead* **h81**

CAPE STORMER (IRE) 10 b.g. Be My Native (USA) – My Sunny South (Strong Gale) [2004/5 c114, h–: c21d2 c21m4 c24g6 c21s Apr 7] workmanlike gelding: fairly useful hunter chaser: successful twice in points in 2005: best short of 3m: raced mainly on good going or firmer. *Mrs C. M. Gorman* **c101 h–**

CAPITANA (GER) 4 ch.f. Lando (GER) – Capitolina (FR) (Empery (USA)) [2004/5 16s6 16spu 16s3 16g* Mar 27] ex-German filly: sister to useful 2m hurdler/chaser Caracciola: placed up to around 1¼m on Flat for P. Rau: modest form over hurdles: won minor event at Plumpton in March: likely to prove best around 2m with emphasis on speed. *N. J. Henderson* **h85**

CAPPADRUMMIN (IRE) 8 ch.g. Bob Back (USA) – Out And About (Orchestra) [2004/5 h101: c25sF Feb 5] rather leggy gelding: bumper winner/maiden hurdler: fell in hunter on chasing debut. *O. R. Dukes* **c– h–**

CAPPANRUSH (IRE) 5 gr.g. Medaaly – Introvert (USA) (Exbourne (USA)) [2004/5 F16d F16s3 F17g4 Apr 7] angular gelding: first foal: dam ran twice: fair form in bumpers: left D. ffrench Davis before final start. *A. Ennis* **F94**

CAPRICORN 7 b.g. Minster Son – Loch Scavaig (IRE) (The Parson) [2004/5 17d 24v Feb 2] leggy gelding: maiden hurdler: wears cheekpieces/blinkers: sold 2,500 gns Doncaster May Sales. *W. McKeown* **h–**

CAPRIOLO (IRE) 9 ch.g. Priolo (USA) – Carroll's Canyon (IRE) (Hatim (USA)) [2004/5 h97§: 20d* 20g May 16] sturdy gelding: modest hurdler: won claimer at Fontwell in May: barely stays 2¾m: acts on good to firm and heavy going: wears headgear: irresolute. *P. G. Murphy* **h86 §**

CAPTAIN AUBREY (IRE) 6 b.g. Supreme Leader – Hamers Girl (IRE) (Strong Gale) [2004/5 F17d4 F16d F16g Apr 19] €40,000 3-y-o, €46,000 4-y-o: first foal: dam unraced daughter of useful hurdler/chaser up to 3m Hamers Flame: best effort in bumpers in maiden at Exeter on debut: likely to be suited by further than 2m. *J. A. B. Old* **F92**

CAPTAIN CAN CAN (IRE) 5 b.g. Hernando (FR) – Can Can Lady (Anshan) [2004/5 F17d F16m Nov 26] 1,500 4-y-o: second foal: half-brother to 2m hurdle winner Robbie Can Can (by Hernando): dam, fair 6f to 9f winner, half-sister to useful 7f and 1m winner Setteen: no show in maiden bumpers. *C. J. Teague* **F–**

CAPTAIN CLOUDY 5 b.g. Whittingham (IRE) – Money Supply (Brigadier Gerard) [2004/5 16g 18s 16g5 Mar 14] leggy gelding: half-brother to 2 poor hurdlers: modest maiden on Flat (stays 1¼m): tailed off in novice company over hurdles: joined D. Flood. *M. Madgwick* **h–**

CAPTAIN CORELLI 8 b.g. Weld – Deaconess (The Parson) [2004/5 h97, F96: 16d4 c19v2 c22d3 c23v* c22s* c21gpu Mar 17] good-topped gelding: fair novice hurdler, not at all knocked about on reappearance: useful form over fences: successful in maiden at Leicester and novice handicap at Haydock (beat Nas Na Riogh 11 lengths) in February: let down by jumping in valuable novice handicap at Cheltenham final outing: will probably stay 3m: acts on heavy going. *M. Pitman* **c130 h99 +**

CAPTAIN HARDY (IRE) 5 b.g. Victory Note (USA) – Airey Fairy (IRE) (Alzao (USA)) [2004/5 h88: 17g6 17g c16s4 c16gF c16mpu Mar 21] close-coupled gelding: modest hurdler: hasn't convinced with jumping over fences, poor form on only completed start: raced around 2m: acts on soft going. *G. Brown* **c82 h–**

CAPTAIN MACHELL (IRE) 7 b. or br.g. King's Ride – Flying Silver (Master Buck) [2004/5 F16g 20s Nov 5] 12,500 4-y-o: good sort: ninth foal: half-brother to 4 winners, including chaser Gee Aker Malayo (by Phardante), stays 25f: dam, winning 2m **h– F–**

hurdler/chaser, half-sister to dam of useful staying chaser Keep Talking: won maiden on last of 5 starts in Irish points in 2004: well held in bumper and novice hurdle. *J. S. King*

CAPTAIN MILLER 9 b.g. Batshoof – Miller's Gait (Mill Reef (USA)) [2004/5 16g 16d 16d^{3} 16s Apr 20] small, sturdy gelding: fair handicap hurdler: form in 2004/5 only when third at Wincanton: raced around 2m, likely to stay further: acts on soft going: tongue tied on reappearance. *N. J. Henderson* **h105**

CAPTAIN MOONLIGHT (IRE) 9 b.g. Religiously (USA) – Next Adventure (IRE) (Denel (FR)) [2004/5 c111, h–: 24v c24d c22s* c21v c24v c28v^{R} c20s^{pu} c24d c20s^{2} c20d^{5} c24v^{2} Apr 10] compact gelding: winning hurdler: fairly useful handicap chaser on his day: won conditional jockeys event at Thurles in December: stays 3m: raced on going softer than good (acts on heavy): tried blinkered: often races prominently: sketchy jumper. *T. J. O'Mara, Ireland* **c117 x h–**

CAPTAIN MURPHY (IRE) 7 b.g. Executive Perk – Laura Daisy (Buckskin (FR)) [2004/5 F96: F18m^{6} May 1] tall gelding: fairly useful form in bumpers. *J. I. A. Charlton* **F96**

CAPTAIN RAWLINGS 6 ch.g. Lancastrian – Coombesbury Lane (Torus) [2004/5 h–, F–: 24d 26s Mar 7] lengthy gelding: first foal: dam, modest hurdler who stayed 3m, from family of smart Norwegian performer up to 9.5f Martellian: well held in bumper and over hurdles. *H. D. Daly* **h–**

CAPTAIN RON (IRE) 9 b.g. Marju (IRE) – Callas Star (Chief Singer) [2004/5 c–, h–: 20m c24g Mar 3] leggy gelding: no worthwhile form outside points, left R. Phillips before final start. *Shaun Lycett* **c– h–**

CAPTAIN'S LEAP (IRE) 9 ch.g. Grand Plaisir (IRE) – Ballingowan Star (Le Moss) [2004/5 h81: 20v^{pu} 16v 20s^{pu} Mar 19] sturdy gelding: maiden hurdler: lame final start: will prove better at 3m than shorter. *L. Lungo* **h–**

CAPTAINS TABLE 12 b.g. Welsh Captain – Wensum Girl (Ballymoss) [2004/5 c–: c19g^{2} c20s^{2} c18d^{4} c19d^{4} c24g c16g Apr 14] workmanlike gelding: fairly useful chaser at best: off 12 months, best efforts in 2004/5 when runner-up in handicaps: stays 2½m: acts on soft and good to firm going. *F. Jordan* **c106**

CAPTAIN SUNSHINE (IRE) 7 ch.g. Bob Back (USA) – Elite (Lord Gayle (USA)) [2004/5 F109: F16g^{3} 20v^{2} 20v* 20d^{F} Mar 10] lengthy gelding: useful form in bumpers: fairly useful form over hurdles: won 23-runner maiden at Naas in February by 1½ lengths from No Complications: close second when fell fatally 4 out in Grade 3 novice at Thurles: stayed 2½m. *N. Meade, Ireland* **h117 F109**

CAPYBARA (IRE) 7 b.g. Commanche Run – The Pledger (Strong Gale) [2004/5 24d^{2} c27d^{2} 24s^{2} Mar 10] £11,500 4-y-o: second foal: brother to winning pointer: dam lightly-raced maiden: won maiden point in March 2004: bought 21,000 gns Doncaster May Sales: fair form in novice hurdles: second in maiden at Sedgefield on chasing debut: stays 27f. *H. P. Hogarth* **c101 h109**

CARACCIOLA (GER) 8 b.g. Lando (GER) – Capitolina (FR) (Empery (USA)) [2004/5 c141, h131+: 20d^{6} c21d^{pu} c16g^{3} c16s^{pu} Apr 7] leggy gelding: useful hurdler: smart chaser: back to best when 6 lengths third to Fota Island in Grand Annual (Handicap) at Cheltenham: never travelling well in valuable handicap at Aintree final start: best form at 2m: acts on good to firm and good to soft going. *N. J. Henderson* **c147 h–**

CARAMAN (IRE) 7 ch.h. Grand Lodge (USA) – Caraiyma (IRE) (Shahrastani (USA)) [2004/5 16s^{pu} 16s 16s^{F} 16d^{2} 16d* 16d^{3} 17d^{6} 16d Jan 8] smallish, workmanlike horse: half-brother to 6f winner Carallia (by Common Grounds): dam, fair 9f winner, sister to smart middle-distance performer Cajarian, from family of smart 2m to 2¾m hurdler Chirkpar: fairly useful hurdler: claimed from C. Roche £6,000 third start: improved after, winning maiden at Newcastle in November: raced mainly around 2m on ground softer than good (acts on heavy): tried in headgear: has had tongue tied. *D. Carroll* **h116**

CARAPUCE (FR) 6 ch.g. Bigstone (IRE) – Treasure City (FR) (Moulin) [2004/5 h122: c16s^{2} c20v^{3} c16s* c21v^{5} 20v^{pu} 18s^{6} Apr 3] good-topped gelding: fairly useful hurdler at best: none too fluent over fences, even when winning 3-finisher maiden at Ayr in December: effective around 2m to 3m: raced on good going or softer (acts on soft): wore cheekpieces on debut. *L. Lungo* **c107 h–**

CARBONADO 11 b.g. Anshan – Virevoite (Shareef Dancer (USA)) [2004/5 c97, h–: c25s^{pu} c24g Apr 15] well-made gelding: fair pointer, successful in March: maiden hunter chaser: stays 25f: acts on soft and good to firm going: has worn tongue strap: unreliable. *H. R. Tuck* **c– § h–**

Ballymore Properties Champion Stayers Hurdle, Punchestown—
outsider Carlys Quest is about to pull well clear of the weakening Homer Wells (who finished fourth)

CARBURY CROSS (IRE) 11 b. or br.g. Mandalus – Brickey Gazette (Fine Blade (USA)) [2004/5 c138d, h–: c24d³ Mar 11] smallish, close-coupled gelding: very smart chaser at one time, generally disappointing since 2001/2: should stay beyond 3¼m: best form on good/good to firm going (ran poorly on heavy): often blinkered: ungenuine. *Jonjo O'Neill* **c– § h– §**

CARDINAL MARK (IRE) 11 b.g. Ardross – Sister of Gold (The Parson) [2004/5 c82, h94: c25g⁴ c21g³ Jul 14] leggy gelding: modest handicap hurdler: poor chaser: let down by jumping both starts in 2004/5: stays 3¼m: acts on any going: tried blinkered: difficult ride. *Mrs S. J. Smith* **c80 x h–**

CARDINAL SINN (UAE) 4 ch.g. Gulch (USA) – Ines Bloom (IRE) (Sadler's Wells (USA)) [2004/5 F16g Mar 16] €9,000 3-y-o: seventh foal: dam, won in Japan at 2 yrs, half-sister to very smart performer up to 1½m Flame of Tara, herself dam of Salsabil and Marju: eighth of 11 in bumper at Huntingdon on debut. *M. Pitman* **F79**

CARDINGTON 6 b.g. Saddlers' Hall (IRE) – Passionelle (Nashwan (USA)) [2004/5 h98p, F95: 20d³ May 6] lengthy gelding: has scope: in frame all 3 starts over hurdles, fair form when third in novice at Wetherby in May: stays 2½m: has hung/jumped right. *Mrs S. J. Smith* **h104**

CAREFREE LOVE (IRE) 11 ch.g. Carefree Dancer (USA) – Eau d'Amour (Tall Noble (USA)) [2004/5 c26gᵖᵘ Apr 27] poor pointer: blinkered, well beaten in novice hunter chase. *G. Chambers* **c–**

CARIBBEAN COVE (IRE) 7 gr.g. Norwich – Peaceful Rose (Roselier (FR)) [2004/5 c–, h100: c21d⁶ c20d² c20s⁴ c20m³ c21d* c16v² c20d⁴ c20gᶠ c21d* c18m* c20d Apr 9] close-coupled gelding: winning hurdler: fair chaser: won handicap at Sedgefield in December and novice handicaps at Fakenham in March and Newbury in April: stays 21f: acts on any going: wears cheekpieces/blinkers nowadays: often makes mistakes. *R. C. Guest* **c100 x h–**

CARLOVENT (FR) 10 b.g. Cadoudal (FR) – Carlaya (FR) (Carmarthen (FR)) [2004/5 c–x, h112x: 24d⁴ May 4] angular gelding: reportedly blind in one eye: useful hurdler at one time, well held since 2002/3: stays 25f: acts on heavy and good to firm going: blinkered once, visored nowadays: sketchy jumper: ungenuine. *M. C. Pipe* **c– § h107 §**

CARLTON CRACKER 13 b.g. Primitive Rising (USA) – Miss Cracker Jack (Ancient Monro) [2004/5 c–, h–: c22mᵖᵘ c21m⁴ c21gᵘʳ Jul 16] big, rather leggy gelding: **c85 h–**

veteran chaser: form in 2004/5 only when fourth in handicap at Southwell: stays 25f: acts on good to firm and good to soft ground: headstrong. *Mrs J. R. Buckley*

CARLUCCIOS QUEST 7 b.g. Terimon – Jindabyne (Good Times (ITY)) [2004/5 F–: 24spu Apr 16] no show in bumper or novice hurdle: runner-up on first of 2 starts in points in between. *Mrs H. Dalton* **h–**

CARLYS QUEST 11 ch.g. Primo Dominie – Tuppy (USA) (Sharpen Up) [2004/5 h104+: 24s* 21d* 22g3 24m2 22v2 24s* 24v2 25s4 23s3 24g5 24d Apr 8] leggy gelding: useful hurdler: vastly improved, successful in handicaps at Chepstow (amateurs) and Huntingdon in May and Chepstow again in December: took advantage of below-par rivals when winning Grade 1 Ballymore Properties Champion Stayers' Hurdle at Punchestown in late-April, beating Kadoun by 9 lengths: stays 25f: acts on heavy and good to firm going: tried blinkered/visored: has worn tongue strap: held up, and usually left with plenty to do: consistent. *Ferdy Murphy* **h140**

CARNEYS CROSS (IRE) 7 b.g. Kahyasi – Cityjet (IRE) (Orchestra) [2004/5 c113, h–: c20g4 24s c19s* c24d4 c20s2 c24vF c19v* c18s5 18s6 19s Mar 27] stocky gelding: fair hurdler: fairly useful handicap chaser: won at Naas in October and January: effective at 19f, will stay beyond 3m: raced on good going or softer (acts on heavy). *S. J. Treacy, Ireland* **c118 h101**

CARN RIVERS (IRE) 10 ch.g. Over The River (FR) – Carnowen (Deep Run) [2004/5 h–: 20g c16g3 Jul 14] angular gelding: little sign of ability. *Mrs S. J. Smith* **c– h–**

CAROUBIER (IRE) 5 ch.g. Woodborough (USA) – Patsy Grimes (Beveled (USA)) [2004/5 h96: 16s4 16d2 16d 19d 17s Feb 7] leggy gelding: fair on Flat (stays 11f): modest hurdler: will prove best around 2m with emphasis on speed: usually wears headgear. *J. Gallagher* **h93**

Ms L. Neville's "Carlys Quest"

Dr P. J. Moriarty Novices' Chase, Leopardstown—
the Jessica Harrington-trained pair Carrigeen Victor and Well Presented (spotted cap)
dominate the finish of a substandard renewal

CARPENTERS BOY 5 b.g. Nomination – Jolly Girl (Jolly Me) [2004/5 F81: F17s Jan 10] little worthwhile form in bumpers. *Mrs A. M. Thorpe* **F–**

CARRAIG BLUE (IRE) 6 b.g. Roselier (FR) – It's All Taboo (Smartset) [2004/5 22d^3 24s 22v* 22s^3 24v^2 22v* 24s^6 Mar 28] ninth foal: half-brother to 2m hurdle winner Dolphins Peak (by Aristocracy): dam unraced: won completed start in Irish points in 2004: once-raced in bumpers: useful novice hurdler: won at Limerick (maiden) in December and Clonmel (beat Oulart 17 lengths) in February: also ran well when second to Sweet Kiln at Fairyhouse: stays 3m: raced on going softer than good (acts on heavy): front runner/races prominently. *E. Sheehy, Ireland* **h134**

CARRAIG BROL (IRE) 11 b.g. Cataldi – Davy's Hall (Weavers' Hall) [2004/5 c–: c25d^{pu} Apr 11] poor maiden pointer: tried in cheekpieces. *W. S. Coltherd* **c–**

CARRAVANISH 5 b.m. Terimon – Proverbial Rose (Proverb) [2004/5 F17v F16v^6 Feb 13] sixth foal: sister to fairly useful chaser Flinders Chase, stays 2½m, and half-sister to smart bumper winner Karanja (by Karinga Bay): dam, won 4 points, out of half-sister to very useful jumper Potentate: well held in bumpers. *J. K. Magee, Ireland* **F–**

CARRIAGE RIDE (IRE) 7 b.g. Tidaro (USA) – Casakurali (Gleason (USA)) [2004/5 h86: c25v^3 c24d^2 c25v^2 c25v^{pu} c31s Apr 22] angular gelding: modest novice hurdler: similar form when placed first 3 starts over fences: stays 25f: acts on heavy going. *N. G. Richards* **c97 h–**

CARRIGEEN VICTOR (IRE) 7 b.g. Old Vic – Carrigeen Kearia (IRE) (Kemal (FR)) [2004/5 c19v^F c20v* c21s* c20s Mar 29] well-made gelding: first foal: dam, winning hurdler/fairly useful chaser who stayed 25f, out of useful 2m to 3m chaser Carrigeensharragh: well held in bumper on debut: excellent start over fences, winning first 2 completed outings, 10-runner novice at Gowran in January by 10 lengths from Pay It Forward and Grade 1 Dr P.J. Moriarty Novices' Chase at Leopardstown by length from Well Presented: failed to settle when well held in Grade 1 at Fairyhouse final start: will stay beyond 21f: raced on soft/heavy going over fences. *Mrs J. Harrington, Ireland* **c133**

CARRYONHARRY (IRE) 11 gr.g. Roselier (FR) – Bluebell Avenue (Boreen Beag) [2004/5 c114x, h–: c25d* c25d^2 c24d c25s^3 c24d c24d c24g c24g c20g^{pu} Apr 22] leggy gelding: fairly useful handicap chaser: won at Ludlow in November by 27 lengths from Midnight Gunner: ran creditably after when placed: stays 25f: acts on good to firm and heavy going: visored: usually let down by jumping. *M. C. Pipe* **c121 x h–**

CARTE DIAMOND (USA) 4 ch.c. Theatrical – Liteup My Life (USA) (Green Dancer (USA)) [2004/5 16d* 16d^3 16m* 17g^{pu} Mar 18] leggy colt: smart middle-distance **h123 +**

stayer on Flat, successful 3 times in 2004, sold out of M. Johnston's stable 105,000 gns Doncaster October Sales: good start over hurdles, winning juveniles at Newcastle in November and Musselburgh (made all despite mistakes to beat Credit 2½ lengths) in February: similar form when third to Salut Saint Cloud in Grade 2 at Lingfield in between: pulled up lame after all but falling last in Triumph Hurdle at Cheltenham, weakening at time having held every chance 2 out when one of several mistakes: will stay beyond 2m: acts on good to firm and good to soft going: tongue tied last 2 starts. *B. Ellison*

CARTHYS CROSS (IRE) 6 ch.g. Moscow Society (USA) – Sweet Tarquin (Lucifer (USA)) [2004/5 F16d* F16g 17d^3 17d^5 16d* Apr 3] well-made gelding: half-brother to winning Irish pointer by Duky: dam ran once: third in maiden Irish point in 2004: better effort in bumpers when winning at Southwell in May, despite pulling hard: off 4 months, much improved over hurdles when winning novice at Wincanton by 2½ lengths from Allumee: hung wide on bends at Newton Abbot on hurdling debut: will stay beyond 2m. *T. R. George* **h112** **F99**

CARTIER OPERA 5 ch.g. Zilzal (USA) – Slipper (Suave Dancer (USA)) [2004/5 20m Jun 5] ex-French gelding: dam half-sister to fair hurdler A Bit of Fun: successful over 1m (at 2 yrs) and 10.5f on Flat in France for Mlle V. Dissaux, useful form: well beaten in maiden on hurdling debut. *Miss Venetia Williams* **h–**

CARTMEL PRINCESS 5 b.m. Mistertopogigo (IRE) – Miss Cashtal (IRE) (Ballacashtal (CAN)) [2004/5 22d^{pu} 16m^{pu} 16d^{ur} Oct 3] sparely-made mare: fifth foal: dam, winning hurdler, stayed 2½m: no sign of ability. *D. Burchell* **h–**

CARVILLA (IRE) 10 b.g. Cardinal Flower – Villawood (Quayside) [2004/5 c20d c21m^{pu} May 19] ex-Irish gelding: poor maiden jumper: tried in cheekpieces: sold £3,300 Ascot October Sales. *N. W. Padfield* **c–** **h–**

CASAS (IRE) 8 b.g. Tenby – Clodagh (Thatching) [2004/5 18m 16d^3 17d 20g^{pu} 16v^6 16v^4 20s^3 Mar 19] leggy ex-Irish gelding: poor maiden hurdler, left H. Kirk after reappearance: probably best around 2m: tried in cheekpieces: sometimes tongue tied. *J. R. Norton* **h80**

CASAYANA 5 b.m. Sir Harry Lewis (USA) – Five And Four (IRE) (Green Desert (USA)) [2004/5 h–, F–: 16d^{pu} May 6] no form: sold £2,000 Ascot June Sales. *D. McCain* **h–**

CASE OF POTEEN (IRE) 9 b. or br.m. Witness Box (USA) – On The Hooch (Over The River (FR)) [2004/5 c82, h95: 24f c21d^6 c20v^5 c20m^{ur} c21s^2 c24g^3 Dec 29] medium-sized mare: winning hurdler: little impact over fences: stays 3m: acts on heavy going: wore cheekpieces final outing. *Mrs S. C. Bradburne* **c–** **h–**

CASH AND CARRY (IRE) 7 b.g. Norwich – Little And Often (IRE) (Roselier (FR)) [2004/5 18g 16s^2 16d^2 16s^3 18v 16s^3 16s 16s^2 Apr 13] useful-looking gelding: chasing type: second foal: dam, poor maiden hurdler, half-sister to fairly useful hurdler/winning 3m chaser Saddler's Choice: bumper winner: fair maiden hurdler: flattered when third of 6 in listed novice at Haydock fourth outing: bred to stay beyond 2m: raced on good going or softer (bumper form on heavy). *E. J. O'Grady, Ireland* **h104**

CASH AND NEW (IRE) 6 b.m. Supreme Leader – Shannon Lough (IRE) (Deep Run) [2004/5 F16v* Feb 20] fifth foal: half-sister to fairly useful 2m hurdler Drumlin (by Glacial Storm) and winning pointer/fair maiden jumper Lough Dante (by Phardante), stays 3m: dam once-raced half-sister to useful chaser up to 3m Woodville Star, from family of smart staying jumper Time For A Run: won mares bumper at Towcester on debut by 5 lengths from Retro's Girl. *R. T. Phillips* **F89**

CASH BONANZA (IRE) 5 ch.g. Beneficial – Vulcash (IRE) (Callernish) [2004/5 20s^3 22s^5 Apr 3] eighth foal: brother to fair chaser Roofing Spirit, effective at 2m to 23f, and half-brother to 2 winners by Roselier, including one-time fairly useful staying chaser Silver Streak: dam unraced half-sister to smart chaser up to 3m Kilkilowen and to dam of high-class staying chaser Couldnt Be Better: won maiden point on debut in February: modest form in novice hurdles, third of 17 to Overserved at Carlisle: may yet do better. *N. G. Richards* **h99 +**

CASH CONVERTER (IRE) 7 ch.g. Houmayoun (FR) – Golden Symphony (Le Moss) [2004/5 F95: 20v^{pu} 22v^2 Apr 22] fairly useful in bumpers: left E. Hales and off 17 months, better effort in maiden hurdles (bled from nose in first) when 29 lengths second of 6 to The Duckpond at Newton Abbot. *R. T. Phillips* **h85 ?**

CASHEL DANCER 6 b.m. Bishop of Cashel – Dancing Debut (Polar Falcon (USA)) [2004/5 h86: 17g^6 20s 17v^{pu} 16g^2 16s^5 16d* 16d^2 19m^6 Apr 17] lengthy, angular mare: modest handicap hurdler: won at Ludlow in February: stays easy 2½m: acts on good to firm and good to soft going, below form on softer. *S. A. Brookshaw* **h99**

CASHEMA (IRE) 4 b.f. Cape Cross (IRE) – Miss Shema (USA) (Gulch (USA)) [2004/5 17d 16m^{5} 16g^{pu} 16v Mar 5] lengthy, sparely-made filly: well held on Flat: no form in juvenile hurdles: sold out of Mrs P. N. Dutfield's stable 5,000 gns Doncaster October Sales after second outing. *D. R. MacLeod* **h–**

CASH IN HAND (IRE) 5 b.g. Charente River (IRE) – Fern Fields (IRE) (Be My Native (USA)) [2004/5 F17s^{6} F16s aF16g^{5} 19d Jan 28] good-topped gelding: second foal: dam, winning 2m hurdler, also 9.5f winner on Flat: modest form in bumpers: tailed off in novice on hurdling debut. *C. J. Mann* **h– F85**

CASH KING (IRE) 5 b.g. Beneficial – On The Bridle (IRE) (Mandalus) [2004/5 F16s^{5} Feb 26] €10,000 3-y-o, €26,000 4-y-o: good-topped gelding: third foal: dam ran twice: 6 lengths fifth to Glasker Mill in slowly-run bumper at Kempton on debut: sold 30,000 gns Doncaster May Sales. *P. R. Webber* **F100**

CASH 'N' CREDIT 7 b.m. Homo Sapien – Not Enough (Balinger) [2004/5 c74, h–: 22m^{5} 24g Jul 7] leggy mare: poor chaser/maiden hurdler: stays 25f: acts on good to firm going: wore cheekpieces/visor 5 of last 6 starts. *R. Dickin* **c– h63**

CASH ON FRIDAY 4 b.g. Bishop of Cashel – Til Friday (Scottish Reel) [2004/5 F16g Mar 16] third foal: dam winning hurdler, stayed 21f: well beaten in bumper on debut. *R. C. Guest* **F–**

CASH RETURN 6 b.m. Bob's Return (IRE) – We're In The Money (Billion (USA)) [2004/5 h–: 16g Apr 19] lengthy mare: no form. *Mrs S. Lamyman* **h–**

CASISLE 4 ch.f. Wootton Rivers (USA) – Isle Maree (Star Appeal) [2004/5 16s^{pu} Nov 21] eighth foal: half-sister to 2 winning hurdlers, including modest 2m winner Miss Greenyards (by Stalker): dam unraced: showed nothing in juvenile hurdle on debut. *Mrs Mary A. Meek* **h–**

CASPERS CASE 12 gr.g. Neltino – Casket (Pannier) [2004/5 c23g^{F} Apr 12] fair pointer, successful in March: fell sixth in novice hunter. *R. Barber* **c–**

CASPER TOM 7 b.h. Perpendicular – Secret Dynasty (Dynastic) [2004/5 F16d 16d^{pu} Jun 1] first foal: dam of little account: no form in bumper or maiden hurdle (tongue tied). *M. A. Barnes* **h– F–**

CASPIAN DUSK 4 b.g. Up And At 'em – Caspian Morn (Lugana Beach) [2004/5 16v* 16s^{5} 17d* 16d^{6} 19m^{5} Apr 9] fair on all-weather on Flat (stays 1¾m): similar standard over hurdles: won juvenile claimer at Chepstow in January and amateur handicap at Exeter in March: probably stays 19f: acts on good to firm and heavy going. *W. G. M. Turner* **h99**

CASSANOS (IRE) 4 b.g. Ali-Royal (IRE) – I'm Your Girl (Shavian) [2004/5 17m Apr 9] poor maiden on Flat (stays 1½m): well beaten in seller on hurdling debut. *D. G. Bridgwater* **h–**

CASSIA GREEN 11 gr.g. Scallywag – Casa's Star (Top Star) [2004/5 c20s^{4} c21s Apr 7] big, lengthy, angular gelding: modest chaser: won points in January and February: probably stays 21f: sound jumper. *P. H. Morris* **c89**

CASSIA HEIGHTS 10 b.g. Montelimar (USA) – Cloncoose (IRE) (Remainder Man) [2004/5 c116, h–: c25g c24d c27s c24s^{5} c24d^{pu} c25m^{2} Apr 13] tall gelding: fair handicap chaser: back to near best when second to Lords Best at Cheltenham: stays 31f: acts on soft and firm going: tongue tied: sound jumper. *S. A. Brookshaw* **c113 h–**

CASTANET 6 b.m. Pennekamp (USA) – Addaya (IRE) (Persian Bold) [2004/5 h84: 20g* 20g^{2} 21d^{pu} 16g 19s Jan 5] lengthy mare: modest hurdler: won mares novice at Uttoxeter in June: ran poorly all 3 starts after 4-month break: stays 21f: acts on firm and soft going. *A. E. Price* **h96**

CASTERFLO 6 b.m. Primitive Rising (USA) – Celtic Sands (Celtic Cone) [2004/5 F16v 20d^{pu} 16g 18v^{6} 16v^{pu} 16s 17v^{pu} Mar 15] sturdy mare: no form. *W. S. Coltherd* **h– F–**

CASTLEBOY (IRE) 7 b.g. King's Ride – Bissie's Jayla (Zambrano) [2004/5 F–: 20d^{pu} 17g^{5} 16g^{ur} 16g Mar 11] lengthy gelding: no form. *P. J. Hobbs* **h–**

CASTLEDIVA 8 ch.m. Carlingford Castle – Bivadell (Bivouac) [2004/5 h–: 16d^{pu} 18m^{6} 22m^{pu} 24g^{pu} Jul 7] poor maiden pointer: no form over hurdles: tried visored: sold £1,300 Ascot July Sales. *B. N. Pollock* **h–**

CASTLE FOLLY (IRE) 13 b.g. Carlingford Castle – Air Plane (Arratos (FR)) [2004/5 c–: c20d^{6} May 3] winning chaser, little sign of retaining ability in 2004: usually blinkered. *R. M. Stronge* **c76 ?**

CASTLEFORD (IRE) 7 b.g. Be My Native (USA) – Commanche Bay (IRE) (Commanche Run) [2004/5 c89, h85: c25g^{pu} c25g^{3} Oct 24] medium-sized gelding: modest **c84 h–**

maiden hurdler/chaser: won points in March and April: will stay beyond 3¼m: acts on soft ground. *P. J. Hobbs*

CASTLEMAINEVILLAGE (IRE) 5 b.g. Supreme Leader – Jennys Castle (Carlingford Castle) [2004/5 F16g Apr 19] 10,000 4-y-o: fifth foal: dam placed in point: seemed in need of experience when eighth of 17 in maiden bumper at Towcester on debut. *M. R. Bosley* **F84**

CASTLEMORE (IRE) 7 b.g. Be My Native (USA) – Parsonetta (The Parson) [2004/5 h97, F88: 24d^3 21g^{ur} 21d* 24g^2 Mar 19] fair hurdler: landed odds in novice at Huntingdon in October: stays 3m: yet to race on extremes of going. *P. J. Hobbs* **h107**

CASTLE PRINCE (IRE) 11 b.g. Homo Sapien – Lisaleen Lady (Miner's Lamp) [2004/5 c121?, h–: c17g^{pu} c16g^{pu} Jul 28] tall gelding: fairly useful 2m chaser: took no interest either outing in 2004/5: acts on firm and soft going: held up: sold £4,500 Ascot October Sales, in frame in points in 2005. *R. J. Hodges* **c– § h–**

CASTLE RIVER (USA) 6 b.g. Irish River (FR) – Castellina (USA) (Danzig Connection (USA)) [2004/5 h94: 16m 16g^5 16g 16g* 16g^3 16m 17f^4 16s Oct 21] close-coupled gelding: modest handicap hurdler: won at Stratford in July: raced around 2m: acts on firm going: wore cheekpieces fourth/fifth outings. *O. O'Neill* **h94**

CASTLESHANE (IRE) 8 b.g. Kris – Ahbab (IRE) (Ajdal (USA)) [2004/5 h127: 16m 16g^3 16m 16d^2 16g^2 16g^6 16d 16d c16d^{ur} 16s^3 17g Mar 18] tall, quite good-topped gelding: useful handicap hurdler: well held in valuable events 3 of last 4 starts: tended to jump right before unseating seventh in novice at Doncaster on chasing debut: raced mainly around 2m: acts on firm and soft going: blinkered/in cheekpieces once: usually front runner. *S. Gollings* **c– p h130**

CATALPA CARGO (IRE) 11 b.g. Buckskin (FR) – Money For Honey (New Brig) [2004/5 c128, h115: c24s^F c24v^4 c21s^5 c20v^4 Feb 12] big, rangy, deep-girthed gelding: useful chaser: creditable efforts all 4 starts in 2004/5: will stay beyond 3m: acts on heavy and good to firm going. *E. Sheehy, Ireland* **c134 h–**

CATCHABIRD (IRE) 7 ch.m. Flying Spur (AUS) – Magic Bird (IRE) (Bluebird (USA)) [2004/5 16s 16d^{pu} Feb 9] no form on Flat or in maiden (for Mrs A. Naughton) and selling hurdle: tried tongue tied. *K. G. Wingrove* **h–**

CATCHATAN (IRE) 10 b.g. Cataldi – Snowtan (IRE) (Tanfirion) [2004/5 c–, h–: c20v^{pu} Feb 2] lengthy gelding: winning chaser: no form since 2002/3: usually tongue tied. *P. R. Webber* **c– h–**

CATCHTHEBUG (IRE) 6 b.g. Lord Americo – Just A Maid (Rarity) [2004/5 F17d* 19s^5 16v^2 Nov 25] sturdy gelding: sixth foal: half-brother to bumper winner Wicked Weasel (by Religiously) and winning pointer by Over The River: dam maiden: pulled up in maiden Irish point: twice-raced in bumpers, fairly useful form when winning at Killarney in May: sold out of M. Kenirons' stable 40,000 gns Doncaster August Sales: better effort over hurdles when second in novice at Uttoxeter: should improve further. *Jonjo O'Neill* **h103 p F99**

CATCH THE PERK (IRE) 8 b.g. Executive Perk – Kilbally Quilty (IRE) (Montelimar (USA)) [2004/5 c74, h–: 16g^2 c16g* 18g^3 c20d* c20m^3 c21g* c20s* c24d* c24d c20v^5 c22d^{pu} c24d^3 24s* 23s^2 c27g^2 Apr 15] medium-sized gelding: much improved handicap chaser, winning at Hexham in May and June, Southwell in July and Perth in August and September: also improved over hurdles, winning handicap at Ayr in March and second in novice at Wetherby 10 days later: stays 27f: acts on soft and good to firm going: wore cheekpieces until last 3 starts: a credit to connections. *Miss Lucinda V. Russell* **c112 h112**

CATECHIST (IRE) 10 b.g. Cataldi – Emily Bishop (IRE) (The Parson) [2004/5 c24g^5 Apr 30] fair pointer: fifth of 9 finishers in novice hunter at Bangor. *Miss A. Nolan* **c90**

CATERHAM COMMON 6 b.g. Common Grounds – Pennine Pink (IRE) (Pennine Walk) [2004/5 16g^{pu} Mar 9] half-brother to winning pointer by Saddlers' Hall: poor on Flat (should stay 1¼m): lame early on hurdling debut. *D. W. Chapman* **h–**

CATHERINE'S WAY (IRE) 13 b.g. Mandalus – Sharp Approach (Crash Course) [2004/5 c–, h–: c16v^{pu} May 10] compact gelding: winning chaser, retains little ability in points: tried in cheekpieces. *Martin Ward* **c– h–**

CATHY COME HOME (IRE) 8 br.m. Bob's Return (IRE) – Colour Clown (Random Shot) [2004/5 c23s^{pu} 17d 23s^6 Nov 11] rather sparely-made mare: poor maiden pointer: tried visored/tongue tied. *C. L. Tizzard* **c– h–**

CATILINE (IRE) 4 b.g. Nashwan (USA) – Mild Intrigue (USA) (Sir Ivor (USA)) **F97**
[2004/5 F14d² F16v⁶ Jan 9] €25,000Y: useful-looking gelding: half-brother to several winners, including Irish Oaks winner Margarula (by Doyoun) and useful 1998 staying 2-y-o Wild Heaven (by Darshaan): dam 1¼m winner from good middle-distance/staying family: easily better effort in bumpers when second to Vertical Bloom in 3-y-o event at Warwick. *M. J. Grassick, Ireland*

CAUCASIAN (IRE) 7 gr.g. Leading Counsel (USA) – Kemal's Princess (Kemal (FR)) [2004/5 h–, F–: 20d 22dᵖᵘ Dec 16] lengthy gelding: no form. *Ian Williams* **h–**

CAUGHT AT DAWN (IRE) 11 b.g. Supreme Leader – Pharisee (IRE) (Phardante (FR)) [2004/5 c25s* c25s² c21s² Apr 7] workmanlike gelding: prolific winning pointer: useful hunter chaser: won at Cheltenham in April 2004: best effort when 1½ lengths second to Katarino in Fox Hunters' at Aintree: stays 25f: acts on soft going. *M. H. Weston* **c123**

CAULKLEYS BANK 5 b.g. Slip Anchor – Mayroni (Bustino) [2004/5 F17d* F16d³ F16g⁴ Dec 16] good-topped gelding: half-brother to winners abroad by Batshoof and Glint of Gold: dam, placed at 1¾m, sister to very smart 1½m winner Bustomi and half-sister to dam of useful chaser up to 21f Scots Grey: won bumper at Market Rasen on debut in October: best effort (useful form) when 7 lengths third of 16 to Rasharrow at Wetherby. *M. W. Easterby* **F106**

CAVEAT GRAECI (IRE) 10 b.m. Ilium – Carrigconeen (Beau Charmeur (FR)) [2004/5 19mᵖᵘ Sep 1] has failed to complete in points and novice hurdle. *R. Williams* **h–**

CAWKWELL MEG 5 ch.m. Afif – Cawkwell Patricia (Boco (USA)) [2004/5 20gᶠ May 29] fourth foal: dam winning pointer: has failed to complete in novice hurdle and points. *F. Jestin* **h–**

CAYMANAS BAY 5 ch.g. Karinga Bay – Carribean Sound (Good Times (ITY)) [2004/5 20g Feb 27] tenth foal: dam, 7f winner, half-sister to fairly useful hurdler up to 3m Mariners Haven: well beaten in novice hurdle on debut. *A. Parker* **h–**

CEDAR 8 gr.g. Absalom – Setai's Palace (Royal Palace) [2004/5 c–, h73: 16m⁴ 24mᵖᵘ 19d c16s³ c19s⁵ c28sᶠ 19v c16s³ c16s⁵ c19v³ Mar 29] sturdy gelding: poor maiden hurdler/chaser: form mainly around 2m: acts on good to firm and heavy going: visored 2 of last 3 starts. *R. Dickin* **c72 h70**

CEDAR CHIEF 8 b.g. Saddlers' Hall (IRE) – Dame Ashfield (Grundy) [2004/5 c–§, h–§: c24d⁵ Mar 11] stocky gelding: winning pointer: poor hurdler/maiden chaser: stays 3m: acts on any going: needs blinkers: hard ride. *K. Tork* **c– § h– §**

CEDAR MASTER (IRE) 8 b.g. Soviet Lad (USA) – Samriah (IRE) (Wassl) [2004/5 h98: 22m⁶ 20mᵖᵘ Jun 27] modest hurdler: barely stays 2¾m: acts on good to firm going: blinkered/visored last 6 starts, tongue tied last 4. *J. R. Boyle* **h93**

CEDAR RANGERS (USA) 7 b.g. Anabaa (USA) – Chelsea (USA) (Miswaki (USA)) [2004/5 h72: 17d 19g³ 16m² Jun 29] angular gelding: poor maiden hurdler: probably best up to 19f: acts on firm and good to soft going: races freely. *G. F. Edwards* **h76**

CELEBRATION MARCH 14 b.g. Sousa – Boundless Grace (Flandre II) [2004/5 24s Oct 30] good-topped gelding: poor maiden hurdler/pointer, very lightly raced. *M. J. Coombe* **h–**

CELEBRATION TOWN (IRE) 8 b. or br.g. Case Law – Battle Queen (Kind of Hush) [2004/5 h97: 16gᵖᵘ 17sᵖᵘ 16g* 16m c17f⁴ Sep 28] lengthy gelding: modest hurdler: left J. O'Neill, won seller at Stratford in July: fourth of 5 finishers in novice at Exeter on chasing debut: best at easy 2m: acts on good to firm and good to soft going: blinkered second outing: has refused/been reluctant to line up. *Miss E. C. Lavelle* **c85 h94**

CELESTIAL GOLD (IRE) 7 br.g. Persian Mews – What A Queen (King's Ride) [2004/5 c133: c20d* c26g* c24d³ c26g Mar 18] **c161**

Horses from Pond House stables dominated Cheltenham's Open meeting once again. Its seven winners over the three days were all ridden by Timmy Murphy, six of them—including a four-timer on the Saturday—for the stable's biggest owner David Johnson who had been forced to look for another jockey after Tony McCoy's departure at the end of the previous season. After discussions with Richard Johnson and approaches to Ruby Walsh and Barry Geraghty, Johnson finally signed Murphy. 'He wasn't a unanimous choice,' Johnson told *Pacemaker* magazine in a frank interview in March, by which time Murphy was firmly established in his new job.

*Paddy Power Gold Cup Chase (Handicap), Cheltenham—
the highlight of a memorable meeting for connections as Celestial Gold
beats Thisthatandtother (right), Monkerhostin (virtually hidden) and Ollie Magern*

Murphy was, in all honesty, something of a surprise replacement for McCoy, his usually quiet style in sharp contrast to that of his more forceful predecessor, and there were some teething problems early on as the Pond House string struggled for consistency, the focus falling on Murphy who told one interviewer he was 'tired and fed up of being compared with AP.' In fact, Murphy didn't ride the Johnson-owned Contraband at the Open meeting, 'jocked off' in favour of McCoy after connections decided McCoy's style 'would suit Contraband's needs best.' The previous weekend, Murphy had ridden Beef Or Salmon at Down Royal rather than another Johnson-owned novice Comply Or Die in the Rising Stars at Wincanton. Murphy's performances at the Open meeting, however, ensured that he wouldn't be watching any of the top Johnson horses from the weighing room again and he went on to enjoy a splendid season, riding 143 winners to finish second to McCoy in the championship, Murphy's mounts in the process picking up £2,068,120 in first-three prize money, more than any other rider. Unfairly labelled by some as a one-dimensional waiting jockey, Murphy demonstrated the full range of his talents at Cheltenham. He made just about all on Comply Or Die, judging the pace well and being clear from a good way out; showed tremendous persistence to get Stormez home after a mistake-riddled round; and displayed his strength in a finish on Team Tassel (unfortunately picking up a two-day riding ban for using the whip with excessive force).

The Murphy-ridden Celestial Gold, a 12/1-shot apparently running as a substitute for the sidelined Our Vic, provided trainer Martin Pipe with his sixth winner in nine years of the feature two-and-a-half-mile handicap at the Open meeting, and his seventh in all. Pipe won the 1987 edition with Beau Ranger when it was still known as the Mackeson Gold Cup, its title between 1960 and 1995. The race has had three guises since, Pipe victories coming with Challenger du Luc and Cyfor Malta in the four years of the Murphy's Gold Cup; with Lady Cricket, Shooting Light and Cyfor Malta again in all three runnings as the Thomas Pink Gold Cup; and now with Celestial Gold in the second Paddy Power Gold Cup. Celestial Gold received a vintage Murphy ride, held up in the rear and moving well through the

Hennessy Cognac Gold Cup Chase (Handicap), Newbury—
front runner Ollie Magern again provides tough opposition as this notable double
is landed for the first time since 1980; also pictured is third-placed Royal Auclair

race before making good headway with three to jump and being produced to lead at the last. Celestial Gold kept on well to win by a length and three quarters and five lengths from Thisthatandtother and Monkerhostin, second and third also coming from off the pace in a truly-run race. The form of the fourteen-runner Paddy Power looked well up to standard and Celestial Gold's performance represented significant improvement on his efforts in the previous season when he had developed into a useful novice, winning two of his five starts and finishing second in the four-mile National Hunt Chase at the Cheltenham Festival. Celestial Gold won three out of four starts in points in 2003 for David Pipe before joining the main Pond House string, but the Paddy Power was only his sixth race over fences and there seemed scope to do better again, especially as he was still only six.

With the step back up in trip looking unlikely to trouble him, Celestial Gold had strong claims under a 6-lb penalty in the Hennessy Cognac Gold Cup at Newbury at the end of November. The field of fourteen was significantly smaller than in the two previous years and only one of the runners—First Gold—was on a BHB mark above 150. The first four in the betting finished clear in a well-run race, the patiently-ridden favourite Celestial Gold gradually creeping into contention on the final circuit and staying on strongly to lead just after the last. Celestial Gold, one of four winners (including three for Johnson) on the card for Murphy, held the renewed challenged of the Paddy Power fourth Ollie Magern by a length and a half, with Royal Auclair another length and a quarter back in third and Lord Transcend, having only his second outing over fences, a further seven lengths away fourth.

The lacklustre performance of the only Irish-trained challenger in the Hennessy, the pulled-up Nil Desperandum, who drifted to 9/1 after being a big ante-post gamble, caused some controversy. A post-race veterinary examination and a routine dope test failed to reveal any explanation for his poor run. Controversy rumbled on, incidentally, over the disqualification of the Irish-trained winner of the race in 2002, Be My Royal, the most high profile of a spate of horses in Britain and Ireland who showed traces of morphine in urine samples in November and December of that year. The challenge by Be My Royal's trainer, supported by Connolly Red Mills, manufacturers of a batch of contaminated feed thought to be responsible, reached the High Court and had still to be resolved at the end of the latest season.

Given the different distances, not many attempt the Paddy Power/Hennessy double—the three latest had been Challenger du Luc (fell), the 1999 winner The Outback Way (pulled up) and Lady Cricket (fourth)—and Celestial Gold became only the third to achieve it in the same season, following Bachelor's Hall in 1977 and Bright Highway in 1980 (Red Candle won the 1972 Mackeson and the 1973 Hennessy). Bachelor's Hall went on to add the King George VI Chase at Kempton and finish fourth in the Cheltenham Gold Cup. Bright Highway damaged a tendon and didn't run again in the 1980/1 season but was among the favourites for the Gold Cup until his injury. Celestial Gold's combination of speed and stamina, his generally sound jumping and his progressive form made him an interesting contender for the Cheltenham Gold Cup for which he started second favourite at 9/2 behind Kicking King. He ran once between the Hennessy and the Gold Cup, finishing a close third, after looking the likely winner for much of the straight, to Farmer Jack and Strong Flow, returned to Newbury for the AON Chase in February. Celestial Gold again finished a place behind Strong Flow at Cheltenham where both ran below form, finishing sixth and seventh respectively behind Kicking King. Celestial Gold, looking very well but taken noticeably steadily to post, made early mistakes and was beaten a fair way from home. Celestial Gold is only seven and there may yet be more to come from him, and he could figure more prominently in the Gold Cup another year.

Celestial Gold (IRE) (br.g. 1998)	Persian Mews (b 1983)	Persian Bold (br 1975)	Bold Lad
			Relkarunner
		Tawny Owl (ch 1968)	Faberge II
			Owlet
	What A Queen (b 1984)	King's Ride (b 1976)	Rarity
			Ride
		What A Honey (b 1962)	Vulgan
			What A Daisy

The tall Celestial Gold is the seventh foal out of the unraced What A Queen whose only other winner is Trimmer Wonder (by Celio Rufo), successful in a

Mr D. A. Johnson's "Celestial Gold"

bumper and a point. Celestial Gold was among his stable's Grand National entries and his family has been regularly represented in that race, notably by dual Gold Cup winner L'Escargot, successful at Aintree in 1975, who was out of the great grandam of Celestial Gold, What A Daisy. L'Escargot ran four times in all in the National, placed on his other completed starts, in 1973 and 1974. What A Daisy produced another Grand National regular in The Pilgarlic, who made the frame three times from four attempts from 1977 to 1980. He was joined in the race by his brothers What A Buck (sixth) in 1977 and Flitgrove (pulled up) in 1979. What A Daisy's grandam Duchess of Pedulas was the dam of the 1958 National winner Mr What (by Grand Inquisitor, also What A Daisy's sire). Mr What ran in the next five Nationals and was placed twice more. Celestial Gold's grandam What A Honey is another to produce a Grand National runner, in the fairly useful staying chaser Wolverhampton, though he was pulled up when a 25/1-chance in 1974. Whether Celestial Gold ever gets the opportunity to contest the Grand National would seem open to doubt since connections were inclined to put his Gold Cup failure down to lack of stamina, an odd conclusion given that the horse has won a Hennessy and finished second in a National Hunt Chase. On the evidence of Celestial Gold's performances overall, he is very versatile so far as distance goes, proven over four miles and fully effective at much shorter distances. He acts on soft and good to firm going. *M. C. Pipe*

CELESTIAL HEIGHTS (IRE) 6 b.g. Fourstars Allstar (USA) – Aon Dochas (IRE) (Strong Gale) [2004/5 F82: 20m³ 20d 18s c24gᵖᵘ Apr 15] poor form over hurdles: lacklustre effort on chasing debut. *O. Sherwood* **c– h83**

CELESTIAL WAVE (IRE) 5 b.m. Taipan (IRE) – Blossom World (IRE) (The Parson) [2004/5 F16s* F19d³ Mar 20] third foal: dam ran once: fairly useful form in 2 bumpers at Limerick in March, beating Haydens First 2 lengths in mares event on debut. *Adrian Maguire, Ireland* **F100**

CELIA'S HIGH (IRE) 6 br.g. Hymns On High – Celia's Fountain (IRE) (Royal Fountain) [2004/5 F16s 24vᵖᵘ c20vᵖᵘ 16d 16sᵖᵘ Apr 22] lengthy gelding: first foal: dam unraced, from family of top-class chaser up to 3m Wayward Lad: won maiden Irish point in 2004: sold 8,500 gns Doncaster May Sales: no sign of ability otherwise. *F. P. Murtagh* **c– h– F–**

CELIOSO (IRE) 8 b.g. Celio Rufo – Bettons Rose (Roselier (FR)) [2004/5 c122, h–: 16d* c32m 22g c23m⁴ c23g³ c22g Sep 25] lengthy gelding: fairly useful handicap chaser at best: fair hurdler: justified good support with plenty in hand in 2m handicap at Hexham in June: below form after: best form at 3½m+: acts on good to firm and good to soft going: sometimes soon off bridle. *Mrs S. J. Smith* **c110 h107**

CELTA VIGO (IRE) 7 b.m. Executive Perk – Alice Freyne (IRE) (Lancastrian) [2004/5 h–, F–: 22vᵖᵘ Oct 30] no sign of ability. *Mrs L. B. Normile* **h–**

CELTIC BLAZE (IRE) 6 b.m. Charente River (IRE) – Firdaunt (Tanfirion) [2004/5 h95§: 17d⁴ 16m³ 22g⁶ 21m 20m² 20s⁵ 20d⁴ 23d* 24v⁶ 23sᵘʳ 23s⁴ Mar 22] small, sturdy mare: modest hurdler: won novice at Wetherby in December: stays 23f: acts on good to firm and good to soft going, possibly not on softer: wears cheekpieces and tongue strap: unreliable. *B. S. Rothwell* **h95 §**

CELTIC BOY (IRE) 7 b.g. Arctic Lord – Laugh Away (Furry Glen) [2004/5 h91, F71: 20d³ 22s⁴ c24g³ c19v⁵ c24g³ Jan 17] quite good-topped gelding: fair hurdler: modest form in maiden chases: stays 3m: raced on good going or softer (probably acts on heavy). *P. Bowen* **c94 h105**

CELTIC DUKE 13 b.g. Strong Gale – Celtic Cygnet (Celtic Cone) [2004/5 c92, h–: c24d* c24dᵖᵘ May 11] sturdy gelding: fair hunter chaser: won at Fakenham (for second year in succession) in May: stays 3½m: acts on firm and good to soft going (possibly not on heavy): jumps well. *J. M. Turner* **c98 h–**

CELTIC FLOW 7 b.m. Primitive Rising (USA) – Celtic Lane (Welsh Captain) [2004/5 c63, h64: 23s 24d⁶ c24g³ c27vᵖᵘ c24g⁶ Jan 21] leggy mare: poor maiden hurdler/chaser: stays 25f: acts on good to soft going: tried blinkered/in cheekpieces. *C. R. Wilson* **c– h65**

CELTIC JEM (IRE) 5 b.g. Norwich – Running Board (IRE) (Deep Run) [2004/5 F17v⁵ F16d Mar 10] €95,000 3-y-o: rangy, useful-looking gelding: fifth foal: half-brother to fair Irish hurdler/chaser up to 2¾m Again An Again (by Montelimar): dam unraced sister to Champion Hurdle winners Morley Street and Granville Again: well held in bumpers. *P. Bowen* **F76**

CELTIC LEGEND (FR) 6 br.g. Celtic Swing – Another Legend (USA) (Lyphard's Wish (FR)) [2004/5 c71, h–: c16s^{6} c21s^{pu} c20m^{4} c21d^{2} c20m* c19g^{5} c20g* c20d^{3} c24m^{F} Feb 6] tall, leggy gelding: maiden hurdler: modest chaser: won handicaps at Musselburgh in December (amateurs) and January: should stay easy 3m: acts on good to firm and good to soft going: tried tongue tied: patiently ridden: has carried head high/hung right. *K. G. Reveley* **c89 h–**

CELTIC MAJOR (IRE) 7 br.g. Roselier (FR) – Dun Oengus (IRE) (Strong Gale) [2004/5 h94, F100: 16d 20s^{pu} Dec 17] sturdy gelding: runner-up in bumper on debut: modest form at best in novice hurdles, not knocked about both outings in 2004/5: should stay at least 2½m. *Jonjo O'Neill* **h–**

CELTIC PRIDE (IRE) 10 gr.g. Roselier (FR) – Grannie No (Brave Invader (USA)) [2004/5 c99, h–: c24d^{4} 22s^{pu} c25s^{5} c24s* c24v* c26v^{pu} c24v^{3} c31s^{pu} Apr 22] tall gelding: winning hurdler: fair handicap chaser: left P. Bowen and off over 17 months prior to reappearance: back in form when winning at Newcastle in January and February: should stay beyond 3m: raced mainly on good going or softer (acts well on soft/heavy): visored last 6 outings. *Mrs J. Candlish* **c105 h–**

CELTIC PRINCE (IRE) 7 gr.g. Old Vic – No Slow (King's Ride) [2004/5 F16v Dec 28] 15,000 4-y-o: half-brother to fair hurdler/chaser up to 23f Stratco (by Satco): dam unraced, from family of fairly useful staying chaser Boom Docker: failed to complete 4 of 5 starts in maiden points: well beaten in bumper. *Miss H. Lewis* **F–**

CELTIC ROMANCE 6 b.m. Celtic Swing – Southern Sky (Comedy Star (USA)) [2004/5 17m 16m 16d^{3} 16d^{3} 19d 16g^{pu} 16s^{4} Mar 13] leggy mare: half-sister to 3 winning hurdlers: poor on Flat (stays 1m): poor maiden hurdler: sold out of Mrs M. Reveley's stable 1,600 gns Doncaster August Sales after debut. *Ms Sue Smith* **h72**

CELTIC RUFFIAN (IRE) 7 b.g. Celio Rufo – Candid Lady (Arctic Lord) [2004/5 h–, F70?: 20m 22d^{4} 25s^{2} c21s^{pu} 25g^{5} 25g^{pu} Mar 27] poor maiden hurdler: bled from nose on chasing debut: stays 25f: acts on soft going. *R. Rowe* **c– h70**

CELTIC SAMMY (IRE) 5 b.g. Beneficial – Sip of Orange (Celtic Cone) [2004/5 F16d^{2} F16v Dec 26] good-topped gelding: sixth reported foal: half-brother to 3 winners, including fairly useful 2½m chaser Jaffa (by Kind of Hush): dam useful staying hurdler: easily better effort in bumpers when second to Albert Mooney at Fairyhouse in November. *N. Meade, Ireland* **F103**

CELTIC SON (FR) 6 b.g. Celtic Arms (FR) – For Kicks (FR) (Top Ville) [2004/5 F101: 17g^{5} 17s^{5} 19g 22s* 20v^{2} 24s* 24d* 25s* 24d* 24d^{2} 20g^{3} 22g^{pu} Apr 16] **h135**

The Jockey Club moved from Portman Square to Shaftesbury Avenue in December, the change of premises coinciding with implementation of a decision to open some hearings of the Jockey Club's disciplinary panel to the media. Champion trainer Martin Pipe was among the first to experience the court-room atmosphere of an open hearing, summoned in January after being automatically referred by the Exeter stewards following a handicap win there by Celtic Son on his fourth outing over hurdles after being unplaced on his first three. The running of Celtic Son in a novice hurdle there three months before his win drew particular attention in Shaftesbury Avenue, though the stewards on the day had not thought it worthy of note. The Jockey Club hearing eventually took place in mid-February, by which time Celtic Son had left that Exeter form—an eye-catching fifth to Salsalino—well behind and was prominent in ante-post betting on the (Brit Insurance) Spa Novices' Hurdle and the Pertemps Final at the Cheltenham Festival.

Celtic Son very much caught the eye again when eighth in a similar event at Newbury on his next start after Exeter, a run which qualified him for a BHB handicap mark. He made a mockery of the modest mark he was allotted when winning a novices' handicap back at Exeter in early-January and added further handicaps at Taunton, Newbury (conditional jockeys) and Warwick (Pertemps series qualifier) in the space of thirteen days, rising 23 lb in the weights between Exeter and Warwick. Celtic Son's impressive progress, coinciding with the fitting of a tongue strap and a step up to longer distances, and interrupted only by defeat at the hands of another progressive hurdler Basilea Star, highlighted his Cheltenham Festival prospects. Celtic Son travelled particularly strongly in a good renewal at Warwick, jumping well and quickening smartly to assert two out, again winning with a fair bit in hand. Celtic Son added a further victory, six days before the Shaftesbury Avenue inquiry, in a novice event at Kempton, landing the odds

Pertemps Handicap Hurdle (Qualifier), Warwick—
a fourth win in just thirteen days for Celtic Son,
though a high-profile ban prevented him from contesting the Final at Cheltenham

impressively without having to run anywhere near the form he had been showing in handicaps.

The Jockey Club's disciplinary panel considered Pipe and conditional jockey Jamie Moore—riding Celtic Son for the only time—guilty of being party to not allowing Celtic Son to run on his merits at Exeter, finding Pipe in breach of rule 155(ii) (which deals with a duty to give adequate instructions to a rider) and Moore in breach of rule 157(d) (dealing with a rider intentionally concealing the true ability of a horse or affecting the result of a race). Pipe was fined £3,000, Moore suspended for twenty-one days and the horse banned from running for forty days. The hearing lasted nearly three hours but, after the panel took just ten minutes to reach its verdict, Pipe accused its members of 'making up their minds before they went in.' The panel found that Moore had 'intentionally restrained the gelding after the third last to the winning post.' Moore asserted he had hit Celtic Son six times in the home straight but the panel 'was of the view that any contact was minimal.' Press coverage of the Celtic Son case seemed, in the main, sympathetic towards Pipe and Moore, questioning whether the evidence was damning enough for a conviction. Neither Pipe nor Moore appealed, Moore's suspension ending just in time to allow him to resume riding at the Cheltenham Festival. Moore won the Grade 1 totesport Chase at Lingfield on It Takes Time for Celtic Son's connections just before the suspension took effect, but had only two other mounts—from seventeen for the Pipe stable—on the horses belonging to Celtic Son's owner David Johnson between Cheltenham and the end of the season. He is to ride freelance in 2005/6.

Media sympathy for Pipe was less evident when he was dealt with more severely by the Jockey Club's disciplinary panel in early-March, after falling foul of the rules of racing a week after the Celtic Son inquiry by refusing to allow the Johnson-owned Tanterari to enter the sampling unit at Haydock after he had run a lacklustre race when odds on in a handicap chase. Around ten per cent of all runners are routinely tested (equating at present to around 8,800 tests a year) and Pipe apparently felt strongly that horses faced a heightened risk of infection while in the sampling units, especially as horses who had run badly accounted for a good proportion of those tested. It was reported that Pipe had had his runners the previous weekend at Sandown and Lingfield tested in their stable boxes, after which the Jockey Club faxed a letter to the trainer informing him that if he refused to allow any horse to enter the sampling unit, as required, he would be referred to the Stewards of the Jockey Club who had the power to invoke rule 2(ii)(c) and refuse to accept entries and allow horses from the stable to run for a period of time, as well as imposing financial penalties. Such penalties put refusal to allow a horse to enter a sampling unit on a par with those for deliberately administering a prohibited substance.

Bans in high profile cases in athletics—Greek sprinters Konstantinos Kenteris and Ekaterina Thanou—and in football—England international Rio Ferdinand—emphasised that missing a dope test was treated just as seriously in most sports as testing positively. A repentant Martin Pipe, who gave an assurance that he would toe the line on dope-testing procedures, escaped the suspension of his licence—which a Jockey Club spokesman said was 'not on the table this time round'—and was fined £7,500, towards the middle of the range available to the stewards. Pipe's concerns over the cleanliness of the sampling boxes on racecourses were genuinely held, and his defence included written statements of support from trainers including Henrietta Knight, but, for the good of the integrity of racing, trainers cannot be allowed to dictate the terms of dope tests, or be given any grounds for refusing them. Allowing dope-testing to be carried out anywhere else than in the controlled environment of a designated sampling unit would inevitably leave the way open for legal argument over possible contamination of samples.

Celtic Son's owner and trainer, incidentally, also featured in newspaper coverage of a well-orchestrated coup—no rules were broken—executed with the three-year-old There Is No Doubt, backed down from 28/1 to 5/2 favourite, on his racecourse debut in a bumper at Exeter in December. It was said that Pipe sold the French-bred a month before the race, after which its name was changed from Le Saadien; 'shrewd faces close to the Pipe yard' were alleged to have supported There Is No Doubt heavily at Exeter, David Johnson saying he needed 'to think seriously about who I bet with in future' after *The Mail On Sunday* published details of reported winnings of £96,000. Incidentally, the Johnson-owned, Pipe-trained runner in the bumper, Oasis Banus, a 4/1-shot, unseated his rider Jamie Moore after jinking as the tapes went up. Oasis Banus was the subject of a stewards' inquiry after finishing down the field in a maiden hurdle at Ludlow in February, his rider that day Timmy Murphy given a seven-day suspension for breaching rule 158 (at the lower end of the scale among the so-called 'non-triers' rules).

To return to Celtic Son's racing record. He appeared three more times after returning from his ban, putting up a useful effort—his best to date—when nine lengths second of twenty-two behind Holland Park in a listed handicap at Aintree. Had Celtic Son been able to record a similar performance in the Spa at Cheltenham—in which stable-companion Over The Creek was second—it would probably have got him into the frame. Celtic Son was turned out on successive days at Ayr but the meeting probably came too soon after his hard race at Aintree the previous week; he trailed in last of three behind Mephisto in a novice hurdle on the Friday and was pulled up, reluctant to line up and losing touch after four out, in the handicap won by Ladalko on the Saturday.

Celtic Son (FR) (b.g. 1999)	Celtic Arms (FR) (b 1991)	Comrade In Arms (b 1982)	Brigadier Gerard
			Girl Friend
		Amour Celtique (ch 1977)	Northfields
			Apoplexy
	For Kicks (FR) (b 1984)	Top Ville (b 1976)	High Top
			Sega Ville
		Insistance (b 1971)	Sir Gaylord
			Aesthetic

The sturdy Celtic Son is a half-brother to several winners out of Flat winner For Kicks, a half-sister to a smart French jumper at up to twenty-five furlongs, Summit, who won the Grand Steeple-Chase d'Enghien and was twice placed in the big hurdle race at that track. Four of the other winners produced by For Kicks have won over jumps: For More (by Sanglamore) showed fairly useful form at up to two and a half miles over hurdles in France and also ran for Henrietta Knight; Dame Foraine (by Rahotep) won a two-and-a-quarter mile chase in France; Sun Kicks (by Saumarez) won at two and a quarter miles over hurdles in France; and the useful staying hurdler Sonevafushi (by Ganges) took well to fences in the latest season for Venetia Williams. It would be no surprise to see Celtic Son put over fences in the next season. He looks just the type to enjoy a successful campaign in novice chases. He stays twenty-five furlongs and has so far been raced on good going or softer (acts on heavy). *M. C. Pipe*

CELTIC STAR (IRE) 7 b.g. Celtic Swing – Recherchee (Rainbow Quest (USA)) [2004/5 c–, h99§: c21g^4 c21d^{pu} 17g* 20m^3 c16d^2 c21m^4 c20m* c26g^3 c20g^F c19g^2 c20s^4 Mar 31] lengthy gelding: modest hurdler: won claimer (claimed from Miss K. George £8,000) at Newton Abbot in August: similar form over fences, winning novice handicap at Plumpton in September: sold out of J. O'Shea's stable 10,000 gns Doncaster October Sales before final start: stays 21f: acts on firm and soft going: effective with visor/cheek-pieces or without: has hung left under pressure. *Mrs L. Williamson* **c96** **h91 §**

CELTIC TANNER (IRE) 6 b.g. Royal Abjar (USA) – Mills Pride (IRE) (Posen (USA)) [2004/5 h–: 19g^{pu} Sep 30] medium-sized gelding: little sign of ability. *D. J. Wintle* **h–**

CELTIC VISION (IRE) 9 b.g. Be My Native (USA) – Dream Run (Deep Run) [2004/5 c96x, h–: 22m 22s^6 19m Nov 25] rather leggy gelding: winning hurdler/maiden chaser: tried in headgear: sometimes tongue tied. *M. Appleby* **c– x** **h–**

CENKOS (FR) 11 ch.g. Nikos – Vincenza (Grundy) [2004/5 c163, h128: c16g* c16d^{ur} c16d^4 c16v^6 c16s c16g^5 c16g^{pu} Mar 16] strong, lengthy gelding: winning hurdler: high-class chaser at best, successful in Tingle Creek and twice in Celebration Chase at **c157** **h–**

Warwick Castle Chase, Warwick—Cenkos gains a third win in the race

Sandown, also in frame 3 times in Queen Mother Champion Chase at Cheltenham: won 4-runner minor event at Warwick (for third time in 4 years) in May, making all and beating Kadarann 7 lengths: creditable effort after only when fourth to Moscow Flyer in Tingle Creek at Sandown: best around 2m: had form on soft/heavy going, possibly ideally suited by less testing conditions: blinkered once (ran badly): usually a fluent jumper: reportedly retired. *P. F. Nicholls*

CENTO (IRE) 12 b.g. Shernazar – Callianire (Sir Gaylord) [2004/5 c24d² c24m⁴ c24spu Feb 10] angular gelding: winning pointer, including in 2005: best effort in hunter chases when second in ladies event at Huntingdon: stays 3m: acts on soft and firm going: usually blinkered, wore cheekpieces final start. *Mrs Sarah Faulks* **c90 h–**

CENTRAL COMMITTEE (IRE) 10 ch.g. Royal Academy (USA) – Idle Chat (USA) (Assert) [2004/5 h–: 22g 26g 24g 22m³ 22f² 20s⁴ 26s⁴ 24d 26g 27mpu Apr 21] leggy gelding: modest handicap hurdler: stays 3¼m: acts on firm and soft going: blinkered once: has had tongue tied. *R. T. Phillips* **h87**

CENTRAL HOUSE 8 b.g. Alflora (IRE) – Fantasy World (Kemal (FR)) [2004/5 c140, h108: c20s⁵ c16s² c16s² c17v* c17v* c20s² c16s* c16g⁶ c17s³ Mar 29] **c153 h–**

What a difference a year makes. When Central House unseated his rider, up with the leaders and still full of running, at the fourth last in the 2004 Arkle Trophy, it seemed reasonable to conclude that with a clear round he would at least have finished a respectable third to Well Chief and Kicking King. Returned to the Cheltenham Festival a year later for the Queen Mother Champion Chase, Central House was a 25/1-shot, very much up against it taking on the exceptional trio Moscow Flyer, Azertyuiop and the vastly improved Well Chief. Central House had around two stone to find to make a race of it with the big three, though his career had gone anything but badly in the interim. Far from it. He had enjoyed a lucrative campaign in pattern events in Ireland and lined up at Cheltenham as the winner of three of his last four races, including the Grade 1 Paddy Power Dial-A-Bet Chase at Leopardstown's Christmas fixture. The problem was that Central House had had to show form no better than smart in picking up his three pattern chases, his Leopardstown victory coming against only three rivals after the late withdrawal of Moscow Flyer who would have been long odds on.

Central House had not won since taking the Denny Gold Medal Novices' Chase—in which Kicking King fell when leading two out—at the same meeting twelve months earlier. He was fitted with blinkers for the first time in the Dial-A-Bet Chase. They seemed to sharpen him up and, after dictating the pace, he held on well from Native Scout, Native Upmanship and a below-par Rathgar Beau, only four and a half lengths separating first and last. Given the limited opportunities in weight-for-age events for smart two-mile chasers in Britain, it is surprising there are not more British-trained challengers for the programme in Ireland. Kadarann and Cenkos, for example, chasers of similar merit to Central House, also lined up for the Queen Mother Champion Chase, but had between them recorded only one win in eleven outings in the current season before the Festival.

Paddy Power Dial-A-Bet Chase, Leopardstown—
Central House makes all in blinkers first time to beat the ill-fated Native Scout

Central House followed up his Leopardstown win in the John Keogh Car Sales Norman Grove Chase, a Grade 2 event at Fairyhouse in mid-January, winning by twelve lengths, though he would have had to work harder had Native Scout not fallen fatally at the second last when almost on terms and going at least as well. After a reverse against Rathgar Beau in the Kinloch Brae Chase over two and a half miles at Thurles, Central House brought his earnings for the season in win money alone to £84,987 when landing the odds in an uncompetitive Paddy & Helen Cox Memorial Newlands Chase, a Grade 2 at Naas in February, in command a long way out against three inferior opponents. Central House faced uphill work in his two races after Cheltenham where he was beaten thirty-three lengths into sixth behind Moscow Flyer after helping force the pace to three out. Central House ran close to his best when third to Ground Ball and Ulaan Baatar under top weight in the Dan Moore Memorial Handicap at Fairyhouse and then managed only fifth, ridden with more restraint than usual and making no impression when ridden four out, behind Rathgar Beau and Moscow Flyer in the Kerrygold Champion Chase at Punchestown just after the end of the British season.

Central House (b.g. 1997)	Alflora (IRE) (b 1989)	Niniski (b 1976)	Nijinsky
			Virginia Hills
		Adrana (ch 1980)	Bold Lad
			Le Melody
	Fantasy World (ch 1986)	Kemal (b 1971)	Armistice III
			Ilrem
		Rockford Lass (b 1977)	Walshford
			Rock Forest

The tall, rather leggy Central House is from the second crop of British-based stallion Alflora who is covering well over two hundred mares a year nowadays and looks set to exert a major influence on jumping (the ill-fated Farmer Jack and Hand Inn Hand were from his first crop). Central House's dam Fantasy World was also represented in the latest season by the fair six-year-old mare Central Arch (by Dilum), successful in a bumper and a maiden hurdle over nineteen furlongs, and the year-younger Cloud Venture (by Cloudings), who was well held in a bumper on his debut. Fantasy World was a fair hurdler at up to three miles, and is out of Rockford Lass who didn't win but is a sister to the useful Carigeensharragh, a winner over hurdles and fences and placed in the Kerry National and the Troytown Chase. Carigeensharragh also finished fourth in a Galway Plate and sixth in an Irish National. Central House's great grandam Rock Forest, successful over hurdles and fences, is also the third dam of Irish Grand National winner The Bunny Boiler. There is plenty of stamina in Central House's pedigree but he has shown his very best form at around two miles, though he stays two and a half. He acts on heavy going and has yet to encounter going firmer than good over fences (ran creditably only outing on good to firm over hurdles). He is a good jumper who seems best making the running. Effective tongue tied or not, he wore blinkers on all his starts from the Dial-A-Bet Chase onwards. Ridden mostly by Paul Carberry, he ran well for 5-lb claiming amateur Mr Roger Loughran in the Dan Moore. *D. T. Hughes, Ireland*

CEOL NA SRAIDE (IRE) 6 b.m. King's Theatre (IRE) – My Lady's Key (USA) (Key To The Mint (USA)) [2004/5 h92: 17d^{F} 17d 16v^{pu} 16v^{pu} 16d Jan 28] sparely-made mare: maiden hurdler: no form in 2004/5: tried in cheekpieces. *B. S. Rothwell* **h–**

CEOPERK (IRE) 6 ch.m. Executive Perk – Golden Mela (Golden Love) [2004/5 F17s* F16s^{6} F16d^{2} F16d Mar 19] 5,000 4-y-o: rather unfurnished mare: half-sister to several winners, including modest hurdler Kaygebe (by Moscow Society) and fair hurdler/modest chaser Tory Bush (by Tale Quale), both stayed 21f: dam, winning pointer, in frame in maiden hurdle in Ireland: fair form in bumpers: won mares event at Folkestone in November by 8 lengths from Lamp's Return. *D. J. Wintle* **F92**

CERESFIELD (NZ) 9 br.m. Westminster (NZ) – Audrey Rose (NZ) (Blue Razor (USA)) [2004/5 c106, h–: c17g* c16g^{3} c16m^{3} c17d c17d^{2} c17g c17d^{pu} 16d Jan 29] leggy mare: fair handicap chaser: won at Southwell in May: maiden hurdler: best around 2m on good ground or firmer: wears cheekpieces: usually tongue tied: front runner. *R. C. Guest* **c100 h–**

CERIUM (FR) 4 b.g. Vaguely Pleasant (FR) – Tantatura (FR) (Akarad (FR)) **h135**
[2004/5 16s* 16d* 16v 16d* 17g4 16s Apr 7]

Since 1997, trainer Paul Nicholls has run just four horses in the Triumph Hurdle, all of them French-bred. Sud Bleu and Vol Solitaire were eighth and tenth respectively in 2002, Le Duc sixth in 2003 and Cerium fourth in 2005. Both Vol Solitaire and Le Duc were sent over fences in the following season, Vol Solitaire showing smart form and winning five times, Le Duc finishing third in the Arkle behind Well Chief and Kicking King. Sud Bleu didn't encounter fences until the latest season, showing useful form in beating Lacdoudal on his debut before dropping dead on the gallops. It will be disappointing if Cerium, who is tall and quite good topped and very much a chaser on looks, fails to make an impact if, as seems likely, he is sent over fences in 2005/6.

Cerium showed useful form over hurdles, certainly on a par with Le Duc's efforts as a juvenile and significantly better than Sud Bleu's. He started third favourite in the Triumph and held every chance nearing the last before being beaten over nine lengths by Penzance, unable to find any extra. Cerium won three of four starts in Britain before Cheltenham (he ran once in France for Jean-Pierre Totain prior to the British season), a juvenile maiden at Kempton, a Grade 2 juvenile at Cheltenham (in which he beat the subsequent Triumph fifth Phar Bleu) and a novice at Wincanton. Cerium failed to give his running when favourite for the Finale at Chepstow and was also well held in another Grade 1 after Cheltenham, the Anniversary at Aintree. Cerium shaped as if amiss at Chepstow and was probably past his best at Aintree, so the testing ground at each may not necessarily have contributed to his performances. Cerium is the fourth foal out of the unraced Tantatura. The first three have also won, including Apple Crumble (by Apple Tree),

B. Fulton, T. Hayward, S. Fisher, L. Brady's "Cerium"

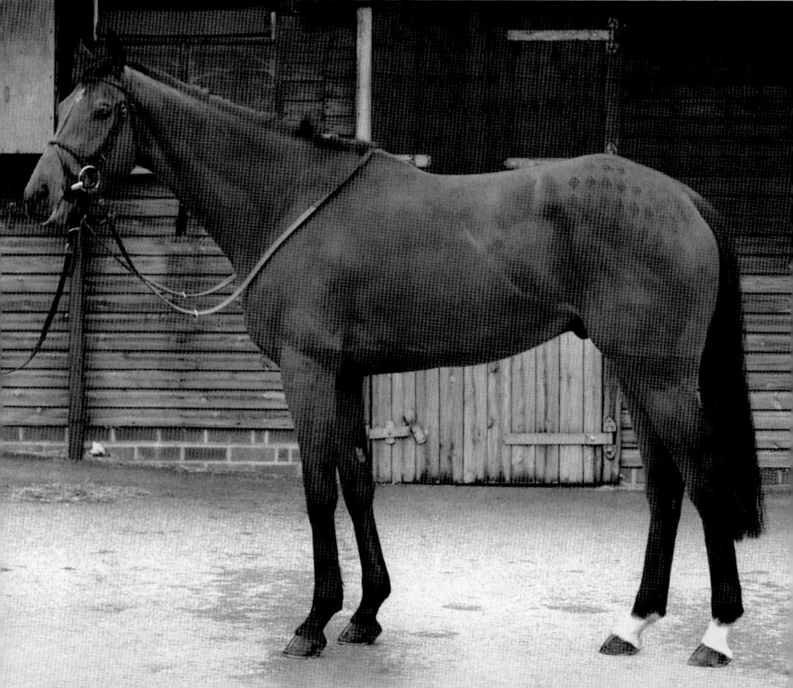

who has been successful over hurdles and fences at around two miles. Before being sent hurdling, Cerium won at a mile and a quarter on his Flat debut at Mont-de-Marsan. *P. F. Nicholls*

CERTIFIABLE 4 b.g. Deploy – Gentle Irony (Mazilier (USA)) [2004/5 16g Jan 24] fairly useful on all-weather, fair on turf on Flat (stays 1m), successful twice in 2004, claimed from A. Reid £11,000 in December: bled from nose on hurdling debut. *Miss S. J. Wilton* **h–**

CERULEAN 7 ch.g. Polar Falcon (USA) – Billie Blue (Ballad Rock) [2004/5 16d^6 22d^5 21g Nov 11] no sign of ability. *A. J. Wilson* **h–**

CETTI'S WARBLER 7 gr.m. Sir Harry Lewis (USA) – Sedge Warbler (Scallywag) [2004/5 h94: c20d c16d* c22d^4 c22s^F c20s^5 c21d* Mar 19] tall mare: modest hurdler: fair over fences, winning mares novices at Leicester in November and Uttoxeter (listed handicap, jumped well when beating Barton May a length) in March: will stay 3m: acts on heavy going. *Mrs P. Robeson* **c109 h–**

CHABRIMAL MINSTER 8 b.g. Minster Son – Bromley Rose (Rubor) [2004/5 h105: c24s^F Apr 2] leggy gelding: lightly raced: winning hurdler: off another 11 months, jumped soundly until falling twelfth in maiden on chasing debut: stays 3m. *R. Ford* **c– p h–**

CHA CHA CHA DANCER 5 ch.g. Groom Dancer (USA) – Amber Fizz (USA) (Effervescing (USA)) [2004/5 h98?: 16m^5 20g^5 17g^2 20v* Nov 6] strong gelding: modest handicap hurdler: won novice event at Ayr in November: stays 2½m: acts on heavy going. *G. A. Swinbank* **h92**

CHAIN OF HOPE (IRE) 4 ch.g. Shinko Forest (IRE) – Fleeting Smile (IRE) (Bluebird (USA)) [2004/5 16f^{pu} Sep 26] modest maiden at 2 yrs, well beaten on Flat in 2004: jumped poorly in juvenile on hurdling debut. *D. E. Cantillon* **h–**

CHAKRA 11 gr.g. Mystiko (USA) – Maracuja (USA) (Riverman (USA)) [2004/5 h–: 17g^4 17g^6 17g* 16g 17d^6 16m 17g 17g^6 Oct 14] modest hurdler: won novice at Newton Abbot in July: raced around 2m. *C. J. Gray* **h89**

CHAMACCO (FR) 5 b.g. Cadoudal (FR) – Awentina (FR) (Caerwent) [2004/5 F16d 19d 19g^{pu} Mar 4] leggy gelding: third foal: dam 15f hurdle winner: seventh in bumper at Huntingdon on debut: no form in novices hurdles, looking green on completed start: sold 3,200 gns Doncaster May Sales. *K. G. Reveley* **h– F83**

CHAMOSS ROYALE (FR) 5 ch.m. Garde Royale – Chamoss (FR) (Tip Moss (FR)) [2004/5 h119p: 22d^3 c21g^F 24s^3 24d^3 24d* 22d^2 24g 21g^3 Apr 14] angular mare: useful handicap hurdler: won at Kempton in January by 1½ lengths from Kadara: good efforts all 3 starts after: still going well when falling 4 out in mares novice at Wincanton on chasing debut: stays 3m: raced on good going or softer. *P. F. Nicholls* **c– p h132**

Tattersalls (Ireland) European Breeders Fund Mares' Novices' Chase Final (Handicap), Uttoxeter—25/1-shot Cetti's Warbler jumps well to beat Barton May in a race dominated by outsiders

CHAMPAGNE HARRY 7 b.g. Sir Harry Lewis (USA) – Sparkling Cinders (Netherkelly) [2004/5 h128: c25g^{2} c23s^{3} c24g^{2} c24s^{4} c24g c24g^{pu} 24d Apr 8] workmanlike gelding: fairly useful novice hurdler in 2003/4: not as good over fences, often let down by jumping: stays 3m: acts on any going: has run well sweating. *N. A. Twiston-Davies* **c111 h–**

CHAMPAGNE KING 6 b.g. Prince Sabo – Champagne Season (USA) (Vaguely Noble) [2004/5 24m^{pu} 17g 16m 20g^{pu} Aug 14] modest form at 2/3 yrs on Flat for P. Harris: no form over jumps, including in points. *Mrs A. M. Thorpe* **h–**

CHAMPAGNE LIL 8 gr.m. Terimon – Sparkling Cinders (Netherkelly) [2004/5 c–, h105: 24g^{6} 24d* 24g^{5} 22d Nov 6] leggy mare: let down by jumping in 3 starts over fences: fair handicap hurdler: won at Perth in September: stays 3m: acts on good to firm and good to soft going, possibly unsuited by soft. *N. A. Twiston-Davies* **c– h109**

CHAMPAGNE LOU LOU 7 b.m. Supreme Leader – Highfrith (Deep Run) [2004/5 F–: F16v^{2} Jan 22] leggy, workmanlike mare: poor in bumpers. *J. Parkes* **F69**

CHAMPAGNE NATIVE (IRE) 11 b.g. Be My Native (USA) – The Race Fly (Pollerton) [2004/5 c21s Apr 7] tall, useful-looking gelding: winning hurdler/chaser: won 2 Irish points in 2005: well held in Fox Hunters at Aintree and valuable similar event at Punchestown in April: should stay beyond 21f: acts on heavy going: tried blinkered/in cheekpieces: inconsistent. *D. Broad, Ireland* **c80 h–**

CHAMPAGNE SUNDAE (IRE) 7 b.g. Supreme Leader – Partners In Crime (Crofthall) [2004/5 F81: 19d 21s^{pu} 18s 18s 16d^{4} 16d^{pu} Apr 17] poor novice hurdler: should stay beyond 2¼m: raced on good going or softer: has shaped as if amiss. *P. Winkworth* **h67**

CHAMPETRE (FR) 7 b.g. Pursuit of Love – Fermiere (FR) (General Holme (USA)) [2004/5 h76: 20s 16f^{F} 16m^{6} 22m Jun 13] poor maiden hurdler: best at 2m: ungenuine. *Miss Victoria Roberts* **h– §**

CHANCE FLIGHT 5 b.m. Busy Flight – Castle Maid (Castle Keep) [2004/5 F–: F17g Apr 27] well held in bumpers. *R. J. Hodges* **F–**

CHANCE MEETING 7 b.m. Overbury (IRE) – Pepper Star (IRE) (Salt Dome (USA)) [2004/5 h–, F–: 20g^{pu} Jun 10] sparely-made mare: no form in bumper or 2 mares novice hurdles. *A. King* **h–**

CHANCERS DANTE (IRE) 9 b.g. Phardante (FR) – Own Acre (Linacre) [2004/5 c–, h92: c27d^{pu} c25v^{pu} Dec 15] angular gelding: modest hurdler: no form over fences: stays 27f: has form on heavy going, possibly better on good/good to firm: tried blinkered. *Ferdy Murphy* **c– h–**

CHANGE AGENT 9 br.g. Royal Fountain – Flashy Looks (Impecunious) [2004/5 c26d^{4} c24s^{pu} c26v^{6} c24d* c20s* Mar 13] big gelding: won both starts in points in 2002: improved form when winning novice handicap chases at Kempton (by 22 lengths) and Warwick in March: stays 3m: acts on soft going: races up with pace: capable of better still. *R. Dickin* **c99 p**

CHANNAHRLIE (IRE) 11 gr.g. Celio Rufo – Derravarragh Lady (IRE) (Radical) [2004/5 c99, h–: c25g^{5} c25g^{3} c25m^{5} c19d^{4} Apr 22] tall, angular gelding: modest handicap chaser: stays 3½m: acts on soft and firm going: wears cheekpieces/visor. *R. Dickin* **c91 h–**

CHANTICLIER 8 b.g. Roselier (FR) – Cherry Crest (Pollerton) [2004/5 h111: c24s^{pu} c23v^{pu} c16g^{F} Mar 4] well-made gelding: fair maiden hurdler, lightly raced: failed to complete all 3 starts over fences: should stay beyond 21f. *K. C. Bailey* **c– h–**

CHANTILLY LADY 12 ch.m. Rising – Ladiz (Persian Bold) [2004/5 c19s^{pu} Jan 3] tall mare: lightly-raced novice hurdler: no show on belated chasing debut. *M. J. Weeden* **c– h–**

CHANTOUE ROYALE (FR) 6 b. or br.m. Cadoudal (FR) – Royal Blessing (Phaeton) [2004/5 c18d* c20m^{3} Jun 8] ex-French mare: seventh foal: sister to smart 1¼m filly Royale Chantou and half-sister to useful miler Royale Bobbe (by Kaldoun): dam won up to around 1½m on Flat: placed up to around 1½m on Flat: fair winning hurdler: left B. Barbier, won maiden chase at Fontwell in May: stays 2½m: acts on heavy and good to firm ground. *Mrs L. J. Mongan* **c97 h–**

CHAOS THEORY 10 b.g. Jupiter Island – Indian Orchid (Warpath) [2004/5 c25d^{4} Apr 11] rangy gelding: winning hurdler/chaser: successful twice in points in 2005: should stay beyond 2½m: acts on heavy going: has worn blinkers: often let down by jumping. *R. C. Guest* **c86 x h– §**

CHAPARRO AMARGOSO (IRE) 12 b.g. Ela-Mana-Mou – Champanera (Top Ville) [2004/5 c–x, h–: c20s^{pu} Mar 31] has stringhalt: winning 2m chaser: little sign of retaining ability in points/hunters: visored twice: has had tongue tied: sketchy jumper. *F. L. Matthews* **c– x h–**

CHAPEL BAY 5 b.m. Alflora (IRE) – Jack It In (Derrylin) [2004/5 F16s Mar 13] third foal: dam unraced half-sister to useful hurdler/chaser up to 2½m Silver Wind: tongue tied, seventh of 18 in mares maiden bumper at Warwick on debut. *Mrs H. Dalton* **F78**

CHAPEL TIMES (IRE) 6 b.g. Supreme Leader – Dippers Daughter (Strong Gale) [2004/5 F87: F16g* May 1] tall gelding: fair form in 2 bumpers, winning at Uttoxeter in May by neck from Bonny Grey. *H. D. Daly* **F90**

CHAPELTOWN (IRE) 13 b.g. Denel (FR) – Lady Dunsford (Torus) [2004/5 c108, h–: c19d* Apr 29] well-made gelding: useful hurdler at one time: fair form over fences: won novice at Hereford (reportedly broke down) in April 2004: stays 19f: acts on soft and good to firm going. *N. J. Henderson* **c108 h–**

CHAPNERS CROSS 9 b.g. Primitive Rising (USA) – Holly (Skyliner) [2004/5 c21d^{pu} May 17] poor winning pointer. *A. W. Congdon* **c–**

CHAPTER HOUSE (USA) 6 b.g. Pulpit (USA) – Lilian Bayliss (IRE) (Sadler's Wells (USA)) [2004/5 h92: 17g^3 16g^{pu} 17m Sep 28] good-topped gelding: modest maiden hurdler: will prove best around 2m: acts on soft going: tried blinkered. *M. W. Easterby* **h90**

CHARALAMBOUS (USA) 8 b.g. Hermitage (USA) – Hula Lei (USA) (State Dinner (USA)) [2004/5 c19m^{pu} May 11] sturdy gelding: maiden hurdler: no show on chasing debut: raced mainly around 2m on good going or softer (acts on heavy). *C. J. Down* **c– h–**

CHARIOT (IRE) 4 ch.g. Titus Livius (FR) – Battle Queen (Kind of Hush) [2004/5 17d 16d^2 17m 17m^{ur} Apr 23] sturdy gelding: half-brother to modest 2m hurdler Celebration Town (by Case Law) and winning staying chaser in Czech Republic by Prince Rupert: fair maiden at 2 yrs: poor maiden hurdler: let down by jumping last 2 starts. *M. R. Bosley* **h77**

CHARLATAN (IRE) 7 b.g. Charnwood Forest (IRE) – Taajreh (IRE) (Mtoto) [2004/5 h–: c16g^{pu} c20g^{ur} Aug 1] of no account. *Mrs C. A. Dunnett* **c– h–**

CHARLESTON 4 ch.g. Pursuit of Love – Discomatic (USA) (Roberto (USA)) [2004/5 16d 17s^{pu} 18s 19m^6 Apr 2] smallish, angular gelding: fair maiden on Flat (stays 1½m), sold out of J. Gosden's stable 20,000 gns Doncaster August Sales: no form in juvenile hurdles. *R. Rowe* **h–**

CHARLESTOWN LASS 8 b.m. Bob Back (USA) – Prepare (IRE) (Millfontaine) [2004/5 21g^5 May 23] poor form over hurdles: would have won point in April 2004 but for running out last: should stay 3m: tried visored. *C. Roberts* **h83**

CHARLIE BEAR 4 ch.c. Bahamian Bounty – Abi (Chief's Crown (USA)) [2004/5 16d 17s 16g^4 Mar 16] angular colt: fair maiden on Flat (effective at 7f/1m), sold out of E. Dunlop's stable 25,000 gns Newmarket Autumn Sales: trained on hurdling debut by P. Bowen: modest form when fourth in maiden at Huntingdon. *W. K. Goldsworthy* **h87**

CHARLIE CASTALLAN 5 gr.g. Wace (USA) – Castle Cary (Castle Keep) [2004/5 F–: F16g F16g 17d^4 24g^{pu} 17d^6 19d^5 17d 18s 20v^{pu} 16g Mar 18] no worthwhile form: wore cheekpieces final start. *D. W. Thompson* **h– F–**

CHARLIE CHAPEL 6 b.g. College Chapel – Lightino (Bustino) [2004/5 F89: F16v^6 17s^5 16s^3 17s^{ro} 16g^6 Apr 19] sturdy gelding: modest at best in bumpers: modest novice hurdler: wayward. *W. M. Brisbourne* **h88 § F–**

CHARLIE EDWARDS (IRE) 7 b.g. Ridgewood Ben – Princess Citrus (IRE) (Auction Ring (USA)) [2004/5 F16s 17d^{pu} Mar 26] lengthy gelding: third foal: half-brother to modest hurdler/chaser Tobesure (by Asir), stays 25f, and winner around 1m Muskerry Princess (by College Chapel): dam unraced: no show in bumper and novice hurdle. *J. I. A. Charlton* **h– F–**

CHARLIEMOORE 9 ch.g. Karinga Bay – Your Care (FR) (Caerwent) [2004/5 c18s^5 c20s^{pu} Feb 10] strong, lengthy gelding: poor hurdler: no show over fences after lengthy absence. *G. L. Moore* **c– h–**

CHARLIES BRIDE (IRE) 10 b. or br.m. Rich Charlie – Nordic Bride (IRE) (Nordico (USA)) [2004/5 h–: 17g^5 16f Jun 6] poor maiden hurdler: tongue tied nowadays. *M. A. Barnes* **h60**

CHARLIE'S CROSS (IRE) 7 gr.g. Roselier (FR) – Estuary View (Prince Rheingold) [2004/5 22s c22s^{pu} c19s c24s^{pu} 24d^{pu} Mar 8] medium-sized gelding: fifth foal: dam unraced: placed both starts in maiden Irish points in 2004: bought 15,000 gns (privately) Doncaster May Sales: no form over hurdles or in chases: tried in blinkers/cheekpieces: ungenuine. *J. G. Portman* **c– § h– §**

CHARLIES DOUBLE 6 b.g. Double Eclipse (IRE) – Pendil's Niece (Roscoe Blake) [2004/5 F79: 17g^{ur} 18s 16s 17v^{6} 24v^{pu} Feb 20] better effort in bumpers when third on polytrack at Lingfield: no form over hurdles: blinkered final start. *J. R. Best* **h–**

CHARLIES FUTURE 7 b.g. Democratic (USA) – Faustelerie (Faustus (USA)) [2004/5 c101, h105: c20g^{4} c19d^{2} c19s^{3} c24g^{F} c24s^{2} c27s^{6} c24v^{2} c24d^{5} c19s* Mar 27] tall gelding: winning hurdler: fair novice chaser: won handicap at Towcester in March: stays 3m: acts on heavy ground: consistent. *S. C. Burrough* **c110 h–**

CHARLIESMEDARLIN 14 b.g. Macmillion – Top Cover (High Top) [2004/5 c84, h–: c23g^{pu} Jul 7] workmanlike gelding: veteran handicap chaser: stays 3m: acts on firm going: visored once: has had tongue tied. *Mrs Barbara Waring* **c– h–**

CHARLIES MEMORY 6 b.g. Blushing Flame (USA) – Hat Hill (Roan Rocket) [2004/5 h90, F84: 16s^{4} 23v^{5} c16s^{4} c25s^{F} c20s^{6} c16v Mar 17] good-topped gelding: modest novice hurdler: no show over fences: stays 2½m: raced only on good going or softer: tried tongue tied. *M. W. Easterby* **c76 ? h76**

CHARLIE STRONG (IRE) 12 b.g. Strong Gale – The Village Vixen (Buckskin (FR)) [2004/5 c–: c21d^{3} Apr 28] strong gelding: fairly useful hunter chaser at one time: runner-up in point in January: should stay beyond 23f: acts on firm and soft going. *R. Kelvin-Hughes* **c93**

CHARLIE TANGO (IRE) 4 b.g. Desert Prince (IRE) – Precedence (IRE) (Polish Precedent (USA)) [2004/5 16m^{4} Dec 1] quite good-topped gelding: fair on Flat (stays 11f): fourth of 10 in juvenile at Catterick on hurdling debut: should do better. *N. Tinkler* **h91 p**

CHARLOTTE LAMB 5 gr.m. Pharly (FR) – Caroline Lamb (Hotfoot) [2004/5 F–: F17g^{4} May 23] medium-sized mare: little show in 2 bumpers. *Miss S. E. Hall* **F–**

CHARLTON KINGS (IRE) 7 b.g. King's Ride – Grove Gale (IRE) (Strong Gale) [2004/5 c24s^{F} 16s* 17v^{2} 22g^{2} Apr 17] first foal: dam, lightly-raced maiden, sister to high-class chaser up to 25f Speaker Weatherill and useful 2m/2½m chaser Certainly Strong: successful in Irish points in 2003 and 2004: beaten when fell 2 out in hunter chase at Thurles in January for P. Cashman: fair form in novice hurdles: won at Towcester in March: better form when runner-up after: stays 2¾m: acts on heavy going. *R. J. Hodges* **c– h107**

CHARLY BOMBER 7 ch.g. Lancastrian – Charlycia (Good Times (ITY)) [2004/5 F–: F17d May 12] no form in 2 bumpers: sold £1,700 Ascot October Sales. *Miss M. Bragg* **F–**

CHARMING FELLOW (IRE) 5 b.g. Taipan (IRE) – Latest Tangle (Ragapan) [2004/5 F16d^{3} F16d^{2} F16d^{3} F17d Apr 9] tall, useful-looking gelding: eighth foal: half-brother to 2 winning staying chasers, including fair Keeponthesunnyside (by Parole): dam never ran: third in maiden point on debut in 2004: fairly useful form when placed in bumpers: ran as if amiss in Grade 2 at Aintree final start. *Miss H. C. Knight* **F95**

CHARM OFFENSIVE 7 b.m. Zieten (USA) – Shoag (USA) (Affirmed (USA)) [2004/5 h79: 22f^{4} 26s 16v 16v c25d^{2} 24g Apr 7] poor hurdler: jumped slowly when beaten distance in 2-finisher novice on chasing debut: should stay beyond 3m: best efforts on good going: has worn cheekpieces. *C. J. Gray* **c– h64**

CHARNWOOD STREET (IRE) 6 b.g. Charnwood Forest (IRE) – La Vigie (King of Clubs) [2004/5 h68§: 24g^{3} 22g^{5} 22m^{4} 24d^{6} 23s 20d^{2} 20s 24d 20s^{pu} Feb 24] close-coupled gelding: poor maiden hurdler: stays 3m: acts on soft and good to firm going: visored: ungenuine. *D. Shaw* **h75 §**

CHARTER ROYAL (FR) 10 gr.g. Royal Charter (FR) – Tadjmine (FR) (Tadj (FR)) [2004/5 c–§, h–: 20d^{5} 22s Dec 5] compact gelding: poor handicap chaser: maiden hurdler: stays 3m: acts on good to firm and heavy going: tried blinkered: unreliable. *A. R. Dicken* **c– § h– §**

CHASE THE SUNSET (IRE) 7 ch.g. Un Desperado (FR) – Cherry Chase (IRE) (Red Sunset) [2004/5 h96+: 21d^{3} c20s^{2} c24g^{3} c18g Nov 28] useful-looking gelding: modest maiden hurdler: fair form when placed over fences: stays 3m: acts on soft going: often finds little. *Miss H. C. Knight* **c103 h96**

CHASING THE BRIDE 12 b.g. Gildoran – Bride (Remainder Man) [2004/5 c107: c22d^{4} c23s^{ur} Mar 11] quite good-topped gelding: fairly useful hunter chaser: stays 25f: acts on firm and good to soft going: formerly tongue tied. *Miss A. Goschen* **c103 +**

CHASING THE LEAD 6 ch.m. Pursuit of Love – Fairlead (Slip Anchor) [2004/5 F17d May 15] fourth foal: half-sister to fair hurdler Follow Me (by Keen), stays 3m, and fair 19f hurdle winner Queen Soraya (by Persian Bold): dam 1m winner: very slowly away in mares bumper on debut. *Miss H. C. Knight* **F–**

CHASTLETON BOY (IRE) 6 b.g. Muroto – Noon Hunting (Green Shoon) [2004/5 F16s^4 Mar 27] 16,000 4-y-o: half-brother to several winners, including fairly useful hurdler/chaser Lordberniebouffant (by Denel), stayed 3¼m, and fair chaser Major Kinsman (by Nepotism), stayed 2½m: dam unraced half-sister to dams of top-class staying chasers The Grey Monk and Grey Abbey: shaped like a stayer in bumper at Towcester on debut. *R. T. Phillips* **F81**

CHATEAU ROUGE (IRE) 4 b.c. Tiraaz (USA) – Carolina Rua (USA) (L'Emigrant (USA)) [2004/5 F17d Mar 26] €9,000 3-y-o: second foal: half-brother to 6f/7f winner La Tavernetta (by Magical Wonder), later successful up to 1¼m in Holland: dam lightly raced, including in points: no show in bumper on debut. *M. D. Hammond* **F–**

CHATER FLAIR 8 b.g. Efisio – Native Flair (Be My Native (USA)) [2004/5 h–: 22g^F Sep 25] maiden hurdler: third on completed start in points in 2005: tried visored. *B. D. Leavy* **h–**

CHAUVINIST (IRE) 10 b.g. Roselier (FR) – Sacajawea (Tanfirion) [2004/5 c121p, h–: c16d* c20d^2 c20s^4 c20d* c20d^3 c25d^{pu} Apr 8] compact gelding: useful hurdler in 2002/3: similar form over fences, made most when winning novices at Aintree in November and Sandown (by 11 lengths from Manly Money) in February: much better effort after when good third to Supreme Prince in very valuable handicap at Newbury in March: stays 2½m: raced on good going or softer (acts on heavy): usually on toes. *N. J. Henderson* **c138 h–**

CHEEKY LAD 5 b.g. Bering – Cheeky Charm (USA) (Nureyev (USA)) [2004/5 20d^{pu} 20d^{pu} 17m^{pu} May 23] well beaten in 2 maidens on Flat at 2/3 yrs, sold out of B. Hills's stable £1,100 Ascot June Sales: no form over hurdles: won maiden point in April. *R. C. Harper* **h–**

CHEF DE COUR (FR) 4 b.g. Pistolet Bleu (IRE) – Cour de Rome (FR) (Cadoudal (FR)) [2004/5 F14s* F12d^6 F14s^4 16v^3 Mar 5] lengthy, rather unfurnished gelding: seventh foal: half-brother to several winners on Flat, including 11.5f to 17f winner Fructus (by Northern Fashion): dam placed around 1½m: fairly useful form in bumpers, successful at Ayr in December: raced freely when third to Andre Chenier in juvenile at Kelso on hurdling debut: should progress. *L. Lungo* **h91 p F95**

CHEF TARTARE (FR) 5 b.g. Nikos – Rive Tartare (FR) (Riverquest (FR)) [2004/5 16d^F 17s^2 17s^4 c17g^3 c19m^F 17s^2 17d^2 20s^3 c16v* c16s^2 c16d^6 c20s* Apr 22] big, useful-looking gelding: third foal: brother to 21f hurdle winner Mascara and half-brother to 11.5f winner Jolie Tartare (by Bulington): dam 11f to 17f winner on Flat: fair form over hurdles and fences, left G. Macaire after fifth start: won novice handicap chases at Chepstow in February and Perth in April: stays 2½m: acts on heavy going: tongue tied last 4 starts: suited by waiting tactics: ungenuine: sold to N. Shutts 46,000 gns Doncaster May Sales. *P. F. Nicholls* **c109 § h112 §**

CHELSEA'S DIAMOND 5 b.m. Man Among Men (IRE) – Sharp Thistle (Sharpo) [2004/5 F–: F18g May 9] no sign of ability. *J. Akehurst* **F–**

CHEM'S TRUCE (IRE) 8 b.g. Brief Truce (USA) – In The Rigging (USA) (Topsider (USA)) [2004/5 h111: c16f^2 c16m^{pu} c17d^{pu} c22d^4 Dec 7] leggy, close-coupled gelding: fair handicap hurdler: modest form over fences only when second in maiden at Worcester on chasing debut: raced mainly around 2m: acts on soft and good to firm going. *Miss Venetia Williams* **c92 h–**

CHERGAN (IRE) 12 b.g. Yashgan – Cherry Bright (IRE) (Miner's Lamp) [2004/5 c123, h–: c25g^5 c25v^3 c21s^4 c16g^4 c20s^{pu} Apr 20] lengthy gelding: fairly useful chaser: effective at 2m to easy 25f: acted on any going: won/placed on 14 of 15 starts at Musselburgh: very sound jumper: dead. *Mrs S. C. Bradburne* **c115 h–**

CHEROKEE BAY 5 b.m. Primo Dominie – Me Cherokee (Persian Bold) [2004/5 h93: 16g* 17d* Nov 2] fair novice hurdler: won mares events at Plumpton in May and Folkestone in November: raced around 2m on good ground or softer. *G. L. Moore* **h103**

CHERRY GENERATION (IRE) 6 ch.m. Anshan – Cherished Princess (IRE) (Kemal (FR)) [2004/5 F16s^3 F16s^2 21d 24v^{pu} Jan 21] lengthy mare: fourth foal: half-sister to fairly useful staying hurdler Woodlands Genpower (by Roselier): dam, winning Irish pointer, half-sister to fairly useful staying chaser Cherry Field: fair form in 2 bumpers: seventh of 22 in maiden at Warwick on hurdling debut: lame next time. *P. A. Pritchard* **h73 F85**

CHERRY GOLD 11 b.g. Rakaposhi King – Merry Cherry (Deep Run) [2004/5 c105x, h93: c25s^F c26g^F c24d* Apr 22] winning hurdler: fairly useful hunter chaser: back to form when winning hunter at Chepstow in April (for third successive year): should **c100 x h–**

stay beyond 3m: acts on good to firm and good to soft going: has worn cheekpieces: front runner: sometimes let down by jumping. *Evan Williams*

CHERRY HUNTER (IRE) 9 b.g. Treasure Hunter – Clever Cherry (Decent Fellow) [2004/5 c16s* Mar 13] tall gelding: fair hurdler: off 11 months, improved form over fences when winning handicap at Naas: effective at 2m to 3m: acts on heavy going: tried tongue tied. *J. T. R. Dreaper, Ireland* **c112 h–**

CHERRY VALLEY (IRE) 8 ch.m. Phardante (FR) – Cherrydawn (Pollerton) [2004/5 F20g4 F16m3 F16m2 F17g* 18g5 24m* Aug 2] 4,200 3-y-o: fifth foal: half-sister to 3 winners, including fair hurdler/chaser In The Rough (by Strong Gale), stayed 29f: dam unraced half-sister to useful chaser up to 2½m Ice Plant: improved form in bumpers when winning at Bellewstown in July: again made all when successful in 3-finisher 3m maiden hurdle at Cork in August. *W. J. Austin, Ireland* **h104 p F100**

CHERUB (GER) 5 b.g. Winged Love (IRE) – Chalkidiki (GER) (Nebos (GER)) [2004/5 h134: 16g* 17s* 16s2 16g 17g3 16d2 Apr 20] compact gelding: useful hurdler, winning Grade 1 4-y-o event at Punchestown in April 2004: successful in amateur novice at Market Rasen in November: best effort in 2004/5 when 4 lengths second to Marcel in Grade 2 novice at Windsor next time: raced around 2m: acts on soft going, yet to race on firmer than good: tongue tied since debut: takes good hold. *Jonjo O'Neill* **h131**

CHETWIND MUSIC (IRE) 7 b.g. Aristocracy – Mariners Music (Black Minstrel) [2004/5 20g 16ssu 16v 16v2 20s Apr 7] strong gelding: fifth foal: dam once-raced half-sister to fairly useful staying chaser Backstreet Guy: successful 3 times in points: fell both starts in hunter chases: easily best effort over hurdles (fair form) when second in novice at Thurles: should be suited by further than 2m (well out of depth in Grade 2 at Aintree final start). *William Coleman O'Brien, Ireland* **c– h105**

CHEVALIER BAYARD (IRE) 12 br.g. Strong Gale – Flying Pegus (Beau Chapeau) [2004/5 c21s5 c19m* c20gpu c17m* Jul 29] rangy gelding: modest handicap chaser: won at Hereford in June and Stratford in July: effective around 2m to 21f: acts on soft and good to firm going: usually blinkered/visored nowadays. *B. G. Powell* **c97 h–**

CHEVALIER ERRANT (IRE) 12 b. or br.g. Strong Gale – Luminous Run (Deep Run) [2004/5 c109, h–: c20g3 Apr 30] tall, good sort: fair handicap chaser: probably stays easy 3m: acts on good to firm and heavy going. *M. Todhunter* **c100 h–**

CHEVET BOY (IRE) 7 b.g. Welsh Term – Sizzle (High Line) [2004/5 27d4 21d6 20v4 20s3 Feb 19] tall, leggy, angular gelding: half-brother to several winners, including useful hurdler/winning chaser up to 2½m Hot Stuff (by Satco): dam once-raced half-sister to smart staying chaser Brown Windsor: fair form in novice hurdles: should stay beyond 2½m. *J. Howard Johnson* **h105**

CHEVIN 6 ch.m. Danzig Connection (USA) – Starr Danias (USA) (Sensitive Prince (USA)) [2004/5 16d 17d 20dpu Dec 6] leggy mare: modest on Flat (stays 2m): no form over hurdles. *R. A. Fahey* **h–**

CHEVRONNE 5 b.g. Compton Place – Maria Isabella (FR) (Young Generation) [2004/5 16g6 16g* 18m2 16g6 Oct 27] compact gelding: half-brother to fairly useful hurdler around 2m Rain In Spain (by Unfuwain): fair maiden on Flat (stays 1½m), sold out of L. G. Cottrell's stable £9,600 Ascot July Sales: modest hurdler: won maiden at Worcester in August: raced around 2m: acts on good to firm going. *B. Llewellyn* **h98**

CHICAGO BREEZE (IRE) 8 b.m. Lord Americo – Anguillita (IRE) (King of Clubs) [2004/5 c–, h–: c25s4 c25vpu c24vpu 26s4 Jan 5] maiden hurdler/chaser: wore cheekpieces final outing: sold 900 gns Doncaster May Sales. *Ferdy Murphy* **c– h–**

CHICAGO BULLS (IRE) 7 b.g. Darshaan – Celestial Melody (USA) (The Minstrel (CAN)) [2004/5 c128, h127: 23m 24g3 24d Jan 1] compact gelding: fairly useful handicap hurdler: best effort in 2004/5 when third to Tanterari at Bangor: mainly let down by jumping and looked hard ride over fences: stays 25f: acts on heavy going, below form on good to firm: tried blinkered. *A. King* **c– h126**

CHICAGO VIC (IRE) 6 b.m. Old Vic – Clearwater Glen (Furry Glen) [2004/5 19f* 20f6 17d3 18m 20m* 19g3 20sF 20s2 20v 16v* 22s* 20d3 16d4 Mar 20] €9,000 3-y-o: sixth reported foal: half-sister to useful but thoroughly ungenuine chaser Montana Glen (by Montelimar), stayed 3m: dam unraced, out of useful 2m hurdler The Very Thing: modest form in bumpers: much improved last 3 starts over hurdles, winning handicap at Thurles and in frame in similar event there and listed mares novice at Limerick: earlier won maiden at Kilbeggan and 2 handicaps at Tramore (second for lady riders): will stay beyond 2¾m: has won on firm and heavy going, best form on soft/good to soft. *Mrs Marian Flavin, Ireland* **h124**

Mr M. J. Tuckey's "Chilling Place"

CHICHELE COLLEGE 4 b.g. Komaite (USA) – Myumi (Charmer) [2004/5 F16g Mar 16] second foal: dam unraced half-sister to fairly useful hurdlers Centaur Express, best at 2m, and Ferrers, stayed 23f: well beaten in bumper on debut. *Mrs P. Sly* **F–**

CHICKAPEAKRAY 4 b.f. Overbury (IRE) – Nevermind Hey (Teenoso (USA)) [2004/5 F14d F13s 16v^F 16v^4 17s^6 19m^5 Mar 21] leggy, close-coupled filly: first foal: dam, modest hurdler, stayed 27f: no form in bumpers/over hurdles. *D. McCain* **h– F–**

CHICUELO (FR) 9 b.g. Mansonnien (FR) – Dovapas (FR) (Paseo (FR)) [2004/5 c138x, h130: c32m^{pu} Jun 27] compact gelding: useful handicap hurdler/chaser in 2003/4: tongue tied, lame only outing in 2004/5: stays easy 25f: probably acts on any going: tried blinkered, visored nowadays: usually let down by jumping over fences. *M. C. Pipe* **c– x h–**

CHIEF DAN GEORGE (IRE) 5 b.g. Lord Americo – Colleen Donn (Le Moss) [2004/5 F16s Apr 22] seventh foal: half-brother to 3 winners by Mandalus, including one-time very smart chaser Macgeorge, stays 3¼m: dam never ran: tailed off in bumper. *D. R. MacLeod* **F–**

CHIEF MOUSE 12 b.g. Be My Chief (USA) – Top Mouse (High Top) [2004/5 c–§, h–: c24g^5 Mar 9] workmanlike gelding: winning chaser: of little account outside points nowadays: tried blinkered/in cheekpieces: has had tongue tied: moody. *Steve Isaac* **c– § h–**

CHIEF PREDATOR (USA) 11 ch.g. Chief's Crown (USA) – Tsavorite (USA) (Halo (USA)) [2004/5 c25v^3 May 10] angular gelding: maiden chaser: winning pointer: stays 3¼m: probably acts on any going: tried blinkered/visored. *Mrs D. C. Faulkner* **c73 h–**

CHIEF YEOMAN 5 b.g. Machiavellian (USA) – Step Aloft (Shirley Heights) [2004/5 h132: 16d 16d^2 Nov 6] close-coupled gelding: useful hurdler: easily better effort in 2004/5 when 7 lengths second to Perouse in Grade 2 limited handicap at Wincanton: likely to stay beyond 17f: acts on soft and good to firm going. *Miss Venetia Williams* **h141**

CHILLING PLACE (IRE) 6 ch.g. Moscow Society (USA) – Ethel's Dream (Relkino) [2004/5 16g* 17s* 17d* 16d³ 16g⁶ 20sᵖᵘ Apr 7] lengthy gelding: chasing type: second foal: dam poor form in bumpers: won maiden Irish point in May: useful novice hurdler: won at Wincanton in October, Exeter in November and Cheltenham in December: good efforts in Grade 1 events both completed starts after (lame final outing), 6 lengths third of 9 to Marcel in Tolworth Hurdle at Sandown and 11¾ lengths sixth of 20 to Arcalis in Supreme Novices' Hurdle at Cheltenham: should stay beyond 17f: raced on good going or softer: races prominently: genuine. *P. J. Hobbs* **h132**

CHILLY MILLY 4 b.f. Shambo – Phrase'n Cold (IRE) (Strong Statement (USA)) [2004/5 F16v⁶ F16s Mar 13] fourth foal: dam ran in 3 Irish points: never a factor in mares bumpers. *V. Smith* **F–**

CHINA CHASE (IRE) 6 b.g. Anshan – Hannies Girl (IRE) (Invited (USA)) [2004/5 F68: F16g 16m 17mᵖᵘ 16v 16s Mar 13] sturdy gelding: poor in bumpers: no form over hurdles: tried in cheekpieces. *J. L. Spearing* **h–** **F–**

CHINA JACK (IRE) 7 b.g. West China – Camp Bay (IRE) (Classic Secret (USA)) [2004/5 F16g aF16g 17m Nov 25] first foal: dam never ran: more signs of temperament than ability. *Ms J. S. Doyle* **h– §** **F–**

CHINA MISS 5 b.m. Thowra (FR) – Sherdon Hutch (New Member) [2004/5 F16gᶜᵒ F18s 21sᵖᵘ Jan 20] fourth foal: dam winning staying chaser: no form in bumpers (carried out on debut) or maiden hurdle. *M. Scudamore* **h–** **F–**

CHIQITITA (IRE) 4 b.f. Saddlers' Hall (IRE) – Funny Cut (IRE) (Sure Blade (USA)) [2004/5 16f 17g 16dᶠ Apr 22] poor maiden on Flat: no form over hurdles. *Miss M. E. Rowland* **h–**

CHITA'S FLIGHT 5 gr.m. Busy Flight – Chita's Cone (Celtic Cone) [2004/5 F–: 17g⁴ 19s⁶ 17s 19mᵖᵘ 22dᵖᵘ Apr 3] poor novice hurdler: should stay beyond 19f. *S. C. Burrough* **h73**

CHIVALRY 6 b.g. Mark of Esteem (IRE) – Gai Bulga (Kris) [2004/5 h128: c16d⁴ 16d 16g³ 16d Apr 9] well-made gelding: useful hurdler: seemingly best effort when third to Self Defense in muddling listed race at Sandown: well-held last of 4 finishers behind Chauvinist in novice at Aintree on chasing debut: likely to prove best at 2m: blinkered last 4 starts over hurdles: not a fluent jumper: attitude under suspicion: sold to join R. C. Guest 50,000 gns Doncaster May Sales. *J. Howard Johnson* **c107** **h142 ?**

CHIVES (IRE) 10 b.g. Good Thyne (USA) – Chatty Actress (Le Bavard (FR)) [2004/5 c–, h–: c24s² c24d* c29v³ c24v c28sᵖᵘ c24g⁴ c33g Apr 16] well-made gelding: usually impresses in appearance: smart chaser: left Miss H. Knight and off a year before **c154** **h–**

Tommy Whittle Chase, Haydock—Chives gains a first win since his novice chase campaign

reappearance: back to near best when winning Tommy Whittle Chase at Haydock in December by 6 lengths from Sir Rembrandt: not discredited after when in frame in Welsh National at Chepstow (third to Silver Birch) in December and valuable handicap at Cheltenham (fourth to Kelami) in March: stays 29f: acts on heavy going: usually sound jumper: has broken blood vessels, ran as if amiss fourth and fifth starts. *Mrs S. J. Smith*

CHIVITE (IRE) 6 b.g. Alhaarth (IRE) – Laura Margaret (Persian Bold) [2004/5 h115: 20g^{5} 19d* 20g* 19g^{ur} 20s 20s 20d^{pu} 20m Apr 23] small, angular gelding: fairly useful handicap hurdler: won at Newton Abbot in May and Worcester in August: best form around 2½m: acts on soft and good to firm going: usually races prominently. *P. J. Hobbs* **h130**

CHIVVY CHARVER (IRE) 8 ch.g. Commanche Run – Claddagh Pride (Bargello) [2004/5 20d^{pu} 16g^{2} 16d^{4} 22s 20s^{3} Apr 10] leggy gelding: poor novice hurdler: left G. A. Swinbank and off 23 months before reappearance: should stay at least 2½m: acts on soft going. *A. C. Whillans* **h74**

CHOCKDEE (FR) 5 b.g. King's Theatre (IRE) – Chagrin d'Amour (IRE) (Last Tycoon) [2004/5 h113: 16d^{3} 16v^{2} 16g* 16g^{2} 16d^{5} 16d 17g^{5} 19m^{5} Apr 23] useful-looking gelding: fairly useful hurdler: won maiden at Cheltenham in October: raced mainly around 2m on good going or softer: patiently ridden: weak finisher. *P. F. Nicholls* **h118 §**

CHOCOLATE SOLDIER (IRE) 7 ch.g. Mister Lord (USA) – Traditional Lady (Carlingford Castle) [2004/5 h66, F101: 16d 20m Jun 27] fairly useful form when winning 2 bumpers: little form over hurdles: should stay beyond 2m: has worn blinkers: usually front runner. *Evan Williams* **h–**

CHOCSTAW (IRE) 8 b.g. Mtoto – Cwm Deri (IRE) (Alzao (USA)) [2004/5 20s^{4} Oct 22] close-coupled gelding: modest maiden hurdler in 2001/2: well beaten in novice only start since: should stay beyond 2m: acts on soft going. *Mrs P. Robeson* **h77 ?**

CHOISTY (IRE) 15 ch.g. Callernish – Rosemount Rose (Ashmore (FR)) [2004/5 c87, h–: c25d* c28g^{2} May 21] close-coupled gelding: modest handicap chaser: won at Hereford in April 2004: stays 29f: acts on soft and good to firm going: sometimes let down by jumping. *H. E. Haynes* **c91 x** **h–**

CHOMOLUNGA (FR) 5 b.g. Video Rock (FR) – Siesta (FR) (Prove It Baby (USA)) [2004/5 F17s Mar 10] sixth foal: brother to winning hurdler up to 3m Jexel and 1½m winner Lorkelle, and half-brother to Glorielle (by Lute Antique), winner 3 times around 1½m on Flat in France: dam, won 3 times up to 1½m on Flat in France, half-sister to dam of useful staying chaser Edmond (by Video Rock): tailed off in bumper on debut. *K. G. Reveley* **F–**

CHRIS AND RYAN (IRE) 7 b.g. Goldmark (USA) – Beautyofthepeace (IRE) (Exactly Sharp (USA)) [2004/5 h–, F–: 17v 20v^{5} 21s^{4} 27v^{2} c16v^{pu} Apr 17] form only when distant second in selling handicap hurdle at Sedgefield. *Mrs L. B. Normile* **c–** **h55**

CHRISTMAS TRUCE (IRE) 6 b.g. Brief Truce (USA) – Superflash (Superlative) [2004/5 h78: 20d^{pu} 17s^{4} 21s 22d 19d^{4} 20s^{5} 17m^{4} Apr 9] good-topped gelding: poor maiden hurdler: stays 21f: acts on good to firm and heavy ground: usually wears cheek-pieces. *Ian Williams* **h75**

CHRISTOPHER 8 gr.g. Arzanni – Forest Nymph (NZ) (Oak Ridge (FR)) [2004/5 c111, h108: c20s^{2} c20s* c21d^{2} c24d^{6} 22s* c22v^{6} c21g Mar 17] close-coupled gelding: fairly useful handicap hurdler/chaser: improved form in 2004/5, winning over fences at Aintree in November: took advantage of much lower mark over hurdles at Wincanton in January: probably stays 3m: acts on any going. *P. J. Hobbs* **c128** **h126**

CHRISTY BEAMISH (IRE) 8 b. or br.g. Jolly Jake (NZ) – Ballinatona Bridge (Black Minstrel) [2004/5 c26v^{4} Apr 22] progressive pointer: successful on 4 of 5 starts, including in 2005: favourite, shaped better than result suggests in novice hunter chase at Newton Abbot, travelling strongly long way: capable of better. *P. Jones* **c95 p**

CHRISTY JNR (IRE) 11 b.g. Andretti – Rare Currency (Rarity) [2004/5 c–, h–: 20d^{pu} 21g^{5} 24g^{5} 20m^{3} 20d^{5} 20s^{pu} 20d^{pu} 17v Jan 11] lengthy gelding: bad maiden hurdler/chaser: wears cheekpieces/blinkers. *C. J. Teague* **c–** **h57**

CHROMBOY (GER) 5 ch.g. Kornado – Chroma (GER) (Torgos) [2004/5 17s^{pu} Nov 18] placed several times up to around 1¼m on Flat in Germany for A. Trybuhl: no show in amateur novice on hurdling debut. *N. B. King* **h–**

CHUNKY LAD 5 ch.g. Karinga Bay – Madam's Choice (New Member) [2004/5 F16g F17g^{5} Oct 14] half-brother to fair hurdler Madam Flora (by Alflora), stays 2¾m, and 2 winning pointers by Impecunious: dam unraced: well beaten in 2 bumpers. *W. G. M. Turner* **F–**

CHURCHILL FLYER 7 b. or br.g. Sulaafah (USA) – Sally's Song (True Song) [2004/5 F16m Apr 25] first foal: dam maiden pointer: no show in bumper/point. *T. R. Greathead* **F–**

CHURCHINFORD 8 ch.g. Safawan – Eider (Niniski (USA)) [2004/5 17dpu 22gpu May 27] 5,000 3-y-o: eighth foal: half-brother to useful hurdler/fairly useful chaser Ledgendry Line, stays 25f, and useful chaser up to 25f Foundry Lane (both by Mtoto): dam fair 2-y-o 9f winner: no show in novice hurdles. *G. A. Ham* **h–**

CIACOLE 4 b.f. Primo Dominie – Dance On A Cloud (USA) (Capote (USA)) [2004/5 16d 16sF 18dpu 16v 17d Mar 26] close-coupled filly: half-sister to 2¼m hurdle winner Dardanus (by Komaite): poor on Flat (stays 1½m), sold out of R. Thompson's stable 3,400 gns Doncaster August Sales: no form over hurdles. *Mrs B. K. Thomson* **h–**

CIARA'S RUN (IRE) 5 ch.m. Topanoora – Rugged Run (Deep Run) [2004/5 F16d F16v Jan 3] sixth foal: half-sister to fair hurdler Poachers Run (by Executive Perk), stays 23f: dam unraced, from family of top-class staying chaser Jodami: well held in 2 bumpers. *G. M. Moore* **F–**

CICATRICE 4 ch.g. Wolfhound (USA) – Capricious Lady (IRE) (Capricorn Line) [2004/5 17g6 Mar 19] modest on Flat (stays 1¼m), successful in January (claimed from I. Wood £5,000): no show on hurdling debut. *D. R. Gandolfo* **h–**

CIDER MAN 10 b.g. Romany Rye – Champagne Peri (The Malster) [2004/5 c24s2 Mar 14] winning pointer: second in novice hunter chase at Stratford. *Mrs J. Hughes* **c82**

CIGARILLO (IRE) 7 br.g. Vestris Abu – Rose-Anore (Roselier (FR)) [2004/5 h104, F89: 20d3 c19m2 c20m* c20d2 c24g4 c20g4 Dec 26] rather leggy gelding: fair hurdler: fairly useful chaser: won novice at Huntingdon in June: creditable efforts in handicaps after: stays 3m: acts on soft and good to firm going: sound jumper. *Noel T. Chance* **c119 h104**

CILLAMON 8 b.m. Terimon – Dubacilla (Dubassoff (USA)) [2004/5 F75: c21gur c21dpu c19dpu c16sF Jan 20] leggy mare: poor form in 2 bumpers for L. G. Cottrell: yet to complete over fences. *K. Bishop* **c–**

CILL CHURNAIN (IRE) 12 b.g. Arctic Cider (USA) – The Dozer (IRE) (Bulldozer) [2004/5 c121, h126: 23m May 1] small, plain gelding: fairly useful handicap hurdler/chaser: tailed off only start in 2004/5: stays 25f: acts on heavy and good to firm going: races prominently. *Mrs S. J. Smith* **c– h–**

CILL UIRD (IRE) 7 ch.m. Phardante (FR) – Sandy Run (IRE) (Deep Run) [2004/5 20d5 17m 22d3 16s 17d2 c27d4 20v c17vF 16s c18d Feb 27] IR £3,700 3-y-o: fourth foal: dam unraced half-sister to dam of one-time useful chaser Another Raleagh: won mares maiden on completed start in points in 2003: poor maiden hurdler: little show in chases: stays 27f: often makes running: signs of temperament. *J. J. Lambe, Ireland* **c88 ? h78**

CIMARRONE COVE (IRE) 10 gr.g. Roselier (FR) – Sugarstown (Sassafras (FR)) [2004/5 c79§, h–: c25gur c30d2 May 11] well-made gelding: fair hunter nowadays: fourth in point in January: stays 3¾m: acts on heavy going: has been blinkered/visored. *M. W. Easterby* **c98 h–**

CIMMAROON (IRE) 6 b.g. Synefos (USA) – Bayalika (FR) (Kashtan (FR)) [2004/5 16g 19g6 19s 24d3 c24s3 22dpu Apr 17] workmanlike gelding: half-brother to fairly useful chaser Un Jour A Vassy (by Video Rock), stays 25f: dam once-raced half-sister to good French jumpers Bayonnet and Bayolidaan: successful 4 times from 9 starts in points in 2004: fair novice hurdler: similar form when third in novice handicap at Huntingdon on chasing debut: broke leg next time: stayed 3m: raced on good going or softer. *M. C. Pipe* **c103 h102**

CINNAMON LINE 9 ch.g. Derrylin – Cinnamon Run (Deep Run) [2004/5 h97: 27gpu c19d2 c24d* c24v2 Mar 29] tall, good sort: modest maiden hurdler in 2003/4: left R. Alner and off 10 months after first outing: fair form when winning maiden chase at Chepstow in March: let down by jumping other 2 starts over fences: stays 3m: raced on good going or softer (acts on heavy): has bled from nose. *R. Lee* **c103 h–**

CINQUE (IRE) 8 b. or br.g. Roselier (FR) – Hazy Hill (Goldhill) [2004/5 24vpu Jan 21] IR 7,500 4-y-o: brother to Irish point/bumper winner Hazy Rose and half-brother to winning 2½m hurdler Chapel Hill (by The Parson): dam unraced half-sister to dams of useful jumpers up to 3m Vanilla Man and Superior Risk and NH Chase winner Hazy Dawn: completed once from 7 starts in maiden Irish points: no show in maiden hurdle. *C. Roberts* **h–**

CINTRA RUBY (IRE) 7 b.m. Phardante (FR) – Ardfallon (IRE) (Supreme Leader) [2004/5 h78: 16m2 16m 16gpu Jul 6] leggy, sparely-made mare: pulled up in 2 points in 2003: poor hurdler: bred to stay at least 2½m: sold £700 Ascot November Sales. *W. K. Goldsworthy* **h71**

CIONN MHALANNA (IRE) 7 b.g. Corrouge (USA) – Pennyland (Le Bavard (FR)) [2004/5 h80?, F–: 23s c25s* c23d^4 c23v^2 c24g^6 c24v^{pu} Mar 20] strong gelding: maiden hurdler: modest form over fences: won maiden at Hexham in November: ran as if amiss final start: stays 25f: acts on heavy ground: tried in cheekpieces. *P. Beaumont* **c96 h–**

CIRCLE OF WOLVES 7 ch.g. Wolfhound (USA) – Misty Halo (High Top) [2004/5 h87: 22d 20d^{pu} 16s^2 16s^3 19d 20s^6 22s^4 16v c24g^{pu} Apr 17] close-coupled gelding: poor hurdler: sold out of M. Gingell's stable £3,200 Ascot August Sales after second start: jumped poorly and looked unwilling on chasing debut: stays 2¾m: acts on soft and good to firm going: tried in cheekpieces, usually visored nowadays. *H. J. Manners* **c– h79**

CIRCUS MAXIMUS (USA) 8 b.g. Pleasant Colony (USA) – Crockadore (USA) (Nijinsky (CAN)) [2004/5 c106§, h109§: 20d^4 May 3] compact gelding: winning hurdler/chaser: stays 3m: acts on good to firm and heavy going: usually blinkered: unreliable: won point in April. *Ian Williams* **c– § h73 §**

CISCO 7 b.g. Shambo – School Run (Deep Run) [2004/5 h–: 22g^{pu} 24m^{pu} Jun 5] well-made gelding: maiden hurdler: stays 2¾m: tried blinkered. *B. Mactaggart* **h–**

CISTERCIAN (IRE) 6 b.m. Anshan – Monks Lass (IRE) (Monksfield) [2004/5 F16g^5 Dec 9] seventh foal: half-sister to fairly useful hurdler/chaser Carmelite and fair hurdler/chaser Hardly (both by Good Thyne), both of whom stay 2½m: dam unraced, out of half-sister to Grand National runner-up Churchtown Boy: fifth of 11 in mares bumper at Ludlow on debut. *Miss H. C. Knight* **F77**

CITY AFFAIR 4 b.g. Inchinor – Aldevonie (Green Desert (USA)) [2004/5 17g 16f 18s^6 17d^5 16g^4 17m^2 19s^4 19v Apr 22] modest maiden on Flat (stays 7f): poor form over hurdles: claimed from Mrs L. Jewell £6,000 sixth start: stays 19f: acts on soft going: visored fifth start, wore cheekpieces final one: has been withdrawn after refusing to line up. *C. J. Down* **h81 §**

CITY GENT 11 b.g. Primitive Rising (USA) – Classy Lassy (Class Distinction) [2004/5 c88, h–: c19g^4 c16s^{pu} Mar 19] well-made gelding: maiden hurdler: poor handicap chaser: best around 2m: acts on good to firm and heavy going: tried blinkered/in cheekpieces: has had tongue tied. *N. Wilson* **c74 h–**

CITY HALL (IRE) 11 gr.g. Generous (IRE) – City Fortress (Troy) [2004/5 c20g^6 c20m^3 c18m* c17f^2 c17d* c17m^{ur} 16g c19s^5 c17s^2 c16s^2 c16d c17d Nov 28] tall, leggy gelding: has reportedly been pin-fired: smart hurdler at one time: fairly useful chaser: won handicaps at Punchestown in May and Killarney in July: creditable efforts after when runner-up: best around 2m: acts on firm and soft going: blinkered/visored: has had tongue tied: usually races up with pace. *Paul Nolan, Ireland* **c123 h–**

CITY OF SAILS (IRE) 6 br.g. Flemensfirth (USA) – Palmrock Donna (Quayside) [2004/5 16d^5 16s^3 18s^3 16v^6 16d^3 16g^4 19s* Mar 27] €7,000 4-y-o: rather leggy gelding: fourth foal: dam, bumper winner, half-sister to one-time useful hurdler/fairly useful chaser Champagne Native, stays 21f: fair hurdler: improved form when winning maiden at Cork in March: good third to Mansony in listed handicap at Punchestown month later: better form around 2½m than 2m and will stay further: raced on good going or softer (acts on soft). *A. J. McNamara, Ireland* **h110**

CITY PALACE 4 ch.g. Grand Lodge (USA) – Ajuga (USA) (The Minstrel (CAN)) [2004/5 16d^{ur} 16d 16d Jan 28] sturdy gelding: half-brother to fairly useful hurdlers Bangalore (by Sanglamore), stays 2½m, and Hyderabad (by Deploy), around 2m: fairly useful on Flat (should be suited by 1¼m+), sold out of B. Hills's stable 25,000 gns Doncaster August Sales: amiss both completed starts in juvenile hurdles: sold 5,000 gns Doncaster May Sales. *S. Gollings* **h–**

CITY POSER (IRE) 10 b.g. Posen (USA) – Citissima (Simbir) [2004/5 22d^5 c23s^{pu} c24d^3 c24d^3 c25d^6 c31s^{pu} Apr 22] close-coupled gelding: fair handicap hurdler in 2002/3 for S. Earle: fair maiden chaser: stays 25f: acts on good to firm and heavy going: has had tongue tied. *Miss Venetia Williams* **c100 h–**

CITY SPRINGS 5 b.m. Parthian Springs – City's Sister (Maystreak) [2004/5 F17g^6 F16s F16d 20v^{pu} Dec 17] half-sister to several winners, including smart staying jumper Better Times Ahead (by Scallywag) and fair staying hurdler/winning 2m chaser Sweet City (by Sweet Monday): dam, winner up to 13f on Flat, half-sister to useful chaser Another City: modest form in bumper on debut: no show subsequently, including on hurdling debut. *Mrs L. Williamson* **h– F77**

CITY VENTURE 8 ch.g. Pursuit of Love – City of Angels (Woodman (USA)) [2004/5 16d 16d^{pu} Apr 20] leggy gelding: fairly useful bumper winner: off nearly 4 years, no form over hurdles in 2004/5. *R. S. Brookhouse* **h–**

CLAIM TO FAME 4 b.g. Selkirk (USA) – Loving Claim (USA) (Hansel (USA)) [2004/5 F14d 16s^{pu} 16d 17s^{6} 16s Jan 27] 4,200 2-y-o: well-made gelding: second foal: half-brother to 1¼m winner First Celebration (by Cadeaux Genereaux): dam, Prix Marcel Boussac winner who stayed 1¼m, half-sister to July Stakes winner City On A Hill: little show in bumper (hung right) and juvenile hurdles. *M. Pitman* **h– F–**

CLAN LAW (IRE) 7 b.g. Danehill (USA) – My-O-My (IRE) (Waajib) [2004/5 F–: 20d^{5} 16v^{4} 18d^{pu} 16s^{pu} 16s^{pu} Apr 22] little form: wore cheekpieces final start. *Mrs L. B. Normile* **h77 ?**

CLAN LEADER (IRE) 5 b.g. Supreme Leader – Curraheigh (IRE) (Carlingford Castle) [2004/5 F16d^{4} Dec 5] useful-looking gelding: first foal: dam poor maiden jumper: looked a stayer when fourth of 20 in bumper at Warwick on debut: will do better. *Jonjo O'Neill* **F89 p**

CLAN ROYAL (FR) 10 b.g. Chef de Clan II (FR) – Allee du Roy (FR) (Rex Magna (FR)) [2004/5 c139, h–: 24g^{4} c36d^{co} Apr 9] **c? h105 +**

Another reminder of the unpredictability of the Grand National was provided by the ignominious departure of Clan Royal and champion jockey Tony McCoy at second Becher's in the latest edition. The hard-pulling Clan Royal—who at times seemed to test the restraining powers even of McCoy—had taken the lead at the Chair, after being waited with in mid-field, and was still five lengths up and travelling strongly when baulked by the riderless Take The Stand and given no chance of jumping the fence. Fortunately, Clan Royal was far enough clear of those heading the rest for their riders to take evasive action, otherwise there could have been an incident similar to that in 2001 when the field was reduced by nearly a quarter after the riderless Paddy's Return caused chaos at the first Canal Turn by veering across the fence on the take-off side. That was the year McCoy finished third on Blowing Wind after remounting and setting off again when his mount was stopped in his tracks by another riderless horse at the nineteenth.

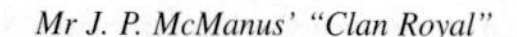

Mr J. P. McManus' "Clan Royal"

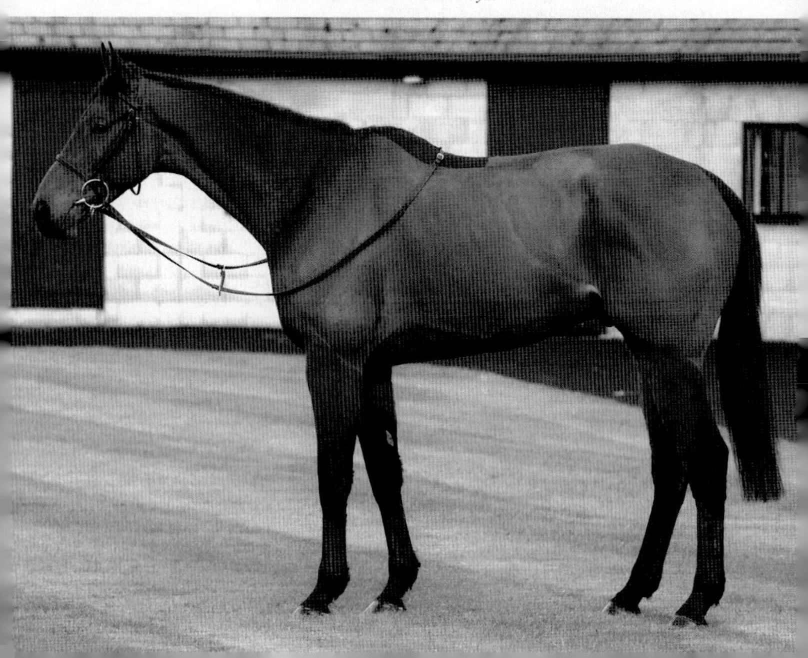

McCoy must be thinking he is fated never to win a National, though whether Clan Royal—his tenth mount and eighth non-completion in the race—would have lasted home and beaten easy winner Hedgehunter, after taking such a keen hold, must be open to some doubt (he was reportedly favourite-in-running at around 3/1 on the betting exchanges just before departing). Clan Royal will be trained for the race again, with a similarly light campaign on the cards. He was seen out only once before the National in the latest season, keeping on without threatening the leaders when fourth in a handicap hurdle at Bangor in December. His trainer had intended to get another run into Clan Royal before Aintree but the horse caught a mild dose of the illness that afflicted the Jackdaws Castle string over the winter, and completed his National preparation at home. Clan Royal used to be a sketchy jumper of fences at one time but his exuberant display demonstrated his affinity for the big, unusual Aintree fences over which he has scarcely put a foot wrong, winning a Topham and a Becher Chase, as well as finishing runner-up to Amberleigh House in the National (his rider that day Liam Cooper was forced to retire in late-September). The tall Clan Royal, a French-bred whose pedigree was covered in *Chasers & Hurdlers 2003/04*, will again be one for the Grand National shortlist. He stays four and a half miles and acts on soft and good to firm going. *Jonjo O'Neill*

CLARAS PRIDE (IRE) 13 b.g. Be My Native (USA) – Our Hollow (Wolver Hollow) [2004/5 20m Jun 5] winning pointer: maiden hurdler/chaser: stays 2½m. *M. S. Wilesmith* **c– h–**

CLARENDON (IRE) 9 ch.g. Forest Wind (USA) – Sparkish (IRE) (Persian Bold) [2004/5 c87, h95: c16d4 c19m6 c16spu c19gpu Dec 30] sturdy gelding: winning hurdler: modest maiden chaser: raced mainly around 2m: acts on heavy and good to firm going: poor jumper. *P. J. Hobbs* **c87 x h–**

CLASSIC ADDITIONS 5 ch.g. Classic Cliche (IRE) – Whatagale (Strong Gale) [2004/5 F16d F16d Mar 14] £6,000 4-y-o: workmanlike gelding: fifth foal: dam, fair chaser, stayed 25f: tailed off in 2 bumpers. *Miss I. E. Craig* **F–**

CLASSICAL BEN 7 ch.g. Most Welcome – Stoproveritate (Scorpio (FR)) [2004/5 h84p, F99: 20g3 20v2 22s3 20v4 20v5 19d3 24v* Mar 17] lengthy gelding: dual bumper winner: fair novice hurdler: won 3-runner event at Hexham in March: stays 3m: acts on heavy going: blinkered sixth start. *R. A. Fahey* **h103**

CLASSICAL LOVE 5 b.m. Classic Cliche (IRE) – Hard Love (Rambo Dancer (CAN)) [2004/5 F16g6 F17s F16v 24s 22g3 Apr 10] unfurnished mare: second foal: dam, 1¼m winner, half-sister to fairly useful 2m jumpers Bettyknowes and Stay Awake: well held in bumpers: in cheekpieces, poor form when third in mares novice hurdle at Newton Abbot. *C. J. Down* **h76 F–**

CLASSIC APPROACH (IRE) 5 b.g. Luso – Vital Approach (IRE) (Pauper) [2004/5 F17d4 Nov 20] third foal: dam, maiden pointer, half-sister to Whitbread winner Harwell Lad: won maiden point on debut in 2004: well beaten in bumper at Aintree. *J. Queally, Ireland* **F–**

CLASSIC CALVADOS (FR) 6 b.g. Thatching – Mountain Stage (IRE) (Pennine Walk) [2004/5 h79: 17d5 16m4 17m5 17g4 17s5 19m2 16d3 20d Jan 7] good-topped gelding: modest maiden hurdler: stays 19f: acts on good to firm and good to soft going: ran poorly in cheekpieces final start: tongue tied. *P. D. Niven* **h90**

CLASSIC CAPERS 6 ch.g. Classic Cliche (IRE) – Jobiska (Dunbeath (USA)) [2004/5 F99: 20s4 20d* 23dpu 20v5 19d* 20dpu Mar 12] tall gelding: will make a chaser: bumper winner: fair novice hurdler: won at Wetherby (maiden) in November and Catterick in February: should stay beyond 2½m: raced on going softer than good. *J. M. Jefferson* **h109**

CLASSIC CHINA 8 ch.m. Karinga Bay – Chanelle (The Parson) [2004/5 h85: c20mur 22fpu 20d4 24s6 c25d* c19d3 c28s6 24s c23s4 Mar 22] rather leggy mare: modest hurdler: better form first 2 completed starts over fences, won weakly-contested mares maiden at Folkestone in November: failed to convince with jumping or attitude afterwards: should stay beyond 25f: acts on soft and good to firm going: wears cheekpieces. *J. W. Mullins* **c99 h86**

CLASSIC CLOVER 5 ch.g. Classic Cliche (IRE) – National Clover (National Trust) [2004/5 F17s F18m6 Apr 21] 20,000 3-y-o: well-made gelding: half-brother to several winners, notably top-class staying chaser Go Ballistic (by Celtic Cone): dam, very useful pointer, daughter of Welsh National winner Clover Bud: better effort in bumpers when sixth of 10 at Fontwell. *C. L. Tizzard* **F84**

CLASSIC CROCO (GER) 4 ro.g. Croco Rouge (IRE) – Classic Light (IRE) (Classic Secret (USA)) [2004/5 16d 16g³ 17g³ Apr 7] workmanlike ex-German gelding: successful 3 times on Flat (stays 1½m) in 2004, at Dortmund in April and Duindigt and Mijas (€100,000 Spanish Derby) in May: modest form over hurdles: left C. Von Der Recke after debut: raced only around 2m on good/good to soft ground. *Ms Bridget Nicholls* **h90**

CLASSIC EAGLE 12 b.g. Unfuwain (USA) – La Lutine (My Swallow) [2004/5 16d 21d May 11] lengthy gelding: of no account nowadays. *M. Wigham* **c– h–**

CLASSIC EVENT (IRE) 4 ch.g. Croco Rouge (IRE) – Delta Town (USA) (Sanglamore (USA)) [2004/5 16d* 16m² 19d² 16vᶠ 16g* Mar 5] well-made gelding: half-brother to fairly useful 2m hurdler Kentucky Blue (by Revoque): modest maiden on Flat (stays 1½m): fair form over hurdles: won juvenile at Newcastle in November and novice handicap at Doncaster in March: stays 19f: acts on good to firm and heavy going. *T. D. Easterby* **h105**

CLASSIC FABLE (IRE) 13 b.m. Lafontaine (USA) – Rathmill Syke (True Song) [2004/5 c16sᵖᵘ Apr 28] of little account: tongue tied. *J. L. Needham* **c– h–**

CLASSIC JAZZ (NZ) 10 br.g. Paris Opera (AUS) – Johnny Loves Jazz (NZ) (Virginia Privateer (USA)) [2004/5 19gᵖᵘ Jan 17] strong, rangy gelding: lightly raced: no show over hurdles since 2001. *R. Bastiman* **h–**

CLASSIC LASH (IRE) 9 b.g. Classic Cheer (IRE) – Khaiylasha (IRE) (Kahyasi) [2004/5 c99, h–: 21vᵖᵘ 21vᵖᵘ Jan 25] winning hurdler/chaser: no show in 2004/5: stays 3m: acts on firm and soft going: blinkered once. *P. Needham* **c– h–**

CLASSIC NATIVE (IRE) 7 b. or br.g. Be My Native (USA) – Thats Irish (Furry Glen) [2004/5 h110: c24v* c28v⁵ c33gᵖᵘ Mar 17] tall, good sort: fair maiden hurdler: fairly useful form when winning handicap at Bangor in November by 8 lengths from The Villager, easily best effort over fences: best at 3m+: acts on heavy ground: strong-galloping sort. *Jonjo O'Neill* **c120 h–**

CLASSIC NOTE (IRE) 10 b.m. Classic Secret (USA) – Fovea (IRE) (Sarab) [2004/5 16f* 16g* 16m 16g⁶ 16sᵖᵘ Oct 21] fair handicap hurdler: won at Cork and Gowran in June: should stay 2½m: acts on firm and good to soft going, not on soft. *Mrs P. Dobbs, Ireland* **h108**

CLASSIC QUART (IRE) 4 b.f. Classic Cliche (IRE) – Ganpati (IRE) (Over The River (FR)) [2004/5 F12g F13s⁴ F17s² F16s* F16d⁴ Mar 12] leggy filly: first foal: dam fair staying hurdler: fair form in bumpers: won mares event at Huntingdon in February by neck from Accordello: shapes like a stayer. *M. Scudamore* **F94**

CLASSIC REVIVAL 7 ch.g. Elmaamul (USA) – Sweet Revival (Claude Monet (USA)) [2004/5 h–, F–: c16mᵘʳ c16m⁶ c20sᵖᵘ Mar 31] no sign of ability. *Mrs A. Price* **c– h–**

CLASSIC ROCK 6 b.g. Classic Cliche (IRE) – Ruby Vision (IRE) (Vision (USA)) [2004/5 h73: 20d⁶ 24mᵖᵘ Jun 5] lengthy gelding: won weak novice on hurdling debut in 2003/4: no form in 3 handicaps subsequently: bred to stay beyond 19f. *J. W. Unett* **h–**

CLASSIC ROLE 6 b.g. Tragic Role (USA) – Clare Island (Connaught) [2004/5 16s² Mar 6] leggy gelding: half-brother to fairly useful hurdler/chaser Alqairawaan (by Ajdal), stayed 3m: fairly useful on Flat (stays 13f) for R. Ingram: ran to similar level when neck second of 16 to Briareus in novice at Kempton on hurdling debut. *L. Wells* **h117**

CLASSIC RUBY 5 b.m. Classic Cliche (IRE) – Burmese Ruby (Good Times (ITY)) [2004/5 F–: F16d⁶ F17d⁴ F16s⁵ Feb 10] leggy mare: modest form in bumpers: will stay beyond 17f. *M. R. Bosley* **F80**

CLASSIC SIGHT 5 ch.m. Classic Cliche (IRE) – Speckyfoureyes (Blue Cashmere) [2004/5 F16s² F16d⁶ F16v⁶ F16v² 16s 22s³ Mar 6] compact mare: eighth foal: half-sister to fair staying hurdlers Lorgnette (by Emperor Fountain) and Sword Lady (by Broadsword): dam, winning hurdler who stayed 2½m, from family of high-class staying chaser Stearsby: modest form in bumpers: upped in trip, better effort in novice hurdles (didn't impress with attitude on first occasion) when third at Market Rasen: blinkered last 3 starts. *C. C. Bealby* **h80 F80**

CLASSIC VIC (IRE) 5 ch.g. Old Vic – Grangeclare Rose (IRE) (Gianchi) [2004/5 F16v* F16s² 16s³ Nov 19] fifth foal: half-brother to useful hurdler/chaser Scarthy Lad (by Magical Wonder), effective at 2m to 3m: dam unraced half-sister to fairly useful staying chaser Thinking Cap: fairly useful form in bumpers at Down Royal, winning on debut in May: 3 lengths third to Guest Artist in maiden at Fairyhouse on hurdling debut, running on. *Mrs J. Harrington, Ireland* **h103 p F101**

CLASSIFY 6 b.g. Classic Cliche (IRE) – Slmaat (Sharpo) [2004/5 h108: 22s^{pu} Oct 28] fair form in bumpers and over hurdles: won 3 times in points in 2005. *P. F. Nicholls* **h–**

CLASSI MAUREEN 5 ch.m. Among Men (USA) – Hi-Hannah (Red Sunset) [2004/5 h–: 17d 20m May 26] soundly beaten over hurdles: third in maiden point in March. *Mrs S. M. Johnson* **h–**

CLAUDE GREENGRASS 9 ch.g. Shalford (IRE) – Rainbow Brite (BEL) (Captain's Treasure) [2004/5 c91p, h105: 17g 16g 16d^{5} 19g^{4} 16g^{4} 20f^{pu} 19s* c18g^{pu} c20d^{pu} Dec 11] sturdy gelding fair handicap hurdler: won at Exeter in October: thrice-raced over fences, moody efforts last 2 starts: stays 19f: acts on heavy going, ran poorly only 2 outings on firmer than good: tried in cheekpieces, possibly best in blinkers: not a fluent jumper. *Jonjo O'Neill* **c– § h105**

CLAWICK CONNECTION (IRE) 10 b.g. Torus – Katie Lowe (IRE) (Pollerton) [2004/5 c24g c34g^{3} c20f c25d c24s c34m^{F} c24s^{6} c31d c20v^{4} Jan 29] strong ex-Irish gelding: poor maiden chaser: left J. Lennon before final start: stays 4¼m: acts on soft going. *J. N. R. Billinge* **c82**

CLAYDON CAVALIER 6 b.g. Regal Embers (IRE) – Marsdale (Royal Palace) [2004/5 F–: F17g^{pu} F16g Jul 20] no form in 3 bumpers. *J. R. Jenkins* **F–**

CLAYMILLS (IRE) 5 b.g. Presenting – Merry Watt (Last Fandango) [2004/5 F16v^{5} F16d F16g Mar 26] lengthy gelding: half-brother to winning hurdler around 2m Hobbs (by Phardante): dam maiden: well held in bumpers. *P. Beaumont* **F–**

CLAYMORE (IRE) 9 b.g. Broadsword (USA) – Mazza (Mazilier (USA)) [2004/5 c133, h137: c20g^{2} 20v^{2} 20v^{4} 16d Feb 12] leggy, lengthy gelding: useful handicap hurdler/chaser: better than ever in 2004/5, second to Supreme Prince in well-contested event over fences at Newbury and to Olney Lad over hurdles at Wetherby: needs further than 2m nowadays, and stays 3m: acts on heavy going: usually races prominently: prone to odd mistake over fences: reliable. *O. Sherwood* **c141 h145**

CLAYPHENTO 7 b.m. Lyphento (USA) – Canny Member (New Member) [2004/5 h–: 19m^{4} 18m^{4} c19d^{F} Oct 28] no form over hurdles: jumped poorly on chasing debut: tried blinkered. *M. C. Pipe* **c– h–**

CLEAR AWAY (IRE) 8 b.g. Clearly Bust – Twinkle Bright (USA) (Star de Naskra (USA)) [2004/5 c24g^{F} Jul 1] won maiden point in 2004: running to modest level on chasing debut when falling fatally. *Evan Williams* **c91 h–**

CLEAR DAWN (IRE) 10 b.g. Clearly Bust – Cobra Queen (Dawn Review) [2004/5 c102, h–: c22g^{4} c24d^{6} c25m^{5} c20s^{4} 24m^{4} 25g^{pu} 24d^{6} 24g^{2} 20m 24g Feb 27] well-made gelding: fair handicap chaser at his best: modest handicap hurdler: should stay beyond 3m: unraced on firm going, acts on any other: usually front runner: inconsistent. *J. M. Jefferson* **c93 h86**

CLEARLY OSCAR (IRE) 6 b.g. Oscar (IRE) – Clear Bid (IRE) (Executive Perk) [2004/5 F16g^{2} F16f Aug 1] second foal: dam bumper winner: much better effort in bumpers when second of 9 at Perth. *J. J. Lambe, Ireland* **F82**

CLEAR THINKING 5 b.g. Rainbow Quest (USA) – Coraline (Sadler's Wells (USA)) [2004/5 16d* 21s^{6} 16d Mar 14] leggy, lengthy gelding: smart up to 15.5f on Flat, successful twice in minor events and placed several times in group company, though didn't always convince with attitude (tail swisher): sold out of A. Fabre's stable 62,000 gns Newmarket Autumn Sales: made all and jumped fluently when winning novice at Newbury in February on hurdling debut by neck from Prins Willem: well held in handicaps: should stay beyond 2m. *Miss Venetia Williams* **h117**

CLEOPATRAS THERAPY (IRE) 8 b.g. Gone Fishin – Nec Precario (Krayyan) [2004/5 h88?, F–: 22d^{6} 24g^{pu} 20v^{4} 20s^{5} 20s^{6} 24v^{pu} Jan 18] good-topped gelding: little form over hurdles. *T. H. Caldwell* **h85 ?**

CLEVER FELLA 6 ch.g. Elmaamul (USA) – Festival of Magic (USA) (Clever Trick (USA)) [2004/5 c25s^{ur} Nov 5] won maiden point in 2004: unseated eleventh on chasing debut. *Mrs K. Walton* **c–**

CLEVER THYNE (IRE) 8 b.g. Good Thyne (USA) – Clever Milly (Precipice Wood) [2004/5 c–, h99: c25s^{pu} c24g* c24d^{pu} c24d^{pu} Mar 24] good-topped gelding: modest hurdler: much improved when winning novice at Huntingdon in January, only completed start over fences: stays 3¼m: raced on good going or softer: has had tongue tied (often runs as if amiss). *H. D. Daly* **c111 h–**

CLEW BAY COVE (IRE) 5 ch.g. Anshan – Crashrun (Crash Course) [2004/5 F18spu F16s* F19s6 F16g5 Mar 16] €26,000 3-y-o: lengthy gelding: seventh foal: half-brother to fair hurdlers My Name's Not Bin (by Good Thyne), stays 3m, and Cumbrian Knight (by Presenting), stays 2½m: dam unraced: won maiden bumper at Leopardstown in February: easily best effort when 5 lengths fifth to Missed That in 24-runner Champion Bumper at Cheltenham, making most: will stay at least 2½m: tongue tied after debut. *C. A. Murphy, Ireland* **F118**

CLEYMOR HOUSE (IRE) 7 ch.g. Duky – Deise Lady (Le Bavard (FR)) [2004/5 c59, h–: 22d 19d2 22s c23mpu c22gpu Apr 19] lengthy gelding: little form over hurdles and fences: has looked hard ride. *John R. Upson* **c– h71**

CLICHY 5 b.m. Classic Cliche (IRE) – Kentucky Tears (USA) (Cougar (CHI)) [2004/5 F82: 16dpu 20v4 20d 21vpu Mar 15] leggy mare: little form over hurdles. *Mrs S. J. Smith* **h82 ?**

CLIFFORD T WARD 5 b.g. Silver Wizard (USA) – Moonduster (Sparkler) [2004/5 F16d3 Mar 19] sturdy gelding: tenth foal: half-brother to winning pointer Roly Prior (by Celtic Cone): dam modest 2m winner: 2¼ lengths third of 16 to Barton Legend in bumper at Uttoxeter on debut. *D. McCain* **F91**

CLIP ON 4 b.f. Past Glories – Scalby Clipper (Sir Mago) [2004/5 F16d F16d Jan 29] unfurnished filly: sixth foal: dam lightly-raced daughter of useful hunter Lady Annapurna: well held in 2 bumpers. *P. T. Midgley* **F–**

CLIQUEY 6 b.g. Muhtarram (USA) – Meet Again (Lomond (USA)) [2004/5 h88: 17d 20m2 Jul 21] modest hurdler: stayed 2½m: acted on good to firm going: successful blinkered and tongue tied or not: dead. *R. H. Buckler* **h86**

CLODAGH VALLEY (IRE) 10 b.g. Doubletour (USA) – Raise A Princess (USA) (Raise A Native) [2004/5 c25spu Feb 5] winning pointer: no form otherwise over jumps: tried blinkered. *R. J. Hewitt* **c– h–**

CLONEYBRIEN BOY (IRE) 5 ch.g. Mister Lord (USA) – Lougheagle (Deep Run) [2004/5 F16d F16g F16s6 19vpu 16s Mar 23] workmanlike gelding: seventh foal: half-brother to winning pointer by Supreme Leader: dam, winning hurdler, sister to smart staying chaser Aquilifer: little sign of ability, sold out of D. Thompson's stable 8,000 gns Doncaster October Sales after second outing. *Mrs A. M. Thorpe* **h– F83 ?**

CLONSHIRE PADDY (IRE) 9 gr.g. Roselier (FR) – Gusserane Princess (Paddy's Stream) [2004/5 c34dpu May 15] good-topped gelding: novice hurdler/chaser: successful twice in points in 2004: should stay beyond 25f: acts on heavy going: tried visored/blinkered. *Mrs C. A. Coward* **c– h–**

CLOONE RIVER (IRE) 9 b. or br.g. Un Desperado (FR) – Grangemills (Strong Gale) [2004/5 h121: 16g* c16v* c17g* Sep 5] **c130 p h129**

Clan Royal wasn't the only horse whose connections waited a year to try to go one better in a big race. Cloone River's connections were successful. The gelding had been beaten three quarters of a length by Sabadilla, caught close home, in the 2003 Guinness Galway Hurdle and reappeared a year later to land quite a gamble in the 2004 renewal. His 2003 appearance had been his first over hurdles for eight months and was preceded by two outings on the Flat. Again in 2004, he made two appearances on the Flat in his build-up for Galway, placed in competitive middle-distance handicaps at the Curragh and Down Royal (showing useful form in the Ulster Derby). Having been available at 12/1 ante-post for the Galway Hurdle, Cloone River was heavily backed down to 7/2 favourite in a field of twenty-four. A record Tote turnover for a single race in Ireland and over €3.3m wagered with bookmakers during the afternoon (another record), gives some indication of the weight of money needed to shorten Cloone River. More patiently ridden this time, Cloone River was produced to lead after the last and won going away by two lengths from Gemini Guest. Cloone River gave trainer Paul Nolan his second win in three years in this most competitive of handicaps, having landed the prize with Say Again in 2002. Nolan's comments after the race gave an indication of his feelings and perhaps the size of the gamble: 'I could feel a tightness across my chest and I thought I was going to have a heart attack. Then my arms seized up with pins and needles. I had a check-up for the same thing once before and I was okay, so it must be all in the mind.'

Say Again went straight over fences after his success at Galway and so too did Cloone River, in his case with immediate success. Although the opposition was

Mrs K. Gillane's "Cloone River"

nothing out of the ordinary, the manner of his victories in a maiden at Tralee and a novice at Galway suggested he was going to make an even better chaser than he had a Flat horse or hurdler. After his victory over Always at Galway, where he again really impressed with his jumping, his trainer reported Cloone River likely to have only one more run before a crack at the Arkle at Cheltenham. Unfortunately, a recurrence of a minor injury in February prevented his appearing again. He was among the market leaders for Cheltenham at the time and, provided all is well, he has every prospect of making a smart chaser on his return. Cloone River is by Un Desperado out of Grangemills, who won a bumper and stayed two miles on the Flat, and should stay beyond two miles over jumps, though he has done nearly all his racing at the minimum trip and certainly is not short of speed. He has won on both firm and heavy going, though his very best efforts have been on good or good to soft and he is regarded by connections as not being ideally suited by very soft going. *Paul Nolan, Ireland*

CLOTH OF GOLD 8 b.g. Barathea (IRE) – Bustinetta (Bustino) [2004/5 h–: 24d² 24d³ 24g² c24g³ c23g³ Oct 6] rather leggy gelding: fairly useful handicap hurdler: fair form when third in novice company over fences: won points in March and April: stays 3m: acts on good to soft and good to firm going: blinkered/in cheekpieces 3 of last 4 starts: not an easy ride. *Lady Herries* **c105 h117**

CLOUD CATCHER (IRE) 4 br.f. Charnwood Forest (IRE) – Notley Park (Wolfhound (USA)) [2004/5 16d⁶ 16vpu Dec 17] small filly: no sign of ability on Flat or over hurdles. *M. Appleby* **h–**

CLOUDINA 4 b.f. Cloudings (IRE) – Lucia Forte (Neltino) [2004/5 F16d F17g⁵ Apr 14] smallish filly: third foal: dam, useful hurdler who stayed 3m, sister to top-class 19f to 3½m chaser Teeton Mill and half-sister to useful staying hurdler/chaser Ashfold Copse: poor form on second of 2 starts in bumpers. *P. T. Dalton* **F69**

CLOUDING OVER 5 gr.m. Cloudings (IRE) – Wellwotdouthink (Rymer) [2004/5 F67: 17d^{6} 19m 19g^{6} 20d^{3} 20s^{3} 20g^{F} 16s* 19g^{2} 16s^{pu} 20s^{2} Apr 22] rather leggy mare: fair hurdler: won mares novice handicap at Catterick in March: may prove best short of 2½m when conditions are testing: acts on soft going: held up. *K. G. Reveley* **h100**

CLOUDINGSWELL 4 b.f. Cloudings (IRE) – L'Ancressaan (Dalsaan) [2004/5 17d 17g^{pu} 16m 18m Sep 21] lengthy, shallow-girthed filly: half-sister to winning hurdler/ fairly useful chaser Mr Cospector (by Cosmonaut), stays 3¼m: poor maiden on Flat (stays 11f): no form in juvenile hurdles. *D. L. Williams* **h–**

CLOUDLESS DAWN 5 b.m. Cloudings (IRE) – Charlotte's Emma (Oats) [2004/5 F16d^{4} F16g^{5} F16s F17m^{3} Apr 23] 10,000 4-y-o: tall mare: fourth foal: dam, fair hurdler/ chaser who stayed 3¼m, half-sister to useful chaser up to 21f Thosewerethedays: modest form in bumpers: bred to stay well. *P. Beaumont* **F83**

CLOUDMOR (IRE) 4 b.g. Cloudings (IRE) – Glen Morvern (Carlingford Castle) [2004/5 F16s Apr 22] 5,500 3-y-o: fourth foal: brother to bumper winner Treasured Memories and half-brother to 17f chase winner The Miner (by Hatim): dam 2¼m hurdle winner: tenth of 18 in bumper at Perth on debut. *Miss S. E. Forster* **F75**

CLOUDS OF GOLD (IRE) 4 b.f. Goldmark (USA) – Tongabezi (IRE) (Shernazar) [2004/5 16v^{pu} 16d 17g Apr 3] leggy, close-coupled filly: little form on Flat: no show over hurdles. *J. S. Wainwright* **h–**

CLOUD VENTURE 5 gr.g. Cloudings (IRE) – Fantasy World (Kemal (FR)) [2004/5 F16s Feb 5] fourth foal: half-brother to 2 winning jumpers, notably smart chaser around 2m Central House (by Alflora): dam, fair hurdler up to 3m, from family of useful Irish hurdler/chaser up to 3m Carrigeensharragh: well held in bumper on debut. *S. E. H. Sherwood* **F–**

CLOUDY BAYS (IRE) 8 ch.g. Hubbly Bubbly (USA) – Bellteen (Beau Charmeur (FR)) [2004/5 c150, h105: 20m 22v^{2} 24v^{4} 20v* c20s^{4} c24s^{3} c20s^{2} c24d^{5} c24v^{4} c22v* 24v* c25s^{4} c24s^{3} Feb 6] rather leggy gelding: smart chaser: won listed event at Tramore in January by distance from Satco Express: well held in good company last 2 starts, reportedly knocked himself when third to Rule Supreme in Grade 1 at Leopardstown: useful handicap hurdler: won at Listowel in September and Leopardstown in January, beating Christmas River 6 lengths in 24-runner event at latter: stays 3m: acts on any going: tried blinkered, often wears cheekpieces: has had tongue tied: makes running: tough. *Charles Byrnes, Ireland* **c151 h131**

CLOUDY BLUES (IRE) 7 ro.g. Glacial Storm (USA) – Chataka Blues (IRE) (Sexton Blake) [2004/5 F–: F17d F16v 19s^{pu} 22s^{pu} 24g c18s^{4} c18m^{F} c25g^{pu} Apr 17] lengthy, good-topped gelding: no form. *R. H. Buckler* **c– h– F–**

CLOUDY GREY (IRE) 8 gr.g. Roselier (FR) – Dear Limousin (Pollerton) [2004/5 h138p: 20s 19d^{ur} 16s^{F} Feb 5] big, lengthy gelding: smart bumper winner: most encouraging start to hurdling career when winning novice at Ascot: missed remainder of 2003/4 due to fractured fetlock and looked in need of first 2 starts back, shaping as if retaining all his ability on second occasion: fell fourth next time: bred to stay 3m. *Miss E. C. Lavelle* **h132 ?**

CLOUDY SKY (IRE) 9 b.g. Sadler's Wells (USA) – Dancing Shadow (Dancer's Image (USA)) [2004/5 20d* May 15] useful form for Sir Michael Stoute at 3 yrs, well held only subsequent outing on Flat: won novice at Uttoxeter on hurdling debut, making virtually all: dead. *Simon Earle* **h110**

CLOVER DOVE 6 b.m. Overbury (IRE) – Coney Dove (Celtic Cone) [2004/5 F17g F17d Oct 17] fourth foal: half-sister to winning 2½m hurdler Scratch The Dove (by Henbit): dam, 21f hurdle winner, half-sister to 1994 Champion Hurdle winner Flakey Dove: tailed off in 2 bumpers. *A. E. Price* **F–**

CLUB ROYAL 8 b.g. Alflora (IRE) – Miss Club Royal (Avocat) [2004/5 c75, h78: c17g^{pu} 19g^{6} 16s^{5} 22v Feb 15] good-topped gelding: poor maiden chaser: poor hurdler: sold out of D. McCain's stable £6,200 Ascot October Sales after second outing: better at 21f than shorter: acts on soft going: tried blinkered. *R. A. Harris* **c– h75**

CLYDEONEEYED 6 b.g. Primitive Rising (USA) – Holly (Skyliner) [2004/5 F16d 20s^{pu} 16s^{F} 16g 19v^{4} 26s^{pu} 21g^{4} 16d^{ur} 16g Apr 19] third foal: brother to winning pointer Chapners Cross: dam unraced: little sign of ability. *K. F. Clutterbuck* **h– F–**

CLYFFE HANGER (IRE) 5 b.g. Taipan (IRE) – French Thistle (Kemal (FR)) [2004/5 F17g* Apr 12] €22,000 4-y-o: sixth foal: dam unraced, out of useful staying chaser Tarthistle: 40/1, won 8-runner bumper at Exeter on debut by 6 lengths from Ballybough Jack, quickening clear 1f out. *R. H. Buckler* **F101 +**

CMEWIN (IRE) 9 ch.g. Le Bavard (FR) – Copper Dash (Copper Gamble) [2004/5 c20v c20g c16g c16m c20g6 c25d4 c24m6 Oct 6] seventh foal: brother and half-brother to winning pointers: dam unraced: poor maiden hurdler/chaser: won points in Britain in January and April: stays 25f: acts on heavy going: tried blinkered/in cheekpieces. *A. J. Martin, Ireland* **c65 h–**

COACH LANE 4 b.g. Barathea (IRE) – Emplane (USA) (Irish River (FR)) [2004/5 16d5 16s3 16d 16s2 Jan 27] useful-looking gelding: second foal: dam, 1m winner, sister to smart 1¼m performer Boatman out of half-sister to Irish 1000 Guineas winner Al Bahathri, dam of 2000 Guineas winner Haafhd: twice-raced on Flat, sold out of M. Zilber's stable 16,000 gns Doncaster August Sales after winning over 11f at Le Touquet: fair form when placed twice from 4 starts in juvenile hurdles: raced at 2m on good to soft/soft going. *Miss Venetia Williams* **h100**

COACHMAN (IRE) 7 b.g. King's Ride – Royal Shares (IRE) (Royal Fountain) [2004/5 h–: 17g May 25] rather leggy gelding: of no account: tried blinkered. *A. J. Lockwood* **h–**

COASTGUARD (IRE) 11 b.g. Satco (FR) – Godlike (Godswalk (USA)) [2004/5 c81x, h87: 20d c22s5 c24v3 c23dpu c24spu c23dpu 20vpu Feb 15] compact gelding: winning hurdler/chaser, little form since early-2003/4: stays 3m: acts on good to firm and heavy going: usually wears blinkers/cheekpieces: sketchy jumper. *D. Pearson* **c72 ? h–**

COAST TO COAST (IRE) 6 ch.g. Moscow Society (USA) – Madame Vitesse (Le Bavard (FR)) [2004/5 c20s2 c24vur c20s3 c20sR Mar 29] dam winning pointer: won point on debut in 2003: sixth in bumper: fair form over hurdles, won maiden at Thurles in 2003/4: fair form both completed starts over fences, 14 lengths third of 5 finishers to Well Presented in Grade 2 novice at Naas: likely to stay 3m: raced on going softer than good. *E. J. O'Grady, Ireland* **c114 h–**

COAT OF HONOUR (USA) 5 gr.g. Mark of Esteem (IRE) – Ballymac Girl (Niniski (USA)) [2004/5 20m* 16m* 16g* 16g2 Apr 15] good-topped gelding: dam won twice over 21f over hurdles, also successful in points: useful on Flat (stays 13f) for Sir Mark Prescott, successful twice in 2004: won first 3 starts over hurdles, maiden at Musselburgh in November and novices at Musselburgh again (blinkered) and Kempton (beat Chockdee by 2½ lengths) in December: off nearly 4 months, stayed on too late when 1½ lengths second of 4 to Cornish Sett in falsely-run novice at Ayr: stays 2½m: raced on good/good to firm going: not a fluent jumper: remains unexposed over hurdles. *J. Howard Johnson* **h125 p**

COBBET (CHR) 9 b.g. Favoured Nations (IRE) – Creace (CZE) (Sirano (CZE)) [2004/5 c121, h–: c16d2 c16m* 17f3 c16d c17g6 c16d2 Dec 26] leggy gelding: fairly useful handicap chaser: won strongly-run event at Uttoxeter in June: fair handicap hurdler, first run in that sphere for 2 years when third to Made In France at Exeter in September: barely stays 21f: acts on firm and good to soft going: sound jumper: genuine and consistent. *T. R. George* **c129 h109**

COBRECES 7 b.g. Environment Friend – Oleada (IRE) (Tirol) [2004/5 c112§, h–: c25d* c23s* c24d* c21sur Apr 7] tall, useful-looking gelding: fairly useful chaser: raced with more zest than usual when winning hunters at Ludlow, Leicester and Ludlow again in March: mistakes and losing position when unseating 5 out in Fox Hunters' at Aintree: stays 25f: unraced on firm going, acts on any other: tried blinkered: has had tongue tied. *Mrs L. Borradaile* **c115 h–**

COCCOLONA (IRE) 7 b.m. Idris (IRE) – Fair Siobahn (Petingo) [2004/5 16m 17g4 20m 17gpu Aug 14] poor on Flat at 4 yrs for D. Haydn Jones: no form over hurdles, lame final start. *R. Williams* **h–**

COCKATOO RIDGE 8 ch.g. Riverwise (USA) – Came Cottage (Nearly A Hand) [2004/5 h98: 17d6 19mF 22m May 30] sturdy gelding: novice hurdler, well below best both completed starts early in 2004/5: stays 3m: acts on good to soft going (won bumper on firm). *N. R. Mitchell* **h–**

COCK OF THE NORTH (IRE) 8 b.g. Supreme Leader – Our Quest (Private Walk) [2004/5 16g 16s Jan 6] thrice-raced over hurdles, well held in 2004/5. *C. R. Egerton* **h–**

COCK OF THE ROOST (IRE) 8 b.g. Executive Perk – Sly Maid (Rapid River) [2004/5 c–, h–: c19d c23m5 Jun 5] lengthy gelding: of no account: tried blinkered: has had tongue tied. *S. T. Lewis* **c– h–**

COCTAIL LADY (IRE) 5 ch.m. Piccolo – Last Ambition (IRE) (Cadeaux Genereux) [2004/5 h86: 19m 20gpu 16gpu Jul 18] sparely-made mare: winning hurdler: no form in **h–**

2004/5: unlikely to stay beyond 2m: raced mainly on good going or firmer: blinkered last 2 outings: usually tongue tied. *B. W. Duke*

CODE (IRE) 4 b.g. Danehill (USA) – Hidden Meaning (USA) (Gulch (USA)) [2004/5 F14d F12d3 F13s4 Jan 31] third foal: dam unraced half-sister to very smart Irish 7f to 1¼m performer Fair Judgment: fair form in bumpers. *Miss Z. C. Davison* **F89**

CODE SIGN (USA) 6 b.g. Gulch (USA) – Karasavina (IRE) (Sadler's Wells (USA)) [2004/5 h96: 17g2 17m* 17m2 19g3 c18m2 c20mF c17f2 19g6 Oct 6] leggy gelding: fair handicap hurdler: won at Hereford in June: second in maiden at Fontwell, first and better effort on completed starts over fences: stays 2½m: acts on firm going: blinkered once. *P. J. Hobbs* **c104 h110**

CODY 6 ch.g. Zilzal (USA) – Ibtihaj (USA) (Raja Baba (USA)) [2004/5 h79: 22gpu 21g2 20s6 21d 20s5 Apr 16] close-coupled gelding: poor maiden hurdler: left G. Ham after third outing: stays 3m: acts on good to soft going: tried visored: has worn tongue strap. *James Moffatt* **h71**

COERCION (IRE) 7 b.g. Ilium – Nicholas Ferry (Floriferous) [2004/5 h–, F–: 24g5 26g5 May 26] little sign of ability: tried in cheekpieces: sold £2,600 Ascot October Sales. *R. F. Fisher* **h67 ?**

COGOLIE (FR) 5 ch.m. Cyborg (FR) – Concinna (FR) (Esprit du Nord (USA)) [2004/5 F16m Nov 26] sixth foal: half-sister to 4 winners, including 17f hurdle winner Caracolo (by Sarhoob) and 19f hurdle winner Calamar (by Galetto): dam unraced half-sister to very smart middle-distance performer Cadoudal: well held in maiden bumper on debut. *J. P. L. Ewart* **F–**

COLCA CANYON (IRE) 8 b.g. Un Desperado (FR) – Golden Flats (Sonnen Gold) [2004/5 c137, h113p, F96: c16gF c20d* c20d2 c22mbd c24s* c24s5 c20dpu c21g6 c21d Apr 8] big, lengthy gelding: winning hurdler: useful chaser: beat Risk Accessor ½ length when winning minor event at Killarney in May and Anglo Irish Bank Munster National (Handicap) at Limerick in October: below form after except when sixth to Liberthine in valuable handicap at Cheltenham: in cheekpieces, acted as pacemaker in Grade 1 at Punchestown in late-April: stays 3m: acts on soft and good to firm going. *Mrs J. Harrington, Ireland* **c141 h–**

COLD ENCOUNTER (IRE) 10 ch.g. Polar Falcon (USA) – Scene Galante (FR) (Sicyos (USA)) [2004/5 c92d, h63: c25gpu c24mpu c23mpu c21dpu Aug 9] lengthy, angular gelding: modest staying handicap chaser, made all 3 times in autumn 2003: no form since: tried in headgear. *R. M. Stronge* **c– h–**

COLESHILL LAD 5 br.g. Wizard King – Hallowed Ground (IRE) (Godswalk (USA)) [2004/5 h–, F–: 16m 16d3 Nov 1] more sign of temperament than ability. *J. Joseph* **h–**

COLLEGE CITY (IRE) 6 b.g. College Chapel – Polish Crack (IRE) (Polish Patriot (USA)) [2004/5 h68: 17d2 c16m 17d6 c20v3 c16vF c20v3 17v5 Mar 28] poor handicap hurdler: similar form over fences: stays 2½m: acts on heavy going: tried in cheekpieces. *R. C. Guest* **c80 h81**

COLLEGE CRACKER 7 b.m. Environment Friend – Primo Panache (Primo Dominie) [2004/5 F–: 16d 16g 16d 19d 22s6 17g6 Apr 3] leggy mare: signs of only a little ability: should stay 2½m. *J. F. Coupland* **h62 ?**

COLLIERS COURT 8 b.g. Puget (USA) – Rag Time Belle (Raga Navarro (ITY)) [2004/5 h–: 16d c17d3 c17d5 c16m4 c16m6 c17g c17m4 c17gF c18m2 c16s* c16g* c16s* c16g* c16d3 c16d4 Jan 29] twice-raced over hurdles: fairly useful chaser: much improved, winning handicaps at Ludlow in October and November and novices at Windsor later in November and Ludlow again in December: best around 2m: acts on soft and good to firm going: headstrong front runner. *Mrs L. Williamson* **c119 h–**

COLLIERS QUAY (IRE) 9 b.g. Warcraft (USA) – Francois's Crumpet (IRE) (Strong Gale) [2004/5 h–: 24spu 26m 22d4 22s5 24s5 Oct 21] fair hurdler at best, no form since 2002/3: sold out of Miss V. Williams' stable £2,800 Ascot June Sales after first outing: tried in cheekpieces: has had tongue tied. *W. K. Goldsworthy* **h66**

COLMCILLE (IRE) 5 ch.g. Desert Story (IRE) – Lasting Peace (IRE) (Pennine Walk) [2004/5 16g c16f* 16v6 c17s5 19g 22d2 22d 26g 22m Apr 23] compact gelding: maiden on Flat: better effort over fences when winning maiden at Tramore in August: modest handicap hurdler: sold out of M. Holden's stable 12,000 gns Doncaster October Sales after fourth start: stays 2¾m: acts on firm and soft going: often tongue tied. *C. C. Bealby* **c82 h88**

Woodlands Park 100 Poplar Square Chase, Naas—
Colnel Rayburn still has ground to make up on John James jumping the last, with runner-up Central House a little further back

COLNEL RAYBURN (IRE) 9 b.g. Un Desperado (FR) – Super Boreen (Boreen (FR)) [2004/5 c123+, h–: c16s* c24vpu c17v² c28v³ c20v⁵ c36dpu Apr 9] tall gelding: useful chaser: won Grade 3 Woodlands Park 100 Poplar Square Chase at Naas in November, idling when beating Central House 1½ lengths: ran well when placed at Fairyhouse (Grade 2) and Punchestown (third to What Odds in handicap) in January: lost confidence after short of room and blundered second Becher's when pulled up in Grand National at Aintree: effective at 2m to 3½m: acts well on soft/heavy going: tried in cheekpieces: usually held up: has his quirks. *Paul Nolan, Ireland* — **c136 h–**

COLNE VALLEY AMY 8 b.m. Mizoram (USA) – Panchellita (USA) (Pancho Villa (USA)) [2004/5 h–: 16g 17gpu 20m 22m Jun 27] no form over hurdles. *Mrs S. J. Smith* — **h–**

COLNSIDE BOBBIN 7 b.m. Afzal – Khatti Hawk (Hittite Glory) [2004/5 F16g⁶ F16s Oct 20] tall mare: eighth foal: dam sister to Triumph Hurdle winner Saxon Farm: tailed off in 2 bumpers. *B. G. Powell* — **F–**

COLNSIDE BROOK 6 br.m. Sovereign Water (FR) – Armagnac Messenger (Pony Express) [2004/5 h89p, F85: 22g³ May 7] quite good-topped mare: second in bumper on debut: not knocked about in 3 novice hurdles, never-nearer third of 10 at Wincanton in May: looked capable of better, but wasn't seen out again. *B. G. Powell* — **h82 +**

COLOMBE D'OR 8 gr.g. Petong – Deep Divide (Nashwan (USA)) [2004/5 c20gpu c20gpu c16spu c16m c21gpu Apr 10] no longer of any account: tried blinkered. *C. J. Leech* — **c– h– §**

COLONEL FRANK 8 b.g. Toulon – Fit For Firing (FR) (In Fijar (USA)) [2004/5 c128, h–: c20d² c24d* c25d* c24d* c24sF Feb 26] — **c145 p h–**

The bold-jumping front runner Colonel Frank made rapid progress through the chasing ranks in the latest season before he disappointed in the Racing Post Chase, well held when falling two out. After finishing second to the well handicapped Oneway on his reappearance over an extended two and a half miles at Worcester in October, Colonel Frank was returned to three miles and progressed into a smart chaser, making all to defeat a field of useful handicappers at Sandown on only his fourth start over fences (he had got off the mark in a three-runner maiden chase at Fontwell the previous January, after which he wasn't seen again until Worcester). A facile win at Wincanton followed his win at Sandown, before a most impressive display, on good to soft ground over three miles back at Sandown, where he won quite a valuable intermediate chase from a field including Calling Brave and Lord Sam, albeit receiving 10 lb from those two rivals. Colonel Frank was sent off favourite for the Racing Post Chase at Kempton despite an absence of nearly three months (and missing an intended outing the previous week at Wincanton). Ridden with more restraint than previously, in a race with more competition for the lead, he was unable to make full use of his bold jumping and his performance

williamhill.co.uk Future Stars Chase (Intermediate), Sandown—
Colonel Frank is much more fluent at the last than Calling Brave

is probably best forgiven. Colonel Frank is the first foal of the fair staying chaser Fit For Firing and, by the 1991 St Leger winner Toulon, has plenty of stamina in his pedigree. He will probably stay beyond twenty-five furlongs. Untried on firm ground, he acts on any other, his most effective displays having come on good to soft. Colonel Frank was unable to run after his fall as his off-hind hock became swollen, ruling out a possible Grand National tilt. He is still relatively inexperienced and starts the next campaign off a good handicap mark. The Hennessy could be on the agenda for this likeable sort. *B. G. Powell*

COLONEL MONROE (IRE) 8 b. or br.g. Lord Americo – Fairy Blaze (IRE) (Good Thyne (USA)) [2004/5 c17d^F c16s* c20v^{pu} c20v^3 c18s^4 c21v^3 c24s^3 Mar 26] well-made gelding: fairly useful hurdler in 2002/3: similar form over fences, off 18 months before reappearance: won novice at Gowran in December by neck from Fota Island, pair long way clear: effective at 2m to 3m: acts on heavy going. *E. J. O'Grady, Ireland* **c120 h–**

COLONIAL SUNSET (IRE) 11 b.g. Lancastrian – Thai Nang (Tap On Wood) [2004/5 c–, h–: 21m^4 c20g^5 c19s* c19s^6 c22d^3 c25s^{pu} c18s 16v^3 16d c16v^5 c19v^4 Mar 29] rather sparely-made gelding: poor hurdler: modest chaser: won selling handicap at Chepstow in October: stays 21f: acts on heavy going: tried in blinkers/cheekpieces: has worn tongue strap: inconsistent. *A. J. Whiting* **c88 h64**

COLOPHONY (USA) 5 ch.g. Distant View (USA) – Private Line (USA) (Private Account (USA)) [2004/5 16d^5 16m^3 16g^3 16g^6 Mar 16] close-coupled gelding: fair at 3 yrs on Flat (stays 10.5f) for H. Cecil: poor form over hurdles: likely to prove best around 2m: usually tongue tied. *K. A. Morgan* **h81**

COLORADO FALLS (IRE) 7 b.g. Nashwan (USA) – Ballet Shoes (IRE) (Ela-Mana-Mou) [2004/5 h111: 16g* 16g 16g^3 Jul 1] leggy gelding: fairly useful on Flat (stays 2m): fairly useful handicap hurdler: won conditional jockeys event at Kelso in May: should stay beyond 17f: acts on soft going. *P. Monteith* **h116**

COLORADO PEARL (IRE) 4 br.f. Anshan – Flying Silver (Master Buck) [2004/5 F16d 20d^5 Apr 20] €6,000 3-y-o: rather unfurnished filly: eleventh foal: half-sister to 4 winners, including chaser Gee Aker Malayo (by Phardante), stays 25f: dam, winning 2m hurdler/chaser, half-sister to dam of useful staying chaser Keep Talking: well held in bumper on debut: signs of ability when fifth of 16 in maiden hurdle at Worcester. *Miss G. Browne* **h77 F–**

Andy Peake & David Jackson's "Colourful Life"

COLOURFUL LIFE (IRE) 9 ch.g. Rainbows For Life (CAN) – Rasmara (Kalaglow) [2004/5 c–x, h118: 23m^{ur} 22g c24g* c21v^{3} c26d* c26s^{6} c24d* c24g^{F} c33g^{pu} Apr 16] big, lengthy gelding: fairly useful handicap hurdler: left Mrs M. Reveley after second outing: improved on return to fences, winning handicaps at Bangor in October, Newton Abbot in November and Great Yorkshire Chase (Handicap) at Doncaster in January, useful form when beating Tikram 7 lengths at last-named: showed himself still prone to mistakes in valuable events last 2 outings (bled final one): stays 3¼m: acts on good to firm and heavy going: tried in cheekpieces: usually held up, and tends to carry head awkwardly under pressure: consistent. *P. F. Nicholls* **c137 h114**

COLQUHOUN 11 b.g. Rakaposhi King – Red Rambler (Rymer) [2004/5 c101x, h–: c24m* c26g^{F} Mar 18] good-topped gelding: fair chaser: won hunter at Stratford in May: left D. Pipe, won point in February: stays 3m: acts on good to firm and good to soft going: often let down by jumping (well behind when fell sixteenth in Foxhunter at Cheltenham). *Mrs O. C. Jackson* **c107 x h–**

COLTSCROFT 5 b.g. Teenoso (USA) – Marquesa Juana (Lepanto (GER)) [2004/5 F16d F16d^{3} F16m Apr 2] £6,000 4-y-o: useful-looking gelding: third foal: dam unraced half-sister to fairly useful 2m chaser Auburn Castle: fairly useful form first 2 starts in bumpers: has pulled hard. *J. C. Fox* **F95 +**

COLUMBUS (IRE) 8 b.g. Sadler's Wells (USA) – Northern Script (USA) (Arts And Letters (USA)) [2004/5 h117: 26g* 27g^{5} 24s c24g^{2} c25d^{ur} c24s^{4} c24d^{6} c25m^{pu} Apr 23] angular gelding: fairly useful handicap hurdler: won at Southwell in May: remote second in novice there on chasing debut, let down by jumping and temperament after: stays 27f: acts on firm and soft going: blinkered/visored: usually gets behind/looks none too keen. *Mrs J. Candlish* **c110 § h120 §**

COLWYN JAKE (IRE) 6 b. or br.g. Jolly Jake (NZ) – Maggie's Beauty (IRE) (Seclude (USA)) [2004/5 20v^{pu} 17s 18s^{4} Jan 1] second foal: dam unraced half-sister to **h75 +**

useful chaser around 2½m Multum In Parvo: poor form on third outing over hurdles. *Ian Williams*

COMANCHE WAR PAINT (IRE) 8 b.g. Commanche Run – Galeshula (Strong Gale) [2004/5 c121, h92: c23m^6 c31d^5 24g* c31d^F 24m* 27s Apr 22] useful-looking gelding: has reportedly been pin-fired: fairly useful chaser: finished distressed when fifth in cross-country event at Cheltenham (reportedly subsequently had breathing operation): making ground when falling twenty-seventh in similar event there in March: fair hurdler: won novices at Taunton in March and Cheltenham (handicap, by ½ length from McKelvey) in April: stays 3¾m: probably acts on any going. *P. F. Nicholls* **c121 h110**

COMBAT DRINKER (IRE) 7 b.g. Mandalus – Auburn Park (Sonnen Gold) [2004/5 c23s^{pu} c23d^F 20v 26s^2 20v^6 Jan 22] 14,000 3-y-o: tall, useful-looking gelding: fifth foal: dam unraced: won maiden point on debut in 2004: let down by jumping both starts in chases: modest form over hurdles, claimed from P. Nicholls £10,000 fourth outing: breathing problem final one. *D. McCain* **c– h87**

COMBE FLOREY 6 ch.m. Alflora (IRE) – Celtic Slave (Celtic Cone) [2004/5 21d^5 19d^5 20m^3 Apr 10] sturdy mare: sister to winning hurdler/chaser Alpine Slave, stays 3¼m, and half-sister to smart hurdler/chaser Young Spartacus (by Teenoso), barely stays 25f, and fairly useful hurdler Rakalackey (by Rakaposhi King), stays 21f: dam, fair hurdler/fairly useful chaser, stayed well: pulled up in maiden point on debut: poor form over hurdles: will stay 3m. *H. D. Daly* **h84**

COMBINED VENTURE (IRE) 9 b.h. Dolphin Street (FR) – Centinela (Caerleon (USA)) [2004/5 c69, h–: c17g c16d^6 May 8] sparely-made horse: little form over hurdles or fences: tried tongue tied. *P. T. Dalton* **c– h–**

COME BYE (IRE) 9 b.g. Star Quest – Boreen Dubh (Boreen (FR)) [2004/5 h76, F86: c20m c20g^{pu} 18m^6 18m^6 16g^2 16g^5 17d^3 16g^4 18d^2 20s* 17s* 18s* 20s^4 18g^{pu} Mar 20] medium-sized gelding: no form in 2 chases: fair hurdler: much improved, winning handicaps at Fontwell (novice and intermediate) and Folkestone (in between) in December and January: effective at 2m to 2¾m: acts on soft going: tried visored, usually blinkered: tongue tied: front runner/races prominently. *Miss A. M. Newton-Smith* **c– h105**

COME ON GEORGE (IRE) 9 b.g. Barathea (IRE) – Lacovia (USA) (Majestic Light (USA)) [2004/5 c–x, h–: 24d^{pu} May 12] angular gelding: winning pointer, no form otherwise (sketchy jumper). *S. E. H. Sherwood* **c– x h–**

COMEONSHE 4 ch.f. Commanche Run – Zajira (IRE) (Ela-Mana-Mou) [2004/5 F13d F16s Apr 10] third foal: half-sister to winning 2½m hurdler Arijaz and bumper winner Stagecoachsapphire (both by Teenoso): dam, fair hurdler/chaser, stayed 2½m: well held in bumpers. *J. Howard Johnson* **F–**

COMETE DU LAC (FR) 8 b.m. Comte du Bourg (FR) – Line du Nord (FR) (Esprit du Nord (USA)) [2004/5 c–§, h78§: 16d^{pu} 20d^{pu} c17s^{pu} 17v^{pu} 16s^{pu} 17v^3 16v^{pu} Feb 19] leggy mare: won handicap hurdle in 2003/4: little other form in Britain: stays 21f: acts on any going: usually blinkered/visored: tried tongue tied: best left alone. *Mrs N. Macauley* **c– § h66 §**

COMFORTABLE CALL 7 ch.g. Nashwan (USA) – High Standard (Kris) [2004/5 h75: 20d* 21g* 20d^3 22g^3 20m^{pu} 24d^{pu} 19g 19g 21v^5 Mar 28] lengthy gelding: modest handicap hurdler: won sellers at Wetherby and Sedgefield very early in season: stays 21f: acts on soft and good to firm going: tongue tied. *H. Alexander* **h93**

COMING AGAIN (IRE) 4 b.g. Rainbow Quest (USA) – Hagwah (USA) (Dancing Brave (USA)) [2004/5 16d^5 16d^4 16d^2 17g^5 17g^2 17g Apr 7] sparely-made gelding: fairly useful maiden on Flat (should stay 1½m), sold out of B. Hills's stable 22,000 gns Doncaster October Sales: best effort in juvenile hurdles when second to Dont Call Me Derek at Catterick third outing: suffered overreach final start: raced around 2m on good/good to soft ground: tongue tied. *D. McCain* **h103**

COMMANCHE HERO (IRE) 12 ch.g. Cardinal Flower – Fair Bavard (Le Bavard (FR)) [2004/5 c103, h90: c23m c25g^2 c24m^3 c24g^3 Jun 10] workmanlike gelding: maiden hurdler: modest handicap chaser: stays 3¾m: acts on heavy and good to firm going: temperamental: sold 11,000 gns Doncaster November Sales, won 2-runner point in March. *R. J. Price* **c97 § h– §**

COMMANCHE JIM (IRE) 9 b.g. Commanche Run – On A Dream (Balinger) [2004/5 c113, h–: c24s^{pu} c24g^4 c26d^5 c32d^{bd} c24s^3 c29s^6 c25s^3 c24d^{pu} c24s* c26v^3 Apr 22] sturdy gelding: modest handicap chaser: won at Chepstow in March: should stay beyond 3¼m: acts on heavy going: tried blinkered/visored: races lazily: unreliable. *R. H. Alner* **c96 § h–**

COMMANCHE KATE 5 ch.m. Commanche Run – Spardante (IRE) (Phardante (FR)) [2004/5 F16d Dec 9] smallish, good-bodied mare: first foal: dam unraced: well beaten in bumper on debut. *C. P. Morlock* **F–**

COMMANCHE LAW (IRE) 12 b.g. Commanche Run – Laurenca (Laurence O) [2004/5 c24d* May 11] workmanlike gelding: winning hurdler/pointer: won ladies hunter at Huntingdon in May: stays 3m: acts on heavy going: has been visored/blinkered. *W. T. Reed* **c92 h–**

COMMANCHE SPIRIT (IRE) 11 b.g. Commanche Run – Emmett's Lass (Deep Run) [2004/5 c–: c27vpu Mar 15] lengthy gelding: no form in chases. *Mrs Sue Bell* **c–**

COMMANCHE WIND (IRE) 10 b.g. Commanche Run – Delko (Decent Fellow) [2004/5 h–: 20g3 24f Jun 6] lengthy gelding: winning hurdler, lightly raced nowadays: stays 21f: acts on good to firm and good to soft going. *E. W. Tuer* **h83**

COMMASARRIS 13 gr.g. Joli Wasfi (USA) – Lucy Aura (Free State) [2004/5 c21mpu May 19] fair pointer: maiden chaser: stays 21f: acts on good to firm going: tongue tied. *Mrs G. Drury* **c–**

COMMEMORATION DAY (IRE) 4 b.g. Daylami (IRE) – Bequeath (USA) (Lyphard (USA)) [2004/5 16d 16s2 16d 16d 17d4 25s 16s5 Apr 10] good-topped gelding: modest maiden on Flat (stays 1½m), sold out of J. Given's stable 6,000 gns Doncaster August Sales: easily best effort over hurdles when second in juvenile at Haydock in November: unlikely to stay 3m: blinkered/visored after debut: edgy sort. *M. E. Sowersby* **h93**

COMMERCIAL FLYER (IRE) 6 ch.g. Carroll House – Shabra Princess (Buckskin (FR)) [2004/5 h96: 16d2 16d3 17d* 19g* 24g* 20s* 27s* 20m5 Apr 23] **h143**

It was a pity that publicity for the achievements of the horses, jockeys and trainers on a gripping final day of the season was diluted by media coverage of the remarks of an equine consultant of the RSPCA who claimed it was 'outrageous' that a horse should run three days in a row. The Jockey Club's veterinary director

Enjoy New totesport Betting Shop Today Conditional Jockeys' Handicap Hurdle, Perth—Commercial Flyer does his bit towards a fifteenth trainers' championship for Martin Pipe, completing a five-timer with this second win in less than twenty-four hours

weighed in with an even more unfortunately-timed contribution—considering his now-lengthy tenure of the post—that horses which race over jumps should not appear on consecutive days. The horse at the centre of the controversy, the Martin Pipe-trained Commercial Flyer, was a ridiculous example to choose. In fact, his performances provided compelling evidence against more regulation. The fast improving Commercial Flyer was not only starting his third race in three days in the opening handicap on Betfred Gold Cup day, for which he was sent off co-favourite, but was having his fifth run in twelve days. The only reason he didn't make it five wins in those five outings (and six wins in a row in all) was that he faced a much stiffer task at Sandown, racing off a BHB mark of 141, 21 lb higher than in handicaps (one of them for conditional jockeys) at Perth on the two previous days. Commercial Flyer's winning streak began at Newton Abbot towards the end of March when he won off a lowly mark of 106 on his third run in handicap company, following creditable placed efforts—four months apart—at Warwick and Newbury. When Commercial Flyer finally found his form, there was no stopping him. He followed up his Newton Abbot victory at Exeter, making light of a mark 7 lb higher, and was then a most decisive winner under a penalty at Ayr—giving his owner his hundredth winner of the season, the first owner to achieve the feat over jumps—before going on to record his two victories at Perth. Commercial Flyer's fifth behind Yes Sir in a field of seventeen at Sandown, travelling smoothly into contention and going second two out before eventually being beaten six and a half lengths, represented easily his best form and he may be capable of a little better over hurdles in the next season before being sent over fences.

Commercial Flyer (IRE) (ch.g. 1999)	Carroll House (ch 1985)	Lord Gayle (b 1965)	Sir Gaylord / Sticky Case
		Tuna (ch 1969)	Silver Shark / Vimelette
	Shabra Princess (b or br 1983)	Buckskin (b 1973)	Yelapa / Bete A Bon Dieu
		Random View (b or br 1977)	Random Shot / Rising View

Commercial Flyer, incidentally, was examined by a Jockey Club vet before leaving Perth and again on his arrival at Sandown. The Jockey Club has powers that it can invoke if a horse is considered unfit to run, which made the remarks of its veterinary director even more puzzling. Commercial Flyer was one of ten declarations for the Sandown race from the Pipe stable—engaged in a close tussle with the Nicholls yard for the trainers' title—and three of these were withdrawn on the day, one with a vet's certificate and two withdrawn after Pipe, who thought they were 'not quite right', requested that the Jockey Club vet have a look at them. Another of those that did make the line-up was Sindapour who trailed in last, turned out less than twenty-four hours after a last-flight fall in gruelling conditions at Newton Abbot where he lay winded for some time. If Sindapour's participation had caused as much controversy as Commercial Flyer's, his stable would have had more of a case to answer. If the Jockey Club has to respond to a formal approach by the RSPCA, it is to be hoped that a thorough examination of all the evidence takes place before any rules are changed. The lengthy, angular Commercial Flyer, a half-brother to the smart hurdler/very smart chaser Our Vic (by Old Vic), is clearly tough, as well as very useful. Tongue tied on his last five starts, Commercial Flyer stays twenty-seven furlongs and prior to Sandown had been raced on good going or softer (acts on heavy). He is usually patiently ridden. *M. C. Pipe*

COMMONCHERO (IRE) 8 b.g. Desert of Wind (USA) – Douala (GER) (Pentathlon) [2004/5 c121, h121: c16g^{2} c16m* May 14] sparely-made gelding: fairly useful hurdler: progressive form over fences, won handicap at Cork (beat Ichi Beau 4 lengths) in May: raced around 2m: acts on firm and soft going: successful with or without tongue strap: usually held up. *M. J. P. O'Brien, Ireland* **c135 h–**

COMMON GIRL (IRE) 7 gr.m. Roselier (FR) – Rumups Debut (IRE) (Good Thyne (USA)) [2004/5 F76: 20d^{5} 19v^{4} 21d^{4} 21s^{6} 16g^{2} 16g^{6} 16g^{3} 21g^{4} 21m^{3} Apr 13] lengthy, workmanlike mare: modest novice hurdler on balance: probably flattered when third to Prins Willem at Cheltenham final start: will be suited by 3m: acts on good to firm and heavy going. *O. Brennan* **h92 +**

COMMONWEALTH (IRE) 9 b.g. Common Grounds – Silver Slipper (Indian Ridge) [2004/5 h84: 16s^5 Dec 4] sturdy gelding: winning 2m hurdler, very lightly raced nowadays: usually tongue tied. *Mrs J. Candlish* **h77**

COMPADRE 7 gr.g. Environment Friend – Cardinal Press (Sharrood (USA)) [2004/5 c88, h80: c17s^F c16g^6 c16v^3 c16v^3 c16v^4 20g^5 c16g^2 c16s^2 c16d^3 c17d^3 c16s^5 Apr 22] tall gelding: poor maiden hurdler/chaser: probably best at 2m: unraced on firm going, acts on any other: consistent. *P. Monteith* **c83 h64 +**

COMPLETE OUTSIDER 7 b.g. Opera Ghost – Alice Passthorn (Rapid Pass) [2004/5 h–, F92: 22s^5 17d^2 17d 19s^2 Jan 31] stocky gelding: modest novice hurdler: should stay 2½m: acts on soft going, won bumper on firm: refused to go to start intended second outing. *Nick Williams* **h95**

COMPLY OR DIE (IRE) 6 b.g. Old Vic – Madam Madcap (Furry Glen) [2004/5 h143: c20g* c24g^2 c21d* c24d* c24g^F c24g^2 c33g^{pu} c29g^6 Apr 23] **c148 h–**

Five-times leading owner David Johnson's policy of buying French breds has paid good dividends through such as Cyfor Malta, Lady Cricket, Or Royal, Champleve and Challenger du Luc, but he says he was 'soured' by the flop of the £325,000 purchase in 2001 of Magnus (the most expensive jumper sold at public auction at the time). As he explained in 2004: 'If Martin and A. P. McCoy had their way, we'd still do all of our shopping in France. Martin wants to win today and A.P. wants to win the day before. It was Magnus that put me off France. I paid a fortune for him but he bled the day he got home to Martin's and he kept doing it. He wasn't the only one either.' Johnson has continued to buy French-breds—the leading French four-year-old hurdler Don't Be Shy was acquired for an undisclosed sum in June—but has also turned his attention to buying stores. 'I'm looking for horses to progress to the top and, if you want to go to the top, you need good chasers that have got a bit of size, whatever their pedigree.' Buying stores can also be a frustrating experience. Johnson calls them 'horses with hope' and says that 'for every three or four decent ones, there are about twenty that turn out more suitable for a riding school because they haven't got the speed for anything else.'

When it comes to store horses, Irish dealer Tom Costello has almost certainly sold more top chasers to British owners than anyone else. Arthur Stephenson was his first big customer in Britain—'I sold him fifty horses a year unseen [including Gold Cup winner The Thinker] and he never sent one back'—and the Dickinsons also became major clients, though they did most of their own buying

totescoop6 Rising Stars Novices' Chase, Wincanton—
Comply Or Die leads (from left) First Ballot, Distant Thunder, Ross River and Red Devil Robert

Steel Plate And Sections Novices' Chase, Cheltenham—
a third win over fences and his most impressive display yet

from around the mid-'seventies when son Michael became involved. Graduates of the Costello academy reputedly include the winners of eight Gold Cups, most recently the three won by Best Mate (for the record, Midnight Court, Cool Ground, Cool Dawn and Imperial Call are the others not mentioned so far). Among those Costello has provided for David Johnson are Our Vic, whom Costello was quoted at the time as saying was 'the best horse I have ever sold', and Comply Or Die, who arrived at Pond House as an unraced three-year-old. It is fair to say that neither has yet fulfilled the highest expectations held for them but both are still young, Our Vic only seven and Comply Or Die (named as a result of a competition for the broker clients of the owner's Commercial First Mortgages) only six.

The pair have started favourite for the last two editions of the Royal & SunAlliance Chase, the so-called 'novices' Gold Cup' at the Cheltenham Festival, Our Vic finishing third and Comply Or Die second. Front-running Comply Or Die turned in an excellent round of jumping and stuck on well to go down by three lengths to Trabolgan in a fairly ordinary renewal which attracted only nine runners. Comply Or Die was having his first outing since taking a heavy fall in a Grade 2 novice at Newbury in November, a rare mistake in his first season over fences. Some splendid jumping was the hallmark of his performances in the autumn in which he looked every inch a SunAlliance type. After landing the odds impressively in a maiden chase at Bangor in October, Comply Or Die went down to Ollie Magern, another exciting recruit to chasing, at Cheltenham later the same month, before picking up the winning thread with all-the-way wins at Wincanton (totescoop6 Rising Stars Novices' Chase by a length and a quarter from Distant Thunder) and Cheltenham (Steel Plate And Sections Novices' Chase, by twenty lengths). It is perhaps significant that Comply Or Die had much more use made of him for those wins. Incidentally, the Rising Stars was run for the first time at

Wincanton, as Chepstow no longer wished to stage it. Comply Or Die's efforts after the SunAlliance were very disappointing by comparison. He folded tamely and was pulled up four out, beaten too soon to blame lack of stamina, in the Scottish Grand National on his first start out of novice company, and was again below form when sixth of thirteen finishers, ridden more patiently than usual but still doing best of the seven Johnson-owned and Pipe-trained runners, in the Betfred Gold Cup on the last day of the season.

Despite his last two runs, Comply Or Die may have further improvement in him. Connections still hold him in very high regard and there could well be a good staying handicap in him during the autumn, the valuable three-mile, three-furlong event on Paddy Power Gold Cup day at Cheltenham (a race won twice in the past three years by one of Johnson's French imports Stormez) and the Hennessy Gold Cup at Newbury among those that spring to mind. Whatever his future, Comply Or Die has already shown himself at least as good over fences as he was over hurdles when he proved himself one of the better staying novice hurdlers of the 2003/4 season, winning three times before finishing an excellent fourth in a good renewal of the Royal & SunAlliance Novices' Hurdle at Cheltenham.

Comply Or Die (IRE) (b.g. 1999)	Old Vic (b 1986)	Sadler's Wells (b 1981)	Northern Dancer
			Fairy Bridge
		Cockade (b 1973)	Derring-Do
			Camenae
	Madam Madcap (b 1987)	Furry Glen (b 1971)	Wolver Hollow
			Cleftess
		Quick Miss (b 1974)	Royal Buck
			Lady Flame

The tall, rather unfurnished Comply Or Die is a non-thoroughbred by Kicking King's sire Old Vic. Old Vic's early produce since being switched to breeding purposely for the jumping game are displaying clear signs that he is going to prove a fair influence for stamina. Comply Or Die is the third foal out of the unraced Madam Madcap, whose first foal Paumafi (by Shardari) got off the mark in the latest season, showing modest winning form in handicaps at up to two and a half miles over hurdles in Ireland. Madam Madcap is a half-sister to the dam of the useful two-and-a-half to three-mile chaser Midland Flame. The best horse produced by the family in recent times before Comply Or Die was the smart two-mile hurdler and winning chaser Flame Creek, with whom Comply Or Die shares his third dam, Lady Flame. Lady Flame was a half-sister to the dour staying chaser Fort Knight who was runner-up in the Welsh National and also ran in the 1968 Grand National. Generally speaking, with the exception of Flame Creek, the best members of Comply Or Die's family on the distaff side have been stayers, and Comply Or Die should prove fully effective over further than twenty-five furlongs, his last two runs almost certainly not representative of what he is capable of at longer distances. He is usually ridden for stamina, making the running or racing prominently, which also allows him to exploit his fine jumping to the full. He acts on soft and good to firm going. *M. C. Pipe*

COMPTON AMICA (IRE) 9 gr.m. High Estate – Nephrite (Godswalk (USA)) [2004/5 c23d c20v^F c19g^5 c18s^2 c16s^2 c20s* Feb 16] neat mare: poor handicap hurdler, missed 2003/4: modest form over fences: won handicap at Leicester in February: stays 2½m: acts on heavy going: blinkered fifth outing: reliable. *K. Bishop* **c91 h–**

COMPTON AVIATOR 9 ch.g. First Trump – Rifada (Ela-Mana-Mou) [2004/5 h–: c16d^{pu} 16g^6 Nov 11] sturdy gelding: modest on Flat (stays 1½m): poor form over hurdles: pulled up on chasing debut: tongue tied all 3 outings. *A. W. Carroll* **c– h70**

COMPTON COMMANDER 7 ch.g. Barathea (IRE) – Triode (USA) (Sharpen Up) [2004/5 h87: 24g^{pu} 21m^2 Jul 26] quite good-topped gelding: fairly useful at best but ungenuine on Flat (stays 1¾m): modest maiden hurdler: should stay 3m: yet to race on extremes of going: tried visored: not a straightforward ride. *Ian Williams* **h90**

COMPTON EAGLE 5 b.g. Zafonic (USA) – Gayane (Nureyev (USA)) [2004/5 17g^5 16d^F 17g 17m* Aug 6] modest form on first of 3 starts over 7f on Flat at 3/4 yrs for G. Butler: dropped markedly in class, first form over hurdles when winning selling handicap at Sedgefield: will prove best around 2m with emphasis on speed. *J. J. Lambe, Ireland* **h68**

COMPTON ECLAIRE (IRE) 5 ch.m. Lycius (USA) – Baylands Sunshine (IRE) (Classic Secret (USA)) [2004/5 17d6 16dF Nov 29] fair but ungenuine on Flat (stays 2m), successful at 4 yrs for G. Butler: not fluent in novice on hurdling debut: blinkered, weakening when fell 3 out next time. *B. Ellison* **h–**

COMPTON PRINCESS 5 b.m. Compton Place – Curlew Calling (IRE) (Pennine Walk) [2004/5 16v 17d 16s Dec 5] half-sister to 2½m hurdle winner Trevaisci (by Dilum): poor maiden on Flat (stays 7f), sold out of Mrs A. Duffield's stable 1,400 gns Doncaster October Sales: no show over hurdles. *Miss S. E. Forster* **h–**

COMPTON STAR 5 ch.g. Compton Place – Darakah (Doulab (USA)) [2004/5 17m 16g 16d4 16s 19g 19m2 17v5 17g4 16d5 Apr 17] half-brother to fair 2m to 3m hurdler Bodfari Signet (by King's Signet): little form on Flat: poor maiden hurdler: stays 19f: acts on good to firm going, ran poorly on soft/heavy. *R. J. Hodges* **h76**

COMTE DE CHAMBORD 9 gr.g. Baron Blakeney – Show Rose (Coliseum) [2004/5 c–x, h–: c21dpu 24spu 22s 23spu Mar 22] medium-sized gelding: no form over hurdles or fences (poor jumper): tried in cheekpieces. *Mark Campion* **c– x h–**

CONCERT HOUSE (IRE) 5 b.m. Entrepreneur – Classic Heights (Shirley Heights) [2004/5 F16mpu F16v Dec 31] 19,000F, 8,500Y: angular mare: seventh foal: closely related to 2 winners abroad by Saddlers' Hall and half-sister to winner in Italy by Orpen: dam unraced sister to high-class 1½m performer Head For Heights: no form in 2 bumpers (saddle slipped on debut). *H. J. Collingridge* **F–**

CONCERT PIANIST 10 b.g. Rakaposhi King – Divine Affair (IRE) (The Parson) [2004/5 c25spu 25s c23sF c21s3 c26v2 c26sF 27spu Apr 22] stocky gelding: useful hurdler at one time: off 3 years prior to 2004/5: best effort over fences (jumps less than fluently) when second in novice at Warwick: stays 3¼m: raced on good going or softer (acts on heavy): blinkered final outing (weakened quickly 4 out). *P. Winkworth* **c107 x h–**

CONCHITA 8 b.m. St Ninian – Carnetto (Le Coq d'Or) [2004/5 F95+: 20dF Dec 6] good-topped mare: dual bumper winner: held when falling 2 out in mares novice on hurdling debut. *Miss R. Brewis* **h–**

CONFLUENCE (IRE) 4 gr.c. Linamix (FR) – River Swan (Nashwan (USA)) [2004/5 17v Nov 26] useful on Flat (stays 12.5f), successful in July, sold out of D. Smaga's stable 140,000 gns Newmarket Autumn Sales: favourite, seventh of 13 in juvenile at Bangor on hurdling debut, not knocked about after losing place 3 out: should do better. *Jonjo O'Neill* **h– p**

CONNA CASTLE (IRE) 6 b.g. Germany (USA) – Mrs Hegarty (Decent Fellow) [2004/5 F18m F16m F18s* F19d* Mar 20] €12,500 4-y-o: fourth reported foal: half-brother to one-time fairly useful chaser Lord North (by Mister Lord), stays 2½m: dam, second in bumper, half-sister to useful hurdler/chaser up to 2¾m Abbot of Furness: useful form in bumpers when winning at Thurles (dead-heated with Dr Willie Martin) in February and Limerick (beat Of Course a head) in March, held up each time. *James Joseph Mangan, Ireland* **F110**

CONNAUGHT LADY (IRE) 6 b.m. Flemensfirth (USA) – Finnuala Supreme (IRE) (Supreme Leader) [2004/5 F16m F16g5 Jul 1] first foal: dam, winning Irish pointer, sister to fairly useful hurdler around 2½m Jessica One: poor form on second outing in bumpers: whipped round at start on debut. *Ferdy Murphy* **F66**

CONNEMARA MIST (IRE) 10 ch.g. Good Thyne (USA) – Rainys Run (Deep Run) [2004/5 c22fpu c21d4 c21d4 Mar 24] ex-Irish gelding: poor handicap chaser: successful at Thurles in 2003/4: little other form for long time, left J. J. Walsh after reappearance: stays 3m: acts on soft ground (well beaten on firm): blinkered. *Mrs N. S. Sharpe* **c–**

CONOR'S PRIDE (IRE) 8 ch.g. Phardante (FR) – Surely Madam (Torenaga) [2004/5 c–, h97, F–: 16f Jun 6] winning hurdler: once-raced over fences: stays easy 19f: best form on good to firm/firm going. *B. Mactaggart* **c– h–**

CONROY 6 b.g. Greensmith – Highland Spirit (Scottish Reel) [2004/5 h100, F76: 16d5 16d 16g* 16d 16m* Apr 17] leggy gelding: fair hurdler: won handicaps at Southwell in January and Stratford (novice event) in April: raced around 2m: best efforts on good/good to firm going. *F. Jordan* **h106**

CONSTANTINE 5 gr.g. Linamix (FR) – Speremm (IRE) (Sadler's Wells (USA)) [2004/5 h110: 18d* 16d6 16g 16s 16d 18s2 20s4 18s* Mar 30] good-topped gelding: fair hurdler: won 4-y-o event in May and handicap (blinkered) in March, both at Fontwell: probably stays 2½m: acts on soft going: difficult ride. *G. L. Moore* **h114**

CONTAS (GER) 5 b.h. Lomitas – Cocorna (Night Shift (USA)) [2004/5 16g4 16g 16d 16dpu Apr 3] ex-German horse: half-brother to useful hurdler Cardenas (by Acatenango), **h77**

stays 2½m: successful at 7f (at 2 yrs) and 1¼m on Flat in Germany for P. Rau: poor form over hurdles: has had tongue tied. *M. F. Harris*

CONTINENTAL (IRE) 7 ch.g. Rashar (USA) – Twilight Katie (Stubbs Gazette) [2004/5 F90: 22g⁴ 19g Nov 10] fair form on second of 2 outings in bumpers 17 months apart: folded tamely in 2 novice hurdles. *P. J. Hobbs* **h–**

CONTRABAND 7 b.g. Red Ransom (USA) – Shortfall (Last Tycoon) [2004/5 h138: c16s² c16d² c16d* c16v³ c16g* c16d c16g³ Apr 23] **c150 h–**

Martin Pipe is edging ever closer to Fulke Walwyn's record of forty Cheltenham Festival winners. Pipe's score moved up to thirty-four—clear in second place—with the victories of Contraband and Fontanesi, both owned by David Johnson whose record-breaking season is discussed under Well Chief. The owner/trainer combination of Johnson and Pipe has now won the top two-mile novice chase, the Irish Independent Arkle Challenge Trophy, four times in the last eight runnings, Contraband's success following those of Or Royal, Champleve and Well Chief. While Or Royal and Champleve were imported from France and Well Chief from Germany, Contraband arrived at Pond House through the medium of that longer-established source of potential jumpers, the Newmarket Autumn Sales (Inglis Drever and No Refuge were other winners at the latest Festival bought there). Waiting in the unsaddling enclosure for the outcome of a stewards' inquiry into the Arkle, Pipe recounted the story of how he bought Contraband. A useful if lightly-raced handicapper, who had finished sixth and fifth in successive runnings of the Ebor for Willie Haggas, Contraband was a horse Pipe had had his eye on for a while. Offers to buy the horse privately met with no success, and when Contraband came up at the 2003 Autumn Sales Pipe was attending the premiere of the movie *Seabiscuit*. Pipe made the purchase by phone, buying Contraband through an intermediary for 64,000 guineas ('I'd already offered nearly three times that before the sale!'). As well as the Arkle prize money, Contraband's owner, who freely admits to being a 'big-hitting' punter, is reputed to have made the horse his

Sodexho Prestige Henry VIII Novices' Chase, Sandown—
Contraband gets the better of The Last Cast to claim a first win over fences

Irish Independent Arkle Challenge Trophy Chase, Cheltenham—a mistake at the last by Ashley Brook contributes to a fourth Arkle win for owner and trainer, David Johnson and Martin Pipe

bet of the week. A visit to the cinema can rarely have had such a financially rewarding outcome!

Contraband began his career over jumps with a successful campaign as a novice hurdler in the 2003/4 season, winning four times and going down by a neck to Royal Shakespeare in the Top Novices' Hurdle at Aintree. With the prospect of being handicapped up to the hilt if he remained over hurdles, Contraband looked an interesting proposition for novice chases. A free-going sort on the Flat and a front runner over hurdles, Contraband set off in the same vein over fences. He went down by two lengths to the more experienced River City in a new race at Aintree in October, sticking to his task after going into a clear lead. More patient tactics were adopted after an eight-length defeat when Contraband was readily outpaced by Fundamentalist in the November Novices' Chase at Cheltenham. The Sodexho Prestige Henry VIII Novices' Chase at Sandown in December usually turns out to be a significant pointer and it established Contraband among the season's leading two-mile novice chasers. Ridden more conservatively by Murphy—who had found himself 'jocked off' in favour of McCoy the time before—Contraband had more left after the last than the eventual second and third, The Last Cast and Made In Japan, and drew clear to win by five lengths and the same. A third to My Will and Ashley Brook in the Lightning Chase (switched from Ascot to Uttoxeter because of redevelopment) was a creditable effort on heavy ground, on which Contraband had run below form over hurdles. He was sent off 7/1 second favourite for the Arkle, behind the well-backed Irish challenger War of Attrition, winner of both his starts over fences, with another Irish challenger Watson Lake, who had won three out of three, the only other runner to start at shorter than 10/1. River City, unbeaten in five runs over fences, was at 10/1, My Will, Ned Kelly and Ulaan Baatar 12/1, Mariah Rollins 14/1, Made In Japan 16/1 and Ashley Brook 20/1 in a nineteen-runner field, equalling the line-up in 1987. The same number also went to post in 1982.

Notwithstanding the joint-record field, the latest renewal of the Arkle looked a shade below standard and Contraband managed to find the necessary improvement to continue his stable's excellent record in the race. Patiently ridden again, and still on the bridle after the second last, Contraband touched down in front at the final fence where front-running Ashley Brook pitched on landing and lost some momentum. Contraband crossed Ashley Brook on the run-in—hence the stewards' inquiry—but was always holding him and won by a length. River City finished a further four lengths back in third, with a further length and a half to Watson Lake, a neck in front of the fifth My Will; War of Attrition managed only seventh, a place in front of Made In Japan. With the latest Cheltenham Festival taking place against a background of worries over future Channel 4 television coverage, the station's well-crafted broadcasts were spoiled for some by the continued use of 'instant' post-race interviews of jockeys before they had reached the unsaddling enclosure. It would be fairer to give a jockey a little time to recover from his exertions and gather his thoughts. In any event, shouldn't connections be the first to hear a jockey's comments? So-called 'ambush' interviews usually involve banal questions that rarely enlighten the viewer anyway. 'How important was that last jump?' was the one posed to Murphy on Contraband. Murphy and backers of Contraband were, however, almost certainly reflecting on his mount's leftward manoeuvre early on the run-in and the impending announcement of a stewards' inquiry. After Cheltenham, Contraband could manage only seventh of nine finishers to Ashley Brook, jumping none too fluently, in the Maghull at Aintree, one of several runners from the Pipe stable who were a long way below their best at the meeting. Contraband then gave some indication of how much improvement would be needed to trouble the very best two-milers in 2005/6. One of five Pipe-trained runners in the Celebration Chase at Sandown on the last day of the season, Contraband finished third of nine, beaten four lengths and ten by stable-companion Well Chief and Azertyuiop. That was not far behind the best performance by a novice chaser all season but still suggested that early quotes after the Arkle for the 2006 Champion Chase of 12/1 about Contraband were poor value.

Contraband (b.g. 1998)	Red Ransom (USA) (b 1987)	Roberto (b 1969)	Hail To Reason
			Bramalea
		Arabia (b 1977)	Damascus
			Christmas Wind
	Shortfall (b 1991)	Last Tycoon (b 1983)	Try My Best
			Mill Princess
		Upend (b 1985)	Main Reef
			Gay Charlotte

Mr D. A. Johnson's "Contraband"

The good-topped Contraband is by Red Ransom, sire of numerous good-class winners on the Flat and one of three sons of Roberto—Lear Fan (sire of Arcalis) and Bob Back (sire of Thisthatandtother) being the others—to sire a winner at the Cheltenham Festival. The Pipe stable's other winner Fontanesi was by Sadler's Wells whose sons Old Vic (sire of Kicking King) and In The Wings (sire of Inglis Drever) also enjoyed Festival success. Specialist jumps sires Roselier and Supreme Leader dominated the end-of-season tables, but stallions regarded as essentially Flat sires make an important contribution to jumping nowadays, the mighty Sadler's Wells himself finishing fifth in the earnings table in the latest season, when Old Vic (now switched to jump breeding) and the deceased In The Wings also made the top ten. The Flat-bred Contraband is the first foal of Shortfall, a useful middle-distance performer who later won in the States. Shortfall's next two foals, Parachute (by Hector Protector) and Fall In Line (by Linamix) who won six times in thirteen days on the all-weather in 2004, proved fairly useful on the Flat, winning at up to thirteen furlongs for Sir Mark Prescott. Contraband's grandam Upend won the Galtres Stakes and the St Simon Stakes, both at a mile and a half, and is a half-sister to the dam of Royal Gait, a top-class long-distance horse who won the Prix du Cadran and Prix Royal-Oak before, after a three-year absence from the track, winning the Champion Hurdle as a novice on only his fourth outing over timber. Upend has produced several other winners, though none better than Shortfall. Her sole winner over jumps is Ashnaya, who showed fair form over fences at up to twenty-five furlongs in the latest season. Despite the stamina on the dam's side of his pedigree, Contraband seems likely to be kept at around two miles, for the time being at least. He acts on heavy and good to firm going but seems ideally suited by conditions which place the emphasis on speed, his very best performances coming on good ground. He is effective forcing the pace or held up. *M. C. Pipe*

CONTRACT SCOTLAND (IRE) 10 br.g. Religiously (USA) – Stroked Again (On Your Mark) [2004/5 c23d* c20s³ c22s⁴ c25dpu 22d Apr 11] deep-girthed gelding: modest handicap hurdler: modest chaser: won novice at Wetherby in April 2004: effective at 2½m to 27f: raced mainly on good going or softer. *L. Lungo* **c93 h93**

CON TRICKS 12 b.g. El Conquistador – Dame Nellie (Dominion) [2004/5 c99+, h–: c24dpu c24spu Jan 10] tall gelding: lightly raced: modest chaser: no show both starts in 2004/5: stays 27f: raced on good going or softer (acts on soft). *J. W. Mullins* **c– h–**

CONTROL MAN (IRE) 7 ch.g. Glacial Storm (USA) – Got To Fly (IRE) (Kemal (FR)) [2004/5 h130: c19s* c21d* c24gur c25s* c24s² c28spu c33g³ c25dpu c33gpu Apr 16] angular, sparely-made gelding: useful hurdler: useful novice chaser: won at Chepstow (maiden) and Cheltenham (beat Joes Edge 9 lengths) in December and Exeter in January: ran creditably when second to L'Ami in quite valuable novice at Warwick: poor efforts after, let down by jumping in valuable handicaps sixth and final starts: stays 25f: raced on good going or softer (acts on heavy): usually races prominently: sometimes looks tricky ride (visored nowadays). *M. C. Pipe* **c138 h–**

COOKIES BANK 7 b.g. Broadsword (USA) – Kitty Come Home (Monsanto (FR)) [2004/5 h89: 22spu May 11] little form over hurdles: runner-up in point in April. *Mrs S. D. Williams* **h–**

COOLAMILL (IRE) 13 b.g. Millfontaine – Cheeky Chic (Laurence O) [2004/5 16gpu Dec 18] good-topped gelding: winning hurdler: off 4½ years before only start in 2004/5. *J. J. Quinn* **h–**

COOLAWARRA (IRE) 6 b.g. Accordion – Cool Virtue (IRE) (Zaffaran (USA)) [2004/5 F16g* F17d Apr 9] €28,000 4-y-o: big, good-topped gelding: second foal: dam, bumper winner, out of half-sister to useful chaser up to 25f Arctic Beau: green, won bumper at Catterick on debut by neck from Bayside: well held in Grade 2 at Aintree month later. *D. M. Forster* **F95**

COOLBYTHEPOOL 5 b.g. Bijou d'Inde – Alchi (USA) (Alleged (USA)) [2004/5 h73: 16mpu 17m³ May 23] poor form over hurdles: joined M. Gingell. *Ian Williams* **h82**

COOL CARROLL (IRE) 7 b.m. Carroll House – Sohot Whyknot (IRE) (Macmillion) [2004/5 c27vpu c20d⁶ c21v³ Mar 28] first foal: dam unraced: won mares maiden Irish point in 2004: form in chases only when third in maiden at Sedgefield. *J. Howard Johnson* **c73**

COOL CHILLI 7 gr.g. Gran Alba (USA) – Miss Flossa (FR) (Big John (FR)) [2004/5 c16s^{pu} c16g^{3} c16g* c16g^{3} Mar 28] workmanlike gelding: modest form over fences: won maiden at Catterick in March: raced mainly at 2m on good ground or softer: usually tongue tied nowadays. *N. J. Pomfret* **c87 h–**

COOL CONNIE (IRE) 6 b.m. Commanche Run – Cool Thistle (IRE) (Mandalus) [2004/5 20g^{pu} Jun 10] €3,400 3-y-o: first foal: dam unraced sister to fairly useful 2¾m hurdler Chilled and half-sister to prolific winning pointer/useful hunter chaser Copper Thistle: showed more temperament than ability in mares novice hurdle on debut. *W. K. Goldsworthy* **h–**

COOL COSSACK (IRE) 8 ch.g. Moscow Society (USA) – Knockacool Breeze (Buckskin (FR)) [2004/5 16s 20s^{2} 20s 20v c25d^{2} c25s* c22g^{4} Mar 26] lengthy gelding: modest form over hurdles, off 18 months before reappearance: fair form over fences, winning maiden at Catterick in March: stays 25f: raced on good going or softer (acts on soft). *Mrs S. J. Smith* **c105 h88**

COOL DANTE (IRE) 10 b.g. Phardante (FR) – Mum's Girl (Deep Run) [2004/5 c16m^{F} c16g* 20m c19g^{3} c19s^{pu} Nov 4] ex-Irish gelding: poor hurdler/modest chaser, trained by M. Hourigan before 2004/5: improved effort over fences when winning handicap at Perth in July: stays 2½m: acts on firm ground: has had tongue tied. *T. R. George* **c91 h78**

COOL DESSA BLUES 6 br.m. Cool Jazz – Our Dessa (Derek H) [2004/5 24d^{pu} 27d^{2} 27v^{pu} Dec 31] second foal: dam, lightly-raced maiden hurdler/chaser, half-sister to fairly useful hurdler up to 2½m Brodessa: form over hurdles only when second in novice at Sedgefield, not fluent other starts. *W. Amos* **h72**

COOLDINE KING (IRE) 6 b.g. Germany (USA) – Tara's Serenade (IRE) (Orchestra) [2004/5 h95, F89: c16d^{pu} c19m^{5} 16s^{2} 18s^{3} 20d^{2} 16d^{3} Mar 12] rather leggy gelding: fair novice hurdler: similar form when fifth to El Vaquero at Taunton on completed start in maiden chases: probably stays 21f: acts on soft and good to firm ground: visored last 5 outings. *P. R. Webber* **c103 h103**

COOLE ABBEY (IRE) 13 b.g. Viteric (FR) – Eleanors Joy (Sheer Grit) [2004/5 c24g^{2} c21s^{2} c21s^{4} Apr 7] rangy, good sort: fairly useful hunter chaser: off 2 years, creditable efforts all starts in 2004/5: stays 25f: acts on soft and firm going: sound-jumping front runner. *W. Amos* **c108**

COOLEFIND (IRE) 7 b.g. Phardante (FR) – Greavesfind (The Parson) [2004/5 c24d* May 11] IR £10,000 3-y-o: sixth foal: half-brother to modest hurdler Bali Strong (by Strong Gale): dam unraced, from family of very smart staying chaser Drumadowney: prolific winning pointer: won hunter at Huntingdon in May on chasing debut by 13 lengths from King's Hero: should improve. *W. J. Warner* **c106 p**

COOLE GLEN (IRE) 9 b.g. Executive Perk – Cailin Liath (Peacock (FR)) [2004/5 c20d^{6} c21d^{2} Mar 28] fair pointer, successful in April: better effort in novice hunter chases when second at Fakenham. *W. J. Warner* **c86**

COOLERS QUEST 6 b.m. Saddlers' Hall (IRE) – Lucidity (Vision (USA)) [2004/5 c–, h–: 16f May 18] leggy, workmanlike mare: little sign of ability outside points (successful twice in 2005). *P. C. Ritchens* **c– h–**

COOLE VENTURE (IRE) 11 b.g. Satco (FR) – Mandavard (IRE) (Mandalus) [2004/5 c102: c24g^{2} c24d^{4} c28g^{pu} May 21] winning pointer: fair hunter chaser: stays 3½m: acts on good to soft going: tried blinkered. *Mrs Edward Crow* **c99**

COOLFORE JADE (IRE) 5 ch.m. Mukaddamah (USA) – Cashel Princess (IRE) (Fayruz) [2004/5 16s Nov 28] modest on Flat (stays 13f), successful in February and March for R. Harris: well held in seller on hurdling debut. *N. E. Berry* **h–**

COOLING CASTLE (FR) 9 ch.g. Sanglamore (USA) – Syphaly (USA) (Lyphard (USA)) [2004/5 h80: 17g^{5} 18m^{3} 20g^{3} c16f^{6} 16v^{pu} Oct 16] angular gelding: poor hurdler: jumped poorly on chasing debut: best around 2m: acts on good to firm and good to soft going. *Evan Williams* **c– h80**

COOL MONTY (IRE) 11 ch.g. Montelimar (USA) – Rose Ground (Over The River (FR)) [2004/5 c122, h–: c17d^{3} c20f^{6} c16d c20d* c21s* Jan 6] close-coupled gelding: fairly useful handicap chaser: back in form when winning at Leicester in December and Wincanton in January: stays 21f: acts on soft and good to firm going: best form on right-handed tracks. *A. M. Balding* **c124 h–**

COOLNAHILLA (IRE) 9 gr.g. Roselier (FR) – Reoss (King's Ride) [2004/5 c113, h–: c22g c21d^{6} c19s^{4} c28s^{6} c20d^{ur} c20v^{3} c24v^{3} c22v* c20s^{2} c29s^{5} Mar 28] workmanlike gelding: fairly useful handicap chaser: better than ever in 2004/5, winning at Punches- **c124 h–**

town in February by ½ length from Berkley: ran really well from 5 lb out of weights when fifth to Numbersixvalverde in Irish National at Fairyhouse in March: creditable second to No Half Sessions at Punchestown in late-April: effective at 2½m to 29f: raced on good going or softer (acts on heavy): tried in headgear: consistent. *W. J. Burke, Ireland*

COOLOURKID (IRE) 5 b.g. Zaffaran (USA) – Vintage Classic (IRE) (Orchestra) [2004/5 F18s 21d 19m Apr 9] lengthy gelding: chasing type: first foal: dam, Irish point winner, out of sister to useful chaser up to 25f Good Crack: well held in bumper and over hurdles. *M. Scudamore* **h– F–**

COOL ROXY 8 b.g. Environment Friend – Roxy River (Ardross) [2004/5 h119: 16m 20f[F] 19v[2] 20s[6] 18d* 19d[3] 16g[6] 20d[5] 16v[3] Feb 25] stocky gelding: fairly useful handicap hurdler: won at Fontwell in November, beating Flying Spirit by 3 lengths: stays easy 23f: acts on soft and good to firm going: races prominently: has gained 5 of 6 wins at Fakenham: genuine and reliable. *A. G. Blackmore* **h122**

COOLSAN (IRE) 10 b.g. Insan (USA) – Coolreagh Princess (Raise You Ten) [2004/5 c23g[pu] May 16] well-made gelding: fair hurdler: off 15 months, showed little on chasing debut: stays 25f: raced on good going or softer: tongue tied once. *R. H. Alner* **c– h–**

COOL SONG 9 ch.g. Michelozzo (USA) – Vi's Delight (New Member) [2004/5 c71, h–: c23d c23s[5] Feb 16] strong gelding: maiden hurdler/poor chaser: stays 25f. *Miss I. E. Craig* **c– h–**

COOL SPICE 8 b.m. Karinga Bay – Cool Run (Deep Run) [2004/5 h119: 19g[pu] 21g Apr 14] smallish mare: fairly useful hurdler: ran as if amiss both starts in 2004/5 11 months apart: stays 19f: acts on firm and good to soft going: patiently ridden. *P. J. Hobbs* **h–**

CO OPTIMIST 8 b.g. Homo Sapien – Tapua Taranata (IRE) (Mandalus) [2004/5 27d[5] c20g[3] c23s[5] c19s[3] c24d* c24s[4] c24v[F] Mar 29] good-topped gelding: modest maiden hurdler: similar form over fences: won handicap at Lingfield in February: stayed 3¼m: raced on good going or softer (acted on soft): dead. *N. A. Twiston-Davies* **c96 h96**

COPELAND 10 b.g. Generous (IRE) – Whitehaven (Top Ville) [2004/5 c101p, h144: 16m 16d[6] 16d 16v[5] 16g[5] 16d 20d[2] 17g 16d[4] 16g[4] 16m[5] Apr 22] smallish, sturdy gelding: useful hurdler nowadays: mainly creditable efforts in 2004/5, including when 4 lengths second to Blue Canyon in Grade 2 at Fontwell: stays 2½m, raced mainly over shorter: acts on heavy and good to firm going: usually wears headgear: often races up with pace. *M. C. Pipe* **c– h137**

COPPER COIN (IRE) 11 b.g. Mandalus – Two-Penny Rice (Reformed Character) [2004/5 c20d[5] c25v[pu] c24s[pu] Jan 10] lengthy gelding: winning hurdler/chaser: off nearly 3 years, well held only completed start in 2004/5: lame final outing: should stay beyond 3m: acts on good to firm and good to soft going. *R. N. Bevis* **c100 h–**

COPPERMALT (USA) 7 b.g. Affirmed (USA) – Poppy Carew (IRE) (Danehill (USA)) [2004/5 16g 16f 16m 16g[4] 16v[3] 16g 16d 16g c16g[4] c20d[5] Apr 18] leggy gelding: poor maiden hurdler: mistakes both starts over fences: raced mainly at 2m: acts on firm going. *R. Curtis* **c63 x h68**

COPPER SHELL 11 ch.g. Beveled (USA) – Luly My Love (Hello Gorgeous (USA)) [2004/5 c75x, h–: c25g[3] c25d[3] c26v[4] c25s c24d[pu] Apr 22] leggy, plain gelding: poor handicap chaser: stays 25f: acts on heavy going: wears headgear: tongue tied: sketchy jumper. *Miss A. M. Newton-Smith* **c73 x h–**

COPPLESTONE (IRE) 9 b.g. Second Set (IRE) – Queen of The Brush (Averof) [2004/5 h94: 22m[3] 20g[2] 22s[pu] 21d 16g 21v[6] 19d 24g 20g Feb 27] compact gelding: modest handicap hurdler: lost form after second outing: stays 2¾m: acts on heavy and good to firm going: usually wears cheekpieces (visored final start): unreliable. *W. Storey* **h85 §**

COPSALE LAD 8 ch.g. Karinga Bay – Squeaky Cottage (True Song) [2004/5 h120+: c19g[ur] c20d[2] c20s[4] c21g[bd] c20d[3] Apr 9] strong, lengthy gelding: fairly useful hurdler: similar form over fences: good effort when 3 lengths third to Joes Edge in amateur handicap at Aintree: travelling well behind leaders when brought down 4 out in valuable handicap won by King Harald at Cheltenham: will stay 3m: acts on soft and good to firm going: room for improvement in jumping. *N. J. Henderson* **c126 + h–**

COPYBOOK 6 b.g. Danehill (USA) – Easy To Copy (USA) (Affirmed (USA)) [2004/5 16d[pu] Jun 1] modest maiden on Flat for H. Cecil in 2002: poor form in points in 2004: little show in maiden on hurdling debut. *J. B. Walton* **h–**

COPYERSELFON (IRE) 6 b. or br.g. Right Win (IRE) – Cedarbelle (IRE) (Regular Guy) [2004/5 F16d F17d 17d[pu] 19v[pu] Feb 13] tall gelding: second foal: dam winning **h– F–**

pointer: no show in bumpers (for J. Jenkins) or novice hurdles: blinkered final start. *P. Wegmann*

CORALBROOK 5 b.g. Alderbrook – Coral Delight (Idiot's Delight) [2004/5 F–: F16d 16g^4 19d^5 21d Mar 4] tall gelding: well held in 2 bumpers: modest form at best in novice hurdles: should stay beyond 2m. *Mrs P. Robeson* **h88** **F–**

CORAL ISLAND 11 b.g. Charmer – Misowni (Niniski (USA)) [2004/5 c–, h–: c20d^4 c17g^4 c18g^5 c20s^4 c26g^5 Mar 14] useful-looking gelding: winning hurdler/chaser: little form since 2002/3: stays 2¾m: acts on firm and soft going: tried blinkered earlier in career. *R. M. Stronge* **c–** **h–**

CORALS LAUREL (IRE) 6 b.g. Accordion – Bold Tipperary (IRE) (Orchestra) [2004/5 F16v* F16s^5 Jan 15] €50,000 3-y-o, €52,000 4-y-o: lengthy, unfurnished gelding: first foal: dam fair hurdler, stayed 2½m: better effort in bumpers when winning at Warwick in December by 4 lengths from Down's Folly. *R. T. Phillips* **F98**

CORAZONADO (FR) 5 b.g. Pistolet Bleu (IRE) – Heleda (FR) (Zino) [2004/5 F–: F18g May 9] well held in 2 bumpers. *R. H. York* **F–**

CORBIE ABBEY (IRE) 10 b.g. Glacial Storm (USA) – Dromoland Lady (Pollerton) [2004/5 c17d^2 c16d^3 Jun 30] rangy gelding: poor maiden hurdler/chaser: best efforts at 2m: acts on good to firm and good to soft going. *B. Mactaggart* **c66** **h–**

CORDILLA (IRE) 7 b.g. Accordion – Tumble Heather (Tumble Wind) [2004/5 h104+: c20s^{ur} c19v^{pu} c20v* c25s^F c24v^2 c25g^{pu} Apr 16] big gelding: fair hurdler: won maiden at Ayr in January, but generally let down by jumping over fences: running best race when falling 4 out in handicap at same course: should stay 25f: raced mainly on soft/heavy going: has shown high head carriage. *N. G. Richards* **c116 x** **h–**

CORE OF SILVER (IRE) 6 b.g. Nucleon (USA) – My Silversmith (IRE) (Cyrano de Bergerac) [2004/5 h64, F–: 16m c16d^5 c17g Jul 15] big gelding: little form. *P. Monteith* **c–** **h–**

CORK HARBOUR (FR) 9 ch.g. Grand Lodge (USA) – Irish Sea (Irish River (FR)) [2004/5 h90: 16g 17g^4 18m^5 Sep 21] poor hurdler: raced mainly around 2m: acts on good to firm going: blinkered. *P. Bowen* **h75**

CORLANDE (IRE) 5 br.g. Teamster – Vaguely Deesse (USA) (Vaguely Noble) [2004/5 16d 21s* 20s^2 20g Mar 26] lengthy ex-Irish gelding: type to make a chaser: half-brother to 2m hurdle winner Bang In Trouble (by Glenstal) and fair chaser up to 3m New Era (by Distinctly North): dam ran once: fair form in bumpers in 2003/4 for P. Rothwell: fair novice hurdler: won at Sedgefield in February: best effort when second to Thames at Haydock: stays 21f: acts on soft going. *Mrs S. J. Smith* **h112**

CORN GENERAL 9 br.g. Governor General – Corncrop (Mycropolis) [2004/5 c20s^{pu} Mar 31] of no account: blinkered and tongue tied in hunter. *Mrs B. Brown* **c–**

CORNISH GALE (IRE) 11 br.g. Strong Gale – Seanaphobal Lady (Kambalda) [2004/5 c–, h102: c19g* Apr 19] well-made gelding: winning hurdler: left P. Nicholls, successful in point in March and hunter at Towcester (beating Longstone Boy 7 lengths) in April: stays 2¾m: best efforts on good/good to firm going: has had tongue tied: of suspect temperament. *D. McCain Jnr* **c104** **h–**

CORNISH GOLD 4 b.f. Slip Anchor – Sans Diablo (IRE) (Mac's Imp (USA)) [2004/5 16d^{pu} Dec 13] maiden on Flat, poor form for I. Wood and D. Thompson in 2005: no show in juvenile on hurdling debut. *N. J. Henderson* **h–**

CORNISH ORCHID (IRE) 4 ch.g. Be My Guest (USA) – Nilousha (Darshaan) [2004/5 16f 16g Nov 10] 11,000 3-y-o: fourth foal: half-brother to bumper winner Makeabreak (by Anshan): dam won 2m hurdle and at 1¾m on Flat: well held in juvenile hurdles (troublesome in preliminaries on debut). *C. J. Down* **h–**

CORNISH REBEL (IRE) 8 br.g. Un Desperado (FR) – Katday (FR) (Miller's Mate) [2004/5 h148: c20g* c24g* c25d* c21s^3 c24g^3 c33g^2 Apr 16] **c146** **h–**

Ruby Walsh disproved the old saying that jockeys are the worst judges when almost completing a unique grand slam of the Welsh National, the Irish National, the Grand National and the Scottish National. The horses who gave him his first three victories, Silver Birch, Numbersixvalverde and Hedgehunter, came from three different stables, Silver Birch one of three saddled at Chepstow by Paul Nicholls, the Martin Brassil-trained Numbersixvalverde selected in preference to several other mounts in the Irish National offered to Walsh, and Hedgehunter trained by Willie Mullins with Walsh presumably also having the pick of some

cantorsport.co.uk Worcester Novices' Chase, Newbury—deputising jockey Tony McCoy delays his challenge on the quirky Cornish Rebel (noseband) to defeat Distant Thunder

of the four Nicholls-trained National runners, among others. Best Mate's younger brother, the Nicholls-trained novice Cornish Rebel was entrusted with making history for Walsh in the Scottish Grand National at Ayr in April. The race looked within Cornish Rebel's grasp after the patient Walsh moved him up steadily on the final circuit and reached a challenging position two out. Cornish Rebel didn't have much room at that point but was produced with apparently perfect timing to lead on the flat, only to idle and allow fellow novice Joes Edge, who had jumped into the lead at the second last, to fight back and snatch the race in the very last stride. The Channel 4 commentator detailed to 'ambush' Walsh on the way in and pose the inevitable 'How do you feel?' received an understandably terse response. 'The winner's over there!' said Walsh as the microphone was thrust under his nose. The look on Walsh's face told its only story, as did that on the face of trainer Nicholls to

Ian Williams' Owners Novices' Chase, Cheltenham—
Ruby Walsh is back to do the coaxing for his hat-trick win

whom the short-head defeat made a difference of £43,448 in a very close battle with Martin Pipe for the trainers' championship, a contest which wasn't resolved in Pipe's favour until the final day of the season.

Walsh's post-mortem—'He just pricked his ears and struggled to hang on in the last hundred yards'—was kind on the quirky Cornish Rebel who has plenty of ability but is of suspect temperament. He made up into a smart novice hurdler in 2003/4 when he gained a Grade 1 win in the Challow Hurdle, but seemed to down tools when tailed-off last in the Sefton Novices' Hurdle at Aintree on his final start. Cornish Rebel won his first three starts over fences, all before the turn of the year—a maiden chase at Lingfield, the cantorsport.co.uk-sponsored Worcester Novices' Chase at Newbury and a novice event at Cheltenham—but he carried his head high and threatened to refuse at the last two at Lingfield, then needed a few sharp reminders after wandering on the run-in at Newbury and again idled in front at Cheltenham. Cornish Rebel didn't win again but put up smart performances when third, under top weight of 11-12, in the Timeform Novices' Handicap Chase at Cheltenham at the end of January and when filling the same position, beaten three lengths and the same by Trabolgan and Comply Or Die, in the Royal & SunAlliance Chase at the Festival meeting. Cornish Rebel ran a little in snatches and found less than expected when beaten five lengths and a neck by Lacdoudal and Joes Edge in the first-named event, but he stuck on pretty well after being the first of the SunAlliance principals to come under pressure. Cornish Rebel had no problem getting the trip in the Scottish National and would be an interesting contender if trained for Aintree in the next season. He has been raced only on good going or softer (acts on soft) and does best patiently ridden.

Cornish Rebel (IRE) (br.g. 1997)	Un Desperado (FR) (b 1983)	Top Ville (b 1976)	High Top
			Sega Ville
		White Lightning (gr 1970)	Baldric II
			Rough Sea
	Katday (FR) (br 1987)	Miller's Mate (b 1982)	Mill Reef
			Primatie
		Kanara (b 1973)	Hauban
			Alika

The rangy, good-topped Cornish Rebel is Katday's third foal—Best Mate was her first and the useful but temperamental handicap chaser Inca Trail (also by Un Desperado) her second—and her fourth and fifth foals are also winners, though the better of them Inexorable (by Roselier), a useful novice hurdler in 2003/4, fell fatally on his debut over fences in the latest season. An expanded account of the family was given in the essay on Cornish Rebel in last year's Annual. As for Ruby Walsh, he landed one other National in 2004/5, apart from the three mentioned, riding Banasan to victory in the Kerry version at Listowel. He finished third in two Midlands Nationals, on Howdydoody at Uttoxeter and Thari at Kilbeggan, and failed to complete in the Summer National at Uttoxeter and the Cork National at, well, Cork. Walsh's failure to acquire a ride in the Borders, Devon, Durham, Highland, Munster, Southern, Sussex or Ulster versions suggests four wins just scratches the surface. He couldn't do much about the Lincolnshire and North Yorkshire being abandoned. *P. F. Nicholls*

CORNISH SETT (IRE) 6 b.g. Accordion – Hue 'n' Cry (IRE) (Denel (FR)) [2004/5 F17g^{ur} F16g* 16d^{2} 16s* 17d* 20d^{4} 16g* Apr 15] €58,000 3-y-o, 40,000 4-y-o: rather unfurnished gelding: fifth foal: half-brother to fairly useful chaser Major Sponsor (by Strong Gale), stays 21f, and fair chaser Scarborough Fair (by Synefos), stays 25f: dam unraced half-sister to Rhyme 'N' Reason out of half-sister to Hallo Dandy: successful at Ludlow on completed start in bumpers in May: fairly useful form over hurdles: won maiden at Chepstow in December, 20-runner novice handicap at Cheltenham (beat Dom d'Orgeval 2½ lengths) in January and novice at Ayr (beat Coat of Honour by 1½ lengths in falsely-run 4-runner event) in April: stays 2½m: raced on good ground or softer. *P. F. Nicholls* **h127 F101**

CORONADO FOREST (USA) 6 b.g. Spinning World (USA) – Desert Jewel (USA) (Caerleon (USA)) [2004/5 16g^{pu} May 21] fair on Flat (stays 1¼m) at best, poor nowadays: bled from nose on hurdling debut. *M. R. Hoad* **h–**

CORPORATE EXPRESS (IRE) 5 b.g. Sri Pekan (USA) – Sandy Fitzgerald (IRE) (Law Society (USA)) [2004/5 18m* 16f* 16m 16d^{4} Aug 16] dam half-sister to fairly **h110**

useful 2m hurdler Creux Noir: 1¾m winner at 3 yrs on Flat, well held in 2004: fair form over hurdles: won maiden at Downpatrick and 4-y-o minor event at Limerick in May: raced around 2m: yet to race on soft/heavy going, acts on any other. *M. Halford, Ireland*

CORPORATE PLAYER (IRE) 7 b.g. Zaffaran (USA) – Khazna (Stanford) [2004/5 h100: c16g4 c18d Dec 29] rangy, useful-looking gelding: fair hurdler: not fluent when well-held fourth of 6 to Made In Japan in novice at Kempton on chasing debut: always behind in similar event at Newbury next time: should stay beyond 2m: tongue tied 4 of 6 starts. *Noel T. Chance* **c100 ? h–**

CORRECT AND RIGHT (IRE) 6 b.m. Great Commotion (USA) – Miss Hawkins (Modern Dancer) [2004/5 16f* 16m2 20mF 20g c16g* c21g2 c21gpu c21dpu c17f3 24g c25d2 c19g Apr 15] angular mare: modest handicap hurdler: off 13 months, won conditional jockeys mares event at Towcester in May: similar form over fences, winning maiden at Newton Abbot in July: best form up to 21f: acts on firm and soft going: usually wears cheekpieces. *J. W. Mullins* **c94 h90**

CORRIB DRIFT (USA) 5 ch.g. Sandpit (BRZ) – Bygones (USA) (Lyphard (USA)) [2004/5 F16f F18m3 F18g aF16g3 Feb 19] eleventh foal: half-brother to fair sprinter Elapse (by Sharpen Up) and several winners in North America: dam, won up to 9f in USA, half-sister to useful 1986 2-y-o 6f and 7f winner At Risk: left T. Walsh and off 6 months, best effort in bumpers when third to Royal Stardust on polytrack at Lingfield, dictating pace. *Jamie Poulton* **F91**

CORRIB LAD (IRE) 7 b.g. Supreme Leader – Nun So Game (The Parson) [2004/5 h–: 20v5 20s5 17s* 24s3 Mar 11] well-made gelding: chasing type: modest handicap hurdler: well backed, confirmed promise of previous start when winning at Carlisle in February: may prove best short of 3m when conditions are testing: raced on good going or softer: may do better yet. *L. Lungo* **h92**

CORRIGEENROE (IRE) 5 b.g. Revoque (IRE) – Amenity (FR) (Luthier) [2004/5 F16v* Dec 26] half-brother to several winners, including useful jumpers Boarding School (by Glenstal), stayed 25f, and Clifton Beat (by Danzatore), stayed 2½m: dam, fair 10.4f winner, half-sister to smart middle-distance colt Art Bleu: won 23-runner bumper at Leopardstown on debut by 9 lengths from Patsy Hall, going clear straight despite hanging right: useful prospect. *N. Meade, Ireland* **F106 p**

CORTON (IRE) 6 gr.g. Definite Article – Limpopo (Green Desert (USA)) [2004/5 21g 20d4 Apr 20] good-topped gelding: fairly useful on Flat (stays 2m) for P. Cole, tailed off last 2 starts in 2004: modest form in maiden hurdles: may still do better. *Jonjo O'Neill* **h92 +**

COSI CELESTE (FR) 8 b.g. Apeldoorn (FR) – Lemixikoa (FR) (Mendez (FR)) [2004/5 h83?: 24d4 21g 25s4 23g2 26g Mar 16] good-topped gelding: failed to complete in 2 points in 2003: modest maiden hurdler: stays 3m: raced on good going or softer. *John Allen* **h85**

COSI FAN TUTTE 7 b.g. Inchinor – Bumpkin (Free State) [2004/5 19d3 16m Aug 30] medium-sized gelding: fair on Flat (stays 1½m) in 2004, pulled up lame in December: modest form first 2 starts over hurdles nearly 2 years apart, mistakes both times: visored: tongue tied in 2004/5. *M. C. Pipe* **h85**

COSMIC CASE 10 b.m. Casteddu – La Fontainova (IRE) (Lafontaine (USA)) [2004/5 h110: 20d3 16g3 16m4 16d5 18v4 20m4 17g 24d5 24g* Jan 21] angular mare: modest at 1½m to 1¾m on Flat: modest handicap hurdler: reportedly retired after winning race named in her honour at Musselburgh in January: stayed 2½m: acted on good to firm and heavy going: tried visored: held up: tough. *J. S. Goldie* **h95**

COSMIC RANGER 7 b.g. Magic Ring (IRE) – Lismore (Relkino) [2004/5 c–, h56: 16d4 17g 20dpu Jun 20] workmanlike gelding: bad maiden hurdler: little form over fences: raced mainly around 2m: acts on good to firm and heavy going: tongue tied last 2 outings, also blinkered on second occasion. *H. Alexander* **c– h–**

COSMOCRAT 7 b.g. Cosmonaut – Bella Coola (Northern State (USA)) [2004/5 h98: c16s3 c19spu c16v3 c16d* c16d5 c16sF c16d4 Mar 26] rangy gelding: modest handicap hurdler: fair chaser: won novice at Ludlow in January: raced mainly around 2m: acts on heavy going. *R. Lee* **c108 h–**

COSSACK DANCER (IRE) 7 b.g. Moscow Society (USA) – Merry Lesa (Dalesa) [2004/5 F99: 16g* 17d2 16s4 Dec 17] third in bumper: good start over hurdles, winning novice at Ludlow in November and second to Countess Point in similar event at Newton Abbot: didn't set so strong a pace when last of 4 to Marcel in Grade 2 novice at Windsor: likely to prove best around 2m for time being: wore cheekpieces in 2004/5: hasn't looked straightforward ride. *M. Bradstock* **h114**

COSTA DEL SOL (IRE) 4 ch.g. General Monash (USA) – L'Harmonie (USA) (Bering) [2004/5 16gpu Dec 8] lengthy gelding: poor and ungenuine maiden on Flat (stays easy 1m), sold out of J. Bridger's stable £2,400 Ascot October Sales: no potential over hurdles. *Miss Victoria Roberts* **h–**

COTSWOLD ROSE 5 b.m. Sovereign Water (FR) – Rosehall (Ardross) [2004/5 F17g3 F16s aF16g Feb 19] first foal: dam, poor hurdler who stayed 21f, out of useful hurdler up to 21f Coral Delight: modest form at best in bumpers. *N. M. Babbage* **F76**

COTTAGE HILL 6 b.m. Primitive Rising (USA) – Celtic Lane (Welsh Captain) [2004/5 h–, F–: c21vbd c20dpu c25spu Mar 1] lengthy mare: no form in varied events. *C. R. Wilson* **c– h–**

COTTAM GRANGE 5 b.g. River Falls – Karminski (Pitskelly) [2004/5 h91: 23s6 17v3 17d3 24v2 20sF 23v2 24v 16g4 22g2 22m* Apr 23] medium-sized gelding: fair hurdler: several good placed efforts prior to winning handicap at Market Rasen in April: effective around 2m (given test) to 3m: acts on good to firm and heavy going. *M. W. Easterby* **h107**

COTTAM KARMINSKI 4 b.f. River Falls – Karminski (Pitskelly) [2004/5 17m 17g Aug 21] little sign of ability on Flat or over hurdles. *J. S. Wainwright* **h–**

COTTY'S ROCK (IRE) 6 ch.g. Beneficial – Its Good Ere (Import) [2004/5 F–: 17d* 20spu 19d Feb 4] good-topped gelding: won novice at Sedgefield in November on hurdling debut, only form: races freely: joined P. Roche in Ireland. *J. Howard Johnson* **h92**

COULD BE ALRIGHT (IRE) 6 b.g. Witness Box (USA) – Some Gossip (Le Bavard (FR)) [2004/5 F16v2 Mar 29] €14,000 4-y-o: seventh foal: half-brother to winning pointer by Mandalus: dam unraced, from family of good chasers Golden Freeze and Sparky Gayle: neck second to Royal Coburg in bumper at Chepstow on debut, clear of remainder: staying type. *Noel T. Chance* **F99**

COULD BE CLASS 6 b.m. Gildoran – Olympic Rose (IRE) (Roselier (FR)) [2004/5 F–: F18s 21vpu Jan 17] no form in bumpers or novice hurdle. *A. Ennis* **h– F–**

COULDN'T BE PHAR (IRE) 8 ch.g. Phardante (FR) – Queenford Belle (Celtic Cone) [2004/5 h76?: 21gpu 19g6 22d2 24s5 c24dF 26spu 27m3 Apr 21] medium-sized gelding: poor maiden hurdler: fell eighth on chasing debut: probably stays 27f: blinkered/visored after reappearance. *D. R. Gandolfo* **c– h82**

COUNSEL 10 ch.g. Most Welcome – My Polished Corner (IRE) (Tate Gallery (USA)) [2004/5 h–: 26m 24s2 22d6 Nov 2] smallish gelding: winning pointer: poor hurdler: stays 3m: acts on soft and good to firm going: wore cheekpieces last 2 starts. *J. C. Tuck* **h78**

COUNTBACK (FR) 6 b.g. Anabaa (USA) – Count Me Out (FR) (Kaldoun (FR)) [2004/5 h66, F–: 16m3 17d3 16s2 20s3 19vpu 20d2 c20mpu Apr 10] sturdy gelding: modest maiden on Flat: poor maiden hurdler: showed nothing on chasing debut: stays 2½m: acts on soft and good to firm going: tried blinkered, wears cheekpieces nowadays. *C. C. Bealby* **c– h75**

COUNT CAMPIONI (IRE) 11 br.g. Brush Aside (USA) – Emerald Flair (Flair Path) [2004/5 c110, h122: c24d5 c25d2 c29v Dec 28] lengthy gelding: winning hurdler: fair handicap chaser: stays 3¼m: acts on heavy and good to firm going: tried blinkered/visored. *M. Pitman* **c105 h–**

COUNT DRACULA 4 b.g. Dracula (AUS) – Chipaya (Northern Prospect (USA)) [2004/5 16m Sep 4] rather leggy gelding: fair on Flat (stays 1m), sold out of A. Balding's stable 5,500 gns Newmarket July Sales: blinkered, well beaten in juvenile on hurdling debut. *Jean-Rene Auvray* **h–**

COUNTESS POINT 7 ch.m. Karinga Bay – Rempstone (Coronash) [2004/5 F101: 17d2 17d* 21dF Dec 29] tall mare: bumper winner: second start over hurdles, won novice at Newton Abbot in November: bled from nose next time: should be suited by further than 17f. *C. L. Tizzard* **h101**

COUNT FOSCO 7 b.g. Alflora (IRE) – Carrikins (Buckskin (FR)) [2004/5 h85, F83: 16m 20dpu 20s4 17g 20d* 20m* 24g6 Mar 5] fair hurdler: sold out of T. Fitzgerald's stable 15,000 gns Doncaster May Sales after second start: won handicaps at Musselburgh in January (novice) and February: should stay 3m: acts on soft and good to firm going. *M. Todhunter* **h104**

COUNT OSKI 9 b.g. Petoski – Sea Countess (Ercolano (USA)) [2004/5 c93, h–: c25g6 Apr 26] tall gelding: modest chaser, lightly raced nowadays: should stay beyond 3m: best efforts on good/good to soft ground: blinkered once. *M. J. Ryan* **c– h–**

COUNTRYWIDE STAR (IRE) 7 ch.g. Common Grounds – Silver Slipper (Indian Ridge) [2004/5 h–: c16m^{pu} c16m^{pu} c16s^{4} c16g^{F} c16s^{pu} c16g^{5} 16d c19g c18g^{ur} 16d c20m Apr 10] sturdy gelding: little form: tried visored: has had tongue tied. *C. N. Kellett* **c– h–**

COUNT THE COST (IRE) 6 ch.g. Old Vic – Roseaustin (IRE) (Roselier (FR)) [2004/5 h87: 17v 20d^{5} 27v^{3} 27v^{2} 25s^{3} 27d* Apr 5] workmanlike gelding: likely to make a chaser: progressive hurdler: won handicap at Sedgefield in April: suited by good test of stamina: raced on good going or softer: wore cheekpieces last 3 starts: reliable. *J. Wade* **h104**

COUNT TONY 11 ch.g. Keen – Turtle Dove (Gyr (USA)) [2004/5 c–, h118: 22s^{4} 24s^{4} 24d 21d 19g Apr 12] close-coupled gelding: fairly useful handicap hurdler: below form last 3 outings after 3-month absence: stays 3m: acts on any going: blinkered (ran poorly) once, wears cheekpieces nowadays. *Mrs D. A. Hamer* **c– h116**

COUNT WALEWSKI 5 b.g. Polish Precedent (USA) – Classic Beauty (IRE) (Fairy King (USA)) [2004/5 16g 16m Jun 13] fair on Flat (stays 1m) at 3 yrs for J. Dunlop, well beaten both starts in 2004: no show in novice hurdles at Stratford. *S. Dow* **h–**

COUNTY CLASSIC 6 b.m. Noble Patriarch – Cumbrian Rhapsody (Sharrood (USA)) [2004/5 h91, F91: 16d^{2} 17d* 20d^{6} 20s^{4} 21v^{3} 21v^{3} 19d^{3} 22s^{2} Mar 6] leggy mare: modest hurdler: won mares maiden at Sedgefield in November: probably stays 2¾m: acts on heavy going: consistent. *T. D. Easterby* **h98**

COUNTY DERRY 12 b.g. Derrylin – Colonial Princess (Roscoe Blake) [2004/5 c125: c33s* c34d^{2} c26d^{3} c26g Mar 18] strong gelding: smart hunter chaser at best: won at Cheltenham very early in season: won twice in points in 2005 prior to well held in Foxhunter at Cheltenham: suited by 3m+: has won on good to firm going, probably suited by more testing conditions (acts on heavy): usually wears cheekpieces nowadays: sometimes makes mistakes. *J. Scott* **c116**

COUNTY FINAL (IRE) 6 b.g. Norwich – Soul Lucy (Lucifer (USA)) [2004/5 F16s^{2} F16v^{4} Dec 28] €25,000 3-y-o: useful-looking gelding: half-brother to several winners, including useful hurdler/chaser up to 3m The Carrig Rua and useful but temperamental staying chaser Sister Stephanie (both by Phardante): dam winning 2m hurdler: easily better effort in bumpers when ¾-length second to Travino, well clear of remainder, at Naas on debut: hung left next time: tongue tied. *N. Meade, Ireland* **F113**

COURAGEOUS DOVE 4 gr.g. Overbury (IRE) – Mazzelmo (Thethingaboutitis (USA)) [2004/5 F16s^{4} F17d^{6} F17g^{6} Mar 19] leggy gelding: first foal: dam, fair hurdler, won up to 2¼m on Flat: poor form in bumpers. *A. Bailey* **F71**

COURAGE UNDER FIRE 10 b.g. Risk Me (FR) – Dreamtime Quest (Blakeney) [2004/5 c109, h–: c25s^{pu} c22d* c23s^{pu} c22s^{3} 23d^{5} Mar 28] good-topped gelding: maiden hurdler: fair handicap chaser: successful at Market Rasen (has won 3 of 6 outings over fences there) in February: stays 3¼m: raced on good going or softer (acts on heavy): usually blinkered, in cheekpieces final start: usually races prominently. *C. C. Bealby* **c105 h–**

COURANT D'AIR (IRE) 4 b.g. Indian Rocket – Red River Rose (IRE) (Red Sunset) [2004/5 17g^{6} 17d^{5} 17g* 16g^{3} 17s* 16d^{4} 16d 17g 17g 16s 16m Apr 17] small gelding: poor 7f winner on Flat: fair juvenile hurdler: won claimer (claimed from P. Haslam £5,000) at Taunton in October and handicap at Market Rasen in November: well held last 5 starts (twice out of depth): likely to prove best around 2m: acts on soft going: often races prominently: has found little. *Mrs Lucinda Featherstone* **h105**

COURSING RUN (IRE) 9 ch.g. Glacial Storm (USA) – Let The Hare Run (IRE) (Tale Quale) [2004/5 c119, h–: c24v^{4} c24d^{pu} c24v^{2} c30s^{6} c29s* Mar 13] smallish, angular gelding: fairly useful handicap chaser: won at Warwick in March: stays 29f: raced only on going softer than good (acts on heavy): visored once (badly let down by jumping): inconsistent. *H. D. Daly* **c121 § h–**

COURT ALERT 10 b.g. Petoski – Banbury Cake (Seaepic (USA)) [2004/5 c24m^{5} Jun 13] winning pointer: no form otherwise: tried blinkered. *Lady Connell* **c– h–**

COURT AWARD (IRE) 8 b.g. Montelimar (USA) – Derring Lass (Derring Rose) [2004/5 21d^{6} 21d Dec 13] IR 22,000 3-y-o: seventh foal: brother to winning hurdler around 2m Jack Robbo and bumper winner Valiant Melody: dam lightly-raced Irish maiden: maiden pointer: well beaten in novice hurdles. *B. G. Powell* **h–**

COURT EMPRESS 8 ch.m. Emperor Fountain – Tudor Sunset (Sunyboy) [2004/5 h75: 19m^{pu} 17d Feb 1] poor novice hurdler: will stay 2½m. *P. D. Purdy* **h–**

COURT LEADER (IRE) 7 b.m. Supreme Leader – Droichidin (Good Thyne (USA)) [2004/5 F17d^{3} F16m^{5} F16m^{6} F20v^{2} F16d^{4} 19s^{6} 20d^{3} 20s^{3} 19s^{5} 19v^{2} 18s^{2} 24s^{5} 16v* 21g 20s Mar 27] angular mare: fifth foal: dam, placed in Irish point, sister to **h108 F92**

top-class hurdler Mighty Mogul: fair form in bumpers: fair novice hurdler: easily justified favouritism in maiden at Leopardstown in March: stiff task, fourteenth of 20 to No Refuge in Grade 1 at Cheltenham next time: barely stays 3m when conditions are testing: acts on heavy going. *Thomas Mullins, Ireland*

COURTLEDGE 10 b.g. Unfuwain (USA) – Tremellick (Mummy's Pet) [2004/5 c–, h–: c21d^{3} c21m^{3} c22m^{pu} c16m^{3} c21m^{6} c21g^{pu} 22g^{6} 26f Sep 26] lengthy gelding: maiden hurdler: poor handicap chaser, left M. Gingell after sixth start: stays 3m: acts on good to firm and heavy going: tried in cheekpieces/visor: has had tongue tied. *Mrs C. A. Dunnett* **c65 h–**

COURT LENEY (IRE) 10 b.g. Commanche Run – Dont Call Me Lady (Le Bavard (FR)) [2004/5 c–, h–: 25g 21m^{3} May 27] of little account outside points: tried in cheekpieces. *G. Prodromou* **c– h–**

COURT NANNY 11 ch.m. Nicholas Bill – Tudor Sunset (Sunyboy) [2004/5 20d^{pu} May 3] lengthy mare: has stringhalt: possesses more temperament than ability. *P. D. Purdy* **h– §**

COURT OF JUSTICE (USA) 9 b.g. Alleged (USA) – Captive Island (Northfields (USA)) [2004/5 c76, h106: 19s^{5} 16s* Mar 31] leggy, angular gelding: fair hurdler at best: didn't need to be near that to win claimer at Ludlow in March: well held in novice only start over fences: stays 2½m: raced on good going or softer (acts on heavy): has worn cheekpieces, including when successful: has carried head awkwardly. *K. A. Morgan* **c– h76**

COURT ONE 7 b.g. Shareef Dancer (USA) – Fairfields Cone (Celtic Cone) [2004/5 20m^{6} 16g^{ur} 17d 16d Dec 5] small, sparely-made gelding: brother to useful hurdler Court Shareef: modest on Flat (stays 2m): poor form over hurdles: should stay beyond 2m. *R. J. Price* **h71**

COURT SHAREEF 10 b.g. Shareef Dancer (USA) – Fairfields Cone (Celtic Cone) [2004/5 h141: 23m^{F} May 1] compact gelding: useful hurdler: would have stayed 3m: acted on firm going (below form on good to soft): held up: dead. *R. J. Price* **h–**

COURT STORM (IRE) 6 b.g. Flemensfirth (USA) – Storm Court (IRE) (Glacial Storm (USA)) [2004/5 F16s^{3} F16s* Dec 4] €25,000 4-y-o: second foal: half-brother to useful bumper winner Davenport Democrat (by Fourstars Allstar): dam unraced, from family of smart 2m to 2½m chaser Brockley Court and smart 3m chaser Glyde Court: fairly useful form when winning 20-runner bumper at Gowran by length from Feathered Bury, looking very much a stayer. *F. Flood, Ireland* **F108**

COUSIN NICKY 4 ch.g. Bob Back (USA) – Little Red Spider (Bustino) [2004/5 F12g^{3} F14d^{4} F17s^{3} 18s^{2} 20d 17m^{4} Mar 21] £1,050 3-y-o: workmanlike gelding: first foal: dam, bumper winner, half-sister to useful hurdler around 2½m Abu Kadra: in frame all 3 starts in bumpers: best effort over hurdles when second in juvenile at Fontwell: should stay at least 2½m: acts on soft going, probably on good to firm. *H. E. Haynes* **h103 F96**

COUSTOU (IRE) 5 b.g. In Command (IRE) – Carranza (IRE) (Lead On Time (USA)) [2004/5 h–: 16m^{5} 16d^{4} 16v^{4} 16d 16g^{2} 16d^{3} 17s^{3} 19g^{3} 20g^{5} 20s^{3} 16g Mar 27] medium-sized gelding: fair on Flat (stays 1½m), successful in April: poor maiden hurdler: left A. Dicken after fifth outing: stays 2½m: acts on soft going: effective with or without headgear: patiently ridden (has found little). *R. M. Stronge* **h83**

COVENT GARDEN 7 b.g. Sadler's Wells (USA) – Temple Row (Ardross) [2004/5 h128: 24d 22g^{5} 21g^{4} Mar 16] sturdy gelding: fairly useful handicap hurdler, lightly raced: creditable efforts at Sandown and Cheltenham last 2 starts, niggled along from early stage but stayed on best of all when 16 lengths fourth of 29 to Idole First in Coral Cup at latter: stays easy 3m: acts on firm and good to soft going, unraced on soft/heavy: may benefit from headgear. *J. Howard Johnson* **h125**

COVERDALE 9 b.g. Lapierre – Better Try Again (Try My Best (USA)) [2004/5 20g^{5} May 29] well beaten in novice hurdle: poor form in points. *M. D. Hammond* **h–**

COWBOYBOOTS (IRE) 7 b.g. Lord Americo – Little Welly (Little Buskins) [2004/5 c97, h109: c26d* c24m^{6} 25g^{5} c28d* c25d^{pu} c29s^{F} Jan 15] well-made gelding: fair hurdler: well below form after 5-month break third outing: fairly useful chaser: won twice at Fontwell, novice in May and handicap in November (made all): best at 3m+: acts on heavy going: has hinted at temperament. *L. Wells* **c121 h–**

COXWELL COSSACK 12 ch.g. Gildoran – Stepout (Sagaro) [2004/5 c–, h–: 16m^{4} 20m^{pu} 16m^{F} 16g 20g^{5} 19g^{5} 20g^{3} 22g 16g^{3} Oct 6] sturdy gelding: fair hurdler at best, poor nowadays: effective at 2m (given test) to 2¾m: acts on firm and soft going: wore cheekpieces third start. *Mark Campion* **c– h81**

COY LAD (IRE) 8 ch.g. Be My Native (USA) – Don't Tutch Me (The Parson) [2004/5 h77: c21g^{5} 20s^{pu} 19g^{3} Mar 9] useful-looking gelding: poor maiden hurdler: well-beaten fifth of 9 finishers in novice handicap on chasing debut: should stay beyond 19f. *T. J. Fitzgerald* **c– h79**

COYOTE LAKES 6 ch.g. Be My Chief (USA) – Oakbrook Tern (USA) (Arctic Tern (USA)) [2004/5 F–: F18g 20m^{pu} 22m^{6} 22m^{5} Apr 21] leggy gelding: little sign of ability, left Mrs L. Jewell after third start: tried tongue tied. *M. J. McGrath* **h– F–**

CRAANFORD MILL 6 b.g. Vettori (IRE) – Northern Bird (Interrex) [2004/5 F16m F16f* F16g^{2} Jun 24] fourth foal: brother to fair but ungenuine maiden Spinning Dove, stays 1m, and half-brother to 6f/7f winner Xipe Totec (by Pivotal): dam fair 5f to 7f winner, stayed 1m: won 15-runner bumper at Tralee in June easily by 6 lengths from Golden Moon: useful form when ½-length second to The Alamo at Tipperary later in month. *W. P. Mullins, Ireland* **F107**

CRACBOUMWIZ (FR) 5 b.g. Baby Turk – Ellapampa (FR) (Pampabird) [2004/5 F16g* F17d Apr 9] €80,000 3-y-o: tall gelding: second foal: dam, winning hurdler/chaser up to 19f, half-sister to outstanding 2m chaser Azertyuiop (by Baby Turk) and useful hurdler/very smart chaser Bipbap, stayed 27f: won slowly-run bumper at Huntingdon on debut in March by ½ length from Hibernian: looked short of experience when thirteenth to The Cool Guy in Grade 2 at Aintree. *Mrs H. Dalton* **F94**

CRACKADEE 6 b. or br.g. Alflora (IRE) – Carnetto (Le Coq d'Or) [2004/5 24s^{pu} Apr 10] second foal: half-brother to bumper winner Conchita (by St Ninian): dam fair staying hurdler: won maiden point on debut in February: tailed off when pulled up in novice hurdle. *Miss R. Brewis* **h–**

CRACKED ICE 9 b.g. Arctic Lord – Crackingham (Trimmingham) [2004/5 c21m c24g^{4} c20s^{F} Oct 21] workmanlike gelding: maiden pointer: tongue tied, no form in chases. *M. Sheppard* **c–**

CRACKING DAWN (IRE) 10 b.g. Be My Native (USA) – Rare Coin (Kemal (FR)) [2004/5 c–, h–: 24s c20s^{3} c22v^{3} Jan 8] well-made gelding: fair hurdler/chaser, very lightly raced: will stay beyond 3m: raced on good ground or softer (acts on heavy). *R. H. Alner* **c111 h–**

CRACKINGTON (FR) 5 gr.g. Linamix (FR) – Ta Awun (USA) (Housebuster (USA)) [2004/5 F16v F16g F17v Mar 20] 6,000 4-y-o: tall gelding: third foal: half-brother to fairly useful 7.5f to 1¼m winner Shafeeq (by Halling): dam, useful 1¼m winner, half-sister to one-time fairly useful hurdler up to 2½m Mumaaris: well held in bumpers. *H. Alexander* **F–**

CRACKLEANDO 4 ch.g. Forzando – Crackling (Electric) [2004/5 19s^{3} 19s* 21g^{2} Mar 27] close-coupled gelding: fair up to 17f on Flat for N. Littmoden: best effort in novice hurdles when winning at Hereford in March: should stay beyond 19f. *A. King* **h110**

CRACOW (IRE) 8 b.g. Polish Precedent (USA) – Height of Secrecy (Shirley Heights) [2004/5 22d^{2} 24d^{6} 19v Apr 22] smallish, angular gelding: poor on Flat in 2004, sold out of A. Hales's stable 1,200 gns Doncaster August Sales: poor maiden hurdler: twice-raced over fences: stays 2¾m: tried blinkered: not a fluent jumper: ungenuine. *W. K. Goldsworthy* **c– h66 §**

CRAFTY LADY (IRE) 6 b. or br.m. Warcraft (USA) – Kilmana (IRE) (Castle Keep) [2004/5 F18m^{2} Apr 21] €2,000 4-y-o: fourth foal: half-sister to one-time useful hurdler Kings Castle (by King's Ride), stays 25f: dam unraced: length second to Sun Pageant in bumper at Fontwell on debut. *Miss Suzy Smith* **F90**

CRAFTY MISS (IRE) 6 b. or br.m. Warcraft (USA) – Mrs Rumpole (IRE) (Strong Gale) [2004/5 F–: 16d^{pu} 22s^{pu} Feb 10] no sign of ability. *C. J. Down* **h–**

CRAGG PRINCE (IRE) 6 b.g. Roselier (FR) – Ivory Queen (Teenoso (USA)) [2004/5 F96: F17g F16v 19d 24s^{6} Mar 10] useful-looking gelding: modest form in bumpers: tailed off in novice hurdles: should stay beyond 17f. *Mrs S. J. Smith* **h– F76**

CRAOBH RUA (IRE) 8 b.g. Lord Americo – Addies Lass (Little Buskins) [2004/5 h86, F74: 16m c17f^{5} 16f^{4} 19d^{3} 16s 16d^{F} Jan 6] modest maiden hurdler: last of 5 finishers in novice at Exeter, only start over fences: sold out of R. Alner's stable 7,400 gns Doncaster November Sales after fourth outing: probably stayed 2½m: acted on firm and good to soft ground: headstrong: dead. *A. E. Price* **c84 h85**

CRASHTOWN LEADER (IRE) 6 b.g. Supreme Leader – Crashtown Lucy (Crash Course) [2004/5 F16s* 21d^{3} 22s^{3} Jan 3] well-made gelding: chasing type: sixth foal: half-brother to Irish bumper winner Jodi and fair 17f chase winner Jodante (both by Phardante): dam, won 2m chase in Ireland, sister to top-class staying chaser Jodami: won **h104 F98**

bumper at Uttoxeter on debut in November by 2½ lengths from Barton Park: fair form when third in novice company over hurdles: will stay 3m. *C. Tinkler*

CRATHORNE (IRE) 5 b.g. Alzao (USA) – Shirley Blue (IRE) (Shirley Heights) [2004/5 16d² 16d³ 17s⁶ Feb 9] rather leggy gelding: fair on Flat (stays 2m) nowadays, sold out of J. Bethell's stable 14,000 gns Newmarket Autumn Sales: modest form when placed in novice hurdles: hampered third and not unduly knocked about final start: may still do better. *M. Todhunter* **h91**

CRAZY HORSE (IRE) 12 b.g. Little Bighorn – Our Dorcet (Condorcet (FR)) [2004/5 c–, h141: 16d³ 16d⁴ 20vᵖᵘ 16s 18s³ Apr 3] smallish, plain gelding: very smart hurdler at best, fairly useful nowadays: stays easy 23f: acts on good to firm and heavy going: finds little. *L. Lungo* **c–** **h125 §**

CRAZY LIKE A FOOL (IRE) 6 b.g. Charnwood Forest (IRE) – Shanghai Girl (Distant Relative) [2004/5 F16dᵖᵘ May 13] breathing problem when pulled up both starts in bumpers: well beaten in seller on Flat. *B. Mactaggart* **F–**

CRAZY MAZIE 8 b.m. Risk Me (FR) – Post Impressionist (IRE) (Ahonoora) [2004/5 h72: 20g* May 1] angular mare: poor hurdler: won selling handicap at Uttoxeter in May: best form around 2½m: acts on soft going: inconsistent. *K. A. Morgan* **h75**

CREAM CRACKER 7 b.m. Sir Harry Lewis (USA) – Cream By Post (Torus) [2004/5 F72: 17g⁴ 16d⁴ 16d² 16d 19m³ 19g⁴ Apr 15] modest maiden hurdler: stays 19f: acts on good to firm and good to soft going. *Ms Bridget Nicholls* **h92**

CREATE A STORM (IRE) 5 b. or br.m. Bob Back (USA) – Elag (Strong Gale) [2004/5 F16v F16d Mar 12] workmanlike mare: third foal: dam, winning Irish hurdler up to 21f, half-sister to dam of high-class chaser up to 2½m Function Dream: prominent long way in 2 mares bumpers. *J. G. Portman* **F74**

CREATIVE TIME (IRE) 9 b.g. Houmayoun (FR) – Creative Princess (IRE) (Creative Plan (USA)) [2004/5 c96, h–: c23s c24g⁵ c24g⁵ Nov 11] rangy gelding: modest handicap chaser: likely to stay beyond 3m: acts on soft going: inconsistent: sold 7,500 gns Doncaster May Sales. *Miss H. C. Knight* **c92** **h–**

CREDIT (IRE) 4 b.g. Intikhab (USA) – Tycooness (IRE) (Last Tycoon) [2004/5 16m² 17g* Feb 16] useful on Flat (stays 1½m), won twice in 2004, sold out of R. Hannon's stable 65,000 gns Newmarket Autumn Sales: 11/8-on, confirmed promise of hurdling debut when winning quite valuable juvenile at Musselburgh by 1¾ lengths from Rehearsal: remains open to improvement. *J. Howard Johnson* **h114 p**

CREGG HOUSE (IRE) 10 ch.g. King Persian – Loyal River (Over The River (FR)) [2004/5 c114§, h–§: c20g⁶ c17d* c19v⁶ c17s⁴ c21d* Apr 8] tall gelding: fairly useful handicap chaser on his day: won at Fairyhouse in November and Aintree in April: 50/1, beat Haut de Gamme by length in 30-runner John Smith's And Spar Topham Chase at latter, always going well and leading shortly after last: effective at 2m to 25f (held when refusing both starts over further): acts on heavy going: tried blinkered/in cheekpieces: has had tongue tied: temperamental. *S. Donohoe, Ireland* **c129 §** **h– §**

CREGG ROSE (IRE) 15 br.m. Henbit (USA) – Buckscastle (Buckskin (FR)) [2004/5 c27gᵖᵘ May 25] stocky mare: of little account: tried blinkered/visored. *E. M. Caine* **c– x** **h–**

CREINCH 4 b.g. Overbury (IRE) – Kingsfold Blaze (Mazilier (USA)) [2004/5 F12d* F16d Feb 12] lengthy gelding: first foal: dam, modest maiden, out of half-sister to top-class staying chaser Flashing Steel: won 4-y-o bumper at Newbury on debut by neck from Le Galactico: well held in Grade 2 event there following month. *O. Sherwood* **F100**

CRESSWELL GOLD 8 b.m. Homo Sapien – Running For Gold (Rymer) [2004/5 h–: 16mᵖᵘ 22s⁵ 20g 27d* 26m 26f⁴ 26dᵖᵘ 22dᵖᵘ Nov 14] smallish mare: winning pointer: poor hurdler: won handicap at Newton Abbot in August: stays 27f: acts on good to soft going: tried in cheekpieces: usually tongue tied in 2003/4. *D. A. Rees* **h60**

CRESTED PENGUIN 7 b.g. Rock Hopper – Welsh Secret (Welsh Captain) [2004/5 17g 20v⁵ Oct 29] 5,800 4-y-o: third foal: half-brother to fair 5f winner Secret Voucher (by Vouchsafe): dam fairly useful sprinter: well beaten both outings over hurdles: won maiden point in April. *R. Ford* **h–**

CRIAIRE PRINCESS (IRE) 7 b.m. Tidaro (USA) – Lough Borough (IRE) (Orchestra) [2004/5 h114, F89: 24sᵖᵘ 20d⁴ Nov 14] fair hurdler: stays 3m: acts on good to firm and heavy going: front runner. *Eugene Cleary, Ireland* **h110**

CRISTOFORO (IRE) 8 b.g. Perugino (USA) – Red Barons Lady (IRE) (Electric) [2004/5 h94: 17v^pu Jan 28] lengthy, good-topped gelding: did very well on Flat in 2004, successful on 5 of 6 starts: progressive form over hurdles in 2003/4: beaten long way out on return: will prove best around 2m: acts on good to firm going. *B. J. Curley* **h–**

CRISTOPHE 7 b.g. Kris – Our Shirley (Shirley Heights) [2004/5 c–, h75: 25g* 24g 26m* 24d⁵ Jun 23] lengthy gelding: pulled up only outing over fences: progressive handicap hurdler: won 4 of last 6 starts, including at Plumpton in May and Hereford in June: stays 3¼m: acts on good to firm and heavy going: tried in headgear. *Mrs A. M. Thorpe* **c– h101**

CRITICAL STAGE (IRE) 6 b.g. King's Theatre (IRE) – Zandaka (FR) (Doyoun) [2004/5 19d² 17s* 16d³ 17v⁵ 16d 17g⁴ Apr 10] compact gelding: fair on Flat (stays 1½m), successful early in 2004 for John Berry: fair novice hurdler: won at Newton Abbot in November: stiff task fourth and fifth outings: raced mainly around 2m: acts on soft going. *J. D. Frost* **h101**

CROAGHNACREE (IRE) 8 b.m. Mister Lord (USA) – Castle Flame (IRE) (Carlingford Castle) [2004/5 h–: 24m^pu Oct 1] workmanlike mare: of no account: tried in cheekpieces. *S. J. Marshall* **h–**

CROCADEE 12 b.g. Rakaposhi King – Raise The Dawn (Rymer) [2004/5 c–, h120: 24d^pu May 4] tall, useful-looking gelding: useful hurdler/chaser at best, very lightly raced since 2001: stays easy 23f: acts on good to firm and heavy going: races freely. *Miss Venetia Williams* **c– h–**

CROC AN OIR (IRE) 8 ch.g. Treasure Hunter – Cool Mary (Beau Charmeur (FR)) [2004/5 c88, h75: c25m³ c22g^ur c26g* c25g² c24g* c25g* c24m c24g⁶ Oct 9] good-topped gelding: twice-raced over hurdles: fair handicap chaser: won at Cartmel in July and Bangor and Market Rasen in August: stays 3¼m: well held on soft going. *Miss Venetia Williams* **c106 h–**

CROC EN BOUCHE (USA) 6 b.g. Broad Brush (USA) – Super Cook (USA) (Best Turn (USA)) [2004/5 F–: F16m Feb 6] no form in bumpers. *D. W. Thompson* **F–**

John Smith's And Spar Topham Chase (Handicap), Aintree—
50/1-shot Cregg House (stars) comes to head the eventual fifth Impek

CROCIERA (IRE) 4 b.g. Croco Rouge (IRE) – Ombry Girl (IRE) (Distinctly North (USA)) [2004/5 $16s^{pu}$ 17s Jan 18] modest maiden on Flat (stays 1¼m): no show in 2 outings over hurdles: tried tongue tied: sold 2,000 gns Newmarket February Sales. *M. H. Tompkins* **h–**

CROFT COURT 14 b.g. Crofthall – Queen of Dara (Dara Monarch) [2004/5 c–: $c24s^{5}$ $c24v^{4}$ Apr 17] winning chaser: little form in hunters: stays 3¼m: tried blinkered. *Miss M. Bayliss* **c82**

CROFTON ARCH 5 b.g. Jumbo Hirt (USA) – Joyful Imp (Import) [2004/5 $16d^{pu}$ $17d^{pu}$ Nov 9] second foal: dam poor 2m novice hurdler: pulled up in 2 novice hurdles: tried tongue tied. *M. A. Barnes* **h–**

CROGHAN LOCH (IRE) 8 b.g. Mister Lord (USA) – Croghan Katie (Croghan Hill) [2004/5 $24s^{pu}$ $c20d^{5}$ $c19v^{pu}$ c24d Jan 26] IR £8,500 4-y-o: lengthy gelding: second foal: dam maiden pointer: no sign of ability. *P. G. Murphy* **c–** **h–**

CROIX DE GUERRE (IRE) 5 gr.g. Highest Honor (FR) – Esclava (USA) (Nureyev (USA)) [2004/5 h107: 19g* 17d* $20f^{2}$ $16d^{4}$ $20s^{2}$ 21d $16d^{4}$ $21g^{4}$ $21d^{2}$ $c20d^{3}$ $c16v^{pu}$ c19g* Apr 7] tall gelding: fairly useful hurdler: landed odds in maiden at Stratford in July and novice at Southwell in August: better form in handicaps after, running best races behind Famous Grouse and Supreme Serenade at Kempton eighth and ninth starts: thrice-raced in maiden chases, winning at Taunton by 7 lengths from Tonic du Charmil: stays 21f: acts on soft and firm going, laboured effort on heavy: blinkered: consistent, though has looked ungenuine. *P. J. Hobbs* **c113** **h125**

CROKER (IRE) 10 ch.g. Rainbows For Life (CAN) – Almagest (Dike (USA)) [2004/5 c–§, h–§: 19g $16s^{6}$ $17g^{pu}$ $19d^{6}$ 21s 16s Feb 3] workmanlike gelding: once-raced maiden chaser: winning hurdler: tried in headgear: one to leave alone. *S. T. Lewis* **c– §** **h– §**

CROMABOO COUNT 7 b.g. Makbul – La Belle Epoque (Tachypous) [2004/5 $c20m^{pu}$ Jun 6] half-brother to poor 2m hurdler Cromaboo Crown (by Crowning Honors): dam ran once: runner-up on completed start in maiden points in 2004: mistakes and pulled up in maiden on chasing debut. *B. D. Leavy* **c–**

CROMWELL (IRE) 10 b.g. Last Tycoon – Catherine Parr (USA) (Riverman (USA)) [2004/5 c85, h–: c20d $c20m^{pu}$ Apr 23] workmanlike gelding: poor handicap chaser: off 15 months, no encouragement either outing in 2004/5: stays 3½m: acts on any going: usually blinkered: has gone in snatches/jumped none too fluently: has won 8 times at Market Rasen. *M. C. Chapman* **c–** **h–**

CROOKED MILE (IRE) 8 b.g. Be My Native (USA) – Extra Mile (Torus) [2004/5 h113, F92: 16g $18m^{3}$ c17s $c17v^{3}$ $c18d^{F}$ $c19v^{ur}$ $c17v^{F}$ 18s Mar 13] fair hurdler: similar form at best in maiden chases, though often let down by jumping: raced mainly around 2m: acts on soft and good to firm going. *J. A. O'Connell, Ireland* **c113 x** **h109**

CROOKED THROW (IRE) 6 b. or br.g. Anshan – Mary's View (IRE) (Phardante (FR)) [2004/5 $F16g^{5}$ $16s^{2}$ $16d^{4}$ $16d^{2}$ 16s* $16m^{2}$ 16s $16v^{3}$ Mar 24] second foal: dam unraced: little impact in bumpers: fair hurdler: won maiden at Wexford in November: raced at 2m: acts on soft and good to firm going: consistent. *C. F. Swan, Ireland* **h107** **F–**

CROOKSTOWN CASTLE (IRE) 7 gr.g. Castle Keep – Moorstown Rose (IRE) (Roselier (FR)) [2004/5 h89, F95: 20d* $22d^{4}$ $20s^{3}$ $24d^{F}$ Jan 12] rangy gelding: modest hurdler: off 10 months, won conditional jockeys handicap at Sandown in November: stays 2¾m: acts on soft going. *Noel T. Chance* **h92**

CROSBY DANCER 6 b.g. Glory of Dancer – Mary Macblain (Damister (USA)) [2004/5 h–: $16g^{ur}$ 17m 16d $16g^{F}$ Feb 27] no form over hurdles. *W. S. Coltherd* **h–**

CROSBY DON 10 b.g. Alhijaz – Evening Star (Red Sunset) [2004/5 c–, h–: $c20d^{pu}$ 25g c16v $c20v^{4}$ Feb 15] leggy gelding: maiden hurdler/chaser, little form for long time: stays 2¾m: acts on firm and soft going. *J. R. Weymes* **c57** **h–**

CROSBY WALTZER 5 b.m. Terimon – Mary Macblain (Damister (USA)) [2004/5 F16s Nov 5] third foal: dam 1m winner: well beaten in bumper and claimer on Flat: sold 800 gns Doncaster March Sales. *John A. Harris* **F–**

CROSSBOW CREEK 7 b.g. Lugana Beach – Roxy River (Ardross) [2004/5 h106, F99: $16d^{4}$ $16d^{F}$ $16v^{2}$ 16d* 16d* $16d^{4}$ $17g^{5}$ $16d^{3}$ Apr 9] rangy gelding: will make a chaser: useful handicap hurdler: much improved in 2004/5, winning twice at Kempton in January, beating Torrid Kentavr 3½ lengths in totesport Lanzarote Hurdle and McBain by 2½ lengths in 11-runner race despite idling: better form again in valuable events at Sandown, Cheltenham and Aintree last 3 starts: raced at 2m on good ground or softer **h133**

(acts on heavy): reliable: a credit to connections: one to follow in novice chases in 2005/6. *M. G. Rimell*

CROSS RIVER 10 b.g. Reprimand – River Maiden (USA) (Riverman (USA)) [2004/5 c–, h–: c21gpu c26g* May 31] lengthy, good-topped gelding: winning pointer: tongue tied, first form otherwise when winning maiden hunter at Cartmel: sold 5,000 gns Doncaster October Sales. *Joss Saville* **c89 h–**

CROSS THE HIGHMAN (IRE) 7 b.g. Un Desperado (FR) – Adabiya (IRE) (Akarad (FR)) [2004/5 17m* 21d3 20g* Aug 24] ex-Irish gelding: second foal: half-brother to modest hurdler Tony The Piler (by Tidaro), stays 3m: dam, well held in 2 bumpers, half-sister to smart hurdler/useful chaser Ventana Canyon, stayed 2½m: bumper winner: fair hurdler: left C. Roche, won seller at Southwell (looked less than keen) in July and novice at Worcester (blinkered) in August: stays 21f: acts on good to firm and good to soft ground. *Jonjo O'Neill* **h103**

CROWN AGENT (IRE) 5 b.g. Mukaddamah (USA) – Supreme Crown (USA) (Chief's Crown (USA)) [2004/5 16dpu 20vpu 16d Mar 10] good-topped gelding: fair maiden on Flat (stays 12.6f): no form in 3 starts over hurdles. *A. M. Balding* **h–**

CROWN TRIX (IRE) 6 b.g. Riverhead (USA) – Ballagh Trix (IRE) (Buckskin (FR)) [2004/5 F16v F17g Mar 19] third foal: dam unraced: well held in bumpers, bit slipped second start. *C. W. Moore* **F–**

CRUISE LEADER (IRE) 10 b.g. Supreme Leader – Ormskirk Mover (Deep Run) [2004/5 c120p, h–: c20sF c25d* c25s3 Dec 26] good-topped gelding: type to carry condition: lightly raced: fairly useful chaser: won 3 of 4 completed starts over fences, all at Wetherby, including when beating Flying Instructor 6 lengths in November: stays 25f: raced on going softer than good (acts on heavy). *C. Grant* **c120 h–**

CRUISE THE FAIRWAY (IRE) 9 b.g. Insan (USA) – Tickhill (General Assembly (USA)) [2004/5 c–, h–: c24d5 c24dpu c24dF c29spu c23mpu Apr 10] tall gelding: fairly useful chaser at best: failed to complete all starts after reappearance, running as if amiss last 2 outings: stays 3m: acts on heavy going. *B. G. Powell* **c106 d h–**

CRUISING ALONG 7 gr.m. Thethingaboutitis (USA) – Cruising On (Cruise Missile) [2004/5 F–: 17d May 15] no sign of ability. *P. T. Dalton* **h–**

CRUISING CLYDE 6 ch.g. Karinga Bay – Bournel (Sunley Builds) [2004/5 F95: 20s4 Oct 20] stocky gelding: bumper winner for E. Retter: fourth of 15 in novice at Chepstow on hurdling debut. *C. J. Mann* **h88**

CRUISING HOME 7 b.g. Homo Sapien – Fast Cruise (Cruise Missile) [2004/5 22gpu Apr 12] 5,200 4-y-o: first foal: dam, winning hurdler/chaser, stayed 3½m: no show in novice hurdle on debut. *D. A. Rees* **h–**

CRUISING RIVER (IRE) 6 b.g. Over The River (FR) – Jellaride (IRE) (King's Ride) [2004/5 21d3 24g4 Apr 1] sturdy gelding: second foal: half-brother to winning hurdler/most progressive chaser Lord of Illusion (by Mister Lord), stays 3¼m: dam, in frame in point, sister to fairly useful chaser up to 3m Ounavarra Creek: twice-raced in Irish points, won maiden in January on completed start: shaped promisingly on hurdling debut when 1¾ lengths third of 17 to dead-heaters Bengo and Il Duce in novice at Newbury: only fourth to Bowleaze in similar event there next time: should stay 3m: may still do better. *Miss H. C. Knight* **h113**

CRUMBS 5 b.m. Puissance – Norska (Northfields (USA)) [2004/5 F–: F16d May 13] well beaten in bumpers. *B. Mactaggart* **F–**

CRUNCHY (IRE) 7 ch.g. Common Grounds – Credit Crunch (IRE) (Caerleon (USA)) [2004/5 h91: 16g5 17mpu Jun 9] small gelding: maiden hurdler, modest at best: stays 19f: acts on good to firm and good to soft ground: tried in cheekpieces: usually tongue tied: unreliable. *B. Ellison* **h69 §**

CRUSSET (IRE) 7 b.g. Petardia – Go Flightline (IRE) (Common Grounds) [2004/5 16gpu 16d 17f 16g 16v3 Oct 16] good-topped ex-Irish gelding: 1½m winner on Flat: fairly useful 2m hurdler at best, poor nowadays, claimed £6,000 final start: acts on heavy ground: tried blinkered: often tongue tied prior to 2004/5. *S. T. Lewis* **h80**

CRUSTY MISS 6 b.m. Chaddleworth (IRE) – Miss Crusty (Belfort (FR)) [2004/5 19dpu Dec 16] third foal: half-sister to 2 modest sprint winners: dam 1m winner: no show in novice hurdle on debut: well beaten in claimers on Flat. *M. Sheppard* **h–**

CRYSTAL D'AINAY (FR) 6 b.g. Saint Preuil (FR) – Guendale (FR) (Cadoudal (FR)) [2004/5 c–, h160: $25s^2$ $24g^2$ $25s^2$ $24s^4$ 24s* $24g^{pu}$ $c25s^3$ Apr 7] **c135** **h156**

Crystal d'Ainay's prospects don't look quite so sparkling as they appeared at the end of the 2003/4 season, during which he developed into a high-class hurdler and won two races at Cheltenham, notably the Cleeve Hurdle in which he beat Hardy Eustace by three lengths. That Crystal d'Ainay would go on to win more good prizes kept to hurdling seemed one obvious conclusion at the time. Another was that if returned to chasing—he had won a three-year-old chase in France before joining his present stable—there was every chance of his reaching a similar standard and proving just as successful. Unfortunately, doubts about Crystal d'Ainay's attitude now cloud the issue and make it impossible to be anything like so positive about his future. A tendency to idle became more marked as the latest season wore on, while he seemed to lose interest when blinkered on his penultimate start and didn't race with too much enthusiasm when tried over fences for the first time in Britain on his final one. Crystal d'Ainay showed earlier in the season that he retains virtually all his ability, and it is to be hoped that his temperament doesn't prevent him from making full use of it when he returns to action, though he may not be easy to place in 2005/6.

Crystal d'Ainay occupied the runner-up spot in his first three races in the latest season. Beaten a length and a half by Telemoss, after looking all over the winner, in the West Yorkshire Hurdle at Wetherby, Crystal d'Ainay then came up against Baracouda in both the Long Distance Hurdle at Newbury and the Long Walk Hurdle at Windsor, beaten three quarters of a length each time. Crystal d'Ainay was handed the advantage at the last at Windsor, when the winner stumbled, but he himself then idled and nearly lost second place to Rule Supreme. Crystal d'Ainay could finish only fourth when attempting a repeat win in the now three-mile Cleeve Hurdle, and after idling once again it came as no surprise when connections decided to fit him with a visor on his next appearance, in the betfair.com Rendlesham Hurdle at Kempton in February. As had been the case twelve months

betfair.com Rendlesham Hurdle, Kempton—
Crystal d'Ainay, with the aid of a visor, defeats Monet's Garden for his sole success of 2004/5

earlier, the Grade 2 Rendlesham was transferred to Kempton's Saturday card following the abandonment of its Friday meeting. It attracted just five runners, all of whom had also met Crystal d'Ainay in the Cleeve Hurdle, namely the winner Patriarch Express, fifth-placed Monet's Garden, seventh-placed Royal Rosa and the tailed-off Quick. Royal Rosa, expected to be all the better for what had been his first run of the season, was sent off favourite to turn the tables on the other principals, and Crystal d'Ainay came next in the betting. With Royal Rosa going lame and Patriarch Express running well below form, it was left to Monet's Garden to provide the main threat to Crystal d'Ainay, but Crystal d'Ainay won convincingly. Travelling strongly from the off, Crystal d'Ainay was clearly going best three out and saw his race out well after hitting the front at the next, going on to win by three and a half lengths. The replacing of the visor with blinkers in the World Hurdle at Cheltenham, in which he had finished third the previous year, didn't have the same effect. Far from it, in fact, with Crystal d'Ainay seeming to lose interest after meeting interference at the seventh, dropping away before three out and pulled up at the next. There was no headgear involved when Crystal d'Ainay tackled fences on his final outing of the season, thrown in at the deep end somewhat in the Betfair Bowl Chase at Aintree. Surprisingly, given his inexperience, Crystal d'Ainay's jumping proved not to be too much of a problem up against some good-class chasers, so it was disappointing that he should lose his place so easily in the back straight, dropping right out of contention before staying on past tiring rivals late on to finish third, twenty-nine lengths behind the winner Grey Abbey.

Crystal d'Ainay (FR) (b.g. 1999)	Saint Preuil (FR) (gr 1991)	Dom Pasquini (gr 1980)	Rheffic
			Boursonne
		Montecha (br 1972)	Montevideo II
			Chasseresse
	Guendale (FR) (b or br 1992)	Cadoudal (br 1979)	Green Dancer
			Come To Sea
		Rose Sanguine (ch 1982)	Sang Bleu
			Rosa d'Estrees

Crystal d'Ainay, whose pedigree was dealt with comprehensively in last year's Annual, is the second foal of the maiden Guendale. He is a brother to one minor winner over hurdles and fences in France and half-brother to the mare Etoile d'Ainay (by Dom Alco), who won a listed hurdle at Auteuil shortly after the end of the British season. Guendale's fourth foal Le Galactico (by Sleeping Car), a stable-companion of Crystal d'Ainay, showed fairly useful form when placed on all three of his starts in bumpers in the latest season. Crystal d'Ainay stays twenty-five furlongs and acts on soft ground (untried on firmer than good). A tall, good-topped gelding, he probably took the eye in the paddock more than any other horse during the season, our reporters invariably commenting on how he looked in the pink of condition. *A. King*

CRYSTAL DANCE (FR) 5 gr.g. Loup Solitaire (USA) – Somptueuse (FR) (Crystal Palace (FR)) [2004/5 c95, h92: 16d^{pu} 20d May 6] leggy gelding: maiden hurdler/chaser, poor form over hurdles in Britain: raced mainly around 2m on good ground or softer. *C. Grant* **c– h–**

CRYSTAL GIFT 13 b.g. Dominion – Grain Lady (USA) (Greinton) [2004/5 h111: 20v^{pu} 20s^{4} 16s^{5} 20d 20s^{2} Apr 21] small, sparely-made gelding: fair hurdler: stays 3m: raced mainly on good going or softer (acts on heavy). *A. C. Whillans* **h108**

CRYSTAL RUNNER 5 b.m. Glacial Storm (USA) – Swift Run (Deep Run) [2004/5 F16s F16v F16g Feb 16] 4,000 4-y-o: second foal: dam, bumper winner, half-sister to fairly useful chaser up to 3m Shining Willow, out of half-sister to top-class 2m to 2½m jumper Buck House: well held in bumpers: cocked jaw and ducked right on debut. *E. J. Jamieson* **F–**

CUDGLEY (IRE) 7 b.g. Lapierre – Vanessa's Lass (IRE) (King's Ride) [2004/5 24m 20d c22g c18g c25s^{pu} c20m Dec 12] 10,000 3-y-o: third foal: dam unraced: no sign of ability: usually tongue tied. *Ronald O'Leary, Ireland* **c– h–**

CULBANN (IRE) 6 b.m. Religiously (USA) – Persian Gem (IRE) (Persian Heights) [2004/5 F86: F16s F16v 19s 16g 20s Mar 22] smallish mare: fourth in bumper on debut in 2003/4: has shown nothing since, including over hurdles. *C. Rae* **h– F–**

CULCABOCK (IRE) 5 b.g. Unfuwain (USA) – Evidently (IRE) (Slip Anchor) [2004/5 h91: 18m^{6} 16g 16m^{4} 22s^{2} 22v^{3} 21d^{3} 20s* 16v^{2} 20v^{4} 20v^{2} 18d^{5} Feb 3] leggy gelding: fair handicap hurdler: won at Ayr in December: probably best up to 2½m: acts on heavy and good to firm going: consistent. *P. Monteith* **h106**

CULLEN ROAD (IRE) 7 b.g. Wakashan – My Wings (Erin's Hope) [2004/5 h63: 16m^{2} 16m^{2} 16m^{pu} 20m^{3} 20g^{4} 16g 16g 16d Mar 24] leggy gelding: maiden hurdler, poor on balance of form: left J. Jenkins after sixth outing: stays easy 2½m: acts on good to firm going: tried in cheekpieces. *P. Wegmann* **h87**

CULLIAN 8 b.m. Missed Flight – Diamond Gig (Pitskelly) [2004/5 c88, h92: 21m^{3} 22g^{2} 24d^{6} May 12] good-topped mare: modest handicap hurdler: similar form on completed outing over fences: stays 2¾m: acts on soft and good to firm going: has won in cheekpieces, also tried blinkered: has had tongue tied. *J. G. M. O'Shea* **c– h95**

CUMBRIAN KNIGHT (IRE) 7 b.g. Presenting – Crashrun (Crash Course) [2004/5 h109: 17g 16s^{3} 17s^{6} 19d c19d^{6} c16s c19g^{2} c17g^{3} Mar 19] good-topped gelding: fair handicap hurdler: modest form over fences: effective at 2m to 2½m: raced mainly on good going or softer (acts on soft): blinkered third outing. *J. M. Jefferson* **c96 h109**

CUMWHITTON 6 b.m. Jumbo Hirt (USA) – Dominance (Dominion) [2004/5 17m^{ur} 17d 16d^{5} 16g^{4} 17m^{rtr} 17m^{rtr} Aug 6] sister to 2 winning hurdlers: dam unraced half-sister to useful 2m hurdler Surrey Dancer, from family of top-class hurdlers French Holly and Deano's Beeno: poor on Flat (stays 11f): similar standard over hurdles: refused to race last 2 starts (in cheekpieces on second occasion): one to leave well alone. *R. A. Fahey* **h73 §**

CUNNING PURSUIT 4 b.g. Pursuit of Love – Mistitled (USA) (Miswaki (USA)) [2004/5 16d* 17g^{2} 17m^{2} Mar 21] modest on Flat (barely stays 11.5f) for M. Bell: fair form over hurdles, winning juvenile at Wincanton in December: runner-up after at Taunton (conditional jockeys handicap) and Hereford. *N. J. Henderson* **h106**

CUPBOARD LOVER 9 ch.g. Risk Me (FR) – Galejade (Sharrood (USA)) [2004/5 22s Jan 1] rather leggy gelding: fairly useful handicap hurdler in 2002/3: off nearly 2 years, well held at Fontwell: stays easy 21f: acts on soft and good to firm going. *N. J. Henderson* **h–**

CURLY SPENCER (IRE) 11 br.g. Yashgan – Tim's Brief (Avocat) [2004/5 c109, h–: c25s^{3} c22d^{6} Feb 24] leggy, quite good-topped gelding: fair chaser: won point in March: stays 25f: best efforts on going softer than good (acts on heavy). *R. J. Hewitt* **c106 h–**

CURRAGH GOLD (IRE) 5 b.m. Flying Spur (AUS) – Go Indigo (IRE) (Cyrano de Bergerac) [2004/5 h78: 17f 19d^{pu} 19s^{pu} c16g^{pu} Mar 3] poor maiden hurdler: mistakes when pulled up on chasing debut: stays easy 19f: acts on good to firm going: tried in headgear. *Mrs P. N. Dutfield* **c– h70**

CURTINS HILL (IRE) 11 b.g. Roi Guillaume (FR) – Kinallen Lady (IRE) (Abednego) [2004/5 c111, h–: c24g^{3} c24d^{2} c21d^{F} c24d^{2} c26d^{2} Mar 26] lengthy gelding: fair handicap chaser: placed all 4 completed starts in 2004/5: stays 3¼m: acts on soft and good to firm going: patiently ridden: has found little. *T. R. George* **c112 h–**

CUSP 5 b.m. Pivotal – Bambolona (Bustino) [2004/5 h76: 21g 16g 16s 20v^{pu} c16v* c16s c16s^{pu} Apr 10] tall mare: poor maiden hurdler: better form when winning maiden at Hexham in March on chasing debut: saddle slipped final start: best form at 2m: acts on heavy going. *C. W. Thornton* **c84 h66**

CUSTOM DESIGN 4 ch.g. Minster Son – Scotto's Regret (Celtic Cone) [2004/5 F14s^{3} F13g^{5} Jan 17] leggy gelding: fifth foal: brother to fair staying hurdler Micklow Minster: dam poor maiden hurdler: better effort in bumpers when third of 6 in slowly-run 3-y-o event at Ayr. *G. A. Harker* **F92**

CUTHILL HOPE (IRE) 14 gr.g. Peacock (FR) – Sicilian Princess (Sicilian Prince) [2004/5 c–, h–: c25m^{pu} c20d Jun 1] good-topped gelding: veteran handicap chaser: little form since 2002/3: stays 25f: acts on heavy going, probably on good to firm: tried visored. *A. C. Whillans* **c– h–**

CUTINA 11 b.m. Tina's Pet – Cute Pam (Pamroy) [2004/5 c24d May 15] small, sturdy mare: maiden chaser: winning pointer, in frame in 2005: stays 3m: acts on heavy going: makes mistakes. *P. A. Jones* **c– x h–**

CUTTHROAT 5 ch.g. Kris – Could Have Been (Nomination) [2004/5 F86: F16g^{6} 16m^{F} 17g^{4} 17s^{5} Feb 17] workmanlike gelding: better effort in bumpers on debut in 2003/4: sold out of T. Tate's stable 13,000 gns (privately) Doncaster May Sales: fair **h102 F74**

form over hurdles when fourth to Manorson in novice at Taunton: likely to stay 2½m. *P. J. Hobbs*

CYANARA 9 b.m. Jupiter Island – Shamana (Broadsword (USA)) [2004/5 c?, h–: c26g* c21d4 c20d c25sur c20dpu c20d c24d Apr 22] compact mare: winning hurdler: poor novice chaser: won weak maiden at Newton Abbot in June: stays 3¼m: acts on soft and good to firm going. *Dr P. Pritchard* **c76 ? h–**

CYBELE ERIA (FR) 8 b.m. Johann Quatz (FR) – Money Can't Buy (Thatching) [2004/5 c–, h95§: 16g3 19vpu 16d4 20d3 c16d6 16d 17s2 Apr 2] close-coupled mare: winning hurdler/chaser: left N. Henderson, modest form at best after first outing: raced mainly around 2m: acts on soft going: weak finisher. *John Allen* **c– § h100 d**

CYBORG DE SOU (FR) 7 b.g. Cyborg (FR) – Moomaw (Akarad (FR)) [2004/5 h93, F–: 16d4 16d 16s2 16g 21d* 20v3 c19d c21s2 c24gpu c20s5 c16vpu Mar 17] tall gelding: fairly useful hurdler: didn't need to be near best to win claimer at Huntingdon in December: modest form over fences, bled from nose final outing: should stay 3m: raced on good going or softer (acts on heavy): none too fluent over fences. *G. A. Harker* **c96 h115**

CYBORSUN (FR) 8 ch.g. Cyborg (FR) – Kaprika (FR) (Cadoudal (FR)) [2004/5 c119, h99: c22gpu c24g2 c23mpu 20g* c20spu c25dF c23sF c20gpu Apr 17] well-made gelding: modest form when winning selling hurdle (sold from J. O'Neill 10,500 gns) at Worcester in August: fairly useful chaser, form in hunters (for C. Leech) and handicaps in 2004/5 only on second outing (first after leaving A. Moore): stays 3m: acts on heavy going: bled from nose final start: unreliable. *M. F. Harris* **c116 d h99**

CYINDIEN (FR) 8 b. or br.g. Cyborg (FR) – Indiana Rose (FR) (Cadoudal (FR)) [2004/5 c–, h97: 22g5 19g5 25g 24m Apr 10] rather sparely-made gelding: no show in 2 handicap chases: modest maiden hurdler: sold out of Ms B. Nicholls' stable 18,000 gns Doncaster May Sales after first outing: form in 2004/5 only when fifth in novice at Stratford only start for Mrs A. Thorpe: stays 25f: acts on soft going: tried blinkered/in cheekpieces: temperamental. *D. E. Cantillon* **c– § h87 §**

CYRIUM (IRE) 6 b.g. Woodborough (USA) – Jarmar Moon (Unfuwain (USA)) [2004/5 F84: F16g3 22s2 22s5 21d Dec 13] big, rangy gelding: best effort in bumpers on reappearance: form over hurdles only when runner-up in novice: has failed to see race out both starts since: stays 2¾m. *C. J. Mann* **h84 F88**

CYRLIGHT (FR) 5 ch.g. Saint Cyrien (FR) – Yellow Light (FR) (Lightning (FR)) [2004/5 c143p, h?: c20s* c20s* c20s* c22s* 20s2 19v* 20v* Apr 17] **c150 p h148 p**

Cyrlight is much the most exciting jumper in France at present, exciting not only to watch in action, but also because of his untapped potential. Cyrlight has been beaten only twice in fifteen career starts, while he has yet to meet with defeat, or even remotely look like being beaten, in the ten races he has run over fences. The French press and his own connections are struggling to find new ways to describe him, 'crack', 'phenomene' and even 'extra-terrestre' among the labels that have been applied to him. He was the obvious choice when votes were cast for the jumps Horse of the Year title in France at the end of 2004. But, strictly on bare form, on what he has actually achieved to date, Cyrlight cannot yet be rated quite so highly as those aforementioned epithets suggest, though, given the right circumstances, there is every chance that Cyrlight will prove himself a high-class horse. The ease of his wins makes him less straightforward to assess, while the relatively low standard of opposition that he has faced at Auteuil, the fact that he has only taken on fellow three- or four-year-olds over fences, and that he was receiving weight for his wins over hurdles, are all factors in his rating being lower than it might otherwise be.

By the first half of 2004, Cyrlight had stamped himself as being head and shoulders above the rest of his generation over fences at Auteuil, and another three easy wins against fellow four-year-olds in the autumn only served to ram the point home. His wins—giving weight in the Group 3 Prix Edmond Barrachin and Prix Orcada, and on level terms in the Group 1 Prix Maurice Gillois—were gained by five, ten and four lengths respectively, though his winning margins were pretty academic, with Cyrlight coasting home unchallenged each time in familiar style, making the running at a relentless gallop, establishing a clear lead and leaving most of his rivals toiling some way from home. For the most part, Cyrlight jumps his fences with plenty of zest, though he is by no means foot-perfect, tending to jump out to his right on occasions, and in the Prix Orcada he survived a notable mistake at the big open ditch. By winning the Prix Maurice Gillois in November, Cyrlight completed a Group 1 double, following his success in the Prix Ferdinand Dufaure in May, Mysoko chasing him home in both races. Winning both the top chases for four-year-olds has proved surprisingly difficult, the last to do so before Cyrlight being As des Carres back in 1991, and, before him, Katko in 1987. Neither of those horses dominated their respective generations as four-year-olds to the same extent as Cyrlight though, each gaining their only other big success that year in the Prix Orcada. Katko, however, went on to become one of the best, as well as the most popular, French chasers in recent times, winning three consecutive editions of the Grand Steeple-Chase de Paris in the years that followed.

Cyrlight might have been expected to be aimed at the Grand Steeple-Chase himself after the turn of the year, but his attentions were next switched to hurdles and he would remain over the smaller obstacles for the rest of the campaign. Having taken so little out of himself in the Maurice Gillois, Cyrlight was turned out just thirteen days later for the equivalent championship event of the autumn for four-year-old hurdlers, the Prix Renaud du Vivier. His only previous outing over hurdles had been a winning debut at Vichy as a three-year-old. The Renaud du Vivier was the most intriguing race of the season in France, pitching Cyrlight against Maia Eria, the filly who was in a class of her own among the four-year-olds over hurdles to much the same extent as Cyrlight was over fences. Adding further spice to the confrontation, Maia Eria had the same catch-me-if-you-can style of racing. Although the filly was the established hurdler of the pair Cyrlight started odds on. Neither horse's usual tactics were amended in any way for the clash, and they were soon bowling along twenty-five lengths or so clear of the main body of the field, initially racing on opposite sides of the course but virtually matching strides down the back straight. Rounding the final turn, Maia Eria gained the upper hand and Cyrlight wasn't persevered with once clearly held, doing just enough to keep second place behind the twenty-length winner. The defeat had two consequences.

Prix Leon Rambaud-Chambre du Commerce Franco-Irlandaise Et de L'Office du Tourisme Irlandais, Auteuil—Cyrlight, foot perfect, is out on his own

Firstly, Cyrlight was ruled out of the King George VI Chase at Kempton which had been opened to four-year-olds expressly because Cyrlight was talked of as an intended runner. Had he run, Cyrlight would have been the second four-year-old to run in the King George, Priorit, who had won the Grand Steeple-Chase des Quatre Ans, being pulled up in the 1948 running on his debut for Ryan Price. Cyrlight was not considered mature enough to take on his elders over fences. The second consequence of his defeat in the Renaud du Vivier was that Phillipe Sourzac was replaced as Cyrlight's rider.

By the time Cyrlight returned in the spring, Maia Eria had been retired to stud, while her regular rider, perennial champion Christophe Pieux, had been taken on as retained jockey to Cyrlight's owner Sean Mulryan. The older horses available to contest the top hurdles at Auteuil were a substandard lot and, at least in his first two meetings with them, Cyrlight treated them in the same manner with which he had been dispatching his rivals over fences. He gave an impressive fifteen-length beating to Grande Haya (a Group 1 winner in the autumn) in the Group 3 Prix Hypothese in March, and followed up with an almost solo performance (and a more fluent round of jumping) in the Group 2 Prix Leon Rambaud, in which the runner-up, El Paradiso, was the only rival within twenty lengths of the winner for much of the way. The Grande Course de Haies now looked well within Cyrlight's grasp, with the main trial, the Prix La Barka in late-May, widely expected to be a mere formality beforehand; Cyrlight started at 10/1-on on the pari-mutuel, with the previous year's Grande Course de Haies winner Rule Supreme and El Paradiso the only others in the thirteen-strong field at shorter than 30/1. However, Cyrlight met with a shock defeat, going down by two lengths to the unconsidered Rock And Palm, not dominating to the usual extent and unable to quicken when ridden at the last. It came to light afterwards that an unspecified problem with a foot had confined Cyrlight to his box for a week before the race, while unusually firm conditions by Auteuil standards (the ground was good rather than the usual soft or heavy) may not have helped matters. Worse was to follow when it was announced that Cyrlight would have to miss the Grande Course de Haies with a foot abscess. Rock And Palm was also unable to run in the Grande Course. His trainer Yann Porzier, who also trained Maia Eria, was under investigation by the French police over the use of prohibited substances and his licence had been suspended by France-Galop, the French Jockey Club.

The angular Cyrlight is by the Grand Criterium winner Saint Cyrien, while his dam, Yellow Light, also failed to win after the age of two, gaining her only win in a maiden at Argentan over just short of a mile and a quarter. She has produced three other winning jumpers, including Mansonnia (by Mansonnien), whose wins included the Grande Course de Haies de Vichy, and Roscoff (by Start Fast), a useful chaser and fairly useful hurdler at up to two and a half miles for Cyrlight's connections, as well as the mile and nine-furlong winner Maria Thai (by Siam). Yellow Light is one of three winners out of the French nine-furlong winner Maria Star. There is plenty of 'black type' further back in Cyrlight's pedigree, much of it earned at listed level, but the name that stands out is that of Sandpit who shares his great grandam with Cyrlight. The high-class Sandpit was a multiple Grade 1 winner, first in Brazil and then in the United States, who might be best remembered by followers of the sport in Britain for his third place behind Singspiel in the Dubai World Cup.

Cyrlight (FR) (ch.g. 2000)	Saint Cyrien (FR) (b 1980)	Luthier (br 1965)	Klairon
			Flute Enchantee
		Sevres (b 1974)	Riverman
			Saratoga
	Yellow Light (FR) (ch 1989)	Lightning (b 1974)	Kashmir
			Fidra
		Maria Star (ch 1981)	Pharly
			Suffisante

Cyrlight has yet to race beyond two and three quarter miles, but he should stay at least three, particularly now that he is considered less of a tearaway as he has matured. In the words of his owner's racing manager, 'il ne court plus comme un chien fou'—he no longer runs like a mad dog. Whether he stays over hurdles or is switched back to fences, Cyrlight should be more than a match for anything he might meet at Auteuil in the foreseeable future. Hopefully though, connections will take up the challenge of a run in the British Isles at some stage, having successfully tested the water with Ambobo at Cheltenham in the latest season. Cyrlight would be a fine sight over British fences, and a campaign involving some of the top chases might also be the best way of finding out how good he really is. *A. Chaille-Chaille, France*

D

DABARPOUR (IRE) 9 b. or br.g. Alzao (USA) – Dabara (IRE) (Shardari) [2004/5 c–, h90: 17g May 25] good-topped gelding: winning hurdler around 2m: no show only start in 2004/5: acts on firm and good to soft going: tried in cheekpieces/visor: usually tongue tied. *M. A. Barnes* **c– h–**

DABIROUN (IRE) 4 b.g. Desert Prince (IRE) – Dabaya (IRE) (In The Wings) [2004/5 16v² 16s² 16s⁵ 16g* 16s⁵ Apr 7] **h136**

As one name disappeared in 2005 from those which grace the races at the Cheltenham Festival, two more were added. Out went the family name of the architect of Cheltenham as the home of National Hunt racing, Frederick Cathcart, the Cathcart Chase relinquishing its long-standing place at the fixture in favour of the Daily Telegraph Chase. In came the name of another important administrator, Johnny Henderson, father of trainer Nicky, added to the title of the Grand Annual. The creation of new races to accommodate the first four-day Festival was used to provide a timely opportunity to commemorate another notable name, one whose influence at Cheltenham came on the track, Fred Winter, probably the greatest participant National Hunt racing has known, joining the Queen Mother, Lord Anthony Mildmay, Arkle, Fulke Walwyn and Vincent O'Brien among other iconic figures acknowledged in race titles at the fixture. Winter, who died in April 2004, aged seventy-seven, reached equal heights as a jockey and as a trainer, and holds a special place in the Cheltenham record books as the only man to have ridden and then trained the winner of the Champion Hurdle and the Gold Cup, a feat he also accomplished in the Grand National. Champion jockey four times between 1953 and 1958 and champion trainer on eight occasions between 1971 and 1985, Winter partnered three Champion Hurdle winners and two Gold Cup winners in all and went on to saddle four winners of the Champion Hurdle to go with his one success as a trainer in the Gold Cup.

With a generous first prize of £43,500—only two handicaps at the meeting were worth more—a maximum field of twenty-four lined up for the inaugural Fred Winter Juvenile Novices' Handicap Hurdle run over an extended two miles as the last race on the opening day of the Festival. All bar three of the runners were already winners over hurdles, favourite among them at 4/1 the Irish-trained Ease The Way, but it was one of the exceptions that came out on top in most convincing fashion. Runner-up twice in juvenile maidens at Limerick before finishing a close fifth to Strangely Brown in the Grade 2 Cashmans Hurdle at Leopardstown, Dabiroun showed much improved form at Cheltenham, making smooth headway to lead at the last and quickening right away once shaken up on the run-in to beat At Your Request by eight lengths, his jockey Nina Carberry having time to wave her whip in celebration at the line. Twenty-year-old Carberry's victory on Dabiroun on her first Festival ride made her only the second woman to partner a winner at the meeting against professional riders, following on from Gee Armytage, successful on Gee-A in the Mildmay of Flete Chase in 1987, her second winner at that year's Festival after triumphing against fellow amateurs in the Kim Muir on The Ellier. Armytage is one of the few lady riders to have ridden with regular success outside the amateur ranks over jumps, but Carberry, daughter of Gold Cup winning rider Tommy, and sister of professional riders Paul, runner-up on Harchibald in the Champion Hurdle a couple of hours before Dabiroun's win, and Philip, appears to be far and away the most polished lady recruit so far, destined for a good career if she decides to relinquish her amateur status.

*Fred Winter Juvenile Novices' Handicap Hurdle, Cheltenham—
Dabiroun heads the blundering grey At Your Request*

Fears that the staging of an additional race for four-year-olds at the Festival would take something away from the quality and competitiveness of the Triumph Hurdle—worth only £58,000 to the winner itself—proved largely unfounded. The majority of runners in the Fred Winter Hurdle looked exposed as being in the second rank of juveniles beforehand, and only Dabiroun and the filly Miss Academy, who finished fourth, carrying 11-12, among them did enough to suggest the Triumph would have been significantly the stronger for their participation. Dabiroun's effort in outclassing the opposition under 11-9 would have been good enough to see him finish third in the Triumph, and he started at only 6/1 in a field of twelve when stepped up to Grade 1 company in the Anniversary Hurdle at Aintree the following month. With Carberry unable to claim her 5-lb allowance, Dabiroun was re-united with stable-jockey John Cullen, but he failed to run his race back on softer ground, soon beaten at the third last after travelling well again, finishing a remote fifth behind Triumph runner-up Faasel. On his final outing, shortly after the end of the British season at Punchestown, Dabiroun bypassed the fixture's Champion Four Year Old Hurdle in favour of a minor hurdle for four-year-olds run twenty-four hours earlier, but, with the going again on the soft side, despite looking very well beforehand, he once more failed to reproduce his Cheltenham form, having every chance when ten lengths third to Strides of Fire.

Dabiroun has already proved a bargain for the €20,000 he cost when bought out of John Oxx's stable at the Goffs October Sale. He looked cheap even at the time, having shown useful form in only three starts on the Flat, following a successful debut in a mile maiden at the Curragh as a three-year-old with second place in listed events over seven furlongs and a mile and a quarter, beaten ten lengths by Yeats, Derby favourite at the time, in the Ballysax Stakes at Leopardstown over the latter distance. Dabiroun was bred by the Aga Khan. His dam Dabaya gained her only win at a mile and a quarter, but showed useful form to be placed in listed company at up to a mile and three quarters. Dabaya is out of Dabiliya, a half-sister to the Aga's Prix du Jockey Club winner Darshaan as well as two above-average

Donal O'Gorman's "Dabiroun"

Dabiroun (IRE) (b.g. 2001)	Desert Prince (IRE) (b 1995)	Green Desert (b 1983)	Danzig
			Foreign Courier
		Flying Fairy (ch 1983)	Bustino
			Fairy Footsteps
	Dabaya (IRE) (b 1995)	In The Wings (b 1986)	Sadler's Wells
			High Hawk
		Dabiliya (b or br 1984)	Vayrann
			Delsy

hurdlers, the smart stayer Daraydan, who also won over fences, and Darialann, who was useful at one time. Best at two miles, Darialann was second in the Galway Hurdle in 2000. This is also the family of the smart bumper winner Dawadari, who is out of a half-sister to Dabiliya. Dabiroun is likely to prove best at around two miles over hurdles. He raced only on soft/heavy ground on the Flat, but seems to have more speed than stamina and his best effort over jumps so far came on the one occasion he tackled good ground. A compact gelding, he has a fair way to go to be up to taking on the best hurdlers, but he should pay his way in valuable handicaps when conditions are in his favour. *Paul Nolan, Ireland*

DABUS 10 b.g. Kris – Licorne (Sadler's Wells (USA)) [2004/5 c–, h89§: 17d 17d 16m $17m^3$ $19d^{pu}$ $17g^2$ 17d* 16g $17d^4$ 16s $22v^{pu}$ $16s^3$ $16d^5$ 17s* $21d^{ur}$ $22s^{pu}$ $17d^2$ 16s* 17d $c16g^5$ $c16g^6$ $c16v^3$ $c16g^2$ $c16d^3$ $c16d^6$ $c17d^4$ $c16s^3$ $c16s^3$ $c16g^F$ Mar 4] small gelding: modest handicap hurdler: won at Cartmel, Market Rasen and Leicester before turn of year: fair form over fences: barely stays 19f: acts on any going: takes good hold: has refused to race, virtually did so final circuit eleventh outing. *M. C. Chapman* **c101 § h96 §**

DAD'S ELECT (GER) 6 b.g. Lomitas – Diamond Lake (USA) (Cox's Ridge (USA)) [2004/5 c?, h109: 17g* $16m^5$ $16g^5$ $16g^{ur}$ 16d $16d^{pu}$ 16d $16d^6$ $c20g^2$ Apr 3] good-topped gelding: fairly useful hurdler: won intermediate at Southwell in May: below form after **c100 p h125**

third outing, left C. Mann after sixth: second start over fences, fair form when second in maiden at Market Rasen: at least as effective over 2m as 2½m: probably acts on any going: wore blinkers/cheekpieces fourth to seventh outings: will probably do better over fences. *Ian Williams*

DADS GIFT 7 ch.g. Ajjaj – Lyricist (Averof) [2004/5 F69: 17m 20s6 Nov 24] little sign of ability. *R. L. Brown* **h–**

DADS LAD (IRE) 11 b.g. Supreme Leader – Furryvale (Furry Glen) [2004/5 c100: c28s2 c28sur c29d2 c30sur c28s4 c27spu Jan 20] fair handicap chaser: thorough stayer: raced on good going or softer (acts on heavy): blinkered. *Miss Suzy Smith* **c100**

DAFFODIL THYNE (IRE) 6 ch.m. Good Thyne (USA) – Mandys Gale (IRE) (Strong Gale) [2004/5 F16g4 F16s3 F17d4 20d Dec 9] €6,000 3-y-o, €3,500 4-y-o: lengthy mare: first foal: dam unraced: poor form in bumpers: soundly beaten in mares novice on hurdling debut. *J. R. Jenkins* **h– F67**

DAGUYDA (FR) 6 b.g. Northern Crystal – La Domizia (FR) (Tip Moss (FR)) [2004/5 F16m6 F16m 22spu 21g5 16v5 21g4 c19gur c21v2 c24d5 Jan 28] rather leggy gelding: third foal: half-brother to winning hurdler/chaser up to 2½m Palm Beach (by Great Palm) and winning 2m chaser Starting (by Start Fast): dam placed around 2m over hurdles: twice-raced in bumpers: modest novice hurdler: similar form over fences when second in maiden at Sedgefield: stays 21f: acts on heavy going. *Ferdy Murphy* **c90 h90 F78**

DAILY RUN (IRE) 7 b.g. Supreme Leader – Rugged Run (Deep Run) [2004/5 h–, F–: 16d 16g Dec 18] leggy gelding: no sign of ability: visored and tongue tied final start. *G. M. Moore* **h–**

DAISY DALE 7 gr.m. Terimon – Quetta's Girl (Orchestra) [2004/5 h72?, F–: 16g 16d Dec 26] little form over hurdles. *S. C. Burrough* **h–**

DAISYS RAINBOW 6 b.g. Dreams End – Daisy Miller (Daring March) [2004/5 F17m4 Jun 9] first foal: dam maiden who stayed 1m: pulled up in 3 maiden points in 2004: fourth of 14 in bumper at Hereford on debut. *Mrs D. A. Hamer* **F75**

DAJAZAR (IRE) 9 b.g. Seattle Dancer (USA) – Dajarra (IRE) (Blushing Groom (FR)) [2004/5 c–, h–: 21dpu 24m5 25gpu Dec 16] sturdy gelding: fair hurdler at one time, little form since 2002: stays 3m: acts on any going: has worn blinkers: tried tongue tied. *Mrs K. Walton* **c– h82**

DALARAM (IRE) 5 b.g. Sadler's Wells (USA) – Dalara (IRE) (Doyoun) [2004/5 h124: 16m 16d* 21d3 16d 16g3 Apr 16] rather leggy gelding: useful hurdler: won quite valuable 4-y-o handicap at Chepstow in October: ran well after when third to Lough Derg in minor event at Cheltenham and Genghis in valuable handicap at Ayr: effective at 2m to 21f: acts on good to firm and good to soft going: effective tongue tied or not. *J. Howard Johnson* **h139**

DALAWAN 6 b.g. Nashwan (USA) – Magdala (IRE) (Sadler's Wells (USA)) [2004/5 F93: F16v5 Jan 29] twice-raced in bumpers, off 17 months before well held on second occasion. *Mrs J. C. McGregor* **F77**

DALBLAIR (IRE) 6 b.g. Lake Coniston (IRE) – Cartagena Lady (IRE) (Prince Rupert (FR)) [2004/5 h88: 16g 19g 22spu Mar 11] sturdy gelding: novice hurdler, modest form at best. *M. Todhunter* **h81**

DALCASSIAN KING (IRE) 12 b.g. King's Ride – Niagara Lass (Prince Hansel) [2004/5 c75?, h–: c21g4 c23g5 c20m5 Jun 5] tall gelding: maiden hurdler/chaser: tried blinkered/in cheekpieces. *P. Wegmann* **c69 ? h–**

DALIADOT 5 ch.g. Jendali (USA) – Miss Polkadot (Beveled (USA)) [2004/5 F17g Apr 7] second foal: dam unraced: last of 12 in bumper on debut. *Miss M. Bragg* **F–**

DALIAN DAWN (IRE) 7 ch.g. Topanoora – Lovely Deise (IRE) (Tate Gallery (USA)) [2004/5 c17g4 c16m2 c16mF c20dF 16v4 Dec 19] half-brother to fairly useful hurdlers Dyrick Daybreak (by Ali-Royal), stays 2½m, and Tate Tirol (by Tirol), raced mainly at 2m: dam lightly-raced maiden: fair hurdler, ran as if needing race final start: fairly useful form when second in novice chase at Punchestown in May: let down by jumping subsequently: raced mainly around 2m: acts on heavy and good to firm going. *David A. Kiely, Ireland* **c116 h94 +**

DALIDA 4 ch.f. Pursuit of Love – Debutante Days (Dominion) [2004/5 17g5 17g 16v4 Dec 17] second foal: dam useful 2m hurdler: poor maiden up to 1m on Flat, has found little: well held in juvenile hurdles. *P. C. Haslam* **h62 +**

DALKEYS LAD 5 b.g. Supreme Leader – Dalkey Sound (Crash Course) [2004/5 F88: 16d^{4} 16s^{6} 20v^{4} 24s^{4} 20s Apr 20] sturdy gelding: fair form in bumpers: poor novice hurdler: stays 2½m: raced only on going softer than good. *Mrs L. B. Normile* **h74**

DALLAS ALICE 5 ch.m. Sir Harry Lewis (USA) – Run On Stirling (Celtic Cone) [2004/5 F17g^{4} Apr 3] fourth foal: half-sister to dual bumper winner Little Feat (by Terimon): dam poor 2m novice hurdler: fourth in mares bumper at Market Rasen on debut. *Ian Williams* **F84**

DALLIGAN (IRE) 11 b.g. Executive Perk – Comeragh Queen (The Parson) [2004/5 c24m^{F} c22g^{5} c21g^{5} c17g^{6} Sep 12] workmanlike gelding: winning chaser: little show in 2004/5: stays 3m: raced mainly on good ground or firmer: amateur ridden. *G. R. Pewter* **c–**

DALMARNOCK (IRE) 4 ch.g. Grand Lodge (USA) – Lochbelle (Robellino (USA)) [2004/5 19m^{pu} Apr 23] thrice-raced maiden on Flat (stays 1m) for B. Smart: jumped poorly in novice on hurdling debut. *P. D. Niven* **h–**

DALON (POL) 6 b.g. Winds of Light (USA) – Dikte (POL) (Babant (GER)) [2004/5 21g^{5} 22d^{5} 20d^{6} Nov 19] won 3 times on Flat (stays 1¼m) in Poland, including twice at 4 yrs, modest form at best in Britain in 2004: tailed off in 3 novice hurdles, blinkered last 2. *D. B. Feek* **h–**

DALRIATH 6 b.m. Fraam – Alsiba (Northfields (USA)) [2004/5 h82: 17g^{F} 17g^{4} 17d^{6} 17d^{pu} 16d^{5} 16g^{pu} 16g* 16d 16d^{5} 16d^{6} 16s^{2} 16g^{ur} 16g^{bd} Mar 9] lengthy mare: poor on Flat (stays 1½m): modest hurdler: won maiden at Catterick in December: will prove best at 2m: raced on good going or softer (acts on soft): saddle slipped fourth and sixth outings: makes running. *M. C. Chapman* **h88**

DALTON (FR) 4 ch.c. Bering – Divination (FR) (Groom Dancer (USA)) [2004/5 16v^{2} 16v* 16s^{6} 16g Mar 15] rather leggy colt: fairly useful maiden on Flat (stays 1½m), sold out of F. Head's stable €25,000 Goffs (France) October Sale: fair juvenile hurdler: won at Gowran in January: raced around 2m on good going or softer (acts on heavy). *E. J. O'Grady, Ireland* **h110**

DALUS PARK (IRE) 10 b.g. Mandalus – Pollerton Park (Pollerton) [2004/5 c98: c22s^{2} c24v^{4} c24v^{4} c30v^{2} c24s^{pu} c24s^{2} c24v^{4} Mar 19] good-topped gelding: modest handicap chaser: thorough stayer: acts on heavy going: ran poorly in cheekpieces fifth outing. *C. C. Bealby* **c94**

DALVENTO (IRE) 7 b.g. Monsun (GER) – Dream of You (GER) (Music Boy) [2004/5 16d 21s* 16v^{F} 24g Mar 18] good-topped gelding: second foal: dam 9f/1¼m winner in Germany: won 4 times up to 1½m from 16 starts on Flat in Germany for U. Suter, well beaten both starts in 2004: 50/1, won minor hurdle at Thurles in December by 3½ lengths from Hedgehunter: stiff task and no show next 2 starts: stays 21f. *John Joseph Murphy, Ireland* **h108**

DALYAN (IRE) 8 b.g. Turtle Island (IRE) – Salette (Sallust) [2004/5 17m 17g^{6} 21m^{pu} Jul 26] tall gelding: of little account. *A. J. Lockwood* **h–**

DAMARISCO (FR) 5 b.g. Scribe (IRE) – Blanche Dame (FR) (Saint Cyrien (FR)) [2004/5 h–: 16s 16s^{4} 19v^{6} 16s^{6} 17v* 17g* 19v^{2} Apr 22] angular gelding: modest hurdler: won novice handicaps at Exeter in March (conditional jockeys) and April: best form around 2m: raced on good ground or softer (acts on heavy). *P. J. Hobbs* **h94**

DAME BEEZIL 6 b.m. Man Among Men (IRE) – Cuillin (Emarati (USA)) [2004/5 F17d^{6} F16d 19s^{pu} Jan 31] lengthy mare: first foal: dam no sign of ability: well held in 2 bumpers and novice hurdle: tongue tied final outing. *K. Bishop* **h– F–**

DAME NOVA (IRE) 4 b.f. Definite Article – Red Note (Rusticaro (FR)) [2004/5 17d^{pu} Jul 17] sparely-made filly: poor maiden on Flat: none too fluent in juvenile on hurdling debut. *P. C. Haslam* **h–**

DAMIEN'S CHOICE (IRE) 13 b.g. Erin's Hope – Reenoga (Tug of War) [2004/5 c99§, h79§: 18m^{pu} 16m^{F} 17s^{pu} 16m c16g^{5} c17d^{pu} c16m 17v c21d c16s^{6} 16v^{6} 16d 16s^{4} 16d Apr 9] tall gelding: winning hurdler/chaser: retains little ability: has worn visor/cheekpieces: not one to trust. *Dr P. Pritchard* **c62 § h66 §**

DAMIENS PRIDE (IRE) 15 b.g. Bulldozer – Riopoless (Royal And Regal (USA)) [2004/5 c89: c21g^{pu} Apr 27] veteran chaser: stays 3¼m: acts on firm going. *Mrs S. J. Batchelor* **c–**

DAMUS (GER) 11 b.g. Surumu (GER) – Dawn Side (CAN) (Bold Forbes (USA)) [2004/5 c111§, h–: 18m 20d^{pu} 16f 16g^{F} c20s^{5} c16g^{pu} Sep 23] leggy gelding: no longer of any account: wears headgear. *Mrs J. C. McGregor* **c– h–**

DANAW (FR) 4 b.g. Lomitas – Damanka (IRE) (Slip Anchor) [2004/5 16s* 16s* 17s* 17s 17g Mar 18] tall gelding: fairly useful middle-distance maiden on Flat: unbeaten first 3 starts over hurdles, fairly useful form when winning Group 3 Prix General de Saint-Didier at Enghien in November impressively by 2 lengths from King's Daughter: earlier won at Fontainebleau and Enghien: well held after in Grade 2 juvenile and Triumph Hurdle at Cheltenham: raced around 2m: acts on soft going: has had tongue tied. *F. Doumen, France* **h124**

DANBURY (FR) 5 b.g. Lost World (IRE) – Dany Ohio (FR) (Script Ohio (USA)) [2004/5 F18d Apr 18] 40,000 4-y-o: sixth foal: half-brother to fairly useful hurdler/chaser Reizeiger (by Balleroy), stays 2½m, and 2¼m chase winner Sarrohio (by Sarhoob): dam unraced half-sister to useful French hurdler up to around 2½m Ray Cupid: seventh of 10 in maiden bumper at Plumpton on debut. *O. Sherwood* **F85 ?**

DANBYS GORSE 13 ch.g. Presidium – Dohty Baby (Hittite Glory) [2004/5 c24spu Mar 10] workmanlike gelding: veteran chaser: stays 3m: acts on good to firm and heavy going: tried visored, usually blinkered. *Miss Louise Todd* **c– h–**

DANCE OF LIFE 6 b.m. Shareef Dancer (USA) – Regan (USA) (Lear Fan (USA)) [2004/5 h73: 16m* 17m4 c16g c18m4 20m6 16g Oct 4] poor hurdler: won selling handicap at Worcester in June: no show over fences: raced mainly around 2m: acts on good to firm going: tried in cheekpieces, usually blinkered. *Mrs L. Wadham* **c– h67**

DANCE PARTY (IRE) 5 b.m. Charnwood Forest (IRE) – Society Ball (Law Society (USA)) [2004/5 19vpu 17d* 16v* 16v6 20v5 16v6 Mar 17] rather leggy mare: modest maiden on Flat (stays 1½m), sold out of A. Balding's stable 7,500 gns Newmarket July Sales: modest form over hurdles: won mares maiden at Sedgefield in November and novice at Hexham in December: stays 2½m: raced on going softer than good (acts on heavy). *M. W. Easterby* **h99**

DANCER KING (USA) 4 b.g. King of Kings (IRE) – Tigresa (USA) (Tejano (USA)) [2004/5 16m5 Dec 1] sturdy gelding: modest maiden on Flat (should stay 1¼m): well beaten in juvenile on hurdling debut. *T. P. Tate* **h–**

DANCER LIFE (POL) 6 b.g. Professional (IRE) – Dyktatorka (POL) (Kastet (POL)) [2004/5 h110: 20m5 20mpu 16g* 16g3 20gpu Aug 24] angular gelding: fair handicap hurdler: back to form when winning at Perth in July: should stay beyond 2m: unraced on extremes of going: tried blinkered/visored, better form when not: has looked reluctant. *Jonjo O'Neill* **h110**

DANCER POLISH (POL) 7 b.g. Professional (IRE) – Doloreska (POL) (Who Knows) [2004/5 h–: 17dpu c16mpu c24f2 19g c25s4 Oct 29] close-coupled gelding: no form since 2002/3: usually blinkered nowadays. *A. Sadik* **c– h–**

DANCE WITH WOLVES (FR) 5 ch.g. Tel Quel (FR) – La Florian (FR) (River Mist (USA)) [2004/5 16v 16g 16s2 16v3 17spu 17d Feb 11] leggy ex-French gelding: first foal: half-brother to 11f winner Time Flies (by Turgeon): dam won several times up to around 11f on Flat: 11.5f winner on Flat at 3 yrs, left R. Pritchard-Gordon in early-2004: modest form when placed in novice hurdles: raced around 2m on good ground or softer (acts on heavy): wears blinkers/cheekpieces. *D. P. Keane* **h91**

DANCING BAY 8 b.g. Suave Dancer (USA) – Kabayil (Dancing Brave (USA)) [2004/5 h127: 16m2 17d 21g2 24s5 Apr 7] sturdy gelding: developed into smart performer on Flat in 2004: useful hurdler: good efforts when runner-up in valuable handicaps at Haydock (beaten 2½ lengths by Macs Joy) in May and Cheltenham (beaten 5 lengths by Idole First) in March: ran as if amiss in Grade 2 at Aintree final start: stays 21f: acts on soft and good to firm going: sweated badly when running poorly second outing: held up. *N. J. Henderson* **h144**

DANCING DOLPHIN (IRE) 6 b.m. Dolphin Street (FR) – Dance Model (Unfuwain (USA)) [2004/5 16s6 16d 16v Dec 17] lengthy mare: poor maiden on Flat/over hurdles. *Julian Poulton* **h80 ?**

DANCING FOSENBY 9 b.g. Terimon – Wave Dancer (Dance In Time (CAN)) [2004/5 c73+, h–: c25vR c26m* May 19] prolific winning pointer: won novice hunter at Folkestone in May: refused fourth previous outing: stays 3¼m: acts on good to firm ground: tried blinkered: races freely. *Miss P. C. Lownds* **c89 h–**

DANCINGINTHESTREET 5 b.g. Groom Dancer (USA) – Usk The Way (Caerleon (USA)) [2004/5 16s 16s 16v3 Mar 29] good-topped gelding: fairly useful on Flat (stays **h88**

2m) at 3 yrs, sold out of J. Given's stable only 2,500 gns Newmarket Autumn (2003) Sales: modest form over hurdles: will stay beyond 2m. *J. L. Flint*

DANCING PARTNER (USA) 4 b.g. Distant View (USA) – Bold Ballerina (Sadler's Wells (USA)) [2004/5 F16v* Feb 19] fifth foal: half-brother to fairly useful 2001 2-y-o 7f winner Ballet Fame (by Quest For Fame): dam, second at 1m in France, half-sister to Lowther winner Kingscote out of smart performer up to 1m Bold Fantasy: sold unraced out of B. Hills's stable 3,500 gns Doncaster August Sales: won bumper at Uttoxeter on debut by 6 lengths from A Few Kind Words. *M. W. Easterby* **F98**

DANCING PEARL 7 ch.m. Dancing Spree (USA) – Elegant Rose (Noalto) [2004/5 h114: 16s² 16d³ 16d² 16g* 17g 20m Apr 23] smallish, leggy mare: fairly useful handicap hurdler: better than ever in 2004/5, winning mares event at Doncaster (for second consecutive year) in February by 2½ lengths from Norma Hill: raced mainly around 2m: acts on soft going, probably on good to firm: genuine and consistent. *C. J. Price* **h120**

DANCING ROCK 7 b.g. Dancing High – Liblet (Liberated) [2004/5 F16d* 16d⁵ 19g³ 20s* 24g² Apr 1] tall, angular gelding: should make a chaser: first foal: dam of little account in points: won bumper at Perth in May on debut: sold out of J. I. A. Charlton's stable 45,000 gns Doncaster August Sales: fairly useful form over hurdles: won maiden at Wetherby in March by 10 lengths from Love That Benny: better effort when 3½ lengths second to Bowleaze in novice at Newbury: stays 3m: acts on soft going. *P. J. Hobbs* **h119 F99**

DANCING SHIRLEY 7 b.m. Dancing Spree (USA) – High Heather (Shirley Heights) [2004/5 17g 20gpu 16g⁶ 18d³ Nov 14] poor hurdler: probably best short of 2½m. *T. P. McGovern* **h73**

DANCING TILLY 7 b.m. Dancing Spree (USA) – L'Ancressaan (Dalsaan) [2004/5 h–: 16g Mar 28] modest at best on Flat (stays 11f): little form over hurdles: wore cheekpieces last 2 starts. *R. A. Fahey* **h–**

DAN DE LION 6 b.g. Danzig Connection (USA) – Fiorini (Formidable (USA)) [2004/5 16spu 16d 16v 17g Apr 3] lengthy gelding: no sign of ability on Flat: poor form over hurdles. *R. C. Guest* **h70**

DAN DE MAN (IRE) 14 br.g. Phardante (FR) – Slave De (Arctic Slave) [2004/5 c67§, h69§: 20d Apr 25] lengthy gelding: veteran handicap chaser/hurdler: stays 21f: acts on heavy going, probably on good to firm: best held up: unreliable. *Miss L. C. Siddall* **c– § h– §**

DANEBANK (IRE) 5 b.g. Danehill (USA) – Snow Bank (IRE) (Law Society (USA)) [2004/5 h–: 19g 19g³ Dec 16] modest on Flat (stays 1¾m), successful in July: easily best effort over hurdles when third to Stan in novice at Catterick. *J. Mackie* **h108**

DANELOR (IRE) 7 b.g. Danehill (USA) – Formulate (Reform) [2004/5 16sur 16g Nov 15] sturdy gelding: fairly useful on Flat (stays 11f), successful in February and March: well held but not knocked about on completed start over hurdles: likely to do better. *R. A. Fahey* **h– p**

DANGEROUSDANMAGRU (IRE) 9 b.g. Forest Wind (USA) – Blue Bell Girl (Blakeney) [2004/5 c20d³ c16sur c19s² c16v* c20v⁴ c16d⁴ c20dF Apr 9] ex-Irish gelding: fair handicap hurdler in 2002/3: fair chaser: won handicap at Listowel in September, final outing for N. Glynn: stays 2½m: raced on good going or softer (acts on heavy). *A. E. Jones* **c104 h–**

DANGEROUS DAN MCGO (IRE) 7 b.g. Un Desperado (FR) – Sharnad (IRE) (Shardari) [2004/5 F95: 21v 17s 16d 16s Mar 23] tall gelding: fairly useful form in bumper on debut: well beaten over hurdles, racing freely: should stay at least 2½m. *M. C. Pipe* **h– p**

DANGEROUSLY GOOD 7 b.g. Shareef Dancer (USA) – Ecologically Kind (Alleged (USA)) [2004/5 h125: 16d³ 22d* Dec 26] leggy gelding: useful hurdler: best effort when winning handicap at Wincanton by 8 lengths from Glacial Sunset: stays 2¾m: acts on good to firm and good to soft going: wears headgear: held up. *G. L. Moore* **h131**

DANIAN (IRE) 6 b.g. Fourstars Allstar (USA) – Ruby Belle (IRE) (Strong Gale) [2004/5 F16s³ F16s Mar 22] sturdy gelding: second foal: dam, winning pointer, third in Irish 2¼m bumper: much better effort in bumpers when third in maiden at Catterick on debut. *N. Wilson* **F90**

DANIEL'S DREAM 5 b.g. Prince Daniel (USA) – Amber Holly (Import) [2004/5 F16v F16g Mar 9] smallish, sturdy gelding: first foal: dam poor hurdler: tailed off in bumpers. *J. E. Dixon* **F–**

DANIELS HYMN 10 b.g. Prince Daniel (USA) – French Spirit (FR) (Esprit du Nord (USA)) [2004/5 c106, h113: c24s^{F} c18g^{2} c23d^{3} 20d c20d^{3} c24g^{4} c21d^{6} Dec 11] well-made gelding: fair hurdler/chaser, below best in 2004/5: stays 21f: acts on good to soft and good to firm going: usually blinkered: not a fluent jumper. *Ms F. M. Crowley, Ireland* **c101 x h–**

DANISH DECORUM (IRE) 6 ch.g. Danehill Dancer (IRE) – Dignified Air (FR) (Wolver Hollow) [2004/5 h82: 16g^{6} 16m c16g^{5} c16m* c19m^{F} c16m* c19g^{2} Sep 30] angular gelding: maiden hurdler: fair chaser: won maiden at Sedgefield in August and conditional jockeys handicap at Uttoxeter in September: likely to stay beyond 19f: acts on good to firm going: front runner. *Evan Williams* **c108 + h–**

DANLEE 6 ch.g. Rock Hopper – Kentucky Tears (USA) (Cougar (CHI)) [2004/5 F17m^{pu} Jun 25] 5,000 4-y-o: eighth foal: half-brother to winning hurdler around 2m Noble Colours (by Distinctly North) and 2 winners on Flat: dam unraced: pulled up in bumper on debut. *N. Wilson* **F–**

DANNY DOLITTLE (IRE) 12 ch.g. Denel (FR) – Tactique (FR) (Anne's Pretender (USA)) [2004/5 c23g^{pu} Apr 12] sparely-made gelding: of little account outside points nowadays. *M. S. Sweetland* **c–**

DANNY LEAHY (FR) 5 b.g. Danehill (USA) – Paloma Bay (IRE) (Alzao (USA)) [2004/5 h83: 20d^{pu} 20d^{pu} 20s^{pu} 20s^{pu} 22m Apr 23] leggy gelding: maiden hurdler: visored final start: has had tongue tied: has looked moody. *M. D. Hammond* **h–**

DAN'S MAN 4 ch.g. Zaffaran (USA) – Solo Girl (IRE) (Le Bavard (FR)) [2004/5 F16g^{2} Apr 19] fourth foal: half-brother to useful hurdler Over The Creek (by Over The River), stays 3m: dam, lightly raced, from family of Grand National winner Rubstic and top-class staying chaser Kildimo: favourite but green, short-head second to Regal Heights in maiden bumper at Towcester on debut: will be suited by further than 2m. *N. A. Twiston-Davies* **F92**

DANS PRIDE (IRE) 7 b.g. Presenting – Mindyourown (IRE) (Town And Country) [2004/5 F91: aF16g* aF16g^{3} Nov 11] tall gelding: fair form in bumpers: won on polytrack at Lingfield in October. *Noel T. Chance* **F94**

DANTE CITIZEN (IRE) 7 ch.g. Phardante (FR) – Boreen Citizen (Boreen (FR)) [2004/5 c98, h93: c24d^{ur} c24d^{2} c22v^{pu} c24g^{6} c22s* c25d* c25m^{4} Apr 9] sturdy gelding: modest novice hurdler: fair handicap chaser: won weakly-contested events at Market Rasen and Wincanton in March: stays 25f: acts on soft going. *T. R. George* **c104 h–**

DANTECO 10 gr.g. Phardante (FR) – Up Cooke (Deep Run) [2004/5 c86x, h–: c25g^{F} 24d^{2} 21m^{pu} 24g^{pu} 27m^{pu} Jul 26] big gelding: modest handicap hurdler/chaser: stays 3m: acts on firm and good to soft going: has worn cheekpieces: headstrong, and often makes running: sketchy jumper of fences. *Miss Kate Milligan* **c– x h90**

DANTE'S BACK (IRE) 7 b.g. Phardante (FR) – Jordans Pet (IRE) (Vision (USA)) [2004/5 26d^{2} 24d^{2} 24d^{3} 24d^{pu} 21g Apr 1] IR 3,000 3-y-o: tall gelding: fourth foal: half-brother to 2½m chase winner Hits And Memories (by Accordion): dam unraced half-sister to fairly useful 23f hurdle winner Moment of Glory: placed twice from 5 starts in maiden Irish points: best effort over hurdles when second to Football Crazy in maiden at Uttoxeter on second start: looks a thorough stayer. *N. A. Twiston-Davies* **h109**

DANTE'S BATTLE (IRE) 13 b.g. Phardante (FR) – No Battle (Khalkis) [2004/5 c–x, h86: 20m* 20m^{5} 20g^{5} 20m^{5} Sep 5] veteran jumper: successful in claiming hurdle at Wetherby in May: pulled up in point in March: stays 21f: acts on good to soft and good to firm going: often let down by jumping over fences. *Miss K. Marks* **c– x h87**

DANTE'S BROOK (IRE) 11 ch.g. Phardante (FR) – Arborfield Brook (Over The River (FR)) [2004/5 c67, h–: c16m^{4} c16g^{2} c16m* c16d* Oct 9] strong, lengthy gelding: has been hobdayed: modest chaser: made all in handicap and novice at Hexham in October: best around 2m: acts on firm and good to soft going: effective tongue tied or not. *B. Mactaggart* **c86 h–**

DANTE'S HONOUR (IRE) 8 b.g. Phardante (FR) – Wild Fantasy (IRE) (Cataldi) [2004/5 c24m^{pu} 22d^{pu} 17g^{ur} 20d^{6} 22g^{6} Jul 15] won maiden Irish point in May: has shown very little otherwise: tried blinkered. *J. J. Lambe, Ireland* **c– h–**

DANTE'S PORRIDGE (IRE) 9 b.g. Phardante (FR) – Canal Street (Oats) [2004/5 h93: 20g^{2} 24m^{pu} c17g^{4} 23v^{pu} c16v^{F} c16g^{ur} c20s^{bd} Mar 10] workmanlike gelding: poor hurdler/chaser on balance: best effort at 2m on good to firm ground. *Mrs S. J. Smith* **c79 h73**

DANTES REEF (IRE) 9 b.g. Phardante (FR) – Thousand Flowers (Take A Reef) [2004/5 c121p, h123+: c16v^F c20s^2 c17v^F c18s* Feb 10] fairly useful handicap hurdler/chaser: successful over fences at Thurles by 6 lengths from Oh Be The Hokey: stays 2½m: acts on heavy going: makes mistakes over fences. *A. J. Martin, Ireland* **c123 x h–**

DANTES VENTURE (IRE) 8 b.g. Phardante (FR) – Fast Adventure (Deep Run) [2004/5 c83, h100: 26d* 24g^4 26m* 24d^4 22d^5 24d 24s Jan 20] sturdy gelding: once-raced over fences: fair hurdler: won maiden and conditional jockeys novice (tongue tied) at Hereford early in season: stays 3¼m: acts on heavy and good to firm going: usually visored. *Miss I. E. Craig* **c– h101**

DANTIE BOY (IRE) 9 br.g. Phardante (FR) – Ballybride Gale (IRE) (Strong Gale) [2004/5 c118, h113: c23d^3 c24g^5 Apr 7] lengthy gelding: winning hurdler: fairly useful chaser at best: won point in March: probably stays 3m: raced mainly on good going or firmer (acts on firm) *A. W. Congdon* **c91 h–**

DANZIG CONQUEST 5 ch.g. Danzig Connection (USA) – Seren Quest (Rainbow Quest (USA)) [2004/5 F17v^3 F16d F16s^3 F17g^6 Apr 12] sturdy gelding: fourth foal: half-brother to one-time smart 1½m winner Saddler's Quest (by Saddlers' Hall) and useful middle-distance stayers Conquestadora (by Hernando) and Seren Hill (by Sabrehill): dam fair 1¼m winner: fair form at best in bumpers. *Mrs A. T. Cave* **F92**

DARAB (POL) 5 ch.g. Alywar (USA) – Damara (POL) (Pyjama Hunt) [2004/5 h–: 16m^4 16d^F 16m^3 16g^3 16g^3 17s 20v 25d* 25d Feb 4] sparely-made gelding: modest hurdler: left T. George after fifth start: won novice at Catterick in January: stays easy 25f: acts on good to firm and good to soft going: tried in cheekpieces. *Mrs S. J. Smith* **h97**

DARA CAPALL (IRE) 5 b.g. Simply Great (FR) – She's Pretty (Furry Glen) [2004/5 F84p: F16s^3 19g^{pu} Dec 10] useful-looking gelding: fair form in bumpers: broke leg on hurdling debut: dead. *K. G. Reveley* **h– F85**

DARAK (IRE) 9 b.g. Doyoun – Dararita (IRE) (Halo (USA)) [2004/5 c17m^3 Jun 9] sturdy gelding: of little account outside points nowadays. *Mrs K. J. Tutty* **c– h–**

DARAMOON (IRE) 4 b.f. Darazari (IRE) – Yellow Moon (IRE) (Executive Perk) [2004/5 F16d Apr 20] leggy filly: first foal: dam unraced: well held in bumper on debut. *D. J. S. ffrench Davis* **F–**

DARCEY MAE 7 b.m. Afzal – Belhelvie (Mart Lane) [2004/5 F17g^2 21d^5 21s^5 16s^5 22d^4 22s^5 24s^{pu} Feb 17] third foal: half-sister to fair pointer St Helier (by Gildoran): dam winning pointer: won maiden point in 2004: second in bumper at Taunton: poor novice hurdler: should stay 3m. *Mrs H. M. Bridges* **h74 F63**

DARCY 11 ch.g. Miswaki (USA) – Princess Accord (USA) (D'Accord (USA)) [2004/5 17v 16s^6 21d^{pu} Apr 18] of little account nowadays. *D. C. O'Brien* **c– h–**

DARDANUS 7 ch.g. Komaite (USA) – Dance On A Cloud (USA) (Capote (USA)) [2004/5 c102, h–: c24m c20m^F May 25] medium-sized gelding: lightly raced: winning hurdler/maiden chaser: not sure to stay 2½m: acts on good to firm going: blinkered (ran poorly) once: sold 4,500 gns Doncaster August Sales. *C. J. Mann* **c89 h–**

DARETOBEDIFFERENT (IRE) 7 ch.g. Aristocracy – Telmary (Guillaume Tell (USA)) [2004/5 c25s* c24d^4 c26v^3 Feb 25] rangy gelding: no form over hurdles: off 21 months, fair form over fences, winning maiden at Wincanton in January: will stay beyond 3¼m: sold 8,500 gns Doncaster May Sales. *Miss H. C. Knight* **c112 h–**

DARE TOO DREAM 6 b.g. Thowra (FR) – Dubacilla (Dubassoff (USA)) [2004/5 F17s^2 F17v^2 F17g Apr 12] big, rangy, good sort: third foal: half-brother to bumper winner Mister Quasimodo (by Busy Flight) and winning pointer by Terimon: dam, top-class staying chaser, half-sister to Grand National runner-up Just So: fairly useful form when 6 lengths second to Ain't That A Shame in maiden bumper at Exeter on debut: much better than bare result next 2 starts: bred to stay at least 2½m. *K. Bishop* **F97**

DARGAVILLE (NZ) 6 br. or bl.g. Sakti (NZ) – Oak Invasion (NZ) (Oak Ridge (FR)) [2004/5 16d^6 16s^2 19g 16g^3 17g Mar 19] runner-up once over 9.5f from 6 starts in maidens on Flat in New Zealand: modest form over hurdles. *R. C. Guest* **h92**

D'ARGENT (IRE) 8 gr.g. Roselier (FR) – Money Galore (IRE) (Monksfield) [2004/5 c148, h116+: c20s^F c25d c24d^5 c29s^2 c33d^{ur} Mar 19] leggy, useful-looking gelding: smart chaser: upped in trip, back to best when 2½ lengths second to Baron Windrush in valuable handicap at Warwick in January: leading narrowly when blundered and unseated 3 out in **c148 h–**

similar event at Uttoxeter won by Philson Run next time: will stay extreme distances: acts on soft and good to firm going: sometimes let down by jumping: best form over fences on left-handed tracks. *A. King*

DARGHAN (IRE) 5 b.g. Air Express (IRE) – Darsannda (IRE) (Kahyasi) [2004/5 16vpu Dec 18] fair on Flat (stays 9f): tongue tied, pulled up on hurdling debut. *P. D. Evans* **h–**

DARIALANN (IRE) 10 b.g. Kahyasi – Delsy (FR) (Abdos) [2004/5 20d 22g2 20m* 20d6 16d 21d Dec 9] compact gelding: modest form over fences: no better over hurdles nowadays: won conditional jockeys seller at Huntingdon in August: stays 2¾m: acts on soft and good to firm going: formerly often blinkered: tongue tied once. *O. Brennan* **c– h87**

DARING NEWS 10 b.g. Risk Me (FR) – Hot Sunday Sport (Star Appeal) [2004/5 c17g4 Jul 18] good-topped gelding: of little account nowadays. *O. O'Neill* **c– h–**

DARJEELING (IRE) 6 b.m. Presenting – Afternoon Tea (IRE) (Decent Fellow) [2004/5 F–: 19s5 19m2 17g2 16s* 22d2 19m3 22s2 22s* 22d3 Feb 19] angular mare: fair novice hurdler: won at Stratford in October and Wincanton in February: will stay beyond 2¾m: acts on soft and good to firm going: has looked no easy ride but is consistent: sold 39,000 gns Doncaster May Sales. *Mrs S. Gardner* **h112**

DARK ALL OVER 6 b. or br.m. Overbury (IRE) – The Dark Walk (Kemal (FR)) [2004/5 aF16g F17m4 20s Dec 4] second foal: dam, winning pointer, half-sister to dam of one-time smart chaser/useful hurdler Promalee, stays 3m: no form in bumpers or novice hurdle (jumped badly). *W. K. Goldsworthy* **h– F–**

DARK BEN (FR) 5 b.g. Solar One (FR) – Reine d'Auteuil (FR) (Cap Martin (FR)) [2004/5 F74: 16g3 16d2 17d* 16s4 18d 17v* 18s4 Apr 3] fair form over hurdles: won twice at Sedgefield, novice in October and handicap in March: raced around 2m on good going or softer (acts on heavy): genuine. *Miss Kate Milligan* **h105**

DARK CUT (IRE) 5 b.g. Ali-Royal (IRE) – Prima Nox (Sabrehill (USA)) [2004/5 17d6 16spu 16gpu 17vpu Jan 11] poor on Flat (should stay 1¼m): no show over hurdles. *H. Alexander* **h–**

DARK HUNTER 9 ch.g. Mon Tresor – Beaver Skin Hunter (Ballacashtal (CAN)) [2004/5 23dpu Apr 25] angular gelding: fifth foal: half-brother to winner in Greece by Distant Relative: dam winner in Belgium, including at 2 yrs: no show in maiden on hurdling debut. *M. J. Gingell* **h–**

DARK ISLAND 10 b.g. Silver Season – Isle Maree (Star Appeal) [2004/5 c–, h–: c25g4 c22s4 Oct 12] lengthy, rather sparely-made gelding: of no account. *Mrs Mary A. Meek* **c– h–**

DARK MANDATE (IRE) 7 b. or br.m. Mandalus – Ceoltoir Dubh (Black Minstrel) [2004/5 c–, h–: c16g c21dpu c21dpu Nov 9] of no account. *J. S. Haldane* **c– h–**

DARKNESS 6 ch.g. Accordion – Winnowing (IRE) (Strong Gale) [2004/5 F97: F18s* 20s2 21s* 21v2 19s* 21g Mar 16] tall, lengthy gelding: fairly useful in bumpers, won at Plumpton in December: useful novice hurdler: landed odds at Plumpton in January and Towcester (beat Jaunty Times 11 lengths despite hanging left) in February: blinkered, tailed off in Royal & SunAlliance Novices' Hurdle at Cheltenham final start: will stay at least 2¾m: raced mainly on soft/heavy going: not a straightforward ride. *C. R. Egerton* **h134 F99**

DARK'N SHARP (GER) 10 b.g. Sharpo – Daytona Beach (GER) (Konigsstuhl (GER)) [2004/5 20v c25gpu Apr 8] sturdy gelding: useful hurdler/smart handicap chaser in 2002/3: off nearly 2 years, no sign of retaining ability: should stay beyond 2m: acts on soft and good to firm going: patiently ridden. *R. T. Phillips* **c– h–**

DARK ROOM (IRE) 8 b.g. Toulon – Maudlin Bridge (IRE) (Strong Gale) [2004/5 c118: c21dpu c26g4 c24d c25m Apr 13] lengthy gelding: fair handicap chaser: stays 3¼m: acts on heavy going: often let down by jumping. *Jonjo O'Neill* **c109 x**

DARK SHADOWS 10 b.g. Machiavellian (USA) – Instant Desire (USA) (Northern Dancer) [2004/5 h92: c24dpu c24gpu c25spu 18s 22dpu Apr 11] smallish gelding: maiden hurdler: no show in 2004/5, including over fences: stays 3m: acts on good to firm and good to soft going: wore cheekpieces final start: not a fluent jumper. *W. Storey* **c– h–**

DARKSHAPE 5 b.g. Zamindar (USA) – Shapely (USA) (Alleged (USA)) [2004/5 16gpu 17gpu Dec 30] leggy gelding: fairly useful on Flat (stays 11f), successful at Amiens on last of 4 starts at 3 yrs in France, sold out of M. Zilber's stable 18,000 gns Newmarket Autumn (2003) Sales: failed to settle both starts in novice hurdles. *Miss Venetia Williams* **h–**

DARK SLANEY (IRE) 10 b.g. Meneval (USA) – Black Valley (IRE) (Good Thyne (USA)) [2004/5 h–: 20d5 22g* 27m3 Jul 26] poor hurdler: won selling handicap at Cartmel in July: stays 2¾m. *P. D. Niven* **h71**

DARK SOCIETY 7 b.g. Imp Society (USA) – No Candles Tonight (Star Appeal) [2004/5 16g* 17v* 16g6 16s4 16g* Jan 19] modest novice hurdler: won handicaps at Kempton (conditional jockeys) and Bangor in November and Fakenham in January: raced around 2m: acts on heavy going: held up: fair on Flat, successful in February. *A. W. Carroll* **h89**

DARK THUNDER (IRE) 8 br.g. Religiously (USA) – Culkeern (Master Buck) [2004/5 c–, h–: c27vpu c27v 27v3 27v* c27v3 27d3 24s Apr 20] modest hurdler: won selling handicap at Sedgefield in March by distance: first form over fences when third in handicap at same course: stays 27f: acts on heavy going: may do better again over fences. *Ferdy Murphy* **c67 + h87**

DARNAY BOY (IRE) 5 b.g. Darnay – Mumtaz Queen (IRE) (Emmson) [2004/5 F17s6 Apr 2] second foal: dam no sign of ability: tailed off in bumper on debut. *Mrs P. Ford* **F–**

DARNAYSON (IRE) 5 b.g. Darnay – Nakuru (IRE) (Mandalus) [2004/5 F17s2 F16v2 19d 19s3 24d4 Mar 8] 9,000 3-y-o: tall gelding: fourth foal: half-brother to useful hurdler/fairly useful chaser Prominent Profile (by Mazaad), stays 3m: dam, placed in bumper, half-sister to dam of useful hurdler/chaser Storm Damage, stayed 31f: runner-up in bumpers at Hereford and Uttoxeter (carried head awkwardly): best effort in novice hurdles when fourth at Exeter: stays 3m: has raced freely: type to do better over fences. *N. A. Twiston-Davies* **h100 F91**

DARNLEY 8 b. or br.g. Henbit (USA) – Reeling (Relkino) [2004/5 c100, h95: c16g5 16g Sep 23] tall gelding: modest hurdler/fair chaser: below form both starts in 2004/5: raced around 2m: acts on soft and good to firm going. *J. N. R. Billinge* **c– h85 +**

DARRIAS (GER) 4 b.g. Sternkoenig (IRE) – Dark Lady (GER) (Lagunas) [2004/5 16d5 16s6 17g* Apr 15] lengthy gelding: successful once over 1¼m from 6 starts on Flat for H. Blume in Germany in 2004: fair form in juvenile hurdles: won at Taunton by 2½ lengths from Master Mahogany: will prove best at 2m: free-going sort: sure to progress further. *P. F. Nicholls* **h105 p**

DARYAL (IRE) 4 b.c. Night Shift (USA) – Darata (IRE) (Vayrann) [2004/5 16s 17s* 16g2 16d2 16g Mar 15] good-topped colt: half-brother to fair hurdler Darbela (by Doyoun), stays 2½m: fairly useful on Flat, placed 4 times up to around 1½m from 5 starts in 2004 for A. de Royer Dupre: fairly useful juvenile hurdler: won novice at Taunton in January: ran well after when runner-up at Sandown and Newbury: likely to stay beyond 17f. *A. King* **h115**

DASH FOR COVER (IRE) 5 b.g. Sesaro (USA) – Raindancing (IRE) (Tirol) [2004/5 16g 17d6 16d 18s Mar 9] angular gelding: fair at one time on Flat (stays 9.7f), sold out of R. Hannon's stable 10,000 gns Newmarket Autumn Sales: poor form over hurdles. *J. G. Portman* **h78**

DASH FOR GLORY 6 ch.g. Bluegrass Prince (IRE) – Rekindled Flame (IRE) (Kings Lake (USA)) [2004/5 17gpu Aug 21] poor maiden on Flat (stays 1¼m): no show on hurdling debut. *J. S. King* **h–**

DASHING CHARM 6 b.g. Charmer – New Cruiser (Le Solaret (FR)) [2004/5 h–, F–: 24spu 21d Oct 31] stocky gelding: of little account outside points. *G. F. Bridgwater* **h–**

DASHING DOLLAR (IRE) 14 b.g. Lord Americo – Cora Swan (Tarqogan) [2004/5 h61§: 20spu 24d5 16s5 24g6 19dpu Jan 7] smallish, workmanlike gelding: veteran handicap hurdler: stays 3m: acts on heavy going: ungenuine. *J. R. Payne* **h63 §**

DASHING HOME (IRE) 6 b.g. Lahib (USA) – Dashing Rose (Mashhor Dancer (USA)) [2004/5 h119: 16gbd 16g 16d5 Nov 27] tall gelding: will make a chaser: useful up to 1½m on Flat, successful twice in 2004: fairly useful handicap hurdler: not sure to stay beyond 2m: acts on good to firm and heavy going. *N. Meade, Ireland* **h119**

DASH OF MAGIC 7 b.m. Magic Ring (IRE) – Praglia (IRE) (Darshaan) [2004/5 17d 20m Dec 12] leggy mare: modest on Flat (should stay 1¾m), successful 3 times in 2004: little form over hurdles. *J. Hetherton* **h–**

DATITO (IRE) 10 b.g. Over The River (FR) – Crash Call (Crash Course) [2004/5 h102: c24spu c24s* c23dpu Apr 20] tall gelding: thrice-raced over hurdles: only comple- **c100 ? h–**

tion in novice chases when beating Sea Ferry by distance in match at Newcastle in March, making numerous mistakes: seems to stay 3m. *R. T. Phillips*

DAT MY HORSE (IRE) 11 b.g. All Haste (USA) – Toposki (FR) (Top Ville) [2004/5 cxx, h97: 24g 20g^{pu} 20m^{pu} Aug 19] big, workmanlike gelding: winning staying hurdler: has finished tamely: bad jumper over fences. *Evan Williams* **cxx h–**

DAUNTED (IRE) 9 b.g. Priolo (USA) – Dauntess (Formidable (USA)) [2004/5 16d Feb 9] fair on Flat (stays 2m), successful 5 times in 2004: little form in 3 starts over hurdles. *P. A. Blockley* **h–**

DAVENPORT MILENIUM (IRE) 9 b.g. Insan (USA) – Society Belle (Callernish) [2004/5 h148: c20s^{ur} c16s^{2} c20s^{pu} Mar 29] useful-looking gelding: smart hurdler in 2003/4, reportedly underwent wind operation and off a year: clearly best effort over fences when 5¾ lengths third to Forget The Past in Grade 2 novice at Punchestown in late-April: will stay 3m: raced on good going or softer (won bumper on heavy). *W. P. Mullins, Ireland* **c136 h–**

DAVIDS LAD (IRE) 11 b.g. Yashgan – Cool Nora (IRE) (Lafontaine (USA)) [2004/5 c138, h–: 24g^{6} c20d^{3} 22m* 22g^{5} c19s^{3} c16s c19s c21d c18s 18s^{4} c21g Mar 17] strong, lengthy gelding: fair hurdler: won handicap at Kelso in May: smart chaser at best, little form in 2004/5 before winning cross-country event at Punchestown in late-April by 4½ lengths from Shady Lad: reportedly fractured pedal bone when pulled up there 48 hrs later: stays 29f: acts on any going: effective tongue tied or not: held up: usually sound jumper. *A. J. Martin, Ireland* **c138 d h109**

DAVNIC 5 ch.m. Weld – Lahtico VII (Damsire Unregistered) [2004/5 F16g F16g F16g Sep 12] lengthy, unfurnished mare: fourth foal: dam never ran: no form in bumpers. *P. Morris* **F–**

DAVOSKI 11 b.g. Niniski (USA) – Pamela Peach (Habitat) [2004/5 c122, h–: c20d^{5} c21d^{5} c16m c20g^{4} c16g^{pu} 20d^{5} 16g c20d* c16g c20d^{5} Apr 8] angular gelding: winning hurdler: fair handicap chaser nowadays: sold out of Ms B. Nicholls' stable 7,800 gns Doncaster May Sales after second outing: 50/1-winner at Cheltenham in November: stays 21f: acts on good to firm and heavy going: tried in cheekpieces: often jumps poorly: ungenuine. *Dr P. Pritchard* **c113 § h100 ?**

DAVY JO 6 b.g. Jumbo Hirt (USA) – Morepatience (North Briton) [2004/5 20m^{pu} 16m^{ur} Jun 5] third foal: dam unraced: tongue tied, no show in 2 novice hurdles. *M. A. Barnes* **h–**

DAWADARI (IRE) 5 b.g. Indian Ridge – Dawala (IRE) (Lashkari) [2004/5 F16m F16s^{4} F16m* F16g* F16s* F16s^{2} F16v^{3} Apr 17] leggy gelding: half-brother to 3 winners, including useful hurdler up to 3¼m Darapour (by Fairy King): dam, French 1½m winner, closely related to Darshaan and half-sister to smart staying hurdler Daraydan and one-time useful 2m hurdler Darialaan: smart bumper performer, completed hat-trick at Down Royal when beating Classic Vic by 14 lengths in November: below form after, including in Grade 1 won by Refinement at Punchestown in April: reportedly lame sixth start: makes running. *S. J. Mahon, Ireland* **F118**

DAWN DEVOY (IRE) 6 b.g. Supreme Leader – Dawn Hunt (IRE) (Architect (USA)) [2004/5 F16v F16d 18v^{5} 21v^{3} 20s^{2} Apr 20] lengthy gelding: third foal: dam, winning pointer, from family of Dawn Run: won maiden Irish point in 2004: well held in 2 bumpers: modest form over hurdles when runner-up in maiden at Perth. *Miss V. Scott* **h92 F–**

DAWN FROLICS 4 gr.f. Silver Patriarch (IRE) – Mighty Frolic (Oats) [2004/5 aF13g F12g Dec 8] 1,500 3-y-o: sturdy filly: fourth foal: dam, fairly useful hunter, stayed 3½m: well beaten in 3-y-o bumpers: pulled hard and hung badly on debut. *M. J. Gingell* **F–**

DAWN'S COGNAC (IRE) 12 b.g. Glacial Storm (USA) – Misty Venture (Foggy Bell) [2004/5 c–x: c24d^{3} Apr 22] rangy gelding: little form outside points, successful 4 times in 2005: often let down by jumping. *D. Brace* **c74 x**

DAWN WALK (IRE) 4 b.f. Kahyasi – Lautrea (IRE) (Danehill (USA)) [2004/5 F16d^{6} Feb 18] second foal: dam unraced: well held in mares bumper on debut. *N. A. Twiston-Davies* **F–**

DAWTON (POL) 7 br.g. Greinton – Da Wega (POL) (Who Knows) [2004/5 h–: 16g 17g* 16g* 16d^{5} 17g^{2} 16g^{2} 16d Nov 12] compact gelding: fairly useful novice hurdler: won at Newton Abbot in June and Perth in July: good efforts when runner-up after, beaten 6 lengths by Goblet of Fire in handicap at Cheltenham on second occasion: out of depth **h117**

and possibly amiss final start: likely to stay beyond 2m: unraced on extremes of going over hurdles: races prominently. *T. R. George*

DAY DU ROY (FR) 7 b.g. Ajdayt (USA) – Rose Pomme (FR) (Rose Laurel) [2004/5 c115, h110: c20d* c17m^{5} 19d^{6} c17d^{2} c17g^{2} c16m^{5} 22d^{6} 20d^{3} 19d 20g^{6} Mar 26] rather leggy gelding: fairly useful handicap chaser: won at Southwell in May: sold out of J. O'Neill's stable 20,000 gns Doncaster October Sales after sixth start: fair handicap hurdler: stays 2½m: acts on good to soft and good to firm going: below form both runs in blinkers: has had tongue tied: held up and often finds little. *Miss L. C. Siddall* **c123 § h103 §**

DAYENOO (FR) 5 b.g. Subotica (FR) – La Cenomane (FR) (Master Thatch) [2004/5 F83: F17d^{5} F17v 20s Oct 31] medium-sized gelding: form in bumpers only on debut: no show on hurdling debut: won point in March. *M. W. Easterby* **h– F–**

DAYS OF GOLD 6 ch.m. Past Glories – Flira (Lir) [2004/5 F17g^{pu} Jul 12] second foal: dam never ran: looked reluctant in bumper on debut. *Ms Sue Willcock* **F–**

DAYTIME ARRIVAL (IRE) 7 ch.g. Lucky Guest – Daymer Bay (Lomond (USA)) [2004/5 h–: 20d^{pu} 16g c16g^{F} c17g c16m c16g^{6} c16d^{pu} Oct 9] angular gelding: won 2-runner point in March, of little account otherwise: tried blinkered. *K. S. Thomas* **c– x h–**

DAZZLING RIO (IRE) 6 b.g. Ashkalani (IRE) – Dazzling Fire (IRE) (Bluebird (USA)) [2004/5 h87d: 17m^{F} May 19] lengthy gelding: maiden hurdler: fell fatally at Sedgefield: stayed easy 21f: unraced on extremes of going: tried in cheekpieces. *G. M. Moore* **h–**

DBEST (IRE) 5 b.g. Woodborough (USA) – Leopard Lily (IRE) (Belmez (USA)) [2004/5 16m^{2} 16m* 16m^{2} Jul 26] fair on Flat (stays 1¼m): fair handicap hurdler: won at Roscommon in June: good second at Galway following month: well held at Punchestown in late-April: likely to prove best around 2m: acts on good to firm going. *Ms J. Morgan, Ireland* **h111**

DD'S GLENALLA (IRE) 8 b.m. Be My Native (USA) – Willowho Pride (Arapaho) [2004/5 h89: c23d^{pu} 21g^{6} 20d^{5} 24v 25v* 26s^{5} 26s^{ur} 26g Mar 16] leggy, quite good-topped mare: jumped poorly on chasing debut: modest handicap hurdler: won conditional jockeys event at Warwick in December: stays 3¼m: acts on good to firm and heavy going: has looked temperamental. *N. A. Twiston-Davies* **c– h96**

DEAD-EYED DICK (IRE) 9 b.g. Un Desperado (FR) – Glendale Charmer (Down The Hatch) [2004/5 c90, h–: c16d^{5} c26m* c25g* c23s^{5} c25d^{ur} Nov 22] tall, quite good-topped gelding: modest handicap chaser: won at Newton Abbot in September and Exeter in October: stays 3¼m: acts on soft and good to firm going: sometimes runs as if amiss. *Nick Williams* **c99 h–**

DEAD MANS DANTE (IRE) 7 ch.g. Montelimar (USA) – Great Dante (IRE) (Phardante (FR)) [2004/5 F16m^{2} F16f^{3} 20g^{pu} 20m^{2} 20s^{5} 24m Nov 26] first foal: dam fair bumper winner: best effort in bumpers for A. Mullins when second at Punchestown: poor novice hurdler: stays 2½m: free-going sort. *Ferdy Murphy* **h82 F96**

DEALER'S CHOICE (IRE) 11 gr.g. Roselier (FR) – Cam Flower VII (Damsire Unregistered) [2004/5 c111§, h95§: 26g^{pu} c25g^{pu} c24s^{3} c24d^{4} c20d^{3} Feb 9] quite good-topped gelding: modest hurdler: fair handicap chaser: stays 27f: acts on soft going: tried blinkered/in cheekpieces: usually let down by jumping/temperament. *Miss Victoria Roberts* **c108 § h– §**

DEAR DEAL 12 b.g. Sharp Deal – The Deer Hound (Cash And Carry) [2004/5 c122, h–: c24d^{4} c24d^{F} c25d^{4} c26g^{ur} c25d^{2} c24g^{5} c30d c25d^{2} c25d^{4} Apr 3] lengthy gelding: fairly useful handicap chaser: running very well when falling 2 out in race won by Gunther McBride at Kempton second start: no comparable form after: stays at least 4m: acts on soft and firm going: tried blinkered: has had tongue tied. *C. L. Tizzard* **c127 d h–**

DEAR SIR (IRE) 5 ch.g. Among Men (USA) – Deerussa (IRE) (Jareer (USA)) [2004/5 h84: 19g^{6} 17g^{2} 16g 17f^{5} 16g 17d^{5} c16d^{pu} c19g^{ur} Apr 7] tall gelding: modest hurdler: best effort when second in handicap at Newton Abbot: no show in maiden chases: raced mainly around 2m on good going or firmer. *Mrs P. N. Dutfield* **c– h92**

DEARSON (IRE) 4 b.g. Definite Article – Petite Maxine (Sharpo) [2004/5 F13s F12d^{5} 16g^{6} Mar 11] 17,000Y: fifth foal: half-brother to several winners, including fairly useful sprinter Pipadash (by Pips Pride) and 11.6f winner Pont Neuf (by Revoque): dam, maiden who stayed 7f, half-sister to dam of useful 2m to 21f jumper Chief's Song: sold unraced out of E. O'Neill's stable 6,500 gns Newmarket July Sales: fair form second start **h82 F89**

in bumpers: none too fluent when sixth of 9 in novice at Sandown on hurdling debut. *C. J. Mann*

DEBATABLE 6 ch.g. Deploy – Questionable (Rainbow Quest (USA)) [2004/5 F105: 19d^pu 16g 22g^pu Apr 17] won bumper for P. Webber on debut: off 18 months, no show over hurdles. *N. J. Hawke* **h–**

DEBBIE 6 b.m. Deploy – Elita (Sharpo) [2004/5 h85: 16d* 16g² 16g³ 16g* 16g³ 16g⁴ 17d* 16g⁴ 16d 16d* 16d⁶ Jan 29] close-coupled mare: fairly useful hurdler: won novices at Wetherby (conditional jockeys) in May, Uttoxeter in July and Hereford in October and handicap at Catterick (much improved when beating Stan by 17 lengths) in January: likely to prove best around 2m: raced on good/good to soft ground over hurdles: held up. *B. D. Leavy* **h119**

DE BLANC (IRE) 5 b.m. Revoque (IRE) – Queen's Share (Main Reef) [2004/5 h108: 17g³ 16g³ 16g* 17d* 16s 16d³ 16d⁴ 16g² 16g^F 16g⁴ Apr 15] good-topped mare: fairly useful handicap hurdler: won at Ludlow (mares) and Exeter in December: ran well sixth to eighth outings: raced around 2m: acts on good to soft ground: often leads/races prominently: sold 35,000 gns Doncaster May Sales. *Miss Venetia Williams* **h123**

DECKIE (IRE) 10 b.g. Be My Native (USA) – Shannon Spray (Le Bavard (FR)) [2004/5 c24d* Mar 28] angular gelding: winning hurdler/chaser: bought out of C. Roche's stable 5,500 gns Doncaster May (2004) Sales: successful 4 of first 6 starts in points in 2005: also won hunter at Fakenham in March, beating only other finisher a distance: stays 3m: acts on firm and soft going: effective tongue tied or not. *D. J. Kemp* **c105 h–**

DECODED 9 ch.g. Deploy – Golden Panda (Music Boy) [2004/5 c–, h–: c22s^pu c25m^pu May 19] compact gelding: winning hurdler/chaser: of little account nowadays: often wears cheekpieces. *Mrs Sarah L. Dent* **c– h–**

DEDRUNKNMUNKY (IRE) 6 b. or br.m. Rashar (USA) – Rostoonstown Lass (IRE) (Decent Fellow) [2004/5 F16g⁶ 21s^pu 16d^F 21s³ 26m³ 24m Apr 10] angular mare: sixth foal: half-sister to winning pointer by Dromod Hill: dam unraced: won mares maiden Irish point in 2004: bought 17,000 gns Doncaster May Sales: sixth to The Mick Weston in bumper at Cheltenham: poor form over hurdles: looks a thorough stayer: sold 9,200 gns Doncaster May Sales. *N. A. Twiston-Davies* **h83 F83**

DEE PEE TEE CEE (IRE) 11 b.g. Tidaro (USA) – Silver Glimpse (Petingo) [2004/5 16d⁵ 17v Dec 31] good-topped gelding: winning 2m hurdler: very lightly raced since 2000: acts on soft going. *M. W. Easterby* **h94**

DEEP KING (IRE) 10 b. or br.g. King's Ride – Splendid Run (Deep Run) [2004/5 c85: c20g³ c17g* c16g* c16d³ c16m² c20d³ Oct 14] lengthy gelding: fair handicap chaser: improved jumper, won at Southwell in May and Newton Abbot in June: effective at 2m to 23f: acts on firm and good to soft going: has had tongue tied. *J. W. Mullins* **c110**

DEEP SIGH 8 b.g. Weld – At Long Last (John French) [2004/5 c–x, h73x: 16m^R May 16] good-topped gelding: little form over hurdles: failed to complete in 2 novice chases: untrustworthy. *D. R. Gandolfo* **c– x h– x**

DEEP WATER (USA) 11 b.g. Diesis – Water Course (USA) (Irish River (FR)) [2004/5 c120, h–: c16d⁴ c20d² c20s⁴ c19d⁴ c21d⁶ c20s⁶ c20s^pu Apr 20] leggy gelding: fairly useful handicap chaser: lost form final 3 starts: barely stays 2¾m: acts on good to firm and heavy going: visored twice. *M. D. Hammond* **c119 h–**

DEER DANCER 5 b.g. Tamure (IRE) – Anatomic (Deerhound (USA)) [2004/5 h101, F94: 17d² 19s 21d c19d³ c19d^F Mar 8] fair hurdler: modest form when third in maiden on completed start over fences: stays 19f: raced on going softer than good. *J. D. Frost* **c90 h102**

DEEWAAR (IRE) 5 b.g. Ashkalani (IRE) – Chandni (IRE) (Ahonoora) [2004/5 h–: 16d 16m³ 16d Nov 1] lengthy, sparely-made gelding: untrustworthy maiden on Flat: poor form over hurdles: likely to prove best at 2m: free-going sort *J. C. Fox* **h73**

DEFANA 4 b.g. Defacto (USA) – Thalya (Crofthall) [2004/5 16s^pu Feb 14] modest on Flat (stays 1½m), successful in September, sold out of M. Dods's stable 1,800 gns Doncaster October Sales: no show in juvenile on hurdling debut. *D. C. O'Brien* **h–**

DEFERLANT (FR) 8 ch.g. Bering – Sail Storm (USA) (Topsider (USA)) [2004/5 c–§, h96§: 22g⁵ 22m² 22m* 26g 22s* 24s^F 24g 22s⁴ 21d 20v 22d Feb 20] close-coupled gelding: fair handicap hurdler: won at Fontwell in September and October: stays 2¾m: acts on soft and good to firm going: formerly visored, wears cheekpieces and tongue strap nowadays: moody. *K. Bell* **c– § h101 §**

John Smith's Extra Smooth Handicap Hurdle, Aintree—
Definate Spectacle beats Say What You See to become the third Irish-trained winner of this race in as many years

DEFINATE SPECTACLE (IRE) 5 b.g. Spectrum (IRE) – Silver Bubble (USA) (Silver Hawk (USA)) [2004/5 h124p: 16g* 16vpu 16s 16s 16s 16sur 16d* Apr 9] sturdy gelding: fairly useful hurdler: won minor event at Punchestown in April 2004: improved effort when winning valuable 18-runner handicap at Aintree by 8 lengths from Say What You See: will prove best at 2m: raced on good going or softer. *N. Meade, Ireland* **h126 +**

DEFINITE APPROACH (IRE) 7 b.g. Presenting – Crash Approach (Crash Course) [2004/5 24d2 24d3 Mar 8] useful-looking gelding: eighth foal: half-brother to smart 2m hurdler/winning chaser Adamant Approach (by Mandalus): dam unraced half-sister to Hennessy winner Approaching: fourth in bumper at Punchestown in October 2003 for E. Hales: better effort in novice hurdles when third to Laska de Thaix at Exeter: will stay beyond 3m. *R. T. Phillips* **h103**

DEFINITE GUEST (IRE) 7 gr.g. Definite Article – Nicea (IRE) (Dominion) [2004/5 16m Aug 30] leggy gelding: fairly useful on Flat (stays 1¼m), successful twice at 5 yrs: favourite, let down by jumping and finished distressed in maiden on hurdling debut. *R. A. Fahey* **h–**

DEJA VU (IRE) 6 b.g. Lord Americo – Khalkeys Shoon (Green Shoon) [2004/5 h85: 21d5 21d* 21v* 20vpu 21v3 27d4 Apr 5] sturdy gelding: fair hurdler: won minor event and handicap at Sedgefield in December: stays 21f: raced on good going or softer (acts on heavy). *J. Howard Johnson* **h105**

DELAWARE BAY 6 ch.g. Karinga Bay – Galacia (IRE) (Gallic League) [2004/5 c71, h82: c19mur 22d* 22s 22s4 24d 22d4 22s2 24gpu Apr 1] useful-looking gelding: poor form on completed start over fences: fair handicap hurdler: won amateur event at Exeter in **c– h101**

December: lame final outing: should stay 3m: acts on heavy going: has looked difficult ride. *R. H. Alner*

DELAWARE (FR) 9 b.g. Garde Royale – L'Indienne (FR) (Le Nain Jaune (FR)) [2004/5 24g 27g 17g4 20m6 27d4 26m 26m3 17fur 19g4 24g5 19d6 17d2 19v4 Apr 22] leggy, angular gelding: modest hurdler nowadays: left M. Pipe after eleventh outing: probably stays 27f, effective at much shorter: acts on heavy and good to firm going: sometimes used to wear visor/cheekpieces: ungenuine. *H. S. Howe* **c– § h85 §**

DELFINIA 4 b.f. Kingsinger (IRE) – Delvecchia (Glint of Gold) [2004/5 16mF 16spu 16m 16d 16g 17d6 16s6 Apr 10] sturdy filly: well held on Flat, sold out of H. S. Howe's stable £1,100 Ascot August Sales: little show over hurdles. *N. Waggott* **h76 ?**

DELGAY LAD 7 b.g. Homo Sapien – Sloe Hill (Le Moss) [2004/5 F17s F18d 19s6 19g 16s5 Mar 5] 13,000 4-y-o: well-made gelding: second foal: dam, winning pointer, half-sister to useful hurdler/chaser up to 25f Moondigua: well held in 2 bumpers: sixth to It's Just Harry at Hereford, best effort in novice hurdles: should do better granted more of a test of stamina. *Jonjo O'Neill* **h89 p F–**

DELICEO (IRE) 12 b.g. Roselier (FR) – Grey's Delight (Decent Fellow) [2004/5 c101§, h–§: c20d* c20d* c24s c19vpu c20d c20d4 c23m3 c19d Apr 22] leggy gelding: fair handicap chaser: won at Huntingdon in October and Ludlow in November: stays 25f: acts on any going: usually held up: inconsistent. *M. Sheppard* **c103 § h– §**

DELIGHTFUL CLICHE 4 b.g. Classic Cliche (IRE) – Ima Delight (Idiot's Delight) [2004/5 F16m2 Apr 10] third foal: dam, fair hurdler, stayed 2¾m: 1½ lengths second to Young Dude in 19-runner maiden bumper at Worcester on debut: likely to stay 2½m. *Mrs P. Sly* **F86**

DELIGHTFULLY 4 b.f. Definite Article – Kingpin Delight (Emarati (USA)) [2004/5 16m Apr 2] angular filly: fair on Flat (stays easy 13f), sold out of B. Hills's stable £5,700 Ascot October Sales: eighth of 15 in novice hurdle at Newbury, not knocked about when unable to reach leaders: likely to improve. *Jean-Rene Auvray* **h82 p**

DELIGHTFUL PET 8 b.m. Tina's Pet – Majestic Golfe (Majestic Maharaj) [2004/5 20mpu Jun 27] first foal: dam poor staying hurdler: no show in maiden hurdle on debut. *P. Bowen* **h–**

DEL LA ROSA 7 ch.h. Sabrehill (USA) – Song Test (USA) (The Minstrel (CAN)) [2004/5 16mpu Jun 13] successful 3 times up to 7.5f on Flat in Germany: winning hurdler/chaser in France and Italy: left E. Leenders and off 14 months, no show in handicap hurdle on British debut: raced mainly around 2m. *B. G. Powell* **c– h–**

DELL FARM BOY 7 b.g. Lancastrian – Wild Sap (Sapsford) [2004/5 F16g May 1] third foal: dam, winning pointer, half-sister to top-class staying chaser Rushing Wild: tailed off in bumper on debut. *G. J. Smith* **F–**

DELPHI 9 ch.g. Grand Lodge (USA) – Euridice (IRE) (Woodman (USA)) [2004/5 h–: 22d6 May 3] smallish gelding: maiden hurdler: should stay beyond 2½m: acts on soft and good to firm going: tried blinkered/visored. *B. G. Powell* **h–**

DELPHINE 6 ch.m. Old Vic – Oh So Bright (Celtic Cone) [2004/5 F84: F16d F17g 16spu 22dpu Mar 24] unfurnished mare: modest in bumpers: pulled up both starts over hurdles. *T. R. George* **h– F76**

DEL TROTTER (IRE) 10 b.g. King Luthier – Arctic Alice (Brave Invader (USA)) [2004/5 c88, h87: 17gpu c16d4 c21d c16spu c16vpu c22sR c21v4 c25s6 Apr 10] maiden hurdler/winning chaser: little impact in 2004/5, sold out of J. H. Johnson's stable 2,300 gns Doncaster May Sales after first outing: stays 19f: acts on heavy going: tried blinkered/in cheekpieces: has looked tricky ride. *M. E. Sowersby* **c82 d h–**

DEMARCO (IRE) 7 ch.g. Old Vic – Peas (IRE) (Little Wolf) [2004/5 F114: 18s* Feb 4] medium-sized gelding: useful bumper performer: off over 10 months, promising start over hurdles when winning novice at Fontwell by 12 lengths from Escompteur: will be suited by 2½m+. *N. J. Henderson* **h130 p**

DEMASTA (NZ) 14 ch.g. Northerly Native (USA) – Hit It Gold (AUS) (Hit It Benny (AUS)) [2004/5 c112, h–: c17mpu May 22] compact gelding: veteran chaser: won point in January: tried in cheekpieces: bold-jumping front runner. *Ms A. E. Embiricos* **c– h–**

DEMI BEAU 7 b.g. Dr Devious (IRE) – Charming Life (NZ) (Sir Tristram) [2004/5 h133: 17g 16g5 16g Apr 16] tall gelding: useful handicap hurdler in 2003/4: easily best effort after year's absence when fifth to Pardishar at Newbury: raced around 2m: yet to race on extremes of going: often shapes as if amiss. *C. J. Mann* **h120**

Sunderlands Novices' Chase, Sandown—
Dempsey keeps the jumping errors to a minimum as he proves too strong for Mambo

DEMPSEY (IRE) 7 b.g. Lord Americo – Kyle Cailin (Over The River (FR)) [2004/5 h121, F104: 16g c17s^{F} c21d^{pu} c16d^{2} c16s* c16d^{ur} c16d* c16d^{3} Apr 9] good-topped gelding: fairly useful hurdler: better over fences, won maiden at Ludlow in January and novice at Sandown (beat Mambo comfortably by 4 lengths) in March: respectable third to Ashley Brook in Grade 1 novice at Aintree, jumping more fluently and weakening after 3 out having tried to take on winner: raced mainly at 2m, only on good going or softer over jumps (won bumper on good to firm). *M. Pitman* **c133 h–**

DENADA 9 ch.g. Bob Back (USA) – Alavie (FR) (Quart de Vin (FR)) [2004/5 c24s^{F} Apr 2] lengthy gelding: fair form only 2 completed starts in chases: off over 2 years, would probably have finished second in weak maiden at Bangor but for falling last: likely to stay beyond 3¼m. *Mrs Susan Nock* **c94 ?**

DENARIUS SECUNDUS 8 ch.g. Barathea (IRE) – Penny Drops (Sharpo) [2004/5 22v 22v^{4} 20v 20s^{4} Mar 30] disappointing maiden on Flat for M. Tregoning: poor novice hurdler, left J. Brassil after third outing: stays 2¾m: raced mainly on soft/heavy ground. *N. R. Mitchell* **h60**

DENARIUS (USA) 10 b.g. Silver Hawk (USA) – Ambrosine (USA) (Mr Prospector (USA)) [2004/5 17v^{6} 25v^{pu} 21v 16v Feb 20] good-topped gelding: modest handicap hurdler in 2002/3 for G. A. Swinbank: no sign of retaining ability: tried in cheekpieces: has had tongue tied: ungenuine: sold £850 Ascot April Sales. *J. G. M. O'Shea* **c– § h– §**

DENISE BEST (IRE) 7 ch.m. Goldmark (USA) – Titchwell Lass (Lead On Time (USA)) [2004/5 17s 20g c16s^{5} 16d c19g^{6} 19s^{3} Jan 10] stocky mare: poor novice hurdler: similar form both outings over fences: probably stays 2½m: wears headgear. *Miss K. M. George* **c74 h62**

DENNIS THE MENNIS (IRE) 6 b.g. Fourstars Allstar (USA) – Farm Approach (Tug of War) [2004/5 F–: F16g 24g^{pu} 16s 16s 20s* 24v^{5} 24v^{5} 21v* 20s Apr 10] well beaten in bumpers: poor hurdler: sold out of Mrs A. Thorpe's stable 1,100 gns Doncaster **h75 F–**

October Sales after second outing: won conditional jockeys selling handicaps at Newcastle in January and Sedgefield in March: may prove best short of 3m when conditions are testing: raced on good going or softer (acts on heavy). *R. Johnson*

DENVALE (IRE) 7 b.g. Denel (FR) – Brackenvale (IRE) (Strong Gale) [2004/5 c23s² c24s* c26g⁵ Apr 14] IR £14,500 3-y-o: tall, angular gelding: first foal: dam poor maiden hurdler: fairly useful pointer, successful in February: good start in hunter chases, won at Towcester in March in good style: possibly amiss next time. *Mrs Caroline Bailey* **c111**

DEO GRATIAS (POL) 5 b.h. Enjoy Plan (USA) – Dea (POL) (Canadian Winter (CAN)) [2004/5 18mur 22g⁴ 16m⁴ 20m Sep 19] angular horse: successful over 1m and 9f on Flat in Poland: poor form over hurdles. *M. Pitman* **h78**

DEPTFORD (IRE) 6 ch.g. Un Desperado (FR) – Katty London (Camden Town) [2004/5 F88: 16g³ 19g⁴ 19s³ 20g Feb 5] rather unfurnished gelding: fair form in novice hurdles: lame final outing: should be suited by 2½m+. *P. R. Chamings* **h101**

DEPUTY FAIRFAX (IRE) 7 b. or br.g. Posen (USA) – Rainbow Gurriers (IRE) (Buckskin (FR)) [2004/5 c20dpu c26vpu Oct 29] ex-Irish gelding: no form in bumpers or chases, left J. Mangan after reappearance: won points in March and April: tried blinkered. *D. Brace* **c–**

DEPUTY LEADER (IRE) 13 b.g. Florida Son – Larne (Giolla Mear) [2004/5 c–, h–: c17d May 29] rangy gelding: winning pointer. *J. K. Hunter* **c–** **h–**

DERAINEY (IRE) 6 b.g. Farhaan – Hurricane Hazel (Lorenzaccio) [2004/5 F16d 20vpu Feb 2] lengthy gelding: seventh foal: half-brother to fair sprinter Wild Honour (by Fayruz) and winner in Italy by Petardia: dam poor maiden: no sign of ability: tongue tied on hurdling debut. *R. Johnson* **h–** **F–**

DERAMORE (IRE) 8 b.g. Hollow Hand – Leaney Kamscort (Kambalda) [2004/5 24g c20f⁴ c22m c25d⁴ c24s c23d c24gpu c16dpu 16d Feb 18] lengthy ex-Irish gelding: brother to winning hurdler/fair chaser Son of Light, stays 3¼m: dam unraced: poor maiden hurdler/chaser: sold out of D. T. Hughes's stable 8,000 gns Doncaster October Sales, no form in 3 starts in Britain: stays 25f: acts on firm going: sometimes blinkered, also tried in cheekpieces: usually tongue tied. *B. N. Pollock* **c–** **h–**

DERE LYN 7 b.g. Awesome – Our Resolution (Caerleon (USA)) [2004/5 19g* 24d⁴ 22d³ 22d⁶ 24g 24d 20v* 20v⁶ 17v* 24d⁶ 21s⁴ Mar 31] smallish, rather leggy gelding: modest handicap hurdler, off over 2 years before reappearance: won at Hereford (66/1, final start for D. Burchell) in September, Leicester (hung right) in January and Hereford again in February: needs testing conditions around 2m, stays 3m: acts on heavy going: effective in headgear and tongue tied or not. *Mrs D. A. Hamer* **h97**

DERIVATIVE (IRE) 7 b. or br.g. Erins Isle – Our Hope (Dancing Brave (USA)) [2004/5 h121: 23m May 1] smallish gelding: fairly useful handicap hurdler: below best only outing in 2004/5: stays 3m: acts on heavy going: tried blinkered: not an easy ride. *Miss Venetia Williams* **h113**

DERRAVARRA EAGLE (IRE) 5 br.g. Flemensfirth (USA) – Rathcolman Queen (IRE) (Radical) [2004/5 F16s* Nov 26] third foal: half-brother to winning hurdlers Derravarra Breeze, stays 2½m, and Derravarra Sunset (both by Supreme Leader), at 2m, latter also successful at 1¾m on Flat: dam unraced half-sister to useful chaser up to 3m Greenwood Lad: weak 7/1-chance, useful form when winning 16-runner bumper at Wexford on debut by 4 lengths from Avoca Mist, held up and leading over 1f out. *N. Meade, Ireland* **F106**

DERRING DOVE 13 b.g. Derring Rose – Shadey Dove (Deadly Nightshade) [2004/5 c–§, h–: c24d⁵ Apr 22] angular gelding: winning pointer: maiden chaser: stays 3¼m: acts on good to firm and heavy going: tried visored: unreliable. *H. W. Lavis* **c– §** **h–**

DERRINTOGHER YANK (IRE) 11 b.g. Lord Americo – Glenmalur (Black Minstrel) [2004/5 c119, h108: c24g⁴ Apr 7] rangy gelding: winning hurdler: fairly useful chaser: shaped as if in need of race, only outing in 2004/5: stays 3m: raced mainly on good going or softer: front runner. *Miss R. S. Reynolds* **c101 +** **h–**

DERRY DICE 9 b.g. Derrylin – Paper Dice (Le Dauphin) [2004/5 h79: 20d Nov 13] lengthy gelding: poor novice hurdler: stays 3m: blinkered. *C. T. Pogson* **h–**

DERWENT (USA) 6 b.g. Distant View (USA) – Nothing Sweeter (USA) (Darby Creek Road (USA)) [2004/5 20vpu 17g Apr 7] useful at best on Flat (stays 1¼m, usually **h–**

blinkered), fair in 2004, sold out of J. Bethell's stable 13,000 gns Newmarket Autumn Sales: no form in maiden hurdles. *R. H. Buckler*

DESAILLY 11 ch.g. Teamster – G W Superstar (Rymer) [2004/5 c132, h–: c24d² c26g² c29v^F Dec 28] strong, lengthy gelding: useful handicap chaser: good second to Colonel Frank at Sandown (final start for G. Balding) and Willie John Daly at Newbury (bled from nose): headway when falling 4 out in Welsh National at Chepstow: best at 2¾m+ (should stay long distances): raced on good going or softer (acts on soft): sound jumper: patiently ridden, has finished weakly. *J. A. Geake* **c134 h–**

DESERT AIR (JPN) 6 ch.g. Desert King (IRE) – Greek Air (IRE) (Ela-Mana-Mou) [2004/5 h108: 17d² 19g 19g* 16g⁵ 16d 17d⁶ 16d⁴ 16d 17g Mar 18] angular gelding: fairly useful handicap hurdler: won at Exeter in October: stays 19f: raced on good going or softer: usually visored prior to last 4 starts: tongue tied: difficult ride.. *M. C. Pipe* **h124**

DESERT CITY 6 b.g. Darnay – Oasis (Valiyar) [2004/5 16g 16s 16d 16s Jan 20] good-topped gelding: little form over hurdles: sold out of P. Webber's stable 3,200 gns Doncaster November Sales after second start: tried blinkered/visored: sold £1,100 Ascot February Sales. *M. Sheppard* **h–**

DESERT IMAGE (IRE) 4 b.g. Desert King (IRE) – Identical (IRE) (Machiavellian (USA)) [2004/5 16d^pu Jan 26] fair on Flat (stays 11.7f): tongue tied, saddle slipped early on hurdling debut. *C. Tinkler* **h– p**

DESERTMORE CHIEF (IRE) 6 b.g. Broken Hearted – Mangan Lane (Le Moss) [2004/5 F16s 19s^F 20d Apr 20] €11,000 3-y-o: sixth foal: half-brother to winning hurdler/chaser up to 27f Polo Pony (by The Noble Player): dam ran once in bumper: well beaten in bumper and on completed start over hurdles. *B. De Haan* **h– F–**

DESERT SPA (USA) 10 b.g. Sheikh Albadou – Healing Waters (USA) (Temperence Hill (USA)) [2004/5 h–: 19m³ 20m⁵ 20g 19m⁶ 19d 17s* 16s⁴ 19s⁶ 17s⁴ 17m⁶ Apr 9] lengthy gelding: poor hurdler: won selling handicap at Hereford in November: stays easy 2½m: acts on soft and good to firm going. *G. E. Jones* **h78**

DESERT TOMMY 4 b.g. Desert King (IRE) – Flambera (FR) (Akarad (FR)) [2004/5 16g^ur 17d* 17m² 17g^pu Sep 25] rather leggy gelding: half-brother to useful 2m hurdler Far Pavilions (by Halling): soundly beaten all 3 starts on Flat, sold out of T. Mills's stable £2,700 Ascot February Sales: modest form in juvenile hurdles: 66/1-winner at Market Rasen in July: lame final outing. *Evan Williams* **h93**

DESLA'S DEVIL 13 b.g. Devil To Play – Miss Desla (Light Thrust) [2004/5 16f^pu Sep 5] big, lengthy gelding: no form over hurdles or fences: tried blinkered: has had tongue tied. *Ms Sue Smith* **c– x h–**

DE SOTO 4 b.g. Hernando (FR) – Vanessa Bell (IRE) (Lahib (USA)) [2004/5 F16d³ F16g² Mar 16] **F122**

For the third time in four years the winning margin in the Champion Bumper was no more than half a length. Liberman beat Trabolgan by that margin in 2003 while in 2002, when Pizarro got the better of Rhinestone Cowboy in a controversial finish, and 2005, when Missed That beat De Soto, the margin was only a neck. Like Trabolgan, De Soto was a maiden, though one that had looked highly promising on his only previous appearance, and clearly the subsequent exploits of Trabolgan and Rhinestone Cowboy suggest De Soto is no forlorn hope to make quite an impact when he goes over jumps. It was clear from De Soto's first run that he was very well regarded, as he not only contested the Grade 2 at Newbury in February, usually one of the hottest bumpers of the season, but was also backed into third favourite at 6/1. Approaching two furlongs out, the gamble looked as if it might be landed, but in the end De Soto couldn't stay on so well as either Karanja or Be Be King. Nevertheless, De Soto finished well clear of the remainder and even better was to come at Cheltenham. This time, with a race under his belt, he saw out the trip more thoroughly, responding after being tapped for foot to challenge in the final furlong but finding the winner pulling out more close home.

Given that he's only four, connections of De Soto might consider keeping him for bumpers again in 2005/6, perhaps following the example of the 2004 Champion Bumper runner-up Refinement. De Soto is a Flat type on looks and breeding. A leggy gelding, he is from the family of the disqualified Oaks winner Aliysa and top-class middle-distance colt Alamshar, his dam Vanessa Bell being

Mr P. A. Deal's "De Soto"

out of a half-sister to the former, who in turn is the grandam of the latter. De Soto is his dam's third foal. The first, Cent Prime (also by Hernando), is a fair hurdler at around two miles in France while the second Angelica Garnett (by Desert Story) won over a mile and a half. De Soto's year-younger half-brother Pagan Sword (by Selkirk) has shown progressive form at a mile and a quarter on the Flat in 2005. *P. R. Webber*

DESPALIN (IRE) 8 ch.m. Un Desperado (FR) – Satlin (IRE) (Satco (FR)) [2004/5 $16s^{pu}$ $18m^{pu}$ Apr 21] smallish, angular mare: first foal: dam unraced half-sister to smart hurdler up to 2½m Neblin: no show in mares events over hurdles. *Mrs S. J. Humphrey* **h–**

DESTINO 6 ch.g. Keen – Hanajir (IRE) (Cadeaux Genereux) [2004/5 h–, F83: $16g^{ur}$ $17m^4$ $19g^4$ $20g^2$ $20g^4$ Sep 12] poor maiden hurdler: stays 2½m: room for improvement in his jumping. *Mrs S. J. Smith* **h82**

DEVIL'S RUN (IRE) 9 b.g. Commanche Run – She Devil (Le Moss) [2004/5 c108, h–: $c20d^4$ $c25s^4$ $c20g^5$ c25v* c27v* $c32v^3$ Mar 5] strong gelding: fairly useful handicap chaser: won at Wetherby and Sedgefield in January: good third to Malek in valuable event at Kelso final start: stays 4m: raced on good going or softer (acts on heavy). *J. Wade* **c117 h–**

DEVIL'S TEARDROP 5 ch.g. Hernando (FR) – River Divine (USA) (Irish River (FR)) [2004/5 h–: $18m^{pu}$ $16g^4$ $17g^4$ 16d $16m^2$ 16f Oct 7] small gelding: modest novice hurdler: will prove best around 2m: acts on good to firm going. *C. J. Mann* **h94**

DEVITO (FR) 4 ch.g. Trempolino (USA) – Snowy (FR) (Wollow) [2004/5 $16g^5$ $18m^5$ $17m^6$ $16v^2$ 16v* $17d^4$ $22g^5$ $20s^{pu}$ Apr 16] thrice-raced on Flat, modest form on first of 2 **h90**

starts around 1½m in 2004: modest juvenile hurdler: sold out of A. King's stable £1,700 Ascot October Sales after third outing: won novice claimer at Leicester in February: seems to stay 2¾m: acts on heavy going: visored second start: has looked hard ride. *G. F. Edwards*

DEVON BLUE (IRE) 6 ch.m. Hubbly Bubbly (USA) – Tuney Blade (Fine Blade (USA)) [2004/5 F16g³ F17m⁴ Sep 1] €5,000 3-y-o: eighth foal: half-sister to 3 winners, including fairly useful 23f chase winner Trust Fund (by Rashar): dam unraced: modest form when in frame in bumpers, off bridle throughout on debut. *J. S. Moore* **F84**

DEVON VIEW (IRE) 11 b.g. Jolly Jake (NZ) – Skipaside (Quayside) [2004/5 c132: 21s* Dec 1] tall gelding: useful handicap chaser in 2003/4: off 12 months, easily won novice claimer at Plumpton in December on hurdling debut: stays 21f: unraced on firm going, acts on any other: consistent: sold only 900 gns Doncaster March Sales. *P. F. Nicholls* **c– h100 +**

DEVOTE 7 b.g. Pennekamp (USA) – Radiant Bride (USA) (Blushing Groom (FR)) [2004/5 h90: 17s² 17m⁶ 17d² 16s⁴ Nov 24] close-coupled gelding: poor hurdler: stayed 19f: acted on heavy going: often blinkered/in cheekpieces: dead. *J. D. Frost* **h81**

DEWASENTAH (IRE) 6 b.m. Supreme Leader – Our Sioux (IRE) (Jolly Jake (NZ)) [2004/5 F90: F16s⁶ F16d 20d 21v² 20s 16g⁵ 16v³ 20s⁵ Apr 10] tall, rather unfurnished mare: bumper winner: modest novice hurdler: stays 21f: raced on good going or softer (acts on heavy). *J. M. Jefferson* **h94 F83**

DEXTER GORDON (IRE) 14 gr.g. Bar Dexter (USA) – Sabev (USA) (Saber Thrust (CAN)) [2004/5 c24d⁴ Apr 22] ex-Irish gelding: winning pointer, including in 2005: maiden chaser: tried blinkered: has had tongue tied. *Malcolm Tucker* **c– h–**

DHARKAN (USA) 5 b.g. King of Kings (IRE) – Meritorious (USA) (St Jovite (USA)) [2004/5 17s Jan 20] won maiden at 2 yrs, sold out of E. Dunlop's stable 8,800 gns Newmarket Autumn (2002) Sales and successful several times in Spain since: showed little on hurdling debut. *G. L. Moore* **h–**

DHAUDELOUP (FR) 10 ch.g. Mister Sicy (FR) – Debolouve (FR) (Yours) [2004/5 c20d² c16gF 16d² c16s² c16v² 22s⁵ Jan 18] tall, plain gelding: useful handicap hurdler in 2000/1: off over 3 years, modest form over hurdles and fences in 2004/5, reluctant in preliminaries third outing (claimed from R. Fahey £6,000): best around 2m: acts on good to firm and heavy going: free-going sort, often makes running. *A. G. Juckes* **c99 h93**

DHEHDAAH 4 b.g. Alhaarth (IRE) – Carina Clare (Slip Anchor) [2004/5 16d⁶ 16d⁴ 16d² 16d⁴ 20vpu 16d² Feb 17] angular gelding: fair on Flat (stays 1½m), sold out of N. Graham's stable 14,000 gns Doncaster August Sales, successful in March: fair juvenile hurdler: should stay beyond 2m: acts on good to soft going. *Mrs P. Sly* **h101**

DIAGON ALLEY (IRE) 5 ro.g. Petong – Mubadara (IRE) (Lahib (USA)) [2004/5 17g 16v 16v³ 17m Apr 23] of no account on Flat: little form over hurdles. *K. W. Hogg, Isle of Man* **h69 ?**

DIAMANIKOS (FR) 9 b.g. Nikos – Diamarella (FR) (Rose Laurel) [2004/5 20dpu May 15] no show in bumper or novice hurdle over 2 years apart. *R. T. Phillips* **h–**

DIAMOND COTTAGE (IRE) 10 b.g. Peacock (FR) – Sea Bright (IRE) (King's Ride) [2004/5 c16vpu c27vpu c20v³ c27v* c26vpu Apr 17] good-topped gelding: novice hurdler: off over 2 years prior to reappearance: poor form when winning handicap chase at Sedgefield in March: stays 27f: raced on going softer than good (acts on heavy): tried tongue tied. *S. B. Bell* **c73 h–**

DIAMOND DARREN (IRE) 6 ch.g. Dolphin Street (FR) – Deerussa (IRE) (Jareer (USA)) [2004/5 h–: 19s 22dpu Apr 17] modest juvenile hurdler in 2002/3: lightly raced and little form since: tongue tied last 4 starts. *Miss Victoria Roberts* **h–**

DIAMOND HALL 12 b.g. Lapierre – Willitwin (Majestic Maharaj) [2004/5 c–, h–: c17d⁵ c16spu c20spu c19gpu c16g⁶ Jan 17] good-topped gelding: winning hurdler/maiden chaser: no longer of any account: tried blinkered. *R. D. Tudor* **c– h–**

DIAMOND JIM (IRE) 5 ch.g. Lord of Appeal – Smash N Lass (Crash Course) [2004/5 22s⁶ 20s Apr 20] fifth foal: half-brother to 3¼m hunter chase winner Monty's Lass (by Montelimar): dam won 2½m chase in Ireland: no show over hurdles. *Mrs R. L. Elliot* **h–**

DIAMOND JOSHUA (IRE) 7 b.g. Mujadil (USA) – Elminya (IRE) (Sure Blade (USA)) [2004/5 h–: 20d⁶ 16g⁵ 17m³ 16g⁴ 20g² 17d⁵ 22m 21mbd 20s* 21d⁴ Oct 27] smallish gelding: modest hurdler nowadays, claimed from M. Scudamore £6,000 fifth **h89**

outing: won conditional jockeys seller at Uttoxeter in October: stays 21f: acts on soft going: blinkered once, often visored nowadays: formerly tongue tied. *J. Hetherton*

DIAMOND MERCHANT 6 ch.g. Vettori (IRE) – Tosca (Be My Guest (USA)) [2004/5 F87: 19g^F 17d^2 19s^pu 19d Jan 28] angular gelding: runner-up in bumper on debut: fair form first 2 outings in novice hurdles. *A. King* **h101**

DIAMOND MICK 5 ch.g. Pivotal – Miss Poll Flinders (Swing Easy (USA)) [2004/5 h90: 16s* 20v^6 16v* 18d 16s^2 16d 16s^6 Apr 20] close-coupled gelding: fair hurdler: won maiden in December and novice in January, both at Kelso: likely to prove best around 2m: raced on going softer than good (acts on heavy): tried in cheekpieces: usually races prominently. *Mrs R. L. Elliot* **h101**

DIAMOND MONROE (IRE) 9 ch.g. Treasure Hunter – Star of Monroe (Derring Rose) [2004/5 c94, h96: 22g^4 24g 24d c21d c25g^6 Mar 9] lengthy, angular gelding: modest handicap hurdler/novice chaser: below form in 2004/5 after first outing, sold out of N. Henderson's stable 8,000 gns Doncaster August Sales after second: stays 3m: acts on soft and good to firm going: tried blinkered: usually let down by jumping: sold 2,400 gns Doncaster May Sales. *Mrs S. E. Grant* **c– x** **h94 x**

DIAMOND ORCHID (IRE) 5 gr.m. Victory Note (USA) – Olivia's Pride (IRE) (Digamist (USA)) [2004/5 h109: 16m* 20m^6 16m^4 21d* 25d^5 Jan 1] modest on Flat (stays 2m): similar standard over hurdles: won claimer at Ludlow in April 2004: left P. D. Evans, won novice there in November: stays 21f: acts on good to soft and good to firm going: usually visored for former stable: not an easy ride. *A. L. Forbes* **h99 §**

DIAMOND SAL 7 b.m. Bob Back (USA) – Fortune's Girl (Ardross) [2004/5 F103: 16s^2 20s^2 20g* 21m^pu Apr 2] close-coupled mare: fairly useful form in bumpers: fair form over hurdles, didn't need to be at best when winning novice at Musselburgh in March: not fluent when favourite for valuable mares novice handicap at Newbury final start: should stay 21f: acts on soft going, possibly not on good to firm. *J. Howard Johnson* **h104**

DIAMOND'S FIRST 6 b.g. Naskracker (USA) – Diamond Express (Pony Express) [2004/5 F16d^pu Dec 26] first foal: dam unraced: showed nothing in bumper on debut. *N. R. Mitchell* **F–**

DIAMOND SONG (IRE) 6 gr.m. Carroll House – April Gold (King's Leap) [2004/5 F18s^pu 16d^pu Mar 10] €1,600 4-y-o: eighth foal: dam, lightly raced in bumpers/over hurdles, from family of Danoli: no show in mares bumper or maiden hurdle. *N. J. Gifford* **h–** **F–**

DIAMONDS WILL DO (IRE) 8 b.m. Bigstone (IRE) – Clear Ability (IRE) (Be My Guest (USA)) [2004/5 h97: 20s^5 22s Jan 1] rather leggy mare: modest handicap hurdler: below form both starts in 2004/5: probably stays 3m: acts on soft and good to firm going. *Miss Venetia Williams* **h–**

DIAMOND VEIN 6 b.g. Green Dancer (USA) – Blushing Sunrise (USA) (Cox's Ridge (USA)) [2004/5 h–: 21g 20v^5 20g^pu 20v^pu 19g Mar 9] bumper winner: little form over hurdles: tongue tied first outing. *S. P. Griffiths* **h–**

DIBBLE'S BARN 5 b.m. Thowra (FR) – Colette's Choice (IRE) (Alzao (USA)) [2004/5 17g^pu 17d 22g^pu Apr 10] no sign of ability. *R. J. Hodges* **h–**

DICEMAN (IRE) 10 b.g. Supreme Leader – Henry's Gamble (IRE) (Carlingford Castle) [2004/5 c122, h–: c20m Jun 25] lengthy gelding: fairly useful handicap chaser: again let down by jumping only 2004/5 start: should stay beyond 2½m: raced mainly on good going or softer (acts on soft). *Mrs S. J. Smith* **c–** **h–**

DICKENSBURY LAD (FR) 5 b.g. Luchiroverte (IRE) – Voltige de Cotte (FR) (Saumon (FR)) [2004/5 h110: 22g* 24d^4 May 13] fair form over hurdles: won intermediate at Kelso in April 2004: stays 2¾m: acts on soft going: has jumped none too fluently. *N. A. Twiston-Davies* **h105**

DICKENS (USA) 5 ch.g. King of Kings (IRE) – Dellagrazia (USA) (Trempolino (USA)) [2004/5 h113: 16d^2 24v^6 21d c24d^2 c24d^3 c24g^3 c22s^F c24s* Apr 2] workmanlike gelding: fair winning hurdler: modest form over fences, won very weak 2-finisher maiden at Bangor, jumping right and looking unwilling when left clear last: probably stays 3m: raced on good going or softer: wore cheekpieces third outing, visored last 2: temperamental. *Miss Venetia Williams* **c86 §** **h102 §**

DICKIE DEADEYE 8 b.g. Distant Relative – Accuracy (Gunner B) [2004/5 16s^5 17v 20s Mar 9] half-brother to useful hurdlers up to 3m Accipiter (by Polar Falcon) and Brave Tornado (by Dominion): dam fairly useful though temperamental staying hurdler: fair on Flat (stays 13f), successful in April: modest form on debut over hurdles (trained by G. Balding): let down by jumping second start: possibly doesn't stay 2½m. *J. A. Geake* **h98**

DICK MCCARTHY (IRE) 13 b.g. Lancastrian – Waltzing Shoon (Green Shoon) [2004/5 c–§, h–§: c25m^{ur} May 19] medium-sized gelding: veteran chaser: winning pointer, including twice in 2005: stays 3¼m: acts on any going: tried blinkered/in cheekpieces: unreliable. *Mrs G. M. Gladders* **c– § h– §**

DICK THE TAXI 11 b.g. Karlinsky (USA) – Another Galaxy (IRE) (Anita's Prince) [2004/5 c101, h–: c16d^{pu} May 8] good-topped gelding: fair hurdler/chaser at best: jumped poorly only start in 2004/5: raced around 2m: acts on heavy and good to firm going: held up, and races freely. *R. J. Smith* **c– h–**

DICTUM (GER) 7 ch.g. Secret 'n Classy (CAN) – Doretta (GER) (Aspros (GER)) [2004/5 h127: 16s^{3} 20s Dec 4] good-topped gelding: fairly useful hurdler: creditable third of 5 to easy winner Rigmarole in quite valuable minor event at Kempton, better effort in 2004/5: should be suited by further than 2m: acts on heavy going: jumps far from fluently. *Mrs Susan Nock* **h128**

DIDCOT 6 ch.g. Roselier (FR) – Astromis (IRE) (Torus) [2004/5 F90: F17d 25m^{3} May 27] modest form in bumpers: remote last of 3 finishers in intermediate on hurdling debut. *J. Rudge* **h– F79**

DIDIFON 10 b.g. Zafonic (USA) – Didicoy (USA) (Danzig (USA)) [2004/5 c101, h–: c16d^{5} c16m^{6} Nov 26] compact gelding: fair handicap chaser: off a year, well held both starts in 2004/5: should stay 2½m: acts on heavy going: tried blinkered, usually wears cheekpieces. *N. P. McCormack* **c– h–**

DIEGO CAO (IRE) 4 b.g. Cape Cross (IRE) – Lady Moranbon (USA) (Trempolino (USA)) [2004/5 16d* 16d^{2} 16d* 17g Mar 18] sturdy gelding: useful on Flat (stays 1¼m), successful in April (sold out of A. Fabre's stable 6,500 gns Newmarket July Sales) and September: useful juvenile hurdler: won at Huntingdon in November and Sandown in January, leading 2 out and responding well to beat stable-companion Nation State ¾ length at latter: good seventh of 23 to Penzance in Triumph Hurdle at Cheltenham: raced around 2m on good/good to soft going: genuine. *G. L. Moore* **h130**

DIEGO GARCIA (IRE) 5 b.g. Sri Pekan (USA) – Chapel Lawn (Generous (IRE)) [2004/5 h121: 16g^{6} 16g* May 12] rangy gelding: fairly useful hurdler: won minor event at Ballinrobe in May by 1½ lengths (value more) from Rapide Plaisir: not seen out again: raced at 2m. *W. P. Mullins, Ireland* **h118**

DIFFERENT CLASS (IRE) 6 b.g. Shardari – Hollygrove Cezanne (IRE) (King's Ride) [2004/5 F16v^{3} Dec 17] €34,000 4-y-o: first foal: dam unraced sister to top-class 2m to 3m hurdler Mister Morose and half-sister to smart 2½m chaser Southolt: third to Back Among Friends in bumper at Uttoxeter on debut: will be suited by further than 2m. *Jonjo O'Neill* **F90**

DIFFERENTGEAR 4 b.g. Robellino (USA) – Garconniere (Gay Mecene (USA)) [2004/5 F13d F16g Apr 19] half-brother to several winners, including bumper winner Saif Majrour (by Darshaan) and useful Italian 7f and 1m winner Giselle Penn (by Cozzene): dam ran twice in France: well held in 2 bumpers. *P. C. Haslam* **F–**

DIGGING DEEP 9 ch.m. Scorpio (FR) – Two Travellers (Deep Run) [2004/5 h–: 23d^{pu} Apr 25] good-topped mare: no show in 2 starts over hurdles. *N. J. Pomfret* **h–**

DIGITALIS 12 ch.m. Henbit (USA) – Vulpine Lady (Green Shoon) [2004/5 c19g^{pu} May 12] winning pointer, completed once from 4 starts in 2004: blinkered, mistakes when pulled up in novice hunter. *Miss Emma Oliver* **c– x**

DIKLERS ROSE (IRE) 6 gr.m. Roselier (FR) – Diklers Run (Deep Run) [2004/5 F75: F16d^{6} F16s^{2} F16v* F16d^{5} 22s^{2} Apr 3] sturdy mare: fair form in bumpers, winning at Newcastle in February by 1¾ lengths from General Hardi: 7 lengths second to Wild Cane Ridge in novice at Kelso on hurdling debut, not knocked about once held: will stay 3m: likely to improve. *K. G. Reveley* **h98 p F93**

DILETIA 8 b.m. Dilum (USA) – Miss Laetitia (IRE) (Entitled) [2004/5 c23s^{ur} c24d^{4} c25d^{5} c19d^{5} 24s^{2} 26g* 21g Apr 14] leggy mare: modest handicap hurdler: won at Huntingdon in March: let down by jumping/temperament most starts over fences: stays 3¼m: acts on firm and soft going: often soon off bridle. *R. H. Alner* **c92 h96**

DIM DOT 7 b.g. Inzar (USA) – Plucky Pet (Petong) [2004/5 19g^{ur} 16s 16g^{pu} Dec 9] poor form at 2 yrs for B. Palling: no impact in 3 outings over hurdles, left R. Williams after debut. *P. D. Evans* **h–**

DIMINUTIVE (USA) 12 b.g. Diesis – Graceful Darby (USA) (Darby Creek Road (USA)) [2004/5 20d^{pu} May 9] close-coupled gelding: very lightly raced and little form over hurdles. *Miss M. E. Rowland* **h–**

DIMITRI (IRE) 8 gr.g. Roselier (FR) – Treidlia (Mandalus) [2004/5 c–§, h89§, F79: 24d[5] May 9] compact gelding: maiden hurdler: no show on chasing debut: tried blinkered: ungenuine: sold 6,000 gns Doncaster May (2004) Sales. *S. Gollings* **c– § h– §**

DIMPLE CHAD 6 b.g. Sadler's Wells (USA) – Fern (Shirley Heights) [2004/5 17s[ur] 16v Feb 15] rather leggy gelding: fairly useful on Flat (should be suited by at least 1½m) at 3 yrs, well held only start at 4 yrs, sold out of L. Cumani's stable 7,500 gns Newmarket Autumn (2003) Sales: no show on completed outing over hurdles. *W. Storey* **h–**

DINAN (IRE) 13 gr.g. Step Together (USA) – Nobodys Lady (Nobody Knows) [2004/5 c25g[pu] Mar 9] ex-Irish gelding: maiden hurdler: no form in chases (refused to race once), placed in maiden points in Britain: tried blinkered: has had tongue tied. *Mrs Joanne Brown* **c– h–**

DINARELLI (FR) 6 gr.g. Linamix (FR) – Dixiella (FR) (Fabulous Dancer (USA)) [2004/5 h87: 17d* 16d[4] 17d[2] 17g[3] 16f[3] 17s[3] 16g 17g[6] 19s[pu] 17d 17s 19v[pu] Apr 22] modest handicap hurdler: won novice at Hereford very early in season: lost form after sixth outing: raced mainly around 2m: acts on firm and good to soft going: effective visored or not: tongue tied last 3 starts: has shown signs of temperament. *M. C. Pipe* **h99 §**

DING DONG BELLE 6 ch.m. Minster Son – Corn Lily (Aragon) [2004/5 F16g[3] F16g 17d[3] 19d[4] 16d 23d Nov 24] fifth foal: sister to fairly useful hurdler Cathedral Belle, stayed 25f: dam, fair 2m hurdler, half-sister to useful 2m hurdler Cardinal Flower: third in bumper on debut, very reluctant to race next time: nearly ducked out fourth when third in novice on hurdling debut: well held after: bred to stay well beyond 17f. *Mrs S. J. Smith* **h82 F77 §**

DINGLE FUN GUY (IRE) 7 b.g. Dolphin Street (FR) – Lhotse (IRE) (Shernazar) [2004/5 c20g[ur] 16g[6] 16m[2] 20v c16d[5] c24s c20s[pu] Nov 26] fourth foal: half-brother to modest hurdler up to 3m Lobuche (by Petardia): dam maiden: maiden pointer: poor maiden hurdler/chaser: tried in cheekpieces. *J. G. Carr, Ireland* **c76 h71**

DINGO DANCER 12 b.g. Dancing High – Some Shiela (Remainder Man) [2004/5 c16g[6] c17m[2] c16m c21m c20g[pu] c19d[5] Jan 1] tall gelding: modest handicap chaser, no form after second start: stays easy 2¾m: acts on good to firm and good to soft going, possibly not on soft. *J. P. Dodds* **c99 d h–**

DINOFELIS 7 b.g. Rainbow Quest (USA) – Revonda (IRE) (Sadler's Wells (USA)) [2004/5 h71§: 16m 17d[F] 16d[6] 16m[4] 17m[4] 16g[6] 16g 20g[6] 22d[pu] 16s Mar 31] leggy gelding: poor hurdler: raced mainly around 2m: acts on firm and good to soft going: usually wears cheekpieces, tried visored: has had tongue tied: unreliable. *C. W. Moore* **h71 §**

DINSEY FINNEGAN (IRE) 10 b.g. Fresh Breeze (USA) – Rose of Solway (Derring Rose) [2004/5 c86, h–: c21d[F] Apr 28] winning pointer: maiden hunter chaser: usually wears cheekpieces/visor. *Simon Bloss* **c– h–**

DIRECT ACCESS (IRE) 10 ch.g. Roselier (FR) – Spanish Flame (IRE) (Spanish Place (USA)) [2004/5 c–, h–: c25s* c24g[4] Feb 17] tall, rangy, angular gelding: fairly useful chaser: won handicap at Ayr in December by 5 lengths from Lord Capitaine: should stay beyond 25f: acts on heavy going, not discredited on good to firm: tried blinkered. *N. G. Richards* **c127 h–**

DIRECT BEARING (IRE) 8 b.g. Polish Precedent (USA) – Uncertain Affair (IRE) (Darshaan) [2004/5 c126, h132: c17m* c22m[4] Jul 28] well-made gelding: useful hurdler/chaser: won 4-runner minor event over fences at Tipperary in July by 4 lengths from Stage Affair: very good fourth of 22 to Ansar in Galway Plate (Handicap): effective at 2m to 2¾m: acts on good to firm and heavy going: blinkered once. *D. K. Weld, Ireland* **c134 h–**

DIRECT DESCENDANT (IRE) 6 ch.g. Be My Guest (USA) – Prague Spring (Salse (USA)) [2004/5 h82: 16m Jun 12] workmanlike gelding: poor hurdler: well held only start in 2004/5: best around 2m: raced mainly on good going or firmer: tried visored. *J. J. Quinn* **h–**

DIRECT FLIGHT (IRE) 7 ch.g. Dry Dock – Midnight Mistress (Midsummer Night II) [2004/5 h89, F96: 22s* 20s* 21d[6] 22s Jan 1] tall, useful-looking gelding: fair hurdler: won novices at Kelso (conditional jockeys) and Fakenham in October: stays 2¾m: acts on soft going: tongue tied final outing. *Noel T. Chance* **h113**

DIRECTION 7 b.m. Lahib (USA) – Theme (IRE) (Sadler's Wells (USA)) [2004/5 h–: 20d[5] May 5] medium-sized mare: little show over hurdles: tried in cheekpieces: sold 18,000 gns Doncaster May (2004) Sales. *K. A. Morgan* **h–**

DIRECT MANDATE (USA) 5 b.g. Woodman (USA) – Dangora (USA) (Sovereign Dancer (USA)) [2004/5 17m[pu] Aug 31] 6,000 3-y-o: seventh foal: half-brother to 7f winner Corsini (by Machiavellian) and fair sprinter Delegate (by Polish Precedent): dam **h–**

2-y-o 6f winner, closely related to smart miler Zaizafon, herself dam of Zafonic: no show in novice hurdle on debut. *P. D. Niven*

DIRK COVE (IRE) 11 ch.g. Montelimar (USA) – Another Miller (Gala Performance) [2004/5 c94§, h–: c26s² Oct 12] angular gelding: modest handicap chaser: stays 4m: acts on any going: usually blinkered/in cheekpieces: ungenuine. *R. Rowe* **c91 § h–**

DISCORD 4 b.g. Desert King (IRE) – Lead Note (USA) (Nijinsky (CAN)) [2004/5 F13g F16s Feb 5] good-topped gelding: seventh foal: half-brother to 1m winner Notecard (by Zafonic) and 1¼m winner in Germany by Selkirk: dam, 2-y-o 1m winner on only start, half-sister to top-class middle-distance colt Rainbow Quest: well held in 2 bumpers. *T. H. Caldwell* **F–**

DI'S DILEMMA 7 b.m. Teenoso (USA) – Reve En Rose (Revlow) [2004/5 h83: 16d² 16s² 16v² 17s³ 16s³ 16s⁶ Mar 27] small mare: modest maiden handicap hurdler: stays 21f: acts on heavy going. *C. C. Bealby* **h89**

DISGRACE 5 b.g. Distinctly North (USA) – Ace Girl (Stanford) [2004/5 h80: 19d⁵ c21sᵖᵘ Feb 7] poor form over hurdles: no show on chasing debut: likely to prove best around 2m: has raced freely. *Mrs S. J. Smith* **c– h–**

DISH 6 b.m. Distant Relative – Shalati (FR) (High Line) [2004/5 F16g 17d 17g 16s 16dᵘʳ 16g Mar 28] sister to useful 1¼m winner Kewarra and half-sister to several winners, including useful 7f/1m winner Shalad'or (by Golden Heights): dam French 1m winner: no sign of ability. *Miss C. J. E. Caroe* **h– F–**

DISPOL FOXTROT 7 ch.m. Alhijaz – Foxtrot Pie (Shernazar) [2004/5 16vᶠ Jan 14] sturdy mare: fair on Flat (stays 11f), successful in April: no form in 3 starts over hurdles. *Miss V. Scott* **h–**

DISTANT PROSPECT (IRE) 8 b.g. Namaqualand (USA) – Ukraine's Affair (USA) (The Minstrel (CAN)) [2004/5 h120p: 16g* 21g Mar 16] angular gelding: useful on Flat (stays 21f) and over hurdles: improved form when winning Gerry Feilden Hurdle (Limited Handicap) at Newbury in November by ½ length from Albuhera: well-backed favourite, laboured effort when only ninth to Idole First in Coral Cup at Cheltenham in March: should be suited by further than 2m: unraced on extremes of going over hurdles. *A. M. Balding* **h136**

DISTANT ROMANCE 8 br.m. Phardante (FR) – Rhine Aria (Workboy) [2004/5 c–, h–: c17m² c16gᶠ⁴ c16m⁵ 16d c17sᵖᵘ Jan 2] tall mare: second in novice chase at Exeter, virtually only form. *Miss Z. C. Davison* **c76 ? h–**

DISTANT THUNDER (IRE) 7 b.g. Phardante (FR) – Park Breeze (IRE) (Strong Gale) [2004/5 h121: c21d² c24g² c24d² c24g⁴ c22s² c24d* c24d* Feb 19] **c142 h–**

A routine blood test the week before that was not 'quite one hundred per cent' meant Distant Thunder was ruled out of his bid to emulate his half-brother Fork Lightning by winning the William Hill Handicap Chase at the Cheltenham Festival. Distant Thunder had already shown in novice company form on a par with Fork Lightning's the previous season and he was disputing favouritism in the ante-post book when he was scratched. The problem is very unlikely to be a long-term one and there is every chance that Distant Thunder will make an impact in good staying handicaps in 2005/6.

It was clear from the start of the campaign that Distant Thunder was expected to achieve quite a bit over fences and he made his first four appearances in graded company. Although he failed to win any of those races he acquitted himself well each time and the list of horses that beat him makes quite impressive reading. Distant Thunder finished second in Grade 2 novices at Wincanton, Newbury and Lingfield behind Comply Or Die, Cornish Rebel and L'Ami respectively, then took fourth in the Grade 1 Feltham Novices' Chase at Kempton behind Ollie Magern, Trabolgan and Quazar. Those performances suggested any maiden or ordinary novice was at his mercy but not, as it turned out, the one he contested next at Fontwell. Starting at 13/8-on, he went down by half a length to the 100/1-chance Bubble Boy. While he might be forgiven some one-paced finishes in graded company, Distant Thunder looked to be outbattled on this occasion and his season was in danger of becoming disappointing. However, he managed to put things right on his last two starts, beating some useful opposition, headed by Sixo, comfortably in a novice at Newbury and finally landing a graded success, in the transferred Reynoldstown Novices' Chase at Lingfield (from Ascot) in February, in which he beat the ill-fated Persian Waters three lengths.

Telectronics Reynoldstown Novices' Chase, Lingfield—Distant Thunder takes advantage of a substandard renewal to justify favouritism from Persian Waters

Although Fork Lightning missed 2004/5 through a leg injury, Distant Thunder's dam Park Breeze had two other winners to represent her, Moving Earth (by Brush Aside), who won a three-mile chase, and The Listener (like Fork Lightning, by Roselier), a promising hurdler in the same stable as Distant Thunder. The unraced Park Breeze is a sister to the La Touche Cup legend Risk of Thunder and stamina is certainly the strong suit in the family. The lengthy Distant Thunder is sure to stay beyond three miles. He has raced on good going or softer and acts on soft. *R. H. Alner*

DIVA DANCER 5 ch.m. Dr Devious (IRE) – Catina (Nureyev (USA)) [2004/5 h–: 17g May 31] little sign of ability on Flat or over hurdles. *J. Hetherton* **h–**

DIVERSITY (IRE) 7 ch.g. Over The River (FR) – Ballymas (Martinmas) [2004/5 c–, h87: 22m^pu Jun 13] modest form at best over hurdles, seemingly amiss only start in 2004/5: no show only outing over fences: likely to stay beyond 3¼m: raced mainly on good ground or softer. *Jonjo O'Neill* **c– h–**

DIVET HILL 11 b.g. Milieu – Bargello's Lady (Bargello) [2004/5 c122, h100: 22m³ c16d⁴ c25g* c24f c20m 20d Mar 26] good-topped gelding: fair hurdler: fairly useful handicap chaser: best effort when winning quite valuable event at Kelso in May by 10 lengths from Kock de La Vesvre: stays 25f: acts on firm and good to soft going: front runner. *Mrs A. Hamilton* **c127 h100**

DIVEX (IRE) 4 b.g. Taipan (IRE) – Ebony Countess (IRE) (Phardante (FR)) [2004/5 F16s Mar 12] first foal: dam unraced half-sister to fairly useful 2m hurdler Miss Daisy Dee: raced freely when eighth of 16 in bumper at Ayr on debut. *M. D. Hammond* **F80**

DIVULGE (USA) 8 b.g. Diesis – Avira (Dancing Brave (USA)) [2004/5 c–§, h81§: c17g^F Aug 9] leggy gelding: poor maiden hurdler: lightly raced over fences: best at sharp 2m: acted on soft and good to firm going: tried in cheekpieces/visor: sketchy jumper: dead. *P. Bowen* **c– § h– §**

DIX BAY 10 b.g. Teenoso (USA) – Cooks Lawn (The Parson) [2004/5 c–x, h103: 20g 16d² 17d⁴ 20m² 16d 16d⁶ 16d² 16v⁵ 16v c19d² 19s 19gF Mar 4] good-topped gelding: fair hurdler: jumped more fluently and first form over fences when second in maiden at Catterick: effective at 2m to 2½m: acts on soft and good to firm going: usually blinkered: sometimes finds little and not one to trust. *M. W. Easterby* **c103 § h105 §**

DIX HUIT CYBORG (FR) 4 ch.g. Cyborg (FR) – Dix Huit Brumaire (FR) (General Assembly (USA)) [2004/5 F14g³ F16v Jan 15] 25,000 3-y-o: tall gelding: fourth foal: dam unraced half-sister to smart 2m hurdler Mounamara: much better effort in bumpers when third to The Duke's Speech in 3-y-o event at Newcastle. *J. Howard Johnson* **F91**

DIZZY'S DREAM (IRE) 7 b.g. Shernazar – Balingale (Balinger) [2004/5 h115: 16g³ c18g* c20sF c20s² c17v⁶ c19v* Jan 2] tall gelding: fairly useful hurdler: similar form over fences: won maiden at Punchestown in September and novice at Naas (collapsed and died) in January: effective at 2m to 2¾m: acted on heavy ground. *N. Meade, Ireland* **c124 h113**

DJANGO (IRE) 6 ch.g. Glacial Storm (USA) – Rathtrim (Strong Gale) [2004/5 F16s* F16d⁴ 16s⁶ 18v 16v² 18g* Mar 12] €48,000 4-y-o: half-brother to modest hurdler/ fairly useful chaser Millcroft Riviera (by Henbit), stays 21f: dam unraced half-sister to high-class hurdler Kesslin and smart hurdler/useful chaser Rathconrath: fairly useful in bumpers, successful at Punchestown in October: fair form in maiden hurdles, made all when beating So Determined by 3½ lengths at Downpatrick. *Mrs J. Harrington, Ireland* **h107 F99**

D J FLIPPANCE (IRE) 10 b.g. Orchestra – Jane Bond (Good Bond) [2004/5 22v* c24d Mar 26] rangy gelding: fair chaser: off over 2 years, first success over hurdles in handicap at Kelso in March: ran poorly returned to fences later in month: stays 3¾m: raced mainly on going softer than good (acts on heavy). *A. Parker* **c– h87**

DMITRI 5 b.g. Emperor Jones (USA) – Shining Cloud (Indian Ridge) [2004/5 17dpu 17g 16d 16vpu Mar 29] fairly useful on Flat (stays 1m) at 3 yrs, sold out of M. Bell's stable 23,000 gns Newmarket February (2004) Sales: no show over hurdles. *J. D. Frost* **h–**

DOCE VIDA (IRE) 7 b.m. Montelimar (USA) – Miss The Post (Bustino) [2004/5 h95, F95: 16g² 20g* 20mF 17d⁴ 19g* 21d 19d Jan 29] angular mare: fair handicap hurdler: won at Uttoxeter in June and Doncaster in December: stays 2½m: raced mainly on good going or softer. *A. King* **h106**

DOCK COPPER'S GIRL 5 b.m. Thowra (FR) – Reeling (Relkino) [2004/5 F17d F16g Dec 16] small mare: third foal: half-sister to modest hurdler/fair chaser around 2m Darnley (by Henbit): dam winning 2m hurdler/chaser: well held in bumpers. *J. N. R. Billinge* **F–**

DOCTOR LINTON (IRE) 6 b.g. Norwich – Alannah Rose (IRE) (Roselier (FR)) [2004/5 F16d F16v² F16v³ 16s* 20s* 20d 16s⁵ Mar 28] good-topped gelding: third foal: dam unraced half-sister to useful 2m chaser Town Crier: fairly useful form when placed in bumpers: promising start over hurdles, winning maiden at Thurles and novice at Down Royal (comfortably, by 2 lengths from Romaha) in February: well held in more competitive company subsequently: stays 2½m: raced on going softer than good. *M. J. P. O'Brien, Ireland* **h115 F96**

DOCTOR WOOD 10 b.g. Joligeneration – Ladywood (Doctor Wall) [2004/5 16d* Mar 24] leggy gelding: modest novice hurdler: much improved when winning handicap at Wincanton on return from 2-year absence: stays 19f: acts on heavy going: amateur ridden. *Miss V. A. Stephens* **h93**

DODGER MCCARTNEY 7 ch.g. Karinga Bay – Redgrave Girl (Deep Run) [2004/5 F90: F16g⁴ Jul 7] fair form in 2 bumpers 11 months apart: tongue tied. *K. Bishop* **F86**

DOE NAL RUA (IRE) 8 b.g. Mister Lord (USA) – Phardante Girl (IRE) (Phardante (FR)) [2004/5 c103, h85: c24dpu c25d³ c23d³ c25d² c25g³ c24g* c20g³ c22d⁵ Feb 8] big, rangy gelding: fair handicap chaser: won at Musselburgh in December: stays 25f: acts on heavy going: probably best ridden prominently: has found little. *T. D. Easterby* **c102 h–**

DOESHEKNOW (IRE) 10 b. or br.g. Insan (USA) – Maeves Invader (Brave Invader (USA)) [2004/5 c120, h–: c16m c18m c20gpu c16s⁵ c24s* c21d⁵ c28s c24dur 18s c20d⁵ c24vpu Dec 27] maiden hurdler: fair handicap chaser: won at Listowel in September: stays 3m: acts on soft and good to firm going: blinkered final start. *P. A. Fahy, Ireland* **c112 h–**

DOES IT MATTER 8 b.g. Carlingford Castle – Flopsy Mopsy (Full of Hope) [2004/5 c–, h–: c16spu c24vpu c19gF 16vpu Feb 2] of no account. *C. N. Kellett* **c– h–**

DO KEEP UP 8 b.g. Missed Flight – Aimee Jane (USA) (Our Native (USA)) [2004/5 16d 16d⁵ 16d c19d c16dF c16dpu c20v² Feb 15] leggy gelding: poor maiden hurdler/ chaser: stays 2½m: acts on heavy going. *J. R. Weymes* **c73 h70**

DO L'ENFANT D'EAU (FR) 6 ch.g. Minds Music (USA) – L'Eau Sauvage (Saumarez) [2004/5 h130: 16s⁴ c17s³ c19s* c16v⁴ c18m⁵ Apr 2] compact gelding: fairly useful hurdler: just fair form over fences, winning maiden at Exeter in January: stays 21f: acts on soft going, possibly unsuited by good to firm: sold only 5,200 gns Doncaster May Sales. *P. J. Hobbs* **c108 h127**

DOLLAR LAW 9 ch.g. Selkirk (USA) – Western Heights (Shirley Heights) [2004/5 16dpu 16g³ 16s⁶ 16s⁴ 17d c16v³ c16d³ c16d³ c16v³ c19d⁴ c16v* c19d³ c17gpu Mar 19] angular, close-coupled gelding: modest hurdler: fair form over fences: won maiden at Leicester in March: lame final outing: stays 19f: acts on heavy going: wears cheekpieces and tongue strap: has been let down by jumping: waited with. *R. J. Price* **c108 h101**

DOLLY BELL (IRE) 7 b.m. Commanche Run – Rosey Park (Boreen (FR)) [2004/5 h–, F–: 19dpu Apr 29] lengthy mare: no form in bumpers or over hurdles: tried blinkered: sold £1,700 Ascot June Sales: runner-up completed start in points in March. *J. G. M. O'Shea* **h–**

DOLMUR (IRE) 5 b. or br.g. Charnwood Forest (IRE) – Kawanin (Generous (IRE)) [2004/5 h112: 16s 17d³ 20m³ 20g³ 21d 26m* 26m² Apr 9] angular ex-Irish gelding: fair hurdler: left A. Mullins after reappearance: won conditional jockeys handicap at Hereford in March: stays 3¼m: acts on soft and good to firm going: has worn cheekpieces, including last 2 starts. *Ferdy Murphy* **h104**

DOLPHIN SQUARE (IRE) 12 b.g. Phardante (FR) – Clarahill (Menelek) [2004/5 c25g⁴ May 1] fair pointer: fourth in maiden hunter chase at Hexham. *W. A. Bethell* **c81**

DOLZAGO 5 b.g. Pursuit of Love – Doctor's Glory (USA) (Elmaamul (USA)) [2004/5 h–: 18m* 17d³ 17g 16m* Sep 19] fair on Flat (stays 13f): modest form over hurdles, winning novice at Fontwell in May and handicap at Plumpton in September: will stay 2½m: acts on good to firm going, probably unsuited by softer than good: blinkered 3 of 4 starts in 2004/5. *G. L. Moore* **h99**

DOMART (POL) 5 gr.g. Baby Bid (USA) – Dominet (POL) (Dixieland (POL)) [2004/5 17s 17d 16d 17m⁵ 21g Mar 28] good-topped gelding: successful 5 times up to 11f on Flat in Poland, well held on British debut in June: poor novice hurdler: should stay beyond 2m. *M. Pitman* **h77**

DOM D'ORGEVAL (FR) 5 b.g. Belmez (USA) – Marie d'Orgeval (FR) (Bourbon (FR)) [2004/5 h–, F–: 22gpu 19g⁶ 19g* 17m* 16v* 19g² 17d² 16v* 20v² 16d⁵ Mar 14] leggy gelding: fairly useful hurdler: most progressive, winning handicaps at Newton Abbot in July and September, Stratford (ladies) in October and Uttoxeter in January: stays 2½m: acts on good to firm and heavy ground: tried visored: patiently ridden. *Nick Williams* **h116**

DOMENICO (IRE) 7 b.g. Sadler's Wells (USA) – Russian Ballet (USA) (Nijinsky (CAN)) [2004/5 h115: 17g 17d 16m⁶ 20m 21g⁶ 16s⁴ 16s⁶ 16gur 16d³ c16spu 17d⁶ 16s 16g Mar 16] good-topped gelding: modest handicap hurdler: no show on chasing debut: should stay 2½m: acts on good to firm and heavy going: tried visored/in cheekpieces: tongue tied final outing: inconsistent. *J. R. Jenkins* **c– § h95 §**

DOMINICAN MONK (IRE) 6 b.g. Lord Americo – Ballybeg Katie (IRE) (Roselier (FR)) [2004/5 F102: 17gur 17m* 16m⁵ 17g² 16m² 17d* 17m² 16g² 16d³ Dec 2] smallish gelding: fairly useful hurdler: won novices at Hereford in May and Bangor in September: largely better form when placed: bred to stay well beyond 17f: yet to race on extremes of going. *C. Tinkler* **h118**

DOMINIKUS 8 b.g. Second Set (IRE) – Dolce Vita (GER) (Windwurf (GER)) [2004/5 c119, h–: c25m⁵ c24fpu Jun 6] leggy gelding: fairly useful handicap chaser at best: in cheekpieces, lame final outing: stays 3¼m: acts on firm and good to soft going. *Ferdy Murphy* **c113 h–**

DOMNUL ADMIRAL (IRE) 7 ch.g. In The Wings – Folkboat (Kalaglow) [2004/5 16v 20m 16m³ 20f² 20f* 20g* 20v* 21d 24spu 20s Feb 26] leggy, quite good-topped gelding: fourth live foal: brother to fairly useful hurdler up to 21f Admiral Wings: dam twice-raced half-sister to smart middle-distance stayer Dry Dock and smart miler Showboat and to dam of high-class 1m to 1½m horse Norse Dancer: fair novice hurdler: won at Tralee (maiden, final start for A. Gannon) in June and Galway and Listowel (beat Master Ofthe Chase by 25 lengths in 3-runner event) in September: stays 2½m: acts on any going. *K. J. Condon, Ireland* **h111**

DONALD (POL) 5 b.g. Enjoy Plan (USA) – Dahira (POL) (Dakota) [2004/5 22g⁵ 22g* 20m 21g³ 21s* 19d 24dpu Dec 11] leggy gelding: won 2 races in Poland up to 1m, modest form on Flat in Britain in 2004: modest novice hurdler: won at Stratford (maiden) **h99**

in September and Ludlow (handicap) in October: should stay 3m: acts on soft going. *M. Pitman*

DON AND GERRY (IRE) 4 ch.f. Vestris Abu – She's No Tourist (IRE) (Doubletour (USA)) [2004/5 F16s* F16v⁵ F16d Mar 12] angular filly: second foal: dam of little account: best effort in bumpers when winning conditional jockeys event at Ludlow on debut in January. *P. D. Evans* **F87**

DONATUS (IRE) 9 b.g. Royal Academy (USA) – La Dame du Lac (USA) (Round Table) [2004/5 h62: 17s³ 17g⁶ 19g⁴ c16g* Jul 14] neat gelding: poor hurdler: fortunate to win 3-finisher maiden at Uttoxeter on chasing debut, soon long way behind but staying on to lead between last 2 as others fell or faltered: stays easy 2½m: acts on soft and good to firm going, probably on firm: wears headgear: often finds little. *Miss K. M. George* **c64 ? h62**

DON IDO (ARG) 9 b.g. Lazy Boy (ARG) – She's Got You (ARG) (Indalecio (ARG)) [2004/5 h–: 17dF 16m 19gpu 16g 17m³ Sep 1] good-topped gelding: poor maiden hurdler: raced mainly around 2m: acts on firm going: has looked none too keen. *J. A. B. Old* **h77**

DONNABELLA 8 b.m. Bustino – Howanever (Buckskin (FR)) [2004/5 21spu Mar 10] angular mare: very lightly raced and no sign of ability. *John R. Upson* **h–**

DONNA'S DOUBLE 10 ch.g. Weldnaas (USA) – Shadha (Shirley Heights) [2004/5 20m⁴ 16g² 16g⁵ 16d 20g⁴ 16g 16d² Apr 11] rather leggy gelding: brother to listed chase winner in Germany Last Corner, stayed 25f: modest on Flat (probably stays 1½m): modest novice hurdler, trained first 4 starts by D. Eddy: stays easy 2½m: acts on good to soft ground. *Karen McLintock* **h95**

DONNYBROOK (IRE) 12 ch.g. Riot Helmet – Evening Bun (Baragoi) [2004/5 c–, h–: c20g⁶ c20d⁴ c19s* c24s⁵ c25s⁶ c22d³ c21s Apr 7] tall gelding: modest chaser on balance nowadays: won 4-runner handicap at Towcester in October: stays 3m: acts on good to firm and heavy going: tried blinkered, sometimes wears cheekpieces. *R. D. E. Woodhouse* **c89 h–**

DONOVAN (NZ) 6 b.g. Stark South (USA) – Agent Jane (NZ) (Sound Reason (CAN)) [2004/5 c–, h76, F78: 17g⁴ 16m* 17g³ 17g* 20d² 20g⁵ 16g⁴ 16v* 19d⁵ 16s⁴ Mar 22] close-coupled gelding: pulled up only outing over fences: fair handicap hurdler: won novice events at Kelso in May and Bangor (conditional jockeys) in August and 11-runner race at Wetherby in January: improved effort when beating Crossbow Creek 6 lengths at last-named: stays 2½m: acts on good to firm and heavy going: wears cheekpieces: held up. *R. C. Guest* **c– h104**

DON ROYAL 11 b.g. Rakaposhi King – Donna Farina (Little Buskins) [2004/5 c89: c28g⁴ c20gpu c24s* Mar 14] tall gelding: fair hunter chaser: won 3-finisher novice at Stratford in March: best form around 3m: acts on soft going. *J. Scott* **c89**

DON RUBINI 7 b.g. Emarati (USA) – Emerald Ring (Auction Ring (USA)) [2004/5 c–: 16gpu Jun 10] of no account: tried tongue tied. *W. K. Goldsworthy* **c– h–**

DON'T ASK ME (IRE) 4 b.g. Spectrum (IRE) – Ediyrna (IRE) (Doyoun) [2004/5 aF13g⁴ 16gF 16s 16s 16s Jan 27] quite good-topped gelding: third foal: half-brother to fair 2m hurdler Swift Spirit (by Lake Coniston): dam unraced half-sister to useful performer up to 9f Eymir: fourth of 8 in 3-y-o bumper on polytrack at Lingfield on debut: no form in juvenile hurdles. *M. C. Pipe* **h– F84**

DON'T BE BITIN (IRE) 4 b.g. Turtle Island (IRE) – Shonara's Way (Slip Anchor) [2004/5 16s* 16d² 16v² 16s⁴ 16s² 17g Mar 18] leggy, angular gelding: dam, fair hurdler, stayed 3m: fair on Flat (stays 1½m): fairly useful juvenile hurdler: won maiden at Cork in November: in frame in graded company next 4 starts: jumped poorly in Triumph Hurdle at Cheltenham in March, but back to form when fifth to United in Grade 1 at Punchestown in late-April: raced around 2m on good going or softer (acts on heavy): makes running. *E. Griffin, Ireland* **h123**

DON'T BE SHY (FR) 4 b.g. Trempolino (USA) – Be Claimed (FR) (Al Nasr (FR)) [2004/5 15s² 17sF 17d* 18s³ 18s² 18s² 18s³ 18s² 18v* Apr 2] rather leggy gelding: second foal: dam 1¼m winner: useful juvenile hurdler, raced exclusively at Auteuil: won 3 of 12 starts, minor event in June, Group 3 Prix de Pepinvast in April and Group 2 Prix Amadou in early-May: beat Kiko for last 2 successes, showing greater resolution in muddling race on second occasion: will stay 2½m: raced mainly on soft/heavy going: sold privately, to join M. Pipe. *T. Trapenard, France* **h129**

DONT CALL ME DEREK 4 b.g. Sri Pekan (USA) – Cultural Role (Night Shift (USA)) [2004/5 16d* 16v* 16s² Mar 19] good-topped gelding: fairly useful on Flat (stays 1½m), successful 4 times in 2004, sold out of S. Williams' stable 55,000 gns Newmarket Autumn Sales: soon of similar standard over hurdles, winning juvenile at Catterick and **h126**

novice at Newcastle in February: better form still when 1¼ lengths second to Torkinking in handicap at Newcastle: raced at 2m on going softer than good. *J. J. Quinn*

DON'T MATTER 5 b.m. Petong – Cool Run (Deep Run) [2004/5 16vpu 16dpu Mar 3] half-sister to fairly useful hurdler up to 19f Cool Spice (by Karinga Bay): lightly-raced maiden on Flat, no form since 2 yrs: showed nothing in 2 novice hurdles. *Mrs S. M. Johnson* **h–**

DONTNOCK'ER (IRE) 7 br.m. Naheez (USA) – Castlemagner (IRE) (Hatim (USA)) [2004/5 21spu 20s 22s5 c22s6 c26vR c24vR 24s 20d c16d4 c17gF Mar 28] fourth foal: dam 1½m winner: won 3 Irish points in 2004: bought 9,000 gns (privately) Doncaster May Sales: no form over hurdles or in chases: often wears headgear: has refused twice over fences. *R. H. Buckler* **c– h–**

DON'T PUSH IT (IRE) 5 b.g. Old Vic – She's No Laugh Ben (USA) (Alleged (USA)) [2004/5 F16d3 Dec 5] well-made gelding: sixth foal: half-brother to 1m/1¼m winner Larifaari (by Lashkari): dam lightly raced: useful form when 3 lengths third of 20 to Netherley in bumper at Warwick on debut, hanging left. *Jonjo O'Neill* **F109**

DON'T SIOUX ME (IRE) 7 b.g. Sadler's Wells (USA) – Commanche Belle (Shirley Heights) [2004/5 h113: 16m 16g 16g5 22v3 20s Nov 4] lengthy, angular gelding: fair hurdler in 2003/4: below form in 2004/5: stays 19f: acts on soft and good to firm going: usually tongue tied: tends to sweat: usually free-going front runner. *C. R. Dore* **h102**

DON'T TELL JR (IRE) 11 b.g. Mister Lord (USA) – Middle Third (Miner's Lamp) [2004/5 c24s2 c24vpu c21spu 27v5 c24d* Feb 18] tall gelding: little form over hurdles: modest handicap chaser: won at Fakenham in February: stays 29f: raced on good going or softer (acts on heavy): wore cheekpieces fourth start: has been let down by jumping. *J. A. Supple* **c90 h–**

DONT TELL SIMON 4 ch.g. Keen – Circumnavigate (Slip Anchor) [2004/5 17dpu 17gpu Jul 30] angular, plain gelding: no form on Flat or over hurdles. *M. E. Sowersby* **h–**

DON VALENTINO (POL) 6 ch.g. Duke Valentino – Dona (POL) (Dakota) [2004/5 h106: c17m3 c21dpu c20m5 Jun 8] tall, close-coupled gelding: fair hurdler: let down by jumping over fences, would probably have finished second but for almost falling last in novice final start (blinkered): stays 2½m: acts on soft and good to firm going. *T. R. George* **c92 h–**

DOOBERRY FIRKIN 7 b.m. Presenting – Shipley Bridge (Town And Country) [2004/5 h–, F81: 22f2 c24dpu Oct 28] quite good-topped mare: form over hurdles only when second in amateur handicap: ran as if amiss in maiden on chasing debut: stays 2¾m: acts on firm going. *A. E. Jones* **c– h81**

DOODLE ADDLE (IRE) 9 ch.g. Good Thyne (USA) – Call Trish (IRE) (Callernish) [2004/5 c16d3 c22d3 c20s* c19v2 c21s3 c21v2 c20s4 c24v4 Apr 10] IR 5,200 3-y-o: lengthy gelding: third foal: dam unraced: in front when fell 3 out in maiden point on debut: winning hurdler in 2002/3, then off 20 months: fairly useful novice chaser: won maiden at Navan in December, beating G V A Ireland a head: generally creditable efforts in better company after: probably stays 2¾m: raced on going softer than good (acts on heavy). *J. T. R. Dreaper, Ireland* **c124 h–**

DOOF (IRE) 5 b.g. Old Vic – Ashpark Rose (IRE) (Roselier (FR)) [2004/5 F17d6 16gF 17s5 19s6 22v* Apr 22] €10,500 3-y-o: sparely-made gelding: second foal: dam, 2m hurdle winner, half-sister to useful 2m chaser Town Crier: 11/10 on, sixth in bumper on debut: fair form over hurdles, won handicap at Newton Abbot in April, soon allowed to build long lead and never challenged: stays 2¾m: acts on heavy going: has raced freely. *M. C. Pipe* **h104 F87**

DOON RUN (IRE) 11 ch.g. Commanche Run – Paupers Spring (Pauper) [2004/5 22mur 22g c20dpu c20m 22g 27g5 26d2 20m5 26d4 Aug 22] workmanlike gelding: maiden chaser: poor hurdler nowadays: finished lame only start in point in 2005: stays 27f: acts on good to firm and heavy going: tried blinkered: not one to rely on. *B. G. Powell* **c– h82 §**

DOOR OF KNOWLEDGE (USA) 5 b.g. Theatrical – Mynador (USA) (Forty Niner (USA)) [2004/5 h83: 17g4 16g4 16m2 16g5 Jul 11] rather leggy, workmanlike gelding: modest maiden hurdler: raced around 2m: acts on good to firm going: blinkered/visored: tongue tied: joined Miss V. Williams. *M. F. Harris* **h98**

DORA CORBINO 5 b.m. Superpower – Smartie Lee (Dominion) [2004/5 19g 21g4 Oct 7] half-sister to winning hurdlers Norma Hill (by Polar Prince), fairly useful at 2m, and Miss Lacroix (by Picea), stayed 3m: poor maiden on Flat (stays 2¼m): little show in novice hurdles, jumping poorly on debut. *R. Hollinshead* **h–**

DORANS LANE 7 b.m. Gildoran – Snitton Lane (Cruise Missile) [2004/5 F16g 20m Apr 10] second foal: dam, useful chaser, stayed 2½m: no sign of ability. *W. M. Brisbourne* **h– F–**

DORANS MAGIC 10 b.g. Gildoran – Mearlin (Giolla Mear) [2004/5 c102x, h–: c25d* c34d³ May 15] strong, workmanlike gelding: fairly useful hunter chaser: won at Wetherby in May: stays 4¼m: raced on good going or softer (acts on heavy): usually a sketchy jumper. *Miss A. Armitage* **c102 x h–**

DORISIMA (FR) 4 ch.f. Mark of Esteem (IRE) – Suhaad (Unfuwain (USA)) [2004/5 16d Nov 12] well beaten in maidens on Flat: tailed off in juvenile on hurdling debut: sold 500 gns Doncaster November Sales. *M. W. Easterby* **h–**

DORMY TWO (IRE) 5 b.m. Eagle Eyed (USA) – Tartan Lady (IRE) (Taufan (USA)) [2004/5 h78: 16m³ 21m² 17d 20s³ Oct 24] leggy mare: modest maiden hurdler: stays 21f: acts on soft and good to firm ground: has worn cheekpieces. *J. S. Wainwright* **h87**

DOROOSS (IRE) 5 b.g. Charnwood Forest (IRE) – Catherinofaragon (USA) (Chief's Crown (USA)) [2004/5 F80: F16d 16m⁴ Jun 6] mid-field in 2 bumpers: well-held in novice on hurdling debut. *Ian Williams* **h– F79**

DOUBLE AGENT 12 ch.g. Niniski (USA) – Rexana (Relko) [2004/5 c–, h91: 22s⁵ 22s 21v³ 22v 22s⁴ 25g 25g³ Mar 27] sturdy gelding: poor hurdler: stays 25f: acts on soft and good to firm going: tried blinkered/in cheekpieces. *Miss A. M. Newton-Smith* **c– h82**

DOUBLE ANGE (FR) 7 b.g. Double Bed (FR) – La Mesange (FR) (Olmeto) [2004/5 17s⁴ c21d³ Feb 18] fourth foal: half-brother to one-time smart chaser/useful hurdler up to 21f Mister Ange (by Mister Jack): dam in frame on Flat/over jumps in France: fair hurdler/fairly useful chaser at best: left J-P. Gallorini, third to Sleeping Night in hunter at Fakenham on British debut: stays 23f: acts on heavy going: tried blinkered. *Mrs Katie Baimbridge* **c103 h105**

DOUBLE BLADE 10 b.g. Kris – Sesame (Derrylin) [2004/5 c–, h108§: c16g³ c16d³ c16m³ c17g* c16d⁶ c16d³ c16d⁵ c16g³ Mar 4] strong, lengthy gelding: fair hurdler: modest chaser: left clear 2 out when winning maiden at Cartmel in July: best around 2m: acts on firm and good to soft going: has won 5 times at Sedgefield: often held up: usually finds little. *N. Wilson* **c98 § h– §**

DOUBLE BOGEY BLUES (IRE) 9 b.g. Celio Rufo – Belmount Star (IRE) (Good Thyne (USA)) [2004/5 c81x, h–: c25g* c25d³ c25g⁴ 26d⁵ c30sᶠ Dec 15] angular gelding: winning hurdler: modest handicap chaser: won at Towcester in April 2004: stays 3¼m: acts on soft and good to firm going: often let down by jumping. *M. Mullineaux* **c88 x h87**

DOUBLE DIZZY 4 b.g. Double Trigger (IRE) – Miss Diskin (IRE) (Sexton Blake) [2004/5 F12g F13s⁶ F18s⁴ F16s 18g⁴ 16g² Mar 28] second foal: dam, winning hurdler/fairly useful staying chaser, half-sister to fairly useful 2m hurdler Derrynap and fairly useful 2m to 21f chaser Perknapp: modest form in bumpers and over hurdles: bred to stay 3m+. *R. H. Buckler* **h93 ? F80**

DOUBLE GEM (IRE) 6 ch.g. Grand Plaisir (IRE) – Thatilldofornow (IRE) (Lord Americo) [2004/5 F17g⁵ F16m³ F16g² F16m³ 16g⁵ 16d³ Apr 11] €10,500 4-y-o: first foal: dam winning pointer: fairly useful in bumpers: modest form over hurdles: likely to prove best at 2m. *J. I. A. Charlton* **h89 F97**

DOUBLE GIN 5 gr.g. Double Trigger (IRE) – Belmore Cloud (Baron Blakeney) [2004/5 F16d F17d² Mar 26] 7,800 4-y-o: leggy gelding: second foal: dam, fair hurdler, stayed 21f: easily better effort in bumpers when neck second to Flintoff at Carlisle. *W. Amos* **F95**

DOUBLE HEADER (IRE) 6 b.g. Old Vic – Ballybeggan Lady (IRE) (Le Bavard (FR)) [2004/5 F95: 17s⁵ 17d* 19vᵖᵘ 19g 20d² 24g³ 22g⁵ Apr 12] compact gelding: fair novice hurdler: won at Exeter in December: ran well after when placed: stays 3m: acts on good to soft going: races prominently. *Mrs S. D. Williams* **h113**

DOUBLE HELIX 6 b.g. Marju (IRE) – Totham (Shernazar) [2004/5 h81: 17d³ 16mᵖᵘ 17d⁴ 17m³ Aug 31] poor maiden hurdler: probably best around 2m with emphasis on speed: acts on good to firm and good to soft going: blinkered/visored: races prominently: has high head carriage. *M. E. Sowersby* **h79**

DOUBLE HONOUR (FR) 7 gr.g. Highest Honor (FR) – Silver Cobra (USA) (Silver Hawk (USA)) [2004/5 c140, h133: c25m³ c26g* c24d³ c25d⁵ c27s⁴ c25d⁴ c29s³ c28s² c36dᵘʳ c33g⁴ Apr 16] close-coupled gelding: useful handicap chaser: won at Newton Abbot in July: mostly creditable efforts after, in frame in valuable events at Warwick, Haydock (second to Forest Gunner) and Ayr (third to Joes Edge in Scottish National) last 3 completed outings: still prominent when unseating twenty-first in Grand National at Aintree: stays 33f: acts on soft and good to firm going: tricky ride, but raced more sweetly in blinkers last 4 starts: often makes running nowadays: tough and consistent. *P. J. Hobbs* **c140 h–**

DOUBLE LAW 5 ch.g. Double Trigger (IRE) – Sister-In-Law (Legal Tender) [2004/5 F16d³ F17g⁴ Apr 12] sixth foal: half-brother to fair hurdler Tisho (by Sir Harry Lewis), **F94**

stays 21f: dam, novice hurdler who stayed 2¾m, from family of high-class 2½m chaser Townley Stone and 1991 Grand National third Auntie Dot: better effort in bumpers when third to Noland in maiden at Wincanton on debut: carried head awkwardly under pressure next time. *P. R. Webber*

DOUBLE LEO (FR) 4 br.g. Double Bed (FR) – Miss Planette (FR) (Tip Moss (FR)) [2004/5 F16g Mar 5] 36,000 3-y-o: fourth foal: half-brother to bumper winner The Weaver (by Villez): dam placed up to 21f over fences in France: seventh of 15 in bumper at Doncaster on debut. *Ferdy Murphy* **F80**

DOUBLE MAGNUM 5 b.g. Double Trigger (IRE) – Raise The Dawn (Rymer) [2004/5 F16g^4 F16d^2 F16d F16s Feb 26] unfurnished gelding: seventh foal: half-brother to several winners, notably useful hurdler/chaser Crocadee (by Rakaposhi King), best around 2½m: dam, of little account, half-sister to useful hurdler/chaser up to 2½m Silver Wind: best effort in bumpers when second to Karanja at Sandown: sold 7,500 gns Doncaster May Sales. *Jamie Poulton* **F94**

DOUBLE ROYAL (IRE) 6 b.g. Ali-Royal (IRE) – Royal Wolff (Prince Tenderfoot (USA)) [2004/5 16f 20v 18s^3 16v^4 16s^{pu} 16d^2 19s^{ur} 19d^3 Mar 14] tall gelding: fair on Flat (stays 1¼m) at 4 yrs for J. O'Gorman: poor maiden hurdler: left P. Nolan after fifth outing: stays 19f: acts on soft going: tried blinkered/in cheekpieces: tongue tied third to fifth starts. *J. G. M. O'Shea* **h80**

DOUBLE SPEY 6 b.g. Atraf – Yankee Special (Bold Lad (IRE)) [2004/5 h–: 16d 17g^6 21m^{pu} 17m^{pu} Aug 31] workmanlike gelding: lightly raced and little form over hurdles nowadays: tongue tied final start. *Miss Kate Milligan* **h74 ?**

DOUBLE YOU CUBED 11 b.g. Destroyer – Bright Suggestion (Magnate) [2004/5 c85, h67: c24d* c25v^{pu} c24d c25s^{pu} c20v^{pu} c21v* Jan 29] leggy gelding: poor hurdler: modest handicap chaser: won in small fields at Perth in May and Ayr in January: little show in between: effective at 2½m to 3m: acts on heavy ground. *J. S. Goldie* **c92 h–**

DOUCEUR DES SONGES (FR) 8 b.m. Art Francais (USA) – Ma Poetesse (FR) (Sorrento (FR)) [2004/5 c–§, h87§: c21d^5 c16d^{bd} c20s^{pu} c16s^{pu} 16d^6 16g 20s^5 Nov 13] leggy, lengthy mare: maiden chaser/winning hurdler: little sign of retaining ability: tried in headgear: ungenuine. *A. L. Forbes* **c– § h– §**

DOUGLA 11 b.m. Dancing High – Elisetta (Monsanto (FR)) [2004/5 20d^{pu} Jun 30] third foal: dam, winner over 1m, stayed 11f: showed nothing in mares maiden hurdle on belated debut. *J. S. Haldane* **h–**

DOVEDALE 5 b.m. Groom Dancer (USA) – Peetsie (IRE) (Fairy King (USA)) [2004/5 F77: F17d F16m^6 Jun 29] lengthy mare: little impact in bumpers: fair form on Flat. *Mrs Mary Hambro* **F–**

DOVER CREEK 5 b. or br.m. Dover Patrol (IRE) – Up The Creek (IRE) (Supreme Leader) [2004/5 F16v F16g 19v Feb 13] first foal: dam poor novice hurdler: tailed off in bumpers and claiming hurdle. *Miss M. E. Rowland* **h– F–**

DOWER HOUSE 10 ch.g. Groom Dancer (USA) – Rose Noble (USA) (Vaguely Noble) [2004/5 16s^4 16d^{ur} Nov 13] rather leggy gelding: fairly useful on Flat (stays 1½m), successful 3 times on all-weather in 2005: very lightly raced over hurdles: fair form when fourth in handicap at Wetherby: probably best around 2m: raced only on going softer than good over hurdles (winner on firm on Flat). *Andrew Turnell* **h111**

DOW JONES (GER) 7 b.g. Temporal (GER) – Dahsa's Dream (IRE) (Pitpan) [2004/5 19f^3 16g^2 20d 20s 24s Nov 7] won twice around 1¼m at 4 yrs on Flat in Germany for R. Rohne: fair hurdler: stays 19f: possibly unsuited by going softer than good. *M. Halford, Ireland* **h111**

DOWNING STREET (IRE) 4 b.g. Sadler's Wells (USA) – Photographie (USA) (Trempolino (USA)) [2004/5 16d^5 16s^5 17g^5 Apr 7] fair form in maidens around 1m at 2 yrs, sold out of A. Balding's stable 6,000 gns Doncaster October Sales: modest form over hurdles: not knocked about in maiden final start: raced around 2m on good ground or softer: blinkered: capable of better. *Mrs J. Candlish* **h93 p**

DOWNPOUR (USA) 7 b.g. Torrential (USA) – Juliac (USA) (Accipiter (USA)) [2004/5 h130: 16g^4 c20g^3 c19s^5 c16s^2 16g Apr 1] useful-looking gelding: useful handicap hurdler at best, respectable effort on reappearance: fair form over fences: best effort when fifth in maiden at Hereford: stays 19f: raced on good going or softer. *Ian Williams* **c106 h117**

DOWN'S FOLLY (IRE) 5 b.g. Darnay – Pils Invader (IRE) (Carlingford Castle) [2004/5 F16v^2 17d 19s 22g^2 Apr 17] €25,000 4-y-o: useful-looking gelding: second foal: dam, winning pointer/modest hurdler up to 2½m, sister to fairly useful hurdler up to 2½m **h94 + F94**

Disputation: runner-up in bumper on debut: best effort over hurdles when second to Shining Light in novice at Wincanton: stays 2¾m: may improve further. *H. D. Daly*

DOWNTHEREFORDANCIN (IRE) 5 b.g. Groom Dancer (USA) – Merlin's Fancy (Caerleon (USA)) [2004/5 h111§: 16d* 17g 19g^{6} 18s^{5} 19s 20s^{rtr} 22s^{6} 16d^{5} 17s^{4} 17d^{5} 17m^{4} 19d^{5} 19v 22m^{rtr} Apr 23] leggy gelding: modest hurdler: won seller at Ludlow in May: stays 19f: acts on firm and soft going: formerly visored, usually wears cheekpieces nowadays: thoroughly temperamental. *M. C. Pipe* **h§§**

DOWN THE STRETCH 5 b.g. Rakaposhi King – Si-Gaoith (Strong Gale) [2004/5 c20g^{5} c16g^{5} c16g^{2} c16s^{4} c21g^{5} c20d 18g^{6} 21d^{pu} Apr 18] tall gelding: ninth foal: brother to fair hurdler Some Judge, stays 21f: dam unraced half-sister to fairly useful 3m hurdle winner Mount Hillary: won maiden Irish point in 2004: poor maiden chaser: no show over hurdles. *A. Ennis* **c78 h–**

DOWN TO THE WOODS (USA) 7 ch.g. Woodman (USA) – Riviera Wonder (USA) (Batonnier (USA)) [2004/5 h–: 16m^{pu} May 27] modest on Flat (stays 1¼m): no show over hurdles. *R. D. E. Woodhouse* **h–**

DRAGON HUNTER (IRE) 10 b.g. Welsh Term – Sahob (Roselier (FR)) [2004/5 c96, h–: c26g^{4} May 9] modest novice chaser: best at 3m+: raced on good ground or softer: has bled from nose: sold 4,500 gns Doncaster May (2004) Sales. *C. R. Egerton* **c83 h–**

DRAGON KING 13 b.g. Rakaposhi King – Dunsilly Bell (London Bells (CAN)) [2004/5 c104, h–: c25d^{4} c25m^{5} c25m^{4} c22m* c25m^{5} c21m^{2} c20g^{2} c21f^{2} c18d^{3} c19s^{4} c20m^{6} Apr 23] sturdy gelding: fair handicap chaser: won at Market Rasen in June: stays 27f: acts on any going: tried in cheekpieces, usually blinkered nowadays: front runner: tends to jump right: tough. *P. Bowen* **c100 h–**

DRAGON PRINCE 5 b.g. Zamindar (USA) – Nawafell (Kris) [2004/5 h–: 17d^{F} 16m 16d Aug 15] smallish gelding: little form over hurdles: likely to need sharp 2m. *R. C. Guest* **h–**

DRAGUT TORGHOUD (IRE) 9 b.g. Persian Mews – Artist's Jewel (Le Moss) [2004/5 h–: 22m^{2} 26f^{5} 24d^{5} 24d* Apr 20] leggy gelding: poor novice hurdler: fortunate to win conditional jockeys novice handicap at Worcester in April (leader clear when fell last): will stay further than 3m: acts on good to firm and good to soft going. *N. M. Babbage* **h83**

DRAMATIC QUEST 8 b.g. Zafonic (USA) – Ultra Finesse (USA) (Rahy (USA)) [2004/5 16s* 16s^{2} 16s^{2} 16s* 16d* c20s^{4} c22g^{2} Apr 19] good-topped gelding: fair performer on Flat nowadays: modest hurdler: won sellers (claimed from I. Williams £6,000 second start) at Stratford and Leicester (2) between October and December: easily better effort over fences when second in maiden at Towcester: probably stays 2¾m: raced on good ground or softer (acts on soft): tried blinkered, wore cheekpieces last 7 outings. *A. G. Juckes* **c83 h98**

DRAT 6 b.g. Faustus (USA) – Heresy (IRE) (Black Minstrel) [2004/5 F86: F16g F16d 20v 22v^{5} 19s^{4} 20d Feb 17] sturdy gelding: fair form in bumpers: just poor form over hurdles: stays 2½m. *R. Mathew* **h78 F83**

DR BILLY (IRE) 11 b.g. Dry Dock – Carrigconeen (Beau Charmeur (FR)) [2004/5 c21m May 19] little form, including in points: blinkered once: tried tongue tied. *W. Storey* **c– h–**

DR CERULLO 4 b.g. Dr Fong (USA) – Precocious Miss (USA) (Diesis) [2004/5 16d^{4} Dec 5] medium-sized gelding: fairly useful on Flat (should stay beyond 1½m): fourth to Woody Valentine in juvenile at Warwick on hurdling debut: should do better. *C. Tinkler* **h90 p**

DR CHARLIE 7 ch.g. Dr Devious (IRE) – Miss Toot (Ardross) [2004/5 h97: 22g* 21d^{6} 22g^{pu} 22s^{5} 22d 22d^{pu} Apr 17] angular gelding: modest handicap hurdler: won at Wincanton in May: stays 2¾m: acts on good to firm and heavy going: tried blinkered. *Miss C. Dyson* **h99**

DR DEDUCTIBLE 13 b.g. Derrylin – Tantrum (Leading Man) [2004/5 c88: c24v^{ur} c25d^{F} Apr 11] winning pointer, runner-up in March: failed to complete in hunters in 2004/5: stays 3¼m: acts on good to soft going: often blinkered/in cheekpieces. *Ian Stark* **c–**

DREAM ALLIANCE 4 ch.g. Bien Bien (USA) – Rewbell (Andy Rew) [2004/5 F12g^{4} Nov 10] lengthy gelding: third foal: dam of little account: fourth in 3-y-o bumper at Newbury on debut: will be suited by greater test of stamina. *P. J. Hobbs* **F91**

DREAM FALCON 5 br.g. Polar Falcon (USA) – Pip's Dream (Glint of Gold) [2004/5 h102: 16g 16g^{3} 24g* 24s^{4} 24s^{2} 24g^{2} 24v^{pu} 21d^{6} 22g Feb 5] lengthy gelding: fairly useful handicap hurdler: won steadily-run event at Taunton in October: stays 3m: acts on soft going. *R. J. Hodges* **h115**

DREAMING AWAY (IRE) 5 b.g. Un Desperado (FR) – Little Treat (Miner's Lamp) [2004/5 F17g^5 F17d^2 Aug 22] €22,000 3-y-o: fifth foal: half-brother to fair chaser Three Days Reign (by Camden Town), stays 3m, and useful pointer Evan's Collier Boy (by Supreme Leader): dam once-raced, from family of Carvill's Hill: better effort in bumpers at Newton Abbot (wandered and carried head high on debut) when runner-up: bred to stay well beyond 17f. *M. C. Pipe* **F83**

DREAM MAGIC 7 b.g. Magic Ring (IRE) – Pip's Dream (Glint of Gold) [2004/5 16d^6 Nov 9] good-topped gelding: half-brother to fairly useful hurdler Dream Falcon (by Polar Falcon), stays 3m: fairly useful on Flat (stayed 13f), successful in February: sixth of 15 in novice at Huntingdon on hurdling debut: dead. *M. J. Ryan* **h83**

DREAM OF MY LIFE (USA) 12 gr.g. Danzatore (CAN) – Sureya (Sharpen Up) [2004/5 c20g^{pu} c24g^{pu} Feb 16] fair pointer, successful in April: little show in hunters, tongue tied on first occasion. *Alan Balmer* **c– h–**

DREAM ON WILLIE (IRE) 8 b.g. Synefos (USA) – Mrs Mahon's Toy (IRE) (Roselier (FR)) [2004/5 c102, h–: c20m^5 c20m^2 Jun 12] maiden hurdler: fair handicap chaser: best efforts around 2½m: acts on soft and good to firm going: blinkered in 2004/5: weak finisher. *E. A. Elliott* **c105 h–**

DREAMS FORGOTTEN (IRE) 5 b.m. Victory Note (USA) – Sevens Are Wild (Petorius) [2004/5 16s 16d^5 16s 18s^{pu} Dec 21] modest maiden on Flat (stays 1¼m): poor form over hurdles. *P. R. Hedger* **h64**

DREAMS JEWEL 5 b.g. Dreams End – Jewel of The Nile (Glenstal (USA)) [2004/5 F17d* F16d Nov 14] first foal: dam, poor maiden, out of half-sister to smart stayer Tug of War: better effort in bumpers when winning weakly-contested maiden at Hereford in October, flashing tail and hanging right. *A. G. Newcombe* **F80**

DREAM WITH ME (FR) 8 b.g. Johann Quatz (FR) – Midnight Ride (FR) (Fast Topaze (USA)) [2004/5 c102, h–: 19g 16s 16d 21d^4 20s^5 19g Apr 12] sturdy gelding: fair novice chaser in 2003/4 for M.Pipe: fair handicap hurdler: stays 21f: acts on firm and good to soft going, possibly not on soft: well below form in blinkers/visor: tongue tied. *J. A. Geake* **c– h114**

DRIFT AWAY (USA) 5 b.m. Dehere (USA) – Flying Blind (IRE) (Silver Kite (USA)) [2004/5 h104: 16d 18m 18m^2 16s^3 16m 24d^{pu} Sep 22] fair hurdler, generally well below form in 2004/5: raced mainly around 2m: acts on good to firm going, probably not on softer than good: tried blinkered/in cheekpieces. *J. J. Lambe, Ireland* **h97**

DRIZZLE 4 ch.g. Hector Protector (USA) – Rainy Sky (Rainbow Quest (USA)) [2004/5 16g 16g 16g^{pu} Mar 28] poor maiden on Flat: no show over hurdles: visored final start. *M. J. Gingell* **h–**

DR MANN (IRE) 7 b. or br.g. Phardante (FR) – Shuil Le Laoi (IRE) (Lancastrian) [2004/5 24m 24f^4 24g^5 Oct 14] IR £2,000 3-y-o: first foal: dam, winning pointer, out of half-sister to Scottish Grand National winner Baronet and dam of very smart staying hurdler Liss A Paoraigh: won maiden Irish point in 2004: little form in novice hurdles. *Miss G. Browne* **h87 ?**

DRONGO 4 b.g. Sure Blade (USA) – Ardeola (Ardross) [2004/5 F16g Apr 19] second foal: dam unraced: tailed off in maiden bumper on debut. *Mrs P. Robeson* **F–**

DROUMLEIGH LAD (IRE) 10 b.g. Jurado (USA) – Myra Gaye (Buckskin (FR)) [2004/5 20d^{pu} 16m 16g^2 17m 18m^6 20m 18m* 17f^2 c16s^6 c16s^5 c17s^{pu} c21g^{pu} c17g^4 Mar 27] small ex-Irish gelding: poor hurdler/maiden chaser: sold out of N. Richards' stable 1,800 gns Doncaster August Sales after fourth start: won selling handicap over hurdles at Fontwell in September: sold out of Miss G. Browne's stable £2,200 Ascot November Sales after ninth: best around 2m: acts on firm going: blinkered once: has had tongue tied, including most outings in 2004/5. *Miss Z. C. Davison* **c– h85**

DR SHARP (IRE) 5 ch.g. Dr Devious (IRE) – Stoned Imaculate (IRE) (Durgam (USA)) [2004/5 h97: 22v^6 Nov 25] good-topped gelding: fairly useful on Flat (stays 2¼m), successful in April: only modest form over hurdles, generally let down by jumping: should stay 2½m+. *T. P. Tate* **h–**

DRUIDS CONFEDERACY (IRE) 7 ch.m. Great Marquess – Winsome Blends (IRE) (Zaffaran (USA)) [2004/5 h100, F97: 16s^3 Nov 14] lengthy, rather leggy mare: fair form over hurdles, last of 3 finishers in mares handicap at Haydock in November: should be suited by much further than 2m: raced on soft/heavy going. *C. R. Egerton* **h111**

DRUMAVISH LASS (IRE) 6 b. or br.m. Oscar (IRE) – Fraulein Koln (IRE) (Mandalus) [2004/5 F16m* F16m* F16s^6 Oct 3] third foal: half-sister to winning hurdlers up to **F100**

2¾m Bowling Green (by Bowling Pin) and Koln Stars (by Fourstars Allstar): dam lightly raced: fairly useful form when winning bumpers at Cork in May and July: well held on softer ground final start. *P. R. Lenihan, Ireland*

DRUMBEATER (IRE) 5 b.g. Supreme Leader – Ballydrummund (IRE) (Henbit (USA)) [2004/5 F16d F16d^4 F16s^3 19g 20s^6 19g^3 Apr 15] €24,000 3-y-o: rather unfurnished gelding: first foal: dam, twice-raced in bumpers, from family of top-class 2m to 2½m jumper Buck House: fair form in bumpers: well held in novice company over hurdles. *P. J. Hobbs* **h– F87**

DR WILLIE MARTIN (IRE) 5 b. or br.g. Dr Massini (IRE) – Patchouli's Pet (Mummy's Pet) [2004/5 F16s F18s* Feb 24] rather unfurnished gelding: fifth living foal: dam, winning but temperamental staying hurdler, from family of useful but temperamental hurdler around 2½m Abu Kadra: easily better effort in bumpers when dead-heating with Conna Castle at Thurles in February. *C. F. Swan, Ireland* **F105**

DRY OLD PARTY (IRE) 6 ch.g. Un Desperado (FR) – The Vine Browne (IRE) (Torus) [2004/5 F–: 18s^{pu} 17v^{pu} 16g Mar 28] more signs of temperament than ability in bumpers and over hurdles: blinkered last 2 starts. *P. Winkworth* **h–**

DUAL PURPOSE (IRE) 10 b.g. Rainbows For Life (CAN) – Gracieuse Amie (FR) (Gay Mecene (USA)) [2004/5 19g^{pu} Sep 30] brother to fair hurdler Nadisha, stays 2½m: poor on Flat, made debut at 9 yrs: in cheekpieces, no show on hurdling debut. *C. Roberts* **h–**

DUAL STAR (IRE) 10 b.g. Warning – Sizes Vary (Be My Guest (USA)) [2004/5 c90§, h–: c16g^5 c16g^{ur} c21s^4 c16g^6 c21g 16m c16d c19g c19d^5 c19g^{pu} c18s^{pu} c16d^{pu} c19g^{pu} Apr 15] sparely-made gelding: winning hurdler/chaser: no longer of any account: tried blinkered/visored: usually tongue tied. *L. Waring* **c– h–**

DUBAI ACE (USA) 4 b.g. Lear Fan (USA) – Arsaan (USA) (Nureyev (USA)) [2004/5 16g^6 16d^2 18s^4 16s^4 16g Mar 15] smallish gelding: half-brother to Allgrit (by Shadeed), fairly useful juvenile hurdler in 1998/9: modest form in two 1¼m maidens in 2004, sold out of J. Bolger's stable 5,200 gns Newmarket July Sales: fair juvenile hurdler: tongue tied last 4 starts: tail flasher. *Miss S. West* **h103**

DUBAI SEVEN STARS 7 ch.m. Suave Dancer (USA) – Her Honour (Teenoso (USA)) [2004/5 h89§: 19g^F Dec 9] leggy mare: modest hurdler nowadays: fell last (would probably have finished second) in seller at Taunton in December: stays 3m: raced on good going or softer (acts on soft): visored: unreliable. *M. C. Pipe* **h90 §**

DUB DASH (USA) 5 b.g. Siphon (BRZ) – Thesky'sthelimit (USA) (Northern Prospect (USA)) [2004/5 16d 16s 16m Dec 12] twice-raced over 1½m at 3 yrs, winning on second occasion: sold out of S. Williams' stable 10,000 gns Doncaster March Sales: no form over hurdles: tongue tied final start. *R. C. Guest* **h–**

DUBLIN HUNTER (IRE) 9 br.g. Treasure Hunter – Cutty Sark (Strong Gale) [2004/5 24g^5 c22d c23d^6 c17d^2 c23s^3 c16v^4 c22v^2 c20s^3 c22s* Mar 27] good-topped gelding: fair hurdler: fairly useful novice chaser: won maiden at Fairyhouse in March and quite valuable amateur riders handicap at Punchestown (made all when beating Howaya Pet 7 lengths) in late-April: stays 4m: acts on heavy ground: often blinkered. *D. T. Hughes, Ireland* **c115 h105**

DUBONAI (IRE) 5 ch.g. Peintre Celebre (USA) – Web of Intrigue (Machiavellian (USA)) [2004/5 16s^4 17d^3 16d Nov 29] leggy, angular gelding: modest on Flat (stays 1½m): modest form when in frame in novice hurdles, has been let down by jumping. *Andrew Turnell* **h92**

DUCHAMP (USA) 8 b.g. Pine Bluff (USA) – Higher Learning (USA) (Fappiano (USA)) [2004/5 c123, h–: c17g^2 c19d* c17g^3 c18m^6 c20g^2 Apr 17] tall, leggy gelding: fairly useful handicap chaser: won at Taunton in February: creditable efforts when placed after: stays 21f: acts on good to firm and heavy ground: wears headgear: front runner. *A. M. Balding* **c118 h–**

DUGGLEBY 5 b.g. Tamure (IRE) – Glorious Romance (Ra Nova) [2004/5 21g^{pu} 16m^2 May 27] first foal: dam ran once: better effort over hurdles when second in novice at Wetherby: won point in April. *G. P. Kelly* **h93**

DUKE OF BUCKINGHAM (IRE) 9 b.g. Phardante (FR) – Deselby's Choice (Crash Course) [2004/5 c144: 16m* 16g^5 c17m c16d 16d^2 c16d^6 c17g^3 16d^6 c16s^{pu} Apr 7] lengthy, good sort: easily landed odds in novice hurdle at Stratford in June: better form when fifth to Accordion Etoile in minor event at Tipperary next time: useful chaser: best effort in 2004/5 when third to impressive Great Travel in handicap at Newbury: best at 2m: best form on good going or firmer (acts on firm): formerly front runner, held up nowadays: usually sound jumper. *P. R. Webber* **c134 h114**

DUKE ORSINO (IRE) 5 b.g. Old Vic – Deselby's Choice (Crash Course) [2004/5 16s 16s³ Mar 11] €27,000 3-y-o: fourth foal: half-brother to winning hurdler/useful chaser around 2m Duke of Buckingham (by Phardante): dam winning chaser up to 2½m: much better effort over hurdles when third in maiden at Ayr: will stay beyond 2m: should improve again. *Miss Lucinda V. Russell* **h81**

DUMADIC 8 b.g. Nomadic Way (USA) – Duright (Dubassoff (USA)) [2004/5 c20d⁵ c19g³ c16g c21v⁵ c27v² c25sᵖᵘ c25g* c25s³ c25g³ Apr 16] tall gelding: fair novice chaser: won handicap at Catterick in March: stays 25f: acts on heavy going: has found little. *R. E. Barr* **c102 h–**

DUMFRIES 4 ch.g. Selkirk (USA) – Pat Or Else (Alzao (USA)) [2004/5 16d 16s⁴ 17g 17m 17g 17m Apr 13] good-bodied gelding: fairly useful on Flat (will stay 1¾m), sold out of J. Gosden's stable 30,000 gns Doncaster August Sales: poor juvenile hurdler: raced around 2m. *T. H. Caldwell* **h79**

DUN AN DORAS (IRE) 9 b.g. Glacial Storm (USA) – Doorslammer (Avocat) [2004/5 c99, h99: 19d c21g⁴ c20d² c21v⁴ c17s* c16s² c18d² c19d⁵ Feb 1] leggy gelding: modest hurdler: fair handicap chaser: won at Stratford in October: stays 2¾m: acts on any going. *J. D. Frost* **c112 h95**

DUNASKIN (IRE) 5 b.g. Bahhare (USA) – Mirwara (IRE) (Darshaan) [2004/5 16gᶠ Feb 27] dam half-sister to useful hurdler up to 3m Mirjan and fairly useful hurdler/chaser Mirpour, stays 2¾m: useful on Flat (stays 1½m): joint favourite, clear second when fell last in maiden won by Rehearsal at Musselburgh on hurdling debut: should prove capable of better. *Karen McLintock* **h108 p**

DUNCANBIL (IRE) 4 b.f. Turtle Island (IRE) – Saintly Guest (What A Guest) [2004/5 17d 16d Sep 22] poor maiden on Flat, soundly beaten for J. Bridger in 2005: well held in 2 juvenile hurdles: sold £2,700 Ascot October Sales. *R. F. Fisher* **h–**

DUNCLIFFE 8 b.g. Executive Perk – Ida Melba (Idiot's Delight) [2004/5 c92: c18d⁵ c21d⁴ c24g* c20g* c20d* c20s³ Feb 26] well-made gelding: useful novice chaser: won maiden at Taunton and handicap at Kempton (beat True Mariner 15 lengths) in December and novice at Leicester in January: easily better subsequent effort when 7¾ lengths fourth to Forget The Past in Grade 3 novice at Punchestown in late-April: stays 3m: acts on good to soft ground: front runner/races prominently. *R. H. Alner* **c138**

stanjamesuk.com Novices' Handicap Chase, Kempton—Duncliffe en route to the middle leg of a three-timer

DUNCRIEVIE GALE 8 gr.g. Gildoran – The Whirlie Weevil (Scallywag) [2004/5 c75?, h–: c24d^{4} c20s^{pu} Mar 10] big gelding: little form. *Miss Lucinda V. Russell* **c65 h–**

DUNDRIDGE NATIVE 7 b.m. Be My Native (USA) – Fra Mau (Wolver Hollow) [2004/5 F74: F17s^{5} aF16g 21d 18s 24g^{5} Mar 3] poor form in bumpers and novice hurdles: will prove suited by thorough test of stamina. *M. Madgwick* **h76 F–**

DUNEDEN (IRE) 5 ch.g. Dr Devious (IRE) – Suaad (IRE) (Fools Holme (USA)) [2004/5 F16f^{4} F16m* F19f* 16m^{3} 20s^{3} 20m^{ro} 22s Nov 5] fourth foal: dam fairly useful 2-y-o 7f winner: useful form in bumpers, winning at Naas and Kilbeggan in June: promising third in maiden at Galway on hurdling debut following month: disappointing subsequently: tongue tied, ran out 4 out sixth start: lame next time: possibly unsuited by soft going. *N. Meade, Ireland* **h101 F107**

DUNGARVANS CHOICE (IRE) 10 ch.g. Orchestra – Marys Gift (Monksfield) [2004/5 c–, h126?: c16v* c16v^{F} c24d^{3} c24d^{pu} Mar 19] sturdy, useful-looking gelding: fairly useful hurdler: similar form on completed starts over fences in 2004/5, winning maiden at Uttoxeter in December and third to Distant Thunder in Grade 2 novice at Lingfield in February: likely to prove best short of 3m: raced on good going or softer (acts on heavy): edgy sort. *N. J. Henderson* **c126 h–**

DUNGUAIRE LADY (IRE) 6 ch.m. Toulon – Why Me Linda (IRE) (Nashamaa) [2004/5 F16v^{4} F18m^{5} F20m F16g 16m 20d^{6} 16g 20s^{2} 20s 22s 16v^{6} 22g^{5} Mar 12] third foal: dam, placed over 7f, out of half-sister to smart 2m hurdler Athy Spirit: poor form in bumpers and over hurdles: stays 2½m: acts on heavy going: usually tongue tied. *T. Hogan, Ireland* **h82 F74**

DUNKERRON 8 b.g. Pursuit of Love – Top Berry (High Top) [2004/5 c82, h73: 16g 20m^{4} 20s 19d^{pu} 16s^{pu} Feb 14] compact gelding: winning chaser: poor handicap hurdler: stays 2½m: acts on good to firm and good to soft going: failed to settle in blinkers. *J. Joseph* **c– h71**

DUNLEA DANCER 4 b.g. Groom Dancer (USA) – Be My Lass (IRE) (Be My Guest (USA)) [2004/5 16d* 16s^{3} 16s 16g Mar 15] rather leggy gelding: fair on Flat (should stay 1¾m), sold out of M. Johnston's stable 25,000 gns Newmarket July Sales: fair form over hurdles: made all in juvenile at Wincanton in December: tongue tied final start: takes good hold. *P. J. Hobbs* **h107**

DUNLEA (IRE) 9 b.g. Common Grounds – No Distractions (Tap On Wood) [2004/5 c100?, h91: c18m 20g^{6} c20f^{pu} 26d^{pu} c20f^{ur} 16g^{pu} c24f^{3} c17v^{3} Oct 16] angular gelding: winning hurdler/maiden chaser: no form in 2004/5: sold out of J. Carr's stable 4,200 gns Doncaster August Sales before fourth start: tried in headgear: untrustworthy: sold 500 gns Doncaster October Sales. *M. J. Gingell* **c– § h– §**

DUN LOCHA CASTLE (IRE) 10 b.g. Cataldi – Decent Preacher (Decent Fellow) [2004/5 c24d^{5} c24s^{pu} c26d^{3} c26s* c24s^{2} c29s^{4} c24s^{2} c26v^{pu} c24v^{2} c25s^{4} c24d^{6} c26d* c24s^{3} c25d^{3} c25g^{pu} Apr 17] workmanlike gelding: modest handicap chaser: left J. Brassil after reappearance: won at Plumpton (amateurs) in December and Chepstow in March: stays 3¼m: acts on heavy ground: tried in blinkers/cheekpieces. *N. R. Mitchell* **c86 h–**

DUNNET HEAD (IRE) 6 ch.g. Shernazar – Kabarda (Relkino) [2004/5 F108: F16s^{6} Nov 7] big, strong gelding: twice-raced in bumpers, well below debut form on only start in 2004/5. *L. Lungo* **F80 +**

DUNNICKS FIELD 9 b.g. Greensmith – Field Chance (Whistlefield) [2004/5 c19s^{pu} c19d^{4} c24s^{5} c24g^{F} Mar 3] plain gelding: no form over hurdles: form over fences only when fifth in maiden at Taunton: needs to improve jumping. *F. G. Tucker* **c85 x h–**

DUNOWEN (IRE) 10 b.g. Be My Native (USA) – Lulu Buck (Buckskin (FR)) [2004/5 c91x, h91: 20s* 20d^{3} 20d^{pu} Apr 20] lengthy gelding: winning chaser: modest hurdler: off a year, won handicap at Huntingdon in February: reportedly bled from nose final start: stays 21f: raced on good going or softer (acts on heavy): tried visored, usually blinkered: poor jumper of fences. *J. M. P. Eustace* **c– x h92**

DUNRAVEN 10 b.g. Perpendicular – Politique (Politico (USA)) [2004/5 c70x, h86: 16m^{2} 19m^{pu} May 23] workmanlike gelding: poor hurdler: poor maiden chaser (often let down by jumping): stays 2½m: acts on heavy and good to firm going: wears visor/cheekpieces: unreliable. *M. J. Gingell* **c– x h79 §**

DUNRIG (IRE) 10 b.g. King's Ride – Belon Brig (New Brig) [2004/5 c31m^{pu} May 19] winning pointer/hunter chaser: tried blinkered: temperamental. *J. M. Turner* **c– §**

DUN ROSE 11 b. or br.m. Roscoe Blake – Dun Gay Lass (Rolfe (USA)) [2004/5 c25d* Apr 11] fair pointer: won maiden hunter at Kelso on chasing debut. *Mrs P. Claxton* **c79 h–**

DUNSEMORE 5 b.m. Prince Daniel (USA) – Admire-A-More (Le Coq d'Or) [2004/5 F–: F16f^2 F16s^3 16g^4 Sep 23] poor form in bumpers: more encouragement when fourth in novice at Perth on hurdling debut. *P. Monteith* **h90** **F72**

DUNSFOLD DUKE 5 b.g. Cloudings (IRE) – Rositary (FR) (Trenel) [2004/5 F16s^2 F16s Mar 23] tall, useful-looking gelding: sixth foal: brother to winning pointer: dam useful staying hurdler/winning chaser: much better effort in bumpers when 6 lengths second of 15 to Mendo at Sandown on debut. *P. Winkworth* **F105**

DUNSHAUGHLIN (IRE) 8 b.g. Supreme Leader – Russian Gale (IRE) (Strong Gale) [2004/5 h83p, F87: 16g^3 16v 20g 16g^4 Apr 19] useful-looking gelding: will make a chaser: easily best effort in novice hurdles when third at Towcester: should be suited by 2½m+. *J. A. B. Old* **h97**

DUNSTER CASTLE 10 ch.g. Carlingford Castle – Gay Edition (New Member) [2004/5 c106+, h–: c24m^2 c23f* c27d c25s^{pu} c26d^5 Mar 26] workmanlike gelding: fairly useful handicap chaser: won at Exeter in September: stays 3¼m: best efforts on good going or firmer: front runner: has looked awkward/found little under pressure. *P. J. Hobbs* **c118** **h–**

DUNSTON BILL 11 b.g. Sizzling Melody – Fardella (ITY) (Molvedo) [2004/5 c107, h–: c24s^{pu} May 5] workmanlike gelding: winning chaser: useful pointer nowadays, successful on all 4 completed starts in 2005: stays 3m: acts on heavy and good to firm going: blinkered. *C. J. Mann* **c–** **h–**

DUNSTON DURGAM (IRE) 11 b.g. Durgam (USA) – Blazing Sunset (Blazing Saddles (AUS)) [2004/5 19m 21m^{pu} 20g 24g^3 Jul 30] bad hurdler. *Ms Sue Smith* **h55**

DURAID (IRE) 13 ch.g. Irish River (FR) – Fateful Princess (USA) (Vaguely Noble) [2004/5 h–: 17d Dec 7] workmanlike gelding: very lightly raced over hurdles. *D. W. Thompson* **h–**

DURANTE (IRE) 7 ch.g. Shernazar – Sweet Tune (Welsh Chanter) [2004/5 F–: 20s^5 25s^3 16d 21v^4 20d^2 Feb 17] good-bodied gelding: best effort over hurdles when second in novice handicap at Sandown: stays 25f: raced on good going or softer. *J. A. B. Old* **h100**

DURHAM DANDY 9 b.g. Inchinor – Disco Girl (FR) (Green Dancer (USA)) [2004/5 c87d, h–: c21g^5 Mar 18] angular gelding: winning pointer: maiden hurdler/chaser: tried blinkered, often wears cheekpieces. *Miss J. E. Foster* **c–** **h–**

DURLSTON BAY 8 b.g. Welsh Captain – Nelliellamay (Super Splash (USA)) [2004/5 22d c20s^{pu} c24g^6 c20d^4 c20d* c22g^{pu} Apr 1] sturdy gelding: winning hurdler, off 2½ years before reappearance: modest form over fences, won novice handicap at Sandown in March: lame final outing: probably stays 3m: acts on firm and good to soft going. *S. Dow* **c97** **h–**

DURNOVARIA (IRE) 5 b.g. Fourstars Allstar (USA) – Solar Jet (Mandalus) [2004/5 F16s F16d Mar 10] well-made gelding: sixth foal: half-brother to several winners, including fairly useful hurdler/winning chaser Spring Double (by Seclude), stayed 3m: dam unraced: breathing problem when well held in maiden bumpers: tongue tied second start. *D. P. Keane* **F–**

DUSIT DOWN (IRE) 6 b.g. Anshan – Windy Road (Strong Gale) [2004/5 F16s^4 F16v 24g^F 22g^F Apr 12] sturdy gelding: fourth foal: dam unraced: fourth in bumper on debut: no form after, including over hurdles. *V. R. A. Dartnall* **h–** **F89**

DUSKY DAME 5 ch.m. Sir Harry Lewis (USA) – Red Dusk (Deep Run) [2004/5 F16s Mar 22] 11,000 4-y-o: sturdy mare: seventh foal: half-sister to winning 2m hurdler Spud One and useful bumper winner Dusky Lord (both by Lord Americo): dam, poor novice hurdler who stayed 2½m, sister to high-class 2m to 2½m chaser Deep Sensation: no show in bumper on debut. *S. B. Bell* **F–**

DUSKY DAWN (IRE) 4 b.g. Desert Style (IRE) – Kaaba (Darshaan) [2004/5 F14g Dec 18] third foal: half-brother to smart 1¼m winner Lady's Secret (by Alzao): dam unraced close relation to smart 1½m performer Konigsberg: mid-field in 3-y-o bumper at Newcastle on debut. *J. M. Jefferson* **F81**

DUSKY LORD 6 b.g. Lord Americo – Red Dusk (Deep Run) [2004/5 F80: F18d* F16d^3 F17d Apr 9] sturdy gelding: useful form in bumpers: won maiden at Plumpton in November by 4 lengths from Netherley: easily better effort in Grade 2 events after when third to Earth Man at Newbury following month. *N. J. Gifford* **F111**

DUSKY WARBLER 6 br.g. Ezzoud (IRE) – Bronzewing (Beldale Flutter (USA)) [2004/5 16s* 20v^3 17v* 16g^3 16d^2 Apr 8] **h137**

Paying 68,000 guineas to buy Dusky Warbler out of Michael Bell's stable at the Newmarket Autumn Sales represented quite a gamble on the part of his new connections, but he justified their investment in his first season over hurdles by showing useful form and reaching a place in both the Supreme Novices' at Cheltenham and the Top Novices' at Aintree. With his potential beyond two miles not yet tested fully, there may well be more to come and Dusky Warbler could well make an impact in good handicaps in 2005/6. Dusky Warbler had been a smart stayer on his day on the Flat, notably at four years, when he was placed behind Persian Punch in a listed race at Sandown and in the Doncaster Cup, but he hadn't won since his fourth start at three (his only other success coming via the stewards on his debut at two) and his five-year-old campaign had been largely disappointing, not wholly redeemed by a respectable effort at Maisons-Laffitte shortly before he was sold. Further, he is from the final crop of Ezzoud, whose best Flat performer, Ela Athena, and jumper, Stormez, were both typically quirky progeny of the sire.

Dusky Warbler won two of his first three starts once sent over hurdles in the New Year, novices at Leicester and Folkestone. He put up a useful performance when beating Jair Ohmsford ten lengths at Folkestone and went on to better the form at Cheltenham and Aintree, finishing just behind the runner-up Wild Passion when third to Arcalis at 20/1 for the Supreme, and then coming home a long way clear of the remainder when beaten half a length by the highly promising Mighty Man when favourite at Aintree. While he might have carried his head awkwardly, there was no caste lost in defeat on either occasion. Dusky Warbler is one of nine winners out of Bronzewing, the others including the Dee Stakes winner Merry Merlin and the smart miler Snow Goose (both by Polar Falcon) and two other winning hurdlers, Minivet (by Midyan), who was fairly useful at one time, and the modest Snowy Petrel (by Petorius). Both Minivet and Snowy Petrel stay or stayed two and three quarter miles and lack of stamina is unlikely to be the reason for Dusky Warbler's one disappointing effort over hurdles. He was beaten at odds on over two and a half miles at Leicester on his second start, some poor hurdling and a steady pace the chief reasons for the defeat. A lengthy gelding, Dusky Warbler has raced on good going or softer over hurdles but acts on good to firm on the Flat. *G. L. Moore*

DUSTY BANDIT (IRE) 7 ch.g. Un Desperado (FR) – Marble Miller (IRE) (Mister Lord (USA)) [2004/5 h98: 22s[3] 24v[F] 22v* 24d[6] 24s[6] Apr 2] tall, good-topped gelding: will make a chaser: fair hurdler: fortunate to win amateur handicap at Exeter in February, left in front 2 out: stays 3m: acts on heavy ground: tongue tied 4 of last 5 starts. *P. F. Nicholls* **h105**

DUSTY CARPET 7 ch.g. Pivotal – Euridice (IRE) (Woodman (USA)) [2004/5 18d Dec 7] angular gelding: lightly raced and little worthwhile form over hurdles. *M. J. Weeden* **h–**

DYRICK DAYBREAK (IRE) 6 ch.m. Ali-Royal (IRE) – Lovely Deise (IRE) (Tate Gallery (USA)) [2004/5 h111§: 16m[2] 16m[2] 20f* 17g[4] 16g[6] 16g[2] Sep 5] angular mare: fairly useful hurdler: simple task when winning 3-runner intermediate at Fairyhouse in July: stays 2½m: probably acts on any going: usually tongue tied: refused to race once. *David A. Kiely, Ireland* **h118 §**

E

EAGLES HIGH (IRE) 6 ch.g. Eagle Eyed (USA) – Bint Al Balad (IRE) (Ahonoora) [2004/5 h108§: 24d[6] 24v[2] 24v 24v[3] 24s[2] Feb 20] smallish gelding: fair handicap hurdler: effective at 2m to 3m: raced mainly on going softer than good (acts on heavy): has refused/been reluctant to race. *P. O. Brady, Ireland* **h112 §**

EAGLE'S LANDING 7 b.m. Eagle Eyed (USA) – Anchorage (IRE) (Slip Anchor) [2004/5 17s[6] 20d 20s[3] 26m[pu] 22v[4] Apr 22] half-sister to useful hurdler Barneys Lyric (by Hector Protector), stays 3m: poor on Flat (stays 1¾m), sold out of D. Ivory's stable £2,200 Ascot February (2004) Sales: little form over hurdles: wore cheekpieces and tongue strap final start. *W. K. Goldsworthy* **h–**

EARCOMESANNIE (IRE) 5 ch.m. Anshan – Play It By Ear (IRE) (Be My Native (USA)) [2004/5 F16g[4] F16g F16s[6] 16g[pu] 19s[6] 20m[6] Apr 10] first foal: dam thrice-raced, from family of very smart 2m to 3m chaser Opera Hat: fourth in mares bumper at Towcester on debut: little other form. *P. A. Pritchard* **h67 ? F83 ?**

EARL OF BUCKINGHAM 7 b.g. Alderbrook – Arctic Oats (Oats) [2004/5 F16g Oct 27] IR £10,000 3-y-o, 30,000 4-y-o: workmanlike gelding: fourth foal: brother to bumper winner Arctic Echo: dam, fair hurdler, stayed 3m: well beaten in bumper on debut: successful twice in points in 2005. *S. J. Gilmore* **F–**

EARL OF FORESTRY (GER) 4 b.g. Dream For Future (IRE) – Effelie (FR) (Son of Silver) [2004/5 F18d^2 Apr 18] first foal: dam, third both starts over hurdles, half-sister to top-class 2m to 21f chaser Fadalko and fairly useful staying chaser Historg: 1½ lengths second to Argent Ou Or in maiden bumper at Plumpton on debut. *P. F. Nicholls* **F94**

EARL OF MERCIA 5 b.g. Mistertopogigo (IRE) – Lady Godiva (Keen) [2004/5 17s 16g 16s 17m Apr 23] first foal: dam, fair 1m winner at 2 yrs, modest novice hurdler: no form over hurdles. *B. N. Pollock* **h–**

EARL OF SPECTRUM (GER) 4 b.g. Spectrum (IRE) – Evry (GER) (Torgos) [2004/5 16s^5 16d 16d Feb 19] sturdy ex-German gelding: placed 3 times up to 1¼m from 7 starts on Flat at 3 yrs for H. J. Groschel: modest novice hurdler: likely to prove best at 2m. *O. Sherwood* **h81**

EARLSFIELD RAIDER 5 ch.g. Double Trigger (IRE) – Harlequin Walk (IRE) (Pennine Walk) [2004/5 h104: 20d^6 18d 16s 17v^3 21g^2 Mar 28] leggy gelding: fair handicap hurdler: will stay 3m: acts on heavy and good to firm going: blinkered fourth outing. *G. L. Moore* **h111**

EARL SIGURD (IRE) 7 ch.g. High Kicker (USA) – My Kind (Mon Tresor) [2004/5 h100: 17v 17v^{pu} 16s c16s^3 Apr 10] leggy gelding: fair handicap hurdler, out of sorts in 2004/5: poor form when third in novice at Hexham on chasing debut: best form around 2m: acts on good to firm and good to soft going: tried in cheekpieces. *L. Lungo* **c78 h–**

EARL'S KITCHEN 8 ch.g. Karinga Bay – Rempstone (Coronash) [2004/5 21s^5 20s^3 19d c20d^6 c26d* c33g Mar 17] deep-girthed gelding: chasing type: fairly useful form in bumpers: off 20 months before reappearance: best effort over hurdles when third in novice at Chepstow: better form over fences, winning handicap there in February by 8 lengths from Howdydoody: stays 3¼m: raced on good going or softer: tongue tied last 2 starts. *C. L. Tizzard* **c109 h101**

EARLS ROCK 7 b.g. Gunner B – Will Be Wanton (Palm Track) [2004/5 h82, F68: 19g 19v 20s^5 Mar 22] smallish gelding: poor form in bumpers: has shown little over hurdles. *J. K. Cresswell* **h–**

EARLY EDITION 9 b.g. Primitive Rising (USA) – Ottery News (Pony Express) [2004/5 c87, h94: c26g^2 c16g^4 c26m^{pu} Sep 1] tall gelding: winning hurdler: fair handicap chaser: lame final outing: stays 3¼m: acts on good to soft going: tried tongue tied: often makes mistakes. *O. J. Carter* **c101 h–**

EARLY RIVERS 6 b.m. Teenoso (USA) – Cherry Morello (Bargello) [2004/5 F–: 17g^{pu} 19m^{pu} Sep 1] no sign of ability. *C. J. Down* **h–**

EARLY START 7 ch.m. Husyan (USA) – Gipsy Dawn (Lighter) [2004/5 h111: 19v^6 21s* 21m^2 Apr 2] lengthy mare: fair novice hurdler: won mares event at Towcester in March: better form when second to Penneyrose Bay in valuable mares handicap at Newbury: will probably stay 3m: acts on soft and good to firm going. *J. W. Mullins* **h111**

EARNEST (IRE) 5 b.g. Oscar (IRE) – Unassisted (IRE) (Digamist (USA)) [2004/5 F16d F17g Apr 7] €9,000 3-y-o: second foal: dam, 2m hurdle winner, from family of very smart hurdler/chaser up to 3m Bunker Hill and Irish 2000 Guineas winner Furry Glen: no show in 2 bumpers. *W. W. Dennis* **F–**

EARN OUT 4 b.g. Sovereign Water (FR) – Tudor Spartan (Spartan General) [2004/5 16v^6 17s 19s 22s^2 17m^{pu} 16g^{pu} 16d^{pu} Apr 18] sixth foal: dam unraced half-sister to useful staying hurdler Celtic Rambler, from family of very smart 2m to 3m chaser Clear Cut: form over hurdles only when second in 2¾m selling handicap at Fontwell: visored last 4 starts: ungenuine. *M. C. Pipe* **h83 §**

EARTH MAN (IRE) 6 b.g. Hamas (IRE) – Rajaura (IRE) (Storm Bird (CAN)) [2004/5 F93+: F17d* F16d* F16d 16d^3 16g* Apr 17] good-topped gelding: won bumpers at Newton Abbot in November and Newbury in December, useful form when beating Netherley 1½ lengths in Grade 2 at latter: fair form in 2 novice hurdles at Wincanton, beating Allumee by ½ length in April: not sure to stay much beyond 2m. *P. F. Nicholls* **h111 F114**

EARTHMOVER (IRE) 14 ch.g. Mister Lord (USA) – Clare's Crystal (Tekoah) [2004/5 c135, h–: c34d* c28m^{bd} c26d* c26g^6 c26g^3 Apr 14] rangy gelding: smart chaser in his prime: twice won Foxhunter Chase at Cheltenham: successful in 2004/5 in hunter chases at Uttoxeter in May and Fontwell in February: below par when remote sixth to Sleeping Night in latest renewal of Foxhunter penultimate start: best at 3m+: acted on **c117 h–**

any going: prone to mistakes: thoroughly game and genuine and a credit to connections: reportedly retired. *P. F. Nicholls*

EARTH MOVING (IRE) 5 ch.g. Anshan – Jacks Sister (IRE) (Entitled) [2004/5 F17s F16v^{pu} Mar 29] €20,000 4-y-o: third foal: half-brother to modest chaser Jack Fuller (by Be My Native), stays 3m: dam unraced half-sister to smart 2m hurdler/useful chaser Native Mission, useful hurdler/chaser up to 3¼m Joss Naylor and useful chaser around 2½m Jack Doyle: reportedly bled from nose in bumper on debut: distressed next time. *P. F. Nicholls* **F–**

EASBY BLUE 13 b.g. Teenoso (USA) – Mellie (Impecunious) [2004/5 c16v^{ur} May 10] workmanlike gelding: maiden chaser: no form in points in 2004: tongue tied last 4 starts: has bled from nose: weak finisher: not one to rely on. *Miss Stephanie Reading* **c– § h– §**

EASBY MANDARIN 4 b.g. Emperor Fountain – Beijing (USA) (Northjet) [2004/5 F13g^{3} F14s^{3} F16s Mar 12] brother to fairly useful stayer Oriental Empress and half-brother to several winners, including useful but temperamental hurdler Danjing (by Danehill): dam, won from 1½m to 2m, half-sister to very smart stayer Protection Racket: fair form in 4-y-o bumpers, best effort second start. *C. W. Thornton* **F89**

EASE THE WAY 4 b.g. Nashwan (USA) – Desert Ease (IRE) (Green Desert (USA)) [2004/5 16v^{6} 16v^{2} 16v* 16g Mar 15] rather leggy gelding: half-brother to modest 2m hurdle winner Outside Investor (by Cadeaux Genereux): fairly useful form in maidens on Flat, successful over 1½m at Gowran in August: fair juvenile hurdler: won at Tramore in January: well-backed favourite, only fourteenth of 24 in valuable handicap at Cheltenham 2 months later: raced at 2m: blinkered after debut. *D. K. Weld, Ireland* **h109**

EASIBROOK JANE 7 b.m. Alderbrook – Relatively Easy (Relkino) [2004/5 h109: c26d^{F} c25d^{4} c20d^{4} c21d^{pu} c24v^{5} Mar 29] tall mare: fair novice hurdler in 2003/4: let down by jumping all starts over fences, blundering last when looking probable winner of mares novice at Ludlow third outing: should stay 3m: acts on good to firm and heavy going. *C. L. Tizzard* **c82 x h–**

EASTERN DAGGER 5 b.g. Kris – Shehana (USA) (The Minstrel (CAN)) [2004/5 17g^{pu} 16d 16g^{5} Aug 24] sturdy gelding: half-brother to winning 2m hurdlers by Ahonoora and Elmaamul: fair at 3 yrs on Flat (stays 1m), well held for several trainers in 2004: no form over hurdles: trained on debut by J. Turner. *Miss L. V. Davis* **h–**

EASTERN FAITH 4 ch.g. Perugino (USA) – Bright Fountain (IRE) (Cadeaux Genereux) [2004/5 16s 17s^{pu} 17v^{pu} 19v^{pu} 19m^{6} Mar 21] rather leggy gelding: modest maiden (stays 7f) at 2 yrs for Mrs L. Stubbs: no form over hurdles: tongue tied on debut. *C. W. Moore* **h61**

EASTERN POINT 11 b.m. Buckskin (FR) – Deep Creek (Deep Run) [2004/5 c94: c25s^{3} c24g^{4} c23s^{3} Mar 11] lengthy mare: fair hunter chaser: below form in 2005, hinting at temperament more than once. *P. York* **c85**

EASTERN TRIBUTE (USA) 9 b.g. Affirmed (USA) – Mia Duchessa (USA) (Nijinsky (CAN)) [2004/5 c105, h–: c16s^{pu} 16s^{3} 20s^{6} 16d^{6} 20v c20s^{pu} 16s^{pu} 18s^{pu} Apr 3] sturdy gelding: winning chaser: fair handicap hurdler: mainly below par in 2004/5: barely stays 2¾m: raced on good going or softer (acts on heavy): in cheekpieces final outing. *A. C. Whillans* **c– h111**

EASTER PRESENT (IRE) 6 br.g. Presenting – Spring Fiddler (IRE) (Fidel) [2004/5 h104, F100: 19s^{4} 17s^{4} 21g^{2} Mar 28] useful-looking gelding: bumper winner: novice hurdler, just modest form in 2004/5 after 11-month absence: should stay at least 2½m: acts on soft going. *Miss H. C. Knight* **h98**

EAST HILL (IRE) 9 b.g. Satco (FR) – Sharmalyne (FR) (Melyno) [2004/5 h107: 18s 20d^{pu} Mar 28] workmanlike gelding: chasing type: fair handicap hurdler: left G. Balding and off a year, no form in 2 starts in 2005: likely to stay 3m: acts on good to firm and good to soft going, possibly not on soft. *J. J. Best* **h–**

EAST LAWYER (FR) 6 b.g. Homme de Loi (IRE) – East Riding (FR) (Fabulous Dancer (USA)) [2004/5 h116d: c19d* c16g* c19s^{2} c16g^{4} c16s^{4} Apr 21] good-topped gelding: has reportedly had breathing operation: winning hurdler: fairly useful form over fences: won maiden at Chepstow in February and novice handicap at Taunton (beat Silvergino 4 lengths) in March: stays 19f: raced on good going or softer (acts on heavy): tried blinkered: tongue tied once. *P. F. Nicholls* **c116 h–**

EAST TYCOON (IRE) 6 ch.g. Bigstone (IRE) – Princesse Sharpo (USA) (Trempolino (USA)) [2004/5 h121: c17g* 19g^{2} Sep 25] tall, angular gelding: fairly useful hurdler: well-backed favourite, good second to Football Crazy in valuable handicap at Market Rasen: impressive start to chasing career when winning maiden at Bangor by 19 lengths from Saspys Lad: likely to prove best short of 2½m: yet to race on extremes of going: **c120 P h123**

blinkered twice (won first time): open to plenty of improvement over fences. *Jonjo O'Neill*

EASTWELL VIOLET 5 b.m. Danzig Connection (USA) – Kinchenjunga (Darshaan) [2004/5 h–: 16m 19g⁵ 19g³ 22m² 22d⁴ 22mpu 19m⁴ 22dpu 21d Apr 18] poor maiden hurdler: claimed from R. Phillips £6,000 third outing: stays 2¾m: acts on good to firm going. *Mrs A. M. Thorpe* **h71**

EASY SQUEEZY 8 b.g. Alflora (IRE) – Easy Horse (FR) (Carmarthen (FR)) [2004/5 c–x, h83§: 20g* c26gpu Aug 2] poor hurdler: off 11 months, won selling handicap at Worcester in July: no form over fences, reportedly lame final outing: should stay at least 3m: acts on good to soft going: has worn blinkers: has been reluctant to race/attempted to run out. *N. A. Twiston-Davies* **c– x h83 §**

EATON HALL (IRE) 5 b. or br.g. Saddlers' Hall (IRE) – Lady Bow (Deep Run) [2004/5 F16v² F16d Feb 12] lengthy, rather unfurnished gelding: seventh foal: half-brother to modest hurdler/chaser Foxbow (by Mandalus), stays 3m: dam, modest Irish maiden hurdler, half-sister to Supreme Novices' Hurdle winner Hartstown: twice-raced in Irish points in 2004, third on completed start: easily better effort in bumpers when second to It's In The Stars at Uttoxeter on debut. *N. A. Twiston-Davies* **F90**

EAU DE COLOGNE 13 b.g. Persian Bold – No More Rosies (Warpath) [2004/5 c122, h–: c24mpu Jun 13] good-topped gelding: veteran chaser: stays 25f: acts on any going: wears headgear nowadays. *B. G. Powell* **c– h–**

EAU PURE (FR) 8 b.m. Epervier Bleu – Eau de Nuit (Kings Lake (USA)) [2004/5 c–, h100: 20s 20d⁴ 18s³ 20v⁶ 22v 22g* 21d² Apr 18] angular mare: winning chaser: modest handicap hurdler: won at Fontwell in March: stays 23f: acts on soft ground: tried in cheekpieces. *G. L. Moore* **c– h87**

EBAC (IRE) 4 ch.g. Accordion – Higher Again (IRE) (Strong Gale) [2004/5 F16g Apr 16] €160,000 3-y-o: seventh foal: half-brother to 2 winners, including fairly useful hurdler/chaser Hersov (by Roselier), stays 33f: dam unraced half-sister to Champion Hurdle winners Morley Street and Granville Again: tongue tied, soundly beaten in bumper on debut. *J. Howard Johnson* **F–**

EBINZAYD (IRE) 9 b.g. Tenby – Sharakawa (IRE) (Darshaan) [2004/5 c–, h122: 18m* 19g⁴ c19d* c24g* 21g c16g² Apr 15] angular gelding: useful handicap hurdler: won at Kelso in April 2004: successful first 2 completed starts over fences, in maiden at Catterick in January and novice at Musselburgh in February: much better form when second to Locksmith in novice at Ayr: stays easy 3m: acts on any going. *L. Lungo* **c132 h132**

EBONY JACK (IRE) 8 b. or br.g. Phardante (FR) – Ebony Jane (Roselier (FR)) [2004/5 c27v⁴ c24v⁵ c24d c26g⁴ Mar 27] 12,000 4-y-o: second foal: brother to 2½m hurdle winner Bolt Action and half-brother to winning pointer by Flemensfirth: dam, useful staying chaser, won Irish Grand National: won maiden point in 2004: little form in chases. *Mrs Tracey Barfoot-Saunt* **c–**

EBONY LIGHT (IRE) 9 br.g. Buckskin (FR) – Amelioras Daughter (General Ironside) [2004/5 c126, h–: c24g³ c24d² c26spu c25d³ c28v³ c22v² c24s² c24d² c24g³ c24d² c24s³ Apr 16] tall gelding: fairly useful handicap chaser: placed all completed starts in 2004/5: ideally needs 3m+ nowadays: acts on good to firm and heavy going: wore cheekpieces last 7 starts: sound-jumping front runner: sometimes races lazily, but is consistent. *D. McCain* **c118 h–**

ECCENTRICITY 7 b.m. Emarati (USA) – Lady Electric (Electric) [2004/5 h80: 17s 17m 17dpu Mar 26] poor novice hurdler: likely to prove best around 2m: races freely. *Mrs S. D. Williams* **h75**

ECO WARRIOR (IRE) 12 ch.g. Be My Native (USA) – Kerry Minstrel (Black Minstrel) [2004/5 c25gur May 1] modest pointer, placed twice in 2005: let down by jumping both starts in hunter chases: stays 25f: raced on good going or softer (acts on heavy): has had tongue tied. *Nick Bell* **c– h–**

EDE'IFF 8 b.m. Tragic Role (USA) – Flying Amy (Norwick (USA)) [2004/5 c104, h89: c20d³ c16s⁴ c16g² c17d⁶ c16g⁵ 16g⁵ c24g⁴ c21d² c24g² Apr 7] leggy mare: modest hurdler: fair handicap chaser: stays easy 3m: acts on firm and soft going: tongue tied prior to last 2 starts: takes good hold. *W. G. M. Turner* **c104 h89**

EDENDERRY (IRE) 6 ch.g. Dock Leaf – Orwell Annie (Risk Me (FR)) [2004/5 F16s Apr 10] third foal: dam raced twice on Flat in Ireland: well held in bumper on debut. *J. Hetherton* **F–**

EDE'S 5 ch.g. Bijou d'Inde – Ballagarrow Girl (North Stoke) [2004/5 h86: 16d 16g Jan 19] winning hurdler: well held both starts in 2004/5: should stay beyond 2m: acts on soft and good to firm going. *W. G. M. Turner* **h–**

EDGAR GINK (IRE) 11 ch.g. Step Together (USA) – Turbo Run (Deep Run) [2004/5 c71+, h–: c21dF Mar 10] lengthy gelding: maiden hunter chaser: stays 25f: acts on firm going: has had tongue tied. *L. Corcoran* **c– h–**

EDGAR WILDE (IRE) 7 b.g. Invited (USA) – Ou La La (IRE) (Be My Native (USA)) [2004/5 16g4 21g 21d2 Apr 18] good-topped gelding: second foal: brother to winning pointer Wild Edgar: dam never ran: placed in maiden Irish points: best effort over hurdles when second in maiden at Plumpton: stays 21f. *R. Rowe* **h96**

EDGEHILL (IRE) 4 b.g. Ali-Royal (IRE) – Elfin Queen (IRE) (Fairy King (USA)) [2004/5 16m 18s4 Oct 12] fair maiden on Flat (stays 1¼m): well held in juvenile hurdles: failed to settle in blinkers second start: capable of better. *C. R. Egerton* **h84 p**

EDGEMOOR PRINCESS 7 b.m. Broadsword (USA) – Stubbin Moor (Kinglet) [2004/5 F–: 24dpu 17g 19mpu Apr 9] no form in bumpers or over hurdles. *R. J. Armson* **h–**

EDMO HEIGHTS 9 ch.g. Keen – Bodham (Bustino) [2004/5 c103, h124: c16d5 c16s5 c19g6 c21d3 Mar 19] smallish, leggy gelding: fairly useful hurdler: fair handicap chaser: stays 21f: acts on good to firm and heavy going: races prominently. *T. D. Easterby* **c106 h–**

EDMO YEWKAY (IRE) 5 b. or br.g. Sri Pekan (USA) – Mannequin (IRE) (In The Wings) [2004/5 h115: 19v 20s4 21dF 22s 19d c16v2 c16g4 c19d3 c20v* c24s4 c19s2 c22g5 c20d4 c20s2 Apr 22] useful-looking gelding: fairly useful juvenile hurdler in 2003/4, well below form in handicaps in 2004/5: fair chaser: won 2-finisher novice at Wetherby in January: will stay beyond 2½m: acts on heavy going: tried blinkered. *T. D. Easterby* **c108 h–**

EDREDON BLEU (FR) 13 b.g. Grand Tresor (FR) – Nuit Bleue III (FR) (Le Pontet (FR)) [2004/5 c169, h–: c17s6 c24g 21d4 c25dpu c21gpu Mar 17] useful-looking gelding: top-class chaser, successful on 24 out of 47 starts, most notably in 2000 Queen Mother Champion Chase and 2003 King George VI Chase: thrice-raced over hurdles, fair form when fourth in novice at Kempton: stayed easy 3m: acted on firm and good to soft going, possibly not at best on soft/heavy: tongue tied: went well fresh: bold-jumping front runner: reportedly retired. *Miss H. C. Knight* **c– h114**

EFFECTUAL 12 b.g. Efisio – Moharabuiee (Pas de Seul) [2004/5 c–, h115: 27g May 21] compact gelding: winning chaser: fairly useful handicap hurdler: well held only start in 2004/5: stays 3¼m: acts on any going: sometimes swishes tail. *Miss Venetia Williams* **c– h–**

EFRHINA (IRE) 5 ch.m. Woodman (USA) – Eshq Albahr (USA) (Riverman (USA)) [2004/5 16mpu Jun 6] fair on Flat (stays 1½m), successful twice in early-January: no show on hurdling debut: subsequently joined Stef Liddiard. *Miss K. Marks* **h–**

EGGMOUNT (IRE) 7 b.g. Riberetto – Brigade Leader (IRE) (Supreme Leader) [2004/5 F109: 24d4 c21d5 c19vpu c24dpu Feb 18] strong, good sort: useful bumper winner: remote fourth in maiden at Uttoxeter on hurdling debut: fair form (still looked inexperienced) when fifth to Control Man in well-contested novice at Cheltenham on chasing debut: amiss both starts after. *T. R. George* **c108 ? h82 +**

EHAB (IRE) 6 b.g. Cadeaux Genereux – Dernier Cri (Slip Anchor) [2004/5 h80: 16g5 20d3 18m6 16s 16d6 16d c16s5 16dpu Feb 18] tall gelding: poor maiden hurdler: tailed off in maiden only outing over fences: likely to prove best short of 2½m: tried blinkered: has been let down by jumping. *G. L. Moore* **c– h82**

EI EI 10 b.g. North Briton – Branitska (Mummy's Pet) [2004/5 c142, h114: 16g6 c21m3 19mF Jun 9] sturdy gelding: useful handicap hurdler/chaser: long way clear when fell fatally last in handicap hurdle at Market Rasen: stayed 21f: acted on firm and soft going: headstrong front runner who jumped boldly: very tough and thoroughly genuine. *M. C. Chapman* **c136 h135**

EIFFEL TOWER (IRE) 8 b.g. Wakashan – My Wings (Erin's Hope) [2004/5 17g 21m 22d3 17d4 Aug 30] poor maiden hurdler: refused only start in chase: thoroughly temperamental. *J. J. Lambe, Ireland* **c– § h71 §**

EIGHT ELLINGTON (IRE) 4 b.g. Ali-Royal (IRE) – Where's Charlotte (Sure Blade (USA)) [2004/5 17g 16g6 Mar 14] modest on Flat (stays 9.4f), successful in January, sold out of Miss G. Kelleway's stable 800 gns Newmarket February Sales: well held over hurdles, looking wayward in claimer second start. *R. M. Stronge* **h–**

EIGHT FIFTY FIVE (IRE) 5 gr.g. Wood Chanter – Electric View (IRE) (Electric) [2004/5 F17s4 Mar 10] €3,800 4-y-o: first foal: dam unraced: runner-up in maiden Irish point on debut in 2004: fourth of 11 in bumper at Carlisle. *R. T. Phillips* **F87**

EIGHT (IRE) 9 ch.g. Thatching – Up To You (Sallust) [2004/5 h74: 16d c19gpu Mar 5] compact gelding: poor on Flat (stays 1¾m) nowadays: similar form over hurdles: jumped sketchily on chasing debut. *J. M. P. Eustace* **c– h–**

EILEENS COMET 5 br.m. Cosmonaut – Starnina (IRE) (Caerleon (USA)) [2004/5 F16g F16s Apr 10] second foal: dam unraced, from family of high-class 1¼m filly Kartajana: tailed off in bumpers. *P. Beaumont* **F–**

EILLENRIDGE (IRE) 5 br.m. Balla Cove – Just A Maid (Rarity) [2004/5 F16m⁶ Sep 24] seventh foal: half-sister to bumper winners Wicked Weasel (by Religiously) and Catchthebug (by Lord Americo) and winning pointer by Over The River: dam maiden: well held in bumper on debut. *Mrs H. Dalton* **F–**

EISENHOWER (IRE) 6 b.g. Erins Isle – Lyphard Abu (IRE) (Lyphard's Special (USA)) [2004/5 c–, h–: c23dpu c21d Oct 27] good-topped gelding: fourth in point in March, little sign of ability otherwise: blinkered last 3 starts. *J. Wade* **c– h–**

ELA FIGURA 5 ch.m. The West (USA) – Chili Bouchier (USA) (Stop The Music (USA)) [2004/5 16spu 17m 17spu Apr 2] angular mare: 5f maiden on Flat: no form over hurdles. *K. J. Burke* **h–**

ELA JAY 6 b.m. Double Eclipse (IRE) – Papirusa (IRE) (Pennine Walk) [2004/5 h104: 19m* Jun 9] medium-sized mare: fair form over hurdles: left H. Morrison, fortunate to win handicap at Market Rasen, left in front after clear leader fell last: should be suited by 2½m+: acts on good to firm going. *M. G. Rimell* **h101**

EL ANDALUZ (FR) 5 b.g. Baby Turk – Elise L'Ermitage (FR) (Quart de Vin (FR)) [2004/5 16v 16g Jan 17] leggy gelding: fourth foal: dam ran once: no show in novice hurdles. *M. Todhunter* **h–**

ELA RE 6 ch.g. Sabrehill (USA) – Lucia Tarditi (FR) (Crystal Glitters (USA)) [2004/5 h107: 16g 17d 16s 16d 16g 16d 20v² 20vpu 16d³ 20d Apr 20] sparely-made gelding: fair handicap hurdler: stays 2½m: acts on heavy and good to firm going: has looked difficult ride. *C. R. Dore* **h102**

EL BANDITO (IRE) 11 ch.g. Un Desperado (FR) – Red Marble (Le Bavard (FR)) [2004/5 c106, h–: c20g* c19s* c20g⁴ c19s⁴ c24d c16s² c19d⁵ c24spu Apr 16] well-made gelding: fairly useful handicap chaser: won at Worcester in May and Chepstow in October: poor efforts last 2 starts: stays 2¾m: acts on soft going. *R. Lee* **c115 h–**

ELBDOUBLEU 5 ch.m. Classic Cliche (IRE) – Bowling Fort (Bowling Pin) [2004/5 F17m⁶ F17d* Aug 22] fifth foal: half-sister to fairly useful but temperamental staying hurdler/chaser King Pin (by King's Ride): dam unraced, from family of very smart staying chaser Fort Fox: better effort in bumpers (trained by S. Brookshaw on debut) when winning at Newton Abbot. *C. J. Down* **F80**

EL CORDOBES (IRE) 14 b.g. Torus – Queens Tricks (Le Bavard (FR)) [2004/5 c90, h72: c22g Jul 4] lengthy gelding: veteran chaser: well held only 2004/5 start: stays easy 3m: acts on firm and soft going: front runner. *Mrs J. R. Buckley* **c– h–**

ELECTRIQUE (IRE) 5 b.g. Elmaamul (USA) – Majmu (USA) (Al Nasr (FR)) [2004/5 h103p: 16s Nov 20] leggy gelding: twice-raced over hurdles, well held on second occasion: likely to prove best with emphasis on speed around 2m. *Mrs S. J. Smith* **h–**

ELEGANT ACCORD (IRE) 7 b.m. Accordion – Swan Bridge (IRE) (Supreme Leader) [2004/5 F–: 24gpu May 16] no sign of ability. *Mrs P. Ford* **h–**

ELENAS RIVER (IRE) 9 br.g. Over The River (FR) – Elenas Beauty (Tarqogan) [2004/5 c116, h–: c24m* c32mpu Jun 27] rather sparely-made gelding: winning hurdler: fairly useful chaser: completed hat-trick in novice at Stratford in June: jumped markedly right throughout when running poorly in valuable handicap at Uttoxeter next time: stays 3¼m: acts on firm and soft going: usually jumps soundly: front runner. *P. J. Hobbs* **c116 ? h–**

ELFEET BAY (IRE) 10 b.g. Yashgan – Marjoram (Warpath) [2004/5 c73, h–: 17g⁵ Aug 14] poor maiden hurdler/chaser: off 13 months before only start in 2004/5: should stay beyond 17f: acts on soft going: tried blinkered/in cheekpieces. *Mrs L. Williamson* **c– h–**

ELFKIRK (IRE) 6 b.m. Zaffaran (USA) – Winter Sunset (Celio Rufo) [2004/5 F88: F16d⁴ 23s³ 22g⁴ 21v³ 20v* 21s⁵ 21m Apr 2] leggy mare: fair bumper winner: bought out of J. I. A. Charlton's stable 60,000 gns Doncaster August Sales: best effort over hurdles when winning mares novice at Chepstow in February: should stay beyond 2½m: acts on heavy ground. *R. H. Buckler* **h92 F85**

EL GIZA (USA) 7 ch.g. Cozzene (USA) – Gazayil (USA) (Irish River (FR)) [2004/5 h–: 16g 20g⁵ 16m Aug 6] maiden on Flat, well held in 2005 for Miss J. Tooth: little form over hurdles: reluctant at start second outing. *J. M. Bradley* **h–**

EL HAMRA (IRE) 7 gr.g. Royal Abjar (USA) – Cherlinoa (FR) (Crystal Palace (FR)) [2004/5 19d6 Mar 26] lightly raced and no form on Flat since 2002: well held both starts over hurdles. *T. R. George* **h–**

ELHEBA (IRE) 6 b. or br.g. Elbio – Fireheba (ITY) (Fire of Life (USA)) [2004/5 h98§: 19d 17m2 19m4 19g4 Apr 15] modest hurdler: likely to prove best around 2m: acts on good to firm going: tried blinkered: has refused to race. *C. J. Down* **h92 §**

EL HOMBRE DEL RIO (IRE) 8 ch.g. Over The River (FR) – Hug In A Fog (IRE) (Strong Gale) [2004/5 c108, h–: c26dpu c26g4 c24g2 c28dR c24d2 c24d c24v* c24s6 c26d6 Feb 26] rangy gelding: fair handicap chaser: won at Chepstow in January: stays 3½m: yet to race on firm going, acts on any other: visored/blinkered last 4 starts: hard ride (refused fourth start) and not one to trust. *R. H. Alner* **c110 § h–**

ELITHA 6 b.m. Glacial Storm (USA) – Daddy's Darling (Mummy's Pet) [2004/5 F17dpu May 15] fifth foal: dam 1½m winner/novice hurdler, stayed 2½m: pulled up in mares bumper at Bangor: dead. *M. Appleby* **F–**

ELJUTAN (IRE) 7 b.g. Namaqualand (USA) – Camarat (Ahonoora) [2004/5 16s Feb 18] workmanlike gelding: fair juvenile hurdler in 2001/2 for R. O'Sullivan: no sign of retaining ability. *J. Joseph* **h–**

ELLANDSHE (IRE) 5 b. or br.g. Topanoora – Fox Glen (Furry Glen) [2004/5 F16d F16m5 Apr 10] €20,000 3-y-o: ninth foal: half-brother to fairly useful hurdler/useful chaser around 2m Sir OJ (by Be My Native): dam, placed over hurdles in Ireland, from family of Grand National winner Last Suspect: better effort in bumpers when fifth at Worcester. *P. R. Webber* **F86**

ELLAS RECOVERY (IRE) 5 b.g. Shernazar – Nancys Wood (IRE) (Doubletour (USA)) [2004/5 F18s 24s3 20d Apr 20] €3,200 3-y-o: compact gelding: first foal: dam maiden: won maiden Irish point on debut in 2004: tailed off in bumper: better effort over hurdles when third in novice at Kempton, jumping poorly. *D. B. Feek* **h83 ? F–**

ELLE ROSEADOR 6 b.m. El Conquistador – The Hon Rose (Baron Blakeney) [2004/5 F–: F18s* 20spu 22sur 16dpu 24gF 22gpu Apr 17] rather unfurnished mare: fair form in bumpers, successful in mares event at Fontwell in January: sketchy jumper and failed to complete all starts over hurdles: should stay at least 2½m: blinkered last 2 starts. *M. Madgwick* **h– x F88**

ELLERSLIE DE HOOCH 5 b.m. Cosmonaut – Oleron (Darshaan) [2004/5 F16g Mar 28] third foal: dam, poor maiden, stayed 1½m: last in bumper on debut: sold 1,600 gns Doncaster May Sales. *O. Brennan* **F–**

ELLO OLLIE (IRE) 10 b.g. Roselier (FR) – Kayanna (Torenaga) [2004/5 c–x, h77: 24d5 26m2 24m5 Jun 5] close-coupled gelding: poor hurdler: stays 3¼m: acts on soft and good to firm going: sometimes blinkered: sold 2,500 gns Doncaster August Sales. *Andrew Turnell* **c– x h73**

EL LUTE (IRE) 9 b.g. Abednego – Much Obliged (Crash Course) [2004/5 c25sur c24dur Mar 28] won maiden Irish point in 2002: little form otherwise, let down by jumping in chases. *Mrs E. M. Collinson* **c– x h–**

ELLWAY PROSPECT 5 ch.m. Pivotal – Littlemisstrouble (USA) (My Gallant (USA)) [2004/5 h78: 22s3 22s 21d6 Feb 11] lengthy mare: poor novice hurdler: should stay beyond 2¾m: raced on good going or softer: wore cheekpieces final start. *Miss I. E. Craig* **h82**

EL MAGNIFICO 4 b.g. Forzando – Princess Poquito (Hard Fought) [2004/5 16g Jul 11] half-brother to poor 2m hurdler Magic Box (by Magic Ring) and winning pointer by Emarati: maiden on Flat (stays 1¼m), well beaten in 2005: well held in juvenile on hurdling debut. *P. D. Cundell* **h–**

EL PEDRO 6 b.g. Piccolo – Standard Rose (Ile de Bourbon (USA)) [2004/5 h–: 16s 16s Nov 28] leggy, lengthy gelding: poor on Flat (stays easy 1½m): well held over hurdles. *N. E. Berry* **h–**

ELTRINGHAM 5 b.m. Milieu – Whosgotsillyssense (Pragmatic) [2004/5 F–: F16s Mar 1] leggy mare: well beaten in 2 bumpers. *C. R. Wilson* **F–**

ELUSIVE SKY (IRE) 5 b.g. Sabrehill (USA) – Aneen Alkamanja (Last Tycoon) [2004/5 F17g May 23] first foal: dam never ran: tailed off in bumper on debut: fell in point in March. *M. W. Easterby* **F–**

ELUVAPARTY 5 b.g. El Conquistador – Ruby Celebration (New Member) [2004/5 F16d Mar 19] tall, useful-looking gelding: sixth foal: dam, maiden, sister to smart staying **F87 p**

chaser Country Member: seventh of 16 at Uttoxeter in bumper on debut, keeping on not knocked about: likely to improve. *D. P. Keane*

EL VAQUERO (IRE) 7 ch.g. Un Desperado (FR) – Marble Fontaine (Lafontaine (USA)) [2004/5 h125: $c17s^{pu}$ c19m* $c21d^{F}$ $c21d^{2}$ c20g* Feb 5] **c143 + h–**

Henrietta Knight's fondness for the stock of Un Desperado would be understandable, even if he wasn't the sire of Best Mate. Many of Un Desperado's offspring are athletic sorts with scope, just the type to make better chasers than hurdlers and thus just the type Knight has made her speciality as a trainer. No fewer than sixteen of the eighty-nine horses listed under her care in *Horses In Training 2005* are by the sire, a high-class mile-and-a-quarter winner in France who died in 2000 in his tenth season at stud in Ireland. It's clearly long odds against any of the fifteen others being nearly so good as the triple Cheltenham Gold Cup winner but another of the group, El Vaquero, gave the Knight stable its biggest success of the season, when winning the totesport Scilly Isles Novices' Chase at Sandown in February. El Vaquero ('the cowboy' in Spanish) was unable to run as planned at Aintree but reportedly all was well with him and he should make an impact in good handicaps at two and a half miles or more in 2005/6, when he will be trained by Howard Johnson, having been bought on behalf of Andrea and Graham Wylie in the summer.

It was clear early on that El Vaquero was held in some regard. After showing fairly useful form to win a bumper at Huntingdon on his debut, he was sent to contest the Grade 2 bumper at Aintree's Grand National meeting. El Vaquero wasn't up to the task at that stage, finishing ninth to Classic Native after being flat out at halfway. He wasn't the only subsequent Grade 1 novice chase winner in the field, with Ashley Brook and the 2004 Scilly Isles winner Patricksnineteenth also among the also-rans. El Vaquero went on to show fairly useful form over hurdles in 2003/4, though it took him until his fifth and final start to get off the mark, winning a novice at Wincanton in April from Red Devil Robert. Though pulled up when in need of the run on his debut over fences behind Ashley Brook, El Vaquero soon showed form well in advance of that achieved in bumpers and over hurdles. He won

totesport Scilly Isles Novices' Chase, Sandown—
El Vaquero (right) stays on too strongly for Le Passing (centre), Lacdoudal (grey) and Ashley Brook

at the second attempt, landing a maiden at Taunton in November when a switch to front-running tactics and some quick if low jumping enabled him to get the better of two other promising sorts in Le Passing and Lacdoudal. El Vaquero's next two outings resulted in defeats at Cheltenham, though he was going strongly and disputing the lead with the winner Control Man when falling four out in a well-contested novice there in December and, with stable-jockey Jim Culloty riding him for the first time over fences, wasn't seen to best advantage when second to My Will, the pair the only finishers, in the Dipper Novices' Chase the following month.

Everything came right a month later at Sandown. Just five went to post for the Scilly Isles, a small field even by the standards of a race which sometimes struggles to justify its status as a championship event. The opposition included both Le Passing and Lacdoudal. Le Passing had won both his starts since Taunton, while Lacdoudal had won three times and started the shortest odds of the trio, though the favourite was another old rival Ashley Brook (See You Sometime made up the field). With Ashley Brook as usual making the running, and Lacdoudal helping, El Vaquero was patiently ridden. After getting tapped for foot over the railway fences, he was back on the bridle after three out and ran on too strongly on the flat for Le Passing, winning by two lengths with Lacdoudal (like the first two, filling the same position as at Taunton) and Ashley Brook, who hit the last, close behind. Le Passing wasn't at his best subsequently but the three others went on to better things, Lacdoudal finishing second in the valuable new novice handicap at the Cheltenham Festival, Ashley Brook taking second in the Arkle and winning the Maghull, and See You Sometime running gallant races in defeat, including when second to Like-A-Butterfly at Aintree. For El Vaquero, though, the season was over.

El Vaquero (IRE) (ch.g. 1998)	Un Desperado (FR) (b 1983)	Top Ville (b 1976)	High Top
			Sega Ville
		White Lightning (gr 1970)	Baldric II
			Rough Sea
	Marble Fontaine (b 1987)	Lafontaine (b 1977)	Sham
			Valya
		Marble Owen (b 1972)	Master Owen
			Ossians Marble

The rangy El Vaquero is the third foal and second winner out of Marble Fontaine, who was awarded a two-mile hurdle in Ireland. Her first foal Alota Baby (by Satco) won at two and a half and two and three quarter miles over hurdles in 2004/5. The grandam Marble Owen produced five winners, including the fairly useful hurdler The Papparazi, who stayed three miles, and the fairly useful French chaser Agissez, but the family's most notable performer in recent years before El Vaquero came along is another by Un Desperado, the useful two-mile hurdler Unarmed, who won the Jameson Gold Cup for Paddy Mullins. Unarmed is out of a half-sister to Marble Owen. El Vaquero will stay three miles and acts on good to firm and good to soft going (also ran creditably at the time on soft over hurdles). He is clearly effective either held up or making the running. *Miss H. C. Knight*

ELVERYS (IRE) 6 b.g. Lord Americo – Paddy's Babs (Little Buskins) [2004/5 F16v4 Jan 3] €28,000 4-y-o: good-topped gelding: has scope: sixth foal: brother to fair hurdler Little Duke, stayed 2½m, and half-brother to dam of fairly useful hurdler up to 3m Priests Bridge: dam maiden pointer: 4½ lengths fourth of 17 to Notaproblem in bumper at Wetherby on debut. *R. A. Fahey* **F93**

EL VIEJO (IRE) 8 b.g. Norwich – Shuil Na Gale (Strong Gale) [2004/5 24gpu c25s4 c24d5 Jan 15] rangy, useful-looking gelding: winning hurdler: ran as though amiss on return from 2-year absence: modest form both starts over fences: should stay 3m: raced on good going or softer. *L. Wells* **c93 h–**

ELZEES 4 b.g. Magic Ring (IRE) – White Flash (Sure Blade (USA)) [2004/5 20d 19mpu Apr 9] leggy gelding: half-brother to bumper winner Hi Humpfree (by Thowra): fair maiden on Flat (should have stayed 1½m), sold out of D. Elsworth's stable £3,600 Ascot February Sales: no form over hurdles: dead. *Miss J. S. Davis* **h–**

EL ZITO (IRE) 8 b.g. Mukaddamah (USA) – Samite (FR) (Tennyson (FR)) [2004/5 19d 17s Nov 18] workmanlike gelding: fairly useful hurdler at one time, no sign of retaining ability: formerly tongue tied. *D. Burchell* **h–**

EMANATE 7 ch.g. Nicholas Bill – Sleepline Princess (Royal Palace) [2004/5 F81: 22g^{6} Oct 24] rangy gelding: modest form in bumpers: not fluent when tailed off in novice hurdle: sold 3,000 gns Doncaster November Sales. *P. F. Nicholls* **h–**

EMANIC (FR) 5 b.g. Video Rock (FR) – Una Volta (FR) (Toujours Pret (USA)) [2004/5 h115: c20d^{F} c16d^{2} 16d 16s^{pu} 16s^{4} Feb 10] leggy, useful-looking gelding: fairly useful hurdler: similar form when falling 2 out in well-contested novice at Huntingdon on chasing debut: probably stays 2½m: raced on good going or softer: blinkered last 2 starts: patiently ridden: weak finisher: not one to trust. *P. F. Nicholls* **c116 § h116 §**

EMERALD EXPRESS 6 b.m. Bigstone (IRE) – Nashkara (Shirley Heights) [2004/5 F87: 17g^{5} 16d* 19m^{5} 16d^{pu} 16d 16s^{4} c20d^{pu} Mar 3] lengthy, angular mare: fair form in bumpers: won mares maiden hurdle at Southwell in November: disappointing after, including on chasing debut (bled from nose): not certain to stay much beyond 2m: wore headgear 4 of last 5 starts: front runner: ungenuine: sold 10,000 gns Doncaster March Sales. *P. R. Webber* **c– h93 §**

E MINOR (IRE) 6 b.m. Blushing Flame (USA) – Watch The Clock (Mtoto) [2004/5 16g 16d Dec 8] leggy mare: modest on Flat (stays 2m): little show over hurdles. *T. Wall* **h–**

EMKANAT (IRE) 4 ch.f. Unfuwain (USA) – Raaqiyya (USA) (Blushing Groom (FR)) [2004/5 F12g F12g F16g^{4} F16g^{2} Feb 16] 3,500 2-y-o: leggy filly: sixth foal: half-sister to Irish 6f winner Samawi (by Pennekamp): dam unraced half-sister to very good French fillies up to 1m Maximova, Navratilovna and Vilikaia: progressive form in bumpers, second in mares event at Musselburgh. *K. A. Morgan* **F86**

EMMASFLORA 7 b.m. Alflora (IRE) – Charlotte's Emma (Oats) [2004/5 20v^{5} 24v^{5} 20s^{5} Feb 9] leggy mare: third foal: dam, fair hurdler/chaser who stayed 3¼m, half-sister to useful chaser around 2½m Thosewerethedays: poor form in novice hurdles. *Miss P. Robson* **h72**

EMOTIONAL ARTICLE (IRE) 5 ch.g. Definite Article – Cairo Lady (IRE) (Persian Bold) [2004/5 F103: 16s 16s^{2} 16d^{2} 16s* 16v* 16v^{F} 16s^{F} Mar 29] bumper winner: fair form over hurdles, winning handicap at Gowran (most impressive) and 4-y-o minor event at Limerick in December: let down by jumping in 3 valuable handicaps after: raced at 2m on going softer than good (acts on heavy). *T. J. Taaffe, Ireland* **h114 x**

EMOTIONAL MOMENT (IRE) 8 b.g. Religiously (USA) – Rosceen Bui (IRE) (Phardante (FR)) [2004/5 c131, h135: c25g^{F} 20v 20s^{4} 16d^{5} 24d^{3} 24v* 24v* 24v* 24g^{pu} Mar 17] leggy gelding: useful form over fences, though generally let down by jumping: smart hurdler: won in small fields Grade 2 woodiesdiy.com Christmas Hurdle at Leopardstown (by distance from Yogi) in December, Grade 3 Alo Duffin Memorial Galmoy Hurdle at Gowran (beat Homer Wells 25 lengths) in January and Grade 2 McCabe **c– h149**

woodiesdiy.com Christmas Hurdle, Leopardstown—
Emotional Moment gains the first of three wins during a profitable winter

Builders Ltd Boyne Hurdle at Navan in February: ran as if amiss in Grade 1 events at Cheltenham in March and Punchestown in late-April: stays 3m: raced on good going or softer (acts on heavy). *T. J. Taaffe, Ireland*

EMPEROR ROSCOE 10 b.g. Roscoe Blake – Royal Celt (Celtic Cone) [2004/5 c–: c24dpu May 11] winning pointer, successful twice in 2005: pulled up in 2 hunter chases. *A. A. Day* **c–**

EMPEROR ROSS (IRE) 10 b. or br.g. Roselier (FR) – Gilded Empress (Menelek) [2004/5 c114, h114: c24dpu c24g4 c20g* c21sur c22g4 Apr 1] useful-looking gelding: has reportedly had 3 wind operations: fair hurdler: useful hunter chaser: successful in point in January and hunter at Sandown in February, beating Satchmo by 7 lengths in latter: will prove best at 2¾m+: acts on good to firm and good to soft going: tongue tied prior to 2004/5: usually jumps well. *N. G. Richards* **c113 h–**

EMPERORS GUEST 7 b.g. Emperor Jones (USA) – Intimate Guest (Be My Guest (USA)) [2004/5 c127, h–: c16g3 17d c16g4 c16dpu c17g c16sur c16g* 16g5 c16gpu Apr 14] tall gelding: winning hurdler: fairly useful handicap chaser: sold out of T. Mullins' stable 25,000 gns Doncaster May Sales after second start: won 4-runner event at Fakenham in January: lame final outing: raced mainly around 2m: acts on heavy going: in cheekpieces/blinkers last 5 appearances: has been let down by jumping. *C. J. Mann* **c125 h96**

EMPEROR'S MONARCH 6 ch.g. Emperor Fountain – Shalta (FR) (Targowice (USA)) [2004/5 F88: F17d2 22v5 20d5 19d6 20v6 16s* 21d5 Apr 5] leggy gelding: best effort in bumpers on reappearance: modest novice hurdler: won maiden at Ayr in March: finished distressed final outing: likely to prove best up to 2½m: raced on good going or softer (acts on heavy). *J. Wade* **h91 F92**

EMPHATIC (IRE) 10 ch.g. Ela-Mana-Mou – Sally Rose (Sallust) [2004/5 h107: 25g6 24g5 c24d4 c26dpu 24d 26s4 26g 26mF Mar 21] small gelding: fair handicap hurdler: creditable effort in 2004/5 only on second outing: let down by jumping over fences: stays 3¼m: acts on heavy and good to firm going: blinkered/visored: tongue tied final start: races prominently: lazy. *J. G. Portman* **c– x h102**

EMPRESS OF IRELAND (IRE) 6 b.m. King's Ride – My Lovely Rose (IRE) (Orchestra) [2004/5 F16s Nov 5] €13,000 3-y-o, €10,000 4-y-o: fourth foal: dam unraced half-sister to top-class staying chaser Life of A Lord: eighth of 17 in bumper at Hexham on debut. *R. A. Fahey* **F–**

EM'S GUY 7 b.g. Royal Fountain – Gaelic Empress (Regular Guy) [2004/5 h–, F–: 16v 16vpu 20spu c21vpu c21dpu Apr 5] lengthy gelding: no sign of ability: wore cheekpieces final start. *A. Parker* **c– h–**

EM'S ROYALTY 8 b.g. Royal Fountain – Gaelic Empress (Regular Guy) [2004/5 h98: 22v 24v2 24v4 24v2 24v4 24vF 24v2 24s5 Apr 10] fair novice hurdler: stays 3m: raced on going softer than good (acts on heavy). *A. Parker* **h102**

ENCORE CADOUDAL (FR) 7 b.g. Cadoudal (FR) – Maousse (FR) (Labus (FR)) [2004/5 h113: c16v3 c16vpu c16d2 c16s* Apr 21] leggy gelding: fair hurdler: similar form over fences: won handicap at Perth in April by 2 lengths from Island Faith: best around 2m: acts on heavy going: none too fluent over fences: seems best held up. *H. P. Hogarth* **c113 h–**

ENCOUNTER 9 br.g. Primo Dominie – Dancing Spirit (IRE) (Ahonoora) [2004/5 16m 16g5 Feb 27] modest on Flat (stays 1¼m): little encouragement in 2 starts over hurdles. *J. Hetherton* **h70**

ENDLESS POWER (IRE) 5 b.g. Perugino (USA) – Charroux (IRE) (Darshaan) [2004/5 F16s* F16d6 F16v3 F16s Apr 22] tall gelding: first foal: dam, third from 3 outings at 1¼m, half-sister to Gold Cup winner Gildoran out of half-sister to Arc winner Detroit: 33/1, won bumper at Ayr on debut in November by 8 lengths from Notaproblem: similar form next 2 starts. *Mrs L. B. Normile* **F97**

END OF AN ERROR 6 b.m. Charmer – Needwood Poppy (Rolfe (USA)) [2004/5 h93: 21g6 24f 27m 21v 19d 21d Apr 5] small, leggy mare: modest hurdler in 2003/4: well held in 2004/5: stays 25f: acts on firm and good to soft going: gets behind, and not one to trust. *Mrs E. Slack* **h82 §**

END OF SAGA 6 ch.g. Endoli (USA) – Super Saga (Sagaro) [2004/5 F16g F16s4 Aug 25] first foal: dam of little account: tailed off in 2 bumpers, tried to run out on debut. *J. B. Walton* **F–**

EN EL EM FLYER 10 b.g. Seymour Hicks (FR) – Sound 'n' Rhythm (Tudor Rhythm) [2004/5 c68, h–: c24spu Oct 13] poor chaser/maiden hurdler: again let down by jumping only start in 2004/5: stays 25f: acts on heavy going. *C. Tinkler* **c– h–**

ENGLISH JIM (IRE) 4 b.g. Saddlers' Hall (IRE) – Royal Folly (IRE) (King's Ride) [2004/5 F18s⁵ F18s⁴ F16d 21gpu Mar 27] first foal: dam unraced, out of half-sister to smart chaser up to 3m Hard Case and useful staying chaser Sound Judgement: modest form in bumpers: jumped erratically in novice on hurdling debut. *T. P. McGovern* **h– F80**

ENGLISHTOWN (FR) 5 b.g. Mark of Esteem (IRE) – English Spring (USA) (Grey Dawn II) [2004/5 16m 20m² 17s⁴ 16d⁶ c17v³ 20d⁴ Dec 4] leggy, close-coupled gelding: half-brother to fair hurdler/modest chaser Spring To Glory (by Teenoso), stays 3m: useful on Flat (stays 1½m) at 3 yrs, sold out of J. Oxx's stable 130,000 gns Newmarket Autumn (2003) Sales: modest form over hurdles: mistakes when well held on chasing debut: may prove best around 2m: tried blinkered. *Jonjo O'Neill* **c72 h96 +**

ENHANCER 7 b.g. Zafonic (USA) – Ypha (USA) (Lyphard (USA)) [2004/5 F–: 16s³ 16s² 16s 17g* Apr 14] good-topped gelding: fairly useful bumper performer: fair form over hurdles, left Mrs L. Jewell after second start: won falsely-run novice at Cheltenham in April by ¾ length from Mister Mustard. *M. J. McGrath* **h112**

ENITSAG (FR) 6 ch.g. Pistolet Bleu (IRE) – Rosala (FR) (Lashkari) [2004/5 c93, h101§: c21g⁶ c20dF c21d³ c20sur Mar 31] leggy gelding: winning hunter chaser, below best in 2004/5: won point in April: stays 21f: acts on soft going, probably on firm: tried in headgear: sketchy jumper. *S. Flook* **c82 x h– §**

ENNEL BOY (IRE) 12 ch.g. Torus – Golden Symphony (Le Moss) [2004/5 c112, h–: c24g⁶ c25gpu Apr 12] close-coupled gelding: winning hurdler/chaser: off 16 months, little sign of retaining ability in 2004/5: stays 27f: acts on firm and good to soft going: has run well in cheekpieces. *N. M. Babbage* **c– h–**

ENTERTAINER (IRE) 9 b.g. Be My Guest (USA) – Green Wings (General Assembly (USA)) [2004/5 c–, h101: 24d May 12] good-topped gelding: fairly useful hurdler at best, largely disappointing since 2001: probably stays 2¾m: acts on soft and good to firm going: tried blinkered: of suspect temperament. *A. R. Dicken* **c– h–**

ENVIOUS 6 ch.g. Hernando (FR) – Prima Verde (Leading Counsel (USA)) [2004/5 h79: 16g⁶ 16dpu 16g⁶ 20gF Jul 14] good-topped gelding: modest hurdler: improved form and would probably have won handicap at Worcester in July but for falling 2 out: stays 21f: acts on firm and good to soft ground: usually wears cheekpieces. *R. Allan* **h89**

ENVIRONMENT AUDIT 6 ch.g. Kris – Bold And Beautiful (Bold Lad (IRE)) [2004/5 h–: 16gpu 16m 17d⁴ 16g Oct 4] good-topped gelding: bad mover: modest juvenile hurdler in 2002/3: little form since: tried in cheekpieces/visor. *J. R. Jenkins* **h70 ?**

ENZO DE BAUNE (FR) 8 b.g. En Calcat (FR) – Pure Moon (FR) (Pure Flight (USA)) [2004/5 c114: c20d⁶ c23g³ c20dpu c19d* c19g⁵ c16g⁴ c20g³ Apr 22] good-topped gelding: fairly useful handicap chaser: won at Catterick in February by 3 lengths from Welcome To Unos: ran well when in frame in races won by Andreas at Cheltenham and Tikram at Sandown last 2 starts: effective at 2m to 21f: acts on soft and firm going: tried blinkered, wore cheekpieces last 4 outings: free-going front runner: bold jumper, though has tended to go right. *G. A. Harker* **c122**

EPICURE (FR) 8 b. or br.g. Northern Crystal – L'Epicurienne (FR) (Rex Magna (FR)) [2004/5 h88: 24gpu Jul 4] fair hurdler at best, little form since early-2002/3: won point in 2004: stays 2½m: acts on soft and good to firm going: has worn visor. *M. C. Pipe* **h–**

EPITRE (FR) 8 b.g. Common Grounds – Epistolienne (Law Society (USA)) [2004/5 h73: 22spu 16d 19m⁵ 16s² 16g² 16s⁶ 18gF Mar 20] leggy gelding: modest maiden handicap hurdler: should be suited by further than 2m: acts on soft going: tried visored. *A. King* **h99**

EPSILO DE LA RONCE (FR) 13 b. or br.g. Le Riverain (FR) – India Rosa (FR) (Carnaval) [2004/5 c105, h–: c20g⁵ c20s⁴ c16m c21s Apr 7] medium-sized gelding: veteran hunter chaser, sold out of C. A. Ramsay's stable 6,000 gns Doncaster August Sales after first outing: raced mainly around 2½m: acts on any going: blinkered once: has found little. *P. Morris* **c97 h–**

ERIC'S CHARM (FR) 7 b.g. Nikos – Ladoun (FR) (Kaldoun (FR)) [2004/5 h143: c20gF c25g* c23d² c20s* c21g⁶ Mar 17] tall, angular gelding: smart novice hurdler in 2003/4: only fairly useful over fences, though won maiden at Folkestone (by 3 lengths from Hirvine) in December and novice at Kempton (easily) in March: likely to stay beyond 25f: acts on soft going, won only start on good to firm: free-going front runner. *O. Sherwood* **c128 h–**

ERIN ALLEY (IRE) 12 ch.g. Be My Native (USA) – Cousin Flo (True Song) [2004/5 c71, h–: 21g³ c21spu 21g Jul 16] sparely-made gelding: poor maiden hurdler/handicap **c– h67**

chaser: stays 21f: acts on heavy going: sold 1,200 gns Doncaster August Sales, no form in points in 2005. *D. J. Wintle*

ERINS LOVE (IRE) 4 b. or br.f. Double Bed (FR) – Erintante (IRE) (Denel (FR)) [2004/5 F16d Mar 19] unfurnished filly: first foal: dam useful hurdler up to 21f: tongue tied, dropped right out final 2f in bumper on debut. *F. Doumen, France* **F–**

ERISKAY (IRE) 9 b.g. Montelimar (USA) – Little Peach (Ragapan) [2004/5 h–: 20vpu c24gpu Dec 18] strong gelding: fair hurdler in 2001/2: lightly raced and no form since, including on chasing debut: stays 2¾m: acts on soft going. *L. Lungo* **c– h–**

ERNEST LLEWELLYN 8 b.g. Afzal – Little Gift (Broadsword (USA)) [2004/5 24dpu Mar 8] no sign of ability. *P. W. Hiatt* **h–**

ERRIS EXPRESS (IRE) 7 ch.g. Definite Article – Postie (Sharpo) [2004/5 c70?, h–: c16g5 c21gpu c20m4 May 27] lengthy gelding: won maiden point in March: little form otherwise: visored nowadays. *J. R. Jenkins* **c– h–**

ERROL 6 ch.g. Dancing Spree (USA) – Primo Panache (Primo Dominie) [2004/5 h–: 16d 16g6 17s 16g2 16g 16d* 17d2 16g 16s 16m Apr 17] compact gelding: modest novice hurdler: won 20-runner conditional jockeys handicap at Doncaster in January: likely to prove best at 2m: acts on good to soft going. *J. F. Coupland* **h92**

ERSAAL (USA) 5 ch.g. Gulch (USA) – Madame Secretary (USA) (Secretariat (USA)) [2004/5 16gpu 19g 17m Sep 8] modest on Flat (stays 1½m): sold out of J. Jay's stable 1,400 gns Doncaster August Sales: first form over hurdles when seventh in seller final outing: blinkered time before: tongue tied. *Evan Williams* **h68**

ERTE 4 ch.g. Vettori (IRE) – Cragreen (Green Desert (USA)) [2004/5 16d 16d Jan 7] modest maiden on Flat (stays 1½m), claimed from M. Channon £6,000 in July: tailed off both outings over hurdles. *V. Thompson* **h–**

ESCALADE 8 b.g. Green Desert (USA) – Sans Escale (USA) (Diesis) [2004/5 16gpu Oct 3] stocky gelding: modest on Flat (stays 1½m, tends to find little): jumped poorly and pulled up after fourth on hurdling debut: sold 2,200 gns Doncaster March Sales. *W. M. Brisbourne* **h–**

ESCAYOLA (IRE) 5 b.g. Revoque (IRE) – First Fling (IRE) (Last Tycoon) [2004/5 19gF 19m4 Apr 23] useful on Flat (stays 2¼m) for W. Haggas: better effort in novice hurdles when fourth to Queen Soraya at Market Rasen: tongue tied: room for improvement in jumping. *P. F. Nicholls* **h106 +**

ESCOMPTEUR (FR) 5 b.g. Poliglote – Escopette (FR) (Tourangeau (FR)) [2004/5 c17s2 c17d2 c20s4 c20sur 17g* 21g* 19sF 16d 18s2 16d 20d 17v* 16s2 Apr 21] sturdy ex-French gelding: eighth foal: half-brother to several winners, including fair 15f hurdle winner Excusez Moi (by Kadrou) and fairly useful chaser around 2½m Escorteur (by Roi de Rome): dam middle-distance winner: fair maiden chaser: fairly useful hurdler: left G. Cherel, won novices at Bangor and Plumpton in October and Exeter (jumped left, didn't need to be at best) in March: fair form over fences: stays 21f: raced on good ground or softer (acts on heavy): free-going sort. *M. C. Pipe* **c114 h129**

ESCORT 9 b.g. Most Welcome – Benazir (High Top) [2004/5 h–: 20dpu 20g* 20dpu 24gpu Jun 10] sturdy gelding: poor handicap hurdler: made all at Bangor in April 2004, only form for long time: stays 3m: acts on good to firm and heavy going: usually visored. *W. Clay* **h73**

ESENDI 10 b.g. Buckley – Cagaleena (Cagirama) [2004/5 c91, h–: c24gpu May 27] tall, leggy gelding: lightly raced: maiden hurdler/chaser: won point in 2004: stays 3m: acts on soft going. *Mrs Anna Brooks* **c– h–**

ESHER COMMON (IRE) 7 b.g. Common Grounds – Alsahah (IRE) (Unfuwain (USA)) [2004/5 h–: 20g3 20dpu May 9] lightly raced: poor maiden hurdler: stays 2½m: acts on soft going: usually tongue tied: headstrong. *A. E. Price* **h76**

ESKIMO JACK (IRE) 9 ch.g. Glacial Storm (USA) – Covette (Master Owen) [2004/5 c22m5 c24vpu c22d4 c20s c17v5 c16s c20d3 Mar 31] useful-looking gelding: useful chaser in 2002/3, fairly useful at best on return from lengthy absence in 2004/5: probably needs further than 2m nowadays (stays 3m): acts on heavy going. *A. L. T. Moore, Ireland* **c119 h–**

ESKIMO PIE (IRE) 6 ch.g. Glacial Storm (USA) – Arctic Verb (Proverb) [2004/5 F97: 20d2 16v2 20s* 20v* 23s5 Feb 19] good-topped gelding: fair novice hurdler: won at Haydock in November and December: should stay beyond 2½m: raced on good going or softer (acts on heavy). *C. C. Bealby* **h112**

ESP HILL 7 ch.m. Moscow Society (USA) – Heatheridge (IRE) (Carlingford Castle) [2004/5 h–, F62: 20g^{pu} 17g^{5} 16f 20m 20d^{6} 21m 24s^{3} Aug 25] of little account: tried in cheekpieces. *J. N. R. Billinge* **h–**

ESPLENDIDOS (IRE) 6 b.m. Beneficial – Index Lady (Decent Fellow) [2004/5 17s^{4} 16d^{3} 20s^{3} Jan 24] €4,250 3-y-o: seventh foal: half-sister to winning hurdler/chaser Altregan Lady (by Roselier), stays 2¾m, and bumper winner Twentyfivequid (by Phardante): dam won 2 Irish points: upped in trip, best effort in novice hurdles when third in mares event at Fontwell: likely to stay beyond 2½m. *D. P. Keane* **h94**

ESPRESSO FORTE (IRE) 6 ch.g. Anshan – Symphony Express (IRE) (Orchestra) [2004/5 21g 24s^{5} 21s^{3} 23g^{5} 24d^{5} 26s* Mar 7] useful-looking gelding: chasing sort: fourth foal: half-brother to prolific winning pointer/winning hunter Involved (by Macmillion), stays 27f: dam never ran: won completed start in maiden Irish points in 2004: fair hurdler: upped in trip, improved form when winning novice handicap at Hereford: will stay beyond 3¼m: raced on good going or softer (acts on soft): tongue tied fifth outing: open to further progress. *Miss H. C. Knight* **h101 p**

ESREEN 4 ch.f. Bijou d'Inde – Audeen (Keen) [2004/5 F16d F14s F16s Mar 1] small, plain filly: second foal: dam, no form on Flat, from family of high-class 1½m colt Acatenango: well beaten in bumpers. *D. W. Barker* **F–**

ESSENNBEE 5 ch.g. Carlingford Castle – Polly B (Distinct Native) [2004/5 F17m Apr 23] first foal: dam unraced: well held in bumper on debut. *Mrs J. R. Buckley* **F–**

ESSEX BIRD 6 b.m. Primitive Rising (USA) – L'Hawaienne (USA) (Hawaii) [2004/5 h–, F–: 27g^{5} Apr 27] well held all starts, including in point. *Mrs S. D. Williams* **h–**

ESSEX (IRE) 5 b.g. Sadler's Wells (USA) – Knight's Baroness (Rainbow Quest (USA)) [2004/5 h126: 16g^{3} 16v* 16d* 16g Mar 15] **h152 +**

On the front page of its pre-Cheltenham edition, *The Irish Field* led with a photo montage, under the title 'The Magnificent Seven', of the seven Irish horses who were dominating the Champion Hurdle betting. Each of the septet was given a suitably wild-west style soubriquet. The *Racing Post* chose exactly the same theme for its front page on Champion Hurdle day a few days later and when it came to finding a nickname for Essex, the choice of both papers was the same. As the junior member, at the age of five, and the least experienced after just five runs over hurdles, Essex was naturally enough dubbed 'The Kid'. Not that that seemed to put

Pierse Hurdle (Extended Handicap), Leopardstown—
hot favourite Essex belies his inexperience over hurdles to land one of Ireland's biggest prizes

too many people off, because Essex started as the 9/1 fifth choice for the Champion Hurdle, though that did underestimate the amount of improvement he needed to find. Barry Geraghty, however, who had partnered Essex to his two wins earlier in the season, preferred to stick with another of his regular mounts, 'The Preacher' Macs Joy (by the sire Religiously). Ridden by Tony McCoy, Essex wasn't up to the task and beat only the two no-hopers.

Essex was alone among 'The Magnificent Seven' in graduating to the Champion Hurdle straight from handicaps. He had won two of the most competitive such events of the season on his last two outings. First up was the Pierse Hurdle at Leopardstown in January for which Essex started the 5/1 favourite. With the only British entry Claymore a non-runner, former winner Adamant Approach was left at the top of the handicap on 11-1, with more than a third of the twenty-one runners out of the weights. That still left an open-looking race in which Essex's fellow five-year-olds Al Eile, Emotional Article and Silk Screen were next in the betting. The ground was heavy but, even so, the pace was surprisingly steady by the race's usual standards. Essex was prominent throughout and took up the running after the third last. Sent for home in earnest rounding the home turn, Essex opened up a five-length lead, but a slow jump at the last meant he was soon joined by the only challenger to emerge from the pack, Mansony. Essex pulled out more in the closing stages to win by a length, with a dozen lengths back to Al Eile and Adamant Approach.

No horse had managed to follow success in Ireland's top handicap hurdle with victory in its British counterpart, at Newbury, now goldless and renamed the totesport Trophy Hurdle. For Auction had come closest, finishing fourth, beaten under five lengths, the month before winning the 1982 Champion Hurdle. In the ten previous years, only Graphic Equaliser and Grinkov among the Leopardstown winners had gone on to Newbury. Essex was put up 13 lb by the Turf Club handicapper after Leopardstown, but a difference in the scale used by the BHB meant that he effectively had to race off a mark 21 lb higher at Newbury. Essex's participation seemed in doubt when the weights went up by more than a stone following the defection of top weights Rooster Booster, Westender and Accordion Etoile, but Essex stood his ground with only Geos, twice a winner of the race, above him in the weights. Essex went off the well-backed 4/1 favourite ahead of 11/2-shot Tamarinbleu, the Ladbroke winner at Sandown and one of seven Martin Pipe runners. Next came the well-treated novice Roman Ark at 7/1. The Pierse third Al Eile on 10/1 was one of three other Irish-trained challengers, all of them prominent in the betting in the field of twenty-five. As at Leopardstown, the pace wasn't as furious as might have been expected, and once again that was very much in favour of the prominently-ridden Essex, making things more difficult for those coming from further behind. Geraghty delayed his challenge until the final flight on this occasion and, having shaken off another of the Pipe runners Bongo Fury, Essex went clear on the run-in for a three-length success, well on top at the finish. Al Eile stayed on from the rear, just failing to snatch second from Bongo Fury, with the main body of the field tightly grouped just behind. Essex was the second Irish-trained winner of the totesport Trophy in three years after Spirit Leader in 2003. Spirit Leader had

totesport Trophy Hurdle (Handicap), Newbury—
in defiance of a mark 21 lb higher, Essex becomes the first to complete this big handicap double;
outsider Bongo Fury (visor) fares best of the rest

finished only fifth in the Pierse before winning at Newbury, but she went on to win the County Hurdle at Cheltenham and earlier that season had won another valuable handicap in Britain, the William Hill at Sandown. Essex's trainer Michael O'Brien had met with success in another big handicap at Newbury before, though that had been back in 1980 when Bright Highway won the Hennessy Gold Cup. Bright Highway also won the Mackeson Gold Cup that year. Other notable wins for O'Brien include three Irish Nationals (King Spruce in 1982, Vanton in 1992 and Glebe Lad in 1999), a Galway Plate (Dovaly in 2000), two Champion Four Year Old Hurdles (Shawiya in 1993 and Shaihar in 1995) and a Triumph Hurdle (also with Shawiya). O'Brien had been champion rider over jumps in the States until being trampled on so badly in the 1974 Carolina Cup after his mount suffered a heart attack that he was left paralysed from the chest down.

Essex (IRE) (b.g. 2000)	Sadler's Wells (USA) (b 1981)	Northern Dancer (b 1961)	Nearctic
			Natalma
		Fairy Bridge (b 1975)	Bold Reason
			Special
	Knight's Baroness (b 1987)	Rainbow Quest (b 1981)	Blushing Groom
			I Will Follow
		Knights Beauty (b 1977)	True Knight
			Broadway Beauty

By Sadler's Wells out of the Irish Oaks winner Knight's Baroness, Essex could certainly boast the choicest pedigree in the Champion Hurdle field, though his breeding had evidently been of academic interest only when he was offered at the Newmarket Autumn Sales as a three-year-old. A 460,000-guinea yearling, he had shown no better than fair form in four starts in maidens for Sir Michael Stoute.

B. P. S. Syndicate's "Essex"

Reportedly introduced in the sales ring as a weaver and windsucker, Essex joined Michael O'Brien's stable for just 8,000 guineas, a pittance compared to the sums that regularly change hands for prospective hurdlers out of top Flat yards (Essex is not the first bargain O'Brien has had from the Stoute yard, as he bought the thrice-raced Knife Edge for 35,000 guineas before winning eleven races over jumps with him, eight of them at graded level). Knight's Baroness has bred four other winners besides Essex, all on the Flat, the best of them her very first foal Riyadian (by Polish Precedent) who was an even better racehorse than his dam, winning the Cumberland Lodge Stakes and the Jockey Club Stakes and finishing second in the Champion Stakes. Wales (by Caerleon), a useful winner up to a mile and a half, is the best of the dam's other winners, though he was one of two to end up with a Timeform squiggle. Knight's Baroness, who was also third in the Oaks, was her dam's only winner in a short stud career which followed a busy racing career in the States for Knights Beauty, during which she won twelve of her seventy-six starts over five seasons, three of them minor stakes events. Knights Beauty's half-brother Geisway was second in the Royal Lodge Stakes, won the Predominate Stakes, and ended up winning a couple of times over hurdles.

As a juvenile hurdler, Essex won his first two starts before running a close third to Cherub and Made In Japan in the Champion Four Year Old Hurdle at Punchestown. Before resuming over hurdles in the latest season, he was given three outings on the Flat, getting off the mark in the Irish Cesarewitch at Leopardstown at the expense of another good hurdler, Solerina. Essex has raced only at two miles over hurdles, but the fact that he has now won at that trip on the Flat suggests he will stay further. He has raced only on good going or softer and acts on heavy. Essex has worn cheekpieces, 'to get him to run at his hurdles' according to his trainer, though they were left off for his two appearances in Britain. Given his lack of experience over hurdles, Essex may still have some improvement in him, though life will obviously be tougher for him in handicaps from now on. There are unlikely to be any easy pickings among Ireland's top weight-for-age hurdles either in the foreseeable future, with the first five home in the Champion Hurdle all Irish trained. *M. J. P. O'Brien, Ireland*

ESSIE 8 b.m. Ezzoud (IRE) – Safari Park (Absalom) [2004/5 19g 22g³ 26mpu Aug 30] angular mare: maiden on Flat: little encouragement over hurdles: sweated badly and pulled very hard second outing. *Miss M. E. Rowland* **h–**

ESS OF NORWAY (FR) 6 gr.g. Linamix (FR) – Tres de Cem (NOR) (Rainbow Quest (USA)) [2004/5 19g 21d* 20v⁴ Jan 8] good-topped gelding: modest novice hurdler: off 20 months prior to reappearance: landed gamble at Plumpton in December: should stay 3m: acts on good to soft going, tailed off on heavy. *J. C. Tuck* **h98**

ESTEBAN 5 b.g. Groom Dancer (USA) – Ellie Ardensky (Slip Anchor) [2004/5 17g⁶ 17m Aug 6] half-brother to useful hurdler Pole Star (by Polar Falcon): modest maiden at best on Flat (stays 11f): well held in novice company over hurdles. *J. J. Quinn* **h–**

ESTERELLE (USA) 10 ch.m. Trempolino (USA) – Duck Flighting (USA) (Far North (CAN)) [2004/5 20s⁴ 27s² 22g⁶ 22g⁵ 27g* 24m² 26m³ 26m² 24m 26g³ 24v² 24s³ Nov 2] narrow, angular mare: unplaced in points in 2004: modest handicap hurdler: won at Newton Abbot in July: stays 27f: acts on good to firm and heavy going: blinkered once. *H. J. Manners* **h92**

ESTERS BOY 7 b.g. Sure Blade (USA) – Moheli (Ardross) [2004/5 h–: 17d⁴ 16g³ 21dpu 19dpu 16s 24m Apr 10] maiden hurdler, modest form at best: probably stays 3m. *P. G. Murphy* **h95**

ESTRELLA LEVANTE 5 ch.g. Abou Zouz (USA) – Star of Modena (IRE) (Waajib) [2004/5 16m Sep 19] poor maiden on Flat (stays 1m): always behind in novice hurdle. *R. M. Flower* **h–**

ESTUPENDO (IRE) 8 b.g. Tidaro (USA) – Spendapromise (Goldhill) [2004/5 c26vF c25g³ c21dpu c26dpu c29spu 22s⁶ 21v⁴ c22s 19s⁵ 23d⁴ 22m Apr 23] temperamental and little form, left L. Wells after eighth start: often wears headgear: poor jumper of fences. *M. J. Gingell* **c76 x h– §**

ETCHED IN STONE (IRE) 6 gr.g. Roselier (FR) – Wilton Castle (IRE) (Monksfield) [2004/5 F16v⁶ F16d⁵ F16s* Jan 3] €22,000 4-y-o: fourth foal: dam unraced, out of half-sister to useful chaser up to 3m Doubleuagain: third start in bumpers, useful form **F107**

when winning 7-runner event at Cork, making all to beat Ray Boy 8 lengths: likely to be suited by further than 2m: joined N. Richards. *John Joseph Murphy, Ireland*

ETENDARD INDIEN (FR) 4 b.g. Selkirk (USA) – Danseuse Indienne (IRE) (Danehill (USA)) [2004/5 16d* 16d^{5} 17g^{pu} Mar 18] angular gelding: smart on Flat (stays 15f) for A. Fabre, successful twice in 2004: won juvenile at Kempton on hurdling debut in February impressively, jumping fluently in main and making all to win by 12 lengths from Reservoir: disappointing both starts after, particularly so when blinkered in Triumph Hurdle at Cheltenham. *N. J. Henderson* **h116**

ETERNAL NIGHT (FR) 9 b.g. Night Shift (USA) – Echoes of Eternity (USA) (Cougar (CHI)) [2004/5 c?, h–: 20m^{pu} 20m 16s 16v^{6} 24g^{pu} Dec 30] good-topped gelding: maiden chaser: fairly useful hurdler at one time, has lost his way completely: tried blinkered/in cheekpieces. *Mrs N. S. Sharpe* **c– h–**

ETERNAL SPRING (IRE) 8 b.g. Persian Bold – Emerald Waters (Kings Lake (USA)) [2004/5 20s^{pu} 24d^{F} Jan 1] workmanlike gelding: useful hurdler at one time, failed to complete last 4 outings (off nearly 2 years before reappearance): stays 21f: acts on heavy going: tried tongue tied. *J. R. Fanshawe* **h–**

ETHAN SNOWFLAKE 6 b.g. Weld – Snow Child (Mandrake Major) [2004/5 h71: 20s^{pu} 16s* 17d^{4} 16d 16g 16s^{6} Feb 24] leggy gelding: modest hurdler: 50/1-winner of novice handicap at Fakenham in November: raced mainly around 2m: acts on soft going. *N. B. King* **h87**

ETTRICK (NZ) 10 b.g. Hereward The Wake (USA) – Kardinia (NZ) (Creag-An-Sgor) [2004/5 17d 16g 20d^{ur} Apr 22] workmanlike gelding: poor hurdler: no form in 2004/5 after near 3-year absence: blinkered once: has shown signs of temperament. *Mrs Barbara Waring* **c– h–**

EURO AMERICAN (GER) 5 b.g. Snurge – Egyptale (Crystal Glitters (USA)) [2004/5 h–: 17g 16m^{4} 16m^{3} 17g^{3} 16g 17g^{3} Feb 16] fair novice hurdler, left B. Powell after fifth outing: likely to prove best around 2m: usually waited with. *Noel T. Chance* **h102**

EURO BLEU (FR) 7 b.g. Franc Bleu Argent (USA) – Princess Card (FR) (Gift Card (FR)) [2004/5 h108: c20s^{F} c26v^{pu} c18d 20v 16v^{4} 16d^{4} 16s 20d Apr 20] useful-looking gelding: modest maiden hurdler: well beaten only completed outing over fences: stays 2½m: acts on heavy ground: blinkered last 2 starts. *Mrs L. Wadham* **c– h95**

EUROCHANCER (IRE) 6 b.g. Eurobus – Woodfield Lass (IRE) (Bustineto) [2004/5 F16s c20s^{F} c22v^{pu} 16s^{4} 18s* 20v^{F} 22v* 20s 22d 24v Apr 2] €9,000 3-y-o: workmanlike gelding: fourth foal: half-brother to winning pointer by Mister Lord: dam unraced: modest form in bumpers: winning pointer: failed to complete in 2 chases: fair hurdler: won maiden in December and handicap in January (beat Sixtino by 6 lengths in 20-runner event), both at Navan: stiff task, probably flattered when seventh to Ambobo in Grade 2 novice at Cheltenham: poor efforts in handicaps both starts after: stays 2¾m: acts on heavy ground: races prominently. *Joseph Fox, Ireland* **c– h113 F86**

EURO LEADER (IRE) 7 b.g. Supreme Leader – Noreaster (IRE) (Nordance (USA)) [2004/5 h120, F108: 24m^{4} c20d* c20s Mar 29] fairly useful hurdler: favourite, won maiden at Limerick in March on chasing debut by 3½ lengths from Jakers: contested Grade 1 novices after, much better effort when fourth of 5 finishers to War of Attrition at Punchestown in late-April: may prove best short of 3m: acts on heavy and good to firm going. *W. P. Mullins, Ireland* **c126 h120**

EUROPA 9 b.g. Jupiter Island – Dublin Ferry (Celtic Cone) [2004/5 c125, h–: 16g c20s^{pu} c20g* c20g^{3} c21d^{3} c21d^{F} c21s c21g^{bd} c36d Apr 9] big, well-made gelding: winning hurdler: useful handicap chaser: sold out of T. Tate's stable 33,000 gns Doncaster August Sales before second start: back to best after, winning at Kempton in November: third to Supreme Prince and Monkerhostin in well-contested races at Newbury and Cheltenham next 2 starts: should stay 3m: acts on heavy going, probably on good to firm. *Ferdy Murphy* **c138 h–**

EUROTREK (IRE) 9 ch.g. Eurobus – Orient Jewel (Pollerton) [2004/5 c25s* c25s^{pu} Nov 21] tall gelding: very lightly raced: good start to hurdling career in 2001/2, winning novice at Newbury and second in Grade 2 at Warwick: left R. Alner, promising chasing debut when winning novice at Market Rasen nearly 3 years later, jumping soundly and readily pulling 3½ lengths clear of Smiths Landing: odds on, bled from nose when pulled up at Aintree 2 weeks later: stays 25f: evidently hard to train. *P. F. Nicholls* **c117 h–**

EURYALUS (IRE) 7 ch.g. Presenting – New Talent (The Parson) [2004/5 h–, F83: 20v^{pu} Feb 2] sturdy gelding: no form in 3 novice hurdles: headstrong. *R. F. Fisher* **h–**

EURYDICE (IRE) 5 b. or br.m. Heron Island (IRE) – Little Thunder (Whistling Deer) [2004/5 F16s Apr 22] third foal: dam unraced, from family of useful hurdler/chaser at 2½m+ Cloone Bridge: showed little in bumper on debut. *Ferdy Murphy* **F–**

EUWILUWIL (IRE) 7 b.g. Eurobus – Market Romance (African Sky) [2004/5 26m^{pu} Jul 2] IR £16,000 3-y-o: sixth foal: half-brother to winning pointer by Orchestra: dam maiden half-sister to smart 2m to 21f chaser Native Charm and useful chaser up to 3m Sir Dante: won 2 of 3 starts in points in Britain in 2004: reportedly lame on hurdling debut. *M. C. Pipe* **h–**

EVA PERON (IRE) 5 b.m. Alzao (USA) – High Flying Adored (IRE) (In The Wings) [2004/5 16d^{pu} May 6] poor and ungenuine on Flat in 2004: pulled up in seller on hurdling debut. *W. G. M. Turner* **h–**

EVA SO CHARMING 7 ch.g. Karinga Bay – Charming Gale (Strong Gale) [2004/5 h109: c26g* c24g^{pu} c26d^{2} c26d^{2} c29d^{2} c28s^{pu} c25s^{3} c26s^{3} c33g c25g^{3} Apr 17] strong gelding: fair hurdler: similar form over fences, winning maiden at Southwell in May: stays 29f: raced on good going or softer (acts on heavy): below form in blinkers final outing: temperament under suspicion: sold to join H. Hogarth 30,000 gns Doncaster May Sales. *Miss H. C. Knight* **c113 h–**

EVEN MORE (IRE) 10 b.g. Husyan (USA) – Milan Moss (Le Moss) [2004/5 c104: c25g^{4} c25g^{pu} c24d^{2} c24d^{4} c24d^{4} c27m* c25d^{5} c25s^{3} c24s^{ur} c24d c25s* c24g Apr 7] workmanlike gelding: fair handicap chaser: won at Taunton in November and Wincanton in February: barely stays 3¾m: acts on soft and good to firm going. *R. H. Alner* **c112**

EVEON (IRE) 5 b.m. Synefos (USA) – Lovely Grand (Le Bavard (FR)) [2004/5 F16d F16d Mar 14] €14,000 4-y-o: medium-sized mare: sixth foal: dam unraced sister to dam of one-time top-class staying chaser Lord Noelie: well held in 2 bumpers. *Ian Williams* **F–**

EVER AN OPTIMIST 8 b.g. Alflora (IRE) – Sweet Optimist (Energist) [2004/5 c24g^{ur} Mar 3] half-brother to fairly useful hurdler Miss Optimist (by Relkino), stayed 2½m: dam, winning hurdler, half-sister to useful staying chaser Bold Agent and dams of useful hurdlers at 2½m+ Yes Sir and Camden Venture: unseated in point in 2003 and in maiden chase (numerous mistakes). *Miss H. C. Knight* **c–**

EVERDEANE 5 b.m. Overbury (IRE) – Winnow (Oats) [2004/5 F16s Dec 22] second foal: dam, poor chaser, stayed 3m: tailed off in bumper on debut. *A. W. Carroll* **F–**

EVER PRESENT (IRE) 7 ch.g. Presenting – My Grand Rose (IRE) (Executive Perk) [2004/5 h108: 20s^{3} Mar 12] fairly useful hurdler in 2002/3: left A. King and only second outing since, encouraging third to Broken Knights in handicap at Ayr, keeping on not knocked about: should prove better suited by 2½m than 2m: acts on soft going. *N. G. Richards* **h109 +**

EVERREADY 7 b.g. Afzal – Sister Shot (Celtic Cone) [2004/5 h85: 21g^{4} 23m* 26m* 26m^{F} 20m* 22m^{pu} c16s^{ur} c16v^{F} Jan 15] tall gelding: progressed into fairly useful hurdler early in 2004/5, winning novice handicaps at Fakenham and Huntingdon in May and novice at Worcester (made virtually all to beat Thyne For Intersky 6 lengths) in July: left M. Quinlan, would probably have finished fifth but for unseating last in maiden won by The Screamer at Thurles on chasing debut: fell first next time: stayed 3¼m: acted on good to firm going: dead. *P. F. Cashman, Ireland* **c107 h119**

EVERY NOTE COUNTS 5 b.g. Bluegrass Prince (IRE) – Miss Mirror (Magic Mirror) [2004/5 17g^{5} 17m^{5} 20g^{6} 16g^{4} 16g 16d^{4} Mar 28] sparely-made gelding: half-brother to poor chaser Constant Husband (by Le Solaret), stays 2½m: modest on Flat (stays 1½m) in 2004: poor maiden hurdler: best efforts around 2m: tried in cheekpieces. *J. J. Quinn* **h76**

EVERYTIME 5 b.g. Vettori (IRE) – Flamingo Times (Good Times (ITY)) [2004/5 F17g^{5} 20d 20d 19s^{5} Nov 18] fifth foal: half-brother to 6f and 7f winner Miss Jingles (by Muhtarram) and French 1½m winner Kaigani (by Pharly): dam 1½m winner: beat only one in bumper and 3 starts over hurdles. *M. W. Easterby* **h71 ? F82 ?**

EVIYRN (IRE) 9 b.g. In The Wings – Evrana (USA) (Nureyev (USA)) [2004/5 h71§: 16g^{6} 21m^{5} 21d 22d^{5} Nov 2] medium-sized gelding: poor handicap hurdler: stays 2½m: acts on heavy going: wears headgear: irresolute. *J. R. Jenkins* **h69 §**

EWAR BOLD 12 b.g. Bold Arrangement – Monaneigue Lady (Julio Mariner) [2004/5 20s^{6} 20g 24m^{pu} 22g c23g^{pu} 22m^{pu} 26f^{3} 26d 24s c26d^{pu} Dec 5] leggy gelding: winning hurdler, little form in 2004/5: no show in 2 maiden chases: tried blinkered: usually tongue tied. *K. G. Wingrove* **c– h66**

EWE BEAUTY (FR) 5 b.m. Phantom Breeze – Baie de Chalamont (FR) (Balsamo (FR)) [2004/5 F–: F17d5 17d4 20dF 21v5 16v3 20s Feb 9] leggy mare: has shown only a little ability in bumpers and over hurdles. *Ferdy Murphy* **h87 ? F69**

EXCELLENT VIBES (IRE) 7 b.g. Doyoun – Hawait Al Barr (Green Desert (USA)) [2004/5 h84: 24d 24g6 27g 26m5 24g4 Oct 14] poor hurdler: stays 3¼m: acts on firm going: tried in blinkers/visor: tongue tied last 2 outings: has looked less than keen. *P. A. Pritchard* **h73**

EXCLUSIVE AIR (USA) 6 ch.g. Affirmed (USA) – Lac Dessert (USA) (Lac Ouimet (USA)) [2004/5 16g 17m 21s6 16spu 16dpu 17dpu 16d Apr 18] stocky gelding: fair on Flat (stays 1½m) at 4 yrs for T. D. Barron: of little account nowadays: in cheekpieces sixth start, tongue tied on fourth. *H. H. G. Owen* **h–**

EXECUTIVE DECISION (IRE) 11 ch.g. Classic Music (USA) – Bengala (FR) (Hard To Beat) [2004/5 c105§, h106§: 16d2 c16d* c16g3 Mar 26] rangy gelding: fair handicap hurdler/chaser: won over fences at Sandown in March by length from Super Nomad: best around 2m: acts on heavy and good to firm going: has worn blinkers, visored nowadays: held up: usually finds little, and not one to trust. *Mrs L. Wadham* **c113 § h104 §**

EXECUTIVE PARK (IRE) 9 br.g. Executive Perk – Brave Park (Brave Invader (USA)) [2004/5 c104: c24dF Mar 24] thrice-raced in hunter chases: off nearly 2 years, 4 lengths down on winner Cobreces when fell heavily last at Ludlow: stays 3m: acts on soft going. *C. R. Egerton* **c107**

EXIT FAST (USA) 4 ch.g. Announce (USA) – Distinct Beauty (USA) (Phone Trick (USA)) [2004/5 16d6 Jan 13] workmanlike gelding: fourth foal: half-brother to fairly useful 6f winner Prince Dayjur (by Dayjur): dam, 8.5f winner in USA, out of half-sister to high-class miler Last Fandango: well held in juvenile seller on hurdling debut. *N. Wilson* **h–**

EXIT SWINGER (FR) 10 b.g. Exit To Nowhere (USA) – Morganella (FR) (D'Arras (FR)) [2004/5 c139, h–: 24d Jun 23] angular gelding: useful chaser: didn't get home over hurdles only start in 2004/5: stays 25f when emphasis is on speed: acts on good to firm and heavy going: usually held up. *P. F. Nicholls* **c– h–**

EXIT TO WAVE (FR) 9 ch.g. Exit To Nowhere (USA) – Hereke (Blakeney) [2004/5 c135, h–: c26d3 c24gpu Apr 7] small, strong gelding: useful handicap chaser in 2003/4: third to Tremallt in hunter at Chepstow: bled from nose next time: stays 3m: acts on heavy going, seemingly not on firmer than good: blinkered once: usually tongue tied. *P. F. Nicholls* **c100 h–**

EXODOUS (ARG) 9 ch.g. Equalize (USA) – Empire Glory (ARG) (Good Manners (USA)) [2004/5 h93: 18g 20g* 20g5 20m Jun 29] angular gelding: modest hurdler: won handicap at Worcester in May: fourth in 2 points in 2005: needs good test around 2m, should stay beyond 2½m: acts on soft ground. *J. A. B. Old* **h97**

EXOTIC DANCER (FR) 5 b.g. Turgeon (USA) – Northine (FR) (Northern Treat (USA)) [2004/5 h119: 16gF 21d2 20d 24g 20d3 Apr 9] rather leggy gelding: much improved over hurdles in 2004/5, apparently very smart effort when length third to Al Eile in slowly-run Grade 1 at Aintree, pulling hard long way: earlier 8 lengths second to Lough Derg in Relkeel Hurdle and seventh to Inglis Drever in Ladbrokes World Hurdle fourth start, both at Cheltenham: likely to prove best short of 3m: raced on good going or softer: in cheekpieces last 2 starts. *Jonjo O'Neill* **h158**

EXPENSIVE FOLLY (IRE) 7 b.g. Satco (FR) – Tarasandy (IRE) (Arapahos (FR)) [2004/5 F–: F16d 19g Dec 30] leggy gelding: no sign of ability: bought £2,500 Ascot June Sales. *A. J. Chamberlain* **h– F–**

EXPLODE 8 b.g. Zafonic (USA) – Didicoy (USA) (Danzig (USA)) [2004/5 h–: 16s5 16d 16g 16g Mar 5] medium-sized gelding: little form over hurdles. *Miss L. C. Siddall* **h86 ?**

EXPLOSIVE FOX (IRE) 4 ch.g. Foxhound (USA) – Grise Mine (FR) (Crystal Palace (FR)) [2004/5 16vpu Feb 20] fair maiden on Flat (stays 1¾m): failed to settle in novice on hurdling debut. *V. Smith* **h–**

EXPRESSWAY (IRE) 7 b.g. Insan (USA) – Artic Squaw (IRE) (Buckskin (FR)) [2004/5 F17g 20g4 Jun 3] fifth foal: half-brother to winning hurdler/chaser Brave Lord, stays 3m, and fair pointer Lively Lord (both by Mister Lord): dam unraced daughter of half-sister to very smart staying chaser Arctic Call: no form in varied events. *M. Scudamore* **h– F–**

EXSTOTO 8 b.g. Mtoto – Stoproveritate (Scorpio (FR)) [2004/5 c112p, h109: c25m2 c24fF c32m2 Jun 27] angular gelding: fair handicap hurdler: quickly developed into much better chaser, 2 lengths second to Take The Stand in valuable handicap at Uttoxeter **c128 h–**

final start: stays 4m: acts on firm and soft going (pulled up only run on heavy): genuine. *R. A. Fahey*

EXTRA CACHE (NZ) 12 br.g. Cache of Gold (USA) – Gizmo (NZ) (Jubilee Wine (USA)) [2004/5 c93, h–: c16f5 c20d3 c21d3 c20g5 c24d5 c24gur c21d6 22mpu Apr 23] leggy gelding: winning hurdler/chaser, on the downgrade: stays 21f: acts on any going: tried in headgear. *O. Brennan* **c76 d h–**

EXTRA PROUD 11 ch.g. Dancing High – Spring Onion (King Sitric) [2004/5 c84, h93: c25g* May 20] modest hurdler: fair handicap chaser: off 5 months, won at Kelso in May: stays 25f: acts on soft and good to firm going, probably on firm: tongue tied: sometimes let down by jumping. *W. Amos* **c105 h–**

EXTRA SMOOTH 4 br.g. Cloudings (IRE) – Miss Ondee (FR) (Dress Parade) [2004/5 F16v4 F17v4 Feb 15] 15,000 3-y-o: first foal: dam winning 2m hurdler: better effort in bumpers when fourth to Von Origny at Wetherby on debut. *C. C. Bealby* **F87**

EXTREMIST (USA) 6 b.g. Dynaformer (USA) – Strumming (IRE) (Ballad Rock) [2004/5 h85: 19gpu 20s 16s 20spu Apr 16] useful-looking gelding: maiden hurdler, no show since third start in 2003/4: tried in cheekpieces. *K. C. Bailey* **h–**

EYE CANDY (IRE) 4 b.g. Princely Heir (IRE) – Timissa (IRE) (Kahyasi) [2004/5 16s3 16s 16s 16d2 16s* Apr 3] angular gelding: fairly useful on Flat (stays 1½m), successful in July: fairly useful juvenile hurdler: won maiden at Tramore in April: clearly best effort when 13 lengths fourth of 7 to United in Grade 1 at Punchestown later in month: raced at 2m on good to soft/soft going. *Mrs Sandra McCarthy, Ireland* **h123**

EYE ON THE BALL 6 b.g. Slip Anchor – Elaine Tully (IRE) (Persian Bold) [2004/5 F16fsu F16d* F16s2 F16g Mar 16] 20,000 3-y-o: good-topped gelding: third foal: brother to winning hurdler up to 2½m Maiden Voyage: dam fairly useful hurdler who should have stayed beyond 2¾m: won bumper at Roscommon in August: useful form after, 4½ lengths second to Merdeka at Leopardstown (final outing for T. Hyde) and 11 lengths ninth to Missed That in Grade 1 at Cheltenham. *M. F. Morris, Ireland* **F112**

EYES TO THE RIGHT (IRE) 6 ch.g. Eagle Eyed (USA) – Capable Kate (IRE) (Alzao (USA)) [2004/5 h–: 16m2 17d3 17d3 17g 16g 19d 16s4 17m* 17s5 16g Dec 9] leggy gelding: poor hurdler: claimed from A. Chamberlain £6,000 on reappearance: won selling handicap at Taunton in November: will prove best around 2m: acts on soft and good to firm going. *D. Burchell* **h70**

EZZ ELKHEIL 6 b.g. Bering – Numidie (FR) (Baillamont (USA)) [2004/5 h–: 16s6 Feb 18] medium-sized gelding: fair but ungenuine on Flat (stays easy 2m): no form over hurdles, looked reluctant in blinkers only 2004/5 start. *J. R. Jenkins* **h–**

F

FAASEL (IRE) 4 b.g. Unfuwain (USA) – Waqood (USA) (Riverman (USA)) [2004/5 16v* 16d* 16v* 18v2 17g2 16s* Apr 7] **h144 p**

Howard Johnson flew the flag for northern stables at the Cheltenham Festival, ending the meeting with three winners and awarded the leading trainer title, but it was Nicky Richards who led the way at the Grand National fixture at Aintree, with a treble on the first day. Richards, long-standing assistant before taking over the licence from his late father Gordon, who trained National winners Lucius and Hallo Dandy, enjoyed the biggest day of his career at Aintree, sending out Monet's Garden, Faasel and Turpin Green to win the Liverpool Hurdle, the Anniversary Hurdle and the Mersey Novices' Hurdle respectively, each of them under stable-jockey Tony Dobbin. All three winners look to have good futures, the four-year-old Faasel having better prospects than most leading juvenile hurdlers of recent years of making the grade in the top flight of two-milers.

Not before time, the John Smith's Anniversary Hurdle was upgraded to Grade 1 status in 2005, giving the race the standing it deserves judged on the fields it has tended to attract, as well as ironing out an anomaly in the pecking order of the top events for four-year-olds. In its guise as a Grade 2, both Made In Japan in 2004 and Spectroscope in 2003 were beaten narrowly at Aintree under a 4-lb penalty for Grade 1 success in the Triumph Hurdle, and, bizarrely, especially given the respective status of the races at the time, it would have taken a better performance for

John Smith's Anniversary 4-Y-O Novices' Hurdle, Aintree—
Faasel (visor) proves far too strong for Phar Bleu

them to win at Aintree than they had needed to put up at Cheltenham. Ironically, a further increase in the difference in prize money between the two events, a difference which rose from £5,800 to £11,600 in favour of Aintree, failed to attract the Triumph winner in 2005, denying the race a rematch at level weights between the first two home at Cheltenham. In the absence of Triumph winner Penzance, runner-up Faasel, who still looked in peak condition beforehand, started favourite at 11/4 at Aintree, though he might have been expected to go off at still shorter odds given that second favourite Cerium, backed from 5/1 to 7/2 on the day, had been over nine lengths behind him when fourth at Cheltenham. Third favourite Dabiroun, a clear-cut winner under a big weight of the inaugural Fred Winter Juvenile Novices' Handicap Hurdle at the Festival, arguably looked a bigger danger, going off at 6/1, but in the event neither he nor Cerium gave their running. In a well-run race, Faasel had only Triumph-fifth Phar Bleu to beat as he improved in the testing conditions approaching the second last. As at Cheltenham, Faasel briefly looked to hang fire once asked to tackle the leader, but he responded to firmish handling so well after the last that he was seven lengths clear at the line, with Triumph sixth Strangely Brown nine lengths further back in third.

Faasel wore a visor at Aintree, having been fitted with one for the first time over hurdles at Cheltenham, despite doing little wrong previously (he also wore blinkers on his last three starts on the Flat). Sent after easy pickings to start with in the New Year, Faasel landed the odds with little fuss in novice events at Kelso twice and Ayr before confirming himself a well-above-average recruit to jumping when suffering a narrow defeat at the hands of the six-year-old Mephisto in the valuable totesport Premier Kelso Hurdle, a Grade 2 novice event, going down by a head as the pair pulled twenty-five lengths clear. Faasel's effort against Mephisto was the best by a juvenile hurdler prior to the Cheltenham Festival, and Faasel started second favourite at 7/1 in a field of twenty-three for the Triumph, only the unbeaten Akilak preferred in the betting at 7/2. Patiently ridden in a well-run race, Faasel went down by a head, coming eight lengths clear of Akilak in third, and was arguably unlucky not to prevail. Still going well a little out of his ground, as Penzance was sent past Cerium approaching the last, Faasel looked slightly hesitant as Penzance jumped the final flight the better with a length or so lead. Faasel's rider Tony Dobbin seemed intent on waiting until the run-in to commit Faasel who was still closing at the line.

Faasel (IRE) (b.g. 2001)	Unfuwain (USA) (b 1985)	Northern Dancer (b 1961)	Nearctic
			Natalma
		Height of Fashion (b 1979)	Bustino
			Highclere
	Waqood (USA) (ch 1991)	Riverman (b 1969)	Never Bend
			Washah
		Saffaanh (b 1984)	Shareef Dancer
			Give Thanks

By the top-class mile-and-a-half performer Unfuwain, Faasel was bred by Hamdan Al Maktoum's Shadwell Estate. The dam Waqood, a half-sister to Harayir, winner of the One Thousand Guineas in the Sheikh's colours, has produced five winners on the Flat, the best of them the useful Mutawaqed (by Zafonic), successful at six furlongs to a mile. Waqood was a maiden herself, her career comprising placed efforts at up to a mile and a half, being tried in blinkers. This is obviously a Flat-oriented family, though the third dam, the very smart middle-distance filly Give Thanks, the Irish Oaks winner, produced two winners over jumps, including the Lanzarote Hurdle winner Shahrur. A winner at seven furlongs and a mile as a two-year-old, Faasel, who also raced in Sheikh Hamdan's colours, won three races at around a mile and a half on the Flat at three for Kevin Prendergast in Ireland, the last two of them in blinkers, and also showed useful form when placed over two miles. At 230,000 guineas, he was the top lot at the Newmarket Autumn Sales in October, two of the next three being Mephisto (220,000 guineas) and No Refuge (180,000 guineas). All three have shown themselves to be smart novices over hurdles with the potential to do better still, and Faasel for one shouldn't be underestimated when he tackles stronger company in 2005/6. Still a little clumsy at times, he probably has more improvement to make in his jumping than Penzance, but his somewhat lazy style of racing in the closing stages suggests strongly that he has still to show the full extent of his ability. Top juveniles usually find the open championship races too big a step at five, but it wouldn't be a surprise to see Faasel make into a realistic Champion Hurdle contender, though he will also be effective at two and a half miles. A strong, close-coupled gelding with 'a bit more growing to do' according to his trainer, he will reportedly be lightly raced prior to Cheltenham. He has raced on good ground or softer over hurdles, though has won on good to firm on the Flat. *N. G. Richards*

FABLE (USA) 9 b.g. Hansel (USA) – Aragon (Raconteur (USA)) [2004/5 c111, h–: c20g c21g6 c18m4 c20f* c20g2 c22mF c17m c20g c18d Nov 13] strong gelding: carries condition: fairly useful handicap chaser: won at Kilbeggan in June: little form after next outing: stays 21f: acts on firm and soft going: blinkered after third start: usually tongue tied. *N. Meade, Ireland* **c117 d h–**

FABREZAN (FR) 6 b.g. Nikos – Fabulous Secret (FR) (Fabulous Dancer (USA)) [2004/5 h117: 24spu 21s 20spu 21v2 22g2 Apr 10] smallish gelding: fairly useful hurdler in 2003/4: modest form at best in 2004/5: stays 3¼m: acts on firm and soft going: wore cheekpieces/blinkers last 4 starts: sold £8,500 Ascot April Sales. *B. J. Llewellyn* **h97**

FABRIAN 7 b.g. Danehill (USA) – Dockage (CAN) (Riverman (USA)) [2004/5 16dpu Apr 20] lengthy gelding: maiden on Flat, sold out of D. Arbuthnot's stable £1,800 Ascot November Sales: pulled up in point in March: failed to settle in novice on hurdling debut. *R. J. Price* **h–**

FABULOUS JET (FR) 5 ch.g. Starborough – Jetty (FR) (Fabulous Dancer (USA)) [2004/5 17m6 Nov 25] dam sister to smart hurdler up to 2½m Cagney: useful on Flat **h– p**

(stays 1½m, best efforts on ground softer than good), successful 4 times at 3 yrs, sold out of M. Channon's stable 60,000 gns Newmarket Autumn (2003) Sales: badly hampered first and failed to settle in maiden at Taunton on hurdling debut: should do better. *Miss Venetia Williams*

FACE THE LIMELIGHT (IRE) 6 b.g. Quest For Fame – Miss Boniface (Tap On Wood) [2004/5 h–: 20dpu 16m 17m Jul 26] no show over hurdles: sold 1,000 gns Doncaster May Sales. *Jedd O'Keeffe* **h–**

FACTOR FIFTEEN 6 gr.g. Hector Protector (USA) – Catch The Sun (Kalaglow) [2004/5 c–, h106: 20d2 19g4 19s2 Mar 1] angular gelding: fair maiden hurdler: unseated third only start over fences: stays 19f: acts on soft and good to firm going: tried in cheekpieces: temperament under suspicion: joined J. Tuck. *J. Howard Johnson* **c– h107**

FADDAD (USA) 9 b.g. Irish River (FR) – Miss Mistletoes (IRE) (The Minstrel (CAN)) [2004/5 h61: 16g3 20d4 16g3 16g* 16g4 16m6 17m* 18m5 17g Sep 25] angular gelding: poor hurdler: claimed from D. O'Brien £5,000 first start: won selling handicaps at Uttoxeter in July and Sedgefield in August: probably best around 2m: acts on good to firm going: tongue tied after second outing. *Mrs A. M. Thorpe* **h76**

FADOUDAL DU COCHET (FR) 12 b.g. Cadoudal (FR) – Eau de Vie (FR) (Dhaudevi (FR)) [2004/5 c142, h–: c16s4 Nov 7] well-made gelding: winning hurdler: useful chaser: well held, not knocked about, in Grade 2 won by Moscow Flyer at Navan only start in 2004/5: raced mainly around 2m, only on good going or softer (acts on heavy): wore cheekpieces once. *A. L. T. Moore, Ireland* **c120 + h–**

FAGIN 8 b.g. Formidable (USA) – Rich Pickings (Dominion) [2004/5 16gpu Oct 6] half-brother to winning 2m hurdler Mrs Bossy Boots (by Mystiko): maiden on Flat: poor handicap hurdler: raced mainly around 2m: acts on good to firm and heavy going: sold 600 gns Doncaster October Sales. *A. J. Martin, Ireland* **h–**

FAIRFIELDS LAD (IRE) 6 b.g. Norwich – Fahoora (IRE) (Orchestra) [2004/5 h–: 16g May 8] no form over hurdles. *J. Howard Johnson* **h–**

FAIRLY HIGH (IRE) 5 b.m. Sri Pekan (USA) – Ecco Mi (IRE) (Priolo (USA)) [2004/5 17g 26s6 21dpu 17s2 17v4 17g6 Apr 12] modest on Flat (stays 1½m) at 3 yrs, sold out of P. Murphy's stable 600 gns Doncaster October (2003) Sales: poor form over hurdles: wore cheekpieces last 3 starts. *N. G. Ayliffe* **h76**

FAIRLY SMART 6 b.m. Good Thyne (USA) – Smart Chick (True Song) [2004/5 h–: 21d 16v* 16v2 19s4 21d c22gpu Mar 20] poor handicap hurdler: won mares event at Chepstow in January: always behind in mares maiden on chasing debut: probably stays 21f: raced on good going or softer. *M. F. Harris* **c– h79**

FAIRMORNING (IRE) 6 b.g. Ridgewood Ben – The Bratpack (IRE) (Mister Majestic) [2004/5 h84: 16g4 16v6 18s6 22s5 20s6 16g Dec 28] angular gelding: poor maiden on Flat and over hurdles. *C. N. Kellett* **h–**

FAIR QUESTION (IRE) 7 b.g. Rainbow Quest (USA) – Fair of The Furze (Ela-Mana-Mou) [2004/5 h107: 22g 20f* Jun 6] leggy, useful-looking gelding: fair hurdler: better effort in novices in 2004/5 when winning at Perth in June: stays 21f: acts on firm and good to soft going. *Miss Venetia Williams* **h107**

FAIR SPIN 5 ch.g. Pivotal – Frankie Fair (IRE) (Red Sunset) [2004/5 16d 16v3 16v 16s* 17d* Mar 26] angular gelding: fair on Flat (stays 1¼m): fair novice hurdler: visored, won at Newcastle and Carlisle in March: raced around 2m on going softer than good (acts on heavy). *M. D. Hammond* **h109**

FAIRTOTO 9 b.g. Mtoto – Fairy Feet (Sadler's Wells (USA)) [2004/5 c–, h82: c20g c26m3 22f Sep 28] good-topped gelding: has been tubed: poor hurdler: no form in chases: runner-up in point in April: should stay beyond 2¾m: acts on firm and soft going: blinkered: has had tongue tied: ungenuine. *D. J. Wintle* **c– § h– §**

FAIR TOUCH (IRE) 6 b.g. Air Display (USA) – Anns Touch (IRE) (Ragapan) [2004/5 F16g2 F16f2 F16d 19g 16g 16d Mar 3] sixth foal: half-brother to winning 2m hurdler Touch Supreme and 2¾m hurdle winner Birmayne (both by Supreme Leader): dam unraced half-sister to high-class 2m to 3m chaser Travado: failed to complete in 2 Irish points: fair in bumpers, sold out of L. Whitmore's stable 31,000 gns Doncaster August Sales after second start: well held in novice hurdles: sometimes tongue tied. *C. P. Morlock* **h– F92**

FAIR WIND (IRE) 13 b.g. Strong Gale – Corcomroe (Busted) [2004/5 c96: c23d2 c24v5 c25s6 Mar 22] workmanlike gelding: fair hunter chaser: won point in February: stays 3¼m: acts on heavy going: tried blinkered. *Mrs H. Bartlett* **c96**

FAIRWOOD HEART (IRE) 8 b. or br.g. Broken Hearted – Bowery Lass (IRE) (Abednego) [2004/5 c109, h121: 24vpu 24s6 24g Mar 17] workmanlike gelding: fair handicap hurdler: fair form over fences: stays 3m: acts on soft going. *P. J. Rothwell, Ireland* **c– h112**

FAIRWOOD NICKLE (IRE) 6 b.g. Shernazar – Hop Picker (USA) (Plugged Nickle (USA)) [2004/5 24v 20vpu 17s 20s4 Mar 19] sixth foal: half-brother to fair hurdler/chaser Palouse (by Toulon), stays 3m, and fair chaser around 2½m Tom Costalot (by Black Minstrel): dam, winning hurdler, stayed 2½m: third in maiden Irish point on debut in 2004: bought 7,000 gns Doncaster May Sales: tongue tied, no show over hurdles. *Miss Lucinda V. Russell* **h–**

FAIRWOOD PRESENT (IRE) 7 ch.g. Presenting – Lady's Wager (Girandole) [2004/5 h124, F92: 20g 16m3 20g* 16s3 21g6 20d Apr 9] tall, quite good-topped gelding: fairly useful hurdler: won minor event at Bellewstown in June: ran well next 2 starts, sixth to Idole First in Coral Cup at Cheltenham on second occasion: likely to stay beyond 21f: acts on soft and good to firm going (won bumper on heavy). *P. J. Rothwell, Ireland* **h124**

FAIRY SKIN MAKER (IRE) 7 ch.g. Nomadic Way (USA) – Malvern Madam (Reesh) [2004/5 h97, F96: 16g4 21m* 17d2 18v2 21d3 20v 21v2 Mar 15] plain gelding: fair handicap hurdler: won at Sedgefield in September: stays 21f: acts on good to firm and heavy going: often held up, and has idled: consistent. *G. A. Harker* **h110**

FAITES VOS JEUX 4 b.f. Foxhound (USA) – Desert Bloom (FR) (Last Tycoon) [2004/5 16vpu 16dpu Jan 13] sparely-made filly: poor sprint maiden on Flat: no show over hurdles. *C. N. Kellett* **h–**

FAIT LE JOJO (FR) 8 b.g. Pistolet Bleu (IRE) – Pretty Davis (USA) (Trempolino (USA)) [2004/5 16m 20d6 16g* Oct 18] rather leggy gelding: useful hurdler at best: won claimer (claimed by A. Juckes £11,000) at Plumpton in October: winning chaser, often let down by jumping: raced mainly around 2m: acts on firm and soft going. *P. J. Hobbs* **c– h115**

FALCHION 10 b.g. Broadsword (USA) – Fastlass (Celtic Cone) [2004/5 c105?, h100: 22v c20s* c21s* c20g c25v* c25vpu c24spu c24vur c24d4 c28s4 Apr 3] quite good-topped gelding: winning hurdler: fair handicap chaser: won at Carlisle in November and Ayr (twice, novice on first occasion) in December: stays 25f: raced mainly on going softer than good (acts on heavy): tongue tied. *J. R. Bewley* **c109 h–**

FALLOUT (IRE) 4 b.f. Goldmark (USA) – Tearful Reunion (Pas de Seul) [2004/5 F14d5 F12g6 F16d2 F16d Mar 12] €3,500Y: lengthy filly: seventh foal: half-sister to winner in South Africa by Emarati: dam poor maiden: fair form at best in bumpers. *J. W. Mullins* **F85**

FALMER FOR ALL (IRE) 7 b.g. Warcraft (USA) – Sunset Walk (Le Bavard (FR)) [2004/5 F18d F18s6 21s6 24v 18s5 22g 21dpu Apr 18] signs of ability in bumpers and over hurdles, off 19 months before reappearance: blinkered final outing. *T. P. McGovern* **h– F–**

FAME 5 ch.g. Northern Amethyst – First Sapphire (Simply Great (FR)) [2004/5 17m* 17g Dec 9] lightly-raced maiden on Flat: won maiden at Taunton on hurdling debut in November by 6 lengths from San Hernando: pulled hard and jumped poorly in novice there next time. *P. J. Hobbs* **h107**

FAMFONI (FR) 12 b.g. Pamponi (FR) – India Rosa (FR) (Carnaval) [2004/5 c–x, h–: c31d6 c31d6 c31dpu Mar 15] quite good-topped gelding: fairly useful chaser on his day: contested only cross country events at Cheltenham in 2004/5, best effort when sixth to Spot Thedifference on reappearance: stays 31f: acts on any going: tried in headgear: far from fluent jumper: reluctant. *K. C. Bailey* **c119 § h–**

FAMILY VENTURE (IRE) 8 br.g. Montelimar (USA) – Well Honey (Al Sirat) [2004/5 c105, h–: c25v3 c25m3 c24m* c24g2 c24g4 Jan 17] fairly useful handicap chaser: won at Musselburgh in December by 2 lengths from Gangsters R Us: stays 25f: acts on good to firm and heavy going: wore cheekpieces last 3 starts: often tongue tied. *Ferdy Murphy* **c115 h–**

FAMOUS GROUSE 5 b.g. Selkirk (USA) – Shoot Clear (Bay Express) [2004/5 h107: 20s* 21g* 24d4 21s3 22dF Mar 19] useful-looking gelding: useful on Flat (stayed 1¼m): bought out of R. Charlton's stable 23,000 gns Newmarket Autumn Sales: improved form over hurdles in 2004/5, winning handicaps at Aintree in November and Kempton in December: stayed 3m: raced on good going or softer: wore cheekpieces final start: dead. *P. Bowen* **h121**

FANDANGO DE CHASSY (FR) 12 b.g. Brezzo (FR) – Laita de Mercurey (FR) (Dom Luc (FR)) [2004/5 c–, h–: 24s5 24s Nov 27] good-topped gelding: veteran staying hurdler/chaser, lightly raced and no form since 2002/3: wears headgear: has had tongue tied. *Mrs L. Wadham* **c– h–**

FANDANI (GER) 5 b.g. Lomitas – Fainting Spell (FR) (Top Ville) [2004/5 16d^{2} Feb 19] angular gelding: fairly useful on Flat, successful 3 times up to around 1½m in Germany for P. Rau, including in 2004: promising 5 lengths second to Cerium in novice at Wincanton on hurdling debut: likely to prove best around 2m. *C. J. Mann* **h116**

FANION DE NOURRY (FR) 12 ch.g. Bad Conduct (USA) – Ottomane (FR) (Quart de Vin (FR)) [2004/5 c75, h–: c25v^{4} c22g^{pu} c25m^{3} Jun 9] workmanlike gelding: hunter chaser, retains little ability: tried in cheekpieces. *E. Haddock* **c– h–**

FANTASMIC 9 ch.g. Broadsword (USA) – Squeaky Cottage (True Song) [2004/5 c16d* c16g Apr 14] good-topped gelding: left A. Hales and off 19 months, better effort in handicap chases when winning 4-runner event at Lingfield in November: stays 21f: acts on soft and good to firm going. *O. Sherwood* **c102 h–**

FANTASTIC ARTS (FR) 5 b.g. Royal Applause – Magic Arts (IRE) (Fairy King (USA)) [2004/5 h104: 16d 17g^{4} 16v^{pu} 17g^{2} Apr 7] rather leggy, close-coupled gelding: fair novice hurdler: likely to prove best around 2m, with emphasis on speed. *Miss Venetia Williams* **h101**

FANTASTIC CHAMPION (IRE) 6 b.g. Entrepreneur – Reine Mathilde (USA) (Vaguely Noble) [2004/5 h117: 23d* 24g^{2} 24m^{3} 24g* 19g c24v^{4} c24g^{4} c24s^{pu} 19d c23d^{3} c16v^{F} c24g^{4} c24g^{5} Apr 17] strong, close-coupled gelding: fairly useful hurdler: won novices at Fakenham in May and Worcester in July: sold out of Mrs L. Wadham's stable 18,000 gns Doncaster August Sales after fourth start, badly out of sorts afterwards: stays 3m: acts on good to firm and good to soft going: tried blinkered: moody. *J. R. Cornwall* **c– § h116 §**

FANTASTICO (IRE) 5 b.m. Bahhare (USA) – Minatina (IRE) (Ela-Mana-Mou) [2004/5 h82: 16d 20d 20d* 24d^{4} 23s^{3} 24d 24d Apr 20] angular mare: modest hurdler: won mares maiden at Perth in June: best at 2½m+: acts on soft going: wore cheekpieces 4 of last 5 starts. *Mrs K. Walton* **h89**

FANTASY PARK 8 b.g. Sanglamore (USA) – Fantasy Flyer (USA) (Lear Fan (USA)) [2004/5 16m^{bd} 20d^{pu} Jun 23] workmanlike gelding: maiden hurdler: off 2½ years, no show in 2004/5: tried blinkered/visored. *D. J. Wintle* **h–**

FARAWAY ECHO 4 gr.f. Second Empire (IRE) – Salalah (Lion Cavern (USA)) [2004/5 17d^{6} 17d^{5} 16m^{3} 16v^{ur} 17s^{4} Nov 7] modest on Flat (stays 1½m): poor form in juvenile hurdles: raced around 2m: acts on soft and good to firm going. *James Moffatt* **h75**

FARCEUR (FR) 6 b. or br.g. Anabaa (USA) – Fabulous Account (USA) (Private Account (USA)) [2004/5 c–, h99: 16v 25v^{6} 19v Apr 22] thrice-raced over fences: maiden hurdler, little show in Britain: stays 19f: acts on soft going: tried blinkered in France. *M. C. Pipe* **c– h–**

FARD DU MOULIN MAS (FR) 12 b. or br.g. Morespeed – Soiree d'Ex (FR) (Kashtan (FR)) [2004/5 c–, h94: 22g 20s 19g* 19g^{5} Apr 12] good-topped gelding: modest hurdler nowadays, won handicap at Doncaster in January: stays 3m: acts on soft going. *M. E. D. Francis* **c– h93**

FARFIELDS PRINCE 13 b.g. Weldnaas (USA) – Coca (Levmoss) [2004/5 c20g^{pu} May 13] leggy gelding: winning hurdler/chaser: no longer of any account: often blinkered/visored. *Mrs L. E. Murray* **c– § h– §**

FAR FROM TROUBLE (IRE) 6 b.g. Good Thyne (USA) – Derry Girl (Rarity) [2004/5 F16m* 18d^{5} 24s* 22v^{2} Apr 2] good sort: type to make a chaser: brother to top-class staying hurdler Bannow Bay and half-brother to 2 winners, including smart staying hurdler/useful hunter chaser Mighty Moss (by Moscow Society): dam, tailed off on only start, half-sister to useful 2m hurdler Timoney: won 27-runner bumper at Fairyhouse on debut in May, overcoming trouble in running: again looked promising second and third starts over hurdles, winning maiden at Naas in March and neck second to Tasman in novice at Navan in April: will stay beyond 3m: useful prospect for novice chases in 2005/6. *C. Roche, Ireland* **h125 F104**

FARINEL 9 b.g. In The Wings – Dame de L'Oise (USA) (Riverman (USA)) [2004/5 c109, h–: c25g c24v* c32m^{4} c22g 24s c28s c24d^{F} c21d^{5} c24d^{4} Mar 5] good-topped gelding: winning hurdler: fairly useful handicap chaser: won at Down Royal in May: left A. Moore after seventh start: stays 4m: acts on heavy and good to firm going: tried blinkered/in cheekpieces. *Jonjo O'Neill* **c115 h–**

FARINGTON LODGE (IRE) 7 b.g. Simply Great (FR) – Lodge Party (IRE) (Strong Gale) [2004/5 h76: c24v^{2} c25g^{F} Mar 9] leggy gelding: poor maiden hurdler: runner-up in point in January: modest form when third to subsequently-disqualified The Butterwick Kid in hunter at Newcastle. *Niall Saville* **c84 h–**

FARLINGTON 8 b.g. Alflora (IRE) – Annapuma (Rakaposhi King) [2004/5 c104: c21g[2] c20g* c20g* c24s Feb 10] tall gelding: fair chaser: left J. H. Johnson after first outing: successful in maiden and novice at Market Rasen in August: stays 21f: probably acts on soft going. *P. Bowen* **c113**

FARMER BROWN (IRE) 4 b.g. Bob Back (USA) – Magic Moonbeam (IRE) (Decent Fellow) [2004/5 F16s* Apr 10] €40,000 3-y-o: third foal: half-brother to bumper winner Majestic Moonbeam (by Supreme Leader): dam, Irish bumper winner, out of half-sister to smart 2m to 2¾m hurdler Troyswood: well-backed 11/2-chance, won valuable 17-runner bumper at Limerick on debut by 2 lengths from Wild Ocean, patiently ridden and leading over 2f out. *P. Hughes, Ireland* **F101**

FARMER JACK 9 b.g. Alflora (IRE) – Cheryls Pet (IRE) (General Ironside) [2004/5 c146, h–: c20s* c20d[F] c20d[2] c21d[F] c21s[4] c24d* c24s* Feb 26] **c162 h–**

It was the best of times, it was the worst of times. Filled for the most part with anticipation and excitement, out of the blue the season stopped abruptly for the connections of Farmer Jack. Farmer Jack's rise up the rankings was brought to a sudden end in March when, with the Festival already in full swing, news broke of his death from a suspected heart attack on the gallops at routine exercise the Wednesday prior to the Gold Cup. Farmer Jack's victories the month before, in the AON Chase at Newbury and under top weight in the Racing Post Chase at Kempton, were among the most striking of the season, both gained with bold jumping and resolute galloping. The improved form he showed in the process would have made Farmer Jack well worth his place in an already depleted field at Cheltenham.

Farmer Jack arrived at Newbury in February with his season in danger of petering out in anti-climax. After a spell largely in the doldrums in 2003/4 following a wind operation, he began 2004/5 with victory in the totesport Wigan Chase, a limited handicap at Aintree in October, a new race which replaced the Desert Orchid Chase at Wincanton in the pattern. In making all to beat Take A Stand by eleven lengths he revived memories of his novice days. Allowed to dominate

totesport Wigan Chase (Limited Handicap), Aintree—
Farmer Jack gets back on track with an all-the-way win over Take The Stand

AON Chase, Newbury—a game performance sees off the Cheltenham Gold Cup hopefuls Strong Flow (centre) and Celestial Gold (right)

against only six rivals, Farmer Jack's jumping was good over the Mildmay course, albeit over fences which looked more forgiving than in recent years, but he fell at the fence before the straight in much more competitive fields in the Paddy Power and the Bonusprint Gold Cups at Cheltenham afterwards, close up but looking held when coming down on each occasion. Beaten twenty lengths into second by Le Roi Miguel in the Peterborough Chase at Huntingdon in between, and only a creditable fourth in the Ladbrokes Trophy Handicap, returned to Cheltenham in January, Farmer Jack started a 12/1-shot when stepped up in class for the AON at Newbury. Entered for the race only after it was re-opened, Farmer Jack was one of the outsiders in a market dominated by Gold Cup aspirants Celestial Gold and Strong Flow. Stepping up to three miles, Farmer Jack sprang a surprise, helping to increase a steady pace from five out, looking held as the market leaders went on approaching three out, the final ditch, but then getting himself back into contention with good jumps there and at the second last. Another one at the final fence took him to the front, and the game Farmer Jack held Strong Flow and Celestial Gold by a length and a half and a head, the three well clear of a below-par Sir Rembrandt.

Farmer Jack escaped a penalty in the Racing Post Chase as he was already set to shoulder the maximum weight allowed under the race conditions. Carrying 11-12, he conceded between 8 lb and 26 lb to his fifteen rivals. All the same, his BHB mark would have been 11 lb higher had the handicapper been able to take his Newbury running into account, and the only runner preferred to 5/1-shot Farmer Jack in the betting was the progressive Colonel Frank at 4/1. Turned out so quickly, Farmer Jack might have been expected to be feeling the effects of his Newbury run a fortnight earlier, but he showed tremendous zest again in the testing conditions. Kept wide, but in close touch, in a race that was not overly-strongly run despite the presence of several habitual front runners, Farmer Jack challenged the long-time leader Banker Count from the fourth last. As the field finally became stretched, Farmer Jack jumped to the front two out and again ran on gamely, the race won at the last. At the line, Farmer Jack had six lengths to spare over Iznogoud, third in the race twelve months earlier, with thirteen-year-old Banker Count keeping on to hold Tikram for fourth. Farmer Jack was a fourth winner of the race in the last six

Racing Post Chase (Handicap), Kempton—
a final win, maintaining Richard Johnson's fine record in the race

runnings for his jockey Richard Johnson, also successful on Gloria Victis in 2000, Young Spartacus in 2001 and Gunther McBride in 2002, and a third in the last seven for trainer Philip Hobbs, following Dr Leunt in 1999 and Gunther McBride.

Good weight-carrying efforts have been quite common among the winners of the Racing Post Chase since Desert Orchid put up a majestic effort to score by eight lengths under 12-3 in 1990. None has been in that league, but Docklands Express in 1992 put up a very smart performance and Val d'Alene in 1995 and Gloria Victis both showed top-class form in winning, Docklands Express and the outstanding novice Gloria Victis doing so under 11-10. Farmer Jack's effort confirmed him a high-class chaser, and, as things turned out, with Best Mate and Kingscliff also among the Gold Cup absentees, a repeat of his Kempton form would probably have been good enough to see him placed in that race. At the time of his death, Farmer Jack was as low as 9/1 for Cheltenham, though a trip to Japan for the extremely valuable Nakayama Grand Jump had been under discussion until the decision was taken to pay £17,500 to supplement him for Cheltenham as others fell by the wayside. Had Farmer Jack made it to Cheltenham, it would have been his fourth Festival. Ninth in the Royal & SunAlliance Novices' Hurdle as a six-year-old, he had been fourth in the Arkle Chase the following year and down the field in the Mildmay of Flete in 2004.

Farmer Jack (b.g. 1996)	Alflora (IRE) (b 1989)	Niniski (b 1976)	Nijinsky
			Virginia Hills
		Adrana (ch 1980)	Bold Lad
			Le Melody
	Cheryls Pet (IRE) (b 1988)	General Ironside (gr 1973)	Sea Hawk II
			Come Dancing
		Kilmanahan (b 1970)	Arctic Slave
			Saucy Vic

Farmer Jack's loss must have been felt all the harder by his owner Peter Partridge who also bred him. Partridge, a retired beef and dairy farmer, named the horse after his father, who was known as 'farmer Jack', the horse being foaled on the father's birthday. Farmer Jack was one of only two horses his owner had in training in the latest season, the other being his brother Harry's Dream, a point winner and successful twice over fences at up to two and three quarter miles in 2003/4. The pair's dam Cheryls Pet was bought as a maiden by Farmer Jack's owner out of a claiming hurdle and went on to win novice events at Ludlow and Taunton at up to twenty-one furlongs, also reaching the frame over fences. A workmanlike gelding, Farmer Jack made his debut at Taunton at the end of 2000/1 season, winning a bumper for Richard Mitchell. He joined Seamus Mullins before winning twice as a novice hurdler in 2001/2, and won three novice chases for him the following season before being transferred to Philip Hobbs. In all, Farmer Jack won ten of his twenty-seven races. Although he spent much of his career tackling shorter, he was clearly at least as effective at three miles as things turned out.

Effective held up or making the running, he acted well on soft ground and gained his bumper win on firm. Like some bold jumpers, Farmer Jack was inclined to make the odd mistake, but he was a fine sight when he met the fences right, and a fine servant to connections. *P. J. Hobbs*

FARMER JOSH 11 b.g. Dancing High – Millie Duffer (Furry Glen) [2004/5 c–x, h–: 25m[5] 20v[5] Oct 29] of little account: tried blinkered. *Miss L. V. Davis* **c– x h–**

FARMER TOM (IRE) 5 br.g. Lord Americo – Churchtown Mist (Modern Dancer) [2004/5 aF16g Feb 19] €5,500 4-y-o: sixth foal: half-brother to winning pointer by Roselier: dam unraced, from family of Grand National runner-up Churchtown Boy: tailed off in bumper on debut. *C. C. Bealby* **F–**

FARNAHEEZVIEW (IRE) 7 b.g. Naheez (USA) – Sweet View (King's Ride) [2004/5 h109, F92: c24d[3] c27g[5] c25s[3] Jan 6] compact gelding: fair novice hurdler: mistakes all starts over fences, apparently easily best effort when fifth of 6 finishers in steadily-run handicap at Ludlow: thorough stayer: raced on good going or softer. *O. Sherwood* **c115 x h–**

FARNE ISLE 6 ch.m. Midnight Legend – Biloela (Nicholas Bill) [2004/5 h87: 17g[5] 20g* 19d[6] 21v[3] 21v[2] 24v[pu] 16g[4] 21v[4] Mar 15] smallish, sparely-made mare: fair hurdler: easily won novice handicap at Leicester in November: should stay 3m: raced mainly on good going or softer (acts on heavy): tried in cheekpieces: has had tongue tied. *G. A. Harker* **h103**

FAR PAVILIONS 6 b.g. Halling (USA) – Flambera (FR) (Akarad (FR)) [2004/5 h118: 17g* 16d 16g[F] Apr 16] useful-looking gelding: useful on Flat (stays 2m), successful in April and May (2): fairly useful hurdler, off 20 months before reappearance: won handicap at Musselburgh in February by 4 lengths from Alrafid: will stay beyond 2m: acts on good to firm and good to soft going. *G. A. Swinbank* **h122 +**

FAR TWO FRIENDLY 6 ch.m. Environment Friend – Four Friends (Quayside) [2004/5 F–: F17d May 15] no form in mares bumpers. *Ms Deborah J. Evans* **F–**

FASGO (IRE) 10 b.g. Montelimar (USA) – Action Plan (Creative Plan (USA)) [2004/5 c130, h–: c27d[5] c27s Nov 21] tall, leggy gelding: fairly useful handicap chaser: thorough stayer: acts on heavy going, below form on good to firm: blinkered once: has idled/gone in snatches. *P. F. Nicholls* **c123 h–**

FASHION SHOOT 4 b.f. Double Trigger (IRE) – Paris Fashion (FR) (Northern Fashion (USA)) [2004/5 F16d Mar 3] first foal: dam winning 2½m chaser: no show in bumper on debut. *P. Kelsall* **F–**

FASHIONS MONTY (IRE) 9 ch.m. Montelimar (USA) – Fashions Side (Quayside) [2004/5 c87, h–: c28g[3] c20s* c27d* c20v* c25d* c29s[5] Jan 15] sturdy mare: fairly useful handicap chaser: vastly improved in 2004/5, winning at Hexham twice (conditional jockeys and mares event), Sedgefield (in between) and Wetherby in November and December: creditable fifth to Baron Windrush in valuable event at Warwick: effective at 2½m (given a test) to 29f: acts on heavy ground: usually tongue tied: races prominently. *Ferdy Murphy* **c121 h–**

FASTAFFARAN (IRE) 4 b.g. Zaffaran (USA) – Break Fast (Prince Tenderfoot (USA)) [2004/5 F14s F16g[5] Apr 16] 5,500 3-y-o: tall gelding with scope: sixth foal: half-brother to 2 winners, including fair hurdler/chaser Double Tempo (by Orchestra), stays 2½m: dam, fair 2m hurdle winner, also won at 1m on Flat: better effort in bumpers when fifth to Rasharrow at Ayr. *I. McMath* **F88**

FAST CINDY (USA) 6 b.m. Fastness (IRE) – Forever Cindy (ARG) (Forever Sparkle (USA)) [2004/5 22g[5] 22g[6] Sep 12] leggy mare: fair on Flat (stays 2m) at 4 yrs: well held over hurdles. *P. Morris* **h–**

FAST KING (FR) 7 b.g. Housamix (FR) – Fast Girl (FR) (Gay Minstrel (FR)) [2004/5 c–, h–: c20g[pu] 16s[3] 18s[pu] 22s 16v 17s 16d 18g[3] 16d Apr 3] leggy gelding: thrice-raced over fences: poor hurdler: stays 2½m: used to wear blinkers. *Dr P. Pritchard* **c– h82**

FAST LANE (IRE) 6 ch.g. Hamas (IRE) – Rainstone (Rainbow Quest (USA)) [2004/5 16s 16s Oct 30] lengthy, sparely-made gelding: no form on Flat or in 2 novice hurdles: blinkered final start. *J. S. Wainwright* **h–**

FAST MIX (FR) 6 gr.g. Linamix (FR) – Fascinating Hill (FR) (Danehill (USA)) [2004/5 h114: 17d[3] 16g[F] 16d* 16s* 16d[3] 17s* 16s 16d 18s[5] 19g Apr 12] angular gelding: fair hurdler: won sellers at Ludlow and Chepstow in November and handicap at Taunton in January: barely stays 19f: probably acts on any going: wears visor/cheekpieces: sketchy jumper: unreliable. *M. C. Pipe* **h114 §**

FATEHALKHAIR (IRE) 13 ch.g. Kris – Midway Lady (USA) (Alleged (USA)) [2004/5 c–, h–: c28g^{pu} Apr 30] sparely-made gelding: useful hurdler/fairly useful chaser in his prime, gained all 13 jumps wins at Sedgefield: stayed easy 3½m, effective at much shorter: acted on any going: reportedly retired. *B. Ellison* **c– h–**

FATHER ABRAHAM (IRE) 7 b.g. Idris (IRE) – Mothers Blessing (Wolver Hollow) [2004/5 c–, h103d: c17g^{4} c21g^{4} c24d* c20d^{3} c22d^{6} c25s^{pu} c24d^{5} c25d^{4} Mar 24] useful-looking gelding: winning hurdler: modest chaser: won handicap at Lingfield in November: stays 3m: acts on soft going: tried blinkered: races prominently: has hinted at temperament. *J. Akehurst* **c92 d h–**

FATHER MANSFIELD (IRE) 11 b.g. Phardante (FR) – Lena's Reign (Quayside) [2004/5 c25s^{4} Mar 22] rangy gelding: fairly useful pointer: well held in hunter chase. *Mrs S. Prouse* **c– h–**

FATHER MATT (IRE) 7 br.g. King's Ride – Honeydew (IRE) (Persian Mews) [2004/5 F18v^{3} F19s^{5} F19s* Mar 26] first foal: dam unraced half-sister to useful 2m hurdlers Alekhine, Carobee (both by King's Ride) and Winter Squall: fairly useful in bumpers: won at Cork in March: fair form in 2 starts over hurdles in late-April, winning maiden there and fourth to Piercing Sun in minor event at Punchestown: will stay beyond 2½m: raced only on soft/heavy going: may yet do better over hurdles. *N. Meade, Ireland* **h110 F104**

FATHEROFTHEBRIDE (IRE) 9 gr.g. Roselier (FR) – Trendy Princess (Strong Gale) [2004/5 h108, F105: c20m^{4} c22g^{6} c22g* c25m^{pu} c24d* c24s^{3} c22g^{2} c24v^{2} c22v^{2} c28s^{3} c24v^{5} c24s^{5} c24v Dec 27] fair hurdler: took well to fences in 2004/5, winning maiden at Galway in July and handicap at Roscommon in August: generally creditable efforts afterwards: best at 2¾m+: acts on heavy going: usually blinkered: usually races prominently. *Joseph Crowley, Ireland* **c113 h–**

FATHER PADDY 10 ch.g. Minster Son – Sister Claire (Quayside) [2004/5 c87, h–: c21g^{2} c24d^{4} Oct 31] good-topped gelding: modest maiden hurdler/chaser: sold out of T. Fitzgerald's stable £3,600 Ascot July Sales after first outing: stays 21f: acts on good to firm and good to soft going. *A. J. Chamberlain* **c95 h–**

FATHOM 7 ch.g. Zafonic (USA) – River Lullaby (USA) (Riverman (USA)) [2004/5 h–: 16v^{pu} 16s^{pu} Apr 21] sturdy gelding: no form: headstrong. *Mrs L. B. Normile* **h–**

FAUGERE 9 ch.g. Jupiter Island – Pinch (Ardross) [2004/5 24m^{pu} Jun 29] lengthy gelding: little form, including in points. *N. R. Mitchell* **h–**

FAVOURITE SON (FR) 7 gr.g. Linamix (FR) – Hot Favourite (FR) (Fast Topaze (USA)) [2004/5 h115: 17d 16g^{6} 16v^{pu} 16s^{2} 16s Nov 6] fair hurdler: easily best effort in handicaps in 2004/5 when second at Gowran: stays 2½m: acts on firm and soft going. *E. J. O'Grady, Ireland* **h114**

FAYRWAY RHYTHM (IRE) 8 b.g. Fayruz – The Way She Moves (North Stoke) [2004/5 c89§, h–§: c24d^{pu} c21v^{pu} c16s c20s^{pu} c20v^{pu} Mar 17] winning hurdler: novice chaser: no form in 2004/5: barely stays 2½m: acts on soft and good to firm going: blinkered/visored: tried tongue tied: ungenuine. *Ian Emmerson* **c– § h– §**

FEANOR 7 b.m. Presidium – Nouvelle Cuisine (Yawa) [2004/5 c–, h98: 18m^{5} 16m* 17g^{5} 17d^{2} 16m 20g Mar 26] leggy mare: pulled up only outing over fences: fair handicap hurdler: won at Hexham in June: best around 2m: acts on soft and good to firm going: held up. *Mrs S. A. Watt* **c– h100**

FEARLESS FOURSOME 6 b.g. Perpendicular – Harrietfield (Nicholas Bill) [2004/5 16s 16v 16v 16s^{4} 16s^{2} Apr 22] first foal: dam never ran: poor maiden hurdler: bred to stay at least 2½m: raced on soft/heavy going. *N. W. Alexander* **h91**

FEARLESS MEL (IRE) 11 b.g. Mandalus – Milan Pride (Northern Guest (USA)) [2004/5 c23s^{pu} c26d^{4} c24d^{3} c24g* c24s c23s^{F} c25m^{F} Apr 23] lengthy gelding: modest chaser: won handicap at Taunton in December: stays 3m: acts on good to firm and good to soft going: tongue tied last 2 starts: often races prominently. *Mrs H. Dalton* **c97**

FEAR SIUIL (IRE) 12 b.g. Strong Gale – Astral River (Over The River (FR)) [2004/5 c120, h–: c21m^{ur} c20g^{3} c16g^{4} c21d c24m^{6} c24g^{pu} c21g^{4} Apr 10] lengthy gelding: fairly useful handicap chaser, generally disappointing in 2004/5: stays 3m: acts on good to firm and good to soft going, probably on firm: tongue tied: often finds little. *Nick Williams* **c113 d h–**

FEATHARD LADY (IRE) 5 b.m. Accordion – Lady Rolfe (IRE) (Alzao (USA)) [2004/5 F16f* F16g* 16s* 16s* Dec 18] first live foal: dam unraced half-sister to smart French hurdler up to 3m Invite d'Honneur: unbeaten in 4 starts, winning bumpers at Limerick in May and Punchestown in September and over hurdles at Naas (maiden) in October and Navan (4-y-o minor event by 4 lengths from Inch Island) in December: missed remainder of season after suffering minor fracture in February. *C. A. Murphy, Ireland* **h122 p F96**

FEEL THE PRIDE (IRE) 7 b.m. Persian Bold – Nordic Pride (Horage) [2004/5 h125: c19d^4 c16v^4 c17g^3 21g^{pu} Apr 14] leggy mare: fairly useful hurdler at best: modest form over fences, though not knocked about: raced mainly around 2m: acts on any going: usually blinkered over hurdles: patiently ridden: will do better over fences. *Jonjo O'Neill* **c95 p h–**

FELIX DARBY (IRE) 10 b.g. Buckskin (FR) – Cool Anne (Orchardist) [2004/5 c87, h–: c25g^4 c26m^4 c26s* c24s^6 c31d c31d c29s^{pu} c26d Mar 12] workmanlike gelding: modest handicap chaser: won at Fontwell in October: suited by 3m+: acts on soft and good to firm going. *Miss G. Browne* **c87 h–**

FELIXRDOTCOM 9 ch.g. Gran Alba (USA) – Golden Curd (FR) (Nice Havrais (USA)) [2004/5 h87: 22d^F c20g^{pu} Oct 30] sturdy gelding: fair hurdler at best: broke leg on chasing debut: stayed 23f: acted on soft ground: dead. *N. J. Gifford* **c– h–**

FELIX REX (GER) 5 ch.g. Tempeltanz (GER) – Figlia d'Oro (GER) (Luigi (GER)) [2004/5 F16d 20s^5 Dec 28] leggy gelding: first foal: dam 9.5f to 11f winner in Germany: no promise in bumper and novice hurdle (jumped less than fluently). *M. J. Gingell* **h– F–**

FELIX THE GREAT (IRE) 7 b. or br.g. Hamas (IRE) – Sonya's Pearl (IRE) (Conquering Hero (USA)) [2004/5 h118, F–: 16m^5 16f^2 17d 16g^5 c17s^5 c18v Oct 31] fairly useful hurdler: just modest form on first of 2 starts over fences: raced mainly around 2m: acts on firm going, won bumper on soft: has worn cheekpieces. *M. Halford, Ireland* **c92 h123**

FELONY (IRE) 10 ch.g. Pharly (FR) – Scales of Justice (Final Straw) [2004/5 h–: 16m c21g^{pu} c23m^{pu} c20m^{pu} Aug 6] compact gelding: winning hurdler/maiden chaser, retains no ability: tried in cheekpieces: tongue tied: temperamental. *L. P. Grassick* **c– § h– §**

FENCOTE GOLD 5 ch.g. Bob's Return (IRE) – Goldaw (Gala Performance) [2004/5 F83: F16d F16v Feb 19] good-topped gelding: modest in bumpers: likely to be suited by test of stamina. *P. Beaumont* **F78**

FENCOTE (IRE) 8 b.g. Norwich – Primrose Forest (Menelek) [2004/5 h87: 17s^3 16d^2 Apr 11] good-topped gelding: chasing type: modest novice hurdler: needs to settle to stay 2½m. *P. Beaumont* **h93**

FEN GYPSY 7 b.g. Nashwan (USA) – Didicoy (USA) (Danzig (USA)) [2004/5 h–: 16d Jun 23] lengthy gelding: fair on Flat (stays 1¼m), successful 3 times in 2004: no form over hurdles: tongue tied both outings in 2002/3. *P. D. Evans* **h–**

FENIX (GER) 6 b.g. Lavirco (GER) – Frille (FR) (Shareef Dancer (USA)) [2004/5 h122: 20s 16d 16s^6 16d^F 16d^6 16d 16d^2 20d^6 Apr 9] good-topped gelding: useful handicap hurdler: best effort when 3½ lengths second to Medison in valuable event at Sandown: not discredited stepped back up to 2½m next time: problem with saddle when pulled up at Punchestown in late-April: raced on good ground or softer (acts on soft): blinkered/visored after second start: reliable. *Mrs L. Wadham* **h130**

FENNEY SPRING 5 b.m. Polish Precedent (USA) – Sliprail (USA) (Our Native (USA)) [2004/5 F89: F17d^3 16d 17s 16s 16g Mar 16] fair bumper winner: little form over hurdles: likely to prove best at 2m: tongue tied final start. *W. Jenks* **h62 + F89**

FERGAL THE PILER 6 b.g. Jendali (USA) – Dorado Beach (Lugana Beach) [2004/5 h–: 16s 16v 17v^5 Jan 11] no form over hurdles. *N. G. Richards* **h–**

FERIMON 6 br.g. Terimon – Rhyming Moppet (Rymer) [2004/5 F106: 17v^F 16s* 19s^3 16v^3 24d* 24d^{pu} 24s^5 Apr 21] sturdy, good sort: bumper winner: fairly useful novice hurdler: won at Towcester in December and Newbury (improved form, beat Get My Drift 1½ lengths) in March: will stay beyond 3m: raced on going softer than good: has tended to hang left. *H. D. Daly* **h120**

FERNENST YOU (IRE) 7 ch.g. Polykratis – Film Lighting Girl (Persian Bold) [2004/5 c16g^{pu} c21v^{pu} Mar 28] ex-Irish gelding: comfortably more temperament than ability. *F. P. Murtagh* **c– § h– §**

FERZAO (IRE) 8 b.g. Alzao (USA) – Fer de Lance (IRE) (Diesis) [2004/5 17m* Jul 2] has reportedly had leg trouble: fair form at best over hurdles: off 2 years and left C. Mann, won novice at Southwell in July: will prove best around 2m: raced on good/good to firm ground over hurdles: tongue tied. *C. R. Egerton* **h97 +**

FESTIVAL FLYER 10 b.g. Alhijaz – Odilese (Mummy's Pet) [2004/5 22d^{pu} 22d^5 24s 22v^{pu} Feb 13] compact gelding: winning hurdler up to 3m: little sign of retaining ability in 2004/5. *Miss M. Bragg* **h–**

FESTIVE CHIMES (IRE) 4 b.f. Efisio – Delightful Chime (IRE) (Alzao (USA)) [2004/5 16s 16g^2 16g^6 18m^4 Apr 21] poor maiden on Flat, sold out of J. Quinn's stable 1,200 gns Newmarket December Sales: modest form at best over hurdles: jumps none too fluently. *N. B. King* **h85**

FFIZZAMO GO 4 b.g. Forzando – Lady Lacey (Kampala) [2004/5 17mpu 19spu Mar 23] brother to winning hurdlers Lord Fernando, at 2m, and Breezer, at 19f: no form on Flat or over hurdles: tried visored. *Mrs A. J. Hamilton-Fairley* **h–**

FIALLI 6 b.m. Samim (USA) – Fabriana (Northern State (USA)) [2004/5 F16g Sep 12] small mare: first foal: dam, modest maiden hurdler, fair 6f winner at 2 yrs: no show in bumper on debut. *C. A. Dwyer* **F–**

FIBRE OPTICS (IRE) 5 b.g. Presenting – Hooch (Warpath) [2004/5 F17g* Jul 12] 31,000 3-y-o: ninth foal: half-brother to fair hurdler Watchowillie (by Un Desperado), stays 3m: dam, maiden hurdler, sister to 3 winners including hurdler/chaser Carouser: favourite, won maiden bumper at Newton Abbot on debut by 5 lengths from Island Pearl. *Jonjo O'Neill* **F91 +**

FIDDLER CRAB 7 br.g. Prince Daniel (USA) – Sea Sand (Sousa) [2004/5 23vpu Jan 26] rather sparely-made gelding: eighth foal: half-brother to winning 3m chaser Rusty Blade and winning 2½m jumper Triggerfish (both by Broadsword): dam poor maiden jumper: pulled up in 2 maiden points in 2004 and on hurdling debut. *Mrs A. F. Tullie* **h–**

FIDDLERS CREEK (IRE) 6 b.g. Danehill (USA) – Mythical Creek (USA) (Pleasant Tap (USA)) [2004/5 h78: 16m 16s4 16s3 16s3 16g Feb 27] fairly useful on all-weather, modest on turf on Flat (stays 1½m): modest maiden hurdler: raced around 2m: acts on soft going: wore cheekpieces/visor after reappearance: tried tongue tied. *R. Allan* **h87**

FIDDLES MUSIC 4 b.f. Fraam – Fiddles Delight (Colmore Row) [2004/5 16d 18d 16d 17s2 16v 16s* 16s 18s Mar 9] small, close-coupled filly: modest on Flat (stays 1¼m), successful twice in 2004: improved effort over hurdles when winning mares novice at Plumpton in February: likely to stay beyond 2m: acts on soft going: takes good hold. *Miss S. West* **h86**

FIELDING'S HAY (IRE) 9 b.m. Supreme Leader – Kates Fling (USA) (Quiet Fling (USA)) [2004/5 c89, h–: c25m4 c24g5 c21m5 c24f6 Sep 26] good-topped mare: modest handicap chaser: lame final outing: stays 3¼m: acts on soft and good to firm going: has been visored: sold 5,000 gns Newmarket February Sales. *Jennie Candlish* **c87 h–**

FIELDINGS SOCIETY (IRE) 6 ch.g. Moscow Society (USA) – Lone Trail (IRE) (Strong Gale) [2004/5 F–: F16s Nov 13] workmanlike gelding: well beaten in bumpers 13 months apart: tried in cheekpieces. *Jennie Candlish* **F–**

FIELD MASTER (IRE) 8 ch.g. Foxhound (USA) – Bold Avril (IRE) (Persian Bold) [2004/5 17d 19mur 24d 19s5 19s4 22g Mar 20] medium-sized gelding: missed 2003/4: poor handicap hurdler nowadays: stays 21f: acts on firm and soft going. *C. J. Gray* **h77**

FIELD OF BLUE 6 b.g. Shambo – Flashing Silks (Kind of Hush) [2004/5 h–, F–: 16s3 22spu 17m c20g5 c25dR Apr 3] no sign of ability: tried visored: has had tongue tied. *C. L. Tizzard* **c– h–**

FIELD POWER (USA) 4 b.g. Gulch (USA) – Dreamy Jovite (USA) (St Jovite (USA)) [2004/5 F13g F14s 17g 17g Apr 3] 22,000 2-y-o: rather leggy gelding: second foal: dam maiden: well beaten in bumpers and juvenile hurdles. *Mrs S. J. Smith* **h– F–**

FIELD ROLLER (IRE) 5 ch.g. High Roller (IRE) – Cathedral Road (Hardboy) [2004/5 20d 21d 19s* 19d5 24sbd Apr 16] sixth foal: dam unraced: runner-up in 4-y-o maiden Irish point on debut in 2004: fair form over hurdles: 12/1 from 20/1, won novice at Exeter in January: should stay beyond 19f: may yet do better. *M. C. Pipe* **h100 +**

FIELDS OF HOME (IRE) 7 b.m. Synefos (USA) – Homefield Girl (IRE) (Rahotep (FR)) [2004/5 c113: c21d5 c26dF c22dpu c22v3 c33dpu Mar 19] tall, leggy mare: fairly useful chaser: form in handicaps in 2004/5 only on fourth outing (tongue tied): should stay 3m: acts on heavy going: has flashed tail under pressure. *J. Howard Johnson* **c115**

FIER GOUMIER (FR) 10 b.g. Chef de Clan II (FR) – Azilal (FR) (Rex Magna (FR)) [2004/5 c101§, h–: c17g4 c22mpu c20d2 c16g2 c16g3 c17m6 c17g5 20m Aug 30] leggy gelding: maiden hurdler: modest handicap chaser: stays 21f: acts on firm and good to soft going: tried blinkered/in cheekpieces: has had tongue tied: ungenuine. *Jonjo O'Neill* **c91 § h– §**

FIER NORMAND (FR) 6 b.g. Cyborg (FR) – Moomaw (Akarad (FR)) [2004/5 F18s* Dec 15] fifth foal: brother to fairly useful hurdler Cyborg de Sou, stays 21f, and useful bumper winner L'Antartique: dam won up to 2½m over hurdles and at 1¼m on Flat in France: well backed, won bumper at Downpatrick on debut comfortably by 4½ lengths from Kings Advocate: will stay 2½m. *J. F. C. Maxwell, Ireland* **F107 +**

FIERY PEACE 8 ch.g. Tina's Pet – Burning Mirage (Pamroy) [2004/5 c111, h91: c20m3 c16m2 c17g* c17d4 17g3 c18s5 c16s2 Dec 22] good-topped gelding: modest **c113 h97**

maiden hurdler: fair handicap chaser: won at Market Rasen in July: effective at 2m to 2½m: acts on soft and good to firm going: possibly best on right-handed tracks: consistent. *H. D. Daly*

FIERY RING (IRE) 10 b.g. Torus – Kakemona (Kambalda) [2004/5 c126, h–: c16g³ c16s c16s³ c18d c17d⁵ c17v⁴ c16v⁵ c18d⁵ c17s⁵ Mar 29] strong, well-made gelding: fairly useful chaser on his day, in-and-out form in 2004/5: stays easy 2½m: probably acts on any going: has had tongue tied: front runner. *J. R. H. Fowler, Ireland* **c124 h–**

FIESTY MADAM 4 ch.f. Bien Bien (USA) – Riverine (Risk Me (FR)) [2004/5 F12d F16s 17g 21dᵖᵘ Apr 18] workmanlike filly: fourth foal: half-sister to 7f/1m winner Pango (by Bluegrass Prince): dam twice-raced, out of half-sister to Yorkshire Oaks winner Hellenic: no sign of ability. *Miss I. E. Craig* **h– F–**

FIFE AND DRUM (USA) 8 b. or br.g. Rahy (USA) – Fife (IRE) (Lomond (USA)) [2004/5 16m Jun 8] angular gelding: modest on Flat (stays 1½m): no form over hurdles. *Miss J. Feilden* **h–**

FIFTEEN REDS 10 b.g. Jumbo Hirt (USA) – Dominance (Dominion) [2004/5 c–, h74: 24s² 24dᵖᵘ 24dᵖᵘ 20sᵖᵘ Nov 5] leggy gelding: well held only start over fences: poor handicap hurdler: stays 27f: acts on firm and soft going: tried visored/in cheekpieces: unreliable. *J. C. Haynes* **c– h70 §**

FIFTH GENERATION (IRE) 15 b.g. Bulldozer – Fragrant's Last (Little Buskins) [2004/5 c–, h–: 20g 20gᵖᵘ May 16] workmanlike gelding: veteran hurdler: stays 3¼m: seems to act on any going: tried blinkered: front runner. *Dr P. Pritchard* **c– h–**

FIFTY QUID SHORT (IRE) 5 ch.g. Glacial Storm (USA) – Park Princess (IRE) (Phardante (FR)) [2004/5 F16d 24dᵖᵘ Mar 8] lengthy gelding: has scope: second foal: dam unraced, out of sister to dam of very smart 3m chaser Irish Hussar, from family of very smart staying hurdler Shuil Ar Aghaidh: in need of race in bumper: not fluent when pulled up in novice on hurdling debut. *C. J. Mann* **h– F–**

FIGARO DU ROCHER (FR) 5 ch.g. Beyssac (FR) – Fabinou (FR) (Cavan) [2004/5 h97: 17g³ 16g⁵ 17m⁴ 19gᶠ 19m⁴ 16g* c16dᶠ 24sᵖᵘ c16g* c16d* c16v² c16d⁴ c18d³ c16g c16g³ c20gᵖᵘ Apr 22] smallish gelding: fair hurdler: landed odds in seller at Leicester in November: fairly useful chaser: won novice handicaps at Doncaster and Warwick in January: better form when placed after, third to Andreas in handicap at Cheltenham fifteenth outing: best up to 19f: acts on heavy and good to firm going: formerly visored: tongue tied: sound-jumping front runner. *M. C. Pipe* **c123 h106**

FIGAWIN 10 b.g. Rudimentary (USA) – Dear Person (Rainbow Quest (USA)) [2004/5 c91, h–: c24d⁴ c28g⁴ Mar 20] leggy gelding: lightly raced nowadays: modest handicap chaser: stays 3m: acts on soft and good to firm going. *John A. Harris* **c88 h–**

FIGHT THE FEELING 7 ch.g. Beveled (USA) – Alvecote Lady (Touching Wood (USA)) [2004/5 16v³ 16s 16d⁶ 17g 16s⁴ 21dᵖᵘ Mar 24] medium-sized gelding: brother to poor hurdler Tsunami, stays 21f: modest on Flat (stays easy 2m): modest form over hurdles: should be suited by further than 2m. *J. W. Unett* **h85**

FILLE DETENTE 5 ch.m. Double Trigger (IRE) – Matoaka (Be My Chief (USA)) [2004/5 F81: 16s⁶ 19s⁶ 19d 17s 16v² 17g Apr 3] plain mare: little form over hurdles: should be suited by further than 2m. *Mrs P. Sly* **h66 ?**

FILLE D'HONFLEUR 4 ch.f. Classic Cliche (IRE) – M I Babe (Celtic Cone) [2004/5 17d 17sᶠ 16s³ 16s⁴ 15v² 17g³ 16d* 18vᵖᵘ Apr 2] half-sister to 2 winners, including fair hurdler Just Kate (by Bob's Return), stays 2¾m: dam, winning hurdler/chaser who stayed 19f, half-sister to Grand National winner Red Marauder: runner-up once over 10.5f from 4 starts on Flat: modest novice hurdler: won mares event at Lingfield in February, length up when left clear last: raced around 2m: has worn blinkers. *E. Danel, France* **h89**

FILSCOT 13 b.g. Scottish Reel – Fililode (Mossberry) [2004/5 c90, h–: c21dᴿ c20g² c24gˢᵘ May 27] compact gelding: fair hunter chaser: stays 25f: acts on firm and soft going: tried in headgear: unreliable. *Mrs S. S. Harbour* **c91 § h–**

FINAL BELLE 6 ch.m. Alflora (IRE) – B Final (Gunner B) [2004/5 F17g Oct 9] fourth foal: dam unraced, out of half-sister to Champion Hurdle winner Royal Gait (by Gunner B): bought £2,700 Ascot June Sales: no sign of ability in point or mares bumper. *S. C. Burrough* **F–**

FINAL COMMAND 8 ch.g. Gildoran – Fine Fettle (Final Straw) [2004/5 h–: 19s 22g⁵ 22s 21d 22s Mar 22] strong, lengthy gelding: form over hurdles only on second outing. *J. C. Tuck* **h87 ?**

FINAL DEAL (IRE) 6 b.g. Rashar (USA) – Cute Boro (IRE) (Borovoe) [2004/5 h–: 22g^ur 19f^pu 16g^pu 17d^pu Oct 28] no form in novice hurdles: tried blinkered: has had tongue tied: placed in maiden points in 2005. *C. J. Down* **h–**

FINAL LAP 9 b.g. Batshoof – Lap of Honour (Final Straw) [2004/5 h–: 17d^5 16s 19d Jan 1] smallish gelding: no longer of much account: tried in headgear. *H. H. G. Owen* **h–**

FINBAR'S REVENGE 10 b.g. Gildoran – Grotto Princess (Pollerton) [2004/5 c100, h–: c28g^3 c21d^4 c23s^F c24g^2 c25d^pu c25d^6 Jan 13] lengthy gelding: fair handicap chaser: left S. Sherwood after fifth outing: stays 3m: acts on soft and good to firm going: blinkered/visored nowadays: inconsistent. *B. G. Powell* **c100 § h–**

FIN BEC (FR) 12 b.g. Tip Moss (FR) – Tourbrune (FR) (Pamponi (FR)) [2004/5 c119, h–: c22s^3 c22s^2 c23g c24d Jan 8] strong, lengthy gelding: fair handicap chaser: stays 3½m: acts on any going: usually blinkered, has worn cheekpieces: front runner: often let down by jumping. *A. P. Jones* **c111 x h–**

FINCHES LANE (IRE) 11 b.g. Le Bavard (FR) – Alice Mann (Mandalus) [2004/5 h–: c24d^3 May 8] angular gelding: lightly raced and little sign of ability: tried tongue tied. *Miss Victoria Roberts* **c– h–**

FIND ME ANOTHER (IRE) 9 b.g. Shardari – Naujwan Too (Kafu) [2004/5 c87: c20d^2 c24g* May 27] fairly useful pointer/hunter chaser: won at Huntingdon in May: stays 3m. *Mrs Caroline Bailey* **c104**

FINE ENOUGH (IRE) 6 br.g. Florida Son – Lodge Party (IRE) (Strong Gale) [2004/5 F18s F16m Apr 2] €7,500 4-y-o: third foal: dam maiden half-sister to dams of high-class 2m hurdler King Credo and smart 2m to 3m chaser Comeragh King: well beaten in 2 bumpers. *R. Rowe* **F–**

FINE FRENZY (IRE) 5 b.m. Great Commotion (USA) – Fine Project (IRE) (Project Manager) [2004/5 h76: 16m 17s^pu Nov 30] leggy mare: poor on Flat (stays 7f): little form over hurdles: needs sharp 2m: has looked tricky ride. *Miss S. J. Wilton* **h–**

FINELY TUNED (IRE) 6 b.g. Lord Americo – Gusserane Princess (Paddy's Stream) [2004/5 F95: F16s^2 16s^2 16s^3 19s^6 18g^5 Mar 20] useful-looking gelding: fairly useful in bumpers: best effort over hurdles when second to Reveillez in novice at Windsor: poor efforts last 2 starts, geed up in preliminaries on first occasion: bred to be suited by 2½m+. *M. Pitman* **h108 F95**

FINGER ONTHE PULSE (IRE) 4 b.g. Accordion – Quinnsboro Ice (IRE) (Glacial Storm (USA)) [2004/5 F16v* Jan 9] first foal: dam, fell only start in points, half-sister to fairly useful hurdler/chaser up to 3m Quadco: created good impression when winning bumper at Leopardstown on debut by 1½ lengths from Kinger Rocks, always prominent. *T. J. Taaffe, Ireland* **F105**

FINNFOREST (IRE) 5 ch.g. Eagle Eyed (USA) – Stockrose (Horage) [2004/5 16v 16g 16d 17m^5 Nov 25] leggy gelding: maiden on Flat: well held in novice company over hurdles: has sweated: headstrong. *Mrs A. J. Bowlby* **h80**

FINZI (IRE) 7 b.g. Zaffaran (USA) – Sporting Talent (IRE) (Seymour Hicks (FR)) [2004/5 h78: c24d^3 c21m^2 c25d^3 c26v^2 c22s* c29d^3 Dec 5] good-topped gelding: poor maiden hurdler: modest chaser: won handicap at Haydock in November: stays 29f: acts on heavy and good to firm going. *M. Scudamore* **c89 h–**

FIONN MAC CUMAILL (IRE) 6 ch.g. Sabrehill (USA) – North Gale (Oats) [2004/5 F–: F17d Oct 27] tailed off in bumpers. *J. J. Quinn* **F–**

FIONNULA'S RAINBOW (IRE) 10 ch.m. Rainbows For Life (CAN) – Bon Retour (Sallust) [2004/5 c–§, h–§: 16s^pu 16s Mar 27] close-coupled mare: winning hurdler/chaser, lightly raced and no form since 2002/3: tried blinkered: moody. *S. T. Lewis* **c– § h– §**

FIORI 9 b.g. Anshan – Fen Princess (IRE) (Trojan Fen) [2004/5 c122, h–: c20s^6 c21s^5 c17d c16g* Apr 19] close-coupled gelding: impresses in appearance: fairly useful chaser at best, off 20 months prior to reappearance: won handicap at Towcester in April: stays 2½m: acts on good to firm and heavy going: usually races prominently: jumps soundly. *P. C. Haslam* **c107 h–**

FIREAWAY 11 b.g. Infantry – Handymouse (Nearly A Hand) [2004/5 c82, h–: 20d^4 19g c24d* c20g^6 c20g^2 c25m^pu Apr 23] lengthy gelding: fair hurdler: modest chaser: upped in trip, fortunate to win maiden at Fakenham in February: stays 3m: acts on firm and soft going: has hung/jumped left under pressure. *O. Brennan* **c98 h102**

FIREBALL MACNAMARA (IRE) 9 b.g. Lord Americo – Glint of Baron (Glint of Gold) [2004/5 c–, h107: c20g^pu c16g* c21m^F 19d^3 16d Apr 9] useful-looking gelding: **c116 h107**

fair hurdler: fairly useful handicap chaser: won strongly-run event at Newton Abbot in July: effective at 2m to 2¾m: has won on firm going, raced mainly on good or softer. *M. Pitman*

FIRE DRAGON (IRE) 4 b.g. Sadler's Wells (USA) – Cattermole (USA) (Roberto (USA)) [2004/5 17g* 17d* 16m* 16d^{3} 16d^{6} 16g Mar 15] useful-looking gelding: closely related to smart 2m hurdler Rigmarole (by Fairy King): fairly useful 1½m winner on Flat for D. Wachman: landed odds with something in hand in juvenile hurdles at Bangor in July, Newton Abbot in August and Stratford in September: well beaten in blinkers last 2 starts, also tongue tied final one. *Jonjo O'Neill* **h118**

FIRE RANGER 9 ch.m. Presidium – Regal Flame (Royalty) [2004/5 h82: 21g^{2} 19s^{3} 19s^{6} 16s^{4} 18s^{5} 17v 19v^{pu} Apr 22] poor novice hurdler: stays 21f: acts on soft going (bumper form on good to firm). *J. D. Frost* **h83**

FIRESIDE LEGEND (IRE) 6 b.g. College Chapel – Miss Sandman (Manacle) [2004/5 h–§: 16g 16d^{2} 16d^{pu} 17g^{4} 16d* Apr 18] leggy gelding: poor hurdler: won selling handicap at Plumpton in April: raced mainly around 2m: acts on soft going: usually blinkered/visored: has had tongue tied: temperamental. *Miss M. P. Bryant* **h69 §**

FIRION KING (IRE) 5 b.g. Earl of Barking (IRE) – Miss Tan A Dee (Tanfirion) [2004/5 F16m Sep 24] sixth foal: half-brother to fair 2m hurdler Adradee (by Ajraas): dam winning hurdler: tailed off in bumper on debut. *T. H. Caldwell* **F–**

FIRLE PHANTASY 12 ch.g. Pharly (FR) – Shamasiya (FR) (Vayrann) [2004/5 21g^{ro} 16g 16f 16m c16g^{R} Jul 7] of no account and temperamental to boot: usually blinkered. *G. F. Bridgwater* **c– § h– §**

FIROZI 6 b.m. Forzando – Lambast (Relkino) [2004/5 h80: 17g^{ur} Aug 26] smallish mare: modest on Flat (stays 1¼m): poor form over hurdles: needs sharp 2m. *R. A. Fahey* **h82**

FIRST ADARE (IRE) 5 ch.g. Un Desperado (FR) – First Mistake (Posse (USA)) [2004/5 h–, F–: 16s 20v^{pu} 16g Feb 27] no form: tried in cheekpieces: sold 1,800 gns Doncaster May Sales. *Miss Lucinda V. Russell* **h–**

FIRST BALLOT (IRE) 9 b.g. Perugino (USA) – Election Special (Chief Singer) [2004/5 h130: c17m^{pu} c17m* c21g* c24g* c20m* c21d^{4} Nov 6] tall, leggy gelding: useful handicap hurdler: successful first 4 completed starts over fences, in novices at Bangor, Newton Abbot, Stratford and Bangor again (beat eased Undeniable in 4-runner event) between May and July: virtually pulled up after seeming to go amiss before running on again straight despite jumping left in Grade 2 novice at Wincanton final outing: effective at 2m to 3m: acts on firm and soft going: usually forces pace. *D. R. C. Elsworth* **c130 h–**

FIRST BOY (GER) 6 b.g. Bering – First Smile (Surumu (GER)) [2004/5 h102: 16g^{4} 17g* May 26] fair form over hurdles: favourite, won maiden at Cartmel in May, in front when left well clear last: likely to prove best around 2m: in cheekpieces in 2004/5. *D. J. Wintle* **h102**

FIRST DE LA BRUNIE (FR) 4 ch.g. Mansonnien (FR) – Samisti (BEL) (Mistigri) [2004/5 18s^{6} c17v^{3} 19s^{5} 19s^{5} 16s^{4} 17s Mar 22] second foal: dam prolific winning jumper up to 21f: third in 3-y-o chase at Le Pin-Au-Haras, final start for G. Macaire: modest form over hurdles. *A. King* **c? h90**

FIRST DOWN JETS (IRE) 8 b.g. Arctic Lord – Kentish Town (Camden Town) [2004/5 c24s^{5} c22s^{F} c26g^{ur} c25s* c24v^{2} Apr 6] useful hunter chaser: won at Fairyhouse in March by head from Good Step: ran well after when second to same horse at Gowran and fourth to General Montcalm at Punchestown: stays 25f: acts on heavy going: tried blinkered. *W. J. Burke, Ireland* **c112 h–**

FIRST DYNASTY (USA) 5 br. or b.g. Danzig (USA) – Willow Runner (USA) (Alydar (USA)) [2004/5 h91: 17d^{4} 16g^{3} 17g^{ur} 16s^{4} Nov 4] leggy gelding: fair on Flat (stays 1¼m): modest novice hurdler: will prove best at 2m with emphasis on speed: wore cheekpieces last 2 outings. *Miss S. J. Wilton* **h96**

FIRSTFLOR 6 b.m. Alflora (IRE) – First Crack (Scallywag) [2004/5 F93: 17g^{ur} 16s 20d 19s^{pu} Mar 27] rather leggy mare: bumper winner: no form over hurdles. *F. Jordan* **h–**

FIRST GOLD (FR) 12 b.g. Shafoun (FR) – Nuit d'Or II (FR) (Pot d'Or (FR)) [2004/5 c165, h121+: c25g^{3} c26g c24g^{5} c24v^{2} c20d^{pu} c25s^{2} Apr 7] tall gelding: top-class chaser in his prime: very smart nowadays, 10 lengths second to Lord Transcend in valuable handicap at Haydock in January: downed tools mid-race in Grade 1 at Punchestown in late-April: stays 29f: raced on good going or softer (acts on heavy): usually blinkered nowadays: sound jumper: usually makes running. *F. Doumen, France* **c159 h–**

FIRST JUDGEMENT (IRE) 9 b.g. Leading Counsel (USA) – Star Gold (Bonne Noel) [2004/5 c23mpu Sep 24] good-topped gelding: very lightly raced: fatally injured on chasing debut. *J. W. Mullins* **c– h–**

FIRST LOVE 9 br.g. Bustino – First Romance (Royalty) [2004/5 c113, h–: c19v c16d6 Feb 18] good sort: fairly useful chaser at best: no form since 2003, usually let down by jumping: stays 3m: raced on good going or softer (acts on heavy): free-going sort. *N. J. Henderson* **c– x h–**

FIRST TRUTH 8 b.g. Rudimentary (USA) – Pursuit of Truth (USA) (Irish River (FR)) [2004/5 h–: 17vpu Nov 26] smallish gelding: fair hurdler at best: very lightly raced and no form since 2002. *W. M. Brisbourne* **h–**

FIRTH OF FORTH (IRE) 5 b.g. Flemensfirth (USA) – Penny Star (IRE) (Al Hareb (USA)) [2004/5 F17v* F16s* Mar 5] **F117 p**

It is not hard to imagine, whilst not knowing the actual figures, that a fair few euro changed hands in the aftermath of the Rockview (Qualified Riders) INH Flat race at Gowran in February. Jack Ingham, like his brother Nick Dundee and half-brother Ned Kelly, trained by Edward O'Grady and in the colours of Mrs John Magnier, started odds on but was eclipsed by a couple with less celebrated backgrounds. The 7/1-chance Firth of Forth and 16/1-shot Some Touch came twenty lengths clear in the straight, Firth of Forth overcoming greenness to get the better of his once-raced rival by six lengths. Some Touch made the move from Trevor Horgan to Howard Johnson after being purchased on behalf of Andrea and Graham Wylie, while Firth of Forth remained in the care of Joe Crowley after being bought for J.P. McManus. Firth of Forth was the first to appear in his new colours, starting a well-backed favourite and landing a winners-of-one bumper in good style at Navan in March, forging clear in the last two furlongs after briefly coming off the bridle before the straight. The win at Navan earned Firth of Forth a 12/1 quote for the Champion Bumper at Cheltenham and he would certainly have been worth his place in the field there. His trainer, however, suggested that Firth of Forth's sire's progeny are best served by soft ground, so Cheltenham and the remainder of the season went by without Firth of Forth. Some Touch went on to finish second in the Grade 2 bumper at Aintree while those beaten at Navan generally upheld the form in their subsequent efforts. Were Firth of Forth to run again in a bumper, he could well be capable of bettering the smart form he has shown to date. As it is, a campaign in novice hurdles seems much more likely, and he looks a leading prospect in that sphere for 2005/6. Firth of Forth was originally bought for just €7,000 at the 2003 Derby Sale and is the second foal out of the unraced Penny Star. The first Run For Help (also by Flemensfirth) has been placed in bumpers and won a maiden point. This isn't a particularly distinguished family in recent times, though Firth of Forth's grandam is a half-sister to the high-class hurdler Corporal Clinger, who won the Bula and the Swinton. *Joseph Crowley, Ireland*

FISHER STREET 10 gr.g. Tigani – Pricket Walk (Amboise) [2004/5 c24dpu c25d6 c17vpu c27dpu c24d Nov 27] leggy gelding: maiden hurdler: winning chaser: no form in 2004/5: stays 25f: acts on good to firm and heavy going: tried in headgear. *Mrs C. J. Kerr* **c– h–**

FISHKI'S LAD 10 b.g. Casteddu – Fishki (Niniski (USA)) [2004/5 c–, h97: 22d* 24s4 21d2 Apr 5] leggy, lengthy gelding: fair handicap hurdler: off 13 months (reportedly had leg problem), won handicap at Market Rasen in February: stays 3m: acts on heavy and good to firm going: usually wears headgear. *E. W. Tuer* **c– h102**

FITZ THE BILL (IRE) 5 b.m. Mon Tresor – In The Sky (IRE) (Imp Society (USA)) [2004/5 h–: 21m5 Jun 8] no form over hurdles. *N. B. King* **h–**

FIVE ALLEY (IRE) 8 gr.g. Roselier (FR) – Panel Pin (Menelek) [2004/5 24dro 24v3 16v4 c24d5 c20g2 c24g3 c26v4 Apr 22] ex-Irish gelding: fair form in novice hurdles: modest maiden chaser: suited by test of stamina: acts on heavy going: refused in hunter chase (blinkered), also ran out on hurdling debut. *R. H. Buckler* **c86 h101**

FIVE COLOURS (IRE) 5 b. or br.g. Lord Americo – Thousand Springs (IRE) (King's Ride) [2004/5 21gpu Oct 18] first foal: dam well beaten over hurdles: third in 4-y-o maiden Irish point on debut in 2004: sold £31,000 Cheltenham April Sales: weakened after 4 out in novice at Plumpton on hurdling debut. *A. King* **h–**

FIVE GOLD (IRE) 4 b.g. Desert Prince (IRE) – Ceide Dancer (IRE) (Alzao (USA)) [2004/5 16d^6 16d 16g^3 20g^4 16d^4 Apr 11] leggy gelding: fair 1m winner at 2 yrs, no form on Flat in 2004, sold out of B. R. Millman's stable only 1,100 gns Doncaster October Sales: modest form over hurdles: may prove best around 2m: raced only on good/good to soft ground: front runner: often races freely. *A. C. Whillans* **h88**

FIVE PENCE 9 b.g. Henbit (USA) – Le Saule d'Or (Sonnen Gold) [2004/5 h95: c20s^{pu} c22d^3 c26d c20s Feb 10] leggy gelding: maiden hurdler: form over fences only when third in novice handicap at Newbury: stays 2¾m: raced mostly on good to soft/soft going. *R. T. Phillips* **c97 h–**

FIZZYWIZ 5 b.m. Wizard King – Edina (IRE) (The Parson) [2004/5 F16g F16s Mar 13] third foal: dam, maiden jumper, out of half-sister to smart 2½m chaser Malya Mal: well held in mares bumpers: sold 1,000 gns Doncaster May Sales. *P. R. Webber* **F–**

FLAGSHIP QUEEN (USA) 8 b.m. Northern Flagship (USA) – Alleged Queen (USA) (Alleged (USA)) [2004/5 16g^4 22g^4 Sep 25] modest handicap hurdler: stays 2¾m: acts on good to firm ground: tried blinkered. *A. J. Martin, Ireland* **h86**

FLAGSHIP UBERALLES (IRE) 11 br.g. Accordion – Fourth Degree (Oats) [2004/5 c163, h–: c17s^5 c16s^5 c16s c16g Mar 18] rangy gelding: formerly top-class 2m chaser, gaining notable successes in Champion Chase at Cheltenham, Tingle Creek Chase (3 times) at Sandown and BMW Chase at Punchestown: lost way in 2004/5 and reportedly retired: acted on soft going, below best on good to firm: well held only run in blinkers: went well fresh: usually sound jumper: carried head high. *P. J. Hobbs* **c– h–**

FLAHIVE'S FIRST 11 ch.g. Interrex (CAN) – Striking Image (IRE) (Flash of Steel) [2004/5 c109, h–: c16d^4 c17g* c16g^2 c20m^3 c16m c20g^2 c21g^4 c21g^5 c17d^3 c17m^3 Sep 4] sparely-made gelding: winning hurdler: fair handicap chaser: won at Cartmel (for sixth time) in May: stays 21f: acts on soft and good to firm going. *D. Burchell* **c103 h–**

FLAKE 5 ch.g. Zilzal (USA) – Impatiente (USA) (Vaguely Noble) [2004/5 h103: 17m 20m^2 24d^3 17s^4 20d^3 c21v* c16s^2 c21v^2 Mar 15] smallish, close-coupled gelding: fair maiden hurdler: similar form over fences: won maiden at Sedgefield in December: stays 21f: acts on heavy going, probably on good to firm: headstrong: has hinted at temperament. *Mrs S. J. Smith* **c101 h99**

FLAME CREEK (IRE) 9 b.g. Shardari – Sheila's Pet (IRE) (Welsh Term) [2004/5 c114p, h149: 17d^F Dec 11] tall, leggy gelding: unbeaten in 3 starts but failed to convince with jumping over fences: smart hurdler: reportedly injured bone above shoulder when falling heavily first in Grade 2 at Cheltenham: should prove as effective at 2½m as 2m: successful on firm going, raced mainly on good or softer (acts on heavy). *Noel T. Chance* **c– h–**

FLAME OF ZARA 6 ch.m. Blushing Flame (USA) – Sierra Madrona (USA) (Woodman (USA)) [2004/5 17v^5 Nov 25] angular mare: fairly useful form in bumpers in 2002/3: modest maiden on Flat, sold out of Mrs M. Reveley's stable 10,000 gns Doncaster May Sales: fifth of 13 in novice at Carlisle on hurdling debut, not at all knocked about: will stay beyond 2m: carries head awkwardly: should do better over hurdles. *James Moffatt* **h84 p**

FLAME PHOENIX (USA) 6 b.g. Quest For Fame – Kingscote (Kings Lake (USA)) [2004/5 h107, F97: 16d^5 16g* 17g^2 17m* 17d* 19g^{pu} 16g* 16g^5 16g^6 Mar 26] sturdy gelding: fairly useful novice hurdler: won at Kelso, Sedgefield (first start after sold out of P. Webber's stable 9,500 gns Doncaster August Sales), Bangor (handicap) and Towcester in first half of season: raced mainly around 2m: acts on good to firm and good to soft going. *D. McCain* **h119**

FLAMING CHEEK 7 b.g. Blushing Flame (USA) – Rueful Lady (Streetfighter) [2004/5 h94: 21g^4 19m* May 22] good-topped gelding: fair hurdler: won amateur handicap at Stratford in May: stays 19f: acts on soft and good to firm going. *A. G. Blackmore* **h102**

FLAMING HECK 8 b.g. Dancing High – Heckley Spark (Electric) [2004/5 h83: c16d c16s^3 c20v^5 c20s* c21v^3 c22s^{pu} c20v^{pu} Mar 17] novice hurdler: modest chaser: won handicap at Newcastle in January: stays 2½m: acts on heavy ground: often let down by jumping. *Mrs L. B. Normile* **c96 x h–**

FLASH HENRY 8 b.g. Executive Perk – Running Valley (Buckskin (FR)) [2004/5 h–, F–: 16v^{pu} Oct 16] workmanlike gelding: no show in bumper or over hurdles. *J. L. Needham* **h–**

FLASHY FILLY 5 b.m. Puissance – Tempted (IRE) (Invited (USA)) [2004/5 F16m^{pu} 17d^{pu} 16g Dec 28] second foal: dam 17f hurdle winner: more signs of temperament than ability. *J. C. Haynes* **h– F–**

FLASHY SIR 6 ch.g. Weld – Manx Princess (Roscoe Blake) [2004/5 F16g4 F16g4 aF16g Nov 11] third foal: dam, maiden on Flat, once-raced over hurdles: little form in bumpers. *M. Appleby* **F–**

FLAT STANLEY 6 b.g. Celtic Swing – Cool Grey (Absalom) [2004/5 h–: c26g3 May 31] no show over hurdles: winning pointer: third in maiden hunter chase at Carlisle. *P. Grindrod* **c77 h–**

FLEETFOOT MAC 4 b.g. Fleetwood (IRE) – Desert Flower (Green Desert (USA)) [2004/5 16sur 16g4 16s5 16v* 19s 20s 20s 24spu Apr 20] medium-sized gelding: fair on Flat (stays 1½m): modest juvenile hurdler: won seller (sold from P. D. Evans 7,400 gns) at Uttoxeter in December: form only at 2m: acts on heavy going: usually visored/blinkered. *B. Storey* **h94**

FLEETWOOD FOREST 5 b.g. Fleetwood (IRE) – Louise Moillon (Mansingh (USA)) [2004/5 F90: F16g 16d6 20d* 22spu 24gpu Mar 19] unfurnished gelding: fair form on first of 3 starts in bumpers: fair form over hurdles, winning novice at Fontwell in December: stays 2½m. *A. King* **h102 F–**

FLEMINGSTONE (IRE) 5 b.m. Flemensfirth (USA) – Philly Athletic (Sit In The Corner (USA)) [2004/5 F16s5 F16s6 F16s Apr 10] small mare: eighth foal: half-sister to winning pointer by Glacial Storm: dam modest hurdler up to 3m: best effort in bumpers when fifth at Catterick on debut. *J. R. Norton* **F79**

FLEMMING (USA) 8 ch.g. Green Dancer (USA) – La Groupie (FR) (Groom Dancer (USA)) [2004/5 h–: 27dpu 23d4 21d 19g 25d6 17v2 23v 19d* 16v5 19s2 27vpu Mar 15] sturdy gelding: poor hurdler: won conditional jockeys selling handicap at Catterick in January: stays 19f: acts on heavy going: tried in blinkers/cheekpieces: has worn tongue strap. *I. A. Brown* **h65**

FLETCHER 11 b.g. Salse (USA) – Ballet Classique (USA) (Sadler's Wells (USA)) [2004/5 22d4 17g3 19d Jan 7] close-coupled gelding: modest on all-weather on Flat (stays 2m): poor hurdler: stays 21f: raced on good going or softer. *H. Morrison* **h80**

FLEURENKA 7 br.m. Alflora (IRE) – Tochenka (Fine Blue) [2004/5 F–: 16d 21dpu Dec 5] tall, plain mare: no show in bumpers or over hurdles. *D. G. Bridgwater* **h–**

FLEURETTE 5 b.m. Alflora (IRE) – Miss Wrensborough (Buckskin (FR)) [2004/5 F16s 19d6 Mar 8] lengthy mare: seventh foal: dam bumper winner/winning Irish pointer: eighth of 14 in bumper on debut: sixth in mares novice at Exeter on hurdling debut, jumping right early and not at all knocked about: capable of better. *D. R. Gandolfo* **h77 p F69 +**

FLEXIBLE CONCIENCE (IRE) 10 br.g. Glacial Storm (USA) – Philly Athletic (Sit In The Corner (USA)) [2004/5 16s Feb 3] good-topped gelding: lightly raced: modest form at best over hurdles: will be suited by 3m. *J. A. B. Old* **h–**

FLICK EM OFF 5 b.m. Turtle Island (IRE) – Spark (IRE) (Flash of Steel) [2004/5 F–: F16m Apr 25] no show in bumpers. *J. M. Bradley* **F–**

FLIGHT COMMAND 7 ch.g. Gunner B – Wing On (Quayside) [2004/5 h105, F86: 20d2 c23dF c25d2 c20s* c25s3 c20v* c19s2 c20g4 Apr 16] big, good-topped gelding: fair hurdler: better over fences, winning novices at Bangor in December and Wetherby (by 2 lengths from Onyourheadbeit) in January: stays 25f: raced on good going or softer (acts on heavy): sound-jumping front runner. *P. Beaumont* **c117 + h105**

FLIGHT HEARTED (IRE) 7 ch.m. Broken Hearted – Amid Birds of Prey (Over The River (FR)) [2004/5 F16d 20dpu Dec 6] tall mare: first foal: dam 19f hurdle winner: no form in varied events. *N. Wilson* **h– F–**

FLINDERS 10 b.m. Henbit (USA) – Stupid Cupid (Idiot's Delight) [2004/5 c82, h–: c22m5 c25d* c26s c24s5 c26dur c26d6 Apr 18] leggy mare: poor handicap chaser: won 3-runner mares event at Hereford in October: stays 3¼m: acts on firm and soft going: front runner: none too reliable. *R. Rowe* **c84 h–**

FLINDERS BAY (IRE) 5 b. or br.g. Luso – McMufins Princess (Decent Fellow) [2004/5 F16d4 F16s* F16d F16g5 Mar 28] €25,000 3-y-o: good sort: fifth foal: dam, lightly raced in points, half-sister to fairly useful staying chaser Indian Tonic: best effort in bumpers when winning at Ludlow in December, not extended to beat The Cool Guy 5 lengths: likely to be suited by further than 2m. *Miss H. C. Knight* **F105**

FLINDERS CHASE 10 gr.g. Terimon – Proverbial Rose (Proverb) [2004/5 c119, h–: c21d3 c19s3 c20sur Dec 28] workmanlike gelding: fairly useful handicap chaser: creditable efforts on completed starts in 2004/5, behind Forest Gunner in Grand Sefton at Aintree and Mouseski at Chepstow: has form up to 3m, raced mainly over shorter nowadays: raced on good going or softer (acts on heavy). *C. J. Mann* **c124 h–**

FLINTOFF (USA) 4 ch.g. Diesis – Sahibah (USA) (Deputy Minister (CAN)) [2004/5 F16g[4] F14s[2] F16g F17d* F17d Apr 9] $250,000Y: rather leggy gelding: fourth foal: half-brother to winner in USA by Quest For Fame: dam unraced half-sister to useful 1m and 9f winner Badawi (by Diesis): sold unraced out of J. Gosden's stable 16,000 gns Newmarket July Sales: best effort in bumpers when winning at Carlisle in March by neck from Double Gin. *R. C. Guest* **F94**

FLIRTAWAY 6 ch.m. Master Willie – Coquette (Gildoran) [2004/5 F17m[6] 16s[pu] Oct 13] second foal: dam unraced: little show in bumper or novice hurdle: sold £1,600 Ascot February Sales. *D. McCain* **h– F–**

FLITE OF ARABY 8 b.g. Green Desert (USA) – Allegedly Blue (USA) (Alleged (USA)) [2004/5 c–, h–: 16g 17d 17s 17s[5] 16g[6] 16g[5] Mar 28] sturdy gelding: once-raced over fences: poor maiden hurdler: raced around 2m. *R. J. Price* **c– h65**

FLOODGATE 8 b.g. Bin Ajwaad (IRE) – Miss Haversham (Salse (USA)) [2004/5 22s[pu] 16s[pu] Oct 28] workmanlike gelding: won maiden point in 2002: no sign of retaining ability over hurdles. *D. L. Williams* **h–**

FLORAGALORE 4 b.f. Dr Fong (USA) – Valagalore (Generous (IRE)) [2004/5 F12g[5] F12g aF16g[6] Feb 19] second foal: half-sister to 1¾m winner The Varlet (by Groom Dancer): dam, 1¾m winner, half-sister to top-class sprinter Mozart: modest form in bumpers: well held on Flat debut in April: sold 5,800 gns Doncaster May Sales. *B. I. Case* **F84**

FLORAL DREAM 6 b. or br.m. Alflora (IRE) – Cauchemar (Hot Brandy) [2004/5 F16s Mar 13] sixth foal: dam, winning hurdler/chaser, stayed 25f: never in contention in mares maiden bumper on debut. *N. J. Henderson* **F–**

FLORA LOU 5 b.m. Double Trigger (IRE) – Upton Lass (IRE) (Crash Course) [2004/5 F17d Nov 16] first foal: dam poor maiden pointer: tailed off in bumper on debut. *R. H. Buckler* **F–**

FLORANZ 9 br.m. Afzal – Tuesday Member (New Member) [2004/5 h67: 22s[3] 19g[2] 19s Nov 18] poor maiden hurdler: stays 2¾m: acts on soft and good to firm going. *Mrs M. Evans* **h72**

FLOREANA (GER) 4 b.f. Acatenango (GER) – Frille (FR) (Shareef Dancer (USA)) [2004/5 15g[2] 15g* 16v[3] 16g* 21d[2] 22s[2] Mar 9] leggy filly: half-sister to fairly useful hurdler Fenix (by Lavirco), probably stays 2½m: maiden on Flat (stays 1¼m): thrice-raced over hurdles in Italy, winning at Merano in September: left P. Schiergen, won fillies juvenile at Fakenham in January: fairly useful form when runner-up after at Kempton and Fontwell: stays 2¾m: acts on soft ground. *C. J. Mann* **h115**

FLORIDA COAST (IRE) 10 b.g. Florida Son – Deep Peace (Deep Run) [2004/5 h136: 24g[6] 20s[3] 20d[5] Nov 28] smallish, sturdy gelding: useful hurdler: creditable third to impressive stable-companion Solerina in Grade 2 at Navan in November: best at 2½m+: acts on heavy going. *James Bowe, Ireland* **h136**

FLORIDA DREAM (IRE) 6 b.g. Florida Son – Ice Pearl (Flatbush) [2004/5 h75, F–: 20d* 23v* 21d 20d 24s Apr 2] well-made gelding: type to make a chaser: fair hurdler: much improved when winning novice at Newcastle in November and handicap at Haydock (by 2½ lengths from Huka Lodge) in December: disappointing in handicaps after: stays 23f: raced on good going or softer (acts on heavy). *N. A. Twiston-Davies* **h110**

FLORIDA VALLEY (IRE) 6 b.m. Florida Son – La Lucilla (IRE) (Over The River (FR)) [2004/5 F17v F16m Feb 6] second foal: dam unraced half-sister to fairly useful hurdler up to 3m Maid For Dancing: tailed off in 2 bumpers. *J. S. Haldane* **F–**

FLORRIES SON 10 b.g. Minster Son – Florrie Palmer (Deadly Nightshade) [2004/5 c108, h–: c25m[6] 24d[pu] 25d[pu] Feb 4] tall gelding: fairly useful hurdler/fair chaser at best: no form in 2004/5, shaping as if amiss: stays 25f: acts on good to firm going, simple task on heavy. *M. Todhunter* **c– h–**

FLOWER OF PITCUR 8 b.g. Alflora (IRE) – Coire Vannich (Celtic Cone) [2004/5 h97: c16g[F] c16s[3] c16s[pu] c17g Mar 14] angular gelding: modest hurdler: little form over fences: best around 2m: raced on good going or softer. *T. R. George* **c88 ? h–**

FLOWING RIVER (IRE) 7 ch.g. Over The River (FR) – Minature Miss (Move Off) [2004/5 F75: F16m[6] 20g[6] 19d 16v[5] 25s[5] 24v[pu] Mar 20] small gelding: sixth in bumpers: poor form over hurdles: trained by D. Eddy until after third start: should stay 3m. *Karen McLintock* **h76 F76**

FLUFF 'N' PUFF 11 ch.g. Nicholas Bill – Puff Puff (All Systems Go) [2004/5 c89, h–: c20m[5] c21d[2] c25s* c24s[3] c24m[4] c16s[2] Mar 23] strong gelding: modest handicap **c91 h–**

chaser: won 2-finisher event at Ludlow in October: left J. King after next outing: effective at testing 2m to 25f: acts on good to firm and heavy going: tried in blinkers, usually wears cheekpieces: usually races prominently: sometimes finds little. *D. P. Keane*

FLURRY 6 gr.m. Terimon – Queen's Favourite (Sunyboy) [2004/5 F–: F16m Apr 10] angular mare: modest form on second of 2 outings in bumpers. *C. J. Down* **F77**

FLY FOR PADDY 7 b.g. Michelozzo (USA) – Tirley Pop Eye (Cruise Missile) [2004/5 19spu 21g6 22gur Apr 17] won first of 2 starts in points in 2004: sixth in maiden on completed outing over hurdles: broke leg next time. *M. Pitman* **h84**

FLYING BOLD (IRE) 10 ch.g. Persian Bold – Princess Reema (USA) (Affirmed (USA)) [2004/5 h–: 22s 20gpu Jul 14] angular gelding: poor hurdler: lightly raced and no form since 2002: tried blinkered: has had tongue tied. *N. G. Ayliffe* **h–**

FLYING DRUID (FR) 5 b.g. Celtic Swing – Sky Bibi (FR) (Sky Lawyer (FR)) [2004/5 F86: F16m2 F16d6 F16v3 16s 16v4 17g Apr 7] fair form in bumpers: best effort over hurdles when fourth of 14 in maiden at Chepstow. *Evan Williams* **h86 F86**

FLYING ENTERPRISE (IRE) 5 b.g. Darshaan – Flying Kiss (IRE) (Sadler's Wells (USA)) [2004/5 18v 19d2 18s* 19sF 17s 16d2 16s4 17g* Apr 10] first foal: half-brother to fairly useful 2004 2-y-o 6f winner Sun Kissed (by Sunday Silence): dam, ran twice in France, sister to Racing Post Trophy winner Commander Collins, and closely related to Breeders' Cup Sprint winner Lit de Justice and Derby third Colonel Collins: in frame 3 times from 6 starts up to 13f on Flat: fairly useful hurdler: won 4-y-o handicap at Auteuil in September and, having left J. Bertran de Balanda €42,000 Goffs (France) November Sale after next start, novice at Newton Abbot in April with plenty to spare: best effort in Britain when second to Medison in novice at Ludlow: stays 19f: raced on good going or softer: blinkered last 3 starts in France. *Miss Venetia Williams* **h119**

FLYING FORTUNE (IRE) 9 b.g. Jolly Jake (NZ) – Dynamite Flyer (USA) (Explodent (USA)) [2004/5 c24d2 c24d c26gpu Apr 10] tall gelding: fair novice hurdler in 2002/3: off 22 months, similar form on first of 3 outings over fences: stays 3m: acts on good to firm and good to soft going. *N. M. Babbage* **c103 h–**

FLYING FUSELIER 6 ch.g. Gunner B – Wing On (Quayside) [2004/5 F–: F16m F17g4 Jul 12] sturdy gelding: modest form on last of 3 outings in bumpers: sold 9,000 gns Doncaster August Sales. *P. J. Hobbs* **F83**

FLYING HIGH (IRE) 10 b.g. Fayruz – Shayista (Tap On Wood) [2004/5 17gpu c21m5 c16m 16d c17g6 c21gpu c21m5 21d6 c20g c21m2 25m Oct 13] compact gelding: poor chaser/maiden hurdler, little form in 2004/5: stays 21f: acts on firm and good to soft going: tried in blinkers/visor, often wears cheekpieces. *R. Johnson* **c64 h–**

FLYING INSTRUCTOR 15 gr.g. Neltino – Flying Mistress (Lear Jet) [2004/5 c131, h–: c25d2 c25dpu c24d Dec 29] workmanlike gelding: very smart chaser in his prime, won 11 times in all over fences: stayed 3¼m when conditions weren't testing: acted on any going: raced prominently: jumped soundly: genuine: reportedly retired. *P. R. Webber* **c121 h–**

FLYING PATRIARCH 4 gr.g. Silver Patriarch (IRE) – Flying Wind (Forzando) [2004/5 16s3 16g 16d3 16s2 16d6 16g 16g5 16d Apr 22] workmanlike gelding: dam half-sister to useful 2m hurdlers Roll A Dollar and Mersey Beat: well held on Flat: fair juvenile hurdler: raced at 2m on good ground or softer: blinkered last 5 starts: races prominently: temperamental. *G. L. Moore* **h103 §**

FLYING PENNANT (IRE) 12 gr.g. Waajib – Flying Beckee (IRE) (Godswalk (USA)) [2004/5 19m 19g Jun 15] small gelding: maiden hurdler: winning pointer, including on completed start in 2005 (usually let down by jumping): has worn blinkers/cheekpieces. *I. R. Brown* **h–**

FLYING SPIRIT (IRE) 6 b.g. Flying Spur (AUS) – All Laughter (Vision (USA)) [2004/5 h119: 16m* 17m3 16gur 18d2 16g Nov 27] medium-sized gelding: fairly useful on Flat (stays 1½m), successful 3 times in 2004: fairly useful handicap hurdler: won at Stratford in May: stays 19f: acts on firm and good to soft going: wore cheekpieces last 3 starts: fluent jumper. *G. L. Moore* **h125**

FLYING TRIX (IRE) 9 b.g. Lord Americo – Bannow Drive (IRE) (Miner's Lamp) [2004/5 c100, h–: c24g3 c30dF c32dpu 24d Jan 1] sturdy gelding: fair handicap hurdler/chaser: should stay beyond 3¼m: acts on good to firm and heavy going: not a straightforward ride. *M. Pitman* **c100 h–**

FLYINGWITHOUTWINGS 6 b.g. Komaite (USA) – Light Slippers (IRE) (Ela-Mana-Mou) [2004/5 F16d Mar 24] second foal: dam ran twice in bumpers: seventh of 15 in bumper at Wincanton on debut. *A. King* **F90**

FLY KICKER 8 ch.g. High Kicker (USA) – Double Birthday (Cavo Doro) [2004/5 h97: 16g 16g Sep 23] modest handicap hurdler in first half of 2003/4: well held both starts on return: best around 2m: acts on firm going: wears cheekpieces. *W. Storey* **h–**

FOLLOW THE BEAR 7 ch.g. Weld – Run Lady Run (General Ironside) [2004/5 F88: 22gpu 19s3 21s6 19d 21g2 20gF 22dpu Apr 17] tall gelding: modest form at best over hurdles: stays 21f: blinkered after first outing: jumps none too fluently: temperament under suspicion. *D. R. Gandolfo* **h92**

FOLLOW THE FLOW (IRE) 9 ch.g. Over The River (FR) – October Lady (Lucifer (USA)) [2004/5 c90d: c25g3 c26d2 c25mpu c24m2 c26d* c24d* c25s* c24s* c29d* c23s3 c24s* c25g Apr 12] lengthy gelding: modest handicap chaser: had excellent 2004/5, winning at Warwick (2), Towcester (2) and Hereford in November and December and Towcester again in March: suited by 3m+: acts on heavy and good to firm going: races prominently: sound jumper. *P. A. Pritchard* **c99**

FOLLOW UP 7 b.g. Phardante (FR) – Dashing March (Daring March) [2004/5 16d 16d 24d5 21dpu Apr 18] good-topped gelding: fairly useful form in bumpers in 2002/3: off over 2 years, no form over hurdles: sold 4,500 gns Doncaster May Sales. *N. J. Henderson* **h–**

FOLLOW YOUR HEART (IRE) 5 b. or br.g. Broken Hearted – Souled Out (IRE) (Noalto) [2004/5 F18s3 F16d5 F17g3 Apr 12] €18,000 3-y-o: second foal: half-brother to fair hurdler Isellido (by Good Thyne), stays 2½m: dam unraced half-sister to useful staying jumpers Woodgate and Gola Cher, out of sister to smart staying chaser Master Spy: fair form in bumpers: bred to stay well. *N. J. Gifford* **F91**

FOLY PLEASANT (FR) 11 ch.g. Vaguely Pleasant (FR) – Jeffologie (FR) (Jefferson) [2004/5 c148, h124: c20s2 c26g2 c36dF Apr 9] sturdy gelding: smart chaser at best for Miss H. Knight: won point in January: also second in 2 hunters for N. Shutts, much better effort when beaten ¾ length by Sleeping Night in Foxhunter at Cheltenham on second occasion: mid-field when fell twentieth in Grand National at Aintree: stays 3¼m: acts on heavy and good to firm going: usually tongue tied: usually sound jumper: genuine. *Miss K. Marks* **c136 h–**

FOND FAREWELL (IRE) 10 b.m. Phardante (FR) – Doorslammer (Avocat) [2004/5 27m5 Apr 21] poor maiden hurdler: similar form only chase start: fell all 3 outings in points in 2005: better around 3m than shorter: acts on soft going, probably on good to firm. *K. C. Bailey* **c– h66**

FONDMORT (FR) 9 b.g. Cyborg (FR) – Hansie (FR) (Sukawa (FR)) [2004/5 c161, h–: c20d c21d c24g c21g2 c36dpu Apr 9] rather leggy gelding: high-class chaser in 2003/4: near best when ½-length second to Thisthatandtother in Grade 2 at Cheltenham, leading ninth until close home: never in contention in Grand National at Aintree following month: effective at 2½m to easy 3m: acts on good to firm and heavy going: tried blinkered, not since 1999/00: usually goes well fresh. *N. J. Henderson* **c157 h–**

FONTANESI (IRE) 5 b.g. Sadler's Wells (USA) – Northern Script (USA) (Arts And Letters (USA)) [2004/5 h115: 16d* 16g2 18g* 17d 22dpu 16d6 19v6 21g 21d 19d4 16s 17g* 16d2 20d 16g6 20m3 Apr 23] smallish, sparely-made gelding: useful hurdler: won intermediates at Ludlow and Kelso in May and handicap at Cheltenham (beat Stance 2 lengths in 30-runner Vincent O'Brien County Handicap) in March: stays 2½m: acts on **h134 §**

Vincent O'Brien County Handicap Hurdle, Cheltenham—
Grande Jete's last-flight blunder lets in Fontanesi (far left) to beat Stance (No.27) and Borora (grey)

good to firm and good to soft ground: visored first 7 starts in 2004/5: has looked unenthusiastic. *M. C. Pipe*

FOODBROKER FOUNDER 5 ch.g. Groom Dancer (USA) – Nemea (USA) (The Minstrel (CAN)) [2004/5 17s* 16s^{6} Mar 6] useful-looking gelding: useful on Flat (stays 1¼m) at 3 yrs, lost his form in 2004: won maiden at Taunton on hurdling debut in February by 6 lengths from Master Mahogany: favourite, sixth of 16 in novice at Kempton following month. *D. R. C. Elsworth* **h111 +**

FOOLING AROUND 7 ch.m. Jester – Scribble Along (Supergrey) [2004/5 F17g^{pu} Apr 27] first foal: dam headstrong maiden pointer: pulled up in bumper on debut. *C. J. Down* **F–**

FOOL ON THE HILL 8 b.g. Reprimand – Stock Hill Lass (Air Trooper) [2004/5 h129: 18g^{2} c17s^{4} c16d^{3} c18d^{4} c17d^{F} c20g^{F} c19g* 17g c18m* c20g^{3} Apr 16] rather leggy gelding: fairly useful hurdler: useful form last 2 starts over fences, winning handicap at Newbury in April by 6 lengths (value extra) from Powder Creek and third to Locksmith in Grade 2 novice at Ayr: earlier won maiden at Doncaster with plenty in hand: stays easy 2½m: acts on good to firm and good to soft going: often makes mistakes over fences. *P. J. Hobbs* **c132 h121**

FOOTBALL CRAZY (IRE) 6 b.g. Mujadil (USA) – Schonbein (IRE) (Persian Heights) [2004/5 h113: 24d* 24m* 24m* 24m* 22d^{2} 19g* 25g* 20s^{3} 20d^{2} 20s 24d^{3} 24d^{3} Apr 8] sturdy, lengthy gelding: useful novice hurdler: made excellent progress in 2004/5, winning in first half of season at Uttoxeter, Market Rasen (twice), Worcester (twice, one a handicap) and Cheltenham: gained most valuable success when beating East Tycoon 5 lengths in handicap at Market Rasen sixth start: prominent long way when third of 17 to Asian Maze in Grade 1 novice at Aintree after 4-month absence final outing: effective at 19f to easy 25f: acts on good to firm and good to soft going (below best on soft): tried in headgear (not when successful): a credit to connections. *P. Bowen* **h135**

FORAGER 6 ch.g. Faustus (USA) – Jolimo (Fortissimo) [2004/5 F93: 16d 20s* 21s* 21g 20s^{ur} Apr 7] angular gelding: off 18 months after winning bumper on debut: quickly showed himself useful over hurdles on return, winning maiden at Windsor in December and novice at Kempton (by neck from Ladalko) in February: well held on completed outing in graded company: will stay beyond 21f: acts on soft going. *M. J. Ryan* **h131**

FORBEARING (IRE) 8 b.g. Bering – For Example (USA) (Northern Baby (CAN)) [2004/5 h105: 16m^{5} 19m 16g^{2} 20m^{6} 17v^{5} 16d Feb 9] angular gelding: fair hurdler: left M. Pipe, well held last 2 starts, downed tools in seller (blinkered) final one: best around 2m: acts on soft going: tried in cheekpieces, usually visored. *F. Jordan* **h104**

Blue Square Casino Handicap Hurdle, Market Rasen—novice Football Crazy maintains his fine start to 2004/5 with victory in the inaugural running of this valuable event

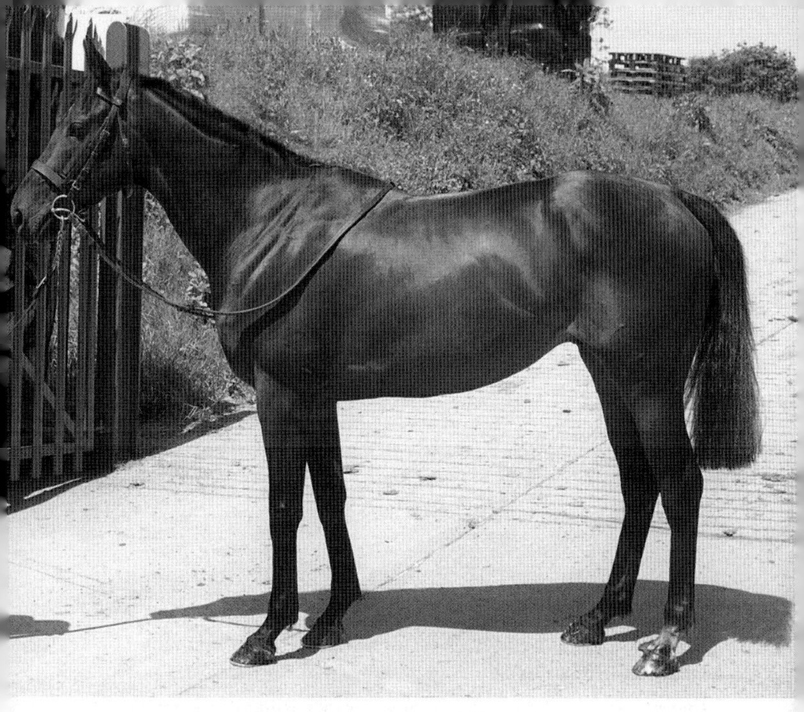

Ken Bevan, Stuart Brain's "Football Crazy"

FORCE TWELVE (IRE) 7 b.g. Magical Wonder (USA) – Gale Force Nine (Strong Gale) [2004/5 c71, h56: c18mpu c23spu Oct 19] sturdy gelding: maiden chaser: little form over hurdles: stays 3¼m: lazy sort, tried in headgear: sold £4,400 Ascot November Sales, won maiden point in March. *P. R. Hedger* **c– h–**

FORDINGBRIDGE (USA) 5 b.g. Diesis – Souffle (Zafonic (USA)) [2004/5 F88: F17m² 19g⁵ 19d 17s⁶ 19g* Apr 7] angular gelding: runner-up in bumper: fair form over hurdles: off 3 months, won handicap at Taunton in April: will be suited by 2½m+. *P. J. Hobbs* **h103 F89**

FOREMAN (GER) 7 ch.g. Monsun (GER) – Fleurie (GER) (Dashing Blade) [2004/5 h155: c18d² c17v² Jan 23] **c145 p h–**

A bout of colic the week before Cheltenham denied Foreman the chance of contesting the Arkle, for which he had been around a 10/1-chance. That was a pity, as he had already, in just two runs over fences, shown form good enough, with every prospect of more to come, to have made him a likely contender for at least a place in the first three. Foreman was one of the best hurdlers sent over fences in the latest season, having finished fourth to Hardy Eustace in the 2004 Champion Hurdle. As he didn't win either of his starts in 2004/5, Foreman seems sure to make a major impact in good novice chases in 2005/6, provided all is well. Foreman made his chasing debut at Newbury in December, in a race which looked a grade or two better than its class C status. The headlines went to another chasing debutant Kauto Star but, in running the impressive winner to nine lengths and beating the useful Sleep Bal fifteen lengths into third, Foreman made a most promising start. Connections were reportedly more than satisfied, as indicated by Foreman's presence the following month in the Grade 1 Arkle at Leopardstown. Foreman had won the AIG

Europe Champion Hurdle on the corresponding day in 2004 and started a warm favourite in the Arkle. He was again beaten nine lengths, by Ulaan Baatar this time, jumping soundly and rallying to challenge going to the last but staying on nowhere nearly so well as the winner on the testing ground. There's every chance Foreman would have been better served by the truer pace and good going at Cheltenham (he has form on soft and heavy going in France but has raced mainly on good or good to soft in Britain and also won on his only start on good to firm). Foreman, a lengthy, angular gelding who usually impresses in appearance, is bred to stay beyond twenty-one furlongs, though most of his races in the last two seasons have been at short of two and a half miles. He wore blinkers in his last four races over hurdles. *T. Doumen, France*

FOREST CHIEF (IRE) 9 b.g. Forest Wind (USA) – Cryptic Gold (Glint of Gold) [2004/5 16d³ 16d 16g* 16g* 19m⁶ 17g 16d⁵ c16d³ c16s² Mar 31] small gelding: half-brother to fairly useful hurdler Handy Money (by Imperial Frontier), stays 19f, and bumper winner Cryptic Myth (by Carlingford Castle): won up to 1¼m on Flat: fair hurdler: won claimer (claimed from E. Doyle £5,000) at Plumpton in October and handicap at Leicester in November: not fluent both starts in maiden chases in small fields: raced mainly at 2m (stamina stretched at 19f): acts on good to firm and good to soft going: wore cheekpieces final outing: tongue tied over hurdles. *Evan Williams* **c92 h99**

FOREST DANTE (IRE) 12 ch.g. Phardante (FR) – Mossy Mistress (IRE) (Le Moss) [2004/5 c96, h–: c23g² c25m² c25g⁴ c25g* c19d³ c24v Feb 2] big, lengthy gelding: modest handicap chaser: ridden more positively than usual when winning at Catterick (fourth course success) in December: effective at 19f to 3¼m: acts on good to firm and heavy going: blinkered once, usually wears cheekpieces: tends to idle. *F. Kirby* **c95 h–**

FOREST FAUNA 5 b.m. El Conquistador – Busy Mittens (Nearly A Hand) [2004/5 F16d F18s³ F16v 19d 22gᵖᵘ Apr 10] £2,100 4-y-o: sturdy mare: fourth foal: sister to winning hurdler/fair chaser Kentford Fern, stays 3¼m, and half-sister to modest hurdler/winning pointer Kentford Busy B (by Petoski), stays 2¾m: dam, fairly useful hunter, stayed 25f: signs of ability only when third in weak bumper at Fontwell. *J. W. Mullins* **h– F76**

FOREST GREEN FLYER 9 b.m. Syrtos – Bolton Flyer (Aragon) [2004/5 h56§: 20g⁵ 20sᵖᵘ c22gᶠ 16m 20g³ 16m 16sᶠ 16v⁵ 19m 16g Apr 19] angular mare: bad hurdler: fell sixth on chasing debut: stays 2½m: acts on heavy going: tried in headgear: has had tongue tied: unreliable. *O. O'Neill* **c– h57 §**

FOREST GUNNER 11 ch.g. Gunner B – Gouly Duff (Party Mink) [2004/5 c122, h–: c21d* c28s* c36d⁵ Apr 9] **c139 h–**

Baron Pierre de Coubertin, founder of the modern Olympics, said: 'Women have but one task, that of crowning the winner with garlands.' How attitudes change. Ellen MacArthur's yachting epic in 2005, a solo round-the-world voyage in a record seventy-one days, fourteen hours and eighteen minutes, placed her among the great British sailors. The major maritime records have largely been a male preserve, non-stop circumnavigation not being achieved by a woman until 1987/8. By coincidence, 2005 saw another Derbyshire-born female make a valiant effort to succeed in a traditionally male-dominated sphere, steeplechasing. Carrie Ford, who won the Fox Hunters' for amateurs over the Grand National fences in 2004, ten weeks after giving birth, returned twelve months later on the same horse Forest Gunner to tackle the world's most famous steeplechase the Grand National. Ford's participation created a media frenzy that would have built—had she been successful—to a crescendo almost equalling that which accompanied MacArthur's return to Falmouth (though probably without a Downing Street 'fast-tracked' damehood).

Back in the 'sixties, when the sea-going feats of Francis Chichester, Alec Rose and Robin Knox-Johnston (completed the first non-stop solo circumnavigation in 312 days) made them household names, women were not even allowed to ride under rules in Britain. Legal action by Mrs Florence Nagle forced the Jockey Club to recognise women trainers in 1966 but it was a further six years before the first race for lady riders, the Goya Stakes for amateurs on the Flat at Kempton, was won by Meriel Tufnell on 50/1-shot Scorched Earth. The first woman professional to ride a winner in Britain was Lorna Vincent—over jumps—in 1978, shortly before Karen Wiltshire achieved the same distinction on the Flat. Flat jockey Alex

betfair.com Grand Sefton Handicap Chase, Aintree—
Forest Gunner sails over Becher's en route to his second win over the National fences

Greaves, who retired in March, is Britain's most successful female professional rider, becoming the first female apprentice to ride out her claim, the first to ride in the Derby and the first to ride a Group 1 winner in Britain when dead-heating in the 1997 Nunthorpe. Greaves, who started as an amateur, kept up a steady flow of winners in a fifteen-year career, ending with a total in Britain and overseas of 289 and paving the way for such as Lisa Jones and Hayley Turner, who are among those now trying to carve out successful careers on the Flat in Britain.

Female riders are no strangers to success around the world. Examples include Julie Krone, who made a big name for herself in North America, with over 3,500 wins, including a Breeders' Cup success, and Lisa Cropp who ran away with the jockeys' title in New Zealand in the 2004/5 season, beating the previous record for a woman rider in that country set by another centurion Cathy Treymane in 1997/8, and also passing the record 193 winners set by Lance O'Sullivan in 2001/2 (Cropp ended the season on 197 but one of her winners is subject to an inquiry and could lose the race). Cathy Gannon was champion apprentice in Ireland in 2004, Anne-Sophie Madelaine twice won the Grade 1 Grand Prix d'Automne on Mon Romain, and Mrs Ann Ferris won the Irish Grand National on Bentom Boy and the Sweeps Hurdle on Irian, but women have not made a similar mark in good races over jumps in Britain, and no woman has reached the first four in the Grand National, a point made by outspoken Ginger McCain who labelled Ford a 'broodmare' and said that 'having kids doesn't get you fit to ride Grand Nationals.' Ford and her husband Richard, trainer of Forest Gunner, both rode for McCain as amateurs and the remarks were made tongue in cheek, though they were published widely in the run up to the National. Mrs Ford's response, incidentally, was that no taxi driver had won the National until Red Rum came along for McCain.

Nina Carberry—riding Dabiroun over hurdles—became the first woman to win against professional riders at the Cheltenham Festival since Gee Armytage in 1987 and Carrie Ford struck another blow for lady riders over jumps on Forest Gunner in the National. She was the fourteenth individual woman to line up (including Judy Davies in the 1993 void race) and became only the third to complete, following Geraldine Rees on the tailed-off Cheers (in 1982, on the first of two attempts by Rees) and Rosemary Henderson on Fiddlers Pike. No woman had contested the race since Mrs Henderson's fifth of six finishers on Fiddlers Pike in 1994, outpaced from second Valentine's and beaten over fifty-five lengths by the winner. Forest Gunner's credentials gave his rider, who only returned from retirement a month before and had just three rides before Aintree, the best chance a lady rider has had in the National and, reunited with Forest Gunner for the first time since the Fox Hunters', Carrie Ford took the precaution of taking out a professional licence to ensure that she would receive her percentage of any prize money (money won by amateurs goes to the British Horseracing Board).

Forest Gunner had won both his outings in the current season, ridden each time by claimer Peter Buchanan who was committed to another well-backed contender on National day, Strong Resolve. Forest Gunner easily bettered his Fox Hunters' form when returned to Aintree for the betfair.com Grand Sefton Handicap over the big fences in November. Forest Gunner has been fairly lightly raced over the years and the Sefton was just his seventh start over fences. Up there all the way and jumping well, Forest Gunner drew clear before the second last to win by eight lengths from Asparagus. Three months elapsed before Forest Gunner lined up for the Red Square Vodka Gold Cup at Haydock and he showed further improvement to defy a 10-lb rise in his BHB handicap mark. Forest Gunner made the running as usual, his excellent jumping again a feature, and pulled out extra to hold Double Honour and Kelami by a length and a half and half a length.

Forest Gunner started 8/1 second favourite (backed from 10/1 on the day) for the Grand National and ran with credit. Ridden a little more patiently than usual, and making a rare mistake at the eleventh, Forest Gunner still had a chance of writing a National fairytale when bang there in the leading group three out. He jumped the last fence in third but couldn't find any extra on the run-in, eventually finishing fifth, beaten just over twenty-seven lengths by the winner Hedgehunter. Forest Gunner's fifth was expensive for totesport and the many other bookmakers who paid out each-way on the first five places in a widely-publicised National promotion, though none of Ladbrokes, Hills (who claimed the 'best National service'), Coral or Stanleybet offered the concession, which must have confused and disappointed many once-a-year punters.

Forest Gunner was bought privately from former jockey Reg Crank and his wife, who bred him, for just £4,000 (the purchasers also had the choice of the

Red Square Vodka Gold Cup Chase (Handicap), Haydock—Peter Buchanan is again aboard Forest Gunner as they get the better of a race-long duel with Double Honour (blinkers)

Forest Gunner and Carrie Ford

then-unnamed Iris's Gift who was in the same field). After showing modest form in bumpers for Richard Bevis, Forest Gunner was switched to the Fords' stables near Tarporley, a yard once occupied by Eric Cousins where top Flat owner Robert Sangster had his first horses. Forest Gunner didn't get off the mark until his second season with the Fords when he won novice hurdles at Aintree, Market Rasen and Wetherby, the last two amateur events in which he was ridden by Mrs Ford. The association continued in 2002/3 when Forest Gunner showed himself even better over fences, winning twice in novice company before being sidelined for fourteen months with tendonitis, returning for a short campaign in hunters which included the Fox Hunters' at Aintree where Mrs Ford rode him for the only time in three starts that season. She has ridden him to five of his eight victories. However, if Forest Gunner has another crack at the National in 2006, it looks very likely that the owners will be looking for another rider. 'That's definitely it for my riding career,' said Ford after the National. 'If he returns next year, it will be without me.'

Forest Gunner (ch.g. 1994)	Gunner B (ch 1973)	Royal Gunner (ch 1962)	Royal Charger
			Levee
		Sweet Councillor (b 1968)	Privy Councillor
			Sugarstick
	Gouly Duff (b 1976)	Party Mink (b 1967)	Pardal
			Lavandou Mink
		Gypsy Dance (b 1961)	Buckhound
			Romany Dance

The leggy Forest Gunner, who is on the small side for a chaser, is a non-thoroughbred out of Gouly Duff who was placed in points. Gouly Duff has also bred the fair staying hurdler Noble Scamp and the winning hunter chaser Freddie Fox (both by Scallywag). The reliable Forest Gunner probably stays four and a half miles and has raced mainly on good going or softer (acts on soft). He usually makes the running or races prominently and is a good jumper. *R. Ford*

FOREST HEATH (IRE) 8 gr.g. Common Grounds – Caroline Lady (JPN) (Caro) [2004/5 h79: 16m 16g 16gpu Aug 24] medium-sized gelding: poor maiden hurdler: tried in cheekpieces: has been tongue tied. *H. J. Collingridge* **h66**

FOREST MAZE 9 b.m. Arzanni – Forest Nymph (NZ) (Oak Ridge (FR)) [2004/5 h64: 17d c21gF c23mpu Jul 21] leggy mare: winning pointer: poor form over hurdles: no show in 2 chases: probably stays 2¾m: tried blinkered. *A. J. Whiting* **c– h–**

FOREST RAIL (IRE) 5 b.m. Catrail (USA) – Forest Heights (Slip Anchor) [2004/5 16s 16s 16gpu 16spu 17spu Mar 6] 5f winner at 2 yrs, disappointing on Flat since: no form over hurdles: headstrong: sold £800 Ascot April Sales. *John A. Harris* **h– §**

FOREST SPRITE 5 b.m. Sir Harry Lewis (USA) – Formal Affair (Rousillon (USA)) [2004/5 F16g4 F18m F17g 21spu Jan 20] fourth foal: dam, winning 2m hurdler, half-sister to high-class hurdlers Anzum, a stayer, and Jazilah, best at 2m: modest form on first of 3 starts in bumpers: no show on hurdling debut: sold £1,200 Ascot February Sales. *R. T. Phillips* **h– F77**

FOREVER DREAM 7 b.g. Afzal – Quadrapol (Pollerton) [2004/5 h110: 16m2 16m2 17f2 16gF 16d2 c17dF 16d 16s3 c16d2 Mar 24] useful-looking gelding: fairly useful handicap hurdler: second of 4 finishers in maiden at Wincanton on completed start over fences, jumping badly left 3 out when looking likely winner: stays 19f: acts on firm and soft going: usually held up: consistent, though has hung under pressure more than once. *P. J. Hobbs* **c93 + h115**

FOREVER EYESOFBLUE 8 b.g. Leading Counsel (USA) – Forever Silver (IRE) (Roselier (FR)) [2004/5 h82+: 24g* 24d 24d 27d* c20s6 c21sF c25v c25dpu 25d 22v 27dpu 27s4 Apr 22] lengthy gelding: let down by jumping over fences: fair handicap hurdler: won at Hexham in May and Sedgefield (amateurs) in October: stays 27f: raced on good going or softer (acts on soft). *A. Parker* **c94 x h102**

FOREVER POSH 8 b.m. Rakaposhi King – B Final (Gunner B) [2004/5 F–: 19s6 17g May 27] leggy mare: no sign of ability. *G. F. Edwards* **h–**

FOREVER WAYWOOD 6 ch.g. Rakaposhi King – I'm Fine (Fitzwilliam (USA)) [2004/5 F–: 24gpu 20gpu 16mpu May 27] no sign of ability. *P. Beaumont* **h–**

FORGE LANE (IRE) 4 b.g. Desert Style (IRE) – March Fourteenth (USA) (Tricky Creek (USA)) [2004/5 16d Oct 2] sturdy gelding: modest maiden on Flat (stays 1¼m): tailed off in juvenile on hurdling debut: sold £800 Ascot October Sales. *G. L. Moore* **h–**

FORGET THE PAST 7 b.g. Past Glories – Worth Matravers (National Trust) [2004/5 c20s* c22d* c20d2 c24v* c20s2 Mar 29] **c148 h–**

If trainer Michael O'Brien is correct, a lot more will be heard of Forget The Past in the next few seasons. After the horse won the Ellier Developments Novices' Chase at the Punchestown Festival, shortly after the end of the British season, he said: 'He's a real staying chaser and should improve over the summer. None of the

Ascon/Rohcon Novices' Chase, Leopardstown—
in gruelling conditions, Forget The Past (checked cap) collars front runner Leading The Way at the last

Ellier Developments Novices' Chase, Punchestown—
improved form to claim his fourth win as a novice, beating British raider Quazar (white face)

rest of his family has been any good until they were eight or nine.' Forget The Past, at the age of seven, showed himself one of the best novice chasers in Ireland, so even average improvement, particularly at three miles or more, could make him a serious contender in the top handicaps or even good conditions races.

Forget The Past started the season with just one win to his name, in a two-finisher point in May 2003. He made a promising start over hurdles the following year, finishing third to Point Barrow, but was then twice a beaten favourite. He soon made amends when sent over fences, winning his first two starts, a maiden at Limerick in October (completing a long-range double for his owner, whose Cyrlight won at Auteuil the same afternoon) and a Grade 3 novice at Punchestown the following month, in the latter gaining his revenge on Point Barrow. Three outings in Grade 1 novice events followed, the first two both in their way gruelling contests. In the first, the Drinmore at Fairyhouse later in November, Forget The Past went down by three lengths to Watson Lake in a race over some of the most demanding fences seen on an Irish racecourse in quite a while. The fences contributed to both making mistakes and ending up having hard races.

A month later, very testing ground rather than stiff fences resulted in another hard race. The venue this time was Leopardstown and the Ascon/Rohcon Novices' Chase, formerly the William Neville. This, in truth, was not a race of any great quality and bore no comparison with the Feltham, a race in theory of the same standing at Kempton two days previously. Mark The Man, who had looked impressive in lesser company, started odds on, with Forget The Past second favourite at 7/2 in a field of seven. The conditions were barely raceable, but Forget The Past admirably slugged it out with the outsider Leading The Way on the flat to win by three quarters of a length, out on his feet after hitting the second last and then forfeiting the lead at the final fence. Mark The Man failed to finish, as did all but one of the others.

After Leopardstown, Forget The Past was reported likely to be aimed at the Irish Grand National, a race in which his trainer has a notable record. Forget The Past's next appearance duly came at Fairyhouse in March, but it came in the Powers Gold Cup, the Grade 1 novice over a trip more than a mile shorter than the National twenty-four hours earlier. The favourite Like-A-Butterfly gained the day, though Forget The Past, beaten just half a length in second, was probably unfortunate not to win. Kicked clear in the straight after leading four out, Forget The Past held a three-length advantage and was going to take some catching when he belted two out. With McCoy riding at his very best on Like-A-Butterfly, Forget The Past was caught close home. Compensation came at Punchestown, at least for owner, trainer and horse (Barry Geraghty, who was publicly criticized by O'Brien, lost the mount to Timmy Murphy who had previously ridden just twice for the stable). Penalised for his Grade 1 success and giving weight away all round, Forget The Past avoided serious error this time and, sent on four from home, crossed the line comfortably on top, five lengths ahead of his market rival Quazar, who had shown his well-being by winning a Grade 2 limited handicap at Cheltenham two weeks before.

Forget The Past (b.g. 1998)	Past Glories (b 1983)	Hittite Glory (b 1973)	Habitat
			Hazy Idea
		Snow Tribe (b 1972)	Great Nephew
			Cold Storage
	Worth Matravers (ch 1980)	National Trust (b 1964)	Relic
			Fortune's Darling
		Sandy's Ellie (ch 1961)	Coup de Myth
			Demon's Well

Forget The Past is a proper, old-fashioned chaser on looks and was well bought for just 8,000 guineas at the Doncaster May Sales in 2002. While his trainer's comment about the late development of the family contains some truth, there was not a lot to encourage would-be purchasers in Forget The Past's pedigree. His sire Past Glories was a top-class two-mile hurdler but had limited opportunities at stud, easily the best of his other offspring, the useful chaser at short of three miles Thosewerethedays. Forget The Past's dam Worth Matravers was a thorough stayer who showed little over hurdles but won twice in points at nine, while the grandam Sandy's Ellie also took time to show her merit, developing into a fair chaser at up to two and a half miles at eight and nine. Even more late-maturing is Worth Matravers' first foal Mouseski (by Petoski) who was much improved in 2004/5, showing himself a useful chaser at up to two and a half miles at the age of eleven. Forget The Past is his dam's third foal, the year-younger El Nombre (by El Conquistador) becoming another winner out of her when landing a maiden point for his breeder in April. Sandy's Ellie produced two other winners, apart from Worth Matravers: Jillikins, a rare hurdles winner in the family, and Free Sandy, a winning chaser as a nine-year-old who stayed two and a half miles. Although this is not a family particularly noted for stamina in recent generations, Forget The Past showed he stayed a testing three miles at Leopardstown and is likely to stay further. Go back half a century or more, though, and there is a noteworthy staying chaser to be found, as the third dam Demon's Well is out of a half-sister to the 1951 Welsh Grand National winner Skyreholme. *M. J. P. O'Brien, Ireland*

FORMAL CLICHE 6 b.g. Classic Cliche (IRE) – Formal Affair (Rousillon (USA)) [2004/5 F–: F16d^5 19g 16s 20v^{pu} 24g^3 Feb 27] useful-looking gelding: poor form in bumpers and over hurdles: stays 3m: sometimes tongue tied. *K. G. Reveley* **h69 F74**

FORSAIL (IRE) 8 br.g. Good Thyne (USA) – Off You Sail (IRE) (Stetchworth (USA)) [2004/5 c24g c32m^{pu} c25g 20s^{pu} 24v^5 22s^{pu} Dec 5] good-topped ex-Irish gelding: modest chaser: won handicap at Kilbeggan in May 2003: no form since including over hurdles, sold out of Mrs J. Harrington's stable 3,400 gns Doncaster May Sales after third outing: stays 25f: acts on soft ground: tried blinkered: has had tongue tied. *P. Spottiswood* **c– h–**

FORTANIS 6 gr.m. Alflora (IRE) – Sister's Choice (Lepanto (GER)) [2004/5 F16s F16m 18m^{pu} Apr 21] €11,000 4-y-o: third foal: sister to modest hurdler/chaser Little Flora, stays 21f: dam unraced, out of sister to smart hurdler up to 2½m Path of Peace: little sign of ability. *P. C. Ritchens* **h– F–**

FORT CHURCHILL (IRE) 4 b.g. Barathea (IRE) – Brisighella (IRE) (Al Hareb (USA)) [2004/5 16d 16s 16g^6 16d^5 16g^5 Jan 21] useful-looking gelding: fairly useful on **h81 p**

Flat (will stay 2m), successful in September (claimed from M. Tompkins £31,000): poor form over hurdles, though held up and not at all knocked about: will be suited by further than 2m: blinkered and tongue tied last 2 starts: likely still to do better, and one to note if there's a market move in his favour. *B. Ellison*

FORTHRIGHT 4 b.g. Cadeaux Genereux – Forthwith (Midyan (USA)) [2004/5 16m^2 Apr 2] leggy gelding: fairly useful on Flat (stays 1¼m) at 3 yrs, sold out of C. Brittain's stable 18,000 gns Doncaster October Sales: caught the eye when 11 lengths second to Briareus in novice at Newbury on hurdling debut, travelling well in rear and finishing strongly once shaken up: type to win races in 2005/6. *G. L. Moore* **h113**

FORTINO 4 ch.g. Abou Zouz (USA) – Blazing Sunset (Blazing Saddles (AUS)) [2004/5 16d 16g 18d 16m^5 Feb 6] workmanlike gelding: no form at 2 yrs (for M. Hammond) or in juvenile hurdles. *Miss S. E. Forster* **h–**

FORTO (GER) 9 ch.g. Acatenango (GER) – Flunder (Nebos (GER)) [2004/5 c23m^2 Jun 16] medium-sized gelding: fair hurdler in 2001/2 for D. L. Williams: second in maiden chase at Worcester, only subsequent outing: stays 3m, at least when conditions aren't testing: acts on soft and good to firm going. *Ian Williams* **c77 h–**

FORT ROYAL (IRE) 6 b.g. Commanche Run – Grainne Geal (General Ironside) [2004/5 F16g^6 Jul 7] brother to 2 winning pointers and half-brother to winning hunters Hall's Mill and What Chance (both by Buckskin): dam maiden Irish pointer: won last of 3 starts in maiden Irish points in 2004: sixth of 15 in bumper at Worcester: probably needs more of a test of stamina. *G. R. Pewter* **F76**

FORTUNA FAVENTE (IRE) 5 b.m. Supreme Leader – La Grande Dame (Niniski (USA)) [2004/5 F16s^3 F16d F17g^3 Apr 3] €27,000 3-y-o: sturdy, useful-looking mare: ninth foal: sister to fair hurdler Reine des Reines, stays 2½m, and half-sister to fair hurdler/chaser Conagher Boy (by Le Moss) and fair hurdler We Three (by Brush Aside), both of whom stayed 21f: dam, fair hurdler, stayed 2½m: fair form in mares bumpers: will be suited by greater test of stamina. *J. Howard Johnson* **F88**

FORTUNE ISLAND (IRE) 6 b.g. Turtle Island (IRE) – Blue Kestrel (IRE) (Bluebird (USA)) [2004/5 h97: 22s 17v^{pu} 19s* Mar 7] leggy gelding: fair hurdler: back to form when winning handicap at Hereford in March: should stay 2¾m: raced on good going or softer: visored: tongue tied last 2 starts. *M. C. Pipe* **h110**

FORTUNE POINT (IRE) 7 ch.g. Cadeaux Genereux – Mountains of Mist (IRE) (Shirley Heights) [2004/5 h93: 16m* c16g^3 c16d^5 Nov 28] angular gelding: fair but unreliable on Flat: modest hurdler: made all in novice at Wetherby in May: similar form when third in novice at Leicester on chasing debut: seemed to take little interest next time: raced at 2m: acts on soft and good to firm ground. *A. W. Carroll* **c98 h94**

FORTUNE'S FOOL 6 b.g. Zilzal (USA) – Peryllys (Warning) [2004/5 h67: 16g 16g^{pu} 17g 17m Apr 23] little form over hurdles: headstrong. *I. A. Brown* **h–**

FORUM CHRIS (IRE) 8 ch.g. Trempolino (USA) – Memory Green (USA) (Green Forest (USA)) [2004/5 c92, h–: c20d^6 c22s^5 c23d^{pu} 21d^5 c20d^{pu} Jan 7] sturdy gelding: winning hurdler: poor form in claimer fourth outing: little form over fences (has jumped poorly): should stay 3m: acts on soft and good to firm going: often front runner: tail swisher. *James Moffatt* **c– h72**

FORZACURITY 6 ch.g. Forzando – Nice Lady (Connaught) [2004/5 h97: 16v^{pu} 19m^{pu} Apr 17] leggy gelding: modest hurdler: left D. Burchell and off 13 months, no show in handicaps in 2004/5: raced mainly around 2m: acts on good to firm and heavy ground: tried in cheekpieces. *M. Sheppard* **h–**

FOTA ISLAND (IRE) 9 b.g. Supreme Leader – Mary Kate Finn (Saher) [2004/5 c–, h151: 16g^3 c20s^3 c17s^2 c17v* c16s^2 c16g* c16s* Apr 7] **c151 p h–**

Fota Island's attempt to complete a hat-trick at the Cheltenham/Aintree/Punchestown Festivals in the same year, last achieved in 1999 by Istabraq, ended when he made a mistake and unseated his rider at the fifth in the Swordlestown Cup, a race run shortly after the end of the British season. In the same ownership as Istabraq, though not quite in the same league, Fota Island is a smart performer, both over hurdles and fences, although it took longer than might have been expected for him to show that form as a chaser. The useful winner of both his starts in bumpers in 2001/2, Fota Island was sent straight over fences the following season, but his jumping proved a cause for concern and, after three runs, connections decided to send him hurdling. Fota Island coped better with the smaller obstacles, winning twice as a novice then going on to show much improved form when raced almost exclusively in Grade 1 events the following campaign, including when sixth to Hardy Eustace in the Champion Hurdle at Cheltenham and third to the same horse in the Emo Oil Champion Hurdle at Punchestown. Nearly six months later, Fota Island was given another opportunity to show what he could do over fences and, following an unpromising start, he gradually began to get the hang of things.

No one who saw Fota Island finish a remote third in an ordinary novice chase over two and a half miles at Cork in October could have envisaged that he would become one of the leading contenders for the Grade 1 Swordlestown Cup in April, and there is no doubt that the step back to two miles was a major factor in the improvement he showed subsequently. On his second appearance after Cork, Fota Island finally got off the mark over fences, though his jumping in a novice event at Navan again gave cause for concern, a mistake at the last almost putting paid to his chance. While his jumping was safe enough when he narrowly failed to land the odds in a similar race at Gowran Park next time, Fota Island still hardly looked equipped to cope with the test which faced him when returned to Cheltenham in March to make his debut in a handicap, in a highly competitive renewal of the Johnny Henderson Grand Annual Chase, a long-established event now named in honour of one of the architects of Racecourse Holdings Trust which had its origins at Cheltenham whose future was safeguarded when Henderson, who died in 2003, got together a group of investors in the early-'sixties to buy the course for £240,000. Johnny Henderson's son Nicky saddled three of the twenty-four runners, the same number as Paul Nicholls, the latter responsible for the top weight Armaturk and the favourite L'Ange Au Ciel. Nine were unable to race off their correct marks, including Fota Island who was 2 lb out of the handicap, but despite that, and the doubts about his jumping, Fota Island was one of only three at single-figure odds, sent off the third favourite at 7/1. A good pace placed plenty of emphasis on jumping, and this time Fota Island, partnered by Paul Carberry for the first time, was foot perfect apart from a mistake four out. Hampered by a loose horse from before two out, where he took up the running still travelling strongly, until approaching the last, Fota Island soon put the issue beyond doubt once clear, running on strongly to win going away by five lengths from Bambi de L'Orme. Caracciola and Tysou took third and fourth for the Henderson yard.

Almost three weeks later, the first two renewed rivalry in the fifteen-runner John Smith's Red Rum Handicap at Aintree, for which Fota Island started a clear favourite, even though racing off a mark 12 lb higher than at Cheltenham (incidentally, the higher weight meant Tony McCoy could take the ride). In defying the rise, Fota Island stepped up to the level of form he had shown in his later races over hurdles, shaping as though capable of even better. Fota Island won by a length from the close finishers Kadount and Bambi de l'Orme, all out to hold on as he began to

Johnny Henderson Grand Annual Chase Challenge Cup (Handicap), Cheltenham—Paul Carberry conjures an improved round of jumping from the novice Fota Island; the grey Bambi de L'Orme chases him home

John Smith's Red Rum Handicap Chase, Aintree—
Tony McCoy takes over for another convincing win, with Kadount (centre) splitting the pair this time

tire in the conditions, but he was much more convincing than the bare result implies, travelling strongly after surviving a couple of early mistakes, disputing the lead on the bridle three out and sent clear between the last two. There are more valuable prizes to be won with Fota Island, though clearly he will need to improve a good deal more yet if he is to make his presence felt at the very highest level.

Fota Island (IRE) (b.g. 1996)	Supreme Leader (b 1982)	Bustino (b 1971)	Busted
			Ship Yard
		Princess Zena (b 1975)	Habitat
			Guiding Light
	Mary Kate Finn (b 1984)	Saher (b 1976)	Great Nephew
			Another Chance
		Cailin Donn (ch 1978)	London Gazette
			Sunny Gal

Fota Island, who is named after the championship golf course near Cork, is a big, good sort who looked in particularly good shape in the paddock at Punchestown. He had been through the sale-ring twice before making his belated racecourse debut at the age of six, fetching IR 20,000 guineas as a three-year-old and IR 38,000 guineas as a four-year-old. He is the third foal of Mary Kate Finn, a mare who achieved little when racing on the Flat and over hurdles, and who would be faring no better at stud had it not been for Fota Island. Her latest foal to reach the racecourse, a brother to Fota Island named Kings Hill Leader, has shown only poor form in novice hurdles so far, and also refused to race once. Another brother, the unraced five-year-old Bobdaman, was sold for just 4,500 guineas at the Doncaster May Sales. Mary Kate Finn is a half-sister to three winners, including the well-above-average hurdlers Castlekellyleader and Cailin Supreme, both of whom are also by Fota Island's sire Supreme Leader: the former was useful at up to three miles, the latter showed useful form at two to two and a half miles. Their dam Cailin Donn, out of the unraced Sunny Gal, won a bumper in Ireland. Fota Island acts on heavy going and has yet to race on firmer than good. He has shown his best form at two miles and is effective making the running or waited with. *M. F. Morris, Ireland*

FOUND GOLD 6 gr.g. Saddlers' Hall (IRE) – Madiyla (Darshaan) [2004/5 16m 20d* 19d^4 16m^4 c16g^{pu} c16g^6 Dec 8] workmanlike gelding: seventh foal: half-brother to winning pointer by Formidable and to 3 winners on Flat, including smart French miler Lethals Lady (by Rudimentary): dam, 1½m winner, half-sister to fairly useful staying hurdler Premier Princess: bumper winner: modest hurdler: won maiden at Sligo in August: left C. Roche after third outing (in cheekpieces): sixth of 7 in novice handicap at Leicester on completed start over fences: stays 2½m: acts on soft and good to firm going. *Jonjo O'Neill* **c90 h97**

FOUNTAIN BRIG 9 b. or br.g. Royal Fountain – Lillies Brig (New Brig) [2004/5 c21s^2 c25s^5 c20v^2 c16v^3 Feb 13] poor maiden hurdler/chaser: stays 3m: raced on going softer than good (acts on heavy). *N. W. Alexander* **c82 h–**

FOUNTAIN HILL (IRE) 6 b.g. King's Theatre (IRE) – Highest Land (FR) (Highest Honor (FR)) [2004/5 h126, F94: 22g^2 21g 24d^{pu} Apr 8] good-topped gelding: has scope: **h134**

useful hurdler: good efforts in valuable handicaps at Sandown (beaten neck by Supreme Serenade) and Cheltenham (shaped as though in need of stiffer test of stamina when eighth of 29 to Idole First) first 2 starts: should prove as effective at 3m+ as 2¾m: raced mainly on good going: type to do well over fences in 2005/6. *P. F. Nicholls*

FOUNTAIN STREET (IRE) 12 b.g. Sharp Charter – Maylands (Windjammer (USA)) [2004/5 c–§: c22mpu Jun 25] unreliable pointer: little form in chases. *T. R. Kinsey* **c– §**

FOURBOYSTOY (IRE) 6 ch.g. Roselier (FR) – Little Twig (IRE) (Good Thyne (USA)) [2004/5 F–: 19v* 20dpu Mar 19] lengthy, rather unfurnished gelding: made most when winning maiden at Market Rasen on hurdling debut in October: dropped right away in stronger contest 5 months later: will stay 3m. *C. C. Bealby* **h101**

FOUR CANDLES 5 b.m. Perpendicular – Skyers Tryer (Lugana Beach) [2004/5 h–: 17vpu 16d 16s 17d Feb 11] no form over hurdles: lame final start. *B. P. J. Baugh* **h–**

FOUR MELONS (IRE) 6 b.g. Anshan – Four Shares (The Parson) [2004/5 F16d5 20s3 27v2 20vpu Feb 13] €60,000 3-y-o: half-brother to 4 winners, including 2m hurdler Adjutant General (by Strong Gale): dam, winning hurdler/chaser, sister to useful hurdler Book of Gold: fifth of 18 in bumper on debut: fair form when placed in novices first 2 starts over hurdles: stays 27f: raced on going softer than good: sold 7,000 gns Doncaster May Sales. *L. Lungo* **h100 F88**

FOUR OF DIAMONDS (IRE) 6 b.g. Fourstars Allstar (USA) – Wine Rock Diamond (IRE) (Actinium (FR)) [2004/5 F16d Dec 5] £2,400 4-y-o: good-topped gelding: third foal: dam unraced, out of half-sister to smart chaser up to 3m The Illywhacker: tailed off in bumper on debut. *Miss Victoria Roberts* **F–**

FOUR ON THE TROT 9 b.g. Totem (USA) – Poppadom (Rapid River) [2004/5 16f2 16m c20m3 19d 16mF 16s c20g2 Oct 7] bumper winner: maiden on Flat: modest handicap hurdler: easily best effort over fences when third in maiden at Kilbeggan: stays 2½m: suited by good going or firmer. *M. Hourigan, Ireland* **c93 h98**

FOXCHAPEL QUEEN (IRE) 7 b.m. Over The River (FR) – Glencairn Lass (Buckskin (FR)) [2004/5 21d 22s2 21spu 21mpu Apr 2] leggy mare: fair form in bumpers: off 20 months, easily best effort in mares novice hurdles when second at Wincanton: lame final start. *N. J. Henderson* **h85 +**

FOX IN THE BOX 8 b. or gr.g. Supreme Leader – Charlotte Gray (Rolfe (USA)) [2004/5 c113p, h–: c23s2 c26g3 c25spu Jan 22] strong gelding: winning hurdler: fairly useful handicap chaser, improved form when short-head second to Tresor de Mai at Exeter and third to Willie John Daly at Newbury: laboured effort final start: stays 3¼m: acts on soft and good to firm ground. *R. H. Alner* **c124 h–**

FOX JOHN 6 b.g. Ballet Royal (USA) – Muskerry Miss (IRE) (Bishop of Orange) [2004/5 F86: 22g3 21s Nov 3] fair form in bumpers in 2003/4: well held in novice hurdles: should stay at least 2½m. *H. J. Manners* **h–**

FOXMEADE DANCER 7 b.g. Lyphento (USA) – Georgian Quickstep (Dubassoff (USA)) [2004/5 c–, h65: 17d2 19m 17s2 17g 16s* 20vpu 19s4 17s3 17v3 19v6 Apr 22] good-topped gelding: poor hurdler: won seller at Leicester in December: pulled up both outings over fences: stays 2¾m: acts on heavy going: tends to find little. *P. C. Ritchens* **c– h80**

FOXTON BROOK (IRE) 6 br.g. Presenting – Martins Times (IRE) (Bulldozer) [2004/5 F89: F16g 21d5 21gpu Apr 1] well-made gelding: fair form on first of 2 starts in bumpers: much better effort over hurdles when fifth to dead-heaters Bengo and Il Duce in novice at Newbury. *N. J. Henderson* **h96 F–**

FOXTROT YANKEE (IRE) 6 b.g. Lord Americo – Derby Fox (IRE) (King's Ride) [2004/5 F16d5 aF16g F16g F14m4 Mar 21] angular gelding: second foal: dam unraced half-sister to fairly useful 2m chaser Belstone Fox, from family of smart chaser Wild Fox and County Hurdle winner Java Fox: best effort in bumpers when fifth of 14 at Wincanton on debut. *J. S. King* **F91**

FRAMBO (IRE) 4 b.f. Fraam – Wings Awarded (Shareef Dancer (USA)) [2004/5 16g 17m* 17g4 16v6 17s2 16s5 Nov 16] poor maiden on Flat (stays 2m): in-and-out form over hurdles, won seller at Hereford in September: will stay beyond 17f: acts on soft and good to firm going: wore cheekpieces after debut: tried tongue tied. *J. G. Portman* **h83**

FRAMLINGHAM 10 gr.g. Out of Hand – Sugar Hall (Weatherbird) [2004/5 h–: c24vpu c26gF 16dpu Apr 18] workmanlike gelding: no form over hurdles/fences: tried in cheekpieces. *R. Curtis* **c– x h–**

FRANCIS BAY (USA) 10 b.g. Alleged (USA) – Montage (USA) (Alydar (USA)) [2004/5 c–, h95+: c16d* 16m Jun 13] good-topped gelding: fairly useful hurdler/chaser on his day: very lightly raced since 2001/2, but as good as ever when winning handicap chase at Wetherby in May by 7 lengths from Jericho III: effective around 2m to 2¾m: unraced on firm going, acts on any other: usually blinkered when trained in Ireland. *Mrs S. J. Smith* **c125 h–**

FRANCIS FLUTE 7 b.g. Polar Falcon (USA) – Darshay (FR) (Darshaan) [2004/5 16g^pu Sep 23] modest on Flat (probably best at 7f/1m): failed to settle on hurdling debut. *B. Mactaggart* **h–**

FRANCKEN (ITY) 6 ro.g. Petit Loup (USA) – Filicaia (Sallust) [2004/5 h67: 23d^6 21m^4 16g 20s^2 21v^4 19d^4 16v^ur 19s^3 16g^5 17d Apr 5] sturdy gelding: poor maiden hurdler: stays 21f: acts on heavy and good to firm going: wore cheekpieces/blinkers after second start. *Lady Susan Watson* **h70**

FRANCO (IRE) 7 b.g. Rashar (USA) – Market Thyne (IRE) (Good Thyne (USA)) [2004/5 c25s^F Mar 7] tall ex-Irish gelding: second foal: dam unraced: easily best effort over hurdles when fourth in 4-y-o novice at Navan in 2002/3: sold out of C. Swan's stable 5,000 gns Doncaster May (2003) Sales: fair pointer in Britain, successful 3 times in 2004: fell ninth in hunter chase. *Mrs Anna Brooks* **c– x h–**

FRANCOLINO (FR) 12 b.g. Useful (FR) – Quintefeuille II (FR) (Kashtan (FR)) [2004/5 c71§, h–§: c26d^pu c25s^5 c26v^pu c20s^3 c24s^6 Mar 27] well-made gelding: poor chaser: stays 3¼m: tried in headgear: ungenuine. *Dr P. Pritchard* **c73 § h– §**

FRANKINCENSE (IRE) 9 gr.g. Paris House – Mistral Wood (USA) (Far North (CAN)) [2004/5 h85: 21g^6 27m^5 21d 17v^3 19d^5 19s^pu 21v^2 17d^4 Apr 5] close-coupled gelding: poor handicap hurdler: barely stays testing 27f: acts on heavy going: wore cheekpieces final outing: usually races prominently. *A. J. Lockwood* **h76**

FRANKSKIPS 6 b.g. Bishop of Cashel – Kevins Lady (Alzao (USA)) [2004/5 c18d^6 Nov 14] modest on Flat (stays 1¼m) for Miss B. Sanders in 2004: bled from nose in maiden on chasing debut. *A. Ennis* **c–**

FRAZERS FORTUNE 5 ch.g. Environment Friend – Safidar (Roan Rocket) [2004/5 h–: 19s^pu Mar 27] no form on Flat or in 2 starts over hurdles. *H. J. Manners* **h–**

FRED ASTOR (FR) 4 b.g. Baryshnikov (AUS) – Mary Astor (FR) (Groom Dancer (USA)) [2004/5 16s^4 17s 16d^5 18s Feb 4] leggy gelding: fifth foal: half-brother to 1m/8.5f winner in Germany by Barathea: dam won several times up to around 1½m on Flat: successful twice up to 15f on Flat in 2004: modest form in juvenile hurdles. *F. Doumen, France* **h94**

FREDDIE ED 4 b.g. Makbul – Miss Mirror (Magic Mirror) [2004/5 F14d^4 F16g Jan 24] seventh foal: half-brother to winning chaser up to 2½m Constant Husband (by Le Solaret) and several winners on Flat, including useful Scandinavian winners up to 1¼m Magic Fact (by Factual) and Tragic Love (by Tragic Role): dam 1m winner: better effort in bumpers when fourth of 9 in slowly-run 3-y-o event at Wetherby, making running. *R. N. Bevis* **F76**

FREDDIE'S COMET (IRE) 9 b.g. Freddie's Star – Baltimore Bay (Bishop of Orange) [2004/5 17d 16m^pu 19m^pu Jun 9] compact gelding: poor hurdler: no form in 2004/5 after 20-month absence. *John R. Upson* **h–**

FREDERIC FOREVER (IRE) 7 b.g. Exit To Nowhere (USA) – Sarooh's Love (USA) (Nureyev (USA)) [2004/5 c74, h109: c21g^2 c22m^2 c23g^4 c26m^2 c26m* c26m^5 c25f^pu Oct 7] compact gelding: fair handicap hurdler on his day: modest novice chaser: made all in weak handicap at Fontwell in September: lame final outing: stays 3¼m: acts on soft and good to firm going: blinkered once: irresolute. *P. J. Hobbs* **c86 § h– §**

FREDERICK JAMES 11 b.g. Efisio – Rare Roberta (USA) (Roberto (USA)) [2004/5 17d^pu Oct 17] half-brother to 2 winning hurdlers: of little account on Flat nowadays: mistakes in novice on hurdling debut. *H. E. Haynes* **h–**

FRED'S IN THE KNOW 10 ch.g. Interrex (CAN) – Lady Vynz (Whitstead) [2004/5 c117, h116: 20g^pu May 1] tall gelding: fairly useful hurdler/chaser, lost his form in spring 2004: stays 21f: acts on heavy going: held up. *N. Waggott* **c– h–**

FREE 10 ch.g. Gone West (USA) – Bemissed (USA) (Nijinsky (CAN)) [2004/5 c24d^pu May 11] leggy, sparely-made gelding: winning hurdler/chaser: fairly useful pointer **c– § h– §**

nowadays, won twice in 2004: stays 3¼m: acts on firm and good to soft going: has worn headgear: moody. *P. Hutchinson*

FREEDOM FIGHTER 14 b.g. Fearless Action (USA) – Zuleika Hill (Yellow River) [2004/5 c90§: c26s^{3} c25v* c24s^{3} c24s^{pu} Mar 27] sturdy gelding: fair hunter chaser: won 4-runner event at Towcester in May: best at 3m+: acts on heavy and good to firm going: unreliable. *Mrs Rosemary Gasson* **c89 §**

FREEDOM NOW (IRE) 7 b.g. Sadler's Wells (USA) – Free At Last (Shirley Heights) [2004/5 h89: 20d^{2} 17m* 21m* 20g* 24m* 21d 16d^{4} 22g^{4} Apr 10] close-coupled gelding: fair hurdler: won novices at Sedgefield (2) in August and Hexham in September and October for M. Hammond: trained next outing only by C. Tizzard: effective at 2m to 3m: acts on good to firm and good to soft going. *R. H. Alner* **h105**

FREE GIFT 7 b.g. Presenting – Gladtogetit (Green Shoon) [2004/5 c21m* c25s^{2} c26g Mar 18] lengthy gelding: successful all 7 starts in points, including in well-contested event in January: also made winning hunter chase debut in novice at Folkestone in May: better form when second to Paddy For Paddy at same course: made a few mistakes when well held in Foxhunter at Cheltenham: stays 25f. *Mrs S. Alner* **c110**

FREELINE FURY 5 b.g. Sir Harry Lewis (USA) – Queen's Favourite (Sunyboy) [2004/5 F18s^{5} F16s^{3} Mar 31] 18,000 4-y-o: fifth foal: dam no sign of ability: better effort in bumpers when third of 7 at Ludlow. *P. R. Webber* **F86**

FREE STRIKE (NZ) 8 ch.g. Straight Strike (USA) – Ansellia (NZ) (Nassipour (USA)) [2004/5 h93?: c16m^{4} c20m^{4} Jun 8] leggy, plain gelding: modest form at best in novice hurdles: poor form in 2 novice chases. *P. Mitchell* **c82 h–**

FREE TO RUN (IRE) 11 b.g. Satco (FR) – Lady Oats (Oats) [2004/5 c103, h–: c28g^{pu} c25m^{3} c25d^{3} c25s^{pu} c24d^{5} c28s^{2} c28s^{6} c25g^{6} c27v^{5} c30s^{pu} c23v^{5} c28g^{5} Mar 26] workmanlike gelding: fair handicap chaser: stays 3½m: acts on firm and soft going: often races prominently: unreliable. *Mrs S. J. Smith* **c103 d h–**

FREETOWN (IRE) 9 b.g. Shirley Heights – Pageantry (Welsh Pageant) [2004/5 c–, h114: 20v^{5} c25v* c32v^{F} Mar 5] tall, leggy gelding: handicap hurdler: best effort since 2001/2 when fifth of 7 finishers at Haydock on reappearance: third outing over fences and heavily backed, won handicap at Wetherby (cheekpieces) in January by 1¾ lengths from Jungle Jinks, having jumped far from fluently and got behind: well beaten when falling last in quite valuable handicap at Kelso: suited by 3m+: acts on heavy going, ran poorly only outing on firmer than good. *L. Lungo* **c128 h128 +**

FREE WILL 8 ch.g. Indian Ridge – Free Guest (Be My Guest (USA)) [2004/5 16m^{4} 17g^{5} 17d^{ur} 17m^{4} Aug 6] rather leggy gelding: no show only outing over fences: poor maiden hurdler: bought 1,000 gns Doncaster January (2004) Sales: best at 2m: acts on good to firm and good to soft going. *R. C. Guest* **c– h79 +**

FRENCH ACCORDION (IRE) 5 b.g. Accordion – Royal Thimble (IRE) (Prince Rupert (FR)) [2004/5 16v^{4} 16v^{4} 20d 16s^{5} Mar 29] good-topped gelding: has scope: third foal: brother to high-class 2m hurdler Accordion Etoile: dam fair 2m hurdler: fair form over hurdles: best effort when fifth to Justified in Grade 2 novice at Fairyhouse: possibly doesn't stay 2½m. *Paul Nolan, Ireland* **h112**

FRENCH BEY (IRE) 5 b.m. Beyssac (FR) – Cerise de Totes (FR) (Champ Libre (FR)) [2004/5 20v^{pu} 16d 16g 23s^{pu} Mar 22] fifth foal: half-sister to winning hurdler/chaser Hussard (by Concorde Jr), stays 3m, and winning cross-country chaser Isidora Bleue (by Fill My Hopes), stays 2¾m: dam unraced: no form over hurdles. *N. J. Pomfret* **h–**

FRENCH CAT (USA) 7 b. or br.g. Storm Cat (USA) – Shannkara (IRE) (Akarad (FR)) [2004/5 17d^{ur} Aug 22] half-brother to fair 2m hurdler Swan Knight (by Sadler's Wells): of little account on Flat: unseated first in seller on hurdling debut. *P. R. Johnson* **h–**

FRENCH CEDAR 9 b.g. Jupiter Island – Another Rumour (The Parson) [2004/5 20v^{pu} 22v c24d^{4} c25d^{pu} Apr 11] big, well-made ex-Irish gelding: maiden hurdler: modest chaser: won maiden at Down Royal in 2003: stays 3m: acts on firm ground: tried tongue tied. *P. Monteith* **c– h–**

FRENCH DIRECTION (IRE) 6 ch.g. John French – Shelikesitstraight (IRE) (Rising) [2004/5 h74: 19d^{pu} 19g 16d^{6} c16g^{6} c18s^{F} Jan 24] poor form over hurdles, makes mistakes: well beaten on completed start in chases. *R. Rowe* **c– h80 x**

FRENCH EXECUTIVE (IRE) 10 br.g. Beau Sher – Executive Move (IRE) (Executive Perk) [2004/5 c113§, h–§: c28g^{6} c26g* c29d* c31d^{2} c31d^{6} c25m Apr 13] lengthy, **c127 § h– §**

angular gelding: fairly useful handicap chaser: won at Plumpton (has good record there) in October and November, beating Dads Lad by 4 lengths in quite valuable event on second occasion: good second to Spot Thedifference in cross-country event at Cheltenham, hanging left under pressure: stays 31f: acts on any going: tried blinkered: has had tongue tied: often let down by jumping/looks none too keen: unreliable. *P. F. Nicholls*

FRENCHGATE 4 br.g. Paris House – Let's Hang On (IRE) (Petorius) [2004/5 F13d[5] F13g Jan 17] third foal: dam, poor maiden hurdler, half-sister to useful staying hurdler Aahsaylad: poor form on first of 2 starts in 13f bumpers at Doncaster. *M. E. Sowersby* **F75**

FRENCH MANNEQUIN (IRE) 6 gr.m. Key of Luck (USA) – Paris Model (IRE) (Thatching) [2004/5 h97: 16g[5] c16m[6] 16m 17g[pu] 16d[rtr] Feb 9] angular mare: modest on Flat, successful in February/March: modest handicap hurdler: refused to race final outing: showed little on chasing debut: best around 2m: acts on soft and firm going: tried blinkered: temperamental. *Mrs A. J. Hamilton-Fairley* **c– § h91 §**

FRENCHMAN'S CREEK 11 b.g. Emperor Fountain – Hollow Creek (Tarqogan) [2004/5 c23d[3] c26g[pu] c25d[3] c26d[4] c24g c36d[ur] Apr 9] big, useful-looking gelding: smart handicap chaser in 2001/2, reportedly sprained tendon final start: useful form at best after 2½-year absence, running moodily last 3 completed outings: probably stays 29f: acts on good to firm and heavy going: tried in cheekpieces: usually sound jumper (unseated first in Grand National): one to treat with caution. *H. Morrison* **c139 § h–**

FRENCH TUNE (FR) 7 ch.g. Green Tune (USA) – Guerre de Troie (Risk Me (FR)) [2004/5 h91: 20s 20d[6] Mar 26] good-bodied gelding: lightly-raced maiden hurdler, modest form at best. *Miss S. E. Hall* **h–**

FRENCH VENTURE 8 b.g. Saddlers' Hall (IRE) – Tafila (Adonijah) [2004/5 19m[pu] Dec 1] tall gelding: sixth foal: brother to fairly useful stayer Quitte Le France, closely related to fair 1¼m winner Include Me Out (by Old Vic) and half-brother to 3 other Flat winners: dam, useful 1m and 1¼m winner, half-sister to useful 2m to 2½m chaser Bright November and Poule d'Essai des Poulains third Tay Wharf: runner-up in maiden on completed start in points in 2004: showed nothing in novice hurdle. *J. J. Quinn* **h–**

FRENTZEN 8 b.g. Golden Heights – Milly Black (IRE) (Double Schwartz) [2004/5 c82, h77: c23m[4] c23g[3] c23m[2] c24g[pu] c23f* c25m* c26m[4] Sep 19] workmanlike gelding: maiden hurdler: fair handicap chaser: won at Worcester and Hereford (novice) within 4 days in September: stays 27f: acts on firm going: ran poorly in cheekpieces fourth start: has had tongue tied: has looked unwilling. *Miss E. C. Lavelle* **c102 h–**

FREYDIS (IRE) 7 b.m. Supreme Leader – Lulu Buck (Buckskin (FR)) [2004/5 F75: 24d[2] 24g[2] 25d* 21s[pu] 24d[6] 21m[pu] Apr 2] tall, lengthy mare: type to make a chaser: modest form in novice hurdles: won at Warwick in November: best at 3m+: acts on good to soft going: wore cheekpieces final outing. *S. Gollings* **h86**

FRIEDHELMO (GER) 9 ch.g. Dashing Blade – Fox For Gold (Glint of Gold) [2004/5 c–, h112: 16g 17g 16g 17d* 17d[4] c16g c16g[6] 17g[6] c20g[pu] 16m 16g 16s[pu] Apr 20] strong, lengthy gelding: winning chaser, usually let down by jumping: fair handicap hurdler on his day: won at Southwell in August: best around 2m: acts on soft and good to firm going: often tongue tied: unreliable. *P. D. Niven* **c88 § h111 §**

FRIENDLY FELLOW 6 gr.g. Environment Friend – Good Fetch (Siberian Express (USA)) [2004/5 h87, F87: 21g* 21d 20d[4] 16m 20d[4] 16d Nov 1] rangy gelding: poor hurdler: easily won weak seller (sold from M. Pipe 9,200 gns) at Towcester very early in season: left M. Harris prior to well beaten at Munich and Warwick last 2 starts: stays 2¾m: acts on soft going, bumper form on good to firm. *C. Von Der Recke, Germany* **h84**

FRIENDLY GIRL (IRE) 6 b.m. King's Ride – Royal Patrol (IRE) (Phardante (FR)) [2004/5 F17d[5] F18s[6] 19s[pu] 20m[pu] Apr 10] 3,500 4-y-o: second foal: half-sister to bumper winner Bubba Boy (by Anshan): dam lightly raced, out of half-sister to useful staying chaser Shuil Donn and useful chaser up to 3m Shuilaris: little sign of ability. *N. J. Hawke* **h– F83 ?**

FRIENDLY REQUEST 6 b.m. Environment Friend – Who Tells Jan (Royal Fountain) [2004/5 h–: 17m 20d* 20g[3] Jul 6] poor hurdler: first form when winning novice handicap at Worcester in June: should stay beyond 2½m. *N. J. Hawke* **h77**

FRIEND'S AMIGO (IRE) 8 b.g. Accordion – Lady Sipash (Erin's Hope) [2004/5 c107p, h121: 20s[3] c22s* c22d[4] c20s[6] c20v[2] c20s[ur] Feb 20] big, well-made gelding: fairly useful hurdler: creditable third to Khetaam in minor event at Tipperary on reappearance: fair form over fences: won maiden at Cork (idled) in November: stays 2¾m: acts on heavy and good to firm going: wore cheekpieces/blinkers 4 starts prior to final one: not a fluent jumper of fences. *P. M. J. Doyle, Ireland* **c108 h125**

FRIXOS (IRE) 5 ch.g. Barathea (IRE) – Local Lass (Local Suitor (USA)) [2004/5 h75§: $16d^{pu}$ $22g^{pu}$ Aug 15] good-topped gelding: maiden hurdler: tried blinkered: ungenuine. *M. Scudamore* **h– §**

FROMRAGSTORICHES (IRE) 9 b.g. Supreme Leader – Family Birthday (Sandalay) [2004/5 h102: $23d^{ur}$ $24g^{2}$ $25m^{pu}$ May 27] good-topped gelding: lightly raced: fair novice hurdler: stays 3m: acts on good to soft going. *Mrs S. J. Smith* **h102**

FRONTENAC (IRE) 9 ch.g. Mister Lord (USA) – Daffydown Dolly (IRE) (The Parson) [2004/5 c24m $c24g^{6}$ $c26v^{F}$ Apr 22] ex-Irish gelding: no form in hunter chases: sold out of Miss M. Hallahan's stable 4,500 gns (privately) Doncaster August Sales after first outing: successful twice in points in 2005. *Mrs Mandy Hand* **c–**

FRONTIER 8 b.g. Indian Ridge – Adatiya (IRE) (Shardari) [2004/5 h105: $17g^{2}$ 17g* 17g* 16g $16d^{3}$ 16g Nov 28] medium-sized gelding: fairly useful on Flat (stays 11.6f), won in June: fair hurdler: won maiden at Newton Abbot (easily) in July and handicap at Bangor in October: likely to prove best around 2m: raced on good going or softer over hurdles: tongue tied. *B. J. Llewellyn* **h113**

FRONT RANK (IRE) 5 b.h. Sadler's Wells (USA) – Alignment (IRE) (Alzao (USA)) [2004/5 h92p: $16d^{3}$ $16d^{2}$ $22s^{2}$ $16v^{3}$ 20g 20d 20g Mar 26] sturdy horse: fair maiden hurdler: well held in handicaps last 3 starts: stays 2¾m: raced on good going or softer (acts on heavy): tried blinkered/in cheekpieces. *K. C. Bailey* **h106**

FROSTY RUN (IRE) 7 b.g. Commanche Run – Here To-Day (King's Equity) [2004/5 h80, F86: $24m^{pu}$ 26m* Aug 30] sturdy gelding: much improved over hurdles when winning handicap at Huntingdon in August: stays 3¼m: acts on good to firm going. *Mrs H. Dalton* **h104**

FROSTY'S COUSIN (IRE) 6 b.g. Arctic Lord – Farojina (IRE) (Farhaan) [2004/5 $F16s^{6}$ $F16s^{4}$ $20v^{6}$ $24d^{5}$ 24d Mar 5] 15,000 4-y-o: big, workmanlike gelding: fifth foal: half-brother to winning pointer by Aristocracy: dam unraced: modest form in 2 bumpers: form over hurdles only when fifth of 6 finishers in steadily-run novice at Kempton. *P. R. Webber* **h91 ?** **F77**

FRUIT DEFENDU (FR) 8 b.g. Exit To Nowhere (USA) – Pauvresse (FR) (Home Guard (USA)) [2004/5 h89§: $19g^{2}$ $20d^{4}$ May 15] good-topped gelding: modest hurdler: runner-up on last of 3 starts in points in 2005: stays 19f: acts on heavy going: usually blinkered and tongue tied: ungenuine. *P. F. Nicholls* **h89 §**

FU FIGHTER 4 b.g. Unfuwain (USA) – Runelia (Runnett) [2004/5 $16f^{5}$ 16d 16d $16d^{6}$ Jan 6] sturdy gelding: fair maiden on Flat (stays 1¾m), claimed from J. Osborne £9,000 in September: poor form over hurdles: will be suited by further than 2m: joined E. Williams. *C. L. Popham* **h77 +**

FULGERE (IRE) 7 b.g. Old Vic – Moppet's Last (Pitpan) [2004/5 h–p, F70: $c19s^{pu}$ Dec 4] signs of ability in bumper and novice hurdle: raced freely and jumped poorly on chasing debut: will stay beyond 2½m. *K. C. Bailey* **c–** **h–**

FULLARDS 7 b.g. Alderbrook – Milly Kelly (Murrayfield) [2004/5 h102: $c21s^{3}$ 24s* $c24v^{2}$ $c22s^{pu}$ $25s^{5}$ $c24s^{2}$ $c24g^{5}$ Mar 18] sturdy gelding: fair handicap hurdler: improved form when winning at Uttoxeter in November: similar form over fences, though has been let down by jumping: stays 3¼m: raced on good going or softer (acts on heavy). *Mrs P. Sly* **c110** **h108**

FULL AS A ROCKET (IRE) 4 b.g. Foxhound (USA) – Taysala (IRE) (Akarad (FR)) [2004/5 F14g $F13g^{2}$ $F16s^{3}$ Feb 5] useful-looking gelding: half-brother to 1m to 2m winner Tiyoun (by Kahyasi) and 2004 2-y-o 7f/1m winner Chavela (by Second Empire): dam unraced, out of half-sister to Princess Royal Stakes winner Tashtiya and smart 1m to 1¼m performer Tassmoun: best effort in bumpers when neck second to Giovanna at Doncaster: well held on Flat debut in March. *D. Nicholls* **F100**

FULL EGALITE 9 gr.g. Ezzoud (IRE) – Milva (Jellaby) [2004/5 $16g^{6}$ May 9] no form over hurdles: has looked temperamental in points: blinkered. *B. R. Johnson* **h–**

FULL HOUSE (IRE) 6 br.g. King's Theatre (IRE) – Nirvavita (FR) (Highest Honor (FR)) [2004/5 h109: $c17g^{F}$ c20m* $c17m^{ur}$ $c16g^{3}$ $c20m^{pu}$ $c21g^{3}$ $c19m^{F}$ c20g* Apr 22] leggy gelding: fair hurdler: better over fences, winning maiden at Stratford (made all) in June and novice handicap at Sandown (improved form when beating Indien Royal 5 lengths) in April: would also have won novice at Hereford but for falling last: stays 21f: raced mainly on good/good to firm going. *P. R. Webber* **c125** **h–**

FULL IRISH (IRE) 9 ch.g. Rashar (USA) – Ross Gale (Strong Gale) [2004/5 c131, h–: c16d* 16d $20s^{6}$ $16v^{4}$ c16g* Apr 16] sturdy gelding: fairly useful handicap hurdler: **c142 +** **h123**

useful chaser: won intermediate at Perth in May and quite valuable handicap at Ayr (better than ever when beating Bleu Superbe 3 lengths) in April: effective at 2m to 21f: raced on good going or softer (acts on heavy). *L. Lungo*

FULL ON 8 b.g. Le Moss – Flighty Dove (Cruise Missile) [2004/5 c100, h81: c19d6 c20s2 c20gF c23s2 c24g4 Jan 14] useful-looking gelding: maiden hurdler: fair novice chaser: ran creditably when runner-up in 2004/5: stays 23f: raced on good going or softer: sold 13,000 gns Doncaster May Sales. *A. M. Hales* **c101 h–**

FULLOPEP 11 b.g. Dunbeath (USA) – Suggia (Alzao (USA)) [2004/5 c91, h–: c21dpu 24mpu Apr 10] sturdy gelding: winning hurdler/chaser: no show in hunter or handicap hurdle in 2004/5: stays 3m: acts on good to firm and good to soft going. *J. R. Holt* **c– h–**

FULL TIME (IRE) 6 b.g. Bigstone (IRE) – Oiche Mhaith (Night Shift (USA)) [2004/5 h–: 17d Aug 22] well held over hurdles. *N. Waggott* **h–**

FULWELL HILL 7 b.m. Anshan – Finkin (Fine Blue) [2004/5 F73: 19spu 24vpu 17d c20mpu c23dpu Apr 20] lengthy mare: poor form in 2 bumpers in 2003: off 19 months, no form over hurdles or fences: tongue tied final start. *Ian Williams* **c– h–**

FUNDAMENTAL 6 ch.g. Rudimentary (USA) – I'll Try (Try My Best (USA)) [2004/5 h124: 19v4 16g6 Nov 28] fairly useful handicap hurdler: better effort in 2004/5 when sixth to Green Tango at Newbury: stays 2½m: acts on soft and good to firm going: makes running. *Jonjo O'Neill* **h114 +**

FUNDAMENTALIST (IRE) 7 b.g. Supreme Leader – Run For Shelter (Strong Gale) [2004/5 h147p: c20g* c16d* c20g2 c21dur Jan 1] **c154 p h–**

And then there were none. At the turn of the year, trainer Nigel Twiston-Davies looked to have three novice chasers capable of making a major impact in some of the top races in March and April, but injuries to Baron Windrush, Fundamentalist and Ollie Magern put paid to their seasons before then. Fundamentalist, the most exciting prospect in the Twiston-Davies yard, was the first casualty.

Albion Drilling Services Ltd Novices' Chase, Perth—
little more than a schooling round for 7/1-on shot Fundamentalist

Thought to have had sore shins when failing to complete the course at Cheltenham on New Year's Day, Fundamentalist was back in work when a tendon problem was discovered later in January, the prognosis twelve months on the sidelines. Twiston-Davies, who won a Welsh National and a Grand National with Earth Summit after an absence of twenty-one months with a serious injury, expects Fundamentalist to make a full recovery. It is very much to be hoped that he does so, as he has the potential to go right to the top over fences.

The well-made Fundamentalist, a winner of three points in Ireland before joining his present stable, always looked the sort to make a chaser and connections probably regarded the success he achieved when sent hurdling in 2003/4 as a bonus. Some bonus. Fundamentalist won two of his three starts, notably the Royal & SunAlliance Novices' Hurdle at Cheltenham in which he beat Inglis Drever by half a length. A more low-key venue was chosen for Fundamentalist's first appearance over fences. Perth in September staged a novice event which offered Fundamentalist just about the perfect introduction to chasing, and he made short work of four decidedly ordinary opponents, whilst gaining valuable experience, jumping adequately though tending to go to the left. His next race was also a five-runner novice chase at Cheltenham, one which provided a far sterner test, seemingly likely to be all the more demanding as it was to be over two miles, Fundamentalist not having previously raced short of two and a half. The Grade 2 November Novices' Chase, sponsored by Independent Newspapers, numbered Azertyuiop and Best Mate among its recent winners, and Fundamentalist, who started second favourite, wasn't the only one in the field with the potential to become one of the season's

Independent Newspapers November Novices' Chase, Cheltenham—
shades of Best Mate and Azertyuiop as he successfully concedes weight to Contraband (left) and My Will

leading novices. The favourite was My Will, impressive winner of his two completed starts over fences, while next in the betting came useful hurdler Contraband, who had shaped well when second on his only previous start over fences. Both were receiving weight from him, but neither troubled Fundamentalist who, in winning by eight lengths and the same from Contraband and My Will, created as good an impression in the race as Azertyuiop and Best Mate had done. The drop in trip posed no problems for Fundamentalist, who took a good hold, led from before the fifth and galloped on strongly. Apart from a slight error three out his jumping was good. Such was the impression created that Fundamentalist was quoted at 11/1 for the King George and 16/1 for the Cheltenham Gold Cup afterwards, as well as being promoted to favouritism for both the Arkle and the SunAlliance Chase, in the latter dislodging Iris's Gift.

At Newbury thirteen days later, up against Vodka Bleu and See You Sometime in another Grade 2 event, Fundamentalist started at 3/1-on to complete his hat-trick, and almost certainly would have done had his rider allowed him to stride on after taking up the running at the ninth. Although Fundamentalist was still on the bridle, his advantage remained a narrow one, and he handed the race to Vodka Bleu when going markedly out to the left at the last, failing by half a length to regain the initiative, also having to be switched right late on the run-in. In a muddling race (two lengths covered the three runners at the line) rider Carl Llewellyn blamed himself for the defeat, calling it 'pilot error'. New Year's Day was Fundamentalist's only subsequent appearance. Once again he was sent off at odds on, but his jumping had already given cause for concern before he blundered and unseated his rider at the tenth. It came as no surprise to learn that he was found to be lame afterwards. The race was won by My Will. Fundamentalist's performance in the November Novices' was as good as any produced by a novice in 2004/5. The Arkle Trophy, the intended target for Fundamentalist at the Cheltenham Festival, was won by Contraband. At the time of his injury Fundamentalist featured in ante-post lists for races as diverse as the Victor Chandler, the Champion Chase and the Cheltenham Gold Cup. He was also quoted a 10/1-chance for the Daily Telegraph Trophy. A season that was a case of what might have been.

Fundamentalist (IRE) (b.g. 1998)	Supreme Leader (b 1982)	Bustino (b 1971)	Busted
			Ship Yard
		Princess Zena (b 1975)	Habitat
			Guiding Light
	Run For Shelter (b 1983)	Strong Gale (br 1975)	Lord Gayle
			Sterntau
		Falcade (b 1971)	Falcon
			Perpelia

Fundamentalist's pedigree was dealt with in depth in *Chasers & Hurdlers 2003/04*, and all that requires repeating here is that he is out of a maiden half-sister to the outstanding two-mile chaser Badsworth Boy and is a half-brother to three winning chasers, the fairly useful Wilde Music (by Orchestra), who stayed twenty-three furlongs, and temperamental La Brigantine (by Montelimar) and Run For Cover (by Lafontaine), both fair winners at around two miles. Fundamentalist's year-younger half-brother Joe McHugh (by Topanoora) won his final start in maiden points in March and was sold to join Charlie Mann's stable for 25,000 guineas at Doncaster in May. An Accordion four-year-old half-brother fetched €19,000 at the Goffs Land Rover Sale in June. Fundamentalist is versatile as regards distance, effective at two miles to three miles. He has raced only on good and good to soft ground. *N. A. Twiston-Davies*

FUNNY TIMES 4 b.f. Silver Patriarch (IRE) – Elegant City (Scallywag) [2004/5 F14s^2 F16s* F16d* F17s^5 Apr 7] workmanlike filly: first foal: dam, 2m hurdle winner, sister to smart staying jumper Better Times Ahead: fairly useful form in bumpers: won mares events at Newcastle in January and Sandown in March, beating Heltornic by 7 lengths in listed race at latter: favourite, only respectable fifth to Senorita Rumbalita in listed mares event at Aintree: will stay beyond 2m. *N. G. Richards* **F104**

FUSION OF TUNES 7 b.m. Mr Confusion (IRE) – Daleria (Darshaan) [2004/5 h–, F70: 20d 20m^2 20g^5 24m^{pu} 21g^4 20d Nov 13] poor form over hurdles. *Mrs K. Walton* **h70**

G

GABLA (NZ) 9 b.g. Prince of Praise (NZ) – Dynataine (NZ) (Centaine (AUS)) [2004/5 c–, h97: 21m^{ur} c16g* c20d^5 c16f^F c16m^4 c17g^3 c16g^6 c16d^3 c16d^4 c16d^6 c16d^{ur} Jan 13] leggy gelding: modest hurdler: fair chaser: won handicap at Hexham in May: generally out of form subsequently: raced mainly around 2m: acts on good to firm going, probably on firm: wears headgear. *R. C. Guest* **c100 h–**

GABOR 6 b.g. Danzig Connection (USA) – Kiomi (Niniski (USA)) [2004/5 h109: 16m^{pu} 16g* c17m^4 c16g^2 c20m^6 c20m^2 c17g^F Oct 4] good-topped gelding: didn't have to be near best to win claiming hurdle at Plumpton in May: modest form at best over fences, not impressing with jumping or attitude: probably stays 2½m: acts on good to firm going: tried in eyeshields/blinkers: temperamental. *G. L. Moore* **c93 § h80 §**

GADZ'ART (FR) 11 b.g. Art Bleu – Naftane (FR) (Trac) [2004/5 25s^{pu} c20g^5 c22d^5 c20s* Mar 11] workmanlike gelding: winning hurdler: left R. Phillips after reappearance: fairly useful hunter chaser nowadays: won 5-runner event at Leicester in March by ½ length from Red Guard: stays 25f: raced on good going or softer (acts on heavy): has worn blinkers: tried tongue tied. *Shaun Lycett* **c102 h–**

GAEILGEOIR (IRE) 8 b.g. Erins Isle – Amparo (IRE) (Taufan (USA)) [2004/5 23d^{pu} Apr 25] IR £1,400 4-y-o: workmanlike gelding: third living foal: half-brother to 1½m winner/19f hurdle winner Arts Project (by Project Manager): dam, Irish 2-y-o 5f/6f winner, out of half-sister to dam of top-class sprinter Lake Coniston and useful 2m hurdler Newlands Gold: won maiden Irish point on debut in 2002: sold €8,500 Goffs February (2003) Sale: soon struggling in maiden on hurdling debut. *Mrs P. Sly* **h–**

GAELIC FLIGHT (IRE) 7 b. or br.g. Norwich – Ash Dame (IRE) (Strong Gale) [2004/5 F100: 17m* 16g^4 16d^3 16m^4 18g^3 17m^{pu} Apr 9] rangy gelding: bumper winner: fair novice hurdler: won at Hereford in May: should stay at least 2½m: acts on good to firm and good to soft going: often makes mistakes. *Noel T. Chance* **h99 x**

GAELIC JIG 6 ch.g. Dancing High – Gaelic Charm (IRE) (Deep Run) [2004/5 F16d F17m^5 Apr 23] workmanlike gelding: second foal: dam lightly-raced novice hurdler: tongue tied, poor form on second of 2 outings in bumpers. *J. I. A. Charlton* **F74**

GAELIC MUSIC (IRE) 6 b.g. Accordion – Cuilin Bui (IRE) (Kemal (FR)) [2004/5 F92: 19d^{pu} 24d^2 24g^3 24g Mar 18] sturdy, workmanlike gelding: chasing type: won bumper on debut: easily best effort in novice hurdles when 2½ lengths second to Blue Business at Taunton in February: let down by jumping there next time: stiff task in Grade 2 at Cheltenham final start: stays 3m. *M. Bradstock* **h120**

GAELIC PARK (IRE) 5 b.g. Erins Isle – American Mint (USA) (Key To The Mint (USA)) [2004/5 16m^{ur} 17m^{pu} Sep 28] fair maiden at 2 yrs, left J. Bolger after well beaten only start in 2003: unseated first on hurdling debut: fatally injured next time. *Noel T. Chance* **h–**

GAETANO (IRE) 10 ch.g. Executive Perk – Bright News (Buckskin (FR)) [2004/5 20g^{pu} Aug 14] won maiden Irish point in 2001, no sign of ability otherwise. *Mrs H. Dalton* **h–**

GAIAC (FR) 11 b.g. Passing Sale (FR) – Ustitine (FR) (Moshi (GER)) [2004/5 c21d c20s^5 Feb 11] fairly useful hurdler/useful chaser at one time: left S. Kalley after reappearance: fair form in points in Britain in 2005, let down by jumping in hunter chase at Bangor: stays 2¾m: acts on heavy ground: usually blinkered. *Ms Nicky Hugo* **c94 h–**

GAINING GROUND (IRE) 5 ch.g. Presenting – Lorglane Lady (IRE) (Lancastrian) [2004/5 F16d F17d^6 Nov 2] first foal: dam ran once: tailed off in 2 bumpers. *John R. Upson* **F–**

GALA FESTIVAL (IRE) 6 b.m. Supreme Leader – Noon Performance (Strong Gale) [2004/5 F72: 22g^6 May 7] tall mare: poor form in bumpers: sixth of 9 finishers in steadily-run novice at Wincanton on hurdling debut. *Mrs P. N. Dutfield* **h74 ?**

GALANT EYE (IRE) 6 ch.g. Eagle Eyed (USA) – Galandria (Sharpo) [2004/5 h91: 20m Jun 27] compact gelding: modest hurdler: well held in handicap at Uttoxeter only start in 2004/5: stays 19f: acts on good to firm and good to soft going. *A. E. Jones* **h–**

GALAPIAT DU MESNIL (FR) 11 b.g. Sarpedon (FR) – Polka de Montrin (FR) (Danoso) [2004/5 c94, h–: c31d^{pu} c24g^2 c26s^2 Apr 21] leggy, angular gelding: formerly useful chaser: best effort since 2002 when second to Sir d'Orton in hunter at Taunton **c113 h–**

second start: stays 31f: acts on good to firm and heavy going: usually races prominently. *P. F. Nicholls*

GALA QUEEN 5 gr.m. Accondy (IRE) – Miss Jedd (Scallywag) [2004/5 F16s F16m Nov 26] good-bodied mare: first foal: dam, poor winning hurdler, stayed 2½m: tailed off in bumpers. *W. G. Young* **F–**

GALAXY SAM (USA) 6 ch.g. Royal Academy (USA) – Istiska (FR) (Irish River (FR)) [2004/5 h96: c24g^F c21s 21d^F 22d 22v^pu Mar 30] tall gelding: winning hurdler: still to be asked for effort when falling 3 out in novice at Huntingdon on chasing debut: also let down by jumping after, including back over hurdles: will stay beyond 3m: raced on good going or softer (acts on soft). *N. J. Gifford* **c107 ? h–**

GALEN (IRE) 14 br.g. Roselier (FR) – Gaye Le Moss (Le Moss) [2004/5 c64, h–: c26g^pu May 23] compact gelding: veteran chaser: stays 3¾m: acts on heavy and good to firm going: blinkered earlier in career: difficult ride. *Mrs S. J. Smith* **c– h–**

GALERO 6 b.g. Overbury (IRE) – Rare Luck (Rare One) [2004/5 16d 19d* 20g* Feb 16] 21,000 3-y-o: useful-looking gelding: fourth foal: half-brother to fair hurdler/fairly useful chaser Muck Savage (by Homo Sapien), stays 3m, and modest chaser Four Mile Clump (by Petoski), stays 3¼m: dam, modest chaser, suited by test of stamina: won maiden Irish point on debut in 2004: successful on 2 of 3 starts over hurdles, in novices at Catterick in January and Musselburgh in February, beating Another Deckie by neck in handicap event at latter: will stay beyond 2½m: capable of further improvement. *J. Howard Johnson* **h109 p**

GALE STAR (IRE) 12 b.g. Strong Gale – Fairly Deep (Deep Run) [2004/5 c20g 24f^5 20f^3 24f^5 c22f^3 c20f* c25m^2 c25d^2 c24s^pu Nov 21] ex-Irish gelding: modest hurdler: poor handicap chaser: won conditional jockeys event at Wexford in July: sold out of D. Hughes' stable 4,000 gns Doncaster October Sales: pulled up on British debut: stays 25f: probably acts on any going: has worn blinkers: tongue tied. *O. Brennan* **c81 h87**

GALEY RIVER (USA) 6 ch.g. Irish River (FR) – Carefree Kate (USA) (Lyphard (USA)) [2004/5 h81: 16g^2 16m* 16g* 19g 16s^3 21d^2 Jan 26] leggy gelding: modest on Flat (stays 1¾m): fair hurdler: won maiden at Huntingdon in August and handicap at Stratford in September: stays 21f: acts on soft and good to firm going. *J. J. Sheehan* **h111**

GALILEO (POL) 9 b.g. Jape (USA) – Goldika (POL) (Dakota) [2004/5 h134§: c24d^F c24m* c23d^3 Jun 23] workmanlike gelding: smart hurdler at best, won Royal & SunAlliance Hurdle in 2001/2: modest form at best in 3 chases: won novice at Perth in June: would have stayed beyond 3m: best run on soft ground: tried visored, blinkered 4 of last 5 starts: became hard ride: reportedly retired. *T. R. George* **c97 § h– §**

GALLANT APPROACH (IRE) 6 ch.g. Roselier (FR) – Nicks Approach (IRE) (Dry Dock) [2004/5 16d^5 Feb 17] rangy gelding: first foal: dam unraced half-sister to Whitbread Gold Cup winner Harwell Lad: won second of 2 starts in Irish points in 2004: some promise when fifth of 7 to Sea Captain in novice at Sandown on hurdling debut: will be suited by much further than 2m: will improve. *C. R. Egerton* **h105 p**

GALLANT HERO 6 b.g. Rainbow Quest (USA) – Gay Gallanta (USA) (Woodman (USA)) [2004/5 h105: 17d^3 16g^ur May 20] smallish gelding: fair form at best over hurdles: let down by jumping both starts in 2004/5: raced around 2m: best effort on good to firm going. *P. J. Hobbs* **h96**

GALLEON BEACH 8 b.g. Shirley Heights – Music In My Life (IRE) (Law Society (USA)) [2004/5 20g^4 Oct 9] successful up to 2¼m on Flat, lightly raced nowadays: second start over hurdles, modest form when fourth in novice at Bangor: visored and tongue tied on debut. *B. D. Leavy* **h93**

GALLERY GOD (FR) 9 ch.g. In The Wings – El Fabulous (FR) (Fabulous Dancer (USA)) [2004/5 16m^2 18s* 20s* 20d^5 22s* 22g^3 Feb 5] good-topped gelding: useful at one time on Flat: similar standard over hurdles, making all in novices at Fontwell in October, November and December: best effort when beating Rotheram by 15 lengths for final success: creditable third to Supreme Serenade in valuable handicap at Sandown, racing close up in strongly-run event: will stay 3m: front runner: reportedly cracked cannonbone in March. *S. Dow* **h130**

GALLIK DAWN 7 ch.g. Anshan – Sticky Money (Relkino) [2004/5 h72, F–: c21d^4 c21g^2 c22g* c23d^pu c24g c24d^2 c24d^pu c33g^F c25m^2 Apr 9] sturdy gelding: poor maiden hurdler: fair novice chaser: won weak maiden at Uttoxeter in May: stays 25f: acts on good to firm and good to soft going. *A. Hollingsworth* **c101 h–**

GALLION'S REACH (IRE) 10 b.g. Good Thyne (USA) – Raise Our Hopes (IRE) (Salluceva) [2004/5 c33spu c25m* Jun 9] workmanlike gelding: poor chaser: left Mrs S. Leech, made all in handicap at Hereford in June: stays 25f: acts on good to firm and heavy going: tried blinkered, including at Hereford: usually tongue tied: makes mistakes over fences. *Ian Williams* **c81 x** **h–**

GALLIUM 8 gr.m. Terimon – Genie Spirit (Nishapour (FR)) [2004/5 c–, h–: 16mpu Jun 16] of no account. *M. Scudamore* **c–** **h–**

GALLOP RHYTHM (IRE) 9 ch.g. Mister Lord (USA) – Kiltannon (Dalsaan) [2004/5 c19dpu Oct 2] big, angular gelding: little form over hurdles: no show in 2 novice chases. *R. H. Alner* **c–** **h–**

GALLOWGATE (IRE) 5 b.g. Nucleon (USA) – Duky Lady (IRE) (Corrouge (USA)) [2004/5 F17m Jun 25] first foal: dam unraced, out of sister to smart staying chaser Handy Trick: no show in bumper on debut. *P. D. Niven* **F–**

GALTEE VIEW (IRE) 7 b.g. Namaqualand (USA) – Miss Dolly (IRE) (Alzao (USA)) [2004/5 h99, F92: 16f* 16f* 16g2 20m2 16g5 16vF 19v c16s c17s c16s c20s Mar 6] useful-looking gelding: fair handicap hurdler: won at Limerick in May and Ballinrobe in June: no form over fences: effective at 2m to 3m: acts on firm ground: tried in cheekpieces: has had tongue tied. *C. Roche, Ireland* **c–** **h108**

GALWAY BREEZE (IRE) 10 b.g. Broussard (USA) – Furena (Furry Glen) [2004/5 c16g c17f5 c17g* c17d* c16g5 c16d3 c20s* c20spu c16s c16g c20s c17d Apr 11] big gelding: fair chaser: successful in maiden at Ballinrobe in July and handicaps at Cartmel (first start after sold out of A. Moore's stable 8,000 gns Doncaster Sales) in August and Wetherby (novice) in October: stays 2½m: acts on firm and soft going: tried tongue tied. *Mrs K. Walton* **c110** **h–**

GAMBLERS DREAM (IRE) 8 b.g. Executive Perk – Tinkers Lady (Sheer Grit) [2004/5 h–: 16g 24mpu 20d c16g6 Jul 14] winning pointer: no form over hurdles or on chasing debut (looked unwilling): sold £4,200 Ascot August Sales. *P. J. Hobbs* **c–** **h–**

GAME ON (IRE) 9 b.g. Terimon – Nun So Game (The Parson) [2004/5 c90, h–: 20m c17g* c16s2 c17s* c16g2 c16d2 c17d* c17s3 Mar 6] maiden hurdler: fair handicap chaser: won at Market Rasen in August, November and February: stays 2½m: acts on soft and good to firm ground: tried tongue tied: reliable. *B. N. Pollock* **c108** **h–**

GAMMA-DELTA (IRE) 10 b.g. Alphabatim (USA) – Hardy Polly (Pollerton) [2004/5 c16d4 c16d5 23vpu 20vpu 21s2 19s3 20g5 21d4 20s 22mpu Apr 23] workmanlike ex-Irish gelding: modest hurdler: off 2½ years before reappearance: no form over fences: stays 3m: acts on soft going. *C. T. Pogson* **c–** **h85**

GANDALF THE GREY 6 gr.g. Atraf – Kalogy (Kalaglow) [2004/5 F16d F18d 16d Apr 3] big, plain gelding: second foal: dam, fairly useful hurdler, stayed 21f: no form in bumpers and novice hurdle. *M. Madgwick* **h–** **F–**

GAN EAGLA (IRE) 6 b.g. Paris House – Mafiosa (Miami Springs) [2004/5 h91: 16dpu 20g3 22g2 20d3 19d* 16d 17s* 16spu 21d* Mar 24] angular gelding: fair handicap hurdler: made all at Hereford in October (conditional jockeys) and November (amateur) and Ludlow in March: effective at 2m to 2¾m: acts on soft going: wears blinkers/cheekpieces nowadays. *Miss Venetia Williams* **h101**

GANERO (GER) 6 b.g. Lavirco (GER) – Ghashia (GER) (Prince Ippi (GER)) [2004/5 16dpu 17m 20g4 19g 25m6 Oct 13] successful up to around 1½m on Flat in Germany for P. Rau, including twice in 2004: no form over hurdles: left C. Von Der Recke after debut: tongue tied final outing. *M. F. Harris* **h–**

GANGSTERS R US (IRE) 9 br.g. Treasure Hunter – Our Mare Mick (Choral Society) [2004/5 c104, h–: c24d2 c22v6 c24d4 c24m2 c24gpu c20d3 c24g3 c25s2 c17dpu Apr 11] tall gelding: modest handicap chaser: stays 25f: acts on any going: sometimes hangs/runs as if amiss. *A. Parker* **c98** **h–**

GAORA BRIDGE (IRE) 7 b.g. Warcraft (USA) – Miss Good Night (Buckskin (FR)) [2004/5 h102: 16g2 May 13] fair form over hurdles: will be suited by 2½m+. *C. J. Mann* **h106**

GAORA GALE (IRE) 5 b.g. Anshan – Dancing Gale (Strong Gale) [2004/5 24g6 Apr 1] €11,000 4-y-o: rangy gelding: sixth foal: half-brother to winning pointer by Toulon: dam bumper winner: runner-up in maiden Irish point on debut in January: not knocked about in novice at Newbury on hurdling debut. *P. F. Nicholls* **h90 p**

GARDE BIEN 8 br.g. Afzal – May Lady (Deep Run) [2004/5 c78: c22f* c20g3 c16d* c16d* c19d6 c19d6 Jan 28] lengthy gelding: fair chaser: won novice at Towcester in May **c101**

and handicaps at Sedgefield and Doncaster (novice) in November: effective at 2m to 2¾m: acts on firm and good to soft going. *Ferdy Murphy*

GARDEN PARTY II (FR) 11 br.g. Argument (FR) – Betty Royale (FR) (Royal Charter (FR)) [2004/5 c72, h–: c17m^4 c16d^3 c16m^6 c16d Sep 22] strong gelding: poor maiden chaser: effective at 2m to 3m: acts on heavy and good to firm going. *Mrs J. C. McGregor* **c69 h–**

GARDEN SHED REBEL 5 b.g. Tragic Role (USA) – Clare Island (Connaught) [2004/5 F16s Apr 10] 7,000 4-y-o: brother to fairly useful middle-distance winner Classic Role and half-brother to 7 winners, including fairly useful hurdler/chaser Alqairawaan (by Ajdal), stayed 3m: dam, 7f and 8.5f winner, half-sister to Coronation Cup winner Caliban: well beaten in bumper on debut: sold 2,000 gns Doncaster May Sales. *M. D. Hammond* **F–**

GARDOR (FR) 7 b.g. Kendor (FR) – Garboesque (Priolo (USA)) [2004/5 h90: 17g^4 24m Aug 6] leggy gelding: maiden hurdler: lightly raced in points: raced mainly around 2m: has had tongue tied. *R. Bastiman* **h77**

GARGOYLE GIRL 8 b.m. Be My Chief (USA) – May Hills Legacy (IRE) (Be My Guest (USA)) [2004/5 h88: 16d 20m* 20s* 24d^3 c17v* c20v^4 24m c16v^{pu} c20s^{pu} c21d Mar 19] good-topped mare: modest handicap hurdler: won at Perth (not out of first 3 in 7 starts there) in June and August: won 4-finisher mares novice at Kelso on chasing debut in October: lost her form afterwards: effective around 2m to 3m: acts on heavy and good to firm going: below form in visor/blinkers, effective with/without cheekpieces. *J. S. Goldie* **c99 h97**

GARNETT (IRE) 4 b.g. Desert Story (IRE) – In Behind (IRE) (Entitled) [2004/5 16f* 16d 16g Jan 14] good-topped gelding: half-brother to modest 2m hurdler Shaunas Vision (by Dolphin Street): fair on Flat (stays 2m), successful 3 times in February and March: form over hurdles only when winning juvenile at Wincanton in October on debut: sold out of A. King's stable 14,000 gns Newmarket Autumn Sales after second start. *D. E. Cantillon* **h100**

GAROLSA (FR) 11 b.g. Rivelago (FR) – Rols du Chatelier (FR) (Diaghilev) [2004/5 c107, h–: c24s^3 c25g^2 c25m* c26g* c26g^3 c26g^2 c24d^3 c29d^{pu} c25d^3 c24d^{pu} c24v c26s^4 c16g Apr 17] useful-looking gelding: fair handicap chaser: won at Towcester in May and Newton Abbot in June: stays 29f: acts on good to firm and heavy going: usually wears headgear and tongue strap. *C. L. Tizzard* **c105 d h–**

GARRIGON 4 b.g. Hector Protector (USA) – Queen of The Keys (Royal Academy (USA)) [2004/5 16d^F Feb 11] lengthy, angular gelding: modest maiden on Flat (stays 13f): soon behind in juvenile on hurdling debut. *N. P. Littmoden* **h–**

GARRUTH (IRE) 11 gr.g. Good Thyne (USA) – Lady Sipash (Erin's Hope) [2004/5 c107§, h–: c26s* c25g^2 May 7] medium-sized gelding: fairly useful hunter nowadays: won at Cheltenham in April 2004 by 19 lengths from Victoria's Boy: best at 3m+: successful on good to firm going, best form on more testing ground (acts on heavy): has worn blinkers, including both starts in 2004/5: tried tongue tied: jumps far from fluently: lazy. *R. Barber* **c113 § h–**

GARRYVOE (IRE) 7 b.g. Lord Americo – Cottage Theme (Brave Invader (USA)) [2004/5 c23d* c20v^2 25v^2 25v^2 c33g^6 Mar 17] €7,000 4-y-o: strong gelding: sixth foal: half-brother to winning pointer by Buckskin: dam placed in bumpers and once over fences: thrice-raced in Irish points, won maiden in 2004: fair form in chases, winning maiden at Leicester in December: similar form when runner-up in 2 novice hurdles: stays 25f: acts on heavy going. *T. R. George* **c109 h112**

GARVIVONNIAN (IRE) 10 b.g. Spanish Place (USA) – Garvivonne (Belfalas) [2004/5 c129, h–: c20g c20d^4 16g c24v^4 c19s^6 c28s* c24v c24v c28v^F c25s^3 c29s^{pu} Mar 28] rather leggy gelding: winning hurdler: useful handicap chaser: won Pierse Group Cork Grand National Handicap Chase in November by 6 lengths from Star Clipper: stays 3½m: acts on good to firm and heavy going. *Edward P. Mitchell, Ireland* **c133 h–**

GARW VALLEY 6 b.m. Mtoto – Morgannwg (IRE) (Simply Great (FR)) [2004/5 h80: 16m 17g 19g 16m^6 19m^4 20m^5 17g^6 20g^5 16s 16d* 16d 20s^{ur} 16d 16s^{pu} Dec 22] poor hurdler: won mares handicap at Huntingdon in October: probably stays easy 2½m: acts on good to firm and good to soft going: tried tongue tied: amateur ridden. *M. Wigham* **h73**

GARY'S PIMPERNEL 6 b.g. Shaddad (USA) – Pennine Star (IRE) (Pennine Walk) [2004/5 h83+, F99: 20m* 16s^2 16v^2 20d^6 18v^3 c16s^3 c20v* Mar 20] fair hurdler: won novice at Hexham in October: twice-raced over fences, winning 2-finisher event at Car- **c100 p h107**

lisle in March with ease: stays 2½m: acts on heavy and good to firm going: likely to progress over fences. *M. W. Easterby*

GASTORNIS 7 ch.g. Primitive Rising (USA) – Meggies Dene (Apollo Eight) [2004/5 h–: 17v c16v^{ur} Dec 15] lengthy, angular gelding: fair hurdler in 2002/3, lightly raced and no form since: unseated first on chasing debut: should stay beyond 2½m: acts on good to firm going: usually tongue tied. *M. W. Easterby* **c–** **h–**

GATE EXPECTATIONS 7 b.m. Alflora (IRE) – Dorazine (Kalaglow) [2004/5 h73: 17g 16g 18m^{2} 17g 16g Oct 7] poor maiden hurdler: raced around 2m: best efforts on good to firm going: tried in cheekpieces: tongue tied final start. *R. J. Price* **h73**

GATEJUMPER (IRE) 7 b.g. Zaffaran (USA) – Nelly Don (Shackleton) [2004/5 h93: c25g^{ur} c21g^{4} c22d^{F} Dec 7] leggy gelding: modest hurdler: fourth in novice at Folkestone on completed start over fences: bred to stay 3m+: raced on good going or softer (acts on heavy). *R. H. Alner* **c100** **h–**

GATHERING STORM (IRE) 7 gr.g. Roselier (FR) – Queen of The Rock (IRE) (The Parson) [2004/5 h–, F94: 16g 21g May 8] good-topped gelding: fair form in bumpers: well held over hurdles: should be suited by 2½m+: wore cheekpieces final outing. *P. R. Hedger* **h–**

GATORADE (NZ) 13 ch.g. Dahar (USA) – Ribena (NZ) (Battle-Waggon) [2004/5 c105, h–: c20g^{6} c21m^{3} c24f^{2} c25m^{2} c24d* c25s^{F2} c20d^{2} c25s^{2} c20s* c20v^{3} c19d^{2} c20d c21d^{2} c20s^{4} Apr 2] leggy gelding: fair handicap chaser, rarely out of frame: won at Carlisle in October and Wetherby in December: stays 25f: acts on any going: wears cheekpieces: has broken blood vessels: held up: tough and reliable. *R. C. Guest* **c115** **h–**

GATSBY (IRE) 9 gr.g. Roselier (FR) – Burren Gale (IRE) (Strong Gale) [2004/5 c100, h–: c26g^{5} c21s^{ur} c24s^{3} Apr 16] lengthy gelding: useful hunter chaser: best effort when fifth to Sleeping Night in Foxhunter at Cheltenham: unseated eighth in Aintree Fox Hunters' next time: stays 3¼m: acts on soft and good to firm going. *J. Groucott* **c113** **h–**

GAUCHO 8 b.g. Rambo Dancer (CAN) – Sioux Be It (Warpath) [2004/5 c86, h–: c17d^{ur} c21m^{pu} c16g c20s^{5} c16v^{4} c16v^{6} c16g^{3} c16s c16d^{pu} Apr 5] strong, compact gelding: winning pointer: maiden chaser, little form in 2004/5: probably stays 2½m: raced mainly on good going or softer (acts on heavy): wears cheekpieces. *Miss T. Jackson* **c80 ?** **h–**

GAVROCHE COLLONGES (FR) 11 b.g. Video Rock (FR) – Amazone Collonges (FR) (Olmeto) [2004/5 c21g^{pu} 20d 17d^{5} 16g Aug 24] of little account nowadays: tried blinkered: has had tongue tied. *Mrs J. A. Saunders* **c–** **h–**

GAY ABANDON 10 ch.m. Risk Me (FR) – School Dinners (Sharpo) [2004/5 17m^{pu} May 23] of no account. *D. Burchell* **c– x** **h–**

GAYBLE 7 b.g. Good Times (ITY) – High Kabour (Kabour) [2004/5 c16m^{4} Sep 1] workmanlike gelding: fourth of 6 in bumper on debut for P. Nicholls in 2002: poor form in maiden points: soundly beaten on chasing debut: sold 800 gns Doncaster October Sales. *J. D. Frost* **c–**

GAYCZAR 5 b.g. Double Trigger (IRE) – Indomitable (FR) (Indian King (USA)) [2004/5 F17d F17d Feb 1] rather unfurnished gelding: third foal: half-brother to fair hurdler/fairly useful chaser Gaysun (by Lir), stayed 3¼m: dam, of little account, half-sister to useful stayer Mubarak of Kuwait: well beaten in 2 bumpers. *J. D. Frost* **F–**

GAYE DREAM 7 b.g. Gildoran – Gaye Fame (Ardross) [2004/5 h–: 22d^{2} 26s^{4} 22d^{pu} 21d^{pu} Mar 3] lengthy, angular gelding: poor form over hurdles, left Mrs J. Caro after reappearance: stays 2¾m: has shown signs of temperament. *M. Scudamore* **h81**

GAYE TRIGGER 7 ch.g. Karinga Bay – Gaye Memory (Buckskin (FR)) [2004/5 h101: 25d^{4} c23d^{5} c19s c24s^{F} c20s^{5} Mar 14] big, lengthy gelding: fair hurdler in 2003/4: disappointing in 2004/5, including over fences: should stay 3m+: blinkered fourth start: sold 2,500 gns Doncaster May Sales. *J. L. Spearing* **c91 ?** **h82 +**

GAY GLADYS 5 b.m. Ridgewood Ben – Ovideo (Domynsky) [2004/5 F16s^{2} F16s* F17s Apr 7] compact mare: half-sister to several winners, including fairly useful miler Cool Temper (by Magic Ring) and fair sprinter Aintnecessarilyso (by So Factual): dam, 2-y-o 7f winner, half-sister to smart middle-distance winner Captain Horatius: confirmed debut promise when winning mares maiden bumper at Warwick in March by 7 lengths from What A Vintage: sold out of D. Elsworth's stable £38,000 Cheltenham April Sales: well held at Punchestown in late-April. *T. H. Caldwell* **F98**

GAY KINDERSLEY (IRE) 7 ch.g. Roselier (FR) – Ramble Bramble (Random Shot) [2004/5 h–, F90: 20s c24d^{5} Nov 27] tall, useful-looking gelding: fair form in bumper on **c–** **h–**

debut: well held in 2 novice hurdles and novice chase: bred to be suited by at least 2½m. *K. G. Reveley*

GAY MILLENIUM 5 ch. or gr.m. Silver Owl – Gay Abandon (Risk Me (FR)) [2004/5 F16g Nov 11] first foal: dam no form on Flat or over jumps: tailed off in bumper on debut. *W. K. Goldsworthy* **F–**

GAY OSCAR (IRE) 6 b. or br.g. Oscar (IRE) – Deep Inthought (IRE) (Warcraft (USA)) [2004/5 F91: F17g* F17d² 20d Nov 13] quite good-topped gelding: fairly useful form in bumpers: won at Southwell in May by 6 lengths from Rouge Et Noir: well held in maiden on hurdling debut: should stay 2½m: should do better. *Mrs K. Walton* **h– p F98**

GAZA STRIP (IRE) 6 b.m. Hamas (IRE) – Maratona (Be My Guest (USA)) [2004/5 F16m⁵ F16m F18s* 19v* 19s⁵ 16d³ Mar 20] half-sister to 9 winners on Flat in Britain and USA: dam twice-raced half-sister to Oh So Sharp: fairly useful in bumpers, winning mares event at Fairyhouse in November: won mares maiden at Limerick on hurdling debut following month: much better form when third to Blazing Liss in listed mares novice again at Limerick: stays 19f. *G. M. O'Neill, Ireland* **h113 F99**

GAZUMP (FR) 7 b.g. Iris Noir (FR) – Viva Sacree (FR) (Maiymad) [2004/5 h80: 21d* 24d² 20g* 19g⁶ c20g* c21dᵖᵘ c18d⁶ c18d* Mar 5] rangy gelding: fair hurdler: made most when winning novice handicaps at Ludlow in May and Perth in September: fairly useful over fences, winning novice handicaps at Cheltenham (by 2½ lengths from Lord of Illusion) in October and Newbury (by 1¾ lengths from Glengarra) in March: effective around 2½m, probably stays 3m: raced on good going or softer: free-going sort, races up with pace. *N. A. Twiston-Davies* **c124 h103**

GEBORA (FR) 6 ch.g. Villez (USA) – Sitapanoki (FR) (Houston (FR)) [2004/5 h100: c16g³ c21sᵖᵘ c16g 17g² 22g 20gᵖᵘ 16s Jan 11] compact gelding: none too fluent in 3 handicap chases: fair hurdler at best: has gone the wrong way, sold out of M. Pipe's stable only 1,500 gns Doncaster October Sales after sixth outing: barely stays 21f: best form over hurdles on good to firm going (won bumper on soft): usually visored: one to leave alone. *B. R. Foster* **c90 ? h75**

GEE AKER MALAYO (IRE) 9 b.g. Phardante (FR) – Flying Silver (Master Buck) [2004/5 h76: 16g c16dᶠ c21d⁴ c25s* c26sᵖᵘ c24vᴿ c20d* Apr 20] strong, lengthy gelding: poor maiden hurdler: modest form over fences: won handicaps at Folkestone in February and Worcester in April: stays 25f: acts on soft going: tried blinkered: temperament under suspicion. *R. T. Phillips* **c92 h–**

GEILL SLI (IRE) 7 b.g. Charente River (IRE) – Lumiere (USA) (Northjet) [2004/5 F117: F16g* 16s 16v³ Feb 15] good-topped gelding: has reportedly had wind operation: smart bumper performer: won in Grade 1 Champion INH Flat at Punchestown: better effort in maiden hurdles there (jumped badly and reportedly made a noise on debut) when third to Teeming Rain: best bumper form on good/good to soft going. *N. Meade, Ireland* **h106**

GEMI BED (FR) 10 b.g. Double Bed (FR) – Gemia (FR) (King of Macedon) [2004/5 c89§, h71: c19g c19dᵖᵘ c18d⁵ c16d³ c18s c21s Jan 18] modest on Flat (stays 2m): maiden hurdler: winning chaser: little form in 2004/5: should stay beyond 17f: acts on good to firm and good to soft going: blinkered: ungenuine. *G. L. Moore* **c65 § h–**

GEMINEYE LORD (IRE) 8 b.g. Mister Lord (USA) – Mum's Eyes (Al Sirat) [2004/5 h81: 19gᵖᵘ Mar 9] rangy gelding: poor form in novice hurdles: off 13 months, ran as if amiss only start in 2004/5: probably stays 3m. *Mrs S. J. Smith* **h–**

GEMINI DANCER 6 b.g. Glory of Dancer – Lamloum (IRE) (Vacarme (USA)) [2004/5 h–, F72: 16g⁴ Apr 17] off a year, better effort in novice hurdles at Wincanton when fourth to Earth Man. *C. L. Tizzard* **h80 +**

GEMINI GUEST (IRE) 9 ch.g. Waajib – Aldhabyih (General Assembly (USA)) [2004/5 h112: 16g² 22m* Jul 31] fairly useful handicap hurdler: ran well both starts in 2004/5, second to Cloone River in Galway Hurdle and successful in valuable event there 2 days later: effective at 2m to 2¾m: acts on soft and good to firm going. *P. Hughes, Ireland* **h119**

GEMINI LADY 5 b.m. Emperor Fountain – Raunchy Rita (Brigadier Gerard) [2004/5 16sᶠ 16v 16d 16gᶠ 24s⁶ Apr 20] modest maiden on Flat (stays 1¼m) for Mrs G. Rees: let down by jumping and only poor form over hurdles: raced mainly around 2m, failed to stay 3m. *Mrs J. C. McGregor* **h79 x**

GEMS BOND 5 b.g. Magic Ring (IRE) – Jucinda (Midyan (USA)) [2004/5 17m 16s⁵ 16d Jan 26] fair on Flat (stays 1m): well held over hurdles. *J. S. Moore* **h–**

GENERAL 8 b.g. Cadeaux Genereux – Bareilly (USA) (Lyphard (USA)) [2004/5 c100§, h–: 17s^pu Oct 31] good-topped gelding: fairly useful 2m hurdler/fair chaser at best, has lost his form: raced on good going or softer (acts on heavy): has worn blinkers: moody. *C. R. Dore* **c– § h– §**

GENERAL CARATS 11 b.g. Cotation – Madam Carats (Mandrake Major) [2004/5 24m^pu Jun 16] poor pointer: blinkered, no show in maiden hurdle. *Mrs J. A. Saunders* **h–**

GENERAL CLAREMONT (IRE) 12 gr.g. Strong Gale – Kasam (General Ironside) [2004/5 c120§, h97§: c33s² c31m* c32m^ur c26g⁴ c25d^pu c26g Mar 18] workmanlike gelding: winning hurdler: fairly useful chaser at one time, on downgrade: won hunter at Folkestone in May: stays 33f: acts on soft and firm going: tried blinkered: has had tongue tied: weak finisher: not one to trust. *P. F. Nicholls* **c107 § h– §**

GENERAL CUSTER (IRE) 11 b.g. Buckskin (FR) – Cottage Theme (Brave Invader (USA)) [2004/5 c–, h74: 26d⁴ 24d c22g⁴ c24m³ c26g^F 24g 22g⁶ Aug 15] rangy gelding: maiden outside points, little form in 2004/5: tried blinkered. *F. M. Barton* **c– h–**

GENERAL DUROC (IRE) 9 ch.g. Un Desperado (FR) – Satula (Deep Run) [2004/5 h114: 22d^pu 24g 22d⁶ c26v^pu 24d 22d^pu 24s 22d⁴ Apr 17] well-made gelding: fair handicap hurdler in 2003/4: no show in 2004/5 until final outing: jumped poorly on chasing debut: should stay beyond 3m: raced on good ground or softer over jumps: in cheekpieces/blinkers last 3 starts, tongue tied final one. *R. T. Phillips* **c– h95**

GENERAL GOSSIP (IRE) 9 b. or br.g. Supreme Leader – Sno-Sleigh (Bargello) [2004/5 c–p, h93: c23s* c23s³ c24v* c29s^pu 24s* Apr 16] sturdy gelding: fairly useful chaser: won novice at Leicester in December and 4-runner handicap at Newcastle in February: fair form when winning handicap hurdle at Bangor in April: stays 25f: raced on good ground or softer (acts on heavy): tried tongue tied. *R. T. Phillips* **c116 h105**

GENERAL GREY (IRE) 5 gr.g. Fourstars Allstar (USA) – Tara The Grey (IRE) (Supreme Leader) [2004/5 F16d⁴ 17d 22s^pu 19d⁴ 21d² 22d² 24m^ur Apr 13] good-topped gelding: first foal: dam poor form in bumpers: fourth of 16 in slowly-run bumper at Ludlow on debut: fair form over hurdles: stays 2¾m: acts on good to soft going. *Miss H. C. Knight* **h101 F87**

GENERAL HARDI 4 b.g. In Command (IRE) – Hardiprincess (Keen) [2004/5 F14s⁴ F14g² F16v² Feb 2] sturdy gelding: fourth foal: half-brother to modest performer around 1¼m Anne-Sophie (by First Trump): dam ran twice: fair form in bumpers, in frame all 3 starts. *J. Wade* **F94**

GENERAL JAKE (IRE) 8 b.g. Jolly Jake (NZ) – Moscow Lady (IRE) (Moscow Society (USA)) [2004/5 c21g³ May 31] first foal: dam unraced, out of half-sister to useful staying chaser Wont Be Gone Long: won maiden point in 2004: distant third of 4 finishers in maiden chase at Cartmel. *Miss S. E. Forster* **c69 ?**

GENERAL MONTCALM (IRE) 7 b.g. Roselier (FR) – Pamela's Princess (Black Minstrel) [2004/5 c119: c25g^ur c24m^F c24s^ur c22s* c26g^pu c25s Mar 29] good-topped gelding: useful hunter chaser: won at Fairyhouse in February by 10 lengths from Van Ness and Punchestown in late-April by neck from Industrious: stays 25f: acts on soft ground: often let down by jumping. *E. J. O'Grady, Ireland* **c118 x**

GENERAL O'KEEFFE 8 b.g. Alflora (IRE) – Rosie O'Keeffe (IRE) (Royal Fountain) [2004/5 c24d⁴ c23s⁵ c25s³ c26d^ur c24s⁴ c26g² Apr 10] modest maiden chaser: stays 3¼m: raced on good going or softer (acts on soft). *R. H. Alner* **c87 h–**

GENERAL OLIVER (IRE) 5 b.g. General Monash (USA) – Sea Idol (IRE) (Astronef) [2004/5 F16d^pu Apr 20] second foal: dam maiden, stayed 6f: pulled up in bumper on debut. *K. G. Wingrove* **F–**

GENERALS LASTSTAND (IRE) 7 b.g. Little Bighorn – Our Dorcet (Condorcet (FR)) [2004/5 21d 19d Jan 12] useful-looking gelding: won bumper on debut: blinkered, well beaten in novice company over hurdles after 2-year absence: should stay at least 2½m. *Ms J. S. Doyle* **h–**

GENERAL SMITH 6 b.g. Greensmith – Second Call (Kind of Hush) [2004/5 16d Apr 22] half-brother to winning 2m hurdler Alphacall (by Forzando): dam winning hurdler/chaser up to 2½m: 5f winner on Flat, little form in 2004 for G. Harker: soon behind in maiden on hurdling debut. *H. J. Evans* **h–**

GENERAL TANTRUM (IRE) 8 b.g. Ilium – Barna Havna (Crash Course) [2004/5 c–, h–: 21d⁵ c24s⁶ c24g⁶ c26g^pu c28g* Mar 20] strong, lengthy gelding: 13 lb out of weights, first form when winning handicap chase at Fontwell in March: stays 3½m: wears cheekpieces: tongue tied last 3 outings. *A. Ennis* **c79 h–**

GENEREUX 12 ch.g. Generous (IRE) – Flo Russell (USA) (Round Table) [2004/5 c25m^4 c25m^{pu} May 11] poor pointer/hunter chaser nowadays: stays 3m: acts on good to firm and good to soft going: usually wears visor/cheekpieces: tongue tied: sold £3,700 Ascot June Sales. *Mrs A. Price* **c62 h–**

GENEROUS SPIRIT (IRE) 4 ch.c. Cadeaux Genereux – Miss Rossi (Artaius (USA)) [2004/5 16s 16d Feb 9] modest maiden on Flat (stays 7f) for J. Osborne: well beaten in novice and selling hurdles. *O. Sherwood* **h–**

GENEROUS WAYS 10 ch.g. Generous (IRE) – Clara Bow (USA) (Coastal (USA)) [2004/5 c–, h82: c20m c16m^4 c16g^4 20m 17g^5 Aug 14] sturdy gelding: poor hurdler/maiden chaser: should stay beyond 2m: acts on good to firm going: visored third start: tongue tied: sold £3,800 Ascot August Sales. *R. Lee* **c77 h71**

GENGHIS (IRE) 6 br.g. Persian Bold – Cindy's Baby (Bairn (USA)) [2004/5 20s^2 17g^6 19d^6 17v* 16d* 20d* 16g* Apr 16] **h146 +**

Genghis didn't manage to crush all who came up against him in his first campaign over jumps but, for a two-month spell from mid-February, he did prove unstoppable in handicap hurdles, winning four in succession at Exeter, Chepstow, Aintree and Ayr, the last gained from a mark 32 lb higher than the first. Front-running tactics played no small part in his success. Allowed to stride on from the start, having pulled too hard under restraint on his first three outings, Genghis was a revelation at Exeter, jumping more fluently than previously and winning by nineteen lengths. A blunder two out was the only blemish on his performance at Chepstow, and then it was on to Aintree where Genghis was one of twenty who lined up for a listed event on Grand National day. Genghis, whose wins had come at around two miles, wasn't ridden so forcefully back over two and a half at Aintree, but he did lead from the sixth and stayed on very strongly, despite some sloppy jumping in the closing stages, to win by six lengths from Tamarinbleu. A further 7-lb rise and a return to two miles could not prevent Genghis completing a four-timer in the Samsung Electronics Scottish Champion Hurdle at Ayr. There

John Smith's No Nonsense Handicap Hurdle, Aintree—the progressive Genghis routs a competitive field

*Samsung Electronics Scottish Champion Hurdle (Limited Handicap), Ayr—
a second valuable prize on consecutive weekends*

was a bigger field than usual for this limited handicap, but Genghis was sent off favourite at 5/2 to account for twelve rivals, including the previous year's winner Copeland. In the first two from the start, Genghis took command off the home turn and quickened between the last two flights, going around six lengths clear on the extended run-in—what should have been the last flight was omitted because of damage on the previous circuit—then eased slightly nearing the line, which he passed with four lengths to spare over nearest pursuer Royal Shakespeare. Despite a further 10-lb rise, Genghis also went off favourite when attempting a five-timer in the Stanleybet Handicap Hurdle at Haydock, formerly the Swinton, after the end of the season. However, this time he managed only sixth, just over twelve lengths behind the winner Coat of Honour, giving the impression that the exertions of his busy spell, rather than the handicapper, had finally caught up with him. He wasn't far below form and did shape a bit better than the bare result, headed by Coat of Honour after a mistake three out but still only three lengths behind that horse jumping the last. Genghis will find it much more difficult to win races if kept to hurdling and there is a likelihood that he will be switched to fences. Tony McCoy, who rode him on all bar his third and fifth starts, is of the opinion that Genghis is an exciting chasing prospect, yet it has to be said that the rather leggy Genghis is hardly a chaser on looks, and still has a bit to learn about jumping hurdles.

Genghis was a 35,000-guinea yearling who fetched 30,000 guineas when next going through the sale-ring as a five-year-old at Doncaster in October. In between, he ran ten times on the Flat for Paul Webber and Hughie Morrison, showing fairly useful form at up to a mile and three quarters without managing to get his head in front. The fourth foal of Cindy's Baby, a maiden who finished in the frame in a couple of seven-furlong handicaps in Ireland as a three-year-old, Genghis is a brother to the fair winner at up to a mile and a quarter Karakul, and a half-brother to winners in Italy by Paris House and Priolo. Genghis' grandam Miss Cindy, a sister

Khan Partners' "Genghis"

Genghis (IRE) (br.g. 1999)	Persian Bold (br 1975)	Bold Lad (b 1964)	Bold Ruler
			Barn Pride
		Relkarunner (b or br 1968)	Relko
			Running Blue
	Cindy's Baby (ch 1989)	Bairn (ch 1982)	Northern Baby
			Lady Mouse
		Miss Cindy (br 1975)	Mansingh
			Iridium

to the high-class sprinter Petong, was a useful two-year-old who stayed seven furlongs. Miss Cindy has produced numerous winners, notably the smart sprinter Two Clubs and Gipsy Fiddler, the latter a brother to Cindy's Baby and winner of the 1990 Windsor Castle Stakes at Royal Ascot when trained by Jonjo O'Neill. Genghis is effective at two miles but did not give the impression at Aintree that two and a half miles is the limit of his stamina. He acts on heavy going and has yet to race on ground firmer than good over hurdles, though he has run well on firm on the Flat. *P. Bowen*

GENSCHER 9 b.g. Cadeaux Genereux – Marienbad (FR) (Darshaan) [2004/5 c–, h–: 18m 16d 21g^{4} 24d^{pu} 20g^{4} 21m^{pu} 20s^{pu} 16d 22m Oct 3] winning hurdler/maiden chaser, little form since 2001/2: tried in headgear: has had tongue tied. *R. Allan* **c– h63**

GENTLE BEAU 7 b.g. Homo Sapien – Tapua Taranata (IRE) (Mandalus) [2004/5 h102, F95: 16d Apr 17] quite good-topped gelding: fair hurdler: well held in handicap after 13-month absence: stays 19f. *P. J. Hobbs* **h–**

GENTLEMAN JIMMY 5 b.g. Alderbrook – Irish Orchid (Free State) [2004/5 F16d^{5} Feb 19] good-topped gelding: fifth foal: brother to fair 2m hurdle winner Orchid Bay: **F82**

dam, poor novice hurdler, half-sister to Desert Orchid: 15 lengths fifth of 16 to Yaboya in bumper at Wincanton on debut. *H. Morrison*

GENTLEMANS RELISH 8 b.g. Sir Harry Lewis (USA) – Relishing (Relkino) [2004/5 c20g4 c20s* c20s4 Mar 31] lengthy gelding: maiden pointer: won maiden hunter at Leicester in March. *Mrs F. Kehoe* **c100**

GENTLE WARNING 5 b.m. Parthian Springs – Manx Princess (Roscoe Blake) [2004/5 16vpu 16dpu 16vpu 16d6 Apr 20] plain, sparely-made mare: no form on Flat or over hurdles. *M. Appleby* **h–**

GENUINE ARTICLE (IRE) 9 ch.g. Insan (USA) – Rosemount Rose (Ashmore (FR)) [2004/5 c115, h–: c17m* c16gpu 16g* 16m* 16g Oct 30] sturdy gelding: fairly useful handicap chaser: successful at Stratford in May: fair hurdler: won at same course in July and September, taking unbeaten record there to 5 when making all on latter occasion: best form up to 19f: acts on firm and good to soft going: has been let down by jumping over fences. *M. Pitman* **c115 h105**

GEOGRAPHY (IRE) 5 ch.g. Definite Article – Classic Ring (IRE) (Auction Ring (USA)) [2004/5 h–: 16g 18s5 22d* 22s 20s 22s3 25v4 21s* 22d 25g 21gpu Mar 28] good-topped gelding: modest hurdler: won handicaps at Folkestone (selling) in November and Plumpton in February: stays 25f: acts on any going: tried visored, wears cheekpieces nowadays: tried tongue tied: inconsistent. *P. Butler* **h88**

GEORDIE PEACOCK (IRE) 6 gr.g. Roselier (FR) – Cotton Call (IRE) (Callernish) [2004/5 F16g5 Apr 19] second foal: dam, fairly useful 2m hurdler, half-sister to useful chaser around 2½m Cameron Bridge: 2¼ lengths fifth of 17 to Regal Heights in maiden bumper at Towcester (reportedly unruly beforehand) on debut. *Miss Venetia Williams* **F91**

GEORDIES EXPRESS 13 b.g. Tina's Pet – Maestroes Beauty (Music Maestro) [2004/5 c102: c25m* c26gur c27v4 c25d6 Apr 11] leggy, lengthy gelding: fair hunter chaser: won at Kelso in May: also successful in point in March: stays 27f: probably acts on any going. *G. T. Bewley* **c99**

GEORGES GIRL (IRE) 7 b.m. Montelimar (USA) – Keshia (Buckskin (FR)) [2004/5 h146: 16g 16s5 16v6 Jan 23] leggy mare: smart hurdler in 2003/4: off 8 months, not discredited when fifth of 6 to Macs Joy in Grade 1 at Leopardstown: ran poorly in similar event there following month: raced mainly around 2m: acted on heavy going: reportedly retired to stud. *F. Flood, Ireland* **h140**

GEORGIAN HARRY (IRE) 8 b.g. Warcraft (USA) – Solo Player (Blue Refrain) [2004/5 c22dF 22d 21g5 Mar 28] rather leggy, useful-looking gelding: modest novice hurdler: off nearly 3 years, fell sixth on chasing debut: should stay beyond 19f: acts on good to firm going: tongue tied final outing (raced freely). *R. T. Phillips* **c– h88**

GEORGIC BLAZE 11 b.g. Petoski – Pooka (Dominion) [2004/5 c–, h63x: 24spu 17d 16g 16v Nov 25] sparely-made gelding: unseated second both starts over fences: poor hurdler: no show in 2004/5 after long absence: visored final outing: not a fluent jumper. *G. A. Ham* **c– h– x**

GEORGIE GIRL DOVE 5 b.m. Busy Flight – Emerald Dove (Green Adventure (USA)) [2004/5 F16d Mar 3] second foal: dam, of little account, out of fairly useful hurdler up to 25f Nimble Dove: well beaten in mares bumper on debut. *C. J. Price* **F–**

GEOS (FR) 10 b. or br.g. Pistolet Bleu (IRE) – Kaprika (FR) (Cadoudal (FR)) [2004/5 c–, h149: 16d 25s 16d 20d6 17g 16g5 Apr 16] smallish, strong gelding: smart hurdler: won Tote Gold Trophy Hurdle (Handicap) at Newbury for a second time in 2003/4: struggled to make an impact subsequently, best effort in 2004/5 when twelfth to Essex in corresponding race third start: well held in Grade 2 at Auteuil in May: stayed 2½m, at least with emphasis on speed: acted on heavy going, possibly unsuited by good to firm: reportedly retired. *N. J. Henderson* **c– h147**

GERALDINE 4 br. or b.f. Minster Son – Church Leap (Pollerton) [2004/5 F13d3 F13s Dec 13] sixth foal: half-sister to fairly useful hurdler Vicars Destiny (by Sir Harry Lewis), stays 3m, and fair hurdler up to 19f Vicar's Vase (by Montelimar): dam, won 3m hurdle, half-sister to fairly useful staying hurdler Hopeful Saint: poor form in 3-y-o bumpers. *Mrs S. Lamyman* **F71**

GERRARD (IRE) 7 b.g. Jurado (USA) – Vienna Waltz (IRE) (Orchestra) [2004/5 h–, F84: 21s c23d4 c20g2 Mar 9] lengthy gelding: no form in 3 starts over hurdles: visored, poor form in novice handicap chases: lame final outing: stays 23f: signs of temperament. *Mrs A. Barclay* **c84 h–**

GERT THE FLIRT 7 ch.m. Manhal – Ardross Kala (Ardross) [2004/5 16g^{pu} May 16] showed nothing in seller on Flat or in novice hurdle. *H. J. Manners* **h–**

GETAWAY GIRL 7 b.m. Perpendicular – Viowen (IRE) (Denel (FR)) [2004/5 F–: F17g May 23] well beaten in 2 bumpers. *O. Brennan* **F–**

GETINBYBUTONLYJUST 6 b.g. King's Ride – Madame President (IRE) (Supreme Leader) [2004/5 h–, F–: 22s^{4} 22s^{6} 24v* 24s^{2} 24v^{3} 20s^{2} 24s^{5} Apr 20] modest handicap hurdler: made all at Ayr in January: stays 3m: raced on good going or softer (acts on heavy): usually races prominently. *Mrs Dianne Sayer* **h90**

GET MY DRIFT (IRE) 6 b.g. Beneficial – Boreen Bro (Boreen (FR)) [2004/5 c24s^{2} c25d^{pu} 24d^{2} Mar 5] €95,000 3-y-o: tall gelding: fifth foal: half-brother to fair hurdler/fairly useful chaser Kings Valley (by Castle Keep), stays 29f, and 2 winners by Roselier, smart staying hurdler/chaser Royal Emperor and useful chaser up to 4m A Piece of Cake: dam once-raced, from family of top-class chaser Kinloch Brae: won all 3 completed starts in Irish points in 2004: plenty of encouragement when second in maiden chase at Chepstow (to Limerick Leader) and novice hurdle at Newbury (behind Ferimon): tongue tied when disappointing in between: will stay beyond 3m: likely to win races. *P. F. Nicholls* **c119 p h113 +**

GETON (IRE) 5 b.g. Glacial Storm (USA) – Monavale (IRE) (Strong Gale) [2004/5 F18d^{4} 17d* 16d 20g Feb 5] rather unfurnished gelding: first foal: dam, poor maiden hurdler, out of half-sister to Champion Hurdle winners Morley Street and Granville Again: fourth to Dusky Lord in maiden bumper at Plumpton on debut: won novice at Newton Abbot on hurdling debut in November: disappointing after: should be suited by 2½m. *M. C. Pipe* **h99 F97**

GET THE POINT 11 b.g. Sadler's Wells (USA) – Tolmi (Great Nephew) [2004/5 c93, h–: c22s^{pu} c16s c16v c18s^{4} c17d^{6} c18g* c18s^{4} c19d^{pu} Apr 22] compact gelding: modest chaser: bought out of G. Brown's stable £4,200 Ascot October Sales: won handicap at Fontwell in March: stays 2¾m, effective at much shorter: acts on good to firm and heavy going: tried in cheekpieces: has had tongue tied: inconsistent. *Dr P. Pritchard* **c88 h–**

GHADAMES (FR) 11 b.g. Synefos (USA) – Ouargla (FR) (Armos) [2004/5 c110, h97: c16s* c16s* c16s^{2} c21g c18m^{3} c21d Apr 8] lengthy gelding: winning hurdler: fairly useful handicap chaser: left M. Todhunter, better than ever in 2004/5, winning at Sedgefield and Leicester in February: stays 21f: acts on any going: wore cheekpieces first 5 starts: has broken blood vessels in past. *R. C. Guest* **c125 h–**

GHOST BUSTER 6 ch.g. Opera Ghost – Venetian Storm (Glacial Storm (USA)) [2004/5 20d^{pu} 17v^{pu} 20v Feb 2] €7,000 4-y-o: first foal: dam, poor novice hurdler, out of half-sister to Galway Plate winner Master Player: fourth in maiden Irish point in 2004: bought 14,000 gns Doncaster May Sales: no form in 3 novice hurdles: tried in cheekpieces. *Mrs L. B. Normile* **h–**

GIANLUCA (IRE) 11 br.g. Un Desperado (FR) – Belwood Girl (Ballymore) [2004/5 18m* 16m^{6} Oct 3] very difficult to train but successful on 3 of 5 starts, including in handicap hurdle at Fontwell in August after 2-year absence: raced around 2m: tongue tied in 2004/5. *C. R. Egerton* **h105**

GIELGUD 8 b.g. Faustus (USA) – Shirl (Shirley Heights) [2004/5 c111d, h93: c26d^{2} c21g^{3} c24m^{4} c23m* c24g^{ur} c26m^{4} Aug 19] strong, sturdy gelding: winning hurdler: fair handicap chaser: won at Worcester in June: sold out of N. Twiston-Davies' stable 25,000 gns Doncaster August Sales after next outing: lame final one: stays 3m: acts on soft and good to firm going: often tongue tied prior to 2004/5. *B. G. Powell* **c110 h–**

GIFTED WAY 11 b.m. Teenoso (USA) – Walnut Way (Gambling Debt) [2004/5 20m^{pu} 16g 16m^{pu} Jun 16] lengthy mare: no form: wears cheekpieces: has had tongue tied. *A. E. Price* **h–**

GIFTNEYEV (FR) 6 b. or br.g. Goldneyev (USA) – Girl's Gift (FR) (Gairloch) [2004/5 h–: 16g 24d^{pu} 22d^{pu} Mar 26] no form over hurdles: tried tongue tied. *C. P. Morlock* **h–**

GIFT OF LIFE (FR) 5 b.m. Android (USA) – Teardrops Fall (FR) (Law Society (USA)) [2004/5 26s^{pu} 19s^{pu} Jan 10] half-sister to 3 winning hurdlers around 2m: well beaten on Flat, including in claimer on British debut: no show in 2 starts over hurdles. *C. J. Gray* **h–**

GIFT VOUCHER (IRE) 4 ch.g. Cadeaux Genereux – Highland Gift (IRE) (Generous (IRE)) [2004/5 16s* 16s Feb 26] tall gelding: fairly useful form on Flat (should stay 1¾m), successful in maiden in August, sold out of Sir Michael Stoute's stable 70,000 gns Newmarket Autumn Sales: won juvenile at Warwick on hurdling debut: soundly beaten in Grade 2 juvenile at Kempton following month. *P. R. Webber* **h101**

GIG HARBOR 6 b.g. Efisio – Petonica (IRE) (Petoski) [2004/5 16g May 21] compact gelding: useful on all-weather, fairly useful on turf on Flat (stays 1½m), successful in January and March for P. Chamings: well held in 2 starts over hurdles. *Miss E. C. Lavelle* **h–**

GIGONDAS (IRE) 7 b.g. Zaffaran (USA) – Summit Else (El Conquistador) [2004/5 20g^{4} 20d 24v^{pu} 16d 26s 26m Apr 9] good-topped gelding: first foal: dam, no sign of ability, half-sister to 1998 Grand National winner Earth Summit: little form over hurdles: bled from nose second and third starts. *N. A. Twiston-Davies* **h75**

GIGS GAMBIT (IRE) 8 ch.g. Hubbly Bubbly (USA) – Music Slipper (Orchestra) [2004/5 c100, h–: c26d^{pu} Feb 20] well-made gelding: trained by M. Pitman, won first 2 completed starts over fences in 2003/4: disappointing since: stays 3¼m: acts on soft and good to firm going: tried in cheekpieces. *Peter Guest* **c– h–**

GILDED ALLY 5 b.g. Gildoran – Allyfair (Scallywag) [2004/5 F–: F17s 17d^{pu} 22s^{F} 17v^{pu} Mar 30] lengthy gelding: no form. *A. E. Jones* **h– F–**

GILDORANS SPICE 7 gr.m. Gildoran – Sea Spice (Precipice Wood) [2004/5 c17s^{pu} c20s^{pu} c21g^{ur} c21d c24v^{F} 21s^{pu} Jan 20] lengthy, angular mare: no sign of ability: tried visored. *D. L. Williams* **c– h–**

GILFOOT BREEZE (IRE) 8 b.g. Forest Wind (USA) – Ma Bella Luna (Jalmood (USA)) [2004/5 h75: c16d^{pu} Oct 9] compact gelding: poor maiden hurdler: jumped badly on chasing debut: best around 2m: acts on good to firm and good to soft going: tried tongue tied. *A. Robson* **c– h–**

GILOU 9 b.m. Midyan (USA) – Lunagraphe (USA) (Time For A Change (USA)) [2004/5 h86: 20g^{pu} May 29] modest hurdler: folded tamely only start in 2004/5: stays 3m: raced mainly on good going or firmer: often makes running. *C. W. Fairhurst* **h–**

GIMLI'S AXE (IRE) 6 b.g. Shernazar – Neasham (Nishapour (FR)) [2004/5 F20g* 20g* 20d Mar 10] €13,000 4-y-o: half-brother to 4 winners, including fair 2m to 2½m hurdler/chaser Toulouse (by Toulon): dam maiden, suited by 1¼m+: won first 2 starts, bumper in May and maiden hurdle (made all) in July, both at Roscommon: ran as if in need of race in Grade 3 novice at Thurles 8 months later: remains capable of better. *Ms F. M. Crowley, Ireland* **h111 p F99**

GIMME SHELTER (IRE) 11 ch.m. Glacial Storm (USA) – Glen Dieu (Furry Glen) [2004/5 c82x, h–: c20v^{pu} 24v^{pu} c25d^{pu} 24v^{3} c26s^{5} c32v* c28s^{2} c31s^{2} Apr 22] lengthy, sparely-made mare: winning hurdler: modest chaser: won handicap at Hexham (for second time in 3 years) in March: stays 4m: acts on heavy going: tried in cheekpieces: sketchy jumper of fences. *S. J. Marshall* **c91 x h75**

GIMMICK (FR) 11 b.g. Chamberlin (FR) – Jaida (FR) (Alfaro) [2004/5 c–, h116: 16m* 17m* c20d^{F} Jul 17] good-topped gelding: useful handicap hurdler: better than ever when winning at Stratford and Market Rasen in June, defying penalty at latter in emphatic fashion by 5 lengths from Code Sign: fair form on completed outings over fences (needs to jump better): stays 2½m: acts on any going: blinkered once: usually waited with. *Jonjo O'Neill* **c– h133**

GINGEMBRE (FR) 11 ch.g. Le Nain Jaune (FR) – Teuphaine (FR) (Barbotan (FR)) [2004/5 c24d^{5} c24g^{pu} c33d^{pu} c33g^{pu} Apr 16] workmanlike gelding: has reportedly been fired: very smart handicap chaser in his prime: off nearly 2 years, long way below that level in 2004/5: stays 33f: acts on soft and good to firm going: tongue tied second outing. *Mrs L. C. Taylor* **c– h–**

GINGERBREAD 4 ch.g. Pharly (FR) – Gay Sarah (Last Fandango) [2004/5 F14g F16g Jan 21] leggy gelding: ninth foal: brother to 6f winner Ladychatterly and half-brother to sprint winner in Greece by Botanic and to 2 winners in Belgium: dam winner in Belgium: no encouragement in 2 bumpers. *B. Ellison* **F–**

GINGERBREAD HOUSE (IRE) 7 b.g. Old Vic – Furun (IRE) (Deep Run) [2004/5 h113: c22s* c25s^{2} c25s^{4} Jan 3] lengthy gelding: won first of 2 starts over hurdles in 2003/4: fairly useful form when winning novice handicap at Kelso in November on chasing debut by 2½ lengths from Your A Gassman: again made mistakes next time: should stay 25f: acts on soft going. *R. T. Phillips* **c119 h–**

GINGER ICE 5 ch.g. Bahamian Bounty – Sharp Top (Sharpo) [2004/5 16g Mar 16] half-brother to useful hurdler/chaser Polar Red (by Polar Falcon), stays 21f: poor maiden on Flat (stays 1¼m): finished lame in maiden on hurdling debut. *G. G. Margarson* **h–**

GINGKO 8 b.g. Pursuit of Love – Arboretum (IRE) (Green Desert (USA)) [2004/5 h87: c16g^{pu} 16m^{pu} May 22] well-made gelding: fairly useful on all-weather on Flat (stays 1½m), successful in February and March: novice hurdler: jumped poorly on chasing debut: raced around 2m: acts on soft going. *P. R. Webber* **c– h–**

GIN 'N' FONIC (IRE) 5 ch.g. Zafonic (USA) – Crepe Ginger (IRE) (Sadler's Wells (USA)) [2004/5 17gpu 17s4 17g2 19g3 17g6 21s 17m4 17s Nov 30] workmanlike gelding: fair on Flat (stays 1½m), sold out of H. Cyzer's stable 11,500 gns Newmarket Autumn (2003) Sales: modest maiden hurdler: stays easy 19f: best efforts on good/good to firm going: wore cheekpieces last 3 starts. *J. D. Frost* **h87**

GINSKI 9 b.g. Petoski – Upham Lass (Sula Bula) [2004/5 h–: 20mpu May 26] of no account: sometimes tongue tied. *C. J. Drewe* **h–**

GIOCOMO (IRE) 7 ch.g. Indian Ridge – Karri Valley (USA) (Storm Bird (CAN)) [2004/5 c110, h–: c20s4 c20dpu c20dpu c21dpu Feb 19] sturdy gelding: fairly useful hurdler at best: fair over fences, out of form in 2004/5: left F. Murtagh after second start: stays 2½m: raced on good going or softer (acts on soft): tried in blinkers/cheekpieces: patiently ridden. *M. Pitman* **c– h–**

GIOLLA DE (IRE) 6 b.g. Glacial Storm (USA) – Deep Inagh (Deep Run) [2004/5 F102: F16v3 F16s4 16v4 16v* 16v6 20s 18s Mar 13] well-made gelding: fairly useful in bumpers: slightly disappointing over hurdles, though won 29-runner maiden at Navan by 5 lengths from High Priestess: should stay at least 2½m: raced on going softer than good (acts on heavy): type to make a better chaser. *F. Flood, Ireland* **h105 F101**

GIORGIO (IRE) 7 b.g. Presenting – Billys Pet (Le Moss) [2004/5 h84: 20m2 20m3 16g* c17m2 c16m* c16d3 c16s* c16d4 c21s2 c21gpu c24g Apr 7] fair hurdler: successful in maiden at Worcester in August: similar form over fences, winning maiden at Towcester in October and, having left P. Hobbs after next start, novice there in November: stays 2½m: acts on soft and good to firm going: ungenuine. *Ms Bridget Nicholls* **c109 § h103 §**

GIOVANNA 4 b.f. Orpen (USA) – Red Leggings (Shareef Dancer (USA)) [2004/5 F13s2 F13g* F16d* F17s4 Apr 7] small filly: second foal: half-sister to 5f to 9f winner in Greece by Bahhare: dam, fair up to 1¼m, half-sister to fairly useful hurdler up to 3m Barneys Lyric: fairly useful form in bumpers: won at Doncaster in January and Ludlow (beat Ceoperk impressively by 6 lengths in mares event) in March: best effort when fourth to Senorita Rumbalita in 17-runner listed mares contest at Aintree. *R. T. Phillips* **F100**

GIPSY CRICKETER 9 b.g. Anshan – Tinkers Fairy (Myjinski (USA)) [2004/5 c76, h–: c21dpu c18mpu 16m5 c21mpu c23gpu Jul 14] winning chaser/maiden hurdler, of little account nowadays: has had tongue tied. *M. Scudamore* **c– h–**

GIPSY GIRL 10 b.m. Motivate – Young Gipsy (The Brianstan) [2004/5 c21dF 20s 26m4 Apr 9] winning pointer: would have won maiden hunter chase at Uttoxeter but for falling heavily 2 out: poor form over hurdles. *D. O. Stephens* **c91 h72 +**

GIRL BAND (IRE) 7 b.m. Bluebird (USA) – Bandit Girl (Robellino (USA)) [2004/5 16m Apr 28] no form in 3 outings over hurdles. *E. A. Elliott* **h–**

GIULIANI 5 b.g. Sadler's Wells (USA) – Anka Germania (Malinowski (USA)) [2004/5 h83p: 23d* 23m* 16s 25gF Dec 16] useful-looking gelding: fair form over hurdles: won maiden and novice at Wetherby early in season: will stay 3m+. *J. Howard Johnson* **h106**

GIUST IN TEMP (IRE) 6 b.g. Polish Precedent (USA) – Blue Stricks (Bluebird (USA)) [2004/5 h79: 16f4 16m Sep 19] sparely-made gelding: poor maiden hurdler: will prove best at 2m: raced on good going or firmer. *P. W. Hiatt* **h72**

GIVE HIM CREDIT (USA) 5 b.g. Quiet American (USA) – Meniatarra (USA) (Zilzal (USA)) [2004/5 17d6 17g Aug 14] fair 7f winner at 3 yrs: disappointing since, including over hurdles: wears cheekpieces. *Mrs A. Duffield* **h–**

GIVE ME LOVE (FR) 5 ch.g. Bering – Cout Contact (USA) (Septieme Ciel (USA)) [2004/5 18v3 19d 19d4 18s 18s3 17s* 18s 19s* 18v* 20d6 21s4 17v2 21s4 21g 22g6 Apr 16] leggy gelding: second foal: dam, useful sprinter, out of sister to smart sprinter King's Signet, from family of top-class sprinter Sigy: 11f winner on Flat: fairly useful hurdler: won claimers at Enghien in October and Auteuil (claimed from F. Belmont €13,000) in November, and handicap at Auteuil later in November: left Y. Porzier after next start: stays 21f: acts on heavy ground: tried in blinkers/cheekpieces: tongue tied 5 of 6 outings in Britain. *P. F. Nicholls* **h116**

GIVEN A CHANCE 4 b.g. Defacto (USA) – Milly Molly Mango (Mango Express) [2004/5 16spu 17g5 17g5 Apr 3] poor maiden on Flat (stays 1¼m): easily best effort over hurdles when fifth to Admiral in juvenile at Market Rasen final start. *Mrs S. Lamyman* **h92**

GLACIAL DANCER (IRE) 12 b.g. Glacial Storm (USA) – Castleblagh (General Ironside) [2004/5 c77, h–: c27gpu May 25] lengthy gelding: winning pointer: maiden chaser: pulled up in hunter only start in 2004/5: stays 3m: raced on good going or softer (acts on heavy). *Mrs E. J. Clark* **c– h–**

GLACIAL DELIGHT (IRE) 6 b.g. Glacial Storm (USA) – Annagh Delight (Saint Denys) [2004/5 F81: 20s 19dpu Dec 16] big gelding: winning pointer: not knocked about once held in novice at Haydock on hurdling debut: probably found next race coming too soon. *Miss E. C. Lavelle* **h80 +**

GLACIAL EVENING (IRE) 9 b. or br.g. Glacial Storm (USA) – Cold Evening (IRE) (Strong Gale) [2004/5 h99: 24g 26g* 24s5 c25sur c24dpu Feb 9] sturdy gelding: fair handicap hurdler: won at Huntingdon in October: failed to complete in maiden chases: stays 3¼m: acts on soft ground. *R. H. Buckler* **c– h112**

GLACIAL RIVER (IRE) 12 ch.g. Glacial Storm (USA) – Lucky Trout (Beau Charmeur (FR)) [2004/5 c–, h–: c26g2 c26gpu c24gpu Jun 3] lengthy gelding: maiden hurdler/chaser: successful in maiden point in February: stays 29f: acts on soft and good to firm going: tried in blinkers/visor. *D. J. Caro* **c95 ? h–**

GLACIAL SUNSET (IRE) 10 ch.g. Glacial Storm (USA) – Twinkle Sunset (Deep Run) [2004/5 h118: 24dpu 24spu 24g* 22d2 Dec 26] workmanlike gelding: fairly useful hurdler: twice ran as if amiss before winning handicap at Kempton in November by 3 lengths from Lord Nellsson: good second to Dangerously Good in similar event at Wincanton: stays 3¼m: acts on firm and good to soft going. *C. Tinkler* **h123**

GLACIAL SYGNET (IRE) 12 ch.g. Glacial Storm (USA) – Barnhill Rose (Lucifer (USA)) [2004/5 c22gpu c21m2 c22g4 Jul 4] ex-Irish gelding: winning hurdler: modest handicap chaser nowadays: sold out of J. J. Mangan's stable 2,500 gns Doncaster January (2004) Sales: stays 3m: probably acts on any going: usually blinkered and tongue tied, has worn cheekpieces. *J. L. Gledson* **c90 h–**

GLACIAL VALE (IRE) 6 b.m. Glacial Storm (USA) – Anna Valley (Gleason (USA)) [2004/5 F16sro F16v5 Feb 20] third foal: dam, fair staying hurdler, half-sister to fairly useful hurdlers around 2½m Robin Goodfellow and The Decent Thing: no form in mares bumpers, ran out on debut. *J. A. Geake* **F–**

GLADIATEUR IV (FR) 11 b.g. Useful (FR) – Friga (FR) (Montevideo) [2004/5 c21m* c20dur c21d2 c22g4 c24d5 c24dpu Oct 23] lengthy, rather sparely-made gelding: useful handicap chaser: off 20 months, won at Stratford in May by 5 lengths from Polar Red: best effort after when second to impressive Take The Stand in valuable event at Newton Abbot in August: stayed easy 3m: acted on firm and good to soft going: visored once: tried tongue tied: dead. *M. C. Pipe* **c132 h–**

GLADIATORIAL (IRE) 13 b.g. Mazaad – Arena (Sallust) [2004/5 c–, h–: c23d* c21dpu c24g5 Mar 3] fair hunter chaser: won at Exeter in May: probably stays 3m: acts on soft and good to firm going: tried visored: has had tongue tied: often let down by jumping. *Mrs Frances Bishop* **c92 h–**

GLADTOKNOWYOU (IRE) 12 ch.g. Over The River (FR) – Jonsemma (IRE) (Denel (FR)) [2004/5 c108: c25spu Feb 15] lengthy gelding: lightly raced: fair chaser: placed in points in 2005, no show in hunter at Folkestone: stays 2¾m: acts on soft going. *Mrs A. Blaker* **c– h–**

GLADYS GERTRUDE 4 ch.f. Double Trigger (IRE) – Nour El Sahar (USA) (Sagace (FR)) [2004/5 F16d Feb 18] eighth foal: half-sister to winner around 1½m Ben Kenobi (by Accondy) and to winners abroad by Peking Opera and Chief Singer: dam French 7.5f winner: tailed off in mares bumper on debut. *M. J. Gingell* **F–**

GLANAMANA (IRE) 9 b.g. Be My Native (USA) – Brides Choice (Cheval) [2004/5 c24dpu c24d c23s2 c26d c24d6 c26dpu c24spu c19spu Mar 23] rangy gelding: modest handicap chaser, form in 2004/5 only on third outing: stays 3¼m: acts on soft going: ran as if amiss in blinkers last 2 starts: races up with pace. *B. G. Powell* **c93 h–**

GLANWORTH (IRE) 4 ch.g. Woodman (USA) – Leo Girl (USA) (Seattle Slew (USA)) [2004/5 16spu Mar 23] little sign of ability on Flat at 3 yrs, sold out of N. Callaghan's stable 3,000 gns Newmarket July Sales: no show in novice on hurdling debut. *Miss M. Bragg* **h–**

GLASHEDY ROCK (IRE) 8 b.g. Shernazar – Classical Lady (IRE) (Orchestra) [2004/5 h–: c19g4 c24g5 c24dF c23spu Mar 22] lengthy gelding: winning pointer: maiden hurdler: off 14 months, modest form in chases first 2 starts: will stay beyond 3m: sold 6,000 gns Doncaster May Sales. *Miss H. C. Knight* **c96 h–**

GLASKER MILL (IRE) 5 b.g. Old Vic – Lucey Allen (Strong Gale) [2004/5 F16s* F17d Apr 9] good sort: eighth foal: half-brother to 27f hurdle winner Moonlite Magic (by Phardante): dam, lightly-raced maiden pointer, half-sister to useful but temperamental staying chaser Sister Stephanie: won maiden Irish point on debut in November: useful **F106**

form when winning slowly-run bumper at Kempton by 4 lengths from Promise To Be Good in February: not knocked about when mid-field in Grade 2 event at Aintree: useful prospect. *Miss H. C. Knight*

GLASS NOTE (IRE) 7 b.m. Spectrum (IRE) – Alice En Ballade (Tap On Wood) [2004/5 h–: 17dpu 24m3 19m5 c23mpu c24mF c17gpu 17spu 19g 19spu 16d Jan 6] of no account: tried blinkered: has had tongue tied. *S. T. Lewis* **c– h–**

GLENCOYLE (IRE) 5 b.g. In The Wings – Lucky State (USA) (State Dinner (USA)) [2004/5 h109: 16dF 22m3 May 19] smallish gelding: fair form over hurdles: stays 2¾m: tends to hang left: sold only 2,000 gns Newmarket Autumn Sales. *N. J. Henderson* **h105 ?**

GLENDEVON GREY 6 gr.g. Karinga Bay – Sandy Etna (IRE) (Sandalay) [2004/5 h–, F–: c24d5 c25dpu Apr 11] workmanlike gelding: no sign of ability. *G. M. Moore* **c– h–**

GLENELLY GALE (IRE) 11 b. or br.g. Strong Gale – Smart Fashion (Carlburg) [2004/5 c143, h103: c24s4 c24s6 18v c17v3 c16v4 c18d3 c36dpu c20g Apr 22] big, lengthy gelding: winning hurdler: useful chaser: creditable efforts when third to Central House in Grade 2 at Fairyhouse and Mossy Green in minor event at Thurles: left A. Moore before final outing: effective at 2m to easy 3m: acts on any going. *M. W. Easterby* **c131 h–**

GLENFARCLAS BOY (IRE) 9 b.g. Montelimar (USA) – Fairy Blaze (IRE) (Good Thyne (USA)) [2004/5 c97§, h–: c16d5 20m6 c16d2 c22v5 c20s3 18s c20v5 c21v5 c20d2 c16v2 Apr 17] good-topped gelding: maiden hurdler: modest handicap chaser: stays 21f: acts on heavy and good to firm going: usually wears cheekpieces: often let down by jumping: inconsistent. *Miss Lucinda V. Russell* **c94 § h72 §**

GLENFINN CAPTAIN (IRE) 6 br.g. Alderbrook – Glenfinn Princess (Ginger Boy) [2004/5 F16s* Mar 26] first foal: dam fair hurdler/chaser, stayed 4m: won bumper at Down Royal on debut easily by 11 lengths from Dead Sound: likely to improve. *W. J. Lanigan, Ireland* **F101 p**

GLENGARRA (IRE) 8 ch.g. Phardante (FR) – Glengarra Princess (Cardinal Flower) [2004/5 h82: c21g3 c16d2 c17g3 c16g4 c17m4 c20g3 c20f4 c18d2 Mar 5] deep-girthed gelding: maiden hurdler: modest novice chaser: stays 2½m: acts on good to soft going: often finds little. *D. R. Gandolfo* **c97 § h–**

GLENHAVEN BOY (IRE) 7 br.g. Satco (FR) – Dunabell Lady (Garda's Revenge (USA)) [2004/5 h–: c26dF c22gpu 21gpu Oct 27] won Irish point in 2003: no form otherwise: tried blinkered. *K. C. Bailey* **c– h–**

GLENMOSS ROSY (IRE) 6 gr.m. Zaffaran (USA) – Rosy Posy (IRE) (Roselier (FR)) [2004/5 22v 20vpu 20s4 24s2 24vpu Mar 20] good-topped mare: sixth foal: sister to bumper winner Go White Lightning and 25f chase winner Greyton and half-sister to fairly useful bumper winner Dobbiesgardenworld (by Great Marquess): dam unraced half-sister to smart 2m hurdler Honeygrove Banker: modest form over hurdles: will prove suited by thorough test of stamina. *N. G. Richards* **h86**

GLENOGUE (IRE) 7 b.m. Hushang (IRE) – Glenamal (Kemal (FR)) [2004/5 h98: c20g5 Oct 27] tall mare: modest novice hurdler: last of 5 finishers in novice handicap at Cheltenham on chasing debut: probably stays 3m: raced on good going or softer. *K. C. Bailey* **c97 h–**

GLEN ORCHY 7 b.m. Mazaad – Royal Pocket (True Song) [2004/5 F16g Sep 12] medium-sized mare: third reported foal: dam winning pointer: tailed off in bumper on debut: failed to complete in 3 points in 2005. *P. W. Hiatt* **F–**

GLENSAN (IRE) 8 b.g. Insan (USA) – Strikes Glen (Le Moss) [2004/5 c25s4 24dpu c24d6 c24spu c25s5 c25g4 Mar 9] sturdy gelding: winning pointer: first form in chases when fourth in novice handicap at Catterick. *M. E. Sowersby* **c64 h–**

GLEN THYNE (IRE) 5 b.g. Good Thyne (USA) – Glen Laura (Kambalda) [2004/5 F16s Jan 27] €15,000 3-y-o, resold €8,000 3-y-o: seventh foal: dam unraced half-sister to useful chaser Zeta's River: green, well held in bumper on debut. *K. C. Bailey* **F–**

GLEN WARRIOR 9 b.g. Michelozzo (USA) – Mascara VII (Damsire Unregistered) [2004/5 h118: c21d2 c21g* 22d4 c24d5 c26v4 c24d* c23v3 Mar 30] tall gelding: fairly useful hurdler: similar form over fences: won maiden at Cartmel in May and novice handicap at Uttoxeter (beat Beau Supreme by 6 lengths in good style) in March: likely to prove best at 3m+: raced on good going or softer (acts on heavy): patiently ridden: reliable. *J. S. Smith* **c127 h121 +**

totescoop6 Summer Plate (Handicap Chase), Market Rasen—
the lightly-raced Glinger upsets Irish raider Colca Canyon (noseband)

GLINGER (IRE) 12 b.g. Remainder Man – Harilla (Sir Herbert) [2004/5 c104, h91: 20d^6 c20m* c20d* Jul 17] workmanlike gelding: maiden hurdler: fairly useful handicap chaser: much improved when making most to beat Broadgate Flyer 3 lengths at Perth in June and Colca Canyon 5 lengths in totescoop6 Summer Plate at Market Rasen in July: stays 2¾m: acts on good to firm and good to soft going: sound jumper. *N. G. Richards* **c119 h78 +**

GLOBAL CHALLENGE (IRE) 6 b.g. Sadler's Wells (USA) – Middle Prospect (USA) (Mr Prospector (USA)) [2004/5 h104§: 22d* 22m^2 24m^2 22s^2 24g* Jul 1] sturdy gelding: fairly useful hurdler: won maiden at Newton Abbot in May and novice at Perth in July: stays 3m: acts on soft and good to firm going: often blinkered/in cheekpieces: has had tongue tied: hard ride and one to treat with caution. *Jonjo O'Neill* **h119 §**

GLOBE DREAM (IRE) 5 b.m. Eagle Eyed (USA) – Scenic Villa (Top Ville) [2004/5 F17g Apr 3] half-sister to fairly useful hurdler Globe Runner (by Adbass), stayed 2¾m, and fair 2m hurdler Pirandello (by Shalford): dam poor maiden: soundly beaten in mares bumper on debut. *F. P. Murtagh* **F–**

GLOBE PEARL (IRE) 5 b.m. Oscar (IRE) – Wolver Top (Wolver Heights) [2004/5 F16m F16d Jan 13] compact mare: sixth foal: dam unraced: well held in 2 bumpers. *F. P. Murtagh* **F–**

GLORIOUS WELCOME 7 b.g. Past Glories – Rest And Welcome (Town And Country) [2004/5 h–: 22g 25g 24m^{pu} Jun 5] of no account: visored: has had tongue tied. *Jane Southcombe* **h–**

GLORY BE 5 ch.m. Gunner B – Geoffreys Bird (Master Willie) [2004/5 F16d^3 Nov 22] seventh foal: half-sister to winner up to 1¼m in Spain by King's Signet: dam unraced half-sister to smart 6f and 7f performer Mac's Fighter: third in maiden bumper at Ludlow on debut. *Miss Venetia Williams* **F83**

GLORY OF LOVE 10 b.g. Belmez (USA) – Princess Lieven (Royal Palace) [2004/5 h–: 16s^6 18d^{pu} Nov 14] lengthy gelding: very lightly raced: maiden hurdler: tried visored. *J. A. Supple* **h–**

GLOSTER GUNNER 6 ch.g. Gunner B – Blue Empress (Blue Cashmere) [2004/5 h–, F–: c16s^6 c20m^{pu} 22g^{pu} Oct 6] of little account: left Dr P. Pritchard after second outing. *Miss J. S. Davis* **c– h–**

GLOWING EMBER 5 b.m. Blushing Flame (USA) – California Dreamin (Slip Anchor) [2004/5 F–: aF16g^3 aF16g^6 aF16g 17g 16g^5 17d Mar 26] poor form in bumpers and over hurdles: left D. Feek after fourth outing. *J. F. Panvert* **h77 F75**

GLYNN DINGLE (IRE) 12 b.g. Millfontaine – Banner Lady (Milan) [2004/5 c127, h96: c25g c25g^3 c24f^2 c22m c22g^{pu} Sep 25] workmanlike gelding: maiden hurdler: fairly **c122 x h–**

useful handicap chaser: creditable efforts first 3 starts: stays 25f: acts on firm and soft ground: sometimes makes mistakes. *A. J. Martin, Ireland*

GNILLISH 5 b.g. Bob's Return (IRE) – Spring Flyer (IRE) (Waajib) [2004/5 F17d Nov 16] fifth foal: half-brother to fairly useful hurdlers up to 3m Miss Tango (by Batshoof) and Roveretto (by Robellino), latter also winning 2m chaser: dam, fair 7f to 9f winner, half-sister to smart sprinter A Prayer For Wings: tailed off in bumper on debut: sold 1,200 gns Doncaster May Sales. *M. C. Pipe* **F–**

GOBLET OF FIRE (USA) 6 b.g. Green Desert (USA) – Laurentine (USA) (Private Account (USA)) [2004/5 h99: 16d² 16g* 17d³ 16s⁴ 17g² 16d 16d⁵ 21m³ 22m* Apr 21] good-topped gelding: fairly useful hurdler: won handicap at Cheltenham (by 6 lengths from Dawton) in October and novice at Plumpton (retried in blinkers) in April: stays 2¾m: acts on soft and good to firm going: has had tongue tied: not a straightforward ride (has raced freely). *P. F. Nicholls* **h121**

GOBLIN 4 b.g. Atraf – Forest Fantasy (Rambo Dancer (CAN)) [2004/5 16d⁶ 16s⁴ 16m² 16d* 16g* 16m Feb 6] leggy gelding: fair on Flat (stays 1½m): similar standard over hurdles: won novice and juvenile handicap (beat A Bit of Fun 8 lengths) at Musselburgh in January: let down by jumping in handicap there final start: will prove best at sharp 2m: acts on good to firm and good to soft going. *D. E. Cantillon* **h110**

GO CLASSIC 5 b.m. Classic Cliche (IRE) – Edraianthus (Windjammer (USA)) [2004/5 17d 16sᵖᵘ 16g⁴ 19m⁵ Mar 14] half-sister to useful hurdler Edwarda (by Safawan), stayed 2½m, and winning 2m hurdler Border Run (by Missed Flight): fair maiden on Flat (should stay 2m): form over hurdles only when fourth in maiden at Southwell: should stay beyond 2m. *A. M. Hales* **h88**

GODFATHER (IRE) 7 ch.g. Insan (USA) – Lady Letitia (Le Bavard (FR)) [2004/5 h–, F–: 20m 17s 17g⁶ c16s⁵ c25vᵖᵘ c28gᵖᵘ Mar 20] tall gelding: no worthwhile form. *M. Pitman* **c–** **h–**

GODS TOKEN 7 gr.g. Gods Solution – Pro-Token (Proverb) [2004/5 h115: 16d³ 16g* 17g³ May 23] good-topped gelding: fairly useful hurdler: won intermediate at Ludlow in May by 2 lengths from Gaora Bridge: will stay beyond 17f: acts on soft going: tongue tied in 2004/5: sometimes jumps none too fluently. *Miss Venetia Williams* **h115**

GOFAGOLD 10 ch.g. Tina's Pet – Golden Della (Glint of Gold) [2004/5 c83, h82: c16sᵘʳ c16v⁵ c16s⁴ c20v⁴ Mar 17] well-made gelding: poor maiden hurdler/chaser: should stay 2½m: raced on good going or softer (acts on heavy): prone to mistakes. *A. C. Whillans* **c81** **h–**

GO FOR BUST 6 b.g. Sabrehill (USA) – Butsova (Formidable (USA)) [2004/5 F83: 16d⁶ 20s⁴ 22s 20s* 21d* 24g² 24m⁴ Apr 13] compact gelding: fairly useful hurdler: won handicaps at Huntingdon in February and Ludlow (novice) in March, significant improvement when beating General Grey by 19 lengths at latter: challenged on bridle last when 3¾ lengths fourth to Comanche War Paint in novice handicap at Cheltenham final start: stays 3m: acts on soft and good to firm going: ridden by 7-lb claimer last 4 starts. *N. J. Henderson* **h125**

GO GREEN 4 ch.f. Environment Friend – Sandra Mac (Marju (IRE)) [2004/5 16g⁵ 17sᶠ 16s⁴ 16s⁶ Jan 20] modest on Flat (stays 1¼m): little form over hurdles, stamina limitations: visored final outing: tongue tied. *P. D. Evans* **h61**

GO GWENNI GO 6 b.m. Bold Fox – Landsker Pryde (Nearly A Hand) [2004/5 F16m⁵ F16g Aug 18] first foal: dam won 2¾m hurdle: soundly beaten in 2 bumpers. *P. Bowen* **F–**

GO HARVEY GO (IRE) 6 b.g. Supreme Leader – Python Wolf (IRE) (Jolly Jake (NZ)) [2004/5 aF16g Feb 19] €21,000 4-y-o: first foal: dam, dual bumper winner, out of half-sister to useful 2m to 2½m chaser Hoh Warrior: eighth of 14 in bumper on polytrack at Lingfield on debut. *R. T. Phillips* **F80 +**

GOLA CHER (IRE) 11 b.g. Beau Sher – Owen Money (Master Owen) [2004/5 c131, h–: 24d⁵ May 8] rangy gelding: useful hurdler/chaser at best: won twice in points in 2005: will stay beyond 3½m: raced on good going or softer (acts on heavy): tried blinkered/in cheekpieces: lazy. *A. King* **c–** **h–**

GOLANO 5 gr.g. Linamix (FR) – Dimakya (USA) (Dayjur (USA)) [2004/5 16g⁵ 16v* 16s⁴ 16d* 16d Dec 9] leggy gelding: fairly useful on Flat (stays 1½m), successful in February: fair form over hurdles: won maiden at Stratford in October and novice at Warwick in November: raced at 2m: acts on heavy going: wore cheekpieces last 2 starts. *P. R. Webber* **h112**

GOLA SUPREME (IRE) 10 gr.g. Supreme Leader – Coal Burn (King Sitric) [2004/5 c–, h109: 24s^{pu} 24g^{3} 24s^{pu} 24s* 24g c19s^{6} c23d^{4} c25s^{4} c24g^{6} c24s^{2} Mar 27] workmanlike gelding: fair handicap hurdler: won at Towcester in November: modest novice chaser: should stay beyond 3m: acts on heavy going: effective tongue tied or not: none too consistent. *R. Lee* **c93 h110**

GOLD AGAIN (IRE) 7 b.g. Old Vic – Thomastown Girl (Tekoah) [2004/5 F75: F16g^{2} F17g* 16g^{6} 17g^{5} 19d Jan 12] lengthy gelding: progressive form in bumpers, useful form when making all at Southwell in May: best effort in novice hurdles when sixth to Marcel at Newbury: should stay 2½m: blinkered in 2004/5: races prominently. *Noel T. Chance* **h98 F108**

GOLDAMIE (IRE) 6 ch.m. Zaffaran (USA) – Keeping Company (King's Company) [2004/5 h–, F79: 19d^{5} Apr 29] well held in mares novice hurdles: likely to be suited by good test of stamina. *M. Scudamore* **h–**

GOLDBROOK 7 b.g. Alderbrook – Miss Marigold (Norwick (USA)) [2004/5 h118: c17s^{4} c19m^{4} c16d^{4} c16d^{pu} c16d^{3} c17s^{pu} c16d^{F} c16d^{6} c19g^{pu} Apr 7] good-topped gelding: fairly useful hurdler: similar level over fences: stays 19f: unraced on firm going, acts on any other: ran as if amiss 3 times in 2004/5 (bled from nose final one): unreliable. *R. J. Hodges* **c122 § h–**

GOLDEN ALPHA (IRE) 11 b.g. Alphabatim (USA) – Gina's Love (Golden Love) [2004/5 c145, h–: c16d^{3} c16s^{4} c16s c16g Apr 23] well-made gelding: winning hurdler: useful handicap chaser: 12 lb out of weights, good fourth to Well Chief in valuable event at Cheltenham in January: best around 2m: acts on firm and soft going (bumper winner on heavy): tried visored: front runner: has found little. *M. C. Pipe* **c142 h–**

GOLDEN AMBER (IRE) 6 ch.g. Glacial Storm (USA) – Rigton Angle (Sit In The Corner (USA)) [2004/5 h–: 20d 24d^{pu} c23v^{pu} c23m^{pu} Apr 10] no sign of ability. *John R. Upson* **c– h–**

GOLDEN BAY 6 ch.m. Karinga Bay – Goldenswift (IRE) (Meneval (USA)) [2004/5 F88: 21d^{3} 21s^{3} 20d^{2} 21s* 24d 21d^{3} 22d Mar 11] medium-sized mare: fair novice hurdler, trained on debut by G. Balding: won mares event at Ludlow in December: should stay 3m: raced only on soft/good to soft going over hurdles. *J. A. Geake* **h103**

GOLDEN CHALICE (IRE) 6 ch.g. Selkirk (USA) – Special Oasis (Green Desert (USA)) [2004/5 17g 16s 17v 17g^{3} 17m* 16m^{2} Apr 17] useful on Flat (stays 1m), sold out of A. Balding's stable 16,000 gns Newmarket Autumn Sales: fair form over hurdles: won handicap at Taunton in March: would also have won similar event at Stratford final start but for blundering last: best with emphasis on speed around 2m: acts on good to firm ground. *Miss E. C. Lavelle* **h106**

GOLDEN CLICHE 4 ch.f. Classic Cliche (IRE) – Hop The Twig (Full of Hope) [2004/5 18m^{pu} Sep 21] sixth foal: half-sister to fairly useful hunter chaser Kestick (by Roscoe Blake): dam winning hurdler: no show in juvenile hurdle on debut. *Mrs L. Williamson* **h–**

GOLDEN CREW 5 b.h. Busy Flight – Goldenswift (IRE) (Meneval (USA)) [2004/5 F16d Mar 5] tall horse: has scope: second foal: half-brother to fair 21f hurdle winner Golden Bay (by Karinga Bay): dam, fair hurdler/chaser, stayed 3m: backward and very green when tailed off in bumper at Newbury on debut. *J. A. Geake* **F–**

GOLDEN CRUSADER 8 b.g. Gildoran – Pusey Street (Native Bazaar) [2004/5 h98?: 16d^{5} 16g^{6} c16s^{F} c16s^{3} c16s^{5} c16s* c16s^{2} c16d^{3} c18m Apr 2] tall gelding: maiden hurdler: fair chaser: won maiden at Hereford in February: best at 2m: acts on soft and good to firm going: headstrong front runner. *J. W. Mullins* **c109 h87 +**

GOLDEN DUAL 5 b.g. Danehill (USA) – Golden Digger (USA) (Mr Prospector (USA)) [2004/5 17g^{6} 17g^{3} Aug 2] modest maiden on Flat (stays 13f) for S. Dow: blinkered, better effort over hurdles when third in claimer at Newton Abbot. *C. L. Tizzard* **h75**

GOLDEN DUCK (IRE) 5 b.g. Turtle Island (IRE) – Mazeeka (IRE) (Glow (USA)) [2004/5 F16d^{2} F18g^{3} 19s 22v^{4} 21d^{pu} 16v^{5} 19s^{pu} 21d^{pu} Mar 24] sturdy gelding: fourth foal: dam 5f (at 2 yrs) to 1m winner: placed both starts in bumpers: poor form over hurdles: free-going sort. *N. A. Twiston-Davies* **h82 F82**

GOLDEN EXCHANGE (IRE) 5 ch.g. Polar Falcon (USA) – Melting Gold (USA) (Cadeaux Genereux) [2004/5 16d^{4} 16s^{2} 16v* 16s^{2} 16s Mar 29] €80,000 3-y-o: lengthy, angular gelding: fifth foal: half-brother to 3 winners, including useful 6f and 7f filly Caveral (by Polar Falcon): dam, useful 2-y-o 7f winner, out of half-sister to 2000 Guineas **h110**

winner Shadeed: twice-raced in bumpers: fair novice hurdler: won maiden at Limerick in December: good second to Arc En Ciel in minor event at Thurles next time: raced at 2m on going softer than good (acts on heavy). *D. Wachman, Ireland*

GOLDEN FIELDS (IRE) 5 b.m. Definite Article – Quickstep Queen (FR) (Pampabird) [2004/5 h–: 17g^{rtr} 17g 20g^{rtr} Aug 26] rather leggy mare: poor on Flat (stays 1½m): maiden hurdler: bought out of A. Jones's stable £2,800 Ascot July Sales: has worn visor: refused to race twice in 2004/5 and one to avoid. *Jennie Candlish* **h§§**

GOLDEN FITZ (ARG) 6 ch.g. Fitzcarraldo (ARG) – Good Last (ARG) (Good Manners (USA)) [2004/5 16d^{pu} 17d^{pu} Oct 17] leggy gelding: won 7f maiden in UAE at 4 yrs, well held both starts in 2004 (for E. Charpy): no show in novice hurdles, blinkered and tongue tied second outing: sold £1,500 Ascot November Sales. *D. P. Keane* **h–**

GOLDEN HAZE 8 ch.m. Safawan – Hazel Hill (Abednego) [2004/5 h62§: 17g^{pu} 17g 22g 20d^{pu} 27v^{pu} Dec 31] chunky mare: little sign of ability: ungenuine. *Miss T. Jackson* **h– §**

GOLDEN KEY 4 b.g. Rainbow Quest (USA) – Keyboogie (USA) (Lyphard (USA)) [2004/5 17s^{pu} 16d^{pu} Dec 2] well held in two 1¼m maidens in 2004, sold out of Sir Michael Stoute's stable 4,500 gns Doncaster August Sales: no show in 2 juvenile hurdles, gave trouble at start on second occasion. *J. S. Smith* **h–**

GOLDEN LAW 7 b.m. Gildoran – Sister-In-Law (Legal Tender) [2004/5 F82: F17d 17d 23s^{pu} Nov 11] modest form in bumper on debut in 2003/4: no show since, including over hurdles. *P. R. Webber* **h–** **F–**

GOLDEN MEASURE 5 b.g. Rainbow Quest (USA) – Dawna (Polish Precedent (USA)) [2004/5 F95: F17v* F16d F16g^{2} Dec 29] good-topped gelding: fairly useful form in bumpers: won maiden at Market Rasen in October by short head from Va Vavoom. *G. A. Swinbank* **F97**

GOLDEN MILLENIUM (GER) 4 b.c. Monsun (GER) – Gluckskind (GER) (Mister Rock's (GER)) [2004/5 16v^{2} 16v 16d^{3} Jan 12] tall, leggy colt: useful on Flat (stays 1¼m), successful in April 2004 for T. Hanson: beaten neck in juvenile at Pisa on hurdling debut: better effort in Britain when third to Papini at Newbury. *C. Von Der Recke, Germany* **h110**

GOLDEN ODYSSEY (IRE) 5 ch.m. Barathea (IRE) – Opus One (Slip Anchor) [2004/5 F106: 19d* 19d^{2} 21d^{4} 20g* 20g^{3} 21g^{6} Apr 14] unfurnished mare: successful 3 times in bumpers: fair novice hurdler: won at Market Rasen in October and Musselburgh (beat Simply Mystic by 3 lengths) in January: looked less than keen final start: stays 21f: yet to race on extremes of going. *K. G. Reveley* **h111**

GOLDEN RAMBLER (IRE) 9 br.g. Roselier (FR) – Goldiyana (FR) (Glint of Gold) [2004/5 h103+: c24d* c26d* c24f^{F} c22s^{pu} c24d^{pu} c25g^{F} Apr 16] good-topped gelding: winning hurdler: landed odds in novice chases at Southwell and Uttoxeter in May: failed to complete subsequently: suited by 3m+: acts on soft going. *Jonjo O'Neill* **c115 d** **h–**

GOLDEN REWARD (SAF) 7 ro.g. Goldmark (SAF) – Enticement (SAF) (Capture Him (USA)) [2004/5 h94p: 16g 16m^{5} 17g Jul 15] angular gelding: novice hurdler: no form in 2004/5, let down by jumping final start. *Miss Venetia Williams* **h–**

GOLDEN SHELL 6 ch.m. Hatim (USA) – Sonnenelle (Sonnen Gold) [2004/5 16d^{pu} Oct 9] no form on Flat or on hurdling debut. *A. C. Whillans* **h–**

GOLDEN STORM (IRE) 8 ch.g. Magical Wonder (USA) – Independent Woman (IRE) (Carmelite House (USA)) [2004/5 c127, h–: c25g^{4} c24s^{5} c22g* c24v^{pu} c28s^{4} c24v^{3} c29d^{ur} c24s c24v c24v^{3} c24v^{5} c21v^{bd} c29s Mar 28] smallish, rather leggy gelding: fairly useful handicap chaser: won listed event at Galway in September: in-and-out form after: stays 29f: acts on heavy going: usually blinkered. *Joseph Crowley, Ireland* **c127** **h–**

GOLDEN TINA 7 ch.m. Tina's Pet – Gold 'n Soft (Whistling Deer) [2004/5 F16g F16v^{4} 19v^{pu} 17g Mar 9] first foal: dam, winning selling hurdler, stayed 2½m: no form in mares bumpers or novice hurdles. *A. E. Price* **h–** **F–**

GOLD FERVOUR (IRE) 6 b.g. Mon Tresor – Fervent Fan (IRE) (Soviet Lad (USA)) [2004/5 16s^{6} 16g 16d 16s Jan 20] half-brother to modest 2m hurdler Lemagurut (by Mukaddamah): poor maiden on Flat (stays 1m): non-stayer over hurdles. *W. M. Brisbourne* **h–**

GOLD FOR ME (FR) 6 b.g. Solar One (FR) – Volcania (FR) (Neustrien (FR)) [2004/5 F16s^{4} 19s^{pu} 17s^{5} 19v^{5} 24m^{6} 20d^{F} Apr 22] has scope: fourth foal: half-brother to one-time smart hurdler Magnus (by Roakarad), stays 3m, and middle-distance winners **h89** **F93**

Cosmographie (by Lomitas) and King Volcano (by Bon Sang): dam unraced, from family of high-class hurdler around 2½m Rockeby Basie: fourth in bumper on debut: modest form over hurdles: should stay 2½m: sold 2,600 gns Doncaster May Sales. *M. C. Pipe*

GOLDHORN (IRE) 10 b.g. Little Bighorn – Stylish Gold (IRE) (Tumble Gold) [2004/5 h–: 16g Dec 11] medium-sized gelding: bumper winner: little impact in 2 novice hurdles 9 months apart. *O. Brennan* **h81 ?**

GOLD KRIEK 8 b.g. High Kicker (USA) – Ship of Gold (Glint of Gold) [2004/5 c24g* c25d³ c21g² c24m* c24gᵖᵘ Aug 14] good-topped gelding: modest chaser: won novice handicaps at Uttoxeter (11 lb out of weights) in June and Stratford in July: broke down final start: stays 3m: acts on good to firm going and good to soft: often makes mistakes. *B. J. Llewellyn* **c92 h–**

GOLD MEDALLIST 5 ch.g. Zilzal (USA) – Spot Prize (USA) (Seattle Dancer (USA)) [2004/5 19d* 24d* 20s* 21g⁵ 24dᵖᵘ Apr 8] **h144**

The ranks of the novices and juvenile hurdlers included a strong intake from the Flat in the latest season. Among the smart performers who switched codes were the winners of three of the most prestigious Flat handicaps, Mephisto (Ebor), Arcalis (John Smith's Cup) and Carte Diamond (November Handicap), the stayers Pole Star (placed in a Gold Cup and an Ebor) and Dusky Warbler (a Doncaster Cup runner-up), as well as No Refuge who had won a listed race in Germany and foreign imports Olaso (a Group 2 winner in Germany), Etendard Indien (a Group 3 winner in France) and Clear Thinking (placed in French pattern races). Just about the pick on Flat form, however, was Gold Medallist who had been considered good enough to contest the St Leger the year before and had had the winner of that race, Brian Boru, as well as the previous year's Derby runner-up The Great Gatsby, behind him when winning the Group 2 Prix Kergorlay at Deauville as a four-year-old. Inevitably, not all those named lived up to their Flat form over hurdles, but they all managed to win at least once and the majority did prove at least as good over hurdles as they had been on the Flat.

Bought privately out of David Elsworth's stable to join Philip Hobbs, Gold Medallist was one of those to make the grade. He wasted no time in showing that he was going to be one of the season's leading novices when making a winning debut in a novice at Exeter in December. Starting favourite ahead of the previous season's best bumper horse Secret Ploy, Gold Medallist showed useful form with a length and a quarter victory over the second favourite, the pair pulling twenty-three lengths clear. Gold Medallist found plenty when challenged after racing prominently from the off and jumping particularly fluently for a newcomer. By the time Gold Medallist was turned out again, the well-held fourth and fifth at Exeter had both won. Only three rivals turned up to take on Gold Medallist over three miles at Kempton in January, and Gold Medallist didn't have to repeat his earlier form, having the race won a long way out. More significant than Gold Medallist's own performance on the day was his stable's feat of completing a five-timer on the card.

By the time of the Kempton race, Gold Medallist had already been made ante-post favourite for the Royal & SunAlliance Hurdle and he was given a bit more experience before Cheltenham when contesting the Sidney Banks Memorial Novices' Hurdle at Huntingdon in February. Once again, Gold Medallist frightened off all bar three rivals, though the fact that one of them was Pole Star ensured that Gold Medallist didn't have things all his own way. The pair pulled a distance clear of their two four-year-old rivals, Gold Medallist making all and responding well to maintain a half-length advantage over Pole Star on the run-in. Gold Medallist shared favouritism at Cheltenham with the Irish-trained Royal Paradise and ran up to the best of his previous form. That, however, was only good enough to secure Gold Medallist fifth place, around three and a half lengths behind the winner No Refuge and a neck behind Pole Star this time. Although soon in front, Gold Medallist was always being strongly pressed and was headed after two out, his jumping less fluent than it had been in his earlier races. Gold Medallist was returned to three miles for the Sefton Novices' Hurdle at Aintree but proved disappointing, ridden more patiently but never on terms and eventually pulled up after two out when very tired. Despite looking well, it is possible the Cheltenham race had left

*Braybrook Racing Sidney Banks Memorial Novices' Hurdle, Huntingdon—
Gold Medallist is pushed hard by Pole Star to maintain his unbeaten start over hurdles*

its mark. Gold Medallist was not the only one of the principals from the Royal & SunAlliance to underperform subsequently.

Gold Medallist was bred and formerly owned by Jeff Smith of Persian Punch fame and had looked a natural successor to that horse for his connections in the Cup races. After the Kergorlay (a race Persian Punch had won in the past), there was even talk of Gold Medallist's contesting the Melbourne Cup, a race in which Persian Punch twice finished third. Persian Punch would doubtless have made a fine hurdler himself, and it looked at one stage in his career as though hurdling was under serious consideration for him, though, with his owner reportedly not keen on the idea, the plan was shelved. Smith did send his other good Flat stayer Grey Shot, who finished second in the Kergorlay, over hurdles, and with some success, though he eventually sold him on.

Gold Medallist is by the top-class miler Zilzal whose best jumper for now remains Latalomne, based on what he looked like achieving when disputing the lead and falling two out in two consecutive Champion Chases. Gold Medallist's dam Spot Prize gained her only win over five furlongs as a two-year-old but showed much better form in defeat over longer distances, finishing second in the Musidora and fourth in both the Oaks and Ribblesdale. Her failure to win in lesser company from several attempts thereafter meant she needed treating with caution, but there has been nothing wrong with her record as a broodmare. Besides Gold Medallist, Spot Prize has produced the useful mile-and-a-quarter listed winner Premier Prize (by Selkirk), the fairly useful stayer Prize Dancer (by Suave Dancer), the fairly useful mile-and-a-half winner Stage Right (by In The Wings) and another winning hurdler, Prize Ring (by Bering), also successful on the Flat in selling company. The next two dams on the bottom line of Gold Medallist's pedigree, Lucky Brook and

Mrs D. L. Whateley's "Gold Medallist"

Gold Medallist (ch.g. 2000)	Zilzal (USA) (ch 1986)	Nureyev (b 1977)	Northern Dancer
			Special
		French Charmer (ch 1978)	Le Fabuleux
			Bold Example
	Spot Prize (USA) (ch 1991)	Seattle Dancer (b 1984)	Nijinsky
			My Charmer
		Lucky Brook (br 1980)	What Luck
			Brookward

Brookward, won four and five races respectively in the States where both have bred several winners. Another of Brookward's winners was Watertight, a one-time pacemaker for Gold Cup winner Sadeem, who went on to win both over hurdles and fences, showing fairly useful form in the former sphere. The good-topped Gold Medallist stays three miles and acts on soft ground, while he had plenty of form under much firmer conditions on the Flat. His background is hardly typical of a chaser, but he has the size to jump fences, and his stable has already successfully nurtured a smart stayer from the Flat, Double Honour, into one of almost equal standing over fences. *P. J. Hobbs*

GOLD NATIVE (IRE) 7 br.g. Be My Native (USA) – Goldiyana (FR) (Glint of Gold) [2004/5 h70: $21g^F$ May 1] poor maiden hurdler. *B. Ellison* **h–**

GOLD RING 5 ch.g. Groom Dancer (USA) – Indubitable (Sharpo) [2004/5 $16s^F$ $16g^6$ 16d* Mar 10] leggy gelding: half-brother to winning pointer by Then Again: dam half-sister to fairly useful hurdler Accuracy, dam of useful hurdlers Accipter and Brave Tornado: useful on Flat (stays 1¾m) for G. Balding, successful in July, runner-up in Ebor following month: in narrow lead when falling 2 out in novice at Windsor won by Reveil- **h115**

lez on hurdling debut: much better effort after when winning maiden at Wincanton by 2½ lengths from Bonny Grey: will stay 2½m: room for improvement in jumping. *J. A. Geake*

GOLDSEAM (GER) 6 gr.g. Neshad (USA) – Goldkatze (GER) (Czaravich (USA)) [2004/5 h–: 17g Oct 14] no form over hurdles: bought out of C. Mann's stable £3,200 Ascot July Sales. *S. C. Burrough* **h–**

GOLD SPEAR (IRE) 7 ch.g. Torus – Rosel Chris (Roselier (FR)) [2004/5 22v* 22m² c22g² c20d* c22g³ Sep 6] seventh foal: half-brother to useful hurdler/chaser up to 3m Satco Express (by Satco) and bumper winner Abbey Prince (by Tanfirion): dam unraced: modest hurdler: won amateur maiden at Down Royal in May: much better form over fences, winning maiden at Tralee in August: improved again when close third to Windsor Boy in novice at Galway, despite jumping and hanging left: should stay 3m: unraced on firm going, acts on any other: tried tongue tied. *E. Sheehy, Ireland* **c117 h97**

GOLD STANDARD (IRE) 7 ch.g. Goldmark (USA) – Miss Audimar (USA) (Mr Leader (USA)) [2004/5 16g Jul 14] leggy gelding: twice-raced over hurdles: off over 2 years, no show in maiden at Worcester: sold £2,200 Ascot August Sales. *P. J. Hobbs* **h–**

GOLFAGENT 7 b.g. Kris – Alusha (Soviet Star (USA)) [2004/5 h96§: c16s^ur Mar 11] small, close-coupled gelding: modest hurdler: won point in March: held in third when hampered and rider unseated last in hunter chase at Leicester: effective at 2m to 3m: acts on soft and good to firm going: tried visored: tongue tied: unreliable. *Nick Shutts* **c91 h– §**

GOLLY (IRE) 9 b.g. Toulon – Tor-Na-Grena (Torus) [2004/5 c97, h89: c22m^pu c19m^pu Jun 9] angular gelding: modest form only start over hurdles: modest chaser: pulled up both starts in 2004/5: stays 2¾m: acts on firm and good to soft going: difficult ride. *D. L. Williams* **c– h–**

GONDOLIN (IRE) 5 b.g. Marju (IRE) – Galletina (IRE) (Persian Heights) [2004/5 16d 19d 17s 20d Apr 22] tall gelding: fairly useful on Flat (stays 10.5f) for G. Butler, well held both starts in 2004: no form over hurdles. *G. Brown* **h–**

GONE FAR (USA) 8 b.g. Gone West (USA) – Vallee Dansante (USA) (Lyphard (USA)) [2004/5 h124: c17m² c16f³ c21g⁴ c21m³ 16v 19m Apr 17] leggy gelding: fairly useful hurdler in 2003/4: fair form first 2 starts over fences: best around 2m: acts on firm and soft going: usually visored/blinkered nowadays. *M. C. Pipe* **c101 h–**

GONE LOCO 4 b.f. Piccolo – Missed Again (High Top) [2004/5 16m^pu Sep 4] leggy filly: half-sister to fairly useful hurdler Knighted (by Bigstone), stays 25f: little sign of ability on Flat: temperamental display in juvenile on hurdling debut. *H. S. Howe* **h–**

GONE MISSING 6 b.g. Early Edition – Tom's Little Bet (Scallywag) [2004/5 F17d⁵ F16d F17d 21d Dec 5] workmanlike gelding: second foal: dam, fairly useful hurdler who stayed 2¾m, half-sister to smart 2½m to 3m chaser Tom's Little Al: well held in bumpers and on hurdling debut: trained first 2 starts by O. Carter. *Ms Bridget Nicholls* **h– F–**

GONE TOO FAR 7 b.g. Reprimand – Blue Nile (IRE) (Bluebird (USA)) [2004/5 h109: c17g² c16d² c16m* c16d⁴ c16g^F c16d³ c16d⁴ c16s c16m⁵ Nov 26] lengthy, angular gelding: winning hurdler/fair chaser: won weak handicap at Hexham in June: stays 19f: acts on firm and good to soft going: blinkered/visored: better than ever when winning on Flat in June. *P. Monteith* **c110 h–**

GO NOMADIC 11 br.g. Nomadic Way (USA) – Dreamago (Sir Mago) [2004/5 c97: c25g² c21d c27v⁶ c27v³ c24s² c25d⁴ c32v^pu Mar 17] lengthy gelding: modest handicap chaser: stays 31f: acts on heavy going (below best on good to firm): tried in cheekpieces: usually tongue tied. *P. G. Atkinson* **c89**

GOODANDPLENTY 7 b.g. Sovereign Water (FR) – Our Wilma (Master Willie) [2004/5 h–, F91?: 20d^pu 20f^pu Jun 6] no show over hurdles. *Mrs J. C. McGregor* **h–**

GOODBADINDIFERENT (IRE) 9 b. or br.g. Mandalus – Stay As You Are (Buckskin (FR)) [2004/5 c20s⁴ c25s³ c24g^F c25d c25s⁶ c25s⁵ c20s⁴ Apr 22] half-brother to useful staying chaser Stormtracker and modest chaser Gale Force (both by Strong Gale): dam unraced half-sister to fairly useful chasers Knockbrack, best at 2m, and General Highway, a stayer: apparently running easily best race over fences when falling last in novice at Newcastle: modest form at best on completed starts, all on soft/good to soft going: stays 25f: has been let down by jumping. *Mrs J. C. McGregor* **c95 ?**

GOOD BONE (FR) 8 b.g. Perrault – Bone Crasher (FR) (Cadoudal (FR)) [2004/5 c83: c25m³ c22m³ c22m* c21g³ c25d⁴ c22g c26g^pu Apr 14] tall gelding: modest chaser: won novice handicap at Market Rasen in June: left L. Wells and off 8 months, probably flattered when fourth in hunter at Ludlow: stays 25f: acts on good to soft and good to firm going. *S. Flook* **c86**

Blue Square Chase (La Touche Cup), Punchestown—
Good Step (hoops) tracks the grey Andrewjames on his way to his first cross-country win

GOODBYE CHEMO 7 b.g. Greensmith – Bajina (Dancing Brave (USA)) [2004/5 F17m 20gpu 17s 19s 16d Apr 17] 5,000 (privately) 4-y-o: fourth foal: half-brother to 2m hurdle winner Naked Oat (by Imp Society) and winner up to 1¼m in France Tibbie Shiels (by Deploy): dam unraced daughter of useful 1987 2-y-o sprinter Babita: no form: tried tongue tied. *Evan Williams* **h– F–**

GOOD CITIZEN (IRE) 5 b.g. Good Thyne (USA) – Citizen Levee (Monksfield) [2004/5 17d³ 19g⁴ 20d⁴ 20d Mar 12] workmanlike gelding: second foal: dam winning chaser up to 3m: twice-raced in Irish points in 2004, third on completed start: fair form over hurdles, apparently best effort on debut: will stay beyond 2½m. *T. R. George* **h113**

GOOD COMMUNICATOR 5 b.g. Compton Place – Mira Lady (Henbit (USA)) [2004/5 F16m Apr 25] half-brother to several winners, including temperamental hurdler Eric's Bett (by Chilibang): dam won in Germany: seventh of 12 in bumper at Ludlow on debut. *P. D. Evans* **F73**

GOOD FRIEND 6 b.m. Environment Friend – Gunner Be Good (Gunner B) [2004/5 F17dpu F17g F16g⁶ F16m⁴ Sep 24] second foal: dam modest 2m hurdler: no form in bumpers. *J. K. Cresswell* **F–**

GOOD HEART (IRE) 10 ch.g. Be My Native (USA) – Johnstown Love (IRE) (Golden Love) [2004/5 c–, h–: c20g⁴ c21mpu May 19] sturdy, lengthy gelding: maiden hurdler/chaser: winning pointer: possibly best up to 2½m: acts on good to soft going: tried visored: has had tongue tied. *Mrs K. L. Caldwell* **c90 h–**

GOOD JUDGEMENT (IRE) 7 b.g. Good Thyne (USA) – Loch Na Mona (IRE) (King's Ride) [2004/5 16s* Dec 13] €32,000 4-y-o: fifth foal: half-brother to winning 2½m hurdler Tempting Touch (by Welsh Term): dam unraced half-sister to useful staying chasers Hard Case and Sound Argument: won novice hurdle at Towcester on debut by 5 lengths from Monsieur Georges: will be suited by further than 2m: will do better. *Jonjo O'Neill* **h105 p**

GOOD LORD LOUIS (IRE) 7 br.g. Presenting – Ash Queen (IRE) (Altountash) [2004/5 h90: c19m³ c19g* Sep 30] angular gelding: lightly raced: modest form over hurdles: much better effort over fences when winning 4-runner novice handicap at Hereford: should stay beyond 19f. *P. J. Hobbs* **c123 h–**

GOOD LORD MURPHY (IRE) 13 br.g. Montelimar (USA) – Semiwild (USA) (Rumbo (USA)) [2004/5 c–§, h84§: 21mpu Apr 25] tall gelding: veteran hurdler/chaser: stays 27f: acts on heavy going: tried blinkered/in cheekpieces: ungenuine. *Dr P. Pritchard* **c– § h– §**

GOOD MAN AGAIN (IRE) 7 b.g. Arctic Lord – Amari Queen (Nicholas Bill) [2004/5 F18m* 20sbd 24d³ 20s⁵ 25v³ 26s² Mar 7] tall gelding: second foal: dam, won 2m hurdle, half-sister to useful 2½m hurdler Halmajor and good Italian middle-distance stayer Celio Rufo: won bumper at Downpatrick in August: modest form over hurdles: sold out of C. Roche's stable 4,000 gns Doncaster October Sales after third start: stays 3¼m: acts on heavy going. *Evan Williams* **h97 F95**

GOOD OUTLOOK (IRE) 6 b.g. Lord Americo – I'll Say She Is (Ashmore (FR)) [2004/5 c89, h75: 22g^6 c24g^6 Aug 15] sturdy gelding: thrice-raced hurdler: sold out of M. Pipe's stable 5,000 gns Doncaster May Sales after first start: winning chaser, but often let down by jumping: should stay 3m: acts on good to firm going: prone to breaking blood vessel: takes good hold. *R. C. Guest* **c86 x h76**

GOOD SAMARITAN (IRE) 6 ch.g. Insan (USA) – Ballymave (IRE) (Jareer (USA)) [2004/5 F94: F16s F18s^2 17v^{pu} Jan 28] good-topped gelding: fair form in bumpers: breathing problem on hurdling debut. *M. Pitman* **h– F89**

GOOD STEP (IRE) 7 ch.g. Be My Native (USA) – Shuil Alainn (Levanter) [2004/5 c24g^6 c23s^2 c22v* c24s c22s^3 c25s^2 c24v* Apr 6] strong, compact gelding: half-brother to several winners, including fair staying chasers Turnberry Dawn (by Fair Turn) and The Pennys Dropped (by Bob's Return): dam, 2m hurdle winner, half-sister to Scottish National winner Baronet and dam of very smart 2m to 2½m hurdler Liss A Paoraigh: winning pointer: fair chaser: won hunters at Limerick (maiden) in December and Gowran in April and La Touche Cup at Punchestown (beat Shady Lad ½ length) later in April: suited by test of stamina (stays 4¼m): raced mainly on soft/heavy going: effective with or without blinkers: has had tongue tied. *E. Bolger, Ireland* **c110**

GOOD THYNE JOHNNY (IRE) 11 b.g. Good Thyne (USA) – Wiasma (Ashmore (FR)) [2004/5 h72: 20d^6 20d* 21m* 24g^6 20m Jun 27] angular gelding: modest handicap hurdler: won selling events at Uttoxeter and Huntingdon in May: stays 25f: acts on soft and good to firm going: takes good hold and usually makes running. *Jennie Candlish* **h86**

GOODTIMELADY (IRE) 11 b. or br.m. Good Thyne (USA) – Peppardstownlady (Gleason (USA)) [2004/5 c–, h91: 24g^{pu} Jul 4] tall mare: twice-raced chaser: modest hurdler: stays 25f: acts on heavy going: tried blinkered, wore cheekpieces only start in 2004/5. *D. G. Bridgwater* **c– h–**

GOOD TIMING 7 bl.g. Timeless Times (USA) – Fort Vally (Belfort (FR)) [2004/5 h–: 17g^6 17m^5 16g Jul 6] sparely-made gelding: poor maiden on Flat (stays 9.4f): poor selling hurdler: barely stays 2m: sold £3,500 Ascot August Sales. *J. Hetherton* **h63**

GO PETE (NZ) 6 ch.g. Senor Pete (USA) – Lillibet (NZ) (First Norman (USA)) [2004/5 20s^{pu} 20m 16d Nov 29] in frame up to around 1¼m on Flat in New Zealand: no show over hurdles. *R. C. Guest* **h–**

GORDON HIGHLANDER 6 b.m. Master Willie – No Chili (Glint of Gold) [2004/5 h–: 21g^{pu} 17g^2 22d* 22g^{ur} Apr 17] lengthy mare: modest hurdler: won mares novice at Wincanton in March: stays 2¾m: raced on good going or softer: tongue tied last 4 starts. *Mrs P. Robeson* **h95**

GORDY'S JOY 5 b.m. Cloudings (IRE) – Beatle Song (Song) [2004/5 h–: 19s^{pu} 16d^{pu} Apr 22] of little account: tried blinkered. *G. A. Ham* **h–**

GO ROGER GO (IRE) 13 b.g. Phardante (FR) – Tonto's Girl (Strong Gale) [2004/5 c146, h–: c31d c16s c22v^{pu} Jan 1] rangy, good sort: smart chaser at best: off a year, no form in 2004/5: barely stayed 2¾m: acted on good to firm and heavy going: dead. *E. J. O'Grady, Ireland* **c– h–**

GORTINARD (IRE) 7 b.g. King's Ride – The Lady's Last (IRE) (Brush Aside (USA)) [2004/5 24v Jan 9] first foal: dam unraced half-sister to useful 2m hurdler Hansel Rag: fairly useful hurdler: well-backed favourite on only second outing in over a year, won 25-runner handicap at Punchestown in late-April by length from Kings Advocate: stays 3m: acts on soft and good to firm going. *Charles Byrnes, Ireland* **h116**

GOSPEL SONG 13 ch.g. King Among Kings – Market Blues (Porto Bello) [2004/5 h86: 20v 16v* 16s^3 20v^6 20s^5 16s^2 Apr 20] small gelding: modest handicap hurdler: won conditional jockeys event at Wetherby (for second year running) in January: probably best up to easy 2½m: acts on heavy going: tried tongue tied: free-going sort: genuine. *A. C. Whillans* **h94**

GOSS 8 gr.g. Linamix (FR) – Guillem (USA) (Nijinsky (CAN)) [2004/5 c112, h125: 16m 16m 16g^F 16s^5 16g 16d^6 Dec 11] tall ex-Irish gelding: fair chaser/useful hurdler at best: little form and looked none too keen in 2004/5: raced around 2m: acts on good to firm and heavy going: has had tongue tied. *Jonjo O'Neill* **c– h111 §**

GOSS HAWK (NZ) 5 br.g. Senor Pete (USA) – Stapleton Row (NZ) (Long Row) [2004/5 F–: F16d 24s^{pu} 25v^{pu} 21d^{pu} 16g^6 Mar 28] medium-sized gelding: no form in bumpers and over hurdles: tongue tied final outing. *Jonjo O'Neill* **h– F–**

GOTHAM ABBEY (IRE) 8 gr.m. Gothland (FR) – Abbeyside (Paddy's Stream) [2004/5 h–: 17m^{pu} 22m^{pu} Jun 13] leggy mare: no form over hurdles: runner-up in point in April. *H. W. Lavis* **h–**

GOTHAM (IRE) 8 gr.g. Gothland (FR) – Inchriver (IRE) (Over The River (FR)) [2004/5 c101, h–: c16g^{4} c19s^{ur} c20d^{6} c21d^{pu} 19g Apr 7] lengthy gelding: winning hurdler/novice chaser, form in 2004/5 only on reappearance: should be suited by further than 2m: acts on soft and good to firm going. *R. H. Alner* **c86 h–**

GOTNO DESTINATION (IRE) 4 ch.g. Accordion – Slaney Pal (IRE) (Supreme Leader) [2004/5 F12d^{3} F16s^{3} Apr 10] lengthy, useful-looking gelding: third foal: dam unraced from family of smart but unreliable 2m hurdler/chaser Redundant Pal: fairly useful form in bumpers at Cheltenham (third to Openide in listed 4-y-o event) and Limerick. *T. J. Taaffe, Ireland* **F98**

GOT NO SHADOW 6 b.g. Terimon – Run On Stirling (Celtic Cone) [2004/5 F16g F16m^{4} F16m^{6} Jul 21] third foal: brother to bumper winner Little Feat: dam poor 2m novice hurdler: modest form in bumpers. *N. B. King* **F79**

GOTTA GET ON 4 br.f. Emperor Fountain – Lonicera (Sulaafah (USA)) [2004/5 16d^{pu} 19d^{pu} 22g^{6} 18m^{6} Apr 21] lengthy filly: second foal: dam modest 2m hurdler: no sign of ability. *R. H. Alner* **h–**

GOVERNMENT (IRE) 4 b.g. Great Dane (IRE) – Hidden Agenda (FR) (Machiavellian (USA)) [2004/5 16d^{ur} 16s 20s^{4} 16d^{pu} Apr 20] leggy gelding: half-brother to winning 2½m hurdler Sting Like A Bee (by Ali-Royal): poor maiden on Flat: no form over hurdles. *M. C. Chapman* **h–**

GOVERNOR DANIEL 14 b.g. Governor General – Princess Semele (Imperial Fling (USA)) [2004/5 c–, h101: 20m^{pu} Aug 6] sturdy gelding: a grand servant to connections, winning 14 times over hurdles and 5 over fences: thought by rider to be lame only outing in 2004/5: stays easy 21f: acts on firm and soft going: has had tongue tied: usually races prominently: sometimes let down by jumping over fences: tough and consistent. *Ian Williams* **c– h–**

GO WHITE LIGHTNING (IRE) 10 gr.g. Zaffaran (USA) – Rosy Posy (IRE) (Roselier (FR)) [2004/5 c101, h–: c26d^{pu} c33g^{4} Mar 17] leggy gelding: fair maiden chaser: 100/1, dictated steady pace when fourth to Another Rum in National Hunt Chase at Cheltenham, probably flattered: stays 33f: acts on soft going: free-going front runner: often shapes as if amiss. *M. Bradstock* **c108 ? h–**

GRACE DIEU 4 br. or gr.f. Commanche Run – Race To The Rhythm (Deep Run) [2004/5 F12g F17s 19s^{pu} 19m 16g Apr 19] leggy filly: third foal: dam poor novice staying hurdler: no form in bumpers or over hurdles: virtually refused to race fourth outing. *M. Scudamore* **h– § F–**

GRACEFUL DANCER 8 b.m. Old Vic – Its My Turn (Palm Track) [2004/5 c77, h78: 26s^{2} 22v* Mar 30] good-topped mare: poor form on completed outing over fences: fair hurdler: left C. Morlock and off a year, improved form in 2004/5, winning handicap at Exeter with plenty in hand: stays 3½m: raced on good going or softer (acts on heavy): blinkered (looked unwilling) once, usually visored for former stable. *B. G. Powell* **c– h103**

GRACILIS (IRE) 8 b.g. Caerleon (USA) – Grace Note (FR) (Top Ville) [2004/5 h110: 24d^{3} 24v^{pu} 16s^{3} 20d^{6} 16v^{pu} 16d Jan 1] sturdy gelding: fairly useful on Flat (stays 21f) at best, well beaten in 2004: fair hurdler: ran as if amiss last 2 starts: stays 3m: raced on going softer than good (acts on soft): tried in cheekpieces: sold 4,200 gns Doncaster May Sales. *G. A. Swinbank* **h114**

GRADUAND (IRE) 6 br.g. Executive Perk – Right Then Rosie (IRE) (Callernish) [2004/5 F16v^{4} F19v* F19s^{2} 24d^{3} Mar 20] €9,200 4-y-o: second foal: half-brother to bumper winner/winning pointer Quarryfield Lass (by Lord Americo): dam maiden pointer: useful in bumpers: won at Naas in January: ½-length second, staying on well, to Mister Top Notch there following month: 4 lengths third to Gayle Abated in 3m maiden at Limerick on hurdling debut: will improve over hurdles. *Ms F. M. Crowley, Ireland* **h99 p F111**

GRAFFITI TONGUE (IRE) 12 b.g. Be My Native (USA) – Lantern Line (The Parson) [2004/5 24m^{4} 22f* 24f^{6} 24m^{6} 20d^{5} 20v^{5} 24s 24d^{2} 26s* 24d^{2} 27m* Apr 21] ex-Irish gelding: poor maiden chaser: fair handicap hurdler: won at Kilbeggan (conditional jockeys) in June and, having left P. Heffernan after sixth start, Huntingdon in January and Fontwell in April: stays 27f: acts on any going: has worn headgear: tried in tongue strap: difficult ride and best with strong handling. *Evan Williams* **c– h100**

GRAFTON TRUCE (IRE) 8 gr.g. Brief Truce (USA) – Grafton Street (GER) (Pentathlon) [2004/5 20g 16d c16dF Jun 30] workmanlike gelding: winning 2m hurdler in Switzerland, well held in handicaps in 2004/5: third on first of 2 starts in points in 2003: tailed off when falling 3 out in novice on chasing debut: acts on soft and good to firm going: tried tongue tied. *Miss Lucinda V. Russell* **c– h–**

GRALMANO (IRE) 10 b.g. Scenic – Llangollen (IRE) (Caerleon (USA)) [2004/5 c–, h139: 24sF Apr 7] sturdy gelding: fairly useful on Flat: successful both starts in novice chases: useful hurdler: well beaten when falling 3 out in Grade 2 at Aintree, only outing in 2004/5: stays 25f with emphasis on speed: acts on firm and soft going: genuine. *K. A. Ryan* **c– h–**

GRAND DAUM (FR) 4 b. or br.g. Double Bed (FR) – Maousse (FR) (Labus (FR)) [2004/5 F16d Feb 24] 15,000 3-y-o: ninth foal: half-brother to 5 winners, including fair hurdler/chasers around 2m Maousse Honor (by Hero's Honor) and Encore Cadoudal (by Cadoudal): dam won 6 times around 1¼m on Flat in France: raced freely when eighth of 10 in bumper at Haydock on debut. *T. P. Tate* **F73**

GRANDE BRETAGNE (FR) 6 b.g. Legend of France (USA) – L'Epicurienne (FR) (Rex Magna (FR)) [2004/5 h–, F–: 17dpu May 4] good-topped gelding: no form in bumper or over hurdles: tongue tied last 2 outings: sold 4,000 gns Doncaster May Sales: in frame in maiden points in 2005. *Ian Williams* **h–**

GRANDE CREOLE (FR) 6 b.g. Byzantium (FR) – Sclos (FR) (Direct Flight) [2004/5 F88: F17d F16s4 19v3 24g2 24s4 Apr 16] rather unfurnished gelding: fair form in bumpers: best effort in novice hurdles when second to Comanche War Paint at Taunton: will prove suited by good test of stamina. *P. F. Nicholls* **h100 F89**

GRANDEE LINE 10 gr.g. Gran Alba (USA) – Judys Line (Capricorn Line) [2004/5 c92, h–: c21g c22s5 c23spu c18g6 c22sF c19d3 Apr 22] sturdy gelding: poor maiden handicap chaser: should stay beyond 2½m: often let down by jumping. *R. H. Alner* **c81 x h–**

GRANDE JETE (SAF) 8 ch.g. Jallad (USA) – Corps de Ballet (SAF) (Truely Nureyev (USA)) [2004/5 h114: 17g4 16d Apr 9] rather leggy gelding: won novice hurdle in 2003/4: off over 13 months, best effort when fourth to Fontanesi in 30-runner valuable handicap at Cheltenham quickening impressively to lead after 2 out but no extra after blundering last: will prove best around 2m with emphasis on speed. *N. J. Henderson* **h132**

GRAND FINALE (IRE) 8 b.h. Sadler's Wells (USA) – Final Figure (USA) (Super Concorde (USA)) [2004/5 h122: 20g2 22dpu Dec 26] compact horse: fairly useful hurdler: poor efforts on 3 of last 4 starts: stays 2½m: acts on soft going: has raced lazily. *Miss Venetia Williams* **h125**

GRAND LASS (IRE) 6 b.m. Grand Lodge (USA) – Siskin (IRE) (Royal Academy (USA)) [2004/5 h–: 17gur 16mpu 19mpu Sep 8] modest on Flat (should stay 1¾m, banned from racing from stalls in 2004): no form over hurdles: tried in cheekpieces: sold €1,500 Goffs February Sale. *A. Sadik* **h–**

GRAND MANNER (IRE) 5 b.g. Desert Style (IRE) – Reacted (IRE) (Entitled) [2004/5 16d 16g 16g5 19s4 16g* 20s Apr 22] IR 25,000F, IR 66,000Y, 6,500 3-y-o: leggy gelding: fifth foal: half-brother to winner in Turkey: dam unplaced in bumpers: poor form over hurdles: won selling handicap at Huntingdon in March: should stay 2½m: acts on soft going. *K. G. Reveley* **h77**

GRAND MUSIC (IRE) 5 b.g. Grand Lodge (USA) – Abury (IRE) (Law Society (USA)) [2004/5 22dpu Nov 2] no show in maidens on Flat or novice hurdle (cheekpieces). *J. J. Sheehan* **h–**

GRAND OPINION (IRE) 6 b.g. Grand Plaisir (IRE) – Cousin Rose (Track Spare) [2004/5 F–: 20s 25dpu c24g5 c25s c26dF Dec 5] good-topped gelding: no form: tried blinkered. *B. W. Duke* **c– h–**

GRAND PRAIRIE (SWE) 9 b.g. Prairie – Platonica (ITY) (Primo Dominie) [2004/5 h88: 19d 17g6 17s2 16s6 16v2 16s4 16g2 16d4 Apr 18] sturdy gelding: poor hurdler: probably best around 2m: acts on heavy going: wore cheekpieces last 4 starts: weak finisher: not one to rely on. *G. L. Moore* **h84 §**

GRAND PROMPT 6 ch.g. Grand Lodge (USA) – Prompting (Primo Dominie) [2004/5 h91§: 20d6 18m3 May 26] angular gelding: modest hurdler at best: stays 2½m: best form on good going or firmer: usually wears headgear: ungenuine. *Mrs L. J. Mongan* **h77 §**

GRANGEHILL DANCER (IRE) 4 ch.f. Danehill Dancer (IRE) – Bella Galiana (ITY) (Don Roberto (USA)) [2004/5 16m² 16s² 16s³ 16d² 16d⁴ 16s² 16v* 16s² 16s* Apr 10] angular filly: fair around 1m on Flat, won at Tralee in August: fair juvenile hurdler: won at Punchestown (maiden) in December and Hexham (odds on) in April: raced at 2m: acts on heavy and good to firm going: front runner: consistent. *P. J. Rothwell, Ireland* **h105**

GRANGEWICK FLIGHT 11 b.g. Lighter – Feathery (Le Coq d'Or) [2004/5 c94§: c25d² c25m⁴ c20d³ c25d Apr 11] workmanlike gelding: modest chaser: left N. Wilson and off 10 months, ran poorly in hunter final start: stays 25f: unraced on firm going, acts on any other: effective with or without cheekpieces/blinkers: sometimes let down by jumping: ungenuine. *Mrs H. D. Marks* **c92 §**

GRANIT D'ESTRUVAL (FR) 11 b.g. Quart de Vin (FR) – Jalousie (FR) (Blockhaus) [2004/5 c133, h–: c26sᵖᵘ c26s³ c29dᵘʳ c24g³ Feb 5] tall, useful-looking gelding: useful handicap chaser: back to best when third to Innox in valuable event at Sandown final start: stays 33f: raced on good going or softer (acts on heavy): tongue tied on reappearance: genuine. *Ferdy Murphy* **c133 h–**

GRANITE STEPS 9 gr.g. Gran Alba (USA) – Pablena (Pablond) [2004/5 c–, h110: 20d c26v⁴ c24d⁶ Jan 15] lengthy gelding: fair handicap hurdler: returned to former trainer, weakened quickly 3 out on reappearance: disappointing over fences: stays 25f: raced on going softer than good (acts on heavy): sold 5,400 gns Doncaster May Sales. *Ferdy Murphy* **c– h–**

GRANNY ANNIE 6 b.m. Minster Son – Castle Fountain (Royal Fountain) [2004/5 h–: 24gᵖᵘ May 1] looked wayward in 2 novice hurdles. *W. Amos* **h– x**

GRANRICH 5 ch.m. Alflora (IRE) – Weareagrandmother (Prince Tenderfoot (USA)) [2004/5 h–, F–: 16s 17gᵖᵘ Dec 30] leggy mare: no show over hurdles. *P. M. Rich* **h–**

GRAN ROMANY 5 gr.g. Gran Alba (USA) – Gipsy Rew (Andy Rew) [2004/5 F17gᵖᵘ Apr 12] first foal: dam no sign of ability over hurdles: soon detached in bumper on debut. *R. J. Hodges* **F–**

GRAPHIC APPROACH (IRE) 7 b.g. King's Ride – Sharp Approach (Crash Course) [2004/5 h125, F103: c19s* c24g* c24d³ c21gᵘʳ Mar 17] strong, lengthy gelding: fairly useful hurdler: quickly as good over fences, landing odds in maiden at Hereford and novice at Southwell in January, jumping fluently in main both times: upped in class, 24 lengths third of 6 to Distant Thunder in novice at Newbury: stays 3m: acts on soft going. *C. R. Egerton* **c128 h–**

GRASIA (IRE) 6 b.g. Glacial Storm (USA) – Bar Flute (IRE) (Orchestra) [2004/5 F16d Dec 29] first foal: dam won 2½m hurdle in Ireland: won maiden on last of 3 starts in Irish points in 2004: bought 36,000 gns Doncaster May Sales: eighth of 15 in Grade 2 bumper at Newbury. *K. C. Bailey* **F91**

GRATOMI (IRE) 15 b.g. Bustomi – Granny Grumble (Politico (USA)) [2004/5 c91?, h–: c22sᵖᵘ c24g May 27] workmanlike gelding: veteran chaser: stays 3m: acts on any going. *Mrs A. E. Lee* **c– h–**

GRATTAN LODGE (IRE) 8 gr.g. Roselier (FR) – Shallow Run (Deep Run) [2004/5 c114, h–: c26s* c24v* c29sᵖᵘ Jan 15] lengthy gelding: successful 9 of last 10 completed outings: developed into useful chaser, winning handicaps at Carlisle in October and November (beat Malek a short head): disappointed in valuable handicap at Warwick final start: should stay beyond 27f: acts on heavy going. *J. Howard Johnson* **c138 h–**

GRATTAN SQUARE (IRE) 6 b.m. Broken Hearted – Out The Nav (IRE) (Over The River (FR)) [2004/5 F18m² F16v² F16d* Nov 13] second foal: half-sister to winning hurdler/chaser Camdenation (by Camden Town), stays 2¾m: dam maiden hurdler: fairly useful in bumpers: won at Punchestown in November: best effort when second at Galway previous start. *J. E. Kiely, Ireland* **F102**

GRAVE DOUBTS 9 ch.g. Karinga Bay – Redgrave Girl (Deep Run) [2004/5 h132: 19gᶠ 16d 17g Mar 18] good-topped gelding: useful handicap hurdler in 2003/4: well held both completed outings in 2004/5: raced mainly around 2m: acts on firm and good to soft going: tongue tied. *K. Bishop* **h–**

GRAY KNIGHT (IRE) 8 gr.g. Insan (USA) – Moohono (IRE) (Roselier (FR)) [2004/5 c21m* May 19] sturdy gelding: novice hurdler: successful twice in points in 2004: won maiden hunter at Folkestone in May: will stay 3m. *Mrs T. J. Hill* **c85 h–**

GRAY'S EULOGY 7 b.g. Presenting – Gray's Ellergy (Oats) [2004/5 h72: c22s² c22dpu c24d* c24d* Feb 18] sturdy gelding: poor form over hurdles: fair novice chaser: blinkered, won handicaps at Huntingdon in January and Sandown (much improved) in February: likely to prove best at 3m+: raced on good going or softer (acts on soft). *D. R. Gandolfo* **c101 h–**

GREAT AS GOLD (IRE) 6 b.g. Goldmark (USA) – Great Land (USA) (Friend's Choice (USA)) [2004/5 h119: 23m⁵ May 1] fair stayer on Flat: fairly useful hurdler: stays 3m: acts on good to firm and good to soft going: wears cheekpieces. *B. Ellison* **h119**

GREAT BENEFIT (IRE) 6 ch.g. Beneficial – That's Lucy (IRE) (Henbit (USA)) [2004/5 F–: 16g 20d Dec 7] well held in bumper and novice hurdles. *Miss H. C. Knight* **h–**

GREAT COMPTON 5 b.g. Compton Place – Thundercloud (Electric) [2004/5 17d⁶ 16f 16g 16d 17dpu 16d⁶ 16s⁴ 17s⁶ Mar 22] medium-sized gelding: half-brother to fairly useful hurdler Moving On Up (by Salse), stays 21f: fairly useful on Flat (stays 1½m) at 3 yrs, well held only outing in 2004: poor novice hurdler: sold out of D. Weld's stable 21,000 gns Newmarket July Sales after second outing (blinkered): raced around 2m. *B. J. Llewellyn* **h84**

GREAT CRUSADER 13 ch.g. Deploy – Shannon Princess (Connaught) [2004/5 c87, h111d: 24s⁴ 24f² 26m⁶ 22d Dec 3] small, sturdy gelding: generally let down by jumping over fences: veteran staying hurdler, very much on downgrade: acts on heavy going. *M. J. Hogan* **c– h84**

GREATEST BY PHAR 4 b.g. Pharly (FR) – Greatest Friend (IRE) (Mandalus) [2004/5 18d⁴ 16s 16d 19spu Jan 31] close-coupled gelding: well held in 2 maidens on Flat early in 2004 for J. Akehurst: poor form on hurdling debut, regressed. *D. P. Keane* **h80**

GREAT EXPENSE 6 b.g. Shambo – Zoes Pet (Cisto (FR)) [2004/5 F16gpu F16gpu F16g Oct 5] first foal: dam winning pointer: more temperament than ability in bumpers: tried visored. *G. R. Pewter* **F– §**

GREAT GAME 5 b.g. Indian Ridge – Russian Grace (IRE) (Soviet Star (USA)) [2004/5 16gF 17g⁶ 17g Jul 28] fair maiden at 2 yrs, well held on Flat in 2003, sold out of B. Rothwell's stable £1,500 Ascot November Sales: no show over hurdles: unlikely to stay 2m. *E. Retter* **h–**

GREAT MAN (FR) 4 b.g. Bering – Great Connection (USA) (Dayjur (USA)) [2004/5 16gF Mar 14] fourth foal: brother to 7f and 1m winner Great News and half-brother to winner around 1m Guana (by Sillery): dam unraced: fair on Flat for C. Laffon-Parias: remote third when falling last in novice at Plumpton on hurdling debut: should do better. *Noel T. Chance* **h– p**

GREAT OAKS 11 b.g. Sylvan Express – Springdale Hall (USA) (Bates Motel (USA)) [2004/5 c79x, h75: 16f⁶ 20m⁶ c18m⁵ c19m⁵ 21m³ c20gF Oct 4] lengthy gelding: poor maiden hurdler: mistakes and little form over fences: stayed 2½m: acted on good to firm and heavy going: dead. *Miss Z. C. Davison* **c– x h64**

GREAT OVATION (FR) 6 ch.m. Boston Two Step (USA) – Baldiloa (No Lute (FR)) [2004/5 h83: 16dpu 16d⁴ 18s² 17m² 17s² 17m³ 19m⁴ Mar 21] lengthy mare: poor maiden hurdler: raced mainly around 2m: acts on soft and good to firm going: tongue tied once. *R. T. Phillips* **h78**

GREAT TRAVEL (FR) 6 b.g. Great Palm (USA) – Travel Free (Be My Guest (USA)) [2004/5 c110, h104: c16d* c17g* c16g³ c16gF Mar 18] good-topped gelding: useful 2m chaser: much improved in 2004/5, winning handicaps impressively at Kempton in October and Newbury in November, and third to Oneway in similar event at Sandown, though found little at last-named: tongue tied, fatally injured when falling first at Cheltenham: acted on soft going. *P. F. Nicholls* **c144 h–**

GRECIAN STAR 13 b.g. Crested Lark – Grecian Lace (Spartan General) [2004/5 c90: c33s⁶ c25v² May 10] strong, deep-girthed gelding: winning hunter chaser: placed in points in 2005: stays 33f: acts on firm and good to soft going. *G. J. Tarry* **c80**

GRECO (IRE) 8 b.g. Dolphin Street (FR) – Fabulous Deed (USA) (Shadeed (USA)) [2004/5 c21sur Apr 7] good-topped gelding: winning hurdler/chaser: left N. Meade, placed twice from 4 starts in Irish points: tongue tied, soon trailing and unseated 4 out in Fox Hunters' at Aintree: should stay beyond 2½m: acts on good to soft going, probably on firm: has worn blinkers. *David Christie, Ireland* **c– h–**

GREEK STAR 4 b.g. Soviet Star (USA) – Graecia Magna (USA) (Private Account (USA)) [2004/5 16m² 16s⁴ 17s 24g⁶ 22dpu Feb 8] workmanlike gelding: half-brother to 3 winners over jumps, including useful 2m chaser Theseus (by Danehill) and fairly useful hurdler/chaser Polydamas (by Last Tycoon), stays 2½m: little worthwhile form on Flat: modest form over hurdles: stays easy 3m. *K. A. Morgan* **h88**

GREENACRES BOY 10 b.g. Roscoe Blake – Deep Goddess (Deep Run) [2004/5 c–, h–: 17d 17g* 26m⁵ 20dpu Apr 20] leggy gelding: poor hurdler: form only when winning 17f selling handicap at Sedgefield in May: failed to complete in 3 chases: tried blinkered, usually wears cheekpieces nowadays: headstrong. *M. Mullineaux* **c–** **h61**

GREENAWN (IRE) 6 ch.g. Anshan – Arctic Bead (IRE) (Le Moss) [2004/5 16s⁵ 16s³ 16v⁵ Dec 18] angular gelding: fifth foal: half-brother to fair hurdler/fairly useful chaser Asparagus (by Roselier), stayed 29f: dam unraced half-sister to fairly useful hurdler/chaser up to 21f Redgrave Devil: modest form on second of 3 starts in novice hurdles: raced around 2m on soft/heavy ground. *M. Sheppard* **h88**

GREEN BELT FLYER (IRE) 7 b.g. Leading Counsel (USA) – Current Liability (Caribo) [2004/5 h125: 16g c17vF c16v⁴ c16v* c16v⁴ c16s* c17s Mar 29] useful-looking gelding: fairly useful hurdler: bit disappointing over fences, though won maiden at Tramore in January and novice at Naas (easily best effort, beat Davenport Milenium 4 lengths) in March: blinkered, well held in handicap at Punchestown in late-April: best at 2m: acts on good to firm and heavy going. *Mrs J. Harrington, Ireland* **c122** **h–**

GREENCARD GOLF 4 b.g. Foxhound (USA) – Reticent Bride (IRE) (Shy Groom (USA)) [2004/5 16m 16d 17vpu Nov 26] 1,400 3-y-o: good-topped gelding: sixth foal: half-brother to several winners, including useful hurdler/fairly useful chaser Palua (by Sri Pekan), stays 3m: dam, Irish 6f winner, sister to Lowther winner Miss Demure: no form in juvenile hurdles. *Jennie Candlish* **h–**

GREEN FALCON 4 b.g. Green Desert (USA) – El Jazirah (Kris) [2004/5 18m Sep 21] half-brother to bumper winner Joy Box (by Unfuwain): modest maiden on Flat (stays 1½m), ran creditably for Mrs S. Lamyman in March: let down by jumping in juvenile at Fontwell on hurdling debut. *J. W. Hills* **h–**

GREENFIELD (IRE) 7 ch.g. Pleasant Tap (USA) – No Review (USA) (Nodouble (USA)) [2004/5 h109: 19g⁶ 21g 20v³ 20s³ 22d² Mar 11] good-topped gelding: fair handicap hurdler: finished lame final start: stays 2¾m: raced on good ground or softer (acts on heavy): blinkered nowadays. *R. T. Phillips* **h113**

GREEN FINGER 7 b.g. Environment Friend – Hunt The Thimble (FR) (Relkino) [2004/5 c16g* c17m² c20g Oct 27] workmanlike gelding: fourth foal: half-brother to 3 winners, including fairly useful hurdler/fair chaser Roi de La Chasse (by Royal Vulcan), stayed 3m: dam unraced: won maiden Irish point in 2002: maiden hurdler: fair chaser, won maiden at Ballinrobe in May: should stay 2½m: acts on good to firm and good to soft going. *A. L. T. Moore, Ireland* **c111** **h–**

GREENFIRE (FR) 7 ch.g. Ashkalani (IRE) – Greenvera (USA) (Riverman (USA)) [2004/5 h–, F84?: 16v⁵ 18spu Dec 5] little form: has had tongue tied. *Mrs Dianne Sayer* **h–**

GREEN GAMBLE 5 gr.g. Environment Friend – Gemma's Wager (IRE) (Phardante (FR)) [2004/5 h86?, F–: 16g³ 16g² 16d² 20s 16g⁴ 16d³ c16g* c20d² Apr 18] good-topped gelding: modest maiden hurdler: won novice handicap at Huntingdon in March on chasing debut: likely to prove best around 2m: acts on good to soft going. *D. B. Feek* **c87** **h87**

GREEN GO (GER) 7 ch.g. Secret 'n Classy (CAN) – Green Fee (GER) (Windwurf (GER)) [2004/5 c87, h88: c26d* 26g³ c24d⁴ c26g c24g⁴ c24g⁵ c21d* Aug 30] angular gelding: poor hurdler: modest handicap chaser: won weak races at Cartmel (all 4 successes over fences there) in May and August: stays 3¼m, at least as effective at shorter: acts on good to firm and good to soft going: has shaped as if amiss more than once: front runner. *A. Sadik* **c95** **h82**

GREENHALL RAMBLER (IRE) 6 ch.m. Anshan – Gentle Pressure (Sharpo) [2004/5 h115, F–: 18m² 16g 17d⁴ 16g³ 19s Mar 27] tall, angular mare: fair hurdler: stays 2½m: acts on good to firm and good to soft going: consistent. *P. A. Fahy, Ireland* **h113**

GREENHILL BRAMBLE (IRE) 5 b.g. Supreme Leader – Green Thorn (IRE) (Ovac (ITY)) [2004/5 F17d* F16d Feb 12] well-made gelding: fifth foal: brother to 2m hurdle winner Monte Rosa: dam unraced: useful form when winning bumper at Newton Abbot on debut by 14 lengths from Rutland: never a factor in Grade 2 at Newbury 3 months later. *P. J. Hobbs* **F109**

GREENHOPE (IRE) 7 b.g. Definite Article – Unbidden Melody (USA) (Chieftain) [2004/5 h129: 16g c16g^{2} 16d c17s^{2} c17s* c16g^{6} c16g^{3} Apr 15] good-topped gelding: fairly useful handicap hurdler in 2003/4: useful form over fences: won 4-runner maiden at Plumpton in February by 12 lengths from Mondul: clearly better effort after when sixth to Fota Island in Grand Annual (Handicap) at Cheltenham: will stay 2½m: acts on soft and good to firm going: jumped markedly left on chasing debut: usually races up with pace. *N. J. Henderson* **c133 h–**

GREEN IDEAL 7 b.g. Mark of Esteem (IRE) – Emerald (USA) (El Gran Senor (USA)) [2004/5 c108§, h–: c16s^{2} c16v^{ur} c16s^{2} c16v^{4} c16s^{4} c20v^{F} c21s^{ur} c21s^{6} c21v* c21v* Mar 28] compact gelding: fair chaser: won novice and handicap at Sedgefield in March: stays 21f: acts on heavy going: tried in cheekpieces, wore blinkers last 5 starts: has had tongue tied. *Ferdy Murphy* **c108 h–**

GREEN MASTER (POL) 5 bl.g. Who Knows – Green Fee (GER) (Windwurf (GER)) [2004/5 16f 20v^{pu} 20s^{6} 16d 16s Nov 21] half-brother to winning hurdler/chaser Green Go (by Secret 'n Classy), stays 3¼m: successful twice around 6f on Flat (blinkered) in Poland, including in 2004 for J. Siwonia: no show over hurdles: tried in cheekpieces: has had tongue tied. *A. Sadik* **h–**

GREENMOOR HOUSE (IRE) 7 b.g. Denel (FR) – No Reason (Kemal (FR)) [2004/5 22g^{6} Apr 12] fourth foal: brother to winning pointer: dam unraced: sixth of 16 to Standin Obligation in novice hurdle at Exeter on debut, getting hang of things late on: should improve. *V. R. A. Dartnall* **h92 p**

GREEN 'N' GOLD 5 b.m. Cloudings (IRE) – Fishki (Niniski (USA)) [2004/5 h87p: 22d* 21m^{2} 23s^{2} 23d^{F} 21v 20v^{pu} 20s Apr 10] modest on Flat (stays 2¼m): modest novice hurdler: won weak mares race at Cartmel in August: will stay 3m: acts on soft going. *M. D. Hammond* **h92**

GREEN PROSPECT (FR) 5 b.g. Green Tune (USA) – City Prospect (FR) (Diamond Prospect (USA)) [2004/5 17m* 19g^{2} Jul 4] ex-French gelding: second foal: half-brother to 1m winner by Loup Solitaire: dam French 7f winner: placed over 1½m on Flat: winning chaser: fair form over hurdles: made all in novice at Bangor on British debut in May: stays 19f: acts on soft and good to firm going. *M. C. Pipe* **c– h110**

GREENSMITH LANE 9 br.g. Greensmith – Handy Lane (Nearly A Hand) [2004/5 h96: 16g^{4} 17g* 16m^{3} 17f^{pu} 16d^{5} 16d^{6} 16d^{F} Apr 3] fair handicap hurdler: won at Newton Abbot in August: left G. Balding after fourth outing: stayed 2½m: won on soft going, best efforts on good/good to firm: usually wore cheekpieces: dead. *J. J. Best* **h105**

GREEN TANGO 6 br.g. Greensmith – Furry Dance (USA) (Nureyev (USA)) [2004/5 h122+, F103: 16g 16g* 16d 16d 16d 16d Apr 9] good-topped gelding: fairly useful handicap hurdler: won at Newbury in November by 2 lengths from Haditovski: ran creditably in valuable/well-contested events next 3 starts: best at 2m: raced on good going or softer: likely to do well in novice chases in 2005/6. *H. D. Daly* **h123**

GREENWICH 11 br.g. Handsome Sailor – Praise The Lord (Lord Gayle (USA)) [2004/5 c88, h–: c26g* c25d^{5} c26g^{4} c24g^{4} c24m^{F} Oct 6] tall gelding: modest chaser: won maiden at Plumpton in May: also successful in point in March: suited by 3m+: best form on good/good to firm going: usually front runner. *M. Scudamore* **c94 ? h–**

GREGORIAN (IRE) 8 b.g. Foxhound (USA) – East River (FR) (Arctic Tern (USA)) [2004/5 c–, h96: 16d 17s^{pu} 17m 16m 16d^{2} 19s^{2} 16d^{2} 16s 17s 19s^{pu} 17v^{6} 17g 16s Mar 13] neat gelding: won only completed start over fences: modest hurdler: claimed from J. O'Shea £6,000 seventh start: little form after: best around 2m: acts on good to firm and heavy going. *Ian Williams* **c– h88**

GREGORIO (FR) 11 b.g. Passing Sale (FR) – Apside (FR) (Mistigri) [2004/5 c114, h–: c22s^{4} Dec 2] ex-Irish gelding: thrice-raced hurdler: fairly useful chaser at best, little form since 2002/3: stays 2½m: acts on good to firm and heavy going: tried blinkered. *Ian Williams* **c96 + h–**

GRENFELL (IRE) 6 br.m. Presenting – Arumah (Arapaho) [2004/5 F16s* F17s Apr 7] €12,000 3-y-o: good-topped mare: ninth foal: half-sister to one-time fairly useful chaser up to 3m Shining Light (by Crash Course) and useful bumper winner Brave King (by King's Ride): dam unraced half-sister to useful staying chaser Castle Warden: won maiden bumper at Kempton on debut in March by ½ length from Gay Gladys: raced freely when well beaten in listed mares event at Aintree month later. *R. T. Phillips* **F88 +**

GREY ABBEY (IRE) 11 gr.g. Nestor – Tacovaon (Avocat) [2004/5 c159, h116: c25s* c25s* c26g5 c25s* Apr 7] **c168 h–**

The sight of the strong-galloping, sound-jumping Grey Abbey in full flight is guaranteed to quicken the pulse of even the most imperturbable follower of steeplechasing. The zestful Grey Abbey has come a very long way since starting his career in bumpers as a five-year-old, improving with virtually every season and making the transition over the last two from useful handicapper to top-class chaser.

Grey Abbey established a fine record for his first trainer Barry Murtagh, but has not looked back since joining Howard Johnson, his one defeat in six starts over fences for the stable coming in the Cheltenham Gold Cup. He included the Scottish Grand National under 11-12 (his sixth win at Ayr) among three victories from four starts (the other a prep run over hurdles) in his first season with Johnson and progressed further in the latest, his defeat in the Gold Cup coming under conditions which placed considerably more emphasis on speed than they did in the three races which he won. Stamina is Grey Abbey's strong suit and he is ridden to make the best use of it, usually forcing the pace. Front running also brings Grey Abbey's superb jumping technique fully into play and he cuts a dashing figure out in front. There has been talk of retirement but Grey Abbey's legion of fans will be hoping connections decide to give him one more season. If Grey Abbey is retired, he can certainly be said to have gone out at the top. He began the latest season with a typical, all-the-way win in the bet365 Charlie Hall Chase at Wetherby in October, jumping really well and responding gamely in the home straight to beat the Gold Cup runner-up Sir Rembrandt, who started favourite, by three lengths, with a distance back to Royal Emperor, the only other finisher. The performance represented a further progression in Grey Abbey's form, though it was three months before he was seen out again. The absence affected him not a jot as he gained a fifth victory in a row in the Pillar Property Chase, a race often billed as a dress rehearsal for the Gold Cup. Though it hasn't had much bearing during the Best Mate era, previously Master Oats, See More Business and Looks Like Trouble contested it on their way to Gold Cup success.

The Pillar featured on a tremendous card at Cheltenham at the end of January. If Well Chief's brilliant weight-carrying effort in the Victor Chandler was arguably the highlight, Grey Abbey's demolition of six rivals in the Pillar wasn't far behind. With Grey Abbey and Cloudy Bays setting a really good pace, the race provided a thorough test at the trip, with the soft ground also helping to bring out Grey Abbey's superior stamina. Grey Abbey galloped on in great style to win by sixteen lengths and twelve from Therealbandit and Royal Auclair, both of whom tired noticeably in the closing stages, exaggerating Grey Abbey's superiority. The form didn't have to be taken strictly at face value, however, to give Grey Abbey a

bet365 Charlie Hall Chase, Wetherby—
Grey Abbey enters the Cheltenham picture with victory over 2004 Gold Cup runner-up Sir Rembrandt

Pillar Property Chase, Cheltenham—there will be sixteen lengths back to Therealbandit come the line

fair chance—he was as low as 6/1 in ante-post betting afterwards—if the Gold Cup took place on soft or heavy ground. Unfortunately for Grey Abbey, who was also chasing a £100,000 bonus if the Charlie Hall winner landed the Gold Cup, soft ground is much rarer than it once was at the Festival meeting. Grey Abbey started 15/2 fifth favourite but couldn't hold his place when the winner Kicking King pressed on three out and finished fifth, two places behind 12/1-shot Sir Rembrandt and one behind 40/1-shot Royal Auclair.

An injury scare had put Grey Abbey's participation in the Gold Cup in some doubt for a time and his trainer had said that—left to him—the horse would have gone straight to Aintree ('He's better on a flatter track'). Grey Abbey seemed the perfect horse for the 2005 Grand National in which he would have been one of the favourites, his supporters looking for a weight-carrying performance to rival the likes of Suny Bay and Crisp that would have put him into the history books. An announcement just over a week before the race that Grey Abbey would not be in the National line-up came as a surprise. After schooling Grey Abbey over Aintree-style fences, his trainer reported that the horse had been 'a bit frightened by them'. 'He's so extravagant with his jumping that I couldn't see him maintaining it for four and a half miles anyway with top weight.' Even more surprisingly, his usually far-from-fluent stable-companion Ballybough Rasher got the go-ahead to run but predictably jumped lamentably and eventually refused at second Becher's. So much for the schooling session. Grey Abbey would make plenty of appeal for the National were connections to take a different view in 2006. As it was, after considering waiting for another tilt at the Scottish National, Grey Abbey ran instead over the Mildmay fences at Aintree, in the Betfair Bowl over a distance a mile and three furlongs shorter than that for the National. Grey Abbey was impressive once more, making all and typically jumping well. His rider stepped up the tempo on the final circuit,

Betfair Bowl Chase, Aintree—
a superb leap two out puts paid to the challenge of former dual winner First Gold

gradually seeing off his rivals and sealing victory with a terrific jump two out. Grey Abbey was well on top at the line, winning by twelve lengths and seventeen lengths from the favourite First Gold, a dual winner of the event, and Crystal d'Ainay.

Grey Abbey (IRE) (gr.g. 1994)	Nestor (gr 1980)	Nishapour (gr 1975)	Zeddaan
			Alama
		Meadow Rhapsody (ch 1967)	Ragusa
			Meadow Music
	Tacovaon (ch 1985)	Avocat (ch 1969)	Relko
			Pourparler
		No Hunting (b 1971)	No Time
			Hunter's Hut

The lengthy Grey Abbey, who had a wind operation as an eight-year-old, is out of the unraced Tacovaon, a half-sister, among others, to unraced Ballybeg Maid, the dam of another top-class grey chaser renowned for his bold jumping, The Grey Monk. The pair are easily the best horses to come from the family, though Ballybeg Maid also bred the very useful Princess Casilia, a tough Irish mare who won the Jameson Gold Cup at Fairyhouse. None of the mares on the bottom line of Grey Abbey's pedigree ever ran. The best of Tacovaon's other offspring is the fairly useful but error-prone staying chaser Mister Dave's (by Bluffer), though Grey Abbey's sisters, Scathach and Little Brockwell, won in points. Grey Abbey stays extremely well, acts on good to firm and heavy going, and is thoroughly game and genuine. *J. Howard Johnson*

GREY BROTHER 7 gr.g. Morpeth – Pigeon Loft (IRE) (Bellypha) [2004/5 h117p: 22g* Apr 27] sturdy gelding: lightly-raced hurdler: won handicap at Newton Abbot in April 2004 by 2½ lengths from Polar Scout: will stay 3m: raced mainly on good going or softer: looked likely to progress further but not seen out again: joined P. Hobbs. *J. D. Frost* **h117 p**

GREY CISEAUX (IRE) 10 gr.g. Mujtahid (USA) – Inisfail (Persian Bold) [2004/5 c79§, h75§: c26g^{3} c26g^{4} c26g^{3} Aug 10] angular gelding: poor hurdler/chaser: stays 27f: acts on firm going: has worn blinkers, in cheekpieces nowadays: ungenuine. *A. E. Jones* **c77 §** **h– §**

GREY MISTRAL 7 gr.m. Terimon – Winnowing (IRE) (Strong Gale) [2004/5 18s^{6} 16s^{pu} Feb 3] good-topped mare: second foal: half-sister to useful hurdler Darkness (by Accordion), stays 21f: dam, winning hurdler who stayed 2½m, out of half-sister to top-class hurdler Aonoch: no show in 2 novice hurdles. *P. R. Chamings* **h–**

GREY PRINCE 4 gr.g. Samraan (USA) – Scallys Queen Jay (Scallywag) [2004/5 F18d Apr 18] second foal: dam never ran: tailed off in maiden bumper on debut. *G. Prodromou* **F–**

GREY REPORT (IRE) 8 gr.g. Roselier (FR) – Busters Lodge (Antwerp City) [2004/5 h143: 24s⁴ 25d^ur 24d^pu c22d⁴ c20v^F c20s* Mar 14] compact gelding: smart novice hurdler in 2003/4: became most temperamental in 2004/5, though did win maiden chase at Stratford in March, despite again jumping left: stays 3m well: acts on good to firm and heavy going: front runner: attempted to pull himself up with circuit to go third to fifth starts: one to avoid. *P. J. Hobbs* **c120 § h– §**

GREY SAMURAI 5 gr.g. Gothenberg (IRE) – Royal Rebeka (Grey Desire) [2004/5 F–: F16d May 8] lengthy gelding: soundly beaten in 2 bumpers and on Flat. *P. T. Midgley* **F–**

GREY SHARK (IRE) 6 gr.g. Roselier (FR) – Sharkezan (IRE) (Double Schwartz) [2004/5 h70?, F–: 22s² 22d³ 20s 22s^pu Jan 6] angular gelding: modest form over hurdles: will stay beyond 2¾m: sold 7,200 gns Doncaster May Sales. *D. P. Keane* **h88**

GRIFFENS BROOK 5 b.g. Alderbrook – Ima Delight (Idiot's Delight) [2004/5 F–: 20s^pu 20d Feb 18] no sign of ability. *Mrs P. Sly* **h–**

GRIFFIN'S LEGACY 6 b.g. Wace (USA) – Griffin's Girl (Bairn (USA)) [2004/5 F–: F16d* F17s 20s 17s 17g Apr 10] medium-sized gelding: 66/1-winner of weak bumper at Chepstow in October: well held in novice company over hurdles: has carried head high. *N. G. Ayliffe* **h– F81**

GRIMES 12 b.g. Reprimand – Diva Madonna (Chief Singer) [2004/5 c120+, h–: 16g² 16g c21d^pu 16s⁴ Oct 3] tall, imposing gelding: top-class hurdler/useful chaser at one time: easily best effort in 2004/5 when second to Accordion Etoile in minor hurdle at Tipperary: effective at 2m to 2¾m: has form on soft going, used to go particularly well on good/good to firm: tried blinkered: often none too fluent over fences. *C. Roche, Ireland* **c– h133**

GRIMSHAW (USA) 10 ch.g. St Jovite (USA) – Loa (USA) (Hawaii) [2004/5 c–, h85: 16g 19g² 19g³ 19m⁴ 22g² 19g^pu 16v^pu Oct 16] rather sparely-made gelding: no form over fences: poor hurdler: stays 2¾m: acts on good to firm and heavy going: tried blinkered/in cheekpieces: has had tongue tied: races prominently. *Mrs D. A. Hamer* **c– h83**

GRITTI PALACE (IRE) 5 b.g. Duky – Glittering Grit (IRE) (Sheer Grit) [2004/5 F16v⁵ F16s⁴ F16v⁵ Mar 29] third foal: dam unraced: poor form in bumpers: very much a staying type. *John R. Upson* **F74**

GRIZZLY ACTIVEWEAR (IRE) 11 ch.g. Camden Town – Boro Cent (Little Buskins) [2004/5 h91: 24g* 26d³ 24g^F 26m Sep 8] leggy gelding: modest hurdler: won selling handicap at Market Rasen in July: lame final outing: stays 27f: acts on soft and good to firm going: none too consistent. *B. D. Leavy* **h86**

GROESFAEN LAD 8 b.g. Casteddu – Curious Feeling (Nishapour (FR)) [2004/5 16m 22s^pu 16g² 17m⁴ 19m² 19g Sep 30] half-brother to poor hurdler Tui (by Tina's Pet), stayed 3m: poor on Flat (stays 1¼m) at 5 yrs for J. M. Bradley: modest form over hurdles: probably stays 19f: acts on good to firm going: tongue tied last 4 starts. *Evan Williams* **h87**

GROUND BALL (IRE) 8 b. or br.g. Bob's Return (IRE) – Bettyhill (Ardross) [2004/5 c137, h121: c20d 16v* 16v* c20v² c16g^ur c17s* Mar 29] well-made gelding: fairly useful hurdler: won listed event at Thurles and handicap at Leopardstown (dictated pace and beat Kilbeggan Lad 4½ lengths) in December: smart chaser: won Dan Moore Memorial Handicap Chase at Fairyhouse in March by ½ length from Ulaan Baatar: better than ever when 5 lengths fourth to Rathgar Beau in Grade 1 at Punchestown in late-April: needs good test at 2m and likely to stay 2¾m: raced on good going or softer (acts on heavy): reliable. *C. F. Swan, Ireland* **c150 h127 +**

GROUND BREAKER 5 b.g. Emperor Jones (USA) – Startino (Bustino) [2004/5 F92: F17g³ 17s³ 17s^F 16v^pu 16g Jan 17] fair form in bumpers: third to Cherub in amateur novice at Market Rasen on hurdling debut: ran poorly last 2 outings: likely to stay beyond 17f. *M. W. Easterby* **h97 F87**

GROUSE MOOR (USA) 6 b.g. Distant View (USA) – Caithness (USA) (Roberto (USA)) [2004/5 h96, F69: 16d* 17s² 21v⁴ 18s⁴ 16d³ 16d Mar 24] sturdy gelding: fair handicap hurdler: had breathing operation before winning at Plumpton in November: should stay 2½m: raced on going softer than good over hurdles (bumper form on good to firm): tried tongue tied. *P. Winkworth* **h108**

GROUVILLE 4 b.g. Groom Dancer (USA) – Dance Land (IRE) (Nordance (USA)) [2004/5 18s^pu 16d 16g⁴ 16d⁶ Jan 15] rather leggy gelding: half-brother to fairly useful hurdler Dariole (by Priolo), stays 2½m: won 1m maiden on debut, well held both other **h87**

starts on Flat (tried blinkered), sold out of B. Meehan's stable 14,000 gns Newmarket July Sales: modest form in juvenile hurdles: likely to prove best at 2m. *C. J. Mann*

h– **GROVE JULIET (IRE)** 6 ch.m. Moscow Society (USA) – Cloona Lady (IRE) (Duky) [2004/5 F–: 20m^{pu} 20d Dec 9] well-made mare: no sign of ability. *B. G. Powell*

c101 h– **GRUMPY STUMPY** 10 ch.g. Gunner B – Moaning Jenny (Privy Seal) [2004/5 c24m^{4} c24s^{F} c24s* c22d* c24d^{3} c26d^{4} Apr 18] good-topped gelding: fair handicap chaser: off nearly 2 years before reappearance: won handicaps at Towcester (amateurs) and Newbury in December: will prove best at 3m+: best efforts on going softer than good (acts on heavy). *N. A. Twiston-Davies*

h113 F107 **GUANTAMA BAY (IRE)** 6 b. or br.g. Roselier (FR) – Life's Treasure (IRE) (Brush Aside (USA)) [2004/5 F16d* F16v^{4} 20d^{4} 24s* 22v^{5} 22v 20s Mar 27] €23,000 4-y-o: first foal: dam fell in point, only start: won bumper at Roscommon on debut in October: better form when fourth to The Fingersmith at Galway later in month: best effort over hurdles when winning maiden at Gowran in December by length from Southern Vic: ran as if amiss all subsequent starts: stays 3m. *N. Meade, Ireland*

c– § h85 § **GUARD DUTY** 8 b.g. Deploy – Hymne d'Amour (USA) (Dixieland Band (USA)) [2004/5 c103§, h–§: 21g^{ur} 19g^{4} 16s 22s^{2} 22s^{3} 24d 24d^{pu} 21s^{6} 26m Mar 21] leggy gelding: winning chaser: poor hurdler nowadays: claimed from M. Pipe £6,000 first outing: stays 25f: acts on heavy going: often visored/blinkered nowadays: usually tongue tied: held up: ungenuine. *D. M. Lloyd*

c– h– **GUE AU LOUP (FR)** 11 gr.g. Royal Charter (FR) – Arche d'Alliance (FR) (Pamponi (FR)) [2004/5 c93, h–: c20d c17g^{4} c17g^{ur} c16m^{ur} c20s^{F} c25d^{F} Mar 3] tall gelding: winning chaser: no form in 2004/5, left B. Ellison after fourth start. *G. C. Evans*

c97 h– **GUIGNOL DU COCHET (FR)** 11 ch.g. Secret of Success – Pasquita (FR) (Bourbon (FR)) [2004/5 c98, h–: c21g* c20g^{6} c24g* c24d^{4} c21s^{bd} c24g^{5} Apr 15] tall gelding: fair hunter chaser: won at Newton Abbot (handicap) and Stratford early in season: below form after 8-month absence: stays 3m with emphasis on speed: acts on soft and good to firm going: tried blinkered/visored and tongue tied earlier in career. *S. Flook*

c97 **GUILSBOROUGH GORSE** 10 b.g. Past Glories – Buckby Folly (Netherkelly) [2004/5 c96: c21m* c20d^{2} c22g^{pu} c16m c20m^{2} Apr 23] lengthy gelding: modest handicap chaser: won at Fakenham in May: effective at 2½m to 25f: acts on firm and soft going: tried blinkered/in cheekpieces. *T. D. Walford*

h89 F89 **GULABILL** 6 b.g. Safawan – Gulsha (Glint of Gold) [2004/5 F76: F16s^{2} 20s^{4} 20d^{5} 23s^{3} 24m^{pu} Apr 13] lengthy gelding: much better effort in bumpers when second to Villon at Haydock on reappearance, making running: modest form on hurdling debut, went wrong way. *N. A. Twiston-Davies*

c114 h114 **GUMLEY GALE** 10 b.g. Greensmith – Clodaigh Gale (Strong Gale) [2004/5 h90: 22g* 24d* 24d^{6} c23m^{2} c23g* c23m^{2} c24d^{4} c24d^{6} Mar 24] sturdy gelding: fair hurdler: back to form in 2004/5, winning 2 handicaps at Exeter very early in season: similar form over fences, winning maiden at Worcester in August: stays 3m: acts on good to firm and good to soft going: tongue tied nowadays. *K. Bishop*

c– h78 ? **GUNNER ROYAL** 7 b.g. Gunner B – Loadplan Lass (Nicholas Bill) [2004/5 h–: c16v^{5} c16v^{pu} c16v^{pu} 21s^{3} Feb 7] good-topped gelding: little form over hurdles or fences: tried in cheekpieces. *J. Wade*

c138 **GUNNER WELBURN** 13 ch.g. Gunner B – Vedra (IRE) (Carlingford Castle) [2004/5 c142: c24s^{5} c26s^{3} c25s^{5} c22v^{2} c24m^{3} c24s* Apr 16] strong, lengthy gelding: veteran chaser: proved himself still useful when winning handicap at Bangor in April by 14 lengths from Jaoka du Gord: best form up to 3¼m: acts on heavy and good to firm going: ran poorly in cheekpieces third outing: usually sound jumper. *A. M. Balding*

c118 x h– **GUN'N ROSES II (FR)** 11 gr.g. Royal Charter (FR) – Offenbach II (FR) (Ermitage (FR)) [2004/5 c115, h–: c22d* c31d^{F} c21s^{ur} Apr 7] rangy gelding: useful hunter chaser: won at Haydock (for second year running) in February by 12 lengths from The Butterwick Kid: stays 3m: raced mainly on good going or softer (acts on heavy): blinkered nowadays: front runner: often let down by jumping. *D. P. Keane*

c– h– **GUNSON HIGHT** 8 b.g. Be My Chief (USA) – Glas Y Dorlan (Sexton Blake) [2004/5 h78?: c16g^{5} c25m^{pu} Oct 1] won poor novice hurdle in 2003/4, no other form: has had tongue tied. *M. Todhunter*

*Worthington's Creamflow Neville Crump Memorial Handicap Chase, Doncaster—
Gunther McBride provides Paddy Brennan with his fourth winner
on an afternoon which saw Doncaster's fences take their toll*

GUNTHER MCBRIDE (IRE) 10 b.g. Glacial Storm (USA) – What Side (General Ironside) [2004/5 c132, h–: c24d* c25d² c26g⁵ c26g* c24s Feb 26] good-topped gelding: useful handicap chaser: won quite valuable events at Kempton (fourth win from 6 starts there) in October and Doncaster in December, making all when beating Lord of The River 20 lengths at latter: also ran well when second to Royal Auclair in listed contest at Wincanton: rare poor effort final start: stays 33f: acts on any going: races prominently: game and consistent. *P. J. Hobbs* **c139 h–**

GURU 7 b.g. Slip Anchor – Ower (IRE) (Lomond (USA)) [2004/5 h110: 16g* Oct 30] leggy gelding: fairly useful handicap hurdler: looked still on upgrade when winning at Lingfield in October with something in hand, but not seen out again: probably best around 2m: acts on soft and good to firm going. *G. L. Moore* **h120 +**

GUS BERRY (IRE) 12 ch.g. Montelimar (USA) – Eurolink Sea Baby (Deep Run) [2004/5 c73, h–: c27vᵖᵘ Mar 15] smallish, angular gelding: poor chaser: won point in March: stays 27f: raced on good going or softer (acts on heavy): often blinkered prior to 2002/3: has had tongue tied. *Mrs Alison Christmas* **c– h–**

GUS DES BOIS (FR) 11 ch.g. Lampon (FR) – Fiacina (FR) (Fiasco) [2004/5 c99§, h–: c21f⁶ c19s³ c17d³ c17g² c18d² c16d³ c21d³ c20d* c22s³ Dec 21] strong gelding: modest handicap chaser: won at Plumpton in December: effective at 2m to 3m: acts on heavy going: visored/blinkered: usually front runner: consistent, but often looks none too resolute. *R. H. Alner* **c94 § h–**

GUTHRIE (IRE) 7 ch.g. Mister Lord (USA) – Nephin Far (IRE) (Phardante (FR)) [2004/5 F87: 22gᵖᵘ 21s⁴ 22sᵖᵘ c24d⁴ c24g² c25dᵘʳ c24g² Mar 28] lengthy gelding: poor form only completed start over hurdles: easily best effort over fences when second in maiden at Doncaster fifth outing: stays 3m: hasn't always impressed with jumping or attitude: sold 15,500 gns Doncaster May Sales. *A. King* **c101 h80**

GUZZLE 5 b.m. Puget (USA) – Convamore Queen (IRE) (Carlingford Castle) [2004/5 F16d 17s 16s 21dF Mar 4] leggy mare: first foal: dam of little account: no sign of ability. *R. Dickin* **h– F–**

G V A IRELAND (IRE) 7 b.g. Beneficial – Dippers Daughter (Strong Gale) [2004/5 h127: 24m* c17v6 c16s4 c20s2 c24v2 c22v* c24s c20g3 c24s* c24v6 Apr 10] good-topped gelding: fairly useful hurdler: similar form over fences, winning maiden at Punchestown in February and 5-runner listed event at Cork (by 9 lengths from Joueur d'Estruval) in March: poor efforts in Grade 3 novice at Limerick and valuable novice handicap at Punchestown in April: needs good test at 2½m and stays 25f: acts on heavy going. *F. Flood, Ireland* **c125 h–**

GWEN 6 ch.m. Beveled (USA) – Taffidale (Welsh Pageant) [2004/5 F–: F16g May 16] tailed off in bumpers. *B. L. Lay* **F–**

GWENS GIRL 5 b.m. Wizard King – Russian Project (IRE) (Project Manager) [2004/5 F–: F17m Sep 8] lengthy mare: no form in bumpers. *S. T. Lewis* **F–**

GYPSY LEE (IRE) 7 b.m. Blues Traveller (IRE) – Hollyberry (IRE) (Runnett) [2004/5 16v 16dpu Oct 9] little form on Flat, none over hurdles: tried tongue tied. *J. G. Carr, Ireland* **h–**

H

HAADEF 4 b.c. Sadler's Wells (USA) – Taqreem (IRE) (Nashwan (USA)) [2004/5 17d6 16v 17g6 20s4 Apr 22] half-brother to winning 2m hurdler Jayed (by Marju): useful on Flat (stays 1½m), successful in June, sold out of J. Gosden's stable 85,000 gns Newmarket Autumn Sales: only poor form over hurdles, jumps none too fluently: tried blinkered: has looked none too keen. *J. Howard Johnson* **h84**

HAAFEL (USA) 8 ch.g. Diesis – Dish Dash (Bustino) [2004/5 c97, h–: c17d2 c20d4 c16s2 c18sF c16s* c19spu Mar 23] angular gelding: fair chaser: won 2-finisher novice at Huntingdon in March: stays 21f: acts on firm and soft going: effective blinkered or not. *G. L. Moore* **c105 h–**

HABIHAT (IRE) 6 ch.g. Sabrehill (USA) – Fur Hat (Habitat) [2004/5 F16g* F16m* May 20] half-brother to 2 winning hurdlers, including fair Be My Habitat (by Be My Guest), stayed 21f, and several winners on Flat, including Chester Cup winner Merit (by Rainbow Quest): dam unraced sister to Sun Chariot winner Topsy, dam of top-class 1m to 1½m colt Most Welcome, and half-sister to top-class 1½m colt Teenoso: useful form in bumpers, winning at Clonmel and Tipperary in May, beating The Screamer 1½ lengths, pair well clear, at latter: likely to stay 2½m: missed remainder of season due to injury, but type to do well in novice hurdles in 2005/6 if fully recovered. *Thomas Mullins, Ireland* **F108**

HABITUAL DANCER 4 b.g. Groom Dancer (USA) – Pomorie (IRE) (Be My Guest (USA)) [2004/5 16d6 16d6 16d* 16v3 18d* 18v3 Mar 5] quite good-topped gelding: fair on Flat (stays 2¼m): progressive form in juvenile hurdles: won at Newcastle in December and Kelso in February, rallying gamely to lead again run-in when beating Regal Setting by length, pair long way clear, at latter: stiff task when third behind Mephisto and Faasel in Grade 2 novice at Kelso final start: will stay 2½m: raced on going softer than good over hurdles (acts on heavy): front runner/races prominently: genuine. *Jedd O'Keeffe* **h121**

HACHLEY (FR) 10 b. or br.g. Grand Tresor (FR) – Tess Bowl (FR) (Rolling Bowl (FR)) [2004/5 c20dpu May 11] lightly-raced winning pointer, pulled up all starts since 2002. *M. G. Hazell* **c– h–**

HADEQA 9 ch.g. Hadeer – Heavenly Queen (Scottish Reel) [2004/5 c–x, h–: c21g Mar 18] compact gelding: fair but temperamental pointer nowadays, tends to make mistakes: well held on completed start in hunter chases: has had tongue tied. *M. J. Brown* **c– § h–**

HADITOVSKI 9 b.g. Hatim (USA) – Grand Occasion (Great Nephew) [2004/5 c110, h–: 20gpu 16s 16d4 16g2 16d 16v4 16d 16d 16spu Apr 20] compact gelding: fair chaser in 2003/4: similar form at best in handicap hurdles in 2004/5: stays 2½m: used to act well on ground softer than good: visored: usually ridden up with pace. *J. Mackie* **c– h111**

HAGGLE TWINS (IRE) 5 b.g. Thowra (FR) – Orwell Gaye (IRE) (Strong Gale) [2004/5 F16v2 F16s* 16s* 16s2 22v3 24v Apr 2] third foal: dam unraced half-sister to high-class staying chaser Kingsmark, from family of top-class 2m to 3m hurdler Gaye Brief and very smart staying jumper Gaye Chance: fairly useful form in bumpers, win- **h110 F104**

ning 20-runner event at Down Royal in November: won 20-runner maiden at Gowran on hurdling debut month later: better form when second in novice again at Gowran: should be suited by further than 2m: raced only on soft/heavy going. *Ms F. M. Crowley, Ireland*

HA HA HA 7 b.g. Sure Blade (USA) – Crownego (Abednego) [2004/5 h–, F–: 21d^ur 16f^pu May 18] no form over hurdles, makes mistakes: tried in visor/cheekpieces. *K. F. Clutterbuck* **h– x**

HAIKAL 8 b.g. Owington – Magic Milly (Simply Great (FR)) [2004/5 h81: c21g^pu 22m^5 22g Jun 7] strong, workmanlike gelding: poor handicap hurdler: out of sorts early in 2004/5, including on chasing debut: stays easy 3m: acts on any going: tried blinkered. *R. H. Buckler* **c– h–**

HAILE SELASSIE 5 b.g. Awesome – Lady of The Realm (Prince Daniel (USA)) [2004/5 h90: 16d^3 17m^4 17d^6 16g 17g^5 21s^pu Oct 21] close-coupled gelding: modest maiden hurdler: may prove best at 2m: acts on good to soft and good to firm ground: blinkered fifth outing: sold £2,100 Ascot February Sales. *W. Jenks* **h90**

HAIL THE KING (USA) 5 gr.g. Allied Forces (USA) – Hail Kris (USA) (Kris S (USA)) [2004/5 h90: 17g^pu 18d^5 16m 16g^4 16s^5 17m^3 16d^2 16d^4 16g^5 16d* Apr 17] leggy gelding: modest hurdler: won conditional jockeys handicap at Wincanton in April: will prove best around 2m: acts on good to firm and good to soft going, below form on soft: held up: none too consistent. *R. M. Carson* **h95**

HALCON GENELARDAIS (FR) 5 ch.g. Halcon – Francetphile (FR) (Farabi) [2004/5 18d^2 20v^2 22d* 20d* Mar 19] workmanlike gelding: will make a chaser: sixth foal: dam, ran 3 times on Flat, half-sister to dam of useful French hurdler Kingphil: once-raced on Flat: in frame twice from 4 starts over hurdles for J. L. Pelletan: looked useful prospect in Britain, winning novices at Fontwell in February and Uttoxeter (ran on well when beating Double Header 8 lengths) in March: will stay 3m. *A. King* **h127 p**

HALCYON MAGIC 7 b.g. Magic Ring (IRE) – Consistent Queen (Queen's Hussar) [2004/5 16g Jan 24] half-brother to 2 winning hurdlers: modest on Flat (stays easy 1½m), successful in April: well held in maiden on hurdling debut. *M. Wigham* **h–**

HALEXY (FR) 10 b.g. Iron Duke (FR) – Tartifume II (FR) (Mistigri) [2004/5 c119, h–: c22d^4 Nov 28] tall, good sort: fairly useful chaser in 2002/3 for Miss V. Williams: finished weakly only 2 subsequent outings: has won at 3m, best form over shorter: raced mainly on good going or softer: bold jumper who races with plenty of zest. *Jonjo O'Neill* **c110 h–**

HALFAJOBJONES 6 b.m. Tina's Pet – Hop The Twig (Full of Hope) [2004/5 F16v 19v^pu 17g 24s^pu Apr 16] medium-sized mare: third foal: half-sister to fairly useful hunter chaser Kestick (by Roscoe Blake): dam winning hurdler: no show in bumper or novice hurdles. *C. W. Moore* **h– F–**

HALF AN HOUR 8 b.g. Alflora (IRE) – Country Mistress (Town And Country) [2004/5 c–, h–: c24d^4 c21g^2 c24g^4 c21m^2 c21g* c21g^pu c21m^2 c21f c20d^6 Nov 9] well-made gelding: fair chaser: won novice handicap at Stratford in July: stays 2¾m: acts on firm and good to soft going (won bumper on soft): visored last 5 starts: inconsistent. *A. King* **c112 h–**

HALF BARRELL (IRE) 13 br.g. Lord Americo – Araybeam VII (Damsire Unregistered) [2004/5 c117, h–: c21g c17d^4 c17m^6 c20v^3 c22g^3 c19s c21d Oct 11] winning hurdler: veteran handicap chaser, still capable of fair form in 2004: stays 3m well: acts on heavy going: has won 4 times at Galway: inconsistent. *V. T. O'Brien, Ireland* **c113 h–**

HALF INCH 5 b.m. Inchinor – Anhaar (Ela-Mana-Mou) [2004/5 16d^4 16g^2 16m^4 17g^3 16f^2 16m^3 16s* 16m Apr 17] leggy mare: half-sister to several winners over jumps, including fairly useful hurdler Four Aces (by Forzando), stays 2¾m: fair on Flat (stays 1¼m): modest hurdler: won handicap at Fakenham in October: raced around 2m: acts on soft and good to firm going. *B. I. Case* **h99**

HALLAND 7 ch.g. Halling (USA) – Northshiel (Northfields (USA)) [2004/5 h93p: 16g 20v^2 16d 19g^2 18s^6 21g^6 Mar 28] workmanlike gelding: modest novice hurdler: left N. Littmoden after third outing: likely to prove best up to 2½m: raced on good going or softer. *A. King* **h95**

HALLEM HALL 8 ch.g. Little Wolf – Oneninefive (Sayyaf) [2004/5 F–: 26d^pu Apr 29] no form in Grade 2 bumper or maiden hurdle (cheekpieces). *Mrs E. B. Scott* **h–**

HALLRULE (IRE) 11 ch.g. Be My Native (USA) – Phantom Thistle (Deep Run) [2004/5 c74, h–: c25g^4 24s* 20v^4 Nov 25] sturdy gelding: poor hurdler/chaser: won amateur novice handicap over hurdles at Carlisle in October: probably best at 3m+: acts on heavy going: visored last 5 outings. *Miss P. Robson* **c74 h76**

HALLYARDS GAEL (IRE) 11 br.g. Strong Gale – Secret Ocean (Most Secret) [2004/5 c129, h112: c25m* c22g* May 5] strong, lengthy gelding: fair hurdler: useful handicap chaser: successful twice at Kelso very early in season, beating Benrajah by 9 lengths on second occasion: stays 25f: acts on good to firm and good to soft going: wore cheekpieces last 4 starts in 2003/4. *L. Lungo* **c135 h–**

HAMADEENAH 7 ch.m. Alhijaz – Mahbob Dancer (FR) (Groom Dancer (USA)) [2004/5 h87: 17m^2 16g^2 17m* 17d* 16g^4 18s^{pu} 17s^5 19g^2 20d^6 Apr 20] leggy mare: fair hurdler: claimed from D. Wintle £6,000 on reappearance, back with D. McCain next 2 runs: won claimer (claimed £10,000) at Sedgefield in September and handicap at Taunton in October: stays 19f with emphasis on speed: acts on soft and good to firm going. *C. J. Down* **h101**

HAM STONE 7 b.g. Picea – Blushing Belle (Local Suitor (USA)) [2004/5 h–: 19m^5 c24g^{pu} Jul 11] good-bodied gelding: of no account. *B. J. M. Ryall* **c– h–**

HANBRIN ROSE 8 gr.m. Lancastrian – Rymolbreese (Rymer) [2004/5 c71, h65: c23d^6 c20m^2 c20s^6 c16d^4 c19s^3 Mar 23] leggy mare: poor maiden hurdler/chaser: stays easy 3m: acts on good to firm and good to soft going: wore cheekpieces/blinkers in 2004/5. *R. Dickin* **c68 h–**

HANDA ISLAND (USA) 6 b.g. Pleasant Colony (USA) – Remote (USA) (Seattle Slew (USA)) [2004/5 h84: 16s^6 Dec 26] useful on Flat (stays 2m) at 3 yrs for H. Cecil: failed to see race out both outings over hurdles. *M. W. Easterby* **h–**

HAND INN HAND 9 b.g. Alflora (IRE) – Deep Line (Deep Run) [2004/5 c162, h134+: 16d^5 c20d^4 c24v^5 c20d^3 c20d^5 c21g^4 c25g^3 Apr 8] close-coupled, workmanlike gelding: useful hurdler, well held though not knocked about in handicap on reappearance: high-class chaser in 2003/4: not quite in same form in 2004/5, typically not finding great deal when fourth to Thisthatandtother in Grade 2 at Cheltenham sixth outing: stays 25f: unraced on firm going, acts on any other. *H. D. Daly* **c156 h–**

HANDS DOWN (IRE) 7 b.g. Old Vic – Kissowen (Pitpan) [2004/5 F17s 17s^6 Dec 2] €71,000 4-y-o: sturdy gelding: seventh foal: half-brother to smart bumper performer Alexander Milenium (by Be My Native) and fair hunter chaser Wise Prince (by Denel): dam unraced half-sister to smart 2½m to 3m chaser Kissane: green, seventh of 14 in bumper at Exeter on debut: well held in novice hurdle 6 weeks later. *Jonjo O'Neill* **h– F82**

HANDY MONEY 8 b.g. Imperial Frontier (USA) – Cryptic Gold (Glint of Gold) [2004/5 h115: 16d* 16d* 16d^5 Apr 9] workmanlike gelding: fairly useful handicap hurdler: left M. Ryan and off 16 months, won twice at Wincanton in March, improved effort when beating Fontanesi comfortably by 1¾ lengths on second occasion: stays 19f: acts on heavy going. *A. King* **h126**

HANNAH MONTER (IRE) 6 b.m. Topanoora – Katie Daly (IRE) (Lord Americo) [2004/5 F16g Apr 26] first foal: dam ran twice: well held in mares bumper on debut. *T. P. McGovern* **F–**

HANOVER SQUARE 9 b.g. Le Moss – Hilly-Down Lass (Deep Run) [2004/5 c84, h93: c24s^3 c26v^{ur} 24s^6 25v 24d Jan 12] leggy, angular gelding: modest handicap hurdler at best, well held last 3 starts: often let down by jumping and only poor form over fences since 2002/3: thorough stayer: raced mainly on going softer than good (acts on soft): unreliable. *N. A. Twiston-Davies* **c71 § h– §**

HANSAN BUOY (IRE) 5 b. or br.g. Anshan – Miss Tagalie (IRE) (Cyrano de Bergerac) [2004/5 F16d 24m^{pu} Apr 10] €9,000 3-y-o: fourth foal: dam unraced: no show in bumper or novice hurdle (lame). *J. W. Mullins* **h– F–**

HAPPY BOY (IRE) 4 b.g. Victory Note (USA) – Pepper And Salt (IRE) (Double Schwartz) [2004/5 F16v^6 F14s 16g 20s 16s^5 Apr 3] 800 3-y-o: sturdy gelding: third foal: half-brother to useful miler Unshakable (by Eagle Eyed) and winning 2m hurdler Northern Raider (by College Chapel): dam unraced: well held in bumpers and over hurdles. *M. A. Barnes* **h– F67**

HAPPY HUSSAR (IRE) 12 b.g. Balinger – Merry Mirth (Menelek) [2004/5 c–x, h89: 22g^5 24d 24d 21g c24d^4 c25d c21s^2 c25s* c19v^F c28g^2 c25g Apr 8] workmanlike gelding: has stringhalt: modest handicap hurdler/chaser: won over fences at Exeter in January: stays 3½m: acts on any going: sketchy jumper of fences. *Dr P. Pritchard* **c94 x h85**

HAPTHOR 6 ch.m. Zaffaran (USA) – My Goddess (Palm Track) [2004/5 F16g Apr 16] ex-Irish mare: sixth foal: dam, winning pointer, half-sister to dam of useful hurdler Ingletonian, stayed 2¾m: little sign of ability in points and bumpers. *F. Jestin* **F–**

HARAPOUR (FR) 7 b.g. Valanour (IRE) – Haratiyna (Top Ville) [2004/5 h118: 20g^6 c20s^4 c20d^3 c20s* c20v^F c19d* c24d^{pu} c20g^3 Apr 15] useful-looking gelding: fairly useful hurdler in 2003/4: at least as good over fences despite jumping none too fluently at times, winning maiden at Plumpton in December and handicap at Chepstow in March: stays 2¾m: raced on good going or softer: has hinted at temperament. *P. F. Nicholls* **c128 h–**

HARBEN (FR) 6 ch.g. Luchiroverte (IRE) – Dixia (FR) (Altayan) [2004/5 F–: 20m^5 22g 20g^2 20d^{pu} 20g 16s^3 c16v^3 c20s^6 c16v^{pu} 20s^{pu} Mar 10] rather leggy gelding: poor maiden hurdler: left R. Guest after fifth start, D. McCain after eighth: form over fences only when third of 4 in novice at Uttoxeter on debut: should stay beyond 2m: acts on heavy going. *M. A. Barnes* **c93 ? h70**

HARBOUR BOUND (IRE) 6 b.g. Sadler's Wells (USA) – Argon Laser (Kris) [2004/5 17m 17d 19g* 22g* 21m^3 24f^5 20d Oct 2] lengthy gelding: fairly useful 12.5f winner on Flat, sold out of A. O'Brien's stable 28,000 gns Newmarket Autumn (2002) Sales, resold £1,300 Ascot April (2004) Sales: fair novice hurdler: won twice at Newton Abbot in August: failed to impress with attitude last 2 starts, visored final one: stays 2¾m: acts on good to firm going: lazy. *Evan Williams* **h109**

HARBOUR KING (FR) 6 b.h. Darshaan – Zinarelle (FR) (Zino) [2004/5 17s^{pu} Jan 10] half-brother to fair 2m hurdler Zapateado (by Galetto): ran once on Flat at 3 yrs for F. Head: bought 2,000 gns Newmarket July (2002) Sales: no show in novice on hurdling debut. *N. I. M. Rossiter* **h–**

HARBOUR PILOT (IRE) 10 b.g. Be My Native (USA) – Las-Cancellas (Monksfield) [2004/5 c168, h–: c25g^2 c24s^4 c20s^{pu} Dec 5] rangy gelding: winning hurdler: top-class chaser, twice placed in Cheltenham Gold Cup: unsuited by steadily-run race when fourth to Beef Or Salmon in Grade 1 at Down Royal in November: reported to be clinically abnormal after folding tamely at Punchestown final start: reported in January to have suffered leg injury and missed rest of season: will stay beyond 3¼m: thorough stayer: raced on good going or softer (acts on heavy): usually blinkered nowadays: tends to jump left, and prone to the odd bad mistake. *N. Meade, Ireland* **c165 h–**

HARBOUR POINT (IRE) 9 b.g. Glacial Storm (USA) – Forest Jem (Croghan Hill) [2004/5 h86: 19s 22d 20d Mar 28] lengthy gelding: bumper winner: maiden hurdler, no form in 2004/5: should be suited by further than 2½m: visored final outing. *Miss I. E. Craig* **h–**

HARBOUR ROCK (IRE) 6 b.g. Midhish – Annie's Glen (IRE) (Glenstal (USA)) [2004/5 F73: F17g^3 Jul 12] compact gelding: fair form when third in maiden bumper at Newton Abbot. *D. J. Wintle* **F86**

HARCHIBALD (FR) 6 b.g. Perugino (USA) – Dame d'Harvard (USA) (Quest For Fame) [2004/5 h144: 16g^4 16s^3 16d* 16d* 16g* 16g^2 Mar 15] **h164 §**

The close co-operation between trainers and jockeys and those who work on the racecourse for the media has some obvious advantages for both groups, and for racing generally, but it does sometimes seem to lead to the stifling of criticism. Unfortunately, in such a closely-knit world, there is always a danger that an over-critical reporter could find himself denied access to some of the people who provide him with the interviews and information upon which he relies for his livelihood. The quotes of the top jockeys, in particular, are seen as essential by many broadcasting and newspaper racing editors, which begs a question about those who orchestrated the defence of Paul Carberry's riding of Harchibald in the Champion Hurdle. Would they have acted the same if the horse had been ridden by a less well known jockey or by a Frenchman—say Thierry Doumen whose exaggerated waiting tactics on Baracouda were much criticised at times? Attempts to hold Carberry to account for what some considered an ill-judged piece of riding were largely left to contributors to the letters columns.

Any idea, however, that the motionless Carberry had tried to be too clever after cruising into contention, and had left it too late to shake up Harchibald, was immediately rejected as the media closed ranks behind the view that criticism was misplaced. 'Any of you criticising Paul Carberry, wash your mouth out with soap,' John McCririck told Channel 4 viewers. 'You don't know what you're talking about, you don't know about racing.' McCririck seems to have changed his mind about exaggerated waiting tactics since the days of The Fellow, his regular criticism of the French-based Pole Adam Kondrat's riding of that horse being described as 'particularly bombastic' in *Chasers & Hurdlers 1992/93*. Alastair Down in the

Mongey Communications Morgiana Hurdle, Punchestown—
Paul Carberry oozes confidence on Harchibald (noseband) as Back In Front is dispatched with ease

Racing Post labelled critics of Carberry's ride as 'imbeciles'. Down described it as 'a ride that was on nodding terms with genius and nobody else would have got Harchibald so close.' It was Down who had led the chorus of disapproval of the owner of Azertyuiop for having the temerity to criticise Ruby Walsh's riding when he was beaten by Moscow Flyer in the Tingle Creek Chase in December. Down described the horse's owner on that occasion as a 'pooper at the party . . . [who] let himself down with his snivelling complaints about Ruby Walsh's riding of Azertyuiop, a spoilt man's jarring analysis of a job he would not be able to do if he lived to be Methuselah.' Azertyuiop's owner had merely expressed the view—as he had every right to do—that his horse might have done better had Walsh pressurised Moscow Flyer earlier in the race. His solicited remark—given in answer to a question from a journalist—was, in fact, refreshingly honest by the usual standards of post-race interviews and certainly didn't deserve the spiteful reprimand it received. If it is possible for Down, self evidently no jockey, to recognise a ride of genius, it must also be possible for someone with similarly limited experience of raceriding to take a reasonably critical view.

There are a number of ways a horse can lose a race that should be won, and the blame for some of them can be laid firmly at the door of the jockey. In others the only reasonable conclusion may well be that the horse turned it in, threw away a winning opportunity. We broadly take the view that Harchibald did not go through with his effort in the Champion Hurdle against a very game opponent. The matter, though, is not clear cut by any means and the racegoers and punters who criticised Carberry's riding in the Champion Hurdle were perfectly entitled to their say. Harchibald was a much improved performer in the latest season and had won three races in a row before the Champion Hurdle, including the 'Fighting Fifth' and the Christmas Hurdle, both Grade 1 events. Harchibald looked to be in a winning position all the way up the run-in in the Champion, soon alongside the under-pressure leader Hardy Eustace after the last and still on the bridle a hundred yards from the line. Carberry is coolness personified and his daring can look like brilliance when it comes off. His ride on Loyal Focus at Fairyhouse in January, when he effectively checked his mount halfway up the run-in before easing him to the front near the line, was an extreme example, one few jockeys would have had the temerity to execute. It was audacious, and it can be viewed as brilliant, but, as at Cheltenham, by delaying his final effort for so long, Carberry left himself wide open to criticism if the tactics didn't come off. It worked at Fairyhouse, as it has on so many other occasions, but many thought he overdid it at Cheltenham, so that, when he finally got down to brass tacks, Harchibald was left with the task of accelerating past a fully opened out Hardy Eustace who was galloping on very strongly to the line. Carberry didn't exercise the option of picking up his whip until virtually on the line (he said afterwards that Harchibald would have 'stopped' if he had hit him), tactics consistent with those employed on Harchibald earlier in the season.

So was Carberry guilty of a misjudgement in expecting Harchibald to respond almost instantaneously when push came to shove in the last fifty yards? Well, if he was, there were extenuating circumstances. He himself had passed a late fitness test after injuring his rib cage out hunting, and, more pertinently, there were the worries expressed by the stable about Harchibald's 'terrible' gallop after racing at Navan ten days before Cheltenham. Trainer Noel Meade said: 'He worked terrible. He emptied very badly and just stopped'. Perhaps Carberry might have felt, contrary to the impression of those in the stands, that Harchibald was coming to the end of his tether. Furthermore, Harchibald had demonstrated weakness in a finish in the past. As a juvenile he had finished weakly on several occasions, tending to carry his head high. At the Festival twelve months earlier, he had also failed to go through with his effort when fifth in the County Hurdle after looking all over the winner. 'The later you come the better with him, so I won't be in any hurry to hit the front,' Carberry was reported as saying before the latest Festival, confirming his fears about committing Harchibald too soon up Cheltenham's stiff final hill.

But there is yet another angle. Given Carberry's own view about the desirability of coming late on Harchibald, was he not actually guilty of arriving there too soon? Would Harchibald's cause have been better served if Carberry had lain further back and brought Harchibald to challenge later, executing the classic waiting ride? By ranging alongside Hardy Eustace, Harchibald arguably played into the hands of his spirited rival and allowed Hardy Eustace's rider valuable time to build up momentum in his mount. It could still be argued that, having got there too soon, Carberry might have done better to have sent on Harchibald early on the run-in and trusted that the advantage secured would have served him to the line. That is a view not shared by many, certainly not by Carberry and not by Harchibald's trainer Noel Meade, who said afterwards 'Had Paul passed him at the last, the other horse would have gone past him again.' Which brings us to the horse himself. Was Harchibald largely responsible for his own downfall? His trainer took exception to some of the things written about Harchibald's supposed lack of resolution—'gutless' and 'a thief' were among the terms that appeared in print—and claimed that the horse 'simply got tired'. 'If he's a rogue, a thief or gutless, I wish to God they'd send me ten more like him!' Notwithstanding considerations about tactics and timing, Harchibald's response when let down left something to be desired. Though beaten only a neck, Harchibald was clearly held by Hardy Eustace at the line and wouldn't have won with further to go. Whether Carberry's tactics contributed to his defeat, or whether all the blame attached to Harchibald himself, is virtually impossible to prove one way or the other, though, as we have said, Harchibald has a history of shirking it. However, those who took a dogmatic approach afterwards would have been better served by trying to persuade the racing public of their view, rather than by talking down to them. Insulting the intelligence of readers,

Pertemps 'Fighting Fifth' Hurdle, Newcastle—home-trained Champion Hurdle hopefuls Inglis Drever, Royal Shakespeare (partially hidden) and Intersky Falcon (blinkers) meet with a similar fate

Stan James Christmas Hurdle, Kempton—
the grey Rooster Booster's lead is rapidly diminishing between the final two flights

viewers or listeners is as risky for a journalist or broadcaster as upsetting those upon whose co-operation he or she relies for stories.

After the reports of his gallop at Navan, Harchibald was sent off 7/1 joint third favourite in the Champion Hurdle. He had been vying for ante-post favouritism before his lacklustre display in the public workout with four other stable companions. Nothing untoward came to light when Harchibald was examined afterwards but public confidence was still dented. Harchibald returned from a wind operation (tongue tied earlier in his career) to show improved form in handicaps in the second half of 2003/4 and to finish fourth to Hardy Eustace in the Emo Oil Champion Hurdle at Punchestown in April on effectively his final outing of that campaign. Returned to action in October, connections having considered sending him novice chasing, Harchibald ran as though the race was needed when a well-beaten third to Solerina at Tipperary, after which he was as long as 40/1 for the Champion Hurdle. Sharpened up, Harchibald then won the Mongey Communications Morgiana Hurdle at Punchestown in November by a length and a half and a head from Back In Front (who conceded 5 lb) and Macs Joy who had dominated the betting. Stalking the leaders and produced to take over at the last, 10/1-shot Harchibald was not hard pressed to maintain his advantage on the run-in. Down to as low as 16/1 for Cheltenham after the Morgiana, Harchibald was cut to 4/1 favourite with Hills after another impressive victory in the Pertemps 'Fighting Fifth' Hurdle at Newcastle in November, the first running of the race as a Grade 1. Cruising into contention after travelling strongly under restraint, Harchibald touched down just in front at the last and won by two lengths and the same, from Inglis Drever and Royal Shakespeare, asserting himself without Carberry having to do much in the saddle.

With an excellent programme in Ireland over the Christmas period, it is unusual to see Irish-trained challengers for Kempton's big Boxing Day card. Florida Pearl won the King George VI Chase in 2001 and 20/1-shot Afrostar was successful in a novice hurdle in 1999 but they were rare occurrences. The Irish landed both the King George (with Kicking King) and the Stan James Christmas Hurdle in the latest season, Harchibald landing the odds in the latter. As at Newcastle, Harchibald won without Carberry drawing his whip, consolidating his position at the head of the Champion Hurdle betting after reeling in the runaway leader Rooster Booster who was over twenty lengths up by halfway and even further clear three out. Harchibald reduced the gap to twelve lengths two out, and then to four at the last, before leading a hundred yards out and winning by a length and a half. The first two finished twenty lengths clear. Carberry's ride at Kempton could be said to have been every bit as exaggerated as the one at Cheltenham. But the course and the mettle of the opposition were very different on this occasion.

Harchibald by-passed the AIG Europe Champion Hurdle in January and wasn't seen out again until Cheltenham. The Emo Oil Champion Hurdle at Punchestown, shortly after the end of the British season, was Harchibald's only other race. With Hardy Eustace sidelined, he started odds on in a small field against the Champion Hurdle third Brave Inca, who had finished only a neck behind Harchibald, and the Champion Hurdle fifth Macs Joy. A farcical early pace—the field took fifteen seconds longer to reach the third flight than the leaders in the novice hurdle later on the card—meant the race developed into a sprint. The tactics adopted on Harchibald, who was very much the paddock pick, were broadly similar to those at Cheltenham, though Harchibald never looked to be travelling with the supreme ease of Cheltenham. Carberry could certainly not be blamed for the fact that Harchibald was beaten again, finding little in a tight finish, after coming to lead at the last. Harchibald went down by a head to Brave Inca, who lived up to his name under a typically strong ride from Tony McCoy, replacing regular jockey Barry Cash. With Macs Joy only a length further away in third, the result confirmed that there was very little between the top two-mile hurdlers in the latest season. The race also confirmed that, although the consistency of his performances cannot be questioned, Harchibald is not one to trust.

Harchibald (FR) (b.g. 1999)	Perugino (USA) (b 1991)	Danzig (b 1977)	Northern Dancer
			Pas de Nom
		Fairy Bridge (b 1975)	Bold Reason
			Special
	Dame d'Harvard (USA) (gr 1994)	Quest For Fame (b 1987)	Rainbow Quest
			Aryenne
		Bridge Table (ro 1978)	Riva Ridge
			Grey Table

Mr D. P. Sharkey's "Harchibald"

The lengthy, useful-looking Harchibald has the scope to make a chaser, though another, similar campaign over hurdles seems more likely. No doubt he will find further races where everything falls into place, though connections of his opponents must be wise to his failings and are again likely to employ tactics to exploit them. Harchibald is by Perugino, a once-raced (won over six furlongs at two) close relative of Sadler's Wells, Fairy King and Tate Gallery. Perugino is now at stud in Australia where he has sired a champion sprinter in Testa Rossa, among others. The very smart sprinter The Tatling is his best known offspring on the Flat in Britain. Harchibald's dam Dame d'Harvard, out of an unraced half-sister to the good American horse Quiet Little Table, was a French two-year-old five-furlong winner who finished fourth in the Prix de la Salamandre. Harchibald is her first foal and she is also the dam of French mile winner Jeu de Dame, a sister to Harchibald, and Dametori (by Vettori) who won over nine furlongs in France as a three-year-old. Harchibald showed useful form over middle distances on the Flat for Bernard Goudot in France—winning at up to twelve and a half furlongs—before being sold to present connections as a three-year-old for €90,000 at Goffs' Arc Sale. Harchibald is raced at around two miles over hurdles and has shown his best form on ground ranging from soft to good to firm. *N. Meade, Ireland*

HARDI DE CHALAMONT (FR) 10 gr.g. Royal Charter (FR) – Naita II (FR) (Dom Luc (FR)) [2004/5 c72x, h76: 20d 24d^5 21g^2 20s^6 21g^3 20s^3 Apr 16] leggy gelding: poor handicap hurdler/chaser, often let down by jumping over fences: stays 3m: acts on soft and good to firm going: tried in headgear: not one to trust. *Jennie Candlish* **c– x h84 §**

HARDRADA (IRE) 6 b.g. Entrepreneur – Alamiya (IRE) (Doyoun) [2004/5 18g^{pu} 22d c23d^{pu} 24s Jan 10] good-topped gelding: fairly useful maiden on Flat (should stay 1½m) at 3 yrs for R. Charlton: winning hurdler: sold out of N. Meade's stable 7,000 gns Doncaster May Sales after first start: no form in 2004/5, including on chasing debut: stays 2¾m: acts on soft ground: often blinkered: tried tongue tied. *N. J. Hawke* **c– h–**

HARDWICK 6 br.g. Oscar (IRE) – Paper Tigress (IRE) (King's Ride) [2004/5 F18d^2 F16d^2 F19s^6 Mar 26] first foal: dam tailed off on completed start in bumpers: fourth start in points when winning maiden in February: fairly useful form when second in bumpers at Downpatrick and Thurles (beaten 3½ lengths by Avoca Mist). *Adrian Maguire, Ireland* **F100**

HARDY DUCKETT (IRE) 6 br.g. Key of Luck (USA) – Bramdean (Niniski (USA)) [2004/5 h121, F101: 16g^2 16g^3 16s* 21s^5 16v^3 16v^5 16s^4 Mar 6] close-coupled gelding: fairly useful hurdler: landed odds in minor event at Cork in November: stays 2½m: raced on good going or softer over hurdles (acts on heavy). *D. T. Hughes, Ireland* **h116**

HARDY EUSTACE (IRE) 8 b.g. Archway (IRE) – Sterna Star (Corvaro (USA)) [2004/5 h167: 16g* 20s^2 16s^3 16v^3 16v* 16g* Mar 15] **h165**

'Golden age—the period when a specified art, skill or activity is at its peak; *the golden age of cinema*.' What has become known as 'the golden age of hurdling' can be identified, retrospectively, as the period from the first of Persian War's three Champion Hurdle victories in the 1967/8 season to the second of Sea Pigeon's Champion Hurdle wins in the 1980/1 season. Bula dethroned Persian War in the 1971 Champion Hurdle and won the race again in 1972. Comedy of Errors, the only horse to regain the crown, and Lanzarote accounted for the three renewals after Bula before Night Nurse—the best hurdler in Timeform's experience—won successive editions, a feat then equalled first by Monksfield, then by Sea Pigeon, both of whom were in the frame behind Night Nurse when he won for the second time. Also racing at this time was one of the best hurdlers never to win a Champion Hurdle, Bird's Nest, runner-up in Night Nurse's first Champion and third to Sea Pigeon and Monksfield in 1980. Bird's Nest won the Bula three times, the Scottish Champion twice and was first past the post in the 'Fighting Fifth' four times. The rivalry between Bird's Nest and Sea Pigeon was one of the features of the 'the golden age of hurdling', the pair meeting on no fewer than fourteen occasions, including five times in the Champion Hurdle, in which Sea Pigeon finished ahead of Bird's Nest every time. Two of the renewals in which they took part where those in 1977 and 1978 which also featured both Night Nurse (the winner in 1977) and Monksfield (the winner in 1978). The four also met on May Day 1978 in the inaugural Royal Doulton Handicap Hurdle at Haydock, which attracted twenty runners and was by far the most valuable handicap hurdle ever staged in Britain up

Red Mills Trial Hurdle, Gowran—Hardy Eustace completes his Cheltenham preparations

to that time (and the fourth-biggest prize on offer in the season after the Grand National, the Gold Cup and the Champion Hurdle). Monksfield, Sea Pigeon and Night Nurse had filled the first three places in the Champion Hurdle, with Bird's Nest back in seventh. Monksfield and Night Nurse, conceding the winner Royal Gaye 28 lb and 23 lb respectively, finished second and third in a thrilling race in which the course record was lowered by over seven seconds. Monksfield won a particularly memorable battle with Sea Pigeon at Cheltenham the following season (with Bird's Nest fifth). He then came first for the third time (including a famous dead-heat with Night Nurse) in what is now known as the Aintree Hurdle, before winning the Welsh Champion Hurdle (from Bird's Nest) and then finishing an exceptionally game runner-up to the top-class Beacon Light, again under 12-0, in the Royal Doulton whose first prize had overtaken that for the Champion Hurdle.

Dessie Hughes, who rode Monksfield to the second of his Champion Hurdle victories, drew parallels between that race and the latest edition won by Hardy Eustace, whom he trains. 'I'd won the Aintree race twice on Monksfield, including the dead-heat, and thought he was probably better at around two and a half than at two. I made my mind up to make the running, as there were no stamina doubts, and when Sea Pigeon joined me at the last we still had a bit left.' *Chasers & Hurdlers 1978/79* recounts the finish: 'Facing up to the last flight it looked all Lombard Street to a china orange against Monksfield; O'Neill was sitting with a double handful on Sea Pigeon; Hughes had already picked up his stick and was hard at work on Monksfield. The pair touched down together, both having jumped it equally well. For a few strides Sea Pigeon took the lead but Monksfield, head thrust forward in typical fashion, refused to give in and it was not long before Sea Pigeon was off the bridle. In a thrilling battle to the line, Monksfield gradually edged ahead, showing the determination for which he is justly renowned to struggle home by three quarters of a length. There were no more gallant performances seen all season than Monksfield's and Sea Pigeon's at Cheltenham. For let no-one think that Monksfield's victory owed anything to any lack of resolution on Sea Pigeon's part; both horses ran their heart out and neutrals admitted afterwards to more than a twinge of sympathy for Sea Pigeon. The Champion Hurdle is the race likely to be remembered above all others in the most recent season.'

Any similarities between the 1979 Champion Hurdle and the latest edition apply only to the way the two races unfolded. The winner and runner-up in 2005, Hardy Eustace and Harchibald, were just about the two best hurdlers around, but they bear no comparison with Monksfield and Sea Pigeon who were among the most popular horses in the history of jumping and achieved legendary status. Third-placed Beacon Light finished fifteen lengths behind Sea Pigeon in the 1979 renewal. There was a broad parallel at the last flight where front-running Hardy Eustace, who had quickened the pace after three out, was joined by Harchibald, who was cantering and looked to have plenty left. Harchibald's effort was delayed a bit longer than Sea Pigeon's and he was still on the bridle a hundred yards out. The controversy over Harchibald's performance is discussed fully in his essay and there is no need to go into it again here. It could not be said, however, as it was of Sea Pigeon, that he ran his heart out. Suffice to say that Hardy Eustace responded most gamely to pressure, after looking sure to be beaten, and kept on very strongly to win by a neck from Harchibald, the smallest winning margin in the race since 1955 when Clair Soleil beat Stroller by a head. Brave Inca was only a neck away third, with less than six lengths covering the first six home. Accordion Etoile and Macs Joy completed a clean sweep of the first five places by Irish-trained horses, with the previous year's third Intersky Falcon sixth. It was not a vintage Champion Hurdle and may end up being remembered as much for being a race Harchibald lost, as for being one which Hardy Eustace won.

The current generation of two-mile hurdlers lacks an outstanding performer but the latest Champion Hurdle was thoroughly representative of the best available. Reigning champion Hardy Eustace, who had been a 33/1-chance in 2004, and the Bula Hurdle winner Back In Front were joint favourites, ahead of Harchibald, winner of the 'Fighting Fifth' and the Christmas Hurdle, and Macs Joy, winner of the December Festival Hurdle and the AIG Europe Champion Hurdle. Brave Inca, successful in the Supreme Novices' Hurdle the previous year, had been beaten a short head by Macs Joy in the AIG Europe Champion, in which Hardy Eustace had finished a head away third, with Accordion Etoile fifth. The progressive handicapper Essex, successful in the Pierse Hurdle and the totesport Trophy, was also in the fourteen-strong Champion Hurdle line-up, as was the 2003 winner Rooster Booster who had been beaten on all five of his starts in the current season. The winning time of 3m 51.40sec was faster than that for the other two-mile hurdles on the opening day of the Festival but, considering the relative merits of the horses involved, the Champion Hurdle time did not compare well, indicative of the fact that Hardy Eustace set not much more than a fair pace in the first part of the race. For the

Smurfit Champion Hurdle Challenge Trophy, Cheltenham—the blinkers are back on as Hardy Eustace prevails in a three-way thriller from Harchibald (centre) and Brave Inca

second year running, Conor O'Dwyer was allowed to dictate the pace on Hardy Eustace, sending him straight into the lead, then steadying the tempo after jumping the first two flights before gradually stepping things up from three out. Hardy Eustace still had something in reserve when O'Dwyer had to call on him to pull out all the stops on the run-in. Hardy Eustace's tenacity played a big part in the victory but the Champion Hurdle was also the story of two jockeys riding different types of waiting races. O'Dwyer rode his waiting race from the front and executed the tactics in copybook fashion. Hardy Eustace was never headed, emulating the achievement of Night Nurse in 1976 and Make The Stand in 1997 (Blaris in the inaugural running in 1927 and Victor Norman in 1936 are the only others thought to have made all in a Champion Hurdle). Hardy Eustace was headed for a stride or two after the last by Rooster Booster in 2004. Hardy Eustace was the only one of the four major winners from the previous year's Festival to retain his title. Stayers' Hurdle winner Iris's Gift—for whom a chasing campaign had been planned—and Gold Cup winner Best Mate were both sidelined, while Azertyuiop's winning chance effectively went in the Champion Chase with a mistake at the sixth fence, the water.

Hardy Eustace took a couple of races to reach his peak in the latest season. Having followed up his 2004 Champion Hurdle victory by repeating his Cheltenham form with Rooster Booster in the Emo Oil Champion Hurdle at Punchestown, it was intended that Hardy Eustace would reappear after a summer's break in the Hatton's Grace Hurdle at Fairyhouse in November, but he missed that with a mucus problem. Hardy Eustace was beaten by Solerina in the Tara Hurdle at Navan in December, but he had that mare a place behind him when third to Macs Joy and Brave Inca in the December Festival Hurdle at Leopardstown two and a half weeks later. Hardy Eustace wore blinkers in the Festival Hurdle (as he had for his Champion Hurdle wins at Cheltenham and Punchestown) but they were left off again when the prominently-ridden Hardy Eustace kept on splendidly when just touched off in the AIG Europe Champion Hurdle on heavy going at Leopardstown in January. He had his final outing before Cheltenham—again without headgear—in the Red Mills Trial Hurdle at Gowran, landing odds of 6/1-on by twenty-five lengths. The blinkers were back on at Cheltenham where the value of Hardy Eustace's form was virtually on a par with the previous year.

The two Champion Hurdle victories stand out on Hardy Eustace's record, in terms of form as well as importance, with his efforts in defeat without blinkers in the Tara Hurdle and the AIG Europe Champion Hurdle representing slightly better form than his run when blinkered in the December Festival Hurdle. The original aim of fitting blinkers—before Hardy Eustace's first Champion Hurdle win—was said to have been 'to help sharpen him up', according to his trainer. Blinkers seem sure to continue to play a part in Hardy Eustace's career, though punters shouldn't be unduly put off him in races when they are not fitted. He is both game and reliable. He does seem to come to his best in the spring, however, and is clearly suited by Cheltenham with its undulations and, particularly, its stiff uphill finish. Hardy Eustace acts on heavy going but the ground has been good for both his Champion Hurdle victories, which, as has been said, represent the best efforts of his career. He is effective at two miles to twenty-one furlongs, the distance of the Royal & SunAlliance Novices' Hurdle which he won as a six-year-old. If Hardy Eustace retains his Champion Hurdle crown in 2006, he will emulate Istabraq—easily the best two-mile hurdler since 'the golden age of hurdling'—who also won the Royal & SunAlliance before his Champion Hurdle victories. See You Then (1985, 1986 and 1987) is the only other triple Champion Hurdle winner since Persian War.

The pedigree of the good-topped Hardy Eustace has been covered in detail in the last two Annuals. He is from the last Irish crop of the smart sprinter Archway who has since made a name for himself in Australia (Perugino, another stallion now going well in Australia, is the sire of Champion Hurdle runner-up Harchibald). Archway was put down after a suspected heart attack in July 2004. Hardy Eustace's dam Sterna Star gained her only victory in a ladies race over a mile and a half. She was also represented on the racecourse in the latest season by the six-year-old Ca Na Trona (by Accordion) who won a novice hurdle at Taunton in November; the gelding by Accordion out of Sterna Star who fetched €160,000 as an unbroken three-year-old at the 2004 Derby Sale and subsequently named Bill Cody has yet to

Mr Laurence Byrne's "Hardy Eustace"

Hardy Eustace (IRE) (b.g. 1997)	Archway (IRE) (ch 1988)	Thatching (b 1975)	Thatch
			Abella
		Rose of Jericho (b 1984)	Alleged
			Rose Red
	Sterna Star (b or br 1984)	Corvaro (b 1977)	Vaguely Noble
			Delmora
		Star Girl (b 1973)	Sovereign Gleam
			Sterna

reach the racecourse. Sterna Star's next foal, by Pistolet Bleu, was bought by Hughes as a yearling for €60,000. Sterna Star had to be put down in 2004 after breaking a hock. Hardy Eustace's half-sister Forgotten Star (by Don't Forget Me) is now at stud and her first foal, Star Award (by Oscar), is reportedly to join Nicky Henderson after making £50,000 at the Cheltenham April Sales. Both Hardy Eustace's grandam Star Girl and great grandam Sterna bred nine winners, the latter being the dam of Eclipse and Prix de l'Arc de Triomphe winner Star Appeal and also the grandam of Strong Gale, the predominant jumps sire of the 'nineties. *D. T. Hughes, Ireland*

HARDY RUSSIAN (IRE) 8 b.g. Moscow Society (USA) – Catchmekiss (IRE) (Executive Perk) [2004/5 c19s^{pu} c26v^{pu} c23s^{pu} Jan 31] workmanlike gelding: first foal: dam once-raced, out of sister to very smart 2m to 21f hurdler Dunaree and close relative of Grand National winner Rag Trade: lightly-raced maiden Irish pointer, in frame twice in 2004: bought £2,600 Ascot October Sales: no form in maiden chases. *P. R. Rodford* **c–**

HAREM SCAREM (IRE) 14 b.g. Lord Americo – River Rescue (Over The River (FR)) [2004/5 c61, h–: c16g⁴ c20m⁶ c17g³ c21d² c20g² c23f⁴ c20g* c16m³ c16m³ c24s⁶ c20s² c20g⁴ c20vᵘʳ c21sᵘʳ c16s⁶ c20vᵖᵘ Mar 17] tall, workmanlike gelding: poor handicap chaser: won amateur event at Hexham in September: stays 21f: acts on good to firm and heavy going: tried blinkered earlier in career. *Mrs L. Williamson* **c73** **h–**

HARIK 11 ch.g. Persian Bold – Yaqut (USA) (Northern Dancer) [2004/5 c107, h–: c20d* c20g c20m⁶ c17g⁵ c21g⁶ c17g⁴ c18s* Mar 30] workmanlike gelding: modest on all-weather, poor on turf on Flat (stays 17f) nowadays: fair handicap chaser: won at Fontwell in May and March (sixth course success): stays 2½m: acts on any going: has won in visor, usually blinkered/tongue tied. *G. L. Moore* **c110** **h–**

HARLEQUIN CHORUS 15 ch.g. Jester – Raise The Dawn (Rymer) [2004/5 16gᵖᵘ Apr 19] winning hurdler/maiden chaser, off 4 years before return: blinkered twice: has had tongue tied. *H. E. Haynes* **c–** **h–**

HARLEY 7 ch.g. Alderbrook – Chichell's Hurst (Oats) [2004/5 h–, F–: 21s 20v⁴ 20d* 19s³ 16v 20s⁵ 19g² Apr 1] lengthy gelding: modest hurdler: won novice handicap at Wetherby in December: stays 2½m: raced on good ground or softer (acts on heavy): races prominently: not a fluent jumper. *Mrs P. Sly* **h86 x**

HARLOV (FR) 10 ch.g. Garde Royale – Paulownia (FR) (Montevideo) [2004/5 c110, h–: c24d³ c26sᵖᵘ c24v³ c27g⁴ c25v⁴ c30s* c32v⁴ c28sᶠ Apr 3] well-made gelding: fair handicap chaser: won at Bangor in February by 6 lengths from Legatus: in process of running best race when falling 2 out at Kelso: stays 3¾m: acts on heavy going: blinkered once, wears cheekpieces nowadays: reliable. *A. Parker* **c111 +** **h–**

HARMONY BRIG (IRE) 6 ch.g. Accordion – Bridges Daughter (IRE) (Montelimar (USA)) [2004/5 16sᶠ 16v² Dec 30] well-made gelding: second foal: dam, bumper winner, out of useful staying hurdler Mayobridge: fair form when second to Baby Run in novice at Haydock on completed start over hurdles: likely to be suited by further than 2m: should do better. *N. G. Richards* **h107 p**

HARNAGE (IRE) 10 b.g. Mujadil (USA) – Wilderness (Martinmas) [2004/5 c–, h–: c21g⁶ c23m³ c26g² c26m³ Aug 19] leggy, close-coupled gelding: winning pointer: poor maiden chaser: stays 3¼m: acts on soft and good to firm going: tongue tied final start: tends to make mistakes: weak finisher. *Jean-Rene Auvray* **c73 x** **h–**

HARPASGON DE L'OMBRE (FR) 10 b.g. Mbaiki (FR) – Undress (FR) (Signani (FR)) [2004/5 c20d³ c24d² Jan 6] sturdy gelding: modest chaser: off 21 months before reappearance, back to best when second to Radcliffe in handicap at Ludlow: stays 3m: acts on firm and soft going: tried blinkered. *O. Sherwood* **c93**

HARPOON HARRY (IRE) 8 ch.g. Alphabatim (USA) – Procastrian (IRE) (Lancastrian) [2004/5 h95: 20d⁵ May 6] twice-raced over hurdles, let down by jumping on second occasion: bred to stay beyond 2½m. *K. C. Bailey* **h–**

HARPS HALL (IRE) 11 ch.g. Yashgan – Parsons Glen (IRE) (Glen Quaich) [2004/5 21dᵖᵘ Dec 5] workmanlike gelding: maiden pointer: no show in maiden on belated hurdling debut. *N. I. M. Rossiter* **h–**

HARRINGAY 5 b.m. Sir Harry Lewis (USA) – Tamergale (IRE) (Strong Gale) [2004/5 F85p: 21d³ 20d³ 16d⁴ 19s³ 21m Apr 2] lengthy, useful-looking mare: bumper winner: modest form at best in mares novice hurdles: stays 21f: has had breathing problems/found little. *Miss H. C. Knight* **h93**

HARRIS BAY 6 b.g. Karinga Bay – Harristown Lady (Muscatite) [2004/5 F106: 16d 19gᵖᵘ 20s⁴ 17d 20d 16g Apr 17] rangy gelding: bumper winner: disappointing hurdler, often shaping as if amiss: should prove best beyond 2m. *Miss H. C. Knight* **h–**

HARRIVAL 5 ch.g. Hazaaf (USA) – Departure (Gorytus (USA)) [2004/5 F17g F17m³ F17s⁵ F17v⁶ Feb 13] medium-sized gelding: first foal: dam, winning hurdler/pointer, stayed 25f: modest in bumpers: will be suited by further than 2m. *Miss M. Bragg* **F75**

HARROVIAN 8 b.g. Deploy – Homeoftheclassics (Tate Gallery (USA)) [2004/5 h74+: 24g* 24d² 22s c24d* c25v* c22d⁴ c25s³ c25s² Apr 3] fair hurdler: landed odds in novice at Hexham in May: better over fences: won novice at Musselburgh and handicap at Kelso in January: creditable efforts all starts after: will stay beyond 25f: raced on good going or softer (acts on heavy). *Miss P. Robson* **c117** **h101**

HARRY BLADE 6 b.g. Karinga Bay – Sparkling Cinders (Netherkelly) [2004/5 F16g² F17m* 16g² Nov 17] 4,500 3-y-o: rangy gelding: half-brother to several winners, including fairly useful hurdler Champagne Harry (by Sir Harry Lewis), stays 3m, and fair chaser Prancing Blade (by Broadsword), stays 3¼m: dam, poor staying maiden **h105 p** **F88**

hurdler/chaser, sister to useful 2½m chaser Fu's Lady: fair form in bumpers, winning at Hereford in September: 15 lengths second to Lord Henry in novice at Kempton on hurdling debut: will be suited by further than 2m: looked likely to progress but not seen out again. *N. A. Twiston-Davies*

HARRY BRIDGES 6 ch.g. Weld – Northern Quay (Quayside) [2004/5 F–: 21d 19s 20d^{pu} Apr 22] lengthy gelding: no sign of ability. *R. Lee* **h–**

HARRYCAT (IRE) 4 b.g. Bahhare (USA) – Quiver Tree (Lion Cavern (USA)) [2004/5 16s^{4} 16d^{2} 18s^{6} 16s^{pu} Feb 14] fair maiden on Flat (stays 1½m): best effort in juvenile hurdles when second to Nation State at Plumpton: may prove best at sharp 2m. *V. Smith* **h104**

HARRY COLLINS 7 ch.g. Sir Harry Lewis (USA) – Run Fast For Gold (Deep Run) [2004/5 h85: 25g^{4} c21d^{2} c22s^{2} c22d c20s^{F} c24g* c21g^{F} Apr 14] workmanlike gelding: modest maiden hurdler: fair form over fences: won maiden at Fakenham in March: barely stays 25f: acts on heavy going: tongue tied once: reliable. *B. I. Case* **c108 h83**

HARRYCONE LEWIS 7 b.g. Sir Harry Lewis (USA) – Rosie Cone (Celtic Cone) [2004/5 c110, h–: 21g^{2} 26g^{3} c22s* c23d^{pu} 25g^{2} c24d* c24d^{2} Mar 5] fair maiden hurdler: better over fences, winning handicaps at Market Rasen in November and Huntingdon in January: best effort when ½-length second to Zeta's River in well-contested handicap at Newbury final start, prominent throughout in strongly-run race: stays 3¼m: raced on good going or softer (acts on soft): wore cheekpieces first 2 starts, blinkered last 3. *Mrs P. Sly* **c125 + h105**

HARRY FLASHMAN 4 ch.g. Minster Son – Youandi (Silver Season) [2004/5 F16s* F16g^{4} Apr 16] second foal: dam, winning 2m hurdler, out of half-sister to smart 2½m to 3m chaser Bishop's Pawn: fairly useful form in bumpers at Ayr, winning 16-runner event in March by 7 lengths from Arctic Minster and fourth of 15 to Rasharrow in April. *D. W. Whillans* **F96**

HARRY HARESTONE 10 b.g. Miner's Lamp – Slipalong (Slippered) [2004/5 c22d^{pu} c19s^{pu} c19v^{pu} c19s^{pu} Mar 23] workmanlike gelding: winning hurdler/chaser: off nearly 3 years, no sign of retaining ability. *P. J. Jones* **c– h–**

HARRY HOOLY 10 b.g. Lithgie-Brig – Drummond Lass (Peacock (FR)) [2004/5 27d^{3} 20v* 20v^{3} 24v^{3} 21v^{6} c21s^{5} c20s^{3} c20v^{ur} c24d^{4} 20s Apr 10] leggy gelding: fair handicap hurdler: won at Hexham (fourth course success) in November: form over fences only when third in maiden at Carlisle: needs good test around 2½m and stays 27f: raced mainly on going softer than good (acts on heavy). *Mrs H. O. Graham* **c97 h101**

HARRY POTTER (GER) 6 b.g. Platini (GER) – Heavenly Storm (USA) (Storm Bird (CAN)) [2004/5 24v^{5} 24d^{5} 16v Mar 29] fairly useful on Flat (stays 9f), successful 4 times in 2004 for K. Burke: placed once from 3 starts around 2m over hurdles in Germany in 2003/4: little form in Britain, amiss last 2 starts. *Evan Williams* **h– p**

HARRY'S DREAM 8 b.g. Alflora (IRE) – Cheryls Pet (IRE) (General Ironside) [2004/5 c109, h93: c21d^{F} c24d^{5} Nov 3] leggy, workmanlike gelding: maiden hurdler: fair chaser: stays 3m: acts on soft and good to firm going: sometimes makes mistakes. *P. J. Hobbs* **c109 h–**

HARRY'S GAME 8 gr.g. Emperor Jones (USA) – Lady Shikari (Kala Shikari) [2004/5 h74: 16s 16g 16d^{F} 16g^{2} 16d^{pu} Apr 18] sturdy gelding: poor hurdler: raced around 2m on good ground or softer: tongue tied once. *A. P. Jones* **h76**

HARTIGAN (IRE) 9 b. or br.g. Be My Native (USA) – My Sunny Glen (Furry Glen) [2004/5 16m^{5} 17d^{3} 16g^{4} c16d^{pu} Oct 17] fair hurdler, off 2½ years prior to reappearance: left C. Roche after second start: let down by jumping in novice on chasing debut: will stay 2½m: acts on soft and good to firm going: blinkered third start: tried tongue tied. *Jonjo O'Neill* **c– h104**

HARVIS (FR) 10 b.g. Djarvis (FR) – Tirana (FR) (Over) [2004/5 c109§, h–: c20g^{3} May 16] smallish, angular gelding: winning hurdler: handicap chaser, on downgrade: stays 3m: acts on heavy and good to firm going: often fails to impress with jumping/attitude: sold 6,500 gns Doncaster August Sales: fourth in point in January. *G. B. Balding* **c99 § h–**

HASANPOUR (IRE) 5 b.g. Dr Devious (IRE) – Hasainiya (IRE) (Top Ville) [2004/5 h98: 20s^{5} 20s* 24s^{5} 24v^{pu} 17v 20s c16d^{3} c16s^{3} Mar 26] good-topped gelding: fairly useful on Flat (stays 13f): fair hurdler: won minor event in large field at Navan in November: well below best after next start: modest form when third in maiden chases: stays 2½m: acts on soft going. *C. F. Swan, Ireland* **c92 h110**

HASHID (IRE) 5 b.g. Darshaan – Alkaffeyeh (IRE) (Sadler's Wells (USA)) [2004/5 17d^{3} 16g^{6} 16d^{3} 19d* 20s^{2} 21d^{5} Mar 4] useful-looking gelding: half-brother to fairly useful hurdler Ambry (by Machiavellian), stays 25f: fair maiden on Flat (will stay 1¾m): fair novice hurdler: left clear last when fortunate to win at Lingfield in December: stays 21f: acts on soft going. *P. C. Ritchens* **h103**

HAS SCORED (IRE) 7 b.g. Sadler's Wells (USA) – City Ex (Ardross) [2004/5 h–: c27d^{6} c24g^{4} c25d* c25s^{4} Mar 11] sturdy gelding: well held only start over hurdles: fair form over fences: won maiden at Catterick in January: should stay beyond 25f: raced on good going or softer. *Ferdy Murphy* **c107 h–**

HASTY PRINCE 7 ch.g. Halling (USA) – Sister Sophie (USA) (Effervescing (USA)) [2004/5 h150: 16g c16v^{ur} c20g* c20s^{3} Dec 18] leggy, sparely-made gelding: smart hurdler in 2003/4 useful form over fences: easily won novice at Ludlow in December: third of 4 finishers to See You Sometime in Grade 2 novice at Windsor 9 days later: effective at 2m to 2½m: acts on soft and good to firm going: may still improve over fences, but needs to brush up jumping. *Jonjo O'Neill* **c133 h–**

HATCH A PLAN (IRE) 4 b.g. Vettori (IRE) – Fast Chick (Henbit (USA)) [2004/5 17d^{3} 16d Feb 17] angular gelding: fairly useful on Flat (stays 1½m), sold out of R. Beckett's stable 22,000 gns Newmarket Autumn Sales: better effort over hurdles when third to Manorson in novice at Taunton. *Mrs A. J. Hamilton-Fairley* **h96**

HATCH GATE 12 gr.g. Lighter – Yankee Silver (Yankee Gold) [2004/5 c79: c26d^{pu} Apr 28] winning pointer/hunter chaser: stays 3m: acts on good to firm going: ungenuine. *P. York* **c– §**

HATHLEN (IRE) 4 b.g. Singspiel (IRE) – Kameez (IRE) (Arazi (USA)) [2004/5 16d^{3} 20s^{4} 16g^{5} Mar 28] rather leggy gelding: fair on Flat (stays 2m), sold out of M. Channon's stable 17,000 gns Doncaster October Sales: modest form over hurdles: stays 2½m: carried head high final start. *G. L. Moore* **h91**

HATSNALL 7 b.g. Mtoto – Anna of Brunswick (Rainbow Quest (USA)) [2004/5 c–, h79: 21g 24m^{3} 20d 16s 22d^{pu} 16s^{6} 20d^{3} c20v^{2} c20s^{6} Feb 16] good-topped gelding: poor maiden hurdler: lightly raced over fences, better effort in 2004/5 when second in handicap at Leicester: stays 3m: acts on heavy and good to firm going. *Miss C. J. E. Caroe* **c87 h74**

HATTERAS (FR) 6 b.g. Octagonal (NZ) – Hylandra (USA) (Bering) [2004/5 h97: 18s^{2} 16v 16g^{2} 21d^{3} Apr 18] modest maiden hurdler: claimed from P. Nicholls £6,000 on reappearance: broke blood vessel second start: stays 21f: acts on soft ground. *Miss M. P. Bryant* **h94**

HATTINGTON 7 b.g. Polish Precedent (USA) – Ruffle (FR) (High Line) [2004/5 16g^{2} 16d^{5} 17s^{3} 16s* 22g^{6} Apr 3] fair on Flat (barely stays 14.6f) for M. Todhunter in 2003: fair novice hurdler: claimed from N. Richards £6,000 third start: improved effort when winning handicap at Towcester in March: stays 2¾m: acts on soft going: patiently ridden. *M. F. Harris* **h100**

HAT TRICK MAN 4 gr.c. Daylami (IRE) – Silver Kristal (Kris) [2004/5 16s 17s 24v^{pu} 17g Mar 3] fair maiden on Flat (stays 11.5f), sold from J. Akehurst £6,000 in November: no form over hurdles, tongue tied final start. *Evan Williams* **h–**

HAUNTED HOUSE 5 ch.g. Opera Ghost – My Home (Homing) [2004/5 F17v^{4} Feb 13] 18,000 4-y-o: sturdy gelding: half-brother to modest hurdler Handson (by Out of Hand), stayed 19f: dam 5f winner: still looked green when fourth of 14 in bumper at Exeter on debut. *H. D. Daly* **F77**

HAUTCLAN (FR) 6 b.g. Chef de Clan II (FR) – Haute Tension (FR) (Garde Royale) [2004/5 24s^{3} 24d^{2} 24d^{4} 24g Mar 17] workmanlike ex-French gelding: first foal: half-brother to fairly useful hurdler/chaser Positive Thinking (by Nikos), stays 2½m, and half-brother to 11.5f winner Good Spirit (by Smadoun): dam, won over hurdles on only start, sister to dam of useful hurdler around 2½m/useful Flat stayer Heros Fatal: successful up to 1½m on Flat: useful hurdler/chaser, won 4-y-o events at Auteuil (fences) and Bordeaux (hurdles) in 2003/4 for G. Macaire: creditable efforts all starts in handicap hurdles in 2004/5: stays 3m: raced on good ground or softer. *Jonjo O'Neill* **c– h132 +**

HAUT DE GAMME (FR) 10 ch.g. Morespeed – Chantalouette (FR) (Royal Charter (FR)) [2004/5 c24m^{4} c24v^{pu} c20v* c31d^{4} c19s^{5} c20g c19v^{3} c22d^{3} c22v^{pu} c22v* c21d^{2} Apr 8] sturdy ex-French gelding: winning hurdler: one-time smart chaser for J-P. Totain: useful form in Britain: won handicaps at Ayr in November and Kelso (easily beat Strong Resolve 3½ lengths) in March: best effort when length second of 30 to Cregg House in Topham Chase at Aintree: best form up to 2¾m: raced mainly on going softer than good (acts on heavy). *Ferdy Murphy* **c136 h–**

HAVANTADOUBT (IRE) 5 ch.m. Desert King (IRE) – Batiba (USA) (Time For A Change (USA)) [2004/5 h–: 16g 16s^{pu} Oct 28] no form over hurdles: tried tongue tied: sold £2,000 Ascot November Sales. *M. R. Bosley* **h–**

HAVE-NO-DOUBT (IRE) 11 b.g. Glacial Storm (USA) – Lady Kas (Pollerton) [2004/5 c–, h–: 26g^{pu} c21g^{3} c26g^{pu} c20m^{3} c17m^{pu} Sep 19] no longer of any account. *L. A. Dace* **c– h–**

HAVING A PARTY 7 b.m. Dancing High – Lady Manello (Mandrake Major) [2004/5 F95: 24g^{2} 20v^{pu} Jan 15] sturdy mare: bumper winner: better effort over hurdles when second to eased Lord Gale in novice at Worcester. *J. Mackie* **h94**

HAWADETH 10 ch.g. Machiavellian (USA) – Ghzaalh (USA) (Northern Dancer) [2004/5 h133: 21g 16d 16g* 16d^{5} 16d^{4} Feb 12] compact gelding: useful handicap hurdler: won at Doncaster in December by 8 lengths from Castleshane: ran well both starts after, best effort when 4¼ lengths fourth of 25 to Essex in totesport Trophy Hurdle at Newbury: stays 2½m, at least when emphasis is on speed: unraced on firm going, acts on any other: has worn blinkers, effective with or without cheekpieces: consistent, though sometimes soon off bridle or gets behind. *V. R. A. Dartnall* **h144**

HAWICK 8 b.g. Toulon – Slave's Bangle (Prince Rheingold) [2004/5 h–, F99: 22s Apr 3] fairly useful form in bumpers: off 15 months, no show in novice on completed outing over hurdles. *D. W. Whillans* **h–**

HAWKIT (USA) 4 b.g. Silver Hawk (USA) – Hey Ghaz (USA) (Ghazi (USA)) [2004/5 16g^{6} Oct 7] fairly useful on Flat (stays 1¼m), back to best for A. Bailey in 2005: tongue tied, well held in juvenile maiden on hurdling debut. *P. D. Evans* **h–**

HAWK'S LANDING (IRE) 8 gr.g. Peacock (FR) – Lady Cheyenne (Stanford) [2004/5 c125, h117: 24s^{3} c20s^{ur} c20g c24s^{pu} Dec 18] well-made gelding: fairly useful hurdler: winning chaser, usually let down by jumping: probably stays 3m: raced on good going or softer (acts on heavy): not a fluent jumper of fences. *Jonjo O'Neill* **c– x h122**

HAXTON 5 b.g. Sadler's Way – Ember (Nicholas (USA)) [2004/5 F16m Apr 25] first foal: dam modest maiden on Flat/poor over hurdles: no show in bumper on debut. *P. W. Hiatt* **F–**

HAYDENS FIELD 11 b.g. Bedford (USA) – Releta (Relkino) [2004/5 h120: 24v^{4} 21d 20v^{4} 24d 22g^{F} Apr 10] angular gelding: fairly useful handicap hurdler in 2003/4: left P. Rich and off 13 months, below form in 2004/5: stays 25f: raced on good going or softer (acts on heavy): front runner. *Miss H. Lewis* **h100**

HAYDENS FIRST (IRE) 5 b.m. Flemensfirth (USA) – Womenofninetyeight (IRE) (Buckskin (FR)) [2004/5 F16s^{2} Mar 3] €28,000 4-y-o: first foal: dam unraced half-sister to useful chaser up to 3m Corymandel: promising start in bumpers when 2 lengths second to Celestial Wave in mares event at Limerick in March. *T. Cooper, Ireland* **F99**

HAYLEY'S PEARL 6 b.m. Nomadic Way (USA) – Pacific Girl (IRE) (Emmson) [2004/5 h–, F–: 16d 19s^{pu} 17v^{pu} Feb 13] of no account. *Mrs P. Ford* **h–**

HAYS MEWS (IRE) 7 b.g. Lion Cavern (USA) – Classic Design (Busted) [2004/5 aF16g Dec 11] eighth foal: half-brother to 3 winners, notably very smart 5f performer Eveningperformance (by Night Shift): dam unraced half-sister to 2000 Guineas winner Tirol: never a factor in maiden bumper on debut. *J. R. Best* **F–**

HAYSTACKS (IRE) 9 b.g. Contract Law (USA) – Florissa (FR) (Persepolis (FR)) [2004/5 h99§: 22g^{4} 24s^{pu} Apr 16] leggy gelding: fair handicap hurdler: stays 25f: acts on firm and good to soft going: often visored, also successful in cheekpieces: has carried head awkwardly and found little. *James Moffatt* **h103 §**

HAYTON BOY 11 ch.g. Gypsy Castle – Young Christine VII (Damsire Unregistered) [2004/5 h–: c16g c16d^{F} c17g^{pu} c16m^{pu} Aug 6] of no account: tried tongue tied. *S. G. Chadwick* **c– h–**

HAZEL FLIGHT 5 ch.m. Hazaaf (USA) – Sapphire Flight (Scallywag) [2004/5 F–: F16g^{6} May 16] poor form in bumpers. *Miss M. Bragg* **F72**

HAZELJACK 10 b.g. Sula Bula – Hazelwain (Hard Fact) [2004/5 c109?, h–: c21g^{6} c20m^{6} c24s^{2} c20s^{2} c24v^{2} c24v* c25s^{pu} c24d^{6} c23v* c24s^{4} Mar 14] tall gelding: modest chaser: won handicaps at Warwick in December and Leicester in March: stays 3m: acts on heavy going: sound jumper. *A. J. Whiting* **c97 h–**

HAZEL MERE 5 b.m. Gildoran – After Time (Supreme Leader) [2004/5 F17m Jun 25] first foal: dam well beaten in bumper: tailed off in bumper on debut. *M. C. Chapman* **F–**

HEAD FOR THE HILLS 12 ch.g. Scottish Reel – Merry Cherry (Deep Run) [2004/5 c25s5 c22dpu Feb 24] close-coupled gelding: winning hurdler: off nearly 5 years, fifth in on completed outings in hunter chases: suited by good test of stamina. *Niall Saville* **c85 h–**

HEADLINER (IRE) 6 ch.g. Topanoora – Fairy River (Over The River (FR)) [2004/5 17d5 17d 20v c24v* c24sF c25v* c23vF c30d4 c25g2 Apr 12] angular gelding: sixth foal: half-brother to 2¾m hurdle winner Artic Native (by Be My Native): dam, winning Irish pointer, half-sister to useful chaser at 2½m+ Arctic Stream: runner-up in 4-y-o maiden Irish point in 2003: thrice-raced hurdler: fairly useful chaser: won handicaps at Uttoxeter (novice) in January and Exeter in February: mainly badly let down by jumping otherwise but avoided serious error when ¾-length second to Twisted Logic in similar event at latter course final start: stays 3¾m: raced on good going or softer (acts on heavy). *M. C. Pipe* **c118 x h–**

HEADS ONTHE GROUND (IRE) 8 br.g. Be My Native (USA) – Strong Wings (Deep Run) [2004/5 c17d3 c25dpu c24vpu Dec 27] rangy gelding: fairly useful hurdler: placed first 4 starts over fences, best effort when third to Cregg House in handicap at Fairyhouse on reappearance: pulled up both subsequent outings: effective around 2m and stays 3m: acts on heavy ground. *D. T. Hughes, Ireland* **c116 h–**

HEADS YOUR GRAY 4 gr.g. Atraf – Port Hedland (Then Again) [2004/5 17dpu Jul 17] big gelding: signs of only a little ability in 3 races at 2 yrs for D. Morris: no show on hurdling debut. *Mrs L. Wadham* **h–**

HEAD TO KERRY (IRE) 5 b.g. Eagle Eyed (USA) – The Poachers Lady (IRE) (Salmon Leap (USA)) [2004/5 16d6 Jan 26] half-brother to useful hurdler Pembroke Square (by Tenby), stayed 3m: modest on Flat (stays 2m): sixth to Penzance in muddling novice at Huntingdon on hurdling debut. *D. J. S. ffrench Davis* **h90**

HEALY'S PUB (IRE) 9 b.g. Accordion – Valary (Roman Warrior) [2004/5 c16dF c17dF c17v4 c16v2 c20s2 c16spu 22s* 20d Apr 9] workmanlike gelding: fairly useful handicap hurdler: won at Fairyhouse in March by ¾ length from Tasman: easily best effort over fences (fell first 2 starts) when second to easy winner War of Attrition in Grade 2 novice at Naas fifth start: stays 2¾m: acts on heavy and good to firm going: blinkered final outing. *Oliver McKiernan, Ireland* **c122 h122**

HEARTACHE 8 b.g. Jurado (USA) – Heresy (IRE) (Black Minstrel) [2004/5 c91, h–: c16g6 c16s c20s3 c22dpu c20g c24vpu c23spu Feb 16] tall gelding: little form over hurdles: maiden chaser, largely out of sorts in 2004/5: stays 2½m: has worn cheekpieces. *R. Mathew* **c80 h–**

HEARTBREAKER (IRE) 5 b.g. In Command (IRE) – No Hard Feelings (IRE) (Alzao (USA)) [2004/5 h78: 17dpu Aug 1] fifth on first of 2 starts over hurdles, only sign of ability. *M. W. Easterby* **h–**

HEART MIDOLTIAN (FR) 8 gr.g. Royal Charter (FR) – Pride of Queen (FR) (Saint Henri) [2004/5 c126, h120: c20gpu c20spu c24gpu c20g Apr 22] long-necked gelding: winning hurdler: fairly useful chaser: out of form in 2004/5, left S. Neville after second start: stays 2¾m: acts on firm and soft going: visored last 2 starts: usually tongue tied. *M. C. Pipe* **c– h–**

HEARTOFMIDLOTHIAN (IRE) 6 ch.g. Anshan – Random Wind (Random Shot) [2004/5 F76: F16d5 F16d Dec 9] workmanlike gelding: modest form first 2 starts in bumpers. *K. C. Bailey* **F82**

HEATHERLEA SQUIRE (NZ) 7 b.g. His Royal Highness (NZ) – Misty Gleam (NZ) (Gleam Machine (USA)) [2004/5 16s3 17g 20vpu Feb 15] successful twice over 1m on Flat in New Zealand: well beaten on completed start over hurdles. *D. J. Wintle* **h–**

HEATHYARDS FRIEND 6 b.g. Forest Wind (USA) – Heathyards Lady (USA) (Mining (USA)) [2004/5 h69: 19gpu 16d Feb 26] leggy gelding: poor hurdler: no show in 2004/5: raced mainly around 2m, on good/good to soft going: tongue tied first start. *B. Forsey* **h–**

HEATHYARDS SWING 7 b.g. Celtic Swing – Butsova (Formidable (USA)) [2004/5 h81: 17g2 May 26] poor form over hurdles: wears cheekpieces/blinkers. *James Moffatt* **h81**

HEAVENLY KING 7 b.g. Homo Sapien – Chapel Hill (IRE) (The Parson) [2004/5 h72: 19m4 Apr 9] quite good-topped gelding: poor maiden hurdler: off nearly 2 years before reappearance: stays 19f: acts on good to firm ground: wears blinkers/cheekpieces. *P. Bowen* **h77**

HEAVENLY PLEASURE (IRE) 6 b.m. Presenting – Galynn (IRE) (Strong Gale) [2004/5 F76?: F18m6 May 26] little form in bumpers. *C. Roberts* **F–**

HEAVENLY STRIDE 9 b.g. Karinga Bay – Chapel Hill (IRE) (The Parson) [2004/5 16s^{2} 16v^{6} 16s^{pu} 20s^{2} 24s^{2} 21d^{pu} Apr 18] good-topped gelding: winning chaser: fair hurdler: off 20 months before reappearance: claimed from D. McCain £8,000 fourth start: stays 2½m: raced mainly on soft/heavy going. *P. Bowen* **c– h107**

HECKLEY CLARE GLEN 7 b.m. Dancing High – Heckley Spark (Electric) [2004/5 F88: 16s^{pu} 21s^{pu} 19s^{pu} Jan 10] bumper winner: no show over hurdles: blinkered final start: sold £2,000 Ascot February Sales. *C. J. Mann* **h–**

HEDGE FUND 8 b.g. Slip Anchor – Burnished (Formidable (USA)) [2004/5 17s c16s^{pu} Mar 11] half-brother to winning 2m chaser Chain Shot (by Pas de Seul) and winning 2m hurdler Charly Pharly (by Pharly): successful 6 times up to 11f on Flat, including twice in 2004 for J-Y. Artu: modest form over hurdles: little show both starts over fences, including in hunter on British debut: stays 2½m: acts on heavy ground. *R. Summers* **c– h95**

HEDGEHUNTER (IRE) 9 b.g. Montelimar (USA) – Aberedw (IRE) (Caerwent) [2004/5 c144, h–: 24s 21s^{2} 24d^{4} 24v 24v^{6} c25s* c36d* Apr 9] **c157 + h?**

At times, it is just possible to be persuaded that Flat racing at the top end is as much about making money as about earning glory. The empires of such as Coolmore and Godolphin, with their vast racing and breeding interests, seem to bear out the old saying that money begets money. Jumping, by contrast, is a financial non-starter for an owner, the potential rewards slight in comparison to the costs. Yet it seems that more and more of the super rich are being drawn to the sport, their presence and rivalry a boon at a time when jumping's very foundations still remain under some threat from a heralded 'explosion' in winter all-weather Flat racing. The latest Grand National—an event often described as 'the people's race'—was almost as much of a rich man's playground as the classics and major Flat championship races. Seventeen of the maximum forty runners in the National were owned by people who appeared in the *Sunday Times* Rich List in 2004 or 2005.

J. P. McManus, reportedly the twelfth richest person in Ireland with a fortune estimated at £400m, had six National runners trained by four different trainers,

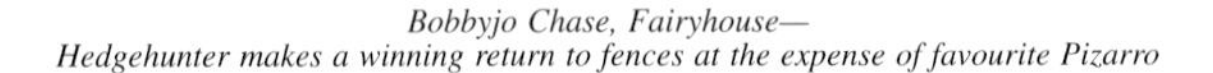

Bobbyjo Chase, Fairyhouse—
Hedgehunter makes a winning return to fences at the expense of favourite Pizarro

John Smith's Grand National Chase (Handicap), Aintree—plenty of mistakes but Frenchman's Creek (No.22) and 2004 third Lord Atterbury (next right, far side of the grey) are the only casualties at the first

headed by top weight Le Coudray, a faller at second Becher's the previous year, and also including the previous year's runner-up Clan Royal, the mount of champion jockey Tony McCoy, and French-trained Innox, bought by McManus since winning the Agfa Diamond Chase at Sandown on his last start. Risk Accessor and Spot-thedifference, who had contested three previous Nationals between them, were others in the McManus colours. Clan Royal, 9/1 co-third favourite, and 16/1-shot Innox were the shortest-priced among the McManus sextet. On the same odds as Innox were the previous year's winner Amberleigh House, owned by a company set up by John Halewood (£65m according to the 2004 Rich List), and Joly Bey, a 240,000-guinea purchase at the 2003 Doncaster May Sales by John Dunsdon (£120m) for his son David who rode him in the National. Joly Bey had fallen four out when in the lead and looking all over a winner in the Topham, ridden by his owner, the previous year.

Among the others with experience of the National fences—there were sixteen in all—were the 2002 National winner Bindaree, contesting his fourth National and owned by Raymond Mould (£62m in the 2004 Rich List), the chairman of Pillar Property, sponsors of the big chase at Cheltenham's January meeting. Back for a third crack at the National was Ad Hoc, owned by Sir Robert Ogden (£120m) and unluckily brought down when on the heels of the leaders in Bindaree's year. Among the top weights with no previous experience of the National fences was Fondmort owned by William Brown, chairman of Lloyd's insurance broker Walsham Brothers who, with his family, has reported assets of £98m. Fondmort's trainer is a supporter of the theory that good two and a half mile chasers who jump soundly can make National horses, his stable having saddled similar types in Classified and The Tsarevich, both of whom reached a place. The Earl Cadogan (family motto 'He who envies is the lesser man') heads the eighteenth-richest family in the country, with assets estimated at £1,650m. He was represented in the National by the useful handicapper Jakari, while a little further down the weights came Polar Red in the colours of Lady Clarke, widow of Sir Stanley whose assets were worth £128m when he died, and Native Emperor, owned by three members of the Hitchens family including Jonathan Hitchens, chairman of the Robert Hitchens Group with family assets said to be worth £95m. Native Emperor was brought in as a reserve when Turnium, one of two no-hopers set to represent Judith and Fergus Wilson (£75m), was pulled out the day before the race. Fergus Wilson, who reportedly built a fortune in property after winning the pigeon Grand National in 1973, described Turnium and National runner Astonville—useful performers at one time

The Chair—Clan Royal and Glenelly Gale (noseband) lead the way . . .

in France bought out of claimers because their handicap marks were thought high enough to secure a place in the National field—as 'cheap lottery tickets.' Both had contested the Champion Hurdle, starting at 500/1, and Astonville had gone on to complete the course, tailed off at 500/1, in the Gold Cup at Cheltenham three days later.

David Johnson, out in front in the owners' championship and headed for his fifth title, has never appeared in a *Sunday Times* Rich List but he reportedly sold igroup, which employed around a thousand, for 216m in 2002. He was doubly represented in the National by 18/1-shot It Takes Time, winner of the Grade 1 totesport Chase at Lingfield over two and a half miles, and the previous year's National third Lord Atterbury who started at 25/1. Both were trained by Martin Pipe (also trainer of Polar Red) whose four National runners were well down on his annual totals of ten, eight and seven (twice) between 2001 and 2004. Paul Nicholls also saddled four, Ad Hoc joined by Cheltenham Gold Cup fourth Royal Auclair (Gold Cup runner-up Take The Stand was also in the line-up), Heros Collonges and the six-year-old mare L'Aventure, the eighth (none of whom, incidentally, has started shorter than 50/1) to take advantage of a lowering of the minimum age from seven introduced after conditions barred Cyfor Malta after he won the Topham as a five-year-old in the 1997/8 season. Jonjo O'Neill, whose stable had been largely out of sorts since being closed down for the best part of two months after Christmas because of a virus, was also four-handed, Clan Royal, Shamawan (also among the 'McManus six') and Native Emperor joined in the line-up by the consistent Simply Gifted, another who had done much of his racing at around two and a half miles.

A reminder that the smaller stables can triumph in the Grand National was provided, not only by the presence of the McCain-trained Amberleigh House, but by that of 2003 winner Monty's Pass, having his third run in the race for the County Cork yard of Jimmy Mangan, listed in the 2005 edition of *Horses In Training* as having only seven National Hunt horses. Monty's Pass, owned by the five-man Dee Racing Syndicate, was among several syndicate-owned horses in the latest National line-up. They also included the Fair City Flyers, twelve Perth racing enthusiasts who owned 9/1 co-third favourite Strong Resolve, runner-up in the Welsh National to the Nicholls-trained Silver Birch who had been one of the ante-post favourites for Aintree until being ruled out in early-March with a leg injury. The Thatch (Ferns) Racing Syndicate had the well-supported, Irish-trained 20/1-shot Colnel Rayburn. Strong Resolve's regular rider, claimer Peter Buchanan, had also won twice during the season on 8/1 National second favourite Forest Gunner who was reunited in the National with Carrie Ford, his jockey when winning the Fox Hunters' over the National fences twelve months earlier.

Until the latest season, only three favourites—Grittar, Rough Quest and Earth Summit—had won the National since 9/1-shot Red Rum got his head in front in the last few strides to touch off the other joint favourite Crisp in the never-to-be-forgotten race of 1973. Favourite at 7/1 for the latest renewal was Hedgehunter, owned by another of jumping's biggest owners, Trevor Hemmings, sixtieth-equal in the *Sunday Times* Rich List with a fortune estimated at 730m. Mr Hemmings, who was also represented in the latest National by Europa, worked his way up the Pontin's holiday business as a young man and says a dream to win the National was inspired by Specify's victory for Fred Pontin in the 1971 running. Mr Hemmings was instrumental in the sale of Pontin's to Scottish & Newcastle Breweries (in which he still has a substantial stake) and is said to have had a role in the £4m sponsorship deal agreed by Aintree with that company to sponsor the National for three years. The John Smith's brand is one of several under the Scottish & Newcastle banner to be associated with sponsorship in sport (Kronenbourg 1664 is a major golf sponsor, Scrumpy Jack among the backers of the England cricket team). John Smith's racing sponsorships also include the John Smith's Cup at York (which was previously the John Smith's Magnet Cup, the first big, commercially-sponsored Flat handicap when it was inaugurated in 1959), and the Northumberland Plate, as well as an important handicap on the Flat at Newbury in the autumn and the Midlands Grand National.

Mr Hemmings, the owner of Blackpool Tower, has made his money in the field of property and leisure and is a major shareholder in Arena Leisure, owners of Britain's first three all-weather courses Lingfield, Southwell and Wolverhampton, as well as Folkestone and Windsor. One of the Hemmings' companies bought the Littlewoods pools business, which includes Bet Direct, for £161m in 2000. The record of Hemmings-owned horses in the Grand National before the latest running was three finishers from fourteen starters. The Last Fling achieved the highest placing when seventh in 2000, two years before he fell fatally in the race, to be

. . . but it's the end of the race for Leighton Aspell and Take The Stand; runner-up Royal Auclair (noseband) has yet to make a move

Second Becher's—Tony McCoy's Grand National bad luck continues as the riderless Merchant's Friend (cheekpieces) and Take The Stand force Clan Royal out . .

followed the next year by another fatality, that of Goguenard, trained like The Last Fling by Sue Smith. Two other high-profile acquisitions were Beau, whose rider was unseated in a freak accident in 2002 and ran just once more, and Young Kenny, who was fatally injured in his prep race when ante-post favourite in 2001. None of the three Hemmings-owned runners (from different yards) completed the course in the 2004 National—the Smith-trained Artic Jack a first-fence faller—but Hedgehunter looked sure to finish in the frame before coming down at the last when held in third, after leading for a long way. Coincidentally, Hedgehunter would have become the first finisher in the National for his trainer Willie Mullins, none of whose three other runners had got further than the eighteenth.

David Casey rode Hedgehunter in the 2004 National but lost the ride to Ruby Walsh in the latest edition, Casey suffering a double blow, very shortly after the announcement at the end of March, when fracturing a bone in his neck and suffering a dislocated hip in a fall from Emotional Article at Fairyhouse. With Casey out of action for three months earlier in the season with a broken leg, Hedgehunter had five different jockeys in five outings over hurdles between November and the end of January. He is nothing like so good over hurdles as over fences and ran his best race in his spell over the smaller obstacles when fourth of seventeen in a handicap at Fairyhouse in December. Once connections had decided against a second tilt at the Hennessy Gold Cup at Newbury in November, Hedgehunter was trained with the single objective of being at his peak for the early part of April. He did not appear over fences until shortly after the Grand National weights were announced and, by the time he lined up for the Grade 3 Bobbyjo Chase at Fairyhouse in February, Casey was back from injury to resume the partnership. Hedgehunter recorded as good an effort as he had produced in his career, making all and jumping well, and then holding off the very smart Pizarro by a length and a half.

'He is a stronger horse and will benefit from last year's experience so I'd say we are pretty hopeful,' said Mullins after the Bobbyjo. 'But you cannot legislate for the luck you need.' It wasn't revealed until after the National that, a week before Aintree, Mullins had been braced to withdraw Hedgehunter because of sickness symptoms. 'We kept it between four people, including our vet, and it's fantastic to know our stable security is good,' said Mullins. 'I was dreading a call to ask me why he was drifting on Betfair!' Mullins and his vet took the view that Hedgehunter had nothing more serious than a runny nose, and three days before the National Hedgehunter was duly 'back on his toes'. Mullins revealed that he told neither owner nor jockey about the eleventh-hour hiccup ('You can never be sure but I was convinced Hedgehunter had come right'). The orders given to Ruby Walsh were different to those to which Casey had ridden the year before. Casey himself had been convinced, with the benefit of hindsight, that the pace he set on the free-going Hedgehunter and the strong headwind in the finishing straight drained the gelding's reserves and contributed to his fall. Walsh, who won the National when only twenty on Papillon in 2000 and has a good record over the big fences, set out to be more patient, tactics which—bearing in mind the trainer's remark about the need for luck in a National—paid off in more than one respect.

In a last-minute change, Aintree ran the John Smith's Grand National, the most valuable race of the season with a first prize of £406,000, twenty-five minutes later than originally scheduled, as the fifth race on the card rather than the fourth, as intended. The move was designed to maximise the build-up on BBC1, the first four races switched to BBC2 because of extensive coverage on the main channel of the wedding of the Prince of Wales and Camilla Parker Bowles, which itself had been postponed by a day because of the funeral of the Pope. It was not the first time, incidentally, that a Camilla had been involved in a late start to the National. The mare Princess Camilla came last of seventeen finishers after delaying the start with some fractious behaviour in 1974—the year of Red Rum's second victory.

Runners with a royal name naturally came in for plenty of support in the latest edition, with mixed results. Clan Royal and Royal Auclair were towards the middle of the field on the run to first Becher's where amateur-ridden 150/1-shot Glenelly Gale, Double Honour, Astonville, Colnel Rayburn, Forest Gunner and Monty's Pass led the way. The pace steadied after the traditional good gallop down to Becher's and the strong-pulling Clan Royal began to close on the leading group from first Valentine's, jumping into second behind Glenelly Gale at the eleventh. The time to the Chair, where Take The Stand parted company with his rider, was over six seconds slower than the previous year (on similar going). Clan Royal was in front by this time, and was followed out into the country for a second time by Glenelly Gale, Double Honour, Colnel Rayburn, Hedgehunter (who had steadily made ground, kept to the inner), Monty's Pass, Forest Gunner, Innox, Just In Debt, Ad Hoc, Fondmort, Simply Gifted, Royal Auclair, Heros Collonges, Joly Bey and It Takes Time. No fewer than thirty-two were still in the race, with Strong Resolve,

. . . the rest avoid the hazard, Hedgehunter (right) with Innox (hoops) and Joly Bey leading the way; Nil Desperandum (left) survives a blunder, but Ad Hoc (centre) is not so lucky

Second Canal Turn—fancied runners Colnel Rayburn (hooped sleeves) and Strong Resolve (grey) are already beaten, whilst 2004 winner Amberleigh House (right) never reaches a challenging position

who made a bad mistake at the first and lost a lot of ground with another at the water, Bindaree and Amberleigh House among those even further back. Double Honour unseated his rider at the twenty-first, after which Hedgehunter's rider seemed briefly to lose an iron on the flat.

Clan Royal was travelling strongly in a five-length lead when he was baulked by the riderless pair Merchants Friend and Take The Stand and prevented from jumping second Becher's, taken sharply left across the fence on the take-off side, McCoy thrown out of the saddle as Clan Royal was brought to a halt near the inside running rail. If Clan Royal was the unlucky horse in the race, some of those in the chasing group were also affected, Just In Debt, Monty's Pass and Colnel Rayburn making mistakes after being distracted, the last-named doing well to negotiate the fence at all. Ad Hoc was trying to work his way into contention when coming down at Becher's. The prominent Hedgehunter jumped it safely, though Walsh admitted to 'doing a fair bit of panicking . . . Hedgehunter was very brave to go and jump it with several horses running around.' Joly Bey, towards the outside, touched down in the lead from Innox and Hedgehunter, but Hedgehunter was soon in front, much earlier than intended but clearly moving very well. At the second Canal Turn, he led from Innox, Joly Bey (who went wide), Just In Debt, Royal Auclair, Glenelly Gale, Simply Gifted, Heros Collonges, Monty's Pass and Forest Gunner. Glenelly Gale and Monty's Pass steadily weakened from Valentine's but It Takes Time, Nil Desperandum and Polar Red all made ground to be among a closely-bunched group of eleven at the third last.

Barely four lengths covered the eleven crossing the Melling Road with two still to jump, reminiscent of 1978 (Lucius) and 1999 (ten-length winner Bobbyjo), and indeed of Specify's year, when eight were still in with a chance turning into the final straight. The smooth-travelling Hedgehunter looked the likeliest winner, though Polar Red made eye-catching headway into the first three jumping the second last, briefly threatening to pull off a major shock. By the final fence, Hedgehunter had stretched nearly four lengths clear, with Royal Auclair second, Forest Gunner third and Simply Gifted fourth, ahead of the weakening Innox and the running-on Nil Desperandum and It Takes Time. Hedgehunter quickened impressively once shaken up after the last and turned the race into a procession, as Monty's Pass had done two years earlier, pulling right away towards the finish to win by fourteen lengths from Royal Auclair, with Simply Gifted a head away third, and a further four lengths back to fourth-placed It Takes Time. Forest Gunner couldn't find any extra on the run-in and finished nine lengths behind It Takes Time in fifth, just holding off Nil Desperandum. The next home, Innox, Heros Collonges and Just In Debt, were followed by Amberleigh House, completing a race over the National fences for the eighth consecutive time (he was among nine put right out of the race when a riderless horse veered sharply across the first Canal Turn in the

2001 National, his only other start over the course). Bindaree was eleventh, Polar Red thirteenth, Joly Bey fourteenth, Monty's Pass sixteenth and Strong Resolve seventeenth as twenty-one got round. The winning time was 9m 20.86sec, only slightly slower than 2004, though Hedgehunter had been a full eleven seconds slower at the final fence than last-fence leader Clan Royal the year before, indicative not only of how much Hedgehunter had left at that stage, but also of the effects of the overly-strong pace in 2004.

Hedgehunter was the last National winner to be unsaddled in Aintree's famous weatherboarded winner's enclosure, though one unfortunate consequence of the lead-in for the new sponsors was the absence of branding on the winning jockey's breeches. Not allowed to wear their own sponsors' logo, a few riders felt the fee they were offered (reportedly around £100) for sporting John Smith's was not enough. Walsh was among them. As part of a £16m rebuilding programme at Aintree, the course will have new saddling boxes, pre-parade ring, parade ring, weighing room and unsaddling enclosure for the 2006 National, with a further £14m to be spent on a new grandstand to be ready for the 2007 running. Most of the existing buildings will remain, the unsaddling enclosure and weighing room set to be changed into either a museum or brasserie bar, retaining the original character (the various plaques in the unsaddling area and weighing room are to stay and will be supplemented by other artefacts currently on display in the course's visitor centre). Aintree's new weighing room will be built next to the paddock stables, with the combined paddock and unsaddling enclosure stretching from the weighing room steppings to Red Rum's statue.

Improvements over the years at Aintree have gone hand in hand with increasing attendances and the crowds were up again in 2005, an official total of 151,660 attending the three days, with the National day crowd at 70,739. The television viewing figures were also healthy at 9.5m, more people watching the National than the royal wedding. Betting on the National eclipses that on any other horse race in Britain but many once-a-year punters who supported Carrie Ford must have been puzzled by the fact that, while totesport and many independents paid out each-way on fifth-placed Forest Gunner, the 'big four', Ladbrokes, Hills (who claimed 'the best National service'), Coral and Stanleybet, did not. 'First four are our trading terms and our prices are framed on that basis,' said Mike Dillon of Ladbrokes, though the move was described as 'cynical' by Channel 4's betting pundit John McCririck. The major bookmakers, however, have come a long way since they were dependent on big events like the National. The abolition of betting tax has seen enormous growth in low-margin products such as fixed-odds betting terminals, featuring virtual roulette. Twenty-four-hour betting over the internet on racing and sport around the world, and on virtual racing, means that a punter can now lose his shirt even if he is not wearing one.

The National's safety record has been broadly good in recent years, the relatively steady pace for a long way contributing to the fact that the latest running was fairly free of incident by National standards. No horses or jockeys were seriously injured and there were only five fallers among the nineteen who failed to

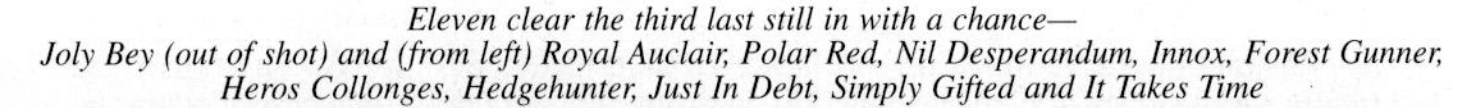
Eleven clear the third last still in with a chance—
Joly Bey (out of shot) and (from left) Royal Auclair, Polar Red, Nil Desperandum, Innox, Forest Gunner, Heros Collonges, Hedgehunter, Just In Debt, Simply Gifted and It Takes Time

The last—Hedgehunter is still on the bridle;
placed horses Royal Auclair (noseband) and Simply Gifted (right) are also in shot

complete. The number of finishers was only two short of the record of twenty-three in 1984 (twenty-two finished in 1963, 1987 and 1992). The toe boards on the take-off side of all the Grand National fences were increased to around ten inches before the latest running to ensure a stronger ground line. Some changes were also made to Becher's, where the ditch on the landing side was fitted with a wooden cover with a non-slip rubber top, making it impossible for any horse to fall back into the ditch. There was talk in the media about a reduction in the height of some of the National fences but the Aintree management was adamant that all were at least the published height, Becher's itself built to five feet, as opposed to its official four feet ten inches. Although Grey Abbey, First Gold and Sir Rembrandt were late absentees, the latest National field was, in theory at least, of good quality. Two of the first four in the Cheltenham Gold Cup were in the line-up and all forty of the runners had shown useful form or better, though some had questionable credentials, being either seemingly on the downgrade or out of form, uncertain to stay or none too fluent jumpers. That said, a Jockey Club panel, first set up after three horses were killed in the 1998 National, still monitors Grand National entries for jumping ability at the entry stage and has the power of veto. Also introduced at the same time was a compulsory pre-race veterinary check of every runner.

In recent years, the BHB's senior jumps handicapper Phil Smith, the man responsible for the National weights, has tried to reshape the National, consciously treating some of the top entries leniently in an attempt to entice connections to run more high-class chasers in the race. In the latest National, some of the top dozen or so in the original handicap, ranging from Grey Abbey on 11-12 to those on 11-4, were set to race off marks lower than their BHB handicap marks at the time (Grey Abbey, for example, had a current mark of 166 but was allotted one of 158 in the National). Such discrimination is justified by the BHB partly on the grounds that most of the form of those at the top of the handicap has been shown at around three miles, but 'they have to carry this weight over four and a half miles.' Why the extra distance should have such an effect only on those at the top of the handicap was not explained. Interestingly, the Turf Club handicapper treated Beef Or Salmon with similar leniency in the original handicap for the latest Irish Grand National, though he did not run. Le Coudray and Royal Auclair were the only ones near the top of the handicap to make the Grand National line-up, but the treatment of those who headed the original weights resulted in a compressing of the handicap. From an increased entry of one hundred and fifty-two, ninety-two were originally set to run off 10-0 or more, making it unlikely that any of the eventual runners would be 'out of the handicap'. On the day, none of the forty carried less than 10-5, among those failing to secure a place the first and second in the previous year's Topham, Cassia Heights and Longshanks, the 2003 National runner-up Supreme Glory, Smarty (third in the latest Becher Chase) and Gunner Welburn, the last two having finished in the frame three times over the National fences, and, further down the weights, the Hemmings-owned Kim Muir winner Juveigneur and the Singer & Friedlander winner Whereareyounow, who had finished a creditable third over the National fences in the 2003 Sefton Chase.

The BHB handicapper apparently took pride in the fact that all the runners were in the handicap. 'This is the best year we've had for strength in depth,' Mr Smith said. 'There is no doubt that the standards have risen over the past six years.' Making the National a race for better horses does not automatically make it a better race, but Mr Smith seems hell bent on raising the standard of the National runners. 'What would really make me overjoyed would be if a top weight could win again,' he said in an interview in *The Guardian*. 'When that happens, I'll know that we've done what we set out to achieve'. What every BHB handicapper should be trying to do, of course, is to equalise the chances of the horses, not favour the best ones. No top weight has succeeded in the Grand National since Red Rum won with 11-8 in 1977. Indeed, Hedgehunter—who would probably have had a few pounds more if the handicapper had been able to take into account his Fairyhouse victory—was the first to carry 11-0 or more to victory since Rhyme 'N' Reason in 1988. Grittar (11-5 in 1982) and Corbiere (11-4 in 1983) are the only National winners since Red Rum's era to carry more than 11-0 to victory. L'Escargot carried 11-3 when beating Red Rum (12-0) in 1975 and then Red Rum, after finishing second under 11-10 to Rag Trade, won his third National carrying 11-8. Horses have carried big weights into the frame in the Grand National in the interim, most recently Suny Bay, What's Up Boys, Kingsmark and Monty's Pass, which should provide some encouragement for owners of the top-class chasers the race is trying to attract.

Desert Orchid never contested the Grand National (nor did Arkle), but his connections seriously considered it at one time. The handicapper leant over backwards to attract Desert Orchid, assessing him more favourably—to the tune of 6 lb in 1990—than he would in any race away from Aintree. However, there was a public outcry at the prospect of Desert Orchid being 'risked' at Aintree—the *Daily Mail* conducted a poll of its readers on the subject, nine thousand being against his running and only forty-eight in favour—and in the end his connections decided against. It is arguable that the death of Alverton in the 1979 National put off many in the 'eighties, and the prospect of running an outstanding chaser in the race has undoubtedly been an emotive subject at times—with Best Mate's connections, for example. But the organisers of the National have made great efforts, continued since Desert Orchid's day, to make the course safer, without having too much of an effect on its unique character. Decisions about running the top horses in the National deserve to be taken on the merits of each case (lenient handicapping

The run-in—fourteen lengths clear at the line as Ruby Walsh celebrates his second Grand National win

Mr Trevor Hemmings' "Hedgehunter"

obviously being one factor). There still isn't a tougher race anywhere, and there is no denying that the risks are almost certainly still greater than in any other steeplechase. Since 1996 no reigning Gold Cup winner or runner-up had run in the race until Take The Stand did so. The risk is, however, only a matter of degree. Risks are inseparable from steeplechasing and the severity of the National is not a good enough reason in itself to shun the race. For an experienced and accomplished staying chaser—like Best Mate, for example—the risks at Aintree nowadays are, in all probability, not very much greater than those he faces every time he sets foot on a racecourse.

Plans to run Hedgehunter in the Grand Steeple-Chase de Paris at Auteuil in May had to be shelved when he failed to recover quickly enough from his exertions at Aintree. He was said in early-May to be still suffering muscular stiffness in his shoulders. Hedgehunter is a useful-looking gelding and he often spoils his appearance by sweating before his races. His trainer purchased him privately before he had raced, 'one of the cheaper ones among a lorry load from Tom Costello.' Owned initially by Niall Quaid, a friend of the O'Learys, who had Florida Pearl, among others, with Willie Mullins, Hedgehunter was acquired on behalf of Trevor Hemmings when his Canadian-based, Irish owner reportedly found he could no longer travel to see the horse run. Hedgehunter won twice for Mr Quaid, finishing second five times in bumpers and twice in maiden hurdles before getting off the mark, stepped up considerably in distance, on his tenth start, in a three-mile maiden hurdle on heavy ground at Clonmel as a six-year-old. Sent chasing the following season, Hedgehunter won the National Trial over three and a half miles at Punchestown, relishing his stiffest test yet and making all under 7-lb claimer Sam Curling to win by eleven lengths. Hedgehunter had his first race in the

Hemmings colours in the National Hunt Chase at the 2003 Cheltenham Festival and was travelling like a winner when blundering and all but unseating his rider two out. He finished in the frame in the Hennessy Cognac Gold Cup at Newbury and in the Coral Welsh National, before a return to front-running tactics saw him run away with the Goulding Thyestes Chase at Gowran on his final outing before a first crack at the Grand National in 2004.

Hedgehunter (IRE) (b.g. 1996)	Montelimar (USA) (b 1981)	Alleged (b 1974)	Hoist The Flag
			Princess Pout
		L'Extravagante (br 1973)	Le Fabuleux
			Fanfreluche
	Aberedw (IRE) (b 1990)	Caerwent (b 1985)	Caerleon
			Marwell
		Secret Hideaway (b 1983)	Key To The Mint
			Turning Bold

Hedgehunter's sire, the now-deceased Montelimar, had five runners in the latest Grand National, all of whom got round. In addition to Hedgehunter, they were It Takes Time, Just In Debt, Monty's Pass and nineteenth-placed Arctic Copper. If Cassia Heights had made the cut, Montelimar's representation would have been six. He was also represented in the latest season by the Powers Gold Cup winner Like-A-Butterfly, among others. Hedgehunter's dam Aberedw, whose first foal he is, was a modest maiden on the Flat and over hurdles for Aidan O'Brien. Her only other winner is the fair Merlyn's Monty, a brother to Hedgehunter, who has gained his only successes so far in a bumper at Tipperary and a two-and-a-half mile maiden hurdle at Cork. Hedgehunter's grandam Secret Hideaway was unraced but bred several winners on the Flat, the best of them the useful Lagoon (by Common Grounds), who was successful at up to a mile. Being half-sisters to the dam of a Grand National winner is the main claim to fame so far of two of Secret Hideaway's daughters, the maidens Nutley Queen (by Eagle Eyed) and Secret Mint (by Victory Note) who were lightly raced without success over hurdles in Britain and Ireland respectively in the latest season. A younger daughter, Missperon (by Orpen), won a six-furlong maiden at Pontefract in 2004. Hedgehunter, who has sometimes hung right and found little, seemed best when allowed to bowl along over fences, but he settled and jumped well for Walsh in the latest National. He has been raced on good going or softer and acts on heavy. The handicap mark of Monty's Pass in the National went up by 14 lb after his wide-margin win, but he still made the frame behind Amberleigh House. Hedgehunter is unlikely to receive any favours from the handicapper if he is returned to Aintree—though he will be near the top of the weights, so who knows—but, if he gets there fit and well, he looks sure to give another good account. *W. P. Mullins, Ireland*

HEEZ A WONDER (IRE) 6 b.g. Naheez (USA) – Honey Wonder (Winden) [2004/5 F17d F16s^{3} F16s* 16s^{3} 19v* 20v^{2} 20s^{6} 22s Mar 28] €17,000 4-y-o: half-brother to 3 winners around 2m, including useful hurdler Honeydew Wonder (by Idiot's Delight): dam unraced half-sister to useful hurdler up to 2½m Walnut Wonder: best effort in bumpers when winning at Clonmel in November: fair form over hurdles, winning 6-runner maiden at Naas in January: stays 2½m: raced on going softer than good (acts on heavy). *F. Flood, Ireland* **h108 F101**

HEGARTY (IRE) 6 gr.g. Topanoora – Banderole (FR) (Roselier (FR)) [2004/5 17g^{6} 16d^{2} 16g^{2} 16d* 17d* 16s^{5} Oct 3] workmanlike gelding: third foal: half-brother to smart hunter chaser Never Compromise (by Glacial Storm), stays 3¼m: dam unraced half-sister to useful hurdler up to 25f Sip of Orange: fairly useful hurdler: made all in maiden at Sligo and novice handicap at Newton Abbot (beat Kalambari ¾ length) in August: raced around 2m on good going or softer: blinkered final start: tongue tied. *C. Roche, Ireland* **h118**

HEHASALIFE (IRE) 8 b.g. Safety Catch (USA) – America River (IRE) (Lord Americo) [2004/5 c112, h103: c17m c21s^{pu} 20g^{6} c20m^{pu} Apr 23] tall, shallow-girthed gelding: fair hurdler/chaser: no form in 2004/5: stays 3m: acts on firm and soft going: tried in cheekpieces/blinkers: tongue tied third start. *Mrs H. Dalton* **c– h–**

HEIDI III (FR) 10 b.g. Bayolidaan (FR) – Irlandaise (FR) (Or de Chine) [2004/5 c112, h–: c25g^{pu} c22g^{pu} c25v* c23s^{3} c25s^{2} Mar 22] close-coupled gelding: fairly useful handicap chaser: left Mrs L. Williamson after second start: won at Wetherby in January by 4 lengths from Ossmoses: stays 25f: acts on good to firm and heavy going: wears headgear nowadays: races prominently. *M. D. Hammond* **c113 h–**

HEIR TO BE 6 b.g. Elmaamul (USA) – Princess Genista (Ile de Bourbon (USA)) [2004/5 24d^2 21d* 25s^2 Dec 18] sturdy gelding: half-brother to fairly useful hurdler around 2½m Ela Mata (by Dancing Brave): fair on Flat (stays 2m) for J. Dunlop: similar standard over hurdles: won 22-runner maiden at Warwick in December: stays 25f. *Mrs L. Wadham* **h111**

HELENSBURGH (IRE) 4 ch.c. Mark of Esteem (IRE) – Port Helene (Troy) [2004/5 16g* 16d* Nov 13] fair form on first of 3 starts at 2 yrs for M. Johnston: successful in juveniles at Punchestown both starts over hurdles, by 1½ lengths from Kentucky Charm in September and 4 lengths from Rolling Home in November, idling both occasions: respectable effort on Flat in between: open to further improvement. *P. Hughes, Ireland* **h119 p**

HELLO BABY 5 b.g. Jumbo Hirt (USA) – Silver Flyer (Silver Season) [2004/5 F91: 16d 22v 24d^6 22s 20s* Apr 10] leggy gelding: poor hurdler: won novice handicap at Hexham in April: stays 2½m: acts on soft going. *A. C. Whillans* **h75**

HELL OF A TIME (IRE) 8 b.g. Phardante (FR) – Ticking Over (IRE) (Decent Fellow) [2004/5 h–, F–: 24d^{pu} Mar 8] workmanlike gelding: no show both starts over hurdles 16 months apart. *Mrs N. S. Sharpe* **h–**

HELLO ROSCREA (IRE) 12 b.g. Homo Sapien – Waterpark Lady (IRE) (Jamesmead) [2004/5 c26g^{pu} Apr 27] winning pointer: no show in novice hunter chase. *Mrs S. Brown* **c–**

HELM (IRE) 4 b.g. Alhaarth (IRE) – Pipers Pool (IRE) (Mtoto) [2004/5 18d^F 18s^4 20s^3 19m^5 Apr 2] useful-looking gelding: half-brother to modest hurdler Dudeen (by Anshan), stays 2¾m: fair maiden on Flat (will stay 2m): best effort over hurdles when third to Mister Mustard in maiden at Fontwell: probably better suited by 2½m than shorter: wore cheekpieces final start. *R. Rowe* **h97**

HELTORNIC (IRE) 5 ch.m. Zaffaran (USA) – Majestic Run (Deep Run) [2004/5 F16d* F16d^2 F17s^3 Apr 7] leggy mare: sixth foal: sister to 3 winning hurdlers, notably fairly useful Glenmoss Tara, stays 21f: dam won poor 17f novice hurdle: fairly useful form in mares bumpers: made all at Fakenham on debut in February: placed in listed events at Sandown and Aintree subsequently: will stay 2½m. *M. Scudamore* **F99**

HELVETIUS 9 b.g. In The Wings – Hejraan (USA) (Alydar (USA)) [2004/5 c97, h89: c21d* c21g^{pu} 22g^{pu} c22m^{pu} c24g^4 c20g^2 c24m^2 c24g^3 Feb 16] leggy gelding: winning hurdler: modest handicap chaser: won at Newton Abbot in May: left P. Ritchens after fourth start: stays 3¼m: acts on any going: has worn cheekpieces/blinkers: tried tongue tied. *W. T. Reed* **c97 h–**

HENRIANJAMES 10 b.g. Tina's Pet – Real Claire (Dreams To Reality (USA)) [2004/5 c113, h–: c16d^3 c17m^3 May 22] strong gelding: fair handicap chaser: raced around 2m: acts on firm and good to soft going. *Mrs M. Reveley* **c108 h–**

HENRIETTA (IRE) 7 b.m. Hushang (IRE) – Jennie's First (Idiot's Delight) [2004/5 h97: 24g^3 c22d^{pu} c25s^2 c25s^4 c22g^{ur} Apr 1] workmanlike mare: fair hurdler: better effort on completed starts over fences when 24 lengths second of 4 finishers to Even More in handicap at Wincanton: may prove best up to 3m: acts on soft going: visored last 3 starts: has run as if amiss. *M. C. Pipe* **c88 h102**

HENRY ISLAND (IRE) 12 ch.g. Sharp Victor (USA) – Monterana (Sallust) [2004/5 21d^{pu} 21d^{pu} Jan 26] leggy gelding: winning hurdler: no show in 2004/5: stays 21f: acts on good to firm and heavy going: has twice refused to race. *Mrs A. J. Bowlby* **h– §**

HENRY'S LUCK PENNY (IRE) 5 br.g. Muroto – Lady Sallyanna (IRE) (Be My Native (USA)) [2004/5 20d 16g^{pu} 24s Apr 16] first foal: dam unraced, out of half-sister to useful hurdler/chaser up to 25f Moondigua: no form over hurdles. *Mrs H. Dalton* **h–**

HENRY'S PRIDE (IRE) 5 ch.g. Old Vic – Hightown Girl (IRE) (Over The River (FR)) [2004/5 F16s^5 F16v^3 20v Feb 2] has scope: second foal: half-brother to fair 2½m chase winner Carroll Encore (by Carroll House): dam unraced: fair form both starts in bumpers, trained on debut by Miss H. Knight: eighth of 15 in novice on hurdling debut. *Mrs H. Dalton* **h80 F93**

HERACLES 9 b.g. Unfuwain (USA) – La Masse (High Top) [2004/5 c102, h–: c20d^{pu} c21g^{pu} c16g^2 Jul 28] leggy gelding: winning hurdler: fair handicap chaser: stays 23f, effective at much shorter: acts on soft and good to firm going: tried blinkered: sold 8,000 gns Doncaster August Sales: won and twice runner-up from 3 starts in points in 2005. *R. H. Buckler* **c105 h–**

HERACLITEAN FIRE (IRE) 8 b.g. Norwich – Mazovia (FR) (Taufan (USA)) [2004/5 c99, h90: c16s^3 c20d^6 c16d^F c20s^4 c17v^6 20s^3 Feb 16] workmanlike gelding: **c96 h90**

modest handicap chaser: maiden hurdler: effective at 2m to 2¾m: acts on soft going: blinkered once: sometimes let down by jumping. *J. J. Lambe, Ireland*

HERE COMES HARRY 9 ch.g. Sunley Builds – Coole Dolly Day (Arctic Lord) [2004/5 h76: 20d Apr 22] poor hurdler: off 16 months before only start in 2004/5: will stay 3m: acts on good to firm going. *C. J. Down* **h–**

HERES HARRY 5 b.h. Most Welcome – Nahla (Wassl) [2004/5 F–: F18g May 9] tailed off in 2 bumpers and at 5f on Flat: sold £1,100 Ascot July Sales. *Ms J. S. Doyle* **F–**

HERE WE GO (IRE) 6 b.g. Bob Back (USA) – Bold Lyndsey (Be My Native (USA)) [2004/5 F16s[2] F17g[3] Dec 15] €44,000 3-y-o: tall, good-topped gelding: seventh foal: brother to bumper winner Park's Pet and half-brother to winning pointer Bold Tactics (by Jurado): dam won over hurdles around 2m: better effort in bumpers when second to Blushing Bull at Chepstow on debut. *Jonjo O'Neill* **F99**

HERIOT 4 b.g. Hamas (IRE) – Sure Victory (IRE) (Stalker) [2004/5 16f 16g[pu] 16g[6] 16d[4] 17d 19s[pu] 17g Apr 15] compact gelding: lightly raced and little form on Flat, sold out of H. Candy's stable £1,700 Ascot August Sales: poor juvenile hurdler: unlikely to stay much beyond 2m: blinkered on debut: tongue tied last 5 outings: often soon off bridle. *S. C. Burrough* **h– §**

HERITAGE CASTLE 6 b.g. Past Glories – Castle Claire (Carlingford Castle) [2004/5 19m[pu] 17g[pu] 17s c20d Apr 18] rather unfurnished gelding: first foal: dam no sign of ability: no form: in cheekpieces last 2 starts. *A. E. Jones* **c– x h–**

HERMANO CORDOBES (IRE) 5 b.g. Un Desperado (FR) – Queens Tricks (Le Bavard (FR)) [2004/5 F16v Jan 3] €26,000 4-y-o: half-brother to useful staying chaser Numbersixvalverde (by Broken Hearted) and modest chaser El Cordobes (by Torus), stays 3m: dam unraced: always rear in bumper on debut. *Mrs J. R. Buckley* **F–**

HERMITAGE COURT (USA) 4 ch.g. Out of Place (USA) – Russian Act (USA) (Siberian Express (USA)) [2004/5 17m[pu] Apr 13] big, workmanlike gelding: fairly useful on Flat (stays 1¼m) at 3 yrs for B. Meehan: no show in juvenile on hurdling debut. *M. J. McGrath* **h–**

HERNANDITA 7 b.m. Hernando (FR) – Dara Dee (Dara Monarch) [2004/5 h98: 22g[3] 22m[3] 20f* 21g* 20d* 21g 22d[6] 22d c19g[6] Apr 12] small, leggy mare: fair handicap hurdler: won at Huntingdon in September and Plumpton and Worcester in October: bled from nose when well held in maiden on chasing debut: stays 2¾m: acts on any going: visored once: has looked difficult ride: often makes running. *Miss E. C. Lavelle* **c– h112**

HERNANDO'S BOY 4 b.g. Hernando (FR) – Leave At Dawn (Slip Anchor) [2004/5 17d[3] 16d[2] 16m* 16m* 16s[5] Oct 30] good-topped gelding: fair maiden on Flat (stays 2m): fairly useful juvenile hurdler: won at Kelso and Wetherby in October: will be suited by 2½m+. *K. G. Reveley* **h114**

HERNE BAY (IRE) 5 b.g. Hernando (FR) – Charita (IRE) (Lycius (USA)) [2004/5 20m[5] 17d[2] 16s[5] 24s[6] 16s[4] 19d* Mar 14] leggy gelding: fair on Flat (stays 2m well): trained by A. Bailey on hurdling debut: well backed, won seller (sold 9,000 gns) at Stratford by 14 lengths from Lewis Island: may prove best around 2½m. *D. Burchell* **h101**

HERODOTUS 7 b.g. Zafonic (USA) – Thalestria (FR) (Mill Reef (USA)) [2004/5 16s[pu] 19d[pu] 17s[pu] Feb 17] tall gelding: half-brother to fair hurdlers Amazon Express (by Zafonic) and Pomme Secret (by Assert): useful at one time on Flat (stays 1½m), of little account nowadays: no form over hurdles: tongue tied on debut. *K. O. Cunningham-Brown* **h–**

HEROIC (IRE) 9 b.g. War Hero – Happy Patter (Pitpan) [2004/5 c113, h–: c28s c29d[3] c28v c33d[ur] c29s[pu] Mar 28] sturdy gelding: fair handicap chaser: form in 2004/5 only when third of 4 finishers to Howaya Pet at Fairyhouse in November: stays 29f: acts on soft ground. *C. F. Swan, Ireland* **c113 h–**

HEROICUS (NZ) 8 ch.g. Heroicity (AUS) – Glenford (NZ) (Sackford (USA)) [2004/5 c–, h–: 16g[pu] 20s[pu] Mar 22] workmanlike gelding: of little account. *F. Kirby* **c– h–**

HEROS COLLONGES (FR) 10 b.g. Dom Alco (FR) – Carmen Collonges (FR) (Olmeto) [2004/5 21s[5] c25d* c24g[pu] c36d Apr 9] tall, close-coupled gelding: useful chaser: left G. Macaire and off 3 years (reportedly suffered tendon injury) prior to reappearance: won 4-runner listed event at Wincanton in February easily by 4 lengths from Bathwick Annie: weakened quickly after travelling well to 3 out in Grand National at Aintree final start: stays 25f: raced on good going or softer. *P. F. Nicholls* **c134 + h–**

HERSOV (IRE) 9 gr.g. Roselier (FR) – Higher Again (IRE) (Strong Gale) [2004/5 c125, h125: 24g^{pu} c28s^{pu} c24v c24v^{2} c28v c24s^{6} c33d^{5} c21d Apr 8] rangy gelding: winning hurdler: fairly useful chaser: best effort in 2004/5 when second to Marcus du Berlais in valuable event at Leopardstown: stays 33f: raced on good ground or softer (acts on heavy): tried blinkered/in cheekpieces. *Paul A. Roche, Ireland* **c119 h–**

HERVEY BAY 7 b.m. Primitive Rising (USA) – Macusla (Lighter) [2004/5 c25g^{6} c20d^{5} c20g^{3} c21s^{F} Mar 11] 5,800 4-y-o: seventh foal: half-sister to winning staying hurdlers Akulite (by Rakaposhi King) and Minulsa (by Minster Son) and winning pointer by Henbit: dam, fair 2m hurdler/winning chaser, half-sister to dams of useful chasers up to 3m Flaxley Wood and Mr Baxter Basics: winning pointer: poor maiden hunter chaser: tongue tied last 2 starts. *William Goldie* **c64**

HE'S A LEADER (IRE) 6 b.g. Supreme Leader – Raise The Bells (Belfalas) [2004/5 h–, F–: 19s* 19d* 22s* Nov 29] progressive hurdler: unbeaten in 3 handicaps in November, at Hereford (novices), Warwick and Folkestone (beat Front Rank 3½ lengths): stays 2¾m: raced on good going or softer: looked likely to progress further, but not seen out again. *M. C. Pipe* **h107 +**

HESCONDIDO (FR) 10 gr.g. Dadarissime (FR) – Vahine de Prairie (FR) (Brezzo (FR)) [2004/5 c–x, h–: c24s c24m^{6} May 25] good-topped gelding: useful chaser in 2001/2, no form since: second in point in February: stays 3m: acts on heavy going: blinkered once: poor jumper: sometimes weak in finish. *Miss Venetia Williams* **c– x h–**

HE'S HOT RIGHT NOW (NZ) 6 b.g. Pentire – Philadelphia Fox (NZ) (Dahar (USA)) [2004/5 16d 16s^{6} 16m^{6} 17v 16g^{pu} 16d 16g 16g^{3} Mar 16] lengthy gelding: successful from 6.5f to around 1¼m on Flat in Australia: poor novice hurdler: likely to prove best around 2m: in cheekpieces final start (ran well). *R. C. Guest* **h82**

HE'S MY MAN (IRE) 7 b.g. Be My Native (USA) – That's The Bonus (IRE) (Executive Perk) [2004/5 20d^{pu} 20d^{2} 22v^{4} 20v^{3} 16m Feb 6] €125,000 4-y-o: first foal: dam unraced half-sister to useful 2m hurdlers Thats My Man and Spirit Leader: fair maiden hurdler: stays 2½m: acts on soft going, possibly not on heavy. *C. F. Swan, Ireland* **h100**

HE'S THE BIZ (FR) 6 b.g. Nikos – Irun (FR) (Son of Silver) [2004/5 h90: c16m^{3} c21m^{6} c23g^{4} c23s^{F} c26d^{2} c16d c26g* Apr 10] good-topped gelding: modest handicap hurdler: similar form over fences: jumped better when winning novice handicap at Newton Abbot in April: stays 3¼m: acts on good to firm and good to soft going: sometimes flashes tail. *Nick Williams* **c94 h–**

HE'S THE BOSS (IRE) 8 b.g. Supreme Leader – Attykee (IRE) (Le Moss) [2004/5 h125: c24s^{3} c21d^{pu} Dec 11] workmanlike gelding: fairly useful form in novice hurdles in 2003/4: better effort over fences when third to Limerick Leader in maiden at Chepstow: stays 21f: raced on good going or softer. *R. H. Buckler* **c112 h–**

HE'S THE GAFFER (IRE) 5 b.g. Oscar (IRE) – Miss Henrietta (IRE) (Step Together (USA)) [2004/5 F16d F16s^{2} F16d F16d 22g^{4} Apr 17] sixth foal: half-brother to fairly useful chaser Tollbrae (by Supreme Leader), stays 2½m: dam, lightly-raced hurdler, from family of top-class 2m to 2½m jumper Buck House: fair form in bumpers: no show in novice on hurdling debut. *R. H. Buckler* **h– F86**

HE'S THE GUV'NOR (IRE) 6 b.g. Supreme Leader – Love The Lord (IRE) (Mister Lord (USA)) [2004/5 h–, F88: 27g^{6} 21g^{4} 22d^{2} 22s^{2} 21v* 21s* 24d^{pu} Feb 12] workmanlike gelding: fair hurdler: won handicap at Towcester and minor event at Warwick in January: should stay at least 3m: acts well on soft/heavy going. *R. H. Buckler* **h104**

HESTHERELAD (IRE) 6 b.g. Definite Article – Unbidden Melody (USA) (Chieftain) [2004/5 19g 17d^{3} 21m^{4} Aug 31] brother to useful 2m hurdler/chaser Greenhope and half-brother to winning 2m hurdler Muhandam (by Common Grounds): no form on Flat at 4 yrs for C. Teague: poor form on second start in novice hurdles. *R. Johnson* **h76 ?**

HETLAND HILL 9 ch.g. Secret Appeal – Mohibbah (USA) (Conquistador Cielo (USA)) [2004/5 h–: 16g^{pu} 16m^{pu} Oct 1] more temperament than ability over hurdles. *L. Lungo* **h–**

HEVERGOLF PRINCESS (IRE) 10 ch.m. Petardia – High Profile (High Top) [2004/5 h–: 16d^{pu} May 6] of no account. *B. Bousfield* **h–**

HEVER ROAD (IRE) 6 ch.g. Anshan – The Little Bag (True Song) [2004/5 21d^{3} 21s^{2} 24v^{pu} Jan 21] sixth foal: half-brother to 17f hurdle winner Little Veralyn (by Good Thyne) and winning pointer by Supreme Leader: dam fair pointer/hunter chaser: in frame in maiden points in 2004: modest form both completed starts in novice hurdles. *M. C. Pipe* **h98**

HEY BOY (IRE) 6 b.g. Courtship – Make Me An Island (Creative Plan (USA)) [2004/5 F87: F16s^{6} 22s 18s 16g^{3} Mar 28] fair form in bumpers: first form over hurdles when third in maiden at Plumpton: should be suited by further than 2m. *C. J. Mann* **h92 F84**

HIALEAH 4 ch.g. Bal Harbour – Tommys Dream (Le Bavard (FR)) [2004/5 F16g^{3} F16s Mar 22] lengthy gelding: ninth foal: half-brother to modest hurdler/winning pointer Preston Brook (by Perpendicular), stays 3m: dam, fair hurdler, successful from 2m to 25f: better effort in bumpers when third to Coolawarra at Catterick on debut. *M. W. Easterby* **F86**

HIAWATHA (IRE) 6 b.g. Danehill (USA) – Hi Bettina (Henbit (USA)) [2004/5 17d^{pu} Feb 1] smallish gelding: fair on Flat (stays 1¼m): jumped poorly in novice on hurdling debut: sold 3,500 gns Doncaster March Sales. *P. A. Blockley* **h–**

HIBERNIAN (IRE) 5 br.g. Supreme Leader – Tullahought (Jaazeiro (USA)) [2004/5 F16g^{2} F16d^{4} Apr 20] 25,000 4-y-o: half-brother to fair 2m hurdler Frances Street (by Be My Native) and winning pointer by Broken Hearted: dam, fair 2m to 2½m hurdler, half-sister to prolific 2-y-o winner Spindrifter and fairly useful 2m to 2½m hurdler Sand-Dollar: fair form in 2 bumpers: will stay beyond 2m. *O. Sherwood* **F94**

HICKLETON CLUB 7 b.g. Aragon – Honest Opinion (Free State) [2004/5 h–, F–: 16v^{pu} Jan 14] of no account. *R. M. Clark* **h–**

HI CLOY (IRE) 8 b.g. Be My Native (USA) – Thomastown Girl (Tekoah) [2004/5 c152, h120: c20g^{2} 19v^{5} c16v^{3} Jan 30] rangy, well-made gelding: winning hurdler: smart novice chaser in 2003/4: below-form third of 5 to Moscow Flyer in Grade 3 at Punchestown final start: reportedly suffered tendon injury in February and missed rest of season: has won at 2m and 3m, best form around 2½m: raced on good going or softer (acts on soft). *M. Hourigan, Ireland* **c136 + h–**

HIDDEN BOUNTY (IRE) 9 b.g. Generous (IRE) – Sought Out (IRE) (Rainbow Quest (USA)) [2004/5 h124: 22s 19d c24g* c24s^{4} c16s c24d^{4} c25s* Apr 3] lengthy, rather leggy gelding: fairly useful handicap hurdler: similar form over fences: won maiden at Newcastle (by short head from King Harald) in December and novice at Kelso (by 7 lengths from Harrovian) in April: stays 25f: acts on soft and good to firm going: patiently ridden. *K. G. Reveley* **c125 h112 +**

HIDDEN SMILE (USA) 8 b.m. Twilight Agenda (USA) – Smooth Edge (USA) (Meadowlake (USA)) [2004/5 h77: 16g^{pu} Apr 19] tall mare: poor maiden hurdler: off 12 months before return: raced around 2m: yet to race on extremes of going. *F. Jordan* **h–**

HIDDEN STORM (IRE) 6 br.m. Jamesmead – Hidden Play (IRE) (Seclude (USA)) [2004/5 22s 21g Mar 28] first foal: dam placed once over hurdles: won mares maiden on last of 7 starts in Irish points in 2004: no show in maiden hurdles. *Mrs S. J. Humphrey* **h–**

HIDDEN WEAPON 8 b.g. Charmer – Bustellina (Busted) [2004/5 24d^{pu} Oct 3] half-brother to several winners, including fair hurdler/chaser Dawn Mission (by Dunbeath), stays 21f: dam 1m winner: won maiden on second of 2 starts in Irish points in 2002: not knocked about once weakening in novice at Market Rasen on hurdling debut. *L. Wells* **h–**

HIERS DE BROUAGE (FR) 10 b.g. Neustrien (FR) – Thalandrezienne (FR) (Le Correzien (FR)) [2004/5 c105, h–: c23s^{4} c21d* c19s* c22v^{pu} c21s^{pu} c21d^{pu} c25d^{pu} Mar 24] tall, rangy gelding: fair handicap chaser: won at Wincanton and Chepstow in November: badly lost form after: barely stays 3m: acts on soft and good to firm going: wears cheekpieces: tongue tied final start. *J. G. Portman* **c105 h–**

HI FI 7 b.g. Homo Sapien – Baroness Orkzy (Baron Blakeney) [2004/5 h109: 17d 16g c20d^{5} c18g^{3} c18g^{4} c21s^{5} c20g^{3} c19g^{3} Apr 12] leggy gelding: winning hurdler: fair maiden chaser: stays 2½m: acts on soft ground. *Ian Williams* **c107 h–**

HIGH ACTION (USA) 5 ch.g. Theatrical – Secret Imperatrice (USA) (Secretariat (USA)) [2004/5 h72: 16m* 16g^{2} May 30] sturdy gelding: useful on Flat (effective at 1½m to 2¼m), back to very best when winning in 2005: modest form over hurdles: won handicap at Wetherby in May: raced around 2m, likely to stay at least 2½m: acts on good to firm ground: has reportedly suffered breathing problems. *Ian Williams* **h97 +**

HIGH ALTITUDE (IRE) 4 b.g. Alhaarth (IRE) – Delphini (IRE) (Seattle Dancer (USA)) [2004/5 F12g^{2} F14d^{3} F12d 16d^{4} 16d^{4} Mar 10] 40,000Y: leggy gelding: first foal: dam, 1m winner, half-sister to very smart 1¼m performer Mister Monet and Irish 1000 Guineas winner Tarascon: placed in 3-y-o bumpers at Newbury and Warwick: fair form when fourth over hurdles at Wincanton in novice won by Cerium and maiden by Gold Ring: not sure to stay much beyond 2m. *A. King* **h102 F96**

HIGH BIRD HUMPHREY 6 ch.g. Nomadic Way (USA) – Miss Kewmill (Billion (USA)) [2004/5 F81: 21g 21d^F Dec 13] mid-field in 2 bumpers and on completed outing over hurdles: visored final start. *P. R. Webber* **h82**

HIGH BOUNCE (USA) 5 ch.g. Trempolino (USA) – Top Hope (High Top) [2004/5 16s 19g Dec 9] half-brother to winning 2m hurdler Cobo Bay (by General Assembly): tailed off in maiden for I. Balding on debut: no sign of ability in selling hurdles. *R. J. Hodges* **h–**

HIGH CLASS PET 5 b.m. Petong – What A Pet (Mummy's Pet) [2004/5 F–: 16d^5 17d^4 17d 16v 20g^ur 16s^pu Mar 1] poor novice hurdler: looked unwilling in blinkers final start. *F. P. Murtagh* **h73**

HIGH COTTON (IRE) 10 gr.g. Ala Hounak – Planalife (Beau Charmeur (FR)) [2004/5 c112§, h–: c25s^2 c29d^3 Nov 21] useful-looking gelding: fair maiden chaser: suited by 3m+: raced on good going or softer (acts on heavy): tried blinkered: irresolute. *K. G. Reveley* **c102 § h–**

HIGH DRAMA 8 b.g. In The Wings – Maestrale (Top Ville) [2004/5 h102: c23d^F c21m^pu 22d^2 c20m^4 Aug 6] smallish gelding: poor on Flat (stays 2¼m): fair handicap hurdler: very much let down by jumping over fences: stays 2¾m: acts on firm and good to soft going. *P. Bowen* **c– x h100**

HIGHEST OFFER 6 b.g. Puissance – Scoffera (Scottish Reel) [2004/5 F–: F16f Jun 6] no form in bumpers: tongue tied in 2004/5. *W. S. Coltherd* **F–**

HIGH EXPECTATIONS (IRE) 10 ch.g. Over The River (FR) – Andy's Fancy (IRE) (Andretti) [2004/5 c83: c17g c25g^3 c21g^pu c25v^5 c25d^3 Apr 11] workmanlike gelding: winning pointer: poor maiden chaser: stays 25f: acts on good to soft going. *J. S. Haldane* **c83**

HIGH GEAR (IRE) 7 br.g. Accordion – Holly Grove Lass (Le Moss) [2004/5 22m^3 24m^2 c26m^3 Sep 21] IR £25,000 3-y-o, €15,000 4-y-o: fourth known foal: dam maiden half-sister to top-class hurdler up to 3m Mister Morose and smart staying hurdler The Proms: once-raced in bumpers: modest maiden hurdler: left C. Swan, similar form when third in novice handicap at Fontwell on chasing debut: stays 3¼m: acts on firm and soft going: tried blinkered/in cheekpieces: ungenuine. *Jonjo O'Neill* **c93 § h88 §**

HIGH KICK 4 gr.g. Sadler's Wells (USA) – High Tern (High Line) [2004/5 F16m* F16g^3 F17d^5 Apr 9] close-coupled gelding: half-brother to several winners, including Derby winner High-Rise (by High Estate) and fairly useful hurdler up to 2½m Gamekeeper (by Mujtahid): dam, 1¾m/2m winner, half-sister to very smart stayer High Hawk, herself dam of In The Wings (by Sadler's Wells): sold unraced out of M. Bell's stable 13,000 gns Newmarket Autumn (2004) Sales: won bumper at Musselburgh on debut in February by 1¼ lengths from Love Supreme: progressed after, useful form after when fifth to The Cool Guy in Grade 2 event at Aintree. *R. A. Fahey* **F109**

HIGHLAND BRIG 9 b.g. Homo Sapien – Birniebrig (New Brig) [2004/5 c71: c25v^2 c25d^4 Apr 11] leggy, lengthy gelding: fair pointer/hunter chaser: will stay beyond 25f: acts on heavy going. *Tim Butt* **c92**

HIGHLAND ISLAND 9 b.m. Jupiter Island – Close Call (Nearly A Hand) [2004/5 c–, h76?: c27d^3 c27d^6 c25v^5 c21v^pu Jan 11] little form outside points: tried tongue tied. *L. Lungo* **c57 h–**

HIGHLAND TRACKER (IRE) 10 ch.g. Indian Ridge – Track Twenty Nine (IRE) (Standaan (FR)) [2004/5 c–, h87: c21g^pu May 1] close-coupled gelding: very lightly raced: winning hurdler/maiden chaser: stays 2¾m: acts on soft and good to firm going. *Miss M. E. Rowland* **c– h–**

HIGHLIGHT GIRL 4 ch.f. Forzando – Norska (Northfields (USA)) [2004/5 16m 16f^5 16s Nov 4] angular filly: half-sister to several winners, including fairly useful hurdler/winning chaser Eponine (by Sharpo), stays 21f, and winning hurdler Titus Bramble (by Puissance), stays 2¾m: little sign of ability on Flat or over hurdles. *A. W. Carroll* **h–**

HIGH PADDY 6 b.g. Master Willie – Ivy Edith (Blakeney) [2004/5 h89: 20d^4 May 15] lengthy, rather sparely-made gelding: lightly raced: maiden hurdler: well held only start in 2004/5: should stay 2½m. *R. Ingram* **h–**

HIGH PEAK 8 b.g. Alflora (IRE) – High Heels (IRE) (Supreme Leader) [2004/5 c19s^pu c24d^pu c24d^ur Mar 11] sturdy gelding: winning pointer: no form in chases: probably stays 2½m: raced on good going or softer: has worn visor: poor jumper. *J. W. Mullins* **c– x h–**

HIGHPOINT (GER) 7 b.m. Acatenango (GER) – Holly (GER) (Cortez (GER)) [2004/5 c22d c21s^pu c22s^3 c20v^F Mar 1] tall mare: modest hurdler: off 22 months, similar form at best over fences: stays 2¾m: raced on going softer than good. *Mrs L. Wadham* **c86 h–**

HIGH RANK 6 b.g. Emperor Jones (USA) – Hotel Street (USA) (Alleged (USA)) [2004/5 h105, F–: 20v^3 20d 21d^3 25v c19g^3 Mar 5] tall, close-coupled gelding: modest maiden hurdler on balance: similar form when third in maiden at Doncaster on chasing debut: stays 21f: acts on good to soft going: often tongue tied. *J. Mackie* **c89 h86**

HIGH TECH MADE (FR) 5 br.g. Nononito (FR) – Home Made (FR) (Appiani II) [2004/5 F103: F16g^3 F16g Mar 16] leggy gelding: fairly useful form in bumpers: bred to stay at least 2½m. *C. R. Egerton* **F102**

HIGHWAY ROBBERY 8 b.g. Un Desperado (FR) – Drivers Bureau (Proverb) [2004/5 c89, h94: 20g 22d^6 May 29] maiden hurdler/chaser: well held in early-2004/5: probably stays 25f: yet to race on extremes of going: in cheekpieces second start: sold £3,100 Ascot July Sales: in frame in points in 2005. *Jennie Candlish* **c– h–**

HIGH WINDOW (IRE) 5 b.g. King's Theatre (IRE) – Kayradja (IRE) (Last Tycoon) [2004/5 F17d^6 F16g F16d Jan 13] IR 18,000F, 17,000Y: tall gelding: fifth foal: half-brother to 2 winners abroad by Distinctly North, including Italian 5f and 7f winner Nicolo Fly: dam unraced half-sister to useful performer up to 1¼m Kayfa: modest form in bumpers. *S. Gollings* **F85**

HIHO SILVER LINING 4 gr.f. Silver Patriarch (IRE) – By Line (High Line) [2004/5 F13s^2 F17s Apr 7] rather leggy filly: half-sister to smart bumper winner/useful maiden hurdler Secret Ploy (by Deploy) and fairly useful bumper winner The Thunderer (by Terimon): dam fair hurdler up to 19f: much better effort in bumpers when 2 lengths second to Wishin And Hopin at Exeter on debut. *H. Morrison* **F89**

HI HUMPFREE 5 b.g. Thowra (FR) – White Flash (Sure Blade (USA)) [2004/5 F16s F16d F16m* Apr 2] stocky gelding: half-brother to winners up to 1m by Magic Ring in Spain and Serbia: dam, poor maiden, out of half-sister to St Leger winner Bruni: green first 2 starts: clear best effort when winning 21-runner bumper at Newbury, beating Le Galactico 1¼ lengths: sold 43,000 gns Doncaster May Sales. *D. R. C. Elsworth* **F101**

HIJACKED 11 b.g. True Song – Scamper (Abwah) [2004/5 c33s^pu c25v^3 May 10] winning pointer: poor hunter chaser. *A. Hollingsworth* **c70**

HILARIOUS (IRE) 5 b.m. Petorius – Heronwater (IRE) (Ela-Mana-Mou) [2004/5 16d^3 16d^2 16d 17d^6 17g Apr 12] maiden on Flat: poor form over hurdles: likely to prove best at 2m. *Dr J. R. J. Naylor* **h77**

HI LILY 9 b.m. Jupiter Island – By Line (High Line) [2004/5 c79, h–: c21d c16m^F c18m^5 c20s^pu c16s^3 c21d c20g^5 c16g^6 Apr 19] tall mare: poor maiden hurdler/chaser: stays 21f: unraced on firm going, acts on any other. *Miss Z. C. Davison* **c79 d h–**

HILL FORTS HENRY 7 ch.g. Karinga Bay – Maggie Tee (Lepanto (GER)) [2004/5 h79: 22d^6 26s^6 22d^6 Apr 3] poor maiden hurdler: stays 3¼m: acts on firm and soft going. *J. W. Mullins* **h72**

HILL PORT (IRE) 8 ch.g. Port Lucaya – Minstrelsdaughter (Black Minstrel) [2004/5 c–§, h114§: 22v 16s 20s^2 24d* 20v^3 Dec 31] leggy gelding: twice-raced chaser: fairly useful handicap hurdler: back to form when good second to impressive Tumbling Dice at Punchestown in November: won at Fairyhouse following month readily by 4 lengths from Christmas River: stays 27f: acts on heavy going: usually blinkered prior to 2003/4: formerly ungenuine. *S. McConville, Ireland* **c– h121**

HILLS OF RAKAPOSHI 6 ch.m. Rakaposhi King – Hilly Path (Brave Invader (USA)) [2004/5 h–, F–: 16d May 11] medium-sized mare: little sign of ability over hurdles: placed on completed starts in points in 2005. *R. Fielder* **h–**

HILLS OF VIEW 7 b.g. Sea Raven (IRE) – Hardwick Sun (Dieu Soleil) [2004/5 h–, F–: 20v^pu 16g Mar 5] big, lengthy gelding: no sign of ability. *J. M. Jefferson* **h–**

HILLTIME (IRE) 5 b.g. Danetime (IRE) – Ceannanas (IRE) (Magical Wonder (USA)) [2004/5 h102: 17m^3 16d Nov 27] angular gelding: modest maiden on Flat (stays 1m): fair hurdler: likely to prove best at 2m: acts on good to firm going: races prominently. *J. J. Quinn* **h105**

HILLY BE 4 b.f. Silver Patriarch (IRE) – Lolita (FR) (Hellios (USA)) [2004/5 16d 16d 17d Nov 15] workmanlike filly: no sign of ability on Flat/in juvenile hurdles. *J. R. Jenkins* **h–**

williamhill.co.uk Marathon Chase (Handicap), Sandown—
Historic lands a weakish race for the money

HIM OF DISTINCTION 6 br.g. Rainbow Quest (USA) – Air of Distinction (IRE) (Distinctly North (USA)) [2004/5 h87: 16g Apr 26] compact gelding: thrice-raced novice hurdler, well held only start in 2004/5: may prove best around 2m. *R. T. Phillips* **h–**

HIPPY DIPPY DREAMS 5 b.m. Dreams End – Virginia Stock (Swing Easy (USA)) [2004/5 F17g 21s^{pu} Jan 20] first foal: dam little sign of ability: no encouragement in bumper or mares maiden hurdle. *C. J. Hemsley* **h–** **F–**

HIRED GUN (IRE) 6 b.g. Needle Gun (IRE) – Monahullen Rose (IRE) (Fayruz) [2004/5 F–: 16d^{F} 18g^{pu} Mar 20] workmanlike gelding: no sign of ability: sold £1,100 Ascot April Sales. *V. R. A. Dartnall* **h–**

HIRT LODGE 14 ch.g. Jumbo Hirt (USA) – Holly Lodge (Rubor) [2004/5 c–, h–: c23d^{ur} c25d^{pu} 24s^{5} Mar 11] workmanlike gelding: veteran hurdler: no show over fences, poor jumper: retains little ability: tried in cheekpieces. *J. E. Dixon* **c– x** **h–**

HI RUDOLF 10 b.g. Ballet Royal (USA) – Hi Darlin' (Prince de Galles) [2004/5 c80, h–: 22g^{pu} c20g* c21m^{4} c22m^{F} c20d^{4} 24g c21g^{3} c21g^{3} 22g^{4} 20g^{2} c19g^{5} c26s^{ur} c19s^{F} c19g^{4} Apr 19] small gelding: modest maiden hurdler: poor chaser: won point in March: stays 25f: acts on soft and good to firm going: claimer ridden: often let down by jumping. *H. J. Manners* **c88 x** **h85**

HIRVINE (FR) 7 ch.g. Snurge – Guadanella (FR) (Guadanini (FR)) [2004/5 h123p: 23m 22g^{2} c24s^{4} c22s^{3} c25s^{4} c25g^{2} c23d* c24s* 23s^{2} 24g 24d^{F} Apr 8] good-topped gelding: useful handicap hurdler: ran well last 2 completed starts, including when eighth to Oulart in valuable 22-runner event at Cheltenham in March: fairly useful novice chaser: won at Leicester and Newcastle in January, beating Meneur de Jeu a short head at latter: will stay beyond 25f: raced mainly on good going or softer (acts on heavy): in cheekpieces last 3 outings: needs to brush up jumping over fences. *P. Bowen* **c129** **h138**

HISAR (IRE) 12 br.g. Doyoun – Himaya (IRE) (Mouktar) [2004/5 c69, h–: c16m^4 c16g^5 c17m^3 c20g^{pu} c19d^4 c16s^{pu} c18s^4 c16d^F c16s^4 c16s* c20m^{pu} c16g Apr 19] leggy gelding: poor handicap chaser: won conditional jockeys event at Chepstow in March: best around 2m: unraced on heavy going, acts on any other: tried blinkered: often tongue tied: unreliable. *P. C. Ritchens* **c68 § h–**

HIS NIBS (IRE) 8 b.g. Alflora (IRE) – Mrs Jennifer (River Knight (FR)) [2004/5 c–, h131: 23m 24d^5 Jan 31] workmanlike gelding: refused first only outing over fences: useful handicap hurdler: much better effort in 2004/5 when fifth to Chamoss Royale at Kempton: stays 25f: acts on good to firm and heavy going. *Miss Venetia Williams* **c– h133**

HISTORG (FR) 10 b.g. Cyborg (FR) – Kalliste (FR) (Calicot (FR)) [2004/5 c20s^3 c23d^4 c22s^3 c26s c29s c24d^{pu} c26v^{pu} Feb 19] leggy, useful-looking gelding: fairly useful handicap chaser: off 20 months before reappearance: out of form after third outing: suited by 2¾m+: acts on heavy and good to firm going: wore cheekpieces sixth start. *Ferdy Murphy* **c116 h–**

HISTORIC (IRE) 9 b.g. Sadler's Wells (USA) – Urjwan (USA) (Seattle Slew (USA)) [2004/5 c124, h–: c24d c29d* c29s^{pu} c24g c21d^F Apr 8] good-topped gelding: impresses in appearance: useful chaser: form in 2004/5 only when winning listed handicap at Sandown in December by 5 lengths from Innox: will stay beyond 29f: acts on heavy going: tried blinkered: races prominently. *T. R. George* **c130 h–**

HIT AND RUN (FR) 10 ch.g. River Mist (USA) – La Dunanerie (FR) (Guadanini (FR)) [2004/5 c–, h–: 16m c16g^5 Jun 7] leggy gelding: smart hurdler/fairly useful handicap chaser in his prime: lightly raced and no form since 2002: usually blinkered/visored. *M. C. Pipe* **c– h–**

HI TECH 6 b.g. Polar Falcon (USA) – Just Speculation (IRE) (Ahonoora) [2004/5 h93: 16g^6 27m^{pu} 20g^4 20m^5 17d* 20f* 17d^4 22d^3 16s^2 20d^4 Jan 1] smallish, angular gelding: modest hurdler: won seller at Southwell in August and handicap at Worcester in September: effective around 2m to 3m: acts on soft and firm going: front runner. *Dr P. Pritchard* **h99**

HIT ROYAL (FR) 10 ch.g. Montorselli – Valse Royale (FR) (Cap Martin (FR)) [2004/5 c106x, h–: c20d^6 c20m* c21g^2 c17d* c17g^3 Sep 12] workmanlike gelding: fair handicap chaser: won at Stratford in June and August: collapsed and died after finishing third there in September: successful at 3m, better over shorter: acted on good to firm and heavy going. *P. R. Webber* **c112 h–**

HIYAH (IRE) 6 ch.g. Petardia – Stairway To Heaven (IRE) (Godswalk (USA)) [2004/5 16d 16m^{pu} 16m 22g 20m 20m 17m Aug 31] good-topped gelding: winning hurdler: no form in 2004/5, including in point in April: usually in headgear: ungenuine. *John R. Upson* **h– §**

HOBBS HILL 6 b.g. Alflora (IRE) – Rim of Pearl (Rymer) [2004/5 F16d* Jan 31] 12,500 4-y-o: tall, good sort: fifth foal: half-brother to useful bumper winner Posh Pearl (by Rakaposhi King): dam, poor maiden hurdler, half-sister to dam of top-class 2m chaser Pearlyman: easily better effort in bumpers (trained by E. Hales on debut in 2003) when winning 18-runner event at Kempton by 9 lengths from Autumn Red: open to further improvement. *C. R. Egerton* **F107 p**

HOBBYCYR (FR) 10 b.g. Saint Cyrien (FR) – Sauteuse de Retz (FR) (Funny Hobby) [2004/5 c33s^3 c34d^{pu} May 15] tall gelding: winning pointer: fairly useful hunter chaser: better effort in 2004 when third to County Derry at Cheltenham: stays 33f: acts on soft going. *R. Kelvin-Hughes* **c104 h–**

HODGSON'S CHOICE (IRE) 6 b.m. Fourstars Allstar (USA) – Waterland Lady (Strong Gale) [2004/5 h–, F79: 19d 19v 16d^5 c16s^{ur} c16s^{pu} Jan 18] workmanlike mare: form only in bumper on debut: dead. *M. J. Ryan* **c– h63**

HOH NELSON 4 b.g. Halling (USA) – Birsay (Bustino) [2004/5 16f^3 16d^F 16d^5 19s^6 19s^6 23d* 24s^3 Mar 6] lengthy gelding: fair maiden on Flat (stays 2¼m) for H. Morrison: fair hurdler: won handicap at Fakenham in February: stays 3m: acts on firm and soft going: blinkered after debut: has carried head awkwardly/swished tail under pressure: room for improvement in jumping. *C. J. Mann* **h100**

HO HO HILL (IRE) 7 b.g. Beneficial – Bale Out (Shackleton) [2004/5 22s^6 24v^4 24d^6 19m^3 16d^5 c18m^{ur} c24g^F c20m^3 Apr 23] £14,000 3-y-o: rangy gelding: eighth foal: half-brother to fair 2m hurdler Sirmoor Rifles (by Be My Native): dam Irish bumper winner: won maiden Irish point in 2003: modest novice hurdler: similar form on com- **c88 h89**

pleted start in chases: stays easy 3m: acts on soft and good to firm going: tongue tied when failing to complete over fences: has taken good hold. *P. F. Nicholls*

HOH TEL (IRE) 11 ch.g. Montelimar (USA) – Party Dancer (Be My Guest (USA)) [2004/5 c90x, h–: c25gF c26gpu May 31] lengthy gelding: maiden chaser/fair pointer: stays 25f: acts on soft and good to firm going: usually wears headgear: makes mistakes. *G. F. White* **c– x h–**

HOLDERNESS GIRL 12 b.m. Lapierre – Isobel's Choice (Green God) [2004/5 17d 17gpu May 31] of no account. *M. E. Sowersby* **h–**

HOLD ON HARRY 9 ch.g. Endoli (USA) – Hold On Tight (Battlement) [2004/5 c26gpu c21g2 Apr 10] winning pointer: second in novice at Newton Abbot on completed start in hunter chases. *Ms C. Williams* **c95**

HOLD THE LINE 4 b.g. Titus Livius (FR) – Multi-Sofft (Northern State (USA)) [2004/5 16d 16g3 16d4 16m* 16d Dec 13] stocky gelding: fair on Flat (stays 1m): fair juvenile hurdler: won handicap at Musselburgh in November: wore cheekpieces after debut: has looked difficult ride. *W. G. M. Turner* **h97**

HOLLAND PARK (IRE) 8 gr.g. Roselier (FR) – Bluebell Avenue (Boreen Beag) [2004/5 h121: c20dF c19vF 23s 24d 22d* 24d* Apr 8] workmanlike gelding: useful hurdler: won handicaps at Uttoxeter (by 1¼ lengths from Nick's Choice) in March and Aintree in April, further improvement when winning 22-runner listed event by 9 lengths from Celtic Son at latter: fell both starts over fences, still disputing lead when going 3 out in maiden at Lingfield won by Trabolgan on first occasion: suited by test of stamina: raced on going softer than good. *Mrs S. D. Williams* **c– p h137**

HOLLOW FLIGHT (IRE) 7 b.g. Hollow Hand – Gers Pet (IRE) (Baragoi) [2004/5 c24gpu c24g6 c20v3 c25s5 Mar 11] first foal: dam maiden chaser: runner-up on first of 2 starts in points in 2004: no other form. *J. N. R. Billinge* **c– h–**

HOLLOWS MILL 9 b.g. Rudimentary (USA) – Strawberry Song (Final Straw) [2004/5 h92: 20dpu 17d c17d4 c16s2 c20m6 c21d4 c19gpu c16s* c16s* c20v4 c17d Apr 11] workmanlike gelding: winning hurdler: fair handicap chaser: won at Carlisle in February and March: stays 2½m: acts on firm and soft going: has finished weakly. *F. P. Murtagh* **c106 h–**

HOLLOWS MIST 7 b.g. Missed Flight – Joyfulness (FR) (Cure The Blues (USA)) [2004/5 h89, F84: 16d Oct 16] modest maiden hurdler: raced around 2m on good going or softer: usually tongue tied. *F. P. Murtagh* **h–**

HOLLY PARK 7 b.m. Syrtos – Mapleline (Shy Groom (USA)) [2004/5 22mur 19mpu Apr 23] third foal: half-sister to winning pointer by Puget: dam well behind in 2 races on Flat: completed only once in 5 starts in maiden points in 2004: no show in 2 novice hurdles. *C. N. Kellett* **h–**

John Smith's Extra Cold Handicap Hurdle, Aintree—
Holland Park survives a mistake at the last to beat hot favourite Celtic Son and The Dark Lord (centre)

HOLLY ROSE 6 b.m. Charnwood Forest (IRE) – Divina Luna (Dowsing (USA)) [2004/5 h–: 16m Aug 30] sturdy mare: modest and temperamental on Flat (stays 11f): in cheekpieces, well held in maiden hurdles a year apart. *D. E. Cantillon* **h–**

HOLLY WALK 4 ch.f. Dr Fong (USA) – Holly Blue (Bluebird (USA)) [2004/5 16d⁵ 16m² 16mF 16s⁶ 17s⁶ 16g² 16v³ 16v⁵ Jan 21] sturdy filly: poor maiden on Flat (should stay 1¾m): modest form over hurdles: claimed from M. Dods £6,000 sixth start: raced around 2m: acts on soft and good to firm going: tried in cheekpieces. *A. G. Juckes* **h89**

HOLLYWEST (FR) 5 ch.g. Sillery (USA) – Hollywood Trick (USA) (Caro) [2004/5 h84: 20dpu 22gpu Aug 14] poor hurdler, no show in 2004/5: probably best around 2m: acts on soft going: tried blinkered: front runner. *M. E. Sowersby* **h–**

HOLLYWOOD 4 b.f. Bin Ajwaad (IRE) – Raaha (Polar Falcon (USA)) [2004/5 F12g⁴ F16d² F16d⁵ F17g³ Apr 14] leggy filly: third foal: dam, 7f/1m winner, half-sister to smart 1¼m to 2m performer Labirinto, from family of useful staying jumper Robbo: fair form when in frame in bumpers. *V. R. A. Dartnall* **F86**

HOLLYWOOD CRITIC (USA) 4 b.g. Theatrical – Lyphard's Starlite (USA) (Lyphard (USA)) [2004/5 16spu 16s Apr 10] modest maiden on Flat (stays 11f): no show over hurdles. *P. Monteith* **h–**

HOMBRE 10 ch.g. Shernazar – Delray Jet (USA) (Northjet) [2004/5 c85, h–: c19g⁵ c21v⁵ Mar 28] leggy gelding: poor handicap chaser: stays 3m: acts on any going: tried blinkered. *M. D. Hammond* **c– h–**

HOMEBRED BUDDY 6 ch.g. Environment Friend – Royal Brush (King of Spain) [2004/5 h–, F–: 21s Jan 2] of no account. *P. Bowen* **h–**

HOMEBRED STAR 4 ch.g. Safawan – Celtic Chimes (Celtic Cone) [2004/5 17spu 16s Jan 2] dam won 2m hurdle: no sign of ability on Flat or in juvenile hurdles. *P. Bowen* **h–**

HOME BY SOCKS (IRE) 6 ch.m. Desert King (IRE) – Propitious (IRE) (Doyoun) [2004/5 17d 17g 17dpu 17m⁵ 19g⁶ c17g³ c21d⁶ c21d⁴ c22vpu c21s⁴ c25spu 20g c16s² c16d³ c16g Dec 8] poor maiden hurdler/chaser: seems best around 2m: acts on soft going: has had tongue tied: sold 500 gns Doncaster March Sales. *M. C. Chapman* **c72 h66**

HOME JAMES (IRE) 8 b.g. Commanche Run – Take Me Home (Amoristic (USA)) [2004/5 h114: c21d³ c21g⁶ c24g³ c23s* c24s³ c24s* Feb 10] sturdy gelding: fairly useful hurdler: useful chaser: won handicaps at Exeter in January and Huntingdon (novice, beat Fullards by ½ length) in February: should stay beyond 3m: raced on good going or softer (acts on heavy). *A. King* **c130 h–**

HOMELEIGH MOONCOIN 10 ch.g. Jamesmead – Super Sol (Rolfe (USA)) [2004/5 h115: c26g⁵ c24mR 24gpu Apr 14] angular gelding: winning hurdler: well held in maiden chases and points for various stables in 2004/5: stays 3¼m: acts on good to soft going. *B. G. Powell* **c– h–**

HOMELIFE (IRE) 7 b.g. Persian Bold – Share The Vision (Vision (USA)) [2004/5 16v 16g⁵ Jan 24] compact gelding: fairly useful at one time on Flat (stays 2m), well held in 2003: better effort over hurdles when fifth in maiden at Southwell: should stay beyond 2m. *Mrs J. A. Saunders* **h82**

HOME MADE 7 b.g. Homo Sapien – Inch Maid (Le Moss) [2004/5 c77x, h–: c24dpu Feb 9] tall gelding: little form outside points, successful in March: often let down by jumping. *Miss H. Brookshaw* **c– x h–**

HOMER (IRE) 8 b.g. Sadler's Wells (USA) – Gravieres (FR) (Saint Estephe (FR)) [2004/5 h–: c16spu c16sR 17s³ 16s Dec 13] close-coupled gelding: winning hurdler, little form since 2001/2: failed to complete over fences: stays 2½m: acts on soft and good to firm going: tried tongue tied: ungenuine. *N. M. Babbage* **c– § h66 §**

HOME RULE 5 b.m. Wizard King – Pastures Green (Monksfield) [2004/5 F16s F16s F18m Apr 21] small mare: third foal: dam lightly-raced half-sister to high-class staying chaser Scotton Banks: no sign of ability. *G. P. Enright* **F–**

HOMER WELLS (IRE) 7 b.g. Arctic Cider (USA) – Run And Shine (Deep Run) [2004/5 h–, F108: 19s* 24s* 20v* 24v² 20s² 20s³ Mar 27] lengthy, useful-looking gelding: useful hurdler: successful in maiden at Naas in November, Grade 3 O'Connell Transport Stayers Novice Hurdle at Cork in December and Grade 2 Woodlands Park 100 Slaney Novice Hurdle at Naas (beat Sweet Kiln by head) in January: creditable efforts **h133**

Woodlands Park 100 Slaney Novices' Hurdle, Naas—
Homer Wells (centre) stays on best in gruelling conditions to beat Sweet Kiln and Petertheknot (left)

next 3 starts but below best in Grade 1 Champion Stayers' Hurdle at Punchestown in late-April: stays 3m: raced mainly on soft/heavy going: type to make useful novice chaser in 2005/6. *W. P. Mullins, Ireland*

HONAN (IRE) 6 b.g. College Chapel – Medical Times (IRE) (Auction Ring (USA)) [2004/5 F103: 22g³ 16m³ 17g³ 16d⁴ 16s² 19g 19s 16s³ 17d³ 17v² 16s 20s Apr 22] leggy gelding: bumper winner: modest maiden hurdler: may prove best around 2m: acts on heavy going: tried in visor. *M. C. Pipe* **h91**

HONEST ENDEAVOUR 6 b.g. Alflora (IRE) – Isabeau (Law Society (USA)) [2004/5 F68: 16m* 16s* 17s² 16v 16m Feb 6] well-made gelding: fair novice hurdler: won at Hexham and Uttoxeter in October: ran poorly in handicaps last 2 starts: will stay 2½m: acts on soft and good to firm going. *J. M. Jefferson* **h99**

HONEST INJUN 4 b.c. Efisio – Sioux (Kris) [2004/5 16s 16s Nov 21] small, compact colt: fairly useful on Flat (should stay 1¼m), claimed from B. Hills £20,000 in August: poor form in juvenile hurdles: likely to prove best at sharp 2m. *J. G. M. O'Shea* **h69**

HONEST YER HONOUR (IRE) 9 b.g. Witness Box (USA) – Castle Duchess (Abednego) [2004/5 h120: c24sᵖᵘ c24dᶠ Mar 24] sturdy ex-Irish gelding: fairly useful hurdler: won twice in points in 2005: failed to complete in hunters at Huntingdon (ran as if amiss) and Ludlow: stays 2½m: acts on soft going. *Mrs C. J. Robinson* **c–** **h–**

HONEY'S GIFT 6 b.m. Terimon – Honeycroft (Crofter (USA)) [2004/5 h86: 16s⁴ 16s² 16g³ 18s* 19s 16g⁶ 21d 18s* 18g Mar 20] compact mare: fair handicap hurdler: won at Fontwell in December (mares) and March: should stay 2½m: acts on heavy and good to firm going. *G. G. Margarson* **h101**

HONNEUR FONTENAIL (FR) 6 ch.g. Tel Quel (FR) – Fontanalia (FR) (Rex Magna (FR)) [2004/5 c65, h–: c21sᵖᵘ c21gᵖᵘ c24mᶠ c23g Jul 7] angular gelding: won very weak maiden chase in 2003/4, little sign of ability otherwise: in cheekpieces/blinkers in 2004/5. *N. J. Hawke* **c–** **h–**

HONOR ROUGE (IRE) 6 ch.m. Highest Honor (FR) – Ayers Rock (IRE) (In The Wings) [2004/5 20g^{ur} 19g^{4} 16g* 17g^{5} 16m^{6} 19g Sep 30] fairly useful on Flat (stays 1½m) at 4 yrs, sold out of P. Harris' stable 12,000 gns Newmarket Autumn (2003) Sales: modest hurdler: won maiden at Worcester in July: may prove best around 2m: sold 7,000 gns Newmarket February Sales. *D. G. Bridgwater* **h89**

HOOISE 8 b.g. Welsh Captain – The Last Tune (Gunner B) [2004/5 16g 16s 24d^{pu} 16d^{pu} Jan 28] sturdy gelding: second foal: brother to modest hurdler Captain O'Neill, stays 3m: dam, winning hurdler, stayed 2½m: no sign of ability. *A. W. Carroll* **h–**

HOOKEDONAFEELING (IRE) 7 ch.m. Shernazar – Fireblends (IRE) (Phardante (FR)) [2004/5 F16s c21v^{F} c17v* c22v^{pu} c18d^{2} c21d c17v^{4} c20s^{F} Apr 13] 26,000 3-y-o: lengthy mare: first foal: dam, lightly raced in points, half-sister to useful hurdler/chaser up to 25f Mixed Blends and dual Whitbread Gold Cup winner Topsham Bay: maiden hurdler: won mares maiden point in 2004: well held in bumpers: modest novice chaser: won mares maiden at Fairyhouse in January: should stay 2½m: acts on heavy ground: tried tongue tied. *Michael Cunningham, Ireland* **c95 h– F–**

HOOPZ 5 gr.m. Linamix (FR) – Pearl Venture (Salse (USA)) [2004/5 16s^{pu} Nov 3] lightly-raced maiden on Flat: soon behind in novice on hurdling debut. *L. A. Dace* **h–**

HO PANG YAU 7 b. or br.g. Pivotal – La Cabrilla (Carwhite) [2004/5 h–: 16d* 16d^{ro} 16m 16d^{2} 16d^{pu} 18s^{F} 16g^{F} 16d 16g Feb 27] close-coupled gelding: poor handicap hurdler: 50/1-winner of amateur event at Wetherby in April 2004: will prove best around 2m: acts on good to soft ground: difficult ride: inconsistent. *Mrs R. L. Elliot* **h77 §**

HOPBINE 9 ch.m. Gildoran – Haraka Sasa (Town And Country) [2004/5 h106: 26g^{5} 21m^{4} 20d^{pu} 20d 22d^{5} 19g^{2} 21s 20g 22g* Apr 3] small, sturdy mare: fair hurdler: won handicap at Market Rasen in April: stays 3¼m: acts on heavy going: blinkered/in cheek-pieces last 6 outings: unreliable. *J. L. Spearing* **h102 §**

HOPEFUL CHANCE (IRE) 8 b.g. Machiavellian (USA) – Don't Rush (USA) (Alleged (USA)) [2004/5 c77, h85: c17g c16d^{3} c16s^{4} Oct 31] close-coupled gelding: modest handicap hurdler: poor maiden chaser: stays 2½m: acts on soft going: tried visored: often tongue tied. *J. R. Turner* **c80 h–**

HOPEFUL MISSION 4 b.g. Bien Bien (USA) – Tiama (IRE) (Last Tycoon) [2004/5 aF13g^{6} Nov 24] fourth foal: half-brother to 1m and 1½m winner Hot Love (by Blushing Flame): dam maiden who should have been suited by further than 7f: well held in 3-y-o bumper on debut: little form on Flat in 2005. *K. R. Burke* **F75**

HOPESARISING 6 b.g. Primitive Rising (USA) – Super Brush (IRE) (Brush Aside (USA)) [2004/5 h87, F–: 22g^{pu} 20g^{3} 20v c16s^{4} c20s^{3} c20v^{3} Mar 1] workmanlike gelding: poor maiden hurdler: modest form over fences, though jumps none too fluently: likely to stay 3m. *P. R. Johnson* **c88 h83**

HOPE SOUND (IRE) 5 b.g. Turtle Island (IRE) – Lucky Pick (Auction Ring (USA)) [2004/5 h98: 21g^{2} 20d^{2} 24g* 22d^{4} 20d 27d^{pu} c16g^{5} c21v* c24d^{pu} c19d c20s^{pu} 24s^{6} Mar 6] sturdy gelding: modest hurdler: won maiden at Uttoxeter in June: best effort over fences when winning maiden at Sedgefield in January: stays 3m: acts on heavy going: often wears headgear. *B. Ellison* **c99 h99**

HOPE VALUE 10 b.g. Rock City – Folle Idee (USA) (Foolish Pleasure (USA)) [2004/5 c26g^{4} Jun 7] good-topped gelding: winning hurdler: no longer of much account. *G. F. Edwards* **c– h–**

HOP FAIR 6 ch.m. Gildoran – Haraka Sasa (Town And Country) [2004/5 F16m* Apr 25] fifth foal: sister to fair hurdler Hopbine, stays 3¼m: dam behind in novice hurdles: green when winning bumper at Ludlow on debut by ½ length from Flying Druid in April 2004. *J. L. Spearing* **F83**

HORCOTT BAY 5 b.m. Thowra (FR) – Armagnac Messenger (Pony Express) [2004/5 F–: F18s 16s^{2} 16v^{6} 21s^{4} 22g Apr 12] workmanlike mare: tailed off in 2 bumpers: poor novice hurdler: probably stays 2¾m. *M. G. Rimell* **h73 F–**

HORDAGO (IRE) 5 gr.g. Highest Honor (FR) – Mirmande (Kris) [2004/5 16f 20m^{2} 20v* 22s 21d* 21v^{2} 24v^{pu} 22s^{2} 19s* Mar 27] big, leggy gelding: fourth foal: half-brother to fairly useful winner around 1m Eric Le Beau (by Great Commotion): dam maiden half-sister to smart 1¼m performer Dartrey: fair handicap hurdler: won at Tralee in August, Cheltenham (by 8 lengths from Brigadier Brown) in November and Cork (beat Kilbeggan Lad 4 lengths in 21-runner listed event) in March: should stay 3m: acts on heavy going. *E. McNamara, Ireland* **h106**

HORIZON HILL (USA) 5 b.g. Distant View (USA) – Accadia Rocket (CAN) (Bold Ruckus (USA)) [2004/5 16m 16f^{2} 16d^{3} 16f 18f^{6} 16s^{6} 16m 19g 16g^{6} Oct 7] modest maiden on Flat (stays 7f) at 3 yrs for Mrs J. Ramsden: poor maiden hurdler: runner-up in point in Britain in March: raced mainly around 2m: acts on firm and good to soft going: tried blinkered: not one to trust. *M. Hourigan, Ireland* **h80 §**

HORIZONTAL (USA) 5 ch.g. Distant View (USA) – Proud Lou (USA) (Proud Clarion) [2004/5 16g 16d^{6} Nov 22] modest maiden on Flat (probably best short of 1m) for several trainers: tailed off in 2 selling hurdles. *N. A. Twiston-Davies* **h–**

HORS LA LOI (FR) 9 ch.g. Exit To Nowhere (USA) – Kernia (IRE) (Raise A Cup (USA)) [2004/5 c101p, h115: c16m^{2} 16g^{6} 16g^{pu} c17m^{2} c16m* c16d c17g^{4} Nov 27] close-coupled gelding: fairly useful handicap hurdler/chaser: successful over fences at Worcester in September by 1¾ lengths from Deep King: easily better effort after when fourth to Great Travel at Newbury: raced around 2m: acts on good to firm and heavy going: bled from nose on reappearance. *Ian Williams* **c122 h–**

HORUS (IRE) 10 b.g. Teenoso (USA) – Jennie's First (Idiot's Delight) [2004/5 c142: c24d^{pu} c24s* c24d^{6} c24d c24g^{6} c24s c20d^{2} c25g Apr 8] good-topped gelding: smart handicap chaser: off 6 months, won Edward Hanmer Memorial Chase (Limited Handicap) at Haydock in November by 6 lengths from Chives: creditable effort after (tended to make mistakes otherwise) only when ½-length second to Supreme Prince in very valuable event at Newbury in March: effective at 2½m to easy 3¼m: acts on soft and good to firm going: tried visored, including last 2 starts. *M. C. Pipe* **c148 x**

HOT AIR (IRE) 7 b.g. Air Display (USA) – Lyraisa (Tumble Wind) [2004/5 F76: F17d 20v^{pu} Feb 2] lengthy gelding: little form in bumpers: no show in novice on hurdling debut: tried tongue tied. *J. I. A. Charlton* **h– F–**

HOTFOOT HARRY 6 ch.g. King's Signet (USA) – Castle Maid (Castle Keep) [2004/5 F17d F17m^{6} Sep 1] fourth foal: dam 5f winner: looked temperamental in bumpers: sold £3,000 Ascot October Sales: failed to complete in points in 2005. *W. G. M. Turner* **F–**

HOT GIRL 7 b.m. State Diplomacy (USA) – Hundred Islands (Hotfoot) [2004/5 F–: F17m Jun 25] plain mare: no form in bumpers. *S. P. Griffiths* **F–**

HOT LIPS PAGE (FR) 4 b.f. Hamas (IRE) – Salt Peanuts (IRE) (Salt Dome (USA)) [2004/5 16s^{3} 16g* 16m^{pu} Apr 17] fair on Flat (stays 1m): modest form over hurdles, winning maiden at Huntingdon in March: likely to prove best at 2m. *N. P. Littmoden* **h94**

HOT PLUNGE 9 b.g. Bustino – Royal Seal (Privy Seal) [2004/5 c83, h–: c16s^{2} c20d^{5} c21m^{2} c20g c16s^{bd} c16m* c21s^{F} Apr 7] good-topped gelding: winning pointer: fair hunter chaser: won at Hereford in March: stays 21f: acts on soft and good to firm going. *Mrs J. P. Lomax* **c96 h–**

HOT PRODUXION (USA) 6 ch.g. Tabasco Cat (USA) – Princess Harriet (USA) (Mt Livermore (USA)) [2004/5 h103§: 20d^{2} c19g^{2} c20g^{6} Apr 3] compact gelding: fair maiden hurdler: better effort in maiden chases when second to Oso Magic at Catterick: stays 2½m: acts on soft and good to firm going: tried visored/in cheekpieces: not a fluent jumper or an easy ride. *J. Mackie* **c97 h103 §**

Edward Hanmer Memorial Chase (Limited Handicap), Haydock—
Horus (noseband) has the measure of third-placed Keen Leader

HOT SHOTS (FR) 10 b.g. Passing Sale (FR) – Uguette IV (FR) (Chamberlin (FR)) [2004/5 c146, h131: 16g* c17s^4 c20d^3 c24g 16d 16g c20g^{pu} Apr 22] good-topped gelding: smart chaser: creditable efforts when fourth to Azertyuiop in limited handicap at Exeter and third to Le Roi Miguel in Grade 2 at Huntingdon: useful handicap hurdler: won at Huntingdon by 1¼ lengths from Winsley in October: little show last 4 starts: raced mainly around 2m, effective at 2½m: acts on good to firm and heavy going: held up. *M. Pitman* **c146 h130 +**

HOT TODDY (IRE) 10 b.g. Glacial Storm (USA) – Technical Merit (Gala Performance) [2004/5 c23s^3 c23g^{ur} c26v^F Apr 22] fairly useful pointer, successful twice in 2005: similar form when third in maiden hunter chase at Leicester: will stay beyond 3m. *G. L. Landau* **c99**

HOT WELD 6 b.g. Weld – Deb's Ball (Glenstal (USA)) [2004/5 h97: 20s^2 27d* 24d* 24d^2 24d^{pu} 27s^5 Apr 22] sturdy gelding: fair hurdler: won novices at Sedgefield in November and Newcastle in December: best at 3m+: acts on soft going. *Ferdy Murphy* **h112**

HOUGHTON BAY (IRE) 10 b.g. Camden Town – Royal Bavard (Le Bavard (FR)) [2004/5 c99, h100: 20s Oct 20] workmanlike gelding: fairly useful hurdler at one time: maiden chaser: won point in April: stays 3m: acts on good to firm and heavy going: tried in blinkers/cheekpieces. *R. H. Buckler* **c– h–**

HOUSEPARTY (IRE) 7 b. or br.g. Grand Lodge (USA) – Special Display (Welsh Pageant) [2004/5 h104: 16d^3 16g 20m* 20g^2 19g^{pu} Aug 2] well-made gelding: modest hurdler: won conditional jockeys handicap at Worcester in June: stayed 2½m: acted on firm and good to soft going: dead. *J. A. B. Old* **h98**

HOUSE WARMER (IRE) 6 ch.g. Carroll House – Under The Duvet (IRE) (Brush Aside (USA)) [2004/5 h–: c23d^3 c26g^{pu} Mar 27] sturdy gelding: little sign of ability: tongue tied last 3 outings. *A. Ennis* **c77 ? h–**

HOWABOYS QUEST (USA) 8 b.g. Quest For Fame – Doctor Black (USA) (Family Doctor (USA)) [2004/5 c64, h80: 20d 23m^3 22g c20g^5 c21m^3 24s^4 20g^{pu} c20d^4 Nov 28] winning hurdler/maiden chaser, largely below form in 2004/5: stays 21f: acts on firm and good to soft going: usually blinkered/in cheekpieces. *Ferdy Murphy* **c85 h82**

HOWARD'S LASS 4 ch.f. Compton Place – Al Guswa (Shernazar) [2004/5 F13d Nov 28] 10,000Y: eighth foal: half-sister to several winners, including useful 7f to 1½m winner Tough Leader (by Lead On Time) and fairly useful 1¼m to 2¼m winner King Flyer (by Ezzoud): dam Irish 1m (at 2 yrs) and 1¼m winner: never a factor in 3-y-o bumper on debut. *I. Semple* **F–**

HOWARDS ROCKET 4 ch.g. Opening Verse (USA) – Houston Heiress (USA) (Houston (USA)) [2004/5 16s^{pu} 16d Nov 27] little form on Flat: no show in 2 juvenile hurdles. *J. S. Goldie* **h–**

HOWAYA PET (IRE) 9 br.m. Montelimar (USA) – Sarahs Music (IRE) (Orchestra) [2004/5 c25g* c24v^6 c21d^F c22v^5 c24s^4 c29d* c24s^4 c24v^6 c28v^4 c26v^3 c29s^4 c25g^6 Apr 8] useful-looking mare: fairly useful handicap chaser: won at Punchestown in April 2004 and Fairyhouse (beat Mullacash 11 lengths) in November: improved further after, fourth rallying strongly after bad mistake 5 out, to Numbersixvalverde in 29f Irish Grand National at Fairyhouse in March and second to Dublin Hunter in amateur event at Punchestown in late-April: suted by thorough test of stamina: raced on good going or softer (acts on heavy): tongue tied: tough and genuine. *G. Keane, Ireland* **c127 h–**

HOWDYDOODY (IRE) 9 b.g. Hawkstone (IRE) – Larry's Law (IRE) (Law Society (USA)) [2004/5 c118, h100: c26d^2 c33d^3 c24s^{pu} Apr 16] lengthy gelding: fair hurdler: fairly useful handicap chaser: off 13 months, good efforts when placed at Chepstow and Uttoxeter, 8 lengths third to Philson Run in valuable event at latter: stays 33f: acts on soft and good to firm going: tried blinkered: tongue tied: often soon off bridle: sold 15,000 gns Doncaster May Sales. *P. F. Nicholls* **c119 h–**

HOW GREAT THOU ART 9 b.g. Almoojid – Mamamere (Tres Gate) [2004/5 h74: 19m* 22d^3 19g^{pu} Apr 1] big, lengthy gelding: modest hurdler: won conditional jockeys handicap at Hereford in September: stays 2¾m: acts on good to firm and good to soft going. *P. J. Hobbs* **h91 +**

HOWLE HILL (IRE) 5 b.g. Ali-Royal (IRE) – Grandeur And Grace (USA) (Septieme Ciel (USA)) [2004/5 h133: 16m 16m^3 16d^3 16g^3 16d Feb 12] leggy gelding: smart on Flat (stays 1¼m), successful in January: useful handicap hurdler: good efforts when third to Perouse at Wincanton and Distant Prospect at Newbury third and fourth starts: ideally suited by emphasis on speed at 2m: acts on good to soft and good to firm going: patiently ridden. *A. King* **h140**

HOW RAN ON (IRE) 14 br.g. Mandalus – Kelly's Bridge (Netherkelly) [2004/5 c76x, h–: c16g^{pu} c18m^{6} c16m^{2} Jun 8] poor handicap chaser: raced mainly around 2m nowadays: acts on any going: tried in cheekpieces: tongue tied once: front runner. *Mrs L. Williamson* **c69 h–**

HOWSHAM LAD 6 b.g. Perpendicular – Sherwood Hope (Eborneezer) [2004/5 F–: F16g F17v^{4} F17m^{pu} Apr 23] smallish gelding: no form in bumpers. *G. P. Kelly* **F–**

HUCKLEBERRY FINN 5 b.g. Sadler's Wells (USA) – Cruising Height (Shirley Heights) [2004/5 F16d F16d F17s^{4} F17s 16s Dec 13] sturdy gelding: eighth foal: half-brother to 3 winners, including very smart middle-distance stayer High And Low and smart stayer Corradini (both by Rainbow Quest): dam, 10.5f and 1½m winner, half-sister to Park Hill winner Trampship: bought unraced out of G. L. Moore's stable £10,500 Ascot June Sales: no form in bumpers or in novice on hurdling debut: wore cheekpieces last 2 starts. *R. J. Price* **h– F–**

HUE 4 ch.g. Peintre Celebre (USA) – Quandary (USA) (Blushing Groom (FR)) [2004/5 16d^{3} 17g^{4} 16g^{3} Feb 27] small, close-coupled gelding: half-brother to winning 2m hurdler Predicament (by Machiavellian): in frame all 3 starts on Flat in France, sold out of Mme C. Head-Maarek's stable 27,000 gns Newmarket Autumn Sales: best effort over hurdles when fourth to Credit in juvenile at Musselburgh: room for improvement in his jumping. *B. Ellison* **h103**

HUGO DE GREZ (FR) 10 b.g. Useful (FR) – Piqua Des Gres (FR) (Waylay) [2004/5 c127d, h–: c26s^{4} c26s^{5} c25s^{3} Dec 5] close-coupled gelding: useful chaser at one time, nowhere near so good nowadays: stays 3½m: acts on heavy going: effective tongue tied or not: has won 6 times at Carlisle. *A. Parker* **c115 h–**

HUGO DE PERRO (FR) 10 b.g. Perrault – Fontaine Aux Faons (FR) (Nadjar (FR)) [2004/5 c–x, h131§: 22m^{rtr} 23s 20v 20s^{5} 20d 22d^{pu} Apr 11] leggy gelding: winning hurdler/chaser: left P. Monteith after first outing: stays 3m: acts on heavy and good to firm going: wears cheekpieces nowadays: has refused to race 5 times: thoroughly untrustworthy. *Miss Lucinda V. Russell* **c– x h100 §**

HUKA LODGE (IRE) 8 ch.g. Roselier (FR) – Derrella (Derrylin) [2004/5 h100: c20s^{ur} c25v* c21s^{F} 23v^{2} c24s^{3} 24s^{5} c24v* Apr 17] fair handicap hurdler: fairly useful chaser: won novice handicaps at Hexham in November and Carlisle (beating Tom Fruit 16 lengths) in April: stays 25f: raced on going softer than good (acts on heavy): whipped round start fifth outing. *L. Lungo* **c120 h101**

HUMDINGER (IRE) 5 b.m. Charnwood Forest (IRE) – High Finish (High Line) [2004/5 19d Nov 28] fair on Flat (stays 1¾m) at 3 yrs: no form since, including on hurdling debut. *D. Shaw* **h–**

HUMID CLIMATE 5 ch.g. Desert King (IRE) – Pontoon (Zafonic (USA)) [2004/5 h103: 17s^{5} 16m^{3} 16g^{6} 16m^{4} Apr 17] strong, good-bodied gelding: fairly useful 1¼m winner on Flat, well beaten in 2004: modest maiden hurdler: raced around 2m: has carried head awkwardly. *R. A. Fahey* **h99**

HUM (IRE) 4 ch.f. Cadeaux Genereux – Ensorceleuse (FR) (Fabulous Dancer (USA)) [2004/5 16g^{pu} 21g Mar 28] poor maiden on Flat: no show in 2 starts over hurdles. *Miss D. A. McHale* **h–**

HUMMING 8 b.g. Bluebird (USA) – Risanda (Kris) [2004/5 h–: 20d Apr 22] leggy gelding: lightly raced: poor hurdler: should stay at least 2½m: tried tongue tied. *Miss M. E. Rowland* **h–**

HUNCA MUNCA (IRE) 6 b.m. Presenting – Tulladante (IRE) (Phardante (FR)) [2004/5 F16g Apr 26] €12,000 3-y-o: fourth foal: dam unraced sister to dam of smart staying hurdler Emotional Moment: winning pointer, including in March: no show in mares bumper. *N. J. Pomfret* **F–**

HUNCHEON SISS (IRE) 8 b.m. Phardante (FR) – Parsons Term (IRE) (The Parson) [2004/5 h–: 20g^{3} c21m^{4} May 19] good-topped mare: modest maiden hurdler: poor form when fourth in novice at Sedgefield on chasing debut: stays 2½m: acts on soft going: usually tongue tied. *J. Howard Johnson* **c74 h89**

HUNORISK (FR) 4 b.f. Mansonnien (FR) – La Vie Immobile (USA) (Alleged (USA)) [2004/5 18s* 18s^{2} 18s^{ur} 16d^{3} 16v^{6} 18v* 18v^{3} Apr 17] lengthy, angular filly: sister to fair 2m hurdle winner Life Is Life: dam unraced half-sister to leading 1999/00 juvenile hurdler Grand Seigneur (by Mansonnien): 1½m winner on Flat: fairly useful juvenile hurdler: won at Auteuil in September and March: creditable efforts when placed, staying-on third to Calomeria at Sandown fourth outing: unbeaten in 3 starts over fences, at Compiegne **c120 h110**

and Auteuil (twice), completing hat-trick in Group 3 Prix La Perichole in June: will stay beyond 2½m: raced on ground softer than good. *G. Macaire, France*

HUNTER PUDDING 5 b.m. Shambo – Pudding (Infantry) [2004/5 F17s⁴ 16v³ Jan 8] first foal: dam winning pointer: beaten long way in mares bumper and novice hurdle: sold £3,100 Ascot April Sales. *B. I. Case* **h– F–**

HUNTERS TWEED 9 ch.g. Nashwan (USA) – Zorette (USA) (Zilzal (USA)) [2004/5 c138, h–: c25d² c22vpu 20d⁶ c21gpu c24spu Apr 21] leggy gelding: useful handicap chaser: form over fences in 2004/5 only when second to Joe Blake at Wetherby: winning hurdler: fair form when sixth to Spring Pursuit in handicap at Haydock: stays 25f: acts on heavy and good to firm going: wore blinkers/cheekpieces 4 of last 5 starts: usually races prominently. *P. Beaumont* **c134 d h113**

HUNTING YUPPIE (IRE) 8 ch.g. Treasure Hunter – Super Yuppie (Belfalas) [2004/5 h108: 24g* 24g* c20g² Oct 9] robust gelding: fairly useful hurdler: won novices at Bangor and Worcester (beat Fromragstoriches 2½ lengths) very early in season: 2½ lengths second to Comply Or Die in maiden at Bangor on chasing debut: stays 3m: raced on good going or softer: looked likely to improve over fences but not seen out again. *N. A. Twiston-Davies* **c114 h116**

HURDLE (FR) 10 gr.g. Dadarissime (FR) – Ulisa II (FR) (Pot d'Or (FR)) [2004/5 18s 18d c17gpu 16g 16g⁶ 20d Dec 8] angular gelding: successful up to 11f on Flat: fairly useful hurdler/chaser: successful 7 times in French Provinces prior to winning 2 handicaps and 2 claimers at Auteuil in 2003/4: claimed from P. Cottin €16,100, little impact in Britain: stays 21f: acts on soft going: wore blinkers/cheekpieces last 3 outings. *Miss A. M. Newton-Smith* **c– h108 ?**

HURLERS CROSS (IRE) 7 b.g. Jurado (USA) – Maid of Music (IRE) (Orchestra) [2004/5 c83, h72: c25dpu c25g c26m⁴ c28d³ c24spu c27mpu c26g* Mar 28] poor maiden hurdler: modest handicap chaser: off 4 months and left M. Appleby, won handicap at Plumpton in March: stays 3¼m: acts on good to soft going: has worn blinkers/cheekpieces: sketchy jumper. *Mrs H. Dalton* **c88 x h–**

HURRICANE ALLEY (IRE) 4 b.g. Ali-Royal (IRE) – Trumped (IRE) (Last Tycoon) [2004/5 16s² 16d 16s³ 16v* Apr 14] dam half-sister to fair hurdler up to 3m Morning Blush: fairly useful on Flat (stays 11f): similar standard over hurdles, won maiden at Tipperary easily by 12 lengths, soon clear: creditable fifth to Strides of Fire in minor event at Punchestown later in month: raced at 2m on going softer than good. *G. M. Lyons, Ireland* **h121**

HURRICANE BAY 9 ch.g. Karinga Bay – Clodaigh Gale (Strong Gale) [2004/5 c82, h71: 24d 26g⁴ c25mpu 25m⁴ 20d⁶ c30dpu 25g Dec 28] lengthy gelding: winning chaser/maiden hurdler, little show in 2004/5: suited by 3m+: tried blinkered/in cheekpieces, including last 4 starts: has had tongue tied. *P. D. Niven* **c– h68**

HURRICANE DIPPER (IRE) 7 b.g. Glacial Storm (USA) – Minnies Dipper (Royal Captive) [2004/5 h–: c23gpu c20s² c21d⁶ c25g c21spu c26v⁵ c25s⁵ c26g² Mar 14] tall gelding: bad maiden hurdler/chaser: stays 3¼m: wore cheekpieces after reappearance. *Miss A. M. Newton-Smith* **c56 h–**

HURRY BOB (IRE) 10 b.g. Bob Back (USA) – Dundovail (Dunphy) [2004/5 24g* 22m 22m* 24s⁵ 20d⁴ 24s c20sbd c16s⁵ c18d c20d³ Mar 31] tall gelding: fairly useful handicap hurdler: won at Punchestown in April 2004 and Cork (tongue tied) in August: only modest form in novice company over fences: stays 3m: acts on any going. *Thomas Mullins, Ireland* **c96 h115**

HUSKY (POL) 7 b.g. Special Power – Hallo Bambina (POL) (Neman (POL)) [2004/5 h79: 16m² 16g 16d 16m 16gF Mar 18] sturdy gelding: modest on Flat in Britain, stays 1¼m: poor maiden hurdler: will prove best at sharp 2m: acts on good to firm going: wears cheekpieces: usually front runner. *R. M. H. Cowell* **h79**

HUSSARD COLLONGES (FR) 10 b.g. Video Rock (FR) – Ariane Collonges (FR) (Quart de Vin (FR)) [2004/5 c158, h–: 20d c24g⁵ c24g c33gpu Apr 16] useful-looking gelding: impresses in appearance: top-class chaser at best: reportedly cracked pelvis and off 14 months, little show in handicaps in 2004/5, including over hurdles: should stay beyond 3¼m: raced on good going or softer (acts on heavy). *P. Beaumont* **c– h–**

HUTCH 7 b.g. Rock Hopper – Polly's Teahouse (Shack (USA)) [2004/5 h92: 16g³ 16g⁴ 17d* May 29] lengthy gelding: modest hurdler: won novice at Cartmel in May: raced mainly around 2m on good going or softer. *P. Beaumont* **h98**

HUW THE NEWS 6 b.g. Primo Dominie – Martha Stevens (USA) (Super Concorde (USA)) [2004/5 h–, F–: 17s 17m^{6} 16v^{5} 17g Apr 12] little sign of ability. *S. C. Burrough* **h75 ?**

HUXLEY (IRE) 6 b.g. Danehill Dancer (IRE) – Biddy Mulligan (Ballad Rock) [2004/5 h85: 16g 16d Nov 9] leggy gelding: fairly useful on Flat (stays 1¼m), successful in September: poor maiden hurdler: tongue tied last 2 starts: headway. *M. G. Quinlan* **h76**

HYLIA 6 ch.m. Sir Harry Lewis (USA) – Lady Stock (Crofter (USA)) [2004/5 h78, F78: 20g 21g^{2} 22d^{3} Apr 17] unfurnished mare: modest hurdler: stays 2¾m: acts on good to soft going. *Mrs P. Robeson* **h87**

HYPARK (IRE) 6 br.m. Oscar (IRE) – La Ronde (Common Grounds) [2004/5 F16g Aug 18] first foal: dam unraced half-sister to useful jumper up to 3m Palette: unseated rider leaving paddock prior to well held in bumper on debut. *C. Roberts* **F–**

I

IACACIA (FR) 9 b. or br.g. Silver Rainbow – Palencia (FR) (Taj Dewan) [2004/5 c95, h85: c21d^{ur} Feb 18] small, sparely-made gelding: winning chaser/maiden hurdler: reportedly lame in point in March: stays 2¾m: acts on soft and good to firm going: tried blinkered. *G. F. Edwards* **c– h–**

IADORA 10 br.m. Gildoran – Combe Hill (Crozier) [2004/5 c–, h–: c24d May 15] rather leggy mare: winning pointer: poor maiden hurdler/chaser: seems to stay 25f: acts on heavy going. *Patrick Thompson* **c– h–**

IAMBE DE LA SEE (FR) 9 b.m. Useful (FR) – Reine Mati (SWI) (Matahawk) [2004/5 h97: c20d^{2} c16s^{4} c16d^{F} c16d^{5} c16v^{2} c17g^{3} Mar 27] useful-looking mare: modest hurdler: fair chaser: 10 lengths clear when fell last in mares novice at Leicester in November: raced mainly around 2m on good going or softer (acts on heavy): free-going front runner. *N. J. Henderson* **c102 h–**

I AM SAID I (IRE) 7 b.g. Presenting – Moonlight Romance (Teenoso (USA)) [2004/5 c24m* c23m c24g^{3} c25s^{pu} c24g Apr 15] half-brother to fair chaser Seven Mile Gale (by Strong Gale), stays 2½m: dam ran 3 times on Flat in Ireland: winning pointer: won maiden at Uttoxeter in July on chasing debut: sold out of M. Pipe's stable 24,000 gns Doncaster August Sales after next start: best effort in hunters when third at Taunton. *C. J. Bennett* **c92**

IAN'S BOY 9 ch.g. Current Edition (IRE) – Lady Verdi (USA) (Monteverdi) [2004/5 26m^{pu} Jun 9] winning pointer: looked temperamental on hurdling debut. *W. K. Goldsworthy* **h–**

IBAL (FR) 9 b.g. Balsamo (FR) – Quart d'Hekla (FR) (Quart de Vin (FR)) [2004/5 c–, h–: c17g^{pu} c16s^{3} c20s^{pu} c17s^{pu} c20v* c20s Apr 2] big, useful-looking gelding: useful chaser in 2002/3: left Mrs N. Smith, form since only when winning handicap at Leicester in March: best form up to 2½m (finished very tired when winning at 3¼m): raced on good going or softer (acts well on heavy): tongue tied last 2 starts: usually front runner. *P. F. Nicholls* **c111 h–**

IBERUS (GER) 7 b.g. Monsun (GER) – Iberica (GER) (Green Dancer (USA)) [2004/5 h–: 17s^{2} 17d* 16d^{5} Nov 27] angular gelding: fair on Flat in 2004: fair hurdler: won ladies handicap at Sedgefield in November: raced around 2m: acts on soft going: tried in cheekpieces/visor. *S. Gollings* **h107**

IBIN ST JAMES 11 b.g. Salse (USA) – St James's Antigua (IRE) (Law Society (USA)) [2004/5 c99, h–: 24v^{4} Feb 20] sturdy gelding: winning chaser: poor hurdler: stays 29f: acts on soft going: blinkered nowadays: temperament under suspicion. *M. Bradstock* **c– h83**

IBIS ROCHELAIS (FR) 9 b.g. Passing Sale (FR) – Ta Rochelaise (FR) (Carmont (FR)) [2004/5 c125, h–: c24s^{ur} May 5] big, lengthy gelding: fairly useful handicap chaser: appeared to suffer serious injury only start in 2004/5: stays 3m: acts on soft going: has reportedly broken blood vessels. *A. Ennis* **c– h–**

ICANNSHIFT (IRE) 5 b.g. Night Shift (USA) – Cannikin (IRE) (Lahib (USA)) [2004/5 16m Aug 30] compact gelding: half-brother to winning hurdler around 2m Canni Thinkaar (by Alhaarth): modest on Flat (stays 11f), joined T. Jones before final start in 2004: well held in maiden on hurdling debut. *S. Dow* **h–**

ICARE D'OUDAIRIES (FR) 9 ch.g. Port Etienne (FR) – Vellea (FR) (Cap Martin (FR)) [2004/5 h105: c26g^{2} May 9] workmanlike gelding: fair handicap hurdler: modest **c93 h–**

form on chasing debut when second in maiden at Plumpton: best at 2½m+: acts on heavy going: visored once: sold 12,000 gns Doncaster May Sales, resold £9,000 Ascot July Sales. *C. L. Tizzard*

ICARUS DREAM (IRE) 4 ch.g. Intikhab (USA) – Nymphs Echo (IRE) (Mujtahid (USA)) [2004/5 16m* 16s^5 17d* 16g^3 Nov 18] leggy gelding: half-brother to winning 2¼m hurdler Kirov King (by Desert King): fair maiden at best on Flat (stayed 9f) for D. Weld: modest form over hurdles: won juveniles at Plumpton in September and Folkestone (handicap) in November: dead. *P. R. Hedger* **h89**

ICE AND FIRE 6 b.g. Cadeaux Genereux – Tanz (IRE) (Sadler's Wells (USA)) [2004/5 h–: 16g^5 16g^3 16g 17g 16g Jan 14] medium-sized gelding: modest form at best over hurdles, left B. Leavy after third start: barely stays 2m: raced on good/good to soft ground. *J. T. Stimpson* **h84**

ICEBERGE (IRE) 9 b.g. Glacial Storm (USA) – Laura Daisy (Buckskin (FR)) [2004/5 22g^{pu} Sep 12] lengthy gelding: modest hurdler in 2002/3 for I. Williams: off 17 months, let down by jumping in handicap at Stratford on return: stays 3¼m: acts on heavy going, probably on good to firm. *Jonjo O'Neill* **h– x**

ICE BUCKET (IRE) 5 ch.g. Glacial Storm (USA) – Tranbu (IRE) (Buckskin (FR)) [2004/5 F17s^3 F16d^6 Mar 14] second foal: dam unraced half-sister to useful hurdler/chaser up to 3m Tryfirion: signs of ability in bumpers, not knocked about after having plenty to do second start. *Miss H. C. Knight* **F83**

ICE COOL LAD (IRE) 11 b.g. Glacial Storm (USA) – My Serena (No Argument) [2004/5 c87, h–: c25g c24d^{pu} c20s^{pu} c28g^6 Mar 20] sturdy gelding: modest handicap chaser at best: no show in 2004/5: stays easy 3½m: acts on heavy going: blinkered once. *R. Rowe* **c–** **h–**

ICE CREAM (FR) 4 ch.f. Cyborg (FR) – Icone (FR) (Nikos) [2004/5 F13g F16d Feb 12] 13,500 3-y-o: unfurnished filly: first foal: dam, 15f hurdle winner, half-sister to very smart 2m hurdler/useful chaser Santenay: better effort in bumpers when seventh of 18 at Doncaster on debut: well held in Grade 2 at Newbury next time. *M. E. D. Francis* **F76**

ICE CRYSTAL 8 b.g. Slip Anchor – Crystal Fountain (Great Nephew) [2004/5 h–: 25g 22s^2 22d^2 24s^2 24s^4 24g^6 24d^3 25s^{pu} 25s* 22d^2 24d^5 c25d^2 c24v^4 c23m Apr 10] leggy gelding: fair handicap hurdler: won at Warwick in January: modest form at best in maiden chases (let down by jumping last 2 starts): thorough stayer: acts on heavy going: tried in cheekpieces/blinkers: hard ride. *W. K. Goldsworthy* **c97 §** **h112 §**

ICE RAIN (IRE) 5 gr.g. Zaffaran (USA) – Turbet Lass (IRE) (Carlingford Castle) [2004/5 F–: F17g^3 F17m^3 21g^4 16v 20s 22d Nov 14] strong, lengthy gelding: poor form in bumpers: soundly beaten all 4 starts over hurdles: blinkered first 2 starts, visored final one: tried tongue tied. *Evan Williams* **h–** **F70**

ICE SAINT 10 gr.g. Ballacashtal (CAN) – Sylvan Song (Song) [2004/5 c–, h–: 22g^{pu} Sep 12] good-topped gelding: winning hurdler: unseated only start over fences: should stay 3m: acts on heavy and good to firm going. *Mrs C. A. Dunnett* **c–** **h–**

ICHI BEAU (IRE) 11 b.g. Convinced – May As Well (Kemal (FR)) [2004/5 c123, h116: c16m^2 May 14] sturdy, deep-bodied gelding: fairly useful hurdler/chaser: barely stays 2½m: acts on heavy and good to firm going: tried in cheekpieces: usually tongue tied: effective held up or making running: bold jumper of fences, though inclined to make odd mistake. *A. J. Martin, Ireland* **c123** **h–**

ICY BLAST (IRE) 6 b.g. Glacial Storm (USA) – Fair Lisselan (IRE) (Kemal (FR)) [2004/5 F94: 16g^3 20s^2 Nov 24] rangy gelding: bumper winner: better effort over hurdles (fair form) when second in novice at Chepstow: stays 2½m. *P. R. Webber* **h101**

ICY PROSPECT (IRE) 7 ch.g. Glacial Storm (USA) – Prospect Lady (IRE) (Boreen (FR)) [2004/5 F16g* 20g* 25g^4 24d 25v^4 24d^{pu} Mar 12] €10,000 4-y-o: angular gelding: first foal: dam modest maiden hurdler: won maiden on completed start in Irish points: won bumper at Perth in September and novice hurdle at Bangor in October: folded tamely last 2 starts: should stay beyond 2½m. *N. A. Twiston-Davies* **h98** **F91**

IDAHO D'OX (FR) 9 b.g. Bad Conduct (USA) – Queseda (FR) (Quart de Vin (FR)) [2004/5 c126, h123: 20g 16d 16d 16d 24d^4 24g^2 20m^{pu} Apr 23] sparely-made gelding: winning chaser: fairly useful handicap hurdler: mostly creditable efforts in 2004/5, particularly so when in frame at Aintree and Cheltenham in April: stays 3m: acts on any going: formerly blinkered/visored: difficult ride. *M. C. Pipe* **c–** **h116**

IDEAL DU BOIS BEURY (FR) 9 b. or br.g. Useful (FR) – Pampa Star (FR) (Pampabird) [2004/5 c94, h–: c17v c16v4 c16v2 c20spu Mar 12] leggy gelding: winning hurdler: modest maiden chaser: stays 2½m: acts on any going: tried visored: held up. *P. Monteith* **c87 h–**

IDEAL JACK (FR) 9 b.g. Agent Bleu (FR) – Nuit Des Fanges (FR) (Trac) [2004/5 c17sur c21spu c19dpu c16s4 c19g3 c21s5 c19d2 c19mur c16d5 c19g Apr 15] good-topped gelding: winning hurdler: modest maiden chaser on balance: stays 2¾m: acts on firm and soft going: tried visored: makes mistakes. *G. A. Ham* **c85 x h–**

IDEALKO (FR) 9 b.g. Kadalko (FR) – Belfaster (FR) (Royal Charter (FR)) [2004/5 c101, h–: c20d2 c19g3 17d c20s3 c20d5 c19g 20g Mar 26] leggy gelding: maiden hurdler: fair handicap chaser: stays 2½m: acts on soft and good to firm going: tried blinkered, in cheekpieces first start: not a fluent jumper. *Ian Williams* **c101 x h–**

IDIOME (FR) 9 b.g. Djarvis (FR) – Asterie L'Ermitage (FR) (Hamster (FR)) [2004/5 c114, h–: 21d5 20v5 20s3 Mar 23] leggy gelding: fair chaser/hurdler: stays 21f: yet to race on firm going, acts on any other: has bled from nose. *Mrs L. C. Taylor* **c– h110**

IDLE JOURNEY (IRE) 4 b.g. Mujadil (USA) – Camassina (IRE) (Taufan (USA)) [2004/5 17s 16d6 16s5 16d Feb 24] rather leggy gelding: modest on Flat (stays 8.5f), successful in June for R. Donohoe: best effort over hurdles when fifth to Dusky Warbler in novice at Leicester: raced around 2m on good to soft/soft ground, likely to prove at least as effective with greater emphasis on speed. *M. Scudamore* **h95 +**

IDLE TALK (IRE) 6 br.g. Hubbly Bubbly (USA) – Belon Breeze (IRE) (Strong Gale) [2004/5 24s* 24d4 23d* 24dpu Apr 8] strong gelding: will make a chaser: second foal: dam ran once: won maiden Irish point in 2004: fairly useful form over hurdles, winning maiden at Chepstow in October and novice at Lingfield (made all when easily beating Theatre 7 lengths) in February: disappointing in Grade 1 novice at Aintree final start: raced around 3m: acts on soft going. *T. R. George* **h127**

IDLEWILD (IRE) 10 br.g. Phardante (FR) – Delia Murphy (Golden Love) [2004/5 c–§, h–§: 21v5 19d 16v* 19g6 20d 16g4 c16d4 Apr 5] workmanlike gelding: modest hurdler: improved form when making all in novice seller at Uttoxeter in February: poor form on first completed outing in chases: should stay beyond 2m: acts on heavy going: tried blinkered: formerly ungenuine. *C. T. Pogson* **c78 h91**

IDOLE FIRST (IRE) 6 b.g. Flemensfirth (USA) – Sharon Doll (IRE) (Shahrastani (USA)) [2004/5 h114: 16d* 16d6 16v2 16d6 21g* 24s4 Apr 7] **h144**

The Cheltenham Festival victories of Idole First in the Coral Cup and King Harald in the Jewson Novices' Handicap Chase both produced a ticklish situation for Jockey Club officials. Idole First ran in the colours of Direct Sales UK Limited, the banner used by owner Dean Shakespeare who had been asked to co-operate with a Jockey Club investigation (still on-going at the time of going to press) into the running of one of his horses, the Ian Williams-trained Wild Power, who was narrowly beaten in a conditional jockeys handicap hurdle at Taunton in March 2004. Wild Power's rider Willie Worthington was banned for fourteen days for making insufficient effort, *Timeform Perspective* labelling it 'as bad a case of its

Coral Cup (Handicap Hurdle), Cheltenham—
outsider Idole First (left) stays on much too strongly for Dancing Bay and Tumbling Dice (No.11)

sort seen in a long time.' Investigations were reopened in July 2004 when it was reportedly discovered that Wild Power had been laid by an individual—unconnected with the horse—whose activities 'interested' the Jockey Club. Wild Power's owner fell foul of the Jockey Club by not handing over his telephone records, reportedly claiming business confidentiality, as well as saying that he used a system which did not produce individual billing records. No further action has yet been taken in the Wild Power case but the rider of King Harald, Mattie Batchelor, had been fined £2,500 after a seven-hour hearing the week before Cheltenham for deliberately misleading Jockey Club officials looking into race-fixing allegations involving warned-off punter John McCracken. Batchelor claimed he did not know McCracken well and did not speak to him regularly, but inspection of his telephone records revealed regular calls to a number used by McCracken (Batchelor claimed the conversations were with an associate of McCracken). Batchelor had been interviewed—denying any impropriety—in connection with the defeats of Tollbrae at Leicester in February 2004 and Ice Saint at Fontwell in March that year. Batchelor had not ridden in either race and the jockeys of Tollbrae and Ice Saint, Marcus Foley and Sean Fox, had also come under investigation. Enquiries cleared Foley of any wrongdoing and Fox—originally banned for twenty-one days after controversially parting company with Ice Saint—was cleared on appeal of deliberately jumping off his mount. Batchelor's punishment could have been stiffer. Dale Jewett, an amateur rider who featured in another much publicised case which virtually collapsed—that of the Flat performer Hillside Girl, pulled up at Carlisle in June 2003—had received a three-month suspension for hindering and obstructing Jockey Club investigators.

Direct Sales UK Ltd's "Idole First"

Idole First's victory at 33/1 in the Coral Cup was one of the biggest upsets at the Festival, but an explanation for his improvement was not hard to find. A fair novice hurdler in 2003/4, Idole First progressed again on his reappearance to make a successful switch to handicap company in a fairly valuable event at Huntingdon in December, jumping noticeably more fluently. Idole First was kept to two miles in the latest season until stepped up to two miles five furlongs for the first time in the Coral Cup. He recorded creditable efforts in two of the season's most valuable handicaps, finishing sixth in the Ladbroke Handicap Hurdle at Sandown in January and in the totesport Trophy at Newbury in February, in between recording his best effort—under conditions which placed more emphasis on stamina—when beaten a length and a quarter by Dom d'Orgeval at Uttoxeter. Idole First consistently shaped as if he would do better over further and he proved extremely well suited by the extra distance in the twenty-nine-runner Coral Cup, chasing the leaders and staying on strongly from two out to lead on the flat and win by five lengths and six from Dancing Bay and Tumbling Dice. Idole First repeated the form when fourth to Monet's Garden, facing a stiffer task, in the three-mile Liverpool Hurdle on his only subsequent start.

Idole First (IRE) (b.g. 1999)	Flemensfirth (USA) (b 1992)	Alleged (b 1974)	Hoist The Flag
			Princess Pout
		Etheldreda (ch 1985)	Diesis
			Royal Bond
	Sharon Doll (IRE) (b 1991)	Shahrastani (ch 1983)	Nijinsky
			Shademah
		Ah Ya Zein (b 1983)	Artaius
			Come True

The smallish, angular Idole First joined his present stable as a four-year-old after winning four times on the Flat for Richard Chotard in France at up to thirteen and half furlongs. His sire the very smart Flemensfirth, one of Coolmore's current band of extremely busy National Hunt sires, was trained by John Gosden but ran his best races in France, gaining his most important win in the now-defunct Prix Lupin, and also winning the Prix Dollar twice. Idole First's dam Sharon Doll won at eight and a half furlongs and a mile and a quarter in France. Her other offspring include Kedic (by General Holme), a winner three times at up to a mile and a half, and Lorainovich (by Verbier), successful on the Flat at eight and a half furlongs, and first past the post in juvenile hurdles at Fontwell and Enghien in the latest season when he also won at Cagnes-sur-Mer on his chasing debut. Idole First stays three miles and acts on heavy going. *Miss Venetia Williams*

IDRIS (GER) 4 ch.c. Generous (IRE) – Idraak (Kris) [2004/5 F12g aF13g* F13s^5 16d 18s^3 16d Mar 4] £6,000 3-y-o: sturdy colt: sixth foal: closely related to smart 1½m performer Iscan (by Caerleon) and half-brother to useful Irish 1¼m winner Legacy (by Carnegie) and fairly useful 1½m winner Idrica (by Rainbow Quest): dam, French middle-distance maiden, half-sister to Oaks winner Snow Bride, herself dam of Lammtarra: fair form in 3-y-o bumpers, made all on polytrack at Lingfield in November: easily best effort in juvenile hurdles when third at Fontwell. *G. L. Moore* **h103** **F93**

I D TECHNOLOGY (IRE) 9 ch.g. Commanche Run – Lady Geeno (IRE) (Cheval) [2004/5 h102: 16d^2 18m^2 17d^2 Jul 17] rangy gelding: modest hurdler: likely to stay 2½m: acts on good to firm and good to soft going. *G. L. Moore* **h98**

IFRANE BALIMA (FR) 9 ch.g. Video Rock (FR) – Balima Des Saccart (FR) (Quart de Vin (FR)) [2004/5 c90, h–: 19d^{bd} c16g^F Nov 11] rather leggy gelding: modest hurdler: similar form on only completed start over fences: raced mainly around 2m: acts on soft and good to firm going: visored once, blinkered both outings in 2004/5. *P. F. Nicholls* **c–** **h94**

IGLOO D'ESTRUVAL (FR) 9 br.g. Garde Royale – Jalousie (FR) (Blockhaus) [2004/5 c113x, h95§: c25g 24d* 27g^3 24s* Nov 2] lengthy, useful-looking gelding: winning chaser: fairly useful handicap hurdler: won at Exeter in May and November: stays 3¾m: acts on soft going: usually visored before last 3 starts: sketchy jumper of fences. *Mrs L. C. Taylor* **c– x** **h115**

IGLOUX ROYAL (FR) 9 b.g. Lights Out (FR) – Onde Royale (FR) (Danoso) [2004/5 c21d^F May 15] no show in bumper or maiden hunter chase 2½ years apart. *Mrs S. Smith-Kellard* **c–**

I GOT RHYTHM 7 gr.m. Lycius (USA) – Eurythmic (Pharly (FR)) [2004/5 h96: 22d 19m 20m 24d^3 24g^F 20m 20g 19g^3 16g* 16s^5 20s^6 Apr 21] angular mare: modest hurdler: won seller at Catterick in March: effective 2m to 3m: acts on soft and good to firm going. *K. G. Reveley* **h97**

I HAVNT A CENT (IRE) 8 b.g. Unfuwain (USA) – Miss Gris (USA) (Hail The Pirates (USA)) [2004/5 c22v^5 c20s^F c20s^6 c22s^3 Apr 13] half-brother to several winners, including smart 7f to 1m winner Mahoob (by Marju) and fairly useful 2m hurdler Elflaa (by Sure Blade): dam very smart 2-y-o, won at up to 10.5f: fairly useful bumper winner: no form over hurdles: fair form in maiden chases: stays 2¾m. *S. Donohoe, Ireland* **c102 h–**

I HEAR THUNDER (IRE) 7 b.g. Montelimar (USA) – Carrigeen Gala (Strong Gale) [2004/5 c99, h79: c24d^F 21g^3 c23s^5 c22s^2 c23d^3 c25d^3 c20v^3 c25s^2 c21s^4 c21s* c22g^2 Mar 4] lengthy gelding: modest maiden hurdler: fair chaser: won maiden at Folkestone in February: stays 25f: raced on good going or softer (acts on soft). *R. H. Buckler* **c114 h92**

IKDAM MELODY (IRE) 9 b.g. Ikdam – Music Slipper (Orchestra) [2004/5 24g 24m^6 c22f* c24f^3 c25d^3 Apr 11] sturdy ex-Irish gelding: fair hurdler at best: won maiden at Wexford on chasing debut in May: sold out of M. Halford's stable 17,000 gns Doncaster August Sales after fourth start: successful in point in March: stays 25f: acts on firm and soft ground: tried in cheekpieces. *Miss J. E. Foster* **c100 h94**

IKTITAF (IRE) 4 b.g. Alhaarth (IRE) – Istibshar (USA) (Mr Prospector (USA)) [2004/5 16s^4 Feb 19] fairly useful on Flat (will stay 1½m), sold out of J. Gosden's stable 85,000 gns Newmarket Autumn Sales: around 13 lengths fourth to Majlis in Grade 3 juvenile at Fairyhouse on hurdling debut, travelling comfortably until 2 out. *N. Meade, Ireland* **h110**

ILABON (FR) 9 ch.g. Secret Haunt (USA) – Ahuille (FR) (Haltea (FR)) [2004/5 h114: 22g^2 Apr 28] angular gelding: fair hurdler: found little in amateur novice at Exeter only start in 2004/5: stays 2½m: acts on soft and good to firm going: visored last 3 starts. *M. C. Pipe* **h91 +**

IL'ATHOU (FR) 9 b.g. Lute Antique (FR) – Va Thou Line (FR) (El Badr) [2004/5 c–, h98: c24d^3 c20s^F c24v^5 c19d^4 Mar 12] tall, lengthy gelding: winning hurdler: useful handicap chaser at best, generally disappointing since 2002/3: best form at 2½m: acts on heavy going: tends to get on toes: bold-jumping front runner who races freely. *S. E. H. Sherwood* **c126 h–**

IL CAPRICCIO (IRE) 5 b.g. Windsor Castle – Brogeen View (Kambalda) [2004/5 F16d Mar 10] 18,000 4-y-o: fifth foal: half-brother to winning 2m hurdler Boston Melody (by Phardante) and fairly useful pointer Lord of The Mist (by Mister Lord): dam once-raced sister to fairly useful chaser up to 3¼m Buck Willow: never a factor in maiden bumper on debut. *B. J. M. Ryall* **F74**

IL CAVALIERE 10 b.g. Mtoto – Kalmia (Miller's Mate) [2004/5 h121x: c24d^2 c22d^F c17v^4 19d 21d^4 23s^6 c24m^2 c24g^2 c25s^3 c20g^{ur} Mar 16] sturdy gelding: fairly useful hurdler in 2003/4, well below best in 2004/5: fair novice chaser: stays easy 3m: acts on firm and good to soft going: usually held up: tends to make mistakes. *K. G. Reveley* **c101 h103 x**

IL DE BOITRON (FR) 7 b.g. Sheyrann – Ilkiya (FR) (Red Regent) [2004/5 16d^4 20d c17s^2 c19v^4 c16v^2 c16d c17v* c20v^4 c18s c24s c20g^4 c20d^4 Apr 3] IR £11,000 3-y-o: good-topped gelding: second foal: dam once-raced half-sister to smart middle-distance performers Ifrad and Istikal: maiden hurdler: fairly useful novice chaser: won maiden at Limerick in December: ran well when fourth to Carrigeen Victor at Gowran next time: stays 2½m: raced mainly on going softer than good (acts on heavy): tried blinkered. *T. G. O'Leary, Ireland* **c119 h–**

IL DUCE (IRE) 5 br.g. Anshan – Glory-Glory (IRE) (Buckskin (FR)) [2004/5 F17g^5 F16d^2 aF16g* 16g^2 16d^2 21d* 24d^{pu} 20d* Apr 22] €10,500 3-y-o: tall, useful-looking gelding: will make a chaser: first foal: dam lightly-raced, out of half-sister to useful chaser up to 25f Yorkshire Gale: won bumper on polytrack at Lingfield in December: fairly useful form over hurdles, dead-heated with Bengo in novice at Newbury in March and beat same rival by 9 lengths in similar event at Chepstow in April: reportedly lost action in Grade 1 novice at Aintree in between: stays 21f: acts on good to soft going. *A. King* **h121 + F103**

ILE DE PARIS (FR) 6 b.g. Cadoudal (FR) – Sweet Beauty (FR) (Tip Moss (FR)) [2004/5 h98: 21g* 23d^6 c24d^2 c23d^2 c23s* c24d^{pu} Mar 3] leggy gelding: fair novice hurdler: won at Warwick in May: similar form over fences, winning maiden at Exeter in January: stays 3m: raced on good going or softer. *P. J. Hobbs* **c112 h106**

ILE FACILE (IRE) 4 b.g. Turtle Island (IRE) – Easy Pop (IRE) (Shernazar) [2004/5 17d^5 Feb 1] leggy gelding: fair on Flat (stays 1½m), successful twice in 2004, sold out of N. Littmoden's stable 20,000 gns Newmarket Autumn Sales: pulled hard when fifth to Noble Request in novice at Taunton on hurdling debut: may do better. *B. De Haan* **h87 +**

IL EN REVE (FR) 7 b.g. Denham Red (FR) – Itaparica (FR) (Kind of Hush) [2004/5 22m^3 24f* 24f^5 c20f* 24m^3 c22g^2 c20s^5 c20s* c24s^5 c22d^3 c20v^2 c21s^4 c24v^5 c24s Mar 5] IR £5,000 3-y-o: lengthy gelding: fifth foal: half-brother to winning chaser up to 21f Ithuriel and winning cross-country chaser around 3m Itapasquini (both by Dom Pasquini): dam lightly-raced maiden on Flat: fair hurdler: won intermediate at Kilbeggan in May: fairly useful novice chaser: won at Wexford (maiden) in July and Cork (by 25 lengths from Big King) in October: ran well when fourth to Carrigeen Victor in Grade 1 at Leopardstown: stays 3m: acts on firm and soft going: tried in blinkers/cheekpieces. *S. J. Treacy, Ireland* **c117 h106**

ILIOS 6 b.g. Grand Lodge (USA) – Ilanga (IRE) (Common Grounds) [2004/5 17m^{pu} May 23] fairly useful 1m winner on Flat: poor over hurdles for B. Nolan: lame only start in 2004/5: tried tongue tied. *C. J. Mann* **h–**

I'LL CALL YOU BACK (IRE) 6 b.g. Zaffaran (USA) – Ben Tack (Lucifer (USA)) [2004/5 F16g^2 F18d* 19s^4 20d^2 18d^4 20v^4 20v^4 16v* 16s^6 16s Mar 29] good-topped gelding: sixth reported foal: dam unraced half-sister to fairly useful hurdler/chaser up to 2½m Stigon: fairly useful in bumpers, won at Downpatrick in October: fairly useful hurdler, won novice at Tramore in January: in process of showing improved form (3 lengths clear) when falling last in handicap won by Stutter at Punchestown in late-April: stays 2½m: raced on good going or softer (acts on heavy). *Mrs J. Harrington, Ireland* **h123 F102**

I'LL DO IT TODAY 4 b.g. Mtoto – Knayton Lass (Presidium) [2004/5 16d 16d 17d Feb 8] workmanlike gelding: half-brother to fair hurdler Mrs Jodi (by Yaheeb), stayed 2½m: twice-raced on Flat: no sign of ability in juvenile hurdles. *J. M. Jefferson* **h–**

I'LL FLY 5 ch.g. Polar Falcon (USA) – I'll Try (Try My Best (USA)) [2004/5 h78: 16d 16g Jan 19] poor novice hurdler. *J. R. Fanshawe* **h–**

ILLINEYLAD (IRE) 11 b.g. Whitehall Bridge – Illiney Girl (Lochnager) [2004/5 c66, h–: 20d Jun 23] sparely-made gelding: poor chaser: maiden hurdler: stays 25f: acts on good to firm and good to soft going: visored once. *Mrs N. S. Sharpe* **c– h–**

ILLUSIVE GAIT 5 b.g. Cloudings (IRE) – Miller's Gait (Mill Reef (USA)) [2004/5 16m^{pu} Oct 1] half-brother to several winners, including useful 2m hurdler Bold Gait (by Persian Bold) and fairly useful 2m hurdler Captain Miller (by Batshoof): dam half-sister to Champion Hurdle winner Royal Gait: well beaten in 3 maidens on Flat at 3 yrs: no show on hurdling debut. *T. D. Easterby* **h–**

ILNAMAR (FR) 9 b.g. Officiel (FR) – Quillemare (FR) (Le Pontet (FR)) [2004/5 20d^3 25s 16d 21g 21m^4 16m^6 Apr 22] good-topped gelding: high-class hurdler in 2001/2: reportedly suffered tendon strain after only outing in 2002/3: off 22 months, useful form in 2004/5 only when in frame behind Monet's Garden in Grade 2 at Windsor and Lough Derg in handicap at Cheltenham: should stay 3m: acts on good to firm and heavy going: tried visored: races prominently. *M. C. Pipe* **c– h135**

ILONGUE (FR) 4 b.f. Nononito (FR) – Marie de Geneve (FR) (Nishapour (FR)) [2004/5 F13g F16v 20m 16d Apr 22] 9,500 3-y-o: ninth foal: half-sister to 3 winners, including one-time fair hurdler/chaser up to 21f Pornic (by Shining Steel): dam maiden: well held in bumpers and maiden hurdles. *R. Dickin* **h– F–**

ILOVETURTLE (IRE) 5 b.g. Turtle Island (IRE) – Gan Ainm (IRE) (Mujadil (USA)) [2004/5 h86: 17d^5 17g^2 17m^3 17m^5 17g^5 17g^3 24d^2 16d 17s^6 20s^2 20d^4 Dec 8] leggy gelding: modest maiden hurdler: stays 2½m: acts on soft and good to firm going. *M. C. Chapman* **h90**

IMAGINAIRE (USA) 10 b.g. Quest For Fame – Hail The Dancer (USA) (Green Dancer (USA)) [2004/5 c101, h–: c20d^3 c17g* c21d c16s^3 c20d^6 c16s* Mar 5] angular gelding: fair handicap chaser: won weak events at Newbury in November and Huntingdon in March: effective at 2m to 23f: acts on heavy going, possibly unsuited by good to firm: has had tongue tied: weak finisher and not one to trust. *Miss Venetia Williams* **c110 § h–**

IMAGO II (FR) 9 b.g. Chamberlin (FR) – Pensee d'Amour (FR) (Porto Rafti (FR)) [2004/5 c–, h–: c20g* c16m c20g^4 c16m^3 Mar 21] tall gelding: poor chaser: won handicap at Market Rasen in August: left I. Williams after fourth start, back to form when third in hunter chase at Hereford final start: stays 2¾m: acts on soft and good to firm going: has worn blinkers: not fluent over fences and attitude under suspicion. *R. Summers* **c86 h–**

IMAZULUTOO (IRE) 5 b.g. Marju (IRE) – Zapata (IRE) (Thatching) [2004/5 h126: 16d 16s 16v² 16s Mar 29] good-topped gelding: fairly useful hurdler: off a year before reappearance: form in 2004/5 only when 1½ lengths second to Escrea in handicap at Leopardstown: raced at 2m on good going or softer (acts on heavy). *Mrs J. Harrington, Ireland* **h117**

I'M BART (IRE) 6 b.g. Norwich – Swanbistersister (IRE) (Roselier (FR)) [2004/5 F16s² Mar 13] £5,400 4-y-o: first foal: dam unraced sister to fairly useful staying jumper Swanbister: fairly useful form when neck second to Khudabad in bumper at Naas on debut. *A. Oliver, Ireland* **F99**

I'M DREAMING (IRE) 11 ch.g. White Christmas – Suffolk Bells (London Bells (CAN)) [2004/5 c89: c25s^pu c20d May 11] medium-sized gelding: winning pointer: maiden hunter chaser: has had tongue tied. *Andrew J. Martin* **c–**

I'M FOR WAITING 9 ch.g. Democratic (USA) – Faustelerie (Faustus (USA)) [2004/5 h78: 24s³ 26g⁶ c20d⁴ c24d⁵ c24s² Apr 2] small gelding: poor maiden hurdler/chaser: stays 3m: acts on heavy going: blinkered once. *John Allen* **c80 ? h78**

I'M INNOCENT 4 b.g. Silver Patriarch (IRE) – Lady Confess (Backchat (USA)) [2004/5 F17g Apr 7] second foal: dam, fair hurdler up to 19f, half-sister to fairly useful 2½m chaser Secret Walk: well held in bumper on debut. *P. J. Hobbs* **F–**

IMMOLA (FR) 9 b. or br.g. Quart de Vin (FR) – Jessica (FR) (Laniste) [2004/5 h–: c19s^pu Jan 3] tall, useful-looking gelding: lightly-raced winning hurdler: ran as if amiss in maiden at Exeter on chasing debut. *Miss E. C. Lavelle* **c– p h–**

I'M NO FAIRY 6 b.g. Efisio – Fairywings (Kris) [2004/5 21d Dec 7] first foal: half-brother to fairly useful sprinter Trojan Flight (by Hector Protector): dam, fairly useful around 1¼m on Flat, out of half-sister to one-time useful 2m hurdler Papua: won completed start in points in 2004: well held in novice on hurdling debut. *P. Beaumont* **h–**

I MOVE EARTH 8 b.m. Bandmaster (USA) – Lady of Milton (Old Jocus) [2004/5 h–: 20d^pu 22g^pu Jul 20] lengthy mare: modest form in bumpers: pulled up all 4 starts in novice hurdles: tried tongue tied. *C. J. Down* **h–**

IMPACT CRUSHER (IRE) 5 b.g. Sri Pekan (USA) – Costume Drama (USA) (Alleged (USA)) [2004/5 F16m⁶ F17d⁶ 20d Nov 12] first foal: half-brother to 2004 2-y-o 1m winner Widely Accepted (by Mujadil): dam unraced: little show in bumpers or novice hurdle. *J. Wade* **h– F–**

IMPARTIAL 4 b.c. Polish Precedent (USA) – Always Friendly (High Line) [2004/5 16s* 16s Mar 29] dam half-sister to fairly useful hurdler Hawkes Run, barely stays 3m: third in 1m maiden at 2 yrs, sold out of P. Cole's stable 3,000 gns Newmarket Autumn Sales: won juvenile at Thurles on hurdling debut in February: well held both subsequent starts. *S. J. Mahon, Ireland* **h114**

IMPEK (FR) 9 b.g. Lute Antique (FR) – Attualita (FR) (Master Thatch) [2004/5 c157, h–: c20s⁴ c21d⁶ 16g⁴ c16g² c16g⁵ c21d⁵ c20g² Apr 22] rather leggy gelding: useful hurdler, 22 lengths equal-fourth to Harchibald in Grade 1 at Kempton in December: smart chaser: mainly creditable efforts in 2004/5, second to Oneway at Sandown and fifth to Fota Island in Grand Annual at Cheltenham fourth and fifth starts: probably best short of 3m: acts on soft and good to firm going: blinkered once (ran poorly): edgy sort, has given trouble at start: jumps well: weak finisher. *Miss H. C. Knight* **c146 h137**

IMPERATIVE (USA) 5 ch.g. Woodman (USA) – Wandesta (Nashwan (USA)) [2004/5 h88: 16s 16s c20s⁴ c18g^ro c17g⁴ c20m^pu Apr 10] angular gelding: little form for various trainers since hurdling debut: ran out second outing over fences: races freely. *M. J. Gingell* **c– h–**

IMPERIAL CROWN (FR) 4 ch.f. Highest Honor (FR) – Imperial Prospect (USA) (Imperial Falcon (CAN)) [2004/5 F12g³ Dec 8] third foal: dam once-raced on Flat and in bumpers: 7½ lengths third to Senorita Rumbalita in 3-y-o fillies bumper at Newbury. *J. J. Sheehan* **F88**

IMPERIAL DE THAIX (FR) 9 b.g. Roi de Rome (USA) – Soiree d'Ete (FR) (Prove It Baby (USA)) [2004/5 c113, h115: 27g² May 21] leggy, close-coupled gelding: fairly useful handicap hurdler/fair handicap chaser, has not won since 2001/2: stays 27f: acts on heavy and good to firm going: visored last 5 starts: tongue tied: has been let down by jumping: looks hard ride. *M. C. Pipe* **c– h115**

IMPERIAL DREAM (IRE) 7 b.g. Roselier (FR) – Royal Nora (IRE) (Dromod Hill) [2004/5 h89: 19d³ c21d² c21d² c20d* c24d* c25d⁴ c22g³ c25g* Apr 16] tall gelding: maiden hurdler: left Miss H. Knight after first outing: fairly useful novice chaser: won at **c118 h89**

Newcastle in November and December and Ayr (blinkered, beat Zeta's River a neck in quite valuable handicap) in April: will stay beyond 25f: raced on good going or softer. *H. P. Hogarth*

IMPERIAL LINE (IRE) 11 ch.g. Mac's Imp (USA) – Ellaline (Corvaro (USA)) [2004/5 c–, h–: c26g⁵ May 31] tall gelding: poor hunter chaser: stays 3¼m: acts on good to firm and good to soft going: tongue tied. *H. L. Thompson* **c66 h–**

IMPERIAL ROCKET (USA) 8 b. or br.g. Northern Flagship (USA) – Starsawhirl (USA) (Star de Naskra (USA)) [2004/5 h87: 16m⁴ 17m⁴ 22gF c17m⁴ 19g² Dec 9] strong, lengthy gelding: modest hurdler: last of 4 finishers in maiden at Plumpton on chasing debut: not sure to stay much beyond 2¼m: acts on good to firm going: tried in cheekpieces: sold £750 Ascot February Sales. *Mrs A. L. M. King* **c86 + h85**

IMPERIAL ROYALE (IRE) 4 ch.g. Ali-Royal (IRE) – God Speed Her (Pas de Seul) [2004/5 17s 17g Apr 3] modest on Flat (probably best at 1½m), successful in January: well held both starts over hurdles. *P. L. Clinton* **h–**

IMPERO 7 b.g. Emperor Jones (USA) – Fight Right (FR) (Crystal Glitters (USA)) [2004/5 h62: 16g 21g³ 19m⁵ 24s⁶ 20v 17s⁶ 16s 19s² 16d 16v³ 19vF 17d 16s⁶ Mar 13] medium-sized gelding: poor maiden hurdler, left W. Clay after third outing: stays 2¾m: acts on heavy going: usually visored/blinkered: has had tongue tied. *G. F. Bridgwater* **h64**

IMPERTIO 11 b.g. Primitive Rising (USA) – Silly Beggar (Silly Prices) [2004/5 c99§, h–§: c25s c22d c20v² c20v² c20v² Mar 20] strong gelding: modest chaser: stays 3½m: raced mainly on good going or softer (acts on heavy): has worn blinkers/cheekpieces: jumps soundly in main: weak finisher. *P. Beaumont* **c90 § h– §**

IMPISH JUDE 7 b.m. Imp Society (USA) – Miss Nanna (Vayrann) [2004/5 h91: 20m⁴ 16v³ 18d⁴ Feb 3] rather leggy mare: modest handicap hurdler: probably best around 2m: acts on heavy going. *J. Mackie* **h88**

IMPORTANT BOY (ARG) 8 ch.g. Equalize (USA) – Important Girl (ARG) (Candy Stripes (USA)) [2004/5 h–: 17d 17d 16g 22g³ 22g 22g⁵ 22g² 22g⁵ 22s Oct 19] compact gelding: poor maiden hurdler: stays 2¾m: acts on firm going: has been visored: tongue tied after third outing: ungenuine. *D. D. Scott* **h71 §**

IMPS WAY 10 br.m. Nomadic Way (USA) – Dalton's Delight (Wonderful Surprise) [2004/5 c73: c25g⁵ c25dpu c24spu c25g² c27v³ Mar 15] leggy mare: winning pointer: fair hunter chaser: stays 25f: acts on soft ground. *Mrs T. Corrigan-Clark* **c88**

IMPULSIVE BID (IRE) 4 b.f. Orpen (USA) – Tamburello (IRE) (Roi Danzig (USA)) [2004/5 16d 16d² 16v² 16s⁴ 16v* Feb 19] leggy filly: modest maiden on Flat (stays 7f): fair juvenile hurdler: won handicap at Uttoxeter in February: raced around 2m on going softer than good (acts on heavy). *Jedd O'Keeffe* **h102**

I'M SMART 7 b.m. Relief Pitcher – Sunylyn (Sunyboy) [2004/5 F18g Oct 18] sixth foal: half-sister to bumper winner Smithlyn (by Greensmith) and to 2 winning pointers: dam, fairly useful hunter chaser, sister to smart staying chaser Elmboy: no show in maiden bumper or in points. *J. Gallagher* **F–**

I'M THE MAN 14 ro.g. Say Primula – Vinovia (Ribston) [2004/5 c–§, h–§: c25s⁴ Apr 3] workmanlike gelding: veteran staying chaser: inconsistent. *J. M. B. Cookson* **c– § h– §**

IMTIHAN (IRE) 6 ch.g. Unfuwain (USA) – Azyaa (Kris) [2004/5 h112: 20g 22gpu 19g 19s 22s 16s Feb 10] compact gelding: fair handicap hurdler at best: no show in 2004/5: stays 2¾m: acts on good to firm and good to soft going: tried tongue tied: sold 6,000 gns Doncaster May Sales. *S. C. Burrough* **h–**

I'M YOUR MAN 6 gr.g. Bigstone (IRE) – Snowgirl (IRE) (Mazaad) [2004/5 F79: F16m⁴ F16s⁶ 20s⁶ 22s⁶ 24s⁴ Apr 10] workmanlike gelding: modest form in bumpers: form over hurdles only when sixth in novice at Kelso fourth start: stays 2¾m: acts on soft ground. *Mrs Dianne Sayer* **h95 ? F83**

IN ACCORD 6 ch.g. Accordion – Henry's True Love (Random Shot) [2004/5 F96: 20s⁴ 22v² 21s³ 19sbd Mar 27] good-bodied gelding: fair form when placed in novice hurdles at Uttoxeter and Kempton: likely to stay 3m. *H. D. Daly* **h106**

INARO (IRE) 4 b.g. Bahhare (USA) – Doo Han (IRE) (Doulab (USA)) [2004/5 F12g* Nov 10] leggy gelding: third foal: dam modest maiden who stayed 7.8f: stayed on well to win 23-runner 3-y-o bumper at Newbury on debut by 2½ lengths from High Altitude: joined J. O'Neill. *E. U. Hales, Ireland* **F100**

INCANDESCENCE (IRE) 4 b.g. Insatiable (IRE) – Glowing Embers (Nebbiolo) [2004/5 F16d Mar 19] angular gelding: half-brother to several winners, including fairly **F–**

useful 1m and 1¼m winner Valley of Fire (by Dancing Brave) and fair hurdler/chaser Monterey Bay (by Montelimar), stays 25f: dam, useful 7f and 1¼m winner, half-sister to Kalaglow: no show in bumper on debut. *Mrs P. Robeson*

INCA TRAIL (IRE) 9 br.g. Un Desperado (FR) – Katday (FR) (Miller's Mate) [2004/5 c96, h131: c19d^3 c25g^2 c24g* c21g^2 c25d* c27g^6 c24d* c29g Apr 23] tall, good sort: winning hurdler: progressed into useful handicap chaser in 2004/5 despite looking difficult ride, winning at Ludlow in November, Wincanton in December and Sandown (produced on run-in to beat Boy's Hurrah by ¾ length) in March: always behind in Betfred Gold Cup at Sandown final start: stays 25f: acts on soft and good to firm going: blinkered nowadays: tried tongue tied: temperamental. *P. F. Nicholls* **c133 §** **h–**

INCH' ALLAH (FR) 9 b.g. Royal Charter (FR) – Cadoudaline (FR) (Cadoudal (FR)) [2004/5 h95?: 21d^2 23d^{pu} Nov 24] lightly raced: modest novice hurdler: stays 21f: raced on good going or softer. *Jennie Candlish* **h92**

INCHING CLOSER 8 b.g. Inchinor – Maiyaasah (Kris) [2004/5 c121, h–: 25s^4 Oct 30] tall, leggy gelding: winning chaser: smart hurdler in his prime, only fairly useful form when fourth to Telemoss in Grade 2 at Wetherby in October: stays 27f: acts on soft going: tried blinkered. *J. Howard Johnson* **c–** **h125**

INCHINNAN 8 b.m. Inchinor – Westering (Auction Ring (USA)) [2004/5 h93: 22g^6 16d^5 16d^5 21d^3 Apr 5] close-coupled mare: modest on Flat (stays 1½m): modest maiden hurdler: stays easy 21f: acts on soft going. *James Moffatt* **h85**

INCH PRIDE (IRE) 6 b.m. Beneficial – Stradbally Bay (Shackleton) [2004/5 F17d F20g F16s* 20s* 16s* 21g 22g* 21g* 24s^2 Apr 21] leggy mare: eighth foal: sister to smart bumper performer Lennon and half-sister to modest hurdler Goodnight Irene (by Crash Course), stays 3m, and to 2 winning pointers: dam unraced: won both starts in Irish points in 2004: thrice-raced in bumpers for W. Burke, winning at Clonmel in December: fairly useful over hurdles: won mares novices at Fontwell, Towcester and Newton Abbot between January and April, and listed mares handicap at Cheltenham later in April by 3 lengths from Silver Charmer: should stay 3m: acts on soft going. *M. C. Pipe* **h122** **F110**

INCOADY 7 gr.g. Aydimour – Fallonetta (Tachypous) [2004/5 20v^{pu} 19s 20v^{pu} Feb 15] lengthy gelding: ninth foal: half-brother to fair up to 1¾m Big Pat (by Backchat): dam bad maiden plater: no sign of ability. *B. N. Pollock* **h–**

IN COMPLIANCE (IRE) 5 b.g. Old Vic – Lady Bellingham (IRE) (Montelimar (USA)) [2004/5 F16g F16d* 16v^2 16v* 20s^2 Mar 28] €36,000 3-y-o: well-made gelding: has scope: first foal: dam unraced, from family of smart 3m chaser Cavity Hunter: won bumper at Fairyhouse in November: quickly developed into useful hurdler, winning maiden at Punchestown in January and short-head second, 20 lengths clear, to Major Vernon in minor event at Fairyhouse: also ran well when 2 lengths third of 8 to Wild Passion in Grade 1 novice at Punchestown in late-April: will stay beyond 2½m. *M. J. P. O'Brien, Ireland* **h130** **F106**

IN CONTRAST (IRE) 9 b. or br.g. Be My Native (USA) – Ballinamona Lady (IRE) (Le Bavard (FR)) [2004/5 c–, h148d: 16m c23g^{ur} c21g^5 May 23] leggy gelding: smart hurdler at best: eleventh to Macs Joy in valuable handicap at Haydock in May: well held only completed outing over fences: stays 21f: acts on good to firm and good to soft going: hangs left under pressure: held up and suited by truly-run race. *P. J. Hobbs* **c–** **h130**

INCURSION 4 b.g. Inchinor – Morgannwg (IRE) (Simply Great (FR)) [2004/5 17m^2 16g^3 17v^{pu} Nov 26] sturdy gelding: half-brother to 3 winning hurdlers, including modest around 2m Penybont (by Unfuwain) and Welsh Dream (by Mtoto): fairly useful on Flat (stays 2m): modest form in juvenile hurdles: visored last 2 outings. *A. King* **h92**

INDALO (IRE) 10 b.g. Lord Americo – Parson's Princess (The Parson) [2004/5 c22v^3 c24d c21s^3 c23s* c24d* c24g c24d* Mar 26] compact gelding: useful handicap chaser, off 20 months before reappearance: won at Leicester and Haydock in February and Carlisle (beat Ebony Light ½ length) in March: stays 3m: acts on heavy and good to firm going: has been let down by jumping: takes strong hold and usually races up with pace. *Miss Venetia Williams* **c131** **h–**

INDEED TO GOODNESS (IRE) 10 b.m. Welsh Term – Clare's Sheen (Choral Society) [2004/5 c113, h102: c26s^4 Mar 13] tall mare: fair hurdler/chaser in 2003/4: successful in point in January: soundly beaten in hunter at Warwick: stays 3¼m: acts on heavy going: sometimes let down by jumping. *Mrs K. Smyly* **c–** **h–**

IN DEEP 4 b.f. Deploy – Bobbie Dee (Blakeney) [2004/5 16d 17d^4 Nov 30] fair maiden on Flat (stays 1¼m): well held in juvenile and novice hurdle. *Mrs P. N. Dutfield* **h–**

INDEMINI 5 ch.m. Elmaamul (USA) – Hills' Presidium (Presidium) [2004/5 F18m May 26] fifth foal: sister to fairly useful 1½m winner Barabaschi and half-sister to useful middle-distance stayer Saltrio (by Slip Anchor): dam 5f to 1m winner: tailed off in bumper on debut. *J. J. Bridger* **F–**

INDEMNITY (USA) 6 b.g. Kris S (USA) – Interim (Sadler's Wells (USA)) [2004/5 20gpu 16m* Jul 28] lightly-raced maiden on Flat, sold out of A. Fabre's stable 42,000 gns Newmarket Autumn (2002) Sales: fairly useful hurdler, lightly raced: much improved when winning minor event at Galway by 2 lengths from Rockstown Boy: reportedly suffered cardiac irregularity previous start: both wins at 2m on good to firm going. *M. J. P. O'Brien, Ireland* **h121**

INDIAN BEAT 8 ch.g. Indian Ridge – Rappa Tap Tap (FR) (Tap On Wood) [2004/5 h70: 24m3 24g4 24g4 Aug 18] poor hurdler: stays 3m: acts on firm and good to soft going: tried blinkered: tail flasher. *C. L. Popham* **h70**

INDIAN CHANCE 11 b.g. Teenoso (USA) – Icy Miss (Random Shot) [2004/5 c116, h–: c25dpu c24d Jan 12] useful-looking gelding: fairly useful handicap chaser: off a year, well held in 2004/5: stays 25f: acts on good to firm and heavy going. *Dr J. R. J. Naylor* **c– h–**

INDIAN CHASE 8 b.g. Terimon – Icy Gunner (Gunner B) [2004/5 c–§, h–, F83: 22d Nov 14] lengthy gelding: well held over hurdles and fences: ungenuine. *Dr J. R. J. Naylor* **c– § h– §**

INDIAN LABURNUM (IRE) 8 b.g. Alphabatim (USA) – St Cristoph (The Parson) [2004/5 c82x, h–: c24s2 c26v* c24s4 c24vpu c27v4 c24v2 c25spu Mar 22] sturdy gelding: modest chaser: won novice handicap at Uttoxeter in October: stays 3¼m: acts on heavy going: ran poorly in cheekpieces last 2 starts: often let down by jumping. *C. C. Bealby* **c88 x h–**

INDI ANO STAR (IRE) 4 b.g. Indian Rocket – Audriano (IRE) (Cyrano de Bergerac) [2004/5 16d Nov 12] poor maiden on Flat (stays 1m): well beaten in juvenile on hurdling debut. *D. Carroll* **h–**

INDIAN RAIDER (IRE) 11 b.g. Commanche Run – Borecca (Boreen (FR)) [2004/5 c26gpu Apr 27] winning pointer: well held on completed start in hunter chases: tried in cheekpieces. *R. G. Chapman* **c–**

INDIAN SOLITAIRE (IRE) 6 b.g. Bigstone (IRE) – Terrama Sioux (Relkino) [2004/5 h94: 16m4 17g6 16dpu Nov 13] leggy gelding: fair on Flat (stays 1¾m) in 2004: modest maiden hurdler: sold out of R. Fahey's stable 9,000 gns Newmarket July Sales, ran poorly both subsequent starts: raced around 2m: acts on soft and good to firm going, probably on heavy: tried in cheekpieces. *B. P. J. Baugh* **h96**

INDIAN SQUAW (IRE) 6 br.m. Supreme Leader – Kemchee (Kemal (FR)) [2004/5 F16g3 F16m4 16s6 22g 19s5 17d Mar 26] eighth foal: sister to fair hurdler Riothamus, stays 3m, and half-sister to several winners, including fairly useful hurdler/chaser Indian Scout (by Phardante), stays 25f: dam, winning 2m hurdler, sister to smart jumper up to 3m Kissane: third in mares bumper at Towcester on debut: poor form over hurdles: tongue tied last 2 starts. *B. De Haan* **h72 F85**

INDIAN STAR (GER) 7 b.g. Sternkoenig (IRE) – Indian Night (GER) (Windwurf (GER)) [2004/5 h80: 16d3 16d4 Mar 24] leggy gelding: poor hurdler: stays 19f: acts on good to soft going: tongue tied in 2004/5. *J. C. Tuck* **h83 +**

INDIAN SUN 8 ch.g. Indian Ridge – Star Tulip (Night Shift (USA)) [2004/5 h100: 19g c16m5 c26gpu Jun 7] compact gelding: fair hurdler in 2003/4: not fluent both starts over fences: best around 2m: acts on good to firm and heavy going: blinkered once: usually tongue tied. *Mrs A. M. Thorpe* **c– h–**

INDIAN TOM (IRE) 11 b. or br.g. Cataldi – Dame Sue (Mandamus) [2004/5 c20g* c22g c18d5 c18d5 c18v c16v2 c20g c16d c22s c20s Mar 6] workmanlike gelding: winning hurdler: poor handicap chaser: won at Ballinrobe in May: stays 2¾m: acts on any going: tongue tied. *T. Hogan, Ireland* **c66 h–**

INDIBAR (IRE) 4 b.g. Indian Ridge – Barbara Frietchie (IRE) (Try My Best (USA)) [2004/5 16d3 16d 16dpu 26spu Jan 5] half-brother to winning hurdler around 2m Little Tobias (by Millkom): tailed off in maiden on Flat, sold out of A. Turnell's stable 1,200 gns Doncaster August Sales: no form over hurdles: tried visored. *Evan Williams* **h–**

INDIEN DU BOULAY (FR) 9 ch.g. Chef de Clan II (FR) – Radesgirl (FR) (Radetzky Marsch (USA)) [2004/5 c89§, h–§: c25mF c25g4 c26g5 c24d2 Mar 11] leggy, useful-looking gelding: fair hunter chaser: stays 25f: acts on good to firm and heavy going: has worn headgear: ungenuine. *Major General C. A. Ramsay* **c86 § h– §**

INDIENNE EFI (FR) 9 b. or br.m. Passing Sale (FR) – Udine Bowl Efi (FR) (Rolling Bowl (FR)) [2004/5 16s^F 16g^pu c24g^ur c24s^pu Jan 19] smallish mare: twice-raced on Flat: won 2 cross-country events around 21f at Vichy in 2002 for G. Macaire: no form over hurdles or fences in Britain: tongue tied final outing. *J. P. L. Ewart* **c– h–**

INDIEN ROYAL (FR) 6 b.g. Dauphin du Bourg (FR) – Royale Nabeysse (FR) (Beyssac (FR)) [2004/5 c21d² c16v² c16s² c18d⁴ c17g⁴ c25d* c26d⁴ c17s* c20g² Apr 22] good-topped gelding: has reportedly been fired: winning hurdler: fairly useful novice chaser: won at Wincanton (weak maiden) in March and Bangor (by 3 lengths from Roofing Spirit) in April: good second to Full House in handicap at Sandown final outing: has won at 25f, best form over shorter: acts on heavy and good to firm going: tried blinkered: tongue tied last 5 starts. *P. F. Nicholls* **c124 h–**

INDIGO SKY (IRE) 4 gr.c. Adieu Au Roi (IRE) – Urban Sky (FR) (Groom Dancer (USA)) [2004/5 16g 17m Mar 21] leggy colt: half-brother to winning hurdler/chaser around 2m Sea To Sky (by Take Risks): fair on Flat (stays 1¼m), sold out of M. Grassick's stable 20,000 gns Newmarket Autumn Sales: well held in 2 juvenile hurdles. *B. G. Powell* **h–**

IN DISCUSSION (IRE) 7 b.g. King's Theatre (IRE) – Silius (Junius (USA)) [2004/5 17m* 17g² c17m* c21d* c17g* c22g^pu Sep 25] medium-sized gelding: closely related to useful sprinter Dairine's Delight (by Fairy King) and half-brother to poor chaser Balla d'Aire (by Balla Cove): dam, Irish Cambridgeshire winner, half-sister to dam of Racing Post Trophy winner Seattle Rhyme: modest hurdler: left C. Roche, won selling handicap at Market Rasen in June: unbeaten first 3 starts over fences, in handicaps at Bangor in July, Newton Abbot in August and Stratford (improved again despite several mistakes when beating Kety Star 2 lengths) in September, first 2 for novices: ran poorly in valuable event final outing: stays 21f: acts on good to firm and good to soft ground: tongue tied for former stable. *Jonjo O'Neill* **c121 h93**

INDUCEMENT 9 ch.g. Sabrehill (USA) – Verchinina (Star Appeal) [2004/5 16d 16v 16s 16s Feb 24] strong, useful-looking gelding: fair handicap hurdler in 2002/3: well beaten all starts after 2-year absence: stays 19f: acts on firm and soft going: has found little. *R. M. Stronge* **c– h–**

INDUSTRIAL STAR (IRE) 4 ch.c. Singspiel (IRE) – Faribole (IRE) (Esprit du Nord (USA)) [2004/5 F16g⁴ F17m* Apr 23] 115,000 2-y-o: leggy colt: sixth foal: half-brother to 3 winners, notably smart middle-distance stayer Hilbre Island (by Halling) and useful miler Date (by Cadeaux Genereaux): dam French 1¼m winner: sold unraced out of L. Cumani's stable 6,000 gns Newmarket Autumn Sales: fairly useful form in bumpers, winning at Market Rasen in April by 3 lengths from Panama Venture. *M. D. Hammond* **F102**

INDUSTRIOUS 6 b.g. Flemensfirth (USA) – Miss Redlands (Dubassoff (USA)) [2004/5 c20v⁴ Apr 6] €130,000 3-y-o: strong gelding: seventh foal: half-brother to 5 winning staying jumpers, including top-class chaser See More Business (by Seymour Hicks) and useful hurdler Blue Business (by Roselier): dam of little account: won in March on second of 2 starts in maiden points: second start in hunter chases, looked very promising when neck second to General Montcalm in valuable event at Punchestown in late-April: will stay long distances: sure to improve and win races. *Mrs D. A. Love, Ireland* **c119 p**

INDY MOOD 6 ch.g. Endoli (USA) – Amanta (IRE) (Electric) [2004/5 F92: 16g² 22v* 24d* 20v* 24d² 23s 18v^ur Mar 5] workmanlike gelding: fairly useful hurdler: won novices at Kelso in October and Newcastle in November and handicap at Newcastle again in January: good second of 5 to Bewley's Berry in Grade 2 novice at Doncaster: stays 3m well: acts on heavy going. *Mrs H. O. Graham* **h120**

INFIDEL (IRE) 5 b.g. Spectrum (IRE) – Implicit View (Persian Bold) [2004/5 18d⁴ 17g* 18s⁵ 16d 16d Dec 2] strong ex-Irish gelding: half-brother to bumper winner Master Tumnus (by Bob Back): well beaten in 3 maidens on Flat: sold out of C. O'Brien's stable 8,000 gns Newmarket Autumn (2003) Sales: modest form first 2 starts over hurdles, won 4-y-o novice at Cartmel in May: out of sorts after. *C. J. Mann* **h91**

INFLUENCE PEDLER 12 b.g. Keen – La Vie En Primrose (Henbit (USA)) [2004/5 c–, h–: c25m^pu Jun 9] smallish, well-made gelding: modest handicap chaser in 2002/3: lightly raced and no form since, including over hurdles: tried visored: has had tongue tied. *Miss K. M. George* **c– h–**

INFLUENTIAL (IRE) 9 b.g. Spanish Place (USA) – More Drama (Pragmatic) [2004/5 c17d* c20d³ c16g Jul 1] poor form over hurdles: winning pointer, including **c76 h–**

twice in 2004: poor chaser: won novice handicap at Cartmel in May: best around 2m: acts on firm and good to soft going: tried blinkered. *J. J. Lambe, Ireland*

INFRASONIQUE (FR) 9 b.g. Teresio – Quatalina III (FR) (Chateau du Diable (FR)) [2004/5 c116d, h–: c20g[4] c25g[bd] May 12] good-topped gelding: handicap chaser, very much on downgrade: stays easy 25f: acts on heavy and good to firm going: tried in cheekpieces/visor. *Mrs L. C. Taylor* **c95 h–**

INGLEMOTTE MISS 7 ch.m. Hatim (USA) – Phantom Singer (Relkino) [2004/5 17m[R] May 19] no form on Flat: maiden pointer, failed to complete in 3 starts in 2004: soon tailed off and refused fourth in novice on hurdling debut. *Ms Liz Harrison* **h–**

INGLEWOOD 5 ch.g. Fleetwood (IRE) – Preening (Persian Bold) [2004/5 h87: 16d 22d[F] Apr 11] winning hurdler: left C. Thornton, well held on completed start in handicaps in 2004/5. *Miss Kate Milligan* **h–**

INGLIS DREVER 6 b.g. In The Wings – Cormorant Creek (Gorytus (USA)) [2004/5 h152: 16d[2] 17d[2] 16v* 16d* 24g* 20d[2] Apr 9] **h162**

One significant event which determined the outcome of the Ladbrokes World Hurdle at the Cheltenham Festival took place, not during the race, but three weeks previously at the end of the Rendlesham Hurdle at Kempton. Royal Rosa, one of the leading novice hurdlers the previous season, finished lame when having his final run before Cheltenham and was ruled out for the remainder of the season. Had he not finished lame then it seems highly likely that Inglis Drever, who is in the same ownership, that of Andrea and Graham Wylie, would not have run in the World Hurdle, and might even not have run at Cheltenham at all. Rather like Ian McKellen rehearsing a role in The Vagina Monologues, only to be told on the opening night he is playing King Lear, Inglis Drever spent the winter trying to shape up as a plausible Champion Hurdle candidate before the call came to step up to three miles in the World Hurdle. In four starts at around two miles, Inglis Drever made a good fist of a role that really didn't look his forte. Indeed he won two of the more important British trials for the Champion Hurdle before really coming into his own when stepped up in trip at Cheltenham.

The World Hurdle, which, under its former name of the Stayers' Hurdle, was the main supporting race on the third and final day at Cheltenham had top billing for the first time on the third and penultimate day of the newly expanded Festival. Prize money was increased significantly, with the winner's connections pocketing £116,000 compared to the £81,200 landed by those of Iris's Gift in 2004. Such largesse was never likely to strengthen the quality of a race that had, in the previous couple of years, been truly memorable, in terms of merit arguably the best two runnings of the race. The 2003 Stayers' Hurdle was one of the finest races at the Festival in recent years and the increased prize money and heightened focus for the latest edition served only to give the race the prominence it merited. Iris's Gift, second in that epic contest as well as the winner a year later, was a notable absentee from the latest renewal of the championship race for three-mile hurdlers, neither entered when the race closed in January nor supplemented much nearer the time. Solerina, fourth in 2004, had been in excellent form over shorter distances in 2004/5, but connections opted not to have a second try with her, while rumours that her stable companion, the 2000 runner-up and 2003 third Limestone Lad, would be making a comeback in 2004/5 came to nothing. Patriarch Express, winner of the Cleeve Hurdle, was another not entered for the race. Just twelve were left in at the five-day declaration stage but all stood their ground overnight, resulting in a field slightly bigger than in the two previous years. As in the three preceding renewals, the race revolved around Baracouda. He stood out on his best form and had won two of the more significant staying hurdles of the season, at Newbury on Hennessy day and the Long Walk Hurdle at Windsor. Even though both were rather muddling affairs, Baracouda still looked the one to beat and was sent off favourite at 6/5. Crystal d'Ainay, second to Baracouda at both Newbury and Windsor, and Rule Supreme, third at Windsor, were again in the line-up, though Rule Supreme, the Grande Course de Haies winner running in preference to contesting the Gold Cup, was emphatically preferred in the betting, sent off 4/1 second favourite against odds of 10/1 for the Rendlesham winner Crystal d'Ainay. Four of the field started at 150/1 or longer, others who could be given a chance including the Martin Pipe-

Axminster Kingwell Hurdle, Wincanton—
Inglis Drever's tendency to jump left prompts a last-flight blunder but he recovers to see off Perouse

trained pair Westender, the 2003 Champion Hurdle second, and Korelo and the Irish challenger Emotional Moment, who had completed a hat-trick in graded company. Inglis Drever, very much the unknown quantity in the race, was third favourite at 5/1. His form at two miles was little behind the best staying form shown by the opposition, with the exception of Baracouda, and there was every reason to think that Inglis Drever would be at least as effective at three miles.

The World Hurdle couldn't match the 2003 Stayers' for excitement from start to finish, but it was certainly a race for the connoisseur, the tactics played out fascinating to watch. Baracouda had a pacemaker in a bid to prevent a falsely-run contest like those at Newbury and Windsor, but Knife Edge, travelling freely fitted with blinkers for the first time, was largely ignored by the principals. By three out, none of the market leaders had made a move, and Westender, who had taken over the lead at halfway, held a healthy advantage. Westender was still four lengths up two out, though by now Rule Supreme was beginning his effort and Baracouda, going best, was creeping closer. Inglis Drever, in contrast, was looking an unlikely winner but he responded to pressure and, when Baracouda failed to quicken as expected in the straight, Inglis Drever came through to lead at the last before extending his advantage over Baracouda and Rule Supreme on the flat, crossing the line three lengths ahead of Baracouda with three quarters of a length further to Rule Supreme. Westender, possibly flattered, held on for fourth two lengths further back, with Korelo, who never really got in a blow, fifth and three of the longshots completing the finishers. Crystal d'Ainay, who took little interest after meeting interference, and Emotional Moment, possibly amiss, were among those pulled up.

Inglis Drever defeated Baracouda by twice the distance of Iris's Gift's triumph twelve months previously. Iris's Gift clearly produced a top-notch performance, yet taking the latest edition as a whole, rather than just on the runner-up, Inglis Drever showed form of a somewhat lower order. Ignoring the two previous years, however, Inglis Drever's performance was well up to standard for the race, on a par or better than all winners in the last decade of the old century apart from Dorans Pride and King's Curate. King's Curate won the Stayers' Hurdle when it was staged as the race following the Champion Hurdle, the race starting before the final flight and taking in over two complete circuits of the Old Course. Since it moved to the Thursday the Stayers' has been started at the beginning of the back straight and takes in under two full circuits of the New Course. The official distance, which was remeasured in 2001 and reduced by half a furlong, is shorter by a furlong, race distances being measured to the nearest half-furlong, though times suggest the actual difference may be even larger. Whatever the real difference, the times recorded for the Stayers' when it was run on the Old Course, compared to

Ladbrokes World Hurdle, Cheltenham—
a marked change of trip reaps dividends as Inglis Drever lowers the colours of Baracouda (centre), with Rule Supreme (left) taking third

those since it was moved to the New Course, demonstrate that it now provides much less of a test of stamina than it used to. The prevalence of good ground for the Festival nowadays, compared to the usually much softer conditions in the past, may be a factor, but the Stayers' between 1980 and 1992 never took less than 6m 28.10sec to run, while the Stayers' has only twice been run in more than 5m 52sec since its move. The slowest of the last dozen renewals is the 6m 03.26sec it took Dorans Pride on soft ground in 1995. Bacchanal in 2000 took just 5m 36.54sec. Now that the Pertemps Final has made the same move to the New Course, and from Tuesday to Thursday, and the new (Brit Insurance) Spa Hurdle is staged on the New Course on the final day, all three staying hurdles are staged over the same course and distance. It would be desirable to make the World Hurdle different, stage it over the New Course if needs be, but start the race before the final flight and make it more of a race for true stayers; the Gold Cup is over an extended three and a quarter miles, so why not have the equivalent race for hurdlers over the same distance?

And another thing. The name. Presumably such a change was important to the sponsors, putting up money for a race with a well-established name, from which their branding might conveniently be dropped without any loss of recognition to the race. 'World' must have seemed like a good idea, though no plausible explanation was offered as to why the name was appropriate, nor does there appear to have been much of an attempt in the first year to make it so by, for example, inviting the best hurdlers from Japan, Australia, the States or those raced in France to take part. Given the trip, the different nature of the obstacles and the time of year, it might be difficult to attract an international field, but it must be worth the effort, if for no other reason than to help the race live up to a name that otherwise seems mystifyingly inappropriate.

After Cheltenham, Inglis Drever was aimed at Aintree, a meeting which might have been his main target but for Royal Rosa's injury. With the choice between the three-mile Liverpool Hurdle and the more valuable Aintree Hurdle over half a mile shorter, connections opted for the latter, though the deciding factor seemed to be the prospect of landing the inaugural BHB Order of Merit and the £250,000 prize that went with it, £50,000 for being top hurdler and £200,000 for being the overall winner. The main intention with the Order of Merit is to increase the field sizes for the top races and to encourage the better horses to run more frequently, the one complementing the other, also giving a 'narrative' to the season and spreading the focus beyond Cheltenham and the Festival. If the Order of Merit has the last effect then it will have done plenty of good. It was certainly well received by owners, trainers and stable staff (who receive a share of the money) and the BHB team kept the Order of Merit in the media spotlight. Points were awarded in all graded races over hurdles and fences apart from those confined to novices and juveniles. The points were structured to give a good chance in the overall standings to those that ran often without necessarily winning. There were moments when the name given to the project seemed particularly ill-named (Farmer Jack's twenty-length defeat at the hands of Le Roi Miguel in the Peterborough Chase gave his position in the early standings a significant boost), but to see it as an unnecessary reward for those that run early and run often would be churlish.

Inglis Drever, then, took his chance in the Aintree Hurdle. He didn't win but came mighty close, a neck second to Al Eile proving good enough to land the Order of Merit. In contrast to Cheltenham, Inglis Drever made the running in a muddling race, rousted along to increase the tempo after halfway. He found plenty in the straight and only just lost the lead close home. Less than fluent jumps at the seventh and eighth didn't hinder him much at Aintree and his jumping had not prevented his finishing first or second in his four races at around two miles much earlier in the season. In his race before Cheltenham, the Axminster Kingwell Hurdle, in which he ran in preference to the two-and-a-half mile National Spirit Hurdle at Fontwell the following day, Inglis Drever jumped left throughout, badly so in the latter stages, though he still managed to beat Perouse by five lengths. The time before, in the Commhoist Logistics Champion Hurdle Trial at Haydock, run on heavy ground, Inglis Drever had to work hard to reel in Mister McGoldrick, though he eventually won by eight lengths. Neither performance suggested a horse that would be at home under the usual Champion Hurdle conditions, nor did his second places before Christmas to Harchibald in the 'Fighting Fifth' at Newcastle or to Back In Front in the Bula at Cheltenham. Indeed, had he faced any of the strong Irish-trained contingent of two-mile hurdlers at either Haydock or Wincanton, Inglis Drever might have struggled to win those as well.

Andrea & Graham Wylie's "Inglis Drever"

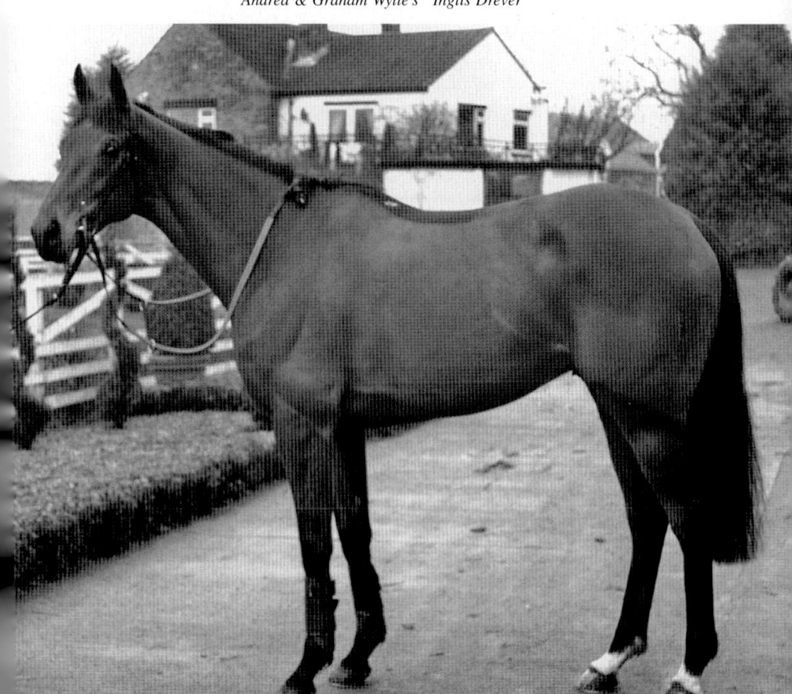

Inglis Drever (b.g. 1999)	In The Wings (b 1986)	Sadler's Wells (b 1981)	Northern Dancer
			Fairy Bridge
		High Hawk (b 1980)	Shirley Heights
			Sunbittern
	Cormorant Creek (b 1987)	Gorytus (b 1980)	Nijinky
			Glad Rags
		Quarry Wood (b 1968)	Super Sam
			Phrygia

Inglis Drever was essentially bred for the Flat, like Balasani, Karshi and Bacchanal, three other winners of the Stayers' since the race was switched to the New Course. Along with Iris's Gift, Karshi and Anzum, Inglis Drever is one of four British-bred winners of the race over that period, the British for once matching the Irish in this area, the French also having managed four wins. Inglis Drever showed useful form at up to a mile and three quarters for Sir Mark Prescott on the Flat, though he isn't the only winning hurdler out of his dam Cormorant Creek in what is something of a dual-purpose family. Inglis Drever's brother Bodfari Creek is fair at up to three miles, while the fair Far Removed (by Distant Relative) and fairly useful Spartan Royale (by Shareef Dancer) are two-milers. Cormorant Creek is also half-sister to a high-class if quirky hurdler in River Ceiriog, as well as the Champion Stakes winner Cormorant Wood, herself dam of the equally quirky Rock Hopper, who won the Yorkshire Cup and the Hardwicke Stakes twice. Their dam Quarry Wood was a sister to the useful staying hurdler Super Trojan and half-sister to the smart two- to two-and-a-half-mile hurdler and Great Metropolitan Handicap winner Cullen. She was also half-sister to the dam of the high-class staying chaser Young Hustler. The sturdy, close-coupled Inglis Drever will presumably be kept over hurdles in 2005/6, with a campaign focussed on the World Hurdle next time round. Inglis Drever has raced on good going or softer over hurdles, though his best form on the Flat was on good to firm. He is effective making the running or held up, although his rider at Wincanton felt front-running tactics were possibly a factor in his jumping left. It may be more likely that the right-handed track was not ideal, Inglis Drever having, with one other exception, raced as a novice on left-handed ones. He is genuine and reliable and should continue to do well in the top conditions hurdles for a while yet. *J. Howard Johnson*

IN GOOD FAITH 13 b.g. Beveled (USA) – Dulcidene (Behistoun) [2004/5 c–, h81: 21g 23m[2] 24d[6] 17d 21d[pu] 16m 19g[2] 19d[4] 20s[5] Jan 19] leggy gelding: poor handicap hurdler: stays 23f: acts on any going: has worn cheekpieces. *R. E. Barr* **c– h76**

IN GOOD FAITH (USA) 4 b. or br.f. Dynaformer (USA) – Healing Hands (Zafonic (USA)) [2004/5 17g 17d[5] Mar 26] fairly useful up to 10.5f on Flat, sold out of C. Laffon-Parias' stable 45,000 gns Newmarket Autumn Sales: only poor form both starts in maiden hurdles. *N. J. Henderson* **h82**

INLAND RUN (IRE) 9 b.g. Insan (USA) – Anns Run (Deep Run) [2004/5 h92: 21g[6] 20m* c23s[pu] c23d[2] c27d[pu] c24d[pu] Feb 11] well-made gelding: third start over hurdles, won weak novice at Wetherby in May: modest form only completed outing over fences: bred to stay at least 3m. *R. T. Phillips* **c89 h75**

INMATE (IRE) 4 b.g. Needle Gun (IRE) – Highland Spirit (Scottish Reel) [2004/5 F16d F16m F16g Mar 9] sixth foal: half-brother to 3 winning 2m hurdlers, including fair Langwaki Island (by Never So Bold) and Conroy (by Greensmith): dam, fairly useful 2m to 2½m hurdler, also won at 6f and 7f at 2 yrs: well held in bumpers. *Mrs E. Slack* **F–**

INNER SANCTUM (IRE) 8 ch.g. Bob's Return (IRE) – Princess Wager (Pollerton) [2004/5 h–: c24d[F] c22m[pu] 26g[pu] Jul 16] sparely-made gelding: no form since hurdling debut, including over fences. *Miss Venetia Williams* **c– h–**

INN FROM THE COLD (IRE) 9 ch.g. Glacial Storm (USA) – Silver Apollo (General Ironside) [2004/5 h–: 20d* 24s[4] 20v* Nov 25] strong gelding: poor handicap hurdler: won novice at Hexham (well backed) in June and amateur event at Carlisle in November: stays 2½m: raced on good going or softer (acts on heavy). *L. Lungo* **h84**

INNOCENT REBEL (USA) 4 ch.g. Swain (IRE) – Cadeaux d'Amie (USA) (Lyphard (USA)) [2004/5 18s[2] 16d[4] 16s[6] Feb 26] lengthy, angular gelding: fair maiden on Flat (seems to stay 1¾m), sold out of E. Dunlop's stable 14,000 gns Newmarket Autumn Sales: best effort in juvenile hurdles when fourth to Redi at Sandown: has taken good hold. *A. King* **h91**

Agfa Diamond Handicap Chase, Sandown—the biggest of three winners on the card for Robert Thornton, standing in for flu-struck Tony McCoy on Innox

IN NO HURRY (IRE) 4 b.g. Supreme Leader – South Quay Lady (Quayside) [2004/5 F16d Mar 19] workmanlike gelding: seventh foal: half-brother to winning chaser Jolly Side (by Jolly Jake), stays 2¾m: dam bumper/2m hurdle winner: well held in bumper on debut. *M. G. Quinlan* **F–**

INNOX (FR) 9 b.g. Lute Antique (FR) – Savane III (FR) (Quart de Vin (FR)) [2004/5 c136: c21v6 c22s6 c22g c20s3 c27d c29d2 c24g* c36d Apr 9] good-topped gelding: useful handicap chaser: heavily backed, won Agfa Diamond Chase at Sandown in February by 9 lengths from Lou du Moulin Mas: found little going to last when seventh to Hedgehunter in Grand National at Aintree next time: stays 29f: raced on good going or softer (acts on heavy): blinkered: inconsistent. *F. Doumen, France* **c139 §**

INSHARANN (FR) 6 b.g. Sheyrann – My Last Chance (FR) (Tiffauges) [2004/5 F–: F17d May 12] no form in bumpers: sold £1,300 Ascot October Sales. *N. J. Henderson* **F–**

INSURRECTION (IRE) 8 b.g. Un Desperado (FR) – Ballycahan Girl (Bargello) [2004/5 h–, F–: c19gpu Dec 30] no form outside points. *J. D. Frost* **c–** **h–**

INTAVAC FLIGHT 5 b.g. Tamure (IRE) – Mossfield (Le Moss) [2004/5 F16v F16d Mar 19] 5,000 4-y-o: compact gelding: ninth foal: half-brother to winning pointers by Mandalus and Buckskin: dam unraced, from family of very smart staying chaser The Benign Bishop: well held in bumpers. *C. W. Thornton* **F–**

INTENSITY 9 b.g. Bigstone (IRE) – Brillante (FR) (Green Dancer (USA)) [2004/5 h92+: 16mpu Oct 3] lengthy gelding: modest hurdler in 2003/4 for P. Blockley: breathing problem only outing in 2004/5: stays easy 3m: acts on good to soft going: has had tongue tied. *S. B. Bell* **h–**

INTERDIT (FR) 9 b. or br.g. Shafoun (FR) – Solaine (FR) (Pot d'Or (FR)) [2004/5 c110, h–: c25m3 c28gur c27g* c24f5 24d6 27m6 c22v* c25s2 c28s4 Nov 18] leggy gelding: winning hurdler: fair handicap chaser: won at Sedgefield in May and Kelso (has good **c113** **h91**

record there) in October: stays 4m: acts on any going: effective blinkered or not: usually races prominently: tough. *Mrs B. K. Thomson*

INTERSKY FALCON 8 ch.g. Polar Falcon (USA) – I'll Try (Try My Best (USA)) [2004/5 h158: 16d4 16g6 20d Apr 9] leggy gelding: has reportedly had breathing operation: very smart hurdler: best effort in 2004/5 when sixth of 14 behind Hardy Eustace in Champion Hurdle at Cheltenham, held up and never nearer: stays 2½m when conditions aren't testing: acts on firm and soft going: blinkered: tongue tied 5 of last 6 starts: has idled: effective held up or making running. *Jonjo O'Neill* **h158**

INTERSKY SOVEREIGN (IRE) 7 b.g. Aristocracy – Queen's Prize (Random Shot) [2004/5 h65: 20gpu c25spu Nov 5] little form over hurdles: tongue tied, pulled up in maiden chase. *J. Howard Johnson* **c–** **h–**

INTERSTICE 8 b.g. Never So Bold – Mainmast (Bustino) [2004/5 16d 16g3 16m5 16g c16fpu c16mpu Sep 19] half-brother to fair hunter chaser Northern Bluff (by Precocious): fair at best on all-weather on Flat (stays 1½m), sold out of A. Newcombe's stable 2,500 gns Doncaster May Sales: probably flattered when third in maiden hurdle at Worcester, only form over jumps. *M. J. Gingell* **c–** **h82**

IN THE FRAME (IRE) 6 b.g. Definite Article – Victorian Flower (Tate Gallery (USA)) [2004/5 h108: 16gpu 16g 16s c19g3 Apr 7] rather leggy gelding: fair hurdler: out of form in 2004/5, left P. Hobbs and off 5½ months before chasing debut: raced mainly around 2m: acts on soft going. *Evan Williams* **c– p** **h–**

IN THE HAT (IRE) 9 br.g. Roselier (FR) – Cotton Gale (Strong Gale) [2004/5 21dpu 22spu 20s 20sF Feb 24] bumper winner: fair hurdler: left C. Swan and off 2½ years, no form in 2004/5: stays 3m. *J. R. Jenkins* **h–**

IN THE HIGH GRASS (IRE) 4 b.g. In The Wings – Gale Warning (Last Tycoon) [2004/5 F18d* Feb 27] seventh foal: half-brother to several winners including useful 1½m/1¾m winner Takwin (by Alzao): dam French 2-y-o 6f winner: favourite, won maiden bumper at Downpatrick on debut by ¾ length from Hardwick: should improve. *T. J. Taaffe, Ireland* **F101 p**

IN THE PARK (IRE) 8 gr.g. Roselier (FR) – Gay Seeker (Status Seeker) [2004/5 h–, F87: 20d 16d c20gpu c26g5 Apr 10] leggy gelding: bumper winner: no form over hurdles or fences, generally none too fluent: tried blinkered. *Jonjo O'Neill* **c–** **h–**

INTITNICE (IRE) 4 b.g. Danehill Dancer (IRE) – Gathering Place (USA) (Hawaii) [2004/5 16dpu Oct 2] sturdy gelding: half-brother to winning 2m hurdler Night Time (by Night Shift): modest maiden at 2 yrs, well beaten on Flat in 2004: no show in juvenile hurdle. *Miss K. M. George* **h–**

INTO BATTLE 11 b.g. Daring March – Mischievous Miss (Niniski (USA)) [2004/5 h–: 21dpu Dec 7] lengthy gelding: poor handicap hurdler in 2001/2: no show only 3 outings since: has had tongue tied. *J. J. Quinn* **h–**

INTO THE SHADOWS 5 ch.m. Safawan – Shadows of Silver (Carwhite) [2004/5 F101: 16d3 16g* Dec 11] angular mare: fairly useful form in bumpers and on Flat: second start over hurdles, won novice at Doncaster in December comfortably by 2½ lengths from Donna's Double: open to improvement. *K. G. Reveley* **h96 p**

INTREPID MOGAL 8 b.g. Terimon – Padrigal (Paddy's Stream) [2004/5 c97, h–: c24dpu May 1] workmanlike gelding: winning chaser: largely out of form in early part of 2004: stays 3¼m: acts on heavy going. *N. J. Pomfret* **c–** **h–**

INTRODUCTION 4 b.g. Opening Verse (USA) – Cartuccia (IRE) (Doyoun) [2004/5 16m4 18m6 Sep 21] lengthy gelding: half-brother to winning 2m hurdler Cheyenne Chief (by Be My Chief): of little account on Flat: well held in juvenile hurdles. *R. J. Price* **h–**

INVER LADY (IRE) 7 b.m. Phardante (FR) – Shean Hill (IRE) (Bar Dexter (USA)) [2004/5 16f2 16m* 16g3 16d6 Aug 5] sister to bumper winner Resistance: poor 1¼m winner on Flat: poor handicap hurdler: won at Roscommon in July: best efforts at 2m on good going or firmer: tongue tied after reappearance. *A. J. Martin, Ireland* **h84**

INVESTMENT AFFAIR (IRE) 5 b.g. Sesaro (USA) – Superb Investment (IRE) (Hatim (USA)) [2004/5 16g6 16d4 16s2 16s* 16v 16s6 17g5 Dec 29] tall gelding: half-brother to fairly useful chaser Cool Investment (by Prince of Birds), stayed 29f, and modest 2m hurdler Investment Force (by Imperial Frontier): fair on Flat (should stay 1¼m) at 3 yrs, sold out of M. Johnston's stable 2,000 gns Newmarket Autumn (2003) Sales: fair novice hurdler: won at Haydock in November: raced around 2m: acts on soft going (well held on heavy). *D. McCain* **h106**

INVESTOR RELATIONS (IRE) 7 b.g. Goldmark (USA) – Debach Delight (Great Nephew) [2004/5 c–, h90: c17m³ c16s⁵ 19g Jun 15] angular gelding: winning 17f hurdler: no form in 3 starts over fences: tried visored. *N. J. Hawke* **c– h–**

INVIRAMENTAL 9 b.g. Pursuit of Love – Corn Futures (Nomination) [2004/5 h–: 17d⁶ c23gᵘʳ 19m c20mᵖᵘ May 30] maiden hurdler: lightly raced and no form since 2001/2, including over fences. *R. Williams* **c– h–**

INVOLVED (IRE) 9 b.g. Macmillion – Symphony Express (IRE) (Orchestra) [2004/5 c25v* c27v² c24s⁴ Apr 16] angular gelding: fair pointer, successful all 5 completed starts in 2003: won novice hunter at Kelso in March: better form when fourth to Ask The Natives at Bangor: suited by 3m+: acts on heavy ground. *Mrs Edward Crow* **c106**

IOWA (IRE) 5 b.g. Sadler's Wells (USA) – Puzzled Look (USA) (Gulch (USA)) [2004/5 F16g F16g⁴ F16m⁶ 16g⁶ 16v 17s 21dᵖᵘ Mar 3] 6,500 4-y-o: second foal: brother to fairly useful 2001 2-y-o 7f winner Ballet Score and useful performer up to 1½m Temple Place: dam, minor sprint winner in USA, half-sister to smart performer up to 1½m Winged Victory: modest form in bumpers, none over hurdles. *M. F. Harris* **h– F78**

IPLEDGEALLEGIANCE (USA) 9 b.g. Alleged (USA) – Yafill (USA) (Nureyev (USA)) [2004/5 19d* 18d² 17s⁵ 20g⁶ c16v⁴ c21v⁴ c16s⁴ Apr 10] sparely-made gelding: poor on Flat (stays 2m) nowadays, left D. Chapman after final start in 2004: modest handicap hurdler: 50/1-winner of 17-runner event at Catterick in January: poor form over fences: stays 19f: acts on heavy going: often tongue tied. *N. Waggott* **c78 h90**

IRANOO (IRE) 8 b.g. Persian Bold – Rose of Summer (IRE) (Taufan (USA)) [2004/5 h55: 20dᵖᵘ 16g 17g May 25] maiden hurdler, retains little ability: usually tongue tied. *R. Allan* **h–**

IRBEE 13 b.g. Gunner B – Cupids Bower (Owen Dudley) [2004/5 c110§, h–§: c21d⁴ c20g³ May 8] tall, well-made gelding: fairly useful hunter chaser nowadays: effective at 2½m to 3¼m: acts on good to firm and heavy going: blinkered: irresolute. *P. F. Nicholls* **c105 § h– §**

IRELAND'S EYE (IRE) 10 b.g. Shareef Dancer (USA) – So Romantic (IRE) (Teenoso (USA)) [2004/5 h101d: 20v² 20d* 20v⁶ 20v⁵ 24s⁶ 20s⁶ Apr 10] small gelding: modest handicap hurdler: won at Leicester in December: well below form last 3 starts: stays 2½m: raced on going softer than good (acts on heavy): visored final outing. *J. R. Norton* **h97**

IRENE KATE 6 b.m. Bob's Return (IRE) – Shean Deas (Le Moss) [2004/5 F66: F17d⁴ 21mᵖᵘ Jun 8] poor form in bumpers: reportedly lost action on hurdling debut: sold 7,400 gns Doncaster August Sales. *P. R. Webber* **h– F72**

IRILUT (FR) 9 br.g. Lute Antique (FR) – Patchourie (FR) (Taj Dewan) [2004/5 c–: c25sᵖᵘ Apr 28] fair pointer, successful in February and April: in cheekpieces, pulled up both starts in hunter chases. *R. Waley-Cohen* **c–**

IRIS BLEU (FR) 9 ch.g. Beyssac (FR) – Dear Blue (FR) (Cyborg (FR)) [2004/5 c24g² c24g c33g c29g Apr 23] stocky gelding: smart handicap chaser in 2002/3, pulled up badly lame in Grand National final start: promising return when second to Joly Bey at Sandown: well held in valuable events after: stays 29f: acts on heavy and good to firm going. *M. C. Pipe* **c139 h–**

IRISH BLESSING (USA) 8 b.g. Ghazi (USA) – Win For Leah (USA) (His Majesty (USA)) [2004/5 h63: 21m² 24gᵖᵘ 16sᵖᵘ 22s³ 20s³ 19d⁵ 16d⁴ 20d* 20s² Mar 30] smallish gelding: poor hurdler: won selling handicap at Chepstow in March: stays 2¾m: acts on soft and good to firm going: tried in blinkers, wears cheekpieces nowadays: tongue tied last 4 starts: has failed to impress with attitude. *F. Jordan* **h72 §**

IRISH DISTINCTION (IRE) 7 b.g. Distinctly North (USA) – Shane's Girl (IRE) (Marktingo) [2004/5 h102: 16d² 16d c16g³ c17d⁴ c16g⁴ Aug 2] leggy gelding: fair handicap hurdler: similar form on first of 3 outings over fences: best around 2m: acts on good to firm and good to soft going: headstrong. *T. R. George* **c100 h98**

IRISH FASHION (USA) 10 ch.g. Nashwan (USA) – L'Irlandaise (USA) (Irish River (FR)) [2004/5 c–, h–: 16d c16s⁵ c16d⁶ 22d c17v³ c24vᶠ c24vᵖᵘ 24d Feb 26] sturdy gelding: fair handicap hurdler at one time: retains little ability, including over fences: tried in cheekpieces. *A. J. Whiting* **c81 h–**

IRISH GROUSE (IRE) 6 b.g. Anshan – Another Grouse (Pragmatic) [2004/5 F–: 16gᵖᵘ 20s 22s 19s Jan 31] no show in bumper or over hurdles: tongue tied final outing. *Miss H. C. Knight* **h–**

IRISH HUSSAR (IRE) 9 b.g. Supreme Leader – Shuil Ard (Quayside) [2004/5 c154, h–: c24g³ Mar 15] tall, useful-looking gelding: very smart chaser: off 12 months, **c157 h–**

ran as well as ever when 3¼ lengths third to Kelami in valuable handicap at Cheltenham, travelling strongly long way: should stay beyond 25f: raced on good going or softer (won bumper on heavy): has been let down by jumping. *N. J. Henderson*

IRISHKAWA BELLEVUE (FR) 7 b. or br.g. Irish Prospector (FR) – Strakawa (FR) (Sukawa (FR)) [2004/5 h99: 22m c23d[2] c21g[5] c20m[3] 20s c21f 20d Nov 6] modest hurdler/maiden chaser: mainly out of sorts in 2004/5: stays 23f: acts on good to firm and good to soft going: usually blinkered, ran poorly only start in cheekpieces. *Jean-Rene Auvray* **c85 h–**

IRISH LEGEND (IRE) 5 b.g. Sadler's Wells (USA) – Wedding Bouquet (Kings Lake (USA)) [2004/5 21d[2] 20s[F] 22s[3] 18s[ur] 19d[4] 21d* 24g[4] 21s* Mar 31] smallish gelding: fair on Flat (stays 1¾m), sold out of C. O'Brien's stable 5,000 gns Newmarket Autumn Sales: fair hurdler: successful at Ludlow in novice in February and handicap in March, improved form when beating Mini Dare 4 lengths in latter: stays 3m: raced on good going or softer (acts on soft). *C. Roberts* **h111**

IRISHMAN (IRE) 11 b.g. Bob Back (USA) – Future Tense (USA) (Pretense) [2004/5 c74, h–: c21s[pu] c26g[6] c23g[pu] Jul 7] lengthy, workmanlike gelding: poor handicap chaser: no show in 2004/5: stays 3m: acts on firm and good to soft ground: tried blinkered/in cheekpieces. *Miss I. E. Craig* **c– h–**

IRISH PREACHER (IRE) 6 br.g. Presenting – Cherl Bo-A (Charlaw) [2004/5 F16d[4] Dec 9] €22,000 3-y-o: useful-looking gelding: half-brother to winning pointers by Mummy's Luck and Lord Americo: dam unraced: 5¼ lengths fourth to Bugle Major in bumper at Huntingdon on debut. *P. R. Webber* **F93**

IRISH PRINCE (IRE) 9 b.g. Fresh Breeze (USA) – Kilivarig (Crozier) [2004/5 h71§: 20s[pu] May 5] sturdy gelding: maiden hurdler: usually visored/blinkered: pulls hard: has looked none too keen: sold £2,100 Ascot June Sales. *J. G. M. O'Shea* **h– §**

IRISH SEA (USA) 12 b.g. Zilzal (USA) – Dunkellin (USA) (Irish River (FR)) [2004/5 c91x, h82: c21d[pu] Feb 18] neat gelding: winning hurdler/chaser: pulled up in hunter and points in 2004/5: stays 3m: acts on any going: tried blinkered/in cheekpieces: often let down by jumping. *Mrs S. Bowman* **c– x h–**

IRISH TOTTY 6 b.m. Glacial Storm (USA) – Elver Season (Vital Season) [2004/5 F17s[2] F16d F16s Mar 13] fourth foal: half-sister to winning pointer by Miner's Lamp: dam fairly useful hunter chaser who stayed 25f: best effort in mares bumpers when second at Taunton on debut. *C. J. Down* **F78**

IRIS'S DREAM 5 ch.g. Gunner B – Miss Shaw (Cruise Missile) [2004/5 F16g[5] Sep 23] first foal: dam poor novice chaser – well held in bumper on debut. *Jonjo O'Neill* **F–**

IRIS'S GIFT 8 gr.g. Gunner B – Shirley's Gift (Scallywag) [2004/5 h172: 24g[2] c20d[5] Feb 19] **c128 P h–**

No sooner had *Chasers & Hurdlers 2003/04* gone to print in August than news broke that the season's champion staying hurdler Iris's Gift—winner of the Stayers' Hurdle at Cheltenham and the Liverpool Long Distance Hurdle—had suffered two hairline fractures of a cannon bone on the gallops. For the team at Jackdaws Castle the troubles were just beginning. A tremendous start—coinciding with the arrival of champion jockey Tony McCoy—produced sixty-eight winners and prize money of £454,022 by the end of October, putting the stable third in the table, but the flow of winners began to dry up in November before coming to a virtual halt in December. The rest of the campaign was blighted by the effects on some of the horses of a serious viral infection which led to the shutting down of the stable for a time. 'The virus', a term used widely in racing, is not one disease but a whole group, mostly affecting the respiratory system, with new strains appearing from time to time. The effects are not always obvious. The Jackdaws Castle runners in November, for example, showed no overt signs of sickness, the effects of 'the virus' only apparent from their performances. The situation was complicated by the fact that recovery with some of the horses seemed short-lived and they became re-infected, hence the closure of the yard. Even the most scrupulously maintained stables can be ravaged by 'the virus', despite advances in veterinary science and general improvement in stable procedures. Another complication with some viral infections is that they suppress the immune system to aid their own survival, leaving the host exposed to other infections, as well as to a recurrence of the same virus. The biggest threat to the health of a racing stable is from horses coming from other yards or from the sale-ring. Jackdaws had a sizeable intake, including horses in training, over the summer. Newcomers are usually isolated at first and another nearby racing yard has now been purchased and added to the magnificent facilities at Jackdaws. Mixing with other horses at the races, or in horseboxes on the way to the races, also spreads 'the virus', and the latest season saw champion trainer Martin Pipe in trouble with the authorities after refusing to let some of his horses enter the dope-testing boxes at the races, a subject dealt with in the essay on Celtic Son.

Iris's Gift (gr.g. 1997)	Gunner B (ch 1973)	Royal Gunner (ch 1962)	Royal Charger
			Levee
		Sweet Councillor (b 1968)	Privy Councillor
			Sugarstick
	Shirley's Gift (gr 1986)	Scallywag (gr 1973)	Sea Hawk II
			Scammell
		Earlsgift (b 1976)	Dusky Boy
			Austrian Girl

Iris's Gift made a speedier than expected recovery from his cannon bone injuries and was taking swimming and walking exercise again by mid-October. It was thought that he was on course to make his eagerly-awaited debut over fences just before Christmas, but plans were shelved when his work failed to satisfy. By the time Iris's Gift was seen out, in the totesport Chase at Lingfield on February 19th, he was among the first batch of runners sent out from Jackdaws Castle since Boxing Day. With the Cheltenham Gold Cup on the agenda, the rescheduled totesport Chase, a Grade 1 usually run at Ascot, provided the opportunity to pitch Iris's Gift in at the deep end. It wasn't a vintage renewal but, if Iris's Gift was to be ready for the Gold Cup, he had to perform well against the likes of Hand Inn Hand, the previous year's winner, and Ollie Magern, the season's leading staying novice. Iris's Gift was sent off favourite but came back last of five finishers behind It Takes

Mr Robert Lester's "Iris's Gift"

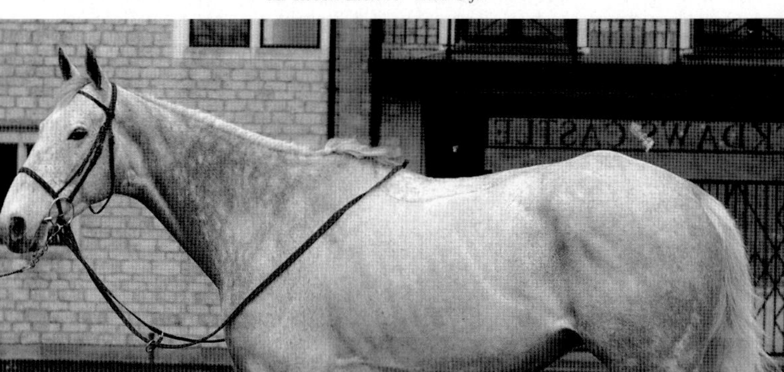

Time. The most pleasing aspect of Iris's Gift's performance was that he jumped soundly, but he was beaten some way out and was clearly not going to be ready for Cheltenham. 'We're two months behind with him,' said O'Neill, confirming that Iris's Gift would miss the Gold Cup. It was mooted that Iris's Gift might revert to hurdling for Aintree and Punchestown but, in the end, he was roughed off to resume his career over fences, starting in novice events, in 2005/6. He still has plenty of time to make up into a high-class chaser and the three and a quarter miles of the Cheltenham Gold Cup will suit him admirably if he makes the grade. On his final start of the 2003/4 campaign Iris's Gift went down by seven lengths to his top-class stablemate Rhinestone Cowboy in the Champion Stayers' Hurdle at Punchestown. Rhinestone Cowboy also went on to have his problems in the autumn, picking up a leg injury which put him out for the season. The big, workmanlike Iris's Gift, very much a chasing type in appearance, acts on good to firm and heavy going. He has hung on occasions but is a thoroughly genuine racehorse who has excellent prospects over fences. *Jonjo O'Neill*

IRIS'S PRINCE 6 ch.g. Gunner B – Colonial Princess (Roscoe Blake) [2004/5 F16g² F17m* 22g* 23s^pu Mar 22] big, leggy gelding: chasing type: sixth foal: half-brother to smart hunter chaser County Derry and fair staying hurdler Brush A King (both by Derrylin): dam winning pointer: fair in bumpers, winning at Market Rasen in June: landed odds in novice at Uttoxeter on hurdling debut following month: left J. O'Neill and off 8 months, ran poorly final outing: should be suited by 3m+. *A. Crook* **h104 F99**

IRIS'S QUEEN 5 b.m. Bob's Return (IRE) – Colonial Princess (Roscoe Blake) [2004/5 F16d 17d^F 17g^pu Mar 9] rather leggy mare: seventh foal: half-sister to smart hunter chaser County Derry and fair staying hurdler Brush A King (both by Derrylin) and bumper/2¾m hurdle winner Iris's Prince (by Gunner B): dam winning pointer: no show in bumper or novice hurdles. *D. McCain* **h– F–**

IRON BUCK 12 gr.g. Buckley – Rusty To Reign (General Ironside) [2004/5 c–: c19g^ur c24d^pu c22f³ c16m^pu Oct 6] of no account outside points. *W. Davies* **c–**

IRON EXPRESS 9 b.g. Teenoso (USA) – Sylvia Beach (The Parson) [2004/5 c98§, h–: c20m c26g⁴ c26d* c28d⁴ c28s⁴ c27d⁴ c32v^pu Mar 17] sparely-made gelding: modest handicap chaser: won weakly-contested event at Southwell in August, typically looking hard ride: stays 4m: acts on heavy and good to firm going: tried blinkered, wore cheekpieces last 5 outings: unreliable. *G. M. Moore* **c96 § h–**

IRON MAN (FR) 4 ch.g. Video Rock (FR) – Key Figure (FR) (Fast Topaze (USA)) [2004/5 15v⁶ 17s 16s² 16s* 16d² 16d³ 16g* 17g² 20s^ur Apr 21] leggy gelding: fifth foal: half-brother to 17f hurdle winner Foreighner (by Adieu Au Roi): dam useful jumper up to around 2½m: fairly useful juvenile hurdler: trained first 2 starts by G. Cherel in France: won at Ayr (7/2-on) in November and Sandown (made most when beating Daryal 8 lengths) in February: running well in handicap at Perth final start when hampered and unseated 2 out: probably stays 2½m: raced on good going or softer: races prominently. *J. Howard Johnson* **h121**

IRONMAN MULDOON (IRE) 8 gr.g. Roselier (FR) – Darjoy (Darantus) [2004/5 20s* 24g^pu Apr 1] IR £25,000 4-y-o: sturdy gelding: brother to 1995 Grand National winner Royal Athlete and fairly useful staying chaser Tipsy Mouse and half-brother to several winners, including useful staying chaser Tennessee Twist (by Buckskin): dam unraced, from family of 1986 Grand National winner West Tip: won novice hurdle at Chepstow on debut in October by neck from Kilgowan: ran poorly when next seen over 5 months later: bred to be suited by 3m+. *M. Pitman* **h95**

IRON N GOLD 13 b.g. Heights of Gold – Southern Dynasty (Gunner B) [2004/5 c95, h–: c21d⁶ c24g 19g* 20g Aug 14] good-topped gelding: poor hurdler/chaser nowadays: made most when winning amateur selling handicap hurdle at Newton Abbot in June: stays 25f: acts on good to firm and heavy going: visored once: has reportedly bled: often finds little. *B. G. Powell* **c80 + h78**

IRONSIDE (IRE) 6 b.g. Mister Lord (USA) – The Helmet (IRE) (Riot Helmet) [2004/5 21g^pu 21s² 22v³ 25v⁵ Feb 25] €11,000 4-y-o: sturdy gelding: second foal: dam unraced sister to Hennessy winner Coome Hill: modest form over hurdles: will stay beyond 25f. *H. D. Daly* **h86**

IRON WARRIOR (IRE) 5 b.g. Lear Fan (USA) – Robalana (USA) (Wild Again (USA)) [2004/5 h–: 20d 20s⁵ Mar 10] rather sparely-made gelding: maiden on Flat: modest form on last of 3 outings over hurdles. *G. M. Moore* **h92**

ISAM TOP (FR) 9 b.g. Siam (USA) – Miss Sic Top (FR) (Mister Sic Top (FR)) [2004/5 c68, h83: 16d^3 18m 17g^6 16g 18s^4 c18d^4 c20d^3 c16g^5 c18s^6 c17v^4 c18g^R 16d Apr 3] compact gelding: poor hurdler/maiden chaser: best around 2m: acts on soft and firm going: blinkered twice: tried tongue tied. *M. J. Hogan* **c65 h81**

ISARD DU BUARD (FR) 9 b.g. April Night (FR) – Upsala du Buard (FR) (Un Numide (FR)) [2004/5 h–: 19s^4 19d^3 c18g c24v^3 c25s^{pu} c20v* c19s^3 c20d^2 Apr 20] leggy gelding: modest maiden hurdler: fair chaser: won novice handicap at Leicester in March: finished badly lame final start: stays 2½m: acts on heavy going (bumper form on good to firm). *S. E. H. Sherwood* **c100 h93**

ISARD III (FR) 9 gr.g. Royal Charter (FR) – Aurore d'Ex (FR) (Mont Basile (FR)) [2004/5 c120, h115: 23m^3 22g 24d c21g* c21g^F c21g* c20d* c22g^3 c20g^3 Apr 22] tall, angular gelding: fairly useful hurdler: best effort when third to Kivotos in handicap at Haydock in May: similar form over fences, winning in novice company at Newton Abbot in July and August and Bangor in September: stays easy 23f: acts on soft and good to firm going: has been let down by jumping over fences. *M. C. Pipe* **c126 h122**

ISELLIDO (IRE) 6 b. or br.m. Good Thyne (USA) – Souled Out (IRE) (Noalto) [2004/5 16d^3 20s^5 20s^4 20v^F 17d* 16v* 20v 16d 16v^2 20d^6 21m Apr 2] smallish mare: first foal: dam unraced half-sister to useful staying jumpers Gola Cher and Woodgate, out of sister to smart staying chaser Master Spy: failed to complete in 3 mares maiden Irish points in 2004: fair hurdler: improved form when winning handicaps at Sedgefield (novice) and Hexham in December: bred to stay beyond 2½m: acts on heavy going: has raced freely. *R. C. Guest* **h107**

ISHKA BAHA (IRE) 6 ch.m. Shernazar – Briongloid (Callernish) [2004/5 F16g F16d 21d 21s^3 19v^3 22d^3 21m Apr 2] €14,000 4-y-o: workmanlike mare: fifth foal: half-sister to winning 2½m hurdler Our Rob (by Be My Native): dam fair hurdler up to 3m: mid-division in 2 bumpers: poor novice hurdler: stays 2¾m: acts on heavy going. *T. R. George* **h83 F72**

ISIDORE BONHEUR (IRE) 4 b.g. Mtoto – Way O'Gold (USA) (Slew O' Gold (USA)) [2004/5 17d 16g Apr 16] useful on Flat (stays 1½m), in 2004, sold out of B. Hills's stable 47,000 gns Newmarket Autumn Sales: no show in juvenile hurdles. *J. Howard Johnson* **h–**

ISLAND FAITH (IRE) 8 b. or br.g. Turtle Island (IRE) – Keep The Faith (Furry Glen) [2004/5 c113§, h–: c16s* c16s^5 c16s^{pu} c16s^2 Apr 21] strong, compact gelding: fairly useful chaser: left F. Murphy, won handicap at Warwick in January easily by 2 lengths from Mouseski: form after only when good second to Encore Cadoudal in similar event at Perth: best form at 2m: acts on heavy going, possibly unsuited by good to firm: usually weak finisher: unreliable. *J. Howard Johnson* **c125 § h–**

ISLAND FORTRESS 6 ch.m. Infantry – Misty Fort (Menelek) [2004/5 c94, h89: c17m^F Apr 28] sturdy mare: novice hurdler/chaser, modest form at best: raced around 2m: acts on soft going: has been let down by jumping over fences. *H. D. Daly* **c94 ? h–**

ISLAND OF MEMORIES (IRE) 5 ch.m. Beneficial – Coronea Sea Queen (IRE) (Bassompierre) [2004/5 21d Dec 29] €9,500 3-y-o: fifth foal: half-sister to winning pointer by Hallowed Turf: dam unraced half-sister to smart 2½m to 3m chaser The Illywhacker: always behind in mares novice hurdle on debut. *D. P. Keane* **h–**

ISLAND PEARL (IRE) 6 ch.m. Definite Article – Iolanta (IRE) (Danehill (USA)) [2004/5 F17g^2 Jul 12] first foal: dam, fair maiden with best form at 1m, out of half-sister to smart 1995 2-y-o 6f winner Kahir Almaydan: carried head high when second in maiden bumper at Newton Abbot on debut. *Miss K. B. Boutflower* **F81**

ISLAND SOUND 8 b.g. Turtle Island (IRE) – Ballet (Sharrood (USA)) [2004/5 c93+, h115: 19g^3 16g^5 16s* 16d Mar 5] angular gelding: useful on Flat (raced mainly at 1¼m nowadays): winning chaser: fairly useful handicap hurdler: won at Wincanton in January readily by 1¾ lengths from Kildee Lass: stays 19f: acts on heavy going: not a fluent jumper of fences: races prominently: none too resolute. *D. R. C. Elsworth* **c– h126**

ISLAND STREAM (IRE) 6 b.g. Turtle Island (IRE) – Tilbrook (IRE) (Don't Forget Me) [2004/5 h103: 16d* 19m^5 c16m^3 c19g^F 16g^2 16s^{ur} 18d 16d* Dec 2] strong gelding: none too fluent both starts over fences: left J. Jenkins in between: fairly useful handicap hurdler: won at Southwell in May and Wincanton in December, best effort when beating Man From Highworth 1¼ lengths at latter: would also have won at Kempton sixth outing but for unseating 2 out: raced mainly around 2m: acts on heavy going, not at best on good to firm: blinkered/visored over hurdles in 2004/5. *P. F. Nicholls* **c103 h116**

ISLAND WARRIOR (IRE) 10 b.g. Warcraft (USA) – Only Flower (Warpath) [2004/5 16v^{pu} 19g Mar 3] workmanlike gelding: winning hurdler: off 2½ years, well held in 2004/5: stays 2¾m: acts on firm going: tried blinkered/in cheekpieces: has had tongue tied. *B. P. J. Baugh* **c– x h–**

ISLEOFHOPEANTEARS (IRE) 6 b.g. College Chapel – Fontaine Lodge (IRE) (Lafontaine (USA)) [2004/5 16g 17m 17m 16g Mar 18] tall, angular gelding: first foal: dam, fairly useful hurdler up to 2½m, half-sister to smart middle-distance performer Artan: no form in bumper or over hurdles: pulled hard in cheekpieces third outing. *A. E. Jones* **h–**

ISMENE (FR) 9 b.m. Bad Conduct (USA) – Athena de L'Isle (FR) (Quart de Vin (FR)) [2004/5 20d^{F} 20v^{pu} 22g^{6} Apr 10] close-coupled mare: fell on only start over fences: fair hurdler in 2002/3: no form on return: should stay 3m: acts on heavy going: wore blinkers final start: temperamental. *Miss Venetia Williams* **c– h–**

ISOU (FR) 9 ch.g. Dom Alco (FR) – Aghate de Saisy (FR) (Rhapsodien) [2004/5 c26d^{3} c24s^{4} c24v^{pu} c24s^{5} Mar 23] sturdy gelding: modest chaser: off nearly 2 years, form in 2004/5 only when fourth in handicap at Towcester: stays 3¼m: probably acts on any going. *V. R. A. Dartnall* **c84 ? h–**

ISTANBUL (IRE) 6 b.g. Revoque (IRE) – Song of The Glens (Horage) [2004/5 h93?: 16d^{pu} May 8] leggy, angular gelding: little form over hurdles: blinkered only start in 2004/5: difficult ride. *C. J. Mann* **h–**

ITALIAN COUNSEL (IRE) 8 b.g. Leading Counsel (USA) – Mullaghroe (Tarboosh (USA)) [2004/5 c–, h116: 19m^{2} c20f^{2} Sep 5] angular gelding: fairly useful handicap hurdler: left L. Dace after first outing: best effort over fences when second in novice handicap at Worcester: stays easy 2½m: acts on any going: tried in cheekpieces: has had tongue tied: has drifted left. *P. J. Hobbs* **c98 + h108**

ITALIANO 6 b.g. Emperor Jones (USA) – Elka (USA) (Val de L'Orne (FR)) [2004/5 F16g^{5} F16m^{3} 16g^{2} 16g 19d^{2} 19s* 16d^{6} Apr 11] well-made gelding: seventh reported foal: half-brother to winner in Italy by Midyan: dam, French 1¼m winner, half-sister to smart sprinter West Man: twice-raced in 2 bumpers: sold out of C. Thornton's stable 17,000 gns Doncaster October Sales: fair form over hurdles, winning novice at Catterick in March: likely to prove best up to 2½m: free-going sort. *P. Beaumont* **h107 F88**

ITCHEN MILL 8 b.m. Alflora (IRE) – Treble Chance (Balinger) [2004/5 h–: 24s^{pu} May 5] signs of only a little ability over hurdles: winning pointer, including in January. *R. H. Alner* **h–**

ITCHINTOGO (IRE) 7 b.g. Namaqualand (USA) – Lamp of Phoebus (USA) (Sunshine Forever (USA)) [2004/5 h–, F–: 24g^{pu} 19m Jun 9] no sign of ability: tried visored. *L. A. Dace* **h–**

I TINA 9 b.m. Lycius (USA) – Tintomara (IRE) (Niniski (USA)) [2004/5 h70§: 16v^{pu} 20d^{F} 16g^{6} 17s^{4} Apr 2] leggy mare: poor hurdler: no show in 2004/5: raced mainly around 2m: acts on soft and good to firm going: usually visored/blinkered: irresolute. *A. G. Juckes* **h– §**

ITS A CRACKER (IRE) 6 br.g. Roselier (FR) – Lilliput Queen (IRE) (Drumalis) [2004/5 17s 16g 17s^{bd} Nov 2] €25,000 4-y-o: sturdy gelding: third foal: dam, won up to 2½m over hurdles, also 1½m winner on Flat: well beaten in maiden Irish point: no form over hurdles. *M. C. Pipe* **h–**

Goffs Land Rover Bumper, Punchestown—
sole British raider Its A Dream lands this valuable contest, formerly staged at Fairyhouse

Mrs R. Murdoch & David Murdoch's "Its A Dream"

ITS A DREAM (IRE) 5 b.g. Oscar (IRE) – Gra-Bri (IRE) (Rashar (USA)) [2004/5 F18s³ F17v* Feb 15] €31,000 4-y-o: tall gelding: has scope: first foal: dam, placed in points, sister to smart hurdler at 2½m+ Rash Remark: won at Folkestone in February: better form when winning 25-runner event at Punchestown in late-April, leading in straight and beating Virginia Preuil by 4 lengths. *N. J. Henderson* **F110**

ITSALF 7 ch.g. Afzal – Sail On Sunday (Sunyboy) [2004/5 h–, F–: 25mᵖᵘ May 27] angular gelding: little sign of ability, even in points. *J. Rudge* **h–**

ITSALLUPINTHEAIR 9 b.g. Lion Cavern (USA) – Flora Wood (IRE) (Bob Back (USA)) [2004/5 20sᵖᵘ c21dᶠ c19vᵖᵘ Dec 28] tall gelding: winning pointer: no show in novice hurdle/maiden chases, let down by jumping. *Mrs A. M. Thorpe* **c–** **h–**

ITS A MYSTERY (IRE) 6 b.m. Idris (IRE) – Blue Infanta (Chief Singer) [2004/5 h–: 20gᵖᵘ Jun 10] rather leggy mare: no sign of ability. *R. J. Smith* **h–**

IT'S A PLEASURE (IRE) 5 b.g. Lord Americo – Kiria Mou (USA) (To-Agori-Mou) [2004/5 F16d 21d⁴ 21s⁴ Jan 2] well-made gelding: seventh foal: brother to fairly useful Irish 2¾m chase winner Lord Heavens and half-brother to 2 winners, including fair 2½m to 3m chaser Come In Moscow (by Over The River): dam lightly-raced maiden: fourth in maiden Irish point on debut: eighth of 14 in bumper at Wincanton: poor form in novice hurdles: likely to be suited by good test of stamina. *Miss H. C. Knight* **h85** **F79**

ITSASURETHING 5 b.g. Sure Blade (USA) – Ginka (Petoski) [2004/5 h–, F–: 20d May 5] little sign of ability. *J. W. Mullins* **h–**

IT'S A WIZARD 5 b.g. Wizard King – Axed Again (Then Again) [2004/5 h–: 17dʳᵒ Oct 8] no show over hurdles. *M. A. Barnes* **h–**

IT'S BERTIE 5 b.g. Unfuwain (USA) – Legend of Aragon (Aragon) [2004/5 F16v F16d² Feb 4] €17,000 3-y-o, 7,000 4-y-o: rather leggy gelding: second foal: half-brother **F93**

to 1¼m winner Spanish Bells (by Robellino): dam 2-y-o 5f winner who stayed 1m: better effort in bumpers when second to Malt de Vergy at Catterick. *Mrs S. J. Smith*

IT'S BLUE CHIP 4 b.g. Polar Falcon (USA) – Bellateena (Nomination) [2004/5 16s* 18s⁵ 16d 18s* Mar 30] fair on Flat (stays 1½m), successful twice in 2004 for P. D'Arcy: fair form over hurdles: won juvenile at Plumpton in January and novice at Fontwell (by 12 lengths from Nuit Sombre) in March: should stay 2½m. *Miss H. C. Knight* **h107**

ITS CRUCIAL (IRE) 5 b.g. Beneficial – Balda Girl (IRE) (Mandalus) [2004/5 F16d 16v⁴ 17s* 16d³ 17g 20d 16s Apr 20] compact gelding: fourth foal: dam unraced: runner-up on completed start in Irish points: seventh of 20 in bumper at Warwick: won novice hurdle at Hereford in February: disappointing in handicaps last 3 starts, albeit twice highly tried: should stay beyond 2m. *N. A. Twiston-Davies* **h122 F80**

IT'S DEFINITE (IRE) 6 b.g. Definite Article – Taoveret (IRE) (Flash of Steel) [2004/5 h–p: 22g⁴ 24g³ 24g⁴ 19m* 20m 19d⁴ 24g* 24d* 24s Nov 3] sturdy gelding: fair hurdler: won novices at Hereford in June and Market Rasen in August (made all) and October: stays 3m: acts on good to firm and good to soft ground: usually wears cheekpieces. *P. Bowen* **h112**

ITSDOWNTOBEN 4 b.g. Karinga Bay – Martins Lottee (Martinmas) [2004/5 F16g Mar 26] compact gelding: fifth foal: dam unraced half-sister to high-class middle-distance stayer Funny Hobby: ninth of 12 in bumper at Haydock on debut. *D. McCain* **F80**

IT'S EJ 7 b.g. Karinga Bay – Merry Marigold (Sonnen Gold) [2004/5 F86: 20m³ 20m 19m Apr 23] fair form in bumper on debut: off 10 months, improved effort over hurdles when seventh of 8 finishers in novice at Market Rasen final start, not unduly knocked about. *Mrs S. J. Smith* **h93**

IT'S GOT BUCKLEYS 6 b.g. El Conquistador – Saucey Pup (The Parson) [2004/5 F–: F17d c23gᶠ 16s 19d 22sᵖᵘ Dec 21] very little sign of ability in bumpers or over hurdles: fell first on chasing debut. *L. A. Dace* **c– h– F–**

IT'S GWENDOLENE 5 ch.m. Bedford (USA) – Built In Heaven (Sunley Builds) [2004/5 F16d F16s F18s 21d Apr 18] angular mare: second foal: sister to fair hurdler up to 21f Its Wallace Jnr: dam showed little: well held in bumpers and maiden hurdle (jumped poorly). *Miss S. West* **h– F–**

IT'S HARRY 7 b.g. Aragon – Andbracket (Import) [2004/5 h99, F86: 20d⁴ 20s⁵ 20sʳᵒ c21s⁶ Feb 7] quite good-topped gelding: modest maiden hurdler: tailed off in maiden on chasing debut: should stay 3m: acts on soft and good to firm ground: ran out third outing. *Mrs S. J. Smith* **c– h91**

IT'S IN THE STARS 5 b.g. Teenoso (USA) – Sail By The Stars (Celtic Cone) [2004/5 F16v* F16d F16d Apr 20] has scope: first foal: dam, useful staying chaser, from family of top-class 2½m chaser Dublin Flyer: best effort in bumpers when winning at Uttoxeter on debut in January, signs of greenness before beating Eaton Hall 3½ lengths: will be suited by 2½m+. *H. D. Daly* **F93**

IT'S JUST HARRY 8 b.g. Tragic Role (USA) – Nipotina (Simply Great (FR)) [2004/5 h107p: 19s* 19g* 16d² Jan 8] sturdy, lengthy gelding: lightly raced: won novice hurdles at Hereford (impressive when beating The Market Man 14 lengths) in November and Taunton (easily landed odds) in December: useful form when 2 lengths second to Marcel in Grade 1 novice at Sandown, staying on well after tapped for speed: will stay beyond 19f: raced on good going or softer: reportedly injured at Sandown, but remains open to improvement. *C. R. Egerton* **h132 p**

IT'S JUST SALLY 8 b.m. Kylian (USA) – Hush It Up (Tina's Pet) [2004/5 21d Dec 29] well held in 3 outings over hurdles. *B. G. Powell* **h–**

IT'S MUSIC (IRE) 6 b.g. Accordion – Leadon Lady (Monksfield) [2004/5 c93, h93: c24gᵖᵘ c21s³ c23sᶠ c20d* c20v 21g* 21dᵖᵘ Apr 5] tall gelding: modest form over hurdles: first start after leaving M. Pipe, won novice at Plumpton in March: lame final outing: fair form over fences: won weakly-contested handicap at Warwick in January: stays 25f: acts on heavy going: visored second to fifth starts: usually let down by jumping over fences. *B. G. Powell* **c108 x h93**

ITSMYBOY (IRE) 5 br.g. Frimaire – Hawkfield Lass (IRE) (The Parson) [2004/5 F101: F16g F17d Apr 9] rather unfurnished gelding: won bumper at Fontwell on debut in 2003/4: smart form when 7½ lengths seventh of 24 to Missed That in Grade 1 at Cheltenham 11 months later: badly hampered 6f out when well held at Aintree following month: will stay 2½m. *M. C. Pipe* **F115**

IT'S MY PARTY 4 b.g. Danzero (AUS) – Addicted To Love (Touching Wood (USA)) [2004/5 F12g^{ro} F14d^{6} Nov 23] tall, lengthy gelding: fifth foal: half-brother to 3 winners on Flat, including 7.5f to 1¼m winner Can't Buy Me Love (by Bijou d'Inde): dam, fair middle-distance stayer, half-sister to smart 6f and 7f performer Red Carpet: sixth of 14 in bumper at Warwick: ran out early on debut. *W. G. M. Turner* **F86**

ITSMYTURNNOW (IRE) 10 b.g. Glacial Storm (USA) – Snuggle (Music Boy) [2004/5 c92?: c21m c26s^{pu} c26g^{pu} Mar 27] tall gelding: winning hunter chaser: no form in 2004/5: should stay beyond 3¼m: acts on firm going. *M. J. Roberts* **c–**

ITSONLYME (IRE) 12 b.g. Broken Hearted – Over The Arctic (Over The River (FR)) [2004/5 c130, h–: c24v^{pu} c24g* c24d^{pu} c24g^{pu} c21d Apr 8] useful-looking gelding: fairly useful handicap chaser: won at Doncaster in January, only form since 2003: stays 25f: acts on soft and good to firm going: has found little. *Miss Venetia Williams* **c119 h–**

ITS ONLY POLITE (IRE) 9 b.g. Roselier (FR) – Decent Debbie (Decent Fellow) [2004/5 c103+, h–: c26s^{ur} c28s* Nov 18] workmanlike gelding: lightly raced: has won 3 of 6 starts over fences, fair form when beating Free To Run 5 lengths in handicap at Market Rasen in November: stays 3½m: raced on going softer than good (acts on heavy). *C. Tinkler* **c114 h–**

IT'S RUMOURED 5 ch.g. Fleetwood (IRE) – Etourdie (USA) (Arctic Tern (USA)) [2004/5 h88: 16s^{3} 21v^{3} 22v^{2} 18s Mar 9] modest handicap hurdler: stays 2¾m: acts on good to firm and heavy going. *Jean-Rene Auvray* **h89**

ITS THE BOSS (IRE) 10 b.g. Supreme Leader – Polar Bee (Gunner B) [2004/5 c16m c20g^{F} c20d^{5} Aug 29] winning hurdler: poor chaser, won handicap at Tipperary in 2003/4: effective at 2m to 3m: acts on firm and good to soft going: sold 500 gns Doncaster October Sales. *A. J. Martin, Ireland* **c73 h–**

ITSUKATE 5 b.m. Makbul – Kilvarnet (Furry Glen) [2004/5 F16d F16d Mar 28] half-sister to several winners, including fair hurdler/middle-distance mare McGillycuddy Reeks (by Kefaah): dam fair winner up to 7.6f: well beaten in mares bumpers. *J. Rudge* **F–**

ITSUPTOHARRY (IRE) 6 b.g. Old Vic – Celtic Gale (Strong Gale) [2004/5 17m^{2} 17d^{pu} 17d^{5} 16d^{pu} Feb 24] £3,800 4-y-o, £3,300 5-y-o: fourth foal: half-brother to modest hurdler Paddy The Duke (by Phardante), stays 2½m: dam fair hurdler: left M. Barnes, easily best effort over hurdles when fifth in novice at Bangor. *D. McCain* **h93**

IT'S WALLACE 12 b.g. Bedford (USA) – Rua Batric (Energist) [2004/5 c–, h102: 22d^{pu} 21g^{2} 18m^{2} 20m* 19d* 25g* 24s^{2} 24g^{6} 21g 21v^{F} 21d 16d^{6} Feb 19] leggy gelding: fair hurdler: won claimer at Fontwell in September and seller at Stratford and handicap at Plumpton in October: little impact last 5 starts: stays 25f: acts on good to firm and heavy going: formerly blinkered, tried in cheekpieces: has won 6 times at Plumpton. *Miss S. West* **c– h115**

ITS WALLACE JNR 6 b.g. Bedford (USA) – Built In Heaven (Sunley Builds) [2004/5 h107: 21g* May 9] leggy gelding: fairly useful handicap hurdler: better than ever when winning amateur event at Plumpton (tongue tied) in May by 4 lengths from It's Wallace: not seen out again: stays 21f: best efforts on good going. *Miss S. West* **h116**

IT TAKES TIME (IRE) 11 b.g. Montelimar (USA) – Dysart Lady (King's Ride) [2004/5 c143?, h–: c20d^{5} 24g^{5} 25s^{4} c26d^{3} c20d* c20d c36d^{4} c24s^{2} Apr 21] **c154 h155**

The name of this horse could easily serve as a motto for anyone involved in owning or breeding jumpers. Compared to Flat racing, the rewards are generally longer in coming, particularly for chasers. At least, that has traditionally been the case, though the phenomenal success enjoyed by owner David Johnson and trainer Martin Pipe has not—mainly at any rate—come from a policy based on 'playing the long game'. But at the age of eleven, some five years after his debut for those connections in the Champion Bumper at Cheltenham, and now one of the senior members of the stable, It Takes Time gained the biggest success of his career and showed his best form over fences. A useful bumper horse and then a very smart staying hurdler, It Takes Time had looked an interesting chasing prospect after showing plenty of ability in his novice season. But his jumping let him down badly in the 2003/4 campaign, his season ending after just three starts, the last of them when pulled up in the King George VI Chase at Kempton.

It Takes Time began the latest season with his jumping showing little sign of improvement, and seemingly with some doubt about what direction the rest of his campaign might take. He reappeared in the Paddy Power Gold Cup at Chelten-

totesport Ascot Chase, Lingfield—a welcome win for connections in the wake of the Celtic Son affair, with It Takes Time (spotted cap) proving too strong for Ollie Magern and Hand Inn Hand (noseband)

ham in which a bad mistake three out put paid to any chance he had, though, unlike the previous year, he did at least get round, finishing fifth. With the winner of that race Celestial Gold joining Our Vic, Well Chief and Therealbandit among David Johnson's string of good younger chasers, It Takes Time was briefly sent back over hurdles. He proved no match for Baracouda at either Newbury or Windsor, though he wasn't beaten far in a muddling race when fourth in the Long Walk Hurdle at the latter course. Back over fences in a handicap at Cheltenham on New Year's Day, It Takes Time's jumping was better, but this time his stamina seemed to give out in finishing a well-held third over the Gold Cup trip.

It Takes Time was, therefore, an unconsidered 14/1-shot in the Grade 1 Ascot Chase in February, sponsored by totesport and transferred to Lingfield. Most of the attention was focussed instead on the chasing debut of the top-notch hurdler Iris's Gift who edged out the previous year's winner Hand Inn Hand and the leading novice Ollie Magern for favouritism. The Pipe stable looked to have a better candidate than It Takes Time in Seebald, though he was pulled up after halfway after striking into himself. The three market leaders led It Takes Time into the straight where Iris's Gift was the first to crack. Despite tending to hang left, It Takes Time responded to pressure and was produced between the leading pair on the run-in, running out a two-length winner from Ollie Magern, with Hand Inn Hand another two and a half lengths back in third. As well as providing It Takes Time's most valuable success, it was the biggest win so far for his young rider Jamie Moore, and a timely one too, coming just days after he received a twenty-one day ban for his riding of the same connections' Celtic Son earlier in the season, details of which can be found in the essay on that horse.

Despite adding a Grade 1 win to his name, it had not taken any better than a smart performance to win the Lingfield race, and It Takes Time was returned to handicap company for his remaining starts. He ran creditably without threatening off his reassessed mark when a close seventh to Supreme Prince in the Vodafone Gold Cup at Newbury, before taking his chance in the Grand National. On paper, It Takes Time looked well treated off his old mark (13 lb lower than at Newbury), though stamina doubts and jumping worries tempered enthusiasm about his chances. Whilst the National was not one of It Takes Time's better efforts on form, he jumped round safely and saw the trip out better than most, creeping into contention to join the leading pack late in the race, but then unable to quicken when ridden at the last, finishing around eighteen lengths behind Hedgehunter in fourth. Back in 2001/2, It Takes Time had put the owners' championship beyond doubt for David Johnson when winning on the final day of the season at Sandown. With another owners' championship long since wrapped up, It Takes Time was pressed into service in the last days of the season again, this time as part of his trainer's all-out title defence. It Takes Time did his bit by finishing a good second, conceding upwards of 16 lb all round, to Kock de La Vesvre in the most valuable event at Perth's April meeting.

It Takes Time (IRE) (b.g. 1994)	Montelimar (USA) (b 1981)	Alleged (b 1974)	Hoist The Flag
			Princess Pout
		L'Extravagante (b 1973)	Le Fabuleux
			Fanfreluche
	Dysart Lady (br 1984)	King's Ride (b 1976)	Rarity
			Ride
		Dalystown (b 1974)	Royal Chet
			Lynn Lady

Although he hadn't shown an abundance of stamina prior to the Grand National, It Takes Time's pedigree gave encouragement for his staying long dist-

Mr D. A. Johnson's "It Takes Time"

ances. For a start, he shares his sire, Montelimar, with Hedgehunter and another recent National winner Monty's Pass, while his half-brother Bright Approach (by Roselier) has wins at beyond four miles in hunter chases to his name. Their dam Dysart Lady has had a rather patchy breeding record since those first two foals, though a potential third winner is her fifth foal Lusatani (by Luso), fourth on his debut in a maiden point in Ireland in March. Like her son, It Takes Time's dam won both over hurdles and fences, as well as in points and a bumper prior to that, showing fairly useful form and winning at up to three miles. The angular It Takes Time's best efforts remain at between two and a half and three miles one furlong, and he acts on heavy and good to firm going. He failed to take the eye when sweating up before his two runs over hurdles in the latest season, though that didn't stop him from running well at Windsor. His jumping has seemingly improved, and he looks more of a straightforward ride nowadays than he used to be. *M. C. Pipe*

IVANOPH (FR) 9 b.g. Roi de Rome (USA) – Veronique IV (FR) (Mont Basile (FR)) [2004/5 c125§, h–: c24d^{5} c16m^{ur} c19v^{pu} Mar 30] tall, sparely-made gelding: fairly useful handicap chaser at best: sold out of P. Nicholls' stable 23,000 gns Doncaster May Sales after first outing: failed to complete in points/hunter chases after: stays 3m: acts on any going: often finds little: unreliable. *J. J. Boulter* **c– § h–**

IVERAIN (FR) 9 b.g. Le Riverain (FR) – Ursala (FR) (Toujours Pret (USA)) [2004/5 c122, h–: c24d^{5} c20s^{5} c20s^{5} c20d^{2} Jan 7] good-topped gelding: fairly useful handicap chaser at one time, has deteriorated: stays 25f: acts on good to soft and good to firm going: blinkered once (well below form). *Sir John Barlow Bt* **c102 h–**

IVORSAGOODUN 6 b.m. Piccolo – Malibasta (Auction Ring (USA)) [2004/5 h88: 17g^{2} 18m 22g^{5} 20m^{pu} Jul 21] leggy mare: modest maiden hurdler: seems to stay 3m: acts on good to firm going: tried visored: hard ride. *N. R. Mitchell* **h88**

IVORY FORT 5 ch.g. Bold Fort – Ivory Girl (IRE) (Sharp Victor (USA)) [2004/5 F–: F17d 17m 18m^{pu} May 30] no form in bumpers or novice hurdles. *R. Williams* **h– F–**

IVORY VENTURE 5 b.m. Reprimand – Julietta Mia (USA) (Woodman (USA)) [2004/5 h–: 16d 17m 16g^{pu} May 30] no form over hurdles: tried blinkered: sold £900 Ascot July Sales. *I. R. Brown* **h–**

IZNOGOUD (FR) 9 br.g. Shafoun (FR) – Vancia (FR) (Top Dancer (FR)) [2004/5 c140, h–: c21s c24s^{2} c21g c36d Apr 9] tall, leggy gelding: has a markedly round action: winning hurdler: useful handicap chaser: placed in race for second year running when 6 lengths second to Farmer Jack in Racing Post Chase at Kempton in February: bad mistake first in Grand National: effective at 2½m to easy 29f: acts on good to firm and heavy going: visored twice (departed early both times). *M. C. Pipe* **c143 h–**

IZZY GETS BUSY (IRE) 5 b.m. Flemensfirth (USA) – Builders Line (IRE) (Sheer Grit) [2004/5 F16v F16s Mar 13] second foal: dam winning pointer: tailed off in mares bumpers: tried in cheekpieces. *G. F. Bridgwater* **F–**

IZZYKEEN 6 b.g. Keen – Washita (Valiyar) [2004/5 F85: F16g^{3} F17g^{3} F16m^{4} 16g^{4} 20g^{5} 20m* 22d^{4} 19m* Dec 1] smallish, angular gelding: in frame all 4 starts in bumpers: modest novice hurdler: won at Uttoxeter in September and Catterick in December: stays easy 2½m: acts on good to firm going. *Mrs S. J. Smith* **h95 F88**

J

JABIRU (IRE) 12 b. or br.g. Lafontaine (USA) – Country Glen (Furry Glen) [2004/5 c101, h–: c21g^{2} c28m^{6} c26g* c24g* c26g c25s^{ur} c24g^{pu} Apr 7] good-topped gelding: fairly useful hunter chaser: successful at Newton Abbot (third successive win in race) in May and Taunton (third course win) in March: stays 3½m: best efforts on good ground or firmer (acts on firm): usually blinkered. *Mrs K. M. Sanderson* **c104 h–**

JABO ORIGNY (FR) 8 gr.g. Royal Charter (FR) – Coralline (FR) (Iron Duke (FR)) [2004/5 16m^{6} Aug 6] smallish gelding: lightly-raced novice hurdler: seemed not to stay 2½m. *Miss Venetia Williams* **h68**

JABOUNE (FR) 8 ch.g. Johann Quatz (FR) – Seasonal Pleasure (USA) (Graustark) [2004/5 c120, h129: 19g^{5} 20g^{5} c17m^{4} c17g^{pu} 22d^{pu} Dec 26] compact gelding: type to carry condition: fairly useful hurdler/chaser at best: out of form in 2004/5: stays 19f: acts **c111 h–**

on good to firm and good to soft going, possibly not on soft: tried visored: has had tongue tied. *A. King*

JAC AN REE (IRE) 9 b.g. Supreme Leader – Nic An Ree (IRE) (King's Ride) [2004/5 h87: 21g^pu May 1] useful-looking gelding: lightly-raced novice hurdler: won points in February and April. *A. King* **h–**

JACARADO (IRE) 7 b.g. Jurado (USA) – Lady Mearba (IRE) (Le Bavard (FR)) [2004/5 h–, F–: 19s c21v^4 Jan 28] good-topped gelding: no sign of ability. *R. Dickin* **c– h–**

JACCOUT (FR) 7 b.g. Sheyrann – Jacottiere (FR) (Dom Racine (FR)) [2004/5 c–, h80: 21d^4 16d 17v^3 16s 17s* 16s^5 17v* 18s c16v^3 Apr 17] winning chaser in France: modest hurdler: made all in handicaps at Sedgefield in February and March: stays 2½m: acts on heavy going: usually wears headgear and tongue strap: probably best when able to dominate: unreliable. *R. Johnson* **c– h89 §**

JACDOR (IRE) 11 b.g. Be My Native (USA) – Bellalma (Belfalas) [2004/5 c119, h105: c24g Mar 19] tall gelding: fairly useful handicap hurdler/chaser: well beaten on return from 13-month absence: stays 25f: acts on good to firm and heavy going: blinkered/visored: tried tongue tied. *R. Dickin* **c– h–**

JACK DAWSON (IRE) 8 b.g. Persian Bold – Dream of Jenny (Caerleon (USA)) [2004/5 h120: 16m^6 22g* 17d^4 21g^pu 20d^5 20m^4 Apr 23] smallish gelding: fairly useful on Flat: useful handicap hurdler: won at Kelso in May by length from Hirvine: creditable efforts all 3 completed starts after: stays 2¾m: acts on good to firm and good to soft going: normally patiently ridden: genuine. *John Berry* **h131**

JACK DORAN 5 ch.g. Gildoran – Faustelerie (Faustus (USA)) [2004/5 F–: F16s^pu 16d 16s^pu Mar 5] unfurnished gelding: no form in bumpers (saddle slipped twice) or novice hurdles (looked temperamental): tried visored. *J. R. Jenkins* **h– § F–**

JACK DURRANCE (IRE) 5 b.g. Polish Precedent (USA) – Atlantic Desire (IRE) (Ela-Mana-Mou) [2004/5 h–: 17s^5 May 11] smallish gelding: no form over hurdles. *G. A. Ham* **h–**

JACKEM (IRE) 11 b. or br.g. Lord Americo – Laurence Lady (Laurence O) [2004/5 c–x, h–: c25s^pu c23d* c25s^3 c23s^6 c24g^4 Mar 19] useful-looking gelding: modest chaser: won handicap at Leicester in January: stays 25f: acts on heavy going, probably on good to firm. *Ian Williams* **c89 h–**

JACK FLUSH (IRE) 11 b.g. Broken Hearted – Clubhouse Turn (IRE) (King of Clubs) [2004/5 h–: 20d^5 20m^pu 16g 20s^3 21v 19d 19s 27v^pu 21v^3 Mar 28] leggy gelding: poor hurdler: stays 21f: acts on heavy going: usually blinkered/visored and tongue tied: unreliable. *M. E. Sowersby* **h64 §**

JACK FULLER (IRE) 8 b.g. Be My Native (USA) – Jacks Sister (IRE) (Entitled) [2004/5 c94, h–: c16g^2 c19s^2 c21g^3 c24g c24d^4 c20s^2 c24s* c25m^pu Apr 9] tall gelding: modest handicap chaser: won at Towcester in March: stays 3m: acts on soft and good to firm going: often wears headgear. *P. R. Hedger* **c99 h–**

JACK HIGH (IRE) 10 br.g. Erdelistan (FR) – Lyntim (Fidel) [2004/5 c108, h127: c22v^3 c18d c24v* c24v^4 c24v c24s^4 20s^6 c29s^2 c29g* Apr 23] **c134 h120 +**

Sandown is already regarded by many as Britain's finest dual-purpose course and it must have won still more converts with its action-packed finale to the latest jumps season. Well Chief's defeat of Azertyuiop in the Celebration Chase helped to clinch a very tight trainers' championship for Martin Pipe over his great rival Paul Nicholls. Champion jockey Tony McCoy secured his two-hundredth winner of the season on Yes Sir, the sixth time he has reached that figure in a season. And the day's most valuable event, the showpiece Gold Cup, a staying handicap chase run for the second time under the Betfred banner, produced one of those turnarounds on the flat for which Sandown has become famous. Irish-trained Jack High produced a strong burst under pressure from the last, despite edging right, to get up near the finish, pulling off a 16/1 surprise and in the process saving the race's sponsor from a potential £250,000 bonus payout if either of the Cheltenham Festival winners who finished second and third, Juveigneur and Kelami, had won. Fourth-placed Whitenzo, representing the Nicholls stable, also played his part, leading from four out and battling on when challenged strongly by the runner-up from the last, before Jack High came through, with Kelami also finishing strongly. The first four were clear, with sixth-placed Comply Or Die faring best from a seven-strong challenge by the Pipe stable (all seven owned by Well Chief's owner David Johnson).

Stanleybet Troytown Handicap Chase, Navan—Jack High is in little danger

Jack High was 5 lb out of the weights in the Betfred Gold Cup and had done most of his racing before Sandown under much more testing conditions in Ireland. Trained until his death in 2003 by Northern Ireland trainer Willie Rock, with whom Tony McCoy started, the late-developing Jack High was Rock's last winner, making his mark as a novice hurdler in the 2002/3 season, in which he progressed well in handicaps before finishing second to Nobody Told Me in the Menolly Homes Champion Novices' Hurdle at Punchestown. Jack High seemed to lack the size for steeplechasing and his first season with his present trainer (who rode Willie Rock's first winner) produced only one victory—in a maiden at Navan—in six outings over fences, Jack High failing to get round in three of them. Jack High was given more opportunity to bring his stamina into play in the latest season and, stepped up to three miles over fences for the first time, he won the Stanleybet Troytown Handicap on heavy going at Navan in November, showing much improved form and winning by six lengths from Jaquouille. Runs in two of Ireland's most competitive handicaps came next, easily the better effort being his fourth, with Jaquouille

Betfred Gold Cup Chase (Handicap), Sandown—the runner-up Juveigneur (white face) and fourth-placed Whitenzo (noseband) are set to be reeled in; third-placed Kelami is also just in shot

second, to Keepatem in the thirty-runner Paddy Power Chase at Leopardstown. Then, in keeping with the sometimes unconventional planning of his trainer, Jack High was pitched in against Rule Supreme and company in the Hennessy Cognac Gold Cup over the same course in February (starting at 66/1 he was beaten forty-nine lengths into fourth by the winner). A run over hurdles completed Jack High's preparation for the Irish Grand National in which he was down among the 10-0 brigade (he had also been entered at Aintree but was too far down the weights to have any real hope of getting a run). The further step up in distance at Fairyhouse suited Jack High admirably and, leading before the last after being patiently ridden, he was caught on the flat and beaten three quarters of a length by the Ruby Walsh-ridden Numbersixvalverde after drifting left. Jack High was unexposed over very long distances before his improved effort in the Irish National and would have had a higher mark in the Betfred Gold Cup if the BHB handicapper had been able to take his Fairyhouse run into account. Though on the small side for tackling the big Aintree fences, Jack High should be just about high enough in the handicap to secure a run in the Grand National in the next season (his trainer won the race with Papillon who twice finished in the frame in the Irish National).

Jack High (IRE) (br.g. 1995)	Erdelistan (FR) (br 1987)	Lashkari (b or br 1981)	Mill Reef
			Larannda
		Eunomia (br 1975)	Abdos
			Iroma
	Lyntim (br 1983)	Fidel (b 1968)	Relko
			Cuba
		Viacandella (b 1967)	Cantab
			Fire Forest

Jack High, a smallish gelding, is by the very smart mile-and-a-half performer Erdelistan, a product of the Aga Khan Studs, out of the fairly useful hurdler and

Miss Brenda Ross's "Jack High"

fair chaser for Willie Rock, Lyntim. Lyntim—whose name was a combination of the names of Rock's children—is a sister to Rock's useful jumpers Eddie Wee and Helynsar, all three closely related to the smart two-mile chaser Thumbs Up, by the one-eyed Fidel out of daughters of Fire Forest. Thumbs Up's dam Misclaire was unraced while Viacondella, the dam of Lyntim, Eddie Wee and Helynsar, was an Irish hunter chaser. Eddie Wee and Helynsar were best known as two-milers but stayed two and a half. Lyntim probably stayed three miles, while Viacondella was a sister to the fairly useful staying chaser Cantabet. Jack High, who is held up, stays three miles five furlongs well and may get further. He acts on heavy going. *T. M. Walsh, Ireland*

JACKIE BOY (IRE) 6 b.g. Lord Americo – Riverpauper (IRE) (Over The River (FR)) [2004/5 F17g* F17d^2 21d 19s^6 19v^4 22g Apr 12] €6,200 4-y-o: second foal: dam unraced half-sister to fairly useful hurdler Team Tassel: very green but still won bumper at Hereford on debut in September: modest form at best in novice hurdles: should stay beyond 19f. *N. A. Twiston-Davies* **h87 F89**

JACKLIGHTE BELLEVUE (FR) 8 b.g. Saint Cyrien (FR) – Kalighte (FR) (Light Butterfly) [2004/5 c23d^{pu} Jun 23] good-topped gelding: winning hurdler/maiden chaser, pulled up only start since 2002/3: stays 21f: acts on heavy going. *Mrs H. Dalton* **c– h–**

JACK LYNCH 9 ch.g. Lancastrian – Troublewithjack (Sulaafah (USA)) [2004/5 16s^4 20v^F 24v^6 24v* Feb 2] modest form over hurdles, off 2½ years before reappearance: won conditional jockeys handicap at Newcastle in February: will stay beyond 3m: raced only on soft/heavy ground over hurdles. *Ferdy Murphy* **h96**

JACK MARTIN (IRE) 8 ch.g. Erins Isle – Rolling Penny (IRE) (Le Moss) [2004/5 h119, F94: c22s^5 c16d* c16s^F 20v^{pu} 20v^3 20v^3 16v^4 22d 20s^{pu} Apr 10] leggy gelding: fairly useful handicap hurdler, below form last 3 outings: won 2-finisher novice chase at Haydock in December: close up when falling 4 out in handicap next time: will stay 3m: acts on heavy going. *S. Gollings* **c107 h118**

JACK OF KILCASH (IRE) 11 br.g. Glacial Storm (USA) – Candora (Cantab) [2004/5 c–: c21m^6 May 19] modest pointer: well beaten in 2 hunter chases. *Nigel Benstead* **c–**

JACK OF SPADES (IRE) 9 b.g. Mister Lord (USA) – Dooney's Daughter (The Parson) [2004/5 c–: 21d 16s^{pu} c16s c20s c26d^2 c25s^4 c23m* Apr 10] good-topped gelding: no show in 2 starts over hurdles: modest form over fences: won handicap at Worcester in April: stays 3¼m: acts on good to soft and good to firm going. *R. Dickin* **c91 h–**

JACK POT II (FR) 8 ch.g. Luchiroverte (IRE) – Roxane II (FR) (Signani (FR)) [2004/5 h97: c25g^2 c23g^{pu} c28s^{pu} 24s^{pu} 22d^{pu} 20v^{pu} c25s^{pu} Apr 10] useful-looking gelding: modest hurdler: second in novice at Hexham on chasing debut: sold out of L. Lungo's stable 12,000 gns Doncaster May Sales: out of sorts subsequently, left M. Sheppard before final outing: best around 3m: raced on good ground or softer (acts on heavy): tried in cheekpieces/blinkers: has worn tongue strap: makes mistakes. *G. R. I. Smyly* **c88 x h–**

JACKS CRAIC (IRE) 6 b.g. Lord Americo – Boleree (IRE) (Mandalus) [2004/5 h99, F92: 21d^F 17d^3 17s^3 20s^3 16s^5 17v* 17s^2 16s^2 16s^4 Mar 6] good-topped gelding: fairly useful hurdler: won handicap at Folkestone in January: stays 2½m: acts on heavy going (bumper form on good to firm): reliable. *J. L. Spearing* **h112**

JACKS HELEN 8 b.m. Lancastrian – Troublewithjack (Sulaafah (USA)) [2004/5 23v^{pu} 21s^{pu} 20d^{pu} Apr 20] angular mare: fifth foal: half-sister to winning pointer Fisherman Jack (by Carlingford Castle): dam poor maiden, stayed 11f: no sign of ability. *G. J. Smith* **h–**

JACKS JEWEL (IRE) 8 b.g. Welsh Term – September Daydream (IRE) (Phardante (FR)) [2004/5 h81, F–: c20d^F c20v^{pu} c19s^3 c19s^5 c19m^3 c24g^{ur} Apr 15] poor form over hurdles/fences: stays 21f: acts on soft and good to firm going. *C. J. Down* **c81 x h–**

JACK'S LAD (IRE) 6 ch.g. High Roller (IRE) – Captain's Covey (Captain James) [2004/5 F17s* F17g^5 19s^{pu} 16d 16d* 17g^4 Apr 14] workmanlike gelding: seventh foal: half-brother to 1991 2-y-o 5.3f winner Dollar Wine (by Alzao) and winner in Czech Republic by Astronef: dam maiden: better effort in bumpers when winning at Hereford in November: fair form over hurdles: much improved when winning maiden at Ludlow in February by neck from Mister Mustard. *Mrs S. M. Johnson* **h114 F93**

JACKSON (FR) 8 b.g. Passing Sale (FR) – Tynia (FR) (Djarvis (FR)) [2004/5 c–, h–: c24g^{ur} c24s^2 22g^3 24d^2 22v^2 22s 24g 22g^2 Apr 12] sturdy gelding: winning pointer: runner-up on completed start in hunter chases: left Mrs H. Dalton, fairly useful form in novice hurdles: stays 3m: raced on good going or softer: has had tongue tied. *A. King* **c77 h122**

JACKSONVILLE (FR) 8 b.g. Petit Montmorency (USA) – Quinine Des Aulnes (FR) (Air du Nord (USA)) [2004/5 c93, h–: c25d^{pu} 20d^{5} c20s^{3} 22s^{5} c22v^{5} c20v^{3} c25v^{3} c25d^{pu} c26s^{pu} c32v^{2} c27v^{pu} c25s* c26v^{5} Apr 17] sturdy gelding: maiden hurdler: modest handicap chaser: won amateur selling event at Hexham in April: should stay beyond 25f: raced on good going or softer (acts on heavy): usually blinkered/in cheekpieces nowadays: tongue tied eleventh start: inconsistent. *A. Parker* **c91 § h79**

JACK WHITE 8 b.g. Teenoso (USA) – Frabjous Day (Broadsword (USA)) [2004/5 16g 23s^{pu} 19s Mar 1] 6,000 4-y-o: useful-looking gelding: third foal: dam, winning pointer, out of sister to useful staying chaser Roman Holiday and half-sister to very smart staying chaser Master H and useful 2m chaser Master Eye: poor form on first of 3 outings over hurdles. *Mrs S. J. Smith* **h79**

JACQUEMART COLOMBE (FR) 8 gr.g. Royal Charter (FR) – Tanie (FR) (Kashmir Ring) [2004/5 c24g^{2} c26g^{pu} c26d* c24d^{6} c26g^{3} c25g^{3} Apr 12] sturdy gelding: second foal: half-brother to 21f chase winner Isope Colombe (by Roi de Rome) and fairly useful 2½m chase winner Meneur de Jeu (by Sleeping Car): dam winning chaser around 2m in France: won twice over fences in French Provinces at 4 yrs: left G. Macaire and off over 2 years, fairly useful form in handicap chases in Britain: won at Newton Abbot in August: stays 3¼m: acts on soft going. *P. Bowen* **c115**

JADEERON 6 b.g. Green Desert (USA) – Rain And Shine (FR) (Rainbow Quest (USA)) [2004/5 16d^{pu} 16d Nov 23] smallish gelding: fair on Flat (stays 2m), successful in December: showed little in 2 runs over hurdles. *Miss D. A. McHale* **h–**

JADES DOUBLE 4 b.f. Double Trigger (IRE) – Jaydeebee (Buckley) [2004/5 F17s^{4} F16v F16d^{6} F18d^{4} Apr 18] third foal: dam, ran 3 times in bumpers, half-sister to Cheltenham Gold Cup winner Master Oats: modest form in bumpers: will be suited by 2½m+. *M. Madgwick* **F81**

JAFFA 13 ch.g. Kind of Hush – Sip of Orange (Celtic Cone) [2004/5 c104: c20s^{2} c20g* Apr 3] well-made gelding: fairly useful handicap chaser: better than ever aged 13, winning at Market Rasen in April: best around 2½m: acts on soft going. *Miss J. Wormall* **c117**

JAHIA (NZ) 6 br.m. Jahafil – Lana (NZ) (Tristrams Heritage (NZ)) [2004/5 h–: 17g^{pu} 17d^{6} 17g 16g^{pu} Oct 4] no form over hurdles, left R. Guest before final start: tried tongue tied: modest on Flat (stays 1m), won in March. *M. Madgwick* **h–**

JAIR OHMSFORD (IRE) 6 b.g. Hamas (IRE) – Harry's Irish Rose (USA) (Sir Harry Lewis (USA)) [2004/5 16s^{2} 17v* 17v^{2} 17s* 20g^{3} Mar 26] sturdy gelding: fairly useful on Flat (stays 1½m), successful 3 times in 2004: fairly useful novice hurdler: won at Folkestone in January and Market Rasen in March: best effort when third to Kilgowan in handicap at Haydock: stays 2½m: raced on good going or softer (acts on heavy). *W. J. Musson* **h128**

JAKARI (FR) 8 b.g. Apeldoorn (FR) – Tartifume II (FR) (Mistigri) [2004/5 c141, h–: c21s c24g^{5} c36d^{pu} Apr 9] rather leggy gelding: useful handicap chaser: easily best effort in 2004/5 when creditable fifth to Kelami in valuable event at Cheltenham in March, making most until hitting 4 out and rallying: jumped with little confidence in Grand National at Aintree: stays 3m: acts on soft and good to firm going: races prominently. *H. D. Daly* **c140 h–**

JAKE BLACK (IRE) 5 b.g. Definite Article – Tirhala (IRE) (Chief Singer) [2004/5 h94: 16s* 16s^{3} 16m^{6} 16g 16v^{3} Jan 3] close-coupled gelding: fair on Flat (seems to stay 1½m): fairly useful handicap hurdler: won intermediate event at Wetherby in October by 23 lengths: best at 2m: acts on heavy and good to firm going. *J. J. Quinn* **h116 +**

JAKERS (IRE) 8 b.g. Jolly Jake (NZ) – Catchthegoose (Tug of War) [2004/5 19g^{2} 18s* 20s 16v* 20v^{4} c22v^{4} c24s^{2} c20d^{2} c20s^{4} Mar 26] fourth foal: dam half-sister to fairly useful hurdler/chaser up to 3m Liver Bird: placed all 4 outings in bumpers: fairly useful hurdler: won maiden at Thurles and novice at Tramore (by 4 lengths from Pacolet) in December: fair form when in frame all 4 starts over fences: probably stays 3m: acts on heavy going. *P. A. Fahy, Ireland* **c103 h116**

JAKE'S CASTLE 6 b.g. Shambo – Brass Castle (IRE) (Carlingford Castle) [2004/5 F16d^{3} May 8] 15,000 4-y-o: useful-looking gelding: fifth foal: half-brother to fair hurdler/useful chaser Longshanks (by Broadsword), stays 3m: dam unraced, from family of top-class staying chaser Teeton Mill, high-class 2m hurdler Celtic Ryde and high-class 2m chaser Noddy's Ryde: 2¾ lengths third to Carthys Cross in bumper at Southwell on debut: looking very much a stayer. *Mrs H. Dalton* **F95**

JAKE THE JUMPER (IRE) 8 b.g. Jolly Jake (NZ) – Princess Tino (IRE) (Rontino) [2004/5 h97: 23d^{2} 24g^{pu} May 16] workmanlike gelding: lightly raced: modest maiden **h97**

hurdler: seemed to go amiss final start: stays 3¼m: acts on firm and soft going. *Miss G. Browne*

JALLASTEP (FR) 8 b.g. Boston Two Step (USA) – Balladine (FR) (Rivelago (FR)) [2004/5 h92: c17g^{6} c20m^{3} c20d* c21s^{3} c21s^{ur} c20g c24g^{5} c16d^{2} Jan 7] lengthy, workmanlike gelding: modest handicap hurdler: fair form over fences: won novice handicap at Perth in June: stays 21f: acts on good to firm and good to soft going: tried in cheekpieces/visor. *J. S. Goldie* **c101 h–**

JALONS STAR (IRE) 7 b.g. Eagle Eyed (USA) – Regina St Cyr (IRE) (Doulab (USA)) [2004/5 c86, h–: 22m^{3} Sep 1] workmanlike gelding: maiden chaser: winning hurdler: best around 2m: probably acts on any going. *M. R. Channon* **c– h67**

JALOUSIE DREAM 4 b.f. Easycall – Forest Maid (Thatching) [2004/5 16m 16g^{6} Nov 15] leggy filly: no form on Flat or over hurdles: tongue tied final start. *G. M. Moore* **h–**

JALOUX D'ESTRUVAL (FR) 8 b.g. Kadalko (FR) – Pommette III (FR) (Trac) [2004/5 c125x, h103+: c26d^{2} c32d^{F} 23v^{5} 21v* Jan 17] tall gelding: useful handicap chaser: good second to Colourful Life at Newton Abbot: fair handicap hurdler: fitted with hood, won at Plumpton in January: will probably stay beyond 3¼m: raced on good going or softer (acts on heavy): has worn net muzzle: often let down by jumping over fences. *Mrs L. C. Taylor* **c130 x h110**

JALPREUIL MALTA (FR) 8 gr.g. Saint Preuil (FR) – Alzira (FR) (Numbi (FR)) [2004/5 c20g^{4} c22d^{pu} c20d^{4} Dec 11] workmanlike gelding: winning cross-country chaser: left P. Nicholls and off 20 months, best effort in handicaps in 2004/5 when fourth to Europa at Kempton on reappearance: may prove best around 2½m. *J. R. Best* **c96 ? h–**

JAMAL (POL) 5 b.h. Who Knows – Jugoslawia (POL) (Danish Fort) [2004/5 17d 24f^{pu} Sep 5] successful at 1m and 9f on Flat in Poland for B. Mazurek: no sign of ability in 2 outings over hurdles. *A. Sadik* **h–**

JAMEROSIER (FR) 8 b.g. The Wonder (FR) – Teuphaine (FR) (Barbotan (FR)) [2004/5 c113, h–: c28s^{pu} c30d^{pu} c24d^{5} c24d c26v^{3} c25s c26s^{4} Feb 14] strong gelding: reportedly tubed: fair maiden chaser: likely to prove best at 3m+: raced on going softer than good (acts on heavy): tried visored/in cheekpieces: has had tongue tied: lazy. *Mrs L. C. Taylor* **c93 § h–**

JAMES VICTOR (IRE) 7 b.g. Be My Guest (USA) – Antakiya (IRE) (Ela-Mana-Mou) [2004/5 c17f* c17s^{4} c16g^{4} Nov 18] leggy gelding: well held in bumper: fell in point in 2004: easily best effort in chases when fortunate winner of novice at Exeter in September: acts on firm going: free-going sort. *N. R. Mitchell* **c95**

JAMIE BROWNE (IRE) 8 ch.g. Sayaarr (USA) – Glowing Embers (Nebbiolo) [2004/5 c–: 21m^{pu} 20g^{pu} 22v^{pu} 20s^{pu} Nov 5] winning pointer: no show in novice hunter chase/over hurdles: tried tongue tied. *W. G. Young* **c– h–**

JAMORIN DANCER 10 b.g. Charmer – Geryea (USA) (Desert Wine (USA)) [2004/5 c84§, h–§: 17g^{6} 17g^{pu} 16d 17d 16g^{5} c16m c16m c20m^{ur} c16s^{5} Mar 10] sturdy gelding: maiden hurdler/winning chaser: little form in 2004/5: tried blinkered, usually wears cheekpieces: irresolute. *S. G. Chadwick* **c– § h55 §**

JANBRE (IRE) 6 br.g. Zaffaran (USA) – Black Gayle (IRE) (Strong Gale) [2004/5 F96: 22d^{2} 24s^{3} 24d^{2} 24s^{4} 23s^{pu} c24s^{pu} Apr 2] useful-looking gelding: modest form over hurdles: lame on chasing debut: stays 3m: raced on good ground or softer (bumper form on heavy): tried visored. *M. Scudamore* **c– h96**

JANDAL 11 ch.g. Arazi (USA) – Littlefield (Bay Express) [2004/5 c–, h–: 22g^{5} 17g c21g^{ur} c16g^{3} c21g^{pu} c21g^{4} c21d^{4} c23f^{2} c23g^{5} c19s^{ur} c19d^{ur} 19d c24g^{6} c19g Dec 30] poor maiden hurdler/chaser: stays 23f: acts on firm going, possibly unsuited by softer than good: tried in cheekpieces. *B. Scriven* **c82 h–**

JANGO MALFOY (IRE) 4 ch.g. Russian Revival (USA) – Sialia (IRE) (Bluebird (USA)) [2004/5 17g^{6} 17m Sep 8] modest maiden at 2 yrs, out of form on Flat in 2004: tongue tied, little form over hurdles. *B. W. Duke* **h–**

JANORAMIC (FR) 8 b.g. Panoramic – Victoire V (FR) (Nellio (FR)) [2004/5 c–, h–: 16d^{6} 22g^{5} May 26] sturdy gelding: failed to complete both starts over fences: modest novice hurdler: stays 19f: acts on good to firm and good to soft going. *T. J. Fitzgerald* **c– h84**

JANSUE CHARLIE 11 ch.g. Ardar – Kincherinchee (Dunbeath (USA)) [2004/5 c20s^{pu} c20v^{6} c25s^{4} c20v^{4} c24s^{5} c20v^{5} c26s^{pu} 24v^{pu} c25s^{3} c26v Apr 17] lengthy gelding: winning hurdler: little form since 2001, including over fences: stays 2¾m: acts on heavy going: has worn blinkers/cheekpieces. *R. Nixon* **c– h–**

JAOKA DU GORD (FR) 8 b.g. Concorde Jr (USA) – Theorie du Cochet (FR) (Franc Ryk) [2004/5 c–, F84: c22s^4 c24s^{pu} c23s^{pu} c20d^2 c22d^3 c22g^4 c24g* c24s^2 Apr 16] good-topped gelding: fair handicap chaser: won at Bangor in March: stays 3m: raced on good going or softer (acts on soft). *P. R. Webber* **c107**

JAOLINS 4 b.f. Groom Dancer (USA) – On The Top (High Top) [2004/5 16s^{pu} 16d^{pu} 17g Apr 15] leggy, angular filly: poor up to 1m on Flat, sold out of P. Murphy's stable £400 Ascot December Sales: no form over hurdles: headstrong. *M. Appleby* **h–**

JAQUOUILLE (FR) 8 b.g. Agent Bleu (FR) – Topeka (FR) (Italic (FR)) [2004/5 c22s* c24v^2 c24v^2 20s c29s Mar 28] winning hurdler: useful handicap chaser: won at Down Royal in November: better form when second in valuable handicaps won by Jack High at Navan later in month and Keepatem at Leopardstown in December: failed to stay when well held in Irish Grand National at Fairyhouse final start: stays 3m: acts on heavy and good to firm going. *A. L. T. Moore, Ireland* **c130 h93**

JARDIN DE BEAULIEU (FR) 8 ch.g. Rough Magic (FR) – Emblem (FR) (Siberian Express (USA)) [2004/5 c122, h–: c20s^4 c20d^5 c21d^{pu} c25s^{pu} c23m^2 Apr 10] well-made gelding: fairly useful handicap chaser at best: dropped long way in weights and tongue tied, second at Worcester in April: stays 23f: acts on soft and good to firm going: has worn headgear. *Ian Williams* **c104 h–**

JARDIN FLEURI (FR) 8 ch.g. Cyborg (FR) – Merry Durgan (FR) (Le Nain Jaune (FR)) [2004/5 c–, h86: 20d^5 May 15] winning hurdler: let down by jumping on chasing debut: stays 2¾m: acts on soft going. *M. C. Pipe* **c– h74**

JAROD (FR) 7 b.g. Scribe (IRE) – Somnambula (IRE) (Petoski) [2004/5 h79, F84: c23d^{pu} May 4] sturdy gelding: poor form over hurdles: no show on chasing debut: tried blinkered: sold 2,000 gns Doncaster May Sales, won point in March. *P. J. Hobbs* **c– h–**

JARRO (FR) 9 b.g. Pistolet Bleu (IRE) – Junta (FR) (Cariellor (FR)) [2004/5 c–, h–: c16d^3 c16s* c16d^3 c16d^5 c16g^5 c16g^2 c16s Apr 21] workmanlike gelding: fairly useful handicap chaser: won at Windsor in December by ½ length from Batswing: best effort after when second to Runner Bean at Wincanton: best around 2m: acts on good to firm and heavy going: free-going sort. *Miss Venetia Williams* **c120 h–**

JARVO 4 b.g. Pursuit of Love – Pinkie Rose (FR) (Kenmare (FR)) [2004/5 16g^{pu} Oct 26] fair maiden on Flat (stays 1¼m) in 2004: modest form in 2005: no show in juvenile on hurdling debut: sold to join M. Salaman's stable 2,000 gns Newmarket February Sales. *N. P. Littmoden* **h–**

JASEUR (USA) 12 b.g. Lear Fan (USA) – Spur Wing (USA) (Storm Bird (CAN)) [2004/5 c–, h105§: 21m^6 24s^6 24s 24s^{pu} 17s^3 19s^5 16s^F Dec 13] angular, rather leggy gelding: mistakes both starts over fences: winning hurdler, poor in 2004/5: stays 3¼m: acts on any going: usually wears headgear: ungenuine. *S. T. Lewis* **c– h82 §**

JASMIN D'OUDAIRIES (FR) 8 b.g. Apeldoorn (FR) – Vellea (FR) (Cap Martin (FR)) [2004/5 c123, h–: c20g^3 c16g c19s^3 c20d* c17d c22v^3 c19v^2 c20v^3 16s^3 20s* 19s Mar 27] compact gelding: useful chaser: won minor event at Clonmel in November by 3½ lengths from Be My Better Half: better than ever when winning 23-runner handicap **c133 h116**

S. M. Morris Ltd Handicap Chase, Punchestown—
Jasmin d'Oudairies (No.8) is poised to challenge three out behind Kymandjen and John James

at Punchestown in late-April by 5 lengths from Kymandjen: fairly useful over hurdles: won 18-runner listed handicap at Navan in March by 6 lengths from One Four Shannon: likely to stay 3m: raced on good going or softer over jumps (acts on heavy). *W. P. Mullins, Ireland*

JASMIN GUICHOIS (FR) 8 ch.g. Dom Alco (FR) – Lady Belle (FR) (Or de Chine) [2004/5 c115, h–: c22d^ur Nov 28] compact gelding: fairly useful handicap chaser: well held when unseating only start in 2004/5: stays 21f: acts on good to firm and heavy going. *Miss Venetia Williams* **c– h–**

JASPER ROONEY 6 b.g. Riverwise (USA) – Miss Secret (El Conquistador) [2004/5 F–: 19d^pu 22s^pu Jan 6] no form in bumper or 2 novice hurdles. *C. W. Mitchell* **h–**

JAUNTY TIMES 5 b.g. Luso – Jaunty June (Primitive Rising (USA)) [2004/5 F84: F16d^2 19s^3 19s^2 19v^2 22d^4 20d^3 Apr 20] good-bodied gelding: chasing type: fair form in bumpers, sold out of B. Eckley's stable 30,000 gns Doncaster August Sales after first start: fair novice hurdler: stays 2¾m: raced on going softer than good over hurdles. *H. D. Daly* **h113 F91**

JAVA DANCER 4 b.g. Danehill Dancer (IRE) – Evasive Step (Batshoof) [2004/5 17v^pu Nov 26] well held in 3 maidens around 1m on Flat in 2004: no show in juvenile on hurdling debut. *T. D. Easterby* **h–**

JAVELIN 9 ch.g. Generous (IRE) – Moss (Alzao (USA)) [2004/5 c92, h107: 20f 22g 24s^3 21d* 17g 21v^5 24d 21s^4 24d 22d 19s^pu Mar 23] sturdy, lengthy gelding: twice-raced chaser/modest hurdler nowadays: won selling handicap (sold from I. Williams 7,000 gns) at Sedgefield in November: lost form after: stays 2½m: acts on good to firm and good to soft going: wears headgear nowadays. *N. J. Hawke* **c– h97 d**

JAVELOT D'OR (FR) 8 b. or br.g. Useful (FR) – Flika d'Or (FR) (Pot d'Or (FR)) [2004/5 c–, h–: c16f^3 20g^pu c17d^4 Apr 11] smallish, lengthy gelding: lightly raced over hurdles: poor chaser: left Miss V. Williams after first outing: raced mainly around 2m: probably acts on any going: tongue tied last 2 starts. *Mrs B. K. Thomson* **c78 h–**

JAWAD (IRE) 4 b.g. Kahyasi – Mystic Charm (Nashwan (USA)) [2004/5 16s^6 16d 17v^pu 16d Dec 11] modest maiden on Flat (stays 1½m): no form over hurdles: tongue tied first 2 starts. *Ms J. Morgan, Ireland* **h–**

JAWWALA (USA) 6 b.m. Green Dancer (USA) – Fetch N Carry (USA) (Alleged (USA)) [2004/5 h84§: 16d^5 20m^pu 24d^R Nov 7] leggy mare: poor maiden hurdler: has refused to race/pulled herself up: usually wears headgear: thoroughly ungenuine. *J. R. Jenkins* **h§§**

JAYBEEDEE 9 b.g. Rudimentary (USA) – Meavy (Kalaglow) [2004/5 c–, h86: c16g^6 c24d^5 c21d^pu 20v^5 c16v^6 19g Mar 3] good-bodied gelding: winning 2m hurdler: little form since 2002, including over fences: tried in cheekpieces. *Dr P. Pritchard* **c– h–**

JAY BEE ELL 8 b.g. Pursuit of Love – On Request (IRE) (Be My Guest (USA)) [2004/5 h–: 22d^2 21g 24s^6 18d Nov 14] sturdy gelding: modest hurdler: sold out of A. King's stable 1,400 gns Doncaster August Sales after second start: should stay 3m: acts on good to soft going. *B. N. Pollock* **h96**

JAYBEJAY (NZ) 10 b.g. High Ice (USA) – Galaxy Light (NZ) (Balios) [2004/5 c117§, h–: c20g^F c20m^5 c26d^pu c24g^pu c19s^pu c23g Dec 8] smallish gelding: fairly useful handicap chaser in 2003/4, has lost his way: stays 21f: acts on soft and good to firm going: visored/in cheekpieces nowadays: often let down by jumping: temperamental. *M. C. Pipe* **c111 § h–**

JAY BE JUNIOR 5 br.g. J B Quick – Staggering (IRE) (Daring March) [2004/5 F17s* F17m* F16g Oct 27] sturdy gelding: first foal: dam, poor novice hurdler who stayed 2½m, half-sister to useful hurdler up to 25f Sip of Orange: fairly useful in bumpers, winning at Market Rasen in May and Hereford in June: off 4 months, finished lame at Cheltenham final start. *G. A. Harker* **F104 +**

JAYED (IRE) 7 b. or br.g. Marju (IRE) – Taqreem (IRE) (Nashwan (USA)) [2004/5 h77: 16m^5 16s^3 16d^2 16d* Feb 18] modest hurdler: won selling handicap at Fakenham in February: best at sharp 2m: acts on good to firm and good to soft going: headstrong front runner. *M. Bradstock* **h91**

JAZIL 10 b.g. Nashwan (USA) – Gracious Beauty (USA) (Nijinsky (CAN)) [2004/5 24s^pu Oct 21] workmanlike gelding: let down by jumping over fences: fair hurdler at best: no show in seller only start in 2004/5: tried visored: tongue tied. *K. A. Morgan* **c– h–**

Northwest Racing Club Novices' Chase, Haydock—the grey Jazz d'Estruval has already taken the measure of eventual third Sonevafushi as that one blunders two out

JAZZ D'ESTRUVAL (FR) 8 gr.g. Bayolidaan (FR) – Caro d'Estruval (FR) (Caramo (FR)) [2004/5 h129: c21v* c22v* c25s^2 c24s^3 Apr 20] strong, useful-looking gelding: fairly useful hurdler: off a year, useful form when winning novice chases at Ayr (by 10 lengths from Tribal Venture) in December and Haydock (4-runner event, beat Trabolgan 9 lengths easing down) in January: let down by jumping both starts after, several bad mistakes when remote third to My Will at Perth: stays 25f: raced on good ground or softer (acts on heavy): needs to brush up jumping if he's to fulfil potential. *N. G. Richards* **c144 h–**

JAZZ DU FOREZ (FR) 8 b.g. Video Rock (FR) – Ophyr du Forez (FR) (Fin Bon) [2004/5 c60, h60: c26g^6 c20s^3 c25g^2 c24g^{wo} c24g Jan 19] smallish gelding: poor chaser: walked over at Doncaster: stays 25f: acts on heavy and good to firm going: tried blinkered. *John Allen* **c70 h–**

JAZZ NIGHT 8 b.g. Alhijaz – Hen Night (Mummy's Game) [2004/5 c82, h–: c16s^{pu} c16s^{pu} c16m^2 Mar 21] good-topped gelding: fair hunter chaser: best form at 2m: acts on good to firm going. *Shaun Lycett* **c91 h–**

JBALLINGALL 6 b.g. Overbury (IRE) – Sister Delaney (Deep Run) [2004/5 h–, F–: 20d^{pu} 20v^{pu} c27v^3 c21s^3 c24g^{pu} c20v^{ur} c21d^3 c20v* Apr 17] lengthy gelding: no show in bumper or over hurdles: poor chaser: won novice handicap at Carlisle in April: should stay beyond 21f: raced on good going or softer (acts on heavy): blinkered last 3 starts. *N. Wilson* **c75 h–**

JEALOUS MEAD (IRE) 4 ro.g. I'm Supposin (IRE) – Spindle's (Gran Alba (USA)) [2004/5 F17s^5 16g^{pu} Mar 9] leggy gelding: first foal: dam, little promise over hurdles, half-sister to fairly useful hurdler up to 2½m Silver Shred: no show in maiden bumper or novice hurdle. *J. Howard Johnson* **h– F–**

JEEPERS CREEPERS 5 b.g. Wizard King – Dark Amber (Formidable (USA)) [2004/5 F–: F16g Dec 16] workmanlike gelding: tailed off in bumpers 12 months apart. *Mrs A. M. Thorpe* **F–**

JEFERTITI (FR) 8 ch.g. Le Nain Jaune (FR) – Nefertiti (FR) (Tourangeau (FR)) [2004/5 c102, h–: c24g² c20gᵖᵘ c20s² c16g* c16s³ c16s* c16d⁶ c16gᶠ Jan 14] rangy, good sort: fair chaser: made running when winning handicaps at Perth in September and Ayr in November, beating Polyphon both times: stays 2½m: acts on good to firm and heavy going: free-going sort. *Miss Lucinda V. Russell* **c102 h–**

JENAVIVE 5 b.m. Danzig Connection (USA) – Promise Fulfilled (USA) (Bet Twice (USA)) [2004/5 h74: 18m 17m 19m⁶ 22d 19d Dec 3] good-topped mare: poor maiden hurdler: stays 2½m. *N. J. Hawke* **h74 ?**

JENGA 8 ro.m. Minster Son – Maybe Daisy (Nicholas Bill) [2004/5 c105, h–: c24gᵖᵘ c23vᵖᵘ c26dᵖᵘ Apr 18] medium-sized mare: winning hurdler/chaser: left K. Bailey and off 15 months, no sign of retaining ability. *O. Sherwood* **c– h–**

JENKO (FR) 8 b.g. Cadoubel (FR) – Maika d'Ores (FR) (Gaur) [2004/5 c21g⁴ c26gᵖᵘ Aug 2] tall gelding: poor maiden hurdler in 2002/3: little form over fences: stays 21f: acts on soft ground: tried tongue tied. *C. J. Gray* **c– h–**

JERICHO III (FR) 8 b.g. Lute Antique (FR) – La Salamandre (FR) (Pot d'Or (FR)) [2004/5 c92, h–: c20m⁵ c16d² c17mʳᵒ c17gᵘʳ c17g³ c17sᶠ c16d² c16m² c16d² c19g⁶ c17v* c16d* c16v* c16s* c16d⁵ c16g c16g Mar 26] leggy gelding: fairly useful handicap chaser: much improved in 2004/5, winning at Kelso, Leicester (conditional jockeys) and Ayr in January and Towcester (made all to beat Compton Amica 6 lengths) in February: would also have won at Kelso third start but for running out after last: best around 2m: acts on good to firm and heavy going: wears headgear: tried tongue tied: bold jumper: free-going front runner. *R. C. Guest* **c117 h–**

JERINGA 6 b.g. Karinga Bay – Jervandha (Strong Gale) [2004/5 F17s* F16g⁴ F17v³ Mar 20] 5,000 4-y-o: good-topped gelding: fifth foal: dam, no form over hurdles, half-sister to fairly useful chaser up to 2½m Buckland Lad: fairly useful form in bumpers: won maiden at Sedgefield on debut in February, making all to beat The Wife's Sister 12 lengths: will stay 2½m. *J. Wade* **F95**

JEROME JEROME 13 b.g. Arctic Lord – Polaris Song (True Song) [2004/5 c30dᵖᵘ May 11] of little account outside points: tried blinkered. *B. G. Clark* **c– h–**

JEROPINO (IRE) 7 b.g. Norwich – Guillig Lady (IRE) (Hatim (USA)) [2004/5 h94: 17d² c17mᵖᵘ c16s⁴ c16g⁵ c18g c16s³ c16gᶠ Mar 9] quite good-topped gelding: maiden hurdler/chaser, fair form at best: best form around 2m: free-going sort. *J. Mackie* **c103 h108**

JESNIC (IRE) 5 b.g. Kahyasi – Fur Hat (Habitat) [2004/5 16g 19s 17d c16m⁵ c23d³ Apr 20] €2,500 3-y-o: strong, stocky gelding: half-brother to several winners, including fair hurdler Be My Habitat (by Be My Guest), stayed 21f, and useful bumper winner Habihat (by Sabrehill): dam unraced sister to Sun Chariot winner Topsy, dam of top-class 1m to 1½m colt Most Welcome, and half-sister to top-class 1½m colt Teenoso: first sign of ability when third in novice handicap chase at Worcester: tried visored: has had tongue tied. *R. Dickin* **c76 h–**

JESPER (FR) 8 b.g. Video Rock (FR) – Belle Des Airs (FR) (Saumon (FR)) [2004/5 h86: 19d⁶ 20v 19g 21g* 23d* 24m Apr 13] smallish gelding: modest hurdler: won handicaps at Huntingdon (seller) and Fakenham (novice) in March: stays 23f: acts on good to soft going: tongue tied last 3 starts. *R. T. Phillips* **h95**

JESSINCA 9 b.m. Minshaanshu Amad (USA) – Noble Soul (Sayf El Arab (USA)) [2004/5 16m⁵ 19d⁴ 16s³ 16gᵖᵘ 17s Jan 3] poor on Flat (barely stays 1¼m): poor novice hurdler: unlikely to stay beyond 2m. *A. P. Jones* **h77**

JETHRO TULL (IRE) 6 b.g. Witness Box (USA) – Country Project (IRE) (Project Manager) [2004/5 F16s³ F16d⁴ 16s 20v Dec 27] lengthy gelding: first foal: dam, no sign of ability on Flat, half-sister to fairly useful winner up to 1¼m Family Project: won 2½m maiden point in 2004: in frame in bumpers: not knocked about either start in novice hurdles at Ayr, banned under non-triers rule on first occasion: capable of better. *G. A. Harker* **h79 + F89**

JET MAGIC (IRE) 5 b.g. Semillon – Kerry Minstrel (Black Minstrel) [2004/5 24d⁵ 20v³ 20d² 20gᵖᵘ Mar 26] useful-looking gelding: seventh foal: half-brother to winning pointer by Be My Native: dam lightly raced in bumpers/points: runner-up in maiden Irish point on debut: bought £56,000 Cheltenham April Sales: form over hurdles only when second in maiden at Chepstow: should stay beyond 2½m: raced on good ground or softer. *A. King* **h104**

JIDIYA (IRE) 6 b.g. Lahib (USA) – Yaqatha (IRE) (Sadler's Wells (USA)) [2004/5 h–, F95: 16d 16s Dec 4] lengthy, good-topped gelding: bumper winner: fair on Flat (stays 2m), successful in January and March: little form over hurdles: tried blinkered. *S. Gollings* **h–**

JIMBOY (IRE) 8 b.g. Jimmys Pixie (IRE) – Caitrionas Joy (IRE) (Royal Fountain) [2004/5 19spu 19spu 24m 22mF Apr 17] pulled up in maiden Irish point in 2003: no form over hurdles: dead. *T. P. Walshe* **h–**

JIM DORE (IRE) 10 b. or br.g. Mac's Imp (USA) – Secret Assignment (Vitiges (FR)) [2004/5 h–: 20dpu 17m 19m6 24mpu Jun 16] no sign of ability: tried tongue tied. *R. Williams* **h–**

JIM (FR) 8 b.g. Glaieul (USA) – Beautywal (FR) (Magwal (FR)) [2004/5 c138, h115: c16s c20s6 16s* c21v* c25s5 Apr 7] lengthy, well-made gelding: fairly useful hurdler: won handicap at Naas in February: useful handicap chaser: won quite valuable event at Leopardstown in March by 4½ lengths from Lord Who: out of depth next time, held up at Punchestown when below form in late-April: best up to 21f: raced on going softer than good (acts on heavy): usually front runner. *J. T. R. Dreaper, Ireland* **c138 h128**

JIM JAM JOEY (IRE) 12 ch.g. Big Sink Hope (USA) – Ascot Princess (Prince Hansel) [2004/5 c–, h106: 24s2 c24s* c24s2 c29vpu c24v5 Jan 21] angular gelding: fair hurdler/chaser: won novice handicap over fences at Chepstow in October: best at 3m+: acts on heavy going: blinkered: takes plenty of driving and sometimes none too fluent. *Miss Suzy Smith* **c100 h103**

JIM LAD 5 b.g. Young Ern – Anne's Bank (IRE) (Burslem) [2004/5 h77§: 20g5 26m4 May 27] poor maiden hurdler: probably stays 3¼m: acts on soft and good to firm going: usually visored/blinkered: ungenuine. *Dr J. R. J. Naylor* **h70 §**

JIMMY BEDNEY (IRE) 4 b.g. Simply Great (FR) – Double Token (Furry Glen) [2004/5 F12d F16d Mar 5] angular gelding: seventh foal: dam, winning hurdler, half-sister to fairly useful staying chaser Noosa Sound: well held in bumpers. *Mrs D. A. Hamer* **F–**

JIMMY BYRNE (IRE) 5 ch.g. Red Sunset – Persian Sally (IRE) (Persian Bold) [2004/5 16m2 16dur 16s4 17s Nov 18] leggy gelding: fairly useful on Flat (stays 10.5f): modest form at best over hurdles: hung left under pressure on debut: needs to improve jumping. *B. Ellison* **h91 x**

JIMMY CRICKET 8 ch.g. Primitive Rising (USA) – Norton Gale (IRE) (Le Bavard (FR)) [2004/5 c24s4 c25sur Mar 7] winning pointer: fourth in novice at Huntingdon on completed outing in hunters: thorough stayer. *Ms Caroline Walker* **c87**

JIMMY JUMBO (IRE) 12 ch.g. Dragon Palace (USA) – Sail On Lady (New Member) [2004/5 c78, h–: 24gpu Jul 7] workmanlike gelding: winning pointer: little form otherwise: tried tongue tied. *M. Sheppard* **c– h–**

JIMMYS DUKY (IRE) 7 b.g. Duky – Harvey's Cream (IRE) (Mandalus) [2004/5 h–: c21d4 c24d3 c21v3 c24s3 c24spu Feb 9] no show over hurdles: poor chaser on balance: stays 3m: raced on good going or softer (acts on heavy). *D. M. Forster* **c75 h–**

JIMMY TENNIS (FR) 8 b. or br.g. Video Rock (FR) – Via Tennise (FR) (Brezzo (FR)) [2004/5 c134x, h–: c26s c25dpu c24g6 c24d c24g2 c24s4 Apr 16] leggy, lengthy gelding: useful handicap chaser in 2003/4, just fair form at best in 2004/5: best up to 3m: raced mainly on good going or softer (acts on heavy): tried blinkered: usually let down by jumping. *Miss Venetia Williams* **c114 x h–**

JINFUL DU GRAND VAL (FR) 8 b.g. Useful (FR) – Marine (FR) (African Joy) [2004/5 c–: c20dpu May 13] winning pointer: no show in maiden or hunter chases. *N. W. Alexander* **c–**

JIVAROS (FR) 8 br.g. Video Rock (FR) – Rives (FR) (Reasonable Choice (USA)) [2004/5 c102, h–: c25gF May 12] leggy gelding: fair handicap chaser: will prove best at 3m+: raced mainly on good/good to soft ground. *H. D. Daly* **c– h–**

JIVATY (FR) 8 b.g. Quart de Vin (FR) – Tenacity (FR) (Prove It Baby (USA)) [2004/5 h109: 27g2 24g4 c23d3 c19v4 c23s4 c22s5 c16d c22m2 Apr 21] leggy gelding: fair hurdler: similar form over fences: left M. Pipe after fifth start: stays 27f: acts on heavy and good to firm going. *B. G. Powell* **c110 d h109**

JIVER (IRE) 6 b.g. Flemensfirth (USA) – Choice Brush (IRE) (Brush Aside (USA)) [2004/5 F84: 22s5 21g* 26d* 24d 24s3 24d 24d 24s5 Apr 2] rather unfurnished gelding: **h107**

fair hurdler: won maiden at Ludlow and handicap at Huntingdon in November: will stay extreme distances: raced on good going or softer (acts on soft). *M. Scudamore*

JOAACI (IRE) 5 b.g. Presenting – Miss Sarajevo (IRE) (Brush Aside (USA)) [2004/5 c24v* c27g* c24s² c26vF Apr 22] second foal: dam ran once in points: won second of 2 starts in maiden Irish points in 2005: highly encouraging start in chases, easily winning maiden at Chepstow in March and handicap at Ayr in April: much improved form when head second to My Will in novice at Perth: found race coming too soon final outing: stays 27f: acts on heavy going. *M. C. Pipe* **c130 +**

JOB SHOP 4 b.g. Dancing Spree (USA) – Kathy Fair (IRE) (Nicholas Bill) [2004/5 F17v Feb 13] fourth foal: half-brother to fair but temperamental performer up to 1¼m Quite Remarkable (by Danzig Connection): dam, ungenuine maiden hurdler, half-sister to smart stayer Silence In Court: more temperament than ability in bumper on debut. *A. D. Smith* **F–**

JOCKER DU SAPIN (FR) 8 br.g. Franc Parler – Nymphe Rose (FR) (Rose Laurel) [2004/5 c90, h–: c19s* c22sF Nov 27] easily best effort over fences when winning novice handicap at Towcester in November by distance (actual margin 50 lengths): stays 2½m: acts on soft going. *A. J. Whitehead* **c107 h–**

JOCKIE WELLS 7 b.g. Primitive Rising (USA) – Princess Maxine (IRE) (Horage) [2004/5 h–: c25dF Apr 11] no sign of ability: headstrong. *Miss Lucinda V. Russell* **c– h–**

JOCKSER (IRE) 4 b.g. Desert Story (IRE) – Pupa Fiorini (ITY) (Indian Ridge) [2004/5 16d 16v 17s⁶ 16s² 16s* 16d 17d³ 19m² Apr 17] close-coupled gelding: fairly useful on Flat (stays 9f) for G. Lyons: fair hurdler: won handicap at Huntingdon in February: stays 19f: acts on soft and good to firm going. *J. W. Mullins* **h107**

JODANTE (IRE) 8 ch.g. Phardante (FR) – Crashtown Lucy (Crash Course) [2004/5 c95p, h89: c17g³ c17g* c16s² c16g⁴ c17spu c16g² c16g⁶ Mar 26] strong, lengthy gelding: good mover: fair chaser: won maiden at Kelso in May: raced around 2m: acts on heavy going. *P. Beaumont* **c105 h–**

JOE BLAKE (IRE) 10 b.g. Jurado (USA) – I've No Idea (Nishapour (FR)) [2004/5 c132: c25d* c24f⁴ Jun 6] big, workmanlike gelding: useful handicap chaser: won at Wetherby in April 2004 by 2¼ lengths from Hunters Tweed: respectable fourth to Montreal at Perth over month later: stays 3¼m: probably acts on any going: has been let down by jumping. *L. Lungo* **c138**

JOE DEANE (IRE) 9 ch.g. Alphabatim (USA) – Craic Go Leor (Deep Run) [2004/5 c105, h–: c25g² c21d² c21d c25dF Dec 26] strong, lengthy gelding: fair handicap chaser: stays 3¼m: raced mainly on good going or softer (acts on heavy). *T. R. George* **c110 h–**

JOE DI CAPO (IRE) 10 b.g. Phardante (FR) – Supreme Glen (IRE) (Supreme Leader) [2004/5 c82x, h–: c25g³ c21mur c27g² c27vpu Mar 15] lengthy, angular gelding: poor maiden chaser: sold out of T. Easterby's stable 3,200 gns Doncaster August Sales after third start: fourth in point in March: stays 27f: acts on heavy and good to firm going: has worn headgear: poor jumper. *S. J. Robinson* **c78 x h–**

JOELY GREEN 8 b.g. Binary Star (USA) – Comedy Lady (Comedy Star (USA)) [2004/5 h–: c20spu c24g³ Mar 28] good-topped gelding: modest and unreliable on Flat (probably stays 19f): winning hurdler: jumped poorly both starts over fences: tried blinkered. *N. P. Littmoden* **c– h–**

JOE MALONE (IRE) 6 br.g. Rashar (USA) – Bucktina (Buckskin (FR)) [2004/5 F85: 17d Mar 26] tall, rather unfurnished gelding: fair form in bumper on debut for C. Bealby: off a year, looked to need run when mid-field in novice at Carlisle on hurdling debut. *N. G. Richards* **h83**

JOE PUBLIC (IRE) 7 b.g. Actinium (FR) – Cool Boreen (Boreen (FR)) [2004/5 h–, F–: 16gpu Apr 26] no sign of ability: sold £2,200 Ascot November Sales. *T. P. McGovern* **h–**

JOES EDGE (IRE) 8 b. or br.g. Supreme Leader – Right Dark (Buckskin (FR)) [2004/5 h111: 20d⁵ c20s* c25s² c21d² c21s² c21gpu c20d* c33g* Apr 16] **c144 h–**

Twelve months on from the disappointment of seeing Granit d'Estruval crash out at the last in the Scottish National, Ferdy Murphy experienced the other side of the coin when winning this very valuable handicap chase with Joes Edge. Murphy, who in 2000 had won the race with another eight-year-old, Paris Pike, wasn't at Ayr to witness Joes Edge's thrilling victory. The meeting coincided with an end-of-season sale in Dubai, and Murphy was there looking for additions to his string. Paris Pike, like Joes Edge, also won the Scottish National (in 2000) in his

John Smith's Novices' Handicap Chase (Amateur Riders), Aintree—
Joes Edge thwarts the grey Schuh Shine's bid for a five-timer

first season over fences and looked capable of going on to even better things. The Scottish National proved the high point of Paris Pike's career, as he missed the following season through injury and was a shadow of his former self when he returned to action, failing to win again. Joe's Edge isn't quite so good as Paris Pike was at the same stage, but he is a smart novice nevertheless and, all being well, he should continue to do well in the top staying handicaps. A sound jumper, Joes Edge could well prove an ideal type for the Grand National itself in 2006.

Joes Edge began his career with Murphy and was successful at Carlisle on the first of two starts in bumpers in April, 2002, before a tendon injury then kept him off the course until November, 2003, by which time he had been transferred to Venetia Williams' yard. After one season with Williams, during which he won novice hurdles at Ascot and Carlisle, Joes Edge was returned to Murphy, and made a successful start to his chasing career in a novice event at Ayr in November. Win number two didn't arrive until April, at Aintree, though he did run well in between when second twice over twenty-one furlongs at Cheltenham, splitting Lacdoudal and Cornish Rebel in the Timeform Novices' Handicap Chase on the second occasion. Joes Edge didn't need to improve to account for nine rivals in a similar event for amateur riders at Aintree, but a lot more was required if he was to follow up a week later in the Gala Casinos Daily Record Scottish Grand National, in which he was set to race off a mark 10 lb higher than at Aintree over a distance around a mile and a half further than that over which he had done most of his racing. The Scottish National attracted a field of twenty, though it wasn't so competitive as it might have been, the presence of the Gold Cup runner-up Take The Stand resulting in over half of the field being out of the handicap, including Joes Edge who was 5 lb out despite a penalty for his win at Aintree. Patiently ridden in a race run at just a fair pace, Joes

Gala Casinos Daily Record Scottish Grand National Handicap Chase, Ayr—fellow novice Cornish Rebel flatters to deceive as Ruby Walsh just misses out on a grand slam of Nationals

Edge was in the last two, along with Cornish Rebel, in the early stages but made up his ground gradually to be one of no more than five still in with a chance after the fifth last, where Double Honour was still forcing the pace. At the second last Joes Edge jumped past Double Honour and was then pressed by Cornish Rebel, the pair now beginning to draw clear. Cornish Rebel took a narrow lead early on the run-in but he began to idle, whereas Joes Edge, defying any stamina doubts, found extra under pressure and regained the advantage close home to win a thrilling race by a short head, confirming placings despite terms 8 lb worse than at Cheltenham. Joes Edge led a clean sweep of the placings for novices (Another Rum was third) and was the seventh to win the Scottish National since 1979. It was a tremendous effort by both Joes Edge and by his relatively inexperienced rider Keith Mercer, the partnership denying Cornish Rebel's jockey Ruby Walsh a clean sweep of four major Grand Nationals in the same season. Mercer, who claims the 3-lb allowance, grew up on Merseyside but first came to prominence as a rider in Ireland, one of his earliest wins coming on Liberman in a bumper at the Punchestown Festival in 2002. The following year Mercer joined Murphy's stable and his career really blossomed in the latest season, forty wins taking him into third in the conditional jockeys' championship. Mercer paid a return visit to Punchestown later in April and teamed up with Joes Edge again, this time in a valuable novice handicap. Mercer had won the Champion Stayers' Hurdle there the previous day on the Murphy-trained Carlys Quest, and Joes Edge went close to completing a notable double for trainer and jockey, showing further improvement under another penalty to finish two lengths second to Pay It Forward. Again waited with, Joes Edge was still going well when none too fluent at the second last, after which he could make no further impression on the winner. It was Joes Edge's third outing in three weeks, and bouncing back from such a hard race at Ayr demonstrated just what a tough customer he is.

Joes Edge (IRE) (b. or br.g. 1997)	Supreme Leader (b 1982)	Bustino (b 1971)	Busted
			Ship Yard
		Princess Zena (b 1975)	Habitat
			Guiding Light
	Right Dark (b or br 1984)	Buckskin (b 1973)	Yelapa
			Bete A Bon Dieu
		Right Performance (b 1976)	Gala Performance
			Cherry Princess

The well-made Joes Edge is the seventh foal produced by Right Dark, who finished down the field in a bumper at Killarney on her only start, and is her only winner to date. Right Dark, a half-sister to the useful staying jumper Do Be Brief, is a daughter of the lightly-raced maiden Right Performance and granddaughter of the unraced Cherry Princess. The last-named is the dam of the smart staying chaser Omerta, who in 1991 was runner-up in the Scottish National at the age of eleven, having won the Irish National three weeks earlier. Joes Edge, a sound jumper, acts on soft going and has yet to encounter ground firmer than good over jumps. He was well held on good to firm on his second start in bumpers. *Ferdy Murphy*

JOE SNIPE 6 ch.g. Jendali (USA) – Lady Blues Singer (Chief Singer) [2004/5 F17g F16m Jun 12] half-brother to 1m winner in Italy by Clantime: dam maiden who seemed to stay 7f: soundly beaten in 2 bumpers. *Miss L. C. Siddall* **F–**

JOEY DUNLOP (IRE) 11 br.g. Maelstrom Lake – Middle Verde (USA) (Sham (USA)) [2004/5 c24v² c24m⁵ c25f³ c25d⁶ c24gᵖᵘ Jul 1] successful in 5 Irish points, including in 2004: poor maiden chaser: stays 3m: probably acts on any going: has shown signs of temperament, including when blinkered final start. *J. J. Lambe, Ireland* **c73 h–**

JOFI (IRE) 6 b.g. Shernazar – Giolla Donn (Giolla Mear) [2004/5 F–: 22sᵖᵘ 16v Jan 10] strong gelding: no sign of ability. *Miss Lucinda V. Russell* **h–**

JOHANN DE VONNAS (FR) 8 b.g. Cadoudal (FR) – Diana de Vonnas (FR) (El Badr) [2004/5 h84: 20d⁴ c19d* c22d* c22s³ Jan 1] leggy gelding: poor form over hurdles: fair form over fences, winning minor event at Towcester in November and novice at Fontwell in December: stays 2¾m: acts on soft going: tongue tied last 3 starts: sold 8,500 gns Doncaster May Sales. *N. J. Henderson* **c100 h76**

JOHN BUILDER 9 b.g. Nader – My Molly (Averof) [2004/5 c20gᵖᵘ May 13] of little account. *G. Ivall* **c–**

JOHN JAMES (IRE) 9 b.g. Bravefoot – Glitter Grey (Nishapour (FR)) [2004/5 c122, h88: c18g² c16s³ c20s⁵ c18v⁴ 17v c18v⁵ c18d⁴ c20g* c20d* c21d Apr 8] angular gelding: winning hurdler: fairly useful chaser: won minor events at Tramore and Clonmel (by 5 lengths from Quadco) in March: stays 2½m: acts on soft going: wore cheekpieces once: usually front runner. *J. H. Scott, Ireland* **c128 h–**

JOHNJOE'S EXPRESS (IRE) 8 gr.g. Moscow Society (USA) – Abigail's Dream (Kalaglow) [2004/5 h103, F95: 16g 18m* c21sᵘʳ c20g* c20s⁴ c20dᶠ Nov 13] workmanlike gelding: fair hurdler: made all in handicap at Galway in August: similar form over fences, winning maiden at Kilbeggan following month: probably stayed 2¾m: acted on soft and good to firm going: dead. *Mrs J. Harrington, Ireland* **c107 h109**

JOHN JORROCKS (FR) 6 br.g. Chamberlin (FR) – Caryatide (FR) (Maiymad) [2004/5 F72: 17s 19sᵖᵘ 20d 22d Mar 10] rangy, rather unfurnished gelding: little sign of ability. *J. C. Tuck* **h–**

JOHNNY ALLJAYS (IRE) 4 b.g. Victory Note (USA) – It's Academic (Royal Academy (USA)) [2004/5 17dᵖᵘ Jul 17] good-bodied gelding: poor on Flat (stays 1½m), successful twice in March for P. Blockley: in cheekpieces, showed nothing in juvenile on hurdling debut: sold £1,300 Ascot August Sales. *J. S. Moore* **h–**

JOHNNY GRAND 8 b.g. Kasakov – Richesse (FR) (Faraway Son (USA)) [2004/5 c21m³ c17g* c20f⁶ c20m⁵ c19gᵘʳ c16dᶠ Nov 7] leggy gelding: form only when winning novice handicap chase at Southwell in August: sold out of D. P. Keane's stable £2,000 Ascot Sales later in month: blinkered once. *D. W. Lewis* **c72 h–**

JOHNNY REB 7 b.g. Danehill (USA) – Dixie Eyes Blazing (USA) (Gone West (USA)) [2004/5 h66: 20dᵖᵘ 17gʳᵒ May 26] poor maiden hurdler: has twice run out: headstrong. *Mrs S. J. Smith* **h– §**

JOHNNY WILKIE 6 b.g. Shambo – Kelly's Maid (Netherkelly) [2004/5 F18s Dec 1] eighth foal: dam, maiden chaser, sister to useful chaser up to 3¼m Kelly's Honor: well held in bumper on debut: sold £580 Ascot February Sales. *M. Pitman* **F–**

JOHN OLIVER (IRE) 7 gr.g. Lure (USA) – Glitter Grey (Nishapour (FR)) [2004/5 h117: c16sᶠ c16vᵖᵘ c18v* c16s⁵ Mar 13] big, well-made gelding: winning hurdler: fair form over fences, successful in maiden at Gowran in February: raced around 2m on good going or softer (acts on heavy): sometimes runs as if amiss. *J. Queally, Ireland* **c112 h–**

JOHN RICH 9 b.g. Mesleh – South Lodge (Current Magic) [2004/5 c68§, h–§: 23dᵖᵘ Apr 25] lengthy, sparely-made gelding: poor chaser: no show over hurdles: not one to trust (has refused/run out). *M. E. Sowersby* **c– § h– §**

JOHNS LEGACY 10 gr.g. Almoojid – Flying Joker (Kalaglow) [2004/5 c88?: c26g² c26d⁴ c21g* Apr 10] fairly useful hunter chaser: won novice at Newton Abbot in April by 7 lengths from Hold On Harry: stays 3¼m: prone to the odd mistake. *Miss S. E. Robinson* **c108**

JOHN THE MOLE (IRE) 7 ch.g. Glacial Storm (USA) – City Dame (Golden Love) [2004/5 c–§, h–§: c25gpu May 8] compact gelding: maiden hurdler: no form in chases: won maiden point in February: tried in cheekpieces/visor: temperamental. *M. D. Hammond* **c– § h–**

JOHNYYOURONLYJOKEN (IRE) 9 gr.g. Roselier (FR) – Badsworth Madam (Over The River (FR)) [2004/5 c24sF c24vpu c21s5 Jan 18] ex-Irish gelding: winning pointer: little form in chases, left N. Glynn after reappearance: often wears blinkers/cheekpieces: has had tongue tied. *A. E. Jones* **c70 ?**

JOINT AUTHORITY (IRE) 10 b.g. Religiously (USA) – Highway's Last (Royal Highway) [2004/5 c111, h89: 16d5 16g5 c28s4 c20s4 c24d5 c24d5 c24g2 c24d6 c29gpu Apr 23] workmanlike gelding: maiden hurdler, left L. Lungo after first outing: fair chaser: stays 3m: raced on good going or softer (acts on soft): amateur ridden for present stable. *D. L. Williams* **c106 h81**

JOIZEL (FR) 8 b.g. Fill My Hopes (FR) – Anne de Boizel (FR) (Dhausli (FR)) [2004/5 h–: 25g6 22s4 22d4 22d2 22spu 19s4 Feb 17] chunky gelding: poor maiden hurdler: sold out of R. Alner's stable 3,600 gns Doncaster August Sales after first outing: stays 2¾m: acts on soft going: tried blinkered in France. *V. G. Greenway* **h69**

JOKE CLUB 4 b.g. Inchinor – Kicka (Shirley Heights) [2004/5 F13d2 F17d Apr 9] 9,000F, €16,000Y, 16,000 3-y-o: rather leggy gelding: first foal: dam, maiden in Italy, out of close relation to Derby runner-up Glacial Storm: fairly useful form in bumpers, second to There Is No Doubt in 3-y-o event at Exeter and twelfth to The Cool Guy in Grade 2 at Aintree, eased after making running in latter. *V. R. A. Dartnall* **F99**

JOLEWIS 7 ch.m. Sir Harry Lewis (USA) – Askwood (IRE) (Gunner B) [2004/5 F–: 21mpu 20g6 26mpu Jul 2] no form in bumper or novice hurdles. *E. W. Tuer* **h–**

JOLI BREEZY 4 b.f. Thowra (FR) – Pedrosa (IRE) (Petardia) [2004/5 F16d F16s Mar 13] second foal: dam unraced: tailed off in bumpers: sold £1,200 Ascot April Sales. *R. J. Hodges* **F–**

JOLIKA (FR) 8 b.m. Grand Tresor (FR) – Unika II (FR) (Rolling Bowl (FR)) [2004/5 h93: 20d5 21v3 c16v* c20spu 24s3 Apr 20] leggy mare: modest handicap hurdler: easily better effort over fences when winning novice handicap at Ayr in February: effective at testing 2m to 3m: acts on heavy going. *L. Lungo* **c96 h93**

JOLI SADDLERS 9 b.m. Saddlers' Hall (IRE) – Vitality (Young Generation) [2004/5 c–, h–: 22fpu Oct 7] winning hurdler: well held when falling on chasing debut: lame only outing in 2004/5: has had tongue tied. *R. J. Hodges* **c– h–**

JOLITAN 10 b.g. Joligeneration – Tanber Lass (New Member) [2004/5 c–: c23gpu Apr 12] winning pointer: blinkered, pulled up in 2 novice hunter chases: temperamental. *P. Greenwood* **c– §**

JOLLY BOY (FR) 6 b.g. Franc Bleu Argent (USA) – Lady Charrecey (FR) (Fin Bon) [2004/5 c16vF 19spu 19g Mar 4] good-topped gelding: eleventh foal: half-brother to 5 winners, including fairly useful hurdler Slooghy (by Missolonghi), stays 3m: dam unraced: fair form when fifth in minor hurdle at Auteuil on sole start for E. Lemartinel: fell second on chasing debut: folded tamely both outings back over hurdles. *Miss Venetia Williams* **c– h–**

JOLLYSHAU (IRE) 7 b.g. Jolly Jake (NZ) – Escheat (Torus) [2004/5 h78: 24g4 21d c25g4 c24d* c24s3 c25sR c24gpu Mar 16] workmanlike gelding: maiden hurdler: modest novice chaser: won handicap at Huntingdon in December: will stay beyond 25f: acts on soft going. *Miss A. M. Newton-Smith* **c91 h–**

JOLLYS PRIDE 4 b.g. Orpen (USA) – Greek Night Out (IRE) (Ela-Mana-Mou) [2004/5 F12g Nov 10] 5,000 3-y-o: third foal: half-brother to 2 winners by Tragic Role, including fair hurdler up to 3m Midnight Creek: dam, modest on Flat, stayed well: always rear in 3-y-o bumper on debut: poor form on Flat. *K. F. Clutterbuck* **F–**

JOLY BEY (FR) 8 ch.g. Beyssac (FR) – Rivolie (FR) (Mistigri) [2004/5 c147, h128p: 20s c25d5 c21d4 c24g* c24gpu c36d c29g Apr 23] tall, angular gelding: fairly useful form over hurdles, not knocked about in valuable handicap at Chepstow on reappearance: smart handicap chaser: best effort when winning at Sandown in February by 6 lengths from Iris Bleu, making most: badly hampered twelfth (saddle slipped) at Cheltenham next time, raced freely and failed to stay in Grand National at Aintree sixth outing: stays **c145 h128 p**

25f: raced on good going or softer (acts on heavy): tongue tied last 4 starts: fluent jumper: owner ridden nowadays. *N. J. Gifford*

JO MAXIMUS 13 b.g. Prince Sabo – Final Call (Town Crier) [2004/5 c16m^pu Mar 21] 6f and 7f winner on Flat: off nearly 6 years, no show in hunter chase. *Mrs E. Newman* **c–**

JONALTON (IRE) 6 b.g. Perugino (USA) – Vago Pequeno (IRE) (Posen (USA)) [2004/5 h99: 22g 20s 20s^6 26g^pu c23m^pu Apr 10] plain gelding: modest hurdler at best: no form in 2004/5: left C. Dore, jumped poorly on chasing debut (lame): stays 3m: acts on firm and soft going: tried tongue tied. *M. J. Gingell* **c– h–**

JONANAUD 6 b.g. Ballet Royal (USA) – Margaret Modes (Thatching) [2004/5 h111, F71: 20s^6 21s* 21d 24s^5 22d^pu 16v^5 20s^2 Mar 23] leggy gelding: fairly useful handicap hurdler: won at Towcester in November: stays 3m: acts on heavy ground. *H. J. Manners* **h117**

JONCHEE (FR) 8 ch.m. Le Thuit Signol (FR) – Dame d'Onze Heures (FR) (Noble Cake (USA)) [2004/5 25g^5 c22s^pu 22s^6 Feb 10] sturdy mare: second foal: half-sister to 17f hurdle winner Lotier (by Dress Parade): dam unraced half-sister to very smart staying chaser Gingembre: little sign of ability: jumped poorly both starts over hurdles. *Mrs L. C. Taylor* **c– h–**

JONES'S ROAD (IRE) 7 ch.g. Be My Native (USA) – Hill Blends (IRE) (Glacial Storm (USA)) [2004/5 c20g^5 c20s* c24g^ur 17d^6 c22g^3 Apr 1] workmanlike gelding: second foal: dam unraced half-sister to useful hurdler/chaser up to 25f Mixed Blends and dual Whitbread winner Topsham Bay: winning hurdler: fairly useful chaser: left T. Taaffe and off 6 months, improved form when winning handicap at Windsor in November: stays 3m: acts on soft and good to firm going. *Jonjo O'Neill* **c117 h82**

JONGLEUR COLLONGES (FR) 8 gr.g. Royal Charter (FR) – Soubrette Collonge (FR) (Saumon (FR)) [2004/5 c97, h–: c22s* c20d^2 c24g^pu c20d^6 Mar 11] tall, useful-looking gelding: maiden hurdler: modest chaser: off nearly a year (reportedly had wind operation), made all in intermediate handicap at Towcester in October: poor efforts last 2 starts: stays 3m: acts on good to firm and heavy going: jumps soundly. *R. H. Alner* **c97 h–**

JONNY'S KICK 5 b.g. Revoque (IRE) – Prudence (Grundy) [2004/5 F84: F17v^3 19s^4 23d^3 24v^3 20v^3 16g Jan 17] big, strong, lengthy gelding: third twice in bumpers: modest form in novice hurdles: stays 23f: acts on heavy going. *T. D. Easterby* **h95 F84**

JONTYS'LASS 4 b.f. Tamure (IRE) – Gay Muse (Scorpio (FR)) [2004/5 F16g F17g Apr 3] first foal: dam poor form in bumpers: well held in bumpers. *A. Crook* **F75**

JORDANS LAD (IRE) 9 b.g. Camden Town – Clockonocra (Shall We Dance) [2004/5 c18m^4 c16g c20s^4 c24v c20v c20v* c20v^2 c17v^2 c20v c19v* c20v^F c24d^4 c19s^3 c22g^2 24m* Apr 10] tall ex-Irish gelding: fair hurdler: well backed, won handicap at Worcester in April: at least as good over fences, trained until after second outing by P. Nolan: won handicaps at Tramore in December and Towcester (first start after leaving E. Sheehy) in February: stays 3m: acts on heavy and good to firm going: tried blinkered/ in cheekpieces in Ireland. *M. Scudamore* **c113 h102**

JORDAN'S RIDGE (IRE) 9 br. or b.g. Indian Ridge – Sadie Jordan (USA) (Hail The Pirates (USA)) [2004/5 c127, h102: 16s^5 c20d^4 c25s^5 c20g c22d^2 c22v^4 20g 22d* Apr 11] sparely-made gelding: fairly useful handicap chaser, in decline in 2004/5: fair handicap hurdler: won narrowly at Kelso in April: stays 25f: has form on heavy going, best efforts under less testing conditions (acts on good to firm): tried blinkered: has had tongue tied: doesn't always impress with attitude. *P. Monteith* **c119 d h106**

JORIS DE VONNAS (FR) 8 ch.g. Dear Doctor (FR) – Carine de Neuvy (FR) (Shelley (FR)) [2004/5 22g c25s^pu c24s* c24s^pu 24m^4 Apr 10] fourth foal: dam unraced, out of half-sister to useful staying chaser Jivago de Neuvy: once-raced on Flat: fair hurdler/ chaser in France for G. Cherel: off almost 2 years, second once from 2 starts over fences in 2003/4 for Mrs S. Bramall: only modest form in Britain, winning handicap chase at Huntingdon in March: stays 3m: acts on heavy and good to firm going. *Ian Williams* **c85 h85**

JORN DU SOLEIL (FR) 8 ch.g. Murmure (FR) – Ina du Soleil (FR) (Or de Chine) [2004/5 c–, h–: c16s^ur Nov 7] well-made gelding: type to carry condition: lightly-raced maiden chaser. *Mrs J. C. McGregor* **c– h–**

JOROBADEN (FR) 5 gr.g. Poliglote – Mercalle (FR) (Kaldoun (FR)) [2004/5 17s^2 17s* 16v^3 20d Apr 9] leggy gelding: useful on Flat (should stay 2m), successful twice in 2004, sold out of C. Wall's stable 17,000 gns Newmarket Autumn Sales: favourite, won **h120**

steadily-run novice hurdle at Carlisle in February: fairly useful form when third to Pay Attention in similar event at Towcester: should be suited by further than 17f: acts on heavy going. *Mrs H. Dalton*

JOSH MOR 7 b.g. Chaddleworth (IRE) – Little Morston (Morston (FR)) [2004/5 20gpu c17fpu 22spu Oct 19] medium-sized gelding: third in seller at 2 yrs for G. L. Moore: runner-up in 2½m maiden point in 2003: pulled up in novice hurdles and chase. *C. J. Down* **c– h–**

JOSHUA'S BAY 7 b.g. Karinga Bay – Bonita Blakeney (Baron Blakeney) [2004/5 h113: 24d6 16g4 23spu 22s 21d 18s c19gpu 21m6 Apr 13] sturdy gelding: fair handicap hurdler: mistakes when pulled up in maiden on chasing debut: stays 23f: acts on any going: has worn visor. *J. R. Jenkins* **c– h113**

JOSHUAS BOY (IRE) 5 ch.g. Bahhare (USA) – Broadway Rosie (Absalom) [2004/5 16d3 16g 16g Dec 28] workmanlike gelding: poor maiden on Flat: ran to similar level on first of 3 outings over hurdles. *K. A. Ryan* **h82**

JOSHUA'S VISION (IRE) 14 b.g. Vision (USA) – Perle's Fashion (Sallust) [2004/5 c–, h–: c25mpu Apr 25] workmanlike gelding: winning pointer: maiden hurdler/chaser: tried visored/in cheekpieces: usually tongue tied. *Lady Susan Brooke* **c– h–**

JO'S SALE (IRE) 6 b.g. Germany (USA) – Clonmeen Lodge (IRE) (Buckskin (FR)) [2004/5 F16g6 16vpu 16g Apr 17] third foal: half-brother to winning Irish pointer by Mister Lord: dam unraced: distant second in maiden Irish point on debut: sold 11,000 gns Doncaster May Sales: sixth of 21 in bumper at Worcester: no show in 2 starts over hurdles. *Evan Williams* **h– F82**

JOUEUR D'ESTRUVAL (FR) 8 gr.g. Perrault – Alrose (FR) (Kalyan (FR)) [2004/5 c121, h108: c25g5 21s 16d5 18s3 c20s3 c24vpu 20s2 16v4 20s* 16s* c24s2 Mar 26] leggy, useful-looking gelding: fairly useful hurdler/chaser: won over hurdles at Thurles (handicap) in February and Clonmel (minor event) in March: ran well over fences next 2 starts, including when third to Jasmin d'Oudairies in handicap at Punchestown in late-April: effective at 2m to 25f: acts on soft going. *W. P. Mullins, Ireland* **c125 h124**

JOUNG ISLANDER (POL) 5 b.g. Tioman Island – Joung Girl (POL) (Valiant Heart (FR)) [2004/5 20dpu 17m5 May 25] successful up to 1½m and runner-up in 1¾m St Leger on Flat in Poland for M. Melnicki: no show in novice company over hurdles. *T. R. George* **h–**

JOUR DE MEE (FR) 8 ch.g. Beyssac (FR) – Une de Mee (FR) (Sarpedon (FR)) [2004/5 c22spu c24vpu 16s2 16s c18s3 c16s4 16s3 16d c19s* Mar 23] good-topped ex-French gelding: fifth foal: half-brother to several winners, including Grand Steeple-Chase des Flandres winner Gailoorn de Mee (by Apeldoorn): dam won up to 13f on Flat in France: once-raced on Flat: winning hurdler: left M. Rolland and off over 2 years before reappearance: best effort in Britain when winning handicap chase at Towcester in March: stays 2½m: raced on going softer than good (acts on soft): tried blinkered: has had tongue tied. *Mrs H. Dalton* **c98 ? h69**

JOURNAL PRINCESS (IRE) 6 b.m. Zaffaran (USA) – Bramble Hatch (Pry) [2004/5 F16d 16vpu 19v 17g Mar 9] eighth foal: sister to 2½m hurdle winner Mullahoran and half-sister to useful chaser Major Summit (by Callernish), stayed 3m, and fairly useful staying hurdler/winning chaser Warner For Players (by Good Thyne): dam poor performer: first signs of ability in mares novice hurdle final start: bred to be suited by lot further than 2m. *M. Scudamore* **h– F–**

JOY BOX 5 ch.g. Unfuwain (USA) – El Jazirah (Kris) [2004/5 F–: F16m* 20sF 16vpu Feb 15] won bumper at Hexham in June: going well in mid-field when falling 4 out in novice there on hurdling debut: lost action next time: will stay 2½m. *T. D. Easterby* **h– F98**

JOYE DES ILES (FR) 8 b.g. Mont Basile (FR) – Titjana (FR) (Quart de Vin (FR)) [2004/5 c–, h–: c25s c24dpu Mar 6] tall gelding: won 2½m maiden point in 2003: little form in chases in Britain: blinkered. *N. J. Henderson* **c– h–**

JOYFUL ECHO 6 ch.m. Jumbo Hirt (USA) – Joyful Star (Rubor) [2004/5 F17v Mar 20] sister to winning hurdler/chaser Jumbo's Dream, stays 27f: dam modest staying chaser: well beaten in bumper on debut. *J. E. Dixon* **F–**

JOYFUL JADE (FR) 8 b.m. Useful (FR) – Devon Orchid (Brianston Zipper) [2004/5 22s6 22gpu Jul 12] poor pointer: no show in novice hurdles. *J. D. Frost* **h–**

JUDAIC WAYS 11 b.g. Rudimentary (USA) – Judeah (Great Nephew) [2004/5 c96, h–: c24d³ Mar 24] lengthy gelding: modest chaser: off 16 months, creditable third to Cobreces in hunter at Ludlow: stays 3m: acts on firm and soft going: prone to odd bad mistake. *H. D. Daly* **c96 h–**

JUDGE'N'THOMAS 5 b.g. Sadler's Way – Stapleford Lady (Bairn (USA)) [2004/5 F18d Feb 20] lengthy gelding: first foal: dam, winning hurdler/chaser, stayed 2½m: tailed off in bumper on debut. *M. R. Bosley* **F–**

JUDY'S LAD 6 ch.g. Master Willie – Flexwing (Electric) [2004/5 F17m Jun 9] £4,200 4-y-o: second foal: half-brother to fair hurdler Snipe (by Anshan), stays 2½m: dam modest form in bumpers: last of 3 finishers in 2½m maiden, ran out both other starts in points in 2004: well beaten in bumper. *Jane Southcombe* **F–**

JUG OF PUNCH (IRE) 6 ch.g. In The Wings – Mysistra (FR) (Machiavellian (USA)) [2004/5 h77: 19d² 22mᵖᵘ 16sᵖᵘ Jan 20] poor form over hurdles: stays 21f: acts on good to soft going. *S. T. Lewis* **h77**

JULANDI 6 ch.m. Southern Music – Dull'un (True Song) [2004/5 F79?: 16dᶠ 17g 16s Mar 23] signs of ability in bumpers: no form over hurdles. *M. Sheppard* **h–**

JULIES BOY (IRE) 8 b.g. Toulon – Chickmo (IRE) (Seclude (USA)) [2004/5 c86, h72: c21sᵖᵘ c22vᶠ c25gᵖᵘ c25s⁴ c23d c19v* c16g c20g² Mar 14] sturdy gelding: maiden hurdler: poor chaser: made all in novice handicap at Hereford in February: stays 25f: acts on heavy going: tongue tied last 4 starts. *T. R. George* **c80 h–**

JULIUS CAESAR 5 b.g. Sadler's Wells (USA) – Stiletta (Dancing Brave (USA)) [2004/5 17dᵘʳ 20s⁶ 16v³ 21d* 24v* 20d* Mar 12] 13,000 3-y-o: compact gelding: fourth foal: half-brother to fairly useful 1¼m winner Articulation (by Machiavellian): dam **h122 +**

European Breeders Fund Sunderlands National Hunt Novices' Handicap Hurdle Final, Sandown—
Flat-bred Julius Caesar (hooped cap) stays on well despite mistakes to beat
(from left) Billyvoddan, Rebel Rhythm and Cornish Sett

unraced sister to Derby winner Commander In Chief and half-sister to Warning, Deploy and Dushyantor: most progressive over hurdles, winning last 3 starts, novices at Sedgefield and Newcastle and Grade 3 EBF Sunderlands NH Novices' Handicap Hurdle at Sandown, again not fluent when beating Billyvoddan by head in 18-runner race at last-named: likely to stay beyond 3m: raced on going softer than good (acts on heavy): may do better yet back over longer trip. *J. Howard Johnson*

JUMBO'S DREAM 14 b.g. Jumbo Hirt (USA) – Joyful Star (Rubor) [2004/5 c74, h–: c25g5 c27d5 c27vpu c21v3 c25d3 c25vur c20v* c20d Mar 26] deep-girthed gelding: winning hurdler: poor handicap chaser: won at Hexham in March: stays 27f: unraced on firm going, acts on any other: tried blinkered, wears cheekpieces nowadays. *J. E. Dixon* **c78 h–**

JUMIEGES (FR) 8 b.g. Grand Tresor (FR) – Chamad (FR) (Maiymad) [2004/5 c20s6 c22s* c20spu Dec 15] tall ex-French gelding: first foal: half-brother to winning chaser up to 21f Kepi Blanc II (by Kadalko): dam maiden: twice-raced on Flat: fair hurdler/chaser: left T. Trapenard, won maiden chase at Market Rasen in November: broke down badly next time: stays 2¾m: acts on soft ground. *Ian Williams* **c110 h–**

JUMP FOR PADDY 6 b.g. Michelozzo (USA) – Tudor Spartan (Spartan General) [2004/5 F14mpu Mar 21] fifth foal: dam unraced, out of half-sister to very smart 2m to 3m chaser Clear Cut: placed all 3 starts in maiden points in 2004: looked temperamental when pulled up in maiden bumper at Hereford, making running but hanging badly left after 4f. *M. Pitman* **F–**

JUMPTY DUMPTY (FR) 8 b.g. Chamberlin (FR) – Caryatide (FR) (Maiymad) [2004/5 c–, h–: 22dpu c20g Jan 14] tall gelding: winning cross-country chaser/hurdler, no form since 2002: tried tongue tied. *J. C. Tuck* **c– h–**

JUNE'S RIVER (IRE) 12 ch.g. Over The River (FR) – June Bug (Welsh Saint) [2004/5 c96x, h–: 25g Oct 26] rather leggy gelding: modest handicap chaser in 2003/4 for Mrs M. Reveley: lightly raced over hurdles: stays 2½m: acts on heavy going: often let down by jumping: unreliable. *Dr P. Pritchard* **c– x h–**

JUNGLE JIM 4 b.g. Atraf – Enchanting Melody (Chief Singer) [2004/5 F12g Nov 10] good-topped gelding: sixth foal: half-brother to 3 winners, including dual bumper winner First Harmony (by First Trump): dam maiden, should have stayed 1m: well beaten in 3-y-o bumper on debut: modest form in 2 maidens on Flat. *Miss Gay Kelleway* **F–**

JUNGLE JINKS (IRE) 10 b.g. Proud Panther (FR) – Three Ladies (Menelek) [2004/5 c123, h–: c25d5 c24d* c27sF c25v2 c22vpu c25s5 Mar 11] smallish, workmanlike gelding: fairly useful handicap chaser on his day: off 6 months, won at Haydock in October: should stay 3½m: acts on heavy going: inconsistent. *G. M. Moore* **c122 h–**

JUNIOR FONTAINE (FR) 8 b.g. Silver Rainbow – Blanche Fontaine (FR) (Oakland (Fr)) [2004/5 c120, h–: c16g* c22m5 c20s4 16v c16sbd Apr 7] workmanlike gelding: winning hurdler: fairly useful handicap chaser: won at Punchestown in April 2004: best effort when fifth of 22 to Ansar in Galway Plate: effective at 2m to 2¾m: acts on any going. *A. L. T. Moore, Ireland* **c125 h–**

JUNKANOO 9 ch.g. Generous (IRE) – Lupescu (Dixieland Band (USA)) [2004/5 19g 20v 21d* 26s2 Feb 10] tall, workmanlike gelding: fairly useful handicap hurdler, off 21 months before reappearance: won at Huntingdon in January: better form when second to Graffiti Tongue, pair clear, there following month: stays 3¼m: raced mainly on going softer than good (acts on heavy): none too reliable: successful on Flat in April. *K. G. Reveley* **h117**

JUPITER DE BUSSY (FR) 8 b. or br.g. Silver Rainbow – Tosca de Bussy (FR) (Le Riverain (FR)) [2004/5 20v6 20vpu 18d 20spu Mar 12] well-made gelding: chasing type: fair hurdler in 2002/3: no form in handicaps since 20-month lay-off: should stay beyond 2m: raced on good going or softer: visored (pulled hard) final start. *L. Lungo* **h–**

JUPITER JO 9 b.g. Jupiter Island – Marejo (Creetown) [2004/5 c16gpu c16d5 Apr 5] sturdy gelding: winning pointer: little form in chases. *J. B. Walton* **c68**

JUPITER'S FANCY 10 ch.m. Jupiter Island – Joe's Fancy (Apollo Eight) [2004/5 c65, h–: c25gF c20d3 c20g c25spu c24g4 c25g c21g4 Mar 18] modest hunter chaser: stays 25f: has worn cheekpieces. *M. V. Coglan* **c84 h–**

JUPON VERT (FR) 8 b.g. Lights Out (FR) – Danse Verte (FR) (Brezzo (FR)) [2004/5 c95, h–: c17d4 c16gpu c16gur c17s3 c19s* c16d* c16gpu c16s c20spu c16d c24g5 c19g5 Apr 15] leggy gelding: fair handicap chaser: won at Hereford and Warwick in November: **c102 h–**

probably stays easy 3m, effective at much shorter: acts on firm and soft going: formerly tongue tied. *R. J. Hodges*

JUPSALA (FR) 8 ch.g. Video Rock (FR) – Belle d'Avril V (FR) (Quart de Vin (FR)) [2004/5 c25v[F] Mar 5] smallish gelding: placed in maiden points in 2005, no other form: tried blinkered. *J. Burke* **c– h–**

JURADO EXPRESS (IRE) 9 b.g. Jurado (USA) – Express Film (Ashmore (FR)) [2004/5 c119, h–: c16g c17m* c20d[4] c19s c16d[3] Nov 19] workmanlike gelding: fairly useful chaser: won minor event at Clonmel in May: sold out of A. Moore's stable 20,000 gns Doncaster October Sales after fourth outing: raced mainly around 2m: acts on soft and good to firm going. *Miss Venetia Williams* **c122 h–**

JURALAN (IRE) 10 b.g. Jurado (USA) – Boylan (Buckskin (FR)) [2004/5 c126, h103: c16s[3] c19g[6] Dec 11] tall, good sort: winning hurdler: fairly useful handicap chaser: good third to Winchester at Wetherby: stays 21f: raced mostly on good going or softer over jumps. *H. P. Hogarth* **c128 h–**

JURANCON II (FR) 8 b.g. Scooter Bleu (IRE) – Volniste (FR) (Olmeto) [2004/5 c148, h–: c29v c33d[pu] c25m c29g[pu] Apr 23] tall, leggy gelding: smart handicap chaser in 2003/4: out of form in 2004/5: stays 4m: acts on good to firm and heavy going: visored final start. *M. C. Pipe* **c– h–**

JUST ANVIL (IRE) 7 ch.g. Baron Blakeney – Amy Just (IRE) (Bustomi) [2004/5 c–: c26m[2] c25s[F] c26s[3] c26s[4] c21s[4] c26v* c25v* Jan 28] poor handicap chaser: made most when winning at Plumpton and Folkestone in January: stays 3¼m: acts on heavy and good to firm going: game. *L. Wells* **c79**

JUST ASK 5 ch.m. Busy Flight – Last Shower (Town And Country) [2004/5 F16v F16m Apr 10] fifth foal: dam poor half-sister to smart 1m and 9f winner Sign of Hope: little show in bumpers. *N. R. Mitchell* **F–**

JUST A SPLASH (IRE) 5 ch.g. Synefos (USA) – Guitane Lady (IRE) (Commanche Run) [2004/5 F16s F16s[5] 16m Apr 2] rangy, useful-looking gelding: third foal: dam no form: not knocked about in 2 bumpers: no show in novice at Newbury on hurdling debut. *N. J. Gifford* **h– F79**

JUST A TOUCH 9 ch.g. Rakaposhi King – Minim (Rymer) [2004/5 c90, h90: c16g* c16f[2] c17s[2] c17v[5] Jan 17] workmanlike gelding: winning hurdler: modest novice chaser: won handicap at Towcester in April 2004: probably best around 2m: acts on any going. *P. Winkworth* **c95 h–**

JUST BARNEY BOY 8 b.g. Past Glories – Pablena (Pablond) [2004/5 c–, h–: c24v[ur] c25v[3] Mar 5] no form outside points. *S. Waugh* **c– h–**

JUST BETH 9 ch.m. Carlingford Castle – One For The Road (Warpath) [2004/5 h79: 21g[3] 24d[3] 21g* 22m[4] 24g[2] 24d* 24d[3] 24g[2] 25s[6] 21d 20v[2] 20v[5] 24g[3] 22d[3] 24s[4] 21g[4] Apr 14] angular mare: fair handicap hurdler: won at Southwell (conditional jockeys) in May and Ludlow in November: stays 25f: acts on good to firm and heavy going: tried blinkered: tough and consistent. *G. Fierro* **h111**

JUST BRYAN 6 ch.g. Southern Music – Prospect of Whitby (True Song) [2004/5 F–: F16g 24s[pu] 20s[pu] 16s[pu] 19v[pu] Feb 13] of no account. *P. A. Pritchard* **h– F–**

JUST CLIQUOT 9 b.m. Gunner B – Formidable Lady (Formidable (USA)) [2004/5 c24g* c26g[ur] c26g Mar 18] 4,600 4-y-o: quite good-topped mare: fifth foal: sister and half-sister to winning pointers: dam, winning 2m hurdler, half-sister to smart 2m to 2½m chaser Young Benz and smart 2m to 3m hurdler Sprowston Boy: winning pointer, including in 2005: won novice hunter at Bangor in April 2004: seventh to Sleeping Night in Foxhunter at Cheltenham in March: stays 3¼m. *Mrs A. C. Swarbrick* **c94**

JUST FILLY (IRE) 4 ch.f. Woodborough (USA) – Good Aim (IRE) (Priolo (USA)) [2004/5 16m Sep 19] behind in 1m maiden at 2 yrs: sold out of A. Jones's stable £6,000 Ascot July Sales: no show on hurdling debut. *Miss C. J. E. Caroe* **h–**

JUST FOR FUN (IRE) 7 b.g. Kahyasi – Copper Breeze (IRE) (Strong Gale) [2004/5 h77?: 24g[2] 27m* 22d[4] c20s[pu] c20m[F] c24d[3] c27v[F] c24g[pu] Feb 16] smallish gelding: poor hurdler: won handicap at Sedgefield in May: similar standard over fences, though often let down by jumping: stays 27f: acts on good to firm and heavy going: in cheekpieces/ blinkers 6 of last 7 starts. *Ferdy Murphy* **c82 x h82**

JUSTIFIED (IRE) 6 b. or br.g. Leading Counsel (USA) – Monkeylane (Monksfield) [2004/5 F104p: F16v* 16s[2] 16v* 16s[2] 16d[4] 16s* 16v* 16g 16s* Mar 29] **h139 F99**

It is a pity that Justified failed to show to best advantage in either of the Grade 1 novice hurdles he contested, for he did not need to improve much on his best form to have gone close in both the Royal Bond at Fairyhouse in November and the Supreme Novices' at the Cheltenham Festival. Justified started 7/1 second favourite at Cheltenham in a very open renewal of the championship event for two-mile novices, but he found conditions insufficiently testing, racing on good ground for the first time, and couldn't quicken once headed after making most to two out. Justified finished eighth, beaten over thirteen lengths by the winner Arcalis. Justified might well have been better served by contesting the longer Royal & SunAlliance Novices' Hurdle at Cheltenham, the possibility having been mooted after he won the Grade 2 Byrne Group plc Novices' Hurdle at Punchestown at the end of January. With the promising Leopardstown maiden winner Akshar very weak in the betting, Justified was sent off favourite in a field of eight and made the most of a well-run race on testing ground. Racing second and turning in a polished round of jumping, Justified was sent on after the third last and was by no means flat out to draw fourteen lengths clear of the mare Blazing Liss at the post, with Akshar well held in fourth. This was not an especially strong race but the performance was the best by an Irish-trained novice hurdler all season before Asian Maze won the Sefton at Aintree.

The Punchestown race was Justified's sixth over hurdles. He had won twice previously, a maiden at Galway in October, when Blazing Liss had also finished runner-up, and a listed event at Punchestown in December when he didn't have to be at his best to defeat seven opponents in a tactical affair. In between those two wins, Justified finished behind Wild Passion in both a Grade 3 at Navan and in the Royal Bond. Justified was beaten by Wild Passion in all three races in which they faced one another (Wild Passion finished second in the Supreme), but, in our view, Justified was marginally the better novice on the pick of his form, his performance in the Grade 2 at Punchestown rating better than anything achieved by Wild Passion.

After Cheltenham, Justified was seen out only once, two weeks later, in the Grade 2 Menolly Homes Novices' Hurdle at Fairyhouse. Still at two miles, but back on soft ground, Justified was seen in a much better light, going a long way towards repeating the form of his Punchestown win. Again holding a prominent position, he was ridden to lead after two out and once more stayed on well, defeating the

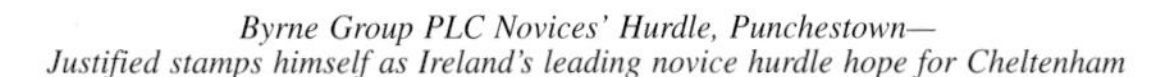

Byrne Group PLC Novices' Hurdle, Punchestown—
Justified stamps himself as Ireland's leading novice hurdle hope for Cheltenham

Menolly Homes Novices' Hurdle, Fairyhouse—
Cheltenham disappointments are banished with victory over The Railway Man (left)

Deloitte runner-up The Railway Man, who was receiving 6 lb, by two lengths, with his old rival Blazing Liss third. That was it for the season for Justified, but those in the frame behind him all ran at the Punchestown Festival, neither The Railway Man nor the fourth Petertheknot really boosting the form.

Justified (IRE) (b. or br.g. 1999)	Leading Counsel (USA) (br 1982)	Alleged (b 1974)	Hoist The Flag
			Princess Pout
		Society Column (br 1969)	Sir Gaylord
			Journalette
	Monkeylane (b 1986)	Monksfield (b 1972)	Gala Performance
			Regina
		Stoirin (ch 1980)	Mart Lane
			Sagosha

Strangely, Justified's most notable relative also gained his most significant win on heavy ground at Punchestown, though the day Big Matt put up a high-class performance, to land the BMW Handicap Chase at the 1998 Festival, Noah was on standby. Big Matt, a half-brother to Justified's dam Monkeylane, was a smart chaser on balance of form and his other major win also came at two miles, in the Victor Chandler Chase, though he was effective at around two and a half. Monkeylane and Justified's grandam Stoirin were maidens, raced both over hurdles and on the Flat, and neither of Monkeylane's two other foals to race, both by Jurado, have shown any ability. To find another winner in the family, it is necessary to go back to the third dam Sagosha, a fair winner at up to a mile and a half-sister to the Yorkshire Oaks winner Condessa. More significantly here, Condessa is also the grandam of the ill-fated top hurdler Valiramix. The lengthy, angular Justified gives the impression he will be suited by a step up in trip, and therein lies his best hope of showing improvement if he is kept over hurdles. However, it would be no surprise to see him sent chasing in 2005/6. Prior to going hurdling, Justified ran twice in bumpers, winning the second of them at Sligo in effectively the last week of the Irish 2003/4 season. *E. Sheehy, Ireland*

JUST IN DEBT (IRE) 9 b. or br.g. Montelimar (USA) – No Debt (Oats) [2004/5 c132, h120: c20m c24d* c27s² 20spu c36d Apr 9] useful-looking gelding: winning hurdler: useful handicap chaser: in cheekpieces, won 4-runner event at Newcastle in November by ½ length from Rosie Redman: good second to Silver Birch in Becher Chase at Aintree 9 days later: failed to get home after travelling strongly to 3 out when ninth in Grand National at Aintree final start: stays 27f: acts on soft and firm going. *M. Todhunter* **c136 h–**

JUST IN TIME 10 b.g. Night Shift (USA) – Future Past (USA) (Super Concorde (USA)) [2004/5 c–, h123: 24dpu 17d 20g³ 20f⁵ 24g³ 24s⁴ 16s 24d 20v Jan 10] leggy gelding: winning chaser: fairly useful handicap hurdler: left P. Hobbs and out of form after sixth start: stays 3m: acts on soft and firm going. *Mrs L. B. Normile* **c– h118**

JUST JED 6 b.g. Presidium – Carrapateira (Gunner B) [2004/5 h–, F–: 20gpu Sep 12] chunky gelding: no show over hurdles: runner-up in point in March. *R. Shiels* **h–**

JUST JIMBO 9 ch.g. Karinga Bay – Ruby Green VII (Damsire Unregistered) [2004/5 c16d² c20spu c16spu c19mpu Mar 14] tall, angular gelding: novice hurdler: form over fences only when runner-up in conditional jockeys handicap: should stay beyond 17f: acts on heavy going: has broken blood vessels. *R. J. Hodges* **c63 h–**

JUST JOLLY (IRE) 10 b.g. Jolly Jake (NZ) – Bulgaden Gypsy (Ballinamona Boy) [2004/5 c22g⁴ 16v⁶ c24d* c24d² c30d⁴ c22s* c24d⁴ c22dpu c24d⁵ c20v⁴ c24s⁶ c19vpu c24g⁵ c20g Apr 3] good-topped gelding: winning Irish pointer: well held over hurdles: modest chaser: won handicaps at Huntingdon (novice) in October and Market Rasen in December: effective at 2½m to 3¾m: raced mainly on going softer than good. *J. R. Cornwall* **c93 h–**

JUST KATE 6 b.m. Bob's Return (IRE) – M I Babe (Celtic Cone) [2004/5 h81, F81: 21g² 22m* 20m⁶ 21d³ 22d* 22s* Jan 1] fair handicap hurdler: won at Fontwell in May (left Mrs H. Dalton after next start) and January and Exeter in December: will stay 3m: acts on soft and good to firm going. *A. King* **h110**

JUST LARK 11 b.g. Rubicund – Shelley's Lark (Sir Lark) [2004/5 c21m³ May 19] modest pointer, successful twice in 2005: well held in maiden hunter at Folkestone. *Mrs V. K. Rickcord* **c68**

JUST LIBBI 5 b.m. Cloudings (IRE) – Tibbi Blues (Cure The Blues (USA)) [2004/5 F17d May 15] fourth foal: dam won over 1m in France: well beaten in mares bumper on debut. *Ferdy Murphy* **F–**

JUST MAYBE (IRE) 11 b.g. Glacial Storm (USA) – Purlace (Realm) [2004/5 c–x, h99: 23s* 26s⁵ c31dur c33d c23v 24s Apr 2] good-bodied gelding: winning chaser: fair hurdler, form in 2004/5 only when winning handicap at Wetherby in February: suited by 23f+: acts on heavy going: wears blinkers/visor: tongue tied once: jumps none too fluently: sold 4,000 gns Doncaster May Sales. *Miss Venetia Williams* **c– x h109**

JUST MIDAS 7 b.g. Merdon Melody – Thabeh (Shareef Dancer (USA)) [2004/5 h83: 17d* 17d⁵ 18m⁴ c16g 17m 16g 16g Sep 12] leggy, sparely-made gelding: poor hurdler: won selling handicap at Hereford in April 2004: left M. Pipe before final outing: not fluent and never dangerous only outing over fences: best around 2m: acts on firm and good to soft going: tongue tied fifth and sixth starts, also in cheekpieces in latter. *N. M. Babbage* **c– h83**

JUST MUCKIN AROUND (IRE) 9 gr.g. Celio Rufo – Cousin Muck (IRE) (Henbit (USA)) [2004/5 c88, h–: c22s² c19vpu c24mpu c16d* c18mF Apr 21] lengthy gelding: modest chaser: won handicap at Newton Abbot in March: stays 2¾m: acts on heavy going. *R. H. Buckler* **c95 h–**

JUST MY PAL 5 b.g. Paris House – Renshaw Wood (Ascertain (USA)) [2004/5 F16d⁵ F17spu Apr 2] fourth foal: dam, poor hurdler/chaser, stayed 3m: fifth of 10 in bumper at Haydock on debut: finished lame next time. *P. Beaumont* **F83**

JUST NICHOLAS 5 ch.g. Magic Ring (IRE) – Just Sidium (Nicholas (USA)) [2004/5 F17m Nov 11] first foal: dam, poor maiden, form only at 5f: tailed off in bumper on debut. *R. J. Hodges* **F–**

JUST OFFALY (IRE) 8 b.g. Supreme Leader – Head of The Gang (Pollerton) [2004/5 c20dpu 24spu Mar 6] 2,000 3-y-o, 1,400 5-y-o: sturdy gelding: fifth foal: brother **c– h–**

to winning hurdler around 2m Brancepeth Belle: dam, runner-up in Irish bumpers, sister to Supreme Novices' Hurdle winner Tourist Attraction: no show in novice chase and hurdle. *M. Appleby*

JUST PERCY 5 b.g. Then Again – Persistent Gunner (Gunner B) [2004/5 F17g F16d Mar 24] workmanlike gelding: second foal: half-brother to winning hurdler La Marette (by Karinga Bay), stays 2½m: dam, poor hurdler who stayed 19f, half-sister to useful 2m hurdler Teletrader: well held in 2 bumpers. *R. J. Hodges* **F–**

JUST POSIN 4 ch.f. I'm Supposin (IRE) – We're In The Money (Billion (USA)) [2004/5 F14d6 F13g Jan 17] leggy filly: fourth foal: dam, winning hurdler/chaser who stayed 25f, out of half-sister to smart performer up to 7f Superlative: well held in 2 bumpers. *Mrs S. Lamyman* **F–**

JUSTPOURIT (IRE) 6 b.g. Glacial Storm (USA) – Gale Choice (IRE) (Strong Gale) [2004/5 F18d5 F16s2 F16v2 F16s2 F19s2 Mar 26] €27,000 4-y-o: second foal: dam unraced half-sister to fairly useful 19f and 2¾ hurdle winner Collier County: fairly useful bumper performer: runner-up last 4 starts, beaten neck by Father Matt at Cork final one. *D. T. Hughes, Ireland* **F103**

JUST REUBEN (IRE) 10 gr.g. Roselier (FR) – Sharp Mama VII (Damsire Unregistered) [2004/5 c89, h–: c16d6 c22m3 c20m4 c25fur c23sur c19g c22s4 c21s6 c22s4 Feb 4] leggy gelding: poor handicap chaser: stays 3¼m: acts on any going: tried blinkered/visored: sometimes let down by jumping. *C. L. Tizzard* **c86 d**

JUST RUBY 4 ch.f. Gunner B – First Crack (Scallywag) [2004/5 F16m Apr 10] third foal: half-sister to bumper winner Firstflor (by Alflora): dam, fair hurdler, stayed 3m: well held in maiden bumper on debut. *F. Jordan* **F–**

JUST SAL 9 b.m. Silly Prices – Hanim (IRE) (Hatim (USA)) [2004/5 h86: 18m 16g 16m 16g 16d 17s 16s 16d 18s5 16g c19dpu 20s6 24v6 24s Apr 20] workmanlike mare: poor handicap hurdler: let down by jumping on chasing debut: stays 2¾m: acts on heavy going: tried in cheekpieces/blinkers: untrustworthy. *R. Nixon* **c– § h75 §**

JUST SCOOBY 4 b.c. Makbul – Cute Wedding (Remainder Man) [2004/5 F17d Mar 26] sturdy colt: first foal: dam ran once in point: no show in bumper on debut. *M. D. Hammond* **F–**

JUST SERENADE 6 ch.m. Factual (USA) – Thimbalina (Salmon Leap (USA)) [2004/5 h–: 16m 20dpu May 15] medium-sized mare: lightly-raced winning hurdler: no form since 2002: tried in cheekpieces. *T. P. Walshe* **h–**

JUST SOOTY 10 br.g. Be My Native (USA) – March Fly (Sousa) [2004/5 c100, h–: c20d3 c20d* c25gpu Dec 16] big, useful-looking gelding: fair handicap chaser: won at Hexham in October: stays 21f: acts on soft going. *N. G. Richards* **c109 h–**

JUST STRONG (IRE) 12 b. or br.g. Strong Gale – Just Dont Know (Buckskin (FR)) [2004/5 c69: c21m4 c27g4 c24g3 c27m3 c25m4 c24s5 c27d2 c30d4 c28gpu Mar 26] good-topped gelding: poor handicap chaser: lame final outing: stays 3¾m: acts on good to firm and good to soft going: tried in cheekpieces. *Mrs A. M. Naughton* **c69**

JUST SUPERB 6 ch.g. Superlative – Just Greenwich (Chilibang) [2004/5 h100: 20d4 20d 16d2 20s6 16g Jan 24] smallish gelding: fair handicap hurdler: best up to 19f: acts on soft going: usually races prominently. *P. A. Pritchard* **h101**

JUST TEN MINUTES 5 ch.g. Atraf – Sabeel (Local Suitor (USA)) [2004/5 F16s Mar 31] second foal: dam, poor novice hurdler, half-sister to fairly useful hurdler Shu Gaa, stayed 3m: no show in bumper on debut. *M. Scudamore* **F–**

JUST THE JOBE 7 gr.g. Roselier (FR) – Radical Lady (Radical) [2004/5 h111: c23d3 c25gF May 1] leggy gelding: fair hurdler: let down by jumping over fences, fatally injured when falling at Hexham: should have stayed 3m: raced on good going or softer over jumps: wore cheekpieces last 4 starts over hurdles. *R. C. Guest* **c– h–**

JUST TOM 10 ch.g. Primitive Rising (USA) – Edenburt (Bargello) [2004/5 27dF Oct 27] tall, quite good-topped gelding: lightly-raced maiden hurdler/chaser: off 2 years, fell second in amateur handicap hurdle only start in 2004/5: should be suited by further than 2m. *M. D. Hammond* **c– h–**

JUST WIZ 9 b.g. Efisio – Jade Pet (Petong) [2004/5 16d* 16s4 Mar 31] half-brother to winning 2m hurdler Jade Warrior (by Sabrehill): poor on Flat (stays 1½m): better effort over hurdles when winning seller at Ludlow in February. *N. P. Littmoden* **h86**

Fulke Walwyn Kim Muir Challenge Cup Handicap Chase (Amateur), Cheltenham—Nicky Henderson-trained runners dominate, with French import Juveigneur too strong for veteran Lord of The River

JUVEIGNEUR (FR) 8 ch.g. Funny Baby (FR) – Azurea (FR) (On My Way (USA)) [2004/5 c20g* $c21g^F$ $c20s^3$ c20d* $c21v^5$ $c24d^2$ $c24d^2$ c24g* c21d $c29g^2$ Apr 23] close-coupled, good-topped gelding: second foal: dam unraced: useful chaser: successful 4 times in France, including at Craon in September and Durtal in November: left G. Macaire, improved form when winning 24-runner Fulke Walwyn Kim Muir Challenge Cup Handicap (Amateur Riders) at Cheltenham in March by 1¼ lengths from Lord of The River: again ran well when 1¼ lengths second to Jack High in Betfred Gold Cup (Handicap) at Sandown: let down by jumping in Topham Chase at Aintree in between: stays 29f: acts on soft going. *N. J. Henderson* **c137**

K

KABOOBI (IRE) 5 ch.g. Anshan – Conna Dodger (IRE) (Kemal (FR)) [2004/5 F16m Jul 21] fourth foal: half-brother to fair chaser Commanche Quest (by Commanche Run), stays 25f: dam, won Irish point, half-sister to useful staying jumper St Mellion Fairway and useful hurdler up to 2½m Native Player: no show in bumper on debut. *D. Brace* **F–**

KADAM (IRE) 5 b.g. Night Shift (USA) – Kadassa (IRE) (Shardari) [2004/5 h80p: $19s^{pu}$ $17d^5$ 19d 16s 22d* $19g^2$ 20d* Apr 22] big, lengthy gelding: fair hurdler: won handicaps at Newton Abbot (novice) and Chepstow in April: stays 2¾m: acts on good to soft going: blinkered last 3 starts: tongue tied on debut: tends to make mistakes. *P. F. Nicholls* **h107**

KADARA (IRE) 6 b.m. Slip Anchor – Kadassa (IRE) (Shardari) [2004/5 h124: $c23s^F$ $22d^5$ $24g^3$ $25s^6$ $24d^2$ 24g Mar 17] tall, useful-looking mare: type to make a chaser: usually looks very well: useful hurdler: mainly creditable efforts in 2004/5, particularly so when 3¾ lengths third to Baracouda in Long Distance Hurdle at Newbury (after building up huge lead) and when second to Chamoss Royale in handicap at Kempton: looked to need **c101 p** **h131**

race and would have finished fourth but for falling 2 out in maiden at Exeter on chasing debut: stays 3m: acts on heavy going, probably on good to firm: likely to do better over fences. *R. H. Alner*

KADARANN (IRE) 8 b.g. Bigstone (IRE) – Kadassa (IRE) (Shardari) [2004/5 c157, h–: c16g² c17s³ c16v² c16s³ c17d⁵ c16g⁵ c20d⁴ c16g⁶ Apr 16] tall, close-coupled gelding: very smart chaser, bit below best in 2004/5, including when fifth to Moscow Flyer in Champion Chase at Cheltenham: tailed off last 2 outings, in Melling Chase at Aintree and handicap at Ayr (blinkered): best around 2m: acts on heavy and good to firm going: usually races prominently. *P. F. Nicholls* **c151 h–**

KADITO 9 b.g. Petoski – Kadastra (FR) (Stradavinsky) [2004/5 c19s³ c20s⁴ c16vpu 19m Apr 9] leggy gelding: winning hurdler/chaser: off 20 months, no show in 2004/5: should stay 2½m: acts on soft going: visored (pulled hard) final outing. *R. Dickin* **c– h–**

KADLASS (FR) 10 b.g. Kadounor (FR) – Brave Lass (Ridan) [2004/5 h89: 16s 16dpu Apr 17] compact gelding: winning hurdler: no sign of retaining ability after 2-year lay-off. *Mrs D. Thomas* **h–**

KADOUN (FR) 6 gr.g. Sleeping Car (FR) – Dea de Chalamont (FR) (Royal Charter (FR)) [2004/5 c115, h110: 21gF c16gF c20sF Nov 21] leggy gelding: fairly useful chaser/ fair hurdler: fell all 3 starts in 2004/5: stays 2½m: raced on good going or softer (acts on heavy): tried blinkered: tongue tied over hurdles in Britain: has found little. *H. D. Daly* **c– h109 ?**

KADOUN (IRE) 8 b.g. Doyoun – Kumta (IRE) (Priolo (USA)) [2004/5 c141, h138: 20s* c26d² c29s Mar 28] leggy gelding: useful handicap hurdler/chaser: successful over hurdles at Fairyhouse in February by neck from Leaders Way: 9 lengths second to Carlys Quest in below-par renewal of Champion Stayers' Hurdle at Punchestown in late-April: let down by jumping both starts over fences in 2004/5: effective at 2m to 3m: acts on heavy going, probably on good to firm: has worn headgear: formerly none too keen. *M. J. P. O'Brien, Ireland* **c115 x h138**

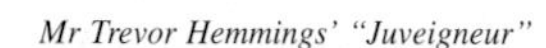

Mr Trevor Hemmings' "Juveigneur"

KADOUNT (FR) 7 b.g. Our Account (USA) – Une de Lann (FR) (Spoleto) **c141**
[2004/5 h130: c16s^{2} c20d^{2} c21d^{3} c17s* c16v^{4} c16d* c16g^{ur} c16s^{2} Apr 7] **h–**

The useful novice chaser Kadount was somewhat unfortunate not to have a better tally than two wins from eight starts over fences. His victories came in a five-finisher novice at Plumpton in January and the two-finisher Grade 2 coralpoker.com Kingmaker Novices' Chase at Wincanton in February, a race transferred from Warwick after that meeting was lost. The Kingmaker was in some ways the least meritworthy of Kadount's performances, though that was hardly his fault and he beat the outsider Roofing Spirit with something to spare. In three starts in maidens Kadount had run into Town Crier, Trabolgan, and Patches and Lacdoudal, useful novices all, and even at Plumpton he had to defeat another useful pair Greenhope and Limerick Boy to get off the mark. Kadount's one outing between Plumpton and Wincanton saw his only finish outside the first three, but his fourth to My Will, Ashley Brook and Contraband in another Grade 2 novice at Uttoxeter wasn't far off his best effort to that point.

While the Grand Annual arguably looked a better option at the Cheltenham Festival than the Arkle for Kadount, connections opted for the novice championship race and were getting a good run for their money until Kadount unseated rider four from home. At least the Arkle didn't ruin his handicap mark and only an even better treated novice in Fota Island denied him a big payday at Aintree. The pair started first and second favourite for the Red Rum Handicap and came home ahead of the field, Kadount going down by a length.

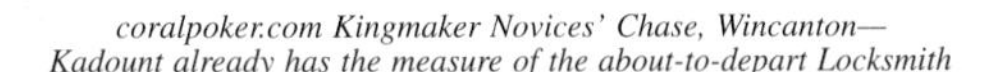

coralpoker.com Kingmaker Novices' Chase, Wincanton—
Kadount already has the measure of the about-to-depart Locksmith

Kadount began his career in France, winning four times in non-thoroughbred races at four and five at around a mile and a half. Kadount then won his first three races over hurdles after coming to Britain, before failing to come up to expectations in two valuable handicaps. Kadount always seemed likely to make a better chaser than a hurdler—he is a strong, good-bodied gelding—and there may well be more to come in handicaps in his second season over fences. It wouldn't be a surprise to see him aimed at the valuable intermediate handicap at Windsor (switched from Ascot). Kadount is effective at two miles to twenty-one furlongs and has raced on good going or softer (acts on heavy). *A. King*

KAHUNA (IRE) 8 b.g. Mister Lord (USA) – My Baloo (On Your Mark) [2004/5 h127: 16g5 c16dF c17dF c18s2 c17v2 c16v2 c17s5 Mar 28] tall, angular gelding: fairly useful hurdler: similar form over fences: clear when coming down last in maiden at Clonmel: runner-up in similar events next 3 outings, beaten 11 lengths by Ulaan Baatar at Punchestown on last occasion: best around 2m: acts on heavy and good to firm going: usually front runner (held up when jumping poorly final start). *E. Sheehy, Ireland* **c121 + h–**

KAID (IRE) 10 b.g. Alzao (USA) – Very Charming (USA) (Vaguely Noble) [2004/5 c81§, h–§: 20g4 c21s6 20s4 16s 26s 21v6 Jan 25] angular gelding: poor maiden chaser/winning hurdler: stays 21f: acts on good to firm and heavy going: tried blinkered/visored: unreliable. *R. Lee* **c– § h– §**

KAIKOVRA (IRE) 9 ch.g. Toulon – Drefflane Supreme (Rusticaro (FR)) [2004/5 h89: 16d May 6] modest hurdler: behind in handicap only outing in 2004/5: stays 19f with emphasis on speed: acts on good to firm going (won bumper on soft): races freely up with pace: sometimes finishes weakly. *M. F. Harris* **h–**

KALAMBARI (IRE) 6 b.g. Kahyasi – Kalamba (IRE) (Green Dancer (USA)) [2004/5 h86§: 16g4 17m3 17m2 19g* 17d2 16g3 19v5 16g6 Oct 27] leggy, angular gelding: fair hurdler: given fine ride by P. Brennan when winning novice handicap at Stratford in July: should stay beyond 19f: acts on good to firm and good to soft ground, probably on soft: blinkered: ungenuine. *P. J. Hobbs* **h105 §**

KALANISHA (IRE) 5 ch.g. Ashkalani (IRE) – Camisha (IRE) (Shernazar) [2004/5 16v5 Oct 16] lengthy gelding: half-brother to fair hurdler Berkeley Bay (by Fit To Fight), stays 2½m: poor maiden on Flat (should stay 1½m): fifth of 7 finishers in selling hurdle at Stratford, mistakes first 2 and early reminders: sold £700 Ascot February Sales. *John Berry* **h78**

KALCA MOME (FR) 7 b.g. En Calcat (FR) – Belle Mome (FR) (Grand Tresor (FR)) [2004/5 c128, h–: c18g5 c16g5 c16s2 c17g c19g* c16d c16s4 16v* 16d c20s2 Apr 2] leggy gelding: useful handicap chaser: won at Doncaster (beat Captains Table 4 lengths) in December: fairly useful handicap hurdler: won at Warwick in February by 4 lengths from Tamarinbleu: stays 2½m: acts on heavy ground, probably on good to firm: often let down by jumping over fences. *P. J. Hobbs* **c132 x h129**

KALDOUAS (FR) 4 bl. or br.g. Kaldou Star – Popie d'Ecorcei (FR) (Balsamo (FR)) [2004/5 F16m6 Apr 2] 180,000 3-y-o: useful-looking gelding: has scope: tenth foal: half-brother to very smart chaser Poliantas (by Rasi Brasak), stayed 2½m, and winning 2m hurdler Lucky d'As (by Sheyrann): dam, winning hurdler/chaser, stayed 25f: needed experience when 9½ lengths sixth of 21 to Hi Humpfree in bumper at Newbury on debut: should improve. *P. F. Nicholls* **F90 p**

KALEXANDRO (FR) 7 b.g. Michel Georges – Dalexandra (FR) (Quain (FR)) [2004/5 c24vF c20g4 21d c20spu c20g4 Mar 28] tall, useful-looking gelding: first foal: half-brother to 14.5f winner Malexandro (by Beyssac): dam no sign of ability: second in 5-y-o non-thoroughbred chase at Fontainebleau on completed start in France for T. Civel: still going well when falling eleventh on British debut but disappointing after, including over hurdles. *C. J. Mann* **c72 h–**

KALIC D'ALM (FR) 7 b.g. Passing Sale (FR) – Bekaa II (FR) (Djarvis (FR)) [2004/5 h–: 20d 16s 16g6 16d4 16v5 16v3 16s 16d5 Apr 11] tall gelding: poor maiden hurdler on balance: will probably prove best at 2m: raced on good going or softer (acts on heavy). *W. S. Coltherd* **h77**

KALI DES OBEAUX (FR) 7 b.m. Panoramic – Alpaga (FR) (Le Pontet (FR)) [2004/5 c–x, h100: c20g4 May 9] compact mare: modest chaser/novice hurdler: stays easy 3m: acts on soft and good to firm going: has been let down by jumping over fences: sold 4,800 gns Doncaster August Sales, unplaced in 2 points in 2005. *Mrs L. C. Taylor* **c97 x h–**

KALOU (GER) 7 b.g. Law Society (USA) – Kompetenz (IRE) (Be My Guest (USA)) [2004/5 h71: 16d² 17d* 18m² 16m⁴ c17g⁴ c16d⁴ c16d² c16s⁶ c20m³ Apr 23] good-topped gelding: modest hurdler: won handicap at Market Rasen in May: similar form over fences, left B. Curley after fifth outing: stays easy 2½m: acts on good to firm and good to soft going, probably on soft: has finished weakly. *C. Grant* **c99 h90 §**

KANDJAR D'ALLIER (FR) 7 gr.g. Royal Charter (FR) – Miss Akarad (FR) (Akarad (FR)) [2004/5 c136d, h94: c20s* c20s* c21d³ c21s² Jan 29] leggy gelding: maiden hurdler: useful handicap chaser: left M. Harris, back to best in 2004/5, winning at Plumpton and Windsor in December: good second to Buckby Lane in valuable event at Cheltenham following month: stays 21f: acts on heavy going. *A. King* **c137 h–**

KANSAS CITY (FR) 7 b.m. Lute Antique (FR) – Tenacity (FR) (Prove It Baby (USA)) [2004/5 c–, h–: 20d 16m 16g⁶ 16s⁵ c17s² c16d² c16s⁴ c20g c20v⁵ 19sᵖᵘ c25v⁴ c19v³ c23v³ c26d c20s² Mar 31] lengthy mare: poor maiden hurdler/chaser: sold out of M. Harris' stable 3,500 gns Doncaster May Sales after first outing, left P. Johnson after seventh: barely stays testing 23f: acts on heavy going: tried visored, usually wears cheek-pieces nowadays: has had tongue tied, including last 4 outings. *T. Wall* **c77 h–**

KAPAROLO (USA) 6 ch.g. El Prado (IRE) – Parliament House (USA) (General Assembly (USA)) [2004/5 h113: 16g³ 18d² 19d 17d 17g³ 17mᵖᵘ Apr 9] strong gelding: fair hurdler: below best in 2004/5, left Mrs A. Perrett after second outing: stays 2¾m: acts on good to firm and good to soft going. *John A. Harris* **h98**

KAPPELHOFF (IRE) 8 b.g. Mukaddamah (USA) – Miss Penguin (General Assembly (USA)) [2004/5 h–: 21d c16sᵖᵘ c25sᵖᵘ c21sᵖᵘ c22s³ c24dᵖᵘ c22s* c26m⁵ Apr 21] leggy gelding: no form over hurdles: poor chaser: won weakly-contested handicap at Fontwell in March: stays 2¾m: form only on soft going: blinkered last 5 starts: makes mistakes. *Mrs L. Richards* **c71 x h–**

KAPSKA (FR) 7 b.g. Silver Rainbow – Chapska (FR) (Le Pontet (FR)) [2004/5 h–: 23m³ May 16] no sign of ability. *M. J. Roberts* **h–**

KARADIN (FR) 11 b.g. Akarad (FR) – In River (FR) (In Fijar (USA)) [2004/5 c25dᵖᵘ Apr 29] workmanlike gelding: winning hurdler/chaser up to 21f: fair pointer nowadays, successful in April. *Mrs M Hand* **c– h–**

KARAGHAN (IRE) 5 b.g. Darshaan – Kadissya (USA) (Blushing Groom (FR)) [2004/5 F16d* F16s⁴ F16v⁴ F16s³ F16g Mar 16] workmanlike gelding: half-brother to 1988 Derby winner Kahyasi (by Ile de Bourbon) and several other winners, including fairly useful hurdler Kadiskar (by Ashkalani), stays 2½m: dam, 1¼m listed winner, sister to dam of useful staying hurdler Great Easeby: useful form in bumpers: won 4-y-o event at Fairyhouse in November: best effort when third to Firth of Forth at Navan: tongue tied, mid-field in Grade 1 at Cheltenham final start: will stay beyond 2m. *S. J. Mahon, Ireland* **F105**

KARAJAN (IRE) 8 b.g. Fairy King (USA) – Dernier Cri (Slip Anchor) [2004/5 c94, h–: c20m* c22m⁴ c25g⁶ Aug 21] angular gelding: modest novice chaser: fortunate to win handicap at Huntingdon in May: stays 3m: acts on heavy and good to firm going: prone to breaking blood vessels: sold 500 gns Doncaster October Sales. *G. M. Moore* **c92 h–**

KARAKAR (FR) 5 b.g. Ashkalani (IRE) – Karikata (IRE) (Doyoun) [2004/5 F16d Jun 23] fifth foal: half-brother to 8.5f winner Karani (by Distinctly North): dam, useful 1¼m to 1½m winner, half-sister to smart 5f performer Proud Native: last of 13 in bumper on debut. *N. A. Twiston-Davies* **F–**

KARAKUM 6 b.g. Mtoto – Magongo (Be My Chief (USA)) [2004/5 h71: 16g⁵ 16g⁵ 19g² 16s 17m⁴ 19g⁴ 19s⁴ Jan 10] poor maiden hurdler: stays 19f: acts on firm going, below form all 3 starts on soft. *A. J. Chamberlain* **h75**

KARANJA 6 b.g. Karinga Bay – Proverbial Rose (Proverb) [2004/5 F16d* F16s* F16d* F16gᵘʳ Mar 16] **F128**

There were some encouraging results for British National Hunt breeders in the latest season. Ollie Magern, Baron Windrush (both by Alderbrook), the French-foaled Mighty Man (by Sir Harry Lewis), Central House, Farmer Jack and Senorita Rumbalita (all by Alflora) were all notable performers bred in Britain, while Missed That (by Overbury) became the first winner of the Champion Bumper at Cheltenham to be bred in Britain, rather than in Ireland. Alderbrook, Alflora, Anshan and Karinga Bay all sired the winners of at least twenty-five races in Britain and Ireland in 2004/5, though it is a sign of the economics of National Hunt breeding that both Alderbrook and Anshan, along with Overbury, now stand in Ireland.

totesportcasino.com Standard Open National Hunt Flat, Newbury—Karanja maintains his unbeaten record by beating Be Be King (right) and subsequent Cheltenham runner-up De Soto

However, Alflora and Karinga Bay, like Alderbrook a son of Ardross, remain in Shropshire and, with their oldest offspring just nine, there is clearly potential for plenty more success. Unlike Alflora, the leading British-based sire, who is also responsible for Hand Inn Hand, Karinga Bay has yet to sire a Grade 1 winner, though his son Karanja is the highest-rated bumper performer in 2004/5 and was most unfortunate not to get the chance to show what he could do in the Champion Bumper, as he was baulked and unseated his rider at the start.

Karanja started second favourite behind Missed That at Cheltenham, having won his three previous races, at Sandown in November, Windsor in December (incidentally, just the second bumper ever staged there, following one the previous month) and Newbury in February. There was plenty to like about Karanja's first two performances but it is his win in the Grade 2 totesportcasino.com Standard Open NH Flat at Newbury which earns him his elevated position among his contemporaries. This race, under its various guises, has quickly established itself as one of the most significant bumpers of the season, with Iris's Gift winning in 2002 and Cornish Rebel in 2003. Seven of the first nine in 2003 have shown themselves useful or better over jumps, while the first six home the following year all showed plenty of ability over hurdles in 2004/5 (the seventh Corrib Eclipse went on to show useful form on the Flat, winning the Queen Alexandra Stakes). Secret Ploy, who showed useful form over hurdles without winning, produced the best performance in a bumper in 2003/4 when winning that renewal.

Seventeen went to post for the latest running, with Be Be King, an impressive winner on his only start, a well-supported favourite. Mr Pointment and Greenhill Bramble were other leading contenders who had been impressive in winning their only start, while Lutea and Earth Man were dual winners with useful form. There was plenty of support too for the Flat-bred newcomer De Soto. Karanja was sent off at 14/1 and, even though just about the pick of the weights, improvement was clearly going to be needed with so many promising sorts in the line-up. The race was well run and played to Karanja's strengths, as he had shown plenty of stamina when asserting in the latter stages at both Sandown and Windsor. Racing in touch, Karanja was being asked to improve into the straight and took until over a furlong out to get to the front, staying on well once there and beating Be Be King by three and a half lengths with De Soto third a further length and three quarters away, the trio pulling ten lengths clear of the remainder headed by Mr Pointment. Be Be King, surprisingly, was sent for a novice hurdle (in which he disappointed) shortly after Cheltenham rather than taking his chance in the Champion Bumper but De Soto went down only by a neck to Missed That in that championship event. Karanja had been ridden at Newbury by the highly promising amateur Nina Carberry and she retained the ride at Cheltenham, even though, for the first time, riders were unable to claim their allowance in the Champion Bumper. De Soto's performance suggests Karanja would have taken some beating. Although Karanja was denied the chance, others further behind at Newbury went on to boost the form and Karanja, on 128, is rated behind only Quadco (129) among bumper horses since such ratings were first published in *Chasers & Hurdlers* in 1993/4 (Montelado, the inaugural winner of the then Festival Bumper, is credited with a rating of 130, though that was not published at the time).

Karanja (b.g. 1999)	Karinga Bay (ch 1987)	Ardross (b 1976)	Run The Gantlet
			Le Melody
		Handy Dancer (ch 1977)	Green God
			Miss Golightly
	Proverbial Rose (b 1982)	Proverb (ch 1970)	Reliance II
			Causerie
		Agapantha (b 1970)	Pampered King
			Potentilla

Quadco was a wide-margin winner of the Grade 2 bumper at Aintree in 2000 but never fulfilled the promise of that win, showing no better than fairly useful form in a lengthy career over jumps and on the Flat. Injury severely restricted Montelado's subsequent appearances and he was seen just twice more over hurdles after trouncing the opposition in the 1993 Supreme Novices' Hurdle. It is to be hoped that Karanja fares rather better. He certainly has the physique—he is rangy and useful looking—and the pedigree to make a significant impact over hurdles and fences in seasons to come. Karanja is the fifth foal out of the winning pointer Proverbial Rose and one of four winners. The pick of the others is Flinders Chase

Mr D. G. Staddon's "Karanja"

(by Terimon), a fairly useful chaser and winning hurdler with form at up to three miles. Karanja's close relative Bansha House (by Ardross) won a two-and-a-half-mile hurdle, while Vicar's Lad (also by Terimon) won a point in the latest season. The grandam Agapantha and third dam Potentilla were both successful on the Flat, though Potentilla is the dam of one useful jumper, Potentate, and grandam of another, the ill-fated Thetford Forest. Potentate, not to be confused with a more recent runner of the same name, finished second in the Imperial Cup and won the Scilly Isles Novices' Chase in the early-'seventies while Thetford Forest won the 1992 Sun Alliance Hurdle. All told, Potentilla produced eleven winners, the best apart from Potentate being the useful stayer Potent Counsellor, who was placed in the Queen Alexandra Stakes. It would be no surprise to see Karanja have the Royal & SunAlliance Hurdle as his long-term target in 2005/6, though there should be plenty of success before that race is reached. Karanja, by the way, maintains a botanical theme in his family begun before the Second World War, as a karanja is a tree which grows commonly in India. *V. R. A. Dartnall*

KARATHAENA (IRE) 5 b.m. Barathea (IRE) – Dabtara (IRE) (Kahyasi) [2004/5 19v6 19s* 17s4 19d* 20d5 16vpu 19d Jan 29] medium-sized mare: disappointing maiden on Flat, sold out of J. Hills's stable 2,800 gns Newmarket July Sales: fair form over hurdles: won novices at Market Rasen and Doncaster in November: stays 19f: raced on going softer than good. *M. E. Sowersby* **h104**

KARAWA 6 ch.m. Karinga Bay – Lady Buck (Pollerton) [2004/5 F16s F17g2 Apr 14] workmanlike mare: half-sister to several winners, including fairly useful chaser Shining Willow (by Strong Gale), stayed 3m, and fair 2m hurdler Lord Buckingham (by Carroll House): dam unraced half-sister to top-class 2m to 2½m jumper Buck House: easily better effort in bumpers when 15 lengths second to Knockara Luck in mares event at Cheltenham, looking a stayer. *C. L. Tizzard* **F87**

KARELIAN 4 gr.g. Linamix (FR) – Kalikala (Darshaan) [2004/5 16v2 16d* 16s2 16s* 16s6 Apr 7] quite good-topped gelding: fair on Flat (likely to stay 1½m), successful in June, sold out of A. Fabre's stable 105,000 gns Newmarket July Sales: fairly useful juvenile hurdler: won at Doncaster (by 3 lengths from Nation State) in January and Ayr (long odds on) in March: best effort when 1½ lengths second of 6 to Akilak in quite valuable event at Haydock: seemed to lose interest final outing: raced at 2m on going softer than good. *K. A. Ryan* **h123**

KARIBLUE 7 ch.m. Imp Society (USA) – Kadastra (FR) (Stradavinsky) [2004/5 F–: F16d 16d Nov 23] smallish mare: well held in bumpers and novice hurdle. *R. Dickin* **h– F–**

KARLINE LADY 5 b.m. Thowra (FR) – Logical Lady (Tina's Pet) [2004/5 F17v Feb 13] workmanlike mare: third foal: dam fair 2m hurdler/1¼m winner: well held in bumper: dead. *W. S. Kittow* **F–**

KARO DE VINDECY (FR) 7 b.g. Mollicone Junior (FR) – Preves du Forez (FR) (Quart de Vin (FR)) [2004/5 c66, h–: c21dF c21g2 c20m4 c21m* c21m* c17d4 c21m5 c20m5 Apr 23] leggy gelding: poor handicap chaser: won at Sedgefield in July and August stays 21f: acts on good to firm and good to soft going: tongue tied: free-going sort. *M. D. Hammond* **c81 h–**

KAROO 7 b.g. Karinga Bay – Cupids Bower (Owen Dudley) [2004/5 F74: 17d5 22d2 19dur 20s5 22d6 22d6 Dec 2] sturdy gelding: fourth in point: modest form first 2 starts over hurdles: stays 2¾m: acts on good to soft ground: headstrong. *P. F. Nicholls* **h94**

KA ROSE (FR) 7 b.g. Missolonghi (USA) – Quelle Etoile V (FR) (Mitsoupam (FR)) [2004/5 27vpu Dec 31] no show in bumper and novice hurdle over 2½ years apart. *Ferdy Murphy* **h–**

KARYON (IRE) 5 b.m. Presidium – Stealthy (Kind of Hush) [2004/5 h71: 17mpu 17dpu 16m 16gpu 19d 19spu 17d Apr 5] smallish mare: poor hurdler: form only when winning juvenile seller at Catterick in 2003/4: tried in cheekpieces/blinkers. *Miss Kate Milligan* **h–**

KASSEL (USA) 5 ch.g. Swain (IRE) – Gretel (Hansel (USA)) [2004/5 h–, F–: 20gpu Aug 14] no sign of ability. *Ian Williams* **h–**

KASTHARI (IRE) 6 gr.g. Vettori (IRE) – Karliyka (IRE) (Last Tycoon) [2004/5 h109: 20d6 20m3 19d* 21gpu Mar 16] tall gelding: smart stayer on Flat, won Doncaster Cup (dead-heated with Millenary) in September: largely progressive over hurdles, winning handicap at Doncaster in January, jumping more fluently than often the case and beating Lord of Beauty 15 lengths: possibly amiss in Coral Cup at Cheltenham next time: stays 2½m: acts on soft and good to firm going. *J. Howard Johnson* **h136**

*John Smith's Fox Hunters' Chase, Aintree—
a family success as Katarino provides young amateur Sam Waley-Cohen
with his second big Festival win in three weeks*

KATARINO (FR) 10 b.g. Pistolet Bleu (IRE) – Katevana (FR) (Cadoudal (FR)) [2004/5 c21s* Apr 7] leggy gelding: has had breathing operation: smart hurdler/useful chaser at one time for N. Henderson: unbeaten in 2005 in points and 30-runner John Smith's Fox Hunters' Chase at Aintree: 100/30 favourite, beat Caught At Dawn by 1½ lengths at Aintree, nearly unseating Canal Turn but continuing to travel well, leading 3 out and idling after last: stays 3m: acts on good to firm and heavy going. *R. Waley-Cohen* — **c131 h–**

KATE'S GIFT 4 b.g. Supreme Leader – Ardentinny (Ardross) [2004/5 F16d Mar 5] 55,000 3-y-o: unfurnished gelding: second foal: dam, fair bumper winner, half-sister to fairly useful staying chaser Fox In The Box (by Supreme Leader): needed experience when ninth of 18 in above-average bumper at Newbury on debut. *P. R. Webber* — **F85 +**

KATHAKALI (IRE) 8 b.g. Dancing Dissident (USA) – Shes A Dancer (IRE) (Alzao (USA)) [2004/5 h94: 16g^{6} 16m^{6} Jun 13] modest hurdler: best at 2m: acts on good to firm going: has worn cheekpieces, blinkered nowadays. *C. J. Bennett* — **h91**

KATHIES PET 10 b.m. Tina's Pet – Unveiled (Sayf El Arab (USA)) [2004/5 16d^{6} 16d* 17g^{5} 20d^{3} 21g^{5} 24g Apr 7] poor handicap hurdler: won conditional jockeys seller at Chepstow in February: stays 2½m: acts on any going: reliable. *R. J. Hodges* — **h73**

KATIE KAI 4 b.f. Cayman Kai (IRE) – Yemaail (IRE) (Shaadi (USA)) [2004/5 16d 16d 16d^{4} 17s^{5} 16v^{ur} 16v^{4} 16s^{4} Apr 10] leggy filly: half-sister to modest hurdler/fair chaser Ross Comm (by Minster Son), stays 3m: tailed off only outing on Flat: poor form over hurdles: raced around 2m on going softer than good. *Miss S. E. Forster* — **h67**

KATIES DOLPHIN (IRE) 7 ch.m. Dolphin Street (FR) – Kuwah (IRE) (Be My Guest (USA)) [2004/5 c–, h–: 16g^{5} 17g^{3} 16f 20d^{ur} 17m 20d 21g^{3} c20g^{4} 21d^{5} Aug 22] poor maiden hurdler: no show in 2 chases: stays 21f: acts on soft going: wears headgear: usually tongue tied. *R. Johnson* — **c– h64**

KATIES HERO 7 b.g. Pontevecchio Notte – Kindly Lady (Kind of Hush) [2004/5 h83: 19d 17g May 27] novice hurdler: won maiden point in March: probably stays 2½m: tried blinkered in bumpers. *J. D. Frost* — **h–**

KATIKI (FR) 8 b.g. Cadoudal (FR) – Tikiti Dancer (FR) (Fabulous Dancer (USA)) [2004/5 c16d^{4} c20d^{rtr} c25g^{ur} Dec 14] compact gelding: smart hurdler in 2003/4, winning Group 2 Grand Prix d'Automne at Auteuil by ¾ length from Karly Flight: left J-P. Gallorini, successful on Flat at Royan in June: inadequate trip when fourth of 5 finishers in maiden at Sandown, only completed start over fences: stays 25f: raced mainly on soft/heavy going: tried blinkered/in cheekpieces: has refused to race on several occasions (banned from racing over jumps in France), and one to steer clear of. *G. Macaire, France* — **c111 § h§§**

KATINKA 12 b.m. Rymer – Millymeeta (New Brig) [2004/5 h–: c21g4 c20dF May 13] lengthy mare: winning pointer: no form otherwise: tried tongue tied. *A. M. Thomson* **c– h–**

KATMANDU 6 b.g. Sadler's Wells (USA) – Kithanga (IRE) (Darshaan) [2004/5 h101: 20d2 24v2 23s 20vpu Jan 10] leggy, useful-looking gelding: fair hurdler: sold out of J. H. Johnson's stable 20,000 gns Doncaster November Sales, below form both subsequent starts: stays 3m: raced on going softer than good over hurdles (acts on heavy): has worn cheekpieces/blinkers: has carried head awkwardly. *J. R. Turner* **h113**

KATOOF (USA) 7 b.g. Silver Hawk (USA) – The Caretaker (Caerleon (USA)) [2004/5 F–: F16s Oct 13] tailed off in 2 bumpers. *J. A. B. Old* **F–**

KATTEGAT 9 b.g. Slip Anchor – Kirsten (Kris) [2004/5 c–, h95: 27g6 27m5 26d3 Oct 17] leggy gelding: modest handicap hurdler: stays 27f: acts on heavy going: wears blinkers/cheekpieces nowadays: not straightforward (has carried head awkwardly), usually ridden by Miss L. Bridges. *Mrs H. M. Bridges* **c– h86 §**

KATY JONES 5 b.m. Alderbrook – Just Jodi (IRE) (Good Thyne (USA)) [2004/5 F16d Feb 12] rather unfurnished mare: first foal: dam unraced: tongue tied, tailed off in Grade 2 bumper at Newbury on debut. *Noel T. Chance* **F–**

KATY'S CLASSIC (IRE) 5 b.g. Classic Cliche (IRE) – Mrs Jennifer (River Knight (FR)) [2004/5 F16g Apr 19] 40,000 4-y-o: fifth foal: half-brother to 3 winning hurdlers, including smart stayer Splendid Thyne (by Good Thyne) and useful performer up to 25f His Nibs (by Alflora): dam, poor novice hurdler, from family of top-class staying chaser Brown Chamberlin: seemed in need of experience when twelfth of 17 in maiden bumper at Towcester on debut. *K. C. Bailey* **F79**

KATY THE DUCK (IRE) 10 br.m. Over The River (FR) – Zagliarelle (FR) (Rose Laurel) [2004/5 c–, h61: 21mpu May 27] angular mare: poor hurdler: probably stays 21f: acts on good to soft going: tried visored. *R. J. Price* **c– h–**

Mr Robert Waley-Cohen's "Katarino"

KATZ PYJAMAS (IRE) 4 b.f. Fasliyev (USA) – Allepolina (USA) (Trempolino (USA)) [2004/5 16d 16s 17vpu Feb 13] small, sparely-made filly: poor and unreliable sprint maiden on Flat: no potential as a hurdler. *G. F. H. Charles-Jones* **h–**

KAUSSE DE THAIX (FR) 7 ch.g. Iris Noir (FR) – Etoile de Thaix (FR) (Lute Antique (FR)) [2004/5 c–: c16d5 c19d3 c24dpu c22d5 c24s* c24s* c24d3 c28g3 Mar 26] lengthy, useful-looking gelding: modest chaser: won handicaps at Towcester in January and February: stays 3½m: acts on soft going. *O. Sherwood* **c98**

KAUTO STAR (FR) 5 b.g. Village Star (FR) – Kauto Relka (FR) (Port Etienne (FR)) [2004/5 h136: 19s* c18d* c17sF2 Jan 31] **c150 p** **h136 +**

'There are fools, damn fools, and those who remount in a steeplechase.' Nobody can do much about those who fall into the first two categories, but the practice of remounting came under close scrutiny in the latest season. Bill Whitbread, in his famous quote, evidently had a jockey's well-being in mind when questioning the sanity of a rider who gets back on a horse that has come to grief, but the issue in the latest season was principally one of horse welfare. The race that sparked the debate was a three-runner novice chase at Exeter in January which should have been a cakewalk for the then ante-post favourite for the Arkle, Kauto Star. It looked like being just that for the 11/2-on shot until he came down when thirteen lengths clear at the second last of his only remaining rival. With both horse and rider back on their feet immediately after the tumble, Ruby Walsh jumped back into the saddle and, without irons, set off in pursuit of Mistral de La Cour, who was still about ten lengths up at the final fence. Kauto Star rapidly cut back the deficit on the run-in and went down only by a short head. Whilst the immediate reaction was to praise Kauto Star's rider's quick thinking which almost pulled the race of the fire, Walsh's actions looked less heroic when X-rays of Kauto Star, described by his trainer as 'stiff and sore' afterwards, revealed a small fracture to his near-hind. There was no way of knowing for sure whether the injury was sustained in the fall or not.

The RSPCA, which had aired its concerns over remounting with the Jockey Club in 2004, brought the issue up again after the Exeter race, even before Kauto Star's injury came to light, though, initially at least, the Jockey Club stood by the existing arrangements. 'There is a key safeguard for the welfare of the horse in instruction H18,' said a spokesman, '. . . the onus is therefore on the jockey, as a horseman, to make a judgement as to whether the welfare of the horse could be compromised by continuing.' Regardless of whether a horse falls or not during a race, the instruction makes it a jockey's responsibility to act in the best interests of his mount. There are penalties that can be invoked for riders who persevere with horses that are patently lame, distressed or exhausted, but it says much for the good sense of jockeys that they have to be applied only very seldom. That should be sufficient. There are always going to be cases of horses picking up injuries, even quite serious ones, during a race, Flat or jumps, that do not come to light until afterwards. Banning remounting is not going to reduce injury to any worthwhile degree, only a tiny proportion of fallers actually being remounted in any case; the circumstances are very rare in which it is both possible, and then worthwhile, for a rider to remount. However, after a meeting with RSPCA officials, by which time support for a modification to the rule had come from other quarters, the Jockey Club seemed forced to backtrack on its original statement, admitting instead that 'this is a more complex issue than it might appear at first sight.' After consultation with the National Trainers' Federation and the Racehorse Owners Association, the Jockey Club was expected to announce a decision in late-summer.

Kauto Star's injury was reportedly not serious as fractures go, though it was enough to rule him out of the Arkle and the rest of the season. His absence was all the more regrettable because he looked one of the most exciting novice chasers of the season, making a most impressive winning debut over fences on his first appearance in Britain at Newbury in December. Kauto Star had been the subject of glowing reports at home and he started joint favourite with another chasing debutant, Foreman, winner of the previous season's AIG Europe Champion Hurdle at Leopardstown. The field also included Locksmith and Sleep Bal, useful hurdlers who had made promising chasing debuts when first and second respectively at Plumpton, and the 2002 Champion Hurdle runner-up Marble Arch. After tracking

Western Daily Press Race Club Novices' Chase, Newbury—
French import Kauto Star makes a hugely impressive start over fences

the leaders, Kauto Star effectively sealed matters with a really good leap three out, and was not at all hard pressed to draw clear, despite showing a slight tendency to hang left. Foreman was beaten nine lengths into second, with Sleep Bal another fifteen lengths away third. The form worked out well, with Sleep Bal, Mixsterthe-trixster (fourth) and Locksmith (seventh) all winning next time out, while Foreman was second in the Arkle at Leopardstown on his only subsequent start.

Kauto Star (FR) (b.g. 2000)	Village Star (FR) (ch 1983)	Moulin (ch 1976)	Mill Reef
			High Fidelyty
		Glitter (br 1976)	Reliance
			Glistening
	Kauto Relka (FR) (b 1993)	Port Etienne (b 1983)	Mill Reef
			Sierra Morena
		Kautorette (br 1981)	Kautokeino
			Verdurette

Unraced on the Flat, Kauto Star was first past the post on his first four starts over hurdles in France (demoted on his debut) as a three-year-old and subsequently spent much of his time at Auteuil in pattern races in vain pursuit of the best filly of his generation, Maia Eria. Kauto Star caught her on an off day when winning the Group 3 Prix de Longchamp in May 2004, and is pictured doing so in the 'Top Horses in France' section of last year's Annual. That turned out to be Kauto Star's final outing for Serge Foucher, before joining Paul Nicholls. Kauto Star is potentially the best horse sired by Village Star who died in 2003. Village Star was a late developer who ended his four-year-old season with third place in the Breeders' Cup Turf and was even better at five when winning the Grand Prix de Saint-Cloud and finishing a close fifth to Tony Bin in the Arc. Village Star has Mill Reef as his paternal grandsire and so too does Kauto Star's unraced dam Kauto Relka. Kauto Star is his dam's fourth foal and second winner after Kauto Lumen Dei (by Useful)

Mr Clive D. Smith's "Kauto Star"

who won at nine furlongs on the Flat and at around two miles over both hurdles and fences. Kauto Karolyna, a year-younger sister to Kauto Star, has been placed over fences in the Provinces, and his three-year-old half-brother, Kauto Dancer (by Jeune Homme), was second on his hurdling debut. Grandam Kautorette was kept much busier and ran more than sixty times in the Provinces, winning eleven races at up to around eleven furlongs on the Flat and another two over hurdles. She has bred several winners, including the four-year-old Kauto Ray (by Saint Cyrien), a promising winner over hurdles and fences already for Guillaume Macaire. The angular Kauto Star will lack experience over fences when he returns, but remains a very exciting chasing prospect. Until his mishap, he had jumped soundly in the Exeter race, as he had at Newbury. He stays nineteen furlongs and has raced only on good to soft or soft ground, and has been tongue tied on both starts in Britain. *P. F. Nicholls*

KAVI (IRE) 5 ch.g. Perugino (USA) – Premier Leap (IRE) (Salmon Leap (USA)) [2004/5 h91: 22g Jun 7] neat gelding: fair on all-weather, modest on turf on Flat (stays easy 13f), successful twice in February: modest hurdler: seems not to stay 2¾m: raced on good/good to firm going over hurdles: tried blinkered. *Simon Earle* **h91**

KAWAGINO (IRE) 5 b.g. Perugino (USA) – Sharakawa (IRE) (Darshaan) [2004/5 16g 17g* Jun 15] half-brother to useful hurdler/chaser Ebinzayd (by Tenby), stays easy 3m: fairly useful maiden up to 1m on Flat for Mrs P. N. Dutfield: second start over hurdles, won 5-runner novice at Newton Abbot impressively in June: not seen out again: will prove best around 2m with emphasis on speed. *J. W. Mullins* **h114 +**

KAYCEECEE (IRE) 4 b.g. Mister Mat (FR) – Maid of Glenduragh (IRE) (Ya Zaman (USA)) [2004/5 F16s³ Mar 5] 26,000 3-y-o: third foal: dam, fair hurdler up to 2½m, also **F83**

won at 13f on Flat: favourite but green, 5 lengths third of 5 in bumper at Huntingdon on debut. *H. D. Daly*

KAYLEIGH (IRE) 7 b.m. Kylian (USA) – Easter Baby (Derrylin) [2004/5 25s^6 22s^4 24v^2 22s^4 26s Mar 7] third known foal: sister to 2m winner Kintbury: dam winning 2m hurdler: won once from 4 starts in points in 2004: sold £5,200 Ascot June Sales: modest form at best over hurdles: should stay beyond 3m: raced only on soft/heavy going. *P. R. Rodford* **h82**

KAYSA (GER) 6 b.m. Second Set (IRE) – Kaytiggy (Busted) [2004/5 h–: 16m Jul 21] no form over hurdles: has had tongue tied. *A. J. Whiting* **h–**

KEEN AND ABLE 5 ch.m. Keen – Four Thyme (Idiot's Delight) [2004/5 F–: 17d Nov 23] lengthy mare: no form in bumpers or maiden hurdle. *N. G. Richards* **h–**

KEEN LEADER (IRE) 9 b.g. Supreme Leader – Keen Gale (IRE) (Strong Gale) [2004/5 c167, h–: c24s^3 c24g^2 Mar 15] tall, angular, rather raw-boned gelding: has stringhalt: high-class chaser, successful on 4 of 9 completed starts over fences: creditable placed efforts in valuable handicaps at Haydock (6½ lengths third of 5 finishers to Horus) and Cheltenham (1¼ lengths second to Kelami) in 2004/5: should stay beyond 25f: raced on good going or softer: strong-running sort, inclined to make the odd mistake. *Jonjo O'Neill* **c164** **h–**

KEEN ROYAL 4 ch.f. Keen – Ropsley High Style (Superlative) [2004/5 F16d Feb 18] fifth foal: dam unraced: always behind in mares bumper on debut. *Miss Suzy Smith* **F–**

KEEN TO GO 5 b.m. Keen – Popping On (Sonnen Gold) [2004/5 F16g F16s Nov 5] seventh foal: half-sister to useful hurdler Just Nip (by Lord Bud), stayed 3m, and poor hurdler up to 27f Nip On (by Dunbeath): dam won 2½m hurdle: last in mares bumpers. *J. R. Turner* **F–**

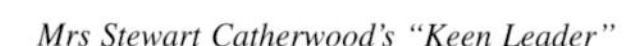

Mrs Stewart Catherwood's "Keen Leader"

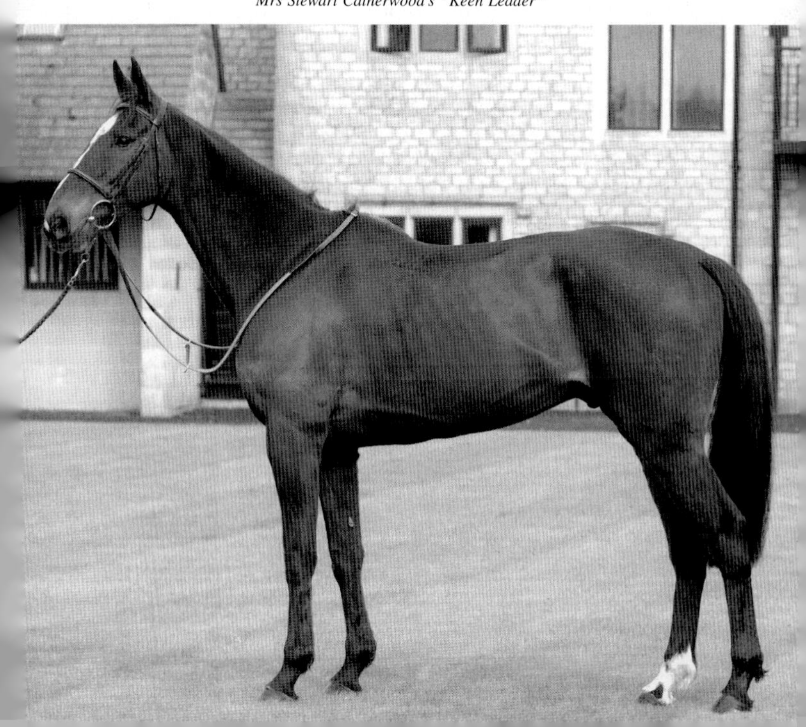

KEEN WARRIOR 5 gr.g. Keen – Briden (Minster Son) [2004/5 F16g F16s Mar 22] **F77**
tall gelding: first foal: dam of little account: mid-division in bumpers. *Mrs S. Lamyman*

KEEPATEM (IRE) 9 ch.g. Be My Native (USA) – Ariannrun (Deep Run) **c132**
[2004/5 h126: c18v^5 c17d^4 c23d* c18s^5 c24v* c21v^3 c33g Mar 17] **h–**

The fairly useful staying hurdler Keepatem made a successful transition to fences in the latest season, gaining two wins from seven starts, the more notable victory coming in one of Ireland's richest handicaps, the Paddy Power at Leopardstown's Christmas meeting. The Paddy Power has quickly established itself as a target for any fairly useful or useful three-mile chaser in Ireland (part of its appeal has been that anything smart or better is too good to be qualified) and it invariably attracts a huge and intriguing field.

By the time he contested the Paddy Power, Keepatem had run four times over fences, and it is true to say that, on the bare form shown on three of those occasions, he could not be given much chance at Leopardstown. However, all three runs had been at an unsuitably short trip, two and a quarter miles at most, and on the other, the third of the four, racing over a much more suitable trip in a maiden at Downpatrick, he showed form more in keeping with his efforts over hurdles. Keepatem beat another formerly useful hurdler Calladine by three quarters of a length with subsequent Irish National winner Numbersixvalverde third. Had he been raced in Britain, Keepatem could have expected a mark pretty close to that he had over hurdles. As it was, connections must have been pleasantly surprised by a mark 12 lb below his hurdles mark, which represented a decidedly low view of the form at Downpatrick. Keepatem's first chance to take advantage came at Gowran early in December. However, the drop of five furlongs in trip was unlikely to be in his favour and, sent off an uneasy favourite, he managed only fifth, beaten over ten lengths. He was, though, not at all knocked about once unable to quicken after getting smoothly into contention four out. The added experience was clearly going to be an advantage in the hustle and bustle of the Paddy Power.

Paddy Power Chase (Extended Handicap), Leopardstown—the well-backed novice Keepatem (hoops) wins a strong renewal from Jaquouille and the weakening Kymandjen (No.12)

Despite the generous prize money, no British-trained runners featured in a maximum field of thirty for the latest Paddy Power (just eleven have crossed the Channel since the race started, though two have won, Calling Wild and World Wide Web). Keepatem was not a market drifter this time, well supported ante-post and then backed down to 7/2 favourite at the off. Those who backed him had few anxious moments. Patiently ridden, Keepatem cut through the field into the straight, untroubled by having to be switched approaching the last, and led on the flat before drawing away to beat Jaquouille by four lengths. Keepatem was a second winner of the Paddy Power for his trainer Mouse Morris, who won the initial running with New Co, and a third win in the race for his owner J. P. McManus, successful previously with Time For A Run and World Wide Web.

After the Paddy Power, Keepatem's principal target was Cheltenham with a choice of one of the handicaps, the Royal & SunAlliance Chase and the National Hunt Chase. Keepatem's one run between Leopardstown and Cheltenham was a creditable third behind Newmill in a Grade 2 novice at Leopardstown, in which a three-furlong shorter trip and steadier pace proved his undoing, though he made up nearly seven lengths on the winner from early on the run-in. With Like-A-Butterfly to represent his owner in the SunAlliance, Keepatem was sent for the four-miler —now, pedantically speaking, the four-mile-and-one-furlonger—at Cheltenham but did not distinguish himself. Starting second favourite at 9/2, he made numerous mistakes and only the sedate pace kept him in with a chance until three from home. He finished eighth of the thirteen to complete, nearly thirty lengths behind the winner Another Rum.

Keepatem (IRE) (ch.g. 1996)	Be My Native (USA) (br 1979)	Our Native (b or br 1970)	Exclusive Native
			Our Jackie
		Witchy Woman (ch 1972)	Strate Stuff
			Witchy Norma
	Ariannrun (ch 1986)	Deep Run (ch 1966)	Pampered King
			Trial By Fire
		Mawbeg Holly (ch 1979)	Golden Love
			Hansels Pride

Keepatem has a classical jumping pedigree, being by Be My Native out of a Deep Run mare Ariannrun who was herself a sister to three winners, including the useful staying chaser Dakyns Boy. This is a family full of the progeny of the leading jumping sires: Ariannrun produced six other foals, the two by Strong Gale including the fairly useful staying hurdler/chaser Shore Party, the one by Supreme Leader being the fairly useful two-mile hurdler Poachin Again. Her only foal not to have won is the 1998 filly by Presenting. This is generally not a family where the mares tend to be raced and none of the four dams at the bottom of Keepatem's pedigree did so, though his fourth dam Slave Light was a sister to the dam of Dawn Run. The grandam Mawbeg Holly also produced six winners, the best of them apart from Dakyns Boy being the fairly useful two-mile chaser Holly's Pride, though the ill-fated Give It Holly (by Be My Native) was a leading candidate for the Champion Bumper before being fatally injured. Mawbeg Holly is also the grandam of the promising hurdler Overserved. The third dam Hansels Pride produced three winning hurdlers and two winning pointers, none of any great note, but was a half-sister to the high-class three-mile chaser Simon Legree and to the dam of the useful staying hurdler Friendship and the useful hurdler/chaser Boneyarrow. The workmanlike Keepatem should stay beyond three and a quarter miles. He has raced on good going or softer and acts on heavy. Despite his age, there may be more to come over fences for Keepatem and he could well make an impact in valuable staying handicaps in Ireland in 2005/6. *M. F. Morris, Ireland*

KEEPERS KNIGHT (IRE) 4 b.c. Sri Pekan (USA) – Keepers Dawn (IRE) (Alzao (USA)) [2004/5 16d Mar 4] workmanlike colt: modest on Flat (stays 1½m), claimed to join Karen McLintock £10,000 in April: tongue tied, not fluent when eighth of 14 in juvenile on hurdling debut. *P. F. I. Cole* **h75 +**

KEEPERS MEAD (IRE) 7 ch.g. Aahsaylad – Runaway Pilot (Cheval) [2004/5 h107: 21s^2 23s* 26d^3 22d^5 25s^{pu} 24d^4 22d^5 22v^{pu} Mar 30] useful-looking gelding: type to make a chaser: fair handicap hurdler: won at Lingfield in November: stays 3¼m: acts on soft going, detached from halfway on heavy final start. *R. H. Alner* **h111**

KEEP IT DARK (IRE) 8 b. or br.g. Castle Keep – Fairhill Lady (Strong Gale) [2004/5 19m^{rtr} May 22] ex-Irish gelding: half-brother to winning pointer by Camden Town: dam never ran: little form over hurdles (refused to race on British debut): runner-up on completed start in Irish points in 2004: tried blinkered in bumper. *M. J. Gingell* **h– §**

KEEP ON SKI 7 b.g. Petoski – Keep On Dancing (Crooner) [2004/5 24g^{pu} c22s^{pu} Dec 13] sturdy gelding: no sign of ability: tried visored. *P. G. Murphy* **c–** **h–**

KEEP SMILING (IRE) 9 b.g. Broken Hearted – Laugh Away (Furry Glen) [2004/5 c–x, h94: 22s^5 20d^5 17g^F c21m Jul 26] tall, rather sparely-made gelding: winning chaser, usually let down by jumping: maiden hurdler: out of form early in 2004/5, sold out of Miss V. Williams' stable 4,500 gns Doncaster May Sales after first outing: stays 2¾m: acts on good to soft going. *Mrs C. J. Kerr* **c– x** **h–**

KEEPTHEDREAMALIVE 7 gr.g. Roselier (FR) – Nicklup (Netherkelly) [2004/5 h103p, F97: 21g* 21g* 20d^F 24d 21d^3 24d 16g^3 Mar 11] rather leggy gelding: fairly useful novice hurdler: won at Plumpton (easily) and Cheltenham in October: generally much stiffer tasks after, creditable third in Challow Hurdle at Newbury and novice at Sandown: should stay at least 3m: raced on good going or softer: has jumped right. *R. H. Buckler* **h121**

KEEP THE PEACE (IRE) 7 br.g. Petardia – Eiras Mood (Jalmood (USA)) [2004/5 h–: 16d^{pu} 16m 16m 16g Jul 29] no form over hurdles: tried blinkered: has had tongue tied. *K. G. Wingrove* **h–**

KEIRAN (IRE) 11 b.g. Be My Native (USA) – Myra Gaye (Buckskin (FR)) [2004/5 c127, h–: c26s^6 24s^6 Nov 13] sturdy gelding: winning hurdler: fairly useful handicap chaser, tired closing stages on reappearance: stays at least 25f: acts on good to firm and heavy going: effective blinkered or not. *H. P. Hogarth* **c118 +** **h–**

KELAMI (FR) 7 b.g. Lute Antique (FR) – Voltige de Nievre (FR) (Brezzo (FR)) [2004/5 c130, h–: 20s c19s c23v c25s^3 c25d^F c29s^4 c28s^3 c24g* c29g^3 Apr 23] **c141** **h110 +**

Francois Doumen has been making successful raids on Britain's top jumps races for the best part of twenty years and the latest season turned out to be one of the most lucrative yet for the stable this side of the Channel. Baracouda was the flagship of the operation again but Blue Canyon, Innox, Kelami, L'Ami and Moulin Riche also all went away with at least one good prize apiece, contributing to a stable total of almost £270,000 in win money, and not far short of £450,000 with place money taken into account as well. Kelami's prize money for third in the Betfred Gold Cup at Sandown, for which he started favourite, was a good sum in its own right but represented a fraction of what he would have earned had he won the race. He was one of two horses in the race (the other being runner-up Juveigneur) eligible for the sponsor's bonus of £250,000 to any Cheltenham Festival winner successful in the Betfred Gold Cup.

Kelami put himself in line for the bonus by winning the William Hill Trophy at Cheltenham. Fourth in the race the year before, when he failed to last home after having too much use made of him. Kelami faced a much bigger field this time, though he was one of a minority among the twenty runners who came into the race with some good recent efforts behind him. In an open market, Kelami started at 8/1, with Iris Bleu sent off the 11/2 favourite after his recent Sandown second to another leading contender Joly Bey. Kelami was always in touch and gradually took closer order, surviving slight mistakes three out and two out to take the lead off top weight Keen Leader before the last. Kelami then idled somewhat up the hill and held on by a length and a quarter from Keen Leader, with two others near the top of the handicap, Irish Hussar and Chives, staying on to complete the frame. Robert Thornton, who had never ridden for the Doumen stable prior to standing in for the flu-struck Tony McCoy at Sandown in February, was on board both the stable's winners at Cheltenham. The partnership could well develop in the coming years—Doumen's son Thierry has retired to concentrate on training, while a brief spell with Dean Gallagher as stable jockey ended in acrimony in the winter.

Kelami had begun the season with a four-race autumn campaign in France, starting with a pipe-opener over hurdles. He ran much his best race on his final start there when third to course specialist Northerntown in the Grand Steeple-Chase d'Enghien at the end of October. On his return to British fences Kelami fell four out at Cheltenham, when moving into contention, in quite a valuable handicap in December, but he then ran well to make the frame in two of the season's most

William Hill Trophy Handicap Chase, Cheltenham—lightly-weighted Kelami holds on from the two at the top of the handicap, Keen Leader (white face) and Irish Hussar

valuable staying handicaps after the turn of the year. Following his fourth to Baron Windrush in the totesport Classic Chase at Warwick, Kelami stayed on well to be beaten only two lengths into third behind Forest Gunner in the Red Square Vodka Gold Cup at Haydock, a race sponsored by his owners. Kelami was prominent in the Grand National betting after his Cheltenham win but, with the previous year's winner Amberleigh House representing his owners at Aintree and the lure of the bonus at Sandown, Kelami was kept for the Betfred instead. He had carried only 10-2 at Cheltenham and, in the event, wouldn't have been high enough in the weights to get into the Grand National field. Off a mark 6 lb higher at Sandown, Kelami ran his best race yet to finish less than four lengths behind the winner Jack High.

The tall Kelami is related to two more stable companions who were successful in Britain in the latest season. His year-younger brother L'Ami was one of the leading staying novice chasers, winning at Lingfield and Warwick and finishing fourth in the Royal & SunAlliance Chase. The other is Innox (like Kelami and L'Ami, by Lute Antique) who didn't run badly in the Grand National after winning the Agfa Diamond Handicap Chase at Sandown. Kelami and L'Ami are the two winners to date (from four runners) out of their once-raced dam Voltige de Nievre, a half-sister to the fairly useful French jumper Belami and the winning pointer Ultrason IV. Grandam Jivati ran only in chases and cross-country events, with alarming results judging from her form figures (FFFPR04) and finished in front of only one rival in her two completed starts. As well as being a sister to Innox's grandam, Jivati is a half-sister to Noubatous, a winner of Belgium's big jumps race, the Grand Steeple-Chase des Flandres. This is one of the most flourishing and successful French non-thoroughbred families, and its other members to have made a name for themselves in Britain include the high-class hurdler Valfinet, the Doumen-trained Royal & SunAlliance Chase third Fulip and the Eider Chase winner Domaine de Pron. Another important member of this particular clan is Italic, sire of the top-class brothers Al Capone II and The Fellow.

The term 'non-thoroughbred' has rather pejorative undertones in Britain, where the very small number of horses ineligible for the *General Stud Book* that compete against their thoroughbred 'cousins' are indeed generally much inferior. The situation is very different in France, where the well-established and purpose-bred 'AQPS' horses (autres que de pur-sang, or 'other than thoroughbred', a term which covers several different breeds, notably the selle francais or French saddle-bred) have their own races, Flat and jumps. They are, however, more than capable of holding their own against thoroughbred jumpers. Francois Doumen in particular owes much of his success as a jumps trainer to members of the selle francais race—First Gold, Nupsala, Algan and his three musketeers The Fellow, Ubu III and

Ucello II are all selle francais. In addition, as well as Al Capone in France, the likes of Edredon Bleu, Azertyuiop, Hors La Loi III and Gloria Victis have done much to advertise and popularise the French non-thoroughbred on the British side of the Channel. In recognition of their success, and to ensure the breeds' standards are maintained, the French ministry of agriculture has approved the creation of an AQPS stud book in 2006.

Kelami (FR) (b.g. 1998)	Lute Antique (FR) (b 1985)	No Lute (b 1978)	Luthier
			Prudent Miss
		Sweet Annie (ch 1980)	Pharly
			Beronaire
	Voltige de Nievre (FR) (br 1987)	Brezzo (b 1979)	Gift Card
			Brezette
		Jivati (ch 1975)	Laniste
			Une Veine

Won three times by French-bred thoroughbreds before the First World War (Alcibiade, Reugny and Lutteur III), the Grand National is one big race in Britain that has so far eluded a French non-thoroughbred—Clan Royal came close to breaking the duck in 2004—though Kelami appeals as one who could put that right in future. He has already tackled the race in fact, but was hampered and parted company with his rider at the first as a six-year-old in 2004 when probably too young for the race in any case. With more experience behind him and his stamina now proven more fully, Kelami is unlikely to be a 66/1-chance if lining up again. He has yet to race on ground firmer than good and acts on heavy. Kelami was blinkered in the Triumph Hurdle in his younger days (when leased to run in the Queen Mother's colours) and has sometimes been tongue tied, including on his last three outings. *F. Doumen, France*

KELANTAN 8 b.g. Kris – Surf Bird (Shareef Dancer (USA)) [2004/5 c102, h95: c24v^{4} c25d^{2} c25s^{2} c24s* c30d Mar 8] tall gelding: won completed outing over hurdles: fair handicap chaser: won at Huntingdon in February: stays 25f: acts on soft going: often wears cheekpieces nowadays. *K. C. Bailey* **c102 h–**

KELLY PRIDE 8 b.g. Alflora (IRE) – Pearly-B (IRE) (Gunner B) [2004/5 c62, h82: c25v^{pu} Mar 5] smallish gelding: poor maiden hurdler: left Mrs S. Smith, runner-up in point in February: little show in 2 chases: stays 3¼m: acts on good to firm and good to soft going. *Niall Saville* **c– h–**

KELLY (SAF) 8 b.g. Ethique (ARG) – Dancing Flower (SAF) (Dancing Champ (USA)) [2004/5 h103+: 17g* 16d^{4} 20d 16v^{6} 20g^{F} 16d^{2} 22d c24g* c21g^{F} Apr 14] strong gelding: fair hurdler: won maiden at Cartmel in July: won 4-runner maiden at Huntingdon on chasing debut in March: looked held when falling 4 out in novice handicap at Cheltenham next time: stays easy 3m: acts on good to soft and good to firm going. *Miss Venetia Williams* **c105 h103**

KELLYS FABLE 5 b.g. Thowra (FR) – Kellys Special (Netherkelly) [2004/5 F73: F17g 20s^{pu} 17s 19d^{F} 24v^{pu} 22g^{5} Apr 17] tall gelding: poor form in bumpers, none over hurdles: tried in cheekpieces. *J. W. Mullins* **h– F73**

KELREV (FR) 7 ch.g. Video Rock (FR) – Bellile II (FR) (Brezzo (FR)) [2004/5 c134, h116: c21g^{2} c20d c19g c16s^{3} 17v^{2} c20s^{3} Feb 26] leggy, angular gelding: fairly useful hurdler: useful handicap chaser: below best after reappearance: stays 21f: acts on heavy going: weak finisher. *Miss Venetia Williams* **c134 § h115**

KELTIC BLUE (IRE) 6 b.g. Blues Traveller (IRE) – White Caps (Shirley Heights) [2004/5 h–: 17m 24v^{pu} 19d^{pu} Feb 8] no form over hurdles. *R. Dickin* **h–**

KELTIC HERITAGE (IRE) 11 gr.g. Roselier (FR) – Peek-A-Step (IRE) (Step Together (USA)) [2004/5 c118d, h82: c23m^{pu} c26s^{F} Oct 12] workmanlike gelding: winning hurdler: fairly useful handicap chaser at best, well below form since second start in 2003/4: stays 3½m: acts on soft and good to firm going: usually tongue tied: sound-jumping front runner. *L. A. Dace* **c– h–**

KELTIC ROCK 6 ch.g. Bigstone (IRE) – Sibley (Northfields (USA)) [2004/5 F80: F17d^{2} 17d^{2} 19d^{3} 19d^{5} 22s^{4} 21d^{3} 24g Mar 18] tall gelding: progressive form in bumpers for G. Balding: fair novice hurdler: stays 2¾m: raced mainly on good to soft/soft going. *J. A. Geake* **h111 F96**

KEMPSKI 5 b.g. Petoski – Little Katrina (Little Buskins) [2004/5 F72: F16v⁶ 20vᵖᵘ 20v² 16s² 22sᵖᵘ 16d 20s Apr 20] unplaced in 4 bumpers: poor form over hurdles: should prove suited by 2½m+. *R. Nixon* **h81 F–**

KEN SCOTT (FR) 7 b.g. Kendor (FR) – Scottish Bride (FR) (Owen Dudley) [2004/5 h100: c16d⁶ 18d³ 16d* 16dᵖᵘ 16d⁴ 18s³ Mar 30] good-topped gelding: fair handicap hurdler: won at Lingfield in December: last of 6 finishers in maiden on chasing debut: best around 2m: raced on good going or softer (acts on soft). *P. Winkworth* **c93 h103**

KENTFORD GREBE 6 b.m. Teenoso (USA) – Notinhand (Nearly A Hand) [2004/5 h107: c20d* 22d c19d² 16d c24d³ c21gᵖᵘ c21gᵖᵘ Apr 14] sturdy mare: fair hurdler in 2003/4: in-and-out form in 2004/5, winning novice over fences at Ludlow in May: stays easy 3m: acts on good to soft and good to firm going. *J. W. Mullins* **c105 h–**

KENTFORD LADY 4 b.f. Emperor Fountain – Kentford Duchess (Jupiter Island) [2004/5 F12g⁵ F17s F17v⁶ F16d Mar 12] tall filly: first foal: dam unraced half-sister to useful chaser around 2½m The Land Agent: form in bumpers only when fifth at Newbury on debut. *J. W. Mullins* **F85**

KENTISH WARRIER (IRE) 7 b.g. Warcraft (USA) – Garden County (Ragapan) [2004/5 h–: 21g 24sᵖᵘ Oct 21] workmanlike gelding: no sign of ability: tongue tied. *B. I. Case* **h–**

KENTMERE (IRE) 4 b.g. Efisio – Addaya (IRE) (Persian Bold) [2004/5 16s 16d³ 16d Nov 9] good-topped gelding: half-brother to 2½m hurdle winner Castanet (by Pennekamp): fair on Flat (stays 1¼m), successful on all-weather in June, sold out of W. Haggas' stable 34,000 gns Newmarket July Sales: best effort in juvenile hurdles when third in maiden at Huntingdon. *P. R. Webber* **h97**

KENT (POL) 7 ch.h. Freedom's Choice (USA) – Kalambia (POL) (Lord Hippo) [2004/5 20gᵖᵘ 16dᵖᵘ Oct 3] angular horse: successful up to 9f on Flat (sometimes blinkered) in Poland: no show in maiden or seller (blinkered) over hurdles. *A. G. Juckes* **h–**

KENTUCKY CHARM (FR) 4 gr.g. Linamix (FR) – Kentucky Kaper (USA) (The Prime Minister (USA)) [2004/5 16sᶠ 16g² 16d* 16dᶠ 16v⁵ Dec 26] leggy, useful-looking gelding: fairly useful on Flat (stays 13f): similar standard in juvenile hurdles, winning maiden at Clonmel in November by 20 lengths from Grangehill Dancer: well held in handicap at Punchestown in late-April: will stay beyond 2m: acts on good to soft going. *E. J. O'Grady, Ireland* **h118**

KEN'TUCKY (FR) 7 b.g. Video Rock (FR) – La Salamandre (FR) (Pot d'Or (FR)) [2004/5 h99: c25g* Sep 30] leggy gelding: modest hurdler for N. Henderson in 2003/4 (reportedly lame final outing): made all in 4-runner maiden at Hereford on chasing debut in September: stays 3¼m: acts on good to soft going (bumper form on good to firm): seemed likely to progress over fences, but wasn't seen out again. *A. King* **c112 h–**

KENTUCKY KING (USA) 5 b.g. Tale of The Cat (USA) – Anna's Honor (USA) (Alleged (USA)) [2004/5 17s 17sʳᵗʳ 16d Jan 6] leggy gelding: fairly useful on Flat (stays 1¼m): refused/reluctant to race all starts over hurdles, left P. Hiatt after second: tried in cheekpieces: one to avoid. *Mrs D. A. Hamer* **h§§**

KENZO III (FR) 7 ch.g. Agent Bleu (FR) – Kelinda (FR) (Pot d'Or (FR)) [2004/5 c24d* c24mᵖᵘ Apr 2] 11,500 4-y-o: tall, angular gelding: ninth foal: half-brother to several winners, including fairly useful hurdler/fair chaser Decyborg (by Cyborg), stayed 3¼m: dam middle-distance maiden: runner-up in maiden point in 2003: won maiden at Ludlow on chasing debut by 17 lengths from Dickens, despite tending to hang after left clear 4 out: very stiff task, pulled hard and weakened 5 out in handicap at Newbury 2 months later. *N. J. Henderson* **c111**

KERCABELLEC (FR) 7 b. or br.g. Useful (FR) – Marie de Geneve (FR) (Nishapour (FR)) [2004/5 h106: c17vᵘʳ c16dᵖᵘ c16g c16dᶠ c16g⁵ c16d⁶ c16s⁵ c16v³ c20sᵘʳ 16g c20g⁴ Apr 3] lengthy gelding: winning hurdler: modest novice chaser: raced mainly around 2m on good going or softer: tried tongue tied: headstrong. *J. R. Cornwall* **c87 h–**

KERRES NOIRES (FR) 7 b.g. Noir Et Or – Viagara (FR) (Mont Basile (FR)) [2004/5 c21dᶠ c20g⁶ May 8] ex-French gelding: third foal: dam maiden on Flat: 1¾m winner on Flat: winning hurdler: fairly useful form over fences, winning non-thoroughbred event at Auteuil in 2002/3: left F. Nicolle, well held only completed start in points and hunter chases in Britain: stays 21f: acts on soft going. *R. Waley-Cohen* **c– h–**

KERRISTINA 4 b.f. So Factual (USA) – Arch Angel (IRE) (Archway (IRE)) [2004/5 16dᵖᵘ Dec 2] no show on Flat (for D. ffrench Davis) or on hurdling debut. *G. F. H. Charles-Jones* **h–**

KERRS WHIN 5 b.g. Past Glories – Dreamago (Sir Mago) [2004/5 F16v^2 F16d Jan 29] big, leggy gelding: fourth foal: half-brother to fair hunter/chaser Go Nomadic, stays 31f, and winning pointer Nomadic Star (both by Nomadic Way): dam modest pointer: much better effort in bumpers when second to Von Origny at Wetherby. *P. G. Atkinson* **F93**

KERRYHEAD WINDFARM (IRE) 7 br.g. Bob Back (USA) – Kerryhead Girl (IRE) (Be My Native (USA)) [2004/5 F101: F16v^4 20s 16d 16v^2 20d* 20v^5 16s^2 24s^4 22v^2 20v* 22v^4 20d 24s^3 Mar 28] good-topped gelding: failed to complete in 2 points in 2003: bumper winner: useful novice hurdler: won maiden in November and minor event in January, both at Punchestown: improved effort when second to eased Asian Maze in Grade 1 at same course in late-April: likely to prove best at 2½m+: raced on going softer than good (acts on heavy). *M. Hourigan, Ireland* **h130 F80**

KERRY LADS (IRE) 10 ch.g. Mister Lord (USA) – Minstrel Top (Black Minstrel) [2004/5 c124x, h107: c26s^5 c26s^4 c25s^3 23v c25s* c33g^5 Apr 16] workmanlike gelding: winning hurdler: fairly useful handicap chaser: won at Ayr in March by 8 lengths from Gangsters R Us: prominent in race for third year running when fifth to Joes Edge in Scottish Grand National at same course following month: stays 33f: acts on good to firm and heavy going: usually wears cheekpieces nowadays: often let down by jumping over fences. *Miss Lucinda V. Russell* **c126 x h–**

KERRY MAGIC 5 b.g. Vettori (IRE) – Cailin Ciarrai (IRE) (Danehill (USA)) [2004/5 F16g Mar 5] second foal: dam unraced, out of half-sister to dam of one-time very smart 2m hurdler Copeland: behind in bumper on debut. *L. R. James* **F–**

KERRY ZULU WARRIOR 8 ch.g. Aspect (USA) – Kerry Blue Nun (Fine Blue) [2004/5 21d^{pu} Nov 22] second foal: dam unraced: won maiden on last of 3 completed starts in points in 2004: went off far too fast on hurdling debut. *Evan Williams* **h–**

KERSTINO TWO 8 b.g. Cruise Missile – Cresswell (Push On) [2004/5 c24g^{ur} c25s^{pu} Mar 22] fairly useful pointer, successful in January and February: let down by jumping both starts in hunter chases. *Mrs Caroline Keevil* **c–**

KETTONG (IRE) 5 b.m. Among Men (USA) – Kettenblume (Cagliostro (GER)) [2004/5 F–: F16s 17g Mar 9] no sign of ability: tried tongue tied. *M. D. Hammond* **h– F–**

KETY STAR (FR) 7 b.g. Bojador (FR) – Danystar (FR) (Alycos (FR)) [2004/5 c121, h93: c20d^{pu} c16g^5 c21d^5 c17g^2 c22g c20d^4 c20d^4 c20d^3 c21g^5 16s^{pu} Feb 3] leggy gelding: maiden hurdler: fairly useful handicap chaser: in-and-out form in 2004/5, left Miss V. Williams before final outing: probably best up to 2½m: acts on good to firm and good to soft going. *A. W. Carroll* **c121 h–**

KEW JUMPER (IRE) 6 b.g. Mister Lord (USA) – Pharisee (IRE) (Phardante (FR)) [2004/5 h91: 16d^2 16m^5 c20g* c20s c16g^2 c24d^2 c21s^F c20g* c22g^2 Apr 1] tall, good-topped gelding: modest maiden hurdler: fairly useful novice chaser: won at Huntingdon in October (4-runner handicap) and March: best effort when second to Colliers Court in handicap at Ludlow fifth start: will probably prove best short of 3m: acts on good to firm and good to soft going. *Andrew Turnell* **c115 h95**

KEY PHIL (FR) 7 ch.g. Beyssac (FR) – Rivolie (FR) (Mistigri) [2004/5 c18s c18s^3 c21s^F c17s* c21s c18s^4 c19s^4 c21d c17s* c20s^3 Apr 20] good-topped gelding: eighth foal: brother to 3 winners, including smart chaser Joly Bey, stays 25f, and useful hurdler up to 2½m Feyssac: dam unraced: ran once on Flat: twice-raced over hurdles: fairly useful chaser: won minor event at Auteuil in September and handicap at Bangor (second outing after leaving N. Madamet) in April: stays 2½m: acts on soft going. *D. J. Wintle* **c120 h–**

KEY TO THE KINGDOM (IRE) 5 br.g. Key of Luck (USA) – Admiralella (Dominion) [2004/5 16d^4 16s 16v^6 16v 20v^6 23g^6 Jan 19] fair on Flat (stays 1½m): easily best effort over hurdles when fourth in 4-y-o maiden at Ballinrobe: sold out of D. Gillespie's stable €22,000 Goffs October Sale before next outing: wore cheekpieces/blinkers last 3 starts. *Eoin Doyle, Ireland* **h96**

KHAIRABAR (IRE) 11 gr.g. Shernazar – Khairkana (IRE) (Darshaan) [2004/5 17d^2 16g c16s c18d^4 c16d^6 Nov 23] good-topped gelding: claimed from C. Roche €5,500 after winning 11.9f claimer on Flat in August: winning hurdler/chaser, modest form at best in 2004/5: stays 2½m: acts on firm and soft going: tried in blinkers/cheekpieces: has had tongue tied. *J. J. Lambe, Ireland* **c78 h90**

KHALADJISTAN (IRE) 7 br.g. Tirol – Khaladja (IRE) (Akarad (FR)) [2004/5 c82, h83: c20d c21g^6 c16m^6 c21g^{pu} c20g^{pu} c19g^4 c20d^4 c20g c19g^3 Mar 4] useful-looking gelding: winning hurdler: poor handicap chaser: stays 2½m: acts on good to firm and good to soft going: wears headgear: tongue tied. *Miss S. J. Wilton* **c77 h–**

KHALYANEE (IRE) 4 b.f. Prospector J (USA) – Dead End (USA) (Cox's Ridge (USA)) [2004/5 16gpu Jul 18] no show in 2 outings at 2 yrs or on hurdling debut. *L. A. Dace* **h–**

KHARAK (FR) 6 gr.g. Danehill (USA) – Khariyda (FR) (Shakapour) [2004/5 h108: c20d3 Oct 8] good-bodied gelding: fair handicap hurdler: similar form when third in maiden at Carlisle on chasing debut: stays 3m: acts on any going: tried visored/in cheek-pieces: reliable. *Mrs S. C. Bradburne* **c108 h–**

KHAYAL (USA) 11 b.g. Green Dancer (USA) – Look Who's Dancing (USA) (Affirmed (USA)) [2004/5 c88?, h–: c26gpu c24m4 Jul 6] sturdy gelding: maiden hurdler/chaser: modest pointer nowadays, won 2-runner event in 2004: tried visored. *C. J. Down* **c– h–**

KHAYSAR (IRE) 7 b.g. Pennekamp (USA) – Khaytada (IRE) (Doyoun) [2004/5 h96: 20d 21d3 19m 21m* 16m2 Aug 30] smallish, sturdy gelding: fair handicap hurdler: won at Huntingdon in June: stays 21f: acts on soft and good to firm going. *N. B. King* **h101**

KHUDABAD (IRE) 4 ch.g. Ashkalani (IRE) – Kozana (Kris) [2004/5 F16s F18d3 F16s* F16s4 F17d Apr 9] €6,000 3-y-o: angular gelding: brother to 1m winner Khanata and half-brother to several winners, including useful Irish 1992 2-y-o 7f winner Khoraz (by The Minstrel) and 1¾m and 2m winner Kauser (by Vaguely Noble): dam, high-class filly up to 1¼m, half-sister to Prix du Cadran winner Karkour, out of Poule d'Essai des Pouliches winner Koblenza: fairly useful form in bumpers: won maiden at Naas in March: best effort when fourth to Avoca Mist at Fairyhouse. *Frederick John Bowles, Ireland* **F94**

KICASSO 6 b.g. Environment Friend – Merry Jane (Rymer) [2004/5 F79+: 20d6 16d 21d5 c19s3 c24dpu c19m4 Apr 9] rangy gelding: poor form over hurdles: better efforts on completed starts over fences: stays 21f: joined D. Bridgwater. *Miss H. C. Knight* **c88 h79 +**

KICKHAM (IRE) 9 b.g. Supreme Leader – Knocknagow (Buckskin (FR)) [2004/5 c–, h117, F106: c20m* c17g3 c17d* c20s2 c17v2 c16d3 Nov 14] tall gelding: winning hurdler: fairly useful chaser: won at Tipperary (maiden) in July and Ballinrobe (minor event) in August: ran well when placed in graded novices last 3 starts, third to Sir OJ at Punchestown final one: stays 2½m: acts on good to firm and heavy going: effective ridden prominently or held up. *E. J. O'Grady, Ireland* **c125 h–**

KICKING KING (IRE) 7 b.g. Old Vic – Fairy Blaze (IRE) (Good Thyne (USA)) [2004/5 c151, h–: c16gbd c20s* c24s2 c20s* c24g* c26g* Mar 18] **c182 h–**

A new young star staying chaser emerged in 2004/5 from among the previous season's novice crop, yet it was not one that had immediately suggested itself at the end of 2003/4. It was not Strong Flow, Therealbandit, Lord Sam, Our Vic, nor even Pizarro or Calling Brave, who might all have seemed more obvious candidates for such a role, but Kicking King, whose highpoint as a novice came chasing home Well Chief in the Arkle. Not only did Kicking King outshine all those named and complete the rare double of winning the King George VI Chase and the Cheltenham Gold Cup in the same season, but he also enjoyed a full campaign, racing regularly from October right through to the Punchestown Festival, shortly after the end of the British season. He won three of his four other races in that period, including two other Grade 1 events, the John Durkan Memorial Punchestown Chase and the Punchestown Guinness Gold Cup. Kicking King showed himself potentially a better chaser than any since Desert Orchid, for it is by no means certain that the best of him has yet been seen. Although the Gold Cup is regarded as the blue riband of steeplechasing, Kicking King ran to a higher level of form in the King George, a race which might, if the original plans had been followed, have been run at Kempton for the last time in 2004.

The King George was born out of the unprecedented popularity of National Hunt racing in the period immediately after the Second World War. Attendances were high, prize money was on the increase, there were new owners coming into the sport, leading to more competitive racing. The interest shown in the sport by the Queen Mother and by the Queen, the expansion of riding and pony clubs and the popularity of show jumping and point-to-point racing, from which an interest in NH racing followed, were all credited as factors in the sport's growth. Valuable new races were added to a programme overwhelmingly dominated by the Grand National and more recently by the Cheltenham Gold Cup. As the *Bloodstock Breeders' Review* recorded in 1954: 'The prosperity of steeplechasing has not been achieved without considerable hard work and planning by the authorities concerned

National Lottery Agent Champion Chase, Gowran—
a highly satisfactory start to the campaign by Kicking King

with the promotion of the sport. New races, introduced to bridge the gap between the New Year and the big spring meetings at Cheltenham and Aintree, have succeeded in ensuring a continuity in the NH Calendar which is so important if the interest of the racegoing public is to be maintained. The Calendar is now sprinkled with well-funded events, ranging from the Grand Sefton at Aintree in November to the newly-promoted Queen Elizabeth Chase at Hurst Park in June.' It went on to report on the second running of the latter, a valuable three-mile handicap chase, in which the second and third in the Gold Cup ran: 'There was an enormous crowd, a part of whose pleasure it was to cheer the Queen and that other great supporter of National Hunt sport, Queen Elizabeth the Queen Mother.'

Other notable races inaugurated during the immediate post-war years included the Mildmay Memorial at Sandown and the Great Yorkshire Chase at Doncaster. The second half of 1947 saw two important and valuable races for three-mile steeplechasers, a new race, the Emblem Chase at Manchester in November and the King George VI Chase at Kempton on Boxing Day, which had been run twice before the War, but in February or March, and with a much smaller prize. The Emblem Chase had a value to the winner of over £1,000, not far below that of the Cheltenham Gold Cup. The King George was even more valuable, the first running worth nearly £2,300 to the winner. Only the Grand National, which in 1947 was worth just over £10,000 to the winner, was worth more. The Emblem Chase was won in its first two years by Silver Fame, who went on to win the Gold Cup in 1951, each Manchester success gained over the latest Cheltenham Gold Cup winner, Fortina and Cottage Rake respectively, Silver Fame receiving weight on each occasion. Like the Emblem, the King George was a conditions race with various penalties. The inaugural Christmas running went to that year's Scottish Grand National winner Rowland Roy, with Fortina, conceding 6 lb, among his rivals. The 1948 renewal went to that year's Gold Cup winner Cottage Rake, who was conceding between 5 lb and 17 lb to his rivals. It would be difficult any longer for the *Bloodstock Breeders' Review* to say that December was 'always a dull month for all except cross-country diehards.'

Both the Emblem and the King George were instant successes, though one matured better than the other. The Emblem, which evolved into a fairly valuable three-mile handicap run in October rather than November, was staged for the last time in 1962, the year before Manchester racecourse closed. The King George VI

Chase continues to attract the cream of the three-mile chasers. It became a level-weights contest in 1982 and is universally acknowledged as the mid-season championship event for staying chasers. Some would even argue that it is a better guide to the merit of the top performers in this division than the Gold Cup, though it is no longer the second most valuable steeplechase of the season. The Cheltenham Gold Cup has long since reclaimed that position, in 2004/5 being worth £212,268 to the winner compared to the King George's £116,000. The latest King George turned out to be a vintage contest, all the more satisfying since it had not looked likely to do so. The Gold Cup winner Best Mate was never a likely runner, connections choosing for the second year running to send him to Ireland for the Grade 1 Lexus Chase two days later. There was much talk early in the autumn of Moscow Flyer, the outstanding two-mile chaser, running in the King George. However, after he won the Tingle Creek at Sandown early in December, connections decided to keep Moscow Flyer to 'what he knows best'. Neither the leading Irish-trained stayer Beef Or Salmon, nor the Gold Cup runner-up Sir Rembrandt was even entered for the race. There was a further blow when the highly promising Our Vic was ruled out following a last-fence fall at Cheltenham two weeks previously. Of the thirteen that eventually lined up for the Stan James-sponsored event, three were top-class chasers at the tail-end of their careers, the 2003 first three Edredon Bleu, Tiutchev and First Gold (also the winner in 2000). Fondmort (fourth), Le Roi Miguel (weakening fifth when falling last) and Seebald (unseated rider thirteenth) were also back for their second crack. Three of the other runners were leading novices from the previous season who had yet to show themselves up to figuring prominently in races like the King George: Therealbandit, who had won a handicap at Cheltenham last time out, and Calling Brave and Lord Sam, second and third in an intermediate chase at Sandown early in the month. Of these nine, seven started at 20/1 or shorter, Therealbandit at only 6/1. If any of these were to win, it seemed very unlikely that the latest King George would be out of the ordinary as a championship race.

If this were to be a vintage King George, it seemed reliant on the three other serious runners producing something special. Azertyuiop was undoubtedly the horse in the race with the best form, having won the Champion Chase at Chelten-

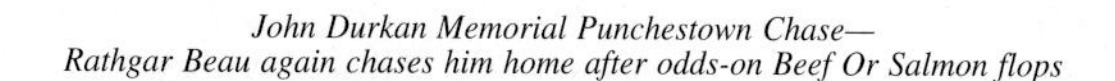

John Durkan Memorial Punchestown Chase—
Rathgar Beau again chases him home after odds-on Beef Or Salmon flops

ham and twice finished second to Moscow Flyer in the Tingle Creek, but there was a doubt about whether he had the necessary stamina, even on good going on a flat track. Kingscliff had looked a really exciting prospect the previous year but he hadn't run since finishing second in the Peter Marsh at Haydock eleven months previously. Kicking King had finished second to Well Chief in the Arkle at Cheltenham in March and had won twice from three starts on his return, including in the John Durkan Memorial Punchestown Chase the time before, but he had been beaten pretty comprehensively by Beef Or Salmon in the James Nicholson at Down Royal on his only attempt at three miles. It was to be hoped that one of these could produce a top-class performance. That all three of them did surpassed expectations and made this one of the most significant runnings of the King George VI Chase in all its long history.

In a well-run race, First Gold took the field along with Kicking King in a handy position. When Barry Geraghty sent Kicking King on at the twelfth of the nineteen fences, most of those not already being urged along were soon in trouble. Turning down the back straight, only Azertyuiop looked a danger, so that when Kicking King got him off the bridle after four out, before stamina should have become an issue, it was clear that an outstanding chaser had arrived on the scene. Going to the last, Kicking King was eight lengths up and storming home from the staying-on Kingscliff. Then calamity almost overtook him. He made a mistake which would have unseated his rider much more often than not (it was reminiscent of Barton Bank's departure there in 1994), but Geraghty was able to haul himself off the horse's neck and gather Kicking King together sufficiently to win by two and a half lengths from Kingscliff. Still more to his credit, Geraghty blamed himself for the error which almost cost victory. Azertyuiop was third, a length and a quarter away, with twenty-four lengths to Le Roi Miguel in fourth. Kicking King's performance was one of the best seen in the race since Desert Orchid's day.

Had he not made the mistake at the last, Kicking King might well have won the King George by ten lengths or more. That he was not immediately made a short-priced favourite for the Cheltenham Gold Cup would have been surprising were it not for two factors—Best Mate had won the Gold Cup for the three previous years and not even defeat at the hands of Beef Or Salmon in the Lexus could shift him from the head of the market, and Kicking King's connections indicated that the new Daily Telegraph Festival Trophy, a revamped Cathcart Chase open to allcomers, was being seriously considered as an alternative to the Gold Cup at Cheltenham. After all, the Gold Cup is run on a stiffer track over a two-and-a-half furlong longer trip than the King George and some doubts were still to be overcome regarding Kicking King's stamina. With neither Best Mate nor Kicking King (nor indeed Kingscliff, whose King George performance, slightly surprisingly, earned as much attention so far as the Gold Cup was concerned) scheduled to make an appearance between Christmas and the Gold Cup, the main trial races were left to

Stan James King George VI Chase, Kempton—three out, and top-notch two-miler Azertyuiop has been dealt with even before his stamina becomes a real issue

others. Not many other contenders can be said to have enhanced their claims. The Pillar Chase at Cheltenham was won impressively by Grey Abbey, who until then had seemed more a Grand National candidate, with Therealbandit well held in second; the AON Chase at Newbury saw Strong Flow and Celestial Gold, the latter winner of the Paddy Power and the Hennessy, beaten by Farmer Jack who was not even entered for Cheltenham; and the Irish Hennessy went to Rule Supreme, with odds-on Beef Or Salmon flopping. As February gave way to March, the ante-post market for the Gold Cup had Best Mate favourite at around 11/4, with Kingscliff at 6/1 and Kicking King 7/1, then Strong Flow and Beef Or Salmon, with Grey Abbey, Celestial Gold and Rule Supreme all also available at no bigger than 16/1. Yet, within twenty-four hours, Kicking King was seemingly out of the Gold Cup. He worked badly in a racecourse gallop at Punchestown, recorded an unsatisfactory scope afterwards and looked like requiring a course of antibiotics. His owner reported: 'With Cheltenham just around the corner, there is no way he's going to make it . . . to rush him there would not be right.' Kicking King was to wait for Punchestown at the end of April. So that seemed to be that.

Seven days later, activity on the betting exchange Betfair suggested that matters were by no means so cut and dried. Laid at 999/1 after his absence was announced (horses are not removed from the list in the way they would be with a traditional bookmaker), Kicking King was back to under 14/1 before the High Street firms reintroduced him into their Gold Cup market at around 8/1. Trainer Tom Taaffe was not altogether forthcoming as to whether Kicking King was back on course or not, merely saying that a statement about the horse's condition was to be made two days later, while confirming that Kicking King had improved since the Punchestown gallop. Two days later duly came and Kicking King was confirmed back to himself and an intended runner at Cheltenham. The news, though, earned hardly a mention in the next-day papers—Best Mate was now out. Had the story about Best Mate's absence not broken, Kicking King's trainer might have received more criticism than he actually did for, albeit unintentionally, presenting a misleading impression to the public. Crucially, Kicking King had not been put on antibiotics, instead being allowed to recover in his own time, which he clearly did much more quickly than had been anticipated. Had he been treated with antibiotics so close to Cheltenham, Kicking King would have been unable to run, yet this crucial information was late coming out, some time after the rumours had taken flight.

Although by this stage it was just a week to the Gold Cup, there was still time for several other twists in the plot, so far as the make-up of the Gold Cup field was concerned. Farmer Jack was supplemented, the novice Ollie Magern, who might have run in the Royal & SunAlliance anyway, and the new favourite Kingscliff (ostensibly for the same reason as Kicking King, working badly) were ruled out, Rule Supreme was switched to the World Hurdle and then Farmer Jack dropped dead on the gallops. Fifteen still went to post and Kicking King was supported down to favourite at 4/1, though on his form he was surely entitled to be close to odds on, looking to have 10 lb in hand of anything else in the race, with only two others within a stone of him on their best recent form. Celestial Gold and Strong Flow were just behind Kicking King in the betting, despite having even more to find with him. Therealbandit and Pizarro looked to have a stiff task too, Beef Or Salmon and Grey Abbey (who had had his own fitness scare since the Pillar) seeming the main threats to Kicking King judged on form shown on the racecourse. Previous runners-up Sir Rembrandt and Truckers Tavern did not look so good as they were, Take The Stand, Royal Auclair and Ballycassidy appeared just smart handicappers, and Tiutchev had plenty to prove after pulling up lame in the King George. Vanity runners Astonville and Venn Ottery, who earlier at the meeting had been found wanting in the Champion Hurdle and Champion Chase respectively, completed the field. The outcome of the Gold Cup revolved around Kicking King: if he was in anything like the same form as at Kempton he would win and win handsomely.

Grey Abbey took the totesport Gold Cup field along, followed by Ballycassidy and Sir Rembrandt. Kicking King, Strong Flow and Celestial Gold all travelled well in mid-field while Beef Or Salmon was held up in rear. It was clear as early as the fifth that Beef Or Salmon was having another off-day, though only Truckers Tavern was detached with a circuit to go, indicative of a pace less strong

totesport Cheltenham Gold Cup Chase—Kicking King and runner-up Take The Stand (second left) take over from Grey Abbey three out; Sir Rembrandt (left) is placed for the second year running

than usual. Jumping the water, early on the final circuit, Geraghty moved Kicking King smoothly into third, behind Grey Abbey and the flat-out Sir Rembrandt. Of those behind, only Strong Flow and Take The Stand, who had survived mistakes at the first two, looked capable of mounting much of a challenge. At the top of the hill, four out, Grey Abbey was still just in front, though by now pushed along and a sitting duck for Kicking King poised behind. Only Take The Stand was now keeping pace, Strong Flow and the outpaced Sir Rembrandt both making hard work of it. Kicking King jumped to the front at the next and, as Grey Abbey faded, drew clear with Take The Stand. There was little in it two out but Kicking King was going much the better and by the last was two lengths clear, extending the advantage to five, well on top, by the line. Sir Rembrandt plugged on for third, a further eight lengths back and just ahead of the never-dangerous Royal Auclair. Grey Abbey finished fifth, ahead of Strong Flow and Celestial Gold. In all, ten completed, Astonville a distance behind the ninth. The only faller was Pizarro, Beef Or Salmon among those pulled up.

The King George had been a vintage edition, but the Gold Cup was nothing of the sort. Take The Stand must be regarded as having shown marked improvement, but the proximity of the thoroughly exposed Royal Auclair led to a low view being taken of the form. Though Kicking King won with something to spare, the bare form of the latest Gold Cup makes it the poorest running since Desert Orchid's day. Had the field for the Gold Cup been stronger, however, there is every reason to believe Kicking King could have pulled out more. Victory for Best Mate, had he turned out, would have been no foregone conclusion.

Those who regard the King George as the more reliable championship race suggest that the Gold Cup places too much emphasis on stamina, though it would be laughable to describe Best Mate and Kicking King as plodders. See More Business, another to win both races in recent times, though not in the same season, was regarded as more of a staying type, yet was able to produce his very best form at Kempton, given softish ground for his second King George win. Accurate jumping and a turn of foot were just as much the hallmark of his performance that day as they were of Best Mate's first two wins in the Gold Cup, or Kicking King's wins at both Kempton (the last fence excepted) and Cheltenham. So far as identifying the season's best staying chaser, there is little to choose between the two races. Using the annual ratings during the life of the *Chasers & Hurdlers* series, the King George is two ahead of the Gold Cup, with three 'best staying chasers' winning both and five winning neither. For the record, the last-named group are: Bannow Rambler, who was brought down when favourite for the 1977 Gold Cup but had beaten the winner Davy Lad a neck conceding 11 lb in the Leopardstown Chase on his previous start; Burrough Hill Lad, who won the Rehearsal and Gainsborough Chases before missing the 1986 Gold Cup due to injury; Desert Orchid, who was surprisingly beaten by Nupsala in the 1987 King George and ran in the Champion Chase at Cheltenham but won the Whitbread under 11-11; Carvill's Hill, who won the 1991 Welsh National in stunning fashion by twenty lengths under top weight; and Suny Bay, whose performance in winning the Edward Hanmer at Haydock from, among others, the season's Gold Cup winner See More Business, was the best of 1998/9. Burrough Hill Lad won the Gold Cup and the King George in different seasons.

Best Mate, in 2002/3, and Kicking King are the only King George winners since Desert Orchid in 1988/9 also to win the Cheltenham Gold Cup in the same season. They, in turn, are the only three to have completed that double since Arkle in 1965/6. Only three other King George winners have completed the double in the same season, Cottage Rake in 1948/9, Limber Hill in 1955/6 and Saffron Tartan in 1960/1. Pendil, in 1973, and The Fellow, in 1992, were King George winners beaten a short head at Cheltenham. Wayward Lad was denied by Dawn Run and the weight-for-sex allowance in the epic 1986 Gold Cup. The exploits of Arkle and Desert Orchid are very well documented and the career of Cottage Rake was touched on in the essay on Best Mate in *Chasers & Hurdlers 2003/04*. Limber Hill and Saffron Tartan are less well remembered today. Both were classified as superior winners of the Gold Cup by John Randall and Tony Morris in *A Century of Champions*, superior being roughly equivalent to a Timeform rating between 175 and 179. Saffron Tartan, the last of Vincent O'Brien's great jumpers, was forced to miss the 1959 Cheltenham Gold Cup after coughing badly on the morning of the race when a hot favourite but came back in 1961, by then trained in Britain, to defeat the previous year's winner Pas Seul and Mandarin, who won the Gold Cup the following year. Saffron Tartan's strengths, like those of most top-class chasers, were his sound jumping and his turn of foot. Limber Hill was rather different, a one-off. He was home bred, his owner Mr Davey saying that the dam 'had weak hocks and bad forelegs and proved impossible to breed from until finally, in desperation, I mated her with a carthorse.' Limber Hill, the mare's second foal, was brought up in the hunting field, though, his owner reported that he tended to stop in turnip fields and start tearing up roots. Successful in the Emblem on his previous start, Limber Hill may have been fortunate to win the King George, as Fred Winter was clear on 1953 winner Galloway Braes but looked the wrong side on the flat and was caught near the finish. However, in the Gold Cup, with the track suiting him better, Limber Hill gained a most authoritative victory. Tom Nickalls, in *The Sporting Life*, described him: 'He is an astonishing individual, as broad as a bus, not outstandingly tall but with bone of the finest quality that must measure well over nine inches. Against some of the more high-quality chasers in the paddock on this occasion he looked a trifle common, with a Roman nose . . . But he is a sort that we seldom see nowadays and would carry 15 stone out hunting.' Limber Hill's outing after his Cheltenham Gold Cup success ended in defeat, though he was conceding 34 lb over two and a half miles to the winner. It is not hard to picture smelling salts being required if such a task was suggested as suitable for some recent Gold Cup winners.

Indeed, top chasers are rarely asked to go to the well so often these days, but Kicking King went to Punchestown at the end of April for another contest at level

. . . Barry Geraghty has matters under control at the last

Punchestown Guinness Gold Cup—another smooth success;
King George runner-up Kingscliff (No.4) proves a big disappointment

weights, this time the Guinness Punchestown Gold Cup. Kingscliff, reportedly over his problems, was in the field of six, but turned out to be clearly not himself, Rule Supreme providing the only company for Kicking King in the closing stages. Company but not opposition. Kicking King looked the winner a long way out and sauntered home, three lengths to the good. It was the perfect end to a full and near-faultless campaign, one which, the weeks before the Gold Cup apart, reflected great credit on his connections. Inevitably, the trainer's link to Arkle, ridden by his father Pat, was widely commented on. Surprisingly, there were few references to the outstanding chaser that Pat Taaffe trained, Captain Christy, who won the Cheltenham Gold Cup in 1974 and the King George VI Chase of that year and the next. That Kicking King can already be regarded as being as good a chaser as Captain Christy must give Tom Taaffe great satisfaction.

Kicking King's two victories over two and a half miles in the early part of the season had both been gained at the main expense of Rathgar Beau. He beat him by eleven lengths in the John Durkan Memorial at Punchestown, in which Beef Or Salmon started odds on but disappointed, and by two and a half lengths on his return from a summer break in the National Lottery Agent Champion Chase at Gowran in October. Kicking King's performance that day was impressive and, while acknowledging the truth of Damon Runyon's oft-quoted saying that it is the difference of opinion that makes horseracing, it is perhaps best to spare the blushes of the journalist who wrote after Gowran: 'I'm predicting a pretty thin season for Kicking King from now on.'

The Gowran race is again likely to be the starting point for Kicking King's season in 2005/6. After that, though, there is a new contest to tempt connections. Half a century or more on from the Emblem, Lancashire will again stage a race to tempt the very best three-mile chasers in November. The Betfair Chase at Haydock, which replaces the Edward Hanmer and Tommy Whittle Chases staged there, carries Grade 1 status, along with a £1m bonus if the winner goes on to collect the King George VI Chase and the Cheltenham Gold Cup. Connections of both Kicking King and Best Mate have said that they are likely to target the race, and presumably any others with pretensions to winning the last two races are likely to have a go at Haydock. Giving the season a narrative and maintaining interest from at least October to April, and perhaps beyond, are as important as they were fifty years ago. The King George meanwhile will be staged at Sandown (as it was in 1995/6, when Kempton was unable to race due to the weather), though that is due to be a one-off. Flat racing on turf, rather than National Hunt racing, has made way for the new all-weather track at the Middlesex venue and the King George will be back home in 2006/7, with the jumps course situated on the old Flat track. More widely, the dangers that threatened jumping in an unregulated fixture free-for-all a couple of seasons previously appear to have receded, for the time being at least.

Though Newbury is also on course to open an all-weather track in 2006 and Wetherby and, perhaps, Aintree are considering racing on the Flat on turf, the future of jumping looks, surprisingly, almost as bright as it did to that writer in the *Bloodstock Breeders' Review* in the 'fifties. Significantly, the British Horseracing Board appears to have grasped with enthusiasm that jump racing is a great asset to the overall racing 'product' and that it is important that it has a proper structure.

Kicking King (IRE) (b.g. 1998)	Old Vic (b 1986)	Sadler's Wells (b 1981)	Northern Dancer
			Fairy Bridge
		Cockade (b 1973)	Derring-Do
			Camenae
	Fairy Blaze (IRE) (b 1991)	Good Thyne (br 1977)	Herbager
			Foreseer
		Fairy Tree (ch 1970)	Varano
			Precision Time

Kicking King's pedigree has been dealt with comprehensively in previous Annuals, though there are some updates on his dam Fairy Blaze. She had two other winners representing her in 2004/5, Colonel Monroe (by Lord Americo), who showed fairly useful form at two miles to three over fences, and Fairy Dawn (by Kicking King's sire Old Vic) who was successful in a bumper at Tipperary on her only start, though she returned to her breeder and was due to be covered by Luso in 2005. Fairy Blaze's first foal Glenfarcas Boy (by Montelimar) was second three times over fences in 2004/5. Since Fairy Dawn, Fairy Blaze has had colt foals by Lord Americo and Old Vic in 2001 and 2003, the former now in training with Paul Nolan in Ireland, and fillies by Carroll House in 2002 and Old Vic in 2004 and 2005. Fairy Blaze was covered again by Old Vic and has reportedly scanned in foal. Kicking King is very much in the mould of the modern chaser, being rangy and well made. Other than on his chasing debut, when he finished fifth, Kicking King has finished first or second on all his completed starts over jumps. Apart from Beef Or Salmon and Well Chief, Hi Cloy has also beaten him over fences, having half a

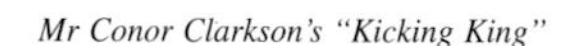
Mr Conor Clarkson's "Kicking King"

length to spare in the Powers Gold Cup at Fairyhouse. Over hurdles, only Solerina and Back In Front managed to get the better of him. Kicking King is effective at two and a half miles to three and a quarter. He has raced on good going or softer, though has yet to race on heavy other than in a bumper, his very best performances coming on good or good to soft. Kicking King ended the 2004/5 season a class apart from his rivals in the staying chase division and, still only seven, it will surely take a considerable reversal in fortune to prevent him continuing in the same vein in 2005/6. *T. J. Taaffe, Ireland*

KIDITHOU (FR) 7 b.g. Royal Charter (FR) – De Thou (FR) (Trebrook (FR)) [2004/5 h102: 20v^pu 24d 24g c24s^3 c25s^ur c25s* c24d^2 c27g^F Apr 15] medium-sized gelding: fair hurdler, out of sorts first 3 starts in 2004/5: fair form over fences, winning maiden at Ayr in March: stays 27f: acts on heavy going: often makes mistakes. *W. T. Reed* **c103 h–**

KIDS INHERITANCE (IRE) 7 b.g. Presenting – Princess Tino (IRE) (Rontino) [2004/5 h93: c16d^4 c17d^3 c17v^3 c16s^5 c20d^6 c16g^pu c16d* c19d^5 c16s^4 c16s^2 c17d^2 Apr 11] good-topped gelding: modest hurdler: fair handicap chaser: won novice event at Catterick in January: best effort when second to Powder Creek at Kelso final start: stays 19f: acts on heavy going: jumped poorly in cheekpieces sixth outing. *J. M. Jefferson* **c110 h–**

KID'Z'PLAY (IRE) 9 b.g. Rudimentary (USA) – Saka Saka (Camden Town) [2004/5 20d* 17d* 20s^5 17v^4 16s* Apr 20] sturdy gelding: fair on Flat (stays 13f): formerly temperamental but much improved over hurdles in 2004/5, winning maiden at Perth in September, novice at Carlisle in October and handicap at Perth (beat Gospel Song 6 lengths) in April: stays 2½m: raced on going softer than good (acts on heavy): front runner. *J. S. Goldie* **h120**

KIEV (IRE) 5 b.g. Bahhare (USA) – Badrah (USA) (Private Account (USA)) [2004/5 F76: 17s 16s 21g Mar 28] leggy gelding: signs of ability in bumpers: well beaten on 3 starts over hurdles: visored final one: ungenuine. *D. G. Bridgwater* **h– §**

KIFTSGATE 8 ch.g. Kris – Blush Rambler (IRE) (Blushing Groom (FR)) [2004/5 16d 16s 20d^3 Nov 19] leggy gelding: useful form on Flat (stays 1½m) at 3 yrs for Sir Michael Stoute: poor form in novice hurdles. *Mrs P. Robeson* **h77**

KIKIS GIRLS (IRE) 4 b.f. Spectrum (IRE) – Jane Heller (USA) (Halo (USA)) [2004/5 16f^pu Sep 26] showed nothing in 2 maidens on Flat in 2004 and on hurdling debut. *M. Wigham* **h–**

KILBREADY BOY (IRE) 10 ch.g. Beau Sher – Ginger Dee (Le Moss) [2004/5 c24v* c25s* c23g^pu Apr 12] rangy gelding: very lightly raced: left L. Wells and off 3 years, successful in hunter chases at Warwick in February and Exeter (beat Bengal Bullet 3 lengths) in March: in touch going well when pulled up lame 5 out at latter course final outing: stays 25f: acts on heavy going. *Mrs Laura J. Young* **c112**

KILCASKIN GOLD (IRE) 10 ch.g. Ore – Maypole Gayle (Strong Gale) [2004/5 c93: c25s^ur c25d^pu Apr 11] fair pointer: winning hunter, usually fails to complete: should stay beyond 25f: acts on good to soft going: tried blinkered. *R. A. Ross* **c–**

KILDEE LASS 6 gr.m. Morpeth – Pigeon Loft (IRE) (Bellypha) [2004/5 h87: 16g^4 19m* 17g^4 16s^2 16d^5 16v^3 Mar 29] leggy, angular mare: fair handicap hurdler: won at Taunton in November: stays easy 19f: acts on soft and good to firm going. *J. D. Frost* **h100**

KILDONNAN 6 b.g. Bob's Return (IRE) – Celtic Tore (IRE) (Torus) [2004/5 F16s^5 F16v^3 F16s Mar 10] 35,000 4-y-o: sturdy gelding: third foal: half-brother to useful 1m winner Bettergeton (by Rakaposhi King): dam unraced: fair form first 2 starts in bumpers. *J. A. B. Old* **F94**

KILDORRAGH (IRE) 11 b.g. Glacial Storm (USA) – Take A Dare (Pragmatic) [2004/5 c113d: c24s^pu c24s^pu Mar 10] tall, useful-looking gelding: winning staying chaser: left L. Wells after first outing and just modest pointer subsequently: has worn blinkers/cheekpieces: moody: sold 3,000 gns Doncaster May Sales. *Miss H. M. Irving* **c– §**

KILDYSART LADY (IRE) 9 b.m. King of Shannon – Raj Kumari (Vitiges (FR)) [2004/5 c21d^4 May 17] lengthy mare: modest pointer: well held on completed start in chases: tried blinkered. *Mrs C. M. Budd* **c– h–**

KILGOWAN (IRE) 6 b.g. Accordion – Gaiety Lass (Le Moss) [2004/5 20s^2 20s* 17d^F 20v^6 21d^5 20g* 19g^4 Apr 1] sturdy gelding: fifth foal: half-brother to winning 2m hurdler/chaser Knockrigg (by Accordion): dam fair hurdler/winning chaser up to 2½m: modest form in bumpers for F. Flood: fair novice hurdler: won at Leicester in November **h108**

and Haydock (handicap, by 1½ lengths from Montgermont) in March: stays 21f: acts on soft going, best effort on good. *Ian Williams*

KILGWRRWG 10 b.g. Shaab – Watch Lady (Home Guard (USA)) [2004/5 21dpu Jan 6] half-brother to winning 2½m chaser Pit Pony (by Hittite Glory) and fairly useful pointer Watchit Lad (by El-Birillo): dam ran twice: no show in maiden hurdle on belated debut. *Miss K. B. Boutflower* **h–**

KILINDINI 4 gr.g. Silver Patriarch (IRE) – Newlands Corner (Forzando) [2004/5 18s3 17g3 Apr 15] fair maiden on Flat (should stay 1½m): modest form in juvenile hurdles 6 months apart. *Miss E. C. Lavelle* **h99**

KILKILIAN (IRE) 5 b.g. Norwich – Vultang Lady (Le Bavard (FR)) [2004/5 F17d3 Feb 1] rangy, useful-looking gelding: eighth foal: half-brother to 3 winners, including fairly useful hurdler Snapper Creek (by Castle Keep), stays 2½m: dam unraced sister to dam of high-class staying chaser Couldnt Be Better and half-sister to smart chaser up to 3m Kilkilowen: 11 lengths third of 14 to Venice Road in maiden bumper at Taunton on debut. *B. G. Powell* **F89**

KILLARNEY PRINCE (IRE) 6 b.g. Lord Americo – Henry Woman (IRE) (Mandalus) [2004/5 F89: 16d 20d Apr 20] plain gelding: third in maiden bumper on debut: off a year, no show in maiden hurdles: should stay beyond 2m. *Mrs J. M. Mann* **h–**

KILL DEVIL HILL (IRE) 5 b.g. Carroll House – Home In The Glen (Furry Glen) [2004/5 F16s4 18v5 20v2 20v* 20s 20s2 Mar 27] **h132 F93**

Kill Devil Hill came within two short heads of landing graded novice hurdles at the Fairyhouse Irish National and Punchestown Festival meetings in the spring. It will be no surprise if he makes ample amends at that level when he goes over fences in the next season. At Fairyhouse, in the Grade 2 Festival Novices' Hurdle over two and a half miles, Kill Devil Hill failed to hold off Sher Beau only in the final stride after having a lead of a length early on the flat. In the Grade 1 Evening Herald Champion Novices' Hurdle at Punchestown, shortly after the end of the British season, Kill Devil Hill ran even better. Running at a bare two miles for the first time over hurdles, he came from the rear to put in a strong challenge at the final flight and only just failed to best the Supreme Novices' runner-up Wild Passion. Kill Devil Hill, who ran just once in a bumper, had four outings over hurdles prior to Fairyhouse. On the second of them, he finished a distance clear of the remainder when second in a maiden to Washington Lad and on the third he beat another subsequent graded winner Teeming Rain to land a similar event at Clonmel easily by ten lengths. He ran too badly to be true at Down Royal on his start before Fairyhouse and was later reported to have a respiratory tract infection. Kill Devil Hill, bought for 36,000 guineas at the Doncaster May Sales as a three-year-old, is by Carroll House out of the winning pointer Home In The Glen. His dam has bred two other winners, the more notable the useful hurdler/chaser Tana River (by Over The River), who won the valuable EBF Novices' Handicap Hurdle Final in 2002/3. Kill Devil Hill is a strong sort who will make a cracking chaser and is likely to stay three miles. He has raced only on going softer than good. *Paul Nolan, Ireland*

KILLEANEY (IRE) 8 b.g. Classic Memory – Welsh Duchy (Welsh Saint) [2004/5 20s3 22m3 20s2 20s* 24s* 24s* 22v* 22s5 22s3 24d2 24s Mar 28] IR 2,300 3-y-o: workmanlike gelding: fourth foal: dam, maiden, out of half-sister to Champion Four-Year-Old Hurdle winner Clarinbridge: poor form on completed start over fences: fair hurdler: won handicaps at Wexford (novice) in November and Gowran, Navan and Limerick in December: best efforts when placed after: stays 3m: acts on heavy going: tried in cheekpieces. *J. G. Carr, Ireland* **c– h110**

KILLENAULE (IRE) 5 b.g. Bob Back (USA) – Party Woman (IRE) (Sexton Blake) [2004/5 aF16g3 21d4 Mar 4] €38,000 3-y-o: lengthy, rather unfurnished gelding: third foal: dam, fairly useful hurdler, stayed 2½m: third in maiden Irish point on debut: shaped well when making frame in bumper on polytrack at Lingfield and novice hurdle at Newbury (staying-on fourth to dead-heaters Bengo and Il Duce): open to improvement. *B. G. Powell* **h108 p F91**

KILLER CAT (FR) 4 b.g. Lost World (IRE) – Heat Storm (USA) (Storm Cat (USA)) [2004/5 F16s 16d 16g5 17m Mar 21] sturdy gelding: eighth foal: brother to 2¼m hurdle winner Fighter Cat and half-brother to several winners up to around 1¼m on Flat: dam **h94 F74**

never ran: well held in bumper on debut: best effort over hurdles when fifth to Mighty Man in novice at Sandown: capable of better. *M. C. Pipe*

KILLER (FR) 7 ch.g. Cupidon (FR) – Kaoutchka (FR) (Bakst (USA)) [2004/5 c20d^{pu} c16v c16v^{pu} Feb 13] workmanlike gelding: no form in novice hurdle or chases: wore cheekpieces final start: tried tongue tied. *Miss Lucinda V. Russell* **c– h–**

KILLINEY BAY (IRE) 9 b.g. Mister Lord (USA) – Tatlock (Paico) [2004/5 c24s^{pu} Feb 10] fair pointer: no show in novice hunter chase. *R. Gurney* **c–**

KILLING JOKE 5 b.h. Double Trigger (IRE) – Fleeting Vision (IRE) (Vision (USA)) [2004/5 20d^{6} Sep 22] fairly useful on Flat (stays 2m) at 3 yrs, below form both starts in 2004, sold out of J. Given's stable 4,000 gns Newmarket July Sales: tailed off in maiden on hurdling debut. *J. J. Lambe, Ireland* **h–**

KILLING ME SOFTLY 4 b.g. Kingsinger (IRE) – Slims Lady (Theatrical Charmer) [2004/5 16g^{F} 16g^{pu} 16g^{4} 16s* 17s^{2} 16v^{4} 16s* 16s Apr 20] modest on Flat (stays 10.9f): similar standard over hurdles: won handicaps at Leicester (seller) in January and Huntingdon (novice) in March: raced around 2m: acts on heavy going: wore headgear after debut: races prominently. *J. Gallagher* **h96**

KILLOCH PLACE (IRE) 4 b.g. Compton Place – Hibernica (IRE) (Law Society (USA)) [2004/5 16m 16m 16d 16g^{pu} 19s^{pu} Mar 1] rather leggy gelding: poor sprint maiden on Flat: no form over hurdles: tongue tied last 3 starts. *W. Storey* **h–**

KILLONE MOONLIGHT (IRE) 6 b.m. Moonax (IRE) – Killone Brae (King's Ride) [2004/5 23s^{4} c22s^{pu} 21g Mar 28] lengthy mare: seventh foal: sister to fairly useful 2¾m hurdle winner King Killone and half-sister to 2 winners, including bumper winner Lord Bacchus (by Insan): dam ran twice: won second of 2 starts in mares maiden Irish points in 2004: bought 13,500 gns Doncaster May Sales: poor form on first of 3 outings over hurdles. *D. R. Stoddart* **c– h72**

KILLULTAGH STORM (IRE) 11 b.g. Mandalus – Rostrevor Lady (Kemal (FR)) [2004/5 c140, h109: c16g^{5} c25g c16d c17g c21d^{ur} c20s^{2} Dec 18] strong, lengthy gelding: useful chaser, left W. Mullins and off 6 months after second start: first show subsequently when second to Noisetine in handicap at Warwick: effective at 2m to 25f: acts on heavy and good to firm going: tried blinkered, usually wears cheekpieces nowadays. *Noel T. Chance* **c118 h–**

KILLWILLIE (IRE) 6 b.g. Carroll House – Home In The Glen (Furry Glen) [2004/5 F90: F16g F16v F16g Apr 16] rangy gelding: form in bumpers only on debut. *J. I. A. Charlton* **F–**

KILLY BEACH 7 b.g. Kuwait Beach (USA) – Spiritual Lily (Brianston Zipper) [2004/5 c73, h–: c19m^{2} c22f^{2} c23m^{3} Jun 16] leggy gelding: poor maiden chaser: barely stays 23f: raced mainly on going firmer than good over jumps: sold £6,400 Ascot October Sales, fifth on completed starts in points. *J. W. Mullins* **c73 h–**

KILMACKILLOGE 6 b.g. Lancastrian – Garjun (IRE) (Orchestra) [2004/5 F16s Apr 22] second foal: brother to winning pointer: dam ran once: eighth of 18 in bumper at Perth on debut. *M. Todhunter* **F81 +**

KILMUCKLIN GIRL (IRE) 6 ch.m. Gone Fishin – Actuate (IRE) (Shardari) [2004/5 F17d 22g^{pu} 17g Oct 14] angular mare: third foal: dam never ran: no sign of ability. *A. E. Jones* **h– F–**

KILT (FR) 7 ch.g. Luchiroverte (IRE) – Unite II (FR) (Toujours Pret (USA)) [2004/5 16d c16s^{pu} Jan 20] of no account: tried tongue tied. *Mrs L. Williamson* **c– h–**

KILVOYDAN (IRE) 10 ch.g. Montelimar (USA) – Vintage Harvest (Deep Run) [2004/5 c26m^{2} May 19] medium-sized ex-Irish gelding: winning pointer: maiden hurdler/chaser: runner-up in novice hunter at Folkestone in May: will stay beyond 3¼m: acts on good to firm and good to soft ground: tried blinkered: has had tongue tied. *David Phelan* **c87 h–**

KIMBAMBO (FR) 7 gr.g. Genereux Genie – Contessina (FR) (Mistigri) [2004/5 h111: 16s 16m^{3} 16g^{pu} 17g 16v* 16s^{2} Feb 5] tall gelding: fairly useful handicap hurdler: won at Kelso in January by head from Oracle des Mottes: raced around 2m: acts on heavy and good to firm going. *J. P. L. Ewart* **h118**

KIM BUCK (FR) 7 b.g. Ambroise (FR) – Darling Jouve (FR) (Some Buck) [2004/5 20d^{pu} c24s^{pu} Nov 21] first foal: dam signs of only a little ability: fourth in maiden Irish point on debut in 2004: pulled up in maiden hurdle and novice chase. *K. A. Morgan* **c– h–**

KIM FONTENAIL (FR) 5 b.m. Kaldounevees (FR) – Fontanalia (FR) (Rex Magna (FR)) [2004/5 h103, F78: 20d^{2} 22d^{4} c19d* c20g^{5} Dec 26] angular mare: fair hurdler: similar form over fences, won mares novice at Exeter on chasing debut in December: likely to prove best up to 2¾m: raced on good going or softer (acts on soft). *N. J. Hawke* **c105 h106**

KIMOE WARRIOR 7 ch.g. Royal Abjar (USA) – Thewaari (USA) (Eskimo (USA)) [2004/5 h83§: c17d^{ur} 17d c17d^{6} c16g 17g c21v c16s c20g^{5} c24g^{3} c24g* Apr 15] leggy gelding: poor handicap hurdler: similar form over fences, winning novice handicap at Taunton in April: stays 3m: acts on any going: tried in cheekpieces, usually blinkered: tried tongue tied: unreliable. *M. Mullineaux* **c78 § h76 §**

KIMONO ROYAL (FR) 7 b. or br.g. Garde Royale – Alizane (FR) (Mourtazam) [2004/5 F96: 16g^{3} 16s^{3} 16g 22g^{6} Dec 14] tall, useful-looking gelding: bumper winner: modest form when placed over hurdles: should be suited by 2½m+. *A. King* **h98**

KIMS PEARL (IRE) 7 b.m. Jurado (USA) – Blushing Pearl (Monksfield) [2004/5 F81: F16d 21s^{pu} 17s 19v^{5} 16d* 19s Mar 7] lengthy, shallow-girthed mare: fourth in bumper on debut: trained by R. Phillips on reappearance: 11 lb out of weights, won handicap hurdle at Chepstow in February: should stay beyond 2m: front runner. *D. Burchell* **h82 F–**

KINBURN (IRE) 6 gr.g. Roselier (FR) – Leadaro (IRE) (Supreme Leader) [2004/5 h65: 24g^{3} 25m* 20v^{3} 20s^{2} Nov 21] good-topped gelding: modest novice hurdler: won handicap event at Wetherby in October: will prove suited by 3m+: acts on soft and good to firm going: room for improvement in jumping. *J. Howard Johnson* **h97**

KINCORA (IRE) 14 b.g. King Persian – Miss Noora (Ahonoora) [2004/5 c73, h–: c26m^{4} May 19] angular gelding: winning pointer: maiden hunter chaser: stays 3m: acts on any going. *Ms Lisa Stock* **c77 h–**

KINDA CRAZY 5 b.g. Petoski – Margaret Modes (Thatching) [2004/5 h84, F–: 17d^{pu} 16s Nov 24] plain gelding: little sign of ability: visored (raced freely) final start. *H. J. Manners* **h–**

KIND SIR 9 b.g. Generous (IRE) – Noble Conquest (USA) (Vaguely Noble) [2004/5 c104, h–: c16g^{4} 20m^{5} c16g^{F} c16s^{5} c20d^{2} c20s^{F} c16d^{4} Mar 12] good-topped gelding: maiden hurdler: fair handicap chaser, generally let down by jumping in 2004/5: stays easy 2½m: acts on good to firm and heavy going: blinkered once: front runner. *A. W. Carroll* **c107 x h–**

KING ALFRED (IRE) 5 b.g. Doubletour (USA) – Society Girl (Shavian) [2004/5 aF16g* F16d Jan 31] angular gelding: second foal: dam, probably stayed 1¼m, half-sister to useful winner up to 13.4f Flossy: 50/1, won 8-runner bumper on polytrack at Lingfield on debut in November: finished lame next time. *Mrs L. Richards* **F84**

KING BAVARD (IRE) 11 b.g. Jurado (USA) – Discerning Lady (Le Bavard (FR)) [2004/5 c24d^{pu} Mar 24] workmanlike gelding: maiden hurdler/chaser: winning pointer: stays 3m: acts on soft going. *P. H. Hogarth* **c– h–**

KING BEE (IRE) 8 b.g. Supreme Leader – Honey Come Back (Master Owen) [2004/5 c109, h–: c24s^{6} May 5] medium-sized gelding: fair chaser: jumped poorly only start in 2004/5: stays 3m: acts on heavy going. *H. D. Daly* **c– h–**

KING CAREW (IRE) 7 b.g. Fairy King (USA) – Kareena (Riverman (USA)) [2004/5 c120, h118: 16g^{3} c17f* 17d* c16m^{5} 16f^{3} 16g 19s Mar 27] useful-looking gelding: useful up to 17f on Flat: fairly useful handicap hurdler/chaser: won over fences at Limerick and over hurdles at Killarney in May: off 8 months before final start: raced mainly around 2m: acts on any going: effective blinkered or not: often races prominently. *M. Hourigan, Ireland* **c128 h126**

KING COAL (IRE) 6 b. or br.g. Anshan – Lucky Trout (Beau Charmeur (FR)) [2004/5 h95: 20s^{pu} 16g 20g 19d Mar 4] tall gelding: chasing type: little impact over hurdles. *R. Rowe* **h–**

KINGCOMBE LANE 5 b.g. Superpower – Starlight Wonder (Star Appeal) [2004/5 F17s F16d 20d Apr 20] close-coupled gelding: second foal: dam poor hurdler who stayed 21f: no show in 2 bumpers and maiden hurdle. *P. W. Hiatt* **h– F–**

KING EIDER 6 b. or br.g. Mtoto – Hen Harrier (Polar Falcon (USA)) [2004/5 h108: 16d* 16d 16d 16d Apr 9] smallish gelding: fairly useful on Flat (stays 2m): fairly useful handicap hurdler: won at Huntingdon in November by 1¼ lengths from Atahuelpa: disappointing in valuable events next 2 starts, bled from nose final one: should stay beyond 2m: acts on good to soft and good to firm going. *B. Ellison* **h118**

KINGFISHER SUNSET 9 b.g. Alflora (IRE) – Jack It In (Derrylin) [2004/5 h–: 20mpu 20dpu 21g2 20g c19gpu c21vpu Mar 15] good-bodied gelding: poor maiden hurdler: jumped poorly both starts over fences. *Mrs S. J. Smith* **c– x** **h78**

KING GEORGES (FR) 7 b.g. Kadalko (FR) – Djoumi (FR) (Brezzo (FR)) [2004/5 h100: 19g3 c20d4 c24g5 c25s5 24d6 24s3 22vpu Apr 22] workmanlike gelding: modest handicap hurdler: better form over fences, though jumping none too fluently: stays 25f: acts on soft ground, well beaten both starts on heavy. *J. C. Tuck* **c107 ?** **h98**

KING HARALD (IRE) 7 b.g. King's Ride – Cuilin Bui (IRE) (Kemal (FR)) [2004/5 c24gF c20sF c24g2 c24d* c25s2 c21g* Mar 17] **c135 +** **h–**

The road which led to King Harald's name entering the record books as the first winner of one of the new races at the expanded Cheltenham Festival, the Jewson Novices' Handicap Chase, had quite a few twists and turns. To begin with, King Harald almost didn't make the line-up, just two away from being ballotted out of an event for which the maximum number of runners allowed was twenty. When it became known that King Harald would get a run, just a few hours before he was due to meet an alternative engagement in the Royal & SunAlliance Chase, his connections scratched him from that particular race, an understandable reaction but one which resulted in a fine of £1,400. With the Jewson worth £46,400 to the winner, it turned out to be a very small price to pay.

King Harald would have been one of the outsiders had he contested the Royal & SunAlliance Chase, in which he was due to meet some of the season's leading staying novices at level weights. He started at shorter odds than all but one of his eighteen rivals (there was one non-runner) in the Jewson, set to receive weight from sixteen of them. Despite being 2 lb out of the handicap in what was a most competitive, good quality contest, those at the top of the handicap well up to competing in graded events, King Harald's chance was obvious judged on his excellent second to Ollie Magern in a Grade 2 novice chase at Wetherby on his previous outing. His performance that day, which followed a win, by a short head from The Bandit, the pair well clear, in a twelve-runner handicap at Newbury in January, underlined that King Harald was at least as good as many of those above him in the handicap at Cheltenham. King Harald had fallen on his first two starts over fences but for most of the way at Cheltenham was foot perfect in a race in which very few managed a trouble-free round, four of his rivals departing four out and several others hampered there. The front-running King Harald, continuing to jump boldly, had seen off all bar one of the top weights, Lacdoudal, by two out, and he looked to have that one's measure until a bad peck at the last, which caused his rider Mattie Batchelor to lose his left iron and allowed Lacdoudal to get on terms. Batchelor, having kicked out his other iron, managed to get his mount back on an even keel, and, to his credit, King Harald responded to his urgings to draw clear

Jewson Novices' Handicap Chase, Cheltenham—King Harald overcomes the grey Lacdoudal, despite Mattie Batchelor riding without irons on the run-in, to land this new race

again and win going away by four lengths. The story of King Harald's Cheltenham Festival win didn't end there, however. When his post-race dope test was returned positive it seemed inevitable that King Harald would be disqualified. However, it transpired that the bottle carrying the sample to the Horseracing Forensic Laboratory had leaked, and, when independent tests were carried out by a German laboratory on a second urine sample, which had not leaked, they proved negative. King Harald's owner was reportedly the first to exercise his right to have an independent test done, and, with the Jockey Club accepting its findings, no inquiry took place into King Harald's victory.

King Harald (IRE) (b.g. 1998)	King's Ride (b 1976)	Rarity (b 1967)	Hethersett
			Who Can Tell
		Ride (b 1966)	Sovereign Path
			Turf
	Cuilin Bui (IRE) (b 1988)	Kemal (b 1971)	Armistice
			Ilrem
		Tullow Performance (b 1977)	Gala Performance
			Maid of Tullow

There should be even better to come from King Harald, who has made just eleven appearances to date, the first five over hurdles in 2002/3, showing fairly useful form when successful on the last of those, in a conditional jockeys handicap at Newbury. Bought for IR £27,000 as a three-year-old, the close-coupled King Harald is the third foal of Cuilin Bui, a fairly useful hurdler herself who stayed three miles. Cuilin Bui has produced three other winners, a winning pointer by Executive Perk and two also trained by Mark Bradstock. Prince Madoc, a brother to King

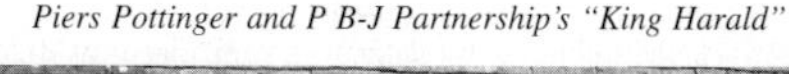

Piers Pottinger and P B-J Partnership's "King Harald"

Harald, won the first of his two starts in bumpers, showing useful form, and was successful in novice hurdles at Exeter and Cheltenham on his only other outings, while Gaelic Music (by Accordion) won a bumper in 2003/4 and showed fairly useful form when second in a three-mile novice hurdle in the latest season. Cuilin Bui is a daughter of Tullow Performance, a mare who won twice in bumpers and also over hurdles, at up to three miles. Tullow Performance has produced several other winners, notably the useful staying hurdler Crank Shaft who also won over fences. Cuilin Bui is also a half-sister to the dam of the smart staying hurdler Emotional Moment and to the grandam of the smart hurdler/chaser War of Attrition. King Harald is effective at twenty-one furlongs and stays twenty-five furlongs, so there should be plenty of opportunities for him in 2005/6, when further valuable handicap chases will surely be on his agenda. A close-coupled gelding, he acts on soft and good to firm going. *M. Bradstock*

KING KILLONE (IRE) 5 b.g. Moonax (IRE) – Killone Brae (King's Ride) [2004/5 F16d* 19d⁴ 22s* 19d² 20d⁵ 24d Apr 8] leggy, lengthy gelding: has scope: eighth foal: brother to winning pointer Killone Moonlight and half-brother to another by Over The River and bumper winner Lord Bacchus (by Insan): dam ran twice: won 4-y-o Irish point in 2004: won maiden bumper at Ludlow in November by 1¼ lengths from Il Duce: fairly useful novice hurdler: successful at Wincanton in January: finished distressed when well held in Grade 1 at Aintree final start: should stay 3m: raced on going softer than good. *Miss H. C. Knight* **h118 F104**

KINGKOHLER (IRE) 6 b.g. King's Theatre (IRE) – Legit (IRE) (Runnett) [2004/5 h102: 16d² 16g⁴ 16s⁴ 16g⁴ Jan 24] fair handicap hurdler: will prove best around 2m: raced on good ground or softer (acts on soft). *K. A. Morgan* **h107**

KING LOUIS (FR) 4 b.g. Nikos – Rotina (FR) (Crystal Glitters (USA)) [2004/5 F16d⁶ F16m⁵ Apr 2] 23,000 3-y-o: rangy, useful-looking gelding: eighth foal: half-brother to several winners, notably smart middle-distance filly Whortleberry (by Starborough) and smart 1m to 1¼m winner Valentino (by Valanour): dam, placed at 10.5f, half-sister to fairly useful 2m hurdler/chaser Running Man: fair form in bumpers at Newbury. *R. Rowe* **F90**

KING OF BARBURY (IRE) 8 b.g. Moscow Society (USA) – Aine's Alice (IRE) (Drumalis) [2004/5 h104: 20g² 21m⁴ 22g⁴ᵈ 21d⁶ 20m 19g² 23d Oct 21] sturdy, lengthy gelding: fair handicap hurdler: stays 2¾m: possibly best on good going or softer: visored second to fourth outings: untrustworthy. *A. King* **h104 §**

KING OF CONFUSION (IRE) 6 br.g. Topanoora – Rich Desire (Grey Desire) [2004/5 F16s⁴ F16d⁴ 24v³ 20v² 20v² Feb 15] has scope: second foal: dam, fairly useful hurdler, stayed 25f: fair form in bumpers: easily best effort over hurdles when second to Victom's Chance in maiden at Folkestone final start. *Ferdy Murphy* **h113 F86**

KING OF GOTHLAND (IRE) 6 b. or br.g. Gothland (FR) – Rose Deer (Whistling Deer) [2004/5 F97: 16s 20sᶠ 19s⁵ 20d Feb 17] tall, good-topped gelding: will make a chaser: fairly useful in bumpers in 2003/4: only poor form over hurdles: best effort in bumpers on good going (raced on softer over hurdles). *K. C. Bailey* **h–**

KING OF MOMMUR (IRE) 10 b.g. Fairy King (USA) – Monoglow (Kalaglow) [2004/5 c98, h–: 18m c20m² c21m⁵ 20g³ c16g⁴ 20m⁴ c17dᵖᵘ Aug 30] leggy gelding: modest hurdler/handicap chaser: claimed from B. Powell £5,000 sixth outing: lame next time: effective at 2m to easy 3m: acts on firm and good to soft going (below form on softer): effective with or without headgear: often front runner. *D. W. Thompson* **c96 h85**

KING OF SCOTS 4 ch.g. Halling (USA) – Ink Pot (USA) (Green Dancer (USA)) [2004/5 F12g F13s Dec 13] fourth foal: half-brother to 2 winners, including fairly useful 2000 2-y-o 6f winner Quink (by Selkirk), later winner up to 1m in Hong Kong: dam maiden half-sister to dam of Imperial Cup winner Scorned: well beaten in 3-y-o bumpers. *R. J. Price* **F–**

KING OF SWING (IRE) 13 b.g. Lancastrian – Romantic Rhapsody (Ovac (ITY)) [2004/5 c19g⁴ May 12] of little account. *Miss E. Webber* **c– h–**

KING OF THE ARCTIC (IRE) 7 b.g. Arctic Lord – Ye Little Daisy (Prince Tenderfoot (USA)) [2004/5 h102, F–: c20s² c16g c21sᵘʳ c16v* c20v* c16s⁴ c21v³ Mar 28] fair hurdler: similar form over fences, winning handicaps at Sedgefield in December and Wetherby in January: effective at 2m to 2½m: yet to race on firm going, acts on any other. *J. Wade* **c107 h–**

KING OF THE CASTLE (IRE) 10 b.g. Cataldi – Monashuna (Boreen (FR)) [2004/5 c97, h–: c16d² c20dpu c17g³ Aug 26] tall gelding: modest maiden chaser: stays 2½m: acts on firm and good to soft going. *B. Mactaggart* **c93 h–**

KING OF THE DAWN 14 b.g. Rakaposhi King – Dawn Encounter (Rymer) [2004/5 c–§, h–: c16v* May 10] angular gelding: modest chaser: won hunter at Towcester in May: stays 2¾m: acts on heavy and good to firm going: irresolute. *Mrs Georgina Worsley* **c85 § h–**

KING OF THE LIGHT 11 b.g. Rakaposhi King – Dawn Encounter (Rymer) [2004/5 16v 19g⁵ c24gpu Mar 18] rather leggy gelding: fair novice hurdler in 2001/2: off nearly 3 years, no show on return, including over fences. *O. Brennan* **c– h–**

KING ON THE RUN (IRE) 12 b.g. King's Ride – Fly Run (Deep Run) [2004/5 c–, h–: c25s⁴ c24g c19v² c24d² c24g⁴ Mar 9] rangy gelding: useful chaser at one time, lightly raced: stays 3m: acts on good to firm and heavy going: has gone well fresh. *Miss Venetia Williams* **c119 h–**

KING PLATO (IRE) 8 b.g. King's Ride – You Are A Lady (IRE) (Lord Americo) [2004/5 c77, h–: 24gpu May 8] poor hurdler/maiden chaser: successful twice in points in 2005: stays 3m: acts on soft going: jumps fences less than fluently: has shown signs of temperament. *M. D. Hammond* **c– h–**

KING REVO (IRE) 5 b.g. Revoque (IRE) – Tycoon Aly (IRE) (Last Tycoon) [2004/5 h127: 21d 19d³ 17d* 16d³ 17g Mar 18] tall, useful-looking gelding: useful handicap hurdler: won at Cheltenham in December by 3½ lengths from Transit: best effort when third to Tamarinbleu in valuable event at Sandown in February: effective at 2m to 21f: raced on good going or softer (acts on heavy): reliable. *P. C. Haslam* **h144**

KINGS ADVOCATE (IRE) 5 b.g. Saddlers' Hall (IRE) – Definitely Maybe (IRE) (Brush Aside (USA)) [2004/5 F18s² 19v³ 16s⁵ 22v* Mar 24] €30,000 3-y-o: lengthy, rather unfurnished gelding: second foal: dam winning pointer: better effort in bumpers when second at Downpatrick on reappearance: fairly useful novice hurdler: won maiden at Thurles in March: much improved form when length second of 25 to Gortinard in handicap at Punchestown in late-April: stays 3m: raced on going softer than good. *T. J. Taaffe, Ireland* **h117 F98**

KINGS BAY 6 ch.m. Beveled (USA) – Storm of Plenty (Billion (USA)) [2004/5 F104: 24d* 22d 24v² 20sF 24g Mar 18] tall, angular mare: bumper winner: fair form over hurdles: won novice at Windsor in November: stays 3m: raced on good going or softer (acts on heavy). *H. Morrison* **h101**

CFR Group (Electrical Services) Handicap Hurdle, Cheltenham—
King Revo (noseband) tackles the driven-along Bongo Fury (visor) and Goblet of Fire at the last

KINGS BLOOM (IRE) 7 b.g. Supreme Leader – Sweet Mignonette (Tina's Pet) [2004/5 F16gpu May 16] second foal: half-brother to bumper winner Reseda (by Rock Hopper): dam, fairly useful 2m hurdler, half-sister to useful 2m hurdler Cardinal Flower: lame in bumper on debut: in frame in points in 2005. *Mrs M. Reveley* F–

KING'S BOUNTY 9 b.g. Le Moss – Fit For A King (Royalty) [2004/5 c104, h–: c20s3 c25v2 c20s2 c22d* c24s6 Mar 14] rangy gelding: fair handicap chaser: won at Kelso in February by ¾ length from Jordan's Ridge: stays 3½m: acts on good to firm and heavy going: blinkered last 3 starts: has looked tricky ride. *T. D. Easterby* **c105 h–**

KINGS BOY (IRE) 11 ch.g. Be My Native (USA) – Love-In-A-Mist (Paddy's Stream) [2004/5 c101, h–: c25gpu Mar 9] good-topped gelding: fair pointer nowadays: should stay beyond 21f: acts on soft and good to firm going: tongue tied last 2 outings: has broken blood vessels. *David M. Easterby* **c– h–**

KINGS BROOK 5 br.g. Alderbrook – Kins Token (Relkino) [2004/5 h83, F81: 16gF 16f 17g4 16g3 16d3 17s 16d 17d6 Mar 26] rather unfurnished gelding: fair novice hurdler: raced around 2m: acts on good to soft ground: irresolute. *Nick Williams* **h106 §**

KINGS CASTLE (IRE) 10 b.g. King's Ride – Kilmana (IRE) (Castle Keep) [2004/5 c100, h–: 19s2 19d2 22g3 Apr 10] compact gelding: useful hurdler at one time, modest nowadays: fair form on completed start in novice chases: stays 25f: acts on good to firm and heavy going. *R. J. Hodges* **c– h98**

KING'S CHAMBERS 9 ch.g. Sabrehill (USA) – Flower Girl (Pharly (FR)) [2004/5 17f 18dF 16dF Feb 9] sparely-made gelding: poor hurdler: stays 19f: acts on good to firm and heavy going: tried blinkered: formerly tongue tied. *N. J. Hawke* **h–**

KINGSCLIFF (IRE) 8 b.g. Toulon – Pixies Glen (Furry Glen) [2004/5 c157p: c24g2 Dec 26] **c175**

In the fourteen months between the 2004 Peter Marsh Chase, in which he finished second, running below expectations, and the 2005 Cheltenham Gold Cup, from which he was withdrawn three days beforehand, Kingscliff ran just once. That was in the King George VI Chase at Kempton in December, an appearance that was enough for him to show that he was every bit as good as his previous performances had suggested he might be. Prior to the Peter Marsh, Kingscliff had won all seven starts, including in the 2003 Foxhunter Chase and handicaps at Ascot and Cheltenham later that year, showing very smart form, his Ascot performance all the more stunning as his rider Andrew Thornton had to cope without a left rein after that snapped at an early stage. In the King George, looking in fine shape after an absence of nearly a year, Kingscliff started fourth favourite in a field of thirteen. Ridden with more restraint than previously, he finished second, beaten two and a half lengths by Kicking King, with Azertyuiop a length and a quarter behind in third. The rest might as well have been in Surrey. So, Kingscliff split one horse rapidly showing himself a top-notch chaser and another who already was, yet his performance, like far too many these days, was viewed through the prism of the Cheltenham Festival. All the talk was of how promising a Gold Cup trial Kingscliff had run. Certainly the ground he made up from five out suggested Cheltenham and a longer trip would have been in his favour, but his performance was more than good enough to have won the majority of runnings of the King George in the last dozen years. In the enthusiasm for Kingscliff's Cheltenham prospects, it was also rather overlooked that Kicking King had been eight lengths clear when blundering at the last.

For the second year running Kingscliff was a significant late absentee from the Cheltenham Gold Cup. In 2004 Kingscliff suffered a recurrence of muscular problems when running below expectations in the Peter Marsh Chase at Haydock in January, and was taken out of the Gold Cup at the five-day declaration stage. In 2005, Kingscliff's being scratched from the Gold Cup came even closer to the day. After his final gallop, on Champion Hurdle day, Kingscliff's trainer Robert Alner said: 'It is a sickener, but Kingscliff's final gallop did not go well at all, and we have no option but to pull him out . . . You have to be spot on for any race, but for the Gold Cup you need to be one hundred percent and to run when any less than that would not be fair to the horse, owner or jockey.' That may well be so, though it's also true that Harchibald was the subject of similarly gloomy reports in the build-up to the Champion Hurdle and Kicking King was effectively declared a non-runner in the Gold Cup after actually recording an unsatisfactory scope, rather than just working badly. At the time of his withdrawal in 2004, Kingscliff had been disputing second favouritism behind Best Mate and, a year on, he was favourite in some books, Best Mate himself having been withdrawn the week before. One reason for Kingscliff's absence between Kempton and Cheltenham was 'a minor back problem' early in the New Year. Alner reportedly considered running Kingscliff in the AON Chase at Newbury, though was concerned because of a risk of further muscular problems so close to Cheltenham. Alner instead took his charge out hunting. The Pillar at Cheltenham, two weeks before the AON, was ruled out as Sir Rembrandt was due to be representing the stable (though withdrawn at the overnight stage after an unsatisfactory blood test). At the end of February, Alner got Thornton to commit himself to one of the pair in the build-up to the Gold Cup. The jockey's choice, after apparently more agonising than might have been expected, was Kingscliff, though in the end he was left with Hobson's choice.

In Kingscliff's absence, Kicking King overcame his illness scare to add the Gold Cup to his haul. The pair met again in the Punchestown Guinness Gold Cup shortly after the end of the British season. With Kicking King on home soil, the betting market entertained few doubts about the outcome—Kingscliff went off 7/2 second favourite—and, after leading after halfway, Kingscliff was quickly beaten once headed four from home and dropped right away after blundering at the next, clambering through the last and beaten eighteen lengths and a distance into fourth. Kingscliff is such a big, rangy, imposing type that he must be difficult to train but it is to be hoped that his performance at Punchestown doesn't signal another lengthy spell off the track.

Kingscliff (IRE) (b.g. 1997)	Toulon (b 1988)	Top Ville (b 1976)	High Top
			Sega Ville
		Green Rock (ch 1981)	Mill Reef
			Infra Green
	Pixies Glen (b 1985)	Furry Glen (b 1971)	Wolver Hollow
			Cleftess
		How Hostile (b 1977)	Tumble Wind
			Pixie Hill

Mr A. J. Sendell's "Kingscliff"

Kingscliff stays three and a quarter miles and he has raced only on good going or softer outside points. His pedigree has been dealt with fully in previous editions of *Chasers & Hurdlers*, the one thing to add being that his half-brother Mister Felix (by Ore) did not progress after showing fair form on his chasing debut. *R. H. Alner*

KINGSCOURT LAD (IRE) 7 b.g. Norwich – Mrs Minella (Deep Run) [2004/5 F16g* F16s F17d5 17s 17v 17gpu Apr 10] €10,000 4-y-o: useful-looking gelding: sixth foal: half-brother to fair hurdler/fairly useful chaser Minella Leisure (by Phardante) and fair chaser Minella Silver (by Roselier), both of whom stay 3m: dam lightly raced in points: fairly useful form in bumpers, trained by Miss F. Crowley on debut in 2003/4: won at Uttoxeter in July: little show in 3 novice hurdles: will be well suited by 2½m+. *Jonjo O'Neill* **h– p F95**

KING'S CREST 7 b.g. Deploy – Classic Beauty (IRE) (Fairy King (USA)) [2004/5 h96: 17v2 20s 16v4 Jan 26] smallish, sturdy gelding: fair on Flat (probably best up to 13f): best effort over hurdles when second in handicap at Carlisle, final start for R. Fahey: likely to prove best around 2m: acts on heavy going. *J. J. Quinn* **h104**

KING'S ECHO 7 b.g. Rakaposhi King – Welgenco (Welsh Saint) [2004/5 h77, F77: 20g 19mpu May 22] good-topped gelding: poor novice hurdler: stays 23f: tried blinkered: sold 4,500 Doncaster May Sales, pulled up in point in February. *S. Gollings* **h–**

KING'S ENVOY (USA) 6 b.g. Royal Academy (USA) – Island of Silver (USA) (Forty Niner (USA)) [2004/5 h–: 16d4 16d 16g2 16s Mar 11] leggy gelding: second in maiden at Musselburgh, little other form over hurdles. *Mrs J. C. McGregor* **h69**

KING'S HERO (IRE) 10 b.g. King's Ride – Dis Fiove (Le Bavard (FR)) [2004/5 c24d2 c25spu c24gpu Mar 4] sturdy gelding: winning pointer: maiden chaser: left Mrs A. Bealby and off 9 months, no show in 2005: stays 3m: sold £2,000 Ascot April Sales. *A. Ennis* **c93 h–**

KINGS HILL LEADER (IRE) 6 b.g. Supreme Leader – Mary Kate Finn (Saher) [2004/5 F–: 16s 24drtr 20d Nov 29] poor form on completed starts over hurdles: refused to race in between. *J. Howard Johnson* **h79 §**

KINGS LINEN (IRE) 9 b.g. Persian Mews – Kings Princess (King's Ride) [2004/5 h72: 24g c23m6 c26dF Aug 9] poor maiden hurdler: similar form on completed start over fences: stays 3¼m: acts on good to firm going. *B. I. Case* **c– h–**

KINGS LOGIC 7 ch.m. King's Signet (USA) – Kalogy (Kalaglow) [2004/5 F16m Jul 21] first foal: dam, fairly useful hurdler, stayed 21f: tailed off in bumper on debut. *R. D. Tudor* **F–**

KING'S MILL (IRE) 8 b.g. Doyoun – Adarika (Kings Lake (USA)) [2004/5 h–: 16g3 Dec 8] small, leggy gelding: fair maiden hurdler, lightly raced: off 15 months, ran well when never-nearer third of 25 to Olaso at Newbury in December: likely to prove best around 2m. *Mrs L. Wadham* **h109**

KINGS MINSTRAL (IRE) 15 ch.g. Andretti – Tara Minstral VII (Damsire Unregistered) [2004/5 c27g5 May 25] plain gelding: veteran chaser: retains little ability. *J. Burke* **c– h–**

KINGSMOOR 9 b.g. Regal Embers (IRE) – Cupids Bower (Owen Dudley) [2004/5 c88, h–: c21g6 May 27] modest handicap chaser: well held only start in 2004/5: stays 2½m: acts on good to firm going. *K. Bishop* **c– h–**

KING'S MOUNTAIN (USA) 5 b.g. King of Kings (IRE) – Statistic (USA) (Mr Prospector (USA)) [2004/5 19gpu 19g5 22g3 27d6 17m 24m Sep 24] fairly useful 1m winner at 2 yrs for D. Wachman, very disappointing on Flat in Britain for Mrs A. King: no form over hurdles: tried in cheekpieces/visor: sold £3,000 Ascot February Sales. *C. J. Gray* **h–**

KING SOLOMON (FR) 6 gr.h. Simon du Desert (FR) – All Square (FR) (Holst (USA)) [2004/5 h118: 16fF Jun 6] close-coupled horse: fairly useful hurdler: fell only start in 2004/5: stays 2½m: raced mainly on good going or softer (acts on heavy): tongue tied last 4 starts. *Miss Venetia Williams* **h–**

KING'S PROTECTOR 5 b.g. Hector Protector (USA) – Doliouchka (Saumarez) [2004/5 16m 16d 16s6 16d4 16g Dec 28] rather leggy gelding: fairly useful winner around 1m at 2 yrs, well held both starts on Flat in 2003: modest form over hurdles: raced at 2m: has taken good hold. *T. D. Easterby* **h96**

KINGS ROCK 4 ch.g. Kris – Both Sides Now (USA) (Topsider (USA)) [2004/5 16d 16d5 16d 16d 16s 16v4 16v2 20g3 19s 20g2 Mar 26] sparely-made gelding: modest on Flat (stays 1m): modest maiden hurdler: stays 2½m: raced on good going or softer (best efforts on good). *Mrs Lucinda Featherstone* **h92**

KINGS SQUARE 5 b.g. Bal Harbour – Prime Property (IRE) (Tirol) [2004/5 h–: 17g4 24dpu 20d* 20s 19g 19d 20g5 24g* Feb 27] poor hurdler: won handicaps at Newcastle in November and Musselburgh in February: stays 3m: acts on good to soft going: tried blinkered: unreliable. *M. W. Easterby* **h81 §**

KINGSTON-BANKER 9 b.g. Teamster – Happy Manda (Mandamus) [2004/5 c104, h–: c26g4 c25m* c25s2 Feb 10] sturdy gelding: fairly useful hunter chaser: won at Folkestone in May: will stay beyond 3¼m: acts on any going. *Mrs S. Alner* **c105 h–**

KINGSTON TOWN (USA) 5 ch.g. King of Kings (IRE) – Lady Ferial (FR) (Carwhite) [2004/5 16g2 16s* 19dF 16v* 16d 20v2 16v4 c19dur Feb 1] close-coupled gelding: modest on Flat (stays 1½m): fairly useful novice hurdler: trained by N. Littmoden on debut: won at Chepstow in October and Uttoxeter (beat Catchthebug 10 lengths) in November: best effort after when second to Eskimo Pie at Haydock: unseated second on chasing debut: stays 2½m: raced on good ground or softer (acts on heavy): front runner. *M. C. Pipe* **c– h118**

KINGSTON VENTURE 9 b.g. Interrex (CAN) – Tricata (Electric) [2004/5 c26gpu Mar 18] good-topped gelding: useful pointer in 2004: stiff task in Foxhunter at Cheltenham on return: stays 2½m: acts on soft and good to firm going: has worn visor/blinkers. *Miss C. Parfitt* **c– h–**

KING'S TRAVEL (FR) 9 gr.g. Balleroy (USA) – Travel Free (Be My Guest (USA)) [2004/5 c85, h71: 22vpu 16d6 19g6 19d4 Mar 26] tall, angular gelding: poor hurdler: similar form in novice chases: best around 2m: raced mainly on good going or softer. *J. D. Frost* **c– h79**

KING SUMMERLAND 8 b.g. Minshaanshu Amad (USA) – Alaskan Princess (IRE) (Prince Rupert (FR)) [2004/5 h–: 17d 17m 16m4 Jun 16] leggy gelding: blinkered, form over hurdles only when fourth in novice claimer at Worcester: sold 1,500 gns Doncaster August Sales: poor form in 2 races on Flat in 2004 for B. Mactaggart: resold 500 gns Doncaster November Sales. *C. J. Mann* **h78**

KINGTOBEE (IRE) 7 b.g. King's Ride – Zephyrelle (IRE) (Celio Rufo) [2004/5 F16v F16v 16v 16vpu Mar 29] rangy gelding: well held in bumpers and over hurdles (not fluent). *J. A. B. Old* **h– F–**

KINKEEL (IRE) 6 b.g. Hubbly Bubbly (USA) – Bubbly Beau (Beau Charmeur (FR)) [2004/5 F17d3 F16g6 16d4 16v 22d 16s 16d Mar 24] €11,000 4-y-o: ex-Irish gelding: fifth foal: dam unraced, out of half-sister to useful staying hurdler Willie Wumpkins: fell in maiden point: third on first of 2 starts in bumpers: easily best effort over hurdles when fourth in novice at Cork: left P. Nolan, not knocked about final start: tried tongue tied. *A. W. Carroll* **h90 F89**

KIPPOUR (FR) 7 b.g. Luchiroverte (IRE) – Obole III (FR) (Signani (FR)) [2004/5 22spu 19d4 c24m4 c16d6 Apr 5] close-coupled, quite attractive gelding: modest form when fourth in 19f novice hurdle at Catterick: well held in 2 maiden chases: blinkered final start. *Ferdy Murphy* **c– h94**

KIRBY'S VIC (IRE) 5 b.g. Old Vic – Just Affable (IRE) (Phardante (FR)) [2004/5 F16s 20vpu 19gpu Mar 4] second foal: dam unraced half-sister to smart chaser up to 2¾m Bells Life: no show in bumper or 2 novice hurdles. *N. A. Twiston-Davies* **h– F–**

KIRKHAM ABBEY 5 b.g. Selkirk (USA) – Totham (Shernazar) [2004/5 16d 16v6 21d2 16s Feb 18] lengthy gelding: fair on Flat (stays 1½m), successful twice in 2004, sold out of M. Jarvis' stable 32,000 gns Newmarket Autumn Sales: modest form over hurdles: possibly amiss final start: stays 21f. *J. J. Quinn* **h95**

KIRKSIDE PLEASURE (IRE) 4 ch.g. Grand Plaisir (IRE) – Caledon Mist (IRE) (Le Moss) [2004/5 F16s4 F16s2 Apr 22] fifth foal: dam unraced: fair form in bumpers at Ayr and Perth. *Mrs S. C. Bradburne* **F93**

KIROV KING (IRE) 5 b.h. Desert King (IRE) – Nymphs Echo (IRE) (Mujtahid (USA)) [2004/5 18m* 18m6 22f4 18gbd 19gpu Apr 7] half-brother to winning 2m hurdler Icarus Dream (by Intikhab): fairly useful on Flat (stays 1½m) at 3 yrs, sold out of D. Weld's stable 18,000 gns Newmarket Autumn (2003) Sales: won novice at Fontwell on hurdling debut in September: no form after. *B. G. Powell* **h92**

KISMET 7 b.m. Tirol – Belamcanda (Belmez (USA)) [2004/5 h–: 21g 20m^{ur} 22g 19m Jun 9] of little account: wore cheekpieces final start. *Lady Susan Watson* **h–**

KIT CARSON (IRE) 5 b.g. Dr Massini (IRE) – Roses Niece (IRE) (Jeu de Paille (FR)) [2004/5 F16s F16s F16d^5 F18d^6 F16g^2 Mar 19] 21,000 3-y-o: first foal: dam, winning 2m hurdler, out of half-sister to Stayers' Hurdle winner Rose Ravine, dam of smart staying jumper Frosty Canyon: fair form in bumpers. *C. F. Swan, Ireland* **F91**

KITIMAT 8 b.g. Then Again – Quago (New Member) [2004/5 c73, h–: c16d^{pu} c23f^{pu} c19s^3 c19d^2 c25s^F c18s^2 Dec 21] rangy gelding: poor handicap chaser: barely stays 25f: acts on good to firm and heavy going: blinkered last 2 outings. *R. H. Buckler* **c64 h–**

KITLEY 4 b.c. Muhtarram (USA) – Salsita (Salse (USA)) [2004/5 16g^5 17m Aug 6] modest maiden on Flat (stays 1m): well held in juvenile hurdles, racing freely. *B. G. Powell* **h66**

KITSKI (FR) 7 b.g. Perrault – Macyrienne (FR) (Saint Cyrien (FR)) [2004/5 F101: F17s^4 21m^{pu} 20g^2 16g 19s^3 24s* 22s^4 19d^2 Feb 8] fairly useful in bumpers: fair hurdler: won handicap at Towcester in November: stays 3m: acts on soft ground: tried blinkered: ungenuine: sold 7,000 gns Doncaster May Sales. *S. Gollings* **h106 § F98 §**

KITTENKAT 11 b.m. Riverwise (USA) – Cut Above The Rest (Indiaro) [2004/5 c94x, h–: c25g^{pu} 27s^6 c23s^3 c26s^4 c28d^{pu} c32d^F c28s^{pu} c25s* c25s^2 c25v^3 c30d^3 c23s* c23v^2 c25g c26v^{ur} Apr 22] lengthy, angular mare: winning hurdler: fair handicap chaser: won at Folkestone in January and Exeter (novice) in March: out-and-out stayer: acts on heavy going, possibly not on good to firm: sketchy jumper. *N. R. Mitchell* **c108 x h–**

KITTYLEE 6 b.m. Bal Harbour – Courtesy Call (Northfields (USA)) [2004/5 h62: 17m^6 17d^6 17d^{pu} Aug 1] rather leggy mare: little form over hurdles. *J. S. Wainwright* **h–**

KITUHWA (USA) 5 br.g. Cherokee Run (USA) – Ruhnke (USA) (Cox's Ridge (USA)) [2004/5 h–: 16m 16g^6 24m^{pu} Jun 5] no form over hurdles. *R. Shiels* **h–**

KIVOTOS (USA) 7 gr.g. Trempolino (USA) – Authorized Staff (USA) (Relaunch (USA)) [2004/5 h123: 23m* May 1] leggy gelding: fairly useful handicap hurdler: won well-contested event at Haydock by 2 lengths from True Lover: stays 3m: unraced on firm going, acts on any other: genuine and reliable: sold to join M. Pipe's stable 150,000 gns Doncaster May (2004) Sales. *A. C. Whillans* **h127**

KIWI BABE 6 b.m. Karinga Bay – Sunshine Gal (Alto Volante) [2004/5 h93, F90: 22g^5 24f^4 20d* 24s 20s* 24d 22d^3 22d 22v^{pu} Apr 22] small, sparely-made mare: fair hurdler: won mares handicap at Folkestone in November and claimer (claimed from P. Nicholls £8,000) at Leicester in January: should stay 3m: acts on soft ground, below form on firm: ran poorly when blinkered/in cheekpieces: hard ride. *P. R. Hedger* **h107 §**

KIWIJIMBO (IRE) 5 b.g. Germany (USA) – Final Touch (IRE) (Orchestra) [2004/5 F17d Mar 26] €36,000 4-y-o: tall gelding: first foal: dam, ran once in point, half-sister to fairly useful chaser Pinkpinkfizz who stayed 29f: tailed off in bumper on debut. *A. C. Whillans* **F–**

KIWI RIVERMAN 5 b.g. Alderbrook – Kiwi Velocity (NZ) (Veloso (NZ)) [2004/5 F–: 17s^{ur} 19s^{pu} 19v^{pu} Feb 13] useful-looking gelding: chasing type: no show in bumpers or over hurdles. *C. L. Tizzard* **h–**

KJETIL (USA) 5 b.g. King of Kings (IRE) – I Wich (FR) (Kris) [2004/5 h105: 16d 16d 20g^2 21d^6 c24d* c25d^{pu} c20m^4 Apr 23] good sort: fair maiden hurdler: won novice at Ludlow on chasing debut in March: stays 3m: acts on good to soft and good to firm going: tried blinkered: tongue tied last 5 outings: ungenuine. *P. F. Nicholls* **c103 § h105 §**

KJJIMMY (IRE) 8 ch.g. Sunley Builds – Cavity (True Song) [2004/5 24d^F 21g Apr 1] workmanlike gelding: no form outside points. *J. W. Mullins* **h–**

KLINE (IRE) 4 b.g. King's Theatre (IRE) – Royal River (Another River) [2004/5 F16g^6 Apr 16] half-brother to useful 2m chaser Billy Bathgate (by Gala Performance) and winning pointer by Camden Town: dam unraced half-sister to top-class 2m to 2½m hurdler Fortune And Fame: green when sixth to 15 to Rasharrow in bumper at Ayr on debut. *N. J. Henderson* **F86 +**

KLONDIKE CHARGER (USA) 11 b.g. Crafty Prospector (USA) – Forever Waving (USA) (Hoist The Flag (USA)) [2004/5 c95§, h–: c17m^4 c18m* c22m^4 c20m^4 c20g^{pu} c24g* c17m c17d^5 c22m^5 c20m^6 c24g^{pu} Apr 7] leggy gelding: modest handicap chaser: won at Fontwell (fourth course success) in May and Stratford in July: left Dr P. Pritchard before final start: stays 3¼m: probably ideally suited by good going or firmer (acts on firm): blinkered once: unreliable. *Miss J. S. Davis* **c98 § h–**

KNIAZ (FR) 7 gr.g. Saint Preuil (FR) – Alberade (FR) (Un Desperado (FR)) [2004/5 h110: 18g4 20mF 20m3 16f2 16m5 Jul 28] workmanlike gelding: fair hurdler: ran creditably all completed starts in 2004/5: stays easy 2½m: acts on firm and soft going. *A. J. Martin, Ireland* **h110**

KNIFE EDGE (USA) 10 b. or br.g. Kris S (USA) – My Turbulent Miss (USA) (My Dad George (USA)) [2004/5 c146, h–: c20s3 c20dpu 24gpu Mar 17] tall gelding: useful chaser nowadays, though hasn't won since 2001/2: left M. O'Brien, form in 2004/5 only when third to Mister McGoldrick in handicap at Wetherby: winning hurdler: blinkered, acted as pacemaker in World Hurdle at Cheltenham final start: stays 2½m: acts on heavy going, possibly not on good to firm: wore cheekpieces last 3 starts in 2003/4. *Jonjo O'Neill* **c141 h–**

KNIGHT OF OLD 10 ch.g. Jupiter Island – Nuns Royal (Royal Boxer) [2004/5 24mpu May 28] fourth foal: dam winning selling hurdler: no show in novice hurdle on belated debut. *J. Rudge* **h–**

KNIGHT OF PASSION 13 b.g. Arctic Lord – Lovelek (Golden Love) [2004/5 c23s4 c24gpu Apr 7] small, angular gelding: fair hunter chaser: won point in February: acts on soft and good to firm going: blinkered once: sometimes makes mistakes. *A. J. Tizzard* **c– h–**

KNIGHT OF SILVER 8 gr.g. Presidium – Misty Rocket (Roan Rocket) [2004/5 c–§, h68§: 17s* 17gpu 16g3 22g 22m2 19g3 24s c19d3 c21spu 17s4 19g 22d5 Apr 17] sparely-made gelding: poor hurdler: won conditional jockeys claimer at Newton Abbot in May: left J. Frost after ninth start: no form over fences: stays 2¾m: acts on soft and good to firm going: tried in headgear: ungenuine. *S. C. Burrough* **c– § h77 §**

KNIGHT OF THE ROAD (IRE) 6 b. or br.g. Lord Americo – Trolly Dolly (IRE) (The Parson) [2004/5 20d 20s c21dpu 24m Apr 10] €19,000 3-y-o: tall, rather unfurnished gelding: third foal: dam, bumper winner, from family of useful 3m chaser Jenniferjo: no sign of ability. *P. G. Murphy* **c– h–**

KNIGHTON LAD (IRE) 5 b.g. Supreme Leader – Tarqueen (IRE) (King's Ride) [2004/5 F17d F16d3 F16g2 Mar 28] third foal: dam unraced half-sister to fairly useful staying chaser Hatcham Boy: fair form in bumpers, shaping like a stayer. *A. King* **F94**

KNIGHTSBRIDGE KING 9 ch.g. Michelozzo (USA) – Shahdjat (IRE) (Vayrann) [2004/5 h94: 20g2 19m 19d2 16s 25s3 23d3 Feb 18] rather sparely-made gelding: modest handicap hurdler: stays 25f, at least as effective at shorter: acts on soft and good to firm going: tried in headgear. *John Allen* **h94**

KNIGHTS CROFT 12 b.g. Henbit (USA) – Bright Tiger-Moth (Funny Man) [2004/5 c–: c20mpu Jun 6] no sign of ability: has had tongue tied. *S. T. Lewis* **c–**

KNOCKANARD (IRE) 13 br.g. Executive Perk – Trianqo (Tarqogan) [2004/5 c–: c23dF Apr 25] tall, sparely-made gelding: winning pointer: no form in chases. *M. J. Gingell* **c–**

KNOCKARA LUCK (IRE) 4 ch.f. Simply Great (FR) – Bonne Atthenagh (IRE) (Rontino) [2004/5 F17g* Apr 14] lengthy filly: fourth foal: half-sister to winning pointers by Broken Hearted and Spanish Place: dam unraced: won mares bumper at Cheltenham on debut impressively by 15 lengths from Karawa: open to improvement. *N. G. Richards* **F101 p**

KNOCKDOO (IRE) 12 ch.g. Be My Native (USA) – Ashken (Artaius (USA)) [2004/5 c–§, h101§: 24vpu 16s 22s6 24s Apr 20] good-topped gelding: winning hurdler, out of form in 2004/5: stays 27f: acts on good to firm and heavy going: tried visored/tongue tied: ungenuine. *J. S. Goldie* **c– § h82 §**

KNOCK DOWN (IRE) 6 b.m. Oscar (IRE) – Bottle A Knock (IRE) (Le Moss) [2004/5 18d 18d2 c22dpu 20s 20s 18s2 20v6 16d c24s c24g c21d Apr 8] lengthy, angular mare: first foal: dam 2¼m chase winner: won up to 12.5f on Flat: useful hurdler/chaser in France: sold out of F. Cottin's stable €60,000 Goffs (France) November Sale after sixth start: little impact in handicaps in Britain: stays 2¾m: acts on heavy ground. *H. D. Daly* **c121 h131**

KNOCK IT BACK (IRE) 13 ch.g. Down The Hatch – Lady Hapsburg (Perhapsburg) [2004/5 c20s Feb 11] ex-Irish gelding: winning hurdler/pointer: stays 2½m: acts on heavy going. *P. C. Handley* **c– h–**

KNOCKRIGG (IRE) 11 ch.g. Commanche Run – Gaiety Lass (Le Moss) [2004/5 c–, h84: 17d6 24dpu 26s 17s Jan 20] good-bodied gelding: winning hurdler/chaser, poor nowadays: stays 2½m: acts on any going: blinkered once. *Dr P. Pritchard* **c– h80**

KNOCK STAR (IRE) 14 gr.g. Celio Rufo – Star of Monroe (Derring Rose) [2004/5 c90?, h–: c26g^{5} c21d^{5} May 17] leggy gelding: winning pointer: maiden hurdler/chaser: stays 3¼m: acts on firm and good to soft ground: tried blinkered. *S. J. Partridge* **c94 h–**

KNOCKTEMPLE LASS (IRE) 6 b.m. Executive Perk – Whats In A Name (IRE) (Le Moss) [2004/5 16d 17g^{3} Apr 10] fifth foal: half-sister to one-time fairly useful hurdler/chaser Another General (by Glacial Storm), stays 25f, and winning pointers by Commanche Run: dam unraced: well beaten in mares maiden points in Ireland: poor form in novice hurdles. *D. P. Keane* **h69**

KNOWHERE (IRE) 7 b.g. Lord Americo – Andarta (Ballymore) [2004/5 20d* 20s* Oct 30] **h136 p**

Those whose interest doesn't turn to jumping until after the November Handicap might well not have heard of Knowhere. His two appearances in Britain came before the end of October and, though a setback at the end of the year ruled him out of the rest of the season, the problem was reportedly not serious and Knowhere should make a big impact over fences when he returns in 2005/6. Both Knowhere's performances over hurdles were impressive. He looked several classes above the usual Hexham winner when landing a novice there by a distance at the

*Royal British Legion Poppy Appeal Persian War Novices' Hurdle, Chepstow—
Knowhere claims some useful scalps*

start of October and then won the Grade 2 Royal British Legion Poppy Appeal Persian War Novices' Hurdle at Chepstow three weeks later. The margin this time was just a neck but his defeat of the useful and more experienced Ladalko at level weights was clearly a highly promising effort. Encouragingly, Knowhere looked to have learned from Hexham, jumping more fluently than he had there, and he showed plenty of resolution in the closing stages. Before coming to Britain, Knowhere had run once in a point in Ireland, looking a decent prospect in winning a maiden. The big, well-made Knowhere looks every inch a chaser. He is a son of Lord Americo and a half-brother to the fair hurdler at up to twenty-one furlongs Pingo Hill (by Salt Dome). Their dam Andarta was a maiden on the Flat and winners in recent generations in the family are otherwise in short supply as well. Knowhere is sure to stay beyond two and a half miles and has raced on soft and good to soft going so far over hurdles. *N. A. Twiston-Davies*

KOBYLA 7 ch.m. Moscow Society (USA) – Jalmaid (Jalmood (USA)) [2004/5 h–, F–: 17g^pu 20d^pu 22g^5 Jul 15] of little account. *H. Alexander* **h–**

KOCK DE LA VESVRE (FR) 7 b.g. Sassanian (USA) – Csardas (FR) (Maiymad) [2004/5 c132, h–: c24d* c25g^2 c24f^3 c22v^3 c24g^6 c24g c25g^5 c24s* Apr 21] leggy, lengthy gelding: useful handicap chaser: won at Uttoxeter (by 1¾ lengths from Longshanks) in May and Perth (for second successive year, beating It Takes Time by ¾ length) in April: stays 3m: acts on any going: blinkered once. *Miss Venetia Williams* **c133 h–**

KOHINOR 6 b.m. Supreme Leader – Always Shining (Tug of War) [2004/5 F91: 20d 24d^3 21s^pu Jan 20] smallish, workmanlike mare: placed twice in bumpers: just poor form over hurdles: in cheekpieces final start. *O. Sherwood* **h84**

KOKO KABANA (IRE) 6 b. or br.m. Glacial Storm (USA) – New Chello (IRE) (Orchestra) [2004/5 c20v^3 c17v^5 c20s c17s c20d^3 c24d Apr 22] €4,000 4-y-o: second foal: dam, maiden pointer, half-sister to fairly useful chaser up to 25f Phar From A Fiddle, out of half-sister to very smart 2m chaser Wolf of Badenoch: won mares maiden point in 2004: poor maiden chaser: stays 2½m: acts on heavy ground. *J. P. Berry, Ireland* **c76**

KOKOPELLI MANA (IRE) 5 b.m. Saddlers' Hall (IRE) – Kachina (IRE) (Mandalus) [2004/5 F17v F16g F16s Apr 10] workmanlike mare: first foal: dam unraced half-sister to useful hurdler/chaser up to 25f Kings Measure: no show in bumpers. *J. M. Jefferson* **F–**

KOMBINACJA (POL) 7 ch.m. Jape (USA) – Komancza (POL) (Dakota) [2004/5 h113: 24d^2 20m^2 Jun 5] big, lengthy mare: fairly useful hurdler: second at Perth both starts in 2004/5: stays 3m: acts on firm and good to soft going. *T. R. George* **h117**

KOMENA 7 b.m. Komaite (USA) – Mena (Blakeney) [2004/5 16d Nov 9] poor on Flat (stays 1m): well beaten on hurdling debut. *J. W. Payne* **h–**

Betdaq Perth Festival Handicap Chase—
a second successive win in the race for Kock de La Vesvre, who pulls clear with It Takes Time

KONFUZIUS (GER) 7 b.g. Motley (USA) – Katrina (GER) (Windwurf (GER)) [2004/5 h–: c20d^{pu} c24g^{pu} Jul 1] no sign of ability: tried in cheekpieces/blinkers. *A. M. Crow* **c– h–**

KONKER 10 ch.g. Selkirk (USA) – Helens Dreamgirl (Caerleon (USA)) [2004/5 c92, h118: 17d^{6} c16g^{5} Oct 26] small, compact gelding: fairly useful 2m hurdler at one time: modest form on first of 2 starts in novice chases: bought out of Mrs M. Reveley's stable 6,000 gns Doncaster August Sales: best on going softer than good: usually held up. *J. R. Cornwall* **c– h–**

KOQUELICOT (FR) 7 ch.g. Video Rock (FR) – Ixia Des Saccarts (FR) (Laniste) [2004/5 c121, h98: 24g* 24s^{6} c23g^{4} c24v^{4} c24d^{2} c24g Mar 16] leggy gelding: modest hurdler, won novice at Worcester in October: fairly useful handicap chaser: best effort in 2004/5 when 3½ lengths second to Longshanks at Kempton: stays 3m: raced on good ground or softer (acts on heavy): tried blinkered: usually jumps soundly. *P. J. Hobbs* **c122 h98**

KORAKOR (FR) 11 ch.g. Nikos – Aniflore (FR) (Satingo) [2004/5 c128d, h–: c16d^{4} c16g c20g^{pu} Apr 22] good-topped gelding: handicap chaser, disappointing since 2003: stays 21f: acts on good to firm and heavy going. *Ian Williams* **c116 h–**

KORELO (FR) 7 b.g. Cadoudal (FR) – Lora du Charmil (FR) (Panoramic) [2004/5 c124x, h136: 24d^{6} 24d* 24s^{2} 24g^{5} 24s^{F6} Apr 7] workmanlike gelding: usually let down by jumping over fences in Britain: very smart hurdler: much improved when winning handicap at Cheltenham in January by short head from Attorney General, despite wandering under pressure: good head second to Patriarch Express in Grade 2 there later in month: never a factor in World Hurdle at same course in March: possibly amiss when sixth to Monet's Garden in Grade 2 at Aintree final start, ridden prominently and well beaten when falling last (remounted): stays 3m: acts on good to firm and heavy going: poor efforts when visored: usually held up. *M. C. Pipe* **c– x h158**

KOSMOS BLEU (FR) 7 ch.g. Franc Bleu Argent (USA) – Fee du Lac (FR) (Cimon) [2004/5 h96: 19f^{2} 19s^{4} c16s* c16d^{3} c16s^{2} c18d^{3} c21s^{2} c22g* c21g^{ur} Apr 10] tall gelding: has reportedly had breathing operation: fair maiden hurdler: better over fences, winning novices at Newton Abbot in November and Newbury (handicap) in March: stays 2¾m: acts on firm and soft going: tongue tied once: usually jumps soundly: consistent. *R. H. Alner* **c113 h100**

KOSSIES MATE 6 b.m. Cosmonaut – Pola Star (IRE) (Un Desperado (FR)) [2004/5 F16d^{pu} F16d Jan 29] 1,200 4-y-o: leggy mare: first foal: dam never ran: no form in 2 bumpers, cocked jaw and hung badly left on debut. *P. W. Hiatt* **F–**

KOUMBA (FR) 7 b.g. Luchiroverte (IRE) – Agenore (FR) (Le Riverain (FR)) [2004/5 h71: 26m^{F} 22d* 20s^{3} 22d^{6} Dec 3] angular gelding: modest handicap hurdler: won at Stratford in October: probably stays 3¼m: acts on soft and good to firm going. *Evan Williams* **h98**

KOUROS DES OBEAUX (FR) 7 b.g. Grand Tresor (FR) – Valse Des Obeaux (FR) (Pot d'Or (FR)) [2004/5 c86, h–: 24d^{3} Nov 22] angular gelding: fair maiden hurdler: winning chaser: barely stays 3¼m: acts on heavy going (looked ill at ease on firm): tried blinkered, visored last 5 outings: temperament under suspicion. *M. C. Pipe* **c– h105**

KOUROSH (IRE) 5 b.g. Anshan – Pit Runner (Deep Run) [2004/5 F17v aF16g Oct 30] 20,000 4-y-o: lengthy gelding: sixth foal: brother to Irish point/bumper winner Bugle Major: dam, 2m hurdle winner, half-sister to fairly useful chaser around 2½m Visible Difference, out of half-sister to high-class 2m to 2½m chaser Travado: little show in 2 bumpers. *C. P. Morlock* **F–**

KRACK DE L'ISLE (FR) 7 b.g. Kadalko (FR) – Ceres de L'Isle (FR) (Bad Conduct (USA)) [2004/5 h–: c16v^{F} Jan 10] lengthy gelding: lightly-raced winning hurdler: off a year, fell first on chasing debut: should stay 3m: raced on going softer than good (acts on heavy). *A. C. Whillans* **c– h–**

KRAKOW BABA (FR) 5 b.g. Sleeping Car (FR) – Babacha (FR) (Latnahc (USA)) [2004/5 19d^{2} 21d 19s 18s* Feb 4] close-coupled gelding: fourth foal: half-brother to useful hurdler/chaser Tribal Venture (by Dom Alco), stays 25f, and winners around 2m over jumps in France by Roi de Rome and Kadalko: dam maiden up to 1½m on Flat: once-raced on Flat: won 4-y-o event at Lyon Villeurbanne on hurdling debut in 2003/4: left M. Boudot after reappearance: easily best effort in Britain when winning handicap at Fontwell by ¾ length from Pardishar: stays 19f: acts on soft going. *Miss Venetia Williams* **h104**

KRISMAS CRACKER 4 b.g. Kris – Magic Slipper (Habitat) [2004/5 F16m Apr 2] 45,000 3-y-o: good-topped gelding: half-brother to several winners, including useful 1994 2-y-o 7f winner Muhab (by Lyphard) and fairly useful hurdler/chaser Thari (by **F–**

Silver Hawk), stays 23f: dam, 1¼m and 11.5f winner, half-sister to Fairy Footsteps and Light Cavalry: well held in bumper on debut. *N. J. Henderson*

KRISTINEAU 7 ch.m. Cadeaux Genereux – Kantikoy (Alzao (USA)) [2004/5 h83: 21g^6 17d^3 17g^4 17m^4 Jul 26] leggy mare: poor maiden hurdler: stays 2½m: acts on good to soft going: in cheekpieces final start: tongue tied nowadays. *Mrs E. Slack* **h83**

KROISOS (IRE) 7 b.g. Kris – Lydia Maria (Dancing Brave (USA)) [2004/5 c76, h60: c26s^{pu} c26d^4 c26g^{pu} c22s^{ur} Mar 30] workmanlike gelding: maiden hurdler: poor chaser: stays 3¼m: acts on soft going: blinkered nowadays. *R. Curtis* **c– x h–**

KRONADO (GER) 7 ch.h. Lomitas – Kadora (GER) (Dashing Blade) [2004/5 17d^3 c17d^5 Jun 12] successful up to 1m on Flat in Germany: twice-raced over jumps in Italy for A. Wohler: modest form when third in novice hurdle at Bangor in May: last of 5 over fences at Krefeld following month. *C. Von Der Recke, Germany* **c– h87**

KUPKA 6 ch.g. Rakaposhi King – Re-Spin (Gildoran) [2004/5 20s* 24v^4 24s^4 20d^{pu} Mar 26] strong, lengthy gelding: second foal: dam unraced half-sister to 1992 Grand National winner Party Politics: runner-up in maiden Irish point in 2004: fair hurdler: won novice at Carlisle in October: lame final outing: stays 3m. *L. Lungo* **h101**

KUPTO (FR) 7 b.g. Luchiroverte (IRE) – Neva (FR) (Danoso) [2004/5 20m Jun 5] fourth foal: dam winning cross-country chaser around 2½m in France: winning pointer: pulled up in 2005: no show in maiden on hurdling debut. *Mrs S. E. Busby* **h–**

KUSTOM KIT FOR HER 5 b.m. Overbury (IRE) – Antonias Melody (Rambo Dancer (CAN)) [2004/5 19v 16g Nov 11] compact mare: modest maiden on Flat (stays 1½m): no show over hurdles. *S. R. Bowring* **h–**

KWAHERI 7 b.m. Efisio – Fleeting Affair (Hotfoot) [2004/5 h–: 17g 16g^5 16g^4 17g 27d Aug 21] little form over hurdles: won maiden point in March. *Mrs P. N. Dutfield* **h–**

KYALAMI (FR) 7 gr.g. Royal Charter (FR) – Reine Margot III (FR) (Trenel) [2004/5 c21d^{bd} c25s^{ur} c24s^{ur} c22g^5 Apr 1] 12,000 4-y-o: good-bodied gelding: third foal (all by Royal Charter): brother to fairly useful 21f chase winner Fier de L'Etre, later prolific cross-country chase winner in Italy: dam won around 1½m on Flat: won both starts in points in 2005: first completion in hunters (left R. Kelvin Hughes after first start) when fifth at Newbury. *B. Tulloch* **c101**

KYBER 4 ch.g. First Trump – Mahbob Dancer (FR) (Groom Dancer (USA)) [2004/5 16g 17d^4 16s^3 Apr 10] workmanlike gelding: half-brother to modest hurdler around 2m Hamadenaah (by Alhijaz): modest maiden on Flat (stays 2m): apparently best effort over hurdles when fourth in novice at Carlisle, making most. *R. F. Fisher* **h90**

KYLE OF LOCHALSH 5 gr.g. Vettori (IRE) – Shaieef (IRE) (Shareef Dancer (USA)) [2004/5 16s 20m 16s^6 20d^{ur} 20m 24g 24s^{pu} Mar 12] leggy gelding: poor on Flat nowadays: little form over hurdles: in cheekpieces and tongue tied final start. *J. S. Goldie* **h71**

KYLIE TIME (IRE) 8 ch.g. Good Thyne (USA) – Miss Kylogue (IRE) (Lancastrian) [2004/5 h85: 16g^3 c22s^F c20m^{pu} c20m^6 c16d^{pu} Feb 4] lengthy gelding: maiden hurdler: no show over fences: tried in cheekpieces. *P. Beaumont* **c– x h83**

KYMANDJEN (IRE) 8 b.g. Un Desperado (FR) – Marble Miller (IRE) (Mister Lord (USA)) [2004/5 c122, h108: c25g c24d^F c24v^3 c24v^2 c20v^5 c29s^6 Mar 28] angular gelding: winning hurdler: useful handicap chaser: numerous creditable efforts in defeat in valuable handicaps in 2004/5, particularly when short-head second to Numbersixvalverde in Thyestes Handicap at Gowran in January and 5 lengths second to Jasmin d'Oudaires at Punchestown in late-April: stays 29f: acts on good to firm and heavy going: front runner: genuine. *Paul Nolan, Ireland* **c132 h–**

KYNANCE COVE 6 b.g. Karinga Bay – Excelled (IRE) (Treasure Kay) [2004/5 h–, F–: 21g^2 20m^3 22s^6 Jun 22] compact gelding: poor maiden hurdler: stays 21f: acts on good to firm going. *C. P. Morlock* **h60**

KYPER DISCO (FR) 7 b.g. Epervier Bleu – Disconea (FR) (Bayolidaan (FR)) [2004/5 19g^{ur} 19g^6 17d 21d 19g^5 Apr 1] well-made gelding: fair maiden hurdler: off 21 months before reappearance: should stay 2½m: raced on good going or softer. *N. J. Henderson* **h103**

KYRTON (CZE) 9 ch.g. Gouriev – Kerty (CZE) (Big Walt (USA)) [2004/5 c22s^4 c29f^5 c29g^F c34m^6 c31d^{pu} Nov 12] lengthy gelding: staying chaser, successful twice in Czech Republic: no show in cross-country event at Cheltenham on only start in Britain. *Pavel Slozil, Czech Republic* **c–**

L

LABEL DU COCHET (FR) 6 b.g. Rahotep (FR) – Astuce du Cochet (FR) (Le Nain Jaune (FR)) [2004/5 18d^rtr 24s^pu Jan 29] good-topped gelding: first foal: dam winning chaser around 2m: won twice on Flat in summer 2004: successful also 3 times over jumps, twice over fences at Pau and over hurdles at Toulouse, but often refuses to race: out of depth only start in Britain: stays 19f: acts on heavy going: tried blinkered: untrustworthy. *A. Chaille-Chaille, France* **c– § h– §**

LABULA BAY 11 b.g. Sula Bula – Lady Barunbe (Deep Run) [2004/5 c101, h–: c22m^6 c24f^pu Sep 26] fair handicap chaser at best: no show in 2004/5: stays 3¼m: acts on soft and good to firm going: tried blinkered: jumps none too fluently: has flashed tail. *B. G. Powell* **c– h–**

LA CALERA (GER) 4 ch.f. Big Shuffle (USA) – La Luce (Niniski (USA)) [2004/5 16g 16g 16v 19d Mar 14] ex-German filly: successful around 7f on Flat: no form over hurdles, left M. Harris after debut: tried blinkered/in cheekpieces. *Mrs Lucinda Featherstone* **h–**

LACDOUDAL (FR) 6 gr.g. Cadoudal (FR) – Belfaster (FR) (Royal Charter (FR)) [2004/5 h123: c16d^2 c16d^2 c19m^3 c21d^2 c19g* c20d* c21s* c20g^3 c20s^2 c21g^2 c25d^4 Apr 8] **c149 h–**

Size matters in a potential chaser but it is nowhere near so important as jumping ability. The smallish, angular Lacdoudal is a good example of a chaser who makes up for any lack of physique by being a most fluent jumper. Lacdoudal won a novice hurdle at Kempton in March 2004 within a few weeks of arriving at Sandhill stables from France, where he had won over eleven furlongs on the Flat before making an encouraging start over hurdles, winning a four-year-old non-thoroughbred event at Pau on his third and final outing for Francois Nicolle. Down the field when highly tried in the Supreme Novices' Hurdle at Cheltenham on his second start in Britain, and then beaten in novice events at Exeter and Cheltenham in April, Lacdoudal was sent straight over fences in the latest season. It took him five races before he got off the mark—in a two-finisher maiden at Doncaster in December—but, from that point until a lacklustre effort in the Mildmay Novices' Chase at Aintree on his final start, he progressed really well, sound jumping the hallmark of his performances as he developed into one of the season's best novices.

Lacdoudal followed up his success at Doncaster with two handicap victories in January, the first over Run For Paddy at Kempton and the second over Joes Edge and Cornish Rebel in the Timeform Novices' Handicap Chase at Cheltenham, where he jumped really well. Creditable efforts followed in graded events at Sandown and Kempton, firstly when a close third to El Vaquero and Le Passing in the Scilly Isles Novices' Chase and then when runner-up to Limerick Boy in the Pendil Novices' Chase. A choice of engagements at the Cheltenham Festival included

Timeform Novices' Handicap Chase, Cheltenham—the grey Lacdoudal proves too strong for the subsequent Scottish National protagonists Joes Edge and Cornish Rebel (noseband)

the Arkle Trophy but, by this stage, two miles under the conditions that tend to prevail at the Festival nowadays looked like proving too much of a test of speed for Lacdoudal. The choice for novice chasers at the Festival meeting was broadened in the latest season by the adding of the Jewson Novices' Handicap over two miles, five furlongs. In earlier years, a novice like Lacdoudal would probably have ended up running against seasoned handicappers in the Mildmay of Flete (which still had twenty-two runners for its latest renewal, only one of them—the eleven-year-old Mouseki—eligible to run in novices), or possibly in the old Cathcart Chase. Lacdoudal carried joint top weight of 11-10 with Le Passing in the nineteen-runner Jewson. His experience stood him in good stead, his sound jumping again a feature as he put up his best effort of the season to finish second to the lightly-weighted King Harald.

Lacdoudal (FR) (gr.g. 1999)	Cadoudal (FR) (br 1979)	Green Dancer (b 1972)	Nijinsky
			Green Valley
		Come To Sea (gr 1971)	Sea Hawk II
			Camarilla
	Belfaster (FR) (gr 1989)	Royal Charter (gr 1982)	Mill Reef
			Royal Way
		Insoumise (b 1974)	Novitur
			Ursule

Lacdoudal is bred for chasing, by Cadoudal out of Belfaster, a winning chaser at up to nineteen furlongs in France. Lacdoudal is Belfaster's fourth foal and closely related to two winners by Kadalko, the fair chasers Keep Me and Idealko, the latter successful at two and a half miles. Lacdoudal's grandam Insoumise and his great grandam Ursule were unraced. Lacdoudal's best form has been shown at around two and a half miles; though he may well have been past his best for the season when disappointing over three miles, one furlong at Aintree, he weakened quickly before the last, giving the impression lack of stamina was also probably a factor. Lacdoudal acts on heavy and good to firm going and is tough, genuine and consistent, as well as being a good jumper. He takes a good hold and is usually ridden handily. *P. J. Hobbs*

LA CONCHA (IRE) 4 b.g. Kahyasi – Trojan Crown (IRE) (Trojan Fen) [2004/5 16g 18m 16m^2 16f 16d^3 Apr 18] no form on Flat: form over hurdles only when second in juvenile at Plumpton: left Mrs L. Jewell before final start. *M. J. McGrath* **h82**

LADALKO (FR) 6 b.g. Kadalko (FR) – Debandade (FR) (Le Pontet (FR)) [2004/5 c116, h–: 20s^2 20d* 21d^2 20s^5 21s^2 22g* Apr 16] tall, useful-looking gelding: won maid- **c– h136**

William Hill Winter Novices' Hurdle, Sandown—despite being none too fluent himself at the last, the consistent Ladalko takes advantage of a mixed round of jumping from runner-up No Refuge

Mr Paul D. Barber & Mrs M. Findlay's "Ladalko"

en on chasing debut in 2003/4: let down by jumping over fences subsequently: useful novice hurdler: won Grade 2 William Hill Winter Novices' Hurdle at Sandown (by 1½ lengths from No Refuge) in December and handicap at Ayr (by length from Basilea Star) in April: ran creditably all other starts: likely to stay 3m: raced on good going or softer: has found little. *P. F. Nicholls*

LADE BRAES (IRE) 4 b.g. Luso – Madamme Highlights (Andretti) [2004/5 F16s Apr 22] €36,000 3-y-o: seventh foal: half-brother to modest hurdler/fair chaser Prince Highlight (by Lord Americo), stays 27f, and winning pointer by Royal Fountain: dam unraced: soundly beaten in bumper on debut. *J. Howard Johnson* **F–**

LADIES FROM LEEDS 6 b.m. Primitive Rising (USA) – Keldholme (Derek H) [2004/5 F–: F16s 20d[6] 20v[pu] 20g[5] Jan 21] no form in bumpers and novice hurdles. *A. Crook* **h– F–**

LA DOLFINA 5 b.m. Pennekamp (USA) – Icecapped (Caerleon (USA)) [2004/5 16g[bd] 16d[3] 16d[F] Nov 9] leggy mare: half-sister to useful 2m hurdler Have Merci (by High Estate) and bumper winner Roomtoroom Express (by Faustus): fairly useful on Flat (stays 1¼m) at 3 yrs, sold out of H. Morrison's stable 39,000 gns Newmarket Autumn (2003) Sales: modest form when third at Haydock on completed start in novice hurdles: may yet do better. *P. J. Hobbs* **h99 +**

LADY ACCORD (IRE) 5 b.m. Accordion – Lady of Tara (Deep Run) [2004/5 F16v* F17s Apr 7] lengthy mare: has scope: fourth foal: half-sister to modest hurdler Cap It If You Can (by Capitano), stays 3m: dam winning Irish hurdler: better effort in **F88**

bumpers when winning at Thurles on debut in March by 2 lengths from Lady Kate Ellen. *W. P. Mullins, Ireland*

LADY ALDERBROOK (IRE) 5 b.m. Alderbrook – Madame President (IRE) (Supreme Leader) [2004/5 F–: 19v4 19dpu 17dF 22g5 Apr 10] leggy, angular mare: well held in bumpers: poor form at best in mares novice hurdles, usually jumping poorly. *C. J. Down* **h–**

LADY ARNICA 6 b.m. Ezzoud (IRE) – Brand (Shareef Dancer (USA)) [2004/5 c–, h–: c20dF 21g6 c18mpu 16m6 22mpu Jun 13] lengthy mare: seemingly no longer of any account: tried blinkered. *A. W. Carroll* **c– h–**

LADY AT LEISURE (IRE) 5 ch.m. Dolphin Street (FR) – In A Hurry (FR) (In Fijar (USA)) [2004/5 h–: 16m May 27] poor on Flat (stays 1¼m): no show over hurdles. *M. J. Ryan* **h–**

LADY BARONETTE 8 b.m. Baron Blakeney – Rueful Lady (Streetfighter) [2004/5 c–: c25dur c30d4 c24sF c24s Mar 27] winning pointer: generally let down by jumping in hunter chases, left Andrew Martin after second start. *Mrs Elizabeth Howe* **c85 x**

LADY BLADE (IRE) 4 b.f. Daggers Drawn (USA) – Singhana (IRE) (Mouktar) [2004/5 16dF 17m Apr 9] half-sister to modest hurdler Singh Street (by Dolphin Street), stays 2½m: poor maiden on Flat (stays 1¼m): no show in 2 selling hurdles: visored final start. *P. D. Evans* **h–**

LADY BLAZE 6 ch.m. Alflora (IRE) – Lady Elle (IRE) (Persian Mews) [2004/5 F–: F16g F16d 25vpu Jan 27] big, lengthy mare: no sign of ability: tried tongue tied. *Miss G. Browne* **h– F–**

LADY BLING BLING 4 b.f. Midnight Legend – Slipmatic (Pragmatic) [2004/5 F17s Apr 7] leggy, unfurnished filly: first foal: dam, fair hurdler, stayed 2¾m: soundly beaten in listed mares bumper on debut. *P. J. Jones* **F–**

LADY BOB BACK 8 br.m. Bob Back (USA) – Whimbrel (Dara Monarch) [2004/5 c70, h66: c20d4 c21mpu c25gF May 29] lengthy mare: poor maiden hurdler/chaser: should be suited by 3m+: acts on heavy going: tried in cheekpieces: has had tongue tied: poor jumper: inconsistent. *M. A. Barnes* **c– x h–**

LADY BUSTED 10 b.m. Almoojid – Sindos (Busted) [2004/5 h–: 16g 16m 22ssu 22m3 20g5 Jul 14] poor maiden hurdler: stays 2¾m: wore cheekpieces final start. *D. Burchell* **h61**

LADY DOT (IRE) 12 ch.m. Mister Lord (USA) – Anvil Chorus (Levanter) [2004/5 c21m4 May 19] poor pointer. *D. S. Dennis* **c–**

LADY DYNAMITE 5 b.m. Glacial Storm (USA) – Lady Elle (IRE) (Persian Mews) [2004/5 F82: 16spu 16s6 19d 21spu 17g6 21dpu 19m Apr 9] leggy mare: no form over hurdles: trained by H. Daly/P. Johnson first 4 starts: wore cheekpieces final outing. *T. Wall* **h–**

LADY GERONA 4 b.f. Danzig Connection (USA) – Broom Isle (Damister (USA)) [2004/5 17m 18m 16f 17m5 16vpu Dec 17] third foal: half-sister to fair 2m hurdler Bolshoi Ballet (by Dancing Spree): dam, winning hurdler up to 2½m, also successful up to 15f on Flat: little form over hurdles: tongue tied last 2 starts. *W. G. M. Turner* **h72**

LADY GODSON 6 ch.m. Bold Arrangement – Dreamy Desire (Palm Track) [2004/5 F–: 16s Dec 5] well held in 2 bumpers and maiden hurdle. *B. Mactaggart* **h–**

LADY GUNNER (IRE) 6 br.m. Needle Gun (IRE) – The Foalicule (Imperial Fling (USA)) [2004/5 19dpu Oct 3] seventh foal: half-sister to 2 winning pointers: dam poor half-sister to useful jumpers Homeson, stayed 3m, and Hill's Pageant, best at 2m: no show in novice hurdle on debut. *B. S. Rothwell* **h–**

LADY HARRIET 6 b.m. Sir Harry Lewis (USA) – Forever Together (Hawaiian Return (USA)) [2004/5 h86, F–: c21g3 Nov 18] leggy mare: modest hurdler for N. Gifford in 2003/4: no show on chasing debut: raced mainly at 2m on good going or softer. *C. J. Mann* **c– h–**

LADY JANAL 7 gr.m. Sir Harry Lewis (USA) – Mrs Dawson (Sharrood (USA)) [2004/5 h69, F–: c21g5 22v c21d c16vur c16v5 c16v3 c16v5 c20sF c16d Apr 5] poor maiden hurdler/chaser: stays 21f: acts on heavy going. *Miss S. E. Forster* **c64 h–**

LADY JEANNIE 8 b.m. Emarati (USA) – Cottonwood (Teenoso (USA)) [2004/5 16m5 16g5 16s6 16dpu Nov 21] poor hurdler: raced around 2m: acts on good to firm and heavy going: sold 500 gns Doncaster January Sales. *M. J. Haynes* **h80**

LADY LAMBRINI 5 b.m. Overbury (IRE) – Miss Lambrini (Henbit (USA)) [2004/5 F–: F16m 20m 20g^{3} 17g 20g^{pu} Aug 26] leggy mare: no form in bumpers/over hurdles: placed twice in points in April. *Mrs L. Williamson* **h– F–**

LADY LISA (IRE) 6 b.m. Supreme Leader – Jennyellen (IRE) (Phardante (FR)) [2004/5 16v 16d 20s 20s^{pu} 18s^{3} 20s^{F} 19v* 22m Apr 23] ex-Irish mare: first foal: dam, modest hurdler, stayed 2¾m: left R. Donohoe after fourth outing: improved effort over hurdles when winning handicap at Newton Abbot in April: should stay at least 2½m: best effort on heavy ground. *M. C. Pipe* **h83**

LADY LOVEDAY 4 b. or br.f. Panoramic – Cadal Queen (FR) (Cadoudal (FR)) [2004/5 16m 16v 20v^{6} Feb 5] sturdy filly: first foal: dam winning hurdler/chaser up to 21f in France: little sign of ability. *Nick Williams* **h–**

LADY MARANZI 6 b.m. Teenoso (USA) – Maranzi (Jimmy Reppin) [2004/5 h73: 19m^{bd} Sep 1] little show in 3 novice hurdles. *Mrs D. A. Hamer* **h–**

LADY MISPRINT 9 ch.m. Classic – Miss Primrose (Primitive Rising (USA)) [2004/5 20d 16d^{6} 23g* 17d^{2} Mar 8] won all 3 starts in points in 2004: fair form over hurdles: made all in amateur maiden at Fakenham in January: stays 23f. *J. D. Frost* **h101**

LADY MORDAUNT (IRE) 7 b.m. Mister Lord (USA) – Castle Flame (IRE) (Carlingford Castle) [2004/5 21m^{pu} Jun 8] 2,400 4-y-o: fifth foal: sister to winning 2¾m chaser Whatsgoingonbob and half-sister to winning hunter chaser Boss Murphy (by Supreme Leader): dam unraced: tailed off on hurdling debut: successful in maiden point in February. *R. H. York* **h–**

LADY OF FORTUNE (IRE) 6 b.m. Sovereign Water (FR) – Needwood Fortune (Tycoon II) [2004/5 F93: 19v* 17g^{4} Mar 9] rather unfurnished mare: bumper winner: off 11 months, won mares novice at Hereford on hurdling debut in February by 9 lengths from Safe To Blush: will stay beyond 19f. *N. J. Henderson* **h96**

LADY OF LISLE 7 ch.m. Afzal – Holy Times (IRE) (The Parson) [2004/5 22d^{pu} 21s^{pu} 21g^{4} 24s 25g^{pu} Mar 14] no sign of ability: tried blinkered: has had tongue tied. *C. P. Morlock* **h–**

LADY OF SCARVAGH (IRE) 6 b.m. Zaffaran (USA) – Dim Drums (Proverb) [2004/5 F16m^{3} F16m^{5} F17m^{2} F16g^{6} 21g^{2} 16s 21d^{2} 23d^{pu} 24s^{6} 21d 21s* 21d c22g^{2} 24m^{3} Apr 13] leggy, workmanlike mare: sixth foal: sister to 21f hurdle winner Shelayly and half-sister to bumper winner Did You Know (by Balinger): dam, maiden hurdler/chaser who stayed 3m, half-sister to fairly useful but ungenuine hurdler La Cienaga: placed twice in bumpers: modest novice hurdler: won mares maiden at Ludlow in January: second in mares maiden at Fontwell on chasing debut: stays 3m: acts on soft and good to firm going: tried to duck out at halfway ninth start. *M. Scudamore* **c102 h99 F88**

LADY OF THE ISLE (IRE) 7 b.m. Aristocracy – Smurfette (Baptism) [2004/5 h–, F78: 17g^{ur} 16g May 30] medium-sized mare: no show over hurdles. *B. D. Leavy* **h–**

LADY PAST TIMES 5 b.m. Tragic Role (USA) – Just A Gem (Superlative) [2004/5 16g 16v^{3} 16d 16s 20s* 20s^{4} 24s Apr 20] small mare: modest maiden on Flat (stays 9f) at 3 yrs, sold out of E. Alston's stable 3,400 gns Doncaster October (2003) Sales: poor hurdler: won novice handicap at Newcastle in March: stays 2½m: raced on good going or softer (acts on soft). *D. W. Whillans* **h76**

LADY RACQUET (IRE) 6 b.m. Glacial Storm (USA) – Kindly Light (IRE) (Supreme Leader) [2004/5 F84: 19d* 19s^{F} 19m^{4} 20d^{2} 21d^{6} 22s^{3} 16d 21m^{4} 21g^{pu} Apr 14] angular mare: fair novice hurdler: won mares event at Hereford in April 2004: stays 2¾m: acts on soft and good to firm going. *Mrs A. J. Bowlby* **h103**

LADY RADMORE 6 b.m. Overbury (IRE) – Val's Jem (Golden Love) [2004/5 F17s F17s^{3} F16v 19m 20m Apr 10] sturdy mare: seventh foal: dam probably of little account: third in mares bumper at Taunton, only form. *J. G. M. O'Shea* **h– F73**

LADY SHANAN (IRE) 5 b.m. Anshan – Cothill Lady (IRE) (Orchestra) [2004/5 F–: F16d F16g^{3} 21d 20s 17s Feb 6] leggy mare: modest in bumpers: well held over hurdles. *D. A. Rees* **h– F80**

LADY SHOPPER 5 b.m. Merdon Melody – Young Whip (Bold Owl) [2004/5 16s 16g Dec 8] well held on Flat and over hurdles: sold £1,250 Ascot April Sales. *N. A. Twiston-Davies* **h–**

LADY SPEAKER 4 b.f. Saddlers' Hall (IRE) – Stormy Gal (IRE) (Strong Gale) [2004/5 F13g F17g^{5} F16s^{4} Apr 10] big, workmanlike filly: second foal: dam unraced, out of useful hurdler up to 2½m Buck Up: modest form in bumpers. *T. D. Easterby* **F82**

LADY SPUR (IRE) 6 b.m. Flying Spur (AUS) – Hasaid Lady (IRE) (Shaadi (USA)) [2004/5 F17g Apr 3] second foal: sister to 6f winner Pilgrim Princess: dam, second at 7f at 2 yrs, closely related to smart sprinter Ellens Lad: never a factor in mares bumper on debut. *J. S. Wainwright* **F–**

LADY STRATAGEM 6 gr.m. Mark of Esteem (IRE) – Grey Angel (Kenmare (FR)) [2004/5 h62: 16g⁶ 16f^pu 16d 19s^pu Mar 1] close-coupled mare: temperamental handicap hurdler: raced mainly around 2m: acts on good to firm going. *E. W. Tuer* **h63 §**

LADY TERIMOND 8 br.m. Terimon – Kitty Come Home (Monsanto (FR)) [2004/5 16g⁶ May 7] angular mare: runner-up in bumpers in 2002/3: off 18 months, looked temperamental when well held in novice on hurdling debut. *N. J. Henderson* **h–**

LADY WARD (IRE) 7 b.m. Mujadil (USA) – Sans Ceriph (IRE) (Thatching) [2004/5 h77§: 22g³ 19m² 22g^pu 17m^rtr 22s 19g* 22g^pu 19g^ur Aug 10] poor hurdler: won minor event at Newton Abbot in July: stays 2¾m: acts on soft and good to firm going: tried blinkered: usually reluctant/refuses to race: best left alone. *P. R. Rodford* **h78 §**

LADY WEST 5 b.m. The West (USA) – Just Run (IRE) (Runnett) [2004/5 h–: 16g^pu Jul 11] no show over hurdles: tried tongue tied. *Dr J. R. J. Naylor* **h–**

LADY ZEPHYR (IRE) 7 b.m. Toulon – Sorimak Gale (IRE) (Strong Gale) [2004/5 F106+: F16g* F17d* 16s² 16s* 21d* 20d³ 21s² 21d* 21s² 20s⁴ 24g Mar 18] rangy, useful-looking mare: won 3 of 4 starts in mares bumpers, including at Towcester and **h125 F106**

Mr David Langdon's "Lady Zephyr"

Bangor early in 2004/5: fairly useful novice hurdler: won mares events at Towcester and Warwick in November and Newbury (beat Mistress Banjo 6 lengths) in December: also in frame in 3 Grade 2 events: should stay beyond 21f (didn't look keen over 3m): raced on good ground or softer: has idled, twice throwing race away. *N. A. Twiston-Davies*

LAFFAH (USA) 10 b.g. Silver Hawk (USA) – Sakiyah (USA) (Secretariat (USA)) [2004/5 22g c24m^{4} c22m^{pu} Jun 25] smallish, round-barrelled gelding: winning hurdler: off over 2 years, no sign of retaining ability, including over fences (blinkered): usually tongue tied. *G. L. Moore* **c– h–**

LA FOLICHONNE (FR) 6 b.m. Useful (FR) – Allure Folle (FR) (Kenmare (FR)) [2004/5 F74: F16m 16g^{pu} 21v^{pu} 17s Feb 6] little sign of ability. *James Moffatt* **h– F–**

LAGANSIDE (IRE) 12 b.g. Montelimar (USA) – Ruby Girl (Crash Course) [2004/5 c79§, h–: c24g Feb 16] lengthy gelding: winning chaser: successful in point in March: stays 3m: unraced on firm going, acts on any other: tried visored: has had tongue tied: unreliable. *J. F. W. Muir* **c– § h–**

LAGGAN BAY (IRE) 5 b.g. Alzao (USA) – Green Lucia (Green Dancer (USA)) [2004/5 h73: 17g 17s^{6} 24d Jan 31] smallish gelding: fair on Flat (stays 2m) for J. Fox/ J. S. Moore in 2004: fair form over hurdles: should be suited by 2½m+: blinkered first 2 starts. *P. R. Rodford* **h100**

LA GITANA 5 b.m. Singspiel (IRE) – Iberian Dancer (CAN) (El Gran Senor (USA)) [2004/5 16d^{pu} Feb 19] modest on Flat (stays 13f), successful in February: no show in mares novice on hurdling debut. *A. Sadik* **h–**

LAGO 7 b.g. Maelstrom Lake – Jugendliebe (IRE) (Persian Bold) [2004/5 h87: 20g 22g May 26] compact gelding: modest hurdler at best, well beaten in 2004/5: stays 2¾m: visored/in cheekpieces last 6 starts: tried tongue tied. *James Moffatt* **h–**

LAGO DI LEVICO 8 ch.g. Pelder (IRE) – Langton Herring (Nearly A Hand) [2004/5 20m^{5} 22g 22f^{2} 26d^{pu} Oct 17] close-coupled gelding: modest hurdler: stays 2¾m: acts on firm and good to soft going: not one to trust. *C. J. Down* **h87 §**

LAGO NAM (FR) 6 gr.g. Cardoun (FR) – Rivalago (FR) (Grey Dawn II) [2004/5 h–: 27g Jul 28] no form over hurdles. *M. C. Pipe* **h–**

LAGOSTA (SAF) 5 ch.g. Fort Wood (USA) – Rose Wine (Chilibang) [2004/5 h83: 17g^{6} 20m 22g 17m^{5} 17d^{2} 17g 17d^{5} Oct 3] workmanlike gelding: poor maiden hurdler: possibly best around 2m: acts on good to firm and good to soft going: blinkered last 5 outings. *G. M. Moore* **h81**

LAHARNA 5 b.g. Overbury (IRE) – Royal Celt (Celtic Cone) [2004/5 F18s^{4} 19d^{pu} 16m Apr 2] €6,200 3-y-o: leggy gelding: fourth foal: half-brother to winning pointer by Roscoe Blake: dam lightly-raced maiden jumper: won second of 2 starts in maiden Irish points in 2004: sold 28,000 gns Doncaster May Sales: fair form when fourth in bumper at Plumpton: no show both starts over hurdles. *Miss E. C. Lavelle* **h– F91**

LAHINCH LAD (IRE) 5 ch.g. Bigstone (IRE) – Classic Coral (USA) (Seattle Dancer (USA)) [2004/5 F17d F16s 20v 16d 21d^{6} 20d 22s^{6} 24s 20d^{4} Jan 26] €13,000 3-y-o: fourth foal: half-brother to 2m winner Citrine (by Selkirk): dam unraced, out of half-sister to very smart middle-distance stayers Bright Finish and Shining Finish: well held in 2 bumpers: modest maiden hurdler, left C. Swan after fifth start: stays 2½m. *B. G. Powell* **h87 F–**

LAHOB 5 ch.g. First Trump – Mystical Song (Mystiko (USA)) [2004/5 18s^{5} 16s Jan 11] modest maiden on Flat (stays 1½m), sold out of P. Howling's stable 2,800 gns Newmarket Autumn Sales: well beaten in 2 novice hurdles. *N. B. King* **h–**

LAKE IMPERIAL (IRE) 4 b.g. Imperial Ballet (IRE) – Lakes of Killarney (IRE) (Ahonoora) [2004/5 16d Jan 15] good-topped gelding: no show in maiden on Flat or juvenile on hurdling debut. *Mrs H. Dalton* **h–**

LAKE 'O' GOLD 6 ch.m. Karinga Bay – Ginka (Petoski) [2004/5 h–: 23d^{3} 21m^{2} 22g^{4} May 31] poor maiden hurdler: best efforts around 2½m on good to firm going. *D. W. Thompson* **h77**

LAKIL BOY (IRE) 5 b.g. Presenting – Tinerana Noble (IRE) (Al Hareb (USA)) [2004/5 16d 20s^{5} 22v^{5} 20v^{5} 20m^{5} 24s^{pu} Mar 13] second foal: dam unraced: bumper winner: modest maiden hurdler: stays 2¾m: acts on heavy going, probably on good to firm. *C. F. Swan, Ireland* **h93**

LAKIL HOUSE (IRE) 5 b. or br.g. Accordion – Own Gale (IRE) (Torenaga) [2004/5 F16s* Jan 6] first foal: dam unraced, from family of Irish National winner Garoupe: fairly useful form when winning bumper at Thurles on debut by 3 lengths from Monoceros. *J. Bleahen, Ireland* **F101**

LALAGUNE (FR) 6 b.m. Kadalko (FR) – Donatella II (FR) (Brezzo (FR)) [2004/5 h109: 22d^{6} c20d^{4} c19s^{5} c22s^{4} 22d^{pu} 20d^{pu} Apr 20] good-topped mare: fair hurdler: let down by jumping and just modest form at best over fences: effective at 2m to 2¾m: acts on heavy going. *A. King* **c87 x h108**

LA LAMBERTINE (FR) 4 b.f. Glaieul (USA) – Mesoraca (IRE) (Assert) [2004/5 15s^{3} 15d^{4} 17d* 17g^{5} 17d^{2} 17m^{4} 17m* 16d* 16d^{2} 16s^{2} 16g 21g^{F} Apr 14] leggy filly: sixth foal: half-sister to winning hurdler/chaser around 2m Crystal Clara (by Northern Crystal): dam, 1¼m winner, half-sister to useful 2m hurdler Romancer: no form on Flat: fair hurdler: won claimer at Auteuil (claimed from R. Caget €20,000) in June, juvenile seller at Taunton in November and novice handicap at Sandown in December: best efforts when runner-up subsequently: raced mainly around 2m: has won on good to firm going, best form on softer than good: usually wears headgear: carries head awkwardly: ungenuine. *M. C. Pipe* **h113 §**

LA MARETTE 7 ch.m. Karinga Bay – Persistent Gunner (Gunner B) [2004/5 h83: 21g^{6} 21g^{bd} c16d^{R} 22d^{4} 16s^{2} 19s^{3} 16v^{5} 21s^{5} 19s^{3} 21s^{3} 20s* Apr 16] sturdy mare: handicap hurdler: won at Bangor in April: tailed off when refusing 3 out on chasing debut (in cheekpieces): barely stays 2¾m: acts on any going: has run creditably when tongue tied: reliable. *John Allen* **c– h87**

LA MARIANNE 5 b.m. Supreme Leader – Belle Magello (FR) (Exit To Nowhere (USA)) [2004/5 F16v* F16s^{2} Mar 27] first foal: dam unraced half-sister to several winners, including fairly useful hurdler/chaser up to around 2½m Litchanine and useful French hurdler Grand Patron: fairly useful form in bumpers at Fairyhouse: won mares event on debut by 4½ lengths from Kinger Rocks: neck second to Avoca Mist 2 months later. *J. R. H. Fowler, Ireland* **F103**

LAMBHILL STAKES (IRE) 7 gr.g. King's Ride – Summerhill Express (IRE) (Roselier (FR)) [2004/5 h89: c17g^{5} Apr 30] rangy gelding: maiden hurdler: fifth in novice handicap on chasing debut: stays 3m: acts on heavy going: races freely: sold 16,500 gns Doncaster May Sales, unseated in point in January. *J. M. Jefferson* **c79 + h–**

LAMBRINI BIANCO (IRE) 7 br.g. Roselier (FR) – Darjoy (Darantus) [2004/5 c–, h–: c21m^{pu} c26v^{pu} Apr 17] leggy gelding: bumper winner: no form over hurdles or in chases: placed in points in 2005: should be suited by 2½m+: tried in cheekpieces. *Mrs L. Williamson* **c– h–**

LAMBRINI MIST 7 gr.g. Terimon – Miss Fern (Cruise Missile) [2004/5 h–: 20s c24d^{4} c24s Jan 20] winning pointer: no form over hurdles: possibly flattered when fourth in steadily-run novice chase at Musselburgh: tried in cheekpieces. *Mrs L. Williamson* **c– h–**

L'AMI (FR) 6 ch.g. Lute Antique (FR) – Voltige de Nievre (FR) (Brezzo (FR)) [2004/5 c22g^{F} c21s 20s^{5} c21s^{ur} c17s c21s* c21v^{2} c24d* c24g^{F} c24s* c24g^{4} c25d^{3} Apr 8] **c145 h121**

Going to three out in the Royal & SunAlliance Chase, it still looked possible that second favourite L'Ami could give his dam a notable double at the Cheltenham Festival. His brother Kelami had won the William Hill Handicap the previous day but, in the event, L'Ami wasn't able to match that achievement, proving one paced once ridden and finishing just over six lengths fourth to Trabolgan, nonetheless confirming himself a smart young chaser. Given his age—he is still just six—there may yet be more to come, particularly over further and possibly on softer ground (raced mainly on soft and heavy otherwise), though the SunAlliance was L'Ami's sixteenth start over fences and few runners in that race can ever have been so experienced. L'Ami had done the majority of his racing at Auteuil, his first twelve starts over fences and his one appearance over hurdles all coming at the Paris track, after he had contested four non-thoroughbred races on the Flat (the French version of bumpers), in which he had Lacdoudal, Hautclan and Kadount among his opponents. Having been beaten three quarters of a length on his debut over fences, in September 2003, it took L'Ami fourteen months and eleven runs over fences before he got off the mark, winning a handicap under joint top weight. That was L'Ami's best performance to that point but still represented just fairly useful form

December Novices' Chase, Lingfield—the first of two successful British raids by L'Ami (No.2), chased home by Distant Thunder (No.5) and Tribal Venture

and, though he showed further improvement when second in a minor event next time out, it was not until his attentions were switched to Britain that L'Ami revealed his full merit.

L'Ami ran three times before the SunAlliance and won both completed starts, the Grade 2 December Novices' Chase at Lingfield, in which he started 14/1 and successfully conceded 7 lb to the favourite Distant Thunder, and a novice at Warwick, in which he comfortably defeated Control Man, who had been unbeaten

Friends of Roscoe Harvey Memorial Novices' Chase, Warwick—Control Man (visor) and Home James have nothing left to give two out

on his completed starts over fences. In between the wins, L'Ami had made mistakes before falling at halfway in the Feltham at Kempton. After Cheltenham, L'Ami could manage no more than a respectable effort when favourite in the Mildmay Novices' at Aintree, finishing third to Like-A-Butterfly, travelling well but not finding much after letting the winner have first run. He wasn't seen out subsequently at Auteuil.

L'Ami (FR) (ch.g. 1999)	Lute Antique (FR) (b 1985)	No Lute (b 1978)	Luthier
			Prudent Miss
		Sweet Annie (ch 1980)	Pharly
			Beronaire
	Voltige de Nievre (FR) (br 1987)	Brezzo (b 1979)	Gift Card
			Brezette
		Jivati (ch 1975)	Laniste
			Une Veine

The step up to three miles looked the main reason for L'Ami's improvement on his French form and, with very limited opportunities beyond two and three quarter miles at Auteuil, and, given his connections, a campaign in good staying handicaps in Britain must be on the cards for 2005/6. It may even be that L'Ami will meet his brother over fences, though the pair have already run against one another on L'Ami's sole start over hurdles, L'Ami finishing fifth, three places ahead of Kelami in what was essentially a prep race for chasers in September, at the start of the Auteuil season. *F. Doumen, France*

LAMPION DU BOST (FR) 6 b.g. Mont Basile (FR) – Ballerine du Bost (FR) (Fast (FR)) [2004/5 $16s^{4}$ $20s^{6}$ 20v 19d 18d 16s Mar 11] good-topped ex-French gelding: first foal: dam won twice at 1¾m over hurdles in French Provinces: in frame all 6 starts over fences, winning minor event at Montier-En-Der in 2003/4: left G. Macaire, easily best effort over hurdles in Britain when fourth in novice at Ayr: raced up to 2½m on good going or softer. *A. Parker* **c– h93 d**

LAMPOS (USA) 5 b. or br.g. Southern Halo (USA) – Gone Private (USA) (Private Account (USA)) [2004/5 $16d^{5}$ 16d $19g^{5}$ 20s Dec 26] modest on Flat (stays 2m): well held over hurdles: wore cheekpieces after debut. *Miss J. A. Camacho* **h–**

LAMP'S RETURN 6 ch.m. Bob's Return (IRE) – Lampstone (Ragstone) [2004/5 F95: $F16d^{2}$ $F17s^{2}$ 16d* $16s^{2}$ 19d $16d^{4}$ Apr 3] unfurnished mare: placed all 3 starts in bumpers: modest novice hurdler: won mares event at Wincanton in December: likely to prove best around 2m. *A. King* **h98 F91**

LA MUETTE (IRE) 5 b.m. Charnwood Forest (IRE) – Elton Grove (IRE) (Astronef) [2004/5 h71: $16g^{5}$ $16s^{3}$ 16v 16g Mar 4] lengthy mare: poor maiden hurdler: will prove best around 2m: acts on soft going. *M. Appleby* **h74**

LANCASHIRE LASS 9 b.m. Lancastrian – Chanelle (The Parson) [2004/5 c77, h80: 19d $26m^{4}$ Jun 9] poor maiden hurdler: well held only start over fences: stays 3m: acts on good to firm going: tried blinkered: inconsistent. *J. S. King* **c– h– §**

LANCASTRIAN JET (IRE) 14 b.g. Lancastrian – Kilmurray Jet (Le Bavard (FR)) [2004/5 c107: c25d* $c24s^{2}$ $c24s^{ur}$ c24s Mar 27] rangy gelding: useful hunter chaser nowadays: won at Hereford in April 2004: off 10 months, good second to Balinova at Huntingdon: stays 4m: acts on heavy going: raced right-handed nowadays: front runner. *H. D. Daly* **c112**

LANCE (IRE) 7 b.g. Old Vic – Gaye Le Moss (Le Moss) [2004/5 F100: $19g^{3}$ 22m* 24g* Jul 5] bumper winner: fair form over hurdles: won maiden at Navan in May and novice at Roscommon in July: stays 3m: acts on good to firm going: looked likely to progress but not seen out again. *N. Meade, Ireland* **h111 +**

LANCE TOI (FR) 6 br.g. Lampon (FR) – Devant Spring (FR) (Spring To Mind (USA)) [2004/5 c16g $c18m^{3}$ $c18f^{4}$ $c17g^{2}$ c20f c16v $c16s^{pu}$ Mar 11] ex-Irish gelding: fifth foal: brother to fairly useful chaser around 2½m Depeche Toi and half-brother to winner up to around 1½m Hemaintenant (by Quitte Et Passe): dam lightly-raced maiden: modest novice hurdler/chaser: left E. O'Grady after sixth start: won point in February: stays 2½m: acts on soft and good to firm going. *G. D. Hanmer* **c86 h–**

LANCIER D'ESTRUVAL (FR) 6 ch.g. Epervier Bleu – Pommette III (FR) (Trac) [2004/5 h–, F75: $24g^{pu}$ 16f $21s^{4}$ $22d^{5}$ $21g^{pu}$ $22d^{2}$ Mar 26] rather leggy gelding: first form **h72**

over hurdles when second in novice handicap at Newton Abbot: stays 2¾m: acts on good to soft going. *J. C. Tuck*

LAND OF NOD (IRE) 4 b.f. Barathea (IRE) – Rafif (USA) (Riverman (USA)) [2004/5 16s 16d 16g 17g Apr 15] maiden on Flat, left G. Butler after final start at 3 yrs: well held in juvenile hurdles. *G. Brown* **h–**

LAND ROVER LAD 7 ch.g. Alflora (IRE) – Fililode (Mossberry) [2004/5 h90?, F70: 25g 20d^{3} 23d 20s^{4} c24d^{5} c25v^{6} Jan 28] medium-sized gelding: poor maiden hurdler: well held both starts over fences: stays 2½m: raced on good going or softer: blinkered in 2004/5: unreliable. *C. P. Morlock* **c– § h80 §**

LANGDON LANE 4 b.f. Overbury (IRE) – Snowdon Lily (Town And Country) [2004/5 F17s Apr 7] unfurnished filly: first foal: dam, poor handicap chaser, stayed 3¼m: no show in listed mares bumper on debut. *P. R. Webber* **F–**

L'ANGE AU CIEL (FR) 6 b.g. Agent Bleu (FR) – Epopee II (FR) (Comrade In Arms) [2004/5 c117p, h–: c20s^{F} c16d* c16g c16s c20g^{F} Apr 22] big, good-topped gelding: reportedly chipped a bone and off a year after winning novice chase on British debut in 2003/4: running well when falling 3 out in intermediate handicap won by Massac at Windsor: progressed further when beating Supreme Developer a neck in handicap at Sandown in February, coming from behind in strongly-run race: little impact in better contested handicaps after: should prove effective at 2½m. *P. F. Nicholls* **c133 h–**

LANHEL (FR) 6 ch.g. Boston Two Step (USA) – Umbrella (FR) (Down The River (FR)) [2004/5 F84: F16d Feb 4] workmanlike gelding: modest in bumpers: off over a year before running poorly in February: difficult ride. *J. Wade* **F–**

LANICENE (FR) 6 b.g. Moon Madness – Ocylla (FR) (Medford (FR)) [2004/5 F–: 20v^{6} 16d^{pu} Nov 24] no form in bumper or over hurdles. *Ferdy Murphy* **h–**

LANMIRE GLEN (IRE) 8 b.g. Jurado (USA) – Cool Glen (Furry Glen) [2004/5 c110, h–: c20s^{pu} c24s^{pu} c24v c24v^{4} Jan 9] fairly useful handicap chaser: stays 3½m: acts on heavy going. *F. Flood, Ireland* **c115 h–**

LANMIRE TOWER (IRE) 11 b.g. Celio Rufo – Lanigans Tower (The Parson) [2004/5 c–§, h–: c25g^{pu} 21m^{6} 26g^{6} 21s^{6} 23d^{2} c28s^{pu} c24s^{ro} 21d^{3} c21s^{5} 22s^{3} c22d^{2} c19g* c20s^{2} c21d Mar 24] workmanlike gelding: modest handicap hurdler/chaser nowadays: won over fences at Doncaster in March: effective at 19f to 4m: acts on good to firm and heavy ground: usually wears headgear: has refused to race/run out: not one to trust. *S. Gollings* **c82 h89**

LANNIGANS LOCK 4 b.g. Overbury (IRE) – Lacounsel (FR) (Leading Counsel (USA)) [2004/5 F19s^{3} F16d^{2} F18m^{5} Apr 21] ex-Irish gelding: first foal: dam, lightly-raced maiden on Flat, half-sister to useful chaser/winning hurdler Luzcadou, stays 31f: fairly useful form first 2 starts in bumpers, left M. Kelly after debut. *R. Rowe* **F97**

LANNKARAN (IRE) 12 b.g. Shardari – Lankarana (Auction Ring (USA)) [2004/5 c106, h–: c25d^{pu} Apr 29] useful-looking gelding: veteran chaser, useful at best: tried blinkered. *H. D. Daly* **c– h–**

LANOS (POL) 7 ch.g. Special Power – Lubeka (POL) (Milione (FR)) [2004/5 h84: 16g 16g 16m^{2} 17g 17g 16s^{pu} 17m^{pu} 17s Jan 20] smallish, angular gelding: poor maiden hurdler: raced around 2m: acts on good to firm and soft going: sometimes blinkered/visored: has had tongue tied. *P. Wegmann* **h78**

L'ANTARTIQUE (FR) 5 b.g. Cyborg (FR) – Moomaw (Akarad (FR)) [2004/5 F16v* F16v* F16s^{4} 16v^{2} 16v^{2} 20d Mar 10] €74,000 3-y-o: workmanlike gelding: fourth foal: brother to winning hurdler Cyborg de Sou, stays 21f: dam won at 1¼m on Flat and up to 2½m over hurdles in France: useful in bumpers, winning at Tralee in August and Listowel in September: apparently best effort over hurdles when 25 lengths second of 6 to long odds-on Hardy Eustace in Grade 2 at Gowran fifth start: should stay beyond 2m: acts on heavy going: not straightforward. *Anthony Mullins, Ireland* **h117 F107**

LANTAUR LAD (IRE) 11 b.g. Brush Aside (USA) – Gleann Oge (Proverb) [2004/5 c25g^{pu} c25s^{4} c24d c24s^{pu} c20g Mar 16] useful-looking gelding: novice chaser: off over 2½ years, mostly let down by jumping in 2004/5: stays 3m. *A. King* **c87**

LANTERN LAD (IRE) 9 b.g. Yashgan – Lantern Lass (Monksfield) [2004/5 c–, h–: c26v^{F} c24s* c25v^{F} c24v^{5} c25s^{pu} c20d^{4} c20v* c20v Feb 15] rangy gelding: poor maiden hurdler: poor chaser: won handicaps at Uttoxeter in November and Newcastle in February: should stay beyond 3m: acts on heavy going: tried blinkered, usually in cheekpieces nowadays: inconsistent. *R. Ford* **c84 h–**

LANTERN LEADER (IRE) 10 b.g. Supreme Leader – Lantern Line (The Parson) [2004/5 c89, h102: 24d 24g 22g^{5} 21d^{pu} Aug 9] winning hurdler: maiden chaser: unseated twice in points in February: often wears headgear. *Miss Lucinda V. Russell* **c– h–**

LANZLO (FR) 8 b. or br.g. Le Balafre (FR) – L'Eternite (FR) (Cariellor (FR)) [2004/5 h92: 16d 20s^{6} 20s^{2} 24d^{2} 25d^{ur} 24g^{co} 24g^{3} Apr 15] small, angular gelding: modest handicap hurdler: stays 3m: acts on any going. *James Moffatt* **h95**

LA PERROTINE (FR) 5 b.m. Northern Crystal – Haratiyna (Top Ville) [2004/5 F92: F16s* F16d^{3} 21v* 21v* 21v* 21m^{6} Apr 2] good-topped mare: fair form in bumpers, won mares race at Hexham in November: fair form when successful in mares novices at Sedgefield first 3 starts over hurdles: will stay 3m: acts on heavy going. *J. Howard Johnson* **h111 F94**

LA PROFESSORESSA (IRE) 4 b.f. Cadeaux Genereux – Fellwah (IRE) (Sadler's Wells (USA)) [2004/5 16s^{pu} 17s^{pu} 16d^{4} 16d^{2} 16d^{6} 17d 17d^{pu} Mar 26] leggy filly: modest maiden on Flat (stays 9f): modest juvenile hurdler: raced around 2m on going softer than good: bled from nose final outing. *Mrs P. N. Dutfield* **h83**

LARAD (IRE) 4 br.g. Desert Sun – Glenstal Priory (Glenstal (USA)) [2004/5 17d^{6} Jul 17] compact gelding: half-brother to 2m hurdle winner Lord Alyn (by Topanoora): modest on Flat (stays 13f): in cheekpieces, tailed off in juvenile on hurdling debut. *J. S. Moore* **h–**

L'ARCHER 7 b.g. Lancastrian – Sailors Joy (Handsome Sailor) [2004/5 h–, F71: 20m 19g^{pu} Oct 30] medium-sized gelding: no form over hurdles: tried in cheekpieces: often tongue tied. *A. E. Jessop* **h–**

LARCH (IRE) 5 b.g. Luso – Riah (Furry Glen) [2004/5 F16d^{6} F16d 16d^{F} Apr 3] good sort: eighth foal: half-brother to hunter chase winner Leodotcom (by Safety Catch), stays 25f: dam unraced: modest form in 2 bumpers: fell second on hurdling debut: bred to stay beyond 2m. *Miss H. C. Knight* **h– F79**

LARKSONG 6 ch.m. Opera Ghost – Gipsy Dawn (Lighter) [2004/5 F17g^{6} Oct 14] third foal: half-sister to 3m hurdle winner Alfa Sunrise (by Alflora) and 21f hurdle winner Early Start (by Husyan): dam, winning hurdler, stayed 2½m: tailed off in bumper on debut. *G. B. Balding* **F–**

LA ROSE 5 b.m. Among Men (USA) – Marie La Rose (FR) (Night Shift (USA)) [2004/5 h77: 16g^{pu} 20g^{pu} Jul 14] sturdy mare: maiden hurdler: failed to complete in 2 points. *J. W. Unett* **h–**

L'ARTISTE BELLEVUE (FR) 6 b.g. Start Fast (FR) – Enus du Manoir (FR) (Le Nain Jaune (FR)) [2004/5 F–: 20s^{F} 21d 21d 24v^{pu} Feb 20] leggy gelding: no sign of ability: tried in blinkers/cheekpieces. *Jean-Rene Auvray* **h–**

LASCAR DE FERBET (FR) 6 br.g. Sleeping Car (FR) – Belle de Ferbet (FR) (Brezzo (FR)) [2004/5 F90: 20v^{5} 16v 20v 16d^{6} Jan 28] leggy gelding: fair form in bumpers in 2003/4 for L. Lungo: poor form in novice hurdles. *R. Ford* **h83**

LASKA DE THAIX (FR) 6 gr.g. Saint Preuil (FR) – Orca II (FR) (Danoso) [2004/5 c20s^{6} 19s^{2} 24d^{3} 24d* c33g^{bd} Mar 17] lengthy, well-made ex-French gelding: fifth foal: half-brother to 1¼m/1½m winner Belle Orca (by Mont Basile): dam, winning chaser up to 21f, sister to dam of useful chaser around 2½m Glinka de Thaix: modest maiden hurdler/chaser for G. Cherel: best effort in novice hurdles in Britain, fairly useful form when winning at Exeter in March by 12 lengths from Lord Killeshana: broke leg when brought down in National Hunt Chase at Cheltenham: stayed 3m: dead. *P. J. Hobbs* **c105 h129**

LASKARI (FR) 6 b.g. Great Palm (USA) – Hatzarie (FR) (Cyborg (FR)) [2004/5 h97: 16s^{4} 19s c19s* c19v^{3} c18d^{5} c19m* c20g^{4} Apr 22] tall, workmanlike gelding: modest form in novice hurdles: fair chaser: won novices at Taunton (handicap) in January and Hereford in April: will stay beyond 2½m: acts on heavy and good to firm ground. *Mrs L. C. Taylor* **c114 h97**

LASQUINI DU MOULIN (FR) 6 gr.g. Saint Preuil (FR) – Api (FR) (El Badr) [2004/5 h111, F91: 20m^{3} 20g* Jul 11] fair hurdler: won minor event at Tipperary in July: raced mainly around 2½m: acts on soft and good to firm going. *W. P. Mullins, Ireland* **h111**

LASTING LADY (IRE) 9 b. or br.m. Supreme Leader – Lasting Legacy (Buckskin (FR)) [2004/5 24v^{pu} Dec 15] lightly raced and poor form over hurdles: raced mainly around 2m: dead. *J. Howard Johnson* **h–**

LASTING MELODY (IRE) 4 ch.g. Accordion – Singing Forever (Chief Singer) [2004/5 F16s Mar 22] strong gelding: fifth foal: dam, winning hurdler who stayed 2½m, half-sister to smart 5f to 7f filly Blue Siren: no show in bumper on debut. *T. P. Tate* **F–**

LAST SYMPHONY 8 b.g. Last Tycoon – Dancing Heights (IRE) (High Estate) [2004/5 17g^{pu} Jun 7] leggy gelding: no form over hurdles: sold £1,100 Ascot July Sales: won point in April. *W. J. Reed* **h–**

LATALOMNE (USA) 11 ch.g. Zilzal (USA) – Sanctuary (Welsh Pageant) [2004/5 c144d, h128: c20d^{5} c16d^{5} c16d^{2} c16g c16g^{5} Apr 14] leggy gelding: fairly useful handicap chaser nowadays: best efforts in 2004/5 when second to Bonus Bridge and tenth to Fota Island in Grand Annual, both at Cheltenham: best form around 2m: acts on good to firm and good to soft going: tried blinkered/visored. *N. Wilson* **c120 h–**

LATE ARRIVAL 8 b.g. Emperor Jones (USA) – Try Vickers (USA) (Fuzzbuster (USA)) [2004/5 16d Feb 3] poor on Flat in 2004: no form over hurdles. *M. D. Hammond* **h–**

LATE CLAIM (USA) 5 ch.g. King of Kings (IRE) – Irish Flare (USA) (Irish River (FR)) [2004/5 h96: 20d^{6} May 15] good-topped gelding: fair juvenile hurdler in 2003/4: no show only start in 2004/5: raced mainly around 2m: raced only on good/good to soft going: visored once. *R. T. Phillips* **h–**

LATEEN 10 b.m. Midyan (USA) – Sail Loft (Shirley Heights) [2004/5 c21d^{pu} Feb 18] of little account. *Mrs E. M. Collinson* **c– h–**

LATEFA (IRE) 5 ch.m. Among Men (USA) – Kraemer (USA) (Lyphard (USA)) [2004/5 F–: F17g F17g Jul 12] angular mare: soundly beaten in bumpers, left Mrs L. Taylor after reappearance. *C. A. Horgan* **F–**

LATENSAANI 7 b.g. Shaamit (IRE) – Intoxication (Great Nephew) [2004/5 c90, h–: 19g 20f c24d^{F} 24s^{pu} c22s^{2} c20s^{F} Dec 26] leggy gelding: winning hurdler/chaser: off 15 months before reappearance: best effort in 2004/5 when runner-up in handicap chase at Market Rasen: stays 2¾m: acts on firm and soft going. *Mrs S. J. Smith* **c106 h91**

LATHYRUS (FR) 5 b.g. Roi de Rome (USA) – Provenchere (FR) (Son of Silver) [2004/5 F16s F17d^{5} 17g Apr 7] 12,000 4-y-o: rather unfurnished gelding: first foal: dam won 3 times around 2m over hurdles in France: better effort in bumpers when fifth in maiden at Taunton: seventh of 14 in maiden there on hurdling debut. *H. D. Daly* **h82 F75**

LATIMER'S PLACE 9 b.g. Teenoso (USA) – Pennethorne Place (Deep Run) [2004/5 c20s^{F} c21g* Nov 15] sturdy gelding: winning hurdler: fairly useful novice chaser: off nearly 2 years before reappearance: trained by G. Balding prior to winning at Folkestone in November by 1½ lengths from Inca Trail: stays 21f: raced on good ground or softer. *J. A. Geake* **c121 h–**

LATIN QUEEN (IRE) 5 b. or br.m. Desert Prince (IRE) – Atlantic Dream (USA) (Muscovite (USA)) [2004/5 16s^{4} 17g^{4} 17g^{5} 19s^{2} 17s^{2} 19m* Mar 14] modest on Flat (barely stays 1½m): fair hurdler: landed odds in mares maiden at Taunton in March: best form when second to Medison in novice on same course previous outing: stays 19f: acts on soft and good to firm ground. *J. D. Frost* **h107**

LATITUDE (FR) 6 b.m. Kadalko (FR) – Diyala III (FR) (Quart de Vin (FR)) [2004/5 c116+, h–: c20s^{3} c22d^{3} c19v^{F} c21s c24g^{F} c20s^{3} c24s c26v^{2} Apr 22] angular mare: fairly useful handicap chaser: stays 3¼m: acts on heavy ground: tried blinkered: sometimes let down by jumping. *M. C. Pipe* **c121 h–**

LA TORTUGA 8 b.g. Turtle Island (IRE) – Ville Sainte (FR) (Saint Estephe (FR)) [2004/5 17g^{ur} 16m Jun 13] half-brother to winning hurdler in Italy by Unfuwain: fair at 2 yrs, below form on Flat in 2000 for W. M. Brisbourne/A. Berry: tailed off in 2 novice hurdles. *C. J. Price* **h–**

LATTERLY (USA) 10 b.g. Cryptoclearance (USA) – Latest Scandal (USA) (Two Davids (USA)) [2004/5 c21m^{pu} May 19] angular gelding: bad maiden jumper: tried in blinkers/cheekpieces: usually tongue tied. *I. Bostock* **c– h–**

LATZOD'ALM (FR) 6 b.g. Passing Sale (FR) – Enea d'Alm (FR) (Djarvis (FR)) [2004/5 20s^{2} 23d^{4} 20v^{6} 24v^{3} 22d^{pu} 24d^{5} Mar 8] ex-French gelding: second foal: dam unraced, from family of top-class French chaser Jasmin II: fair maiden hurdler/chaser: left J. Bertran de Balanda prior to reappearance: stays 23f: raced on going softer than good (acts on soft): blinkered final start. *D. P. Keane* **c– h103**

LAUDAMUS 7 ch.g. Anshan – Faint Praise (Lepanto (GER)) [2004/5 F69: 16s 22v^{3} 20d 22s* 22d* 24m^{6} Apr 13] tall, rather sparely-made gelding: modest form over hurdles: won novice handicaps at Exeter in March and Wincanton in April: should stay 3m: acts on soft going. *R. H. Alner* **h97**

LAUDERDALE 9 b.g. Sula Bula – Miss Tullulah (Hubble Bubble) [2004/5 c103, h–: c17m^{pu} c17g^{4} c17v* c16d^{2} c16g^{F} c17v^{4} c16v^{2} c20v* c20s^{3} c16s^{6} c17d Apr 11] good- **c99 h–**

topped gelding: modest handicap chaser: won at Kelso in October and Newcastle (fortunate) in February: effective at 2m (given a test) to 3m: acts on heavy going: usually front runner/races prominently: reliable. *Miss Lucinda V. Russell*

LAUGHERNE BANK (IRE) 5 b.g. Zaffaran (USA) – Cyrano Imperial (IRE) (Cyrano de Bergerac) [2004/5 F16d 16v 22gpu Apr 12] £21,000 4-y-o: unfurnished gelding: third foal: half-brother to bumper winner Beyond The Pale (by Be My Native): dam unraced: no sign of ability. *T. R. George* **h– F–**

LAUNDMOWER 9 br.g. Perpendicular – Sound Work (Workboy) [2004/5 h79: 20dpu Apr 25] maiden hurdler: stays 2½m. *R. Bastiman* **h–**

LAUREL VIEW (IRE) 7 b.g. Arctic Lord – Solmus (IRE) (Sexton Blake) [2004/5 F16m* 16m* 20d* 20s* 20vpu 22s4 Mar 28] fairly useful in bumpers, won at Navan in May: fair hurdler: awarded maiden at Galway in July: successful in similar event at Ballinrobe in August and listed novice at Limerick in October: stayed 2¾m: acted on soft and good to firm going: dead. *N. Meade, Ireland* **h114 F101**

LAUREN'S PRINCE (IRE) 9 ch.g. Roselier (FR) – Miss Doogles (Beau Charmeur (FR)) [2004/5 c23s6 c20v c25vpu c27vco c24m5 c28d5 c29spu Mar 12] no form over hurdles: winning pointer: poor maiden chaser: stays 3½m: acts on good to soft going: tried blinkered: has had tongue tied: probably ungenuine. *Liam Lennon, Ireland* **c81 § h–**

LAURIER D'ESTRUVAL (FR) 6 ch.g. Ragmar (FR) – Grive d'Estruval (FR) (Quart de Vin (FR)) [2004/5 c?, h106: 21d5 16d3 c20spu c20v6 c16v* c16s* Mar 7] maiden hurdler: fair form over fences: won minor event at Leicester and handicap at Hereford in March: best efforts at 2m: raced on going softer than good (acts on heavy): tongue tied third outing. *S. E. H. Sherwood* **c100 h94**

LAVENOAK LAD 5 b.g. Cloudings (IRE) – Halona (Pollerton) [2004/5 F16d F16g 24m6 20d 25spu Dec 18] €15,500 3-y-o, £10,000 4-y-o: lengthy gelding: first foal: dam, fairly useful hurdler who stayed 19f, half-sister to useful hurdler/chaser up to 21f Major Rumpus: no show in bumpers or novice hurdles. *P. R. Rodford* **h– F–**

L'AVENTURE (FR) 6 b. or br.m. Cyborg (FR) – Amphitrite (FR) (Lazer (FR)) [2004/5 c119, h107: c24d* 24s* 25d c26s2 c29v4 c29s6 c28s4 c33d4 c36d Apr 9] leggy, angular mare: useful chaser on her day: won intermediate at Uttoxeter in May: best efforts when runner-up to One Knight and fourth to Silver Birch in valuable handicaps at Chepstow fourth and fifth starts: fairly useful hurdler: much improved when winning handicap at Chepstow in October by 16 lengths from Barneys Lyric: stays 33f: acts on good to firm and heavy going: usually blinkered and tongue tied: not a fluent jumper of fences: hard ride, usually soon off bridle. *P. F. Nicholls* **c137 § h129 §**

LA VITA E BELLA (FR) 6 b.m. Le Nain Jaune (FR) – Fontaine Aux Faons (FR) (Nadjar (FR)) [2004/5 h–, F–: 27gpu 19spu 22dpu May 17] no sign of ability: wore cheekpieces last 2 outings. *G. F. H. Charles-Jones* **h–**

LAWAAHEB (IRE) 4 b.g. Alhaarth (IRE) – Ajayib (USA) (Riverman (USA)) [2004/5 16s 17m4 Nov 25] workmanlike gelding: modest on Flat (stays 1½m), successful in March: better effort in juvenile hurdles when fourth in seller at Taunton. *B. R. Johnson* **h79**

LAWGIVER (IRE) 4 b.g. Definite Article – Marylou Whitney (USA) (Fappiano (USA)) [2004/5 16s6 16d 16g6 17g2 16d* Apr 11] no form on Flat: modest hurdler: won handicap at Kelso in April: will probably prove best at 2m: acts on good to soft going. *T. J. Fitzgerald* **h96**

LAWMAN 7 b. or br.g. Afzal – Discipline (Roman Warrior) [2004/5 F–: F16m Jun 29] smallish, plain gelding: little sign of ability in bumpers: successful in point in April. *A. M. Hales* **F–**

LAWOOD (IRE) 5 gr.g. Charnwood Forest (IRE) – La Susiane (Persepolis (FR)) [2004/5 16g 17s Jan 20] good-bodied gelding: fairly useful on Flat (stays 1½m), sold out of K. Ryan's stable 29,000 gns Newmarket July Sales: poor form in 2 novice hurdles. *C. J. Mann* **h81 +**

LAYASAR 5 br.g. Wizard King – Rasayel (USA) (Bering) [2004/5 F92: F16m5 16spu 16g 16vpu 17s5 Mar 7] fairly useful at best in bumpers for W. M. Brisbourne: no form over hurdles, including in seller: headstrong. *P. F. Nicholls* **h– F80**

LAZY BUT LIVELY (IRE) 9 br.g. Supreme Leader – Oriel Dream (Oats) [2004/5 c109x, h117: 20g6 c26d* 24v3 c24d3 24d* c24v4 23s Feb 19] medium-sized gelding: fairly useful handicap chaser/hurdler: successful over fences at Uttoxeter in May and **c117 x h117**

betfair.com Jockeys' Challenge Handicap Hurdle, Aintree—
a successful return to hurdles for Lazy But Lively, who gets first run on Hautclan (centre)

hurdles at Aintree (8 lb out of weights, beat Hautclan by 2 lengths) in November: stays 3¼m: probably best on going softer than good: often let down by jumping over fences. *R. F. Fisher*

LAZY LENA (IRE) 6 b.m. Oscar (IRE) – Magnum Gale (IRE) (King's Ride) [2004/5 16g 16g $16g^6$ $17m^6$ Apr 23] small mare: first foal: dam unraced: well held in bumpers and over hurdles, left D. Loughnane after reappearance. *Miss L. C. Siddall* **h72**

LEADAWAY 6 b.g. Supreme Leader – Annicombe Run (Deep Run) [2004/5 h–, F–: $16g^6$ $20v^6$ $18s^4$ $19g^4$ Mar 9] leggy gelding: poor maiden hurdler: bred to stay 3m. *A. Parker* **h70 +**

LEADERS WAY (IRE) 10 b.g. Supreme Leader – Mind Me Back (Kambalda) [2004/5 $16d^4$ $18s^5$ 20d* $20s^5$ 16v* $22v^2$ $20s^2$ $20s^5$ $18s^3$ 16s 20s* Apr 13] sturdy gelding: pulled up only start over fences: fairly useful handicap hurdler: won at Fairyhouse in November, January and April: probably best up to 2¾m: raced on good going or softer (acts on heavy): usually wears cheekpieces. *T. K. Geraghty, Ireland* **c– h117**

LEADING LIGHT 5 ch.g. Classic Cliche (IRE) – Rochestown Lass (Deep Run) [2004/5 F16s Oct 13] fifth foal: half-brother to winning hurdler/chaser Madam Mosso (by Le Moss), stays 3¼m: dam fair staying hurdler: tailed off in bumper on debut. *P. T. Dalton* **F–**

LEADING MAN (IRE) 5 b.g. Old Vic – Cudder Or Shudder (IRE) (The Parson) [2004/5 F87: 20s $20v^2$ $20v^4$ $24v^2$ 20s* Apr 20] workmanlike gelding: fair hurdler: won maiden at Perth in April: should stay 3m: raced on going softer than good (acts on heavy). *Ferdy Murphy* **h110**

LEADING RUN (IRE) 6 b.g. Supreme Leader – Arctic Run (Deep Run) [2004/5 F16v* Nov 21] brother to 2¼m hurdle winner Super Run and half-brother to 3 winners, notably smart chaser/useful hurdler Strong Run (by Strong Gale), stays 2½m: dam unraced: won bumper at Navan on debut in November by 4½ lengths from Silent Oscar: looked useful prospect but not seen out again. *N. Meade, Ireland* **F112 p**

LEADING THE WAY (IRE) 8 ch.g. Mister Lord (USA) – Ramble Along (IRE) (Milk of The Barley) [2004/5 c20d c17d* $c20s^4$ $c24v^2$ $c24v^4$ $c16s^{ur}$ Mar 13] IR 40,000 4-y-o: tall gelding: first foal: dam, 2¼m hurdle winner, from family of top-class 3m chaser Marlborough: winning pointer: fairly useful chaser: always close up when winning maiden at Fairyhouse in November: best effort when ¾-length second to Forget **c116**

The Past in Grade 1 novice at Leopardstown: stays 3m: raced on going softer than good (acts on heavy): tongue tied last 3 starts, also in blinkers final one. *Oliver McKiernan, Ireland*

LEAD IN THE HEAD (IRE) 6 ch.g. Carroll House – Vermont River (IRE) (Over The River (FR)) [2004/5 F16g^2 17s^6 Nov 2] €1,900 3-y-o: second foal: dam, poor maiden hurdler, half-sister to fairly useful chaser up to 2¾m Stormin' Native: well beaten in maiden Irish points: staying-on second in bumper at Ludlow on debut: well held in novice hurdle at Exeter following month. *J. D. Frost* **h– F82**

LEAPOGUES LADY (IRE) 9 b.m. Chakiris (USA) – Canhaar (Sparkler) [2004/5 18g^{ur} 16d 18g^6 21d 24s* Apr 20] sparely-made mare: modest handicap hurdler: off a year before reappearance: easily best effort in 2004/5 when winning amateur event at Perth in April: stays 3m: acts on soft and good to firm going. *C. A. McBratney, Ireland* **h94**

LEAP YEAR LASS 5 ch.m. Fleetwood (IRE) – Lady Phyl (Northiam (USA)) [2004/5 h71: 17g^2 19m^4 Jun 9] smallish mare: poor maiden hurdler: stays 19f: acts on soft and good to firm going: sketchy jumper. *C. Grant* **h76**

LEASE 7 ch.g. Lycius (USA) – Risanda (Kris) [2004/5 h102: 20m^4 16g^4 19m^2 20s^3 16m^3 21d 20m^6 24v^{pu} Dec 27] angular gelding: fair handicap hurdler: stays 21f: acts on good to firm and good to soft going: tried blinkered/in cheekpieces: consistent. *J. G. Carr, Ireland* **h106**

LEASE BACK (FR) 6 b.g. Sleeping Car (FR) – Salse Pareille (FR) (Perouges (FR)) [2004/5 24s^2 Apr 16] ex-French gelding: seventh foal: half-brother to 17f chase winner Babati (by Royal Charter): dam maiden half-sister to dam of very smart hurdler/useful chaser up to 2¾m Homme du Jour: won 4-y-o non-thoroughbred chases at Dieppe and Le Lion d'Angers for G. Cherel: fair form when 1½ lengths second to Rowley Hill in novice hurdle at Bangor on British debut: stays 3m: raced on good going or softer. *L. Wells* **c– h106**

LEATHERBACK (IRE) 7 b.g. Turtle Island (IRE) – Phyllode (Pharly (FR)) [2004/5 c26m^{pu} May 19] compact gelding: winning 2m hurdler: successful twice in points in 2005: acts on soft going. *J. M. Turner* **c– h–**

L'EAU DU NIL (FR) 4 b.g. Kadounor (FR) – Lamakara (FR) (Akarad (FR)) [2004/5 17d^3 c17s^4 16s^5 Mar 23] ex-French gelding: fourth foal: brother to fairly useful hurdler/chaser Or d'Eau, probably stays 2½m, and half-brother to 2¾m hurdle winner Eaux Les Coeurs (by Saint Cyrien): dam, 10.5f to 1½m winner, half-sister to smart middle-distance filly La Monalisa: once-raced on Flat: in frame in 3-y-o hurdle and chase at Pau for J-P. Totain: fifth of 15 in novice hurdle at Chepstow on British debut, travelling well long way. *P. J. Hobbs* **c? h103**

LE BIASSAIS (FR) 6 b.g. Passing Sale (FR) – Petite Fanfan (FR) (Black Beauty (FR)) [2004/5 F94: 16s^2 17v^2 16v^2 20v* 20s^2 22s^2 Apr 3] rangy gelding: fair novice hurdler: won at Newcastle in February: stays 2¾m: raced on ground softer than good (acts on heavy). *L. Lungo* **h110**

LE CHATELIER (FR) 6 b.g. Kadalko (FR) – Tulipp d'Avril (FR) (Saumon (FR)) [2004/5 c17g^6 c21s^{pu} c20s^6 c20s^4 c18s^F c20s^3 19s^{pu} 25s^{pu} Jan 27] fifth foal: half-brother to 3 winners, including winning hurdler/very smart chaser up to 2¾m Fulip (by Cap Martin) and useful 2m hurdler Ilico II (by Trebrook): dam 11f winner on Flat: 11.5f winner on Flat: maiden chaser: fair hurdler: sold out of F. Doumen's stable €10,000 Goffs (France) November Sale: pulled up both subsequent starts: stays 2½m: acts on soft ground: tried blinkered. *A. W. Carroll* **c86 h–**

LECHE BOTTES (FR) 6 b.g. Sleeping Car (FR) – Gibelotte (FR) (Royal Charter (FR)) [2004/5 h104: 22g^3 17s^3 17g^2 17g^3 21g^F Oct 4] angular gelding: fair maiden hurdler: rider banned for failing to obtain best possible placing when third in maiden at Newton Abbot on fourth start: running best race when falling 2 out in handicap at Plumpton next time (finished lame): probably stays 21f: ungenuine. *M. C. Pipe* **h108 §**

LE COUDRAY (FR) 11 b.g. Phantom Breeze – Mos Lie (FR) (Tip Moss (FR)) [2004/5 c164, h–: c21v c29s^{pu} c36d^{pu} Apr 9] rangy, good-topped gelding: high-class chaser in 2003/4: off 11 months, no show in handicaps in 2004/5: stays 3m: raced on good going or softer (acts on heavy): tongue tied: held up. *C. Roche, Ireland* **c– h–**

LE COUESNON (FR) 6 ch.g. Esteem Ball (FR) – Sweet Cashmere (FR) (Kashmir II) [2004/5 24f^{pu} Sep 5] half-brother to several winners, including useful hurdler Sun Surfer (by R B Chesne), stays 3m: dam successful twice up to around 1½m on Flat: lightly raced and little sign of ability. *F. Doumen, France* **h–**

LE DUC (FR) 6 b.g. Villez (USA) – Beberova (FR) (Synefos (USA)) [2004/5 c138§, h129§: c20s^4 c20d 20s^4 c24s^{pu} c21d* c21s 20d^3 c20d c21g^F c21d^3 c24s^3 c16g Apr 23] **c141 § h135 §**

tall, good-topped gelding: impresses in appearance: useful hurdler, good efforts both starts in 2004/5: useful handicap chaser: best effort when winning Unicoin Homes Handicap at Cheltenham in January by 4 lengths from Redemption: mainly ran creditably otherwise, taking well to course when 6 lengths third to Cregg House in Topham Chase at Aintree tenth start: stays 21f: acts on good to firm and heavy going: tried blinkered: consistent but doesn't always apply himself fully. *P. F. Nicholls*

LE FOREZIEN (FR) 6 b.g. Gunboat Diplomacy (FR) – Diane du Forez (FR) (Quart de Vin (FR)) [2004/5 c108, h–: 22s^{3} 24g^{3} Jul 14] winning chaser in France: maiden hurdler. *C. J. Gray* **c–** **h–**

LE FRERE (IRE) 10 gr.g. Lord Americo – Rosa Joyner (Roselier (FR)) [2004/5 c20f^{2} c16s^{F} c18s c18v^{4} c16v* c16v^{5} c16v* c16s^{F} c20s^{F} Mar 26] fairly useful handicap chaser: successful at Punchestown in December and Naas in February: stays 2½m: acts on good to firm and heavy going. *P. J. Stokes, Ireland* **c115** **h–**

LEFT BANK (IRE) 9 ch.g. Over The River (FR) – My Friend Fashion (Laurence O) [2004/5 c84§, h–§: c25g^{5} c21m^{F} c20d^{pu} Oct 21] sturdy gelding: ungenuine handicap chaser: in frame in points in 2005: stays 25f: possibly needs good going or firmer: tried in headgear. *K. G. Reveley* **c– §** **h– §**

LEFT TO HIMSELF 7 b.g. Be My Native (USA) – Premier Nell (Mandamus) [2004/5 c17g^{6} c21s Apr 7] €42,000 4-y-o: good-topped gelding: half-brother to fairly useful staying chaser Jimmy O'Dea (by Funny Man): dam unraced daughter of useful staying chaser Matchboard, the grandam of Morley Street and Granville Again: fair bumper winner: successful once from 4 starts in Irish points: no form over hurdles or in chases: has worn cheekpieces: tried tongue tied: sold 9,500 gns Doncaster May Sales. *J. L. Hassett, Ireland* **c–** **h–**

LE GALACTICO (FR) 4 br.g. Sleeping Car (FR) – Guendale (FR) (Cadoudal (FR)) [2004/5 F12d^{2} F16s^{3} F16m^{2} Apr 2] tall, useful-looking gelding with scope: fourth foal: half-brother to 3 winners, notably high-class hurdler/winning chaser Crystal d'Ainay (by Saint Preuil), stays 25f: dam lightly-raced maiden over hurdles: fairly useful form when placed in bumpers. *A. King* **F99**

LEGALIS (USA) 7 ch.g. Gone West (USA) – Loyalize (USA) (Nureyev (USA)) [2004/5 17v^{pu} 16v^{pu} Mar 29] modest on Flat (stays 7f), sold out of K. Ryan's stable 5,500 gns Doncaster March (2004) Sales: no form in 2 starts over hurdles, blinkered on second occasion. *P. Wegmann* **h–**

LEGALITY 5 b.m. Polar Falcon (USA) – Lady Barrister (Law Society (USA)) [2004/5 16d^{pu} Nov 24] half-sister to modest 2m hurdler Edipo Re (by Slip Anchor): poor on Flat (stays 1m): soon struggling in mares novice on hurdling debut. *Julian Poulton* **h–**

LEGAL RIGHT (USA) 12 b.g. Alleged (USA) – Rose Red (USA) (Northern Dancer) [2004/5 c25s^{2} c22d c33g^{pu} Apr 16] high-class chaser in 2001/2 for J. O'Neill: off 3 years, easily better effort in hunters when second to Sleeping Night at Wetherby: pulled up 4 out in Scottish Grand National at Ayr: stays 3¼m: acts on heavy and good to firm going: tongue tied. *Miss Lucinda V. Russell* **c100 +** **h–**

LEGAL SPY 6 b.g. Weld – Run Lady Run (General Ironside) [2004/5 F16d F16v F16d Mar 14] sturdy gelding: seventh foal: half-brother to winning pointer by Roselier: dam placed in points: well held in bumpers. *F. Jordan* **F–**

LEGATUS (IRE) 8 ch.g. Alphabatim (USA) – Take A Guess (IRE) (Carlingford Castle) [2004/5 c95p: c25s^{6} c24g^{2} c24v^{3} c26d^{2} c30s^{2} Feb 11] sturdy gelding: fair chaser: stays 3¾m: raced on good ground or softer (acts on heavy): wears visor: doesn't always jump fluently. *M. C. Pipe* **c103**

LE GRAND ROCHER 8 ch.g. Factual (USA) – Honey Bridge (Crepello) [2004/5 h–: 19g^{pu} Dec 30] workmanlike gelding: very lightly raced: no show in 2 novice hurdles. *Ian Williams* **h–**

LE GRIS (GER) 6 gr.g. Neshad (USA) – Lady Pedomade (GER) (Mondrian (GER)) [2004/5 h82: 16m 17m 19g^{4} 16m 16g^{5} 17v^{4} 16s^{4} 19d 24m Apr 10] neat gelding: modest maiden hurdler, left J. S. Moore after fourth start: ideally suited by 2m: acts on soft and good to firm going: wore blinkers/cheekpieces last 6 starts. *Miss G. Browne* **h86**

LEIGHTON (IRE) 5 b.g. Desert Story (IRE) – Lady Fern (Old Vic) [2004/5 17d^{6} 16s 17m Nov 11] half-brother to modest and temperamental 2m hurdler Hard To Know (by Common Grounds): fairly useful on Flat (stays 1½m): well held in novice company over hurdles: tongue tied last 2 starts: has pulled hard. *R. M. Stronge* **h–**

LEITH HILL STAR 9 ch.m. Comme L'Etoile – Sunnyday (Sunley Builds) [2004/5 c–, h95: 24s c25g* c21d^3 c25s^F c24d c24d^4 Feb 18] angular mare: modest handicap hurdler: similar form over fences: won novice handicap at Folkestone in November: stays 25f: acts on soft and good to firm going. *R. Rowe* **c95 h–**

LEITRIM ROCK (IRE) 5 b.g. Barathea (IRE) – Kilshanny (Groom Dancer (USA)) [2004/5 h–: 17d^{pu} May 9] poor and ungenuine on Flat: none too fluent in 2 starts over hurdles. *A. G. Newcombe* **h–**

LE JAGUAR (FR) 5 b.g. Freeland (FR) – Fee La Maline (FR) (Maalem (FR)) [2004/5 c16d^2 c16d^3 c19v^3 c21s^4 c23s^2 c25v^4 c24d^2 c25d* c25g^F Apr 17] tall, close-coupled gelding: fourth foal: half-brother to 2 winners, including winning hurdler around 2m Feline de La Palis (by Safir): dam 11f/1½m winner: twice-raced on Flat: won once from 2 starts in juvenile hurdles at Pau for X. T. Demeaulte in 2003/4: fairly useful novice chaser: simple task at Wincanton in April: showing improved form when falling 3 out in handicap won by Tom Sayers there next time: stays 25f: raced on good going or softer (acts on heavy): tongue tied last 5 outings. *P. F. Nicholls* **c117 + h–**

LE JOYEUX (FR) 6 br.g. Video Rock (FR) – Agra (FR) (Brezzo (FR)) [2004/5 h86? , F–: c20s^{pu} c24d^R 26s 22g^4 24m^2 Apr 10] strong gelding: no show both starts over fences: best effort over hurdles when second in handicap at Worcester: stays 3m: wore cheekpieces last 3 starts: has had tongue tied. *B. I. Case* **c– h92**

LE MINO (FR) 6 b.g. Noblequest (FR) – Minouche (FR) (Fill My Hopes (FR)) [2004/5 h–: 17d^5 Oct 27] first sign of ability over hurdles when fifth in novice at Sedgefield in October. *C. W. Thornton* **h83**

LE-MONDE (IRE) 7 br.g. Anabaa (USA) – Alexandra Fair (USA) (Green Dancer (USA)) [2004/5 c106, h117: 20g^6 24m^2 May 16] angular gelding: winning chaser: fairly useful handicap hurdler: creditable efforts both starts in 2004/5: effective at 19f to 3m: acts on good to firm and heavy going: wore headgear 5 of last 6 starts. *D. M. Leigh, Ireland* **c– h117**

LENNEL 7 b.g. Presidium – Ladykirk (Slip Anchor) [2004/5 16m^3 20d^4 17m 17g Mar 19] fair on Flat (stays 13f), successful in January: modest form over hurdles: needs to jump better. *A. Bailey* **h86**

LENNON (IRE) 5 b. or br.g. Beneficial – Stradbally Bay (Shackleton) [2004/5 F16d^2 F16m* F16s^2 F16g* F16g Mar 16] €12,000 3-y-o: tall gelding: ninth foal: brother to fairly useful hurdler Inch Pride, stays 2¾m, and half-brother to modest hurdler Goodnight Irene (by Crash Course), stays 3m, and to 2 winning pointers: dam unraced: smart form in bumpers: landed odds at Musselburgh in November (maiden) and February: best effort when 1½ lengths second to Oscar Park in listed event at Warwick in between: well held in Grade 1 at Cheltenham final start: will stay 2½m: sort to do well in novice hurdles in 2005/6. *J. Howard Johnson* **F118**

LEN ROSS 6 b.g. Bob's Return (IRE) – Instabene (Mossberry) [2004/5 F16d F16v F16m^6 Apr 10] fifth foal: dam winning pointer: best effort in bumpers (trained on debut by F. Murphy) when sixth in maiden at Worcester. *R. Lee* **F85**

LEONARDO DE VINCI (IRE) 5 b.h. Sadler's Wells (USA) – Andromaque (USA) (Woodman (USA)) [2004/5 19g* 16d^6 16s* 16v^2 16v^{ur} 20d^6 Mar 10] fairly useful hurdler: won 4-y-o maiden at Kilbeggan in May and 4-y-o minor event at Naas (beat Rocket Ship short head) in November: best effort when 6 lengths second to Royal Paradise in Grade 2 novice at Leopardstown: likely to prove best around 2m: raced on good going or softer: wore cheekpieces once: tongue tied. *E. J. O'Grady, Ireland* **h125**

LEOPARD SPOT (IRE) 7 b.g. Sadler's Wells (USA) – Savoureuse Lady (Caerleon (USA)) [2004/5 20d^2 17d^4 20d^5 c20m^{pu} c17s^4 c21v^4 c25d^4 c24s^5 Apr 20] quite good-topped gelding: modest maiden hurdler, left I. Semple after reappearance: similar form over fences: stays 25f: acts on heavy going: often in cheekpieces nowadays: tongue tied. *Miss Lucinda V. Russell* **c90 h91**

LEOPHIN DANCER (USA) 7 b.g. Green Dancer (USA) – Happy Gal (FR) (Habitat) [2004/5 h85: c16g^4 c17m^F c17m^6 c16f^4 16g^3 Oct 7] rather leggy gelding: poor hurdler/maiden chaser, generally let down by jumping over fences: will stay beyond 2m: acts on firm going: tried tongue tied. *P. W. Hiatt* **c83 h83**

LEOPOLD (SLO) 4 b.g. Solarstern (FR) – Lucera (GER) (Orofino (GER)) [2004/5 17d^3 16v^3 16s^2 16s 16d^5 16m^3 17g^{pu} 18g^6 16d^2 Apr 17] leggy gelding: maiden on Flat: modest juvenile hurdler, left C. Von Der Recke after third start: should stay beyond 17f: acts on soft and good to firm going. *M. F. Harris* **h91**

LEOS SHUIL (IRE) 8 b.m. Good Thyne (USA) – Shuil Tintreach (IRE) (Electric) [2004/5 16f[5] 22d* 18m 20s* Sep 16] lengthy, angular mare: first foal: dam, poor maiden over hurdles after birth of this foal, from family of very smart staying hurdler Shuil Ar Aghaidh: bumper winner: fair hurdler: won handicap at Killarney in July and novice at Tipperary in September: stays 2¾m: acts on soft going. *J. E. Kiely, Ireland* **h111**

LE PASSING (FR) 6 b.g. Passing Sale (FR) – Petite Serenade (FR) (Trac) [2004/5 c–, h136: c16s[3] c16d[3] c19m[2] c19v* c20v* c20g[2] c24d[5] c21g[5] c21v[3] Apr 22] good-topped gelding: useful hurdler: similar form over fences, winning maiden at Chepstow in December and handicap at Uttoxeter (beat The Villager 6 lengths) in January: best effort when second to El Vaquero in Grade 1 novice at Sandown sixth start: stays 2½m: acts on heavy and good to firm going: has twice run as if amiss: usually jumps soundly. *P. F. Nicholls* **c141 h–**

LE PRINCE 10 ch.g. Le Moss – Yuan Princess (Tender King) [2004/5 c24d[4] May 11] lengthy gelding: winning pointer: twice-raced chaser: will stay beyond 3m: raced on good going or softer. *Miss T. Spearing* **c– h–**

LE ROCHELAIS (FR) 6 ch.g. Goldneyev (USA) – Olympiade de Brion (FR) (Night And Day) [2004/5 h98: 17d[2] 20v[3] Nov 25] workmanlike gelding: fair form in novice hurdles: stays 2½m: raced on good going or softer. *R. H. Alner* **h100**

LE ROI MIGUEL (FR) 7 b.g. Point of No Return (FR) – Loumir (USA) (Bob's Dusty (USA)) [2004/5 c159, h–: 20s[5] c20d* c24g[4] c21g[5] c20d[2] c21m[2] c16g[5] Apr 23] tall, useful-looking gelding: high-class chaser: reportedly had wind operation before reappearance: better than ever when winning Grade 2 totesport Peterborough Chase at Huntingdon in November by 20 lengths from Farmer Jack: also ran well when second to Moscow Flyer in Grade 1 at Aintree fifth start: very lightly raced over hurdles, fifth to **c162 h128**

totesport Peterborough Chase, Huntingdon—
Le Roi Miguel is about to pull clear of Farmer Jack (noseband) for his sole win of 2004/5

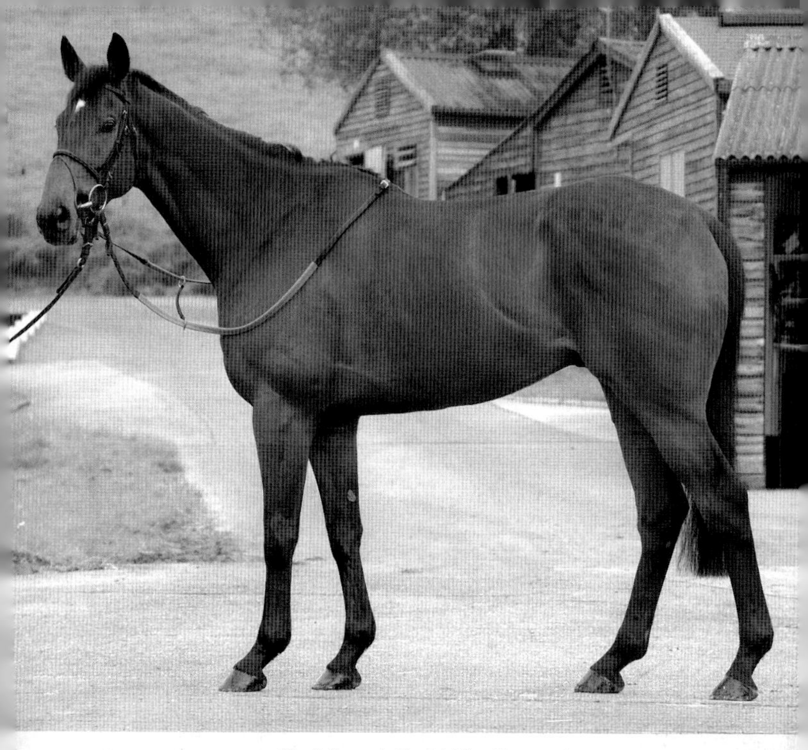

Mrs J. Stewart's "Le Roi Miguel"

Mistanoora in valuable handicap at Chepstow on reappearance: stays 21f: acts on soft and good to firm going: tried tongue tied. *P. F. Nicholls*

LE ROYAL (FR) 6 b.g. Garde Royale – Caucasie (FR) (Djarvis (FR)) [2004/5 h110: c16s⁴ c19gᶠ Dec 11] leggy gelding: fair hurdler: stumbled badly on landing 4 out when still in touch and going well in maiden at Carlisle on chasing debut: beaten when fell 4 out next time: stays 2½m: acts on heavy going: tongue tied on reappearance. *K. G. Reveley* **c111 ? h–**

LEROY'S SISTER (FR) 5 b.m. Phantom Breeze – Loumir (USA) (Bob's Dusty (USA)) [2004/5 F98: 16g⁵ 17d³ 19m² 22s⁶ 22d⁴ 21d³ Apr 18] small, close-coupled mare: modest form at best over hurdles: trained by Miss G. Browne on fifth start only: should stay beyond 19f: blinkered final outing: has hung left: sketchy jumper. *P. F. Nicholls* **h99**

LERUBIS (FR) 6 b.g. Ragmar (FR) – Perle de Saisy (FR) (Italic (FR)) [2004/5 c98d, h104d: 17d 16g⁵ 19d 16v Dec 31] leggy gelding: maiden jumper: poor form over hurdles in Britain: tried blinkered. *F. Jordan* **c– h–**

LES ARCS (USA) 5 br.g. Arch (USA) – La Sarto (USA) (Cormorant (USA)) [2004/5 17d Aug 30] fairly useful on Flat (best form at 7f), sold out of J. Gosden's stable 32,000 gns Newmarket Autumn (2003) Sales, successful in May: got very tired when well beaten in maiden on hurdling debut: likely to have stamina limitations. *R. C. Guest* **h–**

LESCER'S LAD 8 b.g. Perpendicular – Grange Gracie (Oats) [2004/5 h69, F–: 22g⁴ 27m⁶ 25m² c24gᵘʳ Apr 15] tall, lengthy gelding: poor hurdler: sold out of J. Hetherton's stable 5,700 gns Doncaster August Sales: off 11 months, unseated fifth on chasing debut: seems to stay 2¾m. *C. L. Popham* **c– h–**

LESDREAM 8 b.g. Morpeth – Lesbet (Hotfoot) [2004/5 h109: 24d³ 22s³ 24g⁴ 22d² c23spu 24d² 22v³ 22v³ Apr 22] sturdy gelding: fair handicap hurdler: pulled up in maiden on chasing debut: will stay beyond 3m: probably acts on heavy going. *J. D. Frost* **c– h114**

LE SEYCHELLOIS (FR) 5 ch.g. Mansonnien (FR) – Adjirah (FR) (Sicyos (USA)) [2004/5 18v* c16d* c16dF c16dpu Feb 19] rather leggy gelding: second foal: dam placed over 1m/maiden hurdler: fairly useful over hurdles for B. Secly, successful in valuable 4-y-o handicap at Auteuil in May: won 4-runner 4-y-o novice at Warwick on chasing debut in November by 8 lengths from Val du Don: let down by jumping in Grade 2 novices both subsequent starts: raced around 2m on going softer than good (acts on heavy). *P. F. Nicholls* **c116 h124**

LESPRIDE 7 b.g. Morpeth – Lesbet (Hotfoot) [2004/5 h–, F–: 22gpu 22spu 16s⁵ Oct 28] sturdy gelding: no form: blinkered final start. *J. D. Frost* **h–**

L'ETANG BLEU (FR) 7 gr.g. Graveron (FR) – Strawberry Jam (FR) (Fill My Hopes (FR)) [2004/5 c89§, h84§: c16fur 18mpu 18mpu c20m⁴ c17g⁵ c22s³ c19spu c20d⁶ Apr 18] leggy gelding: winning hurdler/maiden chaser, no form in 2004/5: stays easy 2¾m: acts on any going: wears cheekpieces/visor: tongue tied: ungenuine. *P. Butler* **c– § h– §**

LETHEM AIR 7 ch.g. Aragon – Llanddona (Royal Palace) [2004/5 c–: c20dpu May 13] modest pointer: no show in 2 hunter chases. *Tim Butt* **c–**

LETITIA'S LOSS (IRE) 7 ch.m. Zaffaran (USA) – Satin Sheen (Abednego) [2004/5 h90: c17vF 23d* Nov 24] plain mare: fair hurdler: won conditional jockeys handicap at Wetherby in November: fell eighth in mares novice at Kelso on chasing debut: stays 27f: acts on soft going. *N. G. Richards* **c– h100**

LET'S CELEBRATE 5 b.g. Groom Dancer (USA) – Shimmer (Bustino) [2004/5 h86: 16g 16spu Dec 18] leggy, close-coupled gelding: maiden hurdler, poor on balance of form: raced at 2m: acts on firm going. *F. Jordan* **h67**

LET'S FLY (FR) 10 b.g. Rose Laurel – Harpyes (FR) (Quart de Vin (FR)) [2004/5 c25s⁴ c24g³ Apr 7] good-topped gelding: fair pointer, successful twice in 2005: best effort in hunters when third to Sir d'Orton at Taunton: stays 3m: raced on good going or softer (acts on heavy). *Ross Oliver* **c102 h–**

LETS GET BUSY (IRE) 5 ch.m. Presenting – Mindyourown (IRE) (Town And Country) [2004/5 F17s⁶ Nov 29] €6,000 4-y-o: sixth foal: sister to bumper winner Dans Pride: dam unraced from family of useful chaser/smart hurdler up to 3m Forest Sun: soon struggling in mares bumper on debut. *J. W. Mullins* **F–**

LETS GO DUTCH 9 b.m. Nicholas Bill – Dutch Majesty (Homing) [2004/5 h–: c22spu c24s⁶ c25s² c21d c23v⁴ c25g⁴ c26vF Apr 22] workmanlike mare: winning hurdler: fair maiden chaser: will stay further than 25f: acts on heavy going. *K. Bishop* **c102 h–**

LET'S PARTY (IRE) 5 b.m. Victory Note (USA) – Mashoura (Shareef Dancer (USA)) [2004/5 17d Aug 1] fair maiden on Flat (stays 1m) at 3 yrs for P. McEntee: no form since, including in novice on hurdling debut. *P. L. Clinton* **h–**

LETSPLAY (IRE) 5 ch.g. Accordion – Pennine Sue (IRE) (Pennine Walk) [2004/5 F16d F16s⁵ F16g⁴ Mar 28] smallish gelding: second foal: dam poor Irish maiden: first form in bumpers when fourth at Huntingdon. *A. W. Carroll* **F89**

LET'S ROCK 7 b.g. Rock City – Sizzling Sista (Sizzling Melody) [2004/5 19g⁶ 21d 21d⁶ c16s⁵ c19s⁶ c25vpu c16mpu c16s³ Mar 31] £2,100 4-y-o: fourth foal: dam unraced half-sister to Soba: poor maiden pointer: little show over hurdles or in chases: tried in cheekpieces. *Mrs A. Price* **c– h–**

LETTERMAN (IRE) 5 br.g. Presenting – Papoose (IRE) (Little Bighorn) [2004/5 F16g F16d² F16d² 18v² Dec 26] close-coupled gelding: first foal: dam, winning pointer, half-sister to smart chaser Hi Cloy, out of half-sister to 1982 Champion Hurdle winner For Auction: fairly useful form in bumpers, twice runner-up in large-field events at Fairyhouse: promising second to Queen Astrid in maiden at Leopardstown on hurdling debut: soundly beaten in Grade 1 novice won by Asian Maze at Punchestown in late-April. *E. J. O'Grady, Ireland* **h124 F102**

LEVALLOIS (IRE) 9 b.g. Trempolino (USA) – Broken Wave (Bustino) [2004/5 c–, h–: c24s⁵ c24d³ c28s² c27s² c24s c29v⁴ c24s⁵ 20s Mar 23] smallish gelding: winning hurdler: fairly useful chaser nowadays: runner-up to Brave Spirit in handicaps at Fontwell and Taunton in January: stays 3½m: raced mainly on going softer than good (acts on heavy). *P. Winkworth* **c115 x h–**

LEVITATOR 4 b.c. Sadler's Wells (USA) – Cantilever (Sanglamore (USA)) [2004/5 16s* Mar 29] leggy colt: fair on Flat (stays 1¾m), successful in August, sold out of **h114**

Sir Michael Stoute's stable 60,000 gns Newmarket Autumn Sales: won juvenile at Fairyhouse in March on hurdling debut comfortably by 4½ lengths from Tous Les Tables: reportedly suffering from respiratory tract infection when soundly beaten in similar event at Punchestown in late-April. *M. J. P. O'Brien, Ireland*

LEWIS ISLAND (IRE) 6 b.g. Turtle Island (IRE) – Phyllode (Pharly (FR)) [2004/5 c–, h120§: 16g^3 19d^2 Mar 14] well-made gelding: unseated second only start over fences: fairly useful hurdler at best: placed in sellers in 2004/5: stays 2½m: acts on good to firm and heavy going: not one to rely on. *B. Ellison* **c– h88 §**

LEWIS MEAD 6 b.g. Sir Harry Lewis (USA) – Normead Lass (Norwick (USA)) [2004/5 F16g May 16] well held in bumpers. *Stef Liddiard* **F–**

LEWS A LADY 7 ch.m. Sir Harry Lewis (USA) – Pretty Gayle (Midland Gayle) [2004/5 F–: F17d Oct 27] tailed off in bumpers. *D. Eddy* **F–**

LEWSHER 5 b.m. Sir Harry Lewis (USA) – Sheraton Girl (Mon Tresor) [2004/5 F16g F16v 24d^{pu} Mar 24] second foal: dam 7f winner: no sign of ability in bumpers and novice hurdle. *M. Mullineaux* **h– F–**

LEYLAND COMET (IRE) 7 b. or br.g. Roselier (FR) – Firey Comet (IRE) (Buckskin (FR)) [2004/5 F–: 24v^4 24d 24v^4 c27v* c32v^F Mar 17] poor form in novice hurdles: improved effort when winning maiden at Sedgefield in January on completed outing over fences: will stay 4m: acts on heavy going: sold 10,500 gns Doncaster May Sales. *Ferdy Murphy* **c94 h79**

LIATHROIDISNEACHTA (IRE) 5 b.g. Accordion – Anozira Gold (IRE) (Camden Town) [2004/5 F17s^4 F16s* Mar 5] €54,000 3-y-o: sturdy gelding: first foal: dam, dual bumper winner, from family of top-class hurdler/chaser Danoli: very much caught the eye under sympathetic handling in bumper on debut: won 5-runner similar event at Huntingdon 3 months later by short head from Campaign Charlie. *Jonjo O'Neill* **F90**

LIBERIA (FR) 6 b.g. Kadalko (FR) – Unica IV (FR) (Quart de Vin (FR)) [2004/5 20v^5 Dec 30] second foal: dam won twice around 1½m on Flat in France: once-raced on Flat: maiden hurdler, second in 4-y-o event at Auteuil in October 2003, final start for G. Cherel: fifth of 11 in novice at Haydock on British debut. *N. J. Henderson* **h90**

LIBERMAN (IRE) 7 b.g. Standiford (USA) – Hail To You (USA) (Kirtling) [2004/5 h100x: 17d* 17d^{ur} 22g* 22s* 22g 24g^6 Mar 17] progressive form in handicap hurdles in 2004/5, winning at Tralee in August (trained by T. Mullins, also successful on Flat there previous week) and Market Rasen in September and November, beating Patriarch Express by 2 lengths on last occasion: better effort in valuable events after when sixth of 22 to Oulart in Pertemps Final at Cheltenham: stays 3m: acts on soft going, simple task on good to firm: not a fluent jumper. *M. C. Pipe* **h126**

LIBERTHINE (FR) 6 b.m. Chamberlin (FR) – Libertina (FR) (Balsamo (FR)) [2004/5 c107p, h–: c20s^2 c20d^3 c21s c22v^4 c21g* c21d Apr 8] angular mare: useful handicap **c136 h–**

Mildmay of Flete Handicap Chase, Cheltenham—
25/1-shot Liberthine takes over from the fading Brooklyn Breeze;
also pictured are Scots Grey (right), runner-up Banker Count (star on cap) and the about-to-fall Le Duc

Mr Robert Waley-Cohen's "Liberthine"

chaser: won 22-runner Mildmay of Flete Handicap Chase at Cheltenham in March by 7 lengths from Banker Count: badly hampered tenth (Becher's) when never dangerous in Topham Chase at Aintree 3 weeks later: stays 21f: raced on good ground or softer (acts on soft): ridden by Mr S. Waley-Cohen in 2004/5. *N. J. Henderson*

LIBERTINE LADY 8 b.m. Perpendicular – Distant Cherry (General Ironside) [2004/5 16g 19v^pu Oct 17] lengthy mare: third foal: dam, poor novice staying hurdler, half-sister to fairly useful staying chaser Royal Tommy: no show in novice company over hurdles. *H. P. Hogarth* **h–**

LIBERTY BEN (IRE) 5 b.g. Beneficial – Silver Fairy (IRE) (Lancastrian) [2004/5 F16d 17d 19s^5 Jan 31] useful-looking gelding, unfurnished at present: second foal: dam unraced: eighth of 14 in 4-y-o bumper at Newbury on debut: better effort in novice hurdles when fifth to Almah at Exeter. *Miss E. C. Lavelle* **h91 F89**

LIBERTY FLAG (FR) 6 gr.g. Dadarissime (FR) – Ellora du Clos (FR) (Al Riad (FR)) [2004/5 F16g^2 F20f^3 F20g* F20m^3 F16m^2 F16d^5 20g 22s* 20s^2 24v 22s^4 20s^4 Mar 5] second foal: half-brother to 11.5f to 14.5f winner Jelissio (by Dadarissime): dam unraced: fairly useful in bumpers, winning at Gowran in June: fair hurdler: won 20-runner maiden at Down Royal in November: stays 2¾m: acts on soft going (placed in bumper on firm): has broken blood vessels. *P. J. Flynn, Ireland* **h106 F104**

LIBERTY SEEKER (FR) 6 ch.g. Machiavellian (USA) – Samara (IRE) (Polish Patriot (USA)) [2004/5 h115: c16f* c17m* c17g 16m* c16s^F 16g Apr 16] good-topped gelding: modest maiden on Flat: fairly useful hurdler: left P. Niven, improved effort when winning handicap at Kelso in October: earlier won novices at Perth and Market Rasen on first 2 starts over fences: less fluent and little impact in stronger **c114 h126**

company third and fifth outings: will prove best around 2m, probably with emphasis on speed. *P. Monteith*

LIBERTY'S MELODY 8 ch.m. Gildoran – Music Interpreter (Kampala) [2004/5 26dpu 24g May 16] lengthy, plain mare: no form: off 2 years before reappearance. *Mrs S. M. Johnson* **h–**

LIBRE 5 b.g. Bahamian Bounty – Premier Blues (FR) (Law Society (USA)) [2004/5 h68: 17g5 16m5 Sep 19] leggy gelding: fairly useful on Flat (stays 9.4f), successful 3 times in late-2004: poor form over hurdles: blinkered, claimed to rejoin F. Jordan £6,000 final start: also tried in cheekpieces (failed to impress with attitude) and tongue strap. *R. C. Guest* **h69**

LIFE OF A RIVER (IRE) 12 b.g. Over The River (FR) – Myelife (Le Bavard (FR)) [2004/5 c20gur May 13] ex-Irish gelding: winning pointer: maiden hurdler/chaser, formerly trained by E. Macnamara: stays 2¾m: acts on heavy ground. *S. Wynne* **c– h–**

LIFTED WAY 6 b.g. In The Wings – Stack Rock (Ballad Rock) [2004/5 16gpu Mar 16] fairly useful on Flat (raced mainly at 7f/1m), successful twice in 2004: looked non-stayer on hurdling debut. *P. R. Chamings* **h–**

LIGHT DES MULOTTES (FR) 6 gr.g. Solidoun (FR) – Tango Girl (FR) (Tip Moss (FR)) [2004/5 h90x, F99: 19d6 18m2 c20s* c20d* c19s2 c24gpu Mar 16] leggy gelding: modest novice hurdler, has been let down by jumping: left O. Sherwood, successful in novices at Uttoxeter (handicap, idled) in October and Southwell in November on first 2 starts over fences: faltered and caught near line at Hereford next time: stays 2½m: acts on soft and good to firm going: blinkered last 5 outings. *C. R. Egerton* **c109 h84 x**

LIGHTENING RETURNS 6 ch.m. Bob's Return (IRE) – Sally Smith (Alias Smith (USA)) [2004/5 F–: F16g Apr 26] well beaten in bumpers. *S. A. Brookshaw* **F–**

LIGHT HEARTED LILY 6 b.m. Deploy – Darling Splodge (Elegant Air) [2004/5 h76, F79?: 19dpu c24dpu Feb 9] lengthy mare: poor maiden hurdler: no show on chasing debut: stays 23f: acts on soft and good to firm ground. *R. M. Beckett* **c– h–**

LIGHTIN' JACK (IRE) 7 ch.g. Beneficial – Cillrossanta (IRE) (Mandalus) [2004/5 h91: 20v 22s4 c20g4 c22g4 Apr 1] rather leggy gelding: thrice-raced over hurdles, well held in 2004/5: fair form on both starts over fences: stays 3m. *Miss E. C. Lavelle* **c105 h–**

LIGHTNING FORK (IRE) 8 gr.m. Common Grounds – Bahia Laura (FR) (Bellypha) [2004/5 20m4 16m5 20g6 Jun 10] sister to smart 7f/1m performer Amicable and fairly useful Irish 1¼m/1½m winner Bali Breeze: dam, French 10.5f winner, closely related to smart French performer up to 1¼m Benicia: little sign of ability, including in points. *B. I. Case* **h–**

LIGHTNING STAR (USA) 10 b.g. El Gran Senor (USA) – Cuz's Star (USA) (Galaxy Libra) [2004/5 c–, h86: 16v2 18m* 16g* 17s4 17g2 20m2 16m Aug 30] angular gelding: modest hurdler: won seller at Fontwell in May and ladies handicap at Uttoxeter in June: stays 2¾m: acts on any going: blinkered: often looks less than keen. *G. L. Moore* **c– h95**

LIGHT REFLECTIONS 12 b.g. Rainbow Quest (USA) – Tajfah (USA) (Shadeed (USA)) [2004/5 c29spu c25vpu 25gpu Mar 14] tall gelding: maiden hurdler/winning chaser: no sign of retaining ability after near 3-year absence: tried visored/in cheekpieces. *P. G. Murphy* **c– h–**

LIGHTS ON 9 b. or br.g. Young Man (FR) – Lady Eccentric (IRE) (Magical Wonder (USA)) [2004/5 20d5 23m3 c16d5 Jun 1] winning pointer: no other form. *M. W. Easterby* **c– h–**

LIKE A BEE (IRE) 7 b.g. Montelimar (USA) – Dasdilemma (IRE) (Furry Glen) [2004/5 h116, F96: c20s* c22s3 c16s5 c24s2 Mar 5] angular gelding: fairly useful hurdler: fair form over fences: won maiden at Stratford in October: stays 3m: raced only on good to soft/soft going. *C. Roche, Ireland* **c108 h–**

LIKE A BREEZE 6 bl.m. Bob Back (USA) – Whatagale (Strong Gale) [2004/5 F82: F16g5 24dF Mar 12] rather unfurnished mare: modest form in bumpers: 4 lengths down and yet to be asked for effort when falling heavily 3 out in novice at Chepstow on hurdling debut. *C. J. Down* **h– p F82**

LIKE-A-BUTTERFLY (IRE) 11 b.m. Montelimar (USA) – Swifts Butterfly (Furry Glen) [2004/5 c16s* c17vpu c24g5 c20s* c25d* Apr 8] **c136 + h–**

At an age when most mares have long since swapped the racecourse for the paddocks, Like-A-Butterfly returned from more than eighteen months off the track with a tendon injury to embark on a belated novice chasing campaign. Her racing

Powers Gold Cup Chase, Fairyhouse—
Tony McCoy is at his strongest as Like-A-Butterfly (hoops) overhauls Forget The Past

career may be continuing longer than that of most mares, but it had begun later than most as well, Like-A-Butterfly not making her debut in a bumper until after she had turned seven. Already a Grade 1 winner in a bumper and over hurdles, it was perhaps no surprise that connections persevered with Like-A-Butterfly in search of a win at the top level over fences as well. She is a big, rangy mare, one who had always looked a chaser in the making, by a sire, Montelimar, who has been responsible for two of the last three Grand National winners.

The Grade 1 success over fences came eventually, but Like-A-Butterfly had been forced to miss a large part of the season, between Boxing Day and the Cheltenham Festival, with a blood disorder. Her chasing career got off to a fine start when she ran out an impressive winner of a maiden chase at Naas in November and she started a short-priced favourite for the following month's Grade 1 Durkan New Homes Novices' Chase at Leopardstown. Unfortunately, she ran as though clearly sickening for something, dropping away after a mistake five out and eventually being pulled up. The Arkle had been Like-A-Butterfly's intended Festival target, though given her less than ideal preparation she was diverted instead to what looked an easier alternative in the Royal & SunAlliance Chase, even though that meant tackling three miles for the first time. Like-A-Butterfly wasn't obviously beaten by lack of stamina but could only stay on at one pace into fifth, more than eight lengths behind Trabolgan, having been poised behind the leaders three out. It was a useful effort on just her third start over fences, but her trainer gave a prosaic assessment afterwards: 'She's not a patch on the Like-A-Butterfly she used to be . . . you've got to be realistic. She's eleven and retirement is now an option.'

The option was not taken up and, while Like-A-Butterfly failed to better the form she showed at Cheltenham in her two subsequent starts, the next three weeks put a completely different complexion on her season. Less than a fortnight after the Royal & SunAlliance, Like-A-Butterfly was turned out for the Grade 1 Powers Gold Cup at Fairyhouse over two and a half miles, for which she started the 7/2 favourite. It was a competitive thirteen-runner affair, but not a particularly high quality one, despite the presence of three runners who had already won Grade 1 events in Ireland earlier in the season. Two of them, Forget The Past and Watson Lake, ended up chasing Like-A-Butterfly home. Forget The Past kicked clear in the straight with Like-A-Butterfly in pursuit, and it was only going to the last that she closed the gap after the leader had made a crucial mistake two out. Responding to strong pressure, under Tony McCoy at his most persuasive, Like-A-Butterfly led close home to beat Forget The Past half a length, with Watson Lake six lengths back in third. Incidentally, Like-A-Butterfly received only 5 lb as a sex allowance from her male rivals in Ireland compared to 7 lb in the races she contested in Britain.

Like-A-Butterfly looked to have had a hard race at Fairyhouse, but just ten days later she took another good prize, the Grade 2 John Smith's Mildmay Novices' Chase at Aintree over three miles and a furlong. In the absence of the first three from the Royal & SunAlliance, it was L'Ami, who had finished a place ahead of Like-A-Butterfly in that race, who started the 7/2 favourite, with Like-A-Butterfly a 6/1 chance. The placed horses from the Jewson Novices' Handicap at the Festival, Lacdoudal and See You Sometime, were also in the field, and it was the latter, much the longer-priced of the pair, who proved the biggest threat. Like-A-Butterfly improved to take the lead from him two out and ran on strongly, though she had to be kept up to her work on the run-in as the runner-up battled on. Like-A-Butterfly kept on gamely to win by a length and three quarters, with L'Ami beaten another length and a half in third, well clear of Lacdoudal.

In defeating See You Sometime (himself a ten-year-old), Like-A-Butterfly became the oldest winner of the Mildmay since the ten-year-old Delius won in 1988, in fact the oldest winner of a graded novice chase since the first fully-fledged Anglo-Irish pattern was officially adopted in 1999/2000. Like-A-Butterfly is also

John Smith's Mildmay Novices' Chase, Aintree—clearly none the worse for her Fairyhouse exertions as she holds off See You Sometime (noseband) and L'Ami

one of the oldest mares to perform at a high level over fences in recent seasons. Another Irish mare, Opera Hat, showed smart form at the same age in 1999 when fourth in the Melling Chase at Aintree, a race she had won the year before. Three eleven-year-old mares were placed in the Grand National during the twentieth century, the most recent being Eyecatcher who was third (for the second year running) to Red Rum in 1977. She was finally retired a year later after being brought down at the first in the Topham.

Perhaps Like-A-Butterfly's switch to the paddocks would have been hastened if her family background had been one of success at stud, but, as previous Annuals have pointed out, her family was a poor one. Not even Martin Pipe could conjure anything better than poor form out of her dam Swifts Butterfly. One relative not previously mentioned in these pages though is Like A Bee, a fairly useful hurdler who made a winning debut over fences at Stratford in the latest season for Like-A-Butterfly's connections. He is out of a sister to Swifts Butterfly, and is also by Montelimar. Like-A-Butterfly's humble origins are irrelevant now, and thanks to her own efforts on the track she has earned a covering from a top stallion when the time comes. If her offspring inherit just some of her merit and are as genuine, they will be worth looking forward to. But talk of Like-A-Butterfly's stud career would still seem to be premature at this stage. She was due to run at Punchestown shortly after the end of the British season before a pulled muscle ruled her out of that engagement. Her trainer gave no indication, however, that her racing career is to be ended just yet.

Another season's racing for Like-A-Butterfly has the potential for more risks than rewards. Her record means she deserves to be campaigned at the top level, but her form over fences is no better than useful and her mare's allowance (without which, in theory, she wouldn't have won either at Fairyhouse or Aintree incidentally) will not be enough to make up for that. Rising twelve, it is hard to

Mr J. P. McManus' "Like-A-Butterfly"

Like-A-Butterfly (IRE) (b.m. 1994)	Montelimar (USA) (b 1981)	Alleged (b 1974)	Hoist The Flag
			Princess Pout
		L'Extravagante (br 1973)	Le Fabuleux
			Fanfreluche
	Swifts Butterfly (b 1985)	Furry Glen (b 1971)	Wolver Hollow
			Cleftess
		Baloney (ch 1974)	Balidar
			Bay Pearl

think she will improve much, if at all, despite the fact that she has run in just five chases. Like-A-Butterfly has been a credit to her connections, her record now standing at twelve wins from seventeen starts. She is suited by a good test at two miles and stays three miles and a furlong, and she acts on heavy ground whilst yet to run on firmer than good. She is held up and sometimes idles, but there is no question of her being anything other than genuine. *C. Roche, Ireland*

LIKE A LORD (IRE) 7 b. or br.g. Arctic Lord – Likashot (Celtic Cone) [2004/5 h101, F73: 22g² 20g³ 20vpu 21d² Dec 7] angular gelding: fair novice hurdler: will stay 3m: acts on good to soft going, ran poorly on heavy. *Mrs S. J. Smith* **h101**

LIKE THE BUZZ (IRE) 7 b.m. Lord Americo – Crash Course Katie (IRE) (Crash Course) [2004/5 26m⁶ 22g⁴ 22m⁴ c25m⁴ 26f⁶ Sep 26] fourth foal: dam unraced: successful 4 times in points, including 3 in 2004: poor form over hurdles: jumped with little confidence on chasing debut: tried in cheekpieces. *Evan Williams* **c– h61**

LIK WOOD POWER (NZ) 8 b.g. Bigstone (IRE) – Lady Paloma (USA) (Clever Trick (USA)) [2004/5 h100: c19m* c20m* c20m c16m³ 16g² c20d c16m Sep 24] useful-looking gelding: fair maiden hurdler: fairly useful chaser: won maiden at Hereford and handicap at Wetherby in May: well held last 2 starts: should prove at least as effective at 2m as 2½m: acts on good to firm going. *R. C. Guest* **c118 h103**

LILAC 6 ch.m. Alhijaz – Fairfield's Breeze (Buckskin (FR)) [2004/5 h78: 16gF 16vpu 16dpu 26m⁵ 21g Mar 28] smallish mare: poor handicap hurdler: no form in 2004/5, wore cheekpieces last 2 starts: should stay 2½m. *R. J. Price* **h–**

LILAC LADY 8 b.m. Weld – Lilac Wood (Precipice Wood) [2004/5 21g Mar 28] lengthy, angular mare: no form outside points: tried tongue tied. *N. P. Littmoden* **h–**

LILIAN ROSE 6 b.m. Shaddad (USA) – Blennerville (IRE) (General View) [2004/5 F16v Jan 8] first foal: dam winning pointer: showed nothing in bumper on debut. *C. N. Kellett* **F–**

LILIUM DE COTTE (FR) 6 b.g. Ragmar (FR) – Vanille de Cotte (FR) (Italic (FR)) [2004/5 c110+, h–: c20spu 21spu 21g 24dpu Apr 8] good-topped gelding: useful hurdler at best: pulled up both starts over fences after winning on debut: should have stayed beyond 17f: acted on heavy going: dead. *N. J. Henderson* **c– h117**

LILLEBROR (GER) 7 b.g. Top Waltz (FR) – Lady Soliciti (GER) (Solicitor (FR)) [2004/5 h–: 16g* 16spu Jan 2] close-coupled gelding: modest on Flat: form over hurdles only when easily landing gamble in novice handicap at Plumpton in October: possibly unsuited by soft/heavy going. *B. J. Curley* **h96**

LI'L LEES (IRE) 4 ch.g. Lake Coniston (IRE) – Kayrava (Irish River (FR)) [2004/5 17mpu Sep 1] well beaten in maidens at 2 yrs, sold out of I. Semple's stable 1,000 gns Doncaster May (2004) Sales: showed nothing on hurdling debut. *N. J. Hawke* **h–**

LILY GREY (FR) 6 gr.m. Kadalko (FR) – Volmerange (FR) (Grandchant (FR)) [2004/5 F18s⁴ F17s⁵ F16d Mar 12] lengthy mare: fourth foal: dam, maiden on Flat/over jumps in France, half-sister to Gran Premio di Merano winner Norbecour and dam of useful chaser Draborgie: poor form in mares bumpers. *Miss Venetia Williams* **F70**

LILYMAY 5 b.m. Sovereign Water (FR) – Maysimp (IRE) (Mac's Imp (USA)) [2004/5 F16m Sep 24] second foal: dam little form: tailed off in bumper on debut. *B. P. J. Baugh* **F–**

LIMERICK BOY (GER) 7 b.g. Alwuhush (USA) – Limoges (GER) (Konigsstuhl (GER)) [2004/5 h143: c17d³ c17s³ c16d* c16vF c19v² c20s* c16gpu c25dF c21vpu Apr 22] **c141 h–**

The close-coupled Limerick Boy didn't look an obvious candidate to make an impact over fences, particularly given his jumping frailties over hurdles, but he managed to show a useful level of form as a novice in the latest season and won twice, in a maiden at Leicester in January and the Grade 2 Pendil Novices' Chase at

Favourites Racing Pendil Novices' Chase, Kempton—
an improved performance by the sponsors' Limerick Boy, who is a clear-cut winner from Lacdoudal

Kempton in February. The Pendil, which was sponsored by his owners Favourites Racing, was the highpoint of Limerick Boy's season, and he came home twelve lengths clear of the eased Lacdoudal, giving his stable its third win in the race in recent years. Limerick Boy's jumping let him down and he failed to complete subsequently. He was still going well when a bad mistake four out ended his chance in the Arkle at Cheltenham, for which he was a 20/1-chance. Similar errors in the Mildmay at Aintree (where he fell at the eighth) and in a well-contested novice at Newton Abbot came earlier in the race. Unless his jumping improves, Limerick Boy is likely to be held back in handicaps in 2005/6. Limerick Boy, who won the Top Novices' at Aintree and the Lanzarote at Kempton over hurdles, is effective at two to two and a half miles and has raced on good going or softer (acts on heavy). *Miss Venetia Williams*

LIMERICK LEADER (IRE) 7 b.g. Supreme Leader – View of The Hills (Croghan Hill) [2004/5 h128: c24v^2 c24s* c24d^{ur} c23d^2 c29d^F c28v^F 24d^4 c25s^6 c30d c24g^6 Mar 19] useful-looking gelding: useful handicap hurdler: fairly useful form over fences, winning maiden at Chepstow in October: mostly let down by jumping after: should stay beyond 3m: raced on good going or softer: usually blinkered: races lazily. *P. J. Hobbs* **c123 x** **h131**

LIMITED EDITION (IRE) 7 b.g. Parthian Springs – Rosemount Rose (Ashmore (FR)) [2004/5 17g* 16g* 16d^4 Feb 17] rangy gelding: fairly useful novice hurdler: much improved after 20-month absence, winning at Folkestone in December and Doncaster (made all to beat Il Duce a neck) in January: likely to stay 2½m: raced only on good/good to soft going over hurdles. *M. Pitman* **h120**

LINCAM (IRE) 9 b.g. Broken Hearted – Nanogan (Wolver Hollow) [2004/5 20d^5 c24s^2 c22v^5 c22v^F c22s^4 c24s^5 c24s^2 c24v* c24v^2 c28v^F c24v c24v^2 Apr 10] maiden hurdler: fairly useful novice chaser: won maiden at Punchestown in December by 15 lengths from G V A Ireland: good efforts when second to Point Barrow in Grade 2 at Naas next outing and fourth to Pay It Forward in valuable handicap at Punchestown in late-April: stays 25f: raced on good going or softer (acts on heavy). *C. F. Swan, Ireland* **c120** **h81**

LINCOLN PLACE (IRE) 10 ch.g. Be My Native (USA) – Miss Lou (Levanter) [2004/5 c107, h89: c20m^6 c20m^3 c21g^{pu} c22m* c20f^2 Sep 26] sturdy gelding: modest **c111** **h–**

maiden hurdler: fair handicap chaser: won at Fontwell in September: stays 2¾m: acts on firm and good to soft going: none too consistent. *P. J. Hobbs*

LINDBERGH LAW (USA) 5 b.g. Red Ransom (USA) – Not So Shy (USA) (Crafty Prospector (USA)) [2004/5 F16m Dec 12] second foal: half-brother to winning sprinter in US by Defrere: dam won in US: sold unraced out of J. Gosden's stable 6,000 gns Newmarket Autumn (2003) Sales: weakened over 2f out when well held in bumper at Musselburgh on debut. *G. A. Swinbank* **F–**

LIN D'ESTRUVAL (FR) 6 b.g. Cadoudal (FR) – Recolte d'Estruval (FR) (Kouban (FR)) [2004/5 F92: 21s[2] 21d[6] 19d Dec 16] tall gelding: bumper winner: best effort over hurdles when second to Alpha Gioconda in novice at Kempton. *C. P. Morlock* **h98**

LINDSAY (FR) 6 b.g. Chamberlin (FR) – Oliday (FR) (Djarvis (FR)) [2004/5 c96, h?: c20d[ur] c16m Mar 21] winning hurdler/chaser in France: well beaten in point and hunter on completed starts in 2004/5. *G. L. Edwards* **c– h–**

LINGHAM BRIDESMAID 9 b.m. Minster Son – Lingham Bride (Deep Run) [2004/5 h64: 20m Nov 26] small, sparely-made mare: poor maiden hurdler: stays 2½m: acts on good to firm and good to soft going. *Mrs J. C. McGregor* **h–**

LINN BRIDGE (IRE) 4 b.f. City Honours (USA) – Copper Breeze (IRE) (Strong Gale) [2004/5 F12g F16s[6] Feb 10] sixth foal: half-sister to 27f hurdle winner Just For Fun (by Kahyasi) and winning pointer by Erins Isle: dam unraced half-sister to useful staying chaser Sir Leonard, from family of smart jumpers Boro Quarter and Boro Eight: poor form on second of 2 outings in mares bumpers. *J. Nicol* **F73**

LINNING WINE (IRE) 9 b.g. Scenic – Zallaka (IRE) (Shardari) [2004/5 18m[5] Sep 21] good-topped gelding: useful on all-weather, fairly useful on turf on Flat (stays 1½m), claimed to join P. Blockley £12,000 in October: lightly raced and no form in novice hurdles. *B. G. Powell* **h–**

Favourites Racing's "Limerick Boy"

LIONHEART (IRE) 5 ch.g. Rashar (USA) – Greyford River (Over The River (FR)) [2004/5 F16v4 F16s Mar 22] €4,500 4-y-o: lengthy gelding: sixth foal: dam lightly raced over hurdles/in points: well held in bumpers. *M. D. Hammond* **F–**

LION HUNTER (USA) 6 b.g. Quest For Fame – Prodigious (FR) (Pharly (FR)) [2004/5 16g5 16d4 Dec 29] angular gelding: fairly useful on Flat (stays 1¼m): fair form in novice company over hurdles at Newbury. *Miss E. C. Lavelle* **h108**

LIRKIMALONG 12 ch.g. Lir – Kimberley Ann (St Columbus) [2004/5 c–, h–: c19g3 May 12] modest pointer, successful in March and April: third of 4 finishers in weak novice hunter at Exeter. *Miss S. Young* **c69 h–**

LIRSLEFTOVER 13 ch.g. Lir – Full Tan (Dairialatan) [2004/5 c72: c21dpu c26g3 May 27] winning pointer: maiden chaser. *Miss S. Young* **c–**

LIRTA (FR) 6 gr.g. Art Francais (USA) – Sirta (FR) (Le Pontet (FR)) [2004/5 c108, h–: 16g5 16g3 17m2 21s3 16v c17d5 Feb 8] tall, leggy gelding: fair chaser/maiden hurdler: stays 21f: acts on heavy and good to firm going: free-going front runner: has folded tamely (including in visor). *M. C. Pipe* **c– h105**

LISCANNOR LAD (IRE) 7 b.g. Nicolotte – Tinerana Memories (IRE) (Don't Forget Me) [2004/5 c120, h105: c25g* c20d4 c29dur c20s 24v4 Feb 13] rangy gelding: fair hurdler, stiff task final start: fairly useful chaser: won valuable novice handicap at Punchestown in April 2004: stays 25f: acts on good to firm and heavy going. *D. T. Hughes, Ireland* **c120 h–**

LISDANTE (IRE) 12 b.g. Phardante (FR) – Shuil Eile (Deep Run) [2004/5 c110, h–: 24m5 c24g5 c25gpu c27m4 c25v4 Feb 13] sturdy gelding: fair handicap chaser in 2003/4: has gone with little zest since, including on only second start over hurdles: sold out of Mrs S. Smith's stable 800 gns Doncaster October Sales after fourth outing: stays 4m: acts on good to firm and heavy going: tried blinkered. *W. G. Young* **c88 § h–**

LISLAUGHTIN ABBEY 13 ch.g. Nicholas Bill – Kates Fling (USA) (Quiet Fling (USA)) [2004/5 c102, h–: c24m2 c20m c20m2 Jun 13] lengthy, sparely-made gelding: fair handicap chaser: stayed 3m: acted on any going: won 5 times at Fakenham: dead. *O. Brennan* **c102 h–**

LISMEENAN (IRE) 11 ch.g. Be My Native (USA) – Sakanda (IRE) (Vayrann) [2004/5 c24d4 c21d5 c24g c24d6 19g 21g2 22mpu Apr 23] leggy gelding: poor handicap hurdler, lame final outing: lightly-raced novice chaser: stays 21f, at least when conditions aren't testing: acts on soft and good to firm going: blinkered fourth start: has had tongue tied. *C. P. Morlock* **c71 h80**

LISSAHANELODGE 6 br.g. Grand Lodge (USA) – Lissahane Lass (Daring March) [2004/5 17gpu Jul 18] modest on Flat (stays 13.3f), successful on all-weather in 2004: weakening in third when going lame before 2 out in novice at Newton Abbot on hurdling debut. *P. R. Hedger* **h–**

LISSAHANE TURF 5 br.g. Kahyasi – Lissahane Lass (Daring March) [2004/5 F16s6 F16s 21d Apr 18] fourth foal: half-brother to 1½m winner Lissahanelodge (by Grand Lodge): dam fair 2m hurdler: mid-division in 2 bumpers: always behind in maiden on hurdling debut. *P. R. Hedger* **h– F77**

LISSARA (IRE) 7 b.g. Glacial Storm (USA) – Bonnies Glory (General Ironside) [2004/5 F16d5 Dec 29] €23,000 4-y-o: big, well-made gelding: second foal: half-brother to bumper winner Missindependence (by Executive Perk): dam winning pointer: 8 lengths fifth of 15 to Earth Man in Grade 2 bumper at Newbury on debut, staying on well after off bridle long way out: will be suited by greater test of stamina. *Noel T. Chance* **F102**

LISSBONNEY PROJECT (IRE) 7 b.g. Lord Americo – Katie Lowe (IRE) (Pollerton) [2004/5 F20g3 F20f2 F16f2 F16g3 20g5 16d3 16s* 20d3 16vF 16v2 16s2 16s6 Mar 29] £9,000 3-y-o: third foal: dam once-raced half-sister to useful 2m hurdler/chaser Hill's Guard: placed 4 times in bumpers: progressed into fairly useful hurdler: won maiden at Punchestown in October by 2½ lengths from Justified: runner-up in minor events at Navan and Clonmel, beaten 10 lengths by Joueur d'Estruval at latter: stays 2½m: raced on good going or softer over hurdles (form in bumpers on firm): tried tongue tied. *Philip Fenton, Ireland* **h124 F98**

LISSNABRUCKA (IRE) 7 b.m. Lord Americo – Judy Henry (Orchestra) [2004/5 h71: 24s4 20g c24vF Dec 17] good-topped mare: poor form over hurdles: let down by jumping on chasing debut. *Jonjo O'Neill* **c– h76**

LITRON (IRE) 8 b. or br.g. Satco (FR) – Cornamucla (Lucky Guy) [2004/5 22g* 24g5 22g3 21m5 c21d3 21m2 20g6 c20sR Nov 5] half-brother to modest staying hurdler **c95 h86**

Sharp Thyne (by Good Thyne) and fairly useful hunter chaser The Major General (by Pollerton): dam point/bumper winner: won maiden Irish point in 2004: modest novice hurdler/chaser: won maiden over hurdles at Cartmel in May: should stay 3m+: acts on good to soft and good to firm going: refused over fences final start. *J. J. Lambe, Ireland*

LITTLE BEGGAR 7 b.g. North Col – Beggars Lane (Capitano) [2004/5 F16v 16g 21d Mar 4] good-topped gelding: second foal: brother to bumper winner Beggars Balm: dam, poor in bumpers, half-sister to smart hunter chaser Wild Illusion: tailed off in bumper and 2 novice hurdles. *R. Dickin* **h– F–**

LITTLE BIG HORSE (IRE) 9 b.g. Little Bighorn – Little Gort (Roselier (FR)) [2004/5 c109, h89: c20m² c20m* c20dF c20g⁴ 21v² c24d⁴ c24g³ Mar 5] leggy gelding: maiden hurdler: fairly useful handicap chaser: won at Market Rasen in June: good efforts next 3 completed starts: stays 25f: acts on good to firm and heavy going. *Mrs S. J. Smith* **c121 h103**

LITTLE BRAVE 10 b.g. Kahyasi – Littlemisstrouble (USA) (My Gallant (USA)) [2004/5 19s⁴ Mar 7] lightly-raced maiden hurdler. *C. Roberts* **h86**

LITTLE BROWN BEAR (IRE) 11 br.g. Strong Gale – Gladtogetit (Green Shoon) [2004/5 c102, h78+: c28g⁵ c27gF May 25] workmanlike gelding: winning hurdler/chaser: fairly useful form in points in 2005, successful in March: stays 3½m: acts on good to firm and good to soft going: front runner/races prominently. *R. Ford* **c– h–**

LITTLE CHARTRIDGE 7 b.m. Anshan – Auntie Dot (Hallodri (ATA)) [2004/5 F74: c20dpu c20dur c21sF 20m Apr 10] little sign of ability: visored last 3 starts: tongue tied. *P. R. Webber* **c– h–**

LITTLE CLOUD 5 b.m. Cloudings (IRE) – Carousella (Rousillon (USA)) [2004/5 F16g⁵ F16s Oct 22] sixth foal: half-sister to fair hurdler around 2m Galapino (by Charmer): dam, 1m winner, out of smart middle-distance filly Salchow: little show in 2 bumpers, trained by Mrs S. Lamyman on debut. *Mrs J. R. Buckley* **F–**

LITTLE DWARF 5 ch.m. Defacto (USA) – Mirror Four Sport (Risk Me (FR)) [2004/5 F17s F17m⁴ F16g F17g⁶ Aug 26] first live foal: dam, 1m to 11f winner, closely related to useful 6f and 7f performer Madly Sharp: poor form in bumpers, looking awkward under pressure second start. *S. R. Bowring* **F71**

LITTLE ED 7 b.g. Shambo – Edina (IRE) (The Parson) [2004/5 h80?, F73: c22s⁵ c24vpu Feb 5] poor form on completed start over hurdles: off 13 months, no show both outings over fences: sold £2,800 Ascot February Sales. *P. R. Webber* **c– h–**

LITTLE ENAM (IRE) 9 gr.g. Un Desperado (FR) – Black Pheasant (IRE) (Sexton Blake) [2004/5 h–: 23dpu 17dpu May 17] no form over hurdles: blinkered final start. *C. R. Egerton* **h–**

LITTLE FARMER 11 b.g. Little Wolf – Sea Farmer (Cantab) [2004/5 c98, h–: c26s⁴ c25m⁵ May 19] fair hunter: successful twice in points in 2005: barely stays 25f: acts on good to firm ground: front runner. *Mrs D. M. Grissell* **c91 h–**

LITTLE FEAT 10 b.m. Terimon – Run On Stirling (Celtic Cone) [2004/5 20g Aug 14] workmanlike mare: dual bumper winner: remote third in maiden in 2002, only start on Flat: showed little in maiden on hurdling debut. *Ian Williams* **h–**

LITTLE FELLA (IRE) 6 b. or br.g. Kahyasi – Copper Breeze (IRE) (Strong Gale) [2004/5 h–, F86: 17dpu 16g⁶ 20g³ Jun 3] second in bumper on polytrack: little form over hurdles. *B. G. Powell* **h65 ?**

LITTLE FLORA 9 ch.m. Alflora (IRE) – Sister's Choice (Lepanto (GER)) [2004/5 h73: 17gpu c16v² Apr 17] compact mare: poor hurdler nowadays: sold out of Miss V. Scott's stable 8,100 gns Doncaster March Sales: off nearly a year, second in maiden at Carlisle on chasing debut: stays 21f: acts on any going: front runner. *S. J. Marshall* **c85 h–**

LITTLE GRACE 4 b.f. Fleetwood (IRE) – Everdene (Bustino) [2004/5 F12g F17s³ F18d⁴ 18m⁵ Apr 21] quite good-topped filly: seventh foal: half-sister to 3 winners, including fair 2m hurdler Mark It (by Botanic): dam, French 1¼m winner, half-sister to useful sprinter Great Deeds: modest form in bumpers: no show in mares maiden on hurdling debut. *Mrs A. J. Perrett* **h– F81**

LITTLE HERMAN (IRE) 9 b.g. Mandalus – Kilbricken Bay (Salluceva) [2004/5 c70, h–: c23d⁴ c24mpu c25g* 24dpu c24vpu Feb 5] well-made gelding: lightly raced over hurdles: poor handicap chaser: won at Folkestone in November: stays 3¼m: acts on good to soft ground. *J. A. B. Old* **c69 h–**

LITTLE LAURA 9 ch.m. Casteddu – At First Sight (He Loves Me) [2004/5 16d Jun 20] little sign of ability. *K. W. Hogg, Isle of Man* **h–**

LITTLE LIL 6 ch.m. Sula Bula – Sherzine (Gorytus (USA)) [2004/5 h–, F–: 17g^6 Apr 28] little sign of ability. *J. D. Frost* **h–**

LITTLE MICK (IRE) 8 br.g. Mister Lord (USA) – Strong Trump (IRE) (Strong Gale) [2004/5 h74: 21g 22d^F Nov 2] lengthy gelding: lightly raced and little sign of ability. *J. A. B. Old* **h–**

LITTLE MISS PRIM 9 b.m. Gildoran – Laced Up (IRE) (The Parson) [2004/5 h–: 16g^5 Jun 3] small mare: little form. *J. G. O'Neill* **h–**

LITTLE MISTER 9 ch.g. Gran Alba (USA) – Chrissytino (Baron Blakeney) [2004/5 h–: 22d^{pu} 22s^{pu} Mar 9] of no account: tried blinkered/tongue tied. *C. L. Tizzard* **h–**

LITTLE RICHARD (IRE) 6 b.g. Alhaarth (IRE) – Intricacy (Formidable (USA)) [2004/5 17m Nov 25] half-brother to 3 winning hurdlers: modest on Flat (stays 2m), successful twice in March: soon off bridle in maiden on hurdling debut. *M. Wellings* **h–**

LITTLE RORT (IRE) 6 b.g. Ali-Royal (IRE) – Florinda (CAN) (Vice Regent (CAN)) [2004/5 h112: 16g 21s^4 24s^3 19g^5 25v^{pu} 24s^5 24s 26s 19s^{pu} Mar 10] sturdy gelding: handicap hurdler, on downgrade in 2004/5: stays 3m: raced on good ground or softer (acts on heavy): usually tongue tied. *S. T. Lewis* **h87**

LITTLE SALTEE (IRE) 5 ch.g. Anshan – Shuil Na Mhuire (IRE) (Roselier (FR)) [2004/5 F16d^6 F17s* 19d Feb 8] 19,000 3-y-o: medium-sized gelding: first foal: dam, fair chaser, stayed 25f: confirmed debut promise when winning bumper at Taunton in January: well held in novice on hurdling debut. *J. A. B. Old* **h– F92**

LITTLE SAXTEAD (IRE) 5 ch.g. Anshan – Snape (IRE) (Strong Gale) [2004/5 16d 16v 19s^6 Feb 3] lengthy, rather unfurnished gelding: fourth foal: half-brother to 19f hurdle winner Another Promise (by Presenting): dam never ran: no sign of ability. *J. A. Supple* **h–**

LITTLESTAR (FR) 4 b.g. Robellino (USA) – Green Charter (Green Desert (USA)) [2004/5 16s 16d 16m Dec 1] close-coupled gelding: modest maiden on Flat (stays 1¼m), sold out of J. Dunlop's stable 10,000 gns Newmarket July Sales: no form in juvenile hurdles. *A. Dickman* **h–**

LITTLE TASK 7 b.g. Environment Friend – Lucky Thing (Green Desert (USA)) [2004/5 c97?, h75: 16d^6 16d^F 16m^3 20g^4 22m^3 22s^{pu} 20s Nov 4] small gelding: winning chaser: poor hurdler: stays easy 2¾m: acts on firm and good to soft going: tried in headgear. *J. S. Wainwright* **c– h79**

LITTLE TOBIAS (IRE) 6 ch.g. Millkom – Barbara Frietchie (IRE) (Try My Best (USA)) [2004/5 h92§: 20m 25g 16v^6 Jan 15] modest and ungenuine on Flat (stays 2m), sold out of A. Turnell's stable 9,200 gns Doncaster October Sales: winning hurdler: little form since 2002: visored final start: temperamental. *J. S. Wainwright* **h– §**

LITTLETON AMETHYST (IRE) 6 ch.m. Revoque (IRE) – Sept Roses (USA) (Septieme Ciel (USA)) [2004/5 h–: 16s^{pu} 17s^{pu} Nov 18] poor maiden on Flat (barely stays 2m): no form over hurdles. *Mrs P. Ford* **h–**

LITTLETON VALAR (IRE) 5 ch.g. Definite Article – Fresh Look (IRE) (Alzao (USA)) [2004/5 h69: 16g^4 22d* 20m 24g 22g^2 27m^{pu} Jul 26] modest hurdler: best efforts at Cartmel, winning novice handicap in May: stayed 2¾m: acted on good to soft going: dead. *J. R. Weymes* **h91**

LITTLE TRETHEW 6 ch.m. Presidium – Sister Claire (Quayside) [2004/5 F17m F16m F16g Sep 12] 1,600 4-y-o: seventh foal: half-sister to poor chaser Seahawk Retriever (by Treasure Hunter), stays 21f, and bumper winner Father Paddy (by Minster Son): dam won 21f hurdle: tailed off in 3 bumpers. *R. C. Harper* **F–**

LITTLE VILLAIN (IRE) 7 b.g. Old Vic – Party Woman (IRE) (Sexton Blake) [2004/5 20m 21g^6 19d 20d^5 17s^6 20s^2 21g 16v^2 24g^3 21s^{pu} 20d Mar 12] first foal: dam, fairly useful hurdler who stayed 2½m, from family of high-class 2m chaser Wolf of Badenoch: poor maiden hurdler, left T. Kidd after first outing: effective at 2m (given a test) to 3m: acts on heavy going: wore cheekpieces last 5 starts. *T. Wall* **h66**

LITZINSKY 7 b.g. Muhtarram (USA) – Boulevard Girl (Nicholas Bill) [2004/5 h82: 17d^F 19s^{pu} 19s 24v* 25s Mar 1] poor hurdler: bought out of C. Booth's stable £11,500 Ascot June Sales: won handicap at Towcester in February: stays 3m: raced on going softer than good over hurdles (acts on heavy): bled from nose final start. *J. G. M. O'Shea* **h84**

LIVELY DESSERT (IRE) 12 b.g. Be My Native (USA) – Liffey Travel (Le Bavard (FR)) [2004/5 c–, h–: c25g^{pu} 24s^{ur} Oct 31] lengthy gelding: winning chaser: left G. White **c– h–**

after reappearance: runner-up twice in points in April: tried visored/in cheekpieces. *Miss S. E. Forster*

LIVERPOOL ECHO (FR) 5 b.g. Poliglote – Miss Echo (Chief Singer) [2004/5 17d^{2} 19d^{6} c16d^{3} c20d^{2} c19d^{2} c20s^{2} c20d* c21g c25m* Apr 13] stocky gelding: 1m winner on Flat: fairly useful juvenile hurdler in 2003/4, won 3 times: creditable sixth in Group 1 4-y-o event at Auteuil in June, final start for S. Wattel: fairly useful novice chaser: won maiden at Kempton (by 3½ lengths from Copsale Lad) in February and novice at Cheltenham (improved form, beat Red Devil Robert 12 lengths) in April: stays 25f: acts on soft and good to firm going: sold to join Miss K. Marks 83,000 gns Doncaster May Sales. *H. D. Daly* **c128 h120**

LIVIA (IRE) 4 b.f. Titus Livius (FR) – Passing Beauty (Green Desert (USA)) [2004/5 16m 17m 16v^{5} 20d^{pu} Mar 12] modest maiden on Flat (stays 1m): no form over hurdles, left J. Portman after second start: tongue tied third outing, blinkered final one. *R. Flint* **h–**

LIVINGSTONEBRAMBLE (IRE) 9 b.g. Supreme Leader – Killiney Side (General Ironside) [2004/5 c20d^{3} c20s* c20s^{4} c24v^{5} c24v^{F} c17s^{2} Mar 28] compact gelding: useful chaser: won maiden at Wexford in November and valuable novice at Punchestown (by ½ length from Bizet) in late-April: best effort when 2½ lengths second to Strike Back in novice at Fairyhouse: effective around 2m to 3m: raced on good going or softer (acts on heavy). *W. P. Mullins, Ireland* **c134 h–**

LIZZIE BATHWICK (IRE) 6 b.m. Glacial Storm (USA) – Protrial (Proverb) [2004/5 h78: 20v* 20g 25v^{pu} 22s^{5} 19s 22d^{2} 22d Apr 3] modest novice hurdler, won maiden at Uttoxeter in October: should stay beyond 2¾m: raced only on good going or softer (acts on heavy). *D. P. Keane* **h87**

LOADA BALONEY 4 b.g. Jumbo Hirt (USA) – A Sharp (Sharpo) [2004/5 F16v Mar 29] fifth foal: half-brother to fairly useful 1m winner Silken Dalliance (by Rambo Dancer): dam unraced: well beaten in bumper on debut. *Mrs Lucinda Featherstone* **F–**

LOAN MAN (IRE) 11 ch.g. Montelimar (USA) – Miss Daisy Dee (Baptism) [2004/5 c114, h–: c22g c18m^{2} c17f^{3} Jun 12] tall gelding: fair chaser: creditable efforts when placed in handicaps at Punchestown and Cork: stays 2½m: acts on firm and soft going: usually tongue tied. *J. F. O'Shea, Ireland* **c114 h–**

LOBLITE LEADER (IRE) 8 b.g. Tirol – Cyrano Beauty (IRE) (Cyrano de Bergerac) [2004/5 h79+: 21g^{4} Apr 30] good-topped gelding: lightly-raced maiden hurdler: should stay 3m: sold £1,400 Ascot July Sales. *G. A. Swinbank* **h80**

LOCHIEDUBS 10 br.g. Cragador – Linn Falls (Royal Fountain) [2004/5 c90x, h–: c24g c20s^{4} c25v^{4} c23d^{6} c25s^{2} Apr 10] smallish, lengthy gelding: modest chaser: stays 25f: unraced on firm going, acts on any other: tried blinkered, wore cheekpieces 5 of last 6 outings: not a fluent jumper. *Mrs L. B. Normile* **c86 x h–**

LOCH RED 6 ch.g. Primitive Rising (USA) – Lochcross (Lochnager) [2004/5 F–: F16s Mar 22] big, lengthy gelding: tailed off in 2 bumpers. *C. W. Thornton* **F–**

LOCH SOUND 9 b.g. Primitive Rising (USA) – Lochcross (Lochnager) [2004/5 c–, h–: 21g^{2} 24m^{pu} 21m 21m^{pu} Aug 31] close-coupled gelding: poor maiden hurdler: stayed 21f: tongue tied: dead. *Mrs A. M. Naughton* **c– h71**

LOCH TORRIDON 6 b.g. Syrtos – Loch Scavaig (IRE) (The Parson) [2004/5 21m^{5} 24m^{3} Oct 1] no form in bumper or novice hurdles. *James Moffatt* **h–**

LOCKSMITH 5 gr.g. Linamix (FR) – Zenith (Shirley Heights) [2004/5 h133, F100: c17d* c18d c16d* c16d^{F} c16g* c20g* c16g Apr 23] **c139 h–**

Winning a Grade 2 novice chase was presumably not the plan when the mare Zenith, a two-year-old one-mile winner who showed fairly useful form at three when owned by the Queen, was sent to be covered by Linamix in 1999, nor when the resultant foal, named Locksmith, was entered for the 2003 Derby and sent into training with Roger Charlton. That, though, was how things worked out. Locksmith made a winning debut over a mile and a half at Ascot but that came in a three-year-old bumper, nearly six months after Kris Kin's success at Epsom. By that time switched to the stables of Martin Pipe and owned by David Johnson, Locksmith went on to show himself a useful hurdler, finishing second to Trouble At Bay in the Adonis at Kempton and seventh to Brave Inca in the Supreme Novices' at Cheltenham. His Flat pedigree and angular appearance did not obviously suggest improvement would be forthcoming over fences, but in six completed appearances Locksmith won four times and eventually showed even better form than he had

*Ashleybank Investments Future Champion Novices' Chase, Ayr—
Locksmith gains a second win at the two-day meeting*

over hurdles. His successes came in a maiden at Plumpton and a novice at Doncaster and two further novices in successive days at Ayr. Given a two-month break after a fall in a Grade 2 novice at Wincanton in February, Locksmith impressed with both his jumping and his enthusiasm in his wins at Ayr, particularly when battling on most gamely to deny the odds-on My Will by half a length in the Ashleybank Investments Future Champion Novices' Chase on the second occasion. In that event Locksmith also showed unexpected stamina, seeing out the two and a half miles better than anticipated. That will give connections extra options when Locksmith goes into handicaps in 2005/6. Locksmith had one run after Ayr, playing his part in the all-hands-on-deck bid to retain the trainers' title for Pipe. He joined his stable's team of five in the Celebration Chase at Sandown on the final day of the season and started at just 14/1 in a field including Well Chief and Azertyuiop, with smart chasers Armaturk and Seebald at 25/1 and 40/1 respectively. Locksmith was not, however, up to the task, finishing eighth of nine, but that certainly should not be held against him. A free-going sort who usually makes the running, Locksmith raced on good and good to soft going over fences but showed useful form in winning by a wide margin on soft on his hurdling debut. *M. C. Pipe*

LODESTAR (IRE) 8 br.g. Good Thyne (USA) – Let's Compromise (No Argument) [2004/5 c107, h111: 21g c24gpu c25g5 c24d* c24g2 Mar 28] tall gelding: winning hurdler: fair handicap chaser: back to form when winning at Kempton in January: stays 3¼m: acts on good to firm and good to soft going: blinkered last 2 starts. *Ian Williams* **c108 h–**

LOFTY LEADER (IRE) 6 b.g. Norwich – Slaney Jazz (Orchestra) [2004/5 F91: 16vpu 16dpu 16dpu 20g 16s5 16s* Apr 22] modest hurdler: left W. McKeown after second start: won maiden at Perth in April, despite looking quirky under pressure: raced mainly around 2m on good going or softer. *Mrs H. O. Graham* **h94**

LOGGER RHYTHM (USA) 5 b.g. Woodman (USA) – Formidable Dancer (USA) (Danzig (USA)) [2004/5 16s 17m Nov 25] modest maiden on Flat (stays 1½m): tailed off in novice and maiden hurdle. *R. Dickin* **h–**

LOG ON INTERSKY (IRE) 9 ch.g. Insan (USA) – Arctic Mo (IRE) (Mandalus) [2004/5 c135, h–: c20m[5] c16dpu c16d c16g[5] Apr 16] lengthy gelding: useful handicap chaser, well below form in 2004/5: stays 21f: acts on firm and soft going: has had tongue tied: usually races prominently. *J. Howard Johnson* **c118 h–**

L'OISEAU (FR) 6 br.g. Video Rock (FR) – Roseraie (FR) (Quart de Vin (FR)) [2004/5 h92, F93: 21g[5] 22s 16s[3] 20v[5] c16d* c16dF c16s[2] 19m* Apr 9] leggy gelding: modest hurdler: won handicap at Hereford: similar form over fences, winning novice handicap at Musselburgh in January: stays 2½m: acts on good to firm and good to soft ground: has found little. *L. Lungo* **c98 h94**

LOITA HILLS (IRE) 5 b.g. Norwich – Gleann Oisin (IRE) (Le Bavard (FR)) [2004/5 F16d Mar 5] good-topped gelding: fourth foal: half-brother to 2m hurdle winner Oyez (by Jurado): dam lightly-raced half-sister to useful chaser at 2½m+ Connor Macleod: twelfth of 18 in well-contested bumper at Newbury on debut. *P. J. Hobbs* **F–**

LOMICELLI (GER) 5 b.h. Platini (GER) – L'Heure Bleue (IRE) (Kendor (FR)) [2004/5 17g[5] c19dpu 16gF Feb 10] rather leggy horse: successful up to 1¼m on Flat in Germany: well beaten at Rome in December on only completed outing over jumps: joined C. Von Der Relke. *M. Hofer, Germany* **c– h–**

LONE SOLDIER (FR) 9 ch.g. Songlines (FR) – Caring Society (Caerleon (USA)) [2004/5 c–, h79: 20d 17g[6] 19m[3] 17m 16g 17mpu 16g[6] 17g Apr 3] compact gelding: poor hurdler: stays easy 19f: acts on firm and soft going: tongue tied earlier in career. *S. B. Clark* **c– h78**

LONESOME MAN (IRE) 9 ch.g. Broken Hearted – Carn-Na-Ros (Royal Trip) [2004/5 h95: 17d[5] 21d 21spu c16g[5] Mar 28] medium-sized gelding: maiden hurdler: little form in 2004/5: no show on chasing debut: stays 2½m: raced on good going or softer (acts on soft): has had tongue tied. *R. T. Phillips* **c– h85**

LONGDALE 7 b.g. Primitive Rising (USA) – Gunnerdale (Gunner B) [2004/5 20s Mar 10] second foal: dam showed nothing on Flat or over hurdles: fell in maiden point on debut in 2004: well held in novice on hurdling debut. *M. Todhunter* **h–**

LONGHOPE BOY 6 b.g. Rock Hopper – Always A Pleasure (Chauve Souris) [2004/5 F17v F16s[5] Mar 5] first foal: dam twice-raced, out of half-sister to top-class staying chaser Charlie Potheen: well held in 2 bumpers. *W. J. Musson* **F–**

LONG NIGHT 6 b.g. Alflora (IRE) – Twice A Night (Oats) [2004/5 20s 19d 16d Feb 9] 30,000 4-y-o: lengthy, unfurnished gelding: first foal: dam, fair 2m hurdler, out of sister to smart staying jumper Celtic Isle: well beaten in novice company over hurdles. *P. J. Hobbs* **h–**

LONGSHANKS 8 b.g. Broadsword (USA) – Brass Castle (IRE) (Carlingford Castle) [2004/5 c120+, h96+: c24d[2] c20spu c24d* c21d[4] c33g[6] Apr 16] workmanlike gelding: winning hurdler: useful handicap chaser: won at Kempton in January by 3½ lengths from Koquelicot: in frame in Topham Chase at Aintree for second successive year when staying-on fourth of 30 to Cregg House: below form in Scottish Grand National 8 days later: should stay beyond 3m: raced on good going or softer: reportedly amiss second start: sound jumper. *K. C. Bailey* **c133 h–**

LONG SHOT 8 b.m. Sir Harry Lewis (USA) – Kovalevskia (Ardross) [2004/5 h102: 16gF 20mpu Jun 16] leggy mare: fair handicap hurdler: failed to complete both starts in 2004/5: stays 2¾m, possibly not 3m: acts on soft going: has flashed tail. *N. J. Henderson* **h–**

LONGSTONE BOY (IRE) 13 br.g. Mazaad – Inger-Lea (Record Run) [2004/5 c88: c19g[2] Apr 19] good-bodied gelding: fairly useful hunter: successful twice in points in 2005: stays 3m: acts on firm and good to soft going. *E. R. Clough* **c102**

LONGSTONE LADY (IRE) 8 b.m. Mister Lord (USA) – Monamandy (IRE) (Mandalus) [2004/5 19d 16d[5] 19s[2] 24spu c20dpu c19d[4] 17d[4] 22g[2] 22v[3] Apr 22] won maiden point in 2004: poor maiden hurdler: better effort in novice chases (saddle slipped on debut) when fourth at Exeter: stays 2¾m: acts on soft going (tailed off on heavy). *J. D. Frost* **c81 h83**

LONGSTONE LASS 5 b.m. Wizard King – Kamaress (Kampala) [2004/5 h–, F–: 17mpu 17m 20d[6] 20spu 16g[2] 19d* 17v* 20v 16d[4] 16v[5] 16s[6] Mar 1] unfurnished mare: modest handicap hurdler: won at Towcester (amateurs) and Sedgefield (conditional jockeys seller, sold from R. Guest £8,000) in January: may prove best up to 19f: acts **h88**

on heavy going: visored last 3 starts: sometimes hangs left: free-going front runner. *D. Carroll*

LONGTERM (IRE) 8 b.g. Welsh Term – Sahob (Roselier (FR)) [2004/5 16s5 24spu 17s5 Mar 6] good-topped gelding: bumper winner: novice hurdler: off over 2 years before reappearance: should stay beyond 2½m. *Jonjo O'Neill* **h84**

LONG WALK (IRE) 8 b.g. King's Ride – Seanaphobal Lady (Kambalda) [2004/5 c104, h91: c24sF c24gpu Jan 17] tall, useful-looking gelding: maiden hurdler: fair chaser: lame final outing: stays 3m: raced on good going or softer. *H. D. Daly* **c104 ? h–**

LOOK COLLONGES (FR) 6 gr.g. Dom Alco (FR) – Tessy Collonges (FR) (El Badr) [2004/5 c119, h–: c21s c21vpu c24d4 c24d Dec 29] good-topped gelding: fairly useful chaser: form in 2004/5 only when fourth to Mamideos in handicap at Lingfield: stays 3m: acts on soft and good to firm going. *G. Macaire, France* **c119 h–**

LOOKING DOWN 5 ch.m. Compton Place – High Stepping (IRE) (Taufan (USA)) [2004/5 16d 16g* 16d4 20g4 16v5 16s2 16s6 16s5 16g 16s5 21g5 Jan 14] lengthy mare: fairly useful at one time on Flat (stays 1m) for R. Hannon: modest novice hurdler: won seller (sold from P. Haslam 9,000 gns) at Stratford in July: best at sharp 2m: raced on good going or softer over hurdles. *John Allen* **h85**

LOOKING FORWARD 9 b.g. Primitive Rising (USA) – Gilzie Bank (New Brig) [2004/5 c98: c28gpu Apr 30] good-topped gelding: modest handicap chaser: lame very early in season: stays 21f: acts on firm and good to soft going. *Ferdy Murphy* **c–**

LOOKS THE BUSINESS (IRE) 4 b.g. Marju (IRE) – Business Centre (IRE) (Digamist (USA)) [2004/5 16g3 17g4 17g2 17d4 16d3 17g 16g* 17vpu 16dur Apr 17] fair maiden on Flat (stays 1¼m): modest hurdler: won ladies handicap at Huntingdon in March: raced around 2m: acts on good to soft going: usually tongue tied. *W. G. M. Turner* **h93**

LOOK TO THE FUTURE (IRE) 11 b.g. Roselier (FR) – Toevarro (Raga Navarro (ITY)) [2004/5 c87, h100: 20m4 20g4 26d* 26d5 c24d2 c25m5 c19s4 Mar 23] compact gelding: modest hurdler: won seller at Southwell in August: poor maiden chaser: sold out of Mrs S. Smith's stable 2,200 gns Doncaster January Sales before final start: stays 3¼m: acts on heavy and good to firm going. *M. J. M. Evans* **c78 h91**

LOOPY LINDA (IRE) 7 b.g. Simply Great (FR) – Albane (Shirley Heights) [2004/5 h–: 20s 16d 20dpu Dec 4] leggy gelding: fairly useful in bumpers: no show in novice hurdles. *T. D. Easterby* **h–**

L'ORAGE LADY (IRE) 7 ch.m. Glacial Storm (USA) – Commanche Glen (IRE) (Commanche Run) [2004/5 h81, F88: 24g3 22g2 21m2 21dF 24dpu Jan 7] modest handicap hurdler: likely to prove best around 3m: acts on firm going. *Mrs H. Dalton* **h92**

LORAINOVICH (FR) 4 b. or br.c. Verbier (FR) – Sharon Doll (IRE) (Shahrastani (USA)) [2004/5 18m* 16s*dis 16s2 17s5 c17d* c19d3 c19g2 c17s4 Apr 6] fourth foal: half-brother to 2 winners, including useful hurdler Idole First (by Flemensfirth), stays 21f: dam 8.5f and 1¼m winner: twice-raced on Flat in French Provinces (trained by X. Pulero at 2 yrs), successful over 8.5f at Pompadour in July: first past post in juvenile hurdles at Fontwell in August and Enghien (subsequently disqualified due to testing positive for dexamethasone) in October and 3-y-o chase at Cagnes-sur-Mer in December: will stay beyond 19f: blinkered seventh start: has had tongue tied. *Y. Porzier, France* **c112 h113**

LORAMORE 8 ch.m. Alflora (IRE) – Apsimore (Touching Wood (USA)) [2004/5 h–: 17gpu Aug 26] little sign of ability. *J. C. Tuck* **h–**

LORD ANNER (IRE) 6 br.g. Mister Lord (USA) – Anner Lodge (IRE) (Capitano) [2004/5 c23g* Apr 12] 1,000 4-y-o: second foal: dam unraced: progressive pointer, successful all 3 completed starts: favourite, won novice hunter at Exeter on chasing debut by 4 lengths from Beauchamp Oracle. *P. F. Nicholls* **c94**

LORD ATTERBURY (IRE) 9 ch.g. Mister Lord (USA) – Tammyiris (Arapahos (FR)) [2004/5 c133: c28m4 c26g4 c36dF Apr 9] sturdy gelding: smart hunter chaser: fourth to Sleeping Night in Foxhunter at Cheltenham second outing: fell first in Grand National at Aintree (third previous year) next time: stays 4½m: acts on good to soft going: front runner: prone to mistakes. *M. C. Pipe* **c121 +**

LORD ATTICA (IRE) 6 b.g. Mister Lord (USA) – Brief Pace (IRE) (Riot Helmet) [2004/5 24g4 22s 21g c26d2 c26s2 c25v6 c24dpu c25g c26g3 c26gF c26gR Mar 28] €6,000 3-y-o, resold €7,000 3-y-o: angular gelding: fifth foal: half-brother to winning pointer by Husyan: dam winning pointer: won maiden Irish point in 2004: sold 14,000 gns Doncaster May Sales: well held all 3 starts over hurdles: form over fences only when runner-up in handicaps: stays 3¼m: acts on soft going: tried visored/in cheekpieces. *M. F. Harris* **c70 h–**

LORD BEAU (IRE) 9 b.g. Beau Sher – Bonny Joe (Derring Rose) [2004/5 c26d² c26v* Apr 22] winning pointer: won novice hunter chase at Newton Abbot in April: better form when second to Tremallt at Chepstow 2 months earlier: stays 3¼m: acts on heavy going. *A. J. Bateman* **c110**

LORD BLAKE (IRE) 4 ch.g. Mister Lord (USA) – Dalua River (IRE) (Sexton Blake) [2004/5 F16spu Apr 22] 4,800 3-y-o: fifth foal: dam lightly-raced half-sister to useful 2m chaser Billy Bathgate: pulled up in bumper on debut. *I. McMath* **F–**

LORD BROCK 6 b.g. Alderbrook – Mariner's Air (Julio Mariner) [2004/5 F66: F17g* F16g² 21d² 20v* 20s⁵ 24gpu Mar 19] compact gelding: fair in bumpers, landed odds at Bangor in August: fair form over hurdles: won novice at Leicester in January by length from Halcon Genelardais: reportedly lame final outing: not sure to stay much beyond 21f: raced on good going or softer (acts on heavy). *N. A. Twiston-Davies* **h106 F91**

LORD BUCKINGHAM 7 ch.g. Carroll House – Lady Buck (Pollerton) [2004/5 h94: 16d* 17d³ 19g³ 20dpu Mar 12] rangy gelding: will make a chaser: novice hurdler: dictated pace and possibly flattered when winning at Wincanton in November by 1¼ lengths from Cornish Sett: fair form on completed starts after: best form around 2m: yet to race on extremes of going: often tongue tied: races prominently. *N. J. Henderson* **h116 ?**

LORD CAPITAINE (IRE) 11 b. or br.g. Mister Lord (USA) – Salvation Sue (Mon Capitaine) [2004/5 c104: c28g* c25s² c25g* c25d³ c28s⁵ Apr 3] workmanlike gelding: fair handicap chaser: successful at Sedgefield (sixth course success) in April 2004 and Catterick in December: stays 3½m: acts on soft going: tried blinkered: has had tongue tied. *J. Howard Johnson* **c112**

LORD CEBELLINO (IRE) 6 b.g. Lord Americo – Ballyfroary Lady (Pollerton) [2004/5 F16s* Dec 12] €6,200 4-y-o: third reported foal: dam unraced: fairly useful form when winning 23-runner bumper at Cork on debut by neck from Justpourit. *L. Whitmore, Ireland* **F103**

LORD CHESTERS (IRE) 4 b.g. Lord of Appeal – Cherry Chase (IRE) (Red Sunset) [2004/5 F14s⁵ F17s Mar 10] €110,000 3-y-o: sturdy gelding: fourth foal: dam, bumper winner, half-sister to useful staying hurdler Turnpole: better effort in bumpers when fifth to Sotovik at Carlisle on debut. *J. Howard Johnson* **F84**

LORD CODE (IRE) 7 b.g. Arctic Lord – Tax Code (Workboy) [2004/5 h85, F–: c20spu Oct 30] tall gelding: modest form in novice hurdles: no show on chasing debut. *R. H. Alner* **c– h–**

LORD DUNDANIEL (IRE) 8 b. or br.g. Arctic Lord – Killoskehan Queen (Bustineto) [2004/5 h111: 20d² c20s³ c24g² c24g⁶ c20g³ Dec 26] smallish gelding: fair hurdler/novice chaser: likely to prove best short of 3m: acts on soft going. *B. De Haan* **c111 h110**

LORD DUNDEE (IRE) 7 ch.g. Polish Precedent (USA) – Easy To Copy (USA) (Affirmed (USA)) [2004/5 17d Aug 1] half-brother to bumper winner Easy Wonder (by Chief's Crown): fairly useful 1¾m winner on Flat at 4 yrs for H. Cecil: tongue tied, well held in novice on hurdling debut. *R. C. Guest* **h–**

LORD EDWARDS ARMY (IRE) 10 b.g. Warcraft (USA) – Celtic Bombshell (Celtic Cone) [2004/5 c96, h–: c25g⁵ c28mur May 22] strong, lengthy gelding: fair hunter chaser: stays 25f: acts on firm and soft going: sometimes makes mistakes. *W. T. Reed* **c80 x h–**

LORD EURO (IRE) 8 b.g. Lord Americo – Orchards Beauty (IRE) (Miner's Lamp) [2004/5 c21g³ Mar 18] fair pointer: successful in January: third in novice hunter chase at Fakenham in March. *Mrs D. M. Grissell* **c86**

LORD GALE (IRE) 7 b.g. Mister Lord (USA) – Dante Gale (IRE) (Phardante (FR)) [2004/5 F102: 24g* 21gF Oct 27] good-bodied gelding: fairly useful in bumpers: odds on, made all in novice at Worcester on hurdling debut in October: held when falling fatally at Cheltenham: would have stayed beyond 3m. *N. A. Twiston-Davies* **h111**

LORD GREY (IRE) 12 gr.g. Celio Rufo – Clooragh Rose (Boreen (FR)) [2004/5 16gbd 16m* 16m⁴ Aug 2] workmanlike gelding: fairly useful chaser: fair handicap hurdler, off a year before reappearance: won at Navan in May: best form around 2m: goes particularly well on good going or firmer (acts on firm). *D. P. Kelly, Ireland* **c– h112**

LORD GREYSTOKE (IRE) 4 b.g. Petardia – Jungle Story (IRE) (Alzao (USA)) [2004/5 16d 16d 17m 16s⁶ Dec 22] smallish gelding: modest maiden on Flat (stays 7f), well held in 2004: no form in juvenile hurdles: tried blinkered. *C. P. Morlock* **h–**

LORD HALFNOTHIN (IRE) 9 b.g. Mandalus – Midnight Seeker (Status Seeker) [2004/5 c113: c21d^{3} c20d^{4} Dec 2] strong gelding: fair chaser: will stay 3m: acts on firm going. *R. H. Alner* **c102**

LORD HECCLES (IRE) 6 b.g. Supreme Leader – Parsons Law (The Parson) [2004/5 F91: 17s 21d^{2} 20d^{6} Feb 18] well-made gelding: easily best effort over hurdles when second to Ess of Norway in novice at Plumpton: stays 21f. *G. L. Moore* **h97**

LORD HENRY (IRE) 6 b.g. Lord Americo – Auntie Honnie (IRE) (Radical) [2004/5 F17g^{4} 19d* 16g* Nov 17] lengthy gelding: second foal: half-brother to winning chaser Lost In Normandy (by Treasure Hunter), stays 3¼m: dam, well beaten in bumpers, sister to useful staying hurdler/chaser Morgans Harbour and useful 2½m hurdler Red Curate: fourth in bumper at Hereford on debut: won both starts in novice hurdles, at Taunton (travelling strongly when left distance clear 2 out) in October and Kempton (by 15 lengths from Harry Blade, despite running wide and hanging left) in November: looked capable of better when last seen but missed rest of season. *P. J. Hobbs* **h126 +** **F93**

LORD HOPEFUL (IRE) 4 b.g. Lord Americo – Hidden Agenda (Abednego) [2004/5 F16v Mar 29] third foal: dam, winning Irish pointer, half-sister to fairly useful hurdler/chaser up to 3¼m Lordberniebouffant: well held in bumper on debut. *C. P. Morlock* **F–**

LORDINGTON LAD 5 br.g. Terimon – Fit For Firing (FR) (In Fijar (USA)) [2004/5 F16g^{4} Mar 16] fourth foal: half-brother to winning hurdler/smart chaser Colonel Frank (by Toulon), stays 25f: dam fair staying chaser: 3¼ lengths fourth to Cracboumwiz in bumper at Huntingdon on debut: will be suited by greater test of stamina. *B. G. Powell* **F91 +**

LORD JACK (IRE) 9 ch.g. Mister Lord (USA) – Gentle Gill (Pollerton) [2004/5 c124, h–: 24v* c25s* c29v^{pu} c24m^{4} c33g^{pu} Apr 16] workmanlike gelding: first outing over hurdles since 2001/2, won handicap at Ayr in November: fairly useful handicap chaser: won at Kelso in December by 8 lengths from Gatorade: disappointing after: should stay beyond 25f: best on going softer than good (acts on heavy): tried in cheek-pieces: has had tongue tied: sound jumper: tends to run in snatches. *N. G. Richards* **c129** **h114**

LORD JAY JAY (IRE) 5 b.g. Lord of Appeal – Mesena (Pals Passage) [2004/5 F88: F16g 19g 21v^{pu} 21s^{5} 16d^{5} Apr 3] good-bodied gelding: chasing type: twice-raced in bumpers: modest form at best in novice hurdles: likely to prove suited by further than 2m: has taken strong hold. *Miss H. C. Knight* **h92** **F–**

LORD JOSHUA (IRE) 7 b.g. King's Theatre (IRE) – Lady Joshua (IRE) (Royal Academy (USA)) [2004/5 16s^{6} 16d 16g Apr 1] smallish, lengthy gelding: winning hurdler: off nearly 3 years, fair form in handicaps in 2004/5: likely to stay 2½m: raced on good ground or softer. *N. J. Henderson* **h110**

LORD KERNOW (IRE) 5 b.g. Lord Americo – Bramble Ridge (IRE) (Remainder Man) [2004/5 F17g^{3} Apr 7] 7,000 (privately) 4-y-o: third foal: dam unraced half-sister to useful chaser up to 3m Major Summit: fairly useful form when third of 12 to Sunley Shines in bumper at Taunton on debut. *C. J. Down* **F95**

LORD KILLESHANRA (IRE) 6 br.g. Mister Lord (USA) – Killeshandra Lass (IRE) (King's Ride) [2004/5 F100: F16g^{3} 17d^{6} 19s^{6} 21v^{6} 22s^{2} 24d^{2} 16v^{2} 22g^{pu} Apr 17] tall gelding: type to make a chaser: fairly useful in bumpers: fairly useful novice hurdler: best efforts when runner-up at Wincanton (beaten 1½ lengths by Senor Sedona) and Exeter fifth and sixth starts: stays 3m: raced on good going or softer (acts on soft). *C. L. Tizzard* **h119** **F95**

LORD KILPATRICK (IRE) 11 ch.g. Mister Lord (USA) – Running Frau (Deep Run) [2004/5 c24d^{pu} Mar 11] lengthy, workmanlike gelding: winning pointer: lightly raced nowadays, bled from nose in hunter at Sandown on return from another lay-off: stays 3m. *T. R. George* **c–**

LORD LAHAR 6 b.g. Fraam – Brigadiers Bird (IRE) (Mujadil (USA)) [2004/5 17g Dec 15] modest on Flat (stays 13f), sold out of M. Channon's stable 7,500 gns Newmarket Autumn Sales: tailed off in novice on hurdling debut. *M. A. Buckley* **h–**

LORD LAMB 13 gr.g. Dunbeath (USA) – Caroline Lamb (Hotfoot) [2004/5 23s^{pu} 20s^{3} 19g^{5} 24s Apr 20] well-made gelding: winning chaser (sketchy jumper): veteran hurdler, poor nowadays: stays 25f when conditions aren't testing: acts on good to firm and heavy going: irresolute. *K. G. Reveley* **c–** **h81 §**

LORD LEONARDO (IRE) 5 b.g. Norwich – Sue's A Lady (Le Moss) [2004/5 F18d^{5} Apr 18] €20,000 3-y-o: brother to fair hurdler Monsieur Monet and half-brother to 3 winners, including top-class staying chaser Sir Rembrandt (by Mandalus) and useful hurdler/fairly useful chaser up to 3m Audacter (by Strong Gale): dam bumper winner: **F87**

green, 8½ lengths fifth to Argent Ou Or in maiden bumper at Plumpton on debut, losing chance when veering left 1f out. *L. Wells*

LORD LINGTON (FR) 6 b.g. Bulington (FR) – Tosca de Bussy (FR) (Le Riverain (FR)) [2004/5 h101: 17v^{2} 17v^{pu} 16d^{6} Apr 3] rather leggy gelding: fair hurdler: left P. Nicholls after virtually refusing to race second outing: raced around 2m: acts on heavy going: blinkered once: temperamental. *D. J. Wintle* **h107 §**

LORD LUKER (IRE) 9 b.g. Lord Americo – Canon's Dream (Le Bavard (FR)) [2004/5 h77: c20s^{F} c24g^{pu} Nov 11] sturdy gelding: lightly raced: poor form over hurdles: failed to complete both outings over fences: joined J. Allen. *Miss H. C. Knight* **c– h–**

LORD NELLSSON 9 b.g. Arctic Lord – Miss Petronella (Petoski) [2004/5 c89, h85: 20m^{6} 22m^{2} 21s^{2} 24g^{2} 24g^{pu} Dec 9] compact gelding: modest maiden hurdler/chaser: stays 3m: acts on soft and good to firm going: tried in cheekpieces: races prominently. *J. S. King* **c– h94**

LORD 'N' MASTER (IRE) 9 b.g. Lord Americo – Miss Good Night (Buckskin (FR)) [2004/5 c111, h–: c20d c19d^{5} Apr 22] useful-looking gelding: fair handicap chaser: stays 3m: acts on soft and good to firm going: often makes mistakes. *R. Rowe* **c110 h–**

LORD NOELIE (IRE) 12 b.g. Lord Americo – Leallen (Le Bavard (FR)) [2004/5 c143, h–: c24d^{2} c27d^{3} c25d^{pu} c26d^{pu} c31d^{4} c25m^{F} Apr 13] useful-looking gelding: not a good walker: useful handicap chaser: creditable efforts first 2 starts: suited by 3m+: acts on heavy and good to firm going: usually sound jumper. *Ms Bridget Nicholls* **c141 h–**

LORD NORTH (IRE) 10 b.g. Mister Lord (USA) – Mrs Hegarty (Decent Fellow) [2004/5 c102§, h–: c16d^{4} May 6] rangy, good sort: handicap chaser, on the downgrade: stays 2½m: has won on good to firm going, better form on softer: visored 4 of last 6 starts: tongue tied: not one to rely on (often finds little): sold 11,000 gns Doncaster May Sales. *P. R. Webber* **c95 §**

LORD O'ALL SEASONS (IRE) 12 b. or br.g. Mister Lord (USA) – Autumn News (Giolla Mear) [2004/5 c24v^{2} Apr 17] rangy gelding: lightly-raced winning chaser, left N. Henderson after sole outing in 2002/3: won point on return in February: second in falsely-run hunter chase at Carlisle: should stay beyond 3m: acts on heavy going. *Miss M. A. Neill* **c86**

LORD OF BEAUTY (FR) 5 ch.g. Medaaly – Arctic Beauty (USA) (Arctic Tern (USA)) [2004/5 h111: 18d^{2} 20d* 19d* 21g 19d^{2} 20d Apr 9] leggy, angular gelding: fairly useful hurdler: won maiden at Fontwell (easily) and handicap at Doncaster (by 2 lengths from Migration) in November: stays 2½m: raced on good going or softer: sometimes jumps none too fluently. *Noel T. Chance* **h117**

LORD OF ILLUSION (IRE) 8 b.g. Mister Lord (USA) – Jellaride (IRE) (King's Ride) [2004/5 c109, h–: c23m* c24m* c24g^{2} c20g^{2} c24d* c24g* c26d* Jan 1] **c148 p h–**

Lord of Illusion performed a disappearing act after putting himself in the spotlight with an eye-catching display at Cheltenham on New Year's Day, when winning an eleven-runner handicap chase by twelve lengths from another smart novice Baron Windrush. Expected to return to the same venue in March for the Royal & SunAlliance Chase or the William Hill Handicap, he didn't show up for either after failing to please his trainer in a gallop the week before the Festival, and the remainder of the season also went by without him. Lord of Illusion did originally feature on the bill for the opening day of Cheltenham's two-day fixture in April, but another setback resulted in his late withdrawal. It is to be hoped that Lord of Illusion will be able to complete a full season when he returns to action in 2005/6. With only sixteen runs all told under his belt, Lord of Illusion still looks to have a fair amount of improvement in him and is well capable of developing into a good-class staying chaser.

A twice-raced pointer in Ireland, Lord of Illusion won a novice hurdle at Bangor in 2002/3, his first season for his present stable, and then had his attentions turned to chasing. Still in contention when unseating his rider at the last on his debut in a chase, in a novice handicap at Wetherby in November, 2003, Lord of Illusion ran a disappointing race later that month and wasn't seen out again until the following May. He quickly made up for lost time on his return, winning novice events at Wetherby and Stratford; and, after finishing second on his next two starts, he then won three in a row, completing the hat-trick in the Cheltenham handicap after also being successful in a novice event at Ludlow and a novice handicap at Newbury, the long-striding Lord of Illusion benefiting from being allowed to bowl along in front in each of those races. Lord of Illusion faced his stiffest task at Cheltenham, where he was set to take on seasoned handicappers for the first time, off a mark 10 lb higher than at Newbury. The race, run over an extended three and a quarter miles on good to soft ground, also represented the stiffest test of stamina Lord of Illusion had faced. Lord of Illusion, sweating slightly and on his toes, ensured that stamina was at even more of a premium by setting a demanding pace which, coupled with his bold jumping, had most of his rivals in trouble a long way from home, seeing off the remainder as he kept going strongly in the straight to finish well on top at the finish. This already impressive win was made to look even better after the placed horses Baron Windrush and It Takes Time won valuable events next time out. What a pity Lord of Illusion didn't make it to the Cheltenham Festival. He would have been a tough nut to crack in his chosen engagement.

Lord of Illusion (IRE) (b.g. 1997)	Mister Lord (USA) (b 1979)	Sir Ivor (b 1965)	Sir Gaylord
			Attica
		Forest Friend (bl 1966)	Linacre
			Belle Sauvage
	Jellaride (IRE) (br 1990)	King's Ride (b 1976)	Rarity
			Ride
		Swuzzlebubble (br 1976)	Bargello
			Leney Girl

Lord of Illusion is the first foal of Jellaride, a mare who showed only a little ability in Irish points but who already has begun to prove her worth as a broodmare: her second foal, Cruising River (by Over The River) showed promise over hurdles at Newbury after winning a point-to-point in Ireland in January. Jellaride is a sister to Ounavarra Creek, a fairly useful chaser in Ireland at up to three miles. Their dam Swuzzlebubble, who won a maiden hurdle in Ireland, is out of the unraced Leney Girl and is a half-sister to Leney Dual, a useful staying chaser in the 'eighties when trained by David Nicholson. Lord of Illusion, who will stay beyond three and a quarter miles, has won on ground ranging from soft to good to firm. A tall gelding, he jumps well and forcing tactics seem to suit him ideally. He held an entry in the 2005 Grand National and it would be no surprise to see him a leading contender at Aintree another year. *T. R. George*

LORD OF THE BRIDE (IRE) 8 ch.g. Mister Lord (USA) – Carrigan Springs (IRE) (Tale Quale) [2004/5 c71, h–: 24m 22g 22m 26g^{pu} Jul 16] winning Irish pointer: little other form: visored last 3 starts: has had tongue tied: ungenuine. *M. C. Pipe* **c– § h– §**

LORD OF THE GROVE (IRE) 8 b.g. Lord Americo – Come On Lis (Domynsky) [2004/5 16f^3 16m 16m 16d 16g* 18f* 18m^2 16g^3 16s 16s^5 Apr 3] modest handicap hurdler: won twice at Wexford in July: raced mainly around 2m: acts on any going. *M. A. Molloy, Ireland* **h99**

LORD OF THE HILL (IRE) 10 b.g. Dromod Hill – Telegram Mear (Giolla Mear) [2004/5 c98, h–: c16g* c16g^3 c16m^2 c16g^{pu} 19g c16g^5 Apr 17] tall gelding: no form over hurdles: fair handicap chaser: won at Aintree in May: left Mrs H. Dalton after fourth start: stays easy 2½m: acts on good to firm going, possibly not on softer than good: formerly tongue tied: usually front runner. *G. Brown* **c100 h–**

LORD OF THE LAND 12 b.g. Lord Bud – Saint Motunde (Tyrant (USA)) [2004/5 c94, h83: 21g 16g c21m^3 c27g^{ur} c20m 20d^4 24g^3 22g^3 17m^2 17m^6 c20g^4 c21m* c20d^3 c27d^3 c19g 16g^4 c20d^6 Mar 26] leggy gelding: modest hurdler: poor handicap chaser: won weakly-contested event at Sedgefield in September: effective around 2m to 27f: acts on firm and good to soft going (possibly unsuited by soft/heavy): effective with or without cheekpieces/tongue strap. *Mrs E. Slack* **c78 h88**

LORD OF THE LOCH (IRE) 14 b. or br.g. Lord Americo – Loughamaire (Brave Invader (USA)) [2004/5 h92: 20d^2 21g^4 20s^4 20d 16m 20g^F 22s^{pu} 21v^{pu} Mar 28] leggy, rather plain gelding: modest hurdler: lame final outing: stays 21f: acts on good to firm and heavy going. *W. G. Young* **h95**

LORD OF THE MIST (IRE) 11 b.g. Mister Lord (USA) – Brogeen View (Kambalda) [2004/5 c21d^F c24m^2 May 22] fairly useful pointer nowadays, successful 5 times in 2004: mistakes when second at Stratford on completed start in hunter chases: stays 3m. *R. Barber* **c98 h–**

LORD OF THE PARK (IRE) 8 b.g. Lord Americo – Wind Chimes (The Parson) [2004/5 h–, F–: 20v^{pu} c20d^{ur} c20d^{F} c25s^{pu} c21s^{pu} 16v Feb 20] of little account. *John R. Upson* **c– h–**

LORD OF THE REALM (IRE) 9 b.g. Mister Lord (USA) – Traditional Lady (Carlingford Castle) [2004/5 c73: c21g^{F} May 1] rangy gelding: completed only once in 5 chases, running best race when falling 3 out in novice handicap at Southwell (retried in tongue strap) in May: sold 3,200 gns Doncaster Sales later in month. *K. C. Bailey* **c86**

LORD OF THE RIVER (IRE) 13 br.g. Lord Americo – Well Over (Over The River (FR)) [2004/5 c135, h–: c25g c26g c26g^{2} c25v^{3} c24g^{2} c25g^{ur} Apr 8] tall, close-coupled gelding: usually looks well: useful handicap chaser: 50/1, clearly best effort in 2004/5 when 1¼ lengths second of 24 to Juveigneur in valuable amateur event at Cheltenham fifth start, making much of running: stays 25f: has form on good to firm going, raced mainly on good or softer (acts on heavy): probably best ridden up with pace: bold jumper. *N. J. Henderson* **c132 h–**

LORD OF THE ROAD 6 b.g. Gildoran – Ethels Course (Crash Course) [2004/5 22d^{5} 24d^{3} 24s^{2} Mar 31] well-made gelding: sixth foal: brother/half-brother to winning pointers: dam, winning staying hurdler, half-sister to smart staying jumpers Plundering and Triple Witching and useful staying chaser Golden Minstrel: won maiden point on debut in 2004: sold 50,000 gns Doncaster May Sales: best effort in 3 novice hurdles when second to McKelvey at Ludlow: will stay beyond 3m. *P. F. Nicholls* **h95 +**

LORD OF THE SEA (IRE) 4 b.g. Perugino (USA) – Sea Mistress (Habitat) [2004/5 16m^{3} Sep 19] half-brother to fair Irish hurdler Touching Moment (by Pennine Walk): fair maiden at best on Flat (stays easy 1¼m): third of 10 in juvenile at Plumpton on hurdling debut. *Jamie Poulton* **h78**

LORD OF THE SKY 12 b.g. Lord Bud – Fardella (ITY) (Molvedo) [2004/5 16s Nov 10] close-coupled gelding: successful all 5 completed starts over fences in 2000/1: winning hurdler: off nearly 3 years, jumped poorly when mid-field in handicap at Kelso: stays at least 2¾m (simple task at 25f): raced only on going softer than good (acts on heavy): jumps right over fences. *L. Lungo* **c– h–**

LORD OF THE TURF (IRE) 12 b.g. Supreme Leader – Avida Dancer (Ballymore) [2004/5 c131, h–: c24s* c26g c24v^{F} Apr 6] angular gelding: useful handicap chaser at best: successful 3 times in points between October and January, as well as in hunter at Leopardstown in February by 8 lengths from Never Compromise: fell last 2 starts, fatally so at Punchestown: stayed 3m: raced mainly on going softer than good (acted on heavy): tried blinkered. *J. Bleahen, Ireland* **c111 h–**

LORD OLYMPIA (IRE) 6 b.g. Lord Americo – Mooreshill (IRE) (Le Moss) [2004/5 F95: F16s^{3} 22s* 22g^{2} 21s* 20v 20v^{F} 20d^{pu} Mar 12] good-topped gelding: fair form in bumpers: fairly useful hurdler: won maiden at Stratford in October and novice at Towcester in November: ran as if amiss 2 of last 3 starts, on other disputing lead with Always Waining when falling last in novice at Uttoxeter: will stay 3m: acts on soft going, probably on heavy. *Miss Venetia Williams* **h120 F93**

LORD ON THE RUN (IRE) 6 b.g. Lord Americo – Polar Crash (Crash Course) [2004/5 20g^{6} 16d^{3} 20s^{ur} 17d 17d 16s Jan 11] €22,000 3-y-o: good-topped gelding: sixth foal: half-brother to fairly useful hunter chaser Polaris Flame (by Mandalus), stays 25f: dam unraced half-sister to smart 2m hurdler/useful chaser Twinburn: modest form in bumpers (for E. O'Sullivan) and over hurdles. *R. J. Price* **h91**

LORD OSCAR (IRE) 6 b.g. Oscar (IRE) – Americo Rose (IRE) (Lord Americo) [2004/5 F17s^{3} 19g 21g Apr 1] tall gelding: first foal: dam unraced: won maiden point on debut in 2004: favourite, remote third in bumper at Hereford, losing lead when hanging badly left on bend over 4f out: second and better effort over hurdles when eighth to River Phantom in maiden at Newbury, soon in clear lead: headstrong. *M. C. Pipe* **h84 + F–**

LORD PAT (IRE) 14 ch.g. Mister Lord (USA) – Arianrhod (L'Homme Arme) [2004/5 c–, h72: 21g 20d 21d^{5} 19s^{3} 21v Jan 25] small gelding: poor handicap hurdler: stays 21f: acts on heavy going. *Miss Kate Milligan* **c– h63**

LORD ROCHESTER 9 b.g. Distant Relative – Kentfield (Busted) [2004/5 c–x, h81: 21g^{pu} 21m^{pu} 20m Aug 30] close-coupled gelding: maiden chaser, usually let down by jumping: winning hurdler, no form in 2004/5: formerly blinkered, has worn cheekpieces. *K. F. Clutterbuck* **c– x h–**

LORD RODNEY (IRE) 6 b.g. Hatim (USA) – Howcleuch (Buckskin (FR)) [2004/5 F84: F17s F16v^{5} 16v^{5} 19g 20s* 24s^{pu} Apr 10] well-made gelding: chasing type: fair in **h96 F89**

bumpers: best effort over hurdles when winning maiden at Wetherby in March, allowed to dictate in steadily-run race: stays 2½m: acts on soft going. *P. Beaumont*

LORD ROSSKIT (IRE) 5 b. or br.g. Lord Americo – Redstone Lady (IRE) (Buckskin (FR)) [2004/5 24dpu 23vpu 16d4 Apr 11] tall gelding: second foal: dam unraced, out of half-sister to high-class staying chaser Simon Legree: dropped in trip, first sign of ability when fourth of 18 in novice hurdle at Kelso: bred to be suited by much further than 2m. *G. M. Moore* **h79**

LORD SAAR (IRE) 6 b. or br.g. Arctic Lord – Lucycello (Monksfield) [2004/5 20m 20f3 22m4 c17d2 c22v4 Oct 30] €30,000 3-y-o: ex-Irish gelding: seventh foal: brother to fairly useful hurdler/fair chaser up to 3m Hard Winter and half-brother to fairly useful chaser Phar From A Fiddle (by Phardante), stays 25f: dam, placed in points, half-sister to high-class 2m chaser Wolf of Badenoch: best effort over hurdles when third in maiden at Tralee, then sold out of A. Mullins' stable 5,500 gns Doncaster August Sales: modest form both starts in chases: won 2 points in January: stays 2¾m: probably acts on any going. *A. C. Whillans* **c96 h88**

LORD SAM (IRE) 9 b. or br.g. Supreme Leader – Russian Gale (IRE) (Strong Gale) [2004/5 c150p, h–: c20g* c25sF c24d3 c24gpu Dec 26] stocky gelding: successful all 4 outings in novice chases, smart form in Grade 3 at Punchestown in April 2004: creditable third of 5 to Colonel Frank in intermediate at Sandown in December, but badly let down by jumping in stronger company start either side: reported in early-February to have sinus operation and miss remainder of season: will stay beyond 3m: raced on good ground or softer: game. *V. R. A. Dartnall* **c150 x h–**

LORDS BEST (IRE) 9 b.g. Mister Lord (USA) – Ballinlonig Star (Black Minstrel) [2004/5 c118, h–: c27d c26gpu c25dpu c24d2 c24d3 c25m* Apr 13] workmanlike gelding: fairly useful chaser: best effort when winning handicap at Cheltenham (returned lame) in April, racing prominently, left clear 6 out and beating Cassia Heights 13 lengths: probably stays 27f: acts on heavy and good to firm going: has drifted/jumped right under pressure. *A. King* **c126 h–**

LORD SEAMUS 10 b.g. Arctic Lord – Erica Superba (Langton Heath) [2004/5 c102, h–: c25g* c23f3 c24d3 c25spu Feb 10] compact gelding: fair handicap chaser: made all at Exeter in May: stays 4m: acts on firm and soft going: tried in cheekpieces: consistent. *K. C. Bailey* **c110 h–**

LORD STRICKLAND 12 b.g. Strong Gale – Lady Rag (Ragapan) [2004/5 c95x, h103x: c21g* c21g* c21mF c24g3 Oct 14] good-topped gelding: fair handicap hurdler: fairly useful handicap chaser: off a year, won at Newton Abbot (successful there 5 times in all) in May and July: stays 3m: acts on soft and firm going: often let down by jumping. *P. J. Hobbs* **c119 x h– x**

LORD THOMAS (IRE) 7 b.g. Grand Lodge (USA) – Noble Rocket (Reprimand) [2004/5 F–: 16g6 Nov 17] angular gelding: no form: jumped poorly on hurdling debut. *A. J. Wilson* **h–**

LORD TIDDLYPUSH (IRE) 7 b.g. Lord Americo – Ag Rith Abhaile (Carlingford Castle) [2004/5 16dF Apr 20] 10,500 4-y-o: tall, useful-looking gelding: second foal: dam maiden pointer: won last of 3 starts in maiden points in 2003: sold 22,000 gns Doncaster May (2003) Sales: fell second on hurdling debut. *Sir John Barlow Bt* **h–**

LORD TRANSCEND (IRE) 8 gr.g. Aristocracy – Capincur Lady (Over The River (FR)) [2004/5 c117P, h–: c26g4 c25sF c24v* Jan 22] **c150 p h–**

It is to be hoped more is seen of this exciting chaser in the next season than has been so far. Lord Transcend begins his third season over fences with just four chases under his belt, following just five races over hurdles prior to that. Injury has been partly responsible for Lord Transcend's rare visits to the track, but his latest campaign was halted abruptly with the horse seemingly in top form and still with plenty of the season left. Hopefully, the patient approach that has been adopted with Lord Transcend so far will be rewarded with appearances in more top chases over the next few seasons. The performance which left Lord Transcend's supporters wanting more was his superb display in the Peter Marsh Chase at Haydock in January. As well as being much the least experienced member of the seven-runner field, Lord Transcend was also the youngest. He was getting weight from the six others, his more accomplished rivals for the most part struggling to recapture past glories. Take The Stand's finest hour was still to come with his second in the Cheltenham Gold Cup next time out, but the remainder of the field comprised the

Peter Marsh Chase (Limited Handicap), Haydock—
the lightly-raced Lord Transcend resumes his career with an impressive win over First Gold

2000 King George winner First Gold, the 2002 Grand National winner Bindaree, the 2003 Gold Cup runner-up Truckers Tavern and the formerly high-class pair Chives and Hand Inn Hand. Of these, twelve-year-old First Gold was the only one to keep tabs on Lord Transcend, as the favourite gave his rivals a jumping lesson, taking the big Haydock fences boldly and accurately. Leaving the back straight for the final time, Lord Transcend and First Gold had pulled right away from the remainder and, after the last, Lord Transcend galloped on far too strongly for First Gold who passed the post ten lengths behind. Take The Stand fared best of the remainder, another six lengths back in third after jumping persistently left throughout.

After showing smart form over hurdles, Lord Transcend looked sure to take high rank as a novice chaser in 2003/4. He started in the best possible fashion when sauntering to a seventeen-length win at Ayr which, sadly, turned out to be the only race of his novice season. Lord Transcend was subsequently found to have heat in a tendon and, after being fired, it was exactly a year before he was seen out again. He couldn't have had a much sterner examination for only his second race over fences than the Hennessy Cognac Gold Cup at Newbury in November, but Lord Transcend emerged with plenty of credit, leading for much of the final circuit and generally jumping well. It was only going to the final fence that Lord Transcend found the first three going away from him but he finished clear of the remainder in fourth, around ten lengths behind the winner Celestial Gold. The Rowland Meyrick Handicap Chase at Wetherby looked a good opportunity for Lord Transcend to show further progress but his jumping already looked less proficient (under a conditional rider) before he fell on the second circuit. It was reported that he had become stirred up in the preliminaries at Wetherby and, with two handlers, he took proceedings calmly enough at Haydock. Lord Transcend is quite an exuberant type though, and is fitted with a crossed noseband.

		Lord Gayle (b 1965)	Sir Gaylord
	Aristocracy (b 1974)		Sticky Case
		Roxboro (ch 1968)	Sheshoon
Lord Transcend (IRE) (gr.g. 1997)			Sally Stream
		Over The River (ch 1974)	Luthier
	Capincur Lady (gr 1984)		Medenine
		All Put (gr 1968)	Letricolore
			What Ever

Whatever the big, lengthy, angular Lord Transcend goes on to achieve in his own right, his early success as his owners' very first horse was instrumental in Graham and Andrea Wylie rapidly expanding their racing interests to a string that now numbers more than eighty horses. No wonder Lord Transcend is the favourite horse in Howard Johnson's yard! Some of the Wylies' subsequent purchases have made the IR £30,000 paid for Lord Transcend as an unraced four-year-old at the 2001 Derby Sale look peanuts and they may not get a better bargain. Lord Tran-

Andrea & Graham Wylie's "Lord Transcend"

scend stands out in his family, but something that he does have in common with his dam Capincur Lady's other winners is a suitability to both heavy ground and a good test of stamina. His sister Ardnataggle twice contested the Irish Grand National, a test that would have suited her well had she not been two and a half stone out of the handicap on the first occasion and three stone wrong the following year. As that suggests, Ardnataggle was only modest and the dam's other winner, Captain Clooney (by Supreme Leader), was just a fair winner over hurdles in Ireland before winning a weakly-contested amateurs chase over three and a quarter miles at Plumpton. A sister, Lady Transcend, won a mares maiden from three completed starts in points in Ireland in 2005. Further details of Lord Transcend's pedigree were given in *Chasers & Hurdlers 2002/03*. Raced only on good going or softer so far, Lord Transcend looked in his element under the testing conditions at Haydock and he seems well suited to being allowed to bowl along in front. The Charlie Hall Chase at Wetherby (won by stable-companions Ballybough Rasher and Grey Abbey in the last two seasons) would be an obvious starting point for the 2005/6 campaign, with a second attempt at the Hennessy another plausible possibility. *J. Howard Johnson*

LORD TRIX (IRE) 6 b.g. Lord Americo – Up To Trix (Over The River (FR)) [2004/5 h95, F84: 20d^{4} May 5] workmanlike gelding: second in novice at Worcester in late-2003/4, easily better effort on completed outings over hurdles: won points in January and April: should be suited by further than 2m. *P. W. Hiatt* **h–**

LORD VALNIC (IRE) 9 b.g. Mister Lord (USA) – Any Wonder (Hardboy) [2004/5 c–: c22g^{pu} Apr 19] fair pointer: let down by jumping both starts in chases. *Ms A. E. Embiricos* **c– x**

LORD WHO (IRE) 8 b.g. Mister Lord (USA) – Le Bavellen (Le Bavard (FR)) [2004/5 c124, h109: 20s 16s 24v^{3} c24v 24s* c21v^{2} c33d^{6} Mar 19] lengthy, angular gelding: fair hurdler: won handicap at Naas in February: fairly useful chaser: best effort when second to Jim in handicap at Leopardstown: stays 25f: acts on heavy going. *P. M. J. Doyle, Ireland* **c128 h115**

LORD WISHINGWELL (IRE) 4 b.g. Lake Coniston (IRE) – Spirito Libro (USA) (Lear Fan (USA)) [2004/5 16d^{pu} 17d^{ro} Feb 8] poor maiden on Flat (probably stays 7f): no show in juvenile on hurdling debut: ran out second next time: sold 800 gns Doncaster March Sales. *J. S. Wainwright* **h– §**

LORD YOUKY (FR) 11 b.g. Cadoudal (FR) – Lady Corteira (FR) (Carvin II) [2004/5 c107, h–: c24m* c25d^{5} c24g^{ur} Apr 17] useful-looking gelding: fair chaser: won handicap at Stratford in June: sold out of I. Williams' stable 9,500 gns Doncaster August Sales: would probably have won there in hunter but for unseating last: stays 3m: acts on firm and good to soft going: goes well fresh. *Miss J. Hughes* **c114 h–**

LORENZINO (IRE) 8 ch.g. Thunder Gulch (USA) – Russian Ballet (USA) (Nijinsky (CAN)) [2004/5 c112, h112: c24m^{pu} May 25] close-coupled gelding: winning hurdler/chaser, lightly raced and no form since first half of 2003/4: stays easy 3m: acts on firm and soft going: has had tongue tied. *Jonjo O'Neill* **c– h–**

LORGNETTE 11 b.m. Emperor Fountain – Speckyfoureyes (Blue Cashmere) [2004/5 c–, h109: 22d^{pu} 24d 22d 22v^{2} 24s Apr 16] rather sparely-made mare: fair handicap hurdler: didn't convince with jumping when tried over fences: stays 3¼m: acts on any going. *R. H. Alner* **c– h111**

LORIENT EXPRESS (FR) 6 b.g. Sleeping Car (FR) – Envie de Chalamont (FR) (Pamponi (FR)) [2004/5 h–: 16d^{pu} c16m^{5} c17d^{F3} c16s^{ur} c16s^{bd} c16g* c16g^{2} c16s* c17s^{pu} c16d^{6} c16g Mar 3] tall, angular gelding: little form over hurdles for M. Harris: much better over fences, winning novice handicaps at Leicester and Windsor in December: out of sorts last 3 starts: raced around 2m: acts on soft going. *Miss Venetia Williams* **c105 h–**

LORIKO D'AIRY (FR) 6 b.g. Oblat (FR) – Ursali d'Airy (FR) (Marasali) [2004/5 17m^{2} 20d^{pu} 16g c16s^{4} c17s^{2} c17s^{5} Apr 2] good-topped gelding: third foal: half-brother to 19f chase winner Elyauki d'Airy (by Port Lyautey): dam unraced, from family of one-time top-class chaser/high-class hurdler El Paso III: once-raced on Flat: won 4-y-o chase at Pau in 2003/4: runner-up at Libourne on hurdling debut in May: left J. Ortet, form in Britain only when second in handicap chase at Market Rasen: stays 19f: raced mainly on good going or softer: free-going sort. *C. J. Mann* **c107 h109 ?**

LORIO DU MISSELOT (FR) 6 gr.g. Dom Alco (FR) – Byrsa (FR) (Quart de Vin (FR)) [2004/5 F–: 21d^{6} 16d Nov 24] workmanlike gelding: little sign of ability. *Ferdy Murphy* **h–**

L'ORPHELIN 10 ch.g. Gildoran – Balula (Balinger) [2004/5 c81x, h–: c23d^{2} c23g^{4} c21s* c21d* c20s* c22s^{pu} c26v^{pu} 22v^{ur} 22d^{pu} c21g^{3} Apr 10] small, rather plain gelding: little form over hurdles: fair chaser: won handicaps at Newton Abbot in June and November and novice at Fontwell in December: best effort when third of 4 finishers in handicap at Newton Abbot, despite typically making mistakes: stays 21f: acts on soft and good to firm going: tried visored, blinkered 7 of last 8 starts: front runner. *C. L. Tizzard* **c111 x h–**

LOR WEEN (FR) 6 ch.g. Beyssac (FR) – Asterie L'Ermitage (FR) (Hamster (FR)) [2004/5 c20s^{F} c17d^{5} c20s^{2} c16d^{pu} c17s^{pu} Nov 19] fourth foal: half-brother to 4 winners, including fairly useful hurdler/fair chaser Idiome (by Djarvis), stays 2½m: dam, unplaced on Flat/over jumps, half-sister to smart 4-y-o chaser up to 2½m Tamarix: twiced-raced over hurdles: best effort over fences when second in 5-y-o event at Auteuil: stays 2½m: acts on soft ground: tried blinkered. *G. Macaire, France* **c98 h–**

LOSCAR (FR) 6 b.g. General Holme (USA) – Unika II (FR) (Rolling Bowl (FR)) [2004/5 h–, F75: 20d^{4} 16d^{6} 22s^{3} 18s^{3} 20v^{4} Feb 15] poor form over hurdles: stays 2½m: raced only on going softer than good. *L. Lungo* **h71**

LOSING GRIP (IRE) 6 b. or br.m. Presenting – Executive Wonder (IRE) (Executive Perk) [2004/5 F17g Oct 9] second foal: sister to fairly useful staying chaser Out The Black: dam unraced half-sister to fairly useful chaser/hurdler up to 3m Nodform Wonder: awarded last of 4 starts in maiden Irish points in 2004: led until over 3f out when eighth of 16 in mares bumper at Bangor. *Mrs S. J. Smith* **F–**

LOS SAINOS (GER) 6 b.g. Winged Love (IRE) – La Sierra (Connaught) [2004/5 16g 16g 16v^{3} 16d^{4} Dec 4] workmanlike gelding: successful around 1¼m on Flat at 3 yrs in Germany, in frame twice in 2004: modest form over hurdles: not certain to stay beyond 2m: acts on heavy going. *Mrs L. Wadham* **h96**

LOSS OF FAITH (IRE) 7 b.g. Ajraas (USA) – Sharp Mistress (IRE) (Don't Forget Me) [2004/5 c22v³ Oct 25] lengthy gelding: first foal: dam unraced: fairly useful in bumpers: winning hurdler: fairly useful form when third to Cane Brake in maiden at Galway on chasing debut: reportedly had heat in leg and missed rest of season: stays 3m: raced on going softer than good over jumps (acts on heavy). *M. J. P. O'Brien, Ireland* **c119 + h–**

LOST AND FOUND 5 ch.g. Master Willie – Top Cover (High Top) [2004/5 F17v Oct 17] close-coupled gelding: eighth foal: half-brother to modest chaser Charliesmedarlin (by Macmillion), stays 3m, and 7f to 9f winner Marowins (by Sweet Monday): dam ran twice: rear in maiden bumper on debut. *C. Grant* **F–**

LOST BOY (IRE) 6 ch.g. Roselier (FR) – Stranger Still (Cragador) [2004/5 20d² 24d³ Nov 27] €50,000 4-y-o: fourth foal: dam, winning 2m hurdler, half-sister to smart staying hurdler Pertemps Network: modest form when placed both starts in novice hurdles: sold 11,000 gns Doncaster May Sales. *L. Lungo* **h95**

LOST IN NORMANDY (IRE) 8 b.g. Treasure Hunter – Auntie Honnie (IRE) (Radical) [2004/5 c76, h–: c26g c24m² c23g c26g c26gᵖᵘ c24g² Aug 26] lengthy gelding: maiden hurdler: poor handicap chaser: stays 3¼m: acts on good to firm going: blinkered over fences: inconsistent. *Mrs L. Williamson* **c76 h–**

LOST IN THE RAIN (IRE) 6 b.g. King's Theatre (IRE) – Shanira (Shirley Heights) [2004/5 16m⁴ 16m* 16g⁴ Jul 29] sturdy gelding: fairly useful on Flat (stays 1½m) in 2004, won in July: fairly useful hurdler: off 15 months before reappearance, won minor event at Roscommon in June by neck from Dyrick Daybreak: good fourth to Cloone River in Galway Hurdle (handicap): raced at 2m: acts on firm going: effective tongue tied or not. *N. Meade, Ireland* **h121**

LOST THE PLOT 10 b.m. Lyphento (USA) – La Comedienne (Comedy Star (USA)) [2004/5 c99d, h–: c20f⁴ c20mᶠ c20f 20f⁴ 22gᵖᵘ Jul 18] tall, leggy mare: winning hurdler/ novice chaser, no form since very early in 2003/4: stays 2¾m: acts on firm and good to soft going: tried tongue tied. *K. Burke, Ireland* **c– h–**

LOTHIAN EMERALD 8 ch.m. Greensmith – Lothian Rose (Roscoe Blake) [2004/5 22mᵖᵘ Sep 1] workmanlike mare: of no account: tried tongue tied. *R. J. Hodges* **h–**

LOTHIAN FALCON 6 b.g. Relief Pitcher – Lothian Rose (Roscoe Blake) [2004/5 F16d F16g⁵ F16v F16d Apr 20] 8,500 4-y-o: workmanlike gelding: third foal: dam, novice hurdler who stayed 3m, sister to useful chaser up to 3m Lothian Captain: easily best effort in bumpers when fifth to Stagecoach Diamond at Catterick. *P. Maddison* **F88**

LOTUS DES PICTONS (FR) 6 b.g. Grand Tresor (FR) – Ballaway (FR) (Djarvis (FR)) [2004/5 c103, h120: 24d⁵ 21d⁴ c22sᶠ c24dᵖᵘ Feb 9] leggy, close-coupled gelding: fairly useful handicap hurdler: maiden chaser: reportedly broke pelvis when pulled up at Ludlow: stayed 3m: acted on soft ground: inclined to carry head high: dead. *M. C. Pipe* **c– h120**

L'OUDON (FR) 4 ch.g. Alamo Bay (USA) – Stella di Corte (FR) (Lightning (FR)) [2004/5 16s² 16d 16d* 16sᵖᵘ 16g⁶ Apr 16] tall, close-coupled gelding: half-brother to useful hurdler up to 2½m Le Tastevin (by Village Star): dam unraced: fairly useful maiden around 1½m on Flat: second in juvenile at Enghien on hurdling debut for J. Bertran de Balanda: easily best effort after (reportedly struck into second outing) when winning similar event at Newbury in March by 4 lengths from Daryal: raced at 2m on good going or softer: possibly not straightforward ride. *P. F. Nicholls* **h117**

LOU DU MOULIN MAS (FR) 6 b.g. Sassanian (USA) – Houf (FR) (Morespeed) [2004/5 c112, h104: c21g* c23g² 20g² c21g³ 24m² c24g² c24d³ c24d⁶ c24g² c24g² c24g⁶ c25g⁴ Apr 16] rather leggy gelding: novice hurdler: useful chaser: simple task in maiden at Newton Abbot very early in season: best effort when short-headed by Run For Paddy at Doncaster tenth start: stays 3m: acts on soft and good to firm going: tongue tied: sound jumper: reliable. *P. F. Nicholls* **c130 h98**

LOUDY ROWDY (IRE) 14 br.g. Strong Gale – Express Film (Ashmore (FR)) [2004/5 c68?, h–: c25gᶠ May 20] maiden hurdler/chaser: fell fatally at Kelso in May: stayed 25f: raced mainly on good going or softer: visored last 3 starts: tried tongue tied. *Mrs J. K. M. Oliver* **c66 h–**

LOUGHANELTEEN (IRE) 7 b.g. Satco (FR) – Ruths Rhapsody (IRE) (Mandalus) [2004/5 17d⁴ 16m 16v 17v* 16s⁴ Feb 6] useful-looking gelding: second foal: dam unraced: fair handicap hurdler: won at Gowran in January: raced mainly around 2m: acts on any going: tongue tied on debut. *P. J. Rothwell, Ireland* **h113**

LOUGHCREW (IRE) 9 ch.g. Good Thyne (USA) – Marys Course (Crash Course) [2004/5 h–: c20m c16s⁴ c25m* Oct 1] winning hurdler: first form since 2001 when successful in handicap chase at Hexham in October: stays 25f: acts on good to firm going. *L. Lungo* **c87 h–**

Mitie Group Handicap Hurdle, Cheltenham—
a second course-and-distance win of the season for Lough Derg (star on cap),
who beats Unleash and Goblet of Fire (stripes)

LOUGH DANTE (IRE) 7 b.g. Phardante (FR) – Shannon Lough (IRE) (Deep Run) [2004/5 h102: c24d^{3} c23s^{pu} Dec 28] well-made gelding: fair novice hurdler: similar form when third in handicap at Lingfield on completed outing over fences: stays 3m. *H. D. Daly* **c101 h–**

LOUGH DERG (FR) 5 b.g. Apple Tree (FR) – Asturias (FR) (Pistolet Bleu (IRE)) [2004/5 h122: 16g^{5} 21d* 22d^{4} 24s^{6} 21g 21m* Apr 13] rather sparely-made gelding: developed into smart hurdler in 2004/5, winning twice at Cheltenham, Relkeel Hurdle (by 8 lengths from Exotic Dancer) in December and handicap (beat Unleash by 2½ lengths, staying on strongly after last) in April: also ran well when sixth to Patriarch Express in Cleeve Hurdle there in January: stays 3m: acts on soft and good to firm going. *M. C. Pipe* **h147**

LOUGH RYNN (IRE) 7 b.g. Beneficial – Liffey Lady (Camden Town) [2004/5 h79: c20g^{3} c24d^{5} c20s^{2} c24g^{2} c20g Dec 26] tall gelding: thrice-raced hurdler: fair form over fences: stays 3m: raced on good going or softer. *Miss H. C. Knight* **c106 h–**

LOUISIADE (IRE) 4 b.g. Tagula (IRE) – Titchwell Lass (Lead On Time (USA)) [2004/5 16s^{pu} Oct 30] good-topped gelding: fair on Flat (stays 1m), sold 5,500 gns Doncaster January Sales, successful twice in April for K. Ryan: no show in listed juvenile at Wetherby on hurdling debut. *T. D. Easterby* **h–**

LOUP CHARTER (FR) 6 gr.g. Royal Charter (FR) – Easy III (FR) (Perrault) [2004/5 19s* 23d^{3} 20d 24s* 24d* 24d^{pu} Apr 8] well-made gelding: will make a chaser: first foal: half-brother to 13.5f and 2m winner Monty Python (by Video Rock): dam, won 4 times up to 1¾m on Flat, from family of useful 3m chaser Haut Cercy and fairly useful out-and-out staying chaser Rubika: won over 17f at Dieppe on Flat debut at 4 yrs for E. Leenders: fairly useful novice hurdler: won at Exeter in November, Windsor in December and Bangor (beat Reflected Glory 9 lengths) in February: never dangerous in Grade 1 at Aintree final start: will stay beyond 3m: raced on good to soft/soft going. *Miss H. C. Knight* **h128**

LOUSTIC COLLONGES (FR) 6 b.g. Kadalko (FR) – Altesse Collonges (FR) (Quart de Vin (FR)) [2004/5 24v^{pu} 21d 17s^{pu} Feb 9] 44,000 4-y-o: useful-looking gelding: fourth foal: brother to 2 winners, including cross-country chaser Java Collonges and half- **h–**

brother to winner up to 13f Ivresse Collonges (by Video Rock): dam, successful around 1½m, half-sister to fairly useful staying chaser Uranus Collognes: no form in novice hurdles, jumping poorly: sold 6,500 gns Doncaster May Sales. *J. Howard Johnson*

LOVE AT DAWN 11 b.g. Dawn Johnny (USA) – Grafton Maisey (Jimsun) [2004/5 c24s Feb 10] fairly useful pointer: successful in January: let down by jumping on hunter chase debut. *A. J. Mason* **c–**

LOVE DIAMONDS (IRE) 9 b.g. Royal Academy (USA) – Baby Diamonds (Habitat) [2004/5 16gpu 16mpu Aug 6] of little account: has had tongue tied: ungenuine. *Miss C. Dyson* **h– §**

LOVELY LULU 7 b.m. Petrizzo – The Green Girls (USA) (Distinctive Pro (USA)) [2004/5 h–, F–: 17d 17g 17s5 16v 16d2 Apr 18] leggy mare: poor form over hurdles: will stay further than 2m. *J. C. Tuck* **h61**

LOVERS LANE (FR) 5 b.g. Freedom Cry – Leafy Lane (FR) (Garde Royale) [2004/5 F17s4 Apr 2] third foal: half-brother to winner around 7f Idyllic Lane (by Cardoun): dam won around 9f in France: well held in bumper on debut. *M. C. Pipe* **F–**

LOVE'S DESIGN (IRE) 8 b. or br.g. Pursuit of Love – Cephista (Shirley Heights) [2004/5 h–: 16gpu Jul 29] poor on Flat (stays 8.5f): no form over hurdles: has pulled hard: sold £550 Ascot October Sales. *Miss S. J. Wilton* **h–**

LOVE SUPREME (IRE) 5 b.m. Supreme Leader – Tri Folene (FR) (Nebos (GER)) [2004/5 F16m2 F16m5 F16g2 F16m2 F16d4 Mar 10] €21,000 3-y-o: fourth foal: dam, fairly useful chaser, effective from 21f to 27f: fair form in bumpers. *C. F. Swan, Ireland* **F89**

LOVE THAT BENNY (USA) 5 ch.g. Benny The Dip (USA) – Marie Loves Emma (USA) (Affirmed (USA)) [2004/5 17m6 17d5 17s2 16g3 20s2 Mar 22] tall gelding: fairly useful on Flat (stays 11.6f) at 3 yrs, sold out of J. Gosden's stable 24,000 gns Doncaster November Sales, and gelded: fair novice hurdler: best efforts around 2m: acts on soft going. *J. Wade* **h103**

LOVE TRIANGLE (IRE) 4 ch.g. Titus Livius (FR) – Kirsova (Absalom) [2004/5 16d6 17m3 16s2 Dec 22] fair at best on Flat (seems to stay 1¾m): poor form in juvenile hurdles: trained by D. Elsworth first 2 starts: tried tongue tied. *M. C. Pipe* **h83**

LOW CLOUD 5 b.g. Danehill (USA) – Raincloud (Rainbow Quest (USA)) [2004/5 17m* 16d 17d2 Nov 9] angular, close-coupled gelding: fair on Flat (stays 1¼m) for D. Nicholls, has run as if amiss on several occasions: fair novice hurdler: won at Sedgefield in September: raced around 2m: unraced on extremes of going. *J. J. Quinn* **h104**

LOWE GO 5 b.g. First Trump – Hotel California (IRE) (Last Tycoon) [2004/5 h86: 16d6 16m* 17m5 16g 16gur 19d6 18d4 24sF 24s* 24d5 Feb 1] angular gelding: modest handicap hurdler: won at Huntingdon (conditional jockeys seller) in June and Ludlow in January: effective from 2m to 3m: acts on soft and good to firm going. *Miss J. S. Davis* **h91**

LOYAL FOCUS (IRE) 4 ch.g. Definite Article – Temporary Lull (USA) (Super Concorde (USA)) [2004/5 16v* 16s3 17g Mar 18] good-topped gelding: half-brother to useful 2m hurdler/winning chaser Blazing Spectacle (by Sadler's Wells) and Triumph Hurdle winner Rare Holiday (by Caerleon): won 9f maiden at Listowel on second of 2 starts on Flat: changed hands €320,000 Goffs October Sale: fairly useful form over hurdles: won juvenile at Fairyhouse on hurdling debut by short head from Majlis: ran well when third to same horse in Grade 3 there and tenth to Penzance in Triumph Hurdle at Cheltenham (visored), well below form in minor event at Punchestown in late-April. *D. K. Weld, Ireland* **h120**

LOYOLA 5 ch.m. New Reputation – Stay With Me Baby (Nicholas Bill) [2004/5 h80: 22d 22g 22s Jan 3] angular mare: maiden hurdler, no form in 2004/5: stays 2¾m: acts on heavy going: blinkered final start. *Simon Earle* **h–**

LUBINAS (IRE) 6 b.g. Grand Lodge (USA) – Liebesgirl (Konigsstuhl (GER)) [2004/5 h101x: 20d* 20mpu 22v2 21g c20s2 c20v4 c20d3 c20d4 c20s4 c20g3 Apr 3] workmanlike gelding: fair handicap hurdler: won at Uttoxeter in May: similar form over fences: stays 2¾m: acts on heavy going: not a fluent jumper. *F. Jordan* **c106 h107 x**

LUCIFER BLEU (FR) 6 b.g. Kadalko (FR) – Figa Dancer (FR) (Bandinelli (FR)) [2004/5 h107: c17m* c24m3 Jun 5] leggy gelding: fair hurdler: won novice at Exeter in April 2004 on chasing debut: will prove best short of 3m: acts on good to firm and heavy going. *M. C. Pipe* **c100 h–**

LUCKEN HOWE 6 b.g. Keen – Gilston Lass (Majestic Streak) [2004/5 F–: 16g 18vpu 16dpu Apr 11] no sign of ability. *Mrs J. K. M. Oliver* **h–**

LUCK IN RUN'IN 12 b.g. Lapierre – Lady Run (Deep Run) [2004/5 c26g^{ur} May 31] workmanlike gelding: of little account outside points. *R. J. Bevis* **c– h–**

LUCKY AGAIN (IRE) 4 br.g. Be My Guest (USA) – Persian Fantasia (Alzao (USA)) [2004/5 16d 16s Oct 21] small gelding: poor maiden on Flat, sold out of J. Dunlop's stable £3,600 Ascot July Sales: no show in 2 juvenile hurdles: sold £1,300 Ascot November Sales. *J. K. Price* **h–**

LUCKY ARTHUR (IRE) 4 ch.f. Grand Lodge (USA) – Soltura (IRE) (Sadler's Wells (USA)) [2004/5 16s Feb 24] half-sister to winning hurdler/chaser Urban Hymn (by College Chapel), stays 21f: modest maiden on Flat (should stay 1¾m): pulled hard when well beaten in mares maiden on hurdling debut. *J. G. M. O'Shea* **h–**

LUCKY BAY (IRE) 9 b.g. Convinced – Current Liability (Caribo) [2004/5 c129, h–: c24d^{3} c24g^{4} c24d c29g^{pu} Apr 23] well-made gelding: fairly useful handicap chaser: off a year, best effort in 2004/5 when third to Boy's Hurrah at Sandown: should stay beyond 25f: acts on firm and good to soft going. *Ms Bridget Nicholls* **c128 h–**

LUCKY BRUSH (IRE) 11 b.g. Brush Aside (USA) – Luck Daughter (Lucky Brief) [2004/5 c25v^{4} Mar 5] workmanlike gelding: winning pointer, including in February: maiden hunter chaser: stays 25f: jumped poorly when tried in cheekpieces. *N. W. Alexander* **c–**

LUCKY CATCH (IRE) 7 b.g. Safety Catch (USA) – Lucky Monday (Lucky Wednesday) [2004/5 c–x, h–: 17d^{pu} Oct 27] no sign of ability: tried blinkered. *A. Crook* **c– x h–**

LUCKYCHARM (FR) 6 ch.g. Villez (USA) – Hitifly (FR) (Murmure (FR)) [2004/5 h–, F–: 16g 22d 19s c24s^{pu} c16s c24d^{pu} c23d^{4} Apr 20] lengthy, plain gelding: little form over hurdles or fences: tried visored/blinkered. *R. Dickin* **c76 h–**

LUCKY CLOVER 13 ch.g. Push On – Winning Clover (Winden) [2004/5 c101§, h–§: c23g^{5} Jul 7] well-made gelding: veteran staying chaser: acts on firm and good to soft going: tried blinkered: temperamental (needs to dominate). *C. L. Tizzard* **c98 § h–**

LUCKY DO (IRE) 8 b.g. Camden Town – Lane Baloo (Lucky Brief) [2004/5 16f 16m^{2} c20g^{F} c16g^{F} 19s Feb 6] medium-sized gelding: poor maiden hurdler: fell both starts over fences: should stay 2½m. *R. Dickin* **c– h80**

LUCKY DUCK 8 ch.g. Minster Son – Petroc Concert (Tina's Pet) [2004/5 h116: 18m^{2} 16g^{6} 16d^{6} 17s^{6} Oct 31] medium-sized gelding: fair hurdler: off 5 months, below form last 3 outings: should stay 2½m: acts on good to firm and good to soft going: front runner/races prominently. *Mrs A. Hamilton* **h112**

LUCKY JUDGE 8 b.g. Saddlers' Hall (IRE) – Lady Lydia (Ela-Mana-Mou) [2004/5 20s^{F} Nov 4] compact gelding: fair on Flat (stays 2m), successful 3 times in 2004: lightly-raced winning hurdler: stays 25f. *G. A. Swinbank* **h–**

LUCKY LEADER (IRE) 10 b.g. Supreme Leader – Lucky House (Pollerton) [2004/5 c89x: c24s* c23s^{4} c26d^{4} c25d^{5} c23s^{pu} c26v^{pu} c26d^{5} c21d^{3} c25d^{3} c25d^{pu} Apr 3] lengthy gelding: handicap chaser: seemed much improved when winning at Chepstow in May: modest on balance of form: stays 3¼m: raced on good going or softer: often blinkered, not last 3 starts: often let down by jumping. *N. R. Mitchell* **c104 x**

LUCKY LUK (FR) 6 b.g. Lights Out (FR) – Citronelle II (FR) (Kedellic (FR)) [2004/5 F–: 22g^{pu} 25d^{pu} 16d 16g c18g^{4} Mar 20] compact gelding: little impact over hurdles: poor form on chasing debut: tried tongue tied. *K. C. Bailey* **c81 h–**

LUCKY MASTER (IRE) 13 b.g. Roselier (FR) – Golden Chestnut (Green Shoon) [2004/5 c27v^{6} Mar 15] sturdy gelding: winning hurdler/chaser: fair pointer nowadays: probably stays 3¾m: acts on soft and good to firm going. *Miss G. Swan* **c– h–**

LUCKY NOMAD 9 br.g. Nomadic Way (USA) – Daleena (Dalesa) [2004/5 h56: 22g 24m^{3} 27d 24s^{pu} 23d^{pu} 24g^{pu} Dec 30] medium-sized gelding: poor novice hurdler: stays 25f: acts on firm ground: wore cheekpieces/visor last 3 outings. *R. Ford* **h62**

LUCKY PENNY 9 ch.m. Karinga Bay – Redgrave Rose (Tug of War) [2004/5 24m^{4} 22g^{3} Jul 12] workmanlike mare: poor form in 3 starts over hurdles. *K. Bishop* **h72**

LUCKY PETE 8 b.g. Lyphento (USA) – Clare's Choice (Pragmatic) [2004/5 h63, F–: 21d^{2} c21d^{ur} c20d^{F} c18s* c21s^{ur} c18s^{6} c20d* Apr 18] leggy, quite good-topped gelding: poor hurdler: modest chaser: won amateur handicap at Fontwell in December and novice handicap at Plumpton in April: stays 2¾m: acts on soft going: tried in cheekpieces: front runner/races prominently. *P. J. Jones* **c89 h70**

LUCKY PISCEAN 4 b.g. River Falls – Celestine (Skyliner) [2004/5 16s 16d 16d^{5} Dec 6] leggy gelding: little form on Flat in 2004: best effort in juvenile hurdles when fifth of 19 at Newcastle. *C. W. Fairhurst* **h82**

LUCKY SINNA (IRE) 9 b. or br.g. Insan (USA) – Bit of A Chance (Lord Ha Ha) [2004/5 c97, h–: c22s^{2} c21v^{2} c21s^{pu} Feb 10] rangy gelding: modest maiden hurdler/chaser: stays 3m: acts on any going: has had tongue tied: consistent. *B. G. Powell* **c94 h–**

LUCKY UNO 9 b.g. Rock City – Free Skip (Free State) [2004/5 c–, h–: c21g^{pu} May 1] of no account: tried tongue tied. *John A. Harris* **c– h–**

LUDERE (IRE) 10 ch.g. Desse Zenny (USA) – White Jasmin (Jalmood (USA)) [2004/5 h80§: c24v^{F} Dec 17] angular gelding: poor hurdler for B. Llewellyn in 2003/4: showed nothing on chasing debut: stays 3m: acts on any going: tried blinkered/in cheekpieces: moody. *Miss J. S. Davis* **c– § h– §**

LUFTIKUS (GER) 8 ch.g. Formidable (USA) – La Paz (GER) (Roi Dagobert) [2004/5 h80: 20s Dec 21] workmanlike gelding: poor hurdler: stays 3m: acts on good to firm and good to soft ground. *Miss E. C. Lavelle* **h–**

LUGO ROCK (IRE) 5 b. or br.g. Luso – Rocher Lady (IRE) (Phardante (FR)) [2004/5 F16d Apr 20] 20,000 4-y-o: sturdy gelding: first foal: dam Irish bumper winner: well beaten in bumper on debut. *P. R. Webber* **F–**

LUMBACK (IRE) 6 b.g. Desert Style (IRE) – Bellingham Jester (Jester) [2004/5 F16m^{pu} Jun 12] no sign of ability in bumpers or on Flat debut. *N. Wilson* **F–**

LUMINOSO 13 gr.g. Machiavellian (USA) – Light The Sky (FR) (Persepolis (FR)) [2004/5 16g 17d^{5} 16g^{2} 16m^{2} 16s* Dec 13] close-coupled gelding: fair hurdler at best: off nearly 4 years, poor form in 2004/5: won selling handicap at Towcester in December: raced mainly around 2m: acts on soft and good to firm going: tried blinkered. *J. D. J. Davies* **h83**

LUMYNO (FR) 6 b.g. Lute Antique (FR) – Framboline (FR) (Royal Charter (FR)) [2004/5 F–: 17g^{6} 17s 25d^{5} 19s^{pu} Nov 18] has scope: easily best effort when sixth of 15 in novice hurdle at Hereford: tongue tied first 3 outings. *S. E. H. Sherwood* **h88**

LUNAR CRYSTAL (IRE) 7 b.g. Shirley Heights – Solar Crystal (IRE) (Alzao (USA)) [2004/5 16d^{5} 16d^{3} 16g^{2} 16d Apr 9] leggy gelding: fairly useful hurdler: off nearly 2 years, creditable efforts in handicaps first 3 starts: raced around 2m: acts on firm and soft going: tried visored (below form): often makes running. *M. C. Pipe* **h121**

LUNAR DRAM 7 ch.g. Cosmonaut – Moonshine Malt (Superlative) [2004/5 23v^{pu} 19d 17s^{4} 17v^{3} Mar 15] big gelding: off 2 years, modest form over hurdles: form around 2m on soft/heavy going. *M. Dods* **h97**

LUNAR ECLIPSE 5 b.m. Dancing High – Pauper Moon (Pauper) [2004/5 F16s Apr 22] sixth foal: sister to bumper winner Lunar Dancer and winning 23f hurdler Lunar Maxwell: dam untrustworthy winning staying hurdler: mid-division in bumper at Perth on debut. *J. I. A. Charlton* **F72**

LUNAR EXIT (IRE) 4 gr.g. Exit To Nowhere (USA) – Moon Magic (Polish Precedent (USA)) [2004/5 16d^{3} 16d^{4} Dec 3] lengthy gelding: fairly useful on Flat (should stay 1¾m), ran as if amiss 2 of 4 outings in 2004: fair form when in frame in juvenile hurdles: will be suited by further than 2m. *Lady Herries* **h108**

LUNAR FOX 6 b.m. Roselier (FR) – Leinthall Fox (Deep Run) [2004/5 F–: 24d^{pu} 19s Nov 30] small mare: has no tail: no form in mares bumper and novice hurdles. *J. L. Needham* **h–**

LUNAR LEADER (IRE) 5 b.m. Mujadil (USA) – Moon River (FR) (Groom Dancer (USA)) [2004/5 h–: 16g^{3} 18m May 30] fair at best on Flat (stays 1¼m), well held in 2004: no form in 3 starts over hurdles: has worn cheekpieces: tongue tied. *M. J. Gingell* **h–**

LUNAR LORD 9 b.g. Elmaamul (USA) – Cache (Bustino) [2004/5 h89: 19d^{2} 24s^{4} 18d^{5} 16d^{4} 24g^{4} 16s^{5} 17d^{3} 19s^{pu} Mar 10] leggy gelding: modest hurdler: sold out of D. Burchell's stable £1,600 Ascot December Sales after fourth outing: best short of 3m: acts on soft going: tried in cheekpieces. *M. J. M. Evans* **h86**

LUNCH WAS MY IDEA (IRE) 5 b. or br.g. Tawrrific (NZ) – Equity Law (IRE) (Gunner B) [2004/5 F16s^{3} F16s^{6} F16d^{4} F18m^{3} Apr 21] rangy gelding: first foal: dam unraced: fair form when in frame in bumpers. *P. F. Nicholls* **F91**

LUNERAY (FR) 6 b.m. Poplar Bluff – Casandre (FR) (Montorselli) [2004/5 c106, h112: c22s^{pu} c21d^{pu} c21d^{2} c21s^{3} c20s^{pu} c18m^{2} c19d^{6} Apr 22] ex-French mare: fair hurdler/chaser: stays 2¾m: acts on soft going, probably on good to firm: ran poorly in blinkers fifth start, tongue strap first 2. *P. F. Nicholls* **c106 h–**

LUPIN (FR) 6 b.g. Luchiroverte (IRE) – Amarante II (FR) (Brezzo (FR)) [2004/5 h96: 16s^{pu} 19m Apr 17] leggy gelding: winning 2m hurdler: bought out of F. Doumen's stable **h–**

€7,000 Goffs (France) November Sale: little impact in Britain: acts on soft going: tried tongue tied. *A. W. Carroll*

LURID AFFAIR (IRE) 4 b.f. Dr Massini (IRE) – Miss Good Night (Buckskin (FR)) [2004/5 F12g F17s⁶ F16d³ Mar 3] angular filly: ninth foal: half-sister to winning hurdler/ fair chaser Lord 'N' Master (by Lord Americo), stays 3m, and 2 winning pointers, including Gaora Bridge (by Warcraft): dam, placed in bumper, half-sister to useful 2m chaser Cottage Run: modest form on last of 3 outings in bumpers. *Mrs S. Gardner* **F77**

LURISTAN (IRE) 5 b.g. Pennekamp (USA) – Linnga (IRE) (Shardari) [2004/5 h–, F–: 17gʳᵒ 16dᵖᵘ Jan 7] angular gelding: signs of ability only in bumper on debut. *S. T. Lewis* **h–**

LUSCAT (IRE) 5 b.g. Luso – Shuil Shell (IRE) (Cataldi) [2004/5 F16vᵖᵘ Jan 15] 21,000 4-y-o: second foal: dam maiden half-sister to useful chaser up to 27f Good Shuil: pulled up in bumper on debut (gravel in foot). *A. Crook* **F–**

LUSCIOUS (IRE) 5 b.m. Luso – Gaye Chatelaine (IRE) (Castle Keep) [2004/5 F17s⁶ F16d Feb 18] €3,500 3-y-o: first foal: half-sister to bumper winner Wild Ocean (by Old Vic): dam, lightly raced, from family of top-class 2m to 3m hurdler Gaye Brief and very smart staying jumper Gaye Chance: well held in bumpers. *K. C. Bailey* **F–**

LUSHPOOL (IRE) 7 b.m. Supreme Leader – Dawn Hunt (IRE) (Architect (USA)) [2004/5 F16m F16g⁵ 16d Nov 9] angular mare: second foal: sister to winning pointer Dawn Devoy: dam, winning pointer, from family of Dawn Run: modest form on second of 2 outings in bumpers at Worcester for R. J. Smith: last of 15 in novice on hurdling debut. *D. G. Bridgwater* **h– F77**

LUSIMUS 4 ch.g. Piccolo – Bob's Princess (Bob's Return (IRE)) [2004/5 F14d F13d 16dᵖᵘ 16d 18s Feb 4] big, workmanlike gelding: first foal: dam, 2-y-o 7f winner who stayed 1½m, half-sister to useful 7f and 1m performer Biniti: behind all completed outings: tried visored. *J. A. Geake* **h– F–**

LUST FOR LIFE (IRE) 5 br.g. Marju (IRE) – Kariyh (USA) (Shadeed (USA)) [2004/5 16m⁶ Jun 16] ex-Irish gelding: modest maiden at best on Flat at 2 yrs: well beaten over hurdles, formerly trained by N. Madden. *Jonjo O'Neill* **h–**

LUSTRAL DU SEUIL (FR) 6 b.g. Sassanian (USA) – Bella Tennise (FR) (Rhapsodien) [2004/5 h104: 17d³ 17g* 16g⁴ 22s⁴ 16m⁵ Apr 2] tall, useful-looking gelding: fair novice hurdler: won at Folkestone in December: should stay beyond 17f: acts on good to firm going, probably on soft: tends to finish weakly. *N. J. Henderson* **h112**

LUTEA (IRE) 5 ch.g. Beneficial – Francie's Treble (Quayside) [2004/5 F17m* F16d* F16d⁴ F16s³ F16d 16d⁴ Apr 22] leggy gelding: fifth foal: half-brother to winning 3m hurdler Bally Treble (by Balinger) and winning pointer by Remainder Man: dam unraced half-sister to useful 2m hurdler Liscahill Hill and fairly useful staying hurdler Liscahill Fort: useful form in bumpers: won at Taunton and Newbury in November: 4 lengths fourth of 15 to Earth Man in Grade 2 at latter course next time: again raced freely when fourth in maiden at Chepstow on hurdling debut: needs to learn to settle. *M. C. Pipe* **h84 F113**

LUTHELLO (FR) 6 b.g. Marchand de Sable (USA) – Haudello (FR) (Marignan (USA)) [2004/5 F84: 16m⁶ Apr 28] leggy gelding: failed to see race out in bumper and maiden hurdle. *J. Howard Johnson* **h80**

LUTIN DU MOULIN (FR) 6 br.g. Saint Preuil (FR) – Emeraude du Moulin (FR) (Djarvis (FR)) [2004/5 c18s* c20s 16s 16s⁶ 19d 24v c21v⁴ Mar 28] leggy ex-French gelding: first foal: dam, 8.5f winner, out of half-sister to smart chaser up to 2¾m Soliter du Moulin: modest chaser/maiden hurdler: won at Moulins in May, penultimate outing for M. Rolland: stays 21f: acts on heavy ground: has worn blinkers, including when successful: edgy sort. *L. Lungo* **c94 h86**

LUXEMBOURG 6 b.g. Bigstone (IRE) – Princess Borghese (USA) (Nijinsky (CAN)) [2004/5 h–: 24d* 24m² Jun 5] lengthy, angular gelding: poor hurdler: first form when winning handicap at Uttoxeter in May: stays 3m: acts on good to soft and good to firm going: tried visored: not a fluent jumper: hard ride. *N. A. Twiston-Davies* **h84 +**

LUZCADOU (FR) 12 b.g. Cadoudal (FR) – Luzenia (FR) (Armos) [2004/5 c119§, h–: c24g c34gᵖᵘ c34mᴿ c31d³ c31d⁵ c20v⁴ c31d² Mar 15] good-topped gelding: raced in cross-country events in 2004/5 apart from sixth start, seeming to show retains useful level of ability, including when second to Spot Thedifference in Sporting Index Handicap at Cheltenham: stays 31f (had seemed best around 2½m on conventional tracks): acts on heavy going: blinkered/visored: unreliable. *Ferdy Murphy* **c131 ? h–**

LYNRICK LADY (IRE) 9 b.m. Un Desperado (FR) – Decent Lady (Decent Fellow) [2004/5 c94, h106: c26d⁶ c29dᵖᵘ Dec 5] tall mare: fair handicap hurdler: second in novice **c– h–**

in 2003/4, only form in chases: stays 3¼m: acts on heavy going, possibly unsuited by good to firm. *J. G. Portman*

LYNS RESOLUTION 5 b.g. Awesome – Our Resolution (Caerleon (USA)) [2004/5 F16m F17d Aug 22] sixth foal: brother to poor hurdler Dere Lyn, stays 3m, and half-brother to winners up to around 7f in Germany by Distant Relative and Indian Ridge: dam no sign of ability: well held in 2 bumpers: fourth in maiden on Flat in September (refused to enter stalls next intended outing). *D. Burchell* **F–**

LYON 5 ch.g. Pivotal – French Gift (Cadeaux Genereux) [2004/5 F–: 17v⁶ 16g³ Apr 19] well held in bumper: better effort in novice hurdles when third to Standin Obligation at Towcester. *O. Sherwood* **h88**

LYRICAL LILY 7 b.m. Alflora (IRE) – Music Interpreter (Kampala) [2004/5 F72: F16g F16s 21s^pu Jan 20] signs of ability only in bumper on debut in 2003/4: left Mrs S. Johnson after second start. *Mrs A. M. Thorpe* **h– F–**

LYRICAL WAY 6 b.g. Vettori (IRE) – Fortunate (Reference Point) [2004/5 17g⁴ 22m* 19m⁵ 21g³ 19g^pu Apr 15] fair at 1¼m on Flat: poor form over hurdles: won maiden at Fontwell in August: stays 2¾m: raced on good/good to firm going over hurdles: visored last 2 starts. *P. R. Chamings* **h76**

LYRICIST'S DREAM 6 b.m. Dreams End – Lyricist (Averof) [2004/5 F–: F17g⁴ F17d³ 16d 17s⁵ 16g³ 16s^pu Jan 15] sparely-made mare: poor form in bumpers and over hurdles: likely to stay beyond 2m. *R. L. Brown* **h61 F71**

M

MAAREES 4 b.f. Groom Dancer (USA) – Shemaleyah (Lomond (USA)) [2004/5 aF16g⁴ F16d⁴ F18d³ Apr 18] sixth foal: half-sister to 2m hurdle winner Kefaaf (by Lion Cavern) and French 1¼m to 1¾m winner No Win No Deal (by Machiavellian): dam, 1¾m winner, half-sister to high-class 2m hurdler Kingsmill: sold unraced out of M. Tregoning's stable 4,000 gns Newmarket July Sales: best effort in bumpers when third in maiden at Plumpton. *G. P. Enright* **F86**

MABEL RILEY (IRE) 5 b.m. Revoque (IRE) – Mystic Dispute (IRE) (Magical Strike (USA)) [2004/5 16d³ 16m³ 16m³ 17m⁴ 16g⁶ 16m⁵ 17m² 16g⁴ Oct 7] sparely-made mare: modest on Flat (stays 8.5f) at 3 yrs, below form in 2004: poor maiden hurdler: will prove best at 2m with emphasis on speed: sold to join B. Leavy 1,100 gns Doncaster October Sales. *M. A. Buckley* **h73**

MACARONI BEACH 11 ch.m. Jupiter Island – Real Princess (Aragon) [2004/5 c19g² c21d^pu c16m⁵ Mar 21] modest pointer: remote second in weak novice hunter at Exeter: tried blinkered. *Mrs A. L. Tory* **c63**

MACATAQUE (IRE) 6 ch.m. Roselier (FR) – Vulcan Belle (Royal Vulcan) [2004/5 16d 17d^pu Oct 27] third foal: sister to fair chaser Moreluck, stays 3m: dam, tailed off in bumper, sister to very smart chaser Royal Mountbrowne, successful at 2m to 3m: no form in 2 novice hurdles, lame second start. *B. S. Rothwell* **h–**

MACCHIATO 4 br.f. Inchinor – Tereyna (Terimon) [2004/5 16d^ur 16d 16s² 16d³ 16v³ 16s 16s⁶ Jan 27] smallish filly: modest maiden at best up to 11.5f on Flat (tried blinkered), sold out of F. J. Houghton's stable £1,400 Ascot October Sales: poor maiden hurdler on balance: flattered when third to Pay Attention in mares novice at Wetherby fifth outing, able to build clear lead. *I. W. McInnes* **h85**

MACEO (GER) 11 ch.g. Acatenango (GER) – Metropolitan Star (USA) (Lyphard (USA)) [2004/5 c86§, h110§: 16m⁶ 16s 19g⁶ 16d⁵ Dec 4] angular gelding: fair handicap hurdler, below form in 2004/5: little aptitude for chasing: stays 2½m: acts on soft and good to firm going: has run well in blinkers/cheekpieces: held up: often looks unenthusiastic. *K. G. Reveley* **c– § h100 §**

MACGEORGE (IRE) 15 b.g. Mandalus – Colleen Donn (Le Moss) [2004/5 c128, h–: c26d³ c22g² c24d³ c24v³ c26s² c25m³ Apr 9] lengthy gelding: veteran chaser: retains fair level of ability, races mainly in hunters nowadays: stays 3¼m: acts on good to firm and heavy going: races prominently: bold jumper, makes the odd bad mistake: genuine. *R. Lee* **c108 h–**

MACGYVER (NZ) 9 b.g. Jahafil – Corazon (NZ) (Pag-Asa (AUS)) [2004/5 c67, h–: c18m² c16g* c16m² c17g* c17m⁵ c26d³ c16m⁶ 16dᵖᵘ Mar 11] medium-sized gelding: modest chaser: won handicaps at Uttoxeter (novice) in June and Southwell in July: lightly raced over hurdles, lame final outing: best form around 2m: acts on good to firm and good to soft going: formerly headstrong front runner, more settled and ridden with restraint nowadays: usually sound jumper. *D. L. Williams* **c96 h–**

MAC HINE (IRE) 8 b.g. Eurobus – Zoe Baird (Aragon) [2004/5 c111x, h–: c21g³ c20s² c23m* c21dᵘʳ Nov 20] tall gelding: fair chaser: won novice at Worcester (tongue tied) in September: stays 23f: acts on good to firm and heavy going: unreliable. *Jonjo O'Neill* **c108 § h–**

MACHRIHANISH 5 b.g. Groom Dancer (USA) – Goodwood Lass (IRE) (Alzao (USA)) [2004/5 h85§: 20sᵖᵘ May 9] leggy gelding: ungenuine maiden hurdler/pointer. *S. C. Burrough* **h– §**

MACKENZIE (IRE) 9 b.g. Mandalus – Crinkle Lady (Buckskin (FR)) [2004/5 h–: c24d⁴ c20gᵖᵘ c20dᵖᵘ 22s³ 22vᵖᵘ c26sᵖᵘ Apr 21] good-topped gelding: no longer of any account. *Mrs C. J. Kerr* **c– h–**

MACLEAN 4 b.g. Machiavellian (USA) – Celtic Cross (Selkirk (USA)) [2004/5 16g⁴ 16s⁵ 16g³ Mar 28] tall, close-coupled gelding: fairly useful on Flat (stays 1¼m), won twice in 2004, though has looked temperamental: sold out of Sir Michael Stoute's stable 30,000 gns Newmarket Autumn Sales: modest form in juvenile hurdles: likely to prove best over sharp 2m: races freely: needs to brush up his jumping. *G. L. Moore* **h93**

MACMAR (FR) 5 b.g. Ragmar (FR) – Ex Des Sacart (FR) (Balsamo (FR)) [2004/5 c17g³ c20g² c17g* c18d⁴ c18d⁶ c22dᵖᵘ Jan 12] big, good-topped ex-French gelding: first foal: dam, runner-up around 2¾m over fences, half-sister to smart chaser up to 25f Temerson: twice-raced on Flat: won 4-y-o chase at La-Roche-sur-Yon in September: left P. Peltier, little show in 2 novices at Newbury: stays 2½m: has been blinkered, including when successful. *R. H. Alner* **c–**

MACNANCE (IRE) 9 b.m. Mandalus – Colleen Donn (Le Moss) [2004/5 h105: c20d² c20d* c19s² c24s⁵ c21d⁴ c19m³ Apr 9] angular mare: fair hurdler: similar form over fences, winning mares novice at Huntingdon in December: stays 3m: acts on good to firm and heavy going. *R. Lee* **c108 h–**

MACONNOR (IRE) 8 b.g. Religiously (USA) – Door Belle (Fidel) [2004/5 c–, h–: 20d 20s³ 20sᵖᵘ Dec 26] rangy gelding: fell fourth only start over fences: disappointing maiden hurdler, left H. Daly after first outing: should stay beyond 2m: headstrong: sold 1,700 gns Doncaster March Sales. *L. Lungo* **c– h–**

MACREATER 7 b.m. Mazaad – Gold Caste (USA) (Singh (USA)) [2004/5 h–: 20g 19s 20d 19s⁶ 21g 16g² Apr 19] leggy mare: maiden hurdler: in cheekpieces, first form when second in seller at Towcester. *K. A. Morgan* **h65**

MAC'S ELAN 5 b.g. Darshaan – Elabella (Ela-Mana-Mou) [2004/5 16dᵖᵘ 17s³ 16g⁴ Mar 14] leggy gelding: fair maiden on Flat (stays 1½m): best effort in novice hurdles when third to Jair Ohmsford in steadily-run race at Market Rasen, allowed to dictate. *A. B. Coogan* **h77**

MACS FLAMINGO (IRE) 5 br.g. Rashar (USA) – Parkality (IRE) (Good Thyne (USA)) [2004/5 F102: F16s⁵ F16s F18d* 16v* 16v³ 16v* Mar 6] rangy, rather unfurnished gelding: fairly useful form at best in bumpers, won at Downpatrick in November: good start over hurdles, winning 24-runner maiden at Leopardstown (by 8 lengths from In Compliance) in December and minor event there in March: little impact in Grade 1 novice at Punchestown in late-April: will stay at least 2½m. *P. A. Fahy, Ireland* **h123 F91**

MACS GILDORAN 11 b.g. Gildoran – Shamrock Bridge (Golden Love) [2004/5 c29dᵖᵘ c16s 16v² 24v³ 20v³ c16s⁴ c21v³ 20s⁴ Mar 28] good-topped gelding: useful chaser: best effort in 2004/5 when 8 lengths third to Jim in handicap at Leopardstown in March: lightly raced over hurdles, fairly useful form when staying-on fifth to Mansony in listed handicap at Punchestown in late-April: should stay 3m: raced on good going or softer (acts on heavy): tongue tied fifth and sixth starts. *W. P. Mullins, Ireland* **c130 h116 +**

MACS JOY (IRE) 6 b.g. Religiously (USA) – Snob's Supreme (IRE) (Supreme Leader) [2004/5 h132p, F90: 16m* 16s* 16d³ 16s* 16v* 16g⁵ 20d⁴ Apr 9] **h163**

Honours in the top two-mile hurdle races in Britain and Ireland were spread far and wide. Five different horses, all trained in Ireland, shared the seven races carrying Grade 1 status. Solerina beat Accordion Etoile and Harchibald in the John James McManus Memorial Hurdle at Tipperary; Harchibald won both the

Freephone Stanleybet Swinton Handicap Hurdle, Haydock—
Macs Joy takes command from Almaydan and runner-up Dancing Bay at the last

'Fighting Fifth' at Newcastle and the Christmas Hurdle at Kempton, both from almost wholly British-trained opposition; Macs Joy beat Brave Inca, Hardy Eustace and Solerina in the December Festival Hurdle at Leopardstown, before beating the same trio plus Accordion Etoile in the AIG Europe Champion Hurdle at the same course; Brave Inca beat Harchibald and Macs Joy in the Emo Oil Champion Hurdle at Punchestown; and Hardy Eustace beat all those named except Solerina in *the* Champion Hurdle at Cheltenham. So far as status goes, it is a case of some races being more equal than others. The winner of the 'Fighting Fifth' has seldom, in recent times, been required to show even high-class form and the winning performance is almost always inferior to that of the winner of the Grade 2 Bula Hurdle at Cheltenham run shortly before. That said, part of the cause lies with trainers and there is clearly something to be said in favour of a more equitable spread of graded events—not every Grade 1 should be run at Cheltenham. As for the McManus Memorial, this has attracted plenty of top hurdlers in its short history and, if it has not always been that strong a contest, the idea of enticing good horses out earlier in the season has to be commended. As the results indicate, there wasn't a lot to choose between the top two-milers and, on any given day, any one of them might conceivably land the spoils. To say they were all much of a muchness wouldn't be fair. Clearly there are quite a few high-class performers among them, though probably no really top-notch ones. The situation nonetheless made for some exciting races with margins of a head (Emo Oil), two necks (Champion) and a short head and a head (AIG Europe).

Aside from Solerina's four-length success at Tipperary, the widest winning margin in any of the named races came in the December Festival Hurdle at Leopardstown which represented the high water mark of Macs Joy's season. The previous season's Champion Hurdle winner Hardy Eustace started favourite, just ahead of Solerina, who had won three times at two and a half miles since Tipperary, beating a ring-rusty Hardy Eustace last time out, with Brave Inca third in the betting, just ahead of Macs Joy. Macs Joy and Brave Inca had already met earlier in the autumn, in an intermediate hurdle at Down Royal in November, in which Macs Joy, with the benefit of a run on the Flat, had shown too much speed for his rival, though only winning by a length in receipt of 10 lb. Macs Joy went on to show further improvement, though starting odds-on on his first step into graded company when third in the Morgiana at Punchestown nine days later, again receiving weight from his main rivals. That race, however, possibly came too soon and Macs Joy went on to show in a representative field for the December Festival Hurdle that he was indeed a high-class performer. With Solerina setting a decent gallop, Macs Joy travelled smoothly in behind and, after taking over two out, showed his characteristic turn of foot to have the race won by the last, beating Brave Inca by three lengths. Subsequent events suggest neither second, nor third Hardy Eustace, at Leopardstown were quite at their best.

Strange to say, not least of those subsequent events was the AIG Europe Champion Hurdle the following month. Having gone off at 7/1 at Christmas, Macs

Bewleys Hotel December Festival Hurdle, Leopardstown—
Macs Joy takes the step up in class in his stride;
(left to right) Brave Inca, Solerina and Hardy Eustace fight out second

AIG Europe Champion Hurdle, Leopardstown—much closer this time, as Macs Joy is being caught near the line by Hardy Eustace and Brave Inca

Joy was 11/8 to beat largely the same opposition on the same terms. He managed to justify favouritism, but only just, leading by a length at the last but holding on all out at the line from Brave Inca and Hardy Eustace. Macs Joy was in front much earlier this time, at the fifth, and the ground was more testing. However, a more patient ride and good ground at Cheltenham in the Champion Hurdle failed to show Macs Joy to any better effect and he managed only fifth, five lengths behind Hardy Eustace, with Harchibald, Brave Inca and Accordion Etoile also ahead of him. A step up to two and a half miles for the first time, in the Aintree Hurdle, didn't seem likely to show Macs Joy to advantage, for all that he is bred to stay, and he found little after two out when five lengths fourth to Al Eile. Macs Joy was then put away for the season, though was subsequently brought in as an afterthought when it was clear the Emo Oil at Punchestown, shortly after the end of the British season, was going to cut up. In a very slowly-run affair, Macs Joy led fleetingly before the last but was unable to quicken and finished a length behind the first two, Brave Inca and Harchibald.

Macs Joy (IRE) (b.g. 1999)	Religiously (USA) (b or br 1984)	Alleged (b 1974)	Hoist The Flag
			Princess Pout
		Pas de Nom (b 1968)	Admiral's Voyage
			Petitioner
	Snob's Supreme (IRE) (b 1991)	Supreme Leader (b 1982)	Bustino
			Princess Zena
		Boherash Forest (ch 1982)	Proverb
			In The Forest

For a horse whose main target at the start of the season was the totesport Trophy, a haul of three wins, two in Grade 1 contests, isn't bad. Macs Joy had ended his previous campaign in the very early days of the new British season, winning the valuable Swinton Handicap at Haydock. Just as the totesport Trophy is no longer Gold, so the tag Swinton has been consigned to history, the 2005 renewal run solely under the name of the sponsors. Macs Joy, the 4/1 favourite for the 2004 edition, beat Dancing Bay two and a half lengths in a field of nineteen, in which no fewer than twelve, Macs Joy among them, ran off the minimum weight due to the presence of Westender. If he were to run in a handicap again, it could well be Macs Joy keeping the rest on 10-0. With so many opportunities in Grade 1 events, Macs Joy may well not have to contest a handicap again. It would be no surprise if things fell Macs Joy's way in a good race at least once in 2005/6. The compact Macs Joy, who seems more likely to remain over hurdles than be sent novice chasing, has won on ground ranging from good to firm to heavy. There is one thing to add, or rather amend, regarding the details of his undistinguished family recorded in last year's Annual. His dam Snob's Supreme, recorded in the *General Stud Book* as dying in 2001, produced foals by Gone Fishin in 2003 and Old Vic in 2005. No-one is infall-

Mac's J. Racing Syndicate's "Macs Joy"

ible. Readers will note, in the Errata & Addenda, that Vic Toto, previously recorded herein as a gelding, began a career as a stallion in 2005. *Mrs J. Harrington, Ireland*

MAC'S SUPREME (IRE) 13 b.g. Supreme Leader – Merry Breeze (Strong Gale) [2004/5 c30d* c30s* c32v⁶ c33dᵖᵘ Mar 19] good-bodied gelding: fairly useful handicap chaser: rejoined former stable after 3 runs for A. J. Martin in 2003, won handicaps at Newcastle in November and Bangor in December: little impression in valuable events last 2 starts: stays 3¾m: acts on good to firm and heavy going. *Ferdy Murphy* **c116** **h–**

MAC THREE (IRE) 6 b.g. Lord Americo – Le Nuit (Le Bavard (FR)) [2004/5 F16m³ F20g² F20m* 20g³ 24d* 24s² 19s³ 24sᶠ Nov 7] half-brother to 2 winning hurdlers by King's Ride, fairly useful Hi Knight and Regal Knight, both stayed 3m: dam unraced: fairly useful form in bumpers, winning at Roscommon in June: useful novice hurdler: won maiden at Kilbeggan in August: would probably have won listed event at Cork final outing but for falling last: good placed efforts in between, second to Whatareyouhaving in listed handicap at Gowran and third to Royal Paradise at Naas: will prove best at 3m+: acts on soft going, won bumper on good to firm. *N. Meade, Ireland* **h131 +** **F99**

MACY (IRE) 12 ch.g. Sharp Charter – Lumax (Maximilian) [2004/5 c–, h–: c25s Apr 28] good-topped gelding: of little account outside points nowadays, successful in April: has worn visor/cheekpieces. *Martin Jones* **c–** **h–**

MADAAR (USA) 6 b.g. Spinning World (USA) – Mur Taasha (USA) (Riverman (USA)) [2004/5 17d 17gᵖᵘ Aug 14] maiden on Flat: twice refused to race in points in 2004: no show both starts over hurdles. *R. Bastiman* **h–**

MADALYAR (IRE) 6 b.g. Darshaan – Madaniyya (USA) (Shahrastani (USA)) [2004/5 c73, h68: c25mᵖᵘ 17m c16mᶠ Jun 29] angular gelding: poor maiden hurdler/chaser: blinkered second outing. *Jonjo O'Neill* **c–** **h–**

MADAME LUSO (IRE) 5 b.m. Luso – Real Town (IRE) (Camden Town) [2004/5 F17m Jun 9] first foal: dam unraced half-sister to high-class 2m to 2½m hurdler/useful chaser Bonalma: well held in bumper on debut. *C. J. Down* **F–**

MADAM FLORA 8 b.m. Alflora (IRE) – Madam's Choice (New Member) [2004/5 c106, h106: c17s^{2} Oct 19] sparely-made mare: fair hurdler: similar form when second in 2 maiden chases at Exeter: effective at 2m to 2¾m: acts on soft and good to firm going: front runner. *M. J. Weeden* **c109 h–**

MADAM MOSSO 9 b.m. Le Moss – Rochestown Lass (Deep Run) [2004/5 c–, h–: c24d^{5} c26d^{3} c23s^{5} c26v^{ur} c23d^{pu} Jan 25] lengthy, workmanlike mare: winning hurdler: poor handicap chaser, off 13 months before reappearance: will stay beyond 3¼m: acts on good to firm and heavy going. *Mrs A. M. Thorpe* **c85 h–**

MADAM'S MAN 9 b.g. Sir Harry Lewis (USA) – Madam-M (Tina's Pet) [2004/5 c100, h–: c30d^{2} Mar 8] rangy gelding: fair handicap chaser: good second to Toulouse-Lautrec at Exeter in March: stays 3¾m: acts on soft and good to firm going. *N. A. Twiston-Davies* **c108 h–**

MADDY THE HATTER 6 ch.m. Alfie Dickins – Radar Blue (Ardar) [2004/5 F16s Mar 22] lengthy mare: first foal: dam unraced: always behind in bumper on debut. *Miss T. Jackson* **F–**

MADE IN FRANCE (FR) 5 b.g. Luchiroverte (IRE) – Birgonde (FR) (Quart de Vin (FR)) [2004/5 17s 18s c20d^{3} 16m* 17f* 20d^{2} 16s^{4} c16d* 16g c16d^{5} c20g^{6} Apr 22] leggy gelding: third foal: half-brother to 19f chase winner Insoumise (by Royal Charter): dam, lightly-raced maiden, half-sister to fairly useful jumper around 2¼m En Couleurs: placed twice around 1½m from 3 starts on Flat at 3 yrs: sold out of F. Cottin's stable €50,000 Goffs July Sale after third start: fair form over hurdles: won maiden at Worcester in August and handicap at Exeter in September: similar standard over fences: won 3-runner maiden at Newton Abbot in November: stays 2½m: acts on firm and soft going: front runner: carries head high. *M. C. Pipe* **c110 h106**

MADE IN JAPAN (JPN) 5 b.g. Barathea (IRE) – Darrery (Darshaan) [2004/5 h134p: 16g^{2} c16g* c16d^{3} c16d^{4} c16g c16d^{4} c20g^{6} Apr 16] tall, useful-looking gelding: useful hurdler: easily won novice at Kempton on chasing debut in November: failed to progress as well as expected, looked none too keen final start: should stay beyond 2m: raced on good going or softer (acts on soft): blinkered last 2 starts: tends to wander under pressure. *P. J. Hobbs* **c125 h–**

MADE IN MONTOT (FR) 5 b.g. Video Rock (FR) – Deep Turple (FR) (Royal Charter (FR)) [2004/5 17s^{5} 17s* 16d Jan 8] tall, useful-looking gelding: second foal: half-brother to 17f hurdle winner Idylle de Montot (by Luchiroverte): dam, 11f winner, out of half-sister to SunAlliance Chase winner Rolling Ball: placed over 11f on Flat at 3 yrs: thrice-raced over hurdles for J. Bertran de Balanda, improved form when beating Marcel 5 lengths in 4-y-o minor event at Auteuil in May: bled from nose when well held in Grade 1 novice at Sandown on British debut. *P. F. Nicholls* **h116**

MADEMIST SAM 13 b.g. Lord Bud – Mademist Susie (French Vine) [2004/5 c–, h–: c25d^{pu} c20s^{5} Mar 11] workmanlike gelding: winning chaser: modest pointer nowadays: seems to stay 3m: acts on soft and good to firm going: tried blinkered. *M. J. Hill* **c– h–**

MADGE CARROLL (IRE) 8 b.m. Hollow Hand – Spindle Tree (Laurence O) [2004/5 c109, h94: c21d^{2} c24m^{5} May 16] small, sturdy mare: modest hurdler: fair chaser: good second in listed mares handicap at Uttoxeter in May: successful twice in points in 2005: stays 25f: acts on soft and good to firm going. *T. R. George* **c111 h–**

MADGIK DE BEAUMONT (FR) 5 b. or br.g. Sleeping Car (FR) – Matalie (FR) (Danoso) [2004/5 F16d 19g 19m Apr 9] close-coupled gelding: fourth foal: half-brother to winning cross-country chaser D'Italic (by Italic): dam, 1¼m winner, half-sister to dam of useful chaser up to 2¾m Frimeur II: no sign of ability. *Ian Williams* **h– F–**

MADIBA 6 b.g. Emperor Jones (USA) – Priluki (Lycius (USA)) [2004/5 h–: 19d^{5} 17v^{5} 16g Mar 15] leggy gelding: fairly useful on all-weather, modest on turf on Flat (stays 2m): modest novice hurdler: stays 19f. *P. Howling* **h96**

MADISON AVENUE (GER) 8 b.g. Mondrian (GER) – Madly Noble (GER) (Irish River (FR)) [2004/5 h88: 20s^{pu} 21v^{pu} 18s c17s^{F} 18s^{5} 22g 21g^{3} 20s^{3} 16d^{3} Apr 18] leggy gelding: poor hurdler: fell fourth on chasing debut: stays 21f: acts on heavy going: tried blinkered/visored, including last 3 starts. *T. M. Jones* **c– h81**

MADISON DE VONNAS (FR) 5 b.g. Epervier Bleu – Carine de Neuvy (FR) (Shelley (FR)) [2004/5 F–: 16s 16g^{2} 16d^{4} 20d 19g Apr 15] good-topped gelding: modest novice hurdler: should stay beyond 2m: tongue tied after reappearance. *Miss E. C. Lavelle* **h92**

MAD MAX TOO 6 gr.g. Environment Friend – Marnworth (Funny Man) [2004/5 20v^{pu} c27v^{pu} c25s^{pu} c20s^{F} Mar 10] fourth foal: half-brother to winning 2½m hurdler Ragu (by Contract Law): dam, winning pointer, sister to useful staying chasers Riverside Boy and Huntsworth: no sign of ability. *N. Wilson* **c–** **h–**

MAESTRO PLEASE (IRE) 6 b.g. Old Vic – Greek Melody (IRE) (Trojan Fort) [2004/5 F82: 20d 19g 25s 23v^{3} 22v 26s Mar 7] lengthy, rather unfurnished gelding: form over hurdles only when third in amateur novice at Wetherby, probably flattered. *Lady Connell* **h87 ?**

MA FURIE (FR) 5 gr.m. Balleroy (USA) – Furie de Carmont (FR) (Carmont (FR)) [2004/5 h110: 16d^{pu} 16s^{5} 16d^{3} 16d^{pu} 16g 19s^{2} 16d^{F} 19s^{3} 16d^{5} Mar 24] good-topped mare: fair handicap hurdler: stays 19f: acts on soft going: tongue tied 6 of last 7 outings: none too keen: often shapes as if amiss. *Miss H. C. Knight* **h108 §**

MAGALINA (IRE) 6 br.m. Norwich – Pike Review (Dawn Review) [2004/5 h80, F87: 20g^{5} 20d^{2} 20d^{6} 20d^{2} 22s^{pu} 20g^{pu} c19g^{pu} Apr 7] good-topped mare: modest handicap hurdler: pulled up last 3 starts, including on chasing debut: stays 2½m: acts on good to soft going. *D. P. Keane* **c–** **h96**

MAGENKO (IRE) 8 ch.g. Forest Wind (USA) – Bebe Auction (IRE) (Auction Ring (USA)) [2004/5 h77: 22m 22s^{3} 27d^{6} 20d^{3} 27d c21v Jan 11] quite good-topped gelding: poor handicap hurdler: no show in handicap on chasing debut: stays 3m: acts on good to firm and heavy going: tried blinkered: ungenuine. *F. P. Murtagh* **c–** **h76 §**

MAGENTA RISING (IRE) 5 ch.m. College Chapel – Fashion Queen (Chilibang) [2004/5 h72: 16d^{4} 17d 17g^{F} 16f^{5} 17g 17m 17m^{3} 16m^{pu} 17m^{5} 19d^{5} 17d^{pu} Oct 27] small mare: poor maiden hurdler: claimed from D. Burchell £6,000 first outing, left R. C. Guest after sixth: best around 2m: acts on good to firm and good to soft going: tried in cheek-pieces: has had tongue tied. *D. W. Thompson* **h73**

MAGGIE GRAY (IRE) 7 b.m. Erins Isle – Reenoga (Tug of War) [2004/5 F76: 16g^{5} 16d 16g^{5} 17m Aug 31] modest form in 2 bumpers: no show over hurdles: tried in cheek-pieces. *P. D. Niven* **h–**

MAGGIES BROTHER 12 b.g. Brotherly (USA) – Sallisses (Pamroy) [2004/5 c94: c25s^{3} c34d^{4} c24g^{3} c26s^{pu} Mar 13] workmanlike gelding: fairly useful hunter chaser: stays 4¼m: acts on good to firm and heavy going. *R. Shail* **c100**

MAGICAL FUN (IRE) 13 b.g. Magical Strike (USA) – Roundstone Lass (Montekin) [2004/5 c24g Apr 15] ex-Irish gelding: winning hurdler: poor chaser nowadays: placed in points in Britain in 2004: tried blinkered: usually tongue tied. *Mrs J. A. Hayes* **c–** **h–**

MAGICAL KINGDOM 5 b.g. Petoski – Saxon Magic (Faustus (USA)) [2004/5 F16d Mar 24] second foal: dam, winning hurdler, stayed 2½m: tailed off in bumper on debut. *M. Bradstock* **F–**

MAGICAL LEGEND 4 gr.f. Midnight Legend – Alice's Mirror (Magic Mirror) [2004/5 F16d^{4} F17s Apr 7] 70,000 3-y-o: leggy filly: third foal: half-sister to winning 2m hurdler Demesne and bumper winner Magical Wonderland (both by Thowra): dam modest and temperamental hurdler up to 2½m: better effort in bumpers when fourth to Noland in maiden at Wincanton. *B. G. Powell* **F82**

MAGICAL LIAISON (IRE) 7 b.g. Mujtahid (USA) – Instant Affair (USA) (Lyphard (USA)) [2004/5 h70: 21d^{4} 22d^{5} 20d^{3} 24g^{3} 26g^{2} 24g^{6} 26m 24m^{4} c20g^{R} 26d* 21d^{5} Mar 24] rather sparely-made gelding: modest novice hurdler: won handicap at Hereford in October: refused first on chasing debut: stays 3¼m: acts on good to firm and good to soft going: tried in cheekpieces, blinkered nowadays. *W. Jenks* **c–** **h87**

MAGICAL MIMI 4 b.f. Magic Ring (IRE) – Naval Dispatch (Slip Anchor) [2004/5 16m 16m^{pu} Oct 13] angular filly: 6f winner at 2 yrs, disappointing on Flat since: no aptitude for hurdling in 2 juveniles. *Jedd O'Keeffe* **h–**

MAGICAL SHADOWS 6 b.g. Whittingham (IRE) – She Knew The Rules (IRE) (Jamesmead) [2004/5 16d^{pu} 24f^{ro} Sep 5] leggy gelding: poor 5f maiden at 2 yrs for D. Burchell: showed more temperament than ability in 2 novice hurdles. *P. Morris* **h– §**

MAGICAL WONDERLAND 6 br.m. Thowra (FR) – Alice's Mirror (Magic Mirror) [2004/5 h68, F87: 22g^{5} Jul 12] fair bumper performer: some promise in 2 mares hurdles, getting tired over longer trip on only start in 2004/5. *B. G. Powell* **h66 +**

MAGIC BENGIE 6 b.g. Magic Ring (IRE) – Zinzi (Song) [2004/5 h59: 19s^{pu} 16g^{pu} Mar 9] lengthy gelding: bad 2m hurdler: sometimes tongue tied. *F. Kirby* **h–**

MAGIC BOX 7 b.g. Magic Ring (IRE) – Princess Poquito (Hard Fought) [2004/5 h77: 17m 17m* 16s6 17m c16g3 c16d6 Oct 9] angular gelding: poor handicap hurdler: won seller (sold from Miss K. Milligan 3,500 gns) at Sedgefield in July: similar form both starts in novice chases: best around 2m: acts on good to firm and good to soft going (well below form on soft): has worn cheekpieces. *A. M. Crow* **c76 h77**

MAGIC CHARM 7 b.m. Magic Ring (IRE) – Loch Clair (IRE) (Lomond (USA)) [2004/5 h–x: 17m Aug 6] poor on Flat (stays 13f): lightly raced and no form over hurdles: sold 1,400 gns Doncaster January Sales. *Jedd O'Keeffe* **h– x**

MAGIC COMBINATION (IRE) 12 b.g. Scenic – Etage (Ile de Bourbon (USA)) [2004/5 c–, h–: 22dpu 22g 17s3 17v* Nov 8] leggy gelding: fairly useful on Flat, successful in July and August: fair handicap hurdler nowadays: won at Carlisle in November: stays 21f: acts on good to firm and heavy going: tried in cheekpieces/blinkers: usually held up. *L. Lungo* **c– h108**

MAGIC EAGLE 8 b.g. Magic Ring (IRE) – Shadow Bird (Martinmas) [2004/5 17d May 9] poor on Flat (best form at 6f) nowadays: well beaten in maiden on hurdling debut. *P. T. Midgley* **h–**

MAGIC HOUR (IRE) 6 b.g. Weldnaas (USA) – Montohouse (IRE) (Montelimar (USA)) [2004/5 F–: 16gpu 20mpu 26g4 20dpu Jun 20] no form: sold 1,600 gns Doncaster October Sales. *W. McKeown* **h–**

MAGIC MISTRESS 6 b.m. Magic Ring (IRE) – Sight'n Sound (Chief Singer) [2004/5 h117p: 16m2 16g 17d 16d Jan 8] leggy, lengthy mare: fairly useful hurdler: off 6 months, disappointing in handicaps last 3 starts: should stay beyond 2m: acts on good to firm going. *N. J. Henderson* **h121**

MAGICO (NZ) 7 b.g. Casual Lies (USA) – Majica (NZ) (Star Way) [2004/5 12g3 16s2 19s 16s2 16s2 16v3 20v Jan 26] lengthy, angular gelding: won once over 1m on Flat in New Zealand: fair novice hurdler: best efforts at 2m on soft going. *R. C. Guest* **h103**

MAGIC RED 5 ch.g. Magic Ring (IRE) – Jacquelina (USA) (Private Account (USA)) [2004/5 h82: 16dpu 19g Oct 30] workmanlike gelding: modest on Flat (stays 2m), successful twice in 2004: poor novice hurdler: tried in blinkers/cheekpieces. *M. J. Ryan* **h–**

MAGNA 6 ch.g. Cadeaux Genereux – Millyant (Primo Dominie) [2004/5 F16d Feb 12] angular gelding: second foal: dam, 5f performer, half-sister to very smart sprinter Prince Sabo: soundly beaten in bumper on debut. *A. B. Coogan* **F–**

MAGNESIUM (USA) 5 ch.g. Kris S (USA) – Proflare (USA) (Mr Prospector (USA)) [2004/5 16dpu 16s5 16m4 Apr 2] lengthy, useful-looking gelding: half-brother to useful hurdler/chaser Profluent (by Sunshine Forever), stayed 25f: useful on Flat (stays 10.5f), sold out of Mme C. Head-Maarek's stable 60,000 gns Newmarket Autumn Sales: fair form both completed outings in novice hurdles. *B. G. Powell* **h105 +**

MAGNETIC POLE 4 b.g. Machiavellian (USA) – Clear Attraction (USA) (Lear Fan (USA)) [2004/5 16d 16vpu 16g4 Mar 18] useful-looking gelding: fairly useful on Flat (stays 1½m), successful in October, subsequently sold out of Sir Michael Stoute's stable 48,000 gns Newmarket Autumn Sales: tongue tied, first form over hurdles when fourth in maiden at Fakenham. *B. I. Case* **h87**

MAGNIFICENT SEVEN (IRE) 6 ch.g. Un Desperado (FR) – Seven Hills (FR) (Reform) [2004/5 F16d3 19s 20s 16d4 22s Mar 22] well-made gelding: eighth foal: half-brother to winner in Hungary by Satco: dam fair stayer: third to Sea Captain in bumper at Ludlow on debut: modest form over hurdles: stays 2½m. *Miss H. C. Knight* **h94 F92**

MAGNUS MAXIMUS 13 b.g. Takachiho – L'Oraz (Ile de Bourbon (USA)) [2004/5 c20dpu May 11] lengthy gelding: winning pointer: no form otherwise. *Mrs Lynda Lamyman* **c– h–**

MAGOT DE GRUGY (FR) 5 b.g. Tzar Rodney (FR) – Hirlish (FR) (Passing Sale (FR)) [2004/5 21g4 16d5 17m4 16d5 20v4 16s3 17v4 16d3 16s Mar 27] compact ex-French gelding: first foal: dam unraced, from family of top-class chaser up to 29f Oteuil: runner-up twice around 13f on Flat in Provinces for P. Cormier-Martin: modest maiden hurdler: stays 2½m: acts on good to firm and heavy going. *R. H. Alner* **h88**

MAGS BENEFIT (IRE) 5 b.m. Beneficial – Moynetto (Bustineto) [2004/5 F17d4 F16s3 F16g6 F18d3 F16s* F18s3 F16s 16v4 22s5 19s3 18d* 16d2 16g* Apr 15] smallish mare: half-sister to fair 2m hurdler Blazing Arrow and winning 3m chaser Rusnetto (both by Torus): dam unraced sister to fairly useful hurdler up to 21f Court Master: fair form in bumpers, successful at Cork in November: fair hurdler: won handicaps at Thurles in March and Ayr (10 lb out of weights, beat Prairie Moonlight by 2½ lengths in quite **h113 F91**

valuable mares event) in April: best effort when 2½ lengths second to Blazing Liss in listed mares event at Punchestown later in April: bred to stay beyond 2¼m: raced on good ground or softer: tongue tied after third outing. *T. Hogan, Ireland*

MAGS TWO 8 b.g. Jumbo Hirt (USA) – Welsh Diamond (High Top) [2004/5 h71: 20d⁴ 20dᵖᵘ 24g 19sᵖᵘ Mar 1] close-coupled gelding: maiden hurdler: trained by Ms L. Harrison until after second start: stays 2½m: acts on good to firm going. *F. P. Murtagh* **h–**

MAGUIRE (GER) 4 ro.g. Medaaly – Mayada (USA) (The Minstrel (CAN)) [2004/5 16d⁴ 16dᵖᵘ 17gᵖᵘ Apr 3] good-topped gelding: half-brother to winning hurdler/chaser Manoram (by Zinaad), stays 2½m: successful over 7f at 2 yrs in Germany: form in juvenile hurdles only when fourth to Yankeedoodledandy at Sandown. *M. F. Harris* **h87**

MAHARAAT (USA) 4 b.g. Bahri (USA) – Siyadah (USA) (Mr Prospector (USA)) [2004/5 16dᵖᵘ 17g⁴ Mar 19] good-topped gelding: fairly useful form in maidens on Flat, sold out of Sir Michael Stoute's stable 25,000 gns Newmarket July Sales, resold 22,000 gns Newmarket Autumn Sales: better effort in juvenile hurdles when fourth to Mohawk Star at Bangor: tongue tied on debut. *P. J. Hobbs* **h92**

MAHARBAL (FR) 5 b.g. Assessor (IRE) – Cynthia (FR) (Mont Basile (FR)) [2004/5 h107: 18d 17d 19s* Jan 3] good-topped gelding: fairly useful hurdler, improved form when winning handicap at Exeter in January by 2 lengths from Borehill Joker: likely to stay beyond 19f: acts on soft and good to firm going. *N. J. Henderson* **h116**

MAIDEN VOYAGE 7 b.m. Slip Anchor – Elaine Tully (IRE) (Persian Bold) [2004/5 h105: c16d⁴ c19s⁴ c17g⁴ c22m⁵ Apr 21] good-topped mare: fair hurdler: off 17 months, modest form at best over fences: stays 21f: acts on soft and good to firm going: visored: sold 11,500 gns Doncaster May Sales. *P. R. Webber* **c88 h–**

MAID FOR A MONARCH 5 b.m. King's Signet (USA) – Regan (USA) (Lear Fan (USA)) [2004/5 h–: 17m Sep 8] angular mare: no sign of ability. *M. Wigham* **h–**

MAIDSTONE MISTRAL 5 b.g. Slip Anchor – Cayla (Tumble Wind) [2004/5 h–, F82: 20gᵖᵘ May 1] small, close-coupled gelding: modest form in bumpers: headstrong and no form over hurdles. *M. C. Pipe* **h–**

MAIDSTONE MONUMENT (IRE) 10 b.g. Jurado (USA) – Loreto Lady (Brave Invader (USA)) [2004/5 c106, h90: c25g³ c26g c23m⁶ c24g³ 27g c24d c26d⁶ c24dᵖᵘ c26d Apr 18] lengthy gelding: winning hurdler: fair handicap chaser: little form after first outing: stays 3¼m: acts on good to firm and good to soft going: blinkered once: best on left-handed tracks: often front runner: unreliable. *Mrs A. M. Thorpe* **c100 h–**

MAIFUL (FR) 5 b.g. Useful (FR) – Shailann (FR) (Gaspard de La Nuit (FR)) [2004/5 h87: 19s 19d⁶ c16dᵖᵘ Mar 26] leggy gelding: modest novice hurdler: no show on chasing debut: probably stays 19f: acts on good to firm and good to soft going. *P. F. Nicholls* **c– h89**

MAISIEBEL 7 ch.m. Be My Native (USA) – High 'b' (Gunner B) [2004/5 h65: 16s 16d 19sᵖᵘ 21g c22g⁴ Mar 20] rather sparely-made mare: little sign of ability: tried in cheekpieces. *R. N. Bevis* **c– h–**

MAITRE DE MUSIQUE (FR) 14 ch.g. Quai Voltaire (USA) – Mativa (FR) (Satingo) [2004/5 c89x, h–: c27g⁴ May 25] tall gelding: veteran chaser: successful in point in March: stays 27f: acts on good to firm and heavy going: usually tongue tied. *T. P. Tate* **c– x h–**

MAITRE LEVY (GER) 7 b.g. Monsun (GER) – Meerdunung (EG) (Tauchsport (EG)) [2004/5 h90: 17d Apr 29] maiden hurdler: won twice in points in 2005: has had tongue tied: sold 5,800 gns Doncaster May Sales. *M. C. Pipe* **h–**

MAJED (FR) 9 b.g. Fijar Tango (FR) – Full of Passion (USA) (Blushing Groom (FR)) [2004/5 c112, h–: c24s² c25g* c24g⁵ c28d⁴ c31d c27g⁵ Apr 15] compact gelding: fair handicap chaser: won at Wincanton very early in season: sold out of P. Nicholls' stable 22,000 gns Doncaster May Sales: stays 3½m (probably not 4m): acts on good to firm and heavy going: usually blinkered/visored: races prominently: not a straightforward ride, and probably ungenuine. *Mrs L. B. Normile* **c113 § h–**

MAJESTIC BAY (IRE) 9 b.g. Unfuwain (USA) – That'll Be The Day (IRE) (Thatching) [2004/5 c–, h–: 21d³ c24d⁵ 21mᵖᵘ Apr 13] sturdy gelding: fair chaser/maiden hurdler, below form last 2 outings: stays 3m, at least when conditions aren't testing: raced mainly on good going or softer. *J. A. B. Old* **c– h113**

MAJESTIC CLASS (USA) 5 b.g. Majestic Twoeleven (USA) – Miss Count Fleet (USA) (Mr Cockatoo (USA)) [2004/5 F16g⁴ F16v⁶ F17s 16g Mar 16] close-coupled gelding: seventh foal: brother to minor winner in USA: dam ran twice: best effort in bumpers on debut: let down by jumping in maiden on hurdling debut. *M. W. Easterby* **h– F82**

MAJESTIC (IRE) 10 b.g. Belmez (USA) – Noble Lily (USA) (Vaguely Noble) [2004/5 c23m^ur c24m^3 21g^6 24d 25s 21m^pu Apr 13] smallish gelding: useful handicap hurdler in 2002/3: missed 2003/4: form in 2004/5 only when sixth to The Dark Lord at Cheltenham: winning chaser, fairly useful form when third in handicap at Stratford: stays 3m: acts on soft and firm going: blinkered and tongue tied: usually forces pace: often races lazily. *Ian Williams* **c115 h130 d**

MAJESTIC MOONBEAM (IRE) 7 b.g. Supreme Leader – Magic Moonbeam (IRE) (Decent Fellow) [2004/5 c103?, h–: 16m^5 c21s^2 Nov 3] maiden hurdler/chaser: stays 21f: acts on soft ground. *Jonjo O'Neill* **c99 h83**

MAJLIS (IRE) 8 b.g. Caerleon (USA) – Ploy (Posse (USA)) [2004/5 c–, h–: c19d^5 16g^2 18d* 21d^6 18s^4 20v* 22s^5 Feb 4] strong, well-made gelding: let down by jumping both starts over fences: modest hurdler nowadays: won claimer at Fontwell in November and seller at Uttoxeter in January: stays 2½m: acts on heavy going: wears headgear: difficult ride: temperamental. *B. J. Llewellyn* **c– h97 §**

MAJLIS (JPN) 4 b.g. Commander In Chief – Prayer Wheel (CAN) (Conquistador Cielo (USA)) [2004/5 16d^2 16v* 16v^2 16s* 17g Mar 18] strong, compact gelding: fair maiden on Flat (probably stays 1¾m), sold out of A. Fabre's stable 27,000 gns Newmarket July Sales: fairly useful juvenile hurdler: won at Naas (maiden) in January and Fairyhouse (Grade 3, by a neck from Don't Be Bitin) in February: not discredited under less testing conditions in Triumph Hurdle at Cheltenham final outing: will stay beyond 2m: acts on heavy going. *M. J. P. O'Brien, Ireland* **h123**

MAJOR ADAMS 10 b.g. Roscoe Blake – Celtic View (Celtic Cone) [2004/5 c26d^3 c24s^pu Nov 11] sturdy gelding: winning pointer: no show in 2 novice chases: should stay 3m+: acts on soft going. *W. G. M. Turner* **c– h–**

MAJOR BELLE (FR) 6 ch.m. Cyborg (FR) – Mistine Major (FR) (Major Petingo (FR)) [2004/5 c–, h–: 17s^F 19m* 20m 16g^pu 16d^pu c16m^3 16s^5 c16s^pu 16g^pu c20m^pu 17m Apr 23] lengthy mare: poor hurdler: won seller (sold out of M. Pipe's stable 7,250 gns) at Hereford in May: winning chaser, modest form only completion over fences in Britain: stays 19f: acts on heavy and good to firm ground: tried in visor. *M. J. Gingell* **c89 h76**

MAJOR BENEFIT (IRE) 8 b.g. Executive Perk – Merendas Sister (Pauper) [2004/5 c112: c22s^4 Oct 24] strong, workmanlike gelding: fair chaser: below form only start in 2004/5: stays 27f: acts on heavy going. *Miss K. Marks* **c–**

MAJOR BIT 9 b.g. Henbit (USA) – Cute Pam (Pamroy) [2004/5 c26v^pu c24g^pu c24s^pu Apr 16] deep-girthed gelding: little form: usually tongue tied. *S. A. Brookshaw* **c– h–**

MAJOR BLADE (GER) 7 b.g. Dashing Blade – Misniniski (Niniski (USA)) [2004/5 16s 16s^3 Nov 3] good-topped gelding: lightly raced over hurdles, modest form at best. *Mrs H. Dalton* **h83**

MAJOR BLUE 10 ch.g. Scallywag – Town Blues (Charlottown) [2004/5 h92: 24s^4 22d^2 24v^5 c23s^3 c24v^F c26d^4 c24d^3 c33g^pu Mar 17] rangy gelding: fair handicap hurdler: similar form when third in maiden chases: stays 3¼m: acts on good to firm and heavy going: wore cheekpieces last 2 starts. *J. G. M. O'Shea* **c100 h104**

MAJOR BURNS (IRE) 7 b.g. Aahsaylad – Night Matron (IRE) (Hatim (USA)) [2004/5 h118, F98: 20m^2 20m* 20f* Jun 20] fairly useful hurdler: won minor events at Punchestown in May and Navan in June: stays 2½m: acts on firm and soft going: often races prominently. *W. P. Mullins, Ireland* **h118**

MAJOR CATCH (IRE) 6 b.g. Safety Catch (USA) – Inch Tape (Prince Hansel) [2004/5 h–, F107: 22g^3 Apr 12] useful-looking gelding: useful bumper winner: easily better effort in novice hurdles 14 months apart when third at Exeter: will stay 3m: should improve. *N. J. Gifford* **h107 p**

MAJOR EURO (IRE) 8 b.g. Lord Americo – Gold Bank (Over The River (FR)) [2004/5 h111: c19d^4 c19m^4 c21g^5 c20g^2 c19s^4 c20v^pu c20g* c20m^pu Apr 23] good-topped gelding: winning hurdler: fair chaser: won maiden at Market Rasen in April: should stay beyond 2½m: acts on soft and good to firm going. *S. J. Gilmore* **c106 h–**

MAJOR MILLER 4 b.g. Opera Ghost – Millers Action (Fearless Action (USA)) [2004/5 F16s^5 Apr 22] £31,000 3-y-o: third foal: half-brother to useful bumper winner Miller's Bay (by Karinga Bay): dam once-raced half-sister to useful 2m hurdler Bold Gait, out of half-sister to Champion Hurdle winner Royal Gait: fifth of 18 in bumper at Perth on debut. *N. J. Henderson* **F87**

MAJOR OAK (IRE) 4 b.g. Deploy – Mahaasin (Bellypha) [2004/5 F16s^5 Mar 12] 10,000 3-y-o: third foal: half-brother to 5f and 7f winner in Macau by Handsome Sailor: **F84**

dam, poor middle-distance maiden, half-sister to smart middle-distance stayer Fight Your Corner: fifth of 16 in bumper at Ayr on debut. *G. M. Moore*

MAJOR RENO (IRE) 8 b.g. Little Bighorn – Make Me An Island (Creative Plan (USA)) [2004/5 22mpu Jun 13] IR 12,500 4-y-o: ex-Irish gelding: second foal: half-brother to fair 21f chase winner Trotsky (by Jurado) and winning pointer by Courtship: dam winning hurdler/chaser up to 2½m: sold out of Ms F. Crowley's stable £2,100 Ascot February (2004) Sales: won maiden point in May: no other form: tried blinkered. *R. C. Harper* **h–**

MAJOR ROYAL (FR) 5 ch.g. Garde Royale – Majorica Queen (FR) (Kaldoun (FR)) [2004/5 F17d F16g F16g 17d 16d 16s6 Apr 22] close-coupled gelding: fifth foal: half-brother to 3 winners, including fairly useful hurdler/chaser around 2m Six Fois Sept (by Epervier Bleu): dam, 1¼m winner, half-sister to very smart hurdler/chaser up to 2¾m Lute Antique: no better than mid-division in bumpers: well held in novice company over hurdles. *A. Parker* **h– F76**

MAJOR SHARK (FR) 7 b.g. Saint Preuil (FR) – Cindy Cad (FR) (Cadoudal (FR)) [2004/5 h90: 20s2 22g* 27mpu 21m2 21m* 22g* 20g* 22d Apr 11] fair handicap hurdler: won at Cartmel in May, Southwell in July and Newton Abbot and Bangor in August: should stay 3m: acts on soft and good to firm going: wears cheekpieces: races prominently: hard ride, soon off bridle. *Jennie Candlish* **h104**

MAJOR SHARPE (IRE) 13 b.g. Phardante (FR) – Winsome Doe (Buckskin (FR)) [2004/5 24m Sep 24] well-made gelding: maiden hurdler: winning chaser, often let down by jumping. *B. J. M. Ryall* **c– x h–**

MAJOR SPECULATION (IRE) 5 b.g. Spectrum (IRE) – Pacific Grove (Persian Bold) [2004/5 h103: 20m6 May 25] smallish, leggy gelding: winning hurdler: no show in handicap only start in 2004/5: likely to prove best around 2m with emphasis on speed: has worn visor: ungenuine. *M. C. Pipe* **h–**

MAJOR VERNON (IRE) 6 b.g. Flemensfirth (USA) – Rainys Run (Deep Run) [2004/5 F112: F16g* 16d* 16d5 20s5 20d 20s* Mar 28] sturdy gelding: successful 2 of 3 starts in bumpers: useful novice hurdler: won maiden at Clonmel in November and minor event at Fairyhouse in March, beating In Compliance short head, pair 20 lengths clear, in latter: folded tamely in Grade 1 novice at Punchestown in late-April: will stay 3m: raced only on soft/good to soft going over hurdles. *W. P. Mullins, Ireland* **h132**

MAKANDY 6 b.g. Makbul – Derring Floss (Derring Rose) [2004/5 F16s F17m F16g 21vpu Mar 28] first foal: dam, poor maiden hurdler who stayed 25f, half-sister to high-class staying chaser Earth Summit: well beaten in bumpers: no show in novice on hurdling debut. *Miss J. Wormall* **h– F–**

MAKEABREAK (IRE) 6 ch.m. Anshan – Nilousha (Darshaan) [2004/5 F16d5 F16g5 F16d* Mar 28] unfurnished mare: third foal: dam won around 2m over hurdles and 1¾m on Flat: best effort in bumpers when winning mares event at Fakenham by 10 lengths from Retro's Girl: sold 15,000 gns Doncaster May Sales. *R. A. Fahey* **F93**

MAKE HASTE SLOWLY 8 b.g. Terimon – Henry's True Love (Random Shot) [2004/5 h99: 16g5 20m* 20g3 c19d* c20d3 c24g c24s Dec 22] rather leggy gelding: modest hurdler: won maiden at Worcester in June: better over fences: won handicap at Hereford in October: stays 2½m: acts on good to firm and good to soft going: let down by jumping last 3 starts. *H. D. Daly* **c107 x h90**

MAKE IT A DOUBLE (IRE) 7 ch.g. Zaffaran (USA) – La Danse (Le Moss) [2004/5 21g2 Apr 1] 5,800 4-y-o: strong gelding: fourth foal: brother to winning pointer and half-brother to another by Colonel Godfrey: dam unraced: looked in need of race when ¾-length second to River Phantom in maiden at Newbury on hurdling debut, finishing strongly: will stay at least 3m: likely to improve. *Noel T. Chance* **h100**

MAKE IT EASY (IRE) 9 b. or br.g. Alphabatim (USA) – Mammy's Friend (Miner's Lamp) [2004/5 c63, h–: c20g6 c20m3 c16m c21dpu Aug 9] maiden chaser: wears cheekpieces/visor: sold £4,500 Ascot August Sales: successful all 5 starts in points in 2005. *Mrs L. C. Jewell* **c56 h–**

MAKE IT PLAIN 6 b.m. Alflora (IRE) – Gemmabel (True Song) [2004/5 F17g F17gpu F16g 19spu 19spu Mar 7] rather unfurnished mare: first foal: dam unraced: of no account. *A. Hollingsworth* **h– F–**

MAKE MY HAY 6 b.g. Bluegrass Prince (IRE) – Shashi (IRE) (Shaadi (USA)) [2004/5 h67+: 20g6 22dpu 16s3 16s2 16v3 16s6 17g Apr 12] small gelding: modest maid- **h85**

en hurdler: should stay 2½m: raced on good going or softer: blinkered last 5 starts. *J. Gallagher*

MAKE THE CALL 8 b.m. Syrtos – Dawn Call (Rymer) [2004/5 h–: 21g May 23] no form. *John Allen* **h–**

MAKINDI 5 br.m. Makbul – Indian Flower (Mansingh (USA)) [2004/5 17mpu 16dpu Jun 23] half-sister to modest chaser up to 3m Indian Temple (by Minster Son): runner-up in 6f maiden at 2 yrs (has shown signs of temperament): no show in 2 novice hurdles. *J. A. Pickering* **h–**

MAKULU (IRE) 5 b.g. Alzao (USA) – Karinski (USA) (Palace Music (USA)) [2004/5 19g4 16g3 17g4 19s3 20s* 22d6 16s5 18s3 21spu 24mpu Apr 13] leggy gelding: fair on Flat (stays 11.6f) for B. Meehan: fair hurdler: won handicap at Fontwell in November: stays 2½m: acts on soft going: usually races prominently. *C. J. Mann* **h103**

MALAGA BOY (IRE) 8 b.g. Nordic Brave – Ardglass Mist (Black Minstrel) [2004/5 20d 20d6 17v4 Mar 30] good-topped gelding: off 2 years, modest form first 2 starts over hurdles: likely to stay beyond 2½m. *C. L. Tizzard* **h96**

MALAY 8 b.m. Karinga Bay – Malaia (IRE) (Commanche Run) [2004/5 16s3 20m* 16g2 Apr 19] 1,000 7-y-o, resold £1,900 7-y-o: first foal: half-sister to 2m hurdle winner in Italy by Mtoto: dam, fair 2m hurdler, half-sister to smart middle-distance performer Spartan Shareef: progressive form in 3 starts over hurdles, winning mares maiden at Worcester in April: stays 2½m. *Miss K. M. George* **h98**

MALDOUN (IRE) 6 b.g. Kaldoun (FR) – Marzipan (IRE) (Green Desert (USA)) [2004/5 h105: 17m6 17gF 20m4 16g2 16v 17s4 22d 20s 22s* Feb 4] leggy gelding: modest hurdler: in cheekpieces, won seller (sold 5,500 gns) at Fontwell in February: soundly beaten on Flat for R. Hodges later that month: stays 2¾m: acts on soft going: usually visored: ungenuine. *M. C. Pipe* **h99 §**

MALEK (IRE) 9 b.g. Tremblant – Any Offers (Paddy's Stream) [2004/5 c107x, h–: 26g3 c26s* c24v2 c25s2 c32v* c24spu Apr 21] angular gelding: fair hurdler: fairly useful handicap chaser: more fluent and much improved in 2004/5, winning at Carlisle in November and Ashleybank Investment Scottish Borders National at Kelso (beat Ossmoses a length) in March: should also have won Rowland Meyrick Chase at Wetherby fourth start, in command before idling markedly and blundering last when beaten ¾ length by Truckers Tavern: stays 4m: raced on good going or softer (acts on heavy). *K. G. Reveley* **c129 h98 +**

MALETTON (FR) 5 b.g. Bulington (FR) – Reine Dougla (FR) (Faunus (FR)) [2004/5 16s 17s 18s5 18d 18s3 18s 18v* 19s* 19sur Mar 7] ex-French gelding: seventh foal: half-brother to winning Franco-Swiss hurdler/chaser up to 2¾m Fou de La Reine (by Kashneb): dam, in frame over 1½m, from family of smart chaser up to 25f Temerson: ran twice on Flat: fairly useful hurdler: successful in 4-y-o handicaps at Auteuil in October and November (awarded race): left T. Trapenard, still to be asked for effort when unseating sixth in novice at Hereford on British debut: stays 19f: raced on going softer than good (acts on heavy): often blinkered in France. *Miss Venetia Williams* **h120**

MALJIMAR (IRE) 5 b.g. Un Desperado (FR) – Marble Miller (IRE) (Mister Lord (USA)) [2004/5 F90p: 17d6 Dec 10] useful-looking gelding: runner-up in bumper on debut: off 9 months, well held in novice at Cheltenham on hurdling debut, every chance 2 out before weakening quickly: bred to be suited by further. *Miss H. C. Knight* **h90**

MALKO DE BEAUMONT (FR) 5 b. or br.g. Gold And Steel (FR) – Givry (FR) (Bayolidaan (FR)) [2004/5 20d Feb 24] first foal: dam, 1¼m winner, out of half-sister to smart French chaser Gabion: trained by E. Lecoiffier, won both starts up to 13f on Flat in 2004: last of 8 in novice on hurdling debut. *K. C. Bailey* **h–**

MALMO BOY (IRE) 6 gr.g. Roselier (FR) – Charming Mo (IRE) (Callernish) [2004/5 h–, F68: 22gpu 21d* 22s3 22v2 26s3 24v2 Mar 20] lengthy gelding: poor hurdler: won conditional jockeys handicap at Plumpton in November: stays 3m: acts on heavy going. *Mrs H. Dalton* **h81**

MALOY (GER) 5 gr.g. Neshad (USA) – Monalind (GER) (Park Romeo) [2004/5 F–: F16s Mar 23] well held in 2 bumpers. *P. A. Blockley* **F–**

MALT DE VERGY (FR) 5 br.g. Sleeping Car (FR) – Intense (FR) (Roi de Rome (USA)) [2004/5 F16v6 F16d* Feb 4] useful-looking gelding: first foal: dam unraced: well backed, won bumper at Catterick by 1½ lengths from It's Bertie. *L. Lungo* **F99**

MAMBO DES MOTTES (FR) 5 b.g. Useful (FR) – Julie Des Mottes (FR) (Puma Des Mottes (FR)) [2004/5 c18g* c18d* c20d3 c16g c16d Apr 9] neat ex-French gelding: brother to 1½m winner Nippy des Mottes and half-brother to 11.5f winner by Esteem **c114 h–**

Ball: dam unraced half-sister to dam of smart French jumper Echo des Mottes and useful chaser up to 2¾m Disco des Mottes: successful 3 times up to 1½m on Flat: modest form on second of 2 outings over hurdles: won first 2 starts over fences, at Cluny in August and Craon (4-y-o event) in September: left E. Lecoiffier, fair form when third to Chauvinist in 2½m novice at Sandown on British debut, not fluent at times: very stiff task next 2 starts: prominent when fell ninth in novice at Punchestown in late-April: raced on good going or softer. *Miss Venetia Williams*

MAMBO (IRE) 7 b.g. Ashkalani (IRE) – Bold Tango (FR) (In Fijar (USA)) [2004/5 h118: c16d* c16dR c20spu c16d2 c20gpu Apr 15] tall, leggy gelding: fairly useful hurdler: better form when winning maiden at Sandown on chasing debut in November by 4 lengths from Lacdoudal: creditable second to Dempsey in novice there, only subsequent completed start: probably best around 2m: raced on good ground or softer: often runs as if amiss. *N. J. Henderson* **c129 h–**

MAMIDEOS (IRE) 8 br.g. Good Thyne (USA) – Heavenly Artist (IRE) (Heavenly Manna) [2004/5 c103, h–: c25vpu c24gur c24d* c24spu Apr 16] lengthy, useful-looking gelding: fair handicap chaser: won at Lingfield in December, only completed outing in 2004/5: stays 3m: raced on good going or softer (acts on soft): usually tongue tied. *T. R. George* **c108 + h–**

MAMORE GAP (IRE) 7 b.g. General Monash (USA) – Ravensdale Rose (IRE) (Henbit (USA)) [2004/5 16d 16d5 19s 17s6 Mar 6] good-topped gelding: fair on Flat (barely stays 1¼m), sold out of R. Hannon's stable 3,000 gns Doncaster November Sales: poor form over hurdles. *M. E. Sowersby* **h83**

MAN ABOUT TOWN (IRE) 6 b.g. Bob Back (USA) – Pollys Glow (IRE) (Glow (USA)) [2004/5 F97: 16sF 16v* 16d2 16s* 16v3 16v3 16s2 Mar 28] rather leggy gelding: fairly useful novice hurdler: won at Clonmel in October and Navan (handicap, coasted home to beat Almier 10 lengths) in December: generally ran well otherwise, notably when short-head second to Tiger Cry in minor event at Fairyhouse in March: raced at 2m on going softer than good (acts on heavy). *T. J. Taaffe, Ireland* **h126**

MANA-MOU BAY (IRE) 8 b.g. Ela-Mana-Mou – Summerhill (Habitat) [2004/5 h104: 16gpu Jan 24] lengthy gelding: fair hurdler: left B. Ellison and off almost 20 months, led mid-race when pulled up in handicap at Southwell: raced around 2m: acts on good to firm going: has worn cheekpieces: tends to make mistakes. *R. C. Guest* **h–**

MANAWANUI 7 b.g. Karinga Bay – Kiwi Velocity (NZ) (Veloso (NZ)) [2004/5 c104, h94: 22g May 7] sturdy gelding: won both completed outings over fences: modest hurdler: ran poorly only start in 2004/5: stays 2½m: acts on soft going. *R. H. Alner* **c– h–**

MANBOW (IRE) 7 b.g. Mandalus – Treble Base (IRE) (Orchestra) [2004/5 h–, F81: 23d c22m* c23m* c23d* c20d2 c24dpu c25s* Mar 22] very tall gelding: no form over hurdles: very much a chasing type in appearance and won 4 of 6 starts over fences, novice handicaps at Kelso in October and Wetherby in October again, November and March: stays 25f: acts on soft and good to firm going: has idled/carried head high: patiently ridden. *M. D. Hammond* **c108 h–**

MANDHOOR (IRE) 5 b.g. Flying Spur (AUS) – Moy Water (IRE) (Tirol) [2004/5 16g 16s 16sF 16spu Mar 19] ex-Irish gelding: fairly useful on Flat (stays 1¼m), below best in 2004: poor form over hurdles, left D. Weld after second start: has been blinkered and/or tongue tied. *J. Wade* **h–**

MANDICA (IRE) 7 br.g. Mandalus – Mawtvica (Monksfield) [2004/5 F16d4 20s4 20s3 25spu 22v3 c24d2 Mar 6] €31,000 4-y-o: smallish gelding: second foal: dam, maiden hurdler/chaser, from family of top-class chaser Merry Gale: well beaten in maiden Irish points in 2004: fourth in bumper at Worcester: modest novice hurdler: 22 lengths second to Change Agent in novice handicap at Kempton on chasing debut: stays 3m: acts on heavy going. *T. R. George* **c95 h86 F84**

MANDINGO CHIEF (IRE) 6 b.g. Flying Spur (AUS) – Elizabethan Air (Elegant Air) [2004/5 h99: c21s2 c24vpu Mar 19] good-topped gelding: winning hurdler: modest form on completed outing over fences: will stay beyond 3m: acts on heavy going: remains type to do better over fences. *R. T. Phillips* **c95 + h–**

MANDM (IRE) 7 br.g. Air Display (USA) – Hello October (Callernish) [2004/5 F20v6 F18s* F20v2 19v5 24v* 24s Mar 28] third live foal: dam third in bumper: successful twice in points: best effort in bumpers when winning at Cork in November by 25 lengths from Rathvin Raven, always in first 2 and well clear of main body of field: fair form over hurdles, making most when winning at Navan in February: will stay beyond 3m: raced only on soft/heavy going. *P. C. O'Connor, Ireland* **h106 F109**

MANDOOB 8 b.g. Zafonic (USA) – Thaidah (CAN) (Vice Regent (CAN)) [2004/5 h–: 16g4 16g3 16gpu Oct 14] leggy gelding: modest 2m maiden hurdler: acted on heavy going: tried tongue tied: dead. *B. R. Johnson* **h85**

MAN FROM HIGHWORTH 6 b.g. Ballet Royal (USA) – Cavisoir (Afzal) [2004/5 h104, F93: 16g6 16s* 16d6 16d2 16s5 17s6 16d Jan 31] sturdy gelding: fair handicap hurdler: fortunate to win conditional jockeys event at Kempton in November, but improved further after: best at 2m: acts on soft going. *H. J. Manners* **h116**

MANHATTAN JACK 4 ch.g. Forzando – Manhattan Diamond (Primo Dominie) [2004/5 16s 16d 16m5 Dec 1] workmanlike gelding: fair form on Flat (stays 11f): poor form in juvenile hurdles. *G. A. Swinbank* **h79**

MANHUNTER (IRE) 9 b.g. Mandalus – Pinata (Deep Run) [2004/5 h89: 22d5 24mpu 22s c24dpu Apr 22] lengthy gelding: maiden hurdler, modest form at best: left P. Bowen, won points in February and March: weakened quickly straight in hunter chase at Chepstow (tongue tied): stays 25f: acts on good to firm going: has looked difficult ride. *John Moore* **c– h–**

MANIKATO (USA) 11 b.g. Clever Trick (USA) – Pasampsi (USA) (Crow (FR)) [2004/5 h–: 19mpu c16f Sep 5] lightly raced and little sign of ability. *K. G. Wingrove* **c– h–**

MANITOU SPRINGS 8 br.g. Mandalus – Swift Conveyance (IRE) (Strong Gale) [2004/5 19spu Mar 27] tall gelding: tenth in bumper on debut: bled from nose in maiden hurdle 3 years later. *P. Winkworth* **h–**

MANJOE (IRE) 7 b.g. Mandalus – Henris Blaze (IRE) (Mont Basile (FR)) [2004/5 h116: c20m* c24f* c22m3 Jul 28] good-topped gelding: fairly useful hurdler: good start over fences, winning at Cork in May (maiden) and June (minor event): 2 lengths third of 22 to Ansar in Galway Plate: effective at 2m to 3m: acts on firm going, probably on soft. *D. Wachman, Ireland* **c124 h–**

MANLY MONEY 7 b.g. Homo Sapien – Susie's Money (Seymour Hicks (FR)) [2004/5 h111, F91: 19g* c18d2 c19d* c20d2 c20s5 20m Apr 23] lengthy gelding: fairly useful hurdler: won handicap at Hereford in May: fairly useful form over fences, second to See You Sometime in maiden at Fontwell and Chauvinist in novice at Sandown: easily landed odds in maiden at Taunton in between: will probably stay beyond 2½m: acts on soft going. *P. F. Nicholls* **c120 h115**

MAN MURPHY (IRE) 9 b.g. Euphemism – Been About (IRE) (Remainder Man) [2004/5 c–, h–: c20d3 c20g2 c20vpu c19dur Feb 4] sturdy gelding: fair handicap chaser nowadays, often runs as if amiss (bled from nose last 2 starts): should stay beyond 2½m: acts on soft going. *W. McKeown* **c113 h–**

MANNERS (IRE) 7 b.g. Topanoora – Maneree (Mandalus) [2004/5 F90P: F16d* 16d5 Nov 28] **h104 P F118**

Fifth place in a 'National Hunt' maiden hurdle, beaten over twenty lengths, is not normally a performance to merit more than the briefest of entries in *Chasers & Hurdlers*, yet there are good reasons for giving more than the briefest attention to Manners, whose sole outing over hurdles that was. Starting odds on in an eight-runner event at Newbury in November, Manners was travelling smoothly, poised behind the leaders, when he stumbled badly three from home, lost his footing and was allowed to come home in his own time. The 16/1 winner Only Vintage went on to follow up impressively at Hereford, before performing well below expectations in the Supreme Novices', while the runner-up Moonstream was fatally injured next time. What makes Manners' performance all the more interesting is the subsequent exploits of the third and fourth, Secret Ploy and The Listener, who went on to show a useful level of form. With his stable effectively closing down for the main part of the campaign, Manners was not seen out again, preserving his novice status clearly making more sense than bringing him back late in the season.

Manners' starting odds on at Newbury followed two impressive successes in bumpers. The first, at Haydock a year previously, was so eye-catching that he was made one of the favourites for that season's Champion Bumper, even though the seven-runner race he won clearly wasn't much of a contest. As it was, Manners didn't return for a year, contesting a much stronger bumper, one with listed status, at the Open meeting at Cheltenham. He won that nearly as impressively as he had the race at Haydock and showed smart form, defeating Bob Bob Bobbin and The Mick Weston. The third did not show quite the level of form he did either before or after that race, but the runner-up went on to show useful form over hurdles, and

Mr M. Tabor's "Manners"

Manners clearly has the potential to reach a high level as a novice in that sphere. The quite good-topped Manners is a Topanoora half-brother to his connections' Grade 1 bumper winner Refinement (by Oscar), and details of this family can be found in her essay. *Jonjo O'Neill*

MANOLO (FR) 5 b.g. Ragmar (FR) – Coriola (FR) (Brezzo (FR)) [2004/5 17s^{6} 16d^{pu} Mar 3] ex-French gelding: first foal: dam, winning hurdler/chaser around 2m, also won up to 2m on Flat: successful twice up to 1½m on Flat at 4 yrs, sold out M. Rolland's stable €32,000 Goffs (France) November Sale: sixth of 13 in maiden at Taunton on hurdling debut, not knocked about after leading briefly 3 out: lost action next time: remains capable of better. *Ian Williams* **h84 p**

MANORAM (GER) 6 ch.g. Zinaad – Mayada (USA) (The Minstrel (CAN)) [2004/5 h85: c21g^{F} c20m^{3} c16m^{3} c16g* c17m^{2} c17g^{2} c16s^{2} c17g^{4} c16d^{2} c16g* c16g^{3} Nov 11] smallish, sparely-made gelding: winning hurdler: fair novice chaser: won at Worcester (handicap) in July and Cheltenham (sweating) in October: effective at 2m to 2½m: acts on soft and good to firm going: wore headgear after second outing: consistent. *Ian Williams* **c102 h–**

MANORSON (IRE) 6 ch.g. Desert King (IRE) – Familiar (USA) (Diesis) [2004/5 19d^{5} 17g* 17d* 16g 20d Apr 9] strong, compact gelding: useful on Flat (stays 1½m), sold out of M. Magnusson's stable 55,000 gns Newmarket Autumn Sales: fairly useful form in novice hurdles, winning at Taunton in December and February: mid-division in Grade 1 at Cheltenham fourth outing: likely to prove best at 2m: acts on good to soft going. *O. Sherwood* **h125**

MANOR STAR 6 b.m. Weld – Call Coup (IRE) (Callernish) [2004/5 h–, F–: 21s^{pu} 19d Mar 14] angular mare: seems of little account. *B. D. Leavy* **h–**

MANOUBI 6 b.g. Doyoun – Manuetti (IRE) (Sadler's Wells (USA)) [2004/5 h86: 20d* 16d* 17d Oct 8] good-topped gelding: fair form over hurdles: won novices at Perth in June (handicap) and August (unimpressive when long odds on): found nothing final outing: stays 2½m: raced only good to soft going: tried tongue tied. *M. Todhunter* **h100**

Tote Ireland 75th Anniversary Handicap Hurdle, Punchestown—
Mansony clears the last ahead of City of Sails

MANQUE NEUF 6 b.g. Cadeaux Genereux – Flying Squaw (Be My Chief (USA)) [2004/5 h78: 19g 16d^{6} 20s 22s^{6} 21g^{3} 27m^{ro} Apr 21] workmanlike gelding: poor maiden hurdler: ran out early final outing: stays 21f: best efforts on good/good to firm ground: wore cheekpieces last 2 starts. *Mrs L. Richards* **h75**

MANQUE PAS D'AIR (FR) 5 br.m. Kadalko (FR) – Chantalouette (FR) (Royal Charter (FR)) [2004/5 16s 17d^{3} Mar 26] fifth foal: half-sister to 3 winners, including fairly useful chaser up to 2¾m Haut de Gamme (by Morespeed) and fair hurdler/chaser around 2¼m Loi du Plus Fort (by Snurge): dam, 9f winner, half-sister to dam of useful hurdler Image de Marque II: fell in novice hurdle at Pau on debut: left E. Leenders and off nearly 14 months, better effort in mares maidens when third to Be Wise Girl at Newton Abbot: will stay beyond 17f. *T. R. George* **h82**

MAN RAY (USA) 4 b.g. Theatrical – Irtifa (Lahib (USA)) [2004/5 16v^{4} Mar 29] useful on Flat (stays 1½m) for A. de Royer Dupre, successful at Longchamp in September: not fluent when fourth in maiden at Chepstow on hurdling debut: will do better. *Jonjo O'Neill* **h83 p**

MANSEFIELD (IRE) 6 b.g. Un Desperado (FR) – Strong Willed (Strong Gale) [2004/5 F18m* F16m 22s 20s^{2} 24s^{pu} 16s^{4} 16d 20s Apr 13] sixth reported foal: brother to fairly useful 2m hurdler Sanghasta and fair 2½m chaser Hill Fox: dam unraced: better effort in bumpers when successful on debut at Punchestown in May: form over hurdles only when in frame, bled from nose seventh start. *P. J. Rothwell, Ireland* **h112 d F100**

MANSION SPECIAL (FR) 5 b.g. Mansonnien (FR) – Edition Speciale (FR) (Useful (FR)) [2004/5 c18s^{4} c20d^{2} 21d^{pu} 21d 21s^{pu} Feb 26] good-topped gelding: second foal: dam 1½m winner: in frame over 11f on Flat: fair maiden hurdler/chaser for G. Cherel in France: little show in 3 outings in Britain: stays 2½m: acts on soft going: tongue tied final start. *A. King* **c107 h–**

MANSONY (FR) 6 b.g. Mansonnien (FR) – Hairly (FR) (Air de Cour (USA)) [2004/5 h114: 20g 16s 16d^{6} 16v^{2} 16s^{2} Mar 29] tall, rather unfurnished gelding: will make a chaser: useful handicap hurdler: much improved last 3 starts, beaten length by Essex in Pierse Hurdle at Leopardstown and ¾ length by Bon Temps Rouler in valuable event at Fairyhouse: won 25-runner listed event at Punchestown in late-April by length from Raikkonen: stays 2½m: acts on heavy going. *A. L. T. Moore, Ireland* **h136**

MANTEL MINI 6 b.m. Reprimand – Foretell (Tirol) [2004/5 F–: 16d 16d^{pu} Oct 3] lengthy mare: of no account: tried in cheekpieces. *B. A. Pearce* **h–**

MANTILLA 8 b.m. Son Pardo – Well Tried (IRE) (Thatching) [2004/5 h113: c20d^{F} c21g^{6} c21m^{2} c20s^{4} Aug 24] fair hurdler in 2003/4: modest form at best over fences: stays 2¾m: acts on firm and good to soft going: blinkered/visored: has idled. *Ian Williams* **c88 h–**

MANTLES PRINCE 11 ch.g. Emarati (USA) – Miami Mouse (Miami Springs) [2004/5 c–§, h–§: 21d 20v^{4} 19s^{3} 19s 24g^{5} Apr 7] sturdy gelding: very smart hurdler/useful chaser in his prime, poor form in 2004/5: stays 2½m: acts on heavy and good to firm going: tried visored/in cheekpieces: untrustworthy. *A. G. Juckes* **c– § h80 §**

MANTON LASS 6 b.m. Rakaposhi King – My Muszka (Viking (USA)) [2004/5 F16d F17g Dec 15] unfurnished mare: sixth foal: half-sister to winning hurdler around 2½m **F–**

Glenbower (by Primitive Rising): dam winning 2½m hurdler: tailed off in bumpers and claimer on Flat. *M. Mullineaux*

MANX ROYAL (FR) 6 b.g. Cyborg (FR) – Badj II (FR) (Tadj (FR)) [2004/5 h–p: 20m* 19m* 16d⁶ 21d⁵ 24d⁶ 22g* 19m³ Apr 23] big, angular gelding: likely to make a chaser: fairly useful novice hurdler: won at Uttoxeter (maiden) in June, Newton Abbot (6/1-on) in September and Wincanton (improved form, beat Charlton Kings 16 lengths) in April: should stay 3m: acts on good to firm and good to soft going: hung badly right fifth outing. *M. C. Pipe* **h128**

MARALAN (IRE) 4 b.g. Priolo (USA) – Marilaya (IRE) (Shernazar) [2004/5 16v 16v⁶ 16s 16s³ 16s* 16s 16v* Apr 2] fairly useful on Flat (stays 13f), sold out of J. Oxx's stable €56,000 Goffs October Sale: fair novice hurdler: won at Navan in March (juvenile maiden) and April, beating Demesne 1½ lengths on latter occasion: raced at 2m on soft/heavy going: races prominently. *P. O. Brady, Ireland* **h109**

MARATHEA (FR) 4 b.f. Marathon (USA) – Shahmy (USA) (Lear Fan (USA)) [2004/5 16v 16s 16s Feb 24] angular ex-French filly: eighth foal: half-sister to several winners on Flat and fairly useful hurdler Schampus (by Galetto), stays 19f: dam, 1m winner, half-sister to very smart miler Crofter: successful twice up to 1¼m on Flat in 2004, including in claimer at Deauville (claimed from F. Rohaut €28,500) in August: well held in 3 outings over hurdles. *Miss Venetia Williams* **h–**

MARAUD 11 ch.g. Midyan (USA) – Peak Squaw (USA) (Icecapade (USA)) [2004/5 h89: 24g 27d 25gᶠ 20m 23dᵖᵘ Feb 18] smallish gelding: staying handicap hurdler: no form in 2004/5, left L. James after third outing: acts on firm and soft going: tried blinkered/in cheekpieces: usually front runner. *Miss Kariana Key* **h–**

MARBLE ARCH 9 b.g. Rock Hopper – Mayfair Minx (St Columbus) [2004/5 c–p, h–: c18d⁵ 24s 17g Mar 18] leggy gelding: very smart hurdler at best, tailed off in Grade 2 and valuable handicap (in cheekpieces) at Cheltenham last 2 outings: off 13 months after lame on chasing debut, never-dangerous fifth to Kauto Star in novice at Newbury on reappearance, not impressing with jumping: raced mainly around 2m: has won on heavy going, raced mainly under less testing conditions (acts on good to firm): held up: has high head carriage. *H. Morrison* **c122 h–**

MARCEL (FR) 5 b.g. Bateau Rouge – Une Risette (FR) (Air du Nord (USA)) [2004/5 17s² 18s³ 16d* 19d* 19m* 18m* 16s* 16d* 16g* 16s² 16s* 16d* 17v³ 16g 16d⁶ Apr 8] **h137**

After helping himself to a number of starters and moving on to devour several main courses, no wonder Marcel's appetite wasn't quite so healthy when his

Sharp Novices' Hurdle, Cheltenham—Marcel makes it six in a row

sweet trolley—Cheltenham and Aintree—came round. Marcel enjoyed a splendid campaign, one which made a refreshing change from horses of his type for whom a win in the autumn is followed by an announcement that he 'might have another run or two before Cheltenham.' Marcel made at least one appearance every month from August round to April, running thirteen times and winning nine races. Before then, he had been placed in a couple of starts at Auteuil early in the season before joining Martin Pipe from Francois Cottin. Marcel looked a very useful prospect from day one in Britain when making all in quite a good novice hurdle for the time of year at Stratford in August. He proved the point by making short work of all the opposition put before him in the weeks that followed, landing the odds with ease in weak contests at Newton Abbot, Hereford and Fontwell. Marcel's first bigger test looked like coming in a listed event at Kempton in October, but when the other joint favourite Mister Flint made an early exit, Marcel completed his five-timer being eased down.

So much for the hors d'oeuvres. The first of what might be termed Marcel's main courses came in the Sharp Novices' Hurdle, a Grade 2 event at Cheltenham's Open meeting. He was only joint-third in the betting behind recent easy winners The Rising Moon and Nyrche, but Marcel showed further improvement to maintain his unbeaten record in Britain. The front-running Mister Flint was in the field again and stayed on his feet this time, though Marcel, who had himself made the running previously, was not asked to take him on. Instead, Marcel moved up three out to quicken clear with the eventual runner-up Baby Run and was ridden out for a two-and-a-half-length win despite swishing his tail on the run-in. A fortnight later, Marcel wasn't hard pressed to land the odds in another novice on Hennessy Gold Cup day at Newbury, giving upwards of 8 lb all round and winning by six lengths from the smart Flat performer Pole Star. Marcel still looked in good shape when turned out for a listed event at Haydock just seven days after Newbury and was 5/2-on to make it eight out of eight. Making the running but unable to get away when shaken up, he hung left on the run-in before going down to Astronomic by a length and three quarters. This defeat turned out to be no more than a hiccup, any notion that Marcel had had enough for the time being dispelled when he came back for more just two weeks later at Windsor. Facing just three rivals in the bet@bluesq.com Novices' Hurdle (a Grade 2 event better known as the Kennel Gate), Marcel was not at all hard pressed to beat one of the previous season's leading juveniles Cherub by four lengths.

bet@bluesq.com Kennel Gate Novices' Hurdle, Windsor—
Marcel gets the better of Cherub for win number eight

ladbrokes.com Tolworth Hurdle, Sandown—a ninth and final victory for the season; Chilling Place challenges at the last but It's Just Harry gets up for second

By now, Marcel had faced a total of eighty-eight different rivals, only four of whom had finished in front of him. Two of those who had beaten him took him on again in the ladbrokes.com Tolworth Hurdle at Sandown in January. They were Astronomic and Made In Montot, who had beaten Marcel when the latter was making his hurdling debut at Auteuil. Made In Montot was having his first run since, having joined Paul Nicholls in the meantime. Among eight last-time-out winners in the field of nine, the Irish novice Wild Passion looked to be Marcel's chief rival. Whilst Astronomic fell and Made In Montot trailed in last, Marcel's remarkable season reached its high spot, the Grade 1 race his ninth and, as it turned out, final success. Always in touch and going well, Marcel quickened with the leader Chilling Place into the straight and went on before the last for a two-length victory. It's Just Harry stayed on to finish four lengths clear of Chilling Place who stumbled after the last but just held on for third, ahead of Wild Passion.

Marcel's nine wins brought to mind the even more remarkable season enjoyed by another Pipe-trained novice, Make A Stand, in 1996/7. He too won nine races (from twelve starts), though, unlike Marcel, who wasn't tested outside novice company, Make A Stand graduated first to handicaps, winning the William Hill, the Lanzarote and the Tote Gold Trophy, before a leap to championship-standard form—and another magnificent display of front-running—brought him the Champion Hurdle. Marcel was entered for the Champion, and also held the option of going into handicaps, but, rather than contesting the totesport Trophy at Newbury following the Tolworth, Marcel ran in a listed novices' event at Exeter the next day. Despite being beaten thirty-eight lengths into third by the Tolworth fifth My Way de Solzen at Exeter, and finishing out on his feet in desperately testing conditions, Marcel still started favourite for the Supreme Novices' at Cheltenham the following month. It seemed, however, that Marcel had finally had his fill and he never landed a blow at Cheltenham after being held up in rear. Second helpings at Aintree in the Top Novices' Hurdle, before which he was again on his toes, weren't agreeable either, Marcel finishing tailed off.

Marcel's pedigree is certainly an interesting one, though it probably had less of a part to play in his changing stables for €125,000 at Goffs (France) July Sale than the promise shown on his first two starts. Marcel had also finished second from two runs in non-thoroughbred races on the Flat. Seven of Marcel's eight great-grandparents are thoroughbred, the exception being his grandam's sire Le Blizzard who was an anglo-arab. Marcel's own sire Bateau Rouge was trained by

Ian Balding as a two-year-old to win a maiden at Bath and a nursery at Sandown, but he went on to race in pattern company in Italy, winning a Group 3 and finishing third in the Gran Premio di Milano, his last advertised fee in France just €700. Marcel is his dam's fourth foal. Une Risette began her stud career with visits to a couple of much better-known French stallions, Cadoudal and Cyborg. To the latter, she produced Indecise, a winner of a non-thoroughbred event on the Flat in France and successful at two miles over hurdles in Belgium. Her third foal John (by Son of Silver) is yet to win, but he hasn't had much racing and managed to finish fourth in April in France's most valuable handicap chase, the Prix du President de la Republique. Her latest representative, the four-year-old filly Novacella (by Beyssac), was placed twice over hurdles for Cottin before joining Robert Alner's stable. Une Risette enjoyed a very successful racing career, winning three times on the Flat in non-thoroughbred races and another seven times over hurdles and fences at up to two and a half miles. She also picked up good place money, finishing second in the Grand Prix de la Ville de Nice at Cagnes-sur-Mer and in Italy's top chase, the Gran Premio di Merano. Une Risette was the pick of three winners out of Feline II, a mare whose five wins all came in cross-country chases at around two and a half miles.

Marcel is not an obvious chaser on looks—he's a rather leggy gelding—but he was bought with a chasing career in mind and was even entered over fences in the autumn before connections decided to press on with his hurdling campaign. If he takes to fences as well as he did to hurdles, then he could easily be his connec-

Mr D. A. Johnson's "Marcel"

Marcel (FR) (b.g. 2000)	Bateau Rouge (b 1987)	Red Sunset (b 1979)	Red God
			Centre Piece
		Last Gunboat (b 1980)	Dominion
			Sounion
	Une Risette (FR) (b 1986)	Air du Nord (br 1973)	Sadair
			Toe The Line
		Feline II (ch 1971)	Le Blizzard
			Tamagire

tions' Arkle representative in 2006, though don't expect him to run up another sequence beforehand; unlike novice events over hurdles, the structure of novice chases was changed before the latest season and the programme is much tougher. Marcel has raced mainly at around two miles so far, but he stays nineteen furlongs and is bred to stay further still. He acts on soft and good to firm ground and is effective held up or making the running. It goes almost without saying that Marcel is a tough sort and, given time to digest his latest campaign, he'll no doubt be back for more. *M. C. Pipe*

MARCHING PREMIER (IRE) 6 ch.g. Zaffaran (USA) – The Marching Lady (IRE) (Archway (IRE)) [2004/5 F94: 20s^F Nov 5] fair form in 2 bumpers: fell fatally first on hurdling debut. *Noel T. Chance* **h–**

MARCH NORTH 10 b.g. Petoski – Coral Delight (Idiot's Delight) [2004/5 c97, h–: c24s^pu c24d^pu c23d^4 c24d^4 c23d^F c24d^pu c24g Mar 16] compact gelding: handicap chaser, no form in 2004/5: stays 3m: acts on soft and good to firm going, probably on heavy: usually wears cheekpieces/visor. *Mrs P. Robeson* **c– h–**

MARCIANO 9 b.g. Rock Hopper – Raintree Venture (Good Times (ITY)) [2004/5 c21m^5 May 19] workmanlike gelding: maiden hurdler: poor maiden pointer in 2004: tried in headgear: ungenuine. *Miss Louise Allan* **c– h–**

MARCUS DU BERLAIS (FR) 8 gr.g. Saint Preuil (FR) – Rosacotte (FR) (Rose Laurel) [2004/5 c129, h–: c19s c24v c24s^3 c24v* 20s c29s^3 c36d^ur Apr 9] good-topped gelding: winning hurdler: useful handicap chaser: won Pierse Leopardstown Chase in January by 4 lengths from Hersov: placed in last 2 runnings of Irish Grand National at Fairyhouse, stayed on well when 2¼ lengths third to Numbersixvalverde in latest in March: behind until hampered and unseated second Becher's in Grand National at Aintree: should stay beyond 29f: raced on going softer than good (acts on heavy). *A. L. T. Moore, Ireland* **c135 h–**

MARGARETS WISH 5 gr.m. Cloudings (IRE) – Gentle Gain (Final Straw) [2004/5 h69+: 16g^pu 16d* 16s 16d^6 16d^5 16s^5 Mar 31] poor on Flat (stays 1¼m): similar over hurdles: raced exclusively at Ludlow since debut, winning seller in January: likely to prove best around 2m: acts on good to soft going, below form on soft. *T. Wall* **h76**

Pierse Leopardstown Handicap Chase—Marcus du Berlais leads the fading Lanmire Glen over the last

Durkan New Homes Novices' Chase, Leopardstown—
one good turn deserves another . . . Mariah Rollins, who had let in Sir OJ after a blunder the time before, benefits from his last-fence fall

MARIAH ROLLINS (IRE) 7 b. or br.m. Over The River (FR) – Clonloo Lady (IRE) (Nearly A Nose (USA)) [2004/5 h133, F91: c20s* c16d^{2} c17v* c16g^{6} Mar 15] lengthy, narrow mare: useful novice hurdler in 2003/4: soon reached similar level over fences, winning maiden at Down Royal in November and Grade 1 Durkan New Homes Novices' Chase at Leopardstown (looked held when left clear by last-fence fall of Sir OJ) in December: would have beaten Sir OJ in Grade 2 novice at Punchestown on second start but for bad mistake last: good never-nearer sixth to Contraband in Arkle Chase at Cheltenham: ran as if amiss (weakening quickly when fell 3 out) in Grade 1 novice at Punchestown in late-April: should prove suited by 2½m+: unraced on firm going, acts on any other. *P. A. Fahy, Ireland* **c132 h–**

MARIA PIA (IRE) 8 b.m. Bob's Return (IRE) – Blackwater Mist (IRE) (King's Ride) [2004/5 20d c20d^{2} c20s^{F} c20g Mar 19] half-sister to winning hurdler/fairly useful chaser Multeen River (by Supreme Leader), stays 21f: once-raced on Flat: winning hurdler: modest chaser: form in 2004/5 only when second in handicap at Ludlow: stays 2½m: acts on firm and good to soft going. *C. F. Swan, Ireland* **c95 h–**

MARIE DE MARSAL (IRE) 6 ch.m. Zaffaran (USA) – Crabtreejazz (IRE) (Royal Fountain) [2004/5 F18m^{5} F17m^{5} F16g Jul 7] first known foal: dam twice-raced half-sister to fairly useful staying hurdler Ebullient Equiname (by Zaffaran): poor form in bumpers. *L. Wells* **F71**

MARIELLA (GER) 4 br.f. Zinaad – Morgenrote (EG) (Aveiro) [2004/5 16v* 16s^{5} Feb 3] small filly: half-sister to fairly useful hurdler/winning chaser Mondul (by Colon), stays 19f: useful on Flat, successful 4 times up to around 11f in Germany/Czech Republic in 2004: won fillies event at Capannelle on hurdling debut in December: breathing problem at Towcester next time. *C. Von Der Recke, Germany* **h?**

MARINO WEST (IRE) 10 ch.g. Phardante (FR) – Seanaphobal Lady (Kambalda) [2004/5 c–, h–: c25d^{pu} c25m^{3} May 28] well-made gelding: won novice hurdle in 2001/2: little other form outside points. *N. M. Babbage* **c– h–**

MARITIME BLUES 5 b.g. Fleetwood (IRE) – Dixie d'Oats (Alhijaz) [2004/5 16s^{5} 16d 20d^{6} 16g^{4} Mar 27] fair but unreliable 1¼m/1½m handicapper on Flat, won twice in 2004: poor form over hurdles: looked none too keen when blinkered final outing. *J. G. Given* **h77**

MARJINA 6 b.m. Classic Cliche (IRE) – Cavina (Ardross) [2004/5 h104, F85: 22g^{2} 21d^{3} 24v* Jan 21] big, useful-looking mare: fair form over hurdles: fortunate to win maiden at Chepstow in January, looking held when left in front 2 out: stays 3m: raced on good going or softer. *Miss E. C. Lavelle* **h108 +**

MARKED MAN (IRE) 9 b.g. Grand Plaisir (IRE) – Teazle (Quayside) [2004/5 c103+, h106: c16m* c17d^{2} c16g* c16m^{pu} c16d^{2} c16d^{2} c21d c17g^{2} c21g^{F} c21m^{4} Apr 13] good-topped gelding: fair handicap hurdler: fairly useful chaser: won novice at Ludlow and handicap at Uttoxeter early in season: ran well most other starts, but probably flattered when fourth of 5 to Quazar in Grade 2 handicap at Cheltenham: stays 21f: acts on good to soft and good to firm going. *R. Lee* **c126 x h–**

MARK EQUAL 9 b.g. Nicholas Bill – Dissolution (Henbit (USA)) [2004/5 c110, h–: c21d^{pu} c20g* c20d c20g c21g^{4} c18d^{5} c19d^{2} 16s^{2} 19s^{2} 17s^{2} c16g^{6} Apr 14] lengthy gelding: fairly useful handicap chaser: won at Newbury in November: fair handicap hurdler: runner-up all 3 starts in 2004/5: stays 2½m: acts on firm and soft going: tried visored: tongue tied last 5 outings: has hung left/found less than seemed likely. *M. C. Pipe* **c116 h107**

MARKI (FR) 5 b.g. Video Rock (FR) – Payse (FR) (Trenel) [2004/5 16d 16s^{4} 20d Mar 19] lengthy, unfurnished gelding: sixth foal: half-brother to fairly chaser up to around 2¾m Duky (by Iron Duke) and winning 2¼m chaser Flica (by Vorias): dam, well beaten over hurdles, from family of smart staying chaser Fulip: won 17f event on Flat at Dieppe on debut in June for F. Doumen: little show in novice hurdles. *T. Doumen, France* **h–**

MARK THE MAN (IRE) 8 b.g. Supreme Leader – Nuala's Pet (Buckskin (FR)) [2004/5 h116p: c24s* c24v^{pu} c21s^{6} Feb 6] lengthy, good sort: lightly raced: bumper winner: winning hurdler: won novice at Naas on chasing debut in October impressively by 2½ lengths from Prince of Tara, jumping well: ran as if amiss in Grade 1 novices at Leopardstown after: stays 3m: raced on going softer than good. *N. Meade, Ireland* **c117 h–**

Gone West Racing Syndicate's "Mariah Rollins"

MARLBOROUGH (IRE) 13 br.g. Strong Gale – Wrekenogan (Tarqogan) [2004/5 c153, h–: c24g c25g Apr 8] strong gelding: top-class chaser in his prime, winner of 2001 Tote Gold Trophy Chase at Sandown and second in 2002 King George VI Chase: well beaten in valuable handicaps after nearly year off in 2004/5: stayed 3¼m : acted on good to firm and heavy going: tried in cheekpieces: reportedly retired. *N. J. Henderson* **c– h–**

MARLBOROUGH SOUND 6 b.g. Overbury (IRE) – Dark City (Sweet Monday) [2004/5 F–: 17d⁴ Oct 27] well beaten in bumper: fourth of 10 in novice at Sedgefield on hurdling debut: likely to benefit from stiffer test of stamina. *N. G. Richards* **h94 p**

MARREL 7 b.g. Shareef Dancer (USA) – Upper Caen (High Top) [2004/5 h107: 22d³ 22g² 16m⁵ 20m² 20m* 19g* 22d 20f 20m 20d³ 16d⁶ Mar 12] good-topped gelding: fair handicap hurdler: won at Worcester in June and Newton Abbot in July: stays 2¾m: acts on good to firm and good to soft going: usually visored. *D. Burchell* **h114**

MARRON PRINCE (FR) 5 ch.g. Cyborg (FR) – Colombine (USA) (Empery (USA)) [2004/5 F–: 20s 17v 16s⁵ 21gᵖᵘ Mar 28] little sign of ability. *R. Rowe* **h–**

MARSH ORCHID 4 b.g. Lahib (USA) – Majalis (Mujadil (USA)) [2004/5 17sᵖᵘ Jan 18] fair maiden on Flat, sold out of W. Jarvis' stable 11,000 gns Newmarket Autumn Sales: jumped poorly on hurdling debut. *C. C. Bealby* **h–**

MARSH RUN 6 b.m. Presenting – Madam Margeaux (IRE) (Ardross) [2004/5 F108: 16d² 16d⁵ 17d² 20d² 21v⁴ 20s* 24s⁴ Mar 10] angular mare: useful form in bumpers in 2003/4: easily best effort over hurdles when winning mares novice at Carlisle in February: should stay beyond 2½m (in season when tiring markedly over 3m): acts on soft ground (won bumper on good to firm). *M. W. Easterby* **h104**

MARS ROCK (FR) 5 b.g. Video Rock (FR) – Venus de Mirande (FR) (Carmont (FR)) [2004/5 F16d² Mar 19] €30,000 3-y-o: rather leggy gelding: fourth foal: half-brother to fairly useful hurdler/chaser up to 21f Jet Royal (by Garde Royal) and fair 17f hurdle winner Naos de Mirande (by Smadoun): dam second in Grand Steeple-Chase de Paris: 1½ lengths second of 16 to Barton Legend in bumper at Uttoxeter on debut: will stay at least 2½m. *Miss Venetia Williams* **F91**

MARTHA REILLY (IRE) 9 ch.m. Rainbows For Life (CAN) – Debach Delight (Great Nephew) [2004/5 h82: 22g 21g² 27mᵘʳ 22sᵖᵘ 22g³ 22gᵖᵘ 22sᵖᵘ 23s³ 26s 26g⁵ 24s Apr 16] sturdy mare: poor handicap hurdler: stays 3¼m: acts on heavy and good to firm going: tried blinkered/in cheekpieces. *Mrs Barbara Waring* **h82**

MARTHA'S KINSMAN (IRE) 6 b.g. Petoski – Martha's Daughter (Majestic Maharaj) [2004/5 F100: 19g* 16s² Mar 23] won bumper on debut in 2003/4: off a year, successful in novice hurdle at Taunton in March: similar form when second to Charlton Kings at Towcester: likely to stay 2½m: remains open to improvement. *H. D. Daly* **h120**

MARTIN HOUSE (IRE) 6 b.g. Mujadil (USA) – Dolcezza (FR) (Lichine (USA)) [2004/5 h85: 16m 17d⁴ 16sᵖᵘ 21gᵖᵘ Mar 28] mostly well held on Flat since 2002: poor form over hurdles, left Mrs K. Walton after third outing: has pulled hard. *D. W. Thompson* **h80**

MARTOVIC (IRE) 6 b.m. Old Vic – Martomick (Montelimar (USA)) [2004/5 F17v⁶ F17s Apr 7] rather unfurnished mare: second foal: dam smart staying chaser: well beaten in mares bumpers. *K. C. Bailey* **F–**

MARY CHAN 6 b.m. Savahra Sound – Lucky Relikon (Lucky Wednesday) [2004/5 F17m Apr 23] 700 6-y-o: fifth foal: sister to 1½m winner in Norway: dam unraced, out of half-sister to high-class performer up to 1½m Gunner B: tailed off in bumper on debut. *C. W. Fairhurst* **F–**

MARYLAND (IRE) 8 b.m. Executive Perk – Raven Night (IRE) (Mandalus) [2004/5 F94: 20m³ 16d Nov 7] workmanlike mare: bumper winner: better effort over hurdles when third in novice at Fakenham. *O. Brennan* **h87**

MARYLOU DAY (IRE) 6 b. or br.m. Lord Americo – Dark Phoenix (IRE) (Camden Town) [2004/5 F16d F16g Mar 5] €1,500 4-y-o: first foal: dam bumper winner: well held in 2 bumpers. *O. Brennan* **F–**

MARYS MOMENT 5 ch.m. Southern Music – Arley Gale (Scallywag) [2004/5 F16s Mar 27] first foal: dam, little sign of ability, out of half-sister to top-class chaser at 2½m+ Wayward Lad: tailed off in bumper on debut. *P. A. Pritchard* **F–**

MASALARIAN (IRE) 10 b.g. Doyoun – Masamiyda (Lyphard (USA)) [2004/5 c94, h–: c21m* c22g³ c19dᵖᵘ c20dᵘʳ Oct 31] well-made gelding: fair chaser: successful in **c105 h–**

hunter at Folkestone in May: below form after, including back in handicap company: stays 21f: acts on soft and good to firm going: tried blinkered. *Mrs H. M. Bridges*

MA'S CONFUSION 7 b.m. Mr Confusion (IRE) – Spirited Lady VII (Damsire Unregistered) [2004/5 F–: 17d May 9] lengthy mare: no sign of ability. *N. Wilson* **h–**

MASHWE (IRE) 11 b.m. Samhoi (USA) – Glittering Steel (Golden Love) [2004/5 c21gpu Mar 18] fairly useful pointer: no show in novice hunter chase. *H. E. Thorpe* **c–**

MASSAC (FR) 6 b.g. Garde Royale – Mirande (FR) (Tiaia (FR)) [2004/5 c120, h100+: c20s* c20d* c20s* c21dF Dec 11] good-topped gelding: maiden hurdler: useful chaser: won first 3 starts in 2004/5, 5-y-o non-thoroughbred event at Auteuil (final outing for G. Macaire) in May and handicaps at Huntingdon and Windsor in November, fortunate in Grade 2 limited intermediate event at last-named when beating Mondial Jack ½ length, making running but not travelling so well as Non So when left in front again 2 out: fell fatally at Cheltenham: stayed 21f: raced on good going or softer (acted on heavy). *A. King* **c137 h–**

MASSIMO (FR) 5 b.g. Gunboat Diplomacy (FR) – Gitane de L'Allier (FR) (Altayan) [2004/5 F16g* F16d5 16d Feb 19] well-made gelding: first foal: dam unraced: won bumper at Worcester on debut in May, only start for M. Pipe: never a factor in novice on hurdling debut: should do better. *Ian Williams* **h– p F95**

MASTER ACCORD (IRE) 5 b.g. Accordion – Holly Grove Lass (Le Moss) [2004/5 F16g 22g Sep 12] smallish gelding: seventh foal: dam maiden half-sister to top-class hurdler up to 3m Mister Morose and smart staying hurdler The Proms: well held in bumper and maiden hurdle: sold 1,500 gns Doncaster November Sales. *N. A. Twiston-Davies* **h– F–**

MASTER ALBERT (IRE) 7 b.g. Supreme Leader – Mullaun (Deep Run) [2004/5 F117: 16s* 16d* 16d Nov 28] well-made gelding: smart form in bumpers in 2003/4: successful first 2 starts over hurdles, in 23-runner maiden at Cork and 22-runner minor event at Punchestown (impressively by 2½ lengths from Native Stag) in November: presumably amiss in Grade 1 novice at Fairyhouse final outing: will stay beyond 2m: remains capable of better over hurdles. *D. Wachman, Ireland* **h115 +**

MASTER BREW 7 b.g. Homo Sapien – Edithmead (IRE) (Shardari) [2004/5 c72, h87?, F83: c21d6 c21d c26dpu c21spu c24dpu Feb 18] angular gelding: maiden hurdler/chaser: out of sorts in 2004/5: stays 2½m: tried blinkered. *J. R. Best* **c– h–**

MASTER CHIEF (IRE) 11 b. or br.g. Euphemism – Shan's Lass (Mandalus) [2004/5 c–: c21mpu May 19] of little account: tried tongue tied. *D. F. Donegan* **c–**

MASTER CORROUGE (IRE) 7 b.g. Corrouge (USA) – Ballyseskin (Le Bavard (FR)) [2004/5 24dpu c16vpu Jan 10] fourth foal: half-brother to 2 winning pointers: dam winning pointer: in frame in maiden Irish points: no other form: tried blinkered. *Mrs L. B. Normile* **c– h–**

MASTER DJ 6 ch.g. Master Willie – Always Alex (Final Straw) [2004/5 F17d5 Nov 15] third foal: dam, winning selling hurdler who stayed 3¼m, half-sister to dam of top-class 2m hurdler Grimes: well beaten in bumper on debut. *John Allen* **F–**

MASTER D'OR (FR) 5 b.g. Cyborg (FR) – Une Pomme d'Or (FR) (Pot d'Or (FR)) [2004/5 17d5 16s6 16s3 17d c19sF 21d 22d3 21d* 20d2 Apr 22] leggy gelding: second foal: half-brother to 2½m cross-country chase winner L'Etoile d'Or (by Kadrou): dam placed in cross-country chases: fair hurdler: ran once for E. Lecoiffier: improved form when winning conditional jockeys handicap at Plumpton in April by 22 lengths: beaten when fell on chasing debut: stays 2¾m: raced on going softer than good. *P. J. Hobbs* **c– p h106**

MASTER FOX 7 b. or br.g. Puissance – Hill Vixen (Goldhill) [2004/5 F16s 16gpu Apr 17] seventh foal: half-brother to several winners, including useful bumper winner Alpine Fox (by Risk Me) and 2m chaser Floosy (by Governor General): dam, 1½m winner, out of half-sister to useful chaser up to 2½m Ostrich Duck: no form in bumper and novice hurdle. *T. R. George* **h– F–**

MASTER HENRY (GER) 11 b.g. Mille Balles (FR) – Maribelle (GER) (Windwurf (GER)) [2004/5 c99, h–: c16g* c16m2 16dpu c17d2 Oct 5] angular gelding: winning hurdler: fair handicap chaser: won at Newton Abbot in June: ran as if amiss last 2 starts: raced around 2m: acts on good to soft and good to firm going: usually free-going front runner (possibly needs to dominate): has hung right under pressure. *Ian Williams* **c106 h–**

MASTER JACKSON 6 b.g. Jendali (USA) – Fardella (ITY) (Molvedo) [2004/5 h80, F85: 21g 24g4 c19g5 c19spu c24gbd c20g Apr 3] leggy gelding: poor maiden hurdler: no form over fences: seems to stay 3m: tried in cheekpieces. *T. D. Walford* **c– h80**

MASTER JOCK 11 ch.g. Scottish Reel – Mistress Corrado (New Member) [2004/5 c92: c25s^{5} c22g^{pu} c26g^{pu} Apr 14] workmanlike gelding: prolific winning pointer: little impact in hunters since 2003: stays 3m: acts on good to soft going. *P. Jones* **c79**

MASTER MAHOGANY 4 b.g. Bandmaster (USA) – Impropriety (Law Society (USA)) [2004/5 17s^{3} 17d^{4} 17s^{2} 17g^{2} Apr 15] angular gelding: fair on Flat (stays 1¼m), successful in September: fair form over hurdles at Taunton: likely to prove best at 2m: free-going sort. *R. J. Hodges* **h105**

MASTER MARMALADE 4 ch.g. Trempolino (USA) – Miss Picol (Exit To Nowhere (USA)) [2004/5 F16m F16g^{3} Apr 19] medium-sized gelding: first foal: dam, winning hurdler/10.5f winner on Flat, half-sister to useful stayer Raise A Prince: better effort in bumpers when third in maiden at Towcester. *D. Morris* **F92**

MASTER MONEYSPIDER 6 b.g. Regal Embers (IRE) – Mis-E-Fishant (Sunyboy) [2004/5 F17g Dec 15] leggy gelding: second foal: dam winning pointer: tailed off in bumper on debut. *C. J. Price* **F–**

MASTER NIMBUS 5 b.g. Cloudings (IRE) – Miss Charlie (Pharly (FR)) [2004/5 16d 17d Nov 9] leggy gelding: modest sprint maiden on Flat: no show in 2 novice hurdles. *J. J. Quinn* **h–**

MASTER OF STAFFORD 9 b.g. Salse (USA) – Artist's Glory (Rarity) [2004/5 19s^{pu} 19s^{pu} 17g^{pu} Apr 10] lengthy, angular gelding: mid-field in bumper on debut: no form over hurdles after 4-year absence. *A. G. Newcombe* **h–**

MASTER OFTHE CHASE (IRE) 7 b.g. Norwich – Beglawella (Crash Course) [2004/5 F16m^{3} F16m 16f 16m^{5} 17v* 20v^{2} 16s^{3} 16s^{3} Mar 13] well-made gelding: first foal: dam fairly useful hurdler up to 3m: fairly useful bumper winner: fairly useful novice hurdler: won maiden at Tralee in August: should stay beyond 17f: acts on heavy going. *C. F. Swan, Ireland* **h115** **F97**

MASTER OF THE WARD (IRE) 5 ch.g. King Persian – Sara Jane (IRE) (Brush Aside (USA)) [2004/5 F17v^{2} F17s^{3} Apr 2] second foal: dam unraced, out of half-sister to one-time useful chaser up to 3m Exit To Wave: better effort in bumpers when second at Carlisle on debut. *D. McCain* **F93**

MASTER PAPA (IRE) 6 br.g. Key of Luck (USA) – Beguine (USA) (Green Dancer (USA)) [2004/5 h118: 16g c17s^{3} c20d^{4} c16s^{3} c20s^{5} c16g^{3} c19d^{F} c24s^{3} c24g^{6} Apr 7] angular gelding: fairly useful hurdler: fair novice chaser: stays 3m with emphasis on speed: acts on good to firm and heavy going. *N. A. Twiston-Davies* **c106** **h–**

MASTERPOINT 5 ch.g. Mark of Esteem (IRE) – Baize (Efisio) [2004/5 h78: 16d^{pu} 16m Aug 30] sturdy gelding: poor maiden hurdler: barely stays 2m. *R. T. Phillips* **h71**

MASTER REX 10 ch.g. Interrex (CAN) – Whose Lady (USA) (Master Willie) [2004/5 c119, h–: 16m^{3} 16g^{4} c16d* c16d* c16d^{4} c16g c16s^{5} Apr 7] lengthy gelding: fairly useful handicap hurdler: useful handicap chaser: won at Windsor in November and Wincanton (in control when Bambi de L'Orme unseated last) in December: ran well when fourth to Oneway at Sandown next time: not discredited in valuable handicaps at Cheltenham and Aintree last 2 starts: raced around 2m: unraced on heavy going, acts on any other: has refused to line up. *B. De Haan* **c140** **h119**

MASTER RIDE (IRE) 10 b.g. King's Ride – Cahore (Quayside) [2004/5 c109, h113: c24d^{4} c22s^{ur} 22v^{pu} Nov 25] lengthy gelding: fair hurdler/maiden chaser: no form in 2004/5: stays 23f: raced on good going or softer (acts on heavy). *C. Tinkler* **c–** **h–**

MASTER SAM (IRE) 5 b.g. Supreme Leader – Basically (IRE) (Strong Gale) [2004/5 F16d^{3} F17s^{ur} Apr 2] third foal: half-brother to 2m hurdle winner Pharrihy (by Phardante): dam, poor maiden pointer, half-sister to useful hurdler/chaser at 2½m+ Cloone Bridge: fair form when third in bumper at Haydock on debut: hung badly right before running out first bend in similar event at Bangor. *H. D. Daly* **F87**

MASTER SEBASTIAN 6 ch.g. Kasakov – Anchor Inn (Be My Guest (USA)) [2004/5 F96: 20m^{6} 16s^{2} 16s^{4} 16v^{2} 18v* 20d^{4} 16d^{5} Apr 11] smallish gelding: placed twice in bumpers: fair novice hurdler: won at Kelso in January: should stay 2½m: acts on heavy going. *Miss Lucinda V. Russell* **h106**

MASTERS OF WAR (IRE) 8 b.g. Sri Pekan (USA) – Velinowski (Malinowski (USA)) [2004/5 c83, h81: 21g* 22g* 24d^{F} Aug 1] lengthy gelding: let down by jumping both starts over fences: fairly useful hurdler: much improved in 2004/5, winning handicaps at Warwick in May and Newton Abbot (beating Take The Stand 2 lengths) in June: **c–** **h120**

7/1-on, jumped poorly and beaten when fell last in novice at Market Rasen: should stay 3m: raced on good going or softer. *Jonjo O'Neill*

MASTER SPEAKER 7 b.g. Presidium – Miss Ritz (Robellino (USA)) [2004/5 F16d Nov 29] big, lengthy gelding: third foal: half-brother to fairly useful 1997 2-y-o 5f winner Rare Indigo (by Timeless Times): dam 7f winner: well held in bumper on debut. *G. A. Harker* **F–**

MASTER TERN (USA) 10 ch.g. Generous (IRE) – Young Hostess (FR) (Arctic Tern (USA)) [2004/5 c119x, h–: c21v^{6} c24g^{6} Oct 30] big, leggy gelding: shows traces of stringhalt: winning hurdler/chaser: no show in handicap chases in 2004/5 starts: stays 25f: acts on good to firm and heavy going: tried in cheekpieces: patiently ridden: sketchy jumper of fences. *Jonjo O'Neill* **c– x h–**

MASTER T (USA) 6 b.g. Trempolino (USA) – Our Little C (USA) (Marquetry (USA)) [2004/5 h105: c18d^{3} c18m^{2} c17m^{2} c18m^{3} c17g^{4} c17m^{3} c20g^{F2} c19g^{3} c17g* c18m^{4} Apr 21] neat gelding: fair handicap hurdler: similar form over fences: won 4-runner novice at Plumpton in March: best around 2m: acts on firm going: below form in cheekpieces: often let down by jumping over fences: sometimes finds little. *G. L. Moore* **c106 x h–**

MASTER WOOD 14 b.g. Wonderful Surprise – Miss Wood (Precipice Wood) [2004/5 c101, h–: c25g^{pu} May 5] sturdy gelding: veteran chaser: stays 3¼m: acts on heavy going. *C. Grant* **c– h–**

MATELOT (FR) 5 ch.g. Epervier Bleu – Gloria IV (FR) (Video Rock (FR)) [2004/5 F16d^{5} F16s^{6} F18s^{2} F16g Mar 26] lengthy gelding: has scope: first foal: dam, unbeaten in 6 starts up to 1½m on Flat in France, out of half-sister to fairly useful staying jumpers Farfadet V and Uron V: best effort in bumpers when head second, clear of remainder, to Bumper at Fontwell. *F. Doumen, France* **F103**

MATERIAL WORLD 7 b.m. Karinga Bay – Material Girl (Busted) [2004/5 h113, F103: 25g^{2} Oct 18] sturdy mare: has only one eye (wears eyecover): fairly useful hurdler: good second to It's Wallace in handicap at Plumpton in October: stays 25f: acts on soft and good to firm going: jumps none too fluently: reliable. *Miss Suzy Smith* **h117**

MATMATA DE TENDRON (FR) 5 gr.g. Badolato (USA) – Cora Des Tamarix (FR) (Iron Duke (FR)) [2004/5 16d^{6} 16d^{5} 17d^{2} 17s^{6} 17v^{5} 16s^{4} 20s^{4} 21d^{3} Apr 5] good-topped gelding: first foal: dam once-raced on Flat: runner-up once from 5 starts over hurdles in France, sold out of C. Ligerot's stable €16,000 Goffs (France) November Sale: poor form in Britain: stays 21f. *A. Crook* **h81**

MATTHEW MUROTO (IRE) 6 b.g. Muroto – Glenmore Star (IRE) (Teofane) [2004/5 F77: 18m^{4} 22g^{5} 25g^{3} 21d^{pu} c26d^{5} 22s^{6} Dec 21] leggy, lengthy gelding: maiden hurdler: flattered third outing: tailed off in novice at Plumpton on chasing debut: visored third and fourth starts. *C. L. Tizzard* **c– h104 ?**

MATTKAR (NZ) 12 b.g. Kastamoun – Bev's Pride (NZ) (Rapier II) [2004/5 18m^{pu} Aug 19] tall gelding: maiden hurdler: reportedly broke shoulder on return from 4-year absence. *J. C. Tuck* **h–**

MATTYS JOY (IRE) 6 b.m. Beneficial – Moorstown Rose (IRE) (Roselier (FR)) [2004/5 16d 16m^{6} 16f^{5} 16d c16g^{2} c17m^{4} c16f^{3} Aug 14] fourth foal: half-sister to 2½m hurdle winner Crookstown Castle (by Castle Keep): dam unraced half-sister to fairly useful staying chaser Damers Cavalry: brought down in point in 2003: no form over hurdles: poor form in chasers: raced mainly around 2m: acts on firm going: has worn headgear: tried tongue tied. *D. Loughnane, Ireland* **c79 h–**

MAUNBY ROLLER (IRE) 6 b.g. Flying Spur (AUS) – Brown Foam (Horage) [2004/5 c–, h63§: 20s^{6} 19d c20g c24g^{pu} Feb 16] winning hurdler: no form since 2003, including over fences: stays 2½m: acts on good to soft going, probably on good to firm: tried blinkered, usually visored: ungenuine. *K. A. Morgan* **c– h– §**

MAUNSELL'S ROAD (IRE) 6 b.g. Desert Style (IRE) – Zara's Birthday (IRE) (Waajib) [2004/5 h90: 20s Apr 22] angular gelding: modest maiden hurdler: no show only start in 2004/5: stays easy 3m: best efforts on good going: tried visored. *L. Lungo* **h–**

MAXIE MCDONALD (IRE) 12 b.g. Homo Sapien – Lovely Sanara (Proverb) [2004/5 c24g^{3} c27g* c24s^{2} c24d^{3} c24d^{pu} Mar 3] lengthy gelding: modest handicap chaser: won at Ludlow in December: stays 27f: acts on soft and good to firm going. *N. A. Twiston-Davies* **c99 h–**

MAXILLA (IRE) 5 b. or br.m. Lahib (USA) – Lacinia (Groom Dancer (USA)) [2004/5 19s^{ur} 21s^{pu} 17d^{pu} Feb 1] rather unfurnished mare: fair on Flat (stays 1¾m), sold **h–**

out of L. Cumani's stable 24,000 gns Newmarket Autumn Sales: no form over hurdles: tongue tied final start. *Miss J. S. Davis*

MAXIMINUS 5 b.g. The West (USA) – Candarela (Damister (USA)) [2004/5 h84?: 16f 19g^{3} 20d* 19d^{3} 20d^{6} 22d^{pu} 16g^{5} Apr 17] tall, good-topped gelding: modest novice hurdler: won at Windsor in November: stays 2½m: acts on good to firm and good to soft going: has hinted at temperament. *M. Madgwick* **h93**

MAXIMIZE (IRE) 11 b.g. Mandalus – Lone Run (Kemal (FR)) [2004/5 c139§, h–: c32m c26g^{2} c24d c25d c29d c29d^{3} c25d* c29s c24g c28s c24g c29g Apr 23] strong gelding: fairly useful handicap chaser: won at Exeter in December by ½ length from Walter's Destiny: probably stays 33f: acts on any going: tried visored/in cheekpieces: usually sound jumper: temperamental. *M. C. Pipe* **c126 §** **h–**

MAXIMOSS (IRE) 7 b.m. Glacial Storm (USA) – Gi Moss (Le Moss) [2004/5 F16d F16d F16d Mar 12] leggy mare: first foal: dam winning Irish pointer: well held in 3 bumpers. *Dr J. R. J. Naylor* **F–**

MAX THE OBSCURE 5 b.g. Cloudings (IRE) – Princess Maxine (IRE) (Horage) [2004/5 F–: 16g 16m^{pu} 16g^{pu} 16v^{pu} Nov 17] no sign of ability. *Miss Lucinda V. Russell* **h–**

MAXXIUM (IRE) 4 b.g. Orpen (USA) – Florinda (CAN) (Vice Regent (CAN)) [2004/5 16v* 16d 16v^{2} 16s^{6} Feb 19] lengthy gelding: half-brother to one-time fair hurdler around 2m Little Rort (by Ali-Royal): fair on Flat (probably stays 1½m): winning debut in juvenile hurdles in 20-runner maiden at Navan in November: best effort when 5 lengths second to Sky's The Limit at Leopardstown: tried tongue tied. *M. Halford, Ireland* **h115 +**

MA YAHAB 4 ch.g. Dr Fong (USA) – Bay Shade (USA) (Sharpen Up) [2004/5 17s^{5} 16s^{3} 17s 16g* 16d* Mar 24] half-brother to 2m hurdle winner in Italy by Sadler's Wells: fairly useful maiden on Flat (likely to prove best up to 1¼m), sold out of L. Cumani's stable 45,000 gns Newmarket Autumn Sales: fair form over hurdles: won conditional jockeys maiden at Fakenham and handicap at Ludlow in March: likely to prove best at sharp 2m: open to further improvement. *Miss Venetia Williams* **h104 p**

MAYBE A DOUBLE 7 b.m. El Conquistador – Givusashot (Gunner B) [2004/5 c21g^{pu} Apr 10] first foal: dam no sign of ability: modest pointer, successful in March: no show in hunter chase. *Mrs A. L. Tory* **c–**

MAYBESEVEN 11 gr.g. Baron Blakeney – Ninth of May (Comedy Star (USA)) [2004/5 c64, h–: c19m c25f^{3} c25m^{2} c24s c22s* c24d^{3} c24s^{ur} c24s^{5} Mar 27] good-topped gelding: poor handicap chaser: 14 lb out of weights, won weak event at Towcester in November: stays 3¼m: acts on soft going, probably on good to firm: tried blinkered: unreliable. *R. Dickin* **c69 §** **h–**

MAYBE SHE WILL 7 b.m. Tudor Diver – Blue Mischief (Precocious) [2004/5 F82: F16d 16g^{pu} 20s 17d 22s^{pu} Dec 5] bumper winner: no form over hurdles. *D. W. Whillans* **h–** **F–**

MAYERLING 8 b.m. Old Vic – Manon Lescaut (Then Again) [2004/5 c–, h70: 24m^{pu} 22m^{pu} Sep 1] maiden hurdler: left P. Burgoyne and blinkered, lame final outing: jumped slowly and left only start over fences: stays 3¼m: acts on soft going. *A. B. Haynes* **c–** **h–**

MAYEUL (FR) 5 ch.g. Luchiroverte (IRE) – Elbe (FR) (Royal Charter (FR)) [2004/5 17s^{pu} 24s^{3} 20v^{2} 22d^{2} 20g^{5} Mar 26] smallish, leggy gelding: third foal: dam, 1½m winner, half-sister to useful chaser up to 2¾m Frimeur II: placed once around 1½m from 4 starts on Flat in Provinces: fair novice hurdler: stays 3m: acts on heavy going. *F. Doumen, France* **h108**

MAYYAS 5 b.g. Robellino (USA) – Amidst (Midyan (USA)) [2004/5 F16g F16s^{5} Oct 22] 11,000Y: sturdy gelding: third foal: half-brother to 1m and 9f winner Ago (by Rudimentary) and fairly useful 7f winner Aploy (by Deploy): dam fairly useful 6f and 1m winner: well held in bumpers. *C. C. Bealby* **F–**

MAZILEO 12 b.g. Mazilier (USA) – Embroglio (USA) (Empery (USA)) [2004/5 c110, h–: c28g^{pu} c25m* c24d^{F} c25s^{F} c21s^{pu} c24g^{pu} Apr 15] workmanlike gelding: winning hurdler: fair chaser: won handicap at Hereford in June, only completion in 2004/5: stays easy 25f: acts on firm and soft going: has worn cheekpieces, including at Hereford: races prominently: prone to odd blunder: unreliable. *Ian Williams* **c115 d** **h–**

MAZRAM 6 b.m. Muhtarram (USA) – Royal Mazi (Kings Lake (USA)) [2004/5 19v^{pu} Oct 17] leggy, angular mare: no sign of ability. *I. W. McInnes* **h–**

MAZZAREME (IRE) 7 b.g. Supreme Leader – Mazza (Mazilier (USA)) [2004/5 F94: F16d^{4} 22v^{4} 20s* 20v 17s^{5} 21v^{2} Mar 28] good-topped gelding: better effort in **h104** **F88**

bumpers when third on debut: fair novice hurdler: won at Ayr in December: stays 21f: raced on going softer than good. *N. G. Richards*

MAZZINI (IRE) 14 b.g. Celio Rufo – Dontellvi (The Parson) [2004/5 h–: c26g⁵ May 9] useful-looking gelding: winning hurdler up to 2¾m: mistakes on very belated chasing debut. *R. Rowe* **c82 h–**

MCBAIN (USA) 6 br.g. Lear Fan (USA) – River City Moon (USA) (Riverman (USA)) [2004/5 16d⁴ 16s² 17m* 16d 17g³ 16d³ 16d² 16d³ 16d 17g 19g* Apr 15] smallish, angular gelding: fairly useful on Flat (stays 1½m), sold out of F. J. Houghton's stable 26,000 gns Newmarket Autumn (2003) Sales: fairly useful hurdler: easily won maiden in November and novice in April, both at Taunton: best efforts when placed behind Crossbow Creek in handicaps at Kempton sixth and seventh starts: raced mainly around 2m: successful on good to firm going, acts on soft. *P. J. Hobbs* **h123**

MCCRACKEN (IRE) 9 b.g. Scenic – Sakanda (IRE) (Vayrann) [2004/5 c98, h98: 19spu Mar 23] modest hurdler/chaser in 2003/4: pulled up in selling hurdle at Towcester on return from year's absence, though still second turning for home: stays easy 3m: probably acts on any going: wore cheekpieces last 5 starts: usually tongue tied. *R. Ford* **c– h–**

MCGINTY ALL STARS (IRE) 7 b.m. Fourstars Allstar (USA) – Dowdstown Miss (Wolver Hollow) [2004/5 F–: 19d⁶ Apr 29] no sign of ability. *R. J. Price* **h–**

MCKELVEY (IRE) 6 b.g. Anshan – Chatty Actress (Le Bavard (FR)) [2004/5 16v⁵ 20v³ 24v* 24s* 24m² Apr 13] useful-looking gelding: will make a chaser: half-brother to 3 winners, notably very smart chaser Chives (by Good Thyne), stays 29f: dam unraced: most progressive over hurdles, winning maiden at Newcastle (blinkered, final start for S. Donohoe) in February and novice at Ludlow in March: very good second to Comanche War Paint in novice handicap at Cheltenham: will stay beyond 3m: acts on good to firm and heavy going: sure to improve further and win more races. *P. Bowen* **h119 p**

MCMAHON'S BROOK 6 br.g. Alderbrook – McMahon's River (Over The River (FR)) [2004/5 F–: F17v Feb 13] angular gelding: little show in 2 bumpers. *Mrs N. S. Sharpe* **F–**

MCQUEEN (IRE) 5 ch.g. Barathea (IRE) – Bibliotheque (USA) (Woodman (USA)) [2004/5 16s³ 16d³ 17s 19d⁴ Mar 4] angular gelding: fairly useful up to 1¼m on Flat, won 4 times in 2004: modest form over hurdles. *Mrs H. Dalton* **h95**

MEAD (IRE) 8 b.g. Mujadil (USA) – Sweetest Thing (IRE) (Prince Rupert (FR)) [2004/5 16s 19s⁵ 19s⁴ 20spu Apr 16] rather leggy gelding: runner-up in bumpers in 2001/2 for J. Mackie: modest form over hurdles. *D. J. Wintle* **h84**

MEADOW HAWK (USA) 5 b.g. Spinning World (USA) – Sophonisbe (Wollow) [2004/5 16gpu 17d⁶ 17g⁴ 16spu 16g 16d³ 16m³ Apr 17] leggy gelding: half-brother to fair 2m hurdler Sage Dancer (by Green Dancer) and winner over fences in Italy by Shareef Dancer: fair maiden on Flat (stays 1¼m) at 3 yrs: sold out of A. O'Brien's stable 14,000 gns Newmarket July (2003) Sales: modest novice hurdler: likely to prove best around 2m: blinkered/in cheekpieces after debut. *Ian Williams* **h91**

MEANDER (IRE) 10 br.g. Mandalus – Lady Rerico (Pamroy) [2004/5 c24g⁶ Feb 16] useful-looking gelding: winning 3m chaser in 2001/2: lightly raced since, won point in March: tried in cheekpieces: prone to breaking blood vessels. *Mrs K. B. Mactaggart* **c– h–**

MEANDMRSJONES 6 ch.m. Alderbrook – Dunbrody Abbey (Proverb) [2004/5 F–: F16d F17s⁵ 20dur 21spu 20m Apr 10] no form. *J. G. M. O'Shea* **h– F–**

MEASURE OF THE MAN 7 b.g. Dr Devious (IRE) – Run Faster (IRE) (Commanche Run) [2004/5 c16g⁵ c17g⁴ c16mpu c16g² c20g c16m⁵ 16m Sep 19] rather leggy gelding: winning hurdler: modest handicap chaser, formerly trained by C. Roche: seems best around 2m: acts on firm and good to soft going: blinkered last 4 starts: usually tongue tied: unreliable. *Jonjo O'Neill* **c90 § h– §**

MEASURE UP 6 ch.g. Inchinor – Victoria Blue (Old Vic) [2004/5 h96: 21mpu Jul 2] won 2m maiden on hurdling debut for J. M. Bradley: unsuitable trip on return 10 months later. *Mrs A. M. Thorpe* **h–**

MEDALLIST 6 b.g. Danehill (USA) – Obsessive (USA) (Seeking The Gold (USA)) [2004/5 h73: 17g* 16f⁶ c17mrtr 16m 16srtr Oct 28] modest 2m hurdler: won novice handicap at Sedgefield in May: below form after, twice refusing to race, sold out of B. Ellison's stable 2,500 gns Doncaster August Sales after first occasion: tried blinkered/in cheekpieces: has had tongue tied: one to avoid. *Evan Williams* **c§§ h90 §**

MEDA'S SONG 6 ch.m. Master Willie – Cala Conta (Deep Run) [2004/5 F16d F16g[4] Feb 16] half-sister to several winners, including fairly useful staying chaser Warner For Winners (by Roman Warrior): dam maiden sister to very smart hurdler/smart chaser up to 3m Slalom: better effort in bumpers when fourth of 9 in mares event at Musselburgh: will be suited by greater test of stamina. *D. W. Whillans* **F88**

MEDELAI 9 b.m. Marju (IRE) – No Islands (Lomond (USA)) [2004/5 c73, h54: 21g[4] 20g[6] Aug 18] leggy mare: bad maiden hurdler: successful only outing over fences: stays 2½m: acts on firm and soft going: usually blinkered prior to 2004/5: takes strong hold. *A. G. Juckes* **c– h60**

MEDICI (FR) 7 bl.g. Cadoudal (FR) – Marie de Valois (FR) (Moulin) [2004/5 h–, F84: 20mpu 17s[3] 17m[2] 17m* 19s[2] 19g[4] 20dpu 19g[5] Apr 15] leggy gelding: fair novice hurdler: left J. O'Neill after reappearance: won maiden at Taunton in November: stays 19f: acts on soft and good to firm going: free-going sort. *Ms Bridget Nicholls* **h110**

MEDISON (FR) 5 b. or br.g. Video Rock (FR) – Colombia III (FR) (Altayan) [2004/5 16s 16d[3] 17s* 16d* 16d* 16d 16m Apr 22] **h127 +**

While not quite matching his domination of the Paddy Power Gold Cup, Martin Pipe has a record second to none in the Sunderlands Imperial Cup at Sandown in March, and with it the chance at the sizeable bonus for winning at the Cheltenham Festival the following week. When Medison won the latest Imperial Cup it gave Pipe his third win in the race in four years and his sixth in all. He had also had the runner-up in 1997 and 2001, and it is indicative of his reputation in the race that Pipe has trained the favourite seven times in the last nine years. Two of his winners, Olympian in 1993 and Blowing Wind in 1998, collected the bonus with wins in the Coral Cup and County Hurdle respectively but Medison proved too well handicapped and, even under a penalty, missed the cut in the Coral Cup by two. Medison was making his handicap debut at Sandown after just four appearances in novices, the last two winning ones, at Taunton, not fully extended, in January and Ludlow, by a short head after idling, earlier in March. Each time he had looked likely to be well served by the truer pace that might be expected in a handicap and he had been by no means harshly assessed with a BHB mark of 118. Medison started favourite, though at 9/2, rather than the much shorter odds of some of Pipe's earlier 'good things', the odds reflecting the strength of the opposition at Sandown. It wasn't nearly strong enough, however, to prevent Medison from winning with any amount in hand after cruising through the field to challenge on the bridle at the last. For the record, Medison won by three and a half lengths from Fenix with plenty of others with solid form in similar events chasing them home. Medison looked sure to improve considerably on the fairly useful form he showed. That he failed to do so in two subsequent runs probably shouldn't be held against him. There was a clear excuse next time at Aintree, where, in a listed handicap off a mark 16 lb higher, he was still travelling well when stumbling badly three out. On his final start, taking on smart opposition in a minor event back at Sandown, Medison ran too badly to be true on much firmer ground than he had previously encountered.

It will be no surprise if Medison shows himself a useful or better hurdler on his return, though he may well be sent over fences as he has the physique and

Sunderlands Imperial Cup Handicap Hurdle, Sandown—
Medison challenges on the bridle as Fenix fluffs the last; Monte Cinto jumps in third

Mr D. A. Johnson's "Medison"

pedigree for chasing. A tall, angular gelding, Medison is a selle francais, by Video Rock out of a half-sister to Detroit III (by Video Rock), the dam of the Grand Steeple-Chase de Paris runner-up Kamillo, from the family of the high-class French chaser Arenice, who won that race in 1996. As that suggests Medison is bred to stay well beyond the two miles or so he has encountered so far, another reason to think there is plenty more to come. Before joining Pipe's stable, Medison won both starts in non-thoroughbred races over a mile and a half on the Flat for Bernard Secly, at Saint-Cloud and Lyon Parilly in the spring of 2004. He was ridden prominently when well held on his hurdling debut and clearly the subsequent switch to waiting tactics suited him. *M. C. Pipe*

MEEHAN (IRE) 5 b. or br.g. Spectrum (IRE) – Seeds of Doubt (IRE) (Night Shift (USA)) [2004/5 19g² 16m 21s 20d 16sᵖᵘ Dec 22] good-topped gelding: second foal: half-brother to 1¾m winner Irie Rasta (by Desert King): dam unraced close relation to useful 2m hurdler Blazing Spectacle and half-sister to Triumph Hurdle winner Rare Holiday: fair novice hurdler at best, sold out of N. Meade's stable 20,000 gns Doncaster May Sales after first outing: poor form in Britain. *Miss J. S. Davis* **h105 d**

MEGA D'ESTRUVAL (FR) 5 ch.m. Garde Royale – Vocation (FR) (Toujours Pret (USA)) [2004/5 16d² 16d² Dec 8] half-sister to useful chaser Destin d'Estruval (by Port Etienne), stayed 25f: dam unraced: successful 4 times up to 1½m on Flat, including at Longchamp in September, final start for S. Kalley: better effort over hurdles when second in mares novice at Lingfield on debut. *M. C. Pipe* **h90 +**

MEGALALA (IRE) 4 b.g. Petardia – Avionne (Derrylin) [2004/5 F18m Apr 21] half-brother to winning pointers by Most Welcome and Commanche Run: dam prolific winning hurdler around 2m: well held in bumper on debut. *J. J. Bridger* **F–**

MEGAN'S MAGIC 5 b.m. Blue Ocean (USA) – Hot Sunday Sport (Star Appeal) [2004/5 20d 17d^{6} 16d^{4} 16g^{4} 16v^{pu} 16d Jan 28] half-sister to 2 winners by Risk Me, including hurdler/chaser Risky Way, stays 2½m: fair on Flat (stays 1¼m), sold out of W. Storey's stable 3,000 gns Doncaster October Sales: poor novice hurdler. *M. E. Sowersby* **h71**

MEGAPAC (IRE) 7 b.g. Supreme Leader – Mistress Gale (IRE) (Strong Gale) [2004/5 F18g* 21d^{4} 22d^{4} 19m^{3} Apr 9] IR £20,000 3-y-o: lengthy gelding: first foal: dam, poor maiden chaser, sister to useful chaser up to 25f Yorkshire Gale: won bumper at Plumpton on debut in May: modest form in novice company over hurdles: should stay 3m. *Noel T. Chance* **h87** **F96**

MEGGIE'S BEAU (IRE) 9 ch.g. Good Thyne (USA) – Romantic Rose (IRE) (Strong Gale) [2004/5 c19s^{ur} c23v* c24s c23v* c24d^{pu} Mar 19] sturdy gelding: lightly raced: fair form at best over hurdles in 2002/3 (reportedly lame final start): fair form over fences: won twice at Leicester, maiden in February and novice in March: let down by jumping 2 of other 3 outings: stays 23f: raced mainly on soft/heavy ground. *Miss Venetia Williams* **c103** **h–**

MEGGIES GAMBLE (IRE) 8 b.g. Zaffaran (USA) – Glaskerbeg Lady (IRE) (Radical) [2004/5 h123, F–: 22g^{pu} Feb 5] tall gelding: chasing type: fairly useful novice hurdler in 2003/4: dropped out after setting strong pace and jumping less than fluently in valuable handicap at Sandown, only outing in 2004/5: will stay beyond 3m: raced on good going or softer (acts on heavy): front runner. *Miss Venetia Williams* **h–**

MEGGIE'S LAD (IRE) 8 b.g. Beau Sher – Kambaya (IRE) (Kambalda) [2004/5 h103: c25g^{4} c24g^{4} c20s^{4} c16s^{3} c19s^{4} c20g* c21d^{5} Mar 28] rather sparely-made gelding: fair maiden hurdler: modest chaser: won novice handicap at Bangor in March: stays 25f: acts on soft ground: blinkered last 4 starts: free-going sort. *Miss Venetia Williams* **c91** **h–**

MELANGEL 6 br. or b.m. Bob's Return (IRE) – Kellamba (Netherkelly) [2004/5 F16s 17g Mar 9] fourth foal: half-sister to winning 3m chaser Take Aim (by Gunner B) and winning pointer by Rakaposhi King: dam unraced: tailed off in bumper and novice hurdle. *H. D. Daly* **h–** **F–**

MELDRUM STAR (IRE) 8 ch.g. Fourstars Allstar (USA) – Meldrum Lass (Buckskin (FR)) [2004/5 h108: 22d^{5} c24m^{F} Jun 5] sturdy gelding: fair handicap hurdler: fell fatally on chasing debut: should have been suited by further than 21f: acted on good to firm and good to soft going. *Mrs S. J. Smith* **c–** **h97 +**

MELFORD (IRE) 7 br.g. Presenting – Echo Creek (IRE) (Strong Gale) [2004/5 h98: c23s^{4} c24g^{5} c20d* c21s^{pu} c20d^{5} Feb 18] well-made gelding: fair hurdler: similar form over fences, winning novice handicap at Sandown in December: seemed to lose interest final outing: probably stays 3m: acts on good to soft going. *Miss H. C. Knight* **c109** **h–**

MEL IN BLUE (FR) 7 b.g. Pistolet Bleu (IRE) – Calligraphie (FR) (R B Chesne) [2004/5 F16g^{5} 20d^{2} 19g 19g^{5} 19d* 21s* 22g^{4} Apr 3] tall, useful-looking gelding: won bumper at Newbury on debut in 2001/2 for N. Henderson, similar form when fifth of 20 to The Mick Weston at Cheltenham on return (won point in between): progressive hurdler: won handicaps at Newbury (conditional jockeys event, despite mistakes) and Warwick in March: good fourth to Hopbine in similar event at Market Rasen: stays 2¾m: acts on soft going. *R. Waley-Cohen* **h112** **F98**

MELITMA 10 gr.g. Gods Solution – Melsil (Silly Prices) [2004/5 h–: 24g^{pu} Jul 1] no form over hurdles. *R. Nixon* **h–**

MELMOUNT STAR (IRE) 7 b. or br.g. Rashar (USA) – Bucktina (Buckskin (FR)) [2004/5 16v 16v 16g Mar 9] €16,000 4-y-o: leggy gelding: half-brother to several winners, including fairly useful hurdler/fair chaser Beyond Control (by Supreme Leader), stays 3¼m: dam unraced, from family of useful staying chaser Imperial Black: won maiden Irish point on debut in 2003: sold 30,000 gns Doncaster May (2003) Sales: well held all 3 starts in novice hurdles. *J. Howard Johnson* **h–**

MELROSE 6 b. or br.m. Past Glories – Meltonby (Sayf El Arab (USA)) [2004/5 F16g Dec 16] small mare: third foal: sister to poor 2m hurdler/chaser Meltonian: dam fair 6f to 1m winner: seventh of 15 in bumper at Catterick on debut. *J. Hetherton* **F80**

MELTONIAN 8 ch.g. Past Glories – Meltonby (Sayf El Arab (USA)) [2004/5 h84: c16m* c16m^{pu} Jun 8] compact gelding: poor hurdler: successful in weak maiden at Fakenham in May on completed outing over fences, making all despite jumping markedly right throughout: best form up to 21f: acts on good to firm and good to soft going: visored once. *K. F. Clutterbuck* **c72** **h–**

MEMORIES OF GOLD (IRE) 5 b.m. Carroll House – Sweet Harmony (IRE) (Altountash) [2004/5 F16d 19s 24d4 21m Apr 13] tall mare: has scope: first foal: dam unraced: well held in bumper (for Mrs A. Bowlby) and novice hurdles. *O. O'Neill* **h78** **F–**

MEM SCYLLA 6 b. or br.m. Terimon – Occatillo (Maris Piper) [2004/5 F16m F16g5 F16s6 F17d Nov 2] sixth foal: half-sister to fair hurdler up to 3m Memsahib Ofesteem (by Neltino) and poor 2m hurdler Holkam Bay (by Blakeney): dam lightly-raced maiden pointer: well held in bumpers. *N. B. King* **F–**

MENCHIKOV (FR) 5 br.g. Garde Royale – Caucasie (FR) (Djarvis (FR)) [2004/5 F16m4 Apr 2] rather leggy gelding: third foal: brother to fairly useful hurdler Le Royal, stays 2½m: dam, winning 2¼m chaser in France, out of half-sister to useful chaser around 2½m Camitrov: 7¾ lengths fourth of 21 to Hi Humpfree in bumper at Newbury on debut. *N. J. Henderson* **F93**

MENDIP MANOR 7 b.g. Rakaposhi King – Broughton Manor (Dubassoff (USA)) [2004/5 h–: 19s 24d c16dF c19gpu Apr 15] rangy gelding: signs of ability only on chasing debut. *S. C. Burrough* **c92 ?** **h–**

MENDO 5 b.g. Alderbrook – Ina's Farewell (Random Shot) [2004/5 F16s* F17d3 Apr 9] 2,000 3-y-o: good-topped gelding: closely related to 2 winners by Ardross, including fairly useful hurdler/fair chaser Ardrina, stayed 3¼m, and half-brother to winning pointer by Henbit: dam unraced: useful form in bumpers: won at Sandown in February impressively by 6 lengths from Dunsfold Duke on debut: length third of 22 to The Cool Guy in Grade 2 at Aintree (made much of running) in April: will stay at least 2½m: likely to do well in novice hurdles in 2005/6. *Noel T. Chance* **F113**

MENEUR DE JEU (FR) 5 b.g. Sleeping Car (FR) – Tanie (FR) (Kashmir Ring) [2004/5 19s5 c17s2 c20d* c20s4 c20s5 c22s c24s2 c20dF Feb 18] leggy ex-French gelding: fifth foal: half-brother to winning chaser Isope Colombe (by Roi de Rome) and fairly useful chaser up to 3¼m Jacquemart Colombe (by Royal Charter): dam, 17f chase winner, also won up to 1½m on Flat: twice-raced on Flat: thrice-raced over hurdles for E. Clayeux/J. P. Scomparin: better form over fences, winning 4-y-o chase at Auteuil in June: sold out of T. Trapenard's stable €78,000 Goffs (France) November Sale: good second to Hirvine in novice at Newcastle on British debut: mistakes prior to falling twelfth in similar event at Sandown: stays 3m: raced on going softer than good. *M. C. Pipe* **c118** **h?**

MEN OF DESTINY (IRE) 4 b.g. Sadler's Wells (USA) – Caladira (IRE) (Darshaan) [2004/5 F17sro F17d F18d3 Feb 20] €75,000Y: angular gelding: fifth foal: half-brother to Italian 7.5f winner Lady Poison (by Charwood Forest): dam Irish 1½m winner: sold unraced out of C. O'Brien's stable 10,000 gns Newmarket Autumn Sales: modest form in bumpers: would have made winning debut but for hanging left and running out under 2f out at Taunton. *B. G. Powell* **F84**

MENPHIS BEURY (FR) 5 b.g. Art Bleu – Pampa Star (FR) (Pampabird) [2004/5 c? , h96: 20s 21g c20g6 c24d* c24d2 c24sF c23s2 c23mur c25g2 Apr 17] sturdy gelding: maiden hurdler: fair chaser: won novice handicap at Doncaster in January: stays 3m: raced mainly on good going or softer (acts on heavy): has been let down by jumping: carries head high. *H. D. Daly* **c104** **h–**

MENSCH (IRE) 9 ch.g. Husyan (USA) – Floating Dollar (Master Owen) [2004/5 c73, h–: c25m* c25m5 26g* 24g* 24m5 c26m* c24g4 c25m2 Sep 8] modest hurdler/chaser: had good first half of season, winning handicaps over fences at Hereford in May and Fontwell (novice) in August and over hurdles at Southwell (novice) and Bangor (conditional jockeys) in July: finished sore final outing: will probably stay beyond 3¼m: acts on firm going: tried blinkered/in cheekpieces prior to 2004/5. *Evan Williams* **c86** **h86**

MEPHISTO (IRE) 6 b.g. Machiavellian (USA) – Cunning (Bustino) [2004/5 20s3 23s* 18v* 20s3 20g* Apr 15] **h148 p**

It was a measure of the strength of the team of novice hurdlers owned by Andrea and Graham Wylie and trained by Howard Johnson that just about the pick of them, and potentially the best prospect, Mephisto, stayed at home whilst stable-companions Arcalis and No Refuge won the big novice hurdles at the Cheltenham Festival. Mephisto was turned out at Aintree instead, starting odds on to complete a hat-trick in Grade 2 company in the Mersey Novices' Hurdle. The form of Mephisto's earlier wins was working out particularly well. On just his second start over hurdles, Mephisto was a most impressive winner of the Brit Insurance Prestige Novices' Hurdle at Haydock in February, cruising into contention and barely coming off the bridle in beating Moulin Riche three lengths; the runner-up went on to land the three-mile Spa Novices' Hurdle, also sponsored by Brit Insurance, at the Cheltenham Festival. The following month, Mephisto had to work much harder when battling to a head success over the juvenile Faasel in the totesport Premier Kelso Hurdle, the pair pulling twenty-five lengths clear. This time the runner-up went on to finish second in the Triumph Hurdle before winning the John Smith's Anniversary 4-Y-O Novices' Hurdle on the same Aintree card as the Mersey. Mephisto's defeat at Aintree must have come as a big disappointment, though there was a ready explanation for his finishing only a one-paced third to Turpin Green. Mephisto ran far too freely (as he had done on the Flat on occasions) and, having got his tongue over the bit, was reported to have swallowed it. The Aintree result provided further proof of the strength of Mephisto's earlier form. Turpin Green had finished only third behind him at Haydock, while Wild Cane Ridge, fourth in the Prestige, was another from the race to win next time out.

Mephisto made amends quickly for his Aintree defeat by winning at Ayr the following week, this time fitted with an Australian noseband, designed to keep the bit higher in the mouth to prevent him from getting his tongue over it. He ran out an easy winner after setting a steady pace and, with his chief rival Celtic Son nowhere near his best, Mephisto was left with a simple task to beat the only other runner Bagan by five lengths. Mephisto had kept good company right from his very first start over hurdles, the Royal Gloucestershire Hussars Novices' Hurdle at Cheltenham in January. Mephisto very much caught the eye when finishing just over ten lengths third behind Ambobo, giving the distinct impression he would go a long way over hurdles.

Mephisto's Flat career was also going very much the right way before he joined his current yard. Trained by Luca Cumani, Mephisto completed a four-timer in handicaps during the summer and made into a smart performer, his sequence beginning in the Queen Mother's Cup at York on Timeform Charity Day (ridden by the trainer's wife) and ending back at the same course, after a lengthy stewards'

Brit Insurance Prestige Novices' Hurdle, Haydock—
smart novices Mephisto (left) and Moulin Riche over the last together

totesport Premier Kelso Hurdle (Novices')—
an even better performance is needed to get the better of the juvenile Faasel

inquiry and subsequent appeal, in the Ebor. A close-coupled, quite good-topped gelding, Mephisto naturally attracted plenty of interest as a hurdling prospect, and it took a bid of 220,000 guineas to secure him at the Newmarket Autumn Sales, the underbidder being J. P. McManus. As a yearling, Mephisto had been sold for IR 58,000 guineas.

Mephisto's family has created a stir in the sale-ring before. His great grandam, the unraced Super Foxe (out of a half-sister to the Eclipse and Sussex Stakes winner Artaius), was a half-sister to Lichine, the Lyphard colt who in 1980 was sold for the then world-record price for a yearling of $1.7m. Owned by Stavros Niarchos, Lichine proved a smart performer in France. Mephisto's grandam Vice Vixen was also unraced, but his dam Cunning was a smart filly who was beaten only a head in the Prix Vermeille in between wins in the Galtres Stakes and the Princess Royal Stakes. She too was trained by Luca Cumani (and like Mephisto, ridden to victory by Sara Cumani on one occasion) and ran in the colours of the Cumanis' Fittocks Stud. In addition to Mephisto, Cunning has bred another decent jumper, the useful two-mile hurdler/chaser Almaydan (by Marju), also a fairly useful stayer on the Flat, and Ejtithaab (by Arazi), a fairly useful mile winner in Dubai.

Mephisto (IRE) (b.g. 1999)	Machiavellian (USA) (b 1987)	Mr Prospector (b 1970)	Raise A Native
			Gold Digger
		Coup de Folie (b 1982)	Halo
			Raise The Standard
	Cunning (ch 1989)	Bustino (b 1971)	Busted
			Ship Yard
		Vice Vixen (b 1984)	Vice Regent
			Super Foxe

With similar types Inglis Drever and No Refuge in the same ownership, it will be interesting to see how Mephisto is campaigned from now on. He has already proved effective at a range of distances, his impressive win at Haydock coming at

Andrea & Graham Wylie's "Mephisto"

just under three miles. He wasn't at all inconvenienced by the drop back to two and a quarter at Kelso next time, when he put up his best effort in fact. It would be no great surprise were he to be just as effective at two miles and, indeed, he makes some appeal as a prospective Champion Hurdle candidate at the odds of around 33/1 at the time of writing. Mephisto travels strongly in his races and, before Ayr, all his runs had come in the mud, though he also acted on good to firm ground on the Flat. He may be fitted with a tongue strap in future to prevent the breathing problems he experienced at Aintree. Mephisto has the makings of a high-class hurdler, and looks sure to win more good races. *J. Howard Johnson*

MER BIHAN (FR) 5 b.m. Port Lyautey (FR) – Unika II (FR) (Rolling Bowl (FR)) [2004/5 h–: 16d 20vpu Nov 8] light-framed mare: no form over hurdles. *L. Lungo* **h–**

MERCATO (FR) 9 b.g. Mansonnien (FR) – Royal Lie (FR) (Garde Royale) [2004/5 c123, h–: c24d2 c24g5 c24g3 c20spu Mar 6] tall, good-topped gelding: fairly useful chaser at one time: well below best in 2004/5: stays 3m: acts on heavy going: has had tongue tied: usually held up. *J. R. Best* **c99 h–**

MERCHANTS FRIEND (IRE) 10 b.g. Lord Americo – Buck Maid (Buckskin (FR)) [2004/5 c136x, h–: c24d3 c27dpu c28v* c29spu 24d c36dF c29g Apr 23] good-topped gelding: useful handicap chaser: won quite valuable event at Haydock in December by 15 lengths from Tipsy Mouse: generally disappointing otherwise in 2004/5, soundly beaten in handicap hurdle fifth outing: stays 3½m well: raced mainly on good going or softer (acts on heavy): usually wears cheekpieces, blinkered final start: makes mistakes (fell tenth in Grand National). *C. J. Mann* **c134 h–**

MERDEKA (IRE) 5 b.g. Luso – Gentle Reef (IRE) (Orange Reef) [2004/5 F16d^3 F16s* Dec 29] rangy, useful-looking gelding: third foal: dam fair 2m hurdle winner: useful form in bumpers, successful at Leopardstown by 4½ lengths from Eye On The Ball: good prospect. *T. J. Taaffe, Ireland* **F105 p**

MERITOCRACY (IRE) 7 b.g. Lahib (USA) – Merry Devil (IRE) (Sadler's Wells (USA)) [2004/5 h–: 16g 16d c19m^6 c19s^{pu} c16g^{ur} Mar 3] no solid form: tongue tied once: dead. *Miss A. E. Broyd* **c– h–**

MERLINS PROFIT 5 b.g. Wizard King – Quick Profit (Formidable (USA)) [2004/5 16v^6 17d Nov 9] poor maiden on Flat (stays 1¼m): shaped like non-stayer both outings over hurdles. *M. Todhunter* **h–**

MERRYLEA-CONFUSED 6 ch.m. Respect – Merry Mermaid (Bairn (USA)) [2004/5 h–, F–: 16m^{pu} Apr 28] leggy mare: little sign of ability. *Mrs H. O. Graham* **h–**

MERRY MINSTREL (IRE) 12 b.g. Black Minstrel – Merry Lesa (Dalesa) [2004/5 c–: c21d c21d^6 Feb 18] tall gelding: winning chaser: modest pointer nowadays: stays 3m: has high head carriage. *Mrs Jackie Hunt* **c–**

MERRY SHOT (IRE) 13 b.g. Cataldi – Borgina (Boreen (FR)) [2004/5 c24g^4 May 21] strong gelding: maiden chaser: modest pointer: tried blinkered. *C. A. Green* **c78 h–**

MERRY STORM (IRE) 6 b.g. Glacial Storm (USA) – Cap Reform (IRE) (Phardante (FR)) [2004/5 c23v^4 c24v^{pu} Mar 29] €6,000 4-y-o: half-brother to winning 2¼m chaser Canary Tan (by Mister Lord) and to winning pointers: dam, placed in point, half-sister to top-class chaser Merry Gale: won maiden on second of 2 starts in Irish points in 2004: sold £62,000 Cheltenham April Sales: poor form on completed outing in maiden chases. *Miss K. Marks* **c–**

MERRY TINA 10 b.m. Tina's Pet – Merry Missus (Bargello) [2004/5 c64, h–: c16g^4 c16g^3 c17g^3 c16d^4 c16m^4 c16m^{pu} c16s^3 c17d^4 Aug 28] poor novice chaser: best form around 2m: acts on good to soft and good to firm going: tried visored. *J. B. Walton* **c72 h–**

MERRYVALE MAN 8 b.g. Rudimentary (USA) – Salu (Ardross) [2004/5 h104: 16m 16g^4 16d 16g^F 16v^4 16v 16v^5 20v^5 16v^6 20v^2 18d^{ur} 16m 20d^5 22v^4 20s 16s^{pu} 16s^{pu} Mar 22] leggy gelding: fair handicap hurdler, kept busy from December to March: stays 2½m: unraced on firm going, acts on any other: usually races prominently. *Miss Kariana Key* **h106**

MERSEY MIRAGE 8 b.g. King's Signet (USA) – Kirriemuir (Lochnager) [2004/5 h–: 16g 16g 16d^3 Mar 28] bad maiden hurdler: barely stays 2m. *R. C. Guest* **h–**

MESMERIC (IRE) 7 b.g. Sadler's Wells (USA) – Mesmerize (Mill Reef (USA)) [2004/5 16m 20d^2 16g^5 16v^5 24s^3 24g* 21d 24d^6 Feb 11] sturdy gelding: smart at one time on Flat (should stay 1¾m), fair form when winning amateur event in May: fair hurdler: left D. Weld after fourth start: won handicap at Taunton in December: stays 3m: acts on soft going: tried blinkered: has bled from nose. *B. G. Powell* **h111**

MESSAGE RECU (FR) 9 b.g. Luth Dancer (USA) – High Steppe (Petoski) [2004/5 c72, h–: 19s^5 19d 22v Apr 22] workmanlike gelding: fair hurdler/winning chaser, bought privately out of S. Lewis' stable £5,000 Ascot June Sales: stays 3m: acts on soft going, has won on good to firm: blinkered/visored last 2 starts: inconsistent. *K. Bishop* **c– h100**

METAL DETECTOR (IRE) 8 b.g. Treasure Hunter – Las-Cancellas (Monksfield) [2004/5 c106, h112: 20g^{pu} c20d^5 c24d^3 c23g^6 c25s^5 c24d^2 Feb 11] good-topped gelding: winning hurdler: fair chaser: stays 3m: acts on soft and good to firm going: wore cheek-pieces/blinkers after first outing: ungenuine. *K. C. Bailey* **c107 § h–**

METICULOUS 7 gr.g. Eagle Eyed (USA) – Careful (IRE) (Distinctly North (USA)) [2004/5 h–: c17m^4 Jun 9] workmanlike gelding: of little account: tried tongue tied. *M. C. Chapman* **c– h–**

MEVAGISSEY (BEL) 8 b. or br.g. Sula Bula – Fowey (Grand Conde (FR)) [2004/5 F–: 19m^3 19f^6 19g^6 20d^{pu} Jan 26] workmanlike gelding: poor form over hurdles. *J. D. Frost* **h–**

MEXICAN PETE 5 b.g. Atraf – Eskimo Nel (IRE) (Shy Groom (USA)) [2004/5 h98: 16s 18d Nov 14] fairly useful on Flat (stays 1½m): winning hurdler: well beaten in handicaps in 2004/5. *P. W. Hiatt* **h–**

MEXICAN ROCK 9 b.g. Rock City – Pink Mex (Tickled Pink) [2004/5 h74: 16f^4 Sep 5] poor form in 3 starts over hurdles. *N. J. Henderson* **h–**

MEXICAN (USA) 6 b.g. Pine Bluff (USA) – Cuando Quiere (USA) (Affirmed (USA)) [2004/5 c91x, h–: 17d^6 c16d^F c16v^4 c16s^5 c16s^3 c16s^3 c17s^3 Apr 2] rather leggy gelding: **c87 § h80 §**

maiden hurdler: modest handicap chaser: raced around 2m: acts on soft going: wears headgear: ungenuine. *M. D. Hammond*

MIAHEYYUN 9 b.g. Bonny Scot (IRE) – Daunt Not (Kalaglow) [2004/5 16m 16mpu 20gpu 17dpu 16gpu Oct 18] no longer of any account: tried blinkered/in cheekpieces: tongue tied. *C. Roberts* **h–**

MIALYSSA 5 b.m. Rakaposhi King – Theme Arena (Tragic Role (USA)) [2004/5 F17s6 aF16g Feb 19] second foal: dam won around 2m over hurdles/2m winner on Flat: poor form on first of 2 starts in bumpers. *M. R. Bosley* **F–**

MIAMI EXPLORER 5 b.m. Pennekamp (USA) – Elaine Tully (IRE) (Persian Bold) [2004/5 16dF 16g5 16d3 17g2 16m4 16m2 19g5 Sep 30] lengthy mare: half-sister to fair hurdler Maiden Voyage (by Slip Anchor), stays 21f: little form and looked wayward on Flat at 2 and 3 yrs for H. Morrison: modest novice hurdler. *P. R. Webber* **h91**

MICHAELS DREAM (IRE) 6 b.g. Spectrum (IRE) – Stormswept (USA) (Storm Bird (CAN)) [2004/5 h94: 16m3 20g4 17gpu 16gpu Sep 12] modest maiden hurdler: lost action final outing: stays 2½m: acts on firm and soft going: tried visored/blinkered. *J. Hetherton* **h86**

MICHAELS JOY (IRE) 6 br.g. Presenting – Scarteen Lower (IRE) (Royal Fountain) [2004/5 20s3 20spu 20vpu Jan 15] strong, workmanlike gelding: fourth in bumper on debut: off 20 months, third of 16 to Eskimo Pie at Haydock, only completion in 3 novice hurdles. *G. M. Moore* **h86**

MICHIGAN BLUE 13 b.g. Rakaposhi King – Starquin (IRE) (Strong Gale) [2004/5 c17g5 Nov 10] good-topped gelding: fair handicap chaser at best, won 4 times at Hereford in 2001/2: lightly raced since, well beaten on return from 23-month absence: best form at 2m: acts on soft and good to firm going: bold-jumping front runner. *M. J. M. Evans* **c–** **h–**

MICHIGAN D'ISOP (FR) 5 b.g. Cadoudal (FR) – Julie du Berlais (FR) (Rose Laurel) [2004/5 F16d F16s Mar 23] 2,500 4-y-o: useful-looking gelding: first foal: dam winning 2m hurdler in France, also placed over fences: tailed off in bumpers. *B. J. M. Ryall* **F–**

MICKEY CROKE 8 b.g. Alflora (IRE) – Praise The Lord (Lord Gayle (USA)) [2004/5 c–, h114: 20s* 20d3 22v3 Oct 30] rangy, good sort: fell only outing over fences: fair hurdler: odds on, won 5-runner maiden at Perth in August: should stay 3m: raced on good ground or softer. *M. Todhunter* **c–** **h103**

MICKLEY (IRE) 8 b.g. Ezzoud (IRE) – Dawsha (IRE) (Slip Anchor) [2004/5 22s6 20s2 21s4 20s 16d5 Apr 18] close-coupled gelding: poor maiden hurdler: stays 21f: acts on soft and good to firm going: wore cheekpieces last 4 outings. *P. R. Hedger* **h81**

MICK MURPHY (IRE) 8 b.g. Jurado (USA) – Lee Ford Lady (Kemal (FR)) [2004/5 c70, h64: c16g6 17g4 20m 17g3 21m5 Jul 26] big, lengthy gelding: bad maiden hurdler: let down by jumping over fences: stays 2¾m: acts on good to firm and good to soft going: wears cheekpieces: has had tongue tied: sold to join V. Hughes 2,000 gns Doncaster January Sales. *Mrs E. Slack* **c– x** **h58**

MICKTHECUTAWAY (IRE) 13 b.g. Rontino – Le-Mu-Co (Varano) [2004/5 c66, h–: c33spu Apr 28] workmanlike gelding: veteran chaser: won point in 2004: broke down in hunter in April 2004: stays 25f: raced mainly on good going or softer (acts on heavy): usually forces pace. *Daniel Skelton* **c–**

MIDDLEHAM PARK (IRE) 5 b.g. Revoque (IRE) – Snap Crackle Pop (IRE) (Statoblest) [2004/5 h82: 20g3 16g 19s4 21g* 24s6 Apr 16] lengthy gelding: modest maiden on Flat: modest hurdler: sold out of P. Haslam's stable 10,000 gns Doncaster January Sales after third outing: improved form when winning novice at Plumpton in March: stays 21f. *J. W. Mullins* **h94**

MIDDLEHAM ROSE 4 b.f. Dr Fong (USA) – Shallop (Salse (USA)) [2004/5 16g3 17g3 16d6 16v5 16s5 Dec 22] poor maiden on Flat (stays 1½m): modest juvenile hurdler: needs emphasis on speed at 2m. *P. C. Haslam* **h85**

MIDDLE HOUSE 5 b.m. Sayaarr (USA) – Estrela Vermelha (Russian Red) [2004/5 F16d 20fpu Jun 6] £850 3-y-o, resold 500 3-y-o: second foal: dam never ran: tongue tied, no show in bumper and novice hurdle. *W. Amos* **h–** **F–**

MIDDLEMISS (IRE) 5 b.m. Midhish – Teresa Deevey (Runnett) [2004/5 16m Jun 6] poor maiden on Flat: no show in seller on hurdling debut. *J. W. Mullins* **h–**

MIDDLETHORPE 8 b.g. Noble Patriarch – Prime Property (IRE) (Tirol) [2004/5 h111: 16s* 16d 16d* 16d 16s4 Feb 5] workmanlike gelding: fairly useful handicap hurd- **h127**

ler: improved further in 2004/5, winning at Wetherby in October and December (fourth course success, beat Castleshane by head): best around 2m: raced on good going or softer (probably acts on heavy): wears blinkers: not a fluent jumper: consistent. *M. W. Easterby*

MIDDLETON KATE 5 b.m. Thethingaboutitis (USA) – Koritsaki (Strong Gale) [2004/5 F17g Apr 14] smallish mare: seventh foal: sister to winning 3m hurdler Planters Specials and half-sister to winning pointer by Buckley: dam, winning hurdler, stayed 21f: tailed off in bumper on debut. *John R. Upson* **F–**

MIDDLEWAY 9 b.g. Milieu – Galway Gal (Proverb) [2004/5 c68x, h76: c25g^5 c25g* c22m^{pu} c27d^{ur} c21d Dec 7] workmanlike gelding: poor hurdler/chaser: won handicap over fences at Hexham in May: stays 25f: best form on good ground: effective with or without cheekpieces: often let down by jumping over fences. *Miss Kate Milligan* **c68 x h–**

MIDLAND FLAME (IRE) 10 b.g. Un Desperado (FR) – Lathanona (Reformed Character) [2004/5 c134, h–: c26g Nov 27] strong, well-made gelding: usually looks very well: useful handicap chaser: weakened quickly 4 out in very valuable handicap at Newbury, only outing in 2004/5: stays 25f: best efforts on good going: takes strong hold, and probably best ridden up with pace: usually sound jumper. *Miss H. C. Knight* **c– h–**

MIDLEM MELODY 9 b.m. Syrtos – Singing Hills (Crash Course) [2004/5 c86, h–: c17v^4 c20v^F c16m^4 c16d^3 c16g^3 c19g^4 c16v^2 c17v^2 c16s^3 c20d* c17d^5 Apr 11] medium-sized mare: modest handicap chaser: won at Carlisle in March: not discredited considering mistakes in cheekpieces final outing: stays 21f: acts on any going: usually patiently ridden: has swished tail: tough and consistent. *W. S. Coltherd* **c90 h–**

MIDNIGHT ARROW 7 b.m. Robellino (USA) – Princess Oberon (IRE) (Fairy King (USA)) [2004/5 16d^F 17d May 29] fairly useful 5f winner at 2 yrs, lightly raced and no form on Flat subsequently: sold out of I. Balding's stable 8,000 gns Newmarket July (2001) Sales: off 3 years (went to stud), well held on completed outing over hurdles. *R. Johnson* **h–**

MIDNIGHT CREEK 7 b.g. Tragic Role (USA) – Greek Night Out (IRE) (Ela-Mana-Mou) [2004/5 h104§: 21d^F 24d 21g Dec 26] leggy gelding: fair handicap hurdler at best: left Miss V. Williams, no form in 2004/5: stays 3m: raced on good going or softer (acts on heavy): tried in cheekpieces/visor: tongue tied second start: irresolute: joined G. A. Swinbank. *Miss V. Scott* **h– §**

MIDNIGHT GOLD 5 ch.g. Midnight Legend – Yamrah (Milford) [2004/5 F–: F16d F16d^3 F16d 20v 17s 21d^6 24d^2 24d^2 24m Apr 13] medium-sized gelding: best effort in bumpers when third at Chepstow: modest novice hurdler: stays 3m: acts on good to soft going. *L. P. Grassick* **h95 F76**

MIDNIGHT GUNNER 11 b.g. Gunner B – Light Tonight (Lighter) [2004/5 c113, h–: c30d^5 c24g^{pu} c23s c25d^2 c27g^2 c24s^6 c24g^{pu} c26d^3 c29s^3 c25m^{pu} Apr 9] well-made gelding: fair handicap chaser, largely below form in 2004/5: best at 3m+: acts on any going. *A. E. Price* **c105 h–**

MIDNIGHT LORD (IRE) 8 b.g. Mister Lord (USA) – Friary Town (IRE) (Barbarolli (USA)) [2004/5 c24d Mar 11] poor pointer: tailed off in hunter chase. *Nigel Benstead* **c–**

MIDNIGHT SPIRIT 5 b.g. Midnight Legend – West-Hatch-Spirit (Forzando) [2004/5 F–: F16m 22m^4 Apr 17] plain gelding: no show in bumpers and novice hurdle: bought out of S. Burrough's stable £3,500 Ascot February Sales. *H. E. Haynes* **h– F–**

MIDNIGHT SPUR (IRE) 6 b.g. Flying Spur (AUS) – Faramisa (IRE) (Doyoun) [2004/5 F16g* F17s^6 Jan 10] second foal: half-brother to winner in Spain by General Monash: dam thrice-raced hurdler: made virtually all when winning bumper at Huntingdon on debut in October: raced too freely next time. *B. G. Powell* **F94**

MIDNIGHT STAR 4 b.g. Cloudings (IRE) – Blueberry Parkes (Pursuit of Love) [2004/5 F14m^3 Mar 21] second foal: dam, second at 6f from 3 starts, half-sister to useful sprinters Lucky Parkes, My Melody Parkes and Summerhill Parkes: signs of inexperience when 8 lengths third to Post It in maiden bumper at Hereford on debut. *M. Mullineaux* **F82**

MID SUMMER LARK (IRE) 9 b.g. Tremblant – Tuney Blade (Fine Blade (USA)) [2004/5 c82: c25g* c25v^F c24v^{pu} c20d^{pu} Mar 26] second start in hunter chases, won maiden at Hexham in May: failed to complete subsequently, including in handicap: stays 25f: usually wears visor: tongue tied second outing: has attitude/jumping problems. *I. McMath* **c93 x**

MIDY'S RISK (FR) 8 gr.g. Take Risks (FR) – Martine Midy (FR) (Lashkari) [2004/5 c–, h–: c16v^{pu} May 10] lengthy, angular gelding: winning hurdler: little aptitude for fences: tried blinkered/in cheekpieces. *Miss S. J. Davies* **c– h–**

MIGHTY FINE 11 gr.g. Arzanni – Kate Kimberley (Sparkler) [2004/5 c101, h92: 16d 21d^{2} c16d* c17s* c20d^{3} c20d^{5} c16s* c16s* 20d^{2} 18s^{5} 16s^{3} Apr 20] rangy gelding: fairly useful handicap chaser: did well in 2004/5, winning at Sedgefield (fifth course success) and Market Rasen in November and Catterick and Ayr in March: fair handicap hurdler: stays 21f: acts on any going: genuine and reliable. *Mrs E. Slack* **c116 h103**

MIGHTY MAN (FR) 5 b.g. Sir Harry Lewis (USA) – Vanina II (FR) (Italic (FR)) [2004/5 F16g* 17s* 16g* 16d* Apr 8] **h138 p F112**

Mighty Man was one of the most exciting prospects to emerge in 2004/5. He was unbeaten in four starts, culminating in a Grade 2 novice hurdle victory at Aintree and, whether he stays over hurdles or is sent over fences, he looks very much one to keep on the right side in 2005/6.

There was not much sign in the market on his debut that Mighty Man was anything out of the ordinary. Starting off in a sixteen-runner bumper at Worcester in May, he was a 12/1-chance, sixth in the betting, but he crossed the line, coasting, twenty-one lengths ahead of the second Iris's Prince, and it was apparent the sky might well be the limit. The form was soon boosted by the runner-up, who won a bumper and a novice hurdle on his next two starts, though it was February before Mighty Man was seen in public again. The passage of time might well have accounted for Mighty Man's starting third favourite in a thirteen-runner novice at Hereford on his hurdling debut (the two ahead of him in the betting had both been in action the previous month) but he won every bit as impressively as he had in his bumper, requiring minimal assistance to draw seven lengths clear of the recent Folkestone winner Jacks Craic. Even after that, he still didn't start favourite on his next start, in another novice at Sandown the week before Cheltenham, though he faced an opponent in Sea Captain who had also gained an impressive win on his only start over hurdles. As they quickened two out in a steadily-run affair, Mighty Man looked to be going less well than Sea Captain, but he stuck to his task in really genuine fashion and drew away to win by a length after leading at the final flight.

John Smith's Top Novices' Hurdle, Aintree—
the highly promising Mighty Man (right) just gets the better of Dusky Warbler

Mr E. R. Hanbury's "Mighty Man"

Mighty Man and Sea Captain were both in the field for the John Smith's Top Novices' Hurdle at Aintree in April. Only seven in all lined up for the Top Novices', the smallest field in the race's thirty-year history. Dusky Warbler, who had finished third in the Supreme Novices' at Cheltenham, started favourite ahead of Mighty Man and Sea Captain with the recent handicap winner Nyrche and the beaten Supreme Novices' favourite Marcel others at single-figure odds. With the outsider Napolitain setting the pace, nothing much changed until after four out. Nyrche, Sea Captain and Marcel were soon beaten and, as Napolitain gave way three out, Mighty Man and Dusky Warbler had the race between them. Mighty Man led at the next and was always just holding the favourite, winning by half a length with twenty-three lengths back to Napolitain. Afterwards, Mighty Man's trainer Henry Daly was unsure whether hurdles or fences would be the plan in 2005/6 and felt that, whatever course was adopted, the horse first needed to mature further. Mighty Man had been very much on his toes beforehand at Aintree, though again his attitude in the race impressed. The bookmakers took the line that a further season's hurdling might be on the agenda and quoted Mighty Man at around 25/1 for the 2006 Champion Hurdle, which might have trend fetishists shaking their heads. The only previous Champion Hurdle winner on the Top Novices' roll of honour is Granville Again and the thirteen winners of the race between him and Mighty Man were not all that successful in their first campaign out of novice company. Although a few—the ill-fated trio Carobee, Joe Mac and Ilico among them—had very limited opportunities, only three won a race in their second season over hurdles, Midnight Legend successful in the Agfa Hurdle, In Contrast in the

Scottish Champion Hurdle and Limerick Boy in the Lanzarote, while, of the four that ran in the following year's Champion Hurdle, only In Contrast (sixth) finished in the first nine. Mighty Man has the potential to improve that record.

Mighty Man (FR) (b.g. 2000)	Sir Harry Lewis (USA) (b 1984)	Alleged (b 1974)	Hoist The Flag
			Princess Pout
		Sue Babe (b 1978)	Mr Prospector
			Sleek Dancer
	Vanina II (FR) (b 1987)	Italic (b 1974)	Carnaval
			Bagheira
		Pin'hup (b 1981)	Signani
			Julie

The lengthy Mighty Man has shown plenty of speed but is by no means lacking in stamina on breeding. He is the best horse so far by the Irish Derby winner Sir Harry Lewis, whose other significant winners include the useful hurdlers Diamant Noir and Champagne Harry, who both stay three miles, and the fairly useful staying chaser Harrycone Lewis. Mighty Man is the sixth known foal and second winner out of the selle francais mare Vanina II, the first being the useful hurdler Bourbon Manhattan (by Alflora), who won at two and two and a half miles. Vanina was herself a maiden but she is the sister of a notable jumper in Antonin, a very smart staying chaser who won the Racing Post Chase and the National Hunt Handicap and was second in the Whitbread. Mighty Man was due to be sold at the 2003 Doncaster May Sales but returned to his breeder, in whose colours he races. Vanina's 2002 filly by Alflora did find a buyer. She was sold at the same venue in May for 100,000 guineas, purchased on behalf of J.P. McManus. *H. D. Daly*

MIGHTY MAN (IRE) 10 b.g. Mandalus – Mossy Mistress (IRE) (Le Moss) [2004/5 c–, h–: c16m^{3} c20m^{pu} May 27] smallish, strong gelding: won maiden point in March: no other form: tried visored. *O. Brennan* **c– h–**

MIGHTY MATTERS (IRE) 6 b.g. Muroto – Hasaway (IRE) (Executive Perk) [2004/5 F18s^{2} 24d^{pu} Mar 8] €11,000 4-y-o: third foal: half-brother to winning Irish 2m hurdler Call Me Judy (by Beneficial) and bumper winner/fair hurdler up to 2½m Uncle Murt (by Commanche Run): dam unraced from family of high-class 2½m chaser Golden Freeze and smart chaser at 2½m+ Sparky Gayle: fourth in maiden Irish point on debut in 2004: favourite, second of 9 to Pontiff in bumper at Plumpton: possibly amiss on hurdling debut: not sure to stay 3m. *T. R. George* **h– p F92**

MIGHTY MINSTER 8 ch.m. Minster Son – Mighty Fly (Comedy Star (USA)) [2004/5 h–§: 22m^{*dis} 22d 22s Jan 3] lengthy, sparely-made mare: poor hurdler: off 10 months and well backed, first past post (subsequently disqualified on technical grounds) in conditional jockeys selling handicap at Uttoxeter in June, only form since 2002/3: stays 2¾m: acts on good to firm and heavy going: usually wears cheekpieces: temperamental. *A. E. Jones* **h70 §**

MIGHTY STRONG 11 b.g. Strong Gale – Muffet's Spider (Rymer) [2004/5 c128, h–: c21g^{pu} c20g^{2} c22d* Nov 28] sturdy, lengthy gelding: fairly useful handicap chaser: fifth course success and second in particular race when beating Bee An Bee by 7 lengths at Newbury in November: should stay 3m: acts on soft and good to firm going: has bled from nose: races prominently. *N. J. Henderson* **c128 h–**

MIGHTY WILLING 8 br.g. Bollin William – Wild Ling (Mufrij) [2004/5 c90: c25d^{2} c26g^{2} May 31] fair pointer/hunter chaser: stays 3¼m: acts on soft going. *Mrs M. R. Sowersby* **c90**

MIGRATION 9 b.g. Rainbow Quest (USA) – Armeria (USA) (Northern Dancer) [2004/5 17g* 19g* 19g 17d^{2} 16s^{2} 16s^{5} 16s^{3} 19d^{2} 16d 19g 19d Jan 29] tall, useful-looking gelding: fairly useful hurdler: fit from Flat, easily won seller and handicap at Market Rasen in August: better form when second 3 times after, poor efforts last 3 outings: stays 19f: acts on soft going. *Mrs S. Lamyman* **h116**

MIGWELL (FR) 5 b.g. Assessor (IRE) – Uguette IV (FR) (Chamberlin (FR)) [2004/5 h99: 20s^{2} 22v^{3} 22d* 24v^{pu} 16v^{2} 21s* 20d Apr 9] useful-looking gelding: fairly useful hurdler: won handicaps at Sandown in December and Kempton (best effort when beating Mind How You Go by 12 lengths) in February: possibly amiss final outing: should stay 3m: raced on good going or softer (acts on heavy). *Mrs L. Wadham* **h125**

MIJICO (IRE) 9 b.g. Lord Americo – Mijette (Pauper) [2004/5 c83: 20g 20m^{4} 26m c24g^{F} Jan 14] well-made gelding: very tired in third when falling last on chasing debut in 2003/4: no form since, including over hurdles. *Ferdy Murphy* **c– h–**

MIKADO MELODY (IRE) 6 b.g. Supreme Leader – Double Symphony (IRE) (Orchestra) [2004/5 F16s^5 aF16g^4 19g^pu 17d Feb 11] second foal: half-brother to bumper winner Blue Romance (by Bob Back): dam, useful hurdler/chaser, stayed 21f: modest form in bumpers: little encouragement in 2 novice hurdles, mistakes second outing. *A. King* **h– F84**

MIKASA (IRE) 5 b.g. Victory Note (USA) – Resiusa (ITY) (Niniski (USA)) [2004/5 h–: 16d^3 c21m^pu c21d^6 17v c21v^6 c24g^4 c20v^2 c25g^5 c20v^pu c25s^pu Apr 10] poor maiden hurdler/chaser: stays 21f: acts on heavy going: has carried head high. *R. F. Fisher* **c64 h79 ?**

MIKE SIMMONS 9 b.g. Ballacashtal (CAN) – Lady Crusty (Golden Dipper) [2004/5 h73: 20s* 27m^pu Jun 6] leggy gelding: modest handicap hurdler: won at Uttoxeter in May, easily best effort in long time: seems best up to 21f: acts on soft going. *L. P. Grassick* **h93**

MIKO DE BEAUCHENE (FR) 5 b.g. Nashamaa – Chipie d'Angron (FR) (Grand Tresor (FR)) [2004/5 F16d^4 F16d 16v^2 17v^2 19v^2 24s^2 21g^4 24m^pu Apr 13] strong, good sort: will make a chaser: fourth foal: half-brother to fairly useful hurdler Jeannot de Beauchene (by En Calcat), should have stayed 3m, and cross-country chase winner Iris de Beauchene (by Pure Hasard): dam maiden, out of half-sister to dam of useful French chaser Daisy d'Angron: better effort in bumpers when fourth at Wincanton: fair novice hurdler: should stay 3m: acts on heavy going, ran poorly on good to firm. *R. H. Alner* **h110 F94**

MILAN KING (IRE) 12 b.g. King's Ride – Milan Moss (Le Moss) [2004/5 c–, h69§: 17m 17m^3 Aug 6] lengthy gelding: poor hurdler: stays 21f: acts on any going: blinkered twice (pulled up both times): unreliable. *A. J. Lockwood* **c– h63 §**

MILHILLFLYER 10 b.m. Milieu – Hawkes Hill Flyer (Nicholas Bill) [2004/5 22m^pu 22s^pu Nov 7] third foal: dam, of little account, half-sister to top-class 2m hurdler Royal Derbi: showed nothing in 2 novice hurdles. *I. McMath* **h–**

MILLAGROS (IRE) 5 b.m. Pennekamp (USA) – Grey Galava (Generous (IRE)) [2004/5 16g^2 16d* 16g^4 Apr 15] fair on Flat (stays 1¼m): didn't have to repeat debut form over hurdles to win novice at Musselburgh in January: last of 4 in similar event at Ayr next time: likely to prove best at 2m with emphasis on speed. *I. Semple* **h103**

MILLA'S MAN (IRE) 13 b.g. Satco (FR) – Rullahola (Bluerullah) [2004/5 c21d^pu May 17] workmanlike gelding: maiden hurdler/chaser: modest pointer nowadays. *W. W. Dennis* **c– h–**

MILLCROFT SEASCAPE (IRE) 6 b.g. Good Thyne (USA) – Dante's Ville (IRE) (Phardante (FR)) [2004/5 F–: 22g May 7] rather unfurnished gelding: well held in bumpers and novice hurdle. *C. J. Down* **h–**

MILLE ET UNE NUITS (FR) 6 b.m. Ecologist – Migre (FR) (Le Gregol (FR)) [2004/5 F–: F16g May 13] no form in bumpers: hung markedly first 2 starts. *Miss K. Marks* **F–**

MILL EMERALD 8 b.m. Old Vic – Milinetta (Milford) [2004/5 c–, h96d: 20s^5 c20g^pu 24v^6 Mar 17] small mare: lightly raced over fences: winning hurdler: no form since early-2003/4: stays 2½m: acts on any going: tried in blinkers/cheekpieces. *R. Ford* **c– h–**

MILLENAIRE (FR) 6 b. or br.g. Mister Mat (FR) – Mille Perles (FR) (Kashtan (FR)) [2004/5 F111: 16g^3 20s^5 Dec 17] leggy gelding: useful winner but looked temperamental in bumpers in 2003/4: stayed on well and not knocked about unduly when third to ready winner Marcel in novice at Newbury on hurdling debut: badly let down by jumping next time: should stay beyond 2m. *Jonjo O'Neill* **h114 +**

MILLENIUM WAY (IRE) 11 ch.g. Ikdam – Fine Drapes (Le Bavard (FR)) [2004/5 c85, h–: c24d^2 c24d^pu May 11] medium-sized gelding: fair hunter chaser: won 4 times in ladies points between February and April: should stay beyond 3m: acts on any going: tried blinkered. *J. M. Turner* **c85 h–**

MILLENNIUM GOLD 10 ch.g. Be My Chief (USA) – Forbearance (Bairn (USA)) [2004/5 c68x, h–: c34d^pu c22m c24g^4 Jul 11] winning pointer: maiden hurdler/chaser: no form in 2004/5, left M. Frieze after first outing: stays 3¼m: acts on firm and good to soft going: tried in headgear: not a fluent jumper: sold £3,000 Ascot October Sales. *B. J. Llewellyn* **c– x h–**

MILLERBURN (IRE) 6 b.g. Ajraas (USA) – Granalice (Giolla Mear) [2004/5 F16d F16f^3 F16g^4 F16v^4 16s 22s^pu Apr 3] fifth foal: half-brother to fair hurdler/chaser Gran Turismo (by Sovereign Water), stayed 3¼m: dam unraced: poor form in bumpers: no show in 2 races over hurdles. *J. I. A. Charlton* **h– F73**

MILLER'S MONARCH 5 b.g. El Conquistador – Gables Girl (Sousa) [2004/5 F17g^{2} Sep 30] second foal: dam ran twice: green, short-head second to Jackie Boy in bumper at Hereford on debut. *J. S. King* **F86**

MILLIE'S FORTUNE 4 b.f. Classic Cliche (IRE) – Millies Misfortune (IRE) (Hamas (IRE)) [2004/5 F12g F12d^{F} F13g 16v^{pu} 17s^{pu} 19d^{pu} Mar 14] lengthy filly: first foal: dam unraced half-sister to smart 1m to 1¼m colt Lucky Lindy: mid-division on completed starts in bumpers: pulled up all 3 outings over hurdles, including in seller (blinkered, looked reluctant). *R. S. Brookhouse* **h–** **F–**

MILLIGAN (FR) 10 b.g. Exit To Nowhere (USA) – Madigan Mill (Mill Reef (USA)) [2004/5 h129: c20d^{3} c19d^{4} c16v^{F} Jan 26] close-coupled gelding: useful hurdler in 2003: off a year, fair form on completed outings over fences: stays 2½m when emphasis is on speed: acts on soft and good to firm going: usually patiently ridden: sold 4,500 gns Doncaster May Sales. *R. A. Fahey* **c108** **h–**

MILLI WIZZ 5 b.m. Wizard King – State of Love (Northern State (USA)) [2004/5 F16d F16g Dec 9] first foal: dam, no worthwhile form over jumps, half-sister to useful staying chaser Carole's Crusader: soundly beaten in mares bumpers. *W. M. Brisbourne* **F–**

MILLKOM ELEGANCE 6 b.m. Millkom – Premier Princess (Hard Fought) [2004/5 h82: 16d^{6} 17m^{pu} 17d^{6} 19d 19g^{3} 19g^{3} 17m^{2} 19d Mar 26] poor on Flat (stays 1¾m), successful in February: poor hurdler, left K. Ryan after third start: stays 19f: acts on good to firm and good to soft going: usually blinkered/visored. *G. A. Ham* **h83**

MILL LORD (IRE) 12 b.g. Aristocracy – Millflower (Millfontaine) [2004/5 c–, h–: c21m^{2} May 19] good-bodied gelding: winning pointer: maiden chaser: often blinkered. *C. J. Lawson* **c75** **h–**

MILL TOWER 8 b.g. Milieu – Tringa (GER) (Kaiseradler) [2004/5 h–: 16m 16g^{5} 16m^{pu} Jun 5] lengthy, workmanlike gelding: won maiden point in March: no other form. *R. Nixon* **h78 ?**

MILL VALE (IRE) 8 b.g. Good Thyne (USA) – Sales Centre (Deep Run) [2004/5 F16f* F16g^{3} 20m^{3} Jul 6] fifth foal: brother to fair 19f hurdle winner Klohho and half-brother to 4 winners, including Galway Plate winner Stroll Home (by Tale Quale): dam unraced half-sister to smart 2m to 2½m hurdler Potato Merchant: fairly useful form in bumpers, won at Fairyhouse in May by 2 lengths from Come On Ya Star: better effort when 7½ lengths third to The Alamo at Tipperary following month: third in maiden at Roscommon on hurdling debut: likely to do better over hurdles. *J. E. Kiely, Ireland* **h93** **F101**

MILLYHENRY 14 b.g. White Prince (USA) – Milly's Chance (Mljet) [2004/5 c–: c30d^{pu} May 11] smallish, sturdy gelding: veteran chaser: placed in points in 2004: stays 3½m: acts on heavy going: blinkered once. *A. J. Tizzard* **c–**

MILORD LESCRIBAA (FR) 5 b.g. Cadoudal (FR) – Mona Lisaa (FR) (Karkour (FR)) [2004/5 h114p: 17v^{5} 21d 22v^{5} Apr 22] angular gelding: lightly raced: fair hurdler: likely to prove best short of 21f: carries head awkwardly. *M. C. Pipe* **h114**

MILTON MOSS 6 ch.m. Le Moss – Milton Lass (Scallywag) [2004/5 F16s Apr 10] fifth foal: dam signs of a little ability in points: well held in bumper on debut. *Miss S. E. Forster* **F–**

MILTON STAR (IRE) 6 ch.g. Mukaddamah (USA) – Bajan Girl (IRE) (Pips Pride) [2004/5 16v^{3} 16d^{5} 16d^{2} 16d^{F} 16s^{4} 16v^{4} 16v Jan 9] fairly useful on Flat (stays 9f) at 3 yrs: fair maiden hurdler: raced at 2m: acts on heavy going, probably on good to firm. *G. T. Lynch, Ireland* **h105**

MINAT BOY 9 b.g. Gildoran – Childhay Millie (Idiot's Delight) [2004/5 c25s^{5} c20s^{ur} c20s c22s^{3} Mar 23] workmanlike gelding: winning pointer: poor form in chases. *Mrs Tracey Barfoot-Saunt* **c73**

MINDANAO 9 b.m. Most Welcome – Salala (Connaught) [2004/5 h120: c21g^{3} c16d* c22s^{3} c16m^{pu} 16v Dec 15] leggy mare: fairly useful handicap hurdler, well held final outing: fair form over fences: won maiden at Hexham in June: stays easy 2¾m: acts on soft and good to firm going: has been let down by jumping. *L. Lungo* **c107** **h–**

MIND HOW YOU GO (FR) 7 b.g. Hernando (FR) – Cos I Do (IRE) (Double Schwartz) [2004/5 16s^{5} 16s^{3} 21s^{2} Feb 26] sparely-made gelding: fairly useful hurdler, off 20 months prior to reappearance: good placed efforts in handicaps at Wincanton and Kempton: stays 21f: acts on soft ground. *J. R. Best* **h115**

MIND PLAY 4 b.f. Mind Games – Diplomatist (Dominion) [2004/5 17s 16d^{pu} 16v Jan 18] stocky filly: half-sister to winning 2m hurdler Mice Design (by Presidium): of little account: tongue tied after debut, also blinkered final start. *M. E. Sowersby* **h–**

MIND THE GATE 12 b.g. Ardross – Mulloch Brae (Sunyboy) [2004/5 c24v^{pu} Feb 20] rangy gelding: winning pointer: no show on chasing debut: has worn blinkers. *M. G. Rimell* **c– h–**

MINELLA SILVER (IRE) 12 gr.g. Roselier (FR) – Mrs Minella (Deep Run) [2004/5 c24s^{2} c22g^{3} Apr 1] workmanlike gelding: fairly useful pointer/hunter chaser: placed at Towcester (tying up run-in) in March and Newbury (third to Red Brook Lad) 3 weeks later: stays 3m: acts on heavy going: front runner. *G. L. Landau* **c106 h–**

MINERS DANCE (IRE) 12 b.g. Miner's Lamp – Prudent Birdie (Lucifer (USA)) [2004/5 c99, h–: c28d^{2} c32d^{4} c29s Jan 2] angular gelding: modest handicap chaser: suited by thorough test of stamina: acts on heavy going: tried blinkered: broke blood vessel final start last 2 seasons: hard ride (ridden by claimer C. Studd nowadays). *B. G. Powell* **c97 h–**

MINE'S A MURPHYS 9 b.g. Broadsword (USA) – Sparkling Time (USA) (Olden Times) [2004/5 22s^{F} 21g Nov 11] rangy gelding: won bumper on debut in 2001/2 for Miss V. Williams: off nearly 3 years, pulled hard and close up when falling sixth in amateur novice at Exeter on hurdling debut: tailed off next time. *N. E. Berry* **h–**

MINIBALLIST (IRE) 7 b.m. Tragic Role (USA) – Herballistic (Rolfe (USA)) [2004/5 17d 22g* 22d^{5} 19d^{5} 21d 20s^{2} 19s 21d Feb 11] small mare: modest hurdler: won mares novice at Newton Abbot in July: best effort on sixth outing: stays 2¾m: acts on soft ground. *R. T. Phillips* **h98**

MINIBULE (FR) 5 ch.m. Funambule (USA) – Mipour (FR) (Shakapour) [2004/5 17g^{2} 17g^{2} 16g^{4} 19g* 20g^{2} Aug 18] half-sister to 2 winners, including winning hurdler around 2m Hyperion du Moulin II (by Kedellic): dam successful twice up to 1½m on Flat: successful 3 times up to 13f on Flat, including in claimer (claimed from Mme C. Barande Barbe €18,500) in May: modest hurdler: won selling handicap at Newton Abbot in August: claimed to join N. Wilson £6,000 8 days later: stays 2½m: raced only on good going over hurdles: visored: tongue tied last 3 starts. *M. C. Pipe* **h91**

MINI DARE 8 b.g. Derrylin – Minim (Rymer) [2004/5 c91, h87: c23s^{6} 24d* 25v^{4} 24s^{5} 19s^{2} 21s^{2} 24s^{F} Apr 16] good-topped gelding: fair hurdler: won novice handicap at Doncaster in November: modest form over fences, let down by jumping on reappearance: stays 3¼m: acts on heavy going: has run well in blinkers, below form in cheekpieces. *O. Sherwood* **c– h101**

MINI SADDLER (IRE) 6 b.m. Oscar (IRE) – Winnie Wumpkins (IRE) (Roselier (FR)) [2004/5 F16m^{3} F17g 22m^{5} 18m^{2} Sep 21] fifth foal: half-sister to Irish bumper winner Millview Rose (by Glacial Storm) and winning pointer by Wakashan: dam, lightly-raced maiden, from family of useful staying hurdler Willie Wumpkins: modest form in bumpers: better effort over hurdles when second to heavily-eased Marcel in novice at Fontwell: should stay well beyond 2¼m. *G. L. Moore* **h79 F78**

MINI SENSATION (IRE) 12 b.g. Be My Native (USA) – Minorettes Girl (Strong Gale) [2004/5 c–, h–: c24d^{F} c26s c26d^{6} c32d* Dec 3] medium-sized gelding: smart handicap chaser in 2002/3: first form since when winning at Exeter under excellent ride from A. McCoy, soon off bridle in rear: thorough stayer: best form on soft/heavy going: held up: often none too fluent. *Jonjo O'Neill* **c115 h–**

MINIVET 10 b.g. Midyan (USA) – Bronzewing (Beldale Flutter (USA)) [2004/5 c–, h94: 22m^{6} 22d 21g^{3} 20g^{4} 20g^{2} 22g* 20m^{2} 19g^{3} Sep 25] close-coupled gelding: fair hurdler: left T. Easterby, won claimer at Stratford in August: also successful on Flat following month: stays easy 2¾m: acts on soft and good to firm going, possibly not on heavy. *R. Allan* **c– h108**

MINKA 6 b.m. Karinga Bay – Quick Million (Thowra (FR)) [2004/5 F17s Oct 19] rather unfurnished mare: first foal: dam poor maiden on Flat and over jumps: well beaten in bumper on debut (threw rider in paddock). *K. Bishop* **F–**

MINNIE SECRET 6 b.m. Primitive Rising (USA) – Mobile Miss (IRE) (Classic Secret (USA)) [2004/5 h–: 17g^{ur} 20g^{3} 17g Sep 25] rather unfurnished mare: little form over hurdles. *B. N. Pollock* **h–**

MINNIE THE MOOCHER 5 b.m. Karinga Bay – Slippery Fin (Slip Anchor) [2004/5 F16d F17s 19d 22d^{5} 22v^{5} Apr 22] first foal: dam, placed on Flat (up to 1½m) and over hurdles, half-sister to useful French hurdler up to 19f Trait Union: well beaten in bumpers and novice hurdles. *J. W. Mullins* **h– F–**

MINNIGAFF (IRE) 5 b.g. Supreme Leader – Across The Pond (IRE) (Over The River (FR)) [2004/5 F16v[5] 16s Mar 11] €4,500 3-y-o: second foal: dam unraced sister to fairly useful Irish chaser up to 3m Dark Magic and half-sister to smart hurdler/useful chaser Padre Mio, stayed 3m: well held in bumper and maiden hurdle. *N. G. Richards* **h– F–**

MINORA BLUE 7 b.m. Bob Back (USA) – Minora (IRE) (Cataldi) [2004/5 h–, F83: 19m[6] May 23] little show over hurdles. *Ms Bridget Nicholls* **h–**

MINOUCHKA (FR) 5 br.m. Bulington (FR) – Elbury (FR) (Royal Charter (FR)) [2004/5 F16d[3] F16s[4] c20d[3] c21v[3] c16d[2] c17vpu Mar 5] leggy mare: first foal: dam, placed up to 1½m on Flat in France, ran twice over jumps: in frame both starts in bumpers: seemingly easily best effort over fences when second to Locksmith in novice at Doncaster, keeping on off strong pace and probably flattered: probably stays 2½m. *S. H. Shirley-Beavan* **c85 F85**

MINSTER ABBI 5 b.m. Minster Son – Elitist (Keren) [2004/5 F73: F16g 20spu 22spu Apr 3] sturdy mare: poor form in bumpers: no show in 2 novice hurdles. *W. Storey* **h– F–**

MINSTER BLUE 7 b.m. Minster Son – Elitist (Keren) [2004/5 h–: 24spu c20dpu Nov 29] good-bodied mare: no solid form. *F. P. Murtagh* **c– h–**

MINSTER BRIG 6 b.g. Minster Son – Royal Brig (Royal Fountain) [2004/5 F16m 20dpu 22spu 20m 24spu c25dpu Apr 11] second foal: dam unraced: no sign of ability. *F. P. Murtagh* **c– h– F–**

MINSTER FAIR 7 b.m. Minster Son – Fair Echo (Quality Fair) [2004/5 h83: 24s* 22s 22dpu 24s[2] Apr 20] leggy, angular mare: modest hurdler: off 15 months, won conditional jockeys handicap at Ayr in March: better at 3m than shorter: raced on good going or softer (acts on heavy): whipped round start third outing. *A. C. Whillans* **h90**

MINSTER GLORY 14 b.g. Minster Son – Rapid Glory (Hittite Glory) [2004/5 c116, h103: c16dpu c16m[2] c17g[5] c17g[5] Oct 9] tall gelding: fairly useful handicap chaser/fair handicap hurdler, won 5 times in first half of 2003/4: well below form since: stays 19f: acts on soft and firm going: blinkered: races prominently. *M. W. Easterby* **c88 h–**

MINSTER MISSILE 7 b.g. Minster Son – Manettia (IRE) (Mandalus) [2004/5 F90: F16d[6] 23dpu 19d 19d[6] Feb 4] lengthy, useful-looking gelding: won slowly-run bumper on debut in early-2003/4: little impact in novice hurdles, though not knocked about final outing (finished distressed): bred to stay well. *K. G. Reveley* **h– p F80**

MINSTER SHADOW 6 b.g. Minster Son – Polar Belle (Arctic Lord) [2004/5 F94: 20s[3] 24v* 23d[2] 27v* 24v[2] 24dpu 24s[3] Mar 19] tall, rather unfurnished gelding: fair hurdler: won novices at Carlisle in November and Sedgefield in December: thorough stayer: raced only on ground softer than good (acts well on heavy). *C. Grant* **h108**

MINSTER SKY 5 ch.m. Minster Son – Nicola's Princess (Handsome Sailor) [2004/5 F16g[6] F16d 16gpu Dec 10] first foal: dam, 2m selling hurdle winner, also won at 1m on Flat: showed nothing in bumpers and selling hurdle: sold 800 gns Doncaster January Sales. *A. L. Forbes* **h– F–**

MINSTER YORK 11 ch.g. Minster Son – Another Treat (Derring-Do) [2004/5 c106§, h–: c21dpu c24d[2] Mar 28] smallish, angular gelding: fair handicap chaser at best: modest pointer nowadays: stays easy 21f: probably acts on any going: usually wore cheekpieces in 2003/4: tried tongue tied: ungenuine. *J. M. Turner* **c– § h–**

MINSTREL HALL 6 b.m. Saddlers' Hall (IRE) – Mindomica (Dominion) [2004/5 h83: 17mpu Aug 6] tall mare: modest hurdler: appeared likely to win selling handicap at Sedgefield in August when going lame before 2 out: raced around 2m: acts on soft and good to firm going: often tongue tied. *P. Monteith* **h87**

MINSTREL'S DOUBLE 4 ch.g. Jumbo Hirt (USA) – Hand On Heart (IRE) (Taufan (USA)) [2004/5 16m 16g 16v[5] 16s Mar 11] half-brother to modest hurdler Northern Minster (by Minster Son), stays 2½m: no form on Flat or over hurdles. *F. P. Murtagh* **h65**

MINTED (IRE) 8 br.g. Good Thyne (USA) – Sweet Roselier (IRE) (Roselier (FR)) [2004/5 16g[5] 16f[3] 24g[5] Jun 3] first foal: brother to bumper winner Moonzie Laird: dam unraced, out of half-sister to useful staying jumpers Bective Road and Sommelier: modest form on first of 3 outings over hurdles: second in maiden point in January. *B. De Haan* **h88**

MIOCHE D'ESTRUVAL (FR) 5 bl.g. Lute Antique (FR) – Charme d'Estruval (FR) (Mistigri) [2004/5 h102: 16g[5] 22d* 24d[6] 24g[2] 24d[6] 24g[6] Apr 14] angular gelding: fairly useful handicap hurdler: won at Newton Abbot in November: improved again when **h122**

second of 22 to Oulart in Pertemps Final at Cheltenham: stays 3m: acts on soft going: tried visored, including final outing (hung left). *M. C. Pipe*

MIORBHAIL 14 br.g. Wonderful Surprise – Florrie Palmer (Deadly Nightshade) [2004/5 c20g May 29] poor pointer. *Miss C. L. Dennis* **c–**

MIRJAN (IRE) 9 b.g. Tenby – Mirana (IRE) (Ela-Mana-Mou) [2004/5 h128§: 20d* 23m4 22g May 20] angular gelding: useful handicap hurdler: won at Wetherby very early in season by 9 lengths from Moonlit Harbour: stays 23f, at least when emphasis is on speed: acts on good to firm and heavy going: seems best in headgear nowadays: unreliable: lightly raced on Flat, won 2004 Northumberland Plate, good seventh in Cesarewitch. *L. Lungo* **h134 §**

MIRPOUR (IRE) 6 b.g. Turtle Island (IRE) – Mirana (IRE) (Ela-Mana-Mou) [2004/5 h113: 16g3 c16vF c19v* c20s* 20d3 Apr 9] good-topped gelding: fairly useful handicap hurdler: good third in Galway Hurdle in July and quite valuable event at Aintree in April, first run for 6 months when beaten 9½ lengths by Genghis in 20-runner event at latter, finding less than seemed likely: successful both completed starts over fences, in maiden (not keen) at Listowel and Grade 3 novice at Tipperary (by 4 lengths from Kickham): effective at 2m to 2¾m: acts on good to firm and heavy going: tried in cheekpieces, usually blinkered. *E. Griffin, Ireland* **c125 h119**

MISBEHAVIOUR 6 b.g. Tragic Role (USA) – Exotic Forest (Dominion) [2004/5 h75: 16d5 16g5 16s3 16s5 17s 16d 17g2 16s2 16v* 16s5 16s* 16g Mar 27] sparely-made gelding: modest handicap hurdler: left P. Butler after sixth start: mostly good efforts after, winning at Plumpton in January and Warwick (conditional jockeys) in March: best around 2m: acts on heavy going: usually wore visor/cheekpieces prior to last 5 starts. *T. P. McGovern* **h88**

MI SOMBRERO 6 ch.m. Factual (USA) – Rose Elegance (Bairn (USA)) [2004/5 h–: 16mpu Jun 6] pulled up both starts over hurdles. *Mrs B. E. Matthews* **h–**

MISS ACADEMY (FR) 4 ch.f. Video Rock (FR) – Mademoiselle Wo (FR) (Prince Wo (FR)) [2004/5 16s* 17s4 16vF 16g4 16s4 16d* 16d3 Apr 20] leggy ex-French filly: third foal: half-sister to 2 winners, including 2m hurdler La Pommeraie (by Apple Tree): dam winning hurdler around 2m: successful on 5 of 6 starts up to 13f on Flat at 3 yrs for J. Bertran de Balanda: useful juvenile hurdler: easily landed odds in mares maiden at Newcastle in January and juvenile at Plumpton in April: best effort when 11¼ lengths fourth of 24 under top weight to Dabiroun in valuable juvenile handicap at Cheltenham fourth start: raced around 2m on good ground or softer. *M. C. Pipe* **h128**

MISS ARAGONT 6 b.m. Aragon – Uninvited (Be My Guest (USA)) [2004/5 h–: 17mF 16mpu Oct 1] no sign of ability: tried tongue tied. *S. G. Chadwick* **h–**

MISSATTITUDE 4 gr.f. Silver Patriarch (IRE) – Phil's Folly (Glasgow Central) [2004/5 F18s 19g 16gpu Apr 19] first known foal: dam poor maiden on Flat: no show in bumper or novice hurdles. *Miss G. Browne* **h– F–**

MISS CHINCHILLA 9 b.m. Perpendicular – Furry Baby (Furry Glen) [2004/5 h97+: 16g* 20m3 Jun 5] compact mare: successful on 3 of 6 starts over hurdles, including in mares handicap at Warwick in May: finished lame when running another good race next time: effective at 2m to 21f: yet to race on extremes of going. *Miss Venetia Williams* **h114**

MISS COLMESNIL (FR) 5 b.m. Dear Doctor (FR) – Princesse Dolly (FR) (The Wonder (FR)) [2004/5 h98: 18dpu May 3] ex-French mare: modest form in juvenile hurdles for E. Leenders: pulled up both starts in Britain. *A. E. Jessop* **h–**

MISS COSPECTOR 6 ch.m. Emperor Fountain – Gypsy Race (IRE) (Good Thyne (USA)) [2004/5 h–, F82: 24g2 20m4 22d* 24v 20s6 20s2 20v4 20v5 20s4 20g6 22gpu Apr 3] leggy, lengthy mare: modest novice hurdler: won at Uttoxeter in October: stays 3m: acts on heavy going. *T. H. Caldwell* **h98**

MISS DANBYS 10 b.m. Charmer – Dohty Baby (Hittite Glory) [2004/5 16gro 16gpu May 8] maiden pointer: no form over hurdles, temperamental to boot. *J. M. Jefferson* **h– §**

MISS DOUBLET 4 ch.f. Double Trigger (IRE) – Bournel (Sunley Builds) [2004/5 F14d F13d6 20s 16s6 24d6 Mar 8] sturdy filly: second foal: half-sister to bumper winner Cruising Clyde (by Karinga Bay): dam 2¾m hurdle winner who stayed 3¼m: mid-division in 3-y-o bumpers: well beaten in novice hurdles. *J. W. Mullins* **h– F79**

MISSED A NOTE 5 br.g. Missed Flight – Out of Harmony (Song) [2004/5 17mpu 19g Dec 9] poor form at 2 yrs for W. Turner: no show either outing over hurdles. *C. J. Gray* **h–**

MISSED THAT 6 b.g. Overbury (IRE) – Not Enough (Balinger) [2004/5 F18m F16s* F16v* F16g* Mar 16] **F123**

After winning the race four times in five years at the end of the twentieth century, Willie Mullins finally got off the mark in the Champion Bumper in the twenty-first when Missed That got the better of twenty-three rivals in the Weatherbys-sponsored event at Cheltenham in March. Mullins' well-touted Alexander Milenium had pulled up amiss when his sole representative in 2002, while the next two renewals had seen teams of four and five manage a best of eighth and sixth placings respectively. The scattergun technique had worked before, with Joe Cullen in 2000, but it is perhaps significant that Missed That was Mullins' only runner in 2005. Wither Or Which, Florida Pearl and Alexander Banquet were also the stable's sole representative in their winning years. Missed That is not so imposing a type as either Florida Pearl or Alexander Banquet, but his pedigree and background suggest he has a good future over jumps and it would not be a surprise if he followed in the footsteps of his owner's Florida Pearl and was sent straight over fences.

In contrast to the four previous Champion Bumper winners from the stable, who had all run just once in a bumper (Florida Pearl had also won a maiden point), Missed That went to Cheltenham with plenty of experience, relatively speaking. He had made his debut in a maiden point in February 2004, in which he narrowly got the better of Travino, then, having moved to Mullins from the yard of Pat Doyle, contested a useful bumper at Punchestown in May. Gambled on that day (he started 5/2 favourite in a field of twenty-six), he lost his chance at the start but the money, as they say, was only lent. At Clonmel in December, when he started odds on, and at Naas in February he had little trouble justifying his favourite's status. The Naas race had not looked particularly strong at the time, but it worked out better than expected and, by the time Missed That lined up at Cheltenham, he clearly held a leading chance on form. That was more than could be said for the rest of the raiding party, the seven others in the usually strong Irish team looking well short of the standard required. Missed That apart, the pick of the season's Irish-trained bumper horses, Travino, Firth of Forth and Dawadari, were all absent. Two of the best British-trained bumper performers, the sidelined Oscar Park and Be Be King, whose connections wanted softer ground for him, were also missing, but the home team looked the stronger with Karanja, unbeaten in three starts including a Grade 2 impressively at Newbury last time out, and The Mick Weston, who had shown smart form in winning two of his four races, as well as, unusually, the previous year's Champion Bumper runner-up Refinement. Of the eight runners that started at shorter than 20/1, Missed That started favourite at 7/2 but the seven others were trained in Britain.

Weatherbys Champion Bumper (Standard Open National Hunt Flat), Cheltenham—Missed That finds extra to deny De Soto (striped cap) and Rasharrow

If the British challenge for the Champion Bumper looked strong before the start, it was not long before there was a major breach in the defence: Karanja shied at the tapes and unseated Nina Carberry. There was a further setback when The Mick Weston, still in rear but travelling well, lost his rider in scrimmaging at the top of the hill. At this stage Missed That was beginning his move from mid-field, having taken a good hold in what was a truly-run race. He continued to progress and was in front early in the straight. Responding well to pressure, he found extra when tackled by De Soto late on, winning by a neck with Rasharrow three quarters of a length away third. Connections of Karanja, in particular, are entitled to wonder what might have been, as he had beaten De Soto decisively at Newbury.

Neither De Soto nor Karanja ran subsequently, and, by the time Missed That lined up for the Grade 1 bumper at Punchestown, the Cheltenham form had taken a few knocks: the fourth Refinement and seventh Itsmyboy had run below expectations at Aintree while the eighth Mister Top Notch had been well held on heavy ground in a rare bumper at the Curragh and a couple of the also-rans had been well beaten too. The only other to have run, Rasharrow, did not have to match his Cheltenham form to win easily at Ayr. Four of the Cheltenham field lined up at Punchestown, all starting at 10/1 or shorter, with Missed That favourite at 5/4. Missed That ran as if past his best for the season and was well held in fourth behind the rejuvenated Refinement. In contrast to his record at Cheltenham, Willie Mullins has saddled the winner of the Champion INH Flat at Punchestown just once, in 1995.

<table>
<tr><td rowspan="8">Missed That
(b.g. 1999)</td><td rowspan="4">Overbury (IRE)
(br 1991)</td><td rowspan="2">Caerleon
(b 1980)</td><td>Nijinsky</td></tr>
<tr><td>Foreseer</td></tr>
<tr><td rowspan="2">Overcall
(b 1984)</td><td>Bustino</td></tr>
<tr><td>Melodramatic</td></tr>
<tr><td rowspan="4">Not Enough
(ch 1982)</td><td rowspan="2">Balinger
(b 1976)</td><td>Welsh Pageant</td></tr>
<tr><td>Ripeck</td></tr>
<tr><td rowspan="2">Highly Paid
(ch 1970)</td><td>Compensation</td></tr>
<tr><td>Glitter Girl</td></tr>
</table>

Mrs Violet O'Leary's "Missed That"

Missed That was the first British-bred winner of the Champion Bumper, though his sire Overbury now stands in Ireland. Missed That's dam has done well after an unpromising start at stud (her first three foals failed to win), producing three other winners. The Parsons Dingle (by Le Moss) was a fair two-mile chaser at one time, while another winning chaser Cash N Credit (by Homo Sapien) stays twenty-five furlongs. The pick of the trio, however, is Sandy Duff (by Scottish Reel), who was a useful two-mile chaser, though also a bumper winner, fair hurdler and later a prolific winning pointer. Not Enough herself was a novice selling hurdler and a half-sister to three minor winners, out of the once-raced Highly Paid. It is necessary to go back to the third dam Glitter Girl for some more notable names. She herself was a useful two-year-old five-furlong winner and the dam of two useful jumpers, the hurdler Hill Top, who stayed two and a half miles and later won over fences, and the durable two-mile chaser Casbah, who won the Game Spirit (then a handicap) and the Grand Annual at the age of twelve. Although his oldest runners are only seven, Overbury has had several winners over hurdles at two and a half to three miles, and may well prove a reasonably strong influence for stamina. Missed That can be expected to stay two and a half miles. The sturdy Missed That was bought for 15,500 guineas at the Doncaster May Sales in 2002 and presumably cost rather more when changing hands after his point win. Time, however, may well show that he was worth the money. *W. P. Mullins, Ireland*

MISS EGYPT (IRE) 9 br.m. Alphabatim (USA) – Enchanted Queen (Tender King) [2004/5 h74: 18m^{2} 16f^{6} 20g 20g* 20m 24m 18g Sep 17] poor handicap hurdler: won at Sligo in July: stays 2½m: acts on good to firm and good to soft ground: tried blinkered, usually wears cheekpieces nowadays: sold 600 gns Doncaster November Sales. *Lindsay Woods, Ireland* **h74**

MISS ELLIE 9 b.m. Elmaamul (USA) – Jussoli (Don) [2004/5 c–, h–: 17m^{pu} 16s^{2} 24d Sep 22] workmanlike mare: twice-raced chaser: poor hurdler: form since 2001/2 only when second in seller at Perth: tried in cheekpieces. *Mrs C. J. Kerr* **c– h79**

MISS ELOISE 4 b.f. Efisio – Zaima (IRE) (Green Desert (USA)) [2004/5 16s^{6} 17v^{pu} 16d Dec 6] smallish filly: fair on Flat (stays 11f): poor form in juvenile hurdles: sold to join C. Creighton in Spain 2,000 gns Doncaster January Sales, won at Dos Hermanas following month. *T. D. Easterby* **h79**

MISS FAHRENHEIT (IRE) 6 b.m. Oscar (IRE) – Gunner B Sharp (Gunner B) [2004/5 F86: 19s^{5} 17d 20s* 20v* 20v^{3} 24d^{pu} 20s^{6} Mar 23] lengthy, angular mare: fair novice hurdler: easily best efforts when winning at Chepstow in November and December: dislocated pelvis sixth outing: should stay beyond 2½m: raced on good going or softer (acts on heavy). *C. Roberts* **h111**

MISS FIDDLESTICKS (IRE) 5 b.m. First Trump – Tweedling (USA) (Sir Ivor (USA)) [2004/5 F16d Nov 28] leggy mare: half-sister to numerous winners, including modest 2m hurdlers Portscatho (by Common Grounds) and Saffron Rose (by Polar Falcon): dam won around 1m in USA: tailed off in bumper on debut: well held in 2 races on Flat in 2005: sold £600 Ascot April Sales. *J. J. Bridger* **F–**

MISS HOLLY 6 b.m. Makbul – Seraphim (FR) (Lashkari) [2004/5 17d* 20m^{2} 17m^{3} 17m* Jul 26] half-sister to winning hurdler/modest staying chaser April Spirit (by Nomination): fairly useful on Flat (should stay 1¾m) for M. Johnston, won last start in January 2003: modest form over hurdles, winning maiden at Market Rasen in May and mares novice at Sedgefield in July: will prove suited by further than 17f. *Mrs S. J. Smith* **h96**

MISSILE (FR) 5 b.g. Gunboat Diplomacy (FR) – Elysea (FR) (Bad Conduct (USA)) [2004/5 17g May 11] ex-French gelding: second foal: half-brother to bumper winner Nay (by Ragmar): dam, winning hurdler/chaser up to 19f, half-sister to useful chaser around 2½m Jasmin d'Oudaries: runner-up over 12.5f in Provinces on debut in November 2003: sold out of T. Civel's stable €35,000 Goffs Sale later in month: no show in novice on hurdling debut. *N. J. Pomfret* **h–**

MISS JESSICA (IRE) 5 b. or br.m. Woodborough (USA) – Sarah Blue (IRE) (Bob Back (USA)) [2004/5 h–, F–: 19d 19s 21d^{6} 21d^{3} 26s^{pu} 22g 24d^{pu} Apr 20] leggy mare: form only when third in minor hurdle at Sedgefield. *Miss M. E. Rowland* **h75**

MISS KILKEEL (IRE) 7 b.m. Religiously (USA) – Shakiyka (IRE) (Shardari) [2004/5 F16f^{6} 18g^{2} 18g^{bd} 18s 20m^{6} 22v 20v 20v^{5} 16s^{4} 20d Mar 17] first foal: dam un- **h82 F–**

raced, out of half-sister to very smart chaser up to 25f Morceli: poor form in bumper and over hurdles: should stay beyond 2½m. *Roy Wilson, Ireland*

MISS LEHMAN 7 ch.m. Beveled (USA) – Lehmans Lot (Oats) [2004/5 F–: 16g^{6} 17g 20d^{pu} 16d^{4} Feb 9] poor hurdler: left K. Reveley, first form when fourth in seller at Ludlow. *J. D. Frost* **h70**

MISS LEWIS 7 b.m. Sir Harry Lewis (USA) – Teelyna (Teenoso (USA)) [2004/5 h–, F–: 22g* 26m^{3} 22s^{pu} 20g c19d^{6} Mar 8] poor hurdler: won novice at Newton Abbot in May: off 8 months, tailed off in novice on chasing debut: stays 2¾m: tongue tied over hurdles. *C. J. Down* **c– h83**

MISS MAILMIT 8 b.m. Rakaposhi King – Flora Louisa (Rymer) [2004/5 h87, F–: 19d^{2} 21s^{ro} 19s^{F} c20d^{3} c20d^{3} c24s^{3} c24v* c25g^{ur} c24v^{4} Apr 17] leggy mare: modest maiden hurdler: similar form over fences: made all in 2-finisher handicap at Chepstow in March: stays 3m: acts on heavy going: makes mistakes. *J. A. B. Old* **c96 x h89 x**

MISS MATTIE ROSS 9 b.m. Milieu – Mother Machree (Bing II) [2004/5 c99, h–: c25m^{2} c24v^{2} c25v^{pu} Feb 13] medium-sized mare: no form over hurdles: modest chaser: stays 25f: acts on heavy and good to firm going: sometimes let down by jumping. *S. J. Marshall* **c97 h–**

MISS MERENDA 4 b.f. Sir Harry Lewis (USA) – Cool Merenda (IRE) (Glacial Storm (USA)) [2004/5 17s^{2} 16g^{4} 18s 22d^{2} Mar 24] modest maiden on Flat (stays 9.5f): similar standard over hurdles: stays 2¾m: acts on soft going: temperamental. *D. E. Cantillon* **h85 §**

MISS MIA 5 b.m. Merit (IRE) – Alisa Bower (Old Lucky) [2004/5 F–: F17g 19v^{pu} 17d 16s Dec 5] leggy mare: no sign of ability: wore cheekpieces final start. *N. Waggott* **h– F–**

MISS MIDNIGHT 4 b.f. Midnight Legend – Miss Marigold (Norwick (USA)) [2004/5 F17g^{2} Apr 7] third foal: half-sister to fairly useful but temperamental hurdler/maiden chaser Goldbrook (by Alderbrook), stays 2½m: dam, fair but temperamental hurdler/chaser who stayed 3m, half-sister to smart hunter What A Hand: 4 lengths second to Sunley Shines in bumper at Taunton on debut, staying on strongly: will be suited by greater test of stamina. *R. J. Hodges* **F88**

MISS MONARIA (GER) 5 br.m. Alkalde (GER) – Monaria (GER) (Athenagoras (GER)) [2004/5 17d^{6} 17g c16d^{ur} Nov 1] leggy mare: maiden on Flat: last both starts over hurdles: towards rear when unseating seventh in novice at Warwick on chasing debut. *C. Von Der Recke, Germany* **c– h–**

MISS MUSCAT 5 b.m. Environment Friend – Fisima (Efisio) [2004/5 17d 19s 20v Feb 5] fifth foal: dam unraced half-sister to smart chaser up to 3m Voice of Progress: behind in novice hurdles. *Evan Williams* **h–**

MISS OCEAN MONARCH 5 ch.m. Blue Ocean (USA) – Faraway Grey (Absalom) [2004/5 17d Mar 26] lengthy mare: poor and unreliable on Flat (stays 1¼m), left D. Chapman after final start in 2004: well beaten in novice on hurdling debut. *N. Waggott* **h–**

MISSOUDUN (FR) 5 b.g. Esteem Ball (FR) – Lisiana (FR) (Iris Noir (FR)) [2004/5 F16d 20v^{pu} c21v^{5} c25d^{5} c24s^{6} Apr 20] leggy gelding: second foal: dam won 1¾m hurdle in France: little sign of ability. *Ferdy Murphy* **c64 h– F–**

MISS PROSS 5 b.m. Bob's Return (IRE) – Lucy Manette (Final Straw) [2004/5 F16s F16d 16g 16v^{5} 16v^{2} 16g^{2} 19s^{pu} Feb 6] 3,400 4-y-o: lengthy mare: sixth foal: half-sister to 1995 2-y-o 6f winner Zalzie (by Zilzal): dam should have stayed beyond 6f: well beaten in bumpers: modest novice hurdler: best form at 2m: acts on heavy going. *T. D. Walford* **h92 F–**

MISS QUICKLY (IRE) 6 b.m. Anshan – Shari Owen (IRE) (Shardari) [2004/5 h–, F83: 21g 19d^{6} 21d^{pu} 22s^{pu} Jan 3] rather leggy mare: no form over hurdles, left Miss H. Knight after first outing: should stay at least 2½m. *Miss Venetia Williams* **h–**

MISS QUOTE 10 b.m. Cotation – Danax (Jalmood (USA)) [2004/5 17g 16d^{4} Nov 1] third foal: dam well beaten in 2 races on Flat at 3 yrs: last over hurdles on both starts. *J. F. Panvert* **h–**

MISS RIDEAMIGHT 6 b.m. Overbury (IRE) – Nicolynn (Primitive Rising (USA)) [2004/5 F75: 16g 16s 16s^{6} 22s* 22s^{F} 16v^{3} 22v^{5} Feb 15] smallish, lengthy mare: poor hurdler: won selling handicap at Market Rasen in November: stays 2¾m: acts on heavy going. *G. Brown* **h70**

MISS ROYELLO 8 b.m. Royal Fountain – Lady Manello (Mandrake Major) [2004/5 c80: c20v^{3} c27d* c25v* c27v* Dec 31] improved chaser: won 3 times in December, **c98**

maiden at Sedgefield and handicaps at Hexham (novice) and Sedgefield: stays 27f: raced on good going or softer (acts on heavy): usually races prominently. *Mrs A. Hamilton*

MISS SHAKIRA (IRE) 7 b.m. Executive Perk – River Water (Over The River (FR)) [2004/5 19d³ 20m² 24s⁴ Apr 20] second foal: dam winning pointer: wide-margin winner of 2 Irish points: modest form when placed first 2 starts over hurdles: should stay beyond 2½m. *N. A. Twiston-Davies* **h84**

MISS SIRIUS 5 ch.m. Royal Vulcan – Star Shell (Queen's Hussar) [2004/5 F16g Jan 14] compact mare: sister to 4 winners, including very smart chaser up to 3m Royal Mountbrowne and fairly useful 2¾m hurdle winner Senor Sedona, and half-sister to 2 others: dam never ran: pulled hard when well held in bumper on debut. *John R. Upson* **F–**

MISS SKIPPY 6 b.m. Saddlers' Hall (IRE) – Katie Scarlett (Lochnager) [2004/5 F82: F16d⁵ 16g² 16m* 16g² 20g 16m Sep 24] angular mare: modest form in bumpers: second start over hurdles, won novice claimer (claimed from P. D. Evans £6,000) at Worcester in June: best effort next time: tongue tied final outing. *Ms Bridget Nicholls* **h92 F82**

MISS ST ALBANS 4 b.f. Robellino (USA) – Alieria (IRE) (Lomond (USA)) [2004/5 16fᵘʳ Sep 26] well held on Flat: unseated fifth on hurdling debut. *M. Wigham* **h–**

MISS TIDDLYPUSH 4 gr.f. Defacto (USA) – Misty Rocket (Roan Rocket) [2004/5 F17g Apr 3] half-sister to poor staying chaser Supposin (by Enchantment) and 17f hurdle winner Knight of Silver (by Presidium): dam 2½m hurdle winner/1¼m/1½m seller winner on Flat: last in mares bumper on debut. *L. R. James* **F–**

MISS TOULON (IRE) 7 b.m. Toulon – Miss Top (IRE) (Tremblant) [2004/5 F101: F16s⁶ F16s⁶ F16s F16v⁴ F16v² F16v² 16s³ 16g⁴ 16s* Apr 13] bumper winner: useful form when runner-up to Missed That at Naas and Travino at Navan in February: fair form over hurdles: won maiden at Fairyhouse in April: third in minor event at Punchestown later in month: stays 2½m: raced on good going or softer. *Thomas Mullins, Ireland* **h102 F106**

MISS TROOPER 5 b.m. Infantry – Mountain Glen (Lochnager) [2004/5 F77: F16g F18s 16d Feb 9] poor form in bumpers and maiden hurdle. *F. Jordan* **h– F–**

MISSUSLARGE 7 b.m. Contract Law (USA) – Scorpotina (Scorpio (FR)) [2004/5 20mᵖᵘ Jun 27] first foal: dam poor maiden hurdler/pointer: failed to complete in 3 maiden points and maiden hurdle. *T. R. Kinsey* **h–**

MISS WIZADORA 10 ch.m. Gildoran – Lizzie The Twig (Precipice Wood) [2004/5 c75, h–: c20s* c22s² Mar 30] poor handicap chaser: off 11 months, made all at Fontwell in March: should stay 3m: raced on good going or softer (acts on soft): has been let down by jumping. *Simon Earle* **c84 h–**

MISS WOODPECKER 8 b.m. Morpeth – Pigeon Loft (IRE) (Bellypha) [2004/5 19sᵖᵘ 17s 17gᵖᵘ Apr 10] no form in bumper or over hurdles. *J. D. Frost* **h–**

MISSYOUMARY 5 b.m. Petrizzo – Muskerry Miss (IRE) (Bishop of Orange) [2004/5 F17d⁶ F16s Nov 24] third foal: dam winning Irish pointer: well beaten in 2 bumpers. *H. J. Manners* **F–**

MISTANOORA 6 b.g. Topanoora – Mistinguett (IRE) (Doyoun) [2004/5 h140: 20s* 25d² Nov 13] small, leggy gelding: smart handicap hurdler: won totesport Silver Trophy at Chepstow in October by 1½ lengths from Big Moment: again ridden prominently when good second to The Dark Lord in listed event at Cheltenham: stays 25f well: acts on any going: blinkered. *N. A. Twiston-Davies* **h152**

MISTER ARJAY (USA) 5 b.g. Mister Baileys – Crystal Stepper (USA) (Fred Astaire (USA)) [2004/5 h108: 16g³ 17s⁴ 16d 20d³ 16d 16d⁴ 19d Jan 29] small, angular gelding: fair hurdler: stays 2½m: raced on good going or softer: blinkered last 2 starts. *B. Ellison* **h108**

MISTER AUDI (IRE) 13 br.g. Good Thyne (USA) – Symphony Orchestra (Orchestra) [2004/5 c30d⁶ May 11] good-bodied gelding: maiden hurdler/chaser: poor pointer nowadays: tried blinkered. *Martin Ward* **c– h–**

MISTER BOBBY 7 b.g. Manhal – Viola (Extra) [2004/5 F16s F16g May 16] first foal: dam unraced: well beaten in bumpers: sold £1,600 Ascot November Sales. *H. J. Manners* **F–**

MISTER CHISUM 9 b.g. Sabrehill (USA) – Anchor Inn (Be My Guest (USA)) [2004/5 h103d: 16d 16m⁵ 16m 17d³ 16gᶠ 16d 16dᵖᵘ Dec 6] angular gelding: poor handicap hurdler nowadays: lame final outing: raced around 2m: acts on heavy and good to firm going: temperamental. *Miss Kariana Key* **h81 §**

MISTER CLUB ROYAL 9 b.g. Alflora (IRE) – Miss Club Royal (Avocat) [2004/5 c67, h–: 24g c24d^{pu} c24g* Apr 15] good-topped gelding: thrice-raced over hurdles: left D. McCain, seemed to show much improved form over fences when winning hunter at Taunton in April: stays 3m: acts on heavy going, probably on good to firm: tried blinkered: has had tongue tied. *Miss Emma Oliver* — **c95 h–**

MISTER CONE 11 b.g. Long Leave – Miss Cone (Celtic Cone) [2004/5 c21g^{pu} Apr 10] winning pointer, usually fails to complete: tried tongue tied. *I. Hambley* — **c– h–**

MISTER DAVE'S (IRE) 10 ch.g. Bluffer – Tacovaon (Avocat) [2004/5 c105x, h92: 26g c25d^{F} Dec 4] tall, leggy gelding: winning hurdler: fairly useful chaser: has failed to complete last 4 starts over fences, though would have won handicap at Wetherby in December but for falling when clear 3 out: stays 27f: acts on heavy and good to firm going. *Mrs S. J. Smith* — **c122 x h–**

MISTER EL BEE 5 b.g. El Conquistador – Sybillabee (Sula Bula) [2004/5 F16d^{pu} Mar 10] first foal: dam winning pointer: pulled up before halfway in bumper on debut. *B. G. Powell* — **F–**

MISTER FALCON (FR) 8 b.g. Passing Sale (FR) – Falcon Crest (FR) (Cadoudal (FR)) [2004/5 c–§, h–§: c24g c21d^{pu} May 17] sparely-made gelding: winning pointer: no form in hunters: used to wear visor over hurdles: ungenuine. *S. Flook* — **c– § h– §**

MISTER FELIX (IRE) 9 b.g. Ore – Pixies Glen (Furry Glen) [2004/5 h118: 22g^{6} c24g^{3} c24g^{pu} c24g^{5} 21d Mar 4] tall gelding: fairly useful hurdler, well below best in 2004/5: easily best effort over fences when third of 4 finishers in maiden at Kempton: stays 3m: raced on good going or softer (won bumper on heavy). *Mrs Susan Nock* — **c110 h95**

MISTER FLINT 7 b.g. Petoski – National Clover (National Trust) [2004/5 h115, F98: 20m* 19f* 16s^{F} 16d^{6} 17d^{6} 21d^{6} 24m Apr 13] workmanlike gelding: fairly useful hurdler: soon clear when easily winning novices at Worcester and Exeter in September: below form after, distressed final outing: bred to stay beyond 2½m: acts on firm and good to soft going: free-going sort. *P. J. Hobbs* — **h115**

MISTER FRIDAY (IRE) 8 b. or br.g. Mister Lord (USA) – Rebecca's Storm (IRE) (Strong Gale) [2004/5 c104, h–: c22g^{pu} c25s^{pu} c25g* c26g* Apr 14] leggy gelding: winning hurdler: sold out of P. Niven's stable 13,000 gns Doncaster May Sales after first outing: much improved in 2005, winning hunters at Market Rasen and Cheltenham in April, travelling well to lead 2 out and beating Mullensgrove 5 lengths at latter: stays 27f: unraced on firm going, acts on any other: visored nowadays: sound jumper: patiently ridden. *Mrs C. M. Mulhall* — **c126 h–**

MISTER GRAHAM 10 b.g. Rock Hopper – Celestial Air (Rheingold) [2004/5 c–§, h–§: 16m* 16m^{5} 17m 19m 16g^{6} 16s^{4} Oct 22] strong, lengthy gelding: maiden chaser: bad hurdler: won weak selling handicap at Fakenham in May: effective at 2m to 3m: acts on good to firm and good to soft going: tried blinkered/visored, usually wears cheekpieces (didn't when successful): has had tongue tied: ungenuine: sold £1,300 Ascot April Sales. *K. F. Clutterbuck* — **c– § h59 §**

MISTER JULIUS 8 b.g. Mister Lord (USA) – Princess Pool (Push On) [2004/5 22g^{ur} Apr 12] pulled up in 2 maiden points in 2004: unseated second on hurdling debut. *P. Bowen* — **h–**

MISTER KINGSTON 14 ch.g. Kinglet – Flaxen Tina (Beau Tudor) [2004/5 c66: c24m^{4} c23g^{pu} c24m^{pu} c23d^{5} c20g c22s^{6} c24d Apr 22] tall, angular gelding: winning pointer: maiden chaser: stays 25f: acts on good to soft and good to firm going: tried blinkered, usually visored. *R. Dickin* — **c–**

MISTER MAGNUM (IRE) 7 b.g. Be My Native (USA) – Miss Henrietta (IRE) (Step Together (USA)) [2004/5 17m^{3} c16s^{4} Apr 22] leggy gelding: modest form in 3 starts over hurdles: off another 8 months, never-dangerous fourth in novice at Perth on chasing debut: likely to be suited by 2½m+. *P. Monteith* — **c– h84**

MISTER MAGPIE 9 gr.g. Neltino – Magic (Sweet Revenge) [2004/5 c81, h–: c20m^{4} May 25] good-topped gelding: poor chaser: stays 21f: acts on soft going: blinkered once: often let down by jumping. *T. R. George* — **c62 h–**

MISTER MAMBO 5 b.g. Afzal – Elver Season (Vital Season) [2004/5 F17m^{5} F16s Nov 24] fifth foal: half-brother to winning pointer by Miner's Lamp: dam fairly useful hunter chaser, stayed 25f: well beaten in 2 bumpers. *Mrs Jane Galpin* — **F–**

MISTER MCGOLDRICK 8 b.g. Sabrehill (USA) – Anchor Inn (Be My Guest (USA)) [2004/5 c142, h132: c20s* c16d5 16g3 c16v* 16v2 c17d4 c20dF Apr 8] **c156 h142**

Wetherby once again turned out to be a happy hunting ground for Mister McGoldrick. In seven appearances there he has now won six races, split equally between hurdles and fences. Both of Mister McGoldrick's wins in the latest season, his second as a chaser, came at the course, the first in a handicap in October on his reappearance, the second in the skybet.com Castleford Chase in early-January. The transition from novice to open company can sometimes prove tricky, but the bold-jumping Mister McGoldrick, a most likeable individual who races with as much enthusiasm as any horse in training, made light of it. Up against several far more experienced chasers on his return, he didn't put a foot wrong in winning with something to spare by eight lengths from Asparagus, taking up the running before four out. An even stiffer task awaited Mister McGoldrick in the Castleford Chase, a Grade 2 contest which had been rescheduled following the abandonment of the second day of Wetherby's Christmas fixture. The main contenders in the original field of ten were also among the eight declared second time around, the pick of them looking to be the previous season's Arkle Trophy winner Well Chief, who on his previous outing had put up a top-class performance when a close third to Moscow Flyer and Azertyuiop in the Tingle Creek Chase. Well Chief started at odds on and, but for the presence of Mister McGoldrick, the next three in the betting would all have been Paul Nicholls-trained runners, Armaturk, Cenkos and Kadarann, the last-named the winner of the race twelve months earlier. As it was, Mister McGoldrick went off at 6/1, shorter than both Cenkos and Kadarann, in a race which for once lived up to its billing as one of the season's premier two-mile chases. It was also one of the most strongly run. Mister McGoldrick, prominent from the off, took the lead off Kadarann after the fourth last, at which fence Well Chief, around three lengths behind and still to be asked for his effort, came down. The result was never in much doubt once Mister McGoldrick hit the front, and by the time he reached the line he had put eleven lengths between himself and runner-up Kadarann, who finished two lengths clear of third-placed Armaturk. Mister McGoldrick was galloping on so strongly at the end, in what was very testing ground, that it seemed by no means certain, on the face of it, that Well Chief would have pegged him back had he completed the course, though Well Chief is clearly

skybet.com Castleford Chase, Wetherby—
Mister McGoldrick takes advantage after Well Chief has departed four out

much the superior chaser and has beaten Mister McGoldrick the four other times they have met.

Mister McGoldrick showed very smart form in winning the Castleford and, although he failed to run up to it in his other two completed starts over fences in 2004/5, it would be wrong to infer that he isn't so effective away from Wetherby. It is possible that Cheltenham doesn't suit Mister McGoldrick ideally—he was well held in fourth when unseating his rider at the last in the 2004 Arkle and only fifth in a handicap on his second outing in the latest season—but he ran at least respectably on his penultimate start when fourth of six to Azertyuiop in the Game Spirit Chase at Newbury, where the effort of trying to lead against such strong opposition eventually told. Two of Mister McGoldrick's three wins in his first season over fences were gained at Ayr, while he has also won over hurdles at Doncaster and Bangor. Mister McGoldrick did make a couple of appearances over hurdles in the latest season and ran very well at Haydock on the second of them, when eight lengths second to Inglis Drever in the Champion Hurdle Trial. Be it over hurdles or fences, or at Wetherby or elsewhere, Mister McGoldrick looks sure to win more races provided his confidence hasn't been affected by a heavy fall at the third fence in the Melling Chase at Aintree, in which he reportedly sustained an overreach.

Mister McGoldrick (b.g. 1997)	Sabrehill (USA) (ch 1990)	Diesis (ch 1980)	Sharpen Up
			Doubly Sure
		Gypsy Talk (b 1982)	Alleged
			Mazaca
	Anchor Inn (b 1988)	Be My Guest (ch 1974)	Northern Dancer
			What A Treat
		Quiet Harbour (br 1974)	Mill Reef
			Peace

Mister McGoldrick is a brother to the winning two-mile hurdler Mister Chisum and a half-brother to three winners, including the six- and seven-furlong winner Bargash (by Sharpo) and the fair hurdler Master Sebastian (by Kasakov), successful in a two-and-a-quarter-mile novice event at Kelso in January. The dam Anchor Inn had just two outings, both on the all-weather at Lingfield, starting at 50/1 when winning a mile-and-a-quarter claimer on the second occasion. Mister McGoldrick himself won over that trip before he was sent jumping. Anchor Inn, a half-sister to the useful French stayer Cutting Reef, is a daughter of the lightly-raced maiden Quiet Harbour and granddaughter of the well-known broodmare Peace. Peace, winner of the Blue Seal Stakes, produced several good winners, including Quiet Fling (Coronation Cup), Peacetime (Sandown's Classic Trial) and Intermission (Cambridgeshire), as well as appearing in the pedigrees of numerous other good horses. Mister McGoldrick, a workmanlike gelding, is a versatile performer who has shown his form at two and at two and a half miles, on ground ranging from heavy to good to firm. Although a bold jumper, he can make the odd mistake and has fallen early on on both starts at Aintree. He is also effective held up or ridden prominently. *Mrs S. J. Smith*

MISTER MOUSSAC 6 b.g. Kasakov – Salu (Ardross) [2004/5 h–: 21g 16d^{3} 16g^{pu} 17m^{4} 16d^{4} 16m 16g^{2} 20m* 20d* 20m^{4} 19g^{5} 20g^{ro} 22g^{4} 17d 17d^{4} 20f^{6} 20g^{2} 20m^{5} 19g^{5} 21g^{5} 22v^{pu} c20g^{pu} 16g 20d^{pu} Apr 20] lengthy, angular gelding: modest hurdler: won handicap at Worcester and novice at Hexham in June: several mistakes when pulled up on chasing debut: stays 2½m: acts on good to firm and good to soft going, probably on firm: not one to trust. *Miss Kariana Key* **c–** **h101 §**

MISTER MUSTARD (IRE) 8 b.g. Norwich – Monalma (IRE) (Montekin) [2004/5 h115: 16g c16g^{F} c16s^{2} c16d^{4} 16d^{2} 20s* 18g* 20s* 17g^{2} Apr 14] quite good-topped gelding: fair form over fences: fairly useful hurdler: successful in maiden and 2 novices at Fontwell in March: stays 2½m: acts on soft and good to firm going (won bumper on heavy): has found little. *Ian Williams* **c104** **h115**

MISTER PEARLY 8 ch.g. Alflora (IRE) – Pearly Dream (Rymer) [2004/5 c–, F–: c23g^{3} c21g^{5} May 27] sturdy gelding: maiden chaser: tried tongue tied: sold £6,000 (privately) Ascot August Sales, won 3-runner maiden point in March. *J. W. Mullins* **c82**

MISTER PUTT (USA) 7 b. or br.g. Mister Baileys – Theresita (GER) (Surumu (GER)) [2004/5 c90, h–: c18d^{4} c16d^{5} c20s^{3} c17s^{5} c18s^{4} c18s^{5} Feb 4] useful-looking gelding: winning hurdler: modest novice chaser, has been let down by jumping/temperament: **c92** **h–**

not sure to stay beyond 2½m: raced on good going or softer (acts on heavy): wears headgear: has had tongue tied. *Mrs N. Smith*

MISTER QUASIMODO 5 b.g. Busy Flight – Dubacilla (Dubassoff (USA)) [2004/5 F16s* F16s^4 F17v* F16g Mar 16] 20,000 4-y-o: tall gelding: fourth foal: half-brother to winning pointer by Terimon: dam top-class staying chaser: won bumpers at Chepstow in November and Exeter in February, useful form when beating Dare Too Dream 29 lengths at latter: well held in Grade 1 at Cheltenham month later: will stay well. *C. L. Tizzard* **F110**

MISTER RIGHT (IRE) 4 ch.g. Barathea (IRE) – Broken Spirit (IRE) (Slip Anchor) [2004/5 16s^6 16d 16v Mar 29] leggy gelding: half-brother to winning 2½m hurdler Ballintry Guest (by Be My Guest): modest form on Flat (should stay 1¼m): best effort over hurdles when seventh of 14 in juvenile at Newbury: reportedly unsuited by heavy ground next time. *D. J. S. ffrench Davis* **h81**

MISTER TOP NOTCH (IRE) 6 b.g. Mister Lord (USA) – Turn A Coin (Prince Hansel) [2004/5 F16v* F16v^3 F19s* F16g F16v Apr 17] €600 4-y-o: big, rangy gelding: seventh foal: brother to fairly useful chaser Cash Flow, stayed 3m: dam 2¼m hurdle winner: runner-up in point on debut: useful in bumpers: won at Limerick in December and Naas (made most and held on gamely by ½ length from Graduand) in February: geed up, good eighth to Missed That in Grade 1 at Cheltenham fourth outing, short of room then going on well finish. *D. E. Fitzgerald, Ireland* **F114**

MISTER TRICKSTER (IRE) 4 b.c. Woodborough (USA) – Tinos Island (IRE) (Alzao (USA)) [2004/5 16g^6 Jul 11] modest on Flat (stays 1m), successful in June: shaped like non-stayer on hurdling debut. *R. Dickin* **h–**

MISTIFIED (IRE) 4 b.g. Ali-Royal (IRE) – Lough N Uisce (IRE) (Boyne Valley) [2004/5 16g^4 16m 16s^5 17s 20s^2 17d^{ur} 21d^3 Mar 24] modest maiden on Flat (stays 1¾m): modest juvenile hurdler, sold out of Miss I. Oakes' stable €6,000 Goffs October Sale after third outing: stays 21f: acts on soft going: tried in blinkers: has had tongue tied. *J. W. Mullins* **h90**

MISTLETOEANDWINE (IRE) 7 ch.m. Un Desperado (FR) – Crackle Moor (Don) [2004/5 c18s c16s c18d* c17d^2 c16s^3 c18v^5 Jan 6] IR £21,000 3-y-o: sturdy mare: fourth living foal: sister to fair staying hurdler/chaser Christmas Crackle: dam, winning 2m hurdler, also won up to 1½m on Flat: fairly useful chaser: made all in handicap at Punchestown in November: creditable second to Cregg House at Fairyhouse later in month: best form around 2m: raced on going softer than good (acts on heavy). *S. J. Treacy, Ireland* **c117 h–**

MISTLETOE (IRE) 11 gr.m. Montelimar (USA) – Nancy's Sister (The Parson) [2004/5 c23s^{pu} Feb 16] workmanlike mare: fairly useful chaser in 2002/3: left K. Bailey and off 2 years, no encouragement on return: stays 3m: raced on good going or softer (acts on heavy). *O. Sherwood* **c– h–**

MISTRAL BOY (FR) 5 b.g. Port Lyautey (FR) – Une de Mai IV (FR) (Ice Light (FR)) [2004/5 17m^4 16d* 18s^4 c19d* c19g* c17s^2 c17s* c20v^4 17g^3 Dec 14] fifth foal: half-brother to winner around 1¾m Galion Bai (by Shafoun) and 19f chase winner Hunter Gold (by Chamberlin): dam ran twice: fair hurdler/chaser: won over hurdles at Vichy in August and over fences at Nancy (twice) and Auteuil in autumn: creditable third to Lustral du Seuil in novice hurdle at Folkestone on British debut: stays 2½m: acts on good to firm and heavy ground. *G. Macaire, France* **c111 h105**

MISTRAL DE LA COUR (FR) 5 bl.g. Panoramic – Gracieuse Delacour (FR) (Port Etienne (FR)) [2004/5 16d^4 17d^6 17s^{pu} c17v* 16g^5 c16v^3 c17s* c18d^5 c20s^3 c19s^4 16m Apr 2] lengthy, useful-looking gelding: second foal: dam unraced: once-raced on Flat: maiden hurdler: won minor event at Compiegne in October on chasing debut: sold out of J-P. Scomparin's stable €26,000 Goffs (France) November Sale: very fortunate to win 3-runner novice at Exeter in January, just holding on from remounted Kauto Star: best efforts around 2m: acts on heavy going: tried blinkered/in cheekpieces: has been let down by jumping: sold 9,200 gns Doncaster May Sales. *Mrs L. C. Taylor* **c111 h91**

MISTRESS BANJO 5 b.m. Start Fast (FR) – Temperance (FR) (Beyssac (FR)) [2004/5 F93: F16d^2 16d^5 20d^4 21d^2 20s^{pu} 19g^2 Mar 4] lengthy mare: has scope: placed both starts in bumpers: fair maiden hurdler: stays 21f: acts on good to soft going, soon toiling only outing on soft. *A. King* **h109 F86**

MISTRESS COOL 4 b.f. Arctic Lord – Mistress Caramore (IRE) (Moscow Society (USA)) [2004/5 F16d^5 F16d Mar 14] fourth foal: dam unraced half-sister to top-class staying chaser Monsieur Le Cure: little show in 2 bumpers. *Mrs S. Richardson* **F–**

MISTRESS NELL 5 b.m. Thethingaboutitis (USA) – Neladar (Ardar) [2004/5 F18s5 F16s4 F16v3 Mar 29] second foal: dam poor maiden pointer: best effort in bumpers when fourth in mares maiden at Warwick: likely to be suited by further than 2m. *A. J. Lidderdale* **F87**

MISTRESS OFTHEHALL 7 b.m. Son Pardo – Covent Garden Girl (Sizzling Melody) [2004/5 17s 24dpu Mar 24] well held on Flat at 3 yrs: no show over hurdles. *P. D. Evans* **h–**

MISTY BROOK 7 b.g. Alderbrook – Mystic Gale (IRE) (Strong Gale) [2004/5 c26vur Apr 22] first foal: dam, modest hurdler/fair chaser who stayed 3m, sister to useful 2m to 2½m chaser Around The Horn: poor maiden pointer, third on completed start in 2005. *Miss L. Gardner* **c–**

MISTY DANCER 6 gr.g. Vettori (IRE) – Light Fantastic (Deploy) [2004/5 h91+: 16g3 17g4 17m4 Apr 9] fair handicap hurdler: likely to prove best around 2m: acts on soft and good to firm going: tongue tied once: jumps none too fluently. *Miss Venetia Williams* **h106**

MISTY FUTURE 7 b.g. Sanglamore (USA) – Star of The Future (USA) (El Gran Senor (USA)) [2004/5 c119, h92: c24m5 c32mpu Jun 27] sturdy gelding: winning hurdler: fairly useful chaser: well below form in 2004/5: stays 3¼m: acts on firm and good to soft going: blinkered once (finished weakly): has been let down by jumping. *Miss Venetia Williams* **c–** **h–**

MISTY MEMORY 6 b.m. Alderbrook – Misty Sunset (Le Bavard (FR)) [2004/5 h–, F–: 19d 24gpu May 16] no sign of ability. *R. F. Knipe* **h–**

MITCHELDEAN (IRE) 9 b.g. Be My Native (USA) – Pil Eagle (FR) (Piling (USA)) [2004/5 c23mpu Aug 6] good-topped gelding: lightly-raced winning hurdler/chaser: stays 3m: acts on heavy going: blinkered once: poor jumper of fences. *M. Pitman* **c–** **h–**

MITEY PERK (IRE) 6 b.g. Executive Perk – More Dash (IRE) (Strong Gale) [2004/5 h–: 24dpu May 13] no sign of ability in 2 starts over hurdles starts 12 months apart. *J. S. Haldane* **h–**

MITHAK (USA) 11 b.g. Silver Hawk (USA) – Kapalua Butterfly (USA) (Stage Door Johnny (USA)) [2004/5 h–§: 24d 23d Oct 21] leggy gelding: fair handicap hurdler in 2002/3: lightly raced and well held since: stays 3¼m: acts on good to firm and heavy going. *R. T. Phillips* **h–**

MITRASH 5 b.g. Darshaan – L'Ideale (USA) (Alysheba (USA)) [2004/5 16m Oct 1] well held in maidens on Flat and in novice on hurdling debut. *D. McCain* **h–**

MIXED MARRIAGE (IRE) 7 ch.g. Indian Ridge – Marie de Flandre (FR) (Crystal Palace (FR)) [2004/5 h–: 16s Feb 3] leggy gelding: winning hurdler: lightly raced and well held since 2003. *Miss Victoria Roberts* **h–**

MIXSTERTHETRIXSTER (USA) 9 b.g. Alleged (USA) – Parliament House (USA) (General Assembly (USA)) [2004/5 c90, h–: c16g3 c19s2 c18d4 c22d* c24d4 c21g6 c21v* Apr 22] tall, angular gelding: fairly useful novice chaser: successful at Newbury (by neck from See You Sometime) in January and Newton Abbot (by 15 lengths from Wrags To Riches) in April: stays 2¾m: acts on heavy and good to firm going: effective making running or waited with. *Mrs Tracey Barfoot-Saunt* **c135** **h–**

M'LORD 7 b.g. Mister Lord (USA) – Dishcloth (Fury Royal) [2004/5 F–: 19g4 19g5 16d5 Jan 26] workmanlike gelding: modest form in novice hurdles: will stay beyond 19f: may do better if jumping improves. *J. A. Geake* **h96**

MNASON (FR) 5 gr.g. Simon du Desert (FR) – Mincing (FR) (Polyfoto) [2004/5 c18vF 17s6 17d4 19s 16v6 16s2 16d6 16s* 20d 16s3 Mar 10] leggy gelding: ninth foal: half-brother to several winners, including 2m hurdlers Minoen (by Hours After) and Microsbi (by American Stress): dam 7f winner: maiden on Flat: runner-up on first of 2 starts in 4-y-o chases at Pau: fair hurdler, claimed from P. Boisgontier €15,000 third start: won handicap at Towcester in February: should stay beyond 17f: raced on good ground or softer. *S. J. Gilmore* **c–** **h104**

MOBASHER (IRE) 6 b.g. Spectrum (IRE) – Danse Royale (IRE) (Caerleon (USA)) [2004/5 h118: 16g6 16d 20spu Mar 23] leggy gelding: fairly useful hurdler at best: off 9 months, let down by jumping in 2004/5: stays 19f: raced on good going or softer: has looked unenthusiastic. *Miss Venetia Williams* **h106**

MOCHARAMOR (IRE) 7 b. or br.g. Distinctly North (USA) – Oso Sure (IRE) (Sure Blade (USA)) [2004/5 c18g4 c23d5 c20sF c24dpu Nov 22] first foal: dam never ran: **c97** **h–**

won completed start in points in 2003: fair hurdler: modest form at best in 4 starts over fences: stays 2¾m: acts on soft ground. *C. F. Swan, Ireland*

MODAFFAA 5 b.g. Darshaan – Irish Valley (USA) (Irish River (FR)) [2004/5 F16g* Oct 7] half-brother to several winners, including useful 2m hurdler Gaelic Myth (by Nijinsky) and very smart 7f to 9.8f winner Alhaarth (by Unfuwain): dam maiden half-sister to Green Dancer: won bumper at Ludlow on debut, always travelling strongly and beating Lead In The Head 3½ lengths: twice-raced on Flat, winning maiden at Lingfield in November: reportedly finished lame next time. *P. R. Webber* — **F92 +**

MODEL SON (IRE) 7 b.g. Leading Counsel (USA) – Miss Mutley (Pitpan) [2004/5 20g 22m^{pu} 19d^{2} 24g* 24v^{3} 25d c20s^{5} c22v^{F2} 24v Jan 9] workmanlike gelding: fairly useful handicap hurdler: won at Galway in September: better effort over fences when falling last (remounted) in maiden at Limerick, well clear at time: stays 3m: acts on heavy going: should do better over fences. *D. Hassett, Ireland* — **c112 p** **h115**

MODULOR (FR) 13 gr.g. Less Ice – Chaumontaise (FR) (Armos) [2004/5 c–, h–: 23m^{5} 20g^{pu} 24g^{pu} 23d^{6} c26d^{6} c24m^{5} 27v^{pu} Mar 15] small, plain gelding: winning hurdler/chaser, retains little ability: tried in headgear: has had tongue tied *L. R. James* — **c–** **h–**

MOFFIED (IRE) 5 b.g. Nashwan (USA) – Del Deya (IRE) (Caerleon (USA)) [2004/5 F–: F16m 16v Jan 14] soundly beaten in bumpers and novice hurdle. *Mrs L. B. Normile* — **h–** **F–**

MOHAWK STAR (IRE) 4 ch.g. Indian Ridge – Searching Star (Rainbow Quest (USA)) [2004/5 17s^{5} 16s 17s^{5} 17g^{3} 17g* Mar 19] fairly useful on Flat (best form around 1m), sold out of D. Weld's stable 25,000 gns Newmarket Autumn Sales: fair hurdler: won juvenile at Bangor in March: blinkered time before (mistakes): likely to prove best around 2m with emphasis on speed. *Miss Venetia Williams* — **h102**

MOHERA KING (IRE) 13 b.g. King's Ride – Kilbrien Star (Goldhill) [2004/5 c–§, h–: c20d c30d^{R} May 29] sturdy gelding: veteran chaser, retains little ability: acts on good to firm and heavy going: often wears blinkers/cheekpieces: moody. *Ferdy Murphy* — **c– §** **h–**

MOKUM (FR) 4 b.g. Octagonal (NZ) – Back On Top (FR) (Double Bed (FR)) [2004/5 17s^{5} 15s 15s 16s^{5} 18s^{4} 16v 16d^{6} 16v^{2} 16g^{3} 16d^{5} Feb 17] leggy gelding: first foal: dam, placed around 1½m, sister to very smart French hurdler Bedava: maiden up to 1½m on Flat: fair juvenile hurdler: sold out of F. Doumen's stable €10,000 Goffs (France) November Sale after fifth outing: raced around 2m (will stay further) on good going or softer: blinkered on debut: has looked none too keen. *A. W. Carroll* — **h104**

MOLDAVIA (GER) 4 b.f. Lagunas – Moricana (GER) (Konigsstuhl (GER)) [2004/5 17s^{4} 16s Jan 27] runner-up twice from 4 starts on Flat in Germany for P. Schiergen: won over 11f on British debut in January: well held in 2 juvenile hurdles on soft ground: joined M. Chapman. *H. Morrison* — **h–**

MOLLYCARRSBREKFAST 10 b.g. Presidium – Imperial Flame (Imperial Lantern) [2004/5 c80: c19m^{5} c23g^{2} c23g^{2} 27g c20g c23f^{pu} c24d^{6} c24g^{pu} Apr 15] modest handicap chaser: lost form after third outing, left K. Bishop before final one: well beaten only try over hurdles: stays 3m: acts on good to firm going: races prominently. *Miss S. E. Robinson* — **c86 x** **h–**

MOLLYCARRS GAMBUL 6 b.m. General Gambul – Emma's Vision (IRE) (Vision (USA)) [2004/5 c25s^{F} c21d^{4} c26v^{2} Apr 22] no form over hurdles: won maiden point in February: easily best effort in hunter chases when second in novice at Newton Abbot: will stay beyond 3¼m: acts on heavy going: room for improvement in her jumping. *Miss S. E. Robinson* — **c80** **h–**

MOMENT OF MADNESS (IRE) 7 ch.g. Treasure Hunter – Sip of Orange (Celtic Cone) [2004/5 F90: 20d 20d^{4} 19g^{4} 21v^{5} c16d* 20g^{bd} Mar 26] big, lengthy gelding: modest form over hurdles: won novice at Catterick on chasing debut in February: probably stays 2½m: acts on good to soft going. *T. J. Fitzgerald* — **c94 p** **h94**

MOMENTS MADNESS (IRE) 6 b.m. Corrouge (USA) – Treble Clef (IRE) (Supreme Leader) [2004/5 F16d F16m Jun 12] €2,000 4-y-o: first foal: dam, lightly raced in points, from family of smart 2m to 2½m chaser Mossy Moore: no sign of ability in bumpers or maiden point. *Miss S. E. Forster* — **F–**

MONASH GIRL (IRE) 4 b.f. General Monash (USA) – Maricica (Ahonoora) [2004/5 17d^{pu} Nov 15] half-sister to poor chaser J J Baboo (by Be My Guest), stayed 25f: of no account on Flat: no show on hurdling debut. *B. R. Johnson* — **h–**

MONBONAMI (IRE) 8 b.g. Beau Sher – Hard Riche (Hard Fought) [2004/5 c96, h–: c21v^{pu} c24d^{pu} c21s^{4} c19v^{pu} Mar 29] sturdy gelding: winning chaser: no form in 2004/5: tried visored. *Miss K. Marks* — **c–** **h–**

MONDEED 8 b.m. Terimon – House Deed (Presidium) [2004/5 h90, F75: 26m^{5} May 27] smallish mare: modest hurdler: stays 23f: probably acts on any going: effective blinkered or not. *N. B. King* **h86**

MONDIAL JACK (FR) 6 ch.g. Apple Tree (FR) – Cackle (USA) (Crow (FR)) [2004/5 c127, h–: c25m* c20s^{2} c20g^{6} c24s^{3} c26d^{pu} c20d^{F} c21s^{pu} c24s^{pu} c20g Apr 22] leggy, lengthy gelding: winning hurdler: useful chaser: led run-in under really strong ride from A. McCoy when winning 4-runner intermediate at Kelso in May: good efforts in handicaps next 3 starts but out of sorts after: stays easy 25f: acts on soft and good to firm going: wore visor/cheekpieces last 4 outings: sketchy jumper. *M. C. Pipe* **c136 h–**

MONDUL (GER) 5 b.g. Colon (GER) – Morgenrote (EG) (Aveiro) [2004/5 h127: 19s^{3} 19d^{pu} 21d^{6} c16v^{F} c16v^{F} c16v^{5} c17s^{2} c18d* c17v^{3} c16g c20d^{F} 16g c21v^{4} Apr 22] leggy gelding: fairly useful hurdler at best: fair novice chaser: won at Fontwell in February: stays 19f: possibly suited by going softer than good (acts on heavy): has worn off-side pricker: races prominently: sold 36,000 Doncaster May Sales. *M. F. Harris* **c113 h127**

MONET'S GARDEN (IRE) 7 gr.g. Roselier (FR) – Royal Remainder (IRE) (Remainder Man) [2004/5 h138: 20d* 21d^{5} 24s^{5} 24s^{2} 24s* Apr 7] **h160**

A season topped and tailed by victories in Grade 2 events at Windsor and Aintree saw second-season hurdler Monet's Garden progress into a high-class performer and he looks sure to make into a leading staying novice when sent over fences in 2005/6. It was slightly surprising that he was not switched from hurdling

Coloroll Ascot Hurdle, Windsor—
Monet's Garden makes a winning return; Trouble At Bay jumps the last in his wake

John Smith's And Batleys Liverpool Hurdle, Aintree—Monet's Garden signs off in style; runner-up Mr Ed is in cheekpieces

to chasing in 2004/5, but trainer Nicky Richards reported that he felt Monet's Garden was not mature enough and that a few races over hurdles would toughen him up.

Monet's Garden's best performance came on his final start when he won the John Smith's And Batleys Liverpool Hurdle. Run at Aintree for the second time, having formerly been staged as the Long Distance Hurdle at Ascot, the Liverpool Hurdle attracted a field of nine. With the World Hurdle winner Inglis Drever kept for the half-mile shorter and more valuable Aintree Hurdle two days later, the Cheltenham third Rule Supreme started 2/1 favourite. The fourth and fifth from that race, Westender and Korelo, were also in the line-up, the revised weights at Aintree favouring Korelo, who was receiving 8 lb from Rule Supreme and 4 lb from Westender. Monet's Garden, who had missed Cheltenham, reportedly to keep him fresh for Aintree, also had to carry the maximum penalty and looked to have something to find on his best form. As it turned out, Monet's Garden's chance was soon made easier, as approaching the second hurdle, the first away from the stands, the leader Westender slowed right up, ejecting his rider over the hurdle and hampering the following Rule Supreme so badly that Ruby Walsh was unseated. As a result, the pace steadied with the unconsidered Tumbling Dice dictating, before Monet's Garden made his move in the straight, leading after two out and responding well to firm driving to hold off Mr Ed by a length, with ten lengths back to Tumbling Dice in third. Korelo failed to settle and was well held when falling at the last. Even with the effective non-participation of three of the four market leaders, Monet's Garden almost certainly needed to improve considerably to concede 8 lb to the smart Mr Ed. Rule Supreme might have been pushed to beat Monet's Garden even had he completed without mishap.

Nearly five months earlier Monet's Garden had landed another race formerly run at Ascot, the Coloroll Hurdle at Windsor, a race registered as the Ascot Hurdle, and one which had marked the successful return to action of Baracouda in both 2001 and 2002. In this instance, the transfer is only temporary, with the race set to return to Ascot when that course reopens in 2006. Windsor staged both the two-day November and December meetings normally held at nearby Ascot, the fixtures marking a return to jumping action there after a break of six years. Though prize money was generally lower than it would have been had the meeting been held at Ascot, and the very valuable Ladbroke Handicap Hurdle was switched to Sandown instead, the races were well supported in the main and hopefully the resumption at Windsor won't be temporary, as it is planned to be at present. The Coloroll Hurdle was rather overshadowed on the day by Best Mate's return to the fray at Exeter and proved a decidedly muddling race, the seven runners going along at a sedate pace before a sprint developed two from home. In the circumstances Monet's Garden did well to pull four lengths clear of the favourite Monkerhostin, though the form overall does not compare with his later efforts, his Aintree run being preceded by creditable efforts in defeat in the Cleeve Hurdle at Cheltenham and in the Rendlesham at Kempton. At Kempton, Monet's Garden finished second to Crystal d'Ainay at level weights, though sloppy jumping detracted from his performance, as it did also when flopping at odds on in a minor event at Cheltenham on his second start.

Monet's Garden (IRE) (gr.g. 1998)	Roselier (FR) (gr 1973)	Misti IV (br 1958)	Medium
			Mist
		Peace Rose (gr 1959)	Fastnet Rock
			La Paix
	Royal Remainder (IRE) (b 1991)	Remainder Man (ch 1975)	Connaught
			Honerone
		Beyond The Rainbow (b 1977)	Royal Palace
			Villa Marina

Monet's Garden is the first foal out of the unraced Royal Remainder and comes from a family which has only recently become jumping-oriented. Although Royal Remainder is a sister to a winning pointer and a bumper winner (the fairly useful One More Chance), she is also a half-sister to a fairly useful five-furlong two-year-old winner in Heemee, and her grandam Villa Marina was a useful two-year-old sprinter who produced several in similar mould. Cliff Bank and Mary Crocket were useful two-year-old sprinters out of her, with Chalet almost as good, while another of her offspring Overseas Admirer was a useful older sprinter. Villa Marina's only winning jumper was Aniramsky, a sprint maiden who was an early-season firm-ground two-mile jumper of a type hardly ever seen nowadays. The big, good-topped Monet's Garden was bought for IR £35,000 as a three-year-old and has done little but progress since. He won his only start in a bumper, in February 2003, and was beaten just once in his novice season over hurdles. That reverse came in the Grade 2 novice on the same card as the Liverpool Hurdle twelve months before his win. His conqueror that day Garde Champetre was sold for the tidy sum of 530,000 guineas not long afterwards but hasn't been seen since. *N. G. Richards*

MONEY CRAZY (FR) 6 ch.g. Green Tune (USA) – Value For Money (FR) (Highest Honor (FR)) [2004/5 h–: c16m^{6} Jun 8] leggy gelding: little sign of ability except when runner-up in maiden point in March: blinkered last 3 starts. *Ian Williams* **c– h–**

MONEY LINE (IRE) 6 b.g. Roselier (FR) – Pharleng (IRE) (Phardante (FR)) [2004/5 F18s^{2} Dec 1] €31,000 4-y-o: second foal: dam, thrice-raced maiden pointer, half-sister to useful but ungenuine Irish chaser up to 3m Montana Glen: ¾-length second to Darkness in bumper at Plumpton on debut. *Jonjo O'Neill* **F98**

MONGER LANE 9 b.m. Karinga Bay – Grace Moore (Deep Run) [2004/5 c100, h–: c23s c22s^{5} c24d^{6} c25s^{4d} c24s^{4} 21g^{5} Apr 14] tall, good sort: fair handicap hurdler: winning chaser, largely disappointing in 2004/5: should stay 3m: seems best on going softer than good: ungenuine. *K. Bishop* **c93 § h101 §**

MONGINO (GER) 4 b.g. In A Tiff (IRE) – Mondalita (GER) (Alkalde (GER)) [2004/5 F12d F18s 16v^{5} 18g^{F} Mar 20] leggy gelding: first foal: dam, successful around 7f at 2 yrs in Germany, half-sister to fairly useful hurdler Mondul: little sign of ability: tongue tied. *M. F. Harris* **h– F–**

MONITA DES BOIS (FR) 5 b.m. Snurge – Fauvette Grise (FR) (Epervier Bleu) [2004/5 18s^{pu} c22s* c24g^{pu} c17s^{3} Apr 16] leggy, sparely-made mare: second foal: dam, won 6 times up to 9f, half-sister to smart staying chaser Tamarindo and useful hurdler/chaser up to 29f Sun Storm: twice-raced on Flat: fair hurdler: won claimer (claimed from J. Bertran de Balanda €26,000) at Auteuil in late-2003/4: fair novice chaser: easily won mares event at Towcester in February: should stay at least 3m: raced mainly on good to soft/soft going. *Miss Venetia Williams* **c100 h–**

bonusprint.com Gold Cup, Cheltenham—
a close contest is in prospect until Monkerhostin is left clear by Our Vic's fall at the last

MONKERHOSTIN (FR) 8 b.g. Shining Steel – Ladoun (FR) (Kaldoun (FR)) **c144**
[2004/5 c–, h152: c21v* c20d^3 20d^2 c21d* 20d^3 Jan 1] **h148**

Just as Monkerhostin's first season for Philip Hobbs's stable saw marked improvement in his form over hurdles, so his second saw similar progress over fences. Although his season was curtailed by the effects of a virus, Monkerhostin managed five outings between mid-October and New Year's Day, winning twice from three appearances over fences and running respectably in two over hurdles. Monkerhostin's more notable win came in the valuable handicap at Cheltenham's December meeting, run for the only time as the bonusprint.com Gold Cup (it had been the Tripleprint previously and is set to have a new sponsor in 2005/6). It was Monkerhostin's third appearance over fences for the season, after a neck victory over the promising novice Vodka Bleu at Stratford and a third placing, seemingly with no excuses, to Celestial Gold in the Paddy Power Gold Cup at Cheltenham. Running off the same BHB mark as in the Paddy Power, Monkerhostin didn't have to better his form in that race—one of the strongest handicaps run all season—to defeat Thisthatandtother by seven lengths, after he had been left clear by the last-fence fall of Our Vic. Monkerhostin was a length down at that point but finding plenty under pressure and might well have won even if Our Vic had stood up. Monkerhostin's performance suggested there might well be a bit more to come. In his two runs over hurdles, Monkerhostin couldn't quite match the form that had seen him win the Coral Cup the previous season. However, his second to Monet's Garden in a Grade 2 at Windsor came in a muddling affair and he faced a stiffer task than the market suggested when third to Westender at Cheltenham on his final outing. The lengthy Monkerhostin is effective at up to an easy three miles and acts on any going. He tends to take a good hold and is held up. He was tried in a visor and cheekpieces for his former stable but is most reliable. *P. J. Hobbs*

MONKEY OR ME (IRE) 4 b.g. Sri Pekan (USA) – Ecco Mi (IRE) (Priolo (USA)) [2004/5 16s^{pu} Nov 4] lengthy gelding: poor maiden on Flat (stays 8.5f): no show on hurdling debut. *P. T. Midgley* **h–**

MONKS ERROR (IRE) 12 b.g. Eve's Error – Miss Outlaw (IRE) (Lancastrian) [2004/5 c31m^3 c22g* c25m^2 c23m^2 Jun 29] ex-Irish gelding: winning hurdler: fair chaser: won hunter at Uttoxeter in May on second of 2 outings for J. Parfitt: better than ever when runner-up in handicaps at Hereford and Worcester: stays 25f: acts on soft and good to firm ground: tried blinkered/in cheekpieces. *B. J. Llewellyn* **c112 h–**

MONKSFORD 6 b.g. Minster Son – Mortify (Prince Sabo) [2004/5 h71+: 16d* 17d* 16m* 16g^2 16g^2 17d^6 c16d^{pu} 16v 16d^2 16v^2 19m^{pu} Apr 17] fair handicap hurdler: won at Chepstow (novice) and Newton Abbot in May and Uttoxeter (novice) in June: little aptitude for chasing seventh outing: best form around 2m: acted on good to firm and heavy going: wore cheekpieces last 3 outings: dead. *B. J. Llewellyn* **c– h107**

MON MOME (FR) 5 b.g. Passing Sale (FR) – Etoile du Lion (FR) (New Target) [2004/5 16d 16v^{ur} 17v^3 20v^6 20s^2 21g^4 21d^5 Apr 18] first foal: dam won over 10.5f: runner-up over 13.5f on debut for P. Cormier-Martin: modest maiden hurdler: stays 2½m: best form on soft/heavy going. *Miss Venetia Williams* **h99**

MONOLITH 7 b.g. Bigstone (IRE) – Ancara (Dancing Brave (USA)) [2004/5 h107+: 20g^2 24d* 22m* 20s^3 23s^2 Dec 26] compact gelding: progressive hurdler early in season, winning intermediates at Perth and Kelso (useful form, by 4 lengths from Quick) in May: stays 3m: acts on soft and good to firm going: patiently ridden. *L. Lungo* **h133**

MONSAL DALE (IRE) 6 ch.g. Desert King (IRE) – Zanella (IRE) (Nordico (USA)) [2004/5 h70: 20s 22m 17d^2 19g^{ur} c20g^6 16g^5 17g^5 18s^6 22s^5 16s^2 16d^6 16g^6 Mar 27] sturdy gelding: poor hurdler: soundly beaten in handicap on chasing debut: sold out of R. Flint's stable £3,400 Ascot August Sales after fifth outing: best form around 2m: acts on soft going: wore cheekpieces and tongue strap last 6 outings: temperamental. *Mrs L. C. Jewell* **c– h71 §**

MONSIEUR DELAGE 5 b.g. Overbury (IRE) – Sally Ho (Gildoran) [2004/5 F74: F16d F16d^4 F16g^2 Feb 27] good-topped gelding: fair form in bumpers last 2 starts: sold 30,000 gns Doncaster May Sales. *N. Wilson* **F90**

MONSIEUR GEORGES (FR) 5 b.g. Kadalko (FR) – Djoumi (FR) (Brezzo (FR)) [2004/5 c17s^6 c20d^{pu} 22g^5 22d^3 24s^5 16s^2 16d 21g^5 24m^5 Apr 10] good-topped ex-French gelding: third foal: brother to fair hurdler King Georges, stays 25f, and half-brother to fairly useful chaser around 2½m Le Kalinou (by Video Rock): dam won 4 times up to around 1½m on Flat: better effort over fences when sixth in minor event at Auteuil: left G. Cherel, modest form over hurdles in Britain: stays 2¾m: acts on soft ground: tried blinkered. *F. Jordan* **c95 h95**

MONSIEUR MONET (IRE) 6 b.g. Norwich – Sue's A Lady (Le Moss) [2004/5 F102: 16v* Nov 21] useful-looking gelding: winning pointer: bumper winner: evens, won maiden at Navan on hurdling debut in November by 2½ lengths from My Native Lad, making all and jumping soundly: will be well suited by 2½m: seemed sure to progress, but wasn't seen out again. *S. Donohoe, Ireland* **h117 +**

MONSIEUR POIROT (IRE) 8 b.g. Lapierre – Mallia Miss (IRE) (Executive Perk) [2004/5 c74, h74: c17g^4 c20g^{pu} c16d^F c16s^4 c20d^{pu} Nov 29] poor maiden hurdler/chaser: probably stays 3m: acts on heavy going, probably on good to firm: visored. *Mrs S. C. Bradburne* **c71 h–**

MONSIEUR ROSE (IRE) 9 gr.g. Roselier (FR) – Derring Slipper (Derring Rose) [2004/5 h88: c24v^{ur} c22g^4 Apr 19] dipped-backed gelding: lightly-raced novice hurdler: let down by jumping both starts over fences: should stay beyond 3¼m. *N. J. Gifford* **c– x h–**

MONSTER JAWBREAKER (IRE) 6 b.g. Zafonic (USA) – Salvora (USA) (Spectacular Bid (USA)) [2004/5 F17g May 11] 380,000 francs Y, 9,000 3-y-o, 11,500 (priv) 4-y-o: half-brother to several winners, notably US Grade 1 1¼m winner Aube Indienne (by Bluebird) and smart performer up to 1½m Mare Nostrum (by Caerleon): dam French 1¼m winner: never a threat in bumper on debut. *W. M. Brisbourne* **F–**

MONSTER MICK (FR) 7 b.g. Turgeon (USA) – The Dream I Dream (USA) (Theatrical) [2004/5 24v^{pu} 21g^3 20s^2 24m Apr 10] second foal: half-brother to 2 winners, including fair hurdler around 2m Takis (by Villez): dam useful hurdler/chaser up to 2½m: poor form when placed in novice hurdles: should stay 3m: temperament under suspicion. *B. G. Powell* **h77 §**

William Hill Handicap Hurdle, Sandown—
Monte Cinto and the grey Winsley are clear of their rivals at the last

MONTEBANK (IRE) 9 b.g. Montelimar (USA) – Lady Glenbank (Tarboosh (USA)) [2004/5 c–: c20m^{ur} c16g c20d^{ur} c23g^{3} c20g^{4} Aug 14] winning pointer: poor form in chases: often blinkered. *T. R. George* **c62**

MONTE CINTO (FR) 5 br.g. Bulington (FR) – Algue Rouge (FR) (Perouges (FR)) [2004/5 h103: 18d 16d* 17d* 16d* 16d 16d 16d^{3} 17g^{6} Mar 18] leggy gelding: fairly useful handicap hurdler: won at Warwick (flashed tail) and Exeter in November and Sandown (improved again when beating Winsley a length in William Hill Handicap Hurdle) in December: should stay beyond 17f: acts on heavy going. *P. F. Nicholls* **h126**

MONTECORVINO (GER) 4 ch.g. Acatenango (GER) – Manhattan Girl (USA) (Vice Regent (CAN)) [2004/5 F16d^{2} F16g^{2} F16s^{2} 16v^{pu} 19m^{5} Apr 9] good-topped gelding: fifth foal: half-brother to 1999 2-y-o 6f winner Made To Measure (by Platini): dam won 4 times around 7f at 3 yrs in Germany: runner-up in bumpers at Catterick (for M. Hofer), Southwell and Towcester (hung badly left): visored, poor form when fifth in maiden on completed outing over hurdles. *M. F. Harris* **h79 F96**

MONTE CRISTO (FR) 7 ch.g. Bigstone (IRE) – El Quahirah (FR) (Cadoudal (FR)) [2004/5 c120, h–: c20g^{5} c20d* c18s^{2} c16d^{5} c20s^{6} c21d^{pu} 20g^{3} 20d^{4} Apr 20] big, useful-looking gelding: fair hurdler: fairly useful handicap chaser: third win from 5 starts at course when beating Dun An Doras at Stratford in October: stays 2½m: acts on heavy and good to firm going: usually wears headgear: has looked ungenuine. *Mrs L. C. Taylor* **c122 h102**

MONTEFORTE 7 b.g. Alflora (IRE) – Double Dutch (Nicholas Bill) [2004/5 F113: 20s* 22v^{pu} Mar 30] lengthy, good sort: winning pointer: bumper winner: created good impression when winning novice at Chepstow on hurdling debut, making most and not fully extended to beat Genghis 11 lengths: breathing problem in handicap 4 months later: should stay beyond 2½m: may still do better. *J. A. B. Old* **h113**

MONTEL GIRL (IRE) 9 ch.m. Montelimar (USA) – Grassed (Busted) [2004/5 h92: 22m^{2} 20g^{4} 27g^{6} 20s Nov 7] small, angular mare: poor handicap hurdler, left T. McGovern after third outing: stays 27f: acts on good to firm and good to soft ground. *D. Wachman, Ireland* **h83**

MONTE ROSA (IRE) 6 b.m. Supreme Leader – Green Thorn (IRE) (Ovac (ITY)) [2004/5 F90: 16s* Nov 10] runner-up in bumper on debut in 2003/4: favourite, won novice hurdle at Kelso 8 months later by 1½ lengths from Mister Sebastian: seemed sure to progress, but wasn't seen out again. *N. G. Richards* **h100**

MONTESINO 6 b.g. Bishop of Cashel – Sutosky (Great Nephew) [2004/5 h84, F–: 19s^{4} 20s* 21s^{pu} Jan 2] good-bodied gelding: modest novice hurdler: made all in conditional jockeys event at Folkestone in November: stays 2½m: acts on soft going: tried in cheekpieces. *M. Madgwick* **h91**

MONTESSORI MIO (FR) 6 b.g. Robellino (USA) – Child's Play (USA) (Sharpen Up) [2004/5 c77§, h99§: 16m 20m 16m Jun 29] angular gelding: modest hurdler at best, no form early in 2004/5: didn't take to fences: best around 2m: acts on good to firm and good to soft going: usually wore headgear prior to 2004/5: temperamental. *R. A. Fahey* **c– § h– §**

MONTE VISTA (IRE) 8 b.g. Montelimar (USA) – Tarqogan's Rose (Tarqogan) [2004/5 20s* 21d^{2} Nov 14] close-coupled, angular ex-Irish gelding: successful in 27-runner bumper at Punchestown in 2003: left Ms F. Crowley and off 18 months, won novice at Aintree in October on hurdling debut impressively by 13 lengths from Scotch Corner: near useful form when 2½ lengths second to Brewster in similar event at Cheltenham, travelling strongly long way and again jumping soundly in main: bred to stay beyond 21f: capable of better again. *Jonjo O'Neill* **h128 p**

MONTGERMONT (FR) 5 b.g. Useful (FR) – Blowin'in The Wind (FR) (Saint Cyrien (FR)) [2004/5 F16d^{6} aF16g 19d^{3} 17s^{2} 19g^{2} 20g^{2} Mar 26] tall gelding: on weak side: fourth foal: dam placed in 2m hurdle: better effort in bumpers when sixth to Lutea at Newbury: fairly useful novice hurdler: runner-up last 3 starts, beaten 1½ lengths by Kilgowan in handicap at Haydock: likely to stay beyond 2½m: acts on soft going. *Mrs L. C. Taylor* **h117 F93**

MONTICELLI (GER) 5 b.g. Pelder (IRE) – Marcelia (GER) (Priamos (GER)) [2004/5 17g* 16s^{3} 16d^{4} 16d^{bd} Dec 2] good-topped gelding: half-brother to one-time fairly useful hurdler/winning chaser Maragun (by General Assembly), stays 19f: successful on 3 of 4 starts up to around 1¼m on Flat in Germany at 4 yrs for H. Hesse: won novice at Exeter on hurdling debut in October: better form next 2 outings, fourth in handicap at Windsor on second occasion: likely to prove best around 2m. *P. J. Hobbs* **h112 +**

MONTIFAULT (FR) 10 ch.g. Morespeed – Tarde (FR) (Kashtan (FR)) [2004/5 c127d, h–: c24d c25v^{4} c24d* c24v^{4} c21s^{3} Apr 7] lengthy, rather sparely-made gelding: useful chaser in his prime: won hunter at Ludlow in February: weakened markedly late on when third to Katarino in Fox Hunters' at Aintree: stays 3¼m: acts on good to firm and heavy going: jumps soundly: has breathing problem (tried tongue tied): not one to rely on. *P. F. Nicholls* **c121 § h–**

Mr John P. McManus' "Monte Vista"

*Tennents Velvet City of Perth Gold Cup Handicap Chase, Perth—
Montreal defies a rise of 10 lb to complete a hat-trick;
Glynn Dingle and the hidden Kock de La Vesvre take the places*

MONTI FLYER 7 b.g. Terimon – Coole Pilate (Celtic Cone) [2004/5 h96, F89: 22f³ 24s⁴ 24s⁵ c22m⁴ c25mᵖᵘ Apr 23] modest handicap hurdler: similar form on chasing debut: not fluent when pulled up just 2 days later (tongue tied): stays 3m: acts on firm and soft going: sold 3,800 gns Doncaster May Sales. *P. F. Nicholls* **c95 h97**

MONTPELIER (IRE) 12 b.g. Montelimar (USA) – Liscarton (Le Bavard (FR)) [2004/5 c108§, h–: c17m² May 22] rangy gelding: fair handicap chaser: probably stays 3m: acts on good to firm and heavy going: blinkered last 5 starts: idles markedly and often finds little: sold 8,500 gns Doncaster May Sales, third in point in March. *N. J. Henderson* **c108 h–**

MONTREAL (FR) 8 b. or br.g. Chamberlin (FR) – Massada (FR) (Kashtan (FR)) [2004/5 c116, h–: c20d* c24m* c24f* c20d c21d³ c22g c24d⁶ c20g³ c25dᵖᵘ c22d⁶ c24vᵖᵘ c24g c20g⁴ c20g⁵ Apr 22] leggy gelding: fairly useful handicap chaser: won at Bangor (twice) and Perth (quite valuable event, by ¾ length from Glynn Dingle) early in season: generally below form after: stays 3m: acts on any going: tried visored/in cheekpieces: held up, and has idled/found little. *M. C. Pipe* **c128 d h–**

MONTROLIN 5 ch.g. Classic Cliche (IRE) – Charmed I'm Sure (Nicholas Bill) [2004/5 F16s⁴ F16d F16v⁴ Mar 29] rangy gelding: fifth foal: dam winning 2¼m hurdler: fair form in bumpers. *S. C. Burrough* **F87**

MONTU 8 ch.g. Gunner B – Promitto (Roaring Riva) [2004/5 h–: c24d* c23d c24g c24s Mar 23] short-backed gelding: 50/1-winner of maiden at Taunton on chasing debut in October: no other form: stays 3m. *Miss K. M. George* **c89 h–**

MONTY BE QUICK 9 ch.g. Mon Tresor – Spartiquick (Spartan General) [2004/5 h–: 20s 20m⁴ c24g c25sᵖᵘ c16sᵘʳ c24s Feb 17] leggy gelding: poor maiden hurdler: no form in maiden chases: probably stays 2½m: has had tongue tied. *J. M. Castle* **c– h70**

MONTY'S DOUBLE (IRE) 8 b.g. Montelimar (USA) – Macamore Rose (Torus) [2004/5 c99, h–: c21g³ c24d* c23d⁵ c24v² c26d* c24d⁵ Mar 26] workmanlike gelding: fair handicap chaser: won at Windsor in November and Warwick in January: will stay beyond 3¼m: acts on heavy going. *O. Sherwood* **c108 h–**

MONTYS ISLAND (IRE) 8 b.g. Montelimar (USA) – Sea Island (Windjammer (USA)) [2004/5 24g³ 20m³ c20g³ c19m² c20sᶠ c18g⁶ c19sᵖᵘ c18m⁵ c18m³ Apr 21] IR £3,600 4-y-o: good-topped gelding: third foal: half-brother to fair hurdler up to 2¾m Oliver's Island (by Teenoso): dam, fairly useful hurdler/chaser, stayed 27f: in frame in bumpers in 2003/4 for J. A. Berry: third in 2 maiden hurdles: modest novice chaser: stays 3m: acts on good to firm going, bumper form on soft. *C. J. Mann* **c97 h87**

MONTY'S PASS (IRE) 12 b.g. Montelimar (USA) – Friars Pass (Monksfield) [2004/5 c135, h93: 19v³ 16sᶠ c20s 22s c36d Apr 9] sturdy gelding: maiden hurdler: smart chaser at best, won Grand National at Aintree in 2003: little form since except when **c– h97**

fourth in same race following year: stays 4½m: acts on any going: blinkered once (ran poorly): very sound jumper. *James Joseph Mangan, Ireland*

MONTY'S QUEST (IRE) 10 b.g. Montelimar (USA) – A Bit of Luck (IRE) (Good Thyne (USA)) [2004/5 c109, h–: c22g5 c26dpu c25m2 c24g4 c24d* c24g c27v5 c25d* Apr 11] tall gelding: fairly useful chaser: won handicap at Perth in June: sold out of P. Beaumont's stable 10,000 gns Doncaster August Sales after next outing: improved effort when beating Mr Mahdlo 20 lengths in hunter at Kelso in April: stays 25f: acts on good to firm and good to soft going: effective with or without cheekpieces. *Michael Smith* **c117 h–**

MONTY'S SALVO (USA) 6 b. or br.g. Supreme Leader – Likashot (Celtic Cone) [2004/5 21d Mar 4] useful-looking gelding: has scope: third foal: dam, winning 2m hurdler, sister to top-class 2m to 3m hurdler/chaser Celtic Shot: looked in need of experience when well held in novice hurdle at Newbury on debut, jumping poorly and not knocked about. *N. J. Henderson* **h–**

MONTYS TAG (IRE) 12 b.g. Montelimar (USA) – Herbal Lady (Good Thyne (USA)) [2004/5 c24spu c20s3 c22gpu Apr 1] sturdy, lengthy gelding: fairly useful hunter chaser, off nearly 2 years before reappearance: stays 3½m: acts on soft and good to firm going: sound jumper. *S. R. Andrews* **c101**

MONTY'S THEME (IRE) 11 b. or br.g. Montelimar (USA) – Theme Music (Tudor Music) [2004/5 c62: c21spu c23gpu c23g5 c23mpu c21gpu c20g6 c20d 20vpu Dec 17] workmanlike gelding: winning chaser: no longer of any account: tried visored/blinkered. *P. Wegmann* **c– h–**

MOON CATCHER 4 b.f. Kahyasi – Moonlight Saunter (USA) (Woodman (USA)) [2004/5 16g4 17g3 17g4 17g2 16g* 16v* 16d5 17v4 16v 19s 21g Apr 14] angular filly: fifth foal: dam 7f winner: fairly useful on Flat (stays 15f), blinkered when winning at Maisons-Laffitte in May, claimed out of C. Laffon-Parias' stable €26,000 after runner-up in June: fair hurdler: claimed from M. Pipe £5,000 fourth start: won juveniles at Cheltenham (hung left) and Uttoxeter (handicap) in October: should stay beyond 2m: acts on heavy going: visored on debut: usually tongue tied: often fails to impress with attitude. *D. Brace* **h102 §**

MOON EMPEROR 8 b.g. Emperor Jones (USA) – Sir Hollow (USA) (Sir Ivor (USA)) [2004/5 h99: c20d c17dpu Dec 13] close-coupled gelding: fair on Flat (stays 2m) nowadays: fair hurdler: seventh of 8 in slowly-run novice at Huntingdon on completed outing over fences: should prove effective at 2½m: acts on soft going. *J. R. Jenkins* **c99 h–**

MOONHAMMER 6 ch.g. Karinga Bay – Binny Grove (Sunyboy) [2004/5 F16m3 Apr 2] sturdy gelding: fifth foal: brother to winning hurdler/chaser Binny Bay, stays 21f, and half-brother to bumper winner Dorans Grove (by Gildoran): dam bumper winner/ poor novice hurdler: 50/1, 2¾ lengths third of 21 to Hi Humpfree in bumper at Newbury on debut. *N. J. Gifford* **F98**

MOONLIT HARBOUR 6 b.g. Bal Harbour – Nuit de Lune (FR) (Crystal Palace (FR)) [2004/5 h109, F93: 20d2 c16d4 Oct 31] medium-sized gelding: fairly useful hurdler: sold out of M. Easterby's stable 37,000 gns Doncaster August Sales after first start: encouraging fourth in maiden at Huntingdon on chasing debut: will stay beyond 2½m: acts on soft and good to firm going. *Ferdy Murphy* **c110 h117**

MOONLIT KNIGHT 6 gr.g. Sadler's Way – Sunlit (Warpath) [2004/5 F16s5 F17s 20spu Dec 4] workmanlike gelding: eighth foal: half-brother to fair hurdler Brancher (by Lyphento), stayed 2½m: dam stoutly-bred novice hurdler: no form in 2 bumpers or novice hurdle. *H. J. Manners* **h– F–**

MOON MIST 7 gr.m. Accondy (IRE) – Lillies Brig (New Brig) [2004/5 h–: c17v3 c25v4 c24dpu c25v2 c25v3 c25v5 c25dpu c25v* c29s Mar 12] tall mare: little form over hurdles: poor handicap chaser: won at Ayr in February: should stay beyond 25f: raced on going softer than good (acts on heavy). *N. W. Alexander* **c84 h–**

MOON RIVER WONDER (IRE) 9 b.g. Doyoun – Bayazida (Bustino) [2004/5 22gpu Dec 14] smallish gelding: little form over hurdles, off over 4 years prior to only start (visored) in 2004/5: headstrong. *B. G. Powell* **h–**

MOON SHOT 9 gr.g. Pistolet Bleu (IRE) – La Luna (USA) (Lyphard (USA)) [2004/5 c16s6 Dec 28] fairly useful handicap hurdler at one time: still fair on Flat, won early in 2004: last of 6 in novice handicap on chasing debut: raced at 2m: acts on good to soft and good to firm ground: has had tongue tied. *A. G. Juckes* **c– h–**

MOON SPINNER 8 b.m. Elmaamul (USA) – Lunabelle (Idiot's Delight) [2004/5 h81§: 18m 22g4 20mur 20mpu 20g6 16g 16g 24m 20g4 20m2 Aug 30] leggy mare: modest **h92 §**

hurdler on her day: claimed by A. Reid £6,000 final start: stays 21f: acts on soft and good to firm going: has worn cheekpieces: tried tongue tied: weak finisher, and not one to trust. *Mrs A. M. Thorpe*

MOONSTREAM 5 b.g. Terimon – Lunabelle (Idiot's Delight) [2004/5 F102: 16d^{2} 16d^{pu} Dec 29] leggy gelding: won both starts in bumpers: second to Only Vintage in maiden at Newbury on hurdling debut: fatally injured there next time. *N. J. Henderson* **h122**

MOORAMANA 6 ch.g. Alflora (IRE) – Petit Primitive (Primitive Rising (USA)) [2004/5 F93: 19m^{2} 23v^{4} 18v 20s^{6} Apr 20] good-topped gelding: fourth in bumpers: modest form first 2 starts over hurdles: likely to prove best short of 23f. *P. Beaumont* **h88**

MOORE APPEAL 8 b.m. Homo Sapien – Star Leader (Kafu) [2004/5 20m^{rtr} 20g^{pu} Jun 3] sparely-made mare: showed lot more temperament than ability in 2 novice hurdles: one to avoid. *C. W. Moore* **h§§**

MOORESINI (IRE) 5 b.g. Dr Massini (IRE) – Mooreshill (IRE) (Le Moss) [2004/5 F18s^{3} Feb 14] €17,000 4-y-o: fifth foal: half-brother to 2 winning hurdlers by Lord Americo, fairly useful Lord Olympia, stays 2¾m, and fair Moores Light, stayed 2½m: dam unraced half-sister to high-class staying chaser Simon Legree: never-dangerous third in bumper at Plumpton on debut. *N. J. Gifford* **F86**

MOORLAND MONARCH 7 b.g. Morpeth – Moorland Nell (Neltino) [2004/5 h84, F89?: 27g^{pu} 22d 16s^{6} c19s^{2} c20v^{5} Mar 1] poor maiden hurdler: similar form on first of 2 starts in novice chases: stays 2¾m: acts on soft going (bumper form on good to firm). *J. D. Frost* **c75 ? h69**

MOORLANDS AGAIN 10 b.g. Then Again – Sandford Springs (USA) (Robellino (USA)) [2004/5 20s^{co} 21g^{2} 21d^{5} Nov 14] good-topped gelding: fairly useful chaser in 2002/3: ran out in point in 2004: lightly-raced novice hurdler, fair form on completed starts in 2004/5: stays 4m: acts on heavy going: tends to jump right. *T. R. George* **c– h112**

MOORLANDS MILLY 4 b.f. Sooty Tern – Sandford Springs (USA) (Robellino (USA)) [2004/5 F17s^{5} F13s F16d Mar 3] fourth foal: half-sister to 2 winners by Then Again, including fairly useful chaser Moorlands Again, stays 4m, and to bumper winner Moorlands Return (by Bob's Return): dam 11f winner: little form in bumpers. *C. L. Tizzard* **F73**

MOORLANDS RETURN 6 b.g. Bob's Return (IRE) – Sandford Springs (USA) (Robellino (USA)) [2004/5 F98: 21s 21d^{4} 24d^{4} Jan 7] big, workmanlike gelding: won first of 2 starts in bumpers: modest form at best in 3 starts over hurdles: should prove best at 2½m+. *C. L. Tizzard* **h91**

MOOR LANE 13 b.g. Primitive Rising (USA) – Navos (Tyrnavos) [2004/5 c125: c24s^{3} c24d* c24s^{ur} c24s^{5} Apr 16] tall gelding: fairly useful hunter chaser nowadays: won at Sandown in March easily by 18 lengths from Indien du Boulay: should stay beyond 3m: acts on soft and good to firm going: tried visored: usually races prominently. *A. M. Balding* **c104**

MOORLAW (IRE) 4 b.g. Mtoto – Belle Etoile (FR) (Lead On Time (USA)) [2004/5 16m 16f^{2} 16g^{F} 16d^{4} 16g^{pu} 17d^{5} 17g^{2} Mar 9] angular gelding: well held in 1m maiden at 2 yrs for J. Osborne: fair juvenile hurdler: sold out of N. Henderson's stable 15,000 gns Doncaster November Sales after fourth start: best effort when runner-up in maiden at Bangor: raced around 2m: acts on firm and good to soft ground. *D. McCain* **h102**

MOOR SPIRIT 8 b.g. Nomadic Way (USA) – Navos (Tyrnavos) [2004/5 c63, h–, F–: c21d c16d* c20m^{2} c24g* Dec 29] good-topped gelding: no form over hurdles: modest novice chaser: successful at Southwell (handicap) in November and Musselburgh in December: effective at 2m to 3m: acts on good to firm and good to soft going: has worn blinkers: sound jumper. *P. Beaumont* **c99 h–**

MOOSE MALLOY 8 ch.g. Formidable (USA) – Jolimo (Fortissimo) [2004/5 h–§: 17v^{5} 16s^{5} 22s^{6} Nov 18] workmanlike gelding: bad maiden hurdler: tried blinkered/in cheekpieces: ungenuine. *M. J. Ryan* **h– §**

MORAL JUSTICE (IRE) 12 b.g. Lafontaine (USA) – Proven Right (IRE) (Kemal (FR)) [2004/5 c94, h–: c19m^{F} c21m c21g^{6} c21g^{pu} c19m^{5} c24f^{5} Sep 26] good-topped gelding: handicap chaser: no show in 2004/5: stays 25f: raced mainly on good going or firmer (acts on firm): tried visored/in cheekpieces. *S. J. Gilmore* **c– h–**

MORATORIUM (USA) 10 b.g. El Gran Senor (USA) – Substance (USA) (Diesis) [2004/5 h109: 16g 16m 16m Jun 13] close-coupled gelding: handicap hurdler: fair form in 2004/5: best around 2m: acts on firm and good to soft going: formerly blinkered and tongue tied: takes good hold. *N. Meade, Ireland* **h111**

MORE HANKY PANKY (IRE) 7 b.g. King's Ride – Melarka (Dara Monarch) [2004/5 F17s6 21s 19s c20spu Mar 14] 40,000 4-y-o, 5,500 6-y-o: sixth foal: brother to bumper winners No Shenanigans and Kingfisher Flyer, former useful: dam, placed over hurdles/1m winner in Ireland, half-sister to useful hurdler up to 2¾m Koshear: no form in varied events. *R. Lee* **c– h– F–**

MORELUCK (IRE) 9 b.g. Roselier (FR) – Vulcan Belle (Royal Vulcan) [2004/5 c104: c21m6 c26d4 Nov 28] good-topped gelding: fair novice chaser in 2003/4: below form in handicaps in 2004/5: stays 3m: acts on good to soft going: tried in cheekpieces: has twice run as if amiss. *K. C. Bailey* **c95**

MORE RAINBOWS (IRE) 5 b.g. Rainbows For Life (CAN) – Musical Myth (USA) (Crafty Prospector (USA)) [2004/5 h113: 16g 18m* 16fF 16g 16g3 Aug 13] sparely-made gelding: fairly useful on Flat (stays 1½m): similar standard over hurdles, best effort when winning minor event at Navan in May by 6 lengths from Supreme Developer: likely to stay 2½m: acts on firm going. *N. Meade, Ireland* **h116**

MORGAN BE 5 b.g. Alderbrook – Vicie (Old Vic) [2004/5 F16v F16v F16d Jan 29] 15,500 4-y-o: second foal: dam unraced: well held in bumpers. *Mrs L. Williamson* **F–**

MORMOND LASS 5 gr.m. Passing Point (IRE) – Nawtinookey (Uncle Pokey) [2004/5 F16gpu Sep 23] second foal: dam, bad novice hurdler/chaser, stayed 2½m: temperamental display in bumper on debut. *Miss Lucinda V. Russell* **F–**

MORNING PAL (IRE) 6 br.g. Scribano – Morning Clare (IRE) (Over The River (FR)) [2004/5 F17g F17g F16s4 16d 17v5 17g Dec 15] €14,000 3-y-o: workmanlike gelding: second foal: dam unraced, from family of top-class staying chaser Monsieur Le Cure: won maiden Irish point in 2004: well held in bumpers and novice hurdles. *F. Lloyd* **h– F–**

MORRIS PIPER 12 b.g. Long Leave – Miss Cone (Celtic Cone) [2004/5 c–§: c21d6 Mar 10] sturdy gelding: fair pointer, successful in February: little impact in hunter chases since 2000: has had tongue tied. *Mrs R. Partridge* **c– §**

MORSON BOY (USA) 5 b.g. Lear Fan (USA) – Esprit d'Escalier (USA) (Diesis) [2004/5 17d3 16g 19d6 22spu 19s 17g4 16d6 Apr 17] tall gelding: closely related to fairly useful hurdler Spanish John (by Dynaformer), successful up to 3m: smart middle-distance stayer on Flat in 2003, well below best in 2004, left M. Johnston after final start in August: disappointing maiden hurdler: should be suited by further than 19f: raced on good ground or softer: blinkered last 2 starts, also tongue tied final one: weak finisher. *P. F. Nicholls* **h97 §**

MORTAR 6 b.g. Weld – Rockmount Rose (Proverb) [2004/5 aF16g6 F18s Feb 4] fourth foal: dam, modest chaser, stayed 3m: better effort in bumpers when sixth in maiden on polytrack at Lingfield on debut. *J. R. Best* **F79**

MORVERN (IRE) 5 ch.g. Titus Livius (FR) – Scotia Rose (Tap On Wood) [2004/5 h–: c18mpu Sep 21] modest maiden on Flat (stays easy 1½m): no show in juvenile hurdle or maiden chase (finished lame). *J. G. Given* **c– h–**

MOSCOW COURT (IRE) 7 b.g. Moscow Society (USA) – Hogan Stand (Buckskin (FR)) [2004/5 h123, F96: 24m5 c17sur c17s c20dF c20s2 c20dF c24dpu c22s6 Apr 13] fairly useful hurdler in 2003/4: runner-up in maiden at Wexford in November, little other form over fences: stays 3m: probably acts on any going: tongue tied on reappearance: sketchy jumper: sold 16,000 gns Doncaster May Sales. *Mrs J. Harrington, Ireland* **c110 h–**

MOSCOW DANCER (IRE) 8 ch.g. Moscow Society (USA) – Cromhill Lady (Miner's Lamp) [2004/5 h102+: c16v6 18s c16v4 Apr 17] big, strong gelding: fair hurdler: off 15 months, well held in 2004/5, including in 2 maiden chases: should stay beyond 2¼m: raced on good ground or softer (acts on soft). *P. Monteith* **c– h–**

MOSCOW EXECUTIVE 7 b.m. Moscow Society (USA) – Stylish Executive (IRE) (Executive Perk) [2004/5 F17g2 F17m4 F17g5 F16g Dec 9] first foal: dam unraced: modest form in bumpers. *W. M. Brisbourne* **F76**

MOSCOW FIELDS (IRE) 7 ch.g. Moscow Society (USA) – Cloverlady (Decent Fellow) [2004/5 h80: c17d5 Oct 16] tall gelding: poor form in 2 novice hurdles for Miss H. Knight: showed little on chasing debut: has had breathing problems. *K. G. Reveley* **c– h–**

MOSCOW FLYER (IRE) 11 b.g. Moscow Society (USA) – Meelick Lady (IRE) (Duky) [2004/5 c183, h–: c16g* c16s* c16d* c16v* c16g* c20d* Apr 8] **c184 + h–**

'In the 'sixties, I was one of the best players around. You have your moment of glory and then it fades. Mind you, they'll never say that about Muhammad Ali!' BBC golfing commentator Peter Alliss displayed his appreciation of the universal

Ballymore Properties Fortria Chase, Navan—
Moscow Flyer warms up for the campaign; behind, Rathgar Beau is about to depart at the last

truth that all but the legendary sporting heroes eventually fade from the public consciousness. It is rare for sporting fame to endure much beyond its natural span, as it will with Muhammad Ali, or has, to close followers of Alliss' own sport, with such as Harry Vardon, Bobby Jones and Arnold Palmer. Easter Hero, Golden Miller, Arkle, Red Rum and Desert Orchid are among steeplechasers in a similar category. Theirs is the nearest to immortality that a racehorse can achieve. Brilliant performers, however, even of the recent past, are sometimes forgotten and only time will tell whether Moscow Flyer and his three superb contemporaries among the chasers of 2004/5, Azertyuiop, Kicking King and Well Chief, will achieve legendary status. In terms of ability, they deserve to be remembered, as does a season which is unique in the era of *Chasers & Hurdlers* in featuring four horses rated above 180. The best of the quartet, Moscow Flyer, is Timeform's champion jumper and highest rated chaser for the second year running. He is a phenomenon among steeplechasers, winner of nineteen of his twenty completed starts over fences. But for the fact that two-milers do not always get the recognition they deserve, Moscow Flyer would be assured of a place among the all-time greats. On form, only Desert Orchid has stronger claims to that overused mantle 'the greatest steeplechaser since Arkle'.

For those jumping devotees who tend to assume that the glories of the past supersede those of the present, the Timeform view of Moscow Flyer's exalted status may come as a surprise. It will certainly surprise general sports enthusiasts for whom Cheltenham Gold Cup winners and Grand National winners are the be-all and end-all of steeplechasing. Desert Orchid's sparkling career, which included a record four wins in the King George VI Chase, featured numerous performances superior, on form, to his hard-fought victory in the 1989 Cheltenham Gold Cup, yet his duel in the mud with Yahoo was voted the 'greatest race of all time' in a *Racing Post* poll in the latest season (Red Rum's Grand National victory over Crisp came second, Grundy's battle with Bustino in the King George VI and Queen Elizabeth Stakes third). The widespread lament for Best Mate's enforced absence from the latest Gold Cup was further clear evidence of the race's hold on the public imagination. Had a similar fate befallen Moscow Flyer before the Queen Mother Champion Chase, the news would almost certainly have been confined to the racing pages.

It would be trite to reiterate the reasons usually given by those who say it is impossible to compare sporting figures from different eras. One most often used, though, is the difficulty of assessing the quality of the opposition faced by respective protagonists from different generations. There should never be any such reservation about the quality of opposition faced by Moscow Flyer. Like Moscow Flyer himself, Azertyuiop and Well Chief are among the top dozen chasers seen over any distance since the *Chasers & Hurdlers* series began thirty years ago. Using Timeform ratings from the *Timeform Black Book* series between 1962/63 and 1974/75, and ratings compiled on the Timeform scale by Randall and Morris for *A Century of Champions*, it is possible to arrive at an authoritative list of the top chasers since the beginning of the twentieth century. Moscow Flyer, Azertyuiop and Well Chief all make the top twenty (as do Kicking King and, at his peak, Best Mate).

The clash of Moscow Flyer, Azertyuiop and Well Chief in the latest Queen Mother Champion Chase—'the race of the Festival'—would have been even more of a marketing man's dream had it not already taken place at Sandown back in December. Moscow Flyer and Azertyuiop, each an outstanding winner of the Queen Mother Champion Chase, had met twice the previous season, Moscow Flyer beating Azertyuiop convincingly in the Tingle Creek but parting company with his rider at Cheltenham and leaving Azertyuiop to come home a nine-length winner of the Queen Mother Champion Chase, giving one of the best performances in the race in recent times. The question of which was the better looked likely to be settled in the latest William Hill-Tingle Creek, the mid-season championship for the two-milers. Azertyuiop was said by his trainer to have been '12 kilos heavy' when beaten in the race by Moscow Flyer twelve months earlier, but there could be no excuses on the score of fitness this time. Azertyuiop had warmed up for Sandown with a tip-top performance—winning by five lengths under top weight—in the Haldon Gold Cup at Exeter (a limited handicap in which he had slipped and unseated his rider at the first the year before). Moscow Flyer arrived at Sandown, as he had twelve months earlier, with a straightforward victory under his belt at odds on in the Ballymore Properties Fortria Chase at Navan in November (he won by twenty-five lengths after the last-fence departure of closest challenger Rathgar Beau). The betting public sided with the younger Azertyuiop at Sandown, the market going 6/5-on Azertyuiop, 2/1 Moscow Flyer, with the previous year's Arkle winner Well Chief at 6/1, Azertyuiop's stable-companion Cenkos (winner of the race in 2002 when a hampered Moscow Flyer unseated his rider) at 25/1 and 80/1 bar in a field of seven. The race, which carried prize money down to sixth, was reopened after only the four named were originally entered. In a concession to Channel 4's schedule, Sandown dropped the parade stipulated in the conditions, a spectacle popular with racegoers involving the runners being led past the stands before being allowed to canter down.

William Hill-Tingle Creek Trophy Chase, Sandown—
three outstanding chasers; Azertyuiop (right) and Well Chief fight out second

Queen Mother Champion Chase, Cheltenham—
making amends for 2004, Moscow Flyer wins the race for the second time

And so to a race that will live long in the memory of the crowd, at 16,300 one of the biggest in Sandown's history and said to be larger than for any all-jumping card at the course. What was billed as a 'head-to-head' in the Tingle Creek turned into a three-way battle, Well Chief managing to bridge the considerable gap from leading novice to championship contender with a much improved performance which saw him right in contention turning for home. Azertyuiop's jockey had made the first move in the Champion Chase, but he decided to stalk Moscow Flyer in the Tingle Creek, the latter taking over from the front-running Cenkos four out. As in the previous year, Moscow Flyer was never going to be beaten once he established himself in front, especially after being much more fluent than Azertyuiop at the third last. Moscow Flyer produced excellent jumps at the last two fences for good measure and went on to win by a length and a half and a short head, giving the impression he could have found more had it been required. Azertyuiop briefly lost second to Well Chief at the last before rallying on the flat, the first three twenty-five lengths clear of fourth-placed Cenkos in a race that wasn't run at a particularly searching gallop. There was some criticism of Azertyuiop's rider for not harrying Moscow Flyer earlier, but there was no doubt that the best horse on the day had won. Moscow Flyer was simply superb, the first three all putting up performances of outstanding merit in an epic encounter that proved to be the race of the season.

A challenge for the King George VI Chase at Kempton was thought to be on the cards for Moscow Flyer, but prospects receded in the aftermath of the Tingle Creek. Though said to have returned completely unscathed from Sandown ('as if he had never had a race'), a second visit to Britain for a big event in the space of three weeks was considered, on reflection, possibly too much. It was also announced that, with the Champion Chase top of the agenda, it would be best to keep Moscow Flyer at two miles until after the Cheltenham Festival. Plans to run him at Christmas instead for a third successive win in the Paddy Power Dial-A-Bet Chase at Leopardstown were scotched when he was a late withdrawal, a small amount of mucus found in his lungs. Moscow Flyer's only outing between the Tingle Creek and the Cheltenham Festival came in the Byrne Group plc Tied Cottage Chase at Punchestown at the end of January where he completed a simple task in workmanlike fashion, starting at 11/2-on and not needing to run within two stone of his best form against four opponents. Well Chief paid a tremendous compliment to the Tingle Creek form in the Victor Chandler Chase at Cheltenham the same weekend, conceding weight all round and putting up a performance which ranked as one of the best in a handicap in recent times. He won by a length and three quarters from the favourite Thisthatandtother, who was in receipt of 20 lb, a performance even better than Azertyuiop's in the Haldon Gold Cup. Azertyuiop's performance in the previous season's Victor Chandler (at Ascot) had earned him his Timeform rating of 182. In going down by a neck that day, conceding 19 lb to the winner Isio (out of action in the latest season with a recurrence of a joint injury), Azertyuiop put up—by our reckoning—the equal best performance (with Carvill's Hill's in the 1991 Welsh National) seen in a handicap since Desert Orchid's breathtaking eight-length victory under 12-3 in the 1990 Racing Post Chase (worth a rating of 187). Azertyuiop's preparation for the latest Queen Mother Champion Chase took in two races after the Tingle Creek, the first of them a surprise appearance in the King George VI Chase in which the form of his creditable third to Kicking King in a vintage edition would have been good enough to have won five of the seven previous renewals. Azertyuiop was then put back to two miles in the Game Spirit Chase at Newbury in February. Well Chief, in receipt of 4 lb, took him on but Azertyuiop recorded another outstanding performance to beat him by two and a half lengths, the pair a long way clear of the four other runners.

There was a field of eight for the Queen Mother Champion Chase, Moscow Flyer (6/4), Azertyuiop (2/1) and Well Chief (7/2) standing out. The progressive Oneway, unbeaten in five handicaps in the current season, and Central House, winner of the Grade 1 Dial-A-Bet Chase at Christmas in the absence of Moscow Flyer and beaten only once in his last four outings, started at 16/1 and 25/1 respectively, with Venn Ottery (fifth in the race the year before) at 50/1 and Azertyuiop's stable-companions Kadarann and Cenkos (in the frame in the last three editions) at 100/1. One of jumping's most endearing qualities is that its stars tend to be around for longer than their counterparts on the Flat. Although the top jumpers return season after season, however, only Royal Relief had regained the two-mile championship at Cheltenham since it was first run in 1959. He won the Champion Chase as an eight-year-old and, after coming second at nine, won it for a second time at the age of ten (Royal Relief made eight appearances in the race in all, also finishing second on two other occasions and third once). Ten is towards the top of the age range for a Champion Chase winner, but Skymas was eleven when he won in 1976 and Moscow Flyer emulated him when producing another magnificent display in the latest edition. Unfortunately, for the second year running, an eagerly-anticipated close duel between Moscow Flyer and Azertyuiop at Cheltenham did not materialise, Azertyuiop's winning chance effectively ended by a bad mistake at the water, the sixth fence. Moscow Flyer travelled strongly just behind the leaders

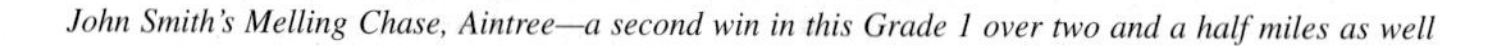

John Smith's Melling Chase, Aintree—a second win in this Grade 1 over two and a half miles as well

Clarkson
4

Kerrygold Champion Chase, Punchestown—even Homer nods: the mistake two out which contributes to Moscow Flyer's first defeat in twenty completed starts over fences

Central House and Kadarann from the start, jumping well except for getting in close four from home (the fence at which he departed the previous year). Leading at the third last, Moscow Flyer was chased all the way from that point by Well Chief, always looking in command and winning by two lengths, with Azertyuiop (subsequently found to have pulled muscles in his abdomen) thirteen lengths behind Well Chief in third and seven lengths ahead of fourth-placed Oneway. Moscow Flyer, mobbed by well-wishers and euphoric Irish racegoers waving the country's tricolour, received a stirring ovation on his return to the unsaddling enclosure where his jockey Barry Geraghty executed a Frankie Dettori-style flying dismount. The celebrations must have gone on well into the night, none presumably more enthusiastic than those at Seven Barrows where Moscow Flyer's trainer was a house guest of Nicky Henderson, whose stable had two winners on the same card.

Moscow Flyer extended his unbeaten record in races completed over fences to nineteen with a second successive victory in Aintree's two-and-a-half-mile Melling Chase, carrying the name of new Grand National sponsors John Smith's for the first time. Moscow Flyer turned the six-runner event into an exhibition, hardly turning a hair in landing the odds by sixteen lengths from Le Roi Miguel. Moscow Flyer misjudged the second fence in the Melling, getting in a shade too close, but it was the only semblance of a mistake that he made. The days when perceived flaws in Moscow Flyer's jumping technique were a hot topic of conversation seemed to be behind him. The Melling was his seventh successive victory since the last hiccup at the 2004 Cheltenham Festival. 'It has taken six years but he has finally got there,' joked Moscow Flyer's trainer after the Melling. 'Barry said he is becoming a nice ride and you can settle him. He was always travelling and jumping superbly.' Mrs Harrington spoke too soon. The Kerrygold Champion Chase at Punchestown, shortly after the end of the British season, was billed as another lap of honour for Moscow Flyer who started at 4/1-on in a field of seven which did not include an overseas challenger. Moscow Flyer would not settle in the race, despite a sound pace, and, in front four out, looked like being strongly pressed by Rathgar Beau even before making a monumental blunder at the second last, the same fence at which he had unseated Geraghty in the race two years previously, at a time when lapses in his jumping were in danger of becoming a little too common. Moscow Flyer stayed on his feet in the latest renewal, after handing the advantage to Rathgar Beau, and he rallied gamely from the last to be beaten only a short head. The judge took longer examining the photo-finish print—the result was very close to being a dead-heat—than the race itself had taken. Because of the width of the chase course, Punchestown does not have 'mirror image' facilities for photo finishes, and it isn't altogether clear from the official print that Moscow Flyer was beaten.

One below-form effort (Moscow Flyer was way below his best at Punchestown) at the end of a full campaign should not be allowed to detract from a season of magnificent achievement. Moscow Flyer will hopefully be back as good as ever in the next season. Azertyuiop is sadly facing a lengthy spell on the sidelines through injury, but Moscow Flyer will still face stiff opposition from Well Chief, who has age on his side. Five years Well Chief's senior, Moscow Flyer will have to be at his peak, if a top-form Well Chief is in the line-up, to record a third victory in the Tingle Creek and in the Champion Chase. He will be twelve when the Cheltenham Festival comes around again but Skymas retained the two-mile championship at that age and Moscow Flyer will still be the one to beat if he keeps his form and steers clear of illness and injury. It must be in his favour that he didn't appear on a racecourse until he was five, incidentally failing to win on any of his four outings in bumpers in his first season. The latest season was only Moscow Flyer's fourth in steeplechases and there were precious few signs of his reaching his limit. In all, he has won twenty-six races from forty-one starts over jumps (including the four in bumpers), covering seven seasons. Moscow Flyer's two seasons over hurdles included victories in the December Festival Hurdle and the Shell Champion Hurdle, in both of which Istabraq fell. Moscow Flyer would have beaten him anyway in the first-named and, though Istabraq had taken his measure on the second occasion, Moscow Flyer still showed form in the Shell Champion Hurdle better than any shown by his contemporaries among the two-mile hurdlers in Britain. Moscow Flyer would have been good enough to win a Champion Hurdle in an average year but he had the physique of a chaser and it was always likely he would be switched to fences sooner rather than later. His record in steeplechases stands at nineteen wins from twenty-five starts. He has fallen twice (which he also did once in his hurdling days) and unseated his rider three times, but he is mostly a fast and accurate jumper. Effective at two miles to two and a half, Moscow Flyer seems unlikely now to get a crack at the King George VI Chase, especially as the next edition has been transferred to Sandown, a stiffer tack than Kempton which is closed temporarily for the development of a new, all-weather track, jumping set to resume in 2006 on the turf course formerly used for Flat racing. Moscow Flyer acts on good to firm and heavy going and, despite having a marked tendency to idle in front, is game and tremendously reliable.

Moscow Flyer (IRE) (b.g. 1994)	Moscow Society (USA) (ch 1985)	Nijinsky (b 1967)	Northern Dancer
			Flaming Page
		Afifa (ch 1974)	Dewan
			Hooplah
	Meelick Lady (IRE) (b 1988)	Duky (ch 1974)	Midsummer Night II
			Frondia
		Quiet Life (b 1972)	No Argument
			Brambling

The pedigree of the strong, lengthy Moscow Flyer has been dealt with thoroughly in earlier Annuals and the only update is that his younger sister Blooming Quick, who fetched €215,000, a record for a store filly, as a three-year-old at the 2002 Derby Sale, belied her name when managing only seventh of twenty-four

Mr Brian Kearney's "Moscow Flyer"

finishers in a bumper at Punchestown in May on her only start so far. The career of Moscow Flyer's sire Moscow Society, who stands in County Limerick, has enjoyed an upturn in recent years and he is now averaging over one hundred and thirty mares a season. Moscow Flyer's dam Meelick Lady, who is now dead, never ran but is from a well-known jumping family, her own dam the winning hurdler/chaser Quiet Life being out of Brambling, a half-sister to the 1959 Champion Hurdle runner-up Ivy Green, the Great Yorkshire Chase winner Bramble Tudor and another winning hurdler/chaser Indicate, the dam of Artic Ale and the unraced Bardicate, dam in turn of the useful-or-better staying chasers Green Bramble, Deviner, Polyfemus and Deep Bramble. Moscow Flyer's breeders now have his Over The River half-sister Meelick Lass at stud. She produced colt foals by Carroll House in 2001 and Lord Americo in 2003. *Mrs J. Harrington, Ireland*

MOSCOW GOLD (IRE) 8 ch.g. Moscow Society (USA) – Vesper Time (The Parson) [2004/5 c–, h–: c16g c20m6 24m Aug 6] big gelding: no form: tried blinkered/in cheekpieces: has had tongue tied. *A. E. Price* **c– h–**

MOSCOW LEADER (IRE) 7 ch.g. Moscow Society (USA) – Catrionas Castle (IRE) (Orchestra) [2004/5 c105, h102: c25gpu c25g4 c21d3 Aug 30] sturdy gelding: fair handicap hurdler/chaser, below form in 2004/5: will stay beyond 3¼m: acts on any going: usually wears cheekpieces. *R. C. Guest* **c90 h–**

MOSCOW WHISPER (IRE) 8 b.g. Moscow Society (USA) – Native Woodfire (IRE) (Mister Majestic) [2004/5 h96: 21d4 22d3 24d2 24d5 c24g2 c22gF Apr 19] lengthy, angular gelding: fair handicap hurdler, often let down by jumping: not fluent when 8 lengths second to Red Devil Robert at Taunton on completed start in maiden chases: stays 3m: acts on good to firm and good to soft going. *P. J. Hobbs* **c95 h110 x**

MOSLOB (IRE) 8 b.g. Black Monday – Musical Millie (IRE) (Orchestra) [2004/5 c–, h–: c20d5 c26dpu Dec 5] good-topped gelding: little form. *Miss J. S. Davis* **c– h–**

MOSSAR (FR) 5 b.g. Passing Sale (FR) – Beatty's (FR) (Sharken (FR)) [2004/5 19g 18s 16gpu Mar 28] close-coupled gelding: third foal: dam, placed over 1½m on Flat, from family of smart 2m chaser Hot Shots and good French chaser French Kankan: no sign of ability. *A. Ennis* **h–**

MOSS CAMPIAN 7 ch.g. Le Moss – Rose Rambler (Scallywag) [2004/5 h–, F–: 16g 22gpu Jul 29] no form outside points. *M. J. Gingell* **h–**

MOSSCOW REALITY 12 ch.m. Le Moss – La Verite (Vitiges (FR)) [2004/5 h–: 24d May 15] lengthy mare: lightly-raced maiden hurdler. *M. D. McMillan* **h–**

MOSS HARVEY 10 ch.g. Le Moss – Wings Ground (Murrayfield) [2004/5 c125, h–: c22g3 c25v* c26s c24sur 23s 20dpu Feb 24] lengthy gelding: winning hurdler: fairly useful handicap chaser: won at Market Rasen in October by 3½ lengths from Boy's Hurrah: no show after, including back over hurdles: stays 25f: raced on good going or softer (acts on heavy): wore cheekpieces fifth start, visor final one: bled from nose final start: has jumped markedly right over fences. *J. M. Jefferson* **c127 h–**

MOSS RUN (IRE) 11 b.g. Commanche Run – Glenreigh Moss (Le Moss) [2004/5 h76: 22d4 22m c21sF 24g 22s4 21g* 21d5 26s3 22dur 26g 21m Apr 13] good-bodied gelding: fell fifth on chasing debut: modest handicap hurdler: won conditional jockeys event at Huntingdon in January: stays 3¼m: acts on soft and good to firm going. *A. E. Jessop* **c– h88**

MOSSY GREEN (IRE) 11 b.g. Moscow Society (USA) – Green Ajo (Green Shoon) [2004/5 c150, h–: c20s2 c20s5 18d* c21dpu c18v3 c18d* 16s3 Mar 28] lengthy, workmanlike gelding: fairly useful hurdler: won minor event at Fairyhouse in November by 3 lengths from Augherskea: better over fences, won similar contest at Thurles in March comfortably by 12 lengths from Alcapone: creditable sixth to Rathgar Beau in Grade 1 at Punchestown in late-April: effective around 2m, will stay 3m: raced on good going or softer (acts on heavy): often front runner: sometimes let down by jumping over fences. *W. P. Mullins, Ireland* **c139 h128**

MOSTAKBEL (USA) 6 b. or br.g. Saint Ballado (CAN) – Shamlegh (USA) (Flying Paster (USA)) [2004/5 F85: F16d Jan 31] tall gelding: fair form in 2 bumpers 17 months apart. *M. D. I. Usher* **F85**

MOTCOMBE (IRE) 7 ch.m. Carroll House – Cooks Lawn (The Parson) [2004/5 h90, F76: 24v5 c26d4 c26dF c25s2 c23v3 c25sur c24v2 Mar 29] good-bodied mare: modest hurdler: similar form on completed starts over fences: stays 3¼m: acts on heavy ground: visored last 2 outings. *R. H. Alner* **c90 h–**

MOTCOMB JAM (IRE) 8 b.g. Frimaire – Flying Flo Jo (USA) (Aloma's Ruler (USA)) [2004/5 c116, h–: c20g^{ur} c20m^{2} c20g^{pu} c21g^{F} Aug 10] rather leggy gelding: fair chaser: well held in point in January: stays 21f: acts on good to soft and good to firm going: wore blinkers/cheekpieces in 2004/5. *C. J. Mann* **c112 h–**

MOTHER SAYS 9 b.g. Landyap (USA) – Miami Blues (Palm Track) [2004/5 19d c24d^{pu} Jan 31] lengthy gelding: no show in novice hurdle or chase. *D. L. Williams* **c– h–**

MOTIVE (FR) 4 ch.g. Machiavellian (USA) – Mistle Song (Nashwan (USA)) [2004/5 16g^{F} 16g^{2} 16g* 16s^{pu} Apr 7] sturdy, lengthy gelding: fairly useful on Flat (should stay 1½m), sold out of Sir Michael Stoute's stable 120,000 gns Newmarket Autumn Sales: best effort over hurdles when winning novice at Catterick in March by 1½ lengths from Beamish Prince: pulled up amiss in Grade 1 juvenile at Aintree: should progress further if none the worse. *J. Howard Johnson* **h109 p**

MOULIN RICHE (FR) 5 b.g. Video Rock (FR) – Gintonique (FR) (Royal Charter (FR)) [2004/5 h118+: 18v^{4} 19d* c17s* c17s^{F} c17s^{6} c19s^{2} c20v* 20s^{6} 23s^{2} 24g* 24d^{4} Apr 8] **c120 p h146**

Novice hurdlers in need of further than two miles now have a choice of engagements at the Cheltenham Festival, with the addition of the Grade 2 three-mile Spa Novices' Hurdle, sponsored by Brit Insurance, to the long-standing Grade 1 Royal & SunAlliance Novices' over three furlongs shorter. The first running of the new race did little to detract from the competitiveness of the SunAlliance and drew eighteen runners, compared to twenty in the shorter event. In terms of quality, the Spa (worth £14,500 less to the winner than the SunAlliance) took a little less winning, but the first four home still showed useful form. Although the SunAlliance has been won by future Champion Hurdle winners Istabraq and Hardy Eustace in recent seasons, it has also been a notable nursery for future chasers over the years, with Alexander Banquet, Behrajan, Bindaree, Farmer Jack, Foxchapel King, Hi Cloy, Irish Hussar, Keen Leader, King's Road, Lord Sam, Pizarro, Puntal and Supreme Prince among those to have contested renewals before going on to greater things over fences. Had the choice then been available to them, it's a near certainty that several of those would have taken up the three-mile option instead. Significantly, the first five home in the first running of the Spa all look the sort to do well over fences, whereas the SunAlliance was unusually sparse in chasing types; indeed, four of the first six home in that race had shown at least useful form on the Flat. That was surely no coincidence and, while it is too soon to conclude that this will happen to the same extent every year, it would be no surprise if the Spa takes over the SunAlliance's mantle as the Festival's race for embryonic staying chasers.

The inaugural winner of the Spa, Moulin Riche, would almost certainly have struggled in the SunAlliance, as it was only when stepped up to three miles that he really came into his own. On his first start in Britain in the latest season, Moulin Riche finished only sixth, not helped by a bad mistake, behind fellow French raider Ambobo in the Royal Gloucestershire Hussars Novices' Hurdle over an extended two and a half miles at Cheltenham. Moved up in trip for another

Brit Insurance Spa Novices' Hurdle, Cheltenham—an exciting inaugural running sees Moulin Riche, Brewster and the grey Bob Bob Bobbin in line at the last; runner-up Over The Creek is out of shot

Grade 2 contest, the Prestige Novices' Hurdle at Haydock, Moulin Riche ran a much better race but was unable to turn the tables on Mephisto (third at Cheltenham), to whom he was conceding weight again, going down by three lengths to the most impressive winner. Mephisto's connections relied on Bewley's Berry instead in the Spa, and he, along with other last-time-out winners Over The Creek and Thames, were preferred in the betting to 9/1-shot Moulin Riche, behind the 9/4 favourite Brewster. Moulin Riche travelled smoothly throughout, held up off a pace that did not really pick up until early on the final circuit. Having avoided the bunching that caused Bewley's Berry's fall at the fifth, Moulin Riche made his only mistake three out but it cost him no momentum and, still going well, he was given a lead round the final turn by Bob Bob Bobbin and Brewster. Taking it up before the last, Moulin Riche was always in control from then on and ran out a two-and-a-half-length winner from the staying-on Over The Creek, with Brewster a neck back in third and Bob Bob Bobbin three lengths away fourth. Moulin Riche gave jockey Robert Thornton a last-day double, after he had won the Triumph Hurdle on Penzance, to go with his win on Kelami, like Moulin Riche also trained by Francois Doumen, in the William Hill Trophy on the opening day of the Festival. Thornton only lost the title of leading rider at the meeting because he had fewer placed rides than Graham Lee. Moulin Riche started favourite when taking on Brewster and Bewley's Berry again in the Sefton Novices' Hurdle at Aintree three weeks later, but a steady pace did not suit him and he finished a remote fourth to the Irish mare Asian Maze, with Brewster second.

Moulin Riche had made a couple of appearances in Britain the previous season, including when seventh in the Triumph Hurdle, but he had spent most of 2004 competing in France. He won a listed handicap hurdle for four-year-olds at Auteuil in June and returned from a summer break to win twice more at the same track from five starts over fences in the autumn. With son Thierry now retired from race riding, Francois Doumen initially took on Dean Gallagher as stable jockey. Now based in France, Gallagher, who had ridden the then Doumen-trained Hors La Loi III to finish second in the 2000 Champion Hurdle, was back from serving an eighteen-month ban after testing positive for cocaine, and Moulin Riche got the new partnership off to a good start when making a successful debut over fences in September. Further successes for the association followed, including with L'Ami in the December Novices' Chase at Lingfield, but the pair split soon afterwards when Gallagher signed a contract to ride for the numerically stronger Francois Cottin stable.

It is little wonder that Moulin Riche has needed a good test of stamina to show his best form, as he is bred on similar lines to the Welsh National winner Edmond. They are both by Video Rock, and Edmond is a half-brother to Moulin Riche's great grandam Nalia. This is a stoutly-bred selle francais family, though each of the mares on the bottom line of Moulin Riche's pedigree did their winning in non-thoroughbred events on the Flat and were given few opportunities over jumps. Moulin Riche's dam Gintonique won four times at up to a mile and three quarters and was placed on her only two outings over hurdles. Moulin Riche, her first foal, won his only start on the Flat before being sent hurdling, and his year-younger half-sister Nilaya (by Ragmar) has also started out on the Flat, being placed on her first three starts in non-thoroughbred races. Gintonique is a half-sister to three winners, the best of them a fairly useful winner over hurdles at Auteuil, Haitza, she too by Video Rock.

Moulin Riche (FR) (b.g. 2000)	Video Rock (FR) (b 1984)	No Lute (b 1978)	Luthier
			Prudent Miss
		Pauvresse (b 1978)	Home Guard
			Misoptimist
	Gintonique (FR) (b 1994)	Royal Charter (gr 1982)	Mill Reef
			Royal Way
		Vodka Tonique (b 1987)	Quart de Vin
			Nalia

The tall, lengthy Moulin Riche gained his second win over fences at Auteuil in a race named the Prix Nupsala in honour of Doumen's 1987 King George VI Chase winner. Surprisingly perhaps, the trainer nominated the King George as a possible race for Moulin Riche in the next season. At this stage, Moulin Riche has a huge amount of improvement over fences to make to warrant a place in the 2005 King George field, though, crucially, he has yet to race beyond two and a half miles over fences and there is every chance that he will prove at least as good a chaser as he is a hurdler when his stamina is tested more fully over the larger obstacles. He has raced only on good going or softer so far and acts on heavy. Moulin Riche has been blinkered a couple of times, the first occasion in the Triumph after he had run out when very short of room on his British debut. *F. Doumen, France*

MOUNSEY CASTLE 8 ch.g. Carlingford Castle – Gay Ticket (New Member) [2004/5 c116, h106: c25gpu c21m6 c24d5 c20g5 c20d c24d6 c24g* Apr 7] good-topped gelding: fairly useful novice chaser in 2003/4: slipped in weights, won handicap at Taunton in April: effective at 2½m to 3m: acts on good to firm and good to soft ground. *P. J. Hobbs* **c108 h–**

MOUNTAIN MIX 5 ch.g. Bigstone (IRE) – Cormorant Bay (Don't Forget Me) [2004/5 F16g May 16] 22,000 3-y-o: half-brother to 3 winners on Flat, including winner up to 1¼m in Germany Dance Again (by Shareef Dancer): dam maiden half-sister to high-class 2m hurdler River Ceiriog and to dam of Inglis Drever: remote seventh in bumper at Worcester on debut. *N. J. Henderson* **F–**

MOUNTAIN SINGER (IRE) 6 b.g. Carroll House – Mountain Grove (Paddy's Stream) [2004/5 F16m F16d F17d F16s 17g Apr 7] good-bodied gelding: fifth foal: half-brother to fairly useful hurdler/chaser Janiste, stayed 3m, and winning 2m hurdler Flaming Lord (both by Lord Americo): dam won up to 2½m over hurdles: well held in bumpers and maiden hurdle. *M. S. Wilesmith* **h– F–**

MOUNT CLARA (IRE) 5 b. or br.g. Norwich – Show M How (Ashmore (FR)) [2004/5 16g 20vpu Feb 2] seventh foal: half-brother to winning staying chasers Alpha Gold (by Alphabatim) and Swansea Gold (by Torus): dam, winning hurdler up to 3m, half-sister to useful middle-distance performer Show-A-Leg: placed once from 4 starts in maiden Irish points in 2004: sold 2,700 gns Doncaster August Sales: no sign of ability in 2 starts over hurdles: sold £600 Ascot April Sales. *F. Kirby* **h–**

MOUNT CLERIGO (IRE) 7 b.g. Supreme Leader – Fair Ava (IRE) (Strong Gale) [2004/5 F121: 16s3 20v* 20v* Jan 15] tall gelding: will make a chaser: smart in bumpers in 2003/4: successful on 2 of 3 starts in novice hurdles, at Uttoxeter in December and Wetherby (beat Secret Ploy 3 lengths) in January: will stay 3m: acts on heavy ground: remains open to improvement. *V. R. A. Dartnall* **h132 p**

MOUNTHENRY (IRE) 5 ch.g. Flemensfirth (USA) – Tudor Lady (Green Shoon) [2004/5 F16v4 F16s5 F18s3 F16s* Mar 28] €26,000 3-y-o: half-brother to several winners, including fairly useful staying chaser/fair hurdler Satshoon (by Satco) and fairly useful hurdler/winning chaser Supreme Lady (by Supreme Leader), stayed 2¾m: dam once-raced, from family of useful chaser up to 3m Church Warden: fairly useful in bumpers: best effort when winning at Cork by 4 lengths from Hurricane Carter: will stay 2½m. *C. Byrnes, Ireland* **F102**

MOUNT KARINGA 7 b.g. Karinga Bay – Candarela (Damister (USA)) [2004/5 h123: c20d2 Nov 13] tall, useful-looking gelding: fairly useful hurdler: promising start over fences when ¾-length second to Vodka Bleu in novice at Cheltenham, tending to jump right: effective at 2m, will stay 3m: acts on good to soft and good to firm going: should progress and win races over fences. *P. F. Nicholls* **c125 + h–**

MOUNT KIMBLE (IRE) 9 b.g. Montelimar (USA) – Sweet Thunder (Le Bavard (FR)) [2004/5 c16g* c16m* c17m5 c20v4 c21g Apr 14] sturdy gelding: fair hurdler: similar form over fences, successful in handicap and novice at Roscommon early in season: sold out of A. Moore's stable 24,000 gns Doncaster November Sales: off 8 months, ran poorly in novice handicap at Cheltenham final start: raced mainly around 2m: acts on good to firm and good to soft ground. *P. Winkworth* **c107 h–**

MOUNT PEKAN (IRE) 5 b.g. Sri Pekan (USA) – The Highlands (FR) (High Line) [2004/5 16s4 16g 16v 16m Dec 1] lengthy, sparely-made gelding: poor maiden on Flat (stays 1m): little worthwhile form over hurdles. *J. S. Goldie* **h–**

MOUNT PRAGUE (IRE) 11 br.g. Lord Americo – Celtic Duchess (Ya Zaman (USA)) [2004/5 c117§, h–: c20m 20m6 c20f5 Sep 26] sturdy gelding: winning hurdler: handicap chaser, below form in 2004/5: stays 3m: acts on heavy and good to firm going: wears cheekpieces: has found little and is not one to rely on. *K. C. Bailey* **c103 § h–**

MOUNTS BAY 6 ch.m. Karinga Bay – Sweet On Willie (USA) (Master Willie) [2004/5 h–, F75: 17g5 22dpu 17s* 17g 19g4 17d3 19d5 19s 16d 19s2 Jan 10] poor hurdler: **h77**

won handicap at Newton Abbot in June: probably stays 19f: acts on soft going: blinkered once. *R. J. Hodges*

MOUNTSORREL (IRE) 6 b.g. Charnwood Forest (IRE) – Play The Queen (IRE) (King of Clubs) [2004/5 h–: c20s^pu Oct 21] no form outside points. *T. Wall* **c– h–**

MOUNT VETTORE 4 br.g. Vettori (IRE) – Honeyspike (IRE) (Chief's Crown (USA)) [2004/5 16m 16g* 16g^4 Jan 21] leggy gelding: fairly useful on Flat (stays 1m), sold out of Mrs J. Ramsden's stable 24,000 gns Newmarket Autumn Sales: modest form in juvenile hurdles: whipped round at start when winning at Musselburgh in December: likely to prove best at sharp 2m. *K. G. Reveley* **h95**

MOUSESKI 11 b.g. Petoski – Worth Matravers (National Trust) [2004/5 c100, h–: c16s* c20g* c24m^F c16s* c18s* c16s^3 c19s* c16s^2 c20s* c20d^6 c21g c21m^5 Apr 13] smallish gelding: winning hurdler: trained by R. Barber first 3 starts, twice successful in hunters at Cheltenham: went on to show considerable improvement in handicap chases, winning at Chepstow (twice), Fontwell and Wetherby (not off bridle to beat Royal Emperor) between October and February: good sixth to Supreme Prince in valuable event at Newbury in March: stays 2½m: acts on soft going. *P. F. Nicholls* **c142 h–**

MOUSTIQUE DE L'ISLE (FR) 5 gr.g. Dom Alco (FR) – Gratiene de L'Isle (FR) (Altayan) [2004/5 F17g^2 F17d^4 20v* 20v^6 25d^3 23v^6 21v^6 Mar 15] 10,000 3-y-o, resold 3,300 3-y-o: leggy, plain gelding: first foal: dam placed up to around 1½m on Flat: in frame in bumpers: modest hurdler: won maiden at Uttoxeter in October: stays 25f: acts on heavy going. *C. C. Bealby* **h92 F87**

MOVIE KING (IRE) 6 ch.g. Catrail (USA) – Marilyn (IRE) (Kings Lake (USA)) [2004/5 16d^6 16g^3 16d^F Jan 13] sturdy gelding: fair on Flat (stays 1¼m): modest form on completed starts in novice hurdles. *S. Gollings* **h89**

MOVING EARTH (IRE) 12 b.g. Brush Aside (USA) – Park Breeze (IRE) (Strong Gale) [2004/5 c124§, h107§: 20d c19s^3 c24d* c24d^3 c24d^2 c24d^6 c24g^5 c20g^6 Apr 17] lengthy gelding: winning hurdler: fairly useful handicap chaser: won at Kempton in November by 2½ lengths from Orswell Crest, despite losing 15 lengths at start: ran well next 2 outings: stays 3m: acts on soft and good to firm going: has had tongue tied: has refused to race several times, and one to treat with caution. *A. W. Carroll* **c121 § h– §**

MOVING ON UP 11 b.g. Salse (USA) – Thundercloud (Electric) [2004/5 19m Apr 17] compact gelding: twice-raced chaser: fairly useful handicap hurdler in 2002/3: off 2 years and left C. Mann, well beaten on return: should stay beyond 21f: acts on heavy and good to firm going: visored once, blinkered nowadays. *C. N. Kellett* **c– h–**

MOYDRUM CASTLE (IRE) 6 b.m. Arctic Lord – Pai-Collect (Paico) [2004/5 F16m^3 16f* 20g^2 24m^2 20m* Aug 8] tenth live foal: half-sister to winning hurdler/chaser up to 3m Wilton Bridge (by Clearly Bust) and winning 2m hurdler Vienna Shop (by Le Johnstan): dam unraced: easily best effort in bumpers when third at Cork on reappearance: improved form over hurdles when winning 4-runner maiden there by 3½ lengths from The Posh Paddy: stays 3m: raced on good going or firmer (acts on firm). *D. Wachman, Ireland* **h110 F93**

MOYGANNON MIST (IRE) 8 b.g. Synefos (USA) – Po Bo Pu (Pollerton) [2004/5 c24g^pu c17g^pu Jul 15] fourth foal: half-brother to one-time fair hurdler/chaser Tom Cobbler (by Zaffaran), stays 27f, and winning hurdler around 2m Bradleys Corner (by Cataldi): dam lightly raced in bumpers: little sign of ability, including in points. *J. J. Lambe, Ireland* **c– h–**

MOYLISCAR 6 b.m. Terimon – Annie Kelly (Oats) [2004/5 c20d^pu c19v^pu c16d^4 c16g^ur c20g^pu c16s^4 Mar 23] lengthy mare: second foal: dam, modest 2m hurdler/chaser, half-sister to dam of fairly useful hurdler Ferimon (by Terimon): unplaced on completed start in Irish points: no form over fences: headstrong. *Capt. J. A. George* **c–**

MR AUCHTERLONIE (IRE) 8 b.g. Mister Lord (USA) – Cahernane Girl (Bargello) [2004/5 h90, F91: 16d 16s c20m^2 c24d^2 c24m^F c20d^pu Mar 26] lengthy gelding: modest maiden hurdler: runner-up in novice chases at Musselburgh in December and January: effective at 2½m, likely to stay beyond 3m: acts on good to firm and good to soft going. *L. Lungo* **c99 h85 +**

MR BABBAGE (IRE) 7 b.g. Carroll House – Winsome Doe (Buckskin (FR)) [2004/5 19s^3 16d 20d* 22s* 20v^4 24s^5 Mar 28] big, rangy gelding: thrice-raced in bumpers: fairly useful hurdler, off 18 months before reappearance: won maiden at Fairyhouse in December and novice at Thurles (by 2½ lengths from Simon) in January: below form after, including in 25-runner handicap at Punchestown in late-April: should stay at least 3m: raced on good going or softer (acts on soft). *W. P. Mullins, Ireland* **h121**

totesport.com Handicap Hurdle, Worcester—Mr Ed has too many guns for the hidden Young American

MR BANKER 10 b.g. Cashwyn – Flaming Fox (Healaugh Fox) [2004/5 c–: c23g4 c21d3 c26d2 c24vpu Feb 5] winning pointer: poor novice chaser: stays 3¼m: acts on good to soft going. *J. C. Tuck* **c80**

MR BAXTER BASICS 14 b.g. Lighter – Phyll-Tarquin (Tarqogan) [2004/5 c129x, h–: c21m5 May 22] tall gelding: veteran handicap chaser: stays easy 3m: acts on any going: makes mistakes: usually weak finisher. *Miss Venetia Williams* **c– x h–**

MR BIGGLESWORTH (NZ) 7 ch.g. Honor Grades (USA) – Panza Anne (NZ) (Sound Reason (CAN)) [2004/5 16d 16g3 16d4 16v2 16s2 16d Apr 11] lengthy gelding: successful up to 10.5f on Flat in New Zealand: fair form over hurdles: raced around 2m on good going or softer. *R. C. Guest* **h101**

MR BOO (IRE) 6 b.g. Needle Gun (IRE) – Dasi (Bonne Noel) [2004/5 h–, F–: 18s4 17d3 16g2 16g* 17dbd 16g3 18g2 20sF3 Mar 30] good-topped gelding: fair novice hurdler: won conditional jockeys handicap at Doncaster in December: will stay 2½m: raced on good going or softer. *G. L. Moore* **h100**

MR BUSBY 12 b.g. La Grange Music – Top-Anna (IRE) (Ela-Mana-Mou) [2004/5 c86, h–: c25gpu c20dpu May 13] strong, lengthy gelding: winning hurdler: maiden chaser: stays 21f: acts on good to firm and heavy going. *Michael Smith* **c– h–**

MR CHRISTIE 13 b.g. Doulab (USA) – Hi There (High Top) [2004/5 c§§, h71§: 24g4 24d2 24d* 23d* 22s4 27d 23v3 26s6 27v6 23sur 24v3 27d5 Apr 5] sturdy gelding: poor handicap hurdler: won at Hexham in June and Wetherby (seller) in November: needs good test of stamina: has form on good to firm going, all wins on softer than good (acts on heavy): tried in headgear: formerly tongue tied: usually gets behind: untrustworthy. *Miss L. C. Siddall* **c§§ h83 §**

MR COOL 11 b.g. Jupiter Island – Laurel Diver (Celtic Cone) [2004/5 c–, h144: 20m Apr 23] workmanlike gelding: winning chaser: useful hurdler in 2003/4: off 14 months, well held in handicap at Sandown: stays 25f: acts on any going: usually forces pace. *M. C. Pipe* **c– h–**

MR COONEY (IRE) 11 b.g. Van Der Linden (FR) – Green Orchid (Green Shoon) [2004/5 h–: c26s^{pu} Apr 21] rangy gelding: winning pointer: no sign of ability otherwise. *James Clements, Ireland* **c–**

MR CRAWFORD 6 b.g. Opera Ghost – Alice Passthorn (Rapid Pass) [2004/5 20g^{pu} 19m^{pu} 22s^{pu} 20v 24d^{pu} Jan 7] sturdy gelding: third foal: brother to bumper winner Complete Outsider: dam no sign of ability: no show in novice hurdles. *Nick Williams* **h–**

MR DINGLAWI (IRE) 4 b.g. Danehill Dancer (IRE) – Princess Leona (IRE) (Naiyli (IRE)) [2004/5 17d^3 18d^3 16s^3 16d^5 18s* 16s* 16g 20s* 21m^4 18s Apr 22] good-topped gelding: lightly-raced maiden on Flat: fairly useful hurdler: won juveniles at Fontwell and Plumpton in February and handicap at Chepstow (best effort, beating Jonanaud by 15 lengths) in March: moody display at Auteuil final start: stays 2½m: acts on soft going. *D. B. Feek* **h124**

MR DON (IRE) 6 b.g. Mister Lord (USA) – Paradiso (IRE) (Phardante (FR)) [2004/5 h–, F–: c26d^{pu} c26d^{pu} Dec 5] tall gelding: no form: tried in cheekpieces. *Mrs A. M. Thorpe* **c– h–**

MR DOW JONES (IRE) 13 b.g. The Bart (USA) – Roseowen (Derring Rose) [2004/5 c113, h110: 27g* 24d^3 27m^2 Jun 6] medium-sized gelding: fair chaser: lightly-raced hurdler, similar form when winning novice at Newton Abbot in April 2004: stays 29f: best form on good going or softer (acts on heavy): tough. *W. K. Goldsworthy* **c– h104**

MR ED (IRE) 7 ch.g. In The Wings – Center Moriches (IRE) (Magical Wonder (USA)) [2004/5 h127+: 24d* 22d* 20s^3 25d 24s^2 Apr 7] tall, good-topped gelding: fairly useful on Flat (stays 2¼m): most progressive hurdler: won well-contested handicaps at Worcester in June and Newton Abbot (by 1½ lengths from Football Crazy) in August, idling both times: off 5 months, smart form when length second to Monet's Garden in Grade 2 at Aintree: effective at 2½m to 3m: acts on firm and soft going: usually wears cheekpieces: patiently ridden. *P. Bowen* **h151**

Mr Gwilym J. Morris' "Mr Ed"

MR FERNET 8 b.g. Mtoto – Francfurter (Legend of France (USA)) [2004/5 16g^{5} 17m^{2} 17m^{4} 16d 19s 19d^{3} 19m^{6} Mar 14] angular gelding: won up to 11f on Flat in Germany for H. Steinmetz: modest novice hurdler: barely stays 19f: acts on good to firm and good to soft going. *C. J. Mann* **h96**

MR FISHER (IRE) 8 ch.g. Toulon – Parthian Opera (Dalsaan) [2004/5 h–: 22g 24s 16d^{3} 23m 19m 16d^{ur} Jun 1] little sign of ability: blinkered last 4 starts: amateur ridden. *Miss E. Hill* **h69**

MR FLUFFY 8 br.g. Charmer – Hinton Bairn (Balinger) [2004/5 h123: 24d 24m^{5} c21m^{2} c21d^{F} c24g* 21g^{ur} 24g^{pu} Apr 14] leggy gelding: fairly useful handicap hurdler, below form in 2004/5: fairly useful form both completed outings over fences, winning 5-runner maiden at Kempton in November by 6 lengths from Champagne Harry: stays 3m: acts on good to soft and good to firm going. *P. J. Hobbs* **c120 h113**

MR FORTYWINKS (IRE) 11 ch.g. Fools Holme (USA) – Dream On (Absalom) [2004/5 17d^{3} 24g^{3} Aug 14] small, sturdy gelding: poor stayer on Flat: better effort in novice hurdles at Market Rasen on debut: should stay beyond 17f. *B. Ellison* **h91**

MR FREEZE (IRE) 5 b.g. Silver Hawk (USA) – Iviza (IRE) (Sadler's Wells (USA)) [2004/5 F16d May 8] good-topped gelding: fourth foal: half-brother to useful but temperamental 1¼m winner Dane (by Doyoun): dam, 2-y-o 7f winner, and second in Ribblesdale Stakes, from family of very smart stayer Distinction: soundly beaten in bumper on debut. *B. D. Leavy* **F–**

MR HICKMAN (IRE) 8 b.g. Montelimar (USA) – Cabin Glory (The Parson) [2004/5 c92, h83: c21m^{5} c22m^{4} Jun 9] once-raced hurdler: modest maiden chaser: suited by 3m+: acts on soft and good to firm going. *G. Prodromou* **c87 h–**

MR JAKE 12 b.g. Safawan – Miss Tealeaf (USA) (Lear Fan (USA)) [2004/5 c–, h–: c25d^{F} 24s^{pu} c23f^{pu} c22s^{pu} c24m^{5} Mar 14] big, workmanlike gelding: winning hurdler/chaser, no longer of any account. *H. E. Haynes* **c– h–**

MR KAAR 8 b.g. Royal Fountain – City Lighter (Lighter) [2004/5 20f^{pu} 16d^{pu} c16d^{pu} c17g^{pu} Jul 15] first foal: dam, of little account, out of useful chaser up to 3m Another City: no sign of ability: tried in cheekpieces. *R. Johnson* **c– h–**

MR LAGGAN 10 b.g. Tina's Pet – Galway Gal (Proverb) [2004/5 c80, h–: c20d^{5} c20m c21m^{pu} c20g^{ro} c25m c20m^{6} Dec 12] workmanlike gelding: poor handicap chaser: no show in 2004/5: stays 25f: has form on soft going, races on firmer nowadays (acts on firm): has worn cheekpieces. *Miss Kate Milligan* **c– h–**

MR LEAR (USA) 6 b.g. Lear Fan (USA) – Majestic Mae (USA) (Crow (FR)) [2004/5 h107: 16v 16d 17m Apr 9] sturdy gelding: fair hurdler: below form in handicaps in 2004/5, left R. Fahey after first start: raced around 2m: acts on heavy going. *J. J. Quinn* **h97**

MR LEWIN 4 ch.g. Primo Dominie – Fighting Run (Runnett) [2004/5 17g^{4} 16s^{4} Mar 27] half-brother to poor 2m hurdler Fencer's Quest (by Bluebird): modest maiden on Flat (stays 9.5f) at 3 yrs for R. Fahey: fair form when fourth in juvenile hurdles, mistakes latter stages on second occasion. *D. McCain* **h99**

MR MAHDLO 11 b.g. Rakaposhi King – Fedelm (Celtic Cone) [2004/5 c86§, h–: c27v* c25d^{2} c26s* Apr 21] leggy, workmanlike gelding: useful hunter chaser: won at Sedgefield in March and Perth (beat Galapiat du Mesnil by 28 lengths) in April: suited by 3m+: acts on heavy going: tried blinkered/in cheekpieces: has had tongue tied. *R. D. E. Woodhouse* **c115 § h–**

MR MCAULEY (IRE) 7 b.g. Denel (FR) – Dusty Lane (IRE) (Electric) [2004/5 F115: 16d^{5} 16v^{3} 18s Feb 6] good sort: smart form in bumpers in 2003/4: best effort over hurdles when third to Akshar in maiden at Leopardstown: will be suited by 2½m+. *M. Halford, Ireland* **h114**

MR MCDELLON (IRE) 8 ch.g. Duky – Erin Brownie (Seclude (USA)) [2004/5 24m Jun 29] fifth foal: brother to winning pointer and half-brother to fairly useful hurdler/chaser around 2m Colins Double (by Doubletour): dam unraced: in frame 3 times in maiden Irish points in 2004: no show on hurdling debut. *J. F. Panvert* **h–**

MR MCDUCK (IRE) 13 ch.g. Denel (FR) – Coldwater Morning (Laurence O) [2004/5 c91, h–: c21g^{bd} c22s^{2} c20g^{6} c22m^{5} Jun 9] winning hunter chaser, left Ms S. Duell before final start: stays 2¾m: acts on soft and good to firm going: tried blinkered. *C. Grant* **c85 h–**

MR MEYER (IRE) 8 b.g. Alphabatim (USA) – Parsons Alert (IRE) (The Parson) [2004/5 c18g^{pu} c16g 16m c20s^{3} c18s* 16v c16s^{2} c16g Apr 14] chunky gelding: winning **c102 h–**

hurdler: fair handicap chaser: won at Punchestown in October: stays 2½m: acts on firm and soft going: usually blinkered prior to last 4 starts: front runner. *S. Donohoe, Ireland*

MR MICKY (IRE) 7 b.g. Rudimentary (USA) – Top Berry (High Top) [2004/5 21g^F 22g Apr 10] workmanlike gelding: winning 2m hurdler: off 2 years, no show in 2 handicaps in 2004/5. *M. B. Shears* **h–**

MR MIDAZ 6 ch.g. Danzig Connection (USA) – Marmy (Midyan (USA)) [2004/5 h78: 20d^{pu} 16g^3 17g^5 16d^2 16d^6 17v* 21v 20g* 18s Apr 3] sturdy gelding: fair handicap hurdler: won at Sedgefield in December and Musselburgh in February: stays easy 2½m: unraced on firm going, acts on any other. *D. W. Whillans* **h95**

MR MISCHIEF 5 b.g. Millkom – Snow Huntress (Shirley Heights) [2004/5 20s^2 16v^3 Jan 26] useful-looking gelding: useful on all-weather, fairly useful on turf on Flat (stays 15f): fair form when placed both starts over hurdles. *P. C. Haslam* **h106**

MR MISTOFFELES (IRE) 8 b.g. Catrail (USA) – Surprise Move (IRE) (Simply Great (FR)) [2004/5 16g^6 21g^{pu} Oct 6] half-brother to winning 2m hurdler Ambushed (by Indian Ridge): maiden on Flat: bumper winner: no form over hurdles: tongue tied last 3 starts. *Eoin Doyle, Ireland* **h–**

MR NEMO (IRE) 9 b.g. Doubletour (USA) – Snowdrifter (Strong Gale) [2004/5 c94§: c20g* c20d^{pu} c21d* c24f* c25m c24s^{pu} c19s^{pu} Jan 20] lengthy gelding: fair chaser: won maiden at Market Rasen in July, handicap at Southwell in August and novice at Huntingdon in September: effective at 2½m to 27f: acts on firm and good to soft going: tried in cheekpieces: usually races up with pace: unreliable. *Evan Williams* **c102 §**

MR PERRY (IRE) 9 br.g. Perugino (USA) – Elegant Tune (USA) (Alysheba (USA)) [2004/5 c–, h77: 22m c21g Jul 11] leggy gelding: winning hurdler, no longer of any account: visored once. *V. Y. Gethin* **c–** **h–**

MR POINTMENT (IRE) 6 b.g. Old Vic – Bettyhill (Ardross) [2004/5 F17g* F16d^4 Feb 12] €32,000 4-y-o: tall gelding: has scope: third foal: half-brother to fairly useful hurdler/smart chaser Ground Ball (by Bob's Return), stays 2½m: dam unraced: useful form in bumpers, won at Bangor on debut impressively by 9 lengths from Valley Ride: 15¼ lengths fourth to Karanja in Grade 2 at Newbury 2 months later: type to do well over hurdles in 2005/6. *C. R. Egerton* **F109**

MR PRESIDENT (GER) 6 b.g. Surako (GER) – Mostly Sure (IRE) (Sure Blade (USA)) [2004/5 h99: 16s* 20s* 16d 21d^3 16s* Feb 18] useful-looking gelding: fairly useful hurdler: won novices at Leicester (2) in December and Sandown in February: beat Enhancer 21 lengths at latter, making all and unchallenged: stays 21f: raced only on good to soft/soft going: not a fluent jumper. *Miss Venetia Williams* **h128**

MR PRICKLE (IRE) 5 ch.g. Carroll House – Auntie Prickle Pin (IRE) (Sexton Blake) [2004/5 F16v^4 F16d^5 F17g^4 F16v^5 19s 17s^4 16s^5 Apr 22] good-topped gelding: has scope: fourth foal: dam maiden half-sister to very smart 2m chaser Wolf of Badenoch: fair form in bumpers: easily best effort over hurdles when fourth in novice. *P. Beaumont* **h87** **F86**

MR RHUBARB (IRE) 7 ch.g. Shardari – Gale Griffin (IRE) (Strong Gale) [2004/5 h81, F89: 22d c23d^{pu} Apr 20] angular gelding: maiden hurdler: no show on chasing debut. *R. T. Phillips* **c–** **h–**

MRS BE (IRE) 9 ch.m. Be My Native (USA) – Kilbrack (Perspex) [2004/5 c97: c26g^3 c28g^3 c26d^2 c31d^3 c24g^2 Apr 17] lengthy mare: winning pointer: placed in hunter chases first 3 starts for Mrs O. Bush: seemingly better form when third to Spot Thedifference in Sporting Index Handicap (Cross Country) at Cheltenham in March, coming from long way off pace: suited by good test of stamina. *J. G. Cann* **c115**

MRS FIZZIWIG 6 b.m. Petoski – Dans Le Vent (Pollerton) [2004/5 F18s F16d^5 Apr 20] lengthy mare: half-sister to several winners, including useful staying chaser up to 3m Air Shot and useful hurdler Flying Gunner (both by Gunner B): dam pulled up in a point: better effort in bumpers when fifth at Worcester. *R. T. Phillips* **F81**

MR SNOWMAN 13 b.g. Lightning Dealer – Eventime (Hot Brandy) [2004/5 c25v* May 10] smallish gelding: useful hunter chaser at best, off over 2 years before return in 2004: won point in April and weak hunter at Towcester in May: stays 3¼m: acts on good to firm and heavy going. *Mrs T. J. Hill* **c76**

MRS PHILIP 6 b.m. Puissance – Lightning Legacy (USA) (Super Concorde (USA)) [2004/5 h75: 17g 19m^2 22d* 19m 19m* Mar 14] modest handicap hurdler: won at Wincanton (conditional jockeys) in November and Taunton in March: stays 2¾m: acts on good to firm and good to soft going. *P. J. Hobbs* **h93**

MRS PICKLES 10 gr.m. Northern Park (USA) – Able Mabel (Absalom) [2004/5 24v^{pu} 20d^{5} c20d^{pu} c22d^{pu} 19d^{4} 16v^{6} 19s* 22v^{pu} 22s^{3} 19s^{4} Mar 23] workmanlike mare: poor handicap hurdler: won mares amateur event at Hereford in February: pulled up both starts over fences: needs thorough test at 2m and stays 3¼m: goes well on soft/heavy going: usually needs plenty of driving. *M. D. I. Usher* **c– h82**

MR SPLODGE 11 b.g. Gildoran – Ethels Course (Crash Course) [2004/5 c75, h–: c20s^{2} Mar 11] lengthy, angular gelding: fairly useful pointer, successful in February and March: second in maiden hunter at Leicester in between: should stay beyond 21f: acts on heavy going. *Mrs T. J. Hill* **c98 h–**

MRS RITCHIE 8 b.m. Teenoso (USA) – Material Girl (Busted) [2004/5 h75: 17m 17d^{5} 17g^{2} 16g^{pu} 16s^{6} 19g^{3} 24g^{3} 22g^{pu} Apr 3] workmanlike mare: modest maiden hurdler: suffered overreach final outing: stays 3m: acts on good to soft going. *Mrs S. Lamyman* **h95**

MR STROWGER 4 b.c. Dancing Spree (USA) – Matoaka (Be My Chief (USA)) [2004/5 16s 16d Mar 14] modest on Flat (stays 13f), successful in December: well beaten in 2 juvenile hurdles, left A. Charlton in between. *J. C. Fox* **h–**

MRS WALLENSKY (IRE) 7 gr.m. Roselier (FR) – Shannon Dee (IRE) (Supreme Leader) [2004/5 F104: 18s^{5} 20v^{2} 22d* 22s^{3} 20v* 20v^{5} 20s^{2} Mar 27] workmanlike mare: fairly useful novice hurdler: won minor event at Fairyhouse in November and handicap at Punchestown (beat Holly Lass 9 lengths) in December: much better effort in Grade 3 events after when 12 lengths second to Asian Maze at Fairyhouse: effective at 2½m given testing conditions, will stay 3m: acts on heavy ground. *Paul Nolan, Ireland* **h119**

MR TENPERCENT 9 gr.g. Gran Alba (USA) – Chatty Corner (Le Bavard (FR)) [2004/5 20v^{4} 16v^{pu} 16s 21s^{6} c25s^{pu} c16s^{5} c25m^{6} Mar 21] 1,700 4-y-o: workmanlike gelding: maiden pointer: poor maiden hurdler: no show in handicap chases: tongue tied after second outing. *M. Sheppard* **c– h–**

MR THURLSTONE 12 b.g. Landyap (USA) – Maywell (Harwell) [2004/5 c26d^{4} c25s^{pu} Mar 7] angular gelding: winning pointer: well beaten only completed start in hunters: has had tongue tied. *Mark Gillard* **c–**

MR TIM (IRE) 7 br.g. Naheez (USA) – Ari's Fashion (Aristocracy) [2004/5 F85: 16d^{6} 16s^{5} 20d^{3} Mar 26] lengthy, useful-looking gelding: fair form in bumpers: not knocked about in 3 novice hurdles: banned for 40 days under non-triers rule on second occasion, and left impression should have won (rider given 10-day ban for making insufficient effort) when third to Pendle Forest at Carlisle: better suited by 2½m than 2m: should prove capable of better. *L. Lungo* **h95**

MR TWINS (ARG) 4 ch.g. Numerous (USA) – Twins Parade (ARG) (Parade Marshal (USA)) [2004/5 16s 16g^{3} 16g^{5} 17m Apr 9] sturdy gelding: 1m winner in Spain at 3 yrs for P. Haley, poor form on 2 starts on Flat in Britain in 2005: poor form over hurdles: blinkered after debut: sold £3,000 Ascot April Sales. *D. B. Feek* **h76**

MR WHIZZ 8 ch.g. Manhal – Panienka (POL) (Dom Racine (FR)) [2004/5 h83+: 16g 16f* c16m^{5} c19m^{3} c16g^{bd} 16g Sep 12] rather sparely-made gelding: modest on Flat (stays 1½m), successful in April: modest hurdler: won novice seller at Towcester in May: well held both completed starts over fences: best at 2m: acts on firm and good to soft going: wears cheekpieces: has had tongue tied. *A. P. Jones* **c89 ? h91**

MR WONG (IRE) 9 br.g. Be My Native (USA) – Adare Boreen (Boreen (FR)) [2004/5 16f^{6} c16f^{6} c16g^{pu} 16d Mar 24] leggy ex-Irish gelding: fair on Flat in 2004: fair hurdler at best: maiden chaser, usually let down by jumping: sold out of Mrs J. Harrington's stable 3,200 gns Doncaster October Sales after second outing: raced around 2m: best efforts on firm/good to firm going. *M. Sheppard* **c– x h91**

MR WOODENTOP (IRE) 9 b.g. Roselier (FR) – Una's Polly (Pollerton) [2004/5 c127, h–: 24d^{pu} 20v^{5} 25d^{6} Feb 4] leggy, close-coupled gelding: fairly useful hurdler/chaser at best: more encouragement than for some time final outing: should stay beyond 25f: acts on heavy and good to firm going: visored on reappearance: has idled. *N. G. Richards* **c– h109**

MR WOODLAND 11 br.g. Landyap (USA) – Wood Corner (Sit In The Corner (USA)) [2004/5 c112, h–: c25s^{5} c19v* c24g^{ur} Apr 7] quite good-topped gelding: fair chaser: back to best when winning hunter at Exeter in March: stays 3m: acts on any going: often makes mistakes. *S. P. Long* **c112 h–**

MS FREEBEE 6 ch.m. Gunner B – Luckifosome (Smackover) [2004/5 F16g F17d F16g F16v 24d^{pu} Mar 24] fourth foal: dam 5f winner: no sign of ability: tried tongue tied. *M. Mullineaux* **h– F–**

MUCKLE FLUGGA (IRE) 6 ch.m. Karinga Bay – Dancing Dove (IRE) (Denel (FR)) [2004/5 h66, F74: 20m² 20d² 20g⁵ 22g 20s* Apr 22] rather unfurnished mare: modest hurdler: won novice handicap at Perth in April: should stay beyond 2½m: acts on soft and good to firm ground. *N. G. Richards* **h86**

MUCKY MAN (IRE) 12 b. or br.g. Exodal (USA) – The Tidy One (Hildenley) [2004/5 c28g⁶ May 21] winning pointer: maiden hunter chaser: stays 3m: acts on good to firm going: tongue tied. *Martin Hurley, Ireland* **c78**

MUFFLER 7 b.h. Next Boom (USA) – Public Offering (Warrshan (USA)) [2004/5 F17s F16v Dec 28] quite good-topped horse: first foal: dam behind in 2 claimers on Flat: well held in bumpers. *J. G. M. O'Shea* **F–**

MUHTENBAR 5 b.g. Muhtarram (USA) – Ardenbar (Ardross) [2004/5 F–: 17s* 19s² 19dpu 20dpu Mar 12] big, good-topped gelding: fair novice hurdler: won at Market Rasen in December: better form when second to Star de Mohaison at Hereford: throat infection third outing: should stay beyond 19f: races prominently. *Miss H. C. Knight* **h107**

MUIR COTTAGE 4 br.g. Chaddleworth (IRE) – Lady Crusty (Golden Dipper) [2004/5 F16v Jan 22] sturdy gelding: seventh foal: half-brother to winning 2½m hurdler Mike Simmons (by Ballacashtal): dam poor selling hurdler, stayed 25f: always rear in bumper on debut. *L. P. Grassick* **F–**

MUKHALIF (IRE) 9 ch.h. Caerleon (USA) – Potri Pe (ARG) (Potrillazo (ARG)) [2004/5 16dpu Jun 23] smart on Flat (stays 1½m) at 3 yrs: useful form at best since, mainly in UAE, sold out of J. Sadler's stable 32,000 gns Newmarket July (2002) Sales: reportedly bled from nose on belated hurdling debut. *M. Pitman* **h–**

MULAN PRINCESS (IRE) 5 b.m. Mukaddamah (USA) – Notley Park (Wolfhound (USA)) [2004/5 h–: 19g 16v⁴ Jan 8] poor on Flat (stays 8.5f) nowadays: no form over hurdles: sold £750 Ascot April Sales. *S. C. Burrough* **h–**

MULKEV PRINCE (IRE) 14 b.g. Lancastrian – Waltzing Shoon (Green Shoon) [2004/5 c110d, h–: c21gpu c21v³ c20g³ c20d⁶ c16s* c16d⁵ c16s c20v c20vpu Mar 1] stocky gelding: poor handicap chaser nowadays: dropped in weights, won at Towcester in January: stays 2½m: acts on good to firm and heavy going: tried tongue tied: has worn off-side pricker: headstrong front runner, prone to odd mistake. *D. Pearson* **c81 h–**

MULLACASH (IRE) 7 b.g. Supreme Leader – The Parson's Line (The Parson) [2004/5 c103, h110: c20g⁴ c21d* c22d³ c29d² c20s² c24vpu c24v⁵ c24v² c21v⁴ c29s c24v⁵ Apr 10] rangy gelding: fairly useful chaser: won handicap at Roscommon in October: good efforts when placed after, kept away from others when third to Pay It Forward in valuable novice handicap at Punchestown in late-April: stays 29f: acts on heavy going: blinkered. *N. Meade, Ireland* **c120 h–**

MULLENSGROVE 11 b.g. Derrylin – Wedding Song (True Song) [2004/5 c117§, h–: c25m² c26d² c22s³ c28m c24d² c25d c24g³ c24d⁵ c20s³ c26g² Apr 14] good-topped gelding: fairly useful hunter chaser on balance: probably flattered when second to Mister Friday at Cheltenham final start: stays 3¼m: acts on soft and good to firm going: hard ride, often takes little interest. *D. Lowe* **c109 § h–**

MULLER (IRE) 5 gr.g. Bigstone (IRE) – Missie Madam (IRE) (Kenmare (FR)) [2004/5 20f⁴ 20dpu 24g⁶ Jul 1] no sign of ability on Flat or over hurdles. *R. W. Thomson* **h–**

MULLIGATAWNY (IRE) 11 br.g. Abednego – Mullangale (Strong Gale) [2004/5 c117, h–: c24d c24dur c24dpu c20v³ c24dpu c26s* c25dpu Apr 3] lengthy, useful-looking gelding: fair handicap chaser: won at Fontwell in March: little other form in 2004/5: stays 3¼m: best efforts on soft/heavy going: tongue tied last 2 starts. *N. J. Gifford* **c108 h–**

MULSANNE 7 b.g. Clantime – Prim Lass (Reprimand) [2004/5 c–, h–: 16m 16d⁴ 16g 19m Sep 8] workmanlike gelding: of little account: tried blinkered. *P. A. Pritchard* **c– h–**

MULTEEN RIVER (IRE) 9 b.g. Supreme Leader – Blackwater Mist (IRE) (King's Ride) [2004/5 c115x, h–: c21m* c20gsu c20d⁴ c16d* c21g Mar 17] tall, useful-looking gelding: fairly useful handicap chaser: won at Uttoxeter in September and Warwick (by length from Marked Man) in December: stays 21f: acts on soft and good to firm going: often fails to impress with jumping/attitude. *Jonjo O'Neill* **c122 x h–**

MULTI TALENTED (IRE) 9 b.g. Montelimar (USA) – Boro Glen (Furry Glen) [2004/5 c113: c28s⁵ c29d⁶ c25s⁴ c26d* c30d⁶ c25mpu c24s⁵ Apr 16] tall gelding: fair handicap chaser: won weak event at Fontwell in February, despite several mistakes: suited by 3m+: acts on heavy going, seems unsuited by firmer than good nowadays: usually blinkered: often looks hard ride, though has run well for amateur/conditional jockey: not one to rely on. *L. Wells* **c105 §**

MUMARIS (USA) 11 b. or br.g. Capote (USA) – Barakat (Bustino) [2004/5 c100, h–: c20d^{3} c16m^{2} c16g^{3} c16m* c17d^{2} c20d* Oct 21] workmanlike gelding: fair handicap chaser: won at Uttoxeter in July and Haydock in October: stays 2½m: acts on any going: effective with or without cheekpieces: usually sound jumper: reliable (out of frame just twice in last 16 starts). *Miss Lucinda V. Russell* **c107 h–**

MUMBLING (IRE) 7 ch.g. Dr Devious (IRE) – Valley Lights (IRE) (Dance of Life (USA)) [2004/5 h109: 19g^{2} Oct 6] compact gelding: lightly raced: fair hurdler: stays 19f. *B. G. Powell* **h110**

MUNNY HILL 5 b.g. Golden Heights – More Laughter (Oats) [2004/5 F–: 18m^{5} 16m^{6} Jun 6] leggy gelding: no sign of ability. *M. Appleby* **h–**

MUNSTER (IRE) 8 b.g. Zaffaran (USA) – Delway (Fidel) [2004/5 c113, h–: c18g^{4} c20s c19v^{4} c18v^{4} c16s c21d^{6} Apr 8] strong, rangy, good sort: fairly useful handicap chaser: 50/1, back to form despite several mistakes when sixth of 30 to Cregg House in Topham Chase at Aintree: stays 21f: acts on heavy going: tongue tied. *A. L. T. Moore, Ireland* **c116 h–**

MUNTASIR 5 b.g. Rainbow Quest (USA) – Licorne (Sadler's Wells (USA)) [2004/5 h80, F–: 21d 19d^{4} 21d^{4} Nov 1] angular gelding: poor novice hurdler: should stay beyond 19f: raced on good going or softer. *P. G. Murphy* **h77**

MURAQEB 5 ch.g. Grand Lodge (USA) – Oh So Well (IRE) (Sadler's Wells (USA)) [2004/5 16d 16g^{6} 16v 20g^{pu} 16s 22d^{pu} Mar 26] compact gelding: modest maiden on Flat (stays 10.3f): no form over hurdles: tried in cheekpieces. *Mrs Barbara Waring* **h–**

MURAT (FR) 5 b.g. Useful (FR) – La Marianne (FR) (Don Roberto (USA)) [2004/5 h102: 17d 16d 17d 16d^{4} Mar 11] leggy gelding: fair form at best over hurdles, often runs as if amiss. *M. C. Pipe* **h–**

MURDINGA 6 br.g. Emperor Jones (USA) – Tintinara (Selkirk (USA)) [2004/5 h94d: 16m^{pu} May 22] form in novice hurdles only on debut in 2003/4: tried in cheekpieces (looked unwilling). *A. M. Hales* **h–**

MURHILL'S PRIDE (IRE) 7 b.g. Great Marquess – Penny's Wishing (Clantime) [2004/5 F70: F16d Jun 23] poor in bumpers: tried in cheekpieces: has looked wayward (ran out on debut). *W. M. Brisbourne* **F–**

MUROTOEVATION (IRE) 6 b.g. Muroto – Toevarro (Raga Navarro (ITY)) [2004/5 F16d Apr 20] €35,000 4-y-o: half-brother to several winners, all by Roselier, including fairly useful staying hurdler/chaser Misty Class: dam bumper winner: always outpaced in bumper on debut. *D. G. Bridgwater* **F–**

MURPHY'S ANGEL 11 br.m. Derrylin – Just A Tipple (IRE) (Roselier (FR)) [2004/5 19d^{pu} Apr 29] no form in bumper or novice hurdle over 3 years apart. *Mrs P. Ford* **h–**

MURPHY'S CARDINAL (IRE) 9 b.g. Shernazar – Lady Swinford (Ardross) [2004/5 c118p, h–: c20s* c24d^{4} c24s^{5} c20d^{pu} Feb 19] tall gelding: has reportedly had pelvic problems: unbeaten first 6 starts, smart form when beating Mossy Green 20 lengths in Grade 3 chase at Down Royal in November: struggled in Grade 1 events last 2 outings, reportedly distressed when pulled up at Lingfield: stays 3m: raced on going softer than good. *Noel T. Chance* **c149 h–**

MURPHY'S NAILS (IRE) 8 b.g. Bob's Return (IRE) – Southern Run (Deep Run) [2004/5 h96: 20v c19g^{ur} c21d^{F} 24m Apr 10] lengthy gelding: second in maiden hurdle in May 2003 for C. Egerton: off 20 months, no form in 2004/5, including over fences: has worn blinkers/cheekpieces. *K. C. Bailey* **c– h–**

MURPHY'S QUEST 9 ch.g. Sir Harry Lewis (USA) – Rondeau (Orchestra) [2004/5 19g^{3} 16d* 19d c16d^{3} Mar 12] tall, angular gelding: off 4 years prior to reappearance (reportedly had tendon problem): easily best effort over hurdles when winning novice at Sandown in December by ½ length from Without A Doubt: similar form when third of 6 to Dempsey in novice chase at same course, not always fluent but not knocked about: will stay at least 2½m: unraced on extremes of going. *Lady Herries* **c112 p h115**

MUSALLY 8 ch.g. Muhtarram (USA) – Flourishing (IRE) (Trojan Fen) [2004/5 c76x, h90: 21m* 20g^{3} 20g^{4} 20f 24g^{4} 16d^{4} Mar 24] angular gelding: usually left down by jumping over fences: modest handicap hurdler: won at Ludlow very early in season: best up to 3m: suited by good going or firmer (acts on firm). *W. Jenks* **c– h98**

MUSCADIER (IRE) 10 ch.g. Roselier (FR) – Banna's Lady (IRE) (Supreme Leader) [2004/5 c20s c25s^{5} c24d^{3} Apr 22] poor hurdler/maiden chaser: winning pointer, has run out: tried blinkered. *E. J. O'Grady, Ireland* **c74 h–**

MUSICAL CAPERS 6 b.m. Piccolo – Canadian Capers (Ballacashtal (CAN)) [2004/5 F17g² F17g⁴ Oct 9] fourth foal: dam, 5.7f (at 2 yrs) and 7.6f winner, probably stayed 1¼m: modest form when in frame in bumpers: third of 4 finishers in maiden point in February. *M. R. Channon* **F85**

MUSICAL GIFT 5 ch.g. Cadeaux Genereux – Kazoo (Shareef Dancer (USA)) [2004/5 16d⁶ May 11] fair on all-weather on Flat (stays easy 1¼m): weakened quickly straight when well held in amateur novice on hurdling debut. *C. N. Allen* **h–**

MUSICAL MAYHEM (IRE) 12 b.g. Shernazar – Minstrels Folly (USA) (The Minstrel (CAN)) [2004/5 24s² 22vᵘʳ Feb 13] leggy gelding: lightly raced: fairly useful hurdler at one time: off nearly 2½ years, second to Celtic Son in handicap at Taunton: stays 25f: best form on good going or softer. *D. J. Wintle* **h109**

MUSICAL STAGE (USA) 6 b.g. Theatrical – Changed Tune (USA) (Tunerup (USA)) [2004/5 h103: 17g³ c16m² c16m* Jun 9] fair hurdler: similar form over fences, winning novice at Hereford in June: raced around 2m: acts on good to soft and good to firm going: tongue tied last 5 starts. *P. R. Webber* **c106 h106**

MUSIC TO MY EARS (IRE) 7 ch.g. Phardante (FR) – Evas Charm (Carlburg) [2004/5 c–, h92: c24dᵖᵘ c22v* Oct 17] workmanlike gelding: winning hurdler: tongue tied, first completion over fences (suffered hair-line fracture on chasing debut) when extremely fortunate to win novice handicap at Market Rasen in October, remote fourth before left ahead in straight: should stay 3m. *Jonjo O'Neill* **c69 ? h–**

MUSIMARO (FR) 7 b.g. Solid Illusion (USA) – Musimara (FR) (Margouillat (FR)) [2004/5 h87: 19g* 20m² 20m* 24d 22g Jul 18] medium-sized gelding: fair hurdler: won seller (sold from O. Sherwood 7,000 gns) at Hereford in May and handicap at Worcester in June: stays 2½m: acts on good to soft and good to firm going: tried blinkered, wears cheekpieces nowadays. *R. J. Price* **h100**

MUSTANG MOLLY 13 br.m. Soldier Rose – Little 'n' Game (Convolvulus) [2004/5 c–: c24g* Apr 17] lengthy, rather sparely-made mare: winning pointer: form in hunters since 2003 only when winning at Stratford in April, left clear last (would probably have finished second): stays 3m: acts on firm and soft going. *Andrew J. Martin* **c85 §**

MUTABARI (USA) 11 ch.g. Seeking The Gold (USA) – Cagey Exuberance (USA) (Exuberant (USA)) [2004/5 h–: 19m May 22] no longer of any account: tried visored/in cheekpieces. *J. L. Spearing* **h–**

Killultagh Properties Ltd Chase, Down Royal—
Murphy's Cardinal puts up a smart effort to defeat some below-par rivals

MUTADARRA (IRE) 12 ch.g. Mujtahid (USA) – Silver Echo (Caerleon (USA)) [2004/5 c75§, h86§: 22g6 c22m4 c20m2 c21gur Jun 15] leggy, lengthy gelding: winning hurdler: poor form over fences: stays 2¾m: acts on firm and good to soft going: has worn cheekpieces: amateur ridden: not one to trust. *J. W. Mullins* **c75 § h– §**

MUTAKARRIM 8 ch.g. Mujtahid (USA) – Alyakkh (IRE) (Sadler's Wells (USA)) [2004/5 c114, h127: 17d c20d* 16g5 c16s6 c24vpu Dec 27] sturdy gelding: useful on Flat (stays 1¾m): fairly useful hurdler/chaser: won minor chase at Killarney in July by 3½ lengths from Quinze: creditable fifth to Cloone River in Galway Hurdle later in month: stays easy 2½m: acts on firm and good to soft going, not at best on softer: usually blinkered, effective when not. *D. K. Weld, Ireland* **c120 h125**

MUTARED (IRE) 7 b.g. Marju (IRE) – Shahaada (USA) (Private Account (USA)) [2004/5 h–: 16g4 Oct 4] no show over hurdles: tried in cheekpieces. *N. P. Littmoden* **h–**

MUTINEER (IRE) 6 gr.g. Highest Honor (FR) – Miss Amy R (USA) (Deputy Minister (CAN)) [2004/5 h129: 24s c24s c16s3 c20d3 c20s3 c24v3 c24v3 c24v6 20s 22s5 Mar 28] good-topped gelding: fairly useful handicap hurdler: below best in 2004/5: fair novice chaser: stays 25f: acts on heavy going: usually blinkered: tongue tied. *D. T. Hughes, Ireland* **c112 h118**

MUTTLEY MAGUIRE (IRE) 6 b.g. Zaffaran (USA) – Alavie (FR) (Quart de Vin (FR)) [2004/5 c23d2 c24s3 c22s3 Jan 24] €40,000 3-y-o: third foal: half-brother to winning pointer by Bob Back: dam won around 2m over fences in France: well beaten on completed start in maiden Irish points: modest form when placed all 3 outings in chases: stays 3m. *B. G. Powell* **c94**

MUZIO SCEVOLA (IRE) 4 ch.g. Titus Livius (FR) – Dancing Sunset (IRE) (Red Sunset) [2004/5 18s Feb 4] modest maiden on Flat: tailed off in juvenile on hurdling debut: sold £1,800 Ascot April Sales. *M. R. Channon* **h–**

MVEZO 7 ch.g. Karinga Bay – Queen of The Celts (Celtic Cone) [2004/5 F82: F17g 24m 20g5 16v Mar 29] never a factor in bumpers and over hurdles. *Evan Williams* **h– F–**

MY ACE 7 b.m. Definite Article – Miss Springtime (Bluebird (USA)) [2004/5 h73: 16d 17d4 16m 17m 22g 17m4 17m2 17m 17m Sep 28] leggy mare: poor hurdler: needs sharp 2m: acts on firm going: blinkered/visored: often tongue tied. *James Moffatt* **h63**

MYANNABANANA (IRE) 4 ch.g. Woodborough (USA) – Raging Storm (Horage) [2004/5 16m6 16g Dec 10] small gelding: half-brother to winning 2m chaser Blazing Storm (by Keen): modest on all-weather, poor on turf on Flat (stays 1¼m): no show over hurdles: sold 500 gns Doncaster January Sales. *J. R. Weymes* **h–**

MY BEST SECRET 6 ch.g. Secret Appeal – Mohibbah (USA) (Conquistador Cielo (USA)) [2004/5 F16m3 Nov 26] brother to modest hurdler around 2m Park Royal: dam 2-y-o 5f winner: 20 lengths third to Lennon in maiden bumper at Musselburgh on debut. *L. Lungo* **F81**

MY BOLD BOYO 10 b.g. Never So Bold – My Rosie (Forzando) [2004/5 c–, h–: c21m c23g6 19spu c23s6 c20m6 Apr 10] sturdy gelding: handicap hurdler: well held over fences: stays 19f: acts on firm and soft going: all 4 wins at Exeter. *K. Bishop* **c– h–**

MY COUNTRY CLUB 8 b.h. Alzao (USA) – Merry Rous (Rousillon (USA)) [2004/5 16f 16g Oct 7] successful up to 7f on Flat in Poland, little form in Britain in 2004: no form in 2 starts over hurdles. *A. G. Juckes* **h–**

MYDANTE (IRE) 10 b.m. Phardante (FR) – Carminda (Proverb) [2004/5 c74, h–: c25g3 c21g* c21d4 Mar 28] workmanlike mare: winning hurdler: fair hunter chaser nowadays, successful in novice at Fakenham in March: stays 27f: acts on soft and firm going: tried visored: has flashed tail. *S. Flook* **c82 h–**

MY FINAL BID (IRE) 6 b.g. Supreme Leader – Mini Minor (IRE) (Black Minstrel) [2004/5 F16g2 Apr 16] €10,000 3-y-o, €3,500 4-y-o: second foal: dam unraced half-sister to fairly useful staying hurdler/chaser Menebuck: 100/1, staying-on second to easy winner Rasharrow in bumper at Ayr on debut. *Mrs A. C. Hamilton* **F94**

MY FLIRTY GERTY 7 ch.m. Tigani – Molly Brazen (Risk Me (FR)) [2004/5 17dpu Aug 1] third foal: sister to 2 poor maidens on Flat: dam, placed once over 6f, half-sister to fairly useful chaser up to 2½m Macarthur: no show in novice hurdle on debut. *R. Johnson* **h–**

MY FLOOSIE 10 b.m. Unfuwain (USA) – My Chiara (Ardross) [2004/5 17gpu Dec 15] sparely-made mare: maiden hurdler: no show on return from over 4-year absence. *P. L. Clinton* **h–**

MY FRIEND FRITZ 5 ch.g. Safawan – Little Scarlett (Mazilier (USA)) [2004/5 F16g[3] Sep 12] stocky gelding: third foal: half-brother to one-time useful sprinter Sundried Tomato (by Lugana Beach): dam 8.5f winner: third of 12 in bumper at Stratford on debut. *P. W. Hiatt* **F70**

MY GALLIANO (IRE) 9 b.g. Muharib (USA) – Hogan Stand (Buckskin (FR)) [2004/5 c89, h99: c16m[3] c16g[3] 17g[5] c16g* c18s[3] 16d Mar 6] sparely-made gelding: modest handicap hurdler/chaser: successful over fences at Huntingdon in January: best around 2m: acts on firm and soft going: free-going sort. *B. G. Powell* **c87 h88**

MY GOOD LORD (IRE) 6 br.g. Mister Lord (USA) – Glenstal Forest (IRE) (Glenstal (USA)) [2004/5 F16s F16v F16d[4] F16g Apr 19] €13,000 3-y-o: workmanlike gelding: first foal: dam maiden half-sister to useful 2m hurdler Joking Aside: best effort in bumpers when fourth at Uttoxeter. *B. D. Leavy* **F88**

MY GOOD SON (NZ) 10 b.g. The Son (NZ) – Meadow Hall (NZ) (Pikehall (USA)) [2004/5 c–, h94: 20m 24g[pu] 24m[6] 26d[2] Aug 22] rather sparely-made gelding: poor hurdler nowadays: no show in points in 2005: stays 3¼m: acts on any going: has worn blinkers/cheekpieces: tongue tied once. *Ian Williams* **c– h84**

MY LADY LINK (FR) 6 bl.m. Sleeping Car (FR) – Cadoudaline (FR) (Cadoudal (FR)) [2004/5 c105, h105: 19s[4] 20m[pu] c20d[pu] 17g[3] 22d c19d[F] Apr 22] fair maiden hurdler/winning chaser in France: poor form in Britain: should stay beyond 2¼m: acts on heavy going: tried blinkered: often let down by jumping over fences: tends to finish weakly. *Miss Venetia Williams* **c– h85**

MY LAST BEAN (IRE) 8 gr.g. Soviet Lad (USA) – Meanz Beanz (High Top) [2004/5 h107: 16s 16m[5] 16g[4] Apr 1] lengthy gelding: modest on Flat (stays 13f, usually blinkered): fair hurdler: sold out of B. Smart's stable 7,200 gns Doncaster January Sales before final start: will stay beyond 2m: acts on good to firm ground. *M. R. Bosley* **h109**

MY LINE 8 b.g. Perpendicular – My Desire (Grey Desire) [2004/5 h112: 22s[pu] Nov 18] sturdy gelding: fair novice hurdler in 2003/4: lame on return: will prove best at 3m+: acts on soft and good to firm going: tried blinkered: not a fluent jumper: difficult ride. *K. G. Reveley* **h–**

MYLO 7 gr.g. Faustus (USA) – Bellifontaine (FR) (Bellypha) [2004/5 h91§: 21g[3] 17d 22s[3] 22g[4] 22g[2] 24g* 22m[ur] 22s* 20d[2] 24s 21d 22v[5] 20d[2] Apr 20] compact gelding: fair handicap hurdler: won in small fields at Market Rasen in August and Newton Abbot in November: stays 3m: acts on soft going: tried in cheekpieces, usually blinkered: sometimes finds little. *Jonjo O'Neill* **h112 §**

MY NATIVE MISS (IRE) 7 b.m. Be My Native (USA) – Explosive Missile (IRE) (Supreme Leader) [2004/5 F18g[rtr] F17d[4] 17m 18m[pu] Apr 21] no sign of ability: refused to race on reappearance: tongue tied last 2 starts. *Mrs L. C. Jewell* **h– F–**

MY NATIVE OGAN (IRE) 10 ch.g. Be My Native (USA) – Cooleogan (Proverb) [2004/5 21g[5] Oct 27] rangy gelding: half-brother to several winners, including fairly useful hurdler/useful chaser Tullymurry Toff (by King's Ride), stays 3m, and useful hurdler/fair chaser Kilcash Castle (by Strong Gale), stays 2¾m: dam, fairly useful hurdler, sister to one-time top-class chaser Marlborough: no show in novice hurdle on belated debut. *J. G. M. O'Shea* **h–**

MYOSS (IRE) 6 b.g. Arctic Lord – Lake Garden Park (Comedy Star (USA)) [2004/5 F17d F16g F17s[3] Feb 7] €15,000 4-y-o: lengthy gelding: fifth foal: brother to fair hurdler/chaser Arctic Sky, stays 21f: dam, ran once at 2 yrs, from family of useful staying chaser Billygoat Gruff: best effort in bumpers (trained by Mrs V. Makin on debut) when third in maiden at Sedgefield, throwing away chance by hanging left. *G. A. Harker* **F83**

MY PAL VAL (IRE) 5 br.g. Classic Cliche (IRE) – Lessons Lass (IRE) (Doyoun) [2004/5 F–: F18d 17d[4] 17g[2] Dec 9] no form in 2 bumpers: better effort over hurdles when runner-up in novice at Taunton: will be suited by greater test of stamina. *Miss H. C. Knight* **h104 F–**

MY RETREAT (USA) 8 b.g. Hermitage (USA) – My Jessica Ann (USA) (Native Rythm) [2004/5 h83: 20d 17s[2] 19s[pu] 16s 16s[pu] 20s 16g[5] Mar 27] close-coupled gelding: modest maiden hurdler: mainly out of form in 2004/5: best around 2m: raced on good going or softer. *R. Fielder* **h94 d**

MY SHARP GREY 6 gr.m. Tragic Role (USA) – Sharp Anne (Belfort (FR)) [2004/5 h94+: 17d May 17] sparely-made mare: modest 2m hurdler: acts on soft and good to firm going: visored once (refused to race). *J. Gallagher* **h–**

MY SKIPPER (IRE) 4 b.g. Old Vic – Nil Faic (IRE) (King's Ride) [2004/5 F16s* Mar 31] third foal: dam maiden half-sister to fairly useful staying chaser Putsometnby: favourite, won bumper at Ludlow on debut easily by 6 lengths from Nevada Red. *Miss H. C. Knight* **F97 +**

MYSON (IRE) 6 ch.g. Accordion – Ah Suzie (IRE) (King's Ride) [2004/5 c83, h–: c21g^{3} c16d^{4} c20d^{2} c22s^{F} c21s* c20s^{2} c20s^{ur} c20g* c20g^{2} c21g^{3} Apr 14] tall gelding: fair handicap chaser: won at Folkestone in January and Plumpton (novice) in March: will probably stay 3m: acts on soft going: patiently ridden: consistent. *D. B. Feek* **c104 h–**

MYSTERI DANCER 7 b.g. Rudimentary (USA) – Mystery Ship (Decoy Boy) [2004/5 h96: 16g 16g^{4} Jul 29] lightly raced: modest handicap hurdler: left P.Hobbs and off a year before reappearance: likely to prove best around 2m. *J. Joseph* **h88**

MYSTERY (GER) 7 br.g. Java Gold (USA) – My Secret (GER) (Secreto (USA)) [2004/5 h81: 16d* 16d^{4} 16g^{3} 17d^{pu} 20d^{3} Apr 20] compact gelding: modest hurdler: off 11 months (reportedly had breathing operation), improved form when winning novice handicap at Wincanton in December: stays 2½m: raced on good going or softer: tongue tied twice. *T. R. George* **h95**

MYSTICAL STAR (FR) 8 b.g. Nicolotte – Addaya (IRE) (Persian Bold) [2004/5 17g^{5} 18m^{4} 16m 16g 21d^{3} 22d^{3} 19d^{2} 20s^{6} Dec 21] half-brother to winning 2½m hurdler Castanet (by Pennekamp): twice-raced on Flat, won over 7f on fibresand in 2003 for J. Sheehan: poor maiden hurdler: stays 2¾m: acts on good to soft ground. *M. J. Hogan* **h66**

MYSTIC GLEN 6 b.m. Vettori (IRE) – Mystic Memory (Ela-Mana-Mou) [2004/5 h69, F77: 16f^{4} 20d 17g^{pu} 17m^{6} 24s^{4} 21d^{5} 24d c20m^{4} Dec 12] poor maiden hurdler: let down by jumping on chasing debut: stays 21f: acts on firm and good to soft going: has worn cheekpieces. *P. D. Niven* **c– h69**

MYSTIC KING 4 b.g. Rakaposhi King – Just Lynn (Legend of France (USA)) [2004/5 16d^{5} 16d^{5} 16s^{pu} 19s Jan 5] fifth foal: dam ran twice at 2 yrs: little sign of ability over hurdles. *M. Scudamore* **h–**

MYSTIC LORD (IRE) 8 br.g. Roselier (FR) – Ash Dame (IRE) (Strong Gale) [2004/5 c25s^{4} c28s^{pu} c24s^{pu} c17d^{pu} Apr 11] fairly useful chaser at best, out of sorts since early-2003: sold out of N. Meade's stable 8,500 gns Doncaster January Sales before final start: should stay beyond 25f: acts on soft going: blinkered once: has had tongue tied. *J. N. R. Billinge* **c– h–**

MYSTIC MOON 4 br.f. First Trump – Misty Moon (Polar Falcon (USA)) [2004/5 16s^{pu} Oct 23] sturdy filly: bad mover: modest maiden on Flat (stays 1¼m): no show on hurdling debut. *J. R. Jenkins* **h–**

MYSTIC NATIVE (IRE) 12 ch.g. Be My Native (USA) – Mystic River (IRE) (Over The River (FR)) [2004/5 c–, h–: c26v^{pu} Oct 29] winning pointer: no form otherwise: tried in cheekpieces. *D. Pearson* **c– h–**

MYSTIC PROMISE (IRE) 4 gr.g. Among Men (USA) – Ivory's Promise (Pursuit of Love) [2004/5 17g^{pu} 16d^{pu} Nov 9] leggy gelding: poor maiden on Flat (stays 1m): no show in juvenile hurdles. *Mrs N. Macauley* **h–**

MY SUNSHINE (IRE) 4 b.f. Alzao (USA) – Sunlit Ride (Ahonoora) [2004/5 16d^{5} 16d 17d^{5} 16g 21v^{3} 16s Apr 10] angular filly: half-sister to Irish bumper winner Couldn't Say (by Tirol): modest maiden on Flat, sold out of B. Hills's stable 1,000 gns Doncaster November Sales: poor juvenile hurdler: stays 21f: acts on heavy going: tried tongue tied. *M. E. Sowersby* **h72**

MYTHICAL KING (IRE) 8 b.g. Fairy King (USA) – Whatcombe (USA) (Alleged (USA)) [2004/5 h117: 20s^{F} 21s 20v^{6} 20v* 23s 21g Mar 16] workmanlike gelding: type to make a chaser: fairly useful handicap hurdler: clearly best effort when winning at Chepstow in February by 20 lengths from Nick's Choice: should stay beyond 2½m: goes particularly well on heavy going: patiently ridden. *R. Lee* **h127**

MY TRUE LOVE (IRE) 6 b.g. Beneficial – Elfi (IRE) (Le Moss) [2004/5 F84: F16g^{2} May 16] fair form in bumpers, not looking easy ride: modest form on Flat. *R. J. Baker* **F89**

MY VALENTINE 6 gr.g. Samim (USA) – Sea Farer Lake (Gairloch) [2004/5 16g 17m^{6} May 23] half-brother to 3 modest winners over jumps, all by Beveled: modest maiden on Flat (stays 9f): well held in 2 novice hurdles: sold £1,300 Ascot August Sales. *P. R. Chamings* **h–**

MY WAY DE SOLZEN (FR) 5 b.g. Assessor (IRE) – Agathe de Solzen (FR) (Chamberlin (FR)) [2004/5 c17g^pu 17s^2 16g* 17g* 16d^5 17v* 16g 20s^2 Apr 7] **c– h144**

'I see him more as a chaser next season than trying anything fancy with him this time.' At least, that was the plan. My Way de Solzen's trainer Alan King was speaking after the French import had made it two out of two for the stable in ordinary novice hurdles at Leicester in November and Bangor in December. There is little doubt that My Way de Solzen is indeed a smashing chaser in the making. A tall, strong type, he took the eye of our racecourse representatives on more than one occasion during the season. But firstly, My Way de Solzen proved himself among the best novices around over hurdles once his sights were raised. After a really impressive performance at Bangor, where My Way de Solzen had seventeen rivals well strung out behind him at the end of a well-run race, his handicap mark left his trainer with little option but to take on the best novices. He did so first in the Grade 1 Tolworth Hurdle at Sandown and acquitted himself well in finishing less than seven lengths behind the prolific winner Marcel, keeping on after being hampered at the fourth flight. All things considered, that wasn't too much of a deficit to make up on the winner, yet Marcel started at 2/1-on and My Way de Solzen at 3/1 when they met again at Exeter in February, heading the betting in the inaugural running of the listed totesport Novices' Hurdle. Conditions were desperately testing and, while Marcel laboured in the ground, My Way de Solzen relished the additional emphasis on stamina, jumping fluently, making the running whilst taking a good hold, and drawing right away in the straight. My Way de Solzen passed the post twenty-seven lengths clear of 33/1-chance Give Me Love who passed the tiring Marcel at the last. With the emphasis much more on speed in the Supreme Novices' Hurdle at Cheltenham on good ground, My Way de Solzen's jumping was relatively less

B. Winfield, A. Longman, J. Wright & C. Fenton's "My Way de Solzen"

accomplished and he failed to do himself justice, starting third favourite and finishing well beaten (Marcel also ran below form, and clearly it is possible conditions at Exeter left their mark). The combination next time of softer ground again and the step up to two and a half miles in the Mersey Novices' Hurdle at Aintree saw My Way de Solzen's best effort over hurdles. Held up, he was initially unable to cover the move made by the eventual winner Turpin Green, but kept on gamely to be beaten six lengths (giving the winner 8 lb), shaping as though likely to stay further still.

My Way de Solzen made his racecourse debut in July in a non-thoroughbreds' race for four-year-olds at Dieppe—over fences. Fortunately for his current connections, he was pulled up, his novice status as a chaser remaining intact. On his only other outing in France for Antoine Lamotte d'Argy, My Way de Solzen finished second over hurdles at Clairefontaine to Ambobo, who put up the best performance by a novice hurdler in 2004/5 when winning at Cheltenham later in the season.

My Way de Solzen (FR) (b.g. 2000)	Assessor (IRE) (b 1989)	Niniski (b 1976)	Nijinsky
			Virginia Hills
		Dingle Bay (b 1976)	Petingo
			Border Bounty
	Agathe de Solzen (FR) (b 1988)	Chamberlin (b 1978)	Green Dancer
			On The Wing
		Nathanaelle (b 1979)	Djarvis
			Idaline

My Way de Solzen is by the very smart Richard Hannon-trained stayer Assessor. He was among the favourites for the 1992 Derby—after winning the Lingfield Trial by seven lengths—but disappointed at Epsom and didn't come into his own until tackling longer distances. Assessor's biggest wins came in the Prix Royal-Oak (on soft ground) at three and the Prix du Cadran (on heavy) the following year, both gruelling contests. His successes also included the Yorkshire Cup and Doncaster Cup and he was second on soft ground in the Gold Cup at Ascot. Saudi Arabia seemed an unlikely place to send a proven mudlark, and he returned from there after a year to his former yard in Britain for another two seasons, without recapturing his old form, before finally being retired to stud in France at the age of eight. Assessor is also responsible for the fairly useful hurdler Migwell in Britain, he too out of a mare by Chamberlin, a stallion best known here as the sire of the top-class but moody chaser Challenger du Luc and also sire of the latest Mildmay of Flete winner Liberthine. There is little to say about My Way de Solzen's family. He is the first foal of his dam, Agathe de Solzen, who was clearly a tough and consistent performer around the French provincial tracks. She ran fifty times all told, winning twice on the Flat in non-thoroughbred races, and won seven chases at up to around two and a half miles, to go with a further fifteen placings over fences. Agathe de Solzen is one of three winners (all by Chamberlin) out of the unraced mare Nathanaelle. *A. King*

MY WEE WOMAN 6 ch.m. Alflora (IRE) – Just A Tipple (IRE) (Roselier (FR)) [2004/5 F16s F16v Jan 29] fifth foal: sister to winning pointer Flora Macdonald: dam unraced half-sister to useful staying hurdler Sip of Orange: no show in 2 bumpers. *Miss V. Scott* **F–**

MY WILL (FR) 5 b.g. Saint Preuil (FR) – Gleep Will (FR) (Laniste) [2004/5 h124: 16g c17v* c16g^{ur} c16d* c16d^{3} c20s^{2} c21d* c16v* c16g^{5} c20g^{2} c24s* Apr 20] **c138 h–**

The Paul Nicholls-trained five-year-old My Will, aided by the weight-for-age allowance, enjoyed a fine first season over fences, winning five times from nine completed starts, including twice in Grade 2 events, and being beaten half a length in two other graded contests. He showed useful form, some way in advance of the level he showed over hurdles. Whether My Will fares quite so well without the allowance in open company is another matter, but he owes connections little. My Will's graded wins came at Cheltenham on New Year's Day, when he beat El Vaquero in the two-finisher 'Dipper' Novices Chase formerly staged at Newcastle, and at Uttoxeter three weeks later, when he got the better of Ashley Brook and Contraband in the Lightning Novices' Chase, a race switched from temporarily-closed Ascot. The latter run was as good as any by My Will, though neither second

Betfred Lightning Novices' Chase, Uttoxeter—
My Will gains a second win in a Grade 2 event, at the chief expense of Ashley Brook

nor third was in the form they showed subsequently and both beat My Will comprehensively when he finished fifth in the Arkle at Cheltenham. My Will's three other wins came in novices, at Market Rasen and Warwick in the autumn, and at Perth at the end of the season. In the last-named, My Will showed plenty of determination, as well as unexpected stamina, on his first attempt at three miles to beat Joaaci a head. My Will was the beaten favourite when runner-up in Grade 2 novices at Windsor (behind See You Sometime) and Ayr (to Locksmith). There was not much wrong with either performance, though he did not jump particularly well at Windsor. The tall, leggy My Will is effective at two miles to three and has raced on good going or softer. He acts on heavy. *P. F. Nicholls*

MY WORLD (FR) 5 b.m. Lost World (IRE) – Fortuna Jet (FR) (Highest Honor (FR)) [2004/5 17d^4 16s^4 21s^4 16d* 16v^5 16v* 16d^5 Mar 12] tall, good-topped mare: chasing type: first foal: half-sister to 11.5f winner New Team (by Green Tune): dam never ran: maiden on Flat: fair hurdler: trained in 2003/4 by P. Montfort: won mares novices at Lingfield in November and Leicester in January: raced mainly around 2m on going softer than good (acts on heavy): tried blinkered. *R. H. Alner* **h102**

N

NAAHIL (IRE) 7 ch.g. Elmaamul (USA) – Nwaahil (IRE) (Nashwan (USA)) [2004/5 18m* 16g 20v^2 22v c20s^5 c16s^6 16v^5 c21v* c20v c24v Feb 13] leggy gelding: third foal: dam unraced half-sister to Istabraq: fair handicap hurdler: won at Kilbeggan in July: modest form over fences: won maiden at Fairyhouse in January: stays 21f: acts on any going: tried blinkered: often amateur ridden. *S. O'Farrell, Ireland* **c93 h111**

NA BAC LEIS 5 ch.g. Bijou d'Inde – Risk The Witch (Risk Me (FR)) [2004/5 20m^{pu} 17v^6 Jan 11] lengthy ex-Irish gelding: poor maiden on Flat, left J. Quinn after final 4-y-o start: no form over hurdles. *R. Johnson* **h–**

NABIR (FR) 5 gr.g. Linamix (FR) – Nabagha (FR) (Fabulous Dancer (USA)) [2004/5 16s⁵ 17m⁶ 20vF 16d 17g 17d 17g Apr 12] angular gelding: seventh foal: brother to 11f winner Nadeema and half-brother to 3 winners on Flat: dam, 1m and 1¼m winner, half-sister to useful 2m hurdler Nahrawali: successful over 9.5f on Flat for A. de Royer Dupre: form over hurdles only on debut: tried tongue tied: ungenuine: sold 4,000 gns Doncaster May Sales. *M. C. Pipe* **h89 §**

NADOVER (FR) 4 br.g. Cyborg (FR) – Djerissa (FR) (Highlanders (FR)) [2004/5 15g² 15g* c17s² c17v⁵ c17s³ 16d⁵ 17v⁴ 16g⁴ Mar 28] close-coupled ex-French gelding: third foal: dam 11f winner: won around 1½m on Flat: won juvenile hurdle at Pompadour in August: fair form in 3-y-o chases at Auteuil: left G. Macaire, similar form over hurdles in Britain: raced around 2m on good ground or softer. *C. J. Mann* **c110 h104**

NAFFERTON HEIGHTS (IRE) 4 b.c. Peintre Celebre (USA) – Gold Mist (Darshaan) [2004/5 17g Sep 25] poor maiden on Flat (stays 1½m): soon well behind on hurdling debut. *M. W. Easterby* **h–**

NAFSIKA (USA) 5 b.m. Sky Classic (CAN) – Exotic Beauty (USA) (Java Gold (USA)) [2004/5 h79: 16vpu 16gpu Apr 19] lengthy mare: no form since hurdling debut, including in points: tried visored. *R. C. Harper* **h–**

NAGANO (FR) 7 b.g. Hero's Honor (USA) – Sadinskaya (FR) (Niniski (USA)) [2004/5 h–: 20spu 16s⁶ c17v² c16g* c16s* c16d² c17g⁵ c16d³ Apr 3] medium-sized gelding: maiden hurdler: fair chaser: won handicaps at Folkestone (novice) and Ludlow in December: best form around 2m: raced on good going or softer (acts on soft). *Ian Williams* **c108 h–**

NAKED FLAME 6 b.g. Blushing Flame (USA) – Final Attraction (Jalmood (USA)) [2004/5 F–: 16s Dec 1] no form in bumpers or novice hurdle (in cheekpieces). *A. G. Blackmore* **h–**

NAKED OAT 10 b.g. Imp Society (USA) – Bajina (Dancing Brave (USA)) [2004/5 h72: 16g³ 20dpu 16mF 17m* 17g⁴ 19g⁶ 20g⁵ 18m⁵ 17g² 17v³ Oct 17] leggy gelding: modest hurdler: won novice handicap at Market Rasen in June: best around 2m with emphasis on speed. *Mrs L. Wadham* **h92**

NAMED AT DINNER 4 ch.g. Halling (USA) – Salanka (IRE) (Persian Heights) [2004/5 16m⁵ 16s² 16d² 16m⁴ 17s⁴ 16v² 16s² 16s³ Apr 3] small gelding: fair maiden (stays 1m) at 2 yrs for B. Meehan, poor form on Flat in 2004: modest juvenile hurdler: claimed from Mrs A. Duffield £6,000 sixth outing: raced around 2m: acts on good to firm and heavy going: wore headgear after debut: front runner. *Miss Lucinda V. Russell* **h86**

NAMELESS WONDER (IRE) 9 b.g. Supreme Leader – Miss Kylogue (IRE) (Lancastrian) [2004/5 h91: 24vpu 20s 20m³ 20gpu Feb 27] lengthy gelding: modest maiden hurdler: lame final outing: stays 2¾m: acts on good to firm and heavy going: tried blinkered/visored. *J. Howard Johnson* **h92**

NANDOO 6 b.m. Forzando – Ascend (IRE) (Glint of Gold) [2004/5 h82§: 21gpu Oct 6] poor and ungenuine winning hurdler: stays 21f: acts on firm going: wears cheekpieces. *A. G. Juckes* **h– §**

NANGA PARBAT (FR) 4 b.g. True Brave (USA) – Celeste (FR) (Amen (FR)) [2004/5 16dF 16s⁶ 17s⁴ 16d* 16d⁶ Mar 24] first foal: dam, no form over jumps, half-sister to very smart French chaser Mister Sy: third over 1¾m on debut on Flat in August for M. Rolland: fair form over hurdles: won novice handicap at Newbury in March: will stay beyond 2m: raced on good to soft/soft going. *P. F. Nicholls* **h104**

NANTUCKET SOUND (USA) 4 b.g. Quiet American (USA) – Anna (Ela-Mana-Mou) [2004/5 18s⁵ 16d Nov 6] fair on Flat (stays 1½m), successful twice in December (claimed by P. Howling £5,000 first occasion): looked temperamental/jumped poorly both starts in juvenile hurdles. *M. C. Pipe* **h– §**

NAPOLITAIN (FR) 4 b.g. Ajdayt (USA) – Domage II (FR) (Cyborg (FR)) [2004/5 18s* 16d⁴ 17d² 18s* 16v⁴ 17s 16g 16d³ 16s* Apr 21] useful-looking gelding: has scope: third foal: dam, won around 2m over hurdles in Italy, half-sister to Gran Premio di Merano winner Ali Baba: placed twice over 1¼m from 4 starts on Flat: fairly useful hurdler: successful in juvenile at Auteuil (final start for F. Cottin) in September and novices at Fontwell in January and Perth in April: stiff task, ran creditably when remote third to Mighty Man in Grade 2 novice at Aintree: will stay 2½m: raced on good going or softer. *P. F. Nicholls* **h121**

NARCISO (GER) 5 b.g. Acatenango (GER) – Notturna (Diu Star) [2004/5 20d⁴ 20s³ 20d³ 24v² 20v* 20v³ Feb 2] leggy gelding: modest maiden on Flat (should stay 2m): fair novice hurdler: won at Wetherby in January: stays 3m: raced on going softer than good (acts on heavy). *M. W. Easterby* **h112**

NARUKHA RAJPUT (FR) 4 b.f. Rajpoute (FR) – French Kiss IV (FR) (Art Francais (USA)) [2004/5 F18d⁵ Feb 20] good-topped filly: third foal: half-sister to fair 17f hurdle winner Ma'am (by Garde Royale): dam unraced, from family of smart chaser up to 23f Ginetta II: well held in bumper on debut. *F. Doumen, France* **F–**

NARWHAL (IRE) 7 b. or br.g. Naheez (USA) – Well Why (IRE) (The Parson) [2004/5 h121: c18dᵖᵘ Nov 14] close-coupled gelding: fairly useful hurdler, lightly raced: lame in maiden on chasing debut: should stay 3m: raced on good going or softer (acts on soft). *N. J. Gifford* **c–** **h–**

NASHVILLE STAR (USA) 14 ch.g. Star de Naskra (USA) – Mary Davies (Tyrnavos) [2004/5 c–§, h–: c20g May 8] no longer of any account: visored: temperamental. *R. Mathew* **c– §** **h–**

NAS NA RIOGH (IRE) 6 b.m. King's Theatre (IRE) – Abstraite (Groom Dancer (USA)) [2004/5 c110p, h114: c21g* c19dᵘʳ c21d⁴ c22s² c21dᵖᵘ Mar 19] tall mare: fairly useful hurdler at best: similar form over fences: idled when winning mares novice at Wincanton in November: best effort when second in novice handicap at Haydock: stays 2¾m: raced on good going or softer (acts on heavy). *N. J. Henderson* **c118** **h–**

NASSAU STREET 5 gr.g. Bahamian Bounty – Milva (Jellaby) [2004/5 17d Feb 1] smallish, angular gelding: half-brother to winning jumper in Italy by Saint Andrews: poor maiden on Flat (stays 9.4f): no show in novice on hurdling debut. *D. J. S. ffrench Davis* **h–**

NASSTAR 4 b.g. Bal Harbour – Prime Property (IRE) (Tirol) [2004/5 F16s Feb 5] fourth living foal: brother to poor hurdler Kings Square, stays 3m, and half-brother to 1½m winner/fairly useful 2m hurdler Middlethorpe (by Noble Patriarch): dam 6f winner: well held in bumper on debut. *M. W. Easterby* **F–**

NATHOS (GER) 8 b.g. Zaizoom (USA) – Nathania (GER) (Athenagoras (GER)) [2004/5 h121: c16d³ c17d* c19dᵖᵘ 17d 16s⁴ 16d 16d³ 17g 16d 18s² Mar 30] close-coupled gelding: fairly useful handicap hurdler: best effort in 2004/5 when 2½ lengths third to Crossbow Creek at Kempton in January: thrice-raced chaser, form only when winning 3-finisher maiden at Plumpton in November: best around 2m: raced on good going or softer: usually waited with: has found little. *C. J. Mann* **c107** **h119**

NATION STATE 4 b.c. Sadler's Wells (USA) – Native Justice (USA) (Alleged (USA)) [2004/5 16d* 16d² 16d² 16g³ Mar 15] useful-looking colt: fairly useful maiden on Flat (stays 15f), sold out of A. Fabre's stable 35,000 gns Newmarket Autumn Sales: fairly useful form in juvenile hurdles: won at Plumpton in December: in cheekpieces, travelled with little fluency but ran well when 9½ lengths third to Dabiroun in valuable handicap at Cheltenham: will stay 2½m. *G. L. Moore* **h121**

NATIVE ALIBI (IRE) 8 b.g. Be My Native (USA) – Perfect Excuse (Certingo) [2004/5 c77: c25dʳᵒ Apr 11] winning pointer: maiden hunter chaser: stays 25f. *S. H. Shirley-Beavan* **c–**

NATIVE BEAT (IRE) 10 b.g. Be My Native (USA) – Deeprunonthepound (IRE) (Deep Run) [2004/5 c109, h–: c24g³ c32m³ c21v c20v c22v c28d* Feb 27] medium-sized gelding: fair chaser: back to best when winning handicap at Downpatrick in February: again in cheekpieces, better effort at Punchestown in late-April when third to David's Lad in cross country event: stays 3½m: acts on any going. *J. R. H. Fowler, Ireland* **c112** **h–**

NATIVE BUCK (IRE) 12 ch.g. Be My Native (USA) – Buckskins Chat (Buckskin (FR)) [2004/5 c–, h–: c24d⁶ 27s c25d⁴ c28sᵘʳ c26s⁶ c30d⁵ Nov 20] leggy gelding: winning hurdler: handicap chaser, little form since 2002/3: stays 3¾m: acts on heavy going: tried blinkered/visored. *M. F. Harris* **c106 d** **h–**

NATIVE CHANCER (IRE) 5 ch.g. Anshan – Native Aughrim (IRE) (Be My Native (USA)) [2004/5 F17g³ F18m F16g F17m² 21gᵖᵘ Oct 7] first foal: dam unraced half-sister to fairly useful hurdler up to 2¾m Apollo King: fair in bumpers: possibly amiss on hurdling debut. *Jonjo O'Neill* **h–** **F87**

NATIVE CORAL (IRE) 7 ch.g. Be My Native (USA) – Deep Coral (IRE) (Buckskin (FR)) [2004/5 c24vᶠ 20v* 24sᵖᵘ Mar 10] €600 4-y-o: first foal: dam unraced, from family of very smart chasers up to around 3m Another Coral and Raymylette: successful twice **c– p** **h104**

from 3 completed starts in Irish points: fell on chasing debut: left K. Riordan, won maiden hurdle at Ayr in February: seemingly amiss next time. *N. G. Richards*

NATIVE CUNNING 7 b.g. Be My Native (USA) – Icy Miss (Random Shot) [2004/5 h75, F78: c23d5 c26v5 c24sur c24spu c25v5 c26d6 c28gpu c26gF c26m6 Apr 21] big, well-made gelding: poor hurdler: form over fences only on debut: should stay beyond 25f: acts on soft going: blinkered 4 of last 5 starts. *R. H. Buckler* **c–** **h–**

NATIVE DAISY (IRE) 10 b.m. Be My Native (USA) – Castleblagh (General Ironside) [2004/5 c–: c26d6 c20g2 c16m2 c21d* c20s4 c20s2 c21g2 c21g* c23d2 Apr 20] workmanlike ex-Irish mare: fair chaser: sold out of K. Burke's stable £5,000 Ascot June Sales after first start: won handicaps at Uttoxeter in October and Cheltenham (novice in April: stays 23f: acts on soft and good to firm going: tried in cheekpieces: has given trouble during preliminaries: front runner/races prominently. *C. J. Down* **c101**

NATIVE EIRE (IRE) 11 b.g. Be My Native (USA) – Ballyline Dancer (Giolla Mear) [2004/5 c83, h–: c21d2 23m6 c27d* Oct 27] tall, angular gelding: winning hurdler: poor handicap chaser: won at Sedgefield in October: stays 27f: acts on heavy going. *N. Wilson* **c89** **h–**

NATIVE EMPEROR 9 br.g. Be My Native (USA) – Fiona's Blue (Crash Course) [2004/5 c137, h–: c27s c26s5 c24gpu c36dF Apr 9] tall, useful-looking gelding: useful novice chaser in 2003/4: little worthwhile form in handicaps in 2004/5: stays 4m: raced on good going or softer (acts on heavy): tongue tied final start: patiently ridden. *Jonjo O'Neill* **c–** **h–**

NATIVE IVY (IRE) 7 b.g. Be My Native (USA) – Outdoor Ivy (Deep Run) [2004/5 h109, F99: 23d2 24s* 24s 23s5 25spu c24g* Mar 4] leggy gelding: fairly useful hurder: won handicap at Kempton in November by 2 lengths from It's Wallace: successful in maiden at Doncaster on chasing debut: stays 25f: raced on good going or softer (acts on soft): tongue tied third start: capable of better over fences. *C. Tinkler* **c108 p** **h119**

NATIVE JACK (IRE) 11 br.g. Be My Native (USA) – Dorrha Daisy (Buckskin (FR)) [2004/5 c144, h126: c24s c24vpu 19v2 c25s5 c29spu Mar 28] tall, lengthy gelding: useful chaser: fairly useful hurdler: well below best in 2004/5: stays 29f: raced on good going or softer (acts on heavy). *A. L. T. Moore, Ireland* **c– x** **h108**

NATIVE LEGEND (IRE) 10 b.g. Be My Native (USA) – Tickhill (General Assembly (USA)) [2004/5 c–, h–: c25vpu c17s5 c25vpu c16d5 Jan 7] leggy, angular gelding: winning hurdler: little form over fences: stays 3m: unraced on firm going, acts on any other: sold 1,050 gns Doncaster May Sales. *Ferdy Murphy* **c74** **h–**

NATIVE PERFORMANCE (IRE) 10 b.g. Be My Native (USA) – Noon Performance (Strong Gale) [2004/5 c117, h110: c25gpu 20f 24f4 24f4 22d c22mpu c24spu c20spu Mar 6] tall, useful-looking ex-Irish gelding: winning hurdler/chaser: form in 2004/5 only when fourth in handicap hurdles at Roscommon and Navan: left M. Hourigan before final start: effective at 2½m to easy 3m: acts on firm and soft ground: tried blinkered. *N. J. Gifford* **c–** **h110**

NATIVE PERSIAN (IRE) 7 b.m. Be My Native (USA) – Wollongong (IRE) (King Persian) [2004/5 c20gpu May 29] ex-Irish mare: second foal: half-sister to fair hurdler up to 19f One More Minute (by Zaffaran): dam bumper winner: won mares maiden point in 2004: well beaten in bumper: broke down 4 out in maiden at Hexham on chasing debut. *P. Monteith* **c–**

NATIVE SCOUT (IRE) 9 b.g. Be My Native (USA) – Carmels Castle (Deep Run) [2004/5 c149, h–: c16gur 17d 16v c16s4 c17v2 16v c17vF Jan 16] close-coupled gelding: useful hurdler at best, no form in handicaps in 2004/5: smart chaser: in cheekpieces, best effort of season when 2 lengths second of 4 to Central House in Grade 1 at Leopardstown in December: challenging when fell fatally 2 out in Grade 2 at Fairyhouse won by same horse: raced mainly around 2m on good going or softer (acted on heavy): blinkered last 2 starts: tongue tied. *D. Hassett, Ireland* **c151** **h–**

NATIVE STAG (IRE) 7 b.g. Be My Native (USA) – Celestial Dance (Scottish Reel) [2004/5 17g 16m 16g5 16v4 16d2 16d* 16v5 16s3 16s5 Mar 29] leggy gelding: fairly useful 1½m winner on Flat: fairly useful handicap hurdler: won at Fairyhouse in November: good second to Stutter in valuable event at Punchestown in late-April: raced mainly around 2m: acts on heavy going. *P. A. Fahy, Ireland* **h117**

NATIVE UPMANSHIP (IRE) 12 ch.g. Be My Native (USA) – Hi'upham (Deep Run) [2004/5 c156, h–: c16g4 c20s4 c17v3 c20s5 c16s2 c21gpu c20v* Apr 2] tall gelding: has stringhalt: top-class chaser at best, smart nowadays: won 3-runner Grade 3 An Uaimh Chase at Navan in April, making all and beating below-par Rathgar Beau by distance: **c154** **h–**

length third to same horse in Kerrygold Champion Chase at Punchestown later in month: probably best around 2½m: acts on good to firm and heavy going. *A. L. T. Moore, Ireland*

NATTERJACK (IRE) 7 b.g. Roselier (FR) – Hansel's Lady (IRE) (The Parson) [2004/5 F90: 22dpu 21d Jan 31] good-topped gelding: fair form in bumpers: well held both outings over hurdles. *A. King* **h–**

NATURAL (IRE) 8 b.g. Bigstone (IRE) – You Make Me Real (USA) (Give Me Strength (USA)) [2004/5 c81, h–: c25g5 16g c16dpu c17d c20dpu 17d c24v* Apr 17] good-topped gelding: winning hurdler: left F. Murtagh before final start: successful in April in point and hunter at Carlisle (tongue tied): stays 3m: acts on heavy going: tried in headgear: has looked less than keen. *Mrs J. Williamson* **c87 h–**

NAUGHTY NOAH 7 b.g. Rakaposhi King – Rockmount Rose (Proverb) [2004/5 17d 16g 17gur 16d 20s5 19vpu 21gpu Mar 27] smallish gelding: third foal: dam, modest chaser, stayed 3m: no sign of ability. *J. R. Best* **h–**

NAUNTON BROOK 6 b.g. Alderbrook – Give Me An Answer (True Song) [2004/5 h103, F85: 26gF c23g* c24dpu Nov 12] leggy gelding: fair hurdler: won novice at Worcester on chasing debut in October: lame next time: better around 3m than shorter: acts on soft going. *N. A. Twiston-Davies* **c118 h–**

NAUTICAL 7 gr.g. Lion Cavern (USA) – Russian Royal (USA) (Nureyev (USA)) [2004/5 h–: 16dpu Oct 2] leggy, angular gelding: fair on Flat, successful in September and October: maiden hurdler, no form in 3 starts since 2002/3: tried tongue tied. *A. W. Carroll* **h–**

NAUTICAL LAD 10 b.g. Crested Lark – Spanish Mermaid (Julio Mariner) [2004/5 c26spu Apr 28] fairly useful pointer, successful twice in 2005. *J. H. Docker* **c–**

NAUTIC (FR) 4 b.g. Apple Tree (FR) – Bella Dicta (FR) (Vayrann) [2004/5 F12d F16s F16s 16s5 17m Apr 13] good-topped gelding: second foal: half-brother to winning hurdler up to 19f/1m winner Ballade En Mer (by Le Balafre): dam placed around 2m over hurdles/fences in France: modest form in bumpers: better effort over hurdles when fifth in novice at Towcester. *R. Dickin* **h89 F78**

NAVADO (USA) 6 b.g. Rainbow Quest (USA) – Miznah (IRE) (Sadler's Wells (USA)) [2004/5 h99: 16m 17g3 Jun 15] modest form at best over hurdles: should prove better at 2½m than shorter: acts on good to soft going. *Jonjo O'Neill* **h–**

NAVARONE 11 b.g. Gunner B – Anamasi (Idiot's Delight) [2004/5 c112, h–: c25d3 c25g2 c32mpu c20m2 c20d3 c21d4 c24mpu Apr 2] tall gelding: fair handicap chaser: stays 25f: acts on good to firm and good to soft going: formerly tongue tied: bold-jumping front runner. *Ian Williams* **c112 h–**

NAWAMEES (IRE) 7 b.g. Darshaan – Truly Generous (IRE) (Generous (IRE)) [2004/5 h114: 16g* 16m* 20d5 16d 17g Mar 18] leggy gelding: useful hurdler: won handicaps at Aintree in May and Wetherby (beat Turgeonev ½ length) in October: well held in valuable handicaps at Newbury and Cheltenham last 2 starts: stays 2½m: acts on good to firm and good to soft ground: wore cheekpieces final start: reliable. *G. L. Moore* **h130**

NAWOW 5 b.g. Blushing Flame (USA) – Fair Test (Fair Season) [2004/5 h96: 19g4 20d Nov 20] compact gelding: fairly useful on Flat (barely stays 2m), successful in January: best effort over hurdles when fourth to Candarli in handicap at Newbury on reappearance: stays 19f: raced on good/good to soft going over hurdles. *P. D. Cundell* **h101**

NAY (FR) 4 b.g. Ragmar (FR) – Elysea (FR) (Shardari)] tall, useful-looking gelding: third foal: dam, winning hurdler/chaser up to 19f, half-sister to useful chaser around 2½m Jasmin d'Oudaries: sweating and on toes, made all in 25-runner bumper at Punchestown on debut in late-April, easily beating Well Mounted by 4 lengths: exciting prospect. *W. P. Mullins, Ireland* **F105 P**

NAZIMABAD (IRE) 6 b.g. Unfuwain (USA) – Naziriya (FR) (Darshaan) [2004/5 16gro 17g4 16g5 16d 20g6 16f c19spu c16v6 c19v6 c16g5 c16m2 Mar 21] half-brother to winning 15f hurdler Nasirabad (by Shahrastani): fairly useful on Flat (should stay 1¾m) at 3 yrs for J. Oxx, generally below form in 2003 for several trainers, sold 3,400 gns Doncaster November Sales that year: poor novice hurdler/chaser, sold out of J. Upson's stable £1,500 Ascot November Sales prior to chasing debut: will prove best around 2m: acts on good to firm going: tongue tied 5 of last 6 starts (breathing problem when not): free-going sort. *Evan Williams* **c78 h77**

NDOLA 6 b.g. Emperor Jones (USA) – Lykoa (Shirley Heights) [2004/5 16d4 16d 16g Dec 8] workmanlike gelding: modest on Flat (stays 11f), successful in February: best effort over hurdles when fourth in novice at Huntingdon on debut. *B. J. Curley* **h87**

NEAGH (FR) 4 b.g. Dress Parade – Carlie II (FR) (Highlanders (FR)) [2004/5 16d^2 Feb 3] first foal: dam runner-up twice around 1½m on Flat: runner-up at 13f on debut: sold out of J. M. Robin's stable €55,000 Goffs (France) November Sale: favourite and ridden by 7-lb claimer, second to Seeyaaj in novice at Kelso on hurdling debut, travelling well long way: should improve. *N. G. Richards* **h94 p**

NEARLY A BREEZE 5 b.m. Thowra (FR) – Nearly At Sea (Nearly A Hand) [2004/5 F16d Nov 6] rather unfurnished mare: first foal: dam fairly useful pointer: no show in bumper on debut. *C. J. Down* **F–**

NECKAR VALLEY (IRE) 6 b.g. Desert King (IRE) – Solar Attraction (IRE) (Salt Dome (USA)) [2004/5 17d^3 16s^4 16v^{pu} Dec 15] fairly useful on Flat (stays 1½m) at 4 yrs, second in minor event in April for R. Whitaker: best effort over hurdles when third in novice at Carlisle on debut. *R. A. Fahey* **h95**

NED KELLY (IRE) 9 ch.g. Be My Native (USA) – Silent Run (Deep Run) [2004/5 c17v^3 c17v^3 c20s* c16g c17s^3 Mar 28] big, strong gelding: high-class hurdler in 2001/2, lame only outing following season: useful novice chaser, contested Grade 1 events 3 of first 4 starts, best effort when 11 lengths third to Ulaan Baatar at Leopardstown (still carrying plenty of condition and heavily bandaged in front) second start: simple task in maiden at Fairyhouse in February: just respectable efforts when ninth in Arkle at Cheltenham and third at Fairyhouse last 2 starts: best at 2m: acts on good to firm and heavy going: has found little. *E. J. O'Grady, Ireland* **c139 h–**

NEEDLE PRICK (IRE) 4 b.g. Needle Gun (IRE) – Emerson Supreme (IRE) (Supreme Leader) [2004/5 F12d F13s F16m Apr 10] €11,000 3-y-o: leggy gelding: sixth foal: dam unraced, out of half-sister to very smart staying chasers Maid of Money and Ten of Spades: mid-division at best in bumpers. *N. A. Twiston-Davies* **F85**

NEEDSMORETIME (IRE) 13 b.g. Strong Gale – Sue's A Lady (Le Moss) [2004/5 c25g^R May 1] of little account nowadays: tried blinkered. *S. J. Robinson* **c– h–**

NEEDWOOD SCOT 4 b.g. Danzig Connection (USA) – Needwood Nymph (Bold Owl) [2004/5 F16g Mar 28] tenth foal: half-brother to 3 winners, including modest hurdler Needwood Spirit (by Rolfe), stays 2½m: dam 1½m winner: well held in bumper on debut. *C. N. Kellett* **F–**

NEEDWOOD SPIRIT 10 b.g. Rolfe (USA) – Needwood Nymph (Bold Owl) [2004/5 h96: 17d^5 16d 17s^{ur} 21d^6 20v 21v^{pu} 19d 16d 20m^4 17s^2 20g 22v^{pu} 20v^4 16d 24s^6 Apr 20] close-coupled gelding: poor handicap hurdler: effective at 2m to 3m: acts on soft and good to firm going. *Mrs A. M. Naughton* **h77**

NEGUS DE BEAUMONT (FR) 4 b.g. Blushing Flame (USA) – Givry (FR) (Bayolidaan (FR)) [2004/5 F16d^6 F16g^4 Apr 19] second foal: half-brother to 11.5f and 13f winner Malko de Beaumont (by Gold And Steel): dam 1¼m winner: better effort in bumpers when 2¼ lengths fourth to Regal Heights in maiden at Towcester: raced freely both starts. *F. Jordan* **F90**

NEIDPATH CASTLE 6 b.g. Alflora (IRE) – Pennant Cottage (IRE) (Denel (FR)) [2004/5 F87: F16s 16s^5 18v 17d^3 20s^5 Apr 20] bumper winner: modest maiden hurdler: should stay beyond 2m: raced on going softer than good (acts on heavy). *A. C. Whillans* **h91 F–**

NELLIE BROWNE (IRE) 5 ch.m. Presenting – Kev's Lass (IRE) (Kemal (FR)) [2004/5 F16g Sep 12] strong mare: fourth foal: dam, won 2m hurdle, half-sister to useful 2m hurdler Impulsive Dream: well held in bumper on debut. *J. A. Supple* **F–**

NELSONS NELL (IRE) 9 b.m. Supreme Leader – Lough Neagh Lady (Furry Glen) [2004/5 c–, h81, F–: 24m^4 17g^4 Aug 14] poor maiden hurdler: no show on chasing debut: stays 2½m: acts on soft going: tried in cheekpieces. *Miss Lucinda V. Russell* **c– h–**

NELTINA 9 gr.m. Neltino – Mimizan (IRE) (Pennine Walk) [2004/5 c20d^F 16d c22g* c21g^2 c20g^5 Apr 22] workmanlike mare: winning hurdler: off 20 months before reappearance: fair form over fences: won mares maiden at Fontwell in March: stays 2¾m: acts on good to soft going. *Mrs J. E. Scrase* **c113 h–**

NEM CON 7 b.g. Alflora (IRE) – Poppy's Pride (Uncle Pokey) [2004/5 19g Nov 10] leggy gelding: seventh foal: half-brother to 3 winners, including modest hurdler around 2m Breeze Home (by Homo Sapien): dam unraced: no show in novice hurdle on debut. *Ian Williams* **h–**

NEMISTO 11 gr.g. Mystiko (USA) – Nemesia (Mill Reef (USA)) [2004/5 c–, h94: c21g^{pu} c16d^{pu} 19m^{pu} Sep 8] good-topped gelding: winning hurdler/maiden chaser: no show after 14-month absence in 2004/5: formerly tongue tied. *B. R. Millman* **c– h–**

NEPHITE (NZ) 11 b.g. Star Way – Te Akau Charmer (NZ) (Sir Tristram) [2004/5 c102§, h–: c17g6 Mar 14] workmanlike gelding: maiden hurdler: fair handicap chaser at best: off 18 months, no show in handicap at Plumpton: raced mainly around 2m: acts on good to firm and heavy going: wears headgear: formerly tongue tied: unreliable. *Miss Venetia Williams* **c– § h–**

NEPTUNE 9 b.g. Dolphin Street (FR) – Seal Indigo (IRE) (Glenstal (USA)) [2004/5 h–: 20m 16s Jan 20] lengthy gelding: modest on Flat (stays 2m): winning hurdler: no show in 3 starts since 2002/3: should stay beyond 17f. *J. C. Fox* **h–**

NERONE (GER) 4 ro.g. Sternkoenig (IRE) – Nordwahl (GER) (Waajib) [2004/5 16d 16v3 18d 17g3 16sur Mar 11] tall, useful-looking gelding: fairly useful up to 1½m on Flat, won twice in Germany in 2004 for U. Stoltefuss: easily best effort over hurdles when third to Credit in juvenile at Musselburgh: likely to prove best at 2m with emphasis on speed: failed to settle first 3 starts. *P. Monteith* **h106**

NERONIAN (IRE) 11 ch.g. Mujtahid (USA) – Nimieza (USA) (Nijinsky (CAN)) [2004/5 20gpu Oct 5] of no account. *G. R. Pewter* **h–**

NESNAAS (USA) 4 ch.g. Gulch (USA) – Sedrah (USA) (Dixieland Band (USA)) [2004/5 16g 16spu 16s Nov 21] medium-sized gelding: fair maiden at 2 yrs, well held on Flat in 2004, sold out of B. Hanbury's stable 10,000 gns Newmarket July Sales: mid-division at best in juvenile hurdles: tongue tied second outing. *M. G. Rimell* **h72**

NETHERLEY (FR) 6 gr.g. Beyssac (FR) – Lessons In Love (FR) (Crystal Palace (FR)) [2004/5 F18d2 F16d* F16d2 Dec 29] tall, useful-looking gelding: fourth foal: half-brother to French middle-distance winners Fast In Love and Stand In Love (both by Fast Topaze) and Thiberline (by Cricket Ball): dam, 1¼m winner, half-sister to very smart middle-distance stayer Dom Pasquini: useful form in bumpers: won 20-runner event at Warwick in December by 3 lengths from Victom's Chance: good 1½ lengths second to Earth Man in Grade 2 at Newbury later in month. *Miss Venetia Williams* **F112**

NETTLETON FLYER 4 b.g. Ajraas (USA) – Mybella Ann (Anfield) [2004/5 F13d F17s F16s Jan 20] sixth foal: dam little sign of ability: tailed off in bumpers: trained on debut by N. Berry. *R. A. Harris* **F–**

NEUTRON (IRE) 8 ch.g. Nucleon (USA) – Balistic Princess (Lomond (USA)) [2004/5 h114: c16s4 c20m5 19g6 Jul 18] angular gelding: winning hurdler, fairly useful at one time: poor form on first of 2 starts over fences: stays 21f: probably acts on any going: tried blinkered, visored nowadays: unreliable. *M. C. Pipe* **c83 § h– §**

NEVADA RED 4 ch.g. Classic Cliche (IRE) – Sovereign Belle (Ardross) [2004/5 F16s2 Mar 31] 2,200 3-y-o: first foal: dam, third in bumper, half-sister to useful staying hurdler Melody Maid: second of 7 to comfortable winner My Skipper in bumper at Ludlow on debut. *D. McCain* **F91**

NEV BROWN (IRE) 9 b. or br.g. Executive Perk – Brandy Hill Girl (Green Shoon) [2004/5 c114, h–: c16dpu 20m c20g3 c16g3 c19g4 c16mpu Mar 21] lengthy, workmanlike gelding: twice-raced hurdler: fair form at best over fences: disappointing in 2004/5: sold out of N. Twiston-Davies' stable 3,000 gns Doncaster November Sales before final start: likely to prove best around 2m: headstrong and often jumps poorly. *Mrs D. C. Faulkner* **c84 x h–**

NEVEN 6 b.g. Casteddu – Rose Burton (Lucky Wednesday) [2004/5 h–: 20g 16m3 17d 16m4 17g 16d3 16g Sep 23] poor maiden hurdler: best at 2m with emphasis on speed: tongue tied. *Miss Lucinda V. Russell* **h70**

NEVER AWOL (IRE) 8 ch.g. John French – Lark Lass (Le Bavard (FR)) [2004/5 c21m6 c24m* c24s4 c24sur c24sur c24spu c23dpu Jan 25] workmanlike ex-Irish gelding: poor handicap chaser: form in 2004/5 only when winning at Towcester in October: stays 3m: acts on good to firm and soft going: has worn blinkers. *B. N. Pollock* **c85**

NEVER CAN TELL 9 ch.g. Emarati (USA) – Farmer's Pet (Sharrood (USA)) [2004/5 h86: 16d 16sF Dec 22] workmanlike gelding: modest handicap hurdler: fell fatally at Ludlow: stayed 19f: acted on firm and soft going: wore cheekpieces once. *B. D. Leavy* **h–**

NEVER COMPROMISE (IRE) 10 br.g. Glacial Storm (USA) – Banderole (FR) (Roselier (FR)) [2004/5 c130, h–: c24s* c24s2 c22s c21sF Apr 7] strong gelding: smart hunter chaser in 2003/4: below best in 2004/5, though made all at Thurles in January: will stay beyond 3¼m: acts on heavy going: tried blinkered. *T. M. Walsh, Ireland* **c113 h–**

NEVER CRIED WOLF 4 b.g. Wolfhound (USA) – Bold Difference (Bold Owl) [2004/5 16g 17m Sep 8] poor maiden around 1m on Flat, sold out of D. Elsworth's stable £1,100 Ascot April Sales: no show in 2 races over hurdles. *T. R. Greathead* **h–**

NEVER (FR) 8 b.g. Vettori (IRE) – Neraida (USA) (Giboulee (CAN)) [2004/5 h117: c20m^F c16g^2d Aug 24] tall, sparely-made gelding: smart hurdler at best: odds on and tongue tied, modest form when second of 3 in novice on completed start over fences (subsequently disqualified on technical grounds): stays 19f: has won on heavy going, best efforts under less testing conditions: usually held up. *Jonjo O'Neill* **c96 h–**

NEVER PROMISE (FR) 7 b.m. Cadeaux Genereux – Yazeanhaa (USA) (Zilzal (USA)) [2004/5 h–: 17d^ur 16d^6 19d 17m 16v^2 16g 19s^pu 16s^pu 16v^4 16s^4 Mar 23] small mare: bad maiden hurdler: raced mainly around 2m: tried visored. *C. Roberts* **h51**

NEVER WONDER (IRE) 10 b.g. John French – Mistress Anna (Arapaho) [2004/5 c24d^3 c25s^5 Jan 18] tall, useful-looking gelding: modest handicap chaser, off 20 months before reappearance: stays 3¼m: raced on good going or softer (acts on soft): usually forces pace. *M. Bradstock* **c94 h–**

NEW BIRD (GER) 10 b.g. Bluebird (USA) – Nouvelle Amour (GER) (Esclavo (FR)) [2004/5 c119, h–: c16m^pu c17m^3 c17g^4 c20f^pu Sep 26] tall gelding: fairly useful handicap chaser: below form in 2004/5: best around 2m: acts on heavy and good to firm going: tongue tied second outing: untrustworthy. *Mrs H. Dalton* **c111 § h–**

NEWBY END (IRE) 11 br.g. Over The River (FR) – Comeallye (Kambalda) [2004/5 c24s^pu c22v^2 c28g^pu May 21] lengthy gelding: maiden hurdler/chaser: stays 25f: acts on heavy going: blinkered once, visored last 5 starts. *D. S. Dennis* **c92 h–**

NEWCLOSE 5 b.g. Barathea (IRE) – Wedgewood (USA) (Woodman (USA)) [2004/5 16g May 16] poor maiden on Flat (stays 11f): tongue tied, well beaten in novice on hurdling debut. *N. Tinkler* **h–**

NEW CURRENCY (USA) 5 b.g. Touch Gold (USA) – Ceirseach (IRE) (Don't Forget Me) [2004/5 h112p: 16g^F 19g^2 16d^4 17g 16d Jan 6] good-topped gelding: fairly useful on Flat (stays 1¼m): fair form in 2 starts over hurdles in Ireland, sold out of J. Bolger's stable 42,000 gns Newmarket July Sales: disappointing subsequently: best at 2m: not a fluent jumper. *M. C. Pipe* **h94**

NEW DIAMOND 6 ch.g. Bijou d'Inde – Nannie Annie (Persian Bold) [2004/5 h–: 16g 17g^6 May 23] no form over hurdles. *Mrs P. Ford* **h–**

NEW ENTIC (FR) 4 b.g. Ragmar (FR) – Entiqua Des Sacart (FR) (Lute Antique (FR)) [2004/5 16d* 16d^2 16d^4 16d^bd 17s 17g Mar 18] well-made gelding: second foal: dam, in frame over jumps around 2m in France, half-sister to fairly useful chaser up to 3m Koquelicot: fairly useful juvenile hurdler: won at Huntingdon in October: best effort when head second to Yankeedoodledandy in quite valuable event there: never a factor when fourteenth to Penzance in Triumph Hurdle at Cheltenham: likely to be suited by further than 2m. *G. L. Moore* **h120**

NEW ERA (IRE) 11 b.g. Distinctly North (USA) – Vaguely Deesse (USA) (Vaguely Noble) [2004/5 c86, h–: c25m^pu May 11] workmanlike gelding: fair chaser in 2000/1: lightly raced and well held since: including in points: stays 3m: acts on good to firm and heavy going. *B. De Haan* **c– h–**

NEW FIELD (IRE) 7 b.g. Supreme Leader – Deep Steel (Deep Run) [2004/5 F102p: 16s* 16s^3 16s^3 18s^5 Feb 6] sturdy, lengthy gelding: bumper winner: fair form over hurdles: won maiden at Fairyhouse in November: will stay at least 2½m. *Patrick Mullins, Ireland* **h113**

NEWGATE SUDS 8 b.m. Kasakov – Newgate Bubbles (Hubbly Bubbly (USA)) [2004/5 19g 17g^6 22d^pu Aug 30] first foal: dam no sign of ability: no better herself. *N. Wilson* **h–**

NEWGATE TIMES 6 b.g. Timeless Times (USA) – Newgate Bubbles (Hubbly Bubbly (USA)) [2004/5 F–: 19g^pu Jul 4] no sign of ability in bumper or novice hurdle. *N. Wilson* **h–**

NEWICK PARK 10 gr.g. Chilibang – Quilpee Mai (Pee Mai) [2004/5 c101, h–: c20g^pu c16d^4 c19d^3 c21d^6 c16v^3 c17g c20g^pu Mar 27] good-topped gelding: fair handicap chaser in 2003/4: mainly out of sorts in 2004/5: stays 21f: acts on good to firm and heavy going: sometimes wears cheekpieces. *R. Dickin* **c94 h–**

NEWMARKET MAGIC (IRE) 9 b.g. Vasco (USA) – Prodical Daughter (Faraway Son (USA)) [2004/5 24s^pu Oct 24] ex-Irish gelding: won both completed starts in points in Britain in 2004: sold £3,400 Ascot July Sales: no show in novice on hurdling debut. *N. B. King* **h–**

NEWMILL (IRE) 7 br.g. Norwich – Lady Kas (Pollerton) [2004/5 h147, F–: c16s^5 c17s* c17v^5 c21v* c21s^{pu} c20s^4 Feb 20] tall, good-topped gelding: smart novice hurdler in 2003/4: useful form over fences, winning maiden at Clonmel (made all) in December and Grade 2 Paddy Fitzpatrick Memorial Novices' Chase at Leopardstown (beat Strong Project 2 lengths) in January: shaped as if amiss last 3 starts, including in Grade 1 novice at Punchestown in late-April (first start after leaving T. O'Leary): stays 21f: acts on heavy and good to firm going. *John Joseph Murphy, Ireland* **c129 h–**

NEW MISCHIEF (IRE) 7 b.g. Accordion – Alone Party (IRE) (Phardante (FR)) [2004/5 h87, F98: 21d^2 Nov 21] big, lengthy gelding: bumper winner: best effort over hurdles when second to Progressive in novice at Plumpton in November: stays 21f: has had tongue tied. *Noel T. Chance* **h102**

NEW PARK (IRE) 5 b.g. Luso – Charleys Lane (IRE) (Remainder Man) [2004/5 17g 17d^5 19s 22v Feb 15] sixth foal: dam unraced: no sign of ability. *R. H. Alner* **h–**

NEW PERK (IRE) 7 b.g. Executive Perk – New Chello (IRE) (Orchestra) [2004/5 c75x, h81: 19m^5 26f^2 20d^{pu} c24g^2 23d^6 c24s^5 c24g^6 c21d^3 Mar 28] close-coupled gelding: poor maiden hurdler/chaser: stays easy 3¼m: acts on firm and soft going: visored once: often let down by jumping. *M. J. Gingell* **c74 x h73**

NEW ROCK (FR) 4 ch.g. Video Rock (FR) – Agathe de Beard (FR) (Faunus (FR)) [2004/5 18s^2 18v^2 15s^2 18v^5 16v* 18s^2 Mar 13] third foal: half-brother to 19f chase winner Little Black (by Lute Antique): dam lightly raced, placed over 11f: useful juvenile hurdler: much improved when winning at Warwick in February by 14 lengths from Phar Bleu, about to take over when left clear by Miss Academy's fall at the last: will stay 2½m: raced on soft/heavy going. *G. Macaire, France* **h129**

NEWS FLASH (IRE) 13 b.g. Strong Gale – Gale Flash (News Item) [2004/5 c78, h–: c21d c25m^4 c28g^2 c24d^{pu} Feb 9] rangy gelding: maiden hurdler/chaser, poor on balance: stays 3½m: acts on good to soft going, probably on good to firm: tends to make mistakes. *Lady Susan Brooke* **c74 h–**

NEW'S FULL (FR) 4 b.f. Useful (FR) – Goldkara (FR) (Glint of Gold) [2004/5 F17s Apr 7] tall, useful-looking filly: sixth foal: half-sister to winning chasers up to around 2½m Windbreaker (by Hellios) and Peesenia (by Passing Sale): dam unraced: in need of race when well held in listed race when well held in listed mares bumper at Aintree on debut. *Ferdy Murphy* **F–**

NEWS MAKER (IRE) 9 b.g. Good Thyne (USA) – Announcement (Laurence O) [2004/5 c100, h–: c24d^F c24d* c24g^{pu} Feb 17] good-topped gelding: fairly useful handicap chaser, lightly raced nowadays: won conditional jockeys race at Kempton in February easily by 11 lengths from Metal Detector: lame at Sandown 6 days later: stays 3¼m: acts on heavy going: usually jumps soundly. *Mrs H. Dalton* **c121 h–**

NEW TIME (IRE) 6 b.g. Topanoora – Fast Time (IRE) (Be My Native (USA)) [2004/5 F80: F16g* 20v^3 17s 19d c20v^{pu} Mar 1] good-topped gelding: second start in bumpers, won at Stratford in September: poor form over hurdles: no show in novice handicap on chasing debut. *Jonjo O'Neill* **c– h– F84**

NEWTOWN 6 b.g. Darshaan – Calypso Run (Lycius (USA)) [2004/5 h–: 17m^5 May 23] poor form only completed start over hurdles. *M. F. Harris* **h73**

NEWTOWN DANCER (IRE) 6 b.m. Danehill Dancer (IRE) – Patience of Angels (IRE) (Distinctly North (USA)) [2004/5 16g 20g 19d 18s 18v 16s^4 16s 16g c18d^3 c18d^F c22d^F Mar 20] smallish, workmanlike mare: modest on Flat (stays 2¼m): modest hurdler: similar form in mares novice on completed outing over fences: should stay 2½m: acts on firm and soft going: has worn cheekpieces: usually tongue tied: front runner. *T. Hogan, Ireland* **c88 h91**

NEW WISH (IRE) 5 b.g. Ali-Royal (IRE) – False Spring (IRE) (Petorius) [2004/5 17g^5 Aug 21] fairly useful on Flat (should stay 1¼m) at 3 yrs, sold out of M. Channon's stable 35,000 gns Newmarket July (2003) Sales, modest nowadays: no show in maiden on hurdling debut. *M. W. Easterby* **h–**

NEXT TO NOTHING (IRE) 8 b.g. Bob's Return (IRE) – Shuil Abhaile (Quayside) [2004/5 c107, h102: c25v* c26s^3 c25g c31s^{pu} Apr 22] sturdy gelding: runner-up in maiden on completed start over hurdles: fair chaser at best: won 5-runner hunter at Ayr in February: below form after, downed tools in handicap final start: should stay beyond 25f: raced on good going or softer (acts on heavy). *N. G. Richards* **c96 h–**

NIAGARA (IRE) 8 b.g. Rainbows For Life (CAN) – Highbrook (USA) (Alphabatim (USA)) [2004/5 c95, h95: c17m^{pu} May 19] medium-sized gelding: modest maiden **c– h–**

hurdler/winning chaser: irregular heartbeat only outing in 2004/5: stays 2½m: acts on firm going: below form when blinkered: front runner/races prominently. *M. H. Tompkins*

NICANOR (FR) 4 b.g. Garde Royale – Uthane (FR) (Baly Rockette (IRE)) [2004/5 F16v^{3} F16s* F16v^{2} Apr 17] €70,000 3-y-o: good-topped gelding: second foal: dam, 21f chase winner/successful up to 1½m on Flat, half-sister to one-time very smart chaser Gadz'art: won maiden bumper at Thurles in February: useful form when placed next 2 starts, at the Curragh (1½ lengths second to Bit of A Gift) and Punchestown (15 lengths third to Refinement) in April. *N. Meade, Ireland* — **F107**

NICE BABY (FR) 4 b.f. Baby Turk – First Union (FR) (Shafoun (FR)) [2004/5 F16v^{6} 19g^{6} 19d 17d 17g 19v^{5} Apr 22] €15,000 3-y-o: second foal: dam, won around 1½m on Flat, sister to smart staying chaser Djeddah and half-sister to smart chaser around 2½m Extra Jack: well held in mares bumper on debut: poor novice hurdler: will stay 2½m. *M. C. Pipe* — **h84** **F–**

NICE HORSE (FR) 4 ch.g. River Bay (USA) – Tchela (FR) (Le Nain Jaune (FR)) [2004/5 F18d* F16g F17d Apr 9] 60,000 3-y-o: leggy gelding: ninth foal: half-brother to several winners, notably very smart hurdler/useful chaser Galant Moss (by Tip Moss), stayed 25f, and useful hurdler/chasers by Garde Royale Iris Royal, stays 3m, and Ma Royale, stays 29f: dam placed around 2m over jumps in France: useful form when winning bumper at Fontwell on debut in February easily by 12 lengths from Aspiring Actor: well held in graded events at Cheltenham and Aintree. *M. C. Pipe* — **F106**

NICELY PRESENTED (IRE) 8 b.g. Executive Perk – Minimum Choice (IRE) (Miner's Lamp) [2004/5 h91: 21g^{4} 16d^{2} 17m^{2} 16m^{F} Jul 21] workmanlike gelding: modest maiden hurdler: stayed 21f: acted on good to firm and good to soft going: dead. *Jonjo O'Neill* — **h96**

NICKIT (IRE) 9 gr.g. Roselier (FR) – Run Trix (Deep Run) [2004/5 c23g^{4} c26v^{pu} Apr 22] quite good-topped gelding: poor maiden hurdler/chaser: winning pointer: stays 23f: acts on soft going: tried blinkered: often sketchy jumper of fences. *Mrs Susan Smith* — **c82** **h–**

NICKLETTE 6 b.m. Nicolotte – Cayla (Tumble Wind) [2004/5 c16d^{pu} Oct 31] 1m winner on all-weather Flat early in 2002: no show in novice chase. *C. N. Allen* — **c–**

NICK'S CHOICE 9 b.g. Sula Bula – Clare's Choice (Pragmatic) [2004/5 h106: 20s^{pu} 16d^{F} 21s^{5} 19s^{3} 17s^{3} 16v^{3} 20v^{2} 20d^{2} c19d^{pu} 22d^{2} 22g* 22v^{2} Apr 22] compact gelding: fair handicap hurdler: won at Newton Abbot in April: less than fluent when pulled up on chasing debut: stays 2¾m: acts on good to firm and heavy going: tried blinkered: genuine and consistent. *D. Burchell* — **c–** **h111**

NICK THE JEWEL 10 b.g. Nicholas Bill – Bijou Georgie (Rhodomantade) [2004/5 c113, h–: 17d^{3} c20m^{pu} Jun 5] tall, angular gelding: fair handicap chaser at best: ran poorly only start over fences in 2004/5: lightly raced over hurdles: best around 2m: acts on soft and good to firm going: usually front runner. *J. S. King* — **c–** **h72**

NICK THE SILVER 4 gr.g. Nicolotte – Brillante (FR) (Green Dancer (USA)) [2004/5 16d^{pu} 16s^{6} 16d 26s* 21s^{2} 20g^{ur} 20d^{pu} 24d^{pu} 21d^{pu} Apr 18] leggy gelding: half-brother to modest hurdler Intensity (by Bigstone), stays 3m: fair form at best on Flat, well held in 2004: modest hurdler: sold out of G. Balding's stable £2,600 Ascot November Sales after third outing: upped markedly in trip, won novice claimer (claimed from E. Williams £10,000) at Hereford in January: lost his way after next 2 starts: stays 3¼m: acts on soft going: tried in cheekpieces/visor: ungenuine. *M. C. Pipe* — **h97 §**

NICOZETTO (FR) 5 b.g. Nicolotte – Arcizette (FR) (Sarhoob (USA)) [2004/5 F16s F16m F16g Jan 21] lengthy gelding: first foal: dam lightly-raced maiden: mid-division at best in bumpers: tried tongue tied. *N. Wilson* — **F86**

NIEMBRO 5 b.g. Victory Note (USA) – Diabaig (Precocious) [2004/5 h90: 20g^{pu} Jun 3] modest hurdler, generally out of form in first half of 2004: seems to stay 19f: acts on good to firm going, possibly not on softer than good. *Mrs T. J. McInnes Skinner* — **h–**

NIFTY ROY 5 b.g. Royal Applause – Nifty Fifty (IRE) (Runnett) [2004/5 16m^{ro} 16g 20s 20v^{3} 20s^{2} 20s Apr 22] angular gelding: modest maiden at 2 yrs for A. Berry, well beaten on Flat in 2004: poor novice hurdler: will stay beyond 2½m: signs of temperament (ran out on debut). *K. W. Hogg, Isle of Man* — **h74**

NIGHT BUSKER (IRE) 7 b.g. Accordion – Toca Time (IRE) (Toca Madera) [2004/5 c20g* c23m* Jul 16] IR 20,000 3-y-o: second foal: dam unraced: bumper winner: fair hurdler: successful on 2 of 3 starts over fences, at Kilbeggan in maiden in May and handicap in July (beat Oh So Lively a length): stays 3m: won bumper on soft, but seems ideally suited by good or firmer (acts on firm): tried blinkered. *D. T. Hughes, Ireland* — **c110 +** **h–**

NIGHT MARKET 7 ch.g. Inchinor – Night Transaction (Tina's Pet) [2004/5 16m^{6} May 27] modest and unreliable on Flat (stays 1¼m) in 2004: well beaten in novice on hurdling debut. *N. Wilson* **h–**

NIGHT PEARL (FR) 4 b. or br.f. April Night (FR) – Tarpeia (FR) (Suvero (FR)) [2004/5 F16s F17v 16d Apr 11] smallish filly: twelfth foal: sister to 11f winner/2m hurdle winner Jalucine and half-sister to several other winners, including 7f to 1½m winner Star du Lore (by Star Maite) and 17f chase winner Hibouver (by Abdonski): dam lightly-raced maiden: well beaten in 2 bumpers and novice hurdle. *B. Storey* **h–** **F–**

NIGHT SIGHT (USA) 8 b.g. Eagle Eyed (USA) – El Hamo (USA) (Search For Gold (USA)) [2004/5 16s^{4} 16s^{6} Nov 21] workmanlike gelding: fair on Flat (stays 1½m) nowadays, successful twice in 2004: lightly raced over hurdles, modest form both starts in 2004/5. *Mrs S. Lamyman* **h88**

NIGHT WARRIOR (IRE) 5 b.g. Alhaarth (IRE) – Miniver (IRE) (Mujtahid (USA)) [2004/5 16g^{pu} 16v Dec 31] lengthy gelding: fairly useful at best on Flat (stays 1½m), has lost his form: showed nothing on completed start in novice hurdles: sold 3,400 gns Doncaster March Sales. *D. Flood* **h–**

NIGHTWATCHMAN (IRE) 6 b.g. Hector Protector (USA) – Nightlark (IRE) (Night Shift (USA)) [2004/5 16s 20d^{4} 16d Mar 3] dam half-sister to useful hurdler around 2½m Call My Guest: fair stayer on Flat, sold out of W. Muir's stable 20,000 gns Newmarket Autumn (2003) Sales: easily best effort over hurdles (needed race on debut) when fourth in novice at Fontwell: sold 4,000 gns Doncaster May Sales. *N. J. Henderson* **h96**

NIKOLAIEV (FR) 4 b.g. Nikos – Faensa (FR) (Fabulous Dancer (USA)) [2004/5 F16g Apr 19] 11,000 3-y-o: fourth foal: brother to middle-distance winner Lamtar and half-brother to 11f to 15f winner Doublon (by General Holme): dam 1m winner: tenth of 17 in maiden bumper at Towcester on debut, travelling best until 2f out. *N. J. Henderson* **F82**

NIL DESPERANDUM (IRE) 8 b.g. Un Desperado (FR) – Still Hoping (Kambalda) [2004/5 c145, h–: c20g^{4} c26g^{pu} c24s^{5} c22v^{su} c20s^{3} c25s^{4} c26d* c36d^{6} Apr 9] useful-looking gelding: smart chaser in 2003/4, rather disappointing in 2004/5, though won minor event at Down Royal in March: kept on steadily when sixth to Hedgehunter in Grand National at Aintree: probably stays 4½m: raced on good going or softer (acts on soft): tried visored/blinkered.(slipped up). *Ms F. M. Crowley, Ireland* **c143** **h–**

NILE MOON (IRE) 4 b.g. Simply Great (FR) – Reasonable Time (IRE) (Reasonable (FR)) [2004/5 F16m Apr 2] €36,000 3-y-o: sturdy gelding: seventh foal: half-brother to bumper/2m hurdle winner Balla Time (by Balla Cove): dam unraced: thirteenth of 21 in bumper at Newbury on debut, failing to settle. *J. Howard Johnson* **F–**

NIMBLE TRAVELLER (IRE) 6 b.m. Blues Traveller (IRE) – Be Nimble (Wattlefield) [2004/5 17g^{ro} 17m^{pu} 17d 17d^{F} 17m Aug 31] little form on Flat at 2/3 yrs for K. Burke: no form over hurdles: wore cheekpieces and tongue strap final start: pulls hard. *R. Johnson* **h–**

NIMVARA (IRE) 9 br.m. Lord Americo – Liskennett Girl (Master Owen) [2004/5 20m 20m 20g 20g 16v 20v^{F} 16d^{ur} 16v^{F} 22s^{5} Mar 22] ex-Irish mare: poor maiden hurdler: left P. Heffernan after seventh outing, trained next one only by J. Motherway: stays 2½m: acts on soft and good to firm ground: has had tongue tied. *Evan Williams* **h72**

NINESTONELAD (IRE) 8 b.g. Montelimar (USA) – Miss Lime (Aristocracy) [2004/5 c24m^{ro} c21f^{5} c20f^{su} c20f c16m^{5} c25d^{5} Oct 9] of little account: tried in cheekpieces: has had tongue tied: sold 2,000 gns Doncaster November Sales. *J. G. Carr, Ireland* **c–** **h–**

NIP ON 11 b.g. Dunbeath (USA) – Popping On (Sonnen Gold) [2004/5 c–, h79: 26g^{5} 24g^{4} 24g^{4} 26d^{pu} 26f Sep 26] little form over fences: poor hurdler: stays 27f: acts on heavy and good to firm going: tried in headgear/tongue tied: sold 600 gns Doncaster November Sales. *M. E. Sowersby* **c–** **h79**

NIPPY DES MOTTES (FR) 4 b.c. Useful (FR) – Julie Des Mottes (FR) (Puma Des Mottes (FR)) [2004/5 16v^{4} 16d^{6} 16d^{3} Apr 22] fifth foal: brother to winning 2¼m chaser Mambo des Mottes and half-brother to 11.5f winner Lido des Mottes (by Esteem Ball): dam unraced half-sister to dam of smart French jumper Echo des Mottes and useful chaser up to 2¾m Disco des Mottes: successful around 1½m on debut at Cluny in July: left E. Lecoiffier, best effort over hurdles when fourth to New Rock in juvenile at Warwick: tongue tied final outing. *P. F. Nicholls* **h107**

NISBET 11 b.g. Lithgie-Brig – Drummond Lass (Peacock (FR)) [2004/5 c90, h–: c25g* c20d* c24g^{pu} c25s^{3} c25d^{pu} Apr 11] fair hunter chaser: won at Kelso and Perth **c95** **h–**

(novice) in May: off 9 months, no form last 3 outings: stays 3¼m: best efforts on good/ good to soft ground: races prominently: usually jumps soundly. *Miss M. Bremner*

NITE FOX (IRE) 6 ch.m. Anshan – New Talent (The Parson) [2004/5 F76: F16g6 16s2 20d 20s6 24s 26g2 25gpu Mar 27] twice-raced in bumpers: modest novice hurdler: stays 3¼m: wore cheekpieces last 2 outings. *Mrs H. Dalton* **h87 F–**

NIZZOLINO 6 b.h. Pennekamp (USA) – Shallop (Salse (USA)) [2004/5 16dF 19d Jan 12] sturdy horse: successful 3 times up to 8.5f on Flat, including at Dusseldorf in October: fell on hurdling debut: left R. Suerland, well beaten in novice at Newbury. *C. Von Der Recke, Germany* **h–**

NOBEL BLEU DE KERPAUL (FR) 4 b.g. Pistolet Bleu (IRE) – Gecika de Kerpaul (FR) (Sarpedon (FR)) [2004/5 F16s F16m Apr 2] tall, close-coupled gelding: first foal: dam, won over hurdles around 2m, also 1½m winner on Flat: green, seventh of 16 in maiden at Kempton, first and better effort in bumpers. *P. Winkworth* **F87**

NOBEL (FR) 4 gr.g. Dadarissime (FR) – Eire Dancer (FR) (Useful (FR)) [2004/5 16sur Apr 3] ex-French gelding: second foal: dam maiden chaser: placed all 6 starts up to 13f on Flat in Provinces at 3 yrs, left C. Le Galliard after winning over 1½m at Nantes in late-October: unseated fourth on hurdling debut. *N. G. Richards* **h–**

NOBLE ACTION 6 ch.g. Mister Lord (USA) – Triggered (Gunner B) [2004/5 F17d* 20s2 Dec 4] 8,500 4-y-o: fourth foal: dam unraced half-sister to useful chaser up to 3m Cherrynut: successful twice from 5 completed starts in points in 2004: won 7-runner bumper at Folkestone in November: 5 lengths second to Yes Sir in novice hurdle at Chepstow: should improve. *P. F. Nicholls* **h109 F104**

NOBLE BARON 9 gr.g. Karinga Bay – Grey Baroness (Baron Blakeney) [2004/5 c–p, h118: c23d4 c23d* c22d2 c24g2 Jan 14] workmanlike gelding: fairly useful hurdler: took advantage of lower mark over fences when winning novice handicap at Exeter (fourth course success) in December: not fluent when second both subsequent outings: stays 3m: acts on soft going: tongue tied last 3 starts. *C. G. Cox* **c110 h–**

NOBLE CALLING (FR) 8 b.g. Caller I D (USA) – Specificity (USA) (Alleged (USA)) [2004/5 h93: 22g* Apr 28] leggy gelding: modest on Flat (stays 17f): modest hurdler: upped in trip, won amateur novice at Exeter very early in season: seemingly better suited by 2¾m than 2m: acts on soft and good to firm going. *R. J. Hodges* **h99**

NOBLE COLOURS 12 b.g. Distinctly North (USA) – Kentucky Tears (USA) (Cougar (CHI)) [2004/5 c–, h–: c21d5 c21mpu c20g3 c22m3 c25s2 c16s4 Oct 24] small gelding: poor chaser nowadays: acts on good to firm and heavy going: has had tongue tied. *P. A. Blockley* **c63 h–**

NOBLE COMIC 14 b.g. Silly Prices – Barony (Ribston) [2004/5 c92, h–: c21g6 Jul 28] good-topped gelding: fair chaser at best, successful 5 times at Newton Abbot: stays 21f: acts on firm and good to soft going, probably not on softer: tried in cheekpieces: has had tongue tied: races prominently. *C. L. Tizzard* **c– h–**

NOBLEFIR (IRE) 7 b.g. Shernazar – Chrisali (IRE) (Strong Gale) [2004/5 h90: 23s4 c20m* c24g2 Dec 29] lengthy, well-made gelding: modest novice hurdler: much better form under less testing conditions when winning novice handicap at Musselburgh on chasing debut in November, making most: jumped less fluently when disappointing there next time: should stay at least 3m: acts on good to firm ground. *L. Lungo* **c118 h91**

NOBLE MIND 4 b.g. Mind Games – Lady Annabel (Alhijaz) [2004/5 16s 16d4 Apr 18] fair maiden on Flat (stays 1½m): well held in juvenile hurdles. *P. G. Murphy* **h–**

NOBLE PASAO (IRE) 8 b.g. Alzao (USA) – Belle Passe (Be My Guest (USA)) [2004/5 16s* 16s 16v3 21d 16s 16s Mar 10] useful-looking gelding: fairly useful on Flat in 2003: fair handicap hurdler: off 15 months, won at Haydock in November: best form at 2m: acts on heavy going: held up. *Andrew Turnell* **h104 d**

NOBLE PURSUIT 8 b.g. Pursuit of Love – Noble Peregrine (Lomond (USA)) [2004/5 16g 16g 16d6 17s6 16g Mar 9] medium-sized gelding: poor and unreliable on Flat (stays 1m): poor form over hurdles: likely to prove best at sharp 2m. *R. E. Barr* **h71**

NOBLE REQUEST (FR) 4 gr.g. Highest Honor (FR) – Restless Mixa (IRE) (Linamix (FR)) [2004/5 16d2 16s 16s2 16d* 16v3 17d* 16v3 16s 16g5 Apr 19] tall, good-topped gelding: chasing type: third foal: half-brother to winning hurdler around 2m Royal Future (by Kendor) and useful filly up to 9f Mes Bleus Yeux (by Exit To Nowhere): dam, 1½m and 13f winner, half-sister to Prix de Diane winner Resless Kara: fairly useful on Flat, successful over 1m at 2 yrs and in 1¼m claimer (claimed from P. Bary €56,000) at **h119**

Longchamp in 2004: similar standard over hurdles: won novices at Towcester in January and Taunton (beat Perfect Storm ½ length) in February: raced around 2m: acts on heavy going: usually front runner/races prominently. *P. J. Hobbs*

NOBLE SPY (IRE) 11 b.g. Lord Americo – Flashey Blond (Buckskin (FR)) [2004/5 c–, h–: c24s³ Mar 14] good-topped gelding: winning hurdler: no form since 2001/2, including over fences: stays 25f: tried visored. *Paul Hamer* **c– h–**

NOBLE TEVIOT 7 b.g. Lithgie-Brig – Polly Peril (Politico (USA)) [2004/5 h–, F–: 22spu 17dF 20s 17d Apr 5] leggy gelding: of little account: tongue tied last 3 starts. *W. Amos* **h–**

NOBLE TIGER (IRE) 4 b.f. Tiger Hill (IRE) – Noble Conquest (USA) (Vaguely Noble) [2004/5 F14s⁶ F16g F16g Feb 16] third foal: half-sister to fair chaser Kind Sir (by Generous), stays 2½m: dam, French 1m winner, half sister to very smart French 2-y-o Noblequest: raced freely when tailed off in bumpers. *Mrs S. C. Bradburne* **F–**

NOBODYS PERFECT (IRE) 5 br.m. Heron Island (IRE) – Likeness (Young Generation) [2004/5 F16d² F16g² 16v 20g⁶ 21v² 24s⁵ Apr 20] unfurnished mare: ninth foal: half-sister to 2 winners on Flat up to 8.5f: dam maiden half-sister to useful staying chaser Sir Peter Lely: runner-up both starts in mares bumpers: form over hurdles only when second in mares novice at Sedgefield: should stay 3m. *Ferdy Murphy* **h83 F94**

NOCATEE (IRE) 4 b.g. Vettori (IRE) – Rosy Sunset (IRE) (Red Sunset) [2004/5 16g* 17d⁴ 17g³ 16d⁴ Sep 22] tall gelding: modest on Flat (stays 1¾m): fair juvenile hurdler: made all at Stratford in July: likely to stay beyond 2m: wore cheekpieces/blinkers last 2 starts: has looked none too keen. *P. C. Haslam* **h99**

NOCKSKY (IRE) 12 b.g. Niniski (USA) – Olivana (GER) (Sparkler) [2004/5 c92, h–: c25d² c24g² c26d² c26mpu Sep 1] leggy, useful-looking gelding: fair handicap chaser nowadays: lame final outing: stays 3¼m: acts on good to firm and heavy going. *M. C. Pipe* **c102 h–**

NO COLLUSION (IRE) 9 b.g. Buckskin (FR) – Miss Ironside (General Ironside) [2004/5 c23dF c21dF Dec 2] well-made gelding: fairly useful novice hurdler in 2002/3: left N. Chance and off 19 months, fell both starts over fences: should prove best at 2½m+: acts on soft going. *Miss H. C. Knight* **c– h–**

NOCTURNALLY 5 b.g. Octagonal (NZ) – Arletty (Rainbow Quest (USA)) [2004/5 F16d³ F16m⁴ Apr 10] 67,000Y: second foal: dam, maiden who stayed 1½m, half-sister to high-class miler Shavian and Gold Cup winner Paean: fair form in frame in bumpers. *V. R. A. Dartnall* **F92**

NOD'S STAR 4 ch.f. Starborough – Barsham (Be My Guest (USA)) [2004/5 18s⁵ 16s⁵ 16g⁵ 18s³ Mar 30] dam half-sister to useful 2m hurdler Arabian Bold: poor maiden on Flat (stays 1¾m) for Miss J. Camacho: first form over hurdles on final outing: likely to stay 2½m: tongue tied last 2 starts. *Mrs L. C. Jewell* **h76**

NOEL'S PRIDE 9 b.g. Good Thyne (USA) – Kavali (Blakeney) [2004/5 c25g⁴ c24g May 27] angular gelding: fairly useful hurdler in 2002/3: lightly-raced chaser, poor form in hunters in 2004: stays 3m: acts on any going: has worn cheekpieces. *Nick Bell* **c76 h–**

NO FORECAST (IRE) 11 b.g. Executive Perk – Guess Twice (Deep Run) [2004/5 c108, h–: c20gpu c24dpu c21mpu Jul 26] tall gelding: maiden hurdler/winning chaser: no form since reappearance in 2003/4: sold out of A. Hales's stable 5,300 gns Doncaster May Sales after first outing: tried blinkered. *J. J. Lambe, Ireland* **c– h–**

NO FURTHER COMMENT (IRE) 5 b.g. Lord Americo – Saltee Star (Arapaho) [2004/5 F18dpu 20dpu c24g² Mar 18] half-brother to winning hurdler around 2m Jervaulx (by Le Bavard) and useful hunter On The Other Hand (by Proverb), stayed 27f: dam unraced half-sister to useful hurdler around 2m Sextant: runner-up on second of 2 starts in maiden Irish points in 2004: first form in Britain when second in maiden chase at Fakenham. *Ms Bridget Nicholls* **c87 h– F–**

NO GLOATING (IRE) 6 b.g. King's Ride – Arctic Gale (IRE) (Strong Gale) [2004/5 F–: F16m 20vpu 19dpu 20gpu Feb 27] rather leggy, workmanlike gelding: no form in bumpers or novice hurdles: tried blinkered/in cheekpieces. *P. D. Niven* **h– F–**

NO GUARANTEES 5 b.g. Master Willie – Princess Hotpot (IRE) (King's Ride) [2004/5 22s⁴ Oct 28] 6,800 3-y-o: fourth foal: dam, fair hurdler/winning chaser, stayed 19f: won maiden Irish point on debut in 2004: raced freely when fourth in maiden hurdle at Stratford. *N. A. Twiston-Davies* **h95 +**

Tattersalls (Ireland) Ltd Pat Taaffe Handicap Chase, Punchestown—
No Half Session wins with plenty to spare

NO HALF SESSION (IRE) 8 ch.g. Be My Native (USA) – Weekly Sessions (Buckskin (FR)) [2004/5 F16d* 20v* 20v^4 22d 24s^5 24v 20v c22v^4 c16s c17v^4 c24d* c20s* Mar 28] rangy gelding: second foal: brother to fairly useful hurdler/chaser Native Sessions, stayed 3m: dam bumper winner: won bumper at Sligo in June: fair hurdler: easily won 18-runner maiden at Listowel in September: often shaped as if amiss after: highly progressive handicap chaser: successful at Limerick and Fairyhouse (novice event, beat Lotomore Lad by 9 lengths) in March and Punchestown (again confidently ridden and just pushed out to beat Coolnahilla by 6 lengths) in late-April: effective around 2½m to 25f: raced on going softer than good (acts on heavy): capable of better yet over fences. *N. Meade, Ireland* **c121 p h112 F102**

NO HESITATION 4 b.g. Terimon – Just A Minute (Derrylin) [2004/5 F14s^5 Dec 6] first foal: dam, placed in points, half-sister to useful chaser up to around 3m Red Ark: tailed off in bumper on debut. *Mrs S. C. Bradburne* **F–**

NOISETINE (FR) 7 ch.m. Mansonnien (FR) – Notabilite (FR) (No Pass No Sale) [2004/5 c112, h–: c21d^6 c16d^3 c20s* c19v^4 c19d* c16s^3 c19g^4 c20s* c20g^5 Apr 15] good-topped mare: fairly useful handicap chaser: won at Warwick in December, Doncaster in January and Bangor (soon clear when beating Kalca Mome 7 lengths) in April: stays 2¾m: has won on good going, best form under more testing conditions. *Miss Venetia Williams* **c128 h–**

NO KIDDING 11 b.g. Teenoso (USA) – Vaigly Fine (Vaigly Great) [2004/5 c97x, h–: c16g c17g^{pu} c16m c16m^5 c17g^{pu} c24m^5 Feb 6] strong, lengthy gelding: modest handicap chaser, out of sorts in 2004/5: stays 2½m: acts on firm and soft going: tried in cheekpieces: sometimes makes mistakes. *J. I. A. Charlton* **c90 x h–**

NOLAND 4 b.g. Exit To Nowhere (USA) – Molakai (USA) (Nureyev (USA)) [2004/5 F16d* F17d^6 Apr 9] good-topped gelding: first foal: dam, runner-up over 1m at 3 yrs on only start, half-sister to dam of top-class 1m to 1¼m filly Bosra Sham and Poule d'Essai des Poulains winners Shanghai and Hector Protector: well-backed favourite, created good impression when winning maiden bumper at Wincanton on debut very easily by 5 lengths from Ballybough Jack: still looked inexperienced when sixth to The Cool Guy in Grade 2 event at Aintree month later: useful prospect. *P. F. Nicholls* **F108**

NOLANS PRIDE (IRE) 8 b.m. Good Thyne (USA) – Saucy Gale (IRE) (Strong Gale) [2004/5 c18v^6 c16d* c20s* c20s^2 c20v^6 c18d^4 c22d^2 c24s^4 Mar 26] 12,000 3-y-o: third foal: dam unraced half-sister to dam of smart staying chasers Calling Brave and Ottowa: bumper winner: fair hurdler/chaser: successful over fences in mares maiden at Wexford and listed mares novice at Clonmel in November: stays 2¾m: acts on soft going: tried in blinkers/cheekpieces: usually tongue tied prior to 2004/5. *W. J. Burke, Ireland* **c113 h–**

NOLIFE (IRE) 9 b.g. Religiously (USA) – Garnerstown Lady (Pitpan) [2004/5 c–, h–: 20d^{4} 26g 24s* 20d* 20v* 24d* Jan 7] leggy gelding: winning pointer: once-raced chaser: progressive hurdler, winning handicaps (first 3 novices) at Perth, Carlisle (2) and Musselburgh between August and January: stays 3m: acts on heavy going: races prominently. *Miss Lucinda V. Russell* **c– h96**

NOMADIC BLAZE 8 b.g. Nomadic Way (USA) – Dreamago (Sir Mago) [2004/5 24v 23v^{6} 24v c25d^{5} c21v^{2} c25d^{ur} Apr 11] leggy gelding: third foal: brother to fair hunter chaser Go Nomadic, stays 31f: dam modest pointer: maiden pointer: well held in 3 outings over hurdles: poor form in maiden chases. *P. G. Atkinson* **c83 h–**

NOMADIC ICE 8 b.g. Nomadic Way (USA) – Icelolly (Idiot's Delight) [2004/5 c–, h–: c23g^{F} 24m^{pu} Jun 29] angular gelding: no sign of ability: sold 2,000 gns Doncaster August Sales. *Miss G. Browne* **c– h–**

NO MORE MONEY 7 b.m. Alflora (IRE) – Cover Your Money (Precipice Wood) [2004/5 h83, F85: 22g May 1] useful-looking mare: modest novice hurdler: should be suited by further than 2½m: tried tongue tied. *Miss H. C. Knight* **h–**

NONANTAIS (FR) 8 b.g. Nikos – Sanhia (FR) (Sanhedrin (USA)) [2004/5 c119, h–: c19v^{pu} 20v^{4} 16d^{4} Feb 19] good-topped gelding: fairly useful hurdler: similar form on first of 3 outings over fences: stays 21f: acts on heavy ground: usually makes running. *M. Bradstock* **c– h115**

NO NEED FOR ALARM 10 ch.m. Romany Rye – Sunley Words (Sunley Builds) [2004/5 c17d^{pu} c17g^{F} c20d^{pu} c16s^{5} c22s^{ur} c16g^{2} c16v^{pu} c16g^{3} Jan 19] rangy, useful-looking mare: fairly useful hurdler/chaser around 2m at one time, little form since 2002/3: trained in 2003/4 by K. Burke in Ireland: tried in cheekpieces: free-going front runner, prone to mistakes when taken on for lead. *R. C. Guest* **c108 x h–**

NONE SO PRETTY 4 ch.f. Tamure (IRE) – Sweet Memory (Lir) [2004/5 F18m^{4} Apr 21] first foal: dam unraced: fourth to Sun Pageant in bumper at Fontwell on debut. *Miss E. C. Lavelle* **F83**

NON SO (FR) 7 b.g. Definite Article – Irish Woman (FR) (Assert) [2004/5 c125p, h–: c20s^{F} c16d^{F} c16s 16d c16s Apr 7] good-topped gelding: useful handicap hurdler: useful chaser: fell first 2 starts, 2 out in valuable intermediate handicap at Windsor (going strongly in share of lead with Massac at time) and 3 out in handicap at Cheltenham (would have finished second at worst behind Bonus Bridge): no form in valuable handicaps after, including back over hurdles: effective at 2m to 2½m: raced on good going or softer (acts on soft): usually patiently ridden: free-going sort. *N. J. Henderson* **c139 h–**

NON STOP AIMS 7 ch.m. Gunner B – Prevada (Soldier Rose) [2004/5 F–: F16g 19d^{pu} Oct 28] no form in bumpers or novice hurdle: sold £1,600 Ascot November Sales: fourth only completed start in points. *J. L. Spearing* **h– F–**

NOPEKAN (IRE) 5 b.g. Sri Pekan (USA) – Giadamar (IRE) (Be My Guest (USA)) [2004/5 h122: 16g^{5} 16d^{pu} 16s^{pu} Oct 21] rather leggy, close-coupled gelding: fairly useful juvenile hurdler in 2003/4 for P. Mullins: no form on Flat or over hurdles subsequently: likely to prove best at 2m with emphasis on speed: acts on soft going: tongue tied final outing. *Miss K. Marks* **h–**

NO PICNIC (IRE) 7 ch.g. Be My Native (USA) – Emmagreen (Green Shoon) [2004/5 h113: 24g^{4} 24s^{2} 20v^{3} 23s 25d^{2} 24d 27s^{6} Apr 22] small, leggy gelding: fair handicap hurdler: thorough stayer: acts on good to firm and heavy going. *Mrs S. C. Bradburne* **h112**

NORAS LEGACY (IRE) 7 b.m. Old Vic – Balda Girl (IRE) (Mandalus) [2004/5 h–, F–: 16d^{3} 16f 20d^{4} Jun 30] smallish mare: poor maiden hurdler. *Miss Lucinda V. Russell* **h68**

NORBERT (IRE) 7 ch.g. Imperial Frontier (USA) – Glowing Reeds (Kalaglow) [2004/5 h–: 17m Apr 9] no form, including in points. *M. F. Harris* **h–**

NORDIC PRINCE (IRE) 14 b.g. Nordance (USA) – Royal Desire (Royal Match) [2004/5 c–, h97: 21g* 27s^{4} c24m^{pu} c24d^{4} c26d^{2} c24v^{6} c24v^{pu} c25s^{4} c24d^{pu} Apr 22] compact gelding: modest hurdler/chaser, won 4-runner selling hurdle at Southwell in May: stays 3¼m: acts on any going: tried visored. *J. G. M. O'Shea* **c96 d h99**

NORDIC WINTER (IRE) 8 b.g. Glacial Storm (USA) – Proverb's Way (Proverb) [2004/5 24g^{pu} 20s Oct 20] IR £11,000 4-y-o: well-made gelding: fifth foal: half-brother to 2¾m chase winner Waydante (by Phardante): dam well beaten in points: no show in 2 novice hurdles: sold £1,600 Ascot November Sales. *D. P. Keane* **h–**

NO REFUGE (IRE) 5 ch.g. Hernando (FR) – Shamarra (FR) (Zayyani) [2004/5 **h147 p**
20d* 20d² 21s* 21g* Mar 16]

A letter received by Graham Wylie on Heath House notepaper began with the writer's reflection that he must be getting old. 'I used to wake up and the first thing I thought about was sex; these days my first waking thought is "I hope Mr Wylie's all right."' Mr Wylie's reply included the advice to 'resume your former pre-occupation'. There is no doubt that a mutually beneficial relationship has grown up between the Wylies and the master of Heath House, Sir Mark Prescott. The Cambridgeshire winner Chivalry, bought out of the Prescott stable as a four-year-old at the Newmarket Autumn Sales for 170,000 guineas in 2003, became the first winner, later that year, to carry the black and beige halved colours of the personable Tyneside software millionaire Graham Wylie and his wife Andrea. The big-spending Wylies have purchased five horses in all from Heath House and all have been successful to varying degrees, the others being Inglis Drever (110,000 guineas), No Refuge (180,000 guineas), Regal Setting (215,000 guineas)—all Newmarket Autumn Sales purchases—and Coat of Honour (bought privately).

No Refuge, an 11,000-guinea yearling, developed into a smart performer on the Flat, his victories including the Tote Gold Trophy at Goodwood, one of four successes at three, and a listed race over fifteen furlongs at Cologne on the first of two outings in blinkers as a four-year-old. No Refuge was relatively lightly raced, proven on soft going and by a sire whose stock-in-trade are later-maturing types, so any number of jumping trainers were likely to be in the market for him. Whether the Wylies and their trainer Howard Johnson were entirely satisfied with their acquisition at first seems debatable. No Refuge's performances on the schooling grounds gave rise to considerable concern. 'Graham Lee came down one day and No Refuge wouldn't go at all,' said the trainer who gives the credit for getting No Refuge going to an ex-showjumper, Lisa Brughan, who reportedly spent a lot of time jumping him over poles. No Refuge's jumping was far from fluent in his first season over hurdles but it did not hold him back. After landing the odds at Aintree in November—in the same two-and-a-half-mile novice hurdle in which Inglis Drever started off the previous year—No Refuge graduated straight into graded company in the Winter Novices' Hurdle at Sandown in early-December. He

betfair.com 0870 90 80 121 Novices' Hurdle, Aintree—
smart Flat recruit No Refuge (No.3) makes a winning start over hurdles

Royal & SunAlliance Novices' Hurdle, Cheltenham—No Refuge collars Racing Demon near the line; Pole Star (No.9) and Gold Medallist will lose third to fast-finishing Our Ben

couldn't emulate Inglis Drever, who also won that race in 2003, but No Refuge still recorded a useful performance, going down by a length and a half, conceding 7 lb to the winner Ladalko, and might well have won had his jumping been more proficient. Improving No Refuge's jumping looked likely to be the key to his progress over hurdles, but the defeat by Ladalko turned out to be the only one he suffered.

No Refuge did not have to improve on his Sandown form to beat Lady Zephyr and three others in the Grade 2 totepool Leamington Novices' Hurdle at Warwick in January—another race contested by Inglis Drever—and he arrived at the Cheltenham Festival as one of the leading contenders for the Royal & SunAlliance Novices' Hurdle, in which his stable companion had started a short-priced favourite and been beaten half a length twelve months earlier. The Wylies—who won the opening race on the first day, the Supreme Novices', with another useful recruit Arcalis—are not the only big owners buying accomplished Flat performers to turn them into successful hurdlers. The latest Royal & SunAlliance line-up contained more ex-Flat horses than it often does, among them, in addition to No Refuge, being Gold Medallist, a smart stayer who had won the Group 2 Prix Kergorlay, and the useful staying handicapper Reveillez. Both had changed hands, while Reveillez's stable-companion Pole Star, in the frame in his time in the Jockey Club Cup, the Sagaro Stakes, the Henry II Stakes and the Gold Cup at Royal Ascot, had also changed hands and had his attentions turned to hurdling. All four named finished in the first six in the Royal & SunAlliance, No Refuge running on tenaciously up the hill to catch Racing Demon, after being only sixth on the home turn and still having around five lengths to make up at the last. The margin of victory was three quarters of a length, with Irish-trained 33/1-shot Our Ben, finishing fastest of all, a further two and a half lengths away third, just ahead of Pole Star, Gold Medallist and Reveillez. Racing Demon and Our Ben had followed a more traditional path to Cheltenham for Royal & SunAlliance contenders, progressing from bumpers.

The rather leggy No Refuge, a Flat type in appearance, is by Prix du Jockey Club winner Hernando, a son of Niniski who is also the sire of Alflora, the most popular sire of jumpers based in Britain. Hernando has himself sired two winners of the Jockey Club, Holding Court and Sulamani, the latter in addition winning the Dubai Sheema Classic, Arlington Million and Turf Classic at four and the Juddmonte International and Canadian International at five. Hernando has had success with his progeny who have found their way into jumping, most notably with the very smart hurdler at up to three miles Sacundai. Sacundai's dam and grandam were both owned by the Aga Khan, as, coincidentally, were the dam and grandam of No Refuge. No Refuge's dam Shamarra, a half-sister to Shantaroun, a smart performer at up to a mile and a half, never ran and was sold out of the Aga Khan's Studs for IR 55,000 guineas, carrying her first foal, a filly by Khayasi, subsequently named Princess Claudia who turned out to be a maiden handicapper on the Flat and only a poor performer over hurdles. Shamarra's second foal

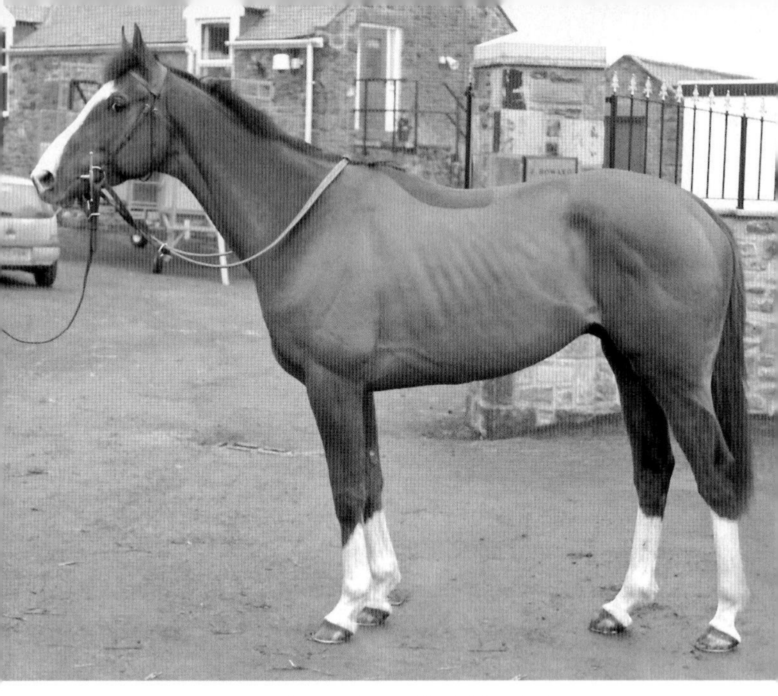

Andrea & Graham Wylie's "No Refuge"

No Refuge (IRE) (ch.g. 2000)	Hernando (FR) (b 1990)	Niniski (b 1976)	Nijinsky
			Virginia Hills
		Whakilyric (b 1984)	Miswaki
			Lyrism
	Shamarra (FR) (gr 1993)	Zayyani (b 1986)	Darshaan
			Zariya
		Shannfara (gr 1977)	Zeddaan
			Shahana

Denmark (by Danehill) was only lightly raced but won over six furlongs as a two-year-old for Sir Mark Prescott. No Refuge is Shamarra's third foal and her fourth, the filly Sweet Home Alabama (by Desert Prince), was a modest maiden. The next foal to reach the racecourse was Proclamation (by King's Best), a top-class performer at up to a mile who won the Sussex Stakes at Goodwood in 2005. No Refuge's grandam Shannfara was a very useful mile- to nine-furlong winner in France, while his great grandam Shahana is the fourth dam of the Aga Khan's top miler Sendawar. The family has produced other performers who have gone on to be useful or better hurdlers including the ill-fated Timber King and Shantarini, who was successful at up to three miles. No Refuge quickly made up into a leading performer over hurdles and, if his jumping becomes more consistently good with experience, he should develop into another leading contender for his stable for the World Hurdle, a race won in the latest season by Inglis Drever. No Refuge will stay three miles and, judged by the gusto with which he tackled the Cheltenham hill at the end of the Royal & SunAlliance, he should improve again when given the chance to tackle a longer trip. He has so far been raced on good going or softer over hurdles and acts on soft. *J. Howard Johnson*

NO REGRETS (FR) 4 b.g. Nononito (FR) – Betty Royale (FR) (Royal Charter (FR)) [2004/5 F16g* F16g^{3} Mar 26] good-topped gelding: seventh foal: half-brother to fairly useful chaser up to 21f Hey Jude and 1½m winner Inchala (both by Argument): dam 11f winner: fairly useful form in bumpers: won at Doncaster by ½ length from Oscardeal: 3 lengths third to Arumun at Haydock later in March. *N. J. Henderson* **F103**

NO REMORSE 7 b.g. Alflora (IRE) – G'Ime A Buzz (Electric) [2004/5 24g Mar 3] second foal: half-brother to 2-y-o 7f winner Cosmic Buzz (by Cosmonaut): dam, winning hurdler, stayed 2½m: thrice-raced in points in 2004, won maiden on completed start: well held in novice on hurdling debut. *R. Lee* **h–**

NO RETREAT (NZ) 12 b.g. Exattic (USA) – Lerwick (NZ) (Thoreau (FR)) [2004/5 c98, h–: c21s^{6} Apr 7] rangy gelding: winning chaser, lightly raced nowadays: fit from points (successful in March), sixth to Katarino in Fox Hunters' at Aintree: probably stays 27f: acts on good to firm and heavy going. *J. Groucott* **c103** **h–**

NO REWARD (IRE) 9 b.g. Persian Mews – Tara's Dream (Polar Jinks) [2004/5 c21m^{4} May 19] modest pointer, won in March: fourth of 5 finishers in novice hunter chase at Folkestone. *Mrs S. J. Hickman* **c66**

NORMA HILL 4 b.f. Polar Prince (IRE) – Smartie Lee (Dominion) [2004/5 17g^{4} 17d^{6} 16g* 16g 17s* 16d^{F} 16s^{6} 16d^{2} 16g^{2} 16d^{4} 17m* Apr 9] leggy filly: half-sister to 3 winners, including poor hurdler Miss Lacroix (by Picea), stays 2¾m: dam, winning hurdler up to 2¾m, also 7f to 1½m winner on Flat: fairly useful hurdler: won juveniles at Ludlow (maiden) in October and Hereford in November and handicap at Hereford (best effort, beat Welsh Man by 5 lengths) in April: raced around 2m: has won on soft going, best form under less testing conditions: races up with pace: tough. *R. Hollinshead* **h118**

NORMANDY SANDS (IRE) 7 b. or br.g. Namaqualand (USA) – Buzz Along (Prince Bee) [2004/5 h82§: 26g^{6} 24d^{3} c24d^{pu} Sep 10] tall gelding: poor maiden hurdler: jumped sluggishly on chasing debut: thorough stayer: acts on heavy and good to firm going: tried in cheekpieces, usually visored: lazy and inconsistent: sold 2,200 gns Doncaster October Sales, won maiden point in April. *Jennie Candlish* **c– §** **h– §**

NORMINSTER 4 ch.g. Minster Son – Delightfool (Idiot's Delight) [2004/5 F17v^{6} F16s Apr 10] first foal: dam bad maiden hurdler/chaser: no encouragement in 2 bumpers. *R. Nixon* **F–**

NORSEMAN CATELINE (FR) 4 b.g. Poplar Bluff – Dame Jaune (FR) (Le Nain Jaune (FR)) [2004/5 16f^{pu} 16d^{5} 17d 16g 16v^{6} 19s^{pu} Jan 31] lengthy gelding: third foal: brother to winner around 1½m Ligne Jaune Cateli: dam, won 2½m chase, also at 1¼m on Flat: fourth both starts on Flat at 3 yrs for J. Barbe: modest form at best over hurdles: visored final start: has been early to post/very unruly at start. *M. Scudamore* **h83**

NORTHAW LAD (IRE) 7 ch.g. Executive Perk – Black Tulip (Pals Passage) [2004/5 h96p, F98: 16g^{2} 20d^{4} 21d^{F} Feb 9] sturdy gelding: bumper winner: fair form at best over hurdles: likely to prove best around 2m. *C. Tinkler* **h100**

NORTHERN DEAL (IRE) 10 b.g. Top of The World – Amberley (Deep Run) [2004/5 c21d^{F} c21m* c19d^{4} c25g* c24d^{2} Nov 12] lengthy gelding: winning pointer: fairly useful novice chaser: won at Stratford in September and Wincanton (handicap, beat Inca Trail comfortably by 5 lengths) in October: ran creditably when 20 lengths second to Comply Or Die in novice at Cheltenham: stays 25f: unraced on extremes of going: races prominently. *Evan Williams* **c128**

NORTHERN ECHO 8 b.g. Pursuit of Love – Stop Press (USA) (Sharpen Up) [2004/5 h53§: 16g^{6} 17g 16d* 21m^{6} 16g^{4} 17m^{6} 16m 20d^{6} 18v^{6} 20s Apr 10] compact gelding: poor hurdler: won amateur novice handicap at Hexham in June: raced mainly around 2m: acts on firm and good to soft going: tried visored/blinkered, wears cheekpieces nowadays: has had tongue tied: ungenuine. *K. S. Thomas* **h68 §**

NORTHERN FLASH 11 b.g. Rambo Dancer (CAN) – Spinster (Grundy) [2004/5 c–, h–: c16g^{5} 17g^{6} 16d^{5} 16m^{5} c16g^{4} 17g^{2} c17g^{6} c16s* c17d^{3} c16s^{ur} c16v^{4} Apr 17] workmanlike gelding: maiden hurdler: poor chaser: finally off mark in handicap at Perth in August: best around 2m: acts on firm and soft going: wears headgear: tongue tied once. *J. C. Haynes* **c71** **h63**

NORTHERN FRIEND 5 b.g. Distinctly North (USA) – Pharaoh's Joy (Robellino (USA)) [2004/5 16s^{pu} 16s^{pu} 16d^{4} 16g 16v 16g 19d Feb 4] sturdy gelding: modest maiden on Flat (stays 1¼m), sold out of J. Glover's stable 4,800 gns Doncaster October (2003) Sales: form over hurdles only when fourth in novice at Wetherby: wore blinkers (raced freely)/cheekpieces last 2 outings. *R. C. Guest* **h79**

NORTHERN LINK (IRE) 6 b.g. Distinctly North (USA) – Miss Eurolink (Touching Wood (USA)) [2004/5 F16m Jun 29] fourth foal: dam, fair hurdler around 2m, half-sister to fairly useful hurdler/chaser up to 27f Sea Island: tailed off in bumper on debut. *Miss G. Browne* **F–**

NORTHERN MADRIK (FR) 4 b. or br.g. Useful (FR) – Belle Des Belles (FR) (Goldneyev (USA)) [2004/5 F17s 20d Feb 26] €16,000 3-y-o: compact gelding: first foal: dam won up to around 11f on Flat: not knocked about when well held in bumper and maiden hurdle: open to improvement. *M. C. Pipe* **h– p F–**

NORTHERN MINSTER 6 b.g. Minster Son – Hand On Heart (IRE) (Taufan (USA)) [2004/5 h75: 16d^{4} 16d 16s 16g^{3} 19d 16s^{pu} 19g* 20v* 20d^{4} 20s^{4} Apr 10] angular gelding: modest handicap hurdler: reportedly underwent breathing operation after sixth start: improved form after, winning at Catterick and Carlisle in March: stays 2½m: acts on any going: tried blinkered. *F. P. Murtagh* **h96**

NORTHERN NEWS (IRE) 5 b.g. Saddlers' Hall (IRE) – Some News (IRE) (Be My Native (USA)) [2004/5 F16s F16g Dec 16] €20,000 3-y-o: sturdy gelding: second foal: dam unraced half-sister to very smart staying chaser Belmont King: shaped like a stayer when well held in bumpers. *G. A. Swinbank* **F–**

NORTHERN RAIDER (IRE) 7 b.g. College Chapel – Pepper And Salt (IRE) (Double Schwartz) [2004/5 c–, h–: c21g^{pu} c20v^{pu} c20v^{pu} Mar 1] sturdy gelding: won juvenile seller in 2001/2, little other form: tried blinkered/in cheekpieces. *Miss T. Jackson* **c– h–**

NORTHERN RAMBLER (IRE) 8 gr.g. Roselier (FR) – Ramble Bramble (Random Shot) [2004/5 c70, h76§: c20v Apr 17] quite good-topped gelding: poor maiden hurdler: twice-raced chaser: in frame both starts in points in 2005: stays 25f: blinkered once (numerous mistakes): has looked temperamental. *K. G. Reveley* **c– h–**

NORTHERN SHADOWS 6 b.m. Rock Hopper – Shadows of Silver (Carwhite) [2004/5 F89: F16d^{4} 16v^{pu} 16v^{3} 16s^{3} 16v^{4} 16g^{6} 21g^{4} Mar 28] sturdy mare: in frame in mares bumpers: modest novice hurdler: stays 21f: acts on heavy going. *K. G. Reveley* **h86 F85**

NORTHERN SPIRIT 4 b.g. Kadeed (IRE) – Elegant Spirit (Elegant Air) [2004/5 17g^{6} Aug 14] modest on Flat (stays 1¾m), sold from K. Ryan 6,200 gns after winning seller in July: no show in juvenile on hurdling debut. *C. W. Moore* **h–**

NORTH (IRE) 7 br.g. Mukaddamah (USA) – Flamenco (USA) (Dance Spell (USA)) [2004/5 h–: 16g^{pu} 26f^{pu} Sep 26] no form: tried blinkered. *A. C. Wilson* **h–**

NORTH LANDING (IRE) 5 b.g. Storm Bird (CAN) – Tirol Hope (IRE) (Tirol) [2004/5 17d 17g 17d^{3} 17g^{3} 16d^{6} 17m^{F} 20g* Aug 14] modest maiden on Flat (stays 1m) for H. McWilliams: modest hurdler: won amateur handicap at Bangor in August: stays 2½m. *R. C. Guest* **h88**

NORTH LODGE (GER) 5 b.g. Grand Lodge (USA) – Nona (GER) (Cortez (GER)) [2004/5 16d 16d^{6} 16s Jan 6] smallish ex-German gelding: useful on Flat (stays 11f) for M. Hofer: best effort in novice hurdles when sixth at Newbury: should stay beyond 2m. *A. King* **h93**

NORTH POINT (IRE) 7 b.g. Definite Article – Friendly Song (Song) [2004/5 h–: 16g 22g^{pu} 20m 16g^{5} 17g Dec 14] smallish, close-coupled gelding: fair hurdler at one time, little impact since 2002/3: best form at 2m: acts on good to firm going: blinkered in 2004/5: sold 1,500 gns Doncaster January Sales. *R. Curtis* **h92 d**

NORTON SAPPHIRE 6 ch.m. Karinga Bay – Sea of Pearls (IRE) (King's Ride) [2004/5 h65, F–: 20d^{6} 21g 16g^{pu} 22m 20g^{4} 22d^{pu} 19g 21g 22s^{pu} 16d^{3} 21g^{6} 16d^{6} Mar 28] smallish mare: bad maiden hurdler: stays 21f: acts on good to soft going: sold £2,600 Ascot April Sales. *M. J. Gingell* **h62**

NORWEGIAN 4 b.g. Halling (USA) – Chicarica (USA) (The Minstrel (CAN)) [2004/5 16d^{6} 16d 16d Mar 14] good-topped gelding: fair on Flat (should stay 1¼m), successful in 2004 for D. Loder: little show in juvenile hurdles. *Ian Williams* **h–**

NOSAM 15 b.g. Idiot's Delight – Socher (Anax) [2004/5 c110, h–: c25m^{5} c22g^{3} c20d^{6} c21m^{6} c20g^{5} Aug 14] sparely-made, close-coupled gelding: veteran chaser: stays 25f: acts on any going: tried visored, usually wears cheekpieces and tongue strap. *R. C. Guest* **c98 d h–**

NO SAM NO 7 b.m. Reprimand – Samjamalifran (Blakeney) [2004/5 c73, h64: 22g^{pu} c21g^{5} 24m* 27d^{3} 24f^{2} Sep 5] leggy mare: winning chaser: poor novice hurdler: won amateurs handicap at Worcester in August: stays 27f: acts on soft and firm going: wears blinkers/cheekpieces nowadays: sold 7,600 gns Doncaster May Sales. *S. C. Burrough* **c– h75**

NO SHENANIGANS (IRE) 8 b.g. King's Ride – Melarka (Dara Monarch) [2004/5 c106: c19m^{2} c20m^{3} Jun 6] strong, good sort: bumper winner: fair form over fences, lightly raced: stays 19f: acts on good to firm and good to soft going: sold only 4,400 gns Doncaster May Sales. *N. J. Henderson* **c109**

NOSHINANNIKIN 11 ch.g. Anshan – Preziosa (Homing) [2004/5 c121x, h110: c17g^{2} c20m^{4} c17m^{ur} c16m^{4} 20d* c20m* 20s^{2} c25d^{F} c20d^{3} 23s^{F} 16s 20v Feb 19] big, strong gelding: fairly useful handicap hurdler/chaser: won over hurdles at Uttoxeter (by 7 lengths from Made In France) and fences at Wetherby (idled when beating Navarone ½ length) in October: stays 2½m: acts on soft and good to firm going: blinkered once: often tongue tied: sketchy jumper of fences. *Mrs S. J. Smith* **c119 x h122**

NOSTRADAMUS (USA) 6 b. or br.g. Gone West (USA) – Madam North (CAN) (Halo (USA)) [2004/5 h91: 18m^{3} 16m Sep 19] good-topped gelding: poor hurdler: raced around 2m: unraced on firm going, acts on any other. *K. Burke, Ireland* **h84**

NOT AMUSED (UAE) 5 ch.g. Indian Ridge – Amusing Time (IRE) (Sadler's Wells (USA)) [2004/5 16g 16g 16s^{6} 16d^{5} 16d 19d Feb 4] sturdy gelding: formerly fairly useful on Flat (stays 11f): sold out of B Hills's stable 26,000 gns Newmarket Autumn (2003) Sales: poor novice hurdler, left I. Williams after fourth outing: likely to prove best around 2m. *C. R. Dore* **h74**

NOTANOTHERDONKEY (IRE) 5 b.g. Zaffaran (USA) – Sporting Talent (IRE) (Seymour Hicks (FR)) [2004/5 F85: F16m^{3} 20s 16d^{6} 17d^{5} Dec 10] tall, unfurnished gelding: modest form in bumpers and over hurdles: should stay well beyond 2m. *M. Scudamore* **h96 ? F85**

NOTAPROBLEM (IRE) 6 b.g. Oscar (IRE) – Smashed Free (IRE) (Carlingford Castle) [2004/5 F16s^{2} F16v^{3} F16v* F16v^{2} 16s^{2} Mar 19] sturdy gelding: fifth foal: dam unraced, out of sister to high-class 2½m chaser Half Free: runner-up in maiden Irish point: fairly useful form in bumpers, winning at Wetherby in January by ½ length from Cantgeton: 1¾ lengths second to Fair Spin in novice at Newcastle on hurdling debut: will stay 2½m. *G. A. Harker* **h102 F97**

NOT A TRACE (IRE) 6 b.g. Gothland (FR) – Copmenow (IRE) (Mandalus) [2004/5 22s^{3} 20d 20v^{6} 24v^{5} 20s^{3} Apr 22] close-coupled gelding: second foal: dam unraced: runner-up in maiden Irish point: poor maiden hurdler: should stay beyond 2½m: acts on soft ground, below form on heavy. *Mrs S. C. Bradburne* **h78**

NOT FOR DIAMONDS (IRE) 5 b.g. Arctic Lord – Black-Crash (Crash Course) [2004/5 F16d Feb 19] €38,000 4-y-o: rather unfurnished gelding: half-brother to useful hurdler up to 2½m Wither Or Which (by Welsh Term) and fairly useful hurdler Total Confusion (by Pollerton), stays 3m, and to dam of top-class staying chaser Alexander Banquet: dam unraced: seventh of 16 in bumper on debut. *Mrs H. Dalton* **F–**

NOT LEFT YET (IRE) 4 b. or br.g. Old Vic – Dalus Dawn (Mandalus) [2004/5 17s 17s^{4} 16d Jan 28] good-topped gelding: fifth foal: dam, bumper winner, half-sister to fairly useful hurdler up to 3m Cullenstown Lady: caught eye when never-nearer fourth to stable-companion Medison in novice hurdle at Taunton: not at all knocked about in juvenile at Doncaster next time: will be suited by further: almost certainly capable of better. *M. C. Pipe* **h102 p**

NOT NOW GEORGE 6 b.g. Sovereign Water (FR) – Threads (Bedford (USA)) [2004/5 h–, F–: 22m^{pu} 20s Oct 31] medium-sized gelding: little sign of ability, including on completed start in points. *Miss S. E. Forster* **h–**

NOTSOTINY 9 b.g. Southern Music – Goodbye Roscoe (Roscoe Blake) [2004/5 h–: 22d^{pu} 20s Nov 21] no sign of ability: tried visored/in cheekpieces. *A. M. Hales* **h–**

NOT TO BE MISSED 7 gr.m. Missed Flight – Petinata (Petong) [2004/5 h68: 16g^{ur} 16f^{2} May 18] poor maiden hurdler: likely to prove best around 2m. *R. Dickin* **h68**

NO TURNING BACK (IRE) 6 b.g. Shernazar – Offaly Rose (IRE) (The Parson) [2004/5 F16g Jan 14] €45,000 3-y-o: third foal: dam ran twice: tongue tied, eighth of 13 in bumper at Huntingdon on debut. *Noel T. Chance* **F73**

NOT YET DECENT (IRE) 12 gr.g. Decent Fellow – Yet (Last Fandango) [2004/5 c24g^{ur} Feb 17] winning pointer. *Mrs R. E. Walker* **c–**

NOUNOU 4 b.c. Starborough – Watheeqah (USA) (Topsider (USA)) [2004/5 16s 16g^{2} 16d^{4} Feb 4] smallish colt: fairly useful on Flat (stays 2m), successful in February and April: modest form when in frame over hurdles: will stay 2½m. *D. J. Daly* **h96**

NOUSAYRI (IRE) 10 b.g. Slip Anchor – Noufiyla (Top Ville) [2004/5 c65, h–: c20g5 c16s* c20s2 Mar 31] leggy gelding: fair hunter chaser nowadays: most fortunate to win 3-finisher event at Leicester in March, held in fourth when left clear last: stays 3m: acts on heavy going: has had tongue tied. *Mrs J. Marles* **c90 h–**

NOVA BEACON 13 b.g. Ra Nova – Ditchling Beacon (High Line) [2004/5 h–: 20m 22m 21gpu 24mpu Aug 6] lengthy gelding: little form over hurdles. *S. J. Gilmore* **h75 ?**

NOVACELLA (FR) 4 b.f. Beyssac (FR) – Une Risette (FR) (Air du Nord (USA)) [2004/5 18s3 18s5 16s3 17s2 Jan 18] ex-French filly: fifth foal: half-sister to useful hurdler Marcel (by Bateau Rouge), stays 19f, and 2m hurdle winner Indecise (by Cyborg): dam, fairly useful chaser/winning hurdler, stayed 2¾m: well held both starts on Flat: fair juvenile hurdler: sold out of F. Cottin's stable €78,000 Goffs (France) November Sale: well below form on British debut: raced only on soft ground. *R. H. Alner* **h101**

NOVATARA 13 ch.g. Ra Nova – Asphaltara (Scallywag) [2004/5 c59x, h85: 26g4 27s5 26m3 24m4 Jul 21] winning chaser: modest maiden hurdler: stays 3¼m: acts on soft and good to firm going: blinkered/visored: poor jumper of fences. *B. G. Powell* **c– x h87**

NOVEL IDEA (IRE) 7 ch.g. Phardante (FR) – Novelist (Quayside) [2004/5 h–, F77: 20d6 24m4 c25dpu 24g6 Jul 7] workmanlike gelding: bad maiden hurdler: jumped poorly on chasing debut: in frame all starts in points in 2005: tried blinkered (raced too freely): sold 4,100 gns Doncaster May Sales. *Mrs H. Dalton* **c– h52**

NOVICE D'ESTRUVAL (FR) 4 gr.g. Kadalko (FR) – Caro d'Estruval (FR) (Caramo (FR)) [2004/5 F13s 19s 21g5 Mar 27] third foal: half-brother to fairly useful hurdler/smart chaser Jazz d'Estruval (by Bayolidaan), stays 25f, and cross-country chase winner Info d'Estruval (by Mistigri): dam twice-raced half-sister to useful chaser up to 2¾m Signal d'Estruval: well held in bumper and 2 novice hurdles (jumped none too fluently). *Mrs L. C. Taylor* **h– F–**

NOVICIATE (IRE) 5 b.g. Bishop of Cashel – Red Salute (Soviet Star (USA)) [2004/5 F16d F17d Feb 1] sturdy gelding: third foal: half-brother to 7f winner in Germany by Blushing Flame: dam unraced, from family of top-class middle-distance filly Northern Trick: well held in 2 bumpers, slowly away on debut. *Simon Earle* **F–**

NOVI SAD (IRE) 7 b.g. Norwich – Shuil Na Gale (Strong Gale) [2004/5 h89§: c20s4 c21g6 c22s* c20g4 Jan 14] workmanlike gelding: modest hurdler/chaser: won handicap over fences at Fontwell in January: stays 25f: acts on soft going: tried in cheekpieces/blinkers: unreliable. *L. Wells* **c98 § h– §**

NOWATOR (POL) 8 ch.g. Jape (USA) – Naradka (POL) (Dakota) [2004/5 h101: c16dF c16g2 c16d* c17v2 c16d4 Nov 28] close-coupled gelding: fair hurdler: better over fences: allowed to dictate when winning novice at Perth in June: may prove best around 2m: acts on heavy going: takes good hold and makes running. *T. R. George* **c120 h–**

NO WAY BACK (IRE) 5 b.g. Eve's Error – Janeyway (Bulldozer) [2004/5 F16s F17g Apr 7] tall, rather unfurnished gelding: fifth foal: half-brother to fair 2½m to 2¾m hurdler Old Kilminchy (by Cashel Court): dam unraced half-sister to fairly useful chaser up to 29f Paco's Boy: modest form on first of 2 starts in bumpers. *Miss E. C. Lavelle* **F79**

NOWBYTHEWAY (IRE) 8 b.g. Wakashan – Gilded Empress (Menelek) [2004/5 c–, h–: 16d4 May 11] little sign of ability outside points. *J. R. Jenkins* **c– h69**

NOWELL HOUSE 9 ch.g. Polar Falcon (USA) – Langtry Lady (Pas de Seul) [2004/5 h123: 16v 16s6 19g4 16s3 16s4 Apr 20] smallish, sparely-made gelding: fair on Flat nowadays (stays 13f): fairly useful hurdler: bit below best in 2004/5: best around 2m: acts on heavy going. *M. W. Easterby* **h115**

NOW THEN AUNTIE (IRE) 4 gr.f. Anshan – Tara's Lady (General Ironside) [2004/5 F14g F16s5 F16s Feb 5] eighth foal: half-sister to winning 2m hurdler Langholm Venture (by Supreme Leader) and winning pointer by Cardinal Flower: dam unraced: modest form on second of 3 starts in bumpers. *Mrs S. A. Watt* **F77**

NOW THEN SID 6 ch.g. Presidium – Callace (Royal Palace) [2004/5 h84: 21m5 21m4 c24dpu 21m* 20g* 21m5 c20d3 c24dF 24g c21v4 c19d c25m5 Apr 23] leggy, lightly-made gelding: modest handicap hurdler: won at Sedgefield (conditional jockeys) in August and Hexham in September: largely disappointing over fences: stays 21f: acts on good to firm and good to soft going. *Mrs S. A. Watt* **c95 h97**

NUCLEAR PROSPECT (IRE) 5 ch.g. Nucleon (USA) – Carraigbyrne (IRE) (Over The River (FR)) [2004/5 h68: 16s 20m 16g5 20m Feb 6] lengthy gelding: poor maiden hurdler: probably best around 2m. *Mrs H. O. Graham* **h–**

NUIT SOMBRE (IRE) 5 b.g. Night Shift (USA) – Belair Princess (USA) (Mr Prospector (USA)) [2004/5 16g 16d* 17g⁶ 17g 18s² Mar 30] compact gelding: half-brother to 2 winning hurdlers around 2m by Linamix: fairly useful on Flat (stays 1¼m), left M. Johnston in June: fair novice hurdler: won at Huntingdon in November by 2½ lengths from Duke of Buckingham: likely to prove best at 2m with emphasis on speed. *N. J. Henderson* **h104**

NUMBERSIXVALVERDE (IRE) 9 b.g. Broken Hearted – Queens Tricks (Le Bavard (FR)) [2004/5 h117: 24g c20s c22v² c23d³ c24s* 24v⁵ c24v* c24v³ c29s* Mar 28] **c136** **h104**

Having started the season with just a maiden hurdle win at Punchestown to his name, Numbersixvalverde earned connections over £150,000 in total prize money with three successes over fences in a consistent campaign, including the prestigious Thyestes Chase at Gowran and the most valuable race run over jumps in Ireland, the Irish Grand National at Fairyhouse. Numbersixvalverde had shown fairly useful form in bumpers, finishing second four times in six outings, and as a hurdler, running his best race in ten starts when third to Jack High in a three-mile novice handicap in 2002/3. Numbersixvalverde was off a year after his final start that season, which delayed his chasing debut until the autumn of 2004, and, initially, the pattern of creditable efforts in defeat continued. On his second and third starts over fences he was placed in maidens behind Cane Brake at Galway and Keepatem and Calladine at Downpatrick, none of whom he was entitled to beat on his form over hurdles. It was only on his next outing that Numbersixvalverde began to reveal his true potential as a chaser. Making his handicap debut off a lenient-looking mark, he made short work of some exposed opposition over three miles at Navan in December, still on the bridle when his nearest challenger Catalpa Cargo capsized at the last fence.

There was clearly more to come and the Paddy Power at Leopardstown might have seemed the obvious target. He did run next in a three-mile handicap sponsored by that firm, but over hurdles rather than fences, performing in satisfactory fashion behind Oulart and not being the only future National winner in the field preserving his mark as Hedgehunter also took part. The Goulding Thyestes Handicap Chase at Gowran in January attracted a field as large as eighteen for only the third time in its fifty-one year history and there can't have been many more competitive renewals. Although Bizet was a well-backed favourite, there were plenty who could be given a chance and quite a few were still in contention as the field turned for home on the final circuit. Numbersixvalverde was still some way back and under pressure at this stage, but moved into fifth three out and challenged between Bizet and the long-time leader Kymandjem at the last. Bizet could find no more but Numbersixvalverde continued to respond and caught Kymandjem on the post to win by a short head.

An even larger field, twenty-six all told, went to post for the Powers Gold Label Irish Grand National at Fairyhouse over two months later, though that was two fewer than the previous year. The Irish Grand National was worth a record €141,500 to the winner (it was the first race over jumps in Ireland with a total prize of €250,000), which was €6,500 more than for the Punchestown Gold Cup, €34,400 than for the Hennessy at Leopardstown and €44,000 more than for the Lexus. Not surprisingly, connections of some of the best chasers in Ireland—there were no British-trained runners—were tempted by the prize money and the Turf Club handicapper adopted a policy of compressing the weights at the top of the handicap, copied from the BHB's approach at Aintree, Beef Or Salmon seemingly at one point a possible runner. In the event, Le Coudray topped the weights and just over half the field had to race from out of the handicap, among them Numbersixvalverde, though he was only 1 lb 'wrong', plus 1 lb overweight. The betting suggested a very open race, with What Odds, not for the first time the subject of a significant gamble, favourite at 8/1, a point ahead of the 2004 runner-up Marcus du Berlais, the Paddy Power second Jaquouille and Numbersixvalverde. The last-named had had one run since the Thyestes, finishing a possibly unlucky third to another leading Irish National fancy Point Barrow in a Grade 3 novice at Navan, where a bad mistake five out cost him more ground than he was beaten by. Numbersixvalverde's jumping again wasn't perfect at Fairyhouse, and mistakes six

*Powers Gold Label Irish Grand National Chase (Handicap), Fairyhouse—
Numbersixvalverde has work to do to catch Jack High at the last*

out and again four from home saw him flat out. Plenty held a chance in the straight after Kymandjem had again made much of the running. He lost the lead to outsider Coolnahilla two out before Jack High led going to the last but, as at Gowran, Numbersixvalverde was responding to pressure and, as the leader drifted badly left, he took over late on the run-in, beating Jack High by three quarters of a length with less than seven lengths between the winner and Kymandjem in sixth. Marcus du Berlais took third, while What Odds and Point Barrow were among those to disappoint. Numbersixvalverde formed the second leg of Ruby Walsh's hat-trick of National wins in 2004/5, in the process denying his father Ted, the trainer of Jack High, a second win in the race.

Numbersixvalverde became the first horse in nearly thirty years to win both the Thyestes and the Irish Grand National in the same season. Five others have achieved the feat, Kerforo (1962), Arkle (1964), Flyingbolt (1966), Dim Wit (1972) and Brown Lad (1976). Kerforo was a smart mare who also won the Leopardstown Chase that year, while Dim Wit showed smart form, though he was outclassed in the same year's Cheltenham Gold Cup and King George VI Chase. Brown Lad was a top-notch performer who won the Irish National three times, was twice second in the Cheltenham Gold Cup and won a Stayers' Hurdle. The other duo's exploits are, of course, widely known. Numbersixvalverde has not yet shown form anywhere nearly as good as any of that quintet, though he progressed again when fifth to Pay It Forward in the valuable novice handicap chase at Punchestown shortly after the

*. . . split by the width of the course;
in between are Kymandjem, Howaya Pet and the greys Coolnahilla and Marcus du Berlais*

end of the British season. With just eight runs over fences, and just one beyond twenty-five furlongs, he probably is not yet fully exposed and may improve further.

Numbersixvalverde is by Broken Hearted, whose best progeny are Pizarro and Ballybough Rasher, while he is also the sire of another Thyestes Chase winner in This Is Serious. Numbersixvalverde is the fifth foal and third winner out of the unraced Queens Tricks, following the modest chaser at up to three miles El Cordobes (by Torus) and the pointer Jonmar (by Mandalus). Both the grandam Queens Folly and third dam Gay Tricks won over hurdles, Gay Tricks good enough to finish third in the 1961 Imperial Cup. She was a sister to the fairly useful chaser Leslie who won at two and a half miles and twice contested the Grand National in the 'sixties. Gay Tricks produced five winners, the best of them the fairly useful chaser at up to two and a half miles Tex, whose finest hour came when beating a below-par Tingle Creek at Worcester. Queens Folly's four winners include a couple of winning chasers effective at up to around three miles, the fair Man of Mystery and fairly useful Fatal Hesitation.

Numbersixvalverde (IRE) (b.g. 1996)	Broken Hearted (b 1984)	Dara Monarch (b 1979)	Realm
			Sardara
		Smash (b 1976)	Busted
			Ash Lawn
	Queens Tricks (b 1985)	Le Bavard (ch 1971)	Devon III
			Lueur Doree
		Queens Folly (br 1967)	King's Bench
			Gay Tricks

Mr O. B. P. Carroll's "Numbersixvalverde"

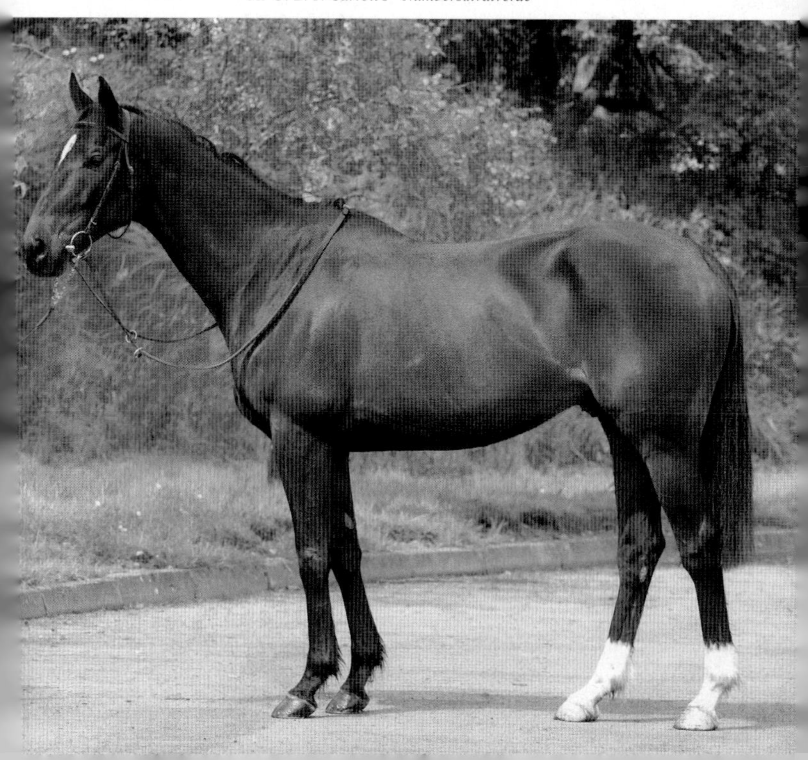

The strong, lengthy Numbersixvalverde, named after his owner's holiday home in Portugal, is a thorough stayer and a genuine sort who has raced almost exclusively on going softer than good. His predecessor as winner of the Thyestes was Hedgehunter and connections may be tempted to make an Aintree bid with Numbersixvalverde one day. Thyestes, who gives his name to the race, was also a National winner of sorts, though not of the same sort as Hedgehunter and Numbersixvalverde. A son of Tetratema, he won the National Breeders' Produce Stakes at Sandown in 1930, a five-furlong race for two-year-olds which was then the most valuable of the year for that age group. *Martin Brassil, Ireland*

NUMITAS (GER) 5 b.h. Lomitas – Narola (GER) (Nebos (GER)) [2004/5 h123: 20g* 22g* 22g* 19g6 21g Oct 26] useful-looking horse: fairly useful novice hurdler: landed odds at Uttoxeter and Stratford in July and Stratford in August: good sixth to Football Crazy in valuable handicap at Market Rasen: will stay 3m: raced on good going since debut: has worn blinkers: has shown signs of temperament (refused on debut): sold to join D. Fout in USA 20,000 gns Doncaster November Sales. *P. J. Hobbs* **h126**

NURZYK (POL) 8 ch.g. Freedom's Choice (USA) – Numeria (POL) (Dakota) [2004/5 h80: 24s 27d6 24s Apr 20] smallish gelding: poor hurdler: off 22 months, well backed but little impact in handicaps in 2004/5: stays 27f: acts on heavy going: jumps none too fluently. *T. R. George* **h–**

NUTCRACKER LAD (IRE) 7 ch.g. Duky – Allercashin Moon (IRE) (Callernish) [2004/5 h62: 20g6 21dpu Aug 9] small, sturdy gelding: bad hurdler: tried in cheekpieces, usually visored. *Mrs C. A. Dunnett* **h–**

NUTLEY QUEEN (IRE) 6 b.m. Eagle Eyed (USA) – Secret Hideaway (USA) (Key To The Mint (USA)) [2004/5 16spu Nov 27] half-sister to winning 2m hurdler Bollington (by Lightning): modest maiden on Flat (stays 1¼m): no show in novice on hurdling debut. *C. N. Kellett* **h–**

NUZUM ROAD MAKERS (IRE) 14 b.g. Lafontaine (USA) – Dark Gold (Raise You Ten) [2004/5 c–, h–: c30dpu c20mpu c20m c24dpu c25spu Apr 10] rangy gelding: no longer of much account: usually blinkered: has had tongue tied. *W. G. Young* **c– h–**

NYCTEOS (FR) 4 ch.g. Chamberlin (FR) – Cynthia (FR) (Mont Basile (FR)) [2004/5 16g5 16d6 16v* 20d3 Apr 22] tall, useful-looking gelding: fourth foal: half-brother to fairly useful hurdler up to 19f Maharbal (by Assessor): dam middle-distance winner: runner-up in 13f maiden at Les Sables on debut for J. M. Robin: easily best effort over hurdles when winning maiden at Chepstow in March: should stay beyond 2m: room for improvement in jumping. *Miss G. Browne* **h108**

NYRCHE (FR) 5 b.g. Medaaly – Thoiry (USA) (Sagace (FR)) [2004/5 h115p: 16d* 16g* 16s* 16d5 16d5 21d6 16g* 16d4 Apr 8] leggy gelding: fairly useful hurdler: easily won novices at Southwell (4-y-o event) and Worcester in May and Wetherby in October: off 3 months, best effort when winning handicap at Haydock in March by 6 lengths from Lunar Crystal: raced mainly around 2m on good going or softer (acts on soft). *A. King* **h128**

O

OAKAPPLE EXPRESS 5 b.g. Alflora (IRE) – Royal Scarlet (Royal Fountain) [2004/5 F16d* Nov 29] close-coupled, quite attractive gelding: seventh foal: half-brother to modest hurdler Captaintwothousand (by Milieu), bumper winner Setatrap (by Lord Bud) and winning pointer by Gunner B: dam poor novice hurdler: won 21-runner bumper at Newcastle on debut by ¾ length from Portavadie. *G. A. Harker* **F89**

OASIS BANUS (IRE) 4 b.g. Shaamit (IRE) – Summit Else (El Conquistador) [2004/5 F13dur F12d5 16vF 17d 16d 19vpu 17g 17m Mar 21] good-topped gelding: fourth foal: dam, no sign of ability, half-sister to 1998 Grand National winner Earth Summit: fifth to Openide in listed event at Cheltenham on completed start in bumpers: no form over hurdles (jockey banned for 7 days for failing to obtain best possible placing fifth start): should be suited by 2½m+: wore cheekpieces last 3 outings. *M. C. Pipe* **h– p F91**

OASIS BLUE (IRE) 4 gr.g. Norwich – Mini Fashion (IRE) (Roselier (FR)) [2004/5 F14d Nov 23] rather leggy gelding: fifth foal: dam maiden: not knocked about when tenth of 14 in 3-y-o bumper at Warwick on debut. *M. C. Pipe* **F81**

OBAY 4 ch.g. Kingmambo (USA) – Parade Queen (USA) (A P Indy (USA)) [2004/5 18d² 18s³ 16g⁶ 21g Mar 28] good-topped gelding: fairly useful on Flat (stays 1½m), sold out of E. Dunlop's stable 28,000 gns Newmarket Autumn Sales: easily best effort over hurdles when runner-up in juvenile at Fontwell on debut: raced freely last 2 starts. *B. G. Powell* **h100**

OCKI 12 gr.g. Octogenarian – Royalty Miss (Royalty) [2004/5 c–, h–: c26mᵖᵘ May 19] lengthy gelding: lightly raced and no form outside points. *Mrs M. R. Eagleton* **c– h–**

OCKLEY FLYER 6 b.g. Sir Harry Lewis (USA) – Bewails (IRE) (Caerleon (USA)) [2004/5 h–: 25g³ 22m³ 26m³ 22d Feb 20] tall gelding: poor maiden hurdler: probably stays 25f: acts on good to firm ground: wore cheekpieces in 2004/5: has had tongue tied: has looked uncooperative. *Miss Z. C. Davison* **h70**

OCRAS MOR (IRE) 7 b. or br.m. Old Vic – Special Trix (IRE) (Torus) [2004/5 16m 16f⁴ 18mᵘʳ 16m² 18g² 16g⁴ 18gᶠ 16s 16dᶠ 19s 16s⁴ 16v² 16v* 16v² 16v² 18d* 20d⁵ 16d² Mar 20] leggy mare: first foal: dam unraced sister to useful hurdler/chaser up to 21f Atone and half-sister to useful chaser around 2½m Music Be Magic: fairly useful hurdler: won maiden at Punchestown in January and mares novice at Downpatrick in February: also runner-up 4 times, including in listed mares novice at Limerick in March: stays 2½m: probably acts on any going. *Miss S. Cox, Ireland* **h119**

OCTAGONAL (IRE) 8 b.g. Woods of Windsor (USA) – Strawberry Belle (IRE) (Vision (USA)) [2004/5 20g 19m⁶ c23mᵘʳ c23mᵖᵘ Jun 16] neat gelding: winning hurdler: no form in 2004/5, including over fences: stays 2½m: acts on firm and soft going: usually blinkered/visored. *Miss K. Marks* **c– h–**

OCTAVIO 4 ch.g. Efisio – Lassoo (Caerleon (USA)) [2004/5 F14g F16v Jan 15] half-brother to temperamental 7f/1m winner Mustang (by Thatching) and 1½m winner Sioux (by Kris): dam, placed up to 11f, half-sister to very smart middle-distance colt Apache and fairly useful hurdler up to 21f Bandelero: well beaten in 2 bumpers. *J. R. Turner* **F–**

OCTOBER MAGIC 6 b.m. Hatim (USA) – Wand of Youth (Mandamus) [2004/5 F–: F16dᵖᵘ F16s⁶ Aug 25] no form in bumpers. *A. R. Dicken* **F–**

OCTOBER MIST (IRE) 11 gr.g. Roselier (FR) – Bonny Joe (Derring Rose) [2004/5 c108, h136d: 23m 19d 16g⁵ 20vᵖᵘ 20vᵖᵘ 19d 24g⁵ 20g⁴ 22dᵘʳ Apr 11] stocky gelding: carries plenty of condition: winning chaser: useful handicap hurdler at best, mainly well held in 2004/5: stays 23f: acts on good to firm and heavy going: tried in cheekpieces: has had tongue tied. *K. G. Reveley* **c– h103**

ODAGH ODYSSEY (IRE) 11 ch.g. Ikdam – Riverside Willow (Callernish) [2004/5 c–, h106: 21m² 17d* 19m² 19m² 16m³ 19f³ 17s³ 16sᵖᵘ Jan 22] sturdy gelding: useful handicap chaser at best: fair novice hurdler, won at Exeter in May: stays 21f: acts on soft and good to firm going: often makes running: has found little. *Miss E. C. Lavelle* **c– h109**

OF COURSE (IRE) 7 ch.g. Montelimar (USA) – Linda's Course (IRE) (Crash Course) [2004/5 F19d² F20v* Apr 14] sturdy gelding: second foal: dam, maiden pointer, half-sister to Midlands National winner Another Excuse: fairly useful form first 2 starts in bumpers, winning at Tipperary by 1½ lengths from Lunar Sea: disappointing at Punchestown later in April. *W. P. Mullins, Ireland* **F103**

OFF BEAT (USA) 4 ch.g. Mister Baileys – Off Off (USA) (Theatrical) [2004/5 17dᵘʳ 16v⁵ 16d 16d⁶ Mar 24] modest on Flat (stays 1¼m), sold out of T. D. Barron's stable 3,200 gns Doncaster January Sales: no form over hurdles. *J. K. Price* **h–**

OFF BROADWAY (IRE) 7 b.g. Presenting – Mona Curra Gale (IRE) (Strong Gale) [2004/5 h90: 21d May 6] rather leggy, close-coupled gelding: modest form at best over hurdles: should stay beyond 21f. *A. King* **h–**

OFF THE EDGE (AUS) 6 br.g. Hatta's Mill – Himalaya Vain (AUS) (Semipalatinsk (USA)) [2004/5 17g 20vᵖᵘ 16v⁶ 16s³ Mar 11] sturdy gelding: second once over 1m from 4 starts on Flat in New Zealand in 2003: poor form over hurdles, trained on debut by R. C. Guest: will prove best at 2m. *N. G. Richards* **h76**

OFF THE HOOK (IRE) 9 b.g. Montelimar (USA) – Hook's Close (Kemal (FR)) [2004/5 c26gᵖᵘ Apr 27] modest pointer nowadays, successful in February and March. *I. Hambley* **c– h–**

OFF THE SEAL (NZ) 9 b.g. Imperial Seal – Grand Countess (NZ) (St Puckle) [2004/5 h68: c17vᵖᵘ 17s 18d⁶ 24d² 22dᵖᵘ c19g² c20g² Jan 14] lengthy gelding: lightly raced: maiden hurdler/chaser, modest form at best over fences. *B. G. Powell* **c92 h82**

O'FLAHERTY'S (IRE) 13 ch.g. Balinger – Deise Lady (Le Bavard (FR)) [2004/5 c–: c21g^{pu} Apr 27] no frm outside points: tried blinkered. *G. D. Blagbrough* **c–**

OH BE THE HOKEY (IRE) 7 b.g. Be My Native (USA) – Lucky Perk (IRE) (Executive Perk) [2004/5 c115, h108, F97: 16s^{3} 20d^{2} c22d* c24v^{4} c24v^{F} 20s* c18s^{2} c24g Mar 16] tall gelding: fairly useful hurdler/chaser: won minor events at Thurles (over fences, by 3 lengths from The Young Bishop) in November and Cork (over hurdles, by length from Joueur d'Estruval) in January: favourite, let down by jumping when eighth in valuable amateur handicap chase at Cheltenham in March: effective around 2m to 3m: raced on good going or softer (acts on heavy). *C. F. Swan, Ireland* **c125 h125**

OH GOLLY GOSH 4 ch.g. Exit To Nowhere (USA) – Guerre de Troie (Risk Me (FR)) [2004/5 16d^{6} Nov 1] workmanlike gelding: modest on Flat (stays 1m): sixth to Scarlet Mix in juvenile at Warwick on hurdling debut. *N. P. Littmoden* **h89**

OH LORDIE BE (IRE) 7 gr.m. Arctic Lord – Beagan Rose (IRE) (Roselier (FR)) [2004/5 F–: F16d 21d Dec 5] well beaten in bumpers and maiden hurdle. *T. P. Walshe* **h– F–**

OH SO BRAVE 8 gr.g. Arzanni – Goodbye Roscoe (Roscoe Blake) [2004/5 h76: 22m* 26m^{2} 21m* 21m^{2} 21d^{2} 19m c24v^{3} Oct 16] medium-sized gelding: modest handicap hurdler: won novices at Stratford in June and Sedgefield in July: jumped poorly in maiden on chasing debut: should stay beyond 2¾m: acts on good to firm and good to soft going: game front runner. *Evan Williams* **c– h89**

OH SO LIVELY (IRE) 7 b.g. King's Ride – Borgina (Boreen (FR)) [2004/5 19g^{6} 16f^{6} 16f c20m c25f c22f* c23m^{2} c25m^{F} c24s* 24g^{4} c24v^{F} 22v c28s^{ro} c20v^{2} c33g Mar 17] sturdy gelding: sixth foal: half-brother to bumper winner Merry Shot (by Cataldi): dam unraced: poor hurdler: fair chaser: won handicaps at Fairyhouse in July and Cork in August: should stay beyond 25f: acts on any going: ran out thirteenth start. *E. J. O'Grady, Ireland* **c108 h84**

OH SO POSH 6 b.m. Overbury (IRE) – Sally Ho (Gildoran) [2004/5 h–, F69?: 22g May 27] workmanlike mare: little sign of ability: tried tongue tied. *B. Llewellyn* **h–**

OH SUNNY BOY (IRE) 4 b.g. Desert Sun – Naivement (IRE) (Doyoun) [2004/5 16m^{6} 16d 16f Oct 7] leggy gelding: poor maiden at 2 yrs for J. S. Moore: no form in 3 juvenile hurdles. *B. G. Powell* **h66**

OH VLO (FR) 6 b. or br.g. Sassanian (USA) – Lady Christine (FR) (Vayrann) [2004/5 c–, h102d: c16d^{5} c20m^{F} Jun 5] rather leggy gelding: maiden hurdler: no form in 3 outings over fences: probably stays 2½m: acts on soft going. *M. C. Pipe* **c– x h–**

OJAYS ALIBI (IRE) 9 b.g. Witness Box (USA) – Tinkers Lady (Sheer Grit) [2004/5 h99: c16s^{4} c19d^{pu} c20s^{2} c16v* c27s c19d^{2} c21g* Apr 10] fair hurdler: similar standard over fences: won 4-runner novice at Uttoxeter in January and handicap at Newton Abbot in April: probably stays 27f: acts on heavy going. *J. D. Frost* **c105 h–**

OKAYMAN (FR) 4 b.g. Mansonnien (FR) – Aykoku Saky (FR) (Baby Turk) [2004/5 16s^{6} 16d 16m Dec 1] leggy gelding: second foal: dam 1m winner: well held in 3 juvenile hurdles. *A. Parker* **h–**

OK SO (IRE) 12 ch.g. Naheez (USA) – Flowering Moss (IRE) (Le Moss) [2004/5 c25s^{pu} c25v^{pu} Jan 28] lengthy gelding: fair hunter chaser in 2001/2: no sign of retaining ability after near 3-year lay-off. *Mrs H. R. J. Nelmes* **c– h–**

OLASO (GER) 6 b.g. Law Society (USA) – Olaya (GER) (Acatenango (GER)) [2004/5 16g* 17s^{2} 21g Mar 16] tall, useful-looking ex-German gelding: smart on Flat (stays 2m), successful 6 times from 15 starts, including at Bremen and Cologne in spring 2004 for P. Vovcenko: won 25-runner maiden at Newbury on hurdling debut in December impressively by 3½ lengths from Allumee: fifteenth of 20 to No Refuge in Grade 1 novice at Cheltenham final start, not knocked about after mistake 3 out: should stay 21f: remains likely to do better. *Jonjo O'Neill* **h121**

OLD BUDDY (IRE) 9 br.g. Roselier (FR) – Tipperary Star (Arcticeelagh) [2004/5 c18s* c20s^{2} c20s^{pu} c23s^{5} Mar 22] IR 50,000 4-y-o: ex-Irish gelding: half-brother to 3 winners, including fair staying hurdler/chaser The Bud Club (by Le Moss): dam unraced: won maiden point in 2001: poor form over hurdles: off over 2½ years (reportedly suffered leg trouble), won novice handicap at Fontwell on chasing debut in January: poor efforts last 2 outings: bred to stay beyond 2½m: raced mainly on soft going. *B. G. Powell* **c88 h–**

OLD FEATHERS (IRE) 8 b.g. Hernando (FR) – Undiscovered (Tap On Wood) [2004/5 22d^{6} 22g* 24d^{2} 21g 24s^{5} 24g 24d^{pu} Apr 8] workmanlike gelding: fair handicap hurdler, off 19 months before reappearance: won at Market Rasen in August: stays 3m: acts on good to firm and heavy going: jumps none too fluently. *Jonjo O'Neill* **h110**

OLD FLAME (IRE) 6 b.g. Oscar (IRE) – Flameing Run (Deep Run) [2004/5 h117, F92: 16g6 c16v* c20s4 c16d2 c20vF c19vpu c20v5 c16v3 c17s4 Mar 28] lengthy, rather unfurnished gelding: fairly useful hurdler: similar standard over fences: won novice at Listowel in September: several creditable efforts after: stays 2½m: acts on heavy going: front runner. *C. F. Swan, Ireland* **c116 h–**

OLD GINGER (IRE) 5 ch.g. Zaffaran (USA) – Most Effective (IRE) (Lancastrian) [2004/5 F16m Apr 10] £25,000 4-y-o: fourth foal: dam, lightly raced in bumpers, half-sister to fairly useful chaser up to 3¼m Little Buck: last of 19 in bumper on debut. *M. Scudamore* **F–**

OLD GOLDEN BAY 5 b.g. Meqdaam (USA) – Modina April (New Member) [2004/5 F16v F16d F16g6 Mar 28] rather unfurnished gelding: second foal: dam once-raced in points: behind in 3 bumpers. *M. Wellings* **F–**

OLD MARSH (IRE) 9 b.g. Grand Lodge (USA) – Lolly Dolly (Alleged (USA)) [2004/5 c118, h–: c21g2 c18m* c16m* c16d5 c17spu c20s4 c19g3 c16g* c16s6 Apr 7] strong gelding: fairly useful chaser: landed odds at Fontwell (maiden) in August and Newton Abbot (novice) in September: left Miss V. Williams after sixth outing: improved form when winning handicap at Haydock in March easily by 7 lengths from Super Nomad: best around 2m: acts on soft and good to firm going: tried blinkered: has had tongue tied: formerly raced prominently, patiently ridden last 2 starts: prone to mistakes. *A. W. Carroll* **c129 h–**

OLD NOSEY (IRE) 9 b.g. Muharib (USA) – Regent Star (Prince Regent (FR)) [2004/5 h84: 22g3 20d2 22m4 24f 24d4 24d 20m 25g 24dF 24g 22s2 22d6 Apr 11] modest handicap hurdler: stays 3m: acts on soft and good to firm going: tried blinkered: doesn't always convince with finishing effort. *B. Mactaggart* **h89**

OLD ROLLA (IRE) 7 b.g. Old Vic – Criswood (IRE) (Chromite (USA)) [2004/5 c82, h82: c25d6 Apr 11] lengthy gelding: poor maiden hurdler/chaser, formerly trained by C. Grant: unbeaten in points in 2005: let down by jumping in hunter chase: stays 27f: raced on good ground or softer (acts on heavy). *C. Storey* **c– h–**

OLD ROWLEY 6 br.g. Supreme Leader – Teeno Nell (Teenoso (USA)) [2004/5 F16v3 19v4 21g6 Mar 14] 15,000 4-y-o: tall, useful-looking gelding: second foal: dam, unraced half-sister to fairly useful staying chaser Jimmy O'Dea, from family of Champion Hurdle winners Morley Street and Granville Again: third to Corals Laurel in bumper at Warwick on debut: easily better effort over hurdles when fourth in novice at Exeter: should be suited by further than 19f. *N. J. Henderson* **h90 F90**

OLE GUNNAR (IRE) 13 b.g. Le Bavard (FR) – Rareitess (Rarity) [2004/5 h–: 26d 24m Jun 5] winning pointer: lightly raced and little form over hurdles: wears cheekpieces. *M. S. Wilesmith* **h–**

OLIMPO (FR) 4 ch.g. Starborough – Emily Allan (IRE) (Shirley Heights) [2004/5 16g6 17m 17d Sep 10] ex-French gelding: fifth foal: half-brother to fairly useful French 1¼m winner Sound of Laughter (by Zafonic): dam, no worthwhile form, half-sister to smart sprinter Whippet: trained by F. Rohaut, thrice-raced on Flat in Provinces at 3 yrs: well held in juvenile hurdles. *P. J. Hobbs* **h–**

OLIVERJOHN (IRE) 8 ch.g. Denel (FR) – Graeme's Gem (Pry) [2004/5 h114: c20d6 16d4 17s5 20vpu c16s3 c25vpu c20v2 c16v4 c24gF c20v2 c20s Apr 22] lengthy gelding: fair hurdler: modest maiden chaser: sold out of M. Hourigan's stable 5,500 gns Doncaster May Sales after first outing: stays 2½m: acts on heavy going: tried in cheekpieces/visor: not a fluent jumper of fences. *Miss Lucinda V. Russell* **c96 x h107**

OLIVIER (USA) 7 ch.g. Theatrical – Izara (USA) (Blushing John (USA)) [2004/5 h89: 20d May 15] useful-looking gelding: lightly-raced maiden hurdler: stays 21f. *Miss Venetia Williams* **h–**

OLLIE MAGERN 7 b.g. Alderbrook – Outfield (Monksfield) [2004/5 h125: c24g* c21s* c24g* c20d4 c26g2 c24g* c25sur c25s* c20d2 Feb 19] **c154 h–**

Whoever wrote the script for the 2005 Cheltenham Festival had been watching too many episodes of *Midsomer Murders*. In the fortnight before the Festival, hardly a day seemed to go by without one big name or another being announced an absentee, as it appeared barely safe for leading fancies to venture onto the gallops. Kicking King, Foreman, Distant Thunder, Best Mate, Lord of Illusion, Baron Windrush, Ollie Magern, Kingscliff, Ambobo and Farmer Jack were just some of those who were reported non-runners in the first half of March alone. Five of that list were potential runners in the Gold Cup, one, of course,

Stan James Feltham Novices' Chase, Kempton—
Ollie Magern leads Trabolgan (right) and Quazar over two out

turning out not to be an absentee at all, a twist Inspector Barnaby might have missed. But the overall toll was particularly heavy among the novices, meaning that events in that division were not nearly so strong as they might have been. Six of Timeform's top twenty novice hurdlers before Cheltenham, including the top two, failed to make it to the Festival, along with more than a dozen of the highest-rated bumper horses, while no fewer than nine of the top twenty novice chasers, including the top three, were absent. Fundamentalist, Ollie Magern, Kauto Star, Foreman, Jazz d'Estruval, Lord of Illusion, Baron Windrush, El Vaquero, Distant Thunder is a considerable list, nearly all of those named near the head of the betting for their target races at Cheltenham. When the likes of Iris's Gift, Sporazene and Cloone River are added, it makes for a salutary warning to ante-post punters.

Ollie Magern might have provided a salutary warning for ante-post punters even if he had turned up at Cheltenham. A long-time market leader for the Royal & SunAlliance Chase, he was still to be committed for either that race or the Gold Cup when he suffered a hairline fracture of an offhind cannon bone on the Friday before the meeting, Best Mate's burst blood vessel the previous day having precipitated another rethink as to Ollie Magern's target. Ollie Magern would have held a first-rate chance had he contested the SunAlliance, having already won the top mid-season staying novice chase, the Feltham at Kempton in December. He had also, however, been regularly campaigned outside novice company, taking in two of the biggest handicaps, a Grade 1 chase and a significant Gold Cup trial. All told, Cheltenham would have been his tenth outing of the season. He won all five of his starts in novice company and ran well when in the frame on his three completed starts outside it. According to his trainer Nigel Twiston-Davies, the prognosis for Ollie Magern making a full recovery from the required surgery is good. If so, he may well be a leading contender for good races again in 2005/6, when his generally sound jumping and zest for racing will stand him in good stead.

Ollie Magern's busy campaign began in early-September, in a novice chase at Stratford. By no means an obvious chaser on looks, Ollie Magern started second favourite to the Martin Pipe-trained Vodka Bleu, a slightly inferior hurdler but already the winner of a maiden chase. However, Ollie Magern showed just how good a chaser he was going to become, putting up a useful performance in beating Vodka Bleu by eight lengths. Successes in similar events at Fakenham and Cheltenham towards the end of the following month confirmed the very favourable impression created at Stratford, Ollie Magern's defeat of another Pipe-trained favourite Comply Or Die at Cheltenham suggesting that, even at that early stage of the season, that Ollie Magern was going to be very near the top of the staying novice chase division in 2004/5.

It might seem slightly odd that Ollie Magern had a gap of forty days between his first two races, followed by a gap of five, but, to a certain extent, that was forced on his trainer. A radical restructuring of the novice chase programme over the last two years meant there were virtually no other races, other than open handicaps, in which Ollie Magern could have run in October, except for two races over a trip short of two and a half miles. In October 2002, there would have been no fewer than twelve at two and three quarter miles or further. No wonder some trainers were complaining about how hard it now was to place novice chasers. Clearly, though, in an era when competitiveness is an overriding priority, something needed to be done. In order to make novice chases more competitive, the majority have been turned into either beginners chases (i.e. maidens open to winners over hurdles), novice handicaps or rating-restricted races. The switch to beginners chases, in 2003/4, removed around a third of the ordinary novice events from the programme in October and further extensions to the novice handicap and beginners chase programmes removed a further third in 2004. In all, though, there were fifty-two events of various types for novices in October 2004 compared to forty-six in 2002; whereas thirty-seven in 2002 were ordinary novices, just sixteen were of similar type in 2004, though only six of those were not restricted to those with a BHB mark of 110 or lower. The trainer of a fairly useful or better hurdler that had won a beginners chase had limited options, but the programme scheduled in 2002/3 was an unaffordable luxury in a world where a minimum of eight runners and an odds-against favourite are the desired goals. Racecourses are penalised for races with fewer than eight runners, under contracts with bookmakers, and all events which regularly fall short of appropriate field sizes will be under threat. In the first season, taking figures from October to December, novices of class C or above, effectively the open events, performed marginally better in terms of runners than class D or below, rating-restricted races and mares-only novices. Both, however, performed poorly, with over three quarters of the races in each category attracting fewer than eight runners. In more than half the open novices the favourite started odds on, while that was the case in only a quarter of the rating-restricted races. Beginners/maidens and novice handicaps performed significantly better in both categories with under sixty percent of races failing to muster eight runners, and the favourite starting at odds on in twenty-nine percent and six percent of the races respectively. It will be no surprise to see an increase in the number of novice handicaps, at the expense of other types, in 2005/6, and the introduction of some

Totty Construction Towton Novices Chase, Wetherby—another smart performance

novice handicaps at the lower end of the scale as well—class E and F races meet the requirements rather more often than those in classes C or D. The trainers of the Ollie Magerns of the future are likely to find their options increasingly restricted.

A balance has to be struck between the demands of the authorities and bookmakers for a suitable 'product' and the need for a proper structure for bringing along inexperienced chasers. Whether rating-restricted races are the answer is another matter. Any non-handicap in which the quality of the runner is determined by an upper rating limit has a built-in, inherent unfairness, since the upper limit (virtually always divisible by five) has to be arbitary. Why 0-105 or 0-110 and never 0-107 or 0-113? In theory, a horse with a BHB mark of 105 could farm such races from October to April, provided its trainer waited for it to be reassessed. Since it would always be meeting inferior rivals on terms better than in a handicap, its mark may, in theory, never have to be raised. Perhaps there is scope within the programme for a limited number of races (not necessarily novices) restricted to those that have won a maximum of once over fences or restricted to those with fewer than three runs over fences.

To return to Ollie Magern. After Cheltenham, the next available opportunities over a suitable trip in novice company came in the Rising Stars at Wincanton and a class B novice at Cheltenham's Open meeting (both races won by Comply Or Die) but connections opted instead for the Paddy Power Gold Cup at the latter fixture. Ollie Magern looked to have been set a very stern task by the BHB handicapper, racing off the same mark as Thisthatandtother, who had won two Grade 2 novice events and started favourite for the Arkle the previous season. Ollie Magern acquitted himself splendidly. Dominating proved more difficult than it had in novices in small fields but Ollie Magern, who jumped particularly well, led from the sixth to before the last and finished nine and a quarter lengths fourth to Celestial Gold, who was receiving 10 lb. Ollie Magern's performance in the Paddy Power would have been good enough to have won all but four runnings of the SunAlliance Chase since the *Chasers & Hurdlers* series began. Two weeks later Ollie Magern and Celestial Gold met again, in the Hennessy Gold Cup at Newbury. Ollie Magern wasn't able to reverse placings, even on terms 6 lb better, but again performed with much credit, up with the pace throughout and keeping on stoutly after Celestial Gold had taken over at the last, beaten a length and a half into second.

After two such competitive handicaps, the Stan James Feltham Novices' Chase seemed almost an easy option, though it is a race which has lived up to its Grade 1 status in recent seasons, with the last five winners including Gloria Victis, Bacchanal, Jair du Cochet and Strong Flow. Ollie Magern stood out on form in a nine-runner field for the latest renewal, with his main opponents looking to be Control Man, who had won both his starts over fences, the December Novices' Chase winner L'Ami and Backbeat, who had shown useful form in winning twice at Exeter. Also in the line-up was the well-regarded Trabolgan and he proved the toughest opponent Ollie Magern faced in his races in novice company. Control Man went at the second, L'Ami at the eleventh. Ollie Magern himself did not jump so well going right handed but he had most in trouble after quickening four out. He looked beaten when headed by Trabolgan early on the run-in but rallied tenaciously to gain the day by a short head. In Ollie Magern's absence, Trabolgan won the SunAlliance Chase ten weeks later, with Comply Or Die second.

Ollie Magern's next appearance featured a rare jumping lapse—he blundered and unseated his rider at the fourth in the Pillar Property Chase at Cheltenham in January—but he made amends a week later in the Grade 2 Totty Construction Towton Novices' Chase at Wetherby where he again got the better of a subsequent Festival winner, this time King Harald by four lengths easing down. Ollie Magern had been raced at three miles or more since the Paddy Power but, for what turned out his final run of the season, he was back at around two and a half miles and in Grade 1 company to boot. The main focus in the totesport Chase at Lingfield was another novice, Iris's Gift, making his chasing debut, but Ollie Magern turned in yet another smart effort, looking every bit as game as he had at Stratford first time out and was only overhauled on the run-in, beaten two lengths into second by It Takes Time. With stable-jockey Carl Llewellyn riding Baron Windrush at Haydock, Ollie Magern was the mount of Antony Evans, who was unable to claim his 3-lb allowance.

Mr Roger Nicholls' "Ollie Magern"

Ollie Magern (b.g. 1998)	Alderbrook (b 1989)	Ardross (b 1976)	Run The Gantlet
			Le Melody
		Twine (ch 1981)	Thatching
			House Tie
	Outfield (b 1986)	Monksfield (b 1972)	Gala Performance
			Regina
		Pedalo (ch 1979)	Legal Tender
			Honey Isle

Although he has made his name over fences at two and a half miles or further, Ollie Magern is unusually bred, by a Champion Hurdle winner out of a mare by a Champion Hurdle winner, being by Alderbrook out of the Monksfield mare Outfield. Ollie Magern is Outfield's third foal, the first two, both by Gildoran, being Doranfield Lady, who was well held in a bumper and on the all-weather, and Only You, an ungenuine selling hurdler who has shown his best form at two and a half miles. A second visit to Alderbrook produced the useful hurdler at up to twenty-five furlongs Petite Margot, who is in a similar mould to her brother. Outfield is one of three winners out of the unraced Pedalo, having won at three miles over hurdles. The others are the fair but inconsistent three-mile chaser Ankles Back and the modest staying chaser The Gallopin' Major. Outfield's trainer was John Webber and that gives the clue to the most notable names in this family, as Pedalo is a half-sister to a notable broodmare, Dream Isle, the dam of Auntie Dot and Townley Stone. Auntie Dot won eighteen races, including an Edward Hanmer, and finished third in the 1991 Grand National, while Townley Stone, who later joined

Nicky Henderson, won twelve and was a high-class chaser at two to two and a half miles. Dream Isle herself was a notably tough and versatile sort, winning twelve races, including five at Towcester, and showing fairly useful form at two miles to beyond three. Clearly some of the family's toughness has resurfaced in Ollie Magern and Petite Margot. The source of their lack of stature (both are smallish in appearance) and that of Outfield, who is small, is presumably the similarly vertically-challenged Monksfield, since other branches in the pedigree aren't wanting for size and scope. Ollie Magern is effective at two and a half miles and will stay beyond three and a quarter. He acts on firm and soft going. It is worth repeating that he is thoroughly game and genuine. *N. A. Twiston-Davies*

OLNEY LAD 6 b.g. Democratic (USA) – Alipampa (IRE) (Glenstal (USA)) [2004/5 h114: 22v^4 20d^4 22d^5 21g^5 20v* 20v* Feb 19] leggy gelding: useful handicap hurdler: improved efforts when winning at Wetherby in January and Uttoxeter in February, making all and eased late on when beating Dom d'Orgeval by 8 lengths in quite valuable event at latter: stays 21f: acts on heavy going: blinkered second to fourth outings. *Mrs P. Robeson* **h131**

OLYMPIAN TIME 5 b.m. Luso – Little Time (Arctic Lord) [2004/5 F16v F16d^4 F17g Apr 14] small mare: first foal: dam once-raced, out of useful 2m to 25f chaser Olympian Princess, herself half-sister to smart staying chaser Bob Tisdall: modest form on second of 3 starts in bumpers. *B. J. Eckley* **F75**

OLYMPIC STORM (IRE) 7 b.g. Glacial Storm (USA) – Philly Athletic (Sit In The Corner (USA)) [2004/5 F–: 20v^{pu} 18v^{pu} 16s 20s^3 22d 20s Apr 22] winning Irish pointer: poor maiden hurdler: stays 2½m: raced on ground softer than good: has shown signs of temperament (ran out in bumper). *N. W. Alexander* **h82**

OMNI COSMO TOUCH (USA) 9 b.g. Trempolino (USA) – Wooden Pudden (USA) (Top Ville) [2004/5 c103§, h§§: c20s^F c23d^3 c25d^3 c24d^{ur} 25d* 24d^2 24g* 21g Mar 16] good-topped gelding: fair maiden chaser: fairly useful handicap hurdler: better than ever, winning at Catterick in February and Doncaster in March, beating Ballybough Rasher 3 lengths despite idling at latter: very good second to Over The Creek at Newbury in between: stays 25f: acts on firm and soft going: tried blinkered: often refuses/reluctant to race: ungenuine. *Mrs S. J. Smith* **c108 §** **h129 §**

'Cream of Mushroom' HBLB Handicap Hurdle, Wetherby—
Olney Lad (near side) gets the better of Claymore

O'MUIRCHEARTAIGH (IRE) 5 b.g. Accordion – Brian's Delight (IRE) (Celio Rufo) [2004/5 F16s² Feb 6] 23,000 4-y-o: has plenty of scope: first foal: dam fairly useful staying chaser: encouraging 4 lengths second to Clew Bay Cove in bumper at Leopardstown on debut, picking up nicely once getting the hang of things without being knocked about: looks sure to do better. *E. J. O'Grady, Ireland* **F99 p**

ON A DEAL 7 b.g. Teenoso (USA) – Gale Spring (IRE) (Strong Gale) [2004/5 h90: 19d⁵ 16d² 22s³ Jan 3] long-backed gelding: modest maiden hurdler: stays 2¾m: acts on soft and good to firm ground. *R. J. Hodges* **h98**

ONAROLL 5 ch.g. Fleetwood (IRE) – New Dawn (Rakaposhi King) [2004/5 F16d Jan 29] lengthy gelding: first foal: dam, bumper winner, sister to useful hurdler/chaser up to 2½m Crocadee: well held in bumper on debut. *O. Brennan* **F–**

ONASSIS 8 b.g. Roselier (FR) – Jack's The Girl (IRE) (Supreme Leader) [2004/5 c–, h88: 19spu 16d³ 21spu Mar 13] sturdy gelding: modest maiden hurdler: no form in 2 starts over fences: stays 3m: acts on soft going: usually blinkered. *R. J. Price* **c– h87**

ONCE SEEN 5 b.g. Celtic Swing – Brief Glimpse (IRE) (Taufan (USA)) [2004/5 h97: 17d² 19g² 22s³ 20v⁴ 19d Mar 8] close-coupled gelding: fair handicap hurdler: barely stays testing 2¾m: raced on good going or softer (acts on soft): tried visored/blinkered: has carried head awkwardly. *O. Sherwood* **h105**

ONE ALONE 4 b.f. Atraf – Songsheet (Dominion) [2004/5 18m⁴ Aug 19] modest maiden on Flat (stays 1½m): fourth in juvenile at Fontwell on hurdling debut. *Jean-Rene Auvray* **h73**

ONEANTHREEQUARTERS (IRE) 13 ch.g. King Luthier – Khaki Kate (Brigadier Gerard) [2004/5 c24d⁶ May 15] rangy gelding: winning chaser: modest pointer nowadays: stays 3¼m: acts on heavy going: tried blinkered. *R. Teague* **c– h–**

ONE CORNETTO (IRE) 6 b.g. Eurobus – Costenetta (IRE) (Runnett) [2004/5 F84: F17d³ 16spu 17d* 18s² 16d 17v⁶ 20d 17m³ Apr 9] lengthy gelding: will make a chaser: fair form in bumpers: fair novice hurdler: won at Folkestone in November: should stay 2½m: acts on good to firm and heavy ground. *L. Wells* **h106 F90**

ONE FIVE EIGHT 6 b.g. Alflora (IRE) – Dark Nightingale (Strong Gale) [2004/5 h65, F95: 19v² 17d² 24d* 20d⁶ 23spu 20vpu Jan 15] workmanlike gelding: modest hurdler: won novice at Southwell in November: stays 3m: acts on heavy going (won bumper on firm): races prominently. *M. W. Easterby* **h98**

ONEFORBERTANDHENRY (IRE) 6 b.g. Rashar (USA) – Roi Vision (Roi Guillaume (FR)) [2004/5 h64, F85: 20dpu May 6] tall, rather unfurnished gelding: novice hurdler, pulled up only start in 2004/5. *G. M. Moore* **h–**

ONE FOR ME 7 br.m. Tragic Role (USA) – Chantallee's Pride (Mansooj) [2004/5 h108: c20d³ c20m⁴ c24gur c20g⁵ 20f Sep 5] fair handicap hurdler in 2003/4: running best race over fences when unseating 2 out in novice at Stratford: stays at least 2¾m: acts on firm going: has had breathing problems. *Jean-Rene Auvray* **c81 h–**

ONE FOR TERRY (IRE) 5 b.m. Saddlers' Hall (IRE) – Crosschild (IRE) (Buckskin (FR)) [2004/5 F16v⁵ F17s Jan 20] 10,000 4-y-o: first foal: dam, 2½m bumper winner, out of half-sister to smart 2m hurdler Raretylo: poor form in bumpers: looks a stayer. *Mrs S. D. Williams* **F–**

ONE KNIGHT (IRE) 9 ch.g. Roselier (FR) – Midnights Daughter (IRE) (Long Pond) [2004/5 c–, h–: c26s* Dec 4] **c155 + h–**

The emerald green and purple colours which had been carried to victory in two races over the National fences by Bells Life, the 1997 John Hughes Chase and the 2000 Fox Hunters' Chase, might well have been figuring prominently in the latest running of the Grand National itself if the same owner's One Knight had not had his season cut short by injury once again. One Knight, successful in the Royal & SunAlliance Chase at Cheltenham on his final outing in the 2002/3 season, when he was beaten only once in five starts, has made just two appearances since. A first-fence fall in the following season's Hennessy Cognac Gold Cup at Newbury resulted in his chipping a bone in a hock, and, although he made a full recovery and returned to win the John Hughes Rehearsal Chase at Chepstow in December, a back problem kept him off the course for the remainder of the season. One Knight, allotted 11-6 among the original entries for the National, still has time on his side and, given a trouble-free season, could well take his place in the field in 2006. His

John Hughes Rehearsal Chase (Handicap), Chepstow—the only curtain call of the season for One Knight

performance in the Rehearsal Chase, a ten-runner handicap in which he faced his stiffest test of stamina to date, showed that One Knight was better than ever. Sent off favourite despite having been off for over a year, One Knight made the running as he usually does, racing with plenty of zest, and was always holding L'Aventure as the pair pulled well clear of the remainder in the straight, a length and a quarter the winning margin. The distance of the Grand National won't be a problem for One Knight and his bold jumping will be an asset around Aintree, although he does need to overcome a tendency to make the odd bad mistake. The Rehearsal, meanwhile, is being moved in 2005/6, with a switch to Newcastle to boost the card on 'Fighting Fifth' day.

One Knight (IRE) (ch.g. 1996)	Roselier (FR) (gr 1973)	Misti IV (br 1958)	Medium
			Mist
		Peace Rose (gr 1959)	Fastnet Rock
			La Paix
	Midnights Daughter (IRE) (ch 1991)	Long Pond (ch 1981)	Rarity
			Raindrops
		Midnight Oil (ch 1976)	Menelek
			Ballinacree

One Knight is the first foal of Midnights Daughter whose only other offspring to reach the racecourse is the five-year-old Medianoche (by Spanish Place). Bought for €62,000 at the 2003 Derby Sale, Medianoche failed to recoup any of his purchase price in two starts in bumpers in Ireland, but he did win a four-year-old maiden point there in November. The unraced Midnights Daughter comes from a splendid jumping family, that of the 1975 Champion Chase winner Lough Inagh. She is a half-sister to four winners over jumps, notably the smart and game front-

Mr R. Gibbs's "One Knight"

running hurdler Shannon Spray who also won once over fences. One Knight, a tall gelding, has raced only on good ground or softer and acts on soft. Still relatively lightly raced, he could show further improvement if he remains sound enough to complete a full season in 2005/6, though we won't see all that much of him even so, his trainer being of the opinion that the gelding does best fresh. One Knight will do well, though, to improve upon his wins-to-runs ratio, fourteen appearances having yielded nine victories. *P. J. Hobbs*

ONEMINUTETOFIVE 8 b.g. Neltino – Island Beat (Jupiter Island) [2004/5 c116p: c24v^F Oct 16] useful-looking gelding: successful on 5 of 6 starts in points and fourth to Earthmover in 2004 Foxhunter at Cheltenham on chasing debut: left D. Pipe, fell fatally eleventh in maiden at Stratford. *M. C. Pipe* **c–**

ONE MORE NATIVE (IRE) 8 ch.g. Be My Native (USA) – Romany Fortune (Sunyboy) [2004/5 h–, F–: 26m^pu Jun 9] angular gelding: modest form in bumpers: failed to complete both starts over hurdles: fourth in maiden point in March. *J. L. Needham* **h–**

ONE NATION (IRE) 10 br.g. Be My Native (USA) – Diklers Run (Deep Run) [2004/5 c122, h–: 17d 21s* 22d Dec 26] big, strong gelding: fairly useful hurdler/chaser when trained by Miss H. Knight: won at Warwick in December, easily best effort in handicap hurdles in 2004/5: should stay beyond 21f: acts on heavy going. *R. S. Brookhouse* **c–** **h115**

ONE NIGHT OUT (IRE) 9 b. or br.g. Jamesmead – Deladeuce (Le Bavard (FR)) [2004/5 c125, h127: 24g^4 c22m* c20f* c22m c21f* c22f* c22g 24s 24d Dec 11] sturdy gelding: fairly useful hurdler/chaser: won over fences at Fairyhouse (maiden) and Punchestown (minor event) in May and Cork (novice) and Tramore (handicap) in August: well held last 3 starts: stays 3m: acts on any going. *W. P. Mullins, Ireland* **c124** **h–**

ONE OF THE BOYS (IRE) 4 ch.g. Shernazar – Easter Morning (FR) (Nice Havrais (USA)) [2004/5 F18s⁴ F16s³ Mar 27] 20,000 3-y-o: half-brother to modest stayer/fair hurdler up to 3m Renaissance Lady (by Imp Society): dam, won 1¾m hurdle in France, half-sister to smart miler Flying Trio: modest form in frame in bumpers. *P. R. Webber* **F82**

ONE OF THEM 6 ch.g. Pharly (FR) – Hicklam Millie (Absalom) [2004/5 h81: 22s⁵ 19d 18s³ 16s c17v⁵ 17sᵘʳ c20vᵖᵘ 20d Mar 12] neat gelding: poor maiden hurdler: mistakes both starts over fences: form only around 2m: raced on good going or softer: usually wore cheekpieces/blinkers in 2004/5: sold £3,100 Ascot April Sales. *Miss G. Browne* **c74 h73**

ONEOFTHEMONGOES (IRE) 9 b.g. Ikdam – Miss Hganavak (Abednego) [2004/5 h67: 16g 20d 16m 24m Jun 16] winning pointer: little form over hurdles: tried in cheekpieces/visor: sold £2,200 Ascot August Sales. *Mrs L. C. Jewell* **h–**

ONE UPMANSHIP 4 ch.g. Bahamian Bounty – Magnolia (Petong) [2004/5 16d 17m Nov 25] rather leggy gelding: fair at best on Flat (stays 1¼m), claimed £6,000 in January: shaped like non-stayer in juvenile hurdles. *J. G. Portman* **h–**

ONEWAY (IRE) 8 b.g. Bob's Return (IRE) – Rendezvous (Lorenzaccio) [2004/5 c105, h–: c20d* c16d* c16d* c16d* c16g* c16g⁴ Mar 16] **c159 h–**

It became much less likely that the name Rimell—last associated with a winner at the Cheltenham Festival when Three Counties, trained by Mercy Rimell and owned and ridden by her granddaughter Kate, took the 1989 Foxhunter—would be on the roll of honour again once Mercy's grandson Mark had decided to run Oneway in the Champion Chase and not the Grand Annual. Oneway would probably have started favourite had he contested the handicap, in which he was set to run off a BHB mark of 149, whereas he went off at 16/1 in the Champion, odds that were far from generous given that he was meeting his seven rivals, who included Azertyuiop, Moscow Flyer and Well Chief, at level weights. Not surprisingly, Oneway was unable to cope with the aforementioned trio, but he did acquit himself very well in finishing fourth, twenty-two lengths behind the winner Moscow Flyer, keeping on from off the pace after hitting four out and three out. Mark Rimell, who owns as well as trains Oneway, was surprisingly downbeat about the gelding's performance but surely any regrets about his decision to run in the Champion Chase, which did come in for criticism in some quarters, might have been tempered by the result of the Grand Annual, which was won in good style by

Gordon Plant Memorial Handicap Chase, Haydock—
Oneway is much improved in defeating the grey Bambi de L'Orne

Sodexho Prestige Handicap Chase, Sandown—
almost hidden on the way to a five-timer as Great Travel and Impek (left) lead over the last

Fota Island. Oneway had been set to give 18 lb to Fota Island, and he would have done very well to get the better of that horse on those terms. Fourth in the Champion Chase netted £12,500, which compares favourably to place prize money for the handicap.

Thanks to Oneway and Crossbow Creek, who won seven races between them, Mark Rimell enjoyed easily his best season to date, from a team of just eight horses, and there should be even better times ahead for a trainer who was successful with his first runner, when Varykinov, whom he also rode, won a hunter chase in April, 1998. Crossbow Creek, whom he also rode prior to 2004/5, developed into a useful hurdler and won two races, including the Lanzarote Handicap at Kempton, while he also ran well at the Cheltenham Festival, finishing fifth in the County Hurdle. It was Oneway who was the star of the show, though. A maiden hurdler whose only success in four starts over fences in 2003/4 had come when partnered by his trainer in an amateur riders' handicap at Lingfield, Oneway, professionally ridden, never stopped improving in his second season as a chaser and was unbeaten in five appearances, all in handicaps, prior to the Champion Chase. The first of those wins came at Worcester in October off a mark of 107, the last at Sandown four months later off 143, which demonstrates clearly the extent of the progress. The Worcester race was over two and a half miles, but Oneway was kept to two miles subsequently, following up at Wetherby, then beating subsequent Grand Annual runner-up Bambi de L'Orme by three and a half lengths at Haydock, where, as is usual, he jumped soundly and travelled strongly under a patient ride. The first of two wins at Sandown came in a nine-runner event by two lengths from Bleu Superbe, the second in a six-runner contest in which he forged ahead on the run-in to beat Impek by a length and a half. Another rise in his BHB mark following his Champion Chase effort will make things a great deal tougher for Oneway from now on.

From the second crop of the St Leger winner Bob's Return, Oneway fetched 20,000 guineas as an unraced four-year-old at the Doncaster May Sales. He is the ninth foal of Rendezvous whose only previous winners are the fair hurdler/chaser

Oneway (IRE) (b.g. 1997)	Bob's Return (IRE) (br 1990)	Bob Back (b 1981)	Roberto
			Toter Back
		Quality of Life (b 1985)	Auction Ring
			Flirting Countess
	Rendezvous (br 1976)	Lorenzaccio (ch 1965)	Klairon
			Phoenissa
		Seam (br 1958)	Nearula
			Coal Board

Countess Veruschka (by Strong Gale), who stayed twenty-five furlongs, and the winning pointer Kamberty. Rendezvous, placed in a couple of races including a seller over hurdles, is a half-sister to numerous winners, among them the smart 1966 staying two-year-old Slip Stitch, the 1983 Triumph Hurdle second Tenth of October and Threadbare, who achieved a remarkable hat-trick at the age of ten when he won a hurdle, a chase and a Flat race in the space of three racing days. Their dam Seam was a useful miler, and their grandam Coal Board is also the grandam of the 1974 Champion Hurdle Lanzarote, who gained a rare victory over Comedy of Errors, the finest hurdler trained by Rimell's grandfather Fred. Oneway, a workmanlike gelding who acts on soft going, finished well held on the two occasions he raced beyond two and a half miles, which included his only start on ground firmer than good. *M. G. Rimell*

ONE WILD NIGHT 5 b.m. Rakaposhi King – Teenero (Teenoso (USA)) [2004/5 F16d F16g^{6} Mar 16] £4,500 4-y-o: leggy, sparely-made mare: first foal: dam once-raced, out of smart staying hurdler Miss Nero: modest form on second start in bumpers. *J. L. Spearing* **F76**

ONIZ TIPTOES (IRE) 4 ch.g. Russian Revival (USA) – Edionda (IRE) (Magical Strike (USA)) [2004/5 16d 16d 17s^{6} Dec 2] poor maiden on Flat (stays 1½m): modest form on first 2 starts in juvenile hurdles: wears cheekpieces. *J. S. Wainwright* **h86**

ONLYBEGONEANHOUR 6 gr.g. Terimon – Phar Too Touchy (Mister Lord (USA)) [2004/5 F16s 20s^{pu} Dec 4] first foal: dam winning pointer: no form in bumper or novice hurdle: sold £4,000 Ascot April Sales. *Jonjo O'Neill* **h–** **F–**

ONLY MILLIE 4 b.f. Prince Daniel (USA) – Deb's Ball (Glenstal (USA)) [2004/5 F16d^{6} F14s Feb 9] unfurnished filly: half-sister to 3 winning hurdlers, including fair Hot Weld (by Weld), stays 27f: dam useful hurdler, stayed 25f: poor form on first of 2 starts in bumpers: tongue tied. *James Moffatt* **F74**

ONLY ONCE 10 b.g. King's Ride – Rambling Gold (Little Buskins) [2004/5 c–, h91p: c25d^{4} c25d^{3} c25v^{pu} c26s^{2} c24v^{3} c21v^{pu} Mar 28] rather leggy gelding: lightly raced: second in novice only start over hurdles: fair handicap chaser: stays 27f: acts on heavy going: wore cheekpieces/blinkers last 4 outings: sold 5,500 gns Doncaster May Sales. *J. Howard Johnson* **c113** **h–**

ONLY ONE MATTY (IRE) 8 b.g. Satco (FR) – Poundworld (IRE) (Orchestra) [2004/5 h106: c21g* 26g^{pu} c21m^{4} c23m^{ur} c24d^{4} c26s c25m^{5} c24m^{4} c25d^{5} Jan 13] workmanlike gelding: fair hurdler: similar form when winning novice at Sedgefield on chasing debut very early in season: disappointing after: stays 3m: acts on soft and good to firm going: blinkered once: tried tongue tied. *Mrs K. Walton* **c106 d** **h–**

ONLY VINTAGE (USA) 5 b.g. Diesis – Wild Vintage (USA) (Alysheba (USA)) [2004/5 F112: 17s^{F} 16d* 19s* 16g 20s^{5} Apr 7] lengthy gelding: fairly useful form when easily winning first 2 completed starts over hurdles, maiden at Newbury (beat Moonstream 4 lengths) in November and novice at Hereford (by 8 lengths from stable-companion Smart Mover) in January: well held in Supreme Novices' at Cheltenham (failed to settle) and Grade 2 novice at Aintree (mistakes) last 2 starts: stays 19f: raced on good ground or softer (acts on soft). *Miss H. C. Knight* **h126**

ONLY WORDS (USA) 8 ch.g. Shuailaan (USA) – Conversation Piece (USA) (Seeking The Gold (USA)) [2004/5 h91: 16d^{3} 16m^{ur} 16d^{5} 19d^{3} 19g^{6} 20g 22g 17s^{2} 19g 17v^{3} 21d Apr 5] workmanlike gelding: modest handicap hurdler: barely stays 2½m: acts on any going: blinkered once. *A. J. Lockwood* **h92**

ONTARIO SUNSET 4 ch.g. Weldnaas (USA) – High Penhowe (Ardross) [2004/5 F17m^{6} Apr 23] first foal: dam poor selling hurdler who stayed 21f: well held in bumper on debut. *G. M. Moore* **F–**

ON THE BONE 13 b.m. Lyphento (USA) – Lydia Languish (Hotfoot) [2004/5 c–, h–: c26g^{pu} May 1] of no account: tried blinkered. *C. N. Kellett* **c–** **h–**

ON THE LEVEL 6 ch.m. Beveled (USA) – Join The Clan (Clantime) [2004/5 16g^{pu} May 21] sprint maiden on Flat: no potential over hurdles. *Mrs N. Macauley* **h–**

ON THE LUCE 8 b.g. Karinga Bay – Lirchur (Lir) [2004/5 c89, h–: 24g^{pu} c24v^{6} c26s^{pu} c24v^{2} c27v^{5} c26v^{pu} Apr 17] good-topped gelding: pulled up both starts over hurdles: handicap chaser, largely out of form in 2004/5: stays 25f: probably acts on heavy going: wore cheekpieces last 3 starts. *Miss P. Robson* **c78 h–**

ON THE OUTSIDE (IRE) 6 ch.m. Anshan – Kate Fisher (IRE) (Over The River (FR)) [2004/5 F75: 20m^{pu} 19g^{2} 17g* 19m^{2} Sep 8] winning Irish pointer: modest form over hurdles, winning mares novice at Market Rasen in August: should stay beyond 19f: tongue tied last 2 starts. *S. E. H. Sherwood* **h95**

ON THE RUN (IRE) 11 ch.m. Don't Forget Me – Chepstow House (USA) (Northern Baby (CAN)) [2004/5 c–, h–: 19m^{4} 16g^{4} 17m c20m^{ur} 20g^{4} 19m^{pu} Sep 8] lengthy, angular mare: poor hurdler/maiden chaser: left D. Wintle before final outing: stays 2½m: acts on firm and good to soft going: tongue tied. *P. M. Rich* **c– h77**

ON THE VERGE (IRE) 7 ch.g. Alphabatim (USA) – Come On Lis (Domynsky) [2004/5 h87?, F94: 21g 20d^{5} 20m^{3} 21d 16m 24m 21g^{2} 24g^{6} Oct 14] workmanlike gelding: poor maiden hurdler: stays 21f: acts on good to firm and good to soft going: visored/blinkered 5 of last 6 outings: temperamental. *J. R. Jenkins* **h84 §**

ON TOP (IRE) 5 b.g. Topanoora – Ballyanne Supreme (IRE) (Supreme Leader) [2004/5 F16v^{6} F16s Jan 27] €13,000 3-y-o: good-topped gelding: second foal: dam won 2m hurdle: well beaten in 2 bumpers. *Mrs S. E. Busby* **F–**

ONTOS (GER) 9 b. or br.g. Super Abound (USA) – Onestep (GER) (Konigsstuhl (GER)) [2004/5 h114: 16g^{5} 16d^{6} Nov 13] leggy, short-backed gelding: fair handicap hurdler: best around 2m: acts on heavy and good to firm going: has finished weakly but is consistent. *Miss V. Scott* **h113**

ONYOURHEADBEIT (IRE) 7 b.g. Glacial Storm (USA) – Family Birthday (Sandalay) [2004/5 h86p, F98: c20s^{2} c24v^{F} c20v^{2} c22d^{3} Feb 24] rangy gelding: bumper winner: once-raced over hurdles: fair form over fences: stays 3m: acts on heavy going: has found little. *K. C. Bailey* **c104 h–**

ON Y VA (FR) 7 b.g. Goldneyev (USA) – Shakna (FR) (Le Nain Jaune (FR)) [2004/5 c–, h126: 22d* 24m^{4} 24s^{3} Apr 16] leggy gelding: last of 6 finishers only start over fences: fair hurdler nowadays: won maiden at Newton Abbot in May: off 10 months before final outing: probably stays easy 3m: unraced on firm going, probably acts on any other: tongue tied in 2004/5: has bled from nose. *R. T. Phillips* **c– h108**

OODACHEE 6 b.g. Marju (IRE) – Lady Marguerrite (Blakeney) [2004/5 h103, F100: 20m^{2} 22m^{4} Jul 31] fair on Flat up to 17f: fair form over hurdles: good efforts when fourth in handicaps at Galway in July and Punchestown (5 lengths behind Mansony) in late-April: will stay 3m: acts on firm and soft going. *C. F. Swan, Ireland* **h113**

OPAL'S HELMSMAN (USA) 6 b.g. Helmsman (USA) – Opal's Notebook (USA) (Notebook (USA)) [2004/5 16g^{F} 17d^{pu} 16v^{2} 16s 24d^{pu} 24g^{4} 24v^{ur} 24v^{pu} 24g 22d^{4} Apr 11] poor maiden hurdler: stays 3m: acts on good to soft going. *W. S. Coltherd* **h83**

OPENIDE 4 b.g. Key of Luck (USA) – Eyelet (IRE) (Satco (FR)) [2004/5 F12d* 17s 16d 17m* Apr 13] compact gelding: second foal: half-brother to bumper winner Oscars Vision (by Oscar Schindler): dam unraced half-sister to Grande Course de Haies d'Auteuil winner Tongan: 66/1, won listed bumper at Cheltenham on debut in January by head from Senorita Rumbalita: fairly useful form over hurdles: won juvenile at same course in April by 1¾ lengths from Papini: creditable sixth to United in Grade 1 4-y-o event at Punchestown later in month: will stay 2½m: bled from nose third outing. *B. W. Duke* **h119 F102**

OPENING HYMN 5 b.m. Alderbrook – Hymne d'Amour (USA) (Dixieland Band (USA)) [2004/5 16d Nov 9] sturdy mare: half-sister to one-time fairly useful hurdler/fair chaser Guard Duty (by Deploy), stays 25f: fifth both starts over 1¼m on Flat at 3 yrs for M. Tregoning: raced freely and not knocked about when well held in novice on hurdling debut. *Miss H. C. Knight* **h–**

OPERA BABE (IRE) 4 b.f. Kahyasi – Fairybird (FR) (Pampabird) [2004/5 16m Sep 4] leggy filly: fair form first 2 starts at 2 yrs, no form on Flat since: well held in juvenile on hurdling debut. *H. S. Howe* **h–**

OPERA HALL 5 b.m. Saddlers' Hall (IRE) – Opera Hat (IRE) (Strong Gale) [2004/5 F86: 16d 21d^{4} 16d 21v^{4} 21d^{5} 19g Apr 7] angular mare: modest novice hurdler: stays 21f: acts on good to soft going: usually finds little. *H. D. Daly* **h86**

OPERASHAAN (IRE) 5 b.g. Darshaan – Comic Opera (IRE) (Royal Academy (USA)) [2004/5 h–: 16v^{ur} Jan 17] lightly-raced maiden on Flat: let down by jumping on 2 starts over hurdles 12 months apart. *G. L. Moore* **h–**

OPPORTUNITY KNOCKS 5 gr.g. Wace (USA) – Madame Ruby (FR) (Homing) [2004/5 F18s^{3} 20d^{6} 20s^{4} 20v 20g^{4} 22d^{pu} Mar 10] fourth foal: half-brother to modest hurdler/chaser Got News For You (by Positive Statement), stays 3m: dam, fair 17f hurdle winner, half-sister to fairly useful 2m hurdler Might Move: third of 4 in slowly-run bumper at Fontwell on debut: poor novice hurdler: should stay beyond 2½m. *N. J. Hawke* **h74 F86 ?**

OPTIMAITE 8 b.g. Komaite (USA) – Leprechaun Lady (Royal Blend) [2004/5 h110: c16m^{2} c16g^{2} 19g^{pu} Aug 21] winning hurdler: better effort over fences when runner-up in novice at Hereford on reappearance: jumped right after badly hampered first next time: raced mainly at 2m: acts on good to firm ground: tongue tied: sold 6,100 gns Doncaster January Sales. *B. R. Millman* **c104 h–**

OPTIMISTIC ALFIE 5 b.g. Afzal – Threads (Bedford (USA)) [2004/5 F17v^{5} F16d Mar 5] has scope: second foal: dam placed twice in bumpers: well held in 2 bumpers. *C. P. Morlock* **F–**

OPTIMO (GER) 4 b.g. Kahyasi – Onanga (GER) (Acatenango (GER)) [2004/5 F16d aF16g 16m Apr 2] €40,000 3-y-o: rather leggy gelding: fourth foal: half-brother to 3 winners in Germany: dam, 8.5f and 9.5f winner, closely related to smart middle-distance stayer Orange Touch: little show in 2 bumpers and novice hurdle. *G. L. Moore* **h– F76**

OPTIMUM NIGHT 6 b.g. Superlative – Black Bess (Hasty Word) [2004/5 16g^{pu} 16g Jul 29] little sign of ability. *P. D. Niven* **h–**

ORACLE DES MOTTES (FR) 6 b.g. Signe Divin (USA) – Daisy Des Mottes (FR) (Abdonski (FR)) [2004/5 h112: 19s^{pu} 16s* 16v^{2} 17v^{3} c16s^{F4} c22g^{co} Apr 19] tall gelding: fairly useful handicap hurdler: won conditional jockeys event at Wincanton in January: would have shown similar form but about to be collared when falling last (remounted) in maiden at Ludlow on chasing debut: tongue tied, carried out eleventh in similar event next time: raced mainly around 2m: acts on any going: has failed to impress with attitude. *P. F. Nicholls* **c112 h115**

OR AIBREAN 5 b.m. Commanche Run – The Angel Leek (Sonnen Gold) [2004/5 F16g May 16] first foal: dam bumper winner: well beaten in bumper on debut. *Jennie Candlish* **F–**

ORANGE STREET 5 b.g. Primitive Rising (USA) – Arctic Oats (Oats) [2004/5 F16d^{6} F18g^{5} F16m^{3} Apr 10] 12,000 4-y-o: good-topped gelding: sixth foal: half-brother to bumper winner Arctic Echo (by Alderbrook): dam, fair hurdler, stayed 3m: better effort in bumpers when third to Young Dude at Worcester. *Mrs L. J. Mongan* **F87**

ORBICULARIS (IRE) 9 b.g. Supreme Leader – Liffey Travel (Le Bavard (FR)) [2004/5 h79: 22s^{2} 22g* 22g^{3} 25g^{pu} Dec 16] sparely-made gelding: fair handicap hurdler: won at Stratford in July: stays 2¾m: acts on soft going. *Mrs A. M. Thorpe* **h100**

ORCHARD FIELDS (IRE) 8 b.g. Lord Americo – Art Lover (IRE) (Over The River (FR)) [2004/5 23d^{4} 20s^{pu} 20v^{pu} 26g^{4} Mar 16] good-topped gelding: modest handicap hurdler: stays 3¼m: raced on good going or softer: often let down by jumping: sold 5,000 gns Doncaster May Sales. *Mrs P. Sly* **h88 x**

ORCHESTRAL DREAM (IRE) 5 ch.g. Flying Legend (USA) – Mill Dancer (IRE) (Broken Hearted) [2004/5 F16m F16v^{3} F16v^{5} 16d 16s^{5} 16v^{3} 20v* Apr 17] first foal: dam, poor on Flat/no form over hurdles, half-sister to useful hurdler up to 3m Spirit Dancer: fair in bumpers: off nearly 4 months and stepped up in trip, much improved when first past post in 2 outings over hurdles in April, maiden at Listowel and 3m minor event at Punchestown (demoted after beating Bright Gas a neck): will stay beyond 3m. *M. Hourigan, Ireland* **h114 F89**

ORCHESTRA'S BOY (IRE) 10 b.g. Homo Sapien – Ballycurnane Lady (Orchestra) [2004/5 c25s^{pu} Mar 6] winning pointer: jumped badly in novice hunter chase. *R. Green* **c– h–**

ORIENTAL MOON (IRE) 6 ch.m. Spectrum (IRE) – La Grande Cascade (USA) (Beaudelaire (USA)) [2004/5 h–: 16d 20d^{pu} May 9] of no account: tried visored. *M. J. Gingell* **h–**

ORIENTAL STYLE (IRE) 11 ro.g. Indian Ridge – Bazaar Promise (Native Bazaar) [2004/5 c24s^{pu} Mar 5] close-coupled gelding: winning chaser/maiden hurdler, lightly raced nowadays. *J. J. Best* **c– h–**

ORIENT BAY (IRE) 10 b.g. Commanche Run – East Link (IRE) (Over The River (FR)) [2004/5 c61, h76: 21d^{5} 16m^{3} 16g^{5} c23f^{3} c19g^{3} 19d c19d^{ur} Oct 28] strong gelding: poor maiden hurdler/chaser: little impact in points in 2005: effective at 2m to 3¼m: acts **c65 h71**

on firm and good to soft going: wears cheekpieces/blinkers: tongue tied: has jumped poorly/hung under pressure. *M. Sheppard*

ORIGINAL SIN (IRE) 5 b.g. Bluebird (USA) – Majakerta (IRE) (Shernazar) [2004/5 16v[5] 21dpu Jan 6] poor maiden on Flat (stays 7f), sold out of S. Dow's stable £700 Ascot February (2004) Sales: no form in 2 outings over hurdles. *I. R. Brown* **h–**

ORIGINAL THOUGHT (IRE) 5 b.g. Entrepreneur – Troyanos (Troy) [2004/5 F16g[3] F16d[3] Apr 20] good-topped gelding: half-brother to several winners, including fairly useful winner around 1½m Summer Pageant (by Chief's Crown): dam unraced half-sister to Oaks and St Leger winner Sun Princess and high-class middle-distance stayer Saddlers' Hall: runner-up in maiden Irish point on debut in 2004: fair form when third in bumpers at Doncaster and Worcester. *B. De Haan* **F95**

ORINOCOVSKY (IRE) 6 ch.g. Grand Lodge (USA) – Brillantina (FR) (Crystal Glitters (USA)) [2004/5 h82: 16g[4] c16f* Sep 5] good-topped gelding: modest on Flat (stays 1¾m): modest form over hurdles: better form when winning maiden at Worcester on chasing debut: raced mainly around 2m: acts on firm going: blinkered once (raced freely). *N. P. Littmoden* **c102 h93**

ORION EXPRESS 4 b.g. Bahhare (USA) – Kaprisky (IRE) (Red Sunset) [2004/5 17g[5] 17g[5] 16m Oct 13] lengthy gelding: modest maiden on Flat (stays 1¼m): poor form in juvenile hurdles: sold 2,400 gns Doncaster March Sales. *M. W. Easterby* **h–**

ORLEANS (IRE) 10 b.g. Scenic – Guest House (What A Guest) [2004/5 c71, h–: c21g[3] c25g[5] Mar 9] tall gelding: winning pointer: maiden hunter chaser: stays 25f: acts on soft and good to firm going: visored/blinkered: has been reluctant to race/refused in points, and is one to treat with caution. *S. J. Robinson* **c83 h–**

ORNELLA SPEED (FR) 5 b.m. Vertical Speed (FR) – Macyrienne (FR) (Saint Cyrien (FR)) [2004/5 17gpu 17d 27d[3] 21d 25gpu 17v c24gF c24g[5] Feb 16] ex-French mare: third foal: half-sister to fair but ungenuine hurdler Kitski (by Perrault), stays 3m: dam unraced: poor novice hurdler: well held on completed start over fences: stays 27f: tried blinkered/in cheekpieces: tongue tied nowadays. *Ferdy Murphy* **c74 ? h69**

ORO STREET (IRE) 9 b.g. Dolphin Street (FR) – Love Unlimited (Dominion) [2004/5 h83: 16m[3] 20d[3] 19m[5] May 23] workmanlike gelding: poor hurdler: lame final start: stays 2½m: acts on good to firm and good to soft going: tried tongue tied: has pulled hard/found little. *G. F. Bridgwater* **h78**

ORSWELL CREST 11 b.g. Crested Lark – Slave's Bangle (Prince Rheingold) [2004/5 c111, h–: c23m[3] c24g c24d[2] c25d[2] c27m[2] c25dpu Mar 24] lengthy gelding: fair handicap chaser: stays 27f: acts on soft and good to firm going: often soon off bridle. *P. J. Hobbs* **c106 h–**

ORTHODOX 6 gr.g. Baryshnikov (AUS) – Sancta (So Blessed) [2004/5 h–: 16m Apr 2] good-topped gelding: no form on Flat in 2005: no show in 2 novice hurdles 16 months apart. *G. L. Moore* **h–**

OSCAR BILL (IRE) 6 b.g. Oscar (IRE) – Forecast Rain (IRE) (Phardante (FR)) [2004/5 F84: F18g[2] 22g[5] Nov 18] stocky gelding: fair form at best in bumpers: well beaten on hurdling debut. *M. J. Coombe* **h– F88**

OSCAR BRUNEL (IRE) 6 b.g. Oscar (IRE) – Pima (IRE) (Commanche Run) [2004/5 20v* 22v[6] 20d 24s[4] Mar 28] first foal: dam second in mares maiden Irish point, only outing: third in bumper at Fairyhouse on debut: fair form over hurdles: won maiden at Fairyhouse in January: raced on going softer than good. *P. M. J. Doyle, Ireland* **h111**

OSCARDEAL (IRE) 6 b.g. Oscar (IRE) – Sleepy Bye Byes (IRE) (Supreme Leader) [2004/5 F17v F16g* F16d[5] F16g[2] F16g Mar 16] 5,000 5-y-o: workmanlike gelding: fifth foal: half-brother to fair hurdler Brave Dream (by Commanche Run), stayed 23f: dam unraced, from family of outstanding 2m chaser Badsworth Boy: useful form in bumpers: won at Southwell in January: ½-length second to No Regrets at Doncaster: well held in Grade 1 at Cheltenham final start: races prominently. *C. T. Pogson* **F105**

OSCAR FOXBOW (IRE) 6 b. or br.g. Oscar (IRE) – Miss Fox Bow (IRE) (King's Ride) [2004/5 F16d[5] F16s[5] F16g* 16d[6] Feb 9] first foal: dam unraced, out of half-sister to dam of 1981 Supreme Novices' Hurdle winner Hartstown: fair form in bumpers: won at Ludlow in November: never a factor but not knocked about in maiden there on hurdling debut. *C. Tinkler* **h– F86**

OSCAR MADISON (IRE) 4 b.g. Petorius – She's Our Lady (IRE) (Scenic) [2004/5 16m Oct 3] last all 4 starts in maidens at 2 yrs and in juvenile on hurdling debut. *B. Mactaggart* **h–**

OSCAR ORANGE (IRE) 5 br.m. Oscar (IRE) – Pappy's Girlfriend (Strong Gale) [2004/5 F18v* Apr 6] second foal: dam unraced, out of half-sister to useful chaser up to 2½m Poets Corner: successful both completed starts in Irish points: won mares bumper at Gowran in April impressively by 6 lengths from Coolgreaney: sure to progress. *J. A. Flynn, Ireland* **F101 p**

OSCAR PARK (IRE) 6 b.g. Oscar (IRE) – Parkavoureen (Deep Run) [2004/5 F16s* F16s* Jan 15] **F120**

A pulled muscle a week before the big day ruled Oscar Park out of the Champion Bumper at the Cheltenham Festival. He would have had to have proved his effectiveness on less testing ground than previously, but his form in winning both his previous starts was not that far behind that of the pick of the field at Cheltenham and he would have been well worth his place there. Although Oscar Park was held up for only a few days, connections called it a day for the season. Oscar Park gained his wins at Windsor in November and in a listed event at Warwick in January. None of the nine behind him at Windsor that ran subsequently managed to win but the style of his victory was impressive. He faced much stronger opposition at Warwick and, under conditions which made for a thorough test of stamina, he and Lennon came a long way clear of the remainder, Oscar Park getting on top in the last hundred yards or so to win by a length and a half. Lennon went on to win a second time at Musselburgh before finishing well held at Cheltenham, while the fourth also won next time out.

Oscar Park should make up for lost time when sent over jumps in the next season and is likely to stay well. His dam Parkavourneen is a bumper winner and half-sister to the useful hurdler/chaser at up to three miles Lanturn and the fairly useful staying chaser Mailcom. Parkavoureen's four other winners from seven foals to race include three successful over two and a half miles or further, the pick of them the fairly useful hurdler and fair chaser Julie's Leader (by Supreme Leader), who stayed at least twenty-seven furlongs. *C. Tinkler*

OSCAR PEPPER (USA) 8 b.g. Brunswick (USA) – Princess Baja (USA) (Conquistador Cielo (USA)) [2004/5 c25gpu c27vpu c24spu Apr 16] fair on Flat (stays 1¼m) for T. D. Barron in 2004: no show (made mistakes) in hunter chases. *M. J. Brown* **c–**

OSCAR'S ADVANCE (IRE) 6 b.g. Oscar (IRE) – Banna's Retreat (Vitiges (FR)) [2004/5 F107: F16g Mar 16] sturdy gelding: useful form in bumpers, successful twice in 2003/4: left Ms M. Mullins and off 18 months, not discredited when tenth to Missed That in Grade 1 at Cheltenham. *C. Roche, Ireland* **F103**

OSCARS LAW 4 b.f. Oscar (IRE) – Eloquent Lawyer (Law Society (USA)) [2004/5 F12g F13s5 F16s Mar 6] leggy filly: first foal: dam, winning pointer, out of half-sister to smart stayer Ivory Fields: modest form in bumpers. *J. L. Spearing* **F81**

OSCARS VISION (IRE) 5 ch.m. Oscar Schindler (IRE) – Eyelet (IRE) (Satco (FR)) [2004/5 h–, F95: 16s2 16s4 16d3 21d 20d 22g Mar 20] angular mare: won only start in bumpers: poor maiden hurdler: probably stays 2¾m. *B. W. Duke* **h79**

OSCAR THE BOXER (IRE) 6 b.g. Oscar (IRE) – Here She Comes (Deep Run) [2004/5 F84: 16v6 19m4 16v4 16d Jan 28] lengthy, useful-looking gelding: poor novice hurdler: will be suited by 2½m+. *J. M. Jefferson* **h80**

OSCAR WILDE 13 b.g. Arctic Lord – Topsy Bee (Be Friendly) [2004/5 c73x: c21m May 19] tall gelding: winning chaser: barely stays 25f: tends to make mistakes. *Mrs S. Alner* **c– x**

OSCATELLO (USA) 5 b. or br.g. Woodman (USA) – Galea Des Bois (FR) (Persian Bold) [2004/5 F16s2 Nov 20] 20,000 2-y-o: first foal: dam 1m winner: staying-on 6 lengths second to Oscar Park in bumper at Windsor on debut. *Ian Williams* **F99**

OSIRIS (IRE) 10 b.g. Orchestra – Merry Servant (Giolla Mear) [2004/5 c20g3 c21f2 c24mF c25fpu c22d5 c22d c24s5 c19g* c20g2 c21s* c22sF c20d3 Mar 11] ex-Irish gelding: winning hurdler: fair handicap chaser: left P. Heffernan after seventh start: won novice handicap at Taunton in December and Wincanton in February: creditable second to Monterey Bay at Punchestown in late-April: stays 25f: acts on any going: tried blinkered/in cheekpieces: tongue tied. *Evan Williams* **c113 h–**

OSOKENDA 5 b.m. Teenoso (USA) – Song of Kenda (Rolfe (USA)) [2004/5 F17d 22dpu Mar 24] sturdy mare: second foal: dam, poor maiden hurdler who stayed 2¾m, **h– F–**

half-sister to useful staying chaser Kendal Cavalier: no show in bumper and mares novice hurdle. *K. Bishop*

OSO MAGIC 7 b.g. Teenoso (USA) – Scottish Clover (Scottish Reel) [2004/5 h85: 20d6 16g4 20s5 16d6 c20d4 c19g* c19g2 c16d3 Feb 4] big, lengthy gelding: modest maiden hurdler: fair form over fences: won maiden at Catterick in December: stays 2½m: raced on good going or softer. *Mrs S. J. Smith* **c112 h84**

OSSMOSES (IRE) 8 gr.g. Roselier (FR) – Sugarstown (Sassafras (FR)) [2004/5 c91, h86: c22v* c25v2 c26v* c32v2 Mar 5] big gelding: once-raced hurdler: fairly useful handicap chaser: won at Haydock in December and Uttoxeter (by ½ length from Toulouse-Lautrec) in February: good second to Malek in valuable event at Kelso final start: stays 4m: raced on going softer than good (acts well on heavy). *D. M. Forster* **c118 h–**

OSTFANNI (IRE) 5 b.m. Spectrum (IRE) – Ostwahl (IRE) (Waajib) [2004/5 17d 16g5 17v3 21s2 20gro Feb 27] fair on Flat (stays 2m), sold out of D. Gillespie's stable 11,000 gns Newmarket July Sales: fair novice hurdler: held when running out final start: stays 21f: acts on heavy going. *M. Todhunter* **h100**

OTAHUNA 9 b.g. Selkirk (USA) – Stara (Star Appeal) [2004/5 19s* c16s6 Mar 23] leggy gelding: modest hurdler: left J. A. Moore and off 2½ years, improved form when winning conditional jockeys handicap at Towcester in March: well held in handicap on chasing debut: will stay beyond 19f: acts on soft ground. *J. W. Mullins* **c– h86**

O'TOOLE (IRE) 6 b.g. Toulon – Legs Burke (IRE) (Buckskin (FR)) [2004/5 F94: 19s3 20s3 19g5 17s* 19g6 Apr 12] lengthy gelding: has scope: fair hurdler: won handicap at Exeter in March: stays 2½m: acts on soft going. *P. J. Hobbs* **h106**

OTTOMAN (AUS) 9 br.g. Grand Lodge (USA) – Cushti (AUS) (Gypsy Kingdom (AUS)) [2004/5 c–, h85: 18m4 20g* 20g3 16m3 22g2 20gF Jul 30] leggy, workmanlike gelding: unseated only outing over fences: fair handicap hurdler: won at Hexham in May: running another good race when falling fatally 2 out at Bangor: stayed 2¾m: acted on good to firm and heavy going: effective with/without cheekpieces: patiently ridden. *R. C. Guest* **c– h106**

OUH JAY 7 ch.m. Karinga Bay – Creeping Jane (Rustingo) [2004/5 F16g4 F16g F17g Sep 30] close-coupled mare: fourth foal: dam fair pointer: modest form on first of 3 starts in bumpers. *P. Bowen* **F79**

OUI EXIT (FR) 4 b.g. Exit To Nowhere (USA) – Forest Hills (FR) (Sicyos (USA)) [2004/5 F13s Jan 31] ninth foal: half-brother to several winners on Flat, including smart around 2m Forestier (by Nikos): dam French maiden: last of 14 in bumper on debut. *M. Scudamore* **F–**

OULART 6 ch.g. Sabrehill (USA) – Gaye Fame (Ardross) [2004/5 F16d4 16d4 16d2 20s* 24v* 24v 22v2 24g* Mar 17] 30,000 4-y-o: lengthy gelding: second foal: half-brother to bumper winner Round The Horn (by Master Willie): dam, modest hurdler who stayed 3m, out of sister to very smart staying chaser Black Humour and half-sister to top-class 2m to 3m hurdler Gaye Brief and very smart staying jumper Gaye Chance: fair **h126 F83**

Pertemps Final (Handicap Hurdle), Cheltenham—the handicapper can pat himself on the back; Oulart leads narrowly at the last with Mioche d'Estruval and Quick (visor) his closest challengers

form in bumpers: progressive hurdler: won maiden at Clonmel and handicap at Leopardstown in December and 22-runner Pertemps Final (Handicap) at Cheltenham (by 2 lengths from Mioche d'Estruval) in March: stays 3m: acts on heavy ground. *D. T. Hughes, Ireland*

OULTON BROAD 9 b.g. Midyan (USA) – Lady Quachita (USA) (Sovereign Dancer (USA)) [2004/5 c–, h101: 16g4 21dF 16s6 19gur c18s2 c19g2 Apr 12] sparely-made gelding: winning hurdler: poor form in 2004/5 (trained second and third outings by M. Gingell): runner-up in maidens on completed starts over fences: stays 23f, effective at much shorter: acts on soft and good to firm going: wears cheekpieces. *F. Jordan* **c85 § h83 §**

OUR BEN 6 ch.g. Presenting – Forest Pride (IRE) (Be My Native (USA)) [2004/5 F99: F16g 16d* 20s3 22v* 24v3 21g3 20s5 Mar 27] **h144**

So far, the 2004 Champion Bumper at Cheltenham has not matched its predecessors as a nursery for the pick of the prospective jumpers. The best hurdler to emerge from the twenty-four-strong field is the sixteenth home Our Ben. He lacked the maturity and probably the speed required when sent over to Cheltenham after just one previous run in 2004, and also finished well held in a well-contested bumper at Punchestown the following month. Our Ben progressed well over hurdles, showing useful form before returning to Cheltenham a year later to take third, finishing strongly, behind No Refuge, in a good renewal of the Royal & SunAlliance Novices' Hurdle, with the Champion Bumper fourth Royal Paradise, the next best hurdler in that field, over seven lengths away in seventh. Our Ben is still unfurnished but if he fills out over the summer he should make at least a similar impact sent over fences, particularly if his stamina is tested more fully than it has been in most of his races so far.

Our Ben won twice from four starts over hurdles prior to Cheltenham, a two-mile maiden at Clonmel on his debut, in which he was not required to show

Mr Trevor J. Hemmings' "Our Ben"

anything like his later form, and a two-and-three-quarter-mile Grade 3 novice at Limerick. In the latter event, with the ground particularly testing, Our Ben produced a strong-galloping display from the front and beat the useful Kerryhead Windfarm by twenty-five lengths. Our Ben was more patiently ridden and couldn't get on terms with Sweet Kiln and Carraig Blue at Fairyhouse on his start before Cheltenham and also failed to show to advantage on two subsequent starts. Back at Fairyhouse, in a Grade 2 novice, just eleven days after the SunAlliance, he wasn't well served by a steady pace and ran below his best in fifth behind Sher Beau. At Punchestown, in the Champion Stayers Hurdle, Our Ben lost his chance when all but falling at the sixth. The unfurnished Our Ben is the third foal out of the two-mile hurdle winner Forest Pride. The second Countess Camilla (by Bob's Return) won twice in bumpers and then showed fairly useful form at up to two and three quarter miles over hurdles in 2003/4. Forest Pride's three-year-old brother to Our Ben made 120,000 guineas at the Doncaster May Sales, bought on behalf of War of Attrition's owner Michael O'Leary. Our Ben should stay three miles. He has raced on good going or softer. *W. P. Mullins, Ireland*

OUR IMPERIAL BAY (USA) 6 b.g. Smart Strike (CAN) – Heat Lightning (USA) (Summer Squall (USA)) [2004/5 h79§: 21gpu 17dpu Aug 1] tall gelding: poor and ungenuine on Flat and over hurdles: sold out of R. Stronge's stable £4,300 Ascot June Sales after first outing: usually wears headgear. *Jennie Candlish* **h– §**

OUR JASPER 5 gr.g. Tina's Pet – Dawn's Della (Scottish Reel) [2004/5 F16g4 F16d 19s6 20spu 17s Apr 2] tall gelding: first foal: dam poor maiden hurdler: signs of ability in bumpers and over hurdles (twice not knocked about). *K. G. Reveley* **h80 F77**

OUR JOLLY SWAGMAN 10 b.g. Thowra (FR) – Queens Dowry (Dominion) [2004/5 c118, h–: c19v6 24d4 c27spu c26dpu c24spu c26d Apr 18] sturdy gelding: fairly useful handicap chaser in 2003/4: off a year, no form in 2004/5, including in novice hurdle: stays 3½m: acts on good to firm and heavy going: usually wears visor/cheekpieces: has won 4 times at Plumpton. *J. W. Mullins* **c– h–**

OUR JOYCEY 4 b.f. Shernazar – Charisse Dancer (Dancing Dissident (USA)) [2004/5 F16g F17g Apr 3] third foal: dam, poor maiden, stayed 1m: mid-division in 2 bumpers. *Mrs K. Walton* **F79**

OUR KEV (IRE) 9 b.g. Be My Native (USA) – Sunbath (Krayyan) [2004/5 c87, h–: c25dpu c25gpu May 12] tall gelding: won conditional jockeys handicap in 2003/4, only form in chases: stays 3m. *B. G. Powell* **c– h–**

OUR LAWMAN 6 b.g. Shareef Dancer (USA) – Motoqua (Mtoto) [2004/5 h–, F77?: 20s c21d 20v c16gpu c20gpu Apr 3] no form over hurdles or fences. *Mrs S. J. Smith* **c– h–**

OUR MAN DENNIS 11 b.g. Arzanni – Pendocks Polly (Grey Steel) [2004/5 c69, h–: c19m6 c26g3 c19m2 c16m5 c26g2 c21d4 Aug 9] lengthy gelding: poor maiden hurdler/chaser: stays 3¼m: acts on good to firm and good to soft going. *Mrs P. Ford* **c76 h–**

OURMAN (IRE) 9 b.g. Good Thyne (USA) – Magic Minstrel (Pitpan) [2004/5 c98, h–: c25s c24vpu c26gpu Mar 18] useful-looking gelding: winning chaser: well held on completed outing in hunters in 2005: stays 27f: acts on heavy going: has had tongue tied. *Nick Bell* **c– h–**

OUR MEN 6 b.g. Classic Cliche (IRE) – Praise The Lord (Lord Gayle (USA)) [2004/5 F–: aF16g F16d6 Mar 10] modest form in bumpers after 21-month absence, blinkered second occasion. *C. R. Egerton* **F82**

OUR PRIMA DONNA (IRE) 7 ch.m. Be My Native (USA) – Stage Debut (Decent Fellow) [2004/5 h91: 24s4 22g3 c24s4 Jan 20] workmanlike mare: modest novice hurdler: not fluent when fourth in novice handicap at Ludlow on chasing debut: should prove better suited by 3m than shorter: raced on good going or softer. *Miss Venetia Williams* **c85 h93**

OUR SAMSON (IRE) 5 b.g. Old Vic – Strong Gale Pigeon (IRE) (Strong Gale) [2004/5 F17d3 20d4 Nov 19] small, close-coupled gelding: second foal: brother to fair hurdler Vic The Piler (by Old Vic), stays 2¾m: dam unraced: won second of 2 starts in maiden Irish points in 2004: sold 39,000 gns Doncaster May Sales: third of 9 in bumper at Folkestone: well-beaten fourth of 9 in novice at Windsor on hurdling debut. *G. L. Moore* **h– F81**

OUR TOMMY 12 ch.g. Ardross – Ina's Farewell (Random Shot) [2004/5 c75: c25m c21g* c21spu c23g* c23fpu Sep 5] poor handicap chaser: won at Uttoxeter in May and Worcester in July: lame final outing: best short of 3m: acts on soft going: usually races prominently. *A. E. Price* **c83**

OUR VIC (IRE) 7 b.g. Old Vic – Shabra Princess (Buckskin (FR)) [2004/5 c150p, h146p: c21dF c21gpu c25spu Apr 7] tall, good-topped gelding: smart hurdler, won 3 of 4 outings: also made very good start in chases, winning twice in 2003/4: in process of showing further improvement when falling in lead at last in valuable handicap won by Monkerhostin at Cheltenham on reappearance: more mistakes when pulled up after in Grade 2 events at Cheltenham and Aintree: stays 3m: raced on good going or softer: not easiest to train. *M. C. Pipe* **c158 h–**

OUTSIDE INVESTOR (IRE) 5 b. or br.g. Cadeaux Genereux – Desert Ease (IRE) (Green Desert (USA)) [2004/5 h83: 22mF 22g 22s4 19d 19m6 16d 16sF Dec 18] workmanlike gelding: poor hurdler: sold out of N. Gifford's stable £6,000 Ascot November Sales after fourth outing: should prove best short of 2¾m when conditions are testing: usually blinkered. *P. R. Rodford* **h83**

OUT THE BLACK (IRE) 7 b. or br.g. Presenting – Executive Wonder (IRE) (Executive Perk) [2004/5 c23g* c24g3 c24g* c23dF c25dF4 Dec 10] rather leggy gelding: first foal: dam unraced half-sister to fairly useful hurdler/chaser up to 3m Nodform Wonder: won 4 of 7 starts in points in 2004: fairly useful form when winning maiden chase at Exeter (beat eased stable-companion Willie John Daly 12 lengths) in October and novice at Ludlow (by 10 lengths from Lord Dundaniel) in November: fell last 2 starts, held in third when coming down at last (remounted) in novice at Cheltenham won by Cornish Rebel: stays 3m. *P. J. Hobbs* **c125**

OVER BOOKED 6 b.g. Overbury (IRE) – Miss Arc (Gildoran) [2004/5 19d Jan 1] 6,500 3-y-o: rather leggy gelding: first foal: dam unraced, out of half-sister to useful hurdler Winston Run: always behind in novice hurdle on debut. *J. Wade* **h–**

OVER BRIDGE 7 b.g. Overbury (IRE) – Celtic Bridge (Celtic Cone) [2004/5 h78§: 20g5 19m6 22m Apr 23] smallish, workmanlike gelding: poor handicap hurdler: stays 19f: acts on good to firm going: ungenuine. *Mrs S. M. Johnson* **h– §**

OVERBURY AFFAIR 6 b.g. Overbury (IRE) – Dara's Course (IRE) (Crash Course) [2004/5 F104p: 16d* Oct 17] successful in bumper on debut: won novice at Cork on hurdling debut by 3 lengths from The Foyle: looked type to progress. *E. J. O'Grady, Ireland* **h107 +**

OVER FLO 6 b.m. Overbury (IRE) – Flo-Jo (DEN) (Pelton Lad) [2004/5 F17m3 F16s2 Aug 25] eighth foal: dam unraced half-sister to high-class 2m to 3m chaser Vodkatini, who later became thoroughly temperamental: poor form when placed in 2 bumpers, looking a stayer. *C. Grant* **F71**

OVERSERVED 6 b. or br.g. Supreme Leader – Divine Comedy (IRE) (Phardante (FR)) [2004/5 h–: 16s4 18v4 20s* 20d* Mar 26] good-topped gelding: chasing type: fair hurdler: successful twice at Carlisle in March, in novice then a handicap: will stay beyond 2½m: raced only on ground softer than good: open to further improvement. *A. Parker* **h105 p**

OVERSTRAND (IRE) 6 b.g. In The Wings – Vaison La Romaine (Arctic Tern (USA)) [2004/5 h131: 16gpu 22g4 Apr 16] lengthy, angular gelding: useful hurdler: left Mrs M. Reveley and off a year, fourth of 7 to Ladalko in handicap at Ayr: effective at 2m to 2¾m: raced on good going or softer: usually held up. *M. Todhunter* **h127**

OVER THE BLUES (IRE) 5 b.g. Bob Back (USA) – Fiona's Blue (Crash Course) [2004/5 17g Dec 15] €105,000 3-y-o: seventh foal: half-brother to several winners, including one-time smart hurdler/useful chaser up to 4m Native Emperor (by Be My Native): dam, lightly-raced Irish maiden jumper, half-sister to useful jumpers Treyford, Dis Train and Deep Heritage: backward, always behind after mistake first in novice hurdle on debut: sort to do better. *Jonjo O'Neill* **h– p**

OVER THE CREEK 6 br.g. Over The River (FR) – Solo Girl (IRE) (Le Bavard (FR)) [2004/5 h102p: 16d* 20s* 20s 24d* 24g2 Mar 18] **h144**

Over The Creek proved as smart a novice over hurdles in the latest season as his owner David Johnson's Comply Or Die had done in the previous one, and there seems no reason why he shouldn't continue to follow Comply Or Die's lead when sent over fences in 2005/6. If he does, Over The Creek will be in for another successful campaign, his stable-companion having made up into one of the best staying novice chasers in 2004/5, when he won three races and finished second in the Royal & SunAlliance Chase. Physically, the tall, lengthy Over The Creek is not unlike Comply Or Die, and is certainly very much a chasing type. For a while it seemed as though Over The Creek might not be up to making a significant impact over hurdles, second place at Wincanton the best he could manage in three outings

totescoop6 Handicap Hurdle, Newbury—
Over The Creek (right) and Omni Cosmo Touch have the race to themselves

in his first season. He was a very different proposition in his second season, though, returning from ten months off to open his account in a novice handicap at Cheltenham in November, then winning open handicaps at Aintree later in the month and at Newbury in February. The only blip on his record in this period came in December at Haydock, where he started at very short odds to complete his hat-trick but ran poorly, without an obvious reason, though it was his third outing in three weeks. Over The Creek bounced back, to put up his best performance to date, when stepped up to three miles at Newbury. Set to give weight to all eleven of his rivals and racing off a mark 24 lb higher than at Cheltenham, Over The Creek won by three and a half lengths from Omni Cosmo Touch with the remainder well beaten off. Patiently ridden as usual, Over The Creek jumped accurately, moved through strongly to challenge two out and didn't need to be put to his best to assert on the run-in. Over The Creek's only subsequent outing came in a non-handicap, the Spa Novices' Hurdle at the Cheltenham Festival, and he acquitted himself well given that conditions didn't place quite enough emphasis on stamina for him, outpaced after three out, then staying on strongly from the next to finish two and a half lengths second to Moulin Riche.

Over The Creek (br.g. 1999)	Over The River (FR) (ch 1974)	Luthier (b or br 1965)	Klairon
			Flute Enchantee
		Medenine (b 1967)	Prudent II
			Ma Congaie
	Solo Girl (IRE) (b 1988)	Le Bavard (ch 1971)	Devon
			Lueur Doree
		Go-It-Alone (br 1977)	Linacre
			Leuze

Over The Creek, who seems certain to stay a good deal further than three miles, is stoutly bred. By Over The River, he is from the family of the 1979 Grand National winner Rubstic and the top-class staying chaser Kildimo, the latter winner of the Sun Alliance Chase in 1987. Rubstic and Kildimo, along with the useful chaser Bennachie and the very smart hurdler and useful chaser Baydon Star, both of whom stayed three miles, are out of Over The Creek's great grandam, the unraced Leuze. One of the very few of Leuze's foals which failed to win was Lettuce, and she made amends at stud with the Lincoln and Royal Hunt Cup winner Mighty Fly and the Derby third Mighty Flutter. Another out of Lettuce was the fairly useful chaser and winning hurdler Mighty Flutter. Over The Creek's grandam Go-It-

Mr D. A. Johnson's "Over The Creek"

Alone won a five-furlong maiden as a two-year-old when trained by Jack Berry and was subsequently placed over hurdles for him, though she showed only poor form and wasn't one to trust. Over The Creek's dam Solo Girl, who is by Le Bavard, the sire of Kildimo, showed a little ability in a bumper but none in five starts in novice hurdles in the 1993/4 season. Over The Creek is Solo Girl's only winner to date, but her fourth foal Dan's Man (by Zaffaran) couldn't have gone any closer to becoming her second when making his debut in a maiden bumper at Towcester in April, beaten a short head. So far, Over The Creek has raced only on good ground or softer, and he acts on soft. He looks one to follow in staying novice chases in 2005/6. *M. C. Pipe*

OVER THE FIRST (IRE) 10 b. or br.g. Orchestra – Ruby Lodge (Peacock (FR)) [2004/5 c124, h–: c16s 20s^5 c18d^4 c20s^4 c24s^3 c22v^F c24v c18s^6 c21v^4 c21d^{ur} Apr 8] rangy gelding: winning hurdler: useful handicap chaser: best effort when fourth to Mistletoeandwine at Punchestown third outing: reportedly made a noise when pulled up there in late-April: stays 3m: acts on heavy going, possibly not on good to firm. *C. F. Swan, Ireland* **c130 h–**

OVER TO JOE 5 br.g. Overbury (IRE) – Flo-Jo (DEN) (Pelton Lad) [2004/5 F16s F17s 21v^{ur} 21d^6 Apr 5] €7,500 4-y-o: good-topped gelding: ninth foal: dam unraced half-sister to high-class 2m to 3m chaser Vodkatini, who later became thoroughly temperamental: no show in bumpers or over hurdles. *C. Grant* **h– F–**

OVER TO YOU BERT 6 b.g. Overbury (IRE) – Silvers Era (Balidar) [2004/5 h–: 16d^F 17s^5 16v^{pu} Oct 16] good-topped gelding: modest on Flat (best at 1m), successful twice in 2004: looks non-stayer over hurdles. *R. J. Hodges* **h–**

OVER ZEALOUS (IRE) 13 ch.g. Over The River (FR) – Chatty Di (Le Bavard (FR)) [2004/5 c91§, h–§: c25g^5 c26d^4 c25f^2 c24m^5 c26s^{pu} c25g^{pu} c24s^3 Mar 27] leggy **c91 § h– §**

gelding: modest handicap chaser: thorough stayer: probably acts on any going: blinkered/ visored: moody. *John R. Upson*

OWEN'S BOY (IRE) 4 b.g. Gulland – Cloughteana (IRE) (Mandalus) [2004/5 16v 16s 16d 19m^{ur} Apr 2] leggy gelding: no sign of ability on Flat (for P. Morris) or over hurdles: tried tongue tied. *R. P. O'Keeffe, Ireland* **h–**

OWN LINE 6 b.g. Classic Cliçhe (IRE) – Cold Line (Exdirectory) [2004/5 16s 16s 20v 20d^2 24g Jan 21] good-topped gelding: half-brother to fair hurdler Give Best (by Dunbeath), stayed 25f: dam, modest 1½m winner, half-sister to high-class hurdler Past Glories: modest on Flat (stays 2m) as 4-y-o: best effort over hurdles when second in novice handicap at Musselburgh: should stay beyond 2½m. *J. Hetherton* **h88**

OXENDALE 12 ch.g. Primitive Rising (USA) – Saucy Moon (Saucy Kit) [2004/5 c26m^6 May 19] modest pointer: blinkered, well held in novice hunters. *Mrs Diane Broad* **c–**

OYSTERHAVEN (IRE) 7 b.g. Mister Lord (USA) – Haven's Glory (IRE) (Supreme Leader) [2004/5 h98, F82: 24s^{pu} 26d^4 22s^3 20s^2 22d Mar 11] useful-looking gelding: chasing type: fair handicap hurdler: stays 3¼m: raced on good going or softer: blinkered last 3 starts: not a fluent jumper. *D. P. Keane* **h106**

OYSTER POINT (IRE) 6 br.g. Corrouge (USA) – Ross Gale (Strong Gale) [2004/5 F16m^4 F16d 20m Dec 12] €18,000 3-y-o: sixth foal: half-brother to fairly useful hurdler/ useful chaser Full Irish (by Rashar), stays 21f: dam won bumper/over hurdles in Ireland: won maiden on last of 5 starts in Irish points in 2004: bought 20,000 gns Doncaster May Sales: modest form on first of 2 outings in bumpers: looked uncooperative on hurdling debut. *Mrs K. Walton* **h–** **F85**

P

PACE STALKER (USA) 9 b.g. Lear Fan (USA) – In The Habit (USA) (Lyphard (USA)) [2004/5 16g 21s^{pu} c18g c17g^5 Mar 28] maiden hurdler: winning chaser (sketchy jumper): no form in 2004/5: tried in blinkers/cheekpieces: has had tongue tied. *M. R. Hoad* **c– x** **h–**

PACHARAN QUEEN 4 b.f. Terimon – Persian Fountain (IRE) (Persian Heights) [2004/5 F12g F14d Nov 23] small filly: fifth foal: sister to one-time fair hurdler/chaser Pertino, stays 2½m, and half-sister to fairly useful 2-y-o 5f winner Annamoe Bay (by Presidium) and 1½m winner Perpetuo (by Mtoto): dam 2-y-o 7.5f winner: well held in 3-y-o bumpers. *V. Smith* **F–**

PACIFIC HIGHWAY (IRE) 6 b.g. Sadler's Wells (USA) – Obeah (Cure The Blues (USA)) [2004/5 F–: F16d 19g 20g^5 20s Mar 22] lengthy gelding: little sign of ability: whipped round at start third outing. *Mrs L. B. Normile* **h–** **F–**

PADAMUL 9 ch.g. Polish Precedent (USA) – Oxslip (Owen Dudley) [2004/5 21g^{bd} c24g Apr 15] of no account: tried blinkered. *J. W. Mullins* **c–** **h–**

PADDINGTON GREEN 7 b.g. Primitive Rising (USA) – Mayfair Minx (St Columbus) [2004/5 h82, F–: 21d^6 May 6] poor form in novice hurdles: stays 23f: raced on good going or softer: blinkered last 3 starts. *H. Morrison* **h82**

PADDY BOY (IRE) 4 br.g. Overbury (IRE) – Arts Project (IRE) (Project Manager) [2004/5 17s 20v^F Feb 15] dam winning 19f hurdler: poor maiden up to 1¾m on Flat: jumped poorly in 2 maiden hurdles: wore cheekpieces second outing. *J. R. Boyle* **h–**

PADDY FOR PADDY (IRE) 11 b.g. Mandalus – Lady Rerico (Pamroy) [2004/5 c–: c30d* c25s* c24s^2 Mar 27] useful hunter chaser: successful at Huntingdon in May and Folkestone (by 6 lengths from Free Gift) in February: stays 3¾m: acts on soft going. *G. L. Landau* **c115**

PADDY'S RETURN (IRE) 13 b.g. Kahyasi – Bayazida (Bustino) [2004/5 27g May 21] close-coupled gelding: top-class hurdler in his prime, successful in Triumph Hurdle at Cheltenham and Long Walk Hurdle at Ascot: useful at best over fences, very lightly raced in recent seasons: stayed 4m: acted on good to firm and heavy going: usually wore blinkers/visor: reportedly retired. *B. G. Powell* **c–** **h–**

PADDY THE OPTIMIST (IRE) 9 b.g. Leading Counsel (USA) – Erne Duchess (IRE) (Duky) [2004/5 c87, h74: c25d* c24m^5 c20m^3 c23m^{pu} c26g^5 c26g^3 c20s^5 c22s^3 c21d c24g^3 c24s^6 c25s^5 c25v^3 c20v^3 c24m^3 c25m* c25m* Apr 9] sturdy gelding: modest chaser: won minor event at Market Rasen in May and handicaps at Hereford in March **c96** **h–**

and April: stays easy 25f: acts on heavy and good to firm going: tried visored, effective with or without blinkers. *D. Burchell*

PADDY THE PIPER (IRE) 8 b.g. Witness Box (USA) – Divine Dibs (Raise You Ten) [2004/5 h134p: c20s^{ur} c20d* c24d^{2} 22g^{3} Apr 16] quite good-topped gelding: useful hurdler: good third to Ladalko in handicap at Ayr: fairly useful form when landing odds in maiden chase at Newcastle in November: let down by jumping (tended to go right) other 2 starts over fences: stays 3m: raced on good going or softer. *L. Lungo* **c123 h135**

PADRE (IRE) 6 b.g. Mister Lord (USA) – Lee Valley Lady (IRE) (Boyne Valley) [2004/5 F16v^{6} 20v^{pu} Feb 15] workmanlike gelding: third foal: dam maiden pointer: no show in bumper and maiden hurdle. *M. Pitman* **h– F–**

PAGAN CEREMONY (USA) 4 ch.g. Rahy (USA) – Delightful Linda (USA) (Slew O' Gold (USA)) [2004/5 16d^{pu} 16v^{pu} 19g^{co} 17g Apr 3] no sign of ability on Flat or over hurdles: sold out of Mrs A. Perrett's stable 1,800 gns Newmarket Autumn Sales: tongue tied last 2 outings. *N. Wilson* **h–**

PAGE POINT (AUS) 7 b.g. Supremo (USA) – She's Fun (NZ) (Racing Is Fun (USA)) [2004/5 16d^{5} 16d^{5} 16s^{3} 20s^{6} 20v 20g^{3} 21g* 19m^{5} Apr 17] compact gelding: successful once over 10.5f from 31 starts on Flat in New Zealand: fair hurdler: won handicap at Huntingdon in March: stays 21f: acts on good to firm and soft going: wore cheekpieces final start: held up. *R. C. Guest* **h105**

PAILITAS (GER) 8 b.g. Lomitas – Pradera (GER) (Abary (GER)) [2004/5 h81: c16m^{pu} Jun 5] rather leggy gelding: poor handicap hurdler: no show on chasing debut: best at sharp 2m: acts on good to firm going: headstrong. *G. A. Swinbank* **c– h–**

PAK JACK (FR) 5 ch.g. Pitchounet (FR) – Miss Noir Et Or (FR) (Noir Et Or) [2004/5 c19d^{pu} c16d* c16d^{5} Jan 29] lengthy gelding: third foal: half-brother to 2 winners, notably Grand Steeple-Chase de Paris winner Sleeping Jack (by Sleeping Car): dam prolific winning cross-country chaser: runner-up all 4 completed starts over jumps in France for C. Aubert: form over fences in Britain only when winning 4-finisher novice at Kempton in January: ran as if amiss start either side: possibly better around 2m than further: raced on going softer than good. *P. J. Hobbs* **c107 h–**

PALACE (FR) 9 b.g. Rahotep (FR) – La Musardiere (FR) (Cadoudal (FR)) [2004/5 c–, h–: 17g 17d^{6} c16g c16s^{pu} Jan 3] of no account: has had tongue tied. *R. H. Buckler* **c– h–**

PALACE PETT 5 ch.m. Alflora (IRE) – Black H'Penny (Town And Country) [2004/5 F17s Jan 18] fourth foal: half-sister to winning pointer by Rakaposhi King: dam, won 2¾m hurdle, half-sister to very smart staying hurdler Simpson: reportedly lost action when tailed off in bumper on debut. *J. R. Best* **F–**

PALAIS (IRE) 10 b.g. Darshaan – Dance Festival (Nureyev (USA)) [2004/5 h–: c25s^{3} c22s^{pu} c24d^{pu} c23s^{pu} Dec 28] leggy gelding: winning hurdler: jumped poorly and no form over fences: stays 3m: acts on good to firm and good to soft going: wore cheekpieces final start. *John A. Harris* **c– x h–**

PALANZO (IRE) 7 b.g. Green Desert (USA) – Karpacka (IRE) (Rousillon (USA)) [2004/5 16d Oct 3] good-topped gelding: useful at one time on Flat (stays 7f), fair and ungenuine nowadays: soundly beaten in seller on hurdling debut. *N. Wilson* **h–**

PALARSHAN (FR) 7 b. or br.g. Darshaan – Palavera (FR) (Bikala) [2004/5 c146, h–: 20s^{5} c21d c21s^{3} c24s^{6} c21g^{pu} Mar 17] tall, good-topped gelding: useful handicap chaser: back to form when third to Buckby Lane in valuable event at Cheltenham in January: not discredited when sixth to Farmer Jack at Kempton: lost action at former course final start: winning hurdler, second outing in Britain when fifth in valuable handicap at Haydock: probably stays 3m: acts on soft and good to firm going. *H. D. Daly* **c143 h125**

PALIETER (BEL) 6 gr. or ro.g. Zeami (IRE) – Just Lady (BEL) (Seclusive (USA)) [2004/5 c21g^{3} 20s 20g Dec 29] third foal: half-brother to French 17f chase winner Calvados (by Welkin) and Belgian 1¾m hurdle winner Samie Bel (by Siam): dam placed up to 9.5f on Flat: successful twice over 11f in Belgium at 3 yrs: modest form over hurdles: third in minor event at Moulins on chasing debut: sold out of R. Martens' stable 7,000 gns Doncaster August Sales: no show in novice/maiden hurdles in Britain. *E. J. Jamieson* **c? h–**

PALISANDER (IRE) 11 ch.g. Conquering Hero (USA) – Classic Choice (Patch) [2004/5 c26g^{2} c20d^{4} c26g^{3} 27g^{4} c25g^{2} c26s^{2} c26g* c25d* c24s^{ur} Oct 22] small gelding: winning hurdler: modest chaser: won weak races at Uttoxeter (conditional jockeys handicap) and Hexham (minor event) in October: stays 3¼m: acts on good to firm and heavy going: tongue tied. *R. Ford* **c87 h73 +**

PALMAC'S PRIDE 5 ch.g. Atraf – Nashwanah (Nashwan (USA)) [2004/5 F–: F17g^pu Oct 14] no sign of ability in bumpers: tried tongue tied. *M. F. Harris* **F–**

PALOUSE (IRE) 9 gr.g. Toulon – Hop Picker (USA) (Plugged Nickle (USA)) [2004/5 c90§, h110§: c20g² c22m² c17m^F c21g* c21d⁴ c19m² c20m* c21f* c24g* c21g⁵ 18d⁵ c25d⁶ Dec 2] tall, leggy gelding: winning hurdler: fair handicap chaser: won at Newton Abbot, Fontwell, Wincanton and Taunton in first half of season: stays 3m, at least when conditions aren't testing: acts on firm and good to soft going (possibly unsuited by softer): formerly blinkered. *R. H. Buckler* **c109 h100 +**

PALUA 8 b.g. Sri Pekan (USA) – Reticent Bride (IRE) (Shy Groom (USA)) [2004/5 c127, h–: c20d^F c20f³ c16d c16d c16d⁶ c16d* c16g Mar 18] lengthy gelding: useful handicap chaser: won at Doncaster in January by 7 lengths from Argento: form otherwise in 2004/5 only on second outing: effective at 2m to 3m: acts on good to firm and heavy ground: races prominently: has found little. *Miss E. C. Lavelle* **c133 h–**

PAMS OAK 7 b.g. Afzal – Kins Token (Relkino) [2004/5 c23m* Apr 10] fourth foal: dam unraced: winning pointer: won maiden at Worcester on chasing debut in April, despite mistakes latter stages. *P. S. Payne* **c93**

PANAMA ROYALE (IRE) 7 ch.m. Aristocracy – Boreen Girl (IRE) (Boreen (FR)) [2004/5 F16d 20v^F Dec 30] leggy mare: first foal: dam never ran: no show in bumper or novice hurdle. *Mrs S. J. Smith* **h– F–**

PANAMA VENTURE (IRE) 6 b. or br.m. Hollow Hand – Venture To Heaven (IRE) (The Parson) [2004/5 F17v² F16v⁴ F17m² Apr 23] third foal: half-sister to winning Irish pointer by Moscow Society: dam, twice-raced half-sister to fairly useful hurdler/chaser up to 21f Regal Venture, from family of high-class hurdler/smart staying chaser Venture To Cognac: fair form when runner-up in bumpers at Sedgefield and Market Rasen. *Mrs S. J. Smith* **F92**

PANCAKE ROLE 5 b.g. Tragic Role (USA) – My Foxy Lady (Jalmood (USA)) [2004/5 16m⁶ Aug 30] lengthy gelding: poor maiden on Flat, well held in 2004: well held in maiden on hurdling debut. *A. W. Carroll* **h–**

PANCHOVILLAS GLEAM (IRE) 11 b.g. Un Desperado (FR) – Shining Spear (Commanche Run) [2004/5 c32m^pu c24d⁴ c26s* c24s⁵ c24d⁵ c22d c20v c25s Mar 27] rangy gelding: winning hurdler: modest handicap chaser: won at Perth in August: stays 3¼m: acts on heavy going: usually wears blinkers, also tried in cheekpieces: has looked ungenuine. *Dermot Day, Ireland* **c90 d h–**

PANDA (IRE) 6 b.m. Glacial Storm (USA) – Inca Rose (IRE) (Strong Gale) [2004/5 18m⁵ 20f 18m c25m^pu Jun 9] third foal: half-sister to winning 2m hurdler Killaloe (by Phardante): dam unraced, out of half-sister to smart chaser Zongalero and dam of Cheltenham Gold Cup winner Garrison Savannah: no sign of ability: left T. Walsh after second start: tried tongue tied. *B. G. Powell* **c– h–**

PANGERAN (USA) 13 b.g. Forty Niner (USA) – Smart Heiress (USA) (Vaguely Noble) [2004/5 c86d, h–: c21m⁶ c19m² c16m⁵ c23m⁶ c26g^pu 26m c27m* c26m⁵ 26f c21s³ c25s⁴ c24s⁶ Nov 21] leggy gelding: maiden hurdler: poor handicap chaser: 20 lb out of weights, won very weak event at Sedgefield in August: stays 27f: acts on firm and soft going: has had tongue tied: not a fluent jumper: unreliable. *N. B. King* **c68 § h–**

PANGLOSS (IRE) 4 ch.g. Croco Rouge (IRE) – Kafayef (USA) (Secreto (USA)) [2004/5 16d 17d² 16d⁶ Dec 3] workmanlike gelding: fair maiden on Flat (probably stays 2m, has looked none too genuine): best effort over hurdles when second in juvenile maiden at Folkestone: visored final start. *G. L. Moore* **h93**

PANHANDLE 11 b.m. Riverwise (USA) – Pallanda (Pablond) [2004/5 c22s^pu c20v⁶ c24v^pu c17s³ Feb 14] workmanlike mare: winning pointer: no form in chases. *N. R. Mitchell* **c– h–**

PANMURE (IRE) 9 b.g. Alphabatim (USA) – Serjitak (Saher) [2004/5 c94, h–: 16d c16d^F c16g⁶ c17g² c16m^F 20g² c17g³ c20d⁶ c17s^ur c17s⁴ c16m c20m³ c20m* Apr 23] good-topped gelding: modest maiden hurdler: fair handicap chaser: would have won but for falling 2 out at Uttoxeter fifth start: successful at Market Rasen in April: stays 2½m: best efforts on good going or firmer: tried blinkered/in cheekpieces: has had tongue tied. *P. D. Niven* **c101 h87**

PAPAWALDO (IRE) 6 ch.g. Presenting – Another Bless (Random Shot) [2004/5 F16s 17d 22s Apr 3] €2,300 5-y-o: half-brother to fairly useful staying hurdler Furry Baby (by Furry Glen) and fairly useful staying chaser Roundwood (by Orchestra): dam **h– F–**

unraced sister to useful hurdler/chaser up to 2½m Another Shot and half-sister to very smart chaser at 2½m+ Straight Jocelyn: well held in bumper and novice hurdles. *R. C. Guest*

PAPERCHASER 5 ch.g. Minster Son – Eye Bee Aitch (Move Off) [2004/5 17d 16s Nov 10] fourth foal: half-brother to fairly useful hurdler/useful chaser Paperising (by Primitive Rising) who stayed 25f: dam winning selling hurdler: well beaten in 2 novice hurdles. *N. G. Richards* **h–**

PAPER CLASSIC 5 ch.m. Classic Cliche (IRE) – Kiniohio (FR) (Script Ohio (USA)) [2004/5 F16v F17s Mar 10] second foal: half-sister to fairly useful hurdler around 2m Tragic Ohio (by Tragic Role): dam fair hurdler around 2m: well held in 2 bumpers. *A. C. Whillans* **F–**

PAPEROUND 7 ch.m. Primitive Rising (USA) – Eye Bee Aitch (Move Off) [2004/5 F–: 16d^{pu} May 12] no show in bumper and maiden hurdle 13 months apart. *N. G. Richards* **h–**

PAPERPROPHET 7 b.g. Glory of Dancer – Living Legend (ITY) (Archway (IRE)) [2004/5 h136: 20s^2 25d^3 20v^4 24d^{pu} Apr 8] leggy gelding: useful handicap hurdler: creditable efforts when placed in quite valuable events at Ayr and Cheltenham (third to The Dark Lord): stays 25f: acts on soft going: looks difficult ride and sometimes soon off bridle. *N. G. Richards* **h130**

PAPILLON DE IENA (FR) 5 ch.g. Varese (FR) – Belle du Chesne (FR) (R B Chesne) [2004/5 h118: 16d^5 17d 22d^3 16d 22v^6 Apr 22] smallish, lengthy gelding: fairly useful hurdler: good effort when third to Dangerously Good in handicap at Wincanton in December: effective at 2m to 2¾m: raced on going softer than good: visored last 2 starts. *M. C. Pipe* **h115**

PAPINI (IRE) 4 ch.g. Lomitas – Pariana (USA) (Bering) [2004/5 16g* 16d^2 16d* 16g 17m^2 Apr 13] well-made gelding: fourth known foal: half-brother to useful performer up to 1¼m Pappus (by Acatenango): dam, lightly-raced German maiden, half-sister to useful miler Page's King: successful once around 1¼m on Flat in Germany for D. Richardson: useful form in juvenile hurdles, winning at Newbury in November and January (by ½ length from At Your Request): good second to Openide at Cheltenham final start: likely to stay beyond 17f: yet to race on extremes of going: front runner/races prominently. *N. J. Henderson* **h125**

PAPUA 11 ch.g. Green Dancer (USA) – Fairy Tern (Mill Reef (USA)) [2004/5 c112§, h–: c17d^6 c16d^4 c17m^6 c16s* c16g^{pu} c17g^3 c16s^6 c18d c19d^6 c19g^4 Apr 15] quite good-topped gelding: fair handicap chaser: won at Uttoxeter (unbeaten in 3 starts there) in October: best around 2m: acts on firm and soft going: usually visored/blinkered: often tongue tied nowadays: front runner: unreliable. *N. J. Hawke* **c113 § h–**

PARABLE 9 b.g. Midyan (USA) – Top Table (Shirley Heights) [2004/5 16s^{pu} 16s^6 16g^{pu} 16v^{pu} Feb 2] good-topped gelding: poor form over hurdles: raced at 2m on good going or softer. *Mrs P. Sly* **h71**

PARACHUTE 6 ch.g. Hector Protector (USA) – Shortfall (Last Tycoon) [2004/5 20v^F Dec 17] half-brother to useful hurdler/smart chaser around 2m Contraband (by Red Ransom): fairly useful on Flat (stays 2m) at 3 and 4 yrs for Sir Mark Prescott: tired when falling 2 out in novice at Uttoxeter on hurdling debut: should do better. *J. A. B. Old* **h–**

PARADISE FLIGHT (IRE) 4 ch.f. In The Wings – Aloft (IRE) (Ela-Mana-Mou) [2004/5 16d^5 16g Dec 29] fair on Flat (stays 2¼m), successful in August (for Ms J. Morgan) and January: better effort in juvenile hurdles when fifth at Wetherby on hurdling debut: will stay 2½m. *K. A. Ryan* **h87**

PARDINI (USA) 6 b.g. Quest For Fame – Noblissima (IRE) (Sadler's Wells (USA)) [2004/5 h90: 21g^3 16v^4 c16s^{pu} c17s^2 c21v* c21s^2 c26d^2 Nov 16] angular gelding: modest maiden hurdler: bit better over fences: fortunate to win handicap at Uttoxeter in October, held in second when left well clear 2 out: stays 3¼m, effective at much shorter: acts on heavy going: tried blinkered. *M. F. Harris* **c98 h88**

PARDISHAR (IRE) 7 b.g. Kahyasi – Parapa (IRE) (Akarad (FR)) [2004/5 h115: 16d^4 16d 16d^4 21v^3 18s^2 21s^2 16g* 19m^3 20m Apr 23] well-made gelding: fairly useful handicap hurdler: won at Newbury in April by 5 lengths from Tighe Caster: good third to The Persuader at Stratford next time: stays 21f: acts on good to firm and heavy going: wore cheekpieces last 3 starts: tongue tied once: signs of temperament. *G. L. Moore* **h116**

PARDON WHAT 9 b.g. Theatrical Charmer – Tree Poppy (Rolfe (USA)) [2004/5 c–x, h77x: 21g* 25g^2 22m^3 c24v^R Apr 17] leggy, lengthy gelding: winning chaser: poor handicap hurdler: won at Southwell in May: left B. Powell, refused first in point and **c– § h89 x**

hunter chase: stays 25f well: acts on heavy and good to firm going: has worn headgear: sketchy jumper: best left alone. *Ferdy Murphy*

PARIS DREAMER 4 b.f. Paris House – Stoproveritate (Scorpio (FR)) [2004/5 16d^{ur} Nov 24] half-sister to fair hurdler/fairly useful chaser Exstoto (by Mtoto), stays 4m, and fair 3m hurdle winner Classical Ben (by Most Welcome): modest on Flat (stays 1¾m), successful in February: no show in juvenile on hurdling debut. *R. A. Fahey* **h–**

PARISH OAK 10 b.g. Rakaposhi King – Poppy's Pride (Uncle Pokey) [2004/5 c21g^{5} c21s^{ur} c20d* c21d* c24v^{pu} c19v^{5} c20v^{3} c21v* 20d^{4} Apr 22] useful-looking gelding: poor hurdler: fair chaser: won minor event at Leicester in November and handicaps at Wincanton (conditional jockeys) in December and Sedgefield in March: stays 21f: acts on heavy going: tried tongue tied. *Ian Williams* **c106 h73**

PARISIAN ROSE (IRE) 6 b.m. Norwich – Magar's Mandy (Mandalus) [2004/5 F16g F17v^{5} F16s Apr 10] third known foal: dam unplaced in Irish bumpers: well beaten in 3 bumpers. *Mrs H. O. Graham* **F–**

PARISIAN STORM (IRE) 9 b.g. Glacial Storm (USA) – Lost In Paris (Deep Run) [2004/5 c96x: 22d^{5} 26m^{2} 26m* 24g^{2} c26d* 24g* c28s^{4} c25g^{pu} Apr 17] fair form over hurdles, winning maiden at Southwell in July and novice at Worcester in August: best effort over fences when easy winner of 2-finisher novice at Southwell earlier in August: stays 3¼m: acts on soft and good to firm going. *Evan Williams* **c112 h112**

PARISIENNE GALE (IRE) 6 b.m. Lapierre – Elegant Gale (IRE) (Strong Gale) [2004/5 h–, F64: 19d^{pu} 16g 17g May 26] no form in novice hurdles, twice shaping as if amiss: successful on first of 2 starts in points in March. *D. McCain* **h–**

PARISI PRINCESS 4 ch.f. Shaddad (USA) – Crambella (IRE) (Red Sunset) [2004/5 17g Apr 15] poor maiden on Flat: well held in juvenile on hurdling debut. *D. L. Williams* **h–**

PARK CITY 6 b.g. Slip Anchor – Cryptal (Persian Bold) [2004/5 h92: 18m^{6} 16g^{5} Jul 18] rather leggy gelding: modest handicap hurdler: should stay 2½m: acts on soft and good to firm going: none too consistent. *J. Joseph* **h86**

PARKETT HILL 6 b.g. Moshaajir (USA) – Young Bella (Young Man (FR)) [2004/5 F16s 17s 20v^{pu} Nov 25] small gelding: first foal: dam never ran: no form in bumper and 2 novice hurdles. *I. McMath* **h– F–**

PARK LANE FREDDIE 7 b.g. Nalchik (USA) – Kathy's Role (Rolfe (USA)) [2004/5 h82: 17m^{rtr} Jun 9] leggy gelding: poor form in novice hurdles: refused to race only start in 2004/5: tried tongue tied. *J. Mackie* **h– §**

PARKNASILLA 5 b.g. Marju (IRE) – Top Berry (High Top) [2004/5 h119: c16v^{3} c16v* c16s^{2} c17v^{ur} c16d^{5} c16s^{2} Apr 22] lengthy gelding: fairly useful juvenile hurdler in 2003/4: won maiden chase at Wetherby in January: easily best effort over fences when short-head second to Through The Rye in novice at Carlisle 2 weeks later: let down by jumping after, out of depth in Grade 1 novice at Aintree fifth start: raced around 2m on good going or softer. *M. W. Easterby* **c120 h–**

PARK SUPREME (IRE) 6 b.m. Supreme Leader – Nic An Ree (IRE) (King's Ride) [2004/5 F17s^{2} Mar 10] fourth foal: dam, lightly raced over hurdles, sister to winning 2m chaser King of The Glen: 8 lengths second to Pinkerton Mill in bumper at Carlisle on debut. *N. G. Richards* **F82**

PAROLE OFFICER 6 b.g. Priolo (USA) – Twosixtythreewest (FR) (Kris) [2004/5 F–: 21g^{pu} Apr 30] no show in bumper or maiden hurdle. *J. Wade* **h–**

PARSIFAL 6 b.g. Sadler's Wells (USA) – Moss (USA) (Woodman (USA)) [2004/5 h88: 16d 16v^{6} 21s 16v^{6} Mar 29] angular gelding: winning pointer: modest maiden hurdler: bought 12,500 gns Doncaster October Sales: no form in 2004/5: visored last 3 starts: headstrong: temperamental. *P. Wegmann* **h–**

PARSON JACK 8 b.g. Bedford (USA) – Scobitora (Thesauros) [2004/5 h–: 21g May 8] no sign of ability. *R. Dickin* **h–**

PARSON PLOUGHMAN 10 br.g. Riverwise (USA) – Pretty Pantoes (Lepanto (GER)) [2004/5 h79: 22g^{4} c21s* c19d^{F} c21d^{pu} c20d^{pu} Apr 18] plain gelding: lightly-raced maiden hurdler: form over fences only when winning novice handicap at Newton Abbot on chasing debut in November: stays 21f: raced on good going or softer. *P. F. Nicholls* **c92 h79**

PARSONS FANCY 7 ch.m. Alflora (IRE) – Preachers Popsy (The Parson) [2004/5 F16s 16d^{ur} 21s^{pu} Mar 10] medium-sized mare: fourth foal: half-sister to winning hurdlers Silk Vestments (by Rakaposhi King), stayed 21f, and Bobby Dazzler (by Bob's Return), **h– F–**

stays 3m, and bumper winner Scarlett Poppy (by Petoski): dam, maiden, out of half-sister to useful chasers up to 25f Colonel Heather and Fudge Delight: no show in bumper (for S. Earle) or mares novice hurdles: tongue tied. *Jane Southall*

PARSONS LEGACY (IRE) **c134 h–** 7 b.g. Leading Counsel (USA) – The Parson's Girl (IRE) (The Parson) [2004/5 h111: c20s* c20g^{3} c23d^{2} c23g* c24d^{6} c24g^{3} c25m^{5} Apr 13] angular gelding: fair hurdler: useful chaser: won maiden at Ludlow in October and handicap at Leicester in December: also ran well when placed, 2¼ lengths third of to Juveigneur in valuable amateur handicap at Cheltenham in March: stays 3m: acts on soft and good to firm going: often races prominently. *P. J. Hobbs*

PARSONS PRIDE (IRE) **c– h–** 9 b.g. Persian Mews – First Prize (IRE) (The Parson) [2004/5 h92: c19m^{pu} c23m^{3} 24m c23g^{5} c20f^{pu} c25m^{5} Sep 8] smallish gelding: winning hurdler: form over fences only on second outing: best at 3m+: acts on firm ground: blinkered final start: tongue tied after reappearance. *J. W. Tudor*

PARSON'S ROSE **c– h–** 8 ch.m. Lancastrian – Sexton's Service (The Parson) [2004/5 16s^{pu} 16s^{6} 24d^{pu} 24v^{pu} 16v^{5} c25s^{pu} c20v^{pu} Mar 1] smallish, angular mare: fifth foal: dam, won 2½m hurdle, half-sister to useful staying chaser Ebony Jane: no sign of ability: blinkered final start. *B. N. Pollock*

PARTE PRIMA **c83 h–** 9 b.g. Perpendicular – Pendle's Secret (Le Johnstan) [2004/5 c88, h–: c21g^{pu} c25m^{3} May 11] modest hunter chaser. *Alan Walter*

PARTY GAMES (IRE) **c– h108** 8 b.g. King's Ride – Shady Miss (Mandamus) [2004/5 c–, h99: 16g^{6} 21g^{5} 16d* 16d^{3} 20s^{4} 20d* 20d^{3} Feb 17] workmanlike gelding: once-raced chaser: fair novice hurdler: won claimer (claimed from D. Feek £8,000) at Plumpton in November and handicap at Huntingdon in January: likely to stay beyond 21f: raced on good going or softer (acts on heavy). *G. L. Moore*

PASSENGER OMAR (IRE) **h91** 7 b.g. Safety Catch (USA) – Princess Douglas (Bishop of Orange) [2004/5 h89: 27s* May 11] modest hurdler: won handicap at Newton Abbot in May: stays 27f: acts on soft going: tongue tied: sometimes soon off bridle: refused to race on debut. *Noel T. Chance*

PASS GO **h82** 4 b.g. Kris – Celt Song (IRE) (Unfuwain (USA)) [2004/5 17m^{3} 16d 16s Nov 5] half-brother to useful hurdler Rebel Rhythm (by Robellino), stays 2½m: fair form only start at 2 yrs, well held on Flat in 2004 for G. Butler: form over hurdles only when third in juvenile at Sedgefield on debut, carrying head awkwardly. *J. J. Lambe, Ireland*

PASS IT ON (IRE) **h95 p** 6 br.g. Accordion – Windswept Lady (IRE) (Strong Gale) [2004/5 17d^{4} Dec 3] second foal: half-brother to 2½m hurdle winner Windswept Leader (by Supreme Leader): dam fair hurdler who stayed 21f: 3 lengths fourth to Double Header in novice hurdle at Exeter on debut: will be suited by further: will improve. *Jonjo O'Neill*

PASS ME A DIME **h108 p F–** 6 b.g. Past Glories – Hand Out (Spare A Dime) [2004/5 aF16g 19s 24d^{4} 20d* Feb 26] rather unfurnished gelding: first foal: dam, poor novice hurdler/chaser, stayed 3m: well held in bumper on debut: fair form over hurdles: best effort when winning maiden at Chepstow in February: likely to prove best short of 3m: should improve again. *C. L. Tizzard*

PASS ME BY **c– h105 §** 6 b.g. Balnibarbi – Errol Emerald (Dom Racine (FR)) [2004/5 h120: c20d^{pu} 20v^{4} 20v 20d^{pu} Mar 26] tall, angular gelding: fairly useful novice hurdler in 2003/4: below form in 2004/5: jumped poorly on chasing debut: should stay beyond 2½m: raced on good going or softer: tried in cheekpieces: unreliable. *T. D. Walford*

PAST HERITAGE **h– F71** 6 b.g. Past Glories – Norman's Delight (IRE) (Idiot's Delight) [2004/5 F17d F17g* 17d 19g^{pu} 17d^{pu} Feb 1] medium-sized gelding: third foal: dam little sign of ability: won weak bumper at Taunton in October: no form otherwise, including over hurdles. *A. E. Jones*

PATCHES (IRE) **c143 + h120** 6 b. or br.g. Presenting – Ballykilleen (The Parson) [2004/5 h107: 22g* 22g* c21d* c24g^{5} Dec 26]

A tongue strap fitted on his final outing in 2003/4 failed to help Patches fulfil the promise he had shown on his hurdling debut, but a subsequent operation to improve his breathing did the trick, and he returned to win the first three of his four starts in the latest season. All three wins came at Wincanton, the first two in novice hurdles in October and November, Patches showing fairly useful form when beating Marjina by six lengths, then Lord Olympia by a short head. The hat-trick was completed on Patches' chasing debut, in what was an above-average maiden in December. Patiently ridden, Patches moved through to track the other market leaders Lacdoudal and Kadount in the back straight, came under pressure after making his only noticeable mistake four out but responded well to challenge Lacdoudal going to the last, the pair having pulled away from Kadount. A good leap sealed victory for Patches, who went on to win by three lengths. Patches, untried beyond two and three quarter miles thus far, was stepped up both in trip and class for what turned out to be his final outing, in the Feltham Novices' Chase at Kempton on Boxing Day. A 14/1-shot, Patches acquitted himself quite well given his inexperience, beaten seventeen lengths by close-finishers Ollie Magern and Trabolgan even though last of the five runners who completed. As at Wincanton, Patches jumped soundly in the main, and he looks the sort to do well in handicap company around three miles when he returns to action. Patches, who won a four-year-old maiden point in Ireland in 2003, has raced only on good and good to soft going. *P. F. Nicholls*

PAT MALONE 5 b.g. Jumbo Hirt (USA) – A Sharp (Sharpo) [2004/5 F16s^5 Mar 31] fourth foal: half-brother to fairly useful 1m winner Silken Dalliance (by Rambo Dancer): dam unraced: well held in bumper on debut. *Mrs Lucinda Featherstone* **F–**

PAT N DEC 6 b.g. Overbury (IRE) – Princess Semele (Imperial Fling (USA)) [2004/5 F79: 16s^5 17m^5 Nov 11] workmanlike gelding: twice-raced over hurdles, fifth in novice at Uttoxeter and maiden at Taunton: likely to be suited by further. *Ian Williams* **h85**

PATRIARCH EXPRESS 8 b.g. Noble Patriarch – Jaydeeglen (Bay Express) [2004/5 h126+: 20s* 22s^2 20s* 20v^F 24s* 24s^4 Feb 26] **h158**

The Byrne Bros Cleeve Hurdle underwent another makeover in the latest season and seemed all the better for it. When downgraded to Grade 2 in 2003/4 after failing to justify its status as a championship contest, it also had its distance reduced by a furlong to two and a half miles. The latest renewal, at Cheltenham in January, took place over three miles and attracted a good quality field. Even without Baracouda, it looked a good trial for the World Hurdle to be run over the same course and distance almost two months later. In an eleven-runner field, Crystal d'Ainay

totesport Handicap Hurdle, Haydock—
Patriarch Express gains a second win from three starts for his new stable;
Petrula (blinkers) and Turtle Soup chase him home

Byrne Bros Cleeve Hurdle, Cheltenham—
further improvement lands this Grade 2 event at the chief expense of Korelo

was sent off favourite to win it for a second successive time, with Royal Rosa, one of the leading novice hurdlers of 2003/4 and making his seasonal reappearance, the second favourite. Also prominent in the betting were the Martin Pipe-trained pair Korelo and Westender, both successful at Cheltenham on their previous starts; and Patriarch Express, an eight-year-old who had quickly made up into a smart performer in what was only his second season over hurdles, winning two of his three completed starts. Those wins had come in handicaps at Wetherby in October and Haydock in December, ten lengths the margin of victory in a very strongly-contested event on the latter course.

Still unproven over as far as three miles, Patriarch Express wasn't ridden in the Cleeve as though there was a doubt about his stamina, racing keenly close up as 50/1-shot Quick, one of two other Pipe runners, set the pace. Patriarch Express took over from that rival five from home. Still travelling well when kicked on two out, he was being strongly pressed at the next by Korelo, who lost momentum when going to the left, and found plenty for pressure to hold on by a head. The pair finished eight lengths clear of third-placed Westender, and there was a further three quarters of a length back to Crystal d'Ainay in fourth. The performance represented further improvement from Patriarch Express who just seven days earlier had failed to complete the course for the only time to date. Normally a quick and accurate jumper, Patriarch Express, started favourite for a limited handicap at Haydock and was close up and travelling strongly when misjudging the fourth last and coming down. Patriarch Express didn't hold an entry for the World Hurdle, and any thoughts of supplementing him for it would have been put to one side after a poor run in the Rendlesham Hurdle at Kempton four weeks after the Cleeve. That tame effort proved to be Patriarch Express' final outing of the season, and when he returns it is likely to be in a new role. Chasing beckons for Patriarch Express, a strong, good sort who certainly looks the type to do well over fences. His stable-companion Royal Emperor, whose form over hurdles wasn't quite so good as that of Patriarch Express, finished second in the 2004 Royal & SunAlliance in his first season over fences, and Patriarch Express has it in him to become a leading contender for the 2006 renewal.

Patriarch Express (b.g. 1997)	Noble Patriarch (b 1987)	Alzao (b 1980)	Lyphard
			Lady Rebecca
		Pampala (b 1979)	Bold Lad
			Pantamerla
	Jaydeeglen (b 1987)	Bay Express (b 1971)	Polyfoto
			Pal Sinna
		Friendly Glen (b 1978)	Furry Glen
			Gay Friend

Patriarch Express and Royal Emperor weren't stable-companions prior to the latest season, Patriarch Express having been with Geoff Harker previously. He would have been a big loss to Harker, for whom he won four races, bumpers at Perth and Cheltenham in 2002/3 and novice hurdles at Newcastle and Haydock the following season. Apart from Patriarch Express, the smart mile-and-a-quarter winner Noble Patriarch hasn't been responsible for much out of the ordinary at stud, while the dam of Patriarch Express, Jaydeeglen, has produced nothing else of note. Jaydeeglen showed fair form on her debut when runner-up in a five-furlong maiden at Wolverhampton at two, but failed to run anywhere near that in seven subsequent appearances. Her dam Friendly Glen, though a half-sister to the fairly useful five-furlong performer Avonmore Glen, won a two-mile novice hurdle at Kelso and a novice chase over half a mile further at Sedgefield. She also produced the useful handicap chaser Armagret, a winner at up to twenty-five furlongs. The third dam Gay Friend was also half-sister to a couple of above-average Flat performers, the fairly useful sprinter Naomi Joy and the useful Tardot, who was effective at up to a mile. Clearly Patriarch Express stays a good deal better than might be anticipated. Genuine and consistent, he has raced only on good ground or softer, apart from when winning the bumper at Cheltenham on good to firm, and he acts on soft. *Mrs S. J. Smith*

PATRIXPRIAL 4 gr.g. Linamix (FR) – Magnificent Star (USA) (Silver Hawk (USA)) [2004/5 16d³ 16d² Dec 11] smallish, lengthy gelding: half-brother to 2 winners over jumps, including fair hurdler/chaser up to 2½m Profiler (by Capote): fairly useful on Flat (stays 1¾m), successful in August: ran to similar level both starts in juvenile hurdles, close third to Yankeedoodledandy at Huntingdon and 4 lengths second to Salut Saint Cloud in Grade 2 event at Lingfield. *M. H. Tompkins* **h115**

PATRIXTOO (FR) 4 gr.c. Linamix (FR) – Maradadi (USA) (Shadeed (USA)) [2004/5 16gᶠ Mar 9] leggy colt: modest maiden on Flat (stays 10.5f), sold out of M. Tompkins' stable 15,000 gns Newmarket Autumn Sales: still to be asked for effort in third when falling 2 out in novice at Catterick on hurdling debut. *T. J. Fitzgerald* **h100 p**

PATS CROSS (IRE) 16 b.g. Abednego – No Hunting (No Time) [2004/5 c22sᵖᵘ May 9] veteran chaser: no longer of any account. *S. J. Goodings* **c– h–**

PATS FUTURE 6 ch.m. King's Signet (USA) – Bedelia (Mr Fluorocarbon) [2004/5 h–, F82: 17m³ 17g⁵ 17g⁵ Aug 2] smallish mare: poor maiden hurdler: will prove best around 2m. *P. R. Rodford* **h68**

PATSY STONE 9 b.m. Jester – Third Dam (Slip Anchor) [2004/5 17sᵖᵘ 16d Feb 9] fair on Flat (stays 1m) in 2001: has been to stud: tongue tied, no show in novice or selling hurdle. *H. J. Manners* **h–**

PATTERSON (IRE) 4 br.f. Turtle Island (IRE) – Richmond Lillie (Fairbairn) [2004/5 18sᵖᵘ Oct 12] well held in maidens on Flat: showed nothing on hurdling debut. *M. Madgwick* **h–**

PAULA LANE 5 b.m. Factual (USA) – Colfax Classic (Jareer (USA)) [2004/5 h–: 16g³ 18s⁵ Mar 30] form over hurdles only when third in novice at Plumpton. *R. Curtis* **h–**

PAULS PLAIN 4 b.g. Young Buster (IRE) – On The Wagon (Then Again) [2004/5 F16v⁴ F16g F16v Feb 19] first foal: dam unraced: well held in bumpers. *C. N. Kellett* **F–**

PAUNTLEY GOFA 9 b.g. Afzal – Gotageton (Oats) [2004/5 19g May 11] tall gelding: fair hurdler/chaser in 2002/3: well held in handicap hurdle after 22-month lay-off: probably stays 2½m: acts on good to soft and good to firm going: usually makes running. *J. L. Spearing* **c– h–**

PAVEY ARK (IRE) 7 b.g. King's Ride – Splendid Run (Deep Run) [2004/5 h–: 20g 22d³ 17g⁶ c21m⁴ c16m² c21m² c21m* Sep 28] tall, lengthy gelding: bad maiden hurdler: modest form over fences at Sedgefield, winning maiden in September: should stay beyond 21f: acts on good to firm going: usually races prominently. *James Moffatt* **c89 h55**

PAVONE QUEST 8 ch.g. Jumbo Hirt (USA) – Gilsan Grey (Grey Ghost) [2004/5 h–, F–: 23dᵖᵘ 21mᵖᵘ 26mᵖᵘ 22g Jul 15] lengthy gelding: little sign of ability: tried tongue tied. *G. M. Moore* **h–**

PAXFORD JACK 9 ch.g. Alflora (IRE) – Rakajack (Rakaposhi King) [2004/5 c22s* c22vᵖᵘ c24s⁵ c23s⁴ c21d³ c24s³ c21d² c25mᵖᵘ Apr 9] lengthy gelding: winning hurdler: fair handicap chaser: off 18 months, won at Towcester in November: should stay beyond 25f: acts on heavy going: blinkered/visored 3 starts prior to final one: races prominently: usually sound jumper. *M. F. Harris* **c109 d h–**

PAY ATTENTION 4 b.f. Revoque (IRE) – Catch Me (Rudimentary (USA)) [2004/5 17s* 16v* 16v* 16d³ 16v* 16d² Mar 14] leggy filly: fair around 1¼m on Flat: very good first season over hurdles, successful between December and February in juvenile at Market Rasen, mares novice at Wetherby and mares handicap and novice (by 1½ lengths from Almah) at Towcester: best effort when 5 lengths second to United in juvenile at Stratford: raced around 2m on going softer than good (acts on heavy). *T. D. Easterby* **h120**

*betfair.com Novices' Handicap Chase, Punchestown—
Pay It Forward shows improved form to defeat Joes Edge*

PAY IT FORWARD 7 b.g. Anshan – Kellsboro Kate (Paddy's Stream) [2004/5 c111, h131: c21v^{bd} c20v^{2} c22v^{3} c23g* Mar 12] well-made gelding: useful hurdler: reached similar level over fences, winning valuable novice handicap at Punchestown in late-April by 2 lengths from Joes Edge: readily landed odds in novice at Downpatrick previous month: stays 25f: acts on heavy and good to firm going. *Mrs J. Harrington, Ireland* **c128 h–**

PAYNESTOWN LAD (IRE) 9 b.g. Bravefoot – Athy Lady (Welsh Captain) [2004/5 h–: 21m^{pu} 22d^{pu} 17v^{pu} 16d^{ur} 21g Mar 16] small, angular gelding: winning hurdler, no form since 2002/3. *Miss C. J. E. Caroe* **h–**

PEACEMAKER (IRE) 13 br.g. Strong Gale – Gamonda (Gala Performance) [2004/5 c70, h–: c21d^{4} c21m c26g May 23] sturdy gelding: poor chaser: stays 25f: acts on firm and soft going: blinkered once: has had tongue tied. *J. R. Cornwall* **c61 h–**

PEACHY (IRE) 10 b.g. Un Desperado (FR) – Little Peach (Ragapan) [2004/5 h–: 21g^{5} May 1] leggy gelding: bumper winner: very lightly raced and modest form over hurdles: probably stays 21f: has jumped less than fluently. *R. T. Phillips* **h88**

PEARCECROFT (IRE) 5 b.g. Grand Lodge (USA) – Tart (FR) (Warning) [2004/5 F16g Aug 18] second foal: half-brother to winner around 11f in Germany by Bigstone: dam, 1¼m and 11.5f winner, from family of good French hurdler Model Man: soundly beaten in bumper on debut. *P. A. Pritchard* **F–**

PEARLY BAY 7 b.m. Karinga Bay – Marina Bird (Julio Mariner) [2004/5 F97: F16v^{3} F16d 18m^{pu} Apr 21] lengthy mare: thrice-raced in bumpers, sold out of M. Rimell's stable 30,000 gns (privately) Doncaster May Sales after winning on debut: jumped poorly and badly outpaced in mares maiden on hurdling debut: will be suited by 2½m. *P. F. Nicholls* **h– F91**

PEARLY JACK 7 ch.g. Weld – Pearly Lady (Tycoon II) [2004/5 20g 20d c20s c16s c18s c16s c18v* c20v^{2} c22v* c16v^{2} c22v^{3} c16s* c24g^{bd} c29s^{ro} c24v^{3} Apr 10] rather leggy gelding: dam unraced, from family of outstanding 2m chaser Pearlyman: bumper winner: fair hurdler: fairly useful chaser: won handicaps at Thurles and Limerick in December and Thurles again in February: rear when ran out 5 out in Irish Grand National at Fairyhouse: effective at 2m to 3m: raced on good going or softer (acts on heavy). *D. E. Fitzgerald, Ireland* **c118 h–**

PEARLY STAR 4 b.g. Bob's Return (IRE) – Pearly-B (IRE) (Gunner B) [2004/5 F16s^{5} F16d Mar 24] £8,000 3-y-o: smallish gelding: sixth foal: brother to 2m hurdle winner What's A Filly: dam unraced, from family of outstanding 2m chaser Pearlyman: fair form in bumpers. *A. King* **F86**

PEARSON GLEN (IRE) 6 ch.g. Dolphin Street (FR) – Glendora (Glenstal (USA)) [2004/5 17d 16d Nov 24] half-brother to 2m hurdle winner Shares (by Turtle Island): modest on Flat (stays 1½m): well held in novice hurdles, not knocked about on debut: joined J. Moffatt. *G. A. Swinbank* **h–**

PEASE BLOSSOM (IRE) 6 b.m. Revoque (IRE) – Saneena (Kris) [2004/5 h90: 18m* 21d^{F} Nov 12] lengthy, leggy mare: modest handicap hurdler: won amateur event at Galway in July: yet to be asked for effort when falling fatally 3 out in conditional jockeys race at Cheltenham: raced mainly around 2m: acted on soft and good to firm ground: tried visored, often wore cheekpieces prior to 2004/5. *Thomas McCourt, Ireland* **h90**

PEBBLE BAY 10 br.g. Perpendicular – Milly L'Attaque (Military) [2004/5 h83?: 21v* 25s* 20g* Mar 26] angular gelding: fair hurdler: left G. Harker and off nearly 14 **h99**

months, improved form in 2004/5, unbeaten in handicaps at Sedgefield (seller) in January and Catterick (novice) and Haydock in March: stays 25f: acts on heavy going: tried blinkered: races prominently. *Mrs S. J. Smith*

PECCADILLO (IRE) 11 br.g. Un Desperado (FR) – First Mistake (Posse (USA)) [2004/5 c132, h–: c23m c20f* c24d² c20d⁵ c20d⁶ c20d⁶ c24d⁵ Mar 12] big, rangy gelding: useful handicap chaser: won at Huntingdon (landed corresponding race in 2002) in September: good second, as in previous year, in quite valuable event at Kempton following month, beaten ¾ length by Gunther McBride: out of form subsequently: stays easy 3m: acts on firm and good to soft going (unsuited by soft): has run well when sweating: races prominently: goes well fresh. *R. H. Alner* **c132 h–**

PEDDARS WAY 6 b.g. Nomadic Way (USA) – Deep Selection (IRE) (Deep Run) [2004/5 F79: F16d² 21d 22s² 24d³ 21sF 22d⁴ 24m³ Apr 10] rather unfurnished gelding: runner-up on second of 2 starts in bumpers: modest novice hurdler: likely to prove suited by 3m+: acts on soft and good to firm going: visored final outing. *A. King* **h96 F96**

PEDINA (IRE) 7 b.g. Toulon – Bilberry (Nicholas Bill) [2004/5 h121, F96: 16v³ 16v⁵ 16spu 18s Mar 13] fairly useful hurdler: best effort in handicaps in 2004/5 when third to The Screamer at Listowel in September: should stay beyond 2m: acts on heavy going: wore cheekpieces third start. *G. M. Lyons, Ireland* **h121**

PEDLER'S PROFILES 5 br.g. Topanoora – La Vie En Primrose (Henbit (USA)) [2004/5 h–: 17s⁴ 16m 16g 17g⁵ 16g² Aug 24] little form on Flat: poor form over hurdles: raced around 2m. *Miss K. M. George* **h74**

PEEJAY HOBBS 7 ch.g. Alhijaz – Hicklam Millie (Absalom) [2004/5 c21spu c23dpu c23v⁴ c23m³ Apr 10] winning hurdler: off over 2 years before reappearance: first solid form over fences when third in maiden at Worcester: stays 23f: best form on good/good to firm going. *C. J. Gray* **c86 h–**

PEEYOUTWO 10 b.g. Golden Heights – Nyika (Town And Country) [2004/5 h84: 22g² Jul 11] modest hurdler: ran well only outing in 2004/5: stays 2¾m: best efforts on good/good to firm ground. *Mrs D. A. Hamer* **h89**

PEGGY SIOUX (IRE) 8 b.m. Little Bighorn – Gayable (Gay Fandango (USA)) [2004/5 h66: 16g⁵ 16m⁵ May 19] sturdy mare: poor maiden hurdler: stays 2½m: acts on firm going. *J. I. A. Charlton* **h68**

PEGGY'S PRINCE 7 b.g. Morpeth – Prudent Peggy (Kambalda) [2004/5 F88: 22d⁴ 17d 16d 22d⁶ Mar 26] lengthy gelding: fair form in bumpers: best effort over hurdles when fourth of 5 finishers in maiden at Newton Abbot: will stay 3m. *J. D. Frost* **h80**

PEN-ALMOZON 9 ch.h. Almoojid – Cornish Mona Lisa (Damsire Unregistered) [2004/5 c25spu Jan 3] no form: tried in cheekpieces. *N. J. Hawke* **c– h–**

PENALTY CLAUSE (IRE) 5 b.g. Namaqualand (USA) – Lady Be Lucky (IRE) (Taufan (USA)) [2004/5 h86: 19m⁶ 21mpu 17m⁵ 17d⁶ 16d Feb 18] leggy gelding: winning 2m hurdler: out of form in 2004/5: acts on good to firm and good to soft ground: tried in headgear: has worn tongue strap. *K. A. Morgan* **h–**

PENDIL'S PRINCESS 6 b.m. Afzal – Pendil's Delight (Scorpio (FR)) [2004/5 F73: 20mpu 19s 21spu Jan 20] little sign of ability. *S. E. H. Sherwood* **h–**

PENDING (IRE) 4 b.g. Pennekamp (USA) – Dolcezza (FR) (Lichine (USA)) [2004/5 16dpu Jan 28] lengthy gelding: half-brother to fair hurdler C'Est Fantastique (by Hernando), stays 2½m: fair maiden at best on Flat (stays 1m), sold out of J. Fanshawe's stable 13,000 gns Newmarket Autumn Sales: failed to settle in juvenile on hurdling debut. *J. Mackie* **h–**

PENDLE FOREST (IRE) 5 gr.m. Charnwood Forest (IRE) – Pride of Pendle (Grey Desire) [2004/5 F87+: F16d³ F16d 19d³ 17sur 20g² 20d* 20s Apr 10] big mare: fair form in bumpers: modest hurdler: won novice at Carlisle in March: stays 2½m: raced on good ground or softer (won bumper on soft). *R. A. Fahey* **h88 F92**

PENDRAGON 13 b.g. Bold Fox – Celtic Royale (Celtic Cone) [2004/5 c–: c24s⁴ c34dpu May 15] rangy gelding: winning pointer: maiden hunter chaser: tried blinkered. *Mrs Sarah Faulks* **c–**

PENLET TOO 10 b.g. Kinglet – Pensun (Jimsun) [2004/5 c20dpu May 11] modest pointer, won in January: no show in hunter chase. *J. I. Pritchard* **c–**

PENNEECK 5 ch.g. Pennekamp (USA) – Orange Hill (High Top) [2004/5 16g⁴ 16g⁵ 20v² 21s Mar 13] workmanlike gelding: half-brother to several winners, including fair **h86**

hurdler/chaser Harding (by Dowsing), barely stayed testing 3m: dam won Cesarewitch: well beaten in two 2-y-o maidens: sold out of N. Graham's stable 2,000 gns Newmarket Autumn (2003) Sales: modest form first 2 starts over hurdles: seems not to stay testing 2½m: takes strong hold. *S. L. Keightley*

PENNEY LANE 4 ch.f. Minster Son – Cullane Lake (IRE) (Strong Statement (USA)) [2004/5 F16s⁵ Apr 10] first foal: dam, 2½m chase winner, half-sister to useful hurdler up to 25f Lake Terreen: achieved little in maiden bumper on debut. *Miss Kate Milligan* **F–**

PENNEYROSE BAY 6 ch.m. Karinga Bay – Pennethorne Place (Deep Run) [2004/5 F79: 16s⁶ 17sᶠ 20s² 21d⁵ 20s⁴ 20d⁵ 19d* 21m* Apr 2] lengthy, rather unfurnished mare: fair novice hurdler: trained by G. Balding until after second start: made all in mares events at Exeter in March and Newbury in April, beating Early Start 3½ lengths in EBF Mares Only NH Novices' Hurdle Final (Limited Handicap) at latter, finding plenty in straight: will stay beyond 21f: acts on soft and good to firm going. *J. A. Geake* **h108**

PENNILLION 5 b.g. Pennekamp (USA) – Brave Princess (Dancing Brave (USA)) [2004/5 h–: 16dᵖᵘ Oct 16] no form in 3 starts over hurdles. *Mrs J. C. McGregor* **h–**

PENNYAHEI 14 b.m. Malaspina – Pennyazena (Pamroy) [2004/5 c106§, h–§: c25m* Apr 25] angular mare: fairly useful hunter chaser on her day: won at Ludlow very early in season: stays 3¼m: acts on good to firm and heavy going: inconsistent. *S. A. Brookshaw* **c97 h–**

PENNY BLUE 6 br.m. Sovereign Water (FR) – Suzy Blue (Relkino) [2004/5 F16d F16g⁵ 21d Nov 22] second foal: dam ran twice: won last of 3 starts in maiden points in 2004: little worthwhile form in bumpers: well held in novice on hurdling debut. *M. Sheppard* **h– F–**

PENNY CHASE 4 b.f. Bien Bien (USA) – Fullfilling (IRE) (Red Ransom (USA)) [2004/5 16sᵖᵘ Oct 23] angular filly: half-sister to 2004 2-y-o 7f winner John Ells (by Vettori): dam unraced, out of close relation to Oaks winner Intrepidity and smart Irish performers Acushla, a sprinter, and Calandra, stayed 1¼m: showed nothing in juvenile hurdle on debut. *M. P. Muggeridge* **h–**

PENNY NATIVE (IRE) 13 ch.g. Be My Native (USA) – Penny Maes (Welsh Saint) [2004/5 c94, h–: c16m Jun 5] sturdy gelding: veteran hurdler/chaser: never a danger in handicap, only outing in 2004/5: stays 3m: acts on any going. *Miss S. E. Forster* **c– h–**

PENNY PICTURES (IRE) 6 b.g. Theatrical – Copper Creek (Habitat) [2004/5 h103: 17g* 16m⁴ 22d³ 22d* 24d 24g 24d 20m² Apr 23] small gelding: fairly useful on Flat in 2004: useful handicap hurdler: generally progressive in 2004/5, winning at Bangor very early in season and Newton Abbot in November: very good second to Yes Sir at Sandown in April: stays 2¾m: acts on soft and good to firm going: patiently ridden. *M. C. Pipe* **h133**

PENNY'S CROWN 6 b.m. Reprimand – Two And Sixpence (USA) (Chief's Crown (USA)) [2004/5 h–, F84: 20m³ 22g⁴ 22g⁶ 22m 21m⁵ 17f 19g² 19g⁶ 16d⁶ 19s* 19s 19s* 19s 22s 17m³ Apr 9] poor hurdler: won sellers at Taunton (conditional jockeys handicap) in January and Hereford in February: stays 2¾m: acts on soft and good to firm going: best form without headgear: tried tongue tied. *G. A. Ham* **h81**

European Breeders Fund Mares' Only 'National Hunt' Novices' Handicap Hurdle, Newbury— Penneyrose Bay leads Early Start (right) and Zaffaran Express at the last

PENNYS FOREVER (IRE) 7 b.m. Arctic Lord – Ballela Maid (Boreen (FR)) [2004/5 F16g F17d May 15] IR £3,200 3-y-o: fifth foal: half-sister to winning 2½m hurdler Super Lucky and 2m winner Moscow Maid (both by Moscow Society): dam unraced sister to fairly useful staying chaser Patrico: well held in mares bumpers. *Jonjo O'Neill* **F–**

PENNYS FROM HEAVEN 11 gr.g. Generous (IRE) – Heavenly Cause (USA) (Grey Dawn II) [2004/5 h69§: 17d 16gpu 17s 19s 16s c16m² c16d Apr 9] compact gelding: poor maiden hurdler: second of 3 in maiden at Taunton on chasing debut: out of depth next time: best around 2m: acts on soft and good to firm going: tried blinkered: headstrong and irresolute. *Mrs Tracey Barfoot-Saunt* **c69 ? h69 §**

PENNY STALL 4 b.f. Silver Patriarch (IRE) – Madiyla (Darshaan) [2004/5 16d⁶ 16d⁴ 17m³ 18m³ Apr 21] tall filly: half-sister to 2½m hurdle winner Found Gold (by Saddlers' Hall) and winning pointer by Formidable: fair maiden on Flat (stays 17f), left J. Dunlop prior to final start in 2004: best effort in juvenile hurdles when third to Reservoir at Hereford penultimate start: will be suited by 2½m+: tongue tied final outing. *Miss E. C. Lavelle* **h92**

PENRIC 5 b.g. Marju (IRE) – Nafhaat (USA) (Roberto (USA)) [2004/5 h89: 17g⁶ 16d 21v⁴ 16vpu 20spu Apr 20] close-coupled gelding: maiden hurdler: below form in 2004/5, sold out of C. Cox's stable 21,000 gns Doncaster May Sales after first outing: should stay beyond 17f: acts on soft going: tried blinkered. *Miss V. Scott* **h81**

PENSTRUMBLY FLOWER 5 b.m. Wild Law – Princess Poppy (Baron Blakeney) [2004/5 F17m F17s 19vpu Feb 13] medium-sized mare: first foal: dam unraced: no sign of ability. *H. S. Howe* **h– F–**

PENTHOUSE MINSTREL 11 b. or br.g. Seven Hearts – Pentameron (Heres) [2004/5 c100, h–: c23m² c21mur c21g⁴ c20m³ c20g⁶ c20g c17s c20dur c19s² c21d c21d* c25d² c19d Apr 22] lengthy gelding: fair handicap chaser: won amateur event at Wincanton (for second successive year) in March: stays 25f: acts on firm and good to soft going: usually visored (not last 3 starts). *R. J. Hodges* **c107 h–**

PENZANCE 4 ch.g. Pennekamp (USA) – Kalinka (IRE) (Soviet Star (USA)) [2004/5 17s* 16d* 16s* 17g* Mar 18] **h144 p**

Even among good winners of the race, graduating from leading juvenile hurdler to top-flight two-miler has been very much the exception rather than the rule for those successful in the Triumph Hurdle. Indeed, 1967 winner Persian War is the only one to go on to victory in the following season's Champion Hurdle, and, of the nine to have tackled the double since Kribensis completed it as a six-year-old at the second attempt in 1990, only Oh So Risky has managed a place in the Champion, finishing second in 1992 as a five-year-old and runner-up again in 1994. Many Triumph winners haven't been good enough, or had the speed, to cope in the Champion Hurdle, which is run on the Old Course, and, historically of late, they have been more likely to make a mark subsequently in the Stayers' Hurdle. However, the Triumph is not, in itself, the test of stamina some perceive it to be. It is run over a longer trip than the Champion Hurdle but representative standard times don't suggest that seventeen furlongs on the New Course is that much more of a test than the half-furlong shorter trip on the Old. The chief reason for the lack of continuity is surely the immaturity of the runners. Just as many leading two-year-olds do not develop into top three-year-olds, so quite a number of leading juveniles simply do not improve enough to make the transition to top open company. While some to have done well in the Triumph in recent years have made more of an impact in staying races, it is worth noting that three of the nine highest-rated performers at two miles, over hurdles and fences, in the history of *Chasers & Hurdlers* were placed in the race. These are Monksfield, Badsworth Boy and Well Chief. Another of those nine, Night Nurse, failed to give his running in the Triumph.

The JCB Triumph, run as the first race on Friday's Gold Cup card at the revamped four-day Festival, suffered little from having another four-year-old hurdle added to the meeting. Nor did it suffer either, incidentally, from its first prize of £58,000 again being smaller than that for the Anniversary Hurdle at Aintree, which also gained Grade 1 status for the first time in 2005. Penzance might well prove different to many Triumph Hurdle winners. Considering the relatively unusual demands of the race, compared to most of the juvenile events that lead up to it, Penzance's victory was all the more encouraging for his future as a two-miler.

Racing Post '100 Favourite Racehorses' Adonis Juvenile Novices' Hurdle, Kempton— Penzance completes a hat-trick; Amarula Ridge is in vain pursuit

His three wins from as many starts over hurdles beforehand were gained on tracks which provide a far greater test of speed than Cheltenham, in novice events at Taunton and Huntingdon in January and in the Grade 2 Adonis Juvenile Hurdle at Kempton in February. Penzance looked promising in the process, scoring readily by a convincing margin each time and putting up his best effort when beating Amarula Ridge by seven lengths at Kempton. That said, Penzance's odds as 9/1 fourth favourite on the day at Cheltenham reflected his potential more than his form. A good number of his rivals in a representative field of twenty-three (the joint-smallest field since Connaught Ranger won the 1978 Triumph, which was run in April) had achieved more on form. The most notable among them was Faasel, a close second to Mephisto in a novice event outside his own age group at Kelso the time before. Faasel went off at 7/1, second favourite behind 7/2-shot Akilak, already successful against a big field over course and distance when making a most impressive hurdling debut in the Finesse Hurdle in January, before following up in the Victor Ludorum Hurdle at Haydock in February. Cerium was at 8/1, with Strangely Brown, unbeaten in three starts in Ireland, including the Cashmans Hurdle at Leopardstown in February, shortest-priced of the overseas challengers at 11/1.

Despite one minor false start, the Triumph was less eventful than usual, all bar two runners completing the course. Only Penzance and Faasel were still travelling strongly as a typically strong pace began to take its toll on the long run from the second last. Despite having made his first mistake two out, Penzance was still moving smoothly as he was sent past Cerium on the inside from the turn. Taking the final flight a length or so to the good over Faasel, who had still be asked for his effort, Penzance put in the better leap and, running on gamely, held on all out, though edging right, winning by a head. Akilak, never nearer, completed a clean sweep of the places for the home-trained runners, eight lengths back in third, over a length in front of the fading Cerium with Phar Bleu fifth and Strangely Brown sixth. Penzance would have found it harder still to hold on had Faasel jumped the last better. It would have been informative had the pair met again, but both did enough in the Triumph to show themselves smart juveniles, among the best of recent years.

While Faasel went on to frank the Triumph form at Aintree, Penzance was put away soon after Cheltenham, making him only the second Triumph Hurdle winner since Kribensis to end the season unbeaten. Commanche Court was the other, though Katarino met his defeat over fences in France rather than over hurdles in Britain or Ireland. In his second campaign, Kribensis won three more races, including the Christmas Hurdle at Kempton, before suffering his first defeat in the Champion Hurdle, briefly looking the winner turning for home, only to fade into seventh on softish going. Generally speaking, five-year-olds have found it hard to win the Champion Hurdle—multiple champions See You Then (1985) and Night Nurse (1976) were the last two—but the best hurdlers around at present do lack an outstanding performer and Penzance may well have to make only normal improvement to be snapping at their heels in 2005/6. Quoted at 33/1 for the Champion Hurdle after Cheltenham, it is easy to see his odds being a good deal shorter on the day.

Penzance's success in the Triumph capped a remarkable twelve months for the sixteen thousand or so members of the Elite Racing Club, in whose name he runs, and for his dam Kalinka, also responsible for the club's high-class miler Soviet Song (by Marju), winner of three Group 1 events as a four-year-old in 2004, the Sussex Stakes at Goodwood, the Falmouth Stakes at Newmarket and the Matron Stakes at Leopardstown. Kalinka is one of a small band of broodmares which form the basis of the breeding side of Elite Racing, whose familiar colours of white with black spots and black cap have been carried to success more than two hundred times on the Flat and over jumps since Kabayil, now another of its broodmares, became its first winner in a novice hurdle at Plumpton in 1993 (Kabayil is the dam of Dancing Bay, second in Club colours in the Coral Cup). Kalinka was acquired for 23,000 guineas as a two-year-old at the Newmarket Breeze-Up Sales after going through the ring unsold as a yearling. Kalinka's only racecourse success came in a seven-furlong maiden at Warwick as a two-year-old and she showed fairly useful form at up to a mile and a quarter before being tried over hurdles twice, finishing fourth on the first occasion. She has been a revelation at stud, her first foal, and only other to race so far, Baralinka (by Barathea), also a fairly useful winner over five and six furlongs. There isn't much jumping influence in Kalinka's pedigree, her dam Tralthee being a smart performer on the Flat, winning the Rockfel Stakes and the Lupe Stakes, but Kalinka's half-brother Tuco was successful in a point, the valuable Goffs Land Rover Bumper at Fairyhouse and two races over hurdles in Ireland, including a Grade 3, before being killed in action. Penzance's sire Pennekamp, winner of the Two Thousand Guineas, has proved a flop on the whole at stud, at least on the Flat, and he was leased to Sweden in 2004 by Sheikh Mohammed's Darley operation before being sold to stand at the Bracklyn Stud in Ireland as a National Hunt stallion, after Penzance's success in March. Penzance's progress hasn't been the only stimulus to Pennekamp's change of direction at stud, another of his sons Rocket Ship showing useful form in the latest season, finishing second to Wild Passion in the Grade 1 Royal Bond Novices' Hurdle at Fairyhouse in November.

JCB Triumph Hurdle, Cheltenham—Faasel (visor) is the main danger at the last; Cerium will lose third to Akilak near the line

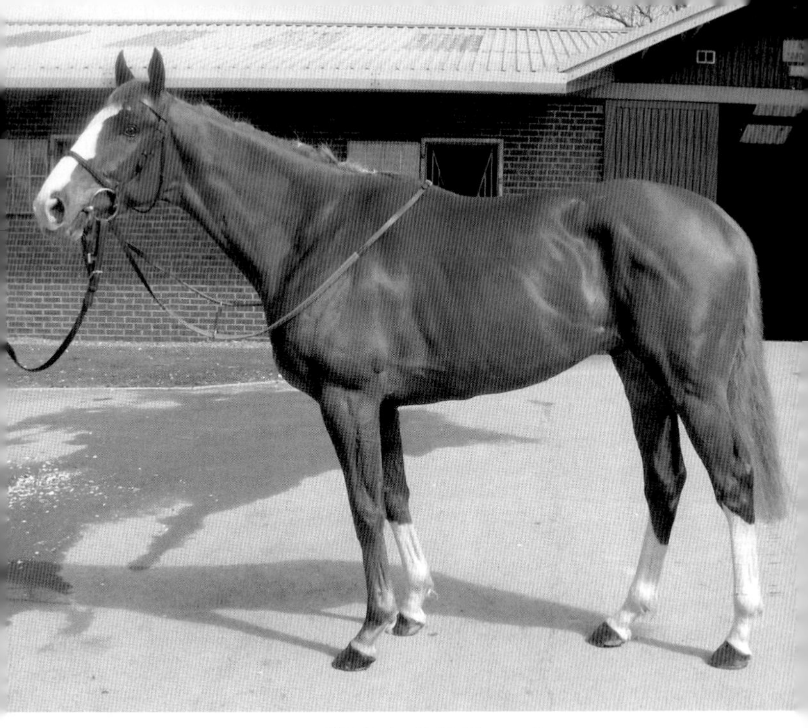

Elite Racing Club's "Penzance"

Penzance (ch.g. 2001)	Pennekamp (USA) (b 1992)	Bering (b 1983)	Arctic Tern Beaune
		Coral Dance (b 1978)	Green Dancer Carvinia
	Kalinka (IRE) (b 1994)	Soviet Star (b 1984)	Nureyev Veruschka
		Tralthee (ch 1983)	Tromos Swalthee

Given the further improvement he is likely to make, Penzance looks to have good prospects of boosting Pennekamp's profile as a jumping stallion further in 2005/6. Successful in a maiden over a mile in September on the first of two starts as a two-year-old, he had only eight races in all on the Flat in his first two seasons, showing fairly useful form in winning a handicap over a mile and a quarter at three, and he is still lightly raced over hurdles. Penzance's jumping generally stood up well among his own age group in his first season—he made a bad mistake at the last at Taunton—but, like most juveniles, the more experience he gains before taking on the established top hurdlers, the better for his prospects. A sturdy gelding, Penzance will prove best at around two miles and has raced only on good ground or softer so far, though his debut win on the Flat came on firm. *A. King*

PEPPERNICK 9 br.g. Alflora (IRE) – Nicolini (Nicholas Bill) [2004/5 c25d^{pu} Apr 11] lightly-raced winning pointer: no show in maiden chase. *Miss R. Brewis* **c–**

PEPPERSHOT 5 b.g. Vettori (IRE) – No Chili (Glint of Gold) [2004/5 h93: 18m^{3} 21d^{F} Apr 18] workmanlike gelding: modest maiden hurdler: off nearly 11 months, **h90**

running well when stumbling and falling last at Plumpton: stays 21f: acts on soft and good to firm going. *G. P. Enright*

PEQUENITA 5 b.m. Rudimentary (USA) – Sierra Madrona (USA) (Woodman (USA)) [2004/5 h94: 16d 18dpu 17s* 16s* 16s3 Mar 31] modest hurdler: sold out of G. L. Moore's stable £6,000 Ascot December Sales: made all in sellers at Taunton and Chepstow next 2 starts: largely temperamental displays otherwise: claimed to join R. Guest £10,000 final outing: raced around 2m on good going or softer: has worn blinkers/cheekpieces. *Miss K. M. George* **h94 §**

PER AMORE (IRE) 7 ch.g. General Monash (USA) – Danny's Miracle (Superlative) [2004/5 c119?, h109: c20gF May 16] medium-sized gelding: fair handicap hurdler: fairly useful chaser: out of contention when falling only outing in 2004/5: stays 21f: acts on any going: tried in cheekpieces, blinkered nowadays. *P. J. Hobbs* **c– h–**

PERANGE (FR) 9 ch.g. Perrault – La Mesange (FR) (Olmeto) [2004/5 c129, h–: c20g Feb 17] close-coupled, workmanlike gelding: fairly useful chaser in 2003/4: left P. Nicholls and fit from point, well beaten in hunter at Sandown: stays 21f: acts on heavy and good to firm going. *R. Barber* **c– h–**

PERCHANCER (IRE) 9 ch.g. Perugino (USA) – Irish Hope (Nishapour (FR)) [2004/5 c88, h–: c22s* May 9] winning hurdler: fit from points, won hunter chase at Market Rasen in May, left disputing lead at last: stays 2¾m: acts on heavy going. *Miss A. Armitage* **c88 h–**

PERCIPIENT 7 b.g. Pennekamp (USA) – Annie Albright (USA) (Verbatim (USA)) [2004/5 h85: 16m 16g5 20spu 16d c16g5 c20g6 c17g2 Mar 28] useful-looking gelding: poor maiden hurdler: blinkered, first form over fences when second in selling handicap at Plumpton, jumping right: will prove best around 2m: acts on soft going. *D. R. Gandolfo* **c71 h78**

PERCY BRAITHWAITE (IRE) 13 b.g. Kahyasi – Nasseem (FR) (Zeddaan) [2004/5 c–, h–: c20d3 c17gpu 24mpu Aug 6] small, angular gelding: winning hurdler/chaser, no form since 2001/2. *Mrs P. Ford* **c– h–**

PERCY JAY (NZ) 6 ch.g. Rainbow Myth (NZ) – Zillah Grace (NZ) (Otehi Bay (AUS)) [2004/5 F16v Jan 3] New Zealand-bred gelding: tailed off in bumper on debut. *W. Jenks* **F–**

PERCY-VERANCE (IRE) 7 ch.g. Dolphin Street (FR) – Sinology (Rainbow Quest (USA)) [2004/5 h81: 20m6 26g5 21m4 Aug 31] compact gelding: runner-up in point: poor maiden hurdler, lightly raced: stays 21f: acts on soft and good to firm going: tried tongue tied. *J. J. Quinn* **h74**

PERERIN 4 b.g. Whittingham (IRE) – Antithesis (IRE) (Fairy King (USA)) [2004/5 16s 16g 16g Mar 18] poor on Flat (stays 1m), sold out of I. Wood's stable £1,000 Ascot November Sales: no form in juvenile hurdles: sold £1,600 Ascot April Sales. *N. B. King* **h–**

PERESTROIKA (IRE) 7 ch.g. Ashkalani (IRE) – Licentious (Reprimand) [2004/5 17d 19s 17s Nov 18] fairly useful at one time on Flat (stays 1¾m), modest in 2004: well held in novice hurdles. *B. Ellison* **h–**

PERFECT BALANCE (IRE) 4 b. or br.g. Shinko Forest (IRE) – Tumble (Mtoto) [2004/5 16s 16d 17s 16d Dec 6] good-topped gelding: modest on Flat (stays 1¼m): no form in juvenile hurdles: visored last 2 starts. *N. Tinkler* **h–**

PERFECT FELLOW 11 b.g. Teamster – G W Supermare (Rymer) [2004/5 c127, h–: c25d4 Nov 6] smallish, sturdy gelding: fairly useful handicap chaser, lightly raced: stays 25f: acts on good to firm and heavy going. *Miss H. C. Knight* **c126 h–**

PERFECT HINDSIGHT (IRE) 4 b.g. Spectrum (IRE) – Vinicky (USA) (Kingmambo (USA)) [2004/5 16spu Oct 23] close-coupled gelding: fair form at 2 yrs, well held on Flat in 2004, left C. Cox before final outing: no show on hurdling debut. *C. J. Gray* **h–**

PERFECT LIAISON 8 b.g. Alflora (IRE) – Connie's Pet (National Trust) [2004/5 h108+: c23sF Oct 19] tall, good-topped gelding: won novice on first of 2 starts over hurdles in 2003/4: fell seventh on chasing debut: will stay 3m. *R. H. Alner* **c– h–**

PERFECT MATCH (IRE) 7 b. or br.g. Un Desperado (FR) – Imperial Blue (IRE) (Callernish) [2004/5 F16s Feb 3] €9,200 4-y-o: useful-looking gelding: first foal: dam unraced: little show in bumper on debut. *Noel T. Chance* **F–**

PERFECT PUNCH 6 b.g. Reprimand – Aliuska (IRE) (Fijar Tango (FR)) [2004/5 16g5 Dec 18] leggy gelding: half-brother to fairly useful 2m hurdlers Altay (by Erins Isle) and Three Mirrors (by Cloudings): fair on Flat (stays 1¾m), sold out of C. Wall's stable **h81**

24,000 gns Newmarket Autumn Sales: not knocked about when fifth of 16 in novice at Newcastle on hurdling debut: should do better. *K. G. Reveley*

PERFECT STORM 6 b.g. Vettori (IRE) – Gorgeous Dancer (IRE) (Nordico (USA)) **h114** [2004/5 17d^{2} 16g Mar 15] smallish gelding: useful on Flat (stays 1½m) for M. Blanshard: favourite, ½-length second to Noble Request in novice at Taunton on hurdling debut: 66/1 and tongue tied, blundered fifth when well held in Grade 1 novice at Cheltenham. *M. C. Pipe*

PERFECT VENUE (IRE) 12 b.g. Danehill (USA) – Welsh Fantasy (Welsh Pageant) **h79 §** [2004/5 h–§: 16m^{4} 16g 16d Feb 18] compact gelding: winning 2m hurdler: lightly raced and poor form at best since 2001: tried blinkered/in cheekpieces: has had tongue tied: unreliable. *A. J. Wilson*

PERHAPS THIS TIME (IRE) 6 b.g. Flemensfirth (USA) – Royal Chapeau (IRE) **h–** (Royal Fountain) [2004/5 F85: 20s 21d^{pu} 20s^{pu} 21s^{5} 22s^{5} 25v 26s Mar 7] sturdy gelding: no form over hurdles, left D. P. Keane after third start. *Miss J. S. Davis*

PERIDA (IRE) 5 b.m. Perugino (USA) – Razida (IRE) (Last Tycoon) [2004/5 19m^{pu} **h–** 17g^{4} 20m^{pu} 19g^{pu} Jul 28] modest maiden at best on Flat (stays 1½m) for C. Swan: no form over hurdles, saddle slipped twice in 2004/5. *B. G. Powell*

PERIWINKLE LAD (IRE) 8 b.g. Perugino (USA) – Bold Kate (Bold Lad (IRE)) **c– x** [2004/5 c81x, h102: 20v^{5} 22d 20s 22d Apr 17] angular gelding: maiden chaser (jumps **h–** ponderously): fair handicap hurdler, well held in 2004/5: stays 3m: acts on any going: tried in blinkers/cheekpieces. *Miss Victoria Roberts*

PEROUSE 7 ch.g. Alderbrook – Track Angel (Ardoon) [2004/5 h140: 16d* 16d^{3} 16d^{6} **h149** 16g^{3} 16d^{2} 17g 16m^{3} Apr 22] sturdy gelding: smart hurdler: reportedly had wind operation before reappearance: won totesport Elite Hurdle (Limited Handicap) at Wincanton in November, making all to beat Chief Yeoman 7 lengths: largely creditable efforts after, third to Rooster Booster in valuable minor event at Sandown final outing: best at 2m with emphasis on speed: usually tongue tied, effective when not. *P. F. Nicholls*

PERSEPHONE HEIGHTS 5 br.m. Golden Heights – Jalland (Jalmood (USA)) **h–** [2004/5 16s^{pu} 16s Dec 1] fair on Flat (should stay 1¾m) at 3 yrs for D. Coakley, lightly raced since: no aptitude in 2 outings over hurdles. *M. Madgwick*

PERSIAN EMBERS 6 gr.m. Blushing Flame (USA) – Podrida (Persepolis (FR)) **h–** [2004/5 24s^{pu} 19g 21s^{pu} Nov 16] leggy mare: fourth foal: dam winning hurdler, stayed 27f: runner-up on first of 3 starts in maidens over 1½m on Flat at 3 yrs for I. Wood: no form over hurdles. *Miss Victoria Roberts*

PERSIAN KING (IRE) 8 ch.g. Persian Bold – Queen's Share (Main Reef) [2004/5 **c–** c115, h115: 20g^{2} 20m^{6} 20d^{4} Oct 2] good-topped gelding: fair handicap hurdler: winning **h114** chaser, let down by jumping both other starts over fences: placed in ladies points in 2005: stays 2½m: raced mainly on good/good to firm going. *J. A. B. Old*

PERSIAN POINT 9 ch.g. Persian Bold – Kind Thoughts (Kashmir II) [2004/5 20s^{2} **h84** 18s^{6} 21v^{2} 20v^{6} 18v^{5} Mar 5] winning pointer: poor maiden hurdler: likely to stay beyond 21f: acts on heavy ground. *Miss S. E. Forster*

PERSIAN WATERS (IRE) 9 b.g. Persian Bold – Emerald Waters (Kings Lake **c135** (USA)) [2004/5 h136: c20d* c21d^{3} c24d^{3} c24d^{2} c24g^{4} Mar 16] leggy gelding: useful **h–** handicap hurdler: off 18 months, similar form over fences: won novice at Huntingdon in November: in frame all 4 starts after, fourth to Juveigneur in valuable amateur handicap at Cheltenham (collapsed and died afterwards): stayed 3m: acted on good to firm and good to soft going: usually raced prominently. *J. R. Fanshawe*

PERSONAL ASSURANCE 8 b.g. Un Desperado (FR) – Steel Typhoon (General **c122 x** Ironside) [2004/5 h120: 23m 24d* c21g* c21g^{2} c26m^{2} c20d^{F6} c26g^{ur} c24d^{pu} c21g^{pu} Apr **h124** 10] rangy gelding: fairly useful handicap hurdler: won at Southwell in May: won maiden there on chasing debut later in month: would have shown fairly useful form in handicap at Huntingdon sixth start, close second when falling last: probably stays 3¼m: yet to race on firm going, acts on any other: has been reluctant at start: poor jumper of fences. *Jonjo O'Neill*

PERSONA PRIDE 11 gr.g. St Enodoc – Le Jour Fortune (Twilight Alley) [2004/5 **c–** c–: c25m^{pu} May 11] angular gelding: of little account outside points. *Mrs B. Brown*

PERTEMPS JOB 4 b.c. First Trump – Happy And Blessed (IRE) (Prince Sabo) **F–** [2004/5 F13d F16d Feb 19] lengthy colt: third foal: dam unraced, out of useful 2-y-o sprinter Bless The Match: well beaten in 2 bumpers: poor form on Flat subsequently. *A. D. Smith*

PERTINO 9 b.g. Terimon – Persian Fountain (IRE) (Persian Heights) [2004/5 c111, h–: c17g4 c17g4 c16m4 c23mpu c16m6 c17v c16v5 Jan 29] good-topped gelding: winning hurdler: fair handicap chaser in 2003/4, below form in 2004/5: stays 2½m: acts on any going: wears headgear. *J. M. Jefferson* **c89 h–**

PERUVIAN BREEZE (IRE) 4 b.g. Foxhound (USA) – Quietly Impressive (IRE) (Taufan (USA)) [2004/5 17gpu Aug 21] modest on Flat (stays 1½m), claimed from J. Gallagher £6,000 in July: raced freely before pulled up (struck into) in juvenile on hurdling debut. *Evan Williams* **h–**

PERUVIAN PRINCESS 6 gr.m. Missed Flight – Misty View (Absalom) [2004/5 F–: F16s Oct 22] small mare: tailed off in 2 bumpers and on Flat debut. *C. N. Kellett* **F–**

PESKI MOOSE 6 b.g. Petoski – Lynemore (Nearly A Hand) [2004/5 F16v F16d 19g 20s Mar 22] lengthy gelding: sixth foal: brother to fair chaser Starting Again, stays 2¾m: dam, fair hurdler/winning chaser who stayed 3m, half-sister to useful 2m to 2½m jumper For Good: well held in bumpers and over hurdles. *Mrs S. J. Smith* **h– F–**

PETANQUE (IRE) 9 b.g. King's Ride – Phargara (IRE) (Phardante (FR)) [2004/5 h118: 20g c16mur c16m4 20m2 16g* 16d6 17g6 17vF Feb 13] tall gelding: modest form completed start over fences: fair hurdler nowadays, sold out of N. Henderson's stable 5,500 gns Doncaster August Sales after third outing: won conditional jockeys seller at Ludlow in November: stays 19f: best form on good/good to soft going. *Evan Williams* **c85 h101**

PETERHOUSE 6 b.g. Persian Bold – Run With Pride (Mandrake Major) [2004/5 h–, F–: 20v6 c27vpu c16v* Jan 10] first sign of ability when winning handicap at Newcastle on second start over fences. *Mrs E. Slack* **c70 h–**

PETER PARKGATE 6 gr.g. Kuwait Beach (USA) – Nellie's Joy VII (Damsire Unregistered) [2004/5 F17s F18m Apr 21] plain gelding: fifth known foal: dam unraced: of no account. *N. R. Mitchell* **F–**

PETER'S DEBT 6 b.g. Arzanni – Another Debt (Pitpan) [2004/5 F16g6 F16s 16d Mar 10] second foal: dam tailed off in 2 bumpers: well beaten in 2 bumpers and maiden hurdle. *T. R. George* **h– F–**

PETER'S IMP (IRE) 10 b.g. Imp Society (USA) – Catherine Clare (Sallust) [2004/5 h73: 22d* 17d* 24s6 17d5 Nov 23] small, good-bodied gelding: modest on Flat (stays 2m), successful in July: poor hurdler: won 2 selling handicaps at Cartmel in August, second for second consecutive year: effective at 17f to 2¾m: acts on good to soft going. *A. Berry* **h89**

PETERSON'S CAY (IRE) 7 b.g. Grand Lodge (USA) – Columbian Sand (IRE) (Salmon Leap (USA)) [2004/5 h78§: c20s3 c20gF Oct 27] lengthy gelding: poor hurdler on balance: didn't convince with jumping when third in novice handicap at Uttoxeter on chasing debut: stays 2½m: acts on soft and good to firm going: tried blinkered: temperamental. *C. L. Tizzard* **c89 § h– §**

PETER'S TWO FUN (FR) 8 b.g. Funambule (USA) – Spinner's Mate (FR) (Miller's Mate) [2004/5 c78, h70§: c23dpu 19g6 22s4 Jun 22] leggy gelding: poor hurdler/chaser: successful in point in March: stays 3¼m: acts on firm and soft going: has worn blinkers/visor: often front runner: not one to rely on. *A. S. T. Holdsworth* **c– h78 §**

PETERTHEKNOT (IRE) 7 ch.g. Beneficial – A Woman's Heart (IRE) (Supreme Leader) [2004/5 h102, F98: 20v5 20s4 19s2 20v2 20s* 20v3 20v 20s4 16s4 Mar 29] good-topped gelding: useful novice hurdler: won Grade 2 Barry & Sandra Kelly Memorial Novices' Hurdle at Navan in December easily by ¾ length from Sweet Kiln: creditable efforts when in frame in similar events after at Naas and Fairyhouse (2, to Justified on second occasion): not discredited when fourth to Asian Maze in Grade 1 at Punchestown in late-April: stays 2½m: raced mainly on soft/heavy going: has run as if amiss/found little. *Patrick Sinnott, Ireland* **h132**

PETE THE PAINTER (IRE) 8 b.g. Detroit Sam (FR) – Rambling Moss (Le Moss) [2004/5 c22g2 c23m* c26dpu c24gur Apr 15] winning pointer, including twice in 2004: poor form in chases, jumped right when winning maiden at Worcester in June: blinkered. *J. W. Tudor* **c77**

PETITE MARGOT 6 b.m. Alderbrook – Outfield (Monksfield) [2004/5 h121, F83: 23mpu 22d* 25s5 20v3 22g 23s 24g Mar 17] smallish mare: useful handicap hurdler: beat Darjeeling ¾ length in quite valuable mares event at Wincanton in November: good efforts at Warwick and Haydock next 2 starts, below form in well-contested events after: will stay beyond 25f: acts on any going: front runner/races prominently: tough. *N. A. Twiston-Davies* **h131**

PETITE SALOU 8 ch.m. Path of Condie – Rock of Ages (Blakeney) [2004/5 16s 16vpu 22s 19s Mar 27] sturdy mare: first foal: dam fair 17f winner/lightly-raced novice hurdler: no form over hurdles. *C. N. Kellett* **h–**

PETOLINSKI 7 b.g. Petoski – Olnistar (FR) (Balsamo (FR)) [2004/5 c79§, h–: c24gF c24g2 Apr 15] winning hurdler: modest maiden chaser: stays 3m: acts on soft going: has worn cheekpieces: has failed to impress with attitude. *Mrs Sue Popham* **c87 h–**

PETROLERO (ARG) 6 gr.g. Perfect Parade (USA) – Louise (ARG) (Farnesio (ARG)) [2004/5 17d4 17m4 17d5 19m 16d3 Jan 7] leggy gelding: modest maiden on Flat (stays 1m), for Stef Liddiard, lightly raced since 2003: poor novice hurdler: will prove best around 2m. *James Moffatt* **h82**

PETROVKA (IRE) 5 b.m. King's Theatre (IRE) – Adjacent (IRE) (Doulab (USA)) [2004/5 F17s F16s F17g6 Apr 14] 22,000 3-y-o: angular mare: sixth foal: half-sister to 3 winning hurdlers: dam fair 1¼m and 1½m winner: little solid form in mares bumpers. *S. Gollings* **F–**

PETRULA 6 ch.g. Tagula (IRE) – Bouffant (High Top) [2004/5 h119: 16s6 16d* 20s2 20v3 16v6 17gF Feb 16] leggy, close-coupled gelding: fairly useful on Flat (best around 1¼m): fairly useful handicap hurdler: won at Wetherby in November by ¾ length from Beseiged, pair clear: good efforts when placed at Haydock next 2 starts: stays 2½m: acts on heavy going, probably on good to firm: usually wears blinkers/cheekpieces. *K. A. Ryan* **h128**

PETWICK (IRE) 6 b. or br.g. Flemensfirth (USA) – Scottish Minnie (IRE) (Farhaan) [2004/5 F84: F16d6 16d 19s5 20s6 Dec 17] sturdy gelding: twice-raced in bumpers: best effort over hurdles when sixth to Forager in maiden at Windsor. *P. G. Murphy* **h100 F–**

PEVERIL PRIDE 7 b.g. Past Glories – Peveril Princess (Town And Country) [2004/5 h98§, F–: 27gpu 22f5 22gpu 24spu Nov 2] workmanlike gelding: maiden hurdler: no show in 2004/5, left M. Weeden after first outing: temperamental (refused to race once). *G. B. Balding* **h– §**

PEWTER LIGHT (IRE) 8 gr.g. Roselier (FR) – Luminous Light (Cardinal Flower) [2004/5 c79, h–: c25m c31dF c25s* c26vpu c25s* Feb 6] sturdy gelding: poor handicap chaser: won at Hereford in January and February, well ridden by P. Brennan on each occasion: should stay beyond 25f: acts on soft going: tried in cheekpieces, blinkered last 3 starts: often races lazily. *B. J. M. Ryall* **c79 h–**

PHAIRY STORM (IRE) 6 b. or br.g. Glacial Storm (USA) – Railstown Phairy (IRE) (Phardante (FR)) [2004/5 19vpu 24g 24d 22d c24gpu Apr 15] compact gelding: second foal: half-brother to 2½m chase winner Il Penseroso (by Norwich): dam unraced, out of half-sister to useful staying hurdler/chaser My View: placed once from 3 starts in maiden Irish points in 2004: no form over hurdles or on chasing debut: tried in cheekpieces. *J. D. Frost* **c– h–**

PHANTOM HAZE 12 gr.g. Absalom – Caroline Lamb (Hotfoot) [2004/5 c–, h–: 20dpu Apr 25] good-topped gelding: maiden hurdler, very lightly raced: pulled up both starts over fences. *J. Parkes* **c– h–**

PHARAGON (IRE) 7 b.g. Phardante (FR) – Hogan (IRE) (Black Minstrel) [2004/5 c–, h–: c21dpu c25dF 16s 22spu 16s Apr 22] no sign of ability. *Mrs C. J. Kerr* **c– h–**

PHARAOH HATSHEPSUT (IRE) 7 b.m. Definite Article – Maid of Mourne (Fairy King (USA)) [2004/5 17g 16g5 16d4 16m 17dpu Nov 23] poor on Flat: no form over hurdles: sold out of J. Moffatt's stable 900 gns Doncaster October Sales before final outing. *W. G. Young* **h–**

PHARAWAY CITIZEN (IRE) 10 ch.g. Phardante (FR) – Boreen Citizen (Boreen (FR)) [2004/5 c120, h–: 24g3 Oct 14] useful-looking gelding: fairly useful handicap chaser in 2003/4: maiden hurdler: stays 3¼m: acts on soft and good to firm going. *T. R. George* **c– h–**

PHARBEITFROME (IRE) 11 b.g. Phardante (FR) – Asigh Glen (Furry Glen) [2004/5 c88, h–: c17gpu c21dpu c24dpu Mar 28] lengthy, workmanlike gelding: winning chaser: pulled up most starts (including points) in 2004/5, left N. Wilson after reappearance: stays 2½m: acts on heavy and good to firm going: tongue tied: makes mistakes. *W. Stone* **c– x h–**

PHAR BLEU (FR) 4 b.g. Agent Bleu (FR) – Guilt Less (FR) (Useful (FR)) [2004/5 16d5 16s3 16d2 16g* 16v* 16d6 16v2 17g5 16s2 Apr 7] **h134**

Juvenile hurdling tends to be dominated—in terms of quality as well as quantity—by ex-Flat racers. Since the *Chasers & Hurdlers* series began, only Upgrade, in 1998, has been successful in the Triumph Hurdle, still the most prestigious event of the season confined to four-year-olds, without having raced on the Flat beforehand. Since then, no horse has been so much as placed at Cheltenham without the benefit of experience on the level. All things considered, therefore, Phar Bleu looks to have a good future with his first season behind him. Bought as an unraced three-year-old in France for €27,000 only in July, Phar Bleu proved the best juvenile of 2004/5 among those untried on the Flat. He improved with virtually every run, winning twice, and climaxed his season with two good efforts in top company, finishing fifth in the Triumph at Cheltenham and second in the Anniversary Hurdle at Aintree.

Phar Bleu's wins both came before the turn of the year. After placed efforts at Wetherby and Cheltenham on his second and third starts, he went off favourite for a juvenile event at Newbury in November and ran out a decisive winner by three and a half lengths from Verasi. Phar Bleu was only third favourite of sixteen behind Cerium for the Grade 1 Finale Juvenile Novices' Hurdle at Chepstow the following month but, with the market leader well below par, he gained a notable success for his small stable, taking command at the fourth last and holding on well to beat 50/1-shot Biscar Two by a length and a quarter. Turned out quickly after Chepstow, Phar Bleu ran his only poor race of the season when tried against his elders in the Tolworth Hurdle at Sandown in January, and he also seemed to have his limitations exposed somewhat when a remote second to New Rock back against his own age group at Warwick in February. As a result, he started at 66/1 in a field of twenty-three for the Triumph, but he belied those odds with an improved effort, doing comfortably best of the three runners not to have been raced on the Flat. Ridden patiently, Phar Bleu was still well back at the third last, but he ran on well from the turn without reaching Penzance and Faasel, beaten just over a length and half a length by Akilak and Cerium for third and fourth, around ten lengths overall by the first two. Reunited with Tony McCoy, who had partnered him to both his successes, Phar Bleu was ridden more enterprisingly in the Anniversary Hurdle at Liverpool the following month. In the absence of Penzance, he started at 11/1 in a market headed by Faasel and was the only one to give the Triumph runner-up a race. Phar

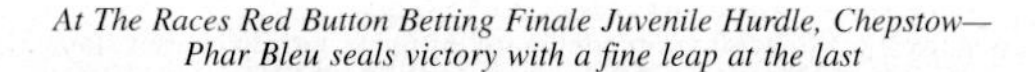

At The Races Red Button Betting Finale Juvenile Hurdle, Chepstow—
Phar Bleu seals victory with a fine leap at the last

Bleu tried to stretch him from the second last before being put well in his place in the end, going down by seven lengths though pulling nine lengths clear of third-placed Strangely Brown, a margin between the pair eight lengths wider than in the Triumph.

Phar Bleu (FR) (b.g. 2001)	Agent Bleu (FR) (b 1987)	Vacarme (b 1981)	Lyphard
			Virunga
		Acoma (b 1973)	Rheffic
			Almyre
	Guilt Less (FR) (b 1994)	Useful (br 1986)	Vorias
			Etoile du Berger II
		Valenda (ch 1982)	French Friend
			Hard To Fight

Along with Bonbon Rose and New Entic, the other Triumph runners not to have raced on the Flat, Phar Bleu was bred in France. His sire Agent Bleu, unraced as a two-year-old, showed smart form there at around a mile and a quarter at three, and has been responsible for several other useful or better performers over jumps, most notably the Grand Steeple-Chase de Paris winner Line Marine. Phar Bleu is the second foal out of the unraced Guilt Less, the first Manon des Bois (by Perrault) being successful over thirteen furlongs on the Flat and second on his only starts over hurdles and fences. Guilt Less is by the non-thoroughbred Useful, her dam Valenda's eight other foals all being by thoroughbred stallions. They include five winners on the Flat, the majority over middle distances. Both Valenda, who ran three times on the Flat, and the third dam Hard To Fight, who ran twice over hurdles, were half-sister to a winning jumper. Phar Bleu's future appears to be as a chaser. A tall, leggy, useful-looking gelding, altogether an athletic-looking sort, he was reportedly to be schooled over fences before his summer break, and may well take a similar path as a five-year-old to his owner's My Will, a winner five times over fences for Paul Nicholls in 2004/5, when he was also fifth in the Arkle. Like My Will, Phar Bleu should be at least as effective beyond two miles. A tough sort, a credit to his young trainer in only her third season with a licence, he raced only on good going or softer in his first season. *Miss G. Browne*

PHAR CITY (IRE) 8 b.g. Phardante (FR) – Aunty Dawn (IRE) (Strong Gale) [2004/5 c97, h–: c25g^{pu} c21d^{2} c19s^{4} c19d^{2} c20s^{4} c26d^{ur} c21d^{4} c17s^{4} c19v^{pu} 21g^{4} c19d^{2} Apr 22] strong, well-made gelding: maiden hurdler: fair handicap chaser: stays 21f: acts on soft and good to firm going: often let down by jumping. *R. H. Buckler* **c100 x h82**

PHAR FAR AWAY 7 b.m. Phardante (FR) – Shannon Juliette (Julio Mariner) [2004/5 h–, F88: 16s Oct 24] good-topped mare: second in bumper on debut: no show in 5 outings over hurdles. *D. R. Gandolfo* **h–**

PHAR FROM CHANCE 10 ch.g. Phardante (FR) – Chancer's Last (Foggy Bell) [2004/5 c25g^{4} May 7] rangy gelding: winning chaser: fair pointer nowadays: stays 3¼m: raced on good going or firmer (acts on firm): has carried head awkwardly. *James Richardson* **c–**

PHAR JEFFEN (IRE) 10 ch.g. Phardante (FR) – Clever Milly (Precipice Wood) [2004/5 c118x, h–: 19g^{5} 19s^{6} 16d 16d* 17g 16s Jan 6] smallish gelding: fairly useful chaser, though let down by jumping most starts in 2003/4: modest hurdler: won weakly-contested handicap at Lingfield in November: effective at 2m to 2½m: unraced on heavy going, acts on any other: blinkered once: races prominently. *R. J. Hodges* **c– h90**

PHARLETTA (IRE) 10 b. or br.m. Phardante (FR) – Vibrant Hue (USA) (Exclusive Native (USA)) [2004/5 16d^{pu} c21m c24m^{6} c20d^{6} c24g^{4} c17g^{F} Jul 15] lengthy, sparely-made mare: maiden hurdler: little show over fences. *Mrs C. J. Kerr* **c– h–**

PHARLY REEF 13 b.g. Pharly (FR) – Hay Reef (Mill Reef (USA)) [2004/5 h79: 16d 17d^{6} 17g May 31] small gelding: handicap hurdler, little impact in 2004: best around 2m: acts on firm and soft going. *D. Burchell* **h69**

PHARLY STAR 11 ch.g. Pharly (FR) – Norapa (Ahonoora) [2004/5 c76: c24g^{F} Apr 17] winning pointer: left Mrs F. Midwood, much improved in maiden chase at Stratford won by Sweet Diversion, jumping well and likely to have finished close second but for falling 2 out: dead. *H. D. Daly* **c100**

PHARMACY'S PET (IRE) 7 b.m. Petardia – Pharmacy (Mtoto) [2004/5 16g^{pu} Jul 11] little form on Flat at 2 and 3 yrs for H. S. Howe: jumped badly on hurdling debut. *R. C. Harper* **h–**

PHARNOON 9 b.g. Pharly (FR) – Mountain Willow (Doyoun) [2004/5 23vpu Jan 26] sturdy gelding: second foal: dam, fair stayer, half-sister to smart stayer Compton Ace (by Pharly), out of Irish St Leger and Cesarewitch winner Mountain Lodge: showed nothing in amateur novice hurdle on belated debut. *E. M. Caine* **h–**

PHAR OUT PHAVORITE (IRE) 6 b.g. Beneficial – Phar From Men (IRE) (Phardante (FR)) [2004/5 F96: 17s6 17g2 19s4 19s3 20s2 19g4 Apr 7] good-topped gelding: has plenty of scope: fair novice hurdler: stays 2½m: raced on good going or softer: visored final outing: has worn net muzzle: consistent, but has looked less than straightforward. *Miss E. C. Lavelle* **h99**

PHARPOST (IRE) 10 b.g. Phardante (FR) – Branstown Lady (Deep Run) [2004/5 c111§, h99§: c24gpu Jun 10] lengthy, deep-girthed gelding: lightly-raced winning hurdler: fair chaser: lost his form in 2004: stays 25f: acts on firm and soft going: tried blinkered: often finds little: joined A. Juckes. *Miss Venetia Williams* **c– § h– §**

PHAR RIVER (IRE) 6 ch.g. Scribano – Down By The River (Over The River (FR)) [2004/5 F16s6 F17g F16v6 F17g4 Mar 19] workmanlike gelding: half-brother to 3m chase winner Broadwater Boy (by Miner's Lamp) and winning pointer by Callernish: dam winning Irish pointer: best effort in bumpers (trained by F. Lloyd first 2 starts) when fourth to Rimsky at Bangor. *W. M. Brisbourne* **F87**

PHARTODANTE (IRE) 8 b.m. Phardante (FR) – Hennywood (IRE) (Henbit (USA)) [2004/5 h–: 16g4 24m6 Jun 16] of little account: tried in cheekpieces/visor: sold £4,000 Ascot August Sales. *Mrs L. C. Jewell* **h–**

PHARVIVA (IRE) 8 gr.g. Phardante (FR) – Stepfaster (Step Together (USA)) [2004/5 18f* 22m* 20g* 20g* Jul 29] IR £27,000 3-y-o: first foal: brother to fair hurdler up to 19f Almier: dam, modest chaser, who stayed 27f, half-sister to fairly useful hurdler/chaser up to 2½m Mister Drum: bumper winner: fairly useful hurdler: unbeaten in 2004/5, winning maiden at Limerick and minor event at Down Royal in May and novices at Tipperary in June and Galway in July: stays 2¾m: acts on firm going: forces pace. *M. Halford, Ireland* **h118**

PHASE EIGHT GIRL 9 b.m. Warrshan (USA) – Bugsy's Sister (Aragon) [2004/5 h67: 24d4 24g* 24d 24g2 27m4 24g5 Aug 21] small mare: poor handicap hurdler: won at Uttoxeter in June: thorough stayer: acts on firm and good to soft going: often soon off bridle. *J. Hetherton* **h81**

PHATIC (IRE) 9 b.g. Alphabatim (USA) – Pharisee (IRE) (Phardante (FR)) [2004/5 c23mpu c20m5 Aug 6] IR 5,000 3-y-o, 6,000 5-y-o: third foal: half-brother to smart hunter chaser Caught At Dawn (by Supreme Leader) and fairly useful 2½m chase winner Kew Jumper (by Mister Lord): dam unraced: well beaten only completed outing (including in points) in maiden chase at Worcester, though going better than most when bad mistake tenth. *R. Williams* **c–**

PHELANS FANCY (IRE) 7 ch.m. Mister Lord (USA) – Forty Quid (IRE) (Exhibitioner) [2004/5 19g 20d 16m c22v3 c20v2 c22d2 c23g* c26g c24v6 Apr 6] IR £2,000 3-y-o: lengthy mare: second foal: sister to winning pointer Lord Rockfield: dam, placed once around 1½m, half-sister to useful miler Dancal: no form over hurdles, left G. Cully after third outing: winning pointer: modest hunter chaser, winning maiden at Downpatrick in March: stays 23f: acts on heavy going. *Michael Winters, Ireland* **c94 h–**

PHILDARI (IRE) 9 b.g. Shardari – Philosophical (Welsh Chanter) [2004/5 c101§, h–: c16m4 c20spu c24gpu Apr 17] lengthy gelding: fair chaser in 2003/4: well held only completed outing in 2004/5, final outing for P. Webber: stays easy 25f: acts on soft and firm going: tried in cheekpieces: tongue tied: weak finisher. *Mrs Jelly O'Brien* **c– § h–**

PHILIPPA YEATES (IRE) 6 b.m. Hushang (IRE) – Miss Bobby Bennett (Kings Lake (USA)) [2004/5 h–: 22spu 16g 16v* 16s3 16g 18spu 16v5 16d 19g4 21g* 20s* 24g Apr 7] rather leggy mare: poor handicap hurdler: won selling events (first 2 conditional jockeys) at Uttoxeter in November and Plumpton and Fontwell in March: stays 21f: acts on heavy ground: visored/in cheekpieces after reappearance: has shown signs of temperament. *M. C. Pipe* **h79**

PHILOMENA 6 b.m. Bedford (USA) – Mandalay Miss (Mandalus) [2004/5 F–: F17d* May 12] twice-raced in bumpers: easily better effort when winning maiden at Exeter in May: will be suited by further. *V. R. A. Dartnall* **F92**

PHILSON RUN (IRE) 9 b.g. Un Desperado (FR) – Isis (Deep Run) [2004/5 c107p: c25dpu c26v* c33d* c33g Apr 16] strong gelding: lightly-raced chaser, successful on 3 of 5 starts, notably in John Smith's Midlands Grand National (Handicap) at Uttoxeter in March when beating Toulouse-Lautrec a length, left in front 3 out and idling: had won **c127 +**

John Smith's Midlands Grand National Chase (Handicap), Uttoxeter—Philson Run takes command three out as D'Argent and Robert Thornton part company; Toulouse-Lautrec is left second

handicap at Chepstow previous month: well held under less testing conditions in Scottish National at Ayr: stays 33f: acts on heavy going: may yet improve further back on softer ground. *Nick Williams*

PHILTRE (IRE) 11 b.g. Phardante (FR) – Forest Gale (Strong Gale) [2004/5 c–: c25m^3 c28m^5 May 22] tall, angular gelding: fair pointer/hunter chaser nowadays: stays 3½m: acts on good to firm going: races prominently. *Mrs H. L. Needham* **c89**

PHOENIX PHLYER 11 b.g. Ardross – Brown Coast (Oats) [2004/5 c93, h–: c21g^4 c20s* c24g^2 Apr 17] fair pointer/hunter chaser: left D. Pipe, won at Ludlow in March: probably stays 3m: acts on soft and good to firm going: often wears headgear, effective without. *Mrs Marilyn Scudamore* **c96 h–**

PHONE BACK (IRE) 6 b.g. Bob Back (USA) – Will Phone (Buckskin (FR)) [2004/5 F–: F18d^6 20d^F 16d Dec 3] tall gelding: better effort in bumpers when sixth in maiden at Plumpton: readily left behind once tempo increased on completed outing over hurdles: will prove suited by 2½m+. *G. L. Moore* **h– F–**

PHRED 5 ch.g. Safawan – Phlirty (Pharly (FR)) [2004/5 h–: 16s^6 Nov 24] angular gelding: fair at best on Flat (stays 1m), has lost his form, sold out of F. J. Houghton's stable 4,000 gns Newmarket Autumn Sales: well held over hurdles: pulls hard. *I. A. Wood* **h–**

PHYSICAL GRAFFITI (USA) 8 b.g. Mister Baileys – Gleaming Water (USA) (Pago Pago) [2004/5 h87: 17s^5 21s 16v* 22d^3 16v^6 16g Apr 19] compact gelding: modest hurdler: won conditional jockeys selling handicap at Leicester in February, easily best effort in 2004/5: stays 19f: acts on heavy going. *J. A. B. Old* **h94**

PICCINI (FR) 5 ch.g. Sillery (USA) – Emblem (FR) (Siberian Express (USA)) [2004/5 F17g^4 24g^6 20s^{pu} Oct 20] good-topped gelding: second foal: half-brother to one-time fairly useful chaser Jardin de Beaulieu (by Rough Magic), stays 2½m: dam, lightly-raced maiden, half-sister to smart 1½m winner Another Dancer: fourth in bumper at Newton Abbot on debut: no form in 2 starts over hurdles or maiden point. *M. C. Pipe* **h– F87**

PICK OF THE CROP 4 ch.g. Fraam – Fresh Fruit Daily (Reprimand) [2004/5 16s Dec 2] fair at best on Flat (stays 7f), has lost his form: tailed off in juvenile on hurdling debut. *J. R. Jenkins* **h–**

PICTURE PALACE 7 ch.g. Salse (USA) – Moviegoer (Pharly (FR)) [2004/5 h97: 22m Apr 28] workmanlike gelding: winning hurdler: lame only outing in 2004/5: stays 3¼m, at least when conditions aren't testing: acts on soft and good to firm going: usually blinkered: has looked irresolute. *T. R. George* **h–**

PIERCING SUN (IRE) 6 b.g. Eagle Eyed (USA) – Out In The Sun (USA) (It's Freezing (USA)) [2004/5 22m 18v^2 20v^5 16v 19s^4 Mar 27] angular gelding: fourth foal: brother to fairly useful 2m hurdler Aquila Oculus and half-brother to fair 2m hurdler Summer Break (by Foxhound): dam, fair 2m hurdler, half-sister to fairly useful hurdler up to 23f Bay Tern: fairly useful hurdler: in cheekpieces third time, won 25-runner minor event at Punchestown in late-April by 7 lengths from Miss Toulon: stays 2½m: acts on heavy going (won bumper on firm): tried tongue tied. *Anthony Mullins, Ireland* **h115**

PIERRE DE LUNE 5 b.g. Double Eclipse (IRE) – Rowlandsons Charm (IRE) (Fayruz) [2004/5 F16d^4 17g 22v^{pu} Jan 28] 1,000 3-y-o: first foal: dam successful on Flat, stayed 2m: little sign of ability in bumper and novice hurdles. *R. H. York* **h– F–**

PIKESTAFF (USA) 7 ch.g. Diesis – Navarene (USA) (Known Fact (USA)) [2004/5 h75: 16m 16d 20g^5 16m^6 24d* 22s 23d^6 24d 22d Apr 11] small gelding: won handicap hurdle at Hexham in October: no comparable form: seemingly better suited by 3m than shorter: acts on good to firm and good to soft going: tongue tied. *M. A. Barnes* **h89**

PILCA (FR) 5 ch.g. Pistolet Bleu (IRE) – Caricoe (Baillamont (USA)) [2004/5 h103: 17d 16d^{pu} 16d^4 16d 16d^5 16d 16s 16s 16g^5 20m 16d^4 Apr 17] small, leggy gelding: fair hurdler: generally below best in 2004/5, trained first start only by Mrs H. Dalton, sold out of I. McInnes' stable 4,500 gns Doncaster March Sales before final outing: raced mainly around 2m: acts on soft and good to firm going: blinkered (looked far from keen) sixth outing. *R. Flint* **h102**

PILGRIMS PROGRESS (IRE) 5 b.g. Entrepreneur – Rose Bonbon (FR) (High Top) [2004/5 h103: 18d^{pu} 16m 20m Dec 12] lengthy gelding: fair hurdler: little impact in 2004/5, sold out of P. Hobbs's stable 3,800 gns Doncaster May Sales before second outing (flattered): should stay beyond 2m: acts on soft and good to firm going: blinkered once. *D. W. Thompson* **h116 ?**

PILIBERTO 5 br.g. Man of May – Briska (IRE) (River Falls) [2004/5 16m^{pu} Apr 25] of little account on Flat: showed nothing on hurdling debut. *G. F. Bridgwater* **h–**

PILLAGING PICT 10 ch.g. Primitive Rising (USA) – Carat Stick (Gold Rod) [2004/5 c–: c22v^5 c20s^4 Apr 20] lengthy gelding: fair handicap chaser: best effort for long time when fourth to Almost Broke at Perth: stays 2¾m: raced on good going or softer (acts on soft). *J. B. Walton* **c109**

PILLAR OF FIRE (IRE) 11 gr.g. Roselier (FR) – Cousin Flo (True Song) [2004/5 c88§, h98§: c24d^{pu} c24m^3 c20s^3 c20s^3 c25m^3 Apr 23] leggy gelding: winning hurdler: poor maiden chaser: stays easy 25f: acts on soft and good to firm going: visored twice: ungenuine. *Ian Williams* **c77 § h–**

PILLAR TO POST 6 b.g. Bluegrass Prince (IRE) – Parisana (FR) (Gift Card (FR)) [2004/5 F–: 19g^{pu} 19g Dec 30] good-topped gelding: no form in bumpers or novice hurdles. *Ian Williams* **h–**

PILOT'S HARBOUR 9 b.g. Distant Relative – Lillemor (Connaught) [2004/5 c–§, h–§: c25m^F May 19] winning hurdler/maiden chaser: no longer of much account. *Mark Hughes* **c– h–**

PINK ECLIPSE 5 b.m. Double Eclipse (IRE) – Caspian Mist (Remainder Man) [2004/5 F–: F16s^5 20m Apr 10] leggy mare: form only in bumper on reappearance. *C. Roberts* **h– F80**

PINKERTON MILL 5 b.m. Rudimentary (USA) – Real Silver (Silly Season) [2004/5 F17v^4 F16g^5 F17s* F17g Apr 14] lengthy, unfurnished mare: sixth foal: half-sister to winners abroad by Music Boy and Northern State: dam, fairly useful 6f and 7f winner, out of half-sister to useful hurdler/staying chaser Fanackapan: easily best effort in bumpers when winning at Carlisle in March by 8 lengths from Park Supreme, soon in clear lead: sold out of Miss S. Forster's stable 12,500 gns Doncaster Sales later in month. *J. T. Stimpson* **F90**

PINK HARBOUR 7 b.m. Rakaposhi King – Let Me Finish (Chantro) [2004/5 h–: 20g^2 16v^3 c20m^5 c20m^4 c17m^{pu} 22d^5 c19g^F 21g* 19g^3 c19d* c16d^2 c16s* c17v* c20d^4 c19g^F c16d^5 19s Feb 6] lengthy mare: poor hurdler/modest chaser: won sellers at Towcester (hurdle) and Taunton (chase) in October and novice handicap chases at Hereford and Bangor in November: stays 21f: acts on heavy going: races prominently. *D. McCain* **c88 h64**

PINK PEARLS (IRE) 5 gr.m. Arzanni – Castle Ceile (IRE) (Castle Keep) [2004/5 F16d F17g^4 aF16g Oct 30] angular mare: second foal: dam unraced: well held in bumpers: tried in cheekpieces: sold £4,000 (privately) Ascot November Sales. *S. C. Burrough* **F–**

PINMOOR HILL 9 b.g. Saddlers' Hall (IRE) – Pennine Pink (IRE) (Pennine Walk) [2004/5 c24s^3 c21d^F c26v^{pu} Apr 22] poor pointer. *Mrs Diane Wilson* **c–**

PINNACLE RIDGE 5 ch.g. Bob's Return (IRE) – Canal Street (Oats) [2004/5 F17d^3 20s 16d^4 16v^4 22d Apr 11] close-coupled gelding: third foal: dam lightly raced: third in bumper at Carlisle on debut: modest form over hurdles: stays 2¾m: raced on going softer than good. *Mrs K. Walton* **h84 F91**

PINTAIL 5 b.g. Petoski – Tangara (Town Crier) [2004/5 F17s 16s Jan 11] lengthy gelding: seventh foal: half-brother to poor hurdler Bellbird (by Bob's Return), stays 19f, **h– F–**

and winning hunter chaser Tanager (by Carlingford Castle): dam unraced: well held in bumper and novice hurdle. *Mrs P. Robeson*

PIPERS BOY 9 b.g. Buckley – Pipers Reel (Palace Music (USA)) [2004/5 17g May 11] failed to complete in 2 points: well beaten in novice on hurdling debut. *D. Burchell* **h–**

PIPERSLAND 8 b.g. Lir – Celtic Mist (Celtic Cone) [2004/5 h–: 17gpu 19g Jul 29] little sign of ability, including in points. *Ms Sue Willcock* **h–**

PIPERS LEGEND 6 b.g. Midnight Legend – Pipers Reel (Palace Music (USA)) [2004/5 F16m5 F16gro F16g Oct 27] compact gelding: second foal: dam 1m winner: well held on completed starts in bumpers (in front when running out in between). *D. Burchell* **F–**

PIP MOSS 10 ch.g. Le Moss – My Aisling (John de Coombe) [2004/5 c–, h–: c20s6 c25dpuc26v3 Apr 17] lengthy, workmanlike gelding: lightly raced: poor form over hurdles and fences: stays 3¼m: raced on going softer than good (acts on heavy). *J. A. B. Old* **c70 h–**

PIRAEUS (NZ) 6 b.g. Beau Zam (NZ) – Gull Mundur (NZ) (Icelandic (IRE)) [2004/5 16v6 16g 21s2 25s4 Mar 1] compact gelding: apparently best effort over hurdles when second to ready winner Corlande in 21f novice at Sedgefield. *R. Johnson* **h91 ?**

PIRANDELLO (IRE) 7 ch.g. Shalford (IRE) – Scenic Villa (Top Ville) [2004/5 h120: 19g 16d4 20d5 21d Jan 26] rather leggy gelding: fairly useful handicap hurdler at best, generally well below form in 2004/5: best around 2m: acts on soft and good to firm going. *K. C. Bailey* **h113**

PIRATE FLAGSHIP (FR) 6 b.g. River Mist (USA) – Sacadu (Tyrant (USA)) [2004/5 F16v4 22g3 Apr 17] leggy gelding: eleventh foal: brother to 3 winners on Flat in France and half-brother to 4 winners, including 17f hurdle winner Karly Lawyer (by Sky Lawyer): dam unraced half-sister to dam of Viking Flagship and Flagship Uberalles: finished tired when fourth to The Mick Weston in bumper at Chepstow on debut: not fluent when 24 lengths third of 8 to Manx Royal in 2¾m novice hurdle at Wincanton: should do better. *P. F. Nicholls* **h93 p F–**

PIROUETTES (IRE) 5 b.m. Royal Applause – Dance Serenade (IRE) (Marju (IRE)) [2004/5 16s4 16g Mar 18] modest on all-weather, poor on turf on Flat (stays easy 1½m), successful in January: poor form in novice on hurdling debut: saddle slipped next time. *E. R. Oertel* **h–**

PISTE BLEU (FR) 5 b.m. Pistolet Bleu (IRE) – Thamissia (FR) (Riverman (USA)) [2004/5 h66: 16gpu Jul 29] modest on Flat (stays 1½m): poor form on completed outing over hurdles. *R. Ford* **h–**

PISTOL KNIGHT 11 b.g. Jupiter Island – Porchester Run (Deep Run) [2004/5 c71: c21mpu c23s6 Mar 11] poor maiden pointer/hunter chaser. *Mrs S. Bowman* **c–**

PITMINSTER 7 b.g. Karinga Bay – Eleanora Muse (Idiot's Delight) [2004/5 h86, F–: 20d6 22s6 19g6 26spu Jan 5] failed to complete in 3 points: maiden hurdler, no form in 2004/5. *P. F. Nicholls* **h–**

PITTON MILL 5 b.g. Millkom – Sea Song (Prince Sabo) [2004/5 20g 21gpu Jul 16] no form on 2 starts on Flat and over hurdles. *W. G. M. Turner* **h–**

PIXLEY 5 ch.g. Saxon Farm – Lady Renton (Rolfe (USA)) [2004/5 F–: F16v Jan 15] well held in 2 bumpers. *Mrs Pippa Bickerton* **F–**

PIZARRO (IRE) 8 ch.g. Broken Hearted – Our Swan Lady (Swan's Rock) [2004/5 c150+, h–: c24d3 c24v3 c24sF c25s2 c26gF Mar 18] workmanlike gelding: smart chaser: best efforts when third to Chives in Grade 2 at Haydock, Beef Or Salmon in Grade 1 at Leopardstown in December and Kicking King in Grade 1 at Punchestown in late-April: stays 25f: acts on heavy going: tried visored: often let down by jumping. *E. J. O'Grady, Ireland* **c154 x h–**

PLACE ABOVE (IRE) 9 b.g. Alphabatim (USA) – Lucky Pit (Pitpan) [2004/5 c–§, h–§: c27dur c27d* c24d* c27v2 c24g* c24d5 c25spu c23mF Apr 10] modest handicap chaser: won at Sedgefield and Newcastle in November and Musselburgh in January: stays 27f: acts on heavy going: refused to race once: front runner/races prominently. *E. A. Elliott* **c98 h–**

PLACID MAN (IRE) 11 br.g. Un Desperado (FR) – Sparkling Gale (Strong Gale) [2004/5 c116, h–: c20g* c28mur c26g3 Mar 18] big, rangy gelding: lightly raced: successful first 3 completed outings in chases, including in hunter at Warwick in May: winning return in point in 2005: ran very well when 11¾ lengths third to Sleeping Night in Foxhunter Chase at Cheltenham, despite mistakes last 3: stays 3¼m: acts on heavy going, probably on good to firm. *Ms A. E. Embiricos* **c128 h–**

PLAIN CHANT 8 b.g. Doyoun – Sing Softly (Luthier) [2004/5 c16m⁴ c16d³ c20m² c20m c23mᵖᵘ Jul 21] leggy gelding: winning pointer: form otherwise only when second in novice handicap chase at Worcester: let down by jumping next 2 starts: wears cheekpieces. *C. Roberts* **c70 x h–**

PLAISANCE (GER) 6 b.m. Monsun (GER) – Pariana (USA) (Bering) [2004/5 h–: 20g May 16] sturdy mare: lightly-raced hurdler, no show both starts since 2002/3. *A. M. Hales* **h–**

PLANTAGENET PRINCE 6 b.g. Lancastrian – Yuan Princess (Tender King) [2004/5 F–: 21d 16s Mar 23] no form in bumper or novice hurdles. *M. Scudamore* **h–**

PLANTERS PUNCH (IRE) 4 br.g. Cape Cross (IRE) – Jamaican Punch (IRE) (Shareef Dancer (USA)) [2004/5 16d Dec 6] useful-looking gelding: half-brother to modest hurdler Oversman (by Keen), stays 2¾m: fair on Flat (stays 1¼m), successful in June, sold out of R. Hannon's stable 30,000 gns Newmarket Autumn Sales: mistakes when only ninth of 19 in juvenile at Newcastle on hurdling debut. *G. M. Moore* **h–**

PLASBELLIN 7 b.g. Mazaad – Troublewithjack (Sulaafah (USA)) [2004/5 24sᵖᵘ Oct 30] workmanlike gelding: sixth foal: half-brother to winning 3m hurdler Jack Lynch (by Lancastrian) and fairly useful pointer Fisherman Jack (by Carlingford Castle): dam poor maiden who stayed 11f: showed nothing in maiden hurdle on debut. *G. J. Smith* **h–**

PLATINUM POINT (IRE) 6 b.g. Norwich – Blackhill Lass (IRE) (King's Ride) [2004/5 F16v⁶ Dec 31] rangy, good sort: second foal: dam unraced, from family of very smart staying chaser Garamycin: in need of experience when sixth of 12 in bumper at Warwick on debut: type to do better. *Noel T. Chance* **F78**

PLAY MASTER (IRE) 4 b.g. Second Empire (IRE) – Madam Waajib (IRE) (Waajib) [2004/5 16s 16g⁶ Jan 24] fair on Flat around 1m in 2004 for D. Haydn Jones: poor form both starts over hurdles: joined D. Morris. *K. A. Morgan* **h79**

PLAY THE MELODY (IRE) 4 b. or br.g. Revoque (IRE) – Dumayla (Shernazar) [2004/5 17v⁵ 16s⁵ 16s⁶ Jan 11] sturdy gelding: twice-raced on Flat, winning 9.7f maiden: raced around 2m on soft/heavy going over hurdles, best effort on second outing. *C. Tinkler* **h87**

PLEASED TO RECEIVE (IRE) 5 ch.g. Beneficial – Cheeney's Gift (Quayside) [2004/5 F16s Mar 27] seventh foal: half-brother to modest hurdler/chaser Brush With Fame (by Brush Aside), stays 3¼m: dam, lightly raced in points, out of half-sister to very smart 2m hurdler Drumikill and smart 2m chaser Jabeg: tailed off in bumper on debut. *A. M. Hales* **F–**

PLENTY 6 b.m. Terimon – Mrs Moneypenny (Relkino) [2004/5 F–: F16d 16d 20m Apr 10] compact mare: soundly beaten in bumpers and over hurdles. *S. J. Gilmore* **h– F–**

PLENTY COURAGE 11 ch.g. Gildoran – Fastlass (Celtic Cone) [2004/5 c–, h81: c20v³ Apr 17] small gelding: poor handicap hurdler in 2003/4: third of 9 in novice handicap at Carlisle on chasing debut: should stay 3m: acts on any going: effective with/without cheekpieces: races prominently. *B. Storey* **c72 h–**

PLUME OF FEATHERS (IRE) 5 b.m. Ali-Royal (IRE) – Feather-In-Her-Cap (Primo Dominie) [2004/5 17gᶠ 17gᵖᵘ Apr 10] well held in 2 maidens on Flat at 3 yrs for L. G. Cottrell: failed to complete both starts over hurdles. *D. P. Keane* **h–**

PLUMIER (FR) 7 b.g. Beyssac (FR) – Plume Rose (FR) (Rose Laurel) [2004/5 c108, h–: c20g⁵ c21d c25vᶠ c20vᵖᵘ c24vᶠ Feb 2] tall, useful-looking gelding: fair chaser: sold out of Ms B. Nicholls' stable 10,000 gns Doncaster May Sales after first outing: stays 3m: acts on heavy going: tongue tied: has been let down by jumping/temperament. *Miss L. C. Siddall* **c108 ? h–**

PLUTOCRAT 9 b.g. Polar Falcon (USA) – Choire Mhor (Dominion) [2004/5 h113+: 22m⁴ 21d* 20m c25dᵘʳ c25sᵖᵘ Mar 11] smallish, angular gelding: fairly useful handicap hurdler: better than ever when winning at Sedgefield in November: let down by jumping after, last twice over fences: barely stays 3m: acts on good to firm and good to soft going (possibly not on softer): usually patiently ridden. *L. Lungo* **c– h123**

POACHIN AGAIN (IRE) 8 b.g. Supreme Leader – Ariannrun (Deep Run) [2004/5 h109: 17g² May 10] strong, stocky gelding: winning hurdler: improved effort (fairly useful form) when second to Sir OJ in intermediate event at Killarney, only outing in 2004/5: bred to stay well beyond 2¼m: raced on good going or softer (acts on heavy). *A. L. T. Moore, Ireland* **h124**

POC FADA (IRE) 8 b. or br.g. Be My Native (USA) – She's Tough (Deep Run) [2004/5 16d* 22d c17d 16v[2] 20d[2] 16v[3] Oct 24] fifth foal: brother to fair hurdler Soldiered Again, stays 2¾m: dam unraced sister to useful staying chaser Gimme Five: bumper winner: fair hurdler: easily won maiden at Sligo in August: eighth of 10 finishers in maiden at Ballinrobe on chasing debut: stays 2½m: raced on going softer than good (acts on heavy): wore cheekpieces last 3 outings. *C. Roche, Ireland* **c88 h108**

POCKET SEVENS (IRE) 5 b.g. Supreme Leader – Flutter (IRE) (Floriferous) [2004/5 16d Jan 7] €10,500 3-y-o: fifth foal: dam unplaced in bumpers and over hurdles: tailed off in novice hurdle on debut. *Miss E. C. Lavelle* **h–**

POETRY AND JAZZ 6 b.g. Nomadic Way (USA) – Indian Crown (Welsh Captain) [2004/5 F–: 17g[pu] 17g 18m[6] 16m[ur] Sep 19] leggy gelding: of no account. *Dr P. Pritchard* **h–**

POGGENIP 6 b.m. Petoski – Princess Tria (Space King) [2004/5 F80: F18g May 9] twice-raced in bumpers, well held on second occasion. *B. G. Powell* **F–**

POILU 7 ch.g. Fearless Action (USA) – Marielou (FR) (Carwhite) [2004/5 h–, F73: 20g[pu] c21m[F] c22m[6] Oct 3] big, short-backed gelding: no form over hurdles: blinkered, let down by jumping both starts over fences: sold 2,300 gns Doncaster November Sales. *J. M. Jefferson* **c– h–**

POINT 8 b.g. Polish Precedent (USA) – Sixslip (USA) (Diesis) [2004/5 16g[4] 20v[4] 17s[6] 24g[4] 24s[6] Apr 16] lengthy gelding: maiden hurdler, fair form at best: possibly best short of 3m: acts on soft going. *W. Jenks* **h99**

POINTALISM (IRE) 6 br.g. Roselier (FR) – Ballinahowna Dream (IRE) (Treasure Kay) [2004/5 h–: 22g[pu] May 1] good-topped gelding: winning Irish pointer: no form in novice hurdles. *Miss H. C. Knight* **h–**

POINT BARROW (IRE) 7 b.g. Arctic Lord – Credit Transfer (IRE) (Kemal (FR)) [2004/5 h126, F100: 20g[5] c24s[4] c22d[2] c25d* c24v* c24v* c33g[5] c29s Mar 28] good-topped gelding: fairly useful hurdler: similar form over fences, best effort when winning Grade 3 Ladbroke Ten Up Novices' Chase at Navan in February by ¾ length from Mullacash: earlier won maiden at Fairyhouse and Grade 2 Woodlands Park 100 Club Novices' Chase at Naas: bit disappointing last 2 starts, in NH Chase at Cheltenham (favourite) and Irish Grand National at Fairyhouse (mistakes): should stay beyond 25f: raced on good going or softer (acts on heavy). *P. Hughes, Ireland* **c130 h–**

POINT OF ORIGIN (IRE) 8 b.g. Caerleon (USA) – Aptostar (USA) (Fappiano (USA)) [2004/5 c92d, h–: c22s[pu] 19s[6] 21g[3] 20g[6] 21g 17g Apr 3] smallish, lengthy gelding: successful on only completion in 5 starts over fences: poor maiden hurdler: stays 21f: acts on soft going: blinkered last 5 outings: has had tongue tied: sold 3,000 gns Doncaster May Sales. *C. C. Bealby* **c– h83**

POITIERS (FR) 6 b.g. Bering – Prusse (USA) (Ogygian (USA)) [2004/5 c103, h106: c16m[2] c21g[4] c17d[5] c17m Jul 30] leggy gelding: fair hurdler: similar form first 2 starts over fences: subsequently lost his way (twice pulled up in points in 2005): stays 21f: acts on any going: visored. *M. C. Pipe* **c103 h–**

POKER 4 ch.g. Hector Protector (USA) – Clunie (Inchinor) [2004/5 16g[pu] Oct 7] modest on Flat (should stay 1¼m), successful in early-2004, sold out of W. Haggas' stable 6,500 gns Newmarket July Sales: temperamental display on hurdling debut: sold 1,500 gns Doncaster October Sales. *Jennie Candlish* **h–**

POLAR CHAMP 12 b.g. Polar Falcon (USA) – Ceramic (USA) (Raja Baba (USA)) [2004/5 c–, h–: c24m[ur] c32m[F] c26g[pu] c26g Mar 18] sturdy gelding: useful hurdler/chaser at best: prolific winning pointer nowadays: unfortunate not to win hunter at Stratford in May, making running and around 4 lengths ahead when unseating last: left D. Pipe, trained next 2 outings by M. Pipe: stays 33f: acts on any going: blinkered twice, visored nowadays: temperamental. *Mrs O. C. Jackson* **c110 § h–**

POLAR FLIGHT 11 br.g. Polar Falcon (USA) – Fine Honey (USA) (Drone (USA)) [2004/5 c24s[pu] c21g[4] Apr 10] tall, useful-looking gelding: winning hurdler: fair pointer nowadays, successful in February: fourth at Newton Abbot on completed outing in novice hunters: stays 21f: acts on any going. *Mrs R. Vickery* **c88 h–**

POLAR GUNNER 8 b.g. Gunner B – Polar Belle (Arctic Lord) [2004/5 h–: c22v[F3] c20s[5] c25v[pu] 16v* c16v[3] c16v* c20v[4] c17s* c17s* 17v[5] c16s[6] Apr 21] good-topped gelding: modest handicap hurdler: won conditional jockeys event at Uttoxeter in December: progressed well back over fences, successful in handicaps at Sedgefield, Bangor and Market Rasen: best form around 2m: acts well on soft/heavy going: has had tongue tied: front runner/races prominently. *J. M. Jefferson* **c108 h91**

POLARNIK (CZE) 6 b.g. Just A Flutter – Polarni Zare (CZE) (Sectori (USA)) [2004/5 c22g[2] c22g* c20g[2] c25g* c22g[3] 21d Nov 14] sturdy, lengthy gelding: maiden on Flat: placed all 5 starts in chases, winning twice at Pardubice: tailed off in novice hurdle at Cheltenham: stays 25f. *Pavel Slozil, Czech Republic* **c? h–**

POLAR PROSPECT 12 b.g. Polar Falcon (USA) – Littlemisstrouble (USA) (My Gallant (USA)) [2004/5 c–, h–: c20g[pu] May 13] workmanlike gelding: smart hurdler/ fairly useful chaser at best: no form in 4 hunters: stays 2½m: acts on good to firm and heavy going: effective blinkered or not. *Miss Sarah George* **c– h–**

POLAR RED 8 ch.g. Polar Falcon (USA) – Sharp Top (Sharpo) [2004/5 c139, h–: c17d* c21m[2] c20d 20v[5] 16d c21g c36d c24s[6] Apr 21] angular gelding: winning hurdler: useful chaser: won intermediate at Bangor in May: well below form after next outing, rapid headway to hold every chance 2 out before dropping away just as quickly when thirteenth of 21 finishers to Hedgehunter in Grand National seventh start: stays 21f: acts on heavy and good to firm going: often visored over hurdles: tongue tied final outing. *M. C. Pipe* **c139 h–**

POLAR SCOUT (IRE) 8 b.g. Arctic Lord – Baden (IRE) (Furry Glen) [2004/5 c97, h96: 22g[2] c21d[3] c21s[ur] c20d[2] c21g* c22s[2] c19d[3] c19g* c20g[3] Apr 17] rather leggy gelding: modest hurdler: fair handicap chaser: won at Folkestone in December and Doncaster in March, aided by omission of 8 fences when beating Undeniable 9 lengths at latter: best up to 2¾m: acts on any going: tongue tied: often let down by jumping over fences: consistent. *C. J. Mann* **c114 x h99**

POLE STAR 7 b. or br.g. Polar Falcon (USA) – Ellie Ardensky (Slip Anchor) [2004/5 16g[2] 19g* 19d* 20s[2] 21g[4] 20s[4] Apr 7] leggy, useful-looking gelding: smart on Flat (stays 2½m), well beaten only start in 2004: useful novice hurdler: easily landed odds **h144**

Mr Paul Green's "Pole Star"

at Doncaster in December and Newbury in January: further improvement next 2 starts, ½-length second of 4 to Gold Medallist at Huntingdon and 3¼ lengths fourth of 20 to No Refuge in Royal & SunAlliance Novices' Hurdle at Cheltenham: lacklustre effort (lost action) at Aintree final outing: will stay beyond 21f: raced on good going or softer (acts on soft). *J. R. Fanshawe*

POLISH BARON (IRE) 8 b.g. Barathea (IRE) – Polish Mission (Polish Precedent (USA)) [2004/5 c89, h88: $c24d^{ur}$ $c24d^{*}$ $c26d^{R}$ May 15] close-coupled gelding: winning hurdler: modest chaser: won 3-runner novice at Fakenham in May: stayed 3m: acted on any going: dead. *J. R. Cornwall* **c89 x** **h–**

POLISH CLOUD (FR) 8 gr.g. Bering – Batchelor's Button (FR) (Kenmare (FR)) [2004/5 h106: $c16s^{*}$ c20m $c17s^{pu}$ 21d $16s^{6}$ 16d Mar 6] medium-sized gelding: fair handicap hurdler: won novice at Newton Abbot on chasing debut in May: ran poorly next 2 starts: effective at 2m to 2¾m: acts on soft going, possibly not on good to firm. *T. R. George* **c105** **h100**

POLISHED 6 ch.g. Danzig Connection (USA) – Glitter (FR) (Reliance II) [2004/5 c85+, h85: $16g^{*}$ $20d^{3}$ 16g $16s^{5}$ $17s^{3}$ $c16v^{2}$ $c20s^{4}$ $c16s^{4}$ Mar 19] leggy gelding: poor hurdler: won handicap at Hexham in May: modest chaser: best around 2m: raced on good going or softer (acts on heavy): wore cheekpieces 6 of last 8 outings: waited with. *R. C. Guest* **c88** **h80**

POLISH LEGEND 6 b.g. Polish Precedent (USA) – Chita Rivera (Chief Singer) [2004/5 h82: $19g^{5}$ $17g^{*}$ $17s^{pu}$ $17g^{5}$ $16g^{6}$ $17g^{3}$ $17d^{rtr}$ 17m $17f^{3}$ $16f^{5}$ $18s^{rtr}$ Nov 5] modest hurdler: won handicap at Newton Abbot in May: sold out of B. R. Millman's stable 2,000 gns (privately) Doncaster October Sales before final outing: raced mainly around 2m: acts on firm and good to soft going: usually blinkered: tongue tied: ungenuine (twice refused to race). *P. Wegmann* **h88 §**

POLISH PILOT (IRE) 10 b.g. Polish Patriot (USA) – Va Toujours (Alzao (USA)) [2004/5 c74, h–: $16d^{6}$ $c17g^{5}$ $c21s^{4}$ $c17s^{3}$ $c16d^{3}$ 16d $c16d^{*}$ $c16g^{5}$ $c16s^{4}$ $c16d^{3}$ $c16s^{5}$ $c20s^{4}$ $c20s^{ur}$ $16s^{3}$ Mar 13] smallish gelding: poor handicap hurdler/chaser: won weak conditional jockeys event over fences at Huntingdon in December: best around 2m: acts on any going: tried blinkered/tongue tied, not since 2001/2: tough. *J. R. Cornwall* **c76** **h72**

POLISH POWER (GER) 5 b.h. Halling (USA) – Polish Queen (Polish Precedent (USA)) [2004/5 17s Feb 17] seemingly useful up to 1½m on Flat in Germany for B. Hellier, fair form in Britain: eighth of 14 in maiden at Taunton on hurdling debut. *J. S. Moore* **h–**

POLISH RHAPSODY (IRE) 4 b.f. Charnwood Forest (IRE) – Polish Rhythm (IRE) (Polish Patriot (USA)) [2004/5 $19m^{pu}$ Mar 21] of little account. *J. A. Supple* **h–**

POLISH ROSE 4 ch.f. Polish Precedent (USA) – Messila Rose (Darshaan) [2004/5 $16s^{F}$ $17s^{pu}$ Jan 20] little form on Flat: no show both starts over hurdles: sold £1,600 Ascot April Sales. *Miss G. Browne* **h–**

POLITICAL CRUISE 7 b.g. Royal Fountain – Political Mill (Politico (USA)) [2004/5 h–: 16m $20d^{3}$ $20f^{3}$ $20d^{5}$ 20d $22s^{6}$ $16v^{3}$ $20s^{*}$ $20v^{4}$ 22s $20v^{4}$ $16v^{6}$ $20v^{5}$ 25s $22s^{5}$ $20v^{2}$ Mar 20] smallish gelding: poor hurdler: won selling handicap at Hexham in November: probably stays 2¾m: acts on heavy ground: blinkered once. *R. Nixon* **h78**

POLITICAL SOX 11 br.g. Mirror Boy – Political Mill (Politico (USA)) [2004/5 c–, h98: $22m^{5}$ $24d^{3}$ 22m $24f^{*}$ $27m^{pu}$ 24d $22v^{6}$ 24v 20v $24m^{*}$ $24d^{5}$ $24g^{5}$ $20v^{pu}$ 25d 17g 22v Mar 5] compact gelding: fair handicap hurdler: won at Perth in June and Musselburgh (conditional jockeys) in November: stays 27f: acts on any going: tried blinkered/in cheekpieces. *R. Nixon* **c–** **h101**

POLKA 10 b.g. Slip Anchor – Peace Dance (Bikala) [2004/5 $c21g^{pu}$ $c26v^{pu}$ Apr 22] maiden hurdler: modest pointer: no show in 2 novice hunters. *V. G. Greenway* **c–** **h–**

POLLENSA BAY 6 b.g. Overbury (IRE) – Cloncoose (IRE) (Remainder Man) [2004/5 h89, F85: $20v^{2}$ 20s 20s $c16v^{4}$ $c24s^{2}$ $c24d^{5}$ $c22d^{4}$ $c20g^{4}$ $c24g^{4}$ Apr 17] smallish gelding: modest maiden hurdler/chaser: stays 3m: raced mainly on good going or softer (acts on heavy) over jumps: tried in visor/cheekpieces. *S. A. Brookshaw* **c83** **h85**

POLLIGANA 9 b.g. Lugana Beach – Pollibrig (Politico (USA)) [2004/5 c88, h86: $c21s^{pu}$ May 11] modest novice hurdler: similar form on first of 3 starts in handicap chases: won maiden point in April: stays 3¼m: acts on good to firm going. *V. R. A. Dartnall* **c–** **h–**

POLLY COME BACK 6 br.m. Bob's Return (IRE) – Brown Coast (Oats) [2004/5 F17d Oct 17] rather unfurnished mare: sixth foal: half-sister to fair hunter chaser Phoenix **F–**

Phlyer (by Ardross), probably stays 3m: dam unraced: little form in points: tailed off in maiden bumper. *W. S. Kittow*

POLLYS ANGEL 6 b.m. Makbul – Wayzgoose (USA) (Diesis) [2004/5 20mpu Apr 10] sister to modest hurdler Rookery Lad, effective from 2m to 2¾m: no show in maidens on Flat or over hurdles (headstrong) nearly 3 years apart. *C. N. Kellett* **h–**

POLLY WHITEFOOT 6 b.m. Perpendicular – Cream O The Border (Meadowbrook) [2004/5 F17d6 F16s* F16g 20vpu 16v5 Jan 10] first foal: dam poor maiden hurdler: easily best effort in bumpers when winning at Perth in August: little show in novice hurdles. *R. A. Fahey* **h– F88**

POLY AMANSHAA (IRE) 13 b. or br.g. Nashamaa – Mombones (Lord Gayle (USA)) [2004/5 c109§, h–: 19g c19d c21g3 c21d4 Mar 28] workmanlike gelding: winning hurdler/chaser, well beaten in 2004/5: stays 21f: acts on firm and soft going. *M. C. Banks* **c85 h–**

POLYPHON (FR) 7 b.g. Murmure (FR) – Petite Folie (Salmon Leap (USA)) [2004/5 c85, h74: c16g2 16m6 c16m5 c16g2 c16m2 c16s2 c16m* c16d5 c16v2 c16s* Apr 10] poor form both outings over hurdles in Britain: fair chaser: won handicap at Musselburgh in November and novice at Hexham (easily) in April: best at 2m: acts on heavy and good to firm going: sound jumper: consistent, though has often found little. *P. Monteith* **c106 h71**

POM FLYER (FR) 5 b.g. Broadway Flyer (USA) – Pomme d'Emeraude (FR) (Margouillat (FR)) [2004/5 F16v 16d 16s5 18v4 16v* 16v2 16s Mar 29] leggy gelding: seventh foal: half-brother to 5 winners, including 17f hurdle/9f winner Pommier Blanc (by Balleroy): dam, won over 6f on only start, out of half-sister to high-class middle-distance colts Apple Tree and Noir Et Or: mid-division in bumper on debut: fairly useful hurdler: easily won 25-runner maiden at Naas in February: better form in similar event and minor contest start either side: let down by jumping last 2 outings, including in valuable novice at Punchestown in late-April: likely to prove best around 2m: raced on going softer than good (acts on heavy). *F. Flood, Ireland* **h117 F78**

POMPEII (IRE) 8 b.g. Salse (USA) – Before Dawn (USA) (Raise A Cup (USA)) [2004/5 h83: 19m 21d4 21vpu 16v5 Jan 15] neat gelding: poor hurdler: stays 21f: acts on firm and soft going: tongue tied once. *A. J. Lockwood* **h76**

PONDERON 5 ch.g. Hector Protector (USA) – Blush Rambler (IRE) (Blushing Groom (FR)) [2004/5 16s Mar 6] lengthy gelding: useful on Flat (stays 2m) at 3 yrs, best effort in 2004 when sixth in Chester Cup, left F. J. Houghton after running as if amiss next time: eighth of 16 in novice at Kempton on hurdling debut: likely to benefit from greater test of stamina. *Mrs P. Robeson* **h103 p**

PONTIFF (IRE) 5 b.g. Alflora (IRE) – Northwood May (Teenoso (USA)) [2004/5 F18s* Feb 14] first foal: dam unraced half-sister to useful hurdler/high-class chaser Hand Inn Hand, stays 25f, from family of Champion Hurdle winners Morley Street and Granville Again: won 9-runner bumper at Plumpton on debut in February, tapped for speed 6f out but staying on to lead 1f out and beat Mighty Matters 6 lengths. *M. Pitman* **F98**

PONTIUS 8 b.g. Terimon – Coole Pilate (Celtic Cone) [2004/5 c104x, h–: c24dpu c24gpu Oct 9] tall, leggy gelding: fair hurdler/chaser: ran as if amiss both starts in 2004/5: stays 27f: raced mainly on good/good to soft going: usually makes mistakes over fences. *N. A. Twiston-Davies* **c– x h–**

POOR TACTIC'S (IRE) 9 b.g. Commanche Run – Hilary's Image (IRE) (Phardante (FR)) [2004/5 21d 20vpu 16v 20v 16v 22g2 Mar 12] won maiden point in 2002: poor maiden hurdler: stays 2¾m: acts on heavy going. *J. J. Lambe, Ireland* **h74**

POP GUN 6 ch.g. Pharly (FR) – Angel Fire (Nashwan (USA)) [2004/5 h75: 17mpu May 23] sturdy gelding: poor novice hurdler. *Miss K. Marks* **h–**

POPSI'S CLOGGS 13 ch.g. Joli Wasfi (USA) – Popsi's Poppet (Hill Clown (USA)) [2004/5 24fpu c26mur c24mR c24dR c18dpu Nov 14] big, lengthy gelding: lightly raced over hurdles: ungenuine winning chaser, no sign of retaining ability. *R. Curtis* **c– § h–**

PORAK (IRE) 8 ch.g. Perugino (USA) – Gayla Orchestra (Lord Gayle (USA)) [2004/5 h–: c16s4 c20sF c17d4 c16d4 Jan 6] close-coupled gelding: fairly useful hurdler at best: off 18 months, considerately handled when fourth of 5 in handicap at Lingfield on chasing debut: let down by jumping after: raced mainly around 2m: acts on soft going. *G. L. Moore* **c103 x h–**

PORLOCK HILL 11 b.g. Petoski – Gay Ticket (New Member) [2004/5 c21gpu Jul 12] tall, angular gelding: winning pointer: little ability otherwise. *C. L. Popham* **c– x h–**

PORNIC (FR) 11 b.g. Shining Steel – Marie de Geneve (FR) (Nishapour (FR)) [2004/5 c80§, h86§: c21d^F c24d³ c21m* c22m³ c16g c16m³ c16d⁴ c20m⁴ c19g^pu c20g⁶ c24m³ c22s² c21v^ur c20g^pu c16v^pu Apr 17] workmanlike gelding: poor handicap chaser: won at Sedgefield in May: probably stays easy 3m: acts on good to firm and heavy going: tried visored, not since 1999/00: ungenuine. *A. Crook* **c82 § h– §**

PORTANT FELLA 6 b.g. Greensmith – Jubilata (USA) (The Minstrel (CAN)) [2004/5 h116: 16g⁴ 16g⁴ 17g² 16g 16g* 16g 16s c17s⁶ Apr 13] rather leggy gelding: fairly useful on Flat (best around 1m), successful twice in 2004: fairly useful handicap hurdler: won at Tramore in August: remote sixth in maiden at Fairyhouse on chasing debut: raced around 2m: acts on firm going, probably on soft: tried tongue tied: usually waited with: should do better over fences. *Ms J. Morgan, Ireland* **c– p h121**

PORTAVADIE 6 b.g. Rakaposhi King – Woodland Flower (Furry Glen) [2004/5 F16s³ F16d² F16v⁴ F16d* 16d* Apr 11] 22,000 4-y-o: lengthy gelding: fourth foal: half-brother to fair hurdler/fairly useful chaser Stamparland Hill (by Gildoran), barely stays 25f: dam winning staying hurdler/chaser: fairly useful form in bumpers, winning at Haydock in February: won 18-runner novice at Kelso on hurdling debut, jumping well, leading on bridle 2 out and beating Fencote 7 lengths with plenty in hand: bred to stay 2½m: sure to improve. *J. M. Jefferson* **h106 p F95**

PORTAVO (IRE) 5 b.g. Luso – Inchriver (IRE) (Over The River (FR)) [2004/5 F16s⁶ 21d^F 19s Jan 3] workmanlike gelding: second foal: half-brother to winning 2m hurdler Gotham (by Gothland): dam unraced, from family of top-class staying chaser Righthand Man: thrice-raced in Irish points in 2004, winning maiden in October: sixth of 12 in bumper at Windsor: considerately handled both starts in novice hurdles: probably capable of better. *Miss H. C. Knight* **h– p F86**

PORT FONTAINE (IRE) 5 b.g. College Chapel – Seaward (Slip Anchor) [2004/5 F16g Oct 5] 7,000 4-y-o: third foal: half-brother to winner in Italy by Dilum: dam, fair maiden on Flat/over hurdles, half-sister to high-class 2m hurdler Intersky Falcon: tailed off in bumper on debut. *M. J. Ryan* **F–**

PORTHILLY BAY 5 b.g. Primitive Rising (USA) – Threewaygirl (Orange Bay) [2004/5 F16d 22s 21d⁴ 24d⁶ 24d⁵ Apr 20] sturdy gelding: has scope: fifth foal: half-brother to 2½m hurdle winner Alderburn (by Alderbrook): dam 2¼m hurdle winner: soundly beaten in bumper: poor form over hurdles: may prove best short of 3m. *H. D. Daly* **h85 + F–**

PORTICHOL PRINCESS 5 b.m. Bluegrass Prince (IRE) – Barbrallen (Rambo Dancer (CAN)) [2004/5 h–: 16s 22s^pu Jan 1] no form: tried tongue tied. *R. M. Stronge* **h–**

PORT MORENO (IRE) 5 b.g. Turtle Island (IRE) – Infra Blue (IRE) (Bluebird (USA)) [2004/5 h93: 17d⁴ 16d² 16v* 17m* 21g 24m² 16m² 21g⁵ Jul 16] modest hurdler: won amateur seller at Towcester and novice at Sedgefield in May: claimed £6,000 final outing (visored): best around 2m: acts on heavy and good to firm going: usually blinkered: temperament under suspicion. *J. G. M. O'Shea* **h96**

POSH CRACK 5 b.m. Rakaposhi King – First Crack (Scallywag) [2004/5 F17g F16g Jan 24] second foal: half-sister to bumper winner Firstflor (by Alflora): dam, fair hurdler, stayed 3m: well held in bumpers. *F. Jordan* **F–**

POSH STICK 8 b.m. Rakaposhi King – Carat Stick (Gold Rod) [2004/5 h65: 16f c20d³ c20d^ur c21d* c22v^F c16v⁶ 16s⁴ c20v* c20d³ c16v* c20s³ Apr 22] sturdy mare: poor maiden hurdler: fair chaser: won maiden at Cartmel in August and handicaps at Carlisle in March and April: stays 21f: acts on heavy going, probably on good to firm. *J. B. Walton* **c102 h67**

POSITIVE PROFILE (IRE) 7 b.g. Definite Article – Leyete Gulf (IRE) (Slip Anchor) [2004/5 h116: c24g^ur c24g^pu c19d^F 25d Feb 4] rather sparely-made gelding: failed to complete in 3 maiden chases, though was staying on just behind leaders when falling 3 out at Catterick: fairly useful hurdler, reportedly suffered hair-line fracture of pelvis final outing: barely stays 25f: acts on good to soft going: carries head high. *P. C. Haslam* **c100 ? h–**

POSSEXTOWN (IRE) 7 b.g. Lord Americo – Tasse du The (Over The River (FR)) [2004/5 c20s³ c20d^pu Nov 29] big, lengthy, good sort: second foal: dam fair hunter chaser: won second of 2 starts in maiden Irish points in 2004: shaped well when third of 4 finishers to Joes Edge in novice at Ayr on chasing debut, jumping well in lead until mistake 2 out: bled from nose next time. *N. G. Richards* **c121**

POST IT 4 b.f. Thowra (FR) – Cream By Post (Torus) [2004/5 F17s F13s F14m* Mar 21] sixth foal: half-sister to bumper winner Mister Wellard (by Sir Harry Lewis): dam, winning hurdler/fair pointer, out of half-sister to useful hurdler/chaser up to 25f Gallaher: **F84**

best effort in bumpers when winning maiden at Hereford in March by length from Zanzibar Boy: bred to stay much further than 1¾m. *R. J. Hodges*

POTOFFAIRIES (IRE) 10 ch.g. Montelimar (USA) – Ladycastle (Pitpan) [2004/5 c24v^{5} c23d^{6} c26v^{3} c27v^{6} Jan 11] good-topped ex-Irish gelding: fair hurdler/maiden chaser: well held in 2004/5, left Mrs S. Bramall after first outing: should stay beyond 3m: raced on good going or softer (acts on heavy): often blinkered. *Miss H. C. Knight* **c– h–**

POTTER'S WHEEL 6 b.g. Elmaamul (USA) – Bewitch (Idiot's Delight) [2004/5 F16d Jan 6] second foal: dam, second from 2 starts in bumpers, half-sister to one-time useful hurdler/chaser First Love, from family of Spanish Steps: failed to complete in 4 maiden points in 2004: tailed off in bumper. *T. Wall* **F–**

POTTS OF MAGIC 6 b.g. Classic Cliche (IRE) – Potter's Gale (IRE) (Strong Gale) [2004/5 F71: F16g 20s 21d 24d Mar 12] poor form in bumpers: well beaten over hurdles. *R. Lee* **h– F–**

POTTSY'S JOY 8 b.g. Syrtos – Orange Spice (Orange Bay) [2004/5 h93, F–: 21g 16s^{5} 19s 24d^{3} 25g* 25s 24s^{pu} Apr 16] workmanlike gelding: modest novice hurdler: won conditional jockeys handicap at Catterick in December: stays 25f: best efforts on good/good to soft going (no form on soft): not a fluent jumper. *Mrs S. J. Smith* **h89**

POUGATCHEVA (FR) 6 ch.m. Epervier Bleu – Notabilite (FR) (No Pass No Sale) [2004/5 h94: 16v* c20d^{5} 19s^{6} c21v^{3} c22s^{ur} c24v^{3} c25s^{3} c24v^{pu} Apr 17] small, close-coupled mare: fair handicap hurdler: won at Towcester in May: only modest form and largely let down by jumping over fences: stays 21f: acts on heavy going, seemingly not on good to firm. *Miss Venetia Williams* **c86 x h102**

POUNSLEY MILL (IRE) 12 b.g. Asir – Clonroche Abendego (Pauper) [2004/5 c96, h–: c20d^{3} c21d^{pu} c20d^{5} c22s^{4} c20s^{5} c22s^{3} c26m^{pu} Apr 21] sturdy gelding: modest handicap chaser: form in 2004/5 only on reappearance: stays 21f: acts on heavy and good to firm going: tried in cheekpieces. *N. J. Gifford* **c90 d h–**

POURQUOI 5 ch.m. King's Signet (USA) – Stravano (Handsome Sailor) [2004/5 F17g Oct 9] second foal: dam no form on Flat: well tailed off in mares bumper on debut. *C. W. Moore* **F–**

POWDER CREEK (IRE) 8 b.g. Little Bighorn – Our Dorcet (Condorcet (FR)) [2004/5 h96: 20d* 16d 20s^{pu} c20d c16g^{4} c25s^{4} c20s^{4} c24s^{pu} c24g^{3} c20s^{4} c16s* c18m^{2} c17d* c20s^{2} Apr 20] well-made gelding: fair hurdler: won novice at Wetherby very early in season: improved form over fences late in season, winning handicaps at Newcastle in March and Kelso in April: stays 2½m: acts on soft and good to firm going: patiently ridden: has finished weakly. *K. G. Reveley* **c113 h109 §**

POWER AND DEMAND 8 b.g. Formidable (USA) – Mazurkanova (Song) [2004/5 19g^{pu} 16m 16m^{6} 16g 16m 16g^{pu} 19d^{2} 17v^{4} 19d^{2} 19g^{5} Mar 9] good-topped gelding: poor maiden hurdler: left K. Wingrove after fourth start: stays 19f: acts on good to soft ground: tried in blinkers: has worn tongue strap: has been reluctant to race. *C. W. Thornton* **h70**

POWER BIRD (IRE) 5 b.m. Bluebird (USA) – Polynesian Goddess (IRE) (Salmon Leap (USA)) [2004/5 16g^{3} 17m^{2} 17g^{3} 20g^{2} 16g 16s^{3} 16d^{pu} Oct 31] sparely-made mare: half-sister to 3m hurdle winner Sea Squirt (by Fourstars Allstar): modest maiden on Flat (stayed 1m): poor novice hurdler, claimed from B. Johnson £6,000 on debut: likely to have proved best around 2m: acted on soft and good to firm going: usually tongue tied: dead. *R. Flint* **h80**

POWER ELITE (IRE) 5 gr.g. Linamix (FR) – Hawas (Mujtahid (USA)) [2004/5 h133: 16g 16d^{5} Feb 12] lengthy, well-made gelding: useful on Flat (signs of temperament), successful both starts in 2004: similar standard over hurdles: best effort when fifth of 25 to Essex in valuable handicap at Newbury: reportedly suffered bruised foot in mid-March: raced at 2m on good going or softer (acts on soft): may be capable of better yet. *N. Meade, Ireland* **h141**

POWERLOVE (FR) 4 b.f. Solon (GER) – Bywaldor (FR) (Magwal (FR)) [2004/5 F16g^{3} F16g^{3} F17s^{6} F16s* Apr 22] lengthy, angular filly: third foal: half-sister to Al Malak (by Scandinavian), successful up to 1½m on Flat/winning 2m hurdler: dam, in frame around 2m over jumps, sister to fairly useful hurdler around 2m Magdor: fair form in bumpers, winning at Perth in April. *Mrs S. C. Bradburne* **F86**

POWER UNIT 10 ch.g. Risk Me (FR) – Hazel Bee (Starch Reduced) [2004/5 c109x, h109: 16g^{3} 16m* 19g^{4} 16d^{3} 16d 16d Mar 14] workmanlike gelding: winning chaser, often let down by jumping: fair hurdler: won novice at Stratford in June: stays 19f: acts on good **c– x h114**

to firm and good to soft going: tried visored, effective with or without cheekpieces: usually races prominently. *Mrs D. A. Hamer*

POWRA 5 b.g. Thowra (FR) – Lake Mariner (Julio Mariner) [2004/5 F16d F17d 17s^ur 20d^pu 19g^pu Mar 3] workmanlike gelding: first foal: dam unraced: lot more temperament than ability: wore cheekpieces final outing. *R. J. Hodges* **h– § F–**

PRAIRIE FIRE 5 b.g. Commanche Run – Light Your Fire (Bay Express) [2004/5 F16g^5 May 13] sixth foal: half-brother to winning sprinter Doris Doors (by Beveled): dam maiden, best at 6f: favourite, fifth of 17 in bumper at Ludlow on debut. *H. D. Daly* **F81**

PRAIRIE MOONLIGHT (GER) 5 br.m. Monsun (GER) – Prairie Princess (GER) (Dashing Blade) [2004/5 16d* 16s^3 16g^pu 16d^5 16g^2 Apr 15] tall, unfurnished mare: successful over 1¼m at Milan on Flat at 3 yrs for M. Trinker: easily won mares novice at Hexham in October on hurdling debut: running well when going lame third outing: will prove best around 2m. *C. J. Mann* **h110**

PRAIRIE SUN (GER) 4 b.f. Law Society (USA) – Prairie Flame (IRE) (Marju (IRE)) [2004/5 17d^2 17d^2 17g^3 16s^4 17s^3 16m^2 16m* Dec 1] leggy filly: modest on Flat (stays 1¾m): fair juvenile hurdler: won at Catterick in December: will stay beyond 17f: acts on soft and good to firm going: consistent. *Mrs A. Duffield* **h99**

PRATO (GER) 5 ch.h. Kornado – Prairie Lila (GER) (Homing) [2004/5 16v* 20d^4 Apr 22] placed several times up to 1½m on Flat prior to winning 8.5f handicap at Dortmund in January: easily won maiden at Chepstow in March on hurdling debut: well held in novice there next time: will prove best around 2m: should still do better. *C. Von Der Recke, Germany* **h103 p**

PRAYERFUL 6 b.m. Syrtos – Pure Formality (Forzando) [2004/5 h81: 20s* 19d^5 24v^pu c20s^3 c21d^2 c22s^3 c18s^bd 22v^pu c22g^3 c26g^ur Apr 10] sturdy mare: maiden chaser: modest hurdler: won selling handicap (sold from R. Flint 8,300 gns) at Chepstow in May: out of form last 3 starts: stays 2½m: acts on good to firm and heavy going: tried in cheekpieces. *R. H. Alner* **c88 h88**

PRECIOUS LUCY (FR) 6 gr.m. Kadrou (FR) – Teardrops Fall (FR) (Law Society (USA)) [2004/5 h–: 17m^2 17m* 19g^4 Aug 2] ex-French mare: steady progress first 4 starts over hurdles, modest form when winning novice handicap at Hereford in June: lame next time. *C. J. Down* **h88**

PRECIOUS MYSTERY (IRE) 5 ch.m. Titus Livius (FR) – Ascoli (Skyliner) [2004/5 h99: 18d^6 Dec 7] leggy mare: fair on Flat (stays 15f), successful in March: fair hurdler as a juvenile: lacklustre display only outing in 2004/5: probably stays 19f: acts on soft going. *A. King* **h–**

PREDICAMENT 6 br.g. Machiavellian (USA) – Quandary (USA) (Blushing Groom (FR)) [2004/5 16s* Dec 1] ex-French gelding: well beaten in 3 races on Flat at 4 yrs, sold out of Mme C. Head-Maarek's stable 22,000 gns Newmarket Autumn (2003) Sales: successful in novice at Plumpton on hurdling debut, rallying to beat Talldark'n'andsome a head: open to improvement. *Jonjo O'Neill* **h111 p**

PREMIER CHEVAL (USA) 6 ch.g. Irish River (FR) – Restikarada (FR) (Akarad (FR)) [2004/5 h–: 22d^pu Feb 20] sturdy gelding: pulled up all 4 starts in novice hurdles. *R. Rowe* **h–**

PREMIER DRIVE (IRE) 12 ch.g. Black Minstrel – Ballyanihan (Le Moss) [2004/5 c–x, h91: 24d^2 23d^3 23d^2 24v^6 23s^5 20d 22d^F Apr 11] workmanlike gelding: winning chaser: modest handicap hurdler: stays 3m: raced mainly on good going or softer (acts on heavy): tried tongue tied: sketchy jumper. *G. M. Moore* **c– x h96 x**

PREMIER ESTATE (IRE) 8 b.g. Satco (FR) – Kettleby (IRE) (Tale Quale) [2004/5 h103: 18d^4 c20s^pu c21v* c18d^3 c18d^4 c22g^5 c22m^3 Apr 21] tall gelding: fair handicap hurdler: similar form in novice chases, winning 4-runner event at Folkestone in January: will stay 3m: acts on heavy going (below form on good to firm). *R. Rowe* **c107 h103**

PREMIER MARBLE (IRE) 7 ch.g. Carroll House – Thyne Please (IRE) (Good Thyne (USA)) [2004/5 21g 20d^pu 20d^ur 16g^2 21m^pu 16m 20g^3 20m^6 16d^2 c20d^6 Oct 9] sturdy ex-Irish gelding: second foal: dam showed little in 3 Irish points: poor maiden hurdler: tailed off on chasing debut: stays 2½m: acts on good to firm and good to soft going: usually tongue tied: sold 2,000 gns Doncaster October Sales, fell both starts in points in 2005. *R. C. Guest* **c– h77**

PREMIER REBEL (IRE) 7 b.g. Borovoe – Gorazhire (Pauper) [2004/5 F16g* F16m^5 F16d^3 F17d^2 F20g^2 20v 20s 16v 18s^5 20d 24d Mar 20] €4,500 4-y-o: third foal: dam placed in point: won bumper at Ballinrobe in July: best effort when runner-up at **h96 F102**

Galway fifth start: modest form in maiden hurdles: has had tongue tied, including last 3 starts. *T. Hogan, Ireland*

PRESENCE OF MIND (IRE) 7 ch.g. Presenting – Blue Rose (IRE) (Good Thyne (USA)) [2004/5 h91, F66: c23s^{pu} c24d^{3} c24g^{F} c24g* c25d^{pu} Apr 3] workmanlike gelding: in frame both completed outings in novice hurdles: modest novice chaser: won handicap at Huntingdon in March: stays 3m: acts on good to soft going, possibly not on softer: visored last 2 starts. *Miss E. C. Lavelle* **c96** **h–**

PRESENT BLEU (FR) 10 b.g. Epervier Bleu – Lointaine (USA) (Lyphard's Wish (FR)) [2004/5 c18d c17g^{4} c17g^{5} c18g^{6} c29v^{pu} c21d^{F} Apr 8] leggy gelding: useful hurdler/chaser in his prime, successful in 2002 Gran Premio di Merano: very much on downgrade: claimed from F. Kronauer €8,000 fourth start: stays 25f: acts on firm and soft going: tried blinkered/visored: has had tongue tied. *M. Scudamore* **c104 ?** **h–**

PRESENT COMPANY (IRE) 7 ch.m. Presenting – Calmount (IRE) (Callernish) [2004/5 19s^{pu} Jan 10] €16,000 4-y-o: second foal: dam unraced, from family of high-class staying chaser Marlborough: no form in 3 bumpers for E. Hales: won maiden point in 2004: failed to settle when pulled up on hurdling debut. *N. A. Twiston-Davies* **h–**

PRESENTER (IRE) 5 ch.g. Cadeaux Genereux – Moviegoer (Pharly (FR)) [2004/5 16d^{pu} 17s^{pu} Feb 17] sturdy gelding: half-brother to 3 winning hurdlers, including fair performers Mane Frame (by Unfuwain), stays 21f, and Picture Palace (by Salse), stays 3¼m: fair form in 2 starts on Flat, sold out of J. Gosden's stable 22,000 gns Newmarket Autumn (2003) Sales, well held on all-weather in 2005: mistakes both outings over hurdles, trained on debut by Mrs J. Caro. *Miss I. E. Craig* **h–**

PRESENT GLORY (IRE) 6 br.g. Presenting – Prudent Rose (IRE) (Strong Gale) [2004/5 F80: F17s^{2} F16v^{6} 22s^{3} Mar 9] lengthy gelding: chasing type: easily best effort in bumpers when second to Barrys Ark at Hereford: encouraging third of 7 to Theatre in novice at Fontwell on hurdling debut, staying on strongly after getting tapped for foot: will stay at least 3m. *C. Tinkler* **h106** **F96**

PRESENTING ALF (IRE) 5 b.g. Presenting – Hilary's Penny (Avocat) [2004/5 F16m^{2} F16s^{6} 20d 19g 19d^{4} 20d^{5} Feb 24] €5,000 3-y-o: rather unfurnished gelding: third foal: dam placed in points: runner-up in 4-runner maiden bumper at Wetherby on debut: sold out of T. Tate's stable 20,000 gns Doncaster May Sales: poor form in novice hurdles: should be suited by 2½m+. *Mrs S. J. Smith* **h85** **F80**

PRESENTING EXPRESS (IRE) 6 b.g. Presenting – Glenbane Express (IRE) (Roselier (FR)) [2004/5 20s 21d^{6} 22s c24d c20s^{3} Feb 10] €12,000 3-y-o: workmanlike gelding: first foal: dam unraced: won last of 3 starts in maiden Irish points in 2004: sold 40,000 gns Doncaster May Sales: well held in 3 starts over hurdles, though not knocked about final one: shaped better than result suggested in handicaps at Huntingdon both outings over fences, blundering 2 out on second occasion: probably capable of better. *Miss E. C. Lavelle* **c84 p** **h– p**

PRESENTINGTHECASE (IRE) 7 b.g. Presenting – Let The Hare Run (IRE) (Tale Quale) [2004/5 c–, h–: c26v^{3} c24s^{pu} c26d^{pu} Nov 23] good-topped gelding: no form: blinkered final outing: mistakes over fences. *Jonjo O'Neill* **c– x** **h–**

PRESIDIO (GER) 10 b.g. Konigsstuhl (GER) – Pradera (GER) (Abary (GER)) [2004/5 c–, h–: c16s^{3} Mar 11] close-coupled gelding: maiden hurdler: no form in chases: sold out of N. Hawke's stable £1,000 Ascot July Sales: runner-up in point in March. *S. Flook* **c–** **h–**

PRESTBURY KNIGHT 5 ch.g. Sir Harry Lewis (USA) – Lambrini (IRE) (Buckskin (FR)) [2004/5 F16g^{2} F16d F17d^{3} F18s^{6} 22s^{pu} 20s Mar 22] £15,000 4-y-o: angular gelding: second foal: dam, poor novice chaser up to 2½m, half-sister to useful but temperamental staying chaser Browjoshy: best effort in bumpers when second to The Mick Weston at Cheltenham on debut: swished tail next time: no encouragement in 2 runs over hurdles. *N. A. Twiston-Davies* **h–** **F91**

PRESTON HALL 4 b.g. Accordion – Little Preston (IRE) (Pennine Walk) [2004/5 18m^{4} 16d^{2} Oct 5] lightly-raced maiden on Flat: poor form when in frame in juvenile hurdles. *Mrs L. C. Jewell* **h74**

PRESUMPTUOUS 5 ch.g. Double Trigger (IRE) – T O O Mamma's (IRE) (Classic Secret (USA)) [2004/5 h106: 16s 16d 16v^{3} 20s 16d Apr 11] fair form in juvenile hurdles in 2003/4 for Mrs S. Smith: largely disappointing in handicaps: should stay beyond 17f. *G. M. Moore* **h97**

PRETTY BOY BLUE 10 gr.g. Portogon – Nicola Lisa (Dumbarnie) [2004/5 c–, h–: c16g 16v4 24g May 16] no sign of ability. *W. Davies* **c– h–**

PRETTY STAR (GER) 5 b.g. Lando (GER) – Pretty Ballerina (Sadler's Wells (USA)) [2004/5 16g 16d2 19g2 20g* 21d* 22d Mar 19] rather leggy gelding: useful on Flat (stays 1½m), successful 3 times in Germany at 3 yrs for E. Groschel, runner-up on British debut in August for M. Johnston: fairly useful novice hurdler: won handicaps at Sandown in February and Newbury (beat Bohemian Boy 2½ lengths) in March: should stay beyond 21f: raced on good/good to soft ground over hurdles. *A. King* **h122**

PREVEZA 6 br.m. Presidium – Ping Pong (Petong) [2004/5 16vpu Oct 30] sister to winning hurdler around 2m Ascari: no sign of ability on Flat or in selling hurdle. *R. Shiels* **h–**

PRIDE OF PENLEE 5 b.g. Pontevecchio Notte – Kindly Lady (Kind of Hush) [2004/5 F–: 16m 19fpu 17g 19d 16s5 Jan 22] no sign of ability. *J. D. Frost* **h–**

PRIDEWOOD DOVE 6 b.m. Alderbrook – Flighty Dove (Cruise Missile) [2004/5 F–: 20mro May 25] temperamental displays in varied company. *R. J. Price* **h– §**

PRIDEYEV (USA) 5 ch.g. Nureyev (USA) – Pride of Baino (USA) (Secretariat (USA)) [2004/5 16mpu Jun 16] modest form on Flat, sold out of Mrs A. Perrett's stable 4,000 gns Newmarket Autumn (2003) Sales: no show in novice claimer on hurdling debut. *B. J. Llewellyn* **h–**

PRIME COURSE (IRE) 16 b.g. Crash Course – Prime Mistress (Skymaster) [2004/5 c26m3 May 19] plain, workmanlike gelding: veteran pointer/hunter chaser: stays 3¼m: acts on good to firm and good to soft going: has had tongue tied. *Mrs A. Farrant* **c86 h–**

PRIME MINISTER 11 ch.g. Be My Chief (USA) – Classic Design (Busted) [2004/5 h70: 17d5 17g c16dpu Oct 17] angular gelding: poor maiden hurdler: no show on chasing debut: stays 19f: acts on soft and good to firm going: tried tongue tied. *G. E. Jones* **c– h–**

PRIMESHADE PROMISE 4 ch.f. Opening Verse (USA) – Bonnie Lassie (Efisio) [2004/5 17spu Nov 18] modest around 1m on Flat: no show in juvenile on hurdling debut. *D. Burchell* **h–**

PRIMITIVE COVE 4 b.g. Primitive Rising (USA) – Katie-A (IRE) (Cyrano de Bergerac) [2004/5 F13g F16s Mar 22] tall gelding: third foal: dam modest sprinter: well held in bumpers. *G. A. Swinbank* **F–**

PRIMITIVE POPPY 6 b.m. Primitive Rising (USA) – Lady Manello (Mandrake Major) [2004/5 F16s6 F16v F16g3 21v5 16d Apr 11] sixth foal: half-sister to 3 winners, including fair staying chaser Miss Royello (by Royal Fountain): dam, placed over hurdles, half-sister to fairly useful chasers up to 25f Sword Beach and Divet Hill: form only when sixth in mares bumper at Newcastle on debut. *Mrs A. Hamilton* **h– F81**

PRIMITIVE REBEL 6 gr.g. Primitive Rising (USA) – Distant Cherry (General Ironside) [2004/5 F17v5 F16s5 Nov 13] rangy gelding: fourth foal: dam, poor novice staying hurdler/chaser, half-sister to fairly useful staying chaser Royal Tommy: modest form on second of 2 outings in bumpers: will be suited by further. *H. P. Hogarth* **F84**

PRIMITIVE RITES 8 b.g. Primitive Rising (USA) – Sun Goddess (FR) (Deep Roots) [2004/5 c–: c25v2 c26dpu c26dur c27vpu Mar 15] workmanlike gelding: winning pointer: second of 5 to Next To Nothing at Ayr, only completion in hunters. *M. J. Brown* **c87**

PRIMITIVE SATIN 10 ch.g. Primitive Rising (USA) – Satinanda (Leander) [2004/5 c–: c25g3 c25dpu c25mpu May 19] modest hunter chaser: stays 25f: acts on good to soft going: wears blinkers. *Mrs R. Tate* **c78**

PRIMITIVE WAY 13 b.g. Primitive Rising (USA) – Potterway (Velvet Prince) [2004/5 c95: c25m2 c25m2 c22v2 c24v3 c21spu Mar 11] sturdy gelding: modest chaser: left Miss S. Forster after third start: runner-up in point in February: ran poorly in 2 hunter chases: stays 3¼m: acts on any going: wears headgear. *C. Storey* **c95**

PRIMROSE PARK 6 b.m. Thowra (FR) – Redgrave Rose (Tug of War) [2004/5 F16m 24g5 Jul 14] fifth foal: half-sister to winning 2m hurdler Redgrave Wolf (by Little Wolf): dam winning staying hurdler/chaser: well held in bumper and novice hurdle. *K. Bishop* **h– F–**

PRINCE ADJAL (IRE) 5 b.g. Desert Prince (IRE) – Adjalisa (IRE) (Darshaan) [2004/5 h90: 16s4 16m6 17v 21v 19d 16v Feb 19] poor handicap hurdler: mainly well held in 2004/5: best at 2m: acts on firm and soft going: headstrong. *G. M. Moore* **h84**

PRINCE ALBERT 7 ch.g. Rock City – Russell Creek (Sandy Creek) [2004/5 16dF Jun 23] poor maiden on Flat (stays 1¼m): thrice-raced hurdler: will probably prove best around 2m. *J. R. Jenkins* **h–**

PRINCE AMONG MEN 8 b.g. Robellino (USA) – Forelino (USA) (Trempolino (USA)) [2004/5 h114: 16g² 16f* 16g² 16g 19g 16m Oct 13] angular gelding: fairly useful handicap hurdler: won at Perth in June by short head from Kniaz: good second to Dancer Life there, only subsequent form: raced mainly around 2m: has form on any going, raced mainly on good or firmer nowadays: tried visored: has idled/found little. *N. G. Richards* **h118**

PRINCE ANGOT 4 b.g. Princely Heir (IRE) – Mam'zelle Angot (Balidar) [2004/5 F13d³ Dec 3] third foal: dam, 8.3f/9.4f winner, half-sister to smart stayer Sir Michael: played up in preliminaries when third to There Is No Doubt in 3-y-o bumper at Exeter on debut. *M. D. I. Usher* **F94**

PRINCE DOMINO 6 b.g. Primo Dominie – Danzig Harbour (USA) (Private Account (USA)) [2004/5 16f⁵ 20m⁶ 17d⁵ 19s⁴ 17s³ 16v³ 16d⁶ 20g* Jan 24] smallish gelding: fair on Flat (stays 8.5f) at 4 yrs, sold out of G. L. Moore's stable £2,000 Ascot February (2004) Sales: modest hurdler: won novice handicap at Southwell in January: stays easy 2½m: acts on heavy ground: tongue tied on debut: has found little. *C. Roberts* **h87**

PRINCE DUNDEE (FR) 10 ch.g. Ecossais (FR) – Princesse Normande (FR) (Belgio (FR)) [2004/5 c16s³ c19vpu Mar 30] angular gelding: winning hurdler/maiden chaser: usually blinkered/visored before 2004/5: has had tongue tied: makes mistakes over fences: ungenuine. *M. Keighley* **c– x** **h– §**

PRINCE DU SOLEIL (FR) 9 b.g. Cardoun (FR) – Revelry (FR) (Blakeney) [2004/5 h75: 16d 16s Nov 21] close-coupled gelding: poor and ungenuine on Flat (stays 1m) nowadays: maiden hurdler: pulls hard. *J. R. Jenkins* **h–**

PRINCE HIGHLIGHT (IRE) 10 b.g. Lord Americo – Madamme Highlights (Andretti) [2004/5 c21s² c24g³ c26m³ c20gpu 23s⁵ c25d* c27g³ c25dF c25sF c30d c23spu c25gpu Apr 17] sturdy gelding: modest hurdler: fair handicap chaser: won weak event at Folkestone in November: stays 27f: acts on heavy and good to firm going: tried blinkered/ in cheekpieces: weak finisher. *Ms Bridget Nicholls* **c105 d** **h–**

PRINCE HOLING 5 ch.g. Halling (USA) – Ella Mon Amour (Ela-Mana-Mou) [2004/5 h–: 16mpu 17m Aug 6] angular gelding: fair on Flat (stayed 1½m) in 2004: jumped poorly and no form over hurdles: left Miss V. Williams before final start: tried tongue tied: dead. *M. Todhunter* **h– x**

PRINCE IVOR 5 b.g. Polar Falcon (USA) – Mistook (USA) (Phone Trick (USA)) [2004/5 h–: 17d 16f 16mpu 18spu 16s 19dpu 24gpu Apr 7] poor and ungenuine maiden on Flat: no form over hurdles, left M. Gingell after fifth start: tried in headgear: has had tongue tied. *P. R. Rodford* **h–**

PRINCE MANDALA (IRE) 8 bl.g. Mandalus – Lady Red (Red Regent) [2004/5 F18s 20m⁴ 18s Dec 18] IR 9,500 3-y-o: half-brother to winning pointer by Tanfirion: dam unraced: placed twice from 7 starts in maiden Irish points: well beaten in bumper: poor form when fourth in maiden at Musselburgh on hurdling debut. *C. A. McBratney, Ireland* **h82 ?** **F–**

PRINCE NASSEEM (GER) 8 b.h. Neshad (USA) – Penola (GER) (Acatenango (GER)) [2004/5 h–: 22spu 21g 16spu 16s Dec 28] good-topped horse: no form over hurdles: wore headgear last 3 starts. *A. G. Juckes* **h–**

PRINCE OF ARAGON 9 b.g. Aragon – Queens Welcome (Northfields (USA)) [2004/5 20g⁶ 16m* c20f⁵ Sep 5] leggy gelding: poor hurdler: won selling handicap at Worcester in August: well held in novice handicap there on chasing debut: stays easy 2½m: acts on good to firm going: tongue tied last 2 starts. *Miss Suzy Smith* **c–** **h73**

PRINCE OF PERILS 11 b.g. Lord Bud – Kumari Peril (Rebel Prince) [2004/5 c–, h79: 20spu 20vpu 21vpu 27vpu Mar 15] sturdy gelding: fell in hunter only start over fences: winning hurdler: no show in 2004/5: stays 27f: raced on going softer than good. *J. S. Haldane* **c–** **h–**

PRINCE OF PERSIA 5 b.g. Turtle Island (IRE) – Sianiski (Niniski (USA)) [2004/5 h97: 16d² 17d² 16m 16dbd 21s³ 16d² 17mpu 20d* Apr 20] leggy, close-coupled gelding: fair handicap hurdler: won at Worcester in April, despite jumping right latter stages: stays 2½m: acts on soft going, poor efforts on good to firm: wears cheekpieces. *R. S. Brookhouse* **h109**

PRINCE OF PLEASURE (IRE) 11 b.g. Spanish Place (USA) – Oronocco Gift (Camden Town) [2004/5 c119, h105: c20g* 20m⁵ 16d² c22m 20d⁵ c19s³ 18s c16s Mar 13] good-topped gelding: modest hurdler: fairly useful handicap chaser: effective at 2m to 2½m: probably acts on any going: front runner. *D. Broad, Ireland* **c118** **h98**

PRINCE OF SLANE 6 b.g. Prince Daniel (USA) – Singing Slane (Cree Song) [2004/5 F84: 20gpu 16g⁵ 20m⁴ 22mpu 20s 19m³ 21d⁵ c19g³ c24g² c24mF c25g² Mar 9] **c90** **h80**

short-backed gelding: poor maiden hurdler: modest form over fences: stays 25f: acts on soft and good to firm going. *G. A. Swinbank*

PRINCE OF TARA (IRE) 8 b.g. Prince of Birds (USA) – Fete Champetre (Welsh Pageant) [2004/5 h127: c24s* 24s c24s^2 Oct 30] strong, workmanlike gelding: fairly useful hurdler in 2003/4: fair form both starts over fences, successful in maiden at Roscommon in September: stays 3m: raced on good going or softer (acts on heavy). *P. O. Brady, Ireland* **c114 h–**

PRINCE OF THE WOOD (IRE) 5 ch.g. Woodborough (USA) – Ard Dauphine (IRE) (Forest Wind (USA)) [2004/5 h85: 20g* 24f* 24s^{pu} 24g^5 Mar 19] strong, close-coupled gelding: modest on Flat (stays 17f): modest hurdler: won maiden at Bangor in August and novice at Worcester in September: stays 3m: acts on firm ground: wore cheekpieces in 2004/5. *A. Bailey* **h93**

PRINCE RENESIS 4 b.g. Mind Games – Stoneydale (Tickled Pink) [2004/5 16d Jan 13] angular gelding: poor maiden on Flat (stays 8.6f): tailed off in juvenile seller on hurdling debut. *I. W. McInnes* **h–**

PRINCE ROSCOE 9 b.g. Roscoe Blake – Standard Breakfast (Busted) [2004/5 16v^4 20s* 18s^2 20s Dec 12] fifth foal: dam 1½m winner on Flat, proved disappointing: bumper winner: no form over fences in 2002/3: fairly useful hurdler: won maiden at Clonmel in November: stays 2½m: acts on heavy going. *D. E. Fitzgerald, Ireland* **c– h117**

PRINCE SANDROVITCH (IRE) 11 b.g. Camden Town – Devon Royale (Le Prince) [2004/5 c–, h–: 24s^{pu} May 5] useful-looking gelding: winning hurdler/pointer: no form in chases: stays 21f: acts on soft going: tried in cheekpieces. *Mrs Jane Galpin* **c– h–**

PRINCE SLAYER 9 b.g. Batshoof – Top Sovereign (High Top) [2004/5 h82: 16s^4 16d^5 16s^2 18s 16g Mar 18] poor maiden handicap hurdler: best at 2m: acts on heavy and good to firm going: tried in blinkers/cheekpieces: has had tongue tied. *T. P. McGovern* **h78**

PRINCESS AIMEE 5 b.m. Wizard King – Off The Air (IRE) (Taufan (USA)) [2004/5 h–: 20m^{pu} 16m 16g^3 17d* 17g^4 18s* 21d^{pu} Nov 1] poor hurdler: won selling handicaps at Market Rasen in August and Fontwell (conditional jockeys) in October: should stay beyond 2¼m: acts on soft going: wore cheekpieces last 4 starts: signs of temperament. *P. Bowen* **h84**

PRINCESSE GREC (FR) 7 b.m. Grand Tresor (FR) – Perimele (FR) (Mon Fils) [2004/5 c70, h–: 19m* 16g^2 20m* c16m* c20m^2 c20g* c24g^2 Oct 7] plain mare: modest handicap hurdler/chaser: left Dr P. Pritchard and much improved, winning over hurdles at Hereford (mares) in May and Hexham (novice) in June, and over fences at Worcester in June (novice) and August: should stay beyond 2½m: acts on soft and good to firm going. *M. Scudamore* **c96 h90**

PRINCESS ISMENE 4 b.f. Sri Pekan (USA) – Be Practical (Tragic Role (USA)) [2004/5 17s^6 17m^6 16d^{pu} Feb 19] leggy filly: poor and temperamental on Flat (barely stays 1¼m): little form over hurdles, trained first 2 starts by M. Appleby: virtually refused to race final outing: best left alone. *Mrs H. Dalton* **h70 §**

PRINCESS PEA 5 b.m. Shareef Dancer (USA) – Super Sol (Rolfe (USA)) [2004/5 F16g^6 F16d^5 F17g Apr 14] smallish mare: sixth foal: half-sister to several winners, including one-time fairly useful hurdler Homeleigh Mooncoin (by Jamesmead), stays 3¼m: dam winning selling hurdler: well held in 3 bumpers. *Mrs L. Wadham* **F–**

PRINCESS STEPHANIE 7 b.m. Shaab – Waterloo Princess (IRE) (Le Moss) [2004/5 h–, F–: c17m^F 18s^6 16s^2 16s 16v 16g^{pu} Dec 28] poor maiden hurdler: in cheekpieces, fell eighth on chasing debut: also tried visored. *M. J. Gingell* **c– h66**

PRINCE VALENTINE 4 b.g. My Best Valentine – Affaire de Coeur (Imperial Fling (USA)) [2004/5 16s^5 16d 16s 16d Apr 18] modest maiden on Flat (stays 1¼m): poor juvenile hurdler: tongue tied last 2 starts. *D. B. Feek* **h78**

PRINCIPE AZZURRO (FR) 4 b.g. Pistolet Bleu (IRE) – Massalia (GER) (Leone (GER)) [2004/5 F16s^4 Feb 18] leggy gelding: second foal: half-brother to fairly useful French hurdler/winner up to 15f on Flat Forges Gold (by Java Gold): dam, successful up to 11f on Flat in Germany, half-sister to Preis der Diana winner Majoritat, dam of useful 2m hurdler Major Lando: staying-on fourth to Mendo in bumper at Sandown on debut. *H. D. Daly* **F99**

PRINS WILLEM (IRE) 6 b.g. Alzao (USA) – American Garden (USA) (Alleged (USA)) [2004/5 16d* 16d^2 16d^2 16g^4 21m* Apr 13] good-topped gelding: useful on Flat (stays 2m): useful novice hurdler: won at Huntingdon in November and Cheltenham (comfortably by 6 lengths from Alderburn) in April: best effort when 10½ lengths fourth **h133**

Mr Chris van Hoorn's "Prins Willem"

to Arcalis in Supreme Novices' Hurdle at Cheltenham, nearest at finish: stays 21f: unraced on extremes of going: tongue tied last 2 outings. *J. R. Fanshawe*

PRIORS DALE 5 b.g. Lahib (USA) – Mathaayl (USA) (Shadeed (USA)) [2004/5 16s^{3} 17g 16v* Jan 17] fair maiden up to 1¼m on Flat for K. Bell: best effort over hurdles when winning novice at Plumpton in January, making most to beat Migwell 8 lengths: likely to prove best around 2m: should progress further. *Miss E. C. Lavelle* **h120 p**

PRISCILLA 7 b.m. Teenoso (USA) – Dubacilla (Dubassoff (USA)) [2004/5 19v^{5} 19d^{4} 19m^{2} 21m^{pu} Apr 2] lengthy mare: second foal: half-sister to winning pointer Cillamon (by Terimon) and useful bumper winner Mister Quasimodo (by Busy Flight): dam, top-class staying chaser, half-sister to Grand National runner-up Just So: modest form at best over hurdles: should be suited by 2½m+. *K. Bishop* **h92**

PRIVATE BENJAMIN 5 gr.g. Ridgewood Ben – Jilly Woo (Environment Friend) [2004/5 h92: 16m^{ur} Sep 19] leggy gelding: modest on Flat (stays 2m): thrice-raced winning hurdler: prominent when unseated 3 out in handicap at Plumpton only start in 2004/5: will prove best around 2m. *Jamie Poulton* **h92 ?**

PRIVATE JESSICA 4 ch.f. Cadeaux Genereux – Rose Bay (Shareef Dancer (USA)) [2004/5 16g^{6} 16d 18d 16s 16g^{3} 17s^{3} 17m^{5} Apr 23] angular filly: modest maiden on Flat (stays 7f), sold out of J. Fanshawe's stable 4,000 gns Newmarket Autumn Sales: poor maiden hurdler: likely to prove best at 2m: acts on soft going, probably on good to firm. *R. C. Guest* **h75**

PRIVATE NOTE 5 b.g. Accordion – Lady Geneva (Royalty) [2004/5 F16d^{6} F17s^{2} Jan 10] half-brother to several winners, including useful 2½m hurdler Arkley Royal (by Ardross) and fairly useful staying hurdler/winning chaser Buck's Palace (by Buckley): dam, placed over hurdles, half-sister to useful 2m jumper Kescast: easily better effort in bumpers when second to Little Saltee at Taunton. *S. Pike* **F81**

PRIZE RING 6 ch.g. Bering – Spot Prize (USA) (Seattle Dancer (USA)) [2004/5 h95: 16d* 17m* 20m³ 17v⁶ 16g Mar 26] leggy gelding: fair handicap hurdler: won at Wetherby and Sedgefield (third course success) in May: stays easy 2½m: acts on good to firm and good to soft going, probably on heavy. *G. M. Moore* **h105**

PROBUS LORD 10 b.g. Rough Stones – Decoyanne (Decoy Boy) [2004/5 h93: 22dᵖᵘ c25sᵖᵘ c25mᵖᵘ 24dᵖᵘ Apr 20] quite good-topped gelding: maiden hurdler: off 18 months, no form in 2004/5, including over fences: stays 27f: acts on soft and good to firm going. *C. J. Down* **c– h–**

PROCREATE (IRE) 5 b.g. Among Men (USA) – Woodbury Princess (Never So Bold) [2004/5 16gᵖᵘ Sep 23] poor maiden on Flat: failed to settle when pulled up in novice on hurdling debut. *P. Monteith* **h–**

PRO DANCER (USA) 7 b. or br.g. Pleasant Tap (USA) – Shihama (USA) (Shadeed (USA)) [2004/5 c17f² c16m³ c18mᵖᵘ 16s⁵ c16s* Oct 17] sturdy gelding: winning hurdler: fair chaser: won listed handicap at Cork in October by 1½ lengths from City Hall: raced mainly around 2m: acts on any going. *P. M. J. Doyle, Ireland* **c111 h96**

PROFOWENS (IRE) 7 b.g. Welsh Term – Cutty Sark (Strong Gale) [2004/5 F89: 20d⁴ 20s⁴ 20d⁶ 22s Dec 5] workmanlike gelding: modest novice hurdler: should stay beyond 2½m: raced on good going or softer: has carried head high. *P. Beaumont* **h95**

PROGRESSIVE (IRE) 7 ch.g. Be My Native (USA) – Move Forward (Deep Run) [2004/5 F109p: 20s⁵ 21d* 16v⁴ Dec 18] won bumper impressively on debut in 2003/4: fair form in novice hurdles, successful at Plumpton in November, despite mistakes last 2: soon plenty to do when only fourth to Roman Ark at Haydock: stays 2½m: raced on going softer than good: probably capable of better. *Jonjo O'Neill* **h103 p**

PROKOFIEV (USA) 9 br.g. Nureyev (USA) – Aviara (USA) (Cox's Ridge (USA)) [2004/5 c113§, h–§: c26d⁴ c28s* c29dᵖᵘ c24gᵖᵘ c24mᵖᵘ Apr 2] angular gelding: fairly useful handicap chaser: frequently takes little interest, form in 2004/5 only when winning at Stratford in October: stays 3½m: acts on good to firm and heavy going: blinkered: has had tongue tied: one to leave alone. *Jonjo O'Neill* **c117 § h– §**

PROMALEE (IRE) 13 b.g. Homo Sapien – Oralee (Prominer) [2004/5 c21sᵘʳ Apr 7] good-topped gelding: formerly smart chaser, lightly raced and nowhere near so good nowadays: winning pointer: unseated first in Fox Hunters' at Aintree: stays 3m: raced on good going or softer (acts on heavy): carries head high under pressure. *J. J. Lambe, Ireland* **c– h–**

PROMINENT PROFILE (IRE) 12 ch.g. Mazaad – Nakuru (IRE) (Mandalus) [2004/5 c122, h–: c24gᶠ c23sᵘʳ c24s² c24d c26v² c26v⁶ c24g⁵ Mar 19] angular gelding: fairly useful handicap chaser: creditable efforts in 2004/5 only when runner-up at Windsor and Chepstow: stays 3¼m: acts on good to firm and heavy going: tried blinkered: front runner: sketchy jumper. *N. A. Twiston-Davies* **c119 x h–**

PROMISES 5 b.m. Nashwan (USA) – Balliasta (USA) (Lyphard (USA)) [2004/5 F76: F16g 16s 17sᶠ Apr 2] modest in bumpers: no aptitude for hurdling. *D. Shaw* **h– F–**

PROMISE TO BE GOOD 4 b.g. Unfuwain (USA) – Kshessinskaya (Hadeer) [2004/5 F16s² F17d Apr 9] good-topped gelding: fourth foal: half-brother to winner up to 1½m abroad by Shareef Dancer: dam useful 11.5f winner: 4 lengths second to Glasker Mill in bumper at Kempton on debut: well held in Grade 2 at Aintree. *N. J. Henderson* **F99**

PROPER POSER (IRE) 9 b.g. Posen (USA) – Dahar's Love (USA) (Dahar (USA)) [2004/5 c23vᵖᵘ c19gᶠ c16g⁵ Mar 9] ex-Irish gelding: poor form over hurdles: left P. Brady and off 3 years, no show over fences. *M. C. Chapman* **c– h–**

PROPER PRIMITIVE 12 gr.m. Primitive Rising (USA) – Nidd Bridges (Grey Ghost) [2004/5 c20gᵖᵘ May 13] leggy mare: no longer of account outside points. *Miss W. M. Bayliss* **c– h–**

PROPER SQUIRE (USA) 8 b.g. Bien Bien (USA) – La Cumbre (Sadler's Wells (USA)) [2004/5 c115x, h–: c25g³ c28g* c24m³ c32m⁶ Jun 27] sturdy gelding: fairly useful handicap chaser: won at Stratford in May by 13 lengths from Choisty: well held off higher mark both starts after: best at 3½m+: acts on soft and good to firm going: tried blinkered/in cheekpieces: often jumps none too fluently. *C. J. Mann* **c125 x h–**

PROTAGONIST 7 b. or br.g. In The Wings – Fatah Flare (USA) (Alydar (USA)) [2004/5 c21m Sep 4] good-topped gelding: fair handicap hurdler in 2002/3: off 20 months, tailed off on chasing debut: will stay beyond 21f: acts on soft going: sold 2,500 gns Doncaster November Sales. *P. R. Webber* **c– h–**

PROTECTIVE 4 ch.g. Hector Protector (USA) – You Make Me Real (USA) (Give Me Strength (USA)) [2004/5 16s³ 16v 16sᵖᵘ Apr 7] rather leggy gelding: half-brother to 3 winning jumpers, including hurdler/chaser Natural (by Bigstone), stays easy 3m: fairly useful on Flat (stays 13f): juvenile hurdler: third of 6 to Akilak in quite valuable event at Haydock on hurdling debut: disappointing next time: out of depth in Grade 1 at Aintree final start. *J. G. Given* **h105**

PROTOCOL (IRE) 11 b.g. Taufan (USA) – Ukraine's Affair (USA) (The Minstrel (CAN)) [2004/5 h88: 21g³ 16d² 17d 17v⁶ 20s³ 19s⁴ 16s² 20s⁵ 20v⁵ 16s⁵ 16v⁵ 16g 16g* 20d Mar 28] compact gelding: poor hurdler nowadays: won selling handicap at Fakenham (for second successive year) in March, making virtually all: reportedly struck into next time: stays 2½m: best efforts on good going or softer: tried visored, has worn cheekpieces (including at Fakenham): usually tongue tied. *Mrs S. Lamyman* **h83**

PROUD PEER (IRE) 7 ch.g. Mister Lord (USA) – Raffeen Pride (Shackleton) [2004/5 F–: 16g³ 17g⁵ 16m* 19vᵖᵘ 17d² 16g Nov 11] sturdy gelding: fair novice hurdler: won 4-runner event at Stratford in September: should stay at least 2½m: acts on good to firm and good to soft going: tongue tied fourth outing. *M. Pitman* **h104**

PROUD TO BE IRISH (IRE) 6 b.g. Brief Truce (USA) – Just Little (Mtoto) [2004/5 F16d 16s³ 18d 16v* 16s² 18s 17g⁶ 16sᵘʳ Mar 27] smallish gelding: first foal: dam useful 2m hurdler: fair form in bumpers: fair novice hurdler: won maiden at Fairyhouse in January: raced around 2m: acts on heavy going. *S. O'Farrell, Ireland* **h106 F85**

PROUD WESTERN (USA) 7 b.g. Gone West (USA) – Proud Lou (USA) (Proud Clarion) [2004/5 17m Sep 28] poor on Flat (stays 1m) nowadays: well held over hurdles: tried tongue tied. *B. Ellison* **h–**

PROVINCE 12 b.g. Dominion – Shih Ching (USA) (Secreto (USA)) [2004/5 c25d² c23d c25sᵖᵘ Mar 22] leggy gelding: winning hurdler: fair pointer nowadays, won twice in 2004: second of 3 finishers to Lancastrian Jet at Hereford, only form in hunter chases: stays 25f: formerly blinkered. *G. Chambers* **c87 h–**

PROVOCATIVE (FR) 7 b. or br.g. Useful (FR) – All Blue (FR) (Noir Et Or) [2004/5 h111: c16sᶠ c16s* c20v² c20vᶠ Jan 26] tall, quite good-topped gelding: fair hurdler: better form over fences: made all in 4-runner maiden at Carlisle in November: looked likely winner when falling heavily 3 out in novice at Wetherby final outing: stays 2½m: raced on good going or softer (acts on heavy). *M. Todhunter* **c121 h–**

PUBLICAN (IRE) 5 b.g. Overbury (IRE) – Night Therapy (IRE) (Mandalus) [2004/5 F16g F16s³ F16v* F16d³ F16s* 16v³ 16s* 16g Mar 15] **h132 p F108 +**

When he made his debut in a thirty-runner bumper at the 2004 Punchestown Festival, only five of the field started at longer odds than Publican. Though he didn't win that day, he turned out to be the best bumper performer in the field and has shown just about the best form over hurdles so far as well. With the physique to make an even better chaser, there could be quite a bit more to come. Publican finished eighth in that initial bumper but went on to show much better form, winning twice, at Galway in October and in a Grade 2 at Navan (where he beat a below-par Dawadari) in December before his attentions were turned to hurdling after the turn of the year. After a promising first run, Publican started odds on for a maiden at Naas confined to those that had not run more than twice over hurdles. He ran out an impressive winner, entries at Cheltenham suggesting he was now held in much higher regard than when making his debut, though perhaps quite how high didn't become clear until he was gambled on down to single-figure odds for the Supreme Novices'. Although he drifted on the day, Publican still went off with only three ahead of him in the market and, though he could not quite match the expectation, he shaped for a long way as if he might, still travelling strongly going to two out, and put up a useful performance in finishing seventh, his lack of experience perhaps the reason for his not finishing the race so well as seemed likely after moving up on the bridle at the second last.

Publican went on to make two appearances at the latest Punchestown Festival, both in Grade 1 events, but on each occasion he was let down by his jumping, decidedly hesitant when well held behind the Supreme Novices' runner-up Wild Passion in the Evening Herald Champion Novices' Hurdle but faring much better until all but falling at the last in the Emo Oil Champion Hurdle three days later. Sent off at 33/1 in a five-runner field, Publican was only four lengths behind the principals when making his mistake, though the race was so slowly run that he

Outback Syndicate's "Publican"

could not be rated with confidence on that performance. A tall, good sort who took the eye at both Cheltenham and Punchestown, Publican is the first foal of the twice-raced Night Therapy, who herself is out of a half-sister to Night Nurse. This is also the family of the Coral Cup winner Big Strand, who is out of another half-sister to the dual Champion Hurdle winner. Publican has so far raced at around two miles on good going or softer. He is likely to be at least as effective over further. *P. A. Fahy, Ireland*

PUCKS COURT 8 b.g. Nomadic Way (USA) – Miss Puck (Tepukei) [2004/5 h–: 16g4 16d 16gpu 17m5 19mpu 16g Dec 28] lengthy gelding: little form. *I. A. Brown* **h–**

PUFF AT MIDNIGHT 5 b.m. Midnight Legend – Sulapuff (Sula Bula) [2004/5 F16g F16d 16d 21d 20v6 16v 24s Feb 17] close-coupled mare: first foal: dam unraced: little impact in bumpers or over hurdles. *D. P. Keane* **h–** **F–**

PULHAM DOWNE 10 ch.g. Baron Blakeney – Dame Nellie (Dominion) [2004/5 c–: c21dpu May 17] modest pointer. *Mrs A. L. Tory* **c–**

PULL YOUR SOCKS UP (IRE) 6 b.g. Needle Gun (IRE) – Crackingham (Trimmingham) [2004/5 16s Dec 13] 30,000 4-y-o: sixth foal: half-brother to winning 2½m hurdler Romanoski (by Minster Son): dam unraced half-sister to useful staying chaser Whats The Crack: tailed off in novice hurdle on debut. *Jonjo O'Neill* **h–**

PUNCHY (IRE) 9 b.g. Freddie's Star – Baltimore Fox (IRE) (Arapahos (FR)) [2004/5 c111, h113: c20m* c22g3 c23m5 c24gbd c24m5 c26gur c25g4 Oct 6] lengthy, workmanlike gelding: winning hurdler: fair handicap chaser: won 4-runner event at Worcester in June, idling run-in: successful at 3¼m, better over shorter: acts on soft and firm going: tried visored/in cheekpieces: irresolute. *M. C. Pipe* **c100 §** **h–**

PUNTAL (FR) 9 b.g. Bering – Saveur (Ardross) [2004/5 c147, h–: c26g6 c25d Dec 10] medium-sized gelding: smart chaser in 2003/4, won 5 times, notably Betfred Gold **c–** **h–**

Cup (Handicap) at Sandown: well-held sixth to Celestial Gold in very valuable handicap at Newbury on reappearance: lost interest next time: effective at 2m to easy 29f: acts on any going: visored once (downed tools): tongue tied last 6 starts: often front runner: has raced lazily. *M. C. Pipe*

PURE BRIEF (IRE) 8 b.g. Brief Truce (USA) – Epure (Bellypha) [2004/5 c–, h–: 16g^{pu} 22g^{6} 17d^{2} 16v^{6} 17d 16m^{4} 17g 16g^{3} Dec 28] angular gelding: little show over fences: poor hurdler, left B. Leavy after fifth outing: best around 2m: acts on good to firm and heavy going: effective blinkered/visored or not. *J. Mackie* **c–** **h70**

PURE MISCHIEF (IRE) 6 b.g. Alhaarth (IRE) – Bellissi (IRE) (Bluebird (USA)) [2004/5 h83: 16d^{F} 16s* 16v^{2} 16d 16d Mar 24] angular gelding: fair on Flat, successful 3 times in 2004, claimed from W. M. Brisbourne £14,000 in June: fair handicap hurdler: won at Ludlow in December: improved again when second at Haydock 8 days later: not knocked about last 2 starts: best around 2m: acts on heavy going. *C. R. Dore* **h103**

PURE PLATINUM (IRE) 7 gr.g. Roselier (FR) – Waterloo Ball (IRE) (Where To Dance (USA)) [2004/5 h–, F89: 16g c24s* c26d* c26d^{pu} Nov 30] medium-sized gelding: no form in 4 starts over hurdles: modest form over fences, winning handicaps at Chepstow in October and Newton Abbot (3-runner novice) in November: lame final outing: stays 3¼m: acts on soft going. *Jonjo O'Neill* **c95** **h–**

PURE PLEASURE (NZ) 6 gr.g. Casual Lies (USA) – Pure Glory (NZ) (First Norman (USA)) [2004/5 14v^{4} 16d^{5} Apr 20] rather leggy gelding: twice-raced in New Zealand in June, unplaced in 1m maiden on Flat and fourth in maiden hurdle: looked in need of run on British debut. *N. M. Babbage* **h–**

PURE SPEED (FR) 4 ch.f. Hamas (IRE) – Nexia (FR) (Linamix (FR)) [2004/5 F13d F16s F16s Feb 5] fourth foal: half-sister to 3 winners, including useful hurdler up to 2½m Malone (by Celtic Arms): dam never ran: well held in bumpers. *J. P. L. Ewart* **F–**

PURE STEEL (IRE) 11 b.g. Miner's Lamp – Mary Deen (Avocat) [2004/5 c25g^{pu} c20g^{2} c20d^{5} c24d^{6} Apr 22] strong gelding: maiden chaser: form in hunters only when runner-up at Hexham in May, final outing for C. Storey: sold out of Miss S. Forster's stable 1,000 gns Doncaster August Sales: won maiden point in March: stays 2½m: acts on soft and good to firm going: has worn cheekpieces. *Miss L. Day* **c70** **h–**

PURPLE PATCH 7 b.m. Afzal – My Purple Prose (Rymer) [2004/5 F88: F18g 22g 22g^{3} 22g^{2} 22s^{3} 21g^{6} 19s^{4} 19s^{2} 24s^{5} 19d^{2} Mar 8] small, leggy mare: failed to complete in 2 points in 2003: fair form first 3 starts in bumpers: modest novice hurdler: stays 2¾m: acts on soft ground. *C. L. Popham* **h87** **F72**

PURR 4 b.g. Pursuit of Love – Catawba (Mill Reef (USA)) [2004/5 17g 18s^{pu} 16d 16s 16s^{3} 16s 16d^{3} 16v^{5} 16s 18s 20s 16s^{5} Mar 5] close-coupled gelding: little form on Flat: poor juvenile hurdler: left T. Clement after second outing: tongue tied on debut. *M. Wigham* **h68**

PUTUP OR SHUTUP (IRE) 9 br.g. Religiously (USA) – Nights Crack (Callernish) [2004/5 24d^{3} 24s^{pu} 21d^{pu} 24s^{4} Apr 16] medium-sized gelding: modest hurdler, off over 2 years before reappearance: stays 3m: raced on going softer than good. *K. C. Bailey* **h96**

Q

QABAS (USA) 5 b.g. Swain (IRE) – Classical Dance (CAN) (Regal Classic (CAN)) [2004/5 h71: 17g* 17d* 18d^{6} 22s^{pu} 17v Feb 13] sturdy gelding: fair maiden on Flat (stays 11.7f, none too genuine), sold out of P. Webber's stable 4,800 gns Doncaster August Sales: fair handicap hurdler: improved form when winning at Market Rasen in September (novice) and October, signs of temperament on latter occasion: likely to prove best around 2m: best efforts on good/good to soft going: wore cheekpieces first 4 outings. *P. Bowen* **h107**

QUADCO (IRE) 11 b.g. Be My Native (USA) – Anega (Run The Gantlet (USA)) [2004/5 c109, h102: c21g^{2} c17m^{2} c24f^{2} c20d^{2} Mar 31] leggy gelding: winning hurdler: fairly useful chaser: runner-up all starts in 2004/5, to John James in minor event at Clonmel final one: stays 3m: probably acts on any going: tried blinkered: has found little. *P. A. Fahy, Ireland* **c121** **h–**

QUAINTON HILLS 11 b.g. Gildoran – Spin Again (Royalty) [2004/5 c98x, h–: c25s^{pu} 23s^{4} 24d^{pu} 16s^{5} 24d^{pu} 20g^{pu} 20s^{pu} Apr 16] medium-sized gelding: winning chaser: poor maiden hurdler: stays 23f: acts on good to firm and heavy going: sketchy jumper. *D. R. Stoddart* **c– x** **h82**

Faucets For Mira Showers Silver Trophy Chase (Limited Handicap), Cheltenham—Quazar grabs the initiative at the last as Le Roi Miguel stumbles

QUALITAIR PLEASURE 5 b.m. Slip Anchor – Qualitair Ridge (Indian Ridge) [2004/5 F87: F16g^2 F17g* 21d^{pu} 20d 16g Dec 28] leggy mare: generally progressive in bumpers, fairly useful form when winning at Bangor in October: shaped as if amiss all starts over hurdles. *J. Hetherton* **h– F97**

QUALITY FIRST (IRE) 12 b.g. Un Desperado (FR) – Vipsania (General Ironside) [2004/5 c117§, h–§: c20d^4 c20g^4 c20m^5 Jun 5] good-topped gelding: winning hurdler: fairly useful handicap chaser: won points in February and April (refused to race once in between): probably best up to 21f: acts on heavy and good to firm going: wore cheek-pieces last 4 outings: ungenuine. *Mrs H. Dalton* **c117 § h– §**

QUARRY ISLAND (IRE) 4 b.f. Turtle Island (IRE) – Last Quarry (Handsome Sailor) [2004/5 17d^2 17m^4 17d^4 16d^3 16d^2 16d^3 16m^3 16s^2 Apr 10] tall filly: poor on Flat (stays 1½m), claimed from P. D. Evans £5,000 after winning in May: modest juvenile hurdler, in frame all 8 starts: raced around 2m: acts on soft and good to firm going. *M. Todhunter* **h94**

QUARRYMOUNT 4 b.g. Polar Falcon (USA) – Quilt (Terimon) [2004/5 16g^3 16d^6 17s Jan 29] sturdy, useful-looking gelding: fairly useful on Flat (stays 1¾m), successful 3 times in 2004, sold out of Sir Mark Prescott's stable 67,000 gns Doncaster October Sales: modest form first 2 starts in juvenile hurdles. *J. A. B. Old* **h95**

QUARTER MASTERS (IRE) 6 b.g. Mujadil (USA) – Kentucky Wildcat (Be My Guest (USA)) [2004/5 c82, h88: 21g^{pu} Apr 30] lengthy gelding: winning hurdler: poor maiden chaser: stays 21f: acts on soft going: tried in cheekpieces: sold 3,500 gns Doncaster May Sales, placed 5 times in points in 2005. *G. M. Moore* **c– h–**

QUARTERSTAFF 11 b.g. Charmer – Quaranta (Hotfoot) [2004/5 c110: c25m^4 c24d^6 Mar 26] lengthy gelding: fair handicap chaser, lightly raced nowadays: stays 25f: best form on good going. *C. R. Wilson* **c–**

QUATRAIN (IRE) 5 ch.g. Anshan – Gray's Ellergy (Oats) [2004/5 F86: 20s^6 21g 21s^4 21d^{pu} Mar 24] good-topped gelding: modest form over hurdles: will stay beyond 21f. *D. R. Gandolfo* **h94**

QUAY WALLOPER 4 b.g. In Command (IRE) – Myrrh (Salse (USA)) [2004/5 16d 20s 23s^{pu} 20s Apr 10] sparely-made gelding: half-brother to fair French 2¼m hurdle winner Luarca (by Robellino): seems of little account. *J. R. Norton* **h–**

QUAZAR (IRE) 7 b.g. Inzar (USA) – Evictress (IRE) (Sharp Victor (USA)) [2004/5 h153: 16g c21m^{3} c16d* c20d* c24g^{3} c21g c21m* Apr 13] strong, compact gelding: smart hurdler in 2003/4: useful chaser: won novices at Perth in September and Wetherby (idled) in December and Grade 2 limited handicap at Cheltenham in April, beating Le Roi Miguel 4 lengths in last-named: creditable second to Forget The Past in Grade 2 novice at Punchestown later in April: barely stays 3m: acts on any going: tried in blinkers/ cheekpieces: tongue tied: tends to idle in front: tough. *Jonjo O'Neill* **c140 h–**

QUEDEX 9 b.g. Deploy – Alwal (Pharly (FR)) [2004/5 h–: 16m^{6} 16d* 17d* May 15] smallish, angular gelding: fair hurdler, off nearly a year before reappearance: won seller at Fakenham (easily) and handicap at Bangor in May: stays 19f: acts on good to firm and good to soft going: has worn cheekpieces: won on Flat in May and July, very good fourth in Cesarewitch in October. *R. J. Price* **h109 +**

QUEEN ASTRID (IRE) 5 b.m. Revoque (IRE) – Talina's Law (IRE) (Law Society (USA)) [2004/5 18v* 19s* 21g 20s Mar 27] unfurnished mare: half-sister to fair 2m hurdler Mujalina (by Mujadil): dam fairly useful hurdler, should have stayed beyond 2m: useful on Flat (will stay 2m): promising start over hurdles, winning maiden at Leopardstown (making all to beat Letterman 6 lengths) in December and mares minor event at Limerick in March: only twelfth of 20 to No Refuge in Royal & SunAlliance Novices' Hurdle at Cheltenham, and well below form back in lesser company: should stay at least 2½m. *D. K. Weld, Ireland* **h125**

QUEEN EXCALIBUR 6 ch.m. Sabrehill (USA) – Blue Room (Gorytus (USA)) [2004/5 16v 16v^{pu} Mar 29] poor maiden on Flat (stays 11f): no encouragement either outing over hurdles: claimed from A. Juckes £5,000 on debut. *C. Roberts* **h–**

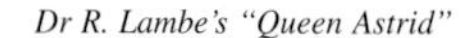

Dr R. Lambe's "Queen Astrid"

QUEEN GUINEVERE 5 b.m. Wizard King – Craft Book Ingot (Ardross) [2004/5 F16g F16g Aug 18] first foal: dam, of little account, half-sister to smart performer up to 1½m Greenwich Papillon: well held in 2 bumpers: hung right on debut. *J. Gallagher* **F–**

QUEEN OF THE SOUTH 8 b.m. Cut The Mustard (IRE) – Kawarau Queen (Taufan (USA)) [2004/5 c–: c25g^{F} May 8] lengthy mare: well beaten only completed outing in chases: tried visored. *L. Lungo* **c–**

QUEENS BRIGADE 13 b.g. K-Battery – Queen of Dara (Dara Monarch) [2004/5 c–, h82: 19g Mar 3] close-coupled gelding: winning chaser: poor handicap hurdler: stays 3m: acts on any going: amateur ridden. *Miss V. A. Stephens* **c– h–**

QUEENS HARBOUR (IRE) 11 b.g. Brush Aside (USA) – Queenie Kelly (The Parson) [2004/5 c24g^{5} c16d^{4} 17d Jan 1] well-made gelding: smart in bumpers in 1998/9: very lightly raced since, no sign of retaining ability in 2004/5. *Dr P. Pritchard* **c– h–**

QUEENS HOUSE 10 b.m. Arctic Lord – Courtlands Girl (Crimson Beau) [2004/5 24m^{pu} Jun 29] placed in maiden points in 2004, no sign of ability otherwise. *N. R. Mitchell* **h–**

QUEEN SORAYA 7 b.m. Persian Bold – Fairlead (Slip Anchor) [2004/5 F96: 16g^{6} 19m* 21s^{3} 16d^{3} 21m^{5} 19m* Apr 23] rather leggy mare: bumper winner: fair form in novice hurdles: won at Taunton (mares, easily) in November and Market Rasen in April: improved effort when making all to beat Aleron 3½ lengths at latter: likely to prove best short of 21f: acts on good to firm and good to soft going. *Miss H. C. Knight* **h114**

QUEL FONTENAILLES (FR) 7 b.g. Tel Quel (FR) – Sissi Fontenailles (FR) (Pampabird) [2004/5 16d 17s^{5} 16d^{F} Jan 26] sturdy gelding: fair on Flat, won on all-weather in March: not fluent and poor form at best over hurdles. *L. A. Dace* **h–**

QUEST ON AIR 6 b.g. Star Quest – Stormy Heights (Golden Heights) [2004/5 16g Oct 30] modest on Flat (stays 1¾m), successful in March: not fluent when well held in novice on hurdling debut. *J. R. Jenkins* **h–**

QUETAL (IRE) 12 ch.g. Buckskin (FR) – Cantafleur (Cantab) [2004/5 c–, h–: c25d^{3} c25m^{2} May 11] rather sparely-made gelding: one-time useful hunter chaser, modest nowadays: stays 3¼m: acts on soft and good to firm going: tends to make mistakes. *Mrs Laura J. Young* **c84 h–**

QUIBBLE 8 ch.g. Lammtarra (USA) – Bloudan (USA) (Damascus (USA)) [2004/5 16v^{4} 16d^{4} c20v^{ro} c17g c20v Apr 17] maiden on Flat: poor form over hurdles and fences, close third when running out 2 out in novice handicap at Leicester on chasing debut: blinkered in 2004/5. *A. Bailey* **c87 ? h84**

QUICK 5 b.g. Kahyasi – Prompt (Old Vic) [2004/5 h128: 22m^{2} 24d* 24d 24s 24s^{5} 24g^{3} 24d 24g^{4} Apr 14] leggy gelding: handicap hurdler: 50/1, won 17-runner event at Cheltenham in December by 17 lengths from Attorney General, soon allowed to build long lead and almost certainly flattered: useful form at best otherwise, again dictated pace when third to Oulart in valuable event there in March: suited by 2¾m+: acts on firm and soft going: visored: usually front runner/races prominently: has looked none too keen. *M. C. Pipe* **h140 +**

QUID PRO QUO (FR) 6 b.g. Cadoudal (FR) – Luzenia (FR) (Armos) [2004/5 F103: 17d* 19g^{2} 19s^{5} 20d 19g^{3} Apr 12] lengthy gelding: bumper winner: fair novice hurdler: won at Taunton in October: should stay beyond 19f. *P. F. Nicholls* **h111**

QUIET MILLFIT (USA) 9 b.g. Quiet American (USA) – Millfit (USA) (Blushing Groom (FR)) [2004/5 20m c23m c20g c20m^{2} c21g^{pu} c19g^{6} Dec 9] ex-Irish gelding: winning hurdler/chaser: left T. J. O'Mara, form in 2004/5 only when second in handicap chase at Fontwell: stays 3m, effective at much shorter: acts on firm and good to soft going: tried blinkered/in cheekpieces: has had tongue tied: inconsistent. *R. Ingram* **c85 h–**

QUIET WATER (IRE) 9 br.g. Lord Americo – Sirana (Al Sirat) [2004/5 c105, h104: 20d^{F} c21d^{4} c19g^{2} c21s^{ur} Jan 6] leggy gelding: fair handicap hurdler/chaser, let down by jumping most starts in 2004/5: stays 21f: acts on soft and good to firm going. *P. J. Hobbs* **c112 h105**

QUILLS (IRE) 6 b.g. Scribano – The Potwalluper (Brave Invader (USA)) [2004/5 F17s 16g 21g Apr 1] €17,000 3-y-o, €20,000 4-y-o: good-topped gelding: ninth foal: half-brother to high-class staying chaser Belmont King (by Kemal) and bumper winner by Executive Perk: dam, winning Irish hunter chaser, half-sister to useful staying chaser King Ba Ba: signs of ability only when eighth of 18 in maiden on hurdling debut. *Miss E. C. Lavelle* **h– F–**

QUINCY'S PERK (IRE) 12 ch.g. Executive Perk – Quincy Bay (Buckskin (FR)) [2004/5 c91?: c25d^{6} c21g^{pu} May 30] lengthy gelding: won maiden chase early in 2004: no form since, including in points: stays 3m: acts on soft going: tried blinkered: sold 800 gns Doncaster August Sales. *C. T. Pogson* **c–**

QUINTOTO 5 b.g. Mtoto – Ballet (Sharrood (USA)) [2004/5 16g^{pu} Jul 14] half-brother to fairly useful 2m hurdler Charlie's Gold (by Shalford) and fair 2m hurdler/chaser Island Sound (by Turtle Island): fairly useful at best on Flat (stays 1¼m), sold out of T. Mills's stable 40,000 gns Newmarket July (2003) Sales, little form in 2004: no show in novice on hurdling debut. *R. A. Fahey* **h–**

QUINZE 12 b.g. Charmer – Quaranta (Hotfoot) [2004/5 c20d^{2} c22m^{4} 22m Jul 31] tall, sparely-made gelding: formerly smart hurdler/chaser: off 3 years before reappearance: fair form when in frame in minor events over fences first 2 starts, tailed off in handicap hurdle final one: stays 2¾m: acts on any going. *P. Hughes, Ireland* **c112 h–**

QUITE REMARKABLE 6 b.g. Danzig Connection (USA) – Kathy Fair (IRE) (Nicholas Bill) [2004/5 h83: 16m^{4} 16g^{pu} 16g^{5} Jul 7] modest form over hurdles: suited by sharp 2m: headstrong. *Ian Williams* **h91**

QUIZZICAL 7 ch.g. Indian Ridge – Mount Row (Alzao (USA)) [2004/5 c76, h84: c24g^{pu} c20f^{5} c24g^{5} 24m^{4} c25d^{5} c22m^{4} 24d^{3} 22s 22s Dec 15] smallish, angular gelding: poor maiden hurdler/chaser: stays 25f: acts on soft and good to firm going: has worn cheekpieces/blinkers. *J. G. Carr, Ireland* **c– h84**

QUIZZLING (IRE) 7 b.g. Jurado (USA) – Monksville (Monksfield) [2004/5 h73, F86: c18d^{pu} c24g^{5} c22d c24s^{pu} c26d^{pu} c25m^{3} c20m^{5} Apr 10] lengthy gelding: poor maiden jumper. *B. J. M. Ryall* **c79 h–**

R

RAB CEE 5 b. or br.g. Tragic Role (USA) – Hilltop Lady (Puissance) [2004/5 F16g Dec 29] 1,100 3-y-o: second foal: dam unraced: showed nothing in bumper on debut. *W. G. Young* **F–**

RABITATIT (IRE) 4 b.f. Robellino (USA) – Coupled (Wolfhound (USA)) [2004/5 16g^{ur} Oct 7] modest on Flat (probably stays 1¼m), successful twice at 2 yrs: well behind when unseating fifth in juvenile on hurdling debut. *J. G. M. O'Shea* **h–**

RACING DEMON (IRE) 5 b.g. Old Vic – All Set (IRE) (Electric) [2004/5 F105p: 16g^{2} 17d* 16d^{3} 19s* 21g^{2} Mar 16] **h146 p**

It may seem curious, given its long-established place in the armoury of those trying to analyse performances in Flat races, that time, and its interpretation, has played such a minor role in Timeform publications when it comes to races over jumps. Timeform was founded, as the name suggests, with time analysis at its core, but it has never published timefigures for National Hunt racing, though they are currently being trialled in-house with a view to publication. There have been reasons for the situation to date—the greater number of steadily-run races; the division of races on a card run over hurdles and, particularly, fences, on different tracks; the effects on official distances of dolling out of courses and the unexpected omission of obstacles; and the deterioration in ground conditions, particularly on softer than good, as the turf becomes churned up during the meeting. The working adjustments required to put a precise figure, to the pound, on every performance in such circumstances may turn out to be of limited value, but that is not to say that time analysis, both of the overall race time (for which reliable Timeform course standards exist) and times for sections of races, is without worth over jumps. Far from it. Just as on the Flat, time analysis is most useful when it identifies a young or inexperienced horse whose performance judged on time appears a fair bit better than conventional analysis of form would indicate. Racing Demon is a good example.

Racing Demon was one of nineteen previous winners over hurdles in a field of twenty for the Royal & SunAlliance Novices' Hurdle at Cheltenham in March, the vast majority of which were lightly raced and had won their final start before the Festival. After defeat at Sandown when odds on in December, on the third of his first four outings in novice hurdles, on the face of it Racing Demon appeared some

williamhillcasino.com Novices' Hurdle, Exeter—
Racing Demon opens his account over hurdles with the first of two wins at the Devon track

way down the pecking order among them on form, but his time performance for the second of his two wins at Exeter in January on his final start before the Festival put a different complexion on things. Favourite that day, as he had been when successful in a similar event on the course in November, Racing Demon showed only quite useful form in coming eleven lengths clear of his rivals, asserting readily from the last. Interestingly, however, taking into account weights carried and the ground, his time performance compared very favourably to the others recorded in the hurdle races on the card at Exeter, suggesting that what he had appeared to achieve on form provided a conservative estimate of his ability. Furthermore, aside from his overall time performance, Racing Demon also covered the last three flights of the contest some five seconds faster than the winner of the handicap later on the card, despite his race being run at the stronger early pace. Considering the ease of Racing Demon's victory as well, all in all, he looked something of a sleeper in form terms in the SunAlliance field at Cheltenham. He all but pulled it off, taken wide throughout, cruising into contention down the hill and looking all over the winner as he went clear approaching the last, only to veer right as he jumped it and be run out of things close home, going down by three quarters of a length to the strong-finishing No Refuge, with Our Ben two and a half lengths away in third.

Racing Demon (IRE) (b.g. 2000)	Old Vic (b 1986)	Sadler's Wells (b 1981)	Northern Dancer
			Fairy Bridge
		Cockade (b 1973)	Derring-Do
			Camenae
	All Set (IRE) (b 1992)	Electric (b 1979)	Blakeney
			Christiana
		Merry Lesa (b 1975)	Dalesa
			Rozeen

Racing Demon's stable-companion Best Mate finished runner-up in the Supreme Novices' Hurdle at the Festival as a five-year-old, and the sky should be the limit for Racing Demon as well when he is sent over fences. By Kicking King's sire Old Vic, Racing Demon is from a largely undistinguished jumping family—he himself cost less than 5,000 guineas when sold as a yearling—but his unraced dam is a half-sister to the top-class chaser Merry Gale, fourth in the Gold Cup and winner of the Martell Cup over twenty-five furlongs at Aintree in 1995. Racing Demon will stay three miles, though he clearly isn't short of speed given the way he travelled for a long way at Cheltenham. A useful-looking, chasing type in appearance, Racing Demon has shown himself a fluent jumper so far, despite his tendency to go right on occasions, and he should take high rank among the season's novices over fences in 2005/6, though there would be a good prize in him too should connections stick to hurdles in the short term. Winner of a bumper at Huntingdon on his only start in 2003/4, and raced only on good ground or softer to date, Racing Demon is altogether a most exciting prospect. *Miss H. C. Knight*

RACING NIGHT (USA) 5 b.g. Lear Fan (USA) – Broom Dance (USA) (Dance Spell (USA)) [2004/5 16s 16v 16g 17s^F Feb 7] fair 9f winner when trained by E. Dunlop, well held both starts on Flat in 2004 for J. Best: no form over hurdles: tongue tied after debut. *W. Storey* **h–**

RADAR (IRE) 10 b.g. Petardia – Soignee (Night Shift (USA)) [2004/5 c–, h101: 16s 17s^4 Feb 7] angular gelding: fair hurdler at best: respectable effort on second of 2 outings in handicaps in 2004/5: raced mainly around 2m: acts on any going. *Miss S. E. Forster* **c– h95**

RADBROOK HALL 6 b.g. Teenoso (USA) – Sarah's Venture (Averof) [2004/5 20s 17d 19g^2 19s^3 22d Feb 20] big, workmanlike gelding: well held in bumper: won maiden point in 2004: modest novice hurdler: will prove suited by 2½m+. *J. W. Mullins* **h95**

RADCLIFFE (IRE) 8 b.g. Supreme Leader – Marys Course (Crash Course) [2004/5 c98, h92: c24s^3 c23g* c29d^4 c28s^3 c24d* c26d^F Feb 20] rather leggy gelding: lightly raced over hurdles: fair handicap chaser: won 2-finisher event at Leicester in November and 6-runner race at Ludlow in January: suited by 3m+: acts on soft going, below form all starts on firmer than good: races prominently. *Miss Venetia Williams* **c104 h–**

RADIANT BRIDE 5 ch.m. Groom Dancer (USA) – Radiancy (IRE) (Mujtahid (USA)) [2004/5 16g Feb 27] modest on Flat (stays 2m), successful 3 times in 2004: folded tamely in maiden on hurdling debut. *Mrs L. B. Normile* **h–**

RADNOR LAD 5 ch.g. Double Trigger (IRE) – Gabibti (IRE) (Dara Monarch) [2004/5 F16d F16s^5 F16d 17s 20d 24d Mar 12] lengthy, rather unfurnished gelding: half-brother to poor hurdler/chaser Multi Franchise (by Gabitat), stays 25f: dam winning sprinter: soundly beaten in bumpers and over hurdles. *R. J. Price* **h– F–**

RAGASAH 7 b.m. Glory of Dancer – Slight Risk (Risk Me (FR)) [2004/5 16s^pu 16g^6 Mar 18] modest on Flat (probably stays 11f), successful in January, no form in 3 starts over hurdles. *E. R. Oertel* **h70**

RAGDALE HALL (USA) 8 b.g. Bien Bien (USA) – Gift of Dance (USA) (Trempolino (USA)) [2004/5 c101, h119: 20m^2 17m^5 22d^3 c20g^pu c19m^3 20m^F Apr 23] medium-sized gelding: fairly useful handicap hurdler: lightly-raced winning chaser: trained by P. Hobbs fourth and fifth starts: barely stays 2¾m: acts on firm and good to soft going: tried blinkered: has had tongue tied. *J. Joseph* **c101 x h117**

RAGING TORRENT 10 b.g. Meadowbrook – Charons Daughter (Another River) [2004/5 c80: c25g^2 c25g^3 c20g^5 May 29] fair maiden hunter chaser: suited by 3m+: sold 7,000 gns Doncaster October Sales, successful in point in March. *S. Waugh* **c89**

RAGU 7 b.m. Contract Law (USA) – Marnworth (Funny Man) [2004/5 h90: 26g 21g^pu c20m^pu 22m^pu 16g Jul 6] leggy mare: modest hurdler: has lost her way: jumped poorly on chasing debut: tried in cheekpieces/visor. *M. J. Gingell* **c– h–**

RAG WEEK (IRE) 8 b.g. Roselier (FR) – Lady Rag (Ragapan) [2004/5 26m^2 c26g* c26g^2 c26d^F c25m^3 Sep 8] IR £15,000 4-y-o: ex-Irish gelding: eighth foal: half-brother to fair hurdler/chaser Lord Strickland, stays 3m, and winning hunter chaser Mill O'The Rags (both by Strong Gale): dam maiden sister to Sweeps Hurdle winner Hansels Rag: well held in bumper: left A. Kennedy, won 3 times in points in Britain in 2004: modest form over hurdles/fences: won maiden chase at Southwell in July: will stay beyond 3¼m: acts on good to firm going: has looked none too keen. *Evan Williams* **c88 h98**

RAIKKONEN (IRE) 5 b.g. Lake Coniston (IRE) – Jour Ferie (IRE) (Taufan (USA)) [2004/5 h116: 16g 16s 20s* 22d^2 24s 20v^4 20v^3 20s^4 22s^3 Mar 28] smallish gelding: fair on Flat (stays 2m), successful in April: fairly useful hurdler: won handicap at Naas in **h120**

October: good second of 25 to Mansony in similar event at Punchestown in late-April: didn't take to course when pulled up in Grade 2 at Auteuil in May: should stay beyond 2¾m: acts on good to firm and heavy going: tongue tied seventh start. *W. P. Mullins, Ireland*

RAINBOW RIVER (IRE) 7 ch.g. Rainbows For Life (CAN) – Shrewd Girl (USA) (Sagace (FR)) [2004/5 h–: 16s 19g 16s⁵ Mar 22] small, close-coupled gelding: fair hurdler in 2002/3: lightly raced and no form since: stays 21f: acts on good to firm going. *M. C. Chapman* **h–**

RAINBOWS AGLITTER 8 ch.g. Rainbows For Life (CAN) – Chalet Waldegg (Monsanto (FR)) [2004/5 c110, h112: 20m* Sep 19] angular gelding: fair chaser: fair handicap hurdler: won at Uttoxeter in September: stays 21f: acts on soft and good to firm going: edgy sort: held up: has found little. *D. R. Gandolfo* **c– h114**

RAINBOW TREE 5 b.g. Rainbows For Life (CAN) – Little Twig (IRE) (Good Thyne (USA)) [2004/5 F17g* 16s⁴ 19s⁵ 17s⁵ 17d⁵ 16g⁴ Mar 5] leggy gelding: second foal: half-brother to 19f hurdle winner Fourboystoy (by Roselier): dam thrice-raced in bumpers: won bumper at Market Rasen on debut in September: modest form over hurdles: stays 19f: raced on good going or softer. *C. C. Bealby* **h90 F89**

RAINSBOROUGH HILL 4 b.g. Groom Dancer (USA) – Ellebanna (Tina's Pet) [2004/5 17d^pu Aug 28] no sign of ability on Flat or in juvenile on hurdling debut. *A. King* **h–**

RAISE A MCGREGOR 9 br.g. Perpendicular – Gregory's Lady (Meldrum) [2004/5 c87, h–: c20m c17g^pu 17g⁴ 16g² c16m^F c17g⁶ c20s^F Nov 5] winning handicap chaser, no form in 2004/5: poor maiden hurdler: stays 2½m: acts on good to firm going. *Mrs S. J. Smith* **c– h69**

RAISEAPEARL 10 b. or br.g. Pocketed (USA) – Little Anthem (True Song) [2004/5 c24g⁴ c24d⁵ c24d² Mar 24] winning pointer: fairly useful hunter chaser, best effort when second at Ludlow: stays 3m: acts on good to soft going. *Patrick Thompson* **c100 h–**

RAISE YOUR GLASS (IRE) 6 b. or br.g. Namaqualand (USA) – Toast And Honey (IRE) (Glow (USA)) [2004/5 h91: 21d Nov 9] sparely-made gelding: modest handicap hurdler: well held only start in 2004/5: should stay beyond 21f: acts on good to firm and good to soft going: usually blinkered: has been reluctant to race. *Miss V. Scott* **h–**

RAJAM 7 b.g. Sadler's Wells (USA) – Rafif (USA) (Riverman (USA)) [2004/5 h102: 19s 17d⁵ 16d Apr 11] sturdy gelding: fair novice hurdler: will stay beyond 17f: raced on good ground or softer (acts on soft). *G. A. Harker* **h103**

RAKALACKEY 7 br.g. Rakaposhi King – Celtic Slave (Celtic Cone) [2004/5 h120: 21g³ Oct 26] medium-sized gelding: fairly useful hurdler: good third to The Dark Lord in handicap at Cheltenham only start in 2004/5: stays 21f: raced mainly on good going: possibly not straightforward. *H. D. Daly* **h127 +**

RAKASSA 7 ch.m. Ballet Royal (USA) – Shafayif (Ela-Mana-Mou) [2004/5 h106: 16g 20s 20d^pu c17s⁵ c22s⁵ c16s* c20d⁵ c24s² c19s* Mar 10] lengthy, plain mare: fair handicap hurdler in 2003/4: of similar merit over fences, winning novices at Folkestone (handicap) in January and Towcester (4 ran) in March: effective at 2m to 3m: acts on soft going. *H. J. Manners* **c104 h–**

RAMBLEES HOLLY 7 ch.g. Alfie Dickins – Lucky Holly (General David) [2004/5 h86: 16d⁵ 24g³ 23m* 16d³ 27m⁵ 21m* 22g³ 17v⁶ 20s* Apr 10] angular gelding: modest handicap hurdler: won at Wetherby (amateur) and Sedgefield in first half of season and Hexham in April: best around 2½m to 2¾m: acts on firm and soft going. *R. S. Wood* **h97**

RAMBLING MINSTER 7 b.g. Minster Son – Howcleuch (Buckskin (FR)) [2004/5 h103p, F102: 20d* 24d* 24g* 24d 19g⁴ 24g Mar 17] tall, good-topped gelding: fairly useful in bumpers: progressed well over hurdles, winning novice at Wetherby in May and handicaps at Newcastle in November and December (beat Just Beth by 3½ lengths): ran creditably when tenth in Pertemps Final (Handicap) at Cheltenham final start: better at 3m than shorter: acts on good to soft ground: patiently ridden: type to do well in novice chases in 2005/6. *K. G. Reveley* **h134**

RANDOLPH O'BRIEN (IRE) 5 b.g. Zaffaran (USA) – Gala's Pride (Gala Performance) [2004/5 h86, F67: 20s⁵ 21d 22v^pu Mar 30] good-topped gelding: modest form over hurdles: bred to be suited by 2½m+: raced on ground softer than good: has raced freely. *N. A. Twiston-Davies* **h88**

RANDOM NATIVE (IRE) 7 br.g. Be My Native (USA) – Random Wind (Random Shot) [2004/5 20s^F 17s⁵ Apr 2] rather leggy gelding: fairly useful bumper winner in 2002/3: off nearly 2 years, jumped poorly but some promise when falling 2 out in maiden **h88**

at Wetherby on hurdling debut: probably found next race coming too soon: should stay 2½m. *T. J. Fitzgerald*

RANDOM PRECISION (IRE) 6 ch.g. Presenting – Rendezvous (Lorenzaccio) [2004/5 h–, F84: 21d^4 16d Dec 26] lengthy gelding: runner-up in bumper on debut: poor form over hurdles: has looked temperamental. *B. G. Powell* **h74**

RANDRICH 8 b.m. Alflora (IRE) – Randama (Akarad (FR)) [2004/5 16d^{pu} Dec 8] no sign of ability. *P. M. Rich* **h–**

RANDWICK ROAR (IRE) 6 b.g. Lord Americo – Le Bavellen (Le Bavard (FR)) [2004/5 h118, F–: 20g^6 c18v^2 c16d^4 c18s^3 c20s^3 c16s^2 c20s^F Mar 27] tall gelding: fairly useful hurdler: similar form over fences, 1½ lengths second to Pearly Jack in handicap at Thurles sixth start: stays 2½m: raced on good going or softer. *P. M. J. Doyle, Ireland* **c119 h–**

RANELAGH GRAY (IRE) 8 gr.g. Roselier (FR) – Bea Marie (IRE) (King's Ride) [2004/5 h101: 19g^4 May 11] leggy gelding: fair hurdler: stays 19f: acts on soft going: races prominently. *Miss Venetia Williams* **h99**

RANSBORO (IRE) 6 br.g. Needle Gun (IRE) – Moylena (Bustomi) [2004/5 20d^2 c18v^3 c17s^{ur} c20s^{ur} c17s c23s^2 c22v^3 c19v* c22v c24s^3 Mar 5] lengthy gelding: third foal: dam, winning pointer, half-sister to useful 2m hurdlers Eddie Wee and Helynsar and to dam of Betfred Gold Cup winner Jack High: bumper winner: fair hurdler: similar form over fences, winning listed handicap at Leopardstown in January: creditable fourth to No Half Session in similar event at Punchestown in late-April: stays 25f, at least as effective at shorter: acts on heavy going. *C. F. Swan, Ireland* **c110 h110**

RAPIDE PLAISIR (IRE) 7 b.g. Grand Plaisir (IRE) – Royal Well (Henbit (USA)) [2004/5 h114: 16g^5 16g^2 20m^3 c16s^6 Mar 13] rather leggy gelding: fair hurdler: never dangerous in 2 novice chases, including valuable event at Punchestown in late-April: stays 2½m: acts on good to firm going. *A. L. T. Moore, Ireland* **c– h114**

RAPT (IRE) 7 b.g. Septieme Ciel (USA) – Dream Play (USA) (Blushing Groom (FR)) [2004/5 h86: 16g c16g^{ur} 16d 17m^{pu} 17d^{pu} Oct 27] leggy gelding: winning hurdler: badly out of sorts in 2004/5: tried in cheekpieces: tongue tied. *M. A. Barnes* **c– h–**

RARE COINCIDENCE 4 ch.g. Atraf – Green Seed (IRE) (Lead On Time (USA)) [2004/5 16s^3 16d^3 16d 16g^6 Jan 21] half-brother to fairly useful 2m hurdler Take Flite (by Cadeaux Genereux): fair on Flat (stays 9f), successful in April: modest form when third in juvenile hurdles. *R. F. Fisher* **h80**

RARE PRESENCE (IRE) 6 b.g. Sadler's Wells (USA) – Celebrity Style (USA) (Seeking The Gold (USA)) [2004/5 h75: 22s^6 24g Jul 4] leggy gelding: poor maiden hurdler: stays 2¾m: raced on good going or softer: tried visored, usually blinkered: tongue tied last 5 starts: temperamental: sold 2,000 gns Doncaster August Sales, fourth on completed starts in points. *C. P. Morlock* **h– §**

RARE SOCIETY (IRE) 7 b.g. Deep Society – Rare Glen (Glen Quaich) [2004/5 c25d^2 Jan 1] rather leggy gelding: second foal: dam maiden pointer: well beaten in 4 maiden Irish points in 2004: 9 lengths second to Has Scored in maiden at Catterick on chasing debut. *Mrs S. J. Smith* **c100**

RARE VINTAGE (IRE) 7 b.m. Germany (USA) – Tatlock (Paico) [2004/5 h–: c16m^3 Apr 25] good-topped mare: no sign of ability. *Miss H. C. Knight* **c– h–**

RASHARROW (IRE) 6 ch.g. Rashar (USA) – Fleeting Arrow (IRE) (Comm-anche Run) [2004/5 F16d* F16g^3 F16g* Apr 16] **F122**

Given his great record as a trainer of bumper winners, it is a little surprising that Len Lungo has had only three runners in the Champion Bumper at Cheltenham. The Bajan Bandit, winner of graded bumpers at Chepstow and Aintree, might well have run in the 2001 renewal had it not been lost to foot and mouth. Crazy Horse, a 10/1-chance in 1998, and 50/1-shot Rose d'April, in 2002, did contest the race and finished well down the field but Rasharrow, his runner in the latest renewal, fared a good deal better in finishing third behind Missed That and De Soto, beaten just a length by the winner. Sent off at 9/1, Rasharrow, who had had just one previous outing, showed his inexperience in the early stages, but he was doing plenty of good work in the straight, staying on well to the line. He shaped like as good a jumping prospect as there was among the finishers at Cheltenham. Rasharrow had made his debut four months previously when beating another well-touted newcomer, Lennon, by five lengths at Wetherby (Lennon was also in the field at Cheltenham but failed to run his race, having won twice from three starts and shown smart form when second on the other in the meantime). Rasharrow was seen out a month after Cheltenham, having little trouble in landing the odds at Ayr on Scottish National day. The useful-looking Rasharrow was bought for €26,000 as a three-year-old, presumably making more appeal on looks than pedigree. His dam, grandam and great grandam were all unraced. His grandam Pollerun Slave has produced just a winning pointer, while the third dam Hurry also has a solitary winner to her name, though that one Hurdante was a promising sort, third in the Mersey Novices' Hurdle and second in the Rising Stars Chase, before injury blighted his career. Hurry was a sister to the useful jumper at two and a half miles or more Belvederian. Rasharrow, who is by the unraced Rashar, is his dam Fleeting Arrow's second foal. He will stay at least two and a half miles. *L. Lungo*

RASH DECISION (IRE) 10 b.g. Rashar (USA) – Lady Nethertown (Windjammer (USA)) [2004/5 c21v^{pu} Mar 15] rangy gelding: winning 2m hurdler/chaser for A. Mullins: lightly raced since 2001: acts on good to firm and good to soft going. *I. W. McInnes* **c– h–**

RASH MOMENT (FR) 6 b.g. Rudimentary (USA) – Ashura (FR) (No Pass No Sale) [2004/5 21g 19g^2 16g 21d^2 21g* Mar 28] close-coupled gelding: fourth foal: half-brother to 2 winners, including winning hurdler around 2m Lady Amanda (by Dom Pasquini): dam well beaten twice on Flat in France: in frame once from 3 starts in maiden points in 2004: fair form over hurdles: best effort when winning maiden at Huntingdon in November: stays 21f: raced on good/good to soft going: sold to join Miss K. Marks 42,000 gns Doncaster May Sales. *H. D. Daly* **h107**

RATHBAWN PRINCE (IRE) 13 ch.g. All Haste (USA) – Ellis Town (Camden Town) [2004/5 c99, h–: c24d^{pu} c26g^6 c24d^5 c21s* c21s^6 c24g c21d Apr 8] good-bodied gelding: smart chaser at best, fairly useful handicapper nowadays, won at Wincanton in January by 4 lengths from Raschal: well held in valuable events at Cheltenham and Aintree (Topham Chase) last 2 starts: stays 29f: acts on good to firm and heavy going: tried in cheekpieces. *Miss H. C. Knight* **c124 h–**

RATHCANNON MAN (IRE) 5 b.g. Anshan – Miss Fern (Cruise Missile) [2004/5 F16g^5 Jan 24] third foal: half-brother to winning pointer Lambrini Mist (by Terimon): dam, winning chaser, stayed 3¼m: poor form when fifth in bumper at Southwell on debut: will be suited by greater test of stamina. *A. King* **F–**

RATHFEIGH LAD 8 gr.g. Phardante (FR) – Par-Bar (IRE) (The Parson) [2004/5 22g^3 22g^3 Sep 12] IR 9,000 3-y-o: workmanlike gelding: first foal: dam, placed over hurdles, winning pointer: second and much better effort over hurdles when third in maiden at Stratford: will stay beyond 2¾m. *Mrs S. M. Johnson* **h93**

RATHFRILAND (IRE) 7 b.m. Supreme Leader – Tassagh Lady (Deep Run) [2004/5 F17d 17v 20s^{pu} Mar 22] 7,000 5-y-o: tall mare: seventh foal: dam winning pointer: well held in bumper and over hurdles. *Miss Lucinda V. Russell* **h– F–**

RATHGAR BEAU (IRE) 9 b. or br.g. Beau Sher – Salerina (Orchestra) [2004/5 c145x, h–: c16g^2 c20s^2 c16s^{ur} c20s* c20s^2 c16s* c17v^4 c20s* c20v* c21g^3 c20v^2 Apr 2] **c158 h–**

If at first you don't succeed . . . the resilient Rathgar Beau, who has more than paid his way thanks to the generous programme of fairly valuable conditions races for smart performers in Ireland, has finally won a Grade 1. He took advantage of Moscow Flyer's being below par to take the Kerrygold Champion Chase at Punchestown shortly after the end of the British season. Moscow Flyer started at 4/1-on and would have won anyway but for blundering when being pressed by Rathgar Beau. With both horses battling on really well, Rathgar Beau just held off the rallying Moscow Flyer by the shortest of short heads, the judge taking longer to decipher the photo-finish print than the race itself had taken. He had not been good enough to threaten Moscow Flyer in four previous encounters but the tough and consistent Rathgar Beau entered the record books as the first to defeat his outstanding rival when that horse completed over fences. The race also provided Rathgar Beau's young trainer with his first Grade 1 win.

Rathgar Beau was better than ever in the latest season, partly because he became generally a more fluent jumper than in his first two seasons over fences, in the first of which he contested some of the top novice events, finishing third in the Arkle Challenge Cup at Leopardstown and the Swordlestown Cup at Punchestown

MacLochlainn Road Markings Limited Kinloch Brae Chase, Thurles—
Rathgar Beau (left) takes the measure of Central House

and falling in between in the Maghull Novices' Chase at Aintree. Rathgar Beau's next crack at Grade 1 company came in the 2004 renewal of Punchestown's championship event for two-mile chasers, then under a different title. He ran very well to finish two lengths second to Moscow Flyer in the Champion Chase on that occasion before being given a well-earned summer break. The Clonmel Oil Chase over two and a half miles in November provided Rathgar Beau with his first victory of the

Kerrygold Champion Chase, Punchestown—a first Grade 1 success for Rathgar Beau
and the first defeat when completing over fences for Moscow Flyer

new season and seemed to mark the start of an improvement in his jumping. He made only one serious mistake—four out—when a creditable runner-up to Kicking King in the Grade 1 John Durkan Memorial Chase in early-December (he had also chased home Kicking King in a Grade 2 at Gowran on their return in the autumn) and his jumping looked much more assured when he beat Central House in both the O'Connell Warehousing Hilly Way Chase at Cork over two miles later in December and the MacLochlainn Road Markings Limited Kinloch Brae Chase over two and a half at Thurles in January.

Rathgar Beau (IRE) (b. or br.g. 1996)	Beau Sher (b 1983)	Ile de Bourbon (br 1975)	Nijinsky
			Roseliere
		Mai Pussy (ch 1975)	Realm
			Broad River
	Salerina (b 1985)	Orchestra (ch 1974)	Tudor Music
			Golden Moss
		Blendwell (br 1968)	Typhoon
			Courtwell

Rathgar Beau missed a good opportunity to win a Grade 1 when—after the late withdrawal of Moscow Flyer—he turned in a rare below-form effort behind Central House when odds on for the newly-elevated Paddy Power Dial-A-Bet Chase at Leopardstown's Christmas fixture. The Red Mills Chase at Gowran in February provided Rathgar Beau, who landed the odds easily, with consolation for his demotion on technical grounds after passing the post first in the same race twelve months earlier. It was also his fourth Grade 2 win of the season. Rathgar Beau's only outing in Britain was at the Cheltenham Festival where the newly-

One-O-Eight Racing Club's "Rathgar Beau"

instituted Daily Telegraph Chase over two miles five furlongs was chosen for him in preference to the Queen Mother Champion Chase, with connections concerned that the less testing ground would make the latter too much of a test of speed. He went down by half a length and two and a half lengths to Thisthatandtother and Fondmort and would have gone close but for hitting the last when challenging and within a length of the leading pair.

The useful-looking Rathgar Beau, who began his career in bumpers as a four-year-old, is by Beau Sher, a splendidly tough, genuine and consistent performer at seven furlongs to a mile and a quarter—reaching his best at the age of six—in the 'eighties. Rathgar Beau, the best offspring of the now-deceased Beau Sher, is the only recorded foal out of the bumper winner Salerina who was sent to Beau Sher after visiting Executive Perk in consecutive years in the mid-'nineties; Salerina died the year after foaling Rathgar Beau. Rathgar Beau was a fairly useful bumper winner and went on to show himself a useful novice hurdler before being switched to steeplechasing. Rathgar Beau, who is held up, is effective at two miles to two miles five furlongs and has been raced mainly on going softer than good (it was good at Cheltenham) and he acts on heavy. He was tried blinkered twice in 2003/4 but is tough, genuine and consistent. Rathgar Beau has been ridden on nineteen of his last twenty starts by Shay Barry, the exception being for his below-par effort in the Dial-A-Bet Chase, when the injured Barry was replaced by Tony McCoy. *E. Sheehy, Ireland*

RATHLIN ISLAND 7 b.g. Carroll House – Mermaid Bay (Jupiter Island) [2004/5 F16g^{5} F18g^{2} F16d 24d^{4} 20s 18v Jan 14] 4,000 4-y-o: ex-Irish gelding: third foal: dam unraced, out of half-sister to very smart staying chaser Everett and dam of high-class hurdler/smart chaser Cab On Target: well beaten on completed start in points: fair form in bumpers, trained by J. A. Berry first 2 starts: form over hurdles only when fourth in novice at Newcastle. *Miss V. Scott* **h– F86**

RATHOWEN (IRE) 6 b.g. Good Thyne (USA) – Owenageera (IRE) (Riot Helmet) [2004/5 F–: F16d^{6} F16s^{2} Apr 10] tall gelding: best effort in bumpers when short-head second to Allegedly So in maiden at Hexham. *J. I. A. Charlton* **F96**

RATTINA (GER) 9 b.m. Motley (USA) – Rottara (GER) (Flotow (GER)) [2004/5 c21s^{pu} c20d^{3} c19s^{4} c16m^{3} c19g Apr 15] ex-German mare: won over 9.5f on first of 2 starts on Flat: successful 4 times around 2m over hurdles, at Gelsenkirchen (3, all at 3 yrs) and Most in Czech Republic (at 5 yrs): runner-up at Bremen at 4 yrs on chasing debut: best effort in Britain when third in maiden at Ludlow on second start: acts on soft ground. *M. F. Harris* **c85 d h–**

RATTY'S BAND 11 ch.g. Gunner B – Arctic Ander (Leander) [2004/5 c62, h–: c17g^{4} c16m* c16g^{pu} Jul 14] maiden hurdler: poor chaser: won handicap at Perth in June: possibly amiss next time: probably best around 2m: acts on good to firm going. *Mrs L. B. Normile* **c75 h–**

RAVENSCAR 7 b.g. Thethingaboutitis (USA) – Outcrop (Oats) [2004/5 20v^{4} c21d^{3} c22s^{F} 24d^{2} 27d^{5} 20v c21v^{2} c24g^{2} c20g^{3} c23v^{2} c24d c20v^{ur} c25s* c21v^{3} c20m* Apr 10] 1,500 4-y-o: workmanlike gelding: first foal: dam no sign of ability: won maiden on last of 7 starts in points in 2004: bought 3,800 gns Doncaster August Sales: modest form over hurdles: fair chaser: won novice at Market Rasen (left alone seventh) in March and conditional jockeys handicap at Worcester in April: stays 3m: acts on good to firm and heavy going. *C. T. Pogson* **c101 h95**

RAVEN'S LAST 6 b.g. Sea Raven (IRE) – Lavenham's Last (Rymer) [2004/5 F102: 16v^{5} 16d 20s^{3} 20s^{pu} Dec 28] useful-looking gelding: fairly useful form in bumpers: form over hurdles only when third to Thames in novice at Haydock: tongue tied last 2 outings: takes strong hold. *R. T. Phillips* **h98**

RAVENSWOOD (IRE) 8 b.g. Warning – Green Lucia (Green Dancer (USA)) [2004/5 23s^{5} 24g 22g^{pu} Apr 10] rather leggy, useful-looking gelding: useful handicap hurdler at best: off nearly 2 years, travelled smoothly long way first 2 starts: lame final outing: stays 25f: best efforts on good/good to firm going: tongue tied. *M. C. Pipe* **h120**

RAVING LORD (IRE) 8 b.g. Lord Americo – Miss Kertina (IRE) (Orchestra) [2004/5 h–: 17m^{F} Aug 6] no show over hurdles: difficult ride. *J. P. Dodds* **h–**

RAW SILK 7 b.g. Rudimentary (USA) – Misty Silks (Scottish Reel) [2004/5 h106: c16s* c16g^{2} c16d^{2} c20v^{3} c16v^{pu} Jan 29] good-bodied gelding: fair handicap hurdler: fair **c106 h–**

novice chaser: off 14 months, won handicap event at Carlisle in October: probably best around 2m: acts on any going: formerly blinkered: tried tongue tied. *M. Todhunter*

RAY BOY (IRE) 6 b. or br.g. Oscar (IRE) – Cappagale (IRE) (Strong Gale) [2004/5 F16s^{3} F16s^{2} 18s* Mar 5] lengthy gelding: first foal: dam unraced, out of half-sister to high-class staying chaser Cahervillahow: useful form in bumpers: won at Cork on debut in 2003/4: favourite, won 26-runner maiden at Navan on hurdling debut: better effort in novices at Punchestown in late-April when 5 lengths third to Snoopy Loopy: will stay at least 2½m. *P. C. O'Connor, Ireland* **h123 F106**

RAY MOND 4 b.g. Midnight Legend – Kinsale Florale (IRE) (Supreme Leader) [2004/5 F16g Jan 24] £3,500 3-y-o: first foal: dam maiden Irish pointer: tailed off in bumper on debut. *M. J. Gingell* **F–**

RAYSHAN (IRE) 5 b.g. Darshaan – Rayseka (IRE) (Dancing Brave (USA)) [2004/5 h113p: 17g 17g 16s* Mar 22] leggy gelding: fairly useful hurdler: improved form when winning handicap at Wetherby in March by 6 lengths from Vigoureux: disappointing in much more competitive race at Punchestown in late-April: should be suited by 2½m+: acts on soft going. *J. Howard Johnson* **h125**

RAY SOURCE (IRE) 10 b.g. Lashkari – Salote (USA) (Forli (ARG)) [2004/5 c98, h93: c26g^{pu} c24g^{2} Aug 14] leggy gelding: modest hurdler/chaser: stayed 3¼m: acted on good to firm and heavy going: blinkered last 3 starts: dead. *Ian Williams* **c92 h–**

RAZZAMATAZZ 7 b.g. Alhijaz – Salvezza (IRE) (Superpower) [2004/5 17d 24m* 21s^{5} 24s Nov 16] modest hurdler: won 3-finisher novice at Towcester in May: stays 3m: acts on good to firm going, below form on softer than good. *R. Dickin* **h85**

REACH FOR THE TOP (IRE) 4 br.g. Topanoora – Burren Gale (IRE) (Strong Gale) [2004/5 F13d^{4} F16g^{6} Mar 26] useful-looking gelding: sixth foal: half-brother to 3 winners, including useful chaser Rosslea, stayed 3m, and useful hunter chaser Gatsby (both by Roselier): dam unraced: fair form in bumpers at Exeter and Haydock: will be suited by further than 2m. *Miss H. C. Knight* **F94 +**

REACH THE CLOUDS (IRE) 13 b.g. Lord Americo – Dusky Stream (Paddy's Stream) [2004/5 c93§, h78: c17d^{4} c16v c17g^{5} c17g* 16d Apr 18] good-topped gelding: winning hurdler: modest chaser: won selling handicap at Plumpton (fourth course success) in March: raced mainly around 2m: acts on heavy and good to firm going: blinkered twice: probably best on left-handed course: usually finds little. *John R. Upson* **c86 § h70 §**

READY TO LAND (IRE) 7 ch.g. Phardante (FR) – Spread Your Wings (IRE) (Decent Fellow) [2004/5 16g^{F} 17g 17s 16g^{pu} Nov 18] IR £15,000 3-y-o: sturdy, lengthy ex-Irish gelding: third foal: dam, modest 2m hurdler, out of half-sister to very smart staying chaser Arctic Call: modest form at best in bumpers for J. A. Berry: no sign of ability over hurdles. *D. R. Gandolfo* **h–**

READY TO RUMBLE (IRE) 10 ch.g. Phardante (FR) – My Only Hope (Brave Invader (USA)) [2004/5 c105, h–: c23d^{pu} c24g^{2} Mar 3] sturdy gelding: winning hurdler: maiden chaser: left N. Chance and fit from points, runner-up in hunter at Taunton: stays 3m: acts on soft going. *J. Scott* **c83 h–**

READY TO RUMBLE (NZ) 8 ch.g. Danasinga (AUS) – Regal Odyssey (NZ) (Vice Regal (NZ)) [2004/5 16d 16s^{6} 20m 16v Dec 27] compact gelding: successful from 6.5f to around 11f on Flat in Australasia: poor form over hurdles. *R. C. Guest* **h79**

REAL CHIEF (IRE) 7 b.g. Caerleon (USA) – Greek Air (IRE) (Ela-Mana-Mou) [2004/5 19s^{pu} 20v 21d^{ur} 20v^{pu} 16d Jan 7] leggy gelding: little sign of ability. *Miss M. E. Rowland* **h–**

REAL CRACKER (IRE) 6 b.g. Lahib (USA) – Loreo (IRE) (Lord Chancellor (USA)) [2004/5 h92p, F91: 17d^{6} 19s 21d 21s^{5} Mar 31] bumper winner: disappointing maiden hurdler: possibly unsuited by soft going. *Miss Venetia Williams* **h85 d**

REAL DEFINITION 6 br.g. Highest Honor (FR) – Segovia (Groom Dancer (USA)) [2004/5 F94: F16s 20v^{pu} 25s^{4} 20d^{5} Apr 22] good-topped gelding: fair form in bumpers, won at Warwick in 2003/4: shaped better than result suggests both completed starts over hurdles: likely to prove capable of improvement, particularly over short of 3m. *D. J. Wintle* **h– p F89**

REAL ESTATE 11 b.g. High Estate – Haitienne (FR) (Green Dancer (USA)) [2004/5 19g Jul 28] compact gelding: handicap hurdler/chaser, tailed off only outing in 2004/5: tried blinkered. *J. S. King* **c– h–**

REAL SHADY 8 b.g. Bob's Return (IRE) – Madam Margeaux (IRE) (Ardross) [2004/5 h104: c17d⁶ c16d³ c16g⁴ c19d* c16d² Jan 13] tall gelding: fair hurdler: similar form over fences, winning handicap at Catterick in January: likely to prove best up to 2½m: raced on good going or softer (won bumper on soft): free-going sort. *M. W. Easterby* **c107 h–**

REAL SHARP (IRE) 7 br.g. Son of Sharp Shot (IRE) – Lady By Chance (IRE) (Never Got A Chance) [2004/5 h–: c21g May 21] lightly raced and little sign of ability: blinkered once: sold 2,200 gns Doncaster August Sales. *S. E. H. Sherwood* **c– h–**

REAP 7 b.g. Emperor Jones (USA) – Corn Futures (Nomination) [2004/5 17s 16g⁵ 16d⁴ 16d Mar 5] tall gelding: fair on Flat (stays 1¼m): apparently best effort in novice hurdles when fourth to Penzance in muddling event at Huntingdon. *J. Pearce* **h92**

REAP THE REWARD (IRE) 5 ch.g. Presenting – Reapers Harvest (Carlingford Castle) [2004/5 F16s³ Apr 22] €31,000 3-y-o: fifth foal: half-brother to winning chaser Live Our Dreams (by Glacial Storm), stays 3m: dam unraced half-sister to useful 2m hurdler The Gatherer: 4¼ lengths third to Powerlove in bumper at Perth on debut: looks a stayer. *L. Lungo* **F89**

REASONABLE RESERVE (IRE) 8 ch.g. Fourstars Allstar (USA) – Alice O'Malley (The Parson) [2004/5 c–x, h107: 26g* c26d² 26dᵖᵘ 22gᵖᵘ Apr 10] fair hurdler: won handicap at Southwell in May: let down by jumping over fences: stays 3¼m: acts on good to firm going: tried blinkered/in cheekpieces: not one to rely on (ran out once in 2003/4). *B. G. Powell* **c– x h108 §**

REASONABLY SURE (IRE) 5 b.g. Presenting – No Reason (Kemal (FR)) [2004/5 F16d 21g⁶ 17g² 16g³ 20dᵘʳ Feb 18] €15,500 3-y-o: well-made gelding: sixth foal: half-brother to winning pointer by Denel: dam unraced: failed to complete in two 4-y-o maiden Irish points in 2004: seventh of 12 in bumper at Chepstow: fair form when placed in novice hurdles: should stay beyond 17f: raced on good/good to soft going: has gone early to post. *O. Sherwood* **h104 F–**

REBEL RHYTHM 6 b.g. Robellino (USA) – Celt Song (IRE) (Unfuwain (USA)) [2004/5 F108: 16s* 16s² 20v* 21d 17d* 20d³ 24dᶠ Apr 8] **h134**

Rebel Rhythm's career is in marked contrast to his two-year-older half-sister Princess Ellen (by Tirol), who won over six and seven furlongs as a juvenile and went on to show smart form at up to a mile and a quarter as a three-year-old, when runner-up in both the One Thousand Guineas and Coronation Stakes. Having been sold untried and unnamed for just 6,000 guineas at the 2003 Doncaster May Sales, Rebel Rhythm is making his name as a jumper, one who has been successful over as far as two and a half miles and is likely to stay three. Unraced on the Flat, Rebel Rhythm showed useful form in bumpers in 2003/4, winning at Wetherby, and also in novice hurdles in the latest season, when successful at Haydock (twice) and Bangor, and he looks the sort who could go on and show himself even better over fences. Whereas the close-coupled, quite attractive Princess Ellen was built for Flat racing, Rebel Rhythm, a big, good-bodied gelding, is very much a chasing type. Rebel Rhythm put up his best performances in the latest season on his third and sixth starts, though a narrow defeat by Turpin Green at Aintree on his second start reads well in hindsight. In the former, over the fixed brush hurdles, he was impressive when landing the odds by fifteen lengths, jumping soundly and drawing clear in the straight; and in the latter he finished third under top weight in the European Breeders' Fund 'National Hunt' Novices' Handicap Hurdle Final at Sandown, beaten around two lengths by the winner Julius Caesar to whom he was conceding a stone. Rebel Rhythm showed in both races that he stays two and a half miles well. He was tried at three miles on his final outing, in the Sefton Novices' Hurdle at Aintree, but took a heavy fall four out when in touch and still travelling well enough. So far, Rebel Rhythm has raced only on ground softer than good, and he acts on heavy. *Mrs S. J. Smith*

RECENT EDITION (IRE) 7 b.g. Roselier (FR) – Hi Millie (Decent Fellow) [2004/5 c25sᶠ c21d⁵ c27dᵖᵘ c24gᵖᵘ c30v* c27v⁴ c26vᵖᵘ Apr 17] third foal: dam won 2½m hurdle: won maiden Irish point in 2004: 15 lb out of weights, form over fences only when winning handicap at Newcastle in January: thorough stayer: wore cheekpieces after debut. *J. Wade* **c82**

RECKLESS RUBY 5 b.m. Keen – Petite Ibnr (IRE) (Phardante (FR)) [2004/5 F16v F17v Mar 20] first foal: dam, modest form in bumper, soundly beaten over hurdles: tailed off in 2 bumpers. *B. Mactaggart* **F–**

RED ACER (IRE) 4 ch.g. Shinko Forest (IRE) – Another Baileys (Deploy) [2004/5 16g^{pu} 16d Dec 2] no form on Flat or 2 starts over hurdles: left P. D. Evans after first outing (tongue tied). *Mrs N. S. Sharpe* **h–**

RED AFGEM 8 ch.m. Afzal – Preacher's Gem (The Parson) [2004/5 h–: 26d Apr 29] sturdy mare: no form. *Mrs S. M. Johnson* **h–**

RED ALERT MAN (IRE) 9 ch.g. Sharp Charter – Tukurua (Noalto) [2004/5 c74?, h–: c22m^{pu} c21g^{4} c21d^{5} c27m^{5} c16m c26g^{2} c24s^{3} c26d* c30d^{5} c24s^{6} c25d^{5} c23s* c32v^{pu} Mar 17] workmanlike gelding: poor handicap chaser: won at Warwick in November and Leicester in February: stays 3¼m: acts on heavy going: tried in cheekpieces, usually wears blinkers. *Mrs L. Williamson* **c65 h–**

RED ALF 6 ch.g. Alflora (IRE) – Red Dust (Saxon Farm) [2004/5 F16g Apr 19] third foal: dam twice-raced half-sister to fairly useful staying hurdler/chaser Sweep Gently: tailed off in bumper on debut. *Miss J. Wormall* **F–**

RED ARK 12 ch.g. Gunner B – Minim (Rymer) [2004/5 c17m^{pu} c23m^{6} Aug 6] good-bodied gelding: has been hobdayed: useful handicap chaser in 2002/3: mistakes both starts on return: stays 23f, effective over much shorter: unraced on firm going, acts on any other: in cheekpieces last 4 starts: tongue tied. *R. C. Guest* **c– h–**

RED AUTUMN 8 ch.g. Nomadic Way (USA) – Naturally Autumn (Hello Gorgeous (USA)) [2004/5 20g^{pu} 16s 27d^{pu} Nov 23] lengthy, rather sparely-made gelding: third foal: half-brother to dual bumper winner Autumn Lord (by Lord Bud): dam, winning staying jumper, half-sister to smart 2m hurdler/useful chaser Aldino: no show in 3 novice hurdles. *C. W. Fairhurst* **h–**

REDBERRY HOLLY (IRE) 7 gr.m. Roselier (FR) – Solvia (IRE) (Persian Mews) [2004/5 c–, h–: c26g c25f^{4} May 18] winning pointer: no form over hurdles or in chases. *R. H. Buckler* **c– h–**

RED BROOK LAD 10 ch.g. Nomadic Way (USA) – Silently Yours (USA) (Silent Screen (USA)) [2004/5 c113, h–: c21g^{pu} c20g^{3} c21d* c22g* Apr 1] leggy gelding: won point in January: useful hunter chaser: successful at Wincanton in March and Newbury (beat Silver Castle 1¼ lengths) in April: stays 25f: acts on firm and good to soft going: tried blinkered over hurdles: improved jumper: patiently ridden. *C. St V. Fox* **c114 h–**

RED CAMPION 5 ch.m. Defacto (USA) – Boulevard Girl (Nicholas Bill) [2004/5 F16s F17g 24s^{pu} Apr 10] angular mare: seventh foal: half-sister to 3m hurdle winner Litzinsky (by Muhtarram), also 2m winner on Flat, and 11f/1½m winner Blenheim Terrace (by Rambo Dancer): dam won at up to 2m: no form in bumpers and novice hurdle. *T. D. Walford* **h– F–**

RED CANYON (IRE) 8 b.g. Zieten (USA) – Bayazida (Bustino) [2004/5 h95: 16g^{3} 22m 20d^{F} 19s 22d^{2} 22d^{3} Nov 18] sturdy gelding: poor handicap hurdler: stays 3m: acts on firm and good to soft going: tried blinkered/visored: usually races prominently. *C. L. Tizzard* **h89**

RED CEDAR (USA) 5 ch.g. Woodman (USA) – Jewell Ridge (USA) (Melyno) [2004/5 16g^{5} Mar 9] small, leggy ex-Irish gelding: half-brother to 1996 Breeders' Cup Distaff winner Jewel Princess (by Key To The Mint): lightly raced on Flat, runner-up in 2 maidens in 2003: modest form over hurdles, left A.Mullins before only outing in 2004/5: raced at 2m on good going or firmer: has had tongue tied. *J. Wade* **h91**

RED CHIEF (IRE) 5 b.g. Lahib (USA) – Karayb (IRE) (Last Tycoon) [2004/5 h83: 16m^{5} 17s^{3} 16s^{5} 16d 21d^{pu} Feb 9] regressive form over hurdles: sold to join Mrs A. Thorpe £1,700 Ascot February Sales. *R. Lee* **h74**

RED DAHLIA 8 b.m. Alflora (IRE) – Redgrave Devil (Tug of War) [2004/5 h–: 16f^{3} 17m^{2} 19g^{pu} 17g^{5} 17d^{5} 21m^{bd} 17g^{ur} 19g* 16s^{4} c19m^{6} 20s^{5} 21d 16v^{5} 24s 21g^{5} Mar 28] rather sparely-made mare: poor handicap hurdler: won conditional jockeys seller at Taunton in October: mistakes when well held on chasing debut: barely stays testing 2½m: acts on good to firm and heavy going. *M. Pitman* **c– h74**

RED DAWN (IRE) 6 ch.g. Presenting – West Tour (Deep Run) [2004/5 F17g May 11] fifth foal: half-brother to fair hurdler Galant Tour (by Riberetto), stayed 2¾m: dam, lightly raced in points, half-sister to Cheltenham Gold Cup winner Cool Dawn: well beaten in bumper on debut. *Miss H. C. Knight* **F–**

Stan James Handicap Chase, Newbury—Red Devil Robert jumps to the front two out; Bee An Bee (left) and Gunner Welburn take the places

REDDE (IRE) 10 ch.g. Classic Memory – Stoney Broke (Pauper) [2004/5 c101, h–: c25dpu 24spu 20vpu 24dpu 24d Feb 26] deep-girthed gelding: one-time fairly useful hurdler/winning chaser: no form in 2004/5, sold out of R. Smith's stable £8,500 Ascot July Sales after second outing: should stay 3¼m: acts on heavy going: tried blinkered. *Mrs J. G. Retter* **c– h–**

RED DEVIL ROBERT (IRE) 7 ch.g. Carroll House – Well Over (Over The River (FR)) [2004/5 h106: c21d³ c24g* c24s* c24m* c25m² Apr 13] good-topped gelding: fair maiden hurdler: progressive form over fences: reportedly had wind operation after reappearance: won maiden at Taunton in March and handicaps at Stratford later in month and Newbury in April, useful form when beating Bee An Bee by 1½ lengths at last-named: not discredited when 12 lengths second to Liverpool Echo in novice at Cheltenham, tending to hang: should stay beyond 25f: acts on soft and good to firm going: may still be capable of improvement. *P. F. Nicholls* **c133 + h–**

RED EMPEROR 11 b.g. Emperor Fountain – Golden Curd (FR) (Nice Havrais (USA)) [2004/5 c–, h–: 21m 24g⁶ May 16] lengthy gelding: winning chaser/maiden hurdler, no longer of any account: formerly often in headgear: has had tongue tied. *Dr P. Pritchard* **c– h–**

REDEMPTION 10 b.g. Sanglamore (USA) – Ypha (USA) (Lyphard (USA)) [2004/5 c142x, h135: 21g c21dur c21d² c21s c24s c21g Mar 17] workmanlike gelding: useful handicap chaser: trained by M. Pipe second and third starts, more fluent than usual when second to Le Duc in valuable event at Cheltenham: well beaten subsequently: useful hurdler, found less than seemed likely on reappearance: stays 21f: acts on heavy and good to firm going: blinkered once (went in snatches): sketchy jumper of fences. *N. A. Twiston-Davies* **c144 x h132**

RED ENSIGN 8 ch.g. Lancastrian – Medway Queen (Pitpan) [2004/5 h–: 22d³ 22d* 22s⁴ 22s⁵ 22s⁴ 22v³ 22g² Mar 20] workmanlike gelding: poor novice hurdler: off over 6 months, won handicap at Fontwell in November: stays 2¾m: raced mainly on going softer than good (acts on heavy): effective with or without cheekpieces. *Mrs L. C. Jewell* **h79**

RED FLYER (IRE) 6 br.g. Catrail (USA) – Marostica (ITY) (Stone) [2004/5 h94: 16d 16m 16d 17d⁴ c16d³ 19m⁵ 20sur 21v³ Jan 25] leggy, quite good-topped gelding: modest handicap hurdler: would have won conditional jockeys seller at Newcastle but for unseating last: similar form on chasing debut: effective at 2m to 21f: acts on heavy going, probably on good to firm. *P. C. Haslam* **c83 h85**

RED GAUNTLET 12 b.g. Wonderful Surprise – Border Minstrel (Menelek) [2004/5 24m^{pu} Jun 5] fair pointer, won twice in 2004: quickly beaten after leading to 4 out in novice on hurdling debut. *Mrs A. C. Hamilton* **c– h–**

RED GENIE 7 ch.g. Primitive Rising (USA) – Marsden Rock (Tina's Pet) [2004/5 h71: 16s^{pu} 17s^{F} 17m 19v^{3} 16v^{ur} 16d 17s 19d^{pu} Mar 26] bad maiden hurdler: stays 2½m: acts on heavy going: has worn cheekpieces: headstrong. *C. J. Gray* **h–**

RED GEORGIE (IRE) 7 ch.g. Old Vic – Do We Know (Derrylin) [2004/5 F17g* F16d* F16d^{5} 20v^{3} 23v^{pu} 23s* 24s* 21g 24s^{4} Apr 21] lengthy, workmanlike gelding: chasing type: half-brother to several winners, including useful hurdler/fair chaser Bo Knows Best (by Burslem), stayed 21f: dam thrice-raced, from family of good Anglo-American jumper Inlander, stayed 3m: useful form in bumpers, winning at Hereford in May and Worcester in October: fairly useful novice hurdler: won at Wetherby (beating Romany Prince 3 lengths) in February and Kempton in March: stiff task, probably flattered when eleventh of 20 in Royal & SunAlliance Novices' Hurdle at Cheltenham eighth start: will stay beyond 3m: raced on good going or softer: races up with pace. *N. A. Twiston-Davies* **h117 F105**

RED GOLD 11 ch.g. Sula Bula – Ruby Celebration (New Member) [2004/5 c75x, h–: c25g^{pu} May 8] workmanlike gelding: poor maiden chaser: stays 25f: acts on heavy going: blinkered only start in 2004/5: has had tongue tied: poor jumper. *Andrew Turnell* **cxx h–**

RED GRANITE 5 gr.g. Rock City – Cherry Side (General Ironside) [2004/5 F16m Apr 2] 14,000 (privately) 4-y-o: compact gelding: half-brother to fairly useful staying chaser Cherokee Boy (by Mirror Boy): dam, winning pointer, from family of useful chaser up to 3m Cherrynut: never-nearer eighth of 21 to Hi Humpfree in bumper at Newbury on debut: likely to benefit from greater test of stamina. *K. C. Bailey* **F90**

RED GUARD 11 ch.g. Soviet Star (USA) – Zinzara (USA) (Stage Door Johnny (USA)) [2004/5 c107§, h–§: c20s^{2} c21s^{pu} Apr 7] workmanlike gelding: ungenuine winning chaser: fit from points, second to Gadz'art in hunter at Leicester, tying up run-in: stays 25f: acts on firm and soft going: has worn blinkers/cheekpieces: weak finisher. *George Hosier* **c102 § h– §**

RED HEATHER 8 b.m. Mistertopogigo (IRE) – That's Rich (Hot Spark) [2004/5 h–: 23d^{pu} Apr 25] sturdy mare: seems of no account. *D. W. Whillans* **h–**

RED HUSTLER (IRE) 9 ch.g. Husyan (USA) – Isoldes Tower (Balliol) [2004/5 c88, h–: c16g^{2} Apr 19] workmanlike gelding: poor handicap chaser: last of 5 finishers on completed outing in points: stays 2¾m: acts on soft and good to firm going: wore cheekpieces/visor last 5 starts in 2003/4. *W. Davies* **c79 h–**

REDI (ITY) 4 b.g. Danehill Dancer (IRE) – Rossella (Shareef Dancer (USA)) [2004/5 16s 16d^{5} 16g* 16d* 16g Mar 15] angular gelding: fair on Flat (stays 1½m), successful in August, sold out of L. Cumani's stable 52,000 gns Newmarket Autumn Sales: fair juvenile hurdler: won at Southwell in January and Sandown in February, dictating steady pace when beating Dhehdaah by 3½ lengths at latter: will stay beyond 2m: tongue tied after debut. *A. M. Balding* **h103**

RED JESTER 4 b.g. Thowra (FR) – Red Ebrel (IRE) (Red Sunset) [2004/5 17d^{pu} Feb 1] sturdy gelding: first foal: dam, poor hurdler, stayed 2½m: no show in novice hurdle on debut. *A. E. Jones* **h–**

RED LION (FR) 8 ch.g. Lion Cavern (USA) – Mahogany River (Irish River (FR)) [2004/5 h–: 20g^{6} c16d^{F} Nov 9] good-topped gelding: maiden hurdler: raced freely and jumped poorly on chasing debut: stays 21f: acts on good to firm and good to soft going: has had tongue tied. *D. McCain* **c– h87**

REDLYNCH SPIRIT (IRE) 5 b.g. Executive Perk – Gently Ridden (IRE) (King's Ride) [2004/5 F17v Feb 13] 6,500 4-y-o: compact gelding: first foal: dam, well held in 2 bumpers, from family of useful staying chasers Harveystown and Deep Moment: well held in bumper on debut. *C. L. Tizzard* **F–**

RED MAN (IRE) 8 ch.g. Toulon – Jamie's Lady (Ashmore (FR)) [2004/5 h106: 21d^{pu} 20s 27d^{pu} 17v^{4} 19d 20s^{2} Mar 12] fair hurdler: back to form in cheekpieces final outing: best efforts at 2½m to 2¾m: probably acts on any going. *Mrs E. Slack* **h103**

RED MARSALA 7 b.g. Tragic Role (USA) – Southend Scallywag (Tina's Pet) [2004/5 c–, h–: c17d 20m^{pu} Jun 12] leggy gelding: no form over hurdles or in chases: tried blinkered, usually wears cheekpieces: sold 1,800 gns Doncaster October Sales: won maiden point in March. *R. C. Guest* **c– h–**

RED MINSTER 8 b.g. Minster Son – Minty Muncher (Idiot's Delight) [2004/5 c–, h–: c25mpu May 11] sturdy, lengthy gelding: winning chaser: no form in 3 outings since 2002/3: stays 2½m: acts on heavy going: usually wears cheekpieces: sold 500 gns Doncaster October Sales. *R. C. Guest* **c– h–**

RED MOOR (IRE) 5 gr.g. Eagle Eyed (USA) – Faakirah (Dragonara Palace (USA)) [2004/5 17g5 Dec 9] half-brother to winning hurdler around 2m Lady of The Inn (by Hamas): modest on Flat (barely stays 14.8f), sold out of R. Hollinshead's stable £7,500 Ascot August Sales: similar form when fifth of 10 in novice at Taunton on hurdling debut. *Mrs D. A. Hamer* **h99**

RED NOSE LADY 8 b.m. Teenoso (USA) – Red Rambler (Rymer) [2004/5 c–§, h82§: 20d3 24g 16g3 16m3 16g* 16g6 17m5 22d2 21m4 24d5 20s* 16d 17g5 16d Feb 24] lengthy mare: no show only outing over fences: modest hurdler: won handicaps at Uttoxeter (seller) in July and Haydock in November: sold out of J. M. Jefferson's stable 4,200 gns Doncaster Sales later in November: effective at 2m to 3m: acts on good to firm and heavy going: usually wears headgear: ungenuine. *G. J. Smith* **c– § h89 §**

RED OR WHITE (IRE) 6 ch.g. Semillon – Sweet Chimes (Orchestra) [2004/5 h112, F74: 24g 20m2 20m* c20mF Jul 8] fair handicap hurdler: won at Fairyhouse in May: still in with chance when fell fatally 2 out in maiden at Tipperary on chasing debut: stayed 2½m: acted on soft and good to firm going. *W. P. Mullins, Ireland* **c82 h112**

RED PERK (IRE) 8 b.g. Executive Perk – Supreme View (Supreme Leader) [2004/5 c87, h76: c25gpu c24gF 24dpu c25d* c25v3 c26s3 c32v3 Mar 17] workmanlike gelding: maiden hurdler: modest handicap chaser: won at Kelso in February: raced mainly at 3m+ (stays 4m): acts on heavy going: usually wears cheekpieces. *R. C. Guest* **c86 h–**

RED RAMPAGE 10 b.g. King's Ride – Mighty Fly (Comedy Star (USA)) [2004/5 c106, h–: c25sR c24v* c32v5 c26s4 c21sF c31s6 Apr 22] good-topped gelding: modest chaser nowadays: awarded hunter at Newcastle in February: stays 31f: acts on heavy and good to firm going: tried visored, blinkered and tongue tied nowadays: often front runner. *H. P. Hogarth* **c98 h–**

RED RAPTOR 4 ch.g. Polar Falcon (USA) – Star Precision (Shavian) [2004/5 F17v Feb 15] first foal: dam, 1m to 13f winner, half-sister to smart staying hurdlers Brave Tornado and Accipiter (by Polar Falcon): last of 8 in bumper on debut. *J. A. Geake* **F–**

RED RED RED (IRE) 9 b.g. Be My Native (USA) – Moppet's Last (Pitpan) [2004/5 24mpu c26mR Aug 19] ex-Irish gelding: winning hurdler: no form in 3 starts over fences: bought out of N. Meade's stable 800 gns Doncaster May Sales: stays 19f: acts on good to firm going, probably on soft. *L. A. Dace* **c– h–**

RED RETURN (IRE) 8 ch.g. Bob's Return (IRE) – Kerrie's Pearl (Proverb) [2004/5 h88: 26d6 25s3 21g6 Jan 14] lengthy gelding: poor novice hurdler. *L. A. Dace* **h76**

RED RUFFLES (IRE) 6 b.g. Anshan – Rosie Ruffles (IRE) (Homo Sapien) [2004/5 h116, F104: 20d2 21g2 21d3 24d 21g Mar 16] unfurnished gelding: fairly useful hurdler: good efforts in handicaps at Cheltenham second to fourth starts: stays 3m: raced on good going or softer. *Noel T. Chance* **h124**

REDSKIN RAIDER (IRE) 9 b.g. Commanche Run – Sheltered (IRE) (Strong Gale) [2004/5 c93, h–: c24g* c24g* c25dpu Mar 24] lengthy gelding: fair chaser: won maiden at Perth in July and novice at Huntingdon (made all) in October: sold out of T. George's stable 15,000 gns Doncaster November Sales: ran no sort of race final outing: stays 25f: best form on good/good to firm going. *Jane Southall* **c104 h–**

RED SOCIALITE (IRE) 8 ch.g. Moscow Society (USA) – Dees Darling (IRE) (King Persian) [2004/5 c100, h–: c20dpu c20gpu Mar 16] tall, angular gelding: winning hurdler: last of 4 finishers only completed outing over fences: stays 21f: acts on good to firm going. *D. R. Gandolfo* **c– h–**

RED SOCIETY (IRE) 7 ch.g. Moscow Society (USA) – Allendara (IRE) (Phardante (FR)) [2004/5 c100, h77: c21d3 22f3 19s2 19dbd 19m* 19m2 19d* 19g* 19s 19d2 c20d3 c19g* Apr 15] angular gelding: fair handicap hurdler/chaser: won over hurdles at Taunton (amateur) in November and Exeter (conditional jockeys) and Taunton in December, and over fences at Taunton again (veered sharply left and hampered runner-up run-in) in April: stays 23f: acts on firm and soft going: usually wears cheekpieces/blinkers: consistent. *P. J. Hobbs* **c106 h107**

REDSPIN (IRE) 5 ch.g. Spectrum (IRE) – Trendy Indian (IRE) (Indian Ridge) [2004/5 h98: 24g2 21gsu 24m4 24g Nov 17] angular gelding: fair on Flat (stays 2½m), **h96 §**

successful in April: modest maiden hurdler: stays 3m: acts on good to firm going: no easy ride (carries head awkwardly). *J. S. Moore*

RED SQUARE LAD (IRE) 9 ch.g. Toulon – Tempestuous Girl (Tumble Wind) [2004/5 h–: c23s* Mar 11] lightly raced: well held in novice hurdle: won maiden point in January: created good impression when winning maiden hunter at Leicester on chasing debut, making most to beat Denvale 6 lengths: should prove as effective over shorter than 23f: open to improvement. *Mrs L. Williamson* **c109 p h–**

REDSTAR ATTRACTION 7 ch.g. Nalchik (USA) – Star Gal (Starch Reduced) [2004/5 F–: F16g³ aF16g⁴ Oct 30] apparently best effort in bumpers when fourth on polytrack at Lingfield, racing freely up with steady pace: sold £2,000 Ascot February Sales. *W. M. Brisbourne* **F80**

RED STRIKER 11 ch.g. Gunner B – Cover Your Money (Precipice Wood) [2004/5 20sᵖᵘ c20d Nov 20] workmanlike gelding: useful handicap chaser in 2002/3: last of 8 in Grade 2 at Huntingdon in November: winning hurdler, backward on reappearance: stays 3m: best form on going softer than good (acts on heavy): usually tongue tied: patiently ridden. *R. C. Guest* **c– h–**

RED SUN 8 b.g. Foxhound (USA) – Superetta (Superlative) [2004/5 h121: 16m May 1] small, leggy gelding: fairly useful handicap hurdler: stiff task at Haydock early in 2004/5: stays 19f: acts on soft and firm going: tongue tied final outing in 2003/4: consistent: won twice on Flat in 2004. *J. Mackie* **h–**

REDVIC 5 b.g. Alhaatmi – Sweet Fortune (Dubassoff (USA)) [2004/5 h–: 24g⁴ 17g 17g c16s c19vᵖᵘ Mar 29] of little account. *G. J. Smith* **c– h–**

RED WILL DANAGHER (IRE) 8 b.g. Glacial Storm (USA) – Clodas Pet (IRE) (Andretti) [2004/5 h85: 19s⁵ 24sᵘʳ Apr 16] workmanlike gelding: maiden hurdler: off 18 months before reappearance: stays 2¾m: temperamental. *John Allen* **h– §**

REEDSMAN (IRE) 4 ch.g. Fayruz – The Way She Moves (North Stoke) [2004/5 16g 17mᵘʳ 17gᵖᵘ 17d 16mᵘʳ 17g 17m Apr 23] brother to modest hurdler Fayrway Rhythm, stays 2½m: disappointing maiden on Flat: no form over hurdles: in headgear after debut: tried tongue tied. *R. C. Guest* **h–**

REEL DANCER 8 b.g. Minshaanshu Amad (USA) – Sister Rosarii (USA) (Properantes (USA)) [2004/5 c105, h–: c21sᵖᵘ c24d³ c26m* Apr 21] sturdy gelding: lightly raced: modest chaser: won handicap at Fontwell in April: stays 3¼m: acts on good to firm and good to soft going: sold 4,700 gns Doncaster May Sales. *N. J. Henderson* **c94 + h–**

REELINGA 6 b.m. Karinga Bay – Reeling (Relkino) [2004/5 F17m aF16g⁵ 17dᶠ 17m⁵ 17s Jan 20] second foal: half-sister to modest hurdler/fair chaser around 2m Darnley (by Henbit): dam, poor around 2m over jumps, half-sister to useful 1m winner Macarthurs Head: signs of only a little ability in bumpers and over hurdles. *G. A. Ham* **h– F73**

REEL MISSILE 6 b.g. Weld – Landsker Missile (Cruise Missile) [2004/5 F109: F16s* 16s² 20s⁵ 20d² 19g* 20g Mar 26] tall, lengthy, angular gelding: will make a chaser: useful at best in bumpers, won at Fakenham in October: fair novice hurdler: won at Doncaster in March by 2½ lengths from Mistress Banjo: stays 2½m: raced on good going or softer: races prominently. *C. T. Pogson* **h114 F103**

REEM TWO 4 b.f. Mtoto – Jamrat Samya (IRE) (Sadler's Wells (USA)) [2004/5 16m⁴ 16g³ 16d⁴ 16d 16g³ 17g³ Mar 19] smallish filly: half-sister to winning 2¾m hurdler Murghob (by Lycius): modest maiden on Flat (stays 1½m): modest novice hurdler: raced around 2m: acts on good to soft ground. *D. McCain* **h95**

REFINEMENT (IRE) 6 b.m. Oscar (IRE) – Maneree (Mandalus) [2004/5 F115: F17d* F16g⁴ F17d⁴ Apr 9] **F121**

As for being an unqualified success at stud, it is not yet clear whether Oscar will or not. No fewer than 130 horses by that stallion ran in Britain and Ireland in 2004/5, the oldest of them six in 2005. This was three times as many as had represented him in 2003/4. Between them they managed forty-one wins, up from twelve in the previous season, but they needed getting on for four times as many runs to record that number and Oscar's wins-to-runs ratio actually fell slightly. As in the previous season, there were clear signs that his stock takes time to mature. The pick of the handful of winners from his 2000 and 2001 crops were the promising hurdler Sea Captain and the useful bumper winner Its A Dream, while his first crop, from 1999, contained half a dozen that are useful or better in bumpers as well. Oscar hasn't yet had a notable performer over jumps, the best of his

Paddy Power Champion INH Flat, Punchestown—blinkers revitalise Refinement, who takes revenge on The Cool Guy (white cap) and Missed That (spotted cap) who had beaten her at Aintree and Cheltenham; Nicanor (hooped cap) splits that pair

hurdlers so far, apart from Sea Captain, being the rather disappointing Augherskea and the fairly useful Arteea and Ray Boy. With Oscar continuing to cover massive books (378 mares in 2004) there is clearly every chance there will be at the very least one really good one in there, though the analogy with chimpanzees at a typewriter producing Shakespeare—or, perhaps, *Lady Windermere's Fan*—springs to mind. Oscar's progeny continued to sell well in 2004, with eight three-year-old and six four-year-old stores by him making €30,000 or the equivalent in guineas. Of the fourteen horses involved, only one has yet raced, €40,000-purchase Sodbuster falling in a maiden point on his debut in April.

As in 2003/4, Oscar's best bumper performer was the mare Refinement. It is very rare for a horse to have two full campaigns in bumpers but Refinement did, and, in keeping with her sire's stock, she improved in her second season. Having chased home another mare Total Enjoyment in the Champion Bumper at Cheltenham in 2004, she contested the three top bumpers in the spring in 2005, putting up an improved performance when winning the Paddy Power Champion INH Flat at Punchestown shortly after the end of the British season. Her appearance at Cheltenham, Aintree and Punchestown was in itself notable, as she was just the third horse to contest all three races, following Burn Out (in 1996) who won at Aintree and King's Road (in 1998) who won at Aintree and Punchestown after finishing sixth at Cheltenham. Until 2005, only two others had run both at Aintree and Punchestown, neither of them successful. Punchestown was Refinement's seventh start in a bumper. She had won three of her first four, including a five-runner event at Aintree in November, but had not been at her best when fourth at Cheltenham, four and a half lengths behind Missed That, or at Aintree, a length closer to the winner that day The Cool Guy, when again finishing fourth. Both those winners were in the nineteen-runner field at Punchestown, with Missed That a short-priced favourite. Refinement, though, was preferred to The Cool Guy in the betting, starting second favourite at 6/1 to his 9/1 (she had been favourite at Aintree). Confidence that she was back to her best proved totally justified. Her turn of foot, which had been lacking previously in the spring, was evident again at Punchestown and Refinement settled matters in strides into the straight. She was by no means all out to beat The Cool Guy by nine lengths, with another six to the third Nicanor, and Missed That some way below his Cheltenham form in fourth. Refinement's was the best performance in a bumper by a mare or filly since Aries Girl won the same Punchestown race in 1994 (Aries Girl had finished second to another mare Mucklemeg in the Festival Bumper at Cheltenham). Blinkers first time may well have played an important part in Refinement's revival at Punchestown, though her trainer Jonjo O'Neill suggested a change of rider might also have played its part. Her work rider Alan Berry, who had won on her at Aintree in the autumn, was back in the saddle, the Punchestown race being for amateurs only, but he could not draw his allowance because of the value of the race. He took over from champion jockeys Kieran

Fallon and Tony McCoy who had ridden her at Cheltenham and Aintree respectively (another champion, Barry Geraghty, rode her when she was beaten in the Champion Bumper in 2004). Fallon, who only took out a National Hunt licence in the week before Cheltenham, was unable to match his predecessor as stable jockey to Aidan O'Brien, Jamie Spencer, who won the Champion Bumper on Pizarro in 2002.

Refinement (IRE) (b.m. 1999)	Oscar (IRE) (b 1994)	Sadler's Wells (b 1981)	Northern Dancer
			Fairy Bridge
		Snow Day (b 1978)	Reliance II
			Vindaria
	Maneree (b 1987)	Mandalus (b 1974)	Mandamus
			Laminate
		Damberee (ch 1975)	Deep Run
			Star O'Meath

Refinement's half-brother Manners (by Topanoora) returned from a year's absence to show smart form to win a listed bumper at Cheltenham in November and then made a highly promising debut over hurdles later in the month before being off the course again. Their dam Maneree, who like them ran in Michael Tabor's colours, was placed in the bumpers at Cheltenham and Aintree before showing fairly useful form over hurdles and winning over fences at up to three miles. Manaree failed to produce another foal after Manners. In the latest season, there were also two other winners out of daughters of Refinement's grandam Damberee, the fairly useful bumper winner Ain't That A Shame and the fair hurdler Jacks Craic, who is out of a sister to Maneree. Other details of this family appeared in *Chasers & Hurdlers 2003/04*. Clearly, in terms of ability, Refinement has the makings of a useful jumper, but there are reasons for doubting whether she will be quite so good as that indicates, most obviously her lack of stature—she's smallish in appearance. That may explain her second campaign in bumpers. French Holly and Rhythm Section were two other notable names to have two bites at the cherry so far as bumpers were concerned. French Holly, placed in successive editions of the Punchestown race, went on to show himself a top-class hurdler but Rhythm Section, winner then fourth in two runnings of the then Festival Bumper at Cheltenham, won just once over hurdles and was a complete flop over fences. *Jonjo O'Neill*

REFLECTED GLORY (IRE) 6 b.g. Flemensfirth (USA) – Clashdermot Lass (Cardinal Flower) [2004/5 23d* 24s2 25v* 24d2 Feb 11] 6,000 4-y-o: tall gelding: half-brother to 3 winners, including fair hurdler/fairly useful chaser Aglish Pride (by Sheer Grit), stayed 2½m: dam unraced, from family of Dorans Pride: won second of 2 starts in 2½m maiden points in 2004: sold 33,000 gns Doncaster May Sales: fairly useful novice hurdler: won at Lingfield in November and Plumpton (beat Garryvoe 2 lengths) in January: stays 25f: acts on heavy going. *P. F. Nicholls* **h120**

REFLEX BLUE 8 b.g. Ezzoud (IRE) – Briggsmaid (Elegant Air) [2004/5 h89§: 24spu 16s 19g Apr 7] angular gelding: winning hurdler: no form in 2004/5: stays easy 21f: acts on firm and good to soft going: usually visored: temperamental. *R. J. Price* **h– §**

REFLEX COURIER (IRE) 13 b.g. Over The River (FR) – Thornpark Lady (Mandalus) [2004/5 c88: c22dpu c22spu Mar 6] good-bodied gelding: handicap chaser: no show both starts in 2004/5: stays 25f: raced on good going or softer (acts on heavy). *John R. Upson* **c–**

REGAL ACT (IRE) 9 ch.g. Montelimar (USA) – Portal Lady (Pals Passage) [2004/5 c–, h–: c26mF 20vpu 20spu 16g 20d 16g Mar 28] maiden hurdler: no form in Britain, including over fences: visored and tongue tied last 3 starts. *Jennie Candlish* **c– h–**

REGAL BANDIT (IRE) 7 b.g. Un Desperado (FR) – Rainbow Alliance (IRE) (Golden Love) [2004/5 h93+, F86: c19m* Nov 11] useful-looking gelding: modest form in novice hurdles: won novice handicap at Taunton on chasing debut in November: will stay 3m. *Miss H. C. Knight* **c96 + h–**

REGAL EXIT (FR) 9 ch.g. Exit To Nowhere (USA) – Regalante (Gairloch) [2004/5 c124, h129: 24d c16d6 c20d3 Nov 9] good-topped gelding: shows traces of stringhalt: winning hurdler: fairly useful handicap chaser: better effort in 2004/5 when sixth to Great Travel at Kempton: probably stays 21f: acts on good to firm and heavy going: has found little. *N. J. Henderson* **c120 h–**

REGAL HEIGHTS (IRE) 4 b.g. Grand Plaisir (IRE) – Regal Hostess (King's Ride) [2004/5 F17d^3 F16g* Apr 19] €15,000 3-y-o: big, good-topped gelding: chasing type: seventh foal: brother to fair hurdler/chaser Star of Caulry, stayed 3m, and half-brother to 2m hurdle winner Ithastobesaid (by Lanfranco): dam unraced: fair form in bumpers: won maiden at Towcester by short head from Dan's Man: likely to stay beyond 2m. *D. McCain* **F94**

REGAL JONES (IRE) 5 b.m. Sovereign Water (FR) – Juleit Jones (IRE) (Phardante (FR)) [2004/5 F–: 16g^5 18m^6 May 30] leggy mare: no sign of ability. *P. Butler* **h–**

REGAL LEADER 6 b.g. Mistertopogigo (IRE) – Princess Zena (Habitat) [2004/5 F16g F17s Feb 7] 2,000 5-y-o: half-brother to several winners, notably very smart 1m to 1¼m winner Supreme Leader (by Bustino): dam, 2-y-o 5f winner, half-sister to dam of Pebbles: no show in 2 bumpers, trained by O. Sherwood on debut. *M. A. Barnes* **F–**

REGAL REPOSE 5 b.m. Classic Cliche (IRE) – Ideal Candidate (Celestial Storm (USA)) [2004/5 17s^{pu} 19m^{pu} Mar 21] modest on Flat (stays 2m) at 3 yrs, well beaten in 2004: no show in 2 novice selling hurdles. *A. J. Chamberlain* **h–**

REGAL RIVER (IRE) 8 b.g. Over The River (FR) – My Friend Fashion (Laurence O) [2004/5 c–, h–: c27d^{pu} c24d^5 c27v^3 c26v^4 c23s^3 Feb 16] close-coupled gelding: poor handicap chaser nowadays: stays 3¼m: raced on good going or softer (acts on heavy). *John R. Upson* **c68 h–**

REGAL SETTING (IRE) 4 br.g. King's Theatre (IRE) – Cartier Bijoux (Ahonoora) [2004/5 16m* 17d^5 18d^2 16g Mar 15] leggy, useful-looking gelding: useful on Flat (will stay 2m), sold out of Sir Mark Prescott's stable 215,000 gns Newmarket Autumn Sales: fairly useful form in juvenile hurdles: 2/1-on, won at Catterick in December by 6 lengths from Classic Event: breathing problems all 3 starts after, running best race when length second to Habitual Dancer at Kelso: tongue tied, well beaten in valuable handicap event at Cheltenham: will probably stay 2½m. *J. Howard Johnson* **h120**

REGAL STATESMAN (NZ) 12 br.g. Vice Regal (NZ) – Hykit (NZ) (Swinging Junior) [2004/5 c–, h–§: c23d^4 c17d^4 c21g^{pu} c16g^{pu} Dec 16] no longer of any account: left O. Brennan before final start. *J. J. Quinn* **c– h– §**

REGAL VINTAGE (USA) 5 ch.g. Kingmambo (USA) – Grapevine (IRE) (Sadler's Wells (USA)) [2004/5 h65: 20d^{pu} 17m^4 22d^{pu} 19m^2 24g Jul 4] little solid form on Flat: poor maiden hurdler: stays 19f: acts on good to firm ground: visored: has had tongue tied: has looked none too keen. *C. Grant* **h67**

REGAL VISION (IRE) 8 b.g. Emperor Jones (USA) – Shining Eyes (USA) (Mr Prospector (USA)) [2004/5 c97§, h–§: c25m^{pu} 24g^5 24m^6 22v^{pu} 26g Mar 16] leggy gelding: winning hurdler/chaser: little show in 2004/5, left C. Mann after first outing: probably stays 3m: acts on firm going, probably on soft: has worn blinkers: ungenuine. *Miss C. Dyson* **c– § h– §**

REGENCY MALAYA 4 b.f. Sri Pekan (USA) – Paola (FR) (Fabulous Dancer (USA)) [2004/5 16m Sep 4] lengthy filly: poor maiden on Flat (stays 1¼m): tongue tied, no show in juvenile on hurdling debut. *M. F. Harris* **h–**

REGENTS WALK (IRE) 7 b.g. Phardante (FR) – Raw Courage (IRE) (The Parson) [2004/5 h101p: 19g* 21g Mar 16] sturdy gelding: fair form in novice hurdles, winning at Newbury in December by 3 lengths from Quid Pro Quo: out of depth final start: should stay beyond 19f. *B. De Haan* **h108**

REGGAE RHYTHM (IRE) 11 b.g. Be My Native (USA) – Invery Lady (Sharpen Up) [2004/5 c82, h–: c24d^5 c17d May 29] angular gelding: winning hurdler/maiden chaser: successful on Flat in March for A. Lidderdale: stays 2½m: acts on heavy going: has worn cheekpieces, visored in 2004/5: not a fluent jumper of fences. *R. N. Bevis* **c– h–**

REGISTANA (GER) 9 br.m. Tauchsport (EG) – Reklame (EG) (Immer (HUN)) [2004/5 c?: c19g* c29f* c19g* c19v* c34m* c31d^{ro} Nov 12] **c128 +**

It is some measure of the impression the race makes, that if one were to ask the average British racing enthusiast to name a jumps race staged outside Britain and Ireland, the most likely answer would be the Velka Pardubicka (or Pardubice's big one), the cross-country steeplechase modelled on the Grand National and staged in sight of the old Semtex factory in the town of Pardubice an hour east of Prague. After some lean years, the race is on the up, with increased prize money (the race, sponsored by Ceske Pojistovny, the leading Czech bank, was worth 4.45 million crowns in 2004, equivalent to over £100,000, compared to 1.8 million in

Velka Pardubicka Ceske Pojistovny, Pardubice—Registana has plenty to spare clearing the ditch at the Taxis on her way to a second win in this famous race

1995) and a crowd of around twenty-five thousand, including many visitors from Britain and Ireland, to see Registana land the race for the second successive year in the 114th running in 2004. The victory made the front page of the leading Czech daily paper *Dnes*, though another paper chose to highlight fatalities in other races on the card, including publishing prominently a picture of a dead horse. The course has a reputation as a most demanding test, though modifications, particularly to the famous Taxis, have made for generally a much fairer one. Having generally looked east for foreign competition during the Communist era, the race's organisers are now seeking to attract runners from the west. Three Irish-trained runners and one from Britain were in the field of seventeen for the latest renewal, though none of them got round.

Registana was a short-priced favourite to follow up her narrow victory over Maskul in 2003. She was on a run of eight starts unbeaten, including one at Pardubice, in a qualifying race for the Velka Pardubicka, in June, and three at Merano in Italy later in the summer. Always in the first two and jumping quickly and nimbly—the course demands agility and guile as much as anything from horse and rider—Registana found plenty as the race began in earnest in the last mile or so, drawing nine lengths clear of Retriever, ridden by the fifty-two-year-old favourite of the home crowd Josef Vana. Registana gave her rider, the German Peter Gehm, a fourth successive win in the race.

After this famous victory, Registana was aimed at the Sporting Index Chase at the Open meeting at Cheltenham, bidding to go one better than Peruan, who was beaten a neck by Fiftysevenchannels in the race in 1997 and went on to win three successive runnings of the Velka Pardubicka. At Cheltenham, Registana again showed what a fine jumper she is and had taken a three-length lead when her rider took the wrong course going to two out. The rider was at fault but Gehm's mistake was understandable: the last two obstacles are placed on the hurdles course, though they would not have been in position when Gehm walked the course before racing, a hurdles race taking place before the cross-country event. Sadly, Gehm won't get the chance to make amends, as he was very badly injured, suffering paralysis, after being thrown while exercising a horse in the New Year. Registana will hopefully be back at Cheltenham in November after an attempt to match Peruan's hat-trick at Pardubice. Her new partner is set to be Jim Crowley, who rides regularly for Registana's trainer Cestmir Olehla. Registana and Crowley made a successful start in a qualifying race at Pardubice in the summer. As well as successes in the Czech

Republic and Slovakia, Crowley and Olehla teamed up to win several of the major jump races in Italy in 2004/5, including the Gran Premio di Merano with Masini.

Registana (GER) (br.m. 1996)	Tauchsport (EG) (b 1972)	Tuny (b 1959)	Zucchero
			Marsyaka
		Tauspur (b 1960)	Asterios
			Taupirsch
	Reklame (EG) (br 1982)	Immer (b 1969)	Imperial
			Margareta
		Reprise (br 1971)	Malmo
			Rebe

The lengthy, rather leggy Registana is a sister to two useful German-trained jumpers, Registano, a prolific winner in the 'nineties, and Regalo, whose victories included one in the Grosses Jagdrennen der GGW, a valuable event for amateur riders over four and a quarter miles. Their half-sister Reseda (by Lavirco) won a mares novice hurdle at Taunton in January. Registana herself stays over four miles cross country, though is effective over much shorter distances. In all, including her win in June, she has won nineteen of her twenty-nine races, ten wins coming at Pardubice, seven at Merano and one each at Bratislava and Svetla Hora. Her wins in the Velka Pardubicka came when the ground was on the firm side, though she also looked effective on good to soft at Cheltenham. *C. Olehla, Czech Republic*

REGULATED (IRE) 4 b.g. Alzao (USA) – Royal Hostess (IRE) (Be My Guest (USA)) [2004/5 18m Aug 19] fair but ungenuine on Flat (stays 1¼m): looked unwilling when well beaten in juvenile on hurdling debut: sold £1,600 Ascot October Sales. *D. B. Feek* **h–**

REHEARSAL 4 b.g. Singspiel (IRE) – Daralaka (IRE) (The Minstrel (CAN)) [2004/5 16d 17g^{2} 16g* 16g^{4} Apr 16] leggy gelding: half-brother to bumper winner Daramsan (by Doyoun): useful on Flat (stays 1¼m) for C. Cox: fair juvenile hurdler: won maiden at Musselburgh in February by 12 lengths from King's Envoy: creditable fourth, despite jumping poorly, to Admiral at Ayr: likely to prove best around 2m with emphasis on speed. *L. Lungo* **h113**

REINE DES REINES (IRE) 7 b.m. Supreme Leader – La Grande Dame (Niniski (USA)) [2004/5 20v^{3} 16v^{2} 18s 20s^{3} 16s* Apr 13] lengthy mare: will make a chaser: eighth foal: half-sister to fair hurdler/chaser Conagher Boy (by Le Moss) and fair hurdler Wee Three (by Brush Aside), both stayed 21f: dam, fair hurdler, stayed 2½m: bumper winner: fair novice hurdler: ran well when 19 lengths third to Asian Maze in Grade 3 mares event at Fairyhouse in March: didn't need to reproduce that form when winning 24-runner maiden there next time: stays 2½m: raced mainly on going softer than good (acts on heavy). *J. E. Kiely, Ireland* **h110**

REIVERS MOON 6 b. or br.m. Midnight Legend – Here Comes Tibby (Royal Fountain) [2004/5 h93: 21g* 21m* 20m 22m* c25d^{3} c24m* c20s^{2} c20g^{4} Apr 15] smallish, leggy mare: fair hurdler: won maiden and novice at Sedgefield very early in season and novice at Kelso in October: similar form over fences, winning maiden at Musselburgh in February: stays 3m: acts on firm and soft going: often races prominently. *W. Amos* **c105 h110**

RELATIVE HERO (IRE) 5 ch.g. Entrepreneur – Aunty (FR) (Riverman (USA)) [2004/5 h–: 17m 16d^{5} 20s^{pu} 16g^{4} 16g^{6} Dec 10] small gelding: modest on Flat (stays 1½m): poor maiden hurdler: wears cheekpieces/visor. *Miss S. J. Wilton* **h67**

RELIANCE LEADER 9 ch.g. Weld – Swift Messenger (Giolla Mear) [2004/5 c17v^{6} c20s c20s^{bd} c25m c22s^{4} c26m^{3} Apr 21] of little account. *D. L. Williams* **c59 h–**

RELIX (FR) 5 gr.g. Linamix (FR) – Resleona (Caerleon (USA)) [2004/5 h–: 20d^{5} 16s 16v^{4} 16d^{2} 20g^{6} 16g^{6} 20s Apr 10] leggy gelding: modest novice hurdler: left F. Murphy before final start: should stay beyond 2m: acts on heavy going. *A. M. Crow* **h90**

REMINGTON (IRE) 7 ch.g. Indian Ridge – Sea Harrier (Grundy) [2004/5 16g 16d Apr 17] smallish gelding: lightly-raced maiden hurdler: well held both starts after 2-year absence. *Mrs A. M. Thorpe* **h–**

REMINISCER (IRE) 8 b. or br.g. Coronado (IRE) – Lady Ghislaine (FR) (Lydian (FR)) [2004/5 22s 16s 16s* Mar 26] sparely-made gelding: first foal: dam winning hurdler/fair chaser up to 21f: fair hurdler: reportedly broke bone in knee and off 2 years before reappearance: in cheekpieces, won handicap at Cork in March by 2½ lengths from Pippin's Ford: stays 2½m: acts on heavy and good to firm going: blinkered once. *Thomas Foley, Ireland* **h110**

RENDARI (IRE) 10 b.g. Shardari – Reneagh (Prince Regent (FR)) [2004/5 h96: 24g² 26g³ May 26] modest hurdler: stays 3¼m: acts on good to soft going. *R. Ford* **h98**

RENO 5 ch.m. Efisio – Los Alamos (Keen) [2004/5 h88: 16d³ 16m* 17m 16s⁶ 16g 17v Dec 31] smallish mare: modest novice hurdler: won mares event at Hexham in June: best around 2m: acts on firm and soft going: usually tongue tied: sold 1,200 gns Doncaster March Sales. *C. W. Thornton* **h88**

REN'S MAGIC 7 gr.g. Petong – Bath (Runnett) [2004/5 h86: 16d 16s Nov 21] close-coupled gelding: form over hurdles only when second in novice in 2003/4: tried visored. *J. R. Jenkins* **h–**

RENVYLE (IRE) 7 b. or br.g. Satco (FR) – Kara's Dream (IRE) (Bulldozer) [2004/5 c108, h98, F100: c28g c25g⁴ 24g² c20s³ 26m* 22v* Oct 17] close-coupled gelding: winning chaser: fairly useful hurdler: blinkered, improved form when winning handicaps at Hereford in September and Market Rasen (beat Lubinas 5 lengths) in October: stays 3¼m: acts on good to firm and heavy going: often let down by jumping/attitude. *Jonjo O'Neill* **c– x** **h116 §**

REPLACEMENT PET (IRE) 8 b.m. Petardia – Richardstown Lass (IRE) (Muscatite) [2004/5 17g 16g 17f⁵ 19g⁵ 17m 16s⁵ 19g Dec 9] modest on Flat (stays 1¼m) in 2003: bad maiden hurdler: usually blinkered and tongue tied. *Mrs S. D. Williams* **h52**

REPULSE BAY (IRE) 7 b.g. Barathea (IRE) – Bourbon Topsy (Ile de Bourbon (USA)) [2004/5 16d⁴ 22m Oct 3] good-bodied gelding: modest on Flat (stays 2m): no form over hurdles: has had tongue tied. *J. S. Goldie* **h–**

RESCATOR (FR) 9 b.g. Saint Estephe (FR) – La Narquoise (FR) (Al Nasr (FR)) [2004/5 h82: c17d⁴ c16g⁶ c21gpu c20mpu 21m Sep 28] workmanlike gelding: poor hurdler: modest form at best over fences, usually let down by jumping: stays 21f: acts on soft and good to firm going: has looked temperamental: sold 1,500 gns Doncaster October Sales. *Mrs S. J. Smith* **c86 x** **h–**

RESCIND (IRE) 5 b.m. Revoque (IRE) – Sunlit Ride (Ahonoora) [2004/5 h78: 16d⁴ 17d² 17v² 16gpu Jan 14] rather leggy mare: fair novice hurdler: lame final start: raced around 2m on good going or softer (acts on heavy). *Jedd O'Keeffe* **h101**

RESEARCHER 6 ch.m. Cosmonaut – Rest (Dance In Time (CAN)) [2004/5 h107: 20d c22s* c21g³ c20d⁵ c21d³ c24d⁵ Mar 24] lengthy mare: fair hurdler: similar form over fences, won mares maiden at Towcester in January: effective at 2m to 3m: raced mainly on good going or softer (acts on soft): room for improvement in jumping over fences: sold 6,000 gns Doncaster May Sales. *Miss Venetia Williams* **c109** **h–**

RESEDA (GER) 6 b.m. Lavirco (GER) – Reklame (EG) (Immer (HUN)) [2004/5 F82: 16s³ 19s* 19d⁶ 16dF 16g 16gF Apr 15] tall, leggy mare: fair novice hurdler: won mares event at Taunton in January: finished weakly last 2 completed starts: stays 19f. *Ian Williams* **h100**

RESEDA (IRE) 8 b.g. Rock Hopper – Sweet Mignonette (Tina's Pet) [2004/5 16d 19g³ 25d² Jan 1] useful-looking gelding: won both starts in bumpers in 2002/3: off over 2 years, modest form in novice hurdles: stays 25f. *R. T. Phillips* **h94**

RESERVOIR (IRE) 4 b.g. Green Desert (USA) – Spout (Salse (USA)) [2004/5 16d² 16s 17m* 16m³ Apr 2] stocky gelding: fairly useful on Flat (stays 1½m), sold out of W. Haggas' stable 30,000 gns Newmarket Autumn Sales: fair hurdler: won juvenile at Hereford in March: raced around 2m. *P. J. Hobbs* **h111**

RESISTANCE (IRE) 8 br.g. Phardante (FR) – Shean Hill (IRE) (Bar Dexter (USA)) [2004/5 h–: c19mbd 20d Jun 23] lengthy gelding: poor novice hurdler: well beaten when brought down on chasing debut: tried visored. *Mrs H. Dalton* **c–** **h–**

RESONANCE 4 b.f. Slip Anchor – Music In My Life (IRE) (Law Society (USA)) [2004/5 16d 16v Jan 22] lengthy filly: fair maiden on Flat (stays 1½m, signs of temperament): tongue tied, poor form when seventh in juvenile at Perth on hurdling debut: well beaten on heavy going next time. *N. A. Twiston-Davies* **h–**

RESPLENDENT KING (USA) 4 b.g. King of Kings (IRE) – Sister Fromseattle (USA) (Seattle Slew (USA)) [2004/5 17m* 18m² Aug 19] fair maiden on Flat (stays 1¼m): modest form in juvenile hurdles, won at Sedgefield in August: looked difficult ride next time. *T. G. Mills* **h92**

RESPLENDENT STAR (IRE) 8 b.g. Northern Baby (CAN) – Whitethroat (Artaius (USA)) [2004/5 17dur 20m² 19d⁴ 19g⁴ Jan 17] fairly useful on all-weather, fair on turf on Flat (stays 1½m) for M. Jarvis: modest form over hurdles: stays 2½m: visored final start. *Mrs L. Wadham* **h96**

RESSOURCE (FR) 6 b.g. Broadway Flyer (USA) – Rayonne (Sadler's Wells (USA)) [2004/5 h85§: 16v² 19m³ 19g² 19spu 17s⁴ Mar 22] leggy gelding: modest maiden hurdler: stays 19f: acts on heavy and good to firm going: blinkered: ungenuine. *G. L. Moore* **h85 §**

RESTLESS WIND (IRE) 13 b.g. Celio Rufo – Trulos (Three Dons) [2004/5 c94§: 22g⁵ 16m c26g³ Oct 3] lengthy gelding: modest chaser: twice-raced hurdler: stays 25f: acts on soft and good to firm going: finds little. *Dr P. Pritchard* **c89 §** **h–**

RETAIL THERAPY (IRE) 5 b.m. Bahhare (USA) – Elect (USA) (Vaguely Noble) [2004/5 h83: 16g 16m Aug 30] leggy mare: won juvenile maiden on hurdling debut in 2003/4: no form since: sold 18,500 gns Newmarket December Sales. *M. A. Buckley* **h–**

RETRO'S GIRL (IRE) 4 ch.f. Zaffaran (USA) – Highland Chain (Furry Glen) [2004/5 F13d⁵ F16v² F16s³ F16d² Mar 28] eighth foal: half-sister to bumper winner Mickey Campbell (by Executive Perk): dam, won 21f hurdle, from family of Grand National winner Last Suspect: modest form in bumpers. *M. Scudamore* **F81**

RETURNED UN PAID (IRE) 8 b.g. Actinium (FR) – Claregalway Lass (Ardross) [2004/5 c75, h67: 21g⁶ 24g⁵ 24g² Jul 7] workmanlike gelding: poor chaser/maiden hurdler: placed in points in 2005: stays 3¼m: acts on good to firm and heavy going: tried blinkered. *Mrs S. J. Smith* **c–** **h77**

RETURN HOME 6 b.g. Bob's Return (IRE) – Walgenco (IRE) (Welsh Saint) [2004/5 F18d 16v 22s 20s 19v Feb 5] sturdy gelding: half-brother to bumper winner Trolly Dolly (by The Parson): dam, won up to 2¾m over jumps, also winning stayer on Flat: well held in bumper (tongue tied) and over hurdles. *C. Roche, Ireland* **h–** **F–**

REVEILLEZ 6 gr.g. First Trump – Amalancher (USA) (Alleged (USA)) [2004/5 16s* 19g* 21g⁶ Mar 16] tall, leggy gelding: useful on Flat (stays 15f), successful twice in 2003: good start to hurdling career, winning novices at Windsor in November and Don- **h143**

Mr J. P. McManus' "Reveillez"

caster in January: much better form when 4 lengths sixth of 20 to No Refuge in Royal & SunAlliance Novices' Hurdle at Cheltenham, wandering under pressure having travelled comfortably long way: stays 21f. *J. R. Fanshawe*

REVELINO (IRE) 6 b.g. Revoque (IRE) – Forelino (USA) (Trempolino (USA)) [2004/5 h72: 17d4 16g3 16m5 17g2 19mF 16g2 19s 19g 16d 19s Mar 7] useful-looking gelding: modest maiden hurdler: stays 19f: possibly better on good/good to firm going than softer: tried in cheekpieces: ungenuine. *Miss S. J. Wilton* **h86 §**

REVIEWER (IRE) 7 b.g. Sadler's Wells (USA) – Clandestina (USA) (Secretariat (USA)) [2004/5 h111: 22dpu 16s 21spu c17g6 c16d* Mar 24] neat gelding: fairly useful hurdler at best, out of form in 2004/5: jumped fluently both starts over fences, winning maiden at Wincanton in March: stays 2¾m: acts on soft going. *M. Meade* **c101 h–**

REYNOLDS ORCHARD 10 ch.g. Henbit (USA) – Wayword Fun (Funny Man) [2004/5 20m4 Jun 5] first foal: dam never ran: fourth of 17 in maiden hurdle at Worcester, only start. *S. T. Lewis* **h79**

RHAPSODY ROSE 4 b.f. Unfuwain (USA) – Haboobti (Habitat) [2004/5 17g* 16s* Mar 27] leggy filly: fairly useful on Flat (stays 1½m), successful in August, sold out of C. O'Brien's stable 62,000 gns Newmarket December Sales: successful in juveniles first 2 starts over hurdles, at Bangor (maiden, sweating and on toes) and Towcester (beat Salut Saint Cloud a length) in March: well beaten in listed mares novice at Punchestown late following month. *P. R. Webber* **h101**

RHEINDROSS (IRE) 10 gr.g. Ala Hounak – Ardcarn Girl (Ardross) [2004/5 c117: c20g4 c24d3 c21d c19v5 c19v3 Jan 23] strong gelding: fair handicap chaser: stays 3m: acts on heavy ground: usually held up: refused to race once. *A. L. T. Moore, Ireland* **c113**

RHETORICAL 4 b.g. Unfuwain (USA) – Miswaki Belle (USA) (Miswaki (USA)) [2004/5 16g 16d 16d 18spu 16dpu Apr 18] workmanlike gelding: poor maiden on Flat, sold out of Sir Mark Prescott's stable 10,000 gns Newmarket Autumn Sales: no form in juvenile hurdles: has worn cheekpieces/visor: tongue tied last 3 starts. *P. Butler* **h–**

RHETORIC (IRE) 6 b.g. Desert King (IRE) – Squaw Talk (USA) (Gulch (USA)) [2004/5 h–: 26mpu Jun 15] angular gelding: poor on Flat: little form over hurdles: tongue tied once: sold to join Miss S. Davies £1,000 Ascot August Sales. *D. G. Bridgwater* **h–**

RHUNA RED 6 ch.m. Good Thyne (USA) – Oh Dear (Paico) [2004/5 F16s6 Apr 10] sixth foal: half-sister to bumper winner Solway Dawn (by Minster Son) and winning pointer by King's Ride: dam runner-up in Irish bumpers: well held in bumper on debut. *J. R. Bewley* **F–**

RICARDO'S CHANCE 6 b.g. Alflora (IRE) – Jims Sister (Welsh Captain) [2004/5 F17m F16g F16m4 16f 16d 17s Feb 6] first foal: dam unraced: poor form in bumpers: well held over hurdles. *O. O'Neill* **h63 F75**

RICCARTON 12 b.g. Nomination – Legendary Dancer (Shareef Dancer (USA)) [2004/5 c84, h–: c16s3 c16g5 c16d c16m2 c17d4 Oct 5] leggy gelding: poor maiden chaser: stays 19f: acts on any going: tried tongue tied. *D. C. Turner* **c84 ? h–**

RICHIE BOY 4 b.c. Dr Fong (USA) – Alathezal (USA) (Zilzal (USA)) [2004/5 16v 17gF Mar 9] leggy colt: fair on Flat (stays 1½m), successful 3 times in 2004 for V. Smith/ P. Blockley: pulled hard and no encouragement both starts in juvenile hurdles. *Jennie Candlish* **h–**

RICHMOND LODGE (IRE) 5 br.g. Sesaro (USA) – Richmond Lillie (Fairbairn) [2004/5 18spu 16g 18spu Dec 21] modest on Flat, won over 1½m at 3 yrs for D. Wachman: no form in 3 starts over hurdles: tried in visor (pulled hard): sold £1,000 Ascot April Sales. *M. Madgwick* **h– §**

RICH SONG (IRE) 7 b.g. Treasure Hunter – Sonnet Lady (Down The Hatch) [2004/5 16s 19s3 19g Dec 10] €2,200 5-y-o: angular gelding: fourth foal: dam unraced: runner-up in maiden point on debut: poor form first 2 starts over hurdles. *Mrs S. J. Smith* **h81**

RICKY MARTAN 4 ch.c. Foxhound (USA) – Cyrillic (Rock City) [2004/5 16dur Dec 5] small, light-framed, dipped-backed colt: poor maiden on Flat (should stay at least 1m): behind when unseating last in juvenile on hurdling debut. *G. C. Bravery* **h–**

RICO HOMBRE (FR) 6 b.g. Cadoudal (FR) – Lady Carolina (FR) (Noir Et Or) [2004/5 F103+: 20v2 Dec 18] won bumper on debut: promising 15 lengths second to Rebel Rhythm in novice at Haydock on hurdling debut 10 months later, jumping soundly: should improve. *N. J. Henderson* **h114 p**

RIDEAWAY ROSE (IRE) 9 b.m. King's Ride – Miss Rockaway (Le Moss) [2004/5 c–, h67: c23d^{pu} 22g^{2} 22g^{2} 22g^{2} 24m^{6} 22g^{F} 22g Aug 2] winning pointer: pulled up both starts in novice chases: poor maiden hurdler: should stay at least 3m: possibly unsuited by going softer than good: wore cheekpieces last 4 starts. *C. J. Down* **c– h84**

RIDERS REVENGE (IRE) 7 b.g. Norwich – Paico Ana (Paico) [2004/5 h88, F84: 16s^{5} 16s^{2} 17d^{bd} 22v^{pu} 19d^{4} 22d^{pu} Apr 17] sturdy gelding: fair maiden hurdler: stays 19f: raced on going softer than good (acts on heavy). *Miss Venetia Williams* **h103**

RIDGEWAY (IRE) 10 b.g. Indian Ridge – Regal Promise (Pitskelly) [2004/5 c101, h–: c26g^{ur} May 26] lengthy gelding: fairly useful hunter chaser: badly hampered and unseated fourteenth at Cartmel in May: stays 25f: acts on good to firm and heavy going: wore cheekpieces last 4 starts. *Miss J. E. Foster* **c– h–**

RIFLEMAN (IRE) 5 ch.g. Starborough – En Garde (USA) (Irish River (FR)) [2004/5 17g^{2} 16s^{3} 16d^{3} 16g 17g^{3} 21d^{3} 22d^{pu} Feb 19] sparely-made gelding: fairly useful at best on Flat (stays 8.5f), well beaten in 2004, sold out of Mrs A. Duffield's stable 25,000 gns Doncaster August Sales: fair novice hurdler: stays 21f: raced on good going or softer: wore cheekpieces last 3 outings: usually soon off bridle and looks ungenuine. *P. Bowen* **h112 §**

RIFT VALLEY (IRE) 10 b.g. Good Thyne (USA) – Necochea (Julio Mariner) [2004/5 c113, h–: 19s 22s 19s 17g 19d 22d* Apr 17] good-topped gelding: winning chaser: fair handicap hurdler: back to form when landing gamble at Wincanton in April: stays 3m: acts on firm and good to soft going: best in visor: jumps right over fences. *P. J. Hobbs* **c– h107**

RIGHT DIRECTION (IRE) 7 b.g. Song of The Woods – Rio Rhythm (Jaazeiro (USA)) [2004/5 F16g^{3} F16s^{pu} F16s Nov 6] third foal: dam placed in bumpers: won maiden point in 2004: poor form on first of 3 outings in bumpers: lame next time. *J. J. Lambe, Ireland* **F74**

RIGHT PROUD 5 gr.g. Morpeth – Pigeon Loft (IRE) (Bellypha) [2004/5 F16d 17v Mar 30] sturdy gelding: sixth foal: brother to fairly useful 2¾m hurdle winner Grey Brother and fair hurdler up to 19f Kildee Lass and half-brother to bumper winner Miss Woodpigeon (by Landyap): dam runner-up in 17f seller, only completed start over hurdles: well held in bumper and novice hurdle. *J. D. Frost* **h– F–**

RIGHTS OF MAN (IRE) 6 b. or br.g. Right Win (IRE) – Stiritup (IRE) (Mandalus) [2004/5 F16s^{4} 18d 20s^{2} 19v^{2} 16v^{2} 19s Mar 27] €1,000: sturdy gelding: third foal: dam, twice-raced in bumpers, half-sister to very smart staying chaser Belmont King: fair form in bumpers: fair maiden hurdler: stays 2½m: acts on soft going. *D. E. Fitzgerald, Ireland* **h112 F94**

RIGHT TO REPLY (IRE) 11 b. or br.g. Executive Perk – Sesheta (Tumble Wind) [2004/5 c109+, h–: c28m^{F} May 22] big, good-topped gelding: useful hurdler in 2000/1: winning chaser: running best race over fences when falling last (upsides winner Torduff Express) in valuable hunter at Stratford: stayed 3½m: acted on heavy and good to firm going: dead. *J. Scott* **c117 h–**

RIGMAROLE 7 b.g. Fairy King (USA) – Cattermole (USA) (Roberto (USA)) [2004/5 c101p, h151: 16s* 16d^{6} 16d 16d 16d^{4} 17g 16g 16m Apr 22] compact gelding: second in maiden only outing over fences: smart hurdler: vastly improved in 2003/4, successful 6 times: won quite valuable minor event at Kempton in October for second successive year, beating Trouble At Bay comfortably by 2½ lengths: little impact after, reportedly had wind operation after fourth outing: best around 2m: acts on soft and firm going: tried blinkered: tongue tied: usually held up. *P. F. Nicholls* **c– h147**

RIGONZA 4 ch.g. Vettori (IRE) – Desert Nomad (Green Desert (USA)) [2004/5 17d Aug 28] fair maiden on Flat (probably stayed 1½m): last of 9 finishers in juvenile hurdle at Cartmel: dead. *T. D. Easterby* **h–**

RIMOSA 10 b.m. Miner's Lamp – Crosa (Crozier) [2004/5 h72: 19d^{F} Oct 28] angular mare: poor maiden hurdler: in front when falling fatally 2 out in amateur handicap at Taunton: raced mainly around 2m: acted on good to firm and good to soft going. *A. P. Jones* **h79**

RIMSKY (IRE) 4 gr.g. Silver Patriarch (IRE) – Mistinguett (IRE) (Doyoun) [2004/5 F16d^{2} F17g* F17d Apr 9] unfurnished gelding: third foal: half-brother to smart hurdler Mistanoora (by Topanoora), stays 25f, and smart stayer Misternando (by Hernando): dam, 2-y-o 1m winner and very smart staying hurdler, out of close relation to dam of Sinndar: won bumper at Bangor in March: best effort when eighth, staying on well, to The Cool Guy in Grade 2 at Aintree: will be suited by 2½m+: sort to make his mark in novice hurdles in 2005/6. *N. A. Twiston-Davies* **F106**

RI NA REALTA (IRE) 10 b.g. King's Ride – Realteen (Deep Run) [2004/5 22g 24s Apr 16] bumper winner: fair form in maiden hurdles in late-2002: left A. Mullins and off 2 years, well beaten both starts in Britain: should be suited by further than 19f. *J. W. Mullins* **h–**

RINCE RI (IRE) 12 ch.g. Orchestra – Mildred's Ball (Blue Refrain) [2004/5 c162, h–: c25g^{4} c25s^{6} c26d^{5} Mar 17] strong gelding: high-class chaser at best: well held last 2 starts after 10-month absence: stays 25f: acts on heavy going, probably on good to firm: tried blinkered: has had tongue tied. *T. M. Walsh, Ireland* **c– h–**

RINCOOLA (IRE) 6 br.m. Warcraft (USA) – Very Tense (IRE) (Orchestra) [2004/5 F–: F16g 23v^{pu} 21v^{5} 20v^{pu} 22s^{4} 21g Mar 16] lengthy mare: signs of only a little ability. *J. S. Wainwright* **h75 ? F–**

RINGSIDE JACK 9 b.g. Batshoof – Celestine (Skyliner) [2004/5 h87: 16m^{4} 16g^{4} 16m^{6} 16v^{5} 17v^{5} 16v^{ur} 20m^{6} 20v^{2} 25s 19g Mar 9] poor novice hurdler: stays 2½m: acts on good to firm and heavy going: visored final outing: takes good hold. *C. W. Fairhurst* **h86**

RINGS OF POWER (IRE) 8 ch.g. Mister Lord (USA) – Rainbow Gurriers (IRE) (Buckskin (FR)) [2004/5 c23d^{pu} c25s^{pu} c24s c25d^{ur} c24d c21d^{5} c19g^{4} Apr 12] IR 15,000 3-y-o: first foal: dam unraced, out of half-sister to smart hurdler up to 2½m Potato Merchant: failed to complete several times in maiden points prior to winning in 2004: no form in chases: poor jumper. *N. R. Mitchell* **c80 x**

RING THE BOSS (IRE) 4 b.g. Kahyasi – Fortune's Girl (Ardross) [2004/5 F16g^{6} F16s^{rtr} Mar 22] tall gelding: fourth foal: half-brother to fairly useful bumper winner/ winning hurdler Diamond Sal (by Bob Back), stays 2½m: dam, fair hurdler who stayed 27f, half-sister to dam of smart 1m to 9.3f winner Mister Sacha: sixth of 15 to No Regrets in bumper at Doncaster on debut: refused to race at Wetherby later in March: will be suited by further than 2m. *K. G. Reveley* **F83 §**

RINGTOWN MINE (IRE) 8 ch.g. Grand Plaisir (IRE) – Your Mine (Push On) [2004/5 c17g c21m^{F} Jul 26] IR £11,000 4-y-o: ninth foal: half-brother to fair hurdler/ fairly useful chaser Compostello (by Erins Isle), stays 21f: dam winning 2m hurdler: runner-up on second of 2 starts in maiden points: pulled up in bumper (reportedly broke blood vessel) for Mrs J. Harrington: no show in 2 maiden chases, virtually refusing to race on first occasion. *J. J. Lambe, Ireland* **c– §**

RIO SAN VIO (IRE) 7 b.g. Phardante (FR) – Grangemills (Strong Gale) [2004/5 F17m* F16m* F16g^{pu} Oct 7] fifth foal: half-brother to fairly useful 2m hurdler/promising chaser Cloone River (by Un Desperado): dam bumper winner, also successful up to 2m on Flat: runner-up once from 3 starts in maiden Irish points: successful at Newton Abbot and Worcester in September on first 2 outings in bumpers, useful form when beating Scalini's by 13 lengths at latter: broke down badly next time. *N. J. Henderson* **F106**

RIPCORD (IRE) 7 b.g. Diesis – Native Twine (Be My Native (USA)) [2004/5 h69: 16m^{2} 16g^{2} 16d^{6} 16g^{pu} Oct 24] sturdy gelding: unreliable maiden on Flat: modest form over hurdles: raced at 2m: temperamental display when visored final outing. *B. R. Johnson* **h89**

RIPNTEAR 6 b.g. Sabrehill (USA) – Sea of Clouds (Soviet Star (USA)) [2004/5 F16g* Dec 29] 4,700 3-y-o, €20,000 4-y-o: third foal: brother to poor 2m hurdler Helenes Hill: dam, French 9.5f winner, half-sister to smart middle-distance stayer Helen of Spain: gave plenty of trouble in preliminaries, won bumper at Musselburgh on debut in November by 8 lengths from Golden Measure, quickening clear final 1f having raced freely when pace was slow. *R. A. Fahey* **F101**

RISETOTHEOCCASION (IRE) 9 b.g. Glacial Storm (USA) – Cute Play (Salluceva) [2004/5 c20d^{4} c24d^{6} c22s^{ur} c22d^{pu} c24s^{pu} 27v* 22s^{3} 24v 27s^{3} Apr 22] poor maiden chaser: fair handicap hurdler: won at Sedgefield in January: stays 27f: acts on heavy ground: tried in cheekpieces. *C. A. McBratney, Ireland* **c84 h102**

RISING GENERATION (FR) 8 ch.g. Risen Star (USA) – Queen's Victory (FR) (Carmarthen (FR)) [2004/5 c–§, h107§: 16d^{2} 16g^{2} 16s* 16g* 16m^{2} 17s* 16s* 16d 16v 17g Feb 16] tall gelding: fairly useful handicap hurdler: better than ever in 2004/5, winning at Perth in August (seller) and September, Carlisle in October and Kelso in November, beating Totally Scottish for last 2 successes: stays 19f: acts on good to firm and heavy going: seems best ridden prominently nowadays. *N. G. Richards* **c– § h118**

RISING TALISKER 12 ch.m. Primitive Rising (USA) – Dialect (Connaught) [2004/5 c–, h–: c22s^{pu} May 9] lengthy, angular mare: maiden hurdler/chaser: modest pointer, won mares maiden in March. *O. R. Dukes* **c– h–**

RISINGTON 7 b.g. Afzal – Barton Rise (Raise You Ten) [2004/5 c23v^5 c16s^{ur} Feb 16] first foal: dam, poor chaser, stayed 3m: won maiden point on debut in 2003: well beaten on completed outing in maiden chases. *Miss Venetia Williams* **c–**

RISK ACCESSOR (IRE) 10 b.g. Commanche Run – Bellatollah (Bellman (FR)) [2004/5 c139, h132: c20d^2 16g^3 c22m^2 c19s* c24s^2 c20s c21g^F c36d^{ur} Apr 9] tall gelding: useful hurdler: smart chaser: easily won minor event at Listowel in September: several good efforts in top handicap company, including when runner-up in Galway Plate (to Ansar) and Munster National at Limerick (beaten ½ length by Colca Canyon) starts either side: effective at 2m to 3m: acts on good to firm and heavy going: often tongue tied: effective held up or ridden prominently (takes good hold): bold jumper, prone to odd bad mistake (failed to get beyond sixth in 2 runnings of Grand National): often weak finisher. *C. Roche, Ireland* **c145 h139**

RISK FACTOR 6 b.g. Classic Cliche (IRE) – Easy Risk (Risk Me (FR)) [2004/5 17v^{pu} 20v^{pu} 19g Jan 17] first foal: dam once-raced: no sign of ability in 3 novice hurdles. *Ian Williams* **h–**

RISK LADY (IRE) 7 b.m. Hollow Hand – Ballinellard Lady (Fine Blade (USA)) [2004/5 24s^4 23s^2 Nov 11] half-sister to 2 winning pointers: dam maiden half-sister to dam of smart 2m to 3m chaser Super Tactics: won mares maiden Irish point in 2004: well held in maiden hunter at Cork on chasing debut: bought out of D. P. Murphy's stable 7,500 gns Doncaster May Sales: better effort in novice hurdles when second in mares event at Lingfield: looks a thorough stayer. *Miss Suzy Smith* **c– h83**

RISKY REEF 8 ch.g. Risk Me (FR) – Pas de Reef (Pas de Seul) [2004/5 h136: 17g Mar 18] lengthy gelding: lightly raced: useful 2m hurdler: travelled strongly long way before squeezed out approaching last in valuable handicap at Cheltenham, only start in 2004/5: raced on good going or softer. *Andrew Lee, Ireland* **h115 +**

RISKY WAY 9 b.g. Risk Me (FR) – Hot Sunday Sport (Star Appeal) [2004/5 c90x, h82: 17g 17m^6 17g^4 c16v^4 c16v^2 c20v^5 16g c20d^5 16d^{pu} Apr 11] leggy, close-coupled gelding: poor hurdler/chaser: sold out of B. Rothwell's stable 800 gns Doncaster August Sales after third outing: stays 2½m: acts on good to firm and heavy going: visored twice, has won with/without cheekpieces. *W. S. Coltherd* **c78 h77**

RIVAL BIDDER 8 ch.g. Arzanni – Beltalong (Belfort (FR)) [2004/5 h95: 20m^5 20m^3 17g^3 c21m* 24g^4 c21d^5 19m^3 25g^6 19g^{pu} Jan 17] close-coupled gelding: modest handicap hurdler: won maiden at Sedgefield on chasing debut in July: let down by jumping only other start over fences: stays 21f: acts on good to firm and good to soft ground. *Mrs S. J. Smith* **c97 h96**

RIVARRIVED 6 b.g. Riva Marquee – Pearly White (Petong) [2004/5 F17m F17g 17s 19v^{pu} Feb 13] first foal: dam poor novice hurdler: seems of no account. *Mrs P. Ford* **h– F–**

RIVELLI (IRE) 6 b.m. Lure (USA) – Kama Tashoof (Mtoto) [2004/5 h–: 17g Jul 30] no show in 2 novice hurdles. *B. R. Foster* **h–**

RIVER ALDER 7 b.m. Alderbrook – River Pearl (Oats) [2004/5 h96+: 20d 16g^3 Apr 15] tall mare: winning pointer: successful in novice on hurdling debut in 2003/4 for Miss S. Forster: better form when third in quite valuable mares handicap at Ayr: should be suited by further than 2m. *J. M. Dun* **h109**

RIVER AMORA (IRE) 10 b.g. Willie Joe (IRE) – That's Amora (Paddy's Stream) [2004/5 c66x, h–: c21d^5 c22m^5 c18m^4 c21s^{pu} c20s^4 c18g^5 c17g^F Mar 28] stocky gelding: poor chaser: left P. Butler after third start: stays 21f: acts on any going: tried visored/in cheekpieces: has had tongue tied: prone to mistakes. *J. J. Best* **c62 x h–**

RIVER BAILIFF (IRE) 9 ch.g. Over The River (FR) – Rath Caola (Neltino) [2004/5 c72: c20g Feb 17] sturdy gelding: winning pointer, including in March: poor maiden chaser: stays 3¼m: tried in blinkers/cheekpieces. *R. Gurney* **c75**

RIVER BANN (USA) 8 ch.g. Irish River (FR) – Spiritual Star (USA) (Soviet Star (USA)) [2004/5 h94: 16g^F Jan 24] modest hurdler: fell heavily only outing in 2004/5: stays 19f: acts on firm and soft going. *B. D. Leavy* **h–**

RIVERBOATMAN (IRE) 4 b.g. Lahib (USA) – Absent Beauty (IRE) (Dancing Dissident (USA)) [2004/5 16s* 16s* 16d^3 16v Dec 26] rangy gelding: fairly useful on Flat (stays 1½m), won twice in 2004: successful at Tipperary (maiden) and Gowran in autumn on first 2 starts in juvenile hurdles: ran as if amiss final outing (blinkered). *Ms F. M. Crowley, Ireland* **h115**

RIVER BUG (IRE) 11 ch.g. Over The River (FR) – Fiona's Wish (Wishing Star) [2004/5 c98§: c24d c29d^5 c29s^5 c25s^{pu} c26s^5 Mar 9] sturdy gelding: winning chaser, on **c70 §**

downgrade: left J. Poulton, broke blood vessel in cross-country event at Punchestown in late-April: thorough stayer: acts on heavy going: often blinkered: hard ride. *John A. Quinn, Ireland*

RIVER CITY (IRE) 8 b.g. Norwich – Shuil Na Lee (IRE) (Phardante (FR)) [2004/5 h121+: 16m c16g* c17g* c16g* c16d* c16s* c16g³ c16d⁶ Apr 9] **c145 h123**

River City ran almost as many times in the latest season, his first over fences, as he had done in the three previous ones when various ailments, including a back problem, restricted him to just nine appearances. The fairly useful winner of a bumper and of three races over hurdles, River City quickly made up into an even better chaser. After upsetting the odds laid on another chasing debutant, the very smart hurdler Westender, in a novice at Worcester in July, River City won similar events at Stratford, Newton Abbot (two of them) and Aintree on his next four outings. He completed the five-timer in a newly-inaugurated four-runner listed contest at Aintree in October, in which he had to concede 4 lb to useful hurdlers Contraband and Le Passing, both of whom were preferred to River City in the betting. It was the front-running Contraband, making his chasing debut, who posed the only threat to River City in the latter stages, but River City had his measure after coming with a steady run to lead between the last two, and he won by two lengths. River City was then given a break, returning in March for the Arkle Trophy at Cheltenham. Although unable to get the better of a more experienced Contraband this time around, River City did show further improvement in finishing five lengths third to that horse, the pair split by Ashley Brook. River City's only disappointing run over fences came on his next start, when only sixth to Ashley Brook in the Maghull Novices' Chase at Aintree, but he bounced back to finish a good second in a minor event at Warwick, which took place shortly after the season had ended, River City beaten only a neck by the useful Bambi de L'Orme who was receiving 10 lb. The rangy River City is the first foal of Shuil Na Lee, the unraced daughter of the useful staying hurdler Gortnalee, herself a half-sister to the Welsh National winner Jocks Cross. This is an excellent family, one of the most successful in the stud book, and one chock-full of stamina, yet River City, who acts on any going,

bonusprint.com Molyneux Novices' Chase, Aintree—
smart novice River City has no trouble completing a five-timer

has done virtually all of his racing at around two miles. He should prove just as effective at two and a half. Incidentally, River City also made a public appearance at the end of May. He was offered for sale at Doncaster, reportedly to dissolve a partnership, but he was led away at 195,000 guineas after failing to make his reserve. He was followed into the ring by stable-companion Mendo but, no doubt to Noel Chance's relief, he was also unsold, at 155,000 guineas. *Noel T. Chance*

RIVER GROUND (IRE) 10 br.g. Lord Americo – Rapid Ground (Over The River (FR)) [2004/5 19g c16g^{ur} 16v c24g^{3} c25s^{6} c26g^{5} Mar 27] ex-Irish gelding: won maiden point in Britain in 2003: upped in trip, form outside that sphere only when third in novice handicap chase at Fakenham. *Miss E. Hill* **c68 h–**

RIVER INDUS 5 b.g. Rakaposhi King – Flow (Over The River (FR)) [2004/5 F17s F16s 21d 16s Mar 23] rangy gelding: first foal: dam fair staying hurdler/chaser: well held in bumpers and novice hurdles. *R. H. Buckler* **h– F79**

RIVER MARSHAL (IRE) 7 b.g. Synefos (USA) – Marshallstown (Callernish) [2004/5 h88, F81: c22v^{pu} c20d^{3} c24s* c26d^{3} c24g^{3} c26d^{2} c25s^{ur} Mar 22] workmanlike gelding: modest form at best in 3 starts over hurdles: tends to make mistakes over fences, though won novice at Fakenham in November despite blundering last: stays 3m: acts on soft going: blinkered once (hung right). *C. C. Bealby* **c98 x h–**

RIVER MERE 11 b.g. River God (USA) – Rupert's Daughter (Rupert Bear) [2004/5 h78: 17g c16g^{2} c16m c20m* c21g^{2} c17m^{3} c20g^{pu} c20f^{3} c21d^{3} c20g^{2} c20s^{6} c16s^{5} c24d^{2} Oct 31] workmanlike gelding: poor hurdler: modest chaser: won novice handicap at Uttoxeter in July: barely stays 3m: acts on firm and good to soft going, below form on softer. *Mrs L. Williamson* **c94 h–**

RIVER MIST (IRE) 6 ch.m. Over The River (FR) – Minature Miss (Move Off) [2004/5 h83, F83: 21g^{3} 24g^{pu} May 14] poor maiden hurdler: should stay at least 3m: raced on good/good to soft ground. *D. Eddy* **h83**

RIVER OF FIRE 7 ch.g. Dilum (USA) – Bracey Brook (Gay Fandango (USA)) [2004/5 16g 20s^{4} 22s 23d 20s^{4} 21d Dec 9] workmanlike gelding: half-brother to bumper winner Brook Dance (by Maashor Dancer): poor on Flat (stays 2m): poor maiden hurdler: visored last 2 outings: sketchy jumper. *C. N. Kellett* **h64 x**

RIVER OF LIGHT (IRE) 5 b.g. Flemensfirth (USA) – Stillbyherself (IRE) (Le Bavard (FR)) [2004/5 20d Mar 19] lengthy gelding: has scope: first foal: dam won 2½m bumper: very green and jumped none too fluently when well held in novice hurdle on debut. *D. P. Keane* **h–**

RIVER OF WISHES 7 b.m. Riverwise (USA) – Wishful Dream (Crawter) [2004/5 19g^{pu} 22d^{F} 22g^{pu} Apr 12] no sign of ability. *C. W. Mitchell* **h–**

RIVER PHANTOM (IRE) 6 b.g. Over The River (FR) – Cathilda (IRE) (Cataldi) [2004/5 F90: 17v^{5} 19g^{4} 21g* Apr 1] good-topped gelding: fair novice hurdler: won maiden at Newbury in April by ¾ length from Make It A Double: stays 21f. *Ian Williams* **h101**

RIVER PIRATE (IRE) 8 b.g. Un Desperado (FR) – Kigali (IRE) (Torus) [2004/5 h106: c16g* c16m^{3} c16g^{2} c16g* c17m^{pu} c20g^{pu} c20d Feb 9] tall gelding: fair hurdler: similar form over fences: won novices at Warwick in May and Worcester in August: best around 2m: acts on good to firm and heavy going: blinkered (looked unenthusiastic) final start: has found little. *N. J. Henderson* **c106 h–**

RIVER QUOILE 9 b.g. Terimon – Carrikins (Buckskin (FR)) [2004/5 c88, h88: c24g^{6} c24d^{4} c24g^{4} Apr 15] workmanlike gelding: winning pointer: maiden hurdler/chaser, modest form at best: stays 25f: acts on firm and good to soft going: tried blinkered: has had jumping problems. *Mrs S. Alner* **c80 h–**

RIVER REINE (IRE) 6 br.m. Lahib (USA) – Talahari (IRE) (Roi Danzig (USA)) [2004/5 h85: 25g^{5} 24f* May 18] leggy, quite good-topped mare: modest hurdler: won weak 5-runner handicap at Towcester in May, but finished badly lame: stays 3m: acts on firm ground. *R. H. Buckler* **h91**

RIVER SHAMROCK (IRE) 11 ch.g. Alphabatim (USA) – High Feather (Nishapour (FR)) [2004/5 c25g^{6} c22m^{4} c30d^{2} c24g^{3} Jul 1] sturdy gelding: winning pointer: maiden hurdler/chaser: stays 3¾m: acts on heavy and good to firm going: tried in cheekpieces, formerly blinkered. *J. J. Lambe, Ireland* **c87 h–**

RIVER TRAPPER (IRE) 6 b.g. Over The River (FR) – Mousa (Callernish) [2004/5 F95: 19g^{6} 21d^{pu} 21s^{6} Feb 26] rangy gelding: has scope: bumper winner: modest form at best over hurdles. *Miss H. C. Knight* **h95**

RIVER TRIX (IRE) 11 b.g. Riverhead (USA) – Game Trix (Buckskin (FR)) [2004/5 c98, h–: c25d^{3} c25g^{bd} c26g c26g^{4} c23f^{5} c19g^{6} Sep 30] useful-looking gelding: maiden hurdler: poor chaser: successful on second of 2 starts in points in 2005: stays 3¼m: acts on good to soft and good to firm going: tried visored: tongue tied once. *M. Scudamore* **c80 h–**

RIYADH 7 ch.g. Caerleon (USA) – Ausherra (USA) (Diesis) [2004/5 20d 20m Dec 12] angular gelding: fair on Flat (stays 2½m): fair juvenile hurdler in 2001/2: very much let down by jumping/temperament since: tried visored. *M. Johnston* **h– §**

ROAD KING (IRE) 11 b.g. Supreme Leader – Ladies Gazette (London Gazette) [2004/5 23m^{4} 22m^{3} Jun 13] good-topped ex-Irish gelding: brother to poor Irish staying chaser Supreme Gazette and half-brother to winning hunter chasers Our Boreen (by Boreen) and The Parish Pump (by Bustineto): dam won 2m hurdle: poor form over hurdles, none in 3 chases: in frame in Irish points in 2004: stays 2¾m: in cheekpieces final outing. *Miss J. Feilden* **c– h77**

ROADWORTHY (IRE) 8 b.m. Lord Americo – Henry Woman (IRE) (Mandalus) [2004/5 h–, F–: 22m^{5} 21v^{6} 24v^{ur} 18d c23g^{6} c20d^{F} 17d^{5} Apr 5] poor maiden hurdler: no show in 2 chases. *J. K. Magee, Ireland* **c– h62**

ROARINGWATER (IRE) 6 b.g. Roselier (FR) – Supreme Cherry (Buckskin (FR)) [2004/5 F16v* 24d^{pu} 16s^{3} 20s Apr 20] €10,000 3-y-o: rather leggy gelding: seventh foal: half-brother to 2 winning pointers: dam lightly-raced, from family of useful chaser up to 3m Cherrynut: won second of 2 starts in maiden Irish points in 2003: useful form when making all in bumper at Hexham in November: lame on hurdling debut, fair form when third in novice at Newcastle: should stay beyond 2m. *R. T. Phillips* **h101 F112**

ROBBER BARON (IRE) 8 ch.g. Un Desperado (FR) – N T Nad (Welsh Pageant) [2004/5 c20g^{pu} c19s^{3} c19s^{4} 21g^{pu} Mar 28] strong, well-made gelding: bumper/hurdle winner: off over 2 years, finished tamely all starts over fences: lame back over hurdles final outing: should stay beyond 19f: acts on soft going. *Miss H. C. Knight* **c107 h–**

ROBBER (IRE) 8 ch.g. Un Desperado (FR) – Christy's Girl (IRE) (Buckskin (FR)) [2004/5 c80, h–: c25s^{2} c24v* c25v^{pu} c26d^{5} c26d* Apr 18] leggy gelding: modest handicap chaser: won at Chepstow in February and Plumpton in April: probably stays 29f: unraced on firm going, acts on any other. *P. Bowen* **c92 h–**

ROBBIE ON TOUR (IRE) 6 b.g. Oscar (IRE) – Mystery Woman (Tula Rocket) [2004/5 h–: 17s^{F} 19s 22s^{2} 22v^{5} 24g Apr 7] angular gelding: poor maiden hurdler: stays 2¾m: tongue tied last 3 outings, visored last 2: probably ungenuine. *M. C. Pipe* **h83 §**

ROBBIE'S ADVENTURE 11 ch.g. Le Coq d'Or – Mendick Adventure (Mandrake Major) [2004/5 c64x, h–: c33s^{5} c31m^{5} c24g c24s^{pu} c24d Apr 22] close-coupled gelding: poor chaser: had several trainers in 2004/5: stays 3¼m: acts on heavy and good to firm going: sometimes wears visor/cheekpieces: often let down by jumping. *D. L. Williams* **c– x h–**

ROBBIE'S RETURN 6 b.g. Bob's Return (IRE) – Si-Gaoith (Strong Gale) [2004/5 F16s 20v 19g Mar 4] well-made gelding: eighth foal: half-brother to 2 winners by Rakaposhi King, including fair hurdler Some Judge, stays 21f: dam unraced half-sister to fairly useful 3m hurdle winner Mount Hillary: well held in bumpers and 2 novice hurdles. *S. E. H. Sherwood* **h– F–**

ROBERT (IRE) 6 ch.g. Bob Back (USA) – Mother Imelda (IRE) (Phardante (FR)) [2004/5 F16v F16s 16s 20v^{2} 24s Mar 28] first foal: brother to bumper winner Square Mile: dam unraced, out of half-sister to useful hurdler/chaser up to 3m Bartres and useful 2m hurdler Dellersbeck: form only when runner-up in maiden hurdle at Leopardstown. *D. T. Hughes, Ireland* **h110 F–**

ROBERT THE BRUCE 10 ch.g. Distinct Native – Kawarau Queen (Taufan (USA)) [2004/5 16v Dec 30] good-topped gelding: very lightly-raced winning handicap hurdler: stays 2½m: acts on soft and good to firm going: clearly difficult to train. *L. Lungo* **h–**

ROBERT THE RASCAL 12 ch.g. Scottish Reel – Midnight Mary (Celtic Cone) [2004/5 c–: c24g^{6} c22g^{pu} c26s^{pu} Mar 13] winning pointer: little form in hunter chases. *Mrs C. M. James* **c91**

ROBERTY BOB (IRE) 10 ch.g. Bob Back (USA) – Inesdela (Wolver Hollow) [2004/5 c119, h–: c29d^{4} c24v^{3} c24s^{3} c23v^{5} Mar 30] good-topped gelding: fairly useful handicap chaser in 2003/4, not so good after 18-month absence in 2004/5: suited by 3m+: raced mainly on going softer than good (acts on heavy): often makes mistakes: lazy. *H. D. Daly* **c114 § h–**

ROBIN HOW (IRE) 8 b. or br.g. Mister Lord (USA) – Joaney How (Crash Course) [2004/5 20d^{pu} Sep 22] ex-Irish gelding: third foal: half-brother to winning pointer by **h–**

Lord Americo: dam bumper winner: failed to complete in 2 points in 2003: has shown nothing in bumper (for M. Hourigan) or maiden hurdle. *J. N. R. Billinge*

ROB LEACH 8 b.g. Robellino (USA) – Arc Empress Jane (IRE) (Rainbow Quest (USA)) [2004/5 18s* 16d 16s* Feb 5] smallish gelding: fairly useful hurdler: off 2 years prior to winning seller at Fontwell in December: back to best when winning handicap at Wetherby in February by 3½ lengths from Kimbambo: would have stayed 2½m: acted on heavy going, probably on good to firm: effective blinkered or not: dead. *G. L. Moore* **h120**

ROBYN ALEXANDER (IRE) 7 ch.m. Sharifabad (IRE) – Flagship Ahoy (IRE) (Accordion) [2004/5 c102, h111: c16g^{pu} c21d^{F} c19s^{ur} 22d 16s^{5} 16s^{4} 16d^{5} 19g^{5} 22d Apr 17] lengthy mare: modest handicap hurdler: winning chaser, though let down by jumping: stays easy 21f: acts on firm and soft going. *P. F. Nicholls* **c– x h97**

ROCINANTE (IRE) 5 b.g. Desert Story (IRE) – Antapoura (IRE) (Bustino) [2004/5 17g^{pu} Jul 15] modest on Flat (stays 8.5f), successful twice in 2004: failed to settle in maiden on hurdling debut. *J. J. Quinn* **h–**

ROCK DE JAY 6 b.g. Mazaad – Kamakaze Girl (Kampala) [2004/5 F16s Oct 22] sixth foal: dam 1m winner: tailed off in bumper on debut. *N. J. Pomfret* **F–**

ROCKERFELLA LAD (IRE) 5 b.g. Danetime (IRE) – Soucaro (Rusticaro (FR)) [2004/5 h65: 16d^{5} 17g^{4} 16d 17d^{6} 16g^{pu} c16d c16v^{6} c20v^{6} c16v Mar 17] quite good-topped gelding: poor maiden hurdler: no show over fences: tried blinkered. *M. Todhunter* **c– h63**

ROCKET BLEU (FR) 5 ch.g. Epervier Bleu – Egeria (FR) (Baly Rockette) [2004/5 h92: 16d 17v^{pu} 16d 17v^{4} 16v^{F} 20s^{pu} Apr 16] good-topped gelding: modest handicap hurdler: sold out of N. Richards' stable 2,100 gns Doncaster January Sales after third start: lost his way: raced around 2m: acts on soft and good to firm going. *D. Burchell* **h91 d**

ROCKET FORCE (USA) 5 ch.g. Spinning World (USA) – Pat Us (USA) (Caucasus (USA)) [2004/5 16g 16d 16g^{3} 16g Mar 5] compact gelding: useful form over 1¼m at 3 yrs, well held in 2004: sold out of E. Dunlop's stable 35,000 gns Newmarket July Sales: modest form at best in novice company over hurdles: room for improvement with jumping. *S. Gollings* **h94**

ROCKET SHIP (IRE) 5 b.g. Pennekamp (USA) – Rock The Boat (Slip Anchor) [2004/5 h109p: 16d* 16s^{2} 16d^{2} 16v^{5} Dec 27] good-topped gelding: useful novice hurdler: easily won maiden at Cork in October: much better form when runner-up next 2 starts, beaten 3 lengths by stable-companion Wild Passion in Grade 1 at Fairyhouse on second occasion, travelling strongly and looking likely winner when bad mistake 2 out: ran poorly on heavy going final start: likely to prove best around 2m: raced on going softer than good over hurdles: free-going sort. *N. Meade, Ireland* **h131**

ROCKFORD (IRE) 9 b.g. King's Ride – Pampered Russian (Deep Run) [2004/5 24m^{pu} 21g^{6} c24m^{2} c26m^{5} Aug 19] tall gelding: runner-up twice in points in 2004: little form over hurdles or in chases: looked no easy ride when visored. *P. W. Hiatt* **c75 h–**

ROCKING SHIP (IRE) 7 b.g. Leading Counsel (USA) – One More Try (Kemal (FR)) [2004/5 24f c22m c17f* c22f^{4} c22m^{F} 19m c25d^{3} c25g* c16s^{3} c20d^{5} Nov 14] winning hurdler: modest handicap chaser: won at Navan in June and Kilbeggan in September: effective at 2m to 25f: acts on firm and soft going: tried blinkered/in cheekpieces: has had tongue tied. *Ms J. Morgan, Ireland* **c99 h–**

ROCKLEY BEACH (IRE) 6 b.g. Tidaro (USA) – Green Fairy (Green Shoon) [2004/5 h–, F87: 22d^{6} May 17] fair form in bumper on debut: no show in 2 starts over hurdles: tried blinkered: sold 2,800 gns Doncaster August Sales. *V. R. A. Dartnall* **h–**

ROCK'N COLD (IRE) 7 b.g. Bigstone (IRE) – Unalaska (IRE) (High Estate) [2004/5 c79, h106: 17g^{3} 20m^{4} Aug 30] lengthy gelding: none too fluent only outing over fences: winning hurdler: off 13 months, in frame in sellers in 2004/5: stays 2½m: acts on good to firm and heavy going: tried visored, often wears cheekpieces. *J. G. Given* **c– h89**

ROCKSPRING HERO 9 b.g. Minster Son – Niel's Crystal (Indiaro) [2004/5 c119, h103: 20d c17d^{4} 20s c24v 19v^{F} c16s c24d Mar 20] sturdy gelding: maiden hurdler: fair handicap chaser: effective at 2m to 3m: acts on heavy going. *John J. Walsh, Ireland* **c113 h–**

ROCKSTOWN BOY (IRE) 7 b.g. Toulon – Palatine Lady (Pauper) [2004/5 h137p: 16g^{4} 16m^{2} 18d^{3} 16v^{F} Dec 28] rangy, useful-looking gelding: twice successful on Flat (stayed 2m) in 2004: useful novice hurdler in 2003/4: below best when placed in minor events in 2004/5: fell fatally third at Leopardstown: would have stayed beyond 2½m: acted on soft going. *C. Byrnes, Ireland* **h128**

ROCKY AGENDA (IRE) 4 b.g. Fort Morgan (USA) – Floating Agenda (USA) (Twilight Agenda (USA)) [2004/5 F14d^5 F14g Dec 18] leggy gelding: first foal: dam 2-y-o 6f winner: modest form in 3-y-o bumpers. *G. A. Harker* **F81**

ROCKY BALBOA 13 b.g. Buckley – Midnight Pansy (Deadly Nightshade) [2004/5 c22v^{pu} May 10] of no account. *W. Davies* **c– h–**

RODBER (USA) 9 ch.g. Rodrigo de Triano (USA) – Berceau (USA) (Alleged (USA)) [2004/5 c113, h78: c16g^2 c16d^6 c16s^3 c17s^2 c16d^{pu} Dec 4] lengthy, angular gelding: maiden hurdler: fair handicap chaser: best form around 2m: raced on good going or softer (acts on soft): wore cheekpieces last 2 starts: has broken blood vessels. *Mrs L. B. Normile* **c111 h–**

RODOLFO 7 b.g. Tragic Role (USA) – Be Discreet (Junius (USA)) [2004/5 h99: c20m^{ur} May 30] tall gelding: winning hurdler: travelling strongly when unseating 5 out in novice on chasing debut: stays 2½m with emphasis on speed. *O. Sherwood* **c– h–**

RO ERIDANI 5 b.m. Binary Star (USA) – Hat Hill (Roan Rocket) [2004/5 h–: 16m^{pu} Jun 12] no form in 2 starts over hurdles. *Miss S. E. Forster* **h–**

RO GEMA RI 7 b.g. Perpendicular – Pretty Soon (Tina's Pet) [2004/5 F–: F17d Oct 3] well beaten in bumpers. *T. D. Walford* **F–**

ROGERO 6 b.g. Presidium – Richesse (FR) (Faraway Son (USA)) [2004/5 h–, F–: 20d^{pu} 17m^{pu} May 19] of no account: sold 1,000 gns Doncaster August Sales, resold £2,500 Ascot October Sales. *R. E. Barr* **h–**

ROGUES GALLERY (IRE) 5 b.g. Luso – Sarah May (IRE) (Camden Town) [2004/5 F16f* F16d^3 F16m^2 20g^2 23s* Mar 22] sturdy gelding: first foal: dam unraced half-sister to useful 2m hurdler Mayasta: fair form in bumpers, won at Punchestown in May, sold out of G. Hourigan's stable 150,000 gns Doncaster Sales later in month: fair form both starts over hurdles, successful in novice at Wetherby in March: stays 23f: acts on soft going (won bumper on firm): open to improvement. *J. Howard Johnson* **h106 p F94**

ROHAN 9 gr.g. Norton Challenger – Acushla Macree (Mansingh (USA)) [2004/5 h87: c23g^5 Apr 12] sturdy gelding: maiden hurdler: won maiden point in March: fifth in novice hunter chase at Exeter: probably stays 23f: acts on soft and good to firm going: tried blinkered. *R. F. Johnson Houghton* **c77 h–**

ROI DE L'ODET (FR) 5 b.g. Grape Tree Road – Fanfare du Roi (Rusticaro (FR)) [2004/5 16s^3 16s 16s^3 24d* Mar 24] leggy ex-French gelding: seventh foal: half-brother to 4 winners on Flat, including 1¼m to 1¾m winner Homme Orchestre (by Homme de Loi): dam 7f to 9f winner: won 5 times from 1m to 11f on Flat at 3 yrs: fairly useful novice hurdler: best effort when 2 lengths third to Briareus at Kempton third start: upped in trip, comfortably landed odds at Ludlow later in month. *N. J. Henderson* **h115**

ROJABAA 6 b.g. Anabaa (USA) – Slava (USA) (Diesis) [2004/5 h–: 16g^2 17g^3 Sep 30] small gelding: poor on Flat (stays 1½m): similar standard over hurdles: raced mainly around 2m: tried blinkered: has had tongue tied. *W. G. M. Turner* **h78**

ROKY STAR (FR) 8 b.g. Start Fast (FR) – Rosydolie (FR) (Dhausli (FR)) [2004/5 h88: c25s^{pu} 22s* 25s^{pu} Jan 27] modest hurdler: won maiden at Fontwell in January: little show on chasing debut: stays 2¾m: acts on heavy ground: tried tongue tied: has finished weakly. *M. R. Bosley* **c– h96**

ROLFES DELIGHT 13 b.g. Rolfe (USA) – Idiot's Run (Idiot's Delight) [2004/5 c84§, h–: c25f* c24g^{ur} Oct 26] workmanlike gelding: poor handicap chaser: off 14 months but well backed, won conditional jockeys event at Wincanton (for second time) in October: unseated first next time: stays 25f: acts on firm going: tried tongue tied: inconsistent and probably best fresh. *A. E. Jones* **c84 § h–**

ROLL ALONG (IRE) 5 b.g. Carroll House – Callmartel (IRE) (Montelimar (USA)) [2004/5 F18s* Oct 12] second foal: dam unraced half-sister to smart staying chaser Nahthen Lad: won 4-runner bumper at Fontwell on debut by ½ length from Yes Sir. *M. Pitman* **F97 +**

ROLLESTON ROCKET 8 ch.m. King's Signet (USA) – Jubilee Line (High Line) [2004/5 16g^{pu} 16m Jun 6] well beaten in 6f seller at 2 yrs for M. Polglase: no sign of ability over hurdles. *P. W. Hiatt* **h–**

ROLLING HOME (IRE) 4 br.g. Key of Luck (USA) – Belike The Wind (IRE) (Marju (IRE)) [2004/5 16g^2 16m* 16d^2 16s* 16v 16g Mar 15] close-coupled gelding: fair on Flat (probably stays 13f): fairly useful juvenile hurdler: won at Tramore in August (final start for K. Prendergast) and Thurles in December: raced at 2m: acts on soft and good to firm going: blinkered last 3 starts. *N. Meade, Ireland* **h112**

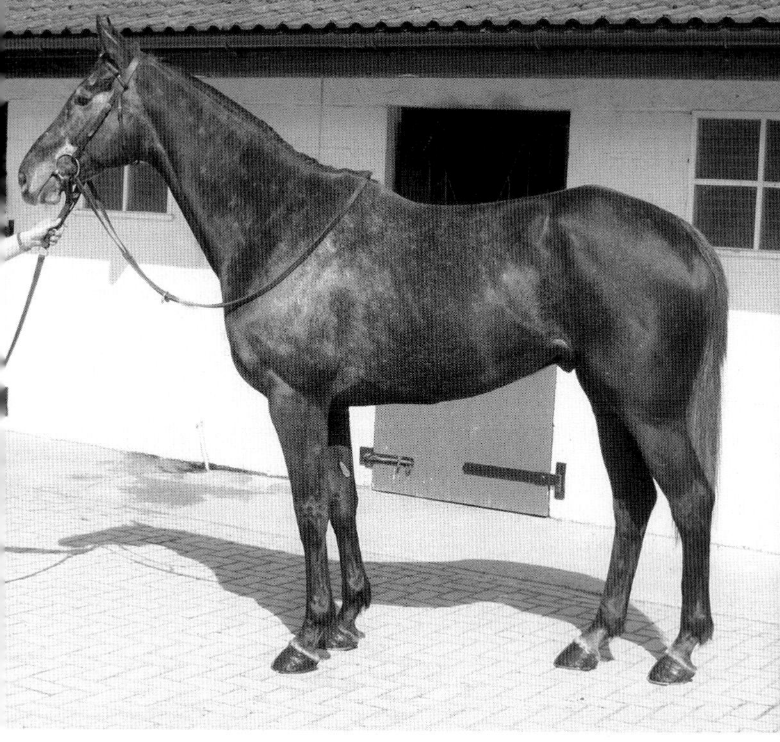

Mr Richard Collins' "Roman Ark"

ROLLO (IRE) 7 gr.g. Roselier (FR) – Comeragh Queen (The Parson) [2004/5 F92: 20d^{F} 24g^{3} 24s^{2} 23s^{3} 22d* c26d^{F} c23d^{pu} 26s 22v^{4} Mar 30] angular gelding: modest hurdler: made all in novice handicap at Exeter in November: failed to complete both starts over fences: will prove best at 3m+: raced on good going or softer: blinkered after second outing: sold 7,500 gns Doncaster May Sales. *P. J. Hobbs* **c– h92**

ROMAN ARK 7 gr.g. Terimon – Larksmore (Royal Fountain) [2004/5 h96: 16d^{2} 17v* 16v* 16v* 16d 21g Mar 16] strong, lengthy gelding: will make a chaser: useful novice hurdler: won at Carlisle in November and Haydock in December and January: easily best effort when beating Baby Run by 8 lengths in Grade 2 Rossington Main Novices' Hurdle on last occasion: below form after in valuable handicap at Newbury and Royal & SunAlliance Novices' Hurdle at Cheltenham: should stay 2½m+: best form on heavy going. *J. M. Jefferson* **h136**

ROMAN CANDLE (IRE) 9 b.g. Sabrehill (USA) – Penny Banger (IRE) (Pennine Walk) [2004/5 h74: 17m 16g 20m^{5} 18m^{5} 26m^{6} Aug 30] lengthy, workmanlike gelding: poor maiden hurdler: stays 2½m: acts on good to firm going. *Mrs Lucinda Featherstone* **h71**

ROMAN CONSUL (IRE) 7 ch.g. Alphabatim (USA) – Stella Romana (Roman Warrior) [2004/5 h–: 24s^{3} 17d^{6} c21d c20v^{pu} Dec 17] workmanlike gelding: poor form over hurdles: no show in 2 handicaps over fences: stays 3m. *Jonjo O'Neill* **c– h83**

ROMAN COURT (IRE) 7 b.g. Witness Box (USA) – Small Iron (General Ironside) [2004/5 h87: 22g^{F} 22d* 22d^{6} 24s 24s 24d^{4} 22d^{5} 22d^{2} Apr 17] smallish gelding: modest hurdler: won novice at Folkestone in November: will stay beyond 25f: acts on firm and good to soft going. *R. H. Alner* **h89**

ROMAN HIDEAWAY (IRE) 7 b.g. Hernando (FR) – Vaison La Romaine (Arctic Tern (USA)) [2004/5 h–: 16g 20d 19d 26s5 Jan 5] poor novice hurdler. *J. A. B. Old* **h66 +**

ROMAN KING (IRE) 10 b.g. Sadler's Wells (USA) – Romantic Feeling (Shirley Heights) [2004/5 20g3 20s3 May 9] leggy gelding: modest hurdler: stays 2½m: acts on heavy going. *B. D. Leavy* **h87**

ROMANOV RAMBLER (IRE) 5 b.g. Moscow Society (USA) – Roses Lady (IRE) (Buckley) [2004/5 F16s Apr 22] €6,500 3-y-o: fourth foal: dam twice-raced half-sister to Galway Hurdle winner/useful 2m chaser Oh So Grumpy: no show in bumper on debut. *Mrs S. C. Bradburne* **F–**

ROMAN RAMPAGE 10 b.g. Perpendicular – Roman Moor (Owen Anthony) [2004/5 h82: 27s 21m6 25g4 Oct 18] medium-sized gelding: lightly-raced winning hurdler: probably stays 27f: acts on heavy going: wore cheekpieces/blinkers last 4 starts. *Miss Z. C. Davison* **h79**

ROMAN REBEL 6 ch.g. Primitive Rising (USA) – Roman Moor (Owen Anthony) [2004/5 F89: 20d 24d5 23v2 24v4 Feb 15] leggy, workmanlike gelding: fair form in bumpers: form over hurdles only when second in maiden at Wetherby: should be suited by 3m+: acts on heavy going. *Mrs K. Walton* **h91**

ROMAN RODNEY 8 b.g. Feelings (FR) – Pohet (Pongee) [2004/5 h–: 20g4 20m5 c20dpu 26dpu Aug 9] no form. *G. M. Moore* **c– h–**

ROMANTIC AFFAIR (IRE) 8 ch.g. Persian Bold – Broken Romance (IRE) (Ela-Mana-Mou) [2004/5 h89: 21g5 19s4 20g6 Feb 5] good-topped gelding: lightly raced: modest novice hurdler: probably stays 21f: raced on good going or softer over hurdles. *Miss H. C. Knight* **h97**

ROMAN WAY 9 ch.g. Gildoran – Olympian Princess (Master Owen) [2004/5 16d6 c24m3 c24g4 c25g3 c25dur Apr 11] maiden pointer: well held in novice hurdle: modest form over fences: will stay beyond 25f. *Miss S. E. Forster* **c90 h–**

ROMANY DREAM 7 b.m. Nomadic Way (USA) – Half Asleep (Quiet Fling (USA)) [2004/5 c–, h–: c17g6 c20m2 c16g3 c16m4 c17mpu c17g4 c21d2 c20m2 c18m* c20s* c16s3 c16d2 c16g4 Dec 8] leggy mare: modest chaser: won maiden at Fontwell in September and mares novice there in November: stays 21f: acts on soft and good to firm going: tried in cheekpieces, usually blinkered: races prominently: virtually refused to race fifth start. *R. Dickin* **c93 h–**

ROMANY PRINCE 6 b.g. Robellino (USA) – Vicki Romara (Old Vic) [2004/5 24d3 23s2 19g3 24g Mar 18] rather leggy gelding: useful on Flat (best form around 2m), sold out of D. Elsworth's stable 60,000 gns Newmarket Autumn Sales: fair form in novice hurdles: stays 3m. *S. Gollings* **h114**

ROMARIC (USA) 4 b.g. Red Ransom (USA) – Eternal Reve (USA) (Diesis) [2004/5 19g 16g Jan 24] small gelding: fairly useful 6f winner for D. Loder at 2 yrs, well held on Flat in 2004: tailed off both starts over hurdles. *J. R. Norton* **h–**

ROMEO JONES 6 bl.g. Roselier (FR) – Juleit Jones (IRE) (Phardante (FR)) [2004/5 F–: F18s4 Oct 12] leggy gelding: tailed off in 2 bumpers: fell fatally on point debut. *B. G. Powell* **F–**

ROMERO 9 b.g. Robellino (USA) – Casamurrae (Be My Guest (USA)) [2004/5 c–§, h88§: 22g4 24d4 22g3 Sep 12] compact gelding: modest handicap hurdler: stays 3m: probably acts on any going: sometimes visored: has had tongue tied: usually races prominently: ungenuine. *P. R. Chamings* **c– § h89 §**

ROMIL STAR (GER) 8 b.g. Chief's Crown (USA) – Romelia (USA) (Woodman (USA)) [2004/5 c–, h101: 19g3 May 11] sturdy gelding: fair hurdler: left G. M. Moore, below form in seller (blinkered) only outing in 2004/5: little show in maiden chases: stays 21f: acts on firm and soft going: often wears cheekpieces: has had tongue tied: fairly useful on all-weather on Flat, successful twice early in 2005. *K. R. Burke* **c– h89**

RONALD 6 ch.g. Karinga Bay – Hy Wilma (Jalmood (USA)) [2004/5 F–: 24gpu 24m5 17d 19vpu Dec 31] tall gelding: no form in bumper or over hurdles. *N. J. Hawke* **h–**

RONANS CHOICE (IRE) 12 b.g. Yashgan – Petite Port (IRE) (Decent Fellow) [2004/5 c99: c23d6 May 4] workmanlike gelding: winning chaser: fair pointer/hunter in 2004: stays 3¼m: acts on good to soft ground: blinkered: tried tongue tied. *Miss Emma Oliver* **c–**

ROOBIHOO (IRE) 6 b.g. Norwich – Griffinstown Lady (Over The River (FR)) [2004/5 h89, F77: 22v4 20v5 21v4 20v* 23s4 20s5 20d3 22d2 Apr 11] rangy gelding: fair **h103**

handicap hurdler: won at Wetherby in January: best efforts last 2 starts: stays 2¾m: raced on good ground or softer over hurdles. *C. Grant*

ROOD BOY (IRE) 4 b.g. Great Commotion (USA) – Cnocma (IRE) (Tender King) [2004/5 16d^2 16s* 17s 16d 17m^5 Mar 21] smallish gelding: modest maiden on Flat (stays 8.5f): fair form first 2 starts over hurdles, winning novice at Wincanton in January: raced around 2m: acts on soft going. *J. S. King* **h102**

ROOFING SPIRIT (IRE) 7 b.g. Beneficial – Vulcash (IRE) (Callernish) [2004/5 h93, F97: c20g^F c21g^3 c23d^3 c16s* c16g^4 c16d^2 c17s^2 Apr 16] rangy gelding: modest maiden hurdler: fair chaser: won maiden at Folkestone in January: effective at 2m to 23f: raced on good going or softer: has flashed tail under pressure. *D. P. Keane* **c111 h–**

ROOFTOP PROTEST (IRE) 8 b.g. Thatching – Seattle Siren (USA) (Seattle Slew (USA)) [2004/5 18s* 16d^5 Nov 13] leggy gelding: half-brother to useful hurdler Ismeno (by Ela-Mana-Mou), stays 2½m, and winning 2¼m hurdler Chimayo (by Sure Blade): fair on Flat (stays 17f), much improved and successful 4 times in 2004: fair hurdler: won handicap at Limerick in October: respectable effort at Cheltenham next time: stays 2½m: acts on heavy going, probably on good to firm: tongue tied in 2004/5. *T. Hogan, Ireland* **h100**

ROOKERY LAD 7 b.g. Makbul – Wayzgoose (USA) (Diesis) [2004/5 h92: 21d^4 16m* 20m c17g^2 c20g^2 c16f^3 c22d^3 c20g^{pu} Oct 27] modest handicap hurdler: made all at Towcester in May: similar form in novice company over fences: stays 2¾m: acts on good to firm and good to soft going: usually front runner. *C. N. Kellett* **c92 h92**

ROOKWITH (IRE) 5 b.g. Revoque (IRE) – Resume (IRE) (Lahib (USA)) [2004/5 h97: 16s 16s^5 16d 16s^2 16v 16v^3 17v Jan 20] workmanlike gelding: modest maiden hurdler: raced around 2m: acts on heavy going: tried visored. *T. G. McCourt, Ireland* **h98**

ROOM TO ROOM GOLD (IRE) 9 b.g. Phardante (FR) – Kiwi Circle (IRE) (Strong Gale) [2004/5 h113, F92: 18m^F 16m^F Jun 13] bumper winner: fairly useful hurdler: fell both starts in minor events in 2004/5: would probably have won but for falling last at Navan on reappearance and travelling best when falling 2 out at Roscommon: raced mainly around 2m: acts on firm going: needs to brush up jumping: joined R. Alner. *M. Halford, Ireland* **h117**

ROONEYRAN 9 br.g. Arctic Lord – Moy Ran Lady (Black Minstrel) [2004/5 c16m Mar 21] poor pointer. *A. P. Morgan* **c–**

ROOSTER 10 b.g. Roi Danzig (USA) – Jussoli (Don) [2004/5 c84, h–: c20d^4 c21m^5 c21d^5 c21g^2 c21d* Mar 28] good-topped gelding: fair hunter chaser: won 5-runner novice at Fakenham in March: stays 21f: acts on good to firm and good to soft going. *Mrs Julie Read* **c91 h–**

ROOSTER BOOSTER 11 gr.g. Riverwise (USA) – Came Cottage (Nearly A Hand) [2004/5 h166: 16g^2 16d^4 17d^4 16g^2 16g^2 16g 20d^5 16m* Apr 22] **h162**

Irish-trained runners outnumbered British-trained by eight to six in the latest Champion Hurdle and included the first seven in the betting. Bookmakers totesport issued additional odds for an 'Irish' Champion Hurdle (with Hardy Eustace 11/4 favourite) and for an 'English' version, with 2003 winner Rooster Booster the 6/4 favourite. Rooster Booster had won only once since his eleven-length Champion Hurdle victory and had finished second on eight of his twelve starts in the interim, including when runner-up to Hardy Eustace in the 2004 Champion. Rooster Booster finished 'second' again in the 'English' version of the latest Champion, two places behind the previous year's third Intersky Falcon, the pair sixth and eighth in a race predictably dominated by the Irish. Rooster Booster isn't so good as he was—he was 16/1 for the latest Champion—but he was left with plenty to do at Cheltenham, the way the race developed, after being held up in last for a long way and then making mistakes at the last two flights.

A plan to give Rooster Booster a second chance of Cheltenham Festival glory under top weight in the County Hurdle on the final day was abandoned after his entry for the race had been confirmed at the five-day stage. Had he been among the final declarations, his weight would have gone up to 12-9 under a rule introduced after the declaration of Rigmarole, eighth in the Champion Hurdle, the previous year prevented the raising of the weights in the County Hurdle. The chief beneficiary was his stable-companion Sporazene who was left heading the weights on 10-13, after Rigmarole's withdrawal through lameness, and duly won the race in which only four others who came under orders in a field of twenty-three were racing from their correct marks. In the latest season, the County Hurdle reverted to a twenty-four-hour declaration (from forty-eight the previous year) and took place three days after the Champion Hurdle rather than two, but the rule stated that, in class A handicaps like the County, any horse that (at the time of declaration) had run within the preceding forty-eight hours, or was declared to run in another race, was disregarded for the purpose of determining the highest weight. Rigmarole carried 11-12 in the latest edition, as he would still have done if Rooster Booster had been declared; at the entries-with-weights stage (before the Champion Hurdle had been run) Rigmarole had been allotted 11-1, with Rooster Booster on 11-12. Rooster Booster's trainer labelled the rule as it applied to the County Hurdle 'totally ridiculous, absolutely crackers', and he had a good point. 'I wouldn't have had to declare Rooster Booster for the County until two days after he had run in the Champion, so I would have known whether he was fit to run,' he said. The rule has since been amended, bringing the time down from forty-eight hours to twenty-four which will solve the particular problem with the Champion Hurdle and the County Hurdle. However, at a time when the BHB is bending over backwards to attract high-class horses to the Grand National by favouring them in the original handicap, it seems inconsistent to have regulations that prevent high-class horses running in the top handicaps in certain circumstances. The Grand National conditions allow for the raising of the weights the day before the race, should any horse be notified as a non-runner after the forty-eight-hour stage. If all Class A handicaps with forty-eight-hour declarations had such a condition, it would ensure that they were as competitive as possible without discriminating against the original top weight.

By the time Rooster Booster lined up for the Concept Hurdle at Sandown on the penultimate day of the season, many had all but written him off as a championship contender. He had run well to finish fourth to Accordion Etoile, to whom he was conceding 20 lb, patiently ridden, in the Greatwood Handicap at Cheltenham in November, on his return from a summer break, but was then some way below form when unfamiliar forcing tactics were employed in the Bula Hurdle (fourth to Back In Front) and in the Christmas Hurdle (reeled in by Harchibald after setting too strong a gallop). He managed only fifth in the Aintree Hurdle, making no impression from three out, on his only start between Cheltenham and Sandown. With no Irish challengers, the nine-runner Concept Hurdle, which also had four Pipe-trained runners and two representing the Nicholls team, was almost a manifestation of totesport's 'English' Champion Hurdle. Intersky Falcon was missing but Self Defense (who beat Rooster Booster in the Agfa Hurdle at Sandown in February) and Royal Shakespeare (a good second in the Scottish Champion Hurdle on his latest start) had finished tenth and eleventh at Cheltenham. Royal Shakespeare was in the lead in the Concept and still going strongly when falling two out. Rooster

Concept Hurdle, Sandown—
Rooster Booster wins for just the second time since the 2003 Champion Hurdle;
Self Defense and Perouse chase him over the last

Booster was poised to challenge at the time and went on to win, after being left in front, by four lengths from the favourite Self Defense. Whether the veteran Rooster Booster would have beaten Royal Shakespeare, had that horse stayed on his feet, is not certain, but he showed no sign of stopping once in the lead on this occasion. Rooster Booster has rather too often displayed a tendency both for idling in front and for not finding much off the bridle, traits which had led to his ending up losing races in which, even at a very late stage, winning looked the likelier outcome. In thirty-eight starts outside his prolific Champion Hurdle-winning season, Rooster Booster has won just four races. Nonetheless, Rooster Booster is widely regarded with affection by jumping followers and was warmly received after the Concept Hurdle. His victory would have been a fitting note on which to bring down the curtain on his career, but he looks set to continue for another season. He was not discredited when fourth under top weight in the Stanleybet Handicap Hurdle (formerly the Swinton) at Haydock shortly after the end of the latest season.

Rooster Booster (gr.g. 1994)	Riverwise (USA) (b 1988)	Riverman (b 1969)	Never Bend
			River Lady
		Village Sass (1982)	Sassafras
			Village Beauty
	Came Cottage (gr 1980)	Nearly A Hand (ch 1974)	Busted
			Petite Chou
		Maybelle (gr 1965)	Perhapsburg
			Tinkling

The sparely-made Rooster Booster was one of four foals to represent the fairly useful pointer Came Cottage on the racecourse in the latest season, all of them by Rooster Booster's sire Riverwise. The modest novice hurdler Cockatoo Ridge, winner of a bumper back in 2002/3, ran three times without reaching the frame; Silkie Pekin showed no sign of ability in bumpers and a mares novice hurdle; and Attitude was never better than mid-field when tenth of fifteen in a mares bumper on her only start. Rooster Booster, who stays an easy two and a half miles and probably acts on any going, is ideally suited by being held up in a truly-run race. He is normally a fluent jumper. *P. J. Hobbs*

ROOSTER'S REUNION (IRE) 6 gr.g. Presenting – Court Town (Camden Town) [2004/5 h105p: 16s^{5} 16d Mar 5] useful-looking gelding: fair hurdler: raced around 2m, on good ground or softer. *D. R. Gandolfo* **h112**

ROPPONGI DANCER 6 b.m. Mtoto – Ice Chocolate (USA) (Icecapade (USA)) [2004/5 h77§: 19m 17m^{6} 17d 17d Aug 22] small mare: poor maiden on Flat and over hurdles: stays 2½m: acts on good to firm going: has worn headgear: usually tongue tied in 2003/4: ungenuine. *Mrs N. Macauley* **h68 §**

ROSADARE (IRE) 7 b.g. Roselier (FR) – Mosephine (IRE) (The Parson) [2004/5 F105: 24s^{pu} 20s^{6} 17s 26s Mar 7] placed in points: fairly useful bumper winner for D. P. Murphy: little form in 4 outings over hurdles. *Miss K. Marks* **h–**

ROSAKER (USA) 8 b.g. Pleasant Tap (USA) – Rose Crescent (USA) (Nijinsky (CAN)) [2004/5 h153: 24g^{3} 20s^{2} 20s^{3} 24v^{pu} 24v^{3} 22s^{6} Mar 28] leggy, rather sparely-made gelding: smart hurdler at best: no match for Solerina when placed in 2½m Grade 2 events at Navan: ran badly after, twice shaping as if amiss: stays 3m: acts on soft and good to firm going. *N. Meade, Ireland* **h144**

ROSALYONS (IRE) 11 gr.g. Roselier (FR) – Coffee Shop (Bargello) [2004/5 c74§, h80d: 20d^{pu} 22m^{6} 22s* 22v* 24d 24g c25d c32v^{pu} 20v^{5} Mar 20] leggy gelding: has stringhalt: poor maiden chaser, often let down by jumping: fair handicap hurdler: won twice at Kelso in October: stays 3¾m: acts on heavy going: tried blinkered/in cheek-pieces: ridden by Miss R. Davidson nowadays. *Mrs H. O. Graham* **c– §** **h103**

ROSCHAL (IRE) 7 gr.g. Roselier (FR) – Sunday World (USA) (Solford (USA)) [2004/5 h79, F85: 19s^{3} c20s* c21s^{2} c20d* c22g^{pu} 21d^{2} 22d^{4} Apr 3] rather leggy gelding: modest maiden hurdler: fair chaser: won handicaps at Ludlow in December (novice) and February: stays 2¾m: acts on soft ground (bumper form on good to firm): blinkered once (well beaten): seems to need right-handed course. *P. J. Hobbs* **c112** **h85**

ROSCOE BURN 13 ch.g. Meadowbrook – Rosecko (White Speck) [2004/5 c–: c27g^{pu} May 25] winning pointer: pulled up in 2 hunters. *Mrs K. Massie* **c–**

ROSEBERRY ROSE 6 ch.m. Keen – Scotch Imp (Imperial Fling (USA)) [2004/5 F–: F16d 24v^{pu} Feb 15] strong mare: no sign of ability. *C. Rae* **h– F–**

ROSECHARMER 8 ch.m. Charmer – Rosie Cone (Celtic Cone) [2004/5 19d^{5} 25v 23v^{5} 23s c24g^{4} Mar 16] smallish, angular mare: poor maiden hurdler: fourth in handicap at Huntingdon on chasing debut: best effort at 19f: acts on good to soft going. *Mrs P. Sly* **c75 h83**

ROSEDALE GARDENS 5 b.g. Fleetwood (IRE) – Freddie's Recall (Warrshan (USA)) [2004/5 F17v F16v Nov 17] good-topped gelding: third foal: half-brother to 6f winner Dear Pickles (by Piccolo) and winner up to 1¼m in Germany by Botanic: dam ran 3 times: well beaten in 2 bumpers. *M. W. Easterby* **F–**

ROSEMAUVE (FR) 5 b.g. Cyborg (FR) – Sweet Jaune (FR) (Le Nain Jaune (FR)) [2004/5 c18d^{2} c17d^{5} 17g^{4} 17g 19g^{6} 26m^{2} 22m* 24m^{2} 24g* 22v* 24d Dec 10] leggy gelding: second foal: dam unraced, out of half-sister to very smart hurdler/smart staying chaser Sweet Duke: fair chaser in France, sold out of M. Rolland's stable €46,000 Goffs July Sale after second start: useful hurdler: won handicaps at Fontwell in September, Ludlow in October and Uttoxeter (by 2½ lengths from Carlys Quest) in November: stays 3¼m: acts on heavy and good to firm going: best in blinkers: not straightforward. *M. C. Pipe* **c115 h131**

ROSE OF THE HILL (IRE) 6 gr.g. Roselier (FR) – Golden Leaf (Croghan Hill) [2004/5 21d^{3} 17s^{5} 17g 25v^{5} 24d 21v^{6} 20s 22m^{5} Apr 23] €21,000 4-y-o: leggy gelding: fifth foal: brother to winning pointer Oak Lodge and bumper winner The Well: dam never ran: won both starts in points in 2004: modest form over hurdles: should be suited by further than 21f. *M. C. Pipe* **h99**

ROSE OF YORK (IRE) 5 b.m. Emarati (USA) – True Ring (High Top) [2004/5 h–: 17m 19m 21g^{F} 24g 16g* Apr 19] rather leggy mare: poor maiden on Flat: first form over hurdles when winning selling handicap at Towcester in April: tongue tied after first outing: poor jumper: signs of temperament. *Mrs A. M. Thorpe* **h64 x**

ROSES ARE WILD (IRE) 7 gr.m. Roselier (FR) – Wild Bramble (IRE) (Deep Run) [2004/5 h–, F–: 20v^{5} 24v 25s^{6} 20s^{pu} 20d^{pu} Mar 26] small mare: no solid form: tried visored: sold 2,800 gns Doncaster May Sales. *Mrs B. K. Thomson* **h–**

ROSE TEA (IRE) 6 ro.m. Alhaarth (IRE) – Shakamiyn (Nishapour (FR)) [2004/5 h89: c23m^{4} c26d^{F} Aug 9] modest winning hurdler: well beaten on completed outing over fences: stays 23f: acts on good to firm going: tried visored. *Miss E. C. Lavelle* **c– h–**

ROSE TINA 8 b.m. Tina's Pet – Rosevear (IRE) (Contract Law (USA)) [2004/5 c100, h75+: 19d^{3} 19m^{3} c20m^{6} c22m^{4} Sep 5] leggy mare: modest chaser/maiden hurdler: stays 2¾m: acts on firm and soft going: usually free-going front runner: ran out once in 2003/4. *B. G. Powell* **c95 h87**

ROSETOWN (IRE) 7 gr.g. Roselier (FR) – Railstown Cheeky (IRE) (Strong Gale) [2004/5 h–, F–: 19d* 22s* 20d^{2} c20g^{3} c21s^{5} c23d^{pu} 26s* 22s* 21s^{3} 26m^{5} Apr 9] smallish gelding: modest hurdler: won handicaps at Exeter (conditional jockeys novice) and Newton Abbot early in season and minor event at Hereford and conditional jockeys handicap at Fontwell in January: poor form first 2 starts over fences: stays 3¼m: acts on soft going: blinkered last 4 outings: tongue tied once. *T. R. George* **c75 h99**

ROSEVILLE (IRE) 5 b.m. Beneficial – Knockhouse Rose (IRE) (Roselier (FR)) [2004/5 F16s F16s F16s F16s Mar 27] €40,000 4-y-o: first foal: dam unraced sister to top-class staying chaser The Grey Monk, from family of Grey Abbey: well beaten in bumpers. *S. T. Lewis* **F–**

ROSIEHAVEAREEF (IRE) 7 b.m. Roselier (FR) – Mirasel (Miramar Reef) [2004/5 F16s 20v^{ur} 21s^{F} 20d^{pu} Apr 20] compact mare: third foal: dam, bumper winner, out of half-sister to Sweeps Hurdle winner Hansel Rag: won maiden Irish point in 2004: well held in bumper: failed to complete all 3 starts over hurdles, left A. Stronge after first one. *R. M. Stronge* **h– F–**

ROSIE REDMAN (IRE) 8 gr.m. Roselier (FR) – Carbia's Last (Palm Track) [2004/5 c105, h95: c21d^{3} c24d^{2} c26d* c26g^{F} c22d^{5} c28s* Apr 3] leggy mare: winning hurdler: fairly useful handicap chaser: won at Doncaster in November and Kelso (left clear 2 out) in April: stays 3½m: raced on good going or softer (acts on soft): front runner/races prominently: game. *J. R. Turner* **c121 h–**

ROSINA COPPER 5 ch.m. Keen – Emilymoore (Primitive Rising (USA)) [2004/5 F16s Mar 1] lengthy mare: third foal: dam, modest novice hurdler, probably stayed 25f: well beaten in bumper on debut. *P. Beaumont* **F–**

ROSITA BAY 4 b.f. Hernando (FR) – Lemon's Mill (USA) (Roberto (USA)) [2004/5 F17g* Apr 3] third foal: dam, smart hurdler/fairly useful chaser who stayed 3¼m, also 1½m winner on Flat: won mares bumper at Market Rasen on debut by 5 lengths from Amalfi Storm. *O. Sherwood* **F96**

ROSNAGOWLOGE (IRE) 7 b.g. Houmayoun (FR) – Ave Lira (Anita's Prince) [2004/5 16d* 16g* 20g3 c18g c16d4 Nov 4] third foal: dam unraced: fair hurdler: won maiden and novice (by 6 lengths from The Screamer) at Limerick in July: better effort in maiden chases when fourth at Thurles: stays 2½m: acts on good to soft ground: tongue tied. *T. Hogan, Ireland* **c100 h110**

ROSSCARBERY GREY (IRE) 7 gr.g. Gothland (FR) – Millroad (Buckskin (FR)) [2004/5 h–: c19gpu Apr 26] lengthy, angular gelding: no sign of ability. *S. T. Lewis* **c– h–**

ROSS COMM 9 gr.g. Minster Son – Yemaail (IRE) (Shaadi (USA)) [2004/5 c20f* Sep 5] angular gelding: winning hurdler/pointer: left G. Stewart, much improved effort in chases when winning novice handicap at Worcester in September: stays 3m: probably acts on any going. *Mrs S. J. Smith* **c102 h–**

ROSS GEE (IRE) 9 gr.g. Roselier (FR) – Miss Leader (Taufan (USA)) [2004/5 c68, h–: c17m4 c21g4 24g 20g c21d3 c21m3 Sep 28] medium-sized gelding: little form, including in points. *Mrs S. J. Smith* **c77 h–**

ROSSLARE (FR) 6 b.g. Lute Antique (FR) – Baie de Chalamont (FR) (Balsamo (FR)) [2004/5 F16v3 Feb 2] first foal: dam, winning chaser up to 21f, from family of very smart French chaser Graal de Chalamont: third of 10 in bumper at Newcastle on debut: sold 4,200 gns Doncaster March Sales. *R. A. Fahey* **F90**

ROSS LEADER (IRE) 8 b.g. Supreme Leader – Emmagreen (Green Shoon) [2004/5 c92: c25d5 c24d* c21g c25mpu Apr 23] workmanlike gelding: modest chaser: off 6 months, won novice handicap at Kempton in November: stays 3m: acts on good to soft going: difficult to keep sound. *Mrs Susan Nock* **c87**

ROSS MOFF (IRE) 12 b.g. Good Thyne (USA) – Miss Kamsy (Kambalda) [2004/5 c132x, h–: c20g c22m2 c19sF Sep 19] good-topped gelding: winning hurdler: one-time useful chaser in his prime: always prone to mistakes and fell fatally 6 out in handicap at Listowel: needed good test at 2m and stayed 25f: acted on good to firm and heavy going: usually tongue tied. *A. J. Martin, Ireland* **c118 x h–**

ROSS RIVER 9 gr.g. Over The River (FR) – Solo Rose (Roselier (FR)) [2004/5 h122: c21d5 c25s* c26vur c20sF Mar 29] lengthy, useful-looking gelding: winning hurdler: fairly useful form when winning maiden chase at Hereford in November by 8 lengths from Whitford Don: generally let down by jumping otherwise over fences, left P. Hobbs after third outing: stays 25f: acts on soft ground. *S. Donohoe, Ireland* **c122 x h–**

ROSTOCK (IRE) 8 br.g. Roselier (FR) – Royal Greenwood (IRE) (Radical) [2004/5 c26gpu May 31] third foal: dam, won bumper/point, half-sister to useful chaser up to 3m Greenwood Lad: progressive pointer, successful 4 times in 2004: up with strong pace until 6 out when pulled up in maiden hunter at Cartmel. *D. Brace* **c–**

ROSTROPOVICH (IRE) 8 gr.g. Sadler's Wells (USA) – Infamy (Shirley Heights) [2004/5 h133§: c20v4 May 3] well-made gelding: useful hurdler: laboured efforts last 4 starts in 2003/4: odds on, only poor form in maiden at Down Royal on chasing debut: stays 3m well: acts on soft and good to firm going: blinkered once, usually wears cheekpieces: tongue tied: none too genuine: joined P. Nicholls. *M. F. Morris, Ireland* **c80 h– §**

ROTHERAM (USA) 5 b.g. Dynaformer (USA) – Out of Taxes (USA) (Out of Place (USA)) [2004/5 22s2 Dec 21] fair on Flat (will be suited by 2m+) at 3 yrs, sold out of P. Cole's stable 3,000 gns Newmarket Autumn (2003) Sales: 15 lengths second to Gallery God in novice at Fontwell on hurdling debut: likely to stay 3m. *C. J. Mann* **h104**

ROUGE ET NOIR 7 b.g. Hernando (FR) – Bayrouge (IRE) (Gorytus (USA)) [2004/5 F90: F17g2 F17m2 20m5 16g5 19d5 Jan 1] fairly useful in bumpers, runner-up on 3 of 4 starts: only modest form on Flat and over hurdles: tried tongue tied: carries head high, tends to find little. *K. G. Reveley* **h92 § F98 §**

ROUGE LADY 7 b.m. Rakaposhi King – Castle Rouge (Carlingford Castle) [2004/5 16v4 May 10] second foal: dam no sign of ability: ran out in maiden point on debut: tailed off in selling hurdle: sold £2,200 Ascot June Sales. *D. McCain* **h–**

ROUND THE BAY 6 b.g. Karinga Bay – Marty's Round (Martinmas) [2004/5 18g Mar 20] £7,700 5-y-o: fifth foal: dam unraced: well held in novice hurdle on debut. *G. L. Moore* **h–**

ROUND THE BEND 13 b.g. Revolutionary (USA) – No Love (Bustiki) [2004/5 c–: c21dpu c21g6 Mar 18] fair pointer, won in March: maiden hunter chaser. *Miss Louise Allan* **c–**

ROUND THE HORN (IRE) 5 ch.g. Master Willie – Gaye Fame (Ardross) [2004/5 F16s* Jan 27] 26,000 4-y-o: third foal: half-brother to fairly useful hurdler Oulart (by Sabrehill), stays 3m: dam, modest hurdler who stayed 3m, out of sister to very smart staying chaser Black Humour and half-sister to top-class 2m to 3m hurdler Gaye Brief and very smart staying jumper Gaye Chance: joint favourite, won bumper at Warwick on debut by 8 lengths from Barclay Boy: likely to improve. *J. A. B. Old* **F102 p**

ROUTE ONE (IRE) 12 br.g. Welsh Term – Skylin (Skyliner) [2004/5 c91, h–: c20g3 c24g5 May 27] rather sparely-made gelding: fair pointer/hunter chaser: stays 3m: acts on good to firm and good to soft going: tried blinkered: best on right-handed track: sometimes let down by jumping. *D. Frankland* **c97 h–**

ROUTE SIXTY SIX (IRE) 9 b.m. Brief Truce (USA) – Lyphards Goddess (IRE) (Lyphard's Special (USA)) [2004/5 c–, h91: 16gpu 16m 16g Feb 27] strong, compact mare: handicap hurdler, no form in 2004/5: best at sharp 2m: acts on good to soft going: often wears cheekpieces nowadays. *Jedd O'Keeffe* **c– h–**

ROVERETTO 10 b.g. Robellino (USA) – Spring Flyer (IRE) (Waajib) [2004/5 c23m4 c20g2 c20m2 c20d6 c21dpu 22s5 24d c27s4 c24gur c21g c25g4 Apr 8] sturdy gelding: useful hurdler at best, well beaten both starts in handicaps in 2004/5: fairly useful handicap chaser: stays 25f: acts on soft and good to firm going: usually visored/blinkered nowadays: temperamental. *M. C. Pipe* **c125 § h– §**

ROWAN CASTLE 9 ch.g. Broadsword (USA) – Brass Castle (IRE) (Carlingford Castle) [2004/5 17g 24d4 20s 20d5 22s3 c20v Apr 17] workmanlike gelding: modest form in novice hurdles, off 3 years before reappearance: last of 9 in novice handicap on chasing debut: stays 2¾m: acts on soft going: should do better over fences. *Sir John Barlow Bt* **c– p h97**

ROWLEY HILL 7 b.g. Karinga Bay – Scarlet Dymond (Rymer) [2004/5 h85, F82: 24m3 26s* 24s* 24s* Apr 16] useful-looking gelding: type to make a chaser: fairly useful hurdler: much improved in spring, winning handicaps at Huntingdon and Towcester and novice at Bangor (beat Lease Back by 1½ lengths): stays 3¼m: best form on soft going. *A. King* **h120 +**

ROYAL ACCENT 8 gr.m. Norton Challenger – Glebes Scallywag VII (Damsire Unregistered) [2004/5 19dpu 21dpu Jan 31] workmanlike mare: fourth foal: dam unraced: no show in 2 novice hurdles. *J. F. Panvert* **h–**

ROYAL ALIBI 11 b.g. Royal Academy (USA) – Excellent Alibi (USA) (Exceller (USA)) [2004/5 c21dpu Feb 18] poor maiden pointer: tongue tied on hunter debut. *J. E. Dillon* **c–**

ROYAL ALPHABET (IRE) 7 b.g. King's Theatre (IRE) – A-To-Z (IRE) (Ahonoora) [2004/5 h140: 16g3 16g4 c16d* Nov 4] won on Flat in May: useful hurdler, respectable fourth to Accordion Etoile in minor event at Tipperary in July: successful in maiden at Thurles on chasing début 4 months later, jumping fluently and beating Aye Aye Popeye easily by 6 lengths: will probably stay 2½m but has plenty of speed: acts on firm and good to soft going, unraced on softer: tongue tied: seemed sure to progress over fences, but presumably met with setback. *W. P. Mullins, Ireland* **c126 + h135**

ROYAL ATALZA (FR) 8 gr.g. Saint Preuil (FR) – Crystalza (FR) (Crystal Palace (FR)) [2004/5 c134, h121: c20m3 c27s6 c26spu c20s3 c20s3 c20d5 c21dur Apr 8] angular gelding: fairly useful handicap chaser: stays 3m: acts on good to firm and heavy going: wears headgear: has poor record over National fences: none too resolute. *G. A. Huffer* **c128 h–**

ROYAL AUCLAIR (FR) 8 ch.g. Garde Royale – Carmonera (FR) (Carmont (FR)) [2004/5 c144, h–: c25d* c26g3 c25d2 c25s3 c25d3 c26g4 c36d2 c29gF Apr 23] **c156 h–**

For a yard noted for its chasers, the Grand National record of Manor Farm stables has become something of a curiosity over the years. Things took a turn very much for the better in the latest edition, with three of the stable's four representatives completing the course and Royal Auclair becoming the first National runner saddled by Paul Nicholls to reach the frame (Montifault, a very tired fifth in 2003, had come closest of only four finishers from twenty-three runners for the stable between 1992 and 2004). Royal Auclair took well to the big, unusual fences, after stumbling at the first, and stayed on to take second behind Hedgehunter on the run-in after being briefly tapped for foot when the pace quickened from the Melling

Badger Ales Trophy (Handicap Chase), Wincanton—
Royal Auclair wins for the first time since the 2003 Cathcart Chase; Gunther McBride is in pursuit

Road. Stable companions Heros Collonges and L'Aventure finished eighth and fifteenth, while Ad Hoc failed to complete for the third time in the race. Still only eight, the consistent Royal Auclair was the first National ride for Christian Williams, one of the season's leading conditional jockeys.

The form of Royal Auclair's Grand National effort matched that of his fourth in the Cheltenham Gold Cup, in which he was also ridden by Williams, on his previous start. The Gold Cup was his fourth consecutive appearance at the Festival, on the first of which, back in 2002 when trained by Martin Pipe, he had won the Cathcart Challenge Cup when still a novice. He made only three racecourse appearances the next season, again for Pipe, making mistakes when ninth in the National Hunt Handicap Chase at the Festival. Switched to his present stable, Royal Auclair enjoyed a full campaign in 2003/4, some good efforts including a third in the National Hunt Handicap and, most notably, a short-head second, touched off on the post by the Pipe-trained Puntal, in the Betfred Gold Cup at Sandown (a race in which he fell at the first on his only outing after the National). Royal Auclair put in a series of smart performances in the latest season, the Badger Ales Trophy at Wincanton on his reappearance (after a wind operation in the summer) providing him with his first success since the Cathcart. The victory was followed by placed efforts, in which he emerged the best horse at the weights, in the Hennessy Cognac Gold Cup at Newbury in November and in a good quality handicap at Cheltenham in December. However, a hard race in the Pillar Chase back at Cheltenham next time seemed to leave its mark and he ran a lifeless race when beaten at odds on in a four-runner conditions event at Wincanton in February and was sent off at 40/1 for the Gold Cup. He returned to his best, staying on past beaten horses in the straight to finish just over thirteen lengths fourth to Kicking King, despite being bumped two out. For the record, in the last thirty years, seven horses have made the frame in both the Gold Cup and the Grand National in the same season. The six prior to Royal Auclair all started at single-figure odds at Aintree, four—Spartan Missile (1981), West Tip (1989), Docklands Express (1992) and Rough Quest (1996, the

Mr Clive D. Smith's "Royal Auclair"

only National winner of the seven) all started favourite. The other pair were the Gold Cup winner Garrison Savannah (1991) and Dubacilla (1995).

Royal Auclair (FR) (ch.g. 1997)	Garde Royale (br 1980)	Mill Reef (b 1968)	Never Bend
			Milan Mill
		Royal Way (gr 1969)	Sicambre
			Right Away
	Carmonera (FR) (ch 1987)	Carmont (ch 1975)	Carmarthen
			Montagne
		Nera (ch 1976)	Hul A Hul
			Novan

The good-topped Royal Auclair began his career as a juvenile hurdler in France before joining the Pipe stable halfway through that season. His dam Carmonera, second over hurdles on her only start, is a half-sister to the useful French hurdler/chaser Poutine. The family contains numerous other jumping performers, Carmonera herself also being the dam of several other winning jumpers, most notably the useful French jumper at up to twenty-one furlongs Dona Carmen (by Dom Pasquini). Two of Carmonera's other winning jumpers have been successful in Britain and Ireland, though both became ungenuine. Canadiane (by Nikos) was a fairly useful handicap hurdler/chaser at up to twenty-one furlongs at her best, trained by Martin Pipe; Coq de Mirande (by Gairloch) was a useful chaser at his best, raced at around two miles. Royal Auclair stays four and a half miles and acts on good to firm and heavy going. He has been tongue tied in all his races for his present stable, and was tried once in blinkers, but he is a dependable sort and rarely runs a bad race. *P. F. Nicholls*

ROYAL BLAZER (IRE) 5 b.g. Barathea (IRE) – Royale (IRE) (Royal Academy (USA)) [2004/5 h79: 17m³ 20m Jun 12] poor novice hurdler: tried visored: sold 1,900 gns Doncaster August Sales, third on completed start in maiden points. *C. Grant* **h72**

ROYAL BUBBEL (IRE) 7 ch.m. Hubbly Bubbly (USA) – Last Royal (Kambalda) [2004/5 h89: 19d⁴ c20d⁵ c21g⁵ 20m Jul 21] modest form on first of 3 outings over hurdles: well beaten both starts in novice chases. *D. R. Gandolfo* **c– h72**

ROYAL CASTLE (IRE) 11 b.g. Caerleon (USA) – Sun Princess (English Prince) [2004/5 c106d, h103d: 22g c30dpu c21m⁴ Jul 26] workmanlike gelding: winning hurdler/chaser: stays 3m: acts on firm and good to soft going, probably on soft: tried blinkered/in cheekpieces: sold 5,000 gns Doncaster August Sales, won twice in points in 2005 (including walkover). *Mrs K. Walton* **c90 h–**

ROYAL CHINA (IRE) 7 b.g. Aristocracy – Luan Causca (Pampapaul) [2004/5 c87x, h–: 21s⁶ c20d⁶ c19d⁵ Nov 19] leggy gelding: poor form over hurdles: maiden chaser, often let down by jumping: stays 21f: acts on soft and good to firm going: has found little. *Miss H. C. Knight* **c– x h–**

ROYAL CLICHE 6 b.g. Classic Cliche (IRE) – Princess Hotpot (IRE) (King's Ride) [2004/5 F16d F16s⁵ Mar 27] 4,500 4-y-o: third foal: half-brother to Irish point winner No Guarantees (by Master Willie): dam, fair hurdler/winning chaser, stayed 19f: better effort in bumpers when fifth at Towcester. *R. T. Phillips* **F81**

ROYAL COBURG (IRE) 5 b.g. Old Vic – Honeyed (IRE) (Persian Mews) [2004/5 F16s⁶ F16v* F16s⁶ Apr 22] €54,000 4-y-o: workmanlike gelding: first foal: dam unraced half-sister to smart 2m hurdler Carobee and useful hurdlers Alekhine and Winter Squall: easily best effort in bumpers when making all at Chepstow in March, beating Could Be Alright by neck: will be suited by further than 2m. *N. A. Twiston-Davies* **F99**

ROYAL CZARINA 8 ch.m. Czaravich (USA) – Sabrata (IRE) (Zino) [2004/5 c21m³ May 19] maiden hurdler: modest pointer, successful twice in 2005: third in novice hunter chase: stays 21f: acts on soft and good to firm going. *J. W. Dufosee* **c72 h–**

ROYALE ACADOU (FR) 7 b. or br.m. Cadoudal (FR) – Girl Vamp (FR) (Kaldoun (FR)) [2004/5 c88, h110: c24dᴿ 16d⁵ 16s c16v³ c20gpu Mar 16] leggy mare: winning hurdler/maiden chaser: modest form at best over fences in Britain: looked thoroughly temperamental final start: probably stays 21f: acts on heavy ground: has worn blinkers/cheekpieces. *Mrs L. J. Mongan* **c95 § h–**

ROYALEETY (FR) 6 b.g. Garde Royale – La Grive (FR) (Pharly (FR)) [2004/5 c133, h122: 20s 20v⁶ 20v⁵ c22v⁵ 21g 20d Apr 9] leggy gelding: fairly useful handicap hurdler: best effort in 2004/5 when seventh to Idole First in Coral Cup at Cheltenham fifth start: bled from nose next time: useful novice chaser in 2003/4: stamina stretched when fifth to Whereareyounow in valuable handicap at Uttoxeter: barely stays 2¾m when conditions are testing: raced on good ground or softer: tried tongue tied. *Ian Williams* **c120 + h126**

ROYAL EMPEROR (IRE) 9 gr.g. Roselier (FR) – Boreen Bro (Boreen (FR)) [2004/5 c153, h136+: c25s³ c27d c25sur c25vpu 20v² c20s² Feb 5] workmanlike gelding: smart hurdler: good second to Blue Canyon in valuable handicap at Haydock: smart novice chaser in 2003/4, let down by jumping in 2004/5: should stay beyond 25f: best form on good going or softer (acts on heavy): front runner. *Mrs S. J. Smith* **c140 x h146**

ROYAL ENCLOSURE (IRE) 7 b.g. Royal Academy (USA) – Hi Bettina (Henbit (USA)) [2004/5 17mpu 16mpu Jun 29] sparely-made gelding: lightly raced and little form over hurdles: tried in visor: has had tongue tied. *C. J. Price* **h–**

ROYALE PEARL 5 gr.m. Cloudings (IRE) – Ivy Edith (Blakeney) [2004/5 h79: 16m 16g Oct 4] poor on Flat (stays 2m): lightly-raced maiden hurdler. *R. Ingram* **h82 ?**

ROYAL EXPOSURE (IRE) 8 b.g. Emperor Jones (USA) – Blue Garter (Targowice (USA)) [2004/5 16sF 19s 17s 17spu 16d⁴ 16g Mar 9] lengthy gelding: won twice around 1¼m in Holland at 4 yrs for Frau E. Verburg: poor maiden hurdler. *H. Alexander* **h61**

ROYAL FASHION (IRE) 5 b.m. Ali-Royal (IRE) – Fun Fashion (IRE) (Polish Patriot (USA)) [2004/5 16vF 16vpu Jan 26] leggy mare: modest on Flat (stays 7f): failed to complete both outings over hurdles. *I. W. McInnes* **h–**

ROYAL FONTENAILLES (FR) 6 ch.g. Tel Quel (FR) – Sissi Fontenailles (FR) (Pampabird) [2004/5 h–: 16g⁴ 16s⁵ 16d 21d 17d⁵ Mar 26] lengthy gelding: fair maiden hurdler: off 13 months, best effort when fourth to Chockdee at Cheltenham: stays 21f. *R. H. Buckler* **h103**

ROYAL FRIEND 6 b.g. Environment Friend – La Princesse (Le Bavard (FR)) [2004/5 19d^pu Feb 8] 6,250 4-y-o: tall gelding: third foal: dam, fair hurdler up to 2¾m, half-sister to Irish Grand National winner Timbera: no show in novice hurdle on debut. *C. R. Wilson* **h–**

ROYAL GILLIE 8 br.m. Royal Fountain – Gilmanscleuch (IRE) (Mandalus) [2004/5 h–, F–: 22g^pu 22g^pu May 31] no sign of ability. *Mrs J. K. M. Oliver* **h–**

ROYAL GLEN (IRE) 7 b.m. Royal Abjar (USA) – Sea Glen (IRE) (Glenstal (USA)) [2004/5 16v 16g 17d Apr 5] lightly-raced maiden hurdler. *W. S. Coltherd* **h74**

ROYAL HECTOR (GER) 6 b.g. Hector Protector (USA) – Rudolfina (CAN) (Pleasant Colony (USA)) [2004/5 h89: 18d* 16d* 17g* 20s* 16v* 16d 20s 21g Mar 16] leggy, good-topped gelding: has reportedly had wind operation: fairly useful handicap hurdler: much improved in 2004/5, winning at Fontwell, Plumpton, Bangor (conditional jockeys), Windsor and Haydock, all in December, beating Pure Mischief ½ length at last-named course: well held in Grade 2 novice and Coral Cup (visored) at Cheltenham last 2 starts: stays 2½m: acts on heavy and good to firm going: held up. *M. C. Pipe* **h125**

ROYAL JAKE (IRE) 11 b.g. Jolly Jake (NZ) – Wee Mite (Menelek) [2004/5 c20g Feb 17] well-made gelding: fairly useful chaser at one time: successful twice in points in 2005: barely stays 25f: acts on good to firm and heavy going: has worn blinkers. *A. G. Hobbs* **c–** **h–**

ROYAL KATIDOKI (FR) 5 b.g. Rochesson (FR) – Miss Coco (FR) (Bay Comeau (FR)) [2004/5 h125: 16g 16v^5 Feb 5] leggy, angular gelding: fairly useful form in juvenile hurdles in 2003/4: disappointing both starts after 10-month absence: raced around 2m: acts on soft going. *N. J. Henderson* **h–**

ROYAL MAID (FR) 7 b.g. Bakharoff (USA) – Swimming Maid (FR) (Esprit du Nord (USA)) [2004/5 h87, F83: 16g^2 16g 16m^pu 21g^5 Oct 6] poor maiden hurdler: stays 19f: acts on soft going: visored final outing: sold 500 gns Doncaster November Sales: pulled up all 4 starts in points. *J. G. M. O'Shea* **h80**

ROYAL MOUNT LOFTUS (IRE) 6 b.m. Un Desperado (FR) – Maudlin Bridge (IRE) (Strong Gale) [2004/5 F20g^5 F20v^4 F16d F18s 19v^5 19s 24d Mar 20] €27,000 4-y-o: second foal: half-sister to fairly useful chaser Dark Room (by Toulon), stays 25f: dam unraced half-sister to dam of useful 2½m to 3m chaser Dun Belle: fair form in bumpers: no show in maiden hurdles. *P. Hughes, Ireland* **h–** **F87**

ROYAL NIECE (IRE) 6 b.m. Rakaposhi King – Sister Stephanie (IRE) (Phardante (FR)) [2004/5 h72, F75: 20d^5 16g 16s^4 16v^2 21d^4 26s^5 22d Apr 3] angular mare: poor maiden hurdler: stays 3¼m: raced on good going or softer (acts on heavy): reluctant to set off and bled from nose second outing. *D. J. Wintle* **h81**

ROYAL PARADISE (FR) 5 b.g. Cadoudal (FR) – Crystalza (FR) (Crystal Palace (FR)) [2004/5 F115: 16d* 19s* 16d^3 16v* 18s* 21g Mar 16] **h137 +**

For the first time in four years, the Grade 1 Deloitte Novices' Hurdle at Leopardstown failed to feature a future winner of a novice hurdle at the Cheltenham Festival. The two from the field of eight that ran at Cheltenham, the winner Royal Paradise and the sixth Black Apalachi, were unable to follow in the footsteps of Like-A-Butterfly, Hardy Eustace (second to Solerina at Leopardstown) and Brave Inca, taking seventh and eighth places respectively behind No Refuge in the Royal & SunAlliance Novices' Hurdle. Although for both this represented a respectable performance in a strong renewal, more might have been anticipated from Royal Paradise as he started joint favourite at 9/2. It turned out afterwards that he had bled internally.

Before Cheltenham, Royal Paradise had won four of his five starts over hurdles after joining Tom Foley's yard in a private deal in the summer. In 2003/4, he had been in the care of Francois Doumen and ran twice in bumpers, winning at Sandown and finishing fourth to Total Enjoyment in the Champion Bumper at Cheltenham. Connections got a quick if modest return on their purchase with successes in novice hurdles at Roscommon and Naas in October. Considering his inexperience, Royal Paradise showed great battling qualities to win narrowly on each occasion, beating Wild Passion by a head at Roscommon and Petertheknot by half a length at Naas. In form terms, Royal Paradise was showing a useful level straight away, which certainly augured well for the season ahead, though things stalled a little on his next appearance, in the Royal Bond at Fairyhouse in November. As at Cheltenham later on, Royal Paradise ran with credit while leaving the

Deloitte Novices' Hurdle, Leopardstown—Royal Paradise lands the odds from The Railway Man

feeling he might have done even better had more use been made of him back at two miles. He finished third behind Wild Passion and Rocket Ship, beaten three lengths and three quarters of a length. Royal Paradise and Rocket Ship met again a month later in the grandly-named paddypower.com Future Champions Novices' Hurdle at Leopardstown. Rocket Ship, considered a shade unlucky at Fairyhouse, started 11/8 favourite but flopped on very testing ground and Royal Paradise, kept to two miles, didn't have to improve on his earlier form to get the better of Leonardo de Vinci by six lengths.

The Deloitte came next. Eight went to post in what was certainly not a vintage field for the race. Justified and Wild Passion were the two most notable absentees, though, overall, the Irish-trained novice hurdlers in 2004/5 were not up to standard. Royal Paradise started odds on and clearly had a leading chance on form over hurdles, though several of the others had been of similar standard in bumpers and had shown some potential over hurdles, chiefly among them the mare Sweet Kiln and Augherskea. With Sweet Kiln also a regular front runner, Royal Paradise raced second before moving up to dispute the running three out, taking over turning for home and keeping on well to win ridden out. He beat the maiden winner The Railway Man by three lengths with Augherskea getting the better of Sweet Kiln for third. After his problem at Cheltenham, Royal Paradise was not seen out again. By the end of the Punchestown Festival, only one of the seven behind Royal Paradise had managed to win another race and the three others in the frame essentially had their limitations exposed in useful novice company. Royal Paradise's winning performance rates around a stone behind the standard for the Deloitte.

Royal Paradise is bred to be good. He is by the leading French jumps stallion Cadoudal out of the prolific winner-producing mare Crystalza. Crystalza wasn't much as a racehorse but her progeny incude seven other winners, five of them at least useful. The best known in Britain is the Howard Johnson-trained Royal Rosa (by Garde Royale) who was a smart staying hurdler in 2003/4. Royal Atalza (by Saint Preuil), who was useful at one time in France, also raced in Britain in the latest season. The pick of Crystalza's winners in France have been Crylza Royal (by Northern Fashion), who was placed in some of the top hurdle races, including the Prix La Barka, and Ytalsa Royale (by Arokar), who won the top four-year-old chase, the Prix Ferdinand Dufaure. Crystalza's latest runner Royale Athenia (by Garde Royale) won the Group 3 Prix de Longchamp at Auteuil in May

Mr P. E. Delaney's "Royal Paradise"

Royal Paradise (FR) (b.g. 2000)	Cadoudal (FR) (br 1979)	Green Dancer (b 1972)	Nijinsky
			Green Valley
		Come To Sea (gr 1971)	Sea Hawk II
			Camarilla
	Crystalza (FR) (gr 1982)	Crystal Palace (gr 1974)	Caro
			Hermieres
		Aldonza (b 1969)	Exbury
			La Bamba

2005. Further back, this is a family more notable for its Flat runners than its jumpers. The third dam La Bamba was a high-class racemare, winning the Prix Jacques le Marois and finishing third in the Oaks and the Arc. La Bamba is the grandam of two Grand Criterium winners Lost World and Fijar Tango, the latter also a high-class middle-distance performer. The lengthy, angular Royal Paradise did not stand out in the paddock before either the Deloitte or the SunAlliance, but he isn't the only member of his family a little lacking in stature and that hasn't held them back. He had looked capable of further progress over hurdles before Cheltenham and may well improve in open company if kept hurdling in 2005/6. He is likely to be more effective at two and a half miles or further than at around two miles. While comparisons were made before Cheltenham with Foley's previous winner of the Deloitte, Danoli, there is clearly quite a gulf in ability between the pair at this stage and Foley himself is reluctant to compare any horse with his iconic former charge. While Royal Paradise wasn't able to match Danoli in winning at Cheltenham, coincidentally, he wasn't the first winner of the Deloitte to finish seventh at Cheltenham. If he can match the subsequent achievements of that horse he won't be doing too badly, as Alexander Banquet became a top-class chaser, winning a Hennessy at Leopardstown and being placed in the Royal & SunAlliance Chase and the Hennessy at Newbury. *Thomas Foley, Ireland*

ROYAL PREDICA (FR) 11 ch.g. Tip Moss (FR) – Girl Vamp (FR) (Kaldoun (FR)) [2004/5 c121, h–: c25g4 c20m* c20d4 c21d c22g c24d 16g Oct 27] good-topped gelding: lightly raced over hurdles: fairly useful handicap chaser: won at Worcester in June by 9 lengths from Motcomb Jam: creditable efforts after when fourth to Glinger and seventh to Bow Strada (fifth start) in valuable events at Market Rasen: stays 25f: acts on any going: formerly blinkered/visored: tongue tied: has been let down by jumping. *M. C. Pipe* **c131 h–**

ROYAL PRODIGY (USA) 6 ch.g. Royal Academy (USA) – Prospector's Queen (USA) (Mr Prospector (USA)) [2004/5 h86§: 19gpu 17d4 16s2 17d4 16s3 17g 24s6 22s6 19s 17s3 19g5 19m2 19g 22dpu Apr 17] modest handicap hurdler: stays 19f: acts on firm and soft going: has worn headgear (cheekpieces last 5 starts): temperamental. *R. J. Hodges* **h92 §**

ROYAL ROSA (FR) 6 ch.g. Garde Royale – Crystalza (FR) (Crystal Palace (FR)) [2004/5 h147: 24s 24s3 Feb 26] good-topped gelding: smart novice hurdler in 2003/4: off 10 months before reappearance: finished lame when 9½ lengths third of 5 to Crystal d'Ainay in Grade 2 at Kempton: stays 3m: raced on good ground or softer (acts on heavy). *J. Howard Johnson* **h144**

ROYAL SHAKESPEARE (FR) 6 b.g. King's Theatre (IRE) – Persian Walk (FR) (Persian Bold) [2004/5 h142: 16g2 16d3 16v4 16g4 16d3 16g 16g2 16mF Apr 22] tall, useful-looking gelding: will make a chaser: smart hurdler: ran well when third to Harchibald in Grade 1 at Newcastle in November on second start and second to Genghis in valuable handicap at Ayr in April: doing so again when falling heavily 2 out in valuable minor event won by Rooster Booster at Sandown, length up and still travelling strongly at time: has won over 19f: raced mainly at 2m: successful on soft going, best form under less testing conditions. *S. Gollings* **h153**

ROYAL SNOOPY (IRE) 12 b. or br.g. Royal Fountain – Lovely Snoopy (IRE) (Phardante (FR)) [2004/5 c22sur c24g4 c24g5 c25g4 Apr 3] lengthy gelding: fairly useful hunter chaser nowadays: left R. Tate after second start: stays 27f: acts on any going: blinkered: front runner: usually makes mistakes/jumps right. *Mrs Sarah L. Dent* **c103 x h–**

ROYAL STARDUST 4 b.g. Cloudings (IRE) – Ivy Edith (Blakeney) [2004/5 F12d5 aF16g* Feb 19] big gelding: third foal: brother to 13f winner Royale Pearl: dam, fairly useful 2m hurdler, half-sister to high-class 2m hurdler Royal Derbi: second start in bumpers, won on polytrack at Lingfield by 1¼ lengths from The Grey Man. *T. G. Mills* **F98**

ROYALTEA 4 ch.f. Desert King (IRE) – Come To Tea (IRE) (Be My Guest (USA)) [2004/5 16v4 16dro 16d6 16d Mar 14] sparely-made filly: half-sister to winning pointer by Henbit: little form on Flat for Ms D. Evans: little impact in novice company over hurdles: ran out second start. *J. T. Stimpson* **h80**

ROYAL TIR (FR) 9 b.g. Royal Charter (FR) – Tirtaine (FR) (Mad Captain) [2004/5 24d May 8] workmanlike ex-French gelding: useful hurdler/chaser at best: left C. Aubert, well held in handicap hurdle at Southwell: stays 3¼m: raced on good ground or softer (acts on heavy): usually blinkered. *P. J. Hobbs* **c– h–**

ROYAL UPSTART 4 b.g. Up And At 'em – Tycoon Tina (Tina's Pet) [2004/5 16g Oct 7] poor maiden on Flat (stays 9.4f): not fluent when well held in juvenile on hurdling debut. *W. M. Brisbourne* **h–**

ROYAL WHISPER 6 b.g. Prince of Birds (USA) – Hush It Up (Tina's Pet) [2004/5 F–: 16dpu Jun 1] no show in bumper and maiden hurdle. *R. Ford* **h–**

ROY MCAVOY (IRE) 7 b.g. Danehill (USA) – Decadence (Vaigly Great) [2004/5 16dpu 16d 16vpu 16spu Apr 21] angular gelding: fair on Flat (stays 7f) at 5 yrs for C. Cyzer, little show in 2004, sold out of Miss G. Browne's stable £6,200 Ascot June Sales: little aptitude for hurdling: tongue tied last 3 starts. *M. A. Barnes* **h–**

ROYMILLON (GER) 11 b.g. Milesius (USA) – Royal Slope (USA) (His Majesty (USA)) [2004/5 c–§, h–§: c25m6 c23mpu Jul 21] leggy gelding: winning hurdler: no form over fences, reportedly lame final start: tried in cheekpieces/blinkers: often gets behind and is not one to trust. *D. J. Wintle* **c– § h– §**

ROZNIC (FR) 7 b.g. Nikos – Rozamie (FR) (Azimut (FR)) [2004/5 F97: 20d5 22s 16v5 16s4 16d5 16d Mar 24] useful-looking gelding: chasing type: modest maiden hurdler: stays 2½m: acts on good to soft ground. *P. Winkworth* **h95**

RUBBERDUBBER 5 b.g. Teenoso (USA) – True Clown (True Song) [2004/5 F98p: 17s3 16d* 16g5 19d6 Feb 8] tall, useful-looking gelding: fairly useful form when winning **h115**

novice hurdle at Newbury in December by neck from Pretty Star, making all: disappointing both subsequent starts: should stay beyond 17f. *C. R. Egerton*

RUBISSIMO (IRE) 12 b.g. Phardante (FR) – Rubydora (Buckskin (FR)) [2004/5 c24g May 27] leggy, lengthy gelding: formerly useful hurdler/very smart chaser for F. Doumen: lightly raced since 2001, showing little in points/hunter: stays 23f: usually blinkered: has looked less than keen. *Miss T. McCurrich* **c– § h– §**

RUBON PRINCE (IRE) 14 ch.g. Kambalda – Oh Clare (Laurence O) [2004/5 c26g^{pu} May 31] workmanlike gelding: of little account: tried blinkered. *J. A. Lytollis* **c– h–**

RUBY FLARE 9 b.m. Nader – Ruby Flame (Tudor Flame) [2004/5 19g 16s^{pu} 16s^{pu} 24g 19m Mar 14] rather sparely-made mare: little sign of ability in points or over hurdles. *J. W. Mullins* **h–**

RUBY GALE (IRE) 9 b.g. Lord Americo – Well Over (Over The River (FR)) [2004/5 c116, h123: c24d^{2} c24d^{3} Nov 12] sturdy gelding: reportedly had wind operation before reappearance: winning hurdler: ungenuine maiden chaser, makes mistakes: stays 2¾m: raced on good/good to soft going: blinkered final outing: has had tongue tied. *P. F. Nicholls* **c88 § h–**

RUBY GATE (IRE) 10 b.g. Rashar (USA) – Vam Cas (IRE) (Carlingford Castle) [2004/5 22s^{4} 22g^{5} 19v^{pu} Feb 13] winning Irish pointer: no other form: tried tongue tied. *N. G. Ayliffe* **h–**

RUBY HARE 4 ch.g. Classic Cliche (IRE) – Five And Four (IRE) (Green Desert (USA)) [2004/5 F16d^{6} Jan 31] 8,000 3-y-o: sturdy gelding: fifth foal: dam, no sign of ability, half-sister to very smart staying hurdler Burgoyne and useful hurdler up to 3m Errand Boy: tongue tied, sixth to Hobbs Hill in bumper at Kempton on debut, looking in need of experience. *Mrs L. Wadham* **F82 p**

RUBYLUV 6 ch.m. Rock Hopper – Hunting Cottage (Pyjama Hunt) [2004/5 F–: 16s 17v Nov 25] no sign of ability. *Miss S. E. Forster* **h–**

RUBY TOO 6 b.m. El Conquistador – Ruby Flame (Tudor Flame) [2004/5 F84: 19g^{4} Sep 30] modest form in bumpers: fourth in novice at Hereford on hurdling debut: likely to be suited by further than 19f. *J. W. Mullins* **h84**

RUDE HEALTH 5 b.m. Rudimentary (USA) – Birsay (Bustino) [2004/5 F16g^{2} F16g^{4} F17g^{3} F16s^{3} 19s 19g Mar 3] third foal: half-sister to 23f hurdle winner Hoh Nelson (by Halling) and 1¼m winner Yanus (by Inchinor): dam unraced sister to useful 1½m to 1¾m winner Baffin Bay: fair form in bumpers: sold out of J. Bethell's stable 15,000 gns (privately) Doncaster November Sales: well held in 2 novice hurdles. *N. J. Hawke* **h– F87**

RUDETSKI 8 b.g. Rudimentary (USA) – Butosky (Busted) [2004/5 c101, h72: c16s^{F} c16d c16g^{6} Apr 17] lengthy gelding: poor form over hurdles: fair chaser: off 13 months, let down by jumping all 3 starts in 2004/5: raced around 2m: acts on good to firm going, probably on soft: tongue tied. *M. Sheppard* **c– h–**

RUDI KNIGHT 10 ch.g. Rudimentary (USA) – Fleeting Affair (Hotfoot) [2004/5 c104x, h–: c20d^{5} c20d 22d^{5} 24g^{3} 24g^{6} c22s^{4} c20g^{5} c25d^{4} c20s* Dec 15] angular gelding: fair handicap hurdler/chaser nowadays: blinkered, made all over fences at Bangor in December despite jumping left: probably stays 3m: acts on heavy and good to firm going: tried in cheekpieces: poor jumper. *Miss Venetia Williams* **c102 x h100**

RUDI'S CHARM 8 b.g. Rudimentary (USA) – Irene's Charter (Persian Bold) [2004/5 h–: 20d 27m^{3} 24m^{6} 24g^{pu} 26g^{pu} 24v^{pu} 27v^{6} c25s^{ur} Apr 10] workmanlike gelding: bad maiden hurdler: unseated eleventh on chasing debut: tried in cheekpieces. *D. W. Thompson* **c– h57**

RUDOLF RASSENDYLL (IRE) 10 b.g. Supreme Leader – Chantel Rouge (Boreen (FR)) [2004/5 c110, h–x: c26d^{pu} 24s^{2} 21s^{4} c24v c24d^{6} c23v^{2} c24s^{pu} Mar 14] workmanlike gelding: fair handicap chaser/modest handicap hurdler: effective around 2½m to 3m: acts on heavy going: often let down by jumping. *Miss Venetia Williams* **c106 x h98**

RUDY'S PRIDE (IRE) 4 ch.g. Anshan – Lisa's Pride (IRE) (Pips Pride) [2004/5 F13d F13s F16d Jan 29] 7,000 3-y-o: second foal: dam, 2-y-o 6f winner, out of half-sister to high-class sprinter Soba: well beaten in bumpers. *C. N. Kellett* **F–**

RUE DU RIVOLI 7 ch.g. Rudimentary (USA) – Lovers Tryst (Castle Keep) [2004/5 F76: 17d^{pu} May 4] good-topped gelding: failed to see races out in bumpers: bled from nose on hurdling debut. *Lady Herries* **h–**

RUFIUS (IRE) 12 b.g. Celio Rufo – In View Lass (Tepukei) [2004/5 c93, h–: c20g^{pu} c23f^{6} c24f^{4} c25g^{6} c19d^{pu} c24v^{pu} c24s^{pu} c25s^{pu} c23s Feb 16] workmanlike gelding: handicap chaser, out of sorts in 2004/5: stays 25f: acts on firm and soft going: blinkered once: usually held up: often fails to impress with attitude. *P. Kelsall* **c– § h–**

RUGGTAH 4 gr.f. Daylami (IRE) – Raneen Alwatar (Sadler's Wells (USA)) [2004/5 19d Jan 1] leggy filly: fair form on Flat at 3 yrs: sold out of M. Channon's stable 10,500 gns Doncaster October Sales: well held in novice on hurdling debut. *P. D. Niven* **h–**

RULE SUPREME (IRE) 9 b.g. Supreme Leader – Book of Rules (IRE) (Phardante (FR)) [2004/5 c149x, h149: c25g⁵ 21s³ 25d* 24s* 20d³ 25s³ c24vF c24s* 24g³ 24sur Apr 7] **c167 x** **h159**

There are better chasers around than Rule Supreme and there are better hurdlers too, but there is no better performer at present able to switch between the two disciplines and hold his own in top company in both. Plenty of good hurdlers have gone on to become good chasers later in their careers, but relatively few horses are asked to lead a double life over hurdles and fences on a regular basis. The odd run over hurdles can be a gentle reintroduction for a chaser returning from an absence or injury (such as Strong Flow in the latest season), or a few runs over hurdles can be a convenient way of a chaser seeing some action without running the risk of his handicap mark going up over fences. All four of Ireland's recent Grand National winners, for example, Rule Supreme's stable-companion Hedgehunter included, ran at least once over hurdles in the season they were successful at Aintree. For most horses who show the level of ability that Rule Supreme had over fences—he had, after all, won the Royal & SunAlliance Chase at Cheltenham in 2004—there wouldn't be much incentive to go back to hurdling. In Rule Supreme's case, however, for all his ability over fences, his jumping has often let him down over the larger obstacles, and hurdling represents a safer option.

French brush hurdles represent a kind of halfway-house between British or Irish hurdles and fences, so perhaps it isn't surprising that Rule Supreme has proved adept over them, winning the Grande Course de Haies d'Auteuil, the misleadingly so-called French Champion Hurdle, in 2004. In fact, there's more similarity between French hurdles and fences than there is between French hurdles and their British counterparts. The word 'haie' means 'hedge' in French, and the French brush 'hurdles' are in effect mini-fences, some of them even forming part of the steeplechase circuit at Auteuil. This also accounts for the reason it is more usual for French jumpers to switch between hurdles and fences. For example, when Rule Supreme won the Grande Course de Haies, he had the dual Grand Steeple-Chase de Paris winner Kotkijet back in third. The leading young French jumper Cyrlight first made a name for himself as a chaser and is due to resume his career over fences at a later date. Prior to Rule Supreme, the last horse capable of mixing performances over both hurdles and fences at such a high level on a regular basis was the French-trained Ubu III. Ubu won his first Grande Course de Haies in 1992, a fortnight after finishing third in the Grand Steeple-Chase, and won it again a year later after winning important chases at Auteuil that spring. Dawn Run can't be left out of the discussion either. Trained by Paddy Mullins and ridden by Tony Mullins, father and

Hennessy Cognac Gold Cup, Leopardstown—Rule Supreme upsets the odds on Beef Or Salmon

brother of Rule Supreme's trainer, Dawn Run added the Grande Course de Haies d'Auteuil (as well as the Prix La Barka beforehand) to her Champion Hurdle win in 1984 and returned to French hurdles for the same two races at Auteuil two years later. In the meantime, she had crowned her brief chasing career by becoming the only horse to win both the Champion Hurdle and Cheltenham Gold Cup. All went well on her return to hurdles in the Prix La Barka in which she finished second, but she suffered a fatal fall in the Grande Course de Haies next time.

Rule Supreme received the same rating over both hurdles and fences in *Chasers & Hurdlers 2003/04*. In the latest season, he showed improved form over both types of obstacle, but it was over fences that he made the greater progress and, when his jumping held up, he proved capable of putting up some top-class efforts. With both hurdles and chases open to him, there was no shortage of races for Rule Supreme, and connections had to choose between hurdling and chasing options at each of the three major Festival meetings in the spring. Perhaps the hardest decision concerned his Cheltenham target. The World Hurdle had been the long-term plan, and that was the race he did contest in the end, though the Gold Cup became a much more tempting proposition after Rule Supreme had shown improved form to land the Hennessy Cognac Gold Cup at Leopardstown, the temptation increasing as intended Gold Cup runners fell by the wayside. The Hennessy was Rule Supreme's second outing of the winter over fences after a fall in the Lexus Chase at Leopardstown in December. His mistake at the last in the Lexus had not been his first in the race, but he had been in the process of showing improved form, challenging Best Mate for second, when coming down. Even so, that still left him with plenty to find to turn the tables on the Lexus winner Beef Or Salmon, who had also beaten Rule Supreme a long way into fifth in the Punchestown Gold Cup back in the spring. As the 11/2 second-favourite for the Hennessy, Rule Supreme looked to be the most likely beneficiary if Beef Or Salmon (15/8-on) were to have an off day. In a rather weak-looking renewal of Ireland's longest-established Grade 1 staying chase, the field was completed by the Lexus third and fourth, Pizarro and Cloudy Bays, British challenger Murphy's Cardinal, and a couple who looked well out of their depth, the future Betfred Gold Cup winner Jack High and Hersov. Crucially, Rule Supreme's jumping held together on the whole, which was more than could be said for that of Pizarro who came down when challenging for the lead five out, hampering Beef Or Salmon in the process. Even before that, however, Rule Supreme had looked to be going better than the favourite and, leading after a mistake three out, Rule Supreme responded when Beef Or Salmon challenged going to the last. Staying on strongly, Rule Supreme came home fourteen lengths clear of an out-of-sorts Beef Or Salmon, who made a mistake at the final fence, with further wide margins back to Cloudy Bays in third and Jack High in fourth.

The Hennessy result was a significant one for his trainer and jockey, as well as for Rule Supreme himself. Willie Mullins was gaining his sixth win in the race in seven runnings after Florida Pearl's four wins spread between 1999 and 2004 and Alexander Banquet's success in 2002. Meanwhile, rider David Casey had only just returned from a three-month absence because of a broken leg, thereby maintaining his record of having partnered Rule Supreme to all his biggest successes. Rule Supreme matched his Hennessy form on his only other outing over fences which came in the Gold Cup at Punchestown, shortly after the end of the British season, rather than at Cheltenham. Making his customary mistakes late in the race, Rule Supreme proved no match for the Cheltenham winner Kicking King, though he finished well clear of the remainder in second.

Over hurdles, Rule Supreme ran well in top company in Ireland, Britain and France, though a major prize eluded him. He did, however, gain something of a surprise win, ridden by stable amateur Jamie Codd, under top weight in a handicap hurdle at Clonmel in November. The Mullins stable fielded three other runners, including favourite Raikkonen, and Hedgehunter who, like Rule Supreme, was making his autumn reappearance. Ten days later, Rule Supreme found the drop back to two and a half miles for the Hatton's Grace Hurdle at Fairyhouse barely enough of a test of stamina when third to Solerina and Brave Inca. Back over further, he was beaten less than a length behind Baracouda and Crystal d'Ainay in the Long Walk Hurdle at Windsor. That represented Rule Supreme's best effort yet over hurdles, even though he finished best of all after giving the first two a start in a muddling contest. Rule Supreme was next seen over hurdles at the Cheltenham Festival, starting second favourite to Baracouda in the World Hurdle. A reproduction of his Windsor form saw him take third place again, beaten under four lengths behind Inglis Drever and Baracouda, after holding every chance before the last. In the absence of Inglis Drever and Baracouda, there were hopes of some consolation for Rule Supreme in the Liverpool Hurdle (the engagement selected at Aintree over the Betfair Bowl over fences) but they were soon dashed when Rule Supreme ran into the back of Westender who had refused at the second flight, causing Ruby Walsh to be unseated.

Rule Supreme's campaign ended at Auteuil with an attempt to retain his Grande Course de Haies title. Like the year before, Rule Supreme prefaced his run in the big one by taking third place in the main trial, the Prix La Barka three weeks beforehand, keeping on behind the shock winner Rock And Palm and the hot favourite Cyrlight. In the absence of both those rivals for the Grande Course de Haies itself, Rule Supreme started odds on and again finished in front of all four of those he had beaten three weeks earlier, but he found Lycaon de Vauzelle four lengths too good on the day. Rule Supreme was below form, giving the impression he might have been over the top at the end of a hard campaign (connections also blamed the heat), while the very sedate pace didn't play to his strengths either.

Rule Supreme (IRE) (b.g. 1996)	Supreme Leader (b 1982)	Bustino (b 1971)	Busted
			Ship Yard
		Princess Zena (b 1975)	Habitat
			Guiding Light
	Book of Rules (IRE) (b 1989)	Phardante (b 1982)	Pharly
			Pallante
		Chapter Four (ch 1971)	Shackleton
			First Edition

Mr John J. Fallon's "Rule Supreme"

There are a couple of updates to first foal Rule Supreme's pedigree details which have appeared in previous Annuals. His dam's next two foals, both by Good Thyne, got off the mark during the latest season, Good Book winning a couple of points, and Tynedale showing fair form in staying novice hurdles. Their unraced dam, Book of Rules, is a half-sister to six winners, including the useful handicap chaser Scribbler, winner of Punchestown's National Trial and third in a Midlands National. Rule Supreme is a well-made gelding who took the eye in appearance on several occasions during the season, and he clearly thrives on racing. He stays very well and goes particularly well on soft and heavy going. For a horse whose jumping often lets him down over fences, Rule Supreme has done well to win a Royal & SunAlliance Chase and an Irish Hennessy. All credit too to his connections for exploiting the lack of strength among the current crop of hurdlers in France with a horse who is a little behind the best stayers racing in Britain and Ireland. *W. P. Mullins, Ireland*

RUMBLING BRIDGE 4 ch.g. Air Express (IRE) – Rushing River (USA) (Irish River (FR)) [2004/5 16d 16d5 17s4 16s6 Mar 27] leggy gelding: modest maiden on Flat (stays 1½m) for J. Dunlop: modest form over hurdles. *H. D. Daly* **h86**

RUM POINTER (IRE) 9 b.g. Turtle Island (IRE) – Osmunda (Mill Reef (USA)) [2004/5 c127, h–: c25gF c24d4 Nov 6] small gelding: fairly useful novice chaser in 2003/4: off 6 months, below form in handicap at Sandown in November: stays 3m: raced on good going or softer (acts on heavy). *R. H. Buckler* **c114 + h–**

RUN ATIM 7 ch.g. Hatim (USA) – Run Pet Run (Deep Run) [2004/5 F89: c25sF Nov 7] fair form on first of 2 outings in bumpers in 2003/4: fell sixth on chasing debut. *K. C. Bailey* **c–**

RUNAWAY BISHOP (USA) 10 b. or br.g. Lear Fan (USA) – Valid Linda (USA) (Valid Appeal (USA)) [2004/5 c91, h70: c25d4 c28d2 c19s2 c22s3 c22s3 c24s3 c24s3 c29d5 c25gur Dec 16] lengthy gelding: maiden hurdler: modest handicap chaser: effective at 19f (given good test) to 29f: acts on any going: effective blinkered/visored or not: usually claimer ridden: has looked temperamental but is consistent. *J. R. Cornwall* **c89 h–**

RUN FOR PADDY 9 b.g. Michelozzo (USA) – Deep Selection (IRE) (Deep Run) [2004/5 c118§, h–: c20d2 c24d3 c24g* Mar 5] useful-looking gelding: useful handicap chaser on his day: back with former stable in 2004/5, winning quite valuable event at Doncaster in March by short head from Lou du Moulin Mas: stays 25f: acts on soft and good to firm going: formerly inconsistent. *M. Pitman* **c133 h–**

RUN FOUR 6 b.g. Runnett – Four M'S (Majestic Maharaj) [2004/5 F17s May 9] £1,500 3-y-o: half-brother to fair hurdler/winning chaser around 2m Argento (by Weldnaas) and winning hurdler/chaser Minioso (by Teenoso), stayed 2¾m: dam winning pointer: well beaten in bumper: poor completion record in points. *C. P. Morlock* **F–**

RUNNER BEAN 11 b. or br.g. Henbit (USA) – Bean Alainn (Candy Cane) [2004/5 c94x, h–: c20m6 c16m* c17g3 c17g2 c16m* c16s4 c16g* c16dur c16s3 c16g* Apr 17] lengthy gelding: fair handicap chaser: had good season, winning at Huntingdon in June and August (fourth course success) and Wincanton in November and April: stays 2½m, raced mainly at shorter: acts on soft and good to firm going: blinkered once (reportedly bled): in frame on all but 2 of 23 completed outings over fences. *R. Lee* **c107 h–**

RUNNING DE CERISY (FR) 11 ch.g. Lightning (FR) – Niloq (FR) (Nikos) [2004/5 c–x, h–: 16d 20dpu May 9] tall, lengthy gelding: winning hurdler/chaser: lightly raced and no form since 2001/2: tried blinkered/in cheekpieces: poor jumper of fences. *P. L. Clinton* **c– x h–**

RUNNING HOT 7 b.g. Sunley Builds – Running Cool (Record Run) [2004/5 c19s3 c19d3 c19v5 c19d5 c23s3 Mar 22] good-topped gelding: third foal: dam, winning pointer, half-sister to dam of useful hurdler up to 2¾m Gravity Gate: twice-raced in points, won maiden in 2004: modest novice chaser: likely to prove best short of 23f: very much on toes second/third outings: headstrong. *N. J. Hawke* **c97**

RUNNING LORD (IRE) 7 b.g. Mister Lord (USA) – Craic Go Leor (Deep Run) [2004/5 F16d 20d 24d Mar 8] 10,000 3-y-o: fourth foal: half-brother to fair chaser up to 3¼m Joe Deane (by Alphabatim): dam, placed in point, sister to useful staying chaser Plenty Crack: well beaten in bumper and over hurdles. *D. A. Rees* **h– F–**

RUNNING MOSS 13 ch.g. Le Moss – Run'n Fly (Deep Run) [2004/5 c–, h–: c25s* Apr 3] lengthy gelding: fair handicap chaser in 2002: first form since when winning **c92 h–**

hunter at Kelso in April, making most: stays 4m: raced on good going or softer (acts on heavy). *A. H. Mactaggart*

RUNNING MUTE 11 b.g. Roscoe Blake – Rose Albertine (Record Token) [2004/5 c98: c25m^pu Apr 28] fair pointer, successful on return in 2005: modest form in chases: stays 3¼m: acts on good to soft going. *S. H. Shirley-Beavan* **c–**

RUNNING QUILL (IRE) 9 ch.g. Commanche Run – Quilty Rose (Buckskin (FR)) [2004/5 20s^pu Oct 31] sixth foal: brother to winning 2½m chaser Take The Lot and half-brother to fairly useful hunter chaser Splash And Dash (by Arcane), stays 3m: dam bumper winner/1¾m winner on Flat: probably amiss on debut. *J. Wade* **h–**

RUNNING TIMES (USA) 8 b.g. Brocco (USA) – Concert Peace (USA) (Hold Your Peace (USA)) [2004/5 c–, h–: 16d^4 18s^F c17s^pu 16s^3 22s^4 16v^4 22s 16d 16s^2 24g^3 20d^5 Apr 22] workmanlike gelding: pulled up in 2 chases: poor hurdler: stays 2¾m: acts on good to firm and heavy ground: usually visored/blinkered. *H. J. Manners* **c– h81**

RUNNINGWITHTHEMOON 9 b.g. Homo Sapien – Ardeal (Ardross) [2004/5 c–, h60: c26g^4 May 23] winning pointer, including in January and April: poor form over hurdles/in chases. *C. C. Bealby* **c68 h–**

RUN OF KINGS (IRE) 7 b.g. King's Ride – Arctic Tartan (Deep Run) [2004/5 c–, h111?: 19s^3 Nov 2] tall gelding: fell fourth only start in chases: fair form in novice hurdles: stays 2¾m: difficult ride. *M. C. Pipe* **c– h97**

RUN RIVER RUN 11 b.m. River God (USA) – Run Lady Run (General Ironside) [2004/5 c–, h–: 21g^5 Apr 26] smallish mare: lightly raced: no longer of any account: tried blinkered: has had tongue tied. *B. D. Leavy* **c– h–**

RUNSHAN (IRE) 5 ch.g. Anshan – Whitebarn Run (Pollerton) [2004/5 F16d Apr 20] lengthy, rather unfurnished gelding: fifth foal: dam runner-up in maiden Irish point: in frame twice from 3 starts in maiden Irish points in 2005: eighth of 17 in bumper at Worcester. *D. G. Bridgwater* **F82**

totescoop6 Grimthorpe Chase (Handicap), Doncaster—
nip and tuck at the last between Run For Paddy (nearer camera) and Lou du Moulin Mas

RUN WITH THE DEVIL 10 ro.m. Thethingaboutitis (USA) – Brenda Blake (Roscoe Blake) [2004/5 22gpu Jul 20] third foal: half-sister to winning pointer Inspector Blake (by River God): dam winning pointer: pulled hard in novice hurdle on belated debut. *P. Morris* **h–**

RUPERT BRUSH 4 b.g. Thornberry (USA) – O K Sohfar (Rolfe (USA)) [2004/5 F17spu F17vpu Feb 13] lengthy, sparely-made gelding: first foal: dam of no account: pulled up in 2 bumpers. *G. F. H. Charles-Jones* **F–**

RUPUNUNI (IRE) 8 b.g. Fourstars Allstar (USA) – Pisa (Carlingford Castle) [2004/5 h117: 16g c18gur c17s c16sF Nov 20] big, good-bodied gelding: fairly useful hurdler: would probably have won maiden at Punchestown on chasing debut but for slipping on landing and unseating last: raced around 2m: successful on soft going, better on firmer (acted on firm): dead. *Francis Ennis, Ireland* **c116 + h–**

RUSHING AGAIN 10 br.g. Rushmere – Saunders Grove (IRE) (Sunyboy) [2004/5 c–, h–: c25s4 c20s4 c24spu Mar 27] workmanlike gelding: winning pointer: maiden hurdler/chaser: tried blinkered/in cheekpieces. *Miss Sarah George* **c– h–**

RUSH'N'RUN 6 b.g. Kasakov – Runfawit Pet (Welsh Saint) [2004/5 F16m Nov 26] little show in bumpers: joined Mrs S. Smith. *D. Carroll* **F–**

RUSSIAN COMRADE (IRE) 9 b.g. Polish Patriot (USA) – Tikarna (FR) (Targowice (USA)) [2004/5 h109d: 20mpu Aug 19] leggy, close-coupled gelding: second in 2m novice hurdle in early-2003/4, virtually only form: tried blinkered/in cheekpieces: thoroughly ungenuine: sold £1,400 Ascot November Sales. *J. C. Tuck* **h– §**

RUSSIAN COURT 9 b.g. Soviet Lad (USA) – Court Town (Camden Town) [2004/5 h98: 20g2 c17g5 19g Sep 30] leggy gelding: fair handicap hurdler: possibly amiss on chasing debut: stays 2½m when conditions aren't testing: acts on heavy and good to firm going: tried in cheekpieces. *S. E. H. Sherwood* **c– h104**

RUSSIAN LORD (IRE) 6 br.g. Topanoora – Russian Gale (IRE) (Strong Gale) [2004/5 F79p: F17v 20spu 21d Jan 31] strong, good sort: signs of ability in bumpers: no show both starts over hurdles, looking temperamental in cheekpieces second occasion. *V. R. A. Dartnall* **h– F–**

RUSSIAN SKY 6 gr.g. Endoli (USA) – Anzarna (Zambrano) [2004/5 h71?: 23d4 24d5 22m5 22g 24f5 24d 24s2 22m2 21d* 22s2 22s4 24g4 22d3 Apr 11] leggy gelding: modest handicap hurdler: won at Sedgefield in October: stays 3m: acts on firm and soft going: front runner/races prominently: consistent *Mrs H. O. Graham* **h97**

RUSTIC CHARM (IRE) 5 b.m. Charnwood Forest (IRE) – Kabayil (Dancing Brave (USA)) [2004/5 h92: 17g* 16m* Jun 6] useful-looking mare: modest hurdler: won mares novice sellers at Cartmel and Stratford (sold to join Miss K. Marks 16,000 gns) early in season: raced around 2m: tried blinkered: pulled up on Flat in September. *C. R. Egerton* **h87**

RUSTIC JOHN 5 ch.g. Afzal – Spartiquick (Spartan General) [2004/5 F18s F16d Jan 31] £11,000 4-y-o: lengthy, unfurnished gelding: half-brother to several winners, including fairly useful 2m to 2½m chaser Newlands-General (by Oats): dam winning chaser: tailed off in bumpers. *H. J. Manners* **F–**

RUSTY FELLOW 15 b.g. Rustingo – Sallisses (Pamroy) [2004/5 c30d5 May 11] workmanlike gelding: winning hunter chaser: poor pointer nowadays: very difficult ride (usually soon off bridle). *R. Shail* **c– §**

RUTLAND CHANTRY (USA) 11 b.g. Dixieland Band (USA) – Christchurch (FR) (So Blessed) [2004/5 h80: 16d6 19s Dec 2] smallish, good-bodied gelding: lightly raced: winning hurdler, well held in 2004/5: raced mainly around 2m: acts on heavy going. *S. Gollings* **h–**

RUTLAND (IRE) 6 b.g. Supreme Leader – I Remember It Well (IRE) (Don't Forget Me) [2004/5 F17d2 F18s 22spu 24d 24s6 Mar 31] sturdy gelding: first foal: dam, fairly useful hurdler up to 2½m, half-sister to useful 2m hurdler Tropical Lake: second in bumper at Newton Abbot on debut: little show after, mostly over hurdles: sold out of A. King's stable £5,400 Ascot February Sales after fourth outing. *Miss K. M. George* **h– F95**

RUTLEDGE RED (IRE) 9 gr.g. Roselier (FR) – Katebeaujolais (Politico (USA)) [2004/5 c–, h–: 20d5 c22d4 c24d3 c25spu c25d4 Apr 11] tall gelding: winning hurdler: off 11 months, tailed-off last of 5 in handicap on reappearance: seemingly best effort over fences when third of 5 finishers in steadily-run novice handicap at Kempton: stays 3m: acts on soft and good to firm going: sold 10,000 gns Doncaster May Sales. *J. M. Jefferson* **c100 h–**

RYALUX (IRE) 12 b.g. Riverhead (USA) – Kings de Lema (IRE) (King's Ride) [2004/5 c–, h–: c25s^4 c25v^4 Jan 15] lengthy gelding: winning hurdler: useful chaser at best, won Scottish Grand National at Ayr in 2002/3: lightly raced and well held subsequently: stayed 33f: probably acted on any going: usually sound jumper: reportedly retired due to pelvic injury. *A. Crook* **c– h–**

RYDERS STORM (USA) 6 b. or br.g. Dynaformer (USA) – Justicara (Rusticaro (FR)) [2004/5 c111, h–§: c16m^{pu} c16m^{ur} c16s^2 c21g^4 c16g^3 c20d^2 c22s^2 Nov 18] workmanlike gelding: fair maiden chaser, left T. George after fifth outing: stays 2¾m: acts on soft and good to firm going: tried visored/in cheekpieces: ungenuine. *Mrs S. J. Smith* **c109 § h– §**

RYDON LANE (IRE) 9 br.g. Toca Madera – Polocracy (IRE) (Aristocracy) [2004/5 c–, h93: 19s 24s^5 22d^5 22d^{pu} 24s 19d* 19g^{pu} Apr 7] useful-looking gelding: fell second only outing over fences: modest handicap hurdler: won at Exeter in March: stays 3m: raced on good going or softer (acts on soft): wore cheekpieces last 2 starts: has raced freely: inconsistent. *Mrs S. D. Williams* **c– h93**

RYE BROOK 8 b.g. Romany Rye – Nearly A Brook (Nearly A Hand) [2004/5 h–, F81: 22d^{pu} May 17] workmanlike gelding: bumper winner: pulled up in 2 maiden hurdles. *P. F. Nicholls* **h–**

RYHALL (IRE) 5 b.m. Saddlers' Hall (IRE) – Loshian (IRE) (Montelimar (USA)) [2004/5 F78: F16g^2 F17d^2 20v^F 21d 20d^3 16s^6 19d^5 25s^{pu} Mar 1] unfurnished mare: fair form when runner-up in mares bumpers: best effort over hurdles when third in mares novice at Newcastle: should stay beyond 2½m: wore cheekpieces final outing. *T. D. Easterby* **h90 F93**

RYMINSTER 6 ch.g. Minster Son – Shultan (IRE) (Rymer) [2004/5 h–: c19g^4 c25d^{ur} c21s^{pu} c24g* c25g^{ur} c25s^2 Mar 22] lengthy gelding: first form when winning handicap chase at Musselburgh in February: stays 25f: acts on soft going. *J. Wade* **c82 h–**

RYMON 5 br.g. Terimon – Rythmic Rymer (Rymer) [2004/5 F–: F16g^5 F16g 16d^{pu} 17d^{pu} Feb 11] good-topped gelding: modest form in bumpers: pulled up in 2 novice hurdles: headstrong. *J. M. Jefferson* **h– F77**

RYOSHI 7 b.m. Rakaposhi King – Rynode (Rymer) [2004/5 F16g^5 May 16] fourth foal: dam, winning chaser who stayed 25f, out of half-sister to fairly useful 2m to 2½m hurdler/chaser Poverty Bonk: fifth of 17 in bumper at Worcester on debut. *Mrs H. Dalton* **F76**

S

SAAFEND ROCKET (IRE) 7 b.g. Distinctly North (USA) – Simple Annie (Simply Great (FR)) [2004/5 h106: 17g^2 16m^5 16s^6 c16g^4 c16g^3 c16s^3 c16s^3 c20d^2 c20d^4 c16s* Mar 31] leggy, sparely-made gelding: fair handicap hurdler: at least as good over fences, won maiden at Ludlow in March: stays easy 2½m: acts on soft and good to firm ground: free-going sort: patiently ridden: reliable. *H. D. Daly* **c113 h106**

SABADILLA (USA) 11 b.g. Sadler's Wells (USA) – Jasmina (USA) (Forli (ARG)) [2004/5 h120: 20g 17d 19f^6 17g^5 16g^{pu} Jul 29] leggy gelding: fairly useful hurdler: best effort in 2004/5 when fifth to Blue Away in handicap at Kilbeggan: reportedly lame in Galway Hurdle final start: best around 2m: acts on soft and good to firm going: held up. *P. Verling, Ireland* **h118**

SABANA (IRE) 7 b.g. Sri Pekan (USA) – Atyaaf (USA) (Irish River (FR)) [2004/5 20m^{pu} 16g^{pu} Oct 3] leggy gelding: modest and unreliable on Flat (best around 6f): most unlikely to stay 2m over hurdles. *J. M. Bradley* **h–**

SABREUR 4 b.g. Thowra (FR) – Sleepline Princess (Royal Palace) [2004/5 F16g^5 Mar 26] unfurnished gelding: half-brother to fairly useful 2m hurdler Sleepline Royale (by Buzzards Bay) and very smart chaser Rockforce (by Rock City), stayed 19f: dam fair 6f winner at 2 yrs, became thoroughly temperamental: 3 lengths fifth of 12 to Arumun in bumper at Haydock on debut, edging left 2f out. *Ian Williams* **F96**

SABY (FR) 7 b. or br.g. Sassanian (USA) – Valy Flett (FR) (Pietru (FR)) [2004/5 c86, h71: c16d* c16g^2 c16g^2 c16g* c16d* c16d* c17d^2 c16g^3 17d c16d^6 c16g Apr 14] tall gelding: poor maiden hurdler: fair chaser: won at Newton Abbot in May (maiden, made all) and August (twice, both handicaps) and Uttoxeter (novice) in October: best at 2m: raced mainly on good/good to soft going. *P. J. Hobbs* **c107 h68**

SACHSENWALZER (GER) 7 ch.g. Top Waltz (FR) – Stairway To Heaven (GER) (Nebos (GER)) [2004/5 h81: 17g^{3} 17m^{ur} 16g^{3} 17g* 16g^{F} 17d^{2} 17m^{pu} 16g^{6} 17s^{pu} Nov 7] fair hurdler: won maiden at Cartmel in July: likely to prove best around 2m: acts on good to soft going. *C. Grant* **h102**

SACRIFICE 10 b.g. Arctic Lord – Kellyann (Jellaby) [2004/5 c93: c19m c16d^{2} c16m^{4} c21f^{3} c19d^{pu} c24d^{4} c24m^{2} c19s^{5} c21d^{2} c19g^{5} c24g^{pu} Dec 30] sturdy gelding: modest handicap chaser: stays easy 3m: acts on firm and good to soft going. *K. Bishop* **c88**

SACSAYHUAMAN 6 b.m. Halling (USA) – La Dolce Vita (Mazilier (USA)) [2004/5 h–: 20d^{pu} 16g Jun 10] no form over hurdles. *D. W. Thompson* **h–**

SACUNDAI (IRE) 8 b.g. Hernando (FR) – Shahdiza (USA) (Blushing Groom (FR)) [2004/5 h153: 20d^{4} Nov 28] good-topped gelding: very smart hurdler at best: off 11 months, needed race when remote fourth of 5 to Solerina in Grade 1 at Fairyhouse: has won at 2m, possibly best at 2½m to 3m: successful on good to firm going, raced mainly on good or softer (acts on heavy). *E. J. O'Grady, Ireland* **h–**

SADDLERS EXPRESS 4 b.f. Saddlers' Hall (IRE) – Swift Conveyance (IRE) (Strong Gale) [2004/5 F16s F17g Apr 14] lengthy filly: fifth foal: dam, modest 2m hurdler, out of half-sister to dam of high-class staying chaser Drumlargan: well beaten in 2 mares bumpers. *H. D. Daly* **F–**

SADDLERS' HARMONY (IRE) 4 b.g. Saddlers' Hall (IRE) – Sweet Mignonette (Tina's Pet) [2004/5 F14g Dec 18] leggy gelding: fourth foal: half-brother to bumper winner Reseda (by Rock Hopper): dam, fairly useful 2m hurdler, half-sister to useful 2m hurdler Cardinal Flower: mid-field in 3-y-o bumper at Newcastle on debut. *K. G. Reveley* **F81**

SADDLER'S QUEST 8 b.g. Saddlers' Hall (IRE) – Seren Quest (Rainbow Quest (USA)) [2004/5 h73: 16m 20g^{4} 16m^{4} 16g^{5} 16d 20d 20s 16v^{4} 19v Dec 31] angular gelding: poor maiden hurdler: trained first 2 starts by A. Deakin: stays 2½m when emphasis is on speed: acts on good to firm going: blinkered once (failed to settle), wore cheekpieces/visor last 3 starts. *B. P. J. Baugh* **h77**

SADIES SPARKLE (IRE) 8 b.m. Synefos (USA) – Canhaar (Sparkler) [2004/5 18d^{ur} 16s 21d^{pu} Apr 5] eighth foal: half-sister to winning hurdler Leapogues Lady (by Chakiris), stays 3m: dam Irish 1½m winner: no sign of ability over hurdles. *C. A. McBratney, Ireland* **h–**

SADLER'S LAMP (IRE) 6 b.g. Pierre – Kyle Lamp (IRE) (Miner's Lamp) [2004/5 20s^{6} 25v^{6} 19v^{6} 22d^{pu} 27d^{2} 24d^{pu} Apr 20] 15,000 4-y-o: sturdy gelding: first foal: dam, twice-raced in points, half-sister to fairly useful staying chaser Ballystone and fairly useful hurdler/chaser up to 3¼m Mr Pickpocket: poor maiden hurdler: stays 27f: raced on going softer than good. *O. Sherwood* **h82**

SADLER'S PRIDE (IRE) 5 b.g. Sadler's Wells (USA) – Gentle Thoughts (Darshaan) [2004/5 20g^{pu} 20m^{3} 20s 16d 17s^{3} 16d Mar 12] smallish gelding: modest maiden on Flat (stays 1¾m): best effort over hurdles when third in steadily-run 17f novice at Carlisle: tongue tied after debut (often runs as if amiss): sold 2,000 gns Doncaster May Sales. *Andrew Turnell* **h100**

SADLER'S ROCK (IRE) 7 b.g. Sadler's Wells (USA) – Triple Couronne (USA) (Riverman (USA)) [2004/5 h–: 17s^{2} 17d^{4} 16g^{pu} Oct 27] good-topped gelding: second in novice at Newton Abbot, easily best effort over hurdles: sold £3,700 Ascot February Sales, pulled up in point following month. *G. L. Moore* **h107**

SADLER'S SECRET (IRE) 10 b.g. Sadler's Wells (USA) – Athyka (USA) (Secretariat (USA)) [2004/5 c–, h115: 17g^{4} 24f^{3} May 18] workmanlike gelding: fair hurdler: stays 27f: acts on any going: usually wears headgear: has had tongue tied: has looked none too keen. *G. J. Smith* **c–** **h115**

SAD MAD BAD (USA) 11 b.g. Sunny's Halo (CAN) – Quite Attractive (USA) (Well Decorated (USA)) [2004/5 c100, h–: c25g^{2} c34d^{5} May 15] workmanlike gelding: fair hunter chaser nowadays: stays 4¼m: acts on good to firm and heavy going: sometimes wears headgear: has raced lazily. *G. Tuer* **c99 §** **h–**

SAFAWI 6 b.m. Safawan – Pejawi (Strong Gale) [2004/5 F16d^{2} Jun 23] 1,500 4-y-o: second foal: dam, winning pointer, half-sister to fairly useful staying hurdler Smith Too: third on completed outing in points: 20 lengths second in bumper at Worcester. *J. G. Cann* **F76**

SAFE ENOUGH (IRE) 9 ch.g. Safety Catch (USA) – Godfreys Cross (IRE) (Fine Blade (USA)) [2004/5 h90: 22d^{F} 21g^{4} c17g^{F} c20g^{6} 24g^{6} Nov 17] workmanlike gelding: modest hurdler: no encouragement either start over fences: stays 21f: acts on soft and good to firm going. *N. J. Gifford* **c–** **h96**

SAFE OASIS 5 b.g. Hector Protector (USA) – Desert Maiden (Green Desert (USA)) [2004/5 F16d aF16g 20s^{pu} 16d Apr 3] £3,000 4-y-o: good-topped gelding: fourth foal: half-brother to 3 winners up to 1¼m on Flat: dam, unreliable 6f winner, half-sister to very smart middle-distance performer Top Class: little show in bumpers or over hurdles. *N. J. Gifford* **h– F77 ?**

SAFE ROUTE (USA) 7 b. or br.m. Farma Way (USA) – Taiki Victoria (IRE) (Caerleon (USA)) [2004/5 h118: 20m^{3} 16m^{3} 19f^{2} 20f* 16g^{pu} 22m 16s Nov 6] fairly useful handicap hurdler: won at Cork in June: no form after: better at 2½m than shorter: acts on firm and soft going: usually races prominently. *W. J. Austin, Ireland* **h118**

SAFE SHOT 6 b.g. Salse (USA) – Optaria (Song) [2004/5 h–: 16d^{6} May 13] leggy gelding: little show on Flat or over hurdles: wears cheekpieces. *Mrs J. C. McGregor* **h–**

SAFE TO BLUSH 7 gr.m. Blushing Flame (USA) – Safe Arrival (USA) (Shadeed (USA)) [2004/5 F80: F16d^{5} F16v^{5} 24v^{6} 19v^{2} 19v^{6} 24d^{pu} 24d^{pu} Apr 20] big mare: modest in bumpers: form in novice hurdles only when second in mares event at Hereford. *P. A. Pritchard* **h88 F81**

SAFFRON SUN 10 b.g. Landyap (USA) – Saffron Bun (Sit In The Corner (USA)) [2004/5 c112, h–: c23m* c20g* c21d c20f^{4} c24d^{5} c23s^{pu} c20g^{5} c21d c21d^{pu} Feb 19] tall, workmanlike gelding: fair handicap chaser: won at Exeter (fourth course success) and Stratford early in season: lost his form: stays 23f: acts on firm and soft going: sometimes makes mistakes. *J. D. Frost* **c114 d h–**

SAFFRONTO (IRE) 6 b.g. Muroto – Saffron Holly (IRE) (Roselier (FR)) [2004/5 20d 21d 20g^{4} 24v Mar 17] big gelding: first foal: dam unraced: won last of 4 starts in maiden Irish points in 2004: sold 36,000 gns Doncaster May Sales: form over hurdles only when fourth in novice at Musselburgh: tongue tied last 2 starts. *Ferdy Murphy* **h90**

SAGARDIAN (FR) 6 b.g. Mister Mat (FR) – Tipnik (FR) (Nikos) [2004/5 h–, F78: 20d 16v 24v c20v^{5} Apr 17] quite good-topped gelding: little show over hurdles: never a factor in novice handicap on chasing debut: tried in cheekpieces. *L. Lungo* **c62 h–**

SAHAAT 7 b. or br.g. Machiavellian (USA) – Tawaaded (IRE) (Nashwan (USA)) [2004/5 16s^{pu} Nov 13] fair on Flat (stays 1¼m) in 2004, below form in 2005: jumped poorly in novice on hurdling debut. *C. R. Dore* **h–**

SAHARA SPIRIT (IRE) 8 b.g. College Chapel – Desert Palace (Green Desert (USA)) [2004/5 17s^{pu} Mar 7] fairly useful on Flat (stays 1m) at 3 yrs for E. Dunlop, well beaten only 2 subsequent starts: no show in novice seller on hurdling debut. *R. J. Baker* **h–**

SAIF SAREEA 5 b.g. Atraf – Slipperose (Persepolis (FR)) [2004/5 16m* 16m^{6} 16v^{4} 17d 16d^{5} Nov 22] compact gelding: half-brother to winning hurdler/chaser Galway Blade (by Faustus), stays 3m: modest maiden at 2 yrs, well beaten on Flat in 2004: modest hurdler: successful in seller (sold from K. Hogg 7,600 gns) at Uttoxeter in September: will prove best around 2m: acts on good to firm and heavy ground. *A. L. Forbes* **h90**

SAILING THROUGH 5 b.g. Bahhare (USA) – Hopesay (Warning) [2004/5 h78: 16m^{3} 16m 17m c16d^{4} c16s^{ur} c16s Nov 30] leggy gelding: fairly useful at best on Flat at 3 yrs: modest maiden hurdler: similar form when fourth in novice at Warwick on chasing debut: raced around 2m: acted on good to firm and good to soft going: dead. *R. Dickin* **c87 h88**

SAILOR A'HOY 9 b.g. Handsome Sailor – Eye Sight (Roscoe Blake) [2004/5 h83: 16g^{4} 17d^{2} 17d^{2} 17s 17g^{6} 16s 16d 21v* 16s 17g c17g^{5} c20g^{5} c23m^{ur} c24s^{6} Apr 16] compact gelding: modest hurdler: won handicap at Sedgefield in January: similar form first 2 starts over fences: should stay 3m: acts on heavy and good to firm going: tried in blinkers/cheekpieces: temperament under suspicion (tried to refuse and unseated thirteenth outing). *M. Mullineaux* **c98 h96**

SAINT ESTEBEN (FR) 6 b.g. Poliglote – Highest Tulip (FR) (Highest Honor (FR)) [2004/5 c114, h–: c16g^{pu} May 8] leggy gelding: winning hurdler: novice chaser: blinkered and tongue tied, jumped poorly only outing in 2004/5: best form around 2m: acted on heavy going, probably on good to firm. *P. F. Nicholls* **c– h–**

SAINT PAR (FR) 7 gr.g. Saint Preuil (FR) – Paris Or (FR) (Noir Et Or) [2004/5 16s^{5} 16s* 21d 16v 20v Feb 19] medium-sized gelding: trained in 2003/4 by T. Trapenard: fair form over fences: fairly useful hurdler: back to best when winning handicap at Leicester in December: stays 21f: acts on good to firm and heavy going: has worn blinkers, visored final start: inconsistent: sold to join Mrs J. Candlish 12,000 gns Doncaster March Sales. *A. King* **c– h116**

SAINT ROMBLE (FR) 8 b.g. Sassanian (USA) – Limatge (FR) (Trac) [2004/5 c91, h–: c19m c21g^{2} May 27] leggy gelding: modest handicap chaser: successful 5 times in **c87 h–**

points between February and April: stays 21f: best efforts on good going or softer (acts on heavy). *P. J. Hobbs*

SAINTSAIRE (FR) 6 b.g. Apeldoorn (FR) – Pro Wonder (FR) (The Wonder (FR)) [2004/5 h140: c17g* c16dpu Apr 9] leggy, useful-looking gelding: useful handicap hurdler: won 4-runner novice at Bangor on chasing debut by 4 lengths from Brown Teddy with something in hand: stable out of sorts when pulled up in Grade 1 novice at Aintree following month: will prove best around 2m: acts on soft going. *N. J. Henderson* **c112 h–**

SAJOMI RONA (IRE) 8 ch.g. Riberetto – Mauma Lady (IRE) (Le Moss) [2004/5 c–x, h–: c21g4 c26d4 May 15] sturdy gelding: no form over hurdles or in chases: has been blinkered/visored: tried tongue tied: sold 3,700 gns Doncaster May (2004) Sales, resold 5,400 gns Doncaster November Sales: winning pointer, runner-up in April. *A. Crook* **c– x h–**

SALAMAN (FR) 13 b.g. Saumarez – Merry Sharp (Sharpen Up) [2004/5 21gpu May 9] sparely-made gelding: winning hurdler: has been blinkered/visored: tried tongue tied: ungenuine. *D. C. O'Brien* **h– §**

SALFORD FLYER 9 b.g. Pharly (FR) – Edge of Darkness (Vaigly Great) [2004/5 h–§: 19g Dec 9] leggy gelding: modest on Flat nowadays: winning hurdler, lightly raced and no show since 1999/00: tried blinkered: ungenuine. *Jane Southcombe* **h– §**

SALIM 8 b.g. Salse (USA) – Moviegoer (Pharly (FR)) [2004/5 c–, h77: c16m c21mF Jul 20] angular gelding: poor maiden hurdler: no form over fences: best efforts around 2m: has had tongue tied. *Miss J. S. Davis* **c– h–**

SALINAS (GER) 6 b.g. Macanal (USA) – Santa Ana (GER) (Acatenango (GER)) [2004/5 h94: 17d5 16d3 17g2 17d* 16g5 17g 21m* 16v2 16g 17s3 16d 17s4 18s6 18s4 16d3 Apr 17] good-topped gelding: modest hurdler: won maiden at Cartmel in August and novice at Sedgefield in September: effective at 2m to easy 21f: acts on good to firm and heavy going: tried visored: front runner. *M. F. Harris* **h96**

SALIX BAY 9 b.g. Karinga Bay – Willow Gale (Strong Gale) [2004/5 23s6 c20spu c21dpu 27m6 Apr 21] no sign of ability: tried in visor/cheekpieces. *P. Butler* **c– h–**

SALLIEMAK 7 b.m. Makbul – Glenbrook Fort (Fort Nayef) [2004/5 h–, F–: 19s6 24d4 23v6 Dec 30] poor maiden hurdler: stays 3m: acts on heavy going. *A. J. Wilson* **h75**

SALLY SCALLY 13 ch.m. Scallywag – Petite Cone (Celtic Cone) [2004/5 c63, h–: c26g2 c26g6 20dpu c24spu c25g6 c25m6 Apr 23] smallish mare: winning pointer: maiden hurdler/chaser: no form after reappearance: stays 3¼m: acts on firm going, possibly unsuited by soft: blinkered once: weak finisher. *Miss T. Jackson* **c77 h–**

SALMON FLY (IRE) 9 b.g. Leading Counsel (USA) – Lola Sharp (Sharpen Up) [2004/5 c23dpu Apr 25] useful-looking gelding: lightly-raced maiden hurdler: off 2 years, no show on chasing debut: tried tongue tied. *N. B. King* **c– h–**

SALOPIAN 5 b.g. Rakaposhi King – Dalbeattie (Phardante (FR)) [2004/5 F16s6 17s 19m Apr 9] fifth foal: half-brother to winning 2m hurdlers Burdens Girl and Burdens Boy (both by Alflora): dam, poor novice hurdler, half-sister to Triumph Hurdle winner Saxon Farm: little sign of ability in bumpers or over hurdles. *H. D. Daly* **h– F–**

SALSALINO 5 ch.g. Salse (USA) – Alicedale (USA) (Trempolino (USA)) [2004/5 16g2 17s* 16d2 21dpu Nov 22] smallish gelding: smart on Flat in 2003, out of sorts in 2004: fairly useful novice hurdler: simple task at Exeter in October: much better form when runner-up other completed starts: would have stayed beyond 17f: dead. *A. King* **h122**

SALTANGO (GER) 6 br.g. Acatenango (GER) – Salde (GER) (Alkalde (GER)) [2004/5 16g2 17g2 16v3 Dec 31] leggy gelding: fair on Flat (stays 1¾m), successful over 1m (at 2 yrs) and 1¼m in Germany for P. Rau: fair form in novice hurdles. *A. M. Hales* **h110**

SALT CELLAR (IRE) 6 b.g. Salse (USA) – Athene (IRE) (Rousillon (USA)) [2004/5 F85: F18g2 20s 21s 17v 16d4 16v Mar 29] medium-sized gelding: fair form when runner-up at Plumpton, third start in bumpers: modest form over hurdles: should stay 2½m: visored last 3 outings: possibly not straightforward. *P. R. Webber* **h99 F94**

SALUTE (IRE) 6 b.g. Muhtarram (USA) – Alasib (Siberian Express (USA)) [2004/5 16g4 16m3 16g* 16d 17d4 Mar 26] fairly useful on Flat (stays easy 1½m), sold out of J. Eustace's stable 30,000 gns Newmarket Autumn (2003) Sales: modest hurdler: won novice at Lingfield in October: raced around 2m. *P. J. Hobbs* **h102**

SALUT SAINT CLOUD 4 b.g. Primo Dominie – Tiriana (Common Grounds) [2004/5 16d* 16d2 16dF 16d* 16v4 17s3 18s 16s2 Mar 27] leggy gelding: fair on Flat (stays 2m): fairly useful juvenile hurdler: won at Chepstow in October and Lingfield in December, beating Patrixprial 4 lengths with plenty to spare in Grade 2 Summit Junior **h123**

Hurdle at latter: easily best effort after when third to Akilak in Grade 2 at Cheltenham: should stay beyond 17f: raced on going softer than good. *G. L. Moore*

SALVAGE 10 b.g. Kahyasi – Storm Weaver (USA) (Storm Bird (CAN)) [2004/5 c89, h–: c16d[5] c20m[pu] c16g[3] c17v[5] c20d[6] c17v[5] c20g[5] c17d c20s[5] Apr 20] angular gelding: poor handicap chaser: stays 2½m: acts on heavy and good to firm going: tried tongue tied much earlier in career. *Mrs J. C. McGregor* **c87 h–**

SAMANDARA (FR) 5 b.m. Kris – Samneeza (USA) (Storm Bird (CAN)) [2004/5 h–: 17d 16d[3] Mar 10] rather leggy mare: off 10 months, first form over hurdles when third to Gold Ring in maiden at Wincanton. *A. King* **h102 ?**

SAMARIA (GER) 4 b. or br.f. Acatenango (GER) – Suanita (GER) (Big Shuffle (USA)) [2004/5 16s[pu] Apr 3] fair maiden on Flat (stayed 13f), left C. Wall after final start at 3 yrs: looked set to make frame when breaking down after 2 out in juvenile at Kelso on hurdling debut: dead. *N. G. Richards* **h–**

SAMIKIN (IRE) 7 b. or br.g. Topanoora – Samika (IRE) (Bikala) [2004/5 16v[3] 17s[4] 20v[pu] Jan 15] workmanlike gelding: second foal: dam unraced half-sister to smart stayer Samourzakan, from family of smart French jumper Sprong: won maiden Irish point in 2004: best effort in novice hurdles when third to Turpin Green at Uttoxeter: amiss final start. *B. N. Pollock* **h106**

SAMMAGEFROMTENESSE (IRE) 8 b.g. Petardia – Canoora (Ahonoora) [2004/5 h75§: 17d 17m[6] c16m[3] c17g[3] Mar 28] angular gelding: poor hurdler: better effort over fences when third in selling handicap at Plumpton final start: best around 2m with emphasis on speed: tried blinkered/in cheekpieces: has had tongue tied: unreliable. *A. E. Jones* **c69 h64 §**

SAMMY SAMBA 7 b.g. Be My Chief (USA) – Peggy Spencer (Formidable (USA)) [2004/5 19g[5] Dec 9] leggy gelding: fair novice hurdler in 2002/3 for P. Hobbs: off over 2 years, fifth in seller at Taunton: will stay 3m: acts on firm ground: tried tongue tied. *R. J. Hodges* **h–**

SAMOLIS (IRE) 4 b.g. College Chapel – Joyful Music (IRE) (Accordion) [2004/5 17d[6] 18d[pu] Dec 7] of no account. *R. Curtis* **h–**

SAMON (GER) 8 ch.g. Monsun (GER) – Savanna (GER) (Sassafras (FR)) [2004/5 c112, h–: 22g[pu] Feb 5] angular gelding: useful handicap hurdler at best: off 19 months, probably amiss in valuable event at Sandown: unbeaten in 3 novice chases in 2003/4: stays 21f: acts on soft and good to firm going. *M. C. Pipe* **c– h–**

SAMSAAM (IRE) 8 b.g. Sadler's Wells (USA) – Azyaa (Kris) [2004/5 h121: 22g[3] 22s[2] 22d 17d[5] Dec 16] lengthy gelding: fairly useful handicap hurdler: stays 2¾m: acts on soft and good to firm going: blinkered/visored: often tongue tied: looks none too keen. *M. C. Pipe* **h116**

SAMSON DES GALAS (FR) 7 b. or br.g. Agent Bleu (FR) – Sarema (FR) (Primo Dominie) [2004/5 h–: 16s Nov 14] quite good-topped gelding: lightly raced and no form over hurdles. *R. Ford* **h–**

SAMS WAY 8 b.g. Nomadic Way (USA) – Samonia (Rolfe (USA)) [2004/5 c25g[4] Mar 9] fifth foal: half-brother to 3 winning pointers: dam, winning hurdler who stayed 25f, half-sister to useful 2m hurdler Windbound Lass: winning pointer, including in 2005: fourth in novice hunter at Catterick. *Mrs S. M. Barker* **c87**

SAMUEL WILDERSPIN 13 b.g. Henbit (USA) – Littoral (Crash Course) [2004/5 c120d, h–: c25g[pu] c25d[6] c25s[3] c24s[4] c26g[pu] Apr 14] rangy gelding: veteran chaser, very much on downgrade: stays 33f: acts on heavy going, possibly not on good to firm: formerly tongue tied: has broken blood vessels. *R. Lee* **c99 h–**

SAN ANTONIO 5 b.g. Efisio – Winnebago (Kris) [2004/5 16v[4] 16g[5] 19s 16v[4] 16v 16g 16s Feb 3] good-topped gelding: useful on Flat (stays 1m), better than ever in 2005: modest novice hurdler. *Mrs P. Sly* **h86**

SANDABAR 12 b.g. Green Desert (USA) – Children's Corner (FR) (Top Ville) [2004/5 h74: 17m[2] 17g[2] May 25] leggy gelding: poor handicap hurdler: best around 2m: acts on firm and good to soft going: usually tongue tied: finds little. *G. A. Swinbank* **h76 §**

SANDAL SAPHIRE 6 b.m. Danzig Connection (USA) – Mudflap (Slip Anchor) [2004/5 F–: F16d Mar 3] no form in bumpers. *Mrs L. Williamson* **F–**

SAN DIMAS (USA) 8 gr.g. Distant View (USA) – Chrystophard (USA) (Lypheor) [2004/5 h92: 20s[pu] 22m 21d 24m 20s[pu] 19g[6] 24d[pu] Jan 7] handicap hurdler, little show in **h78**

2004/5: stays 2¾m: acts on firm and good to soft going, possibly unsuited by soft: wears headgear. *R. Allan*

SANDMARTIN (IRE) 5 b.g. Alflora (IRE) – Quarry Machine (Laurence O) [2004/5 F17g⁵ Apr 12] 19,000 4-y-o: seventh foal: half-brother to winning pointer by Gildoran: dam fairly useful staying hurdler: needed run when fifth to Clyffe Hanger in bumper at Exeter on debut: should do better. *P. J. Hobbs* **F90 +**

SANDOKAN (GER) 4 b.g. Tiger Hill (IRE) – Suivez (FR) (Fioravanti (USA)) [2004/5 16d⁶ 16d 16g 16s⁴ Jan 27] workmanlike gelding: half-brother to fairly useful hurdler Simoun (by Monsun), stays 2½m: modest maiden on Flat: not knocked about all starts in juvenile hurdles: may yet do better, particularly if there's a market move in his favour. *B. J. Curley* **h88 p**

SANDS RISING 8 b.g. Primitive Rising (USA) – Celtic Sands (Celtic Cone) [2004/5 h97: 21d⁶ c20v⁴ c21v⁶ c16v* c16s⁶ c16s c21v³ c21v² c20s⁶ Apr 22] sturdy gelding: fair hurdler/chaser: won novice over fences at Sedgefield in January: ran as if amiss final start: effective at 2m to 3m: raced on good going or softer (acts on heavy): tongue tied 6 of last 7 starts. *R. Johnson* **c105 h–**

SANDY BAY (IRE) 6 b.g. Spectrum (IRE) – Karinski (USA) (Palace Music (USA)) [2004/5 h–: 16m⁴ 17d⁵ 16s 20mᵖᵘ 16vᵖᵘ 17dᵖᵘ Apr 5] angular gelding: poor maiden on Flat: modest maiden hurdler, lost form: left A. Dicken after fifth start: should stay beyond 2m. *W. G. Harrison* **h85 d**

SANDY OWEN (IRE) 9 b.g. Insan (USA) – Daisy Owen (Master Owen) [2004/5 16f* c20dᶠ c18s* c24vᶠ c20s⁵ Mar 29] workmanlike gelding: half-brother to 3 winners, including hurdler Miss Kamsy (by Kambalda), stayed 2½m: dam, bumper winner, from family of useful chaser up to 3m Gee-A: fairly useful on Flat (stays 2m): bumper winner: fair form when winning maiden hurdle at Cork in June: fairly useful form over fences, won maiden at Thurles in November: good 18 lengths fifth to Like-A-Butterfly in Grade 1 novice at Fairyhouse: let down by jumping other starts in chases: will stay 3m: acts on firm and soft going. *P. A. Fahy, Ireland* **c121 h108**

SANDYWELL GEORGE 10 ch.g. Zambrano – Farmcote Air (True Song) [2004/5 h93: c21d⁶ c20mᵘʳ c23m⁵ c20m c23g⁶ 24m Apr 10] good-topped gelding: winning hurdler: little worthwhile form over fences: probably stays 3m: acts on soft and good to firm going: tongue tied: has shown signs of temperament. *L. P. Grassick* **c64 § h–**

SANGATTE (IRE) 7 b.g. Un Desperado (FR) – Mad House (Kabour) [2004/5 h88?, F70: 20dᵖᵘ 16g May 16] rangy gelding: little sign of ability: sold 3,000 gns Doncaster May (2004) Sales. *N. J. Henderson* **h–**

SANGHASTA (IRE) 7 b.m. Un Desperado (FR) – Strong Willed (Strong Gale) [2004/5 F20f⁶ F16f*ᵈⁱˢ 16m 19d⁵ 16m⁵ 18s⁶ 16s* 16s² 16s⁶ Nov 20] fifth reported foal: sister to bumper winner Mansefield and fair 2½m chaser Hill Fox: dam unraced: fairly useful in bumpers, first past post at Roscommon in June (disqualified after testing positive for prohibited substance): fairly useful hurdler: won handicap at Naas in October: best effort when second to Total Enjoyment in Grade 3 mares novice at Down Royal: best form at 2m: acts on soft going (bumper form on firm). *Ms Caroline Hutchinson, Ireland* **h115 F96**

SAN HERNANDO 5 b.g. Hernando (FR) – Sandrella (IRE) (Darshaan) [2004/5 17m² 19d² Dec 11] fair on Flat (stays 2m): runner-up over hurdles in novice company at Taunton and Lingfield: will stay beyond 19f: open to improvement. *D. R. C. Elsworth* **h96 +**

SAN MARCO (IRE) 7 b.g. Brief Truce (USA) – Nuit Des Temps (Sadler's Wells (USA)) [2004/5 c80§, h80§: 24m* 24m² 22g* 20g* Jul 30] thrice-raced chaser: fair hurdler: sold out of Mrs P. Sly's stable 6,200 gns Doncaster March (2004) Sales: much improved, winning handicaps at Worcester (novice) in June and Stratford and Bangor in July: stays 3m: probably acts on any going: wears cheekpieces/blinkers. *M. Sheppard* **c– h112**

SAN PEIRE (FR) 8 b.g. Cyborg (FR) – Shakapoura (FR) (Shakapour) [2004/5 c99, h98§: 20g⁵ May 1] modest hurdler: successful in novice only outing over fences: stays 27f: raced on good going or softer (acts on soft): tried in cheekpieces: not one to trust: sold 10,000 gns Doncaster May (2004) Sales. *J. Howard Johnson* **c– h– §**

SANTA CATALINA (IRE) 6 br.m. Tagula (IRE) – Bui-Doi (IRE) (Dance of Life (USA)) [2004/5 16sᵖᵘ Dec 28] half-sister to fairly useful hurdler/chaser Just Murphy (by Namaqualand), stays 2½m: poor maiden on Flat (stays 1m): no show in seller on hurdling debut. *R. J. Price* **h–**

SANTA LUCIA 9 b.m. Namaqualand (USA) – Villasanta (Corvaro (USA)) [2004/5 c83, h97: c21dᵖᵘ 20d⁴ c17d³ c20mᵖᵘ c20d² c21mᵖᵘ Jul 26] sturdy mare: modest hurdler/ **c86 h95**

maiden chaser: seems best around 2½m: acts on good to firm and good to soft going: wears cheekpieces. *Miss Lucinda V. Russell*

SANTI (FR) 7 b.g. Brief Truce (USA) – Sun River (IRE) (Last Tycoon) [2004/5 c–, h–: c16vpu c24gpu May 27] winning hurdler/chaser in France: no show in points/hunters in Britain: raced mainly around 2m: acts on soft ground: tried blinkered: has had tongue tied. *Mrs K. J. Gilmore* **c– h–**

SAORSIE 7 b.g. Emperor Jones (USA) – Exclusive Lottery (Presidium) [2004/5 h98: 17d5 17m 16g 16g* 16s* 16d 17v 16d 24dpu 16spu 20s6 16d2 16dpu Apr 17] leggy gelding: modest handicap hurdler: won twice at Towcester in October: best around 2m: acts on soft and good to firm going: tried blinkered/in cheekpieces: held up: inconsistent. *J. C. Fox* **h96 §**

SAPOSCAT (IRE) 5 b.g. Groom Dancer (USA) – Dance of Joy (Shareef Dancer (USA)) [2004/5 h–: 17dpu 16gpu Jul 11] of no account: tried in cheekpieces. *W. G. M. Turner* **h–**

SARAGANN (IRE) 10 b.g. Danehill (USA) – Sarliya (IRE) (Doyoun) [2004/5 c112x, h–: c17d5 c18m6 c24m4 16m4 c20gpu 18d c16d5 c17spu c16g Apr 19] leggy gelding: winning hurdler/chaser: little show in 2004/5: sold out of P. Hobbs's stable 6,500 gns Doncaster May Sales after second start, out of J. Price's stable £1,000 Ascot February Sales after eighth: stays easy 2½m: acts on soft and good to firm going: tried blinkered: sketchy jumper. *M. J. M. Evans* **c– x h70**

SARA MONICA (IRE) 8 ch.m. Moscow Society (USA) – Swift Trip (IRE) (Duky) [2004/5 h90, F77: c16spu 16d 24v* 24v2 20v3 Mar 20] sturdy, lengthy mare: fair handicap hurdler: improved form when winning at Hexham in December: ran as if amiss on chasing debut: will prove best at 3m+: raced on going softer than good (acts on heavy). *L. Lungo* **c– p h106**

SARASOTA (IRE) 10 b.g. Lord Americo – Ceoltoir Dubh (Black Minstrel) [2004/5 h80: 22dpu 19s* 20s 18spu Mar 9] angular gelding: modest handicap hurdler: off 19 months before reappearance: best effort when winning at Exeter in January: probably stays 21f: acts on firm and soft going. *P. Bowen* **h90**

SARAWAK 5 b.g. Ashkalani (IRE) – Segovia (Groom Dancer (USA)) [2004/5 F16m Dec 12] fourth foal: half-brother to 2m hurdle winner Govamix (by Linamix) and bumper winner Real Definition (by Highest Honor): dam 1¼m winner who stayed 1½m: always behind in bumper on debut. *P. D. Niven* **F–**

SARDAGNA (FR) 5 gr.m. Medaaly – Sarda (FR) (Funambule (USA)) [2004/5 21g* 16m* 17g* 22d4 16m4 19g5 20d3 16g 16d4 c20d2 c18s* c16s5 c16s* Apr 22] leggy ex-French mare: third foal: half-sister to winner up to 1½m Salinka (by Green Tune): dam maiden: fair maiden on Flat (stays 15.5f), claimed out of J-V. Toux's stable €13,000 in June: fairly useful novice hurdler: successful at Southwell (seller), Worcester and Bangor, all in July: best effort when fourth to Mr Ed in handicap at Newton Abbot next time: fair form over fences: won 4-runner maiden at Fontwell in March and 6-runner novice at Perth (held when clear leader fell last) in April: effective at 2m to 2¾m: acts on soft and good to firm going: visored over hurdles. *M. C. Pipe* **c105 p h121**

SARENA SPECIAL 8 b.g. Lucky Guest – Lariston Gale (Pas de Seul) [2004/5 16vpu 16s 17s4 16s3 Jan 11] neat gelding: 6f winner on Flat: first form over hurdles when third in selling handicap at Leicester: will prove best at 2m. *J. D. Frost* **h75**

SARGASSO SEA 8 gr.g. Greensmith – Sea Spice (Precipice Wood) [2004/5 c–p, h99: 16d4 16sF c16spu 16d2 Apr 22] strong gelding: fair form over hurdles: pulled up both starts in maiden chases: should stay beyond 2½m: raced on good going or softer. *J. A. B. Old* **c– h113 ?**

SARGON 6 b.g. Oscar (IRE) – Syrian Queen (Slip Anchor) [2004/5 16f* 16m3 16m* 20f* 17g 16m c16f4 c16v3 c16m3 c20s5 c22s Apr 13] 15f winner on Flat in France at 3 yrs: fair hurdler: won maiden at Limerick in May and novices at Tralee and Cork in June: poor novice chaser: stays 2½m: acts on firm ground: tried in blinkers. *M. Hourigan, Ireland* **c84 h106**

SAROBAR (IRE) 5 gr.g. Sesaro (USA) – Khairka (IRE) (Tirol) [2004/5 19g5 18d 16s5 16s3 16v 20v 17v 17m Mar 14] angular gelding: fair maiden on Flat (stays 1½m): modest form over hurdles: left T. Doyle after reappearance, sold out of S. Treacy's stable €10,000 Goffs February Sale before final start: raced mainly around 2m: acts on soft ground: tried blinkered. *E. Sheehy, Ireland* **h88**

SASPYS LAD 8 b.g. Faustus (USA) – Legendary Lady (Reprimand) [2004/5 h110: c16spu c16g4 c17g2 c20dpu c16dF c17g2 Oct 9] smallish gelding: fair handicap hurdler: **c102 x h–**

similar form at best over fences: suited by test of speed at 2m: has won on soft going, best form on good/good to firm: needs to brush up jumping over fences. *W. M. Brisbourne*

SATCHMO (IRE) 13 b.g. Satco (FR) – Taradale (Torus) [2004/5 c106: c21m³ c20g² c21s^ur Apr 7] big gelding: impresses in appearance: fairly useful hunter chaser nowadays: successful in point in January: effective at 2½m to 25f: acts on firm and soft going: races prominently: bold jumper. *Mrs D. M. Grissell* **c107**

SATCO EXPRESS (IRE) 9 b.g. Satco (FR) – Rosel Chris (Roselier (FR)) [2004/5 c130, h–: c25g^pu c24v^pu c24v c29d^F c24s⁶ 24v⁴ c22v² c24v Jan 20] strong, well-made gelding: winning hurdler: fairly useful at best over fences in 2004/5: stays 3m, seemingly not 4m: raced on good going or softer (acts on soft): blinkered sixth start: tried tongue tied: often front runner. *E. Sheehy, Ireland* **c121 h–**

SATIVA BAY 6 ch.g. Karinga Bay – Busy Mittens (Nearly A Hand) [2004/5 F84: 22g² May 7] angular gelding: modest in bumpers: 4 lengths second to comfortable winner Supreme Piper in novice at Wincanton on hurdling debut: will stay 3m. *J. W. Mullins* **h91 +**

SATOHA (IRE) 7 br.g. Zaffaran (USA) – Whackers World (Whistling Deer) [2004/5 F100: 16v* 20s^ur 16s 20s⁶ Mar 27] has been fired: fairly useful bumper winner: off a year, won 23-runner maiden at Leopardstown on hurdling debut in January by head from L'Antartique: well held both subsequent completed starts: should be better suited by 2½m than 2m. *F. Flood, Ireland* **h118**

SATTELIGHT 5 b.m. Fraam – Ajig Dancer (Niniski (USA)) [2004/5 F16g⁴ F17d³ F17m⁵ 16d^pu Dec 26] first foal: dam, 5f (at 2 yrs) to 7f winner, out of sister to smart sprinter Puissance: modest form for M. Channon first 2 starts in bumpers: lame on hurdling debut. *B. G. Powell* **h– F77**

SAUCY KING 5 b.g. Amfortas (IRE) – So Saucy (Teenoso (USA)) [2004/5 F16d F16d⁵ 16v 19g 16s⁵ Mar 19] smallish, lengthy gelding: fifth foal: half-brother to 3 winners, including 7f to 2m winner Most-Saucy (by Most Welcome) and middle-distance winner Tidal (by Bin Ajwaad): dam 1¼m and 17f winner: fair form both starts in bumpers: little impact in novice hurdles, though not knocked about. *M. W. Easterby* **h– F85**

SAUCY NIGHT 9 ch.g. Anshan – Kiss In The Dark (Starry Night (USA)) [2004/5 c17g³ 20d⁴ c25s³ c21s* c21s² c22s* c21d² c21d² Mar 10] stocky gelding: poor form over hurdles: fair handicap chaser: off over 2 years before reappearance: won at Folkestone (amateurs) in January and Fontwell in February: stays 2¾m: acts on soft ground: usually sound jumper. *Simon Earle* **c102 h67**

SAVANNAH BAY 6 ch.g. In The Wings – High Savannah (Rousillon (USA)) [2004/5 16g² 21d^pu 19g² 24d Apr 8] good-bodied gelding: half-brother to fairly useful 2m hurdler Smart Savannah (by Primo Dominie): useful on Flat (stays 2½m) for B. Meehan, below best in 2004: best effort over hurdles when 2½ lengths second to Bagan in novice at Doncaster third start: should stay 3m: blinkered last 2 outings. *P. J. Hobbs* **h116**

SAVANNAH MO (IRE) 10 ch.m. Husyan (USA) – Sweet Start (Candy Cane) [2004/5 c–, h72: 24d⁴ May 15] leggy, lengthy mare: poor handicap hurdler: no aptitude for chasing: stays 3m: acts on heavy going. *J. N. R. Billinge* **c– h–**

SAVANNAH RIVER (IRE) 4 b.f. Desert King (IRE) – Hayward (Indian Ridge) [2004/5 16d 16d⁴ 16d^ur 16s 19g 27v³ 20s Apr 10] leggy filly: modest maiden on Flat (stays 1¾m): little solid form over hurdles: wore cheekpieces last 3 starts. *Miss Kate Milligan* **h90 ?**

SAVATI (FR) 5 b.g. Subotica (FR) – Tipsa (FR) (Tip Moss (FR)) [2004/5 F16m⁵ F16v F16s Apr 13] half-brother to several winners, including hurdlers around 2m La Tienta (by Garde Royale) and Trink (by Sir Brink) and 1½m winner Vieux Val (by Galetto): dam, winning 2m hurdler, also successful up to 11.5f on Flat: won 4-y-o maiden point on debut in May 2004: modest form at best in bumpers. *Roy Wilson, Ireland* **F80**

SAXE-COBURG (IRE) 8 b.g. Warning – Saxon Maid (Sadler's Wells (USA)) [2004/5 16v⁵ 16s⁶ 17m Apr 9] fair but ungenuine on Flat (stays 1¾m), sold out of G. Ham's stable £1,000 Ascot December Sales: little form over hurdles: reluctant to race on debut. *K. G. Wingrove* **h66**

SAXON MIST 6 b.g. Slip Anchor – Ruby Venture (Ballad Rock) [2004/5 F92: F17g* F16g Apr 16] strong, close-coupled gelding: fair form in bumpers, winning at Newton Abbot in August by 1½ lengths from Shernatra. *A. King* **F92**

SAY AGAIN (IRE) 9 gr.g. Celio Rufo – Tricias Pet (Mandalus) [2004/5 c135+, h–: c16g* c17v^F 16v⁵ Feb 12] good-topped gelding: winning hurdler, well held in Grade 2 at Gowran in February: useful novice chaser in 2003/4: off 8 months, shaping quite well **c135 ? h–**

when falling 3 out in Grade 2 at Fairyhouse won by Central House: best around 2m: acts on any going. *Paul Nolan, Ireland*

SAYOUN (IRE) 6 gr.g. Primo Dominie – Sarafia (Dalsaan) [2004/5 h–, F–: 16d 22s^{pu} 20m^{pu} 16g^{6} 17g Apr 3] leggy gelding: no sign of ability. *Mrs L. B. Normile* **h–**

SAY WHAT YOU SEE (IRE) 5 b.g. Charnwood Forest (IRE) – Aster Aweke (IRE) (Alzao (USA)) [2004/5 16g* 17s^{2} 17d^{3} 17g* 16d 16d^{2} 16d^{2} 16d^{2} Apr 9] angular gelding: fairly useful on Flat (stays 1¼m) for J. Hills: fairly useful novice hurdler: won at Uttoxeter (by head from Salsalino) in October and Taunton in December: good second to Definate Spectacle in valuable handicap at Aintree final start: will prove best around 2m: raced mainly on good/good to soft ground (below form on soft): visored fifth start: front runner. *M. C. Pipe* **h123**

S B S BY JOVE 12 ch.g. Jupiter Island – Mill Shine (Milan) [2004/5 c–: c21d Apr 28] fair pointer: no show in 2 hunter chases. *Miss L. Blackford* **c–**

SCALINI'S (IRE) 5 ch.g. Peintre Celebre (USA) – Sistadari (Shardari) [2004/5 F16m^{2} Sep 24] half-brother to useful/smart German performers at 1¼m+ Sir Warren (by Warning), Simonas (by Sternkoenig) and Syrakus (by Kris): dam, maiden who stayed 1¼m, out of sister to Bella Colora and half-sister to Colorspin: 5/2-on, runner-up in bumper at Worcester on debut. *Jonjo O'Neill* **F86**

SCALLOWAY (IRE) 5 b.g. Marju (IRE) – Zany (Junius (USA)) [2004/5 h85: 17g^{3} 16g* 16g^{3} 17g^{3} Oct 14] angular gelding: fair hurdler: won maiden at Uttoxeter in June: will prove best at 2m: takes good hold, and races prominently. *D. J. Wintle* **h109**

SCALLYWAGS RETURN 6 b.m. Bob's Return (IRE) – Bee-A-Scally (Scallywag) [2004/5 F–: F16f 16d^{pu} Jan 7] no sign of ability: left Miss L. Russell before hurdling debut: headstrong. *Mrs L. B. Normile* **h– F–**

SCAMP 6 b.m. Selkirk (USA) – Cut And Run (Slip Anchor) [2004/5 F90: 17m 17d 17g^{pu} 17d 19g^{5} 20d Jan 7] leggy mare: bumper winner for H. Daly: bad novice hurdler: sold out of S. Gollings' stable 2,800 gns Doncaster October Sales after third start: free-going sort. *R. Shiels* **h57**

SCAPOLO (IRE) 7 ch.h. Rainbows For Life (CAN) – Tycoon's Catch (IRE) (Thatching) [2004/5 16g^{2} Jul 6] smart on Flat, successful 7 times around 1m in Germany and Spain, including at Leipzig in June: not fluent when second in novice at Uttoxeter on hurdling debut. *C. Von Der Recke, Germany* **h95 +**

SCARFACE 8 ch.g. Hernando (FR) – Scarlatine (IRE) (Alzao (USA)) [2004/5 h80: 16v 21g 22d^{pu} Mar 10] maiden hurdler: left A. Hobbs and off 15 months, no form in handicaps in 2004/5: stays 2¾m: raced on good going or softer over hurdles: visored last 2 outings. *M. C. Pipe* **h–**

SCARLET FANTASY 5 b.g. Rudimentary (USA) – Katie Scarlett (Lochnager) [2004/5 h94: 16v^{F} 20d^{2} 21s^{pu} 16s 24s^{5} 19g Apr 12] fair handicap hurdler: out of form after second outing: stays 2½m: acts on heavy ground. *P. A. Pritchard* **h104**

SCARLET MEMORY 6 b.m. Dancing High – Scarlet Ember (Nearly A Hand) [2004/5 F16s 16d Apr 11] fourth foal: dam no worthwhile form over jumps: well held in mares bumper and novice hurdle. *G. A. Harker* **h– F–**

SCARLET MIX (FR) 4 gr.g. Linamix (FR) – Scarlet Raider (USA) (Red Ransom (USA)) [2004/5 16d* 16d 16g 16d^{2} 16m Apr 17] lengthy gelding: thrice-raced on Flat at 3 yrs, useful form when winning around 1¼m at Chantilly in September, for A. Fabre: made all in juvenile at Warwick in November on hurdling debut: didn't impress with jumping/attitude most starts after, visored last 2. *M. C. Pipe* **h101**

SCARPIA 5 ch.g. Rudimentary (USA) – Floria Tosca (Petong) [2004/5 16d 17s^{3} 17g Apr 7] poor maiden up to 1¼m on Flat: no form over hurdles: tongue tied last 2 outings. *P. R. Rodford* **h–**

SCARROTS 11 b.g. Mazilier (USA) – Bath (Runnett) [2004/5 c22g^{pu} 19g^{5} Jun 15] compact gelding: maiden hurdler/chaser, modest at best: tried in headgear: one to avoid. *J. C. Tuck* **c– § h52 §**

SCARTHY LAD (IRE) 7 ch.g. Magical Wonder (USA) – Grangeclare Rose (IRE) (Gianchi) [2004/5 h138: 16g^{5} c17d* c18v* c17v^{6} c16v^{F} c16s^{3} c20s^{ur} c24v* Apr 10] tall, leggy, close-coupled gelding: useful hurdler: similar form over fences: won maiden at Clonmel (held when left clear last) in November, listed event at Thurles (by 11 lengths from Boneyarrow) in January and Grade 3 Hugh McMahon Memorial Novice Chase at Limerick (beat Lincam easily by 20 lengths) in April: largely let down by jumping otherwise: effective at 2m to 3m: raced on good going or softer (acts on heavy). *T. G. O'Leary, Ireland* **c138 h–**

SCHAPIRO (USA) 4 b.g. Nureyev (USA) – Konvincha (USA) (Cormorant (USA)) [2004/5 17g^{F} 17m* 17g^{2} 16s 16v^{6} 19m* Apr 2] compact gelding: fairly useful on Flat (stays 1½m), successful in June (blinkered), sold out of J. Gosden's stable 130,000 gns Newmarket July Sales: fairly useful juvenile hurdler: won at Newton Abbot (made all) in September and Newbury in April, beating Son of Greek Myth easily by 5 lengths in handicap at latter: stays 19f: acts on good to firm going, well below form on soft/heavy: reportedly lost shoe fourth outing. *Jonjo O'Neill* **h119 +**

SCHINDLERS BEAUTY 5 ch.m. Oscar Schindler (IRE) – Qualitair Beauty (Damister (USA)) [2004/5 F16s F14m Mar 21] first foal: dam little sign of ability on Flat or over hurdles: behind in 2 bumpers: tongue tied second start. *C. Roberts* **F–**

SCHINKEN OTTO (IRE) 4 ch.c. Shinko Forest (IRE) – Athassel Rose (IRE) (Reasonable (FR)) [2004/5 16d 16m^{6} 16g^{4} 16g^{3} Jan 21] workmanlike colt: poor maiden on Flat and over hurdles: unlikely to stay beyond 2m. *J. M. Jefferson* **h79**

SCHNIPP SCHNAPP (FR) 4 b.c. Acatenango (GER) – Selva (IRE) (Darshaan) [2004/5 16d^{ur} 16d 16v^{4} Nov 29] tall, quite good-topped colt: successful over 11.5f at Neuss in December: eighth of 13 finishers in juvenile at Warwick on first completed outing over hurdles: fourth of 12 at Pisa next time. *C. Von Der Recke, Germany* **h?**

SCHOODIC POINT (IRE) 10 ch.g. Roselier (FR) – Madam Beau (Le Tricolore) [2004/5 h83: 23m^{5} 20m^{pu} 19g 16v^{6} 25s^{F} Mar 1] maiden hurdler, no form in 2004/5: stays 3m: headstrong: has looked thoroughly ungenuine in points. *Mrs S. J. Smith* **h–**

SCHOOL CLASS 5 b.m. Classic Cliche (IRE) – School Run (Deep Run) [2004/5 F16d^{5} F17g Apr 14] has scope: ninth foal: half-sister to winning chaser around 2½m Elgar (by Alflora) and winning pointer by Rakaposhi King: dam unraced sister to useful 2m chaser Buckfast Abbey: poor form on first of 2 outings in bumpers. *M. Scudamore* **F74**

SCHOOLHOUSE WALK 7 b.g. Mistertopogigo (IRE) – Restandbejoyful (Takachiho) [2004/5 h93?: 20m^{pu} 22g^{pu} 21v^{pu} c24d^{pu} c22d^{ur} c21v^{5} 21v^{pu} Mar 28] winning hurdler: no form in 2004/5, including over fences: stays 19f: acts on soft going: tried blinkered. *M. E. Sowersby* **c–** **h–**

SCHUH SHINE (IRE) 8 gr.g. Roselier (FR) – Naar Chamali (Salmon Leap (USA)) [2004/5 h103: c24v^{2} c20g* c20d* c22d* c22g* c20d^{2} c20s^{6} Apr 20] robust gelding: fair novice hurdler in 2003/4 for L. Lungo: better over fences, winning handicaps (last 2 novice events) at Southwell (conditional jockeys), Kempton and Haydock and novice at Haydock, all after turn of year: stays 3m: raced on good going or softer: front runner/races prominently. *Miss Venetia Williams* **c117 +** **h–**

SCIENTIST 4 ch.g. Dr Fong (USA) – Green Bonnet (IRE) (Green Desert (USA)) [2004/5 17s^{5} Dec 2] fair form on Flat (stayed 7f), successful in October, sold out of J. Gosden's stable 10,500 gns Newmarket Autumn Sales: fifth of 10 in juvenile hurdle at Market Rasen: dead. *D. Burchell* **h76 +**

SCIPPIT 6 ch.g. Unfuwain (USA) – Scierpan (USA) (Sharpen Up) [2004/5 h83: 17g^{ur} 16m^{6} 16m 17m^{2} 16g^{4} Jul 11] small, compact gelding: poor maiden hurdler: best around 2m with emphasis on speed: tried tongue tied: races prominently: has finished weakly. *N. Waggott* **h76**

SCOLBOA RAINBOW (IRE) 7 b. or br.g. Supreme Leader – Peggy Bull (IRE) (Kemal (FR)) [2004/5 F18s^{2} F18v* Dec 19] €25,000 4-y-o: fourth foal: half-brother to bumper winner Roskem (by Roselier): dam well beaten both starts in bumpers: better effort in bumpers at Thurles when winning 13-runner event in December by 13 lengths from Gandy: will stay at least 2½m. *S. J. Treacy, Ireland* **F102 +**

SCONCED (USA) 10 ch.g. Affirmed (USA) – Quaff (USA) (Raise A Cup (USA)) [2004/5 16d^{4} 16g^{ur} 21v 20g^{2} 24v^{6} 24v^{3} 24g^{4} c20v^{pu} Mar 17] modest maiden hurdler, left M. Polglase and off 16 months prior to reappearance: lost action on chasing debut: stays 3m: acts on heavy going: usually wears blinkers/cheekpieces: has finished weakly. *R. C. Guest* **c–** **h85**

SCOOP THIRTY NINE 7 b.m. Petoski – Welsh Clover (Cruise Missile) [2004/5 h81: 22s^{pu} 17v^{4} 16d 16m^{5} 16g Dec 18] leggy mare: poor handicap hurdler, little show in 2004/5: should stay beyond 19f: acts on soft going: sold 2,800 gns Doncaster January Sales. *Mrs E. Slack* **h70**

SCORCHIO (IRE) 4 b.g. Desert Sun – White-Wash (Final Straw) [2004/5 16g Jul 11] half-brother to modest hurdler Thrashing (by Kahyasi), stays 25f: poor maiden on Flat (stays 11f): tailed off in juvenile on hurdling debut. *M. F. Harris* **h–**

SCOTCH CORNER (IRE) 7 b.g. Jurado (USA) – Quennie Mo Ghra (IRE) (Mandalus) [2004/5 h–, F92: 20g* 20s² 20d⁴ c20g² c20g⁶ c24d³ c24dF c24d⁵ Mar 19] lengthy gelding: fair form in novice hurdles, winning at Huntingdon in October: best effort over fences when second to Hasty Prince in novice at Ludlow: would probably have won but for falling last in maiden at Fakenham: stays 3m: raced on good going or softer: races prominently: sometimes hangs left. *N. A. Twiston-Davies* **c110 h110**

SCOTMAIL (IRE) 4 b.g. Old Vic – Snipe Singer (Tyrnavos) [2004/5 F16d⁴ F16s⁴ F16s⁴ Apr 22] rather unfurnished gelding: half-brother to winning 2m hurdler Just Supposen (by Posen) and 5f winner in Italy by Jareer: dam placed over 7f and 1¼m: fair form when fourth all starts in bumpers. *J. Howard Johnson* **F86**

SCOTMAIL LAD (IRE) 11 b.g. Ilium – Nicholas Ferry (Floriferous) [2004/5 c115d, h–: c20s³ Feb 11] leggy, workmanlike gelding: fairly useful handicap chaser at best for G. M. Moore: remote third in hunter at Bangor: won point in April: effective at 2m to 3m: raced on good going or softer (acts on heavy): usually wears headgear. *Mrs C. M. Mulhall* **c– h–**

SCOTMAIL TOO (IRE) 4 b.g. Saddlers' Hall (IRE) – Kam Slave (Kambalda) [2004/5 F16s F16g Apr 16] quite good-topped gelding: ninth foal: half-brother to 2m hurdle winner Drum A Deal (by Lafontaine): dam winning hurdler: little show in bumpers. *J. Howard Johnson* **F–**

SCOTS GREY 10 gr.g. Terimon – Misowni (Niniski (USA)) [2004/5 c142, h–: c21dur c21d c20d c21g⁵ c24s⁵ Apr 21] sturdy gelding: useful chaser in 2003/4, below best in valuable handicaps in 2004/5: stays 2½m: acts on any going: usually races prominently: usually sound jumper. *N. J. Henderson* **c130 h–**

SCOTTISH ROOTS 10 b.g. Roscoe Blake – Lothian Queen (Scorpio (FR)) [2004/5 c83, h–: c25g³ c21d* c20g* May 29] angular gelding: fair pointer/hunter chaser, successful at Uttoxeter (fortunate) and Hexham in May: stays 25f: probably acts on soft going. *David M. Easterby* **c87 h–**

SCOTTS COURT 5 b.g. Case Law – Pennine Star (IRE) (Pennine Walk) [2004/5 F16g³ Dec 16] sturdy gelding: seventh foal: half-brother to fair hurdler/chaser Gary's Pimpernel (by Shaddad), stays 2½m, and 1m winner Faraude (by Farfelu): dam, 1½m winner, from family of Star Appeal and Strong Gale: 3¼ lengths third of 15 to Stagecoach Diamond in bumper at Catterick on debut, disputing lead. *N. Tinkler* **F90**

SCRAPPY MULDOON 5 ch.g. Komaite (USA) – Stone Madness (Yukon Eric (CAN)) [2004/5 F17dpu May 12] fifth foal: dam poor hurdler: lame on debut. *J. E. Long* **F–**

SCRATCH THE DOVE 8 ch.m. Henbit (USA) – Coney Dove (Celtic Cone) [2004/5 h97: 20s 16d 16g 19s⁵ 24spu 19s² 22vpu 21s⁵ 24sF Apr 16] sturdy mare: modest handicap hurdler: left C. Price after seventh outing (reluctant at start): stays 21f: acts on soft and good to firm going: tried blinkered: inconsistent. *A. E. Price* **h95**

SCURRY DANCER (FR) 9 b.g. Snurge – Fijar Dance (FR) (In Fijar (USA)) [2004/5 c–, h–: c17dpu Aug 15] lengthy gelding: winning hurdler: form over fences only on chasing debut in 2001/2: best efforts around 2m on good/good to firm going: tried in cheekpieces. *S. G. Chadwick* **c– h–**

SEA CAPTAIN 5 b.g. Oscar (IRE) – Calabria (Neltino) [2004/5 F16d* F16d 16d* 16g² 16d⁵ Apr 8] rangy, good sort: will make a chaser: first foal: dam, modest form only outing in bumper, half-sister to useful hurdler/fairly useful chaser up to 2½m Easter Ross: fairly useful form in bumpers, winning at Ludlow on debut in May: ran to similar level first 2 starts in novice hurdles, winning at Sandown in February by 4 lengths from Il Duce and second to Mighty Man, pair clear, there following month: stable out of sorts when running poorly final outing: will stay beyond 2m: should still prove himself capable of better. *N. J. Henderson* **h125 + F100**

SEA COVE 5 b.m. Terimon – Regal Pursuit (IRE) (Roi Danzig (USA)) [2004/5 h80: 22gpu Jul 20] poor maiden on Flat: no form over hurdles since debut. *J. M. Jefferson* **h–**

SEA DIVA (IRE) 5 b.m. Old Vic – Upsail (Top Ville) [2004/5 F16v* 16d 20s⁵ Mar 27] seventh foal: dam, 17f hurdle winner, from family of smart 2m hurdler Sailor's Dance and very smart stayer Longboat: fairly useful form when winning 25-runner bumper at Punchestown on debut in February by ½ length from Ashamdil: better effort over hurdles (not knocked about on debut) when fifth to Asian Maze in Grade 3 mares novice at Fairyhouse. *D. T. Hughes, Ireland* **h104 F100**

SEA DRIFTING 8 b.g. Slip Anchor – Theme (IRE) (Sadler's Wells (USA)) [2004/5 c–, h–: c24d⁵ Nov 6] good-topped gelding: fairly useful hurdler/chaser at best: lightly **c– h–**

raced and well held since 2002/3: stays 3m: acts on firm and soft going, seemingly not on heavy: tried in cheekpieces. *Miss M. E. Rowland*

SEA FERRY (IRE) 9 b.g. Ilium – Nicholas Ferry (Floriferous) [2004/5 20s6 20s 21v 16v c25v4 c25s3 c24s2 c21v c24v5 Apr 17] good-topped gelding: handicap hurdler: left N. Chance and off nearly 2 years, well held in 2004/5: modest form at best over fences: will stay beyond 25f: raced on going softer than good (acts on heavy): tried in cheekpieces/visor. *Miss Lucinda V. Russell* **c88 h–**

SEAFIRE LAD (IRE) 4 b.g. Portrait Gallery (IRE) – Act The Fool (IRE) (Always Fair (USA)) [2004/5 16dpu 18d 16s Apr 3] first foal: dam unraced: no form in juvenile hurdles. *R. Johnson* **h–**

SEAGOLD 4 b.f. Shahrastani (USA) – Raeleen (Jupiter Island) [2004/5 17d 17m Sep 8] no form on Flat (for C. Wall) or in 2 starts over hurdles: tried blinkered. *A. E. Jones* **h–**

SEA GRASS (IRE) 7 b.g. Jolly Jake (NZ) – Furry Dream (Furry Glen) [2004/5 F–: c17gpu 24g4 Aug 14] won maiden Irish point in 2003: no form in varied events otherwise. *N. A. Twiston-Davies* **c– h–**

SEA LAUGHTER (IRE) 7 gr.m. Presenting – Bruna Rosa (Roselier (FR)) [2004/5 F86: 22s2 20v3 23v 24spu 27s Apr 22] big mare: fair form in bumpers: second in novice at Ayr on reappearance, only form over hurdles: should stay 3m. *J. N. R. Billinge* **h86**

SEAL OF OFFICE 6 ch.g. Mark of Esteem (IRE) – Minskip (USA) (The Minstrel (CAN)) [2004/5 16g 16g Mar 28] fairly useful at best on Flat (stays easy 1¼m), has lost his form: well held in maiden hurdles, bled from nose second time. *A. M. Hales* **h–**

SEA MAIZE 7 b.m. Sea Raven (IRE) – Dragons Daughter (Mandrake Major) [2004/5 h65, F–: 22d2 24d5 20dpu 24g5 20v c25g Mar 9] lengthy mare: poor hurdler: no show on chasing debut: stays 3m: usually wears cheekpieces nowadays. *C. R. Wilson* **c– h64**

SEA MARK 9 gr.g. Warning – Mettlesome (Lomond (USA)) [2004/5 c17g2 Jul 15] sturdy gelding: type to carry condition: fair hurdler in early-2002/3 for C. Grant: lightly raced since, but showed retains some ability on Flat and on chasing debut: needs emphasis on speed around 2m: acts on good to firm going: has worn blinkers, including when successful. *B. Ellison* **c87 h–**

SEANIETHESMUGGLER (IRE) 7 b.g. Balla Cove – Sharp Shauna (Sayyaf) [2004/5 F92: F16g3 19s* 21spu 22dpu 16dpu Mar 24] sturdy gelding: winning pointer: fair form in bumpers: off 6 months, successful in novice at Market Rasen on hurdling debut in November, idling markedly: pulled up all 3 subsequent starts: should stay beyond 19f: acts on soft going. *S. Gollings* **h91 F88**

SEAN (IRE) 6 b.g. Arctic Lord – Sextons Road (IRE) (Commanche Run) [2004/5 18m 24mpu Jun 16] first foal: dam unraced daughter of a winning hurdler: showed nothing in 2 races over hurdles. *Mrs L. C. Jewell* **h–**

SEAN NOS (IRE) 4 b.g. Sri Pekan (USA) – Coolaba Princess (IRE) (Danehill (USA)) [2004/5 16d Jan 12] ex-Irish gelding: fair maiden at best on Flat (stays 8.5f), sold out of T. Cooper's stable €3,000 Goffs October Sale: well beaten in juvenile on hurdling debut. *J. W. Mullins* **h–**

SEAPIN 4 b.g. Double Trigger (IRE) – Four-Legged Friend (Aragon) [2004/5 16dpu 16spu Dec 18] half-brother to fairly useful 2m hurdler Cupla Caide (by Double Eclipse) and several winners on Flat: dam sprinter: no show in 2 juvenile hurdles: tried blinkered. *T. J. Fitzgerald* **h–**

SEARCH AND DESTROY (USA) 7 b. or br.g. Sky Classic (CAN) – Hunt The Thimble (USA) (Turn And Count (USA)) [2004/5 c118, h103: c20g* c20m3 20m c19g5 c20s Dec 28] useful-looking gelding: winning hurdler: fair handicap chaser: won at Bangor very early in season: off 6 months, below form last 2 starts: stays easy 2¾m: acts on good to firm and good to soft going, possibly not on soft: blinkered nowadays. *T. R. George* **c113 h–**

SEA SNIPE 8 b.m. King Luthier – Seal Marine (Harwell) [2004/5 c26vF Apr 22] modest pointer, successful twice in 2004: fell seventh in hunter chase. *Mrs R. Kennen* **c–**

SEASQUILL (AUS) 10 bl.g. Squill (USA) – Sea Surge (AUS) (Rolle) [2004/5 c94, h–: c25g4 c21m3 c16g4 c21dF c27dpu Oct 27] leggy gelding: maiden hurdler/chaser: stays easy 21f: acts on firm going: tends to find little. *Ferdy Murphy* **c80 h–**

SEA SQUIRT (IRE) 8 b.g. Fourstars Allstar (USA) – Polynesian Goddess (IRE) (Salmon Leap (USA)) [2004/5 17f 24s* 24g Dec 30] ex-Irish gelding: modest hurdler at best, left E. Hales and off 17 months before reappearance: won seller at Ludlow in **h79**

October: stays 3m: acts on heavy going: ran poorly only try in blinkers: tongue tied in 2004/5. *Miss E. Hill*

SEA THE LIGHT 5 b.g. Blue Ocean (USA) – Lamper's Light (Idiot's Delight) [2004/5 F16s^{3} F16d^{2} F16d^{4} Mar 14] third foal: dam, well beaten in bumper, half-sister to smart 2m chaser Martin's Lamp and useful chaser up to 3m Hurricane Lamp: fair form when in frame in 3 bumpers, hung left final start. *A. King* **F94**

SEATTLE ART (USA) 11 b.g. Seattle Slew (USA) – Artiste (Artaius (USA)) [2004/5 c–§, h–: c18m c18m 24m Jun 5] strong gelding: winning chaser/maiden hurdler, no form since 2002: blinkered once. *Dr P. Pritchard* **c– § h–**

SEATTLE PRINCE (USA) 7 gr.g. Cozzene (USA) – Chicken Slew (USA) (Seattle Slew (USA)) [2004/5 19g^{6} 21s^{5} 19g^{6} 22m^{6} Apr 23] lightly raced on Flat nowadays: poor form over hurdles, not impressing with temperament or jumping. *S. Gollings* **h78**

SEA WARRIOR 7 b.g. Sea Raven (IRE) – Denby Wood (Lord Bud) [2004/5 F16g^{pu} Dec 16] third foal: dam unraced, out of half-sister to very smart middle-distance colt Town And Country: reluctant to race in bumper on debut. *Miss A. Stokell* **F–**

SEA YOU MADAME 6 b.m. Sea Raven (IRE) – Mildame (Milford) [2004/5 F17d^{6} May 12] 3,500 4-y-o: fourth foal: half-sister to 3m chaser Just Adam (by Primitive Rising): dam poor maiden hurdler: sixth of 18 in maiden bumper at Exeter on debut. *C. J. Down* **F85**

SECAM (POL) 6 gr.g. Alywar (USA) – Scytia (POL) (Euro Star) [2004/5 h–: 16v^{pu} Oct 16] stocky gelding: fair up to 1m on Flat, won 3 times on all-weather early in 2005: winning hurdler in Poland: blinkered, no form in 2 starts in Britain, pulling hard. *Mrs P. Townsley* **h–**

SECOND PAIGE (IRE) 8 b.g. Nicolotte – My First Paige (IRE) (Runnett) [2004/5 h108: c20m^{2} c17m^{3} 17d^{6} 20f^{3} 20f^{3} 24g^{2} c16d^{5} 22s^{3} Nov 18] compact gelding: fairly useful handicap hurdler, left N. Graham after third outing: best effort over fences when fifth of 6 finishers in maiden at Huntingdon: effective at 2m to easy 3m: acts on any going: consistent. *Mrs L. Wadham* **c109 h120**

SECRET BLOOM 4 b.g. My Best Valentine – Rose Elegance (Bairn (USA)) [2004/5 19g 16v 17g^{pu} Mar 9] poor on Flat (stayed 9.4f): no form over hurdles: dead. *J. R. Norton* **h–**

SECRET DRINKER (IRE) 9 b.g. Husyan (USA) – Try Le Reste (IRE) (Le Moss) [2004/5 c82, h–: c26d^{4} c30s^{4} c29s^{3} c26v^{2} c24v c24s^{3} 27d^{pu} c26v* Apr 17] useful-looking gelding: winning hurdler: modest chaser: sold out of O. Sherwood's stable 4,200 gns Doncaster March Sales after sixth outing: won handicap at Carlisle following month, making most: stays 29f: raced on good going or softer (acts on heavy): wears cheek-pieces/blinkers: often looks none too keen. *N. P. McCormack* **c85 h–**

SECRET PLOY 5 b.g. Deploy – By Line (High Line) [2004/5 F122: 16d^{3} 19d^{2} 20v^{2} 21g Mar 16] quite attractive gelding: leading bumper performer in 2003/4, unbeaten in 3 starts, including Grade 2 event at Newbury: best effort over hurdles (useful form) when clear second to Gold Medallist in novice at Exeter, spoiling chance by hanging left: off bridle long way out when tenth of 20 to No Refuge in Royal & SunAlliance Novices' Hurdle at Cheltenham: will stay 3m: possibly not at best on heavy going: not a straightforward ride. *H. Morrison* **h131**

SECRET'S OUT 9 b.g. Polish Precedent (USA) – Secret Obsession (USA) (Secretariat (USA)) [2004/5 h81: 16g^{5} 16m^{3} 16g^{6} 17g^{5} 16d Nov 9] leggy gelding: long-standing maiden hurdler: best around 2m: acts on good to soft and good to firm going: effective visored or not. *F. Lloyd* **h84**

SEDGE (USA) 5 b.g. Lure (USA) – First Flyer (USA) (Riverman (USA)) [2004/5 F–: F17g May 23] well held in bumpers: modest on Flat up to 9f, successful in early-February. *P. T. Midgley* **F–**

SEEADOR 6 b.g. El Conquistador – Shepani (New Member) [2004/5 h86, F–: 22g^{4} 22g^{4} 22s^{5} 22d^{4} 22d^{6} 21s^{4} 22v^{F} Feb 13] workmanlike gelding: modest maiden hurdler: looked set to win amateur handicap at Exeter when falling 2 out: will stay 3m: raced on good going or softer (acts on heavy). *J. W. Mullins* **h89**

SEEBALD (GER) 10 b.g. Mulberry (FR) – Spartina (USA) (Northern Baby (CAN)) [2004/5 c152x, h–: c17s^{2} c23d^{2} c24g^{6} c16s^{5} c20d^{pu} c21g^{pu} c16g^{4} Apr 23] leggy gelding: smart chaser: runner-up in valuable events at Exeter first 2 starts, beaten 5 lengths by Azertyuiop in Grade 2 limited handicap and short head by Best Mate in minor event: below par after: stays 23f: acts on any going: visored once: sometimes let down by jumping. *M. C. Pipe* **c154 x h–**

Blue Square 0800 587 0200 Noel Novices' Chase, Windsor—
second-season novice See You Sometime (noseband) makes his experience tell
against the better-fancied My Will and Hasty Prince (hoops)

SEEKING SHELTER (IRE) 6 b.m. Glacial Storm (USA) – Seeking Gold (IRE) (Lancastrian) [2004/5 F–: 24d^{pu} 20v 18v 24v^{ro} Feb 13] lengthy mare: showing first sign of ability when running out 3 out in amateur handicap hurdle at Ayr: stoutly bred. *N. G. Richards* **h– p**

SEE ME 6 ch.g. Nomadic Way (USA) – Ruby Rheims (Paveh Star) [2004/5 F16v^{4} F16s F16s Mar 10] stocky gelding: second foal: half-brother to bumper winner Sunshine Rays (by Alflora): dam lightly raced, out of half-sister to useful 3m chaser Sun Rising: modest form first 2 outings in bumpers. *Mrs H. Sweeting* **F81**

SEE ME THERE 5 b.g. Busy Flight – See-A-Rose (Halyudh (USA)) [2004/5 h–, F81: 19g^{6} 16g^{ur} 17g^{5} 19s^{4} 20g^{4} 20d^{4} 22s^{4} 22d^{pu} Apr 17] useful-looking gelding: modest maiden hurdler: stays 2½m: acts on good to soft going. *J. W. Mullins* **h93**

SEEMMA 5 b.m. Romany Rye – Shepani (New Member) [2004/5 F16d^{3} F16s F16s^{6} F16d Mar 24] unfurnished mare: seventh foal: half-sister to useful hurdler/chaser See You Sometime (by Sharp Deal), stays 3¼m, and bumper winner Seem of Gold (by Gold Dust): dam, maiden Irish pointer, half-sister to Rendlesham Hurdle winner See Enough: seemingly best effort in bumpers when sixth to Glasker Mill in slowly-run event at Kempton. *N. I. M. Rossiter* **F91**

SEE MORE STARS 8 b.g. Seymour Hicks (FR) – China's Way (USA) (Native Uproar (USA)) [2004/5 20g^{5} c23m^{pu} c16m^{pu} c21d^{ur} 21d^{3} 21m^{5} Aug 31] angular gelding: left W. Clay after second outing: signs of a little ability: may prove best around 2m. *J. Mackie* **c– h62**

SEEMORE SUNSHINE 8 br.g. Seymour Hicks (FR) – Temporary Affair (Mandalus) [2004/5 h–: c21m^{5} May 19] tall, lengthy gelding: no sign of ability: headstrong: sold 1,500 gns Doncaster March Sales. *R. Johnson* **c– h–**

SEE RED BILLDAN (IRE) 9 bl.g. Riverhead (USA) – Sweet Mayo (IRE) (Sexton Blake) [2004/5 c–: 24g^{pu} 21v^{pu} c21s^{R} Feb 15] lightly raced: no sign of ability: temperamental. *T. P. McGovern* **c– § h– §**

SEEYAAJ 5 b.g. Darshaan – Subya (Night Shift (USA)) [2004/5 h92: 16d* 16g^{2} 16m^{5} 16g^{5} 20f^{4} 16d 16d* 16d 18v^{pu} Mar 5] good-topped, close-coupled gelding: fair hurdler: won handicap at Ludlow in May and novice at Kelso (first outing after sold out of J. O'Neill's stable 10,000 gns Doncaster November Sales) in February: stays 2½m: acts on firm and good to soft going: tongue tied last 3 starts. *Miss Lucinda V. Russell* **h107**

SEE YOU AROUND 10 b.g. Sharp Deal – Seeborg (Lepanto (GER)) [2004/5 c80, h–: c21g^{pu} c24s^{2} c21s^{4} c24v^{3} c21s^{3} c25v^{3} c25s c24d c21d^{6} Mar 24] compact gelding: poor maiden chaser: stays 3¼m: acts on heavy going: often wears headgear: tried tongue tied. *J. W. Mullins* **c73 h–**

SEE YOU MAN 7 b.g. Young Freeman (USA) – Shepani (New Member) [2004/5 24g^{pu} Mar 3] no show in bumper or novice hurdle 2 years apart. *J. W. Mullins* **h–**

SEE YOU SOMETIME 10 b.g. Sharp Deal – Shepani (New Member) [2004/5 c124+, h–: c18d* c20g^{3} c20s* c21d^{F} c22d^{2} c20g^{5} c24s^{5} c21g^{3} c25d^{2} Apr 8] medium-sized gelding: useful chaser: won maiden at Fontwell in November and Grade 2 Noel Novices' Chase at Windsor (by ½ length from My Will) in December: ran well all completed starts after, third to King Harald in valuable novice handicap at Cheltenham and second to Like-A-Butterfly in Grade 2 novice at Aintree on last 2 outings: effective at 2½m to 3¼m: acts on soft and good to firm going: front runner/races prominently: tough and reliable. *J. W. Mullins* **c140 h–**

SEE YOU THERE (IRE) 6 br.g. Religiously (USA) – Bye For Now (Abednego) [2004/5 24s* 24s^{6} Apr 21] second foal: dam won Irish point: won maiden on last of 4 starts in Irish points in 2004: won novice at Carlisle on hurdling debut in March: stiff task, tailed off next time. *Miss Lucinda V. Russell* **h105**

SEFTON LODGE 6 b.g. Barathea (IRE) – Pine Needle (Kris) [2004/5 h–: 17g 20m^{pu} 16d^{pu} c16g^{ur} c16d c16m^{pu} Oct 1] of no account: tongue tied. *M. A. Barnes* **c– h–**

SEIFI 6 b.g. Hector Protector (USA) – Garconniere (Gay Mecene (USA)) [2004/5 16v^{6} 17s 16g Mar 18] half-brother to bumper winner by Darshaan: fairly useful at one time up to 1¾m on Flat for K. Prendergast, modest form at best in 2003: poor form over hurdles. *B. Ellison* **h75 +**

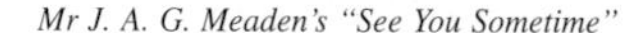

Mr J. A. G. Meaden's "See You Sometime"

Agfa Hurdle, Sandown—Self Defense (right) reverses 2003 placings with the grey Rooster Booster

SEKWANA (POL) 6 b.m. Duke Valentino – Surmia (POL) (Demon Club (POL)) [2004/5 h–: 16m May 27] of no account: usually wears headgear: tried tongue tied. *Miss A. M. Newton-Smith* **h–**

SELASSIE 6 ch.g. Alflora (IRE) – Zanditu (Presidium) [2004/5 h–, F–: $16g^{F}$ $16g^{pu}$ Jul 11] no form over hurdles: won point in April. *M. Scudamore* **h–**

SELBERRY 11 b.g. Selkirk (USA) – Choke Cherry (Connaught) [2004/5 c106d, h–: $c16d^{3}$ $c16g^{3}$ May 27] good-bodied gelding: modest handicap chaser nowadays: has form at 2½m, raced mainly around 2m: acts on heavy and good to firm going: visored once, blinkered nowadays: usually races up with pace. *E. L. James* **c93 h–**

SELF DEFENSE 8 b.g. Warning – Dansara (Dancing Brave (USA)) [2004/5 h140: $16g^{4}$ $16d^{2}$ 16g* 16g $16m^{2}$ Apr 22] sturdy gelding: smart on Flat, better than ever in 2004: of similar merit over hurdles: won Agfa Hurdle at Sandown in February by 3 lengths from Rooster Booster: ran well all other starts, runner-up at same course to Tamarinbleu in valuable handicap and Rooster Booster in valuable minor event: should prove as effective at 2½m as 2m: unraced on firm going, acts on any other. *P. R. Chamings* **h153**

SELVAS (GER) 5 ch.g. Lomitas – Subia (GER) (Konigsstuhl (GER)) [2004/5 h110p: $17m^{pu}$ 17s* 19g* $17g^{3}$ $16d^{2}$ $21d^{4}$ Nov 14] compact gelding: useful hurdler: won first 3 completed starts, including novices at Newton Abbot in June and Market Rasen in July: best efforts last 2 starts, 6 lengths second to Marcel in similar event at Stratford and 4 lengths fourth to Team Tassel in handicap at Cheltenham: stays 21f: raced mainly on good going or softer (acts on soft). *Jonjo O'Neill* **h131**

SEMI PRECIOUS (IRE) 7 ch.g. Semillon – Precious Petra (Bing II) [2004/5 h79, F–: c16s* $c20d^{F}$ c22d $c20d^{pu}$ Jan 27] plain gelding: poor hurdler: better form over fences: won novice handicap at Hereford in November: should stay 2½m: raced on going softer than good: room for improvement in jumping. *D. P. Keane* **c98 h–**

SENDONTHECHEQUE (IRE) 10 b.g. Torus – Miss Riversfield (IRE) (Sandalay) [2004/5 $c16s^{3}$ $c20m^{2}$ $c20s^{5}$ $c24g^{2}$ $c24g^{3}$ Apr 15] poor maiden chaser: probably best short of 3m: acts on soft and good to firm going: tried blinkered: front runner. *R. Ford* **c69 h–**

SENNA DA SILVA 5 gr.m. Prince of Birds (USA) – Impulsive Decision (IRE) (Nomination) [2004/5 h69, F–: 17g² 16f* 17d* 17v³ 16g⁶ 17g² 16v⁶ Jan 18] modest handicap hurdler: won at Wincanton in October and Newton Abbot in November: reportedly suffered irregular heartbeat final start: best at easy 2m: acts on any going: free-going sort, patiently ridden. *J. L. Flint* **h94**

SENOR EDUARDO 8 gr.g. Terimon – Jasmin Path (Warpath) [2004/5 h72p: 16d Nov 9] workmanlike gelding: modest on Flat (stays 1¼m): poor form over hurdles: changed hands 4,000 gns Doncaster November Sales. *S. Gollings* **h–**

SENORITA RUMBALITA 4 b.f. Alflora (IRE) – Lavenham's Last (Rymer) [2004/5 F12g* F12d² F17s* Apr 7] **F113**

'Labour loses safest seat in Wales' ran the headline. In one of the most surprising results—to outsiders at least—of the 2005 general election, a Labour majority of nineteen thousand in the Blaenau Gwent constituency was overturned when the independent candidate Peter Law, a member of the Welsh Assembly, defeated Maggie Jones, the Labour candidate, by over nine thousand votes. Law had effectively resigned from Labour in protest at an all-women shortlist being imposed on the constituency party, and one part of Wales, at least, expressed its own view on interference from London and Cardiff. All-women shortlists had been introduced by Labour in 1993 for half the winnable seats in which a new candidate was required and led to an influx of women MPs in the Labour landslide in 1997. All-women shortlists are seen as patronising in some quarters and aren't favoured by the other main parties, the view being that such a policy allows 'second-rate' candidates to be chosen who otherwise wouldn't make the list. Jump racing has its own version of all-women shortlists in the form of races restricted to fillies and mares, with the breeders heading a vociferous lobby to provide more and more (and better) opportunities. Seemingly not content with the increase in the weight-for-sex allowance from 5 lb to 7 lb, the proponents of more opportunities for mares now have a listed bumper at the Grand National meeting, run for the first time in 2005,

John Smith's HBLB Mares' Only Standard Open National Hunt Flat, Aintree—
Senorita Rumbalita and outsider Accordello (No.11) pull clear in the inaugural running of this race

and have applied some pressure to have a race for mares at the Cheltenham Festival. There are not yet any races above listed status for mares run in Britain but presumably they would be an aim in the longer term, such races already existing in Ireland. Whatever the merits of all-women shortlists for Parliament, there is plenty of evidence that good races for mares being staged at the moment simply aren't worth the status or money allotted them.

Take, for example, the Grade 3 mares novice hurdle run at the Irish Grand National meeting at Fairyhouse, the Mares Novices' Hurdle Championship Final no less. It was won in 2005 by Asian Maze, assuredly a mare quite capable of holding her own against geldings, but only one (Sweet Kiln) in the field had been good enough to win a graded novice not restricted to mares, whilst the only other runner of note was Queen Astrid, a useful performer on the Flat who on her previous start had gone off third favourite in the Royal & SunAlliance Hurdle. Even worse was the 2004 renewal, in which just five of the seventeen runners even contested a graded novice not confined to mares. The even more valuable, restricted Bewleys-sponsored mares bumper at the Punchestown Festival might work as a vehicle for the sales company involved, but the poor standard of the fillies and mares contesting it makes its wider contribution questionable. A total of fifty-seven mares ran in the first two runnings, in 2003 and 2004. They have since won twenty races between them, of which just eleven were not restricted to mares. Five of those were maiden hurdles, the others were three bumpers, a minor hurdle and handicap hurdles off marks of 80 and 83. The valuable mares bumper run at Sandown on Imperial Cup day (and formerly run at Cheltenham in April) is hardly any better. The 2003 and 2004 renewals were contested by thirty-six runners in total, who have since managed twenty-one wins. And while they include the Aintree Grade 2 bumper win by Diamond Sal, only six other wins, all over hurdles, have come outside mares-only events: four novices and two handicaps off marks of 90 and 93. None of these four bumpers, either in Britain or at Punchestown in 2003 and 2004, has featured a mare capable of showing so much as fairly useful form over hurdles. Second rate is a description that hardly begins to convey the mediocrity on display.

While accepting that there should also be room within the programme for trying out valuable new races and looking for fresh ways to boost interest in the sport, the mares bumpers at Punchestown and Sandown are sponsored by sales companies to create a market for a product traditionally considered of limited value. That jumping-bred mares tended to go straight to stud was accepted in days gone by but, in a more commercial era, there is clearly a problem if half the produce is considered to have a much lower value than the other half. There are no equivalents to the One Thousand Guineas and the Oaks, because there is no great tradition of racing fillies and mares over jumps. The number of good mares in recent years has increased slightly but there was not a single mare in the four main championship races at the Cheltenham Festival and the 187 runners in the eight open handicaps included just ten, six over hurdles and four over fences, including Liberthine, winner of the Mildmay of Flete. The impression is that the current programme is failing to identify and bring on a significant number of useful mares. A structure which perhaps caters less for the interests of sales companies and breeders would be more helpful. More bumpers, essentially educational races after all, are not what is required. The development of all-weather Flat racing (which saw a pattern race staged for the first time in 2005) and summer jumping offer examples of what can be done to improve quality. As a start, an intermediate hurdle at one of the main autumn meetings—neither the Open meeting nor the Hennessy meeting, for example, features a race restricted to mares—could provide an early target for the better novice mares of the previous season. A valuable novice or two later in the season, complementing the existing novice programme, might also be appropriate, to be built upon once their worth has been established.

The inaugural John Smith's HBLB Mares' Only Standard Open National Hunt Flat (listed) at Aintree attracted seventeen runners. They had managed to win ten times between them, three of those wins actually coming against geldings. Funny Times, the winner of the Sandown bumper, started favourite and looked the pick on form. Second favourite was Senorita Rumbalita, who had the same chance on form as several others but looked sure to benefit from the step up to two miles and a furlong. She had run twice previously, in so-called junior bumpers over around a mile and a half, winning a fillies-only event at Newbury in December and beaten a head by Openide in a listed event at Cheltenham in January. Senorita Rumbalita was indeed well served by a stiffer test at Aintree and, after cruising into contention despite some bumping into the straight in what was quite a rough race, she led over a furlong out and was always holding the runner-up Accordello, who had also been second to her at Newbury. Senorita Rumbalita won by half a length with fifteen lengths back to the third. Not many of those behind the first two (Accordello, significantly perhaps, is out of the high-class mare Marello) will make much impact in the future, but Senorita Rumbalita did enough to promote the view that she might be capable of holding her own outside mares' company when she goes over hurdles.

Senorita Rumbalita (b.f. 2001)	Alflora (IRE) (b 1989)	Niniski (b 1976)	Nijinsky
			Virginia Hills
		Adrana (ch 1980)	Bold Lad
			Le Melody
	Lavenham's Last (b 1989)	Rymer (b 1971)	Reliance
			Piave
		Lavenham Rose (ch 1969)	Floribunda
			Corn Dolly

The useful-looking Senorita Rumbalita has more about her physically as a potential hurdler than many mares seen in bumpers. She was bought for 11,000 guineas as a three-year-old at the Doncaster May Sales. Her sire Alflora is perhaps

Let's Get Ready To Rumble Partnership's "Senorita Rumbalita"

the main draw in her pedigree, though her dam Lavenham's Last is a half-sister to the high-class staying chaser Cybrandian, who was second to The Thinker in the 1987 Cheltenham Gold Cup. The unraced Lavenham's Last has produced three minor winners as well as Senorita Rumbalita, the pointers Raven's Last (by Sea Raven) and Top of The Dee (by Rakaposhi King), the former also successful in a bumper, and the bumper winner and seventeen-furlong hurdle winner Gohh (also by Alflora). The grandam Lavenham Rose and third dam Corn Dolly both won at three on the Flat and Lavenham Rose produced seven other winners apart from Cybrandian, though none of any great consequence. Senorita Rumbalita will stay two and a half miles. She looked a useful prospect at Aintree. *A. King*

SENOR SEDONA 6 b.g. Royal Vulcan – Star Shell (Queen's Hussar) [2004/5 F95: 20d5 24d5 21d2 22s* 24g Mar 18] tall, useful-looking gelding: will make a chaser: runner-up in 2 bumpers at Ascot: fairly useful novice hurdler: won at Wincanton in February by 1½ lengths from Lord Killeshanra: should stay beyond 2¾m: acts on soft going: tends to swish tail under pressure. *N. J. Gifford* **h120**

SENOR SOL (USA) 5 b.g. El Prado (IRE) – One Moment In Time (USA) (Magesterial (USA)) [2004/5 16g 16g 16s Oct 24] fairly useful on Flat (should stay 1½m), sold out of P. Cole's stable 37,000 gns Newmarket Autumn (2003) Sales: well beaten in novice company over hurdles: tried tongue tied: sold 4,200 gns Newmarket Autumn Sales. *R. T. Phillips* **h–**

SENTO (IRE) 7 ch.g. Persian Bold – Esclava (USA) (Nureyev (USA)) [2004/5 h105: c23g* May 12] good-topped gelding: fair handicap hurdler: off 9½ months, created good impression when winning novice at Exeter on chasing debut, jumping soundly and not extended to beat Lou du Moulin Mas 10 lengths: will stay 3m+: acts on good to firm going: looked sure to improve over fences, but wasn't seen out again. *A. King* **c110 +** **h–**

SEOMRA HOCHT (IRE) 8 b.g. Standiford (USA) – Woodbury Princess (Never So Bold) [2004/5 20m 20g3 22m2 20s2 20g4 24s3 18s4 20s 24d5 Apr 8] leggy gelding: maiden hurdler: 200/1, apparently much improved when fifth of 17 to Asian Maze in Grade 1 novice at Aintree: only modest on balance of form: stays 3m: acts on soft and good to firm going. *William Coleman O'Brien, Ireland* **h96 +**

SEPARATED (USA) 4 b.f. Unbridled (USA) – Lemhi Go (USA) (Lemhi Gold (USA)) [2004/5 16s4 17d2 Mar 26] half-sister to useful hurdler Unleash (by Benny The Dip), stays 2½m: twice-raced in maidens at 2 yrs for E. Dunlop: better effort in mares maiden hurdles when second to Be Wise Girl at Newton Abbot, would have won but for jockey's late reaction to final flight being omitted. *P. J. Hobbs* **h84**

SEPTEMBER MOON 7 b.m. Bustino – Lunabelle (Idiot's Delight) [2004/5 h–: 22g3 22m May 30] angular mare: modest hurdler: will stay 3m: acts on good to firm going: tried in cheekpieces: inconsistent. *Mrs A. M. Thorpe* **h95**

SERAPH 5 ch.g. Vettori (IRE) – Dahlawise (IRE) (Caerleon (USA)) [2004/5 h–: 16m 17d5 Aug 22] poor on Flat (stays 1¾m): little form over hurdles: wore cheekpieces in 2004/5: sold 3,100 gns Doncaster October Sales. *John A. Harris* **h–**

SERGIO COIMBRA (IRE) 6 b.g. Moscow Society (USA) – Across The Pond (IRE) (Over The River (FR)) [2004/5 F16v3 16s6 Mar 11] €36,000 4-y-o: first foal: dam unraced sister to fairly useful Irish chaser up to 3m Dark Magic and half-sister to smart hurdler/useful chaser Padre Mio, stayed 3m: looked a stayer when third to Witch Wind in bumper at Ayr on debut: kept to 2m, one-paced sixth of 15 in maiden hurdle there month later: will do better granted stiffer test of stamina. *N. G. Richards* **h77 p** **F88**

SERIOUS POSITION (IRE) 10 ch.g. Orchestra – Lady Temba (Callernish) [2004/5 c–, h84: c19dpu c24dpu c20dpu c20gpu 20vpu 19s2 16g Apr 19] workmanlike gelding: poor hurdler: pulled up all outings over fences (poor jumper): stays 2¾m: acts on soft and good to firm going: tried blinkered. *D. R. Stoddart* **c– x** **h82**

SERPENTINE ROCK 5 ch.g. Hernando (FR) – Serpentara (Kris) [2004/5 F93: F17s3 23m4 16v* Dec 31] tall, lengthy gelding: fair form in bumpers: sold out of F. Murphy's stable 20,000 gns Doncaster May Sales after hurdling debut: back markedly in trip, won 21-runner novice at Warwick in December by ¾ length from Miko de Beauchene. *P. J. Hobbs* **h111** **F93**

SESAME RAMBLER (IRE) 6 gr.g. Roselier (FR) – Sesame Cracker (Derrylin) [2004/5 F16d6 20d6 22spu 22s4 19s* 20gF Feb 16] 11,000 5-y-o: second foal: dam, maiden pointer, half-sister to Festival Bumper winner Mucklemeg: won maiden Irish point in **h106** **F83**

2004: raced freely in bumper: improved effort over hurdles when winning novice at Taunton in January: should stay beyond 19f: acts on soft going. *G. L. Moore*

SEVENEIGHTSIX (IRE) 5 ch.m. Old Vic – Necochea (Julio Mariner) [2004/5 F16d 17d^ur 16v^pu 21s^pu 16v 16g Apr 19] good-topped mare: sixth foal: half-sister to several winners, including 2 by Good Thyne, fairly useful chaser Talking Cents, stays 2¾m, and fair hurdler/chaser Rift Valley, stays 3m: dam fairly useful but ungenuine staying hurdler: no show in bumper or over hurdles (has jumped poorly): tried blinkered: looked very reluctant final outing. *D. J. Wintle* **h– §** F–

SEVEN UP (IRE) 6 b.g. Executive Perk – Rare Picture (Pollerton) [2004/5 F17s^pu Oct 19] workmanlike gelding: ninth foal: brother to modest chaser Vincent Van Gogh, stays 3m, and half-brother to fairly useful staying chaser Romany Creek (by Trimmingham): dam unraced: pulled up in bumper on debut. *C. P. Morlock* F–

SEVERN AIR 7 b.m. Alderbrook – Mariner's Air (Julio Mariner) [2004/5 h90, F89: 16d 20m^pu Jun 27] winning hurdler: no show either outing in handicaps in 2004/5: will prove best around 2m: raced mainly on good to soft going. *J. L. Spearing* **h–**

SEYMAR LAD (IRE) 5 b.g. Oscar (IRE) – Far And Deep (IRE) (Phardante (FR)) [2004/5 F16v F16s* F16d^5 F16g Apr 16] €42,000 4-y-o: rangy gelding: has plenty of scope: third foal: dam unraced: fairly useful form in bumpers, winning at Wetherby in February by 2 lengths from Summit Up: likely to be suited by 2½m+. *P. Beaumont* **F95**

SHAADIVA 7 b.m. Shaamit (IRE) – Kristal Diva (Kris) [2004/5 h104: 20d c20s^4 c21g^2 c20d* c21d^5 c20m* Apr 23] good-topped mare: fair hurdler, well held in mares handicap on reappearance: fair novice chaser: won at Market Rasen in February (mares) and April (handicap): stays 21f: acts on firm and soft going. *A. King* **c113 h–**

SHAAMIT'S ALL OVER 6 b.m. Shaamit (IRE) – First Time Over (Derrylin) [2004/5 16m 16d^pu Nov 21] poor maiden on Flat (stays 1m): no form in 2 outings over hurdles, jumped poorly in cheekpieces second time. *B. A. Pearce* **h–**

SHAAMIT THE VAAMIT (IRE) 5 b.g. Shaamit (IRE) – Shocker (IRE) (Sabrehill (USA)) [2004/5 F–: F16g F16g 16g^3 19v^3 17g^5 Apr 10] unfurnished gelding: well held in bumpers: modest form in novice hurdles, considerately handled final outing: stays 19f. *M. Scudamore* **h90** F–

SHADBOLT (NZ) 7 gr.g. Heroicity (AUS) – Another Day (NZ) (Open Day) [2004/5 F–: F16s 21d^pu Dec 9] tall gelding: no form in bumpers or claiming hurdle. *L. A. Dace* **h–** F–

SHADOW RIVER (IRE) 7 b.g. Over The River (FR) – Society Belle (Callernish) [2004/5 F94: F17d^3 May 12] fair form when placed in bumpers: will be suited by 2½m+: has looked tricky ride. *P. J. Hobbs* **F94**

SHADY ANNE 7 ch.m. Derrylin – Juno Away (Strong Gale) [2004/5 h78: 20d^3 24d^3 22m^4 17v^2 21g* 16d* 20d^2 17g c24s^pu c23m^4 Apr 10] smallish mare: fair novice hurdler: improved in 2004/5, winning amateur handicaps at Ludlow from The Hairy Lemon in December and January: mistakes and only poor form on completed outing in maiden chases: effective at 2m to 3m: acts on heavy going: wears cheekpieces. *F. Jordan* **c74 h100**

SHADY GREY 7 gr.m. Minster Son – Yemaail (IRE) (Shaadi (USA)) [2004/5 h81: 20m^2 20g^5 16v^5 19v^2 21d^pu Mar 24] poor novice hurdler: claimed from Miss K. Marks £5,000 fourth start: stays 2½m: acts on heavy and good to firm going. *C. J. Mann* **h80**

SHADY LAD (IRE) 8 b.g. Aahsaylad – Pimberley Shades (Pollerton) [2004/5 c24g c34g^2 c30s^5 c25s c24v^pu Apr 10] sturdy gelding: half-brother to thoroughly ungenuine winning jumper Pimberley Place and winning hurdler/pointer Outrigger (both by Spanish Place): dam never ran: fair chaser: apparently best efforts when runner-up in cross-country events at Punchestown in late-April: stays well: acts on heavy going: tried blinkered. *E. Bolger, Ireland* **c104 ? h–**

SHADY MAN 7 b.g. Shaamit (IRE) – Miss Hardy (Formidable (USA)) [2004/5 h90: 16g^pu 19m^pu 19g 19d 19d^pu Feb 4] chunky gelding: winning 17f hurdler: no form in 2004/5, sold out of M. Easterby's stable 1,600 gns Doncaster August Sales after first outing. *J. K. Hunter* **h–**

SHADY MERLIN (IRE) 7 b.g. Shardari – Merillion (Touch Paper) [2004/5 22s^pu Feb 4] ex-Irish gelding: eighth foal: half-brother to fairly useful hurdler Endless Magic (by Zaffaran), stays 2½m: dam lightly raced in bumpers: fifth on last of 3 starts in maidens for C. McCarthy in 2003, only form over hurdles: known as Royal Cruise when running 5 times in points in Britain in 2004, winning maiden in May. *S. Dow* **h–**

SHAFI (IRE) 14 b.g. Reference Point – Azyaa (Kris) [2004/5 c16s^{F} c20g^{pu} May 13] compact gelding: veteran hunter chaser. *Mark Doyle* **c– h–**

SHAH (IRE) 12 b.g. King Persian – Gay And Sharp (Fine Blade (USA)) [2004/5 c77, h–: c20g^{pu} c23f^{pu} c19g^{4} c19s^{pu} c19d^{pu} Oct 28] angular gelding: winning chaser, no form in 2004/5: blinkered once. *P. Kelsall* **c– h–**

SHAKERATTLEANDROLL (IRE) 4 b.g. Dr Fong (USA) – Speedybird (IRE) (Danehill (USA)) [2004/5 F13d aF16g^{5} Feb 19] fifth foal: half-brother to winner in USA by Rahy: dam, 7f winner, out of half-sister to Mill Reef: better effort in bumpers when fifth to Royal Stardust on polytrack at Lingfield. *J. Nicol* **F86**

SHAKWAA 6 ch.m. Lion Cavern (USA) – Shadha (USA) (Devil's Bag (USA)) [2004/5 h83?: 17d^{3} 18s 17v 16d^{pu} Jan 28] tall mare: poor maiden hurdler: best efforts around 2m. *E. A. Elliott* **h78**

SHALAAL (USA) 11 b.g. Sheikh Albadou – One Fine Day (USA) (Quadratic (USA)) [2004/5 19d^{pu} 17g 17d 17d 17v 16s Oct 22] sturdy gelding: winning hurdler, no longer of any account: blinkered once. *M. C. Chapman* **c– h–**

SHALAKO (USA) 7 ch.g. Kingmambo (USA) – Sporades (USA) (Vaguely Noble) [2004/5 h122: c19d^{2} c20m* c20d^{2} c19d^{2} c20d^{2} c20g^{F} c21s^{3} c20s^{4} c19s^{3} Mar 22] angular gelding: fairly useful handicap hurdler: similar form over fences, though hasn't always convinced with jumping/attitude: won maiden at Worcester in August: best efforts on fourth and fifth outings: stays 2½m: acts on soft and good to firm going: tried blinkered/visored. *P. J. Hobbs* **c124 § h–**

SHALATI PRINCESS 4 b.f. Bluegrass Prince (IRE) – Shalati (FR) (High Line) [2004/5 16g^{pu} 16g^{5} 16s 16s^{pu} 16m 16g^{4} Apr 19] leggy filly: poor maiden on Flat and over hurdles. *J. C. Fox* **h70**

SHALBEBLUE (IRE) 8 b.g. Shalford (IRE) – Alberjas (IRE) (Sure Blade (USA)) [2004/5 c–, h102: 17d^{3} 17d^{6} Aug 28] neat gelding: not fluent over fences: fair handicap hurdler in 2003/4, well below form both outings in 2004/5: raced mainly around 2m: acts on heavy and good to firm going: wears headgear: no easy ride. *B. Ellison* **c– h68**

SHAMAN 8 b.g. Fraam – Magic Maggie (Beveled (USA)) [2004/5 h100: 16g 16d 18d^{5} 16s^{3} 16v^{3} 16s 16g^{3} Mar 18] compact gelding: modest handicap hurdler: best around 2m: acts on good to firm and heavy going. *G. L. Moore* **h97**

SHAMAWAN (IRE) 10 b.g. Kris – Shamawna (IRE) (Darshaan) [2004/5 c–, h99+: 22v^{4} c36d Apr 9] leggy gelding: useful chaser at best, reportedly suffered fracture final start in 2002/3: only second outing since, fourth to Rosemauve in handicap hurdle at Uttoxeter, tiring only on run-in: always behind after blunder first in Grand National at Aintree 4½ months later: stays 21f: acts on heavy going: tried tongue tied: takes good hold, and is patiently ridden. *Jonjo O'Neill* **c– h112 +**

SHAMBOLINA 4 b.f. Shambo – Game Dilemma (Sulaafah (USA)) [2004/5 F17s Jan 10] first foal: dam fair 2m hurdler: soundly beaten in bumper on debut. *J. W. Mullins* **F–**

SHAMDIAN (IRE) 5 b.g. Indian Ridge – Shamadara (IRE) (Kahyasi) [2004/5 h105: 17g* 16g^{2} 16d 16m 16d Oct 2] rather leggy gelding: fair hurdler: won novice at Hereford in May: well below form after next outing, shaping as if amiss: will prove best around 2m with emphasis on speed: tongue tied final start: sold 9,500 gns Newmarket Autumn Sales. *N. J. Henderson* **h106**

SHAMELESS 8 ch.g. Prince Daniel (USA) – Level Edge (Beveled (USA)) [2004/5 h–: 20m^{pu} 17m^{ur} 17g Jul 15] leggy gelding: no form on Flat or over hurdles: tongue tied in 2004/5. *H. Alexander* **h–**

SHAMSAN (IRE) 8 ch.g. Night Shift (USA) – Awayil (USA) (Woodman (USA)) [2004/5 c–, h101: 21s^{5} Feb 14] small, sturdy gelding: winning hurdler/chaser: off 16 months, tailed off in handicap hurdle on return: stays easy 2½m: acts on firm and good to soft going: tried blinkered: has had tongue tied: has idled and usually held up. *J. Joseph* **c– h–**

SHAM SHARIF 8 b.m. Be My Chief (USA) – Syrian Queen (Slip Anchor) [2004/5 h82: 19g^{pu} Aug 2] maiden hurdler: raced mainly around 2m: acts on good to soft going: tried visored, blinkered last 4 outings. *C. J. Down* **h–**

SHANAPOVA (IRE) 5 br.m. Anshan – Native Gale (IRE) (Be My Native (USA)) [2004/5 F17g Apr 3] third foal: half-sister to winning 2½m hurdler Whizbang (by Presenting): dam winning 2m hurdler: mid-field in mares bumper on debut. *E. W. Tuer* **F78 +**

SHANESIA (IRE) 6 b.m. Erins Isle – Canadian Project (IRE) (Project Manager) [2004/5 h112: 18m 20d* 22m Jul 31] fair hurdler: form in 2004/5 only when winning handicap at Limerick in July: stays 2½m: acts on good to soft and good to firm going: tongue tied once. *Paul Nolan, Ireland* **h114**

SHANNON QUEST (IRE) 9 b. or br.g. Zaffaran (USA) – Carrick Shannon (Green Shoon) [2004/5 c–, h84§: 20d^{5} 19m^{4} 17m 19g^{2} Aug 10] lengthy gelding: poor maiden hurdler/chaser: won maiden point in April: stays 2¾m: acts on soft and good to firm going: usually blinkered: often finds little. *O. Sherwood* **c– h79 §**

SHANNON'S DREAM 9 b.m. Anshan – Jenny's Call (Petong) [2004/5 22s^{pu} Oct 28] of no account. *P. W. Hiatt* **h–**

SHANNON'S PRIDE (IRE) 9 gr.g. Roselier (FR) – Spanish Flame (IRE) (Spanish Place (USA)) [2004/5 c–, h–: c20d^{4} c21s* c22s^{2} c22d c25s^{4} Apr 3] well-made gelding: winning hurdler: fair chaser: won novice handicap at Ayr in November: might have followed up at Market Rasen but for mistake 3 out: should stay at least 3m: acts on soft going: has shaped as if amiss on several occasions. *N. G. Richards* **c115 h–**

SHANNON WATER'S (IRE) 9 b.m. Moscow Society (USA) – Percy's Pet (Blakeney) [2004/5 c–, h83: c22m* c23m c26g^{5} Jul 18] winning hurdler: modest chaser: won weak handicap at Fontwell in May: well beaten next 2 starts: stays 3¼m: acts on good to firm going, possibly not on softer than good: tongue tied. *M. C. Pipe* **c85 h–**

SHARABAD (FR) 7 b.g. Ela-Mana-Mou – Sharbada (FR) (Kahyasi) [2004/5 h65, F–: 16d^{pu} May 12] little form. *Mrs L. B. Normile* **h–**

SHARAJAN (IRE) 5 b.g. Desert King (IRE) – Balakera (FR) (Lashkari) [2004/5 F16g^{5} F16g^{4} May 16] €11,000 3-y-o: useful-looking gelding: fourth foal: half-brother to winning 2m hurdler Sheer Guts (by Hamas): dam unraced half-sister to dam of top-class staying chaser Behrajan: modest form in bumpers. *A. King* **F81**

SHARED ACCOUNT (IRE) 11 b.g. Supreme Leader – Ribble Rabble (Deep Run) [2004/5 h105: 26g^{5} 22d May 9] sturdy gelding: handicap hurdler, below best both outings in early-2004/5: stays 25f: acts on good to firm and heavy going: tried visored: sold 3,500 gns Doncaster May (2004) Sales, resold 2,000 gns there year later. *P. A. Blockley* **h–**

SHARED EXPECTATION (IRE) 9 ch.g. Husyan (USA) – Calmount (IRE) (Callernish) [2004/5 h–: 20m^{3} Oct 1] lengthy gelding: very lightly raced: first sign of ability when third of 5 in slowly-run novice hurdle at Hexham. *J. M. Jefferson* **h–**

SHAREEF (FR) 8 b.g. Port Lyautey (FR) – Saralik (Salse (USA)) [2004/5 c–, h–: c21s^{2} c21s^{pu} c21d^{4} c21g^{4} Apr 14] good-topped gelding: winning hurdler: fair maiden chaser: stays 2¾m: acts on soft and good to firm going. *A. King* **c112 h–**

SHARES (IRE) 5 b.g. Turtle Island (IRE) – Glendora (Glenstal (USA)) [2004/5 h98+: 17s 16s^{6} 16d^{3} 16v^{5} 18d Feb 3] fair handicap hurdler: will prove best at 2m: raced on good going or softer. *P. Monteith* **h104**

SHARMY (IRE) 9 b.g. Caerleon (USA) – Petticoat Lane (Ela-Mana-Mou) [2004/5 c114, h111: c17g^{3} c16g^{F} c16m c16g* 16d Dec 9] close-coupled gelding: winning hurdler: fairly useful handicap chaser: back to form when winning at Folkestone in November: raced around 2m: acts on soft and good to firm going. *Ian Williams* **c117 h105**

SHARPAMAN 10 b.g. Mandalus – Sharp Glance (IRE) (Deep Run) [2004/5 c26g^{pu} May 31] winning pointer: failed to complete both outings in chases: tried blinkered. *S. H. Shirley-Beavan* **c–**

SHARPASTRIZAM (NZ) 10 b.g. Try To Stop Me – Atristazam (NZ) (Zamazaan (FR)) [2004/5 c97, h–: c16g c16g^{2} c16m^{pu} Jun 5] good-topped gelding: modest chaser: sold out of P. Beaumont's stable 20,000 gns Doncaster May Sales: fatally injured next time: best around 2m: acted on good to soft going, though all wins on good/good to firm: sound jumper. *R. C. Guest* **c93 h–**

SHARP BELLINE (IRE) 8 b.g. Robellino (USA) – Moon Watch (Night Shift (USA)) [2004/5 c92, h90: c26g^{4} 21d^{3} 21d 24d^{2} 24g^{3} 23s* 23s^{4} 22d 24s Apr 2] small, close-coupled gelding: modest form over fences: fair handicap hurdler: won at Wetherby in December: stays 3¼m: acts on firm and soft going: races up with pace: temperamental. *Mrs S. J. Smith* **c87 § h113 §**

SHARP HAND 9 ch.g. Handsome Sailor – Sharp Glance (IRE) (Deep Run) [2004/5 h–: 16d^{5} 17m^{5} 17m^{5} 26m^{4} Jun 15] big, plain gelding: poor maiden hurdler: pulled up in 2 points in 2005: should stay 2½m: acts on good to firm and good to soft going. *J. G. M. O'Shea* **h65**

SHARP JACK (IRE) 7 b.g. Be My Native (USA) – Polly Sharp (Pollerton) [2004/5 h77+, F80: 16s* 16v^{3} Dec 30] fair form in novice hurdles, winning at Uttoxeter in November: likely to stay 2½m. *R. T. Phillips* **h101**

SHARP RALLY (IRE) 4 ch.g. Night Shift (USA) – La Pointe (Sharpo) [2004/5 17s^{pu} Nov 18] ex-French gelding: fourth foal: half-brother to 1¼m to 1½m winner Ganzo **h–**

Novales (by Last Tycoon) and 6f to 7.5f winner in Italy by Turtle Island: dam won up to 13f: successful over 9f on debut at 2 yrs, sold out of H-A. Pantall's stable €9,000 Goffs July Sale: jumped poorly in juvenile on hurdling debut. *A. J. Wilson*

SHARP RIGGING (IRE) 5 b.g. Son of Sharp Shot (IRE) – In The Rigging (USA) (Topsider (USA)) [2004/5 h112: 16g 16g^{6} 16g 16s* 16d^{4} 16d 21g^{F} 20d Apr 9] tall, angular gelding: useful handicap hurdler: won at Windsor in December by 3½ lengths from Thesis: good efforts after in valuable events, disputing lead on bridle when falling 2 out in Coral Cup at Cheltenham: likely to prove best short of 2½m when conditions are testing: acts on soft going: usually races prominently. *A. M. Hales* **h131**

SHARP SINGLE (IRE) 9 b.m. Supreme Leader – Pollyville (Pollerton) [2004/5 c82, h76: c17d^{2} c17v^{F} c16d^{4} c16v^{2} 16s c17d^{6} c16v* Apr 17] workmanlike mare: poor maiden hurdler: modest chaser: won maiden at Carlisle in April: stays 2½m: raced on good ground or softer (acts on heavy). *P. Beaumont* **c90 h–**

SHARVIE 8 b.g. Rock Hopper – Heresheis (Free State) [2004/5 h65: 21g c23m^{4} c26g^{pu} Jul 16] close-coupled gelding: little worthwhile form: wears headgear. *C. J. Hemsley* **c– § h–**

SHAVA 5 b.g. Atraf – Anita Marie (IRE) (Anita's Prince) [2004/5 17g May 11] modest on Flat (stays 7f), trained sole start in 2004 by Mrs B. Waring: well beaten on hurdling debut. *H. J. Evans* **h–**

SHAYADI (IRE) 8 b.g. Kahyasi – Shayrdia (IRE) (Storm Bird (CAN)) [2004/5 h115: c16g* c16f^{F} Jun 6] useful-looking gelding: fairly useful hurdler in 2003/4: won novice at Sedgefield on chasing debut in May by 8 lengths from Spectrometer: fell fatally at Perth: would have stayed beyond 2m: acted on good to firm and good to soft going: tongue tied. *B. Ellison* **c117 h–**

SHAYDEYLAYDEH (IRE) 6 b.m. Shaddad (USA) – Spirito Libro (USA) (Lear Fan (USA)) [2004/5 h72?: 22g 26f Sep 26] angular mare: little form over hurdles: tried in cheekpieces. *M. Wigham* **h–**

SHAYS LANE (IRE) 11 b.g. The Bart (USA) – Continuity Lass (Continuation) [2004/5 c88, h–: c25g^{4} c26d^{pu} c20m* c20g^{pu} c25m^{3} c20d^{5} c25s^{pu} c24d Nov 27] rangy gelding: poor handicap chaser: won at Hexham in June: should stay beyond 25f: acts on good to firm going: blinkered last 6 outings: ungenuine. *Ferdy Murphy* **c80 § h–**

SHAZAL 8 b.m. Afzal – Isolationist (Welsh Pageant) [2004/5 h73: 16g 18v^{5} 18s* 19g 19g^{5} 16v^{2} 22s* Mar 11] smallish, leggy mare: modest handicap hurdler: won at Kelso (amateurs) in December and Ayr in March: effective at 2m to 2¾m: acts on heavy going. *J. N. R. Billinge* **h89**

SHAZANA 4 gr.f. Key of Luck (USA) – Shawanni (Shareef Dancer (USA)) [2004/5 16m^{6} Feb 6] modest form in 3 maidens up to 1¼m for B. Hills: well held in juvenile on hurdling debut. *Mrs L. B. Normile* **h–**

SH BOOM 7 b.g. Alderbrook – Muznah (Royal And Regal (USA)) [2004/5 h149: 25s^{5} 24g^{pu} Mar 17] lengthy, useful-looking gelding: smart hurdler in 2003/4: bit below best when fifth to Baracouda in Grade 1 at Windsor on reappearance: beaten long way out in World Hurdle at Cheltenham 3 months later: stays at least 3m: raced on good going or softer (acts on heavy): usually held up. *Jonjo O'Neill* **h144**

SHEER GUTS (IRE) 6 b.g. Hamas (IRE) – Balakera (FR) (Lashkari) [2004/5 h81§: 20d^{6} 20d 16g^{pu} 16s^{4} 16s 16s^{4} 20s c18d c22s^{pu} Mar 27] leggy gelding: poor hurdler: little form since 2003, including over fences: sold out of J. Harris' stable 1,900 gns Doncaster January Sales after seventh start: form only around 2m: acts on heavy going: sometimes blinkered, has also worn cheekpieces: tried tongue tied: ungenuine. *T. G. McCourt, Ireland* **c– h78 §**

SHEILA MCKENZIE 8 b.m. Aragon – Lady Quachita (USA) (Sovereign Dancer (USA)) [2004/5 c–: c25s^{F} c24s^{F} Feb 10] winning pointer: failed to complete in hunter chases: dead. *Ms Rachel King* **c– x**

SHEKELS (IRE) 14 ch.g. Orchestra – Rare Currency (Rarity) [2004/5 c24m^{6} May 22] strong, lengthy gelding: fairly useful hunter chaser in 2000: lightly raced and well held since: blinkered twice. *A. Wheeler* **c– h–**

SHELEVEN (IRE) 6 ch.g. Accordion – Southcoast Gale (IRE) (Strong Gale) [2004/5 F16g 20s^{3} 22s 20m Nov 26] €48,000 4-y-o: second foal: dam, won point and 19f hurdle, half-sister to useful chaser up to 23f Potter's Gale: modest form in bumper on debut: apparently best effort over hurdles when fourth (promoted) in listed novice at Limerick: joined W. Amos. *C. F. Swan, Ireland* **h86 F79**

SHELLIN HILL (IRE) 11 ch.g. Sharp Victor (USA) – Queenspay (Sandhurst Prince) [2004/5 c66, h–: c21d* c17g^{6} c21g 16g c23f c20g Sep 12] strong, lengthy gelding: **c66 h–**

maiden hurdler: poor handicap chaser: won at Fakenham in May, only form in 2004/5: stays easy 21f: acts on firm and soft going: usually wears cheekpieces: has had tongue tied: none too genuine. *R. J. Price*

SHER BEAU (IRE) 6 b.g. Beau Sher – Welsh Ana (IRE) (Welsh Term) [2004/5 18s* 19v* 20s* Mar 27] useful-looking gelding: first foal: dam unraced, out of half-sister to smart staying chaser Givus A Buck: won second of 2 starts in maiden points in 2004: useful form in novice hurdles: successful first 3 starts, in minor events at Thurles in November and Naas in January and Grade 2 novice at Fairyhouse (beat Kill Devil Hill by short head) in March: jumped poorly when seventh to Asian Maze in Grade 1 novice at Punchestown in late-April (reportedly suffering from upper respiritory tract infection): likely to stay 3m: probably still capable of better. *Philip Fenton, Ireland* **h131 p**

SHERIFF ROSCOE 5 b.g. Roscoe Blake – Silva Linda (Precipice Wood) [2004/5 F16d² Mar 24] 20,000 4-y-o: eighth foal: brother to fairly useful hurdler Rosco, stays 25f, and half-brother to fairly useful chaser Linwood (by Ardross), stayed 3m: dam, half-sister to top-class chaser Brown Chamberlin, won three 2m novice chases: 12 lengths second of 15 to The Cool Guy in bumper at Wincanton on debut. *P. Winkworth* **F95**

SHERKIN ISLAND (IRE) 7 b.g. Shernazar – Tullerolli (IRE) (Barbarolli (USA)) [2004/5 c109p, h96: c16s* c17g⁵ c16d⁶ Dec 11] tall, useful-looking gelding: modest hurdler: fairly useful chaser: won handicap at Lingfield in November: made mistakes and not unduly knocked about both starts after: effective at 2m to 3m: acts on heavy ground. *Jonjo O'Neill* **c118 +** **h–**

SHERNATRA (IRE) 6 b.g. Shernazar – Miss Nancy (Giolla Mear) [2004/5 F17g² F17v³ F16dᵖᵘ Apr 20] €24,000 4-y-o: fourth foal: half-brother to fair hunter chaser Ruperts Choice (by Phardante), stayed 31f: dam lightly-raced half-sister to useful chaser up to 2½m Old Bridge: fair form in bumpers: lost action final start. *J. A. B. Old* **F91**

SHERWOOD FOREST 5 ch.g. Fleetwood (IRE) – Jay Gee Ell (Vaigly Great) [2004/5 16g⁶ Sep 23] modest and inconsistent on Flat (stays 2m): never a factor in novice on hurdling debut. *Miss L. A. Perratt* **h–**

SHERWOOD ROSE (IRE) 9 gr.m. Mandalus – Cronlier (Roselier (FR)) [2004/5 c–x, h68: 20g⁴ Apr 30] sturdy mare: poor maiden hurdler: let down by jumping all 3 starts in chases: stays 2½m: sold 1,800 gns Doncaster May Sales, successful twice in points in 2005. *K. C. Bailey* **c– x** **h56**

SHE'S A FOX 4 b.f. Wizard King – Foxie Lady (Wolfhound (USA)) [2004/5 16d⁴ 16s Oct 21] well beaten in maidens on Flat (refused to enter stall once): tailed off in 2 juvenile hurdles: sold £700 Ascot April Sales. *A. W. Carroll* **h–**

Rathbarry & Glenview Studs Festival Novices' Hurdle, Fairyhouse—
Sher Beau (right) keeps on well to overhaul Kill Devil Hill (centre) and Homer Wells

SHE'S MY GIRL (IRE) 10 ch.m. Arctic Cider (USA) – Sinead's Princess (Sun Prince) [2004/5 24f² 16f* 16f⁴ 20dF 20m³ 19g* 16d⁶ 18s Nov 19] smallish mare: poor hurdler: won handicaps at Perth (mares) in June and Kilbeggan in September: effective at 2m to 3m: acts on any going: no form in blinkers, sometimes wears cheekpieces: front runner. *J. G. Carr, Ireland* **h83**

SHE'S NO MUPPET 5 b.m. Teenoso (USA) – Persian Dream (IRE) (Mazaad) [2004/5 F16d* F16d⁵ F16d F17g Apr 14] good-topped mare: second foal: dam winning 2m hurdler: fair form in bumpers: won 22-runner mares event at Warwick in November on debut: ran as if amiss final start. *Jonjo O'Neill* **F92**

SHE'S OUR DAISY (IRE) 5 b.m. Supreme Leader – Tell A Tale (Le Bavard (FR)) [2004/5 F16d F17s* F17v F16dsu Mar 12] tall mare: fifth foal: dam winning 2½m Irish hurdler: form in bumpers only when winning mares event at Taunton in January: out of depth in Grade 1 at Punchestown in late-April. *S. C. Burrough* **F79**

SHE'S OUR NATIVE (IRE) 7 b.m. Be My Native (USA) – More Dash (IRE) (Strong Gale) [2004/5 h87: 21d c24gF c25d³ c16sF4 c20s² c20d³ c19s* c19v³ c20spu Mar 31] lengthy mare: modest maiden hurdler/novice chaser: left P. Hobbs after first start: won handicap over fences at Hereford in February: lost action final outing: should stay beyond 2½m: probably acts on heavy going: tried visored/blinkered. *Evan Williams* **c91 h–**

SHINING JOY (IRE) 6 gr.g. Be Happy (NZ) – Sexton Gleam (Sexton Blake) [2004/5 F16s Mar 27] first foal: dam awarded point: fell in maiden point on debut: well held in bumper. *E. Sheehy, Ireland* **F–**

SHINING LIGHTS (IRE) 6 b.m. Moscow Society (USA) – Orwell Rose (IRE) (Roselier (FR)) [2004/5 F16g⁶ 20m* 16m³ 20g⁴ c20mF c23f² c24g* c24g⁴ 24v³ c28s³ c25vF c22spu 22d³ 22g* Apr 17] leggy, angular mare: first foal: dam of little account: winning pointer: bumper winner: fair hurdler: won novices at Bangor (mares) in May and, having left M. Pipe after twelfth start, Wincanton in April: fair chaser: easily won mares novice handicap at Ludlow in October: probably stays 3½m: acts on any going: usually visored for former stable: has had tongue tied: moody. *B. G. Powell* **c107 § h104 § F89**

SHINING STRAND 6 ch.g. Karinga Bay – First Romance (Royalty) [2004/5 F104: F16d 16m Apr 2] has scope: twice-raced in bumpers 13 months apart: early to post, kept on not at all knocked about, having pulled hard, when seventh to Briareus in novice at Newbury on hurdling debut: open to improvement. *N. J. Henderson* **h95 p F88**

SHINING TYNE 11 b.g. Primitive Rising (USA) – Shining Bann (Bargello) [2004/5 c70§, h–§: c20s c16d⁴ c24d⁵ c27v⁵ c24s⁴ c25d c20v³ c20vpu Mar 17] lengthy gelding: long-standing maiden chaser: left S. Bell after seventh start: stays 3m: acts on heavy going: has worn cheekpieces/blinkers: often tongue tied: ungenuine. *W. Storey* **c71 § h– §**

SHINY BAY (IRE) 12 ch.g. Glacial Storm (USA) – Raby (Pongee) [2004/5 c–x, h–: c24dpu May 11] compact gelding: one-time fairly useful handicap hurdler: winning chaser, lightly raced outside points nowadays. *Miss Jenny Garley* **c– x h–**

SHIRAZI 7 b.g. Mtoto – Al Shadeedah (USA) (Nureyev (USA)) [2004/5 h101: 21m² Jul 2] leggy gelding: fair form over hurdles: stays easy 21f: acts on good to firm going: has had breathing problem. *D. R. Gandolfo* **h106**

SHIVERMETIMBER (IRE) 7 b.m. Arctic Lord – Cherry Dancer (Monksfield) [2004/5 h114, F94: 24g 24s 22v 24spu c24s c16s³ c20vur c20sF c20v* c24spu c22d* Mar 20] leggy mare: fairly useful hurdler: fair chaser: won mares maiden at Navan in February and Grade 3 mares novice at Limerick (by 3 lengths from Nolans Pride) in March: reportedly clinically abnormal in between: stays 3m: acts on heavy going. *F. Flood, Ireland* **c110 h–**

SHOGOON (FR) 6 b.g. Rangoon (FR) – Touranlad (FR) (Tourangeau (FR)) [2004/5 c57, h–: 17s 21s⁵ Dec 1] close-coupled gelding: winning chaser, but possesses very little ability. *Miss G. Browne* **c– h–**

SHORT CHANGE (IRE) 6 b.g. Revoque (IRE) – Maafi Esm (Polish Precedent (USA)) [2004/5 h103: 16m May 22] workmanlike gelding: fair hurdler: no show only start in 2004/5: raced around 2m: best efforts on good going or firmer. *A. W. Carroll* **h–**

SHOTACROSS THE BOW (IRE) 8 b.g. Warning – Nordica (Northfields (USA)) [2004/5 h–: 17d⁵ 16m 17gpu 17g Apr 12] close-coupled gelding: poor maiden hurdler: raced around 2m: tried tongue tied. *Mrs H. E. Rees* **h–**

SHOTGUN ANNIE 5 b.m. Double Trigger (IRE) – Coh Sho No (Old Vic) [2004/5 F–: 17d Nov 15] small, lengthy mare: no show in bumper or novice hurdle. *S. Dow* **h–**

SHOTGUN WILLY (IRE) 11 ch.g. Be My Native (USA) – Minorettes Girl (Strong Gale) [2004/5 c29v c29spu c33dpu Mar 19] tall, rather sparely-made gelding: has string- **c– h–**

halt: formerly high-class chaser: off 20 months, no show in valuable handicaps in 2004/5: stays 33f: acts on good to firm and heavy going: twice blinkered: has hung/jumped left: sold to join R. C. Guest 16,000 gns Doncaster May Sales. *P. F. Nicholls*

SHOULTON (IRE) 8 br.g. Aristocracy – Jay Joy (Double-U-Jay) [2004/5 c96, h–: c24s⁴ c24g⁶ c24v⁵ Dec 17] workmanlike gelding: maiden chaser, no form in 2004/5. *G. H. Yardley* **c– h–**

SHOVEONTOMMY (IRE) 10 b.g. Odin (FR) – Knockboy Glory (I'm A Star) [2004/5 c20spu Mar 11] winning pointer: tongue tied, no show in maiden hunter chase. *Miss Gina Weare* **c–**

SHOWER OF HAIL (IRE) 5 b.g. Luso – Hail To Home (IRE) (Soughaan (USA)) [2004/5 20s 21d* Apr 18] first foal: dam winning 2m hurdler: won maiden Irish point on debut in 2004: much better effort over hurdles (let down by jumping on debut) when winning maiden at Plumpton in April. *M. C. Pipe* **h101**

SHOW ME THE RIVER 6 b.g. Flemensfirth (USA) – Quare Dream's (IRE) (Strong Gale) [2004/5 F18d³ F16d³ F16v³ F16v* 16s 19s Mar 27] 20,000 4-y-o: second foal: half-brother to bumper winner Tomorrow's Dream (by Be My Native): dam lightly-raced sister to high-class chaser up to around 2½m Function Dream: fairly useful in bumpers, winning at Tramore in January: jumped poorly both starts in maiden hurdles. *Anthony Mullins, Ireland* **h97 p F100**

SHOW NO FEAR 4 b.g. Groom Dancer (USA) – La Piaf (FR) (Fabulous Dancer (USA)) [2004/5 17dF 16d* 16d 16d 16s⁴ 16s⁵ Apr 21] fair on Flat (stays 1¼m), sold out of H. Cecil's stable 12,000 gns Newmarket July Sales: easily best effort over hurdles when making all in juvenile at Perth (reportedly suffered overreach) in September: raced around 2m on going softer than good: tongue tied last 2 outings. *G. M. Moore* **h108 d**

SHOW OF HANDS (IRE) 5 b.g. Zaffaran (USA) – New Technique (FR) (Formidable (USA)) [2004/5 F17s F16v Dec 28] £30,000 4-y-o: sturdy gelding: third foal: dam no form on Flat: little show in bumpers. *J. G. M. O'Shea* **F–**

SHOWTIME LUCY 4 ch.f. Carlingford Castle – Sister Jim (Oats) [2004/5 F13s Dec 13] first foal: dam no sign of ability: tailed off in 3-y-o bumper on debut. *R. J. Price* **F–**

SHRADEN EDITION 8 b.g. Tina's Pet – Star Edition (Leading Man) [2004/5 c93: c25gpu c24s⁶ Feb 10] winning pointer: maiden hunter chaser. *P. A. Jones* **c83**

SHUFFLING PALS (IRE) 8 b.g. Roselier (FR) – Penny Shuffle (IRE) (Decent Fellow) [2004/5 20v c24gpu 25s³ c23dpu Apr 20] IR 10,000 3-y-o, IR £16,500 4-y-o: close-coupled gelding: first foal: dam lightly raced in bumpers: placed in maiden Irish points: remote third in novice hurdle at Warwick: not fluent and no show in 2 chases. *S. E. H. Sherwood* **c– h–**

SHUHOOD (USA) 5 b.g. Kingmambo (USA) – Nifty (USA) (Roberto (USA)) [2004/5 h114: 16m* 16d* 16d³ 20d⁴ 16g 24d⁶ Apr 8] strong, close-coupled gelding: useful novice hurdler: won at Ludlow (4-y-o event) in April and Haydock (beat Roman Ark 5 lengths) in October: better form when in frame in Grade 2 events at Cheltenham and Sandown: below form in Grade 1 events at Cheltenham and Aintree last 2 starts: stays 2½m: acts on good to firm and good to soft going. *P. R. Webber* **h131**

SHUILAN (IRE) 6 b.m. Good Thyne (USA) – Shuil Le Cheile (Quayside) [2004/5 F16g F18s⁵ F16s* 19s* 16v⁵ 20s⁴ 19s³ 16d Mar 20] €15,000 4-y-o: eighth live foal: half-sister to fairly useful chaser up to 3m Burwood Breeze (by Fresh Breeze): dam, maiden half-sister to Welsh National winner Jocks Cross, from very good jumping family: best effort in bumpers when successful in 22-runner mares event at Navan in December: won mares maiden at Limerick on hurdling debut following month: disappointing subsequently: should stay at least 2½m: blinkered final start: races prominently. *E. U. Hales, Ireland* **h113 F99**

SHUIL BOB (IRE) 5 b. or br.m. Bob Back (USA) – Shuil Ar Aghaidh (The Parson) [2004/5 F16s⁵ Mar 13] fifth foal: sister to fair hurdler Bob Ar Aghaidh, stays 3m, and half-sister to bumper winner Top Ar Aghaidh (by Topanoora) and 2m hurdle winner Rith Ar Aghaidh (by Phardante): dam, very smart staying hurdler, half-sister to useful staying jumper Rawhide, from family of very smart hurdler Liss A Paoraigh and Scottish National winner Baronet: fifth to Gay Gladys in mares maiden bumper at Warwick on debut. *C. Tinkler* **F85**

SHUIL TSARINA (IRE) 7 b.m. King's Ride – Shuil Realt (IRE) (Jolly Jake (NZ)) [2004/5 h–, F76: 16d 19d c22vur c27vpu Jan 25] rangy mare: no show over hurdles or fences. *J. M. Jefferson* **c– h–**

SHULMIN 5 ch.m. Minster Son – Shultan (IRE) (Rymer) [2004/5 F16s F17v⁵ Jan 25] second foal: sister to 3m chase winner Ryminster: dam 2¼m chase winner: mid-division in 2 mares bumpers. *J. Wade* **F76**

SIEGFRIEDS NIGHT (IRE) 4 ch.g. Night Shift (USA) – Shelbiana (USA) (Chieftain) [2004/5 17d* 16d 16s* 16d 17s 17d² 17g⁴ 16d⁴ Apr 20] smallish, plain gelding: fair on Flat (stays 14.6f), successful twice in 2004: fair juvenile hurdler: won convincingly at Cartmel in August and Fakenham in November: will stay beyond 17f: raced on good going or softer. *M. C. Chapman* **h106**

SIENA STAR (IRE) 7 b.g. Brief Truce (USA) – Gooseberry Pie (Green Desert (USA)) [2004/5 16g² 16g⁵ 20g⁴ 18m³ 16g⁵ 18d³ 16d Jan 6] close-coupled gelding: fairly useful on Flat (stays easy 1½m), sold out of P. Cole's stable £18,000 Ascot April Sales: modest novice hurdler: may prove best at 2m. *P. Bowen* **h94**

SIGMA TELECOM (IRE) 11 b.g. Be My Native (USA) – Sugar Quay (Quayside) [2004/5 22sᵖᵘ Nov 7] winning pointer: lightly raced over hurdles and in chases. *S.R.B. Crawford, Ireland* **c–** **h–**

SIGNATURE TUNE (IRE) 6 b.g. Gothland (FR) – Divine Affair (IRE) (The Parson) [2004/5 h–, F–: 16g⁴ 16d* 16v⁶ 16d⁶ 17g Apr 12] modest novice hurdler: won at Plumpton in November: no show after: raced around 2m on good going or softer: has bled from nose. *P. Winkworth* **h90**

SIGNED AND DATED (USA) 6 b.g. Red Ransom (USA) – Libeccio (NZ) (Danzatore (CAN)) [2004/5 h–x: 24sᵖᵘ 20s 20s⁴ 16g* 20d⁴ 20v³ 19g 17v⁴ 16dᵖᵘ 17m² Apr 23] workmanlike gelding: poor handicap hurdler: won seller at Catterick in December: barely stays testing 2½m: acts on good to firm and heavy going: wears cheekpieces nowadays: has raced lazily/made mistakes. *Mrs E. Slack* **h79**

SIGN OF THE WOLF 5 b.h. Loup Solitaire (USA) – Sign of The Vine (FR) (Kendor (FR)) [2004/5 16d⁴ 17v Apr 17] useful-looking horse: smart on Flat, successful 6 times up to 1¼m, including at Pau in January: tongue tied, better effort over hurdles when fourth of 5 finishers in novice at Newbury: will prove best around 2m. *F. Rohaut, France* **h98 +**

SIGNORA PANETTIERA (FR) 4 ch.f. Lord of Men – Karaferya (USA) (Green Dancer (USA)) [2004/5 18s⁶ 16s⁶ 19m⁵ Mar 14] half-sister to fair staying hurdler/chaser Karar (by Shardari) and fair hurdler up to 2½m Karakam (by Rainbow Quest): modest and ungenuine maiden on Flat (should stay 1¾m): poor form over hurdles. *M. R. Channon* **h79**

SIGWELLS CLUB BOY 5 b.g. Fayruz – Run With Pride (Mandrake Major) [2004/5 h87: 17g⁵ 16m⁶ 18m³ 20m⁴ 20d² 17g 19g³ 19g² 20g⁵ 17d³ 20m⁴ 19g³ 16s 16s* 17v⁴ Feb 13] angular gelding: modest hurdler: won novice handicap at Warwick in January: stays 2½m: acts on soft and good to firm going, well below form on heavy: tried in cheekpieces: has hung/jumped right. *J. L. Flint* **h99**

SIKANDER A AZAM 12 b.g. Arctic Lord – Shanlaragh (Gaberdine) [2004/5 c115, h–: c20g² c20g⁶ Feb 17] sturdy gelding: useful hunter chaser: stays 21f: acts on soft and good to firm going: free-going sort, patiently ridden nowadays. *David M. Easterby* **c118** **h–**

SIKASSO (USA) 9 b. or br.g. Silver Hawk (USA) – Silken Doll (USA) (Chieftain) [2004/5 20s 24d 16s 23sᶠ 21d* 22m Apr 23] good-topped gelding: modest handicap hurdler: off 19 months before reappearance: won at Sedgefield in April: stays 21f: acts on soft going: tried in cheekpieces. *Mrs K. Walton* **h90**

SILBERWEIDE (GER) 6 ch.m. Motley (USA) – Stairway To Heaven (GER) (Nebos (GER)) [2004/5 17sᵖᵘ Nov 30] lengthy ex-German mare: half-sister to winning hurdler around 2m Sachsenwalzer (by Top Waltz): won 5 times around 1m on Flat in Germany at 4 yrs: no show in seller on hurdling debut. *M. F. Harris* **h–**

SILENCE REIGNS 11 b.g. Saddlers' Hall (IRE) – Rensaler (USA) (Stop The Music (USA)) [2004/5 c118x, h–: c21g⁵ c24mᵘʳ c20s* c22vᵖᵘ c24g² c19v³ Mar 30] sturdy gelding: useful hunter chaser nowadays: off 9 months (reportedly had wind operation), won at Bangor in February by 5 lengths from Foly Pleasant: stays easy 2¾m: acts on soft and good to firm going, probably not on heavy: blinkered: tongue tied second start: often let down by jumping: inconsistent. *P. F. Nicholls* **c117 x** **h–**

SILENCIO (IRE) 4 b.g. Sillery (USA) – Flabbergasted (IRE) (Sadler's Wells (USA)) [2004/5 16g⁴ 17g² 17g* 17g* 17g* 16d* Oct 5] modest maiden on Flat (should stay 1½m): fairly useful juvenile hurdler: won at Bangor, Market Rasen (twice, beat Schapiro 1¼ lengths in quite valuable event second time) and Stratford between August and October: will stay 2½m: tends to race lazily. *A. King* **h125**

SILENT APPEAL 8 b.m. Alflora (IRE) – Silent Surrender (Nearly A Hand) [2004/5 23s^{pu} 21d 16s^{pu} Feb 3] leggy mare: second in bumper on debut: off 22 months, little show in mares novice hurdles in 2004/5. *Ms Bridget Nicholls* **h–**

SILENT GUEST (IRE) 12 b.g. Don't Forget Me – Guest House (What A Guest) [2004/5 h63: 20s^{5} 24d^{3} 24s^{pu} 24g^{5} 19g Mar 3] leggy gelding: poor handicap hurdler: stays 3m: acts on firm and soft going. *J. D. Frost* **h68**

SILENT GUNNER 7 ch.g. Gunner B – Quiet Dawn (Lighter) [2004/5 h–, F68: 20v c24v^{6} c20v^{F} c24s^{2} Mar 23] workmanlike gelding: no form in 3 starts over hurdles: best effort over fences when second in handicap at Chepstow: stays 3m: raced on going softer than good. *J. S. King* **c89 h–**

SILENT OSCAR (IRE) 6 b.g. Oscar (IRE) – Silent Shot (Random Shot) [2004/5 F16v^{2} Nov 21] €13,500: rangy, rather unfurnished gelding: sixth reported foal: half-brother to 2 winning pointers by Buckskin: dam unraced: useful form in bumpers: built on earlier promise (after 5-month absence) when winning 25-runner event at Punchestown in late-April by 2½ lengths from Ballyagran. *C. P. Donoghue, Ireland* **F108**

SILENT VOICE (IRE) 8 ch.g. Unfuwain (USA) – Symeterie (USA) (Seattle Song (USA)) [2004/5 16d 20d 16g Mar 5] workmanlike gelding: little sign of ability: tongue tied in 2004/5. *Sir John Barlow Bt* **h60**

SILISTRA 6 gr.g. Sadler's Wells (USA) – Dundel (IRE) (Machiavellian (USA)) [2004/5 h–: 18s^{6} 20s^{4} 16d^{3} 16d 16s^{6} 16g Jan 14] angular gelding: poor and ungenuine on Flat nowadays: poor maiden hurdler: may prove best short of 2½m: tried visored, usually in cheekpieces: has had tongue tied: not one to trust. *Mrs L. C. Jewell* **h84**

SILJAN (GER) 8 b.g. Darshaan – Schwarzmeer (GER) (Kings Lake (USA)) [2004/5 20s^{4} Dec 28] twice-raced maiden hurdler. *C. R. Egerton* **h–**

SILK APPEAL 5 b.m. Lord of Appeal – Amazing Silks (Furry Glen) [2004/5 F16d Jan 6] fifth foal: half-sister to bumper winner Itsdedfast (by Lashkari): dam winning 2m hurdler: tailed off in bumper on debut. *D. J. Wintle* **F–**

SILKEN JOHN (IRE) 4 ch.g. Grand Lodge (USA) – Lady Ela (IRE) (Ela-Mana-Mou) [2004/5 16g^{ur} 18d Dec 7] poor maiden on Flat: tailed off on completed start in juvenile hurdles. *J. G. Portman* **h–**

SILKEN PEARLS 9 b.m. Leading Counsel (USA) – River Pearl (Oats) [2004/5 h–: 16s* 20v^{6} c22v* 22s c20s^{5} Apr 22] good-topped mare: fair hurdler won handicap at Hexham in November: better effort in novice chases when winning 2-finisher mares event at Kelso in January: needs testing conditions at 2m, and will stay 3m: acts on heavy going. *L. Lungo* **c103 h102**

SILKEN THOMAS 10 b.g. King's Ride – Padykin (Bustino) [2004/5 c–x, h–: c21d^{5} Mar 10] tall, lengthy gelding: maiden hurdler/chaser: won point in March: has hinted at temperament: sketchy jumper. *Miss S. West* **c– x h–**

SILKIE PEKIN 6 gr.m. Riverwise (USA) – Came Cottage (Nearly A Hand) [2004/5 F–: F17d 16d^{F} Dec 26] well held in 2 bumpers: fell third on hurdling debut. *N. R. Mitchell* **h– F–**

SILK ROAD (SWE) 5 b.h. Diaghlyphard (USA) – Princess Persian (Persian Bold) [2004/5 16d^{3} 16s^{5} 16g* 16s^{2} 16g Oct 30] successful over 1m on Flat in Scandinavia: won at Taby in September on third start over hurdles: well backed, no show in novice at Lingfield on British debut. *A. Hyldmo, Norway* **h?**

SILK SCREEN (IRE) 5 b.h. Barathea (IRE) – Sun Screen (Caerleon (USA)) [2004/5 h124: 16g^{4} 19s 16d^{4} 16v 16v^{6} 16s^{4} Mar 29] good-topped horse: fairly useful hurdler: mainly creditable efforts in competitive handicaps in 2004/5, sixth of 25 to Stutter at Punchestown in late-April: best form around 2m: raced on good going or softer (acts on heavy). *W. P. Mullins, Ireland* **h118**

SILK TRADER 10 b.g. Nomadic Way (USA) – Money Run (Deep Run) [2004/5 c96, h109: c20g c16d^{2} c16g* c20s c19d c16s^{4} Mar 1] leggy gelding: fair handicap hurdler: similar form over fences: won 3-finisher handicap at Doncaster in December: stays easy 2½m: acts on heavy and good to firm going: tried tongue tied. *J. Mackie* **c110 h–**

SILKWOOD TOP (IRE) 6 b.g. Norwich – Brave Mum (Brave Invader (USA)) [2004/5 F86: F17s^{4} F17d^{3} 20s 19s 17s^{5} 22d^{6} 22s^{3} Mar 22] good-bodied gelding: fair form in bumpers: modest novice hurdler: stays 2¾m: raced on good going or softer (acts on soft): wore cheekpieces last 3 starts. *V. R. A. Dartnall* **h90 F90**

SILLY MISS OFF (IRE) 4 b.f. Clerkenwell (USA) – Little Hulton (Teenoso (USA)) [2004/5 F13d Nov 28] first foal: dam, lightly-raced half-sister to Hand Inn Hand, from family of Champion Hurdle winners Morley Street and Granville Again: eleventh of 15 in 3-y-o bumper at Doncaster on debut. *M. Scudamore* **F–**

SILVER BIRCH (IRE) 8 b.g. Clearly Bust – All Gone (Giolla Mear) [2004/5 c120, h–: c26s* c27s* c29v* Dec 28] **c137 + h–**

There were only six runners in the five-year-old maiden at the Askeaton point-to-point, County Limerick, in January 2002. But exactly three years later, two of its participants were prominent in the betting for the Gold Cup and the Grand National respectively, each of them having won major handicap chases in Britain in the meantime. In a further twist of fate, the pair have ended up in the same stable. The chasers in question are Strong Flow, who was the winner of the point, and Silver Birch, who fell. Another element common to the career of both horses is that injury stopped both in their tracks at the height of their powers. Like Strong Flow in the previous campaign, Silver Birch was not seen out after the turn of the year. Hopefully, Silver Birch, who was sidelined in early-March when heat was detected in a leg, will make a full recovery, just as Strong Flow did in the latest season from what was by all accounts a much more serious knee fracture. Silver Birch was the slower developer of the pair (though he did go on to win a point), and whilst Strong Flow enjoyed a meteoric rise in his novice chase season, during which he won the Hennessy Cognac Gold Cup at Newbury, Silver Birch made more measured progress. A maiden at Chepstow was the only success in his novice season over fences, though he did take fourth place when starting joint favourite for the four-mile National Hunt Chase at Cheltenham. But it was not until the start of his second season over fences that Silver Birch began to show what he could do.

Silver Birch made a winning reappearance in a four-runner handicap at Newton Abbot in November, getting the better of a stirring finish with Surefast to win by a neck, conceding more than two stone to the runner-up. Less than three weeks later, Silver Birch was at the other end of the weights in quite a competitive renewal of the totesport Becher Handicap Chase at Aintree. He started 4/1 favourite ahead of the 2002 winner Ardent Scout in a field which also included Grand National winner Amberleigh House (another former Becher winner) and the previous season's Topham winner Cassia Heights, among those with experience over the National fences. Silver Birch's lack of experience in that department was belied by a sound display of jumping, the only anxious moment coming for his supporters with a mistake at the water. Left in the lead when Ardent Scout unseated at the next fence, Silver Birch remained in front all the way to the line, finding plenty under pressure on the long run-in to hold outsider Just In Debt by a length, the pair pulling thirteen lengths clear of another with a good completion record over the course, Smarty.

totesport Becher Handicap Chase, Aintree—favourite Silver Birch (No.11) holds off outsider Just In Debt to add to Ruby Walsh's fine record over the big fences

Coral Welsh National (Handicap Chase), Chepstow—the gamble is landed as Strong Resolve (grey), Chives and 2003 winner Bindaree (white face) are held at the last

With the ground soft, the Becher was run at an unusually steady pace for a race over the National course (Silver Birch's rider Ruby Walsh was seen to particularly good effect), but the emphasis was firmly on stamina when Silver Birch lined up as a well-backed favourite to continue his progress in the Coral Welsh National at Chepstow in December, run on heavy ground. The 2002 runner-up and recent Tommy Whittle Chase winner Chives was next in the betting, ahead of Akarus, the more fancied of two Martin Pipe-trained runners, the Nicholls' stable's second-string L'Aventure and a couple of in-form and lightly-weighted northern challengers, Strong Resolve and Lord Jack. Former winners Supreme Glory and Bindaree were also in the field, and it was the latter who, along with Strong Resolve, helped set a sound pace in the conditions, despite having had to be ridden two miles to the course after his horsebox became stuck in traffic near the Severn Bridge. Ridden a bit more patiently than at Aintree, Silver Birch was one of around half a dozen still with a chance going to four out. At that fence, top weight Take A Stand took a heavy fall when looking sure to be involved in the finish, and at the next Silver Birch jumped to the front between the two long-time leaders. Always in control from then on, though tending to idle in front, Silver Birch ran out a two-length winner from Strong Resolve, with Chives and L'Aventure running on to complete the frame ahead of Bindaree, the first five home covered by little more than five lengths. Silver Birch's win was the middle leg of a treble on the card for jockey Ruby Walsh and trainer Paul Nicholls, the latter winning the Welsh National for the first time as a trainer, seventeen years after winning the race as a jockey on Playschool.

Playschool and Silver Birch share a common ancestor in the form of their grandsire Busted. Silver Birch is by his little-used son Clearly Bust and was one of just seven representatives of his to race in Britain and Ireland in the latest season, and the only winner. Clearly Bust was a fairly useful performer on the Flat, winning three times at a mile and a half, and was of similar merit over hurdles, winning five novice events at two miles, though he stayed longer distances under both codes. Clearly Bust comes from a family that has produced its fair share of jumps sires, his dam being a half-sister to the dam of Torus, Rolfe and King Luthier and to the grandam of Dr Massini.

Silver Birch was sold for just IR 2,800 guineas as a yearling and, close up at least, the female side of his pedigree is nothing out of the ordinary. His dam All

Gone had three runs in Irish bumpers without success and her only other winner besides Silver Birch is an Irish point winner by King's Ride, though she is also the grandam of the fairly useful Irish staying chaser Tell Me See. Silver Birch's year-younger brother Limetree Bay showed some promise in a handful of Irish points before a fatal fall in 2004. Silver Birch's grandam Black Barret was placed in Ireland, both on the Flat and over hurdles, and was a half-sister to an unraced mare named Black-Crash, the dam and grandam respectively of the two biggest names in Silver Birch's pedigree, Wither Or Which and Alexander Banquet. This pair won the Champion Bumper at Cheltenham in the late-'nineties, both of them trained by Willie Mullins. Alexander Banquet, incidentally, provided the then 'highly promising Irish amateur' Ruby Walsh with his first winner at the Festival. Injury interrupted Wither Or Which's career subsequently, but Alexander Banquet made into a top-class chaser and, like Silver Birch, held ante-post favouritism for the Grand National for a time, following his win in the 2002 Hennessy Gold Cup at Leopardstown. Stamina looked his forte, but he failed to complete in both his attempts in the Grand National, and again in the Irish version in the latest season when looking a light of other days.

Silver Birch (IRE) (b.g. 1997)	Clearly Bust (b 1980)	Busted (b 1963)	Crepello
			Sans Le Sou
		Crystal Light (ch 1963)	Never Say Die
			Chandelier
	All Gone (b 1981)	Giolla Mear (b 1965)	Hard Ridden
			Iacobella
		Black Barret (b 1970)	Bargello
			Black Grouse

Still only eight, Silver Birch still has time very much on his side as far as the National is concerned. His thorough stamina, sound jumping and style of racing are all points in his favour in any future tilt at Aintree, as is his proven record over the fences. Yet to be proven is Silver Birch's ability to act on ground firmer than good, having raced almost exclusively on softer than good so far; he clearly goes well in heavy ground. Assuming he recovers fully from his setback, Silver Birch may still be capable of better when he returns given that he has had only eight races over fences so far. His tendency to idle led his trainer to suggest that Silver Birch may be fitted with blinkers in future. *P. F. Nicholls*

SILVER CASTLE 9 gr.g. Roscoe Blake – Pendle Princess (Broxted) [2004/5 c24g* c22g^2 Apr 1] lengthy gelding: successful 3 times in points: won hunter chase at Bangor in March by 3 lengths from Upham Lord: better form when second to Red Brook Lad at Newbury: stays 3m. *R. J. Rowsell* **c110**

SILVER CHARMER 6 b.m. Charmer – Sea Dart (Air Trooper) [2004/5 h112: 21g 24d 16d 21g^2 Apr 14] close-coupled mare: fair handicap hurdler: back to form when second to Inch Pride in listed mares event at Cheltenham: stays 21f: acts on good to firm and good to soft going. *H. S. Howe* **h113**

SILVER CHARTER (USA) 6 b.g. Silver Hawk (USA) – Pride of Darby (USA) (Danzig (USA)) [2004/5 c–x, h–x: 24g^2 26s 19g Mar 3] workmanlike gelding: poor hurdler: no form over fences: stays 3m: acts on good to firm and good to soft going: blinkered/visored in 2004/5: sketchy jumper. *Evan Williams* **c– x** **h82**

SILVER CHIEFTAN (IRE) 7 gr.g. Be My Native (USA) – Mystery Rose (Roselier (FR)) [2004/5 h85: 19d^5 20d May 15] tall, angular gelding: little impact in bumper or over hurdles: sold 3,500 gns Doncaster May Sales, pulled up in point in April. *P. J. Hobbs* **h–**

SILVER CITY 5 ro.g. Unfuwain (USA) – Madiyla (Darshaan) [2004/5 17g^6 Apr 7] half-brother to modest hurdler Found Gold (by Saddlers' Hall), stays 2½m: fair on Flat (stays 1½m), sold out of Mrs A. Perrett's stable 20,000 gns Newmarket Autumn Sales: sixth in maiden at Taunton on hurdling debut: likely to do better. *P. J. Hobbs* **h85 p**

SILVER DAGGER 7 gr.g. Dr Devious (IRE) – La Belle Affair (USA) (Black Tie Affair) [2004/5 h–: 16g 16d^4 20d* 20d^6 22g^{pu} 24m 27d^2 26m^{pu} c20m^3 Sep 19] good-topped gelding: poor hurdler: dead-heated with Star of Germany in seller at Uttoxeter in May: well held in novice handicap on chasing debut: stays 27f: acts on soft going, probably on good to firm: blinkered/visored after first outing: has had tongue tied: ungenuine. *Jonjo O'Neill* **c– §** **h81 §**

SILVER DOLLARS (FR) 4 gr.g. Great Palm (USA) – Marie Olga (FR) (Dom Pasquini (FR)) [2004/5 F16m^5 F16s^4 Mar 22] €120,000 3-y-o: sturdy gelding: first foal: **F88**

dam, 17f chase winner, from family of smart chaser Royal Auclair: fair form in bumpers at Musselburgh and Wetherby: carried head awkwardly on debut. *J. Howard Johnson*

SILVER ENTERPRISE 7 gr.m. Jumbo Hirt (USA) – Gilsan Grey (Grey Ghost) [2004/5 F17s^{5} F17g May 23] fifth foal: dam winning staying hurdler/chaser: signs of ability on first of 2 starts in bumpers. *G. M. Moore* **F–**

SILVER GHOST 6 gr.g. Alderbrook – Belmore Cloud (Baron Blakeney) [2004/5 F–: 19g^{5} 20v^{4} 22d^{6} 21s^{pu} Mar 31] good-topped gelding: modest form first 2 starts over hurdles: tried in cheekpieces. *M. Bradstock* **h93**

SILVER GIFT 8 b.m. Rakaposhi King – Kellsboro Kate (Paddy's Stream) [2004/5 c–, h91: 26g 26g^{4} 27m^{F} 24d^{pu} 27g 24g^{4} 26m^{4} 26g^{5} 26d^{4} 24m Apr 10] leggy mare: failed to complete in 2 races over fences: modest handicap hurdler: would have won but for falling last at Stratford in June: stays 27f: best on good going or firmer: tried blinkered: held up: inconsistent. *G. Fierro* **c– h95 §**

SILVERGINO (IRE) 5 b.g. Perugino (USA) – Silvretta (IRE) (Tirol) [2004/5 16m 16d^{5} c16v^{4} c16s^{5} c16g^{2} c19m* c18m^{2} c16g^{3} Apr 17] rather leggy ex-Irish gelding: fair on Flat (stays easy 9f): modest novice hurdler: left D. Wachman after second start: fair chaser: won handicap at Taunton in March: stays 19f with emphasis on speed: acts on good to firm going: sound jumper: races freely: carries head high, but seems genuine. *Ms Bridget Nicholls* **c102 h95**

SILVER HILL LAD 4 gr.g. Petoski – Miss Madelon (Absalom) [2004/5 F17m Apr 23] 4,000 3-y-o: first foal: dam no sign of ability: tailed off in bumper on debut. *C. W. Fairhurst* **F–**

SILVER INNGOT (IRE) 6 gr.g. Gothland (FR) – Hotel Saltees (IRE) (Over The River (FR)) [2004/5 h92: 16d 19d* 19m^{5} c20d^{4} c16s^{3} c20v* c20v^{4} c19d^{2} c22m* Apr 21] tall gelding: modest hurdler: won amateur handicap at Taunton in October: fair chaser: won novices at Plumpton (handicap) in January and Fontwell in April: stays 2¾m: acts on heavy and good to firm going: has hung left: amateur ridden. *R. H. Alner* **c108 h94**

SILVER JACK (IRE) 7 gr.g. Roselier (FR) – Consharon (IRE) (Strong Gale) [2004/5 h84: 16v^{4} 20v^{5} 16v* 16v^{pu} 17s^{4} Feb 9] leggy gelding: modest hurdler: won novice handicap at Ayr in December: effective over testing 2m, and seems to stay 3m: raced on ground softer than good (acts on heavy). *M. Todhunter* **h90**

SILVER JADE 4 b.f. Silver Patriarch (IRE) – Kinraddie (Wuzo (USA)) [2004/5 F13d F16d Jan 29] 1,000Y: small filly: third foal: half-sister to winner in Norway by Emarati: dam won in Norway: tailed off in bumpers. *C. J. Teague* **F–**

SILVER JEWEL (IRE) 6 gr.g. Roselier (FR) – Martin's Pet (IRE) (Deep Run) [2004/5 F16d F16s^{5} F16d^{5} 22s^{pu} Feb 10] 17,500 4-y-o: sturdy gelding: third foal: dam unraced: modest form at best in bumpers: not knocked about once beaten in novice on hurdling debut: needs to learn to settle. *P. F. Nicholls* **h– p F82**

SILVER LAKE (IRE) 11 gr.g. Roselier (FR) – Over The Pond (IRE) (Over The River (FR)) [2004/5 c–, h–: c33s^{pu} c20g^{pu} c26d^{pu} Feb 20] workmanlike gelding: winning pointer: no form in chases, left S. Breen after first outing: wore cheekpieces/visor in 2004/5: tongue tied last 2 starts. *F. R. Jackson* **c– h–**

SILVER ORCHID 6 gr.g. Fourstars Allstar (USA) – Minster Scally (Scallywag) [2004/5 24d^{pu} Nov 7] sixth foal: dam useful pointer/winning hunter: in frame both starts in maiden points in 2004: no show in novice on hurdling debut. *Ms Bridget Nicholls* **h–**

SILVER POT BLACK 10 gr.g. Ron's Victory (USA) – Haunting (Lord Gayle (USA)) [2004/5 c25m^{6} c23g^{6} c26g* c26g^{pu} c26m^{2} c23f^{5} c25f^{3} Oct 7] leggy gelding: modest handicap chaser: won at Newton Abbot in July from 10 lb out of weights: stays 3¼m: acts on firm and soft going: not an easy ride. *P. R. Rodford* **c86 h–**

SILVER PROPHET (IRE) 6 gr.g. Idris (IRE) – Silver Heart (Yankee Gold) [2004/5 h85+: 17m Apr 9] leggy gelding: fair on Flat (stays 1½m): modest hurdler: raced around 2m: has had tongue tied. *M. R. Bosley* **h97**

SILVER SAMUEL (NZ) 8 gr.g. Hula Town (NZ) – Offrande (NZ) (Decies) [2004/5 c–, h95: c24d^{4} c24s^{pu} c24s^{ur} c24v^{pu} c19s^{pu} c24s^{5} 24d^{pu} c25m^{2} c24g^{2} Apr 15] big, lengthy gelding: winning hurdler: poor maiden chaser: stays 25f: acts on heavy and good to firm going: tried in cheekpieces/blinkers: has had tongue tied. *S. A. Brookshaw* **c77 h–**

SILVER SEDGE (IRE) 6 br.g. Aristocracy – Pollyfaster (Polyfoto) [2004/5 h69: 16m 16g 16s^{4} 20d^{F} 21v^{5} 16s^{2} 16v* 16g 16d^{F} Apr 11] modest handicap hurdler, left J. H. Johnson after fourth start: won novice event at Newcastle in February: stays 2½m: acts on heavy going. *Mrs A. Hamilton* **h88 +**

SILVER SEEKER (USA) 5 gr. or ro.g. Seeking The Gold (USA) – Zelanda (IRE) (Night Shift (USA)) [2004/5 16s^F 16v^6 16v^4 17s 16g^4 16s^6 Mar 11] poor on Flat (seems to stay easy 2m) nowadays: poor form over hurdles. *A. R. Dicken* **h75**

SILVER SILENCE (JPN) 4 b. or br.g. Sunday Silence (USA) – Island of Silver (USA) (Forty Niner (USA)) [2004/5 17v^5 Feb 15] fairly useful but inconsistent on Flat (stays 1½m), sold out of J. Bolger's stable 16,000 gns Newmarket Autumn Sales: tailed off in novice on hurdling debut. *V. Smith* **h–**

SILVER STREAK (IRE) 11 gr.g. Roselier (FR) – Vulcash (IRE) (Callernish) [2004/5 c–, h–: c24s^F c25g^2 Apr 3] tall, good-topped gelding: fairly useful chaser at best, sold out of N. Gifford's stable 15,000 gns Doncaster October Sales after first outing: won 3 times in points in 2005: second to Mister Friday in hunter at Market Rasen: should stay beyond 25f: acts on soft and good to firm going. *Milson Robinson* **c96 h–**

SILVER STYX 6 gr.g. Terimon – Sconie's Poppet (Alias Smith (USA)) [2004/5 F16g^5 21d 16g^{pu} 25s^{pu} c24d^F c23m^{pu} Apr 10] third foal: dam unraced: ran 4 times in maiden points in 2004, third in 2½m event on completed start: no sign of ability otherwise. *J. R. Holt* **c– h– F–**

SILVERTOWN 10 b.g. Danehill (USA) – Docklands (USA) (Theatrical) [2004/5 h–: 19g^{pu} 16m^2 20m* 17g* 17g Mar 18] sturdy, lengthy gelding: useful handicap hurdler: better than ever in 2004/5, winning twice at Musselburgh in December, beating Brooklyn's Gold by 1½ lengths on second occasion, making all: stays 2½m: best on good going or firmer: often races up with pace. *L. Lungo* **h137**

SIMBER HILL (IRE) 11 ch.g. Phardante (FR) – Princess Wager (Pollerton) [2004/5 c113d, h–: c25g^4 May 12] lengthy gelding: fairly useful staying chaser at best: modest nowadays, mainly in points: effective blinkered or not: not a fluent jumper: sold 2,000 gns Doncaster May Sales. *P. J. Hobbs* **c89 h–**

SIMIOLA 6 b.m. Shaamit (IRE) – Brave Vanessa (USA) (Private Account (USA)) [2004/5 h–: 17g Apr 14] sturdy mare: no form over hurdles. *S. T. Lewis* **h–**

SIMLET 10 b.g. Forzando – Besito (Wassl) [2004/5 c98, h107: c25g^2 c21m^2 c21d^3 c27d^2 c24d^6 c25g^2 c24g^3 20v 22d^4 21v* 22g 24g^5 Apr 15] good-topped gelding: fair novice chaser: fair handicap hurdler: back to best when winning at Sedgefield in March: stays 27f: acts on firm and soft going: effective with or without cheekpieces: often tongue tied. *E. W. Tuer* **c101 h110**

SIMON 6 b.g. Overbury (IRE) – Gaye Memory (Buckskin (FR)) [2004/5 16d* 24s^2 22s^2 16v^4 18s^2 20d 20s^3 Mar 28] eighth foal: half-brother to 21f hurdle winner Gaye Fame (by Ardross): dam, dual bumper winner and runner-up only outing over hurdles, sister to very smart staying chaser Black Humour and half-sister to top-class 2m to 3m hurdler Gaye Brief and very smart staying jumper Gaye Chance: fairly useful hurdler: won novice at Wexford on debut in November: better form most starts after, second to Barrow Drive in minor event at Thurles fifth start: stays 3m: raced on going softer than good (acts on soft): consistent. *Philip Fenton, Ireland* **h119**

SIMONOVSKI (USA) 4 b.g. Miswaki (USA) – Earthra (USA) (Rahy (USA)) [2004/5 16g 16g^2 16s^4 17s 16d^6 16d^4 17g 19m Apr 2] sturdy gelding: modest maiden on Flat (stays 2m): fair maiden juvenile hurdler: flattered in Triumph Hurdle at Cheltenham seventh outing: should be suited by further than 17f: acts on soft going. *S. C. Burrough* **h99**

SIMON'S HEIGHTS 4 b.g. Weldnaas (USA) – Star Thyme (Point North) [2004/5 F16g 16g 16d Apr 11] third foal: dam poor novice hurdler: well held in bumper and over hurdles. *Miss P. Robson* **h– F–**

SIMONSTOWN 5 ch.g. Pivotal – Watership (USA) (Foolish Pleasure (USA)) [2004/5 F17g F16d F16d Feb 4] 13,500 3-y-o: sturdy gelding: half-brother to several winners, including smart 21f hurdler Lanzerac (by Lycius) and one-time fairly useful but irresolute hurdler up to 19f Renzo (by Alzao): dam maiden half-sister to very smart middle-distance filly Pink Turtle: well held in bumpers: tongue tied final start. *M. D. Hammond* **F–**

SIMON THE POACHER 6 br.g. Chaddleworth (IRE) – Lady Crusty (Golden Dipper) [2004/5 h–: 17g Apr 14] lengthy, plain gelding: bad walker: tailed off both outings over hurdles: pulls hard. *L. P. Grassick* **h–**

SIMOUN (IRE) 7 b.g. Monsun (GER) – Suivez (FR) (Fioravanti (USA)) [2004/5 h123: 20d^{pu} Feb 24] compact gelding: fairly useful novice hurdler in 2003/4: beaten before halfway in handicap on return: stays 2½m: acts on soft going: tongue tied since debut. *M. C. Pipe* **h–**

SIMPLE GLORY (IRE) 6 br.m. Simply Great (FR) – Cabin Glory (The Parson) [2004/5 F16s 21d 24d* 24g Apr 1] sturdy mare: fifth foal: half-sister to 2 winning pointers: dam never ran: won second of 2 starts in maiden Irish points in 2004: mid-division in bumper: best effort in novice hurdles when winning at Chepstow in March: stays 3m. *R. Dickin* **h89 F–**

SIMPLY DA BEST (IRE) 7 b.g. Lake Coniston (IRE) – Sakala (NZ) (Gold And Ivory (USA)) [2004/5 c16m^{pu} 20s^{4} 16d^{pu} c20s c18d^{F} c16d^{pu} c20s^{F} c20v^{bd} 16v 20v c17v^{F} c20s c16s Mar 26] winning hurdler: no form in 2004/5, including over fences: sometimes wears cheekpieces/blinkers: tongue tied once in bumpers. *J. J. Lambe, Ireland* **c– h–**

SIMPLYFORPLEASURE 6 b.g. Simply Great (FR) – Jupiter's Message (Jupiter Island) [2004/5 F16d Dec 26] seventh foal: brother to smart hurdler/very smart chaser up to 3m Bellator and half-brother to fair hurdler Lord Warford (by Bustino), stays 2¾m: dam unraced: well beaten in bumper on debut. *J. A. Geake* **F–**

SIMPLY GIFTED 10 b.g. Simply Great (FR) – Souveniers (Relko) [2004/5 c135, h–: c20g c20s^{5} c24s^{4} c20d^{4} c21g^{3} c36d^{3} Apr 9] well-made gelding: has reportedly had wind operation: useful handicap chaser: generally creditable efforts in 2004/5, particularly when around 14 lengths third to Hedgehunter in Grand National at Aintree: stays 4½m, raced mainly at much shorter: acts on heavy going, below best on good to firm: has worn blinkers/visor. *Jonjo O'Neill* **c138 h–**

SIMPLY MYSTIC 5 ch.m. Simply Great (FR) – Mystic Memory (Ela-Mana-Mou) [2004/5 F84: F17g^{2} 21d^{3} 19d^{3} 20d* 20g^{2} Jan 21] sturdy mare: fair form in bumpers: progressive over hurdles, winning mares novice at Huntingdon in December: good second to Golden Odyssey in similar event at Musselburgh: will stay beyond 2½m: raced on good/good to soft going: usually held up (ridden more prominently at Musselburgh). *P. D. Niven* **h103 F88**

Mr Steve Hammond's "Simply Gifted"

SIMPLY SAM 10 ch.g. Nearly A Hand – Majestic Spider (Majestic Maharaj) [2004/5 c26v^{pu} Apr 22] fair pointer, successful 3 times in 2004: no show in hunter chase. *Dr C. E. Fry* **c–**

SIMPLY SUPREME (IRE) 8 b.g. Supreme Leader – Some Gift (Avocat) [2004/5 c138+, h120: c20s* Oct 31] leggy gelding: winning hurdler: useful chaser: easily landed odds in intermediate at Carlisle in October: reported in January to miss rest of season through injury: stays 25f: acts on heavy going: usually free-going front runner. *Mrs S. J. Smith* **c138 + h–**

SINALCO (USA) 7 b.g. Quest For Fame – Sin Lucha (USA) (Northfields (USA)) [2004/5 h84?, F–: 20m 16v^{F} 21d^{6} Nov 9] signs of a little ability: lame final outing. *Mrs L. B. Normile* **h–**

SINDAPOUR (IRE) 7 b.g. Priolo (USA) – Sinntara (IRE) (Lashkari) [2004/5 h114: 21s^{pu} 22v^{F} 20m Apr 23] lengthy gelding: fair handicap hurdler: disputing second when falling last in race won by Doof at Newton Abbot in April: no show at Sandown following day: will stay 3m: acts on heavy going: tongue tied in 2004/5. *M. C. Pipe* **h113**

SINDERBY 5 b.m. Factual (USA) – Tanoda (Tyrnavos) [2004/5 F17g^{5} Aug 26] fourth foal: dam 5f (at 2 yrs) to 1½m winner: well beaten in bumper on debut. *M. Brittain* **F–**

SINGING SPIRIT 7 b.m. Opera Ghost – Sulamar (Sulaafah (USA)) [2004/5 F17d Oct 17] second foal: dam unraced: favourite, well held in bumper on debut. *M. C. Pipe* **F–**

SINGULARITY 5 b.g. Rudimentary (USA) – Lyrical Bid (USA) (Lyphard (USA)) [2004/5 h–: 17g^{F} 17m 16m^{F} Aug 30] stocky gelding: no form over hurdles: tried in cheekpieces. *K. F. Clutterbuck* **h–**

SINK OR SWIM (IRE) 7 b.m. Big Sink Hope (USA) – Cragreagh VII (Damsire Unregistered) [2004/5 h–, F85: c25s^{5} 16s Mar 31] no form over jumps. *Mrs Lucinda Featherstone* **c– h–**

SINTOS 7 b. or br.g. Syrtos – Sindur (Rolfe (USA)) [2004/5 F77: F16d^{2} aF16g^{2} Oct 30] fair form at best in bumpers, soon off bridle first 3 starts: will be suited by 2½m+. *Miss A. M. Newton-Smith* **F88**

SIP OF BRANDY (IRE) 12 ch.g. Sharp Charter – Manhattan Brandy (Frankincense) [2004/5 c83x: c25m^{F} Apr 25] angular gelding: winning hunter chaser: stays 25f: acts on good to firm and heavy going: has worn blinkers: often let down by jumping. *Miss J. Hughes* **c– x**

SIR ALF 9 ch.g. Alflora (IRE) – D'Egliere (FR) (Port Etienne (FR)) [2004/5 c25g* c25g^{6} Apr 3] good-topped gelding: won maiden point in 2004: successful in novice hunter at Catterick in March: well held month later: stays 25f: tried tongue tied. *Miss Maria D. Myco* **c98 h–**

SIR ALFRED 6 b.g. Royal Academy (USA) – Magnificent Star (USA) (Silver Hawk (USA)) [2004/5 h89: 16m Sep 19] leggy gelding: winning hurdler: fit from Flat, found nothing only outing (visored) in 2004/5: best with emphasis on speed at 2m: excitable sort (has been early to post): sold 5,000 gns Newmarket Autumn Sales. *A. King* **h–**

SIR BOBBY 4 b.g. Kylian (USA) – Ishona (Selkirk (USA)) [2004/5 F14g^{5} Dec 18] good-topped gelding: first foal: dam unraced half-sister to useful German performer up to 11f Abou Lahab: blinkered, 9 lengths fifth of 18 to The Duke's Speech in 3-y-o bumper at Newcastle on debut. *M. Dods* **F84**

SIR BOB (IRE) 13 br.g. Aristocracy – Wilden (Will Somers) [2004/5 c–, h–: c23s^{pu} c26d^{pu} Mar 12] tall gelding: fair chaser at best, no form since 2002/3: blinkered once: lazy. *P. T. Dalton* **c– h–**

SIR BRASTIAS 6 b.g. Shaamit (IRE) – Premier Night (Old Vic) [2004/5 h84p: 17d^{2} 16m^{4} 19g* Sep 30] fair form over hurdles, winning well-run novice at Hereford in September: stays 19f. *K. C. Bailey* **h104**

SIR CUMFERENCE 9 b.g. Sir Harry Lewis (USA) – Puki Puki (Roselier (FR)) [2004/5 c–: c24s^{3} c23d^{3} c24v^{5} c24s^{2} c26v^{4} Apr 17] rangy gelding: modest handicap chaser: left Miss H. Knight and off over a year before reappearance: will stay beyond 3¼m: acts on good to firm and heavy going: blinkered last 2 starts: usually sound jumper. *Miss Venetia Williams* **c91**

SIR D'ORTON (FR) 9 ch.g. Beyssac (FR) – Prime Target (FR) (Ti King (FR)) [2004/5 c113, h–: c24d^{3} c24g* Apr 7] leggy gelding: fairly useful chaser at one time for **c114 h–**

P. Nicholls: much better effort in hunters in 2004/5 when winning at Taunton in April: stays 3¼m: acts on heavy going: tried visored/blinkered: has found little. *A. J. Tizzard*

SIR EDWARD BURROW (IRE) 7 b.g. Distinctly North (USA) – Alalja (IRE) (Entitled) [2004/5 h92: 20v^{6} 20s 21v^{pu} 19d 20v Feb 15] strong, good-topped gelding: maiden hurdler, out of form in handicaps in 2004/5: should stay beyond 2½m: acts on good to firm and good to soft going. *W. Storey* **h–**

SIR FRANK GIBSON 4 b.g. Primo Dominie – Serotina (IRE) (Mtoto) [2004/5 17d^{5} 17m^{6} 17g 16v^{2} 17d^{3} 17s 18d^{6} 16s Jan 20] angular gelding: poor maiden on Flat (stays 11f): poor juvenile hurdler: tongue tied last 5 outings. *Jane Southall* **h76**

SIR FROSTY 12 b.g. Arctic Lord – Snowy Autumn (Deep Run) [2004/5 c115, h–: c28d^{3} c32d^{5} c29v^{pu} c27s c30d^{5} c28g^{3} c31s* Apr 22] lengthy gelding: fair handicap chaser: won at Perth in April: thorough stayer: acts on heavy going: has had tongue tied. *B. J. M. Ryall* **c99**

SIR GORDON 7 ch.g. Hatim (USA) – Sweet Colleen (Connaught) [2004/5 h–: 24d^{pu} 19m c24m^{pu} 24m^{pu} 24g^{pu} 20m^{pu} Sep 19] no sign of ability: left C. Kellett after chasing debut: tried visored/blinkered. *P. T. Dalton* **c–** **h–**

SIR HAYDN 5 ch.g. Definite Article – Snowscape (Niniski (USA)) [2004/5 16s^{6} Oct 23] good-topped gelding: fairly useful on all-weather on Flat (stays 1¼m), successful 3 times in early-2005, fair on turf: not fluent and always behind in listed novice at Kempton on hurdling debut. *J. R. Jenkins* **h–**

SIR HENBUE 9 ch.g. Henbit (USA) – Owena Deep (Deep Run) [2004/5 22s^{pu} Jun 22] big, lengthy gelding: probably of little account. *G. A. Ham* **h–**

SIR HENRIK (IRE) 7 b.g. Tidaro (USA) – Let'shaveaparty (IRE) (Bowling Pin) [2004/5 c21m^{pu} May 19] €5,000 4-y-o: second foal: dam unraced, out of half-sister to Dawn Run: fourth on only completed start in points/hunter chase. *Mrs D. H. McCarthy* **c–**

SIR HOMO (IRE) 11 b.g. Homo Sapien – Deise Lady (Le Bavard (FR)) [2004/5 h78§: 17g 17m 16g^{pu} Sep 12] ungenuine maiden hurdler: tried blinkered. *E. W. Tuer* **h– §**

SIRIUS STORM (IRE) 5 ch.g. Prince of Birds (USA) – Tender Time (Tender King) [2004/5 F16s F18d^{2} F18s^{3} F18v^{2} 16v* Apr 17] half-brother to several winners, including fair 2m hurdler Final Settlement (by Soviet Lad): dam ran twice: fair form when placed in bumpers: won 18-runner maiden at Listowel on hurdling debut by 10 lengths from Practice Match: better form when fifth to Snoopy Loopy in valuable novice at Punchestown 12 days later. *Paul Nolan, Ireland* **h114** **F90**

SIR LAMB 9 gr.g. Rambo Dancer (CAN) – Caroline Lamb (Hotfoot) [2004/5 19d 19g 17v 21v^{pu} Mar 15] strong gelding: winning 2½m hurdler: no form in handicaps in 2004/5: has been visored, including when successful. *Miss S. E. Hall* **h–**

SIR LAUGHALOT 5 b.g. Alzao (USA) – Funny Hilarious (USA) (Sir Ivor (USA)) [2004/5 16g^{2} 16g* 17g^{3} 16g 16d^{5} 16s 16d^{6} 20s^{pu} Feb 18] close-coupled gelding: fair maiden on Flat (stays 1m): fair novice hurdler: won at Stratford in May: will prove best around 2m: acts on good to soft ground. *Miss E. C. Lavelle* **h106**

SIR NIGHT (IRE) 5 b.g. Night Shift (USA) – Highly Respected (IRE) (High Estate) [2004/5 h95: 16d^{pu} 16d 17s 16d 16d^{5} Jan 1] smallish gelding: winning 17f hurdler: no impact in handicaps in 2004/5. *Jedd O'Keeffe* **h–**

SIR NORMAN 10 b.g. Arctic Lord – Moy Ran Lady (Black Minstrel) [2004/5 c101d, h–: c16g^{5} c16d^{5} c21g^{pu} c21m^{4} c20g^{4} 16g^{6} c19g^{2} c24g^{6} c24g^{pu} Apr 15] tall gelding: maiden hurdler: fair handicap chaser at one time, very much on downgrade, left R. Woodhouse after seventh start: best up to 21f: acts on soft and good to firm going: tried in blinkers/cheekpieces: usually tongue tied: front runner. *Ms Alexandra Moller* **c81** **h60**

SIR OJ (IRE) 8 br.g. Be My Native (USA) – Fox Glen (Furry Glen) [2004/5 h116: 17g* c17s* c17v* c16d* c17v^{ur} c17v^{5} c16g c21g^{4} Mar 17] close-coupled gelding: fairly useful hurdler: improved form when winning intermediate at Killarney in May: successful first 3 starts over fences, maiden at Gowran and Grade 3 novice at Galway in October and Grade 2 novice at Punchestown (needed early reminders when beating Mariah Rollins 2 lengths) in November: would also have won Grade 1 novice at Leopardstown next time but for unseating last: ran twice in 3 days at Cheltenham in March, better effort when fourth to King Harald in valuable novice handicap: best form around 2m: raced on good going or softer (acts on heavy): blinkered after fourth outing. *N. Meade, Ireland* **c136** **h126**

Mr A. Hordle's "Sir Rembrandt"

SIR PANDY (IRE) 5 b.g. Taipan (IRE) – Miss Pitpan (Pitpan) [2004/5 F16s Feb 26] €26,000 3-y-o: useful-looking gelding: half-brother to several winners, notably useful chaser Midnight Caller (by Callernish), stayed 3¼m: dam unraced: never a danger when ninth of 13 in slowly-run bumper at Kempton on debut. *R. H. Alner* **F93**

SIR REMBRANDT (IRE) 9 b.g. Mandalus – Sue's A Lady (Le Moss) [2004/5 c169, h–: c25s² c23d⁴ c24d² c24d⁴ c26g³ c25sᵖᵘ Apr 7] big, strong, lengthy gelding: top-class chaser, in 2003/4, second in Cheltenham Gold Cup: very smart form at best in 2004/5, second in Grade 2 events won by Grey Abbey at Wetherby and Chives at Haydock and third to Kicking King in Cheltenham Gold Cup: suited by good test at 3m, and stays 29f: raced on good going or softer: looked unsuited by right-handed track second outing. *R. H. Alner* **c157 h–**

SIRROCO WIND 5 b.g. Oscar (IRE) – Gale (Strong Gale) [2004/5 F16v Feb 13] first foal: dam unraced daughter of useful staying chaser Dalkey Sound: well held in bumper on debut. *Mrs L. B. Normile* **F–**

SIR ROWLAND HILL (IRE) 6 b.g. Kahyasi – Zaila (IRE) (Darshaan) [2004/5 h89, F95: 21d Nov 12] sturdy gelding: bumper winner: fair novice hurdler: ran well only outing in 2004/5: should stay 3m. *Ferdy Murphy* **h101**

SIR STORM (IRE) 9 b.g. Ore – Yonder Bay (IRE) (Trimmingham) [2004/5 c128, h–: c20m c16d c17g c16v⁵ c16s⁵ Jan 15] lengthy gelding: fairly useful handicap chaser in 2003/4, out of sorts in 2004/5: raced mainly around 2m: acts on heavy and good to firm going: wears cheekpieces. *G. M. Moore* **c– h–**

SIR TALBOT 11 b.g. Ardross – Bermuda Lily (Dunbeath (USA)) [2004/5 c115, h113: c21g² c24dᵖᵘ c24d⁴ c23sᵖᵘ Feb 16] quite good-topped gelding: smart hurdler at best: fairly useful handicap chaser, below form after reappearance: stays 21f: acts on soft and good to firm going. *J. A. B. Old* **c119 h–**

SIR TOBY (IRE) 12 bl.g. Strong Gale – Petite Deb (Cure The Blues (USA)) [2004/5 c102, h–: c20d³ c21gᵘʳ c23m⁵ Apr 10] rangy gelding: fair handicap chaser, off over 10 months after first outing: probably best short of 3m: acts on soft and good to firm going: usually sound jumper: races prominently. *R. Rowe* **c102 h–**

SIR WALTER (IRE) 12 b.g. The Bart (USA) – Glenbalda (Kambalda) [2004/5 c–, h94d: 17d⁴ 20g² 19m² 17g⁵ 22g 16g 19g⁵ 16g* 17d* 17v⁵ 19s 16s² Mar 13] leggy gelding: modest handicap hurdler: left A. Hobbs after first start, Mrs A. Thorpe after fifth: won conditional jockeys events at Worcester in August and Market Rasen in October: stays easy 2½m: acts on good to firm and heavy going: tried tongue tied: usually held up: sometimes finds little. *D. Burchell* **c– h87**

SISSINGHURST STORM (IRE) 7 b. or br.m. Good Thyne (USA) – Mrs Hill (Strong Gale) [2004/5 c80, h82: c26dᶠ c23gᵘʳ c24d⁴ c26d³ c23d c22d⁴ c24s⁴ 26m* 24d⁴ Apr 20] workmanlike mare: poor handicap hurdler/chaser: won at Hereford in April: best at 3m+: acts on soft and good to firm going. *R. Dickin* **c75 h82**

SISTER CINNAMON 7 ch.m. Karinga Bay – Cinnamon Run (Deep Run) [2004/5 F95: 16v* 20v² 19vᵖᵘ Feb 13] lengthy mare: bumper winner: landed odds in mares novice at Uttoxeter in January on hurdling debut: similar form next time: likely to stay 3m: acts on heavy ground. *S. Gollings* **h95**

SISTER GRACE 5 b.m. Golden Heights – Black Spring (IRE) (Mister Lord (USA)) [2004/5 F16d Jan 31] useful-looking mare: first foal: dam, poor maiden hurdler/chaser, sister to Champion Bumper winner/unbeaten hurdler Monsignor: little show in bumper on debut. *N. J. Gifford* **F–**

SISTER O'MALLEY (IRE) 6 b. or br.m. Religiously (USA) – Arctic Laura (Le Bavard (FR)) [2004/5 F17d F16f⁴ F16s 19d 20vᵖᵘ 20g 21g Mar 16] €4,000 4-y-o: sturdy mare: fifth foal: sister to 23f hurdle winner Call Me Ash: dam unraced, from family of high-class chaser Ten Plus: no form in bumpers or over hurdles: tongue tied last 2 starts: sold 1,000 gns Doncaster March Sales. *J. I. A. Charlton* **h– F–**

SISTER PHOEBE (IRE) 6 b. or br.m. Germany (USA) – Elea Victoria (IRE) (Sharp Victor (USA)) [2004/5 F16d⁵ 16sᵘʳ 16s⁴ 21dʳᵗʳ 17sʳᵗʳ c18dᶠ 16s c20d⁶ c20sᶠ Mar 27] sturdy, lengthy mare: second foal: dam unraced sister to useful German 1¼m winner Enigma: little form, left B. Powell after fifth outing (refused to race then and time before): one to avoid. *Adrian Maguire, Ireland* **c– h76 § F66**

SITTING DUCK 6 b.g. Sir Harry Lewis (USA) – Fit For Firing (FR) (In Fijar (USA)) [2004/5 F17v⁶ 21sᶠ 19g 16g⁵ 20d Jan 26] rather unfurnished gelding: third foal: half-brother to winning hurdler/smart chaser Colonel Frank (by Toulon), stays 25f: dam fair staying chaser: sixth in maiden bumper on debut: form over hurdles only when fifth in novice at Huntingdon: should prove suited by further than 2m. *B. G. Powell* **h81 F–**

SIXES AND SEVENS (IRE) 9 ch.m. Aristocracy – Eyrefield Rose (Monksfield) [2004/5 16m Jun 6] ex-Irish mare: no form in varied events, mostly points: sold 1,200 gns Doncaster August Sales. *B. N. Pollock* **h–**

SIX OF ONE 7 b.g. Kahyasi – Ten To Six (Night Shift (USA)) [2004/5 h99: 19g² 16g c16s² c20g⁴ c20d⁴ c20d² c19sᵖᵘ c20gᵖᵘ Apr 22] useful-looking gelding: modest maiden hurdler/chaser: stays 2½m: acts on soft going: wore cheekpieces/blinkers last 3 starts. *R. Rowe* **c98 h99**

SIXO (IRE) 8 gr.g. Roselier (FR) – Miss Mangaroo (Oats) [2004/5 h122: 21g³ c26v* c24d² c33gᶠ Mar 17] leggy, close-coupled gelding: useful hurdler: best effort when third in handicap at Kempton on reappearance: won maiden at Chepstow on chasing debut in January by 3 lengths from Sonnant: useful form when 10 lengths second to comfortable winner Distant Thunder in novice at Newbury: fell fourteenth in National Hunt Chase at Cheltenham: will stay beyond 3¼m: raced on good ground or softer (acts on heavy): often front runner over hurdles: remains open to improvement over fences. *M. C. Pipe* **c138 p h138**

SIX PACK (IRE) 7 ch.g. Royal Abjar (USA) – Regal Entrance (Be My Guest (USA)) [2004/5 c97, h88: c17g⁵ c16m⁵ c16s² c20d⁴ c16m* c16g² Dec 16] good-topped gelding: maiden hurdler: fair handicap chaser: won at Catterick in December: best efforts at 2m on good going or firmer. *Andrew Turnell* **c101 h–**

SIXTIES MELODY 11 b.g. Merdon Melody – Balidilemma (Balidar) [2004/5 c20gᵖᵘ May 29] placed in maiden points, has shown little otherwise. *Mrs K. Bewley* **c– h–**

SIYARAN (IRE) 4 ch.c. Grand Lodge (USA) – Sinndiya (IRE) (Pharly (FR)) [2004/5 F16d³ 16v 16d³ 21s Feb 26] €3,500 3-y-o: leggy colt: first foal: dam, 12.5f winner, **h89 F85**

half-sister to top-class 1½m colt Sinndar: third in bumper at Ludlow on debut: easily best effort over hurdles when third in maiden at same course. *D. R. Gandolfo*

SIZER (IRE) 8 ch.g. Eurobus – Costenetta (IRE) (Runnett) [2004/5 16s 17vpu 16gur Dec 18] 4,500 4-y-o: strong gelding: third foal: brother to fair hurdler around 2m One Cornetto: dam unraced half-sister to one-time fairly useful staying chaser Skillwise: winning pointer: no form in 3 novice hurdles: headstrong. *Mrs S. J. Smith* **h–**

SKENFRITH 6 b.g. Atraf – Hobbs Choice (Superpower) [2004/5 h86: 20v 20v* 20v3 20v6 22v5 24s* 24gpu 27s Apr 22] fair handicap hurdler: won at Ayr in December and Newcastle (improved form, beat A Few Bob Back 11 lengths) in March: stays 27f: best efforts on soft/heavy going. *Miss S. E. Forster* **h112**

SKIBEREEN (IRE) 5 b.g. Ashkalani (IRE) – Your Village (IRE) (Be My Guest (USA)) [2004/5 16g6 Apr 17] fair but none too genuine maiden up to 1½m on Flat: tongue tied, little show in novice on hurdling debut. *Mrs A. M. Thorpe* **h–**

SKIDDAW JONES 5 b.g. Emperor Jones (USA) – Woodrising (Nomination) [2004/5 16sF Dec 6] modest on Flat (stays 10.5f) for Mrs L. Perratt: tongue tied, raced freely and well held when fell last in novice on hurdling debut. *M. A. Barnes* **h–**

SKIDDAW ROSE (IRE) 9 gr.m. Terimon – Whimbrel (Dara Monarch) [2004/5 c66, h66x: 16d6 c16g5 c16fbd Jun 6] small mare: poor maiden hurdler/chaser: stays 2½m: acts on firm and good to soft ground: tongue tied last 2 starts: makes mistakes. *M. A. Barnes* **c– x h– x**

SKILLWISE 13 b.g. Buckley – Calametta (Oats) [2004/5 c94§, h–: c25spu Feb 5] big, workmanlike gelding: veteran chaser, little form since early-2002: blinkered once. *T. D. Easterby* **c– § h–**

SKIP 'N' TUNE (IRE) 8 b.m. Mandalus – Molten (Ore) [2004/5 c26g6 Apr 27] IR 4,300 3-y-o, 4,200 4-y-o: sixth foal: half-sister to winning 2¾m hurdler Richter Scale (by Strong Gale): dam unraced half-sister to Whitbread winner Brown Windsor: fairly useful pointer, successful twice in 2005: sixth of 7 finishers in novice hunter at Newton Abbot on chasing debut. *R. N. Miller* **c–**

SKIPPERS CLEUCH (IRE) 11 b.g. Be My Native (USA) – Cloughoola Lady (Black Minstrel) [2004/5 c139, h–: c20spu c24g Feb 17] big, good-topped gelding: useful handicap chaser: no form either start in 2004/5: stays 25f: raced on good going or softer (acts on heavy). *L. Lungo* **c– h–**

SKYCAB (IRE) 13 b.g. Montelimar (USA) – Sams Money (Pry) [2004/5 c133d, h–: c20d3 c29spu c24d3 c24d3 c24g3 Mar 28] useful-looking gelding: veteran chaser, very much on downgrade: stays 25f: acts on soft and good to firm going. *Mrs L. Wadham* **c96 h–**

SKYE BLUE (IRE) 8 b.g. Blues Traveller (IRE) – Hitopah (Bustino) [2004/5 h–: 16g 22d 22dpu 24g Dec 30] strong gelding: winning hurdler, little sign of retaining ability in 2004: blinkered once. *M. J. Weeden* **h–**

SKYHAWK (IRE) 4 b.g. In The Wings – Babushka (IRE) (Dance of Life) [2004/5 16v* 17g Mar 18] close-coupled gelding: fair maiden on Flat (stays 1½m), sold out of M. J. Grassick's stable €21,000 Goffs October Sale: won maiden at Gowran on hurdling debut in February: much better effort after when fourth of 25 to Strides Of Fire in novice at Punchestown in late-April. *H. de Bromhead, Ireland* **h117**

SKY'S THE LIMIT (FR) 4 gr.g. Medaaly – Highness Lady (GER) (Cagliostro (GER)) [2004/5 16v* 16v2 16s5 Feb 19] fairly useful on Flat (stays 1½m, tried blinkered): sold out of E. Libaud's stable €50,000 Goffs (France) October Sale: won juvenile at Leopardstown on hurdling debut in December: best effort when 1½ lengths second to Strangely Brown in Grade 3 juvenile at Punchestown. *E. J. O'Grady, Ireland* **h126**

SKY WARRIOR (FR) 7 b.g. Warrshan (USA) – Sky Bibi (FR) (Sky Lawyer (FR)) [2004/5 c118, h107: c20m* c21m4 22d5 c22v4 c21d4 c24g3 Apr 7] medium-sized gelding: fairly useful handicap chaser: won at Ludlow very early in season: fair hurdler: stays 3m: acts on soft and good to firm going. *Evan Williams* **c120 h107**

SLALOM (IRE) 5 b.g. Royal Applause – Skisette (Malinowski (USA)) [2004/5 16s 19g 24g6 Mar 3] half-brother to fair 2m hurdler Best of All (by Try My Best): fair on Flat (stays 1¼m), sold out of J. Poulton's stable 15,000 gns Newmarket Autumn Sales: well held in novice hurdles: wore cheekpieces on debut. *P. Bowen* **h77**

SLANEY FOX (IRE) 8 b.m. Foxhound (USA) – Mean To Me (Homing) [2004/5 18m 16m 16g 17d 16s5 c20mF Dec 12] smallish mare: winning hurdler: left Mrs J. Harrington after second start: seemed set to make winning debut over fences when **c93 h–**

falling heavily 2 out in novice at Musselburgh: stayed 2½m: probably acted on any going: tried in cheekpieces and tongue tied: dead. *J. K. Magee, Ireland*

SLANEY LASS 11 b.m. Arctic Lord – Deep Cut (Deep Run) [2004/5 24m³ 22gpu c24m³ 24g³ 20g* Aug 26] angular mare: winning pointer: last of 3 finishers in novice handicap on chasing debut: poor novice hurdler: very fortunate to win mares event at Bangor in August, remote second when left in front 2 out: stays 3m: acts on firm going: tried tongue tied. *R. Lee* **c– h81**

SLEEP BAL (FR) 6 b.g. Sleeping Car (FR) – Balle Six (FR) (Balsamo (FR)) [2004/5 h145?: c17d² c18d³ c19v* c18d² c21gpu Mar 17] angular gelding: useful hurdler: similar form over fences, winning novice at Exeter in February by 18 lengths from Limerick Boy: let down by jumping in valuable novice handicap at Cheltenham: stays 2½m: acts on heavy going. *N. J. Henderson* **c139 h–**

SLEEPING NIGHT (FR) 9 b.g. Sleeping Car (FR) – Doll Night (FR) (Karkour (FR)) [2004/5 c–, h120+: c25s* c25sur c21d* c26g* c25g* Apr 8] **c148 h–**

Whatever their status with courses, bookmakers or punters, hunter chases, and indeed points, can seldom have been more popular with owners. Though bookmakers were influential in reducing the number of hunter chases by twenty per cent in April and May 2005 (and staging them late on afternoon cards), maximum fields contested both the Foxhunter at Cheltenham (for the fifth time in six runnings) and the Fox Hunters' at Aintree, the field at Aintree doing much to support the view that such races provide a twilight career for those well past competing in handicaps (fifteen of the thirty were aged eleven or older). The winner at Aintree, Katarino, while not in his dotage, was returning from a lengthy spell on the sidelines after being a smart hurdler and useful chaser in his younger days (he won the Triumph and the Champion Four Year Old Hurdle and was seventh in the 2000 Champion Hurdle). Back after an even more serious interruption was the Foxhunter winner Sleeping Night.

Before his return in 2005, Sleeping Night had run just once in the previous twenty-two months, having been off after injuring a leg, then fracturing his pelvis. He had been even better than Katarino in his younger days, one of the best four-year-old chasers of 2000 in France before finishing second, showing high-class form, to Sackville in the Charlie Hall Chase on his first start for Mary Reveley. He didn't show quite the same form in three further runs in 2001/2 and ran as if needing the outing on his only run in 2003/4, over hurdles at Newbury, after joining Paul Nicholls. Despite that, if he retained anywhere near his old ability, he was likely to make quite an impact in the gentle waters of the hunter chasing field. If that was to include the Foxhunter, Sleeping Night first needed to gain qualification, by finishing in the first two in two hunter chases (points were not an option if he were to remain in Nicholls' yard) before the end of February. He took in the first hunter chase of the year, at Wetherby in early-February, and made short work of sixteen opponents, another former high-class chaser Legal Right finishing seventeen

Christie's Foxhunter Chase Challenge Cup, Cheltenham—the Paul Nicholls stable plunders the top prize for amateurs again as Sleeping Night (star on cap) holds off Foly Pleasant

betfair.com Handicap Chase, Aintree—a successful switch to handicap company for Sleeping Night as he proves too strong for Zeta's River (spotted cap)

lengths back in second. However, Sleeping Night fluffed his lines at Wincanton five days later, unseating his rider, but he was out again a little over a week later. A third appearance in such a short space of time after his lengthy absence proved no handicap and he won by twenty-three lengths at Fakenham. That meeting took place on the day that the Act banning hunting with dogs came into force. The title of the hunter chase advertised the Holkham Country Fair but others on the card left little doubt where Fakenham's sympathies lay, including the 'Hunting Act'—Unworkable Legislation Handicap Hurdle and the For The Fox's Sake Keep Hunting Beginners' Chase.

Qualification gained, Sleeping Night could be prepared for Cheltenham, with the likelihood that he would hold a leading chance on form. Although twenty-three lined up against him, fourteen started at 40/1 or longer and his main opponents looked to be the Martin Pipe-trained Lord Atterbury, the 2004 Grand National third who had been pulled up when favourite for the Foxhunter that year, the dual winner and Sleeping Night's stable-companion Earthmover and another former handicapper, the Irish-trained Lord of The Turf. The much younger Free Gift, trained by Sally Alner, was also prominent in the betting, though had plenty to find on form. Sleeping Night, whose low jumping style had been thought a possible weakness, coped well with the stiff Cheltenham fences and by the top of the hill, no more than four, Sleeping Night and Lord Atterbury among them, were still in serious contention after the front-running The Wipper fell four out. Sleeping Night took over after the next and responded really well when challenged by the little considered Foly Pleasant, holding on by three quarters of a length, with Lord Atterbury tiring into fourth. Foly Pleasant, a chaser almost as good as Sleeping Night in his prime and bought for 100,000 guineas as a Grand National prospect at the Doncaster Sales the previous May, headed for Aintree along with Lord Atterbury, while Sleeping Night went there too. He had not been entered for the National, though, and connections opted for the valuable twenty-five-furlong handicap over the Mildmay course rather than the Topham (rider Ruby Walsh suggested afterwards that Sleeping Night's jumping might not have been ideal for the National fences). Off a BHB mark of 142, Sleeping Night came home ten lengths clear of the promising Zeta's River in what was not that strong a race for the money, though Sleeping Night showed form some way in advance of that he had produced in hunter chases. The penalty value of Sleeping Night's success at Aintree means he won't be eligible for hunter chases in 2006, but, his convalescence complete, a second crack at the Charlie Hall always appeared to be his initial target in the next season.

Sleeping Night (FR) (b.g. 1996)	Sleeping Car (FR) (b 1988)	Dunphy (b 1978)	Riverman
			Dourdan
		Lorelta (br 1977)	Rose Laurel
			Becky
	Doll Night (FR) (b 1987)	Karkour (b or br 1978)	Relko
			Koblenza
		Sobrette (ch 1976)	Montfleur
			Sadore

Sleeping Night, rather leggy, professionally trained and French bred, is hardly a typical winner of the Foxhunter, though he is not a unique one. The rather lightly-made Observe, by the Prix du Jockey Club winner Rheffic out of a useful Franco-Italian jumper, won the race in 1987 for Fred Winter, having been a high-class chaser in his younger days. Sleeping Night's sire was not quite so good as Rheffic, though Sleeping Car, who fell on his sole appearance over hurdles, was a smart performer at up to a mile and a half and won the Prix du Conseil de Paris. He has sired two horses first past the post in the Grand Steeple-Chase de Paris, the 2005 winner Sleeping Jack and Double Car, who lost the race in 2002 after testing positive for a prohibited substance. Sleeping Car is a half-brother to two good jumpers in Force Atlantique, who was twice placed in the Prix Leon Rambaud for Francois Doumen, and the Prix Alain du Breil winner Sarh. Sleeping Night's dam Doll Night won a fifteen-furlong hurdle at Pau and has proved fecund at stud, though her only other winner from her first twelve foals is Vaguely Night (by Vaguely Pleasant), a minor winner over hurdles. Sleeping Night was a possible for the Scottish National at one stage and he is likely to be effective over distances at up to around four miles. He acts on heavy going and ran respectably on his only start on good to firm. Sleeping Night has reduced vision in his right eye and has been raced predominantly left-handed. Much his worst performance in Britain came at right-handed Huntingdon. *P. F. Nicholls*

SLEIGHT 6 ch.m. Bob's Return (IRE) – Jolejester (Relkino) [2004/5 h70: 17g 19s 26g^{6} 24s^{pu} Mar 31] workmanlike mare: poor maiden hurdler. *W. Jenks* **h74**

SLICK (FR) 4 br.g. Highest Honor (FR) – Seven Secrets (Ajdal (USA)) [2004/5 F16s^{6} Mar 6] €35,000 3-y-o: rather leggy gelding: sixth foal: half-brother to 11.5f winner Six Bells (by Slip Anchor) and 1¼m to 11.5f winner Sevens (by Groom Dancer): dam maiden half-sister to very smart 1m to 10.5f filly Secret Form: favourite, sixth of 16 in maiden bumper at Kempton on debut. *N. J. Henderson* **F83**

SLIGHT HICCUP 5 ch.m. Alderbrook – Very Ominous (Dominion) [2004/5 F16d F14m^{5} F16m Apr 10] third foal: dam unraced: no worthwhile form in bumpers. *C. W. Moore* **F–**

SLIM PICKINGS (IRE) 6 b.g. Scribano – Adapan (Pitpan) [2004/5 F20v F16v* 20v^{3} 20v* 20s Mar 28] half-brother to 3 winners, including 3m chaser Allez Toujours (by Castle Keep): dam unraced: best effort in bumpers when winning 6-runner event at Gowran in January: fair form over hurdles, winning maiden at Leopardstown in March by 2½ lengths from Robert: will stay beyond 2½m: raced only on soft/heavy going. *Robert Tyner, Ireland* **h114 F98**

SLINKY MALINKY 7 b.m. Alderbrook – Winnie The Witch (Leading Man) [2004/5 F–: F16g^{5} F17g 16s^{5} 21d Nov 23] lengthy mare: little sign of ability: wore cheekpieces final start. *D. G. Bridgwater* **h– F–**

SLYGUFF RORY (IRE) 7 ch.g. Fourstars Allstar (USA) – Slyguff Rosey (IRE) (Roselier (FR)) [2004/5 24g^{F} 24g 22v 19v^{2} 20v* 20s^{2} 20s^{4} Apr 13] lengthy, angular gelding: fair handicap hurdler: won at Gowran in February: should stay 3m: acts on heavy going: usually blinkered. *Michael McCullagh, Ireland* **h110**

SMALL SHOTS 8 br.g. Roselier (FR) – My Adventure (IRE) (Strong Gale) [2004/5 22m^F Aug 19] smallish, leggy gelding: no show in 2 starts over hurdles nearly 2 years apart. *C. R. Egerton* **h–**

SMART BOY PRINCE (IRE) 4 b.g. Princely Heir (IRE) – Miss Mulaz (FR) (Luthier) [2004/5 16d 16v^3 17d^3 16s^4 16s^3 17m^6 Apr 13] leggy gelding: half-brother to winning hurdler/chaser abroad by Rainbows For Life: modest on Flat (stays 1¼m), had various trainers in 2004, winning twice for P. Blockley: fair juvenile hurdler: raced around 2m on going softer than good. *C. Smith* **h96**

SMART DESIGN (IRE) 10 ch.g. Good Thyne (USA) – Polly's Cottage (Pollerton) [2004/5 c20g^{pu} c21s^3 c19g^{pu} Dec 9] winning hurdler/chaser, poor nowadays: sold out of M. Hourigan's stable 2,500 gns Doncaster May Sales after first outing: stays 21f: acts on heavy going: sometimes tongue tied: usually makes running. *K. Bishop* **c79 h–**

SMART GUY 13 ch.g. Gildoran – Talahache Bridge (New Brig) [2004/5 c79§, h–: c22m^3 c22s* c20g^3 c22s Feb 4] workmanlike gelding: poor handicap chaser: won at Fontwell (all 4 successes there) in December: stays 3m: acts on any going: wears cheekpieces: prone to mistakes: unreliable. *Mrs L. C. Jewell* **c80 § h–**

SMART LORD 14 br.g. Arctic Lord – Lady Catcher (Free Boy) [2004/5 c–, h65: 17d^{pu} c19m^{pu} May 23] angular gelding: maiden hurdler/chaser: fourth on completed start in points in 2005: stays 21f: acts on firm and soft going: tried visored/in cheekpieces: has had tongue tied. *M. R. Bosley* **c– h–**

SMART MOVER 6 b.g. Supreme Leader – Rachel C (IRE) (Phardante (FR)) [2004/5 F17s* 21d^5 19s^2 19v^{pu} 22g^{pu} Apr 17] €30,000 4-y-o: strong, compact gelding: first foal: dam unraced half-sister to useful Irish chaser Master Aristocrat VI and to dam of one-time top-class staying chaser Lord Noelie: won bumper at Exeter on debut in October by 2½ lengths from Ain't That A Shame: easily best effort on completed starts over hurdles (jumped badly on debut) when second to impressive stable-companion Only Vintage in novice at Hereford. *Miss H. C. Knight* **h105 F104**

SMART SAVANNAH 9 b.g. Primo Dominie – High Savannah (Rousillon (USA)) [2004/5 h123: 16m 16g 16g^3 c20s^{pu} c18d^3 Nov 14] rather leggy gelding: fairly useful handicap hurdler: not fluent both starts over fences, better effort when third in maiden at Fontwell: probably best around 2m: acts on soft and good to firm going. *C. Tinkler* **c112 + h127**

SMART THINKER 4 gr.f. Silver Patriarch (IRE) – Smart Rhythm (True Song) [2004/5 F16v^3 F16d F16d Mar 28] first foal: dam winning pointer: well beaten in mares bumpers. *N. J. Pomfret* **F–**

SMARTY BOOTS (IRE) 6 b.m. Arctic Lord – Solmus (IRE) (Sexton Blake) [2004/5 F84: 16d^4 21v 16d 19g Mar 9] poor form over hurdles. *A. M. Crow* **h76**

SMARTY (IRE) 12 b. or br.g. Royal Fountain – Cahernane Girl (Bargello) [2004/5 c108, h–: c26g^2 c27s^3 c29d^6 c31d Mar 15] tall, close-coupled gelding: useful handicap chaser in his prime, one of only 2 to complete course without mishap when second in Grand National in 2001: placed another twice over Aintree fences, including when third to Silver Birch in Becher Chase in November: stayed 3½m: acted on heavy and good to firm going: often wore headgear: sound jumper: reportedly retired. *M. Pitman* **c117 h–**

SMEATHE'S RIDGE 7 b.g. Rakaposhi King – Mrs Barty (IRE) (King's Ride) [2004/5 F–: 21g 24g^5 16s Oct 20] good-topped gelding: little sign of ability. *J. A. B. Old* **h– x**

SMEORACH 4 ch.f. My Generation – Mohican (Great Nephew) [2004/5 17d^{pu} Aug 28] half-sister to winning hurdler/chaser War Whoop (by Mandrake Major), stayed 3¼m: no form on Flat or on hurdling debut. *James Moffatt* **h–**

SMILEAFACT 5 b.g. So Factual (USA) – Smilingatstrangers (Macmillion) [2004/5 16g^{pu} 16m 16g^6 19g 24d Feb 1] tall, angular gelding: half-brother to winning hurdler Frankie Anson (by Anshan), stayed 3m: last in 2 maidens on Flat: no form over hurdles: has worn off-side pricker. *Mrs Barbara Waring* **h–**

SMILE PLEEZE (IRE) 13 b.g. Naheez (USA) – Harkin Park (Pollerton) [2004/5 c75§, h–: c23m^3 c23g* c23m* c23g* 24m c24d c24g^4 c24d* c26d^F c24g c25m^6 Apr 13] smallish gelding: lightly raced over hurdles: fairly useful handicap chaser: in form of life in 2004/5, winning at Worcester in July and August (twice) and Cheltenham (amateur event) in November: probably stays 3¼m: acts on soft and good to firm going: wears cheekpieces: difficult ride (usually soon off bridle). *M. Sheppard* **c117 § h68**

SMILING APPLAUSE 6 b.g. Royal Applause – Smilingatstrangers (Macmillion) [2004/5 h–: 24m^6 Apr 10] little sign of ability: tried visored. *Mrs Barbara Waring* **h77 ?**

SMITHLYN 8 b.g. Greensmith – Sunylyn (Sunyboy) [2004/5 h89, F99: 23mpu c24d6 Nov 9] workmanlike gelding: modest form over hurdles: well beaten on chasing debut: should stay beyond 21f: tried blinkered. *K. C. Bailey* **c– h–**

SMITHS LANDING 8 b.g. Primitive Rising (USA) – Landing Power (Hill's Forecast) [2004/5 h114: 20d5 24d2 c23m* c23d* c22g2 c24gF c25s2 24d3 c26gur Dec 11] medium-sized gelding: fairly useful handicap hurdler: easily won novices at Worcester in June on first 2 outings over fences: much better form when second to Vodka Bleu and Eurotrek in similar events at Market Rasen: stays 25f: acts on soft and good to firm going. *Mrs S. J. Smith* **c126 h126**

SMITH'S TRIBE 7 gr.g. Homo Sapien – Alice Smith (Alias Smith (USA)) [2004/5 F16g3 F17m5 20m 17g2 20gpu 17g6 17d2 16g 16g4 19s2 Nov 18] lengthy gelding: first foal: dam, modest hurdler/chaser, stayed 3m: third at Ludlow on first of 2 starts in bumpers: modest novice hurdler: stays 19f: acts on soft ground: claimer ridden. *B. J. Eckley* **h96 F92**

SMOKESTACK (IRE) 9 b.g. Lord Americo – Chiminee Fly (Proverb) [2004/5 h–: 16d 24dpu 16spu 20v 20d6 Apr 22] sturdy gelding: maiden hurdler, no form since 2002/3: tried tongue tied. *J. A. B. Old* **h–**

SMOKEY ROBOT (IRE) 12 b.g. Riberetto – Smokey Queen (Proverb) [2004/5 c–, h–: c23s5 Mar 11] rather sparely-made gelding: maiden hurdler/chaser, no longer of any account: has had tongue tied/worn a hood. *D. S. Dennis* **c– h–**

SMOKIN GREY 5 gr.m. Terimon – Wollow Maid (Wollow) [2004/5 F93: 16mur 16dpu 16gF 16d Dec 26] lengthy mare: in frame in 3-y-o bumpers for G. Margarson: has shaped as if amiss since, left M. Gingell after second outing: tongue tied last 2. *L. Wells* **h–**

SMOOTHIE (IRE) 7 gr.g. Definite Article – Limpopo (Green Desert (USA)) [2004/5 h76: 17g6 17g2 17m3 Jun 25] fair on Flat (stays 1½m), won twice in 2004: poor form over hurdles: raced around 2m: wore visor/cheekpieces in 2004/5. *Ian Williams* **h75**

SMUDGE (IRE) 8 br.g. Be My Native (USA) – Crash Call (Crash Course) [2004/5 c–, h98: c19sF Feb 6] workmanlike gelding: modest novice hurdler: fell both starts over fences: stays 2½m: acts on good to soft going: tried tongue tied. *P. F. Nicholls* **c– h–**

SMURFIT (IRE) 6 ch.g. Anshan – Williams Girl (IRE) (Be My Native (USA)) [2004/5 20s3 25d3 20s4 c16v5 c23v6 c22g3 Apr 19] workmanlike gelding: first foal: dam maiden: won maiden Irish point in 2004: modest form over hurdles, poor in chases: stays 25f: acts on soft going. *C. C. Bealby* **c77 h91**

SNAILS CASTLE (IRE) 6 b.g. Danehill (USA) – Bean Island (USA) (Afleet (CAN)) [2004/5 h–: 20spu 17g Apr 3] angular gelding: lightly-raced maiden hurdler, modest form at best. *E. W. Tuer* **h–**

SNAKEBITE (IRE) 5 gr.g. Taipan (IRE) – Bee In The Rose (IRE) (Roselier (FR)) [2004/5 F16d3 F16s2 F17v2 F16g Mar 16] good-topped gelding: third foal: dam unraced half-sister to useful staying chaser Stay On Tracks: placed in bumpers, useful form when beaten 1½ lengths by Karanja at Windsor second start. *M. Pitman* **F109**

SNINFIA (IRE) 5 b.m. Hector Protector (USA) – Christmas Kiss (Taufan (USA)) [2004/5 16f* 16m4 17g3 19s4 22s 19s3 19m4 17d 19g6 Apr 15] fair maiden at best on Flat (stays 1¾m): fair hurdler: won maiden at Worcester in September: stays 19f: acts on firm and soft going: has found little. *G. A. Ham* **h100 §**

SNIPE 7 ch.g. Anshan – Flexwing (Electric) [2004/5 h85: 17g3 20d2 20m* 20g* 20g6 16s6 c20d4 Nov 22] lengthy, angular gelding: fair hurdler: won handicap at Bangor in May and novice at Uttoxeter (simple task) in June: fourth in handicap at Ludlow on chasing debut, mistakes latter stages: stays 2½m: acts on good to firm and good to soft going. *Ian Williams* **c96 h101**

SNITTON SALVO 10 b.g. Cruise Missile – Snitton (Rymer) [2004/5 c24mF c26g3 Jul 16] maiden pointer: apparently better effort in chases (would have finished second) when falling last in slowly-run novice at Stratford: visored. *D. G. Bridgwater* **c73**

SNOOPY LOOPY (IRE) 7 ch.g. Old Vic – Lovely Snoopy (IRE) (Phardante (FR)) [2004/5 F108: 20g* 20v3 20v3 24d3 21g Mar 16] leggy gelding: won both completed starts in Irish points in 2004: bumper winner: useful novice hurdler: won maiden at Hexham early in season and 25-runner 2m event at Punchestown (by 2½ lengths from The Railway Man) in late-April: below form over 3m: raced on good ground or softer: sold to join P. Bowen 120,000 gns Doncaster May Sales. *Miss V. Scott* **h132**

SNOOTY ESKIMO (IRE) 13 ch.g. Aristocracy – Over The Arctic (Over The River (FR)) [2004/5 c66, h–: c16s[5] c20d[3] c20g c16g[4] Mar 4] workmanlike gelding: winning pointer: maiden chaser. *W. T. Reed* **c90 ? h–**

SNOW'S RIDE 5 gr.g. Hernando (FR) – Crodelle (IRE) (Formidable (USA)) [2004/5 20s[3] Mar 22] close-coupled gelding: useful on Flat (stays 2m) at 3 yrs, fair in 2004, sold out of W. Muir's stable 21,000 gns Newmarket Autumn Sales: favourite, 16 lengths third to Lord Rodney in maiden at Wetherby on hurdling debut. *M. D. Hammond* **h93**

SNOWY FORD (IRE) 8 b.g. Be My Native (USA) – Monalee Stream (Paddy's Stream) [2004/5 c119, h–: 20g 20s 22v 20s c17d[6] c20s[6] c24d[6] Mar 11] medium-sized gelding: fairly useful hurdler/chaser, largely out of sorts in 2004/5, left P. Nolan before final start: stays 2½m: acts on heavy going: effective blinkered or not. *P. R. Chamings* **c114 h–**

SNOWY (IRE) 7 gr.g. Pierre – Snowy Gunner (Gunner B) [2004/5 h97, F88: 22m* 24v[6] 24d 24g c24d[3] c25d[2] Apr 11] good-topped gelding: modest handicap hurdler: won at Kelso in October: similar form both starts over fences: stays 25f: acts on good to firm and good to soft going, probably on soft. *J. I. A. Charlton* **c95 h100**

SOBER AS A JUDGE 8 b.g. Mon Tresor – Flicker Toa Flame (USA) (Empery (USA)) [2004/5 16d 16s[pu] Nov 28] quite good-topped gelding: little form over hurdles. *C. A. Dwyer* **h–**

SOBRAON (IRE) 6 b.g. Topanoora – Anniepepp (IRE) (Montelimar (USA)) [2004/5 F111: 16d* Oct 16] quite good-topped gelding: useful form in bumpers in 2003/4: 6/4-on, won novice at Kelso on hurdling debut in October, beating Vitelli comfortably by 6 lengths: looked sure to improve, but wasn't seen out again. *N. G. Richards* **h112 +**

SOCARINEAU (FR) 7 b.g. Assessor (IRE) – Samya King (FR) (King of Macedon) [2004/5 c22d[4] c23d[6] c20s c26g[pu] c18s[pu] c21g[ur] c21d[R] Mar 28] maiden on Flat: maiden hurdler/chaser, raced mainly in French Provinces for B. Spieldenner: won 21f point on British debut: failed to complete in 2 novice hunter chases: stays 2¾m: raced on good ground or softer: tried blinkered. *Tim Brown* **c– h–**

SOCIETY BUCK (IRE) 8 b.g. Moscow Society (USA) – Bucks Grove (IRE) (Buckskin (FR)) [2004/5 h108: 22g[2] 21d Nov 14] smallish, lengthy gelding: fair hurdler: will stay 3m: best efforts on good going. *John Allen* **h114**

SO DETERMINED (IRE) 4 b.g. Soviet Star (USA) – Memory Green (USA) (Green Forest (USA)) [2004/5 16d 16v[6] 16s 18g[2] Mar 12] good-topped gelding: half-brother to fair hurdler Forum Chris (by Trempolino), stays 2¾m: modest maiden on Flat (stays 1¼m) for G. Butler: first form over hurdles when second in maiden at Downpatrick. *J. J. Lambe, Ireland* **h96**

SOEUR FONTENAIL (FR) 8 b.m. Turgeon (USA) – Fontanalia (FR) (Rex Magna (FR)) [2004/5 c17d[5] c16g[2] c18g[3] c20s* c16g c23m[6] c20m[pu] Apr 23] big, lengthy mare: winning hurdler: fair handicap chaser, missed 2003/4: won at Kempton in March: breathing problem next 2 starts, seemed to go amiss final one: will prove best up to 2½m: acts on heavy going: tried in cheekpieces: sound jumper: front runner/races prominently. *N. J. Hawke* **c100 h–**

SOFISIO 8 ch.g. Efisio – Legal Embrace (CAN) (Legal Bid (USA)) [2004/5 16g Oct 7] leggy gelding: maiden hurdler, off over 2 years before only outing in 2004/5: tried blinkered: tongue tied. *Miss S. J. Wilton* **h–**

SOHAPARA 10 ch.m. Arapahos (FR) – Mistress Boreen (Boreen (FR)) [2004/5 c75+, h–: c25m* c24g[pu] Jul 11] fairly useful pointer in 2004: won hunter chase at Hereford in May: lame next time: stays 25f: acts on good to firm ground. *Evan Williams* **c85 h–**

SOLARIUS (FR) 8 ch.g. Kris – Nouvelle Lune (FR) (Be My Guest (USA)) [2004/5 20s c20d[4] 19s 18s[2] c19d* 16g[5] 19g* c22v[pu] c17g Mar 4] angular ex-French gelding: 11f winner on Flat: useful hurdler/chaser at best: claimed from J. Bertran de Balanda €20,000fourth outing: won handicap chase and claiming hurdle (claimed from R. Chotard €13,000) at Cagnes-sur-Mer in December: no show in 2 handicap chases in Britain: stays 2½m: acts on heavy ground. *M. Scudamore* **c121 h122**

SOLAR SON 6 gr.g. Roselier (FR) – Polly Washdish (Oats) [2004/5 F16s Mar 23] third foal: half-brother to winning hurdler/useful chaser Billingsgate (by Nicholas Bill), stays 25f: dam never ran: well held in bumper on debut. *A. King* **F–**

SOLAR SYSTEM (IRE) 8 b.g. Accordion – Fauvette (USA) (Youth (USA)) [2004/5 c116, h–: c19s c24d[pu] c20s c20d[ur] c20s* c24v[ur] c24v[pu] c16s[3] c17v* Apr 2] fairly useful handicap chaser: won at Navan in December and April: probably best up to **c117 h–**

2½m: raced on going softer than good (acts on heavy): none too reliable. *T. J. Taaffe, Ireland*

SOL CHANCE 6 ch.g. Jupiter Island – Super Sol (Rolfe (USA)) [2004/5 h79, F79: 20d³ 22m⁵ 24m² 22dᵘʳ 21v² 26s⁶ 24d 22d 22dᵖᵘ 24d Apr 20] rather unfurnished gelding: poor maiden hurdler: stays 3m: acts on good to firm and heavy going: tried in blinkers/cheekpieces: has finished weakly. *R. S. Brookhouse* **h84**

SOLDERSHIRE 8 b.g. Weld – Dishcloth (Fury Royal) [2004/5 h–: 21g⁵ 20m⁵ 22m² 20s 22sᵖᵘ Mar 9] novice hurdler, easily best effort when second over 2¾m at Stratford: acts on good to firm going, seemingly not on soft/heavy: visored final outing. *S. Dow* **h88**

SOLEIL D'HIVER 4 b.f. Bahamian Bounty – Catriona (Bustino) [2004/5 17m⁵ 17d 17g⁵ 16v³ 16v* 16v⁵ 16v³ 19sᶠ 16d⁵ 16s³ 17m⁵ Apr 9] maiden on Flat: poor hurdler: won 3-runner juvenile handicap at Hexham (final start for P. Haslam) in November: raced mainly around 2m: acts on good to firm and heavy ground: wore cheekpieces final outing. *M. Sheppard* **h73**

SOLEIL FIX (FR) 4 b.g. Mansonnien (FR) – Ifaty (FR) (Rose Laurel) [2004/5 F16m Apr 2] rather leggy gelding: first foal: dam, maiden hurdler/chaser, sister to smart French hurdler Lake Powell: green, never a factor in bumper at Newbury on debut. *N. J. Gifford* **F–**

SOLEMN VOW 4 b.f. Zaffaran (USA) – Quick Quick Sloe (Scallywag) [2004/5 F14d F16g F16s Mar 22] 10,000 3-y-o: leggy filly: second foal: dam, winning pointer, from family of very smart chaser at 2½m+ Addington Boy: well held in bumpers. *P. Maddison* **F–**

SOLERINA (IRE) 8 b.m. Toulon – Deep Peace (Deep Run) [2004/5 h149: 16g⁶ 16s* 20s* 20d* 20s* 16s⁴ 16v⁴ 24vᶠ Feb 13] **h157**

It is a pity for racegoers in Britain that Solerina's sole appearance outside Ireland failed to show her to best advantage. She finished fourth to Iris's Gift in the 2004 Stayers' Hurdle at Cheltenham, not jumping nearly so well as is customary and possibly finding the ground insufficiently testing. Granted her optimum conditions—two and a half miles and ground softer than good—she is a match for most of her contemporaries in terms of ability, particularly in receipt of the mares allowance, and more than good enough to beat them when it comes to gameness and resilience. Her latest eight-race campaign, from October through to the Punchestown Festival, brought a run of four successes before Christmas, which included defeats of Accordion Etoile, Brave Inca and Hardy Eustace and, though things didn't go according to plan afterwards over hurdles, two performances on the Flat in the spring suggested she had lost none of her ability.

Solerina started at odds on for all four of her wins in the latest season, the first two of which came in the Grade 1 John James McManus Memorial Hurdle at Tipperary and the Grade 2 Philips Electronics Lismullen Hurdle at Navan. She won the former by four lengths from Accordion Etoile, who wasn't at his best in the testing conditions (nor was Harchibald in a remote third), and the latter by eight lengths from Rosaker. Next up came the Ballymore Properties Hatton's Grace Hurdle at Fairyhouse, in which Solerina's four rivals included Brave Inca, a good second to Macs Joy at Down Royal on his reappearance, and the Grande Course de Haies winner Rule Supreme, successful under top weight in a handicap at Clonmel earlier in the month. Solerina made the running, as she usually does, and the pace she set had both Brave Inca and Rule Supreme in trouble some way from home.

John James McManus Memorial Hurdle, Tipperary—
front-running Solerina lands the odds from race-rusty pair Accordion Etoile and Harchibald

Brave Inca gave chase from three out but could make little impression on Solerina who showed no signs of stopping and passed the post with a six-length advantage. That was Solerina's second successive win in the Hatton's Grace and two weeks later she went for a repeat win in the Giltspur Scientific Tara Hurdle at Navan. Solerina was one of five who turned up for the Tara Hurdle, which on paper looked a match between herself and Hardy Eustace, having his first outing since winning the Emo Oil Champion Hurdle at Punchestown over seven months earlier, a race in which Solerina had finished sixth. Solerina had conditions a good deal more in her favour at Navan than at Punchestown, racing over half a mile further on much softer ground and, given her fitness advantage, the race did look to provide her with an ideal opportunity to turn the tables on Hardy Eustace. Solerina took full advantage of it. Clearly going best when quickening the gallop four out, she needed only to be nudged along after the last to keep Hardy Eustace at bay, two and a half lengths the winning margin.

Solerina's success in the Tara Hurdle completed a four-timer and took Solerina's record over hurdles to fourteen wins from nineteen starts. Unfortunately, by the end of the campaign that read fourteen from twenty-three as the remainder of her season tapered into anti-climax. Solerina could finish only fourth to Macs Joy in a couple of Grade 1 events at Leopardstown, giving the impression that she ideally needs further than two miles nowadays, while a fall at the sixth, the first of her career, put paid to her chance of taking advantage of what looked an easy opportunity in the Boyne Hurdle at Navan; and then, most uncharacteristically, she failed by a long way to give her running in the Champion Stayers' Hurdle at Punchestown. In the Boyne Hurdle, unusually, Solerina was held up, perhaps due to connections' doubts about her effectiveness at three miles. As well as being thoroughly game and genuine, Solerina is also a tough customer and it will be a surprise if she doesn't bounce back to form in the next season, when third successive

Ballymore Properties Hatton's Grace Hurdle, Fairyhouse—
a second successive win in the race for Gary Hutchinson and his tough partner

Giltspur Scientific Tara Hurdle, Navan—
another 2003 win is repeated, this time at the expense of Hardy Eustace

victories in both the Hatton's Grace and the Tara won't be beyond her; a clash with the smart novice Asian Maze, a pea from the same pod, would certainly be one worth seeing.

Solerina (IRE) (b.m. 1997)	Toulon (b 1988)	Top Ville (b 1976)	High Top
			Sega Ville
		Green Rock (ch 1981)	Mill Reef
			Infra Green
	Deep Peace (ch 1984)	Deep Run (ch 1966)	Pampered King
			Trial By Fire
		Bargy Music (ch 1971)	Tudor Music
			Patsy Brown

The only one of the three mares on the bottom line of Solerina's pedigree to make it to the racecourse was her dam Deep Peace, who gained places at around two miles over hurdles in Ireland and probably stayed two and three quarters. Deep Peace has produced just one other runner of any note, Solerina's stable-companion Florida Coast (by Florida Son) who is a fairly useful two-mile winner on the Flat and a useful winner at up to three miles over hurdles. Solerina, a small, leggy mare, has put up her best performances at two and a half miles but probably stays three. She has been ridden for nine of her successes over hurdles by Gary Hutchinson. Unraced on ground firmer than good, she is very well suited by softer and acts on heavy. Incidentally, Solerina's number of wins overall stands at eighteen, including a bumper and three of her five races to date on the Flat. She is a useful stayer in that sphere, as she demonstrated once again when easily winning a minor event at Tipperary in April for the second successive year and when third in a listed event shortly after Punchestown. *James Bowe, Ireland*

SOL MUSIC 13 ch.g. Southern Music – Tyqueen (Tycoon II) [2004/5 c113d, h–: c21g^3 c16v^3 c16g^4 c19m^3 c21s^5 Jun 22] lengthy gelding: useful hunter chaser at one time, has deteriorated: trained first 2 starts by Mrs V. Graham: stays 21f: acts on any going: front runner. *L. G. Cottrell* **c97 h–**

SOLO DANCER 7 ch.m. Sayaarr (USA) – Oiseval (National Trust) [2004/5 h80: 17g^2 19m^{pu} 22g^{pu} 22f^6 16v^{pu} 19d 22v^{pu} 18s^4 21g^F Mar 28] rather sparely-made mare: poor handicap hurdler: stays 21f: acts on soft going: usually wears cheekpieces, blinkered third start. *Mrs H. M. Bridges* **h80**

SOLVE IT SOBER (IRE) 11 b. or br.g. Carefree Dancer (USA) – Haunted Lady (Trimmingham) [2004/5 c67, h–: c19m^5 c24v^{pu} c19v^2 c20m^4 c24d* Apr 22] good-topped gelding: poor chaser: won selling handicap at Chepstow in April: stays 3m: acts on good to soft and good to firm going: tried blinkered/in cheekpieces: has had tongue tied. *S. G. Griffiths* **c70 h–**

SOLWAY BOB 6 b.g. Bob's Return (IRE) – Solway Moss (IRE) (Le Moss) [2004/5 F17v Mar 20] fourth foal: dam unraced: tailed off in bumper on debut. *L. Lungo* **F–**

SOLWAY FLO (IRE) 7 ch.m. Alflora (IRE) – Oh Dear (Paico) [2004/5 F16f 21vpu 20spu Feb 9] fifth foal: half-sister to bumper winner Solway Dawn (by Minster Son) and winning pointer by King's Ride: dam runner-up in Irish bumpers: no sign of ability. *M. Todhunter* **h– F–**

SOLWAY GALE (IRE) 8 b.m. Husyan (USA) – Some Gale (Strong Gale) [2004/5 c73, h73: 24d c22mF 25g5 c24gpu Feb 16] angular mare: poor hurdler/maiden chaser: trained until after second start by Ms L. Harrison: stays 3m: acts on good to firm going. *L. Lungo* **c– h–**

SOLWAY LARKIN (IRE) 7 b.m. Supreme Leader – In Any Case (IRE) (Torus) [2004/5 F65: F17d F16m 20dpu Jun 30] well held in bumpers: lame on hurdling debut. *Ms Liz Harrison* **h– F–**

SOLWAY MINSTREL 8 ch.g. Jumbo Hirt (USA) – Spicey Cut (Cut Above) [2004/5 h99: 24d5 24f4 24d3 24g3 Jul 1] sturdy gelding: fair hurdler: thorough stayer: acts on any going: tough. *Ms Liz Harrison* **h100**

SOLWAY QUEEN (IRE) 7 ch.m. Rakaposhi King – Spicey Cut (Cut Above) [2004/5 20spu Feb 9] lengthy mare: fourth foal: half-sister to fair staying hurdler Solway Minstrel (by Jumbo Hirt) and modest hurdler/chaser Solway Breeze (by King's Ride), stays 3¼m: dam unraced, out of half-sister to smart 3m hurdler Maelkar: no show in novice hurdle on debut. *F. P. Murtagh* **h–**

SOLWAY RAIDER 7 ch.g. Jumbo Hirt (USA) – Lady Mag (Silver Season) [2004/5 F–: 24g4 20d6 24m5 Jun 5] lengthy gelding: little sign of ability. *Ms Liz Harrison* **h69**

SOLWAY SUNSET 6 br. or b.m. Primitive Rising (USA) – Just Jessica (State Diplomacy (USA)) [2004/5 c24v5 Apr 17] second foal: dam of no account: won 2½m maiden on second start in points in 2005: raced freely when tailed off in hunter chase. *Ms Lisa Harrison* **c–**

SOME GO WEST (IRE) 11 b.g. Un Desperado (FR) – Costly Lady (Bold Lad (IRE)) [2004/5 c20gpu May 13] angular gelding: winning chaser: failed to complete last 3 starts in hunters (placed in points in 2004): stays 25f: acts on firm and soft going: tried blinkered/visored: has had tongue tied. *Mrs Caroline Bailey* **c– h–**

SOME JUDGE 8 ch.g. Rakaposhi King – Si-Gaoith (Strong Gale) [2004/5 h85, F95: 21d2 20d* c20mro c20mF Jun 13] rather leggy gelding: fair form over hurdles: improved effort when winning novice handicap at Bangor in May: would probably have won both starts over fences had he completed: ran out approaching straight in novice handicap at Huntingdon and fell when in front 4 out in handicap at Stratford (visored): should stay beyond 21f: acts on soft and good to firm going: sketchy jumper. *Jonjo O'Neill* **c101 x h104**

SOMEMANFORONEMAN (IRE) 11 b.g. Asir – Wintry Shower (Strong Gale) [2004/5 c–§, h–§: 21g2 24g 24g 20mpu 22g4 27d5 22m6 22f4 Sep 28] rangy gelding: poor hurdler nowadays: stays 3m: acts on heavy going: usually blinkered, also tried in cheekpieces: often makes mistakes: on long losing run. *R. S. Brookhouse* **c– § h83 d**

SOME OPERATOR (IRE) 11 b.g. Lord Americo – Rathvilly Flier (Peacock (FR)) [2004/5 h86x: 19dpu c16d4 c16s5 16v4 c16s c16gF Dec 9] sturdy gelding: winning hurdler: little show in 2004/5, mainly over fences: stays 19f: acts on firm going: headstrong front runner: sketchy jumper. *T. Wall* **c– x h– x**

SOMETHING DANDY (IRE) 12 b.g. Brush Aside (USA) – Hawthorn Dandy (Deep Run) [2004/5 c91, h–: c21d3 c23g4 Aug 24] lengthy, angular gelding: winning hurdler: modest chaser: stayed 3¼m: acted on firm and soft going: dead. *J. A. B. Old* **c87 h–**

SOMETHING SPECIAL 7 b.g. Petong – My Dear Watson (Chilibang) [2004/5 16gpu 17dpu Oct 17] of no account. *H. E. Haynes* **h–**

SOME TIMBERING (IRE) 6 b.g. Accordion – Hard Buns (IRE) (Mandalus) [2004/5 F20g4 F16g* 16s2 19g* Nov 10] lengthy ex-Irish gelding: second foal: dam never ran: pulled up in point: better effort in bumpers (trained by E. Sheehy on first outing) when winning at Worcester in August: fair form in novice hurdles, successful at Newbury in November by ¾ length from A Toi A Moi: should stay beyond 19f. *M. Scudamore* **h112 F89**

SOME TOUCH (IRE) 5 b.g. Scribano – Sarahs Touch (IRE) (Mandalus) [2004/5 F16v F17v2 F17d2 Apr 9] €13,000 3-y-o, resold €9,000 3-y-o: sturdy gelding: fourth foal: dam unraced sister to fairly useful hurdler/chaser up to 21f Bob Devani: useful form in bumpers (trained first 2 starts by T. Horgan), second to Firth of Forth at Gowran and **F114**

The Cool Guy in Grade 2 at Aintree, beaten ½ length at latter after travelling best most of way. *J. Howard Johnson*

SOMEWIN (IRE) 5 b.m. Goldmark (USA) – Janet Oliphant (Red Sunset) [2004/5 F85: F16g 16m^{5} 16gp^{u} 16s 16v^{3} 16v^{6} Dec 17] leggy mare: fair form in 2 bumpers for R. Fahey in 2003/4: little show over hurdles: tried in cheekpieces. *Miss K. Marks* **h– F–**

SOMMELIER 5 gr.g. Tamure (IRE) – Dissolve (Sharrood (USA)) [2004/5 F16s^{3} F16s F16s* Mar 23] 11,000 4-y-o: sturdy gelding: second foal: half-brother to fairly useful hurdler Winsley (by Sula Bula), stays 21f: dam, winning hurdler who stayed 2¾m, half-sister to useful filly up to 9f Karla Wyller: fairly useful form in bumpers, winning at Chepstow in March by 5 lengths from Black Hills: will stay at least 2½m. *N. A. Twiston-Davies* **F101**

SONDERBORG 4 b.f. Great Dane (IRE) – Nordico Princess (Nordico (USA)) [2004/5 16d Oct 31] modest maiden on Flat (stays 1¼m): soundly beaten in juvenile on hurdling debut. *Miss A. M. Newton-Smith* **h–**

SONEVAFUSHI (FR) 7 b.g. Ganges (USA) – For Kicks (FR) (Top Ville) [2004/5 h126§: c22s* c21s^{2} c22s* c24s^{2} c24s* c22v^{3} c22s^{3} c21g c25m^{3} Apr 13] leggy, useful-looking gelding: fairly useful but irresolute handicap hurdler: took well to fences and developed into useful performer, winning maiden at Fontwell in October and novices at Haydock (by 17 lengths from Bunkum) in November and Warwick in December: creditable third to Captain Corelli in novice handicap at Haydock seventh start: stays 25f: acts on heavy and good to firm going: usually blinkered over hurdles: good jumper: formerly held up, ridden much more prominently over fences. *Miss Venetia Williams* **c131 h– §**

SONIC SOUND 6 b.g. Cosmonaut – Sophiesue (Balidar) [2004/5 F–: F16d aF16g^{4} F16g* 16d 16m Apr 2] lengthy, rather unfurnished gelding: left Miss C. Caroe after first outing: fair form in bumpers, won at Huntingdon in January: well held both starts in novice company over hurdles. *P. R. Webber* **h88 F90**

SONNANT (FR) 6 ch.g. Cyborg (FR) – Schwarzente (IRE) (Entitled) [2004/5 c23s^{6} c23d^{ur} c26d^{3} c26v^{2} c26v^{2} c26s^{2} c25d^{pu} Mar 10] has scope: second foal: half-brother to middle-distance winner Schlawner (by Neshad): dam unraced half-sister to smart middle-distance colt Sword Local: well beaten all 4 starts over jumps in France for G. Cherel: won 2½m maiden on second of 2 starts in points in 2004: fairly useful novice chaser: lame final start: stays 3¼m: acts on heavy going: has found little. *C. J. Mann* **c115 h–**

SONNYANJOE (IRE) 7 b.g. Roselier (FR) – Carrabawn (Buckskin (FR)) [2004/5 F104: F17d 16d^{4} 17v^{3} 16g 24v^{6} 22d^{5} 22v^{2} 24s^{5} 24s^{2} 20s^{3} 22v^{3} 22v^{4} 20v^{3} 24s^{5} 22s^{6} 20s^{bd} Apr 13] leggy gelding: bumper winner: fair maiden hurdler: stays 3m: acts on heavy going: tongue tied after eighth outing. *T. Hogan, Ireland* **h101 F89**

SONO 8 b.g. Robellino (USA) – Sweet Holland (USA) (Alydar (USA)) [2004/5 h103: 24f^{3} Jun 6] leggy, close-coupled gelding: novice hurdler, fair form at best: stays easy 3m: probably acts on any going: tried in cheekpieces: has jumped less than fluently. *P. D. Niven* **h93**

SON OF ANSHAN 12 b.g. Anshan – Anhaar (Ela-Mana-Mou) [2004/5 c96, h–: c30d^{3} c27g^{2} May 25] rangy, workmanlike gelding: fair hunter chaser: barely stays 3¾m: acts on heavy and good to firm going: tried blinkered: tongue tied. *G. Tuer* **c99 h–**

SON OF FLIGHTY 7 b.g. Then Again – Record Flight (Record Token) [2004/5 c–, h69§: 19d May 4] good-topped gelding: little show only outing in chases: poor and temperamental maiden hurdler: sold £1,400 Ascot November Sales, won maiden point in January: resold £2,800 Ascot April Sales. *R. J. Hodges* **c– h– §**

SON OF GREEK MYTH (USA) 4 b.g. Silver Hawk (USA) – Greek Myth (IRE) (Sadler's Wells (USA)) [2004/5 18s^{2} 16d 16s^{3} 16g^{6} 16s^{2} 16g* 19m^{2} Apr 2] angular gelding: fairly useful form at 2 yrs for J. Gosden, twice-raced on Flat in Germany in 2004, sold out of A. Schutz's stable 12,000 gns Doncaster August Sales: fair juvenile hurdler: won claimer at Plumpton in March: stays 19f: acts on soft and good to firm going: blinkered last 5 starts. *G. L. Moore* **h99**

SON OF LIGHT (IRE) 10 br.g. Hollow Hand – Leaney Kamscort (Kambalda) [2004/5 c25s^{pu} c24d^{3} Nov 7] useful-looking gelding: fair chaser in 2002/3: off 18 months, modest form on completed start in handicaps on return: stays 3¼m: acts on soft and firm going: visored once: has looked none too keen. *Mrs H. Dalton* **c– h–**

SON OF MAN (IRE) 6 b.g. Turtle Island (IRE) – Zagreb Flyer (Old Vic) [2004/5 F16s F17g 22d^{pu} 20s^{5} 20s 20g^{pu} Jan 24] €7,500 3-y-o: leggy gelding: second foal: dam **h– F–**

unraced, out of half-sister to 2000 Guineas winner To-Agori-Mou: little sign of ability: tried in cheekpieces. *B. D. Leavy*

SON OF ROSS 11 b.g. Minster Son – Nancy Ardross (Ardross) [2004/5 c–, h61: 21g 27m^{F} May 19] tall, angular gelding: no form over fences: poor handicap hurdler: stays 27f: acts on firm and good to soft going: wears cheekpieces. *R. W. Thomson* **c– h–**

SON OF SNURGE (FR) 9 b.g. Snurge – Swift Spring (FR) (Bluebird (USA)) [2004/5 h78?: 22g 20m c20d^{R} 22g^{6} 21m^{6} c16m^{pu} 20s^{4} 21m^{F} Aug 31] well-made gelding: maiden hurdler: no show over fences: stayed 3m: tried blinkered, usually wore cheekpieces: tried tongue tied: sketchy jumper: dead. *W. G. Young* **c– h–**

SOPRANO LASS (IRE) 8 ch.m. Black Monday – Kam Country (IRE) (Kambalda) [2004/5 c76?, h–, F–: c26d^{3} c22m^{pu} c24m^{2} c24m^{3} 26m^{5} Jul 2] sturdy mare: twice-raced hurdler: poor maiden chaser: wore cheekpieces last 3 starts: sold 5,000 gns Doncaster August Sales, third on completed outing in points. *J. G. Portman* **c61 ? h–**

SOROKA (IRE) 6 b.g. Sadler's Wells (USA) – Ivy (USA) (Sir Ivor (USA)) [2004/5 20s 21d^{pu} 19d^{4} 16g 20v^{pu} 22m^{pu} Apr 23] lengthy, angular gelding: brother to useful middle-distance performers Ivrea and Iviza, and half-brother to 3 winners, notably Oaks d'Italia winner Ivyanna (by Reference Point): dam placed at 2 yrs in USA: winning hurdler: bought out of D. Wachman's stable 9,000 gns Newmarket July Sales: lost his way: stays 2½m: acts on soft going: wore cheekpieces/visor last 5 starts: tried tongue tied. *Jennie Candlish* **h88**

SORRENTO KING 8 ch.g. First Trump – Star Face (African Sky) [2004/5 c–, h–: c26d^{pu} 24d^{pu} c21g c25m^{5} Jun 9] smallish gelding: winning hurdler/chaser: no form since 2002, including in point: tried blinkered: has had tongue tied. *C. N. Kellett* **c– h–**

SOSSUS VLEI 9 b.g. Inchinor – Sassalya (Sassafras (FR)) [2004/5 c105§, h–: c20d* c20s^{3} c20s^{2} Dec 1] medium-sized gelding: fair chaser: finally got off mark in 4-runner handicap at Plumpton in November: stays 2½m: acts on soft going: tends to carry head high: not one to rely on. *P. Winkworth* **c112 § h–**

SO SURE (IRE) 5 b.g. Definite Article – Zorilla (Belmez (USA)) [2004/5 h98: 17m^{6} 16m* 17g* 17d^{4} 18m Aug 19] smallish gelding: fair hurdler: won seller at Worcester in June and handicap at Southwell in July: will prove best around 2m: acts on firm and good to soft going: wore headgear in 2004/5: below form on Flat return in spring. *J. G. M. O'Shea* **h104**

SOTOVIK (IRE) 4 gr.g. Aahsaylad – Moenzi (IRE) (Paris House) [2004/5 F14s* F17v* Mar 20] €13,000 3-y-o: sturdy gelding: first foal: dam unraced: fairly useful form when winning bumpers at Carlisle in February and March, beating Master of The Ward ½ length in latter. *A. C. Whillans* **F96**

SOUND BLASTER (IRE) 4 ch.g. Zafonic (USA) – Blasted Heath (Thatching) [2004/5 16d^{4} 16d* 16s^{4} 17g Mar 18] workmanlike gelding: lightly raced on Flat, won over 1m at 2 yrs: sold out of A. Balding's stable 9,000 gns Newmarket July Sales: clearly best effort over hurdles when winning juvenile maiden at Fairyhouse in December by length from Majlis with plenty to spare: blinkered, looked none too genuine in Triumph Hurdle at Cheltenham final start: will prove best at 2m: sold 26,000 gns Doncaster May Sales. *L. McAteer, Ireland* **h115**

SOUND LEADER (USA) 5 ch.g. Diesis – Colledge Leader (USA) (Sheikh Albadou) [2004/5 16s 16v^{pu} 16v Jan 14] poor maiden on Flat (stays 11.6f) at 3 yrs for J. Hills: no show over hurdles. *A. C. Whillans* **h–**

SOUND OF CHEERS 8 br.g. Zilzal (USA) – Martha Stevens (USA) (Super Concorde (USA)) [2004/5 c109, h–: c16s c20s^{2} c20d^{4} c20g* c19d^{5} c19d^{3} c17s^{5} c20g^{6} Apr 15] good-topped gelding: fairly useful handicap chaser: won at Newcastle in December: stays 21f: acts on heavy going: tongue tied: sometimes finishes weakly. *F. Kirby* **c116 h–**

SOUNDS EASY (IRE) 7 gr.m. Roselier (FR) – Skinana (Buckskin (FR)) [2004/5 20m^{pu} 26m^{pu} Jul 2] seventh foal: sister to modest chaser up to 2½m Millbrook Lad and winning pointer Take The Odds: dam unraced: won last of 6 starts in mares maiden points in Ireland in 2004: bought 18,000 gns Doncaster May Sales: no form in maiden hurdles or points in Britain. *P. A. Blockley* **h–**

SOUNDTRACK (IRE) 12 b.g. Orchestra – Misty Boosh (Tarboosh (USA)) [2004/5 c101, h–: c26s^{pu} c24d^{3} May 15] rangy gelding: winning hurdler/chaser: modest form on completed start in hunters, successful in point in April: best at 3m+: acts on any going: front runner. *G. D. Hanmer* **c80 x h–**

SOUTHAMPTON JOE (USA) 5 ch.g. Just A Cat (USA) – Maple Hill Jill (USA) (Executive Pride) [2004/5 h–: 17d 17m^{4} 17m^{ur} 16g^{5} Jul 14] poor maiden hurdler: wore cheekpieces final start. *J. G. M. O'Shea* **h76**

SOUTHBOUND (IRE) 6 ch.g. Zaffaran (USA) – Soxess (IRE) (Carlingford Castle) [2004/5 F–: F16g^{3} F16g^{2} 20m^{4} 17d 17s 18s Dec 5] modest form when placed in bumpers: no form over hurdles, left J. H. Johnson after fourth outing: visored final start. *I. McMath* **h– F83**

SOUTH BRONX (IRE) 6 br.g. Anshan – Tender Tan (Tanfirion) [2004/5 F16m 22m^{5} 16s^{3} 20m^{2} 20g* 16d^{2} 18v^{4} 20s^{6} Apr 7] leggy ex-Irish gelding: ninth foal: half-brother to fair 2m hurdler Montetan (by Montelimar): dam unraced: fair at best in bumpers, left N. Brett after first outing: fair novice hurdler: won maiden at Musselburgh in December: stays 2½m: acts on good to firm and heavy going: tongue tied last 5 starts. *Mrs S. C. Bradburne* **h104 F–**

SOUTHERN COMMAND (IRE) 5 b.g. In Command (IRE) – Pretoria (Habitat) [2004/5 F16s^{3} F16d^{4} 16v 18g Mar 12] half-brother to several winners, including winning hurdler/smart staying chaser Aardwolf (by Dancing Brave) and winning hurdler/fairly useful chaser Waterburg (by Sadler's Wells), stays 3m: dam 7f and 1¼m winner: better effort in bumpers when fourth to King Killone in maiden at Ludlow: tongue tied, well held in maiden hurdles. *M. J. Grassick, Ireland* **h– F89**

SOUTHERNCROSSPATCH 14 ch.g. Ra Nova – Southern Bird (Shiny Tenth) [2004/5 c–, h83: 26s 21g 23s 26s 26m^{4} 24g^{6} Apr 7] strong, compact gelding: veteran staying hurdler/chaser, little form in 2004/5: probably acts on any going. *Mrs Barbara Waring* **c– h75**

SOUTHERNDOWN (IRE) 12 ch.g. Montelimar (USA) – Country Melody (IRE) (Orchestra) [2004/5 c83x, h81: c26g^{5} 26m c26g^{ro} c25s^{2} c25s^{3} c24v^{3} c26d^{3} 24m c24d^{2} Apr 22] sparely-made gelding: poor handicap hurdler/chaser: stays 3¾m: acts on any ground: tried blinkered/visored: ran out last on third outing. *R. Lee* **c79 h–**

SOUTHERN FRANCE (IRE) 8 b.g. Toulon – High Fi (High Hat) [2004/5 22g^{6} 26m^{pu} Jul 2] ex-Irish gelding: half-brother to several winners, including fairly useful hurdler Headbanger (by Wassl Merbayah), stayed 2½m, and Mildred's Ball (by Blue Refrain), dam of top-class staying chaser Rince Ri: dam unraced: modest form in 2 bumpers in 2001 for T. Horgan: no form over hurdles after 3-year absence: tried tongue tied. *B. G. Powell* **h–**

SOUTHERN STAR (GER) 5 gr.g. Sternkoenig (IRE) – Sun Mate (IRE) (Miller's Mate) [2004/5 h86: 16m 16m* Sep 24] easily best effort over hurdles when winning novice handicap at Worcester in September: raced around 2m: acts on good to firm going. *R. C. Guest* **h98**

SOUTHERN VIC (IRE) 6 br. or b.g. Old Vic – Hug In A Fog (IRE) (Strong Gale) [2004/5 16v^{4} 24s^{2} 20s* 20v* 20s^{5} Feb 20] third foal: half-brother to fair but temperamental staying chaser El Hombre del Rio (by Over The River): dam unraced half-sister to high-class staying hurdler Pleasure Shared: winning pointer: fairly useful hurdler: won twice at Leopardstown, maiden in December and minor event (by 4 lengths from Arteea) in January: also ran well when around 5 lengths fifth to Black Apalachi in Grade 2 novice at Naas: stays 3m: raced on soft/heavy going. *T. M. Walsh, Ireland* **h125**

SOUTH SANDS (IRE) 4 b.f. Shaamit (IRE) – Mariners Mirror (Julio Mariner) [2004/5 F12g F16v F16v 22g^{pu} Apr 10] big filly: third foal: dam, fair hurdler/fairly useful chaser, stayed 3¼m: signs of ability only when mid-field in 3-y-o fillies bumper at Newbury on debut. *M. Scudamore* **h– F80**

SOUTHWESTERN (IRE) 6 br.g. Roselier (FR) – Catchthegoose (Tug of War) [2004/5 23d^{3} Feb 19] fifth foal: half-brother to fairly useful hurdler Jakers (by Jolly Jake), stays 19f: dam half-sister to fairly useful hurdler/chaser up to 3m Liver Bird: failed to complete both starts in maiden points in 2005: soundly beaten in 4-runner novice on hurdling debut. *Noel T. Chance* **h–**

SOU'WESTER 5 b.g. Fleetwood (IRE) – Mayfair (Green Desert (USA)) [2004/5 h–: 19g 16s^{5} 19v^{2} c16v^{5} c19v^{4} c20v^{F} Mar 1] angular gelding: form over hurdles only when second in novice handicap at Warwick: poor form in handicaps over fences: stays 19f: acts on heavy going: tried tongue tied. *R. Flint* **c66 h79**

SOVEREIGN GIRL 4 b.f. Sovereign Water (FR) – The Quaker (Oats) [2004/5 16s^{ur} 16d^{F} 16v^{5} 16g^{F} Feb 5] tall, lengthy filly: well beaten in 2 starts on Flat in 2004 for B. Doran: no form in juvenile hurdles. *A. W. Carroll* **h–**

SOVEREIGN'S GIFT 9 ch.m. Elegant Monarch – Cadeau d'Aragon (Aragon) [2004/5 h86: 17d^{5} 17d 16v Jan 21] workmanlike mare: winning hurdler: off 19 months, no sign of retaining ability: stays 2¾m: acts on firm and good to soft going. *Mrs S. D. Williams* **h–**

SOVEREIGN STATE (IRE) 8 b.g. Soviet Lad (USA) – Portree (Slip Anchor) [2004/5 h96: 16g^{3} 17m 17d* 16g^{6} 16m^{4} 16m^{5} 19m* 20m^{5} 16m^{4} 16g* Mar 18] fair handicap hurdler: won at Cartmel in May, Catterick (conditional jockeys) in December and Fakenham in March: barely stays 2½m: acts on good to firm and good to soft going: usually visored/in cheekpieces, effective when not. *D. W. Thompson* **h107**

SOVIET COMMITTEE 5 b.g. Presidium – Lady Magician (Lord Bud) [2004/5 F16g^{6} F16d Jan 29] first foal: half-brother to 2004 2-y-o 6f winner Premier Times (by Timeless Times): dam lightly raced: better effort in bumpers when sixth at Catterick on debut. *T. J. Fitzgerald* **F88**

SOVIET JOY (IRE) 4 b. or br.g. Russian Revival (USA) – Danny's Joy (IRE) (Maelstrom Lake) [2004/5 16g^{2} 20v^{6} 16v^{2} 17g^{3} Apr 3] close-coupled ex-Irish gelding: second foal: half-brother to Irish 6f winner Kompressor (by Petorius): dam, maiden who stayed 8.5f, half-sister to useful winner around 7f Sea Storm: fair juvenile hurdler: claimed from Ms J. Morgan £6,500 second start: likely to prove best at 2m: well held on Flat debut. *D. Carroll* **h100**

SOVIET SOCIETY (IRE) 7 b.g. Moscow Society (USA) – Catchmenot (IRE) (Bluebird (USA)) [2004/5 F81: 16g 17g^{pu} 20g^{3} 22m^{6} Jun 13] ran twice in bumpers: no worthwhile form over hurdles: may prove best short of 2½m. *R. C. Guest* **h–**

SPACE COWBOY (IRE) 5 b.h. Anabaa (USA) – Lady Moranbon (USA) (Trempolino (USA)) [2004/5 h95: 16m^{2} 20s^{6} 16d^{3} 18s^{3} 16d 16s^{ur} 16d 16d 16m Apr 17] useful-looking horse: modest maiden hurdler: best around 2m: acts on soft and good to firm going: tried in cheekpieces, sometimes blinkered: ungenuine. *G. L. Moore* **h95 §**

SPACE HOPPER (IRE) 10 ch.g. Mister Lord (USA) – Kilmalooda Lass (Prince Rheingold) [2004/5 24s^{pu} 25s^{pu} 24m Apr 10] lengthy gelding: won maiden point in 2003: no form in novice hurdles: looked ungenuine on debut: wore cheekpieces last 2 starts. *D. G. Bridgwater* **h–**

SPACE STAR 5 b.g. Cosmonaut – Sophiesue (Balidar) [2004/5 h85+: 16m^{2} 16g^{4} 17d^{2} 17g* 17g^{2} 17m^{pu} Apr 9] compact gelding: fair hurdler: won conditional jockeys handicap at Taunton in March: best around 2m with emphasis on speed: acts on good to firm and good to soft going: held up. *P. R. Webber* **h113**

SPAGHETTI JUNCTION 7 ch.m. Sir Harry Lewis (USA) – Up The Junction (IRE) (Treasure Kay) [2004/5 h90: 22g^{pu} Apr 27] sturdy mare: winning hurdler: no show in handicap only start in 2004/5: stays 21f: acts on soft and good to firm going. *R. H. Alner* **h–**

SPAINKRIS 6 b.g. Kris – Pennycairn (Last Tycoon) [2004/5 h86: 16s^{2} 17v^{2} 17v^{5} 16v^{2} 16v^{6} Jan 29] close-coupled gelding: modest handicap hurdler: probably best around 2m: acts on heavy going: blinkered once: tends to race freely/find little. *M. Todhunter* **h94**

SPANCHIL HILL 5 b.g. Sabrehill (USA) – War Shanty (Warrshan (USA)) [2004/5 h–: 20g 18m 24g 24g^{6} 24g^{5} Jul 30] bad maiden hurdler. *L. A. Dace* **h53**

SPANDAU (NZ) 11 br.g. Fiesta Star (AUS) – Koru (NZ) (Diplomatic Agent (USA)) [2004/5 h80§: 17g^{4} 16g^{pu} 20m^{5} Aug 30] well-made gelding: poor hurdler: stays 2½m: probably acts on any going: has worn cheekpieces/visor: has looked hard ride: none too reliable. *J. C. Tuck* **h83**

SPANISH DOLPHIN (IRE) 6 b.g. Dolphin Street (FR) – Alhambra Palace (IRE) (Cyrano de Bergerac) [2004/5 F16s May 5] 7,500 4-y-o: second foal: dam twice-raced half-sister to smart 2m to 2½m hurdler Bank View: won maiden on completed start in points in 2004: well held in bumper. *P. F. Nicholls* **F–**

SPANISH JOHN (USA) 6 b. or br.g. Dynaformer (USA) – Esprit d'Escalier (USA) (Diesis) [2004/5 16m^{4} 20d* 24m* Aug 1] smart stayer on Flat at one time, fairly useful nowadays: fairly useful form over hurdles: won maiden at Killarney in July and handicap at Galway in August: stays 3m: acts on good to firm and good to soft going: looked capable of further progress, but wasn't seen out again. *P. Hughes, Ireland* **h119**

SPANISH MAIN (IRE) 11 b.g. Spanish Place (USA) – Willow Grouse (Giolla Mear) [2004/5 c29v^{3} c30d c31s^{3} Apr 22] tall gelding: fair handicap chaser: off 22 months before **c108 h–**

reappearance: thorough stayer: acts on good to firm and heavy going: tried blinkered/visored: has had tongue tied. *N. A. Twiston-Davies*

SPANISH POINT (IRE) 8 br.g. Un Desperado (FR) – Molly Murphy (IRE) (Phardante (FR)) [2004/5 c102, h93: c24d^{2} Nov 3] rangy gelding: once-raced hurdler: fair form at best over fences: hung left only start in 2004/5: stays 25f. *D. B. Feek* **c97 h–**

SPARKES 7 b.g. Ballet Royal (USA) – Saxon Lass (Martinmas) [2004/5 F17d F16s 16d Apr 22] first foal: dam, little worthwhile form, out of sister to Triumph Hurdle winner Saxon Farm: tailed off in bumpers and maiden hurdle. *H. J. Manners* **h– F–**

SPARKLING SPRING (IRE) 14 b.g. Strong Gale – Cherry Jubilee (Le Bavard (FR)) [2004/5 c–, h86: 24g^{4} 24g* 27m c24f* Sep 26] smallish gelding: modest handicap hurdler/chaser nowadays: won over hurdles at Uttoxeter (conditional jockeys) in July and fences at Huntingdon in September: stays 3½m: acts on firm and good to soft going. *Evan Williams* **c99 h95**

SPARKLINSPIRIT 6 b.g. Sovereign Water (FR) – Emilys Trust (National Trust) [2004/5 F16d Jan 6] second foal: dam winning pointer: well held in bumper on debut. *J. L. Spearing* **F–**

SPARRON HAWK (FR) 5 b.m. Hawker's News (IRE) – In Memoriam (IRE) (Buckskin (FR)) [2004/5 F16g Mar 26] €60,000 4-y-o: leggy mare: sixth foal: half-sister to fairly useful hurdler/chaser La Zingarella (by Phardante), stays 2½m: dam unraced half-sister to dams of Triumph Hurdle winner Snow Drop and one-time very smart chaser Rubissimo: looked green when well held in bumper on debut. *N. G. Richards* **F81**

SPARTAN PLACE 5 b.g. Overbury (IRE) – Pennethorne Place (Deep Run) [2004/5 F16d^{3} 19s^{F} 19d^{2} 18s^{6} 20v^{3} Feb 15] tall, unfurnished gelding: fifth foal: half-brother to fair hurdlers up to 21f Latimer's Place (by Teenoso) and Penneyrose Bay (by Karinga Bay), former also winning chaser: dam, bumper winner/maiden hurdler, stayed 2¾m: third in bumper at Worcester on debut for G. Balding: fair form over hurdles, best effort when second to Pole Star in novice at Newbury: stays 2½m: raced on going softer than good (acts on heavy). *J. A. Geake* **h112 F87**

SPECIAL AGENDA (IRE) 11 b.g. Torus – Easter Blade (IRE) (Fine Blade (USA)) [2004/5 c110x, h87: 16g c16d^{F} 16m^{5} May 28] strong gelding: fairly useful handicap chaser at one time, very much on downgrade: lightly raced over hurdles: best around 2m: acts on heavy going: tried in cheekpieces/blinkers: has had tongue tied: usually let down by jumping. *M. J. M. Evans* **c– x h65**

SPECIAL CONQUEST 7 b.g. El Conquistador – Kellys Special (Netherkelly) [2004/5 h112, F97: 20s^{6} c23d^{ur} c24d^{pu} c22d^{2} 20g Mar 26] big, workmanlike gelding: bumper winner: fair maiden hurdler: similar form only completed start over fences: should stay 3m: raced on good going or softer. *J. W. Mullins* **c111 h103 +**

SPECIAL CONSTABLE 7 b. or br.g. Derrylin – Lavenham's Last (Rymer) [2004/5 c–, h–: c19g^{5} 16m^{4} Jun 16] of little account: tried in blinkers/cheekpieces: has had tongue tied. *B. I. Case* **c– h–**

SPECIAL PROMISE (IRE) 8 ch.g. Anjiz (USA) – Woodenitbenice (USA) (Nasty And Bold (USA)) [2004/5 h–: 20d^{pu} 22m 20g^{5} 20m 20d^{2} 20g^{3} 22g 21m^{6} Aug 6] poor hurdler: stays 21f: acts on firm and good to soft going: visored last 4 starts. *P. Monteith* **h83**

SPECOTIA 4 ch.g. Spectrum (IRE) – Clan Scotia (Clantime) [2004/5 16d^{6} Dec 2] modest form at 2 yrs for M. Pipe: tailed off in juvenile on hurdling debut. *P. F. Nicholls* **h–**

SPECTACULAR HOPE 5 b.m. Marju (IRE) – Distant Music (Darshaan) [2004/5 h–: 16g^{2} 18m^{5} 16d^{6} 19g^{3} 17d 16f^{6} 17f* 16f 19d^{4} Oct 17] poor hurdler: won selling handicap at Exeter in September: stays 19f: acts on firm and good to soft going. *J. W. Mullins* **h75**

SPECTACULAR (IRE) 6 b.g. Spectrum (IRE) – Azra (IRE) (Danehill (USA)) [2004/5 h81: 16d^{4} 17g^{3} 20m^{4} 20d Jun 30] poor maiden hurdler: probably stays 2½m: tried visored. *F. P. Murtagh* **h76**

SPECTESTED (IRE) 4 ch.g. Spectrum (IRE) – Nisibis (In The Wings) [2004/5 16d 16s Oct 30] workmanlike gelding: fair on Flat (stays 2m), successful in January: no show in 2 juvenile hurdles. *A. W. Carroll* **h–**

SPECTROMETER 8 ch.g. Rainbow Quest (USA) – Selection Board (Welsh Pageant) [2004/5 h141: c17g^{F} c17g* c16g^{2} c16g^{F} c20d^{2} c16g* c22g^{5} c20m^{6} c16d^{F} c20d^{F} Dec 4] leggy gelding: useful handicap hurdler: fairly useful chaser: won novices at Kelso in May and Hexham in September: effective around 2m, barely stays 3m: acts on firm and soft **c115 x h–**

going: effective making running or held up: sometimes drifts left: not a fluent jumper over fences: joined I. Williams. *R. C. Guest*

SPECTRUM STAR 5 b.g. Spectrum (IRE) – Persia (IRE) (Persian Bold) [2004/5 h–: 17dpu 21d5 27d5 17s Feb 7] no sign of ability. *F. P. Murtagh* **h–**

SPECULAR (AUS) 9 b.g. Danehill (USA) – Spyglass (NZ) (Sir Sian (NZ)) [2004/5 h139: c17d* c19d4 c16s* Feb 24] smallish, strong gelding: useful hurdler in 2003/4: just fair form over fences, winning maiden at Market Rasen in May and novice at Huntingdon in February: stays 2½m: raced on good going or softer: likely to progress over fences if brushing up jumping. *Jonjo O'Neill* **c112 p h–**

SPECULATIVE 11 b.g. Suave Dancer (USA) – Gull Nook (Mill Reef (USA)) [2004/5 h–: 22spu Jan 1] of no account: tried blinkered. *J. W. Mullins* **h–**

SPECULIGHT 5 b.g. Spectrum (IRE) – Sprite (Fairy King (USA)) [2004/5 F17s6 F17g May 23] first foal: dam, maiden who stayed 8.5f, half-sister to smart performer up to 1m Niche: weakened closing stages both starts in bumpers: sold 1,200 gns Doncaster May Sales. *G. A. Swinbank* **F–**

SPEED KRIS (FR) 6 b.g. Belmez (USA) – Pandia (USA) (Affirmed (USA)) [2004/5 c?, h96: 24d 24d c17dpu c21d c20m5 c20m3 c24d3 c24g5 22v2 20s3 Apr 21] fair hurdler: generally disappointing over fences: stays 3m: acts on heavy going: wears headgear: ungenuine. *Mrs S. C. Bradburne* **c– § h105 §**

SPEED VENTURE 8 b.g. Owington – Jade Venture (Never So Bold) [2004/5 h98: 21g5 17s 17v2 16v5 20v4 17d4 19s Mar 7] sparely-made gelding: modest handicap hurdler: stays 2½m: raced on good going or softer (acts on heavy): often visored/in cheekpieces: tongue tied: has found little. *J. Mackie* **h98**

SPEEDY RICHARD (IRE) 5 ch.g. Zaffaran (USA) – Chadandy (USA) (Fast Enough (USA)) [2004/5 F–: F17d5 16g6 21dpu 17s 20s c17g c18gpu Mar 20] signs of only a little ability. *M. Scudamore* **c84 ? h– F–**

SPES BONA (USA) 4 b.g. Rakeen (USA) – Novelette (Darshaan) [2004/5 16d 16d 19spu Mar 1] workmanlike gelding: poor maiden on Flat (bred to stay beyond 1m) for W. Haggas: no form in novice hurdles. *G. M. Moore* **h–**

SPIDERS WEB 5 gr.g. Linamix (FR) – Cattermole (USA) (Roberto (USA)) [2004/5 16d 16v 16d 16v3 16g2 16g3 Mar 27] compact gelding: half-brother to smart 2m hurdler Rigmarole (by Fairy King) and fair 2m hurdler Fire Dragon (by Sadler's Wells): poor maiden on Flat (stays 8.5f), sold out of T. Keddy's stable 4,000 gns Doncaster August Sales: best effort over hurdles when runner-up in seller (claimed from F. Murphy £6,000) at Catterick: probably suited by sharp 2m: wore cheekpieces/blinkers last 3 outings: has found little. *G. L. Moore* **h86**

SPIKE AND DIVEL (IRE) 7 b.g. Zaffaran (USA) – Lady Go Marching (USA) (Go Marching (USA)) [2004/5 h90, F90: c16g 16f* 20gpu c23spu Oct 19] lengthy gelding: modest hurdler: won steadily-run maiden at Worcester in September: jumped poorly both starts over fences: should stay beyond 2m: acts on firm and good to soft going. *Jonjo O'Neill* **c– h90**

SPIKE JONES (NZ) 7 b.g. Colonel Collins (USA) – Gloss (NZ) (Kaapstad (NZ)) [2004/5 h96, F92: c17sF Jan 2] medium-sized gelding: maiden hurdler: bought out of J. O'Neill's stable 13,000 gns Doncaster October Sales: fell first in novice at Plumpton on chasing debut: raced around 2m: acts on good to soft going, won bumper on good to firm. *M. Pitman* **c– h–**

SPILAW (FR) 9 b.g. Sky Lawyer (FR) – Spinage (FR) (Village Star (FR)) [2004/5 c–, h–: c26dpu c25spu c24d5 Apr 22] angular gelding: winning chaser: no form since 2002/3: stays 3¼m: acts on heavy going: blinkered once. *John Allen* **c– h–**

SPINOFSKI 10 b.g. Petoski – Spin Again (Royalty) [2004/5 c24d3 c21d4 c24d4 c24v* c24d4 c24g5 c25g5 Apr 12] angular gelding: fairly useful handicap chaser, missed 2003/4: won at Haydock in December, making all to beat Monty's Double 7 lengths: stays 3¼m: acts on good to firm and heavy going: wore cheekpieces third start, tongue tied final one: usually sound jumper. *P. R. Webber* **c116 h–**

SPIRITUAL DANCER (IRE) 10 b.g. King's Ride – Arctic Tartan (Deep Run) [2004/5 h88: 21g3 23spu 22s 25s4 c21spu Jan 18] deep-girthed gelding: novice hurdler: no form in 2004/5, including in handicap on chasing debut: thorough stayer: acts on heavy going: tried visored/blinkered. *L. Wells* **c– h–**

SPITFIRE BOB (USA) 6 b.g. Mister Baileys – Gulf Cyclone (USA) (Sheikh Albadou) [2004/5 24d^{pu} 19v 19g 16g^{4} 16g 16d Jan 28] good-topped gelding: fair on Flat (stays 1½m), sold out of T. D. Barron's stable 4,400 gns Doncaster August Sales: modest form at best over hurdles: blinkered (failed to settle) fifth start. *M. E. Sowersby* **h86**

SPLASH AND DASH (IRE) 10 ch.g. Arcane (USA) – Quilty Rose (Buckskin (FR)) [2004/5 c88: c25s^{4} Feb 15] winning hunter chaser: successful in point in April: stays 3m: acts on soft ground: not a fluent jumper. *Mrs S. J. Hickman* **c–**

SPLASH OUT AGAIN 7 b.g. River Falls – Kajetana (FR) (Caro) [2004/5 h104: 22m^{4} Sep 5] useful-looking gelding: fair hurdler, lightly raced: ran as if amiss only outing in 2004/5: stays 2¾m. *P. Bowen* **h–**

SPLENDOUR (IRE) 10 b.g. Broken Hearted – Black Trix (Peacock (FR)) [2004/5 c130, h–: c25g^{6} c21g^{3} c22m c20v* c22g c24v^{5} c24s^{6} c20s^{3} c16s^{4} c24s^{F} c17v^{5} Jan 16] smallish, leggy gelding: fairly useful handicap chaser: won at Tralee in August by 9 lengths from Ballyamber: effective at 2m to 3m: acts on any going. *Miss S. Cox, Ireland* **c129 h–**

SPORAZENE (IRE) 6 gr.g. Cozzene (USA) – Sporades (USA) (Vaguely Noble) [2004/5 h153: c17s* c17s^{F} Nov 2] **c140 p h–**

One of the best hurdlers to go chasing in the latest season was restricted to just two appearances, a leg injury sustained on the gallops in November enough to suspend Sporazene's new career until 2005/6. According to his trainer Paul Nicholls, the injury is similar to the one sustained by his high-class chaser—and another Flat-bred grey—Call Equiname, who returned to win the Queen Mother Champion Chase, and it was reported in the summer that Sporazene has resumed training. That race could be a target for him if all goes well in the next season. His smart hurdling form shows he has the ability to make his mark in good races over fences. What he lacks at the moment is chasing experience. Sporazene, who won three races over hurdles, including the Champion Four Year Old Hurdle at Punchestown and the County Handicap Hurdle at Cheltenham, made his debut over fences in an eight-runner maiden at Exeter in October. A none-too-fluent jumper of hurdles on occasions, Sporazene jumped well in the main at Exeter, albeit a little big at times, and he landed the odds by thirteen lengths with plenty to spare after taking up the running on the bridle four out. Sporazene was again odds on when returned to Exeter two weeks later for a novice chase, but he fell four out when in second place behind all-the-way winner Ashley Brook, eight lengths down at the time, though just beginning to reduce the deficit. That performance looked rather better at the end of the season than it did at the time. All but one of Sporazene's eleven races over jumps have been at around two miles, and he shapes as though he will always be best at that trip. Tried at two and a half miles in the 2004 Aintree Hurdle, Sporazene faced a stiff task and finished last of eleven behind Rhinestone Cowboy. Sporazene, a tall, lengthy, angular gelding who usually impresses in appearance, has raced on good ground or softer, apart from when easily completing a simple task in a juvenile hurdle run on good to firm. *P. F. Nicholls*

SPORTING CHANCE 13 ch.g. Ikdam – Tumbling Ego (Abednego) [2004/5 c76, h–: c21g^{ur} c21d* c21d^{3} c24g^{ur} Apr 7] sturdy gelding: fair hunter chaser: won at Newton Abbot in May: stays 3m: acts on firm and good to soft going: not a fluent jumper. *Mrs Jo Sleep* **c101 x h–**

SPORTING HERO 5 b.g. Safawan – Cryptic Gold (Glint of Gold) [2004/5 h76, F–: 21g^{pu} Apr 30] poor form over hurdles: sold 4,600 gns Doncaster August Sales: successful only completed start in points. *M. W. Easterby* **h–**

SPORTS EXPRESS 7 ch.m. Then Again – Lady St Lawrence (USA) (Bering) [2004/5 h87: 20s^{2} 20v^{2} Nov 6] quite good-topped mare: modest novice hurdler: stays 2½m: acts on heavy going: wore cheekpieces in 2004/5. *Miss Lucinda V. Russell* **h90**

SPORTULA 4 b.f. Silver Patriarch (IRE) – Portent (Most Welcome) [2004/5 17d^{3} Aug 28] well beaten in maidens at 2 yrs, sold out of Mrs A. Perrett's stable 2,100 gns Newmarket July (2004) Sales: not knocked about when third in juvenile at Cartmel on hurdling debut. *C. Grant* **h89 +**

SPOT IN TIME 5 b.m. Mtoto – Kelimutu (Top Ville) [2004/5 F86: 24v^{pu} 21v^{pu} Mar 15] fair form in bumper on debut for J. Pearce: no show both starts over hurdles. *I. W. McInnes* **h–**

SPOT THEDIFFERENCE (IRE) 12 b.g. Lafontaine (USA) – Spotted Choice (IRE) (Callernish) [2004/5 c129, h93: c34g* c19s c31d* c31d* 16v4 c31d* c36d Apr 9] **c146 ? h–**

In the tenth year after McGregor The Third won the inaugural Sporting Index Chase at Cheltenham, a cross-country chase was staged for the first time at the Cheltenham Festival. The Sporting Index Handicap Chase, the fifth race of six on Champion Hurdle day, attracted a maximum field of sixteen with top weight carried by Spot Thedifference, already winner of the two previous races over the course in 2004/5, and with Comanche War Paint starting favourite at 100/30. The Cheltenham executive and sponsors Sporting Index have devoted a good deal of energy and expenditure to reach this point, but it remains to be seen whether cross-country races have anything more than novelty value within National Hunt racing in Britain. The way in which the races are run, the largely ageing profile of the runners and the lack of a tradition of cross-country races all need to be overcome. Cross-country racing is deeply embedded in the racing culture of other countries. At Pardubice, in the Czech Republic, such chases are the norm and the race with the greatest prestige and history is a cross-country event. The same applies at some of the major French tracks outside Paris, such as Pau and Craon, as it does at Punchestown, where until the 'sixties the races were all staged over banks. There seems little prospect of cross-country chasing in Britain spreading beyond Cheltenham, nor of many more than three races being staged there. Right from the start, the cross-country races at Cheltenham have attracted very few up-and-coming runners and plenty of has-beens. The first race included the thirteen-year-old Docklands Express and two fourteen-year-olds, one of them Fiddlers Pike, both good horses in their prime but well past it when they ran at Cheltenham. None of the sixteen who lined up in the first cross-country race at the Festival were that ancient, though all but three were ten or older. Seven of the sixteen had been useful or better in conventional steeplechases at one time, though whether any of them still were was debatable. The way in which races over the course tend to be run probably doesn't help either, a steady pace with the race only taking shape in the closing stages, sometimes as late as two out, having become the norm. Finally, the course itself generally lacks the challenges provided by some of the more demanding fences elsewhere, the Taxis or the double of hedges at Pardubice, the double banks at Punchestown, fences which take some negotiating on the part of both horse and rider. The introduction of a double of hedges to the part of the course nearest the stands in 2005/6 should make the Cheltenham course a little more complex. Perhaps the Cheltenham bars will be a little less crowded for the next Festival running.

Sporting Index Handicap Chase (Cross Country), Cheltenham—
Spot Thedifference leads the field off the bank

Sporting Index Handicap Chase (Cross Country), Cheltenham—
Spot Thedifference (hoops) tracks Lord Noelie and Village King (checked cap)
on the way to his third Cheltenham cross-country win of 2004/5

Spot Thedifference wasn't asked to tackle the cross-country course at Cheltenham until the latest season, though he would almost certainly have done so in the previous one had not the two scheduled races in the autumn been lost to the particularly dry weather. By the start of 2004, Spot Thedifference hadn't won outside of points since the summer of 2001, when he completed a hat-trick in a handicap at Kilbeggan off a mark of 111, and his record, apart from a second to Jurancon II in the 2003 Summer National at Uttoxeter, was singularly disappointing. His appearances in the spring of 2004 suggested he might require a new challenge. He was a remote fifth in both the Foxhunter at Cheltenham, for which he started third favourite, and in the Grand National at Aintree, and then won the La Touche Cup at Punchestown very early in the new British season, having to show just modest form there. Returning from a six-month break, Spot Thedifference was last of fifteen in a handicap chase at Naas, going with little zest, albeit over an inadequate trip. Cheltenham less than two weeks later showed him in a very different light, even if he was fortunate to win the Sporting Index Chase after Registana'a rider Peter Gehm took the wrong course going to two out. Spot Thedifference went on to beat Star Performance by three quarters of a length, and followed up in the two handicaps that complete the series of races, the first at the December meeting. With no Registana in the line-up, Spot Thedifference overcame the efforts of the BHB handicapper to take his measure, beating French Executive four lengths on the first occasion and Luzcadou two and a half lengths on the second. A truer pace than usual probably played into his hands in the race at the Festival, as he ran rather in snatches before staying on to lead at the last. The weights for both of the handicaps in theory favoured those that hadn't previously run on the course, but it didn't turn out like that, confirming the suspicion that cross-country racing is different. Spot Thedifference went some way to confirming the view himself. He ran in the Grand National at Aintree where, in theory, he was well treated off a mark 7 lb lower than at Cheltenham, but he jumped poorly and was soon toiling. Spot Thedifference was due to bid for the La Touche Cup again shortly after the end of the British season, but injury prevented this, along with the chance of winning the bonus for adding the La Touche Cup to the Sporting Index Handicap at the Cheltenham Festival. With his owner reportedly having little interest in the Velka Pardubicka, even though the horse has been entered for the next edition, Spot Thedifference is again likely to be aimed at Cheltenham's cross-country races in 2005/6. The win at the Festival represents the best form of his career so it should not be thought that age and the handicapper are automatically sure to catch up with him. Spot Thedifference was a second Cheltenham Festival winner for his rider John Thomas McNamara, who was seen to good advantage, just as he had been in coaxing home the unwilling Rith Dubh in the National Hunt Chase in 2002.

Spot Thedifference (IRE) (b.g. 1993)	Lafontaine (USA) (b 1977)	Sham (b 1970)	Pretense
			Sequoia
		Valya (b 1965)	Vandale
			Lilya
	Spotted Choice (IRE) (ch 1988)	Callernish (br 1977)	Lord Gayle
			Azurine
		Mourne Lass (ch 1972)	Hereford
			Fine Trix

The tall Spot Thedifference is the first of three foals and only runner out of the unraced Spotted Choice. Her dam Mourne Lass, who was placed over hurdles and in a point, produced five minor winners, including the staying chaser Double Trix. Mourne Lass is half-sister to the dam of the useful staying chaser Torside and to the grandam of another, the Thyestes Chase winner Mweenish. She is also a half-sister to the 1968 Galway Hurdle winner Annalong. The third dam Fine Trix is half-sister to the grandam of some more notable performers, Atone, who won the Ladbroke and the Arkle at Leopardstown, and the useful chaser at up to two and a half miles Music Be Magic. Fine Trix was a half-sister to the smart staying chaser Vultrix. Spot Thedifference is ideally suited by long distances but seems unbeholden to the ground, having shown form on going ranging from good to firm to heavy. He has been tried once each in blinkers and cheekpieces, performing above his recent form at the time on each occasion. *E. Bolger, Ireland*

SPREAD THE DREAM 7 ch.g. Alflora (IRE) – Cauchemar (Hot Brandy) [2004/5 h77: 17s^2 21d^6 19s Feb 17] novice hurdler: best effort when second to easy winner Salsalino at Exeter: should be suited by further than 17f. *N. J. Henderson* **h97**

SPREEJINSKY 7 ch.g. Dancing Spree (USA) – Smooth Flight (Sandhurst Prince) [2004/5 F16g^{pu} F16g^{pu} Sep 12] medium-sized gelding: fifth foal: dam fair 1m winner: no sign of ability: sold £450 Ascot October Sales. *M. J. Gingell* **F–**

SPREE VISION 9 b.g. Suave Dancer (USA) – Regent's Folly (IRE) (Touching Wood (USA)) [2004/5 h82: 16g^4 16d^3 17g^2 16m^2 16d 16s^3 16d* 20v c16v^6 c17v^F Jan 14] smallish gelding: modest hurdler, won claimer at Perth in September: never a factor in maiden on completed start over fences: stays easy 2½m: acts on heavy and good to firm going: visored/blinkered 7 of last 8 starts: has had tongue tied: often finds little. *P. Monteith* **c– § h91 §**

SPREEWALD (GER) 6 b.g. Dulcero (USA) – Spartina (USA) (Northern Baby (CAN)) [2004/5 h78: 19g^5 20g^6 17g^{pu} 16f^6 21s^3 16d^6 c16g^3 Dec 8] rather leggy gelding: poor maiden hurdler: similar form when third in novice handicap on chasing debut: stays 21f: acts on firm and soft going: has worn cheekpieces: tongue tied after third outing. *J. C. Tuck* **c75 h73**

SPRINGALONG (USA) 5 ch.g. Gone West (USA) – Seven Springs (USA) (Irish River (FR)) [2004/5 16g 16g^{pu} Oct 7] modest maiden on Flat (stays 1¼m): no form in 2 starts over hurdles. *P. D. Evans* **h–**

SPRINGAWAY 6 ch.g. Minster Son – Galway Gal (Proverb) [2004/5 F–: F16m^3 F16m 16s^5 19m^5 Dec 1] leggy gelding: probably achieved little in bumpers: poor form in 2 novice hurdles: should be suited by 2½m+. *Miss Kate Milligan* **h72 F75**

SPRING BEE 5 b.m. Parthian Springs – First Bee (Gunner B) [2004/5 h–, F–: 20g 24s 20g^3 17g^6 21d^{pu} 16v Jan 21] poor maiden hurdler: blinkered/visored last 3 starts. *T. Wall* **h65**

SPRINGBROOK GIRL 7 br.m. Alderbrook – Springaleak (Lafontaine (USA)) [2004/5 h81, F67: 19d^3 May 4] sturdy mare: poor form over hurdles: successful twice in points in 2005. *A. G. Hobbs* **h81**

bet@bluesq.com Handicap Chase, Windsor—
Spring Grove proves too strong for Prominent Profile (white face) in a weakish race for the money

SPRING DAWN 10 gr.g. Arzanni – Another Spring (Town Crier) [2004/5 c100, h–: c17g^{2} c16d^{5} May 8] workmanlike gelding: maiden hurdler: modest maiden chaser: form only around 2m: acts on soft going: ran creditably only try in cheekpieces: sold 12,000 gns Doncaster May Sales, successful in maiden point in April. *N. J. Henderson* **c94 h–**

SPRINGFIELD BELLE 6 b.m. El Conquistador – Corrie's Girl (Whistling Deer) [2004/5 F16s^{4} F16d^{4} Nov 1] angular mare: eighth foal: dam ran once: fair form when fourth in bumpers 6 months apart: will be suited by further than 2m. *V. R. A. Dartnall* **F88**

SPRINGFIELD SCALLY 12 ch.g. Scallywag – Ledee (Le Bavard (FR)) [2004/5 h124: 23m May 1] quite good-topped gelding: useful handicap hurdler at his best: stayed 3¼m: had form on good to firm going, probably better under more testing conditions (acted on heavy): usually forced pace: tough: reportedly retired. *S. Gollings* **h–**

SPRINGFORD (IRE) 13 b.g. King's Ride – Tickenor Wood (Le Bavard (FR)) [2004/5 c94, h–: c25g* c28m^{2} May 22] workmanlike gelding: prolific winning pointer, including twice in 2005: useful hunter chaser: won 5-runner event at Wincanton in May by 17 lengths from Garruth: good second to Torduff Express in valuable event at Stratford: stays 3½m: best form on good/good to firm going: sound jumper. *Mrs Caroline Keevil* **c112 h–**

SPRING GAMBLE (IRE) 6 b.g. Norwich – Aurorá Run (IRE) (Cyrano de Bergerac) [2004/5 h95, F90: 17d^{4} 19s^{2} 16v^{4} c19g^{4} Mar 5] modest maiden hurdler: similar form when fourth in maiden on chasing debut: stays 19f: acts on heavy going (bumper form on firm). *G. M. Moore* **c88 h88**

SPRING GROVE (IRE) 10 b.g. Mandalus – Lucy Lorraine (IRE) (Buckskin (FR)) [2004/5 c129, h105: c24d c20g* c20g^{3} c20g^{4} c24s* c21d^{5} c20d^{4} c24g c25m^{3} Apr 13] workmanlike gelding: useful handicap chaser: won at Cheltenham (by ½ length from Better Days) in October and Windsor (beat Prominent Profile 9 lengths in listed event) in December: creditable efforts last 3 starts: barely stays 25f: acts on heavy and good to firm going: has run well when sweating and on toes: usually races prominently. *R. H. Alner* **c134 h–**

SPRINGHILL 10 b.g. Relief Pitcher – Early Call (Kind of Hush) [2004/5 h–: c16g^{F} May 8] strong gelding: maiden hurdler, very lightly raced nowadays: fell sixth in novice at Warwick on chasing debut: stays 2½m: acts on good to soft going. *Mrs Mary Hambro* **c– h–**

SPRING JUNIOR (FR) 4 b.g. Concorde Jr (USA) – Top Spring (FR) (Top Ville) [2004/5 F16g Apr 19] eighth foal: half-brother to winners up to around 1¼m Top River and Top Mist (both by River Mist): dam unraced, out of half-sister to smart middle-distance colt Two Step: soon outpaced once tempo increased in bumper on debut. *P. J. Hobbs* **F–**

SPRING LOVER (FR) 6 b.g. Fijar Tango (FR) – Kailasa (FR) (R B Chesne) [2004/5 c–, h95: c25g^{pu} c18g^{6} c20d* c20s^{2} c20v^{2} c21d* c21g* c20d^{2} Mar 24] smallish gelding: fairly useful handicap chaser: won at Ludlow in January and Wincanton and Fakenham (best effort, beat Walcot Lad by 16 lengths) in March: stays 2¾m: acts on heavy going. *Miss Venetia Williams* **c120 h–**

SPRING LUNAR (IRE) 7 b.g. Parthian Springs – Orospring (Tesoro Mio) [2004/5 26d^{pu} 20d^{pu} 22g 19m 21d^{pu} 23d^{pu} Nov 13] eighth foal: half-brother to winning hurdler **h–**

Cootehill Boy, stayed 3m, and fairly useful hurdler/chaser up to 25f Spring Gale (both by Strong Gale): dam unraced, from family of high-class 2m hurdler King Credo and smart 2½m to 3m chaser Credo's Daughter: unseated in maiden Irish point: no form over hurdles, left Mrs M. Evans prior to final start: tried in cheekpieces/visor. *Evan Williams*

SPRING MARGOT (FR) 9 b.g. Kadalko (FR) – La Brunante (FR) (Chaparral (FR)) [2004/5 c20d* c20g^{5} c24d^{4} c24d^{ur} c20s^{2} c21d^{F} c20g^{4} Apr 22] tall, useful-looking gelding: fairly useful handicap chaser: off 2½ years and left Miss V. Williams, won 3-finisher event at Sandown in November by neck from Shalako: creditable efforts next 3 completed starts: barely stays 3m: acts on good to firm and heavy going. *P. F. Nicholls* **c124 h–**

SPRING PURSUIT 9 b.g. Rudimentary (USA) – Pursuit of Truth (USA) (Irish River (FR)) [2004/5 h104: 19g^{5} 17g^{5} 19v^{3} 20s* 20s 16d^{3} 21d 20s^{4} 16s^{3} 20v^{3} 24s^{6} 20v* 20v^{3} 20d* 21g 16g^{4} Mar 26] neat gelding: fairly useful handicap hurdler: won at Chepstow in October and Leicester and Haydock in February, beating Nick's Choice by 5 lengths at last-named: ran well when fourth to Nyrche at Haydock final start: stays 2½m: acts on heavy going: usually held up: tough. *E. G. Bevan* **h122**

SPRING SURPRISE 4 b.f. Hector Protector (USA) – Tender Moment (IRE) (Caerleon (USA)) [2004/5 16d^{5} Feb 19] half-sister to fairly useful 2m hurdler/winning chaser Bound (by Kris) and modest hurdler Summer Bounty (by Lugana Beach), stays 19f: fairly useful 7f winner at 2 yrs for B. Hills: tailed off in mares novice on hurdling debut. *B. R. Johnson* **h–**

SPRING THE QUE (IRE) 6 b.g. Parthian Springs – Que Tranquila (Dominion) [2004/5 F17d^{6} 16s 19s 20s 16s* 16s^{5} 19s^{3} Mar 27] €11,000 3-y-o: useful-looking gelding: half-brother to 3 winners, including fair 2m hurdler Euro Flyer (by Muharib): dam, ran twice, from family of Pebbles: sixth in bumper on debut: fair hurdler: won maiden at Cork in January by 8 lengths from Dantys Hampsire: ran well in handicaps subsequently: likely to prove best around 2m: raced on going softer than good over hurdles. *Robert Tyner, Ireland* **h112 F–**

SPRINGWOOD WHITE 11 gr.g. Sharkskin Suit (USA) – Kale Brig (New Brig) [2004/5 c71: c26s^{pu} c24m^{3} c24g^{pu} Apr 17] modest hunter chaser: stays 25f: acts on good to firm going: has worn cheekpieces. *Mrs V. Park* **c–**

SPUD ONE 8 b.g. Lord Americo – Red Dusk (Deep Run) [2004/5 16g^{6} Jan 24] lengthy, good-topped gelding: bumper winner/winning hurdler in 2002/3: off 21 months and left O. Sherwood, sixth in handicap at Southwell: raced around 2m: acts on firm and good to soft going: headstrong: has taken little interest. *C. R. Egerton* **h99 +**

SPY BOY (IRE) 9 b.g. Balla Cove – Spy Girl (Tanfirion) [2004/5 c–, h–: c21m^{pu} May 19] no longer of any account: tried visored/blinkered. *Arun Green* **c– h–**

SPYCATCHER (USA) 5 b. or br.g. Dixieland Band (USA) – Secret Seeker (USA) (Mr Prospector (USA)) [2004/5 20g 16g^{pu} Feb 27] fair maiden on Flat (stays 1½m) in Ireland at 3 yrs, sold out of J. Ryan's stable 1,500 gns Doncaster May (2004) Sales: no show in 2 maiden hurdles. *A. C. Whillans* **h–**

SQUANDAMANIA 12 b.g. Ela-Mana-Mou – Garden Pink (FR) (Bellypha) [2004/5 h62: 23d^{5} 20s^{5} 24v^{pu} Dec 15] tall gelding: handicap hurdler, no show in 2004/5: stays 2½m: acts on heavy going: tried in headgear: all 4 wins at Sedgefield. *J. R. Norton* **h–**

SQUANTUM (IRE) 8 b.g. Roselier (FR) – Coole Eile (IRE) (King's Ride) [2004/5 23d^{5} Feb 18] IR £45,000 4-y-o: ex-Irish gelding: first foal: dam unraced sister to useful hurdler/staying chaser Tullymurry Toff, from family of top-class staying chaser Marlborough: poor maiden hurdler/winning chaser: left A. Moore and off nearly 2 years, well held in handicap hurdle: bred to stay beyond 2½m: raced on good going or softer: tongue tied once. *Mrs H. Dalton* **c– h–**

SQUARE DEALER 4 b.g. Vettori (IRE) – Pussy Foot (Red Sunset) [2004/5 F14s F17s Mar 10] half-brother to useful 5f to 1m winner Top Cat (by Be My Chief) and fair 7f winner Anstand (by Anshan): dam fair 5f performer: well held in 2 bumpers. *J. R. Norton* **F–**

SQUARE MILE (IRE) 5 ch.g. Bob Back (USA) – Mother Imelda (IRE) (Phardante (FR)) [2004/5 F16d* F16g* Jul 1] 23,000 3-y-o: second foal: dam unraced, from family of useful chaser up to 3m Bartres: looked good prospect when landing odds in bumpers at Worcester (by 20 lengths from Safawi) in June and Perth in July. *Jonjo O'Neill* **F100 +**

SQUEEZE BOX (IRE) 6 b.m. Accordion – Spread Your Wings (IRE) (Decent Fellow) [2004/5 h74: c17m^{ur} c21g^{pu} Apr 30] poor maiden hurdler: no show in 2 novice chases: stays 2½m: raced freely in cheekpieces. *J. Howard Johnson* **c– h–**

SQUEEZE (IRE) 7 b.g. Old Vic – Petaluma Pet (Callernish) [2004/5 F–: c16s² c16v⁵ c20gᵖᵘ Apr 3] off 18 months, form in maiden chases only when head second to Thieves'-glen at Leicester, closing up late: should be suited by further than 2m. *B. N. Pollock* **c95 ?**

SRAID NA CATHRACH (IRE) 9 ch.g. Insan (USA) – Credo's Campaign (IRE) (Le Moss) [2004/5 c20s⁵ c22d² c20d* c20s c24vᵘʳ Dec 27] IR 20,000 4-y-o: first foal: dam, lightly raced, from family of high-class 2m hurdler King Credo and smart 2½m to 3m chaser Credo's Daughter: modest hurdler in 2002/3: fairly useful form over fences: head second to War of Attrition in maiden at Thurles in November: won similar event at Punchestown later in month: well held on completed start in handicaps after: lame in valuable event at Punchestown in late-April: stays 3m: acts on good to firm and heavy going. *C. Byrnes, Ireland* **c117 h–**

SRIOLOGY (IRE) 4 b.g. Sri Pekan (USA) – Sinology (Rainbow Quest (USA)) [2004/5 16g Mar 18] half-brother to fairly useful hurdler Billy Bonnie (by Anshan), stays 3m: modest maiden on Flat (will stay 1½m): tongue tied, well held in maiden on hurdling debut. *G. Prodromou* **h–**

STACK THE PACK (IRE) 8 ch.g. Good Thyne (USA) – Game Trix (Buckskin (FR)) [2004/5 c21dᶠ c24dᵘʳ c22dᵘʳ 20s⁶ Apr 22] modest form in novice hurdles in 2002/3: off 20 months, failed to complete in 3 novice chases, running to similar level when unseating 3 out at Huntingdon second start: will prove better at 3m than shorter. *T. R. George* **c91 + h79 +**

STAFFORD KING (IRE) 8 b.h. Nicolotte – Opening Day (Day Is Done) [2004/5 h–: 24f³ 21g⁵ 24s⁶ 20s⁶ 19s⁵ 19d Dec 3] workmanlike horse: maiden hurdler, little form since 2002: probably stays 25f: acts on soft and firm going: tried in cheekpieces/visor. *J. G. M. O'Shea* **h70**

STAGE AFFAIR (USA) 11 b. or br.g. Theatrical – Wooing (USA) (Stage Door Johnny (USA)) [2004/5 c117, h–: c17m² c22m³ c17m* c17sᶠ Oct 10] tall gelding: very smart hurdler at best: useful chaser: won handicap at Galway in July by 1½ lengths from Green Finger: still travelling strongly when falling heavily 3 out in minor event at Limerick next time: raced mainly around 2m: acts on good to firm and heavy going: tried blinkered: has had tongue tied. *D. K. Weld, Ireland* **c135 h–**

STAGE BY STAGE (USA) 6 ch.g. In The Wings – Lady Thynn (FR) (Crystal Glitters (USA)) [2004/5 17d⁴ 16d* 16d* 22g* 22g* 20f² 25g² 21d⁶ 24g⁶ 24gᵖᵘ Apr 14] smallish gelding: useful at best on Flat (will probably stay 2m) for M. Bell: fairly useful hurdler: won maiden and novice at Hexham in June and novice at Cartmel and handicap at Uttoxeter in July: best efforts after at Cheltenham, second to Football Crazy seventh start and sixth to Moulin Riche in Grade 2 novice ninth: stays 25f: successful on good to soft ground, best form on good or firmer (acts on firm). *C. R. Egerton* **h121**

STAGECOACH DIAMOND 6 b.g. Classic Cliche (IRE) – Lyra (Blakeney) [2004/5 F16v⁵ F16g* F16g⁴ Mar 5] 3,300 3-y-o: lengthy gelding: half-brother to several winners on Flat, including fairly useful 1m winner Ever So Lyrical (by Never So Bold): dam won 3 races in Belgium: progressive form in bumpers, won at Catterick in December: fairly useful effort when fourth to No Regrets at Doncaster. *Mrs S. J. Smith* **F99**

STAGE DIRECTION (USA) 8 b.g. Theatrical – Carya (USA) (Northern Dancer) [2004/5 20m⁵ Aug 6] leggy gelding: lightly-raced winning hurdler: probably effective at 2½m: acts on good to firm going. *J. D. Frost* **h72**

STAGE FRIENDLY (IRE) 6 ch.g. Old Vic – Just Affable (IRE) (Phardante (FR)) [2004/5 F72: 16g³ 22s 17s 22s⁶ Mar 22] novice hurdler, best effort on debut: should be suited by further than 2m. *N. A. Twiston-Davies* **h88**

STALEY'S QUEEN 4 b.f. Classic Cliche (IRE) – Mesp (IRE) (Strong Gale) [2004/5 F16d Apr 20] angular filly: first foal: dam, maiden hurdler, half-sister to smart staying chasers Calling Brave and Ottowa: no show in bumper on debut. *K. G. Wingrove* **F–**

STAMPARLAND HILL 10 b.g. Gildoran – Woodland Flower (Furry Glen) [2004/5 c120, h–: c16d* c16sᶠ 16v⁶ 19d³ 25d³ 20g² 21v⁴ Mar 15] lengthy gelding: fairly useful handicap chaser: won at Carlisle in October: fair handicap hurdler: barely stays 25f: raced on good ground or softer (acts on soft): free-going sort: makes mistakes over fences. *J. M. Jefferson* **c121 x h103**

STANCE 6 b.g. Salse (USA) – De Stael (USA) (Nijinsky (CAN)) [2004/5 h109: 16g* 17g* 16d* 16d 17g² 16d Apr 9] close-coupled gelding: fairly useful on Flat: progressed into useful hurdler, winning novices at Wincanton and Newton Abbot in May, and **h132**

Vodafone Handicap Hurdle, Newbury—
Stance makes short work of a seemingly competitive field to complete a four-timer

well-contested handicap at Newbury (beat Tighe Caster 4 lengths) in March: best effort when second to Fontanesi in County Hurdle at Cheltenham: raced mainly around 2m: acts on good to soft going. *G. L. Moore*

STAND EASY (IRE) 12 b.g. Buckskin (FR) – Geeaway (Gala Performance) [2004/5 c102§, h–§: c22s⁵ c22s⁶ c24v⁵ c26d⁴ c24s⁴ c26v⁵ c23vᵘʳ c24s⁴ c24s* Mar 10] tall gelding: modest handicap chaser nowadays: won at Towcester in March: will stay beyond 3¼m: acts on heavy and good to firm going: has worn cheekpieces: often none too fluent: temperamental. *J. R. Cornwall* **c88 § h– §**

STANDING APPLAUSE (USA) 7 b. or br.g. Theatrical – Pent (USA) (Mr Prospector (USA)) [2004/5 h84: 20m³ 20m⁵ Jun 29] poor maiden hurdler: stays 2¾m: acts on good to firm going: tongue tied. *Mrs A. J. Hamilton-Fairley* **h80**

STANDING BLOOM 9 ch.m. Presidium – Rosie Cone (Celtic Cone) [2004/5 c92, h–: 23s² 22v⁵ 21v⁵ 23s² c24sᵖᵘ 26g 22g Apr 3] medium-sized mare: modest hurdler/ chaser: stays 3m: acts on heavy going. *Mrs P. Sly* **c– h97**

STANDIN OBLIGATION (IRE) 6 ch.g. Pierre – Clonroche Floods (Pauper) [2004/5 22g* 16g* Apr 19] fifth foal: half-brother to fairly useful 2½m hurdler Tommy Paud (by Asir) and winning pointer by Commanche Run: dam, thrice-raced in Irish points, from family of smart staying hurdler/chaser Birkdale: successful 3 times in Irish points, including both starts in 2005: looked good prospect when winning novice hurdles at Exeter (beat Jackson by neck) and Towcester (jumped left) in April: will stay 3m, though not short of speed: sure to improve. *M. C. Pipe* **h123 p**

STAN (NZ) 6 b.g. Super Imposing (NZ) – Take Care (NZ) (Wham (AUS)) [2004/5 19v³ 16s² 17v⁴ 19g* 16d² 16g Mar 15] compact gelding: ran 4 times on Flat in New Zealand, won over 1¼m in July: progressive hurdler: won novice at Catterick in December by 2 lengths from Aleron: eleventh of 20 to Arcalis in Supreme Novices' Hurdle at Cheltenham final outing: stays 19f: acts on heavy going: patiently ridden. *R. C. Guest* **h115**

STANS MAN CAN 7 gr.g. Arzanni – Tais Toi (Vitiges (FR)) [2004/5 c–, h–: c19dᵖᵘ Apr 29] no sign of ability: tried blinkered. *S. C. Burrough* **c– h–**

STANWAY 6 b.g. Presenting – Nicklup (Netherkelly) [2004/5 h86, F87: 24g⁶ c19g* Apr 12] close-coupled, workmanlike gelding: modest maiden hurdler: better form when winning maiden at Exeter on chasing debut in April: should be suited by 2½m+. *Mrs Mary Hambro* **c106 h–**

STANWICK GYPSY 7 b.m. Nomadic Way (USA) – Stanwick Monument (Grey Ghost) [2004/5 c25s^{pu} 23g^3 20d^4 21s^2 25g^6 24m Apr 10] third foal: dam winning pointer: won maiden on last of 6 starts in points in 2004: badly let down by jumping on chasing debut: best effort over hurdles when second in mares novice at Towcester: stays 21f: acts on soft ground. *Mrs S. J. Humphrey* **c– h90**

STAR ANGLER (IRE) 7 b.g. Supreme Leader – So Pink (IRE) (Deep Run) [2004/5 17d^6 19s^3 19v* 22d 22m^2 Apr 17] useful-looking gelding: will make a chaser: fair novice hurdler: best effort when winning at Exeter in February by 3 lengths from Miko de Beauchene: should stay 2¾m: acts well on heavy going (looked ill at ease on good to firm). *H. D. Daly* **h113**

STARBRIGHT 4 b.g. Polar Falcon (USA) – Treasure Hunt (Hadeer) [2004/5 16m^4 17g 16s^5 Mar 12] soundly beaten in 2 starts on Flat: sold out of Miss S. Hall's stable 500 gns Doncaster October Sales: tailed off in 3 juvenile hurdles. *W. G. Young* **h–**

STARBUCK 11 b.g. Brush Aside (USA) – Clonmello (Le Bavard (FR)) [2004/5 c–, h–: c25g^3 c26g^4 c25s^2 c25d^2 c26s^R Apr 21] tall gelding: fair hunter chaser: stays 25f: acts on soft going: wore cheekpieces last 4 starts. *Miss J. Fisher* **c86 h–**

STAR BUSTER (IRE) 7 b.g. Eurobus – Lucciola (FR) (Auction Ring (USA)) [2004/5 F–: F16s F16v Dec 31] workmanlike gelding: no form in bumpers. *W. Davies* **F–**

STAR CLIPPER 8 b.g. Kris – Anne Bonny (Ajdal (USA)) [2004/5 c118, h–: 20d^6 c28s^2 c24v c29s Mar 28] good sort: fair hurdler: fairly useful chaser: form in 2004/5 only when second to Garvivonnian in valuable handicap at Cork: stays 3½m: acts on heavy going: tried blinkered: tends to find little. *N. Meade, Ireland* **c120 h108 +**

STAR DE MOHAISON (FR) 4 b.g. Beyssac (FR) – Belle de Mohaison (FR) (Suvero (FR)) [2004/5 18s^F 16s^6 18s* 19s* 17s^3 17m^3 Apr 13] tall gelding: will make a chaser: sixth foal: brother to useful hurdler/chaser Billy de Bessac, stays 23f, and half-brother to winning hurdlers around 2m Robor de Mohaison (by Robore) and Lise de Mohaison (by Michel Georges): dam maiden: fairly useful form over hurdles: won 3-y-o event at Auteuil in November and novice at Hereford in January: sold out of F. Cottin's stable €170,000 Goffs (France) November Sale in between: much improved when 3¼ lengths third to Openide in juvenile at Cheltenham final start: will stay beyond 19f: acts on soft and good to firm going. *P. F. Nicholls* **h124**

STAR DIVA (IRE) 9 b.m. Toulon – Kerris Melody (Furry Glen) [2004/5 21s^{pu} 22g^4 Apr 10] bumper winner: off nearly 3 years, well held in mares events over hurdles. *M. Bradstock* **h–**

STAR DIVER (FR) 5 ch.g. Starborough – Swim Dance (USA) (Riverman (USA)) [2004/5 F16s 18v^{pu} Mar 30] small, light-framed gelding: seventh foal: half-brother to 3 winners, including 19f hurdle winner/middle-distance stayer Shadow Dance (by Galetto): dam ran twice: little sign of ability in bumper and 5-y-o hurdle: tongue tied. *T. Doumen, France* **h– F–**

STAR DOUBLE (ITY) 5 ch.g. Bob Back (USA) – Among The Stars (Pharly (FR)) [2004/5 F16s F16d^5 Jan 6] 16,000 4-y-o: good-topped gelding: brother and half-brother to winners on Flat in Italy: dam maiden: half-sister to smart Italian performer up to 1½m Pareo: modest form both starts in bumpers. *N. A. Twiston-Davies* **F80**

STAR FEVER (IRE) 4 b.g. Saddlers' Hall (IRE) – Phenics Allstar (IRE) (Fourstars Allstar (USA)) [2004/5 F12d Jan 12] first foal: dam unraced, from family of very smart staying chaser Golden Friend: eighth of 14 in 4-y-o bumper at Newbury on debut, not knocked about once beaten. *Miss H. C. Knight* **F82**

STAR GALAXY (IRE) 5 b.g. Fourstars Allstar (USA) – Raven Night (IRE) (Mandalus) [2004/5 F16d F17g Apr 7] third foal: half-brother to bumper winner Maryland (by Executive Perk): dam ran once in point: no sign of ability in bumpers. *J. S. King* **F–**

STAR GLOW 11 b.g. Dunbeath (USA) – Betrothed (Aglojo) [2004/5 c24s* Feb 10] poor maiden hurdler: fairly useful pointer: won novice hunter at Huntingdon: stays 3m: tried blinkered. *R. H. York* **c91 h–**

STAR HORSE (IRE) 7 b.g. Toulon – Clerical Lady (IRE) (The Parson) [2004/5 F16m* 18g^2 16f* 16d*^{dis} 16g* 16g^2 Sep 26] third living foal: half-brother to fairly useful hurdler Keltech Grey (by Celio Rufo), would have stayed beyond 2½m: dam unraced half-sister to high-class 2m hurdler/smart chaser Space Trucker: won bumper at Cork on debut in May: first past post on 3 of 5 starts over hurdles in first half of season, in maiden at Wexford, novice at Roscommon (subsequently disqualified after testing positive for prohibited substance) and minor event at Down Royal: fairly useful form when **h125 F111**

beating Banasan by 4 lengths at last-named: raced around 2m: acts on firm and good to soft ground. *Mrs J. Harrington, Ireland*

STAR JACK (FR) 10 b.g. Epervier Bleu – Little Point (FR) (Le Nain Jaune (FR)) [2004/5 c–, h–: c21s* c21s Apr 7] lengthy gelding: winning hurdler: won point in February: won hunter chase at Ayr in March by 3 lengths from Coole Abbey: well-held eighth in Fox Hunters' at Aintree following month, making most until 3 out: barely stays testing 21f: unraced on firm going, acts on any other: has worn cheekpieces: tongue tied: bold jumper. *Dave Parker* **c111 h–**

STARK RAVEN 5 b.g. Sea Raven (IRE) – Hilly Path (Brave Invader (USA)) [2004/5 F16s Feb 26] €22,000 4-y-o: rangy gelding: eighth foal: half-brother to fair staying hurdler Bridal Path (by Teenoso): dam poor novice hurdler: green, eighth to Glasker Mill in slowly-run bumper at Kempton on debut. *Miss E. C. Lavelle* **F94**

STARLIGHT EXPRESS (FR) 5 b.m. Air Express (IRE) – Muramixa (FR) (Linamix (FR)) [2004/5 h89p, F89: 24d^{6} 19s^{5} 22d* 22s^{rtr} 20d^{rtr} 22d^{pu} Feb 20] lengthy mare: modest hurdler: won novice handicap at Wincanton in December: refused to race next 2 starts, mistakes in blinkers final one: stays 2¾m: raced on good ground or softer: one to leave well alone. *Miss E. C. Lavelle* **h90 §**

STARMIX 4 br.g. Linamix (FR) – Danlu (USA) (Danzig (USA)) [2004/5 18d^{6} 17s 19s Mar 1] small, leggy gelding: half-brother to fairly useful hurdler Studmaster (by Snurge), stays 2½m, and fair hurdler/chaser Swing West (by Gone West), stays 25f: fair maiden on Flat (will stay at least 1¼m) for P. Cole: well beaten over hurdles. *G. A. Harker* **h–**

STAR OF GERMANY (IRE) 5 b.g. Germany (USA) – Twinkle Bright (USA) (Star de Naskra (USA)) [2004/5 h70: 20d* 20s^{pu} Nov 28] poor hurdler: dead-heated with Silver Dagger in seller (sold from F. Murphy 13,000 gns) at Uttoxeter in May: no show in novice over 6 months later: stays 2½m: acts on soft going. *R. S. Brookhouse* **h80**

STAR OF RAVEN 8 b.m. Sea Raven (IRE) – Lucy At The Minute (Silly Prices) [2004/5 c102: c25g^{2} c28g^{pu} May 21] winning hunter chaser: stays 25f: acts on soft going: held up. *Joss Saville* **c88**

STAR OF WILLIAM (IRE) 6 ch.g. Idris (IRE) – Fais Vite (USA) (Sharpen Up) [2004/5 20m 16m 22g^{pu} Jul 29] half-brother to fair hurdler/useful chaser Druid's Glen, stays 25f, and winning 2m hurdler Maximus (both by Un Desperado) and several winners on Flat: dam French maiden: placed on completed starts in points: no form over hurdles. *C. Roberts* **h–**

STAR PERFORMANCE (IRE) 10 ch.g. Insan (USA) – Leallen (Le Bavard (FR)) [2004/5 c25g^{5} c24m^{2} c23f* c23m 20s^{5} c25s^{5} c31d^{2} c31d^{4} Dec 10] workmanlike gelding: winning pointer: modest form only start over hurdles: fair chaser on conventional courses: won maiden at Tipperary in June: fairly useful form when in frame in cross-country events at Cheltenham won by Spot Thedifference on last 2 starts: stays 31f: acts on firm and soft going: often blinkered: usually tongue tied. *Oliver McKiernan, Ireland* **c128 ? h92**

STAR PRIZE (IRE) 8 b.g. Fourstars Allstar (USA) – Dipper's Gift (IRE) (Salluceva) [2004/5 h98p, F88: 20v 17s^{3} 21d Mar 3] rather leggy gelding: second in bumper on debut: modest form over hurdles: should be suited by further than 17f. *N. J. Henderson* **h98**

STARRY MARY 7 b.m. Deploy – Darling Splodge (Elegant Air) [2004/5 16g 19g 21s^{5} 20g^{2} 19d 26s^{2} 24d 21s 24s^{3} 26s Mar 7] modest on Flat (seems to stay 2m), sold out of R. Beckett's stable 4,000 gns Newmarket July Sales: poor maiden hurdler: lame final start: stays 3¼m: raced on good going or softer (acts on soft). *R. J. Price* **h76**

STARSHIPENTERPRISE 7 b.g. The Star of Orion VII – Lequest (Lepanto (GER)) [2004/5 c–, h–: c18d^{pu} c20s^{pu} c24s^{3} c27d^{pu} c22s^{pu} c24g^{4} c24d^{2} c24g^{4} Mar 18] poor maiden chaser: left L. Wells after first start: stays 3m: acts on soft going: wore headgear last 6 outings: races prominently. *N. B. King* **c71 h–**

STAR TIME (IRE) 6 b.g. Fourstars Allstar (USA) – Punctual (Lead On Time (USA)) [2004/5 h71§: 24g^{pu} 27d 21m^{6} 19d^{3} 21g^{2} 25m^{3} 27d^{2} 24s^{2} 24s^{3} 24s^{2} 24s 22d^{3} 25v^{6} 19d^{ur} 24s^{3} c24v^{pu} 24v^{pu} 26m^{6} Mar 21] good-bodied gelding: poor maiden hurdler: no show on chasing debut: stays 27f: acts on soft and good to firm going: usually visored, well held only start in cheekpieces: temperamental. *M. Scudamore* **c– h79 §**

STARTING AGAIN 11 b.g. Petoski – Lynemore (Nearly A Hand) [2004/5 c107, h–: c24d^{5} Mar 11] lengthy gelding: fair handicap chaser at best: well beaten in point and hunter in 2005: stays 2¾m: acts on any going. *Capt. J. A. George* **c– h–**

STAR TROOPER (IRE) 9 b. or br.g. Brief Truce (USA) – Star Cream (Star Appeal) [2004/5 c81, h88§: 16s 17d 18s c16v^{5} c16d^{3} c21v^{F} c16s^{5} 16v^{4} 19s^{5} 17d^{2} 16d^{6} Apr 11] **c76 § h73 §**

compact gelding: poor hurdler/maiden chaser: stays 2½m: acts on any going: usually wears blinkers/cheekpieces: not one to trust. *Miss S. E. Forster*

STAR WONDER 5 b.m. Syrtos – Galava (CAN) (Graustark) [2004/5 h–: 19s^{pu} Jan 31] of little account: tried blinkered. *G. R. I. Smyly* **h–**

STASHEDAWAY (IRE) 8 b.m. Treasure Hunter – Mugs Away (Mugatpura) [2004/5 c124, h124: 20g^4 18m* c17s* Oct 10] lengthy mare: fairly useful hurdler/chaser: won listed mares event over hurdles at Punchestown (by 1½ lengths from Greenhall Rambler) in May and minor event over fences at Limerick in October: stays 21f: acts on soft and good to firm going: consistent. *M. J. P. O'Brien, Ireland* **c124 h–**

STATE MEDLAR 14 ro.g. Pragmatic – Lizzie The Twig (Precipice Wood) [2004/5 c23m^4 Jun 16] winning pointer, including in 2005: poor form when fourth in maiden on chasing debut. *W. S. Kittow* **c66**

STATE OF PLAY 5 b.g. Hernando (FR) – Kaprice (GER) (Windwurf (GER)) [2004/5 F94: 19g^5 16d 17s^4 16g^2 Mar 28] rather leggy gelding: bumper winner: modest novice hurdler: will be suited by 2½m+: raced on good going or softer. *P. R. Webber* **h98**

STATION ISLAND (IRE) 8 ch.g. Roselier (FR) – Sweet Tulip (Beau Chapeau) [2004/5 h99: 23m^2 25m* 26g^{pu} Oct 5] close-coupled gelding: fair hurdler: left with simple task in intermediate at Wetherby in May: broke down at Huntingdon next time: stayed 27f: acted on good to firm and heavy going: usually tongue tied: dead. *J. Mackie* **h103**

STATLEY RAJ (IND) 6 b.g. Mtoto – Donna Star (Stately Don (USA)) [2004/5 h–, F83: 17d 18m^4 16g^5 16g 18s*^{dis} 16g^4 17s^{pu} 18s 16s 18s^2 18g 21d^{pu} Apr 18] rather leggy gelding: modest novice hurdler: first past post in minor event at Fontwell (disqualified after testing positive for prohibited substance) in November: should stay beyond 2¼m: acts on soft going: inconsistent. *R. Rowe* **h90**

STATTIN ISLAND (IRE) 6 b.g. Great Marquess – Push Over Lass (Wolverlife) [2004/5 F16s^{pu} F17v 17s^{pu} Mar 22] €1,000 4-y-o: lengthy, rather unfurnished gelding: fifth foal: dam ran once: fifth in maiden Irish point on debut: no sign of ability in bumpers or over hurdles. *J. D. Frost* **h– F–**

ST BARCHAN (IRE) 4 ch.g. Grand Lodge (USA) – Moon Tango (IRE) (Last Tycoon) [2004/5 16s Oct 21] fair on Flat (stays 11f), claimed from W. Jarvis £18,000 after successful in October: tailed off in juvenile on hurdling debut. *J. G. M. O'Shea* **h–**

ST BEE 10 br.g. St Ninian – Regal Bee (Royal Fountain) [2004/5 c–x, h–: c26g May 31] of little account outside points: has worn cheekpieces/blinkers: sketchy jumper. *W. G. Reed* **c– x h–**

STEEL BAND 7 b.g. Kris – Quaver (USA) (The Minstrel (CAN)) [2004/5 h116: 16g^6 20v^6 c17s^F c18v* c16d^5 c17v^2 c17v^{ur} c16v^2 c16v^3 c16g c20d^5 Mar 31] workmanlike gelding: fair handicap hurdler: fairly useful chaser: won novice at Clonmel in October: best efforts when second to Mariah Rollins in Grade 1 novice at Leopardstown and Moscow Flyer in Grade 3 at Punchestown: best around 2m: raced on good going or softer (acts on heavy). *Paul A. Roche, Ireland* **c130 h–**

STEEL MILL (IRE) 10 gr.g. Roselier (FR) – Chatmando (IRE) (Mandalus) [2004/5 c87, h–: c25g^{pu} c25s^{pu} c26s^{pu} c25s^{pu} c22s^6 c25v^{pu} 26s 25g Mar 27] sturdy gelding: maiden hurdler/winning chaser: no form in 2004/5: stays 25f: acts on soft and good to firm going: wore cheekpieces last 4 starts: sketchy jumper. *Miss I. E. Craig* **c– x h–**

STENNIKOV (IRE) 9 b.g. Good Thyne (USA) – Belle Bavard (Le Bavard (FR)) [2004/5 c25f^F Oct 7] rangy gelding: fair novice hurdler in 2002/3: won point in 2004 for Miss E. Baker: held when falling 3 out in conditional jockeys handicap at Wincanton on chasing debut: should stay beyond 2½m: acts on good to soft going, probably on firm: often carries head awkwardly: none too genuine. *P. F. Nicholls* **c91 h–**

STEP IN LINE (IRE) 13 gr.g. Step Together (USA) – Ballycahan Girl (Bargello) [2004/5 16d^2 17d^6 Apr 5] sparely-made gelding: winning chaser: bad maiden hurdler: effective at 2m to 3¼m: acts on firm and soft going. *D. W. Thompson* **c– h57**

STEPPES 10 b.g. Jendali (USA) – Asoness (Laxton) [2004/5 c–, h–: c26d^4 May 3] won weak maiden hurdle in 2002, only form: tried visored. *M. J. Gingell* **c– h–**

STEPPES OF GOLD (IRE) 8 b.g. Moscow Society (USA) – Trysting Place (He Loves Me) [2004/5 h133: 16g* c16v^2 Dec 17] tall gelding: useful hurdler: didn't need to be at best when readily landing odds in intermediate at Kelso in May, final start for N. Richards: fairly useful form when 9 lengths second to Dungarvans Choice in 4-runner **c117 p h126**

maiden at Uttoxeter on chasing debut: raced around 2m on good ground or softer: has carried head high: likely to improve over fences. *Jonjo O'Neill*

STEP QUICK (IRE) 11 ch.g. All Haste (USA) – Little Steps (Step Together (USA)) [2004/5 c85: c21d^{F} c21s* c22m^{6} May 30] tall, angular gelding: modest chaser: won handicap at Newton Abbot in May: sold out of P. Bowen's stable 10,000 gns Doncaster Sales before final start: won twice in points in 2005: stays 25f: acts on soft and firm going: tried in cheekpieces: jumps none too fluently. *Mrs S. E. Busby* **c91 x**

STERLING DOT COM (IRE) 9 b.g. Roselier (FR) – Daddy's Folly (Le Moss) [2004/5 c97x, h–: c23d* c20d^{F} Dec 3] tall gelding: modest chaser: won novice handicap at Exeter in May: should stay beyond 3m: acts on soft going: blinkered once: not a fluent jumper. *A. W. Carroll* **c99 x h–**

STERLING GUARANTEE (USA) 7 b.g. Silver Hawk (USA) – Sterling Pound (USA) (Seeking The Gold (USA)) [2004/5 17g^{pu} 16g^{ur} 20m^{3} 16g^{6} 20g 19g^{ur} 17g^{5} Apr 3] good-topped gelding: modest maiden on Flat (stays easy 1½m), trained in 2004 by D. Nicholls/A. Reid: modest form at best over hurdles. *N. Wilson* **h90**

STERN (IRE) 6 b. or br.g. Executive Perk – Christian Lady (IRE) (Mandalus) [2004/5 F16g^{3} F16d 16m^{6} 20d^{2} Apr 20] sturdy gelding: first foal: dam unraced, from family of high-class chaser around 2½m Golden Freeze and smart chaser up to 25f Sparky Gayle: fair form in bumpers: better effort over hurdles when head second to Cantgeton in maiden at Worcester: will stay beyond 2½m: should improve again. *Miss E. C. Lavelle* **h110 p F89**

STERN LEADER (IRE) 6 b.g. Supreme Leader – Strong Stern (IRE) (Lancastrian) [2004/5 h–, F81: 22s^{6} Oct 28] little impact in 3 starts in novice company over hurdles. *D. J. Wintle* **h–**

STEVE THE FISH (IRE) 9 ch.g. Dry Dock – Country Clothing (Salluceva) [2004/5 c–, h98: 24s^{3} c24v^{R} 25s^{pu} 24v^{pu} c20v^{4} Apr 17] medium-sized gelding: modest handicap hurdler: poor form on completed starts over fences: stays 3m: raced on good going or softer (acts on heavy): tried tongue tied: none too consistent. *J. A. B. Old* **c64 h89**

STEWART'S LAD 8 b.g. Well Beloved – Moneyacre (Veloski) [2004/5 h90: 22g^{pu} c21d^{pu} c21g 19d^{2} 20d* c20d^{pu} Nov 28] workmanlike gelding: modest hurdler: won handicap at Southwell in November: no form in 3 chases: stayed 2½m: acted on soft going: visored once: dead. *B. D. Leavy* **c– h90**

ST GEORGE'S GIRL 4 b.f. Muthahb (IRE) – Nickelodeon (Nickel King) [2004/5 17d 16s^{pu} Dec 2] of little account on Flat: no show in 2 juvenile hurdles. *J. R. Jenkins* **h–**

ST HELIER 10 b.m. Gildoran – Belhelvie (Mart Lane) [2004/5 c25s^{pu} Mar 7] fair pointer: no show in hunter on chasing debut. *D. O. Stephens* **c–**

STICKY END 4 b.g. Endoli (USA) – Carat Stick (Gold Rod) [2004/5 F14g Dec 18] ninth foal: half-brother to fair chasers Pillaging Pict (by Primitive Rising), stays 2¾m, and Posh Stick (by Rakaposhi King), stays 21f: dam fair hurdler/staying chaser: well held in 3-y-o bumper on debut. *J. B. Walton* **F–**

STICKY WICKET 6 b.m. Petoski – Avec Le Vent (IRE) (Strong Gale) [2004/5 19s^{6} 21d^{pu} 19d 16d^{pu} Mar 24] tall mare: first foal: dam unraced: no form in novice hurdles. *P. J. Hobbs* **h–**

STILETTO LADY (IRE) 4 b.f. Daggers Drawn (USA) – Nordic Pride (Horage) [2004/5 16f^{4} 16d 16s 16v^{pu} Dec 17] half-sister to 2 winning hurdlers, including fairly useful 2m performer Feel The Pride (by Persian Bold): modest maiden on Flat (seems to stay 8.5f) for J. Given: has shown more temperament than ability over hurdles. *C. N. Kellett* **h– §**

STILL GOING ON 8 b.g. Prince Sabo – Floppie (FR) (Law Society (USA)) [2004/5 h90: 16m^{3} 16s^{5} 18g^{4} 18d^{4} 16s 16s^{5} 17g^{3} 16g* 16g Jan 19] angular gelding: fair handicap hurdler: easily best effort when successful in 18-runner race at Newcastle in December: raced around 2m: acts on soft ground, probably on firm: often wears blinkers/cheekpieces: usually tongue tied. *Eoin Doyle, Ireland* **h100**

STILL RUNS DEEP 6 b.m. Karinga Bay – Millers Action (Fearless Action (USA)) [2004/5 F17g^{3} F16d F16d 19m Mar 14] second foal: sister to useful bumper winner Miller's Bay: dam once-raced half-sister to useful 2m hurdler Bold Gait, out of half-sister to Champion Hurdle winner Royal Gait: little sign of ability. *Mrs S. M. Johnson* **h– F–**

STILL SPEEDY (IRE) 8 b.g. Toulon – Gorge (Mount Hagen (FR)) [2004/5 h77, F87: 17d 16m^{F} 16m^{5} Jun 16] poor maiden hurdler: raced around 2m: acts on good to firm going: tends to pull hard/carry head high: sold 3,200 gns Doncaster August Sales: failed to complete in 2 points in 2005. *Noel T. Chance* **h68**

STITCH POCKETS (IRE) 7 b.m. Montelimar (USA) – Serpentine Artiste (Buckskin (FR)) [2004/5 19d4 16g3 16f* c16s c17s Mar 3] sister to 2½m hurdle winner Darrens Lass and half-sister to 2 winners, including fairly useful hunter chaser Hillhead (by Aristocracy), stays 25f: dam unraced half-sister to fairly useful chaser up to 3m River Cora: poor hurdler: won weak maiden at Wexford in May: well held in 2 maiden chases: raced mainly around 2m: acts on firm going (bumper form on good to soft). *D. Loughnane, Ireland* **c– h81**

ST JEROME 5 ch.g. Danzig Connection (USA) – Indigo Dawn (Rainbow Quest (USA)) [2004/5 21dur 19d 16v 16d 19mpu Mar 21] good-topped gelding: modest on Flat (stays 1¾m), sold out of N. Littmoden's stable 7,500 gns Newmarket July Sales: signs of ability over hurdles only when seventh in novice on third start. *D. Burchell* **h91 ?**

ST KILDA 8 b.m. Past Glories – Oiseval (National Trust) [2004/5 c–, h65: c24s5 c26v4 c24s3 c25d3 c25spu c26vF c25spu c26g* Mar 14] tall, lengthy mare: poor maiden hurdler: similar standard over fences: in cheekpieces, won weak handicap at Plumpton in March: stays 3¼m: raced on good going or softer (acts on soft): unreliable. *Mrs H. M. Bridges* **c67 § h–**

ST MATTHEW (USA) 7 b.g. Lear Fan (USA) – Social Crown (USA) (Chief's Crown (USA)) [2004/5 20dF 20m2 20m2 c23m* 24g* c26m* 25s3 20s3 c24g3 c20v* c22vur c25sF 23s6 c21g Mar 17] sturdy gelding: useful hurdler: won handicap at Worcester in August: better form after, including when third to Telemoss in Grade 2 at Wetherby seventh start: useful novice chaser: successful at Worcester in July, Uttoxeter (2 finished) in September and Haydock (made all to beat Garryvoe 9 lengths in handicap) in December: stays 3¼m: acts on heavy and good to firm going: tough. *Mrs S. J. Smith* **c130 h134**

STOCK DOVE 7 ch.m. Deploy – Lady Stock (Crofter (USA)) [2004/5 h66, F87?: 20g5 21g3 21s 23g4 24d Feb 1] small mare: modest maiden hurdler: stays 21f: visored (finished lame) final start. *Mrs P. Robeson* **h85**

STOCKS 'N SHARES 9 b.m. Jupiter Island – Norstock (Norwick (USA)) [2004/5 c107, h83+: c21dF May 1] good-topped mare: maiden hurdler: winning chaser: struggling when fell tenth in listed mares handicap at Uttoxeter: stays 2½m: acts on soft and good to firm going: tongue tied. *Noel T. Chance* **c– h–**

STOKESIES BOY 5 b.g. Key of Luck (USA) – Lesley's Fashion (Dominion) [2004/5 h73: 16f4 16m6 17mpu Jun 15] poor maiden hurdler: likely to need sharp 2m. *J. L. Spearing* **h69**

STOLEN GIFT 5 b.m. Zahran (IRE) – Stolen Owl (Bold Owl) [2004/5 F17g F16s Dec 22] fourth foal: dam unraced: tailed off in 2 bumpers. *A. E. Price* **F–**

STOLEN SONG 5 b.g. Sheikh Albadou – Sparky's Song (Electric) [2004/5 h97: 16g5 16g3 20f5 19g4 16s5 16d 24s3 22s6 c20v3 c20d Feb 11] angular gelding: modest handicap hurdler: below form after third outing: showed little both starts over fences: stays 2½m: acts on good to soft going, probably on soft: tried blinkered/visored. *M. J. Ryan* **c– h99 d**

STONE COLD 8 ch.g. Inchinor – Vaula (Henbit (USA)) [2004/5 c99, h–: c20g4 Apr 3] angular gelding: modest handicap chaser: stays 23f: acts on firm and soft going: usually blinkered, tried in cheekpieces: has failed to impress with attitude. *T. D. Easterby* **c92 h–**

STONED (IRE) 5 b.g. Bigstone (IRE) – Lady Celina (FR) (Crystal Palace (FR)) [2004/5 h–, F–: 16m 17g 22gpu 17g 21d4 22m5 20d2 Oct 8] good-topped gelding: first form over hurdles when second in novice handicap at Carlisle: stays 2½m: has worn cheekpieces/visor: sold 10,000 gns Doncaster October Sales. *M. J. Gingell* **h75**

STONEHENGE (IRE) 8 b.g. Caerleon (USA) – Sharata (IRE) (Darshaan) [2004/5 c–, h–: 17dpu Apr 29] angular gelding: winning hurdler, no longer of any account: tried in headgear. *D. Burchell* **c– h–**

STONERAVINMAD 7 ch.g. Never So Bold – Premier Princess (Hard Fought) [2004/5 c–, h–: 20d 18s Dec 5] no sign of ability. *Mrs E. Slack* **c– h–**

STONERIGGS 4 gr.g. Silver Patriarch (IRE) – Maid To Match (Matching Pair) [2004/5 F16s Apr 10] tall gelding: chasing type: third foal: dam winning pointer: well beaten in bumper on debut. *Mrs E. Slack* **F–**

STONERIGGS SILVER 4 gr.g. Silver Patriarch (IRE) – Carole's Crusader (Faustus (USA)) [2004/5 F17mur Apr 23] first foal: dam, useful chaser who stayed 29f, half-sister to useful 2m hurdler Hitman: looked wayward in bumper on debut, tailed off when unseating rider home turn. *Mrs E. Slack* **F–**

STONESFIELD CONEY 5 br.g. Sadler's Way – Rocquelle (Coquelin (USA)) [2004/5 F16d F16d Mar 24] fourth foal: half-brother to modest chaser Ultra Pontem (by Governor General), stayed 21f: dam no worthwhile form over hurdles: tailed off in 2 bumpers. *M. R. Bosley* **F–**

STONEWALL GEORGE (NZ) **h84** 7 ch.g. Stark South (USA) – Mother's Word (Mummy's Pet) [2004/5 16g^{6} 16s^{pu} 17d^{6} Nov 30] smallish gelding: successful over 1m on Flat at 4 yrs in New Zealand: form in novice hurdles only when sixth at Lingfield on debut. *Jonjo O'Neill*

STONEY ROAD GIRL (IRE) **h–** 5 gr.m. Saddlers' Hall (IRE) – No Slow (King's Ride) [2004/5 16s 24s^{pu} Mar 31] 4,200 4-y-o: half-sister to fair hurdler/chaser up to 23f Stratco (by Satco): dam unraced, from family of fairly useful staying chaser Boom Docker: no show over hurdles. *Miss G. Browne*

STONOR LADY (USA) **h–** 4 b. or br.f. French Deputy (USA) – Blush With Love (USA) (Mt Livermore (USA)) [2004/5 16g^{6} Mar 28] poor on Flat (stays 8.5f), sold out of P. D'Arcy's stable 800 gns Newmarket Autumn Sales: little aptitude for hurdling on debut. *Miss S. West*

STOOP TO CONQUER **h112** 5 b.g. Polar Falcon (USA) – Princess Genista (Ile de Bourbon (USA)) [2004/5 21d^{F} 21d^{pu} Feb 9] half-brother to useful hurdler Ela Mata (by Dancing Brave), stayed 21f, and fair hurdler Heir To Be (by Elmaamul), stays 3m: fairly useful on Flat (stays 17f), sold out of J. Dunlop's stable 58,000 gns Newmarket Autumn Sales: 4 lengths down in second when falling last in maiden at Ludlow won by Bagan on hurdling debut: weak favourite, jumped poorly in rear and soon pulled up in novice there following month. *A. W. Carroll*

STOPWATCH (IRE) **c64 h–** 10 b.g. Lead On Time (USA) – Rose Bonbon (FR) (High Top) [2004/5 c–, h–: c18g^{3} c18s^{3} Mar 30] lengthy gelding: poor hurdler/maiden chaser: stays easy 21f: acts on soft and good to firm going: blinkered once, sometimes wears cheekpieces. *Mrs L. C. Jewell*

STORM A BREWING **c– h–** 9 ch.g. Glacial Storm (USA) – Southern Squaw (Buckskin (FR)) [2004/5 h83: c24g^{F} c24g^{pu} 24d Apr 20] lightly-raced maiden hurdler: no show over fences: stays 2¾m. *R. M. Stronge*

STORM AHEAD (IRE) **c– h–** 11 b.g. Glacial Storm (USA) – Little Slip (Super Slip) [2004/5 c–, h–: 20d^{pu} Jun 30] maiden hurdler/chaser: stays 2½m: acts on soft going: tried in cheekpieces: sometimes tongue tied. *S. H. Shirley-Beavan*

STORM CASTLE (IRE) **c92 h–** 13 b.g. Carlingford Castle – Strong Rum (Strong Gale) [2004/5 c25m^{ur} c23d c25m^{4} May 19] sturdy gelding: fair pointer/hunter chaser: stays 3¼m: acts on soft and firm going. *Miss J. Wickens*

STORM CLEAR (IRE) **h65** 6 b.g. Mujadil (USA) – Escape Path (Wolver Hollow) [2004/5 h–: 17d^{6} 16g 16v 16s Mar 13] useful-looking gelding: poor maiden hurdler: raced around 2m: tried tongue tied. *D. J. Wintle*

STORMDANCER (IRE) **h–** 8 ch.g. Bluebird (USA) – Unspoiled (Tina's Pet) [2004/5 h–: 22v^{6} 19s^{pu} Mar 23] of no account: tried in cheekpieces. *J. A. Pickering*

STORMEZ (FR) **c146 § h–** 8 b.g. Ezzoud (IRE) – Stormy Scene (USA) (Storm Bird (CAN)) [2004/5 c145, h132: c27d* c26s^{4} c29s^{pu} c33d c33g^{pu} c29g^{pu} Apr 23] smallish gelding: smart chaser on his day: won Grade 3 handicap at Cheltenham in November (for second time) by 3 lengths from Ballycassidy, aided by omission of numerous fences: typically let down by jumping and looked hard ride subsequently: best at 3m+: unraced on firm going, acts on any other: tried in headgear: tongue tied. *M. C. Pipe*

STORMHILL STAG **c– h–** 13 b.g. Buckley – Sweet Sirenia (Al Sirat) [2004/5 c108d, h–: c24s^{pu} c16m Mar 21] leggy gelding: veteran chaser: little show in 2 hunters: stays 3m, effective at much shorter: acts on good to firm and heavy going: tried blinkered in 2004/5. *Patrick J. Hanly*

STORM OF APPLAUSE (IRE) **F81** 4 b.g. Accordion – Dolce Notte (IRE) (Strong Gale) [2004/5 F17g^{5} Mar 19] second foal: dam won 19f hurdle: fifth in bumper at Bangor on debut. *P. J. Hobbs*

STORM PRINCE (IRE) **h102** 8 ch.g. Prince of Birds (USA) – Petersford Girl (IRE) (Taufan (USA)) [2004/5 h102: 20m^{3} 21m^{pu} Jul 2] smallish gelding: fair handicap hurdler: went amiss final start: stays easy 2¾m: acts on soft and good to firm going: blinkered/visored: tongue tied once: front runner. *J. L. Spearing*

STORMY BEECH **c88 h–** 9 b.g. Glacial Storm (USA) – Cheeny's Brig (New Brig) [2004/5 c88, h88: 16s c16d^{3} c16d^{4} c16v^{2} c16v^{6} c16s^{3} Feb 7] angular gelding: winning hurdler: modest handicap chaser: barely stays 21f: acts on heavy going: usually wears headgear: tried tongue tied: free-going sort: has hung left: none too consistent. *R. Johnson*

STORMY LORD (IRE) 9 br.g. Lord Americo – Decent Shower (Decent Fellow) [2004/5 c16s^F c17s* c16g^3 c20v^2 c16s^3 c17v* c16g^F c16g^{pu} Apr 15] tall gelding: fairly useful hurdler in 2002/3: as good over fences on return, winning 3-runner novice handicap at Market Rasen in December and quite valuable novice at Kelso (by ½ length from Through The Rye) in March: let down by jumping faced with stiff tasks last 2 starts: seems best around 2m: acts on heavy going: has tended to hang/jump left: free-going front runner. *J. Wade* **c118 h–**

STORMY ROW (IRE) 11 b.g. Phardante (FR) – Thistle Chat (Le Bavard (FR)) [2004/5 16g 16d^{pu} Apr 17] of little account: tried tongue tied. *M. B. Shears* **c– h–**

STORMY SKYE (IRE) 9 b.g. Bluebird (USA) – Canna (Caerleon (USA)) [2004/5 c100§, h–§: c18s^3 Mar 30] useful-looking gelding: fair chaser: off 16 months, third of 5 in handicap at Fontwell: stays 25f: acts on soft and good to firm going, probably on heavy: usually blinkered: formerly tongue tied: ungenuine. *G. L. Moore* **c94 § h– §**

STORMY SUNRISE (IRE) 9 b.g. Glacial Storm (USA) – Commanche Maid (Commanche Run) [2004/5 c–, h–: c21g^5 Apr 30] compact gelding: of little account outside points: tongue tied once. *Miss A. Armitage* **c– h–**

ST PIRRAN (IRE) 10 b.g. Be My Native (USA) – Guess Twice (Deep Run) [2004/5 c142, h–: c16g^3 Oct 30] tall gelding: useful handicap chaser: respectable third to stable-companion Armaturk in listed event at Lingfield, only start in 2004/5: best around 2m: acts on soft going: tried blinkered: free-going sort, usually patiently ridden: sold to join R. Guest 10,000 gns Doncaster May Sales. *P. F. Nicholls* **c137 h–**

STRAIGHT TALKER (IRE) 6 b.g. Warcraft (USA) – The Mighty Midge (Hard-green (USA)) [2004/5 16f 21m^F 22g^2 19g^5 c19s^F Oct 20] seventh foal: half-brother to bumper/2½m hurdle winner Mighty Mandy (by Mandalus): dam, middle-distance winner, half-sister to top-class hurdler/chaser Night Nurse and to dam of Coral Cup winner Big Strand: trained by J. J. Murphy until after first start: form over hurdles only when runner-up in novice handicap at Exeter: fell tenth on chasing debut: will stay 3m: visored last 4 starts. *M. C. Pipe* **c– h73**

STRAIT TALKING (FR) 7 b.g. Bering – Servia (Le Marmot (FR)) [2004/5 c–, h–: 16d^6 16g^4 19d Feb 4] leggy gelding: fell heavily only start over fences: poor handicap hurdler: likely to prove best around 2m: acts on soft and good to firm going: wore cheekpieces once. *Jedd O'Keeffe* **c– h71**

STRANGELY BROWN (IRE) 4 b.g. Second Empire (IRE) – Damerela (IRE) (Alzao (USA)) [2004/5 16v* 16v* 16s* 17g^6 16s^3 Apr 7] **h133**

On the same day that Faasel was sold for 230,000 guineas at the Newmarket Autumn Sales, another three-year-old bay gelding, Strangely Brown, was picked up for a small fraction of that amount. Strangely Brown went on to win more prize money than Faasel, even though the latter ended up as one of the season's two top juvenile hurdlers. Strangely Brown made a mere 11,000 guineas at the sales but proved a rare bargain, by the end of his first campaign over hurdles earning just over £150,000, over £38,000 more than Faasal, the main part of his winnings coming from an enterprising raid on Auteuil in the summer. Not that Strangely Brown is as good as Faasel, as the results on the two occasions they met show. In the Triumph Hurdle at Cheltenham, Strangely Brown finished sixth, ten and three quarter lengths behind Faasel who was beaten a head by Penzance; and in the Anniversary Hurdle at Aintree three weeks later, he finished third to Faasel beaten sixteen lengths. Strangely Brown was the first Irish-trained finisher in both races, as he was on the occasion of his only other defeat, when twelve lengths second to United in the Champion Four Year Old Hurdle at Punchestown.

Strangely Brown arrived at Cheltenham with a record of three wins from as many starts over hurdles. He beat another useful juvenile Dabiroun by two and a half lengths in a juvenile maiden at Limerick on his hurdling debut, and followed up in a Grade 3 event at Punchestown, in which he had a length and a half to spare over the runner-up Sky's The Limit. On both occasions, Strangely Brown was ridden by 7-lb claimer Brian Byrnes, but the gelding had fully fledged jockeys on board in his subsequent races, David Casey in the saddle when Strangely Brown completed his hat-trick, in the Grade 2 Cashmans Juvenile Hurdle at Leopardstown in February. Strangely Brown did not look the likely winner turning into the straight at Leopardstown, but then his stamina came into play and he rallied to lead in the last hundred and fifty yards, winning by two lengths from Barati. Up against stronger opposition at Cheltenham, Aintree and Punchestown, Strangely Brown was found wanting for finishing speed over two miles and, on his only subsequent outing, was stepped up to a distance just short of two and a half miles, in the Prix Alain du Breil-Course de Haies d'Ete des Quatre Ans run at Auteuil in mid-June. The longer trip suited Strangely Brown well, though he didn't need to improve to win what is the top race for juvenile hurdlers in France, the French four-year-olds looking a substandard lot, particularly in the absence of Don't Be Shy, who had been sold to join Martin Pipe's stable. Strangely Brown, partnered on this occasion by Ruby Walsh, was ridden to chase the front-running Royale Athenia after two out and stayed on well to collar her in the last hundred metres and win by three lengths, the pair pulling fifteen lengths and more clear of the remainder. The chances are that Strangely Brown will be returning to France in the next season, with the Prix Renaud du Vivier, a Grade 1 hurdle for four-year-olds run at Auteuil in November, mentioned as a possible target.

Strangely Brown (IRE) (b.g. 2001)	Second Empire (IRE) (b 1995)	Fairy King (b 1982)	Northern Dancer
			Fairy Bridge
		Welsh Love (b 1986)	Ela-Mana-Mou
			Welsh Flame
	Damerela (IRE) (b 1990)	Alzao (b 1980)	Lyphard
			Lady Rebecca
		Damana (gr 1981)	Crystal Palace
			Denia

Strangely Brown will prove better at around two and a half miles than two miles, and should stay further. He was suited by a test of stamina on the Flat and won three long-distance handicaps in 2004, when trained by Stuart Williams, showing fair form. Strangely Brown had been purchased by his present handler, former international showjumper Eric McNamara, on behalf of the 'We Didn't Name Him Syndicate', so called because they had had a horse with McNamara called Periwinkle Lad whose name they did not like, and wanted to make it plain they weren't responsible for it. In fact, Strangely Brown owes his nomenclature to Williams, who reportedly is a fan of the *Blackadder* television series, Strangely Brown being one of the people mentioned in conversation during the final episode of the World War I-set *Blackadder Goes Forth*. Strangely Brown is from the first crop of the very smart miler Second Empire who has made a relatively slow start to stud, his best performer to date the smart three-year-old sprinter Beckermet. Damerela, the dam of Strangely Brown, raced in France, gaining her only placing when runner-up over nine furlongs. Strangely Brown is her fourth foal, and her three previous ones were also winners. The fairly useful Cincuenta (by Bob Back) was successful at a mile and a half to two miles in Ireland, while the one-time useful

Cashmans Juvenile Hurdle, Leopardstown—plenty still to play for at the last, with Strangely Brown challenging up the rails to beat Barati (check cap), Arch Rebel and Don't Be Bitin (nearest camera)

*Prix Alain du Breil-Course de Haies d'Ete des Quatre Ans, Auteuil—
Triumph sixth Strangely Brown lands this prestigious prize for Ireland;
Royal Athenia leads him over the last*

pair Crevelli (by Dolphin Street) and Gallant Boy (by Grand Lodge) were winners at seven furlongs and at up to almost a mile and a half respectively. Their grandam Damana won three races for the Aga Khan in France, at up to a mile and three quarters, and is the daughter of a smart half-sister to Raykour, the runner-up in the St James's Palace Stakes and the Hollywood Derby in 1988. Damana, of course, is also the grandam of the Prix du Jockey Club and Prix de l'Arc de Triomphe winner Dalakhani and of Daylami, whose victories included those in the King George VI and Queen Elizabeth Stakes and the Breeders' Cup Turf. If Strangely Brown falls short of Faasal in terms of form, he also compares unfavourably with him in terms of physique, as indeed he does with most of the other leading juveniles, being on the smallish side and sparely made. Others look open to more improvement in their second season and Strangely Brown is likely to find things much tougher, though he has exceeded expectations so far, and who is to say he won't continue to do so. Strangely Brown gained one of his wins on the Flat on good to firm ground, but to date has raced only on good going or softer over hurdles (he acts on heavy). *E. McNamara, Ireland*

STRAVONIAN 5 b.g. Luso – In The Evening (IRE) (Distinctly North (USA)) [2004/5 16g Feb 27] poor and ungenuine maiden on Flat: always behind in maiden on hurdling debut. *D. A. Nolan* **h–**

STREETWISE KID (IRE) 6 b.g. Dolphin Street (FR) – Perfect Answer (Keen) [2004/5 20m 24m^pu Nov 11] of no account. *C. Roberts* **h–**

STRENUE (USA) 5 ch.g. Crafty Prospector (USA) – Shawgatny (USA) (Danzig Connection (USA)) [2004/5 h–§: 19d^pu 27d 22f 19g Oct 14] no sign of ability: usually visored: tried tongue tied: ungenuine. *M. C. Pipe* **h– §**

STRIDES OF FIRE (IRE) 4 b.g. General Monash (USA) – Lagrion (USA) (Diesis) [2004/5 16s 16g 16s 16v 16v^4 16v^2 16v^4 16d^4 16v^3 Apr 14] leggy, lengthy gelding: lightly-raced maiden on Flat: sold out of J. Gosden's stable 6,000 gns Newmarket July Sales: fairly useful juvenile hurdler: best effort when winning valuable 25-runner event **h122**

at Punchestown in late-April by 7 lengths from Afrad: raced at 2m on good going or softer. *John A. Codd, Ireland*

STRIKE BACK (IRE) 7 b.g. Bob Back (USA) – First Strike (IRE) (Magical Strike (USA)) [2004/5 h140, F108: 20g² c17s^F c20s² c20s³ c20v^F c16v* c17v⁴ c17s* Mar 28] useful-looking gelding: useful hurdler: slow learner over fences, but ultimately of similar standard, winning maiden at Tramore in December and novice at Fairyhouse (well ridden when beating Livingstonebramble 2½ lengths) in March: also ran well in frame in Grade 1 novices, fourth to Ulaan Baatar at Leopardstown in between and third to War of Attrition at Punchestown in late-April: stays 2½m: acts on heavy going. *Mrs J. Harrington, Ireland* **c136 h–**

STROLLING VAGABOND (IRE) 6 ch.g. Glacial Storm (USA) – Found Again (IRE) (Black Minstrel) [2004/5 F18d 21d 22s 24v⁵ 25g⁶ 25g⁵ Mar 27] rather unfurnished gelding: fourth foal: dam unraced half-sister to smart chaser Gale Again, stayed 2¾m: well held in bumper: poor novice hurdler: stays 25f. *John R. Upson* **h65 F–**

STROMSTAD (IRE) 4 ch.g. Halling (USA) – Muscadel (Nashwan (USA)) [2004/5 16s* 16d* 16v³ 16v⁶ 16g Mar 15] 10,000 3-y-o: workmanlike gelding: third foal: half-brother to winner in UAE by Quiet American: dam, useful over middle distances in France, out of 1000 Guineas winner Musical Bliss: fairly useful form when successful first 2 starts in juvenile hurdles, maiden at Down Royal and Grade 3 at Fairyhouse (by 4 lengths from Don't Be Bitin) in November: well held after, in valuable juvenile handicap at Cheltenham (blinkered) final outing: raced around 2m. *S. J. Mahon, Ireland* **h120**

STRONG FINISH 10 ch.g. Montelimar (USA) – Atlantic View (Crash Course) [2004/5 24m^pu Aug 6] lengthy, angular gelding: maiden jumper: has had tongue tied. *Mrs Barbara Waring* **c– h–**

STRONG FLOW (IRE) 8 br.g. Over The River (FR) – Stormy Skies (Strong Gale) [2004/5 c156p, h–: 25s³ c24d² c26g⁶ Mar 18] **c161 h125 +**

'This is the first horse with which I've had to attempt a comeback from a knee fracture.' Paul Nicholls' remark about Strong Flow provides some insight into the difficult task facing those at Manor Farm stables after his career-threatening knee injury in the 2003 Feltham Novices' Chase. Strong Flow had looked one of the best prospects seen in a long time, on his previous start winning the Hennessy Cognac Gold Cup at Newbury by fourteen lengths. He is the only horse to win a Hennessy in his first season over fences and, a good sort with a chasing pedigree, had looked set to develop into a top-class staying chaser, one good enough to challenge Best Mate eventually. The Hennessy was only his seventh run under rules—he had also won a maiden on his only start in Irish points—and, up to then, he had had only four outings in a steeplechasing career that was less than seven months old. The serious injury to the knee of his near-fore in December involved several fractures and Strong Flow was clearly going to need plenty of time to recover. However, he was reported by his trainer in late-June to be 'still not right'. Nicholls revealed later than he feared, at around this time, that Strong Flow would never race again. 'The owner sent me an e-mail suggesting we should retire Strong Flow and I could see all my hopes for the horse going up in smoke.' Owner and trainer agreed to seek further veterinary opinion and Strong Flow was sent to Newmarket to be operated on after it was revealed that his continuing lameness was the result of a splinter of bone in the knee. The Strong Flow comeback was back on track and he remained sound during an extended summer break at his owner's home.

Strong Flow wasn't back in the yard until October, very late by normal standards, but, restricted to walking for three weeks, he passed a scan at the end of that month and began a programme of cantering. Strong Flow returned to action, after thirteen months off, in mid-January in the Warwick qualifier in the Pertemps Handicap Hurdle series, running off a mark much lower than the one he had over fences and starting favourite. He finished third, travelling as well as the winner Celtic Son most of the way before being tapped for speed from the final turn. There was time only for one more outing before the Cheltenham Gold Cup and it came in the AON Chase at Newbury in mid-February. Strong Flow started 2/1 joint favourite with the latest Hennessy Gold Cup winner Celestial Gold, but the pair were upstaged by Farmer Jack, who was only entered for the race after it was reopened. Strong Flow is often patiently ridden but his rider Ruby Walsh was under instructions to force the pace in the AON to ensure that the race turned into a full dress rehearsal for Cheltenham. Strong Flow went down by a length and a half to Farmer Jack, the pair disputing or alternating in the lead for most of the way. Celestial Gold was only a head behind Strong Flow in third and, on form, the principals were left with a bit to prove with the Gold Cup only a month away. The most encouraging sign by far about Strong Flow's performance was his jumping. He gave a flawless display, his fluency gaining him ground over his rivals at virtually every fence and banishing the lingering memory of two serious mistakes in the Feltham and another in the Hennessy. Strong Flow had been held up in his work for four days after cutting himself schooling a fortnight before the AON and his trainer said he had not been able to get him as fit as he would have liked, though Strong Flow had not seemed obviously lacking in fitness on paddock inspection. Strong Flow's below-form sixth, two places behind his 40/1 stable-companion Royal Auclair, in the Cheltenham Gold Cup shouldn't result in his being written off as a future winner of the race. He was up there with every chance at the fourth last, after seemingly going very well early on the final circuit, but didn't see the race out. The extra distance of the Gold Cup should have been in his favour but, as his trainer said, it had 'been a rush to get him there' and it is probably best not to judge him too harshly. Strong Flow was found to have 'jarred up his shoulders' on his return home and wasn't seen out again. Starting the next season with a clean bill of health, he should enjoy a much more straightforward preparation for the championship events, in which, still only eight, he has plenty of time to make his mark.

Strong Flow (IRE) (br.g. 1997)	Over The River (FR) (ch 1974)	Luthier (b or br 1965)	Klairon
			Flute Enchantee
		Medenine (b 1967)	Prudent II
			Ma Congaie
	Stormy Skies (br 1987)	Strong Gale (br 1975)	Lord Gayle
			Sterntau
		Perspex-Pride (br 1972)	Perspex
			Pride of Ednego

Mr B. C. Marshall's "Strong Flow"

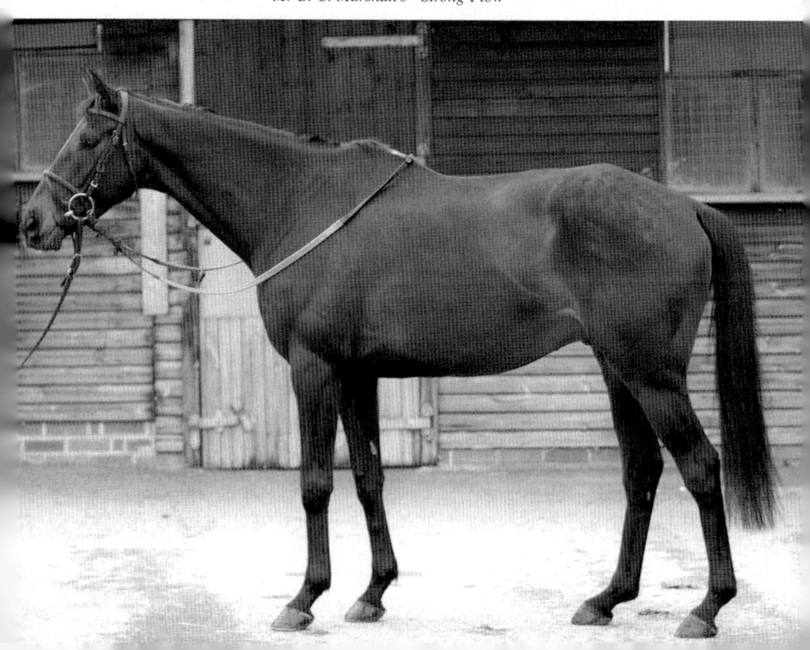

Strong Flow's pedigree was dealt with in last year's Annual. The progeny of his sire Over The River, who died in 2002, include two Gold Cup winners in Cool Ground and Cool Dawn, and he proved a big influence for stamina at stud. Strong Flow's dam Stormy Skies, runner-up in a maiden chase at Fairyhouse, ran in the National Hunt Chase at Cheltenham, unseating her rider, and is a half-sister to the useful staying chaser Plenty Crack. Stormy Skies has been anything but a prolific breeder at stud and her only other foal to reach the racecourse, the fairly useful chaser Ballyconnell, had the misfortune to break his back in a paddock accident in October. Strong Flow is by no means short of speed, but he stays three and a quarter miles well and should get further. Strong Flow won on soft going over hurdles but has done all his racing over fences so far on good going or good to soft, and is most unlikely to be risked on anything less resilient (his participation in the Gold Cup would have been in doubt if conditions had become any firmer). He is a superb jumper in the main. *P. F. Nicholls*

STRONG KING (IRE) 11 b. or br.g. Strong Gale – Mrs Simpson (Kinglet) [2004/5 c24g Apr 30] of little account outside points: tried in visor/cheekpieces. *R. Hirons* **c– h–**

STRONG MAGIC (IRE) 13 br.g. Strong Gale – Baybush (Boreen (FR)) [2004/5 c95, h–: c26dpu c24m3 c21m4 c24g c24s2 c24d* c28s5 c26d2 c22vpu c24d c19v4 c25spu c23s5 c24s2 c25s4 21m Apr 13] workmanlike gelding: fair handicap chaser: won at Southwell in November: lightly-raced hurdler: stays 25f: acts on soft and good to firm going, probably heavy: often races prominently: none too consistent. *J. R. Cornwall* **c102 h–**

STRONG PROJECT (IRE) 9 ch.g. Project Manager – Hurricane Girl (IRE) (Insan (USA)) [2004/5 c–, h126: 24s6 20d3 20s4 c20s3 c19v* c21v2 c21s5 c21v* c20sF Mar 29] workmanlike gelding: fairly useful handicap hurdler: similar form back over fences, winning twice at Leopardstown, maiden in December and novice in March: also ran well there when second in Grade 2 novice won by Newmill: below form in Grade 3 behind Forget The Past at Punchestown in late-April: effective at 19f to 3m: unraced on firm going, acts on any other: has found little: front runner. *C. F. Swan, Ireland* **c127 h127**

STRONG RESOLVE (IRE) 9 gr.g. Roselier (FR) – Farmerette (Teofane) [2004/5 c118, h–: c25g4 c24f6 c24g2 c25v* c23d* c29v2 c22v2 c36d Apr 9] leggy gelding: useful handicap chaser: won at Ayr and Wetherby in November: better form when runner-up to Silver Birch in Welsh National at Chepstow in December and Haut de Gamme at Kelso in March: let down by jumping in Grand National at Aintree: stays 29f: acts on heavy going: usually sound-jumping front runner: genuine and consistent. *Miss Lucinda V. Russell* **c134 h–**

STRONG RUN (IRE) 12 b.g. Strong Gale – Arctic Run (Deep Run) [2004/5 c145, h–: c16g3 c20s3 Oct 8] workmanlike gelding: smart chaser: off 5 months, ran as well as ever when third to Kicking King in Grade 2 at Gowran in October: stays 2½m: raced on good going or softer (acts on soft): tongue tied: carries head awkwardly under pressure. *N. Meade, Ireland* **c151 h–**

STRONG TEA (IRE) 14 b.g. Electric – Cutty Sark (Strong Gale) [2004/5 c76: c25s c24s6 Mar 27] fair pointer, successful in April: maiden hunter chaser: stays 25f. *Miss S. Waugh* **c–**

STRONGTROOPER (IRE) 10 b.g. Doubletour (USA) – Moss Gale (Strong Gale) [2004/5 c106, h–: c20d4 c22m2 c21mpu Jul 2] big, angular gelding: fair handicap chaser: stays 25f: acts on firm and good to soft going: sold 5,500 gns Doncaster August Sales, successful in point in March. *O. Sherwood* **c101 h–**

STROPPY SYD 8 b.g. Shalford (IRE) – Sylvaner (IRE) (Montelimar (USA)) [2004/5 20mpu Sep 24] second foal: half-brother to winner up to 7f in Greece by Bluegrass Prince: dam Irish maiden half-sister to useful sprinter Sizzling Saga: showed nothing in novice hurdle on debut. *Evan Williams* **h–**

ST TROPEZ (IRE) 4 b.f. Revoque (IRE) – Kaziranga (USA) (Lear Fan (USA)) [2004/5 16g 17mpu Sep 8] modest maiden on Flat for B. Powell: no show over hurdles: tried blinkered. *Mrs A. J. Hamilton-Fairley* **h–**

STUDMASTER 5 ch.g. Snurge – Danlu (USA) (Danzig (USA)) [2004/5 16f* 16m2 20g2 16s* Oct 3] half-brother to winning hurdler/chaser Swing West (by Gone West), stays 25f: fair maiden on Flat (stays 2¼m), sold out of P. Cole's stable 7,500 gns Newmarket Autumn (2003) Sales: fairly useful novice hurdler: won at Fairyhouse (maiden) in July and Tipperary (Grade 3, beating Orchid Bay easily by 7 lengths) in October: should stay 2½m: acts on firm and soft going. *Mrs J. Harrington, Ireland* **h118**

STUNNING MAGIC 5 b.g. Magic Ring (IRE) – Absolutelystunning (Aragon) [2004/5 16d^{pu} Feb 12] leggy gelding: of little account on Flat: pulled up in novice on hurdling debut. *Mrs Barbara Waring* **h–**

STURM UND DRANG 11 ch.g. Selkirk (USA) – Historiette (Chief's Crown (USA)) [2004/5 c93, h88: c17d^{pu} c16m^{3} c20m^{F} c17m^{pu} c16g^{pu} 19m^{pu} 17f Sep 28] modest chaser/ maiden hurdler: little show in 2004/5: best around 2m: acts on good to firm and good to soft going: tried blinkered/in cheekpieces. *C. J. Down* **c93 ? h–**

STUTTER 7 ch.g. Polish Precedent (USA) – Bright Spells (Salse (USA)) [2004/5 h102: 18g^{2} 16f^{3} 16m^{6} 16m^{3} 16s Dec 4] sparely-made gelding: fair on Flat (stays 13f): fair hurdler: won 25-runner handicap at Punchestown in late-April by 5 lengths from Native Stag, staying on strongly when left in front at last: will prove best around 2m: acts on soft and firm going: tried in cheekpieces. *J. G. Carr, Ireland* **h111**

ST VITA (FR) 8 ch.m. Vettori (IRE) – St Isadora (Lyphard (USA)) [2004/5 16d^{3} 20s Mar 9] half-sister to several winners, including 1½m winner Akaroa (by Kalaglow): dam French winner around 9f at 4 yrs: poor form on first of 2 starts over hurdles. *N. J. Gifford* **h72**

SUALDA (IRE) 6 b.g. Idris (IRE) – Winning Heart (Horage) [2004/5 16g^{5} Feb 27] fairly useful on Flat (stays 2m): fifth to Admiral in maiden at Musselburgh on hurdling debut: will be suited by stiffer test of stamina. *R. A. Fahey* **h85 +**

SUAVEROF (IRE) 10 ch.g. Suave Dancer (USA) – Mild Intrigue (USA) (Sir Ivor (USA)) [2004/5 c–, h–: c23g^{6} Jul 14] winning hurdler: fair pointer: no form in chases: tongue tied nowadays. *J. Rudge* **c– h–**

SUBADAR MAJOR 8 b.g. Komaite (USA) – Rather Gorgeous (Billion (USA)) [2004/5 20v^{6} c16v^{3} c16d^{F} Jan 11] of no account. *D. McCain* **c– h–**

SUCHWOT (IRE) 4 b.g. Intikhab (USA) – Fairy Water (Warning) [2004/5 16s 16g 16g 16d 16s^{pu} 20d^{pu} Apr 22] modest maiden on Flat (may prove best short of 11f): no form over hurdles: tried in cheekpieces. *F. Jordan* **h76**

SUD BLEU (FR) 7 b.g. Pistolet Bleu (IRE) – Sudaka (FR) (Garde Royale) [2004/5 h135: c18d^{F} c16d* Oct 23] tall, useful-looking gelding: useful handicap hurdler: made nearly all and jumped well when winning maiden at Kempton by ¾ length from Lacdoudal on completed start over fences: best around 2m: raced on good going or softer: held up over hurdles, and suited by well-run race: often weak finisher: dead. *P. F. Nicholls* **c130 h–**

SUGARBABE 4 b.f. Kirkwall – Lightning Legacy (USA) (Super Concorde (USA)) [2004/5 17m Nov 25] half-sister to several winning hurdlers, including Lawahik (by Lahib), fairly useful around 2m: poor maiden at 2 yrs for M. Blanshard: no show in juvenile seller on hurdling debut. *C. L. Popham* **h–**

SUGARBOY 5 b.g. Muhtarram (USA) – Native Flair (Be My Native (USA)) [2004/5 16s^{4} 16v^{F} Dec 15] once-raced at 2 yrs for T. Mills: little show in 2 novice hurdles. *M. F. Harris* **h–**

SUGGEST 10 b.g. Midyan (USA) – Awham (USA) (Lear Fan (USA)) [2004/5 h82: 24g^{6} 26g^{pu} 24d^{5} 22m c20s^{5} c27d^{pu} c24d^{ur} 20s Jan 19] rather leggy gelding: poor handicap hurdler: no form in 2004/5, including over fences: tried visored. *W. Storey* **c– h–**

SUKEY 5 b.m. Sula Bula – Belle VII (Damsire Unregistered) [2004/5 F17s* Jan 18] first foal: dam unraced: won mares maiden bumper at Folkestone on debut by head from Classic Quart, edging ahead 2f out and keeping on. *N. J. Henderson* **F97**

SULAGH RUN 11 b.g. Sula Bula – Brackagh Run (Deep Run) [2004/5 h–: c17g^{5} c20g^{5} c16f^{pu} Jun 6] no form. *R. Nixon* **c– h–**

SULLIVAN'S CASCADE (IRE) 7 b.g. Spectrum (IRE) – Sombre Lady (Sharpen Up) [2004/5 17s Nov 18] ex-Irish gelding: poor maiden on Flat (stays 1¼m): no form over hurdles. *P. A. Blockley* **h–**

SULLIVAN'S GOLD 5 ch.m. Bedford (USA) – Lady Millennium (IRE) (Prince Rupert (FR)) [2004/5 16g^{F} 17g^{pu} 22g^{6} 20m^{pu} Aug 19] no form. *L. A. Dace* **h–**

SULLY SHUFFLES (IRE) 10 b.g. Broken Hearted – Green Legend (IRE) (Montekin) [2004/5 c–p, h107: 22m* 27g* 24m^{4} 24g^{2} Apr 15] angular gelding: fell only start over fences: fairly useful handicap hurdler: won at Kelso and Stratford (beat Imperial de Thaix 3 lengths) early in season: stays 27f: acts on soft and good to firm going. *M. Todhunter* **c– h119**

SUM LEADER (IRE) 9 b.g. Leading Counsel (USA) – Greenodd (Green Shoon) [2004/5 c122, h–: c20g^{3} c20d^{5} c20g^{3} c22m^{ur} c24v^{pu} c20s^{4} c24s Dec 12] lengthy gelding: winning hurdler: fairly useful chaser: lost way after third to Wests Awake in handicap at **c122 h–**

Tipperary in July: stays 3m: acts on good to firm and heavy going: tried tongue tied. *Miss Jane Thomas, Ireland*

SUMMER SPECIAL 5 b.g. Mind Games – Summerhill Special (IRE) (Roi Danzig (USA)) [2004/5 16g^2 17d^2 16s^3 Apr 21] close-coupled gelding: modest maiden on Flat (stays 9f) at 4 yrs for D. Barker: modest form over hurdles. *Mrs S. C. Bradburne* **h96**

SUMMER STOCK (USA) 7 b.g. Theatrical – Lake Placid (IRE) (Royal Academy (USA)) [2004/5 h88: 16f^2 17d 17m 20s Nov 21] smallish gelding: poor maiden hurdler: raced mainly around 2m: acts on good to firm and good to soft going: wore cheekpieces final outing: tongue tied. *J. A. Supple* **h78**

SUMMIT UP (IRE) 5 b.g. Zaffaran (USA) – Summit Else (El Conquistador) [2004/5 F16d F16g^2 F16s^2 Feb 5] lengthy, rather unfurnished gelding: third foal: dam, no sign of ability, half-sister to 1998 Grand National winner Earth Summit: fair form in bumpers: best effort when second to Seymar Lad at Wetherby final start. *M. Scudamore* **F93**

SUNAMI STORM (IRE) 7 b.m. Glacial Storm (USA) – Live It Up (Le Coq d'Or) [2004/5 F16f F20d^3 16v^4 20s* 22s* 20v^2 22v^5 20d^4 20s^4 Mar 27] good-topped mare: sister to fair staying hurdler Sungates: dam unraced sister to useful staying chaser Merry Master: third at Ballinrobe final start in bumpers: fairly useful hurdler: won maiden at Gowran in October and novice at Thurles in November: best effort when fourth to Teeming Rain in Grade 3 novice at Thurles eighth outing: will stay 3m: acts on heavy going. *W. P. Mullins, Ireland* **h120 F88**

SUNDAWN LADY 7 b.m. Faustus (USA) – Game Domino (Derring Rose) [2004/5 h75: 22d^{pu} 19s 24d^{pu} 25g^2 24d^3 Apr 20] medium-sized mare: poor maiden hurdler: stays 25f: acts on good to firm and good to soft going: blinkered last 3 starts. *C. P. Morlock* **h78**

SUNDAY HABITS (IRE) 11 ch.g. Montelimar (USA) – Robertina (USA) (Roberto (USA)) [2004/5 c83§: c26m* c26g^{pu} c26s^6 c20d Nov 14] poor handicap chaser: won at Plumpton in September: stays 3¼m: acts on good to firm going: tried in cheekpieces/visor: has had tongue tied: temperamental. *Dr P. Pritchard* **c83 §**

SUNGATES (IRE) 9 ch.g. Glacial Storm (USA) – Live It Up (Le Coq d'Or) [2004/5 h105+: 22d^{pu} 23s^6 24d* Feb 26] lengthy gelding: fairly useful handicap hurdler: improved form when winning at Chepstow in February: stays 3¼m: raced on good ground or softer. *C. Tinkler* **h110**

SUNISA (IRE) 4 b.f. Daggers Drawn (USA) – Winged Victory (IRE) (Dancing Brave (USA)) [2004/5 16v^4 16d^6 Feb 4] angular filly: fairly useful on Flat (stays 1¼m), sold out of B. Hills's stable 14,000 gns Newmarket Autumn Sales: better effort in juvenile hurdles when sixth at Catterick: tongue tied. *J. Mackie* **h80**

SUN KING 8 ch.g. Zilzal (USA) – Opus One (Slip Anchor) [2004/5 h97: 16d^2 16m^2 May 20] leggy gelding: modest handicap hurdler: stays easy 2½m: acts on soft and good to firm going. *Mrs M. Reveley* **h90**

SUNLEY FUTURE (IRE) 6 b.g. Broken Hearted – The Wicked Chicken (IRE) (Saher) [2004/5 F87: 16d^6 16g^2 16g^3 16m^{pu} Apr 17] useful-looking gelding: modest form over hurdles: raced at 2m: free-going sort: difficult ride and one to treat with caution. *N. J. Henderson* **h93**

SUNLEY SHINES 5 ch.m. Komaite (USA) – Sunley Story (Reprimand) [2004/5 F18s F16d F17g* Apr 7] lengthy, angular mare: second foal: dam unraced: apparently much improved in bumpers when winning at Taunton by 4 lengths from Miss Midnight, unchallenged after pinching big lead at start. *B. G. Powell* **F93 ?**

SUNNYARJUN 7 ch.g. Afzal – Hush Tina (Tina's Pet) [2004/5 h–: 17m 17g* 16s^2 17s^6 16d 16d^5 Mar 24] workmanlike gelding: poor handicap hurdler: won at Folkestone in December: likely to prove best around 2m: acts on soft going. *J. C. Tuck* **h81**

SUNNY BROOK 6 ch.m. Alderbrook – Merry Marigold (Sonnen Gold) [2004/5 F17d^5 F17d Oct 27] 2,400 4-y-o: fourth foal: dam fair 1¼m winner: achieved little in bumpers. *Mrs S. J. Smith* **F–**

SUNNY DAZE 5 ch.g. Unfuwain (USA) – Light Ship (Warning) [2004/5 F16m Apr 25] first foal: dam, lightly-raced maiden, out of Oaks winner Bireme: tailed off in bumper on debut. *D. McCain* **F–**

SUNNYSIDE ROYALE (IRE) 6 b.g. Ali-Royal (IRE) – Kuwah (IRE) (Be My Guest (USA)) [2004/5 h85: 17v^{pu} 16d^6 20v^{pu} 16d Apr 11] leggy, close-coupled gelding: modest on Flat (stays 1¾m): poor handicap hurdler: form only around 2m: acts on soft going: usually tongue tied. *R. Bastiman* **h76**

SUNNY VILLE (IRE) 5 ch.g. Old Vic – Pink Ville (IRE) (Un Desperado (FR)) [2004/5 F16v 22v 20v 20s 20s^{pu} Apr 20] first foal: dam modest maiden hurdler: no sign of ability, including in points: headstrong: sold 2,300 gns Doncaster May Sales. *Liam Lennon, Ireland* **h–** **F–**

SUN PAGEANT 4 ch.f. Double Trigger (IRE) – Summer Pageant (Chief's Crown (USA)) [2004/5 F12g F12g F18m* Apr 21] seventh foal: half-sister to 2 winners by Bishop of Cashel, including fairly useful 6f and 7f performer Cloud Dancer: dam, 1½m winner, out of half-sister to Sun Princess and Saddlers' Hall: best effort in bumpers when winning at Fontwell in April by length from Crafty Lady. *M. G. Rimell* **F91**

SUNRAY 5 b.g. Spectrum (IRE) – Sharkashka (IRE) (Shardari) [2004/5 h118?: 24s^5 24v^5 Dec 28] leggy gelding: fair hurdler on balance in 2003/4: well held in handicaps in 2004/5: stays 3m: acts on soft and good to firm going: tried visored. *Evan Williams* **h–**

SUNRIDGE FAIRY (IRE) 6 b.m. Definite Article – Foxy Fairy (IRE) (Fairy King (USA)) [2004/5 16d 16g Mar 4] small mare: poor on Flat (stays 1¾m): winning 2m hurdler: well held both starts in 2004/5, left A. Lockwood after first: acts on soft and good to firm going. *L. R. James* **h–**

SUNSET LIGHT (IRE) 7 b.g. Supreme Leader – Game Sunset (Menelek) [2004/5 F16v^3 F16s* 20d^6 25s* Mar 13] good-topped gelding: half-brother to several winners, notably useful staying hurdler Goodtime George and fairly useful hurdler/very smart chaser up to 3m Stormyfairweather (both by Strong Gale): dam, winning 2m hurdler/ 2½m winner on Flat, sister to very smart chaser Western Sunset: fairly useful form in bumpers, winning at Towcester in February comfortably by 4 lengths from Montecorvino: much better effort over hurdles when winning novice at Warwick in March by 22 lengths from Woodlands Genpower: likely to prove suited by good test of stamina: should continue to progress. *C. Tinkler* **h122 p** **F104**

SUNSHAN 9 b.g. Anshan – Kyrenia Sunset (CYP) (Lucky Look (CYP)) [2004/5 c82: c19m^3 c24d^2 c21g* c24g^2 c21g^3 c21s^3 c21g^2 c24g^{pu} Aug 15] workmanlike gelding: modest novice chaser: won handicap at Stratford in May: stays 3m: acts on good to firm going, probably on soft: tongue tied earlier in career: often claimer ridden. *R. J. Hodges* **c87**

SUNSHINE RAYS 7 b.m. Alflora (IRE) – Ruby Rheims (Paveh Star) [2004/5 F18m* May 26] first foal: dam lightly raced, out of half-sister to useful chaser up to 3m Sun Rising: won bumper at Fontwell on debut by 2 lengths from The Game Is There. *C. Tinkler* **F83**

SUNSPOT 5 b.g. Peintre Celebre (USA) – Schezerade (USA) (Tom Rolfe) [2004/5 20g* 18s* 17s* 18v* Nov 28] useful form in 3 starts on Flat at 3 yrs for A. de Royer Dupre: unbeaten in 4 starts over hurdles, at Guerlesquin in July, Clairefontaine in August and Enghien and Auteuil in November: useful form when beating Orcantara 4 lengths in quite valuable 4-y-o event at last-named: joined M. O'Brien after, but bruised a bone in December and missed rest of season: stays 2½m: raced on good going or softer: likely to progress further if recovering fully. *A. Chaille-Chaille, France* **h131 p**

SUPER BLUE (IRE) 8 b.m. Supreme Leader – Tip Marie (IRE) (Celio Rufo) [2004/5 h–: 22g^4 19d May 4] useful-looking mare: lightly raced and little sign of ability over hurdles: soundly beaten on completed start in points. *Mrs S. D. Williams* **h–**

SUPER BOSTON 5 b.g. Saddlers' Hall (IRE) – Nasowas (IRE) (Cardinal Flower) [2004/5 F–: 20v^{pu} 16s^6 20v 24v^5 27v^{pu} 19d^3 20s 17g Apr 3] angular gelding: poor maiden hurdler: stays 19f: raced on good going or softer: tried blinkered. *Miss L. C. Siddall* **h67**

SUPERCHARMER 11 ch.g. Charmer – Surpassing (Superlative) [2004/5 c–, h–: c24d^F c24g^2 c20g^6 Jul 4] winning pointer: maiden hunter chaser: left M. Humphreys after second outing: stays 3m: blinkered once over hurdles. *P. T. Midgley* **c98 ?** **h–**

SUPER DOLPHIN 6 ch.g. Dolphin Street (FR) – Supergreen (Superlative) [2004/5 16d c17v^4 c16d^F c17v^{pu} 17m* Apr 23] good-topped gelding: won maiden point in 2004: modest hurdler: sold out of T. Tate's stable 4,200 gns Doncaster August Sales after first outing: improved effort when making all in selling handicap at Market Rasen in April: running best race in chases when falling heavily 2 out in novice handicap at Catterick: raced around 2m: tried tongue tied: has hinted at temperament. *R. Ford* **c82** **h93**

SUPER FELLOW (IRE) 11 b.g. Shy Groom (USA) – Killough (Lord Gayle (USA)) [2004/5 c114, h–: c28g^5 c26g* c32m Jun 27] angular gelding: fair handicap chaser: form in 2004/5 only when winning 4-runner event at Uttoxeter in May: stays 3¼m: acts on any going: effective in headgear or without: moody. *C. N. Kellett* **c112 §** **h–**

SUPERIOR WEAPON (IRE) 11 b.g. Riverhead (USA) – Ballytrustan Maid (IRE) (Orchestra) [2004/5 c84: 17g^{pu} c16g^{4} c16m c17v^{3} c16d* c16d^{5} c19g c17d Apr 11] no show only outing over hurdles: poor handicap chaser: won 4-runner event at Newcastle in November, final start for Mrs A. Hamilton: effective at 2m to easy 3m: acts on soft and good to firm going: tongue tied: usually front runner. *A. Robson* **c81 h–**

SUPER LUCKY (IRE) 9 b.m. Moscow Society (USA) – Ballela Maid (Boreen (FR)) [2004/5 c–, h80: 27m* 21m^{3} Aug 31] modest handicap hurdler: won at Sedgefield in July: stays 27f: acts on good to soft and good to firm going: no show either start in blinkers. *J. J. Lambe, Ireland* **c– h85**

SUPER NOMAD 10 b.g. Nomadic Way (USA) – Super Sue (Lochnager) [2004/5 c119, h–: c16d^{2} c16g^{2} c16s^{3} Apr 21] strong gelding: fairly useful handicap chaser: good efforts all 3 starts in 2004/5, third to Encore Cadoudal at Perth: effective at 2m to 2½m: acts on heavy and good to firm going: ran badly only outing in blinkers: has had tongue tied: sound jumper in main: consistent. *M. W. Easterby* **c125 h–**

SUPER ROAD TRAIN 6 b.g. Petoski – Foehn Gale (IRE) (Strong Gale) [2004/5 h91: 22d 24s^{pu} 22g 27m^{4} Apr 21] poor maiden hurdler: left L. Wells after first outing: stays 27f: has worn cheekpieces: inconsistent. *O. Sherwood* **h76**

SUPERROLLERCOASTER 5 b.g. Classic Cliche (IRE) – Foehn Gale (IRE) (Strong Gale) [2004/5 F18d 21d^{4} 21d^{5} 22d^{3} 21g^{3} Apr 1] strong gelding: second foal: half-brother to bumper winner Super Road Train (by Petoski): dam unraced, out of sister to useful staying hurdler Woodford Prince: seventh in maiden bumper on debut: fair novice hurdler: likely to stay 3m: raced on good/good to soft going. *O. Sherwood* **h100 F–**

SUPER SAMMY 9 br.m. Mesleh – Super Sue (Lochnager) [2004/5 c100, h85: 20s^{4} 17d^{6} 19g 25g^{6} 21v^{2} 27v^{pu} c21s* c21v^{4} c21d^{pu} Apr 5] lengthy mare: modest handicap hurdler: poor form over fences: won maiden at Sedgefield in February: stays 21f: raced mainly on good going or softer (acts on heavy): wore cheekpieces last 5 outings: has bled from nose. *K. A. Ryan* **c80 h97**

SUPERSHOT (IRE) 7 b.g. Son of Sharp Shot (IRE) – One To Two (IRE) (Astronef) [2004/5 F16d^{pu} Nov 29] no show in bumpers nearly 2 years apart. *O. Brennan* **F–**

SUPERSTAR EXPRESS (IRE) 8 br.g. Jurado (USA) – Easter Bee (IRE) (Phardante (FR)) [2004/5 c25g^{pu} May 1] lengthy gelding: of little account outside points: has had tongue tied. *Ms J. M. Findlay* **c– h–**

SUPER TIP (IRE) 7 b.g. Supreme Leader – Tip Marie (IRE) (Celio Rufo) [2004/5 h–, F85: c20g^{3} c21d^{pu} c16s^{pu} c18g Mar 20] lengthy gelding: no form over hurdles or fences: tried blinkered. *P. Winkworth* **c– h–**

SUPPLY AND FIX (IRE) 7 b.g. Supreme Leader – Hannies Girl (IRE) (Invited (USA)) [2004/5 20d^{pu} 17g^{ro} 17m^{pu} c24v^{pu} c23g^{3} Mar 12] first foal: dam, fair chaser around 2m, half-sister to Kerry National winner Desert Lord: poor maiden hurdler: winning pointer: poor form completed start in hunters. *J. J. Lambe, Ireland* **c78 h–**

SUPREME ARROW (IRE) 10 b.m. Supreme Leader – Clover Run (IRE) (Deep Run) [2004/5 c110, h118: c20m^{2} c20m c20g^{5} Jul 11] workmanlike mare: fairly useful handicap hurdler fair handicap chaser: stays easy 3m: acts on soft and good to firm going: tongue tied last 2 starts. *Miss E. C. Lavelle* **c106 h–**

SUPREME BEING (IRE) 8 b.g. Supreme Leader – Parsonetta (The Parson) [2004/5 h108: 20g* 20g^{3} 22m^{2} Jul 31] fair handicap hurdler: ran well when second to Gemini Guest at Galway (reportedly finished lame): stays 2¾m: acts on heavy and good to firm going: usually wears blinkers, also tried in cheekpieces. *Michael Cunningham, Ireland* **h114**

SUPREME BREEZE (IRE) 10 b.g. Supreme Leader – Merry Breeze (Strong Gale) [2004/5 c94§, h–: c25d c26d^{3} c25d* c21m^{3} c23m^{5} c27v^{2} c24s^{2} c26s* c24v* c24d Mar 26] small gelding: fair chaser: won handicaps at Hexham (novice) in June and Carlisle (2, novice on second occasion) in March: stays 31f: acts on heavy going: tried in blinkers/ cheekpieces: generally improved jumping and attitude in 2004/5. *Mrs S. J. Smith* **c112 h–**

SUPREME CATCH (IRE) 8 b.g. Supreme Leader – Lucky Trout (Beau Charmeur (FR)) [2004/5 c127, h–: 24s^{pu} Nov 3] workmanlike gelding: fairly useful handicap chaser in 2003/4: lightly-raced hurdler: will stay beyond 3m: acts on heavy going: patiently ridden. *Miss H. C. Knight* **c– h–**

SUPREME DAWN (IRE) 8 b.g. Supreme Leader – Tudor Dawn (Deep Run) [2004/5 h106, F–: 17d* 19m* 16g^{2} Nov 15] useful-looking gelding: fair hurdler: won maiden at Exeter in May and novice at Hereford in June: should stay beyond 19f: acts on good to firm and heavy ground. *C. Tinkler* **h111**

SUPREME DESTINY (IRE) 7 b.g. Supreme Leader – Shuil Le Gaoth (IRE) (Strong Gale) [2004/5 F79: F16d Nov 13] twice-raced in bumpers, well held in November after 12-month absence. *Miss V. Scott* **F–**

SUPREME DEVELOPER (IRE) 8 b.g. Supreme Leader – Bettys The Boss (IRE) (Deep Run) [2004/5 16g 18m^2 c20d^2 c20d^2 c16g* c16d^2 c16d^2 c16g Mar 15] well-made gelding: fair hurdler: left A. Mullins and off 6 months after second start: fairly useful novice chaser: won at Newcastle in December by 3 lengths from Bold Bishop: good second to L'Ange Au Ciel in handicap at Sandown seventh start: in cheekpieces, well held in Arkle Chase at Cheltenham final start: stays 2½m: acts on soft and good to firm going. *Ferdy Murphy* **c128 h110**

SUPREME GIFT 6 br.m. Supreme Leader – Strong Cloth (IRE) (Strong Gale) [2004/5 F18m^3 May 26] second foal: half-sister to novice hurdler Blank Canvas (by Presenting): dam unraced half-sister to fairly useful staying chaser Parahandy: 8 lengths third in weakly-contested bumper at Fontwell on debut. *R. Curtis* **F75**

SUPREME GLORY (IRE) 12 b.g. Supreme Leader – Pentlows (Sheer Grit) [2004/5 c26g c29v^{pu} c33g^{pu} Apr 16] well-made gelding: formerly useful staying chaser: off 20 months, no sign of retaining ability in valuable handicaps in 2004/5: acts on heavy and good to firm going: sound jumper. *P. G. Murphy* **c–**

SUPREME HILL (IRE) 8 br.g. Supreme Leader – Regents Prancer (Prince Regent (FR)) [2004/5 c–, h88: 22g* May 1] workmanlike gelding: fair form in novice hurdles, won at Uttoxeter in May: fell both starts over fences: stays 2¾m: raced on good going or softer (acts on heavy). *C. J. Mann* **c– h109**

SUPREME HOPE (USA) 6 b.g. Supreme Leader – Flaming Hope (IRE) (Callernish) [2004/5 F98: 16g^6 Mar 16] runner-up in bumper on debut: off 16 months, sixth in maiden at Huntingdon on hurdling debut. *H. D. Daly* **h79**

SUPREME LEISURE (IRE) 8 b.g. Supreme Leader – Maid of Leisure (Le Moss) [2004/5 F103: c21v^{pu} 16v* 24s^5 21v* Mar 28] rangy gelding: pulled up after bad mistake on chasing debut: fair novice hurdler: won at Wetherby in January and Sedgefield in March: ran poorly in between: should stay beyond 21f: raced on ground softer than good (acts on heavy). *J. Howard Johnson* **c– p h112**

SUPREME LOVER 6 b.g. Supreme Leader – Theme Arena (Tragic Role (USA)) [2004/5 17d^{pu} 16d Nov 6] sturdy gelding: first foal: dam won around 2m over hurdles and at 2m on Flat: no show in 2 novice hurdles, jumping very slowly on debut. *Miss H. C. Knight* **h–**

SUPREMELY RED (IRE) 8 b.g. Supreme Leader – Her Name Was Lola (Pitskelly) [2004/5 h–: 26m 24m Sep 24] medium-sized gelding: lightly-raced winning hurdler: well held since 2002; tried visored/blinkered: hard ride. *D. A. Rees* **h81**

SUPREME MISSILE (IRE) 5 b.g. Shernazar – Explosive Missile (IRE) (Supreme Leader) [2004/5 F16g^2 F17s^5 19m^{pu} Apr 9] €12,000: good-topped gelding: fourth foal: dam, twice-raced in points, from family of top-class staying chaser Spartan Missile: fell in maiden Irish point in 2004: better effort in bumpers when runner-up on debut: lost action in maiden at Hereford on hurdling debut: should do better. *Miss H. C. Knight* **h– p F84**

SUPREME NATIVE (IRE) 9 b.g. Be My Native (USA) – Ballough Bui (IRE) (Supreme Leader) [2004/5 17d^6 17d^6 Dec 16] useful-looking gelding: fair novice hurdler in 2001/2: soundly beaten in 2 handicaps after 2-year absence: should stay beyond 19f: acts on firm going: tongue tied on reappearance: not an easy ride. *Ms Bridget Nicholls* **h–**

SUPREME OCEAN (IRE) 5 b.m. Supreme Leader – Shannon Spray (Le Bavard (FR)) [2004/5 F16s^4 F17s Apr 7] rangy, useful-looking mare: half-sister to useful chaser Eirespray (by Executive Perk), stayed 25f, and useful hurdler/chaser Shannon Gale (by Strong Gale), stayed 3¼m: dam, smart hurdler up to 2¾m, half-sister to dams of smart staying chaser One Knight and useful jumpers Direct Access, Sunset Lodge and Atum Re: better effort in mares bumpers when fourth at Huntingdon on debut: bred to stay at least 2½m: tongue tied. *Noel T. Chance* **F87**

SUPREME PIPER (IRE) 7 b.g. Supreme Leader – Whistling Doe (Whistling Deer) [2004/5 h122: 22g^F 22g* 25g^3 21d^6 24s* c24g^4 25s 22d^5 24g Mar 17] useful-looking gelding: fairly useful hurdler: won novice at Wincanton in May and handicap at Windsor (made all, by 5 lengths from Dream Falcon) in November: poor efforts last 3 outings: odds on, numerous mistakes on chasing debut in maiden at Taunton: stays 25f: acts on soft going: sold 17,000 gns Doncaster May Sales. *P. J. Hobbs* **c– p h119**

SUPREME PRINCE (IRE) 8 b.g. Supreme Leader – Strong Serenade (IRE) (Strong Gale) [2004/5 c129, h–: 20s c20s^F c20g* c21d c24d^5 c20d* c21g^F Mar 17] **c146 h141**

The second running of the Vodafone Gold Cup suffered from its proximity to the Cheltenham Festival more than the first had done because of the introduction of the Daily Telegraph Festival Trophy. The Vodafone, run over two and a half miles at Newbury on the first Saturday in March and worth £58,000 to the winner was, however, again a good-quality and very strongly-contested handicap chase. It looks a most welcome addition to the calendar, as in the previous season attracting a field of fifteen. The weights were headed by First Gold, though the best supported runners came from much lower down the handicap, with Buckby Lane, winner of the Ladbrokes Trophy at Cheltenham on his delayed reappearance, the clear favourite at 100/30. Next in the betting at 11/2 came the smart novice Chauvinist, whose trainer Nicky Henderson had saddled Isio, missing through injury in 2004/5, to win the inaugural running when Turgeonev and Hand Inn Hand finished second and fourth respectively, that pair also involved this time around. Third favourite at 7/1 was Supreme Prince, a second-season chaser, as Isio had been, but one who hadn't shown anything like the same aptitude for jumping fences. Supreme Prince had, however, won three chases, including a valuable fifteen-runner handicap over course and distance on Hennessy day in November in which he beat Claymore by three quarters of a length, much more assured than usual at his fences and leading or disputing the lead throughout. Supreme Prince's jumping problems resurfaced at Cheltenham on his next start, but on his only other outing before the Vodafone he jumped soundly and finished a creditable fifth to Colourful Life in the Great Yorkshire Chase at Doncaster, where a testing three miles stretched his stamina.

Supreme Prince's jumping also stood up well to the pressures put on it in the Vodafone, which was run at a sound pace, Buckby Lane one of those who helped force it. When Buckby Lane blundered five out it was Supreme Prince, prominent from the off, who quickened to take the lead. Supreme Prince had most of his rivals off the bridle and seemed to clinch matters when taking a decisive advantage two out, only to idle after the last and let 25/1-shot Horus, one of Martin Pipe's three representatives, in with a chance. Horus was staying on best of all after doing well to survive a blunder at the eighth and, early on the run-in, looked as though he might

Vodafone Gold Cup Handicap Chase, Newbury—
a second valuable course-and-distance success of 2004/5 for Supreme Prince and Paul Flynn

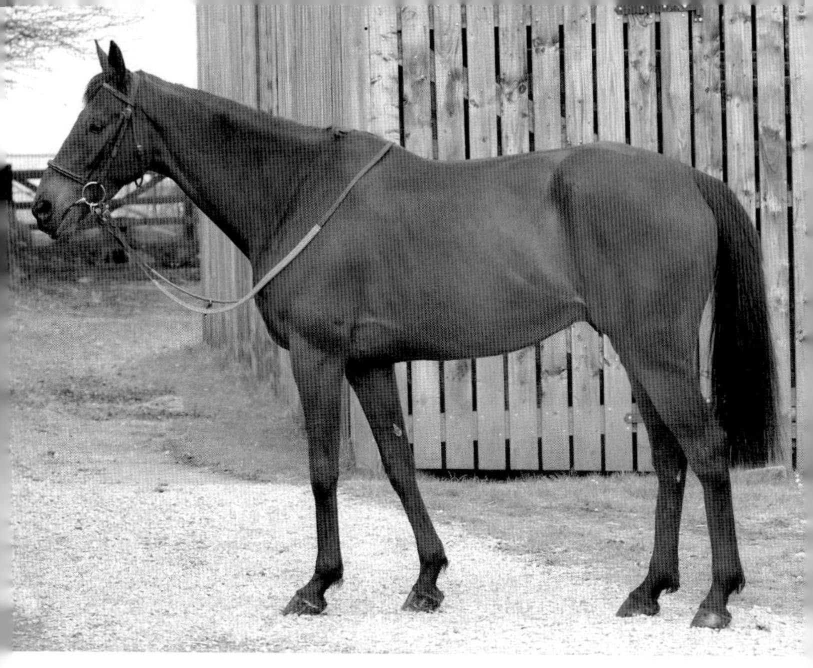

Mrs Karola Vann's "Supreme Prince"

catch Supreme Prince, but the latter found more and held on to win by half a length. Chauvinist was a further two lengths back in third with less than eight lengths covering the first ten home. Five of the runners, including Supreme Prince and fourth-placed Simply Gifted, went on to contest the Mildmay of Flete at Cheltenham, with Simply Gifted faring best in taking third there. Supreme Prince, running under a penalty for his win a Newbury, fell at the eleventh when in touch. Given his record over fences at Cheltenham—his jumping had left a lot to be desired when he was pulled up in the 2004 Royal & SunAlliance Chase—a degree of caution is advised should he turn up in another chase there.

Supreme Prince (IRE) (b.g. 1997)	Supreme Leader (b 1982)	Bustino (b 1971)	Busted
			Ship Yard
		Princess Zena (b 1975)	Habitat
			Guiding Light
	Strong Serenade (IRE) (b 1989)	Strong Gale (br 1975)	Lord Gayle
			Sterntau
		Serenade Run (ch 1983)	Deep Run
			Swift Serenade

Supreme Prince did perform with credit on his only appearance over hurdles at Cheltenham, though. That was in the 2002/3 season when he lined up for the Royal & SunAlliance Hurdle the unbeaten winner of four races, a bumper at Exeter, two novice hurdles at Chepstow, including the Persian War, and one at Wincanton. Supreme Prince finished eighth to Hardy Eustace at Cheltenham, and then showed further improvement when third to Iris's Gift in the Sefton Novices' Hurdle at Aintree. Before his return to Cheltenham for the Royal & SunAlliance Chase, Supreme Prince won a maiden chase at Chepstow and a Grade 2 novice chase at Ascot. Victory in the Vodafone took Supreme Prince's earnings well past the IR 100,000 guineas paid for him as an unraced three-year-old. He would have made plenty of appeal on pedigree when he came up for sale, being by Supreme Leader out of a mare who won a bumper and a two-mile maiden hurdle. The dam Strong Serenade was responsible for one winner before Supreme Prince, That's The Story picking up a bumper and a three-mile handicap hurdle in Ireland; and there have been two since, both of them by Supreme Leader. The seven-year-old Field Marshal won a bumper at Punchestown in 2003, while the six-year-old mare Supreme Serenade, in the same ownership as Supreme Prince, developed into a useful handicap hurdler in the latest season, her two wins including the totescoop6 Sandown Hurdle. Supreme Prince's grandam never ran, but his great grandam Swift Serenade, a half-sister to the smart hurdler at up to three miles Last Serenade, was successful in bumpers and over hurdles. This makes Supreme Prince distantly related to Take The Stand, whose fourth dam Last Serenade is. Supreme Prince, a tall gelding who often takes the eye in the paddock, as he did before the Vodafone, is effective at two and a half miles to three, though the latter distance stretches his stamina. Unraced on ground firmer than good, he acts on soft but has yet to encounter heavy. *P. J. Hobbs*

SUPREME PRIORITY (IRE) 7 b.g. Supreme Leader – Kakemona (Kambalda) [2004/5 h77: 24dpu May 12] lengthy gelding: poor hurdler: pulled up both starts in points: stays 3¼m: probably acts on any going. *C. Roberts* **h–**

SUPREME RETURN 6 b.g. Bob's Return (IRE) – Supreme Wonder (IRE) (Supreme Leader) [2004/5 F83: 16d 20s 19spu 19d 22spu Mar 22] tall gelding: has plenty of scope: modest in bumpers: no form over hurdles. *A. King* **h–**

SUPREME RULLAH (IRE) 8 b.m. Supreme Leader – Trapper Jean (Orchestra) [2004/5 h68, F–: 26s 23d2 Mar 28] easily best effort over hurdles when second in 23f novice handicap at Fakenham: often tongue tied. *Mrs L. Wadham* **h81**

SUPREME SERENADE (IRE) 6 b.m. Supreme Leader – Strong Serenade (IRE) (Strong Gale) [2004/5 h111, F103: 17d3 21d* 22g* 21g Mar 16] good-topped mare: useful handicap hurdler: much improved and won at Kempton (impressively by 1¼ lengths from Croix de Guerre) in January and Sandown in February: beat Fountain Hill a neck in totescoop6 Hurdle at latter, despite blundering last then veering right: below form in Coral Cup at Cheltenham final start: will stay 3m: raced on good going or softer: quirky, and suited by exaggerated waiting tactics in a well-run race. *P. J. Hobbs* **h133**

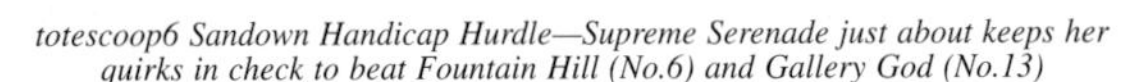

totescoop6 Sandown Handicap Hurdle—Supreme Serenade just about keeps her quirks in check to beat Fountain Hill (No.6) and Gallery God (No.13)

SUPREME SILENCE (IRE) 8 b.g. Bluebird (USA) – Why So Silent (Mill Reef (USA)) [2004/5 c80§, h–§: c20g c27g3 c25s* c26gpu c21d3 c25g5 c24s6 Apr 16] angular gelding: winning hurdler: fair hunter chaser: won 4-runner novice at Market Rasen in March by distance: stays 25f: acts on soft going: tried blinkered/visored: has had tongue tied: ungenuine. *Nick Kent*
c91 § h– §

SUPREME SIR (IRE) 7 b.g. Supreme Leader – Sirrah Madam (Tug of War) [2004/5 c24spu c25spu c26vpu Dec 31] lengthy gelding: fifth foal: half-brother to winning 3m chaser Sirrah Aris (by Buckskin) and winning pointer by Phardante: dam, maiden pointer, sister to useful 2m to 2¾m chaser Sirrah Jay: no sign of ability, including in Irish points. *P. G. Murphy*
c–

SUPREME'S LEGACY (IRE) 6 b.g. Supreme Leader – Lucylet (Kinglet) [2004/5 F111: F16d Nov 29] has scope: useful form when runner-up in bumper on debut in 2003/4: no show in similar event 12 months later. *K. G. Reveley*
F–

SUPREME STORM (IRE) 10 b.g. Supreme Leader – Angolass (Al Sirat) [2004/5 c21d c24g5 Mar 4] strong gelding: winning chaser: well beaten in 2 hunters in 2004/5: should stay 3m: raced on good going or softer. *Mrs D. Buckett*
c– h–

SUPREME TADGH (IRE) 8 b.g. Supreme Leader – Mariaetta (IRE) (Mandalus) [2004/5 20gpu c20v5 22dpu Apr 17] ex-Irish gelding: second foal: dam unraced: maiden hurdler: winning pointer, including in 2005: well held in hunter on chasing debut, final start for W. Burke: stays 2¾m: acts on soft ground. *J. A. Geake*
c86 h–

SUPRENDRE ESPERE 5 b.g. Espere d'Or – Celtic Dream (Celtic Cone) [2004/5 F16d F17g Mar 19] lengthy gelding: third reported foal: half-brother to modest hurdler up to 3m Vert Espere (by Green Adventure): dam bad maiden hurdler/chaser: well held in 2 bumpers. *M. Wellings*
F–

SUREFAST 10 ch.g. Nearly A Hand – Meldon Lady (Ballymoss) [2004/5 c82, h–: c25gF c23s* c26s2 c20s* c26v* c23v4 Mar 1] stocky gelding: modest chaser: won handicap at Exeter in October and minor events at Lingfield (amateur) in November and Plumpton in January: stays 3¼m: acts on heavy going: consistent. *K. Bishop*
c96 h–

SURE FUTURE 9 b.g. Kylian (USA) – Lady Ever-So-Sure (Malicious) [2004/5 c94, h116: 26g6 24s5 21d 20d3 22s2 25s 22d4 24g4 c26g2 c26d2 Apr 18] strong, close-coupled gelding: fair handicap hurdler: modest form over fences (has been let down by jumping): stays 3¼m: acts on heavy and good to firm going: has been blinkered: tried tongue tied. *R. M. Stronge*
c94 h110

SURE RHYTHM 4 b.f. Keen – Rythmic Rymer (Rymer) [2004/5 F16g F16g Mar 9] smallish filly: second foal: dam poor half-sister to useful chaser up to 2½m Anabranch: tailed off in bumpers. *J. M. Jefferson*
F–

SURFBOARD (IRE) 4 ch.g. Kris – Surfing (Grundy) [2004/5 F14m Mar 21] half-brother to several winners, including useful 6f to 9.4f winner Mister Fire Eyes (by Petorious) and ungenuine hurdler/chaser Sea Breaker (by Glow), stayed 3m: dam, maiden who stayed 7f, half-sister to Middle Park winner Bassenthwaite: showed little in maiden bumper on debut. *P. A. Blockley*
F70

SURPRISE GUNNER 15 b.g. Gunner B – Heckley Loch (Lochnager) [2004/5 c–, h–: 16s 24spu 22dpu Dec 16] compact gelding: veteran hurdler: no form over fences. *D. W. Lewis*
c– h–

SURPRISING 10 b.g. Primitive Rising (USA) – Ascot Lass (Touching Wood (USA)) [2004/5 c131, h–: c26gpu Dec 8] lengthy gelding: useful hurdler/fairly useful chaser at best: off over a year, broke blood vessel in handicap chase at Newbury: stays 3½m: acts on any going: has worn blinkers: held up: not an easy ride/has found little. *O. Sherwood*
c– h–

SUSIE BURY 6 b.m. Overbury (IRE) – Susie's Money (Seymour Hicks (FR)) [2004/5 F–: F16d May 6] no form in bumpers. *S. A. Brookshaw*
F–

SUSPENDID (IRE) 12 b.g. Yashgan – Spendapromise (Goldhill) [2004/5 c110§, h–: c20d c20mpu c20mF c20m4 c24g c23m3 Aug 6] sturdy gelding: fair handicap chaser: stays easy 23f: acts on good to firm and good to soft going: tried tongue tied: has broken blood vessels: unreliable. *R. Lee*
c104 § h–

SUSPICIOUS MINDS 4 b.f. Anabaa (USA) – Paloma Bay (IRE) (Alzao (USA)) [2004/5 16m5 16f 16d2 17s 17g Apr 12] half-sister to Triumph Hurdle winner Spectroscope (by Spectrum): well held in maidens on Flat, sold out of G. Bravery's stable 10,000 gns Newmarket July Sales: form over hurdles only when second in juvenile at Wincanton: pulls hard. *J. W. Mullins*
h77

SUSY WELLS (IRE) 10 b.m. Masad (IRE) – My Best Susy (IRE) (Try My Best (USA)) [2004/5 h–: 17s^{pu} Apr 2] of no account: tried in cheekpieces. *C. W. Moore* **h–**

SUTTON BALLAD 11 b.m. Emperor Fountain – Crescent Cottage (Cornuto) [2004/5 h–: 19d Apr 29] no form in 2 starts over hurdles. *P. D. Purdy* **h–**

SVENSON 4 ch.c. Dancing Spree (USA) – Bella Bambola (IRE) (Tate Gallery (USA)) [2004/5 17g^{ur} Aug 21] poor form on Flat: unseated second on hurdling debut. *J. S. Wainwright* **h–**

SWALLOW MAGIC (IRE) 7 b.g. Magic Ring (IRE) – Scylla (Rock City) [2004/5 16f 20f* 20g^{pu} 16s 17d 20d^{6} 20m 24g^{6} Feb 27] well held in 2 races on Flat: won maiden Irish point in 2004: poor hurdler: won maiden at Kilbeggan in June: sold out of L. Whitmore's stable 20,000 gns Doncaster August Sales before next outing: stays 2½m: acts on firm going, probably on good to soft: blinkered final start: tongue tied: usually races prominently. *Ferdy Murphy* **h79**

SWAN KNIGHT (USA) 9 b. or br.g. Sadler's Wells (USA) – Shannkara (IRE) (Akarad (FR)) [2004/5 c102+, h113: 16g 16s^{2} 16s Nov 4] compact gelding: twice-raced chaser: fair handicap hurdler: form in 2004/5 only when runner-up to Middlethorpe at Wetherby: best at 2m: acts on soft and good to firm going. *R. A. Fahey* **c– h106**

SWANSEA BAY 9 b.g. Jurado (USA) – Slave's Bangle (Prince Rheingold) [2004/5 c149, h–: c24d^{4} c25g^{6} 24m* 26d^{2} c25d^{6} c26g c25d c24g c21d^{rtr} Apr 8] lengthy gelding: smart handicap chaser in 2003/4, well below form in 2004/5: took advantage of much lower mark over hurdles when winning at Worcester (unbeaten in 6 starts there) in September: best at 3m+: has form on heavy ground, best efforts on good or firmer: tried in headgear: has had tongue tied: has hinted at temperament (refused to race in Topham Chase at Aintree final start). *P. Bowen* **c– h102**

SWAZI PRINCE 6 b.g. Rakaposhi King – Swazi Princess (IRE) (Brush Aside (USA)) [2004/5 F79: 22d^{F} 24d^{5} 24s^{5} Mar 31] sturdy gelding: would have made winning hurdling debut but for falling last in novice at Uttoxeter in October: disappointing both outings after. *N. A. Twiston-Davies* **h102**

SWEEPING STORM (IRE) 8 ch.g. Glacial Storm (USA) – Sweeping Gold (Quayside) [2004/5 c20g^{4} May 29] poor form in novice hurdle and hunter chase: fair pointer, in frame both starts in 2005. *Mrs Elaine Smith* **c68 h–**

SWEET ARD (IRE) 5 b.m. Zaffaran (USA) – Ard Ri (IRE) (Un Desperado (FR)) [2004/5 F16d* 16v^{4} Jan 3] leggy, useful-looking mare: first foal: dam well beaten in bumper/points: fairly useful form when winning mares bumper at Wetherby on debut in November by 2½ lengths from Nobodys Perfect: favourite, fourth to Pay Attention in mares novice there on hurdling debut: bred to be suited by further than 2m. *N. G. Richards* **h94 F99**

SWEET AUBURN (IRE) 9 b. or br.g. Tidaro (USA) – Sweet View (King's Ride) [2004/5 c82, h78: c16g^{2} 21d^{5} 22m^{6} c20g^{3} 24g^{5} c21m^{2} c20g^{pu} Sep 12] sturdy gelding: poor maiden hurdler/chaser: stays 25f: acts on heavy and good to firm going: tried in headgear: temperament under suspicion. *Mrs B. K. Thomson* **c78 h76**

SWEET AZ 5 b.m. Averti (IRE) – Yen Haven (USA) (Lear Fan (USA)) [2004/5 22g^{4} Aug 10] little form on Flat: in cheekpieces, achieved little in novice on hurdling debut. *S. C. Burrough* **h–**

SWEET CHARIOT 6 b.g. Hatim (USA) – Evening Dusk (IRE) (Phardante (FR)) [2004/5 F–: F17s 19s^{pu} 17g 18s c16g^{pu} Mar 28] sturdy gelding: no sign of ability. *Miss I. E. Craig* **c– h– F–**

SWEET DIVERSION (IRE) 6 b.g. Carroll House – Serocco Wind (Roi Guillaume (FR)) [2004/5 h121, F87: 21d^{5} c19d^{3} c20s^{3} c24g* c21v^{pu} Apr 22] sturdy gelding: fairly useful hurdler: fair form over fences: won maiden at Stratford in April by 3½ lengths from Mrs Be: stays 3m: acts on soft and good to firm going, probably unsuited by heavy final start. *P. F. Nicholls* **c113 h124**

SWEET KILN (IRE) 6 b.m. Beneficial – Miss Pollerton (IRE) (Pollerton) [2004/5 F106+: F16s* 16d^{2} 20v* 20s^{2} 20v^{2} 24v* 18s^{4} 20s^{3} 20d^{2} 20s Mar 27] lengthy mare: progressive form in bumpers, smart form when beating The Alamo by 14 lengths at Tipperary in October: fairly useful novice hurdler: won Grade 3 Tote Exacta Monksfield Novices' Hurdle at Navan (beat Petertheknot 3½ lengths) in November and at Fairyhouse (by length from Carraig Blue, pair distance clear) in January: creditable efforts otherwise until running poorly final start: stays 3m: raced on going softer than good (acts on heavy): front runner: consistent. *James Bowe, Ireland* **h129 F115**

SWEET MILLY 10 b.m. Milieu – Another Joyful (Rubor) [2004/5 h68: 16s^5 Jan 19] poor maiden hurdler: raced mainly around 2m: acts on heavy going. *J. E. Dixon* **h–**

SWEET MINUET 8 b.m. Minshaanshu Amad (USA) – Sweet N' Twenty (High Top) [2004/5 h82: c17g^3 c20s^F c16s^3 c22s^4 c20s^F 22g c20m Apr 10] lengthy mare: poor hurdler/maiden chaser: stays 2¾m: acts on any going: blinkered once. *M. Madgwick* **c84 h–**

SWEET OONA (FR) 6 gr.m. Kendor (FR) – Poplife (FR) (Zino) [2004/5 17m^4 16s^2 16v^2 16d^3 16s^2 16g^2 19s^3 Mar 27] good-topped ex-French mare: second foal: half-sister to winner around 1½m Edward Rabbit (by Le Triton): dam smart French hurdler: 1½m winner on Flat at 3 yrs, placed once from 10 starts at 4 yrs for Mlle V. Dissaux: fair maiden hurdler: should stay beyond 2m: takes strong hold. *Miss Venetia Williams* **h100**

SWEET SHOOTER 5 ch.m. Double Trigger (IRE) – Sweet N' Twenty (High Top) [2004/5 F82: F16s^5 16s^4 20v^4 22d^{pu} Mar 24] angular mare: modest form in bumpers: poor form over hurdles: should stay beyond 2½m: tried visored. *M. Madgwick* **h– F–**

SWEETWATER (GER) 5 b.m. Goofalik (USA) – Safrane (GER) (Mister Rock's (GER)) [2004/5 16m^6 16m^5 16g^{ur} 18m^{pu} Sep 21] successful 3 times over 1¼m on Flat in France, claimed out of M. Rolland's stable €18,000: showed far more temperament than ability over hurdles, claimed by Stef Liddiard £6,000 final start: modest on Flat in Britain, successful in February. *M. C. Pipe* **h73 §**

SWIFT SETTLEMENT 6 br.m. King's Ride – Swift Conveyance (IRE) (Strong Gale) [2004/5 F–: F16g May 13] well beaten in 2 bumpers. *J. Rudge* **F–**

SWIFTS HILL (IRE) 7 ch.g. Executive Perk – Tudor Lady (Green Shoon) [2004/5 F16s^4 20s 20s^{pu} 19m^2 Apr 9] 16,000 4-y-o: sturdy gelding: half-brother to several winners, including fairly useful staying chaser/fair hurdler Satshoon (by Satco) and fairly useful hurdler/winning chaser Supreme Lady (by Supreme Leader), stayed 2¾m: dam once-raced, from family of useful chaser up to 3m Church Warden: well held in bumper on debut: first form over hurdles when second in maiden at Hereford: will stay 3m. *T. R. George* **h88 F–**

SWIFT SWALLOW 7 ch.g. Missed Flight – Alhargah (Be My Guest (USA)) [2004/5 F89: 17d^2 16g^3 19d* 20d^3 16s^4 Mar 23] sturdy gelding: fair novice hurdler: off 9 months, won at Market Rasen in February: stays 2½m: acts on good to soft going. *O. Brennan* **h108**

SWIFTWAY 11 ch.g. Anshan – Solemn Occasion (USA) (Secreto (USA)) [2004/5 c–, h–: c24g* c21s^{ur} c25d^5 Apr 11] workmanlike gelding: winning hurdler: fit from points, won hunter chase at Musselburgh in February by 4 lengths from Coole Abbey: stays 3m: acts on soft and good to firm going: tried blinkered. *Miss J. Fisher* **c101 h–**

SWINCOMBE (IRE) 10 b.g. Good Thyne (USA) – Gladtogetit (Green Shoon) [2004/5 c104§: c25g^3 c23s^2 c24s^F Mar 27] fair chaser, left R. Alner after first outing: successful in point in February: good second to Cobreces in hunter at Leicester following month: stays 3¼m: acts on heavy going: ran moodily when visored. *Mrs S. J. Hickman* **c108 §**

SWISS ROSE 8 ch.m. Michelozzo (USA) – Tic-On-Rose (Celtic Cone) [2004/5 21d^{pu} 19d^{ur} 22d^{pu} Mar 24] sparely-made mare: ninth foal: half-sister to winning pointer Tirley Missile (by Cruise Missile): dam, winning hurdler, sister to useful staying hurdler Celtic Rambler: no sign of ability: has looked temperamental. *J. S. Smith* **h–**

SWORD LADY 7 b.m. Broadsword (USA) – Speckyfoureyes (Blue Cashmere) [2004/5 h104: 21s^F 24s^6 23v 21v^{pu} 24s* 24g* 24s^3 21g Apr 14] leggy mare: fair handicap hurdler: back in form when winning at Taunton (mares amateur event) in February and Bangor in March: stays 3m: acts on heavy going: blinkered last 4 starts: front runner. *Mrs S. D. Williams* **h113**

SWORDPLAY 7 ch.g. Kris – Throw Away Line (Cragador) [2004/5 h130: 16g 16g^6 c17g* c16f* c17s^3 c16s^3 c16d^6 19s Mar 27] leggy gelding: useful hurdler at best: fairly useful form over fences, won novice at Galway in July and 3-runner minor event at Tramore in August: creditable efforts after when third: will prove best at 2m: acts on firm and soft going: tongue tied third to fifth starts. *M. J. P. O'Brien, Ireland* **c121 h–**

SWORN IN (USA) 4 ch.c. Kingmambo (USA) – Under Oath (USA) (Deputed Testamony (USA)) [2004/5 F16d* F16m Apr 2] good sort: brother to smart US winner Queen's Word, second in Grade 1 9f event, and closely related or half-brother to several winners in USA: dam won 15 races in USA, including Grade 3 8.5f event: sold unraced out of J. Gosden's stable 5,000 gns Newmarket December Sales: 50/1, useful form when winning 18-runner bumper at Newbury on debut by 9 lengths from Rimsky: reportedly lost a shoe when only tenth there in March. *N. I. M. Rossiter* **F106**

SWYNFORD PLEASURE 9 b.m. Reprimand – Pleasuring (Good Times (ITY)) [2004/5 16d Nov 9] smallish mare: fair on Flat (stays 1¾m): pulled hard and showed little in novice on hurdling debut. *J. Hetherton* **h–**

SYDNEY (IRE) 5 b.g. Saddlers' Hall (IRE) – Magic Gale (IRE) (Strong Gale) [2004/5 F18d Apr 18] €17,500 3-y-o: fourth foal: dam, placed in points, from family of top-class chaser Buck House: carried head high when eighth of 10 in maiden bumper on debut. *M. Pitman* **F83**

SYLCAN EXPRESS 12 br.g. Sylvan Express – Dercanny (Derek H) [2004/5 24s 16s Jan 11] workmanlike gelding: poor hurdler, off over 2 years before reappearance: tried visored. *O. O'Neill* **c– h60**

SYLPHIDE 10 b.m. Ballet Royal (USA) – Shafayif (Ela-Mana-Mou) [2004/5 c90, h–: 22g^{6} c22m* c25m^{pu} 24g* 26g^{3} 22g^{2} 21s^{2} 16s^{6} 26s^{5} c18s^{pu} c26s^{2} 24m Apr 10] sparely-made mare: modest handicap chaser: won at Fontwell in May: poor hurdler: won novice handicap at Worcester in July: stays 3¼m: acts on soft and good to firm going: held up. *H. J. Manners* **c90 h74**

SYLVAN SHACK (IRE) 7 b. or br.g. Grand Plaisir (IRE) – Caddy Shack (Precipice Wood) [2004/5 c23d^{pu} c26v^{pu} c23v^{pu} 24d^{pu} Feb 11] big, workmanlike gelding: seventh foal: half-brother to fair hurdler Christy's Pride (by Kambalda), stayed 3¼m: dam lightly raced: won 6 of 8 starts in Irish points in 2003: pulled up in 3 maiden chases (jumped poorly) and novice hurdle. *S. J. Gilmore* **c– x h–**

SYLVIAJAZZ 6 b.m. Alhijaz – Dispol Princess (IRE) (Cyrano de Bergerac) [2004/5 h–: 16d^{pu} Nov 22] lightly raced and no sign of ability: tried in cheekpieces. *W. M. Brisbourne* **h–**

SYLVIE D'ORTHE (FR) 4 b.f. Saint Preuil (FR) – Paola Santa (FR) (Son of Silver) [2004/5 15s 17s^{pu} 17d^{2} 17d^{6} 16g 16d^{F} 16s^{2} 16s^{6} Apr 3] seventh foal: half-sister to winning 21f chaser Royal d'Orthe (by Royal Charter) and 11f and 12.5f winner Princhip (by Le Nain Jeaune): dam placed over 11f: juvenile hurdler: claimed from B. Spieldenner €18,700 third start: modest form in Britain, sold out of M. Pipe's stable 1,450 gns Doncaster January Sales before final outing: tried in headgear. *A. C. Wilson* **h86**

SYLVIESBUCK (IRE) 8 b.g. Kasmayo – Sylvies Missiles (IRE) (Buckskin (FR)) [2004/5 c96, h–: c25v^{F} c27v c24v^{3} c24v^{pu} c26s^{pu} c27v^{2} c26v^{6} Apr 17] strong gelding: poor handicap chaser: stays 27f: acts on heavy going: tried blinkered: usually let down by jumping. *G. M. Moore* **c84 x h–**

SYNCOPATED RHYTHM (IRE) 5 b.g. Synefos (USA) – Northern Elation (IRE) (Lancastrian) [2004/5 F17s^{3} 19g 21d 21d 19g^{6} Apr 1] €10,000 3-y-o: rangy gelding: third foal: brother to bumper winner Stanafoss: dam, placed in bumpers, out of sister to Champion Chase winner Another Dolly: third to Smart Mover in bumper at Exeter on debut: little form over hurdles. *N. A. Twiston-Davies* **h– F96**

SYSTEM 6 ch.g. Nashwan (USA) – Vivid Imagination (USA) (Raise A Man (USA)) [2004/5 16s^{pu} 17g^{pu} Dec 14] fair maiden on Flat at 3 yrs, sold out of B. Hills's stable 11,000 gns Newmarket Autumn (2002) Sales: pulled up in 2 novice hurdles: sold £2,100 Ascot February Sales. *P. R. Hedger* **h–**

SZEROKI BOR (POL) 6 b.g. In Camera (IRE) – Szuana (POL) (Five Star Camp (USA)) [2004/5 h102: 16g^{6} 21m* Jun 8] fair form at best over hurdles: landed odds in maiden at Huntingdon in June: stays 21f: acts on soft and good to firm going. *M. Pitman* **h95**

T

TAAKID (USA) 10 b.g. Diesis – Tanwi (Vision (USA)) [2004/5 c105+: c16g^{2} c16m^{4} c17m^{4} c16m^{3} c20g^{3} Aug 18] leggy, angular gelding: fair handicap chaser: stays 21f: acts on good to soft and good to firm ground: has had tongue tied: best form when ridden prominently. *Mrs S. J. Smith* **c108 h–**

TACIN (IRE) 8 b.g. Supreme Leader – Nicat (Wolver Hollow) [2004/5 c–, h–: 21d^{3} 21m^{pu} Apr 13] well-made gelding: fair hurdler, lightly raced: amiss only start over fences: stays 3m. *B. G. Powell* **c– h112**

TACITA 10 ch.m. Gunner B – Taco (High Season) [2004/5 c20s^{pu} Dec 22] lengthy mare: lightly raced: little form over hurdles: seemed to go amiss on chasing debut: should stay 3m. *M. D. McMillan* **c– h–**

TACITUS (IRE) 5 ch.g. Titus Livius (FR) – Idara (Top Ville) [2004/5 16s^4 16s* 16d 16v* 16s Feb 6] good-topped gelding: useful on Flat (stays 1m): fairly useful form over hurdles: won maiden at Fairyhouse in November and novice at Naas (beat Ocras Mor comfortably by 4 lengths) in January: will prove best around 2m: raced on going softer than good over hurdles (acts on heavy): room for improvement in jumping. *D. T. Hughes, Ireland* **h120**

TACOLINO (FR) 11 ch.g. Royal Charter (FR) – Tamilda (FR) (Rose Laurel) [2004/5 c124, h–: c20d c19g^3 c24g^{pu} c16g c20g^{pu} Apr 17] workmanlike gelding: fairly useful handicap chaser: form in 2004/5 only when third at Doncaster: stays 2½m: acts on firm and good to soft ground, probably on heavy: tried blinkered: formerly tongue tied: has bled from nose. *O. Brennan* **c123 h–**

TACTFUL REMARK (USA) 9 ch.g. Lord At War (ARG) – Right Word (USA) (Verbatim (USA)) [2004/5 c96, h111: 16g c16g 17d^4 c17m^5 Sep 4] angular gelding: fair hurdler: lightly raced and modest form over fences: raced around 2m: acts on soft and good to firm going: tried visored: free-going front runner. *M. C. Pipe* **c99 h107**

TAFFRAIL 7 b.g. Slip Anchor – Tizona (Pharly (FR)) [2004/5 h86: 16d 19g^3 20m^{pu} 24m^3 19d^3 19s^6 16d 17g^4 16d^5 20v Feb 5] strong gelding: modest maiden hurdler: stays 3m: acts on good to firm and good to soft going: tried in visor/cheekpieces: ungenuine. *D. Burchell* **h96 §**

TAGULA BLUE (IRE) 5 b.g. Tagula (IRE) – Palace Blue (IRE) (Dara Monarch) [2004/5 16g Dec 11] good-bodied gelding: half-brother to winning hurdler up to 3m Rhapsody In Blue (by Magical Strike): fairly useful on Flat (best around 1m, refused to race once): tongue tied, well held in novice on hurdling debut. *J. A. Glover* **h–**

TAI LASS 5 b. or br.m. Taipan (IRE) – Kerry's Oats (Derrylin) [2004/5 h105: 18d^3 May 3] leggy mare: maiden hurdler, fair form at best: should stay beyond 2m: raced on good going or softer. *P. R. Hedger* **h94**

TAILI 4 b.f. Taipan (IRE) – Doubtfire (Jalmood (USA)) [2004/5 16m^{ro} Oct 3] well beaten on Flat: jumped badly and tailed off when running out in juvenile on hurdling debut. *D. A. Nolan* **h–**

TAILS I WIN 6 b.g. Petoski – Spinayab (King of Spain) [2004/5 F73: 17d^F 16m* 20d^{pu} c24m^5 c20g^{pu} Aug 1] lengthy, plain, sparely-made gelding: won weak novice at Towcester in May, only completed start over hurdles: no show in 2 maiden chases: sold out of J. Mullins' stable £11,500 Ascot July Sales before final outing. *Miss C. J. E. Caroe* **c– h82**

TAIPO PRINCE (IRE) 5 b.g. Entrepreneur – Dedicated Lady (IRE) (Pennine Walk) [2004/5 h80: 16m^2 16m^2 19m^{pu} 16d 16d 16d^{pu} Apr 11] modest maiden hurdler: raced mainly around 2m: acts on good to firm and good to soft going. *Miss Kate Milligan* **h94**

TAKAGI (IRE) 10 b.g. Husyan (USA) – Ballyclough Gale (Strong Gale) [2004/5 c139, h119: c24g^2 c34g^4 c19s^2 c24s^3 c27s^{ur} c21v^5 c29s Mar 28] lengthy gelding: useful chaser: easily best effort in 2004/5 when third to Colca Canyon in Munster National (Handicap) at Limerick: should stay beyond 25f: acts on heavy going: tried blinkered/visored: jumping generally not good enough over National fences/cross-country course at Punchestown. *E. J. O'Grady, Ireland* **c141 h–**

TAKASH (IRE) 5 b.g. Green Desert (USA) – Takarouna (USA) (Green Dancer (USA)) [2004/5 16g^4 17g^2 16m 17g 16g 25g^6 Oct 26] medium-sized ex-Irish gelding: fair maiden up to 1m at 3 yrs for J. Oxx: poor maiden hurdler: bought out of M. Halford's stable 7,500 gns Doncaster May Sales: wore cheekpieces last 3 starts. *C. J. Mann* **h81**

TAKEACHANCEONHIM 7 b.g. Dilum (USA) – Smilingatstrangers (Macmillion) [2004/5 F70: F17d May 12] never a factor in 3 bumpers. *Mrs Barbara Waring* **F–**

TAKE FIVE (IRE) 12 br.g. Satco (FR) – Shan's Moss (Le Moss) [2004/5 c108, h124: 24g 22d 24d Dec 10] tall, leggy gelding: fairly useful hurdler/fair chaser in 2003/4: left J. Kiely after reappearance, always behind in handicap hurdles subsequently: effective around 2m to 3¼m: acts on heavy and good to firm going: has had tongue tied. *Jonjo O'Neill* **c– h–**

TAKE HEED 9 b.g. Warning – Tunaria (USA) (Lyphard (USA)) [2004/5 h–: 16d^{pu} May 12] sturdy gelding: poor hurdler: lightly raced nowadays and little sign of retaining ability: usually tongue tied: sold £1,350 Ascot August Sales. *K. A. Morgan* **h–**

TAKE THE OATH (IRE) 8 b.g. Big Sink Hope (USA) – Delgany Chimes (IRE) (Kafu) [2004/5 c20g^{ur} c20s^{ur} c19g^6 Mar 4] rangy gelding: fair hurdler at one time: poor **c– h–**

maiden chaser: sold out of M. Hourigan's stable €4,200 Goffs October Sale after reappearance: best form around 2m: acts on soft and firm ground: blinkered and tongue tied once. *D. R. Gandolfo*

TAKE THE STAND (IRE) 9 b.g. Witness Box (USA) – Denys Daughter (IRE) (Crash Course) [2004/5 c140, h–: 22g^{2} c32m* c21d* c20s^{2} c20d^{6} c24d^{pu} c29v^{F} c24v^{3} c26g^{2} c36d^{ur} c33g^{pu} Apr 16] **c163 x h122**

Take The Stand, who had progressed in his first season with trainer Peter Bowen from a fairly useful chaser to one nearly two stone better, made marked further progress in 2004/5, showing himself a high-class chaser in winning two of the major prizes of the summer jumping season and finishing runner-up to Kicking King in the Cheltenham Gold Cup. What a pity his jumping sometimes lets him down. Time and again on his other appearances, the fences (or sometimes just a fence) got in the way.

Take The Stand's summer double consisted of the Britannia Building Society English Summer National at Uttoxeter, first run in 2000, and a new race, the Lord Mildmay Memorial Handicap Chase at Newton Abbot. Take The Stand was one of sixteen to line up at Uttoxeter and went off a 14/1 chance, carrying top weight and conceding 10 lb or more to all but two of the field. He had contested the race the year before, falling five from home when bang in contention, and had shown his well-being for the latest renewal by finishing runner-up in a handicap hurdle at Newton Abbot twelve days previously, his first outing in four and a half months. Gradually getting into the marathon contest on the final circuit, Take The Stand led between the last two and won by two lengths from Exstoto. The four-mile race on firmish ground took its toll on the field at Uttoxeter. The runner-up was one of six runners not seen out again over jumps in 2004/5, while apart from the winner only Maximise subsequently won a race. The Lord Mildmay at Newton Abbot nearly two months later, over a trip fully eleven furlongs shorter than at Uttoxeter, again saw Take The Stand under top weight, this time facing ten opponents, on the whole of better quality than at Uttoxeter. Starting 100/30 favourite, Take The Stand demolished the opposition, aided by one of his most assured rounds of jumping, and won by twenty lengths.

Although summer jumping by and large attracts mainly modest horses, it has become well established since the traditional break in June and July was done away with, proving popular with the general public, and boasts several well-endowed feature races. In addition to the two that Take The Stand won (the pair netting connections over £70,000 in prize money), the Summer Festival Handicap Hurdle at Newton Abbot, the Summer Plate and Summer Hurdle at Market Rasen and the City of Perth Gold Cup at Perth were all worth at least £18,000 to the winner in 2004/5. In Ireland, the Galway Plate and Galway Hurdle are among the most valuable handicaps of the whole year, attracting good-quality, competitive fields, and the British races should flourish in similar fashion as they become established. To promote the summer jumping season, the BHB have tried to encourage interest in it as a separate entity, with its own sponsored championship and with *The Sun* as media partner.

Impressive as his performance at Newton Abbot was, Take The Stand did not obviously suggest himself as a Gold Cup candidate at the time, nor did he do much in five subsequent outings to promote the idea either. On his next two, the Wigan Chase at Aintree and the Paddy Power at Cheltenham, he more or less repeated the form shown at Newton Abbot, in attempting to concede 9 lb to Farmer Jack at Aintree and 19 lb to Celestial Gold at Cheltenham facing tasks few, apart from the very top chasers, would manage successfully. Take The Stand's jumping flaws resurfaced over stiffer fences than those at Newton Abbot and became even more of a problem soon after. Landing too steeply and slithering to a halt five out abruptly ended his challenge in the Tommy Whittle at Haydock and he fell heavily four out in the Welsh National at Chepstow, though on neither occasion was he beaten when departing. At Chepstow in particular he looked to hold every chance of winning under top weight. He got round in the Peter Marsh back at Haydock but repeatedly jumped left, which cost him whatever chance he had.

A Cheltenham Gold Cup entry at that point looked highly speculative and, even with several leading candidates falling by the wayside, Take The Stand was a

*Britannia Building Society English Summer National (Handicap Chase), Uttoxeter—
Take The Stand gains ample compensation for his fall twelve months earlier as he defeats Exstoto*

40/1-chance on the morning of the race. But backed down to 25/1, Take The Stand ran the race of his life. After surviving blunders at the first two fences, he became largely fluent and was the only danger as Kicking King went for home four out; Take The Stand held every chance at the second last but couldn't quicken with the winner and went down by five lengths. Much of the credit for Take The Stand's performance should go to his rider Tony Dobbin, who replaced regular partner Seamus Durack, who instead rode stable-companion Ballycassidy in the Gold Cup. Dobbin must have been wondering what he had let himself in for after the first two fences, as the Cheltenham Festival certainly hasn't been his lucky meeting (when asked which was his favourite Festival he said 2001). Since winning the County Hurdle on Dizzy in 1994 on his first ride at the meeting, Dobbin has won just twice in seventy-three more rides, on Master Tern in the 2000 County Hurdle and Freetown in the 2002 Pertemps Final. He was previously second in the Gold Cup on Go Ballistic in 1999, while reverses include a fall from Direct Route in the 1998 Arkle, which kept him out for nearly a month, Hors La Loi III's refusal to race in the 2003 Champion Hurdle and disqualification on Coolnagorna in the same year's Royal & SunAlliance Hurdle.

For all that the latest Gold Cup was far from a vintage renewal, Take The Stand afterwards looked particularly well handicapped for the Grand National. He was cut from 40/1 to just 10/1 by one large bookmaker, though Bowen was in two minds whether to run in the National or in the much less valuable Betfair Bowl. Take The Stand's jumping was an obvious concern, as was the unavailability of Dobbin who was already committed to Just In Debt. In the end, the Grand National proved too tempting not to take a chance and, with Leighton Aspell finally selected to ride, Take The Stand coped better than might have been expected before hitting the Chair and unseating his rider. A week later, Take The Stand lined up for the Scottish Grand National at Ayr. With his Gold Cup form taken into account, Take The Stand was off a mark 15 lb higher than at Aintree and ran as if past his best, left behind on the final circuit and eventually pulled up.

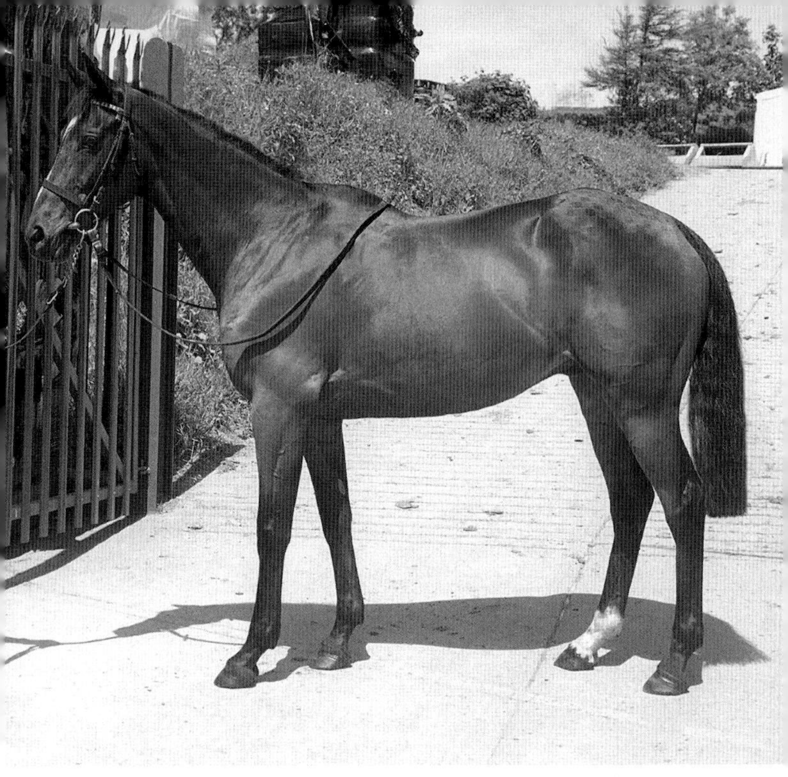

The Courters' "Take The Stand"

Take The Stand (IRE) (b.g. 1996)	Witness Box (USA) (b 1987)	Lyphard (b 1969)	Northern Dancer
			Goofed
		Excellent Alibi (b 1981)	Exceller
			Charming Alibi
	Denys Daughter (IRE) (b 1989)	Crash Course (b 1971)	Busted
			Lucky Stream
		Lady Denys (b 1978)	Saint Denys
			Arctic Serenade

Take The Stand will find winning handicaps difficult off a mark in the 160s and isn't really up to beating the very best chasers at level weights, so further successes may prove difficult to come by. Given that he was bought out of Ian Williams' stable for just 20,000 guineas at the Doncaster May Sales in 2003, he owes connections nothing. The leggy Take The Stand is the only winner so far out of Denys Daughter. Her other foals are two once-raced pointers and Take The Stand's sister Witneses Daughter who was placed twice from five starts in bumpers in Ireland during the latest season. Denys Daughter herself ran twice over hurdles after the birth of her first foal and is a sister to the dam of the useful staying chaser Sheltering. Take The Stand's third dam Arctic Serenade won the Irish Cesarewitch and is the dam of four winners, including Last Serenade, who was smart at up to three miles over hurdles. Take The Stand is versatile with regard to trip and ground. Although all but one of his wins have come on good or good to firm going, he ran well on soft behind Farmer Jack and looked fully effective on heavy in the Welsh National. *P. Bowen*

TAKSINA 6 b.m. Wace (USA) – Quago (New Member) [2004/5 c–, h–: c19m^6 c21s^3 c24g^3 c16s^5 c24s^pu Nov 11] lengthy mare: poor form over fences: probably stays 3m: acts on soft ground. *R. H. Buckler* — **c74 h–**

TALAMA LADY (IRE) 8 b.m. Persian Bold – Talama (FR) (Shakapour) [2004/5 h87, F90: 16g* 16m^2 Jun 12] strong, close-coupled mare: fair form in novice hurdles: won mares event at Uttoxeter in May: likely to prove best around 2m: free-going sort: sold 17,500 gns Doncaster August Sales, resold £2,900 Ascot February Sales. *G. A. Swinbank* — **h104**

TALARIVE (USA) 9 ch.g. Riverman (USA) – Estala (Be My Guest (USA)) [2004/5 h109§: 17d^5 17d^pu 16d^pu 17s 17d^4 16s^4 20v^2 16s^6 17s 20g^pu 21v^4 17d* 16d^3 16s Apr 20] smallish, sturdy gelding: modest handicap hurdler nowadays: won selling event at Sedgefield in April: stays 2½m: acts on heavy going: sometimes wears cheekpieces: tongue tied nowadays: unreliable. *P. D. Niven* — **h97 §**

TALBOT LAD 9 b.g. Weld – Greenacres Girl (Tycoon II) [2004/5 c115, h–: c20m^pu c16s^pu c20d^5 c20d 21d^pu c20d* c20g Apr 17] leggy gelding: maiden hurdler: fair handicap chaser: form in 2004/5 only when winning at Ludlow (12/1 from 25/1) in March: stays 2½m: acts on good to firm and heavy going: usually tongue tied: unreliable. *S. A. Brookshaw* — **c110 § h–**

TALEBAN 10 b.g. Alleged (USA) – Triode (USA) (Sharpen Up) [2004/5 c87, h–: c21m^4 c23m^4 Oct 13] smallish, angular gelding: poor maiden chaser: stays 21f: acts on good to firm and good to soft going: tried blinkered/in cheekpieces. *J. Wade* — **c80 h–**

TALES OF BOUNTY (IRE) 10 b.g. Ela-Mana-Mou – Tales of Wisdom (Rousillon (USA)) [2004/5 c106, h121: c26d^5 c24d^3 Mar 11] lengthy, useful-looking gelding: fairly useful handicap hurdler: fair hunter chaser nowadays: left P. Nicholls after first outing, successful in 2-runner point in January: stays 3m: acts on soft and good to firm going: blinkered last 5 outings. *R. Barber* — **c92 x h–**

TALIKOS (FR) 4 b.g. Nikos – Talaya (FR) (Matahawk) [2004/5 F16d F16d Mar 24] compact gelding: second foal: brother to winning hurdler around 2m Tanika: dam won 2¼m chase in France: tenth of 18 in bumper at Newbury on debut: failed to settle next time. *Miss H. C. Knight* — **F–**

TALKING CENTS (IRE) 8 b.g. Good Thyne (USA) – Necochea (Julio Mariner) [2004/5 c20f* c22m* c22m^pu Jul 31] IR 60,000 3-y-o: good-bodied gelding: fifth foal: brother to fair hurdler/chaser Rift Valley, stays 3m, and half-brother to bumper winner Rhosneigr Bay (by Brush Aside): dam fairly useful but ungenuine staying hurdler: winning pointer: maiden hurdler: promising start to chasing career, winning maiden at Fairyhouse and minor event at Galway (beating Ross Moff 3 lengths) in July: reportedly lame in handicap final start: stays 2¾m: form only on good to firm/firm going: tried in cheekpieces. *S. Donohoe, Ireland* — **c125 h–**

TALLAHASSEE (IRE) 7 ch.g. Moscow Society (USA) – Kemperstrat (The Parson) [2004/5 F–: 24v^pu Dec 15] strong gelding: no sign of ability. *D. R. MacLeod* — **h–**

TALLDARK'N'ANDSOME 6 b.g. Efisio – Fleur du Val (Valiyar) [2004/5 h101p: 16g^pu 16s^2 16v^4 16d^5 Jan 26] medium-sized gelding: fairly useful on Flat (should stay beyond 1¼m) at 4 yrs, well held both starts in 2004: best effort over hurdles when head second to Predicament in novice at Plumpton: likely to prove best around 2m. *N. P. Littmoden* — **h104**

TALLOW BAY (IRE) 10 b.g. Glacial Storm (USA) – Minimum Choice (IRE) (Miner's Lamp) [2004/5 c–, h–: c25d^pu c24s^2 c24s^4 c21s^pu c26v^pu c24d^pu c26d^3 Apr 18] sturdy gelding: poor handicap chaser: stays 3¼m: acts on heavy going, pulled up on firm: tried blinkered/in cheekpieces. *Mrs S. Wall* — **c69 h–**

TALL PAUL 5 b.g. Shaamit (IRE) – Brave Vanessa (USA) (Private Account (USA)) [2004/5 F16g F17m Sep 8] £1,400 3-y-o: fifth foal: brother to 1¼m winner Simiola: dam, 6f winner who stayed 1m, sister to US Grade 2 winner around 1m Topicount: well held in 2 bumpers: sold £2,700 Ascot February Sales. *J. L. Spearing* — **F–**

TAMANGO (FR) 8 gr.g. Klimt (FR) – Tipmosa (FR) (Tip Moss (FR)) [2004/5 c123, h–: c17g^6 c18m^4 Apr 2] leggy, lengthy gelding: fairly useful chaser in 2003/4: off 16 months, better effort in handicaps at Newbury on return when fourth to Fool On The Hill: should stay 2½m: acts on good to firm and heavy going: tried blinkered: often finds little. *P. J. Hobbs* — **c– h–**

Ladbroke Handicap Hurdle, Sandown—Tamarinbleu fares best of Martin Pipe's six-strong contingent as he defeats Self Defense (right) and King Revo (noseband)

TAMARINBLEU (FR) 5 b.g. Epervier Bleu – Tamainia (FR) (Lashkari) [2004/5 h121: 16d* 16d 16v^2 17g 20d^2 16m^4 Apr 22] angular gelding: useful hurdler: won 23-runner Ladbroke Handicap at Sandown in January by 4 lengths from Self Defense: mainly creditable efforts after, second to Genghis in another strongly-contested handicap at Aintree and fourth to Rooster Booster in valuable minor event at Sandown last 2 starts: effective at 2m to 2½m: unraced on firm going, acts on any other: consistent. *M. C. Pipe* **h144**

TAMBO (IRE) 10 b.g. Shardari – Carmen Lady (Torus) [2004/5 c112, h–: c25g* May 14] workmanlike gelding: progressive handicap chaser: fairly useful form when winning at Aintree in May by 7 lengths from Navarone: stays 25f: acts on soft and good to firm going: takes good hold and usually races prominently. *M. Bradstock* **c115 h–**

TAMING (IRE) 9 ch.g. Lycius (USA) – Black Fighter (USA) (Secretariat (USA)) [2004/5 c17g^F Jul 15] compact gelding: fairly useful hurdler in 2002/3: would probably have won maiden chase at Cartmel on only outing since but for falling heavily 2 out: stays 21f: acts on soft and good to firm going: tried tongue tied. *Miss Venetia Williams* **c97 h–**

TAM O'SHANTER 11 gr.g. Persian Bold – No More Rosies (Warpath) [2004/5 c–, h79: 20s^3 27m^2 c27g^3 c25m^4 22m* 24g^2 24g^4 27g^{pu} 24g^F c25s^{pu} 27v^5 24g c24d^6 Apr 22] neat gelding: poor chaser/hurdler: awarded selling handicap hurdle at Uttoxeter in June on technical grounds: stays 27f: acts on firm and soft going: has worn visor/cheekpieces: poor jumper of fences. *J. G. M. O'Shea* **c70 x h80**

TANAGER 10 ch.g. Carlingford Castle – Tangara (Town Crier) [2004/5 c77: c26s^{ur} c22v^{ur} c28g c24s c20g c24g* c26g^{pu} c26g^4 Apr 14] workmanlike gelding: fairly useful hunter chaser: won at Newbury in March by 2½ lengths from Silence Reigns: probably stays 3¼m: acts on heavy going: blinkered: unreliable. *Mrs K. Lawther* **c108 §**

TANA RIVER (IRE) 9 b.g. Over The River (FR) – Home In The Glen (Furry Glen) [2004/5 c25s^{pu} c20s* c20d^2 c21g c23v^{pu} Mar 30] sturdy gelding: fairly useful novice hurdler in 2002/3: off 20 months before reappearance: useful form when winningmaiden chase at Fontwell in January, making most and beating Liverpool Echo 7 lengths: well below that after, jumping poorly final start: should stay 3m: acts on heavy going. *Miss E. C. Lavelle* **c132 h–**

TANDAVA (IRE) 7 ch.g. Indian Ridge – Kashka (USA) (The Minstrel (CAN)) [2004/5 16g^{5} 17d^{2} 16s^{3} 16d^{2} 20s^{2} 20d^{4} 20s^{3} Apr 20] quite good-topped gelding: half-brother to fairly useful hurdler Sharkashka (by Shardari), stays 19f: fair on Flat (stays 17f) for I. Semple: fair novice hurdler: barely stays 2½m: acts on soft going: consistent. *Mrs S. C. Bradburne* **h101**

TANDAWIZI 8 b.m. Relief Pitcher – Arctic Ander (Leander) [2004/5 F71: 16s 20s Feb 9] ran once in bumper: off 18 months, no show in 2 novice hurdles. *Mrs L. B. Normile* **h–**

TANGO BOJANGLES 7 ch.m. Fraam – Hips'n Haws (IRE) (Thatching) [2004/5 h–, F–: 20m 22d^{pu} Oct 3] lengthy mare: no sign of ability: third both completed starts in points. *N. Wilson* **h–**

TANGO ROYAL (FR) 9 gr.g. Royal Charter (FR) – Nazia (FR) (Zino) [2004/5 c136x, h122: 19d^{2} 16m^{6} 20m^{3} 19g^{2} c21d^{4} c22g^{2} 21g^{4} c20g c16g^{F} 16g^{6} c20g^{2} Apr 15] lengthy gelding: useful handicap hurdler/chaser: several creditable efforts in 2004/5, 7 lengths second to Brooklyn Breeze at Ayr final start: effective at 2m to 2¾m: probably acts on any going: tongue tied: usually held up: often makes mistakes over fences: consistent. *M. C. Pipe* **c136 x h132**

TANIKOS (FR) 6 b.g. Nikos – Tamana (USA) (Northern Baby (CAN)) [2004/5 c111, h–: c20d^{6} c20s^{3} c16s^{F} c16d^{5} c17g* c18m^{pu} c20g^{pu} Apr 17] big, workmanlike gelding: fairly useful handicap chaser: best effort when winning at Newbury in March by 12 lengths from Marked Man: let down by jumping afterwards: stays 2½m: acts on soft going: sometimes runs as if amiss. *N. J. Henderson* **c123 h–**

TANK BUSTER 5 b.g. Executive Perk – Macfarly (IRE) (Phardante (FR)) [2004/5 F–: F16g^{3} F16s^{6} Feb 5] good-topped gelding: modest form in bumpers. *Miss E. Hill* **F82**

TANK (IRE) 4 ch.g. Woodborough (USA) – Fiddes (IRE) (Alzao (USA)) [2004/5 16d^{pu} 16d Dec 13] sturdy gelding: well held only start on Flat: no sign of ability in juvenile hurdles. *Miss S. West* **h–**

TANNERS COURT 8 b.g. Framlington Court – True Nell (Neltino) [2004/5 h103: 16d^{6} 20v^{6} 17d^{4} Jan 1] good-topped gelding: fair maiden hurdler: stays 2¾m: acts on soft going: free-going sort, usually races prominently: trainer ridden: consistent. *Miss C. Dyson* **h102**

TANNERS DEN 5 br.g. Abzu – Equilibrium (Statoblest) [2004/5 F18d^{6} F16d Mar 14] compact gelding: fourth foal: dam, 2-y-o 6f winner, half-sister to winning jumper Getting Plenty: tailed off in 2 bumpers. *Miss C. Dyson* **F–**

TANNERS FRIEND 8 b.m. Environment Friend – Glenn's Slipper (Furry Glen) [2004/5 h–: 22g 22d^{pu} 22g^{pu} Jul 20] leggy mare: little sign of ability. *Miss C. Dyson* **h–**

TANTERARI (IRE) 7 b.g. Safety Catch (USA) – Cobblers Crest (IRE) (Step Together (USA)) [2004/5 c?, h93+, F97: 17d^{4} 25s* 22d* 24g* 24v^{pu} c25v* c24s* c24d^{5} c23v c21g^{6} Apr 14] rangy gelding: fair hurdler: favourite, won handicaps at Plumpton (novice), Fontwell (conditional jockeys) and Bangor in December: similar form over fences when winning handicaps at Hereford and Taunton in February: shaped as if amiss all other starts after reappearance, travelling strongly and finding little: stays 25f: raced mainly on going softer than good (acts on heavy): held up. *M. C. Pipe* **c109 h108**

TANTICO (IRE) 8 b.g. Lord Americo – Tanti's Last (Ardoon) [2004/5 h–, F88: 16g Dec 8] well held in 2 novice hurdles: tried tongue tied. *D. J. Wintle* **h–**

TANZANITE DAWN 4 b.f. Gunner B – Quiet Dawn (Lighter) [2004/5 F16s Mar 23] second foal: dam, winning hurdler/chaser who stayed 3¼m, half-sister to useful staying chaser ANC Express: well beaten in bumper on debut. *J. S. King* **F–**

TARANAI (IRE) 4 ch.f. Russian Revival (USA) – Miss Flite (IRE) (Law Society (USA)) [2004/5 16g 16g* 17g^{pu} 16m^{3} 18m^{2} 16f^{4} 16m 17d^{6} 18g^{5} 20d^{6} Mar 28] compact filly: poor maiden on Flat (stays 13f): poor hurdler: won juvenile at Stratford in July: should stay beyond 2¼m: acts on good to firm going: usually tongue tied. *B. W. Duke* **h84**

TARANIS (FR) 4 ch.g. Mansonnien (FR) – Vikosa (FR) (Nikos) [2004/5 15s^{3} 18s^{3} 16s* 17s^{3} Feb 6] first foal: dam fairly useful hurdler/winning chaser around 2m: fairly useful form over hurdles: left G. Macaire, won novice at Wincanton in January readily by 13 lengths from Lamp's Return: good third to Its Crucial in similar event at Hereford next time. *P. F. Nicholls* **h115**

TARBOLTON MOSS 10 b.m. Le Moss – Priceless Peril (Silly Prices) [2004/5 c108, h96: c20v^{2} c30s^{pu} c21v^{2} c29s^{3} Mar 12] winning hurdler: modest handicap chaser: best at 3m+: raced on good going or softer (acts on heavy): unreliable. *M. Todhunter* **c96 § h–**

TARBOUSH 8 b.g. Polish Precedent (USA) – Barboukh (Night Shift (USA)) [2004/5 h96: 16g³ c16m* c16f² c17m² Jun 25] sturdy gelding: fair hurdler: at least as good over fences, easily winning intermediate at Hereford in May: beaten by Liberty Seeker both starts in novices after: needs sharp 2m: acts on firm going: takes good hold. *B. G. Powell* **c110 h101**

TARONGO (FR) 7 b.g. Tel Quel (FR) – Rainbow Rainbow (Vision (USA)) [2004/5 c82, h–: c20d² c17g² c17d* c17v² c16sᵘʳ c17g* c20g* c20g Apr 17] lengthy, rather leggy gelding: fair handicap chaser: won at Stratford in October and twice at Plumpton in March: lame final start: stays 2½m: acts on good to firm and good to soft going: tried visored: usually tongue tied: has jumped none too fluently. *Mrs L. C. Taylor* **c103 h–**

TARSKI 11 ch.g. Polish Precedent (USA) – Illusory (Kings Lake (USA)) [2004/5 h95: 22gᵖᵘ c21gᵖᵘ 20m Aug 6] smallish gelding: modest hurdler: no show in 2004/5, including on chasing debut: barely stays 3m: best form on good to firm/firm going: usually blinkered/visored. *W. S. Kittow* **c– h–**

TARTAN BELLE 5 ch.m. Classic Cliche (IRE) – Elusive (Little Current (USA)) [2004/5 F16d May 6] half-sister to modest hurdler/chaser Playing Truant (by Teenoso), stayed 21f, and poor 2m hurdler Hard To Get (by Rousillon): dam, fairly useful 7f winner at 2 yrs, half-sister to useful hurdlers Hopscotch and Sheriffmuir: well held in bumper on debut. *O. Sherwood* **F74**

TARTAN FLYER 5 b.g. Bonny Scot (IRE) – Run Pet Run (Deep Run) [2004/5 F18d⁶ Apr 18] third foal: dam fair but temperamental staying chaser: sixth of 10 in maiden bumper at Plumpton on debut. *D. B. Feek* **F86**

TARTIRUGA (IRE) 4 b.g. Turtle Island (IRE) – Palio Flyer (Slip Anchor) [2004/5 16d³ 16s 17s Jan 10] modest maiden on Flat (stays 1¼m): form over hurdles only when third in juvenile at Wincanton. *L. G. Cottrell* **h87**

TARWIN 5 b.g. Danzig Connection (USA) – Persian Blue (Persian Bold) [2004/5 F16d F16d⁶ F16s Mar 27] 900 3-y-o, 3,000 4-y-o: small, close-coupled gelding: first foal: half-brother to 5.3f winner Maluti (by Piccolo): dam maiden, stayed 1½m well: modest form at best in bumpers. *J. R. Norton* **F76**

TARXIEN 11 b.g. Kendor (FR) – Tanz (IRE) (Sadler's Wells (USA)) [2004/5 c141, h128: 23m⁶ 24d 24d 22d⁴ 24g 24g⁵ Apr 14] strong, sturdy gelding: formerly useful chaser: fairly useful hurdler, mainly creditable efforts in competitive handicaps in 2004/5: stays 3m: acts on good to firm and heavy going: visored final start: tongue tied. *M. C. Pipe* **c– h128**

TARZAN DU MESNIL (FR) 4 br.g. Turgeon (USA) – Ladies View (FR) (Comrade In Arms) [2004/5 F16s⁴ Mar 6] tall, useful-looking gelding: sixth foal: half-brother to fairly useful hurdler/chaser up to 2½m Gentil du Mesnil (by Nashamaa): dam, winning hurdler/chaser around 2m, half-sister to useful juvenile hurdler/chaser Razzamatazz, dam of useful French jumper Vesuve: better for race, 3½ lengths fourth to Grenfell in maiden bumper at Kempton on debut. *N. J. Hawke* **F89**

TASMAN (IRE) 5 ch.g. Definite Article – Felin Special (Lyphard's Special (USA)) [2004/5 16v* 20d* 20v³ 16s⁵ 22s² 22v* Apr 2] fair maiden on Flat (stays 2m): useful over hurdles: won maiden at Listowel in September, minor event at Cork in October and novice at Navan (beat Far From Trouble by neck) in April: best efforts when third to Sweet Kiln in Grade 3 novice at Navan in November and second to Healy's Pub in handicap at Fairyhouse in March: will stay 3m: raced on going softer than good (acts on heavy). *D. K. Weld, Ireland* **h130**

TASS HEEL (IRE) 6 b.g. Danehill (USA) – Mamouna (USA) (Vaguely Noble) [2004/5 16g 16v⁶ 19m⁶ 22vᵖᵘ Apr 22] half-brother to fairly useful 2m hurdler Darter (by Darshaan): fair on Flat (stays 2m) at 3 and 4 yrs, lightly raced since, sold out of W. Jarvis' stable 12,000 gns Newmarket February Sales: poor form in maiden hurdles. *B. J. Llewellyn* **h80**

TA TA FOR NOW 8 b.g. Ezzoud (IRE) – Exit Laughing (Shaab) [2004/5 c78x, h86: c24d* c24dᵖᵘ c25d⁴ c27d² c28s³ c24m⁴ c29s² c28g c31s⁵ Apr 22] lengthy gelding: modest chaser: won intermediate at Perth in May: stays 29f: acts on soft and good to firm going: tried blinkered/in cheekpieces: inconsistent. *Mrs S. C. Bradburne* **c85 § h–**

TATES AVENUE (IRE) 7 b.g. Zaffaran (USA) – Tate Divinity (IRE) (Tate Gallery (USA)) [2004/5 F67: 16g 16dᵖᵘ 19g⁶ 17v 21d⁴ Apr 18] well-made gelding: chasing type: modest form over hurdles: bred to stay beyond 21f. *N. A. Twiston-Davies* **h94**

TATWEER (IRE) 5 b.g. Among Men (USA) – Sandystones (Selkirk (USA)) [2004/5 16gᵖᵘ Dec 11] modest and wayward on Flat (effective at 5f to 1m): no show in novice on hurdling debut. *D. Shaw* **h–**

TAURUS OATS 6 b.m. Makbul – Aintree Oats (Oats) [2004/5 F17d4 Oct 17] second foal: dam poor maiden pointer: well held in bumper on debut: in frame both starts in points. *J. W. Mullins* **F–**

TAWEELL (IRE) 6 b.g. Mtoto – Kronengold (USA) (Golden Act (USA)) [2004/5 F16g 19vpu 19g 25spu Mar 13] good-topped gelding: fourth foal: dam, middle-distance performer, half-sister to smart German middle-distance performer Komtur: no show in bumper and novice hurdles: tongue tied final start: sold £1,600 Ascot April Sales. *R. T. Phillips* **h– F–**

TEAM CAPTAIN 11 ch.g. Teamster – Silly Sausage (Silly Answer) [2004/5 c99: c25g3 c25mpu c23mpu c23gur c23mpu c25f2 c24d5 c25dpu Dec 2] angular gelding: modest handicap chaser: stays 3½m: acts on firm and good to soft going, pulled up on soft: tried in cheekpieces: has broken blood vessels: unreliable. *C. J. Down* **c97 §**

TEAM RESDEV (IRE) 5 b.m. Zaffaran (USA) – Crabtreejazz (IRE) (Royal Fountain) [2004/5 F16g 20spu Feb 9] second foal: dam twice-raced half-sister to fairly useful staying hurdler Ebullient Equiname (by Zaffaran): showed nothing in bumper or novice hurdle. *F. P. Murtagh* **h– F–**

TEAM TASSEL (IRE) 7 b.g. Be My Native (USA) – Alcmena's Last (Pauper) [2004/5 h109p: 21d* 24d 22g 24g Mar 17] tall gelding: chasing type: fairly useful handicap hurdler: won at Cheltenham in November by short head from Billyvoddan: disappointing in competitive events after: should stay 3m: raced on good/good to soft going: visored final start. *M. C. Pipe* **h123**

TEASDALE HOUSE (IRE) 6 br.g. Carroll House – Mrs Teasdale (Idiot's Delight) [2004/5 F16g Jul 1] €2,700 3-y-o: fifth foal: half-brother to fair 2m chaser Young Chevalier (by Alflora): dam of little account: fell in maiden point in 2004: showed nothing in bumper. *J. I. A. Charlton* **F–**

TEA'S MAID 5 b.m. Wizard King – Come To Tea (IRE) (Be My Guest (USA)) [2004/5 h78?: 16g6 16m5 20d4 22m4 22g5 Jul 29] poor maiden hurdler: claimed from M. Barnes £6,000 fourth start: seems to stay 2¾m: acts on good to firm and good to soft going. *Mrs A. M. Thorpe* **h72**

TECAYA (GER) 6 b.m. Lavirco (GER) – Triple Crown (GER) (Experte (GER)) [2004/5 18g4 16m6 c17g2 c18s c18g3 Jul 25] successful at 1¼m on Flat in Germany for I. Schalter: maiden jumper: placed over fences at Zweibrucken and Bad Harzburg in summer. *C. Von Der Recke, Germany* **c? h83**

TEE-JAY (IRE) 9 ch.g. Un Desperado (FR) – N T Nad (Welsh Pageant) [2004/5 c–, h107: 20g* 20mpu c22mpu c21dpu c20d5 c25vpu 24d Nov 29] workmanlike gelding: maiden chaser, usually let down by jumping: fair handicap hurdler: won at Hexham in May: stays 3m: acts on soft going. *M. D. Hammond* **c– h107**

TEEMING RAIN (IRE) 6 b.g. Supreme Leader – Lady Graduate (IRE) (Le Bavard (FR)) [2004/5 F16d2 F16v* 20v2 16v* 20d* 24d Apr 8] strong, good-topped gelding: will make a chaser: half-brother to modest staying chaser To The Future (by Bob Back): dam unraced half-sister to smart staying chaser Seven Towers, from family of very smart staying chaser Deep Bramble: fairly useful form in bumpers, successful at Down Royal in December: took well to hurdles, winning 22-runner maiden at Punchestown in February and Grade 3 novice at Thurles (beat Sweet Kiln by short head) in March: never dangerous after held up in steadily-run Grade 1 novice at Aintree final start: should stay 3m: raced on going softer than good: may still do better. *C. F. Swan, Ireland* **h131 F101**

TEENAGER 5 b.m. Young Ern – Washita (Valiyar) [2004/5 F71: 16dpu 17m 17m3 17d4 21s5 17d Mar 26] modest form over hurdles, though probably flattered when in frame in steadily-run races: raced mainly around 2m. *P. Wegmann* **h97 ?**

TEEN HOUSE 6 b.m. Teenoso (USA) – Last House (Vital Season) [2004/5 F17s 24spu Dec 18] €3,400 3-y-o: rather leggy mare: third foal: dam, fairly useful staying chaser, out of useful chaser at 2½m+ Parkhouse: no show in mares bumper and novice hurdle. *Miss Suzy Smith* **h– F–**

TEEN LADY 6 b. or br.m. Teenoso (USA) – State Lady (IRE) (Strong Statement (USA)) [2004/5 F16g Apr 26] second foal: dam, no sign of ability over hurdles, from family of top-class 2m chaser Artifice and very smart staying chaser Carbury Cross: eighth of 18 in bumper at Towcester on debut. *Ferdy Murphy* **F79**

TEENO ROSSI (IRE) 7 b.m. Teenoso (USA) – Mistress Ross (Impecunious) [2004/5 h–, F75?: 21vpu 16v Feb 13] small, lightly-made mare: little form. *J. K. Magee, Ireland* **h–**

*John Smith's West Yorkshire Hurdle, Wetherby—
a winning return to hurdles for Telemoss, who beats Crystal d'Ainay (right) and St Matthew (centre)*

TEES MILL 6 b.g. Lugana Beach – Hopperetta (Rock Hopper) [2004/5 F16v Feb 13] 1,500 4-y-o: first foal: dam maiden who probably stayed 1¼m: tailed off in bumper on debut. *D. W. Thompson* **F–**

TEESWATER 5 b.g. Alderbrook – Ewe Lamb (Free State) [2004/5 F16g 19d 24d Mar 5] leggy gelding: half-brother to winning 2¾m hurdler Romney (by Timeless Times): dam winning 2m hurdler: ninth of 15 in bumper at Catterick on debut: no show in 2 novice hurdles. *Mrs P. Sly* **h– F83**

TEETON PRICELESS 10 b.m. Broadsword (USA) – Teeton Frolic (Sunley Builds) [2004/5 c22v* c24s^pu Mar 10] fair pointer, successful in April: only completion in hunter chases when winning at Towcester in April 2004. *Mrs Joan Tice* **c96**

TELEMACHUS 5 b.g. Bishop of Cashel – Indian Imp (Indian Ridge) [2004/5 16v^F 16s^6 Mar 29] useful up to 1¼m on Flat: sold out of J. Given's stable 45,000 gns Newmarket Autumn Sales: still to be asked for effort when falling 2 out in maiden at Punchestown on hurdling debut: 20 lengths sixth to Justified in Grade 2 novice at Fairyhouse next time. *N. Meade, Ireland* **h108**

TELEMOSS (IRE) 11 b.g. Montelimar (USA) – Shan's Moss (Le Moss) [2004/5 c126, h–: 25s* 24g^4 24s 22g^5 Apr 16] rangy, useful-looking gelding: winning chaser: smart hurdler at one time, useful nowadays: won Grade 2 John Smith's West Yorkshire Hurdle at Wetherby in October by 1½ lengths from Crystal d'Ainay: best effort after when fourth of 6 to Baracouda in similar event at Newbury: stays 25f: acts on good to firm and heavy going. *N. G. Richards* **c– h140**

TELIMAR PRINCE (IRE) 9 b.g. Montelimar (USA) – Blakica (Sexton Blake) [2004/5 16d^pu Mar 12] lengthy, angular gelding: formerly useful hurdler for J. Gifford: off over 2 years, no encouragement in valuable handicap on return. *A. King* **h–**

TELL ME SEE (IRE) 9 b.m. Glacial Storm (USA) – Bavards Girl (IRE) (Le Bavard (FR)) [2004/5 c25s^6 c22d^5 c24s* c25v^2 c24v^6 c28v^2 c28d Feb 27] tall, angular mare: fairly useful handicap chaser: won at Naas in November by 2½ lengths from Count Rossini: stays 25f: acts on heavy going: usually owner/trainer ridden. *John Michael Burke, Ireland* **c117 h–**

TELL TALE (IRE) 13 b.g. Tale Quale – Loobagh Bridge (River Beauty) [2004/5 c94+: c26g^3 c31m^2 c30d* c24s^5 c28g^2 c26d* c24g Apr 7] fair handicap chaser: won at Cartmel in May and Newton Abbot in March: stays extreme distances: acts on good to firm and good to soft going. *J. G. Cann* **c104**

TELL THE TREES 4 br.f. Tamure (IRE) – Bluebell Copse (Formidable (USA)) [2004/5 18m* 16d^3 16g^F 16s^3 17d^3 18s 17d 22d* 24m 22v^4 Apr 22] small, sparely-made filly: fair on Flat (stays 2m), sold out of R. Beckett's stable 12,600 gns after winning seller in August: fair form over hurdles: won juvenile in September and handicap in February, both at Fontwell: stays 2¾m: acts on good to firm and good to soft going (below best on soft/heavy): visored third and fourth outings: none too fluent a jumper. *M. C. Pipe* **h105**

TELMAR FLYER 8 b.m. Neltino – Flying Mistress (Lear Jet) [2004/5 h–: 16f^{pu} May 18] of little account: tried tongue tied. *P. R. Webber* **h–**

TEME VALLEY 11 br.g. Polish Precedent (USA) – Sudeley (Dancing Brave (USA)) [2004/5 c88+, h110: c17g^5 16m 21d 16d 16v c16v^{pu} 16g 21d^5 Apr 5] leggy gelding: winning chaser: fair handicap hurdler: stays easy 21f: acts on soft and good to firm going, possibly not on heavy: formerly tongue tied: has won 10 races at Sedgefield. *J. Howard Johnson* **c– h100**

TEMPER LAD (USA) 10 b.g. Riverman (USA) – Dokki (USA) (Northern Dancer) [2004/5 h74: 20g^6 22d^3 21d^6 22s^6 22s^6 19g^2 20d^2 Mar 12] neat gelding: poor handicap hurdler: left J. Joseph after fifth start: stays 2¾m: acts on soft going, probably on firm: tried blinkered: formerly usually tongue tied. *J. D. Frost* **h71**

TEMPLE DOG (IRE) 9 ch.g. Un Desperado (FR) – Shower (Kings Lake (USA)) [2004/5 c110§, h115§: c20s^3 c25d^{pu} 24d^{pu} 20v c25v^{pu} 22v^{pu} 21v^6 Mar 28] workmanlike gelding: fairly useful hurdler/fair chaser at best: has become most temperamental: tried blinkered/in cheekpieces: one to avoid. *Mrs B. K. Thomson* **c– § h– §**

TEMPLE OF ARTEMIS 6 b.g. Spinning World (USA) – Casessa (USA) (Caro) [2004/5 h–: 16g May 16] no sign of ability in 2 novice hurdles. *F. Jordan* **h–**

TEN BOB (IRE) 7 b.g. Jurado (USA) – Rush For Gold (Mugatpura) [2004/5 22s^{ur} Nov 7] 4,000 4-y-o: seventh foal: brother to winning 2m chaser Golden Beacon and half-brother to useful chaser Ten Poundsworth (by Orchestra), stayed 25f: dam winning hurdler/chaser: won both completed starts in points in 2004: joint favourite, unseated second in novice on hurdling debut. *Mrs S. J. Smith* **h–**

TENDER TOUCH (IRE) 10 gr.m. Weldnaas (USA) – Moments Peace (Adonijah) [2004/5 c73, h–: 16g* 16g^3 19m c17g^4 c16m^4 17d^2 16s^6 Nov 5] leggy mare: poor hurdler/chaser: won selling handicap over hurdles at Hexham in May: stays 19f: acts on heavy and good to firm going. *Miss Kate Milligan* **c67 h67**

TENKO 6 ch.m. Environment Friend – Taco (High Season) [2004/5 F16d 20s^{pu} Jan 24] small mare: fourth foal: dam, winning chaser, stayed 25f: no form in bumper or mares novice hurdle. *M. D. McMillan* **h– F–**

TEN PRESSED MEN (FR) 5 b.g. Video Rock (FR) – Recolte d'Estruval (FR) (Kouban (FR)) [2004/5 F95: F16s^3 Dec 18] good-topped gelding: fairly useful in bumpers: third to Karanja at Windsor, only start in 2004/5. *Jonjo O'Neill* **F95**

TENSEESEE (FR) 10 ch.g. Murmure (FR) – Chattannooga Choo (FR) (In The Mood (FR)) [2004/5 c18m^{pu} c23m^F Apr 10] tall, close-coupled gelding: winning hurdler/chaser: off over 3 years, failed to complete in handicap chases in 2004/5: should stay beyond 2½m: acts on good to soft going. *Miss J. R. Tooth* **c– h–**

TENSILE (IRE) 10 b.g. Tenby – Bonnie Isle (Pitcairn) [2004/5 c–, h120: 22s* 22s^2 24d^3 19s* Mar 23] compact gelding: fair hurdler nowadays: had plenty to spare when winning sellers at Folkestone in January and Towcester in March: best effort in 2004/5 when third to Sungates in handicap at Chepstow: stays 3m: acts on any going: has had tongue tied: held up. *R. J. Hodges* **c– h112**

TEORBAN (POL) 6 b.g. Don Corleone – Tabaka (POL) (Pyjama Hunt) [2004/5 h90: 26m^6 21m^3 22d^2 19d^2 21d^{bd} 19g^2 24d Feb 1] stocky gelding: modest maiden hurdler: claimed on Flat from M. Pitman £7,000 after second start: should stay 3m+: acts on good to firm and soft going. *D. J. S. ffrench Davis* **h89**

TERDAD (USA) 12 ch.g. Lomond (USA) – Istiska (FR) (Irish River (FR)) [2004/5 c–§, h88§: 24g 22g^6 22m^4 26f Sep 26] big, rangy gelding: lightly raced and no form over fences: winning hurdler: out of sorts in 2004/5: wears headgear: ungenuine. *J. G. Given* **c– § h– §**

TERIVIC 5 br.g. Terimon – Ludoviciana (Oats) [2004/5 F82: 16d^2 19g Mar 4] compact gelding: twice-raced in bumpers: better effort over hurdles when second to Noble Request in novice at Towcester: should stay beyond 2m. *K. C. Bailey* **h99**

TERLAN (GER) 7 b.g. Medicus (GER) – Taxodium (GER) (Blakeney) [2004/5 16s* 16s^2 16g^6 16v^2 16d^6 16v^3 16g^4 16g^3 16s Apr 20] leggy gelding: successful 6 times up to 1¼m on Flat in Germany for T. Gibson: fair novice hurdler: won at Ayr on debut in November: raced at 2m on good going or softer. *P. Monteith* **h104**

TERMINOLOGY 7 gr.g. Terimon – Rhyming Moppet (Rymer) [2004/5 F88: F16g 16v^5 20v^6 Jan 25] workmanlike gelding: fourth on first 2 starts in bumpers: modest form in 2 novice hurdles: stays 2½m. *K. C. Bailey* **h86 F–**

TERMONFECKIN 7 b.g. Runnett – Crimson Sol (Crimson Beau) [2004/5 16v^{pu} Oct 16] rather leggy gelding: no show in 2 starts over hurdles over 2 years apart. *P. W. Hiatt* **h–**

TERRAMARIQUE (IRE) 6 b.g. Namaqualand (USA) – Secret Ocean (Most Secret) [2004/5 16s 16d^6 16v 16d^6 24v^4 Mar 20] €11,000 3-y-o: seventh foal: half-brother to fair hurdler/useful chaser Hallyards Gael (by Strong Gale), stays 25f, and bumper winner Big Perks (by Executive Perk): dam Irish 7f winner: poor form over hurdles: may prove best around 2½m. *L. Lungo* **h75**

TERRE DE JAVA (FR) 7 b.g. Cadoudal (FR) – Terre d'Argent (FR) (Count Ivor (USA)) [2004/5 h108: c16g^F c16g* c16v^{pu} Feb 5] fair hurdler: hard held when winning 3-finisher maiden at Doncaster in December, only completion over fences: stays 2½m: acts on good to firm and heavy going. *Mrs H. Dalton* **c105 h–**

TERRIBLE TENANT 6 gr.g. Terimon – Rent Day (Town And Country) [2004/5 h–: c19g^3 c19m^4 c21g c16m^5 c16s^2 c19s^4 c17v^5 c16g^3 c21s^5 c16s^{ur} c19s^2 Mar 23] good-topped gelding: twice-raced hurdler: poor maiden chaser: stays 21f: acts on soft going. *J. W. Mullins* **c83 h–**

TESSANOORA 4 b.f. Topanoora – Club Sandwich (Phardante (FR)) [2004/5 F16s^3 F16d^3 Mar 28] first foal: dam, poor form in bumpers, out of half-sister to smart staying chaser Lean Ar Aghaidh: third both starts in mares bumpers, better effort at Huntingdon on debut. *N. J. Henderson* **F87**

TEST OF FAITH 6 b.g. Weld – Gold Pigeon (IRE) (Goldhill) [2004/5 F–: F16s 20s^{pu} 19g 18v 22d Apr 11] little sign of ability. *J. N. R. Billinge* **h– F–**

TEST OF FRIENDSHIP 8 br.g. Roselier (FR) – Grease Pot (Gala Performance) [2004/5 c87, h–, F–: c26g^3 c21d* c21d^3 c24d^{pu} Feb 18] modest chaser: made all in maiden at Sedgefield in November: bred to be suited by test of stamina: has bled from nose. *Mrs H. Dalton* **c91 h–**

TETRAGON (IRE) 5 b.g. Octagonal (NZ) – Viva Verdi (IRE) (Green Desert (USA)) [2004/5 h–: 17s^3 16s 17v Mar 28] compact gelding: poor maiden hurdler: raced around 2m: usually wears headgear and tongue strap. *Miss Lucinda V. Russell* **h69**

TEVIOTINO 4 gr.f. Weldnaas (USA) – Dolitino (Neltino) [2004/5 16d 21v^{pu} 18d^5 20d^{pu} Mar 26] fourth known foal: dam poor novice staying chaser: poor form over hurdles. *W. Amos* **h–**

TEXAS BELLE (IRE) 7 b.m. Glacial Storm (USA) – Cloncannon Bell (IRE) (Creative Plan (USA)) [2004/5 20s^{pu} 20d^{pu} c23m^6 Apr 10] first foal: dam lightly raced: won mares maiden Irish point in 2004: no show in 2 novice hurdles: lost all chance with blunder 5 out in maiden at Worcester on chasing debut. *J. R. Holt* **c– h–**

TEXT 4 b.g. Atraf – Idle Chat (USA) (Assert) [2004/5 16v 17g^4 Apr 15] half-brother to modest hurdler Central Committee (by Royal Academy), stays 3¼m: fair maiden on Flat (stays 7f) at 3 yrs for Stef Liddiard: much better effort over hurdles when fourth in juvenile at Taunton: will prove best around 2m. *C. J. Down* **h99**

THAI TOWN 6 br.g. Afzal – Koo-Ming (Mansingh (USA)) [2004/5 F17g^6 F16d^4 19s 22s 16d Apr 3] fifth foal: half-brother to winning chaser Koo's Promise (by Lepanto), stayed 25f: dam poor maiden on Flat/over hurdles: fair form on second of 2 starts in bumpers: no show in novice hurdles: should be suited by further than 2m. *A. E. Jones* **h– F85**

THAMES (IRE) 7 b.g. Over The River (FR) – Aon Dochas (IRE) (Strong Gale) [2004/5 h105: 20d^3 20s* 20s* 24g^5 Mar 18] strong, lengthy gelding: chasing type: fairly useful novice hurdler: won at Haydock in December and February, beating Corlande easily by 2½ lengths on second occasion: better form other 2 starts, fifth to Moulin Riche in Grade 2 event at Cheltenham: stays 3m: acts on soft going. *N. J. Henderson* **h122**

THARI (USA) 8 b. or br.g. Silver Hawk (USA) – Magic Slipper (Habitat) [2004/5 c125, h–: c25g c17m^4 20d^5 c23m^2 c23m^3 c22m c22g Sep 5] good-topped gelding: **c119 h116**

fairlyuseful hurdler/chaser: should stay 3m: acts on heavy and good to firm going: usually blinkered in 2004/5: sometimes tongue tied. *N. Meade, Ireland*

THAT'S AN IDEA (IRE) 7 b.g. Arctic Lord – Annsgrove Polly (IRE) (Pollerton) [2004/5 F106: 20g* 22s² 20s Feb 20] unbeaten in 2 bumpers for Ms M. Mullins: won maiden at Killarney impressively on hurdling debut in May: better effort after (still looked green) when 1½ lengths second to Sunami Storm in novice at Thurles: will stay 3m. *D. Wachman, Ireland* **h118**

THAT'S FOR SURE 5 b. or br.g. Forzando – Sure Flyer (IRE) (Sure Blade (USA)) [2004/5 F16g* F16g⁵ Aug 18] 2,800 4-y-o: half-brother to several winners, including fair 2m hurdlers Cointosser (by Nordico) and Justupyourstreet (by Dolphin Street) and useful Irish 2-y-o 5f winner Sure Mark (by Goldmark): dam maiden half-sister to smart stayer Jardines Lookout: fair form in bumpers, successful at Worcester on debut in July by neck from Call Me Anything: tongue tied. *Mrs D. A. Hamer* **F93**

THAT'S RACING 5 ch.g. Classic Cliche (IRE) – All On (Dunbeath (USA)) [2004/5 19v 16v⁵ 16v Jan 14] workmanlike gelding: poor maiden on Flat: no form over hurdles. *J. Hetherton* **h61**

THAT'S RHYTHM (FR) 5 b.g. Pistolet Bleu (IRE) – Madame Jean (FR) (Cricket Ball (USA)) [2004/5 F16d⁵ F16s Mar 12] leggy gelding: first foal: dam, 11f winner, half-sister to very smart French hurdler Denham Red and useful 2m hurdler Bongo Fury: better effort in bumpers when fifth of 10 at Catterick on debut. *M. Todhunter* **F88**

THE ALAMO 7 b.g. Supreme Leader – Culinary (Tower Walk) [2004/5 F16g* F16m* F16s² Oct 3] €100,000 4-y-o: brother to fairly useful hurdler Hang 'Em High, stayed 2½m, and fair hurdler/chaser up to 3m Kings Banquet and half-brother to winning pointer by Strong Gale: dam won 2m selling hurdle: useful form in bumpers, won at Tipperary in June and Galway (by 5 lengths from Liberty Flag) in August: will stay 2½m. *A. P. O'Brien, Ireland* **F109**

THE ALLEYCAT (IRE) 14 b.g. Tidaro (USA) – Allitess (Mugatpura) [2004/5 c81, h–: c23m⁴ c21m⁵ Aug 6] veteran handicap chaser: stays easy 21f: raced mainly on good going or firmer (acts on firm): has worn cheekpieces: sold 500 gns Doncaster October Sales. *R. Ford* **c– h–**

THEATRE GROOM (USA) 6 ch.g. Theatrical – Model Bride (USA) (Blushing Groom (FR)) [2004/5 F99: F16d Dec 5] sturdy gelding: fairly useful form in bumpers in 2003/4: no show at Warwick after 15-month absence. *Miss G. Browne* **F–**

THEATRE KNIGHT (IRE) 7 b.g. Old Vic – Musical View (IRE) (Orchestra) [2004/5 16s 20d⁶ Nov 12] rangy gelding: second foal: dam unraced, out of half-sister to smart hurdler/useful staying chaser Interview II: won second of 2 starts in maiden Irish points in 2004: sold 110,000 gns Doncaster May Sales: poor form in 2 novice hurdles. *J. Howard Johnson* **h83**

THEATRE RIGHTS (IRE) 5 ch.g. Old Vic – Deep Perk (IRE) (Deep Run) [2004/5 F16s Mar 1] €10,000 3-y-o: fifth foal: half-brother to fair 2m and 3m winning hurdler Ashleybank House (by Lord Americo): dam ran once: tailed off in bumper on debut. *J. S. Haldane* **F–**

THEATRE TINKA (IRE) 6 b.g. King's Theatre (IRE) – Orange Grouse (IRE) (Taufan (USA)) [2004/5 19g Sep 30] fair on Flat (stays 1¾m): in cheekpieces, well held in novice on hurdling debut. *R. Hollinshead* **h–**

THEATRE (USA) 6 b.g. Theatrical – Fasta (USA) (Seattle Song (USA)) [2004/5 16g⁴ 19dF 21d⁵ 23d² 22s* 22d Mar 19] close-coupled gelding: fairly useful stayer on Flat: fair novice hurdler: won at Fontwell in March by 3½ lengths from Floreana: would also have won at Lingfield on second start but for falling last: will stay beyond 23f: raced on good going or softer: has jumped none too fluently. *Jamie Poulton* **h112**

THE BAG MAN 6 b.g. Alflora (IRE) – Lady Claudia (IRE) (Good Thyne (USA)) [2004/5 F16d⁶ 16d 19m Apr 23] tall, good sort: first foal: dam unraced, from family of one-time very smart 2m to 2½m hurdler/useful chaser Mantles Prince: modest form in bumper on debut: well held in 2 novice hurdles. *P. F. Nicholls* **h– F83**

THE BAILLIE (IRE) 6 b.g. Castle Keep – Regular Dolan (IRE) (Regular Guy) [2004/5 F93: F16s³ Dec 22] modest form in bumpers. *C. R. Egerton* **F80**

THE BAJAN BANDIT (IRE) 10 b.g. Commanche Run – Sunrise Highway VII (Master Owen) [2004/5 c–, h137: 20s 24d 23s* Feb 19] medium-sized gelding: winning **c– h143**

Pertemps Handicap Hurdle (Qualifier), Haydock—a first-time visor works the oracle on The Bajan Bandit, who soon has the measure of Hirvine (cheekpieces)

chaser: useful handicap hurdler: visored, best effort when winning 15-runner event at Haydock in February by 6 lengths from Hirvine: stays 23f: has won on good to firm going, ideally suited by soft/heavy. *L. Lungo*

THE BANDIT (IRE) 8 b.g. Un Desperado (FR) – Sweet Friendship (Alleging (USA)) [2004/5 c128, h99+: c20g^{4} c24d^{2} 21d^{3} c24g^{pu} Mar 16] useful-looking gelding: fair hurdler: useful handicap chaser: best effort when short-head second to King Harald, pair well clear, at Newbury: ran as if amiss in Kim Muir at Cheltenham final start: stays 3m: acts on soft and good to firm going. *Miss E. C. Lavelle* **c134 h109**

THE BAR MAID 7 b.m. Alderbrook – Corny Story (Oats) [2004/5 h88, F70?: 21g* 24s^{2} 21s* 21s^{3} 24v^{4} Jan 18] leggy mare: fair novice hurdler: best form at Towcester, won there in October (handicap) and November (mares): stays 3m: acts on soft going: races up with pace: genuine. *Miss G. Browne* **h103**

THE BATTLIN BISHOP 6 br.g. Bishop of Cashel – Angel Drummer (Dance In Time (CAN)) [2004/5 F–: F16d 16g^{pu} Mar 16] useful-looking gelding: no form in bumpers or maiden hurdle. *Ian Williams* **h– F–**

THE BAY BRIDGE (IRE) 6 b. or br.g. Over The River (FR) – Alamo Bay (Torenaga) [2004/5 F–p: F17s Nov 30] lengthy, useful-looking gelding: well held both starts in bumpers. *Miss E. C. Lavelle* **F–**

THE BEES KNEES 5 b.g. Bijou d'Inde – Dismiss (Daring March) [2004/5 F16s Dec 18] tall gelding: seventh foal: half-brother to fairly useful winner up to 1¼m La Modiste (by Most Welcome) and 7f winner Mystery (by Mystiko): dam, fairly useful 1m and 1¼m winner, sister to useful sprinter Our Jock: tailed off in bumper on debut. *A. P. Jones* **F–**

THE BIKER (IRE) 8 br.g. Arctic Lord – Glenravel (Lucifer (USA)) [2004/5 h–: 16d^{2} 20m Dec 12] tall, workmanlike gelding: disappointing hurdler: should stay beyond 17f: acts on heavy going. *P. Monteith* **h108**

THE BISCUIT 11 ch.m. Nomadic Way (USA) – Not To Worry (USA) (Stevward) [2004/5 h–: 24d^{pu} May 13] lightly raced and little sign of ability: has had tongue tied. *B. Mactaggart* **h–**

THE BOSUN 8 b.g. Charmer – Sailors Joy (Handsome Sailor) [2004/5 F–: 21g^{pu} 22d^{2} 23d^{6} 22s^{5} 24d^{3} 24g Apr 1] workmanlike gelding: poor novice hurdler on balance: stays 3m: tried tongue tied. *A. E. Jessop* **h84**

THE BOYS IN GREEN (IRE) 8 b.g. Shernazar – Mursuma (Rarity) [2004/5 c85, h110, F94: c17s c19s c22s^{4} c18d^{ur} c17v* c21v^{6} 16v^{3} c16s^{2} c17v^{5} Apr 2] well-made **c113 h110**

gelding: fair hurdler/chaser: successful over fences in handicaps at Leopardstown in December and Punchestown (beating Cluain Rua by ½ length) in late-April: effective at 2m to 2¾m: raced on good going or softer (acts on heavy): effective in blinkers/cheek-pieces or without. *C. Roche, Ireland*

THE BUSHKEEPER (IRE) 11 b.g. Be My Native (USA) – Our Little Lamb (Prince Regent (FR)) [2004/5 c24g^F Mar 16] tall gelding: useful handicap chaser in 2001/2, successful in valuable amateur handicap at Cheltenham: shaped as though retaining all his ability in same race on belated return, just a length down when falling 3 out: stays 3¼m: acts on soft going: sound jumper: reportedly hard to train, and very lightly raced. *N. J. Henderson* **c130 ?**

THE BUTTERWICK KID 12 ch.g. Interrex (CAN) – Ville Air (Town Crier) [2004/5 c101, h–§: c25d³ c24v*dis c22d² c22g c24v³ Apr 17] neat gelding: fairly useful hunter chaser: disqualified for taking wrong course after making virtually all at Newcastle in February: effective at 2½m to 25f: acts on good to firm and heavy going: usually visored/blinkered. *T. P. Tate* **c104 h– §**

THE CAD (IRE) 5 gr.g. Broken Hearted – Redondo Beach (Mandalus) [2004/5 17s 21s 16v⁵ 20d⁶ Apr 22] fourth foal: dam won 2½m hurdle in Ireland: form over hurdles only when fifth in maiden at Chepstow. *R. H. Alner* **h–**

THE CAMPDONIAN (IRE) 14 ch.g. Clearly Bust – Not At All (Royal Highway) [2004/5 c24m^ur May 22] compact gelding: winning staying chaser: fair pointer in 2004: has had tongue tied. *Mrs Lucy King* **c– h–**

THECAULOFESKER (IRE) 4 b. or br.g. Imperial Ballet (IRE) – Balance The Books (Elmaamul (USA)) [2004/5 16s 16s² 16s* 16s* 16v⁴ 16s Mar 13] fair on Flat (stays 1¼m): fairly useful juvenile hurdler: won at Thurles (maiden) in November and Gowran in December: raced at 2m on soft/heavy going. *Francis Ennis, Ireland* **h117**

THE COBBLER 6 b.g. Glory of Dancer – Lady Eccentric (IRE) (Magical Wonder (USA)) [2004/5 F16m Jul 21] sixth foal: half-brother to winning pointer by Young Man: dam unraced: well held in bumper on debut. *V. Smith* **F–**

THE COLLECTOR (IRE) 6 ch.g. Forest Wind (USA) – Glowing Reeds (Kalaglow) [2004/5 F–: 27d^pu Nov 23] little sign of ability: tried in cheekpieces. *N. P. McCormack* **h–**

THE CONNOR FELLA 4 b.g. Kris – Flower Fairy (FR) (Fairy King (USA)) [2004/5 F14g F14s F16g³ Feb 27] close-coupled gelding: second foal: half-brother to 1¼m winner King Halling (by Halling): dam unraced half-sister to smart French/US performer up to 10.5f Golden Arches: well held in bumpers. *F. P. Murtagh* **F–**

THE COOL GUY (IRE) 5 b.g. Zaffaran (USA) – Frostbite (Prince Tenderfoot (USA)) [2004/5 F16s² F16d* F17d* Apr 9] **F116**

The useful though unreliable staying chaser Grange Brake won plenty of races, including the Rehearsal Chase, for Nigel Twiston-Davies in the 'nineties, and another member of Grange Brake's family promises to be even more successful for

John Smith's Champion Standard Open National Hunt Flat, Aintree—outsiders The Cool Guy (right) and Some Touch (second right) overhaul long-time leader Mendo close home

Frosby's Four's "The Cool Guy"

the same trainer over the next few years. The Cool Guy, whose grandam is a half-sister to Grange Brake, has shown smart form in bumpers, and looks just the sort to go on and make his mark over jumps. Runner-up at Ludlow in December on his debut, The Cool Guy went one better when next seen three months later at Wincanton; and he was then stepped up in class, taking on twenty-one others, seventeen of whom were also previous winners, in the Grade 2 John Smith's Champion National Hunt Flat race at Aintree in April. Fully-fledged jockeys were able to compete in this race for the first time but, as at Wincanton, 7-lb claimer Steve Crawford partnered The Cool Guy who was sent off at 50/1. The favourite, at 7/4, was Refinement who had finished in the frame in the two previous runnings of the Champion Bumper at Cheltenham. The Cool Guy was still well off the pace as the field turned into the straight at Aintree, but he began to make ground three furlongs out and put in a strong run to lead near the finish and win by half a length and the same from Some Touch and Mendo, with Refinement only fourth. Later that month The Cool Guy and Refinement met again, in a Grade 1 event at Punchestown, but it was the latter, tried in blinkers, who came out on top this time, winning by nine lengths from The Cool Guy who managed to better his Aintree form even so, staying on well to take second after the winner had gone clear. Hennessy Gold Cup winner King's Road won both Aintree and Punchestown races for The Cool Guy's stable in 1998 and The Cool Guy is going to need further than two miles over jumps as well. Given his pedigree, he seems sure to stay three miles. He is by Zaffaran while his unraced dam is a daughter of the useful hurdler Arctic Conditions, who stayed two and three quarter miles. The Cool Guy is a half-brother to two hurdlers who stayed at least two and a half miles, the fairly useful Dramatist (by Homo Sapien) and the fair Professor Cool (by Cataldi), their sires much less of an influence for stamina than Zaffaran. The Cool Guy, a tall gelding who cost €30,000 as a four-year-old, has raced only on good to soft and soft ground. *N. A. Twiston-Davies*

THE COUNT (FR) 6 b.g. Sillery (USA) – Dear Countess (FR) (Fabulous Dancer (USA)) [2004/5 h65§: 16d⁴ 16dpu 16d⁶ Sep 22] temperamental maiden hurdler. *F. P. Murtagh* **h– §**

THE CROPPY BOY 13 b.g. Arctic Lord – Deep Cut (Deep Run) [2004/5 c–x, h–: c23m³ Sep 24] long-standing maiden outside points: poor jumper. *Mrs N. S. Sharpe* **c91 ? h–**

THE CULDEE (IRE) 9 ch.g. Phardante (FR) – Deep Inagh (Deep Run) [2004/5 c112, h–: c25g⁵ c22g* c24vF c28s Nov 7] stocky gelding: modest on Flat (stays 2m): winning hurdler: fair handicap chaser: won at Killarney in May by 3 lengths from Grange Leader: stays 25f: acts on heavy going. *F. Flood, Ireland* **c114 h–**

THE DANCING PHOUNZ 7 b.g. Phountzi (USA) – Lyne Dancer (Be My Native (USA)) [2004/5 F16v 23d⁴ 19spu Mar 23] lengthy gelding: fourth foal: dam tailed off in juvenile hurdle: no sign of ability in bumper or over hurdles: tried in cheekpieces. *Miss Z. C. Davison* **h– F–**

THE DARK FLASHER (IRE) 8 b.g. Lucky Guest – Perpignan (Rousillon (USA)) [2004/5 c105, h113: c17fpu 16m³ c16f² c17d³ Aug 28] leggy gelding: fair hurdler: modest maiden chaser: raced around 2m: acts on good to firm and heavy going: often finds little. *C. F. Swan, Ireland* **c99 h113**

THE DARK LORD (IRE) 8 b.g. Lord Americo – Khalkeys Shoon (Green Shoon) [2004/5 h114: 20g* 21g* 25d* 24d⁵ 24dbd 22g⁶ 24g 24d³ Apr 8] lengthy gelding: progressed into useful handicap hurdler, winning at Uttoxeter in May and Cheltenham in October (by 1¼ lengths from Red Ruffles) and November (led on bridle 2 out when beating Mistanoora 1¼ lengths in listed event): creditable efforts on completed starts after: stays 25f: acts on good to firm and good to soft going: held up: consistent. *Mrs L. Wadham* **h132**

THEDREAMSTILLALIVE (IRE) 5 ch.g. Houmayoun (FR) – State of Dream (IRE) (Carmelite House (USA)) [2004/5 F16d F16v⁵ 19s⁶ 17d⁵ 17s⁶ Feb 6] €6,000 3-y-o: sturdy gelding: second foal: dam unraced, from family of smart 2m hurdler Helenium: won maiden on second of 2 starts in 4-y-o Irish points in 2004: sold 37,000 gns Doncaster May Sales: better effort in bumpers when fifth of 12 at Warwick: poor form in novice hurdles. *J. A. B. Old* **h84 + F89**

Lombard Properties Handicap Hurdle, Cheltenham—
The Dark Lord defeats the blinkered Mistanoora to complete a hat-trick

THE DUCKPOND (IRE) 8 ch.g. Bob's Return (IRE) – Miss Gosling (Prince Bee) [2004/5 16d^{pu} 24v^{F} 22v* Apr 22] tall gelding: fairly useful in bumpers: off 2 years before reappearance: won 6-runner maiden hurdle at Newton Abbot in April by 29 lengths: would have won similar event at Chepstow but for falling 2 out: probably effective at 3m: acts on heavy ground. *J. A. B. Old* **h109 +**

THE DUKE'S SPEECH (IRE) 4 b.g. Saddlers' Hall (IRE) – Dannkalia (IRE) (Shernazar) [2004/5 F13d* F14g* F17d Apr 9] big, well-made gelding: second foal: dam bumper winner: fairly useful form in bumpers, winning 3-y-o events at Doncaster in November and Newcastle in December: creditable ninth of 22 to The Cool Guy in Grade 2 event at Aintree. *T. P. Tate* **F103**

THE EXTRA MAN (IRE) 11 b.g. Sayaarr (USA) – Chez Georges (Welsh Saint) [2004/5 c107, h–: c24d^{2} c21d* c20d^{2} c22d^{5} c22v^{4} c21s^{5} c23v^{3} c19d* Apr 22] tall gelding: fair chaser: won novice at Uttoxeter in May and, having left M. Ryan after sixth start, handicap at Chepstow in April: stays 3m: acts on any going: usually blinkered: usually makes running. *A. King* **c111 h–**

THE FENMAN 7 b.g. Mazaad – Dalgorian (IRE) (Lancastrian) [2004/5 h63: 21g^{4} Apr 26] leggy gelding: poor maiden hurdler: often wears blinkers/cheekpieces: sold 5,800 gns Doncaster May Sales. *R. J. Armson* **h63**

THE FINGERSMITH (IRE) 6 ch.g. Safety Catch (USA) – Dalus Rose (IRE) (Mandalus) [2004/5 F16v* F16v^{6} Feb 13] €3,400 3-y-o: first foal: dam unraced: useful form when winning bumper at Galway on debut in October by 2 lengths from Grattan Square: found little when disappointing in similar event at Navan. *A. J. McNamara, Ireland* **F111**

THE FLYER (IRE) 8 b.g. Blues Traveller (IRE) – National Ballet (Shareef Dancer (USA)) [2004/5 h103d: 22d^{6} 22v^{pu} 23v^{pu} 24s^{2} 24d 24d^{4} 21s^{3} 24s^{3} Apr 16] leggy gelding: fair handicap hurdler: stays 3m: acts on heavy going: usually tongue tied: none too reliable. *Miss S. J. Wilton* **h106**

THE FOOTBALLRESULT 4 b.f. The West (USA) – Bunny Gee (Last Tycoon) [2004/5 17g 18m^{6} 17m^{5} Sep 8] disappointing maiden on Flat: signs of only a little ability over hurdles: blinkered last 2 starts. *Miss G. Browne* **h62**

THE FOYLE (IRE) 5 b.g. Saddlers' Hall (IRE) – Ladycross (Deep Run) [2004/5 F16f* 16d^{2} 18d^{5} Nov 4] eighth foal: half-brother to fair hurdlers Alvine (by Strong Gale), stayed 2½m, and Jacky Flynn (by Phardante), stayed 3m, latter also winning chaser: dam, winning hurdler, half-sister to top-class chaser at 2½m+ Leap Frog: fairly useful form when winning bumper at Ballinrobe in May on debut, only start for P. Doyle: better effort over hurdles (reportedly distressed next time) when second in novice at Cork. *D. Wachman, Ireland* **h90 F103**

THE FRENCH ACTOR (IRE) 7 b.g. Toulon – Actress Mandy (IRE) (Mandalus) [2004/5 F16g May 13] €4,000 4-y-o: fifth foal: half-brother to winning pointer by Montelimar: dam unraced, from family of smart hurdler/chaser up to 2½m Snowtown Boy: no form in bumpers. *W. A. Murphy, Ireland* **F–**

THE FRENCH FURZE (IRE) 11 ch.g. Be My Guest (USA) – Exciting (Mill Reef (USA)) [2004/5 c–, h146: 16m 20s* 16d^{5} 17d^{5} 16v^{3} 24g 16g Apr 16] leggy, close-coupled gelding: useful hurdler: won handicap at Ayr (for second successive year) in November by 3 lengths from Paperprophet: ran well in face of stiffer tasks next 4 starts: stays 21f: acts on heavy and good to firm going: tried blinkered, not since 1999/00. *N. G. Richards* **c– h141**

THE GALWAY MAN (IRE) 8 b.g. Zaffaran (USA) – Nestley River (IRE) (Over The River (FR)) [2004/5 c120p, h–, F–: c24s^{ur} c20s* c24v^{6} c24v c20s^{4} c20v* c20v^{3} Feb 12] rangy, good sort: useful chaser: won minor events at Clonmel in December and February (tongue tied, beat Ground Ball by ½ length): creditable third of 5 to Rathgar Beau in Grade 2 at Gowran final start: barely stays testing 3m: acts on heavy going: sometimes let down by jumping. *Anthony Mullins, Ireland* **c134 x h–**

THE GAME IS THERE (IRE) 6 b.g. Flemensfirth (USA) – Erins Elect (IRE) (Erin's Hope) [2004/5 F18m^{2} 17m^{6} 19g^{F} 18s 16v Dec 27] fourth foal: half-brother to 2¼m hurdle winner Lisa Baker (by Glacial Storm): dam thrice-raced maiden pointer: runner-up in bumper at Fontwell on debut: little impact in novice company over hurdles, left G. L. Moore after third start. *J. F. O'Shea, Ireland* **h81 ? F86**

THE GANGERMAN (IRE) 5 ch.g. Anshan – Ivy Lane (IRE) (Be My Native (USA)) [2004/5 F17s6 F17s4 19s4 19m4 Apr 9] €5,500 4-y-o: leggy gelding: first foal: dam unraced: better effort in bumpers when fourth in maiden at Exeter: poor form on second of 2 starts over hurdles: likely to be suited by good test of stamina. *N. A. Twiston-Davies* **h84 p F90**

THE GENE GENIE 10 b.g. Syrtos – Sally Maxwell (Roscoe Blake) [2004/5 c–, h100: 16g 19m3 19m4 19g4 22d 16s5 Jan 22] workmanlike gelding: modest handicap hurdler: best short of 2¾m: acts on good to firm and heavy going: tried visored: held up. *R. J. Hodges* **c– h100**

THEGEORDIEDUCHESS (IRE) 4 b.f. Revoque (IRE) – Tirhala (IRE) (Chief Singer) [2004/5 F14g F16d Jan 13] 500 3-y-o: leggy filly: fourth living foal: half-sister to winning 2m hurdler/8.5f to 10.5f winner Jake Black (by Definite Article): dam, Irish 2-y-o 6f winner, half-sister to high-class 1¼m performer Timardia: better effort in bumpers when seventh of 18 in 3-y-o event at Newcastle on debut. *G. A. Swinbank* **F76**

THE GLEN 7 gr.g. Mtoto – Silver Singer (Pharly (FR)) [2004/5 h83: 16m5 22g* 19g3 22g6 20g5 16m6 21g* 21sF 21g 22d6 Apr 17] leggy gelding: fair hurdler: won maiden at Newton Abbot in June and novice at Ludlow in October: stays 2¾m: acts on good to firm going. *R. Lee* **h101**

THE GLEN ROAD (IRE) 8 ch.g. Star Quest – Claret Mist (Furry Glen) [2004/5 c20g2 Oct 30] poor pointer, won twice in 2003: 66/1, second to easy winner Cornish Rebel in maiden at Lingfield on chasing debut. *A. W. Carroll* **c95**

THE GRADUATE 11 ch.g. Indian Ridge – Queen's Eyot (Grundy) [2004/5 c24d4 May 11] well held in 2 starts over hurdles: fair pointer, successful in March: last of 4 finishers in hunter chase at Huntingdon. *A. J. Walker* **c– h–**

THE GRANBY (IRE) 11 b.g. Insan (USA) – Elteetee (Paddy's Stream) [2004/5 c110, h–: c21d c24dF May 11] leggy gelding: winning hurdler/chaser: fair pointer nowadays, successful in January: stays 25f: acts on soft and good to firm going. *Miss H. M. Irving* **c– h–**

THE GREY MAN 4 gr.g. Muhtarram (USA) – Lavender Della (IRE) (Shernazar) [2004/5 aF13g2 F12d aF16g2 F16d* Apr 20] smallish, angular gelding: third foal: brother to Austrian middle-distance winner Chiltern Bucks: dam maiden who stayed 1½m: fairly useful form in bumpers, winning at Worcester in April by ½ length from Wogan. *J. W. Mullins* **F97**

THE GROCERS CURATE (IRE) 5 b.g. Anshan – Shining Willow (Strong Gale) [2004/5 21d6 16s3 Mar 23] good sort: chasing type: second foal: dam, fair hurdler/fairly useful chaser who stayed 3m, out of half-sister to top-class 2m to 2½m jumper Buck House: backward, 15 lengths sixth to Bagan in novice hurdle at Kempton on debut: dropped in trip, outpaced in straight when third to Arctic Blue in similar event at Chepstow next time: will stay 3m: remains open to improvement. *N. J. Henderson* **h109 p**

THE HAIRY LEMON 5 b.g. Eagle Eyed (USA) – Angie's Darling (Milford) [2004/5 h–, F–: 16d5 18m 16s5 20s* 16d3 21g2 16s4 16d2 16s2 18s4 16d5 21s4 16s5 Mar 27] quite good-topped gelding: modest handicap hurdler: won amateur race at Uttoxeter in November: good effort next 5 starts: stays 21f: acts on soft going. *M. F. Harris* **h96**

THE HEARTY JOKER (IRE) 10 b.g. Broken Hearted – Furryway (Furry Glen) [2004/5 c86§, h–: c19m* 19d2 19d c19m* c24m3 c21gpu c21gpu c19mpu 21m2 17f6 22g4 18s3 Oct 12] lengthy gelding: poor chaser: won handicap at Exeter and minor event at Towcester early in season: poor maiden hurdler: effective at 19f to 2¾m: acts on firm and good to soft going: tried visored/blinkered: unreliable: sold 900 gns Doncaster November Sales. *B. G. Powell* **c83 § h76 §**

THE HIGHERHO 5 ch.g. Forzando – Own Free Will (Nicholas Bill) [2004/5 F77: F16g May 16] well held in 2 bumpers. *M. W. Easterby* **F–**

THE HOLY BEE (IRE) 6 ch.g. Un Desperado (FR) – Ballycahan Girl (Bargello) [2004/5 F16d6 F16g5 18s3 21dur 21g3 Mar 28] well-made gelding: chasing sort: eighth foal: half-brother to modest chaser Step In Line (by Step Together), stays 3¼m: dam lightly-raced maiden: fair form in 2 bumpers: best effort over hurdles when third to Demarco in novice at Fontwell on debut: should be suited by 2½m+: acts on soft going. *Miss H. C. Knight* **h100 F87**

THE HONEY GUIDE 9 gr.g. Homo Sapien – The Whirlie Weevil (Scallywag) [2004/5 c20dF c16spu c20spu c20g Apr 3] big gelding: no form. *Mrs L. B. Normile* **c– h–**

THE KEW TOUR (IRE) 9 ch.g. Un Desperado (FR) – Drivers Bureau (Proverb) [2004/5 c112, h–: c25gpu c23d2 24g5 c24d4 c24d c22vpu c24d3 Mar 12] big, workmanlike gelding: fair hurdler: fairly useful handicap chaser, in-and-out form in 2004/5: stays 25f: **c119 h100**

acts on soft and good to firm going: front runner/races prominently: has swished tail/ carried head high. *Mrs S. J. Smith*

THE KING OF ROCK 4 b.g. Nicolotte – Lv Girl (IRE) (Mukaddamah (USA)) [2004/5 17g[pu] Apr 10] modest maiden on Flat (stays 1½m): failed to settle in novice on hurdling debut. *A. G. Newcombe* **h–**

THE KIRK (NZ) 7 b.g. Grosvenor (NZ) – Margaux (NZ) (War Hawk) [2004/5 13f[4] 13f[4] 19s[pu] 16d 20s[6] 21g[F] 24m[2] Apr 10] sturdy gelding: unplaced in 5 starts on Flat in New Zealand: modest form in novice hurdles: stays 3m. *M. Madgwick* **h91**

THE KOP END (IRE) 7 b.g. Topanoora – Shermaya (FR) (Shardari) [2004/5 h113, F94: 17d[3] 16s[2] c16s[F] 16s[5] Jan 27] fairly useful hurdler: best effort when second to Athlumney Lad in valuable handicap at Down Royal in November: possibly amiss final start: fell 3 out in maiden at Thurles on chasing debut: raced around 2m on good to soft/ soft going: effective tongue tied or not. *C. Roche, Ireland* **c– p h119**

THE LAIRD'S ENTRY (IRE) 10 b.g. King's Ride – Balancing Act (Balinger) [2004/5 c106, h–: c24d[pu] c20s* Mar 12] big gelding: winning hurdler: fair chaser: won handicap at Ayr in March: stays 21f: acts on heavy going: front runner. *J. Howard Johnson* **c106 h–**

THE LANGER (IRE) 5 b.g. Saddlers' Hall (IRE) – Minigirls Niece (IRE) (Strong Gale) [2004/5 F17s Nov 30] €16,000 4-y-o: sturdy gelding: fourth foal: half-brother to fair hurdler Blue Derby (by Supreme Leader), stays 2¾m, and winning pointer by Be My Native: dam, placed in bumpers/over hurdles, out of half-sister to high-class chaser at 2½m+ Observe and very smart hurdler Minorettes Girl (by Strong Gale), herself dam of one-time high-class staying chaser Shotgun Willy: well held in bumper on debut. *S. T. Lewis* **F–**

THE LAST CAST 6 ch.g. Prince of Birds (USA) – Atan's Gem (USA) (Sharpen Up) [2004/5 h121: 20s[4] c16v* c16d[2] c16s c16g Mar 15] workmanlike gelding: useful handicap hurdler: improved effort when fourth to Mistanoora in valuable event at Chepstow on reappearance: better form again first 2 starts over fences, winning 3-finisher maiden at Uttoxeter in November and 5 lengths second to Contraband in Grade 2 novice at Sandown in December: off 2 months, well beaten last 2 starts, stiff task final one: stays 21f: raced on good going or softer (acts on heavy). *H. Morrison* **c135 h130**

THE LAST MOHICAN 6 b.g. Common Grounds – Arndilly (Robellino (USA)) [2004/5 h74: 16s* 16s* 16s* 21s[2] 16s 16d Feb 26] small gelding: fair hurdler: off 7 months, won sellers at Fakenham (conditional jockeys handicap) in October and Towcester (sold from P. Howling 8,200 gns) in November, and handicap at Leicester in December: stays 21f: acts on good to firm and heavy going. *F. Jordan* **h106**

THE LAST OVER 4 b.f. Overbury (IRE) – Little Serena (Primitive Rising (USA)) [2004/5 F12g F17s 16d[ur] 17g Apr 15] small filly: first foal: dam, modest hurdler who stayed 3¼m, sister to one-time useful 3m chaser Moor Lane: no sign of ability. *N. J. Hawke* **h– F–**

THE LEADER 12 b.g. Ardross – Leading Line (Leading Man) [2004/5 c92, h–: c17v[3] c16v* c16s[4] c16s[2] c17g[3] c18s[5] c16g[5] Apr 19] rangy gelding: modest handicap chaser: successful in 5-runner event (fourth win in equivalent race) at Folkestone in January: stays 3¼m, raced mainly over much shorter: raced on good going or softer (acts on heavy): often weak finisher. *P. R. Chamings* **c94 h–**

THE LISTENER (IRE) 6 gr.h. Roselier (FR) – Park Breeze (IRE) (Strong Gale) [2004/5 F18g[6] 21s 16d[4] 20v[F] 21v* 20v[2] 25v* 20d[su] Mar 12] strong, workmanlike horse: carries condition: brother to fairly useful hurdler/smart chaser Fork Lightning, stays 25f, and half-brother to fairly useful hurdler/useful chaser Distant Thunder (by Phardante), stays 3m, and fairly useful but temperamental chaser/winning hurdler Moving Earth (by Brush Aside), stays 3m: dam unraced sister to useful staying chaser Risk of Thunder: sixth in bumper on debut: useful novice hurdler: won at Plumpton (by 1¼ lengths from Darkness, pair well clear) in January and Warwick (not extended to beat Garryvoe 7 lengths) in February: slipped up after first in valuable novice handicap at Sandown final start: will stay beyond 25f: raced on going softer than good (acts on heavy): good chasing prospect. *R. H. Alner* **h132 p F78**

THE LOCAL 5 b.g. Selkirk (USA) – Finger of Light (Green Desert (USA)) [2004/5 h89: 17g 17v[4] 16s* 16s* 16s* 16v[5] 16d[2] 16d[2] 17m[6] Apr 9] leggy gelding: fair handicap hurdler: left N. Gaselee after first outing: much improved, winning at Warwick in December and Plumpton and Leicester (amateurs) in January: raced around 2m: acts on soft going: blinkered last 3 starts: free-going front runner. *C. R. Egerton* **h111**

THE LONGFELLA 4 b.g. Petong – Miss Tri Colour (Shavian) [2004/5 F14d² F14s⁶ Feb 9] third foal: dam maiden half-sister to useful performer up to 7f Wantage Park: better effort in bumpers when head second of 9 to Troll at Wetherby. *G. M. Moore* **F87**

THELONIUS (IRE) 10 ch.g. Statoblest – Little Sega (FR) (Bellypha) [2004/5 h–: 16m² 16g⁴ 16g⁵ Jul 29] leggy gelding: fair handicap hurdler: best at sharp 2m: acts on firm and good to soft going: usually held up. *C. J. Down* **h105**

THE LORDOF MYSTERY (IRE) 7 b.g. Mister Lord (USA) – Cooline Mist (IRE) (Actinium (FR)) [2004/5 h76: 20m 21d c24spu Jan 7] third in maiden on hurdling debut: no form since, including on chasing debut: left Mrs H. Dalton after first start. *B. G. Powell* **c–** **h–**

THE LORDS CROSS (IRE) 8 b.g. Jolly Jake (NZ) – Deep Chestnut (IRE) (Black Minstrel) [2004/5 20mpu 16g⁶ 19g Jul 29] poor maiden pointer: little show in maiden hurdles. *Mrs D. A. Hamer* **h74**

THE LYME VOLUNTEER (IRE) 8 b.m. Zaffaran (USA) – Dooley O'Brien (The Parson) [2004/5 c105, h–: 26g² 24v⁴ 22d 24v³ c25s³ c30sur c29v² c25s* c24d² c31s Apr 22] useful-looking mare: fair handicap hurdler: similar form over fences: won mares maiden at Hereford in March: suited by 3m+: acts on heavy and good to firm going: tried in cheekpieces/blinkers: has raced lazily: sketchy jumper over fences: sold 20,000 gns Doncaster May Sales. *O. Sherwood* **c104 x** **h108**

THE MAJOR (NZ) 12 ch.g. Try To Stop Me – Equation (NZ) (Palatable (USA)) [2004/5 c106x: c24dpu May 1] tall gelding: veteran chaser: stays 3m: acts on heavy going: idles, and best held up: makes mistakes: sold 5,000 gns Doncaster May Sales, successful all 4 completed starts in points in 2005. *J. R. Cornwall* **c– x**

THEMANFROMCARLISLE 9 br.g. Jupiter Island – Country Mistress (Town And Country) [2004/5 c92, h–: c19d⁴ c24m* c24gF 24spu Apr 20] tall gelding: winning hurdler: fair handicap chaser: won at Musselburgh in February: stays 3m: acts on good to firm going, possibly not on softer than good. *S. H. Shirley-Beavan* **c104** **h–**

THE MANSE BRAE (IRE) 9 b.g. Roselier (FR) – Decent Preacher (Decent Fellow) [2004/5 c24dpu c25d⁵ c24g² c24g⁴ c24g³ c27g³ Apr 15] good-bodied gelding: fair hurdler/chaser: off 20 months before reappearance: should stay beyond 25f: acts on good to firm and good to soft going: has worn cheekpieces, blinkered last 3 starts: hard ride. *J. M. Jefferson* **c110 §** **h–**

THE MARKET MAN (NZ) 5 ch.g. Grosvenor (NZ) – Eastern Bazzaar (IRE) (King Persian) [2004/5 16s* 19s² 16d* Jan 28] medium-sized gelding: successful over 1¼m on Flat at 3 yrs in New Zealand: fairly useful form in novice hurdles: successful at Kempton (by 2½ lengths from McBain) in November and Doncaster (by 15 lengths from Say What You See) in January: should stay beyond 19f. *N. J. Henderson* **h123**

THE MASARETI KID (IRE) 8 b.g. Commanche Run – Little Crack (IRE) (Lancastrian) [2004/5 c–, h83: 19d 20s⁴ 21vpu Jan 25] workmanlike gelding: poor hurdler: stays 27f: acts on firm and soft going: tried in cheekpieces: none too genuine. *G. A. Harker* **c–** **h74**

THE MAYSTONE (IRE) 5 b. or br.g. Thowra (FR) – Peg O The Wood (IRE) (Be My Native (USA)) [2004/5 F16s Mar 12] €23,000 4-y-o: first foal: dam poor novice hurdler: tailed off in bumper on debut. *B. Mactaggart* **F–**

THEME PARK 5 b.g. Classic Cliche (IRE) – Arcady (Slip Anchor) [2004/5 17d Nov 19] good-topped gelding: maiden on Flat, sold out of J. A. Harris' stable 1,200 gns Doncaster March (2004) Sales: tongue tied, no show in novice on hurdling debut. *S. C. Burrough* **h–**

THE MERRY MASON (IRE) 9 b.g. Roselier (FR) – Busters Lodge (Antwerp City) [2004/5 c87§, h–§: c25f* c26gpu c24g* c28d* c23m² c25s* c25vpu c24g* Mar 9] leggy, good-topped gelding: fair chaser: won handicap at Towcester in May: sold out of J. M. Jefferson's stable 7,500 gns Doncaster Sales later in month: successful another 4 times after, in handicaps at Bangor in August and Market Rasen in October, novice at Wetherby later in October and another handicap at Bangor in March: suited by 3m+: acts on firm and soft going, possibly unsuited by heavy: formerly lazy/poor jumper. *Mrs S. J. Smith* **c113** **h– §**

THE MICK WESTON 6 b.g. North Col – Zalina (Tyrnavos) [2004/5 F17s² F16g* F16d³ F16v* F16gur Mar 16] **F122**

Two of the more fancied runners for the Champion Bumper at Cheltenham in March failed to complete the course. Both lost their riders, Karanja at the start and The Mick Weston at the top of the hill when short of room and hitting the rail.

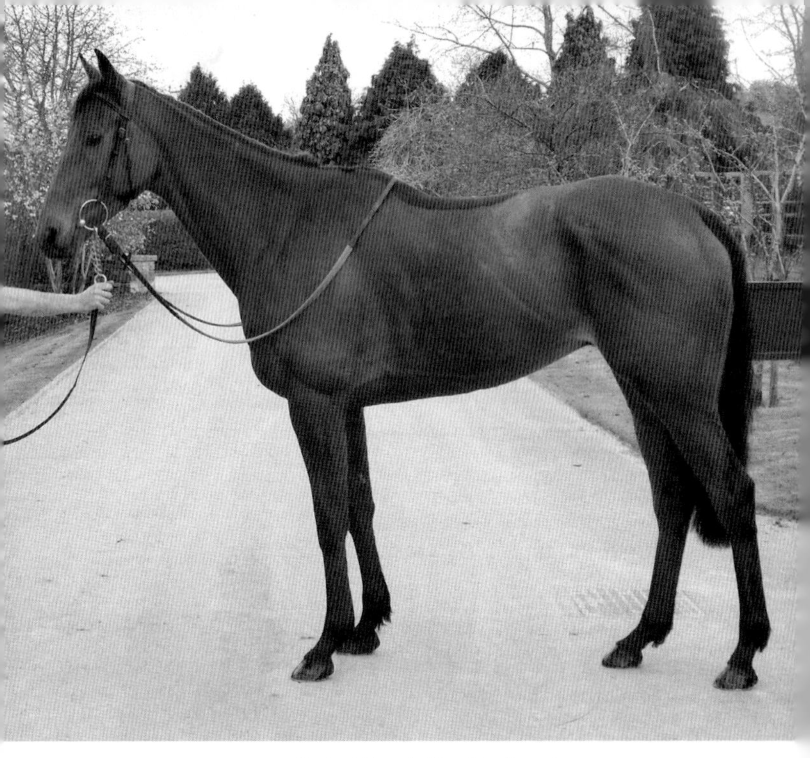

Mr Mick Weston's "The Mick Weston"

The Mick Weston, who had been waited with in rear, was still travelling strongly at the time of the incident and it was most unfortunate that he didn't get the opportunity to show what he could do. A reproduction of the form of his win at Chepstow on his previous outing would have been good enough to involve The Mick Weston in the close finish with the first three Missed That, De Soto and Rasharrow. The Mick Weston had advertised his credentials as a candidate for the Champion Bumper after making a remarkable return to action, following just one run in the spring, at Cheltenham in October. A 25/1-shot in a field of twenty, The Mick Weston produced one of the most impressive performances seen in a bumper, making up his ground effortlessly and quickening in scintillating style into the straight to win by sixteen lengths. The Mick Weston could finish only third at Cheltenham when a hot favourite on his next start, but he did fulfil the promise of that first victory when winning a fifteen-runner event at Chepstow at the end of December. Heavy ground ensured that the race provided more of a test of stamina than most bumpers, and The Mick Weston's opponents were well strung out behind him at the line, which he passed six lengths clear of Victom's Chance after travelling smoothly into contention under a patient ride and soon drawing clear after taking up the running around two furlongs out. The Mick Weston is the second foal of the maiden point winner Zalina, who is out of a winning half-sister to the smart Flat performers Band and Zimbalon. The Mick Weston's sire North Col, a smart winner at up to fifteen furlongs in France, hasn't met with much success at stud so far, but that could change when The Mick Weston goes over jumps. A useful-looking gelding who will be suited by two and a half miles and more, The Mick Weston looks a good prospect. *R. T. Phillips*

THE MIGHTY FLYNN 6 ch.g. Botanic (USA) – Owdbetts (IRE) (High Estate) [2004/5 h–, F–: 16d^5 16v c20m^5 Dec 12] little sign of ability. *P. Monteith* **c– h–**

THE MIGHTY SPARROW (IRE) 12 b.g. Montelimar (USA) – Tamer's Belle (Tamerlane) [2004/5 c82, h85: c18m^F c20g^3 c16g^4 c23m^F c20f^6 19m c19v^{pu} c19g^4 Apr 7] ex-Irish gelding: winning hurdler/maiden chaser: form in 2004/5 only on second outing: left N. Glynn after sixth start: stays 2½m: acts on good to firm and good to soft going: tried blinkered/in cheekpieces. *A. E. Jones* **c84 h–**

THE MILECASTLE (IRE) 6 b.g. Oscar (IRE) – Kiladante (IRE) (Phardante (FR)) [2004/5 F16d Nov 29] 1,000 4-y-o: third foal: dam won 3 bumpers and 1¼m event on Flat: no form in points and bumper. *W. T. Reed* **F–**

THE MINER 7 ch.g. Hatim (USA) – Glen Morvern (Carlingford Castle) [2004/5 h89: c16d^4 c16s^5 c22s^4 c17s* c20v^{pu} c17v^3 c17v^{pu} c17d c16s^3 Apr 22] well-made gelding: poor maiden hurdler: modest chaser: won novice handicap at Kelso in December: probably stays 2½m: acts on heavy going: has been let down by jumping. *Miss S. E. Forster* **c94 h–**

THE MURATTI 7 b.g. Alflora (IRE) – Grayrose Double (Celtic Cone) [2004/5 F94: 21g^{pu} Mar 27] won bumper in 2003/4 for D. Caro: reportedly suffered overreach on hurdling debut. *Miss I. E. Craig* **h–**

THENAMEESCAPESME 5 b.g. Alderbrook – Gaygo Lady (Gay Fandango (USA)) [2004/5 F16d Mar 10] half-brother to 21f chase winner in Switzerland by Glenstal and fairly useful 5f/7f winner Baligay (by Balidar), dam of smart 5f performer Bali-Royal: dam 1m winner: well held, though not knocked about in bumper at Wincanton on debut. *T. R. George* **F– p**

THE NAMES BOND 7 b.g. Tragic Role (USA) – Artistic Licence (High Top) [2004/5 h–: 16d^3 16s^5 16d^5 19s* 20s^2 20v 17s 19g Apr 1] close-coupled gelding: modest hurdler: gained first win in amateur novice handicap at Warwick in December: stays 2½m: acts on soft and good to firm going. *Andrew Turnell* **h96**

THE NEEDLER (IRE) 5 b.g. Needle Gun (IRE) – Monteanna (IRE) (Montelimar (USA)) [2004/5 F16s 16s^6 Mar 23] 7,000 4-y-o: first foal: dam unraced: tailed off in bumper on debut: signs of ability in novice on hurdling debut, though looked very much in need of experience: sold to join B. Pollock 2,600 Doncaster May Sales. *N. A. Twiston-Davies* **h89 ? F–**

THE NEWSMAN (IRE) 13 b.g. Homo Sapien – Miller Fall's (Stubbs Gazette) [2004/5 c121, h101: c20g^6 16m^6 c18s^4 c20s^5 18g^4 c20g^5 Apr 17] tall gelding: veteran handicap hurdler/chaser, fair nowadays: stays 21f: probably acts on any going: tried blinkered: has won 6 times at Fontwell. *G. Wareham* **c106 h104**

THENFORD STAR (IRE) 4 b.f. Zaffaran (USA) – Limavady Lady (IRE) (Camden Town) [2004/5 F16d^6 F16d^5 F17g^4 Apr 14] €8,000 3-y-o: rather unfurnished filly: first foal: dam lightly raced, from family of top-class staying hurdler Bannow Bay and very smart hurdler Mighty Moss: progressive form in bumpers, fourth in mares event at Cheltenham. *J. S. King* **F85**

THE NOMAD 9 b.g. Nomadic Way (USA) – Bubbling (Tremblant) [2004/5 c110, h–: c16s^4 c16d^3 c20d* c20g^6 c22d^6 c16d^{pu} Mar 12] workmanlike gelding: fair handicap chaser: won at Wetherby in December by 4 lengths from Deep Water: stays 21f: acts on heavy and good to firm going: races prominently: sometimes none too fluent. *M. W. Easterby* **c114 h–**

THEOCRITUS (GER) 4 b.g. Trempolino (USA) – Thyatira (FR) (Bakharoff (USA)) [2004/5 17m 16d^6 16g^4 19d^3 19s Jan 31] lengthy, unfurnished gelding: first foal: dam unraced half-sister to useful 2m to 21f hurdler Tryphaena: poor form over hurdles: stays 19f: acts on good to soft going. *Nick Williams* **h84**

THE OUTLIER (IRE) 7 br.g. Roselier (FR) – Shuil A Cuig (Quayside) [2004/5 F96: 16d^4 19d^4 20d^3 23d^3 Mar 28] fair form over hurdles: bred to stay beyond 2½m: takes keen hold and races prominently. *Miss Venetia Williams* **h104**

THE PARISHIONER (IRE) 7 ch.g. Glacial Storm (USA) – Phairy Miracles (IRE) (Phardante (FR)) [2004/5 h130, F94: 20v^3 24s^{pu} Oct 8] useful hurdler: creditable fourth (promoted) to Cloudy Bays in handicap at Listowel: disappointing favourite in listed handicap at Gowran 2 weeks later: should stay 3m: raced on going softer than good. *M. Hourigan, Ireland* **h125**

THE PECKER DUNN (IRE) 11 b.g. Be My Native (USA) – Riversdale Shadow (Kemal (FR)) [2004/5 h85: 24s^6 21v^{pu} 24v^{pu} c24v^{pu} Mar 29] strong gelding: winning hurdler, no form in 2004/5: jumped badly on chasing debut: stays 3m: acts on soft going. *Mrs N. S. Sharpe* **c– h–**

THE PENNYS DROPPED (IRE) 8 ch.g. Bob's Return (IRE) – Shuil Alainn (Levanter) [2004/5 c98, h–: c24dpu c20m* c22m5 c26g2 c25g* Aug 1] sturdy gelding: fair chaser: won handicaps at Bangor (novices) in May and Market Rasen (4-runner event) in August: stays 3¼m: acts on good to soft and good to firm going: visored third start (bled from nose): tongue tied once: makes the odd mistake. *Jonjo O'Neill* **c112 h–**

THE PERSUADER (IRE) 5 b.g. Sadler's Wells (USA) – Sister Dot (USA) (Secretariat (USA)) [2004/5 16d5 17s* 16d4 19m* Apr 17] good-topped gelding: fairly useful up to 1¾m at 3 yrs on Flat, well below form in 2004, left M. Johnston in April: fairly useful form over hurdles: won steadily-run maiden at Taunton in February and handicap at Stratford in April: improved form when beating Jockser 1¾ lengths (value extra) in latter: will stay further than 19f: acts on soft and good to firm going: tongue tied. *P. F. Nicholls* **h116**

THE PLAYER 6 b.g. Octagonal (NZ) – Patria (USA) (Mr Prospector (USA)) [2004/5 17d 17sur Feb 17] good-topped gelding: fair on Flat (probably stays 1m): shaped like non-stayer both starts over hurdles. *A. M. Balding* **h–**

THE POSH PADDY (IRE) 8 b. or br.g. Be My Native (USA) – Dizzy Dot (Bargello) [2004/5 h100p, F112: 16m*dis 20m2 Aug 8] rather leggy gelding: useful bumper winner: fair form over hurdles: first past post in maiden at Galway (subsequently disqualified after testing positive for prohibited substance) in July: stays 2½m: raced mainly on going firmer than good: tongue tied on debut. *Anthony Mullins, Ireland* **h112**

THEPRIDEOFEIREANN (IRE) 6 b.g. Toulon – Slaney Queen (Ballad Rock) [2004/5 F16g 16vpu 16vpu 19g 24dpu Nov 19] €26,000 3-y-o: rangy gelding: eighth foal: dam dual bumper winner: trained by C. Roche when eighth in bumper at Leopardstown on debut in 2003/4: no form in Britain: tongue tied last 2 starts. *Jonjo O'Neill* **h– F–**

THEPUBHORSE 5 ch.g. Endoli (USA) – Lady Insight (Belfort (FR)) [2004/5 F16s F16d Nov 29] unfurnished gelding: first foal: dam little worthwhile form on Flat: well beaten in 2 bumpers: unruly in preliminaries before debut. *Mrs H. O. Graham* **F–**

THE QUADS 13 b.g. Tinoco – Queen's Royale (Tobrouk (FR)) [2004/5 c–, h–: c28spu c31dpu c27sur c31d c30vur c24sur 25dpu 22spu Mar 11] leggy gelding: veteran hurdler/chaser, no longer of any account: usually blinkered and/or tongue tied, has been tried in cheekpieces. *Ferdy Murphy* **c– h–**

THE RAILWAY MAN (IRE) 6 b.g. Shenazar – Sparky Sue (IRE) (Strong Gale) [2004/5 F103: 16s3 16s4 18v* 18s2 16s2 Mar 29] €90,000 3-y-o: well-made gelding: chasing type: useful novice hurder: made all in 23-runner maiden at Leopardstown in December: best effort when second to Royal Paradise in Grade 1 there next time: ran creditably when fifth to Wild Passion in Grade 1 and second to Snoopy Loopy in valuable event, both at Punchestown in late-April: likely to be suited by 2½m: acts on heavy going: often front runner: type to do well in novice chases in 2005/6. *A. L. T. Moore, Ireland* **h131**

THE RAINBOW MAN 5 gr.g. Terimon – Swallowfield (Wattlefield) [2004/5 F16g Jan 14] useful-looking gelding: fourth foal: half-brother to 2m hurdle winner Aerion (by Ardross): dam lightly-raced: last of 13 in bumper on debut. *M. J. Ryan* **F–**

THE RANDY BISHOP 5 b.g. Bishop of Cashel – Fly South (Polar Falcon (USA)) [2004/5 F16v F17g F17s5 Apr 2] second foal: half-brother to 7f and 1m winner Whitgift Rock (by Piccolo): dam unraced: well beaten in bumpers. *T. Wall* **F–**

THEREALBANDIT (IRE) 8 b.g. Torus – Sunrise Highway VII (Master Owen) [2004/5 c155+, h133p: 25d c25d* c24g c25s2 c26g c20d3 c21m3 c29g Apr 23] tall, lengthy, rather sparely-made gelding: useful hurdler: virtually pulled up after setting strong pace in handicap at Cheltenham on reappearance: very smart chaser: won valuable handicap at same course in December by 3 lengths from Royal Auclair, idling after last: generally below best after: stays 27f: acts on soft and good to firm going: visored/in cheekpieces last 3 starts. *M. C. Pipe* **c155 h–**

THE REAL BOSS (IRE) 7 b.g. Grand Plaisir (IRE) – White Beau (Beau Charmeur (FR)) [2004/5 c19vpu c24g3 c24vF c25dur Apr 3] €10,500 4-y-o: sturdy gelding: second reported foal: dam unraced half-sister to useful staying chaser Gay Return: fell both starts in maiden Irish points in 2003: 100/1, modest form when third in maiden at Taunton, only completed outing in chases: needs to brush up jumping. *J. A. Geake* **c95 +**

THE REAL DEAL (IRE) 4 b.g. Taipan (IRE) – Forest Mist (Dalsaan) [2004/5 20d Mar 19] well-made gelding: sixth foal: half-brother to 2½m hurdle winner Dicky's Rock (by Be My Native) and 9f winner in Spain by Rainbows For Life: dam winning 2m hurdler: bit backward and green, signs of ability in well-contested novice hurdle at Uttoxeter on debut: should do better. *Nick Williams* **h– p**

THE REBEL LADY (IRE) 8 br.m. Mister Lord (USA) – Arborfield Brook (Over The River (FR)) [2004/5 c100, h–: c25gpu May 13] tall mare: fair chaser: stays 3m: acts on good to firm and good to soft going: often runs as if amiss. *Miss H. C. Knight* **c– h–**

THE RECIPIENT (IRE) 6 b.g. Eurobus – Saxa Princess (IRE) (Lancastrian) [2004/5 20dpu Nov 12] fifth foal: dam unraced: no sign of ability in 2 maiden Irish points and novice hurdle. *J. Wade* **h–**

THERE GOES WALLY 7 b.g. Lyphento (USA) – Dutch Majesty (Homing) [2004/5 h–, F–: c21sur Oct 22] no sign of ability: tried in cheekpieces. *A. Ennis* **c– h–**

THERE IS NO DOUBT (FR) 4 b.g. Mansonnien (FR) – Ma Chance (FR) (Dancehall (USA)) [2004/5 F13d* F13s* F16s3 F16g Mar 16] useful-looking gelding: second foal: dam, won twice over hurdles at 19f, half-sister to useful hurdler/chaser Chicuelo (by Mansonnien), stays 25f: smart form in bumpers: won 3-y-o events at Exeter (very well backed) and Towcester (beat Giovanna 9 lengths) in December: pulled hard and hung right when well held in Grade 1 at Cheltenham final start. *Mrs H. M. Bridges* **F117**

THE REVEREND (IRE) 5 b. or br.g. Taipan (IRE) – Sounds Classical (IRE) (Over The River (FR)) [2004/5 20s* Oct 31] first foal: dam unraced half-sister to top-class 2m hurdler/smart chaser Classical Charm: dead-heated in maiden Irish point in 2004: impressive start over hurdles when winning novice at Carlisle in October by 4 lengths from Wild Cane Ridge, travelling best and coming clear from last: looked good prospect, but wasn't seen out again. *J. Howard Johnson* **h127 p**

THE RIGHT PEOPLE (IRE) 5 ch.g. Deploy – Marlousion (IRE) (Montelimar (USA)) [2004/5 F16s Mar 12] €24,000 3-y-o, 20,000 4-y-o: third foal: dam lightly-raced half-sister to top-class jumper up to 3m Bradbury Star: never dangerous in bumper at Ayr on debut. *L. Lungo* **F81**

THE RILE (IRE) 11 ch.g. Alphabatim (USA) – Donna Chimene (Royal Gunner) [2004/5 c–, h115: c24dpu c20d c25v5 c17v6 c20vpu Feb 2] strong, lengthy gelding: fairly useful handicap hurdler/chaser at best: out of sorts in 2004/5, left L. Lungo after first start: should stay beyond 21f: raced mainly on going softer than good (acts on heavy): tried in cheekpieces. *Miss P. Robson* **c81 h–**

Mears Group Chase (Handicap), Cheltenham—
Therealbandit sees off top-weight Royal Auclair for his sole win of 2004/5

THE RING (IRE) 5 b.g. Definite Article – Renata's Ring (IRE) (Auction Ring (USA)) [2004/5 20m^{5} 16d^{6} Oct 21] tall gelding: fair on Flat (stays 2m): not knocked about in novice hurdles at Wetherby and Haydock: capable of better. *K. G. Reveley* **h98 +**

THE RIP 4 ch.g. Definite Article – Polgwynne (Forzando) [2004/5 16m 16d^{5} 16d^{4} Nov 27] good-topped gelding: modest maiden on Flat (stays 9f): best effort in juvenile hurdles when fourth in Carte Diamond at Newcastle. *T. D. Easterby* **h81**

THE RISING MOON (IRE) 6 br.g. Anshan – I'm So Happy (IRE) (Miner's Lamp) [2004/5 h–p, F103: 16s* 16d^{4} Nov 12] good-topped gelding: will make a chaser: fairly useful form over hurdles: won maiden at Aintree in October impressively by 10 lengths from Magico: unable to quicken after 3 out when fourth to Marcel in Grade 2 novice at Cheltenham: will be suited by further than 2m: open to improvement. *Jonjo O'Neill* **h116 p**

THE RIVER JOKER (IRE) 9 ch.g. Over The River (FR) – Augustaeliza (IRE) (Callernish) [2004/5 c94§, h80§: 24s^{4} 24s^{4} c26d^{F} c24s^{pu} c26v^{3} 24v^{3} c24s^{pu} Mar 10] lengthy, angular gelding: poor handicap hurdler nowadays: winning chaser, let down by jumping in 2004/5: thorough stayer: acts on heavy going: ungenuine. *John R. Upson* **c77 §** **h82 §**

THE ROOKEN (IRE) 6 b.g. Fourstars Allstar (USA) – Be My Sweetheart (IRE) (Be My Native (USA)) [2004/5 F16s F16g F16m^{6} Feb 6] smallish gelding: first foal: dam never ran: no form in bumpers. *P. Spottiswood* **F–**

THE ROUNDSILLS 11 ch.g. Handsome Sailor – Eye Sight (Roscoe Blake) [2004/5 17g^{pu} Aug 14] maiden hurdler/winning chaser: dead. *M. Mullineaux* **c–** **h–**

THE SAWDUST KID 11 ch.g. River God (USA) – Susie's Money (Seymour Hicks (FR)) [2004/5 c88x, h–: c26m^{2} c25f^{pu} c23s^{5} c26s^{5} c28d^{pu} Nov 14] good-bodied gelding: poor handicap chaser: stays 3¼m: acts on firm going, unsuited by soft/heavy: tried blinkered: sketchy jumper. *R. H. Buckler* **c82 x** **h–**

THE SCREAMER (IRE) 8 b.m. Insan (USA) – Augusta Victoria (Callernish) [2004/5 F16g F16m^{2} 16f* 16f^{2} 16f* 16d^{3} 16g^{2} 16v* 20s 16s c16s* c17s^{2} c20s^{5} 16d 16s Mar 29] leggy mare: bumper winner: fair novice hurdler/chaser: won mares hurdles at Limerick (maiden) in May and Down Royal in June, listed handicap hurdle at Listowel in September and maiden chase at Thurles in December: should stay 2½m: acts on any going. *M. Hourigan, Ireland* **c110** **h109** **F100**

THE SEA CLUB (IRE) 10 b.g. Be My Native (USA) – Furry Slipper (Furry Glen) [2004/5 c–, h–: c20g^{ur} 24m^{pu} 20d^{3} 24s^{6} 20s^{3} 23d^{3} 19s c24g^{F} Dec 29] lengthy gelding: winning pointer: poor maiden hurdler: has failed to complete in chases: stays 2½m: acts on heavy going. *J. S. Wainwright* **c– x** **h66**

THESEUS (IRE) 9 b.g. Danehill (USA) – Graecia Magna (USA) (Private Account (USA)) [2004/5 c130, h–: c16m^{ur} c18m^{3} c17f^{4} c17d^{2} c22m c22g^{6} c19s^{6} c16s^{4} c19s^{5} c18d Nov 13] useful-looking gelding: useful handicap chaser: best efforts when in frame at Cork and Killarney (3 lengths second to City Hall) third and fourth starts: best short of 2¾m: acts on firm and soft going. *P. Hughes, Ireland* **c130** **h–**

THESIS (IRE) 7 ch.g. Definite Article – Chouette (Try My Best (USA)) [2004/5 h138+: 16s^{2} 16d 16d^{F} Jan 31] leggy gelding: useful hurdler: fell fatally 2 out at Kempton: best around 2m: acted on soft and good to firm going. *Miss Venetia Williams* **h133**

THE SISTER 8 b.m. Alflora (IRE) – Donna Farina (Little Buskins) [2004/5 h91: 26g^{2} 26g^{2} c20g^{4} 24v* c21s* c24d^{2} c20v^{2} c20d^{2} c21d^{pu} Mar 19] leggy, workmanlike mare: fair handicap hurdler: successful in mares event at Uttoxeter in October: similar form over fences: won 5-runner handicap at same course in November: stays 3¼m: acts on any going: visored last 6 outings. *Jonjo O'Neill* **c110** **h108**

THE SKY IS BLUE 9 ch.g. Alflora (IRE) – Mistress Boreen (Boreen (FR)) [2004/5 c21m^{pu} May 19] sturdy gelding: of no account outside points: tried tongue tied. *Mrs K. L. Caldwell* **c–** **h–**

THE SLEEPER 9 b.g. Perpendicular – Distant Cherry (General Ironside) [2004/5 c–, h–: c21v^{F} c16v^{pu} c25s^{pu} c25d^{3} Apr 11] strong, workmanlike gelding: little sign of ability: almost certainly flattered when third in falsely-run novice chase at Kelso. *W. S. Coltherd* **c85 ?** **h–**

THESPIAN LADY 4 b. or br.f. Kirkwall – Drama School (Young Generation) [2004/5 F13s F17d 18m^{F} Apr 21] 8,500Y: close-coupled filly: half-sister to several winners, including useful middle-distance winner Rada's Daughter (by Robellino) and bumper winner Dramatic Touch (by Touching Wood): dam maiden who stayed 1m: sold unraced out of A. Balding's stable 7,500 gns Newmarket July Sales: little sign of ability in 2 bumpers and maiden hurdle. *Mrs A. J. Hamilton-Fairley* **h–** **F–**

THE SPOONPLAYER (IRE) 6 b.g. Accordion – Jennie Dun (IRE) (Mandalus) [2004/5 F96: F18d* F16s[5] Dec 29] rather unfurnished gelding: best effort in bumpers when winning slowly-run event at Fairyhouse in November by 7 lengths from The Tinker Murray. *H. de Bromhead, Ireland* **F101**

THE STAGGERY BOY (IRE) 9 b.g. Shalford (IRE) – Murroe Star (Glenstal (USA)) [2004/5 c92, h–: 16m c16s[5] c17d c16v[2] c20s[6] c17g[2] c18g[2] c18m* Apr 21] sturdy gelding: winning hurdler: modest handicap chaser: won at Fontwell in April: best short of 2½m: acts on good to firm and heavy going: has had tongue tied (not since 2002). *M. R. Hoad* **c88 h–**

THE STICKLER 6 ch.g. Weld – Bivadell (Bivouac) [2004/5 F16g 17d[pu] Sep 10] fifth foal: dam maiden pointer: no form in bumper or novice hurdle (lost action): successful in maiden point in April. *B. N. Pollock* **h– F–**

THE SWOPPER 7 b.g. Sovereign Water (FR) – Strathrusdale (Blazing Saddles (AUS)) [2004/5 16v[5] 20v Jan 3] third foal: dam twice-raced in bumpers: well beaten in 2 novice hurdles. *J. Wade* **h–**

THE TALL GUY (IRE) 9 b. or br.g. Zaffaran (USA) – Mullangale (Strong Gale) [2004/5 c103, h–: c25g[pu] May 13] tall gelding: fair chaser: again ran as if amiss in handicap in May: stays 25f: acts on firm and good to soft going: formerly tongue tied. *N. A. Twiston-Davies* **c– h–**

THE TEUCHTER 6 b.g. First Trump – Barefoot Landing (USA) (Cozzene (USA)) [2004/5 h75§: 24s[pu] 22d[5] 16s[5] 24d[6] 25v[5] Jan 27] medium-sized gelding: poor maiden hurdler: effective at 2m to 25f: acts on soft going: tried in cheekpieces/blinkers: ungenuine. *N. A. Dunger* **h78 §**

THETHREERONNIES 5 b.g. Classic Cliche (IRE) – Polly Leach (Pollerton) [2004/5 F16d Dec 26] first foal: dam, 2m hurdle winner, out of useful 2m hurdler Come On Gracie: well beaten in bumper on debut. *B. R. Millman* **F–**

THE THUNDERER 6 gr.g. Terimon – By Line (High Line) [2004/5 F99: 16g Apr 19] rather unfurnished gelding: bumper winner: off 13 months, well held in novice on hurdling debut: should do better. *N. J. Henderson* **h– p**

THE TILE BARON (IRE) 8 b.g. Little Bighorn – Elegant Miss (Prince Tenderfoot (USA)) [2004/5 h79: 16d Nov 29] medium-sized gelding: poor hurdler: stays 2¾m. *L. Lungo* **h–**

THE TINKER 10 b.g. Nomadic Way (USA) – Miss Tino (Relkino) [2004/5 c102x, h–: c22g[6] May 5] fair chaser: effective at 2m to 2½m: acts on good to firm and good to soft going: sometimes let down by jumping. *Mrs S. C. Bradburne* **c– x h–**

THE TROJAN HORSE (IRE) 5 b.g. Ilium – Miss Cynthia (Dawn Review) [2004/5 F–: F17g May 11] tall, rather unfurnished gelding: well held in 2 bumpers. *Miss H. C. Knight* **F–**

THE VARLET 5 b.g. Groom Dancer (USA) – Valagalore (Generous (IRE)) [2004/5 17m[6] 21d 16v 16d 17m 16s[2] Mar 23] close-coupled gelding: fair at best on Flat (should stay 2m), lost form and sold out of B. Case's stable 1,200 gns Newmarket Autumn Sales: poor maiden hurdler: raced mainly around 2m: usually wears cheekpieces/blinkers: tongue tied final start. *D. Burchell* **h69**

THEVENIS 4 ch.c. Dr Fong (USA) – Pigeon Hole (Green Desert (USA)) [2004/5 17m Nov 25] modest maiden on Flat (stays 1m): blinkered, well held in juvenile seller on hurdling debut. *J. S. King* **h–**

THE VILLAGER (IRE) 9 br.g. Zaffaran (USA) – Kitty Wren (Warpath) [2004/5 c123+, h–: c24d[pu] c27d[4] c24v[2] c28v[F] c24v[5] c20v[2] c20d[pu] c21g Mar 17] workmanlike gelding: fairly useful handicap chaser: creditable efforts only when in frame, 6 lengths second to Le Passing at Uttoxeter sixth start: effective at 2½m to 27f: acts on heavy going, won bumper on good to firm: tried tongue tied: often let down by jumping. *M. Scudamore* **c121 x h–**

THE VINTAGE DANCER (IRE) 9 b.g. Riberetto – Strong Swimmer (IRE) (Black Minstrel) [2004/5 c91: c24g[3] c25s[2] Mar 6] fair pointer, successful in January: maiden hunter chaser. *Mrs Nicola Pollock* **c94**

THE WASHERWOMAN 5 b.m. Classic Cliche (IRE) – Olnistar (FR) (Balsamo (FR)) [2004/5 F16d F16d[6] Mar 28] eighth foal: sister to winning pointer Lady of Class and half-sister to winning 2½m hurdler Petolinski (by Petoski) and modest staying hurdler Ardent Lover (by Ardross): dam, fairly useful hurdler up to 25f, half-sister to high-class hurdler/chaser Sabin du Loir: well held in 2 mares bumpers. *B. I. Case* **F–**

THE WEAVER (FR) 6 ch.g. Villez (USA) – Miss Planette (FR) (Tip Moss (FR)) [2004/5 F89: 17d 16s^{5} 16s 20m^{2} 24g^{ur} Feb 27] lengthy gelding: modest form over hurdles: every chance when saddle slipped and unseated last in handicap at Musselburgh: stays easy 3m: acts on good to firm going. *L. Lungo* **h96**

THE WIFE'S SISTER 4 b.f. Classic Cliche (IRE) – Hard Love (Rambo Dancer (CAN)) [2004/5 F17s^{2} 17g^{5} Mar 9] 500F: third foal: dam, 1¼m winner, half-sister to fairly useful 2m jumpers Bettyknowes and Stay Awake: second in maiden bumper at Sedgefield on debut: fifth in mares novice at Bangor on hurdling debut. *D. McCain* **h79 F79**

THE WIPPER (IRE) 9 b.g. Alphabatim (USA) – Musical Millie (IRE) (Orchestra) [2004/5 c24v^{pu} c26g^{F} c24v^{3} Apr 6] sturdy gelding: prolific winning pointer: fairly useful hunter chaser: running excellent race when falling 4 out (had set good pace until then) in Foxhunter at Cheltenham: pulled up in Champion Hunter at Punchestown in late-April: stays 25f: acts on heavy and good to firm going: blinkered after first start: front runner/races prominently. *Sean Aherne, Ireland* **c101 +**

THE YELLOW EARL (IRE) 5 b.g. Topanoora – Sweet Innocence (IRE) (King's Ride) [2004/5 F17d F16v Nov 17] €40,000 3-y-o: first foal: dam poor maiden hurdler: no form in 2 bumpers. *J. M. Jefferson* **F–**

THE YOUNG BISHOP (IRE) 8 b. or br.g. Be My Native (USA) – Gypsy Lass (King's Ride) [2004/5 c111, h–: c18g^{pu} c22d^{2} c16s^{5} Nov 20] tall, useful-looking gelding: winning hurdler: fair chaser: stays 2¾m: acts on soft going. *W. Harney, Ireland* **c114 h–**

THIEVERY 4 b.g. Terimon – Piracy (Jupiter Island) [2004/5 F16d^{2} Feb 24] 23,000 3-y-o: first foal: dam unraced half-sister to useful chaser up to 25f Heist: not knocked about when 1¾ lengths second to Portavadie in bumper at Haydock on debut. *H. D. Daly* **F91**

THIEVES'GLEN 7 b.g. Teenoso (USA) – Hollow Creek (Tarqogan) [2004/5 h110p: 17d c25g^{5} c16s* c18d^{pu} c24d^{pu} 22g^{pu} Apr 12] good sort: maiden hurdler: modest form over fences: won maiden at Leicester in February: stays 25f, effective at much shorter: raced on good ground or softer (acts on soft): shaped as if amiss 2 of last 3 starts. *H. Morrison* **c96 h–**

THINK COMMERCIAL (IRE) 6 b.g. Mister Lord (USA) – Dingle Gal (IRE) (Phardante (FR)) [2004/5 F16d Dec 9] big, lengthy gelding: first foal: dam unraced: won maiden point in 2004: bought 4,000 gns Doncaster May Sales: always behind in bumper. *L. A. Dace* **F–**

THINKING DOUBLE 7 br.g. Homo Sapien – Sheppie's Double (Scallywag) [2004/5 F16d^{6} F16m F16s Nov 13] fifth foal: dam of little account: well held in 3 bumpers. *Mrs D. A. Butler* **F–**

THINK QUICK (IRE) 5 b.m. Goldmark (USA) – Crimson Ring (Persian Bold) [2004/5 16g^{5} 16d^{2} 16v 19d^{5} 16d* Mar 24] half-sister to fair hurdler Fistful of Bucks (by Lochnager), stayed 2½m: poor maiden on Flat (stays 1½m): poor hurdler: won seller at Ludlow in March: best at 2m: acts on good to soft ground, well beaten on heavy. *R. Hollinshead* **h76**

THISISYOURLIFE (IRE) 7 b.g. Lord Americo – Your Life (Le Bavard (FR)) [2004/5 h94, F88: 21s^{3} 21d^{3} c16d^{pu} c23v^{F} 21d^{6} 20g Mar 26] compact gelding: modest novice hurdler: jumped poorly both starts over fences: stays 21f: acts on soft going: free-going sort. *H. D. Daly* **c– h98**

THIS ONE IS A BOY (IRE) 9 b.g. Executive Perk – Belinda Vard (Le Bavard (FR)) [2004/5 24d^{pu} May 9] tall gelding: no form outside points. *M. S. Wilesmith* **h–**

THISTHATANDTOTHER (IRE) 9 b.g. Bob Back (USA) – Baden (IRE) (Furry Glen) [2004/5 c149, h–: c20d^{2} c21d^{2} c16s^{2} c21g* c25s^{4} Apr 7] **c160 h–**

Twelve months on from a second-fence departure when favourite for the Arkle Chase, Thisthatandtother finally won another race when landing the inaugural Daily Telegraph Festival Trophy at Cheltenham in March. Thisthatandtother finished second on all his five appearances between the two Festivals and progressed into a high-class performer, without making the strides of the pair that finished first and second following his tumble, Well Chief and Kicking King. Thisthatandtother had two stabs at a consolation prize as a novice, finishing second to Well Chief in the Maghull at Aintree and to Keltic Bard in a Grade 2 at Ayr. Thisthatandtother appeared not to stay two and a half miles in the latter but events in 2004/5, when he ran just once at two miles, suggest he must simply have been past his best for the season. He was reportedly pinfired over the summer to correct a problem with sore shins.

When Thisthatandtother returned in the autumn, it was in the Paddy Power Gold Cup at Cheltenham's Open meeting. Well supported, he overcame mistakes five out and three out, and then being hampered two out, to chase home Celestial Gold, beaten a length and three quarters, conceding 10 lb to the winner. The winner went on to land the Hennessy under a penalty and those behind Thisthatandtother didn't do the form any harm either, in what was a typically strong renewal of one of the season's major handicaps. Thisthatandtother didn't better his form in the Paddy Power subsequently, though he acquitted himself well in two further valuable handicaps at Cheltenham, the bonusprint.com Gold Cup in December, in which he was left second behind the Paddy Power third Monkerhostin after Our Vic fell at the last, and the Victor Chandler Handicap Chase in January. In the latter, transferred from Ascot, Thisthatandtother had another encounter with Well Chief. It was some measure of their relative progression since the previous spring that Thisthatandtother was set to receive 25 lb from Well Chief, reduced by 5 lb due to 20 lb being the weight range for this limited handicap. Thisthatandtother, the 2/1 favourite, couldn't beat his old rival, but lost little in going down by a length and three quarters.

In previous seasons, the Cathcart Chase would have been the obvious race for Thisthatandtother at the Cheltenham Festival, but that race, confined latterly to novices and those in their first season outside novice company, was replaced by the Festival Trophy in the newly expanded four-day Festival. This new race, granted Grade 2 status straight away and worth nearly twice as much as the last Cathcart, was the fifth most valuable of the whole Festival and attracted twelve runners (more

Daily Telegraph Festival Trophy Chase, Cheltenham—a mistake at the last by Rathgar Beau (right) leaves Thisthatandtother and Fondmort (No.9) to fight out a grandstand finish

than for any Cathcart field in over forty years), all but one of them capable of smart form or better. The favourite was Our Vic, making his first appearance since his fall, with Thisthatandtother and Rathgar Beau, running instead of in the Champion Chase, joint second favourites. Also in the field were the veterans Edredon Bleu and Native Upmanship, the one a winner of the Champion Chase and the other twice a runner-up. For both, the new race seemed likely to have arrived too late. Of the twelve runners, only one other apart from Thisthatandtother and Our Vic would have been qualified to run in the Cathcart. Thisthatandtother was close up all the way and avoided mistakes on this occasion, though it needed a really game effort to edge out the pacemaking Fondmort near the line and win by half a length, with Rathgar Beau two and a half lengths away in third after closing to within a length when belting the last. Hand Inn Hand and Le Roi Miguel also had a chance in the latter stages of what was a well-run and exciting race, but Our Vic was badly let down by his jumping and well out of contention when pulled up late on.

After the meeting, the Cheltenham executive expressed the hope that the Festival Trophy would be swiftly promoted to Grade 1 status. Good though the first running was, such a move might be premature. Connections of Kicking King were reportedly seriously considering the race in preference to the Gold Cup and it is not hard to imagine a situation in which the stars in the future avoid one another by running in different races. In general, though, the new races at the Festival worked as well as could be hoped. Dabiroun and Miss Academy produced performances in the juvenile handicap hurdle which would have seen them close to third in the Triumph, both races overall highly competitive. The new novice handicap chase was an excellent race and clearly attracted runners that previously lacked an opportunity at the meeting. The first three in the three-mile novice hurdle were good enough to have played a part in the Royal & SunAlliance Novices' Hurdle, though all three may well not have shown quite their top form over the shorter trip. Both races were competitive and well supported. The cross-country chase is always likely to be a weaker race compared to most of the others and, if the aim is to make every race either a championship or a highly competitive handicap, its place in the programme is questionable. Cheltenham reportedly have no plans to increase the number of races at the 2006 Festival.

Thisthatandtother was stepped up further in trip for his final start of the season. As at Ayr the previous season, his below-par performance in the Betfair Bowl at Aintree might have been due to his being past his best, though he did perform, on the face of it, as if the testing twenty-five furlongs was beyond him, travelling better than most but fading away four out and beaten over thirty lengths by Grey Abbey. Thisthatandtother is reportedly likely to be campaigned with the King George VI Chase in mind. He needs to improve a bit more to figure in even an average renewal.

Thisthatandtother (IRE) (b.g. 1996)	Bob Back (USA) (br 1981)	Roberto (b 1969)	Hail To Reason
			Bramalea
		Toter Back (ch 1967)	Carry Back
			Romantic Miss
	Baden (IRE) (b 1988)	Furry Glen (b 1971)	Wolver Hollow
			Cleftess
		St Moritz (b 1974)	Linacre
			Machete

Details of Thisthatandtother's family have appeared in previous Annuals. His half-brother Polar Scout (by Arctic Lord) was an improved performer over fences in 2004/5, winning at Folkestone and Doncaster. He is best at up to two and three quarter miles. Their dam Baden has produced seven subsequent foals, five of them fillies, though none of them have raced. Thisthatandtother's sister Baden's Queen went straight to stud and produced fillies by Supreme Leader in 2003 and Moscow Society in 2004. A three-year-old Accordion filly out of Baden was sold for €125,000 at the Derby Sale in June. Baden had a colt foal by Bob Back in May and was due to be covered by the stallion again. Machete, the third dam of Thisthatandtother, is also third dam of a smart chaser at short of three miles in Gale Again. The strong, useful-looking Thisthatandtother tends to take the eye before his races. He acts on soft and good to firm going (unraced on heavy or firm) and is genuine and reliable. *P. F. Nicholls*

THISTLE 4 ch.c. Selkirk (USA) – Ardisia (USA) (Affirmed (USA)) [2004/5 16d^{3} 16g^{4} 16g^{5} Apr 16] half-brother to winning hurdler/chaser Ashgar (by Bien Bien), stays 3¼m: fair around 1m on Flat, sold out of J. Gosden's stable 90,000 gns Newmarket Autumn Sales: modest form in juvenile hurdles: tongue tied last 2 starts. *J. Howard Johnson* **h94**

TH'MOONS A BALLOON (IRE) 11 b.g. Euphemism – Gerti's Quay (Quayside) [2004/5 c89: c23d c19g^{ur} May 12] winning pointer: maiden hunter chaser: tongue tied in 2004/5. *S. J. Partridge* **c–**

THOMO (IRE) 7 b.g. Faustus (USA) – Dawn O'Er Kells (IRE) (Pitskelly) [2004/5 F–: F16v 17s 17g^{2} Apr 10] well held in bumpers: left R. Harris, second in novice hurdle at Newton Abbot. *N. E. Berry* **h95 F–**

THORNBIRD LASS 9 b.m. Alflora (IRE) – Burling Moss (Le Moss) [2004/5 h–: 20s 16s 20s^{6} 16s 16v Mar 17] leggy mare: no sign of ability: tried in headgear: tongue tied third start. *R. Johnson* **h–**

THORNTON CHARLOTTE 4 b.f. Defacto (USA) – Lindrick Lady (IRE) (Broken Hearted) [2004/5 F13d^{4} F14d 16v^{pu} 16d 19s 16g Mar 9] close-coupled filly: first foal: dam, fair 7.5f to 1½m winner, well held over hurdles: little sign of ability. *B. S. Rothwell* **h– F71**

THORNTOUN HOUSE (IRE) 12 b.g. Durgam (USA) – Commanche Song (Commanche Run) [2004/5 c30v^{pu} c21v^{4} c20v c32v^{pu} 24s Apr 20] no longer of any account: usually visored/blinkered. *W. T. Reed* **c– x h–**

THORSGILL 7 ch.g. Denel (FR) – Italian Princess (IRE) (Strong Gale) [2004/5 17d^{pu} Oct 8] second foal: dam twice-raced: third in maiden in 2003, only completed start in points: no show on hurdling debut. *M. Todhunter* **h–**

THOUGHT CONTROL 5 b.g. Kris – Keyboogie (USA) (Lyphard (USA)) [2004/5 F16s^{5} Aug 25] second foal: half-brother to fair 7f winner Mister Sweets (by Nashwan): dam, 1¼m winner, daughter of US Grade 2 9.5f winner Key Dancer: tailed off in bumper on debut. *G. A. Swinbank* **F–**

THOUTMOSIS (USA) 6 ch.g. Woodman (USA) – Toujours Elle (USA) (Lyphard (USA)) [2004/5 h100: 18v* 17v* 20s^{F} Mar 12] fairly useful handicap hurdler: successful at Kelso (conditional jockeys) in October and Carlisle in November: should stay beyond 2¼m: raced on good going or softer (acts on heavy). *L. Lungo* **h115**

THRASHING 10 b.g. Kahyasi – White-Wash (Final Straw) [2004/5 c–, h90: 22g* 24g^{3} 22d^{5} c24g^{pu} c26g^{pu} c24g^{ur} Apr 15] smallish gelding: no form over fences: modest handicap hurdler: won at Newton Abbot in June: stays 25f: best efforts on good going or firmer: tried blinkered/visored, usually wears cheekpieces: tongue tied. *A. E. Jones* **c– h91**

THREAD OF HONOUR (IRE) 8 gr.g. Roselier (FR) – Sharkezan (IRE) (Double Schwartz) [2004/5 h90: 21d Oct 31] good-topped gelding: novice hurdler, modest form at best: should stay beyond 19f. *Miss H. C. Knight* **h–**

THREE COUNTIES (IRE) 4 b.c. Danehill (USA) – Royal Show (IRE) (Sadler's Wells (USA)) [2004/5 F13d F12d^{4} F13s F16g^{3} Mar 28] 360,000Y, 4,500 3-y-o: compact colt: first foal: dam, third at 1¼m on only start, sister to high-class 1½m colt King's Theatre and half-sister to high-class 1988 2-y-o High Estate: fair form in bumpers: has carried head awkwardly. *N. I. M. Rossiter* **F88**

THREE DAYS REIGN (IRE) 11 br.g. Camden Town – Little Treat (Miner's Lamp) [2004/5 c96, h–: c21g* c24d* c20d* c24d^{2} c21d^{5} c24d^{F} c20d^{4} c24d Jan 31] robust gelding: fair handicap chaser: improved form on return from 16-month absence, recording hat-trick at Folkestone (conditional jockeys) and Huntingdon (2) in November: effective at 2½m to 3m: acts on good to firm and good to soft going: tried blinkered. *P. D. Cundell* **c112 h–**

THREE EAGLES (USA) 8 ch.g. Eagle Eyed (USA) – Tertiary (USA) (Vaguely Noble) [2004/5 c110, h110: 24d^{4} c24m^{2} c24m^{2} 24d^{rtr} c20d^{4} Oct 5] small gelding: winning hurdler/chaser: stays easy 3m: acts on any going: tried visored: usually forces pace: has refused/been reluctant to race: ungenuine. *M. Scudamore* **c110 § h– §**

THREE LIONS 8 ch.g. Jupiter Island – Super Sol (Rolfe (USA)) [2004/5 h90§: 20s^{5} 19m^{2} 20m^{3} 20m^{ur} 16s^{6} 19g^{4} 19s^{5} 20s^{F} 19s^{5} 21g Mar 28] leggy gelding: fair handicap hurdler: stays 2½m: acts on soft and good to firm going: wore cheekpieces once: has hinted at temperament. *R. S. Brookhouse* **h102**

THREEPENNY BIT 7 b.m. Safawan – Tuppence In Clover (Petoski) [2004/5 h–, F–: 19d^{pu} 20v^{pu} 16d 16d^{pu} Apr 22] lengthy mare: no sign of ability. *Mrs S. M. Johnson* **h–**

THREES COMPANY (IRE) 10 b.g. Torus – Doonaree Belle (IRE) (Duky) [2004/5 c24s⁵ c25g⁵ c20d⁶ c21s⁶ c25s² c24spu c26gpu Mar 27] compact gelding: poor maiden chaser: stays 25f: acts on soft going: tried tongue tied. *J. R. Best* **c65 h–**

THREE SHIPS 4 ch.g. Dr Fong (USA) – River Lullaby (USA) (Riverman (USA)) [2004/5 16g⁴ 16g⁴ Mar 28] modest maiden on Flat (stays 9.4f): modest form in maiden hurdles, racing very freely. *Miss J. Feilden* **h88**

THREE SPIRES 10 ch.g. Minster Son – Mystic Music (Hansel's Nephew) [2004/5 c24spu c25vpu c24d⁴ c24d⁴ c24gpu c24d⁵ c25d⁶ Feb 3] winning pointer: little form overwise: tried blinkered. *W. T. Reed* **c– h–**

THREE TIMES A LADY 5 b.m. Syrtos – Pure Formality (Forzando) [2004/5 F–: F16d F16g 17m 17g 17d 17m Sep 28] no form. *D. W. Thompson* **h– F–**

THREE WELSHMEN 4 b.g. Muhtarram (USA) – Merch Rhyd-Y-Grug (Sabrehill (USA)) [2004/5 17d³ 16m² 16s⁴ 16d⁴ 16s* 16vpu Dec 28] leggy, plain gelding: modest on Flat (stays 1m) for B. R. Millman: fair juvenile hurdler: best effort when winning 22-runner event at Warwick in December by 1¼ lengths from Arrayou: will prove best at 2m: acts on soft and good to firm going. *D. Burchell* **h107 +**

THRILLING PROSPECT (IRE) 8 b.m. King's Ride – Bail Out (Quayside) [2004/5 h88, F–: 26d³ 16s* 23s* 22d 24d⁵ 20g Mar 26] leggy mare: fair novice hurdler: won mares events at Towcester in October and Lingfield in November: likely to prove best at 3m+: acts on soft going. *R. T. Phillips* **h102**

THROUGH THE RYE 9 ch.g. Sabrehill (USA) – Baharlilys (Green Dancer (USA)) [2004/5 c–, h131: 17g 19d⁶ c16s* c17v² c16d⁴ c16g⁴ Apr 15] strong gelding: useful handicap hurdler in 2003/4, below best in 2004/5: fairly useful form over fences: won novice at Carlisle in February by short head from Parknasilla: raced mainly around 2m on good going or softer (acts on heavy): tongue tied once: has made running over hurdles, ridden more patiently over fences. *E. W. Tuer* **c121 h–**

THUMPER (IRE) 7 b.g. Grand Lodge (USA) – Parkeen Princess (He Loves Me) [2004/5 h98: 17d⁵ 18m* 19m³ 20mpu Jun 29] fair hurdler: won handicap at Fontwell in May: broke leg in similar event at Worcester: should have stayed 2½m: unraced on extremes of going: tried blinkered, visored in 2004/5. *Jonjo O'Neill* **h102**

THUNDERCLAP 6 b. or br.g. Royal Applause – Gloriana (Formidable (USA)) [2004/5 16f 16m³ 16v Oct 30] modest on Flat (stays 1m): best effort over hurdles when third in novice at Hexham: likely to need sharp 2m. *J. J. Quinn* **h87**

Prix Grandak, Auteuil—Tidal Fury rewards the enterprise of connections, landing a juvenile hurdle three months before the first one in Britain

THYNE FOR INTERSKY (IRE) 6 ch.g. Good Thyne (USA) – One Last Chance (Le Bavard (FR)) [2004/5 F105: 20m^{2} 20g 16g^{2} 20d* 21d^{2} 21d^{ro} 24m* Apr 10] sturdy gelding: won both starts in bumpers in 2003/4: fair form over hurdles: won handicap at Bangor in September and novice at Worcester in April: stays 3m: acts on good to soft and good to firm going: blinkered last 2 outings, ran out on first occasion. *Jonjo O'Neill* **h104 +**

THYNE MAN (IRE) 7 br.g. Good Thyne (USA) – Showphar (IRE) (Phardante (FR)) [2004/5 c24d^{2} c24g^{3} c25s^{pu} c25g^{3} c24g^{pu} c25s^{2} c23m^{2} Apr 10] lengthy, angular gelding: second foal: half-brother to winning 19f hurdler Harry Husyan (by Husyan): dam unraced: twice-raced in bumpers in 2002 for P. Cody: won both starts in points in 2004: fair maiden chaser: left P. Jones after second outing: typically none too fluent/less than keen when runner-up last 2 starts: stays 25f: acts on soft and good to firm going: not one to trust. *J. Mackie* **c104 §**

THYNE'S OPTIMIST 6 b.g. Good Thyne (USA) – Sweet Optimist (Energist) [2004/5 19s 20s 21v^{5} 22g Mar 20] sixth foal: half-brother to fairly useful hurdler up to 2½m Miss Optimist (by Relkino): dam, winning hurdler, half-sister to useful staying chaser Bold Agent: well held over hurdles. *B. G. Powell* **h68**

THYNE SUPREME (IRE) 6 b.g. Good Thyne (USA) – Lisfuncheon Adage (Proverb) [2004/5 F18s 21d^{ro} 20s 21g^{6} Mar 27] €9,500 3-y-o, 12,000 4-y-o: eighth foal: brother to winning pointer Themaster's Choice and half-brother to 2¾m chase winner Prime Target (by Never Got A Chance): dam never ran: more signs of temperament than ability in bumper and over hurdles. *A. M. Hales* **h–** **F–**

TIANYI (IRE) 9 b.g. Mujadil (USA) – Skinity (Rarity) [2004/5 c–, h84: 16d 16m^{5} 17m^{3} 16g^{6} Jul 7] angular gelding: poor hurdler: stays 19f: yet to race on heavy going, acts on any other: usually blinkered/visored: often front runner. *M. Scudamore* **c–** **h78**

TIASFOURTH 4 b.f. Contract Law (USA) – Nordic Crown (IRE) (Nordico (USA)) [2004/5 F16g Jan 24] third foal: dam poor hurdler who stayed 2½m: well held in bumper on debut. *A. M. Hales* **F–**

TICKATEAL 5 ch.g. Emperor Fountain – Mary Hand (IRE) (Hollow Hand) [2004/5 F16g^{ro} F16g F17g F16m 17s^{pu} 20s^{5} 21d^{4} 22m^{4} Apr 23] first foal: dam, poor form in points, from family of smart staying chaser Cloudy Bays: temperamental in bumpers: modest form over hurdles: stays 2¾m: acts on soft and good to firm going. *R. D. E. Woodhouse* **h88** **F75 §**

TICKERS WAY 4 gr.g. Cloudings (IRE) – Zany Lady (Arzanni) [2004/5 F16m F16g^{6} Apr 19] first foal: dam poor maiden up to 1¼m on Flat: better effort in bumpers when 2½ lengths sixth to Regal Heights in maiden at Towcester. *C. Drew* **F89**

TICKTON FLYER 7 b.g. Sovereign Water (FR) – Contradictory (Reprimand) [2004/5 h98: c20g^{5} Apr 3] modest hurdler: off a year, similar form when fifth in maiden at Market Rasen on chasing debut: stays 3m: acts on good to soft and good to firm going: blinkered last 3 starts: hasn't always looked an easy ride: will probably do better over fences. *M. W. Easterby* **c92 p** **h–**

TICTAC (FR) 9 ch.g. Beyssac (FR) – Native d'Acres (FR) (Native Guile (USA)) [2004/5 c25m^{pu} Apr 25] ex-French gelding: well beaten only start on Flat: thrice-raced over hurdles, showing fair form: won 4-y-o claimer at Auteuil on chasing debut in 2000 for T. Civel: won both completed starts in points in Britain in 2004: broke down in hunter at Ludlow. *I. Johnson* **c–** **h–**

TIDAL FURY (IRE) 3 b.g. Night Shift (USA) – Tidal Reach (USA) (Kris S (USA)) [2004/5 15v* Apr 17] modest form in 2 maidens at 2 yrs: fairly useful form in 3-y-o hurdles at Auteuil: made all and left clear last in newcomers event in April, and runner-up in listed contest in June (made most when beaten ¾ length by Sunny Winter) in June, jumping left each time. *J. Jay* **h116**

TIDDLE ABOUT (IRE) 4 b.f. In The Wings – Danishkada (Thatch (USA)) [2004/5 F16v^{2} F16s^{2} F16g Mar 16] rather leggy filly: half-sister to smart French sprinter Danakal (by Diesis) and 1m/9f winner in USA by Lyphard: dam won Grand Criterium but failed to train on: fair form in bumpers: never a factor in Grade 1 at Cheltenham: ran as if amiss at Punchestown in late-April. *J. T. Gorman, Ireland* **F95**

TIERKELY (IRE) 10 br.g. Yashgan – Island Dream (Lucifer (USA)) [2004/5 c94: c24m c26d^{pu} c21m^{pu} c26s^{pu} Aug 25] winning chaser: no show in handicaps in 2004/5: tried blinkered/in cheekpieces. *J. J. Lambe, Ireland* **c–**

TIGER CRY (IRE) 7 b.g. Germany (USA) – Dream Academy (Town And Country) [2004/5 h122, F94: 17d² c17s³ c20d⁴ c17v⁶ 16d 16s* Mar 28] well-made gelding: fairly useful hurdler: won minor event at Fairyhouse in March by short head from Man About Town: similar form when third to impressive Watson Lake in maiden at Navan on chasing debut: well held in Grade 1 novices next 2 starts: raced mainly around 2m on good going or softer (acts on soft): best efforts when ridden prominently. *A. L. T. Moore, Ireland* **c124 h128**

TIGER FROG (USA) 6 b.g. French Deputy (USA) – Woodyoubelieveit (USA) (Woodman (USA)) [2004/5 c70, h83: 17g* 17d⁶ 16m² 16g³ 16m* 20f⁴ c16m² c16g* c16s⁴ Dec 28] lengthy gelding: modest handicap hurdler: won at Sedgefield in first half of season and Huntingdon in August: not quite so good over fences, but took advantage of favourable mark at Catterick in December: probably stays easy 2½m: acts on soft and firm going: tried in cheekpieces, blinkered nowadays: has had tongue tied. *J. Mackie* **c85 h99**

TIGER ISLAND (USA) 5 b.g. Grand Slam (USA) – Paris Wild Cat (USA) (Storm Cat (USA)) [2004/5 F17d F16m 16d 16g⁵ 16v 16sᵇᵈ 16s 17sᵖᵘ 17v⁶ Mar 30] ex-Irish gelding: first foal: dam unraced: no show in bumpers: little form over hurdles: left N. Glynn after seventh start. *A. E. Jones* **h77 F–**

TIGER JOHNNY 4 b.g. Tiger Hill (IRE) – Desert Dawn (Belfort (FR)) [2004/5 F16s⁵ F16s 20s 19mᵖᵘ Apr 23] tall, lengthy gelding: tenth foal: half-brother to several winners on Flat: dam useful 5f performer: better effort in bumpers at Wetherby on debut: no form in 2 starts over hurdles. *M. W. Easterby* **h– F83**

TIGERLION (IRE) 7 b.g. Supreme Leader – Avida Dancer (Ballymore) [2004/5 F114: F16g⁴ F16v³ 19s² 20s⁴ 19v⁴ 18s⁴ Feb 24] rangy, good sort: will make a chaser: useful in bumpers: fairly useful novice hurdler: would have won but for mistake last when neck second to Homer Wells in maiden at Naas on debut: best effort when 7¾ lengths fourth to Petertheknot in Grade 2 at Navan in December: seemingly amiss last 2 starts: will stay beyond 2½m. *J. Bleahen, Ireland* **h124 F109**

TIGERS LAIR (IRE) 6 b. or br.g. Accordion – Eadie (IRE) (Strong Gale) [2004/5 F105: 20d² 16g* 16m² 17d⁴ 22s² 16g³ 22s⁴ Nov 18] leggy, rather unfurnished gelding: fair novice hurdler: made all at Aintree in May: creditable efforts last 3 starts: effective at 2m to 2¾m: acts on soft going: blinkered last 2 outings. *Jonjo O'Neill* **h114**

TIGER TALK 9 ch.g. Sabrehill (USA) – Tebre (USA) (Sir Ivor (USA)) [2004/5 c–, h74§: 17m 24g 22g⁵ 22g⁴ 17m 20m⁴ 22g⁴ 22d⁴ 20g 24d 16d⁴ 17d³ 20v⁶ 18s² 19g* 25g² 19d³ 24d⁴ 21v 17s⁵ 24g⁵ 21g³ 20d* c21d⁵ Apr 5] angular gelding: modest handicap hurdler: won at Catterick (amateurs) in December and Fakenham in March: lightly raced and no form over fences: stays easy 25f: acts on good to firm and heavy going: usually wears headgear: tried tongue tied: ungenuine. *R. C. Guest* **c– § h86 §**

TIGER TIPS LAD (IRE) 6 b.g. Zaffaran (USA) – Halens Match (IRE) (Matching Pair) [2004/5 h90, F83: 16g* 21g² May 8] lengthy gelding: progressive form over hurdles: won novice at Towcester in April 2004: neck second to Ile de Paris, pair clear, in similar event at Warwick: probably stays 3m: acts on soft going. *N. A. Twiston-Davies* **h113**

TIGHE CASTER 6 b.g. Makbul – Miss Fire (Gunner B) [2004/5 F83: 21s⁶ 20s⁴ 20s⁵ 16g* 16s* 16d² 16g² 20m Apr 23] good-topped gelding: fairly useful hurdler: won handicaps at Huntingdon (novice) in January and Sandown (conditional jockeys) in February: best effort when 5 lengths second to Pardishar in similar event at Newbury seventh start: best efforts at 2m: raced mainly on good going or softer. *P. R. Webber* **h120**

TIGNASSE (FR) 4 b.f. Double Bed (FR) – Off Guard (FR) (Bakharoff (USA)) [2004/5 16s³ 16g* 18s⁴ Mar 30] modest on Flat (stays 1½m), successful at Fontainebleau in October for A. Hermans: best effort over hurdles when winning maiden at Fakenham in March: carries head awkwardly and possibly none too genuine. *G. L. Moore* **h89**

TIK-A-TAI (IRE) 10 b.g. Alphabatim (USA) – Carrig Ross (Lord Ha Ha) [2004/5 c–, h126: 16m c20d⁵ 20s 16v Jan 22] strong gelding: winning chaser: fairly useful handicap hurdler: off over 5 months, well held last 3 starts, including in handicap chase: stays 3m: acts on soft going: prone to mistakes over fences. *O. Sherwood* **c113 h122**

TIKRAM 8 ch.g. Lycius (USA) – Black Fighter (USA) (Secretariat (USA)) [2004/5 c143, h134: c20d c21d⁵ c16d⁵ c24d² c24s⁴ c24g⁶ c20g* Apr 22] tall gelding: useful handicap chaser: creditable efforts in defeat in valuable contests, including when in frame in valuable event at Doncaster and Racing Post Chase at Kempton, prior to winning at Sandown in April by 2 lengths from Impek: stays 3m: acts on any going: tried in headgear (blinkered at Sandown): not an easy ride (takes plenty of driving), but is tough and consistent. *G. L. Moore* **c142 h–**

TILLA 5 b.m. Bin Ajwaad (IRE) – Tosca (Be My Guest (USA)) [2004/5 22s 21d 16s Feb 24] medium-sized mare: fair on Flat (stays 2m), sold out of H. Morrison's stable 8,500 gns Newmarket Autumn Sales: well held in 3 starts over hurdles. *Mrs A. J. Hamilton-Fairley* **h–**

TIMBERA (IRE) 11 b. or br.g. Commanche Run – Morry's Lady (The Parson) [2004/5 c139, h–: c25g² c26d⁴ Mar 17] lengthy gelding: useful handicap chaser: won 2003 Irish Grand National: blinkered, broke down badly when distant fourth to Nil Desperandum in minor event at Down Royal: would have stayed beyond 4m: raced on good going or softer (acted on heavy): usually tongue tied: usually sound jumper: tended to idle but was genuine: dead. *D. T. Hughes, Ireland* **c– h–**

TIMBERLEY 11 ch.g. Dancing High – Kimberley Rose (Monksfield) [2004/5 c–: c25d⁵ Apr 11] winning pointer, runner-up in March: tongue tied. *Miss R. Brewis* **c74**

TIMBUKTU 4 b.g. Efisio – Sirene Bleu Marine (USA) (Secreto (USA)) [2004/5 16v⁴ Mar 5] half-brother to winning chaser San Francisco (by Aragon), stays 2½m: poor maiden on Flat (stays 13f), sold out of C. Thornton's stable 5,600 gns Doncaster November Sales: poor form when fourth in juvenile at Kelso on hurdling debut. *B. Storey* **h–**

TIME CAN TELL 11 ch.g. Sylvan Express – Stellaris (Star Appeal) [2004/5 c20g c24m⁵ c22g⁴ May 30] well-made gelding: lightly-raced maiden hurdler: in frame in points: well held in hunter chases. *E. A. Thomas* **c– h–**

TIME MARCHES ON 7 b.g. Timeless Times (USA) – Tees Gazette Girl (Kalaglow) [2004/5 h–: 17d³ 16s³ 16d⁴ 16g⁵ 19d* 19d 16v* 19g 21v⁵ Mar 15] leggy gelding: modest handicap hurdler: won selling events at Catterick in January and Newcastle in February: stays 19f: acts on heavy going: tried in cheekpieces: tongue tied first 4 starts: held up. *K. G. Reveley* **h93**

TIMES MONEY 6 b.m. Alflora (IRE) – Third Time (IRE) (Royal Fountain) [2004/5 F16g Jul 20] second foal: dam, winning pointer, out of half-sister to Velka Pardubicka winner It's A Snip: well beaten in bumper on debut. *C. W. Moore* **F–**

TIMES PAST (IRE) 10 b.g. Commanche Run – Orient Moonbeam (Deep Run) [2004/5 c66, h76: 20d May 9] leggy gelding: lightly-raced maiden hurdler/chaser: stays 3m: sold 2,000 gns Doncaster May Sales, successful in point in January. *J. W. Unett* **c– h–**

TIME SPIN 5 b.g. Robellino (USA) – Chiltern Court (USA) (Topsider (USA)) [2004/5 h91: 20s⁴ 20v 24gᵖᵘ Feb 27] modest maiden hurdler: broke leg in handicap at Musselburgh: stayed 2½m: acted on heavy going: dead. *C. Grant* **h98**

Betfred '500 Shops Nationwide' Handicap Chase, Sandown—the consistent Tikram (blinkers) ends 2004/5 on a winning note, beating Impek and Enzo de Baune (cheekpieces)

TIMES UP BARNEY 5 b.g. Alderbrook – Give Me An Answer (True Song) [2004/5 F16v F17g Mar 19] fifth foal: brother to fair hurdler/fairly useful chaser Naunton Brook, stays 25f: dam, winning hurdler, stayed 21f: well held in 2 bumpers. *C. W. Moore* **F–**

TIME TO PARLEZ 14 b.g. Amboise – Image of War (Warpath) [2004/5 c–§, h–: c24s^{pu} c26v^{pu} c25v^{pu} c26g^{4} c24s^{pu} c26m^{pu} Apr 21] veteran chaser: of little account nowadays: blinkered once. *C. J. Drewe* **c– § h–**

TIME TO REFLECT (IRE) 6 ch.g. Anshan – Castlemitchle (IRE) (Roselier (FR)) [2004/5 c–, h96d, F90: 20d^{pu} 20g 21d c21d^{2} c24d* c24d^{4} c25m^{4} 22s c25g^{4} c25d* c20s^{3} c24v^{5} 24v^{5} c23v^{3} c25g^{F} Apr 16] rather leggy gelding: modest hurdler: sold out of M. Pipe's stable 5,500 gns Doncaster May Sales after first outing: fair handicap chaser: won at Bangor (novice) in September and Catterick (second start after reportedly having soft palate operation) in January: stays easy 25f: acts on soft going (won bumper on good to firm): tried visored, wears cheekpieces nowadays. *R. C. Guest* **c108 h73 +**

TIME TO ROAM (IRE) 5 br.g. Darshaan – Minstrels Folly (USA) (The Minstrel (CAN)) [2004/5 16d^{2} 16d^{3} 16g^{2} 18g* 16s* 19g^{F} 17s 18s 17s^{2} 17s* 18s 20s Apr 22] small, sparely-made gelding: half-brother to 2m hurdle winner Marching Orders (by Nashwan) and one-time fairly useful hurdler Musical Mayhem (by Shernazar), stays 25f: fair form at best over hurdles: won maiden at Downpatrick in September (final start for D. Weld), conditional jockeys handicap at Haydock in December and novice seller (sold from M. Pipe 5,500 gns) at Hereford in March: probably stays 19f: raced on good going or softer (acts on soft): wore headgear after debut. *Miss Lucinda V. Russell* **h106**

TIME TO SHINE 6 b.m. Pivotal – Sweet Jaffa (Never So Bold) [2004/5 h113: c20s^{4} c20s^{4} c18d^{6} 16d Mar 5] tall, leggy mare: fairly useful hurdler in 2003/4: modest form at best in 3 starts over fences: stays 2½m: acts on good to firm and heavy going. *Mrs L. J. Mongan* **c– h–**

TIMIDJAR (IRE) 12 b.g. Doyoun – Timissara (USA) (Shahrastani (USA)) [2004/5 h68: 16m 19g^{4} 22m* 17f^{4} 20s^{pu} 24g 16d 20d 21g^{4} 24g* Apr 7] neat gelding: poor handicap hurdler: won conditional jockeys sellers at Stratford in September and Taunton in April: effective at 2m to easy 3m: acts on firm and good to soft going, unsuited by soft: tried blinkered: sometimes finds little. *Mrs D. Thomas* **h75**

TIMOTHY B 6 b.g. Tina's Pet – Dalusaway (IRE) (Mandalus) [2004/5 16m Aug 30] workmanlike gelding: second foal: dam failed to complete in 2 Irish points: no show in maiden hurdle or points. *Jonjo O'Neill* **h–**

TIM'S MOLL 5 b.m. Hatim (USA) – Queen of Dara (Dara Monarch) [2004/5 F17v F16s F17s^{6} F17d Mar 26] small, sturdy mare: seventh foal: half-sister to winning hurdler/ chaser Queen's Brigade (by K-Battery), stays 3m, and 2¾m chase winner Croft Court (by Crofthall): dam poor maiden on Flat: no sign of ability in bumpers: tongue tied last 2 starts. *J. B. Walton* **F–**

TINA COOKE 9 gr.m. Tina's Pet – Up Cooke (Deep Run) [2004/5 c–, h–: c16g^{ur} c20g^{ur} May 29] lengthy mare: little sign of ability: tried in cheekpieces: sketchy jumper. *Miss Kate Milligan* **c– x h–**

TINARANA GALE (IRE) 7 b.m. Mister Lord (USA) – Dozing Gal (IRE) (Bulldozer) [2004/5 F18m F16m Jun 29] £3,800 5-y-o: fourth foal: dam ran once: well beaten in bumpers and a point. *Mrs J. E. Scrase* **F–**

TINA'S SCALLYWAG 8 br.m. Baron Blakeney – Southend Scallywag (Tina's Pet) [2004/5 c27d^{F} c24s^{pu} c27v^{4} 21v^{pu} c25s^{ur} Apr 10] leggy mare: little form over hurdles: running best race over fences when falling last in handicap at Sedgefield: thorough stayer: tried in blinkers/cheekpieces. *H. P. Hogarth* **c69 h–**

TINGSHAW RING (IRE) 5 b.m. Son of Sharp Shot (IRE) – Highest Baby (FR) (Highest Honor (FR)) [2004/5 20v 24g 18g^{4} 16g^{ur} 16g^{2} 16s 16v^{5} 16v Jan 1] half-sister to winning 2½m hurdler Tupgill Tipple (by Emperor Jones): modest maiden on Flat (stays 13f): poor maiden hurdler: raced mainly around 2m: tried in cheekpieces: unreliable. *Eoin Doyle, Ireland* **h81 §**

TINO (IRE) 9 ch.g. Torus – Delphic Thunder (Viking (USA)) [2004/5 c77, h–: c25m^{3} c26g^{6} c26g* c26g* c26m^{R} c26g^{R} Oct 3] sturdy gelding: poor handicap chaser: won twice at Newton Abbot (first conditional jockeys event) in August: well held when refusing last 2 starts: stays 3¼m: acts on firm going: tried blinkered: front runner/races prominently. *J. S. King* **c82 h–**

TINSTRE (IRE) 7 ch.g. Dolphin Street (FR) – Satin Poppy (Satin Wood) [2004/5 17d^{pu} 20s 20d 19g^{6} 20s Dec 21] poor maiden on Flat (stays 11f): no form over hurdles. *P. W. Hiatt* **h78**

TIN STRIKE 8 gr.m. Trifolio – Cawstons Prejudice (Cawston's Clown) [2004/5 19d^{pu} 22m^{pu} 19d^{pu} Oct 5] sixth foal: dam won 1m seller: no sign of ability. *J. D. Frost* **h–**

TIN SYMPHONY 7 ch.m. Opera Ghost – Bronze Age (Celtic Cone) [2004/5 h96: 16g^{2} 16m^{2} 16g^{3} 16g^{3} 16d^{5} 18d c16d^{pu} c16s^{F} c16g^{4} c16d^{3} c19g^{2} Apr 15] medium-sized mare: fair maiden hurdler: similar form over fences: stays 19f: acts on soft going: temperamental (sometimes reluctant to race). *B. J. M. Ryall* **c97 § h100 §**

TIOGA GOLD (IRE) 6 b.g. Goldmark (USA) – Coffee Bean (Doulab (USA)) [2004/5 h–: 20d^{pu} Apr 25] leggy gelding: no form over hurdles. *L. R. James* **h–**

TIOMAN (IRE) 6 b. or br.g. Dr Devious (IRE) – Tochar Ban (USA) (Assert) [2004/5 h–: 16g^{2} 20m* May 26] leggy gelding: modest novice hurdler: claimed from Mary Meek £10,000 after first outing: easily landed odds in weakly-contested novice handicap at Fontwell later in May: stays 2½m. *G. L. Moore* **h94 +**

TIP AWAY (IRE) 7 b.g. Broken Hearted – Jesse Twist (IRE) (Sandalay) [2004/5 20d^{4} 20s 20v^{ur} 22s^{5} 24v^{pu} 22s Mar 22] €7,200 4-y-o: second foal: dam unraced, from family of top-class staying chaser Brown Chamberlin: runner-up on second of 2 starts in Irish points: poor maiden hurdler: should stay 3m: wore cheekpieces final outing. *D. A. Rees* **h73**

TIP KASH (FR) 8 ch.g. Kashtan (FR) – Tipas (FR) (Tip Moss (FR)) [2004/5 c–, h102d: c18d^{2} c20g^{pu} c21g May 21] angular gelding: fair handicap hurdler: modest maiden chaser: stays 2¾m: acts on soft going: blinkered in 2004/5: tried tongue tied: unreliable: sold 6,000 gns Doncaster May Sales. *P. M. Phelan* **c96 § h–**

TIPPERARY ALL STAR (FR) 5 b.g. Highest Honor (FR) – Moucha (FR) (Fabulous Dancer (USA)) [2004/5 16s^{4} 16s^{2} 16v^{3} Dec 27] half-brother to fairly useful hurdler/chaser Tarasco (by Deploy), stays 2½m, and French 17f chase winner by Saint Andrews: dual listed winner on Flat (stays 1½m): in frame all 3 starts in maiden hurdles, best effort when 2 lengths second to Guest Artist at Fairyhouse. *M. Halford, Ireland* **h107**

TIPP TOP (IRE) 8 b.g. Brief Truce (USA) – Very Sophisticated (USA) (Affirmed (USA)) [2004/5 c20f^{5} c25f^{F} c20f^{2} c22g^{2} c25m^{3} c24d c24s^{4} c19g^{2} c24g^{4} c24d^{pu} c22s* c16g^{3} Apr 19] tall gelding: winning hurdler: modest chaser: sold out of D. Hughes's stable 12,000 gns Doncaster October Sales after sixth start: won maiden at Towcester in March: stays 3m: acts on firm and soft ground: blinkered once: often tongue tied. *O. Brennan* **c96 h–**

TIPSY MOUSE (IRE) 9 ch.g. Roselier (FR) – Darjoy (Darantus) [2004/5 c122+, h–: c26s^{3} c21d c28v^{2} c24v^{6} c26v^{3} c24d Mar 26] workmanlike gelding: fairly useful handicap chaser: creditable second to Merchants Friend in quite valuable event at Haydock: below form after: thorough stayer: raced on good going or softer (acts on heavy): usually sound jumper: hard ride (needs plenty of driving). *Mrs S. J. Smith* **c118 h–**

TIQUET 6 b.g. Bedford (USA) – Lady Kay-Lee (Cruise Missile) [2004/5 h82?, F–: 18m^{3} 22g^{pu} 22g Aug 2] medium-sized gelding: maiden hurdler: apparently best effort when third of 6 at Fontwell in May: should stay beyond 2¼m. *N. J. Henderson* **h90**

TIRAILLEUR (IRE) 5 b.m. Eagle Eyed (USA) – Tiralle (IRE) (Tirol) [2004/5 h–: 16d Nov 24] no form over hurdles. *Mrs P. Townsley* **h–**

TIRIKUMBA 9 ch.m. Le Moss – Ntombi (Trasi's Son) [2004/5 h93: 16g^{4} 19m^{4} 22g^{ur} 22g^{4} 19d^{pu} 21g^{3} 21g^{4} 22d^{4} 21s^{4} 19s^{5} 24s^{pu} 24d^{5} 22d* 21g Apr 14] lengthy mare: modest novice hurdler: won handicap at Wincanton in March: should stay 3m: acts on soft and good to firm going: has been blinkered/visored: sketchy jumper. *S. G. Griffiths* **h97 x**

TIRLEY GALE 13 b.g. Strong Gale – Mascara VII (Damsire Unregistered) [2004/5 c82§, h–: c24d^{3} c24g May 27] big, rangy gelding: modest hunter chaser: seems to stay 3m: acts on soft and good to firm going: temperamental (has refused to race). *Mrs N. D. Smith* **c82 § h–**

TIRLEY STORM 10 b.g. Tirley Gale – Random Select (Random Shot) [2004/5 c79, h–: c21m^{pu} c19s^{3} c19g c20g^{4} Mar 27] rangy gelding: poor handicap chaser: should stay 3m: acts on soft and good to firm going: poor jumper. *J. S. Smith* **c79 x h–**

TISN'T EASY (IRE) 7 b.m. Mandalus – Gemini Gale (Strong Gale) [2004/5 h93, F82: c20f 24m^{pu} 24v 22v 22g^{5} Apr 3] well held only start over fences: modest hurdler: left C. Swan after second start: stays 2¾m: acts on soft going (bumper form on good to firm). *D. Carroll* **c– p h95**

TITIAN FLAME (IRE) 5 ch.m. Titus Livius (FR) – Golden Choice (Midyan (USA)) [2004/5 h82: 16g^4 17d^4 17m^5 16f 17d^2 20g^6 18s^F 16v^{pu} 19v* 20v^3 19s 16s 16s Mar 23] modest hurdler: won maiden claimer (claimed from Mrs P. N. Dutfield £6,000) at Hereford in February: stays 19f: acts on heavy going: usually wears cheekpieces. *D. Burchell* **h91**

TIUTCHEV 12 b.g. Soviet Star (USA) – Cut Ahead (Kalaglow) [2004/5 c168, h145: c24g^{pu} c26g^{pu} c25s^{pu} Apr 7] rangy gelding: impressed in appearance: smart hurdler/top-class chaser at best: successful in Arkle, Ascot Chase (twice) and Martell Cup: well held in good company (visored and tongue tied final start) in 2004/5: was effective at 2m to 25f: acted on soft and good to firm going: reportedly retired. *M. C. Pipe* **c– h–**

TIZI OUZOU (IRE) 4 ch.f. Desert Prince (IRE) – Tresor (USA) (Pleasant Tap (USA)) [2004/5 16s* 16g^2 17v^6 16d 16d 17g^6 17m* 16d Apr 17] close-coupled filly: modest maiden on Flat (stays 1¼m), claimed from J. Dunlop £6,000 in September: modest hurdler: won juvenile at Ludlow in November and seller at Taunton in March: raced around 2m: acts on soft and good to firm going: visored last 2 starts: not one to rely on. *M. C. Pipe* **h98 §**

TIZ WIZ 4 b.f. Wizard King – Dannistar (Puissance) [2004/5 16d^{pu} Nov 12] sprint maiden on Flat: saddle slipped early in juvenile on hurdling debut: sold 600 gns Doncaster November Sales. *W. Storey* **h–**

TIZZY MAY (FR) 5 ch.g. Highest Honor (FR) – Forentia (Formidable (USA)) [2004/5 16g^4 Feb 27] useful at best on Flat (stays easy 1½m), out of sorts in second half of 2004: sold out of R. Hannon's stable 30,000 gns Newmarket Autumn Sales: modest form when fourth in maiden at Musselburgh on hurdling debut. *B. Ellison* **h90**

TOAD HALL 11 b.g. Henbit (USA) – Candlebright (Lighter) [2004/5 c63, h–: c16d^{pu} c24m^4 c20d^{pu} c20g^{pu} c24d* c20s^4 c24d^{pu} c20g^3 c25d^{pu} Oct 9] lengthy gelding: poor chaser: form in 2004/5 only when making all in novice at Perth in August: stays 3m: acts on good to firm and good to soft ground: blinkered 5 of last 6 starts. *Mrs L. B. Normile* **c67 x h–**

TOBESURE (IRE) 11 b.g. Asir – Princess Citrus (IRE) (Auction Ring (USA)) [2004/5 c92x, h98: 22m^2 c20m^5 16d 22v^5 24d^6 25g^5 24v^4 22v^3 24v^2 22d^5 Apr 11] sturdy gelding: winning chaser: fair handicap hurdler: stays 25f: acts on any going: tongue tied once: sketchy jumper of fences. *J. I. A. Charlton* **c91 x h100**

TODAYSMYDAY 7 b.g. Homo Sapien – Tuesdaynightmare (Celtic Cone) [2004/5 F16d 16s 16s 16d 16v 20m c16d c17s Apr 13] no sign of ability. *E. Bolger, Ireland* **c– h–**

TODDEANO 9 b.g. Perpendicular – Phisus (Henbit (USA)) [2004/5 24g^{pu} 17g^{pu} May 23] no sign of ability: tried tongue tied. *G. Fierro* **F– h–**

TOD'S BROTHER 11 b.g. Gildoran – Versina (Leander) [2004/5 c–: c26m^5 May 19] winning pointer: let down by jumping both outings in hunters. *Mrs D. M. Grissell* **c–**

TOI EXPRESS (IRE) 9 ch.g. Phardante (FR) – Toi Figures (Deep Run) [2004/5 c115, h112: c16g^3 c16m^5 c16g^3 c17m* c16m^3 c16d^3 c20d^F Nov 14] workmanlike gelding: fairly useful handicap chaser: won at Stratford in September by 1¼ lengths from Hors La Loi: good third after at Worcester and Kempton: stays 19f: acts on firm and good to soft going. *P. J. Hobbs* **c121 h–**

TOJONESKI 6 b.g. Emperor Jones (USA) – Sampower Lady (Rock City) [2004/5 h–: 16v Feb 15] modest on Flat (stays 1¼m): no form over hurdles. *I. W. McInnes* **h–**

TOLEDO STAR 6 br.g. Petong – Shafir (IRE) (Shaadi (USA)) [2004/5 16d Nov 9] leggy gelding: lightly-raced maiden on Flat (has refused to enter stall), sold out of G. Lyons' stable £1,200 Ascot August Sales: well held on hurdling debut: resold £650 Ascot December Sales. *P. S. McEntee* **h–**

TOLEDO SUN 5 b.g. Zamindar (USA) – Shafir (IRE) (Shaadi (USA)) [2004/5 h90: 16m^3 Apr 25] modest on Flat (stays 15f): similar standard over hurdles: raced around 2m: acts on soft and good to firm going. *V. Smith* **h90**

TOLLBRAE (IRE) 8 gr.g. Supreme Leader – Miss Henrietta (IRE) (Step Together (USA)) [2004/5 c110p, h107: c20v^2 c20s^4 Nov 21] sturdy gelding: fair form over hurdles: fairly useful chaser: good second of 4 to Haut de Gamme in handicap at Ayr: stays 2½m: raced on good going or softer. *J. Howard Johnson* **c115 h–**

TOMASINO 7 br.g. Celtic Swing – Bustinetta (Bustino) [2004/5 16d 16s 16s* 16d^4 16d^5 20s Dec 26] medium-sized gelding: half-brother to fair hurdlers Bhutan (by Polish **h100**

Patriot), best around 2m, and Cloth of Gold (by Barathea), stays 3m: fair on Flat (stays 2m) nowadays: fair form over hurdles: won novice at Kelso in November: should stay beyond 2m: acts on soft going: wore cheekpieces fifth start: tongue tied. *K. G. Reveley*

TOM BELL (IRE) 5 b.g. King's Theatre (IRE) – Nordic Display (IRE) (Nordico (USA)) [2004/5 20v^{5} 19s^{F} 19s^{6} 17g^{5} Apr 12] leggy gelding: modest on Flat (stays 17.2f): poor form in novice hurdles: stays 2½m: raced on good going or softer. *J. G. M. O'Shea* **h84 +**

TOM COBBLER (IRE) 11 ch.g. Zaffaran (USA) – Po Bo Pu (Pollerton) [2004/5 c97x, h–§: c31m^{6} May 19] rather sparely-made gelding: winning hurdler/chaser: fair pointer nowadays, successful in February: stays 27f: acts on soft and good to firm going: tried blinkered: sketchy jumper. *Mrs C. S. Hall* **c– x h– §**

TOM COSTALOT (IRE) 10 gr.g. Black Minstrel – Hop Picker (USA) (Plugged Nickle (USA)) [2004/5 c116, h–: c20d^{3} c21g^{ur} c31d c21s^{4} c20d^{3} c21d^{5} Mar 10] good-topped gelding: fair handicap chaser: best around 2½m: acts on soft and good to firm going: none too consistent. *Mrs Susan Nock* **c111 d h–**

TOM FRUIT 8 b.g. Supreme Leader – Forever Mine (IRE) (Phardante (FR)) [2004/5 20m^{4} 16v^{4} 20v^{2} 23v* 23s^{ur} c24g^{pu} c20s^{2} c21v* c24v^{2} Apr 17] tall, quite good-topped gelding: fair novice hurdler, off 19 months before reappearance: won amateur event at Wetherby in January: fairly useful novice chaser: landed odds at Sedgefield in March: best effort when 9 lengths second to Grey Report in maiden at Stratford seventh start: stays 23f: acts on heavy going. *T. D. Easterby* **c115 h112**

TOMICH (IRE) 10 b. or br.g. Lord Americo – Gilt Course (Crash Course) [2004/5 24g^{6} c21d^{5} c24d^{pu} 24d^{pu} Jan 12] sturdy gelding: winning chaser/maiden hurdler: off 2 years, no sign of retaining ability in 2004/5. *Miss A. M. Newton-Smith* **c– h–**

TOMINA 5 b.g. Deploy – Cavina (Ardross) [2004/5 16d^{5} 16g* 16d^{5} 19g* 21m^{F} Apr 13] useful-looking gelding: second foal: half-brother to 3m hurdle winner Marjina (by Classic Cliche): dam, fair 2¾m hurdler, half-sister to dam of top-class staying chaser Bacchanal: fairly useful on Flat (stays 2m): progressive over hurdles: won maiden at Southwell in January and conditional jockeys novice handicap at Newbury in April, fairly useful form when beating Harley 6 lengths in latter: will stay beyond 19f: unraced on extremes of going. *Miss E. C. Lavelle* **h117 +**

TOMMY CARSON 10 b.g. Last Tycoon – Ivory Palm (USA) (Sir Ivor (USA)) [2004/5 c88, h–: c22g* c22m^{2} c22g^{6} c24g* c24d c24d c24d^{pu} c24d^{4} Feb 19] compact gelding: fair handicap chaser: won at Market Rasen in July and Lingfield in October: effective at 2½m to 3m: acts on good to firm and heavy going: tried visored/blinkered, not since 1999/00: hard ride. *Jamie Poulton* **c104 h–**

TOMMY JAY (NZ) 7 b.g. Gold Brose (AUS) – Hey Paula (NZ) (Auk (USA)) [2004/5 F16s Dec 18] rangy gelding: well held in bumper on debut. *Jonjo O'Neill* **F–**

TOMMY SPAR 5 b.g. Silver Owl – Lady of Mine (Cruise Missile) [2004/5 F–: 19m^{3} 20m^{4} 20g 24m^{4} 20g^{3} Aug 14] modest form over hurdles: stays 3m: raced on good going or firmer over hurdles: tongue tied final start. *P. Bowen* **h92**

TOMMY WOLF 9 ch.g. Little Wolf – Oneninefive (Sayyaf) [2004/5 24d^{pu} 17g 17g^{6} 19m Sep 8] of little account. *Mrs E. B. Scott* **h–**

TOM NAIL (IRE) 11 b. or br.g. Be My Native (USA) – Shady Cal (Callernish) [2004/5 c23m^{pu} c21d^{pu} Jan 1] tall, lengthy gelding: fair form in bumpers for N. Meade: off 2 years before reappearance: looked wayward in 2 novice chases, sold out of F. Murphy's stable 2,000 gns Doncaster May Sales in between: has had tongue tied. *Dr P. Pritchard* **c–**

TOM SAYERS (IRE) 7 b.g. Toulon – Jillie James (The Parson) [2004/5 22v^{4} 22s c24s^{6} c24d^{6} c24m* c22g* c25g* Apr 17] €19,000 4-y-o: useful-looking gelding: sixth foal: half-brother to 2½m hurdle winner Strife Leader (by Supreme Leader) and winning pointer by Carlingford Castle: dam unraced: modest maiden hurdler: sold out of M. Morris' stable 23,000 gns Doncaster May Sales after first start: progressive over fences: won minor event at Taunton in March and novice handicaps at Newbury and Wincanton in April: fairly useful form when beating Menphis Beury by 24 lengths at last-named: stays 25f: acts on good to firm and soft ground: tried blinkered: jumps well: races up with pace: capable of better still. *P. J. Hobbs* **c117 p h91**

TOMS GONE GREY (IRE) 6 gr.g. Gothland (FR) – Cpv Lady (Le Moss) [2004/5 h85, F70: 20g^{3} c16s^{F} c24g^{3} c23d^{pu} c20v* c20s* c20s* c19s^{ur} Mar 27] tall gelding: poor maiden hurdler: much better over fences: won 3 handicaps at Leicester in February/ **c117 h82**

March, beating below-par Lanmire Tower 27 lengths in 4-runner amateur event on final occasion: stays 3m: acts on heavy going: front runner/races prominently. *R. H. Alner*

TOMSK (IRE) 5 b.g. Definite Article – Merry Twinkle (Martinmas) [2004/5 h–: 17m Nov 11] poor maiden on Flat: no show both starts over hurdles. *Miss K. M. George* **h–**

TOM'S MAN 11 ch.g. Milieu – Lorna's Choice (Oats) [2004/5 c–, h–: c21g^{pu} Apr 30] little form outside points: usually tongue tied. *G. F. White* **c–** **h–**

TOM'S PRIZE 10 ch.g. Gunner B – Pandora's Prize (Royal Vulcan) [2004/5 c123, h127: 24s^5 c24d^3 c24v^{pu} c24m^6 Apr 2] plain gelding: reportedly hobdayed before final start: fairly useful handicap hurdler/chaser: below form in 2004/5 except on second outing: stays 3¼m: acts on good to firm and heavy going: front runner: usually jumps soundly: game. *J. L. Spearing* **c123** **h–**

TON-CHEE 6 b.g. Vettori (IRE) – Najariya (Northfields (USA)) [2004/5 17d^4 17g^3 17d^5 16g* 20g^4 17s 20v 16v 16s Mar 11] leggy gelding: half-brother to winning hurdler Longcroft (by Weldnaas), stayed 2¾m: poor maiden on Flat (stays 2m): poor hurdler: won novice handicap at Hexham in September: best efforts around 2m on good/good to soft going: free-going sort. *K. W. Hogg, Isle of Man* **h84**

TONIC DU CHARMIL (FR) 5 b.g. Mansonnien (FR) – Thrusting (FR) (Akarad (FR)) [2004/5 18m^2 17g* 19g^2 17g^3 16g^3 19m^3 c16g^F c17g^2 c19g^2 c17s^F c20s^{ur} Apr 22] rather leggy gelding: second foal: dam 1¼m winner: fairly useful maiden chaser, claimed from G. Cherel €22,400) in late-2003/4: fairly useful hurdler: made all in novice at Newton Abbot in July: better form when placed: stays easy 19f: acts on soft and good to firm going: tongue tied last 4 starts: needs to brush up jumping over fences. *M. C. Pipe* **c117 x** **h116**

TONY'S PRIDE 5 b.g. Alderbrook – Lucia Forte (Neltino) [2004/5 F16v Feb 19] second foal: dam, useful hurdler who stayed 3m, sister to top-class 19f to 3½m chaser Teeton Mill and half-sister to useful staying hurdler/chaser Ashfold Copse: well beaten in bumper on debut. *P. T. Dalton* **F–**

TONY THE PILER (IRE) 9 br.g. Tidaro (USA) – Adabiya (IRE) (Akarad (FR)) [2004/5 20d* May 13] small gelding: modest handicap hurdler: off 14 months, improved effort when winning at Perth in May (reportedly finished lame): stays 3m: raced on good going or softer (acts on heavy): has worn cheekpieces. *N. G. Richards* **h87**

TOO FORWARD (IRE) 9 ch.g. Toulon – One Back (IRE) (Meneval (USA)) [2004/5 c20d^4 c25g^3 c25s* c24d^2 c28s c25d^5 Apr 8] tall, leggy gelding: useful hurdler at best in 2001/2: off 19 months, fairly useful form over fences: won maiden at Folkestone in January: best effort when 4 lengths second to Tribal Venture in novice at Kempton: stays 25f: acts on good to firm and heavy going: carries head awkwardly under pressure. *M. Pitman* **c127** **h–**

TOOMEBRIDGE (IRE) 7 b.g. Warcraft (USA) – The Foalicule (Imperial Fling (USA)) [2004/5 h97p: 20s^3 25d^2 22g^4 19g^2 c19s^F c23v^3 c19d^3 21g Apr 1] useful-looking gelding: modest maiden hurdler: fair novice chaser: stays 25f: raced on good going or softer. *J. S. King* **c104** **h99**

TOO POSH TO SHARE 7 b.m. Rakaposhi King – Two Shares (The Parson) [2004/5 16v 16s 16s^4 Feb 3] smallish mare: seventh foal: half-sister to winning 2m hurdler/chaser Knockaulin (by Buckley): dam won 17f hurdle: no form in 3 novice hurdles. *D. J. Wintle* **h–**

TOP ACHIEVER (IRE) 4 ch.g. Intikhab (USA) – Nancy Maloney (IRE) (Persian Bold) [2004/5 16d 16d^2 17s^2 17v^3 16d^4 17s 17v^2 17g^6 17g* 16m^6 Apr 17] smallish gelding: modest maiden on Flat (stays 1½m) for Mrs L. Stubbs: fair hurdler: won handicap at Bangor in March: raced around 2m: acts on heavy and good to firm ground. *C. W. Moore* **h100**

TOPANBERRY (IRE) 6 ch.m. Topanoora – Mulberry (IRE) (Denel (FR)) [2004/5 F90: 16d^2 20d^5 22s^3 24s^3 Apr 20] rather leggy mare: modest novice hurdler: should stay 3m: raced on good going or softer. *N. G. Richards* **h96**

TOP BUCK (IRE) 11 b.g. Top of The World – Orlita (Master Buck) [2004/5 c119, h–: 24g^5 May 13] tall, useful-looking gelding: fairly useful chaser in 2003/4: winning hurdler, well held in handicap in May: effective at 2m to 2¾m: raced on good going or softer (acts on soft): wore cheekpieces last 2 outings. *K. C. Bailey* **c–** **h–**

TOP DANCER (IRE) 5 ch.g. Danehill Dancer (IRE) – Shygate (Shy Groom (USA)) [2004/5 F18s^6 F16s^4 21g^4 Mar 14] sixth foal: half-brother to 2 winners, including 17f hurdle winner Aldwych Arrow (by Rainbows For Life), also successful up to 1¾m on **h82** **F82**

Flat: dam Irish 1½m winner: modest form in 2 bumpers: fourth of 7 in steadily-run novice at Plumpton on hurdling debut. *N. P. Littmoden*

TOP DAWN (IRE) 5 b.g. Topanoora – Andros Dawn (IRE) (Buckskin (FR)) [2004/5 16d Apr 11] €28,000 3-y-o: third foal: dam, maiden hurdler who stayed 3m, from family of Dawn Run: showed nothing in novice hurdle on debut. *L. Lungo* **h–**

TOP DOG (IRE) 6 b.g. Topanoora – Dun Oengus (IRE) (Strong Gale) [2004/5 F74: F17g^5 Sep 30] poor form in bumpers. *L. Wells* **F74**

TOP GALE (IRE) 6 b.m. Topanoora – Amy's Gale (IRE) (Strong Gale) [2004/5 F–: 16g 21g May 8] little sign of ability in bumper or 2 novice hurdles. *R. Dickin* **h–**

TOP OF THE DEE 8 ch.m. Rakaposhi King – Lavenham's Last (Rymer) [2004/5 h–: 16d c17d c16g^5 c19m^4 c20m c20m^3 17g c17d^F c18m^F Sep 21] rangy mare: maiden hurdler/chaser: successful in point in April: stays 2½m: acts on good to firm and heavy going: tried blinkered: often tongue tied: sketchy jumper of fences. *Mrs L. Williamson* **c71 x h–**

TOPOL (IRE) 7 br.g. Topanoora – Kislev (IRE) (Be My Guest (USA)) [2004/5 c94, h–: c16g^{pu} c19d^{pu} c20s c23v^5 Feb 2] rangy, useful-looking gelding: maiden hurdler/chaser: no form in 2004/5: sold 5,800 Ascot April Sales. *Miss H. C. Knight* **c– h–**

TOP PACK (IRE) 6 b.g. Top of The World – Mels Pride (IRE) (Ajraas (USA)) [2004/5 16d 16d 16g^{ur} 21d^{pu} Apr 5] 8,000 4-y-o: leggy gelding: first foal: dam unraced: no sign of ability. *N. G. Richards* **h–**

TOPPING TIME (IRE) 7 b.g. Topanoora – Vampirella (FR) (Cut Above) [2004/5 c19g^{pu} c21v^{pu} Dec 31] 2,100 4-y-o: tall gelding: half-brother to several winners on Flat abroad: dam, won at 3 yrs on Flat in France, half-sister to very smart middle-distance stayer Baby Turk: no sign of ability, including in Irish point: sold £900 Ascot April Sales. *F. Kirby* **c–**

TOP REF (IRE) 5 ch.g. Topanoora – Giveherthewhistle (IRE) (Supreme Leader) [2004/5 16g 16m Aug 30] lengthy, angular gelding: first foal: dam unraced, out of sister to useful chaser up to 3m Gimme Five: little show in 2 maiden hurdles. *Jonjo O'Neill* **h–**

TOP SON 6 b.g. Komaite (USA) – Top Yard (Teekay) [2004/5 16d May 11] well held on Flat in 2003 and on hurdling debut. *D. W. Lewis* **h–**

TOP STRATEGY (IRE) 5 b.g. Hernando (FR) – Sudden Stir (USA) (Woodman (USA)) [2004/5 h132: 16g 20s^2 16s^3 16s^3 16v^3 16v 16v* 21g Mar 16] useful-looking gelding: fairly useful hurdler: won 5-runner minor event at Navan in February by head from Lissbonney Project: stays 21f: acts on heavy going: usually blinkered: has looked none too keen. *T. M. Walsh, Ireland* **h121**

TOP STYLE (IRE) 7 ch.g. Topanoora – Kept In Style (Castle Keep) [2004/5 17s* 20s^{pu} 17g^4 17d^3 Apr 5] ex-Irish gelding: dam winning 2½m hurdler: modest on Flat (seems to stay 1½m): modest hurdler: won novice handicap at Sedgefield in February: should prove at least as effective at 2½m as shorter. *J. Howard Johnson* **h90**

TOP TENOR (IRE) 5 b.g. Sadler's Wells (USA) – Posta Vecchia (USA) (Rainbow Quest (USA)) [2004/5 h–: 16m 16d 16v^6 16d^6 16g^4 Jan 21] signs of ability last 2 starts in novice hurdles. *V. Thompson* **h92 ?**

TOP THE BILL (IRE) 5 b.g. Topanoora – Rio Star (IRE) (Riot Helmet) [2004/5 F84?: F16m^2 22g^5 20d^3 20d^2 19g^5 23v* 27v^{pu} Jan 25] close-coupled gelding: best effort in bumpers when runner-up at Hexham on reappearance: fair hurdler: won maiden at Wetherby in January: stays 23f: acts on heavy going (bumper form on good to firm). *Mrs S. A. Watt* **h103 F93**

TOP TREES 7 b.g. Charnwood Forest (IRE) – Low Line (High Line) [2004/5 h81§: 17f^6 16f Oct 7] modest and unreliable on Flat (stays 17f): poor maiden hurdler: raced mainly around 2m: acts on firm going: tried in cheekpieces: temperamental. *W. S. Kittow* **h69 §**

TORCHE (IRE) 7 b.g. Taos (IRE) – Orchette (IRE) (Orchestra) [2004/5 h101, F–: c23g^4 c24g^2 c30d^2 c26d* c25s* c24d c33g Mar 17] strong gelding: fair hurdler: fairly useful chaser: won maiden at Warwick and 4-runner novice at Wetherby (beat Calvic 5 lengths) in December: dour stayer, should stay extreme distances: acts on soft going: usually visored. *M. Scudamore* **c123 h–**

TORDUFF EXPRESS (IRE) 14 b.g. Kambalda – Marhabtain (Touching Wood (USA)) [2004/5 c104, h–: c26d* c28m* c32m^5 c22d^{pu} Feb 24] rather leggy gelding: **c120 h–**

*Intrum Justitia Cup Champion Hunter Chase, Stratford—
veteran Torduff Express (blinkered) takes advantage of the ill-fated Right To Reply's fall*

useful hunter chaser: won at Cheltenham and Stratford early in season: left clear last when beating Springford by 3 lengths in Intrum Justitia Cup Champion Hunters' Chase at latter: fractured pastern final start: stayed 4m: acted on good to firm and heavy going: sometimes flashed tail under pressure, but was reliable: reportedly retired. *P. F. Nicholls*

TORGIANO (IRE) 4 b.g. Cadeaux Genereux – Delimara (IRE) (In The Wings) [2004/5 F16g Apr 16] second foal: half-brother to 1m winner in Spain by Alhaarth and 15f winner in France by Octagonal: dam, 1m winner in France, out of sister to high-class 1½m performer Scorpio and half-sister to top-class stayer Sagaro: never dangerous in bumper on debut. *P. Monteith* **F79**

TORKINKING (IRE) 6 b.g. Supreme Leader – Nicola's News (IRE) (Buckskin (FR)) [2004/5 17g 17d⁶ 22s⁴ 17v⁶ 20sᵖᵘ 16v⁴ 16s* 16v* 16d* 16s* 18sᵖᵘ Apr 3] €2,500 3-y-o, €1,200 4-y-o, £1,300 5-y-o: first foal: dam unraced half-sister to fairly useful chaser up to 25f Avanti Express (by Supreme Leader): progressive hurdler: recorded 4-timer in handicaps at Newcastle and Ayr in January, Haydock (novice) in February and Newcastle in March: fairly useful form when beating Don't Call Me Derek 1¼ lengths on final occasion: form only around 2m on going softer than good (acts on heavy): tongue tied after debut: free-going front runner. *M. A. Barnes* **h115**

TORKIN WIND 4 ch.g. Chocolat de Meguro (USA) – Helm Wind (North Col) [2004/5 16dᵖᵘ 16vᵘʳ 18d 16g 20sᵖᵘ Mar 10] first foal: dam, poor winning hurdler, stayed 2½m: no sign of ability, including in cheekpieces. *M. A. Barnes* **h–**

TORPICA 9 br.g. Be My Native (USA) – Irish Mint (Dusky Boy) [2004/5 c–, h–: c19g 25gᵖᵘ May 9] no longer of any account: blinkered last 3 starts. *P. Winkworth* **c– h–**

TORRID KENTAVR (USA) 8 b.g. Trempolino (USA) – Torrid Tango (USA) (Green Dancer (USA)) [2004/5 c107, h118: 16m³ c16d* c17g³ 17d³ 16s⁵ 16d 16g⁴ 16d 16d² 16d⁵ c17s⁴ 17g Mar 18] compact gelding: fairly useful chaser: won handicap at Perth in May: useful hurdler: back to best when 3½ lengths second to Crossbow Creek in valuable handicap at Kempton ninth start: best around 2m: acts on soft and good to firm going: free-going sort. *B. Ellison* **c117 h136**

TORY (IRE) 7 gr.m. Roselier (FR) – Doth Protest (IRE) (Dancing Dissident (USA)) [2004/5 24v^pu 21v Mar 28] €3,400 4-y-o: first foal: dam lightly raced on Flat: no sign of ability, including in points. *Willie Lapsley, Ireland* **h–**

TOSAWI (IRE) 9 b.g. Commanche Run – Deep Satisfaction (Deep Run) [2004/5 c–, h96: 22g² 24d⁶ 19m⁴ c19s² c19d⁴ c24s c20s⁵ c16d^pu c19g Apr 15] good-topped gelding: modest handicap hurdler: fair form over fences: stays 21f: acts on heavy and good to firm going: tried in cheekpieces: has bled from nose: ungenuine. *R. J. Hodges* **c105 § h99**

TOTAL ENJOYMENT (IRE) 6 b.m. Flemensfirth (USA) – Oak Court (IRE) (Bustineto) [2004/5 F118: 16s* 16d⁶ 20v⁶ Dec 31] leggy mare: successful in Champion Bumper at Cheltenham in 2003/4: landed odds in Grade 3 mares novice at Down Royal on hurdling debut in November by 3½ lengths from Sanghasta: found little when sixth to Wild Passion in Grade 1 novice at Fairyhouse (reportedly had respiritory tract infection) next time: reported in January to have injured near-fore knee: put down after developing laminitis in April. *T. Cooper, Ireland* **h124**

TOTALLY SCOTTISH 9 b.g. Mtoto – Glenfinlass (Lomond (USA)) [2004/5 h106§: 17s² 16s² 17v³ 16d c21v² 16v 18d³ 19g* 20s³ 20d 18s² Apr 3] rather sparely-made gelding: fair hurdler: ended lengthy losing run in claimer at Doncaster in March: modest form when runner-up in maiden at Sedgefield on chasing debut: stays 21f: probably acts on any going: blinkered and tongue tied on debut: held up. *K. G. Reveley* **c98 h114**

TO THE FUTURE (IRE) 9 ch.g. Bob Back (USA) – Lady Graduate (IRE) (Le Bavard (FR)) [2004/5 c–, h–: c25v⁴ c30d² 27v^pu c25v² c28g^pu Mar 26] tall gelding: maiden hurdler: poor handicap chaser: thorough stayer: raced mainly on going softer than good (acts on heavy): visored final start. *A. Parker* **c82 h–**

TOTHEROADYOUVGONE 11 b.g. Carlingford Castle – Wild Rosie (Warpath) [2004/5 c26g^ro c24f c20f* c25m^ro c20f² c25d^bd c25g⁶ c23f^ur c25g² c24d* c24m* c27m⁴ Nov 25] winning hurdler: modest chaser: won handicaps at Wexford in August and, having left N. Glynn after ninth start, Taunton in October and November (4-runner event): stays 25f: acts on firm and good to soft ground: wears cheekpieces: has been let down by jumping. *A. E. Jones* **c97 h–**

TOTLAND BAY (IRE) 9 br.g. Phardante (FR) – Seanaphobal Lady (Kambalda) [2004/5 c–, h95: c24g^pu c24s^F c21g⁵ Apr 10] lengthy, angular gelding: winning hurdler: last on only completed outing in chases: successful in point in April: stays 2¾m: acts on firm going, possibly not on softer than good: tried tongue tied. *Dr R. D. P. Newland* **c– h–**

TOUCH AND WELD (IRE) 4 ch.f. Weld – Princess Touchee (IRE) (Shernazar) [2004/5 F14m F16d Mar 28] third foal: dam poor form in bumpers: soundly beaten in 2 bumpers. *B. W. Duke* **F–**

TOUCH CLOSER 8 b.g. Inchinor – Ryewater Dream (Touching Wood (USA)) [2004/5 c93, h106: 20v⁴ 22d² 21g⁶ 25s² 22g 24g⁴ 24d Apr 8] angular gelding: once-raced chaser: fairly useful handicap hurdler: much improved in 2004/5, running to best when fourth to Oulart in Pertemps Final at Cheltenham sixth start: stays 25f: acts on heavy going: sold to join P. Bowen 30,000 gns (privately) Doncaster May Sales. *Miss V. Scott* **c– h125**

TOUCH OF EBONY (IRE) 6 b.g. Darshaan – Cormorant Wood (Home Guard (USA)) [2004/5 16g⁵ 19m⁶ 20v² 21g^F 24s 24s⁴ 20v Feb 2] leggy gelding: modest maiden hurdler: stays 3m: acts on heavy going, probably on good to firm: tried in cheekpieces. *C. Roberts* **h98**

TOUCH OF FATE 6 b.g. Sovereign Water (FR) – Coral Delight (Idiot's Delight) [2004/5 17s⁴ 21d⁶ Apr 18] ninth foal: half-brother to several winning hurdlers, including Kino's Cross (by Relkino), fairly useful at 2m: dam, useful hurdler who stayed 21f, sister to useful 2m to 2¾m chaser Our Fun: won completed start in maiden Irish points in 2004: sold 13,000 gns Doncaster May Sales: easily better effort over hurdles when fourth in novice at Folkestone. *R. Rowe* **h100 +**

TOULON ROUGE (IRE) 8 b.m. Toulon – Master Nidee (Master Owen) [2004/5 24v^pu 24s c25d² c20d² c24g^F c22v² c25d* c24v² c21d⁶ c28g^F Mar 26] tall, lengthy mare: winning hurdler: fair chaser: jumped with greater fluency when winning maiden at Kelso in February: running well when falling 2 out in handicap at Haydock final start: stays 3m: acts on heavy going: has looked less than keen. *Ferdy Murphy* **c108 h–**

TOULOUSE (IRE) 8 b.g. Toulon – Neasham (Nishapour (FR)) [2004/5 c100, h–: c16s² c20d^pu c16g² c19s* c21g Apr 14] rangy gelding: fair handicap chaser: won at Hereford in November: stays 19f: acts on soft going. *R. H. Alner* **c109 h–**

Aykroyd's Character Building Handicap Chase, Haydock—
the grey Bambi de L'Orme is about to fall, leaving Town Crier to beat Ghadames (cheekpieces)

TOULOUSE-LAUTREC (IRE) 9 ch.g. Toulon – Bucks Slave (Buckskin (FR)) [2004/5 c107x, h–: 22s* c28s² c29s* c26d⁵ c26v² c30d* c33d² Mar 19] tall gelding: first outing over hurdles since 2001/2, won ladies handicap at Newton Abbot in November: fairly useful handicap chaser: won at Plumpton in January and Exeter (beat Madam's Man a neck) in March: good second to idling Philson Run in valuable event at Uttoxeter final start: stays 33f: raced on going softer than good (acts on heavy): often makes mistakes. *T. R. George* **c122 x h89**

TOUS CHEZ (IRE) 6 b.g. Carroll House – Sixfoursix (Balinger) [2004/5 F16g² F16d³ Jan 13] 12,500 4-y-o: workmanlike gelding: fourth foal: dam bumper winner: placed both starts in bumpers at Catterick, fairly useful form when third to Bayside: likely to benefit from increased test of stamina. *Mrs S. J. Smith* **F95**

TOUS LES TABLES (IRE) 4 ch.g. Alhaarth (IRE) – Nebl (Persian Bold) [2004/5 16v⁵ 16s* 16v⁴ 16s² 16v³ Apr 2] well held at 2 yrs for P. Martin: fairly useful juvenile hurdler: won maiden at Clonmel in December by 7 lengths from Grangehill Dancer: raced at 2m on soft/heavy going. *N. Meade, Ireland* **h117**

TOWN CRIER (IRE) 10 br.g. Beau Sher – Ballymacarett (Menelek) [2004/5 h115: 16d* c16s* c16d² c16dᶠ c16v* c16d³ c16s* c16g c16sᶠ Apr 7] tall gelding: fair hurdler: off 14 months, won 18-runner handicap at Kelso in October: useful over fences: won maiden at Wetherby in October, novice at Newcastle (looked held until left clear by fall of Mondul 2 out) in January and handicap at Haydock (beat Ghadames 3 lengths) in February: should stay beyond 2m: acts on good to firm and heavy going. *Mrs S. J. Smith* **c139 h114**

TRABOLGAN (IRE) 7 b.g. King's Ride – Derrella (Derrylin) [2004/5 h125p: c20d* c24g² c22v² c24g* Mar 16] **c153 h–**

The Cheltenham Festival's two longest-standing sponsorships both began at the 1974 meeting. The three-mile Joe Coral Golden Hurdle became the shorter-distance Coral Cup in 1993, though the longer race was retained under different sponsorship. Meanwhile, the races currently known as the Royal & SunAlliance Chase and the Royal & SunAlliance Hurdle, respectively for five-year-olds and upwards novice chasers and for four-year-old and upwards novice hurdlers, remain largely unchanged. Known simply by the name SunAlliance for most of their existence, they took over from the Totalisator Champion Chase and the Aldsworth Hurdle in 1974—when they were won by Ten Up and Brown Lad—and have been run every year since, with the exception of 2001 when the meeting was abandoned because of foot and mouth. Both races have an impressive history—and an excellent record for producing future stars—with five future Cheltenham Gold Cup winners (Ten Up, Davy Lad, Master Smudge, Garrison Savannah and Looks Like Trouble), plus the disqualified winner Tied Cottage, and the Champion Hurdle winners Istabraq and Hardy Eustace on the roll of honour. However, their supremacy at the Festival had to withstand a challenge in the latest season. Among the races added to extend the meeting to a fourth day were the Spa Novices' Hurdle over three miles and the Jewson Novices' Handicap Chase over two miles five furlongs. The new three-mile novice hurdle did not unduly affect the Royal & SunAlliance Hurdle which is run over a distance three furlongs shorter and attracted twenty runners, though there was a subtle change to the make-up of the field which contained more ex-Flat racers than it often does (they filled four of the first six places). The new novice handicap chase attracted nineteen runners, a few of which would probably have run otherwise in the Royal & SunAlliance over three furlongs further (connections of the winner King Harald were fined, having declared him and then not run him in the previous day's Royal & SunAlliance). The Royal & SunAlliance Chase had a single figure line-up for only the fifth time under the auspices of the current sponsors, only the 1993 edition, when Young Hustler beat seven others, attracting a smaller field. There were, however, extenuating circumstances in the latest season which featured an unusually high rate of absence among the season's leading novices, those who might well have run in the Royal & SunAlliance including the long-time ante-post favourite Ollie Magern, sidelined with a cracked cannon bone, and another injured leading fancy Lord of Illusion. Fundamentalist (winner of the previous year's Royal & SunAlliance Hurdle), Iris's Gift, Jazz d'Estruval, Distant Thunder, Baron Windrush and El Vaquero were other leading novice chasers with pretensions to stay who did not appear at the Festival.

Royal & SunAlliance Chase, Cheltenham—
Trabolgan holds the rally of Comply Or Die in a less-than-vintage renewal

The presence of at least some of those on the missing list would have made for a much stronger Royal & SunAlliance Chase in which the four at the head of the betting filled the first four places in the race itself, though not in market order. Two of the four market leaders, 5/1-shot Trabolgan and 3/1 favourite Comply Or Die had both finished second to Ollie Magern in novice events earlier in the season. Comply Or Die had been despatched by Ollie Magern, who gave him 5 lb, over the SunAlliance course back in October but had won two of his three starts since, though he had not been seen since falling at Newbury at the end of November. Trabolgan, runner-up in the Champion Bumper at Cheltenham as a five-year-old, always looked the type who would come into his own once sent over fences (a knee injury curtailed a campaign in novice hurdles in 2003/4 when he won both his completed starts). He made an impressive start in a maiden chase at Lingfield towards the end of November, jumping soundly and showing the better turn of speed to beat Kadount by two and a half lengths. Trabolgan then took on Ollie Magern and seven others in a notably competitive renewal of the Grade 1 Feltham Novices' Chase at Kempton where, in a thrilling finish after leading briefly on the flat, he was touched off by a short head, despite hitting the second and being hampered at the eleventh. On his only other start before the Cheltenham Festival—where a tilt at the Gold Cup was considered for a time—Trabolgan failed to give his running under extremely testing conditions at Haydock where he was beaten nine lengths by Jazz d'Estruval.

The decision to run Trabolgan in the Royal & SunAlliance, rather than in the Gold Cup, was definitely the right one, despite the rash of late withdrawals from the main event. He had the form to win the Royal & SunAlliance and was ridden out from the last to beat Comply Or Die by three lengths, with Cornish Rebel a further three behind in third, a head in front of fourth-placed L'Ami. Trabolgan quickened into a decisive lead soon after the second last where, clearly going best, he nearly lost his rider when making a bad mistake (he had also made a less serious error at the tenth). Trabolgan's victory and that of Juveigneur in the Fulke Walwyn Kim Muir later in the afternoon (in which the stable also sent out the runner-up) took trainer Nicky Henderson's total of Cheltenham Festival winners to twenty-seven. Liberthine's win in the Mildmay of Flete the next day took the tally to twenty-eight. Henderson's three victories came after two years without success at the meeting by which he largely measures his season, though the stable's form overall in the latest campaign must have been a source of some worry. Problems with a viral infection restricted operations for a time after the turn of the year and ninth place in the trainers' table was the stable's lowest since the 1997/8 season. Trabolgan and Juveigneur, incidentally, provided owner Trevor Hemmings—who won the Grand National with Hedgehunter—with his first Cheltenham Festival winners.

Trabolgan (IRE) (b.g. 1998)	King's Ride (b 1976)	Rarity (b 1967)	Hethersett
			Who Can Tell
		Ride (b 1966)	Sovereign Path
			Turf
	Derrella (br 1985)	Derrylin (b 1975)	Derring-Do
			Antigua
		Kessella (br 1967)	Le Levanstell
			Kessaway

The rangy Trabolgan was not seen out again after Cheltenham. He will have to improve considerably on his Royal & SunAlliance form to make his mark in the top championship events but, with only four steeplechases under his belt, he certainly has the scope to improve and should win more races, good handicaps likely to offer the most lucrative opportunities at first. Trabolgan already ranks among the best progeny of his deceased sire King's Ride who is also the sire of the Jewson Novices' Handicap Chase winner King Harald, both being members of King's Ride's second-last crop. Trabolgan's dam the unraced Derrella is a sister to the high-class two-mile hurdler Kesslin, later successful in the States, and a half-sister to Rathconrath, a smart hurdler and later a useful chaser. The family has produced mainly Flat winners, Trabolgan's great grandam the miler Kessaway being a sister to the smart middle-distance stayer Heswall Honey and a half-sister to Kessall, the dam of high-class miler Roi Soleil. Derrella was also represented on the racecourse in the latest season by the fairly useful staying novice chaser Huka Lodge (by Roselier). Trabolgan will stay beyond three miles and has been raced on good going or softer over jumps. He is a sound jumper of fences in the main. *N. J. Henderson*

TRADE OFF (IRE) 7 b.g. Roselier (FR) – Lady Owenette (IRE) (Salluceva) [2004/5 c94, h90, F82: c25g^{pu} Apr 26] modest maiden hurdler/chaser: visored, lame only 2004/5 outing: stays 3¼m: acts on soft going: sold 6,500 gns Doncaster May Sales: won 4 times in points in 2005. *M. C. Pipe* **c– h–**

TRADINGUP (IRE) 6 b.g. Arctic Lord – Autumn Queen (Menelek) [2004/5 F16d 20s^5 24s^4 22s^6 c24d^5 c24v^3 Mar 29] €9,000 3-y-o: compact gelding: half-brother to several winners, including one-time useful staying chaser Murt's Man (by Be My Native) and fair 2¾m hurdle winner Mickeen (by Le Bavard): dam unraced sister to fairly useful staying hurdler Woodford Prince: third both starts in maiden Irish points in 2004: seventh of 14 in bumper at Wincanton: modest form over hurdles and in chases: will prove best given good test of stamina. *J. S. King* **c91 h91 F80**

TRADITIONAL (IRE) 9 ch.g. Erins Isle – Noorajo (IRE) (Ahonoora) [2004/5 c–, h–: c21g^{pu} Apr 27] close-coupled gelding: winning hurdler/pointer: maiden chaser: stays easy 3m: acts on good to soft and good to firm going: has worn blinkers/cheekpieces: has looked none too keen: sold £7,500 Ascot July Sales. *Miss Chloe Newman* **c– h–**

TRAFALGAR MAN (IRE) 4 b. or br.g. Scribano – Call Over (Callernish) [2004/5 F16s^5 Mar 22] leggy gelding: sixth foal: half-brother to winning pointer by Over The River: dam unraced half-sister to smart 2m to 3m chaser Travelowen and useful chaser around 2½m Socks Downe: modest form when fifth of 21 in bumper at Wetherby on debut. *M. D. Hammond* **F83**

TRANSATLANTIC (USA) 7 gr.g. Dumaani (USA) – Viendra (USA) (Raise A Native) [2004/5 h78: 17m^6 Mar 14] useful miler on Flat in 2002: lightly raced and just poor form over hurdles: needs emphasis on speed at 2m: headstrong. *H. D. Daly* **h71**

TRANSCENDANTALE (FR) 7 b. or br.m. Apple Tree (FR) – Kataba (FR) (Shardari) [2004/5 17g Aug 21] poor on Flat (stays 11.5f) nowadays: always behind in maiden on hurdling debut. *Mrs S. Lamyman* **h–**

TRANSIT 6 b.g. Lion Cavern (USA) – Black Fighter (USA) (Secretariat (USA)) [2004/5 c103+, h89: 17g^2 16d* 16f^5 c17d* 16s 16m^4 17d^2 17g^3 c16d 16m 17g^6 16d* 16g^4 Mar 18] leggy gelding: fair handicap hurdler/chaser: won over hurdles at Perth (intermediate) in May and Sandown (amateurs) in March and over fences at Market Rasen in July: raced mainly around 2m: acts on soft and good to firm going: tried blinkered, usually wears cheekpieces: held up: has looked less than keen. *B. Ellison* **c113 h113**

TRANSLUCID (USA) 7 b.g. Woodman (USA) – Gossamer (USA) (Seattle Slew (USA)) [2004/5 c124, h111+: c19g* c16m* c21g* c23s^F c21s^2 c20g^{pu} Apr 22] angular gelding: fair hurdler: better over fences, winning maiden at Towcester, novice at Huntingdon and listed event at Bremen early in season: stays 21f: acts on firm and soft going: free-going sort: successful on Flat at Bremen in February. *C. Von Der Recke, Germany* **c120 h–**

TRAVEL DEHOUCHE 5 b.m. Defacto (USA) – Travel Mystery (Godswalk (USA)) [2004/5 16f 16d^{pu} 17g 17s Oct 19] angular mare: eighth foal: dam useful 2m hurdler: no sign of ability over hurdles. *Nick Williams* **h–**

TRAVELLING BAND (IRE) 7 b.g. Blues Traveller (IRE) – Kind of Cute (Prince Sabo) [2004/5 h110: 16v 16d Mar 6] angular gelding: fair on Flat (stays 1¼m): fair novice hurdler in 2003/4: sold out of A. Balding's stable 7,500 gns Doncaster October Sales: behind in handicaps in 2004/5: likely to prove best at 2m with emphasis on speed: raced on good going or softer. *J. Mackie* **h–**

TRAVELLO (GER) 5 b.g. Bakharoff (USA) – Travista (GER) (Days At Sea (USA)) [2004/5 h95: 16d 19m 16d^6 c16s^4 c16d^3 c16m^5 Dec 1] rather unfurnished gelding: maiden hurdler, no form in 2004/5: seemingly best effort over fences, though never a factor, when third of 4 to Le Seychellois in 4-y-o novice at Warwick: raced mainly around 2m. *M. F. Harris* **c87 ? h–**

TRAVEL (POL) 5 gr.g. Freedom's Choice (USA) – Transylwania (POL) (Baby Bid (USA)) [2004/5 h–: 16d* 17d^4 17g^3 16g* 16d^2 16m^4 16g^4 16g Oct 27] well-made gelding: fair handicap hurdler: won at Perth (conditional jockeys) in May and Stratford in July: best at sharp 2m: acts on good to firm and good to soft going. *T. R. George* **h105**

TRAVEL SUPREME 5 b.g. Makbul – Celtic Lady (Kabour) [2004/5 F16s Feb 5] **F–**
500 2-y-o: big, good-topped gelding: third foal: dam no sign of ability: well held in bumper on debut. *M. D. Hammond*

TRAVINO (IRE) 6 b. or br.g. Roselier (FR) – Call Catherine (IRE) (Strong Gale) **F123**
[2004/5 F16s* F20v* F16v* Feb 13]

Division 1 of the five-year-old geldings maiden at the Knockanard point-to-point in County Cork on February 15th 2004 must have been quite a race. Not only was the judge's verdict—without benefit of photo finish—given as a head but some observers, including the racereader for *Formcard*, felt that the runner-up had, at least, rejoined the winner on the line. It was hard to separate the two horses involved at the end of the latest season as well, as Missed That and Travino, first and second at Knockanard, were the two best bumper horses seen in Ireland in 2004/5, with nothing between them on form, for all that one contested the Grade 1 bumpers at Cheltenham and Punchestown, while the other kept a lower profile.

Travino's season was over by the time Missed That lived up to his reputation and landed the Champion Bumper. Travino's trainer Mags Mullins considered entering him for Cheltenham but her view on reflection was that, while he might handle good ground, he is so big that she did not want to try him on it at this stage of his career. Travino made three appearances in bumpers, all of them on soft or heavy ground, and won all three. At Naas in November he got the better of the well-touted County Final by three quarters of a length, the pair twenty lengths clear of the rest; at Leopardstown in December he galloped on relentlessly over two and a half miles on heavy ground to beat Mandm by twenty-five lengths; and at Navan in February he was kept up to his work to land the odds by eight lengths from Miss Toulon. At the time, even though it was a winners-of-two bumper, that did not look as good an effort as his form at Leopardstown (the runner-up had had plenty of chances), though subsequently the form looked rather better. All in all, not a bad season for a

Mr P. C. Kilroy's "Travino"

maiden pointer, and there is surely more to come when Travino goes over hurdles and especially fences.

Travino (IRE) (b. or br.g. 1999)	Roselier (FR) (gr 1973)	Misti IV (br 1958)	Medium
			Mist
		Peace Rose (gr 1959)	Fastnet Rock
			La Paix
	Call Catherine (IRE) (b 1988)	Strong Gale (br 1975)	Lord Gayle
			Sterntau
		Brave Intention (b 1977)	Brave Invader
			Marfille

At this stage Travino looks just about the best prospect in the final crop of that tremendous stallion Roselier, which also contains the useful staying hurdlers Carraig Blue and The Listener and the fairly useful Wild Cane Ridge. As few of the crop have had the chance to run over fences yet, there may be one or two others to keep their sire's name in the headlines for a while yet. Roselier is a sire one can almost set one's clock by. Though there are obviously exceptions, the longer the trip and the softer the ground the better his progeny perform. His sire apart, Travino's pedigree could politely be called unpromising. His dam Call Catherine was a maiden in points and, though his grandam Brave Intention won twice, those successes came in a bumper at Limerick and a novice selling chase at Folkestone. The third dam Marfille was a minor winner over hurdles. Call Catherine produced two foals prior to Travino, Cantys Brig (also by Roselier), whose best effort so far was when beaten over thirty lengths in a novice hurdle at Uttoxeter, and De Luain Gorm (by Beneficial), who won a point in 2002 but has not raced since. Brave Intention and Marfille contribute just another winning pointer apiece to the family's tally. Marfille is, though, a half-sister to the dam of the useful chaser at up to twenty-five furlongs Love The Lord and the grandam of the fair staying hurdler Better Bythe Glass. Travino's return is eagerly awaited. Who knows, it may not be that long before he gets the chance to take his revenge on Missed That, with something rather better than a maiden point at stake. *Ms Margaret Mullins, Ireland*

TREASULIER (IRE) 8 gr.g. Roselier (FR) – Flashy Treasure (Crash Course) [2004/5 c26d^{F} c24s^{2} c25s^{5} c25s^{3} c24g^{4} c26d^{3} c26g^{6} Apr 10] IR £28,000 4-y-o: rather leggy gelding: seventh foal: dam unraced half-sister to useful chaser around 2½m Tildarg: well held in bumper for E. O'Grady in 2002/3: won last of 5 starts in maiden points in 2004: bought £3,500 Ascot October Sales: modest novice chaser: stays 3¼m: acts on soft going. *P. R. Rodford* **c93**

TREASURED MEMORIES 5 b.m. Cloudings (IRE) – Glen Morvern (Carlingford Castle) [2004/5 F16m^{5} F16g^{3} F16v* F17s Apr 7] sturdy mare: third foal: half-sister to 17f chase winner The Miner (by Hatim): dam 2¼m hurdle winner: best effort in bumpers when winning at Ayr in January. *Miss S. E. Forster* **F83**

TREASURE TRAIL 6 b.g. Millkom – Forever Shineing (Glint of Gold) [2004/5 h83: 17g^{5} 19g^{6} Apr 7] small, compact gelding: fair on Flat (stays 2m): poor hurdler: stays 2½m. *Ian Williams* **h84**

TREATY STONE 6 b.g. Bigstone (IRE) – Quiet City (True Song) [2004/5 F17m^{3} F17d^{2} 19g Dec 8] 15,000 4-y-o: quite good-topped gelding: third foal: dam winning chaser: fair form when placed in bumpers at Newton Abbot: mid-field in novice at Newbury on hurdling debut. *Jonjo O'Neill* **h88 p F93**

TREBLE VISION (IRE) 11 ch.g. Down The Hatch – General Vision (General Ironside) [2004/5 h–: 16g^{pu} May 1] of no account outside points. *W. G. Young* **h–**

TREETOPS HOTEL (IRE) 6 ch.g. Grand Lodge (USA) – Rousinette (Rousillon (USA)) [2004/5 16m Sep 19] modest on Flat (stays 1¼m): tongue tied, jumped poorly in novice on hurdling debut. *B. R. Johnson* **h–**

TREFOILALIGHT 6 b.m. Morpeth – Imalight (Idiot's Delight) [2004/5 F17s 17d 19d 19g^{pu} Dec 30] angular mare: first foal: dam poor novice hurdler/chaser around 2m: no form in bumper or novice hurdles. *J. D. Frost* **h– F–**

TREGASTEL (FR) 10 b.g. Tel Quel (FR) – Myrtlewood (FR) (Home Guard (USA)) [2004/5 c121, h–: c25s^{pu} c26s^{2} c21d^{F} c23d^{F} 23v c19v^{3} c20v* c20s^{2} c25s^{pu} c24d c31s^{pu} Apr 22] good-topped gelding: winning hurdler: fair chaser: won weak handicap at Plumpton in January: stays 3¼m: raced on good going or softer (acts on heavy): tried in cheekpieces: tongue tied: often let down by jumping over fences. *R. Ford* **c113 x h–**

TREMALLT (IRE) 14 b.g. Henbit (USA) – Secret Romance (Gala Performance) [2004/5 c124, h102: c26d* c21s^F Apr 7] close-coupled gelding: veteran chaser: successful in hunter chase at Chepstow in February, beating Lord Beau 2½ lengths: behind when fell fourteenth in Fox Hunters' at Aintree: stays 3¼m: acts on heavy going, probably on good to firm: visored once: front runner: bold jumper, but prone to odd error: tough. *T. R. George* **c112 h–**

TRENANCE 7 b.g. Alflora (IRE) – Carmel's Joy (IRE) (Carlingford Castle) [2004/5 h88?: c16v⁴ c19s^pu c17s^F c20s² c21d² c31s^pu Apr 22] sturdy gelding: little form over hurdles: modest chaser: stays 21f: acts on soft ground: none too fluent over fences. *T. R. George* **c86 h–**

TRESOR DE MAI (FR) 11 ch.g. Grand Tresor (FR) – Lady Night (FR) (Pompon Rouge) [2004/5 c129x, h–: c21g⁴ c23s* c24v³ c24s⁴ c24d Jan 8] sparely-made gelding: one-time smart chaser, successful in Grade 1 Ascot Chase in 2002: fairly useful in 2004/5: won handicap at Exeter in November by short head from Fox In The Box: stayed 3m: acted on heavy going: wore blinkers until 2002: sketchy jumper: reportedly retired. *M. C. Pipe* **c127 x h–**

TRESOR PREZINIERE (FR) 7 b. or br.g. Grand Tresor (FR) – Rose de Martine (FR) (The Quiet Man (FR)) [2004/5 c108x, h105: 22g³ c21s^pu 19d⁴ 22g⁴ 20m* c21g* c21g² Aug 10] leggy gelding: fair hurdler: won handicap at Uttoxeter in June: similar form over fences: jumped better when winning minor event at Newton Abbot in July: stays 2¾m: acts on heavy and good to firm going: sometimes wears blinkers: has looked none too keen under pressure. *P. J. Hobbs* **c107 h107**

TREYBOR (IRE) 6 br.g. Bob Back (USA) – Ballyvooney (Salluceva) [2004/5 c21d^ur 25d 16v 17s^pu 25s^pu Mar 1] €40,000 4-y-o: tall, leggy gelding: third foal: dam, winning hurdler/chaser who stayed 3m, out of half-sister to dam of smart staying chaser Fauloon: unseated in maiden chase on debut: no form over hurdles, shaping as though amiss: sold 10,000 gns Doncaster May Sales. *J. Howard Johnson* **c– h–**

TRIBAL DANCER (IRE) 11 ch.g. Commanche Run – Cute Play (Salluceva) [2004/5 c109, h99: c23m^pu c25g* 21s³ c25d³ c23g c24s⁴ 24s c25s⁴ 24g⁵ c24g⁴ c25g⁶ Apr 12] leggy, close-coupled gelding: modest handicap hurdler: fair handicap chaser: won at Ludlow in May: stays 25f: acts on soft and good to firm going: tried blinkered: not an easy ride, and often let down by jumping. *Miss Venetia Williams* **c109 d h92**

TRIBAL DISPUTE 8 b.g. Primitive Rising (USA) – Coral Princess (Imperial Fling (USA)) [2004/5 h–: c16v³ c16s⁴ c20s² c16v² c16d* Apr 5] big, useful-looking gelding: winning hurdler: fair chaser: won maiden at Sedgefield in April: best form around 2m: raced on good ground or softer (acts on heavy). *T. D. Easterby* **c106 + h–**

TRIBAL KING (IRE) 10 b. or br.g. Be My Native (USA) – Island Bridge (Mandalus) [2004/5 c21d* c21s⁴ Jan 22] lengthy, good sort: winning hurdler: fairly useful chaser: off nearly 2 years, better effort in handicaps at Wincanton when successful there in December by 19 lengths from Luneray: stays 2¾m: raced mainly on good going or softer (won bumper on soft): takes good hold. *A. King* **c116 h–**

TRIBAL RUN (IRE) 10 ch.g. Be My Native (USA) – Queen's Run (IRE) (Deep Run) [2004/5 c99, h–: c24v² c24s* Mar 10] fairly useful hunter chaser nowadays: won at Towcester in March by 4 lengths from Minella Silver: stays 3¾m: acts on heavy going: tongue tied. *Miss S. A. Loggin* **c108 h–**

TRIBAL VENTURE (FR) 7 gr.g. Dom Alco (FR) – Babacha (FR) (Latnahc (USA)) [2004/5 c25d* c24d³ c21v² c24s^ur c24d* c24s c24g^F c24s⁴ Apr 20] tall, angular gelding: useful hurdler in 2002/3, subsequently off 19 months (reportedly with leg trouble): at least as good over fences, winning maiden at Wetherby in November and novice at Kempton in January: best effort when 3 lengths third to L'Ami in Grade 2 novice at Lingfield in December: let down by jumping last 2 starts: best at 3m+: acts on good to firm and heavy going. *Ferdy Murphy* **c140 h–**

TRICKSTEP 4 b.g. Imperial Ballet (IRE) – Trick of Ace (USA) (Clever Trick (USA)) [2004/5 16d⁶ 16g Mar 18] small, close-coupled gelding: modest up to 13f on Flat: well held both starts over hurdles, trained by I. Semple on debut. *Miss Gay Kelleway* **h78**

TRICKY THYNE (IRE) 6 b.g. Good Thyne (USA) – Cuban Vacation (Ovac (ITY)) [2004/5 h–, F–: 21d^pu 24d^pu Mar 24] unfurnished gelding: no sign of ability: tried tongue tied. *Mrs N. S. Sharpe* **h–**

TRICKY TREVOR (IRE) 12 b. or br.g. Arctic Lord – Chancer's Last (Foggy Bell) [2004/5 c89, h–: c24d³ May 11] rangy gelding: maiden chaser: fair pointer: successful **c– h–**

in March and April: stays 3m: acts on firm and good to soft going: tried blinkered. *Mrs H. J. Cobb*

TRIGGERLINO 5 b.m. Double Trigger (IRE) – Voolino (Relkino) [2004/5 F72: 21s⁶ 19s 21spu 26s⁴ 22d³ 26m³ Apr 9] poor maiden hurdler: stays 3¼m: acts on soft going. *Miss Venetia Williams* **h75**

TRINKET (IRE) 7 b.g. Definite Article – Alamiya (IRE) (Doyoun) [2004/5 h102: 22g⁶ c22spu Nov 4] well-made gelding: very lightly raced: fair hurdler: would have shown improved form in novice at Haydock on chasing debut but for going amiss and pulled up run-in: stays 2¾m. *H. D. Daly* **c113 h–**

TRINK HILL 7 ch.m. Good Times (ITY) – Sweet On Willie (USA) (Master Willie) [2004/5 17g 17d 19dpu 17s 17s Nov 18] no form. *J. D. Frost* **h–**

TRIPLE GLORY (IRE) 6 b.m. Goldmark (USA) – Trebles (IRE) (Kenmare (FR)) [2004/5 c–, h–: c21gpu May 30] angular mare: maiden hurdler/chaser, no form since 2002. *Mrs P. N. Dutfield* **c– h–**

TRIPLE PLAY (IRE) 6 br.g. Tagula (IRE) – Shiyra (Darshaan) [2004/5 h–: 17m⁴ Jun 9] no form in novice hurdles. *Lady Susan Watson* **h–**

TRISONS STAR (IRE) 7 b.g. Roselier (FR) – Delkusha (Castle Keep) [2004/5 F104: F16d² F16f* F17d⁴ 20s 18v² 20v* 24s² 22g 24s* Apr 21] tall gelding: fairly useful form in bumpers, landed odds at Perth in June: fairly useful novice hurdler: won at Ayr in January and Perth (improved effort when beating Inch Pride by 1¼ lengths) in April: will stay beyond 3m: acts on heavy going (bumper form on firm). *Mrs L. B. Normile* **h115 F98**

TRISTAN LUDLOW (IRE) 9 gr.g. Roselier (FR) – Surely Madam (Torenaga) [2004/5 20d 21spu Mar 31] good-topped gelding: fair maiden hurdler for J. O'Neill: off 2 years, no sign of retaining ability in 2004/5. *N. A. Twiston-Davies* **h–**

TRIVIAL (IRE) 13 b.m. Rakaposhi King – Miss Rubbish (Rubor) [2004/5 c–, h–: c25gur c25m³ c26g* May 26] quite good-topped mare: winning hurdler: modest hunter chaser: won at Cartmel in May: fourth in points completed starts in 2005: stays 3¼m: acts on good to firm and good to soft going, possibly not on soft. *J. E. Brockbank* **c82 h–**

TROCHILIDAE (IRE) 9 b.m. Alphabatim (USA) – Quincy Bay (Buckskin (FR)) [2004/5 25dpu Nov 1] of little account. *A. J. Wilson* **h–**

TROEDRHIWDALAR 8 b.m. Gunner B – Delladear (Sonnen Gold) [2004/5 h–: c20mur 24m 22g⁴ 27gpu Jul 28] won point in 2004, little form otherwise: tried visored/in cheekpieces: poor jumper of fences. *Mrs D. A. Hamer* **c– x h71**

TROLL (FR) 4 b.g. Cadoudal (FR) – Miss Dundee (FR) (Esprit du Nord (USA)) [2004/5 F14d* F14g⁴ Dec 18] rangy, good-topped gelding: half-brother to useful bumper/2m hurdle winner Armaguedon (by Garde Royale) and French 12.5f winner Miss Amande (by Vert Amande): dam, fairly useful 2m hurdler, half-sister to useful French hurdler Prestigieux: fairly useful form in 3-y-o bumpers: won at Wetherby on debut in December: better effort when fourth to The Duke's Speech at Newcastle. *L. Lungo* **F97**

TROODOS VALLEY (IRE) 6 b.g. Executive Perk – Valleymay (IRE) (King's Ride) [2004/5 F92: 21d³ 19spu Nov 30] good-topped gelding: fair form at best in bumpers: third of 8 at Huntingdon on completed start in novice hurdles: will benefit from greater emphasis on stamina. *H. D. Daly* **h85**

TROOPER 11 b.g. Rock Hopper – Silica (USA) (Mr Prospector (USA)) [2004/5 c85§, h–§: c27d⁵ c27d³ c25m⁶ c27vpu Dec 31] lengthy gelding: poor handicap chaser: stays 27f: acts on any going: visored/blinkered: ungenuine. *A. Crook* **c65 § h– §**

TROOPER KIT 6 b.g. Petoski – Rolling Dice (Balinger) [2004/5 F–: 21spu 20dpu Nov 19] no sign of ability: tried blinkered. *Mrs L. Richards* **h–**

TROUBLE AHEAD (IRE) 14 b.g. Cataldi – Why 'o' Why (Giolla Mear) [2004/5 c122x, h–: c20s³ Mar 6] quite good-topped gelding: fairly useful handicap chaser: off over 10 months, appeared to run creditably when last of 3 finishers to Soeur Fontenail at Kempton: effective at 2m to 3m: acts on good to firm and heavy going: probably best on right-handed tracks: prone to mistakes. *Miss Venetia Williams* **c118 x h–**

TROUBLE AT BAY (IRE) 5 b.g. Slip Anchor – Fight Right (FR) (Crystal Glitters (USA)) [2004/5 h135: 16s² 16d⁵ 20d⁴ 21d⁴ Dec 11] smallish, close-coupled gelding: useful hurdler: best efforts in 2004/5 when second to Rigmarole in quite valuable minor event at Kempton and fourth to Monet's Garden in steadily-run Grade 2 at Windsor third start: stays 2½m: acts on soft and good to firm going: probably best in well-run race. *A. King* **h140**

skybet.com Rowland Meyrick Handicap Chase, Wetherby—
Truckers Tavern overhauls the blundering Malek for a first win in two years

TRUCKERS TAVERN (IRE) 10 ch.g. Phardante (FR) – Sweet Tulip (Beau Chapeau) [2004/5 c154, h120+: 20s⁴ c24d⁴ c25s* c24v⁴ c28s⁵ c26gᵖᵘ Mar 18] big, well-made gelding: thrice-raced hurdler: smart chaser: won skybet.com Rowland Meyrick Chase at Wetherby in December by ¾ length from Malek, left in front after runner-up slowed and blundered last: ran creditably otherwise in 2004/5 only when fourth to Lord Transcend in Peter Marsh Chase at Haydock next time: suited by 3m+: raced on good going or softer (acts on heavy): tongue tied: effective held up or ridden from front: usually let down by jumping: joined Mrs S. Smith. *Ferdy Murphy* **c146 x h106 +**

TRUE DAWN (IRE) 4 b.f. Luso – Strange But True (IRE) (Heavenly Manna) [2004/5 F16s 20sᵖᵘ Apr 20] third foal: dam, bumper winner, out of half-sister to very smart staying hurdler Trapper John: no sign of ability in bumper or maiden hurdle. *B. Storey* **h– F–**

TRUE LOVER (GER) 8 b.g. Winged Love (IRE) – Truneba (GER) (Nebos (GER)) [2004/5 h123: 23m² May 1] sturdy, close-coupled gelding: fairly useful hurdler: creditable second to Kivotos in well-contested handicap at Haydock: stays 3m: acts on good to firm ground: first run on Flat for 3 years when third in Group 3 at Newmarket in October. *J. W. Mullins* **h121**

TRUE MARINER (FR) 5 b.g. True Brave (USA) – Miss Above (FR) (Houston (FR)) [2004/5 c20v⁵ c20s c17d⁶ 17s³ 18d³ 18s* c16d⁵ c17d³ c19gᶠ c20g² c16dᵖᵘ c20d Feb 11] compact ex-French gelding: second foal: dam maiden: maiden on Flat: fairly useful hurdler: won handicap at Clairefontaine in August (final start for S. Berard): fair chaser: easily best effort in Britain when second to Duncliffe in novice handicap at Kempton: stays 2½m: acts on heavy going: none too fluent over fences. *B. I. Case* **c113 h122**

TRUENO (IRE) 6 b.g. Desert King (IRE) – Stitching (IRE) (High Estate) [2004/5 16s³ 16dᶠ Dec 29] close-coupled gelding: fairly useful on Flat (stays 15f), sold out of L. Cumani's stable 31,000 gns Newmarket Autumn Sales: third in maiden at Chepstow on hurdling debut: stepping up on that form when falling fatally last in novice at Newbury. *N. J. Gifford* **h107**

TRUE NORTH (IRE) 10 b.g. Black Monday – Slip A Loop (The Parson) [2004/5 h–: c21vᵘʳ c21s⁴ Feb 7] workmanlike gelding: one-time fair handicap hurdler: lightly raced since 2003 and little sign of retaining ability, including in 2 starts over fences. *D. R. MacLeod* **c– h–**

TRUE PATRIOT 4 b.g. Rainbow Quest (USA) – High Standard (Kris) [2004/5 17g 18m Aug 19] half-brother to modest hurdler Comfortable Call (by Nashwan), stays 21f: of little account on Flat: well beaten in 2 juvenile hurdles, blinkered in second. *D. R. Gandolfo* **h–**

TRUE TANNER 7 b.g. Lyphento (USA) – True Nell (Neltino) [2004/5 F–: F17s F17s 16v 16v 16g Jan 24] of no account: tried tongue tied. *Miss C. Dyson* **h– F–**

TRULY GOLD (IRE) 6 ch.g. Goldmark (USA) – Truly Flattering (Hard Fought) [2004/5 20m 20s^F Oct 30] fair stayer on Flat, successful in August: fairly useful hurdler: improved form in handicap at Naas on final start, 10 lengths clear when falling last: stays 2½m: acts on good to firm and heavy going: tried blinkered. *R. P. Burns, Ireland* **h116**

TRUST FUND (IRE) 7 ch.g. Rashar (USA) – Tuney Blade (Fine Blade (USA)) [2004/5 c24g⁴ c23d* c24d^pu c26v^pu c24d³ Mar 19] €30,000 4-y-o: rangy gelding: seventh foal: half-brother to 2½m hurdle winner Wild Blade (by Meneval) and 21f hunter chase winner Mid Summer Lark (by Tremblant): dam unraced: winning pointer: fair chaser: won maiden at Exeter in December: ran well only completed subsequent start: likely to prove suited by test of stamina. *R. H. Alner* **c113**

TRUSTING PADDY (IRE) 8 b.g. Synefos (USA) – Homefield Girl (IRE) (Rahotep (FR)) [2004/5 c83, h76: 24m^pu Jun 5] lengthy gelding: poor maiden hurdler: fell both starts over fences: stays 19f: acts on heavy going (bumper form on firm). *L. A. Dace* **c– h–**

TRUST ME (IRE) 6 gr.g. Roselier (FR) – Lady Owenette (IRE) (Salluceva) [2004/5 F17d 19s 19s^pu Mar 27] €41,000 3-y-o, 38,000 4-y-o: sixth foal: half-brother to fairly useful hurdler/winning chaser Castle Owen (by Castle Keep), stayed 25f: dam unraced half-sister to fairly useful staying chaser The Nigelstan: signs of a little ability in bumper and 2 starts over hurdles. *Noel T. Chance* **h– F–**

TRUST SMITH 9 b.m. Greensmith – Loch Chastity (National Trust) [2004/5 22g^pu Jul 12] third foal: dam of little account: no show in mares novice hurdle on debut. *P. C. Ritchens* **h–**

TRY CATCH PADDY (IRE) 7 ch.g. Safety Catch (USA) – Blackwater Rose VII (Damsire Unregistered) [2004/5 F20g F20v* 21d* 23d⁵ 24v^pu 24d 24d³ 27s Apr 22] IR £4,200 3-y-o, 7,000 6-y-o: second foal: dam unraced: won maiden Irish point in 2004: much better effort in 2½m bumpers for J. J. Murphy when winning at Listowel in September: successful in novice at Plumpton on hurdling debut in November by neck from Without A Doubt: disappointing after, bled from nose sixth start: probably stays 3m. *M. C. Pipe* **h120 d F98**

TRY ME AND SEE 11 ch.g. Rock City – Al Raja (Kings Lake (USA)) [2004/5 c–, h–: 16s 21d c16g^pu c21v⁵ Dec 31] good-topped gelding: of little account outside points: tried tongue tied. *A. M. Crow* **c– h–**

TSAR'S TWIST 6 b.g. Presidium – Kabs Twist (Kabour) [2004/5 h–, F81?: c21g^pu 16m 22m⁴ 22g³ 22s Oct 19] leggy, sparely-made gelding: no show on chasing debut: poor maiden hurdler: successful in maiden point in April: stays 2¾m: has worn blinkers. *Mrs S. Gardner* **c– h63**

TSCHIERTSCHEN 5 ch.g. Master Willie – Smocking (Night Shift (USA)) [2004/5 F–: F16g May 16] useful-looking gelding: well held in 2 bumpers. *M. W. Easterby* **F–**

TSUNAMI 9 b.m. Beveled (USA) – Alvecote Lady (Touching Wood (USA)) [2004/5 c–: 20g 20d² 19m⁶ 22m 24g 20g 19d⁴ 26d⁵ 20s⁵ 19d^pu Jan 1] sparely-made mare: no form over fences: poor hurdler: stays 21f: probably acts on any going: tried in headgear: has had tongue tied: not one to trust: sold 1,100 gns Doncaster March Sales. *B. D. Leavy* **c– h68 §**

TUBBER ROADS (IRE) 12 b.g. Un Desperado (FR) – Node (Deep Run) [2004/5 c–: c25s^pu Apr 28] good-topped gelding: formerly useful hunter chaser: no form outside points (successful twice in April) since 2002: blinkered once. *M. G. Hazell* **c–**

TUCACAS (FR) 8 gr.m. Highest Honor (FR) – Three Well (FR) (Sicyos (USA)) [2004/5 c118, h129: c21d^pu May 1] good-topped mare: one-time useful handicap hurdler: fairly useful novice chaser in 2003/4: let down by jumping in listed mares handicap at Uttoxeter only outing in 2004/5: stays easy 2¾m: acts on any going: visored once. *M. C. Pipe* **c– h–**

TUCK IN 8 b.g. Good Thyne (USA) – Always Shining (Tug of War) [2004/5 20s^pu Dec 4] big, imposing gelding: fairly useful form in bumpers in 2001/2: pulled up in novice hurdle on belated return. *P. Winkworth* **h–**

TUDOR BELL (IRE) 4 b.g. Definite Article – Late Night Lady (IRE) (Mujadil (USA)) [2004/5 19s⁴ 17s Feb 17] fairly useful on Flat (stays 1¾m), successful 3 times in 2004: better effort over hurdles when fourth in novice at Exeter: needs to brush up jumping. *J. G. M. O'Shea* **h94**

TUDOR BUCK (IRE) 5 b. or br.g. Luso – Tudor Doe (IRE) (Buckskin (FR)) [2004/5 F16d 16v^{ur} 17g^{6} 16d^{F} Apr 22] 8,500 3-y-o: tall gelding: second foal: dam unraced half-sister to useful hurdler/chaser up to 21f Dawn Leader: well held in bumper on debut: probably flattered only completed start over hurdles. *R. Dickin* **h103 ? F–**

TUDOR KING (IRE) 11 br.g. Orchestra – Jane Bond (Good Bond) [2004/5 c82x, h–§: c22m^{2} c21g^{4} c20g^{5} c26g* 22g* c24d^{3} c25g^{2} c24m^{4} Nov 11] rather sparely-made gelding: poor handicap hurdler/modest chaser: made all in small fields at Plumpton (chase) and Exeter (novice hurdle) within 3 days in October: stays 3¼m: acts on soft and firm going: races prominently: formerly poor jumper/inconsistent. *J. S. King* **c88 h71**

TUDOR STAR 10 b.g. Comme L'Etoile – Tudor Lilly (Domitor (USA)) [2004/5 16v^{pu} 21d^{pu} 20s^{pu} 20d^{pu} Apr 22] sturdy gelding: first foal: dam unraced: no sign of ability. *R. Rowe* **h–**

TUESDAY CLUB (IRE) 6 ch.g. Old Vic – Asfreeasthewind (IRE) (Moscow Society (USA)) [2004/5 F17g^{5} F16s Jan 15] €12,000 4-y-o: workmanlike gelding: first foal: dam, in frame in bumpers, half-sister to useful chaser up to 21f Pete The Parson: modest form on first of 2 starts in bumpers. *J. A. B. Old* **F77**

TUESDAY'S CHILD 6 b.g. Un Desperado (FR) – Amazing Silks (Furry Glen) [2004/5 F16g 17d^{pu} Dec 3] rather unfurnished gelding: fourth foal: half-brother to bumper winner Itsdedfast (by Lashkari): dam winning 2m hurdler: no form in bumper or novice hurdle. *Miss H. C. Knight* **h– F–**

TULACH ARD (IRE) 10 b.g. Erdelistan (FR) – Noon Hunting (Green Shoon) [2004/5 20s^{pu} 23v^{pu} Dec 30] quite good-topped gelding: fair hurdler in 2002/3: no form in handicaps on return: stays 2½m: acts on soft going. *A. Parker* **c– h–**

TULIPA (POL) 6 ch.m. Jape (USA) – Truly Best (POL) (Omen (POL)) [2004/5 16d* 16m* 16d* 17d* 16g 16s^{5} Dec 4] compact mare: successful 6 times from 7f to 13f on Flat (usually blinkered) in Poland for D. Kaluba: fairly useful hurdler: easily won mares intermediate at Perth and novices there, at Worcester (beat Nicely Presented 8 lengths) and Market Rasen between May and July: creditable tenth to Cloone River in Galway Hurdle (Handicap): raced around 2m. *T. R. George* **h119**

TULLIMOSS (IRE) 10 b.m. Husyan (USA) – Ballynattin Moss (Le Moss) [2004/5 h75: 16d 20v^{4} 24m 16d 20s^{5} Apr 22] poor maiden hurdler: stays 2¾m: acts on good to firm and heavy going: has had tongue tied. *J. N. R. Billinge* **h72**

TUMBLEWEED GLEN (IRE) 9 ch.g. Mukaddamah (USA) – Mistic Glen (IRE) (Mister Majestic) [2004/5 c–, h–x: c16d^{5} c20g^{pu} c16s^{5} c16s c25v^{pu} Feb 13] angular gelding: long-standing maiden hurdler/chaser: tried blinkered. *P. Kelsall* **c– h– x**

TUMBLING DICE (IRE) 6 b.g. King's Theatre (IRE) – Eva Fay (IRE) (Fayruz) [2004/5 h110: 20g 16s^{F} 22v^{4} 20d* 20s* 21g^{2} 19v^{F} 21g^{3} 24s^{3} Apr 7] useful-looking gelding: useful hurdler: won handicaps at Punchestown in November and December: good efforts all starts after, third to Idole First in Coral Cup at Cheltenham and to Monet's Garden in Grade 2 at Aintree: stays 3m: raced mainly on good going or softer (acts on heavy): genuine and consistent. *T. J. Taaffe, Ireland* **h143**

TUNES OF GLORY (IRE) 9 b.g. Symboli Heights (FR) – Coxtown Queen (IRE) (Corvaro (USA)) [2004/5 h112, F93: 17g 16g 20s 16g^{4} c16v^{5} c17g* c22g^{6} c17s^{4} Apr 16] good-topped gelding: modest handicap hurdler: similar form over fences, won maiden at Bangor in March: raced mainly at 2m: probably acts on any going: tried tongue tied: has bled from nose. *D. McCain* **c98 h91**

TUPELOV (IRE) 10 b.g. Moscow Society (USA) – Ballela Maid (Boreen (FR)) [2004/5 c20s^{pu} Mar 11] ex-Irish gelding: maiden jumper. *D. S. Dennis* **c– h–**

TUPPENNY CODY (IRE) 6 b.g. Muroto – Alzena (Persian Bold) [2004/5 h120, F105: 16m 16s* 16v^{6} Jan 9] fairly useful hurdler: won minor event at Listowel in September by 10 lengths from Sue N Win: good sixth to Essex in Pierse Hurdle at Leopardstown: raced at 2m: acts on heavy going (won bumper on firm): front runner. *Anthony Mullins, Ireland* **h124**

TURAATH (IRE) 9 b.g. Sadler's Wells (USA) – Diamond Field (USA) (Mr Prospector (USA)) [2004/5 h103§: 20d^{4} 23d^{5} 19m 21d^{2} 20s^{4} 21d 24d* 26s 24d* Mar 3] stocky gelding: fair hurdler: back to best when winning handicaps at Taunton in January and Ludlow in March: stays 3m: acts on good to firm and heavy going: often wears headgear (all wins without): tried tongue tied: not an easy ride and is unreliable. *A. J. Deakin* **h109 §**

TURBO (IRE) 6 b.g. Piccolo – By Arrangement (IRE) (Bold Arrangement) [2004/5 h105: 16g^4 16d 16s^{pu} Jan 22] close-coupled gelding: useful on Flat (stays 1½m): fair form over hurdles: will prove best with emphasis on speed at 2m: in headgear last 5 starts: tongue tied in 2004/5: sold to join T. Mills £21,000 Ascot February Sales. *J. A. Geake* **h106**

TURGEONEV (FR) 10 gr.g. Turgeon (USA) – County Kerry (FR) (Comrade In Arms) [2004/5 c154, h–: 16m^2 c25s^F 20s c16v^4 c16s^6 c20d c21d c16g^4 Apr 16] tall gelding: winning hurdler: smart handicap chaser in 2003/4, below best in 2004/5: barely stays 25f: acts on any going: effective held up or ridden prominently: usually sound jumper. *T. D. Easterby* **c131 h116**

TURKAMA (FR) 8 gr.g. Turgeon (USA) – Whampoa (FR) (Wittgenstein (USA)) [2004/5 16s 22s^{pu} c20d^F c19s^F c19v c21s Mar 23] rather leggy gelding: half-brother to winning hurdlers around 2m Nice Whisky (by Nice Havrais) and Subtil Roa (by Subotica) and winning 2½m chaser Turkoa (by Turgeon): dam maiden: successful 4 times up to 1½m on Flat: fairly useful hurdler/chaser at best: off 18 months, no show in handicap hurdles or chase for G. A. Swinbank before rejoining former trainer after third start: stays 21f: raced on good ground or softer (acts on heavy). *M. Rolland, France* **c113 h–**

TURKS AND CAICOS (IRE) 4 b. or br.g. Turtle Island (IRE) – Need You Badly (Robellino (USA)) [2004/5 16m Dec 1] sturdy gelding: modest on Flat (stays 11f): well held in juvenile on hurdling debut. *P. C. Haslam* **h–**

TURKU 7 b.g. Polar Falcon (USA) – Princess Zepoli (Persepolis (FR)) [2004/5 18s 16d 17s Jan 20] modest on Flat (stays 1m), had several trainers at 5 yrs, sold out of D. Shaw's stable £900 Ascot December (2003) Sales: no form over hurdles. *H. J. Manners* **h–**

TURNIUM (FR) 10 b. or br.g. Turgeon (USA) – Royal Mia (FR) (Kashmir II) [2004/5 c18s^4 18s* 18d^2 16v c28s^{pu} 16g Mar 15] workmanlike ex-French gelding: 11f to 2m winner on Flat: useful chaser/fairly useful hurdler at best in France: successful 7 times at Auteuil, including in claiming hurdle in May: claimed from A. Chaille-Chaille €22,000 third start: off 7 months, no form in good company in Britain: stays 3m: acts on heavy ground: usually blinkered/visored. *M. Scudamore* **c122 h127**

TURNNOCARD (IRE) 6 b.m. Air Display (USA) – Night Blade (Fine Blade (USA)) [2004/5 F16v^5 20d Apr 20] good-topped mare: ninth foal: half-sister to winning 2¾m hurdler Night Thyne (by Good Thyne): dam unraced half-sister to useful hurdler up to 3m Gerry Doyle: won mares maiden Irish point in 2004: no show in bumper or maiden hurdle. *Ian Williams* **h– F–**

TURN OF PHRASE (IRE) 6 b.g. Cadeaux Genereux – Token Gesture (IRE) (Alzao (USA)) [2004/5 h108: 16f^4 20m^{pu} 21m^3 16m^4 19d^6 19d^6 16s^5 16s 20s^3 Apr 10] lengthy gelding: fair on Flat, won in September: fair handicap hurdler: stays easy 21f: acts on good to firm and soft going: usually blinkered/visored (not last 3 outings): ungenuine. *R. A. Fahey* **h106 §**

TURPIN GREEN (IRE) 6 b.g. Presenting – Coolshamrock (IRE) (Buckskin (FR)) [2004/5 16v* 16s* 16v^3 23s^3 20s* Apr 7] **h141**

Monet's Garden isn't the only exciting staying novice chase prospect for 2005/6 to be trained by Nicky Richards. Around three hours after Monet's Garden had put up a high-class performance winning the Liverpool Long Distance Hurdle, the opening event on the first day of Aintree's Grand National meeting, Richards sent out another big chasing type, the year-younger Turpin Green, to win the John Smith's Mersey Novices' Hurdle, capping a memorable day for the stable which also won the Anniversary Hurdle with Faasel. Turpin Green, on what was only his fifth appearance, showed himself a smart novice at Aintree and, given further opportunities, he could well go on and prove as good a hurdler as Monet's Garden. However, with his trainer of the opinion that his achievements over hurdles have been a bonus, it is almost certain that Turpin Green will be switched to fences in the next season, which should give Richards a particularly strong hand in the top staying novice events and a good chance to break his Cheltenham Festival duck with one or other in the Royal & SunAlliance Chase.

It wasn't until the end of October that Turpin Green first appeared on a racecourse, starting at 25/1 in a six-runner novice hurdle at Uttoxeter, evidently having not been showing anything to suggest that his first appearance would be a winning

John Smith's Mersey Novices' Hurdle, Aintree—Turpin Green completes a 364½/1 treble on a red-letter day for trainer Nicky Richards and jockey Tony Dobbin

one. Despite showing his inexperience under pressure, Turpin Green came through to lead at the last and pull four lengths clear. The following month Turpin Green started at 7/1 for a similar event at Aintree, a race which the betting suggested lay between Mount Clerigo, a smart bumper horse making his hurdling debut, and Rebel Rhythm, who had shown useful form in bumpers and made a winning start over hurdles earlier in November. Stepping up appreciably on his Uttoxeter form, Turpin Green won by three quarters of a length from Rebel Rhythm, the pair pulling well clear of Mount Clerigo, Turpin Green rallying gamely, though hanging right, after clipping the last. Turpin Green survived a stewards inquiry, though his rider Tony Dobbin picked up a one-day ban for careless riding. Far from fluent jumping was a major factor in Turpin Green's failing to show any further improvement in Grade 2 novice events at Haydock on his next two starts. On the second occasion, looking sure to benefit from the step up from two miles to three, he managed only third of five to Mephisto, beaten thirteen lengths. Turpin Green didn't look to have an obvious chance of turning the tables on Mephisto, even on terms 12 lb better, in the Mersey Novices' Hurdle, and he started at 14/1 in a nine-runner field, the betting dominated by Mephisto and the Royal & SunAlliance Hurdle fourth Pole Star. With Mephisto swallowing his tongue and Pole Star running a lacklustre race, the contest took less winning than could have been expected, though Turpin Green still deserves plenty of credit for such a convincing success. With little pressure on his jumping, he made no notable errors and battled on well after nosing ahead three out, well on top at the line where he had six lengths to spare over second-placed My Way de Solzen.

Turpin Green (IRE) (b.g. 1999)	Presenting (br 1992)	Mtoto (b 1983)	Busted
			Amazer
		D'Azy (b 1984)	Persian Bold
			Belle Viking
	Coolshamrock (IRE) (b 1992)	Buckskin (b 1973)	Yelapa
			Bete A Bon Dieu
		Arctic Conditions (b 1978)	Lucifer
			Arctic Brilliance

Turpin Green has been raced only on soft or heavy going so far and was staying on so well at the end of the two-and-a-half-mile Mersey Hurdle that it is hard to believe he won't prove at least as effective returned to three miles. There is certainly plenty of stamina in his pedigree. He is by the Derby third Presenting, also the sire of Our Ben and War of Attrition, out of a winning pointer, from the family of the useful but unreliable staying chaser Grange Brake. Turpin Green, bought for €35,000 as an unraced four-year-old, is the first foal of Coolshamrock, who was that age when she won a maiden point in Ireland. Coolshamrock's three-year-old sister to Turpin Green fetched €90,000 at the Derby Sale in June. The next dam Arctic Conditions was also four when she won a point, a bumper, a maiden hurdle and a novice handicap hurdle in Ireland. She went on to show useful form over hurdles and won two more races, including a twenty-one furlong handicap. Arctic Conditions, a half sister to Grange Brake, is out Arctic Brilliance, herself a half sister to the useful hurdler/chaser Bahia Dorada and a winner over both hurdles and fences in Ireland. Turpin Green wasn't the only member of his family to win at Aintree. The winner of the concluding Grade 2 bumper The Cool Guy is out of a half-sister to Coolshamrock. *N. G. Richards*

TURTLE LOVE (IRE) 6 b.m. Turtle Island (IRE) – A Little Loving (He Loves Me) [2004/5 h–: 19g Mar 4] maiden hurdler: tried to refuse only start in blinkers: sold 900 gns Doncaster March Sales. *B. D. Leavy* **h–**

TURTLE RECALL (IRE) 6 b.g. Turtle Island (IRE) – Nora Yo Ya (Ahonoora) [2004/5 h–: 16gpu 16d5 16vpu Feb 2] workmanlike gelding: little solid form over hurdles: wore cheekpieces last 2 outings. *F. Jordan* **h64**

TURTLE SOUP (IRE) 9 b.g. Turtle Island (IRE) – Lisa's Favourite (Gorytus (USA)) [2004/5 h133: 20s 20s3 20v* 20v4 20d4 24dur Apr 8] medium-sized gelding: useful handicap hurdler: won at Haydock in December by 3 lengths from Very Optimistic: still travelling well when badly hampered and unseated 4 out in listed event at Aintree final start: effective at 2½m to 3m: acts on heavy going: races prominently: consistent. *T. R. George* **h138**

TUSCAN TREATY 5 b.m. Brief Truce (USA) – Fiorenz (USA) (Chromite (USA)) [2004/5 16g 16d 16g Mar 28] angular mare: modest on Flat (stays 7f): running best race over hurdles when going lame on home turn in maiden at Plumpton final start. *T. T. Clement* **h83**

TUSCANY BOY (IRE) 5 ch.g. Up And At 'em – Belle Savenay (Coquelin (USA)) [2004/5 18m3 16f 22mpu 18g6 20s 16d 16s6 Apr 21] half-brother to fair chaser Water Font (by Lafontaine), stayed 27f: maiden on Flat: poor form over hurdles: left T. Doyle after first outing: tried blinkered. *C. A. McBratney, Ireland* **h68**

TUSK 5 ch.g. Fleetwood (IRE) – Farmer's Pet (Sharrood (USA)) [2004/5 h121: 16d Nov 6] strong, well-made gelding: fairly useful juvenile hurdler in 2003/4: stiff task, jumped poorly when well held in Grade 2 limited handicap at Wincanton only start in 2004/5: raced around 2m on good going or softer. *Miss H. C. Knight* **h–**

TUXEDO JUNCTION (NZ) 10 br.g. Little Brown Jug (NZ) – Just Kay (NZ) (St Puckle) [2004/5 c88, h–: 22m5 Jun 27] rather leggy gelding: modest handicap chaser: maiden hurdler: stays 21f: acts on soft and good to firm going. *Evan Williams* **c– h73**

TWEED 8 ch.g. Barathea (IRE) – In Perpetuity (Great Nephew) [2004/5 20mpu 21g3 Oct 6] sturdy gelding: maiden hurdler: lightly raced since 2001: tried in blinkers/cheekpieces: ungenuine. *C. Roberts* **h65 §**

TWELI 8 b.g. Deploy – Flying Fantasy (Habitat) [2004/5 h73: 20m4 20gpu 20m Jul 21] lengthy, sparely-made gelding: poor maiden hurdler: stays 2½m: best form on good to firm going: usually wears headgear: tongue tied final start. *I. A. Wood* **h73**

TWENTY BUCKS 11 b.g. Buckley – Sweet N' Twenty (High Top) [2004/5 c92, h–: c17g^{2} Oct 4] workmanlike gelding: modest chaser: should stay 3m: probably acts on any going: prone to mistakes: sold £2,100 Ascot November Sales. *M. Madgwick* **c95 h–**

TWENTY DEGREES 7 ch.g. Beveled (USA) – Sweet N' Twenty (High Top) [2004/5 h106, F103: 16g^{2} 19s^{2} 20s^{2} 16d^{5} 18s^{4} 16d^{3} 16d 16g^{4} Mar 28] good-topped gelding: bumper winner: modest novice hurdler: should stay beyond 2½m: raced on good going or softer: blinkered last 4 starts: temperamental. *G. L. Moore* **h95 §**

TWENTY TO EIGHT 9 b.g. Faustus (USA) – Leilaway (Scallywag) [2004/5 c26v^{pu} c26v^{pu} c24v^{pu} c24d c24v^{6} c24d^{pu} Apr 22] workmanlike gelding: second foal: dam placed over hurdles: won maiden point in 2003: no sign of ability otherwise. *Mrs Tracey Barfoot-Saunt* **c–**

TWENTYTWOSILVER (IRE) 5 ro.g. Emarati (USA) – St Louis Lady (Absalom) [2004/5 h80: 17d^{pu} 16m 17g^{3} 17g^{3} 17d 16f^{3} 16m 16f^{2} 16g^{4} 17d^{6} Oct 28] leggy gelding: modest maiden hurdler: will prove best at 2m: acts on firm and soft going. *N. J. Hawke* **h86**

TWICE AS GOOD (IRE) 11 b.g. Good Thyne (USA) – Twice As Fluffy (Pollerton) [2004/5 c84, h–: 22g^{pu} c25m^{pu} c20g^{F} Oct 7] good-topped gelding: maiden hurdler/chaser: no sign of retaining ability in 2004/5: tried in cheekpieces. *Mrs N. S. Sharpe* **c– h–**

TWIDDEL TURN (DEN) 10 b.h. Lead On Time (USA) – Bint Naas (Lomond (USA)) [2004/5 16g* 16s^{2} 16d* 16s* 16s* 16s^{2} Oct 23] workmanlike horse: successful 12 times up to around 9f on Flat in Scandinavia: won 4 of 5 starts over hurdles at Ovrevoll in 2004/5, including in October: fairly useful form when 2 lengths second to eased Marcel in listed novice at Kempton later in month: raced at 2m: races prominently. *S. E. Lilja, Norway* **h128**

TWILIGHT DANCER (IRE) 7 b.m. Sri Pekan (USA) – Manhattan Sunset (USA) (El Gran Senor (USA)) [2004/5 c20s^{pu} c24d^{pu} Apr 22] maiden on Flat: fair pointer, successful in March: no form in hunter chases. *Miss H. E. Roberts* **c–**

TWISTED LOGIC (IRE) 12 b.g. Tremblant – Logical View (Mandalus) [2004/5 c124, h–: c24d 22s^{3} c23s^{6} c25d^{3} 24d c25v^{5} c30d c23v^{6} c25g* Apr 12] smallish, sturdy gelding: fairly useful handicap chaser: won at Exeter (last 6 wins there) by ¾ length from Headliner: modest maiden hurdler: stays 3¾m: acts on firm and soft going: blinkered once. *R. H. Alner* **c123 h–**

TWIST 'N SHOUT 8 ch.g. Never So Bold – Ravaro (Raga Navarro (ITY)) [2004/5 20d^{4} 16v* 16s 16s^{5} c17s^{2} c16v^{2} c16s* 16v c20g^{2} Mar 19] twice-raced in bumpers: fair hurdler: won maiden at Clonmel in October: better over fences: won maiden at Thurles in February by 4 lengths from Darby Wall: good second to John James in minor event at Tramore final start: stays 2½m: raced on good going or softer (acts on heavy): tried tongue tied. *C. Roche, Ireland* **c116 h107**

TWIST N TURN 5 b.m. Sir Harry Lewis (USA) – Gaye Gordon (Scottish Reel) [2004/5 F17d^{5} 16d^{6} 16v^{pu} 21v^{6} 19d 21g^{5} 17m^{4} Apr 23] rather leggy mare: first foal: dam twice-raced: well held in bumper on debut: bad maiden hurdler. *D. McCain* **h57 F–**

TWIST OF FAITH (IRE) 6 b.g. Fresh Breeze (USA) – Merry And Bright (Beau Chapeau) [2004/5 h–, F–: c25s^{pu} c20s^{2} Mar 6] rangy gelding: winning pointer: tongue tied, 22 lengths second of 4 finishers in novice chase at Kempton: sold 12,000 gns Doncaster May Sales. *N. J. Henderson* **c98 ? h–**

TWO A PENNY 5 b.m. Classic Cliche (IRE) – Pennypot Bay (Suave Dancer (USA)) [2004/5 F–: F18g 17g^{pu} Jul 18] sturdy mare: no form in bumpers and novice hurdle: fourth in point in April. *R. H. York* **h– F–**

TWOEE 5 b.m. El Conquistador – Lady Noso (Teenoso (USA)) [2004/5 F16s 22g^{pu} Apr 10] sturdy mare: second foal: dam, modest novice hurdler, out of half-sister to very smart staying chaser Special Cargo: no show in bumper or mares novice hurdle. *R. J. King* **h– F–**

TWO EWE 6 b.g. Endoli (USA) – Kelsey Lady (Pongee) [2004/5 h–: 20d May 12] no sign of ability. *Mrs H. O. Graham* **h–**

TWO HUGE 7 gr.g. Norton Challenger – Rainy Miss (IRE) (Cheval) [2004/5 h–: 24s 24d^{6} Nov 19] workmanlike gelding: well held in novice hurdles. *N. A. Twiston-Davies* **h–**

TWO OF CLUBS 4 b.g. First Trump – Sulaka (Owington) [2004/5 16g^{pu} 17g^{pu} 17s^{3} 17s^{3} 17g 17s^{2} 17g^{5} Apr 15] fair on Flat (stays 7f), successful in October: modest juvenile **h89**

hurdler: left P. Haslam after second start: raced around 2m: acts on soft going: wore cheekpieces 3 of last 4 starts. *Miss S. J. Wilton*

TWO OF DIAMONDS 11 b.g. Mr Fluorocarbon – Shelleys Rocky Gem (Kemal (FR)) [2004/5 c–: c16v^{pu} c21m May 19] temperamental pointer: no form in hunter chases. *Miss R. Williams* **c–**

TWO RIVERS (IRE) 6 b.g. Over The River (FR) – Clarin River (IRE) (Mandalus) [2004/5 F–: F16s 19s^{pu} Nov 30] sturdy gelding: no form in bumpers or novice hurdle: sold 2,800 gns Doncaster January Sales. *Jennie Candlish* **h– F–**

TWO STEPS TO GO (USA) 6 b.g. Rhythm (USA) – Lyonushka (CAN) (Private Account (USA)) [2004/5 16m 16d 17m 17g^{5} 17m^{6} 17g^{6} 17m^{2} 17g 17v Oct 17] close-coupled gelding: poor and temperamental on Flat (stays 11f): poor maiden hurdler: raced around 2m: acts on good to firm going: blinkered last 4 starts. *E. A. Elliott* **h68**

TWO TEARS 11 gr.g. Silver Owl – Vomero (NZ) (Church Parade) [2004/5 c26d^{pu} c21d^{ur} c24g c21s^{4} c23d^{F} 22v^{4} Feb 13] leggy gelding: maiden hurdler: fair chaser in 2002/3: off over 20 months, little sign of retaining ability. *N. J. Hawke* **c– h–**

TWOTENSFORAFIVE 12 b.g. Arctic Lord – Sister of Gold (The Parson) [2004/5 c85, h73: c21g^{3} c21g* c21d^{pu} Mar 24] angular gelding: maiden hurdler: modest handicap chaser: won at Uttoxeter in July: stays 3m: acts on good to firm and heavy going: tried blinkered: sometimes let down by jumping. *S. C. Burrough* **c87 h–**

TWO TONYS SHAM (IRE) 6 b.g. Fourstars Allstar (USA) – Millies Girl (IRE) (Millfontaine) [2004/5 F17d^{6} 17d^{3} Oct 27] second foal: dam bumper winner: won maiden on last of 5 starts in Irish points in 2004: bought 21,000 gns Doncaster May Sales: not knocked about in bumper: close third to Dark Ben in novice at Sedgefield on hurdling debut, keeping on strongly late: will stay further: looked likely to improve, but wasn't seen out again. *H. P. Hogarth* **h97 + F–**

TYCOON TIM 6 b.g. Alflora (IRE) – Padykin (Bustino) [2004/5 F17v F16s c23m^{pu} Apr 10] rangy, useful-looking gelding: half-brother to 3 winners, including fairly useful hurdler up to 23f Silken Thyne (by Good Thyne) and fairly useful staying chaser Committed Schedule (by Saxon Farm): dam winning staying hurdler: no form in 2 bumpers or maiden chase. *C. C. Bealby* **c– F–**

TYHOLLAND (IRE) 6 br.g. Up And At 'em – Spanish Gypsy (IRE) (Reference Point) [2004/5 16v 20d^{3} 20m^{2} 20g^{4} 22d^{3} 21d 18d Nov 28] leggy gelding: half-brother to 17f hurdle winner in Italy by Namaqualand: modest on Flat (stays 2m): modest maiden hurdler: stays 2¾m: acts on soft and good to firm going: tried in cheekpieces. *R. J. Osborne, Ireland* **h95**

TYNDARIUS (IRE) 14 b.g. Mandalus – Lady Rerico (Pamroy) [2004/5 c114, h–: c28g^{2} c25g^{6} c24d^{2} c25s* c24d^{2} c25d^{4} c26g^{3} c25v^{pu} c30d c25s^{3} Mar 22] strong gelding: fair handicap chaser: left J. Hetherton after third start: only runner to complete without mishap when winning at Aintree in October: went with little zest after, left R. Thompson after eighth start: stays 3½m: acts on heavy going: blinkered once: usually held up: one to treat with caution. *I. W. McInnes* **c114 § h–**

TYNEDALE (IRE) 6 b.g. Good Thyne (USA) – Book of Rules (IRE) (Phardante (FR)) [2004/5 F92: 20d* 24d^{2} 23s^{3} 20v^{2} 24s^{3} 22s^{4} 24s^{2} Apr 10] quite good-topped gelding: fair novice hurdler: won at Newcastle in November: stays 3m: acts on heavy going (bumper form on good to firm): blinkered final start: jumps none too fluently: lazy. *Mrs A. Hamilton* **h111**

TYRRELLSPASS (IRE) 8 b.g. Alzao (USA) – Alpine Chime (IRE) (Tirol) [2004/5 h66: 17d Apr 29] leggy gelding: little form over hurdles: raced around 2m: tongue tied last 4 starts. *J. D. Frost* **h–**

TYSOU (FR) 8 b.g. Ajdayt (USA) – Pretty Point (Crystal Glitters (USA)) [2004/5 c131, h–: 16m c16d^{2} c16d^{3} c16g^{4} Mar 18] smallish, angular gelding: winning hurdler: useful handicap chaser: ran well when third to Armaturk at Cheltenham and fourth to Fota Island in Grand Annual there 4 months later: best around 2m: acts on good to firm and good to soft going, seemingly not on softer: races freely: held up. *N. J. Henderson* **c140 h–**

TYUP POMPEY (IRE) 4 ch.g. Docksider (USA) – Cindy's Baby (Bairn (USA)) [2004/5 16d^{6} 16s 17s 17m^{4} 19g^{2} Apr 15] half-brother to smart hurdler Genghis (by Persian Bold), stays 2½m: modest form only start at 2 yrs for B. Smart, well held in 3 maidens on Flat in 2004, sold out of D. Elsworth's stable £1,900 Ascot November Sales: poor maiden hurdler: seemingly stays 19f. *Miss J. S. Davis* **h74**

U

ULAAN BAATAR (IRE) 8 b. or br.g. Jackson's Drift (USA) – Leinster Lady (IRE) (Lord Chancellor (USA)) [2004/5 h106p, F105: 20m c16v* c17v* c16v^2 c16g c17s^2 Mar 29] **c149 h–**

A broken leg on the gallops towards the end of April brought an untimely end to Ulaan Baatar. He was being prepared for the Swordlestown Cup at Punchestown, and would not have had to improve much on his best form to have gone very close in that event. Ulaan Baatar already had a Grade 1 novice chase success to his name, having landed the Baileys Arkle Challenge Cup at Leopardstown in January. What was all the more notable about that success was that it took place just eight days after Ulaan Baatar had made his chasing debut. Although he had won a seventeen-runner maiden impressively at Punchestown, beating Kahuna eleven lengths and showing useful form, Ulaan Baatar still looked to be flying a bit high in a strong renewal of the Arkle, one of Ireland's top novice chases. The favourite Foreman had shown smart form when chasing home Kauto Star on his chasing debut and, along with the promising Scarthy Lad and Ned Kelly, was a markedly superior hurdler to Ulaan Baatar. So, too, was Ulaan Baatar's stable-companion Strike Back, the mount of stable jockey Robbie Power. Barry Geraghty, who had ridden Ulaan Baatar previously, chose to partner the better fancied Sir OJ. They were all upstaged, however, as Ulaan Baatar coped really well with the testing conditions and, jumping soundly under a patient ride, led at the last and soon went clear when shaken up to win by nine lengths from Foreman. It was one of the best novice chase performances either side of the Irish Sea to that point.

Ulaan Baatar ran three more times but showed form on a par with his Leopardstown success only once. He was found to be suffering from an infection when beaten twenty lengths by Watson Lake in the Flyingbolt at Navan in February and failed to jump at all fluently on much less soft ground when beaten over thirty lengths by Contraband in the Arkle at Cheltenham. Only in the Dan Moore Memorial Handicap at Fairyhouse did Ulaan Baatar show his true merit, going down by half a length to Ground Ball, who was given an inspired ride by Tony McCoy. Ulaan

Baileys Arkle Perpetual Challenge Cup Novices' Chase, Leopardstown—the ill-fated Ulaan Baatar swoops to beat Foreman (hoops), Ned Kelly (almost hidden) and stable-companion Strike Back

Baatar should still almost certainly have won, still on the bridle but nine lengths down three out before managing to make up eight and a half of those lengths, still closing at the line.

Ulaan Baatar showed useful form in bumpers and fair form in three starts over hurdles. All three of his races over hurdles came at two and a half miles and he would have stayed beyond two and a half miles over fences. Ulaan Baatar's pedigree is one of the most obscure for a good jumper in quite a while. His sire Jackson's Drift, whose sole start came over six furlongs at four years, is a half-brother to a Grade 3 winner in the States and has had barely a dozen runners in Britain or Ireland. Only two of those, apart from Ulaan Baatar, have won, the hurdler Jacksons Gold and the ill-fated bumper winner Gentle Drifter. Ulaan Baatar's dam Leinster Lady was unraced, by another little-used sire, the unraced Lord Chancellor, whose only winner is the fairly useful chaser Larry's Lord, and the only foal of Koubana Belle, yet another not to race. The third dam Koubana, who won on the Flat in France, is a half-sister to the dam of the one-time fairly useful hurdler Tidjani.

Ulaan Baatar (IRE) (b. or br.g. 1997)	Jackson's Drift (USA) (b 1986)	Slew O'Gold (b 1980)	Seattle Slew
			Alluvial
		Vain Gold (b 1979)	Mr Prospector
			Chancy Dance
	Leinster Lady (IRE) (b 1990)	Lord Chancellor (ch 1984)	Alydar
			Woodstream
		Koubana Belle (br 1984)	Saher
			Koubana

Strangely, Ulaan Baatar wasn't the only good jumper named after the capital of Mongolia whose career ended in untimely fashion in the latest season. The veteran French chaser Urga, who was twice in the frame in the Grand Steeple-Chase de Paris, fractured a shoulder when falling over hurdles at Auteuil in the autumn. Urga was the original name of Ulaan Baatar (or Ulan Bator) until it became the capital of the newly-founded People's Republic of Mongolia in 1924. Ulaan Baatar in Mongolian means red hero. *Mrs J. Harrington, Ireland*

ULTIMATE LIMIT 5 b.g. Bonny Scot (IRE) – Second Call (Kind of Hush) [2004/5 F18f⁴ 17s 20sF 20s Mar 9] well-made ex-Irish gelding: third foal: half-brother to winning 2m hurdler Alphacall (by Forzando) and 5f winner General Smith (by Greensmith): dam fairly useful hurdler/chaser up to 2½m, half-sister to smart hunter chaser Kerry Orchid: third in 4-y-o 2½m maiden Irish point in 2004: fair form in 2 bumpers, left G. Hourigan after fourth at Limerick in May: no form on soft ground over hurdles: bumper form on good/firm going. *A. Ennis* **h– F89**

ULUNDI 10 b.g. Rainbow Quest (USA) – Flit (USA) (Lyphard (USA)) [2004/5 h–: c17g³ Aug 26] good-topped gelding: very smart on Flat/useful hurdler at best: very lightly raced since 2001: jumped soundly but only modest form when third in maiden on chasing debut: best at sharp 2m: acted on good to firm going: reportedly retired. *P. R. Webber* **c92 h–**

ULUSABA 9 b.g. Alflora (IRE) – Mighty Fly (Comedy Star (USA)) [2004/5 c99, h–: c21mpu c20d c20g* c23d* c23g² c24d* c24d³ c24d³ c24g Mar 16] neat gelding: fairly useful handicap chaser: won at Leicester (twice) in November and Newbury (beat Juveigneur a neck) in December: let down by jumping in valuable amateur event at Cheltenham final start: stays 3m: acts on soft and good to firm going (no form on heavy): usually wears headgear: has had tongue tied: patiently ridden. *Ferdy Murphy* **c117 h–**

UN AUTRE ESPERE 6 b.g. Golden Heights – Drummer's Dream (IRE) (Drumalis) [2004/5 h–: 16g 16g 16g 16gur 17vpu Nov 26] of little account: left T. Wall after first outing. *M. Wellings* **h–**

UNCLE ADA (IRE) 10 ch.g. Phardante (FR) – Park Belle (IRE) (Strong Gale) [2004/5 c24gpu c23s⁶ c24gpu Mar 3] modest pointer, successful twice in 2004: blinkered, no show in 3 maiden chases. *D. J. Minty* **c–**

UNCLE AL (IRE) 6 br.g. Allegoric (USA) – Aunty Rosie (IRE) (Roselier (FR)) [2004/5 16d⁶ 16d Apr 20] smallish gelding: second foal: dam unraced, from family of top-class hunter chasers Animahron and No Other Way and smart hurdler up to 25f Cash Is King: better effort in novice hurdles when sixth at Wincanton on debut: will be suited by further than 2m. *K. Bishop* **h91**

UNCLE BATTY 5 b.g. Bob Back (USA) – Aunt Sadie (Pursuit of Love) [2004/5 F75: 20m^{ur} 16g^{6} 16f^{6} Sep 5] smallish gelding: modest form in bumpers: little show over hurdles. *G. J. Smith* **h–**

UNCLE JOHN 4 b.g. Atraf – Bit O' May (Mummy's Pet) [2004/5 17s^{pu} Nov 18] fair on Flat (stays 1¾m): no show in juvenile on hurdling debut. *S. Kirk* **h–**

UNCLE MAX (IRE) 5 b.g. Victory Note (USA) – Sunset Park (IRE) (Red Sunset) [2004/5 h98: 20d 19m^{pu} 16m^{3} 17m* 16g^{4} 20m* 22g^{4} 22g 19m^{3} Sep 8] leggy, close-coupled gelding: modest hurdler: won seller at Hereford in June and handicap at Worcester in July: stays 2½m: acts on good to firm and good to soft going: blinkered once. *N. A. Twiston-Davies* **h95**

UNCLE MICK (IRE) 10 b.g. Ikdam – Kandy Kate (Pry) [2004/5 c116, h–: c25g^{5} c26g^{2} c32m c26g^{F} c23m^{2} c26d^{3} c23g^{2} c26m^{4} c26m^{3} c21f^{5} c24g^{6} c24d^{6} c27m^{3} c25d^{6} Nov 29] medium-sized gelding: fair handicap chaser: stays 4m: acts on any going: tried visored/blinkered: has had tongue tied: sketchy jumper. *C. L. Tizzard* **c109 x h–**

UNCLE WALLACE 9 b.g. Neltino – Auntie Dot (Hallodri (ATA)) [2004/5 c20s^{pu} c16s* c24d^{4} c16v^{4} c20s* c21d^{6} Mar 10] lengthy, useful-looking gelding: fair chaser: won handicaps at Leicester (novice) in December and Kempton (4-runner event) in February: stays 21f: acts on soft going (bumper form on good to firm). *P. R. Webber* **c110 h–**

UNDENIABLE 7 b.g. Unfuwain (USA) – Shefoog (Kefaah (USA)) [2004/5 h115: c23g^{2} c21m* c20m^{2} c21m* c24g^{5} c20v^{4} c25s^{3} c22s^{5} c19g^{2} c21d* c20d^{5} Apr 9] strong, workmanlike gelding: fairly useful handicap hurdler: fair chaser: won novices at Uttoxeter in June and Sedgefield in August and handicap at Uttoxeter in March: stays 3m: has won on soft going, best form under less testing conditions: tried tongue tied. *Mrs S. J. Smith* **c112 h–**

UNDERLEY PARK (IRE) 11 ch.g. Aristocracy – Even Bunny VII (Damsire Unregistered) [2004/5 c104d, h77: c26d^{pu} May 29] medium-sized gelding: poor maiden hurdler: winning chaser: well held in points in 2005: stays 3¼m: acts on good to firm and heavy going: tried in cheekpieces/blinkers: poor jumper. *R. Ford* **c– x h–**

UNDERWRITER (USA) 5 b.g. With Approval (CAN) – Night Risk (USA) (Wild Again (USA)) [2004/5 16g^{3} 19m* Apr 9] good-topped gelding: well held only start on Flat, sold out of J. Gosden's stable 13,000 gns Doncaster November (2003) Sales: modest form over hurdles: won maiden at Hereford by 5 lengths from Swifts Hill: not discredited in much stronger company behind Snoopy Loopy at Punchestown later in April: stays 19f. *Ferdy Murphy* **h99**

UNEVEN LINE 9 b.m. Jurado (USA) – Altovise (Black Minstrel) [2004/5 c76, h–: c25g^{3} c17v^{ur} c20v^{4} c20m c21v^{4} 24s^{5} Mar 10] winning pointer: poor maiden hurdler/chaser: stays 25f: tried in cheekpieces: often tongue tied. *Miss S. E. Forster* **c76 x h–**

UNGARETTI (GER) 8 b.g. Law Society (USA) – Urena (GER) (Dschingis Khan) [2004/5 c84, h94: c24s c24s^{6} c26d^{5} 25v 24d^{4} c25v^{pu} Jan 28] rangy gelding: handicap hurdler/chaser, form in 2004/5 only on fifth outing: stays 29f: acts on heavy going, possibly not on good to firm: tried blinkered/in cheekpieces: has had tongue tied: inconsistent. *Ian Williams* **c– § h89**

UNGARO (FR) 6 b.g. Epervier Bleu – Harpyes (FR) (Quart de Vin (FR)) [2004/5 F101: 17g^{4} 16s^{F} 20s^{2} 20s^{4} Apr 20] small gelding: bumper winner: modest novice hurdler: will stay beyond 2½m. *K. G. Reveley* **h90**

UNION DEUX (FR) 6 ch.g. Nikos – Sanhia (FR) (Sanhedrin (USA)) [2004/5 h80: 20d 23s* 24s* 23d^{3} 24d 24s^{F} 24v* Mar 20] unfurnished gelding: fair hurdler: won novice handicaps at Wetherby (conditional jockeys) in October and Carlisle in March, and minor event at Towcester in November: will stay beyond 3m: raced on going softer than good (acts on heavy). *Ferdy Murphy* **h101**

UNION WOOD (IRE) 12 ch.g. Un Desperado (FR) – Miss Leone (Milford) [2004/5 c16m^{3} c16g^{5} Jul 1] maiden hurdler: modest handicap chaser: should stay beyond 2¼m: acts on good to soft and good to firm going: usually tongue tied: has flashed tail/idled. *A. J. Martin, Ireland* **c85 h–**

UNITED (GER) 4 b.f. Desert King (IRE) – Una Kasala (GER) (Law Society (USA)) [2004/5 16s* 16d* Mar 14] **h135 p**

Triumph Hurdle winner Penzance wasn't the only leading four-year-old to end the campaign unbeaten. While Penzance made it four wins from four starts with a hard-fought success at the Cheltenham Festival in March, United took her unblemished record to three with a clear-cut victory in Ireland's top race for juveniles, the Grade 1 Colm McEvoy Auctioneers Champion Four Year Old Hurdle at Punchestown in April. United's win in Ireland was gained over a depleted field, also lacking Faasel, successful at Aintree since being runner-up to Penzance at Cheltenham, but it was achieved in most decisive fashion, and there is almost certainly better still to come from United in 2005/6. United provided her trainer Lucy Wadham with the biggest win of her career, better renowned, with a small string in one of Newmarket's few predominantly jumping-oriented yards, for a high strike-rate at the minor tracks.

Colm McEvoy Auctioneers Champion Four Year Old Hurdle, Punchestown— a disappointing field by usual standards, but British raider United is impressive in maintaining her unbeaten record over hurdles

With prize money less than for its counterparts at Cheltenham and Aintree, the Champion Four Year Old Hurdle attracted only seven runners. Another British-trained challenger Akilak dominated the market, going off odds-on after his third behind Penzance and Faasel in the Triumph. Strangely Brown, sixth at Cheltenham before finishing third behind Faasel in the Anniversary Hurdle at Aintree, was second favourite at 7/2, with United, the only other runner at single-figure odds, at 6/1. United had looked worthy of a step up in class when running out an easy winner of her first two starts over hurdles, a mares and fillies maiden at Huntingdon in February and a juvenile event at Stratford, on the eve of Cheltenham, in March, both over two miles. She never looked like relinquishing her unbeaten record at Punchestown, jumping fluently throughout and soon drawing clear after leading on the bridle after the second last, beating Strangely Brown by twelve lengths with her jockey Leighton Aspell easing up. A below-par Akilak finished half a length further away in third. 50/1-shot Eye Candy, in finishing fourth, gave the form a substandard look but United was value for at least another four lengths on the day.

United (GER) (b.f. 2001)	Desert King (IRE) (b 1994)	Danehill (b 1986)	Danzig
			Razyana
		Sabaah (ch 1988)	Nureyev
			Dish Dash
	Una Kasala (GER) (b 1995)	Law Society (br 1982)	Alleged
			Bold Bikini
		Una Primola (ch 1979)	Prince Ippi
			Unwetter

Mr R. B. Holt's "United"

United joins an increasing number of German-bred horses to have made a mark in the major European jumping arenas, among them Well Chief, Foreman, Registana and Seebald, as well as Fenix, placed in the last two runnings of the Imperial Cup for United's stable. United was bought privately off the Flat there after winning twice over ten and eleven furlongs from seven starts for Andreas Trybuhl. United's dam Una Kasala was also successful on the Flat in Germany, where she showed fairly useful form and managed fourth in the Henkel Rennen, the local version of the One Thousand Guineas. United is her first foal. Both grandam Una Primola and third dam Unwetter were successful on the Flat, the latter at listed level, though the most notable performer in the family is the smart middle-distance stayer Ungaro, three times a winner at Group 1 level, who is out of a half-sister to Una Primola. United's sire Desert King was trained by Aidan O'Brien in Ireland, where he won the Two Thousand Guineas and the Derby at the Curragh. Desert King made a limited impact at stud in Europe and after four years of shuttling to and from Australia (where he has been much more successful) he was moved to Japan in 2002, continuing to cover in the Southern Hemisphere as well. His best progeny on the Flat have been Gold Cup winner Mr Dinos, the smart Slovak-trained stayer Darsalam and the mare Makybe Diva, successful in successive runnings of the Melbourne Cup over two miles. As their victories suggest, Desert King has been quite a strong influence for stamina on the Flat, and on balance United should stay beyond two miles over hurdles, though she has shown no lack of speed in that sphere so far. She was due to tackle two miles and three furlongs in the Grand Course de Haies d'Ete des Quatres Ans at Auteuil in June, a race won in her absence by Strangely Brown, but she was ruled out by a hind-leg cut which had to be operated on. The injury will reportedly mean her reappearance is delayed until the New Year, when she will be trained for the Champion Hurdle. She has raced only on good to soft and soft ground so far. *Mrs L. Wadham*

UN JOUR A VASSY (FR) 10 b.g. Video Rock (FR) – Bayalika (FR) (Kashtan (FR)) [2004/5 c127, h–: c25g^{ur} c24d^{ur} c24g* c24d^{5} c31d^{3} c26d^{pu} c31d c25m^{pu} Apr 13] leggy gelding: fairly useful handicap chaser: won amateur event at Cheltenham (for second successive year) in October, beating Bright Approach 1½ lengths: creditable effort after only when third to Spot Thedifference in slowly-run cross-country event there in December: best around 3m on conventional tracks: acts on firm and good to soft going. *P. F. Nicholls* **c124 h–**

UNLEASH (USA) 6 ch.g. Benny The Dip (USA) – Lemhi Go (USA) (Lemhi Gold (USA)) [2004/5 h139p: 21m^{2} Apr 13] leggy gelding: useful handicap hurdler: off 12 months, ran well when 2½ lengths second to Lough Derg at Cheltenham: stays 21f: acts on good to firm going. *P. J. Hobbs* **h140**

UNLIMITED FREE (IRE) 11 ch.g. Ile de Chypre – Merry Madness (Raise You Ten) [2004/5 c103, h–: c24d^{5} c24g^{3} Apr 17] useful-looking gelding: winning hunter chaser: fair pointer, successful in March: stays 25f: acts on soft and firm going: prone to mistakes: seems best when able to dominate. *Mrs S. Alner* **c– h–**

UNSOLICITED 7 b.g. Contract Law (USA) – Islandreagh (IRE) (Knesset (USA)) [2004/5 F17s F17g 19d^{pu} 16g^{pu} Mar 16] first foal: dam no worthwhile form over jumps: no sign of ability. *O. Brennan* **h– F–**

UNTIDY DAUGHTER 6 b.m. Sabrehill (USA) – Branitska (Mummy's Pet) [2004/5 h97: c20d^{3} c21m^{pu} Jul 26] lengthy mare: fair handicap hurdler: similar form when 1½ lengths last of 3 finishers in novice at Market Rasen on chasing debut: broke down soon after start in maiden at Sedgefield: stays 21f: acts on soft and good to firm going: wears cheekpieces: hasn't always impressed with attitude. *B. Ellison* **c100 h–**

UNTWIST (IRE) 6 b.g. Un Desperado (FR) – Pearltwist (Roi Guillaume (FR)) [2004/5 F–: 20m^{5} 24d c25d^{pu} Apr 3] seemingly poor form when well-beaten fifth in novice hurdle at Worcester: looked temperamental when pulled up in novice on chasing debut. *D. R. Gandolfo* **c– h–**

UNUSUAL SUSPECT 6 b.g. Syrtos – Sally Maxwell (Roscoe Blake) [2004/5 F78: F16g 16s 20d^{2} 21s^{5} 19v 20d^{5} 25g* 22s^{pu} 27m^{2} Apr 21] good sort: modest form in bumpers for M. Pitman: similar standard over hurdles: won handicap at Plumpton in March: stays 27f: acts on soft and good to firm ground: blinkered last 4 starts. *G. L. Moore* **h95 F–**

UP AT MIDNIGHT 5 b.m. Midnight Legend – Uplift (Bustino) [2004/5 h88, F88: 16d^{3} 20s^{5} 21d* 16d^{6} Mar 5] compact mare: modest hurdler: won mares novice handicap at Kempton in February: should stay beyond 21f: acts on good to soft ground. *R. Rowe* **h97**

UPGRADE 11 b.g. Be My Guest (USA) – Cantanta (Top Ville) [2004/5 c151, h–: c16d^{4} c20d^{5} c16d^{5} c21d c20v^{5} c16g^{4} c16s^{F} Feb 19] lengthy gelding: smart chaser at best, generally below form in 2004/5: stays 21f: acts on firm and soft going: tried blinkered: often front runner: tends to idle: temperamental. *M. C. Pipe* **c147 § h–**

UPHAM LORD (IRE) 12 b.g. Lord Americo – Top O The Mall (Don) [2004/5 c103, h–: c21d^{F} c24d^{ur} c21m^{2} c21d^{4} c24g^{2} c20g^{3} c20m^{4} Apr 23] tall gelding: fair chaser: effective at 2½m to easy 3m: acts on good to firm and heavy going: effective blinkered or not: front runner/races prominently. *P. Beaumont* **c101 h–**

UP IN THE SKY (IRE) 5 gr.m. Cloudings (IRE) – Littledrunkgirl (Carlingford Castle) [2004/5 F16g F17d Mar 26] leggy mare: seventh foal: half-sister to winning pointer by Gildoran: dam, winning pointer, half-sister to dam of top-class 2m to 3m chaser One Man: well held in bumpers. *Mrs R. L. Elliot* **F–**

UPRIGHT IMA 6 b.m. Perpendicular – Ima Delight (Idiot's Delight) [2004/5 h63, F–: 16g 20d^{2} 20s^{4} 24m^{4} Apr 10] lengthy, angular mare: poor maiden hurdler: stays 3m: acts on soft and good to firm going. *Mrs P. Sly* **h72**

UPSWING 8 b.g. Perpendicular – Moorfield Lady (Vicomte) [2004/5 c73p, h88: 16s 20d^{pu} 17d Dec 7] tall gelding: novice hurdler, little show in 2004/5: once-raced over fences: raced mainly around 2m: raced on good ground or softer: sold 3,500 gns (privately) Doncaster May Sales. *S. B. Bell* **c– h–**

UPTHEDALE (IRE) 4 b.g. General Monash (USA) – Pimpinella (IRE) (Reprimand) [2004/5 17d^{pu} Jul 17] sturdy gelding: poor maiden on Flat (stays 1½m): showed little in juvenile on hurdling debut. *J. R. Weymes* **h–**

UP THE GLEN (IRE) 11 b.g. Tale Quale – Etrenne (Happy New Year) [2004/5 c98, h93: c19g^{2} c20d* c20m* c21g^{pu} c20s^{F} c22s^{3} c20v^{pu} c20g^{5} c19s* c21g^{pu} Apr 14] angular gelding: modest hurdler: fair novice chaser: won at Wetherby (handicap) and Fontwell in May, and Chepstow (handicap) in March: effective around 2½m, barely stays 27f: acts on good to firm and heavy going: makes running/races prominently: bold jumper. *A. W. Carroll* **c102 h–**

UP THE PUB (IRE) 7 ch.g. Carroll House – Brave Ruby (Proverb) [2004/5 c24s^{5} 24d^{6} c20s^{3} c24v^{F4} c24g^{5} c26v^{3} c24v^{4} Feb 5] big, workmanlike gelding: sixth foal: dam winning pointer: runner-up in maiden point in 2004: well held in novice hurdle: modest novice chaser: stays 3m: acts on heavy going: room for improvement in jumping. *R. H. Alner* **c88 h–**

URBAN FREEWAY (IRE) 6 b. or br.g. Dr Devious (IRE) – Coupe d'Hebe (Ile de Bourbon (USA)) [2004/5 22g^{3} May 31] ex-Irish gelding: half-brother to several winners, including poor hurdler Pertemps Boycott (by Indian Ridge), stays 2½m: fair on Flat (stays 2m) in 2002 for K. Prendergast: first run since when third in maiden at Cartmel on hurdling debut: sold £5,800 Ascot July Sales. *C. J. Mann* **h81 +**

URBAN (IRE) 4 b.g. Second Empire (IRE) – Second Revolution (IRE) (On Your Mark) [2004/5 16v* 16v* 16v 16v 22v 16s 20s Apr 13] fairly useful on Flat (stays 1½m): successful on first 2 starts over hurdles, juveniles at Tralee (beat Young Elodie 11 lengths) in August and Listowel (by distance) in September: largely disappointing after: form only at 2m: raced on soft/heavy going. *Joseph Crowley, Ireland* **h111**

URBAN KNIGHT 4 br.g. Dracula (AUS) – Anhaar (Ela-Mana-Mou) [2004/5 16g 17d^{5} 17g^{4} 17s^{5} 19d^{pu} 16v 23g 16g Mar 18] smallish gelding: half-brother to several winners over jumps, including fairly useful hurdler Four Aces (by Forzando), stays 2¾m, and one-time fairly useful hurdler/chaser Son of Anshan (by Anshan), barely stays 3¾m: poor form in maidens at 2 yrs for J. Unett: little form over hurdles: sometimes visored. *M. J. Gingell* **h–**

URQUHARTS ETERNITY 10 b.m. Jendali (USA) – Welsh Fashion (Welsh Saint) [2004/5 20m^{pu} Oct 1] 500 4-y-o: fifth foal: dam unraced: no show in novice hurdle on belated debut. *I. McMath* **h–**

URSIS (FR) 4 b.g. Trempolino (USA) – Bold Virgin (USA) (Sadler's Wells (USA)) [2004/5 16d* Nov 24] fourth foal: dam maiden, out of half-sister to top-class middle-distance performer: successful 3 times from 9.5f (at 2 yrs) to 1½m on Flat in French Provinces for J. Boisnard: most encouraging hurdling debut when winning 23-runner **h117 P**

juvenile at Wetherby with plenty in hand by 5 lengths from Dhehdaah: looked a most exciting prospect. *Jonjo O'Neill*

USEYOURHEAD 4 b.f. Riverhead (USA) – Give Me An Answer (True Song) [2004/5 F16s[6] Mar 31] sixth foal: half-sister to fair hurdler/fairly useful chaser Naunton Brook (by Alderbrook), stays 25f: dam, winning hurdler/twice-raced steeplechaser, stayed 21f: well held in bumper on debut. *C. W. Moore* **F–**

USK VALLEY (IRE) 10 b.g. Tenby – Penultimate (USA) (Roberto (USA)) [2004/5 c75, h85: c25m* c24m* c26g[ur] c23g[pu] c24g[4] c21d[ur] c24g[5] c24g[4] Apr 15] workmanlike gelding: winning hurdler: modest handicap chaser: won at Hereford in May and Huntingdon (intermediate) in June: stays 25f: acts on soft and good to firm going. *P. R. Chamings* **c90 h–**

V

VALANCE (IRE) 5 br.g. Bahhare (USA) – Glowlamp (IRE) (Glow (USA)) [2004/5 h108: 16g[2] 19g Nov 10] sturdy gelding: fairly useful on Flat (stays 2m): similar standard over hurdles, best effort when second to Calatagan in conditional jockeys handicap at Cheltenham: should stay beyond 2m. *C. R. Egerton* **h118**

VAL DU DON (FR) 5 b.g. Garde Royale – Vallee Normande (FR) (Bellypha) [2004/5 h126: c17g* c20s[2] c20s[F] c20s[ur] c16d[2] c22d[5] 25s[pu] Jan 15] leggy gelding: useful juvenile hurdler in 2003/4: won 4-y-o event at Meslay-du-Maine on chasing debut in August: mainly disappointing subsequently: left G. Macaire after fourth start: stays 2½m: raced on good ground or softer (acts on soft): sold 12,000 gns Doncaster May Sales. *N. J. Henderson* **c113 h–**

VALERUN (IRE) 9 b.g. Commanche Run – Glenreigh Moss (Le Moss) [2004/5 h99: 24d[pu] 20m[2] Jun 16] lengthy, rather sparely-made gelding: modest hurdler: stays 3m: acts on firm going (bumper winner on good to soft) sold £3,500 Ascot July Sales. *Miss E. C. Lavelle* **h99**

VALEUREUX 7 ch.g. Cadeaux Genereux – La Strada (Niniski (USA)) [2004/5 h111: 16m c16v Dec 15] tall gelding: modest on Flat (stays 1½m): fairly useful hurdler: mistakes and never dangerous in maiden (finished distressed) on chasing debut: stays easy 21f: acts on heavy and good to firm going: has worn crossed noseband. *J. Hetherton* **c– h–**

VALFONIC 7 b.g. Zafonic (USA) – Valbra (Dancing Brave (USA)) [2004/5 h–§: 20g[pu] 16m May 28] winning hurdler: no form since 2002: tried visored/in cheekpieces: often tongue tied: temperamental. *F. Jordan* **h– §**

VALIANT AIR (IRE) 4 b.g. Spectrum (IRE) – Shining Desert (IRE) (Green Desert (USA)) [2004/5 17g[pu] 16d[pu] Sep 22] poor maiden on Flat (stays 1½m): no show in 2 juvenile hurdles: tried blinkered. *J. R. Weymes* **h–**

VALLEY ERNE (IRE) 14 b.g. King's Ride – Erne Gold VII (Goldhill) [2004/5 c–, h–: c26g[4] 20d 24d 22g Jul 15] lengthy gelding: veteran hurdler/chaser: left N. Sanderson after first outing: tried in cheekpieces. *W. G. Young* **c76 h–**

VALLEY HENRY (IRE) 10 b.g. Step Together (USA) – Pineway VII (General Ironside) [2004/5 c162x, h–: c24d[6] c21g[pu] Mar 17] big, rangy gelding: formerly top-class chaser: generally well below best since 2002/3: stays 3¼m: acts on soft and good to firm going: tried blinkered: usually let down by jumping. *J. Howard Johnson* **c– x h–**

VALLEY RIDE (IRE) 5 b. or br.g. Glacial Storm (USA) – Royal Lucy (IRE) (King's Ride) [2004/5 F17g[2] F16d* 16s* 16g* Mar 14] quite good-topped gelding: fourth foal: brother to 2m winner Glacial Lucy: dam unraced, from family of top-class staying chaser Jodami: fairly useful form in 2 bumpers, winning at Ludlow in January by head from Charming Fellow: successful both starts over hurdles in March, in novices convincingly at Huntingdon and Plumpton, by 4 lengths from Alrafid at latter: raced around 2m: will improve further. *C. Tinkler* **h118 p F100**

VALLEY WARRIOR 8 b.g. Michelozzo (USA) – Mascara VII (Damsire Unregistered) [2004/5 h86, F–§: 23d[4] 22d 22d 21v[pu] 20s 22d[5] Apr 3] lengthy gelding: poor maiden hurdler: should stay beyond 2¾m: blinkered last 2 starts. *J. S. Smith* **h67**

VALLICA 6 b.m. Bishop of Cashel – Vallauris (Faustus (USA)) [2004/5 h92?: 16d[6] 16d 16v 20g[pu] 19s[6] 19v 16d 20d[5] 22g[3] 21g[6] 24d[6] Apr 20] workmanlike mare: poor maiden hurdler: probably stays 3m: raced mainly on good going or softer: tried in cheekpieces. *Mrs A. M. Thorpe* **h83**

VALUABLE (IRE) 8 b.m. Jurado (USA) – Can't Afford It (IRE) (Glow (USA)) [2004/5 h–: 16g* 16d 16g 16m4 17m3 17g 17m3 c16m6 17m4 16g3 17d c17v4 c16g c16d6 20m 17v 17d Apr 5] leggy mare: modest hurdler, won seller at Hexham in May: well held all 4 starts over fences (rider suspended for making insufficient effort on chasing debut): raced mainly around 2m: acts on good to firm going: wore cheekpieces final outing: has had tongue tied. *R. Johnson* **c71 h89**

VALUSO (IRE) 5 b.g. Luso – Regal Grove (IRE) (King's Ride) [2004/5 F16s 17dF 19g 21gpu Apr 1] fourth foal: dam, fairly useful hurdler, stayed 3m: no sign of ability. *Miss H. C. Knight* **h– F–**

VANBRUGH (FR) 5 ch.g. Starborough – Renovate (Generous (IRE)) [2004/5 21d 21g Mar 28] stocky gelding: fairly useful on all-weather, modest on turf on Flat (stays 2m): showed more temperament than ability in maiden hurdles: sold 19,000 gns Doncaster May Sales. *Miss D. A. McHale* **h– §**

VANDAL 5 b.g. Entrepreneur – Vax Star (Petong) [2004/5 h73: 16d6 17mpu 17mpu 17g6 17s 19vpu Dec 31] leggy gelding: little show over hurdles: sold out of Mrs L. Wadham's stable £2,100 Ascot August Sales after fourth start: tried blinkered/visored. *Mrs D. A. Butler* **h–**

VANDANTE (IRE) 9 b.g. Phardante (FR) – Vanessa's Princess (Laurence O) [2004/5 c25g5 c19d3 c22s2 c21d5 Dec 7] ex-Irish gelding: poor handicap chaser: stays 3m: acts on firm and soft going. *R. Lee* **c81**

VANDAS CHOICE (IRE) 7 b.g. Sadler's Wells (USA) – Morning Devotion (USA) (Affirmed (USA)) [2004/5 h117: 16gpu c16d2 c20d* c16s* c20v* c21v3 c25spu c20g5 Apr 16] stocky gelding: fairly useful handicap hurdler: fairly useful novice chaser: won at Carlisle in October and Ayr and Carlisle again (beat Provocative by head) in November: best effort when third to Jazz d'Estruval at Ayr: stays 21f: acts on good to firm and heavy going: sound jumper. *Miss Lucinda V. Russell* **c128 h–**

VANILLA MAN (IRE) 12 b.g. Buckskin (FR) – Ice Cream Girl (Laurence O) [2004/5 c25g c22g3 c21g c24f5 c22m c24d2 Apr 22] lengthy, sparely-made ex-Irish gelding: useful hurdler at one time: winning chaser in 2002/3: sold out of T. Mullins' stable 4,000 gns Doncaster August Sales: placed in points in 2005: second in hunter chase at Chepstow: stays 3m: acts on good to firm and heavy going. *Mrs D. C. Faulkner* **c103 h–**

VANILLA MOON 5 b.m. Emperor Jones (USA) – Daarat Alayaam (IRE) (Reference Point) [2004/5 17d4 16d4 16v4 16d4 Feb 19] close-coupled mare: poor maiden on Flat (stays easy 2m): poor novice hurdler: will stay further than 2m. *J. R. Jenkins* **h79**

VANISHING DANCER (SWI) 8 ch.g. Llandaff (USA) – Vanishing Prairie (USA) (Alysheba (USA)) [2004/5 c21spu c16s6 c19g2 c20d5 Mar 11] tall, leggy gelding: modest handicap hurdler in 2001/2: best effort over fences when second in handicap at Doncaster: stays 2½m: acts on heavy and good to firm going: tongue tied on reappearance: successful on Flat in April. *B. Ellison* **c90 h–**

VANORMIX (FR) 6 gr.g. Linamix (FR) – Vadsa Honor (FR) (Highest Honor (FR)) [2004/5 h117: 19d6 20m4 17s* 20d 21g c23vpu c19g5 Apr 12] sturdy gelding: fair hurdler: landed odds in seller (sold from M. Pipe 8,800 gns) at Hereford in November: little show after, including over fences: stays 21f: acts on heavy and good to firm going: usually visored (also wore eyecover at Hereford). *C. J. Gray* **c79 h110**

VANTAGE (IRE) 4 b.g. Marju (IRE) – Anna Comnena (IRE) (Shareef Dancer (USA)) [2004/5 16dpu Oct 5] half-brother to useful hurdler Sadlers Wings (by In The Wings), stays 21f, and fairly useful hurdler Analogy (by Bahhare), stays easy 3m: fairly useful on Flat (stays 1½m): second when breaking down badly home turn in juvenile at Stratford on hurdling debut. *N. P. Littmoden* **h?**

VA PENSIRO 5 b.g. Lugana Beach – Hopperetta (Rock Hopper) [2004/5 17d 16dpu Mar 3] lengthy gelding: well held in 3 races on Flat at 2/3 yrs for D. Haydn Jones: no form in 2 novice hurdles. *Evan Williams* **h–**

VARUNI (IRE) 4 b.f. Ali-Royal (IRE) – Sauvignon (IRE) (Alzao (USA)) [2004/5 18m5 16f6 16g Mar 14] modest on Flat (stays 13f): folded tamely all 3 starts in juvenile hurdles: sold £1,200 Ascot April Sales. *J. G. Portman* **h–**

VA VAVOOM (IRE) 7 b.g. Supreme Leader – Shalom Joy (Kemal (FR)) [2004/5 F17v2 16s 17d2 21d4 20s 24d3 24g Mar 18] well-made gelding: sixth foal: half-brother to winning pointer by Commanche Run: dam won bumper, up to 2m on Flat and at 2m over **h119 F96**

hurdles: won maiden Irish point in 2003: short-head second in maiden bumper at Market Rasen: fairly useful novice hurdler: best effort when fourth to Brewster in Grade 1 at Newbury: tongue tied, possibly amiss final start: stays 21f: raced on good going or softer. *N. A. Twiston-Davies*

VEDELLE (IRE) 6 b.g. Flemensfirth (USA) – Romitch (Le Bavard (FR)) [2004/5 F18s* Mar 28] fifth foal: dam third in point: successful in maiden point on debut in January: impressive when winning point-to-point bumper at Fairyhouse by 8 lengths from Vic Venturi: useful prospect. *Joseph Crowley, Ireland* **F103 p**

VELERO 6 b.m. Beveled (USA) – Willow Court (USA) (Little Current (USA)) [2004/5 F16f Jun 6] half-sister to 9f winner Media Messenger (by Hadeer) and several winners abroad: dam unplaced in USA: tailed off in bumper on debut. *P. D. Niven* **F–**

VELVET JONES 12 gr.g. Sharrood (USA) – Cradle of Love (USA) (Roberto (USA)) [2004/5 c16m⁵ Sep 1] of little account. *G. F. H. Charles-Jones* **c– h–**

VENICE ROAD (IRE) 4 ch.g. Halling (USA) – Croeso Cynnes (Most Welcome) [2004/5 F17d* Feb 1] leggy gelding: third foal: dam fair sprinter: won maiden bumper at Taunton on debut by 3 lengths from Aspiring Actor. *Miss Venetia Williams* **F97**

VENN OTTERY 10 b.g. Access Ski – Tom's Comedy (Comedy Star (USA)) [2004/5 c148, h–: c16g³ 17g c20dᵖᵘ c16g c26gᵖᵘ c24d⁴ 16d c21s Apr 7] rangy gelding: maiden hurdler: improved rapidly into smart chaser in 2003/4 for P. Nicholls: trained by O. Carter first 2 starts, then off 10 months and reportedly had breathing operation: well held in varied events on completed outings subsequently, including in Champion Chase, Gold Cup, novice hurdle and Fox Hunters' Chase: best at 2m, probably on good going or firmer: usually tongue tied: headstrong: finds little off bridle. *M. C. Pipe* **c132 h90**

VENTUREMORE 9 br.g. Green Adventure (USA) – Admire-A-More (Le Coq d'Or) [2004/5 16vᵖᵘ 17v⁶ 16s Apr 21] tall gelding: maiden hurdler: off 20 months, no sign of retaining ability: raced around 2m: acts on soft and good to firm going: takes strong hold. *Mrs A. F. Tullie* **h–**

VERASI 4 b.g. Kahyasi – Fair Verona (USA) (Alleged (USA)) [2004/5 16d² 16g² 18d* 16v 16dᶠ Apr 18] leggy gelding: fair maiden at best on Flat (stays 1m), lost his way in 2004 (tried blinkered): fair juvenile hurdler: won at Fontwell in December: stays 2¼m: needs to improve jumping. *G. L. Moore* **h109**

VERCHOYLES LAD (IRE) 8 b.g. Treasure Hunter – Lucifer's Way (Lucifer (USA)) [2004/5 c25g² c25g* c25f* 24m* 24g² c17g⁴ c24vᵖᵘ 20d c24m³ Dec 12] IR 8,600 3-y-o: half-brother to 4 winners, including fair hurdler up to 3m The Cushman (by Welsh Term), and to dam of smart hurdler In Contrast: dam, winning 2m hurdler, half-sister to dam of Irish National winner Glebe Lad: winning pointer: fairly useful chaser: won 2 handicaps at Kilbeggan in May: fair novice hurdler: won at Perth in June: effective around 2m to 25f: best efforts on good going or firmer. *J. G. Carr, Ireland* **c123 h108**

VERIDIAN 12 b.g. Green Desert (USA) – Alik (FR) (Targowice (USA)) [2004/5 c–, h–: 20s 24gᵖᵘ 16gᵖᵘ 16gᵖᵘ Aug 24] compact gelding: let down by jumping over fences: useful hurdler at best: no longer of any account: tried blinkered/in cheekpieces. *G. F. Bridgwater* **c– h–**

VERSUS (GER) 5 gr.h. Highest Honor (FR) – Very Mighty (FR) (Niniski (USA)) [2004/5 h102: 16s⁵ 22g* 20s³ 25v³ 24d⁴ 24s Apr 16] well-made horse: fair hurdler: won maiden at Folkestone in December: stays 2¾m: hard ride. *C. J. Mann* **h111**

VERTICAL BLOOM 4 b.f. Perpendicular – Rosie Cone (Celtic Cone) [2004/5 F14d* F13s³ Dec 13] leggy filly: seventh foal: half-sister to several winners, including fair hurdler/fairly useful chaser Harrycone Lewis (by Sir Harry Lewis) and fair hurdler Molsum (by Lord Bud), both of whom stay 3¼m: dam, winning hurdler, probably stayed 3m: won 3-y-o bumper at Warwick on debut by short head from Catiline: better form when third to There Is No Doubt in similar event at Towcester. *Mrs P. Sly* **F98**

VERY OPTIMISTIC (IRE) 7 b.g. Un Desperado (FR) – Bright Future (IRE) (Satco (FR)) [2004/5 h129p: 20s 20v² 23s Feb 19] tall gelding: useful hurdler: easily best effort in handicaps in 2004/5 when 3 lengths second to Turtle Soup at Haydock: should stay 3m: raced on good ground or softer (acts on heavy). *Jonjo O'Neill* **h132**

VERY SPECIAL ONE (IRE) 5 b.m. Supreme Leader – Bright News (Buckskin (FR)) [2004/5 F17s³ 21s⁴ 16s⁵ Feb 24] fifth foal: half-sister to modest hurdler Bright Buck (by Glacial Storm), stayed 3m, and winning pointer by Executive Perk: dam **h80 F84**

unplaced in bumpers/points: won mares maiden Irish point on debut in 2004: modest form when third in mares bumper at Folkestone: poor form in 2 mares maiden hurdles: should be suited by 2½m+. *K. C. Bailey*

VERY TASTY (IRE) 8 ch.g. Be My Native (USA) – Jasmine Melody (Jasmine Star) [2004/5 h–: 22g^{pu} 17g^{3} 17g* 16m^{3} 17m 17g* 17m 17d^{pu} 16g Sep 12] poor hurdler: left Mrs D. Sayer after first outing: won selling handicap (sold from Mrs E. Slack 3,700 gns) in May and novice handicap in July, both at Cartmel: should stay beyond 17f: acts on good to firm going: wore cheekpieces last 6 starts: usually tongue tied. *M. Todhunter* **h76**

VESTA FLAME 4 b.f. Vettori (IRE) – Ciel de Feu (USA) (Blushing John (USA)) [2004/5 16d^{pu} 25s^{pu} 17g 16s Apr 10] compact filly: poor maiden on Flat (will be suited by 1¼m+): no form in juvenile hurdles. *P. T. Midgley* **h–**

VETRANIO (IRE) 8 ch.g. Hubbly Bubbly (USA) – Cool Charm (Beau Charmeur (FR)) [2004/5 26d^{6} 22d^{pu} May 17] well beaten over hurdles. *N. M. Babbage* **h–**

VICARIO 4 gr.g. Vettori (IRE) – Arantxa (Sharpo) [2004/5 17v^{2} 16d^{3} 16v* 17s^{pu} 16d^{4} 19s^{3} 20d 19g^{3} Apr 1] leggy gelding: fair on Flat (stays 2m), sold out of M. Bell's stable 12,000 gns Newmarket Autumn Sales: fair hurdler: won juvenile at Towcester in January: stays 19f: acts on heavy going. *D. McCain* **h104**

VICARS DESTINY 7 b.m. Sir Harry Lewis (USA) – Church Leap (Pollerton) [2004/5 h111: 22d* 25s^{5} 16s^{F} 22s^{5} 21s^{6} 16d^{5} 16d^{4} 20v 24g^{4} Mar 5] leggy mare: fairly useful on Flat (stays 2½m): fairly useful handicap hurdler: won at Market Rasen in May by 11 lengths from Bergamo: stays 3m: best on good going or softer (acts on heavy): usually wears cheekpieces: reliable. *Mrs S. Lamyman* **h120**

VICAR'S LAD 9 b.g. Terimon – Proverbial Rose (Proverb) [2004/5 h101: c24s^{3} c25s^{F3} Mar 6] tall, leggy gelding: fair novice hurdler in 2003/4: fair pointer/novice hunter chaser: stays 25f. *Mrs Jelly O'Brien* **c90 h–**

VICENTIO 6 br.g. Vettori (IRE) – Smah (Mtoto) [2004/5 h72: 20s* 19s^{6} 25g^{3} c24g^{5} 22m^{3} Apr 23] smallish, workmanlike gelding: modest handicap hurdler: won seller at Fakenham in November: jumped none too fluently and not knocked about in novice handicap on chasing debut (breathing problem): stays 25f: acts on soft and good to firm going. *T. J. Fitzgerald* **c75 p h86**

VICIANA 6 b.m. Sir Harry Lewis (USA) – Ludoviciana (Oats) [2004/5 h99, F84: 20d^{2} Nov 13] good-topped mare: modest form in novice hurdles: stays 2½m: acts on soft going (form in bumpers on good to firm). *J. W. Payne* **h99**

VICITY 4 ch.f. Old Vic – Quiet City (True Song) [2004/5 16d Oct 2] small filly: fifth foal: dam fair hurdler/chaser up to 2¾m: tailed off in juvenile hurdle on debut. *R. H. Alner* **h–**

VICKY BEE 6 b.m. Alflora (IRE) – Mighty Frolic (Oats) [2004/5 F16m^{3} F16g^{3} F17d^{6} 16d^{6} 17d 16v Jan 3] good-topped mare: second foal: dam, fairly useful hunter, stayed 3½m: modest form first 2 starts in bumpers: well beaten over hurdles: tongue tied final outing. *M. J. Gingell* **h– F83**

VICOMTE THOMAS (FR) 5 b.g. Highest Honor (FR) – Vigorine (FR) (Shakapour) [2004/5 h–, F–: 16g^{pu} Apr 26] medium-sized gelding: no sign of ability: tried in cheekpieces/blinkers. *R. Dickin* **h–**

VIC THE PILER (IRE) 6 ch.g. Old Vic – Strong Gale Pigeon (IRE) (Strong Gale) [2004/5 16v* 17d^{6} 22s* Apr 3] 25,000 4-y-o: first foal: brother to winning pointer Our Samson: dam unraced: successful on 2 of 3 starts in novice hurdles, at Newcastle in January and Kelso (beat Le Biassais 2 lengths) in April: will stay 3m: open to further improvement. *N. G. Richards* **h112 p**

VICTOM'S CHANCE (IRE) 7 b.g. Old Vic – Lady Swinford (Ardross) [2004/5 F16d^{2} F16v^{2} 20v^{4} 20v* 22s* 24g^{bd} Apr 1] rangy, good sort: will make a chaser: third foal: half-brother to fairly useful hurdler/smart chaser Murphy's Cardinal (by Shernazar), stays 3m: dam won bumper and 2m maiden hurdle: useful form when runner-up in bumpers at Warwick and Chepstow (beaten 6 lengths by The Mick Weston): fairly useful form over hurdles: won maiden at Folkestone (by 4 lengths from King of Confusion) in February and conditional jockeys novice at Market Rasen in March: brought down second in novice at Newbury final start: will stay 3m: should continue to progress. *Noel T. Chance* **h119 p F109**

VICTOR ARGOSY (NZ) 10 b.g. Victory Dance – Fair Clip (NZ) (Lord Ballina (AUS)) [2004/5 c24g^{pu} Jan 17] tall, lengthy gelding: twice-raced on Flat: successful **c–**

twice from 7 starts over fences in New Zealand: pulled up lame after all but falling ninth in handicap at Doncaster on British debut: stays 3m. *M. C. Pipe*

VICTOR BOY (IRE) 12 b.g. Sharp Victor (USA) – Buonas (Orchestra) [2004/5 c16g^{4} c16m* c17f^{5} c17g^{pu} c16v* c16v^{F} c18s c16s c16s* c17d^{pu} c17v^{F} c17v Jan 29] sparely-made gelding: fair handicap chaser: won at Tralee in June and August and Cork (by 6 lengths from Runfar) in November: little form otherwise in 2004/5: raced mainly around 2m: acts on heavy and good to firm going: tongue tied. *G. Keane, Ireland* **c114 h–**

VICTOR FOX TROT 7 b.g. Bold Fox – Vico Equense (Absalom) [2004/5 F17d^{4} Aug 22] seventh foal: dam poor on Flat and over hurdles: runner-up in 2003, only completed outing in points: well held in bumper. *P. Bowen* **F–**

VICTORIA'S BOY (IRE) 12 b.g. Denel (FR) – Cloghroe Lady (Hardboy) [2004/5 c93, h–: c26s^{2} c26g^{3} May 26] strong gelding: fair hunter chaser: stays 3¼m: acts on soft and good to firm going: tried blinkered. *Ms W. Wild* **c94 h–**

VICTORIA'S PET 9 b.g. Kasakov – Lonely Lass (Headin' Up) [2004/5 16g^{ur} Dec 28] fair form on first of 2 starts in bumpers in 2000: unseated fourth in maiden on hurdling debut. *F. P. Murtagh* **h–**

VICTOR ONE (IRE) 5 b.g. Victory Note (USA) – Another Baileys (Deploy) [2004/5 F16m Oct 1] half-brother to 3 winners on Flat, including 5f to 1¾m winner Irish Cream (by Petong): dam 7f winner: tailed off in bumper on debut. *J. Wade* **F–**

VICTORY BELL 7 b.g. Komaite (USA) – Shikabell (Kala Shikari) [2004/5 h–, F–: 21g^{ro} 20d May 3] sturdy gelding: showed more temperament than ability in bumpers and over hurdles: successful in point in February. *A. P. Jones* **h– §**

VICTORY GUNNER (IRE) 7 ch.g. Old Vic – Gunner B Sharp (Gunner B) [2004/5 h101: 22d 24s^{6} 24s^{3} 24s* 24g^{6} 24v* 20v 24d 24g 24d^{5} Apr 8] medium-sized gelding: fairly useful handicap hurdler: successful at Chepstow in November and December, best effort when beating Carlys Quest by 25 lengths in latter: stays 3m: raced mainly on good going or softer (acts on heavy): usually races prominently. *C. Roberts* **h120 ?**

VICTORY SET (GER) 5 ch.g. Second Set (IRE) – Vega Sicilia (Environment Friend) [2004/5 17m^{5} 16d^{6} 16g^{F} 17d Aug 1] unplaced on Flat in Germany at 3/4 yrs for C. Von Der Recke: no form over hurdles: fell in point. *M. F. Harris* **h–**

VICTORY SIGN (IRE) 5 b.g. Forzando – Mo Ceri (Kampala) [2004/5 h77: 16g^{5} 17v^{pu} 16g^{pu} Mar 27] poor maiden hurdler: has worn cheekpieces since debut: carries head awkwardly. *Miss M. P. Bryant* **h63**

VICTORY VENTURE (IRE) 5 b.g. Victory Note (USA) – Shirley Venture (Be My Chief (USA)) [2004/5 16g 16m^{5} 20m Sep 24] smallish, close-coupled gelding: fairly useful on Flat at 3 yrs for M. Johnston, no form in 2004: poor form on second start over hurdles: sold 2,700 gns Newmarket Autumn Sales. *Ian Williams* **h76**

VICTRAM (IRE) 5 b.g. Victory Note (USA) – Lady Tristram (Miami Springs) [2004/5 16s* 16s^{2} 16s 16s* 16d Apr 9] leggy gelding: fairly useful on Flat (stays 1½m): fair handicap hurdler: won at Listowel in September and Naas in March: much stiffer task, not discredited in valuable event at Aintree final start: raced at 2m on going softer than good (acts on soft). *A. McGuinness, Ireland* **h109**

VICTREE (IRE) 6 b.g. Old Vic – Boro Glen (Furry Glen) [2004/5 F16s Feb 26] €19,000 4-y-o: tall gelding: has scope: sixth foal: half-brother to fair chaser Multi Talented (by Montelimar), stays 3¼m: dam, won 2½m hurdle, half-sister to useful 2m to 21f hurdler Killone Abbot and useful 3m chaser Fair Is Fair: yet to be asked for effort when badly hampered in bumper at Kempton on debut. *L. Wells* **F92 +**

VIDI CAESAR (NZ) 10 b.g. Racing Is Fun (USA) – Vidi Vici (NZ) (Roman Empire) [2004/5 c86, h88: c21d^{6} c20g^{4} c16m^{2} c20m^{pu} c16m 17v^{pu} Oct 17] sturdy gelding: maiden hurdler: poor maiden chaser: stays 2½m: acts on soft and good to firm going: usually wears cheekpieces/blinkers: not one to trust. *R. C. Guest* **c72 § h–**

VIGOUREUX (FR) 6 b.g. Villez (USA) – Rouge Folie (FR) (Agent Bleu (FR)) [2004/5 h96: 16s* 16s 17s^{pu} 16d^{6} 16d^{4} 16s^{2} Mar 22] fair handicap hurdler: won at Uttoxeter in October: raced mainly around 2m: acts on good to firm and heavy going: bled from nose second outing: unreliable. *S. Gollings* **h100 §**

VIKING SONG 5 b.g. Savahra Sound – Relikon (Relkino) [2004/5 F16m 16g 16g^{pu} Jan 24] seventh foal: dam, of little account, half-sister to Gunner B: no form in bumpers **h– F–**

and 2 starts over hurdles: sold out of M. Hammond's stable 1,800 gns Doncaster August Sales after hurdling debut. *F. Kirby*

VILLA 9 b.g. Jupiter Island – Spoonhill Wood (Celtic Cone) [2004/5 h93: 25s² Jan 27] good-topped gelding: bumper winner: lightly-raced hurdler: fair form when runner-up in handicap at Warwick in January: stays 25f: raced on good going or softer: visored on hurdling debut: of suspect temperament. *M. C. Pipe* **h101**

VILLAGE COPPER 13 b.g. Town And Country – Culm Valley (Port Corsair) [2004/5 c20d May 11] non-thoroughbred gelding: veteran winning pointer: well held in hunter: in frame completed starts in points in 2005: stays 3m: acts on good to firm going. *Mrs Ruth Hayter* **c–**

VILLAGE KING (IRE) 12 b.g. Roi Danzig (USA) – Honorine (USA) (Blushing Groom (FR)) [2004/5 c137, h–: c31d⁵ c25mᵖᵘ Apr 13] good-bodied gelding: useful chaser at one time, lightly raced nowadays: fairly useful form when fifth in cross-country handicap completed start in 2004/5: probably stays 3½m on conventional track: acts on heavy and good to firm going: blinkered once (ran creditably): sometimes takes little interest. *P. J. Hobbs* **c116 ? h–**

VILLAGO (GER) 5 b.g. Laroche (GER) – Village (GER) (Acatenango (GER)) [2004/5 16s 24d⁵ 19m Apr 9] useful-looking ex-German gelding: fair on Flat (stays 1¾m), sold out of A. Trybuhl's stable 12,000 gns Newmarket Autumn Sales: well held in novice company over hurdles: needs to improve jumping. *C. J. Mann* **h–**

VILLAIR (IRE) 10 b.g. Valville (FR) – Brackenair (Fairbairn) [2004/5 c104, h–: c24s* c26s³ c30d³ c32d⁶ c28s c27s⁵ c30s³ c29sᵖᵘ Mar 13] long-backed gelding: fair handicap chaser: won at Fakenham in October: thorough stayer: raced on good going or softer (acts on heavy): tried in headgear: often let down by jumping: hard ride: not one to trust. *C. J. Mann* **c105 § h–**

VILLA MARA (IRE) 5 b.g. Alflora (IRE) – Claudia Electric (IRE) (Electric) [2004/5 F16s F16d Mar 10] rather unfurnished gelding: first foal: dam, fair 2½m hurdle winner, half-sister to useful 2½m to 3m chaser Killusty: well held in 2 bumpers. *S. Kirk* **F–**

VILLON (IRE) 6 b.g. Topanoora – Deep Adventure (Deep Run) [2004/5 F115p: F16s* 16v* 20v* 16g Mar 15] lengthy, good sort: chasing type: unbeaten in 2 bumpers, beating Gulabill 2½ lengths at Haydock in November, despite hanging left final 2f: successful also on first 2 starts in novice hurdles, at Hexham later in November and Ayr (beat Bewleys Berry 5 lengths, in good style) in December: unsuited by emphasis on speed at trip when well held in Supreme Novices' Hurdle at Cheltenham: stays 2½m: acts on heavy going. *L. Lungo* **h133 F99 +**

VIN DU PAYS 5 b.g. Alzao (USA) – Royale Rose (FR) (Bering) [2004/5 h–: 16m 19f⁵ Sep 28] no form over hurdles: fourth on completed start in points. *M. Blanshard* **h83**

VINGIS PARK (IRE) 7 b.g. Old Vic – Lady Glenbank (Tarboosh (USA)) [2004/5 h105, F105: 22g³ 22s⁴ 21d⁵ 20d³ 16g⁴ c16s⁵ Feb 6] fair novice hurdler: in cheekpieces, fifth of 6 finishers in maiden at Hereford on chasing debut: stays 2¾m: raced on good going or softer: usually tongue tied: usually finds little and not one to rely on. *V. R. A. Dartnall* **c87 h107 §**

VINMIX DE BESSY (FR) 4 gr.g. River Bay (USA) – Hesse (FR) (Linamix (FR)) [2004/5 16g* 16d² Apr 18] second foal: half-brother to 1m winner Bedamix (by Double Bed): dam maiden who stayed 1½m: successful twice up to 8.5f on Flat in France for J-L. Pelletan: easily won maiden at Plumpton on hurdling debut in March: 5 lengths second to Miss Academy (pair clear) in juvenile there next time: may prove best at sharp 2m. *D. B. Feek* **h112**

VINNIE BOY (IRE) 8 b. or br.g. Detroit Sam (FR) – Castle Ita (Midland Gayle) [2004/5 c25s* Feb 10] winning pointer: successful in 5-runner hunter chase at Wincanton, showing fairly useful form to beat Kingston-Banker 1¼ lengths: should stay beyond 25f. *Mrs O. Bush* **c100**

VINTAGE TREASURE (IRE) 6 b.g. Norwich – Bann River (Over The River (FR)) [2004/5 F16s* F16s³ Dec 29] half-brother to a winning pointer by Camden Town: dam unraced half-sister to dam of useful hurdler/chaser Cloone River: won 25-runner bumper at Navan on debut by 2 lengths from Move Yourself: useful form when 7½ lengths third to Merdeka at Leopardstown. *C. Byrnes, Ireland* **F109**

VIRGIN SOLDIER (IRE) 9 ch.g. Waajib – Never Been Chaste (Posse (USA)) [2004/5 c121, h116: c25d⁴ Apr 25] angular gelding: fairly useful hurdler/chaser: let down **c– h–**

by jumping at Wetherby only start in 2004/5: effective at 2m and barely stays 25f: acts on firm and good to soft going. *G. A. Swinbank*

VIRTUS 5 ch.g. Machiavellian (USA) – Exclusive Virtue (USA) (Shadeed (USA)) [2004/5 17d 17d 16g Dec 8] close-coupled gelding: fourth in 1m maiden on debut at 3 yrs, sold out of J. Fanshawe's stable 18,000 gns Newmarket Autumn (2003) Sales: not fluent when well held in novice company over hurdles. *P. J. Hobbs* **h–**

VISCOUNT BANKES 7 ch.g. Clantime – Bee Dee Dancer (Ballacashtal (CAN)) [2004/5 c74, h–: c16s^{4} c16v^{4} c21d^{pu} c16s^{ro} c16m^{4} Mar 21] winning pointer: still just in front and running best race in chases when running out last in hunter at Leicester: raced mainly around 2m: acts on soft going: tried in cheekpieces. *Mrs Rosemary Gasson* **c95 h–**

VISIBILITY (FR) 6 gr.g. Linamix (FR) – Visor (USA) (Mr Prospector (USA)) [2004/5 h129§: 16g c16v* c19v^{4} c16s^{4} 16d 16v^{4} Mar 29] tall, leggy, angular gelding: fairly useful handicap hurdler: best effort in 2004/5 when fourth to Yes Sir at Chepstow: best effort in 3 novice chases when winning at Towcester in January by 7 lengths from Ball O Malt: likely to stay beyond 2m: acts on heavy and good to firm going: often visored: temperamental. *M. C. Pipe* **c121 § h116 §**

VISTA VERDE 7 b.g. Alflora (IRE) – Legata (IRE) (Orchestra) [2004/5 h106, F95: 22g^{5} c16g* Nov 15] useful-looking gelding: fair novice hurdler: off 6½ months, won novice at Leicester on chasing debut in November by 2½ lengths from Raw Silk: effective at 2m to 3m: raced on good going or softer. *A. King* **c109 + h–**

VITAL SPARK 6 b.g. Primitive Rising (USA) – Enkindle (Relkino) [2004/5 F17d* F16s 24d^{4} Dec 6] tall, useful-looking gelding: first foal: dam, poor 2m novice hurdler, half-sister to high-class stayer Recupere: won bumper at Carlisle on debut in October: well held in similar event and novice hurdle after. *J. M. Jefferson* **h– F93**

VITELLI 5 b.g. Vettori (IRE) – Mourne Trix (Golden Love) [2004/5 F94: 16g* 20g* 16d^{2} Oct 16] lengthy gelding: successful in novices at Hexham in May first 2 starts over hurdles, dead-heating with After Galway, then easily beating Dante's Porridge by 25 lengths: off 4½ months, fairly useful form when 6 lengths second to Sobraon in similar event at Kelso: likely to prove best at 2½m+: acts on good to soft going: sold 24,000 gns Doncaster November Sales. *G. A. Swinbank* **h121**

VITELUCY 6 b.m. Vettori (IRE) – Classic Line (Last Tycoon) [2004/5 h85: 16g^{pu} 20g^{5} 22g^{4} 20g^{F} 21d^{2} 21d* 24m 20d Oct 14] smallish mare: modest handicap hurdler: won at Southwell in August: stays 2¾m: acts on good to firm and good to soft going: visored last 5 starts. *Miss S. J. Wilton* **h87**

VIVA FOREVER (FR) 6 br.m. Lando (GER) – Very Mighty (FR) (Niniski (USA)) [2004/5 h–: 16g 20g^{5} 18s^{2} 17s* 16v^{5} 16d Feb 9] lengthy mare: poor hurdler: won mares novice handicap at Folkestone in January: stays 2½m: raced on good ground or softer (acts on soft): blinkered last 3 starts: tongue tied. *A. M. Hales* **h82**

VIVANTE (IRE) 7 b.m. Toulon – Splendidly Gay (Lord Gayle (USA)) [2004/5 F–: 19s 19g 17d 22v^{6} 22g^{4} Apr 17] smallish, lengthy mare: poor maiden hurdler: should stay 2¾m. *A. J. Wilson* **h68**

VIVID IMAGINATION (IRE) 6 b.g. Moonax (IRE) – Sezu (IRE) (Mister Lord (USA)) [2004/5 h–p: c25g^{4} 23v 16s 20v 16d* 16d 24m^{5} Apr 13] sturdy, useful-looking gelding: prolific winning pointer in 2004: fairly useful form when fourth to Eric's Charm in maiden at Folkestone on chasing debut, eased run in: fair hurdler: won handicap at Lingfield in February by 3½ lengths from Executive Decision: effective at 2m to 25f: acts on good to soft and good to firm going. *M. C. Pipe* **c121 h112**

VIVRE AIMER RIRE (FR) 4 b.f. Cyborg (FR) – Badj II (FR) (Tadj (FR)) [2004/5 F14d F12d 20m^{4} 20d Apr 20] small, angular filly: fourth foal: sister to fairly useful hurdler up to 2¾m Manx Royal and winning 2½m hurdler Kampala II: dam, maiden, half-sister to 2002 Champion Hurdle winner Hors La Loi III and high-class hurdler/chaser Cyborgo (both by Cyborg): well held in bumpers: poor form when fourth in maiden at Worcester on hurdling debut. *M. Scudamore* **h75 F–**

VODKA BLEU (FR) 6 b.g. Pistolet Bleu (IRE) – Viva Vodka (FR) (Crystal Glitters (USA)) [2004/5 h118: 22d^{pu} 24m* 22s* 22d^{6} c20m* c24g^{2} c22g* c19d* c21v^{2} c20s^{3} c20d* c20g* Nov 27] leggy, unfurnished gelding: fairly useful hurdler: won maiden at Worcester and novice at Newton Abbot in June: useful chaser: won maiden at Huntingdon in August and novices at Market Rasen in September, Chepstow in October and Cheltenham and Newbury in November: gained final success when beating **c139 h121**

Stan James Fulke Walwyn Novices' Chase, Newbury—
the prolific Vodka Bleu (spotted cap) claims the scalp of Fundamentalist in a muddling race;
also pictured is See You Sometime (noseband)

Fundamentalist ½ length in steadily-run 3-runner Grade 2 Stan James Fulke Walwyn Novices' Chase: ran well when placed in handicaps at Stratford (neck second to Monkerhostin) and Aintree (third to Farmer Jack) ninth and tenth starts: stays easy 3m: acts on good to firm and heavy going: tried visored over hurdles: sound jumper: tough: reported in January to be suffering with heat in a foreleg and missed rest of season. *M. C. Pipe*

VOLCANO SNOW 5 ch.m. Zilzal (USA) – Ash Glade (Nashwan (USA)) [2004/5 h83, F85: 20m^{pu} 16d^{3} 20d^{3} 16g 17g^{6} 16s* 16m 16g^{rtr} 21m^{rtr} 19d 16d 16s 16v Jan 18] angular mare: modest hurdler: won 4-y-o handicap at Perth in August: refused to race eighth and ninth outings: best around 2m: acts on soft going, probably on good to firm: tried blinkered/in cheekpieces: best left alone: sold 4,200 gns Doncaster March Sales. *M. F. Harris* **h87 §**

VON ORIGNY (FR) 4 gr.g. Blushing Flame (USA) – Forza Malta (FR) (Royal Charter (FR)) [2004/5 F16v* 17d^{2} 16s^{2} 17s* Apr 2] first foal: dam, placed over jumps up to 19f, half-sister to top-class chaser Cyfor Malta who stayed 25f: won bumper at Wetherby on debut in January by 4 lengths from Kerrs Whin: fair form in novice hurdles: short-head second to Rebel Rhythm at Bangor on debut: simple task there 2 starts later: will be suited by further than 17f: remains likely to do better. *H. D. Daly* **h108 p** **F97**

VOY POR USTEDES (FR) 4 b.g. Villez (USA) – Nuit d'Ecajeul (FR) (Matahawk) [2004/5 16s^{F} 16s^{3} 17s* 16s^{3} 17s* 16d^{ur} 16d* 16d^{6} 16d^{3} 16g^{3} Apr 16] leggy, angular gelding: eighth foal: half-brother to fairly useful hurdler/chaser Le Pero (by Perrault), stays 21f, and Slovak middle-distance winner Erik d'Ecajeul (by Synefos): dam, won over 15f in France, half-sister to very smart French hurdler Roi d'Ecajeul: useful juvenile hurdler: won at Nancy in October, Enghien in November, and, having left G. Macaire, novice at Huntingdon (beat Prins Willem readily) in January: creditable efforts after, third to Admiral at Ayr final start: will stay beyond 17f: raced on good going or softer: changed hands 106,000 gns Doncaster May Sales. *A. King* **h128**

VRUBEL (IRE) 6 ch.g. Entrepreneur – Renzola (Dragonara Palace (USA)) [2004/5 16s^{5} Dec 2] modest on Flat (stays 1¼m): no form over hurdles. *V. Smith* **h–**

VULCAN LANE (NZ) 8 ch.g. Star Way – Smudged (NZ) (Nassipour (USA)) [2004/5 c72, h75: c16v* c16s^{2} c17s^{3} c16s^{3} c16g^{2} Mar 28] compact gelding: poor hurdler: modest novice chaser: off a year, won handicap at Newcastle in February: raced mainly around 2m: probably acts on any going: wears cheekpieces/blinkers: found little final start. *R. C. Guest* **c87 § h–**

W

WAFTAM 4 ch.f. Compton Place – Wathbat Mtoto (Mtoto) [2004/5 F14d 19d^{pu} Jan 1] 6,000Y, 1,400 3-y-o: small filly: fifth foal: half-sister to fairly useful 1m winner Saladim (by Lahib) and UAE 5.5f/6f winner Wathbat Mujtahid (by Mujtahid): dam fairly useful over middle distances: well held in bumper and novice hurdle. *W. Amos* **h– F–**

WAGES 5 b.g. Lake Coniston (IRE) – Green Divot (Green Desert (USA)) [2004/5 h93: 17g 16s^{4} 16g^{3} 16s 17m^{3} Mar 14] lengthy gelding: modest maiden handicap hurdler: best at sharp 2m: acts on good to firm going: wore cheekpieces final start: tried tongue tied. *A. M. Hales* **h88**

WAGGY (IRE) 9 b.g. Cataldi – Energance (IRE) (Salmon Leap (USA)) [2004/5 h–: c24g^{pu} c16m^{pu} Mar 21] no form over hurdles or in hunter chases: won maiden point in April. *M. Rodda* **c– h–**

WAHIBA SANDS 12 b.g. Pharly (FR) – Lovely Noor (USA) (Fappiano (USA)) [2004/5 c144, h–: c17m^{6} c16m^{6} c19v^{ur} c19g^{3} Apr 19] tall gelding: formerly very smart chaser, nothing like so good nowadays: left M. Pipe after second outing: in frame in points in 2005: stays 21f: acts on heavy and good to firm going: wears visor/cheekpieces: sometimes races lazily. *Mrs H. M. Bridges* **c– h–**

WAIMEA BAY 6 b.m. Karinga Bay – Smart In Sable (Roscoe Blake) [2004/5 h92, F–: 19s^{2} 16g* May 30] modest novice hurdler: won mares event at Uttoxeter in May: likely to prove best around 2m: acts on soft ground: has pulled hard. *P. R. Hedger* **h99**

WAINAK (USA) 7 b.g. Silver Hawk (USA) – Cask (Be My Chief (USA)) [2004/5 h72: 24g^{4} 24d* 24g^{2} Aug 14] close-coupled gelding: modest hurdler: won novice at Market Rasen in August: stays 3m: acts on soft going: tried blinkered/visored, usually wears cheekpieces: hard ride. *Miss Lucinda V. Russell* **h88**

WAINDALE FLYER 6 ch.g. Abzu – Mellouise (Handsome Sailor) [2004/5 F–: F16d May 8] tall, plain gelding: well beaten in bumpers: sold 2,500 gns Doncaster May Sales: has looked temperamental in points. *J. R. Norton* **F–**

WAIN MOUNTAIN 9 b.g. Unfuwain (USA) – Mountain Memory (High Top) [2004/5 c132, h–: c19s^{2} c19v^{2} c29s c20v^{3} c22v^{pu} c21d Apr 8] good-topped gelding: useful handicap chaser: creditable efforts when placed in 2004/5: tongue tied, eighth, never a factor, to Cregg House in Topham Chase at Aintree final start: stays 3¼m: acts on heavy going, possibly unsuited by good to firm: has hung left: tends to flash tail under pressure. *J. A. B. Old* **c133 h–**

WAIT FOR THE WILL (USA) 9 ch.g. Seeking The Gold (USA) – You'd Be Surprised (USA) (Blushing Groom (FR)) [2004/5 h118: c16d^{F} Oct 23] tall gelding: fairly useful on Flat (stays 1¾m) nowadays: fairly useful hurdler: well held when falling 2 out in maiden on chasing debut, only start in 2004/5: raced around 2m: acts on good to firm and good to soft going: usually blinkered. *G. L. Moore* **c– h–**

WAKEUP SMILING (IRE) 7 b.g. Norwich – Blackmiller Lady (Bonne Noel) [2004/5 h120: c19d^{pu} c16g^{4} c21d Dec 11] rangy gelding: fairly useful hurdler: modest form at best in novice chases: stays at least 19f: acts on good to firm going: visored once (pulled up on heavy): has flashed tail. *Miss E. C. Lavelle* **c– h–**

WALCOT LAD (IRE) 9 b.g. Jurado (USA) – Butty Miss (Menelek) [2004/5 c74, h–: c26s^{5} c21s* c21g^{2} c18d* c24s^{4} c18s^{3} c22s^{ur} c20g^{5} c18s* c26d^{3} c20s^{3} c21g^{2} c18s^{2} Mar 30] maiden hurdler: modest handicap chaser: won at Fakenham in October and Fontwell in November (amateurs) and February: stays 3¼m, effective over much shorter: acts on good to firm and heavy going: wears headgear. *A. Ennis* **c89 h–**

WALKING SUNDAY (IRE) 7 b. or br.g. Denel (FR) – Blue Mount (IRE) (Merrymount) [2004/5 c19s^{pu} c23v^{4} 20v c26d^{pu} c26g* c26g^{3} c26m^{4} Apr 21] €16,500 4-y-o: first foal: half-brother to winning pointer by Glacial Storm: dam unraced: maiden Irish pointer: never a factor in maiden at Folkestone on hurdling debut: poor form over fences: **c83 h–**

won novice handicap at Plumpton in March: stays 3¼m: usually wears cheekpieces: has carried head awkwardly. *K. C. Bailey*

WALKMILL (IRE) 4 ch.f. Perugino (USA) – Simply Marilyn (IRE) (Simply Great (FR)) [2004/5 F13g4 Jan 17] well-made filly: sixth foal: dam fair middle-distance stayer: fourth of 18 in bumper at Doncaster on debut: sold 3,200 gns Doncaster May Sales. *J. Parkes* **F77**

WALK ON SEAS (IRE) 10 b.g. Shardari – Over The Seas (North Summit) [2004/5 18s 19s* c21s3 c20d4 Nov 13] leggy, close-coupled gelding: fairly useful hurdler: won 18-runner handicap at Auteuil in October: easily better effort over fences when third in minor event there on debut: stays 21f: raced on good going or softer (acts on heavy). *F. Doumen, France* **c115 h119**

WALLY WONDER (IRE) 7 ch.g. Magical Wonder (USA) – Sally Gap (Sallust) [2004/5 c–, h–: 20d4 17g4 16m 17m 18s4 17d* 16d 20dpu 16d5 19s* 20s Apr 10] close-coupled gelding: no form over fences: poor hurdler: won selling handicaps at Sedgefield in October and Catterick in March: stays 19f: acts on soft and good to firm going: has worn blinkers, including last 6 starts: best form when ridden prominently: inconsistent. *R. Bastiman* **c– h78 §**

WALSINGHAM (IRE) 7 b.g. Presenting – Let's Compromise (No Argument) [2004/5 h–: 22dpu 20g3 22dpu Apr 17] good-topped gelding: poor maiden hurdler: left P. Hobbs after reappearance: should stay beyond 2½m. *Ms Bridget Nicholls* **h81**

WALTER (IRE) 6 ch.g. Presenting – Siberian Princess (Northfields (USA)) [2004/5 F16s F16s Jan 15] big, lengthy gelding: half-brother to several winners, including smart chaser Siberian Gale (by Strong Gale), stayed 3m: dam unraced half-sister to useful 2m hurdler Moody Man: never a factor in 2 bumpers won by Oscar Park. *P. Winkworth* **F–**

WALTER PLINGE 9 b.g. Theatrical Charmer – Carousel Zingira (Reesh) [2004/5 c–, h–: 20g Apr 30] compact gelding: winning hurdler: maiden chaser: pulled up in point in March. *A. G. Juckes* **c– h–**

WALTER'S DESTINY 13 ch.g. White Prince (USA) – Tearful Sarah (Rugantino) [2004/5 c97§, h–: c25g6 c25d4 c25d2 c25d* c25s4 c30d Mar 8] lengthy gelding: modest handicap chaser: won at Wincanton in December: probably stays 3¾m: acts on good to firm and heavy going: lazy and unreliable. *C. W. Mitchell* **c97 § h–**

WALTHAM DOVE 10 br.g. Gypsy Castle – Dovetail (Brigadier Gerard) [2004/5 23dur 20s 21vpu Jan 25] maiden hurdler: lightly raced and no sign of retaining ability. *K. A. Morgan* **h–**

WALTZING ALONG (IRE) 7 b.g. Presenting – Clyduffe Fairy (Belfalas) [2004/5 h–: c16d3 c17s2 Dec 5] lengthy gelding: no form over hurdles: better effort over fences when second in novice handicap at Kelso, looking likely winner before pecking last: should stay beyond 17f. *L. Lungo* **c84 h–**

WALTZING BEAU 4 ch.g. Dancing Spree (USA) – Blushing Belle (Local Suitor (USA)) [2004/5 18s* 16g5 18s* 20s3 Feb 24] tall gelding: modest maiden on Flat (stays 2m): fairly useful juvenile hurdler: successful at Fontwell in October (maiden) and January (beat Innocent Rebel by distance): should stay 2½m: acts on soft going. *B. G. Powell* **h119**

WANANGO (GER) 4 ch.c. Acatenango (GER) – Wanateluthspilgrim (USA) (Pilgrim (USA)) [2004/5 F16v* F16s5 Apr 10] brother to useful middle-distance performer Wala and half-brother to 3 winners on Flat in Germany: dam minor stakes sprint winner in USA: fairly useful form in bumpers: won at Leopardstown in March by 7 lengths from Man of Repute: fifth to Farmer Brown at Leopardstown following month. *T. Stack, Ireland* **F100**

WANDERING LIGHT (IRE) 16 b.g. Royal Fountain – Pleaseme (Javelot) [2004/5 c–, h–: c25v2 May 10] sturdy gelding: veteran chaser: modest form when runner-up in weak 3-finisher hunter at Towcester: well beaten completed start in points in 2005: stays 4m: raced on good ground or softer (acts on heavy). *R. B. Francis* **c78 h–**

WANSBECK 12 b.g. Dancing High – Mother Machree (Bing II) [2004/5 h–: 20dpu May 12] looked of no account in 2 runs over hurdles. *J. S. Haldane* **h–**

WANSFORD LADY 9 b.m. Michelozzo (USA) – Marnie's Girl (Crooner) [2004/5 h–§: 19g Jun 15] more temperament than ability over hurdles: tried tongue tied. *D. W. Lewis* **h– §**

WARBRECK 4 ch.g. Selkirk (USA) – Wigging (Warning) [2004/5 16v Jan 18] modest on Flat (stays 1½m, has looked temperamental), successful in December: blinkered, tailed off in juvenile on hurdling debut. *C. R. Egerton* **h–**

WARDASH (GER) 5 b.g. Dashing Blade – Warusha (GER) (Shareef Dancer (USA)) [2004/5 16d 16s 17g 17m³ Apr 23] ex-German gelding: successful once over 1m at 3 yrs for H. Blume: bad maiden hurdler: likely to need sharp 2m: visored and tongue tied final start. *M. C. Pipe* **h59 +**

WAR DRAGON 8 b. or br.g. Golden Heights – Fortune's Fancy (Workboy) [2004/5 17gpu Aug 14] half-brother to fair sprinter Ballafort (by Ballacashtal): dam, poor sprint winner, out of very smart sprinter Polly Peachum: no show in selling hurdle on debut. *N. A. Twiston-Davies* **h–**

WAREYTH (USA) 6 b. or br.g. Shuailaan (USA) – Bahr Alsalaam (USA) (Riverman (USA)) [2004/5 h–: 16gpu Oct 4] tall gelding: no form over hurdles: runner-up in maiden point in April. *D. P. Keane* **h–**

WARIF (USA) 4 ch.c. Diesis – Alshoowg (USA) (Riverman (USA)) [2004/5 16fpu 16s 16d 20dF Dec 4] small colt: no form on Flat: sold out of E. O'Neill's stable 1,800 gns Newmarket July Sales: no show over hurdles: blinkered (fell first) final start. *M. E. Sowersby* **h–**

WAR OF ATTRITION (IRE) 6 br.g. Presenting – Una Juna (IRE) (Good Thyne (USA)) [2004/5 h147: c22d* c16v* c16g c16d² Apr 9] **c149 h–**

A 33/1-shot when finishing a neck second to Brave Inca in the 2004 Supreme Novices' Hurdle, War of Attrition was a warm order when he turned up at Cheltenham twelve months later to contest the Arkle Trophy. War of Attrition was promoted to favouritism for the race after making it two wins from two starts in chases when beating Healy's Pub by four lengths in a novice event at Naas in early-February, despite his form being well short of that required to win an Arkle. He also came in for strong support on the day, starting clear favourite at 11/4, with Contraband at 7/1 next in the betting. War of Attrition's trainer reportedly considered the six-year-old to be as good, if not better, than any he had trained, praise indeed from someone whose Cheltenham Festival successes included those of Buck House in the 1983 Supreme Novices' Hurdle and 1986 Champion Chase and Trapper John in the 1990 Stayers' Hurdle. Connections must have been most disappointed to see

Swordlestown Cup Novices' Chase, Punchestown—
War of Attrition (No.6) reels in the faltering Watson Lake

War of Attrition finish only seventh behind Contraband. However, in two subsequent outings, War of Attrition at least went some way to justifying his trainer's faith in him, and with time on his side there is still a chance that he could fully justify it one day, especially as a return to further than two miles is likely to suit him well.

Two and three quarter miles is the longest distance War of Attrition has tackled so far, that when winning a maiden at Thurles in November on his chasing debut, reportedly chipping a bone in the process which kept him off the course until Naas. He lacked the speed from three out to make his challenge, at two miles on good ground in the Arkle, after travelling strongly for a long way. More testing conditions did show him in a better light at the trip afterwards. On his next start, in the Maghull Novices' Chase at Aintree, War of Attrition turned the tables on the Arkle first and third, but Ashley Brook, the runner-up at Cheltenham, once again proved too good for him. Ridden with more restraint than in the Arkle, War of Attrition moved into second place three out, but he was flat out to do so and could make no further impression on Ashley Brook, who beat him by sixteen lengths. Another Grade 1 novice chase, the Swordlestown Cup at Punchestown, provided War of Attrition with the opportunity to turn the tables on a couple more who had finished in front of him in the Arkle, namely Watson Lake (fourth) and Mariah Rollins (sixth), and not only did he manage that but he also came out on top overall. Well served by the sound pace and soft ground, which combined to place the emphasis very much on stamina at the trip, War of Attrition looked to have little chance of pegging back the leader Watson Lake following a none-too-fluent jump three out. However, whereas the latter faltered after blundering two out, War of Attrition stayed on well, drawing right away from the third, and collared Watson Lake near the line to win by a length.

War of Attrition runs in the colours of Gigginstown House Stud, which is owned by Michael O'Leary, the boss of the no-frills airline Ryanair and one of the wealthiest men in Ireland. He has built up quite an impressive team of jumpers in the last few seasons—Kill Devil Hill, The Galway Man and Industrious are among his best other prospects—though one of his most promising purchases, Best Mate's half-brother Inexorable, a useful novice hurdler in 2003/4, was killed in a fall on his chasing debut. O'Leary purchased the top-priced store at the Doncaster Sales in May, outlasting Trevor Hemmings and paying 120,000 guineas for a brother to Our Ben, by the same sire are War of Attrition. As some of the names chosen—it's hard to imagine him calling a horse Emollient or Conciliatory—O'Leary has what might politely be called a no-nonsense approach to business, evidently taking the view that, if he upsets a few people along the way, it does at least generate publicity. Purchasing a taxi licence, at the equivalent of £4,000, for his Mercedes so he could use the bus lane between his home and Dublin airport, rather than endure Dublin's perennially clogged roads on the way to work, upset a few people. And when several more traditional airlines joined forces to improve their environmental image, O'Leary declared Ryanair would be increasing its carbon dioxide emissions and any of his passengers so worried about green issues could 'sell your cars and walk'.

War of Attrition (IRE) (br.g. 1999)	Presenting (br 1992)	Mtoto (b 1983)	Busted
			Amazer
		D'Azy (b 1984)	Persian Bold
			Belle Viking
	Una Juna (IRE) (b 1992)	Good Thyne (br 1977)	Herbager
			Foreseer
		An Bothar Dubh (br 1986)	Strong Gale
			Tullow Performance

War of Attrition, by the Derby third Presenting, also has plenty of stamina in the bottom half of his pedigree and may well stay three miles. His dam Una Juna, pulled up in a point on her only start, is a sister to the fairly useful staying chaser Max Pride, while his grandam An Bothar Dubh, a winning hurdler, is a sister to the fairly useful staying hurdler and fair chaser Crank Shaft. War of Attrition is Una Juna's first foal. Her next Fighting Chance (by Germany) won twice in points in 2005 for Sally Alner, having made a promising debut in a bumper the previous year. Una Juna is a half-sister to the dams of the smart staying hurdler Emotional Moment and King Harald, winner of the inaugural Jewson Novices' Handicap

Chase at Cheltenham. War of Attrition, a strong sort, has raced only on good ground or softer and acts on heavy. *M. F. Morris, Ireland*

WARREN PLACE 5 ch.g. Presidium – Coney Hills (Beverley Boy) [2004/5 16m Dec 12] poor maiden on Flat (stays 7f): soundly beaten in novice on hurdling debut. *J. Hetherton* **h–**

WARRENS CASTLE (IRE) 8 b.g. Fourstars Allstar (USA) – Jerusalem Cruiser (IRE) (Electric) [2004/5 h113: c17g c21f* c16f^2 c17d^3 c17g^5 c20g^F c28s^{pu} Nov 7] fair hurdler: fairly useful chaser: won maiden at Punchestown in May: best effort when ¾-length second to Swordplay in 3-runner minor event at Tramore: stays 21f. *W. P. Mullins, Ireland* **c117 h–**

WARRLIN 11 b.g. Warrshan (USA) – Lahin (Rainbow Quest (USA)) [2004/5 c–, h87: 20g 17d^2 16d 16s c19g^{pu} Dec 28] sparely-made gelding: winning chaser: modest hurdler, form in 2004/5 only on second outing: effective around 2m, barely stays 25f: acts on any going: tried visored/blinkered: not one to rely on. *C. W. Fairhurst* **c– h88 §**

WARTORN (IRE) 10 b.g. Warcraft (USA) – Alice Minkthorn (Party Mink) [2004/5 h96: c21g^F Apr 27] workmanlike gelding: modest handicap hurdler: fell in maiden on chasing debut: stays 3m: acts on good to firm and heavy going. *J. S. King* **c– h–**

WAR TUNE 9 b.g. Warrshan (USA) – Keen Melody (USA) (Sharpen Up) [2004/5 c100, h–: c21g^{pu} 20m^{pu} Jun 5] workmanlike gelding: winning chaser/maiden hurdler: ran badly both starts in 2004/5: should stay 3m: acts on soft and good to firm going: tried in cheekpieces: swishes tail under pressure. *Ian Williams* **c– h–**

WAS A DRIVE (IRE) 11 b.g. Yashgan – Alan's Rosalinda (Prefairy) [2004/5 c68, h–: c20m^{ur} c21g^2 c21d^2 c21m^3 Sep 28] good-topped gelding: well held only outing over hurdles: poor handicap chaser: soundly beaten in points in 2005: stays 21f: acts on good to firm and heavy going: tried in cheekpieces, blinkered nowadays. *Miss Kate Milligan* **c68 h–**

WASHBROOK 4 b.g. Royal Applause – Alacrity (Alzao (USA)) [2004/5 16m 16d Feb 4] leggy gelding: modest maiden on Flat (stays 7f), sold out of A. Turnell's stable 1,600 gns Doncaster October Sales: well held in 2 juvenile hurdles. *M. D. Hammond* **h–**

WASHINGTON LAD (IRE) 5 ch.g. Beneficial – Kyle Lark (Miner's Lamp) [2004/5 F16g^2 F16v^3 F16d^2 F16d^4 18v^3 20v* 20v* 24g Mar 18] leggy, quite good-topped gelding: seventh foal: brother to fairly useful hurdler up to 2½m Ardsallagh's Lark: dam unraced **h126 F97**

Building Design Golden Cygnet Novices' Hurdle, Leopardstown—Tony McCoy galvanises Washington Lad after this last-flight mistake to inflict a rare defeat on Asian Maze (No.5)

half-sister to useful hurdler/chaser up to 25f Lake Teereen: fairly useful form in bumpers: successful over hurdles in maiden at Fairyhouse (made all) and Grade 3 novice at Leopardstown (beat Asian Maze 1½ lengths) in January: better effort after (reportedly had lung infection in Grade 2 at Cheltenham) when third to Asian Maze in Grade 1 novice at Punchestown in late-April: should stay 3m: raced on good going or softer (acts well on heavy). *P. A. Fahy, Ireland*

WASHINGTON PINK (IRE) 6 b.g. Tagula (IRE) – Little Red Rose (Precocious) [2004/5 19m5 c21mpu 21m 21m 17d 21d5 20spu 17v5 Nov 8] compact gelding: winning hurdler: off 20 months, no sign of retaining ability, including in maiden chase: visored/in cheekpieces 5 starts prior to final one. *C. Grant* **c– h–**

WASTED TALENT (IRE) 5 b.m. Sesaro (USA) – Miss Garuda (Persian Bold) [2004/5 h112: 19s* 16d2 Oct 2] leggy mare: fairly useful on Flat (stays 1½m): similar form over hurdles: won mares novice at Newton Abbot in May: much better form when ¾-length second to Dalaram in quite valuable 4-y-o handicap at Chepstow (finished lame): likely to stay 2½m: raced on good going or softer over hurdles: in cheekpieces/ blinkers last 5 starts: free-going sort, races prominently. *J. G. Portman* **h119**

WATCHFUL WITNESS 5 ch.h. In The Wings – Eternal (Kris) [2004/5 h94: 16d 25v 24s 20s 24d 25g4 Mar 14] smallish horse: winning hurdler, disappointing in handicaps in 2004/5: stays 25f: acts on soft going: tried blinkered: has failed to impress with attitude. *Dr J. R. J. Naylor* **h77**

WATCH THE DOVE 8 b.g. Afzal – Spot The Dove (Riberetto) [2004/5 c91x, h98: 22g5 c21g4 c20m2 c26d* c26m2 Sep 5] angular gelding: maiden hurdler: modest chaser: won 2-runner maiden at Newton Abbot in August: stays 3¼m: acts on any going: tried in cheekpieces/visor, blinkered last 4 starts: usually front runner: generally let down by jumping over fences. *C. L. Tizzard* **c92 x h80**

WATER JUMP (IRE) 8 b.g. Suave Dancer (USA) – Jolies Eaux (Shirley Heights) [2004/5 16s6 Nov 20] very smart on Flat (stays 13f) at 4 yrs for J. Dunlop: very lightly raced since: none too fluent when well held in novice on hurdling debut. *Miss H. C. Knight* **h–**

WATER KING (USA) 6 b.g. Irish River (FR) – Brookshield Baby (IRE) (Sadler's Wells (USA)) [2004/5 h88: 16s2 18g2 19m2 Apr 9] modest handicap hurdler: stays 19f: acts on soft and good to firm going: has been led to post (refused to line up once). *R. M. Stronge* **h92**

WATERLINE BLUE (IRE) 4 b.g. Mujadil (USA) – Blues Queen (Lahib (USA)) [2004/5 16s 24g 22s6 Mar 9] fairly useful winner at 2 yrs for P. D. Evans, poor efforts on Flat in 2004: no form over hurdles. *P. Bowen* **h–**

WATERLOO SON (IRE) 5 b.g. Luso – Waterloo Sunset (Deep Run) [2004/5 F16v F16d Mar 14] close-coupled gelding: fifth foal: half-brother to bumper winner Waterloo Park (by Alphabatim): dam twice-raced sister to top-class chaser up to 21f Waterloo Boy: signs of ability on second start in bumpers. *H. D. Daly* **F78 +**

WATER QUIRL (GER) 6 ch.g. Dr Devious (IRE) – Water Quest (IRE) (Rainbow Quest (USA)) [2004/5 c125, h?: c17dpu 17g* c22g5 20v5 c21dur 16d 16dur 16v6 16dpu 20d5 17m Apr 9] leggy gelding: winning hurdler/chaser around 2m, including in minor hurdle at Bad Harzburg in July: left C. Von Der Recke after fourth start: modest form at best over hurdles in Britain: tried visored: has had tongue tied. *M. F. Harris* **c? h93**

WATERSHIP DOWN (IRE) 8 b.g. Dolphin Street (FR) – Persian Myth (Persian Bold) [2004/5 19d May 4] leggy gelding: winning chaser: lightly raced over hurdles: stays 23f: acts on firm and good to soft going, possibly not on heavy: has looked none too keen. *B. G. Powell* **c– h–**

WATERSPRAY (AUS) 7 ch.g. Lake Coniston (IRE) – Forain (NZ) (Nassipour (USA)) [2004/5 h97: 20m4 16g3 16m5 16g2 c17m* c17fF c16d2 c16g2 c16g2 c19s* c20d5 Mar 24] small, angular gelding: modest handicap hurdler: fairly useful chaser: won maiden at Plumpton in September and novice handicap at Taunton in January: stays 19f: acts on firm and soft going: races up with pace: consistent. *J. L. Spearing* **c115 h96**

WATER TAXI 4 ch.g. Zafonic (USA) – Trellis Bay (Sadler's Wells (USA)) [2004/5 16v Mar 5] rather leggy gelding: fair form in 1½m maidens on Flat in 2004, sold out of R. Charlton's stable 28,000 gns Doncaster August Sales: tongue tied, tailed off in juvenile on hurdling debut. *Ferdy Murphy* **h–**

WATSON LAKE (IRE) 7 b.g. Be My Native (USA) – Magneeto (IRE) (Brush Aside (USA)) [2004/5 h133: 20g c17s* c20d* c16v* c16g4 c20s3 Mar 29] **c148 + h–**

The first two home in a maiden chase at Navan in early-November had both made a big impact at a far higher level by the time they met up again at Punchestown in late-April, the winner Watson Lake having followed up in Grade 1 and Grade 2 events, while runner-up Fota Island went on to win three races, including major handicaps at Cheltenham and Aintree. The pair were leading contenders for the Swordlestown Cup at Punchestown, but unfortunately Fota Island got no further than the fifth, while Watson Lake could finish only second after looking all over a winner when holding an eight-length lead, still on the bridle, going to the second last. Watson Lake blundered at that fence, faltered when put under pressure and was caught near the line by Fota Island's stable-companion War of Attrition, who beat him a length. No reason for Watson Lake's weak finish came to light immediately after the race and, given that he looked like winning in good style before his blunder, it is possible that he is better than we are able to rate him at present. His trainer Noel Meade thought perhaps the horse had a problem with his wind, and reported that jockey Paul Carberry sensed the horse running out of steam even before the mistake. What isn't in doubt is that Watson Lake was one of the season's best novice chasers, and provided all is well with him he looks sure to pick up more good prizes when he goes into open company.

Watson Lake was a useful performer in bumpers in 2002/3, when successful at Down Royal, and also over hurdles in 2003/4, when winning a maiden at Navan and the Grade 3 Golden Cygnet Novices' Hurdle at Leopardstown, and he quickly showed himself to be an even better chaser. On his second start over fences, Watson Lake won the Grade 1 Pierse Group Drinmore Novices' Chase at Fairyhouse by three lengths from Forget The Past, all out to hold on after looking likely to win impressively before blundering three out and two out. Watson Lake jumped well out in front until those errors, and he was foot perfect throughout when completing his hat-trick in the Flyingbolt Novices' Chase, back at Navan, again making the running and travelling better than odds-on Ulaan Baatar when that rival made a bad mistake three out, Watson Lake drawing clear from that point to win by twenty lengths. Watson Lake had just two more runs before Punchestown and was ridden more patiently in both. He ran creditably when six and a half lengths fourth to Contraband in the Arkle Trophy at Cheltenham, but was below form when third, beaten the same distance, to Like-A-Butterfly in the Powers Gold Cup at Fairyhouse. Having looked in need of a bit more of a test than two miles on good ground

*Pierse Group Drinmore Novices' Chase, Fairyhouse—
Watson Lake on his way to the second of three chase wins*

Mr John Corr's "Watson Lake"

at Cheltenham provided, Watson Lake produced another tame finishing effort over two and a half miles on soft ground at Fairyhouse.

Watson Lake (IRE) (b.g. 1998)	Be My Native (USA) (br 1979)	Our Native (b or br 1970)	Exclusive Native
			Our Jackie
		Witchy Woman (ch 1972)	Strate Stuff
			Witchy Norma
	Magneeto (IRE) (b 1992)	Brush Aside (b 1986)	Alleged
			Top Twig
		Cacador's Magnet (ch 1975)	Chinatown
			Cacador's Darling

Watson Lake, a tall, good sort, fetched IR £70,000 as an unraced three-year-old. There is nothing in his pedigree to suggest two and a half miles should be the limit of his stamina. He is the third foal and only winner to date out of Magneeto, an unraced half-sister to the useful hurdler at up to three miles Truth Be Told. The next dam Cacador's Magnet, a maiden, is a daughter of the unraced Cacador's Darling who has enjoyed a good deal of success at stud. Cacador's Darling herself produced four winners, while one of her daughters, Calamity Jane, is the dam of the Maryland Hunt Cup winner Tom Bob and another, Cacador's Pet, has produced three winners, all useful or better, including the 1988 Galway Plate winner Afford A King and the very smart three-mile chaser Garamycin. This is also the family of the useful but ill-fated staying chaser Smith's Band and the useful two-mile chaser Queen of

Spades. Watson Lake has raced only on good going or softer and acts on heavy. *N. Meade, Ireland*

WAVE BACK (IRE) 9 b.m. Bob Back (USA) – Stormy Wave (Gulf Pearl) [2004/5 21d^{6} 20d 20v^{6} 22s* 27v 22v* 25s 25g^{3} 25g^{4} Mar 27] sturdy mare: winning pointer: poor handicap hurdler: won at Folkestone in January (seller) and February: stays 25f: raced on good going or softer (acts on heavy): none too reliable. *Miss E. Hill* **h76**

WAVENEY LADY 4 ch.f. Dancing Spree (USA) – Tom's Influence (Pitpan) [2004/5 aF13g Nov 24] first foal: dam winning pointer: visored, tailed off in bumper on debut. *M. J. Gingell* **F–**

WAVERLEY ROAD 8 ch.g. Pelder (IRE) – Lillicara (FR) (Caracolero (USA)) [2004/5 h97: 22m 16g^{6} 16d^{3} 16s^{F} 18s^{5} 16s c16g^{6} c20g^{pu} 16d 16d^{6} Apr 18] close-coupled gelding: modest hurdler: well beaten on completed start over fences: should stay beyond 2m: acts on good to soft going: tongue tied eighth outing, blinkered final one. *M. Madgwick* **c–** **h89**

WAVERTREE BOY (IRE) 5 ch.g. Hector Protector (USA) – Lust (Pursuit of Love) [2004/5 17d^{4} Feb 1] compact gelding: half-brother to winning 2m hurdler Lambadora (by Suave Dancer): useful on Flat (should stay 2m) in 2003: over 20 lengths fourth to Manorson in novice at Taunton (banned for 40 days under non-triers rule) on hurdling debut, soon long way behind and steady headway after 4 out without being not at all knocked about: should prove capable of considerably better. *D. R. C. Elsworth* **h98 p**

WAVET 5 b.m. Pursuit of Love – Ballerina Bay (Myjinski (USA)) [2004/5 16s^{pu} Feb 24] modest maiden on Flat (stays 1½m): no show in mares maiden on hurdling debut. *J. Pearce* **h–**

WAYDALE HILL 6 ch.m. Minster Son – Buckby Folly (Netherkelly) [2004/5 F73: 20d 20m 16d 23s^{5} 23d Nov 24] poor maiden hurdler: stays 23f: acts on soft ground: in cheekpieces/blinkers last 2 starts. *T. D. Walford* **h68**

WAYNESWORLD (IRE) 7 b.g. Petoski – Mariners Mirror (Julio Mariner) [2004/5 c84?, h–: 23m^{5} May 16] smallish gelding: maiden hurdler/chaser: won twice in points in 2005: should stay beyond 2½m: acts on good to soft going. *M. Scudamore* **c–** **h–**

WAYWARD MELODY 5 b.m. Merdon Melody – Dubitable (Formidable (USA)) [2004/5 h83: 20d^{2} 22m* 20m 22g 22m^{6} 22s^{3} 20d 22d^{3} 25v 20s 22d 26s^{3} 20d 20d^{3} Apr 22] good-topped mare: modest handicap hurdler: won conditional jockeys event at Fontwell (all 3 wins there) in May: stays 2¾m: acts on soft and good to firm going: tried blinkered/in cheekpieces: ungenuine. *G. L. Moore* **h92 §**

WAZIRI (IRE) 4 b.g. Mtoto – Euphorie (GER) (Feenpark (GER)) [2004/5 16d^{5} 16g^{6} 16d Jan 12] close-coupled gelding: fair on Flat (should stay 1½m): best effort in juvenile hurdles when sixth at Newbury. *H. Morrison* **h–**

WAZIYA 6 ch.m. Hurricane Sky (AUS) – Serration (Kris) [2004/5 16d^{2} 16v Oct 30] half-sister to fair hurdler up to 19f Devon Peasant (by Deploy): little form on Flat at 3 yrs: 2 lengths second of 4 in novice at Perth on hurdling debut: soundly beaten in seller next time. *N. G. Richards* **h68**

WEARERICH 8 ch.m. Alflora (IRE) – Weareagrandmother (Prince Tenderfoot (USA)) [2004/5 h–: 16d Apr 20] workmanlike mare: no form over hurdles. *D. J. Wintle* **h–**

WEAVER GEORGE (IRE) 15 b.g. Flash of Steel – Nephrite (Godswalk (USA)) [2004/5 c110d, h–: c26g* c25g^{3} c25m^{3} c24d^{2} c25d^{2} c28s^{2} c24d^{pu} c25m* c21d^{6} c25g^{F} Dec 16] leggy gelding: grand old campaigner, successful 3 times over hurdles and 19 over fences from 116 starts, including in handicap chases at Southwell in May and Catterick (fourth course success) in December: better at 3m+ than shorter: acted on any going: tried visored/blinkered, wore cheekpieces towards end of career: also won 6 times at Sedgefield and 4 times at Kelso: usually came from off pace: reportedly retired. *W. Storey* **c88** **h–**

WEAVER OF DREAMS (IRE) 5 b.g. Victory Note (USA) – Daziyra (IRE) (Doyoun) [2004/5 h–: 16m Apr 28] well held both starts over hurdles. *G. A. Swinbank* **h–**

WEAVER SPELL 4 b.g. Wizard King – Impy Fox (IRE) (Imp Society (USA)) [2004/5 16d Nov 1] poor maiden on Flat (should stay 7f): no show in juvenile on hurdling debut: sold 600 gns Doncaster November Sales. *J. R. Norton* **h–**

WEBBINGTON LASS (IRE) 4 b.f. Petardia – Richardstown Lass (IRE) (Muscatite) [2004/5 16d^{pu} 17m^{pu} Nov 25] close-coupled filly: no form on Flat or in juvenile hurdles. *Dr J. R. J. Naylor* **h–**

WEB MASTER (FR) 7 b.g. Arctic Tern (USA) – Inesperada (Cariellor (FR)) [2004/5 h93, F–: 26g 24d 27d^{4} c25v^{5} 27d^{2} 23v^{4} c27v 27v 22v 24v^{4} Mar 17] leggy gelding: modest handicap hurdler: little show in 2 outings over fences: stays 27f: acts on heavy going: wore cheekpieces eighth outing: sold 3,500 gns Doncaster May Sales. *C. Grant* **c– h93**

WEDNESDAY CLUB 4 ch.g. Shahanndeh – Fleur de Tal (Primitive Rising (USA)) [2004/5 F13s^{6} F16s Feb 26] angular gelding: third foal: dam, winning 2m hurdler, half-sister to useful winner up to 7f Blakeset: easily better effort in bumpers when sixth of 14 at Exeter. *N. M. Babbage* **F87**

WEE DANNY (IRE) 8 b.g. Mandalus – Bonne Bouche (Bonne Noel) [2004/5 h101: 24d 27m^{3} 24g^{5} 27g^{3} 24g^{5} 26m^{5} 26g^{4} Oct 5] workmanlike gelding: modest handicap hurdler: stays 27f: acts on firm and good to soft going: usually races prominently. *L. A. Dace* **h88**

WEE JUNIOR 9 gr.g. Alflora (IRE) – Sheer Gold (Yankee Gold) [2004/5 c24s^{F} c23g^{pu} Apr 12] winning pointer: failed to complete in hunter chases. *O. A. Little* **c–**

WEE RIVER (IRE) 16 b.g. Over The River (FR) – Mahe Reef (Be Friendly) [2004/5 c–, h–: c16g^{pu} c16m Jun 5] no longer of any account. *J. Barclay* **c– h–**

WEE ROBBIE 5 b.g. Bob Back (USA) – Blast Freeze (IRE) (Lafontaine (USA)) [2004/5 F18s* F16d^{6} F16g Mar 16] 81,000 3-y-o: tall, useful-looking gelding: first foal: dam useful hurdler up to 2½m: fairly useful form in bumpers: won at Plumpton on debut in January: sixth to Karanja in Grade 2 at Newbury and thirteenth in Grade 1 at Cheltenham: will stay at least 2½m. *N. J. Gifford* **F99**

WEE SEAN (IRE) 5 b.g. Rashar (USA) – Mrs Blobby (IRE) (Rontino) [2004/5 16m 17s 22s^{pu} Apr 3] 4,000 4-y-o: third foal: dam, maiden pointer, half-sister to useful chaser Fiftysevenchannels, effective at 2m to 3m and cross country: little show in novice hurdles. *Miss Lucinda V. Russell* **h–**

WEET A HEAD (IRE) 4 b.g. Foxhound (USA) – Morale (Bluebird (USA)) [2004/5 16s^{3} Oct 21] fair on Flat (stays 10.6f): third of 12 in juvenile at Ludlow on hurdling debut. *R. Hollinshead* **h87**

WEE WILLOW 11 b.m. Minster Son – Peak Princess (Charlottown) [2004/5 h79: 24g^{2} 26g^{2} 22s^{4} 27d Oct 27] smallish mare: poor handicap hurdler: attempted to run out twice final start: best at 3m+: acts on heavy going: often front runner. *D. W. Whillans* **h79**

WELCOME TO UNOS 8 ch.g. Exit To Nowhere (USA) – Royal Loft (Homing) [2004/5 h110§: 20d 22v^{5} 17s c16g^{3} c19d c19d^{2} c16s^{bd} Mar 5] sturdy gelding: ungenuine winning hurdler: fair form when placed over fences at Catterick: stays 2½m: acts on good to firm and heavy going: tried visored. *K. G. Reveley* **c107 h– §**

WELL ACTUALLY (IRE) 5 b.g. Luso – Lake Garden Park (Comedy Star (USA)) [2004/5 F16d Feb 12] €85,000 4-y-o: rangy, good sort: sixth foal: half-brother to fair hurdler/chaser Arctic Sky (by Arctic Lord), stays 21f: dam, ran once at 2 yrs, from family of useful staying chaser Billygoat Gruff: tailed off in Grade 2 bumper at Newbury on debut. *B. G. Powell* **F–**

WELLBEING 8 b.g. Sadler's Wells (USA) – Charming Life (NZ) (Sir Tristram) [2004/5 16v^{2} Dec 18] half-brother to useful hurdler Demi Beau (by Dr Devious) and winning hurdler/pointer Rajati (by Chief's Crown): smart up to 1½m on Flat at 3 and 4 yrs for H. Cecil, successful twice in 2002 for P. Bary: curtailed career at stud: shaped with promise when second to Roman Ark in novice at Haydock on hurdling debut: will stay 2½m: open to improvement, especially if brushing up jumping. *P. J. Hobbs* **h108 +**

WELL CHIEF (GER) 6 ch.g. Night Shift (USA) – Wellesiena (GER) (Scenic) [2004/5 c150p, h142: c16d^{2} c16d^{3} c16v^{F} c16s* c17d^{2} c16g^{2} c16g* Apr 23] **c182 h–**

The platitudinous 'Two's company, three's a crowd' seemed an accurate summing-up of the public's anticipation of the Tingle Creek Trophy Chase at Sandown in December. Modern horse racing evolved from early challenge matches and the Tingle Creek was billed, and regarded widely, as a virtual match between the last two winners of the Queen Mother Champion Chase, Irish-trained Moscow Flyer and the reigning British-trained two-mile champion Azertyuiop. Azertyuiop was sent off at 6/5-on with Moscow Flyer at 2/1. Celebrated races apparently involving only two main protagonists, with the rest making up the numbers, often turn out differently—the 1971 Two Thousand Guineas in which Brigadier Gerard upstaged Mill Reef and My Swallow or the 2003 Stayers' Hurdle in which the novice Iris's Gift split Baracouda and Limestone Lad are two particularly notable examples. In both cases the interloper proved every bit as good as the performance suggested, as in the Tingle Creek. Waited with and jumping fluently, the previous year's Arkle Trophy winner Well Chief, contesting only his fifth steeplechase, showed himself a chaser of the highest calibre, narrowly showing in second at the last before going down by a length and a half and a short head to Moscow Flyer and Azertyuiop, with fourth-placed Cenkos, winner of the Tingle Creek two years earlier, twenty-five lengths further back in fourth.

The 'big two' among the two-mile chasers were now definitely the 'big three', anyone doubting the form of the Tingle Creek having only to wait until Well Chief's next completed outing for conclusive proof that, along with Moscow Flyer and Azertyuiop, he ranks among the best two-mile chasers that the sport has ever seen. The latest running of the Victor Chandler Chase—and the sponsor is to be congratulated for not restyling it the vcbet.com Chase—was transferred to Cheltenham's end-of-January fixture because of Ascot's redevelopment. The presence of Well Chief, carrying 11-10, meant that half the field was out of the handicap proper. Well Chief's weight equated to a BHB handicap mark of 176, 8 lb higher than that allotted to Azertyuiop when he was just touched off by Isio in the race the previous year, and 2 lb higher than that allotted to Azertyuiop when winning the Haldon Gold Cup at Exeter on his reappearance. Well Chief himself had been beaten in a handicap (off a BHB mark of 153) on his reappearance, though he all but got up against Armaturk (who was conceding him 1 lb) after being dropped out in last and still having plenty to do two out. When he lined up for the Victor Chandler, Well Chief, who fell four out when seemingly going well in the rescheduled Castleford Chase at Wetherby, was without a win since landing the Arkle/Maghull double in the spring. Easy to back in the Victor Chandler at 5/1, Well Chief came close to repeating the form he showed when a close third in the Tingle Creek, jumping soundly, moving up to lead two out and quickening decisively. His performance in

Victor Chandler Chase (Handicap), Cheltenham—
Well Chief (spotted cap) comes close to repeating his Tingle Creek form as he defies top weight to beat the Paul Nicholls-trained pair Thisthatandtother and Kadarann (noseband)

Betfred Celebration Chase, Sandown—the conclusive blow in the trainers' championship, with Azertyuiop playing second fiddle to his younger rival again

beating Thisthatandtother by a length and three quarters, conceding the runner-up 20 lb, wasn't quite of the calibre—at least the way we looked at the form—of Azertyuiop's cracking effort in the race the previous year, though it was the best handicap performance seen in the latest season, marginally better than Azertyuiop's at Exeter.

The Tingle Creek and Victor Chandler displays established Well Chief as possibly the best horse his trainer has handled in a long and illustrious career, on a par with Carvill's Hill. Carvill's Hill's runaway victory under top weight in the 1991 Welsh National ranks as one of the finest weight-carrying efforts in Timeform's experience. It stood as the best seen in a handicap since Desert Orchid's (rated 187) in the Racing Post Chase at Kempton in 1990 until Azertyuiop equalled it in the 2004 Victor Chandler. Well Chief is owned by Martin Pipe's principal patron David Johnson for whom eighty-two different horses ran in the latest season. Mr Johnson has a string of around forty or fifty in training at any one time and estimates his average monthly training bill at more than £100,000. He was the leading owner over jumps for the fifth time (and the fourth in a row) with 1,2,3 prize money of £1,677,153, shattering his own record set the previous season. As well as becoming the first owner to top the £1m mark in prize money in a season over jumps, he also became the first to win a hundred races in a jumping season, ending the campaign with a total of one hundred and eleven. To put the tremendous season enjoyed by the Johnson horses in perspective, no owner had previously won more than fifty races in a jumping season, a mark set by Dorothy Paget in 1951/2 (Johnson had forty-nine winners in the 2001/2 season). It is surprising that Miss Paget's record, remarkable though it was at the time, should have stood for so long given the steady growth in the number of fixtures down the years. J. P. McManus also surpassed her total—with fifty-eight races—in the latest season. Incidentally, thirty-eight was the best score by Sheikh Ali Abu Khamsin the only other owner to win the title as many as four times over jumps, which he did in the 'eighties. Among the other high profile winners for David Johnson in the latest season were Celestial Gold (Paddy Power Gold Cup and Hennessy Cognac Gold Cup), Contraband (Henry VIII Novices' Chase and Arkle Trophy), Marcel (Tolworth Hurdle among nine victories) and Comply Or Die (Rising Stars Novices' Chase). The essays on some of those horses contain further details about the running of the Johnson operation and the success of its new retained jockey Timmy Murphy. 'It was never the intention to go for any records,' said Johnson. 'We'd lost A. P. [McCoy] and a hundred winners was the furthest thing from my mind, so it all came as a pleasant surprise.'

Well Chief's epic performance in the Victor Chandler provided another good illustration of the potential that the big handicaps have for finding out just how good the top horses are. Azertyuiop earned his rating of 182 the previous year from his performance in defeat in the Victor Chandler, not from his impressive victory in the Queen Mother Champion Chase. Well Chief was handed a chance to take on Azertyuiop in the Game Spirit Chase at Newbury in February, earlier than expected, given it was thought they would not meet again before the Champion Chase. Receiving 4 lb, Well Chief was weighted to reverse Tingle Creek placings, though Azertyuiop just shaded favouritism at the off. Well Chief made a couple of jumping mistakes and didn't quite run to his best, just two weeks after the Victor Chandler, making little impression on Azertyuiop until late on, eventually beaten two and a half lengths, with Armaturk twenty-three lengths away third. The Game Spirit result made it virtually certain that Well Chief would start third favourite in the Champion Chase, behind Moscow Flyer (winner of his only race between the Tingle Creek and the Cheltenham Festival) and Azertyuiop, Ladbrokes having bet 2/1 each of three after the Victor Chandler.

The two-mile championship at Cheltenham was introduced in 1959 and only one six-year-old—Inkslinger in 1973—has been successful. The patiently-ridden Well Chief was never quite able to get to grips with Moscow Flyer but he put up another outstanding performance to be beaten only two lengths, with Azertyuiop, whose winning chance was effectively ended by a bad mistake at the water, thirteen lengths further back in third. Well Chief's rider dropped his whip late on but Well Chief was well held at the time. Well Chief's form, nonetheless, would have been good enough to win him the race virtually any other year and, with time on his side, he must have a fine chance of adding his name to the roll of honour, provided all remains well with him and he retains his form. Well Chief has a good record at Cheltenham where, as well as winning the Victor Chandler, he has finished in the first two in three successive appearances at the Festival, going down by a head in the Triumph Hurdle the year before winning the Arkle (from Kicking King). Well Chief and Azertyuiop met for the fourth time in the Betfred Celebration Chase at Sandown on the last day of the season. The entire field of nine was made up of runners trained by Martin Pipe and by Paul Nicholls whose battle for the trainers' championship was a feature of the last few weeks of the season. Well

Mr D. A. Johnson's "Well Chief"

Chief's owner admitted that, but for the close finish to the trainers' title, Well Chief might not have been pressed into action at Sandown. However, reports passed on through Channel 4's *Morning Line* programme that Well Chief had been confined to his box for four days were categorically denied. Perhaps because of the reports, Well Chief was sent off at 9/4, with Azertyuiop the 11/10 favourite. Next in the betting at 10/1 were Contraband, the latest winner of the Arkle in the Johnson colours, and Le Roi Miguel, runner-up to Moscow Flyer in the Melling Chase at Aintree. The two highest-rated chasers trained in Britain dominated the Celebration Chase, Well Chief drawing level at two apiece in their personal battle when beating Azertyuiop, who reportedly suffered a bad overreach and faces a lengthy absence, by four lengths, with Contraband a further ten behind in third. Well Chief jumped better than he had in the Game Spirit and was ridden clear up the hill after mastering Azertyuiop between the last two fences.

Well Chief (GER) (ch.g. 1999)	Night Shift (USA) (b 1980)	Northern Dancer (b 1961)	Nearctic
			Natalma
		Ciboulette (b 1961)	Chop Chop
			Windy Answer
	Wellesiena (GER) (b 1994)	Scenic (b 1986)	Sadler's Wells
			Idyllic
		Weltkrone (ch 1982)	Lord Udo
			Weltdame

The essay on Comply Or Die gives an insight into changes that have been made in David Johnson's buying policy. He may be on the lookout for more traditional types nowadays—'good chasers that have got a bit of size'—but Well Chief is certainly not in that mould. A Flat-bred son of Coolmore-based Night Shift, bought off the Flat in Germany (where he won in listed company), he is an angular gelding of no more than medium size. What he lacks in inches, however, he certainly makes up for in other ways, showing plenty of zest for the game and being a sound jumper in the main. He was sweating and edgy at Wetherby and had to be led in at the start before the Celebration Chase, but is a game and genuine performer. He is raced at around two miles and acts on soft and firm going. Ridden prominently in his hurdling days, he is more patiently handled over fences. *M. C. Pipe*

WELL CONNECTED (IRE) 5 b.g. Among Men (USA) – Wire To Wire (Welsh Saint) [2004/5 16s^{pu} 16s^{F} Nov 14] tall gelding: half-brother to 2m hurdle winner Wire Man (by Glenstal): modest maiden on Flat (stays 8.5f) for B. Smart: headstrong, and unlikely stayer over hurdles. *P. D. Niven* **h–**

WELLFRANKO (IRE) 10 b.g. Camden Town – Electana (Electrify) [2004/5 h–: 16d^{6} 16m 16m Jun 8] small, angular gelding: winning hurdler in 2001/2: no other form. *Miss Z. C. Davison* **h–**

WE'LL MAKE IT (IRE) 7 b.g. Spectrum (IRE) – Walliser (Niniski (USA)) [2004/5 h104§: c21g c16s^{3} c20s^{5} Jan 1] angular gelding: fair hurdler: little show over fences: stays 21f: acts on soft and firm going: blinkered: irresolute. *G. L. Moore* **c–** **h– §**

WE'LL MEET AGAIN 5 ch.g. Bin Ajwaad (IRE) – Tantalizing Song (CAN) (The Minstrel (CAN)) [2004/5 17g^{4} 16m 19v 16d^{4} 17d^{3} 16g 17v 17s Feb 7] leggy gelding: modest on Flat (stays 1m): poor maiden hurdler: will prove best at 2m. *M. W. Easterby* **h82**

WELLPICT ONE (IRE) 5 b.g. Taipan (IRE) – Emily Bishop (IRE) (The Parson) [2004/5 F16s^{2} F16d^{2} F16v^{4} Feb 19] €15,500 3-y-o: useful-looking gelding: half-brother to fair 2½m hurdler winner Sally Webster (by Norwich) and 2 winning pointers: dam unraced: in frame in bumpers, fairly useful form when second to Bugle Major at Huntingdon second start. *N. A. Twiston-Davies* **F95**

WELL PRESENTED (IRE) 7 ch.g. Presenting – Casualty Madame (Buckskin (FR)) [2004/5 h123, F103: 24g^{3} c20s^{F} c22v^{F} 21d c24s^{2} c25d^{3} c22v* c21s^{2} c20s* c20s^{6} c25d^{6} Apr 8] strong, workmanlike gelding: fairly useful handicap hurdler at best: took time to get hang of fences (has shown tendency to jump right), but won maiden at Fairyhouse in January and Grade 2 Anglo Irish Bank Nas Na Riogh Novices' Chase at Naas (beat Healy's Pub 5 lengths) in February: best effort when sixth to Pay It Forward in valuable novice handicap at Punchestown in late-April: stays 25f: acts on heavy and good to firm going: has had tongue tied: has made running. *Mrs J. Harrington, Ireland* **c132** **h112**

WELL SAID SAM 9 b.g. Weld – Auto Sam (Even Say) [2004/5 c–: c24d^{F} May 15] runner-up in points: failed to complete in 2 hunter chases. *P. C. Handley* **c–**

WELSH AND WYLDE (IRE) 5 b.g. Anita's Prince – Waikiki (GER) (Zampano (GER)) [2004/5 h82: 16d^{3} 19m Sep 8] poor form over hurdles: barely stays 2m: wore cheekpieces final start: has pulled hard. *B. Palling* **h82**

WELSH DANE 5 b.g. Chaddleworth (IRE) – Dane Rose (Full of Hope) [2004/5 F16s^{3} F16s^{4} 17v^{4} 17g 16v 16d 17v^{3} 21d^{pu} Mar 24] sparely-made gelding: first foal: dam poor maiden hurdler: in frame in bumpers: poor form over hurdles: raced mainly around 2m on good going or softer. *M. Sheppard* **h74 F90**

WELSH DOLL (IRE) 6 b.m. Flemensfirth (USA) – Give Me A Name (Pollerton) [2004/5 F16s F17g 20d Apr 22] narrow, unfurnished mare: tenth foal: half-sister to winning pointer by Buckskin: dam unraced half-sister to useful 2m to 2½m chaser Winter Rain and useful chaser up to 3m Donohill: well held in mares bumpers and novice hurdle. *D. Brace* **h– F–**

WELSH DREAM 8 b.g. Mtoto – Morgannwg (IRE) (Simply Great (FR)) [2004/5 h97+: 16s^{5} 16m^{3} 18v^{3} 16d 16d 19d^{2} 18d* 19g^{6} 22d Apr 11] useful-looking gelding: modest handicap hurdler: won at Kelso in February: probably stays 2¾m: acts on heavy going: usually amateur ridden. *Miss S. E. Forster* **h89**

WELSH GOLD 6 ch.g. Zafonic (USA) – Trying For Gold (USA) (Northern Baby (CAN)) [2004/5 h–, F–: 19g^{pu} c19s^{ur} c19s^{pu} Mar 23] no sign of ability. *S. T. Lewis* **c– h–**

WELSH MAIN 8 br.g. Zafonic (USA) – Welsh Daylight (Welsh Pageant) [2004/5 h106: 16m 17m^{2} Apr 9] sturdy gelding: fair handicap hurdler: left F. Jordan after first outing: raced mainly around 2m: acts on good to firm and good to soft going. *Miss G. Browne* **h108**

WEMYSS QUEST 10 b.g. Rainbow Quest (USA) – Wemyss Bight (Dancing Brave (USA)) [2004/5 c108d, h–: c20m c24d^{3} c25g^{3} c26s^{3} c24g^{pu} Nov 11] quite good-topped gelding: winning hurdler/chaser, poor form over fences in 2004/5: stays 25f: acts on firm and good to soft going: often tongue tied. *Ferdy Murphy* **c84 h–**

B. B. Horse Racing Club's "Well Presented"

WENCESLAS (IRE) 5 b.g. Un Desperado (FR) – Lady of The West (IRE) (Mister Lord (USA)) [2004/5 F16d 16g* 16g 21m Apr 13] tall, good sort: chasing type: second foal: dam once-raced sister to useful but error-prone staying chaser Lord of The West: backward in bumper on debut: modest form in novice hurdles, won at Huntingdon in January: should be suited by further than 2m. *Miss H. C. Knight* **h93 +** F–

WENDYS DYNAMO 8 b.g. Opera Ghost – Good Appeal (Star Appeal) [2004/5 c26v^{5} Apr 22] modest pointer, successful twice in 2005. *Mrs Jo Sleep* **c–**

WENGER (FR) 5 b.g. Unfuwain (USA) – Molly Dance (FR) (Groom Dancer (USA)) [2004/5 20d^{pu} 20d^{3} 20s^{6} 16g^{3} 16s^{5} 18g* 16g^{2} Mar 27] tall, useful-looking gelding: second foal: dam never ran: successful 3 times up to 1½m on Flat in France for R. Gibson: modest form over hurdles: won handicap at Fontwell in March: stays 2¼m: best efforts on good/good to soft going: blinkered last 4 outings: signs of temperament. *P. Winkworth* **h89**

WERE IN TOUCH (IRE) 7 b.g. Old Vic – Winterland Gale (IRE) (Strong Gale) [2004/5 20s^{3} c25s^{2} c26v^{4} c24s* c22g^{3} c24g^{4} Apr 7] well-made gelding: bumper winner: off 21 months, third in novice at Chepstow on hurdling debut: fairly useful form over fences: won maiden at Taunton in February: best effort when third of 4 finishers to Kosmos Bleu in novice handicap at Newbury: stays 3m: raced on good going or softer: tongue tied last 5 starts. *P. F. Nicholls* **c118** **h100 +**

WERE NOT STOPPIN 10 b.g. Mystiko (USA) – Power Take Off (Aragon) [2004/5 h83: 20d^{pu} 16m 16d 17m^{pu} c20g^{2} c21d* c22m^{pu} c22v^{pu} c25g^{3} c25m^{2} Apr 23] good-topped gelding: winning hurdler: modest chaser: won weak maiden at Southwell in August: stays 25f: acts on firm and good to soft going: tried in blinkers/cheekpieces. *R. Bastiman* **c86** **h–**

WESLEY'S LAD (IRE) 11 b. or br.g. Classic Secret (USA) – Galouga (FR) (Lou Piguet (FR)) [2004/5 h85: 20s Nov 21] tall gelding: fairly useful handicap hurdler at one time: no show in selling event only start in 2004/5: stays 2½m: acts on soft and good to firm going. *D. Burchell* **h–**

WESTAR LAD (IRE) 9 ch.g. Pips Pride – Mummys Best (Bustino) [2004/5 19g 16m 21m 19d^{pu} Oct 5] sturdy ex-Irish gelding: half-brother to 2½m hurdle winner Take Your Mark (by Goldmark): modest maiden on Flat (best efforts at 6f): no form over hurdles. *S. J. Gilmore* **h–**

WEST ASIDE (IRE) 11 b.g. Brush Aside (USA) – Chancy Belle (Le Bavard (FR)) [2004/5 c–, h–: 20m^{2} 24g 18s 21d^{pu} c25g c26d^{pu} Dec 7] poor maiden hurdler: no form over fences: often blinkered: tried tongue tied. *T. P. McGovern* **c–** **h64**

WEST BAY STORM 5 b.m. Relief Pitcher – West Bay Breeze (Town And Country) [2004/5 F16s F16s Mar 13] first foal: dam poor novice hurdler: well beatens in 2 bumpers. *Mrs H. R. J. Nelmes* F–

WEST COASTER (IRE) 7 gr.g. Be My Native (USA) – Donegal Grey (IRE) (Roselier (FR)) [2004/5 h–: c21g^{5} c24s^{2} c25v^{6} c25s^{pu} c25m^{4} Apr 23] lengthy, good-topped gelding: maiden hurdler/chaser: sold out of Miss H. Knight's stable 14,500 gns Doncaster May Sales after first start, won maiden point in January: left D. Easterby after third start: stays 3m. *M. W. Easterby* **c91** **h–**

WESTCRAFT (IRE) 5 b.g. Warcraft (USA) – Copperhurst (IRE) (Royal Vulcan) [2004/5 aF16g^{2} F16g^{4} F16d F18d Apr 18] €12,000 3-y-o: lengthy, rather unfurnished gelding: first foal: dam, winning hurdler/chaser who stayed 25f, out of sister to useful chaser up to 3m Bold Yeoman: fair form first 2 starts in bumpers. *A. Ennis* F91

WESTENDER (FR) 9 b.g. In The Wings – Trude (GER) (Windwurf (GER)) [2004/5 h158: 16m^{5} c16g^{2} c16g^{R} 16d^{2} 17d^{3} 20d* 24s^{3} 24g^{4} 24s^{R} Apr 7] tall, close-coupled gelding: very smart hurdler: first win since 2001 when beating Big Moment by 9 lengths in minor event at Cheltenham in January: ran creditably there when second to Accordion Etoile in Grade 3 handicap and when fourth to Inglis Drever in World Hurdle: refused second in Grade 2 at Aintree final start: fairly useful form when runner-up to River City in novice at Worcester on chasing debut: refused first next time: stays 3m: acts on good to firm and soft going, probably on heavy: blinkered: not one to trust. *M. C. Pipe* **c117 §** **h157 §**

WEST END PEARL 4 ch.f. The West (USA) – Raghill Hannah (Buckskin (FR)) [2004/5 F12d F13s Jan 31] second foal: dam unraced: well held in 2 bumpers. *C. G. Cox* F73

WESTERN BLUEBIRD (IRE) 7 b.g. Bluebird (USA) – Arrastra (Bustino) [2004/5 h67: 20d 22g^{pu} c21m^{5} Aug 31] leggy gelding: poor hurdler: no show in novice on chasing debut: stays 2½m: sometimes wears blinkers/cheekpieces. *Miss Kate Milligan* **c–** **h–**

WESTERNMOST 7 b.g. Most Welcome – Dakota Girl (Northern State (USA)) [2004/5 h92: 20d 17d^{5} May 29] workmanlike gelding: handicap hurdler, well held both starts in 2004/5: stays easy 21f: acts on heavy and good to firm going: tried in cheekpieces. *M. Todhunter* **h78**

WESTERN RIDGE (FR) 8 b.g. Darshaan – Helvellyn (USA) (Gone West (USA)) [2004/5 h105: 19d^{3} May 17] close-coupled gelding: fair handicap hurdler: pulled up lame on Flat in May: stays 19f: acts on firm and good to soft going: patiently ridden. *B. J. Llewellyn* **h104**

WEST HILL GAIL (IRE) 6 b.m. Roselier (FR) – V'Soske Gale (IRE) (Strong Gale) [2004/5 F17d 24s^{pu} 24d^{pu} Feb 1] 2,000 4-y-o: small mare: second foal: dam, fair hurdler/chaser, stayed 2¾m: no sign of ability in bumper or novice hurdles. *V. R. A. Dartnall* **h– F–**

WEST HILL (IRE) 4 b.g. Gone West (USA) – Altamura (USA) (El Gran Senor (USA)) [2004/5 16s 16s 17d 16s^{3} Mar 5] good-topped gelding: third over 11f on first of 2 starts on Flat at 3 yrs, sold out of A. Fabre's stable 11,500 gns Doncaster August Sales: little sign of ability over hurdles. *D. McCain* **h63**

WESTMEATH FLYER 10 b.g. Deploy – Re-Release (Baptism) [2004/5 c–, h107: 24d* 20s* 18s* 20s^{F} Apr 21] sturdy gelding: fairly useful hurdler: improved in 2004/5, successful in handicap at Perth in May, conditional jockeys claimer at Carlisle in March and handicap at Kelso (by 2½ lengths from Totally Scottish) in April: every chance when fell 2 out at Perth final start: effective at 2¼m to 3m: raced on going softer than good (acts on heavy): consistent. *N. G. Richards* **c– h127**

WESTMERE 5 b.g. Alderbrook – Moonlight Air (Bold Owl) [2004/5 F17g F16m Apr 10] first foal: dam, fair hurdler up to 3m, half-sister to useful 2m hurdler Mariner's Air: well held in 2 bumpers. *J. L. Spearing* **F–**

WESTON MARAUDER 8 b.g. Unfuwain (USA) – Rushing River (USA) (Irish River (FR)) [2004/5 19g^{pu} Jul 4] no sign of ability. *M. J. Gingell* **h–**

WESTON ROCK 6 b.g. Double Eclipse (IRE) – Mossberry Fair (Mossberry) [2004/5 h96, F92: 24g^{3} 21g^{4} 16d^{pu} 19d Jan 13] angular gelding: modest novice hurdler: stays 3m: wore cheekpieces last 3 starts: suffered fibrillating heart third outing. *T. D. Walford* **h96**

WEST PACES (IRE) 11 br.g. Lord Americo – Spanish Royale (Royal Buck) [2004/5 c95, h–: c21d^{2} c22g^{6} Apr 1] medium-sized gelding: fairly useful pointer/hunter chaser: stays 25f: acts on good to firm and good to soft going. *S. Dixon* **c105 h–**

WEST PAL (IRE) 11 ch.g. Lancastrian – Buck And Roll (Buckskin (FR)) [2004/5 c85§, h–: c31m^{pu} c24g^{pu} May 27] workmanlike gelding: winning staying chaser: stays 3¼m: acts on good to firm and good to soft going: blinkered in 2004/5: sold £1,800 Ascot July Sales, no show in points in 2005. *Mrs S. J. Humphrey* **c– § h–**

WESTS AWAKE (IRE) 9 b.g. King's Ride – Letterfore (Strong Gale) [2004/5 c20g* c20m* c21g* 24f^{3} c20g* c22m 24m^{6} 24d^{5} c24v^{pu} Dec 27] fairly useful handicap chaser: won at Clonmel, Fairyhouse and Roscommon in May and Tipperary (beat Fable 1½ lengths) in July: modest maiden hurdler: stays 3m: acts on any going. *I. Madden, Ireland* **c116 h92**

WET LIPS (AUS) 7 ch.g. Grand Lodge (USA) – Kissing (AUS) (Somalia (AUS)) [2004/5 h106: 20d 20g^{3} 22g 17m^{4} 16g^{5} 17d^{2} 19d^{5} 17d^{3} 19g Sep 25] leggy gelding: fairly useful handicap hurdler: best effort when 5 lengths second to Alrida in valuable event at Market Rasen in July: stays 2½m: acts on firm and good to soft going: used to wear cheekpieces, blinkered and tongue tied last 4 starts. *R. C. Guest* **h110**

WHALEEF 7 b.g. Darshaan – Wilayif (USA) (Danzig (USA)) [2004/5 h103: c16m^{F} c16m^{2} c16g^{pu} 16g 18m* 19g^{pu} Sep 25] good-topped gelding: fair hurdler: sold out of P. Webber's stable 7,500 gns Doncaster August Sales after fourth start: form in 2004/5 only when winning handicap at Fontwell in September: found little only completed outing over fences: stays 2¼m: acts on good to firm going: in cheekpieces and tongue tied last 2 starts: inconsistent. *B. J. Llewellyn* **c– h109**

WHAT A CHARMER (IRE) 9 b.g. Be My Native (USA) – Deadly Charm (USA) (Bates Motel (USA)) [2004/5 c22d^{pu} c24s^{pu} Mar 14] 25,000 3-y-o: second foal: dam, fairly useful hurdler/chaser up to 2½m: won maiden point in 2003: no sign of ability otherwise. *J. E. Dillon* **c–**

WHAT A MAN (IRE) 8 b.g. Beau Sher – Cactus Wren (IRE) (Remainder Man) [2004/5 c20d^{4} c24d^{6} c25s^{3} c23v^{2} c24d^{3} Feb 19] winning Irish pointer: fair maiden chaser: blinkered, finished lame when third in handicap at Lingfield final start: stays 25f: raced on going softer than good (acts on heavy). *G. L. Moore* **c107 h–**

WHAT A MONDAY 7 b.g. Beveled (USA) – Raise Memories (Skyliner) [2004/5 h101p, F92: 19d Jan 12] lengthy, angular gelding: bumper winner: never a factor in novice hurdles at Newbury a year apart. *K. Bell* **h–**

WHATAMONKEY 12 gr.g. Thethingaboutitis (USA) – Shrood Biddy (Sharrood (USA)) [2004/5 c25m^pu c26s^pu Mar 13] modest pointer: in cheekpieces, no show in 2 hunter chases. *P. Morris* **c–**

WHAT A MOVER 9 b.m. Jupiter Island – Si-Gaoith (Strong Gale) [2004/5 c25d³ c24g^F Apr 15] fairly useful pointer: third in hunter chase at Ludlow. *Mrs O. Bush* **c98**

WHAT A NIGHT 6 gr.g. Environment Friend – Misty Night (Grey Desire) [2004/5 F16g⁶ 19d 22s Apr 3] sturdy gelding: first foal: dam poor 2m novice hurdler: last of 5 finishers in 2½m maiden on second of 2 starts in points in 2004: well held in bumper and 2 novice hurdles. *Mrs A. C. Hamilton* **h–** **F–**

WHATASHOCK 10 b.g. Never So Bold – Lady Electric (Electric) [2004/5 c78: c21g* c20d² c20m c22m⁶ Jun 25] medium-sized gelding: fair chaser: won novice handicap at Wincanton in May: stays 21f: acts on good to soft going: has folded tamely. *A. King* **c106**

WHAT A VINTAGE (IRE) 5 ch.m. Un Desperado (FR) – The Vine Browne (IRE) (Torus) [2004/5 F16s² Mar 13] €15,000 3-y-o, 6,000 4-y-o: second foal: dam lightly-raced maiden from family of one-time very smart staying chaser Macgeorge and high-class 2m hurdler Deep Idol: 7 lengths second of 18 to Gay Gladys in mares maiden bumper at Warwick on debut: sold 25,000 gns (privately) Doncaster May Sales. *O. Sherwood* **F89**

WHAT DO'IN (IRE) 7 b. or br.g. Good Thyne (USA) – Della Wee (IRE) (Fidel) [2004/5 F96: 22s* 24v³ 20v Jan 3] quite good-topped gelding: won amateur novice at Exeter on hurdling debut in October: below form both subsequent starts: likely to prove better at 3m than shorter. *N. A. Twiston-Davies* **h108**

WHATDO YOU WANT (IRE) 5 b.m. Spectrum (IRE) – Soviet Pretender (USA) (Alleged (USA)) [2004/5 F–: F16s Apr 10] tall mare: well held in bumpers: tried tongue tied. *G. M. Moore* **F–**

WHAT IF (IRE) 8 b.g. Lord Americo – Romany River (Over The River (FR)) [2004/5 h99: c20s c23d c20v⁶ c25s² Mar 11] sturdy gelding: winning pointer: modest maiden hurdler/chaser: stays 25f: acts on heavy and good to firm going. *I. Buchanan, Ireland* **c90** **h–**

WHAT'S A FILLY 5 b.m. Bob's Return (IRE) – Pearly-B (IRE) (Gunner B) [2004/5 F–: F16s 20d^F 16s* 20d Jan 26] 100/1, form only when winning maiden hurdle at Kelso in December: should stay beyond 2m. *R. C. Guest* **h84** **F–**

WHAT'S AHEAD 5 ch.m. Emperor Fountain – Our Wilma (Master Willie) [2004/5 F16s Mar 12] second foal: dam, lightly-raced maiden, half-sister to fairly useful 2m hurdler Top Wave and useful sprinter Flying Squaw: never dangerous in bumper on debut. *Mrs J. C. McGregor* **F–**

WHATS GOOD (IRE) 7 b. or br.g. Religiously (USA) – Islet Time (Burslem) [2004/5 F–: 21d 24d^pu Nov 19] sturdy gelding: no sign of ability: tongue tied both starts in 2004/5. *K. C. Bailey* **h–**

WHAT'SONYOURMIND (IRE) 5 b.g. Glacial Storm (USA) – Granny Clark (IRE) (Remainder Man) [2004/5 F16v* Jan 19] €35,000 4-y-o: first foal: dam unraced sister to Festival Bumper winner/useful hurdler up to 2½m Wither Or Which, and half-sister to dam of one-time top-class staying chaser Alexander Banquet: won bumper at Navan on debut impressively by 14 lengths from Patsy Hall: good prospect. *P. M. J. Doyle, Ireland* **F110 p**

WHAT'S THE COUNT 9 gr.g. Theatrical Charmer – Yankee Silver (Yankee Gold) [2004/5 c91, h–: c19d³ c18d⁵ c17d^ur 20s⁴ 18s 21g 21d^pu Apr 18] lengthy gelding: fair maiden hurdler: modest form over fences: stays 2¾m: acts on heavy going, seemingly not on firmer than good: tried visored/in cheekpieces: usually tongue tied: free-going sort. *B. R. Johnson* **c91** **h100**

WHAT'S UP BOYS (IRE) 11 gr.g. Supreme Leader – Maryville Bick (Malacate (USA)) [2004/5 c123, h–: 21g⁵ 25d⁶ Nov 13] leggy, lengthy gelding: formerly high-class chaser: won Hennessy Gold Cup and runner-up in Grand National in 2001/2, very lightly raced since: winning hurdler: left P. Hobbs, fairly useful form in handicaps in 2004/5: stayed 4½m: acted on good to firm and heavy going: effective blinkered or not: not easiest of rides, jumped none too fluently: reportedly retired. *Miss H. C. Knight* **c–** **h129**

WHATS UP JAKE 9 ch.g. Gunner B – Head Lass (Funny Man) [2004/5 c24dpu Apr 22] won maiden point in March: jumped poorly in hunter chase. *Mrs C. Thomas* **c–**

WHAT YOU KNOW (IRE) 11 b.g. Be My Guest (USA) – Flamme d'Amour (Gift Card (FR)) [2004/5 h80§: 22g3 22g3 20m3 22f3 Oct 7] angular gelding: poor hurdler: stays 3m: acts on firm going: tried in headgear: occasionally tongue tied: has been reluctant to race: one to treat with caution. *Mrs D. A. Hamer* **h83 §**

WHEREAREYOUNOW (IRE) 8 ch.g. Mister Lord (USA) – Angie's Delight (London Gazette) [2004/5 c133, h–: c21d6 c21s c22v* c20d c24g c21d Apr 8] workmanlike gelding: useful handicap chaser: successful in valuable event at Uttoxeter in February by 17 lengths from Gunner Welburn: below form in similar events otherwise in 2004/5: effective at 2½m to 25f: very best efforts on going softer than good (acts on heavy): sound jumper: usually races prominently. *N. A. Twiston-Davies* **c135 h–**

WHEREDIDTHEMONEYGO (IRE) 6 b.m. Anshan – Charmere's Beauty (IRE) (Phardante (FR)) [2004/5 F16g 16m 19f3 24g2 24m4 Jun 16] €25,000 4-y-o: leggy ex-Irish mare: second foal: half-sister to fairly useful hurdler Blue Ride (by King's Ride), stays 25f: dam unraced half-sister to smart chaser up to 25f Jassu: left S. Treacy after third start: form only when second in maiden hurdle at Uttoxeter. *R. H. Alner* **h89 F–**

WHERESBEN (IRE) 6 b.g. Flemensfirth (USA) – Chataka Blues (IRE) (Grange Melody) [2004/5 F16s* F19d5 F16v* F16v4 Apr 17] good-topped gelding: second foal: dam unraced: fairly useful form in bumpers: won at Down Royal (maiden) in February and Navan (beat Money Trix 11 lengths) in April: creditable sixth to Refinement in Grade 1 at Punchestown in late-April. *Seamus Fahey, Ireland* **F103**

WHERE'S SALLY 5 b.m. Polar Prince (IRE) – Mustang Scally (Makbul) [2004/5 F16g Mar 5] first foal: dam modest 2m maiden hurdler: tenth of 15 in bumper on debut. *J. Mackie* **F–**

WHERE'S THE NURSE (IRE) 4 ch.f. Pasternak – African Isle (IRE) (Erins Isle) [2004/5 F16s F16g6 16sF Apr 3] first foal: dam ran 3 times on Flat in Ireland: no show in 2 mares bumpers: fell fatally on hurdling debut. *Mrs R. L. Elliot* **h– F–**

WHERE'S TRIGGER 5 ch.g. Aristocracy – Queens Connection (Bay Express) [2004/5 F–: F16d6 Nov 6] rather unfurnished gelding: easily better effort in bumpers when sixth of 14 to Briery Fox at Wincanton. *N. A. Twiston-Davies* **F90**

WHETHER THE STORM (IRE) 9 b.g. Glacial Storm (USA) – Minimum Choice (IRE) (Miner's Lamp) [2004/5 c92, h–: c21d c23spu c23m4 Apr 10] strong gelding: modest chaser: stays 3m: acts on good to soft going. *Miss I. E. Craig* **c– h–**

WHICH HALF (IRE) 7 b.g. Grand Plaisir (IRE) – Kilnock Lass (Rymer) [2004/5 22d2 22s2 c17sF Nov 18] fifth foal: dam winning 2m hurdler: fair hurdler: left C. Roche, fatally injured when falling 3 out in handicap at Market Rasen on chasing debut: seemed to stay 3m: acted on soft ground, had bumper form on heavy: tried in cheekpieces *Jonjo O'Neill* **c108 h109**

WHICH MOSCOW (IRE) 8 ch.g. Moscow Society (USA) – Beguiled (IRE) (Be My Guest (USA)) [2004/5 22spu c24dpu Oct 28] workmanlike gelding: half-brother to several winners on Flat, including fairly useful 5f to 7f winner Trickery (by Cyrano de Bergerac): dam, disappointing maiden, half-sister to dam of useful 2m hurdler Shirley's Delight: runner-up once from 2 starts in Irish points: bought 2,800 gns Doncaster May (2003) Sales: no form in Britain: tried blinkered. *C. J. Down* **c– h–**

WHINNY BANK 4 b.f. Classic Cliche (IRE) – Edraianthus (Windjammer (USA)) [2004/5 F13g F16g 20spu 16spu Apr 10] rather leggy filly: half-sister to several winners, including useful Franco-American 1m/9f winner Esquive and fairly useful hurdler Edwarda (both by Safawan), stays 2½m: dam maiden, best at 6f: well held in bumpers: no show over hurdles. *M. W. Easterby* **h– F–**

WHISPERED SECRET (GER) 6 b.g. Selkirk (USA) – Wells Whisper (FR) (Sadler's Wells (USA)) [2004/5 h115: 17d* 16g4 18m* 16m2 20g* 17d5 20s5 Apr 21] rather leggy gelding: fair novice hurdler: landed odds at Bangor and Fontwell in May: better form when winning at Worcester in July: stays 2½m: acts on good to firm and good to soft going. *M. C. Pipe* **h112**

WHISPERING HOLLY 6 b.g. Holly Buoy – Stuart's Gem (Meldrum) [2004/5 h–, F–: 23dro 24g6 20g 17g 21m4 17m 21m2 20gF 21m3 Sep 28] poor maiden hurdler: best efforts around 2½m on good/good to firm going: ungenuine. *R. S. Wood* **h82 §**

WHISPERING MOOR 6 br.g. Terimon – Larksmore (Royal Fountain) [2004/5 F86: 16v6 20v4 20s6 22spu 24s2 Apr 20] tall, good sort: fair novice hurdler: stays 3m: raced on going softer than good. *N. G. Richards* **h103**

WHISPERING STORM (IRE) 7 br.g. Good Thyne (USA) – Ballybride Gale (IRE) (Strong Gale) [2004/5 F85: F17d F16g 16d 20spu 21gpu Mar 28] good-topped gelding: fair at best in bumpers: no form over hurdles. *A. King* **h– F–**

WHIST DRIVE 5 ch.g. First Trump – Fine Quill (Unfuwain (USA)) [2004/5 h100: 18d 21g3 20s3 23d2 22g2 22s* Jan 3] fair hurdler: won novice at Folkestone in January: will stay 3m: acts on soft going, probably on good to firm. *Mrs N. Smith* **h107**

WHISTLING FRED 6 b.g. Overbury (IRE) – Megabucks (Buckskin (FR)) [2004/5 F17d2 aF16g2 16g Dec 8] €18,000 4-y-o: lengthy gelding: third foal: half-brother to fair hurdler Turrill House (by Charmer), stayed 21f: dam, fairly useful 2m hurdler/won up to 1½m on Flat, sister to dam of smart hurdler Georges Girl: close second both starts in bumpers, might have won but for interference 3f out when beaten short head on polytrack at Lingfield: soundly beaten in 25-runner maiden at Newbury on hurdling debut. *B. De Haan* **h– F85**

WHITCOMB (USA) 5 b. or br.h. Skip Away (USA) – Whitebread (USA) (Gran Zar (MEX)) [2004/5 16vpu Jan 26] good-topped horse: successful 4 times up to 1¾m on Flat in Spain for J. H. Brown: tongue tied, failed to settle and jumped poorly in novice on hurdling debut. *J. Mackie* **h–**

WHITE DOVE (FR) 7 b.m. Beaudelaire (USA) – Hermine And Pearls (FR) (Shirley Heights) [2004/5 c81, h80: 20d4 16g* 20m3 19d3 16g3 19s* Jan 5] poor hurdler: won mares handicap (conditional jockeys) at Uttoxeter in June and Hereford in January: similar form at best in 3 chases: stays easy 2½m: acts on good to firm and soft going: effective with or without blinkers/visor. *Ian Williams* **c– h87**

WHITEGATES WILLIE 13 b.g. Buckskin (FR) – Whitegates Lady (Le Coq d'Or) [2004/5 c24dpu May 15] workmanlike gelding: winning pointer/maiden chaser: seemingly retains little ability: tongue tied once. *P. H. Morris* **c– h–**

WHITE IN FRONT 14 ch.g. Tina's Pet – Lyaaric (Privy Seal) [2004/5 c16m6 Sep 24] lengthy gelding: winning 2m chaser: formerly blinkered. *Mrs A. Price* **c– h–**

WHITENZO (FR) 9 b.g. Lesotho (USA) – Whitengy (FR) (Olantengy (FR)) [2004/5 c25d3 c25d5 c25s2 c21spu c24g* c24d* c23v* c29g4 Apr 23] tall gelding: winning hurdler: useful chaser, off 18 months before reappearance: won Royal Artillery Gold Cup and Grand Military Gold Cup at Sandown and handicap at Exeter (beat Kittenkat 8 lengths) in February and March: creditable fourth to Jack High in Betfred Gold Cup at Sandown final start: stays 29f: unraced on firm going, acts on any other: blinkered fourth outing: tongue tied last 4 starts. *P. F. Nicholls* **c134 h–**

WHITE PARK BAY (IRE) 5 b.m. Blues Traveller (IRE) – Valiant Friend (USA) (Shahrastani (USA)) [2004/5 h–: 16vF 18g Mar 12] no sign of ability over hurdles. *J. K. Magee, Ireland* **h–**

WHITESTONE 9 b.m. Sula Bula – Flying Cherub (Osiris) [2004/5 h–: 17gpu Apr 28] medium-sized mare: no sign of ability. *Mrs J. G. Retter* **h–**

WHITFIELD WARRIOR 7 ch.g. Husyan (USA) – Valentines Day (Doctor Pangloss) [2004/5 h–: 21gpu c21d4 c25spu c27d5 c25d4 c25dF c27vpu c25mpu Apr 23] workmanlike gelding: little form over jumps: probably flattered on chasing debut: tried visored: sold 1,600 gns Doncaster May Sales. *J. R. Turner* **c– h–**

WHITFORD DON (IRE) 7 b.g. Accordion – Whitford Breeze (Le Bavard (FR)) [2004/5 h109: c25s2 c26v* c26spu c26vF c26v* c33gur c23v* c25dpu Apr 8] well-made gelding: fair hurdler: fairly useful chaser: won maiden at Warwick in December and novices there in February and Exeter (best effort when beating Bubble Boy 8 lengths) in March: will stay beyond 3¼m: raced on good going or softer (acts on heavy): blinkered last 5 starts: temperamental. *P. F. Nicholls* **c127 § h–**

WHIZBANG (IRE) 6 br.g. Presenting – Native Gale (IRE) (Be My Native (USA)) [2004/5 20d3 20s* 24s3 Dec 12] second foal: dam winning 2m hurdler: successful on second of 2 starts in Irish points: won maiden hurdle at Wexford in November by 11 lengths from Cloone Leader: fairly useful form when third to Homer Wells in Grade 3 novice at Cork following month: stays 3m. *E. J. O'Grady, Ireland* **h116**

WHO CARES WINS 9 ch.g. Kris – Anne Bonny (Ajdal (USA)) [2004/5 h100: 21d2 20s3 19g 19spu 16gpu Apr 19] sparely-made gelding: modest handicap hurdler: **h92**

stays 2¾m: acts on soft and good to firm going: wears cheekpieces/visor nowadays. *J. R. Jenkins*

WHO DARES WINS 12 b.g. Kala Shikari – Sarah's Venture (Averof) [2004/5 c91, h–: c25g* c25s c27v^{pu} Mar 15] tall gelding: modest hunter chaser: won at Hexham in May: dour stayer: acts well on soft/heavy going: tried blinkered/cheekpieces. *Ms S. Duell* **c85 h–**

WHOSETHATFOR (IRE) 5 b.g. Beneficial – Native Craft (IRE) (Be My Native (USA)) [2004/5 F16d^{4} Jan 31] €40,000 3-y-o: rather unfurnished gelding: first foal: dam, modest Irish 2m hurdler, from family of top-class 2m to 3m hurdler Mole Board: shaped quite well when fourth to Hobbs Hill in bumper at Kempton on debut. *J. A. B. Old* **F91**

WHO YOU KNOW 5 b.m. Merdon Melody – Dutyful (Bold Owl) [2004/5 F16d F17g 16g 19m Sep 8] fourth foal: sister to winner in Italy: dam won up to 2m: no sign of ability: usually tongue tied. *Mrs D. A. Hamer* **h– F–**

WHY NOT PEARL 8 gr.m. Arzanni – Delta Rose (Swing Easy (USA)) [2004/5 17g Oct 9] seventh foal: dam novice selling hurdler: tailed off in novice hurdle on debut. *D. Burchell* **h–**

WHYSO MAYO (IRE) 8 b.g. Kasmayo – Why Cry (Pry) [2004/5 c24s^{2} c24v* Apr 6] good-topped gelding: half-brother to a winning pointer in Ireland by Arapahos: dam unraced: prolific winning pointer: won maiden hunter chase at Cork by 2½ lengths from Tyrone Trucker: much better form when 2¾ lengths third to General Montcalm in Champion Hunters Chase at Punchestown in late-April. *Raymond Hurley, Ireland* **c116**

WHY THE BIG PAWS 7 ch.m. Minster Son – Springdale Hall (USA) (Bates Motel (USA)) [2004/5 h–: 20d^{pu} 20g^{6} 22m^{4} c20g* 20g^{ur} c21m^{2} c22g^{6} c24g^{3} c25d^{5} c17v^{2} c20s^{3} c24d^{2} c20m* c20v* c25v^{2} c24s* c20s^{3} c21d c28s^{6} Apr 3] angular mare: maiden hurdler: fair novice chaser: won at Hexham (maiden) in May, Musselburgh and Ayr (minor event) in December and Carlisle (handicap) in February: stays 25f: acts on good to firm and heavy going: usually races prominently. *R. C. Guest* **c104 h–**

WHY THE LONG FACE (NZ) 8 ch.g. Grosvenor (NZ) – My Charm (NZ) (My Friend Paul (USA)) [2004/5 h105: c21g^{F} c20d^{4} c20m^{ur} c20d* c20g^{ur} c20d c17d^{6} c21s^{ur} 16d c20g* c20s^{6} c19d c20g^{6} c20m^{ur} Apr 23] leggy gelding: fair hurdler/chaser: won over fences at Hexham (maiden) in June and Leicester (novice) in December: stays 21f: acts on soft going: usually wears cheekpieces: free-going sort: often let down by jumping over fences. *R. C. Guest* **c101 x h–**

WICHWAY NOW (IRE) 6 b.g. Norwich – Proverb's Way (Proverb) [2004/5 F92: 17s^{6} 16g^{pu} Nov 27] lengthy, unfurnished gelding: fair form in 2 bumpers: not knocked about on hurdling debut: showing quite a bit of improvement when pulled up lame before last in novice at Newbury won by Marcel: likely to stay 2½m: likely to prove capable of better if recovering fully from injury. *Miss E. C. Lavelle* **h104**

WICKED NICE FELLA (IRE) 7 b.g. Warcraft (USA) – Down Town To-Night (Kambalda) [2004/5 20m* 19d^{2} Oct 3] €10,000 4-y-o: third foal: dam 2½m hurdle winner: won maiden on last of 4 starts in Irish points in 2004: modest form in 2 novice hurdles, successful at Fakenham in May: will stay beyond 2½m. *C. C. Bealby* **h96**

WICKED WEASEL (IRE) 7 b.g. Religiously (USA) – Just A Maid (Rarity) [2004/5 F99: F16g May 1] lengthy gelding: fairly useful form when successful in bumper on debut: amateur ridden, well held in similar event over 4 months later. *K. C. Bailey* **F77 +**

WIDEMOUTH BAY (IRE) 7 br.g. Be My Native (USA) – Lisaleen River (Over The River (FR)) [2004/5 h112: 21d 16g^{6} c17s^{4} c21g^{4} 24d Feb 12] lengthy gelding: smart bumper performer in 2002/3: disappointing hurdler: little encouragement either outing over fences: should stay at least 2½m: temperamental. *Miss H. C. Knight* **c– § h125 §**

WILD ABOUT HARRY 8 ch.g. Romany Rye – Shylyn (Hay Chas) [2004/5 h–, F–: 22g^{5} c16v c19d^{pu} c25d^{6} c20v^{2} Apr 17] workmanlike gelding: little form over hurdles: runner-up in novice handicap chase at Carlisle. *A. R. Dicken* **c65 h–**

WILD CANE RIDGE (IRE) 6 gr.g. Roselier (FR) – Shuil Na Lee (IRE) (Phardante (FR)) [2004/5 F113: 20s^{2} 20v* 24v* 23s^{4} 22s* Apr 3] leggy, good-topped gelding: fairly useful novice hurdler: won at Carlisle in November, Hexham (by 13 lengths from Narciso) in December and Kelso (by 7 lengths from Diklers Rose) in April: set good gallop when fourth of 5 to Mephisto in Grade 2 at Haydock: will stay beyond 3m: raced on going softer than good (acts on heavy). *L. Lungo* **h126**

WILD CHIMES (IRE) 6 b.g. Oscar (IRE) – Jingle Bells (FR) (In The Mood (FR)) [2004/5 F18g^{3} 21g^{2} 20s^{3} 22s^{2} c19s^{pu} 24d^{6} 24d^{pu} Mar 3] 9,500 4-y-o: workmanlike gelding: tenth foal: half-brother to 4 winners in France, including 15f hurdle winner Djort **c– h97 F93**

(by Pebble): dam won 15f hurdle in France: won maiden on last of 4 starts in points in 2004: third in bumper at Plumpton: modest novice hurdler: stays 3m: raced on good going or softer (acts on soft): blinkered fourth/fifth starts: tongue tied (possibly amiss) final one. *P. F. Nicholls*

WILD EDGAR (IRE) 8 ch.g. Invited (USA) – Ou La La (IRE) (Be My Native (USA)) [2004/5 F–: c21g^F Apr 30] winning pointer: fading when fell 2 out in hunter chase at Sedgefield. *W. T. Reed* **c–**

WILDFIELD RUFO (IRE) 10 b.g. Celio Rufo – Jersey Girl (Hardboy) [2004/5 c100x, h113: c25m* c26g³ c25m* c25d* c25s³ c25v^pu c24v³ c29s⁶ c25s* Mar 22] rangy gelding: fair hurdler/chaser: won handicap chases at Wetherby and Kelso (2) in first half of season, and returned to form when successful at former course in March: stays 25f: acts on heavy and good to firm going: effective in cheekpieces or without. *Mrs K. Walton* **c109 h–**

WILD IS THE WIND (FR) 4 ch.g. Acatenango (GER) – Whirlwind (FR) (Leading Counsel (USA)) [2004/5 16d² 16d 16d³ Mar 4] useful-looking gelding: fourth foal: brother to useful 1m to 10.5f winner Acceleration and half-brother to winners up to 13.5f by Dr Devious and Achille: dam useful around 1m: useful maiden on Flat (stays 1½m) for P. Demercastel: fair form when placed in juvenile hurdles, let down by jumping in between. *Jonjo O'Neill* **h108**

WILD KNIGHT (IRE) 8 b.g. Jurado (USA) – Knight's Maid (Giolla Mear) [2004/5 c108x, h–: c24g³ Apr 15] medium-sized gelding: maiden hurdler: fair chaser at best: successful twice in points in 2005: should stay 3m: acts on good to firm going: takes strong hold: not a fluent jumper of fences. *J. W. Dufosee* **c88 x h–**

WILD OCEAN (IRE) 4 b.g. Old Vic – Gaye Chatelaine (IRE) (Castle Keep) [2004/5 F16s* F16s² Apr 10] €12,000 3-y-o: second foal: dam lightly raced, out of half-sister to top-class 2m to 3m hurdler Gaye Brief and very smart staying jumper Gaye Chance: won 22-runner bumper at Cork on debut in March by short head from Virginia Preuil: better form when 2 lengths second to Farmer Brown at Limerick. *E. Sheehy, Ireland* **F104**

WILD PASSION (GER) 5 b.g. Acatenango (GER) – White On Red (GER) (Konigsstuhl (GER)) [2004/5 h123p: 16d² 16s* 16d* 16d⁴ 16g² Mar 15] **h138**

Although put firmly in his place by Arcalis at Cheltenham, Irish-trained Wild Passion enjoyed a fruitful campaign as a second-season novice, winning three important events in Ireland, two of them Grade 1 contests, gaining rich compensa-

Sharp Minds Betfair Royal Bond Novices' Hurdle, Fairyhouse—second-season novice Wild Passion confirms he's a force to be reckoned with

Evening Herald Champion Novices' Hurdle, Punchestown—Kill Devil Hill (right) pushes the favourite very close; also pictured is third-placed In Compliance (checked cap)

tion for his defeat in the Supreme Novices' Hurdle with victory in the Evening Herald Champion Novices' Hurdle at Punchestown shortly after the end of the British season. Although there was a first prize of €62,000, Wild Passion had only seven rivals. Among them, all bar Publican, five places behind him at Cheltenham, had raced exclusively in Ireland in 2004/5. Publican went off second favourite at 4/1 followed by In Compliance at 9/2 and The Railway Man at 6/1 in a market dominated by Wild Passion at 7/4. The race proved harder fought than the betting suggested it might. Kept in close touch from the outset, Wild Passion briefly looked as though he might win decisively when driven a couple of lengths clear from three out, but he was hard pressed off the turn and had Kill Devil Hill upsides, as In Compliance tried to nose between the pair jumping the last. As the battle intensified, Wild Passion wasn't to be denied, running on slightly the strongest under severe pressure to hold 12/1-shot Kill Devil Hill by a short head, with In Compliance two lengths away in third. The Railway Man was fifth, let down by his jumping, with Publican only sixth.

Wild Passion's first Grade 1 success had come in November in the Sharp Minds Betfair Royal Bond Novices' Hurdle at Fairyhouse. The race drew a good collection of Ireland's most promising novices and Wild Passion was a 6/1-shot in a field of nine, joint second favourite with Royal Paradise, who had beaten him a head in a novice event at Roscommon on his reappearance in October. In the meantime, in the late absence of Royal Paradise, Wild Passion had gained his first victory over hurdles when landing the odds in the Grade 3 Bank of Ireland 'For Auction' Novices' Hurdle at Navan earlier in November, leading three out before holding Justified by a length and a half. Wild Passion was re-opposed by Justified as well at Fairyhouse, in a field which also included the previous season's Champion Bumper winner Total Enjoyment, favourite at 5/4 after a successful debut over hurdles earlier in the month. Wild Passion beat them all decisively in the end. After being held up, he looked up against it at the second last, where 16/1-shot and stable-companion Rocket Ship was still cruising, but Wild Passion was handed the initiative by that rival's blunder, and ran on well to beat him by three lengths, with Royal Paradise third, Justified fourth and Total Enjoyment only sixth. At the time, Wild Passion looked like Ireland's leading contender for the Supreme Novices' Hurdle, but he went off at 10/1 at Cheltenham after finishing just over six lengths fourth to Marcel in the Tolworth Hurdle at Sandown in early-January, several of his stable's runners performing below par in that period. Marcel and Justified were among those preferred to Wild Passion in the market at Cheltenham, but he put his Sandown display behind him with his best effort, leading two out and jumping the last upsides Arcalis, only to go down by six lengths, holding Dusky Warbler by only half a length for second.

Wild Passion (GER) (b.g. 2000)	Acatenango (GER) (ch 1982)	Surumu (ch 1974)	Literat
			Surama
		Aggravate (b 1966)	Aggressor
			Raven Locks
	White On Red (GER) (b 1992)	Konigsstuhl (br 1976)	Dschingis Khan
			Konigskronoung
		Win Hands Down (b 1985)	Ela-Mana-Mou
			Waitotara

Wild Passion was purchased privately by connections after showing useful form on the Flat as a three-year-old in Germany, where he won a maiden and a Group 3 over a mile and a quarter as well as finishing third in the Deutsches St Leger. Wild Passion finished down the field in the Deutsches Derby, a race won by his sire Acatenango during his almost unprecedented domination of the middle-distance scene there in the 'eighties. Acatenango chalked up twelve wins in a row at one point before finishing seventh to Dancing Brave in the Arc de Triomphe in 1986, and he has been responsible at stud on the Flat for leading German performers Borgia and Lando, also winners of the Deutsches Derby among other top races there. Not surprisingly, Acatenango has been less conspicuous as a sire of National Hunt horses, but he has also been represented in Britain by Cardenas, fourth in the 2004 Supreme Novices' Hurdle. Wild Passion's dam White On Red, a winner over seven furlongs and a mile as a two-year-old in Germany, including in

Mr D. P. Sharkey's "Wild Passion"

the leading juvenile contest there, the Preis der Winterkonigin, has produced two other winners on the Flat in Germany. Among them, Wild Power (by Turtle Island), successful at nine furlongs, has since been a winner over hurdles and fences at around two miles in Britain. Wild Power is renowned as a weak finisher, often looking ungenuine, and Wild Passion has shown his quirks too, most notably a tendency to idle in front, though it is hard to question his resolution. He has made the frame on each of his seven completed outings, falling at the second in the 2004 Triumph on the one occasion he failed to do so. His jumping has been sound in the main since. All being well, he should be back at the Festival for a third time in 2005/6, when his target is likely to be the Arkle Trophy Chase, his connections also having Harchibald as a more obvious Champion Hurdle candidate. He would have a long way to go to make a realistic Champion Hurdle contender, but he should take high rank as a novice over fences. A tall, good-topped gelding, a chasing type in appearance, Wild Passion should stay beyond two miles given the chance and has raced only on good ground or softer so far. *N. Meade, Ireland*

WILD POWER (GER) 7 br.g. Turtle Island (IRE) – White On Red (GER) (Konigsstuhl (GER)) [2004/5 c–, h96: 16d5 16g5 c16m3 c17g3 c16m2 c16s3 c16s3 c16s* c17s2 c16d5 Dec 9] modest hurdler/chaser: left I. Williams after third outing: won handicap chase at Fakenham in November: best at 2m: acts on soft and good to firm going: wore headgear last 6 starts: weak finisher, often looks ungenuine. *J. G. M. O'Shea* **c99 § h92 §**

WILD SPICE (IRE) 10 b.g. Mandalus – Curry Lunch (Pry) [2004/5 c98, h–: c26s2 c22s4 c27gF c30s3 c25sur c26s3 c23mur c31s Apr 22] smallish gelding: winning hurdler: modest handicap chaser: stays 27f: best form on good going or softer (acts on heavy): blinkered final outing: often let down by jumping. *Miss Venetia Williams* **c96 x h–**

WILD TEMPO (FR) 10 ch.g. Irish River (FR) – Fast Queen (FR) (Bon Sang (FR)) [2004/5 c19s5 c21s 17d4 19f2 19v 20d6 c31dur c33dpu c21dpu Apr 8] small, compact gelding: prolific winning hurdler/chaser in France, fairly useful form in 2004/5: claimed from J. Ortet €16,500 sixth start: failed to complete in handicap chases in Britain: stays 25f: probably acts on any going: unreliable. *M. Scudamore* **c124 § h121 §**

WILD TIDE 6 b.m. Runnett – Polly Two (Reesh) [2004/5 F–: F16g 16m 19v Oct 17] leggy mare: no sign of ability. *D. W. Thompson* **h– F–**

WILFRED (IRE) 4 b.g. Desert King (IRE) – Kharaliya (FR) (Doyoun) [2004/5 16g2 17g2 17d* 16f* 16g2 Oct 26] useful-looking gelding: half-brother to winning 2m hurdler Adecco (by Eagle Eyed): fair maiden on Flat (should be suited by further than 1m): fair form in juvenile hurdles: won at Bangor and Huntingdon (odds on) in September: blinkered last 3 outings. *Jonjo O'Neill* **h108**

WILFUL LORD (IRE) 8 b.g. Lord Americo – Dotties Girl (IRE) (Remainder Man) [2004/5 16g c21vpu c21v c20vF c16v5 c21v6 c21d* c20v6 Apr 17] tall gelding: no form over hurdles: poor chaser: won handicap at Sedgefield in April: would also have landed gamble in similar event at Newcastle in February but for falling 2 out: stays 21f: raced on good going or softer: tongue tied last 2 outings: makes mistakes. *J. Wade* **c78 x h–**

WILLIE JOHN DALY (IRE) 8 b.g. Mister Lord (USA) – Murphy's Lady (IRE) (Over The River (FR)) [2004/5 h119: c23g2 c23s* c24d2 c26g* c26d5 c24s4 c33g Mar 17] leggy gelding: fairly useful hurdler (none too fluent): better chaser, winning maiden at Exeter in October and handicap at Newbury (beat Desailly by short head) in December: below form after: stays 3¼m: acts on good to firm and heavy going: races prominently. *P. J. Hobbs* **c132 h–**

WILLIES WAY 5 ch.g. Nomadic Way (USA) – Willies Witch (Bandmaster (USA)) [2004/5 F18s6 Feb 4] first foal: dam unraced half-sister to fairly useful hurdler/chaser up to 21f Lets Be Frank: well held in bumper on debut. *C. J. Down* **F–**

WILLIE THE FISH (IRE) 8 b.g. King's Ride – Bricon Lady (Proverb) [2004/5 h85: 23dpu 19s 23d5 c27dF c27v c21v* c20gpu c23vur c25g c21d4 20s4 Apr 16] big gelding: poor maiden hurdler: sold out of J. M. Jefferson's stable 5,500 gns Doncaster May Sales after first outing: poor chaser: won handicap at Sedgefield (4 fences omitted) in January: stays 3m: raced on good ground or softer (acts on heavy): often let down by jumping over fences. *Mrs S. J. Smith* **c79 x h74**

WILL OF THE PEOPLE (IRE) 10 b.g. Supreme Leader – Another Partner (Le Bavard (FR)) [2004/5 h113: 22s 22d4 24s2 Apr 2] well-made gelding: fairly useful handicap hurdler, lightly raced: improved form when ½-length second to Broken Knights at Bangor: stays 3m: acts on soft and good to firm going: races prominently. *M. C. Pipe* **h122**

WILL SHE SPIN 4 b.f. Master Willie – Spinayab (King of Spain) [2004/5 F16d Mar 3] third foal: half-sister to winning 2m hurdler Tails I Win (by Petoski): dam no form on Flat: well beaten in mares bumper on debut. *J. W. Mullins* **F–**

WILL'SILLYSHANKERS 10 b.g. Silly Prices – Hannah's Song (Saintly Song) [2004/5 c–, h–: c24v^{pu} c24g^{pu} Dec 30] quite good-topped gelding: little sign of ability: visored once. *K. Bishop* **c–** **h–**

WILL STEANE 6 ch.g. Master Willie – Deep Pier (Deep Run) [2004/5 F16g May 13] eighth foal: half-brother to one-time useful hurdler/winning chaser Tisrabraq, stays 3m, and bumper winner Tentsmuir (both by Arctic Lord): dam unraced, out of sister to Cheltenham Gold Cup winner Forgive'N Forget: well beaten in bumper on debut. *Lady Connell* **F–**

WILL TELL 7 b.g. Rainbow Quest (USA) – Guillem (USA) (Nijinsky (CAN)) [2004/5 h–, F–: 16d 16d 17d Oct 27] tall gelding: no form over hurdles, often runs as if amiss. *Mrs S. J. Smith* **h–**

WILLY FURNLEY (IRE) 5 b.g. Synefos (USA) – Random Bay (Mandalus) [2004/5 F16s F17s^{2} Apr 2] good-topped gelding: second foal: dam winning Irish pointer: much better effort in bumpers when second to Arnold Layne at Bangor: sold 6,000 gns (privately) Doncaster May Sales. *N. A. Twiston-Davies* **F85**

WILL YOU COME ON (IRE) 7 br.m. Carroll House – Tengello (Bargello) [2004/5 F17s 16d^{pu} Jan 6] €4,200 4-y-o: half-sister to several winners, including fair chaser up to 25f Cumberland Blues (by Lancastrian): dam, winning Irish hurdler, from family of Welsh National winner Kendal Cavalier: no sign of ability, including in points: trained in bumper by Mrs A. Bowlby. *O. O'Neill* **h–** **F–**

WILLYWONT HE 6 b.g. Bollin William – Scalby Clipper (Sir Mago) [2004/5 F79?: 20d 20m^{5} 24m^{6} Jun 9] no form over hurdles: won point in March. *P. T. Midgley* **h–**

WIMBLEDONIAN 6 b.m. Sir Harry Lewis (USA) – Ardent Love (IRE) (Ardross) [2004/5 h86, F–: 24g^{pu} 24v^{6} 24d 19s^{3} 24s^{4} Mar 23] smallish mare: winning hurdler: disappointing in handicaps: should stay 3m: acts on soft going. *R. T. Phillips* **h80**

WIN ALOT 7 b.g. Aragon – Having Fun (Hard Fought) [2004/5 h84: 16s^{pu} 16g 25g^{pu} 19g c20g Apr 3] sturdy gelding: poor handicap hurdler: no show on chasing debut: probably stays 3m: acts on firm going, possibly not on softer than good: inconsistent. *M. C. Chapman* **c–** **h–**

WINAPENNY (IRE) 6 b.g. Right Win (IRE) – Penny Pauper (Pauper) [2004/5 16s^{5} Nov 4] €6,500 3-y-o: rangy gelding: eighth foal: dam maiden: well-beaten fourth in 4-y-o maiden Irish point in 2003: some promise when fifth to Rebel Rhythm in novice at Haydock on hudling debut. *T. D. Easterby* **h88**

WINCHESTER 10 ch.g. Gunner B – Tracy Jack (David Jack) [2004/5 c16s* c20d^{pu} c19g c20s^{2} c16d^{pu} 20d 20s^{4} 21d^{6} Apr 5] good-topped gelding: fair hurdler: fairly useful handicap chaser: off 18 months, won at Wetherby in October: effective at 2m, and stays 25f: raced on good going or softer (acts on heavy): wore cheekpieces last 3 outings. *K. A. Ryan* **c120** **h106**

WINDFOLA 6 b.m. Sovereign Water (FR) – Sainte Martine (Martinmas) [2004/5 h69, F–: 17g^{6} 16m 21m^{3} 26m^{3} 21m^{3} 21m^{3} c23g^{3} c21d^{F} 20g Sep 12] leggy mare: poor maiden hurdler: similar form on completed start over fences: stays 3¼m: acts on good to firm going: has worn headgear. *R. D. E. Woodhouse* **c–** **h73**

WINDING RIVER (IRE) 8 b.g. Montelimar (USA) – Bellora (IRE) (Over The River (FR)) [2004/5 c93p, h95p: c24v^{3} c20g^{6} Jan 24] tall, useful-looking gelding: third in maiden only start over hurdles: fair form over fences: stays 3m. *C. R. Egerton* **c101 +** **h–**

WINDMILL LANE 8 b.m. Saddlers' Hall (IRE) – Alpi Dora (Valiyar) [2004/5 22s^{pu} Jan 24] angular mare: maiden hurdler: sold £780 Ascot February Sales. *J. A. Geake* **h–**

WINDROSS 13 b.g. Ardross – Dans Le Vent (Pollerton) [2004/5 c123, h–: c25g^{pu} May 13] rangy gelding: fairly useful but inconsistent handicap chaser: stays 25f: acts on soft and good to firm going: usually waited with: has found little. *A. King* **c–** **h–**

WINDSOR BEAUTY (IRE) 7 b. or br.g. Woods of Windsor (USA) – Tumble Dale (Tumble Wind) [2004/5 h–: 25g^{pu} 20m May 26] workmanlike gelding: no form over hurdles. *R. Rowe* **h–**

WINDSOR BOY (IRE) 8 b.g. Mtoto – Fragrant Belle (USA) (Al Nasr (FR)) [2004/5 h117: 16g 17d c20d* c17g^{5} c22g* c19s* c16v^{F} Sep 25] fairly useful handicap hurdler at best: similar form over fences, winning novices at Killarney in July and Galway in **c120** **h108**

September and handicap at Listowel (by length from Dangerousdanmagru) later in September: effective at 2m and stays 2¾m, at least when conditions aren't testing: acts on soft and good to firm going. *E. J. O'Grady, Ireland*

WINDSPEED 10 ch.g. Sheerwind – Speed Baby (USA) (Diplomat Way) [2004/5 16dpu Oct 21] lengthy gelding: well beaten in 3 races at 2 yrs for B. Baugh: looked wayward on belated hurdling debut. *M. Mullineaux* **h–**

WINDY HILLS 5 bl.g. Overbury (IRE) – Chinook's Daughter (IRE) (Strong Gale) [2004/5 F16s3 Mar 12] second foal: dam, poor novice hurdler, half-sister to fairly useful staying chaser Highfrith: favourite, 8½ lengths third of 16 to Harry Flashman in bumper at Ayr on debut. *N. G. Richards* **F89**

WINE FOUNTAIN (IRE) 5 b. or br.g. Supreme Leader – Millflower (Millfontaine) [2004/5 F16d* F16v6 F16s6 Mar 27] half-brother to bumper winner by Welsh Term: dam lightly-raced maiden on Flat: successful in bumper at Fairyhouse in December on debut by ½ length from Letterman: well held subsequently. *Ms Margaret Mullins, Ireland* **F103**

WING COMMANDER 6 b.g. Royal Applause – Southern Psychic (USA) (Alwasmi (USA)) [2004/5 17d2 16d 16s4 16d6 16g5 Feb 27] useful at best on Flat (stays 1¼m): modest form over hurdles: likely to prove best at sharp 2m: flashed tail under pressure final start. *R. A. Fahey* **h87**

WINGED LADY (GER) 6 b.m. Winged Love (IRE) – Wonderful Lady (GER) (Surumu (GER)) [2004/5 h66: 21g* May 13] poor hurdler: won conditional jockeys handicap at Ludlow in May: stays 21f. *A. G. Juckes* **h76**

WINGS OF HOPE (IRE) 9 b.g. Treasure Hunter – She's Got Wings (Bulldozer) [2004/5 h–§: 16gpu c23gpu c20mpu c21g c20mpu Aug 30] close-coupled, quite good-topped gelding: winning hurdler: no form in chases: placed in points in 2005: tried blinkered/in cheekpieces: irresolute. *C. J. Hemsley* **c– § h– §**

WINK AND WHISPER 10 b.m. Gunner B – Lady Hannah (Daring March) [2004/5 c25gur May 7] workmanlike mare: winning chaser: successful twice in points in 2005: should stay 3m: acts on soft going. *Mrs H. M. Tory* **c– h–**

WINNERS ENCLOSURE (IRE) 9 b.g. Step Together (USA) – Willabelle (Will Somers) [2004/5 c24s5 May 5] lightly-raced winning pointer: well held in novice hunter on chasing debut. *J. J. Boulter* **c–**

WINNIE FLIES AGAIN 9 b.m. Phardante (FR) – Winnie The Witch (Leading Man) [2004/5 16s6 Nov 4] no sign of ability. *G. F. Bridgwater* **h–**

WINNIE THE POOH 11 br.g. Landyap (USA) – Moorland Nell (Neltino) [2004/5 c–, h–: 22spu 16m c26d2 Aug 22] winning pointer: maiden hurdler: no form in chases: has worn cheekpieces. *J. D. Frost* **c– h–**

WINNING DREAM (IRE) 11 b.g. Hollow Hand – Lottosprite (IRE) (Sandalay) [2004/5 c134, h102: c20g2 c16s c19s c18d c20s 16s c21d Apr 8] strong gelding: useful chaser: off 6 months, disappointing after first outing, including over hurdles: stays easy 29f: acts on soft going. *Oliver McKiernan, Ireland* **c– h101**

WINSABONUS 5 b.g. Defacto (USA) – Heart Broken (Bustino) [2004/5 16dpu 16vpu Feb 2] sturdy gelding: no form on Flat or over hurdles. *P. T. Midgley* **h–**

WINSLEY 7 gr.g. Sula Bula – Dissolve (Sharrood (USA)) [2004/5 h98, F87: 16g2 16s3 17spu 16d2 16d 16d 16g5 Mar 26] good-topped gelding: fairly useful handicap hurdler: 100/1, best effort when length second to Monte Cinto in strongly-run listed race at Sandown fourth start: stays 21f: acts on soft going: tried in cheekpieces/blinkers. *O. Sherwood* **h119**

WINSLOW BOY (USA) 4 b. or br.g. Expelled (USA) – Acusteal (USA) (Acaroid (USA)) [2004/5 16m 16s 16d Nov 12] small, close-coupled gelding: fair on Flat (stays 1¾m) for C. Wall: never dangerous in juvenile hurdles. *P. Monteith* **h64**

WINTER GALE (IRE) 13 b. or br.g. Strong Gale – Winter Fox (Martinmas) [2004/5 c86, h–: c22s4 c24g2 c23g Jul 7] lengthy gelding: modest chaser: stays 25f: acts on good to firm and good to soft going: blinkered once. *T. D. Walford* **c89 ? h–**

WINTER GARDEN 11 ch.g. Old Vic – Winter Queen (Welsh Pageant) [2004/5 c92§: c17m2 c17g3 c17g2 c24m2 c19m2 c24m2 c21m2 c24d3 c24d5 20v c25d* Apr 11] useful-looking gelding: winning hurdler: modest chaser: won 5-finisher maiden at Kelso in April: stays 25f: acts on heavy and good to firm going: tried blinkered, usually wears cheekpieces (not last 2 starts): has has tongue tied: hard to win with and is possibly ungenuine. *Miss Lucinda V. Russell* **c96 § h–**

WINTERS BEAU (IRE) 7 b.g. Star Quest – Tonka Mary (Riot Helmet) [2004/5 21g5 19dpu Oct 28] second foal: dam unraced: no form in 2 novice hurdles: successful in point in April. *G. L. Moore* **h–**

WIN THE TOSS 13 b.g. Idiot's Delight – Mayfield (USA) (Alleged (USA)) [2004/5 c65, h–: c16sur c16v2 c21m6 May 19] leggy, angular gelding: winning hurdler: maiden chaser: placed twice in points in 2005: best up to 2½m: acts on any going: blinkered once: tried tongue tied. *P. York* **c80 h–**

WISCALITUS (GER) 6 b.g. Lead On Time (USA) – Wiscaria (GER) (Ashmore (FR)) [2004/5 17g* 16g3 16s 17d3 19s4 16d Apr 9] good-topped gelding: successful 6 times up to 1½m on Flat, mostly in France in 2003 (useful form) for D. Fechner: fair hurdler: easily won maiden at Market Rasen in August: bit disappointing after: best around 2m. *Miss Venetia Williams* **h110**

WISEGUY (IRE) 6 b.g. Darshaan – Bibliotheque (USA) (Woodman (USA)) [2004/5 h94: 17g May 26] modest form at best over hurdles: failed to settle in maiden on only start in 2004/5: needs treating with caution. *J. Howard Johnson* **h–**

WISE MAN (IRE) 10 ch.g. Mister Lord (USA) – Ballinlonig Star (Black Minstrel) [2004/5 c126, h–: 20vpu 24spu 24v3 c24s4 Apr 21] fairly useful chaser: well-held fourth in handicap at Perth only chase start in 2004/5: modest maiden hurdler: stays 25f: unraced on firm going, acts on any other: has had tongue tied. *N. W. Alexander* **c– h98 ?**

WISE TALE 6 b.g. Nashwan (USA) – Wilayif (USA) (Danzig (USA)) [2004/5 h84§: 16d3 17g* 20g4 19gpu 16gpu 17d Oct 3] sturdy gelding: modest hurdler: won novice handicap at Market Rasen in July: raced mainly around 2m: acts on firm and good to soft going: usually visored: temperamental. *P. D. Niven* **h87 §**

WISHIN AND HOPIN 4 b.g. Danzig Connection (USA) – Trina's Pet (Efisio) [2004/5 aF13g5 F17s5 F13s* F17d Apr 9] smallish, plain gelding: second foal: dam 2-y-o 5f winner: best effort in bumpers when winning at Exeter in January by 2 lengths from Hiho Silver Lining. *A. G. Newcombe* **F95**

WISHWILLOW LORD (IRE) 6 b.g. Lord Americo – The Mrs (Mandalus) [2004/5 F16m2 20f5 16d* 18s5 16s* 20vF 20v6 20s Feb 20] €32,000 4-y-o: big, lengthy gelding: fifth foal: half-brother to fairly useful 2½m chaser Be My Better Half and bumper winner Native Mistress (both by Be My Native): dam winning 21f hurdler: fair form in bumpers: fairly useful form over hurdles: won at Thurles (maiden, beat Sweet Kiln 2 lengths) in November and Gowran (novice) in December: well held both completed starts in Graded novices after: bred to stay 2½m: acts on soft going: often front runner. *L. Whitmore, Ireland* **h123 F92**

WITCH WIND 5 b.g. Accondy (IRE) – Marie Zephyr (Treboro (USA)) [2004/5 F16v2 F16v* F16v* F17d Apr 9] workmanlike gelding: fourth foal: half-brother to 2m hurdle winner Time For A Glass (by Timeless Times): dam maiden who stayed 13f: fairly useful bumper performer: successful at Newcastle in January and Ayr (by 2 lengths from You Do The Math) in February: will be suited by further than 2m. *A. M. Crow* **F97**

WITH OR WITHOUT (IRE) 6 b.m. Ridgewood Ben – Say Thanks (Thatching) [2004/5 26dpu Aug 9] seventh foal: half-sister to 7f to 13f winner Say Wonderful (by Roi Danzig), 1m to 11f winner in Hong Kong by Soviet Lad and 10.5f winner in Sweden by Taufan: dam unraced half-sister to Molecomb Stakes winner Hatta: no show in selling hurdle on debut. *Miss M. E. Rowland* **h–**

WITHOUT A DOUBT 6 b.g. Singspiel (IRE) – El Rabab (USA) (Roberto (USA)) [2004/5 F101: 21g2 21d2 17s* 16d2 16g3 16d 17v3 20d 24g 21m5 Apr 13] leggy gelding: fairly useful novice hurdler: made all at Folkestone in November: mainly creditable efforts after: stays 3m: acts on soft going, below form on good to firm final start. *M. Pitman* **h120**

WITHTHELADS (IRE) 7 b.g. Tidaro (USA) – Quayside Charm (Quayside) [2004/5 h91, F85: 24dpu 23m2 22m4 22g c23g2 c26m* c26s4 c20d3 Nov 1] leggy, angular gelding: modest hurdler: sold out of L. Wells's stable 15,500 gns Doncaster May Sales after third start: similar form over fences, won 5-runner novice handicap at Fontwell in September: stays 3¼m: acts on good to firm going, probably on soft: usually wears headgear nowadays. *P. Bowen* **c98 h98**

WITHYBROOK LASS 7 b.m. Teenoso (USA) – Broadbrook Lass (Broadsword (USA)) [2004/5 F16s6 Oct 20] lengthy mare: first foal: dam, winning chaser, stayed 3m: won mares maiden point in 2004: well held in bumper. *Mrs H. Dalton* **F–**

WITNESS TIME (IRE) 9 b.g. Witness Box (USA) – Lisnacoilla (Beau Chapeau) [2004/5 c–, h–: 26m^2 24s^5 Apr 16] strong, workmanlike gelding: modest hurdler: off 14 months before reappearance: no show in 2 maiden chases: suited by 3m+: acts on heavy and good to firm going. *B. J. Eckley* **c– h99**

WIZARD OF EDGE 5 b.g. Wizard King – Forever Shineing (Glint of Gold) [2004/5 h88: 17g* 19d* 22d^5 22g* 19g^4 Oct 6] workmanlike gelding: fair maiden up to 1½m on Flat: fairly useful hurdler: successful in handicaps at Newton Abbot (intermediate), Exeter (novice) and Stratford between April and September: sold out of G. Balding's stable £22,000 Ascot June Sales after second win: stays 2¾m: raced on good ground or softer. *R. J. Hodges* **h116**

WIZARD OF THE WEST 5 b.g. Wizard King – Rose Burton (Lucky Wednesday) [2004/5 h–: 16g 20m* 20d^4 18m^3 16g 16d 18d^{pu} 22d^{pu} Mar 10] good-topped gelding: poor maiden on Flat (stays 9.4f): modest hurdler: won claimer (claimed from Miss S. West £5,000) at Fontwell in August: form otherwise only when third in novice there in September: stays 2½m: best efforts on good to firm going: visored last 4 starts. *D. P. Keane* **h92**

WIZARDS PRINCESS 5 b.m. Wizard King – Chalice (Governor General) [2004/5 F16d May 13] first foal: dam fair sprinter: well held in bumper and on Flat (for D. Thompson). *R. Allan* **F–**

WIZZICAL LAD 5 ch.g. Selkirk (USA) – Entente Cordiale (USA) (Affirmed (USA)) [2004/5 F16g F16s Oct 22] fifth foal: half-brother to 4 winners, including useful stayers Affaire d'Amour and Bien Entendu, and smart performer up to 1¾m Foreign Affairs (all by Hernando): dam once-raced half-sister to smart 1¼m winner Pegnitz: behind in 2 bumpers: tongue tied on debut. *B. N. Pollock* **F–**

WOGAN 5 b.g. Presenting – Fall About (Comedy Star (USA)) [2004/5 F16d^2 Apr 20] tall, good sort: eighth foal: half-brother to fair hurdler Briery Ann (by Anshan), stays 21f: dam, 1½m winner, half-sister to useful staying hurdler/chaser Ultra Flutter: ½-length second of 17 to The Grey Man in bumper at Worcester on debut: will stay 2½m. *N. J. Henderson* **F97**

WOMAN 7 b.m. Homo Sapien – La Princesse (Le Bavard (FR)) [2004/5 h–, F–: 20s 21g^5 May 13] of little account. *H. J. Manners* **h–**

WONDER BROOK 5 b.m. Alderbrook – Wordy's Wonder (Welsh Captain) [2004/5 F–: F16d Feb 18] no sign of ability in bumpers. *M. J. Gingell* **F–**

WOODBRIDGE QUEST 5 b.h. El Conquistador – Woodbridge Tern VII (Damsire Unregistered) [2004/5 F17d F16s Mar 6] strong horse: first foal: dam never ran: well held in 2 maiden bumpers. *R. H. Alner* **F–**

WOODENBRIDGE DREAM (IRE) 8 b.g. Good Thyne (USA) – Local Dream (Deep Run) [2004/5 21d^R c24g^4 c23d^F c20v^3 c27v^{pu} c20s* c20v^2 c16m* Mar 21] ex-Irish gelding: no form over hurdles: poor chaser: won handicaps at Huntingdon in February and Hereford (novice) in March: stays 2½m: acts on soft and good to firm going: races prominently. *R. Lee* **c81 h–**

WOODENBRIDGE NATIF (IRE) 10 b.g. Be My Native (USA) – Wintry Shower (Strong Gale) [2004/5 c24s^4 c24s^5 27d* 23v^{pu} 27v^4 c26d^4 Mar 12] sturdy ex-Irish gelding: winning hurdler/chaser, has deteriorated, though won handicap hurdle at Sedgefield in December: stays 27f: raced on going softer than good (acts on heavy) over jumps: tried blinkered: tongue tied third to fifth starts: sold 4,400 gns Doncaster May Sales. *R. Lee* **c– h89**

WOODLANDS BEAU (IRE) 13 b.g. Beau Sher – Never Intended (Sayyaf) [2004/5 c98x: c31m May 19] workmanlike gelding: veteran chaser: stays 31f: acts on any going: usually blinkered/visored: sketchy jumper. *Mrs S. Alner* **c– x**

WOODLANDS GENPOWER (IRE) 7 gr.g. Roselier (FR) – Cherished Princess (IRE) (Kemal (FR)) [2004/5 F111: 20s^2 24d^6 25s* 24d* 25v^3 25s^2 Mar 13] quite good-topped gelding: fairly useful novice hurdler: won at Warwick (by 18 lengths from Heir To Be) in December and Towcester in January: suited by good test of stamina: raced on good going or softer (acts on soft): front runner: not a fluent jumper. *P. A. Pritchard* **h116**

WOODLANDS LASS 9 ch.m. Nearly A Hand – Maranzi (Jimmy Reppin) [2004/5 h–: 21g^{pu} 20d^{pu} May 9] of no account: tried tongue tied. *P. A. Pritchard* **h–**

WOOD LORD (FR) 4 b.g. Lord of Men – Genevieve Des Bois (FR) (Diamond Prospect (USA)) [2004/5 15s 15s^F 17d* 17d 17m^5 17d 21g^4 17g^6 16v^4 Oct 29] leggy ex-French gelding: first foal: dam unraced: won juvenile claiming hurdle (claimed from **h97 §**

M. L. Mortier €22,500) at Auteuil in June: modest form at best in Britain: in cheekpieces fourth to sixth starts, tongue tied after: irresolute: sold 900 gns Doncaster January Sales. *M. C. Pipe*

WOODSTOCK EXPRESS 5 b.g. Alflora (IRE) – Young Tess (Teenoso (USA)) [2004/5 17g^{6} 16m^{pu} Aug 6] third foal: dam winning 3¼m hurdler: tailed off all 4 starts on Flat: no form in 2 maiden hurdles. *P. Bowen* **h69**

WOOD STREET (IRE) 6 b.g. Eagle Eyed (USA) – San-Catrinia (IRE) (Knesset (USA)) [2004/5 h82: 17d 16g^{6} Jul 29] poor form over hurdles: needs sharp 2m: wore cheekpieces final start: headstrong. *R. J. Baker* **h–**

WOODVIEW (IRE) 6 ch.g. Flemensfirth (USA) – Marys Bard (Le Bavard (FR)) [2004/5 20s^{5} Oct 31] half-brother to winning 3m hurdler Alpha Two (by Alphabatim): dam unraced: won maiden Irish point in 2004: fair form on second of 2 starts in bumpers for Ms M. Mullins: unseated to post, slow-starting fifth of 8 finishers in novice at Carlisle on hurdling debut. *K. C. Bailey* **h80 +**

WOODWIND DOWN 8 b.m. Piccolo – Bint El Oumara (Al Nasr (FR)) [2004/5 16d^{4d} 16f^{3} Jun 6] modest chaser: poor hurdler: off 20 months before reappearance: stays 2½m: acts on firm and good to soft going: tried blinkered/visored: held up: not an easy ride: successful on Flat in July. *M. Todhunter* **c–** **h82**

WOODY GLEN (IRE) 8 b.g. Wood Chanter – Gipsey Jo (Furry Glen) [2004/5 16m^{2} 20g* 20g* 18m 16s 21d c18s^{pu} c16s c16s c20d^{F} Mar 31] half-brother to useful chaser Man On The Hill (by Mandalus), stays 3m, and fair chaser Fortynineplus (by Torus), stayed 21f: dam lightly-raced maiden hurdler: poor hurdler: won handicaps at Roscommon and Ballinrobe in July: no form over fences: stays 2½m: acts on good to firm going: sometimes tongue tied. *A. J. Martin, Ireland* **c–** **h78**

WOODY VALENTINE (USA) 4 ch.g. Woodman (USA) – Mudslinger (USA) (El Gran Senor (USA)) [2004/5 16d* 16v 16d^{3} 16g Mar 15] leggy gelding: fairly useful on Flat (stays 1¼m): sold out of M. Johnston's stable 30,000 gns Newmarket Autumn Sales: best effort over hurdles (fair form) when successful in juvenile at Warwick in December: probably best with emphasis on speed at 2m: tends to be on toes. *Miss Venetia Williams* **h113**

WORD GETS AROUND (IRE) 7 b.g. King's Ride – Kate Fisher (IRE) (Over The River (FR)) [2004/5 F95: 16m* c16s 16s^{pu} 18v^{pu} Jan 14] lengthy gelding: chasing type: fairly useful in bumpers: successful in 19-runner maiden at Kelso on hurdling debut in April 2004: eased after mistakes when last of 7 in novice handicap on chasing debut: folded tamely last 2 starts: should be suited by further than 2m. *L. Lungo* **c– p** **h91**

WORKAWAY 9 b.g. Alflora (IRE) – Annicombe Run (Deep Run) [2004/5 c96, h86: 16g May 8] modest handicap hurdler/chaser: stays 2½m: acts on good to firm and heavy going: has broken blood vessels: free-going sort: often shapes as if amiss: sold 2,600 gns Doncaster May Sales, resold £4,000 Ascot April Sales. *A. Parker* **c–** **h–**

WORKING GIRL 8 b.m. Morpeth – Workamiracle (Teamwork) [2004/5 h72: 27g^{3} Apr 27] maiden hurdler: seemingly best effort when third in novice at Newton Abbot: successful in maiden point in March. *J. D. Frost* **h88**

WORLABY DALE 9 b.g. Terimon – Restandbethankful (Random Shot) [2004/5 h93: 16s^{4} 16v^{4} 21v 16v^{6} 24s^{5} 20s^{4} Mar 22] workmanlike gelding: poor maiden hurdler: probably stays 3m: raced on going softer than good (acts on heavy). *Mrs S. Lamyman* **h83**

WORLD VISION (IRE) 8 ch.g. Denel (FR) – Dusty Lane (IRE) (Electric) [2004/5 h92: 21m^{4} 24d^{6} c21d* 21d^{2} 27d^{6} c20d* c19d^{6} c24g^{3} Feb 16] big, leggy gelding: modest hurdler: fair form over fences: won novice at Sedgefield in October and handicap at Musselburgh in January: stays 27f: acts on soft and good to firm going: has worn cheekpieces. *Ferdy Murphy* **c112** **h96**

WORLD WIDE WEB (IRE) 9 b.g. Be My Native (USA) – Meldrum Lass (Buckskin (FR)) [2004/5 c128, h–: 24s c24d^{ur} Mar 5] tall, good sort: fairly useful hurdler/chaser: well beaten on completed start in 2004/5: should stay beyond 3m: raced mainly on good going or softer (acts on soft): ran well only try in blinkers. *Jonjo O'Neill* **c–** **h–**

WORTH WAITIN FOR 7 b.m. Casteddu – Grey Sonata (Horage) [2004/5 F18m^{4} F16d^{5} 22g^{pu} Jul 12] first foal: dam, who stayed 2½m, won 2 selling hurdles: poor form in bumpers: no show on hurdling debut: sold 600 gns Doncaster August Sales. *B. G. Powell* **h–** **F71**

WORTHY MAN 8 b.g. Homo Sapien – Marnworth (Funny Man) [2004/5 c–, h–: c16s^{pu} c19g^{pu} 18m^{pu} 16m^{6} 16m^{pu} Jun 6] rangy gelding: no sign of ability: tried tongue tied: sketchy jumper: sold £1,900 Ascot July Sales. *S. T. Lewis* **c– x** **h–**

WOTASHAMBLES (IRE) 4 b.g. Shambo – Rent Day (Town And Country) [2004/5 F16s^4 Feb 26] lengthy gelding: second foal: dam, poor maiden hurdler/chaser who stayed 3m, sister to useful chaser up to 3m The Land Agent: 5¾ lengths fourth of 13 to Glasker Mill in slowly-run bumper at Kempton on debut. *P. R. Webber* **F98**

WOTAVENTURE 5 b.m. Sea Raven (IRE) – Light Venture (Idiot's Delight) [2004/5 F16d Mar 3] sixth foal: dam, poor novice hurdler, stayed 21f: tailed off in bumper on debut. *M. Sheppard* **F–**

WOT NO CASH 13 gr.g. Ballacashtal (CAN) – Madame Non (My Swanee) [2004/5 c74, h–: c18m 26m^5 c20m^5 16m^{pu} c20g^{pu} Sep 12] lengthy gelding: winning chaser: no form in 2004/5, including over hurdles. *R. C. Harper* **c–** **h–**

WOT NO INDIANS 5 b.g. Commanche Run – Shafayif (Ela-Mana-Mou) [2004/5 F16s F18s Dec 1] fourth foal: half-brother to winning hurdler/chaser up to 3¼m Sylphide and fair hurdler/winning chaser Rakassa (both by Ballet Royal), stays 3m: dam, untrustworthy winning 2m selling hurdler, out of smart miler Rare Roberta: no form in 2 bumpers. *H. J. Manners* **F–**

WOTSITOOYA (IRE) 13 b.g. Rashar (USA) – Droppey Loops (Over The River (FR)) [2004/5 c125, h112: c25g* c22m c24s 20d Oct 17] lengthy gelding: fair hurdler: fairly useful handicap chaser: stays 29f: acts on good to firm and heavy going: has worn cheekpieces: easily best efforts on right-handed tracks. *M. J. P. O'Brien, Ireland* **c–** **h107**

WOULD YOU BELIEVE 9 gr.g. Derrylin – Ramelton (Precipice Wood) [2004/5 c112: c24d^4 c25d^5 Apr 3] workmanlike gelding: lightly raced: fair maiden chaser: off a year, folded tamely in handicaps in 2004/5: stays 3m: raced on good going or softer (acts on heavy). *P. J. Hobbs* **c–**

WOZZECK 5 b.g. Groom Dancer (USA) – Opera Lover (IRE) (Sadler's Wells (USA)) [2004/5 h83: 19v^{pu} 16d^3 Mar 24] angular gelding: poor maiden hurdler: tried in cheekpieces: has had tongue tied. *R. H. Buckler* **h77**

WRAGS TO RICHES (IRE) 8 b.g. Tremblant – Clonea Lady (IRE) (Lord Ha Ha) [2004/5 h94, F83: c17f^{ur} c17s^5 c16s^F c16v^2 c19s^2 c21g* c21s^6 c19s* c21v^2 Apr 22] big, good-topped gelding: modest maiden hurdler: fairly useful novice chaser: won at Fakenham in January and Exeter (beat East Lawyer by 12 lengths in 4-runner event) in March: stays 21f: acts on any going: consistent. *J. D. Frost* **c124** **h–**

WREFORD LAKE 5 ch.g. Karinga Bay – Sporting Annie (Teamster) [2004/5 F–: F17g Apr 27] little show in bumpers. *J. D. Frost* **F–**

WRENLANE 4 ch.g. Fraam – Hi Hoh (IRE) (Fayruz) [2004/5 17g^6 Sep 25] fair on Flat (stays 1¼m): well beaten in juvenile on hurdling debut. *R. A. Fahey* **h–**

WRENS ISLAND (IRE) 11 br.g. Yashgan – Tipiton (Balboa) [2004/5 c100: c20g^{pu} c27m^{pu} c21d^{ur} c20d Apr 20] well-made gelding: fair handicap chaser at one time: off 17 months, little sign of retaining ability: wore cheekpieces once. *R. Dickin* **c–**

WUN CHAI (IRE) 6 b.g. King's Theatre (IRE) – Flower From Heaven (Baptism) [2004/5 h91: 22g^{pu} 17s^2 17g 19m^{pu} c21d^4 c19m^{pu} c19s^{pu} 17s^2 c20d^5 c19m^4 c19g^3 Apr 15] compact gelding: modest handicap hurdler: poor novice chaser: stays 19f: acts on soft and good to firm ground: blinkered: inconsistent. *A. E. Jones* **c81** **h89**

WUXI VENTURE 10 b.g. Wolfhound (USA) – Push A Button (Bold Lad (IRE)) [2004/5 c106, h–: c17m* c20d^3 c21d^6 19g c20m^4 c16s^6 c17s^{pu} Nov 18] small, sturdy gelding: winning hurdler: fair handicap chaser: won at Kelso in May: broke leg at Market Rasen: stayed 2½m: acted on soft and good to firm going. *R. A. Fahey* **c112** **h–**

WYLE POST (IRE) 6 ch.g. Mister Lord (USA) – Daffydown Dolly (IRE) (The Parson) [2004/5 24g^{pu} c21d^{ur} c21d^{ur} Aug 28] fifth foal: dam unraced: won maiden Irish point on debut in 2004: bought £65,000 Cheltenham April Sales: little show in maiden on hurdling debut: let down by jumping both starts in chases. *Miss K. Marks* **c– x** **h–**

WYNBURY FLYER 10 ch.g. Risk Me (FR) – Woolcana (Some Hand) [2004/5 c80, h–: c16m^6 c16m^3 c16g c16v^6 c16v^5 Jan 25] workmanlike gelding: poor handicap chaser: stays 2½m: acts on heavy going, probably on good to firm: wore cheekpieces/blinkers last 4 starts. *Ferdy Murphy* **c79** **h–**

WYN DIXIE (IRE) 6 b.g. Great Commotion (USA) – Duchess Affair (IRE) (Digamist (USA)) [2004/5 h93: 16d^2 16g^{pu} 16s^3 Apr 22] sparely-made gelding: modest maiden hurdler: lame second start: will prove best at 2m with emphasis on speed: acts on good to soft going. *P. Monteith* **h89**

WYNYARD DANCER 11 b.m. Minster Son – The White Lion (Flying Tyke) [2004/5 c–, h–: c21g^{ur} c25m^{pu} Oct 1] winning hunter chaser: lightly raced and hasn't completed since 2002: wears cheekpieces. *Miss T. Jackson* **c– h–**

WYOMING 4 ch.f. Inchinor – Shoshone (Be My Chief (USA)) [2004/5 16d 16s 20v^{pu} 16g^{3} Mar 18] modest maiden on Flat (stays 1½m), sold out of J. Toller's stable 7,500 gns Newmarket Autumn Sales: first form over hurdles when third in selling handicap at Fakenham. *Jedd O'Keeffe* **h75**

X

XAIPETE (IRE) 13 b.g. Jolly Jake (NZ) – Rolfete (USA) (Tom Rolfe) [2004/5 c116, h104: c20g^{2} c17g^{2} c20m^{4} 17d^{3} 16m^{2} 16d^{3} c17v^{2} c19d^{2} c20g^{4} c16s^{5} c16s^{F} c20d^{4} c17s^{4} Apr 2] useful-looking gelding: fair handicap hurdler/chaser, rarely out of frame: stays 21f: acts on any going: held up: extremely tough and consistent. *R. C. Guest* **c111 d h102**

XCENTRA 4 b.g. Docksider (USA) – Dicentra (Rambo Dancer (CAN)) [2004/5 aF13g^{3} F12d Jan 12] tall, strong gelding: third foal: half-brother to 6f winner Coracle King (by Compton Place): dam lightly-raced half-sister to smart French middle-distance performer Darine: apparently better effort in bumpers when third in 3-y-o event on polytrack at Lingfield on debut. *B. G. Powell* **F84**

XELLANCE (IRE) 8 b.g. Be My Guest (USA) – Excellent Alibi (USA) (Exceller (USA)) [2004/5 h121: 22g^{6} c21g^{2} c21g* 22d c20d^{3} c20g* 21g c20d* c24d^{3} 21m^{5} 20m^{6} Apr 23] angular gelding: fairly useful handicap hurdler: fair chaser: won novices at Newton Abbot in July, Ludlow in October and Huntingdon (beat Macnance 1¾ lengths) in November: stays easy 3m: acts on firm and good to soft going. *P. J. Hobbs* **c109 h119**

XIXITA 5 ch.m. Fleetwood (IRE) – Conquista (Aragon) [2004/5 h–: 16f^{5} 16m Jun 8] poor maiden on Flat and over hurdles: sold 600 gns Doncaster August Sales, tailed off on completed start in points. *Dr J. D. Scargill* **h63**

XPRESSIONS 4 b.g. Turtle Island (IRE) – Make Ready (Beveled (USA)) [2004/5 16g^{pu} Dec 29] poor on Flat (should stay 1½m): jumped poorly in juvenile on hurdling debut. *R. A. Fahey* **h–**

Y

YABOYA (IRE) 6 b.g. King's Theatre (IRE) – Oh Jemima (Captain James) [2004/5 F16d* F16g Mar 16] rangy gelding: half-brother to several winners, including smart sprinter Oh Bej Oh Bej (by Distinctly North) and winning 2m hurdlers Balmyra (by Digamist) and She's Wonderful (by Magical Wonder): dam placed up to 11f in Ireland: overcame greenness to win bumper at Wincanton on debut in February by 2 lenths from Hollywood: well held in Grade 1 at Cheltenham following month. *P. J. Hobbs* **F98**

YAKAREEM (IRE) 9 b.g. Rainbows For Life (CAN) – Brandywell (Skyliner) [2004/5 c21g^{4} May 30] compact gelding: winning hurdler/chaser: off 18 months before only start in 2004/5: effective at 2m to easy 3m: acts on firm and good to soft going: has had tongue tied: has been reluctant at start. *D. G. Bridgwater* **c72 h–**

YAKIMOV (USA) 6 ch.g. Affirmed (USA) – Ballet Troupe (USA) (Nureyev (USA)) [2004/5 16g May 21] useful winner on Flat (stays 9.7f), sold out of P. Cole's stable 42,000 gns Newmarket Autumn (2003) Sales, out of sorts in 2004: always behind in novice on hurdling debut. *D. J. Wintle* **h–**

YANKEE CROSSING (IRE) 7 b.g. Lord Americo – Ath Leathan (Royal Vulcan) [2004/5 h–: 22v^{6} 20d^{pu} 25d^{4} Jan 1] close-coupled gelding: maiden hurdler: best effort in novice events when fourth of 7 at Catterick. *Ferdy Murphy* **h83**

YANKEEDOODLEDANDY (IRE) 4 b.g. Orpen (USA) – Laura Margaret (Persian Bold) [2004/5 16d* 16d* 17d* 17s^{2} 17g Mar 18] compact gelding: half-brother to fairly useful hurdler around 2½m Chivite (by Alhaarth): fairly useful on Flat (stays 1½m): successful first 3 starts in juvenile hurdles, at Sandown and Huntingdon in November and Cheltenham (by 4 lengths from Napolitain) in December: useful form at Cheltenham last 2 starts, 6 lengths second to Akilak in Grade 2 and eighth to Penzance in **h129**

K. Tyre & Mrs C. Barclay's "Yankeedoodledandy"

Triumph Hurdle: will stay beyond 17f: raced on good ground or softer (acts on soft): genuine. *P. C. Haslam*

YANKEE JAMIE (IRE) 11 b.g. Strong Gale – Sparkling Opera (Orchestra) [2004/5 c–, h97: 16d c22d 22v Mar 5] lengthy, angular gelding: winning hurdler/chaser: well held in handicaps in 2004/5: stays 25f: acts on soft going: reportedly suffers breathing problems. *L. Lungo* **c– h–**

YANN'S (FR) 9 b.g. Hellios (USA) – Listen Gyp (USA) (Advocator) [2004/5 c118, h–: c24s^{4} c24s* c27s^{3} c24g^{2} c24m^{pu} c26v^{5} Apr 22] lengthy, angular gelding: fairly useful handicap chaser: off 8 months, successful at Taunton in January by 9 lengths from Charlies Future: disappointing last 2 starts: stays 27f: acts on heavy going (pulled up only start on good to firm): usually races prominently. *R. T. Phillips* **c121 h–**

YASSAR (IRE) 10 b.g. Yashgan – Go Hunting (IRE) (Abednego) [2004/5 c89, h–: c17g^{4} c23g^{pu} c20m* c19g c23d^{pu} 22v^{pu} c19s^{pu} Mar 27] lengthy gelding: pulled up both outings over hurdles: poor chaser: won novice handicap at Worcester in June: stays 3m: acts on good to firm and good to soft going: often weak finisher. *D. J. Wintle* **c84 h–**

YATTARNA (IRE) 9 b.g. Be My Guest (USA) – Kindpiano (USA) (Fappiano (USA)) [2004/5 c22d^{F} Feb 24] winning hurdler: no longer of any account. *Miss N. L. Elliott* **c– h–**

YDRAVLIS 7 ch.m. Alflora (IRE) – Levantine Rose (Levanter) [2004/5 c19m^{F} May 23] no sign of ability. *D. J. S. ffrench Davis* **c– h–**

YELLOW RIVER (IRE) 5 b.g. Sesaro (USA) – Amtico (Bairn (USA)) [2004/5 h–: 16f Sep 5] no show over hurdles: bought out of R. Curtis' stable £1,500 Ascot June Sales: tried in cheekpieces. *R. Williams* **h–**

YEOMAN LAD 5 b.g. Groom Dancer (USA) – First Amendment (IRE) (Caerleon (USA)) [2004/5 16d 16s^{pu} 18s 23g 16d 16g 16g 16d Apr 18] fairly useful at best on Flat (stays 9f) at 3 yrs, sold out of A. Balding's stable 2,800 gns Doncaster August Sales: no form over hurdles: tried in cheekpieces/visor: sold £600 Ascot April Sales. *M. J. Gingell* **h–**

Betfred 'The Bonus King' Handicap Hurdle, Sandown—
Yes Sir, giving Tony McCoy his two-hundredth winner of the season, sees off the Martin Pipe-trained trio of Penny Pictures (left), Fontanesi (spotted cap) and Commercial Flyer (right)

YEOMAN SAILOR (IRE) 11 gr.g. Roselier (FR) – Liffey Lady (Camden Town) [2004/5 c25s* c24s^2 Apr 16] big, strong, lengthy gelding: useful hunter chaser nowadays: fit from points, won at Hereford in March by 8 lengths from Caught At Dawn: creditable second to Ask The Natives at Bangor: will stay beyond 3¼m: acts on soft and good to firm going. *Grace Muir* **c115 h–**

YEOMAN'S POINT (IRE) 9 b.g. Sadler's Wells (USA) – Truly Bound (USA) (In Reality) [2004/5 c127, h–: c25g^{ur} 24s c20s^{pu} 24g^{pu} Mar 5] good-topped gelding: useful hurdler at one time: fairly useful novice chaser in 2003/4: left C. Roche and off 6 months after first outing, no subsequent form: stays 25f: raced on good going or softer (acts on soft): tried blinkered/in cheekpieces: has had tongue tied. *Jonjo O'Neill* **cxx h–**

YER FATHER'S YACHT (IRE) 5 b.g. Desert Story (IRE) – Alchiea (Alzao (USA)) [2004/5 16m^{pu} 17g^{pu} 22g^{pu} 20g Aug 26] fair maiden on Flat (stays 1½m) at 3 yrs: winning hurdler in 2003/4 for Mrs J. Harrington: no form in handicaps in Britain. *Lady Connell* **h–**

YER 'UMBLE (IRE) 14 b.g. Lafontaine (USA) – Miners Girl (Miner's Lamp) [2004/5 c–, h–: 22m^{pu} Jun 27] stocky gelding: winning hurdler/chaser, lightly raced nowadays: tried blinkered/visored. *J. K. Cresswell* **c– h–**

YES MY LORD (IRE) 6 b.g. Mister Lord (USA) – Lady Shalom (IRE) (Aylesfield) [2004/5 19d 19s 19s^4 Jan 31] first foal: dam ran twice: poor form in novice hurdles, not at all knocked about at Exeter final outing: bred to be suited by 2½m+: jumped none too fluently first 2 starts: almost certainly capable of better. *M. C. Pipe* **h78 p**

YES SES LES 6 b.g. El Conquistador – Kellsboro Queen (Rakaposhi King) [2004/5 F16m F16g F17g^4 24f^F 20m^{pu} Sep 24] £1,800 4-y-o: first foal: dam showed nothing in bumper: little sign of ability. *G. Fierro* **h– F–**

YES SIR (IRE) 6 b.g. Needle Gun (IRE) – Miss Pushover (Push On) [2004/5 F17m^2 F16m^2 F18s^2 F18d^5 17d^{bd} 20s* 20v^5 22s^3 16v* 16d 16v* 20m* Apr 23] ninth foal: half-brother to several winners, including 3¼m chaser Heavenly Citizen (by Ovac): dam unraced half-sister to useful staying chaser Bold Agent: runner-up 3 of 4 starts in bumpers: useful hurdler: won novices at Chepstow in December and February (by 22 lengths from Briareus), and handicaps there in March and Sandown (beat Penny Pictures by 1¼ lengths) in April: stays 2½m: acts on good to firm and heavy ground: usually races prominently: doesn't always jump fluently. *P. Bowen* **h138 F96**

YESYES (IRE) 10 b.g. Supreme Leader – Barton Bay (IRE) (Kambalda) [2004/5 c–, h–: 22d* c23m^3 19s^{pu} c20d^{pu} c20d* c20d^{pu} c20v^5 Jan 17] useful-looking gelding: modest hurdler: won handicap at Fontwell in May: easily best effort over fences when winning novice handicap there in December: stays 2¾m: acts on soft going: has had breathing problem: unreliable. *Miss E. C. Lavelle* **c100 § h96 §**

YOGI (IRE) 9 ch.g. Glacial Storm (USA) – Good Performance VII (Damsire Unregistered) [2004/5 h142: 24s 20s4 24v2 22g 24v2 24g6 24s Mar 28] leggy gelding: useful hurdler: very stiff task, probably flattered when sixth in World Hurdle at Cheltenham in March: laboured efforts after in minor event at Fairyhouse and Champion Stayers' Hurdle at Punchestown: stays 3m: acts on heavy going: below form all starts in blinkers: usually races prominently. *Thomas Foley, Ireland* **h140**

YORK DANCER 4 ch.f. Dancing Spree (USA) – York Street (USA) (Diamond Shoal) [2004/5 F12g Dec 8] leggy filly: eighth foal: half-sister to winning 2m hurdler Coochie (by King of Spain): dam little form at 2 yrs or over hurdles: well beaten in 3-y-o fillies bumper on debut. *A. D. Smith* **F–**

YORK RITE (AUS) 9 ch.g. Grand Lodge (USA) – Amazaan (NZ) (Zamazaan (FR)) [2004/5 c72, h72: 17d c25d4 c20m3 24g c20g2 24m6 c22m2 c23m3 c16g2 c20vur c23s2 c24g2 c19sF Mar 23] strong gelding: poor handicap hurdler/maiden chaser: stays 3m: acts on firm and soft going: tried blinkered, usually wears cheekpieces: often tongue tied: makes mistakes over fences. *R. C. Guest* **c81 x h72**

YOU DO THE MATH (IRE) 5 b.g. Carroll House – Ballymave (IRE) (Jareer (USA)) [2004/5 F16v2 F17s3 Mar 10] €12,000 3-y-o: second foal: dam unraced: fair form when placed in bumpers at Ayr and Carlisle. *L. Lungo* **F88**

YOU GOT ME 6 gr.g. First Trump – Simply Sooty (Absalom) [2004/5 h–: 20dpu May 5] no show in 2 starts over hurdles. *Evan Williams* **h–**

YOUKNOWTHEANSWER 5 b.m. Brief Truce (USA) – Perfect Answer (Keen) [2004/5 F16d F14m Mar 21] second foal: dam once-raced half-sister to useful hurdler Cotteir Chief, stayed 21f: tailed off in 2 bumpers. *Miss L. C. Siddall* **F–**

Ms Y. M. Hill's "Yes Sir"

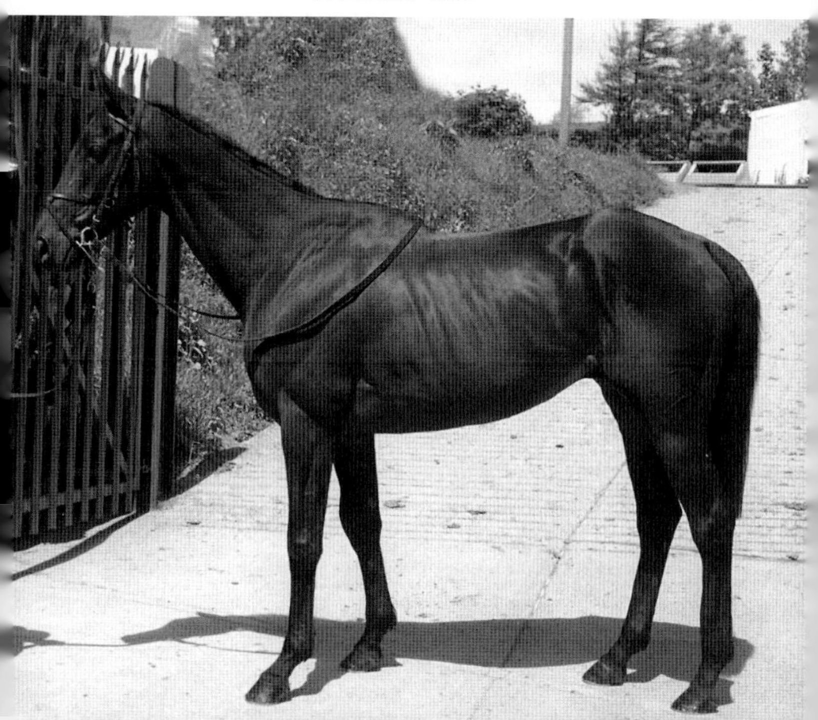

YOUNEVERTOLDME (IRE) 9 b. or br.m. Simply Great (FR) – Royal Daisy (Crash Course) [2004/5 c21d4 May 1] angular mare: winning hurdler: maiden chaser: stays 2¾m: raced on good to soft/soft ground: tried in cheekpieces: signs of temperament. *Mrs J. Harrington, Ireland* **c– h–**

YOUNG AMERICAN (IRE) 9 br.g. Hamas (IRE) – Banana Peel (Green Dancer (USA)) [2004/5 h–: 20g4 27g4 24d2 c21m* c26dR 23s 21d Mar 4] useful-looking gelding: fairly useful handicap hurdler: won 3-finisher maiden at Uttoxeter on chasing debut in July: jumped badly prior to refusing fourth in novice at Southwell next time: probably best up to 3m: acts on good to firm and heavy going: tried blinkered, wore cheekpieces 3 of last 4 starts: one to avoid over fences. *Jonjo O'Neill* **c99 § h116**

YOUNG BOSS 5 b.g. Primitive Rising (USA) – Bossburg (Celtic Cone) [2004/5 F16s F16m Apr 2] good-topped gelding: first foal: dam winning 2m chaser: soundly beaten in 2 bumpers, pulling hard second time. *P. R. Hedger* **F–**

YOUNG BOUNDER (FR) 6 b. or br.g. Septieme Ciel (USA) – Far But Near (USA) (Far North (CAN)) [2004/5 h–, F–: 17m4 16m Jun 13] unfurnished gelding: poor form at best in novice hurdles. *N. A. Twiston-Davies* **h75**

YOUNG CHEVALIER 8 b.g. Alflora (IRE) – Mrs Teasdale (Idiot's Delight) [2004/5 c100, h–: c16sF c16gF Mar 26] rangy gelding: modest handicap chaser: well held when falling both starts in 2004/5: best form around 2m on good/good to soft going. *J. R. Adam* **c– h–**

YOUNG CLAUDE 8 b.g. Le Moss – Deirdres Dream (The Parson) [2004/5 c–, h84: 24dpu 22dpu 22gpu May 31] tall gelding: maiden hurdler/chaser: badly out of sorts in 2004/5: stays 25f: usually blinkered nowadays: probably ungenuine. *P. Beaumont* **c– h–**

YOUNG COLLIER 6 b.g. Vettori (IRE) – Cockatoo Island (High Top) [2004/5 h109: c18g* c18d* Jan 12] tall, useful-looking gelding: has scope: fair hurdler: fairly useful form when winning both starts over fences, handicaps at Newbury in December (by 8 lengths from Barton Hill) and January (by short head from Dun An Doras): should stay beyond 19f: probably capable of better over fences. *J. A. B. Old* **c125 + h–**

YOUNG DANCER (IRE) 7 b.g. Eurobus – Misquested (Lord Ha Ha) [2004/5 h106p: 20g 17g3 20s6 Nov 5] good-topped gelding: novice hurdler, fair form at best: should stay beyond 17f: raced on good going or softer: twice ran as if amiss. *V. R. A. Dartnall* **h–**

YOUNG DUDE (IRE) 6 b.g. Oscar (IRE) – Shuil Realt (IRE) (Jolly Jake (NZ)) [2004/5 F16m* Apr 10] €28,000 4-y-o: second foal: dam unraced, from family of very smart hurdler Liss A Paoraigh and Scottish National winner Baronet: successful in 19-runner maiden bumper at Worcester on debut by 1½ lengths from Delightful Cliche: sure to progress. *Jonjo O'Neill* **F95 p**

YOUNG HARRY 7 b.g. Karinga Bay – Heathfield Gale (Strong Gale) [2004/5 F–: F17g6 21gpu May 8] modest form on second of 2 starts in bumpers: no show in novice on hurdling debut: visored in 2004/5. *M. C. Pipe* **h– F75**

YOUNG JOY 4 ch.f. Captain Maverick (USA) – Sciacca (Dalsaan) [2004/5 16mpu Dec 1] unfurnished filly: fourth foal: dam, modest 2m hurdler, from family of useful 2m hurdler What's The Verdict: bled from nose in juvenile hurdle on debut. *James Moffatt* **h–**

YOUNG LORCAN 9 ch.g. Bay Tern (USA) – Naughty Nessie (Celtic Cone) [2004/5 20dpu c24s2 c24v* 26spu c25v2 c23vur Mar 1] rather leggy gelding: winning hurdler: modest handicap chaser: won at Uttoxeter in November: stays 25f: acts on heavy and good to firm going. *Miss K. Marks* **c95 h–**

YOUNG OWEN 7 b.g. Balnibarbi – Polly Potter (Pollerton) [2004/5 h70: 16m6 16m2 c17d* c17spu Oct 28] rather leggy gelding: poor maiden hurdler: claimed from Mrs L. Normile £6,000 second start: won 5-runner novice at Stratford on chasing debut in October: raced around 2m: acts on soft and good to firm going: headstrong. *A. G. Juckes* **c94 h69**

YOUNG PATRIARCH 4 b.g. Silver Patriarch (IRE) – Mortify (Prince Sabo) [2004/5 17gpu 16d2 17d* 16g 16s 16d3 17g Apr 3] good-topped gelding: half-brother to fair 2m hurdler Monksford (by Minster Son): modest form at 2 yrs for J. Dunlop, disappointing on Flat in 2004 for B. Meehan: fair juvenile hurdler: won maiden at Folkestone in November: raced around 2m: wore cheekpieces after debut: ran as if amiss fourth/fifth starts. *C. J. Mann* **h101**

YOUNG SCOTTON 5 b.g. Cadeaux Genereux – Broken Wave (Bustino) [2004/5 F109: 20dpu 19m6 16d 16gur Feb 27] leggy gelding: useful in bumpers in 2003/4 for K. Ryan: disappointing over hurdles, often shaping as if amiss: blinkered final start. *J. Howard Johnson* **h90**

YOUNG TOMO (IRE) 13 b.g. Lafontaine (USA) – Siege Queen (Tarqogan) [2004/5 c–, h–: c27g^{pu} c24g^{6} Mar 9] sturdy gelding: temperamental pointer/hunter chaser nowadays: wears blinkers/cheekpieces. *Miss C. J. Goodall* **c– § h–**

YOUNG TOT (IRE) 7 b.g. Torus – Lady-K (IRE) (Rock Chanteur) [2004/5 h90, F74: 23d 20g^{5} 17g c16d^{4} c16d^{5} c16d 16m^{3} c16s^{6} Feb 7] poor maiden hurdler/chaser: has form at 2½m, raced mainly around 2m: acts on good to firm and good to soft going: has worn headgear: weak finisher. *Mrs A. Duffield* **c80 h81**

YOUNG WARRIOR (IRE) 4 b.g. Desert Style (IRE) – Arctic Splendour (USA) (Arctic Tern (USA)) [2004/5 16d^{pu} Nov 24] half-brother to winning 2m hurdler Youngblood (by Desert Style): well held in 3 maidens on Flat (has been troublesome at start) for D. Nicholls: no show in juvenile on hurdling debut. *M. D. Hammond* **h–**

YOUNG WILL 6 b.g. Keen – Barkston Singer (Runnett) [2004/5 F16g Oct 27] lengthy gelding: well held in 2 bumpers nearly 2 years apart. *S. G. Griffiths* **F–**

YOU OWE ME (IRE) 8 b.g. Jurado (USA) – Bodyline (Crash Course) [2004/5 h115p: 22d^{6} 21g 24d^{pu} Apr 8] strong, lengthy gelding: chasing type: progressive hurdler in 2003/4: off 14 months, no form in handicaps on return: should stay beyond 21f. *N. A. Twiston-Davies* **h–**

YOUR ADVANTAGE (IRE) 5 b.g. Septieme Ciel (USA) – Freedom Flame (Darshaan) [2004/5 h98: 16d^{2} 20d^{pu} 17d 16s^{2} c20d^{4} 20v c16v^{4} c16v^{ur} c16s^{5} c17v^{4} 20g c16v^{3} Apr 17] good-topped gelding: fair hurdler on his day: generally let down by jumping over fences, sold out of J. O'Neill's stable 12,000 gns Doncaster October Sales after fifth start: best around 2m: acts on good to soft going: tried blinkered: tongue tied last 7 starts. *Miss Lucinda V. Russell* **c100 x h108**

YOUR A GASSMAN (IRE) 7 b.g. King's Ride – Nish Bar (Callernish) [2004/5 h109, F107: 20d* 26g* c22s^{2} c24d* c25s* c24g^{bd} c24d^{6} c33g Mar 17] tall, useful-looking gelding: fair hurdler: won maiden at Perth and novice at Cartmel in May: useful novice chaser: won at Newcastle in November and Kelso (beat Gingerbread House 18 lengths) in December: brought down eleventh in Grade 1 novice at Kempton: well below form after in valuable handicap at Doncaster and National Hunt Chase at Cheltenham: stays 3¼m: raced on good going or softer: bold jumper. *Ferdy Murphy* **c131 h106**

YOU'RE SPECIAL (USA) 8 b.g. Northern Flagship (USA) – Pillow Mint (USA) (Stage Door Johnny (USA)) [2004/5 c125, h–: c20d^{3} c21d* c20s^{5} Dec 17] strong, close-coupled gelding: fairly useful chaser: won conditional jockeys handicap at Cheltenham in December by 5 lengths from Christopher: stays 3¼m, effective at much shorter: acts on soft and good to firm going: has had tongue tied, including all 3 starts in 2004/5: front runner: sound jumper: sold 17,000 gns Doncaster May Sales. *P. C. Haslam* **c125 h–**

YOU'RE THE MAN (IRE) 8 b.g. Lapierre – Another Advantage (IRE) (Roselier (FR)) [2004/5 c–, h71, F–: c16s^{pu} 24v^{pu} 24v^{2} 24g 24v* 27d^{ro} 22m^{pu} Apr 23] lengthy gelding: poor handicap hurdler: won at Hexham (for second successive year) in March: pulled up both starts over fences: will stay beyond 3m: acts on heavy going: usually wears cheekpieces/blinkers: temperamental. *Mrs E. Slack* **c– h81 §**

YOURMAN (IRE) 5 b.g. Shernazar – Lantern Lover (Be My Native (USA)) [2004/5 h74: 17d^{6} 17m^{2} 22m^{su} 20d* 21d^{ur} 22d^{3} 17d 21d^{4} 22s^{F} 24m 22v Apr 22] sparely-made gelding: fair hurdler: comfortably won handicap at Chepstow in October, despite hanging left: stays 2¾m: acts on soft and good to firm going: hasn't always looked straightforward. *M. C. Pipe* **h104**

YOUR SO COOL 8 ch.g. Karinga Bay – Laurel Diver (Celtic Cone) [2004/5 h119: 24s^{pu} 24g^{pu} Dec 15] sturdy gelding: fairly useful hurdler: no show in 2 handicaps in 2004/5: will stay beyond 3m: raced mainly on soft/heavy going: blinkered/visored since debut. *M. C. Pipe* **h–**

YOUWONTCATCHMENOW (IRE) 7 b.m. Old Vic – Sudden Decision (Buckskin (FR)) [2004/5 F16g^{4} F16v* Feb 5] fourth foal: dam, winning hurdler/pointer, half-sister to smart hurdler up to 2½m Cool Decision: better effort in bumpers when winning mares event at Chepstow by 14 lengths from Ballybawn House. *Noel T. Chance* **F99**

YUKON JACK 7 b.g. Tharqaam (IRE) – Spanish Mermaid (Julio Mariner) [2004/5 F17s 23g^{F} Jan 19] seventh foal: half-brother to winning pointer Nautical Lad (by Crested Lark): dam never ran: no show in bumper and maiden hurdle. *Mrs J. A. Saunders* **h– F–**

YVANOVITCH (FR) 7 b.g. Kaldounevees (FR) – County Kerry (FR) (Comrade In Arms) [2004/5 c100, h–: c17d* c18g^{4} c20v^{2} c20s^{pu} c20g^{4} c17g^{2} Mar 27] big, strong **c103 h–**

gelding: maiden hurdler: fair chaser: won handicap at Plumpton in November: stays 2½m: acts on heavy and good to firm going: bled from nose fourth start. *Mrs L. C. Taylor*

Z

ZABADOU 4 b.g. Abou Zouz (USA) – Strapped (Reprimand) [2004/5 16d 16d 16m 16g Dec 10] leggy gelding: no sign of ability. *F. Kirby* **h–**

ZABENZ (NZ) 8 b.g. Zabeel (NZ) – In The Country (NZ) (In The Purple (FR)) [2004/5 17d^4 16d 16d 21s^5 24g^3 Apr 14] sturdy gelding: 1¼m winner on Flat: successful 3 times over hurdles in Australia, and once in USA between June and August in 2002: best effort in handicaps in Britain (useful form) when fourth to King Revo at Cheltenham in December: mainly creditable efforts in competitive events other starts: effective at 2m to 3m: blinkered last 4 outings. *P. J. Hobbs* **h130**

ZACHARY (IRE) 5 b.g. Desert King (IRE) – Amada (IRE) (Sadler's Wells (USA)) [2004/5 F16m^4 F18g 16m^{pu} Jun 6] second foal: dam unraced half-sister to useful 7f and 1¼m winner Santovito: fair form in bumper on debut: tongue tied, pulled up in novice on hurdling debut. *P. R. Webber* **h– F83**

ZADOK THE PRIEST (IRE) 5 b. or br.g. Zafonic (USA) – Valencay (IRE) (Sadler's Wells (USA)) [2004/5 24g^3 22d^3 26g^2 22g^5 26m^{pu} 24g 22d^{pu} Aug 28] modest and ungenuine maiden on Flat (stays 2¼m), sold out of J. Hills's stable 4,000 gns Newmarket Autumn Sales: poor form over hurdles: looked thoroughly temperamental last 4 starts, sold out of C. Mann's stable 4,200 gns Doncaster August Sales before final one: stays 3¼m: tried blinkered/in cheekpieces: one to avoid. *B. S. Rothwell* **h81 §**

ZAFFAMORE (IRE) 9 ch.g. Zaffaran (USA) – Furmore (Furry Glen) [2004/5 c127, h–: c21g^6 c20g c24s* c25s^2 c24s c24s^{pu} Apr 21] strong gelding: fairly useful handicap chaser: won at Ludlow (third course success, beat Maxie McDonald ¾ length) in December: below form otherwise except when second to Bathwick Annie at Wincanton: stays 25f: acts on soft and good to firm going. *Miss H. C. Knight* **c125 h–**

ZAFFARAN EXPRESS (IRE) 6 b.m. Zaffaran (USA) – Majestic Run (Deep Run) [2004/5 F71: F16d^4 19g^F 20g^4 20s^3 17g* 21m^3 Apr 2] close-coupled mare: better effort in bumpers when fourth at Perth: fair form in novice hurdles: won mares event at Bangor in March readily by 10 lengths from Gordon Highlander: not fluent when third to Penneyrose Bay in valuable mares handicap at Newbury final start: stays 21f: may prove best on good going or softer. *N. G. Richards* **h100 F83**

ZAFFAS MELODY (IRE) 5 ch.g. Zaffaran (USA) – Orchette (IRE) (Orchestra) [2004/5 F16v^3 F16d^4 F16d Mar 19] well-made gelding: chasing type: second foal: half-brother to fair hurdler/fairly useful staying chaser Torche (by Taos): dam unraced, from family of smart staying chaser Zeta's Lad: fair form first 2 starts in bumpers: likely to be well suited by further than 2m. *M. Scudamore* **F85**

ZAFFIE PARSON (IRE) 4 b.f. Zaffaran (USA) – Katie Parson (The Parson) [2004/5 F17v^3 F17g Apr 3] third foal: dam, winning pointer, sister to useful staying chaser Boots Madden and half-sister to fairly useful staying chaser Cowboyboots: better effort in mares bumpers when staying-on third at Sedgefield. *G. A. Harker* **F83**

ZAFFINELLO (IRE) 6 ch.g. Zaffaran (USA) – Satin Sheen (Abednego) [2004/5 F17s^5 16s^{ur} 17s^4 19g^5 24m^{pu} Apr 13] well-made gelding: fourth foal: brother to winning pointer/fair hurdler Letitia's Loss, stays 27f: dam, winning pointer, half-sister to smart staying chaser Nuaffe: fifth in bumper at Exeter on debut: fair form in novice hurdles: jumped poorly when amiss in novice handicap at Cheltenham final start: should stay 3m. *Miss H. C. Knight* **h104 F90**

ZAFFISFACTION 5 b.m. Zaffaran (USA) – Anaconda (IRE) (Le Moss) [2004/5 F16s F16d 20d 21g 16g Apr 19] lengthy, rather unfurnished mare: first foal: dam unraced: no sign of ability. *K. C. Bailey* **h– F–**

ZAFFRE D'OR (IRE) 8 b.g. Zaffaran (USA) – Massinetta (Bold Lad (IRE)) [2004/5 20d^5 20s^5 19d 26s^{pu} c20s^{ur} c20g^3 Mar 28] lengthy gelding: no form over hurdles: achieved little when third in maiden chase at Plumpton. *M. Pitman* **c– h–**

ZAFFRE (IRE) 6 gr.m. Mtoto – Zeferina (IRE) (Sadler's Wells (USA)) [2004/5 F86: 17g 19m^3 16s^6 21d 18m* Apr 21] big mare: modest form when winning mares maiden hurdle at Fontwell in April: should stay beyond 2½m: acts on good to firm going. *Miss Z. C. Davison* **h89**

ZAFFRE NOIR (IRE) 9 b.g. Zaffaran (USA) – Massinetta (Bold Lad (IRE)) [2004/5 c98, h98: c23g^{3} c24g^{3} c24m^{2} Jun 13] tall, lengthy gelding: fair hurdler at best: similar form over fences: lame final start: stays 3m: acts on any going. *M. Pitman* **c108 h–**

ZAGGY LANE 13 b.g. Prince of Peace – Meldon Lady (Ballymoss) [2004/5 c95d, h–: c25d^{pu} Apr 29] workmanlike gelding: veteran chaser, lame on only outing in 2004/5: blinkered once. *P. R. Rodford* **c– h–**

ZAHUNDA (IRE) 6 b.m. Spectrum (IRE) – Gift of Glory (FR) (Niniski (USA)) [2004/5 22m^{3} Apr 17] leggy mare: half-sister to fairly useful hurdler up to 2½m Seixo Branco (by Saddlers' Hall): poor on Flat (probably stays 1½m): sold out of W. M. Brisbourne's stable 700 gns Doncaster March Sales: raced freely when third of 4 finishers in novice at Stratford on hurdling debut. *M. J. Gingell* **h80 ?**

ZAKTOO (IRE) 4 b.g. Sri Pekan (USA) – Alpine Symphony (Northern Dancer) [2004/5 18s^{pu} 18s^{6} 22m^{4} Apr 21] well held in 2 maidens at 2 yrs for N. Littmoden: sold £700 Ascot July Sales: no sign of ability over hurdles. *C. J. Drewe* **h–**

ZALDA 4 ch.f. Zilzal (USA) – Gold Luck (USA) (Slew O' Gold (USA)) [2004/5 16d* 17s 16s^{3} 16g Mar 15] leggy filly: fair on Flat (stays 1¾m), successful twice in 2004, sold out of R. Charlton's stable 28,000 gns Newmarket Autumn Sales: fairly useful juvenile hurdler: won at Kempton in January: best effort when seventh of 24 to Dabiroun in valuable handicap at Cheltenham final start: raced around 2m on good ground or softer. *P. J. Hobbs* **h112**

ZALKANI (IRE) 5 ch.g. Cadeaux Genereux – Zallaka (IRE) (Shardari) [2004/5 18s Oct 12] modest on all-weather Flat (stays 1¼m), successful 3 times in December and January: tailed off in novice on hurdling debut. *B. G. Powell* **h–**

ZAMAT 9 b.g. Slip Anchor – Khandjar (Kris) [2004/5 c16s^{F} c16g^{pu} c16v^{6} 16v c16v^{4} Jan 29] lengthy gelding: fair handicap hurdler in 2002/3: modest form on return, mainly over fences: raced mainly around 2m on good going or softer (acts on heavy). *P. Monteith* **c99 h94**

ZAMIR 6 ch.g. Zamindar (USA) – Fairy Flax (IRE) (Dancing Brave (USA)) [2004/5 17d^{pu} Oct 8] showed nothing in 2 starts over hurdles nearly 2 years apart: tried tongue tied. *W. Storey* **h–**

ZANJEER 5 b.g. Averti (IRE) – Cloudslea (USA) (Chief's Crown (USA)) [2004/5 16g* 16d^{F} Jan 13] good-topped gelding: fair on Flat (stays 1m): successful in maiden at Catterick in December on completed start over hurdles: likely to prove best around 2m with emphasis on speed. *N. Wilson* **h100**

ZANZIBAR BOY 6 gr.g. Arzanni – Bampton Fair (Free Boy) [2004/5 F16d^{4} F14m^{2} Mar 21] useful-looking gelding: sixth foal: half-brother to modest hurdler/staying chaser Bay Fair (by Arctic Lord): dam twice-raced daughter of dual Grand National third Eyecatcher: fair form in 2 bumpers, length second to Post It in maiden at Hereford. *H. Morrison* **F93**

ZAPATA HIGHWAY 8 ch.g. Bold Arrangement – Trailing Rose (Undulate (USA)) [2004/5 h–: 17m^{F} 17g Jul 4] of no account: tried in cheekpieces. *R. C. Guest* **h–**

ZARAKASH (IRE) 5 b.g. Darshaan – Zarannda (IRE) (Last Tycoon) [2004/5 h–p: 17d 17d^{pu} May 17] smallish gelding: poor form over hurdles. *Jonjo O'Neill* **h83 +**

ZARNEETA 4 b.f. Tragic Role (USA) – Compton Amber (Puissance) [2004/5 16s 16d 19v^{6} 17s Mar 7] leggy filly: poor maiden on Flat (stays 1¼m): no form over hurdles: wore cheekpieces last 2 starts. *W. de Best-Turner* **h–**

ZEALAND 5 ch.g. Zamindar (USA) – Risanda (Kris) [2004/5 F16g^{3} F16g^{3} 16s^{5} Nov 21] €13,000 3-y-o: fifth foal: half-brother to fairly useful winners around 1¼m Andalish (by Polish Precedent) and Lease (by Lycius), latter fair hurdler up to 2½m: dam unraced half-sister to Cheveley Park winner Prophecy, out of Lancashire Oaks winner Andaleeb: modest form when third in 2 bumpers: tailed off in novice at Aintree on hurdling debut: in frame on Flat in winter. *R. A. Fahey* **h– F77**

ZELENSKY (IRE) 6 b.g. Danehill Dancer (IRE) – Malt Leaf (IRE) (Nearly A Nose (USA)) [2004/5 h–: c16g^{F} c17g^{ur} Mar 28] rather leggy gelding: no form over hurdles and has shown no aptitude for chasing: left G. Brown before final start. *J. W. Mullins* **c– h–**

ZEN (IRE) 10 b.g. Shernazar – Mary Mary (Moulton) [2004/5 c–x, h–: 19d May 4] no longer of any account: blinkered only start in 2004/5. *T. P. McGovern* **c– x h–**

ZEROBERTO (IRE) 5 ch.g. Definite Article – Blazing Soul (IRE) (Common Grounds) [2004/5 h112p: 16m* 16s^{4} Nov 20] thrice-raced hurdler: won 4-y-o novice at Galway in July by 3 lengths from Studmaster: raced at 2m. *D. K. Weld, Ireland* **h110**

Vodafone Handicap Chase, Newbury—
hot favourite Zeta's River is hard pressed to beat long-time leader Harrycone Lewis (blinkers)

ZESTA FIESTA 5 b.g. El Conquistador – Little Lemon (Spartan Jester) [2004/5 F17d Oct 27] second foal: dam winning 27f chaser: well beaten in maiden bumper on debut: successful in maiden point in March: sold 6,200 gns Doncaster May Sales. *C. Grant* **F–**

ZETA'S RIVER (IRE) 7 ch.g. Over The River (FR) – Laurebon (Laurence O) [2004/5 c122: 19d c20d^{2} c24d* c25g^{2} c25g^{2} c29g Apr 23] sturdy gelding: once-raced over hurdles: useful handicap chaser: won at Newbury in March by ½ length from Harrycone Lewis: better form when runner-up next 2 starts, to Sleeping Night at Aintree and Imperial Dream in novice event at Ayr: saddle reportedly slipped when never a factor in Betfred Gold Cup at Sandown: should stay beyond 25f: raced on good/good to soft ground. *M. C. Pipe* **c136 h–**

ZEYDNAA (IRE) 5 b.g. Bahhare (USA) – Hadawah (USA) (Riverman (USA)) [2004/5 F16d 19d 20s^{pu} Mar 10] 22,000F, 29,000Y, 3,500 3-y-o: close-coupled gelding: second foal: half-brother to winner in Turkey by Night Shift: dam, maiden who stayed 1m, half-sister to useful 2-y-o 6f winner Shuhrah, out of half-sister to Lahib: well beaten in bumper and novice hurdles. *C. R. Wilson* **h– F–**

ZIBELINE (IRE) 8 b.g. Cadeaux Genereux – Zia (USA) (Shareef Dancer (USA)) [2004/5 h133p: c21v^{5} c16s^{4} 16d 21g 20d Apr 9] leggy gelding: useful on Flat (barely stays 2¼m): useful hurdler in 2003/4: no form in 2004/5, including in 2 maiden chases: stays 2½m: usually blinkered, tried visored: tongue tied last 2 starts. *B. Ellison* **c– h–**

ZIGGY DAN 5 b.g. Slip Anchor – Nikatino (Bustino) [2004/5 19d^{ur} 17d 18s^{pu} Dec 21] half-brother to winning hurdler around 2m in Italy by Contract Law: well held on Flat, sold out of Ms D. Evans' stable 2,200 gns Doncaster May Sales: looked temperamental over hurdles: blinkered last 2 outings. *R. H. Buckler* **h– §**

ZIGGY'S WAY 10 b.g. Teenoso (USA) – Onaway (Commanche Run) [2004/5 c91, h–: c24s^{2} Oct 30] sturdy, lengthy gelding: fair handicap chaser: ran well but finished lame when second at Chepstow only start in 2004/5: stays 3m: acts on soft going. *Mrs A. Barclay* **c103 h–**

ZIGGY ZEN 6 b.g. Muhtarram (USA) – Springs Welcome (Blakeney) [2004/5 h118: 21g 21d 16d 19d* 17m5 Apr 9] small, close-coupled gelding: fair hurdler: made all in seller at Newton Abbot in March: stays 21f: acts on good to firm and good to soft going. *C. J. Mann* **h106**

ZIMBABWE (FR) 5 b.g. Turgeon (USA) – Razzamatazz (FR) (Always Fair (USA)) [2004/5 16s2 20s6 19g c19s2 24d 22s Mar 22] sturdy gelding: fourth foal: brother to winning hurdler/chaser up to 2¾m Gee Whizz and half-brother to modest 2m hurdler Trinity Belle (by Tel Quel) and fair hurdler/useful chaser up to 2½m Vesuve (by Villez): dam useful 3-y-o hurdler/chaser: modest novice hurdler: jumped poorly but similar form when second in maiden at Exeter on chasing debut: should stay beyond 19f: acts on soft going: well held in cheekpieces final start. *N. J. Hawke* **c87 h87**

ZIPADEA (IRE) 6 b.g. Florida Son – Prudent Princess (Puissance) [2004/5 20spu 21dpu 16s 23vpu Jan 3] workmanlike gelding: first foal: dam poor maiden up to 1m on Flat: no sign of ability. *J. R. Turner* **h–**

ZIPALONG LAD (IRE) 5 b.g. Zaffaran (USA) – Rosy Posy (IRE) (Roselier (FR)) [2004/5 F16s2 F16s6 F16m Apr 10] 18,000 4-y-o: seventh foal: brother to fair chaser Go White Lightning and winning 25f chaser Greyton and half-brother to fairly useful bumper winner Dobbiesgardenworld (by Great Marquess): dam unraced half-sister to smart 2m hurdler Honeygrove Banker: best effort in bumpers when neck second to Billyandi at Towcester on debut. *C. N. Kellett* **F85**

ZOFFANY (IRE) 8 b.g. Synefos (USA) – Shining Green (Green Shoon) [2004/5 c103, h–: c17d3 c16vF Jan 26] lengthy gelding: winning hurdler: fair novice chaser: looked likely winner when falling fatally 3 out in maiden at Wetherby: seemed best at 2m: acted on heavy going. *M. Todhunter* **c105 h–**

ZONERGEM 7 ch.g. Zafonic (USA) – Anasazi (IRE) (Sadler's Wells (USA)) [2004/5 h104p: 16d* 16m* 16s* Oct 21] useful but quirky on Flat (stays easy 1¼m): successful over hurdles in novices at Huntingdon (2, amateurs first time) in May and handicap at Ludlow in October: fairly useful form when beating Candarli 1½ lengths at latter, produced on bridle at last: likely to prove best around 2m: carries head awkwardly. *Lady Herries* **h120**

ZORRO REAL 8 b.g. Rakaposhi King – Sharp Vixen (Laurence O) [2004/5 h–: 16g May 9] workmanlike gelding: lightly raced and no sign of ability. *R. Rowe* **h–**

ZOUAVE (IRE) 4 b.g. Spectrum (IRE) – Lady Windley (Baillamont (USA)) [2004/5 16f3 16s6 Oct 23] good-topped gelding: fairly useful on Flat at 2 yrs, well held in 2004, for B. Meehan: in cheekpieces, set strong pace on testing ground when sixth to Cerium in juvenile maiden hurdle at Kempton: may do better. *C. J. Mann* **h85 +**

ZULETA 4 ch.f. Vettori (IRE) – Victoria (Old Vic) [2004/5 17mpu Apr 9] poor maiden on Flat (stays 1¾m): saddle slipped on hurdling debut. *B. D. Leavy* **h–**

ZUM SEE (IRE) 6 ch.g. Perugino (USA) – Drew (IRE) (Double Schwartz) [2004/5 h126: 16g c17v2 c18d4 Dec 11] well-made gelding: fairly useful hurdler in 2003/4: jumped soundly when 8 lengths second to Fota Island in maiden at Navan on chasing debut: seemingly amiss in similar event at Fairyhouse next time: well held back over hurdles in handicap at Punchestown in late-April: raced around 2m: possibly needs going softer than good. *N. Meade, Ireland* **c115 h–**

ZURS (IRE) 12 b.g. Tirol – Needy (High Top) [2004/5 c–, h–: 17d6 c21g2 c20dpu c20dF c16g c21m5 c20f6 c21m6 c20s* c26d2 c20g2 c24sR Nov 6] leggy gelding: winning hurdler: poor chaser: won weak novice at Perth in August: best form up to 21f: acts on soft and good to firm going: tried visored, in cheekpieces in 2004/5: has been reluctant at start/looked unwilling. *J. J. Lambe, Ireland* **c84 h72**

ZYGOMATIC 7 ch.g. Risk Me (FR) – Give Me A Day (Lucky Wednesday) [2004/5 h83: 21d Dec 7] sturdy gelding: winning hurdler: well beaten in minor event at Sedgefield after 16-month absence: stays 2½m: seems suited by good going or firmer. *R. F. Fisher* **h–**

ERRATA & ADDENDA

'Chasers & Hurdlers 2000/01', '2001/02' & '2002/03'

The Gatherer (Ire)	dam is Reaper's Run (correct in 'Chasers & Hurdlers 1999/2000')

'Chasers & Hurdlers 2002/03' & '2003/04'

Charlie Bubbles (Ire)	is 1998 bay gelding by Red Sunset

'Chasers & Hurdlers 2003/04'

Hawk's Landing (Ire)	did not fall fatally
Hodgson's Choice (Ire)	second outing was over hurdles
Omni Cosmo Touch (USA)	disqualified due to prohibited substance from win at Sedgefield, race awarded to Tor Head
Super Run (Ire)	is a half-brother to Strong Run (by Strong Gale), not as stated
Touch Closer	disqualified due to prohibited substance from win at Kelso, race awarded to Lago
Vic Toto (Fr)	is a horse not a gelding, and retired to stud in 2005
Selected Big Races	back references are omitted from race 198 onwards; all races are listed correctly in the index

Timeform 'Top 100'

P20 The following horses were omitted from the list of the Top 100 Hurdlers: 153–Quazar and Sporazene, 151–Rigmarole, 149–Flame Creek, 147–Big Moment and War of Attrition, 143–Eric's Charm, Grey Report and Mughas, 140–Fleet Street, Perouse, Royal Alphabet, Self Defense and Strike Back, 138–Cardenas, Dromlease Express and Monet's Garden

'Chasers & Hurdlers 2002/03'

Be My Royal (Ire)

P108 The Jockey Club's long-running inquiry into 37 horses which tested positive for morphine in the 2002/3 season concluded in September 2004. In addition to Be My Royal in the Hennessy, the following placed horses under NH rules were disqualified:

Rare Ouzel (Ire)	second at Cheltenham, Nov 15
Classic Note (Ire)	first at Cheltenham, Nov 16, race awarded to Bongo Fury (Fr)
Spree Vision (Ire)	first at Newcastle, Nov 25, race awarded to Middlethorpe
Drama King	first at Uttoxeter, Nov 28, race awarded to Bachelors Pad
River Slave (Ire)	third at Uttoxeter, Nov 28
Royal Beluga (USA)	first at Bangor, Nov 29, race awarded to Bunbury
Lanmire Leader (Ire)	third at Folkestone, Dec 2
Charming Admiral (Ire)	first at Catterick, Dec 4, race awarded to Woodfield Gale (Ire)
Saxon Mill	first at Market Rasen, Dec 5, race awarded to Handy Money
Waterspray (Aus)	third at Doncaster, Dec 14
Barton Nic	first at Plumpton, Feb 10, race awarded to Joshua's Bay

PROMISING HORSES

British-trained horses in *Chasers & Hurdlers* thought capable of noteworthy improvement are listed under the trainers for whom they last ran.

R. H. ALNER
Kadara (IRE) 6 b.m h131 c101p
The Listener (IRE) 6 gr.h h132p F78

JEAN-RENE AUVRAY
Delightfully 4 b.f h82p

A. M. BALDING
Briareus 5 ch.g h124p

C. J. BENNETT
Balinova (IRE) 8 b.g c109p

P. BOWEN
McKelvey (IRE) 6 b.g h119p

SIR JOHN BARLOW BT
Rowan Castle 9 ch.g h97 c—p

JENNIE CANDLISH
Downing Street (IRE) 4 b.g h93p

D. E. CANTILLON
Be Fair 7 br.g h122 c114p

D. CARROLL
Tisn't Easy (IRE) 7 b.m h95 c—p

NOEL T. CHANCE
Great Man (FR) 4 b.g h—p
Southwestern (IRE) 6 br.g h—p
Victom's Chance (IRE) 7 b.g h119p F109

B. J. CURLEY
Be Telling (IRE) 6 b.g h—p
Sandokan (GER) 4 b.g h88p

H. D. DALY
Mighty Man (FR) 5 b.g h138p F112
Von Origny (FR) 4 gr.g h108p F97

V. R. A. DARTNALL
Greenmoor House (IRE) 7 b.g h92p
Mount Clerigo (IRE) 7 b.g h132p

R. DICKIN
Change Agent 9 br.g c99p

C. J. DOWN
Like A Breeze 6 bl.m h—p F82

M. W. EASTERBY
Buttress 6 b.g h—p F95
Gary's Pimpernel 6 b.g h107 c100p
Tickton Flyer 7 b.g h— c92p

C. R. EGERTON
Edgehill (IRE) 4 b.g h84p
Gallant Approach (IRE) 6 ch.g h105p
Hobbs Hill 6 b.g F107p
It's Just Harry 8 b.g h132p

B. ELLISON
Fort Churchill (IRE) 4 b.g h81p

D. R. C. ELSWORTH
Wavertree Boy (IRE) 5 ch.g h98p

A. ENNIS
Beare Necessities (IRE) 6 ch.g h99p

R. A. FAHEY
Danelor (IRE) 7 b.g h—p

T. J. FITZGERALD
Moment of Madness (IRE) 7 ch.g h94 c94p
Patrixtoo (FR) 4 gr.c h100p
Vicentio 6 br.g h86 c75p

R. FORD
Chabrimal Minster 8 b.g h— c—p

J. D. FROST
Grey Brother 7 gr.g h117p

D. R. GANDOLFO
Fleurette 5 b.m h77p F69+

T. R. GEORGE
Lord of Illusion (IRE) 8 b.g h— c148p
Mighty Matters (IRE) 6 b.g h—p F92
Thenameescapesme 5 b.g F—p

N. J. GIFFORD
Joly Bey (FR) 8 ch.g h128p c145
Major Catch (IRE) 6 b.g h107p

S. GOLLINGS
Castleshane (IRE) 8 b.g h130 c—p

R. C. GUEST
Beaver (AUS) 6 b.g h100p
Bergerac (NZ) 7 b.g h80p

N. J. HENDERSON
Brankley Boy 7 ch.g h110p
Bugle Major (IRE) 6 b.g h—p F98
Demarco (IRE) 7 ch.g h130p
Rico Hombre (FR) 6 b.g h114p
Shining Strand 6 ch.g h95p F88
The Grocers Curate (IRE) 5 b.g h109p
The Thunderer 6 gr.g h—p

LADY HERRIES
Murphy's Quest 9 ch.g h115 c112p

P. J. HOBBS
Master d'Or (FR) 5 b.g h106 c—p
Silver City 5 ro.g h85p
Supreme Piper (IRE) 7 b.g h119 c—p
Tom Sayers (IRE) 7 b.g h91 c117p

J. M. JEFFERSON
Portavadie 6 b.g h106p F95

J. HOWARD JOHNSON
Ardynagh (IRE) 6 b.g h81p
Beauchamp Gigi (IRE) 7 b.m h101p
Coat of Honour (USA) 5 gr.g h125p

Credit (IRE) 4 b.g h114p
Galero 6 b.g h109p
Lord Transcend (IRE) 8 gr.g h— c150p
Mephisto (IRE) 6 b.g h148p
Motive (FR) 4 ch.g h109p
No Refuge (IRE) 5 ch.g h147p
Rogues Gallery (IRE) 5 b.g h106p F94
Supreme Leisure (IRE) 8 b.g h112 c—p
The Reverend (IRE) 5 b.g h127p

P. JONES
Christy Beamish (IRE) 8 b.g c95p

D. P. KEANE
Barton Park 5 b.g h78p F95
Eluvaparty 5 b.g F87p

A. KING
Ballistigo (IRE) 6 br.g h101p F89
Halcon Genelardais (FR) 5 ch.g h127p
Penzance 4 ch.g h144p

MISS H. C. KNIGHT
Espresso Forte (IRE) 6 ch.g h101p
Portavo (IRE) 5 b.g h—p F86
Racing Demon (IRE) 5 b.g h146p
Supreme Missile (IRE) 5 b.g h—p F84

MISS E. C. LAVELLE
Immola (FR) 9 b.g h— c—p
Presenting Express (IRE) 6 b.g h—p c84p
Priors Dale 5 b.g h120p
Stern (IRE) 6 b.g h110p F89

L. LUNGO
Bogus Dreams (IRE) 8 ch.g h109p c80p
Brandy Wine (IRE) 7 b.g h96p
Chef de Cour (FR) 4 b.g h91p F95
Sara Monica (IRE) 8 ch.m h106 c—p
Word Gets Around (IRE) 7 b.g h91 c—p

C. J. MANN
Another Native (IRE) 7 b.g h94 c95p

KAREN MCLINTOCK
Dunaskin (IRE) 5 b.g h108p

JAMES MOFFATT
Flame of Zara 6 ch.m h84p

P. MONTEITH
Andre Chenier (IRE) 4 b.g h108p

P. F. NICHOLLS
Aide de Camp (FR) 6 b.g h—p
Andreas (FR) 5 b.g h— c134P
Armariver (FR) 5 ch.g h105p F95
Banchory Two (IRE) 5 b.g h106p F95
Be Be King (IRE) 6 b.g h98p F121
Chamoss Royale (FR) 5 ch.m h132 c—p
Darrias (GER) 4 b.g h105p
Gaora Gale (IRE) 5 b.g h90p
Get My Drift (IRE) 6 b.g h113+ c119p
Kaldouas (FR) 4 bl.g F90p
Kauto Star (FR) 5 b.g h136+ c150p
Pirate Flagship (FR) 6 b.g h93p F—
Silver Jewel (IRE) 6 gr.g h—p F82
Sporazene (IRE) 6 gr.g h— c140p

P. D. NIVEN
Ballyhale (IRE) 7 br.g h81p F93

JONJO O'NEILL
Alright Now M'Lad (IRE) 5 b.g h83p F90
Artane Boys 8 b.g h105 c96p
Bold Bishop (IRE) 8 b.g h— c125p
Catchthebug (IRE) 6 b.g h103p F99
Clan Leader (IRE) 5 b.g F89p
Confluence (IRE) 4 gr.g h—p
Delgay Lad 7 b.g h89p F—
East Tycoon (IRE) 6 ch.g h123 c120P
Feel The Pride (IRE) 7 b.m h— c95p
Good Judgement (IRE) 7 b.g h105p
Iris's Gift 8 gr.g h— c128P
Kingscourt Lad (IRE) 7 b.g h—p F95
Manners (IRE) 7 b.g h104P F118
Man Ray (USA) 4 b.g h83p
Monte Vista (IRE) 8 b.g h128p
Olaso (GER) 6 b.g h121p
Over The Blues (IRE) 5 b.g h—p
Pass It On (IRE) 6 br.g h95p
Predicament 6 br.g h111p
Progressive (IRE) 7 ch.g h103p
Specular (AUS) 9 b.g h— c112p
Steppes of Gold (IRE) 8 b.g h126 c117p
The Rising Moon (IRE) 6 br.g h116p
Treaty Stone 6 b.g h88p F93
Ursis (FR) 4 b.g h117P
Young Dude (IRE) 6 b.g F95p

J. A. B. OLD
Barrys Ark (IRE) 7 b.g h105p F97
Round The Horn (IRE) 5 ch.g F102p

A. PARKER
Overserved 6 b.g h105p

R. T. PHILLIPS
Arnold Layne (IRE) 6 gr.g F101p

M. C. PIPE
Bannow Strand (IRE) 5 b.g h91p
Dangerous Dan McGo (IRE) 7 b.g h—p
Northern Madrik (FR) 4 b.g h—p F—
Not Left Yet (IRE) 4 b.g h102p
Oasis Banus (IRE) 4 b.g h—p F91
Sardagna (FR) 5 gr.m h121 c105p
Sixo (IRE) 8 gr.g h138 c138p
Standin Obligation (IRE) 6 ch.g h123p
Yes My Lord (IRE) 6 b.g h78p

B. G. POWELL
Big Rob (IRE) 6 b.g h88 c121p
Colonel Frank 8 b.g h— c145p
Killenaule (IRE) 5 b.g h108p F91

K. G. REVELEY
Diklers Rose (IRE) 6 gr.m h98p F93
Into The Shadows 5 ch.m h96p
Minster Missile 7 b.g h—p F80

N. G. RICHARDS
Faasel (IRE) 4 b.g h144p
Harmony Brig (IRE) 6 ch.g h107p
Knockara Luck (IRE) 4 ch.f F101p
Marlborough Sound 6 b.g h94p
Native Coral (IRE) 7 ch.g h104 c—p
Neagh (FR) 4 b.g h94p
Seeking Shelter (IRE) 6 b.m h—p

Sergio Coimbra (IRE) 6 b.g h77p F88
Vic The Piler (IRE) 6 ch.g h112p

MRS P. ROBESON
Ponderon 5 ch.g h103p

C. TINKLER
Desert Image (IRE) 4 b.g h—p
Dr Cerullo 4 b.g h90p
Native Ivy (IRE) 7 b.g h119 c108p
Sunset Light (IRE) 7 b.g h122p F104
Valley Ride (IRE) 5 b.g h118p F100

N. TINKLER
Charlie Tango (IRE) 4 b.g h91p

C. L. TIZZARD
Pass Me A Dime 6 b.g h108p F—

N. A. TWISTON-DAVIES
Ardaghey (IRE) 6 b.g h122p F107
Fundamentalist (IRE) 7 b.g h— c154p
Harry Blade 6 b.g h105p F88
Knowhere (IRE) 7 b.g h136p
The Gangerman (IRE) 5 ch.g h84p F90

MRS L. WADHAM
Ruby Hare 4 ch.g F82p
United (GER) 4 b.f h135p

MRS K. WALTON
Gay Oscar (IRE) 6 b.g h—p F98

W. J. WARNER
Coolefind (IRE) 7 b.g c106p

EVAN WILLIAMS
Harry Potter (GER) 6 b.g h—p
In The Frame (IRE) 6 b.g h— c—p

IAN WILLIAMS
Dad's Elect (GER) 6 b.g h125 c100p
Manolo (FR) 5 b.g h84p
Massimo (FR) 5 b.g h—p F95

NICK WILLIAMS
The Real Deal (IRE) 4 b.g h—p

MRS S. D. WILLIAMS
Holland Park (IRE) 8 gr.g h137 c—p

MISS VENETIA WILLIAMS
Fabulous Jet (FR) 5 ch.g h—p
Ma Yahab 4 ch.g h104p

MRS L. WILLIAMSON
Red Square Lad (IRE) 9 ch.g h— c109p

D. J. WINTLE
Real Definition 6 br.g h—p F89

SELECTED BIG RACES 2004/05

Prize money for racing abroad has been converted to £ sterling at the exchange rate current at the time of the race. The figures are correct to the nearest £.

HAYDOCK Saturday, May 1 GOOD to FIRM

1 **Freephone Stanleybet Swinton Hcap Hdle (Gr 3) (A) (161) (4yo+)** £40,600 — 2m (8)

MACS JOY (IRE) *MrsJHarrington,Ireland* 5-10-0^{135} TJMurphy	4/1f		1
DANCING BAY *NJHenderson* 7-9-11^{135} ATinkler^{3}	20/1	2½	2
TORRID KENTAVR (USA) *BEllison* 7-9-7^{135} SJCraine^{7}	25/1	1¼	3
ALMAYDAN *RLee* 6-10-0^{135} MBradburne	12/1	hd	4
Westender (FR) *MCPipe* 8-11-12^{161} (b) APMcCoy	10/1	5	5
Jack Dawson (IRE) *JohnBerry* 7-10-0^{135} JCulloty	20/1	sh	6
Dalaram (IRE) *JHowardJohnson* 4-10-0^{139} GLee	14/1	5	7
River City (IRE) *NoelTChance* 7-10-0^{135} TDoyle	12/1	1¾	8
Smart Savannah *CTinkler* 8-9-11^{135} DCrosse^{3}	20/1	¾	9
Tik-A-Tai (IRE) *OSherwood* 9-9-7^{135} ONelmes^{7}	14/1	sh	10
In Contrast (IRE) *PJHobbs* 8-10-10^{145} RJohnson	10/1	2	11
Merryvale Man *MissKarianaKey* 7-9-7^{135} DGMcGann^{7}	100/1	nk	12
Howle Hill (IRE) *AKing* 4-10-0^{139} RThornton	9/1	nk	13
The French Furze (IRE) *NGRichards* 10-10-6^{141} BHarding	33/1	2½	14
Red Sun *JMackie* 7-9-11^{135} LVickers^{3}	100/1	4	15
Castleshane (IRE) *SGollings* 7-10-0^{135} ADobbin	25/1	1¼	16
Valeureux *JHetherton* 6-9-11^{135} JamesDavies^{3}	100/1	5	17
Copeland *MCPipe* 9-10-10^{148} JEMoore^{3}	10/1	sh	18
Tysou (FR) *NJHenderson* 7-10-4^{139} MAFitzgerald	25/1	1¾	19

Mac's J Racing Syndicate 19ran 3m32.13

UTTOXETER Sunday, Jun 27 GOOD to FIRM

2 **Britannia Building Society English Summer National (Hcap Chase) (B) 0-140(138) (5yo+)** £43,500 — 4m110y (21)

TAKE THE STAND (IRE) *PBowen* 8-11-12^{138} SDurack	14/1		1
EXSTOTO *RAFahey* 7-10-3^{118} PWhelan^{3}	12/1	2	2
BRIGHT APPROACH (IRE) *JGCann* 11-10-2^{121} TJMalone^{7}	16/1	3	3
FARINEL *ALTMoore,Ireland* 8-10-5^{117} APMcCoy	11/2	13	4
Torduff Express (IRE) *PFNicholls* 13-10-2^{119} (b) MrNWilliams^{5}	10/1	7	5
Proper Squire (USA) *CJMann* 7-10-12^{127} DCrosse^{3}	20/1	7	6
Maximize (IRE) *MCPipe* 10-11-7^{133} TJMurphy	8/1	¾	7
Super Fellow (IRE) *CNKellett* 10-10-6^{118} JCullen	25/1	10	8
Uncle Mick (IRE) *CLTizzard* 9-10-2^{114} JTizzard	20/1	5	9
Celioso (IRE) *MrsSJSmith* 7-10-10^{122} DElsworth	5/1jf	7	10
Polar Champ *MCPipe* 11-10-13^{125} (v) JEMoore	25/1		f
General Claremont (IRE) *PFNicholls* 11-10-2^{114} RWalsh	5/1jf		ur
Chicuelo (FR) *MCPipe* 8-11-6^{132} (v+t) RGreene	25/1		pu
Elenas River (IRE) *PJHobbs* 8-10-7^{119} RJohnson	8/1		pu
Misty Future *MissVenetiaWilliams* 6-10-3^{118} SThomas^{3}	33/1		pu
Navarone *IanWilliams* 10-10-1^{113} PaulMoloney	18/1		pu

The Courters 16ran 8m16.80

MARKET RASEN Saturday, Jul 17 GOOD to SOFT

3 **totescoop6 Summer Plate (Hcap Chase) (B) 0-145(138) (5yo+)** £40,600 — 2½m (15)

GLINGER (IRE) *NGRichards* 11-10-2^{114} BHarding	20/1		1
COLCA CANYON (IRE) *MrsJHarrington,Ireland* 7-11-12^{138} BJGeraghty	3/1f	5	2
WUXI VENTURE *RAFahey* 9-10-0^{112} RMcGrath	33/1	½	3
ROYAL PREDICA (FR) *MCPipe* 10-11-9^{135} (t) RJohnson	14/1	8	4
Latalomne (USA) *NWilson* 10-10-9^{126} ACCoyle^{5}	10/1	3½	5
Roveretto *MCPipe* 9-11-4^{130} (v) RGreene	25/1	1½	6
Polar Red *MCPipe* 7-11-12^{138} TScudamore	12/1	30	7
Montreal (FR) *MCPipe* 7-11-7^{133} TJMurphy	10/1	5	8
Gue Au Loup (FR) *BEllison* 10-9-11^{112} PAspell^{3}	33/1	4	9
Lik Wood Power (NZ) *RCGuest* 7-10-5^{117} AThornton	12/1	19	10
Why The Long Face (NZ) *RCGuest* 7-9-9^{112} (s) CBolger^{5}	33/1	25	11
Palua *MissECLavelle* 7-11-9^{135} JAMcCarthy	20/1		f
Little Big Horse (IRE) *MrsSJSmith* 8-10-9^{121} DElsworth	12/1		f
Gimmick (FR) *JonjoO'Neill* 10-10-2^{114} APMcCoy	4/1		f
Gladiateur IV (FR) *MCPipe* 10-11-10^{136} JEMoore	12/1		ur

	Kety Star (FR) *MissVenetiaWilliams* 6-10-9^{124} SThomas^{3}	14/1	pu

Mr James Westoll 16ran 5m07.28

GALWAY Wednesday, Jul 28 GOOD to FIRM

4 **Hewlett-Packard Galway Plate Hcap Chase (Gr 1) (143) (4yo+)** £68,692 2¾m (14)

	ANSAR (IRE) *DKWeld* 8-10-12^{127} DJCasey	10/1	1
	RISK ACCESSOR (IRE) *CRoche* 9-12-0^{143} (t) APMcCoy	20/1	1½ 2
	MANJOE (IRE) *DWachman* 6-10-8^{123} MDGrant	14/1	½ 3
	DIRECT BEARING (IRE) *DKWeld* 7-11-5^{134} MAFitzgerald	11/1	1½ 4
	Junior Fontaine (FR) *ALTMoore* 7-10-10^{125} CO'Dwyer	25/1	nk 5
	Banasan (IRE) *MJPO'Brien* 6-10-11^{126} JCulloty	7/1f	¾ 6
	Wests Awake (IRE) *IMadden* 8-10-4^{119} GLee	9/1	2 7
	Theseus (IRE) *PHughes* 8-10-11^{129} JPElliott^{3}	25/1	1 8
	Prince of Pleasure (IRE) *DBroad* 10-10-6^{121} BMCash	10/1	1¼ 9
	Thari (USA) *NMeade* 7-10-5^{120} (b+t) RMPower	20/1	9 10
	Broadstone Road (IRE) *PaulJohnGilligan* 7-10-7^{125} DJHoward^{3}	16/1	3 11
	Wotsitooya (IRE) *MJPO'Brien* 12-11-0^{129} DNRussell	14/1	4½ 12
	One Night Out (IRE) *WPMullins* 8-10-7^{122} RWalsh	11/1	¾ 13
	Torduff Boy (IRE) *PhilipRedmond* 11-10-7^{129} (s) MrRMMoran^{7}	33/1	sh 14
	Splendour (IRE) *MissSCox* 9-10-7^{125} MFMooney^{3}	25/1	1½ 15
	Glynn Dingle (IRE) *AJMartin* 11-10-10^{125} ADobbin	20/1	nk 16
	Ballyamber (IRE) *WPMullins* 9-11-4^{138} AndrewJMcNamara^{5}	20/1	2½ 17
	Fable (USA) *NMeade* 8-10-6^{121} (b+t) IJPower	25/1	f
3	Colca Canyon (IRE) *MrsJHarrington* 7-11-9^{138} BJGeraghty	9/1	bd
	Sum Leader (IRE) *MissJaneThomas* 8-10-12^{132} DFO'Regan^{5}	16/1	ur
	Rand (NZ) *NMeade* 10-11-1^{130} JRBarry	14/1	pu
	Native Performance (IRE) *MHourigan* 9-10-7^{122} TJMurphy	33/1	pu

Mrs K. Devlin 22ran 5m18.94

GALWAY Thursday, Jul 29 GOOD

5 **Guinness Galway Hcap Hdle (Gr 1) (143) (4yo+)** £72,351 2m (8)

	CLOONE RIVER (IRE) *PaulNolan* 8-10-7^{122} JLCullen	7/2f	1
	GEMINI GUEST (IRE) *PHughes* 8-9-13^{114} JCulloty	12/1	2 2
	MIRPOUR (IRE) *EGriffin* 5-10-2^{117} (b) GLee	16/1	3½ 3
	LOST IN THE RAIN (IRE) *NMeade* 5-10-8^{123} (t) DNRussell	20/1	3½ 4
	Mutakarrim *DKWeld* 7-11-1^{130} (b) DJCasey	16/1	2½ 5
	Dyrick Daybreak (IRE) *DavidAKiely* 5-10-3^{118} (t) RWalsh	14/1	¾ 6
	Callow Lake (IRE) *DWachman* 4-10-1^{118} MDGrant	12/1	sh 7
	Portant Fella *MsJMorgan* 5-10-0^{115} (t) RMPower	25/1	3 8
	Naahil (IRE) *SO'Farrell* 6-9-12^{113} GCotter	25/1	nk 9
	Tulipa (POL) *TRGeorge,GB* 5-10-8^{123} JMMaguire	12/1	1¾ 10
	Mise Rafturai (IRE) *PaulNolan* 6-10-5^{120} (t) APCrowe	33/1	1¼ 11
	Columba (IRE) *DTHughes* 8-9-9^{115} PWFlood^{5}	20/1	3 12
	Batang (GER) *GerardCully* 5-9-10^{114} DJHoward^{3}	12/1	sh 13
	King Carew (IRE) *MHourigan* 6-10-11^{126} (b) TJMurphy	20/1	½ 14
	Dashing Home (IRE) *NMeade* 5-10-6^{121} BJGeraghty	12/1	10 15
	Balapour (IRE) *POBrady* 6-11-0^{132} (t) MFMooney^{3}	20/1	hd 16
	Greenhall Rambler (IRE) *PAFahy* 5-10-1^{116} TPTreacy	25/1	3½ 17
	Prince Among Men *NGRichards,GB* 7-10-8^{123} ADobbin	33/1	4 18
	More Rainbows (IRE) *NMeade* 4-9-11^{117} MrNPMadden^{3}	20/1	nk 19
	Grimes *CRoche* 11-12-0^{143} APMcCoy	20/1	14 20
	Crimson Flower (IRE) *JMorrison* 9-10-0^{115} WSlattery	25/1	ur
	Puck Out (IRE) *CRoche* 6-10-12^{132} MPWalsh^{5}	12/1	pu
	Sabadilla (USA) *PVerling* 10-10-6^{121} (b) JRBarry	14/1	pu
	Safe Route (USA) *WJAustin* 6-10-1^{121} JFLevins^{5}	25/1	pu

Mrs Kathleen Gillane 24ran 3m40.74

NEWTON ABBOT Saturday, Aug 21 GOOD to SOFT

6 **Lord Mildmay Memorial Hcap Chase (B) 0-145(145) (5yo+)** £27,088 2m5f110y (16)

2	TAKE THE STAND (IRE) *PBowen* 8-11-12^{145} SDurack	10/3f	1
3	GLADIATEUR IV (FR) *MCPipe* 10-11-2^{135} RJohnson	7/1	20 2
3	MONTREAL (FR) *MCPipe* 7-10-13^{132} TJMurphy	7/1	2 3
	Tango Royal (FR) *MCPipe* 8-11-8^{141} (t) JMMaguire	10/1	¾ 4
3	Kety Star (FR) *MissVenetiaWilliams* 6-10-2^{121} JTizzard	20/1	2 5
3	Wuxi Venture *RAFahey* 9-9-13^{121} PWhelan^{3}	7/1	4 6
	Fear Siuil (IRE) *NickWilliams* 11-10-0^{119} (t) CLlewellyn	16/1	8 7
	Saffron Sun *JDFrost* 9-10-1^{120} JAMcCarthy	10/1	1 8
3	Royal Predica (FR) *MCPipe* 10-10-9^{135} (t) TJMalone^{7}	17/2	1¼ 9
5	Grimes *CRoche,Ireland* 11-11-7^{140} (b) APMcCoy	6/1	pu
3	Roveretto *MCPipe* 9-10-10^{129} (v) TScudamore	16/1	pu

The Courters 11ran 5m12.60

LISTOWEL Wednesday, Sep 22 HEAVY

7 **Guinness Kerry National Hcap Chase (140) (4yo+)** £61,480 3m (17)

	Horse	SP	Pos
4	BANASAN (IRE) *MJPO'Brien* 6-11-0^{126} RWalsh	7/1	1
	FATHEROFTHEBRIDE (IRE) *JosephCrowley* 8-10-0^{112} (b) DJCasey	10/1	1½ 2
	BARROW DRIVE *AnthonyMullins* 8-12-0^{140} JCulloty	16/1	nk 3
	GARVIVONNIAN (IRE) *EdwardPMitchell* 9-10-10^{127} AndrewJMcNamara^{5}	16/1	1½ 4
4	Splendour (IRE) *MissSCox* 9-11-7^{133} MAFitzgerald	16/1	8 5
	Howaya Pet (IRE) *GKeane* 8-9-13^{111} (t) SPMcCann	10/1	11 6
4	Broadstone Road (IRE) *PaulJohnGilligan* 7-10-12^{124} JLCullen	20/1	f
	The Culdee (IRE) *FFlood* 8-10-6^{118} PCarberry	4/1f	f
	Oh So Lively (IRE) *EJO'Grady* 6-9-10^{108} MrNPMadden	9/1	f
4	Sum Leader (IRE) *MissJaneThomas* 8-11-0^{131} DFO'Regan^{5}	16/1	pu
	Eskimo Jack (IRE) *ALTMoore* 8-11-4^{130} CO'Dwyer	12/1	pu
	Satco Express (IRE) *ESheehy* 8-11-4^{130} BJGeraghty	12/1	pu
	Golden Storm (IRE) *JosephCrowley* 7-10-11^{128} (b) JMAllen^{5}	5/1	pu
	Bassett Tiger (IRE) *WPMullins* 8-10-8^{120} RMPower	20/1	pu
	Haut de Gamme (FR) *FerdyMurphy,GB* 9-10-6^{118} PMoloney	12/1	pu
	Verchoyles Lad (IRE) *JGCarr* 7-10-6^{118} PACarberry	14/1	pu

Mr S. Mulryan 16ran 6m16.49

TIPPERARY Sunday, Oct 3 SOFT

8 **John James McManus Memorial Hdle (Gr 1) (4yo+)** £44,286 2m (11)

	Horse	SP	Pos
	SOLERINA (IRE) *JamesBowe* 7-11-7 GTHutchinson	8/11f	1
	ACCORDION ETOILE (IRE) *PaulNolan* 5-11-12 JLCullen	9/4	4 2
	HARCHIBALD (FR) *NMeade* 5-11-12 PCarberry	4/1	25 3
6	Grimes *CRoche* 11-11-12 CO'Dwyer	10/1	25 4

Mr John P. Bowe 4ran 3m55.80

GOWRAN PARK Friday, Oct 8 SOFT

9 **National Lottery Agent Champion Chase (Gr 2) (5yo+)** £22,448 2½m (14)

	Horse	SP	Pos
	KICKING KING (IRE) *TJTaaffe* 6-11-10 BJGeraghty	11/4	1
	RATHGAR BEAU (IRE) *ESheehy* 8-11-6 JRBarry	9/4f	2½ 2
	STRONG RUN (IRE) *NMeade* 11-11-10 (t) PCarberry	7/1	4 3
	Cloudy Bays (IRE) *CByrnes* 7-11-6 (s) RGeraghty	3/1	nk 4
	Alcapone (IRE) *MFMorris* 10-11-10 CO'Dwyer	12/1	dist 5
	Arctic Copper (IRE) *NMeade* 10-11-8 (s) DNRussell	14/1	1½ 6
	Heart Midoltian (FR) *SNeville* 7-11-6 JLCullen	33/1	pu

Mr Conor Clarkson 7ran 4m56.71

PARDUBICE Sunday, Oct 10 GOOD to FIRM

10 **Velka Pardubicka Ceske Pojistovny (7yo+)** £49,042 4¼m110y

	Horse	SP	Pos
	REGISTANA (GER) *COlehla,CzechRepublic* 8-10-3 PGehm	1/1f	1
	RETRIEVER (GER) *JosefVana,CzechRepublic* 7-10-7 JosefVana		9 2
	DECENT FELLOW (GER) *JosefVana,CzechRepublic* 9-10-7 RHavelka		6 3
	Harry In A Hurry *AndrewLee,Ireland* 7-10-7 NFehily		f
	Clawick Connection (IRE) *JJLennon,Ireland* 9-10-7 KWhelan		f
	Mose Harper (IRE) *TO'Neill,Ireland* 12-10-7 (b) JanRaja		bd
	Luzcadou (FR) *FerdyMurphy,GB* 11-10-7 (b) PMoloney		ref

Staj Wrbna 17ran 9m15.48

AINTREE Sunday, Oct 24 SOFT

11 **totesport Wigan Chase (Ltd Hcap) (Gr 2) (A) (156) (5yo+)** £43,400 2½m (16)

	Horse	SP	Pos
	FARMER JACK *PJHobbs* 8-11-1^{147} PFlynn	14/1	1
6	TAKE THE STAND (IRE) *PBowen* 8-11-10^{156} SDurack	7/2	11 2
	VODKA BLEU (FR) *MCPipe* 5-10-4^{136} TJMurphy	7/4f	2½ 3
	Le Duc (FR) *PFNicholls* 5-10-5^{137} RWalsh	4/1	5 4
	Bold Investor *JonjoO'Neill* 7-10-4^{136} GLee	14/1	f
	Atum Re (IRE) *PRWebber* 7-10-4^{136} MFoley	11/2	ur
	Europa *FerdyMurphy* 8-10-4^{136} ADobbin	50/1	pu

Mr Peter Partridge 7ran 5m15.46

CHELTENHAM Wednesday, Oct 27 GOOD (Old Course)

12 **Ian Williams Owners Nov Chase (B) (5yo+)** £10,840 3m110y (19)

	Horse	SP	Pos
	OLLIE MAGERN *NATwiston-Davies* 6-11-8 CLlewellyn	7/2	1
	COMPLY OR DIE (IRE) *MCPipe* 5-11-3 TJMurphy	8/13f	2½ 2
	OUT THE BLACK (IRE) *PJHobbs* 6-11-5 RJohnson	7/1	dist 3
	Fantastic Champion (IRE) *JRCornwall* 5-10-12 JPMcNamara	50/1	dist 4
	Queens Harbour (IRE) *DrPPritchard* 10-11-0 DrPPritchard	150/1	dist 5

	Smiths Landing *MrsSJSmith* 7-11-8 WMarston	10/1		f

Mr Roger Nicholls 6ran 6m19.74

CHEPSTOW Saturday, Oct 30 SOFT

13 **Royal British Legion Poppy Appeal Persian War Nov Hdle (Gr 2) (A) (4yo+)** £17,400 2½m (11)

	KNOWHERE (IRE) *NATwiston-Davies* 6-11-0 CLlewellyn	2/1f		1
	LADALKO (FR) *PFNicholls* 5-11-0 JTizzard	11/1	nk	2
	FOOTBALL CRAZY (IRE) *PBowen* 5-11-7 (s) WMarston	11/4	19	3
	Brewster (IRE) *IanWilliams* 7-11-0 PaulMoloney	5/1	2	4
	Progressive (IRE) *JonjoO'Neill* 6-11-0 APMcCoy	7/2	dist	5
	Green Master (POL) *ASadik* 4-11-0 (t) JMMaguire	200/1	dist	6

Mr H. R. Mould 6ran 5m03.20

EXETER Tuesday, Nov 2 SOFT

14 **William Hill Haldon Gold Cup Chase (Ltd Hcap) (Gr 2) (A) (174) (5yo+)** £37,700 2m1f110y (12)

	AZERTYUIOP (FR) *PFNicholls* 7-11-10^{174} RWalsh	6/5f		1
	SEEBALD (GER) *MCPipe* 9-10-6^{156} APMcCoy	12/1	5	2
	KADARANN (IRE) *PFNicholls* 7-10-6^{156} JTizzard	6/1	6	3
	Hot Shots (FR) *MPitman* 9-10-4^{154} TJMurphy	9/1	¾	4
	Flagship Uberalles (IRE) *PJHobbs* 10-10-13^{163} RJohnson	11/2	26	5
	Edredon Bleu (FR) *MissHCKnight* 12-11-5^{169} (t) JAMcCarthy	11/2	7	6
	Penthouse Minstrel *RJHodges* 10-10-4^{154} (v) SDurack	250/1	dist	7

Mr J. Hales 7ran 4m30.20

15 **williamhillcasino.com Nov Chase (C) (5yo+)** £10,192 2m1f110y (12)

	ASHLEY BROOK (IRE) *KBishop* 6-10-9 PJBrennan^{3}	9/1		1
	BACKBEAT (IRE) *DRCElsworth* 7-10-9 RYoung^{3}	33/1	25	2
	DO L'ENFANT D'EAU (FR) *PJHobbs* 5-10-12 RJohnson	16/1	11	3
	Goldbrook *RJHodges* 6-10-12 JTizzard	12/1	8	4
	Sporazene (IRE) *PFNicholls* 5-11-4 RWalsh	2/5f		f
	El Vaquero (IRE) *MissHCKnight* 6-10-12 TJMurphy	15/2		pu

Mrs E. K. Ellis 6ran 4m28.90

WINCANTON Saturday, Nov 6 GOOD to SOFT

16 **totescoop6 Rising Stars Nov Chase (Gr 2) (A) (4yo+)** £20,825 2m5f (17)

12	COMPLY OR DIE (IRE) *MCPipe* 5-11-10 APMcCoy	8/13f		1
	DISTANT THUNDER (IRE) *RHAlner* 6-11-6 AThornton	16/1	1¼	2
	RED DEVIL ROBERT (IRE) *PFNicholls* 6-11-6 JTizzard	8/1	21	3
	First Ballot (IRE) *DRCElsworth* 8-11-12 RYoung	7/1	1½	4
	Ross River *PJHobbs* 8-11-6 MAFitzgerald	13/2	24	5
	Mr Fluffy *PJHobbs* 7-11-6 PFlynn	25/1		f
	By Degree (IRE) *RJHodges* 8-11-6 RThornton	22/1		pu

Mr D. A. Johnson 7ran 5m15.18

17 **Badger Ales Trophy (Hcap Chase) (L) (A) 0-150(145) (5yo+)** £46,400 3m1f110y (21)

	ROYAL AUCLAIR (FR) *PFNicholls* 7-11-12^{145} (t) ChristianWilliams	7/2jf		1
	GUNTHER MCBRIDE (IRE) *PJHobbs* 9-11-1^{134} MAFitzgerald	7/2jf	2	2
	WHITENZO (FR) *PFNicholls* 8-10-9^{128} JTizzard	6/1	2	3
	Perfect Fellow *MissHCKnight* 10-10-13^{132} JAMcCarthy	50/1	12	4
	Double Honour (FR) *PJHobbs* 6-11-9^{142} PFlynn	13/2	8	5
	Swansea Bay *PBowen* 8-11-12^{145} (s) AThornton	7/1	6	6
2	Maximize (IRE) *MCPipe* 10-10-12^{131} GSupple	40/1	1	7
	D'Argent (IRE) *AKing* 7-11-10^{143} RThornton	7/1	8	8
	Bounce Back (USA) *MCPipe* 8-10-8^{127} TScudamore	14/1		ur
6	Montreal (FR) *MCPipe* 7-10-10^{129} (s) APMcCoy	12/1		pu

Mr Clive D. Smith 10ran 6m34.05

DOWN ROYAL Saturday, Nov 6 SOFT

18 **James Nicholson Wine Merchant Champion Chase (Gr 1) (5yo+)** £58,333 3m (15)

	BEEF OR SALMON (IRE) *MHourigan* 8-11-10 TJMurphy	1/1f		1
9	KICKING KING (IRE) *TJTaaffe* 6-11-10 BJGeraghty	3/1	3½	2
9	CLOUDY BAYS (IRE) *CByrnes* 7-11-10 (s) DNRussell	12/1	3	3
	Harbour Pilot (IRE) *NMeade* 9-11-10 PCarberry	4/1	½	4
4	Colca Canyon (IRE) *MrsJHarrington* 7-11-10 DJCasey	12/1	dist	5
	Glenelly Gale (IRE) *ALTMoore* 10-11-10 CO'Dwyer	20/1	2	6
	Byron Lamb *DavidChristie* 7-11-10 MDGrant	100/1		f
	Zurs (IRE) *JJLambe* 11-11-10 (s) JLCullen	100/1		ref

Mr B. J. Craig 8ran 6m35.30

CHELTENHAM Friday, Nov 12 GOOD to SOFT (Old Course)

19 Sharp Nov Hdle (Gr 2) (A) (4yo+) £20,300 — 2m110y (8)

	Horse	Odds	Dist	Pos
	MARCEL (FR) *MCPipe* 4-11-7 TJMurphy	5/1		1
	BABY RUN (FR) *NATwiston-Davies* 4-11-0 CLlewellyn	5/1	2½	2
	SHUHOOD (USA) *PRWebber* 4-11-4 TDoyle	10/1	1	3
	The Rising Moon (IRE) *JonjoO'Neill* 5-11-4 APMcCoy	5/2f	14	4
	Nyrche (FR) *AKing* 4-11-7 RThornton	4/1	1¼	5
	Mister Flint *PJHobbs* 6-11-0 MAFitzgerald	15/2	dist	6
	Raven's Last *RTPhillips* 5-11-0 WMarston	33/1	¾	7
	Dawton (POL) *TRGeorge* 6-11-7 JMMaguire	50/1	22	8
	Iloveturtle (IRE) *MCChapman* 4-11-0 ACCoyle	100/1	14	9

Mr D. A. Johnson 9ran 4m02.03

20 Sporting Index Chase (Cross Country) (B) (5yo+) £17,400 — 3m7f (32)

	Horse	Odds	Dist	Pos
	SPOT THEDIFFERENCE (IRE) *EBolger,Ireland* 11-11-8 MrJTMcNamara	6/1		1
	STAR PERFORMANCE (IRE) *OliverMcKiernan,Ireland* 9-11-5 (b+t) GCotter	50/1	¾	2
10	LUZCADOU (FR) *FerdyMurphy* 11-11-8 (b) AO'Keeffe	33/1	hd	3
7	Haut de Gamme (FR) *FerdyMurphy* 9-11-8 KMercer	15/2	10	4
	Comanche War Paint (IRE) *PFNicholls* 7-11-8 RWalsh	11/2	5	5
	Famfoni (FR) *KCBailey* 11-11-8 RThornton	20/1	2	6
	Belski *CLTizzard* 11-11-5 JTizzard	14/1	18	7
	Felix Darby (IRE) *MissGBrowne* 9-11-2 TDoyle	50/1	3	8
10	Clawick Connection (IRE) *JJLennon,Ireland* 9-10-10 KWhelan	66/1	4	9
	Tom Costalot (IRE) *MrsSusanNock* 9-11-5 SStronge	33/1	25	10
	Go Roger Go (IRE) *EJO'Grady,Ireland* 12-11-8 CO'Dwyer	9/1	10	11
	Blazing Batman *DrPPritchard* 11-11-2 DrPPritchard	50/1	dist	12
	Pewter Light (IRE) *BJMRyall* 7-10-10 RYoung	100/1		f
10	Registana (GER) *COlehla,CzechRepublic* 8-11-1 PGehm	9/4f		ro
	The Quads *FerdyMurphy* 12-11-8 (b+t) TJMurphy	16/1		pu
	Kyrton (CZE) *PavelSlozil,CzechRepublic* 8-10-13 PavelSlozil	50/1		pu

Mr John P. McManus 16ran 8m47.50

21 Beards Jewellers Cup (Hcap Chase) (B) (162) (5yo+) £17,400 — 2m (12)

	Horse	Odds	Dist	Pos
	ARMATURK (FR) *PFNicholls* 7-11-4[154] ChristianWilliams	11/2		1
	WELL CHIEF (GER) *MCPipe* 5-11-3[153] TJMurphy	15/8f	hd	2
1	TYSOU (FR) *NJHenderson* 7-9-11[136] ATinkler[3]	9/1	1¼	3
	Upgrade *MCPipe* 10-11-1[151] APMcCoy	16/1	6	4
	Mister McGoldrick *MrsSJSmith* 7-11-0[150] DElsworth	4/1	1¼	5
	Duke of Buckingham (IRE) *PRWebber* 8-10-0[136] TDoyle	14/1	9	6
	City Hall (IRE) *PaulNolan,Ireland* 10-10-0[136] (b) APCrowe	50/1	5	7
	Sir Storm (IRE) *GMMoore* 8-10-0[136] (s) ARoss	66/1	18	8
	Ashgan (IRE) *DrPPritchard* 11-9-4[136] ODayman[10]	100/1	28	9
	Cenkos (FR) *PFNicholls* 10-11-12[162] RWalsh	7/1		ur
	Emperors Guest *CJMann* 6-10-1[137] NFehily	33/1		pu

Mr B. C. Marshall 11ran 3m59.65

CHELTENHAM Saturday, Nov 13 GOOD to SOFT (Old Course)

22 Paddy Power Gold Cup Chase (Hcap) (Gr 3) (A) (160) (5yo+) £63,800 — 2½m110y (15)

	Horse	Odds	Dist	Pos
	CELESTIAL GOLD (IRE) *MCPipe* 6-10-2[136] TJMurphy	12/1		1
	THISTHATANDTOTHER (IRE) *PFNicholls* 8-10-12[146] RWalsh	13/2	1¾	2
	MONKERHOSTIN (FR) *PJHobbs* 7-10-0[134] ADobbin	3/1f	5	3
12	Ollie Magern *NATwiston-Davies* 6-10-12[146] CLlewellyn	8/1	2½	4
	It Takes Time (IRE) *MCPipe* 10-10-9[143] JEMoore	25/1	6	5
11	Take The Stand (IRE) *PBowen* 8-11-7[155] SDurack	25/1	1½	6
	Tikram *GLMoore* 7-10-11[145] LAspell	10/1	13	7
	Ground Ball (IRE) *CFSwan,Ireland* 7-10-6[140] RThornton	14/1	½	8
11	Le Duc (FR) *PFNicholls* 5-10-2[136] JTizzard	20/1	2½	9
	Kelrev (FR) *MissVenetiaWilliams* 6-9-12[135] SThomas[3]	14/1	7	10
	Fondmort (FR) *NJHenderson* 8-11-12[160] MAFitzgerald	9/1	15	11
11	Farmer Jack *PJHobbs* 8-11-8[156] PFlynn	11/1		f
18	Colca Canyon (IRE) *MrsJHarrington,Ireland* 7-10-13[147] BJGeraghty	20/1		pu
	Better Days (IRE) *MrsSJSmith* 8-10-0[134] DElsworth	25/1		pu

Mr D. A. Johnson 14ran 5m04.31

23 Jet UK Juv Nov Hdle (Gr 2) (A) (3yo) £17,400 — 2m110y (8)

	Horse	Odds	Dist	Pos
	CERIUM (FR) *PFNicholls* 3-11-2 RWalsh	10/11f		1
	PHAR BLEU (FR) *MissGBrowne* 3-10-12 BJGeraghty	20/1	3½	2
	FIRE DRAGON (IRE) *JonjoO'Neill* 3-11-2 MAFitzgerald	5/1	8	3
	Courant d'Air (IRE) *MrsLucindaFeatherstone* 3-10-12 JPMcNamara	33/1	1½	4
	Moon Catcher *DBrace* 3-10-13 (t) CLlewellyn	16/1	8	5

	Horse	SP	Dist	Pos
	Calomeria *DMcCain* 3-10-13 ADobbin	12/1	11	6
	Scarlet Mix (FR) *MCPipe* 3-10-12 TJMurphy	13/2	6	7
	Blandings Castle *NickWilliams* 3-10-12 SDurack	100/1	dist	8
	Salut Saint Cloud *GLMoore* 3-10-12 JEMoore	7/1		f
	Maguire (GER) *MFHarris* 3-10-12 RThornton	66/1		pu

B Fulton, T Hayward, S Fisher, L Brady 10ran 4m08.43

CHELTENHAM Sunday, Nov 14 GOOD to SOFT (Old Course)

24 **Independent Newspapers November Nov Chase (Gr 2) (A) (4yo+)** £30,250 — 2m (12)

	Horse	SP	Dist	Pos
	FUNDAMENTALIST (IRE) *NATwiston-Davies* 6-11-9 CLlewellyn	2/1		1
	CONTRABAND *MCPipe* 6-11-5 APMcCoy	7/2	8	2
	MY WILL (FR) *PFNicholls* 4-10-13 RWalsh	13/8f	8	3
12	Queens Harbour (IRE) *DrPPritchard* 10-11-5 DrPPritchard	100/1	dist	4
	Mambo (IRE) *NJHenderson* 6-11-9 MAFitzgerald	7/1		ref

Gripen 5ran 4m00.73

25 **Greatwood Hcap Hdle (Gr 3) (A) (169) (4yo+)** £40,600 — 2m110y (8)

	Horse	SP	Dist	Pos
8	ACCORDION ETOILE (IRE) *PaulNolan,Ireland* 5-10-6^{149} JCullen	10/3f		1
1	WESTENDER (FR) *MCPipe* 8-11-3^{160} (b) APMcCoy	9/1	3	2
	PEROUSE *PFNicholls* 6-10-6^{149} JTizzard	5/1	hd	3
	Rooster Booster *PJHobbs* 10-11-12^{169} TJMurphy	4/1	3	4
	Trouble At Bay (IRE) *AKing* 4-10-0^{143} RThornton	5/1	1¾	5
1	Copeland *MCPipe* 9-10-4^{147} (v) SDurack	20/1	nk	6
	Rigmarole *PFNicholls* 6-11-5^{162} (t) RWalsh	13/2	6	7
	Geos (FR) *NJHenderson* 9-10-10^{153} MAFitzgerald	11/1	3	8
1	Torrid Kentavr (USA) *BEllison* 7-9-7^{143} SJCraine^{7}	25/1	13	9

Banjo Syndicate 9ran 3m58.58

26 **Festival of Food Bumper (Standard Open NHF) (L) (A) (4, 5 and 6yo)** £9,526 — 2m110y

	Horse	SP	Dist	Pos
	MANNERS (IRE) *JonjoO'Neill* 6-11-4 APMcCoy	7/2		1
	BOB BOB BOBBIN *CLTizzard* 5-11-4 JTizzard	11/2	6	2
	THE MICK WESTON *RTPhillips* 5-11-4 WMarston	6/4f	5	3
	Django (IRE) *MrsJHarrington,Ireland* 5-11-4 MAFitzgerald	9/2	6	4
	Etched In Stone (IRE) *JohnJosephMurphy,Ireland* 5-11-0 RThornton	50/1	1½	5
	Ballyhale (IRE) *PDNiven* 6-11-0 RWalsh	16/1	¾	6
	Prestbury Knight *NATwiston-Davies* 4-11-0 CLlewellyn	16/1	2	7
	Royal Mount Loftus (IRE) *PHughes,Ireland* 5-10-7 TJMurphy	33/1	2½	8
	Proud To Be Irish (IRE) *SO'Farrell,Ireland* 5-10-7 MrJPO'Farrell^{7}	66/1	3	9
	Midnight Gold *LPGrassick* 4-10-7 TJMalone^{7}	66/1	13	10
	Dreams Jewel *AGNewcombe* 4-11-4 BJCrowley	50/1	dist	11

Mr M. Tabor 11ran 3m59.55

HAYDOCK Sunday, Nov 14 SOFT

27 **Edward Hanmer Memorial Chase (Ltd Hcap) (Gr 2) (A) (158) (5yo+)** £35,700 — 3m (18)

	Horse	SP	Dist	Pos
	HORUS (IRE) *MCPipe* 9-10-4^{138} JEMoore	4/1		1
	CHIVES (IRE) *MrsSJSmith* 9-10-7^{141} DElsworth	7/2	6	2
	KEEN LEADER (IRE) *JonjoO'Neill* 8-11-10^{158} CO'Dwyer	5/4f	½	3
	Simply Gifted *JonjoO'Neill* 9-10-4^{138} BHarding	16/1	11	4
	Gunner Welburn *AMBalding* 12-10-6^{140} ADobbin	10/1	dist	5
	Moss Harvey *JMJefferson* 9-10-1^{138} FKing^{3}	28/1		ur
	Be My Manager (IRE) *MTodhunter* 9-10-4^{138} (s) GLee	14/1		pu

Mr B. A. Kilpatrick 7ran 6m22.56

PUNCHESTOWN Sunday, Nov 14 GOOD to SOFT

28 **Mongey Communications Morgiana Hdle (Gr 2) (4yo+)** £21,397 — 2m (9)

	Horse	SP	Dist	Pos
8	HARCHIBALD (FR) *NMeade* 5-11-9 PCarberry	10/1		1
	BACK IN FRONT (IRE) *EJO'Grady* 7-12-0 DNRussell	11/10	1½	2
1	MACS JOY (IRE) *MrsJHarrington* 5-11-6 BJGeraghty	9/10f	hd	3
	Kald River (FR) *TJTaaffe* 5-11-3 SMMcGovern	200/1	25	4
	Emotional Moment (IRE) *TJTaaffe* 7-11-12 JRBarry	33/1	4½	5

Mr D. P. Sharkey 5ran 4m01.50

AUTEUIL Sunday, Nov 14 SOFT

29 **Prix Renaud du Vivier (Grande Course de Haies Des 4 Ans) (Gr 1) (4yo)** £78,671 — 2½m110y (12)

	Horse	SP	Dist	Pos
	MAIA ERIA (FR) *YPorzier,France* 4-10-1 CPieux	11/4		1
	CYRLIGHT (FR) *AChaille-Chaille,France* 4-10-6 PSourzac	6/10	20	2
	BABY DU RHEU (FR) *PRago,France* 4-10-6 (b) CGombeau	25/1	1	3

	River Charm (FR) *GCherel,France* 4-10-6 PMarsac	29/1	1½ 4
	Mister Gyor (FR) *BBarbier,France* 4-10-6 LMetais	42/1	10 5
	Ma Royale (FR) *MRolland,France* 4-10-1 CCheminaud	37/1	nk 6
	Psychee du Berlais (FR) *FMCottin,France* 4-10-1 TMajorcryk	38/1	4 7
	Change Partner (FR) *J-PGallorini,France* 4-10-1 SLeloup	38/1	5 8
	Kizit Lo (FR) *RCaget,France* 4-10-6 ELequesne	71/1	1½ 9
	Mesange Royale (FR) *FMCottin,France* 4-10-1 DGallagher	9/1	1 10
	Apanal (GER) *HHack,France* 4-10-6 ADuchene	42/1	11
	Centaure du Clos (FR) *J-PGallorini,France* 4-10-6 RO'Brien	100/1	12

Mr J. P. Dubois 12ran 4m54.00

EXETER Friday, Nov 19 GOOD to SOFT

30 **William Hill Chase (B) (5yo+)** £37,700 — 2m7f110y (17)

	BEST MATE (IRE) *MissHCKnight* 9-11-10 TJMurphy	4/7f	1
14	SEEBALD (GER) *MCPipe* 9-11-6 TScudamore	12/1	sh 2
	FRENCHMAN'S CREEK *HMorrison* 10-11-0 RWalsh	20/1	16 3
	Sir Rembrandt (IRE) *RHAlner* 8-11-6 AThornton	9/4	dist 4

Mr Jim Lewis 4ran 6m02.86

WINDSOR Friday, Nov 19 GOOD to SOFT

31 **Coloroll Ascot Hdle (Gr 2) (A) (4yo+)** £23,200 — 2½m (10)

	MONET'S GARDEN (IRE) *NGRichards* 6-11-0 ADobbin	11/4	1
22	MONKERHOSTIN (FR) *PJHobbs* 7-11-8 CLlewellyn	9/4f	4 2
	ILNAMAR (FR) *MCPipe* 8-11-0 JEMoore	7/2	1¼ 3
25	Trouble At Bay (IRE) *AKing* 4-11-4 RThornton	7/1	hd 4
	Nawamees (IRE) *GLMoore* 6-11-0 LAspell	12/1	12 5
	Caracciola (GER) *NJHenderson* 7-11-0 MAFitzgerald	12/1	12 6
	Keepthedreamalive *RHBuckler* 6-11-0 BHitchcott	25/1	f

Mr David Wesley Yates 7ran 5m13.95

AINTREE Saturday, Nov 20 GOOD to SOFT

32 **betfair.com Grand Sefton Hcap Chase (C) 0-130(130) (5yo+)** £30,670 — 2m5f110y (Nat.) (18)

	FOREST GUNNER *RFord* 10-11-2^{125} PBuchanan^{5}	7/1f	1
	ASPARAGUS (IRE) *MSheppard* 10-11-4^{122} (t) SStronge	11/1	8 2
	FLINDERS CHASE *CJMann* 9-11-4^{122} NFehily	14/1	¾ 3
	Spinofski *PRWebber* 9-10-7^{111} TDoyle	9/1	6 4
2	Farinel *JonjoO'Neill* 8-10-5^{114} MPWalsh^{5}	11/1	1¾ 5
	Bramblehill Duke (IRE) *MissVenetiaWilliams* 12-9-13^{106} PRobson^{3}	33/1	13 6
	Joe Deane (IRE) *TRGeorge* 8-10-5^{109} JMMaguire	15/2	¾ 7
	Tipsy Mouse (IRE) *MrsSJSmith* 8-11-3^{121} DElsworth	8/1	8 8
	Davids Lad (IRE) *AJMartin,Ireland* 10-11-12^{130} (t) BHarding	20/1	28 9
	Rheindross (IRE) *ALTMoore,Ireland* 9-10-9^{113} BMCash	8/1	14 10
	Imaginaire (USA) *MissVenetiaWilliams* 9-10-9^{113} WMarston	28/1	21 11
	Another Joker *JLNeedham* 9-11-4^{122} CLlewellyn	14/1	f
	Tregastel (FR) *RFord* 9-10-1^{105} (t) GLee	14/1	f
	Mac Hine (IRE) *JonjoO'Neill* 7-10-4^{108} TSiddall	12/1	ur
	Dark Room (IRE) *JonjoO'Neill* 7-11-1^{119} MFoley	12/1	pu

Mr John Gilsenan 15ran 5m45.25

HUNTINGDON Saturday, Nov 20 GOOD to SOFT

33 **totesport Peterborough Chase (Gr 2) (A) (5yo+)** £46,400 — 2½m110y (16)

	LE ROI MIGUEL (FR) *PFNicholls* 6-11-0 RWalsh	15/8f	1
22	FARMER JACK *PJHobbs* 8-11-6 AThornton	11/4	20 2
14	HOT SHOTS (FR) *MPitman* 9-11-6 DGallagher	12/1	4 3
	Hand Inn Hand *HDDaly* 8-11-10 MBradburne	11/4	2 4
21	Upgrade *MCPipe* 10-11-4 TScudamore	8/1	17 5
	Enzo de Baune (FR) *GAHarker* 7-11-0 BenOrde-Powlett	50/1	10 6
	Tacolino (FR) *OBrennan* 10-11-0 JAMcCarthy	40/1	3½ 7
	Red Striker *RCGuest* 10-11-0 LMcGrath	66/1	20 8

Mrs J. Stewart 8ran 5m03.75

AINTREE Sunday, Nov 21 SOFT

34 **totesport Becher Hcap Chase (B) (146) (5yo+)** £43,500 — 3m3f (Nat.) (22)

	SILVER BIRCH (IRE) *PFNicholls* 7-10-1^{123} RWalsh	4/1f	1
	JUST IN DEBT (IRE) *MTodhunter* 8-10-6^{128} ADobbin	33/1	1 2
	SMARTY (IRE) *MPitman* 11-10-0^{122} TJMurphy	12/1	13 3
17	Double Honour (FR) *PJHobbs* 6-11-4^{140} PFlynn	14/1	1¼ 4
	Amberleigh House (IRE) *DMcCain* 12-11-10^{146} GLee	12/1	sh 5
	Royal Atalza (FR) *GAHuffer* 7-10-9^{131} (s) CLlewellyn	16/1	10 6

Cassia Heights *SABrookshaw* 9-10-0[122] (t) MFoley ... 20/1 3½ 7
Fasgo (IRE) *PFNicholls* 9-10-3[125] RThornton ... 12/1 9 8
Artic Jack (FR) *MrsSJSmith* 8-11-7[143] DElsworth ... 14/1 dist 9
Native Emperor *JonjoO'Neill* 8-11-4[140] MAFitzgerald ... 7/1 sh 10
Jungle Jinks (IRE) *GMMoore* 9-10-1[123] FKeniry ... 8/1 f
Ardent Scout *MrsSJSmith* 12-9-11[122] LMcGrath[3] ... 5/1 ur
20 The Quads *FerdyMurphy* 12-9-9[122] (s+t) KMercer[5] ... 100/1 ur
Takagi (IRE) *EJO'Grady,Ireland* 9-11-8[144] DNRussell ... 10/1 ur

Mr D. J. Nichols 14ran 7m35.72

NEWBURY Saturday, Nov 27 GOOD

35 Stan James Fulke Walwyn Nov Chase (Gr 2) (A) (5yo+) £20,300 2½m (16)

11 VODKA BLEU (FR) *MCPipe* 5-11-7 TJMurphy ... 7/2 1
24 FUNDAMENTALIST (IRE) *NATwiston-Davies* 6-11-7 CLlewellyn ... 1/3f ½ 2
SEE YOU SOMETIME *JWMullins* 9-11-0 RYoung ... 11/1 1½ 3

Mr D. A. Johnson 3ran 5m06.30

36 Ballymore Properties Long Distance Hdle (Gr 2) (A) (4yo+) £23,200 3m110y (13)

BARACOUDA (FR) *FDoumen,France* 9-11-8 APMcCoy ... 4/9f 1
CRYSTAL D'AINAY (FR) *AKing* 5-11-8 RThornton ... 5/1 ¾ 2
KADARA (IRE) *RHAlner* 5-10-7 AThornton ... 66/1 3 3
Telemoss (IRE) *NGRichards* 10-11-8 ADobbin ... 12/1 7 4
22 It Takes Time (IRE) *MCPipe* 10-11-0 TJMurphy ... 9/1 sh 5
It's Wallace *MissSWest* 11-11-0 JGoldstein ... 66/1 dist 6

Mr John P. McManus 6ran 5m54.19

37 Hennessy Cognac Gold Cup Chase (Hcap) (Gr 3) (A) (163) (5yo+) 3¼m110y (21)
£69,600

22 CELESTIAL GOLD (IRE) *MCPipe* 6-10-5[142] TJMurphy ... 9/4f 1
22 OLLIE MAGERN *NATwiston-Davies* 6-10-9[146] CLlewellyn ... 13/2 1½ 2
17 ROYAL AUCLAIR (FR) *PFNicholls* 7-10-13[150] (t) RWalsh ... 11/2 1¼ 3
Lord Transcend (IRE) *JHowardJohnson* 7-10-0[137] ADobbin ... 6/1 7 4
17 Gunther McBride (IRE) *PJHobbs* 9-10-0[137] RJohnson ... 20/1 17 5
Puntal (FR) *MCPipe* 8-10-12[149] (t) JEMoore ... 14/1 4 6
Lord of The River (IRE) *NJHenderson* 12-10-0[137] MFoley ... 66/1 hd 7
17 Swansea Bay *PBowen* 8-10-3[140] AThornton ... 33/1 20 8
First Gold (FR) *FDoumen,France* 11-11-12[163] APMcCoy ... 16/1 9 9
34 Artic Jack (FR) *MrsSJSmith* 8-10-6[143] DElsworth ... 50/1 ½ 10
Midland Flame (IRE) *MissHCKnight* 9-10-0[137] PFlynn ... 50/1 2½ 11
Supreme Glory (IRE) *PGMurphy* 11-10-2[139] LAspell ... 100/1 7 12
Nil Desperandum (IRE) *MsFMCrowley,Ireland* 7-10-8[145] MAFitzgerald ... 9/1 pu
30 Frenchman's Creek *HMorrison* 10-10-3[140] RThornton ... 11/1 pu

Mr D. A. Johnson 14ran 6m30.51

NEWCASTLE Saturday, Nov 27 GOOD to SOFT

38 Pertemps 'Fighting Fifth' Hdle (Gr 1) (A) (4yo+) £43,500 2m (9)

28 HARCHIBALD (FR) *NMeade,Ireland* 5-11-7 PCarberry ... 9/4jf 1
INGLIS DREVER *JHowardJohnson* 5-11-7 GLee ... 9/4jf 2 2
ROYAL SHAKESPEARE (FR) *SGollings* 5-11-7 TDoyle ... 12/1 2 3
Intersky Falcon *JonjoO'Neill* 7-11-7 (b) RMcGrath ... 3/1 4 4
1 The French Furze (IRE) *NGRichards* 10-11-7 BHarding ... 22/1 8 5
25 Perouse *PFNicholls* 6-11-7 JTizzard ... 11/1 ½ 6
25 Rigmarole *PFNicholls* 6-11-7 (b+t) PJBrennan ... 11/1 11 7
Teme Valley *JHowardJohnson* 10-11-7 ADempsey ... 200/1 dist 8

Mr D. P. Sharkey 8ran 3m50.61

NEWBURY Sunday, Nov 28 GOOD

39 cantorsport.co.uk Worcester Nov Chase (Gr 2) (A) (5yo+) £21,175 3m (18)

CORNISH REBEL (IRE) *PFNicholls* 7-11-2 APMcCoy ... 5/1 1
16 DISTANT THUNDER (IRE) *RHAlner* 6-11-2 AThornton ... 3/1 4 2
ST MATTHEW (USA) *MrsSJSmith* 6-11-2 DElsworth ... 10/1 dist 3
Daniels Hymn *MsFMCrowley,Ireland* 9-11-2 (b) MFoley ... 100/1 12 4
16 Comply Or Die (IRE) *MCPipe* 5-11-8 TJMurphy ... 8/11f f

Mr C. G. Roach 5ran 6m04.50

FAIRYHOUSE Sunday, Nov 28 GOOD to SOFT

40 Sharp Minds Betfair Royal Bond Nov Hdle (Gr 1) (4yo+) £34,331 2m (10)

WILD PASSION (GER) *NMeade* 4-11-7 PCarberry ... 6/1 1
ROCKET SHIP (IRE) *NMeade* 4-11-7 MrNPMadden ... 16/1 3 2
ROYAL PARADISE (FR) *ThomasFoley* 4-11-7 CO'Dwyer ... 6/1 ¾ 3
Justified (IRE) *ESheehy* 5-11-12 JRBarry ... 8/1 2 4

	Major Vernon (IRE) *WPMullins* 5-11-12 RWalsh	7/1	nk 5
	Total Enjoyment (IRE) *TCooper* 5-11-7 BJGeraghty	5/4f	3 6
	Tacitus (IRE) *DTHughes* 4-11-7 PWFlood	33/1	20 7
	Master Albert (IRE) *DWachman* 6-11-12 MrJPMagnier	8/1	10 8
	Mr Babbage (IRE) *WPMullins* 6-11-12 DJCondon	33/1	12 9

Mr D. P. Sharkey 9ran 4m02.40

41 Pierse Group Drinmore Nov Chase (Gr 1) (5yo+) £41,197 — 2½m (16)

	WATSON LAKE (IRE) *NMeade* 6-11-12 PCarberry	4/5f	1
	FORGET THE PAST *MJPO'Brien* 6-11-12 RWalsh	11/4	3 2
	MUTINEER (IRE) *DTHughes* 5-11-9 (b+t) PWFlood	14/1	25 3
	Tiger Cry (IRE) *ALTMoore* 6-11-12 CO'Dwyer	11/2	25 4
	Gayle Abated (IRE) *WPMullins* 5-11-9 BJGeraghty	20/1	pu

Mr John Corr 5ran 5m24.02

42 Ballymore Properties Hatton's Grace Hdle (Gr 1) (4yo+) £41,197 — 2½m (12)

8	SOLERINA (IRE) *JamesBowe* 7-11-7 GTHutchinson	4/5f	1
	BRAVE INCA (IRE) *CAMurphy* 6-11-12 BMCash	7/4	6 2
	RULE SUPREME (IRE) *WPMullins* 8-11-12 RWalsh	8/1	8 3
	Sacundai (IRE) *EJO'Grady* 7-11-12 DNRussell	16/1	25 4
	Florida Coast (IRE) *JamesBowe* 9-11-12 PCarberry	33/1	25 5

Mr John P. Bowe 5ran 5m03.27

WINCANTON Thursday, Dec 2 GOOD to SOFT

43 Guinness Beginners' Chase (D) (5yo+) £5,571 — 2m5f (17)

	PATCHES (IRE) *PFNicholls* 5-11-0 RWalsh	2/1jf	1
	LACDOUDAL (FR) *PJHobbs* 5-11-0 RJohnson	3/1	3 2
	KADOUNT (FR) *AKing* 6-11-0 RThornton	2/1jf	3½ 3
	Duncliffe *RHAlner* 7-11-0 WMarston	50/1	dist 4
	Itsallupintheair *MrsAMThorpe* 8-11-0 ChristianWilliams	200/1	f
	No Collusion (IRE) *MissHCKnight* 8-11-0 SDurack	16/1	f
	Dempsey (IRE) *MPitman* 6-11-0 TJMurphy	7/1	pu
	Knight of The Road (IRE) *PGMurphy* 5-11-0 NFehily	250/1	pu
	Cillamon *KBishop* 7-10-7 PJBrennan	66/1	pu

Mrs Marianne G. Barber 9ran 5m25.05

SANDOWN Friday, Dec 3 GOOD to SOFT

44 William Hill Winter Nov Hdle (Gr 2) (A) (4yo+) £17,400 — 2½m110y (9)

13	LADALKO (FR) *PFNicholls* 5-11-0 RWalsh	5/4f	1
	NO REFUGE (IRE) *JHowardJohnson* 4-11-7 ADobbin	5/2	1½ 2
	LADY ZEPHYR (IRE) *NATwiston-Davies* 6-10-7 CLlewellyn	9/1	½ 3
19	Shuhood (USA) *PRWebber* 4-11-4 TDoyle	5/1	1½ 4
	Gallery God (FR) *SDow* 8-11-0 MAFitzgerald	16/1	10 5
	Give Me Love (FR) *YPorzier,France* 4-11-7 (s+t) DGallagher	33/1	1½ 6
	Loup Charter (FR) *MissHCKnight* 5-11-4 TJMurphy	33/1	10 7

Mr Paul K Barber & Mrs M Findlay 7ran 5m03.91

CHEPSTOW Saturday, Dec 4 SOFT

45 John Hughes Rehearsal Chase (Hcap) (L) (A) (149) (5yo+) £26,100 — 3¼m110y (22)

	ONE KNIGHT (IRE) *PJHobbs* 8-11-9^{146} PFlynn	9/4f	1
	L'AVENTURE (FR) *PFNicholls* 5-10-8^{131} (b+t) PJBrennan	9/1	1¼ 2
27	GUNNER WELBURN *AMBalding* 12-10-13^{136} MBradburne	20/1	22 3
	Stormez (FR) *MCPipe* 7-11-12^{149} (t) TDoyle	14/1	4 4
34	Native Emperor *JonjoO'Neill* 8-10-13^{136} APMcCoy	9/2	½ 5
	Colourful Life (IRE) *PFNicholls* 8-10-9^{132} JTizzard	6/1	4 6
	Jimmy Tennis (FR) *MissVenetiaWilliams* 7-10-6^{132} SThomas^{3}	12/1	½ 7
	Historg (FR) *FerdyMurphy* 9-9-9^{123} KMercer^{5}	10/1	23 8
	Ballybrophy (IRE) *GBrown* 9-10-0^{123} JMogford	25/1	dist 9
34	Royal Atalza (FR) *GAHuffer* 7-10-7^{130} (b) CLlewellyn	20/1	pu

Mr R. Gibbs 10ran 7m13.28

SANDOWN Saturday, Dec 4 GOOD to SOFT

46 Sodexho Prestige Henry VIII Nov Chase (Gr 2) (A) (4yo+) £24,200 — 2m (13)

24	CONTRABAND *MCPipe* 6-11-4 TJMurphy	10/3	1
	THE LAST CAST *HMorrison* 5-11-4 TScudamore	9/2	5 2
	MADE IN JAPAN (JPN) *PJHobbs* 4-10-13 RJohnson	11/10f	5 3
15	Goldbrook *RJHodges* 6-11-4 JamesDavies	66/1	13 4
	Le Seychellois (FR) *PFNicholls* 4-10-13 RWalsh	5/1	f

Mr D. A. Johnson 5ran 3m56.49

47 William Hill - Tingle Creek Trophy Chase (Gr 1) (A) (5yo+) £72,500 — 2m (13)

	MOSCOW FLYER (IRE) *MrsJHarrington,Ireland* 10-11-7 BJGeraghty	2/1	1

14	AZERTYUIOP (FR) *PFNicholls* 7-11-7 RWalsh	5/6f	1½	2
21	WELL CHIEF (GER) *MCPipe* 5-11-7 TJMurphy	6/1	sh	3
21	Cenkos (FR) *PFNicholls* 10-11-7 RJohnson	25/1	25	4
33	Upgrade *MCPipe* 10-11-7 TScudamore	80/1	11	5
20	Blazing Batman *DrPPritchard* 11-11-7 DrPPritchard	300/1	dist	6
	Blackchurch Mist (IRE) *BWDuke* 7-11-0 (t) CStudd	300/1	sh	7

Mr Brian Kearney 7ran 3m52.24

PUNCHESTOWN Sunday, Dec 5 SOFT

48 John Durkan Memorial Punchestown Chase (Gr 1) (5yo+) £40,909 — 2½m (14)

18	KICKING KING (IRE) *TJTaaffe* 6-11-12 BJGeraghty	2/1		1
9	RATHGAR BEAU (IRE) *ESheehy* 8-11-12 JRBarry	8/1	11	2
18	BEEF OR SALMON (IRE) *MHourigan* 8-11-12 TJMurphy	4/5f	6	3
	Native Upmanship (IRE) *ALTMoore* 11-11-12 CO'Dwyer	20/1	sh	4
	John James (IRE) *JHScott* 8-11-12 KWhelan	66/1	dist	5
18	Harbour Pilot (IRE) *NMeade* 9-11-12 (b) PCarberry	9/1		pu

Mr Conor Clarkson 6ran 5m16.12

CHELTENHAM Friday, Dec 10 GOOD to SOFT (New Course)

49 Mears Group Chase (Hcap) (B) (153) (5yo+) £29,000 — 3m1f110y (21)

	THEREALBANDIT (IRE) *MCPipe* 7-11-9^{150} TJMurphy	13/2		1
37	ROYAL AUCLAIR (FR) *PFNicholls* 7-11-12^{153} (t) RWalsh	10/3f	3	2
37	FRENCHMAN'S CREEK *HMorrison* 10-10-11^{138} BJGeraghty	14/1	1½	3
34	Double Honour (FR) *PJHobbs* 6-10-11^{138} RJohnson	12/1	1¼	4
	Joly Bey (FR) *NJGifford* 7-10-10^{140} MrDHDunsdon^{3}	7/1	sh	5
	Baron Windrush *NATwiston-Davies* 6-10-4^{131} CLlewellyn	5/1	18	6
37	Swansea Bay *PBowen* 8-10-8^{135} (v) AThornton	25/1	5	7
37	Puntal (FR) *MCPipe* 8-11-7^{148} (t) JEMoore	16/1	28	8
	Happy Hussar (IRE) *DrPPritchard* 11-9-10^{128} DrPPritchard^{5}	300/1	1¼	9
	Kelami (FR) *FDoumen,France* 6-10-4^{131} DGallagher	8/1		f
	Ballybough Rasher (IRE) *JHowardJohnson* 9-11-6^{147} ADobbin	33/1		ur
	Lord Noelie (IRE) *MsBridgetNicholls* 11-11-1^{142} APMcCoy	9/1		pu

Mr D. A. Johnson 12ran 6m36.69

CHELTENHAM Saturday, Dec 11 GOOD to SOFT (New Course)

50 bonusprint.com Gold Cup (Hcap Chase) (Gr 3) (A) (158) (5yo+) £63,800 — 2m5f (17)

31	MONKERHOSTIN (FR) *PJHobbs* 7-10-2^{134} RJohnson	4/1		1
22	THISTHATANDTOTHER (IRE) *PFNicholls* 8-11-5^{151} RWalsh	7/2	7	2
11	EUROPA *FerdyMurphy* 8-10-3^{135} JMMaguire	25/1	nk	3
21	Armaturk (FR) *PFNicholls* 7-11-12^{158} ChristianWilliams	20/1	4	4
22	Tikram *GLMoore* 7-10-11^{143} JEMoore	20/1	sh	5
	Impek (FR) *MissHCKnight* 8-11-7^{153} ADobbin	33/1	8	6
22	Fondmort (FR) *NJHenderson* 8-11-11^{157} MAFitzgerald	33/1	2	7
33	Farmer Jack *PJHobbs* 8-11-9^{155} PFlynn	28/1		f
	Our Vic (IRE) *MCPipe* 6-11-3^{149} TJMurphy	11/4f		f
	Massac (FR) *AKing* 5-10-12^{144} RThornton	16/1		f
	Redemption *MCPipe* 9-10-10^{142} CLlewellyn	14/1		ur
	Scots Grey *NJHenderson* 9-10-6^{141} ATinkler^{3}	16/1		ur
	Mossy Green (IRE) *WPMullins,Ireland* 10-10-8^{140} BJGeraghty	16/1		pu

Mr M. G. St Quinton 13ran 5m17.45

51 totesport Bula Hdle (Gr 2) (A) (4yo+) £43,500 — 2m1f (8)

28	BACK IN FRONT (IRE) *EJO'Grady,Ireland* 7-11-8 DNRussell	5/2f		1
38	INGLIS DREVER *JHowardJohnson* 5-11-4 ADobbin	7/2	4	2
25	WESTENDER (FR) *MCPipe* 8-11-0 (b) TJMurphy	5/1	¾	3
25	Rooster Booster *PJHobbs* 10-11-8 RJohnson	3/1	½	4
38	The French Furze (IRE) *NGRichards* 10-11-8 BHarding	66/1	16	5
	Knockrigg (IRE) *DrPPritchard* 10-11-0 DrPPritchard	200/1	dist	6
	Flame Creek (IRE) *NoelTChance* 8-11-0 BJGeraghty	13/2		f

NELIUS HAYES 7ran 4m02.34

52 Brit Insurance Bristol Nov Hdle (Gr 2) (A) (4yo+) £20,300 — 3m (12)

13	BREWSTER (IRE) *IanWilliams* 7-11-7 DRDennis	2/1f		1
	JACKSON (FR) *AKing* 7-11-0 RThornton	12/1	12	2
13	FOOTBALL CRAZY (IRE) *PBowen* 5-11-7 WMarston	4/1	sh	3
	Idle Talk (IRE) *TRGeorge* 5-11-0 JMMaguire	7/2	½	4
	Senor Sedona *NJGifford* 5-11-0 JamesDavies	33/1	12	5
	Woodlands Genpower (IRE) *PAPritchard* 6-11-0 MBradburne	7/1	5	6
	Jiver (IRE) *MScudamore* 5-11-4 TScudamore	12/1	4	7
	Icy Prospect (IRE) *NATwiston-Davies* 6-11-4 CLlewellyn	16/1	dist	8

	Alexander Musical (IRE) *STLewis* 6-11-0 PCO'Neill	100/1	28 9
	Donald (POL) *MPitman* 4-11-4 TJMurphy	33/1	pu

Mr & Mrs John Poynton 10ran 6m02.48

LINGFIELD Saturday, Dec 11 GOOD to SOFT

53 **December Nov Chase (Gr 2) (A) (5yo+)** £23,200 3m (18)

	L'AMI (FR) *FDoumen,France* 5-11-7 DGallagher	14/1	1
39	DISTANT THUNDER (IRE) *RHAlner* 6-11-0 AThornton	13/8f	1¾ 2
	TRIBAL VENTURE (FR) *FerdyMurphy* 6-11-4 KMercer	6/1	1¼ 3
	A Glass In Thyne (IRE) *BNPollock* 6-11-4 JPMcNamara	6/1	8 4
	Glen Warrior *JSSmith* 8-11-0 LAspell	25/1	1¾ 5
	What A Man (IRE) *GLMoore* 7-11-0 JTizzard	33/1	dist 6
	Alexanderthegreat (IRE) *PFNicholls* 6-11-7 APMcCoy	9/4	f

Mr Jim McCarthy 7ran 6m15.54

CORK Sunday, Dec 12 SOFT

54 **O'Connell Warehousing Hilly Way Chase (Gr 2) (5yo+)** £26,938 2m (11)

48	RATHGAR BEAU (IRE) *ESheehy* 8-11-10 JRBarry	7/4f	1
	CENTRAL HOUSE *DTHughes* 7-11-12 (t) TJMurphy	6/1	7 2
	MISTLETOEANDWINE (IRE) *SJTreacy* 6-10-13 JLCullen	16/1	4 3
	Native Scout (IRE) *DHassett* 8-11-7 (t) DNRussell	11/2	2 4
14	Flagship Uberalles (IRE) *PJHobbs,GB* 10-11-12 RJohnson	11/4	9 5
5	Mutakarrim *DKWeld* 7-11-4 DTEvans	20/1	5 6
20	Go Roger Go (IRE) *EJO'Grady* 12-11-10 APMcCoy	12/1	2½ 7
9	Alcapone (IRE) *MFMorris* 10-11-12 MDarcy	14/1	3 8
9	Arctic Copper (IRE) *NMeade* 10-11-10 (b) MAFitzgerald	16/1	25 9
	Macs Gildoran *WPMullins* 10-11-4 DCrosse	20/1	20 10

One-O-Eight Racing Club 10ran 4m11.74

NAVAN Sunday, Dec 12 SOFT

55 **Giltspur Scientific Tara Hdle (Gr 2) (4yo+)** £22,448 2½m (11)

42	SOLERINA (IRE) *JamesBowe* 7-11-7 GTHutchinson	4/11f	1
	HARDY EUSTACE (IRE) *DTHughes* 7-11-12 CO'Dwyer	3/1	2½ 2
	ROSAKER (USA) *NMeade* 7-11-10 PCarberry	10/1	20 3
	Yogi (IRE) *ThomasFoley* 8-11-8 RWalsh	33/1	3½ 4
	Glentorpe (IRE) *JJLennon* 5-11-5 BMCash	150/1	dist 5

Mr John P. Bowe 5ran 5m01.31

56 **Barry & Sandra Kelly Memorial Nov Hdle (Gr 2) (4yo+)** £31,428 2½m (11)

	PETERTHEKNOT (IRE) *PatrickSinnott* 6-11-5 CO'Dwyer	7/1	1
	SWEET KILN (IRE) *JamesBowe* 5-11-3 GTHutchinson	5/2	¾ 2
	OUR BEN *WPMullins* 5-11-5 APCrowe	11/1	6 3
	Tigerlion (IRE) *JBleahen* 6-11-5 BJGeraghty	8/1	1 4
40	Major Vernon (IRE) *WPMullins* 5-11-5 RWalsh	7/4f	¾ 5
	Anyportinastorm (IRE) *ThomasMullins* 6-11-5 BMCash	11/1	½ 6
	Jakers (IRE) *PAFahy* 7-11-5 SGMcDermott	16/1	20 7
	Augherskea (IRE) *NMeade* 5-11-5 (t) PCarberry	5/1	3 8
	Prince Roscoe *DEFitzgerald* 8-11-5 MrMJO'Connor	14/1	nk 9

Mr John J. Brennan 9ran 5m15.70

57 **Brian M. Durkan & Co Ltd (Pro-Am) INH Flat (Gr 2) (4yo+)** £15,714 2m

	PUBLICAN (IRE) *PAFahy* 4-11-9 MrPFahey	7/1	1
	DAWADARI (IRE) *SJMahon* 4-11-2 MrKBBowens[7]	7/4f	3½ 2
	RAY BOY (IRE) *PCO'Connor* 5-11-9 MrPTobin[5]	8/1	¾ 3
	L'Antartique (FR) *AnthonyMullins* 4-11-9 MrNPMadden	15/8	¾ 4
	Lovely Present (IRE) *TKGeraghty* 5-11-2 MrSMcGonagle[7]	6/1	3½ 5
	Miss Toulon (IRE) *PatrickMullins* 6-11-2 MrJJFeane[7]	12/1	8 6
	Mags Benefit (IRE) *THogan* 4-10-11 (t) MrEFPower[7]	14/1	10 7
	Executive Paddy (IRE) *JPDempsey* 5-12-0 MrJPDempsey	25/1	dist 8

Outback Syndicate 8ran 4m12.42

EXETER Thursday, Dec 16 GOOD to SOFT

58 **Toby Balding Nov Hdle (D) (4yo+)** £5,753 2m3f (10)

	GOLD MEDALLIST *PJHobbs* 4-10-12 RJohnson	7/4f	1
	SECRET PLOY *HMorrison* 4-10-12 TScudamore	11/4	1¼ 2
	KELTIC ROCK *JAGeake* 5-10-12 MBradburne	16/1	23 3
	King Killone (IRE) *MissHCKnight* 4-10-12 JCulloty	10/1	hd 4
	Manorson (IRE) *OSherwood* 5-10-12 JAMcCarthy	16/1	13 5
	Morson Boy (USA) *PFNicholls* 4-10-12 JTizzard	33/1	½ 6
	Lin d'Estruval (FR) *CPMorlock* 5-10-12 TDoyle	50/1	7 7

	Murphy's Quest *LadyHerries* 8-11-4 LAspell	5/1	19 8
	Yes My Lord (IRE) *MCPipe* 5-10-12 TJMurphy	40/1	dist 9
	Beehawk *PFNicholls* 5-10-12 ChristianWilliams	100/1	¾ 10
	Longstone Lady (IRE) *JDFrost* 7-10-4 TO'Connor[7]	250/1	2½ 11
	Trefoilalight *JDFrost* 5-10-1 CHonour[5]	250/1	1¾ 12
	Debatable *NJHawke* 5-10-9 AHoneyball[3]	33/1	pu
	Gaelic Music (IRE) *MBradstock* 5-10-12 MBatchelor	20/1	pu
	Glacial Delight (IRE) *MissECLavelle* 5-10-12 BFenton	100/1	pu
	Herodotus *KOCunningham-Brown* 6-10-12 BHitchcott	200/1	pu
	Jasper Rooney *CWMitchell* 5-10-12 SDurack	150/1	pu
	Crusty Miss *MSheppard* 5-10-5 JMMaguire	200/1	pu

Mrs D. L. Whateley 18ran 4m39.99

WINDSOR Saturday, Dec 18 SOFT

59 Telectronics Systems Long Walk Hdle (Gr 1) (A) (4yo+) £43,500 3m1f110y (12)

36	BARACOUDA (FR) *FDoumen,France* 9-11-7 APMcCoy	8/13f	1
36	CRYSTAL D'AINAY (FR) *AKing* 5-11-7 RThornton	11/2	¾ 2
42	RULE SUPREME (IRE) *WPMullins,Ireland* 8-11-7 RWalsh	11/2	sh 3
36	It Takes Time (IRE) *MCPipe* 10-11-7 TJMurphy	33/1	1 4
	Sh Boom *JonjoO'Neill* 6-11-7 BJGeraghty	12/1	14 5
36	Kadara (IRE) *RHAlner* 5-11-0 AThornton	50/1	10 6
31	Ilnamar (FR) *MCPipe* 8-11-7 JEMoore	16/1	28 7
25	Geos (FR) *NJHenderson* 9-11-7 MAFitzgerald	33/1	18 8

Mr John P. McManus 8ran 6m51.81

KEMPTON Sunday, Dec 26 GOOD

60 Stan James Feltham Nov Chase (Gr 1) (A) (4yo+) £41,650 3m (19)

37	OLLIE MAGERN *NATwiston-Davies* 6-11-7 CLlewellyn	13/8f	1
	TRABOLGAN (IRE) *NJHenderson* 6-11-7 MAFitzgerald	8/1	sh 2
	QUAZAR (IRE) *JonjoO'Neill* 6-11-7 (t) APMcCoy	20/1	14 3
53	Distant Thunder (IRE) *RHAlner* 6-11-7 AThornton	14/1	1¾ 4
43	Patches (IRE) *PFNicholls* 5-11-7 RWalsh	14/1	1¼ 5
15	Backbeat (IRE) *DRCElsworth* 7-11-7 RYoung	14/1	f
53	L'Ami (FR) *FDoumen,France* 5-11-7 BJGeraghty	15/2	f
	Your A Gassman (IRE) *FerdyMurphy* 6-11-7 BHarding	8/1	bd
	Control Man (IRE) *MCPipe* 6-11-7 (v) TJMurphy	5/1	ur

Mr Roger Nicholls 9ran 6m00.14

61 Stan James Christmas Hdle (Gr 1) (A) (4yo+) £58,000 2m (8)

38	HARCHIBALD (FR) *NMeade,Ireland* 5-11-7 PCarberry	8/11f	1
51	ROOSTER BOOSTER *PJHobbs* 10-11-7 RJohnson	3/1	1½ 2
38	PEROUSE *PFNicholls* 6-11-7 (t) RWalsh	14/1	20 3
	Arcalis *JHowardJohnson* 4-11-7 BJGeraghty	15/2	½ 4
50	Impek (FR) *MissHCKnight* 8-11-7 JCulloty	33/1	dh 4
1	Castleshane (IRE) *SGollings* 7-11-7 TScudamore	66/1	7 6
	Blue Canyon (FR) *FDoumen,France* 6-11-7 APMcCoy	16/1	2 7

Mr D. P. Sharkey 7ran 3m47.32

62 Stan James King George VI Chase (Gr 1) (A) (4yo+) £116,000 3m (19)

48	KICKING KING (IRE) *TJTaaffe,Ireland* 6-11-10 BJGeraghty	3/1f	1
	KINGSCLIFF (IRE) *RHAlner* 7-11-10 AThornton	15/2	2½ 2
47	AZERTYUIOP (FR) *PFNicholls* 7-11-10 RWalsh	4/1	1¼ 3
33	Le Roi Miguel (FR) *PFNicholls* 6-11-10 PCarberry	12/1	24 4
37	First Gold (FR) *FDoumen,France* 11-11-10 (b) APMcCoy	20/1	3½ 5
30	Seebald (GER) *MCPipe* 9-11-10 TScudamore	20/1	1¼ 6
49	Therealbandit (IRE) *MCPipe* 7-11-10 TJMurphy	6/1	1¾ 7
50	Fondmort (FR) *NJHenderson* 8-11-10 MFoley	66/1	7 8
33	Hot Shots (FR) *MPitman* 9-11-10 DGallagher	100/1	24 9
14	Edredon Bleu (FR) *MissHCKnight* 12-11-10 (t) JCulloty	25/1	26 10
	Calling Brave (IRE) *NJHenderson* 8-11-10 MAFitzgerald	10/1	pu
	Lord Sam (IRE) *VRADartnall* 8-11-10 SDurack	12/1	pu
	Tiutchev *MCPipe* 11-11-10 RJohnson	12/1	pu

Mr Conor Clarkson 13ran 5m54.20

LEOPARDSTOWN Sunday, Dec 26 HEAVY

63 Durkan New Homes Nov Chase (Gr 1) (4yo+) £44,521 2m1f (11)

	MARIAH ROLLINS (IRE) *PAFahy* 6-11-7 JLCullen	4/1	1
	STEEL BAND *PaulARoche* 6-11-12 GTHutchinson	40/1	4 2
	NED KELLY (IRE) *EJO'Grady* 8-11-12 DNRussell	8/1	10 3
	Healy's Pub (IRE) *OliverMcKiernan* 8-11-12 PACarberry	33/1	7 4
	Newmill (IRE) *TGO'Leary* 6-11-12 GCotter	9/2	14 5

41	Tiger Cry (IRE) *ALTMoore* 6-11-12 BMCash	20/1	8 6
	Guilt *DTHughes* 4-11-1 (t) PWFlood	16/1	25 7
	Aye Aye Popeye (IRE) *MrsJHarrington* 6-11-12 TPTreacy	20/1	f
	Sir Oj (IRE) *NMeade* 7-11-12 (b) MrNPMadden	9/1	ur
	Like-A-Butterfly (IRE) *CRoche* 10-11-7 CO'Dwyer	11/10f	pu

Gone West Racing Syndicate 10ran 4m28.40

LEOPARDSTOWN Monday, Dec 27 HEAVY

64 Paddy Power Dial-A-Bet Chase (Gr 1) (5yo+) £32,042 — 2m1f (11)

54	CENTRAL HOUSE *DTHughes* 7-11-12 (b) PCarberry	9/2	1
54	NATIVE SCOUT (IRE) *DHassett* 8-11-12 (s+t) DNRussell	6/1	2 2
48	NATIVE UPMANSHIP (IRE) *ALTMoore* 11-11-12 CO'Dwyer	9/2	2 3
54	Rathgar Beau (IRE) *ESheehy* 8-11-12 APMcCoy	8/11f	½ 4

Mr John F. Kenny 4ran 4m33.17

65 Paddy Power Chase (Extended Hcap) 0-145(135) (5yo+) £68,451 — 3m (17)

	KEEPATEM (IRE) *MFMorris* 8-10-8^{115} CO'Dwyer	7/2f	1
	JAQUOUILLE (FR) *ALTMoore* 7-10-12^{119} BMCash	9/1	4 2
	KYMANDJEN (IRE) *PaulNolan* 7-11-3^{124} APCrowe	25/1	10 3
	JACK HIGH (IRE) *TMWalsh* 9-11-4^{125} GCotter	8/1	4 4
	Livingstonebramble (IRE) *WPMullins* 8-10-8^{115} TPTreacy	25/1	nk 5
	The Galway Man (IRE) *AnthonyMullins* 7-11-9^{130} RGeraghty	25/1	hd 6
7	Golden Storm (IRE) *JosephCrowley* 7-11-0^{126} (b) JMAllen^{5}	33/1	½ 7
	Lanmire Glen (IRE) *FFlood* 7-10-2^{116} KTColeman^{7}	40/1	sh 8
	Bennie's Pride (IRE) *MJPO'Brien* 8-10-10^{122} TGMRyan^{5}	14/1	sh 9
	Hersov (IRE) *PaulARoche* 8-10-11^{118} KHadnett	25/1	3 10
7	Garvivonnian (IRE) *EdwardPMitchell* 9-11-7^{135} MJFerris^{7}	33/1	¾ 11
7	Fatherofthebride (IRE) *JosephCrowley* 8-10-9^{116} (b) DJCondon	33/1	hd 12
	Rockspring Hero *JohnJWalsh* 8-10-5^{115} JPElliott^{3}	33/1	1¼ 13
	The Bunny Boiler (IRE) *NMeade* 10-11-3^{129} DFO'Regan^{5}	50/1	15 14
	Boneyarrow (IRE) *WPMullins* 8-11-11^{135} MrJJCodd^{3}	40/1	10 15
	Native Sessions (IRE) *NMeade* 9-11-8^{129} (b) MrNPMadden	33/1	9 16
	Hume Castle (IRE) *MrsJHarrington* 8-11-4^{128} (t) MrDWCullen^{3}	33/1	3 17
	Ride The Storm (IRE) *EJO'Grady* 7-11-3^{124} DNRussell	12/1	¾ 18
	Oh Be The Hokey (IRE) *CFSwan* 6-11-1^{122} APMcCoy	20/1	f
	Carneys Cross (IRE) *SJTreacy* 6-10-1^{115} MrROHarding^{7}	25/1	f
	Sraid Na Cathrach (IRE) *CByrnes* 8-10-12^{119} MDGrant	12/1	ur
	Solar System (IRE) *TJTaaffe* 7-10-7^{117} SMMcGovern^{3}	25/1	ur
	Colnel Rayburn (IRE) *PaulNolan* 8-12-0^{135} JLCullen	10/1	pu
54	Mutakarrim *DKWeld* 7-11-11^{132} (b) DTEvans	25/1	pu
	Joueur d'Estruval (FR) *WPMullins* 7-10-13^{125} MrPCashman^{5}	25/1	pu
	Heads Onthe Ground (IRE) *DTHughes* 7-10-10^{120} PWFlood^{3}	14/1	pu
	Mullacash (IRE) *NMeade* 6-10-12^{119} (b) PCarberry	12/1	pu
4	Wests Awake (IRE) *IMadden* 8-10-8^{118} APLane^{3}	20/1	pu
	Aimees Mark (IRE) *FFlood* 8-10-9^{116} BJGeraghty	12/1	pu
	Doesheknow (IRE) *PAFahy* 9-10-2^{114} (b) AJDonoghue^{5}	50/1	pu

Mr John P. McManus 30ran 6m38.06

66 Paddy Power Christmas Bumper INH Flat (4yo+) £6,813 — 2½m

	TRAVINO (IRE) *MsMargaretMullins* 5-11-9 MrPCashman^{5}	11/10f	1
	MANDM (IRE) *PCO'Connor* 6-11-9 MrROHarding^{5}	9/2	25 2
	SPIDEY (IRE) *CRoche* 5-11-0 MrPRoche^{7}	7/2	3½ 3
	King Johns Castle (IRE) *JohnFO'Neill* 5-11-7 MrPJO'Neill^{7}	8/1	¾ 4
	Powers And Soda (IRE) *PAFahy* 4-11-2 MrPFahey	14/1	dist 5
	Supreme Obsession (IRE) *WPMullins* 6-11-7 MsKWalsh^{7}	8/1	25 6
	Jilted Lover (IRE) *LWDoran* 6-11-0 (t) MissTDoran^{7}	50/1	20 7
	For Orla (IRE) *MichaelPHourigan* 5-10-9 MissLAHourigan^{7}	20/1	sh 8
	Vivace *AnthonyMullins* 4-10-9 MrJJFeane^{7}	14/1	20 9
	Auld Son (IRE) *SJMahon* 5-11-0 MrDJEnglish^{7}	20/1	25 10
	Poker Pal (IRE) *DTHughes* 7-11-7 (t) MrRMHennessy^{7}	12/1	7 11
	Premount (IRE) *PJFHassett* 5-11-0 MrRMMoran^{7}	25/1	dist 12

Mr P. C. Kilroy 12ran 5m43.60

CHEPSTOW Tuesday, Dec 28 HEAVY

67 At The Races Red Button Betting Finale Juv Hdle (Gr 1) (A) (3yo) £29,000 — 2m110y (8)

23	PHAR BLEU (FR) *MissGBrowne* 3-11-0 APMcCoy	9/1	1
	BISCAR TWO (IRE) *BJLlewellyn* 3-11-0 (b) ChristianWilliams	50/1	1¼ 2
	HABITUAL DANCER *JeddO'Keeffe* 3-11-0 BHarding	33/1	9 3
23	Salut Saint Cloud *GLMoore* 3-11-0 BJCrowley	5/2	½ 4
	Beauchamp Prince (IRE) *MScudamore* 3-11-0 TScudamore	20/1	¾ 5
	Hunorisk (FR) *GMacaire,France* 3-10-7 JRicou	14/1	5 6

23	Moon Catcher *DBrace* 3-10-7 (t) TJMurphy	50/1	1	7
	Mokum (FR) *AWCarroll* 3-11-0 CLlewellyn	100/1	1	8
23	Cerium (FR) *PFNicholls* 3-11-0 RWalsh	5/4f	15	9
	Golden Millenium (GER) *CVonDerRecke,Germany* 3-11-0 MAFitzgerald	20/1	2½	10
	Jockser (IRE) *JWMullins* 3-11-0 RYoung	100/1	sh	11
	Woody Valentine (USA) *MissVenetiaWilliams* 3-11-0 RJohnson	11/1	nk	12
	Arrayou (FR) *OSherwood* 3-11-0 (b) LAspell	50/1	4	13
	Verasi *GLMoore* 3-11-0 JEMoore	50/1	25	14
	Three Welshmen *DBurchell* 3-11-0 LStephens	33/1		pu
	23 Calomeria *DMcCain* 3-10-7 ADobbin	20/1		pu

Mrs J. Stewart 16ran 4m12.90

68 Coral Welsh National (Hcap Chase) (Gr 3) (A) (153) (5yo+) £58,000 3m5f110y (22)

34	SILVER BIRCH (IRE) *PFNicholls* 7-10-5^{132} RWalsh	10/3f		1
	STRONG RESOLVE (IRE) *MissLucindaVRussell* 8-9-13^{131} PBuchanan^{5}	8/1	2	2
27	CHIVES (IRE) *MrsSJSmith* 9-11-4^{145} DElsworth	5/1	1¾	3
45	L'AVENTURE (FR) *PFNicholls* 5-10-4^{131} (b+t) PJBrennan	15/2	nk	4
	Bindaree (IRE) *NATwiston-Davies* 10-11-6^{147} CLlewellyn	14/1	1½	5
32	Asparagus (IRE) *MSheppard* 10-9-9^{127} (t) ONelmes^{5}	50/1	2½	6
	Akarus (FR) *MCPipe* 9-10-6^{133} APMcCoy	6/1	7	7
	Shotgun Willy (IRE) *PFNicholls* 10-11-11^{152} JTizzard	20/1	21	8
	Count Campioni (IRE) *MPitman* 10-10-0^{127} ATinkler	50/1	24	9
	Jurancon II (FR) *MCPipe* 7-11-9^{150} TJMurphy	20/1	5	10
22	Take The Stand (IRE) *PBowen* 8-11-12^{153} SDurack	33/1		f
	Be My Royal (IRE) *TRGeorge* 10-10-9^{136} JMMaguire	16/1		f
	Desailly *JAGeake* 10-10-0^{127} MBradburne	14/1		f
37	Supreme Glory (IRE) *PGMurphy* 11-10-5^{132} LAspell	20/1		pu
	Lord Jack (IRE) *NGRichards* 8-10-0^{127} ADobbin	9/1		pu
	Sir Frosty *BJMRyall* 11-10-0^{127} (t) TScudamore	66/1		pu
	Jim Jam Joey (IRE) *MissSuzySmith* 11-9-11^{127} (b) CBolger^{3}	100/1		pu

Mr D. J. Nichols 17ran 8m06.40

LEOPARDSTOWN Tuesday, Dec 28 HEAVY

69 Ascon/Rohcon Nov Chase (Gr 1) (5yo+) £34,331 3m (17)

41	FORGET THE PAST *MJPO'Brien* 6-11-10 MrDWCullen	7/2		1
	LEADING THE WAY (IRE) *OliverMcKiernan* 7-11-10 (t) GCotter	20/1	¾	2
41	MUTINEER (IRE) *DTHughes* 5-11-8 (b+t) PWFlood	11/1	2½	3
	Another Rum (IRE) *IADuncan* 6-11-10 DNRussell	16/1		f
	Sandy Owen (IRE) *PAFahy* 8-11-10 BJGeraghty	7/1		f
	Mark The Man (IRE) *NMeade* 7-11-10 PCarberry	4/7f		pu
	Leodotcom (IRE) *MissNoreenHayes* 7-11-5 SGMcDermott	50/1		pu

Mr S. Mulryan 7ran 6m53.56

70 Lexus Chase (Gr 1) (5yo+) £68,662 3m (17)

48	BEEF OR SALMON (IRE) *MHourigan* 8-11-12 PCarberry	9/4		1
30	BEST MATE (IRE) *MissHCKnight,GB* 9-11-12 JCulloty	9/10f	7	2
	PIZARRO (IRE) *EJO'Grady* 7-11-12 DNRussell	9/1	15	3
18	Cloudy Bays (IRE) *CByrnes* 7-11-12 (s) CO'Dwyer	25/1	7	4
59	Rule Supreme (IRE) *WPMullins* 8-11-12 BJGeraghty	11/2		f
7	Barrow Drive *AnthonyMullins* 8-11-12 (t) RGeraghty	100/1		pu

Mr B. J. Craig 6ran 6m42.20

NEWBURY Wednesday, Dec 29 GOOD to SOFT

71 Western Daily Press Race Club Nov Chase (C) (4yo+) £8,840 2¼m110y (15)

	KAUTO STAR (FR) *PFNicholls* 4-10-7 (t) RWalsh	2/1jf		1
	FOREMAN (GER) *TDoumen,France* 6-11-4 APMcCoy	2/1jf	9	2
	SLEEP BAL (FR) *NJHenderson* 5-11-4 MAFitzgerald	7/1	15	3
	Mixsterthetrixster (USA) *MrsTraceyBarfoot-Saunt* 8-11-4 JTizzard	20/1	2½	4
	Marble Arch *HMorrison* 8-11-4 JCrowley	25/1	6	5
	Macmar (FR) *RHAlner* 4-10-13 AThornton	66/1	23	6
	Locksmith *MCPipe* 4-10-13 TJMurphy	7/2	5	7
	Corporate Player (IRE) *NoelTChance* 6-11-4 (t) TDoyle	40/1	7	8

Mr Clive D. Smith 8ran 4m33.71

72 stanjamesuk.com Challow Nov Hdle (Gr 1) (A) (4yo+) £26,100 2m5f (10)

52	BREWSTER (IRE) *IanWilliams* 7-11-7 DRDennis	3/1		1
44	LADALKO (FR) *PFNicholls* 5-11-7 RWalsh	13/8f	1¾	2
31	KEEPTHEDREAMALIVE *RHBuckler* 6-11-7 BHitchcott	66/1	13	3
	Va Vavoom (IRE) *NATwiston-Davies* 6-11-7 CLlewellyn	20/1	2	4
	Theatre (USA) *JamiePoulton* 5-11-7 MBatchelor	33/1	16	5
19	Nyrche (FR) *AKing* 4-11-7 RThornton	20/1	3	6
	Rebel Rhythm *MrsSJSmith* 5-11-7 DElsworth	10/3	8	7

Bannow Strand (IRE) *MCPipe* 4-11-7 TJMurphy .... 7/1 f
Mr & Mrs John Poynton 8ran 5m08.40

LEOPARDSTOWN Wednesday, Dec 29 SOFT

73 Bewleys Hotels December Festival Hdle (Gr 1) (4yo+) £36,620 2m (8)

28 MACS JOY (IRE) *MrsJHarrington* 5-11-12 BJGeraghty 7/1 1
42 BRAVE INCA (IRE) *CAMurphy* 6-11-12 BMCash 13/2 3 2
55 HARDY EUSTACE (IRE) *DTHughes* 7-11-12 (b) CO'Dwyer 6/4f 2 3
55 Solerina (IRE) *JamesBowe* 7-11-7 GTHutchinson 2/1 3 4
Georges Girl (IRE) *FFlood* 6-11-7 FJFlood 16/1 10 5
Al Eile (IRE) *JQueally* 4-11-7 JCulloty 10/1 25 6
Mac's J. Racing Syndicate 6ran 3m57.91

CHELTENHAM Saturday, Jan 1 GOOD to SOFT (New Course)

74 Cheltenham And Three Counties Race Club Hcap Chase (B) 0-145(141) (5yo+) £16,511 3¼m110y (22)

LORD OF ILLUSION (IRE) *TRGeorge* 8-10-11^{126} MAFitzgerald 11/4f 1
49 BARON WINDRUSH *NATwiston-Davies* 7-11-0^{129} CLlewellyn 15/2 12 2
59 IT TAKES TIME (IRE) *MCPipe* 11-11-12^{141} TJMurphy 8/1 10 3
49 Frenchman's Creek *HMorrison* 11-11-10^{139} (s) RWalsh 4/1 22 4
Willie John Daly (IRE) *PJHobbs* 8-11-6^{135} RJohnson 5/1 3½ 5
Smile Pleeze (IRE) *MSheppard* 13-9-13^{121} (s) LStephens^{7} .... 20/1 f
37 Artic Jack (FR) *MrsSJSmith* 9-11-7^{136} DElsworth .... 16/1 ur
49 Lord Noelie (IRE) *MsBridgetNicholls* 12-11-11^{140} JMMaguire .... 16/1 pu
Mondial Jack (FR) *MCPipe* 6-11-10^{139} APMcCoy .... 12/1 pu
Un Jour A Vassy (FR) *PFNicholls* 10-10-11^{126} PJBrennan .... 20/1 pu
Francolino (FR) *DrPPritchard* 12-10-0^{115} JMogford .... 500/1 pu
Mr P. J. Kennedy 11ran 7m02.66

75 Unicoin Homes 'Dipper' Nov Chase (Gr 2) (A) (5yo+) £26,775 2m5f (17)

24 MY WILL (FR) *PFNicholls* 5-10-12 RWalsh 4/1 1
15 EL VAQUERO (IRE) *MissHCKnight* 7-11-4 JCulloty 9/2 4 2
35 See You Sometime *JWMullins* 10-11-11 AThornton .... 12/1 f
35 Fundamentalist (IRE) *NATwiston-Davies* 7-11-11 CLlewellyn .... 4/7f ur
Tom Nail (IRE) *DrPPritchard* 11-11-4 ODayman .... 200/1 pu
Mrs J. Stewart 5ran 5m30.08

WETHERBY Monday, Jan 3 HEAVY

76 skybet.com Castleford Chase (Gr 2) (A) (6yo+) £29,000 2m (12)

21 MISTER MCGOLDRICK *MrsSJSmith* 8-11-2 DElsworth 6/1 1
14 KADARANN (IRE) *PFNicholls* 8-11-8 PJBrennan 16/1 11 2
50 ARMATURK (FR) *PFNicholls* 8-11-4 ChristianWilliams 9/2 2 3
Turgeonev (FR) *TDEasterby* 10-11-2 DO'Meara 25/1 7 4
21 Sir Storm (IRE) *GMMoore* 9-10-12 (s) FKeniry 200/1 27 5
47 Cenkos (FR) *PFNicholls* 11-11-4 JTizzard 14/1 9 6
47 Well Chief (GER) *MCPipe* 6-11-3 TJMurphy .... 8/13f f
No Need For Alarm *RCGuest* 10-10-5 LMcGrath .... 200/1 pu
Mr Richard Longley 8ran 4m11.94

SANDOWN Saturday, Jan 8 GOOD to SOFT

77 ladbrokes.com Tolworth Hdle (Gr 1) (A) (4yo+) £29,000 2m110y (8)

19 MARCEL (FR) *MCPipe* 5-11-7 TJMurphy 3/1 1
IT'S JUST HARRY *CREgerton* 8-11-7 APMcCoy 6/1 2 2
CHILLING PLACE (IRE) *PJHobbs* 6-11-7 RJohnson 16/1 4 3
40 Wild Passion (GER) *NMeade,Ireland* 5-11-7 PCarberry .... 5/2f hd 4
My Way de Solzen (FR) *AKing* 5-11-7 RThornton .... 10/1 ½ 5
67 Phar Bleu (FR) *MissGBrowne* 4-10-9 CLlewellyn 14/1 30 6
Made In Montot (FR) *PFNicholls* 5-11-7 RWalsh 8/1 11 7
Astronomic *JHowardJohnson* 5-11-7 JCulloty .... 8/1 f
New Entic (FR) *GLMoore* 4-10-9 PHide .... 50/1 bd
Mr D. A. Johnson 9ran 4m06.22

78 Ladbroke Hcap Hdle (L) (A) 0-150(145) (4yo+) £58,000 2m110y (8)

TAMARINBLEU (FR) *MCPipe* 5-10-11^{130} APMcCoy 14/1 1
SELF DEFENSE *PRChamings* 8-11-10^{143} MAFitzgerald 14/1 4 2
KING REVO (IRE) *PCHaslam* 5-10-12^{138} RStephens^{7} .... 14/1 ¾ 3
DESERT AIR (JPN) *MCPipe* 6-10-1^{125} (t) TJMalone^{5} 66/1 1¾ 4
Lunar Crystal (IRE) *MCPipe* 7-10-0^{119} RGreene 66/1 3 5
Idole First (IRE) *MissVenetiaWilliams* 6-10-6^{128} AO'Keeffe^{3} 12/1 3½ 6
Thesis (IRE) *MissVenetiaWilliams* 7-11-4^{137} SThomas 12/1 1¾ 7
Winsley *OSherwood* 7-9-10^{120} ONelmes^{5} 20/1 1½ 8

25	Torrid Kentavr (USA) *BEllison* 8-10-13[132] DGallagher	50/1	sh 9
	Monte Cinto (FR) *PFNicholls* 5-10-8[127] RWalsh	3/1f	½ 10
	Zabenz (NZ) *PJHobbs* 8-10-11[130] (b) RJohnson	9/1	¾ 11
	Escompteur (FR) *MCPipe* 5-10-10[129] TJMurphy	7/1	4 12
25	Copeland *MCPipe* 10-11-12[145] (v) JEMoore	40/1	nk 13
	Idaho d'Ox (FR) *MCPipe* 9-10-6[125] GSupple	66/1	¾ 14
	Emanic (FR) *PFNicholls* 5-10-1[120] ChristianWilliams	33/1	½ 15
	Middlethorpe *MWEasterby* 8-10-11[133] (b) MrTGreenall[3]	66/1	sh 16
	Chivalry *JHowardJohnson* 6-11-3[139] (b) JamesDavies[3]	33/1	¾ 17
	Dream With Me (FR) *JAGeake* 8-10-3[122] (t) SDurack	100/1	5 18
61	Castleshane (IRE) *SGollings* 8-11-2[135] NFehily	100/1	11 19
	Caraman (IRE) *DCarroll* 7-9-9[119] JLevins[5]	100/1	4 20
	Migration *MrsSLamyman* 9-10-2[124] LVickers[3]	66/1	22 21
	Rob Leach *GLMoore* 8-10-1[120] PCarberry	10/1	6 22
	Fenix (GER) *MrsLWadham* 6-10-5[124] (b) LAspell	16/1	f

The Arthur White Partnership 23ran 4m01.54

LEOPARDSTOWN Sunday, Jan 9 HEAVY

79 **Pierse Hdle (Extended Hcap) 0-145(135) (4yo+)** £55,780 — 2m (8)

	ESSEX (IRE) *MJPO'Brien* 5-10-8[123] (s) BJGeraghty	5/1f	1
	MANSONY (FR) *ALTMoore* 6-9-13[114] PACarberry	14/1	1 2
73	AL EILE (IRE) *JQueally* 5-10-10[125] JCulloty	13/2	12 3
	ADAMANT APPROACH (IRE) *WPMullins* 11-11-1[135] (t) AndrewJMcNamara[5]	33/1	½ 4
	Native Stag (IRE) *PAFahy* 7-9-10[111] GCotter	20/1	1½ 5
	Tuppenny Cody (IRE) *AnthonyMullins* 6-10-8[123] MAFitzgerald	14/1	1 6
	Top Strategy (IRE) *TMWalsh* 5-10-6[121] (b) GTHutchinson	16/1	3½ 7
	Beechcourt *MJPO'Brien* 8-9-12[118] TGMRyan[5]	33/1	nk 8
	Experimental (IRE) *GTLynch* 11-9-10[111] DJCondon	50/1	5 9
	Loughanelteen (IRE) *PJRothwell* 7-9-7[111] AJDonoghue[3]	25/1	2 10
	Milton Star (IRE) *GTLynch* 6-9-5[111] TJMalone[5]	50/1	nk 11
	Kilbeggan Lad (IRE) *MHourigan* 7-9-3[111] DFlannery[7]	10/1	nk 12
	Boleyknowsbest (IRE) *RPBurns* 7-10-1[116] TPTreacy	20/1	½ 13
64	Native Scout (IRE) *DHassett* 9-10-11[126] (b+t) CO'Dwyer	25/1	4½ 14
	Athlumney Lad (IRE) *NMeade* 6-10-5[120] PCarberry	12/1	6 15
	Silk Screen (IRE) *WPMullins* 5-10-3[118] RWalsh	8/1	2 16
	Dr Julian (IRE) *MHourigan* 5-9-10[111] TJMurphy	25/1	dist 17
	Dalvento (IRE) *JohnJosephMurphy* 7-9-11[115] PWFlood[3]	33/1	f
	Emotional Article (IRE) *TJTaaffe* 5-9-5[111] JMAllen[5]	7/1	f
	Leonardo de Vinci (IRE) *EJO'Grady* 5-10-4[119] (s+t) DNRussell	10/1	ur
	Supergood (IRE) *IMadden* 7-9-10[111] JAHeffernan	25/1	ur

B. P. S. Syndicate 21ran 4m09.40

WARWICK Saturday, Jan 15 SOFT

80 **Pertemps Hcap Hdle (Series Qual) (B) (135) (5yo+)** £14,019 — 3m1f (12)

	CELTIC SON (FR) *MCPipe* 6-10-12[121] (t) TJMurphy	2/1	1
	TOUCH CLOSER *MissVScott* 8-10-11[120] GLee	25/1	3 2
	STRONG FLOW (IRE) *PFNicholls* 8-10-13[122] RWalsh	15/8f	3 3
	Carlys Quest *FerdyMurphy* 11-11-9[135] KMercer[3]	12/1	7 4
	Petite Margot *NATwiston-Davies* 6-11-12[135] CLlewellyn	16/1	½ 5
	Just Beth *GFierro* 9-9-8[110] DLaverty[7]	12/1	1¼ 6
	Bunkum *RLee* 7-10-13[122] RThornton	66/1	22 7
	Majestic (IRE) *IanWilliams* 10-11-9[132] (b+t) WHutchinson	50/1	7 8
	Concert Pianist *PWinkworth* 10-10-13[122] BHitchcott	100/1	22 9
	Supreme Piper (IRE) *PJHobbs* 7-11-4[127] PJBrennan	18/1	¾ 10
	Sure Future *RMStronge* 9-10-6[115] NFehily	25/1	28 11
	Val du Don (FR) *NJHenderson* 5-11-11[134] MAFitzgerald	50/1	pu
	Native Ivy (IRE) *CTinkler* 7-11-1[124] JMMaguire	22/1	pu
	Ice Crystal *WKGoldsworthy* 8-9-7[109] (b) SWalsh[7]	25/1	pu

Mr D. A. Johnson 14ran 6m26.02

81 **totepool Leamington Nov Hdle (Gr 2) (A) (4yo+)** £23,200 — 2m5f (11)

44	NO REFUGE (IRE) *JHowardJohnson* 5-11-12 GLee	5/6f	1
44	LADY ZEPHYR (IRE) *NATwiston-Davies* 7-10-13 CLlewellyn	9/4	3 2
26	BOB BOB BOBBIN *CLTizzard* 6-11-6 JTizzard	12/1	2 3
44	Give Me Love (FR) *PFNicholls* 5-11-12 PJBrennan	33/1	21 4
	Heros Collonges (FR) *PFNicholls* 10-11-6 RWalsh	8/1	3 5

Andrea & Graham Wylie 5ran 5m20.32

82 **totesport Classic Chase (Hcap) (Gr 3) (A) (152) (6yo+)** £66,700 — 3m5f (22)

74	BARON WINDRUSH *NATwiston-Davies* 7-10-3[129] CLlewellyn	11/1	1
17	D'ARGENT (IRE) *AKing* 8-10-8[134] RThornton	9/1	2½ 2

49	DOUBLE HONOUR (FR) *PJHobbs* 7-10-12^{138} (b) PJBrennan	14/1	16	3
49	KELAMI (FR) *FDoumen,France* 7-10-5^{131} MAFitzgerald	9/1	6	4
	Fashions Monty (IRE) *FerdyMurphy* 9-9-11^{126} (t) NMulholland^{3}	33/1	3½	5
68	L'Aventure (FR) *PFNicholls* 6-10-9^{135} (b+t) RWalsh	9/2f	6	6
	Wain Mountain *JABOld* 9-10-6^{132} WHutchinson	8/1	nk	7
17	Maximize (IRE) *MCPipe* 11-10-0^{131} TJMalone^{5}	40/1	14	8
68	Akarus (FR) *MCPipe* 10-10-7^{133} (v) RGreene	18/1	15	9
45	Historg (FR) *FerdyMurphy* 10-9-11^{126} KMercer^{3}	25/1	27	10
	Cowboyboots (IRE) *LWells* 7-9-12^{131} MrJMorgan^{7}	50/1		f
68	Shotgun Willy (IRE) *PFNicholls* 11-11-12^{152} JTizzard	40/1		pu
45	Stormez (FR) *MCPipe* 8-11-8^{148} (t) TJMurphy	25/1		pu
	Grattan Lodge (IRE) *JHowardJohnson* 8-10-10^{136} GLee	13/2		pu
	Merchants Friend (IRE) *CJMann* 10-10-9^{135} (s) NFehily	14/1		pu
	Historic (IRE) *TRGeorge* 9-10-6^{132} JMMaguire	8/1		pu

The Double Octagon Partnership 16ran 7m40.47

83 Weatherbys Bank Standard Open NHF (L) (A) (4, 5 and 6yo) £10,218 — 2m

	OSCAR PARK (IRE) *CTinkler* 6-11-9 MAFitzgerald	7/2jf		1
	LENNON (IRE) *JHowardJohnson* 5-11-9 GLee	15/2	1½	2
	LUTEA (IRE) *MCPipe* 5-11-12 TJMurphy	7/2jf	19	3
	Mister Quasimodo *CLTizzard* 5-11-9 JTizzard	7/1	14	4
	Corals Laurel (IRE) *RTPhillips* 6-11-9 RThornton	4/1	1½	5
	Lunch Was My Idea (IRE) *PFNicholls* 5-11-5 RWalsh	9/2	dist	6
	Walter (IRE) *PWinkworth* 6-11-5 BHitchcott	66/1	3	7
	Tuesday Club (IRE) *JABOld* 6-11-5 WHutchinson	40/1	dist	8

Mr George Ward 8ran 3m49.80

GOWRAN PARK Thursday, Jan 20 HEAVY

84 Alo Duffin Memorial Galmoy Hdle (Gr 3) (5yo+) £18,210 — 3m (13)

28	EMOTIONAL MOMENT (IRE) *TJTaaffe* 8-11-10 BJGeraghty	8/11f		1
	HOMER WELLS (IRE) *WPMullins* 7-11-10 RWalsh	5/2	25	2
55	ROSAKER (USA) *NMeade* 8-11-10 PCarberry	7/2	25	3
	Calling Classy (IRE) *DenisAhern* 7-11-0 DNRussell	50/1	4	4

Watercork Syndicate 4ran 6m34.55

85 Goulding Thyestes Hcap Chase (Gr B) (132) (5yo+) £34,143 — 3m (16)

	NUMBERSIXVALVERDE (IRE) *MartinBrassil* 9-10-5^{117} MrNPMadden	8/1		1
65	KYMANDJEN (IRE) *PaulNolan* 8-10-13^{125} JLCullen	8/1	sh	2
	BIZET (IRE) *FFlood* 9-10-6^{118} CO'Dwyer	4/1f	3	3
	CATALPA CARGO (IRE) *ESheehy* 11-11-3^{132} MDarcy^{3}	16/1	3½	4
65	Golden Storm (IRE) *JosephCrowley* 8-10-9^{126} (b) JMAllen^{5}	14/1	1½	5
	Tell Me See (IRE) *JohnMichaelBurke* 9-9-9^{114} MrJMBurke^{7}	12/1	1½	6
65	The Bunny Boiler (IRE) *NMeade* 11-10-6^{121} DFO'Regan^{3}	33/1	12	7
65	Jack High (IRE) *TMWalsh* 10-10-13^{125} GCotter	8/1	nk	8
	Over The First (IRE) *CFSwan* 10-10-13^{130} JFLevins^{5}	20/1	4	9
7	Satco Express (IRE) *ESheehy* 9-11-0^{126} (t) JRBarry	20/1	9	10
	Baily Mist (IRE) *MFMorris* 8-10-9^{121} KWhelan	16/1	dist	11
65	Native Sessions (IRE) *NMeade* 10-11-2^{128} PCarberry	20/1	15	12
	Captain Moonlight (IRE) *TJO'Mara* 9-10-3^{115} WSlattery	25/1	8	13
	This Is Serious (IRE) *CFSwan* 11-10-6^{125} DGHogan^{7}	25/1	20	14
65	Livingstonebramble (IRE) *WPMullins* 9-10-3^{115} RWalsh	7/1		f
65	Ride The Storm (IRE) *EJO'Grady* 8-10-11^{123} DNRussell	16/1		ur
	Calladine (IRE) *CRoche* 9-10-4^{116} APCrowe	8/1		ur
	Central Billing (IRE) *MHourigan* 10-10-1^{113} RPMcNally	9/1		pu

Mr O. B. P. Carroll 18ran 6m40.17

HAYDOCK Saturday, Jan 22 HEAVY

86 Commhoist Logistics Champion Hdle Trial (Gr 2) (A) (4yo+) £23,200 — 2m (8)

51	INGLIS DREVER *JHowardJohnson* 6-11-8 GLee	4/5f		1
76	MISTER MCGOLDRICK *MrsSJSmith* 8-11-4 DElsworth	6/1	8	2
51	THE FRENCH FURZE (IRE) *NGRichards* 11-11-12 BHarding	33/1	10	3
38	Royal Shakespeare (FR) *SGollings* 6-11-8 TDoyle	4/1	22	4
78	Copeland *MCPipe* 10-11-8 (v) APMcCoy	7/1	22	5
1	Merryvale Man *MissKarianaKey* 8-11-4 SDurack	200/1	20	6
	Turnium (FR) *MScudamore* 10-11-4 (v) JamesDavies	50/1	27	7

Andrea & Graham Wylie 7ran 3m56.83

87 totesport Co Cup Hdle (Ltd Hcap) (Gr 2) (A) (155) (4yo+) £23,200 — 2½m (10)

61	BLUE CANYON (FR) *FDoumen,France* 7-10-13^{144} APMcCoy	8/1		1
	ROYAL EMPEROR (IRE) *MrsSJSmith* 9-11-0^{145} GLee	14/1	2	2

80	PETITE MARGOT *NATwiston-Davies* 6-10-4^{135} CLlewellyn	7/2	4	3
	Claymore (IRE) *OSherwood* 9-10-13^{144} LAspell	7/2	hd	4
3	Polar Red *MCPipe* 8-10-1^{137} TJMalone^{5}	5/1	22	5
	Mythical King (IRE) *RLee* 8-10-4^{135} TDoyle	50/1	nk	6
	Astonville (FR) *MScudamore* 11-10-1^{135} (v) JamesDavies^{3}	66/1	7	7
	Patriarch Express *MrsSJSmith* 8-11-10^{155} DElsworth	5/2f		f

Mr John P. McManus 8ran 5m14.34

88 Peter Marsh Chase (Ltd Hcap) (Gr 2) (A) (160) (5yo+) £43,500 — 3m (18)

37	LORD TRANSCEND (IRE) *JHowardJohnson* 8-10-4^{140} GLee	9/4f		1
62	FIRST GOLD (FR) *FDoumen,France* 12-11-7^{157} (b) APMcCoy	9/1	10	2
68	TAKE THE STAND (IRE) *PBowen* 9-11-0^{150} SDurack	7/1	6	3
	Truckers Tavern (IRE) *FerdyMurphy* 10-10-9^{148} (t) KMercer^{3}	11/2	1¾	4
33	Hand Inn Hand *HDDaly* 9-11-10^{160} MBradburne	25/1	3½	5
68	Bindaree (IRE) *NATwiston-Davies* 11-10-11^{147} CLlewellyn	7/1	dist	6
68	Chives (IRE) *MrsSJSmith* 10-10-13^{149} DElsworth	11/4	14	7

Andrea & Graham Wylie 7ran 6m37.75

UTTOXETER Saturday, Jan 22 HEAVY

89 Betfred Lightning Nov Chase (Gr 2) (A) (5yo+) £20,300 — 2m (9)

75	MY WILL (FR) *PFNicholls* 5-11-2 RWalsh	11/4jf		1
15	ASHLEY BROOK (IRE) *KBishop* 7-11-7 RGreene	11/4jf	½	2
46	CONTRABAND *MCPipe* 7-11-10 TJMurphy	4/1	4	3
43	Kadount (FR) *AKing* 7-11-7 WHutchinson	4/1	4	4
	Mondul (GER) *MFHarris* 5-10-9 OMcPhail	8/1	21	5
	Jaybeedee *DrPPritchard* 9-11-3 JMogford	200/1	dist	6

Mrs J. Stewart 6ran 4m10.91

LEOPARDSTOWN Sunday, Jan 23 HEAVY

90 Baileys Arkle Perpetual Challenge Cup Nov Chase (Gr 1) (5yo+) £36,364 — 2m1f (11)

	ULAAN BAATAR (IRE) *MrsJHarrington* 8-11-12 TJMurphy	10/1		1
71	FOREMAN (GER) *TDoumen,France* 7-11-12 APMcCoy	13/8f	9	2
63	NED KELLY (IRE) *EJO'Grady* 9-11-12 DNRussell	7/1	2	3
	Strike Back (IRE) *MrsJHarrington* 7-11-12 RMPower	16/1	2½	4
63	Sir Oj (IRE) *NMeade* 8-11-12 (b) PCarberry	5/1	nk	5
	Scarthy Lad (IRE) *TGO'Leary* 7-11-12 BJGeraghty	5/2	20	6
63	Guilt *DTHughes* 5-11-3 (t) PWFlood	50/1	10	7
63	Steel Band *PaulARoche* 7-11-12 KHadnett	20/1		ur

Mr J. P. O'Flaherty 8ran 4m39.89

91 AIG Europe Champion Hdle (Gr 1) (4yo+) £63,112 — 2m (8)

73	MACS JOY (IRE) *MrsJHarrington* 6-11-10 BJGeraghty	11/8f		1
73	BRAVE INCA (IRE) *CAMurphy* 7-11-10 BMCash	7/2	sh	2
73	HARDY EUSTACE (IRE) *DTHughes* 8-11-10 CO'Dwyer	7/1	hd	3
73	Solerina (IRE) *JamesBowe* 8-11-5 GTHutchinson	9/2	11	4
25	Accordion Etoile (IRE) *PaulNolan* 6-11-10 JLCullen	14/1	20	5
73	Georges Girl (IRE) *FFlood* 7-11-5 DNRussell	9/1	15	6

Mac's J. Racing Syndicate 6ran 4m10.98

92 Building Design Golden Cygnet Nov Hdle (Gr 3) (5yo+) £15,934 — 2½m (10)

	WASHINGTON LAD (IRE) *PAFahy* 5-10-12 APMcCoy	10/1		1
	ASIAN MAZE (IRE) *PatrickMullins* 6-11-3 BJGeraghty	11/4f	1½	2
	ARTEEA (IRE) *MHourigan* 6-11-2 TJMurphy	7/1	2	3
40	Mr Babbage (IRE) *WPMullins* 7-11-5 RWalsh	9/2	20	4
	Mrs Wallensky (IRE) *PaulNolan* 7-11-0 JLCullen	6/1	20	5
	Wishwillow Lord (IRE) *LWhitmore* 6-11-5 DNRussell	10/1	25	6
56	Petertheknot (IRE) *PatrickSinnott* 7-11-10 CO'Dwyer	4/1	12	7

Garrafrauns Syndicate 7ran 5m13.39

THURLES Thursday, Jan 27 SOFT

93 Maclochlainn Road Markings Limited Kinloch Brae Chase (Gr 2) (6yo+) £22,604 — 2½m (14)

64	RATHGAR BEAU (IRE) *ESheehy* 9-11-10 JRBarry	6/4f		1
64	CENTRAL HOUSE *DTHughes* 8-11-12 (b) PCarberry	11/4	7	2
37	NIL DESPERANDUM (IRE) *MsFMCrowley* 8-11-12 RWalsh	8/1	4½	3
65	The Galway Man (IRE) *AnthonyMullins* 8-11-5 RGeraghty	14/1	2	4
64	Native Upmanship (IRE) *ALTMoore* 12-11-12 CO'Dwyer	4/1	hd	5
	Darby Wall (IRE) *EBolger* 7-11-5 AndrewJMcNamara	50/1	17	6
	Monty's Pass (IRE) *JamesJosephMangan* 12-11-8 BJGeraghty	20/1	dist	7

One-O-Eight Racing Club 7ran 5m24.80

CHELTENHAM Saturday, Jan 29 SOFT (New Course)

94 Royal Gloucestershire Hussars Classic Nov Hdle (Gr 2) (A) (4yo+) 2½m110y (10) £17,400

	AMBOBO (USA) *AChaille-Chaille,France* 5-11-12 BJGeraghty	14/1		1
72	BREWSTER (IRE) *IanWilliams* 8-11-12 DRDennis	7/4f	2½	2
	MEPHISTO (IRE) *JHowardJohnson* 6-11-5 GLee	8/1	8	3
81	Lady Zephyr (IRE) *NATwiston-Davies* 7-10-12 CLlewellyn	9/2	3	4
72	Ladalko (FR) *PFNicholls* 6-11-12 RWalsh	9/2	2½	5
	Moulin Riche (FR) *FDoumen,France* 5-11-12 LMetais	10/1	1½	6
	Eurochancer (IRE) *JosephFox,Ireland* 6-11-12 RPMcNally	50/1	12	7
72	Va Vavoom (IRE) *NATwiston-Davies* 7-11-5 AntonyEvans	33/1	15	8
	Berengario (IRE) *SCBurrough* 5-11-5 RThornton	100/1	16	9
	Royal Hector (GER) *MCPipe* 6-11-9 TJMurphy	9/1	10	10

Mr S. Mulryan 10ran 5m10.28

95 Timeform Nov Hcap Chase (B) (142) (5yo+) £12,354 2m5f (17)

43	LACDOUDAL (FR) *PJHobbs* 6-11-8^{138} RJohnson	4/1		1
	JOES EDGE (IRE) *FerdyMurphy* 8-10-11^{127} GLee	3/1	5	2
39	CORNISH REBEL (IRE) *PFNicholls* 8-11-12^{142} RWalsh	13/8f	nk	3
	I Hear Thunder (IRE) *RHBuckler* 7-10-0^{116} BHitchcott	7/1	5	4
	Ardashir (FR) *NATwiston-Davies* 6-10-0^{116} CLlewellyn	25/1	3½	5
	Wrags To Riches (IRE) *JDFrost* 8-10-2^{123} CHonour^{5}	12/1	13	6

Mrs R. J. Skan 6ran 5m34.01

96 Victor Chandler Chase (Hcap) (Gr 2) (A) (176) (5yo+) £63,800 2m110y (14)

76	WELL CHIEF (GER) *MCPipe* 6-11-10^{176} TJMurphy	5/1		1
50	THISTHATANDTOTHER (IRE) *PFNicholls* 9-10-4^{156} RWalsh	2/1f	1¾	2
76	KADARANN (IRE) *PFNicholls* 8-10-4^{156} PJBrennan	11/1	7	3
	Golden Alpha (IRE) *MCPipe* 11-10-4^{156} RGreene	50/1	3½	4
62	Seebald (GER) *MCPipe* 10-10-4^{156} APMcCoy	7/1	2½	5
76	Turgeonev (FR) *TDEasterby* 10-10-4^{156} DO'Meara	25/1	2	6
76	Armaturk (FR) *PFNicholls* 8-10-6^{158} (t) ChristianWilliams	11/2	10	7
	Non So (FR) *NJHenderson* 7-10-4^{156} MAFitzgerald	15/2	16	8
76	Cenkos (FR) *PFNicholls* 11-10-9^{161} BJGeraghty	25/1	1¼	9
54	Flagship Uberalles (IRE) *PJHobbs* 11-10-5^{157} RJohnson	16/1	2	10

Mr D. A. Johnson 10ran 4m15.79

97 Byrne Bros Cleeve Hdle (Gr 2) (A) (5yo+) £34,800 3m (12)

87	PATRIARCH EXPRESS *MrsSJSmith* 8-11-0 JCulloty	8/1		1
	KORELO (FR) *MCPipe* 7-11-0 TJMurphy	8/1	hd	2
51	WESTENDER (FR) *MCPipe* 9-11-4 (b) APMcCoy	5/1	8	3
59	Crystal d'Ainay (FR) *AKing* 6-11-8 RThornton	2/1f	¾	4
31	Monet's Garden (IRE) *NGRichards* 7-11-8 ADobbin	14/1	1½	5
	Lough Derg (FR) *MCPipe* 5-11-4 TScudamore	33/1	6	6
	Royal Rosa (FR) *JHowardJohnson* 6-11-4 GLee	10/3	4	7
36	Telemoss (IRE) *NGRichards* 11-11-8 RWalsh	16/1	dist	8
	Quick *MCPipe* 5-11-0 (v) RGreene	50/1	hd	9
71	Marble Arch *HMorrison* 9-11-0 BJGeraghty	50/1	15	10
	Label du Cochet (FR) *AChaille-Chaille,France* 6-11-0 CPieux	100/1		pu

Mr A. P. Muir 11ran 6m11.23

98 Pillar Property Chase (Gr 2) (A) (6yo+) £47,600 3m1f110y (21)

	GREY ABBEY (IRE) *JHowardJohnson* 11-11-10 GLee	10/3		1
62	THEREALBANDIT (IRE) *MCPipe* 8-11-6 TJMurphy	11/4f	16	2
49	ROYAL AUCLAIR (FR) *PFNicholls* 8-11-6 (t) RWalsh	7/2	12	3
70	Cloudy Bays (IRE) *CByrnes,Ireland* 8-11-6 BJGeraghty	10/1	nk	4
	Ballycassidy (IRE) *PBowen* 9-11-5 RJohnson	11/1	dist	5
60	Ollie Magern *NATwiston-Davies* 7-11-5 CLlewellyn	4/1		ur
	Strong Magic (IRE) *JRCornwall* 13-11-0 TSiddall	200/1		pu

The Roper Family and Norman Furness 7ran 6m57.10

99 Wragge & Co Finesse Juv Nov Hdle (Gr 2) (A) (4yo) £17,400 2m1f (8)

	AKILAK (IRE) *JHowardJohnson* 4-11-0 GLee	50/1		1
	YANKEEDOODLEDANDY (IRE) *PCHaslam* 4-11-7 APMcCoy	7/2	6	2
67	SALUT SAINT CLOUD *GLMoore* 4-11-7 BJCrowley	14/1	7	3
	Miss Academy (FR) *MCPipe* 4-10-7 TJMurphy	11/4f	½	4
67	Biscar Two (IRE) *BJLlewellyn* 4-11-0 (b) ChristianWilliams	25/1	1½	5
	Bonbon Rose (FR) *AChaille-Chaille,France* 4-11-7 CPieux	7/1	¾	6
77	New Entic (FR) *GLMoore* 4-11-0 PHide	33/1	5	7
	Openide *BWDuke* 4-11-0 CMStudd	50/1	2	8
	Danaw (FR) *FDoumen,France* 4-11-7 (t) LMetais	7/2	1¼	9
67	Beauchamp Prince (IRE) *MScudamore* 4-11-0 TScudamore	100/1	1	10

	Napolitain (FR) *PFNicholls* 4-11-7 RWalsh	25/1	11	11
	Quarrymount *JABOld* 4-11-0 CLlewellyn	50/1	23	12
	Siegfrieds Night (IRE) *MCChapman* 4-11-4 ACCoyle	100/1	12	13
	Simonovski (USA) *SCBurrough* 4-11-0 MrWPKavanagh	100/1	11	14
	Zalda *PJHobbs* 4-10-11 RJohnson	9/1	3½	15
	Vicario *DMcCain* 4-11-0 ADobbin	66/1		pu

ADA Partnership 16ran 4m17.23

PUNCHESTOWN Sunday, Jan 30 HEAVY

100 Byrne Group plc Nov Hdle (Gr 2) (5yo+) £24,865 — 2m (9)

40	JUSTIFIED (IRE) *ESheehy* 6-11-2 MAFitzgerald	9/4f		1
	BLAZING LISS (IRE) *JEKiely* 6-10-11 DNRussell	7/2	14	2
	MAN ABOUT TOWN (IRE) *TJTaaffe* 6-11-2 APMcCoy	6/1	1½	3
	Akshar (IRE) *DKWeld* 6-11-2 BJGeraghty	5/1	12	4
	Shuilan (IRE) *EUHales* 6-10-11 TJMurphy	14/1	2	5
	Giolla De (IRE) *FFlood* 6-11-2 PCarberry	10/1	10	6
	Maille Blu (FR) *TMWalsh* 5-10-12 RWalsh	6/1	2	7
	Sky To Sea (FR) *MrsAMO'Shea* 7-11-2 AO'Shea	50/1	dist	8

Braybrook Syndicate 8ran 4m03.88

101 Byrne Group plc Tied Cottage Chase (Gr 3) (5yo+) £18,083 — 2m (11)

47	MOSCOW FLYER (IRE) *MrsJHarrington* 11-12-0 BJGeraghty	2/11f		1
90	STEEL BAND *PaulARoche* 7-11-3 GTHutchinson	33/1	2½	2
	HI CLOY (IRE) *MHourigan* 8-12-0 TJMurphy	13/2	3	3
18	Glenelly Gale (IRE) *ALTMoore* 11-12-0 CO'Dwyer	14/1	11	4
	Fiery Ring (IRE) *JRHFowler* 10-11-10 RGeraghty	33/1	sh	5

Mr Brian Kearney 5ran 4m15.11

SANDOWN Saturday, Feb 5 GOOD

102 Sodexho Prestige Hcap Chase (B) (156) (5yo+) £11,867 — 2m (13)

	ONEWAY (IRE) *MGRimell* 8-10-13^{143} GLee	5/2		1
61	IMPEK (FR) *MissHCKnight* 9-11-1^{145} JCulloty	5/1	1½	2
	GREAT TRAVEL (FR) *PFNicholls* 6-10-13^{143} RWalsh	6/5f	½	3
47	Upgrade *MCPipe* 11-11-1^{145} TJMurphy	20/1	14	4
96	Cenkos (FR) *PFNicholls* 11-11-12^{156} ChristianWilliams	16/1	2½	5
	Bleu Superbe (FR) *MissVenetiaWilliams* 10-10-8^{138} SThomas	12/1	4	6

Mr Mark Rimell 6ran 3m54.61

103 Agfa Hdle (L) (A) (5yo+) £17,400 — 2m110y (8)

78	SELF DEFENSE *PRChamings* 8-11-4 RThornton	5/1		1
61	ROOSTER BOOSTER *PJHobbs* 11-11-8 RJohnson	4/5f	3	2
78	CHIVALRY *JHowardJohnson* 6-11-2 (b) GLee	16/1	1¾	3
86	Royal Shakespeare (FR) *SGollings* 6-11-4 TDoyle	7/2	1¼	4
86	Copeland *MCPipe* 10-11-4 (v) TJMurphy	14/1	12	5
	Cool Roxy *AGBlackmore* 8-11-0 CHonour	100/1	26	6

Fraser Miller Racing 6ran 4m06.69

104 totesport Scilly Isles Nov Chase (Gr 1) (A) (5yo+) £29,000 — 2½m110y (17)

75	EL VAQUERO (IRE) *MissHCKnight* 7-11-6 JCulloty	4/1		1
	LE PASSING (FR) *PFNicholls* 6-11-6 RWalsh	5/1	2	2
95	LACDOUDAL (FR) *PJHobbs* 6-11-6 RJohnson	9/4	hd	3
89	Ashley Brook (IRE) *KBishop* 7-11-6 RGreene	2/1f	nk	4
75	See You Sometime *JWMullins* 10-11-6 AThornton	12/1	3½	5

Mr T. M. Curtis 5ran 5m10.65

WETHERBY Saturday, Feb 5 SOFT

105 Totty Construction Towton Nov Chase (Gr 2) (A) (5yo+) £21,440 — 3m1f (18)

98	OLLIE MAGERN *NATwiston-Davies* 7-11-11 CLlewellyn	8/15f		1
	KING HARALD (IRE) *MBradstock* 7-11-4 MBatchelor	8/1	4	2
	UNDENIABLE *MrsSJSmith* 7-11-4 GCarenza	28/1	dist	3
39	St Matthew (USA) *MrsSJSmith* 7-11-8 DElsworth	15/2		f
	Kidithou (FR) *WTReed* 7-11-4 KJohnson	100/1		ur
	Vandas Choice (IRE) *MissLucindaVRussell* 7-11-8 PBuchanan	6/1		pu

Mr Roger Nicholls 6ran 6m28.92

LEOPARDSTOWN Sunday, Feb 6 SOFT

106 Cashmans Juv Hdle (Gr 2) (4yo) £24,694 — 2m (8)

	STRANGELY BROWN (IRE) *EMcNamara* 4-11-3 DJCasey	7/2		1
	BARATI (IRE) *MJPO'Brien* 4-11-0 BJGeraghty	8/1	2	2
	ARCH REBEL (USA) *NMeade* 4-11-6 PCarberry	9/10f	3½	3
	Don't Be Bitin (IRE) *EGriffin* 4-11-0 RWalsh	4/1	hd	4

	Dabiroun (IRE) *PaulNolan* 4-11-0 JLCullen	33/1	½	5
	Dalton (FR) *EJO'Grady* 4-11-0 DNRussell	12/1	8	6

We Didn't Name Him Syndicate 6ran 4m14.52

107 Deloitte Nov Hdle (Gr 1) (5yo+) £35,862 — 2¼m (9)

40	ROYAL PARADISE (FR) *ThomasFoley* 5-11-7 MAFitzgerald	4/5f		1
	THE RAILWAY MAN (IRE) *ALTMoore* 6-11-10 BMCash	5/1	3	2
56	AUGHERSKEA (IRE) *NMeade* 6-11-10 PCarberry	12/1	1½	3
56	Sweet Kiln (IRE) *JamesBowe* 6-11-5 GTHutchinson	9/2	4	4
	New Field (IRE) *PatrickMullins* 7-11-10 CO'Dwyer	16/1	14	5
	Black Apalachi (IRE) *PJRothwell* 6-11-10 DJCasey	9/1	8	6
26	Proud To Be Irish (IRE) *SO'Farrell* 6-11-10 RWalsh	40/1	2	7
	Mr McAuley (IRE) *MHalford* 7-11-10 APLane	16/1	5	8

Mr P. E. Delaney 8ran 4m41.18

108 Dr P.J. Moriarty Nov Chase (Gr 1) (5yo+) £49,310 — 2m5f (14)

	CARRIGEEN VICTOR (IRE) *MrsJHarrington* 7-11-12 RMPower	10/3		1
	WELL PRESENTED (IRE) *MrsJHarrington* 7-11-12 TJMurphy	6/1	1	2
	DOODLE ADDLE (IRE) *JTRDreaper* 9-11-12 DNRussell	20/1	9	3
	Il En Reve (FR) *SJTreacy* 7-11-12 MDarcy	40/1	3	4
	Strong Project (IRE) *CFSwan* 9-11-12 DJCasey	15/2	7	5
69	Mark The Man (IRE) *NMeade* 8-11-12 PCarberry	5/2	25	6
63	Newmill (IRE) *TGO'Leary* 7-11-12 BJGeraghty	9/4f		pu

Mr Richard A. Doyle 7ran 5m50.43

109 Hennessy Cognac Gold Cup Chase (Gr 1) (5yo+) £73,862 — 3m (17)

70	RULE SUPREME (IRE) *WPMullins* 9-11-12 DJCasey	11/2		1
70	BEEF OR SALMON (IRE) *MHourigan* 9-11-12 PCarberry	8/15f	14	2
98	CLOUDY BAYS (IRE) *CByrnes* 8-11-12 DNRussell	20/1	20	3
85	Jack High (IRE) *TMWalsh* 10-11-12 GCotter	66/1	15	4
	Murphy's Cardinal (IRE) *NoelTChance,GB* 9-11-12 TJDoyle	8/1	4	5
65	Hersov (IRE) *PaulARoche* 9-11-12 MAFitzgerald	100/1	dist	6
70	Pizarro (IRE) *EJO'Grady* 8-11-12 BJGeraghty	7/1		f

Mr John J. Fallon 7ran 6m35.75

NEWBURY Saturday, Feb 12 GOOD to SOFT

110 AON Chase (Gr 2) (A) (6yo+) £29,000 — 3m (18)

50	FARMER JACK *PJHobbs* 9-11-6 RJohnson	12/1		1
80	STRONG FLOW (IRE) *PFNicholls* 8-11-6 RWalsh	2/1jf	1½	2
37	CELESTIAL GOLD (IRE) *MCPipe* 7-11-6 TJMurphy	2/1jf	hd	3
30	Sir Rembrandt (IRE) *RHAlner* 9-11-6 AThornton	6/1	14	4
	Gingembre (FR) *MrsLCTaylor* 11-11-0 MBradburne	33/1	23	5
	Valley Henry (IRE) *JHowardJohnson* 10-11-0 BJGeraghty	10/1	22	6
	Ravenscar *CTPogson* 7-11-0 APogson	300/1	3½	7
98	Ballycassidy (IRE) *PBowen* 9-11-5 SDurack	16/1		pu

Mr Peter Partridge 8ran 6m00.11

111 totesport Trophy Hdle (Hcap) (Gr 3) (A) (149) (4yo+) £72,500 — 2m110y (8)

79	ESSEX (IRE) *MJPO'Brien,Ireland* 5-11-6^{144} BJGeraghty	4/1f		1
	BONGO FURY (FR) *MCPipe* 6-10-3^{127} (v) TScudamore	33/1	3	2
79	AL EILE (IRE) *JQueally,Ireland* 5-11-0^{138} JCulloty	10/1	hd	3
	HAWADETH *VRADartnall* 10-10-9^{140} (s) MissNCarberry^{7}	40/1	1¼	4
	Power Elite (IRE) *NMeade,Ireland* 5-11-1^{139} PCarberry	12/1	2	5
78	Idole First (IRE) *MissVenetiaWilliams* 6-10-3^{127} AO'Keeffe	20/1	1	6
78	Fenix (GER) *MrsLWadham* 6-10-0^{124} (v) LAspell	40/1	sh	7
78	Tamarinbleu (FR) *MCPipe* 5-11-4^{142} APMcCoy	11/2	sh	8
	Roman Ark *JMJefferson* 7-10-1^{128} FKing^{3}	7/1	1½	9
78	Monte Cinto (FR) *PFNicholls* 5-10-3^{127} RWalsh	11/1	hd	10
87	Claymore (IRE) *OSherwood* 9-11-6^{144} MBradburne	66/1	¾	11
59	Geos (FR) *NJHenderson* 10-11-6^{149} TJPhelan^{5}	50/1	hd	12
	Sharp Rigging (IRE) *AMHales* 5-10-4^{128} JAMcCarthy	28/1	hd	13
78	Zabenz (NZ) *PJHobbs* 8-10-6^{130} (b) RJohnson	33/1	hd	14
78	Desert Air (JPN) *MCPipe* 6-9-12^{127} (t) TJMalone^{5}	33/1	½	15
1	Howle Hill (IRE) *AKing* 5-11-0^{138} RThornton	14/1	6	16
31	Nawamees (IRE) *GLMoore* 7-10-11^{135} NFehily	50/1	1¼	17
63	Tiger Cry (IRE) *ALTMoore,Ireland* 7-10-3^{127} DJCasey	12/1	¾	18
78	Idaho d'Ox (FR) *MCPipe* 9-10-0^{124} GSupple	100/1	3½	19
96	Non So (FR) *NJHenderson* 7-10-11^{135} MAFitzgerald	12/1	2	20
78	Escompteur (FR) *MCPipe* 5-10-5^{129} TJMurphy	33/1	1¾	21
1	Dalaram (IRE) *JHowardJohnson* 5-10-13^{137} ADobbin	33/1	6	22
103	Copeland *MCPipe* 10-11-5^{143} (s) SDurack	100/1	2	23
87	Polar Red *MCPipe* 8-10-13^{137} (v) JEMoore	50/1	24	24

	Zibeline (IRE) *BEllison* 8-10-11[135] (v) BJCrowley	50/1	13 25

B.P.S. Syndicate 25ran 3m56.41

112 totepool Game Spirit Chase (Gr 2) (A) (5yo+) £34,800 — 2m1f (13)

62	AZERTYUIOP (FR) *PFNicholls* 8-11-10 RWalsh	11/10f	1
96	WELL CHIEF (GER) *MCPipe* 6-11-6 TJMurphy	5/4	2½ 2
96	ARMATURK (FR) *PFNicholls* 8-11-6 ChristianWilliams	33/1	23 3
86	Mister McGoldrick *MrsSJSmith* 8-11-10 DElsworth	7/1	9 4
96	Kadarann (IRE) *PFNicholls* 8-11-10 JTizzard	33/1	6 5
	Get The Point *DrPPritchard* 11-11-0 JamesDavies	200/1	21 6

Mr J. Hales 6ran 4m10.20

113 totescoop6 Hcap Hdle (C) 0-130(129) (4yo+) £6,287 — 3m110y (13)

	OVER THE CREEK *MCPipe* 6-11-12[129] TJMurphy	9/2	1
	OMNI COSMO TOUCH (USA) *MrsSJSmith* 9-11-0[117] DElsworth	10/1	3½ 2
	SNOOPY LOOPY (IRE) *MissVScott* 7-10-10[113] MAFitzgerald	8/1	18 3
49	Ballybough Rasher (IRE) *JHowardJohnson* 10-11-3[120] ADobbin	7/1	½ 4
	Moscow Whisper (IRE) *PJHobbs* 8-10-13[116] RJohnson	3/1f	6 5
	King Georges (FR) *JCTuck* 7-10-2[105] SDurack	40/1	4 6
	Widemouth Bay (IRE) *MissHCKnight* 7-11-6[123] JCulloty	12/1	20 7
	Guard Duty *DMLloyd* 8-9-9[103] (b+t) TJPhelan[5]	66/1	9 8
	Victory Gunner (IRE) *CRoberts* 7-11-8[125] ChristianWilliams	25/1	2 9
	General Duroc (IRE) *RTPhillips* 9-10-13[116] WMarston	40/1	dist 10
	He's The Guv'nor (IRE) *RHBuckler* 6-10-7[110] RThornton	4/1	pu
	Redde (IRE) *MrsJGRetter* 10-10-7[110] JAMcCarthy	100/1	pu

Mr D. A. Johnson 12ran 5m58.40

114 totesportcasino.com Standard Open NH (Gr 2) (A) (4, 5 and 6yo) £12,000 — 2m110y

	KARANJA *VRADartnall* 6-11-3 MissNCarberry[7]	14/1	1
	BE BE KING (IRE) *PFNicholls* 6-11-7 RWalsh	15/8f	3½ 2
	DE SOTO *PRWebber* 4-10-7 TDoyle	6/1	1¾ 3
	Mr Pointment (IRE) *CREgerton* 6-11-7 APMcCoy	9/2	10 4
	Oscardeal (IRE) *CTPogson* 6-11-0 APogson[7]	50/1	6 5
	Wee Robbie *NJGifford* 5-11-7 LAspell	25/1	2½ 6
83	Lutea (IRE) *MCPipe* 5-11-10 TJMurphy	16/1	7 7
	Flinders Bay (IRE) *MissHCKnight* 5-11-7 JCulloty	16/1	2½ 8
	Greenhill Bramble (IRE) *PJHobbs* 5-11-7 PFlynn	7/1	½ 9
	Eaton Hall (IRE) *NATwiston-Davies* 5-11-3 CLlewellyn	50/1	6 10
	Ice Cream (FR) *MEDFrancis* 4-10-3 BJCrowley	100/1	3 11
	Earth Man (IRE) *PFNicholls* 6-11-10 JTizzard	9/1	6 12
	Cappanrush (IRE) *DJSffrenchDavis* 5-11-3 ATinkler	100/1	2½ 13
	Creinch *OSherwood* 4-10-11 JAMcCarthy	14/1	22 14
	Well Actually (IRE) *BGPowell* 5-11-3 MAFitzgerald	50/1	11 15
	Katy Jones *NoelTChance* 5-10-3 (t) WKennedy[7]	25/1	1¼ 16
	Magna *ABCoogan* 6-11-3 SDurack	100/1	dist 17

Mr D. G. Staddon 17ran 3m53.58

GOWRAN PARK Saturday, Feb 12 HEAVY

115 Rockview (QR) INH Flat (5yo) £4,733 — 2m1f

	FIRTH OF FORTH (IRE) *JosephCrowley* 5-11-11 MrKEPower[3]	7/1	1
	SOME TOUCH (IRE) *THorgan* 5-12-0 MrJTMcNamara	16/1	6 2
	THATSYEREMARE (IRE) *TDoyle* 5-11-2 MrBJKelly[7]	20/1	20 3
	Jack Ingham (IRE) *EJO'Grady* 5-11-11 MrJPMagnier[3]	4/6f	1½ 4
	I See Icy (IRE) *DanielMiley* 5-12-0 MrAFitzgerald	16/1	6 5
	Lunar Sea (IRE) *EJO'Grady* 5-11-7 MrRPQuinlan[7]	16/1	1½ 6
	Springvic (IRE) *PCO'Connor* 5-11-9 MrROHarding[5]	10/1	3 7
	Touch Base (IRE) *SeanOO'Brien* 5-11-9 MrSOO'Brien[5]	12/1	8 8
	Supreme Invite (IRE) *MrsJHarrington* 5-11-2 MrRO'Sullivan[7]	10/1	2½ 9
	Bright May Meadows (IRE) *AnthonyJohnBlack* 5-11-2 MrCMotherway[7]	20/1	10 10
	Zululand (IRE) *DTHughes* 5-11-9 (t) MrRLoughran[5]	10/1	1½ 11
	Supreme Deal (IRE) *GerardJO'Keeffe* 5-11-9 MrPTobin[5]	14/1	5 12
	Sycamore House (IRE) *SNeville* 5-11-2 MrPMCloke[7]	20/1	dist 13
	Black Lightening (IRE) *TGO'Leary* 5-11-9 MrNPMadden	10/1	¾ 14
	Glencaraig Joy (IRE) *BrianNolan* 5-11-2 MrAMO'Brien[7]	20/1	2 15
	Zetec (IRE) *PMLynch* 5-11-7 MrPJO'Neill[7]	33/1	dist 16
	Alans Star (IRE) *PHughes* 5-11-4 MissEDoyle[5]	14/1	su
	Baltimore Hill (IRE) *WPMullins* 5-11-11 MrJJCodd[3]	12/1	pu
	Camlin River (IRE) *PAFahy* 5-12-0 MrPFahey	7/1	pu
	Vicar Street (IRE) *IKingston* 5-11-7 MrGMMangan[7]	33/1	pu

Mr J. J. Power 20ran 4m42.19

EXETER Sunday, Feb 13 HEAVY

116 totesport Nov Hdle (L) (A) (4yo+) £13,546 — 2m1f (7)

77	MY WAY DE SOLZEN (FR) *AKing* 5-11-9 RThornton	3/1		1
81	GIVE ME LOVE (FR) *PFNicholls* 5-11-11 (t) PJBrennan	33/1	27	2
77	MARCEL (FR) *MCPipe* 5-11-11 TJMurphy	1/2f	11	3
	Amarula Ridge (IRE) *PJHobbs* 4-10-7 APMcCoy	8/1	19	4
	Critical Stage (IRE) *JDFrost* 6-11-7 CHonour	40/1	25	5
	Katz Pyjamas (IRE) *GFHCharles-Jones* 4-10-0 EDehdashti	300/1		pu

B Winfield,A Longman,J Wright & C Fenton 6ran 4m33.82

NAVAN Sunday, Feb 13 HEAVY

117 Flyingbolt Nov Chase (Gr 2) (5yo+) £20,065 — 2m (10)

41	WATSON LAKE (IRE) *NMeade* 7-11-12 PCarberry	3/1		1
90	ULAAN BAATAR (IRE) *MrsJHarrington* 8-11-12 BJGeraghty	4/5f	20	2
101	STEEL BAND *PaulARoche* 7-11-4 JRBarry	8/1	25	3
	Kopoosha (IRE) *ALTMoore* 7-10-13 SPMcCann	66/1	dist	4
90	Scarthy Lad (IRE) *TGO'Leary* 7-11-4 RWalsh	4/1		f

Mr John Corr 5ran 4m30.59

118 Camlin (Pro-Am) INH Flat (4, 5, 6 and 7yo) £5,916 — 2m

66	TRAVINO (IRE) *MsMargaretMullins* 6-11-12 MrPCashman^{5}	4/5f		1
57	MISS TOULON (IRE) *PatrickMullins* 7-11-2 MrJJFeane^{7}	8/1	8	2
	TOMORROW'S DREAM (IRE) *MHalford* 7-12-0 MrAKWyse	8/1	20	3
	Patsy Hall (IRE) *SJMahon* 5-10-11 MrKBBowens^{7}	12/1	8	4
	You Sir (IRE) *JamesBowe* 5-11-4 SERyder^{7}	8/1	7	5
	The Fingersmith (IRE) *AJMcNamara* 6-11-11 MrKEPower^{3}	4/1	4	6
	Riverside Project (IRE) *EJO'Grady* 7-11-0 MrRPQuinlan^{7}	12/1	sh	7
66	Supreme Obsession (IRE) *WPMullins* 7-11-7 MsKWalsh^{7}	20/1	20	8
	Punta Cana (IRE) *DTHughes* 6-11-0 MrRMHennessy^{7}	20/1	20	9
	Getoutyoubowsey (IRE) *HRogers* 5-10-11 MrPOsborne^{7}	33/1	dist	10
	Rose Border (IRE) *JJCullen* 6-10-9 MrDKelly^{7}	33/1	½	11

Mr P. C. Kilroy 11ran 4m17.84

HAYDOCK Saturday, Feb 19 SOFT

119 Brit Insurance Prestige Nov Hdle (Gr 2) (A) (4yo+) £17,400 — 2m7f110y (12)

94	MEPHISTO (IRE) *JHowardJohnson* 6-11-4 TJMurphy	9/4		1
94	MOULIN RICHE (FR) *FDoumen,France* 5-11-11 MAFitzgerald	4/1	3	2
	TURPIN GREEN (IRE) *NGRichards* 6-11-8 RMcGrath	9/2	10	3
	Wild Cane Ridge (IRE) *LLungo* 6-11-4 ADobbin	2/1f	13	4
	Eskimo Pie (IRE) *CCBealby* 6-11-8 MrSMorris	12/1	dist	5

Andrea & Graham Wylie 5ran 5m56.80

120 Red Square Vodka Gold Cup Chase (Hcap) (Gr 3) (A) (148) (5yo+) £69,600 — 3½m110y (22)

32	FOREST GUNNER *RFord* 11-10-10^{135} PBuchanan^{3}	12/1		1
82	DOUBLE HONOUR (FR) *PJHobbs* 7-11-1^{137} (b) PJBrennan	10/1	1½	2
82	KELAMI (FR) *FDoumen,France* 7-10-8^{130} (t) MAFitzgerald	9/1	½	3
82	L'Aventure (FR) *PFNicholls* 6-10-12^{134} (b+t) RPMcNally	9/1	13	4
88	Truckers Tavern (IRE) *FerdyMurphy* 10-11-4^{147} (t) PCO'Neill^{7}	12/1	1½	5
82	Baron Windrush *NATwiston-Davies* 7-11-3^{139} CLlewellyn	7/2f	11	6
	Too Forward (IRE) *MPitman* 9-10-2^{124} ADobbin	5/1	4	7
82	Maximize (IRE) *MCPipe* 11-10-2^{131} AGlassonbury^{7}	50/1	½	8
88	Chives (IRE) *MrsSJSmith* 10-11-12^{148} DElsworth	10/1		pu
60	Control Man (IRE) *MCPipe* 7-11-5^{141} (v) TJMurphy	4/1		pu
86	Turnium (FR) *MScudamore* 10-10-13^{135} (v) JamesDavies	100/1		pu

Mr John Gilsenan 11ran 7m32.08

LINGFIELD Saturday, Feb 19 GOOD to SOFT

121 Telectronics Reynoldstown Nov Chase (Gr 2) (A) (5yo+) £20,300 — 3m (18)

60	DISTANT THUNDER (IRE) *RHAlner* 7-11-8 AThornton	6/4f		1
	PERSIAN WATERS (IRE) *JRFanshawe* 9-11-8 BJGeraghty	11/2	3	2
	DUNGARVANS CHOICE (IRE) *NJHenderson* 10-11-4 MFoley	9/1	6	3
	Brave Spirit (FR) *CLTizzard* 7-11-8 (s) TScudamore	8/1	nk	4
104	Le Passing (FR) *PFNicholls* 6-11-10 JTizzard	5/2	1½	5
	Hazeljack *AJWhiting* 10-11-4 TDoyle	100/1	dist	6

Old Moss Farm 6ran 6m19.57

122 totesport Ascot Chase (Gr 1) (A) (5yo+) £58,500 — 2½m110y (14)

74	IT TAKES TIME (IRE) *MCPipe* 11-11-7 JEMoore	14/1		1
105	OLLIE MAGERN *NATwiston-Davies* 7-11-7 AntonyEvans	4/1	2	2
88	HAND INN HAND *HDDaly* 9-11-7 MBradburne	10/3	2½	3

	Spring Grove (IRE) *RHAlner* 10-11-7 AThornton	25/1	18	4
	Iris's Gift *JonjoO'Neill* 8-11-7 BJGeraghty	3/1f	7	5
109	Murphy's Cardinal (IRE) *NoelTChance* 9-11-7 TDoyle	11/2		pu
96	Seebald (GER) *MCPipe* 10-11-7 TScudamore	6/1		pu

Mr D. A. Johnson 7ran 5m17.69

WINCANTON Saturday, Feb 19 GOOD to SOFT

123 Axminster Kingwell Hdle (Gr 2) (A) (4yo+) £37,700 — 2m (8)

86	INGLIS DREVER *JHowardJohnson* 6-11-10 APMcCoy	11/10f		1
61	PEROUSE *PFNicholls* 7-11-6 (t) ChristianWilliams	10/1	5	2
103	ROYAL SHAKESPEARE (FR) *SGollings* 6-11-6 JCulloty	11/2	1½	3
38	Rigmarole *PFNicholls* 7-11-10 (t) RWalsh	4/1	12	4
78	Torrid Kentavr (USA) *BEllison* 8-11-2 KRenwick	25/1	4	5
	Voy Por Ustedes (FR) *AKing* 4-10-11 RThornton	6/1	sh	6
	Barton Nic *DPKeane* 12-11-2 (b) NFehily	100/1	dist	7

Andrea & Graham Wylie 7ran 3m46.82

FONTWELL Sunday, Feb 20 GOOD to SOFT

124 totesport National Spirit Hdle (Gr 2) (A) (4yo+) £29,000 — 2½m (10)

87	BLUE CANYON (FR) *FDoumen,France* 7-11-12 APMcCoy	3/1		1
111	COPELAND *MCPipe* 10-11-8 (s) JEMoore	22/1	4	2
22	LE DUC (FR) *PFNicholls* 6-11-4 PJBrennan	8/1	sh	3
	Turtle Soup (IRE) *TRGeorge* 9-11-4 JMMaguire	9/1	15	4
103	Cool Roxy *AGBlackmore* 8-11-4 CHonour	66/1	¾	5
111	Geos (FR) *NJHenderson* 10-11-8 MAFitzgerald	9/2	½	6
	Big Moment *MrsAJPerrett* 7-11-4 LAspell	7/4f	2½	7
	Exotic Dancer (FR) *JonjoO'Neill* 5-11-8 SDurack	20/1	¾	8

Mr John P. McManus 8ran 5m15.20

NAAS Sunday, Feb 20 SOFT

125 Paddy & Helen Cox Memorial Newlands Chase (Gr 2) (5yo+) £29,183 — 2m (10)

93	CENTRAL HOUSE *DTHughes* 8-11-12 (b) PCarberry	4/7f		1
93	NATIVE UPMANSHIP (IRE) *ALTMoore* 12-11-12 CO'Dwyer	7/1	7	2
117	SCARTHY LAD (IRE) *TGO'Leary* 7-11-4 BJGeraghty	7/2	11	3
54	Macs Gildoran *WPMullins* 11-11-4 (t) RWalsh	8/1	15	4

Mr John F. Kenny 4ran 4m17.70

KEMPTON Saturday, Feb 26 SOFT

126 betfair.com Rendlesham Hdle (Gr 2) (A) (4yo+) £23,200 — 3m110y (12)

97	CRYSTAL D'AINAY (FR) *AKing* 6-11-12 (v) RThornton	5/2		1
97	MONET'S GARDEN (IRE) *NGRichards* 7-11-12 ADobbin	11/2	3½	2
97	ROYAL ROSA (FR) *JHowardJohnson* 6-11-8 APMcCoy	2/1f	6	3
97	Patriarch Express *MrsSJSmith* 8-11-12 DElsworth	11/4	30	4
97	Quick *MCPipe* 5-11-4 (v) TJMalone	22/1	dist	5

Mr Tony Fisher & Mrs Jeni Fisher 5ran 6m14.33

127 Racing Post Chase (Hcap) (Gr 3) (A) (152) (5yo+) £58,000 — 3m (19)

110	FARMER JACK *PJHobbs* 9-11-12^{152} RJohnson	5/1		1
	IZNOGOUD (FR) *MCPipe* 9-10-12^{138} TScudamore	20/1	6	2
	BANKER COUNT *MissVenetiaWilliams* 13-10-2^{128} SThomas	12/1	1¾	3
50	TIKRAM *GLMoore* 8-11-0^{140} APMcCoy	14/1	1¾	4
104	See You Sometime *JWMullins* 10-10-12^{138} AThornton	16/1	3	5
	Palarshan (FR) *HDDaly* 7-11-1^{141} MBradburne	9/1	1½	6
27	Horus (IRE) *MCPipe* 10-10-10^{141} TJMalone^{5}	20/1	9	7
53	Tribal Venture (FR) *FerdyMurphy* 7-10-13^{139} BHarding	7/1	4	8
	Zaffamore (IRE) *MissHCKnight* 9-10-2^{128} JCulloty	33/1	16	9
	Knock Down (IRE) *HDDaly* 6-10-11^{137} RThornton	50/1	8	10
50	Redemption *NATwiston-Davies* 10-11-3^{143} CLlewellyn	33/1	14	11
37	Gunther McBride (IRE) *PJHobbs* 10-10-11^{137} PJBrennan	10/1	15	12
	Colonel Frank *BGPowell* 8-11-4^{144} JPMcNamara	4/1f		f
87	Astonville (FR) *MScudamore* 11-11-2^{142} (v) BJCrowley	150/1		pu
74	Mondial Jack (FR) *MCPipe* 6-10-9^{135} (v) ADobbin	33/1		pu
	Be My Better Half (IRE) *ALTMoore,Ireland* 10-10-0^{126} DJCasey	9/1		pu

Mr Peter Partridge 16ran 6m08.06

128 Racing Post '100 Favourite Racehorses' Adonis Juv Nov Hdle (Gr 2) (A) (4yo) £16,240 — 2m (8)

	PENZANCE *AKing* 4-10-12 RThornton	10/11f		1
116	AMARULA RIDGE (IRE) *PJHobbs* 4-10-12 APMcCoy	13/2	7	2
99	ZALDA *PJHobbs* 4-10-9 RJohnson	11/2	1½	3

	Dubai Ace (USA) *MissSWest* 4-10-12 (t) JGoldstein	25/1	5	4
	Maclean *GLMoore* 4-10-12 PHide	20/1	15	5
	Innocent Rebel (USA) *AKing* 4-10-12 WMarston	50/1	¾	6
	Gift Voucher (IRE) *PRWebber* 4-10-12 TDoyle	13/2	3½	7
	Dunlea Dancer *PJHobbs* 4-10-12 PJBrennan	14/1	27	8

Elite Racing Club 8ran 4m04.74

KELSO Saturday, Mar 5 HEAVY

129 totesport Premier Kelso Hdle (Nov) (Gr 2) (A) (4yo+) £20,300 — 2¼m (10)

119	MEPHISTO (IRE) *JHowardJohnson* 6-11-9 WMarston	4/5f		1
	FAASEL (IRE) *NGRichards* 4-10-12 ADobbin	6/4	hd	2
67	HABITUAL DANCER *JeddO'Keeffe* 4-10-8 BHarding	12/1	25	3
	South Bronx (IRE) *MrsSCBradburne* 6-11-2 (t) KMercer	50/1	14	4
	Persian Point *MissSEForster* 9-11-2 MrCStorey	200/1	30	5
	Northern Echo *KSThomas* 8-11-2 (s) GThomas	300/1	dist	6
	Indy Mood *MrsHOGraham* 6-11-6 CEddery	40/1		ur
	Olympic Storm (IRE) *NWAlexander* 7-11-2 RMcGrath	500/1		pu
	Seeyaaj *MissLucindaVRussell* 5-11-2 (t) PBuchanan	66/1		pu

Andrea & Graham Wylie 9ran 4m37.60

NEWBURY Saturday, Mar 5 GOOD to SOFT

130 Vodafone Gold Cup Hcap Chase (L) (A) (156) (5yo+) £58,000 — 2½m (16)

	SUPREME PRINCE (IRE) *PJHobbs* 8-10-12^{142} PFlynn	7/1		1
127	HORUS (IRE) *MCPipe* 10-10-4^{139} (v) TJMalone^{5}	25/1	½	2
	CHAUVINIST (IRE) *NJHenderson* 10-10-8^{138} MAFitzgerald	11/2	2	3
27	Simply Gifted *JonjoO'Neill* 10-10-5^{135} JCulloty	50/1	1	4
122	Hand Inn Hand *HDDaly* 9-11-5^{149} MBradburne	8/1	hd	5
	Mouseski *PFNicholls* 11-10-13^{143} ChristianWilliams	25/1	hd	6
122	It Takes Time (IRE) *MCPipe* 11-11-9^{153} TJMurphy	11/1	1	7
50	Scots Grey *NJHenderson* 10-10-3^{133} ATinkler	16/1	1¼	8
124	Le Duc (FR) *PFNicholls* 6-10-8^{138} RWalsh	8/1	¾	9
	Buckby Lane *PRWebber* 9-10-10^{140} TDoyle	10/3f	¾	10
96	Turgeonev (FR) *TDEasterby* 10-11-5^{149} DO'Meara	25/1	dist	11
	Whereareyounow (IRE) *NATwiston-Davies* 8-10-7^{137} CLlewellyn	12/1	5	12
88	First Gold (FR) *FDoumen,France* 12-11-12^{156} (b) APMcCoy	14/1		pu
	Knife Edge (USA) *JonjoO'Neill* 10-11-1^{145} RJohnson	50/1		pu
	Venn Ottery *MCPipe* 10-11-1^{145} (t) TScudamore	14/1		pu

Mrs Karola Vann 15ran 4m59.60

SANDOWN Saturday, Mar 12 GOOD to SOFT

131 European Breeders Fund Sunderlands NH Nov Hcap Hdle Final (Gr 3) (A) (130) (4, 5, 6 and 7yo) £34,800 — 2½m110y (9)

	JULIUS CAESAR *JHowardJohnson* 5-10-12^{116} GLee	18/1		1
	BILLYVODDAN (IRE) *HDDaly* 6-11-3^{121} RJohnson	15/2	hd	2
72	REBEL RHYTHM *MrsSJSmith* 6-11-12^{130} DElsworth	8/1	2	3
	CORNISH SETT (IRE) *PFNicholls* 6-11-7^{125} RWalsh	10/3f	2½	4
58	King Killone (IRE) *MissHCKnight* 5-11-0^{118} JCulloty	9/1	6	5
	Alderburn *HDDaly* 6-11-6^{124} MBradburne	33/1	½	6
	Florida Dream (IRE) *NATwiston-Davies* 6-10-11^{115} CLlewellyn	18/1	28	7
	Quid Pro Quo (FR) *PFNicholls* 6-11-0^{118} APMcCoy	20/1	½	8
	Without A Doubt *MPitman* 6-11-4^{122} NFehily	25/1	1	9
	One Cornetto (IRE) *LWells* 6-10-9^{113} LAspell	50/1	1¼	10
	Good Citizen (IRE) *TRGeorge* 5-10-11^{115} JMMaguire	25/1	11	11
111	Escompteur (FR) *MCPipe* 5-11-11^{129} TJMurphy	16/1	2	12
	The Listener (IRE) *RHAlner* 6-11-10^{128} AThornton	6/1		su
	Lord Olympia (IRE) *MissVenetiaWilliams* 6-11-3^{121} SThomas	18/1		pu
	Muhtenbar *MissHCKnight* 5-11-1^{119} JAMcCarthy	33/1		pu
	Classic Capers *JMJefferson* 6-10-13^{117} JCrowley	28/1		pu
	Lord Buckingham *NJHenderson* 7-10-11^{115} (t) MAFitzgerald	25/1		pu
	Medici (FR) *MsBridgetNicholls* 7-10-8^{112} RThornton	25/1		pu

Jack Coupe and John Thompson 18ran 5m04.60

132 Sunderlands Imperial Cup Hcap Hdle (L) (A) 0-150(143) (4yo+) £34,800 — 2m110y (8)

	MEDISON (FR) *MCPipe* 5-10-1^{118} TJMurphy	9/2f		1
111	FENIX (GER) *MrsLWadham* 6-10-8^{125} (b) LAspell	12/1	3½	2
111	MONTE CINTO (FR) *PFNicholls* 5-10-10^{127} RWalsh	14/1	6	3
	CROSSBOW CREEK *MGRimell* 7-11-3^{134} GLee	10/1	hd	4
	After Eight (GER) *MissVenetiaWilliams* 5-10-6^{123} JCulloty	25/1	nk	5
	All Star (GER) *NJHenderson* 5-10-0^{117} ATinkler	20/1	7	6
78	Winsley *OSherwood* 7-9-12^{120} ONelmes^{5}	20/1	1	7

	Stance *GLMoore* 6-11-2^{133} DGallagher	6/1	2½ 8
	McBain (USA) *PJHobbs* 6-10-3^{125} RStephens^{5}	20/1	hd 9
	Nathos (GER) *CJMann* 8-9-13^{121} SJCraine^{5}	100/1	4 10
	Far Pavilions *GASwinbank* 6-10-12^{129} JCrowley	6/1	¾ 11
	Papillon de Iena (FR) *MCPipe* 5-10-2^{119} (v) TScudamore	22/1	1½ 12
	Chockdee (FR) *PFNicholls* 5-10-6^{123} ChristianWilliams	40/1	½ 13
	King Eider *BEllison* 6-10-6^{123} SThomas	12/1	hd 14
62	Hot Shots (FR) *MPitman* 10-11-4^{135} NFehily	33/1	13 15
	Kalca Mome (FR) *PJHobbs* 7-11-0^{131} RJohnson	16/1	13 16
	Visibility (FR) *MCPipe* 6-10-5^{127} (v) TJMalone^{5}	66/1	4 17
	Bold Bishop (IRE) *JonjoO'Neill* 8-11-12^{143} APMcCoy	20/1	pu
	Telimar Prince (IRE) *AKing* 9-10-13^{130} RThornton	25/1	pu

Mr D. A. Johnson 19ran 4m01.72

CHELTENHAM Tuesday, Mar 15
GOOD (Old course), Cross-country course: GOOD to SOFT

133 Letheby & Christopher Supreme Nov Hdle (Gr 1) (A) (4yo+) 2m110y (8)
£58,000

61	ARCALIS *JHowardJohnson* 5-11-7 GLee	20/1	1
77	WILD PASSION (GER) *NMeade,Ireland* 5-11-7 PCarberry	10/1	6 2
	DUSKY WARBLER *GLMoore* 6-11-7 JEMoore	20/1	½ 3
	Prins Willem (IRE) *JRFanshawe* 6-11-7 (t) APMcCoy	20/1	4 4
	Aleron (IRE) *JJQuinn* 7-11-7 RGarritty	150/1	sh 5
77	Chilling Place (IRE) *PJHobbs* 6-11-7 RJohnson	9/1	1¼ 6
57	Publican (IRE) *PAFahy,Ireland* 5-11-7 RWalsh	9/1	hd 7
100	Justified (IRE) *ESheehy,Ireland* 6-11-7 JRBarry	7/1	1½ 8
100	Akshar (IRE) *DKWeld,Ireland* 6-11-7 BJGeraghty	14/1	3 9
58	Manorson (IRE) *OSherwood* 6-11-7 JAMcCarthy	22/1	1¾ 10
	Stan (NZ) *RCGuest* 6-11-7 HOliver	200/1	10 11
44	Shuhood (USA) *PRWebber* 5-11-7 TDoyle	33/1	3 12
116	Marcel (FR) *MCPipe* 5-11-7 TJMurphy	13/2f	hd 13
	Cherub (GER) *JonjoO'Neill* 5-11-7 (t) MAFitzgerald	33/1	10 14
116	My Way de Solzen (FR) *AKing* 5-11-7 RThornton	8/1	8 15
	Akhtari (IRE) *DTHughes,Ireland* 5-11-7 CO'Dwyer	33/1	½ 16
	Villon (IRE) *LLungo* 6-11-7 ADobbin	16/1	9 17
	Perfect Storm *MCPipe* 6-11-7 (t) TScudamore	66/1	13 18
	Only Vintage (USA) *MissHCKnight* 5-11-7 JCulloty	12/1	6 19
	Madiba *PHowling* 6-11-7 SDurack	400/1	3 20

Andrea & Graham Wylie 20ran 3m53.02

134 Irish Independent Arkle Challenge Trophy Chase (Gr 1) (A) (5yo+) 2m (12)
£81,200

89	CONTRABAND *MCPipe* 7-11-7 TJMurphy	7/1	1
104	ASHLEY BROOK (IRE) *KBishop* 7-11-7 PJBrennan	20/1	1 2
1	RIVER CITY (IRE) *NoelTChance* 8-11-7 TDoyle	10/1	4 3
117	Watson Lake (IRE) *NMeade,Ireland* 7-11-7 PCarberry	17/2	1½ 4
89	My Will (FR) *PFNicholls* 5-11-2 RWalsh	12/1	nk 5
63	Mariah Rollins (IRE) *PAFahy,Ireland* 7-11-0 DJCasey	14/1	4 6
	War of Attrition (IRE) *MFMorris,Ireland* 6-11-7 CO'Dwyer	11/4f	3 7
46	Made In Japan (JPN) *PJHobbs* 5-11-2 RJohnson	16/1	6 8
90	Ned Kelly (IRE) *EJO'Grady,Ireland* 9-11-7 DNRussell	12/1	½ 9
117	Ulaan Baatar (IRE) *MrsJHarrington,Ireland* 8-11-7 BJGeraghty	12/1	11 10
90	Sir Oj (IRE) *NMeade,Ireland* 8-11-7 (b) MAFitzgerald	25/1	1 11
89	Mondul (GER) *MFHarris* 5-11-2 SDurack	100/1	4 12
	Town Crier (IRE) *MrsSJSmith* 10-11-7 DElsworth	50/1	5 13
	Mambo Des Mottes (FR) *MissVenetiaWilliams* 5-11-2 AO'Keeffe	100/1	5 14
46	The Last Cast *HMorrison* 6-11-7 TScudamore	66/1	9 15
117	Steel Band *PaulARoche,Ireland* 7-11-7 GTHutchinson	66/1	1½ 16
	Supreme Developer (IRE) *FerdyMurphy* 8-11-7 (s) BHarding	50/1	24 17
89	Kadount (FR) *AKing* 7-11-7 RThornton	20/1	ur
	Limerick Boy (GER) *MissVenetiaWilliams* 7-11-7 SThomas	20/1	pu

Mr D. A. Johnson 19ran 3m53.08

135 Smurfit Champion Hdle Challenge Trophy (Gr 1) (A) (4yo+) 2m110y (8)
£174,000

91	HARDY EUSTACE (IRE) *DTHughes,Ireland* 8-11-10 (b) CO'Dwyer	7/2jf	1
61	HARCHIBALD (FR) *NMeade,Ireland* 6-11-10 PCarberry	7/1	nk 2
91	BRAVE INCA (IRE) *CAMurphy,Ireland* 7-11-10 BMCash	10/1	nk 3
91	Accordion Etoile (IRE) *PaulNolan,Ireland* 6-11-10 JCullen	14/1	3 4
91	Macs Joy (IRE) *MrsJHarrington,Ireland* 6-11-10 BJGeraghty	7/1	1½ 5
38	Intersky Falcon *JonjoO'Neill* 8-11-10 (b+t) ADobbin	40/1	½ 6
111	Al Eile (IRE) *JQueally,Ireland* 5-11-10 TJMurphy	25/1	2 7

103	Rooster Booster *PJHobbs* 11-11-10 RJohnson	16/1	3	8
51	Back In Front (IRE) *EJO'Grady,Ireland* 8-11-10 RWalsh	7/2jf	nk	9
103	Self Defense *PRChamings* 8-11-10 RThornton	20/1	1¾	10
123	Royal Shakespeare (FR) *SGollings* 6-11-10 JCulloty	50/1	3	11
111	Essex (IRE) *MJPO'Brien,Ireland* 5-11-10 APMcCoy	9/1	3	12
127	Astonville (FR) *MScudamore* 11-11-10 TScudamore	500/1	17	13
120	Turnium (FR) *MScudamore* 10-11-10 JamesDavies	500/1	20	14

Mr Laurence Byrne 14ran 3m51.40

136 William Hill Trophy Hcap Chase (Gr 3) (A) (157) (5yo+) £46,400 3m110y (19)

120	KELAMI (FR) *FDoumen,France* 7-10-2^{133} (t) RThornton	8/1		1
27	KEEN LEADER (IRE) *JonjoO'Neill* 9-11-12^{157} BJGeraghty	28/1	1¼	2
	IRISH HUSSAR (IRE) *NJHenderson* 9-11-7^{152} MAFitzgerald	33/1	2	3
120	CHIVES (IRE) *MrsSJSmith* 10-11-3^{148} DElsworth	50/1	¾	4
	Jakari (FR) *HDDaly* 8-10-8^{139} RJohnson	25/1	2	5
127	Tikram *GLMoore* 8-10-9^{140} APMcCoy	6/1	1¾	6
122	Spring Grove (IRE) *RHAlner* 10-10-4^{135} AThornton	25/1	1¼	7
	Kock de La Vesvre (FR) *MissVenetiaWilliams* 7-10-3^{134} SThomas	50/1	5	8
	Iris Bleu (FR) *MCPipe* 9-10-9^{140} TJMurphy	11/2f	¾	9
49	Swansea Bay *PBowen* 9-10-1^{132} (s+t) LAspell	33/1	7	10
	Marlborough (IRE) *NJHenderson* 13-11-5^{150} MFoley	66/1	½	11
	Hussard Collonges (FR) *PBeaumont* 10-11-0^{145} RGarritty	33/1	2½	12
74	Frenchman's Creek *HMorrison* 11-10-7^{138} PCarberry	10/1	15	13
130	Whereareyounow (IRE) *NATwiston-Davies* 8-10-6^{137} CLlewellyn	20/1	5	14
47	Blazing Batman *DrPPritchard* 12-9-9^{131} DrPPritchard^{5}	250/1	29	15
45	Colourful Life (IRE) *PFNicholls* 9-10-8^{139} RWalsh	7/1		f
113	Ballybough Rasher (IRE) *JHowardJohnson* 10-11-2^{147} GLee	33/1		pu
49	Joly Bey (FR) *NJGifford* 8-10-13^{147} (t) MrDHDunsdon^{3}	13/2		pu
81	Heros Collonges (FR) *PFNicholls* 10-10-12^{143} ChristianWilliams	10/1		pu
45	Native Emperor *JonjoO'Neill* 9-10-3^{134} ADobbin	25/1		pu

Halewood International Ltd 20ran 6m08.62

137 Sporting Index Hcap Chase (Cross Country) (B) (143) (5yo+) £23,200 3m7f (32)

20	SPOT THEDIFFERENCE (IRE) *EBolger,Ireland* 12-11-12^{143} MrJTMcNamara	4/1		1
20	LUZCADOU (FR) *FerdyMurphy* 12-10-13^{130} (b) AO'Keeffe	22/1	2½	2
	MRS BE (IRE) *JGCann* 9-9-12^{118} MissPGundry^{3}	20/1	6	3
74	LORD NOELIE (IRE) *MsBridgetNicholls* 12-11-8^{139} JMMaguire	14/1	¾	4
	Village King (IRE) *PJHobbs* 12-10-8^{125} RJohnson	9/1	7	5
	French Executive (IRE) *PFNicholls* 10-10-13^{130} PJBrennan	15/2	5	6
	Andrewjames (IRE) *PDMcCreery,Ireland* 11-10-0^{117} DJCasey	12/1	11	7
34	Smarty (IRE) *MPitman* 12-10-0^{117} TJMurphy	20/1	12	8
74	Un Jour A Vassy (FR) *PFNicholls* 10-10-9^{126} ChristianWilliams	16/1	13	9
	Majed (FR) *MrsLBNormile* 9-10-0^{117} (b) NMulholland	33/1	20	10
	Gun'n Roses II (FR) *DPKeane* 11-10-11^{128} (b) NFehily	14/1		f
20	Comanche War Paint (IRE) *PFNicholls* 8-10-3^{120} RWalsh	10/3f		f
	Wild Tempo (FR) *MScudamore* 10-11-2^{133} TScudamore	100/1		ur
	Just Maybe (IRE) *MissVenetiaWilliams* 11-10-6^{123} (v) SThomas	40/1		ur
	Galapiat du Mesnil (FR) *PFNicholls* 11-10-8^{125} JTizzard	33/1		pu
20	Famfoni (FR) *KCBailey* 12-10-0^{117} JCulloty	25/1		pu

Mr John P. McManus 16ran 8m43.81

138 Fred Winter Juv Nov Hcap Hdle (L) (A) (127) (4yo) £43,500 2m110y (8)

106	DABIROUN (IRE) *PaulNolan,Ireland* 4-11-4^{124} MissNCarberry^{5}	20/1		1
	AT YOUR REQUEST *IanWilliams* 4-11-3^{118} DRDennis	33/1	8	2
	NATION STATE *GLMoore* 4-11-4^{119} (s) JEMoore	7/1	1½	3
99	MISS ACADEMY (FR) *MCPipe* 4-11-12^{127} TJMurphy	16/1	1¾	4
67	Arrayou (FR) *OSherwood* 4-10-12^{113} (v) CO'Dwyer	50/1	hd	5
	Alikat (IRE) *MCPipe* 4-10-6^{112} TJMalone^{5}	25/1	sh	6
128	Zalda *PJHobbs* 4-11-1^{116} RJohnson	25/1	4	7
128	Amarula Ridge (IRE) *PJHobbs* 4-11-3^{118} APMcCoy	9/1	sh	8
99	Napolitain (FR) *PFNicholls* 4-11-10^{125} ChristianWilliams	22/1	1¼	9
	Rolling Home (IRE) *NMeade,Ireland* 4-11-3^{118} (b) PCarberry	25/1	2½	10
106	Dalton (FR) *EJO'Grady,Ireland* 4-11-3^{118} DNRussell	33/1	sh	11
	Daryal (IRE) *AKing* 4-11-1^{116} RThornton	13/2	1	12
99	Beauchamp Prince (IRE) *MScudamore* 4-11-0^{115} TScudamore	66/1	1¾	13
	Ease The Way *DKWeld,Ireland* 4-10-13^{114} (b) DJCasey	4/1f	nk	14
	Mr Dinglawi (IRE) *DBFeek* 4-11-0^{115} JamesDavies	50/1	2½	15
128	Dubai Ace (USA) *MissSWest* 4-10-10^{111} (t) JGoldstein	66/1	1¾	16
	La Lambertine (FR) *MCPipe* 4-11-2^{117} (v) GSupple	33/1	½	17
	Redi (ITY) *AMBalding* 4-10-13^{114} (t) BJGeraghty	11/1	1	18
67	Woody Valentine (USA) *MissVenetiaWilliams* 4-11-2^{117} SThomas	33/1	2	19

	Stromstad (IRE) *SJMahon,Ireland* 4-11-7^{125} (b) JPElliott^{3}	33/1	14 20
	Regal Setting (IRE) *JHowardJohnson* 4-11-3^{118} (t) GLee	16/1	15 21
23	Fire Dragon (IRE) *JonjoO'Neill* 4-11-4^{119} (b+t) ADobbin	25/1	3 22
	Papini (IRE) *NJHenderson* 4-11-10^{125} MAFitzgerald	10/1	½ 23
128	Dunlea Dancer *PJHobbs* 4-11-1^{116} (t) PJBrennan	100/1	8 24

Donal O'Gorman 24ran 3m53.99

CHELTENHAM Wednesday, Mar 16 GOOD (Old Course)

139 Royal & SunAlliance Nov Hdle (Gr 1) (A) (4yo+) £58,000 — 2m5f (10)

81	NO REFUGE (IRE) *JHowardJohnson* 5-11-7 GLee	17/2	1
	RACING DEMON (IRE) *MissHCKnight* 5-11-7 JCulloty	14/1	¾ 2
56	OUR BEN *WPMullins,Ireland* 6-11-7 RWalsh	33/1	2½ 3
	Pole Star *JRFanshawe* 7-11-7 RThornton	12/1	sh 4
58	Gold Medallist *PJHobbs* 5-11-7 RJohnson	9/2jf	nk 5
	Reveillez *JRFanshawe* 6-11-7 APMcCoy	9/1	nk 6
107	Royal Paradise (FR) *ThomasFoley,Ireland* 5-11-7 MAFitzgerald	9/2jf	7 7
107	Black Apalachi (IRE) *PJRothwell,Ireland* 6-11-7 JCullen	33/1	9 8
113	Snoopy Loopy (IRE) *MissVScott* 7-11-7 ChristianWilliams	200/1	nk 9
58	Secret Ploy *HMorrison* 5-11-7 BJGeraghty	16/1	nk 10
	Red Georgie (IRE) *NATwiston-Davies* 7-11-7 CLlewellyn	100/1	1¼ 11
	Queen Astrid (IRE) *DKWeld,Ireland* 5-11-0 PCarberry	8/1	hd 12
	Inch Pride (IRE) *MCPipe* 6-11-0 TJMurphy	33/1	1 13
	Court Leader (IRE) *ThomasMullins,Ireland* 7-11-0 RMPower	200/1	8 14
	Olaso (GER) *JonjoO'Neill* 6-11-7 DJCasey	33/1	¾ 15
	Forager *MJRyan* 6-11-7 SDurack	25/1	7 16
	Bagan (FR) *CJMann* 6-11-7 NFehily	16/1	¾ 17
	Darkness *CREgerton* 6-11-7 (b) JAMcCarthy	66/1	2 18
111	Roman Ark *JMJefferson* 7-11-7 ADobbin	25/1	2½ 19
	Regents Walk (IRE) *BDeHaan* 7-11-7 LAspell	66/1	27 20

Andrea & Graham Wylie 20ran 5m00.16

140 Royal & SunAlliance Chase (Gr 1) (A) (5yo+) £81,200 — 3m110y (19)

60	TRABOLGAN (IRE) *NJHenderson* 7-11-4 MAFitzgerald	5/1	1
39	COMPLY OR DIE (IRE) *MCPipe* 6-11-4 TJMurphy	3/1f	3 2
95	CORNISH REBEL (IRE) *PFNicholls* 8-11-4 RWalsh	9/2	3 3
60	L'Ami (FR) *FDoumen,France* 6-11-4 RThornton	4/1	hd 4
63	Like-A-Butterfly (IRE) *CRoche,Ireland* 11-10-11 APMcCoy	9/1	2½ 5
121	Brave Spirit (FR) *CLTizzard* 7-11-4 (s) JTizzard	33/1	dist 6
127	Tribal Venture (FR) *FerdyMurphy* 7-11-4 BHarding	10/1	f
60	Backbeat (IRE) *JHowardJohnson* 8-11-4 GLee	16/1	pu
	Light Des Mulottes (FR) *CREgerton* 6-11-4 (b) JAMcCarthy	100/1	pu

Mr Trevor Hemmings 9ran 6m12.63

141 Queen Mother Champion Chase (Gr 1) (A) (5yo+) £145,000 — 2m (12)

101	MOSCOW FLYER (IRE) *MrsJHarrington,Ireland* 11-11-10 BJGeraghty	6/4f	1
112	WELL CHIEF (GER) *MCPipe* 6-11-10 TJMurphy	7/2	2 2
112	AZERTYUIOP (FR) *PFNicholls* 8-11-10 RWalsh	2/1	13 3
102	Oneway (IRE) *MGRimell* 8-11-10 GLee	16/1	7 4
112	Kadarann (IRE) *PFNicholls* 8-11-10 PJBrennan	100/1	7 5
125	Central House *DTHughes,Ireland* 8-11-10 (b) PCarberry	25/1	4 6
130	Venn Ottery *MCPipe* 10-11-10 (t) JEMoore	50/1	1½ 7
102	Cenkos (FR) *PFNicholls* 11-11-10 JTizzard	100/1	pu

Mr Brian Kearney 8ran 3m54.37

142 Coral Cup (Hcap Hdle) (Gr 3) (A) (147) (5yo+) £43,500 — 2m5f (10)

111	IDOLE FIRST (IRE) *MissVenetiaWilliams* 6-10-10^{131} AO'Keeffe	33/1	1
1	DANCING BAY *NJHenderson* 8-11-1^{136} MAFitzgerald	14/1	5 2
	TUMBLING DICE (IRE) *TJTaaffe,Ireland* 6-11-1^{136} BJGeraghty	16/1	6 3
	COVENT GARDEN *JHowardJohnson* 7-10-7^{128} ADobbin	14/1	5 4
132	After Eight (GER) *MissVenetiaWilliams* 5-10-2^{123} SThomas	33/1	nk 5
	Fairwood Present (IRE) *PJRothwell,Ireland* 7-10-7^{128} JCullen	25/1	1¼ 6
	Royaleety (FR) *IanWilliams* 6-10-10^{131} DRDennis	50/1	½ 7
	Fountain Hill (IRE) *PFNicholls* 6-11-2^{137} PJBrennan	12/1	¾ 8
	Distant Prospect (IRE) *AMBalding* 8-10-8^{129} APMcCoy	10/3f	½ 9
	Lilium de Cotte (FR) *NJHenderson* 6-10-4^{125} ATinkler	100/1	2 10
	Supreme Serenade (IRE) *PJHobbs* 6-11-2^{137} PFlynn	10/1	7 11
87	Mythical King (IRE) *RLee* 8-10-9^{130} RThornton	66/1	hd 12
79	Top Strategy (IRE) *TMWalsh,Ireland* 5-11-1^{136} (b) RWalsh	20/1	1¼ 13
	Spring Pursuit *EGBevan* 9-10-8^{129} ChristianWilliams	50/1	2½ 14
97	Lough Derg (FR) *MCPipe* 5-11-12^{147} TScudamore	40/1	6 15
4	Ansar (IRE) *DKWeld,Ireland* 9-11-7^{142} (b) DJCasey	33/1	1½ 16
111	Zibeline (IRE) *BEllison* 8-11-0^{135} (t) NFehily	50/1	4 17

	You Owe Me (IRE) *NATwiston-Davies* 8-10-4^{125} CLlewellyn	66/1	½ 18
116	Give Me Love (FR) *PFNicholls* 5-10-2^{123} (t) RPMcNally	66/1	7 19
113	Omni Cosmo Touch (USA) *MrsSJSmith* 9-10-7^{128} DElsworth	25/1	5 20
94	Royal Hector (GER) *MCPipe* 6-10-3^{129} (v) TJMalone^{5}	33/1	4 21
59	Ilnamar (FR) *MCPipe* 9-11-4^{139} (v) TJMurphy	12/1	15 22
	Red Ruffles (IRE) *NoelTChance* 6-10-5^{126} TDoyle	33/1	12 23
	Ebinzayd (IRE) *LLungo* 9-10-9^{135} GBerridge^{5}	50/1	5 24
	Anatar (IRE) *MCPipe* 7-10-4^{125} JEMoore	25/1	dist 25
111	Sharp Rigging (IRE) *AMHales* 5-10-7^{128} JAMcCarthy	66/1	f
16	Mr Fluffy *PJHobbs* 8-9-11^{123} RStephens^{5}	50/1	ur
	Kasthari (IRE) *JHowardJohnson* 6-11-5^{140} GLee	14/1	pu
1	Jack Dawson (IRE) *JohnBerry* 8-11-2^{137} JCulloty	20/1	pu

Direct Sales UK Ltd 29ran 5m04.56

143 Fulke Walwyn Kim Muir Challenge Cup Hcap Chase (Amat) (B) 0-140(133) (5yo+) £29,000 — 3m110y (19)

	JUVEIGNEUR (FR) *NJHenderson* 8-11-7^{128} MrRBurton	12/1	1
37	LORD OF THE RIVER (IRE) *NJHenderson* 13-11-5^{126} MrAFitzgerald	50/1	1¼ 2
	PARSONS LEGACY (IRE) *PJHobbs* 7-11-6^{127} MrDerekO'Connor	16/1	1 3
121	PERSIAN WATERS (IRE) *JRFanshawe* 9-11-12^{133} MrTGreenall	11/1	6 4
	Bee An Bee (IRE) *TRGeorge* 8-10-10^{117} (b) MrDHDunsdon	25/1	6 5
	Lou du Moulin Mas (FR) *PFNicholls* 6-10-11^{121} (t) MrCJSweeney^{3}	8/1	nk 6
127	Knock Down (IRE) *HDDaly* 6-11-6^{130} MrAWintle^{3}	100/1	5 7
65	Oh Be The Hokey (IRE) *CFSwan,Ireland* 7-11-3^{124} MrJTMcNamara	9/2f	hd 8
74	Smile Pleeze (IRE) *MSheppard* 13-11-0^{121} (s) MissPGundry	50/1	2½ 9
	Ulusaba *FerdyMurphy* 9-10-7^{117} (s) MrTJDreaper^{3}	14/1	14 10
	Rathbawn Prince (IRE) *MissHCKnight* 13-10-9^{123} MrJJarrett^{7}	33/1	9 11
	Carryonharry (IRE) *MCPipe* 11-10-9^{123} (v) AGlassonbury^{7}	50/1	hd 12
120	Maximize (IRE) *MCPipe* 11-11-5^{131} MrDEdwards^{5}	20/1	2½ 13
17	Montreal (FR) *MCPipe* 8-10-11^{125} MrRQuinn^{7}	33/1	1 14
	Koquelicot (FR) *PJHobbs* 7-10-10^{124} MrTJO'Brien^{7}	16/1	½ 15
	Indalo (IRE) *MissVenetiaWilliams* 10-11-2^{123} MrNWilliams	10/1	24 16
	The Bushkeeper (IRE) *NJHenderson* 11-10-13^{125} MrBKing^{5}	16/1	f
	Latitude (FR) *MCPipe* 6-10-10^{124} MrGWeatherley^{7}	66/1	f
	Pearly Jack *DEFitzgerald,Ireland* 7-10-8^{118} MrMJO'Connor^{3}	16/1	bd
11	Bold Investor *JonjoO'Neill* 8-11-11^{132} MrKEPower	66/1	ur
	The Bandit (IRE) *MissECLavelle* 8-11-9^{130} MrRWidger	14/1	pu
9	Heart Midoltian (FR) *MCPipe* 8-11-5^{126} (v+t) MrGordonElliott	14/1	pu
	Itsonlyme (IRE) *MissVenetiaWilliams* 12-10-11^{125} MrRMcCarthy^{7}	50/1	pu
	Champagne Harry *NATwiston-Davies* 7-10-3^{117} MrGTumelty^{7}	40/1	pu

Mr Trevor Hemmings 24ran 6m16.78

144 Weatherbys Champion Bumper (Standard Open NHF) (Gr 1) (A) (4, 5 and 6yo) £23,200 — 2m110y

	MISSED THAT *WPMullins,Ireland* 6-11-5 RWalsh	7/2f	1
114	DE SOTO *PRWebber* 4-10-12 TDoyle	20/1	nk 2
	RASHARROW (IRE) *LLungo* 6-11-5 ADobbin	9/1	¾ 3
	Refinement (IRE) *JonjoO'Neill* 6-10-12 KFallon	6/1	3½ 4
	Clew Bay Cove (IRE) *CAMurphy,Ireland* 5-11-5 (t) PCarberry	40/1	½ 5
	Buena Vista (IRE) *MCPipe* 4-10-12 JPSpencer	33/1	1¼ 6
	Itsmyboy (IRE) *MCPipe* 5-11-5 TJMurphy	12/1	1¼ 7
	Mister Top Notch (IRE) *DEFitzgerald,Ireland* 6-11-5 MrMJO'Connor	66/1	1½ 8
	Eye On The Ball *MFMorris,Ireland* 6-11-5 CO'Dwyer	20/1	2 9
	Oscar's Advance (IRE) *CRoche,Ireland* 6-11-5 FMBerry	33/1	9 10
	Karaghan (IRE) *SJMahon,Ireland* 5-11-5 (t) MrKBowens	100/1	sh 11
	High Tech Made (FR) *CREgerton* 5-11-5 JAMcCarthy	33/1	nk 12
114	Wee Robbie *NJGifford* 5-11-5 LAspell	100/1	3½ 13
	Tiddle About (IRE) *JTGorman,Ireland* 4-10-5 RHughes	50/1	½ 14
83	Lennon (IRE) *JHowardJohnson* 5-11-5 GLee	14/1	4 15
	Beautiful Vision (IRE) *TJTaaffe,Ireland* 5-11-5 BJGeraghty	20/1	2 16
	Yaboya (IRE) *PJHobbs* 6-11-5 APMcCoy	16/1	¾ 17
114	Oscardeal (IRE) *CTPogson* 6-11-5 APogson	100/1	1¼ 18
	Nice Horse (FR) *MCPipe* 4-10-12 JEMoore	33/1	½ 19
83	Mister Quasimodo *CLTizzard* 5-11-5 JTizzard	40/1	7 20
	Snakebite (IRE) *MPitman* 5-11-5 SDurack	50/1	18 21
	There Is No Doubt (FR) *MrsHMBridges* 4-10-12 MissLucyBridges	66/1	21 22
114	Karanja *VRADartnall* 6-11-5 MissNCarberry	5/1	ur
26	The Mick Weston *RTPhillips* 6-11-5 RJohnson	12/1	ur

Mrs V. O'Leary 24ran 3m52.65

CHELTENHAM Thursday, Mar 17 GOOD (New Course)

145 Jewson Nov Hcap Chase (L) (A) (143) (5yo+) £46,400 — 2m5f (17)

105	KING HARALD (IRE) *MBradstock* 7-10-4^{123} MBatchelor	9/1	1

104	LACDOUDAL (FR) *PJHobbs* 6-11-10[143] RJohnson	12/1	4 2
127	SEE YOU SOMETIME *JWMullins* 10-11-3[136] AThornton	12/1	5 3
134	SIR OJ (IRE) *NMeade,Ireland* 8-10-11[130] (b) PCarberry	18/1	1¾ 4
121	Le Passing (FR) *PFNicholls* 6-11-10[143] RWalsh	22/1	12 5
	Eric's Charm (FR) *OSherwood* 7-11-5[138] LAspell	20/1	1¾ 6
60	Quazar (IRE) *JonjoO'Neill* 7-11-6[139] (t) APMcCoy	14/1	3 7
105	St Matthew (USA) *MrsSJSmith* 7-11-1[134] DElsworth	80/1	½ 8
	Liverpool Echo (FR) *HDDaly* 5-10-6[130] MBradburne	11/1	8 9
	Sonevafushi (FR) *MissVenetiaWilliams* 7-11-0[133] SThomas	50/1	nk 10
85	Bizet (IRE) *FFlood,Ireland* 9-10-6[125] JCullen	10/1	8 11
	Tana River (IRE) *MissECLavelle* 9-11-0[133] NFehily	16/1	14 12
	Ball O Malt (IRE) *RAFahey* 9-10-1[123] PWhelan[3]	25/1	f
	Big Rob (IRE) *BGPowell* 6-10-4[123] JTizzard	16/1	f
	Copsale Lad *NJHenderson* 8-10-7[126] MFoley	25/1	bd
	Graphic Approach (IRE) *CREgerton* 7-10-12[131] JAMcCarthy	25/1	ur
	Captain Corelli *MPitman* 8-10-12[131] TJMurphy	8/1f	pu
95	Joes Edge (IRE) *FerdyMurphy* 8-10-8[127] BHarding	9/1	pu
71	Sleep Bal (FR) *NJHenderson* 6-11-5[138] MAFitzgerald	14/1	pu

Piers Pottinger and P B-J Partnership 19ran 5m12.20

146 Daily Telegraph Festival Trophy Chase (Gr 2) (A) (5yo+) £87,000 — 2m5f (17)

96	THISTHATANDTOTHER (IRE) *PFNicholls* 9-11-3 RWalsh	9/2	1
62	FONDMORT (FR) *NJHenderson* 9-11-0 MAFitzgerald	9/1	½ 2
93	RATHGAR BEAU (IRE) *ESheehy,Ireland* 9-11-3 JRBarry	9/2	2½ 3
130	Hand Inn Hand *HDDaly* 9-11-5 MBradburne	20/1	3½ 4
62	Le Roi Miguel (FR) *PFNicholls* 7-11-3 BJGeraghty	10/1	5 5
71	Mixsterthetrixster (USA) *MrsTraceyBarfoot-Saunt* 9-11-0 JTizzard	200/1	dist 6
4	Risk Accessor (IRE) *CRoche,Ireland* 10-11-0 (t) APMcCoy	25/1	f
62	Edredon Bleu (FR) *MissHCKnight* 13-11-5 (t) JCulloty	33/1	pu
125	Native Upmanship (IRE) *ALTMoore,Ireland* 12-11-3 CO'Dwyer	33/1	pu
50	Our Vic (IRE) *MCPipe* 7-11-3 TJMurphy	7/4f	pu
122	Seebald (GER) *MCPipe* 10-11-3 TScudamore	25/1	pu
110	Valley Henry (IRE) *JHowardJohnson* 10-11-0 (b) GLee	33/1	pu

Mr C. G. Roach 12ran 5m11.67

147 Ladbrokes World Hdle (Gr 1) (A) (4yo+) £116,000 — 3m (12)

123	INGLIS DREVER *JHowardJohnson* 6-11-10 GLee	5/1	1
59	BARACOUDA (FR) *FDoumen,France* 10-11-10 APMcCoy	6/5f	3 2
109	RULE SUPREME (IRE) *WPMullins,Ireland* 9-11-10 DJCasey	4/1	¾ 3
97	Westender (FR) *MCPipe* 9-11-10 (b) TScudamore	33/1	2 4
97	Korelo (FR) *MCPipe* 7-11-10 TJMurphy	14/1	7 5
55	Yogi (IRE) *ThomasFoley,Ireland* 9-11-10 RJohnson	200/1	1 6
124	Exotic Dancer (FR) *JonjoO'Neill* 5-11-10 (s) PCarberry	150/1	1½ 7
86	The French Furze (IRE) *NGRichards* 11-11-10 BHarding	250/1	2½ 8
126	Crystal d'Ainay (FR) *AKing* 6-11-10 (b) RThornton	10/1	pu
84	Emotional Moment (IRE) *TJTaaffe,Ireland* 8-11-10 BJGeraghty	16/1	pu
130	Knife Edge (USA) *JonjoO'Neill* 10-11-10 (b) CO'Dwyer	200/1	pu
59	Sh Boom *JonjoO'Neill* 7-11-10 MAFitzgerald	22/1	pu

Andrea & Graham Wylie 12ran 5m48.21

148 Mildmay of Flete Hcap Chase (Gr 3) (A) (146) (5yo+) £43,500 — 2m5f (17)

	LIBERTHINE (FR) *NJHenderson* 6-10-1[128] MrSWaley-Cohen[7]	25/1	1
127	BANKER COUNT *MissVenetiaWilliams* 13-10-12[132] SThomas	16/1	7 2
130	SIMPLY GIFTED *JonjoO'Neill* 10-11-1[135] APMcCoy	14/1	3 3
	BROOKLYN BREEZE (IRE) *LLungo* 8-11-0[134] ADobbin	9/2f	2 4
130	Scots Grey *NJHenderson* 10-10-13[133] MAFitzgerald	20/1	3 5
22	Colca Canyon (IRE) *MrsJHarrington,Ireland* 8-11-12[146] RMPower	25/1	nk 6
	Christopher *PJHobbs* 8-10-4[124] PJBrennan	20/1	1¼ 7
6	Roveretto *MCPipe* 10-10-0[125] (b) TJMalone[5]	66/1	6 8
32	Davids Lad (IRE) *AJMartin,Ireland* 11-10-5[125] (t) PCarberry	20/1	1¾ 9
	Multeen River (IRE) *JonjoO'Neill* 9-10-6[126] DJCasey	33/1	2½ 10
	The Villager (IRE) *MScudamore* 9-10-0[120] TScudamore	50/1	6 11
127	Redemption *NATwiston-Davies* 10-11-8[142] CLlewellyn	25/1	2½ 12
	Ghadames (FR) *RCGuest* 11-10-5[125] (s) SFox	33/1	9 13
127	Iznogoud (FR) *MCPipe* 9-11-8[142] BJGeraghty	9/1	8 14
130	Mouseski *PFNicholls* 11-11-4[143] MrNWilliams[5]	33/1	2 15
111	Polar Red *MCPipe* 8-11-3[137] TJMurphy	20/1	1¼ 16
130	Supreme Prince (IRE) *PJHobbs* 8-11-12[146] PFlynn	20/1	f
	Marked Man (IRE) *RLee* 9-10-7[127] RThornton	33/1	f
130	Le Duc (FR) *PFNicholls* 6-11-4[138] RWalsh	10/1	f
50	Europa *FerdyMurphy* 9-11-1[135] JMMaguire	20/1	bd
127	Palarshan (FR) *HDDaly* 7-11-6[140] RJohnson	7/1	pu

	Hunters Tweed *PBeaumont* 9-10-11^{131} (b) GLee	20/1		pu

Mr Robert Waley-Cohen 22ran 5m15.52

149 NH Chase Challenge Cup (Amat Nov Chase) (B) (5yo+) £29,000 4m1f (27)

Form	Horse	SP	Dist	Pos
69	ANOTHER RUM (IRE) *IADuncan,Ireland* 7-11-7 MrMJO'Hare	40/1		1
	CAISLEAN UI CUAIN (IRE) *JJLambe,Ireland* 9-11-11 MrJPO'Farrell	150/1	7	2
120	CONTROL MAN (IRE) *MCPipe* 7-12-0 (v) MrGordonElliott	11/1	½	3
	Go White Lightning (IRE) *MBradstock* 10-11-7 MrDHDunsdon	100/1	sh	4
	Point Barrow (IRE) *PHughes,Ireland* 7-12-0 MrDerekO'Connor	10/3f	1	5
	Garryvoe (IRE) *TRGeorge* 7-11-11 MrTGreenall	20/1	18	6
74	Willie John Daly (IRE) *PJHobbs* 8-12-0 MrRWidger	14/1	nk	7
65	Keepatem (IRE) *MFMorris,Ireland* 9-12-0 MrJTMcNamara	9/2	2	8
60	Your A Gassman (IRE) *FerdyMurphy* 7-12-0 MrTJDreaper	7/1	1¼	9
	Torche (IRE) *MScudamore* 7-12-0 (v) MrJMPritchard	40/1	3	10
	Earl's Kitchen *CLTizzard* 8-11-11 (t) MissPGundry	33/1	14	11
	Eva So Charming *MissHCKnight* 7-11-11 MrSMorris	40/1	26	12
7	Oh So Lively (IRE) *EJO'Grady,Ireland* 7-12-0 MrRPQuinlan	50/1	dist	13
	Gallik Dawn *AHollingsworth* 7-11-11 MrGHanmer	150/1		f
	Sixo (IRE) *MCPipe* 8-11-11 AGlassonbury	13/2		f
95	Ardashir (FR) *NATwiston-Davies* 6-11-7 MrGTumelty	100/1		f
	Laska de Thaix (FR) *PJHobbs* 6-11-7 MrTJO'Brien	20/1		bd
	Whitford Don (IRE) *PFNicholls* 7-12-0 (b) MrCJSweeney	16/1		ur
	Classic Native (IRE) *JonjoO'Neill* 7-11-11 MrDWCullen	12/1		pu
	Major Blue *JGMO'Shea* 10-11-7 (s) MrNWilliams	100/1		pu

Ronald Lilley 20ran 8m49.91

150 Pertemps Final (Hcap Hdle) (L) (A) (140) (5yo+) £34,800 3m (12)

Form	Horse	SP	Dist	Pos
	OULART *DTHughes,Ireland* 6-10-2^{121} PCarberry	10/1		1
	MIOCHE D'ESTRUVAL (FR) *MCPipe* 5-10-0^{119} TScudamore	66/1	2	2
126	QUICK *MCPipe* 5-11-0^{140} (v) AGlassonbury^{7}	50/1	4	3
80	TOUCH CLOSER *MissVScott* 8-10-7^{126} MAFitzgerald	66/1	1¼	4
80	Carlys Quest *FerdyMurphy* 11-10-13^{135} KMercer^{3}	20/1	¾	5
	Liberman (IRE) *MCPipe* 7-10-9^{128} BJGeraghty	10/1	nk	6
	Hautclan (FR) *JonjoO'Neill* 6-10-11^{130} APMcCoy	8/1	sh	7
	Hirvine (FR) *PBowen* 7-11-2^{140} (s) TGreenway^{5}	25/1	sh	8
	Basilea Star (IRE) *FerdyMurphy* 8-11-1^{134} (t) GLee	9/1	sh	9
	Rambling Minster *KGReveley* 7-10-13^{132} DJCasey	16/1	½	10
	Chamoss Royale (FR) *PFNicholls* 5-11-1^{134} RWalsh	20/1	½	11
	The Dark Lord (IRE) *MrsLWadham* 8-11-1^{134} LAspell	12/1	½	12
59	Kadara (IRE) *RHAlner* 6-11-2^{135} AThornton	16/1	1	13
	Tarxien *MCPipe* 11-10-3^{127} (t) TJMalone^{5}	33/1	sh	14
	Ravenswood (IRE) *MCPipe* 8-10-6^{125} (t) TJMurphy	7/2f	¾	15
	Penny Pictures (IRE) *MCPipe* 6-11-2^{135} RThornton	50/1	1¼	16
	Fairwood Heart (IRE) *PJRothwell,Ireland* 8-9-10^{120} AJDonoghue^{5}	50/1	2½	17
113	Victory Gunner (IRE) *CRoberts* 7-9-12^{122} LStephens^{5}	100/1	1½	18
	Attorney General (IRE) *JABOld* 6-11-0^{133} WHutchinson	9/1	6	19
	Team Tassel (IRE) *MCPipe* 7-10-7^{126} (v) JEMoore	20/1	1	20
87	Petite Margot *NATwiston-Davies* 6-10-13^{132} CLlewellyn	33/1	hd	21
80	Supreme Piper (IRE) *PJHobbs* 7-10-6^{125} PFlynn	100/1	nk	22

Mr G. T. Pierse 22ran 5m52.84

CHELTENHAM Friday, Mar 18 GOOD (New Course)

151 JCB Triumph Hdle (Gr 1) (A) (4yo) £58,000 2m1f (9)

Form	Horse	SP	Dist	Pos
128	PENZANCE *AKing* 4-11-0 RThornton	9/1		1
129	FAASEL (IRE) *NGRichards* 4-11-0 (v) ADobbin	7/1	hd	2
99	AKILAK (IRE) *JHowardJohnson* 4-11-0 GLee	7/2f	8	3
67	Cerium (FR) *PFNicholls* 4-11-0 RWalsh	8/1	1¼	4
77	Phar Bleu (FR) *MissGBrowne* 4-11-0 JCulloty	66/1	½	5
106	Strangely Brown (IRE) *EMcNamara,Ireland* 4-11-0 DJCasey	11/1	1	6
	Diego Cao (IRE) *GLMoore* 4-11-0 JEMoore	20/1	3	7
99	Yankeedoodledandy (IRE) *PCHaslam* 4-11-0 FKeniry	14/1	1	8
99	Biscar Two (IRE) *BJLlewellyn* 4-11-0 (b) ChristianWilliams	100/1	8	9
	Loyal Focus (IRE) *DKWeld,Ireland* 4-11-0 (v) PCarberry	33/1	1½	10
	Majlis (JPN) *MJPO'Brien,Ireland* 4-11-0 APMcCoy	20/1	1	11
	Admiral (IRE) *RCGuest* 4-11-0 HOliver	33/1	1½	12
99	Simonovski (USA) *SCBurrough* 4-11-0 TDoyle	300/1	1½	13
99	New Entic (FR) *GLMoore* 4-11-0 PHide	100/1	nk	14
	Skyhawk (IRE) *HdeBromhead,Ireland* 4-11-0 DenisO'Regan	100/1	10	15
99	Danaw (FR) *FDoumen,France* 4-11-0 (t) LMetais	25/1	3	16
23	Courant d'Air (IRE) *MrsLucindaFeatherstone* 4-11-0 PJBrennan	200/1	10	17
106	Don't Be Bitin (IRE) *EGriffin,Ireland* 4-11-0 DJCondon	50/1	4	18
	Sound Blaster (IRE) *LMcAteer,Ireland* 4-11-0 (b) DNRussell	66/1	2½	19

99	Bonbon Rose (FR) *AChaille-Chaille,France* 4-11-0 CO'Dwyer	33/1	hd 20
106	Barati (IRE) *MJPO'Brien,Ireland* 4-11-0 BJGeraghty	16/1	½ 21
	Carte Diamond (USA) *BEllison* 4-11-0 (t) RJohnson	11/1	pu
	Etendard Indien (FR) *NJHenderson* 4-11-0 (b) MAFitzgerald	22/1	pu

Elite Racing Club 23ran 4m03.45

152 Brit Insurance Spa Nov Hdle (Gr 2) (A) (4yo+) £43,500 3m (12)

119	MOULIN RICHE (FR) *FDoumen,France* 5-11-7 RThornton	9/1	1
113	OVER THE CREEK *MCPipe* 6-11-7 TJMurphy	5/1	2½ 2
94	BREWSTER (IRE) *IanWilliams* 8-11-7 RJohnson	9/4f	nk 3
81	Bob Bob Bobbin *CLTizzard* 6-11-7 JTizzard	20/1	3 4
	Thames (IRE) *NJHenderson* 7-11-7 MAFitzgerald	13/2	14 5
	Stage By Stage (USA) *CREgerton* 6-11-7 JAMcCarthy	66/1	1¾ 6
131	Without A Doubt *MPitman* 6-11-7 SDurack	66/1	1¼ 7
52	Jackson (FR) *AKing* 8-11-7 WHutchinson	66/1	½ 8
	Romany Prince *SGollings* 6-11-7 PCarberry	33/1	16 9
	Kings Bay *HMorrison* 6-11-0 JCrowley	100/1	17 10
58	Keltic Rock *JAGeake* 6-11-7 MBradburne	100/1	5 11
52	Senor Sedona *NJGifford* 6-11-7 JamesDavies	33/1	1¾ 12
94	Lady Zephyr (IRE) *NATwiston-Davies* 7-11-0 CLlewellyn	14/1	1¼ 13
92	Washington Lad (IRE) *PAFahy,Ireland* 5-11-7 APMcCoy	12/1	6 14
79	Dalvento (IRE) *JohnJosephMurphy,Ireland* 7-11-7 AJMcNamara	100/1	1 15
94	Va Vavoom (IRE) *NATwiston-Davies* 7-11-7 (t) TScudamore	66/1	29 16
58	Gaelic Music (IRE) *MBradstock* 6-11-7 MBatchelor	100/1	sh 17
	Bewleys Berry (IRE) *JHowardJohnson* 7-11-7 GLee	11/2	f

J. C. Seroul 18ran 5m55.80

153 totesport Cheltenham Gold Cup Chase (Gr 1) (A) (5yo+) £212,268 3¼m110y (22)

62	KICKING KING (IRE) *TJTaaffe,Ireland* 7-11-10 BJGeraghty	4/1f	1
88	TAKE THE STAND (IRE) *PBowen* 9-11-10 ADobbin	25/1	5 2
110	SIR REMBRANDT (IRE) *RHAlner* 9-11-10 AThornton	12/1	8 3
98	Royal Auclair (FR) *PFNicholls* 8-11-10 (t) ChristianWilliams	40/1	nk 4
98	Grey Abbey (IRE) *JHowardJohnson* 11-11-10 GLee	15/2	9 5
110	Strong Flow (IRE) *PFNicholls* 8-11-10 RWalsh	5/1	1¼ 6
110	Celestial Gold (IRE) *MCPipe* 7-11-10 TJMurphy	9/2	½ 7
110	Ballycassidy (IRE) *PBowen* 9-11-10 SDurack	80/1	14 8
98	Therealbandit (IRE) *MCPipe* 8-11-10 APMcCoy	16/1	11 9
135	Astonville (FR) *MScudamore* 11-11-10 TScudamore	500/1	dist 10
109	Pizarro (IRE) *EJO'Grady,Ireland* 8-11-10 (v) DNRussell	14/1	f
109	Beef Or Salmon (IRE) *MHourigan,Ireland* 9-11-10 PCarberry	5/1	pu
62	Tiutchev *MCPipe* 12-11-10 RThornton	50/1	pu
120	Truckers Tavern (IRE) *FerdyMurphy* 10-11-10 (t) BHarding	100/1	pu
141	Venn Ottery *MCPipe* 10-11-10 (t) JEMoore	200/1	pu

Mr Conor Clarkson 15ran 6m42.60

154 Christie's Foxhunt Chase Challenge Cup (B) (5yo+) £23,200 3¼m110y (22)

	SLEEPING NIGHT (FR) *PFNicholls* 9-12-0 MrCJSweeney	7/2f	1
	FOLY PLEASANT (FR) *NickShutts* 11-12-0 (t) MrRBurton	20/1	¾ 2
	PLACID MAN (IRE) *MsAEEmbiricos* 11-12-0 MsAEmbiricos	14/1	11 3
	Lord Atterbury (IRE) *MCPipe* 9-12-0 MrGordonElliott	4/1	9 4
	Gatsby (IRE) *JGroucott* 9-12-0 MrJMPritchard	40/1	9 5
	Earthmover (IRE) *PFNicholls* 14-12-0 MissAGoschen	7/1	7 6
	Just Cliquot *MrsACSwarbrick* 9-11-7 MrGHanmer	66/1	9 7
	Cantarinho *DJKemp* 7-12-0 (t) MrDKemp	50/1	6 8
	Lord of The Turf (IRE) *JBleahen,Ireland* 12-12-0 MrDerekO'Connor	11/1	4 9
2	Polar Champ *MrsOCJackson* 12-12-0 (v) MissLucyBridges	66/1	nk 10
	County Derry *JScott* 12-12-0 (s) MrNHarris	25/1	16 11
	Phelans Fancy (IRE) *MichaelWinters,Ireland* 7-11-7 MrMJO'Connor	40/1	1 12
2	General Claremont (IRE) *PFNicholls* 12-12-0 (t) MrLHeard	66/1	5 13
	Free Gift *MrsSAlner* 7-12-0 DJacob	8/1	1 14
	Jabiru (IRE) *MrsKMSanderson* 12-12-0 (b) MrDEdwards	50/1	3½ 15
	Colquhoun *MrsOCJackson* 11-12-0 MrsOliviaJackson	200/1	f
	The Wipper (IRE) *SeanAherne,Ireland* 9-12-0 (b) MrBHassett	28/1	f
	Ballysicyos (FR) *MrsOCJackson* 10-12-0 MrGWeatherley	40/1	ur
	First Down Jets (IRE) *WJBurke,Ireland* 8-12-0 MrRHarding	200/1	ur
	General Montcalm (IRE) *EJO'Grady,Ireland* 7-12-0 MrJTMcNamara	12/1	pu
	Kingston Venture *MissCParfitt* 9-12-0 MrJBarnes	66/1	pu
	Ourman (IRE) *NickBell* 9-12-0 MrNMBell	100/1	pu
	Supreme Silence (IRE) *NickKent* 8-12-0 MrNKent	100/1	pu
	Tanager *MrsKLawther* 10-12-0 (b) MrBKing	50/1	pu

D. J. & F. A. Jackson 24ran 6m50.42

	155 Johnny Henderson Grand Annual Chase Challenge Cup (Hcap) (Gr 3) (A) (156) (5yo+) £43,500		2m110y (14)
	FOTA ISLAND (IRE) *MFMorris,Ireland* 9-10-0^{130} PCarberry	7/1	1
	BAMBI DE L'ORME (FR) *IanWilliams* 6-10-0^{130} GLee	16/1	5 2
31	CARACCIOLA (GER) *NJHenderson* 8-10-12^{142} MFoley	16/1	1 3
21	TYSOU (FR) *NJHenderson* 8-10-6^{136} MAFitzgerald	10/1	1 4
102	Impek (FR) *MissHCKnight* 9-11-1^{145} JCulloty	12/1	3 5
	Greenhope (IRE) *NJHenderson* 7-10-2^{132} ATinkler	20/1	½ 6
	Master Rex *BDeHaan* 10-10-8^{138} NFehily	40/1	3½ 7
102	Bleu Superbe (FR) *MissVenetiaWilliams* 10-10-7^{137} SThomas	66/1	½ 8
112	Armaturk (FR) *PFNicholls* 8-11-12^{156} ChristianWilliams	40/1	½ 9
3	Latalomne (USA) *NWilson* 11-10-0^{130} PRobson	66/1	6 10
	Batswing *GLMoore* 10-10-0^{130} JEMoore	66/1	5 11
	Figaro du Rocher (FR) *MCPipe* 5-9-9^{134} (t) TJMalone^{5}	50/1	sh 12
11	Atum Re (IRE) *PRWebber* 8-10-0^{130} (v) JamesDavies	50/1	1 13
	L'Ange Au Ciel (FR) *PFNicholls* 6-10-7^{137} RWalsh	9/2f	8 14
1	Almaydan *RLee* 7-10-3^{133} RThornton	5/1	2½ 15
	Bonus Bridge (IRE) *HDDaly* 10-10-9^{139} MBradburne	25/1	½ 16
	Jericho III (FR) *RCGuest* 8-9-11^{130} (b+es) LMcGrath^{3}	66/1	14 17
96	Flagship Uberalles (IRE) *PJHobbs* 11-11-8^{152} RJohnson	50/1	1 18
3	Palua *MissECLavelle* 8-10-7^{137} JAMcCarthy	50/1	3½ 19
	Davoski *DrPPritchard* 11-9-9^{130} DrPPritchard^{5}	100/1	¾ 20
102	Great Travel (FR) *PFNicholls* 6-10-13^{143} (t) APMcCoy	12/1	f
6	Tango Royal (FR) *MCPipe* 9-10-7^{137} (t) TJMurphy	28/1	f
	Stormy Lord (IRE) *JWade* 9-10-0^{130} BHarding	66/1	f
22	Ground Ball (IRE) *CFSwan,Ireland* 8-10-6^{136} DJCasey	10/1	ur
	Mr John P. McManus 24ran 4m03.52		

	156 Vincent O'Brien County Hcap Hdle (Gr 3) (A) (154) (5yo+) £37,700		2m1f (8)
	FONTANESI (IRE) *MCPipe* 5-10-0^{128} TJMurphy	16/1	1
132	STANCE *GLMoore* 6-10-0^{128} DJCasey	11/1	2 2
	BORORA *RLee* 6-10-0^{128} TDoyle	200/1	2 3
	GRANDE JETE (SAF) *NJHenderson* 8-10-2^{130} MFoley	14/1	1½ 4
132	Crossbow Creek *MGRimell* 7-10-6^{134} JCrowley	16/1	1¼ 5
132	Monte Cinto (FR) *PFNicholls* 5-10-1^{129} RWalsh	8/1	4 6
111	Desert Air (JPN) *MCPipe* 6-9-9^{128} (t) TJMalone^{5}	20/1	nk 7
124	Geos (FR) *NJHenderson* 10-11-0^{147} TJPhelan^{5}	33/1	½ 8
132	McBain (USA) *PJHobbs* 6-10-0^{128} PFlynn	66/1	3½ 9
5	Balapour (IRE) *POBrady,Ireland* 7-10-9^{137} (t) JCullen	20/1	sh 10
79	Beechcourt *MJPO'Brien,Ireland* 8-10-0^{128} PCarberry	9/2f	½ 11
123	Perouse *PFNicholls* 7-11-6^{148} (t) ChristianWilliams	20/1	2 12
78	King Revo (IRE) *PCHaslam* 5-11-1^{143} FKeniry	10/1	1 13
	Dancing Pearl *CJPrice* 7-10-0^{128} WHutchinson	50/1	5 14
	Its Crucial (IRE) *NATwiston-Davies* 5-10-0^{128} CLlewellyn	200/1	½ 15
123	Torrid Kentavr (USA) *BEllison* 8-10-7^{135} BHarding	33/1	¾ 16
124	Copeland *MCPipe* 10-10-13^{141} (s) JEMoore	40/1	nk 17
123	Rigmarole *PFNicholls* 7-11-12^{154} (t) PJBrennan	50/1	½ 18
	Calatagan (IRE) *JMJefferson* 6-10-3^{131} ADobbin	100/1	sh 19
	Risky Reef *AndrewLee,Ireland* 8-10-8^{136} CO'Dwyer	33/1	1½ 20
111	Tamarinbleu (FR) *MCPipe* 5-11-3^{145} APMcCoy	9/1	1¼ 21
	Grave Doubts *KBishop* 9-10-5^{133} (t) JAMcCarthy	50/1	¾ 22
78	Castleshane (IRE) *SGollings* 8-9-8^{129} (s) WKennedy^{7}	50/1	9 23
	Silvertown *LLungo* 10-10-3^{136} GBerridge^{5}	33/1	1¾ 24
	Fool On The Hill *PJHobbs* 8-10-7^{135} RJohnson	66/1	12 25
97	Marble Arch *HMorrison* 9-11-5^{147} (s) BJGeraghty	66/1	4 26
111	Bongo Fury (FR) *MCPipe* 6-10-5^{133} (v) TScudamore	8/1	1 27
111	Nawamees (IRE) *GLMoore* 7-10-5^{133} (s) MAFitzgerald	40/1	18 28
	Demi Beau *CJMann* 7-10-5^{133} NFehily	16/1	13 29
	Another Dude (IRE) *JHowardJohnson* 8-10-0^{128} GLee	25/1	pu
	Mr D. A. Johnson 30ran 4m01.10		

UTTOXETER Saturday, Mar 19 GOOD to SOFT

	157 John Smith's Midlands Grand National Chase (Hcap) (L) (A) (147) (5yo+) £58,000		4m1f110y (24)
	PHILSON RUN (IRE) *NickWilliams* 9-10-2^{123} PCarberry	14/1	1
	TOULOUSE-LAUTREC (IRE) *TRGeorge* 9-10-0^{121} SDurack	7/1	1 2
	HOWDYDOODY (IRE) *PFNicholls* 9-10-2^{123} (t) RWalsh	8/1	7 3
120	L'AVENTURE (FR) *PFNicholls* 6-10-12^{133} (t) PJBrennan	12/1	3½ 4
109	Hersov (IRE) *PaulARoche,Ireland* 9-10-0^{121} (s) BHarding	14/1	5 5
	Lord Who (IRE) *PMJDoyle,Ireland* 8-10-9^{130} DNRussell	8/1	9 6
82	Stormez (FR) *MCPipe* 8-11-12^{147} (s+t) APMcCoy	16/1	13 7
137	Just Maybe (IRE) *MissVenetiaWilliams* 11-10-4^{125} (v) SThomas	33/1	23 8

74	Artic Jack (FR) *MrsSJSmith* 9-10-10[131] DElsworth	25/1	6 9
82	D'Argent (IRE) *AKing* 8-11-5[140] RThornton	5/1f	ur
	Heroic (IRE) *CFSwan,Ireland* 9-10-0[121] DJCasey	20/1	ur
68	Jurancon II (FR) *MCPipe* 8-11-11[146] TJMurphy	12/1	pu
82	Shotgun Willy (IRE) *PFNicholls* 11-11-10[145] (b) JTizzard	25/1	pu
110	Gingembre (FR) *MrsLCTaylor* 11-11-6[141] AThornton	33/1	pu
137	Wild Tempo (FR) *MScudamore* 10-10-12[133] TScudamore	100/1	pu
	Bathwick Annie *DPKeane* 9-10-11[132] NFehily	12/1	pu
	Mac's Supreme (IRE) *FerdyMurphy* 13-9-11[121] KMercer[3]	33/1	pu
	Fields of Home (IRE) *JHowardJohnson* 7-10-0[121] GLee	20/1	pu

Gale Force One 18ran 9m11.31

FAIRYHOUSE Sunday, Mar 27 SOFT

158 Rathbarry & Glanview Studs Festival Nov Hdle (Gr 2) (4yo+) £21,700 — 2½m (11)

	SHER BEAU (IRE) *PhilipFenton* 6-11-5 DJCasey	5/1	1
	KILL DEVIL HILL (IRE) *PaulNolan* 5-11-3 JLCullen	10/1	sh 2
84	HOMER WELLS (IRE) *WPMullins* 7-11-10 DJCondon	11/4	2 3
92	Petertheknot (IRE) *PatrickSinnott* 7-11-10 APMcCoy	13/2	¾ 4
139	Our Ben *WPMullins* 6-11-8 RWalsh	2/1f	1½ 5
	Satoha (IRE) *FFlood* 7-11-5 TJMurphy	8/1	dist 6
	Guantama Bay (IRE) *NMeade* 6-11-5 PCarberry	12/1	dist 7

Mr N. P. Morrissey 7ran 5m12.88

FAIRYHOUSE Monday, Mar 28 SOFT

159 Powers Gold Label Irish Grand National Chase (Hcap) (Gr A) (153) (5yo+) £98,264 — 3m5f (23)

85	NUMBERSIXVALVERDE (IRE) *MartinBrassil* 9-10-1[126] RWalsh	9/1	1
109	JACK HIGH (IRE) *TMWalsh* 10-10-0[125] GCotter	10/1	¾ 2
	MARCUS DU BERLAIS (FR) *ALTMoore* 8-10-6[134] DJHoward[3]	9/1	1½ 3
7	HOWAYA PET (IRE) *GKeane* 9-10-0[125] (t) JRBarry	33/1	1½ 4
	Coolnahilla (IRE) *WJBurke* 9-10-0[125] DJCondon	33/1	1½ 5
85	Kymandjen (IRE) *PaulNolan* 8-10-4[129] JLCullen	12/1	1½ 6
85	Golden Storm (IRE) *JosephCrowley* 8-9-9[125] (b) JMAllen[5]	20/1	14 7
	What Odds (IRE) *TKGeraghty* 9-10-0[125] RGeraghty	8/1f	nk 8
	Star Clipper *NMeade* 8-10-0[125] APCrowe	50/1	5 9
149	Point Barrow (IRE) *PHughes* 7-10-9[134] JPElliott	10/1	1 10
65	Jaquouille (FR) *ALTMoore* 8-10-0[125] PACarberry	9/1	1½ 11
65	Mullacash (IRE) *NMeade* 7-10-0[125] (b) PCarberry	16/1	3½ 12
	Kadoun (IRE) *MJPO'Brien* 8-11-3[142] APMcCoy	10/1	4½ 13
	Darrens Lass (IRE) *RobertMurphy* 9-10-0[125] MDGrant	100/1	6 14
85	The Bunny Boiler (IRE) *NMeade* 11-10-0[125] GTHutchinson	66/1	½ 15
34	Takagi (IRE) *EJO'Grady* 10-11-2[141] DNRussell	25/1	13 16
85	Native Sessions (IRE) *NMeade* 10-10-0[125] (b) MrNPMadden	50/1	f
143	Pearly Jack *DEFitzgerald* 7-9-11[125] TGMRyan[3]	12/1	ro
	Le Coudray (FR) *CRoche* 11-12-0[153] (t) MrJTMcNamara	25/1	pu
	Alexander Banquet (IRE) *WPMullins* 12-11-9[148] BJGeraghty	25/1	pu
	Native Jack (IRE) *ALTMoore* 11-10-13[138] BMCash	20/1	pu
65	Garvivonnian (IRE) *EdwardPMitchell* 10-10-6[134] AndrewJMcNamara[3]	25/1	pu
65	Hume Castle (IRE) *MrsJHarrington* 9-10-1[126] (t) RMPower	25/1	pu
157	Heroic (IRE) *CFSwan* 9-10-0[125] DJCasey	33/1	pu
	Green River (IRE) *JTRDreaper* 11-9-9[125] RCColgan[5]	66/1	pu
	Lord Alphieross (IRE) *WJBurke* 7-9-11[125] PWFlood[3]	66/1	pu

Mr O. B. P. Carroll 26ran 8m03.60

FAIRYHOUSE Tuesday, Mar 29 SOFT

160 Menolly Homes Nov Hdle (Gr 2) (4yo+) £27,125 — 2m (10)

133	JUSTIFIED (IRE) *ESheehy* 6-11-10 JRBarry	7/2	1
107	THE RAILWAY MAN (IRE) *ALTMoore* 6-11-4 BMCash	15/8f	2 2
100	BLAZING LISS (IRE) *JEKiely* 6-11-2 DNRussell	4/1	4 3
158	Petertheknot (IRE) *PatrickSinnott* 7-11-10 APMcCoy	11/1	2 4
	French Accordion (IRE) *PaulNolan* 5-11-2 JLCullen	16/1	8 5
	Telemachus *NMeade* 5-11-2 PCarberry	7/1	4 6
	Golden Exchange (IRE) *DWachman* 5-11-2 MDGrant	14/1	4 7
	Lenrey *ALTMoore* 5-11-2 DJCasey	33/1	20 8
	Pom Flyer (FR) *FFlood* 5-11-2 FJFlood	14/1	¾ 9
	Impartial *SJMahon* 4-10-8 JPElliott	25/1	8 10
	Pepperwood (IRE) *NMeade* 5-11-2 BJGeraghty	20/1	8 11

Braybrook Syndicate 11ran 4m05.28

161 Powers Gold Cup Chase (Gr 1) (5yo+) £41,319 — 2½m (16)

140	LIKE-A-BUTTERFLY (IRE) *CRoche* 11-11-4 APMcCoy	7/2f	1

69	FORGET THE PAST *MJPO'Brien* 7-11-9 BJGeraghty	7/1	½	2
134	WATSON LAKE (IRE) *NMeade* 7-11-9 PCarberry	5/1	6	3
108	Doodle Addle (IRE) *JTRDreaper* 9-11-9 JLCullen	25/1	9	4
69	Sandy Owen (IRE) *PAFahy* 9-11-9 SGMcDermott	16/1	3	5
108	Well Presented (IRE) *MrsJHarrington* 7-11-9 GLee	6/1	6	6
108	Carrigeen Victor (IRE) *MrsJHarrington* 7-11-9 RMPower	9/2	¾	7
	Euro Leader (IRE) *WPMullins* 7-11-9 JRBarry	20/1	½	8
16	Ross River *SDonohoe* 9-11-9 MrRWidger	33/1		f
108	Strong Project (IRE) *CFSwan* 9-11-9 DJCasey	18/1		f
	Coast To Coast (IRE) *EJO'Grady* 6-11-9 DNRussell	20/1		ref
125	Scarthy Lad (IRE) *TGO'Leary* 7-11-9 JCulloty	12/1		ur
	Davenport Milenium (IRE) *WPMullins* 9-11-9 RWalsh	8/1		pu

Mr John P. McManus 13ran 5m20.16

162 **Bet @ Blue Square Dan Moore Memorial Hcap Chase (152) (4yo+)** £31,646 — 2m1f (13)

155	GROUND BALL (IRE) *CFSwan* 8-10-12^{136} APMcCoy	15/8f		1
134	ULAAN BAATAR (IRE) *MrsJHarrington* 8-11-5^{143} BJGeraghty	4/1	½	2
141	CENTRAL HOUSE *DTHughes* 8-11-9^{152} (b) MrRLoughran^{5}	3/1	1	3
	Cregg House (IRE) *SDonohoe* 10-10-7^{123} RWalsh	12/1	8	4
101	Fiery Ring (IRE) *JRHFowler* 10-10-7^{126} RGeraghty	18/1	13	5
54	Arctic Copper (IRE) *NMeade* 11-10-11^{135} (b) DNRussell	16/1	3½	6
	Green Belt Flyer (IRE) *MrsJHarrington* 7-10-7^{128} RMPower	7/2	10	7

Mr John P. McManus 7ran 4m28.55

AUTEUIL Saturday, Apr 2 HEAVY

163 **Prix Fleuret (Gr 3) (4yo)** £43,750 — 2½m110y (18)

	NEPTUNE COLLONGES (FR) *JOrtet,France* 4-10-6 CPieux	26/10		1
	BALKO (FR) *GMacaire,France* 4-10-10 JRicou	9/10	15	2
	NAROCK (FR) *JBertrandeBalanda,France* 4-10-8 LMetais	9/2	2	3
	Nalexibo (FR) *FDanloux,France* 4-9-13 SBeaumard	53/1	10	4
	Matuvu (FR) *TTrapenard,France* 4-10-1 SDupuis	32/1	3	5
	Korean (FR) *BSecly,France* 4-10-3 BThelier	20/1	3	6
	Targentiel (FR) *FMCottin,France* 4-10-1 DGallagher	19/1	20	7
	Anglican (FR) *GCherel,France* 4-10-1 EChazelle	22/1		f
	Esturgeon du Ranch (FR) *GCherel,France* 4-10-1 (b) PMarsac	16/1		pu

Mme G. Vuillard 9ran 5m35.15

AINTREE Thursday, Apr 7 SOFT

164 **John Smith's And Batleys Liverpool Long Distance Hdle (Gr 2) (A) (4yo+)** £34,800 — 3m110y (13)

126	MONET'S GARDEN (IRE) *NGRichards* 7-11-10 ADobbin	11/2		1
	MR ED (IRE) *PBowen* 7-11-2 (s) APMcCoy	14/1	1	2
142	TUMBLING DICE (IRE) *TJTaaffe,Ireland* 6-11-2 BJGeraghty	14/1	10	3
142	Idole First (IRE) *MissVenetiaWilliams* 6-11-6 AO'Keeffe	9/1	4	4
142	Dancing Bay *NJHenderson* 8-11-2 MAFitzgerald	10/1	dist	5
147	Korelo (FR) *MCPipe* 7-11-2 TJMurphy	9/2	dist	6
	Gralmano (IRE) *KARyan* 10-11-10 GLee	100/1		f
147	Rule Supreme (IRE) *WPMullins,Ireland* 9-11-10 RWalsh	2/1f		ur
147	Westender (FR) *MCPipe* 9-11-6 (b) TScudamore	7/1		ref

Mr David Wesley Yates 9ran 6m31.40

165 **Betfair Bowl Chase (Gr 2) (A) (5yo+)** £89,250 — 3m1f (19)

153	GREY ABBEY (IRE) *JHowardJohnson* 11-11-12 GLee	7/2		1
130	FIRST GOLD (FR) *FDoumen,France* 12-11-2 (b) APMcCoy	3/1f	12	2
147	CRYSTAL D'AINAY (FR) *AKing* 6-11-2 RThornton	7/1	17	3
146	Thisthatandtother (IRE) *PFNicholls* 9-11-12 RWalsh	5/1	2½	4
	Jim (FR) *JTRDreaper,Ireland* 8-11-8 RMPower	16/1	26	5
153	Tiutchev *MCPipe* 12-11-12 (v+t) RJohnson	25/1		pu
153	Sir Rembrandt (IRE) *RHAlner* 9-11-8 AThornton	13/2		pu
146	Our Vic (IRE) *MCPipe* 7-11-7 TJMurphy	13/2		pu

The Roper Family and Norman Furness 8ran 6m38.24

166 **John Smith's Anniversary 4-Y-O Nov Hdle (Gr 1) (A) (4yo)** £69,600 — 2m110y (9)

151	FAASEL (IRE) *NGRichards* 4-11-0 (v) ADobbin	11/4f		1
151	PHAR BLEU (FR) *MissGBrowne* 4-11-0 APMcCoy	11/1	7	2
151	STRANGELY BROWN (IRE) *EMcNamara,Ireland* 4-11-0 PCarberry	7/1	9	3
138	Miss Academy (FR) *MCPipe* 4-10-7 TJMurphy	14/1	5	4
138	Dabiroun (IRE) *PaulNolan,Ireland* 4-11-0 JCullen	6/1	8	5
	Karelian *KARyan* 4-11-0 CLlewellyn	8/1	12	6
151	Courant d'Air (IRE) *MrsLucindaFeatherstone* 4-11-0 JPMcNamara	200/1	5	7
151	Cerium (FR) *PFNicholls* 4-11-0 RWalsh	7/2	11	8

	Horse / Trainer / Age-Weight / Jockey	SP	Pos
	Noble Request (FR) *PJHobbs* 4-11-0 PFlynn	100/1	3 9
	L'Oudon (FR) *PFNicholls* 4-11-0 BJGeraghty	12/1	pu
	Motive (FR) *JHowardJohnson* 4-11-0 GLee	25/1	pu
	Protective *JGGiven* 4-11-0 MAFitzgerald	100/1	pu

Mr Jim Ennis 12ran 4m11.12

167 John Smith's Fox Hunt Chase (B) (6yo+) £20,300 — 2m5f110y (Nat.) (18)

	Horse / Trainer / Age-Weight / Jockey	SP	Pos
	KATARINO (FR) *RWaley-Cohen* 10-12-0 MrSWaley-Cohen	10/3f	1
	CAUGHT AT DAWN (IRE) *MHWeston* 11-12-0 MrTWeston	25/1	1½ 2
	MONTIFAULT (FR) *PFNicholls* 10-12-0 (t) MrCJSweeney	7/1	15 3
	Coole Abbey (IRE) *WAmos* 13-12-0 MrTOates	50/1	2½ 4
	An Capall Dubh (IRE) *MrsEdwardCrow* 9-12-0 MrRBurton	33/1	1 5
	No Retreat (NZ) *JGroucott* 12-12-0 MrWHill	33/1	5 6
153	Venn Ottery *MCPipe* 10-12-0 (t) AGlassonbury	25/1	½ 7
	Star Jack (FR) *DaveParker* 10-12-0 (t) MissPRobson	16/1	12 8
	Cape Stormer (IRE) *MrsCMGorman* 10-12-0 (b) MrMGorman	100/1	7 9
	Champagne Native (IRE) *DBroad,Ireland* 11-12-0 MrACash	100/1	8 10
	Donnybrook (IRE) *RDEWoodhouse* 12-12-0 (s) MrBWoodhouse	100/1	7 11
	Cassia Green *PHMorris* 11-12-0 MrDGreenway	100/1	3 12
	Left To Himself *JLHassett,Ireland* 7-12-0 (s) MrBHassett	100/1	3 13
	Epsilo de La Ronce (FR) *PMorris* 13-12-0 MrPaulMorris	100/1	hd 14
	Arctic Times (IRE) *EugeneMO'Sullivan,Ireland* 9-12-0 (s) MrWMO'Sullivan	25/1	f
	Hot Plunge *MrsJPLomax* 9-12-0 MrJOwen	100/1	f
	Never Compromise (IRE) *TMWalsh,Ireland* 10-12-0 MrDerekO'Connor	8/1	f
	Red Rampage *HPHogarth* 10-12-0 (b+t) MrPKinsella	100/1	f
	Tremallt (IRE) *TRGeorge* 14-12-0 MrTGreenall	10/1	f
	Guignol du Cochet (FR) *SFlook* 11-12-0 MrMWalford	100/1	bd
	Satchmo (IRE) *MrsDMGrissell* 13-12-0 MrGWragg	25/1	ur
	Arctic Challenge (IRE) *DavidMEasterby* 11-12-0 MrOGreenall	100/1	ur
	Beachcomber Bay (IRE) *IJKeeling,Ireland* 10-12-0 MrJTKeeling	40/1	ur
	Cobreces *MrsLBorradaile* 7-12-0 MrJSnowden	15/2	ur
154	Gatsby (IRE) *JGroucott* 9-12-0 MrRHFowler	25/1	ur
	Greco (IRE) *DavidChristie,Ireland* 8-12-0 (t) MissCJMacMahon	100/1	ur
137	Gun'n Roses II (FR) *DPKeane* 11-12-0 (b) DJacob	15/2	ur
	Promalee (IRE) *JJLambe,Ireland* 13-12-0 MrJPO'Farrell	100/1	ur
	Mazileo *IanWilliams* 12-12-0 MrAWintle	66/1	pu
	Red Guard *GeorgeHosier* 11-12-0 TMessenger	100/1	pu

Mr Robert Waley-Cohen 30ran 5m52.09

168 John Smith's Red Rum Hcap Chase (Gr 3) (A) (144) (5yo+) £40,600 — 2m (12)

	Horse / Trainer / Age-Weight / Jockey	SP	Pos
155	FOTA ISLAND (IRE) *MFMorris,Ireland* 9-11-10^{142} APMcCoy	10/3f	1
134	KADOUNT (FR) *AKing* 7-11-5^{137} RThornton	5/1	1 2
155	BAMBI DE L'ORME (FR) *IanWilliams* 6-11-0^{132} BJGeraghty	10/1	nk 3
155	Bonus Bridge (IRE) *HDDaly* 10-11-6^{138} MBradburne	66/1	10 4
155	Master Rex *BDeHaan* 10-11-5^{137} NFehily	25/1	2½ 5
	Old Marsh (IRE) *AWCarroll* 9-10-10^{128} JCulloty	16/1	10 6
155	Bleu Superbe (FR) *MissVenetiaWilliams* 10-11-3^{135} SThomas	25/1	nk 7
155	L'Ange Au Ciel (FR) *PFNicholls* 6-11-5^{137} RWalsh	8/1	10 8
96	Golden Alpha (IRE) *MCPipe* 11-11-12^{144} TJMurphy	16/1	2 9
111	Non So (FR) *NJHenderson* 7-11-8^{140} MAFitzgerald	10/1	½ 10
134	Town Crier (IRE) *MrsSJSmith* 10-11-9^{141} DElsworth	20/1	f
4	Junior Fontaine (FR) *ALTMoore,Ireland* 8-10-8^{126} RMPower	14/1	bd
155	Caracciola (GER) *NJHenderson* 8-11-11^{143} MFoley	14/1	pu
21	Duke of Buckingham (IRE) *PRWebber* 9-10-13^{131} TDoyle	25/1	pu
	Island Faith (IRE) *JHowardJohnson* 8-10-4^{122} GLee	12/1	pu

Mr John P. McManus 15ran 4m09.32

169 John Smith's Mersey Nov Hdle (Gr 2) (A) (4yo+) £29,000 — 2½m (12)

	Horse / Trainer / Age-Weight / Jockey	SP	Pos
119	TURPIN GREEN (IRE) *NGRichards* 6-11-0 ADobbin	14/1	1
133	MY WAY DE SOLZEN (FR) *AKing* 5-11-8 RThornton	12/1	6 2
129	MEPHISTO (IRE) *JHowardJohnson* 6-11-8 GLee	5/6f	2 3
139	Pole Star *JRFanshawe* 7-11-0 APMcCoy	5/2	9 4
133	Only Vintage (USA) *MissHCKnight* 5-11-0 JCulloty	18/1	27 5
129	South Bronx (IRE) *MrsSCBradburne* 6-11-0 (t) MBradburne	200/1	18 6
	Chetwind Music (IRE) *WilliamColemanO'Brien,Ireland* 7-11-0 JCullen	100/1	dist 7
139	Forager *MJRyan* 6-11-3 SDurack	33/1	ur
133	Chilling Place (IRE) *PJHobbs* 6-11-5 RJohnson	12/1	pu

Mr Trevor Hemmings 9ran 5m11.63

170 John Smith's HBLB Mares' Only Standard Open NHF (L) (A) (4, 5 and 6yo f+m) £14,500 — 2m1f

	Horse / Trainer / Age-Weight / Jockey	SP	Pos
	SENORITA RUMBALITA *AKing* 4-10-12 RThornton	9/2	1

Horse	SP	Dist	Pos
ACCORDELLO (IRE) *KGReveley* 4-10-8 TJMurphy	25/1	½	2
HELTORNIC (IRE) *MScudamore* 5-11-4 TScudamore	12/1	15	3
Giovanna *RTPhillips* 4-11-1 WMarston	14/1	¾	4
Funny Times *NGRichards* 4-11-1 ADobbin	5/2f	½	5
Powerlove (FR) *MrsSCBradburne* 4-10-8 MBradburne	100/1	7	6
Gay Gladys *DRCElsworth* 5-11-1 RWalford[3]	7/1	6	7
Lady Accord (IRE) *WPMullins,Ireland* 5-11-4 RWalsh	7/1	2	8
Treasured Memories *MissSEForster* 5-11-1 MrCStorey[3]	100/1	14	9
New's Full (FR) *FerdyMurphy* 4-10-5 KMercer[3]	100/1	3½	10
Langdon Lane *PRWebber* 4-10-8 TDoyle	20/1	1	11
Grenfell (IRE) *RTPhillips* 6-11-4 RJohnson	18/1	6	12
Hiho Silver Lining *HMorrison* 4-10-8 APMcCoy	8/1	16	13
Supreme Ocean (IRE) *NoelTChance* 5-11-0 (t) BJCrowley	33/1	¾	14
Lady Bling Bling *PJJones* 4-10-8 LAspell	100/1	11	15
Magical Legend *BGPowell* 4-10-1 MrWPKavanagh[7]	100/1	21	16
Martovic (IRE) *KCBailey* 6-11-0 JPMcNamara	100/1	28	17

Let's Get Ready To Rumble Partnership 17ran 4m18.62

AINTREE Friday, Apr 8 GOOD to SOFT

171 John Smith's Mildmay Nov Chase (Gr 2) (A) (5yo+) £43,500 3m1f (19)

	Horse	SP	Dist	Pos
161	LIKE-A-BUTTERFLY (IRE) *CRoche,Ireland* 11-11-2 APMcCoy	6/1		1
145	SEE YOU SOMETIME *JWMullins* 10-11-9 AThornton	20/1	1¾	2
140	L'AMI (FR) *FDoumen,France* 6-11-9 RThornton	7/2f	1½	3
145	Lacdoudal (FR) *PJHobbs* 6-11-7 RJohnson	4/1	30	4
120	Too Forward (IRE) *MPitman* 9-11-2 SDurack	33/1	5	5
161	Well Presented (IRE) *MrsJHarrington,Ireland* 7-11-9 RMPower	33/1	3½	6
134	Limerick Boy (GER) *MissVenetiaWilliams* 7-11-9 SThomas	9/1		f
149	Control Man (IRE) *MCPipe* 7-11-7 (v) TJMurphy	11/1		pu
149	Whitford Don (IRE) *PFNicholls* 7-11-7 (b) RWalsh	6/1		pu
130	Chauvinist (IRE) *NJHenderson* 10-11-5 MAFitzgerald	7/1		pu

Mr John P. McManus 10ran 6m26.62

172 John Smith's Top Nov Hdle (Gr 2) (A) (4yo+) £29,000 2m110y (9)

	Horse	SP	Dist	Pos
	MIGHTY MAN (FR) *HDDaly* 5-11-0 RJohnson	3/1		1
133	DUSKY WARBLER *GLMoore* 6-11-0 APMcCoy	15/8f	½	2
138	NAPOLITAIN (FR) *PFNicholls* 4-11-2 RWalsh	25/1	23	3
72	Nyrche (FR) *AKing* 5-11-3 RThornton	7/1	9	4
	Sea Captain *NJHenderson* 5-11-0 MAFitzgerald	5/1	nk	5
133	Marcel (FR) *MCPipe* 5-11-8 TJMurphy	15/2	29	6
77	Astronomic *JHowardJohnson* 5-11-8 GLee	14/1		pu

Mr E. R. Hanbury 7ran 4m01.90

173 John Smith's Melling Chase (Gr 1) (A) (5yo+) £89,250 2½m (16)

	Horse	SP	Dist	Pos
141	MOSCOW FLYER (IRE) *MrsJHarrington,Ireland* 11-11-10 BJGeraghty	4/9f		1
146	LE ROI MIGUEL (FR) *PFNicholls* 7-11-10 RWalsh	9/2	16	2
153	THEREALBANDIT (IRE) *MCPipe* 8-11-10 (v) TJMurphy	9/1	28	3
141	Kadarann (IRE) *PFNicholls* 8-11-10 PJBrennan	40/1	dist	4
155	Davoski *DrPPritchard* 11-11-10 JAMcCarthy	200/1	17	5
112	Mister McGoldrick *MrsSJSmith* 8-11-10 DElsworth	11/1		f

Mr Brian Kearney 6ran 5m01.34

174 John Smith's And Spar Topham Chase (Hcap) (B) 0-150(145) (5yo+) £46,400 2m5f110y (Nat.) (18)

	Horse	SP	Dist	Pos
162	CREGG HOUSE (IRE) *SDonohoe,Ireland* 10-10-5[124] DNRussell	50/1		1
20	HAUT DE GAMME (FR) *FerdyMurphy* 10-10-10[132] KMercer[3]	25/1	1	2
148	LE DUC (FR) *PFNicholls* 6-11-3[136] RWalsh	20/1	5	3
	LONGSHANKS *KCBailey* 8-11-0[133] JPMcNamara	9/2f	nk	4
155	Impek (FR) *MissHCKnight* 9-11-11[144] JCulloty	16/1	2	5
	Munster (IRE) *ALTMoore,Ireland* 8-9-11[119] (t) DJHoward[3]	50/1	2½	6
136	Whereareyounow (IRE) *NATwiston-Davies* 8-10-12[131] CLlewellyn	14/1	4	7
82	Wain Mountain *JABOld* 9-10-11[130] (t) WHutchinson	25/1	4	8
22	Better Days (IRE) *MrsSJSmith* 9-10-9[128] DElsworth	20/1	nk	9
	Winning Dream (IRE) *OliverMcKiernan,Ireland* 11-10-12[131] APMcCoy	20/1	2½	10
148	Colca Canyon (IRE) *MrsJHarrington,Ireland* 8-11-12[145] RMPower	25/1	6	11
143	Itsonlyme (IRE) *MissVenetiaWilliams* 12-10-5[124] SThomas	100/1	6	12
143	Juveigneur (FR) *NJHenderson* 8-11-0[133] MAFitzgerald	11/2	8	13
148	Liberthine (FR) *NJHenderson* 6-10-12[138] MrSWaley-Cohen[7]	10/1	2	14
148	Ghadames (FR) *RCGuest* 11-10-4[123] SFox	100/1	10	15
	Boy's Hurrah (IRE) *JHowardJohnson* 9-10-0[119] GLee	12/1	hd	16
143	Knock Down (IRE) *HDDaly* 6-10-7[126] RJohnson	25/1	2	17
130	Turgeonev (FR) *TDEasterby* 10-11-9[142] DO'Meara	33/1	½	18
143	Rathbawn Prince (IRE) *MissHCKnight* 13-10-2[121] TDoyle	40/1	1¼	19

127	Be My Better Half (IRE) *ALTMoore,Ireland* 10-10-7^{126} CO'Dwyer	25/1	dist 20
157	Hersov (IRE) *PaulARoche,Ireland* 9-10-0^{119} (s) BHarding	40/1	dist 21
48	John James (IRE) *JHScott,Ireland* 9-11-1^{134} KWhelan	16/1	nk 22
82	Historic (IRE) *TRGeorge* 9-10-13^{132} JMMaguire	66/1	f
	Present Bleu (FR) *MScudamore* 10-10-9^{128} JamesDavies	100/1	f
	Spring Margot (FR) *PFNicholls* 9-10-5^{124} ChristianWilliams	25/1	f
136	Swansea Bay *PBowen* 9-10-8^{127} (t) AThornton	33/1	rtr
85	Over The First (IRE) *CFSwan,Ireland* 10-10-8^{127} ADobbin	33/1	ur
45	Royal Atalza (FR) *GAHuffer* 8-10-4^{123} (s) PaulMoloney	50/1	ur
54	Alcapone (IRE) *MFMorris,Ireland* 11-11-5^{138} NFehily	25/1	pu
157	Wild Tempo (FR) *MScudamore* 10-10-6^{125} TScudamore	125/1	pu

Mrs Kathleen Kennedy 30ran 5m31.34

175 John Smith's NUSSL Sefton Nov Hdle (Gr 1) (A) (4yo+) £46,400 3m110y (13)

92	ASIAN MAZE (IRE) *ThomasMullins,Ireland* 6-10-11 RWalsh	7/1	1
152	BREWSTER (IRE) *IanWilliams* 8-11-4 DRDennis	6/1	2½ 2
52	FOOTBALL CRAZY (IRE) *PBowen* 6-11-4 WMarston	33/1	25 3
152	Moulin Riche (FR) *FDoumen,France* 5-11-4 MAFitzgerald	7/2f	1¾ 4
	Seomra Hocht (IRE) *WilliamColemanO'Brien,Ireland* 8-11-4 BJGeraghty	200/1	2½ 5
133	Shuhood (USA) *PRWebber* 5-11-4 TDoyle	66/1	4 6
139	Black Apalachi (IRE) *PJRothwell,Ireland* 6-11-4 JCullen	40/1	11 7
	Teeming Rain (IRE) *CFSwan,Ireland* 6-11-4 APMcCoy	12/1	4 8
131	King Killone (IRE) *MissHCKnight* 5-11-4 TJMurphy	50/1	30 9
131	Rebel Rhythm *MrsSJSmith* 6-11-4 DElsworth	12/1	f
152	Bewleys Berry (IRE) *JHowardJohnson* 7-11-4 GLee	6/1	pu
136	Blazing Batman *DrPPritchard* 12-11-4 DrPPritchard	250/1	pu
	Ferimon *HDDaly* 6-11-4 MBradburne	50/1	pu
139	Gold Medallist *PJHobbs* 5-11-4 RJohnson	11/2	pu
52	Idle Talk (IRE) *TRGeorge* 6-11-4 JMMaguire	16/1	pu
	Il Duce (IRE) *AKing* 5-11-4 RThornton	66/1	pu
44	Loup Charter (FR) *MissHCKnight* 6-11-4 JCulloty	22/1	pu

Mrs C. A. Moore 17ran 6m10.08

176 betfair.com Hcap Chase (B) (154) (5yo+) £29,000 3m1f (18)

154	SLEEPING NIGHT (FR) *PFNicholls* 9-11-0^{142} RWalsh	3/1	1
	ZETA'S RIVER (IRE) *MCPipe* 7-10-0^{128} TJMurphy	5/2f	10 2
146	HAND INN HAND *HDDaly* 9-11-12^{154} MBradburne	11/1	4 3
148	Roveretto *MCPipe* 10-9-9^{128} (b) RStephens^{5}	100/1	2 4
136	Kock de La Vesvre (FR) *MissVenetiaWilliams* 7-10-4^{132} SThomas	13/2	3½ 5
159	Howaya Pet (IRE) *GKeane,Ireland* 9-10-0^{128} (t) JRBarry	16/1	3½ 6
49	Happy Hussar (IRE) *DrPPritchard* 12-9-9^{128} DrPPritchard^{5}	200/1	24 7
136	Marlborough (IRE) *NJHenderson* 13-11-3^{145} MAFitzgerald	40/1	dist 8
130	Horus (IRE) *MCPipe* 10-10-9^{142} (v) TJMalone^{5}	14/1	12 9
143	Lord of The River (IRE) *NJHenderson* 13-10-0^{128} MFoley	6/1	ur
	Dark'n Sharp (GER) *RTPhillips* 10-11-1^{143} RJohnson	50/1	pu
157	Artic Jack (FR) *MrsSJSmith* 9-9-11^{128} KMercer^{3}	16/1	pu

D. J. & F. A. Jackson 12ran 6m24.60

177 John Smith's Extra Cold Hcap Hdle (L) (A) (142) (4yo+) £23,200 3m110y (13)

	HOLLAND PARK (IRE) *MrsSDWilliams* 8-11-0^{130} JTizzard	10/1	1
80	CELTIC SON (FR) *MCPipe* 6-11-5^{135} (t) TJMurphy	2/1f	9 2
150	THE DARK LORD (IRE) *MrsLWadham* 8-11-3^{133} LAspell	16/1	¾ 3
111	IDAHO D'OX (FR) *MCPipe* 9-9-12^{119} TJMalone^{5}	25/1	5 4
150	Victory Gunner (IRE) *CRoberts* 7-9-13^{120} LStephens^{5}	50/1	½ 5
150	Mioche d'Estruval (FR) *MCPipe* 5-10-9^{125} TScudamore	14/1	16 6
	Back To Ben Alder (IRE) *NJHenderson* 8-10-4^{120} MFoley	20/1	¾ 7
143	Champagne Harry *NATwiston-Davies* 7-11-5^{135} CLlewellyn	66/1	17 8
150	Penny Pictures (IRE) *MCPipe* 6-11-3^{133} RThornton	100/1	sh 9
150	Carlys Quest *FerdyMurphy* 11-11-2^{135} (v) KMercer^{3}	10/1	nk 10
150	Touch Closer *MissVScott* 8-10-11^{127} GLee	16/1	7 11
150	Quick *MCPipe* 5-11-5^{142} (v) AGlassonbury^{7}	50/1	dist 12
	Savannah Bay *PJHobbs* 6-10-4^{120} (b) RJohnson	10/1	hd 13
	No Picnic (IRE) *MrsSCBradburne* 7-10-0^{116} MBradburne	100/1	9 14
150	Hirvine (FR) *PBowen* 7-11-5^{140} (s) TGreenway^{5}	33/1	f
124	Turtle Soup (IRE) *TRGeorge* 9-11-0^{140} WMcCarthy^{10}	66/1	ur
142	You Owe Me (IRE) *NATwiston-Davies* 8-10-6^{122} WMarston	66/1	pu
142	Fountain Hill (IRE) *PFNicholls* 6-11-6^{136} RWalsh	11/1	pu
	Ballylusky (IRE) *JonjoO'Neill* 8-11-5^{135} APMcCoy	25/1	pu
	Paperprophet *NGRichards* 7-11-3^{133} ADobbin	7/1	pu
142	Lilium de Cotte (FR) *NJHenderson* 6-10-8^{124} MAFitzgerald	33/1	pu
	Old Feathers (IRE) *JonjoO'Neill* 8-10-0^{116} (b) SDurack	100/1	pu

Mr B. M. Yin 22ran 6m07.49

AINTREE Saturday, Apr 9 GOOD to SOFT

178 John Smith's Extra Smooth Hcap Hdle (L) (A) (143) (4yo+) £29,000 2m110y (9)

	DEFINATE SPECTACLE (IRE) *NMeade,Ireland* 5-10-1^{118} PCarberry	11/1	1
	SAY WHAT YOU SEE (IRE) *MCPipe* 5-10-6^{123} ADobbin	50/1	8 2
156	CROSSBOW CREEK *MGRimell* 7-11-3^{134} JCrowley	16/1	½ 3
156	COPELAND *MCPipe* 10-11-5^{141} (s) TJMalone^{5}	100/1	3 4
	Handy Money *AKing* 8-10-13^{130} RThornton	8/1	½ 5
79	Boleyknowsbest (IRE) *RPBurns,Ireland* 7-9-9^{117} TGMRyan^{5}	33/1	4 6
	Atahuelpa *AKing* 5-10-7^{124} PJBrennan	33/1	3 7
	Victram (IRE) *AMcGuinness,Ireland* 5-9-9^{117} MissNCarberry^{5}	5/1	1¼ 8
156	Stance *GLMoore* 6-11-2^{133} APMcCoy	12/1	4 9
78	Lunar Crystal (IRE) *MCPipe* 7-10-8^{125} TScudamore	33/1	¾ 10
	Fireball Macnamara (IRE) *MPitman* 9-10-0^{117} ATinkler	200/1	½ 11
156	Grande Jete (SAF) *NJHenderson* 8-11-1^{132} MAFitzgerald	9/1	7 12
132	Medison (FR) *MCPipe* 5-11-3^{134} TJMurphy	9/4f	1 13
	Wiscalitus (GER) *MissVenetiaWilliams* 6-10-0^{117} AO'Keeffe	25/1	1 14
103	Chivalry *JHowardJohnson* 6-11-12^{143} (b) GLee	28/1	11 15
132	King Eider *BEllison* 6-10-3^{120} LAspell	16/1	7 16
	Green Tango *HDDaly* 6-10-10^{127} RJohnson	16/1	¾ 17
	Damien's Choice (IRE) *DrPPritchard* 13-9-9^{117} DrPPritchard^{5}	300/1	5 18

Mrs P. Sloan 18ran 4m02.02

179 John Smith's Maghull Nov Chase (Gr 1) (A) (5yo+) £63,800 2m (12)

134	ASHLEY BROOK (IRE) *KBishop* 7-11-4 PJBrennan	3/1	1
134	WAR OF ATTRITION (IRE) *MFMorris,Ireland* 6-11-4 CO'Dwyer	11/4f	16 2
43	DEMPSEY (IRE) *MPitman* 7-11-4 ATinkler	20/1	9 3
134	Made In Japan (JPN) *PJHobbs* 5-11-1 (b) RJohnson	20/1	8 4
	Parknasilla *MWEasterby* 5-11-1 ADempsey	50/1	11 5
134	River City (IRE) *NoelTChance* 8-11-4 TDoyle	7/2	¾ 6
134	Contraband *MCPipe* 7-11-4 TJMurphy	4/1	15 7
134	Mambo Des Mottes (FR) *MissVenetiaWilliams* 5-11-1 AO'Keeffe	100/1	4 8
	Pennys From Heaven *MrsTraceyBarfoot-Saunt* 11-11-4 MrGBarfoot-Saunt	200/1	dist 9
	Saintsaire (FR) *NJHenderson* 6-11-4 MAFitzgerald	11/1	pu

Mrs E. K. Ellis 10ran 3m54.82

180 John Smith's No Nonsense Hcap Hdle (L) (A) (143) (4yo+) £23,200 2½m (11)

	GENGHIS (IRE) *PBowen* 6-10-13^{130} APMcCoy	10/1	1
156	TAMARINBLEU (FR) *MCPipe* 5-11-5^{143} AGlassonbury^{7}	50/1	6 2
5	MIRPOUR (IRE) *EGriffin,Ireland* 6-10-5^{122} (b) GLee	8/1	3½ 3
131	BILLYVODDAN (IRE) *HDDaly* 6-10-11^{128} RJohnson	15/2	1½ 4
142	Jack Dawson (IRE) *JohnBerry* 8-11-4^{135} SDurack	25/1	¾ 5
132	Fenix (GER) *MrsLWadham* 6-10-13^{130} (b) LAspell	14/1	nk 6
142	After Eight (GER) *MissVenetiaWilliams* 5-10-5^{122} JCulloty	12/1	¾ 7
142	Sharp Rigging (IRE) *AMHales* 5-11-3^{134} BJGeraghty	9/1	½ 8
133	Manorson (IRE) *OSherwood* 6-10-8^{125} JAMcCarthy	16/1	2½ 9
142	Fairwood Present (IRE) *PJRothwell,Ireland* 7-10-10^{127} JCullen	28/1	15 10
156	Fontanesi (IRE) *MCPipe* 5-11-5^{136} TJMurphy	16/1	3 11
156	Its Crucial (IRE) *NATwiston-Davies* 5-10-6^{123} CLlewellyn	100/1	1 12
	Lord of Beauty (FR) *NoelTChance* 5-10-5^{122} BJCrowley	40/1	nk 13
142	Royaleety (FR) *IanWilliams* 6-10-13^{130} RWalsh	8/1	10 14
63	Healy's Pub (IRE) *OliverMcKiernan,Ireland* 9-10-6^{123} (b) PACarberry	14/1	1½ 15
	Migwell (FR) *MrsLWadham* 5-10-8^{125} RThornton	11/2f	7 16
142	Zibeline (IRE) *BEllison* 8-11-1^{132} (t) BHarding	33/1	11 17
	Jorobaden (FR) *MrsHDalton* 5-9-12^{122} PMerrigan^{7}	33/1	15 18
70	Barrow Drive *AnthonyMullins,Ireland* 9-10-11^{128} (s+t) CO'Dwyer	20/1	16 19
	Chivite (IRE) *PJHobbs* 6-10-12^{129} PJBrennan	20/1	pu

Khan Partners 20ran 4m52.03

181 Scottish And Newcastle Aintree Hdle (Gr 1) (A) (4yo+) £87,000 2½m (11)

135	AL EILE (IRE) *JQueally,Ireland* 5-11-7 TJMurphy	11/1	1
147	INGLIS DREVER *JHowardJohnson* 6-11-7 GLee	9/4	nk 2
147	EXOTIC DANCER (FR) *JonjoO'Neill* 5-11-7 (s) PCarberry	50/1	¾ 3
135	Macs Joy (IRE) *MrsJHarrington,Ireland* 6-11-7 BJGeraghty	7/1	4 4
135	Rooster Booster *PJHobbs* 11-11-7 RJohnson	16/1	6 5
135	Accordion Etoile (IRE) *PaulNolan,Ireland* 6-11-7 JCullen	16/1	nk 6
124	Blue Canyon (FR) *FDoumen,France* 7-11-7 APMcCoy	12/1	2 7
135	Intersky Falcon *JonjoO'Neill* 8-11-7 (b+t) ADobbin	14/1	hd 8
135	Brave Inca (IRE) *CAMurphy,Ireland* 7-11-7 BMCash	2/1f	ur

Mr M. A. Ryan 9ran 5m09.39

182 John Smith's Grand National Chase (Hcap) (Gr 3) (A) 0-110(155) (6yo+) £406,000 4½m (30)

	HEDGEHUNTER (IRE) *WPMullins,Ireland* 9-11-1^{144} RWalsh	7/1f		1
153	ROYAL AUCLAIR (FR) *PFNicholls* 8-11-10^{153} (t) ChristianWilliams	40/1	14	2
148	SIMPLY GIFTED *JonjoO'Neill* 10-10-6^{135} BHarding	66/1	hd	3
130	IT TAKES TIME (IRE) *MCPipe* 11-10-11^{140} TJMurphy	18/1	4	4
120	Forest Gunner *RFord* 11-10-7^{136} CarrieFord	8/1	9	5
93	Nil Desperandum (IRE) *MsFMCrowley,Ireland* 8-10-11^{140} JCulloty	16/1	½	6
	Innox (FR) *FDoumen,France* 9-10-6^{135} (b) RThornton	16/1	11	7
136	Heros Collonges (FR) *PFNicholls* 10-10-11^{140} JPMcNamara	66/1	3½	8
34	Just In Debt (IRE) *MTodhunter* 9-10-7^{136} ADobbin	33/1	2½	9
34	Amberleigh House (IRE) *DMcCain* 13-11-3^{146} GLee	16/1	5	10
88	Bindaree (IRE) *NATwiston-Davies* 11-11-3^{146} CLlewellyn	33/1	1½	11
148	Iznogoud (FR) *MCPipe* 9-10-9^{138} TScudamore	125/1	1	12
148	Polar Red *MCPipe* 8-10-8^{137} TJMalone	100/1	1¼	13
136	Joly Bey (FR) *NJGifford* 8-10-10^{139} (t) MrDHDunsdon	16/1	9	14
157	L'Aventure (FR) *PFNicholls* 6-10-5^{134} (b+t) RPMcNally	66/1	15	15
93	Monty's Pass (IRE) *JamesJosephMangan,Ireland* 12-11-6^{149} BJGeraghty	33/1	5	16
68	Strong Resolve (IRE) *MissLucindaVRussell* 9-10-6^{135} PBuchanan	9/1	6	17
137	Spot Thedifference (IRE) *EBolger,Ireland* 12-10-7^{136} RMPower	25/1	16	18
162	Arctic Copper (IRE) *NMeade,Ireland* 11-10-6^{135} (s) DNRussell	200/1	17	19
148	Europa *FerdyMurphy* 9-10-6^{135} JMMaguire	150/1	21	20
	Shamawan (IRE) *JonjoO'Neill* 10-10-6^{135} JRBarry	200/1	19	21
154	Foly Pleasant (FR) *MissKMarks* 11-11-0^{143} (t) AThornton	50/1		f
	Ad Hoc (IRE) *PFNicholls* 11-10-12^{141} JTizzard	33/1		f
154	Lord Atterbury (IRE) *MCPipe* 9-10-6^{135} MBradburne	25/1		f
82	Merchants Friend (IRE) *CJMann* 10-10-6^{135} (s) NFehily	80/1		f
136	Native Emperor *JonjoO'Neill* 9-10-5^{134} (t) DElsworth	100/1		f
	Clan Royal (FR) *JonjoO'Neill* 10-10-11^{140} APMcCoy	9/1		co
136	Ballybough Rasher (IRE) *JHowardJohnson* 10-11-4^{147} ADempsey	100/1		ref
153	Take The Stand (IRE) *PBowen* 9-11-5^{148} LAspell	16/1		ur
153	Ballycassidy (IRE) *PBowen* 9-11-5^{148} SDurack	66/1		ur
146	Risk Accessor (IRE) *CRoche,Ireland* 10-11-4^{147} (t) APCrowe	100/1		ur
136	Frenchman's Creek *HMorrison* 11-10-9^{138} JAMcCarthy	50/1		ur
120	Double Honour (FR) *PJHobbs* 7-10-8^{137} (b) PJBrennan	25/1		ur
159	Marcus du Berlais (FR) *ALTMoore,Ireland* 8-10-5^{134} BMCash	25/1		ur
159	Le Coudray (FR) *CRoche,Ireland* 11-11-12^{155} (t) CO'Dwyer	33/1		pu
146	Fondmort (FR) *NJHenderson* 9-11-6^{149} MAFitzgerald	50/1		pu
153	Astonville (FR) *MScudamore* 11-10-13^{142} BJCrowley	100/1		pu
101	Glenelly Gale (IRE) *ALTMoore,Ireland* 11-10-11^{140} MrTGreenall	150/1		pu
136	Jakari (FR) *HDDaly* 8-10-10^{139} RJohnson	33/1		pu
65	Colnel Rayburn (IRE) *PaulNolan,Ireland* 9-10-7^{136} PCarberry	20/1		pu

Mr Trevor Hemmings 40ran 9m20.86

183 John Smith's Nov Hcap Chase (Amat) (B) (129) (5yo+) £19,198 2½m (16)

145	JOES EDGE (IRE) *FerdyMurphy* 8-11-9^{127} MrTJDreaper^{3}	9/2		1
	SCHUH SHINE (IRE) *MissVenetiaWilliams* 8-10-8^{116} MrRMcCarthy^{7}	4/1	2½	2
145	COPSALE LAD *NJHenderson* 8-11-6^{126} MrBKing^{5}	8/1	½	3
	Edmo Yewkay (IRE) *TDEasterby* 5-10-2^{114} MrTJO'Brien^{7}	33/1	4	4
105	Undeniable *MrsSJSmith* 7-10-11^{112} MrTGreenall	8/1	3½	5
	Almost Broke *PFNicholls* 8-11-7^{125} MrCJSweeney^{3}	10/3f	22	6
	Caribbean Cove (IRE) *RCGuest* 7-9-7^{101} (b) MrWPKavanagh^{7}	11/2	23	7
	Cyanara *DrPPritchard* 9-10-0^{101} DrPPritchard	200/1	17	8
134	Mondul (GER) *MFHarris* 5-11-10^{129} MrDHDunsdon	14/1		f
	Dangerousdanmagru (IRE) *AEJones* 9-10-0^{101} MrNPMadden	20/1		f

Chemipetro Limited 10ran 5m09.28

184 John Smith's Champion Standard Open NHF (Gr 2) (A) (4, 5 and 6yo) £17,400 2m1f

	THE COOL GUY (IRE) *NATwiston-Davies* 5-10-11 SCrawford^{7}	50/1		1
115	SOME TOUCH (IRE) *JHowardJohnson* 5-11-4 GLee	33/1	½	2
	MENDO *NoelTChance* 5-11-4 TDoyle	16/1	½	3
144	Refinement (IRE) *JonjoO'Neill* 6-10-11 APMcCoy	7/4f	2½	4
	High Kick *RAFahey* 4-10-12 ARoss	66/1	hd	5
	Noland *PFNicholls* 4-10-12 RWalsh	5/2	1½	6
	Avoca Mist (IRE) *WPMullins,Ireland* 5-10-4 MissKWalsh^{7}	16/1	¾	7
	Rimsky (IRE) *NATwiston-Davies* 4-10-12 CLlewellyn	66/1	1¼	8
	The Duke's Speech (IRE) *TPTate* 4-10-12 JMMaguire	66/1	3	9
	Glasker Mill (IRE) *MissHCKnight* 5-11-4 JCulloty	13/2	2½	10
	Dusky Lord *NJGifford* 6-11-4 LAspell	40/1	5	11
	Joke Club *VRADartnall* 4-10-12 BJGeraghty	25/1	½	12
	Cracboumwiz (FR) *MrsHDalton* 5-10-11 PMerrigan^{7}	50/1	3	13

	Wishin And Hopin *AGNewcombe* 4-10-12 BJCrowley	100/1	nk	14
	Promise To Be Good *NJHenderson* 4-10-12 MAFitzgerald	50/1	22	15
144	Nice Horse (FR) *MCPipe* 4-10-12 TScudamore	100/1	nk	16
	Coolawarra (IRE) *DMForster* 6-11-4 ADobbin	33/1	5	17
	Khudabad (IRE) *FrederickJohnBowles,Ireland* 4-10-7 TGreenway^{5}	100/1	3	18
	Witch Wind *AMCrow* 5-10-11 DMcGann^{7}	50/1	¾	19
144	Itsmyboy (IRE) *MCPipe* 5-11-4 TJMurphy	11/1	2½	20
	Flintoff (USA) *RCGuest* 4-10-5 PCO'Neill^{7}	100/1	6	21
	Charming Fellow (IRE) *MissHCKnight* 5-11-4 SDurack	100/1	10	22

Frosty's Four 22ran 4m14.71

AYR Saturday, Apr 16 GOOD

185 Ashleybank Investments Future Champion Nov Chase (Gr 2) (A) (5yo+) £23,200 — 2½m (17)

71	LOCKSMITH *MCPipe* 5-11-6 TJMurphy	5/1		1
134	MY WILL (FR) *PFNicholls* 5-11-6 RWalsh	10/11f	½	2
156	FOOL ON THE HILL *PJHobbs* 8-11-3 PJBrennan	5/1	3	3
	Flight Command *PBeaumont* 7-11-7 RGarritty	33/1	13	4
105	Vandas Choice (IRE) *MissLucindaVRussell* 7-11-7 PBuchanan	20/1	1¼	5
179	Made In Japan (JPN) *PJHobbs* 5-11-3 (b) RJohnson	6/1	nk	6

Mr D. A. Johnson 6ran 5m00.97

186 Samsung Electronics Scottish Champion Hdle (Ltd Hcap) (Gr 2) (A) (150) (4yo+) £34,800 — 2m (8)

180	GENGHIS (IRE) *PBowen* 6-10-11^{137} APMcCoy	5/2f		1
135	ROYAL SHAKESPEARE (FR) *SGollings* 6-11-8^{148} RThornton	13/2	4	2
111	DALARAM (IRE) *JHowardJohnson* 5-10-11^{137} (t) GLee	8/1	¾	3
178	Copeland *MCPipe* 10-10-10^{141} (s) TJMalone^{5}	10/1	6	4
156	Geos (FR) *NJHenderson* 10-11-5^{145} MAFitzgerald	33/1	hd	5
180	Fontanesi (IRE) *MCPipe* 5-10-10^{136} TJMurphy	12/1	2	6
156	Calatagan (IRE) *JMJefferson* 6-10-4^{130} RJohnson	25/1	2½	7
156	Rigmarole *PFNicholls* 7-11-10^{150} (t) RWalsh	22/1	7	8
	Liberty Seeker (FR) *PMonteith* 6-10-4^{130} ADobbin	20/1	1	9
183	Mondul (GER) *MFHarris* 5-10-9^{135} SDurack	66/1	1	10
147	The French Furze (IRE) *NGRichards* 11-11-4^{144} BHarding	33/1	7	11
156	Demi Beau *CJMann* 7-10-4^{130} NFehily	14/1	dist	12
132	Far Pavilions *GASwinbank* 6-10-4^{130} JCrowley	4/1		f

Khan Partners 13ran 3m38.38

187 Gala Casinos Daily Record Scottish Grand National Hcap Chase (Gr 3) (A) (163) (5yo+) £70,000 — 4m1f (27)

183	JOES EDGE (IRE) *FerdyMurphy* 8-9-11^{137} KMercer^{3}	20/1		1
140	CORNISH REBEL (IRE) *PFNicholls* 8-10-7^{144} RWalsh	9/2	sh	2
149	ANOTHER RUM (IRE) *IADuncan,Ireland* 7-10-0^{137} ARoss	10/1	10	3
182	DOUBLE HONOUR (FR) *PJHobbs* 7-10-5^{142} (b) PJBrennan	20/1	3½	4
	Kerry Lads (IRE) *MissLucindaVRussell* 10-9-11^{137} (s) PBuchanan^{3}	33/1	3	5
174	Longshanks *KCBailey* 8-10-0^{137} CLlewellyn	9/1	17	6
157	Philson Run (IRE) *NickWilliams* 9-10-0^{137} SDurack	12/1	hd	7
136	Iris Bleu (FR) *MCPipe* 9-10-3^{140} TScudamore	16/1	5	8
136	Chives (IRE) *MrsSJSmith* 10-10-11^{148} DElsworth	20/1	28	9
182	Take The Stand (IRE) *PBowen* 9-11-12^{163} RJohnson	12/1		pu
140	Comply Or Die (IRE) *MCPipe* 6-10-10^{147} TJMurphy	4/1f		pu
157	Stormez (FR) *MCPipe* 8-10-8^{145} (b+t) APMcCoy	16/1		pu
136	Colourful Life (IRE) *PFNicholls* 9-10-2^{139} JTizzard	12/1		pu
171	Control Man (IRE) *MCPipe* 7-10-1^{138} (v) RThornton	40/1		pu
136	Hussard Collonges (FR) *PBeaumont* 10-10-0^{137} GLee	28/1		pu
157	Gingembre (FR) *MrsLCTaylor* 11-10-3^{140} AThornton	50/1		pu
68	Lord Jack (IRE) *NGRichards* 9-10-0^{137} BHarding	33/1		pu
	A Piece of Cake (IRE) *JSGoldie* 12-10-0^{137} ADempsey	66/1		pu
	Legal Right (USA) *MissLucindaVRussell* 12-10-0^{137} (t) KRenwick	100/1		pu
68	Supreme Glory (IRE) *PGMurphy* 12-10-0^{137} JCrowley	66/1		pu

Chemipetro Limited 20ran 8m23.77

PERTH Thursday, Apr 21 SOFT

188 Betdaq Perth Festival Hcap Chase (B) (152) (5yo+) £18,298 — 3m (18)

176	KOCK DE LA VESVRE (FR) *MissVenetiaWilliams* 7-10-4^{130} SThomas	11/2		1
182	IT TAKES TIME (IRE) *MCPipe* 11-11-12^{152} TJMurphy	7/1	¾	2
174	LE DUC (FR) *PFNicholls* 6-10-10^{136} RWalsh	4/1f	27	3
	Wise Man (IRE) *NWAlexander* 10-9-11^{126} PBuchanan^{3}	25/1	9	4
148	Scots Grey *NJHenderson* 10-10-5^{131} ATinkler	10/1	26	5
182	Polar Red *MCPipe* 8-10-3^{134} (t) TJMalone^{5}	10/1	24	6
	Malek (IRE) *KGReveley* 9-10-4^{130} RMcGrath	9/2		pu

148	Hunters Tweed *PBeaumont* 9-10-1[127] (s) GLee	8/1		pu
127	Zaffamore (IRE) *MissHCKnight* 9-10-0[126] CLlewellyn	8/1		pu

Mr O. P. Dakin 9ran 6m18.84

189 Betdaq 24 Hour Telebet Hcap Hdle (C) 0-130(129) (4yo+) £7,183 2½m110y (10)

	COMMERCIAL FLYER (IRE) *MCPipe* 6-11-3[120] (t) TJMurphy	1/1f		1
	CRYSTAL GIFT *ACWhillans* 13-10-0[110] MrEWhillans[7]	33/1	2½	2
	SPEED KRIS (FR) *MrsSCBradburne* 6-10-4[107] (s) MBradburne	20/1	nk	3
	Blue Americo (IRE) *PFNicholls* 7-11-3[120] RWalsh	16/1	8	4
	Whispered Secret (GER) *MCPipe* 6-10-11[119] TJMalone[5]	16/1	¾	5
	I Got Rhythm *KGReveley* 7-10-0[103] RMcGrath	33/1	29	6
	Westmeath Flyer *NGRichards* 10-11-12[129] ADobbin	13/2		f
	Iron Man (FR) *JHowardJohnson* 4-11-2[125] GLee	3/1		ur

Mr D. A. Johnson 8ran 5m17.07

PERTH Friday, Apr 22 SOFT

190 Genesis Oil And Gas Nov Chase (C) (5yo+) £8,398 2m (12)

	SARDAGNA (FR) *MCPipe* 5-10-3 TJMalone[5]	10/1		1
179	PARKNASILLA *MWEasterby* 5-11-1 ADempsey	11/4	21	2
	THE MINER *MissSEForster* 7-11-1 MrCStorey[3]	66/1	¾	3
	Mister Magnum (IRE) *PMonteith* 7-10-2 DDaSilva[10]	66/1	7	4
	Compadre *PMonteith* 7-10-12 NMulholland	25/1	4	5
	Andreas (FR) *PFNicholls* 5-11-5 (t) JTizzard	1/2f		f

Mr D. A. Johnson 6ran 4m09.84

SANDOWN Friday, Apr 22 GOOD to FIRM

191 Concept Hdle (B) (4yo+) £29,000 2m110y (8)

181	ROOSTER BOOSTER *PJHobbs* 11-11-10 RJohnson	5/1		1
135	SELF DEFENSE *PRChamings* 8-11-10 MAFitzgerald	7/2f	4	2
156	PEROUSE *PFNicholls* 7-11-8 (t) RWalsh	8/1	1¼	3
180	Tamarinbleu (FR) *MCPipe* 5-11-8 APMcCoy	4/1	6	4
186	Copeland *MCPipe* 10-11-8 (s) JEMoore	33/1	6	5
142	Ilnamar (FR) *MCPipe* 9-11-4 BJGeraghty	33/1	7	6
186	Rigmarole *PFNicholls* 7-11-10 (b+t) ChristianWilliams	33/1	3½	7
178	Medison (FR) *MCPipe* 5-11-8 TJMurphy	13/2	dist	8
186	Royal Shakespeare (FR) *SGollings* 6-11-7 RThornton	4/1		f

Mr Terry Warner 9ran 3m47.70

SANDOWN Saturday, Apr 23 Chase course: GOOD, Hurdles course: GOOD to FIRM

192 Betfred 'The Bonus King' Hcap Hdle (B) 0-140(141) (4yo+) £15,857 2½m110y (10)

	YES SIR (IRE) *PBowen* 6-11-9[135] APMcCoy	13/2cf		1
177	PENNY PICTURES (IRE) *MCPipe* 6-11-5[131] RThornton	11/1	1¼	2
186	FONTANESI (IRE) *MCPipe* 5-11-9[135] TJMurphy	20/1	3½	3
180	JACK DAWSON (IRE) *JohnBerry* 8-11-7[133] GLee	13/2cf	¾	4
189	Commercial Flyer (IRE) *MCPipe* 6-11-10[141] (t) TJMalone[5]	13/2cf	1	5
	Xellance (IRE) *PJHobbs* 8-10-6[123] RStephens[5]	16/1	3½	6
	Tighe Caster *PRWebber* 6-10-8[120] TDoyle	8/1	6	7
	Pardishar (IRE) *GLMoore* 7-10-8[120] (s) JEMoore	12/1	nk	8
180	After Eight (GER) *MissVenetiaWilliams* 5-10-10[122] SThomas	9/1	1¼	9
180	Chivite (IRE) *PJHobbs* 6-11-3[129] RJohnson	25/1	1½	10
	Manly Money *PFNicholls* 7-10-10[122] RWalsh	11/1	½	11
142	Anatar (IRE) *MCPipe* 7-10-13[125] RGreene	25/1	9	12
156	Dancing Pearl *CJPrice* 7-10-12[124] CLlewellyn	20/1	12	13
	Mr Cool *MCPipe* 11-11-5[138] AGlassonbury[7]	40/1	7	14
	Sindapour (IRE) *MCPipe* 7-10-9[121] (t) SDurack	66/1	dist	15
	Ragdale Hall (USA) *JJoseph* 8-10-4[123] SWalsh[7]	66/1		f
177	Idaho d'Ox (FR) *MCPipe* 9-10-8[120] TScudamore	14/1		pu

Ms Y. M. Hill 17ran 4m43.90

193 Betfred Celebration Chase (Gr 2) (A) (5yo+) £58,000 2m (13)

141	WELL CHIEF (GER) *MCPipe* 6-11-10 TJMurphy	9/4		1
141	AZERTYUIOP (FR) *PFNicholls* 8-11-10 RWalsh	11/10f	4	2
179	CONTRABAND *MCPipe* 7-11-10 APMcCoy	10/1	10	3
146	Seebald (GER) *MCPipe* 10-11-6 TScudamore	40/1	½	4
173	Le Roi Miguel (FR) *PFNicholls* 7-11-6 BJGeraghty	10/1	nk	5
155	Armaturk (FR) *PFNicholls* 8-11-6 ChristianWilliams	25/1	8	6
188	Le Duc (FR) *PFNicholls* 6-11-6 MAFitzgerald	40/1	1	7
185	Locksmith *MCPipe* 5-11-3 TJMalone	14/1	2½	8
168	Golden Alpha (IRE) *MCPipe* 11-11-6 RGreene	66/1	2	9

Mr D. A. Johnson 9ran 3m52.48

194 Betfred Gold Cup Chase (Hcap) (Gr 3) (A) (155) (5yo+) £87,000 3m5f110y (24)

159	JACK HIGH (IRE) *TMWalsh,Ireland* 10-10-0[129] GCotter	16/1		1

174	JUVEIGNEUR (FR) *NJHenderson* 8-10-4^{133} MAFitzgerald	14/1	1¼	2
136	KELAMI (FR) *FDoumen,France* 7-10-10^{139} (t) RThornton	4/1f	2½	3
17	WHITENZO (FR) *PFNicholls* 9-9-9^{131} (t) MrJSnowden^{7}	9/1	1	4
182	Ballycassidy (IRE) *PBowen* 9-11-0^{143} RJohnson	16/1	9	5
187	Comply Or Die (IRE) *MCPipe* 6-11-4^{147} TJMurphy	14/1	3½	6
176	Zeta's River (IRE) *MCPipe* 7-9-9^{129} TJMalone^{5}	7/1	1¼	7
143	Maximize (IRE) *MCPipe* 11-10-0^{129} (s) TScudamore	50/1	6	8
182	Merchants Friend (IRE) *CJMann* 10-10-6^{135} (b) NFehily	33/1	1½	9
	Inca Trail (IRE) *PFNicholls* 9-10-6^{135} (b) RWalsh	5/1	7	10
173	Therealbandit (IRE) *MCPipe* 8-11-5^{155} (s) AGlassonbury^{7}	33/1	10	11
182	Joly Bey (FR) *NJGifford* 8-11-1^{147} (t) MrDHDunsdon^{3}	10/1	1¼	12
187	Iris Bleu (FR) *MCPipe* 9-10-11^{140} APMcCoy	14/1	8	13
182	Royal Auclair (FR) *PFNicholls* 8-11-12^{155} (t) ChristianWilliams	12/1		f
187	Stormez (FR) *MCPipe* 8-11-2^{145} (t) BJGeraghty	50/1		pu
157	Jurancon II (FR) *MCPipe* 8-10-11^{140} (v) RGreene	50/1		pu
	Lucky Bay (IRE) *MsBridgetNicholls* 9-9-7^{129} PCO'Neill^{7}	50/1		pu
174	Boy's Hurrah (IRE) *JHowardJohnson* 9-10-0^{129} GLee	40/1		pu
	Joint Authority (IRE) *DLWilliams* 10-9-7^{129} MissLHorner^{7}	200/1		pu

Miss Brenda Ross 19ran 7m22.65

PUNCHESTOWN Tuesday, Apr 26 First 6 races: GOOD to SOFT, Remainder: SOFT

195 Evening Herald Champion Nov Hdle (Gr 1) (5yo+) £42,466 2m (9)

133	WILD PASSION (GER) *NMeade* 5-11-11 PCarberry	7/4f		1
158	KILL DEVIL HILL (IRE) *PaulNolan* 5-11-11 JLCullen	12/1	sh	2
	IN COMPLIANCE (IRE) *MJPO'Brien* 5-11-11 TJMurphy	9/2	2	3
92	Arteea (IRE) *MHourigan* 6-11-12 BJGeraghty	20/1	4	4
160	The Railway Man (IRE) *ALTMoore* 6-11-12 BMCash	6/1	3	5
133	Publican (IRE) *PAFahy* 5-11-11 RWalsh	4/1	2	6
100	Man About Town (IRE) *TJTaaffe* 6-11-12 APMcCoy	10/1	1¾	7
57	Ray Boy (IRE) *PCO'Connor* 6-11-12 CO'Dwyer	16/1	8	8

Mr D. P. Sharkey 8ran 3m58.18

196 Kerrygold Champion Chase (Gr 1) (5yo+) £76,438 2m (11)

146	RATHGAR BEAU (IRE) *ESheehy* 9-11-12 JRBarry	8/1		1
173	MOSCOW FLYER (IRE) *MrsJHarrington* 11-11-12 BJGeraghty	1/4f	sh	2
146	NATIVE UPMANSHIP (IRE) *ALTMoore* 12-11-12 CO'Dwyer	14/1	1	3
162	Ground Ball (IRE) *CFSwan* 8-11-12 APMcCoy	16/1	4	4
162	Central House *DTHughes* 8-11-12 (b) PCarberry	14/1	4	5
50	Mossy Green (IRE) *WPMullins* 11-11-12 RWalsh	25/1	9	6
174	Colca Canyon (IRE) *MrsJHarrington* 8-11-12 (s) RMPower	33/1	10	7

One-O-Eight Racing Club 7ran 4m14.01

197 Ellier Developments Nov Chase (Gr 2) (5yo+) £24,524 2m5f (15)

161	FORGET THE PAST *MJPO'Brien* 7-11-10 TJMurphy	7/4f		1
145	QUAZAR (IRE) *JonjoO'Neill,GB* 7-11-6 (t) APMcCoy	11/4	5	2
161	DAVENPORT MILENIUM (IRE) *WPMullins* 9-11-3 RWalsh	14/1	¾	3
43	Duncliffe *RHAlner,GB* 8-11-6 AThornton	7/1	2	4
161	Strong Project (IRE) *CFSwan* 9-11-3 GLee	12/1	25	5
145	Sir Oj (IRE) *NMeade* 8-11-8 (b) PCarberry	11/2	dist	6
	Feathered Storm (IRE) *MJO'Connor* 7-11-3 JLCullen	33/1		pu
	Talking Cents (IRE) *SDonohoe* 8-11-3 MAFitzgerald	25/1		pu

Mr S. Mulryan 8ran 5m35.75

198 Tote Ireland 75th Anniversary Hcap Hdle (L) 0-140(133) (4yo+) £33,442 2½m (12)

79	MANSONY (FR) *ALTMoore* 6-11-4^{130} MissNCarberry^{5}	10/1		1
	RAIKKONEN (IRE) *WPMullins* 5-10-9^{116} RWalsh	13/2	1	2
	CITY OF SAILS (IRE) *AJMcNamara* 6-9-10^{106} PWFlood^{3}	20/1	sh	3
	OODACHEE *CFSwan* 6-10-1^{113} JFLevins^{5}	10/1	4	4
125	Macs Gildoran *WPMullins* 11-10-9^{116} DJCondon	16/1	1	5
	Hard Shoulder (IRE) *NMeade* 5-9-11^{104} PCarberry	11/1	nk	6
79	Kilbeggan Lad (IRE) *MHourigan* 7-9-6^{106} DFFlannery^{7}	11/1	1¾	7
	Piercing Sun (IRE) *AnthonyMullins* 6-10-6^{113} (s+t) MAFitzgerald	16/1	2	8
	Escrea (IRE) *PaulNolan* 6-10-2^{109} APCrowe	12/1	3	9
150	Basilea Star (IRE) *FerdyMurphy,GB* 8-11-7^{133} (t) KMercer^{5}	14/1	1	10
72	Keepthedreamalive *RHBuckler,GB* 7-11-0^{121} BHitchcott	16/1	2	11
	Leaders Way (IRE) *TKGeraghty* 10-10-9^{116} (s) RGeraghty	16/1	½	12
	One More Minute (IRE) *CFSwan* 5-10-1^{108} GLee	20/1	½	13
	Joint Agreement (IRE) *TMWalsh* 8-9-11^{104} GCotter	9/2f	2	14
	Derawar (IRE) *ALTMoore* 6-9-9^{105} DJHoward^{3}	16/1	11	15
	Doctor Linton (IRE) *MJPO'Brien* 6-10-10^{120} TGMRyan^{3}	20/1	4½	16
	Barrow Walk (IRE) *ThomasMullins* 6-9-3^{103} AFreeman^{7}	25/1	20	17

	Hordago (IRE) *EMcNamara* 5-9-8[108] BCByrnes[7]	16/1	1½	18
	Mocharamor (IRE) *CFSwan* 7-10-4[111] DNRussell	33/1	20	19
100	Giolla De (IRE) *FFlood* 6-9-9[107] KTColeman[5]	20/1	20	20
	Hickory Hill (IRE) *JMotherway* 7-9-12[105] JRBarry	25/1	7	21
	Urban (IRE) *JosephCrowley* 4-9-10[112] JMAllen[3]	16/1	½	22
	Demesne *PaulNolan* 5-9-13[106] TPTreacy	16/1		23
79	Emotional Article (IRE) *TJTaaffe* 5-10-2[109] TJMurphy	12/1		f
	Imazulutoo (IRE) *MrsJHarrington* 5-10-11[118] BJGeraghty	16/1		pu

Mr Michael Mulholland 25ran 5m09.29

199 Goffs Land Rover Bumper (4 and 5yo) £26,267 — 2m

	ITS A DREAM (IRE) *NJHenderson,GB* 5-11-11 MrAFitzgerald	13/2		1
	VIRGINIA PREUIL (FR) *PHughes* 4-11-0 MrNPMadden	5/1	4	2
	TUDORVIC (IRE) *JohnJosephMurphy* 4-10-9 MrRO'Sullivan[5]	20/1	nk	3
	Sir Overbury *DanielO'Connell* 4-11-0 MrJTMcNamara	16/1	3	4
	Macs Mandalus *WPMullins* 5-11-7 MrJJCodd	9/1	2	5
	Sher One Moor (IRE) *JosephCrowley* 4-10-9 MrGJPower[5]	9/1	2	6
	Schindlers Hunt (IRE) *DTHughes* 5-11-2 MrRLoughran[5]	9/2f	2	7
	Major Hayward (IRE) *EJO'Grady* 4-10-11 MrKEPower[3]	8/1	1	8
	The Sham *MHourigan* 5-11-0 MrPTEnright[7]	20/1	3	9
	Artic Web (IRE) *FFlood* 5-11-4 MrDerekO'Connor[3]	16/1	13	10
	Rossmore Castle (IRE) *NMeade* 5-11-0 MrTDCarberry[7]	25/1	2	11
	Johnnybarry *TGO'Leary* 5-11-2 MissNCarberry[5]	12/1	1	12
	Pure Palatial *DTHughes* 4-10-7 (t) MrRMHennessy[7]	14/1	¾	13
	Hey Bob (IRE) *JGMurphy* 4-10-7 MrWJMcLernon[7]	20/1	8	14
	Western Dasher (IRE) *TGO'Leary* 4-11-0 MrAKWyse	16/1	4	15
	Thenford Trout (IRE) *EJO'Grady* 4-10-7 MrRPQuinlan[7]	16/1	3	16
	Steel Duke (IRE) *DBroad* 4-11-0 MrPFahey	25/1	9	17
	Anaczar (IRE) *PJRothwell* 5-11-0 MrDGPorter[7]	20/1	½	18
	Dunlo Society (IRE) *SJTreacy* 4-10-7 MrRMMoran[7]	20/1	½	19
	Erritt (IRE) *JohnCShearman* 5-11-2 MrCJSweeney[5]	20/1	10	20
	Fabro (IRE) *PAFahy* 4-10-2 MrJTCarroll[7]	20/1	2½	21
	Adair Mohr (IRE) *MHourigan* 5-11-0 MrCPHuxley[7]	20/1	7	22
	All Is Bright (IRE) *SJTreacy* 5-11-2 MrROHarding[5]	20/1	25	23
	Thinking of You (IRE) *MosesMcCabe* 5-11-0 MrBOWalsh[7]	33/1	3	24
	Jameson Prince (IRE) *BPGalvin* 5-11-0 MrATDuff[7]	16/1		su

Mrs R. Murdoch &. David Murdoch 25ran 3m59.09

PUNCHESTOWN Wednesday, Apr 27 GOOD to SOFT

200 AON Group/Sean Barrett Bloodstock Insurances Hdle (4yo) £13,775 — 2m (9)

	STRIDES OF FIRE (IRE) *JohnACodd* 4-10-7 MrRMMoran[7]	20/1		1
	AFRAD (FR) *NJHenderson,GB* 4-11-7 MAFitzgerald	4/1	7	2
166	DABIROUN (IRE) *PaulNolan* 4-11-2 MissNCarberry[5]	11/2	3	3
151	Skyhawk (IRE) *HdeBromhead* 4-11-7 RWalsh	12/1	2	4
	Hurricane Alley (IRE) *GMLyons* 4-11-7 SPMcCann	12/1	4½	5
	Articulation *CByrnes* 4-10-11 AndrewJMcNamara[3]	25/1	1½	6
	Dujareva *JPBroderick* 4-10-4 JFLevins[5]	50/1	2½	7
160	Impartial *SJMahon* 4-11-7 PCarberry	20/1	1¼	8
	Under Oath *MrsJHarrington* 4-11-0 (s) ADLeigh[7]	20/1	1¼	9
138	Dalton (FR) *EJO'Grady* 4-11-7 DNRussell	14/1	2½	10
	Double Dizzy *RHBuckler,GB* 4-11-0 AThornton	25/1	7	11
	Levitator *MJPO'Brien* 4-11-4 TGMRyan[3]	11/8f	4	12
	Slightly Shifty (IRE) *JTGorman* 4-10-11 (b) PWFlood[3]	25/1	½	13
	Twofan (USA) *CByrnes* 4-10-7 MJFerris[7]	20/1	7	14
	Connemara Rose (IRE) *FrancisEnnis* 4-10-6 (t) APLane[3]	50/1	7	15
	Kyno (IRE) *MichaelDavidMurphy* 4-11-0 KWhelan	33/1	13	16
	Gun Tote (USA) *PHughes* 4-11-0 JPElliott	20/1	4	17
	Bakhtyar *AJMartin* 4-10-11 MFMooney[3]	33/1	14	18
	Broken River (IRE) *PJRothwell* 4-11-0 JLCullen	50/1	2	19
	Fourpointone *EMcNamara* 4-10-7 BCByrnes[7]	50/1	7	20
	Areba Rocky (IRE) *PJRothwell* 4-10-11 AJDonoghue[3]	66/1	3½	21
	Clearwaterdreamer (IRE) *MartinBrassil* 4-11-0 DTEvans	66/1	1½	22
	Longueville Manor (FR) *NMadden* 4-11-0 CO'Dwyer	50/1	1	23
	Tuckerman *AJMartin* 4-11-0 BMCash	33/1	11	24
	Victory Lap (GNY) *GTLynch* 4-10-2 MTMannion[7]	66/1	nk	25

Make Six Syndicate 25ran 4m01.54

201 Punchestown Guinness Gold Cup (Gr 1) (5yo+) £93,151 — 3m1f (17)

153	KICKING KING (IRE) *TJTaaffe* 7-11-12 BJGeraghty	8/11f		1
164	RULE SUPREME (IRE) *WPMullins* 9-11-12 RWalsh	4/1	3	2
153	PIZARRO (IRE) *EJO'Grady* 8-11-12 DNRussell	20/1	15	3
62	Kingscliff (IRE) *RHAlner,GB* 8-11-12 AThornton	7/2	dist	4

165	First Gold (FR) *FDoumen,France* 12-11-12 (b) APMcCoy	20/1	25 5
182	Arctic Copper (IRE) *NMeade* 11-11-12 (s) PCarberry	66/1	pu

Mr Conor Clarkson 6ran 6m27.07

202 **Paddy Power Champion INH Flat (Gr 1) (4, 5, 6 and 7yo m)** £44,589 — 2m

184	REFINEMENT (IRE) *JonjoO'Neill,GB* 6-11-9 (b) MrAJBerry	6/1	1
184	THE COOL GUY (IRE) *NATwiston-Davies,GB* 5-11-13 MrRWidger	9/1	9 2
	NICANOR (FR) *NMeade* 4-11-6 MrNPMadden	10/1	6 3
144	Missed That *WPMullins* 6-12-0 MrJJCodd	5/4f	4 4
144	Eye On The Ball *MFMorris* 6-11-11 MrKEPower[3]	10/1	4 5
	Wheresben (IRE) *SeamusFahey* 6-12-0 MrJAFahey	25/1	2½ 6
144	Clew Bay Cove (IRE) *CAMurphy* 5-11-13 (t) MrDerekO'Connor	10/1	3 7
	Knight Legend (IRE) *MrsJHarrington* 6-12-0 MrRO'Sullivan	16/1	½ 8
	The Dasher (IRE) *SeanAherne* 6-12-0 MrPTobin	25/1	2 9
184	Avoca Mist (IRE) *WPMullins* 5-11-8 MsKWalsh	25/1	2½ 10
57	Dawadari (IRE) *SJMahon* 5-11-13 MrKBBowens	14/1	20 11
	Dark Artist (IRE) *JEKiely* 6-12-0 MissNCarberry	25/1	4 12
	Skeheenarinky (IRE) *SeanOO'Brien* 5-11-13 MrSOO'Brien	25/1	3½ 13
	Ballintra Boy (IRE) *NMeade* 6-12-0 MrGElliott	14/1	2 14
	Lyical Assassin (IRE) *PaulARoche* 5-11-13 MrDRoche	100/1	½ 15
	Bit of A Gift *ThomasMullins* 7-12-0 MrPFahey	14/1	dist 16
	She's Our Daisy (IRE) *SCBurrough,GB* 5-11-8 MrAFitzgerald	66/1	½ 17
	Dontbebrushedaside (IRE) *RMMoore* 6-12-0 MrDWCullen	66/1	dist 18
	Littlejimmybrown (IRE) *PJFlynn* 7-12-0 MrJTMcNamara	50/1	pu

Mr M. Tabor 19ran 3m55.47

PUNCHESTOWN Thursday, Apr 28 SOFT

203 **Blue Square Chase (La Touche Cup) (5yo+)** £11,147 — 4¼m (27)

	GOOD STEP (IRE) *EBolger* 7-12-3 MrJTMcNamara	11/2	1
	SHADY LAD (IRE) *EBolger* 8-11-7 MissNCarberry[5]	10/1	½ 2
	I'M ON THE LINE (IRE) *MrsDALove* 9-11-0 MrCMMurphy[7]	33/1	14 3
10	Harry In A Hurry *AndrewLee* 8-11-12 KWhelan	20/1	25 4
	Three Mill (IRE) *ThomasCleary* 8-11-2 MrJDMoore[5]	25/1	6 5
137	Andrewjames (IRE) *PDMcCreery* 11-12-0 MrJCash[7]	10/1	7 6
20	Star Performance (IRE) *OliverMcKiernan* 10-11-12 (t) GCotter	7/1	11 7
137	Luzcadou (FR) *FerdyMurphy,GB* 12-11-7 (b) KMercer[5]	6/1	f
	Timucua (IRE) *DTHughes* 6-11-2 MrRLoughran[5]	33/1	f
159	Takagi (IRE) *EJO'Grady* 10-11-12 DNRussell	11/2	ur
20	Clawick Connection (IRE) *JNRBillinge,GB* 10-11-7 RGeraghty	33/1	ur
	Desperately Frisky (IRE) *DBroad* 12-11-7 BMCash	66/1	ref
	Panchovillas Gleam (IRE) *DermotDay* 11-12-7 (b) PACarberry	33/1	pu
148	Davids Lad (IRE) *AJMartin* 11-11-12 (t) PCarberry	9/4f	pu
10	Mose Harper (IRE) *TO'Neill* 13-11-12 (b) JPElliott	66/1	pu
	Pre Ordained (IRE) *MAStafford* 13-11-0 MrRMMoran[7]	33/1	pu

Mr John P. McManus 16ran 10m19.95

204 **Colm McEvoy Auctioneers Champion Four Year Old Hdle (Gr 1) (4yo)** £46,712 — 2m (9)

	UNITED (GER) *MrsLWadham,GB* 4-10-9 LAspell	6/1	1
166	STRANGELY BROWN (IRE) *EMcNamara* 4-11-0 RWalsh	7/2	12 2
151	AKILAK (IRE) *JHowardJohnson,GB* 4-11-0 GLee	8/13f	½ 3
	Eye Candy (IRE) *MrsSandraMcCarthy* 4-11-0 DJCondon	50/1	½ 4
151	Don't Be Bitin (IRE) *EGriffin* 4-11-0 BJGeraghty	14/1	sh 5
99	Openide *BWDuke,GB* 4-11-0 APMcCoy	14/1	5 6
	Maxxium (IRE) *MHalford* 4-11-0 (t) PCarberry	50/1	dist 7

Mr R. B. Holt 7ran 4m03.09

205 **Swordlestown Cup Nov Chase (Gr 1) (5yo+)** £42,466 — 2m (11)

179	WAR OF ATTRITION (IRE) *MFMorris* 6-11-12 CO'Dwyer	3/1	1
161	WATSON LAKE (IRE) *NMeade* 7-11-12 PCarberry	7/4f	1 2
90	STRIKE BACK (IRE) *MrsJHarrington* 7-11-12 RMPower	10/1	20 3
161	Euro Leader (IRE) *WPMullins* 7-11-12 RWalsh	33/1	3 4
108	Newmill (IRE) *JohnJosephMurphy* 7-11-12 AndrewJMcNamara	10/1	dist 5
134	Mariah Rollins (IRE) *PAFahy* 7-11-7 BJGeraghty	13/2	f
168	Fota Island (IRE) *MFMorris* 9-11-12 APMcCoy	4/1	ur

Gigginstown House Stud 7ran 4m23.70

206 **Ballymore Properties Champion Stayers' Hdle (Gr 1) (4yo+)** £72,192 — 3m (14)

177	CARLYS QUEST *FerdyMurphy,GB* 11-11-12 KMercer	25/1	1
159	KADOUN (IRE) *MJPO'Brien* 8-11-12 APMcCoy	14/1	9 2

198	BASILEA STAR (IRE) *FerdyMurphy,GB* 8-11-12 (t) GLee	25/1	2	3
158	Homer Wells (IRE) *WPMullins* 7-11-12 DJCondon	16/1	20	4
91	Solerina (IRE) *JamesBowe* 8-11-7 JRBarry	5/2	7	5
84	Rosaker (USA) *NMeade* 8-11-12 PCarberry	10/1	dist	6
147	Emotional Moment (IRE) *TJTaaffe* 8-11-12 BJGeraghty	9/4f	dist	7
158	Our Ben *WPMullins* 6-11-12 RWalsh	10/3		pu
147	Yogi (IRE) *ThomasFoley* 9-11-12 MAFitzgerald	25/1		pu

Ms L. Neville 9ran 6m16.40

207 Tattersalls (Ireland) Ltd Pat Taaffe Hcap Chase (Gr B) 0-145(135) (5yo+) £24,524 — 3m1f (17)

	NO HALF SESSION (IRE) *NMeade* 8-10-0^{111} PCarberry	9/2f		1
159	COOLNAHILLA (IRE) *WJBurke* 9-10-10^{121} KHadnett	9/1	6	2
159	WHAT ODDS (IRE) *TKGeraghty* 9-11-0^{125} BJGeraghty	10/1	¾	3
	RANSBORO (IRE) *CFSwan* 6-9-13^{110} JRBarry	14/1	nk	4
	Berkley (IRE) *PVerling* 8-9-11^{111} (b) TGMRyan^{3}	14/1	½	5
	Hard Winter (IRE) *DTHughes* 8-9-10^{110} PWFlood^{3}	14/1	2½	6
	Ossmoses (IRE) *DMForster,GB* 8-10-7^{118} DRDennis	12/1	1	7
	Like A Bee (IRE) *CRoche* 7-9-11^{108} APCrowe	10/1	2½	8
	Bob Justice (IRE) *TMWalsh* 9-10-0^{111} (b) GCotter	20/1	13	9
159	Star Clipper *NMeade* 8-10-8^{122} DFO'Regan^{3}	16/1	2	10
159	Garvivonnian (IRE) *EdwardPMitchell* 10-11-6^{134} AndrewJMcNamara^{3}	25/1	¾	11
7	The Culdee (IRE) *FFlood* 9-10-5^{116} DJCondon	12/1		f
	Beau Colina (IRE) *AJMartin* 8-10-1^{112} RWalsh	5/1		f
174	Munster (IRE) *ALTMoore* 8-10-7^{118} (t) GLee	12/1		bd
176	Dark'n Sharp (GER) *RTPhillips,GB* 10-11-10^{135} MAFitzgerald	33/1		pu
161	Ross River *SDonohoe* 9-11-3^{128} MrRWidger	25/1		pu
159	Golden Storm (IRE) *JosephCrowley* 8-10-11^{125} (b) JMAllen^{3}	20/1		pu
159	Hume Castle (IRE) *MrsJHarrington* 9-10-12^{123} (t) RMPower	16/1		pu
85	This Is Serious (IRE) *CFSwan* 11-10-7^{123} JFLevins^{5}	33/1		pu
159	Heroic (IRE) *CFSwan* 9-10-7^{118} CO'Dwyer	16/1		pu
65	Sraid Na Cathrach (IRE) *CByrnes* 9-10-7^{118} DJCondon	7/1		pu

Mr R. D. Murphy 21ran 6m46.41

PUNCHESTOWN Friday, Apr 29 GOOD to SOFT

208 Emo Oil Champion Hdle (Gr 1) (5yo+) £67,123 — 2m (9)

181	BRAVE INCA (IRE) *CAMurphy* 7-11-12 APMcCoy	2/1		1
135	HARCHIBALD (FR) *NMeade* 6-11-12 PCarberry	4/6f	hd	2
181	MACS JOY (IRE) *MrsJHarrington* 6-11-12 BJGeraghty	11/2	1	3
	Bob What (IRE) *ThomasMullins* 11-11-12 (t) RMPower	125/1	dist	4
195	Publican (IRE) *PAFahy* 5-11-11 RWalsh	33/1	25	5

Novices Syndicate 5ran 4m05.04

209 betfair.com Nov Hcap Chase (140) (5yo+) £42,466 — 3m1f (17)

	PAY IT FORWARD *MrsJHarrington* 7-10-5^{121} RMPower	7/1		1
187	JOES EDGE (IRE) *FerdyMurphy,GB* 8-11-7^{140} KMercer^{3}	7/1	2	2
159	MULLACASH (IRE) *NMeade* 7-10-3^{119} (b) PCarberry	16/1	4	3
	Lincam (IRE) *CFSwan* 9-10-4^{120} CO'Dwyer	7/1	1½	4
159	Numbersixvalverde (IRE) *MartinBrassil* 9-11-4^{134} RWalsh	10/3f	nk	5
171	Well Presented (IRE) *MrsJHarrington* 7-11-4^{134} (t) BJGeraghty	9/1	2	6
159	Pearly Jack *DEFitzgerald* 7-10-1^{120} TGMRyan^{3}	14/1	1	7
161	Scarthy Lad (IRE) *TGO'Leary* 7-11-10^{140} APMcCoy	5/1	4	8
	G V A Ireland (IRE) *FFlood* 7-10-10^{126} DNRussell	8/1	25	9
	Ballynattin Buck (IRE) *ALTMoore* 9-10-4^{120} (t) TPTreacy	25/1	15	10
65	Aimees Mark (IRE) *FFlood* 9-9-12^{119} KTColeman^{5}	20/1		ur

Paid Thru The Nose Syndicate 11ran 6m34.70

210 Menolly Homes Champion Nov Hdle (Gr 1) (4yo+) £42,466 — 2½m (12)

175	ASIAN MAZE (IRE) *ThomasMullins* 6-11-7 PCarberry	6/4f		1
	KERRYHEAD WINDFARM (IRE) *MHourigan* 7-11-12 AndrewJMcNamara	25/1	5	2
152	WASHINGTON LAD (IRE) *PAFahy* 5-11-11 APMcCoy	7/1	3½	3
160	Petertheknot (IRE) *PatrickSinnott* 7-11-12 CO'Dwyer	14/1	3	4
139	Bagan (FR) *CJMann,GB* 6-11-12 NDFehily	14/1	½	5
56	Major Vernon (IRE) *WPMullins* 6-11-12 RWalsh	6/1	13	6
158	Sher Beau (IRE) *PhilipFenton* 6-11-12 DNRussell	7/2	nk	7
198	Keepthedreamalive *RHBuckler,GB* 7-11-12 BHitchcott	50/1	hd	8
	Letterman (IRE) *EJO'Grady* 5-11-11 TGMRyan	40/1	3½	9
	Macs Flamingo (IRE) *PAFahy* 5-11-11 BJGeraghty	12/1	9	10
26	Django (IRE) *MrsJHarrington* 6-11-12 RMPower	40/1		pu

Mrs C. A. Moore 11ran 4m56.06

AUTEUIL Sunday, May 8 SOFT

211 **Prix Amadou (Gr 2) (4yo)** £49,315 — 2m3f110y (12)

	Horse	SP	Dist	Pos
	DON'T BE SHY (FR) *TTrapenard,France* 4-10-10 AKondrat	37/10		1
	KIKO (FR) *AChaille-Chaille,France* 4-10-8 CPieux	9/4	1½	2
	KING'S DAUGHTER (FR) *FMCottin,France* 4-10-1 DGallagher	29/4	hd	3
	Aroldo (FR) *JBertrandeBalanda,France* 4-10-3 RSchmidlin	10/1	¾	4
	Gerfaut (FR) *TCivel,France* 4-9-13 SBeaumard	37/1	sn	5
	Sol Roc (FR) *JBertrandeBalanda,France* 4-10-8 LMetais	2/1f	½	6
	Royale Athenia (FR) *BBarbier,France* 4-10-1 CGombeau	22/1	nk	7
	Turthen (FR) *GCherel,France* 4-10-1 PMarsac	37/1	3	8
	Icarro (FR) *J-PGallorini,France* 4-10-1 HGallorini	23/1	10	9
	Prima Note (FR) *PLenogue,France* 4-9-8 (b) RO'Brien	66/1	6	10

Mrs M. A. Berghgracht 10ran 4m59.03

AUTEUIL Sunday, May 29 GOOD

212 **Gras Savoye Hipcover Prix La Barka (Gr 2) (5yo+)** £49,655 — 2m5f110y (14)

	Horse	SP	Dist	Pos
	ROCK AND PALM (FR) *YPorzier,France* 5-9-13 MDelmares	36/1		1
29	CYRLIGHT (FR) *AChaille-Chaille,France* 5-10-6 CPieux	1/10	2	2
201	RULE SUPREME (IRE) *WPMullins,Ireland* 9-10-6 RWalsh	9/1	6	3
	Sphinx du Berlais (FR) *FMCottin,France* 6-10-3 DGallagher	33/1	3	4
	Cheler (FR) *BSecly,France* 6-10-3 LMetais	30/1	2	5
	L'Interprete (FR) *TTrapenard,France* 6-10-6 AKondrat	41/1	¾	6
	Ennemi d'Etat (FR) *MRolland,France* 6-10-6 (b) RSchmidlin	54/1	1½	7
	Prince Dolois (FR) *ABonin,France* 7-10-3 CGombeau	44/1	hd	8
186	Geos (FR) *NJHenderson,GB* 10-10-6 BGicquel	64/1	15	9
206	Homer Wells (IRE) *WPMullins,Ireland* 7-10-6 DJCondon	42/1	½	10
	Phonidal (FR) *MRolland,France* 9-10-6 (b) GAdam	86/1		11
	El Paradiso (FR) *MRolland,France* 8-10-6 (b) PMarsac	14/1		pu
198	Raikkonen (IRE) *WPMullins,Ireland* 5-9-13 SBeaumard	65/1		pu

Mme P. Menard 13ran 5m03.83

213 **Gras Savoye Cinema Prix Ferdinand Dufaure (Gr 1) (4yo)** £83,793 — 2½m110y (18)

	Horse	SP	Dist	Pos
151	BONBON ROSE (FR) *AChaille-Chaille,France* 4-10-6 CPieux	1/1f		1
163	ANGLICAN (FR) *GCherel,France* 4-10-6 EChazelle	51/1	6	2
	WILLDANCE (FR) *FMCottin,France* 4-10-1 DGallagher	7/2	5	3
	Indian Spirit (FR) *LPostic,France* 4-10-6 (b) PBigot	73/1	1	4
	Kauto Ray (FR) *GMacaire,France* 4-10-6 BGicquel	14/1	¾	5
	Le Volfoni (FR) *TTrapenard,France* 4-10-6 PMarsac	40/1	nk	6
	Tevere (FR) *TTrapenard,France* 4-10-6 SDupuis	34/1	1	7
	Rouletabille (FR) *RChotard,France* 4-10-6 JDucout	81/1	8	8
163	Narock (FR) *JBertrandeBalanda,France* 4-10-6 LMetais	15/1	2	9
163	Nalexibo (FR) *FDanloux,France* 4-10-6 SBeaumard	56/1	15	10
	Costic (FR) *MmeIPacault,France* 4-10-6 SMassinot	10/1		ur
163	Balko (FR) *GMacaire,France* 4-10-6 JRicou	13/2		pu
163	Matuvu (FR) *TTrapenard,France* 4-10-6 CGombeau	69/1		pu
	Nymphe de Sivola (FR) *TTrapenard,France* 4-10-1 AKondrat	33/1		pu

Mr S. Mulryan 14ran 5m02.88

214 **Gras Savoye Grand Steeple-Chase de Paris (Gr 1) (5yo+)** £186,207 — 3m5f (23)

	Horse	SP	Dist	Pos
	SLEEPING JACK (FR) *JOrtet,France* 6-10-8 CPieux	3/1		1
29	MA ROYALE (FR) *MRolland,France* 5-9-13 RSchmidlin	5/2	nk	2
	LORD CARMONT (FR) *MmeIPacault,France* 6-10-8 SMassinot	12/1	2	3
	Kamillo (FR) *FCottin,France* 7-10-8 DGallagher	25/4	3	4
	Samson (FR) *MmeLAudon,France* 8-10-8 CGombeau	12/1	2	5
	Double Car (FR) *BdeWatrigant,France* 9-10-8 CCheminaud	12/1	2½	6
	Masini (POL) *COlehla,CzechRepublic* 6-10-8 JCrowley	12/1	4	7
	Jerico Vallis (FR) *GChaignon,France* 8-10-8 DBerra	12/1	8	8
	Ty Benjam (FR) *GLePaysan,France* 9-10-8 SLeloup	86/1	10	9
	Sun Storm (FR) *TCivel,France* 8-10-8 BThelier	55/1	10	10
	Scandor (FR) *FDanloux,France* 11-10-8 SBeaumard	76/1		11
	Louping d'Ainay (FR) *FMCottin,France* 6-10-8 GBrunot	41/1		ur
182	Astonville (FR) *RChotard,France* 11-10-8 LBouldoires	102/1		ref
	Fustrien du Paon (FR) *AChaille-Chaille,France* 9-10-8 (b) GRiviere	29/1		pu
	Hespoir d'Aurelie (FR) *MRolland,France* 10-10-8 PMarsac	66/1		pu
	Batman Senora (FR) *JOrtet,France* 9-10-8 (b) XHondier	45/1		pu
	Milou Des Enceints (FR) *TTrapenard,France* 5-10-3 AKondrat	27/1		pu

Mr R. Temam 17ran 7m04.41

AUTEUIL Saturday, Jun 18 GOOD to SOFT

215 **Prix Alain du Breil - Course de Haies d'Ete Des Quatre Ans (Gr 1) (4yo)** £69,000 — 2m3f110y (12)

	Horse	SP	Dist	Pos
204	STRANGELY BROWN (IRE) *EMcNamara,Ireland* 4-10-6 RWalsh	66/10		1

211	ROYALE ATHENIA (FR) *BBarbier,France* 4-10-1 (b) CGombeau	17/2	3 2
211	AROLDO (FR) *JBertrandeBalanda,France* 4-10-6 RSchmidlin	13/1	15 3
211	Kiko (FR) *AChaille-Chaille,France* 4-10-6 JRicou	15/1	3 4
211	Sol Roc (FR) *JBertrandeBalanda,France* 4-10-6 BChameraud	21/1	3 5
211	Icarro (FR) *J-PGallorini,France* 4-10-6 HGallorini	57/1	4 6
213	Bonbon Rose (FR) *AChaille-Chaille,France* 4-10-6 CPieux	1/2f	2 7
211	King's Daughter (FR) *FMCottin,France* 4-10-1 DGallagher	9/1	10 8
211	Gerfaut (FR) *TCivel,France* 4-10-6 SBeaumard	50/1	pu
	Nooska Tivoli (FR) *PTual,France* 4-10-6 (b) SLeloup	58/1	pu

We Didn't Name Him Syndicate 10ran 4m38.10

216 Grande Course de Haies d'Auteuil (Gr 1) (5yo+) £90,000 3m1f110y (16)

	LYCAON DE VAUZELLE (FR) *JBertrandeBalanda,France* 6-10-8 BChameraud	36/10	1
212	RULE SUPREME (IRE) *WPMullins,Ireland* 9-10-8 RWalsh	4/5f	4 2
214	DOUBLE CAR (FR) *BdeWatrigant,France* 9-10-8 CCheminaud	17/2	3 3
212	Sphinx du Berlais (FR) *FMCottin,France* 6-10-8 DGallagher	9/1	¾ 4
212	Cheler (FR) *BSecly,France* 6-10-8 CPieux	10/1	2½ 5
212	Ennemi d'Etat (FR) *MRolland,France* 6-10-8 (b) RSchmidlin	42/1	3 6
212	Prince Dolois (FR) *ABonin,France* 7-10-8 BThelier	47/1	dist 7
29	Mister Gyor (FR) *BBarbier,France* 5-10-3 CGombeau	7/1	pu

Mr F. Wintz 8ran 6m32.57

INDEX TO SELECTED BIG RACES

TIMEFORM 'TOP HORSES IN FRANCE'

The Grand Steeple-Chase de Paris and the Grande Course de Haies d'Auteuil have seen some top-class winners over the years, naturally enough given their status as the top races in France over fences and hurdles respectively. But recent renewals of both races have been sorely lacking in quality, and it took barely smart form to win both contests in 2005. To put that in a British context, if they reproduced the same form, neither the Grand Steeple winner Sleeping Jack nor the Grande Course de Haies winner Lycaon de Vauzelle, would have made the first seven had they contested the closest equivalent races in Britain, the Cheltenham Gold Cup and the World Hurdle respectively. Another illustration of the difference in quality between the top contests in France and Britain at present is provided by Rule Supreme. He had to put up a career-best effort to take third in the World Hurdle, but despite running about a stone below form, still managed to finish second when sent over for the latest Grande Course de Haies.

Racegoers in Britain do not have to look far to find where the good French jumpers, or at least a large proportion of them, have gone. It is surely no coincidence that the current lack of strength in France's top jumps races has come at a time when the success of French-bred jumpers in Britain has never been greater. Of course, the popularity of French-bred jumpers over here is good news for French breeders and vendors, but sooner or later, with so many young horses crossing the Channel every year, many of the best or most promising jumpers among them, the quality of racing at Auteuil was bound to suffer. Annual statistics published in the *Abrege des courses au galop*, the French breeders' statistical record, show the extent of this trend and how it has developed over the last twenty years or so. Back in 1984, it listed just a dozen French-bred winners over jumps in Britain that year. By 1994, that figure had risen to fifty in Britain (with Klairon Davis the sole example in Ireland), but in 2004 there were more than two hundred and fifty individual French-bred winners over jumps in Britain and another thirty in Ireland. It seems fair to assume that at least that many again raced here but did not win.

Another reason for the lack of quality in Auteuil's top contests is that some of the best French-trained jumpers have been campaigned largely, or exclusively, in Britain in recent seasons. The François Doumen-trained pair **First Gold** and **Baracouda**, both owned by J. P. McManus, were the top French chaser and hurdler respectively in the latest season, but neither have raced at home since 2001. Neither may no longer be capable of the form they showed in their prime, but they were still comfortably better than the pick of their compatriots who performed at Auteuil. In what was a particularly successful season for the Doumen stable in Britain, Cheltenham Festival winners **Kelami** and **Moulin Riche**, plus **Blue Canyon**, **Innox** and **L'Ami** all showed their best form this side of the Channel. Other French-trained horses to perform to a good level in Britain were novice hurdler **Ambobo** (Arnaud Chaille-Chaille), novice chaser **Foreman** (Thierry Doumen) and juvenile hurdler **New Rock** (Guillaume Macaire).

Gras Savoye Grand Steeple-Chase de Paris, Auteuil—a sorry renewal of France's most important jumps race; winner Sleeping Jack (No.15) and runner-up Ma Royale are led over the wall by eventual third Lord Carmont

Prix Georges Courtois, Auteuil—Kario de Sormain shows her rivals the way home

Auteuil's top chases were also much the poorer for the absence of the reigning champion **Kotkijet** and the horse who looks much his most likely successor, **Cyrlight**. Kotkijet, who won his second Grand Steeple in 2004, appeared only once in the latest season, finishing fourth over hurdles in the autumn. He had been entered for the Horses In Training Sales at Newmarket, but an ownership dispute led to his withdrawal, and a recurrence of leg trouble kept him off the track for the rest of the season. Even if he does make another comeback, the ten-year-old Kotkijet looks to have work cut out against Cyrlight, a rival half his age who is much the best chasing prospect in France at present. During the autumn, he mopped up three more group races for four-year-old chasers, including the Group 1 Prix Maurice Gillois, to add to those he had dominated earlier in the year. Now unbeaten in ten starts over fences, Cyrlight was switched back to hurdles after the turn of the year, rather than being aimed at the Grand Steeple, and looked well on course for the Grande Course de Haies instead. He gained easy wins in the Prix Hypothese and Prix Leon Rambaud in the spring but met with a shock defeat next in the Prix La Barka. A foot problem was blamed for his reverse, and he then had to miss the Grande Course de Haies with further foot trouble.

With the top chases for older horses looking wide open, some new names emerged. First to come to the fore in the autumn was the mare **Kario de Sormain**, a free-running type who made all and jumped well under her young lady rider Nathalie Desoutter to win both the Prix Heros XII and the Prix Georges Courtois. Kario de Sormain was not seen out after the turn of the year, but in the latter race she was chased home by a couple of five-year-olds, **Sleeping Jack** and **Lord Carmont** who had been in good form in lesser company during the autumn and went on to better things in the second half of the season. The pair next met in the Prix Murat in April, by which time Sleeping Jack had also won the Grand Prix de Pau, and the Prix Troytown back at Auteuil. He looked all set to win the Murat as well, but was collared by the rallying Lord Carmont close home, going down by half a length but emerging the better horse at the weights. On level terms in the Grand Steeple, Sleeping Jack turned the tables, quickening decisively at the last to leave Lord Carmont back in third this time after the latter had again made the running. This pair were split in the Grand Steeple by the five-year-old mare **Ma Royale**. A sister to the Tripleprint Gold Cup winner Iris Royal, Ma Royale came out of the Grand Steeple with plenty of credit, going down by a neck on what was only her fifth start over fences. She had made her chasing debut less than three months earlier and had won her first four starts over fences, notably the Group 3 Prix Ingre. She could have further progress to make with a bit more experience.

The previous year's Grand Steeple runner-up **Kamillo** made the frame again in fourth and is clearly well suited by the test of stamina the race provides. He had also looked set to be placed in the Group 1 Prix La Haye-Jousselin in the autumn but was carried left and unseated his rider, whose saddle had slipped, just yards from the line. That race went to **Turgot** who failed to make the Grand Steeple line-up after finishing lame in the Murat. Turgot had also finished a good second to Kario de Sormain in the Prix Heros XII and fourth to Lord Carmont in the Troytown, giving weight away both times. Away from Auteuil, **Northerntown** maintained his dominance at Enghien, winning both the track's own Grand Steeple and the top hurdle race there, the Prix Leopold d'Orsetti, for the second year running.

Cyrlight's absence from the Grande Course de Haies has already been noted, and another absentee was **Maia Eria**, the filly who dominated the four-year-olds over hurdles in 2004 in much the same way as Cyrlight had over fences. Maia Eria was retired to stud at the end of 2004 but bowed out over hurdles in a fascinating clash with Cyrlight in the Group 1 Prix Renaud du Vivier, one which she won impressively. Maia Eria had returned earlier in the autumn with two more Group 3 successes, and made her final racecourse appearance when second in a listed race on the Flat eight days after the Renaud du Vivier.

The Grande Course de Haies fell to the non-thoroughbred six-year-old **Lycaon de Vauzelle**. In defeating the previous year's winner, Rule Supreme, he became only the fifth non-thoroughbred to win the race and the first since Ubu III in 1993. He had been no match for Cyrlight in the spring, finishing third behind him twice, but had gained a couple of important victories in the autumn in the Prix Carmarthen (from **Grande Haya**) and the Prix Leon Olry-Roederer. Grande Haya profited from Lycaon de Vauzelle's absence to take the Group 1 Grand Prix d'Automne on only his sixth start over hurdles, ahead of **Great Love**, and returned in the spring to win the Prix Juigne, but was not seen out again after his second to Cyrlight in the Prix Hypothese. Third place in the Grande Course de Haies went to **Double Car**, better known as a chaser, who enjoyed the run of the race, setting a very steady pace. Another important name missing from the Grande Course de Haies line-up, albeit for very different reasons, was **Rock And Palm**, the horse who had inflicted the shock defeat on Cyrlight in the Prix La Barka. His trainer, Yann Porzier (also the trainer of Maia Eria) had his licence suspended in June by the French authorities,

Grande Course de Haies d'Auteuil—four in with a shout at the last–
Lycaon de Vauzelle leads Double Car with Rule Supreme (left) and Sphinx du Berlais just behind

Grand Prix d'Automne, Auteuil—more mist than mellow fruitfulness; the winner Grande Haya is jumping in second as the field reaches halfway

being one of several persons under investigation in connection with an affair concerning the importation and use of banned substances.

The latest contingent of imports to Britain who began the season with French stables included the Fulke Walwyn Kim Muir winner Juveigneur and the good juvenile hurdlers Voy Por Ustedes, Star de Mohaison and Napolitain. But perhaps the most interesting acquisition by a British yard was that of the very promising four-year-old chaser **Neptune Collonges** who will now run in the colours of John Hales for Paul Nicholls' stable. Unbeaten in his first four chases at Pau, Neptune Collonges came to grief on his Auteuil

Gras Savoye Hipcover Prix La Barka, Auteuil—Rock And Palm (left) causes a major upset by defeating 10/1-on chance Cyrlight

debut but jumped well and was most impressive when winning the Prix Fleuret there in April by fifteen lengths from the pair who had finished first and second in both the Prix Congress and Prix Duc d'Anjou beforehand, **Balko** and **Narock**. Neptune Collonges had been sold by the time of the Prix Ferdinand Dufaure and in his absence the Group 1 prize went to **Bonbon Rose**. Representing the same connections—Arnaud Chaille-Chaille and Sean Mulryan—as Cyrlight, Bonbon Rose ran twice over hurdles at Cheltenham but soon made into a better chaser back at Auteuil, completing a hat-trick in the Ferdinand Dufaure from outsider **Anglican** and the Prix Jean Stern winner **Willdance**. At this stage, the still-entire Bonbon Rose looks the best prospect for the top four-year-old chases during the autumn.

Bonbon Rose was odds on to complete a Group 1 double when reverting to hurdles for the Prix Alain du Breil in June but finished only seventh to Irish raider Strangely Brown. A little below the best juveniles in the British Isles, Strangely Brown's victory confirmed earlier impressions that the French four-year-old hurdlers were a substandard lot. The chief absentee from the Alain du Breil was **Don't Be Shy** who had by then joined Martin Pipe and David Johnson. Don't Be Shy had been thereabouts in all the big juvenile hurdles earlier in the season and won the Prix de Pepinvast and Prix Amadou in the spring from old rival **Kiko**. Another of Sean Mulryan's powerful string, Kiko won the top three-year-old hurdle in the autumn, the Prix Cambaceres (with Don't Be Shy third), but as the season wore on his temperament began to look suspect, and he could finish only fourth in the Alain du Breil. The placed horses in the Alain du Breil, **Royale Athenia** and **Aroldo**, had earlier had Kiko a close third when fighting out the finish to the Prix de Longchamp in May. Both are of interest from a British point of view, Royale Athenia being a half-sister to Royal Rosa and Royal Paradise, while Aroldo had passed into Sir Robert Ogden's ownership by then. With little between the leading four-year-old hurdlers, the remaining contests for that age-group during the autumn look very open, and they could prove vulnerable to later developers or perhaps further runners from Britain or Ireland.

The likelihood of stronger representation at Auteuil from British and Irish stables received a big boost with confirmation that the inaugural International Jumps Weekend—plans for which were first outlined in last year's Annual—will take place on November 5th and 6th. Promoted as jumping's equivalent of Arc weekend at Longchamp, just under €2 million will be on offer in total, spread over fifteen races, with the intention of attracting runners from outside France. The Grand Prix d'Automne, a three-mile hurdle, is the most valuable event on the Saturday card, while three more Group 1 contests feature on the Sunday programme: the €400,000 Prix La Haye-Jousselin for chasers over nearly three and

Gras Savoye Vie Et Avenir Prix de Longchamp, Auteuil—
blinkers work the oracle for Royal Athenia as she defeats Aroldo (left) and the odds-on Kiko

a half miles, the Prix Maurice Gillois for four-year-old chasers, and the Prix Cambaceres for three-year-old hurdlers. The meeting falls early in the season for British horses and comes just a week before the Open meeting at Cheltenham, but hopefully British stables will take up the challenge; the combination of good prize money and a less than formidable home defence ought to be enough of an incentive for British trainers to send representatives.

Chasers (5yo+)

159	*First Gold _12_
150p	Cyrlight _5_
148+	Douze Douze _9_
146	Kario de Sormain (f) _7_
145p	*Foreman _7_
145	*L'Ami _6_
145	Northerntown _9_
145	Sleeping Jack _6_
143	Turgot _8_
142	Lord Carmont _6_
141	*Kelami _7_
141	Lorka de Thaix _6_
140	Kamillo _7_
139§	*Innox _9_
138	Garde d'Estruval _11_
138	Gondleen _9_
138	Samson _8_
137	Ma Royale (f) _5_
136	Beau Turgeon _9_
136	Domirome _7_
136	Double Car _9_
136	Hercule Noir _6_
136	L'As de Pembo _6_
135	Jerico Vallis _8_
134	Dukeen _10_
134	Golden Flight _6_
134	Grand Cyborg _7_
134	Hespoir d'Aurelie _10_
133	Cerilly _8_
133	Saint Realise _8_
132	Cheler _6_
132	Jazeb _7_
131	Baby du Rheu _5_
131	Baby Norm _7_
131	Mister Mic _8_
130	Choum _10_
130	Idaos _9_
130	Lord Mirande _6_
130	Mysoko _5_
130	Sphinx du Berlais _6_
130	Thenymon _8_
130§	Royal Beaufort _7_

Hurdlers (5yo+)

159	*Baracouda _10_
149+	*Ambobo _5_
149+	Maia Eria (f) _5_
148p	Cyrlight _5_
147	*Blue Canyon _7_
147	Lycaon de Vauzelle _6_
146	*Moulin Riche _5_
145	Grande Haya _6_
145	Great Love _7_
142	El Paradiso _8_
142	Nousha _11_
141	Double Car _9_
140	Northerntown _9_
140	Rock And Palm _5_
139	Cerilly _8_
139	L'Interprete _6_
139§	El Paso III _13_
138	Batman Senora _9_
138	Ennemi d'Etat _6_
138	Phonidal _9_
137	Mister Gyor _5_
137	River Charm _5_
137	Saute Au Bois _11_
136	Gold Magic _7_
136	Pop Art _5_
135+	Kotkijet _10_
135	Baby du Rheu _5_
134	Sphinx du Berlais _6_
133	Djawack _8_
133	Samson _8_
133	Vesuve _6_
132	Cheler _6_
132	Mesange Royale (f) _5_
132	Royale Cazoumaille (f) _6_
131	Jemykos _5_
130	Fustrien du Paon _9_
130	Joly Precy _6_
130	Pour Dol _5_
130	Prince Dolois _7_
130?	Beau Turgeon _9_

Chasers (4yo)

141p	Neptune Collonges
131	Balko
128p	Bonbon Rose
127	Narock
126	Korean
123	Anglican
121	Esturgeon du Ranch
121	Saint Nono
120	Hunorisk (f)
119	Polivalente (f)
119	Westos
118	Turthen
118	Hyalamo
117	Indian Spirit
117	Kauto Ray
117	Le Volfoni
116	Cayras Style (f)
116	Willdance (f)
115	Nice Doctor Picton
115	Numero Special
115	Ramses Bleu
115	Rexlor
115	Tevere

Hurdlers (4yo)

129	Don't Be Shy
129	*New Rock
128§	Kiko
127	Bonbon Rose
125	Royale Athenia (f)
123	Aroldo
123	Sol Roc
120	Balko
119	Danaw
119	King's Daughter (f)
118	Symphonique (f)
117	King Tune
117	Mid Dancer
117	New Will (f)
117	Willdance (f)
116	Kauto Ray
116	Le Volfoni
116	Nan's Catch (f)
115	Malongo
115	Si Sol

NB Horses marked with an * achieved their best performance in GB or Ireland, otherwise ratings relate to performances in France between July 2004 and June 2005.

There are essays in the main body of the book on Ambobo, Baracouda, Blue Canyon, Bonbon Rose, Cyrlight, Foreman, Kelami, L'Ami and Moulin Riche.

INDEX TO PHOTOGRAPHS

PORTRAITS & SNAPSHOTS

RACE PHOTOGRAPHS

ADDITIONAL PHOTOGRAPHS

The following photographs appear in the Introduction:– Tingle Creek Chase and Kicking King at Punchestown (facing Intro) taken by Ed Byrne; Kicking King at the last in the King George VI Chase–Tom Shaw/Getty Images; Harchibald and Hardy Eustace–Bill Selwyn; jockeys group picture before Grand National–George Selwyn; Brit Insurance Spa Novices' Hurdle–Ed Byrne; totesport Trophy presentation–Ed Byrne; Contraband returning after the Arkle–Bill Selwyn; Paddy Brennan–Bill Selwyn; Jim Culloty–George Selwyn

Timeform Champions of 2004/5–picture of Moscow Flyer by Ed Byrne

All the photographs which appear in Timeform 'Top Horses In France' were taken by Ed Byrne

CHAMPIONS FROM THE 'CHASERS & HURDLERS' SERIES

Best Two-Mile Chaser

75/76	Lough Inagh	**167**	90/91	Desert Orchid	**178**
76/77	Skymas	**156**	91/92	Remittance Man	**173**
77/78	Tingle Creek	**154**	92/93	Katabatic	**161 ?**
78/79	Siberian Sun	**151**	93/94	Viking Flagship	**166**
79/80	I'm A Driver	**163**	94/95	Viking Flagship	**169**
80/81	Anaglogs Daughter	**171**	95/96	Klairon Davis	**177**
81/82	Rathgorman	**170**	96/97	Martha's Son	**177**
82/83	Badsworth Boy	**179**	97/98	One Man	**176**
83/84	Badsworth Boy	**177**	98/99	Direct Route	**166**
84/85	Bobsline	**164 +**	99/00	Flagship Uberalles	**175**
85/86	Dawn Run	**167**	00/01	Flagship Uberalles	**175**
86/87	Pearlyman	**171**	01/02	Flagship Uberalles	**170**
87/88	Pearlyman	**174**	02/03	Moscow Flyer	**170 p**
88/89	Desert Orchid	**182**	03/04	Moscow Flyer	**183**
89/90	Desert Orchid	**187**	04/05	Moscow Flyer	**184 +**

Best Staying Chaser

75/76	Captain Christy	**182**	90/91	Desert Orchid	**178**
76/77	Bannow Rambler	**163**	91/92	Carvill's Hill	**182**
77/78	Midnight Court	**164**	92/93	Jodami	**174 p**
78/79	Gay Spartan	**166**	93/94	The Fellow	**171**
79/80	Silver Buck	**171**	94/95	Master Oats	**183**
80/81	Little Owl	**176**	95/96	One Man	**179**
81/82	Silver Buck	**175**	96/97	One Man	**176**
82/83	Bregawn	**177**	97/98	Cool Dawn	**173**
83/84	Burrough Hill Lad	**175**	98/99	Suny Bay	**176**
	Wayward Lad	**175**	99/00	See More Business	**182**
84/85	Burrough Hill Lad	**184**	00/01	First Gold	**180**
85/86	Burrough Hill Lad	**183**	01/02	Best Mate	**173**
86/87	Desert Orchid	**177**		Florida Pearl	**173**
87/88	Desert Orchid	**177**	02/03	Best Mate	**182**
88/89	Desert Orchid	**182**	03/04	Best Mate	**176 +**
89/90	Desert Orchid	**187**	04/05	Kicking King	**182**

Best Novice Chaser

75/76	Bannow Rambler	**152 p**	92/93	Sybillin	**156**
76/77	Tree Tangle	**159 §**	93/94	Monsieur Le Cure	**156 p**
77/78	The Dealer	**145**	94/95	Brief Gale	**159**
78/79	Silver Buck	**151**	95/96	Mr Mulligan	**154**
79/80	Anaglogs Daughter	**156**	96/97	Strong Promise	**171 +**
80/81	Clayside	**145**	97/98	Escartefigue	**171 p**
81/82	Brown Chamberlin	**147 p**	98/99	Nick Dundee	**164 +**
82/83	Righthand Man	**150**	99/00	Gloria Victis	**172**
83/84	Bobsline	**161 p**	00/01	Bacchanal	**161 p**
84/85	Drumadowney	**159**		Shotgun Willy	**161**
85/86	Pearlyman	**150**	01/02	Moscow Flyer	**159 p**
86/87	Kildimo	**151 p**	02/03	Beef Or Salmon	**165 p**
87/88	Danish Flight	**156 p**	03/04	Strong Flow	**156 p**
88/89	Carvill's Hill	**169 p**	04/05	Ashley Brook	**154 +**
89/90	Celtic Shot	**152 p**		Fundamentalist	**154 p**
90/91	Remittance Man	**153 p**		Ollie Magern	**154**
91/92	Miinnehoma	**152 p**			

Best Two-Mile Hurdler

Season	Horse	Rating
75/76	Night Nurse	**178**
76/77	Night Nurse	**182**
77/78	Monksfield	**177**
78/79	Monksfield	**180**
79/80	Sea Pigeon	**175**
80/81	Sea Pigeon	**175**
81/82	For Auction	**174**
82/83	Gaye Brief	**175**
83/84	Dawn Run	**173**
84/85	Browne's Gazette	**172**
85/86	See You Then	**173**
86/87	See You Then	**173**
87/88	Celtic Shot	**170**
88/89	Beech Road	**172**
89/90	Kribensis	**169**
90/91	Morley Street	**174**
91/92	Granville Again	**165 p**
92/93	Mighty Mogul	**170**
93/94	Danoli	**172 p**
94/95	Alderbrook	**174 p**
95/96	Alderbrook	**174**
96/97	Make A Stand	**165**
97/98	Istabraq	**172 +**
98/99	Istabraq	**177 +**
99/00	Istabraq	**180**
00/01	Istabraq	**180**
01/02	Limestone Lad	**167**
02/03	Rooster Booster	**170**
03/04	Hardy Eustace	**167**
04/05	Hardy Eustace	**165**

Best Staying Hurdler

Season	Horse	Rating
75/76	Comedy of Errors	**170**
76/77	Night Nurse	**182**
77/78	Monksfield	**177**
78/79	Monksfield	**180**
79/80	Pollardstown	**167**
80/81	Daring Run	**171 +**
81/82	Daring Run	**171**
82/83	Gaye Brief	**175**
83/84	Dawn Run	**173**
84/85	Bajan Sunshine	**162**
85/86	Gaye Brief	**167**
86/87	Galmoy	**165**
87/88	Galmoy	**160**
88/89	Rustle	**169**
89/90	Trapper John	**159**
90/91	King's Curate	**164**
91/92	Nomadic Way	**162**
92/93	Sweet Duke	**161**
93/94	Sweet Glow	**162**
94/95	Dorans Pride	**167**
95/96	Pleasure Shared	**163 p**
96/97	Paddy's Return	**164**
97/98	Paddy's Return	**168**
98/99	Deano's Beeno	**165**
	Princeful	**165**
99/00	Limestone Lad	**177**
00/01	Le Sauvignon	**178**
01/02	Baracouda	**169 +**
02/03	Baracouda	**175**
03/04	Iris's Gift	**172**
04/05	Inglis Drever	**162**

Best Novice Hurdler

Season	Horse	Rating
75/76	Grand Canyon	**159**
76/77	Outpoint	**154**
77/78	Golden Cygnet	**176**
78/79	Venture To Cognac	**162**
79/80	Slaney Idol	**143**
80/81	Dunaree	**159**
81/82	Angelo Salvini	**149**
82/83	Dawn Run	**168**
83/84	Desert Orchid	**158**
84/85	Asir	**148 p**
85/86	River Ceiriog	**158 p**
86/87	The West Awake	**153 p**
87/88	Carvill's Hill	**157 p**
88/89	Sondrio	**152 p**
	Wishlon	**152 +**
89/90	Regal Ambition	**151**
90/91	Ruling	**167**
91/92	Royal Gait	**164 p**
92/93	Montelado	**150 P**
93/94	Danoli	**172 p**
94/95	Alderbrook	**174 p**
95/96	Pleasure Shared	**163 p**
96/97	Make A Stand	**165**
97/98	French Holly	**151 P**
98/99	Barton	**153 p**
99/00	Monsignor	**158 p**
00/01	Baracouda	**172**
01/02	Intersky Falcon	**152 p**
02/03	Iris's Gift	**172**
03/04	Inglis Drever	**152**
04/05	Ambobo	**149 +**

Best Juvenile Hurdler

Season	Horse	Rating	Season	Horse	Rating
75/76	Valmony	**157**	91/92	Staunch Friend	**151 p**
76/77	Meladon	**149**	92/93	Shawiya	**141 p**
77/78	Major Thompson	**144**	93/94	Mysilv	**144 p**
78/79	Pollardstown	**141**	94/95	Kissair	**143 p**
79/80	Hill of Slane	**144**	95/96	Escartefigue	**159**
80/81	Broadsword	**144**	96/97	Grimes	**138 p**
81/82	Shiny Copper	**141**	97/98	Deep Water	**149 p**
82/83	Sabin du Loir	**147 p**	98/99	Hors La Loi III	**162 p**
83/84	Northern Game	**142**	99/00	Grand Seigneur	**148 p**
84/85	Out of The Gloom	**151**	00/01	Jair du Cochet	**163**
85/86	Dark Raven	**153 p**	01/02	Scolardy	**147**
86/87	Aldino	**154**	02/03	Nickname	**142**
87/88	Kribensis	**143 p**	03/04	Maia Eria	**143**
88/89	Royal Derbi	**144**	04/05	Faasel	**144 p**
89/90	Sybillin	**138**		Penzance	**144 p**
90/91	Oh So Risky	**149 p**			

Best National Hunt Flat Race Performer

Season	Horse	Rating	Season	Horse	Rating
93/94	Aries Girl	**123**	00/01	The Bajan Bandit	**128**
94/95	Dato Star	**120**	01/02	Pizarro	**123**
95/96	Wither Or Which	**122**		Rhinestone Cowboy	**123**
96/97	Florida Pearl	**124**	02/03	Rhinestone Cowboy	**123**
97/98	Alexander Banquet	**126**	03/04	Secret Ploy	**122**
98/99	Monsignor	**122**	04/05	Karanja	**128**
99/00	Quadco	**129**			

Best Hunter Chaser

Season	Horse	Rating	Season	Horse	Rating
75/76	Otter Way	**143**	91/92	Rushing Wild	**127 p**
76/77	Under Way	**124**	92/93	Double Silk	**122 p**
77/78	Spartan Missile	**133**	93/94	Double Silk	**130 p**
78/79	Spartan Missile	**133 +**		Elegant Lord	**130 p**
79/80	Rolls Rambler	**132**	94/95	Fantus	**139 p**
80/81	Spartan Missile	**169**	95/96	Elegant Lord	**138 p**
81/82	Compton Lad	**142**	96/97	Celtic Abbey	**136 p**
82/83	Eliogarty	**147**		Fantus	**136**
83/84	Venture To Cognac	**149**	97/98	Earthmover	**140 p**
84/85	Further Thought	**141**	98/99	Castle Mane	**148 p**
85/86	Ah Whisht	**148**	99/00	Cavalero	**142**
86/87	Observe	**146**	00/01	Sheltering	**136**
87/88	Certain Light	**147**	01/02	Torduff Express	**130**
88/89	Call Collect	**142 p**	02/03	Kingscliff	**137 P**
89/90	Mystic Music	**143**	03/04	Earthmover	**133**
90/91	Mystic Music	**143 ?**	04/05	Sleeping Night	**148**

HIGHEST TIMEFORM RATINGS

Chasers & Hurdlers 1975/76 was the first in the Timeform annual series but the jumping edition of the weekly Timeform Black Book has been published since the early-'sixties. The following 'annual' ratings are the highest achieved since that time (Timeform ratings for the leading French jumpers were not published regularly until the 'nineties).

Chasers

212 Arkle
210 Flyingbolt
191 Mill House
187 Desert Orchid
186 Dunkirk
184+ Moscow Flyer
184 Burrough Hill Lad
183 Master Oats
182 Azertyuiop, Best Mate, Captain Christy, Carvill's Hill, Kicking King, See More Business, Well Chief
180 First Gold
179 Badsworth Boy, Fortria, One Man
178 Imperial Call, Pendil
177 Bregawn, Kinloch Brae, Klairon Davis, Martha's Son, The Dikler
176 Buona notte, Little Owl, Looks Like Trouble, Suny Bay, Titus Oates
175 Brown Lad, Flagship Uberalles, Kingscliff, L'Escargot, Night Nurse, Rough Quest, Silver Buck, Wayward Lad
174 Barnbrook Again, Bula, Jodami, Pearlyman
173 Al Capone II, Blazing Walker, Captain John, Cool Dawn, Cyfor Malta, Florida Pearl, Remittance Man, Teeton Mill
172 Barton Bank, Bradbury Star, Brown Chamberlin, Crisp, Gloria Victis, Go Ballistic, Katabatic, Rushing Wild, Strong Promise, Valley Henry, Valley Henry, Viking Flagship

Hurdlers

182 Night Nurse
180 Istabraq, Monksfield
179 Persian War
178 Comedy of Errors, Le Sauvignon
177 Lanzarote, Limestone Lad
176 Bird's Nest, Bula, Golden Cygnet
175 Baracouda, Deano's Beeno, Gaye Brief, Salmon Spray, Sea Pigeon
174 Alderbrook, Dramatist, For Auction, Magic Court, Morley Street
173 Dato Star, Dawn Run, Mon Romain, See You Then
172 Anzio, Bannow Rambler, Beech Road, Boreen Prince, Browne's Gazette, Danoli, Flatterer, Iris's Gift, Prideaux Boy
171 Barnbrook Again, Canasta Lad, Captain Christy, Celtic Gold, Chorus, Daring Run, Le Coudray, Moyne Royal, Pollardstown

The following ratings for horses in the pre-Timeform era, compiled by Randall and Morris for 'A Century of Champions', were used by Timeform for an exhibit in Cheltenham's Hall of Fame:

190 Easter Hero
188 Golden Miller
183 Pas Seul, Prince Regent
176 Sir Ken